THE AMERICAN MOVIES REFERENCE BOOK
THE SOUND ERA

PAUL MICHAEL

THE ACADEMY AWARDS: A PICTORIAL HISTORY

HUMPHREY BOGART: THE MAN AND HIS FILMS

Prentice-Hall Presents

THE AMERICAN MOVIES REFERENCE BOOK
THE SOUND ERA

PAUL MICHAEL
EDITOR-IN-CHIEF

JAMES ROBERT PARISH
ASSOCIATE EDITOR

JOHN ROBERT COCCHI   RAY HAGEN   JACK EDMUND NOLAN
CONTRIBUTING EDITORS

PRENTICE-HALL, INC., ENGLEWOOD CLIFFS, N. J.

THE AMERICAN MOVIES REFERENCE BOOK: THE SOUND ERA

© 1969 by Paul Michael

Library of Congress Catalog Card Number: 68-13401
Printed in the United States of America • T
Prentice-Hall International, Inc., London
Prentice-Hall of Australia, Pty. Ltd., Sydney
Prentice-Hall of Canada, Ltd., Toronto
Prentice-Hall of India Private Ltd., New Delhi
Prentice-Hall of Japan, Inc., Tokyo
13-028134-4

ACKNOWLEDGMENTS

The editors wish to extend their thanks to the following for their generous help in the preparation of this volume: Entertainment Copyright Research Co., Inc., 225 West 57th Street, New York, New York, for making available their most complete files on the motion picture industry, for without the extensive library and research facilities of this organization, the book would not have been possible; Lennard DeCarl, for making available his detailed files on all available screen credits of over 1,500 performers, gathered over a period of nearly two decades; Jerry Vermilye, whose career studies of such performers as Jean Arthur, Ida Lupino and Maria Montez have appeared in *Films in Review* and *Screen Facts*, for his tremendous help in the verification of material; Ken Jones, Mrs. Peter Smith, Charles Stumpf, Charles Smith and Harry Wilkinson, for opening their superb collections of photographs for use in all chapters; Marc Ricci, for opening the doors of The Memory Shop and allowing the selection of hundreds of photographs for use in the book.

The editors would also like to thank: William Breen, Samuel Goldwyn Productions; Ted McInerney; Martin A. Grove, American Broadcasting Company; Judith L. Bly, The Walter Reade Organization; Paul Kamey, Universal Pictures Corporation; Harvey Stewart; Leonard Brown, Collectors Book Shop; Jonas Rosenfield, Jr. and Jerry Anderson, 20th Century-Fox; Perry Mandel, Vitaprint; Michael Linden and Joseph Infantino, Motion Picture Association of America; Harold Danziger, Columbia Pictures; Charles Alicoate and Gloria Kravitz, *Film Daily;* Arthur Freed, former President of The Academy of Motion Picture Arts and Sciences; Lorraine Burdick; Mary Fiore and Mark J. Greenberg, *Photoplay* magazine; Florence Solomon; Peter Miglierini; Samuel M. Sherman; Robert Seger, Harshe-Rotman and Druck; Barney Pitkin; Phil Moshcovitz, Famous Fantasy Films; Sig Shore, Video Artists Features; David Bloom, Hollywood Television Service; Erwin Ezzes and Helen Killeen, United Artists Television; Paul Lazarus and Albert Stefanic, National Screen Service; Lou Valentino; Peter Rogers and Ruth Robinson, National Telefilm Associates; Hank Warner, CBS-TV; Marvin Korman, Screen Gems; Phil Saltman, MCA-TV; Emery Austin and Norman Kaphan, Metro-Goldwyn-Mayer; A. Morgan Maree and Earl R. Beaman, The Selznick Company; David Cantor, Magna Pictures Corporation; Lou Edelman, Embassy Film Corporation; Jack Goldstein, Allied Artists Corporation; Leonard Maltin, *Film Fan Monthly;* Albert B. Manski; Jeanne Stein; Mike Berman, Paramount Pictures; Jonas Mekas, *Film Culture* magazine; Henry Hart, *Films in Review;* Homer Dickens; William K. Everson; Jane Gordon, Seven Arts Associated Corporation; Robert W. Fouse, The American Humane Association; Mrs. Rose Cocchi; Lillian Schwartz and her staff at the Academy of Motion Pictures Arts and Sciences, Barbara Browning, Joyce Foreman, Midori Martin, Mildred Simpson; Don Koll; Hilary Knight; Victor Sanjuro; Hanna Henner; the late Walt Disney; Apco Apeda Photos; Diane Giddis, my very patient editor, and hundreds of others in and out of the motion picture industry.

KEY TO ABBREVIATIONS OF PRODUCTION COMPANIES

AA	Allied Artists
AIP	American International
BIP	British International Pictures
BV	Buena Vista
Col.	Columbia Pictures
DCA	Distributing Corporation of America
EL	Eagle Lion Classics
Fox	Fox Picture Corporation
GN	Grand National Pictures
Lip.	Lippert Pictures
MGM	Metro-Goldwyn-Mayer, Inc.
Mon.	Monogram Pictures
Par.	Paramount Pictures
PRC	Producers Releasing Corporation
PRO	Producers Releasing Organization
Rank	J. Arthur Rank
Rep.	Republic Pictures
RKO	RKO Radio Pictures
Tif.	Tiffany
20th	20th Century-Fox Film Corporation
UA	United Artists
Univ.	Universal Pictures, Universal-International
WB	Warner Brothers Pictures and First National Pictures

NOTE ON SCOPE

One of the most difficult tasks in the preparation of *The American Movies Reference Book: The Sound Era*, was the selection of the material to be included in the work. With more than a forty-year period to cover, more than 15,000 films, thousands of players, hundreds of producers and directors, dozens of awards to choose from, it was necessary to be highly selective. It is obvious that it was impossible to include everything and everyone.

The "ground rules" for the selection of the material were arrived at after more than six months of discussion and consultation by the editors with the men and women of the film industry, critics, historians and scholars.

Chapter I is intended as a survey of the sound era. The chapter offers a panoramic view of films, trends and people. Entire volumes have been devoted and will continue to be devoted to many of the individual aspects covered in this chapter, and it was not the intention to be all-inclusive or comprehensive. Rather, the editors have attempted to outline the major developments of the forty-year period to give the reader an idea of the ever-changing pattern of film-making.

The ground rules for the selection of the six hundred players in Chapter II were among the most difficult to determine. Fame was not the only criterion. The superstars are, of course, all included. But so are players whose work has been valuable through the years, even though their names are not well known to the general public. Many of the players who are not remembered today were nevertheless prominent players in their day. By the same token some well-known players whose fame is based more on publicity and personality than on their work in films have been excluded. Players whose careers were primarily in silent films are not generally included unless their career in sound films was also significant. The editors have tried to present a cross-section of dramatic and comedy players, musical performers, featured and supporting players, character men and women, Western stars, and "B" picture perennials. To represent as many different types as possible, certain players on the lower rungs in each category are not

included. Nor have the editors included stars in foreign films unless their success was due in substantial part to their exposure in American films. The biographical material for each player has been carefully checked and the editors have included only the material that could be verified. The editors felt that it was better to have only verifiable material rather than a massive collection of misinformation and half-truths. The list of credits for each player includes only English-language feature sound films. Therefore, although many of the players made silent and/or foreign-language films during their careers, this material does not fall within the scope of this volume.

The just over 1,000 films presented in Chapter III fall into two categories. In the first place, every film that won a major award during the period covered by the book is included. In the second place, the films that had the highest box-office receipts in the year that they were released are also included. It must also be noted that the only films included are American, either produced or financed by an American company. The chapter has also been limited to feature films, so that serials, documentaries, and short subjects are omitted. Films have not been selected on the basis of personal favoritism. If a film is not included, it did not meet the criteria. Of course, a number of films which are the personal favorites of certain readers, and, as a matter of fact, the personal favorites of the editors, have not and could not have been listed.

The producers and directors covered in Chapters IV and V were selected on the basis of their positions as representatives of various styles of film-making as well as their overall contribution to American sound films. All production credits for producers are films that were "personally" produced. Mere purchase of film rights or the general overseeing of a film is not considered a credit for the purposes of this chapter. The producer must actively have worked on the film to be credited. Producers' credits reflect situations where the producer also directed a particular film. As in all chapters. only English-language sound feature films are included in the credits.

CONTENTS

CHAPTER I - THE HISTORY   1

A new and exciting era in American films was born when the movies learned to talk. The industry had to come to grips with a revolution of such gigantic proportions that many thought it could not survive. But instead of collapsing, the industry flourished. Here is the whole panorama of the American sound film from the first almost inaudible syllable to the most recent trends in a multi-billion-dollar industry. Here are the films, the film-makers, the methods, and the techniques that have contributed to America's most popular entertainment medium.

CHAPTER II - THE PLAYERS   40

Here, in alphabetical order, are over 600 actors and actresses who have made their mark in American sound films—not only the top stars and award-winners, but the character men and women, Western stars and sidekicks, mobsters and gun molls, B-picture heroes and heroines — all the players who have given their talents to the medium. For each player there is a brief biography, a complete listing of all his English-language films, and a still from one of the films.

CHAPTER III - THE FILMS   247

Over 1,000 American sound films are presented in alphabetical order. Each entry includes cast and credits, running time, studio, and date of release, as well as many interesting sidelights on the production. Each of these films, either an award-winner or one of the top money-making films of its year of release, is represented by a still.

CHAPTER IV - THE DIRECTORS

Films have been called "the director's medium"—and here are over 50 of the top directors of American sound films. For each director there is a complete chronological listing of his English-language sound feature films, as well as a still from one of the films.

CHAPTER V - THE PRODUCERS

The art of film producing is much misunderstood, for every producer contributes in a different way. Some are in complete command of the production while others act only as business managers. Here are more than 50 top film producers with a listing of their productions, accompanied by a still from one of their great films.

CHAPTER VI - THE AWARDS

A comprehensive, illustrated compilation of film awards: The Academy Awards from the first presentation in 1927 to the present; The New York Film Critics Awards from 1935 to the present; The National Board of Review Awards from 1930 to the present; The Patsy Awards; *Film Daily*'s Ten Best Awards; Photoplay Gold Medal Awards. Also included is a list of the top-grossing films of each year.

BIBLIOGRAPHY

INDEX

The following deaths were reported while the book was in the final stages of production:

Dan Duryea, June 7, 1968
Hunt Stromberg, August 23, 1968
Benedict E. Bogeaus, August 23, 1968
Kay Francis, August 26, 1968
Dennis O'Keefe, August 31, 1968
Franchot Tone, September 18, 1968
Lee Tracy, October 18, 1968
William Perlberg, October 31, 1968
Wendell Corey, November 8, 1968
Walter Wanger, November 17, 1968
Fred Clark, December 5, 1968
Tallulah Bankhead, December 12, 1968

CHAPTER I

THE HISTORY

The screen at the Warner Theater in New York flickered. Al Jolson had just finished singing one of his numbers. "Wait a minute, wait a minute. You ain't heard nothin' yet, folks; listen to this." With this simple bit of dialogue spoken by Jolson to a speakeasy audience in *The Jazz Singer* on October 6, 1927, a revolution started, a revolution that was to change the film industry.

Legend has it that Jolson had ad-libbed those now famous lines during the recording of his musical number and that they had been left in the film at the insistence of Sam Warner. But, whatever the reason for the dialogue, the lines of eager people that awaited each performance of *The Jazz Singer* attested to the fact that the public was ready for sound.

Since movies had first been exhibited to a paying audience in 1895, technicians the world over had tried to devise ways to marry the all-important sound element to film

In 1925 William Fox leased the use of the Swiss Tri-Ergon sound system. The Fox Corporation released a Movietone short featuring sound, January 21, 1926, and then—despite its shortcomings—purchased the American rights to the sound system through March 1927.

But it was not until the four Warner brothers acquired the rights to the Bell Telephone Laboratories sound invention called Vitaphone that sound came to stay. On August 6, 1926, Warner Brothers presented the first public exhibition of talking and musical shorts at the Manhattan Opera House on a bill featuring *Don Juan*, a John Barrymore–Mary Astor silent film with an accompaniment of synchronized music.

However, it was the tremendous success of *The Jazz Singer*, and then Warners' production of *Lights of New York*, the first "all-talking" feature film, that spurred all the major studios into sound production.

But sound equipment was bulky, complicated and costly. Its use meant that no more first features could be produced inexpensively. Moreover, the relative inadequacies of the first recording devices forced audiences to listen attentively, rather than simply sit back and enjoy picture and sound. The intricacies of recording sound on a printed film brought increased importance to the sound engineer; for Metro-Goldwyn-Mayer's "100% talking" *Broadway Melody*, made in 1929, director Harry Beaumont had to use fifteen sound engineers to solve the shooting problems. Moreover, the scriptwriters of original stories rose in stature; stories were no longer extemporized by directors. By the same token, those players whose voices pleased audiences achieved greater popularity than did the less well-spoken players of the silents. Finally, the introduction of sound process led to a temporary diminution of the director's function and to a vast increase in the prestige of the producer, who had to pull together money, talent groups and technicians to achieve a final product within a budget.

1

When Al Jolson said, "You ain't heard nothin' yet, folks; listen to this," the sound era took a giant stride forward. This immortal line in *The Jazz Singer* was the first time that an actor had spoken dialogue in a motion picture. Here are Jolson and May McAvoy in a scene from *The Jazz Singer*.

SOUND'S IMPACT ON CONTENT

For a while, the cumbersome sound equipment chained the camera to one spot; pictures lost most of their motion and were less visually oriented. But this loss was more than balanced by the realism and verisimilitude gained: the sound of raindrops, express trains and the human voice could now be heard, not just imagined. In addition, music began to figure significantly—as in Jolson's *The Jazz Singer* and in Warners' *The Singing Fool* (1928) and *Big Boy* (1930). Sound, even early sound, allowed shooting outdoors. In Paramount's *Applause* (1929), director Rouben Mamoulian was forced to record singer Helen Morgan indoors and then photograph New York City streets. So rapid were the early advances in sound processes that for *City Streets* (1931) the same director and studio recreated the sounds of the city on indoor sets. Similarly, director King Vidor recreated New York City in Hollywood for United Artists' *Street Scene* (1931), portraying tenements and streets plus such "natural" city noises as subways, water swirling in the streets, and footsteps. Sound revolutionized not only photographed realism, but also the cartoon form: Walt Disney became a leading producer through the sound cartoon, of which *Steamboat Willie* (1928) was his first.

Even more important, however, was the change in content as reflected in the choice of actors and thematic material.

Historian Leslie Halliwell believes that fully ninety per cent of the silent stars faded at sound's outset—many because their voices were ill-placed and embarrassing. The most famous such casualty was John Gilbert. The New York City premiere of the MGM film *His Glorious Night* (1929) was jeered by the audience because of his voice, afterwards widely described by critics in such terms as "freakish." Charles Farrell's voice displeased audiences with its "mushy" quality in Fox's *Sunny Side Up* (1929). For similar reasons, such stars as Norma Talmadge and

Even John Barrymore took second billing to Vitaphone in the first years of sound. *Don Juan*, a silent film with a synchronized musical score, was less important on the bill than four Vitaphone short subjects.

After the success of *The Jazz Singer*, which was basically a silent film with a few sequences in sound, Warner Brothers proudly announced the first "all-talking picture," *Lights of New York*. This coming-attractions circular was mailed to exhibitors around the country.

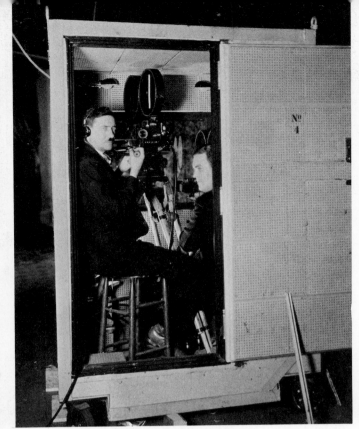

Because, during the early days of sound, the microphone used for talking pictures would pick up the noise of the camera, the camera and cameraman were enclosed in a soundproof booth. Pictured here are cameramen Edwin DuPar and Ray Foster of Warner Brothers.

The revolution that came with the introduction of sound was apparent to the moviegoer in many ways, but significant changes were taking place behind the scenes. The entire physical plant of the industry had to be changed. Tons of steel and concrete, huge two-ton doors and other elaborate details went into the construction of giant soundproof stages at the Metro-Goldwyn-Mayer studios.

One of the early technical problems of the talkies was the fact that the microphone had to be hidden and yet close enough to the action to pick up the dialogue. Here Lloyd Bacon, director of the 1929 production *Say It with Songs*, is shown talking to Al Jolson on the set. Note the traveling microphone over Jolson's head.

Marie Prevost "retired" soon after their recorded voices were heard.

The charm, innocence and whimsy of the silents had vanished and the players who had symbolized these characteristics disappeared with the coming of sound. The passing of innocence meant the passing of such favorites as Mary Pickford, Colleen Moore and Betty Compson. Also fading were the "epic" characterizations of Douglas Fairbanks, Sr., Lon Chaney, Sr., and Gloria Swanson, for the addition of sound made it difficult for the public to believe in the archetypes these players had represented. There was a decline in the moralism and Victorianism of director-scriptwriters such as D. W. Griffith; the need for dialogue swept away the tableaux and themes favored by such men. Also swept aside were Buster Keaton's largely visual brand of comedy, Conrad Nagel's stance and posture, and Richard Barthelmess' projection of the quiet hero.

Because of this impact on content, sound can be seen to have occasioned a greater revolution in entertainment than any other device since the invention of movies themselves.

SOUND'S EFFECT ON MARKETS

The financial effect of sound can be stated most graphically in statistics: in 1927 (the last year in which silent films predominated), American films brought in $60 million in admissions; in 1929 (the first year in which talkies

predominated) they registered $110 million—almost double. Nor did the depression that began in October 1929 cause a drop in admissions. In fact, the widespread unemployment of the early 1930's left enough money in enough homes to make sound movies increasingly profitable. Talkies were lauded (not quite accurately) as a depression-proof industry and they resulted in yearly profit increases through 1946.

But if talkies brought two decades of prosperity to Hollywood, they also spelled the end (at least temporarily) of Hollywood's domination of world film markets. The advent of the spoken word meant that foreign languages had to be employed for successful overseas distribution.

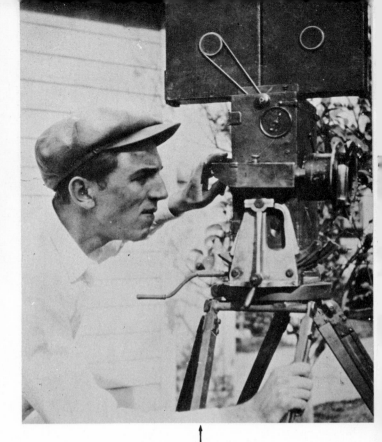

Cecil B. De Mille was not only one of Hollywood's leading producer-directors at the start of the sound era, but a technical innovator as well. De Mille helped to develop the "blimp"—the mechanism that made the motion picture camera noiseless, a tremendous advance in film making. Here he is shown with the camera he used to film his most famous silent films (right), and his newly developed sound camera.

With the advent of sound, Walt Disney became one of the foremost producers in Hollywood. Here is a scene from his first sound cartoon, *Steamboat Willie*, released in 1928.

Once the major European countries had acquired sound facilities (this occurred in 1929-1930, giving Hollywood a two-year lead), feature films had to be in the language of the audience in order to be salable.

Foreign actors in Hollywood became unemployable if their English was too accented. Pola Negri, Vilma Banky and (temporarily) Emil Jannings dropped by the wayside. Even some British players such as May McAvoy were unusable in America's sound industry, so pronounced were their accents. Beginning about 1930, however, Hollywood started to shoot films simultaneously in two or more languages, enabling Jannings, Anna Sten, Fritz Kortner, Charles Boyer and many others to resume their American careers. Despite Hollywood's attempt to defeat the "national cinema" created by sound through these double versions and (later) dubbed films, it was sound itself that enabled the British, German and French industries to grow independently.

THE NEW STARS

If sound destroyed many careers, it created a host of new stars and stimulated the careers of many who had worked in silent films.

Among the silents veterans, Marlene Dietrich gained her first success overseas and later delighted American audiences in Paramount's early sound successes such as *Morocco* (1930), *Dishonored* (1931) and *Blonde Venus* (1932). Because a premium was placed on articulate speech, sophistication and good looks, Joan Crawford bridged the gap into success in early MGM sound films such as *Untamed* (1929), *Our Modern Maidens* (1929) and *Possessed* (1931), as did Ruth Chatterton in Paramount's *The Sins of the Fathers* (1929) and *The Laughing Lady* (1930). At least one famous foreign star, Greta Garbo, made the successful switch to sound films, as exemplified by *Anna Christie* (MGM, 1930).

Male players who most successfully negotiated the transi-

Musicals were an important part of early sound-film fare. Here is a scene from the first "all-talking and singing operetta," *The Desert Song*, released by Warner Brothers in 1929. The exotic dancer (center) is Myrna Loy.

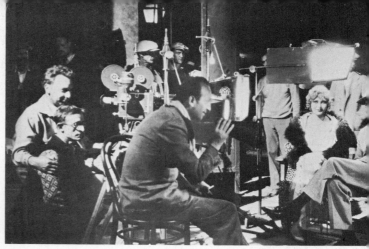

Shooting an early sound film, Michael Curtiz is shown directing Dolores Costello and George O'Brien in *Noah's Ark*.

tion from silent films to sound had been action or Western stars, or alluring sophisticates. William Boyd's screen career had begun right after World War I, yet it blossomed with the coming of sound and continued into the fifties. Gary Cooper had already made several silent Western features but first began to draw audiences in sound features such as Paramount's *Morocco* (1930), *I Take This Woman* (1931) and *A Farewell to Arms* (1932). Jack Holt, whose forte before sound had been action, was a sound success in Columbia's *Submarine* (1928) and *The Donovan Affair* (1929). Edward G. Robinson, who started in silent films in 1923, made his first real impact on audiences in Warner Brothers sound films such as *Little Caesar* (1930), *Five Star Final* (1931) and *The Hatchet Man* (1932).

Charles Boyer had begun in French silent films as early as 1921, but his presence was not really felt until American-made "double versions" from 1930 to 1934, and after 1936 in solely American features. Similarly, Ronald Colman's career began in the silent era, but his box-office breakthrough came with his early sound films for Samuel Goldwyn's United Artists' films *Bulldog Drummond* (1929), *Condemned* (1929), *Raffles* (1930) and *Arrowsmith* (1931). Sophistication was the quality of both Boyer and Colman that brought audiences into the theaters. Among the homegrown sophisticates, Douglas Fairbanks, Jr., succeeded in sound in *The Barker* (Warner Brothers, 1928) and also in *Our Modern Maidens* (MGM, 1929) and *Dawn Patrol* (Warner Brothers, 1930).

Another group of players who found it relatively easy to bridge the gap between silent and sound films were the comedians. Harold Lloyd, who started in silent films in about 1913, was even more successful in such Paramount talkies as *Welcome Danger* (1929) and *Feet First* (1930).

Constance Bennett had appeared in dozens of silent short comedies and then carried on as a vocal comedienne and actress in *Common Clay* (Fox, 1930) and *Born to Love* (RKO, 1931).

Old careers fell by the wayside and new careers were born with the start of the sound era. Although he started in silent films in 1923, Edward G. Robinson gained stardom in such early crime and action films as *Little Caesar*.

Laurel and Hardy, who had been captivating audiences with silent features and shorts for more than ten years, either singly or as a team, found little difficulty in transferring their popularity to the new sound medium. They were bigger hits than ever in such sound films as *Rogue Song* (MGM, 1930) and *Pack Up Your Troubles* (MGM, 1932).

While these players had lasted through the silents to achieve stardom in sound films, another group of stars were creations of sound with little or no silent tradition behind them.

The Marx Brothers would have had little impact in the silents, because so much of their humor was verbal and because Harpo's and Chico's music was an essential element. Their films such as Paramount's *The Cocoanuts* (1929), *Animal Crackers* (1930) and *Monkey Business* (1931) would have been impossible without sound. And a comedienne such as Mae West also needed the sound medium;

Choreographer-director Busby Berkeley at Warner Brothers brought his genius to the musicals of the thirties. Brilliantly conceived dances and multiple-image scenes were a part of the magic he created on the screen.

a brief, early interlude—Latin performers such as Lili Damita and Dolores Del Rio. But more important, sound brought a new type of film, less innocent than the silent film, and it brought new acting talents: Paul Muni, Herbert Marshall, Kay Francis, Fredric March, John Wayne, Walter Pidgeon, Helen Hayes and Fay Wray.

THE THIRTIES

The 1930's were years of depression and recovery for the United States, of President Roosevelt and of gathering war clouds. For Hollywood these years were the first full decade of sound films, and they are still regarded by many as the "golden years."

THE MUSICAL

The brightest new film form brought by sound was the musical. Warners, which had pioneered the sound feature, also led the way with the musical. Choreographer-director Busby Berkeley made huge contributions to *42nd Street* (1933), with his brilliantly conceived dances and rousing finale. In addition, Berkeley added to the spice of the Gold Diggers series that Warners produced—*Gold Diggers of 1933*, which featured Joan Blondell and helped advance the career of Ginger Rogers—and *Gold Diggers of 1935*, which included the brilliant multipiano sequence.

Other studios were quick to follow Warners' lead into the musical field. MGM featured Robert Taylor in its Broadway Melody series directed by Roy del Ruth, and teamed William Powell and Myrna Loy in *The Great Ziegfeld* (1936). Fox followed suit with *George White's Scandals* (1934), featuring Alice Faye, and *George White's Scandals of 1935* (1935), with James Dunn opposite Miss Faye. Paramount began the Big Broadcast series in 1932, of which the 1938 version successfully joined both popular and classical musical themes. Paramount had more success with a nonseries musical, *Sing You Sinners* (1938), which

subtitles could never have conveyed her brash comic style. She scripted or co-scripted her first features: Paramount's *Night After Night* (1932), *She Done Him Wrong* (1933) and *I'm No Angel* (1933).

No less than the comedians, musical "personalities" found sound essential to success. There would have been no point to Maurice Chevalier's presence in silents; he was a creation of the sound era. As surely as Warners' musicals "made" Jolson, those of Paramount "made" Chevalier: *The Love Parade* (1929), *Innocents of Paris* (1929) and *One Hour With You* (1932). The first and last of these three co-starred Jeanette MacDonald, who also made her mark in other early Paramount musicals such as *The Vagabond King* (1930).

Sound also brought a new type of male hero to the screen: naturalistic, modern, and well-spoken. Three such newcomers were Robert Montgomery, Cary Grant and Joel McCrea. Montgomery became popular in such MGM features as *The Single Standard* (1929), *Faithless* (1932) and *Private Lives* (1931). Grant was a product of what only sound could deliver in such Paramount hits as *Blonde Venus* (1932), *She Done Him Wrong* (1933) and *The Devil and the Deep* (1932). McCrea went from sophistication in his early pictures to action films, and he was best represented in *Lightnin'* (Fox, 1930), *Born to Love* and *Kept Husbands* (RKO-Pathé, 1931).

The early sound features still catered to the older generation with such stars as Fanny Brice and Texas Guinan. Child stars such as Shirley Temple and Jackie Cooper were well utilized by the sound films, too, as were—during

Musical series were the rage of the thirties. The Big Broadcast series from Paramount took advantage of the names made famous on radio. Shown here are Gracie Allen, Leila Hyams, Stuart Erwin and Bing Crosby.

Dick Powell and Ginger Rogers reached the top of the popularity ladder in musicals such as *20 Million Sweethearts*.

starred the enormously popular Bing Crosby and cast Donald O'Connor in a child's role.

United Artists was not deeply involved in the musical series race, but its *Roman Scandals* (1933) transported Eddie Cantor back to early Roman days for fine musical numbers, girls, and a great chase ending. Universal confined itself mainly to conservative and "standard" musical fare, such as *Show Boat* (1936) and *One Hundred Men and a Girl* (1937), in which young Deanna Durbin sang with Leopold Stokowski's direction. Warners' principal box-office competition in the musical field was RKO, which enjoyed the services of Ginger Rogers and Fred Astaire. *Flying Down to Rio* (1933) saw the partners dance "The Carioca," and *Top Hat* (1935) was pure escapism, with its magnificent choreography and rain-drenched set for "Isn't This a Lovely Day." Perhaps best was *Follow the Fleet* (1936), with the Rogers–Astaire shipboard dance

Child stars such as Shirley Temple (shown in a scene from *Just Around the Corner* with Charles Farrell) and Deanna Durbin (in a scene from *100 Men and a Girl*) gained tremendous popularity.

Even Samuel Goldwyn produced musicals. Eddie Cantor and Verree Teasdale starred in his production of *Roman Scandals*.

7

routines and fine supporting performances by Randolph Scott and Harriet Hilliard.

Among the child musical stars who flourished in the 1930's was Shirley Temple, who sang in *The Littlest Rebel* (1935) and in the heart-tugging *Heidi* (1937), and gave a nonsinging performance in *Our Little Girl* (1935); all were Fox features. Another young star was Judy Garland, who emerged from MGM's Andy Hardy series to star in the musical fantasy *The Wizard of Oz* (1939) under producer Mervyn LeRoy and director Victor Fleming.

COMEDY

A lasting comedy form that began in the 1930's was the sophisticated style called "screwball." Its roots can probably be seen in such films as Ernst Lubitsch's *Design for Living* (Paramount, 1933) and RKO's *Topaze* (1933), which featured John Barrymore and Myrna Loy.

Screwball comedy, a careful blend of sophistication and slapstick, came into its own, however, in 1934, with Columbia's *Twentieth Century* and *It Happened One Night*. The former starred John Barrymore and Carole Lombard in a zany transcontinental train trip. The latter included the risqué tourist-cabin scene with stars Clark Gable and Claudette Colbert. Frank Capra, director of the Gable–Colbert film, made another classic for Columbia, *Mr. Deeds Goes to Town* (1936), in which a rustic millionaire, played by Gary Cooper, discovers New York and love in the person of Jean Arthur. Capra also produced *You Can't Take It With You* (1938), in which a seedy but congenial family, headed by Lionel Barrymore and including Miss Arthur, creates a bizarre urban Bohemia. Capra was not responsible for all of Columbia's screwball products of the 1930's, however; director Leo McCarey with sophisticated assistance from Cary Grant and Irene Dunne filmed a masterpiece in *The Awful Truth* (1937), a tale of a married couple who come to the edge of divorce before discovering love.

Nor was screwball comedy the exclusive province of Columbia; one of the finest examples of the genre was Howard Hawks' feature *Bringing Up Baby* (RKO, 1938), in which Cary Grant starred as a disoriented student of dinosaurs and Katharine Hepburn as a society girl. United Artists contributed a further classic, the Carole Lombard–Fredric March film *Nothing Sacred* (1937).

Another facet of the screwball movement was represented by the immortal Marx Brothers. Their *Duck Soup* (Paramount, 1933) had Groucho as the dictator of a Ruritanian nation, his brothers as spies, and a marvelous quick-change finish. Even more hilarious was *A Night at the Opera* (MGM, 1935), which was climaxed by Harpo and company turning an operatic performance into a madhouse. The brothers similarly made sport of established institutions in *A Day at the Races* (MGM, 1937) and *Room Service* (RKO, 1938), which parodied both hotel opera-

tion and the theater. The brasher representatives of the era were the Ritz Brothers, whose best work was in *The Gorilla* (Fox, 1939), and their lower-bracket rivals, the Three Stooges.

The 1930's were also rich in gentler forms of homespun comedy. The decade saw the beginnings of such character series as Andy Hardy (MGM), the Mexican Spitfire (RKO), Maisie (MGM), and Blondie (Columbia), all of which represented middle-class stereotypes.

Joan Blondell and Glenda Farrell were among the most popular comedy stars of the era.

ADVENTURE

Musicals and comedies provided almost pure escape, while adventure films occasionally also provided a modicum of education in historical eras and their customs.

The 1930's brought the sound spectacle, with thousands of extras and vast exterior scenes; director Cecil B. De Mille was the undisputed master of the form. In such films as *The Sign of the Cross* (Paramount, 1932), he wedded Biblical themes to frank sexuality. The new Production Code of 1933, at once more Victorian and more liberal, temporarily abolished some of the wilder pictorial excesses but left room for De Mille to include some startling verbal allusions to sex in *The Crusades* (Paramount, 1935).

Another aspect of the adventure feature was the war film. World War I was a prime subject. Lewis Milestone's *All Quiet on the Western Front* (Universal, 1930) presented Lew Ayres and a distinguished cast in a faithful reading of Erich Maria Remarque's novel. Howard Hughes' *Hell's Angels* (United Artists, 1930) featured Jean Harlow and some of the finest aerial-combat footage ever assembled in a fictional feature. *Dawn Patrol* (Warner Brothers, 1930) starred Richard Barthelmess, while *Men With Wings* (Paramount, 1938) featured Ray Milland and Fred MacMurray.

The adventure classic was often a costume film, set in a glamorous past. In John Ford's *The Lost Patrol* (RKO, 1934), a British African force including Victor McLaglen and Boris Karloff was almost wiped out by marauding Arabs. The isolated force vs. attacking Arabs theme continued through the decade and was apotheosized in *Beau Geste* (Paramount, 1939), in which Gary Cooper and Ray Milland were among the besieged legionnaires serving under Brian Donlevy. Other tributes to colonialism included the low-budget, brilliant *Gunga Din* (RKO, 1939), with Sam Jaffe in the title role. Douglas Fairbanks, Jr., Cary Grant and Victor McLaglen represented the British forces in India and Eduardo Cianelli and Abner Biberman led the Kali-worshipers. Among the better costume dramas were *Thunder in the East* (United Artists, 1934), featuring Charles Boyer, and *Mutiny on the Bounty* (MGM, 1935), with the ruthless Captain Bligh (Charles Laughton) harassing the handsome Mr. Christian (Clark Gable).

Unquestionably one of the biggest stars of the 1930's was Errol Flynn, who swashbuckled his way through a host of adventure classics. In *Captain Blood* (Warner Brothers, 1935), Flynn helmed a ship in and out of port and staged a magnificent closing duel; in *The Charge of the Light Brigade* (Warners, 1936) he led the British charge of "the six hundred"; and in *The Adventures of Robin Hood* (Warners, 1938) he represented King Richard against arch-menace Basil Rathbone.

Gary Cooper played in many action movies, the best of which were *Lives of a Bengal Lancer* (Paramount, 1935) and *The General Died at Dawn* (Paramount, 1936). An example of a contemporary, modernized and sophisticated adventure film was *Only Angels Have Wings* (Columbia, 1939), which placed aviator Cary Grant with Jean Arthur in a Latin American "banana republic."

A durable adventure classic was the Tarzan series, which continued from silents until the present day, but reached its apogee at MGM with Johnny Weissmuller starring as the "ape man" and Maureen O'Sullivan as his mate. Another class of adventure film was the serial, many of which were released in the later 1930's and during World

De Mille produced and directed an epic in *Cleopatra*, which starred Claudette Colbert as the *femme fatale*.

War II as features. Serials were the special province of Mascot (later known as Republic), with strong competition from Columbia and Universal.

THE WESTERN

The sound era continued Hollywood's classic Western. Oddly, it was not particularly altered or enhanced by the addition of sound, so archetypal is the form. Early sound Westerns such as *The Big Trail* (Fox, 1930) might as well have been silent.

But the evolution of the big Western stars in the 1930's changed much of that. Gary Cooper was perhaps the biggest; his feature films ranged from Paramount's *The Spoilers* and *The Texan* (both 1930), through De Mille's *The Plainsman* (Paramount, 1936). To a lesser degree of

Gary Cooper made a number of classic Westerns during the thirties. Here he is seen with Jean Arthur and James Ellison in a scene from De Mille's *The Plainsman*.

KAY FRANCIS
Confession

IAN HUNTER · BASIL RATHBONE
JANE BRYAN · DONALD CRISP · MARY MAGUIRE
Directed by Joe May · Original Screen Play by Hans Rameau
Adaptation by Julius J. Epstein and Margaret LeVino
A First National Picture · Presented by Warner Bros.

Women made up a great part of the motion picture audience. Greta Garbo thrilled millions of women as she avoided the attentions of Erich von Stroheim in *As You Desire Me*, while other women identified with the sacrificing Kay Francis in *Confession*.

popularity, Joel McCrea represented the same stalwart type and (usually) the side of the right in *Wells Fargo* (Paramount, 1937) and in De Mille's broad-brush *Union Pacific* (Paramount, 1939). Newcomer Anthony Quinn portrayed somewhat less moral types in both *The Plainsman* and *Union Pacific*. A popular Western figure was Randolph Scott, who starred in *Wild Horse Mesa* (Paramount, 1933) through *Jesse James* (Fox, 1939). James Stewart played in Westerns, too, notably in the half-serious *Destry Rides Again* (Universal, 1939).

However, John Wayne's Westerns (many of them series films) did the most to establish the lasting Western archetype of the right-thinking man. He played in *The Big Trail* and John Ford's *Stagecoach* (United Artists, 1939), and in many lesser films in between. A host of series players gained wide popularity in the decade: Gene Autry, Roy Rogers and, above all, William Boyd, who went from Pathé's *The Painted Desert* (1931) on into Paramount's durable Hopalong Cassidy series.

THE WOMAN'S PICTURE

This genre flourished in the post-Depression years in the United States, when fewer single and married women were employed and many had afternoons to spare that could be spent in moviehouses.

Most of the women's films were glossy, well-accoutered and handsomely mounted, and their heroines were less stereotyped as "good" and "bad" than were the Western heroes of the period. An early example was the David O. Selznick production *What Price Hollywood* (RKO, 1932), directed by the master of the woman's picture, George Cukor. Some films skillfully employed war themes to cater to male interests, yet remained essentially women's products; for example, *Waterloo Bridge* (Universal, 1931). Marlene Dietrich presented the exotic woman at bay in such pictures as *Morocco* (Paramount, 1930) and *Desire* (Paramount, 1936), while her costar Gary Cooper lent Americanized romanticism to both features.

The staple of the woman's picture was the ultradramatic female star herself—someone with whom the audience could readily identify or who might serve as a model for wish fulfillment. Greta Garbo avoided the attentions of Erich von Stroheim in *As You Desire Me* (MGM, 1932), starred with another woman's favorite, Maureen O'Sullivan, in *Anna Karenina* (MGM, 1935), and expired in Robert Taylor's arms in *Camille* (MGM, 1936). Garbo in many ways represented a "foreign" past, as Mary Pickford represented an American past. Janet Gaynor still had a following, as demonstrated by the popular film of a woman's sacrifice and success, *A Star Is Born* (United Artists, 1937). Bette Davis suffered in *Of Human Bondage* (RKO, 1934) and in a host of Warners hits such as *Marked Woman* (1937) and *Dark Victory* (1939). Katharine Hepburn represented the sophisticated (and sometimes predatory) female in *Sylvia Scarlett* (RKO, 1935), while Norma Shearer, Rosalind Russell and Joan Crawford created one of the finest films of the type in *The Women* (MGM, 1939).

One of the most important attractions in women's pictures, from the depths of the Depression until Pearl Harbor, were the clothes worn by the female stars. A string of actresses drew tremendous audiences from the members of their sex because of the jewelry, costumes and fashions they displayed. Some of the clothes were merely exotic, such as those worn by Carlotta King in *The Desert Song* (Warners, 1929) or Dolores Del Rio in *Resurrection* (Universal, 1931). Joan Crawford sparked audiences most with her fashion-consciousness, but there were many who functioned partially as clotheshorses: Jeanne Eagels in *The Letter* (Paramount, 1929), Ruth Chatterton in *Madame X* (MGM, 1929), Norma Shearer in *The Trial of Mary Dugan* (MGM, 1929), Jean Harlow in *Platinum Blonde* (Columbia, 1931), Constance Cummings in *American Madness* (Columbia, 1932) and Kay Francis in *Give Me Your Heart* (Warners, 1936). The first all-color fictional feature was a woman's film, *Becky Sharp* (RKO, 1935), with Miriam Hopkins and Frances Dee.

The late-1930's trend toward the purchase of foreign (particularly British) films for exhibition in the United States was related to the growing custom of employing expensive foreign actresses in women's films. Thus Samuel Goldwyn hired Merle Oberon as well as Britons Laurence Olivier and David Niven for his film treatment of Emily Brontë's *Wuthering Heights* (United Artists, 1939). And, after testing many Americans, Selznick imported Vivien Leigh to play Scarlett O'Hara in *Gone With the Wind* (MGM, 1939) opposite Clark Gable.

AMERICANA

The 1930's were rich in screen celebrations of American *mores;* whether the films were set in the past or the present, they represented a treasury of the familiar with which audiences could identify.

Rural America was seen in several historical films such as John Ford's *Young Mr. Lincoln* (Fox, 1939), in which Henry Fonda starred. Farm life was well represented in pictures such as United Artists' *Our Daily Bread* (1934) and *Of Mice and Men* (1939). Small-town life was reflected in such wide-ranging pictures as *David Harum* (Fox, 1934), Charles Laughton's half-serious Western *Ruggles of Red Gap* (Paramount, 1935), Norman Taurog's *The Adventures of Tom Sawyer* (United Artists, 1938) and an excellent adaptation of Eugene O'Neill's *Ah, Wilderness* (MGM,

Costume dramas were in vogue in the thirties. Such films as *Jezebel*, starring Henry Fonda and Bette Davis, were produced by all studios.

1935). The rural scene was depicted by most studios: by MGM in *Small Town Girl* (1936) and *Boys Town* (1938), by Universal in *Imitation of Life* (1934) and by Fox in *State Fair* (1933).

But the big town was America, too, and several films explored the lives of its citizens. John and Lionel Barrymore and the rest of the sophisticated cast were quite clearly at home in the superglossy *Dinner at Eight* (MGM, 1933). The working classes had some fun amid the monotony in Charles Chaplin's *Modern Times* (United Artists, 1936), but much unhappiness, too, in *Four Daughters* (Warners, 1938).

Two important series began in the 1930's and remained popular for many years. The first was the MGM series about Judge Hardy's family, particularly his son Andy played by Mickey Rooney, which began with *A Family Affair* (1937) and passed through *Judge Hardy's Children* (1938) and *Judge Hardy and Son* (1939) into the Andy Hardy emphasis of the 1940's. The other series was Columbia's "Blondie," which began in 1938 with the title film and, starring Arthur Lake and Penny Singleton, eventually included 28 films. MGM's two "medical" series about

Lew Ayres, Lionel Barrymore and Laraine Day brought audiences into the theaters with a series of Dr. Kildare films from Metro-Goldwyn-Mayer.

doctors Kildare and Gillespie both began in the 1930's, although their main impact came in the 1940's.

MELODRAMA

Melodrama was featured in almost every type of film in the 1930's, though primarily in Westerns, adventure features, and the crime-mystery cycle. Anti-Nazi and anti-dictatorship films produced before the American entry into World War II helped to make the American mass audience politically conscious.

An early study of Germany, *Little Man, What Now?* (Universal, 1934), helped audiences to understand the inflationary pressures in Central Europe. But in the anti-Nazi cycle, as in many other film types, Jack Warner and his company led the way. Together with German-born director William Dieterle, Warners produced two early films against fascism in general: *The Life of Emile Zola* (1937), in which Paul Muni played the French crusader and Joseph Schildkraut played the victim of anti-Semitism, and *Juarez* (1939), which starred Muni as the Mexican rebel who ousts a colonialist regime. Warners continued this type of crusading, notably with *Confessions of a Nazi Spy* (1939), directed by Anatole Litvak and featuring Edward G. Robinson and George Sanders as representations of good and evil. Other studios were also involved in the anti-Fascist cycle: United Artists presented *Blockade* (1938), aimed against Francisco Franco of Spain, while with *Three Comrades* (1938), MGM launched a series of films about Germany which was to grow to a wave in the 1940's.

Of the anti-Communist melodramas of the 1930's, a handful of features stand out, among them Warner Brothers' fine reconstruction of post-revolutionary Russia, *British Agent* (1934), featuring Kay Francis with Leslie Howard as the title character; Warners' *Tovarich* (1937), which transported refugees Charles Boyer and Claudette Colbert from the U.S.S.R. to Paris, where they were besieged by Communist Basil Rathbone; and MGM's *Ninotchka* (1939), in which Ernst Lubitsch used such disparate types as Garbo and Bela Lugosi to etch the story of a Russian agent in Paris who defects to the West. Many B films of the decade dealt with communism at home; one, *Our Leading Citizen* (Paramount, 1939), with its story of labor strife, was only semirealistic.

SOCIAL REALISM

Many films of the 1930's were heavily committed to depicting the causes and effects of the Depression and dealt with such matters as slums, prison and prostitution. At no time (crime films of this coloration excepted) did such films represent a major wave.

"Seriousness" was the prime element of the socially conscious film. Thus women's films such as *Madame X* (MGM, 1929) differed from others of the genre in their serious approach to the problems surrounding marriage. *An American Tragedy* (Paramount, 1931) dealt with illicit sex in a moralistic vein, as did *Marked Woman* (Warners, 1937).

The perils of lynch law were cited in *The Black Legion* (Warners, 1936), with Humphrey Bogart, in the Claude Rains vehicle *They Won't Forget* (Warners, 1937), and in the Spencer Tracy shocker *Fury* (MGM, 1936). Everywhere (and especially at Warners) the social causes of crime were being examined: in *They Made Me a Criminal* (1939) with John Garfield, in *The Petrified Forest* (1936) with Bogart, in *The Amazing Dr. Clitterhouse* (1938) with Edward G. Robinson, in *Bordertown* (1935), and in *Each Dawn I Die* (1939).

MYSTERY

A check of all American features first released in the 1930's would reveal that mystery, gangster, detective and crime films led the field by a wide margin.

Warners spearheaded the movement into the hard-core gangster cycle with Edward G. Robinson's *Little Caesar* (Warner Brothers, 1930) and James Cagney's *Public Enemy* (Warners, 1931). Previous efforts, such as Pathé's *Gang War* (1928), fell short of the 1930's standard. United Artists entered the field with Paul Muni in *Scarface* (1932), while MGM released American, French and German versions of their successful *Big House* (1930). But Warners led the way through the decade—from socially oriented films such as Paul Muni's *I Am a Fugitive from a Chain Gang* (1932) through such Bogart classics as *King of the Underworld* (1939) and *The Roaring Twenties* (1939).

The standard newspaper melodrama was prominent in the 1930's, too, beginning with a flurry of features such as *Five Star Final* (Warner Brothers, 1931) and *The Front Page* (United Artists, 1931). Among the more sophisticated mysteries were the urbane *Crime Without Passion* (Paramount, 1934), featuring Claude Rains, *Night Must Fall* (MGM, 1937), with Robert Montgomery, and the Hedy Lamarr–Charles Boyer love-crime film, *Algiers* (United Artists, 1938).

Many important series mystery characters arose in the 1930's, among them MGM's Thin Man (William Powell), whose first film was thus titled in 1934. The witty and sophistiated Powell–Myrna Loy couple solved mild mysteries well into the 1940's. Twentieth had the dynamic Charlie Chan series, with the Oriental detective played by Warner Oland and Sidney Toler, as well as the popular Mr. Moto series, featuring Peter Lorre. Fox also acquired the rights to another important detective series, Michael Shayne, which had begun in 1940 with Lloyd Nolan but had its major exposure in the later 1940's. Universal's Sherlock Holmes series (which began as two 20th Century-Fox films in the late 1930's) was the most popular movie series of all time—detective or otherwise; Basil Rathbone was hired by Fox

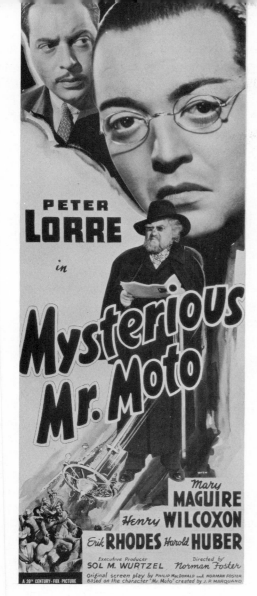

to play Holmes in *The Hound of the Baskervilles* (1939) and quickly wired Nigel Bruce in New York to "come West to play Watson . . ."; after *The Adventures of Sherlock Holmes* (1939), Fox sold the series and its two stars to a very lucky Universal.

FANTASY

Science fiction, horror and fantasy features came to prominence with sound during the 1930's.

The decade saw the growth of the Disney cartoon feature; until Paramount released *Gulliver's Travels* (1939), this form was (in the States) exclusively Disney's. In 1937 he released the first of his masterpieces through RKO: *Snow White and the Seven Dwarfs.*

Other fantasies were features for all ages, such as *Alice in Wonderland* (Paramount, 1933); *Babes in Toyland* (MGM, 1934), featuring Laurel and Hardy; and the all-star *A Midsummer Night's Dream* (Warners, 1935). Fantasy was also employed for other purposes: for dramatic and alienation themes in the Leslie Howard film *Berkeley Square* (Fox, 1933) and the Gary Cooper vehicle *Peter Ibbetson* (Paramount, 1935), in proto-religious features such as *Green Pastures* (Warners, 1936), and in melodramas such as the Ronald Colman feature based on James Hilton's *Lost Horizon* (Columbia, 1937).

But the main use of fantastic themes was in the horror feature, which burgeoned in the early 1930's under Carl Laemmle, Sr., and his son at Universal. In 1931 the Laemmles brought out the two most famous features of the genre, the Boris Karloff–Colin Clive *Frankenstein* and Bela Lugosi in *Dracula.* Sound radically changed the capacity of the horror film to scare an audience: scratchings

Mystery and crime films were turned out by the hundreds. Peter Lorre starred in a series of mysteries as *Mr. Moto* for 20th Century-Fox, while Warner Brothers, the "king of the crime film makers" filmed numberless movies such as *Jailbreak.*

Bela Lugosi frightened a generation of Americans with his chilling portrayal of Count Dracula.

and dust dropping are heard in *Murders in the Rue Morgue* (1932), wrappings glide audibly in the grime in *The Mummy* (1932), and without sound there could have been few indications of *The Invisible Man* (1933). After Universal introduced *The Black Cat* (1934) and *The Werewolf of London* (1935), most of its later hits were reprises of the "families" begun in the first half of the decade, such as Gloria Holden as *Dracula's Daughter* (1936), Elsa Lanchester as the monster's mate in *Bride of Frankenstein* (1935) and Basil Rathbone as *The Son of Frankenstein* (1939).

Other studios rode the horror cycle less effectively. RKO in 1933 released both *King Kong* and *Son of Kong*. Paramount spent more money and used better players in its horror products, as exemplified by the Fredric March version of *Dr. Jekyll and Mr. Hyde* (1932) and the Charles Laughton *Island of Lost Souls* (1933). MGM was responsible for some of the wilder horror features, including Tod Browning's famous *Freaks* (1932), the frequently banned Boris Karloff shocker *The Mask of Fu Manchu* (1932) and the miniaturization classic starring Lionel Barrymore, *The Devil Doll* (1936).

THE FORTIES

All-time film attendance records were set from 1941 to the end of World War II, even though many of the men who had presided at the birth of sound films were beginning to pass from the scene, and many of Hollywood's most talented producers, directors and writers left commercial production to make service films and documentaries.

Theaters remained open for many more hours per day than they had in the 1930's. The affluent but bored home-front audience insured high box-office receipts.

The impact of the war itself brought two major trends in Hollywood film production. The first was a striving for greater realism in fictional accounts of the war; the second, taking place at the very same time, was a major trend toward more escapist fare.

Styles of acting and types of players changed to adapt to both the greater realism and broader fantasy: the heroes portrayed by Gary Cooper in the 1930's and Cagney's gangster types were things of the past. Cooper and Cagney remained; the characters they played did not. Any naïveté that had survived sound was further diminished because of the audience's growing sophistication. A trend toward superstars set in; fewer big stars began to earn more of the big money, while many lesser stars began to find that their employers would no longer abide time-wasting shenanigans; production costs had escalated, and time was money as never before. And, even before TV's impact in the second half of the decade, the series films of the 1930's had begun their decline. Many more features were high-budgeted and ran much longer than ever before.

As the 1940's began, the United States was not yet involved in the war, but the war was reflected in Hollywood films. Several features of 1940 probed the German or Nazi mind for movie audiences: *The Mortal Storm* (MGM), *Four Sons* (20th Century-Fox) and (in a humorous vein) Charles Chaplin's *The Great Dictator* (United Artists), which parodied both Hitler and Mussolini. Perhaps more effective than these melodramas were the anti-Nazi films that went out as mysteries or suspense pictures. Hitchcock's *Foreign Correspondent* (United Artists, 1940) had Joel McCrea as an American reporter traversing Europe to find out if a respected Briton (Herbert Marshall) was really on the Nazi side. Fritz Lang's *Man Hunt* (20th Century-Fox, 1941) had Walter Pidgeon fly to Berchtesgaden to attempt to assassinate the Nazi Führer. Bitterer than these was the Fredric March–Erich von Stroheim drama *So Ends Our Night* (United Artists, 1941), which pitted fugitive workers against the Wehrmacht.

Once America entered the war, Hollywood responded with many pictures about overseas combat. The Pacific theater was the first to which Americans were committed, and it received the major portion of the early film emphasis. Paramount had Brian Donlevy represent Marine traditions in *Wake Island* (1942), lauded American nurses in *So Proudly We Hail!* (1943), had Alan Ladd defeat several thousand Japanese in *China* (1943), and in a De Mille–Gary Cooper collaboration celebrated courage under fire with *The Story of Dr. Wassell* (1944). Robert Taylor gave a moving performance in *Bataan* (1943), as did Spencer Tracy in *A Guy Named Joe* (1943) and Van Johnson in *Thirty Seconds Over Tokyo* (1944), all MGM films. Warners enlisted Humphrey Bogart to oppose Japanese agents led by Sidney Greenstreet in *Across the Pacific* (1942), released the near-documentary *Air Force* (1943), brought the sea war to the Japanese in the Cary Grant–John Garfield action film *Destination Tokyo* (1943) and had Errol Flynn fighting valiantly in *Objective, Burma!* (1945). Twentieth Century-Fox released an early Anthony Quinn effort, *Guadalcanal Diary* (1943) and depicted the sea war brilliantly in *The Sullivans* (1944) and *The Fighting Lady* (1944). Other fine war films were *The Fighting Seabees* (Republic, 1944) and a postwar reconstruction of Pacific combat in *Home of the Brave* (United Artists, 1949).

The war in Europe produced another group of films. Early efforts, such as *Eagle Squadron* (Universal, 1942), were not too realistic. Warners inched into films about Europe with Paul Henreid's portrayal of the anti-Nazi German aided by Bogart and Ingrid Bergman in *Casablanca* (1942); progressed with a fine Bogart–Raymond Massey film about the merchant marine, *Action in the North Atlantic* (1943) and in the same year released a paean to Josef

World War II provided a staple film product of the forties. All studios turned out films of this genre. From 20th Century came Henry Hathaway's spy story, *The House on 92nd Street*, with Harry Belaver (in cap), Signe Hasso and William Eythe; and MGM released *Thirty Seconds Over Tokyo*, starring Van Johnson and Don De Fore.

Stalin in *Mission to Moscow*, featuring Walter Huston as the U.S. ambassador. Twentieth Century-Fox depicted occupied Norway in *The Moon Is Down* (1943), had Hitchcock maneuver Tallullah Bankhead and John Hodiak in *Lifeboat* (1944) and showed a realistic American-occupied Italy in *A Bell for Adano* (1945). Columbia had Zoltan Korda direct Bogart in the period's finest desert film, *Sahara* (1943) and sponsored Garson Kanin's and Carol Reed's documentary, *The True Glory* (1945); it also released its best combat film in the same year, Paul Muni in *Counter-Attack*. United Artists released several of the most realistic films: Fritz Lang's film about the assassination of Reinhard Heydrich, *Hangmen Also Die* (1943); one of Constance Bennett's last pictures, *Paris Underground* (1945); and perhaps the finest combat film of all, William Wellman's *The Story of G.I. Joe* (1945), featuring Burgess Meredith and Robert Mitchum. MGM produced William Wyler's tribute to the British home front, *Mrs. Miniver* (1942), featuring Greer Garson and Walter Pidgeon, and the memorable *Song of Russia* (1943). RKO released Norman Foster's and Orson Welles' fine spy story *Journey Into Fear* (1942), the Samuel Goldwyn–Lewis Milestone tribute to Soviet resistance, *North Star* (1943), and Gregory

Peck's first feature, set on the Soviet combat front, *Days of Glory* (1944). Of Paramount's several fine features, the Fritz Lang–Graham Greene spy film *Ministry of Fear* (1944), featuring Ray Milland and Marjorie Reynolds, was among the best.

THE AMERICAN HOME FRONT

Before America's entry into the war, there were many films that offered a patriotic view of the nation's institutions, among them *Abe Lincoln in Illinois* (RKO, 1940), in which Raymond Massey gave his famous portrayal of of Lincoln. Other films studied the problems of small towns, such as *Our Town* (United Artists, 1940), starring young William Holden, and particularly *Kings Row* (Warners, 1941), with fine performances by Ann Sheridan, Ronald Reagan, Robert Cummings, Maria Ouspenskaya and Charles Coburn. Two 1941 Warners features starring Gary Cooper did much to epitomize the values for which the country would soon fight: Howard Hawks' *Sergeant York*, about the backwoods origins of America's most famous World War I hero, and *Meet John Doe*, in which Cooper portrayed a tramp almost duped by a millionaire Fascist (Edward Arnold).

Once America's commitment to the war had been made, the home front was portrayed in many ways. In MGM's Maisie series, particularly *Swing Shift Maisie* (1943), Ann Sothern displayed how an American working girl helped the war effort. United Artists pioneered in the new trend toward longer films: in *Since You Went Away* (1944), director John Cromwell used Jennifer Jones, Claudette Colbert, Shirley Temple, Guy Madison, Robert Walker and many others to depict the home front and its problems with great realism. In Columbia's *Mr. Winkle Goes to War* (1944), Edward G. Robinson played an over-age clerk who becomes a war hero. Another group of films depicted the hazards of wartime romance and marriage: *Sunday Dinner for a Soldier* (20th, 1944) and *The Very Thought of You* (Warners, 1944).

But the home front was also depicted as infiltrated by spies and agents in a series of films that presumably allowed

Films with a patriotic view of American history gained new popularity. Here, director John Cromwell can be seen standing near camera (with beret) during the filming of *Abe Lincoln in Illinois* as Raymond Massey pulls Harlan Briggs from the river.

15

Even Batman and Robin were enlisted to fight home-front espionage in their popular serialized adventures, released in 1943 by Columbia.

best ones cinematically—combined reality and fantasy: two 1942 Paramount films had Alan Ladd combatting America's enemies effectively, *This Gun for Hire* and *Lucky Jordan*, and John Garfield appeared in *Fallen Sparrow* (RKO, 1943), where he played a Spanish Civil War veteran combatting home-based Nazis Walter Slezak and Maureen O'Hara.

Many films about the home front scarcely noticed that America was at war, and these served the purpose of proving thematic stability: MGM's Andy Hardy series, particularly *Andy Hardy's Blonde Trouble* (1944), or films depicting successful wartime marriages, such as *Claudia* (20th Century-Fox, 1943). Significantly, directors George Seitz and Edmund Goulding, whose popularity had been in the 1930's, were assigned to these.

SOCIAL REALISM

audiences to identify with stay-at-home civilians who were really doing something to help the war effort. Twentieth Century-Fox was responsible for some of the more interesting items, such as *Quiet Please, Murder!* (1942), which had a public library as a locus for Nazi agents; the more documentary approach of *They Came to Blow Up America* (1943), based on a true story of captured Nazi saboteurs (both films starred George Sanders); and the documentary *The House on 92nd Street* (1945), with Signe Hasso representing the Nazis and William Eythe the United States. Other films presented a more fantastic view of home-front espionage, including the major portion of the 1942-1945 serials, such as Columbia's *Batman* (1943, rereleased in 1965 as a feature), and features such as Warners' *All Through the Night* (1942). Warners later took a more realistic approach in such films as *Watch on the Rhine* (1943), with Paul Lukas. Many films of the genre—perhaps the

The realist current that had begun in the "social consciousness" and gangster films in the 1930's was accelerated by the war's impact. With the coming of the 1940's, the movement was in full flower. Many films about city hazards and corruption, such as *The Great McGinty* (Paramount, 1940) and *Invisible Stripes* (Warners, 1940), or about the social causes of crime—*High Sierra* (Warners, 1941)—had paved the way. Other films, such as Anatole Litvak's *City for Conquest* (Warners, 1940), depicted the struggles of youths caught up in a tough labor market. Before World War II, however, it was director John Ford and 20th Century-Fox who sparked the realist movement with two films about rural and farm problems: *The Grapes of Wrath* (20th Century-Fox, 1940), with Henry Fonda leading the Okies to California, and *Tobacco Road* (20th Century-Fox, 1941), with Charley Grapewin and family on a Georgia dirt farm. Ford's kind of realistic portrayal of ordinary people can be seen in such widely disparate films as Preston Sturges' tragicomedy *Sullivan's Travels* (Paramount, 1941) and Ford's own *How Green Was My Valley* (20th Century-Fox, 1941). During the war this kind of realism was temporarily suspended or blended into combat films or those about America's allies at war. But in the postwar era it flourished and was responsible for many features on newly recognized social ills.

The problem of the returning veteran was viewed realistically from sexual and political points of view in *Till the End of Time* (RKO, 1946), while the entire problem of readjustment to civilian life was studied in Goldwyn's and William Wyler's *The Best Years of Our Lives* (RKO, 1946), with Fredric March, Dana Andrews, Virginia Mayo and Myrna Loy. Earning a living was a difficulty for Mark Stevens in *From This Day Forward* (RKO, 1946) and for John Hodiak in *Somewhere in the Night* (20th Century, 1946). The generation that came back accused the generation which stayed (the two represented by Burt

Hollywood personnel did their part on the home front. Here Mrs. Darryl Zanuck, Myrna Loy and Kay Francis distribute warm sweaters to Navy men in San Pedro, California. They also led War Bond drives and entertained the troops around the world.

Lancaster and Edward G. Robinson) in *All My Sons* (Universal, 1948).

Realistic movies began to examine the problems of youth and of racial minorities. Youth was often treated in crime, or near-crime, features such as *They Live By Night* (RKO, 1948), in which Farley Granger and Cathy O'Donnell are almost defeated by the older generation (represented by Howard da Silva), while in *Knock on Any Door* (Columbia, 1949), Humphrey Bogart tries to help young John Derek.

The films about racial minorities were similarly realistic. Anti-Semitism was given a hard look in *Crossfire* (RKO, 1947), with Sam Levene and Robert Ryan, and a harder look in Elia Kazan's *Gentleman's Agreement* (20th Century-Fox, 1947), with John Garfield and Gregory Peck. Several films treated the Negro and his problems: *Intruder in the Dust* (MGM, 1949) as a semi-mystery, *Lost Boundaries* (Film Classics, 1949), with Mel Ferrer, and *Pinky* (20th Century-Fox, 1949), with Jeanne Crain. Paramount's little-known *The Lawless* (1949) depicted the plight of the Mexican minority.

Other social ills were treated realistically in the 1940's: the alcoholic, brilliantly played by Ray Milland in Billy Wilder's *Lost Weekend* (Paramount, 1945); the corruptive force of money in an Italian community represented by

John Ford and 20th Century sparked the realistic movement in films of the forties with such productions as *Tobacco Road* (with Gene Tierney, Ward Bond, Marjorie Rambeau, Elizabeth Patterson and Charles Grapewin) and *How Green Was My Valley*, which starred Maureen O'Hara and Walter Pidgeon.

Producer, director and star Orson Welles broke with tradition in his startling production of *Citizen Kane*. Here is Welles on the set during the filming.

Richard Conte and Edward G. Robinson in Joseph L. Mankiewicz' *House of Strangers* (20th Century-Fox, 1949); and politics itself as practiced by Broderick Crawford in *All the King's Men* (Columbia, 1949).

DRAMA AND MELODRAMA

To these traditional forms the war and the Cold War brought new realism and new acting talents. The impact of the draft and a change in public taste encouraged new actors and acting techniques.

Dramatic features released before America entered the war utilized many of the stars of the 1930's: RKO's *They Knew What They Wanted* (1940), for example, used Carole Lombard and Charles Laughton. Yet by the following year the studio released Orson Welles' *Citizen Kane*, which introduced the acting talents of the director, plus Joseph Cotten, Paul Stewart and Ray Collins. Though the film was largely expressionistic in story and decor, the acting was realistic, with asides, cross-currents in conversations, whispers, etc., all of which represented a radical break with tradition. (Later, at Republic, Welles remade Shakespeare's *Macbeth* as a virtual Western, with similarly imaginative uses of cast and sound.) It was in the new uses of actors that the cinema of the 1940's excelled: in Hedy Lamarr's performance opposite Spencer Tracy's and Clark Gable's in *Boom Town* (MGM, 1940); in relative newcomer Martha Scott's and Fredric March's roles in *One Foot in Heaven* (Warners, 1941); in Jennifer Jones's uncharacteristic playing of the title role in *Song of Bernadette* (20th Century-Fox, 1943); in Bing Crosby's and Barry Fitzgerald's playing of priests in *Going My Way* (Paramount, 1944). Actors were commonly cast out of type, beginning with the wartime cinema: George Sanders, still playing Nazis and detectives in other films, played the Gauguinesque artist in Albert Lewin's *Moon and Sixpence* (United Artists, 1942); Ingrid Bergman

The traditional mystery was quite popular during the forties. One of the best was *Gaslight*, starring Charles Boyer and Ingrid Bergman.

clipped her hair for a magnificent "Maria" in *For Whom the Bell Tolls* (Paramount, 1943); and Bogart moved away from his usual characterizations to play opposite newcomer Lauren Bacall in *To Have and Have Not* (Warners, 1944).

Of all the new talent uncovered during the war and immediately after, Universal's Burt Lancaster proved by his popularity best suited to the temper of the 1940's. His forte was the slightly tarnished adventurer-hero, as in *Desert Fury* (Paramount, 1947) and *Rope of Sand* (Paramount, 1949).

MYSTERY

The realistic mystery film was dominated by the stories and fictional theories of Dashiell Hammett, Raymond

Alfred Hitchcock (left), one of the masters of the mystery film, directs Ingrid Bergman and Gregory Peck in a scene from *Spellbound*.

Chandler and James M. Cain, all of whom had actually worked in Hollywood as scriptwriters.

There was, however, still room for the "standard" mystery. Universal produced the series of Sherlock Holmes films starring Basil Rathbone as Holmes and Nigel Bruce as Dr. Watson. Alfred Hitchcock managed to survive the deluge of the "hard-boiled" school with his highly effective although more traditional productions of *Shadow of a Doubt* (Universal, 1943), with Joseph Cotten and Teresa Wright; *Spellbound* (United Artists, 1945), with Gregory Peck and Leo G. Carroll; *Notorious* (RKO, 1946), starring Cary Grant and Ingrid Bergman; and *Rope* (Warners, 1948), with James Stewart and Farley Granger.

Another traditionalist was Fritz Lang, who utilized Edward G. Robinson, Joan Bennett and Dan Duryea in *The Woman in the Window* (RKO, 1944) and in *Scarlet Street* (Universal, 1945). Other important traditional mysteries were *Gaslight* (MGM, 1944), with Charles Boyer and Ingrid Bergman; *The Red House* (United Artists, 1947), with Edward G. Robinson; *Monsieur Verdoux* (United Artists, 1947), with director-actor Charles Chaplin and Martha Raye; and George Cukor's *A Double Life* (Universal, 1948), featuring Ronald Colman.

But the trend of the times was away from the good, gray, British-oriented mystery that served Hitchcock so well in *Rebecca* (United Artists, 1940) and *Suspicion* (RKO, 1941). The trend was toward the brutal and sex-directed private detective, pursued both by police and by the guilty, whom he in turn pursues. The impassioned private avenger vs. the corrupt policeman was probably first seen in Victor Mature's duels with Laird Cregar over Carole Landis and Betty Grable in *I Wake Up Screaming* (20th Century, 1941); but it was seen more in the screen adaptations of the hard-boiled novelists. Hammett's Sam Spade was played by Humphrey Bogart in *The Maltese Falcon* (Warners, 1941). Ernest Hemingway's short story was the basis of Burt Lancaster's first feature, *The Killers* (Universal, 1946), in which a good-bad hero is defeated by a scheming woman (Ava Gardner) and an insurance investigator (Edmond O'Brien). Edward G. Robinson, playing an insurance agent, dominated James M. Cain's *Double Indemnity* (Paramount, 1944), with Fred MacMurray and Barbara Stanwyck as the "heavies" *and* the lovers. Cain's work was also the basis of *The Postman Always Rings Twice* (MGM, 1946). More than any of these, Raymond Chandler's private eye Philip Marlowe, as played by Dick Powell in *Murder, My Sweet* (RKO, 1944), Bogart in *The Big Sleep* (Warners, 1946), Robert Montgomery in *The Lady in the Lake* (MGM, 1946) and by George Montgomery in *The Brasher Doubloon* (20th Century-Fox, 1947), set the pace for the new and hard-boiled avenger in a jaundiced world.

Other semiofficial private detectives of the hard-boiled era were the Edward G. Robinson U.N. operative in *The*

Stranger (RKO, 1946), the Robert Mitchum detective in *Out of the Past* (RKO, 1947) and Dick Powell as the ex-airman charged with bringing the French Nazi to bay in *Cornered* (RKO, 1945). But more often the heroes worked completely without official sanction, as did Glenn Ford in *Gilda* (Columbia, 1946); Orson Welles in his pursuit of Rita Hayworth in *The Lady From Shanghai* (Columbia, shot 1946, released 1948); Bogart in *Dark Passage* (Warners, 1947), *Dead Reckoning* (Columbia, 1947), *Key Largo* (Warners, 1948) and *Tokyo Joe* (Columbia, 1949); Burt Lancaster's attempts to redress prison wrongs in *Brute Force* (Universal, 1947); and Richard Conte in *Thieves' Highway* (20th Century-Fox, 1949).

In the meantime, the hard-boiled trend influenced the treatment on the screen of actual law-enforcement personnel, who were now often portrayed in a near-documentary vein, probably beginning with the handling of George Sanders as he represented Scotland Yard in its pursuit of Jack the Ripper (Laird Cregar) in *The Lodger* (20th Century-Fox, 1944). Other examples are Thomas Mitchell's policeman in *The Dark Mirror* (Universal, 1946), Brian Donlevy's pursuit of Richard Widmark in *Kiss of Death* (20th Century-Fox, 1947), the Lee J. Cobb character in Elia Kazan's *Boomerang!* (20th Century-Fox, 1947), Barry Fitzgerald's and Don Taylor's policemen in *The Naked City* (Universal, 1948), and Glenn Ford's tax expert in *Undercover Man* (Columbia, 1949).

The few anti-Communist films that began during the last half of the 1940's were seldom realistic or documentary-styled, but those that dealt with the subject in realistic terms remain the best: *The Iron Curtain* (20th Century-Fox, 1948), *Berlin Express* (RKO, 1948) and *We Were Strangers* (Columbia, 1949). Too often, the subject was attacked with a resolute ignoring of reality, as in *Guilty of Treason* (Eagle Lion, 1949) and *The Red Menace* (Republic, 1949) or in low-budget productions such as *Sofia* (Film Classics, 1948) or *Project X* (Film Classics, 1949).

The bravura female performances of the thirties gave way to much truer characterizations. Joan Crawford played the ambitious Mildred Pierce (with Zachary Scott, left, and Ann Blyth) while Jane Wyman gave a sensitive and moving performance as the deaf-mute in *Johnny Belinda* (with Charles Bickford and Lew Ayres).

Mark Hellinger's production of *The Naked City* was a forerunner of stark, realistic and semi-documentary films of the fifties and sixties.

THE WOMAN'S PICTURE

In the 1940's the woman's picture became a blurred concept, no longer capable of attracting a large audience on its own merits.

The pre-war woman had become a thing of the past, and with her the "woman's picture." The naive and merry couple (Ronald Colman and Ginger Rogers) who split

Yankee Doodle Dandy with James Cagney as George M. Cohan was a typical musical of the forties, which tended to smaller casts than the Berkeley extravaganzas of the thirties.

a sweepstakes ticket in *Lucky Partners* (RKO, 1940) could not have been envisioned in the postwar world of realism. The bravura performance given by Bette Davis in *The Letter* (Warners, 1940) or by Joan Crawford in *A Woman's Face* (MGM, 1941) represented obsolescent tastes; in the postwar world Crawford played the ambitious James M. Cain character in *Mildred Pierce* (Warners, 1945) and the indecisive wife in *Daisy Kenyon* (20th Century-Fox, 1947) while Davis became the deprived wife of *Beyond the Forest* (Warners, 1949). Katharine Hepburn shifted from the sophisticated screwball of *The Philadelphia Story* (MGM, 1940) to the struggles of *Sea of Grass* (MGM, 1947). The kind of marriages reflected in Hitchcock's films of the early 1940's—Laurence Olivier–Joan Fontaine in *Rebecca* (United Artists, 1940), Cary Grant–Fontaine in *Suspicion* (RKO, 1941) and Robert Montgomery–Carole Lombard in *Mr. and Mrs. Smith* (RKO, 1941)—were no more in the postwar films. Marriage itself was more realistically depicted in films such as *A Letter to Three Wives* (20th Century-Fox, 1948).

Actresses old and new played women who had been subjected to real hazards. Olivia De Havilland was afflicted with mental disease in *The Snake Pit* (20th Century-Fox, 1948) and with ugliness and disfavor in *The Heiress* (Paramount, 1949). Jane Wyman was a victimized deaf-mute in *Johnny Belinda* (Warners, 1948), Ingrid Bergman a lost girl in Paris in *Arch of Triumph* (United Artists, 1948), Claire Trevor a hapless lover in *Born to Kill* (RKO, 1947), Virginia Mayo the willing accomplice and victim of James Cagney and Steve Cochran in *White Heat* (Warners, 1949). Many of the themes once devoted to women's films were linked to men's action films, especially those involving crime and business. These featured "new" female stars in roles such as Ann Blyth's ambivalent young lover role in *A Woman's Vengeance* (Universal, 1947), Debra Paget's role as a gangster's young but decent girl in *Cry of the City* (20th Century-Fox, 1948), Lilli Palmer's role giving comfort to the prizefighter in *Body and Soul* (United Artists, 1947), Lola Albright's similar role in *Champion* (United Artists, 1949) and Audrey Totter's in *The Set-Up* (RKO, 1949).

THE MUSICAL

The musical came under the sharp influence of big-band jazz during the war years, then returned to more legitimate and filmic forms after the war.

Just before Pearl Harbor there were released a few of the older style musicals, such as the Irving Berlin *Louisiana Purchase* (Paramount, 1941), starring Bob Hope and Vera Zorina, and *Ziegfeld Girl* (MGM, 1941), a lavish and star-studded item featuring Judy Garland, Hedy Lamarr, Lana Turner and James Stewart.

Two factors reduced the wartime musical largely to jazz orientation and smaller scale: the 1940 draft began removing the enormous number of males needed for dancers' ranks, and the 1942 recording ban forced lovers of popular music to the movies for the only newly recorded jazz they could hear for the duration. The lack of extras can be seen in the depleted ranks of dancers in *Yankee Doodle Dandy* (Warners, 1942), and the use of prolonged footage of big bands can be observed in a number of films beginning in 1942, such as *Du Barry Was a Lady* (MGM, 1943).

The use of big-band jazz in early 1940's musicals was perhaps an afterthought; the bands had had their era in the 1930's but now were needed as escapist segments in a variety of films: Jimmy Lunceford's in Anatole Litvak's realistic *Blues in the Night* (Warners, 1941); Glenn Miller's in Milton Berle's first starring film, *Sun Valley Serenade* (20th Century-Fox, 1941) and in *Orchestra Wives* (20th Century-Fox, 1942); Duke Ellington's and others' in *Reveille with Beverly* (Columbia, 1943); and Charlie Barnet's and Louis Armstrong's in *Jam Session* (Columbia, 1944). And big-band jazz paved the way for a healthy new aspect to the musical, providing a medium by which Negro artists could reach Hollywood in unstereotyped and positive roles: Lena Horne and Cab Calloway in *Stormy Weather* (20th Century-Fox, 1943), Ethel Waters in *Cabin in the Sky* (MGM, 1943), and many others.

The current of the "standard" musical was more durable in the 1940's film, however. Material like *Song of the Islands* (20th, 1942), with Victor Mature and Betty Grable, was giving way to more tasteful items, such as the Gene Kelly–Judy Garland classic *For Me and My Gal* (MGM, 1942) and Garland's other big wartime film, *Meet Me in St. Louis* (MGM, 1944). Another important trend was the one-man show of Danny Kaye, who played the double hero of the musical *Wonder Man* (RKO, 1945) and the professor in *A Song Is Born* (RKO, 1948).

The postwar musical can best be seen in the fine films released by MGM. Vincente Minnelli's *Ziegfeld Follies* (1946) presented most of the studio's contract stars and an excellent rendering of "Limehouse Blues"; *Good News* (1947) featured June Allyson in a lively musical; *Summer Holiday* (1948) combined nostalgia with music and featured Gloria De Haven and Mickey Rooney; *Words and Music* (1948) told the Rodgers and Hart story; and even such relatively quiet items as the Frank Sinatra vehicle *The Kissing Bandit* (1948) were smartly mounted.

COMEDY

World War II screen comedy was largely composed of two-man teams who moved through countries and industries in a quest for adventure: Bob Hope (usually with Bing Crosby), Abbott and Costello, and, to a lesser extent, Laurel and Hardy and the Three Stooges.

At Paramount, Hope and Crosby made their famous *Road* pictures, usually accompanied by Dorothy Lamour in exotic locales: *To Singapore* (1940), *To Zanzibar* (1941), *To Morocco* (1942), *To Utopia* (1945) and *To Rio* (1947). Without Crosby, Hope engaged in superlative home-front comedies, usually having to do with the defeat of foreign agents: *My Favorite Blonde* (1942), a Betty Hutton-starring service comedy *Let's Face It!* (1943), *My Favorite Brunette* (1947), and the first of his Western parodies, *Paleface* (1948).

Hope and Crosby spanned three decades of success, but Abbott and Costello were firmly rooted in the 1940's. Their greatest popularity was in their zany early Universal comedies, such as *Buck Privates* (1941) and *In the Navy* (1941), but at the same studio they made a series of less pleasing slapstick vehicles: *Hold That Ghost* (1941), *Pardon My Sarong* (1942), *Ride 'Em Cowboy* (1942). Their prospects brightened again with their horror parodies, beginning with *Abbott and Costello Meet Frankenstein* (1948).

More sophisticated comedy had become neither urbane nor upper class, as it so often had been in the 1930's; the bittersweet *Comrade X* (MGM, 1940), a King Vidor film with Hedy Lamarr and Clark Gable, represented the new taste. W. C. Fields wrote and starred in two prewar classics at Universal, *The Bank Dick* (1940) and *Never Give a Sucker an Even Break* (1941) and ended his days in such episodic films as *Follow the Boys* (Universal,

The Western continued to thrive in the forties, although the emphasis turned to high budgets and top box-office names. David O. Selznick (standing) produced *Duel in the Sun*, starring Jennifer Jones, Gregory Peck and Joseph Cotten.

1944) and *Sensations of 1945* (United Artists, 1944). The only significant newcomers of the 1940's were rapid-fire song-and-dance man Danny Kaye, who burst on the scene in *Up in Arms* (RKO, 1944) and played the dreamer in the largely nonmusical *The Secret Life of Walter Mitty* (RKO, 1947); and Jerry Lewis, who with Dean Martin became a postwar favorite beginning with *My Friend Irma* (Paramount, 1949).

THE WESTERN

In the opinion of many, the big Western saw better days in the 1940's than ever before, while the B-budget Western was not as effective as those of the 1930's.

Twentieth Century-Fox brought out a string of well-acted, high-budget and often "significant" Westerns, beginning the decade with Henry Fonda in the title role of *The Return of Frank James* (1940) and also starring in William Wellman's brilliant anti-lynching testament, *The Ox-Bow Incident* (1943), Joel McCrea's playing of Wellman's *Buffalo Bill* (1944), and John Ford's best all-time reading of the O.K. Corral's gunfight, *My Darling Clementine* (1946). Warners utilized Errol Flynn as General Custer in *They Died With Their Boots On* (1941), and toward the end of the decade presented a Bogart-starring, Mexican-locale, Western-action masterpiece, *Treasure of the Sierra Madre* (1948). RKO under Howard Hawks had Jack Buetel as Billy the Kid playing opposite Jane Russell in *The Outlaw* (shot in 1940, released in 1946); under David O. Selznick used Jennifer Jones, Gregory Peck and Joseph Cotten in *Duel in the Sun* (1946); and under John Ford produced two Henry Fonda films, *The Fugitive* (1947)

The first of the horror film parodies was *Abbott and Costello Meet Frankenstein*, produced by Universal in 1948. This production led to a string of similar films from many studios.

21

and *Fort Apache* (1948), and the John Wayne feature *She Wore a Yellow Ribbon* (1949). Wayne himself had played in a string of high-budget Westerns in the decade, from *The Spoilers* (Universal, 1942) through Howard Hawks' fine film with Joanne Dru and Montgomery Clift, *Red River* (United Artists, 1948).

The 1940's saw stars newly come to the Western, too: Glenn Ford in *Texas* (Columbia, 1941), Sterling Hayden in *Albuquerque* (Paramount, 1948), Arthur Kennedy in *They Died With Their Boots On*, Robert Mitchum in several Hopalong Cassidy features, Robert Taylor in *Billy the Kid* (MGM, 1941), and Richard Widmark in *Yellow Sky* (20th Century-Fox, 1948). The B champion of the decade was unquestionably Randolph Scott, who starred in about two dozen Westerns (as well as other films), from *Virginia City* (Warners, 1940) through the *The Doolins of Oklahoma* (Columbia, 1949).

HORROR, SCIENCE FICTION AND FANTASY

Horror films proliferated in the first half of the 1940's.

Universal had not abandoned its lead in horror production, but the lead in inventiveness went to RKO, mostly under the aegis of producer Val Lewton. Financial data only recently available establishes that Lewton's first RKO "horror," *Cat People* (1942), under director Jacques Tourneur, literally saved RKO after the box-office disaster of the previous year's *Citizen Kane*. Lewton used Tourneur and two other ex-editors, Robert Wise and Mark Robson, to direct most of his wartime horror features, which saw an apogee of quiet, restrained fright in *I Walked With a Zombie* (1943), *The Leopard Man* (1943), *The Seventh Victim* (1943) and *The Curse of the Cat People* (1944).

Universal spanned most of the decade with horror films (if the later Abbott and Costello parodies are counted), with Lon Chaney, Jr., vehicles such as *Man-Made Monster* (1941), *The Wolf Man* (1941) and *Weird Woman* (1944), and with its reworking of older series beginning with Chaney as the *Son of Dracula* (1943) and its "stock company" in *Ghost of Frankenstein* (1942). The revival trend at Universal resulted in such items as *Frankenstein Meets the Wolf Man* (1943), the whole stock company including John Carradine and Boris Karloff in *House of Frankenstein* (1944), *House of Dracula* (1945) and the like.

Other studios during and after the war were far less interested in horror films and followed the trends of milder science fiction or fantasy films. RKO, of course, had the early Disney cartoon features: the memorable *Pinocchio* (1940), the "classic" musical *Fantasia* (1940) and *Dumbo* (1941); some cartoon features combined with photographed action, such as *Saludos Amigos* (1942). RKO tested the fantasy market with its pre-war witchcraft film *All That Money Can Buy* (1941) and shied away from the field. Similarly, the United Artists historical fantasy *One Million B.C.* (1940), with Carole Landis and Victor Mature,

though it resulted in good box office, did not trigger a trend.

The biggest studios largely stayed out of the field in the 1940's, though Columbia had a minor wave of wartime horror products, of which *Cry of the Werewolf* (1944), starring Nina Foch, was perhaps the best. Warners confined most of its efforts to things like the mild Peter Lorre vehicle *The Beast With Five Fingers* (1946), while 20th Century-Fox stayed in its naturalist vein for the Tyrone Power picture *Nightmare Alley* (1947). Paramount released high-cost color films such as *Dr. Cyclops* (1940) and *Lady in the Dark* (1944), but MGM seldom touched the genre unless it was star-laden, such as their Spencer Tracy–Ingrid Bergman film *Dr. Jekyll and Mr. Hyde* (1941).

THE FIFTIES

Although the impact of television, the talent drain overseas and increasing foreign productions had been apparent in the late 1940's, it was in the 1950's that Hollywood most felt these factors economically and adapted to them.

During this decade, TV became more than a fixture of public restaurants and bars; it moved into American homes, and with it came first a trickle, then a flood of old Hollywood movies that the audience could watch at home gratis. Hollywood answered with special wide processes of Cinerama, CinemaScope and VistaVision—processes that could not be duplicated by television. Another visual answer to TV was the 3-D system, which ran its course from mid-1953 to early-1954 and was seldom seen thereafter. The public did not like the polaroid glasses that were then necessary in American three-dimensional systems, and the boom expired.

The flight of talent overseas was sparked by a second series of congressional hearings (1951-1952), a climate of McCarthyism and blacklist, plus tax advantages available to independent producers, packagers and stars operating in Europe.

The overseas companies' products were being felt; the sophisticated and the unsophisticated were talking about and watching foreign films, often not differentiating between the domestic and the foreign (dubbed) product. Hollywood had faced such competition before (in the early 1920's, when Germany's expressionistic drive was designed to break Hollywood's hold on the European market), and the answer was the same in the 1950's: Join them! Hollywood money and the investment bankers who supplied it saw to it that the major studios "bought in" to European-based firms—mostly in England, but by the mid-1950's in France and elsewhere.

The audience was changing; movie-going by habit was a thing of the past; audiences were selective and sparser. The double feature waned, as did the supporting stage

22

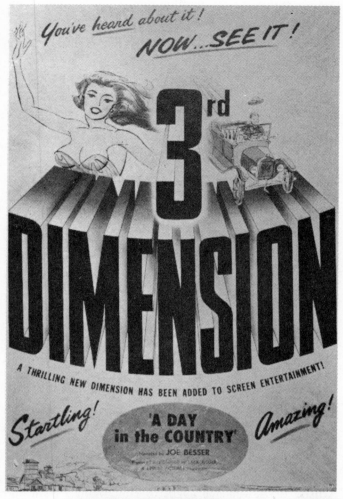

show in the big cities; meanwhile the A films grew longer.

Following the Korean War and at the low point of Hollywood's morale (1954), *Cahiers du Cinema* and a score of European magazines began praising the Hollywood product as unquestionably the best ever, providing a much-needed "psychic lift" to the Coast community.

DRAMA: NEW STARS, NEW THEMES

A retrospective look at the 1950's indicates that the two men most responsible for new thematic material, acting styles and players were the Actors' Studio's Lee Strasberg (who did not work in Hollywood) and director Elia Kazan (who did). At three studios during the decade, Kazan produced and directed several features that reflected Strasberg's dramatic theories as adapted to the motion-picture form. With *Panic in the Streets* (20th Century-Fox, 1950), Kazan utilized Jack Palance and Zero Mostel as New Orleans-based criminals ill with plague and Richard Widmark as the Public Health Service officer who tracks down these "carriers"; shooting scenes in the streets was not new, but the film's offhand, improvised acting style was. In March 1952 Kazan's first two Marlon Brando films were released: *Viva Zapata!* (20th Century-Fox) and *A Streetcar Named Desire* (Warners); the actor had first been seen as a paraplegic veteran in *The Men* (United Artists, 1950), but under Kazan he became extremely popular with mass audiences. In *Streetcar* Kazan used Brando and Kim Hunter in the roles they had played in the stage version of the Tennessee Williams play. Brando's mumbling, scratching and semi-violent working-class hero became a widely imitated stereotype. At Columbia Kazan directed *On the Waterfront* (1954), in which Brando played with Karl Malden and Rod Steiger: these newcomers fitted in with the naturalistic demands, as did oldtimer Lee J. Cobb. For *East of Eden* (Warners, 1955), Kazan used James Dean to tell a modernized Cain and Abel story; for *A Face in the Crowd* (Warners, 1957) he employed Andy Griffith as a hill singer.

These were not the only Kazan features of the 1950's, of course, but they were the most widely imitated and those which, in their break with previous casting customs, encouraged new themes.

The Robe in CinemaScope

The newly created, dimensional curved Miracle Mirror Screen achieves panoramic scope.

Television posed a threat to the motion picture industry in the fifties, and one of Hollywood's answers was, "Find a new process!" Hollywood came up with three-dimensional productions such as Arch Oboler's *Bwana Devil*, and the Lippert featurette *A Day in the Country;* and the CinemaScope production from 20th Century, *The Robe*.

23

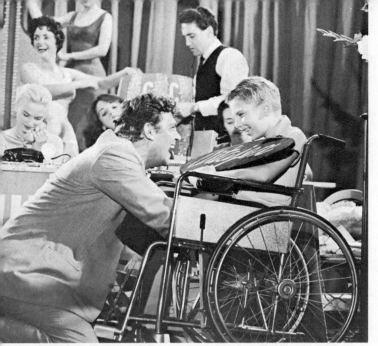

Directors such as Elia Kazan were not afraid to deal with offbeat and downbeat characters and plots. Andy Griffith played a power-mad hill singer in Kazan's production of *A Face in the Crowd*.

Other signal films in the naturalistic wave were *No Way Out* (20th Century-Fox, 1950), with Widmark as a bigot and Sidney Poitier as his main target; *All About Eve* (20th Century-Fox, 1950), which used Anne Baxter as an aspiring actress and Bette Davis as *her* target; Clifford Odets' *Clash by Night* (RKO, 1952), with Barbara Stanwyck, Robert Ryan and Paul Douglas; and the nearly expressionistic Stanley Kramer production of Arthur Miller's play *Death of a Salesman* (Columbia, 1951). The new novelists and playwrights increasingly provided material for the new screen movement: William Inge's *Come Back, Little Sheba* (Paramount, 1952) became the basis for a Burt Lancaster vehicle and James Jones' novel *From Here to Eternity* (Columbia, 1953) for another, the latter film marking the debut of Frank Sinatra as a serious actor. Herman Wouk's novel *The Caine Mutiny* (Columbia, 1954) offered a new role to Bogart, that of the tyrannical

Naturalistic films broke with custom and presented difficult themes. One of the most important of these films was *From Here to Eternity*, starring Burt Lancaster and Montgomery Clift.

Captain Queeg. Inge's *Bus Stop* (20th, 1956) showed the public a different Marilyn Monroe.

In the wake of screen naturalism came easier attitudes toward taboo subjects. The barrier against depicting drug addicts administering narcotics was broken by Otto Preminger for *Man With the Golden Arm* (United Artists, 1955), starring Sinatra. Female sexuality was examined in the Kazan film *Baby Doll* starring Carroll Baker (Warners, 1956), while homosexuality in a military academy was hinted at in *The Strange One*, featuring Ben Gazzara and Pat Hingle (Columbia, 1957).

A number of new dramatic films dealt with the problems of youth. Among the best of these was the Brando feature about motorcyclists, *The Wild One* (Columbia, 1954); James Dean's most famous movie, *Rebel Without a Cause* (Warners, 1955); *The Blackboard Jungle* (MGM, 1955), wherein teacher Glenn Ford tries to cope with problem students; *Somebody Up There Likes Me* (MGM, 1956), with Paul Newman; and *High School Confidential* (MGM, 1958), with Russ Tamblyn among the drug-ridden students. In *Fear Strikes Out* (Paramount, 1957), Anthony Perkins and Karl Malden joined to tell the story of a young baseball player driven to madness.

Also in the 1950's, TV techniques, themes and personnel combined to influence screen drama. TV furnished a source of scriptwriting and directorial talent, and even plots. From TV came *Patterns* (United Artists, 1956), *Dragnet* (Warners, 1954), and *Our Miss Brooks* (Warners, 1956). Henry Fonda starred in *Twelve Angry Men* (United Artists, 1957), which brought to Hollywood TV director Sidney Lumet and writer Reginald Rose. These feature adaptations of TV specials and series were usually not successful at the box office, but they brought to Hollywood much-needed new production talent.

For a while and in certain areas, World War II films absorbed some of the film makers. A hitherto unseen realism was evidenced in such films as *Decision Before Dawn* (20th Century-Fox, 1951), which, in addition to stars Gary Merrill and Richard Basehart, initiated a trend toward hiring European actors such as Hildegarde Neff and Oskar Werner. *Decision* was perhaps the most anti-Nazi film ever shot anywhere; it even aroused a storm of protest in West Germany! Other World War II films were more favorable to Germans: *The Desert Fox* (20th Century-Fox, 1951), with James Mason as General Erwin Rommel, or the John Wayne–Lana Turner vehicle *The Sea Chase* (Warners, 1955). This trend, however, soon faded in favor of films that were both less objective and more realistic: *Attack!* (United Artists, 1956), featuring Jack Palance and Eddie Albert as beleaguered G.I.'s; *Fräulein* (20th Century-Fox, 1958); and *A Time to Love and a Time to Die* (Universal, 1958), which placed its anti-Nazi German hero on the Russian front.

The 1950's were rich in films treating other wars, too. *The Vikings* (United Artists, 1957) combined the spectacular and the war genres in depicting a bygone era; *Something of Value* (MGM, 1957) pitted Rock Hudson and Sidney Poitier against each other in Kenya's struggles; *Paths of Glory* (United Artists, 1958) utilized Kirk Douglas and George MacCready to impugn military traditions during World War I; and Stanley Kramer's *On the Beach* (United Artists, 1959) dealt with civilians facing nuclear obliteration.

In one way, the cinema of the 1950's remained constant in its provision of spectacles: *Quo Vadis* (MGM, 1951) featured Robert Taylor, Deborah Kerr and the burning of Rome; *The Robe*, the first CinemaScope feature (20th 1953), carried on the tradition, and De Mille's all-star *The Ten Commandments* (Paramount, 1956) was the last of that director's big Biblical features. A particularly interesting sub-genre of spectacle in the decade was the "knight cycle," which received a new lease on life with Robert Taylor in *Ivanhoe* (MGM, 1952) opposite Elizabeth Taylor; the studio followed it with other historic pageants such as *Knights of the Round Table* (1953) and *Quentin Durward* (1955). Universal offered *The Black Shield of Falworth* (1954), a Tony Curtis–Janet Leigh spectacular; Warners employed Rex Harrison for *King Richard and the Crusaders* (1954), and 20th Century-Fox, turned out *Prince Valiant* (1954), starring Robert Wagner.

Not all the spectacle of the decade was action-oriented. *War and Peace* (Paramount, 1956) offered a panoramic view of the Napoleonic era; and the outdoor shots of *Carousel* (20th Century-Fox, 1956) made it magnificent spectacle.

But another sort of filmic spectacle was provided by several new systems. The first Cinerama, Inc., production, *This Is Cinerama* (1952), was a triple-wide-screen travelogue and, with its roller-coaster sequence, an exciting experience. The first commercial three-dimensional U.S. feature was producer Arch Oboler's safari film with Robert Stack, *Bwana Devil* (United Artists, 1952), but the trend expired within a year. Todd-AO (a new 70-mm wide-screen process) was first presented in *Around the World in 80 Days* (United Artists, 1956), which featured David Niven and Cantinflas and a galaxy of international stars.

ROMANCE

The 1950's films of love, romance, marriage and sexuality were no longer only women's films; the woman's picture had been blended with elements of realism to attract wider audiences.

Conflict in love was the main theme; but now there was more "bite." Both the Lana Turner and Kirk Douglas characters in *The Bad and the Beautiful* (MGM, 1952) are somewhat alienated from normal life and from each other. Another romantic look at the film industry itself, *The Barefoot Contessa* (United Artists, 1954), starred Ava Gardner and Humphrey Bogart. Moreover, particularly

The problems of youth from dope to delinquency were shown without fear of box-office failure during the fifties. Films such as *The Blackboard Jungle* and *Somebody Up There Likes Me* with Paul Newman and Pier Angeli were important contributions to film making.

in films of the period in which Hollywood examined Hollywood, the ages of the lovers were often disparate, adding to the conflict, as in the Gloria Grahame–Bogart relationship in *In a Lonely Place* (Columbia, 1950) or that of Gloria Swanson–William Holden in *Sunset Boulevard* (Paramount, 1950).

The handling of the romantic triangle was no longer traditional. In *The Snows of Kilimanjaro* (20th Century-Fox, 1952), Susan Hayward attempts to retrieve her husband Gregory Peck from an Ava Gardner no longer present; would-be wife Elizabeth Taylor competes with the memory of Shelley Winters for Montgomery Clift in *A Place in the Sun* (Paramount, 1951); and *Beat the Devil* (United Artists, 1954) has the triangle formed by Jennifer Jones, Gina Lollobrigida and Bogart.

The romantic comedy or drama had always been a suitable entry for new star talent. In the 1950's, Judy Holliday followed her earlier successes with Columbia features like *Born Yesterday* (1950) opposite William

The biblical spectacular was as popular as ever, and Cecil B. De Mille produced his all-star remake of *The Ten Commandments*. Here he directs Martha Scott in a scene, while Charlton Heston studies his script for the next shot.

Hollywood became introspective in the fifties, and in several films took a long look at itself. One such film was *Sunset Boulevard*, with Erich von Stroheim, William Holden and Gloria Swanson.

Holden, *The Marrying Kind* (1952) opposite Aldo Ray, and *It Should Happen to You* (1954) opposite Jack Lemmon. Marilyn Monroe played a kind of old-fashioned vamp in *Niagara* (20th Century-Fox, 1953), an urban temptress in *The Seven Year Itch* (20th Century-Fox, 1955) and a musician-showgirl in *Some Like It Hot* (United Artists, 1959). Kim Novak progressed from Guy Madison's colleague in *Five Against the House* (Columbia, 1955) to the bucolic foil to William Holden in *Picnic* (Columbia, 1955) and the apparent double role in *Vertigo* (Paramount, 1958). Many new talents were unveiled during the decade: Shirley MacLaine in *The Trouble With Harry* (Paramount, 1955) and *Some Came Running* (MGM, 1958); Grace Kelly in *To Catch a Thief* (Paramount, 1955); and Audrey Hepburn in *Roman Holiday* (Paramount, 1953). Sex symbols such as Jayne Mansfield in *The Girl Can't Help It* (20th, 1956) and Anita Ekberg in *Hollywood or Bust* (Paramount, 1956) also made their appearance.

The more traditional players were often cast against type: Bogart and Katharine Hepburn in *The African Queen* (United Artists, 1951), Charles Boyer as the grand oldtimer in *The Happy Time* (Columbia, 1952), Anna Magnani

Although on-location work and realism were taking hold of films in the fifties, studio special-effects men were not out of work. Here a driving rainstorm is simulated for the production of *The African Queen*.

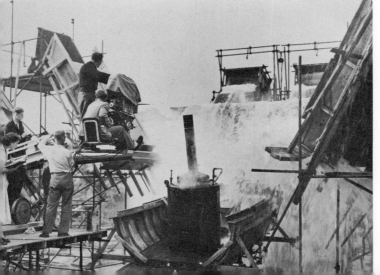

in *The Rose Tattoo* (Paramount, 1955), Burt Lancaster in *Trapeze* (United Artists, 1956), Ann Sheridan in the bittersweet *Come Next Spring* (Republic, 1956), Yul Brynner and Ingrid Bergman in *Anastasia* (20th, 1956) and Gary Cooper in *Love in the Afternoon* (Allied Artists, 1957).

In retrospect, those romantic films that were considered revolutionary at the time now seem the most ordinary by plot standards of the 1930's: as the naturalistic Ernest Borgnine hit *Marty* (United Artists, 1955), the race-obsessed lovers in *Island in the Sun* (20th Century-Fox, 1957), or that long John Ford travelogue pitting husband (John Wayne) against brother (Victor McLaglen) for wife (Maureen O'Hara), *The Quiet Man* (Republic, 1952).

This is not to say that there was no mainstream of standard romantic themes in American features of the 1950's; there was, but it had lessened somewhat in quantity and quality.

THE MUSICAL

Many of the most successful musicals of the 1950's were taken from previous shows or motion-picture successes. From Broadway came *Kiss Me, Kate!* (MGM, 1953), with Kathryn Grayson, Ann Miller and Howard Keel, as well as the Marlon Brando–Frank Sinatra *Guys and Dolls* (MGM, 1955) and Otto Preminger's salutes to the American Negro: *Carmen Jones* (20th Century-Fox, 1954), with Harry Belafonte, and *Porgy and Bess* (Columbia, 1959), with Sidney Poitier. From films themselves (and some from both films and shows) came *My Sister Eileen* (Columbia, 1955); Judy Garland and James Mason in *A Star Is Born* (Warners, 1954); *Silk Stockings* (MGM, 1957), the updated *Ninotchka* with Cyd Charisse in the original Garbo role; and *High Society* (MGM, 1956), which used Bing Crosby, Frank Sinatra and a Cole Porter score to update *The Philadelphia Story*. A few musicals, such as *Gigi* (MGM, 1958), derived more from literary sources than from their stage predecessors.

The better musicals of the decade derived from screen originals, from basic biographical material, or even from songs. Stanley Donen's *Singin' in the Rain* (MGM, 1952) featured Gene Kelly, Debbie Reynolds and Cyd Charisse in one of Hollywood's most inventive looks at itself. Vincente Minnelli's *An American in Paris* (MGM, 1951) also used Kelly together with Oscar Levant, and brilliant tableaux provided an impressionistic backdrop for Gershwin's musical concept of the French capital. *Moulin Rouge* (United Artists, 1952) was a subdued-color view of the same city; although its use of José Ferrer to tell the Toulouse-Lautrec story made it other than pure musical, its can-can sequences and Zsa Zsa Gabor's singing of the title song made it one of the best musicals of the decade. Charles Chaplin's *Limelight* (United Artists, 1952), in theory a British film, took a similar look backward at the London music halls. Other creative new musicals rode a variety of trends: *The Band Wagon* (MGM, 1953) capitalized on Fred Astaire and Cyd Charisse as well as Mickey Spillane for its famous "Girl Hunt Ballet"; *Love Me or Leave Me* (MGM, 1955) had James Cagney plus Doris Day's fine singing of updated standards; and *Les Girls* (MGM, 1957) spotlighted Kay Kendall and Gene Kelly in a series of musical vignettes.

In the process, the "folksy" musical of the past was just about dead; musical features such as *On Moonlight Bay* (Warners, 1951) and *Seven Brides For Seven Brothers* (MGM, 1954) appeared only sporadically in the 1950's. Nor was jazz ordinarily the substance of musicals, as it so often had been in the 1940's. *Young Man With a Horn* (Warners, 1950), with Kirk Douglas as the trumpeter and Doris Day as the vocalist, just about finished jazz as serious film subject matter; the jazz form slipped into background music for films as widely different as *The Wild One* (Columbia, 1954), *Sweet Smell of Success* (United Artists, 1957) and *I Want to Live* (United Artists, 1958). The "standard" Broadway musical adaptations such as *Pajama Game* (Warners, 1957) and *Pal Joey* (Columbia, 1957) were quite successful.

COMEDY

The Jerry Lewis–Dean Martin duo had their big decade in the 1950's. In a series of Paramount films, Lewis (and Martin, until the pair separated) achieved new heights for himself and the studio, from *My Friend Irma Goes West* (1950), which used Marie Wilson in a sequel to their first film, to *The Geisha Boy* (1958), with Marie McDonald. In between, among other films, Lewis and Martin delighted younger audiences (and brought many teenagers into theaters) with the service comedies *At War With the Army* (1950) and *Jumping Jacks* (1952), fare similar to the Abbott and Costello successes of the previous decade.

Until Costello's death, Abbott and Costello continued to work at Universal in the horror parody series and other reprises such as *Abbott and Costello Meet the Keystone Cops* (1955). Bob Hope, by far the most successful of all 1950's comics, reprised other eras, too, in such films as *The Son of Paleface* (Paramount, 1952) and *Road to Bali* (Paramount, 1952); he then worked overseas with less-than-successful results in *The Iron Petticoat* (MGM, 1956) and *Paris Holiday* (United Artists, 1958). Danny Kaye worked in a variety of properties: old-time farce in *On the Riviera* (20th Century-Fox, 1951), children's sentimental comedy such as *Hans Christian Andersen* (RKO, 1952), costume comedy such as *The Court Jester* (Paramount, 1956) or *Merry Andrew* (MGM, 1958) and straight dramatic roles such as *Me and the Colonel* (Columbia, 1958).

The old comedy was dead. Buster Keaton did a few walk-ons in the 1950's; Laurel and Hardy had gone to France to shoot their last film, *Atoll K* (Léo Joannon,

1952); Groucho Marx played in *A Girl in Every Port* (RKO, 1952), then departed for a very successful decade in television. But in the 1950's, little appeared to supplant the lost comedy. The Judy Holliday–Jack Lemmon films were comedic dramas or romantic films, not pure comedies in the more traditional sense of the term. The same can be said of the work of newcomers such as Tony Randall, who made several films in the decade, the best of which was *Will Success Spoil Rock Hunter?* (20th Century-Fox, 1957) with Jayne Mansfield, but whose heavy TV schedule prevented his becoming a major movie comedian.

THE WESTERN

Among all forms, the Western was strongest in the 1950's. Korea, inflation, and the Cold War seemed to augur for the simplistic black and white of Western drama in the movies, and some of America's finest sound Westerns appeared in the decade.

Among the best were *High Noon* (United Artists, 1952) and *Shane* (Paramount, 1953). *High Noon* had sheriff Gary Cooper and wife Grace Kelly stand up against a hostile town. Cooper appeared in other fine Westerns: *Vera Cruz* (United Artists, 1954), *Friendly Persuasion* (Allied Artists, 1956), and *Man of the West* (United Artists, 1958). *Shane* had Alan Ladd in the lead role vanquishing the blackest of recent Western villains, Jack Palance; director George Stevens' use of black and white as color symbols in a color film gave it a hitherto unseen expressionistic quality. Ladd went on to make such great Westerns as *Drum Beat* (Warners, 1954) and *The Badlanders* (MGM, 1958), both films under expert Western director (and relative newcomer) Delmer Daves. Daves had also been responsible for *Broken Arrow* (20th Century-Fox, 1950), with James Stewart and Jeff Chandler, for Glenn Ford's film for Jerry Wald, *Jubal* (Columbia, 1956), and most important of all, for the Ford–Van Heflin masterpiece *3:10 to Yuma* (Columbia, 1957).

Among practiced Western directors operating best in the decade were Anthony Mann and the older John Ford. Mann did some of his best work: the amazing *Devil's Doorway* (MGM, 1950), with Robert Taylor as an Indian war hero; fine James Stewart in *Winchester 173* (Universal, 1950); finer Stewart in *The Man from Laramie* (Columbia, 1955); and the great Henry Fonda vehicle *The Tin Star* (Paramount, 1957), among many others. Ford's skilled hand was brought to bear on such panoramic views of the West as *The Searchers* (Warners, 1956) and *The Horse Soldiers* (United Artists, 1959), which provided that quintessential Fordian interest in Civil War and post-war frontier *mores* among combatants and civilians alike.

But among directors, *the* emergent Western talent of the 1950's was that of Preston Sturges' younger brother John. John Sturges filled the John Ford role of the 1930's, and by using the outlooks and technical processes of the 1950's made many of the period's best Westerns. Among these were the fine William Holden film of beleaguered cavalry, *Escape From Fort Bravo* (MGM, 1953); *Gunfight at the O.K. Corral* (Paramount, 1957), with Burt Lancaster and Kirk Douglas taking over the Wyatt Earp and Doc Holliday roles; and the Douglas–Anthony Quinn *Last Train from Gun Hill* (Paramount, 1959); as well as a "modernized" Western with Spencer Tracy, *Bad Day at Black Rock* (MGM, 1954).

America's favorite Western stars had a field day. John Wayne played in the 3-D *Hondo* (Warners, 1953) and continued in '50's Westerns through Howard Hawks' near-parody *Rio Bravo* (Warners, 1959). Gregory Peck portrayed the title role of *The Gunfighter* (20th Century-Fox, 1950), the courageous Army officer in *Only the Valiant* (Warners, 1951), and the frontier-prodder in *The Big Country* (United Artists, 1958). Richard Widmark played in 20th's *Broken Lance* (1954) and *Warlock* (1959); Robert Taylor in *The Last Hunt* (MGM, 1956), with Stewart Granger, and Glenn Ford in several films, notably *Cowboy* (Columbia, 1958). Newcomers to the A Western during the 1950's included Kirk Douglas in *Along the Great Divide* (Warners, 1951), Burt Lancaster in *Vengeance Valley* (MGM, 1951), and Lee Marvin in *Hangman's Knot* (Columbia, 1952).

In addition to its A Westerns, the decade was rich in B's. Among the best: *The Redhead and the Cowboy* (Paramount, 1950), *Shotgun* (Allied Artists, 1955) and *War Drums* (United Artists, 1957). As during the previous decade, Randolph Scott remained the King of the B's, in films ranging from *Colt .45* (Warners, 1950) through *Westbound* (Warners, 1959).

THE GREAT CRUSADE: KOREA AND ANTI-COMMUNIST FILMS

The screen depictions of Korean combat and its home-front aftermath began with *The Steel Helmet* (Lippert, 1951) and *Fixed Bayonets* (20th Century-Fox, 1951). These early films suffered from lack of attention to detail and were little more than remakes of World War II films about the land war against Japan. With the Frank Lovejoy feature *Retreat, Hell!* (Warners, 1952) and the Robert Mitchum film *One Minute to Zero* (RKO, 1952), the depiction of uniforms, terrain and battle conditions became much more exacting. Realism saw its height in features made after the war had ended, such as *Men in War* (United Artists, 1957) and particularly in Lewis Milestone's semidocumentary use of Gregory Peck and the supporting cast in the superb *Pork Chop Hill* (United Artists, 1959).

A large body of features treated supposed collaboration on the part of brainwashed G.I.'s, including *Prisoner of War* (MGM, 1954), *The Rack* (MGM, 1956), an early Paul Newman film, and particularly *Time Limit* (United Artists, 1957), Karl Malden's first feature as a director.

It was not remarkable that American film producers made many features having to do with the commitment of America and her allies in the Korean War (1950-1954), particularly during the first half of the decade. It *was* remarkable that the wave of films about Korea reinforced a group of films that attacked communism at home and in the U.S.S.R. (in theory, a neutral).

The anti-Communist series covered a broad area. Many of the films dealt with espionage at home or abroad: *The Woman on Pier 13* (RKO, 1949, formerly *I Married a Communist*); *My Son, John* (Paramount, 1952), Robert Walker's last feature performance; *Night People* (20th Century-Fox, 1954), with Gregory Peck and Peter van Eyck; the Richard Widmark near-fantasy *Hell and High Water* (20th Century-Fox, 1954); and *The Fearmakers* (United Artists, 1958), with Dana Andrews. Other films used big stars to illustrate the perils of escaping from Iron Curtain countries: Clark Gable rescues Gene Tierney in *Never Let Me Go* (MGM, 1953); Fredric March and Gloria Grahame escape Adolphe Menjou's Czech network in Elia Kazan's *Man on a Tightrope* (20th Century-Fox, 1953).

Some American features dealt with communism as an intellectual issue; among them were *Trial* (MGM, 1955), in which Glenn Ford bests party types Dorothy McGuire and Arthur Kennedy, and *Storm Center* (Columbia, 1956), with Bette Davis as a librarian beset by political bigots.

MYSTERY AND CRIME

The crime and mystery features of the 1950's were of the serious, semidocumentary and "tough" school. Some of the best were: the Eleanor Parker film *Caged* (Warners, 1950); the Sterling Hayden, Sam Jaffe, Louis Calhern, Marilyn Monroe masterpiece of John Huston, *The Asphalt Jungle* (MGM, 1950); the Shelley Winters film in which John Garfield gave his last feature performance, *He Ran All the Way* (United Artists, 1951); and the Glenn Ford–Alexander Scourby duel of *The Big Heat* (Columbia, 1953). *Kiss Me Deadly* (United Artists, 1955) was much more than a Mickey Spillane property, as had been lesser films such as *I, the Jury* (United Artists, 1953); *Deadly* featured Ralph Meeker as Spillane's detective Mike Hammer and Robert Aldrich's direction, which lifted the mystery film to the level of serious drama. A string of semidocumentary dramas followed: Stanley Kubrick's *The Killing* (United Artists, 1956); Stanley Kramer's *The Defiant Ones* (United Artists, 1958); Robert Wise's *I Want to Live!* (United Artists, 1958), with Susan Hayward as a doomed murderess; and the retelling of the Leopold-Loeb case in *Compulsion* (20th Century-Fox, 1959).

A smaller wave of realistic crime melodramas dealt with corrupt policemen or court officials: the Robert Taylor role in *Rogue Cop* (MGM, 1954), Edmond O'Brien in his first directorial effort, *Shield for Murder* (United Artists, 1954), the Harry Belaver role in *The Brothers Rico* (Columbia, 1957), Orson Welles' cop in *Touch of Evil* (1958), and Taylor's role in *Party Girl* (MGM, 1958).

Meanwhile, the "standard" mystery continued, best exemplified as it had been since the early 1920's by Alfred Hitchcock productions. In *Strangers on a Train* (Warners, 1951) Hitchcock used Farley Granger and Robert Walker as antagonists in a tale of wife murder; the subject of uxoricide was also the director's theme in *Rear Window* (Paramount, 1954), the Grace Kelly film *Dial "M" for Murder* (Warners, 1954) and *Vertigo*. Hitchcock developed other themes, however, such as that of the confession-bound priest (Montgomery Clift) who knows the killer but cannot divulge his name, in *I Confess* (Warners, 1953); jewel robbery on the Riviera with Cary Grant and Grace Kelly in *To Catch a Thief* (Paramount, 1955), and the espionage-travelogue with Grant and Eva Marie Saint, *North by Northwest* (MGM, 1959). Nor did Hitchcock's successful switch to an enormously popular TV series (1955) diminish his feature output; the most one can say of its influence is that it may have sparked the director's interest in documentary mysteries, of which *The Wrong Man* (Warners, 1956) with Henry Fonda remains his sole such feature effort.

Other producer-directors worked in the mystery format as well: Joseph Losey with John Barrymore, Jr.'s expressionistic *The Big Night* (United Artists, 1951), King Vidor with the Ruth Roman–Richard Todd romantic mystery *Lightning Strikes Twice* (Warners, 1951), Lewis Allen with his Sinatra vehicle about a president's would-be assassin, *Suddenly!* (United Artists, 1954), and William Wyler in his Bogart thriller which pitted householders against intruding criminals, *The Desperate Hours* (Paramount, 1955).

FANTASY, SCIENCE FICTION AND HORROR

On a sheer statistical basis, the number of fantasy and horror films of the 1950's (particularly the second half) has not been equaled in any country before or since. Part of this wave was doubtless due to the growing drive-in theater market.

The "pure" science fiction films, though their budgets were the highest in the fantasy films category, did not have particular success. The Eagle Lion feature *Destination Moon* (1950) was typical in its wonderful color effects and in its lack of "big" names, as were *The War of the Worlds* (Paramount, 1953) and *Riders to the Stars* (United Artists, 1954), and such features (without color) as the Patricia Neal–Michael Rennie film *The Day the Earth Stood Still* (20th Century-Fox, 1951), Howard Hawks' and Christian Nyby's *The Thing* (RKO, 1951), and Richard Carlson's (3-D) *It Came From Outer Space* (Universal, 1953). A bit more ambitious were MGM's most expensive science-fiction production up to that time, *Forbidden Planet* (1956), starring Walter Pidgeon; Walt Disney's Buena Vista production from Jules Verne, *20,000 Leagues Under the Sea* (1954); and Universal's *This Island Earth* (1955).

Alfred Hitchcock remained the top producer of film mysteries with productions such as *Vertigo* starring James Stewart and Kim Novak.

The teenage wave began in earnest at American International with *I Was a Teenage Werewolf* (1957), which featured Michael Landon in the title role, and broadened into *I Was a Teenage Frankenstein* (1957), with Whit Bissell, and one of Robert Vaughn's earliest films in the title role of *Teenage Caveman* (1958). That studio was a catalyst in the teenage horror cycle, and so was young director Roger Corman (29 years old in 1955), who added teenage elements to the more "standard" horror-science-fiction films at American International in films such as *Night of the Blood Beast* (1958), at Allied Artists in *Not of This Earth* (1957) and in his own firm's (Filmgroup) releases such as *The Wasp Woman* (1959). Aside from Corman's efforts, teenage tastes were catered to in a variety

Science-fiction films, especially those slanted to teenagers, were tremendously popular and profitable. Here Grant Williams, shrunk to a mere two inches in height, battles a tarantula in the Universal production *The Incredible Shrinking Man*.

29

of films, such as *Gog* (United Artists, 1954), *The Creature from the Black Lagoon* (Universal, 1954), *Tarantula* (Universal, 1955), *Earth vs. the Flying Saucers* (Columbia, 1956) and *The Incredible Shrinking Man* (Universal, 1957).

A new horror stream that began in the 1950's was that of "Vincent Price neo-Gothic," which was eventually to link up under Corman in the 1960's to become an enormously profitable enterprise. Most of Price's roles in the 1940's and earlier had been of sophisticates, but often he had brought a trace of the bizarre to them. With director Andre de Toth's 3-D and color *House of Wax* (Warners, 1953), Price was given a whole new career in the Gothic: his apparel and cultured accent impressed audiences. Price continued the trend in *Mad Magician* (Columbia, 1954) and *The Fly* (20th Century-Fox, 1958).

The 1950's were not years of traditional horror films or gentle fantasies. Older horror themes were occasionally restated in such fine films as Allied Artists' *The Invasion of the Body Snatchers* (1956) and *Frankenstein 1970* (1958), but such films were few. Equally out of fashion were the Disney fantasies, of which the decade's best was *Peter Pan* (RKO, 1953), and the whimsical witchcraft trifle *Bell, Book and Candle* (Columbia, 1958).

THE SIXTIES

This decade will probably prove more profitable for Hollywood than the 1950's.

Not all such profit will derive from theatrically exhibited features, for much will come from Hollywood's production of TV series, of feature films made directly for first exhibition on TV, and from similar earnings from abroad. In the feature category, the 1960's are the decade of the multimillion-dollar budget, of the "hard ticket" feature, and of the blockbuster. The decade, however, has still produced many smallish, well-made features as well as many minor classics that reflect the tastes of a generation shaken by various internal and external factors.

DRAMA: NEW STARS, NEW WAVES

Naturalistic drama of Elia Kazan's type seems to have faded: at least two of this director's films did not register well at the domestic box office—*Wild River* (20th Century-Fox, 1960), which used Montgomery Clift as a TVA representative in the 1930's South, and *America America* (Warners, 1963), a semiautobiographical treatise about a boy's arrival in the New World. More often successful dramas reflected exciting or sensational elements. For example, *Elmer Gantry* (United Artists, 1960) had Burt

Lancaster in the title role as a fraudulent spiritual leader, *Shock Corridor* (Allied Artists, 1964) was set in a mental hospital, and such 1966 features as *An American Dream* (Warners) and *The Wild Angels* (American International) treated sexuality among business executives and maverick motorcyclists, respectively. Films emphasizing triumphant women, such as *Bus Riley's Back in Town* (Universal, 1965) or Stanley Kramer's star-studded *Ship of Fools* (Columbia, 1965), were fashionable. A minor trend of naturalistic films reflected corruption among professional and nonprofessional gamblers: *The Hustler* (20th Century-Fox, 1961), with Paul Newman in the title role and Jackie Gleason as his pool-playing nemesis, and *The Cincinnati Kid* (MGM, 1965), with Steve McQueen as the card hustler and Edward G. Robinson as his nemesis. In a film such as *The Oscar* (Embassy, 1966), Hollywood admitted the possibility of corruption at its own door.

The draining of TV for directors and stars continued. Television film production techniques had transformed all but the biggest stars into malleable and quick-working units, but the directors and writers originating in the small-screen medium, while very fast, were not accustomed to big-studio authority: their products were more often personal dramatic creations. One such was Arthur Penn, who directed the Anne Bancroft–Patty Duke film *The Miracle Worker* (United Artists, 1962), left *The Train* and other films after a few days' shooting, and finally registered well under producer Sam Spiegel with *The Chase* (1966); familiar TV figures such as Victor Jory and E. G. Marshall were often seen in Penn's films. Another TV man, Sidney Lumet, had begun feature direction in the mid-1950's, yet maintained in the 1960's the independence of mind that allowed him to do such dramatic features as the French coproduction about Brooklyn dock workers, *A View from the Bridge* (Cocinor, 1962), *The Pawnbroker* (Allied Artists, 1965), with Rod Steiger as a fugitive from Nazism who has lost his capacity to feel, and *The Group* (United Artists, 1966), which included at least one Lesbian character.

Several other features dealt with religious or racial themes. Otto Preminger's *Exodus* (United Artists, 1960) cast Paul Newman and Sal Mineo as fighters for Israel; Stanley Kramer's *Judgment at Nuremberg* (United Artists, 1961) used an Abby Mann script and such varied players as Spencer Tracy, Burt Lancaster, Judy Garland, Marlene Dietrich and Montgomery Clift to show how Nazism had decimated an entire people in Europe; and *Judith* (Paramount, 1966) used Sophia Loren to describe the rooting-out of secret Nazis who still oppose Israel.

Another group of features began to deal realistically with the plight of the American Negro, and Sidney Poitier appeared in many of the best of these: in the extremely

Religious and racial themes were tackled by Hollywood in many films of the sixties. *Black Like Me* with James Whitmore was a step toward social consciousness.

War films were increasingly used for the dual purpose of spectacle and drama. Darryl Zanuck's production of *The Longest Day* with Stuart Whitman and John Wayne was a good example of the genre.

realistic feature about urban Negroes, *A Raisin in the Sun* (Columbia, 1960), in the somewhat romanticized award-winner *Lilies of the Field* (United Artists, 1963), as the man who would save Anne Bancroft from suicide in *The Slender Thread* (Paramount, 1965), and as the romantic lead in *A Patch of Blue* (MGM, 1965). Some features about the Negro were courageous, yet fell short of the mark, such as TV director Robert Mulligan's *To Kill a Mockingbird* (Universal, 1962), and *Black Like Me* (Lerner, 1964), which cast James Whitmore as a white who "passes." Two independent Cinema V productions were more realistic than any of the above: *One Potato, Two Potato* (Cinema V, 1964), which dealt with interracial love and marriage, and *Nothing But a Man* (Cinema V, 1965), which treated a Negro's family conflicts.

Increasingly, homosexuals were treated maturely: in Preminger's *Advise and Consent* (Columbia, 1962), and in *The Group*, among others.

In the 1960's the war film was increasingly used for the dual purpose of spectacle and drama. The majority of the better war films dealt with World War II: *The Victors* (Columbia, 1963) was perhaps the most realistic of these. Several films treated native resistance to Nazism, such

as *The Train* (United Artists, 1965), while others showed Allied sabotage and invasion units linking up with the resistance, as in *The Guns of Navarone* (Columbia, 1961) or *The Heroes of Telemark* (Columbia, 1965). There was a rash of films about interned Allies escaping Nazi captivity, as the Steve McQueen vehicle *The Great Escape* (United Artists, 1963) and that starring Frank Sinatra, *Von Ryan's Express* (20th Century-Fox, 1965). Most of these were high-budget, in color, and well-acted, and objectivity about the nature of war and its effects on people was the hallmark of all of them. Some films revealed the corrupt inner workings of the Nazi high command, as Sam Spiegel and Anatole Litvak's *The Night of the Generals* (Columbia, 1967).

World War II in Europe was not the only conflict portrayed in major features of the 1960's. The John Saxon film *War Hunt* (United Artists, 1962) viewed the Korean War; *King Rat* (Columbia, 1965) treated the situation of Allied prisoners in the Pacific theater; *The Blue Max* (20th Century-Fox, 1966) covered World War I air combat from the German point of view; and *Lost Command* (Columbia, 1966) was a far-ranging look at the French Special Forces.

Stanley Kramer's production of *Judgment at Nuremberg* told the story of the war crimes trials after World War II with stark realism. Here are Maximilian Schell and Richard Widmark in a scene from the film.

Otto Preminger turned to a war story when he directed *In Harm's Way*.

A trio of important 1964 features dealt, in one way or another, with the possibility that failure of U.S. military personnel to live up to their obligations might lead to nuclear war. The bitterest, yet most comic, among them was Stanley Kubrick's *Dr. Strangelove* (Columbia). Sidney Lumet's *Fail Safe* (Columbia) used Henry Fonda as the U.S. President and told a similar story about technological or human error leading to a nuclear holocaust. John Frankenheimer's *Seven Days in May* (Paramount), set in the future, had a similarly quiescent U.S. President (Fredric March) faced with a general (Burt Lancaster) who would lead a mutiny against the government. These themes, and their responsible handling, would scarcely have been possible ten years earlier.

Drama: Sex, Romance and Love

Romantic screen stories made during the 1960's tended to seek unusual pairings of players, odd aspects of love-making and exotic locales. The overseas location had a twofold purpose of adding the spice of distance to the stories and making possible the use of foreign talent and facilities and jointly owned production firms. Many films emphasized the Gallic touch, such as *In the French Style* (Columbia, 1963), and France was best served visually in Joshua Logan's *Fanny* (Warners, 1961), whose cast included four leads, not one of whom was American— Leslie Caron, Horst Buchholz, Maurice Chevalier and Charles Boyer. Vincente Minnelli's *Two Weeks in Another Town* (MGM, 1962) was shot in Rome with a largely American cast headed by Kirk Douglas and Cyd Charisse, while *Hatari!* (Paramount, 1962) featured John Wayne, an overseas cast and Central African locales. Many films were set in England (where American financial control of local movie production firms was most blatant), such as the Julie Andrews–James Garner film *The Americanization of Emily* (MGM, 1964).

A constant in romantic melodrama was the theme of lovers of disparate ages, such as the Marlon Brando–Anna Magnani interchange in *The Fugitive Kind* (United Artists, 1960) or Lola Albright's role opposite TV star Scott Marlowe in *A Cold Wind in August* (1961). Similarly offbeat couples had populated the U.S. screen in the past, but the 1960's brought a taste for neurotic or outright psychopathic lovers. Some of the more disturbed were to be seen in Universal's *Kitten With a Whip* (1964), in William Wyler's *The Collector* (Columbia, 1965), and in the Richard Burton–Elizabeth Taylor *Who's Afraid of Virginia Woolf?* (1966). Other couples were even institutionalized, such as Keir Dullea and Janet Margolin in *David and Lisa* (Continental, 1963) and the Warren Beatty–Jean Seberg pair in Robert Rossen's last feature, *Lilith* (Columbia, 1964).

Romantic comedies, too, tended to be more offbeat and somewhat sexually permissive. The moods of such 1965 features as *What's New, Pussycat?* (United Artists) and *A Very Special Favor* (Universal) would have been impossible to film in the 1940's. On the other hand, the screen humor of the 1960's did not always require a new permissiveness. The situations in which Glenn Ford found himself in *The Courtship of Eddie's Father* (MGM, 1963) and Rock Hudson in *Strange Bedfellows* (Universal, 1965) might have been seen on the screen of the 1930's.

The homey virtues in romantic drama were shown in a series of Disney's Buena Vista productions, such as the 1964 *Those Calloways* or *A Tiger Walks*, or in such non-Disney films as *Born Free* (Columbia, 1966). Indicating the growing link between features made for theaters and those made for TV (see below), the Disney features were quickly released on the small screen.

There were still many high-budget romantic dramas that could properly be called women's pictures. Among the lead players and roles with whom the woman in the audience still identified were Natalie Wood in *Splendor in the Grass*, (Warners, 1961) directed by Elia Kazan, Marilyn Monroe's playing opposite Clark Gable in *The Misfits* (United Artists, 1961), the Janet Leigh role in *Wives and Lovers* (Paramount, 1963), the Susan Hayward and Bette Davis roles in *Where Love Has Gone* (Paramount, 1964), Elizabeth Taylor in *The Sandpiper* (MGM, 1965) and Sophia Loren in MGM's *Lady L* (1966).

Many spectacles were based on the Bible, most of them wide-screen and in color. *The Story of Ruth* (20th Century-Fox, 1960) was in CinemaScope; the Samuel Bronston–Nicholas Ray production of *King of Kings* (MGM, 1961), in Technirama; while George Stevens' three-years-in-the-shooting *The Greatest Story Ever Told* (United Artists, 1965) in Cinerama featured Swedish star Max von Sydow as Christ. The wide screen and color had become essential to achieve decent domestic grosses; but Biblical films of the 1960's reputedly did proportionally better business in Europe.

Several spectacles set in the same era dealt with Judeo-Christian conflicts, Imperial Rome's problems or related topics. The Technirama feature *Spartacus* (Universal, 1960), as directed by Stanley Kubrick and based on Howard Fast's novel, had pro-Christian and anti-Roman sentiments, allusions to homosexuality, and violence in and out of the arena. An even more violent and spectacular treatment of a similar subject was *Barabbas* (Columbia, 1962), shot by Richard Fleischer in Technirama, with Anthony Quinn and a largely foreign cast; like many of the new spectacles, *Barabbas* was shot (and first released) overseas. Wyler's *Ben-Hur* (MGM, 1959) dressed Lew Wallace's novel in Camera 65 and starred the decade's most heroic actor-symbol of all, Charlton Heston. Heston progressed through many spectacles of the 1960's: in TV director Franklin Schaffner's *The War Lord* (Universal, 1965), he played the title role in a pre-Renaissance Europe beset by invaders and witchcraft, and the title role in *Major Dundee* (Columbia, 1965); in *The Agony and the Ecstasy* (20th Century-Fox, 1965) he played a sensitive and realistic Michelangelo.

The spectacle to end all spectacles was *Cleopatra* (20th Century-Fox, 1963), finally completed by director Joseph L. Mankiewicz after a succession of producers, directors and writers had been forced to leave the three-year production. Stars Richard Burton and Elizabeth Taylor, and a $20-million shooting cost (plus a similar amount for advertising) helped make this Todd-AO production the most expensive and publicized feature of all time.

Less ambitious but no less impressive spectacle films of the 1960's were set in more modern times. These include Richard Brooks' production of *Lord Jim* (Columbia, 1965), a *fin de siècle* tour of the South Seas, with British actor Peter O'Toole in the title role, and Cornel Wilde's directorial-acting effort, *The Naked Prey* (Paramount, 1966), set in the wilds of Africa, and the anti-war film *Beach Red* (United Artists, 1967). A favorite vehicle of contemporary spectacle since the 1930's was the racing-car film; among the worst was Howard Hawks' *Red Line 7000* (Paramount, 1965), and among the best Frankenheimer's *Grand Prix* (MGM, 1966).

MUSICALS AND COMEDIES

"Fewer pictures, but better ones."

In the realm of musicals and comedies, this slogan explains what happened in the 1960's: live and filmed musical shows were everywhere on TV, and theaters had to have better musical attractions in order to draw customers to the box office. Similarly, the A and B comedy series of the past were supplanted by TV's many comedies, so theatrically released comedies became bigger and often better.

Within a year, three of Hollywood's finest musicals were premiered. The earliest of the trio, *Mary Poppins* (1964), was the work of Disney's Buena Vista and had Julie Andrews in the title role opposite TV favorite Dick Van Dyke. A "sleeper," *Mary Poppins* proved one of Hollywood's most popular musicals and most profitable features of any genre. Julie Andrews also starred in *The Sound of Music* (20th Century-Fox, 1965), Robert Wise's splendid version of the Rodgers and Hammerstein musical (and a remake of a West German musical film of almost a decade earlier), which broke all hard-ticket records during its first year and became the biggest box-office success in history. The third major musical hit was *My Fair Lady* (Warners, 1964), in which George Cukor used Audrey Hepburn in the role created by Julie Andrews on stage and Rex Harrison in a repeat of his Broadway success.

The Sound of Music, with the religious aspects of the flight of the Trapp family from Nazi Austria, was related to a musical comedy cycle that was well under way by spring of 1966. *The Singing Nun* (MGM, 1966), with Debbie Reynolds, did well at the box office, as did the comedy

Cleopatra was the spectacle to end all spectacles. This production turned out to be the most publicized and expensive film ever made. Elizabeth Taylor and Rex Harrison were two of the stars of the production.

about nuns and their charges, *The Trouble With Angels* (Columbia, 1966), Ida Lupino's first feature directorial assignment in almost ten years, starring Rosalind Russell.

Other important musicals ranged from the tragic *West Side Story* (United Artists, 1961), through one of the decade's few jazz-oriented musicals, *Paris Blues* (United Artists, 1961) to "standard" dramatic musicals such as *Bye Bye Birdie* (Columbia, 1963). Styles went from formal set pieces such as *Camelot* (Warner Brothers-7 Arts, 1967) to Ross Hunter's corncake and profitable *Thoroughly Modern Millie* (Universal, 1967). The only sure bet of the 1960's musical remained Elvis Presley, who sang in a host of features such as *Frankie and Johnny* (United Artists, 1966) and *Speedway* (MGM).

The realm of screen comedy was also given over in large part to the bigger film. Billy Wilder's *One! Two! Three!* (United Artists, 1961) was filmed at fairly high budget in the United States and Europe and featured James Cagney,

My Fair Lady was brought to Hollywood by Jack Warner, and the production proved that a successful Broadway musical could be made into an equally successful Hollywood musical. Audrey Hepburn played the role originally played on Broadway by Julie Andrews.

33

West Side Story was a new type of musical for Hollywood. The story, dealing with the battles of two teenage gangs on the streets of New York, was directed by Robert Wise and Jerome Robbins. Here, one of the scenes is before the camera.

Horst Buchholz, Arlene Francis and a European supporting cast. Wilder moved into color comedy with the Jack Lemmon–Shirley MacLaine film *Irma La Douce* (United Artists, 1963) and went to black-and-white with Dean Martin and Kim Novak in *Kiss Me, Stupid!* (Lopert, 1964) and to greater sarcasm with *The Fortune Cookie* (United Artists, 1966). Jerry Lewis began the decade by starring in other producer-directors' black-and-white comedies, such as *Visit to a Small Planet* (Paramount, 1960), then moved to his own color efforts, such as *The Nutty Professor* (Paramount, 1963) or his multiroled *The Family Jewels* (1965). Fine sex-and-romance-oriented comedies proliferated; most had big stars, color, and some form of wide screen, and most were remakes of literary or stage properties: *Breakfast at Tiffany's* (Paramount, 1961), *Send Me No Flowers* (Universal, 1964), *The Unsinkable Molly Brown* (MGM, 1964), *Boeing-Boeing* (Paramount, 1965).

Some screen comedies took more offbeat routes, among them Stanley Kramer's all-star *It's a Mad, Mad, Mad, Mad World* (United Artists, 1963) and Blake Edwards' often slapstick *The Great Race* (Warners, 1965). "Sick" or "black" comedy had a field day in the all-star fiasco *The Loved One* (MGM, 1965), the film from Evelyn Waugh's novel with "something to offend everyone" and in *Oh Dad, Poor Dad, Mama's Hung You in the Closet and I'm Feeling So Sad* with Rosalind Russell, Jonathan Winters and Robert Morse (Paramount, 1967). Perhaps the most bizarre comedy of all was *Batman* (20th Century-Fox, 1966), the color feature reprise of the then smash TV show, with TV stars Adam West and Burt Ward and the supporting cast of "villains." *Batman* did fantastic business in one summer month of theatrical exposure.

In many ways, the Western grew bigger, too. A Cinerama Western with three directors and a large cast, and covering a half century of history, was *How the West Was Won*. This fine MGM picture illustrated, however, the technical problems in flattening wide-screen systems for "normal" exhibition: its process shots looked bad in the flattened version. It was released in Europe in 1962, more than a year before its American premiere. The tendency toward sprawling Westerns can be discerned in such films as the half-comic Burt Lancaster film *The Hallelujah Trail* (United Artists, 1965), the outright comedy *Cat Ballou* (Columbia, 1965), and the John Wayne film *The Sons of Katie Elder* (Paramount, 1965).

The decade saw many old favorites back in Western action: Kirk Douglas in *The Last Sunset* (Universal, 1961), the modern *Lonely Are the Brave* (Universal, 1962) and *The War Wagon* (Universal, 1967); Henry Fonda in *The Rounders* (MGM, 1965) and *Welcome to Hard Times* (MGM, 1967); Richard Widmark in John Ford's *Two Rode Together* (Columbia, 1961), with James Stewart, and in the same director's lovely *Cheyenne Autumn* (Warners, 1964); James Stewart in *The Man Who Shot Liberty Valance* (Paramount, 1962), with John Wayne and Lee Marvin, and in *Shenandoah* (1965); Wayne in *The Comancheros* (20th Century-Fox, 1961), *McLintock* (United Artists, 1963) and *El Dorado* (Paramount, 1967); and Joel McCrea and Randolph Scott in *Ride the High Country* (MGM, 1962). As *Hombre* (20th Century-Fox, 1967), Paul Newman impressed critics and audiences alike and threatened to start a new wave in Westerns all his own.

The 1960's brought some players seldom seen in Westerns to the front lines: Red Buttons and Bing Crosby to the remake of *Stagecoach* (20th Century-Fox, 1966), Elvis Presley to *Flaming Star* (20th Century-Fox, 1960), and Linda Darnell in her last feature, *Black Spurs* (Paramount, 1965). The four biggest production companies did not completely neglect the medium-budget Western, which proved itself a profitable staple in such films as MGM's *Son of a Gunfighter* (1966), Paramount's *Stage to Thunder Rock* (1964), 20th's *The Reward* (1965) and Columbia's *The Great Sioux Massacre* (1965). Universal had made the form its feature backbone and 1966 alone brought such fine Western B films as *Incident at Phantom Hill*, *Gunpoint* and *The Rare Breed*. Allied Artists followed this pattern with films such as *Blood on the Arrow* (1964), and Embassy entered the field with *The Bounty Killer* (1965).

MYSTERY AND CRIME

The series mystery was no longer a staple in the 1960's. TV now served these tastes. Attempts to bring back the series detective, such as *The Return of Mr. Moto* (20th Century-Fox, 1965) met with massive failure. Moreover, the element of crime-fighting had entered many other kinds of films: comedies such as *The Great Chase* and *Batman*, dramatic features such as *To Kill a Mockingbird* and *The Chase*, and many science-fiction and horror films. In addition, the main tenets of the mystery—unknown guilty party, clues and pursuit—had been shifted to the more popular espionage film.

Nonetheless, straight mysteries continued to appear. Hitchcock used Tippi Hedren and Sean Connery in *Marnie* (Universal, 1964), after having begun his contribution to the decade with the bizarre Tony Perkins film *Psycho* (Paramount, 1960). Robert Aldrich directed such features as *What Ever Happened to Baby Jane?* (Warners, 1962), with Joan Crawford and Bette Davis, and *Hush . . . Hush, Sweet Charlotte* (20th Century-Fox, 1965), with Davis and Olivia De Havilland before slipping into espionage/sabotage with *The Dirty Dozen* (MGM, 1967). Producer-director William Castle (of the Whistler and Crime Doctor series two decades before) emphasized shock tactics in films such as *Zotz!* (Columbia, 1962), *13 Frightened Girls* (Columbia, 1963) and *I Saw What You Did* (Universal, 1965).

The realistic documentary style of criminal melodrama lost ground in the 1960's due to the competition of such TV series as "Naked City" and "The Defenders." A few good ones appeared nonetheless: John Frankenheimer's *The Young Savages* (United Artists, 1961), with Burt Lancaster as a district attorney and Shelley Winters as a slum mother, and Otto Preminger's *Bunny Lake Is Missing* (Columbia, 1965), with Carol Lynley and Laurence Olivier. Even realism ran the gamut of styles in the 1960's though: Roger Corman recreated the Chicago 1920's in *The St. Valentine's Day Massacre* (20th Century-Fox, 1967); Arthur Penn the 1930's in a nouvelle vague-ish excess starring Warren Beatty and Faye Dunaway which fractured the critics, *Bonnie and Clyde* (WB-7 Arts, 1967); and interregional racial problems were cleverly turned topsy-turvy in Norman Jewison's *In the Heat of the Night* (UA, 1967). One character of realistic crime drama had a minor renaissance—the hardboiled "private eye." Mike Hammer came back, played by his author Mickey Spillane himself in the Roy Rowland Colorama production *The Girl Hunters* (1963). Craig Stevens played *Gunn* in the Paramount feature of the same name (1967), while John Ross MacDonald's detective Lew Archer was retitled *Harper* (Warners, 1966) and played by Paul Newman. Sometimes members of the police force went "hard-boiled" and private to bring justice to the parties, as in Buzz Kulik's *Warning Shot* (Paramount, 1967) and in Gordon Douglas' *Tony Rome* (20th Century-Fox, 1967) starring Frank Sinatra.

THE ESPIONAGE FILM

Impetus for the spy wave were the James Bond British features, which began being released (in England) in 1962 with *Dr. No* (United Artists). Though most of these films employed European actors, half of the production teams and most of the finance behind them were American.

With production and advertising costs recovered in Britain alone, the American releases that followed within six months represented almost pure profit. The main ingredients of these films were sophistication, sexy dialogue and footage and unmotivated violence.

A fair case can be made for the allegation that big-budget American spy features preceded the Bonds. Typically, however, those preceding the Bonds were workmanlike B's about World War II, such as *The Enemy General* (Columbia, 1960), or anti-Communist coproductions shot in black and white, such as Richard Widmark's production *The Secret Ways* (Universal, 1961). When an A budget was risked on an espionage theme, there had to be the assurance of a name cast, as Frank Sinatra, Janet Leigh and Laurence Harvey in Frankenheimer's *The Manchurian Candidate* (United Artists, 1962), or a prime cast plus color as in the William Holden spectacular-travelogue *The Counterfeit Traitor* (Paramount, 1962).

After Bond's impact was felt, American production teams eased into his format: *Mirage* (Universal, 1965) with Gregory Peck, *The Saboteur, Code Name—Morituri* (20th, 1965) with Marlon Brando, and *Father Goose* (Universal, 1965) with Cary Grant used big stars and bigger budgets to tell spy stories. But with *The Satan Bug* (United Artists, 1965) and *36 Hours* (MGM, 1964), American producers moved into the familiar Bond ground of master spies, criminal masterminds and scientific gadgetry. Universal resurrected Bulldog Drummond in a garish color job (shot in Britain), *Deadlier Than the Male* (1967). In 1966 Dean Martin began his characterization of Matt Helm in *The Silencers, Murderer's Row* and *The Ambushers* (Columbia); Rock Hudson and Claudia Cardinale played lovers in flight from agents in *Blindfold* (Universal); Julie Andrews pursued Paul Newman behind the Iron Curtain in *Torn Curtain;* Gregory Peck played a professor and Sophia Loren a spy in *Arabesque* (Universal); and James Coburn

The impact of James Bond on the film world was undeniable. Audiences flocked into the theaters in tremendous numbers. Gimmicks abounded and the superhero was back in action. James Bond made a flying escape in *Thunderball*.

Spies and counterspies were everywhere. Richard Burton made his escape from East Berlin in *The Spy Who Came In From the Cold*, while Claire Bloom failed to get over the wall.

was *Our Man Flint* (20th Century-Fox) and *In Like Flint* (20th Century-Fox, 1967). There were some signs that the Bond cycle was about to turn in on itself, in such films as the bittersweet British-agent characterization by Michael Caine in Universal's *The Ipcress File* (1965) and *Funeral in Berlin* (1966), and particularly in Richard Burton's characterization of a foiled agent in *The Spy Who Came In From the Cold* (1965). But even bitterness and realism were escalated to less than believable heights in Lumet's *The Deadly Affair* (Columbia, 1967) and in the high-budget Frank Sinatra-starrer *The Naked Runner* (Warners, 1967).

FANTASY, SCIENCE FICTION AND HORROR

As with espionage features, American producers took their lead in horror films in the 1960's from the British. The color Hammer films based on Universal properties of the late 1950's—*The Curse of Frankenstein, The Horror of Dracula, The Curse of the Werewolf*—began to be imitated in the United States. Permissiveness of a sadistic variety was apparent in the British features, which were sold with extra footage so that local censors could replace offensive portions with milder ones. As a direct response to the British trends came medium-budget features such as *My Blood Runs Cold* (Warners, 1965) starring Troy Donahue; the William Castle productions *Strait-Jacket* (Columbia, 1963) with Joan Crawford and *The Night Walker* (Universal, 1965) with Robert Taylor and Barbara Stanwyck and outright British coproductions such as Paramount's *The Deadly Bees* and Joan Crawford's *Berserk!* (Columbia, 1967). At American International the Roger Corman-Vincent Price/Edgar Allan Poe cycle hit its stride with *The House of Usher* (1960) and *The Pit and the Pendulum* (1961). Corman used Ray Milland in *X—The*

Man With the X-Ray Eyes (1963) and Boris Karloff in *The Terror* (1963). Despite Corman's short shooting schedules (*The Terror* was shot in less than three days), most of his 1960's hits were uniformly beautiful in color, well acted and fairly savage in content.

The 1960's brought returnees to the horror and science-fiction genre, particularly directors who had not recently worked in it. Robert Wise made *The Haunting* (MGM, 1963); puppetoon veteran George Pal introduced horror elements into his wide-screen *The Wonderful World of the Brothers Grimm* (MGM, 1962) and *The Time Machine* (MGM, 1960), and even Alfred Hitchcock used fantasy and horror throughout *The Birds* (Universal, 1963). Another kind of returnee was that of content: the Golem legend was brought back to the screen after a thirty-year hiatus in *It* (WB-7 Arts, 1967), while dead Nazis represented most of the menace in *The Frozen Dead* (WB-7 Arts, 1967).

In addition, the number of fantasy films was even greater than in the 1950's: these productions ranged from W. Lee Wilder's very inexpensive 58-minute film *Fright* to the enormous budget of Raquel Welch's first-released feature, *Fantastic Voyage* (20th Century-Fox, 1965). Responsible younger directors, who had been working in TV, were absorbed with fantasy: Ray Milland with his fine *Panic in the Year Zero* (American International, 1962), Arthur Penn with the very strange *Mickey One* (Columbia, 1965), and John Frankenheimer with his bizarre Rock Hudson feature *Seconds* (Paramount, 1966). Among contemporary phenomena examined were the hippies in Columbia's *The Love-In* (1967), the world of the psychedelic, *The Trip* (AIP, 1967), and post-adolescent motorcyclers, *Born Losers* (AIP, 1967), *Hell's Angels on Wheels* (U.S. Films, 1967).

TRENDS

As the decade of the 1960's moves toward its close, American sound features seem to show the following trends:

Internationalism. Since about the mid-1950's, Hollywood's men and money have regained control of world production and now have a king-sized stake in much of what is being exhibited the world over. This has been accomplished by (1) direct and indirect ownership of foreign production facilities, financing of those not yet owned, and coproduction; (2) shooting in foreign locations and/or the use of highly refined dubbing techniques; (3) employment of foreign personnel en masse.

But what is new here?

Ownership is the key; both Government and private financial literature reveal an astonishing degree of American control over South American and European heavy and light industry, with the motion picture industry leading most other industries. In the early 1950's, Columbia had its Warwick in Britain, 20th utilized Roxy in West Germany and France to free funds blocked in Europe, etc. Everyone knew of such linkages and no one was surprised by them.

But, by the late 1960's, independent and "house" production packagers in Europe were hard pressed to find *any* continental production facility which was *not* American owned or controlled.

Therefore, American-based production crews routinely shoot footage overseas; and nowadays this includes work on features for theaters, telefeatures, and even TV-series films. Moreover, Hollywoodites, as well as the California and New York banking interests which supply their funds, think in terms of a world audience: much of the product must not only draw the teenager in Toledo, but audiences everywhere.

Some things have not changed: no one is astonished that Richard Fleischer shot *Doctor Dolittle* (20th, 1967) partly in Britain or that Andrew Marton shot *Africa, Texas Style* (Paramount, 1967) at home *and* abroad; such activities routinely occurred in the thirties. But American crews travel in and out of Rome nowadays (e.g., Huston's production of *The Bible* (Laurentis, 1966) as they once did in and out of Balboa, California, and similar U.S. teams work in every major European capital. Even Canada, once terra incognita for American *and* Canadian production, is becoming a major U.S. production site, viz Mark Rydell's *The Fox* (WB-7 Arts, 1968), or the telefeature *Dr. Jekyll and Mr. Hyde* (Dan Curtis Productions, 1968).

Concurrently, American production companies now hire distinguished foreign directors without a second thought, some for features designed mostly for U.S. audiences, some for foreign audiences, and some for world audiences. Such directors include David Lean (*Dr. Zhivago*), Luchino Visconti (*The Leopard*), Claude Chabrol (*The Champagne Murders*), and François Truffaut (*Fahrenheit 451*). An early 1965 symposium of European directors revealed that many believed that, except for some TV work and B products, there might soon be no native feature production.

Interrelationship of Theater Features and TV. Today many features are televised soon after theatrical release. This applies not only to European "spy packages" and "mystery packages" which *never* make U.S. theatres but which are block-sold in thirteen-feature lots direct to U.S. TV networks, but also to American features themselves. At time of writing fewer than 600 English-language sound features had *not* been sold for U.S. televising, and the average lag between theatrical premiere and first televising in the U.S. is down to about a year. While this has hurt theater business, it has also had the effect of triggering a shortage of feature product, which can be filled only by shooting more new features.

The relationship of feature production to TV-film production has not developed via features based on TV series, as was common in the fifties.

Instead, some of those who wished to rent new products to theaters merely spliced together previously televised TV-series segments to make "new" features. Where the series

was of quality, the "feature" was usable, as were the "Man from U.N.C.L.E." features from MGM: *One Spy Too Many* (1966), *The Spy in the Green Hat* (1967), etc., or in the "FBI" series feature *Cosa Nostra* (Warners-7 Arts, 1967). But more often such "assembly job" features were suitable only for European exhibition or for television itself, as, for example, *I Deal In Danger* (20th Century-Fox, 1966), taken from the short-run Robert Goulet TV series, "Blue Light."

Since the relative failure of "Pay-TV" in the decade 1955–1965, other and more prescient moviemakers tried a new tack of producing features directly for TV premiere and for later release in theaters at home and abroad. TV series themselves having replaced the old-fashioned theatrically released "B" series, today's "telefeatures" have had to compete with theatrical films in cast, direction and (sometimes) production values.

The first serious attempt to shoot features for TV was launched by Universal in 1963–1964, which intended to begin its telefeature schedule of two-hour (less commercials) films with Don Siegel's *The Killers*, with Lee Marvin and Angie Dickinson. N. B. C. executives were horrified by Siegel's effort, however, and this first intended telefeature went into theaters instead (1964). Universal's next, *See How They Run*, thus became the first telefeature actually to premiere on the small screen. The date of this historic telecast—October 7, 1964—might ultimately prove of as much significance to Hollywood as the introduction of sound features. Though this telefeature proved unpopular, Universal's next, Don Siegel's *The Hanged Man* (1964), drew large audiences.

Despite the inconclusiveness of the Universal experiment, Telsun Foundation, Inc. pushed into the telefeature race on December 28, 1964 with its two-hour, star-studded *Carol for Another Christmas*, which represented Joseph L. Mankiewicz' first TV effort and featured Peter Sellers, Sterling Hayden and a Rod Serling script. Though Telsun's next two, *Who Has Seen the Wind?* (1965, with Edward G. Robinson) and *Once Upon a Tractor* (1965, directed by Argentinian importee Leopoldo Torre Nilsson), bombed badly, the fourth Telsun effort, *The Poppy Is Also a Flower*, signaled a new and real lesson (and danger) to theater exhibitors. *Poppy* was directed by Bond-specialist Terence Young, had a script based on an Ian Fleming property and featured Yul Brynner, E. G. Marshall, Rita Hayworth and literally dozens of other stars. Premiering on U.S. TV on April 22, 1966, *Poppy* did turnaway business in a Viennese theater the following week and went on to high theatrical profit throughout Europe and back in the United States. In 1966, Columbia meekly entered the telefeature lists with *Scalplock*.

Meantime, Universal slammed back during the 1966–67 TV season with *Fame is the Name of the Game* (a remake of *Chicago Deadline*, Paramount, 1949), which broke all previous feature viewership records on U.S. TV (except for that of the televising of *The Bridge on the River Kwai*) and *The Birds*, until another Universal telefeature, Rod Serling's *Doomsday Flight*, achieved even higher viewership. Though subsequently released 1967 Universal telefeatures tended to just slog along (e.g., *How I Spent My Summer Vacation*, *The Longest Hundred Miles*, *Wings of Fire*, *The Borgia Stick*), the dikes were down and a flood of successful telefeatures really began to make a dent in theater business.

MGM began its telefeatures with *The Dangerous Days of Kiowa Jones* (1966), an inoffensive Western starring Robert Horton, and progressed to the Robert Taylor starrer *Return of the Gunfighter* (1967). With Richard Thorpe's *The Scorpio Letters* (1967), the studio demonstrated that it could apply to a telefeature all the gloss and production values that it had to theatrically destined features. And, like Universal, MGM played the so-called "switch and swap" game with TV networks; some telefeatures (*Hot Rods to Hell*, 1966; *Welcome to Hard Times*, 1967) went into theaters first anyway.

Nor has all been sunny on the telefeature front; Hy Averback's *Chamber of Horrors* (Warners, 1966) proved to be too much of a shocker and it went to theaters and not (yet) to TV. Producer Roy Huggins decided that two of his Universal telefeatures, (*The Scavengers*, *The Adversaries*) would do better if cut up to make TV *series* episodes. Producer-director John Moxey scrapped his telefeature *Dr. Jekyll and Mr. Hyde* and turned it over to a Canadian production crew, who *taped* the "film" for its TV premiere. N. B. C. kicked James Goldstone's *Jigsaw* out of its 1968 schedule because of this telefeature's spotlighting of nudity and psychedelia. And RKO elected to premiere its telefeature *Some May Live* via TV in five cities only (1967), going the theatrical route in the rest of the world.

But the handwriting is on the wall for all to see. Universal's telefeature *Stranger on the Run* (1967) featured Henry Fonda, Anne Baxter, Sal Mineo and the now ubiquitous color—and significantly cut into theater attendance on the night it was telecast (Halloween, as it happened). At time of writing such "names" as Glenn Ford, Bob Hope, and Robert Taylor have completed telefeatures, and virtually every big-name director and scripter in Hollywood has signed on for one TV-film project or another. An actual count of all features shot in the United States by MGM, Universal and C. B. S. *Theatrical* Films (sic!) during the winter of 1967–1968 reveals that just under half are destined for TV premieres.

The Surfacing of Underground Films. There had always been little films shot away from the normal production sources: art films, experimental films, pornographic films, all manner of independently produced films destined for specialized audiences outside the standard theater circuits. Perhaps the 1960's major innovation was that such films were propelled into the mainstream of production and into four-wall theatres.

What happened in the 1960's can be seen as a juncture of the art/experimental film movement with the pornographic movement via virtually standard production/distribution channels.

The art film movement of the sixties was first called the "New American Cinema" and represented the work of painters, poets and other nonprofessionals working on shoestring budgets. Many of the film makers clustered around the editors of New York's *Film Culture* magazine, run by the Mekas brothers and their staff; many of the films were first shown in the city's Film-Makers'. Cinémathèque. The movement had had its American origins in screen poems created by Ben Hecht (*Spectre of the Rose*), Hans Richter (*Dreams That Money Can Buy*) and others back in the forties and in such items as Kenneth Anger's homosexual-oriented *Fireworks* (1947). However, the first Underground feature to be seen by a broad public was certainly Shirley Clarke's *The Connection* (Films-Around-the-World, 1961). This feature was screened in several "standard" locations, as was the director's succeeding feature about Harlem Negroes, *The Cool World* (Cinema V, 1964). In these pictures and in such works as Mekas' *The Brig* (1964) and Anger's film about cyclists, *Scorpio Rising* (1963), offbeat sexual themes had already been limelighted and nonprofessional casts plus deliberately jerky photography been used. At first, few of such "Underground features" could favorably be compared in any way with Hollywood's commercial output.

Another prong of the Underground thrust was the pornographic, or near-pornographic, film. Originally, the blatantly sex-directed features (e.g., William Mishkin's *The Orgy at Lil's Place*, circa 1962) had little in common with the objectives of the art film movement. Gradually, though, the pornographic element was grafted onto some art films. If any one man can be said to have presided most at this Underground wedding, he would be Andy Warhol. Nudity, frank dialogue and outright sexual titillation (to suit *many* tastes) were present in most of Warhol's features, from his slice of life on the split screen, *The Chelsea Girls* (1966), through the hetero/homosexual cheapie *Bike Boy* (1967) and the incredibly frank dialogue and visuals of *The Nude Restaurant* (1967). The Warhol features, like those of the Mekas brothers and Clarke, saw exhibition in some theaters in most of America's largest cities.

A subsidiary category of pornographic feature was that which mixed sexuality with frankly sadist themes. Early features in this pattern, such as James Landis' *The Sadist* (Fairway, 1963) or Herschel G. Lewis' *2,000 Maniacs* (1964) and *Blood Feast* (1965), were unexhibitable in most United States locations and could be seen only privately in Britain. But as the 1960's pressed forward, sexploitation films more generally entered theaters, as did Paul Mart's *Sinderella and the Golden Bra* (1966) and sadist features such as Russ Meyer's *Faster Pussycat, Kill! Kill!* (1967). Early in the 1960's, in a TV interview, producer-director

Otto Preminger pooh-poohed part of the Underground movement with "No one ever made a million dollars from dirty movies." While this is still true, and while there are some signs that pornographic features may cost exhibitors more than they can earn from them, the Underground movement in general has made substantial impact on many professional moviemen. Directors Arthur Penn, Sidney Lumet and Elia Kazan, among many Hollywoodites, have favored Underground experimentation and sung the praises of some of the Underground features as having opened new streams of creativity.

Many "standard" features, such as Joseph Strick's *The Balcony* (Continental, 1963), starring Shelley Winters and Peter Falk, adopted the technology and themes of the movement. Other features, such as Strick's *Ulysses* (Columbia, 1967), have included dialogue impossible only five years before, while others mixed such dialogue with new and extreme sexual situations, as did Anthony Harvey's *Dutchman* (Planet Films, 1967). Other theatrically released features spotlighted themes of sadism, as did Walter Grauman's relatively mild *Lady in a Cage* (Paramount, 1964) and Peter Collinson's *The Penthouse* (Paramount, 1967).

By 1968, the Underground and nudie movements had produced at least one talented director who went on to "straight" features: Francis Ford Coppola, who in his mid-twenties directed Warners features *You're a Big Boy Now* (1967) and *Finian's Rainbow* (1968).

Technological Innovation. The 1960's did not bring anything as new as 3-D or Cinerama.

Warners employed, for use with *Chamber of Horrors* (1966) and other features, the "fear flasher" and "horror horn" as extra-screen additives, but these sensory mechanisms were little more impressive than the contraptions which William Castle had used for several of his 1950's features (the "tingle" effect, a skeleton on wires, etc.). Feel-o-vision and Smell-o-vision have been tried and are promised for the future, but little is expected from these effects.

Perhaps only Spacevision, a three-dimensional system (for which polaroid glasses would still, unfortunately, be needed) developed by Arch Oboler after he sifted two men out of more than one hundred inventors, will prove its merit as *the* new development of the decade. The first Spacevision feature, *The Bubble* (1967), utilized the Spacevision process (as well as Oboler's penchant for macabre stories); its box office results in Midwest tests were encouraging.

CHAPTER II

THE PLAYERS

Nat Pendleton, Bud Abbott and Lou Costello in *Buck Privates*.

ABBOTT AND COSTELLO

BUD ABBOTT (William A. Abbott) Born October 2, 1895, Asbury Park, New Jersey. Married Betty Pratt (1918), children: Bud, Vickie.

LOU COSTELLO (Louis Francis Cristillo) Born March 6, 1908, Paterson, New Jersey. Married Anne Balter (1934), children: Patricia, Carole, Christine. Died March 3, 1959.

Sound Feature Films: *One Night in the Tropics* (Univ., 1940), *Buck Privates* (Univ., 1941), *In the Navy* (Univ., 1941), *Hold That Ghost* (Univ., 1941), *Keep 'Em Flying* (Univ., 1941), *Ride 'Em Cowboy* (Univ., 1942), *Rio Rita* (MGM, 1942), *Pardon My Sarong* (Univ., 1942), *Who*

Done It? (Univ., 1942), *It Ain't Hay* (Univ., 1943), *Hit the Ice* (Univ., 1943), *Lost in a Harem* (Univ., 1944), *In Society* (Univ., 1944), *Here Come the Co-eds* (Univ., 1945), *The Naughty Nineties* (Univ., 1945), *Bud Abbott and Lou Costello in Hollywood* (MGM, 1945), *Little Giant* (Univ., 1946), *The Time of Their Lives* (Univ., 1946), *Buck Privates Come Home* (Univ., 1947), *The Wistful Widow of Wagon Gap* (Univ., 1947), *The Noose Hangs High* (EL, 1948), *Abbott and Costello Meet Frankenstein* (Univ., 1948), *Mexican Hayride* (Univ., 1948), *Africa Screams* (UA, 1949), *Abbott and Costello Meet the Killer* (Univ., 1949), *Abbott and Costello in the Foreign Legion* (Univ., 1950), *Abbott and Costello Meet the Invisible Man* (Univ., 1951), *Comin' Round the Mountain* (Univ., 1951), *Jack and the Beanstalk* (WB, 1952), *Lost in Alaska* (Univ., 1952), *Abbott and Costello Meet Captain Kidd* (WB, 1952), *Abbott and Costello Go to Mars* (Univ., 1953), *Abbott and Costello Meet Dr. Jekyll and Mr. Hyde* (Univ., 1953), *Abbott and Costello Meet the Keystone Kops* (Univ., 1955), *Abbott and Costello Meet the Mummy* (Univ., 1955), *Dance With Me, Henry* (UA, 1956), *The 30 Foot Bride of Candy Rock* (Col., 1959).*

*Without Bud Abbott.

WALTER ABEL Born June 6, 1898, St. Paul, Minnesota. Married Marietta Bitter (1926).

Sound Feature Films: *The Three Musketeers* (RKO, 1935), *The Lady Consents* (RKO, 1936), *Two in the Dark* (RKO, 1936), *The Witness Chair* (RKO, 1936), *Fury* (MGM, 1936), *We Went to College* (MGM, 1936), *Second Wife* (RKO, 1936), *Portia on Trial* (Rep., 1937), *Wise Girl* (RKO, 1937), *Law of the Underworld* (RKO, 1938), *Racket Busters* (WB, 1938), *Men With Wings* (Par., 1938), *King of the Turf* (UA, 1939), *A Miracle on Main Street* (Col., 1940), *Dance, Girl, Dance* (RKO, 1940), *Arise, My Love* (Par., 1940), *Michael Shayne, Private Detective* (20th, 1940), *Who Killed Aunt Maggie?* (Rep., 1940), *Hold Back the Dawn* (Par., 1941), *Skylark* (Par., 1941), *Glamour Boy* (Par., 1941), *Beyond the Blue Horizon* (Par., 1942), *Holiday Inn* (Par., 1942), *Wake Island* (Par., 1942), *Star Spangled Rhythm* (Par., 1942), *So Proudly We Hail!* (Par., 1943), *Fired Wife* (Univ., 1943), *Mr. Skef-*

Shirley Temple, Walter Abel and Katharine Alexander in *Kiss and Tell*.

Iris Adrian, Barry Norton and Betty Blythe in *Murder at Glen Athol*.

fington (WB, 1944), *An American Romance* (MGM, 1944), *The Affairs of Susan* (Par., 1945), *The Hitler Grang* (narrator; Par., 1944), *Duffy's Tavern* (Par., 1945), *Kiss and Tell* (Col., 1945), *The Kid From Brooklyn* (RKO, 1946), *13 Rue Madeleine* (20th, 1946), *The Hal Roach Comedy Carnival* (UA, 1947), *Dream Girl* (Par., 1948), *That Lady in Ermine* (20th, 1948), *So This Is Love* (WB, 1953), *Night People* (20th, 1954), *The Indian Fighter* (UA, 1955), *The Steel Jungle* (WB, 1956), *Bernardine* (20th, 1957), *Raintree County* (MGM, 1957), *Handle With Care* (MGM, 1958), *Mirage* (Univ., 1965).

IRIS ADRIAN (Iris Adrian Hostetter) Born May 29, 1913, Los Angeles, California. Married Charles Over (1935); divorced 1936. Married George Jay.

Feature Films: *Paramount on Parade* (Par., 1930), *Gay Deception* (Fox, 1935), *Rumba* (Par., 1935), *Stolen Harmony* (Par., 1935), *Murder at Glen Athol* (Invincible, 1935), *Our Relations* (MGM, 1936), *Stage Struck* (WB, 1936), *A Message to Garcia* (20th, 1936), *Mister Cinderella* (MGM, 1936), *Lady Luck* (Chesterfield, 1936), *One Rainy Afternoon* (UA, 1936), *Gold Diggers of 1937* (WB, 1936), *One Third of a Nation* (Par., 1939), *Back Door to Heaven* (Par., 1939), *Meet the Wildcat* (Univ., 1940), *Go West* (MGM, 1940), *Road to Zanzibar* (Par., 1941), *Horror Island* (Univ., 1941), *Meet the Chump* (Univ., 1941), *The Lady From Cheyenne* (Univ., 1941), *Wild Geese Calling* (20th, 1941), *New York Town* (Par., 1941), *Too Many Blondes* (Univ., 1941), *Hard Guy* (PRC, 1941), *I Killed That Man* (Mon., 1941), *Sing Another Chorus* (Univ., 1941), *Swing It Soldier* (Univ., 1941), *Roxie Hart* (20th, 1942), *To the Shores of Tripoli* (20th, 1942), *Rings on Her Fingers* (20th, 1942), *Juke Box Jenny* (Univ., 1942), *Broadway* (Univ., 1942), *Fingers at the Window* (MGM, 1942), *Moonlight Masquerade* (Rep., 1942), *Orchestra Wives* (20th, 1942), *Ladies' Day* (RKO, 1943), *The Crystal Ball* (UA, 1943), *Taxi, Mister* (UA, 1943), *Lady of Burlesque* (UA, 1943), *Action in the North Atlantic* (WB, 1943), *Calaboose* (UA, 1943), *Hers to Hold* (Univ., 1943), *Submarine Base* (PRC, 1943), *Spotlight Scandals* (Mon., 1943), *Career Girl* (PRC, 1944), *Million Dollar Kid* (Mon., 1944), *Shake Hands With Murder* (PRC, 1944), *The Singing Sheriff* (Univ., 1944), *Bluebeard* (PRC, 1944), *Alaska* (Mon., 1944), *I'm From Arkansas* (PRC, 1944), *Swing Hostess* (PRC, 1944), *Once Upon a Time* (Col., 1944), *The Woman in the Window* (RKO, 1944), *It's a Pleasure* (RKO, 1945), *Steppin' in Society* (Rep., 1945), *Road to Alcatraz* (Rep., 1945), *The Stork Club* (Par., 1945), *Boston Blackie's Rendezvous* (Col., 1945), *The Bamboo Blonde* (RKO, 1946), *Vacation in Reno* (RKO, 1946), *Cross My Heart* (Par., 1946), *Fall Guy* (Mon., 1947), *Philo Vance Returns* (PRC, 1947), *The Trouble With Women* (Par., 1947), *Smart Woman* (AA, 1948), *Out of the Storm* (Rep., 1948), *The Paleface* (Par., 1948), *Flamingo Road* (WB, 1949), *The Lovable Cheat* (Film Classics, 1949), *Sky Dragon* (Mon., 1949), *Miss Mink of 1949* (20th, 1949), *Trail of the Yukon* (Mon., 1949), *Always Leave Them Laughing* (WB, 1949), *There's a Girl in My Heart* (AA, 1949), *Tough Assignment* (Lip., 1949), *Mighty Joe Young* (RKO, 1949), *My Dream Is Yours* (WB, 1949), *Woman on Pier 13* (RKO, 1949), *Hi-Jacked* (Lip., 1950), *Once a Thief* (UA, 1950), *Blondie's Hero* (Col., 1950), *Joe Palooka in*

Humphrey Takes a Chance (Mon., 1950), *Sideshow* (Mon., 1950), *Stop That Cab* (Lip., 1951), *My Favorite Spy* (Par., 1951), *Varieties on Parade* (Lip., 1951), *G. I. Jane* (Lip., 1951), *The Racket* (RKO, 1951), *Carson City* (WB, 1952), *Take the High Ground* (MGM, 1953), *The Fast and Furious* (American Releasing Corp., 1954), *Crime Wave* (WB, 1954), *Devil's Harbor* (20th, 1954), *Carnival Rock* (Howco, 1957), *The Buccaneer* (Par., 1958), *Blue Hawaii* (Par., 1961), *The Errand Boy* (Par., 1961), *Fate Is the Hunter* (20th, 1964), *That Darn Cat* (BV, 1965).

BRIAN AHERNE (Brian de Lacy Aherne) Born May 2, 1902, King's Norton, Worcestershire, England. Married Joan Fontaine (1939); divorced 1943. Married Eleanor Labrot (1946).

Feature Films: *Song of Songs* (Par., 1933), *What Every Woman Knows* (MGM, 1934), *The Fountain* (RKO, 1934), *The Constant Nymph* (Fox, 1934), *Sylvia Scarlet* (RKO, 1935), *I Live My Life* (MGM, 1935), *Beloved Enemy* (UA, 1936), *The Great Garrick* (WB, 1937), *Merrily We Live* (MGM, 1938), *Captain Fury* (UA, 1939), *Juarez* (WB, 1939), *Lady in Question* (Col., 1940), *Hired Wife* (Univ., 1940), *My Son, My Son* (UA, 1940), *The Man Who Lost Himself* (Univ., 1941), *Skylark* (Par., 1941), *Smilin' Through* (MGM, 1941), *My Sister Eileen* (Col., 1942), *Forever and a Day* (RKO, 1943), *A Night to Remember* (Col., 1943), *First Comes Courage* (Col., 1943), *What a Woman!* (Col., 1943), *The Locket* (RKO, 1946), *Smart Woman* (AA, 1948), *Angel on the Amazon* (Rep., 1948), *I Confess* (WB, 1953), *Titanic* (20th, 1953), *Prince Valiant* (20th, 1954), *A Bullet Is Waiting* (Col., 1954), *The Swan* (MGM, 1956), *The Best of Everything* (20th, 1959), *Susan Slade* (WB, 1961), *Sword of Lancelot* (Univ., 1963), *The Cavern* (20th, 1965), *Rosie!* (Univ., 1968).

Brian Aherne and Louis Hayward in *My Son, My Son*.

Rosemary Lane, Eddie Albert and May Robson in *Four Wives*.

EDDIE ALBERT (Edward Albert Heimberger) Born April 22, 1908, Rock Island, Illinois. Married Margo (1945), children: Edward, Maria.

Feature Films: *Brother Rat* (WB, 1938), *On Your Toes* (WB, 1939), *Four Wives* (WB, 1939), *Brother Rat and a Baby* (WB, 1940), *An Angel From Texas* (WB, 1940), *My Love Came Back* (WB, 1940), *A Dispatch From Reuters* (WB, 1940), *Four Mothers* (WB, 1941), *The Wagons Roll at Night* (WB, 1941), *Thieves Fall Out* (WB, 1941), *Out of the Fog* (WB, 1941), *The Great Mr. Nobody* (WB, 1941), *Treat 'Em Rough* (Univ., 1942), *Eagle Squadron* (Univ., 1942), *Ladies' Day* (RKO, 1943), *Lady Bodyguard* (RKO, 1943), *Bombardier* (RKO, 1943), *Strange Voyage* (Mon., 1945), *Rendezvous With Annie* (Rep., 1946), *The Perfect Marriage* (Par., 1946), *Smash-Up—The Story of a Woman* (Univ., 1947), *Time Out of Mind* (Univ., 1947), *Hit Parade of 1947* (Rep., 1947), *The Dude Goes West* (AA, 1948), *You Gotta Stay Happy* (Univ., 1948), *The Fuller Brush Girl* (Col., 1950), *You're in the Navy Now* (20th, 1951), *Meet Me After the Show* (20th, 1951), *Actors and Sin* (UA, 1952), *Carrie* (Par., 1952), *Roman Holiday* (Par., 1953), *The Girl Rush* (Par., 1955), *Oklahoma!* (Magna, 1955), *I'll Cry Tomorrow* (MGM, 1955), *Attack!* (UA, 1956), *The Teahouse of the August Moon* (MGM, 1956), *The Sun Also Rises* (20th, 1957), *The Joker Is Wild* (Par., 1957), *The Gun Runners* (UA, 1958), *The Roots of Heaven* (20th, 1958), *Orders to Kill* (United Motion Pictures Organization, 1958), *Beloved Infidel* (20th, 1959), *The Young Doctors* (UA, 1961), *The Two Little Bears* (20th, 1961), *Madison Avenue* (20th, 1962), *The Longest Day* (20th, 1962), *Who's Got the Action?* (Par., 1962), *Miracle of the White Stallions* (BV, 1963), *Captain Newman, M.D.* (Univ., 1963), *7 Women* (MGM, 1965), *The Party's Over* (AA, 1968).

LOUISE ALLBRITTON Born July 3, 1920, Oklahoma City, Oklahoma. Married Charles Collingwood (1946).

Robert Paige and Louise Albritton in *Her Primitive Man*.

Feature Films: *Parachute Nurse* (Col., 1942), *Danger in the Pacific* (Univ., 1942), *Not a Ladies' Man* (Col., 1942), *Who Done It?* (Univ., 1943), *Pittsburgh* (Univ., 1942), *It Comes Up Love* (Univ., 1943), *Good Morning, Judge* (Univ., 1943), *Fired Wife* (Univ., 1943), *Son of Dracula* (Univ., 1943), *Follow the Boys* (Univ., 1944), *This Is the Life* (Univ., 1944), *Her Primitive Man* (Univ., 1944), *San Diego, I Love You* (Univ., 1944), *Bowery to Broadway* (Univ., 1944), *The Men in Her Diary* (Univ., 1945), *That Night With You* (Univ., 1945), *Tangier* (Univ., 1946), *The Egg and I* (Univ., 1947), *Sitting Pretty* (20th, 1948), *Walk a Crooked Mile* (Col., 1948), *Don't Trust Your Hasband* (UA, 1948), *The Doolins of Oklahoma* (Col. 1949).,

Sara Allgood and Ginger Rogers in *Roxie Hart*.

SARA ALLGOOD Born October 31, 1883, Dublin, Ireland. Married Gerald Hanson (1917); widowed. Died September 13, 1950.

Feature Films: *Blackmail* (Sono Art-World Wide, 1929), *Riders to the Sea* (Flanagan-Hurst, 1935), *The Passing of the Third Floor Back* (Gaumont-British, 1935), *It's Love Again* (Gaumont-British, 1936), *Storm in a Teacup* (UA, 1937), *Kathleen* (Hoffberg, 1938), *On the Night of the Fire* (GFD, 1939), *That Hamilton Woman* (UA, 1941), *Dr. Jekyll and Mr. Hyde* (MGM, 1941), *Lydia* (UA, 1941), *How Green Was My Valley* (20th, 1941), *Roxie Hart* (20th, 1942), *This Above All* (20th, 1942), *It Happened in Flatbush* (20th, 1942), *The War Against Mrs. Hadley* (MGM, 1942), *Life Begins at 8:30* (20th, 1942), *City Without Men* (Col., 1943), *The Lodger* (20th, 1944), *Jane Eyre* (MGM, 1944), *Between Two Worlds* (WB, 1944), *Keys of the Kingdom* (20th, 1945), *The Strange Affair of Uncle Harry* (Univ., 1945), *Kitty* (Par., 1945), *The Spiral Staircase* (RKO, 1946), *Cluny Brown* (20th, 1946), *The Fabulous Dorseys* (UA, 1947), *Ivy* (Univ., 1947), *Mother Wore Tights* (20th, 1947), *Mourning Becomes Electra* (RKO, 1947), *My Wild Irish Rose* (WB, 1947), *The Girl From Manhattan* (UA, 1948), *One Touch of Venus* (Univ., 1948), *The Man From Texas* (EL, 1948), *The Accused* (Par., 1948), *Challenge to Lassie* (MGM, 1949), *Cheaper by the Dozen* (20th, 1950), *Sierra* (Univ., 1950).

JUNE ALLYSON (Ella Geisman) Born October 7, 1923, Bronx, New York. Married Dick Powell (1945), children: Pamela, Richard; widowed 1963. Married Alfred Glenn Maxwell (1963); divorced 1965. Remarried 1966.

Feature Films: *Best Foot Forward* (MGM, 1943), *Girl Grazy* (MGM, 1943), *Thousands Cheer* (MGM, 1943), *Two Girls and a Sailor* (MGM, 1944), *Meet the People* (MGM, 1944), *Music For Millions* (MGM, 1945), *Her Highness and the Bellboy* (MGM, 1945), *The Sailor Takes a Wife* (MGM, 1945), *Two Sisters From Boston* (MGM, 1946), *Till the Clouds Roll By* (MGM, 1946), *The Secret Heart* (MGM, 1946), *High Barbaree* (MGM, 1947), *Good News* (MGM, 1947), *The Bride Goes Wild* (MGM, 1948), *The Three Musketeers* (MGM, 1948), *Words and Music* (MGM, 1948), *Little Women* (MGM, 1949), *The Stratton Story* (MGM, 1949), *The Reformer and the Redhead* (MGM, 1950),

Right Cross (MGM, 1950), *Too Young to Kiss* (MGM, 1951), *The Girl in White* (MGM, 1952), *Battle Circus* (MGM, 1953), *Remains to Be Seen* (MGM, 1953), *The Glenn Miller Story* (Univ., 1954), *Executive Suite* (MGM, 1954), *Woman's World* (20th, 1954), *Strategic Air Command* (Par., 1955), *The McConnell Story* (WB, 1955), *The Shrike* (Univ., 1955), *The Opposite Sex* (MGM, 1956), *You Can't Run Away From It* (Col., 1956), *Interlude* (Univ., 1957), *My Man Godfrey* (Univ., 1957), *Stranger in My Arms* (Univ., 1959).

Robert Sterling and June Allyson in *The Secret Heart.*

Arleen Whelan and Don Ameche in *Gateway.*

DON AMECHE (Dominic Felix Amici) Born May 31, 1910, Kenosha, Wisconsin. Married Honore Prendergast (1932), children: Ronald, Dominic, Thomas, Lonnie, Bonnie, Connie.

Feature Films: *Sins of Man* (20th, 1936), *Ramona* (20th, 1936), *Ladies in Love* (20th, 1936), *One in a Million* (20th, 1936), *Love Is News* (20th, 1937), *Fifty Roads to Town* (20th, 1937), *You Can't Have Everything* (20th, 1937), *Love Under Fire* (20th, 1937), *In Old Chicago* (20th, 1938), *Happy Landing* (20th, 1938), *Josette* (20th, 1938), *Alexander's Ragtime Band* (20th, 1938), *Gateway* (20th, 1938), *The Three Musketeers* (20th, 1939), *Midnight* (Par., 1939), *The Story of Alexander Graham Bell* (20th, 1939), *Hollywood Cavalcade* (20th, 1939), *Swanee River* (20th, 1939), *Little Old New York* (20th, 1939), *Lillian Russell* (20th, 1940), *Four Sons* (20th, 1940), *Down Argentine Way* (20th, 1940), *That Night in Rio* (20th, 1941), *Moon Over Miami* (20th, 1941), *Kiss the Boys Goodbye* (Par., 1941), *The Feminine Touch* (MGM, 1941), *Confirm or Deny* (20th, 1941), *The Magnificent Dope* (20th, 1942), *Girl Trouble* (20th, 1942), *Heaven Can Wait* (20th, 1943), *Happy Land* (20th, 1943), *Something to Shout About* (Col., 1943), *Wing and a Prayer* (20th, 1944), *Greenwich Village* (20th, 1944), *It's in the Bag* (UA, 1945), *Guest Wife* (UA, 1945), *So Goes My Love* (Univ., 1946), *That's My Man* (Rep., 1947), *Sleep, My Love* (UA, 1948), *Slightly French* (Col., 1949), *A Fever in the Blood* (WB, 1961), *Rings Around the World* (Col., 1966), *Picture Mommy Dead* (Embassy, 1966).

LEON AMES (Leon Waycoff) Born January 20, 1903, Portland, Indiana. Married Christine Gossett (1938), children: Shelley, Leon.

Feature Films:
as **Leon Waycoff** *Murders in the Rue Morgue* (Univ., 1932), *13 Women* (RKO, 1932), *Cannonball Express* (World-Wide, 1932), *Uptown New York* (World-Wide, 1932), *Parachute Jumper* (WB, 1933), *Alimony Madness* (Mayfair, 1933), *The Man Who Dared* (Fox, 1933), *Forgotten* (Invincible, 1933), *Ship of Wanted Men* (Showmen's Pictures, 1933), *The Count of Monte Cristo* (UA, 1934), *I'll Tell the World* (Univ., 1934), *Now I'll Tell You* (Fox, 1934), *Reckless* (MGM, 1935).
as **Leon Ames** *Strangers All* (RKO, 1935), *Mutiny Ahead* (Majestic, 1935), *Get That Man* (Empire, 1935), *Stowaway* (20th, 1936), *Dangerously Yours* (20th, 1937), *Murder in Greenwich Village* (Col., 1937), *Charlie Chan on Broadway* (20th, 1937), *45 Fathers* (20th, 1937), *International Settlement* (20th, 1938), *Walking Down Broadway* (20th, 1938), *The Spy Ring* (Univ., 1938), *Island in the Sky* (20th, 1938), *Come On Leathernecks* (Rep., 1938), *Mysterious Mr. Moto* (20th, 1938), *Strange Faces* (Univ., 1938), *Cipher Bureau* (GN, 1938), *Suez* (20th, 1938), *Secrets of a Nurse* (Univ., 1938), *Risky Business* (Univ., 1939), *I Was a Convict* (Rep., 1939), *Mr. Moto in Danger Island* (20th, 1939), *Panama Patrol* (GN, 1939), *Man of Conquest* (Rep., 1939), *Fugitive at Large* (Col., 1939), *Code of the Streets* (Univ., 1939), *Legion of Lost Flyers* (Univ., 1939), *Calling All Marines* (Rep., 1939), *Thunder Afloat* (MGM, 1939), *East Side Kids* (Mon., 1940), *Marshal of Mesa City* (RKO, 1940), *No Greater Sin* (University Film Products, 1941), *Ellery Queen and the Murder Ring* (Col., 1941), *Crime Doctor* (Col., 1943), *The Iron Major* (RKO, 1943), *Meet Me in St. Louis* (MGM, 1944), *Thirty Seconds Over Tokyo* (MGM, 1944), *The Thin Man Goes Home* MGM, 1944), *Son of Lassie* (MGM, 1945), *Weekend at the Waldorf* (MGM, 1945), *Yolanda and the Thief* (MGM, 1945), *They Were Expendable* (MGM, 1945), *The Postman Always Rings Twice* (MGM,

Fay Wray and Leon Ames in *Murder in Greenwich Village.*

43

1946), *No Leave, No Love* (MGM, 1946), *The Show-off* (MGM, 1946), *The Cockeyed Miracle* (MGM, 1946), *Undercover Maisie* (MGM, 1947), *Song of the Thin Man* (MGM, 1947), *Merton of the Movies* (MGM, 1947), *Alias a Gentleman* (MGM, 1948), *On an Island With You* (MGM, 1948), *A Date With Judy* (MGM, 1948), *The Velvet Touch* (RKO, 1948), *Little Women* (MGM, 1949), *Any Number Can Play* (MGM, 1949), *Scene of the Crime* (MGM, 1949), *Battleground* (MGM, 1949), *Ambush* (MGM, 1949), *The Big Hangover* (MGM, 1950), *The Skipper Surprised His Wife* (MGM, 1950), *The Happy Years* (MGM, 1950), *Crisis* (MGM, 1950), *Cattle Drive* (Univ., 1951), *On Moonlight Bay* (WB, 1951), *It's a Big Country* (MGM, 1951), *Angel Face* (RKO, 1952), *By the Light of the Silvery Moon* (WB, 1953), *Let's Do It Again* (Col., 1953), *Sabre Jet* (UA, 1953), *Peyton Place* (20th, 1957), *From the Terrace* (20th, 1960), *The Absent-Minded Professor* (BV, 1961), *Son of Flubber* (BV, 1963), *The Misadventures of Merlin Jones* (BV, 1964), *The Monkey's Uncle* (BV, 1965).

Stanley Ridges and Dana Andrews in *Canyon Passage*.

DANA ANDREWS

(Carver Dan Andrews) Born January 1, 1912, Collins, Mississippi. Married Janet Murray (1932), child: David; widowed 1935. Married Mary Todd (1939), children: Kathryn, Stephen, Susan.

Feature Films: *The Westerner* (UA, 1940), *Lucky Cisco Kid* (20th, 1940), *Sailor's Lady* (20th, 1940), *Kit Carson* (UA, 1940), *Tobacco Road* (20th, 1941), *Belle Starr* (20th, 1941), *Swamp Water* (20th, 1941), *Ball of Fire* (RKO, 1941), *Berlin Correspondent* (20th, 1942), *Crash Dive* (20th, 1943), *The Ox-Bow Incident* (20th, 1943), *The North Star* (RKO, 1943), *The Purple Heart* (20th, 1944), *Wing and a Prayer* (20th, 1944), *Up in Arms* (RKO, 1944), *Laura* (20th, 1944), *State Fair* (20th, 1945), *Fallen Angel* (20th, 1945), *A Walk in the Sun* (20th, 1945), *Canyon Passage* (Univ., 1946), *The Best Years of Our Lives* (RKO, 1946), *Boomerang* (20th, 1947), *Night Song* (RKO, 1947), *Daisy Kenyon* (20th, 1947), *The Iron Curtain* (20th, 1948), *Deep Waters* (20th, 1948), *No Minor Vices* (MGM, 1948), *The Forbidden Street* (20th, 1949), *Sword in the Desert* (Univ., 1949), *My Foolish Heart* (RKO, 1949), *Where the Sidewalk Ends* (20th, 1950), *Edge of Doom* (RKO, 1950), *The Frogmen* (20th, 1951), *Sealed Cargo* (RKO, 1951), *I Want You* (RKO, 1951), *Assignment Paris* (Col., 1952), *Elephant Walk* (Par., 1954), *Duel in the Jungle* (WB, 1954), *Three Hours to Kill* (Col., 1954), *Smoke Signal* (Univ., 1955), *Strange Lady in Town* (WB, 1955), *Comanche* (UA, 1956), *While the City Sleeps* (RKO, 1956), *Beyond a Reasonable Doubt* (RKO, 1956), *Curse of the Demon* (Col., 1957), *Spring Reunion* (UA, 1957), *Zero Hour* (Par., 1957), *The Fearmakers* (UA, 1958), *Enchanted Island* (WB, 1958), *The Crowded Sky* (WB, 1960), *Madison Avenue* (20th, 1962), *Crack in the World* (Par., 1965), *The Satan Bug* (UA, 1965), *In Harm's Way* (Par., 1965), *Brainstorm* (WB, 1965), *Town Tamer* (Par., 1965), *The Loved One* (MGM, 1965),

Battle of the Bulge (WB, 1965), *Johnny Reno* (Par., 1966), *Spy in Your Eye* (AIP, 1966), *Hot Rods to Hell* (MGM, 1967), *The Frozen Dead* (WB-7 Arts, 1967), *Cobra* (AIP, 1967), *Ten Million Dollar Grab* (RKO, 1968).

Julie Andrews and Max Von Sydow in *Hawaii*.

JULIE ANDREWS

(Julia Welles) Born October 1, 1934, Walton-on-the-Thames, England. Married Tony Walton (1959), child: Emma Kate; divorced 1968.

Feature Films: *Mary Poppins* (BV, 1964), *The Americanization of Emily* (MGM, 1964), *The Sound of Music* (20th, 1965), *Torn Curtain* (Univ., 1966), *Hawaii* (UA, 1966), *Thoroughly Modern Millie* (Univ., 1967), *The Singing Princess* (voice only; Larry Joachim Prod., 1967), *Star* (20th, 1968).

THE ANDREWS SISTERS

(Patty, Maxene, LaVerne)
PATRICIA Born February 16, 1920, Minneapolis, Minnesota. Married Marty Melcher; divorced. Married Wally Wechsler.
MAXENE Born January 3, 1918, Minneapolis, Minnesota. Married Lou Levy (1941), children: Aleda, Peter; divorced 1950.
LAVERNE Born July 6, 1915, Minneapolis, Minnesota. Married Louis A. Rogers (1948). Died May 8, 1967.

Feature Films: *Argentine Nights* (Univ., 1940), *In the Navy* (Univ., 1941), *Buck Privates* (Univ., 1941), *Hold That Ghost* (Univ., 1941), *Give Out, Sisters* (Univ., 1942), *Private Buckaroo* (Univ., 1942), *What's Cookin'?* (Univ., 1942), *Always a Bridesmaid* (Univ., 1943), *How's About It?* (Univ., 1943), *Follow the Boys* (Univ., 1944), *Hollywood Canteen* (WB, 1944), *Moonlight and Cactus* (Univ., 1944), *Swingtime Johnny* (Univ., 1944), *Her Lucky Night* (Univ., 1945), *Make Mine Music* (RKO, 1946), *Road to Rio* (Par., 1947), *Melody Time* (RKO, 1948).

LaVerne, Patti and Maxene Andrews in *Follow the Boys*.

44

Evelyn Ankers and Lon Chaney, Jr., in *The Frozen Ghost.*

EVELYN ANKERS Born August 17, 1918, Valparaiso, Chile. Married Richard Denning, child: Diana.

Feature Films: *Villiers Diamond* (British), *Second Thoughts* (British), *Land Without Music* ("Forbidden Music"—Capitol Films, 1936), *Rembrandt* (London Films, 1936), *Fire Over England* (UA, 1937), *Knight Without Armour* (UA, 1937), *Wings of the Morning* (20th, 1937), *Murder In the Family* (20th, 1937), *Claydon Treasure Mystery* (20th, 1938), *Over the Moon* (London Films, 1939), *Hold That Ghost* (Univ., 1941), *Hit the Road* (Univ., 1941), *Bachelor Daddy* (Univ., 1941), *Burma Convoy* (Univ., 1941), *Sandy Steps Out* (Univ., 1941), *The Wolf Man* (Univ., 1941), *The Ghost of Frankenstein* (Univ., 1942), *North to the Klondike* (Univ., 1942), *Eagle Squadron* (Univ., 1942), *Pierre of the Plains* (MGM, 1942), *Sherlock Holmes and the Voice of Terror* (Univ., 1942), *The Great Impersonation* (Univ., 1942), *Keep 'Em Slugging* (Univ., 1943), *The Mad Ghoul* (Univ., 1943), *You're a Lucky Fellow, Mr. Smith* (Univ., 1943), *All By Myself* (Univ., 1943), *Hers to Hold* (Univ., 1943), *Captive Wild Woman* (Univ., 1943), *Son of Dracula* (Univ., 1943), *His Butler's Sister* (Univ., 1943), *Follow the Boys* (Univ., 1944), *Ladies Courageous* (Univ., 1944), *Pardon My Rhythm* (Univ., 1944), *Invisible Man's Revenge* (Univ., 1944), *Jungle Woman* (Univ., 1944), *The Pearl of Death* (Univ., 1944), *Weird Woman* (Univ., 1944), *Bowery to Broadway* (Univ., 1944), *The Fatal Witness* (Rep., 1945), *The Frozen Ghost* (Univ., 1945), *Queen of Burlesque* (PRC, 1946), *The French Key* (Rep., 1946), *Black Beauty* (20th, 1946), *Spoilers of the North* (Rep., 1947), *The Last of the Redmen* (Col., 1947), *The Lone Wolf in London* (Col., 1947), *Tarzan's Magic Fountain* (RKO, 1949), *Parole, Inc.* (EL, 1949), *The Texan Meets Calamity Jane* (Col., 1950), *No Greater Love* (Brandon Films, 1960).

Ann-Margret and John Forsythe in *Kitten With a Whip.*

ANN-MARGRET (Ann Margret Olson) Born April 28, 1941, Stockholm, Sweden. Married Roger Smith, 1967.

Feature Films: *Pocketful of Miracles* (20th, 1961), *State Fair* (20th, 1962), *Bye Bye Birdie* (Col., 1962), *Viva Las Vegas* (MGM, 1964), *Kitten With a Whip* (Univ., 1964), *Bus Riley's Back in Town* (Univ., 1965), *The Pleasure Seekers* (20th, 1965), *Once a Thief* (MGM, 1965), *Cincinnati Kid* (MGM, 1965), *Made in Paris* (MGM, 1966), *The Swinger* (Par., 1966), *Stagecoach* (20th, 1966), *Murderers' Row* (Col., 1966), *The Tiger and the Pussycat* (Embassy, 1967), *Maggie* (Fairfilm, 1968).

Barton MacLane and Eve Arden in *Big Town Czar.*

EVE ARDEN (Eunice Quedens) Born April 30, 1912, Mill Valley, California. Married Ned Bergen (1939), children: Liza, Constance; divorced (1947). Married Brooks West (1951), children: Duncan, Douglas.

Feature Films:

as **Eunice Quedens** *Song of Love* (Col., 1929), *Dancing Lady* (MGM, 1933).

as **Eve Arden** *Oh, Doctor* (Univ., 1937), *Stage Door* (RKO, 1937), *Cocoanut Grove* (Par., 1938), *Letter of Introduction* (Univ., 1938), *Having Wonderful Time* (RKO, 1938), *Women in the Wind* (WB, 1939), *Big Town Czar* (Univ., 1939), *The Forgotten Women* (Univ., 1939), *Eternally Yours* (UA, 1939), *At the Circus* (MGM, 1939), *A Child Is Born* (WB, 1940), *Slightly Honorable* (UA, 1940), *Comrade X* (MGM, 1940), *No, No, Nanette* (RKO, 1940), *Ziegfeld Girl* (MGM, 1941), *That Uncertain Feeling* (UA, 1941), *She Couldn't Say No* (WB, 1941), *She Knew All the Answers* (Col., 1941), *San Antonio Rose* (Univ., 1941), *Sing for Your Supper* (Col., 1941), *Manpower* (WB, 1941), *Whistling in the Dark* (MGM, 1941), *Last of the Duanes* (20th, 1941), *Obliging Young Lady* (RKO, 1941), *Bedtime Story* (Col., 1941), *Hit Parade of 1943* (Rep., 1943), *Let's Face It* (Par., 1943), *Cover Girl* (Col., 1944), *The Doughgirls* (WB, 1944), *Pan Americana* (RKO, 1945), *Patrick the Great* (Univ., 1945), *Earl Carroll's Vanities* (Rep., 1945), *Mildred Pierce* (WB, 1945), *My Reputation* (WB, 1946), *The Kid From Brooklyn* (RKO, 1946), *Night and Day* (WB, 1946), *Song of Scheherazade* (Univ., 1947), *The Arnelo Affair* (MGM, 1947), *The Unfaithful* (WB, 1947), *The Voice of the Turtle* (WB, 1947), *One Touch of Venus* (Univ., 1948), *Whiplash* (WB, 1948), *My Dream Is Yours* (WB, 1949), *The Lady Takes a Sailor* (WB, 1949), *Paid in Full* (Par., 1950), *Curtain Call at Cactus Creek* (Univ., 1950), *Tea for Two* (WB, 1950), *Three Husbands* (UA, 1950), *Goodbye, My Fancy* (WB, 1951), *We're Not Married* (20th, 1952), *The Lady Wants Mink* (Rep., 1953), *Our Miss Brooks* (WB, 1956), *Anatomy of a Murder* (Col., 1959), *The Dark at the Top of the Stairs* (WB, 1960), *Sgt. Deadhead* (AIP, 1965).

Clancy Cooper, Mary Beth Hughes, Richard Arlen, June Havoc and Edmund MacDonald in *Timber Queen*.

RICHARD ARLEN (Richard Van Mattemore) Born September 1, 1900, Charlottesville, Virginia. Married Jobyna Ralston (1927), child: Richard; divorced 1945.

Sound Feature Films: *The Man I Love* (Par., 1929), *Thunderbolt* (Par., 1929), *Dangerous Curves* (Par., 1929), *The Virginian* (Par., 1929), *Burning Up* (Par., 1930), *Dangerous Paradise* (Par., 1930), *Light of Western Stars* (Par., 1930), *Paramount on Parade* (Par., 1930), *Border Legion* (Par., 1930), *Sea God* (Par., 1930), *Santa Fe Trail* (Par., 1930), *Only Saps Work* (Par., 1930), *The Conquering Horde* (Par., 1931), *Gun Smoke* (Par., 1931), *The Lawyer's Secret* (Par., 1931), *The Secret Call* (Par., 1931), *Caught* (Par., 1931), *Touchdown* (Par., 1931), *Wayward* (Par., 1932), *The Sky Bride* (Par., 1932), *Guilty as Hell* (Par., 1932), *Tiger Shark* (WB, 1932), *The All American* (Univ., 1932), *Island of Lost Souls* (Par., 1933), *Song of the Eagle* (Par., 1933), *College Humor* (Par., 1933), *Three-Cornered Moon* (Par., 1933), *Golden Harvest* (Par., 1933), *Alice in Wonderland* (Par., 1933), *Hell and High Water* (Par., 1933), *Come On Marines* (Par., 1934), *She Made Her Bed* (Par., 1934), *Ready for Love* (Par., 1934), *Helldorado* (Fox, 1935), *Let 'Em Have It* (UA, 1935), *Three Live Ghosts* (MGM, 1935), *The Calling of Dan Matthews* (Col., 1936), *The Mine With the Iron Door* (Col., 1936), *Secret Valley* (20th, 1936), *Silent Barriers* (Gaumont-British, 1937), *Artists and Models* (Par., 1937), *Murder in Greenwich Village* (Col., 1937), *No Time to Marry* (Col., 1938), *Call of the Yukon* (Rep., 1938), *Straight, Place and Show* (20th, 1938), *Missing Daughters* (Col., 1939), *Mutiny on the Blackhawk* (Univ., 1939), *Tropic Fury* (Univ., 1939), *Legion of Lost Flyers* (Univ., 1939), *The Man From Montreal* (Univ., 1940), *Danger on Wheels* (Univ., 1940), *Hot Steel* (Univ., 1940), *The Leather Pushers* (Univ., 1940), *Black Diamonds* (Univ., 1940), *The Devil's Pipeline* (Univ., 1940), *A Dangerous Game* (Univ., 1941), *Lucky Devils* (Univ., 1941), *Mutiny in the Arctic* (Univ., 1941), *Men of the Timberland* (Univ., 1941), *Raiders of the Desert* (Univ., 1941), *Forced Landing* (Par., 1941), *Power Dive* (Par., 1941), *Flying Blind* (Par., 1941), *Torpedo Boat* (Par., 1942), *Wildcat* (Par., 1942), *Wrecking Crew* (Par., 1942), *Alaska Highway* (Par., 1943), *Aerial Gunner* (Par., 1943), *Submarine Alert* (Par., 1943), *Minesweeper* (Par., 1943), *Timber Queen* (Par., 1944), *The Lady and the Monster* (Rep., 1944), *Storm Over Lisbon* (Rep., 1944), *That's My Baby!* (Rep., 1944), *The Big Bonanza* (Rep., 1945), *Identity Unknown* (Rep., 1945), *The Phantom Speaks* (Rep., 1945), *Accomplice* (PRC, 1946), *The French Key* (Rep., 1946),* *Speed to Spare* (Par., 1948), *When My Baby Smiles at Me* (20th, 1948), *Return Of Wildfire* (Screen Guild, 1948), *Grand Canyon* (Screen Guild, 1949), *Kansas Raiders* (Univ., 1950), *Flaming Feather* (Par., 1952), *Silver City* (Par., 1952), *Hurricane Smith* (Par., 1952), *The Blazing Forest* (Par., 1952), *Sabre Jet* (UA, 1953), *Devil's Harbor* (20th, 1954), *Stolen Time* (British Lion, 1955), *Hidden Guns* (Rep., 1956), *The Mountain* (Par., 1956), *Blonde Blackmailer* (AA, 1958), *Warlock* (20th, 1959), *Raymie* (AA, 1960), *The Last Time I Saw Archie* (UA, 1961), *The Young and the Brave* (MGM, 1963), *Thunder Mountain* ("Shepherd of the Hills"—Howco, 1963), *Cavalry Command* (Pano-

rama, 1963), *Law of the Lawless* (Par., 1964), *The Best Man* (UA, 1964), *Young Fury* (Par., 1965), *Black Spurs* (Par., 1965), *The Bounty Killer* (Embassy, 1965), *Town Tamer* (Par., 1965), *The Human Duplicator* (AA, 1965), *Apache Uprising* (Par., 1966), *Johnny Reno* (Par., 1966), *Waco* (Par., 1966), *To the Shores of Hell* (Robert Patrick-SR, 1966), *Red Tomahawk* (Par., 1967), *Fort Utah* (Par., 1967), *Huntsville* (Par., 1967), *Arizona Bushwhackers* (Par., 1968), *Rogue's Gallery* (Par., 1968), *The Frontiersman* (Par., 1968), *Buckskin* (Par., 1968).

*Unbilled guest appearance.

Marjorie Gateson, George Arliss and Patricia Ellis in *The King's Vacation*.

GEORGE ARLISS Born April 10, 1868. Married Florence Montgomery (1899). Died February 5, 1946.

Sound Feature Films: *Disraeli* (WB, 1929), *The Green Goddess* (WB, 1930), *Old English* (WB, 1930), *Millionaire* (WB, 1931), *Alexander Hamilton* (WB, 1931), *The Man Who Played God* (WB, 1932), *Successful Calamity* (WB, 1932), *King's Vacation* (WB, 1933), *Working Man* (WB, 1933), *Voltaire* (WB, 1933), *House of Rothschild* (UA, 1934), *Last Gentleman* (UA, 1934), *Cardinal Richelieu* (UA, 1935), *Iron Duke* (Gaumont-British, 1935), *The Guv'nor* ("Mister Hobo"—Gaumont-British, 1935), *East Meets West* (Gaumont-British, 1936), *Man of Affairs* (Gaumont-British, 1937), *Dr. Syn* (Gaumont-British, 1937).

EDWARD ARNOLD (Guenther Schneider) Born February 18, 1890, New York, New York. Married Harriet Marshall (1917), children: Elizabeth, Jane, William; divorced 1927. Married Olive Emerson (1929); divorced 1948. Married Cleo McClain (1951). Died April 26, 1956.

Sound Feature Films: *Rasputin and the Empress* (MGM, 1932), *Okay America!* (Univ., 1932), *Afraid to Talk* (Univ., 1932), *Whistling in the Dark* (MGM, 1933), *The White Sister* (MGM, 1933), *The Barbarian* (MGM, 1933), *Jennie Gerhardt* (Par., 1933), *Her Bodyguard* (Par., 1933), *Secret of the Blue Room* (Univ., 1933), *I'm No Angel* (Par.,

Purnell Pratt, Edward Arnold and Harry C. Bradley in *Diamond Jim*.

1933), *Roman Scandals* (UA, 1933), *Madame Spy* (Univ., 1934), *Sadie McKee* (MGM, 1934), *Thirty Day Princess* (Par., 1934), *Unknown Blonde* (Majestic, 1934), *Hide-Out* (MGM, 1934), *Million Dollar Ransom* (Univ., 1934), *The President Vanishes* (Par., 1934), *Wednesday's Child* (RKO, 1934), *Biography of a Bachelor Girl* (MGM, 1935), *Cardinal Richelieu* (UA, 1935), *The Glass Key* (Par., 1935), *Diamond Jim* (Univ., 1935), *Crime and Punishment* (Col., 1935), *Remember Last Night?* (Univ., 1935), *Sutter's Gold* (Univ., 1936), *Meet Nero Wolf* (Col., 1936), *Come and Get It* (UA, 1936), *John Meade's Woman* (Par., 1937), *The Toast of New York* (RKO, 1937), *Easy Living* (Par., 1937), *Blossoms on Broadway* (Par., 1937), *The Crowd Roars* (MGM, 1938), *You Can't Take It With You* (Col., 1938), *Let Freedom Ring* (MGM, 1939), *Idiot's Delight* (MGM, 1939), *Man About Town* (Par., 1939), *Mr. Smith Goes to Washington* (Col., 1939), *Slightly Honorable* (UA, 1940), *The Earl of Chicago* (MGM, 1940), *Johnny Apollo* (20th, 1940), *Lillian Russell* (20th, 1940), *The Penalty* (MGM, 1941), *The Lady From Cheyenne* (Univ., 1941), *Meet John Doe* (WB, 1941), *Nothing But the Truth* (Par., 1941), *Unholy Partners* (MGM, 1941), *Design for Scandal* (MGM, 1941), *Johnny Eager* (MGM, 1941), *All That Money Can Buy* (RKO, 1941), *The War Against Mrs. Hadley* (MGM, 1942), *Eyes in the Night* (MGM, 1942), *The Youngest Profession* (MGM, 1943), *Standing Room Only* (Par., 1944), *Janie* (WB, 1944), *Kismet* (MGM, 1944), *Mrs. Parkington* (MGM, 1944), *Main Street After Dark* (MGM, 1944), *Weekend at the Waldorf* (MGM, 1945), *The Hidden Eye* (MGM, 1945), *Ziegfeld Follies* (MGM, 1946), *Janie Gets Married* (WB, 1946), *Three Wise Fools* (MGM, 1946), *No Leave, No Love* (MGM, 1946), *The Mighty McGurk* (MGM, 1946), *My Brother Talks to Horses* (MGM, 1946), *Dear Ruth* (Par., 1947), *The Hucksters* (MGM, 1947), *Three Daring Daughters* (MGM, 1948), *The Big City* (MGM, 1948), *Wallflower* (WB, 1948), *Command Decision* (MGM, 1948), *John Loves Mary* (WB, 1949), *Take Me Out to the Ball Game* (MGM, 1949), *Big Jack* (MGM, 1949), *Dear Wife* (Par., 1949), *The Yellow Cabman* (MGM, 1950), *Annie Get Your Gun* (MGM, 1950), *The Skipper Surprised His Wife* (MGM, 1950), *Dear Brat* (Par., 1951), *Belles on Their Toes* (20th, 1952), *The City That Never Sleeps* (Rep., 1953), *Man of Conflict* (Atlas, 1953), *Living It Up* (Par., 1954), *The Houston Story* (Col., 1956), *The Ambassador's Daughter* (UA, 1956), *Miami Exposé* (Col., 1956).

JEAN ARTHUR (Gladys Georgianna Greene) Born October 17, 1905, New York, New York. Married Julian Anker (1928); divorced 1928. Married Frank Ross (1932); divorced 1949.

Sound Feature Films: *Easy Come, Easy Go* (Par., 1928), *The Canary Murder Case* (Par., 1929), *The Mysterious Dr. Fu Manchu* (Par., 1929), *The Greene Murder Case* (Par., 1929), *The Saturday Night Kid* (Par., 1929), *Half Way to Heaven* (Par., 1929), *Street of Chance* (Par., 1930), *Young Eagles* (Par., 1930), *Paramount on Parade* (Par., 1930), *The Return of Dr. Fu Manchu* (Par., 1930), *Danger Lights* (RKO, 1930), *The Silver Horde* (RKO, 1930), *The Gang Buster* (Par., 1931), *Virtuous Husband* (Univ., 1931), *The Lawyer's Secret* (Par., 1931), *Ex-Bad Boy* (Univ., 1931), *Get That Venus* (Regent, 1933), *The Past of Mary

Charles Arnt, Lee Bowman and Jean Arthur in *The Impatient Years.*

Holmes (RKO, 1933), *Whirlpool* (Col., 1934), *The Defense Rests* (Col., 1934), *Most Precious Thing in Life* (Col., 1934), *The Whole Town's Talking* (Col., 1935), *Public Hero Number One* (MGM, 1935), *Party Wire* (Col., 1935), *Diamond Jim* (Univ., 1935), *The Public Menace* (Col., 1935), *If You Could Only Cook* (Col., 1935), *Mr. Deeds Goes to Town* (Col., 1936), *The Ex-Mrs. Bradford* (RKO, 1936), *Adventure in Manhattan* (Col., 1936), *The Plainsman* (Par., 1936), *More Than a Secretary* (Col., 1936), *History Is Made at Night* (UA, 1937), *Easy Living* (Par., 1937), *You Can't Take It With You* (Col., 1938), *Only Angels Have Wings* (Col., 1939), *Mr. Smith Goes to Washington* (Col., 1939), *Too Many Husbands* (Col., 1940), *Arizona* (Col., 1940), *The Devil and Miss Jones* (RKO, 1941), *The Talk of the Town* (Col., 1942), *The More the Merrier* (Col., 1943), *A Lady Takes a Chance* (RKO, 1943), *The Impatient Years* (Col., 1944), *A Foreign Affair* (Par., 1948), *Shane* (Par., 1953).

Bing Crosby, Joan Caulfield and Fred Astaire in *Blue Skies.*

FRED ASTAIRE (Frederick Austerlitz) Born May 10, 1899, Omaha, Nebraska. Married Phyllis Potter (1933), children: Fred, Ava; widowed 1954.

Feature Films: *Dancing Lady* (MGM, 1933), *Flying Down to Rio* (RKO, 1933), *Roberta* (RKO, 1935), *Top Hat* (RKO, 1935), *Follow the Fleet* (RKO, 1936), *Swing Time* (RKO, 1936), *Shall We Dance* (RKO, 1937), *A Damsel in Distress* (RKO, 1937), *Carefree* (RKO, 1938), *The Story of Vernon and Irene Castle* (RKO, 1939), *Broadway Melody of 1940* (MGM, 1940), *Second Chorus* (Par., 1940), *You'll Never Get Rich* (Col., 1941), *Holiday Inn* (Par., 1942), *You Were Never Lovelier* (Col., 1942), *The Sky's the Limit* (RKO, 1943), *Yolanda and the Thief* (MGM, 1945), *Ziegfeld Follies of 1946* (MGM, 1946), *Blue Skies* (Par., 1946), *Easter Parade* (MGM, 1948), *The Barkleys of Broadway* (MGM, 1949), *Three Little Words* (MGM, 1950), *Let's Dance* (Par., 1950), *Royal Wedding* (MGM, 1951), *The Belle of New York* (MGM, 1952), *The Band Wagon* (MGM, 1953), *Deep in my Heart* (MGM, 1954), *Daddy Long Legs* (20th, 1955), *Funny Face* (Par., 1957), *Silk Stockings* (MGM, 1957), *On the Beach* (UA, 1959), *The Notorious Landlady* (Col., 1962), *Finian's Rainbow* (WB-7 Arts, 1968).

MARY ASTOR (Lucille Vasconcells Langhanke) Born May 3, 1906, Quincy, Illinois. Married Kenneth Hawks (1928); widowed 1930. Married Franklyn Thorpe (1931), child: Marylyn; divorced 1935. Married Manuel del Campo (1936), child: Anthony; divorced 1941. Married Thomas Wheelock (1945); divorced 1955.

Sound Feature Films: *Ladies Love Brutes* (Par., 1930), *The Runaway Bride* (RKO, 1930), *Holiday* (Pathé, 1930), *The Lash* (WB, 1930), *The Sin Ship* (RKO, 1930), *The Royal Bed* (RKO, 1930), *Other Men's Women* (WB, 1931), *Behind Office Doors* (RKO, 1931), *White Shoulders* (RKO, 1931), *Smart Woman* (RKO, 1931), *Men of Chance* (RKO,

Mary Astor and Van Heflin in *Act of Violence.*

1931), *The Lost Squadron* (RKO, 1932), *A Successful Calamity* (WB, 1932), *Those We Love* (World Wide, 1932), *Red Dust* (MGM, 1932), *The Little Giant* (WB, 1933), *Jennie Gerhardt* (Par., 1933), *The Kennel Murder Case* (WB, 1933), *Convention City* (WB, 1933), *The World Changes* (WB, 1933), *Easy to Love* (WB, 1934), *The Man With Two Faces* (WB, 1934), *Return of the Terror* (WB, 1934), *Upper World* (WB, 1934), *The Case of the Howling Dog* (WB, 1934), *I Am a Thief* (WB, 1934), *Man of Iron* (WB, 1935), *Red Hot Tires* (WB, 1935), *Straight From the Heart* (Univ., 1935), *Dinky* (WB, 1935), *Page Miss Glory* (WB, 1935), *The Murder of Dr. Harrigan* (WB, 1935), *The Lady From Nowhere* (Col., 1936), *And So They Were Married* (Col., 1936), *Dodsworth* (UA, 1936), *Trapped by Television* (Col., 1936), *The Prisoner of Zenda* (UA, 1937), *The Hurricane* (UA, 1937), *Paradise for Three* (MGM, 1938), *No Time to Marry* (Col., 1938), *There's Always a Woman* (Col., 1938), *Woman Against Woman* (MGM, 1938), *Listen, Darling* (MGM, 1938), *Midnight* (Par., 1939), *Turnabout* (UA, 1940), *Brigham Young* (20th, 1940), *The Great Lie* (WB, 1941), *The Maltese Falcon* (WB, 1941), *Across the Pacific* (WB, 1942), *In This Our Life* (WB, 1942)* *Young Ideas* (MGM, 1943), *Meet Me in St. Louis* (MGM, 1944), *Blonde Fever* (MGM, 1944), *Claudia and David* (20th, 1946), *Desert Fury* (Par., 1947), *Cynthia* (MGM, 1947), *Fiesta* (MGM, 1947), *Act of Violence* (MGM, 1948), *Cass Timberlane* (MGM, 1948), *Little Women* (MGM, 1949), *Any Number Can Play* (MGM, 1949), *A Kiss Before Dying* (UA, 1956), *The Power and the Prize* (MGM, 1956), *The Devil's Hairpin* (Par., 1957), *This Happy Feeling* (Univ., 1958), *Stranger in My Arms* (Univ., 1959), *Return to Peyton Place* (20th, 1961), *Youngblood Hawke* (WB, 1964), *Hush . . . Hush, Sweet Charlotte* (20th, 1964).

*Unbilled guest appearance

LIONEL ATWILL Born March 1, 1885, Croydon, England. Married Phyllis Ralph (1917); divorced 1919. Married Elsie Mackay (1919),

Lon Chaney, Jr., Anne Nagel and Lionel Atwill in *Man-Made Monster.*

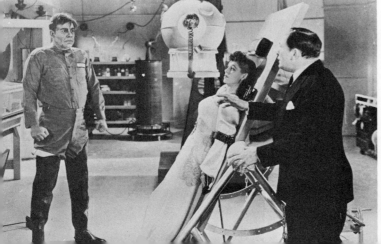

child: John; divorced 1928. Married Louise Stolesbury (1930); divorce 1943. Married Mary Shelstone (1944), child: Lionel. Died April 22 1946.

Sound Feature Films: *Silent Witness* (Fox, 1932), *Dr. X* (WB, 1932), *Vampire Bat* (Majestic, 1933), *Secret of Madame Blanche* (MGM, 1933), *Mystery of the Wax Museum* (WB, 1933), *Murders in the Zoo* (Par., 1933), *The Sphinx* (Mon., 1933), *Song of Songs* (Par., 1933), *Solitaire Man* (MGM, 1933), *Secret of the Blue Room* (Univ., 1933), *Beggars in Ermine* (Mon., 1934), *Nana* (UA, 1934), *Stamboul Quest* (MGM, 1934), *One More River* (Univ., 1934), *Age of Innocence* (RKO, 1935), *Firebird* (WB, 1934), *The Man Who Reclaimed His Head* (Univ., 1935), *Mark of the Vampire* (MGM, 1935), *The Devil Is a Woman* (Par., 1935), *Murder Man* (MGM, 1935), *Rendezvous* (MGM, 1935), *Captain Blood* (WB, 1935), *Lady of Secrets* (Col., 1936), *Absolute Quiet* (MGM, 1936), *Till We Meet Again* (Par., 1936), *The Road Back* (Univ., 1937), *Last Train From Madrid* (Par., 1937), *Lancer Spy* (20th, 1937), *The Wrong Road* (Rep., 1937), *The Great Garrick* (WB, 1937), *High Command* (GN, 1938), *Three Comrades* (MGM, 1938), *The Great Waltz* (MGM, 1938), *The Three Musketeers* (20th, 1939), *Son of Frankenstein* (Univ., 1939), *The Hound of the Baskervilles* (20th, 1939), *The Mad Empress* (WB, 1939), *The Gorilla* (20th, 1939), *The Sun Never Sets* (Univ., 1939), *Mr. Moto Takes a Vacation* (20th, 1939), *The Secret of Dr. Kildare* (MGM, 1939), *Balalaika* (MGM, 1939), *Charlie Chan in Panama* (20th, 1940), *Johnny Apollo* (20th, 1940), *Charlie Chan's Murder Cruise* (20th, 1940), *The Girl in 313* (20th, 1940), *Boom Town* (MGM, 1940), *The Great Profile* (20th, 1940), *Man-Made Monster* (Univ., 1941), *Junior G-Men of the Air* (Univ. serial, 1942), *Ghost of Frankenstein* (Univ., 1942), *Strange Case of Dr. RX*, (Univ., 1942), *Pardon My Sarong* (Univ., 1942), *Cairo* (MGM, 1942), *Night Monster* (Univ., 1942), *Sherlock Holmes and the Secret Weapon* (Univ., 1942), *Mad Doctor of Market Street* (Univ., 1942), *Captain America* (Rep. serial, 1943), *Frankenstein Meets the Wolf Man* (Univ., 1943), *Raiders of Ghost City* (Univ. serial, 1944), *Lady in the Death House* (PRC, 1944), *Secrets of Scotland Yard* (Rep., 1944), *House of Frankenstein* (Univ., 1945), *Fog Island* (PRC, 1945), *Crime, Inc.*, (PRC, 1945), *House of Dracula* (Univ., 1945), *Genius at Work* (RKO, 1946), *Lost City of the Jungle* (Univ. serial, 1946).

GENE AUTRY Born September 29, 1907, Tioga, Texas. Married Ina Spivey (1932).

Feature Films: *In Old Santa Fe* (Mascot, 1934), *Mystery Mountain* (Mascot serial, 1934), *The Phantom Empire* (Mascot serial, 1935), *Tumbling Tumble-weeds* (Rep., 1935), *Melody Trail* (Rep., 1935), *The Sagebrush Troubadour* (Rep., 1935), *The Singing Vagabond* (Rep., 1935), *Red River Valley* (Rep., 1936), *Comin' Round the Mountain* (Rep., 1936), *The Singing Cowboy* (Rep., 1936), *Guns and Guitars* (Rep., 1936), *Oh, Susannah!* (Rep., 1936), *Ride, Ranger, Ride* (Rep., 1936), *The Old Corral* (Rep., 1936), *Round-up Time in Texas* (Rep., 1937), *Git Along, Little Dogies* (Rep., 1937), *Rootin' Tootin' Rhythm* (Rep., 1937),

Smiley Burnette, Charles King, Gene Autry, Tom London, J.P. McGowan, Earle Hodgins and Dorothy Dix in *Guns and Guitars.*

Yodelin' Kid From Pine Ridge (Rep., 1937), *Public Cowboy No. 1* (Rep., 1937), *Boots and Saddles* (Rep., 1937), *Manhattan Merry-Go-Round* (Rep., 1937), *Springtime in the Rockies* (Rep., 1937), *The Old Barn Dance* (Rep., 1938), *Gold Mine in the Sky* (Rep., 1938), *Man from Music Mountain* (Rep., 1938), *Prairie Moon* (Rep., 1938), *Rhythm of the Saddle* (Rep., 1938), *Western Jamboree* (Rep., 1938), *Home on the Prairie* (Rep., 1939), *Mexicali Rose* (Rep., 1939), *Blue Montana Skies* (Rep., 1939), *Mountain Rhythm* (Rep., 1939), *Colorado Sunset* (Rep., 1939), *In Old Monterey* (Rep., 1939), *Rovin' Tumbleweeds* (Rep., 1939), *South of the Border* (Rep., 1939), *Rancho Grande* (Rep., 1940), *Shooting High* (20th, 1940), *Gaucho Serenade* (Rep., 1940), *Carolina Moon* (Rep., 1940), *Ride, Tenderfoot, Ride* (Rep., 1940), *Melody Ranch* (Rep., 1940), *Ridin' on a Rainbow* (Rep., 1941), *Back in the Saddle* (Rep., 1941), *The Singing Hills* (Rep., 1941), *Sunset in Wyoming* (Rep., 1941), *Under Fiesta Stars* (Rep., 1941), *Down Mexico Way* (Rep., 1941), *Sierra Sue* (Rep., 1941), *Cowboy Serenade* (Rep., 1942), *Heart of the Rio Grande* (Rep., 1942), *Home in Wyomin'* (Rep., 1942), *Stardust on the Sage* (Rep., 1942), *Call of the Canyon* (Rep., 1942), *Bells of Capistrano* (Rep., 1942), *Sioux City Sue* (Rep., 1946), *Trail to San Antone* (Rep., 1947), *Twilight on the Rio Grande* (Rep., 1947), *Saddle Pals* (Rep., 1947), *Robin Hood of Texas* (Rep., 1947), *The Last Round-up* (Col., 1947), *The Strawberry Roan* (Col., 1948), *Loaded Pistols* (Col., 1949), *The Big Sombrero* (Col., 1949), *Riders of the Whistling Pines* (Col., 1949), *Rim of the Canyon* (Col., 1949), *The Cowboy and the Indians* (Col., 1949), *Riders in the Sky* (Col., 1949), *Sons of New Mexico* (Col., 1950), *Mule Train* (Col., 1950), *Cow Town* (Col., 1950), *Beyond the Purple Hills* (Col., 1950), *Indian Territory* (Col., 1950), *The Blazing Hills* (Col., 1950), *Gene Autry and the Mounties* (Col., 1951), *Texans Never Cry* (Col., 1951), *Whirlwind* (Col., 1951), *Silver Canyon* (Col., 1951), *Hills of Utah* (Col., 1951), *Valley of Fire* (Col., 1951), *The Old West* (Col., 1952), *Night Stage to Galveston* (Col., 1952), *Apache Country* (Col., 1952), *Barbed Wire* (Col., 1952), *Wagon Team* (Col., 1952), *Blue Canadian Rockies* (Col., 1952), *Winning of the West* (Col., 1953), *On Top of Old Smoky* (Col., 1953), *Goldtown Ghost Riders* (Col., 1953), *Pack Train* (Col., 1953), *Saginaw Trail* (Col., 1953), *Last of the Pony Riders* (Col., 1953), *Silent Treatment* (Ralph Andrews, 1968).

LEW AYRES (Lewis Ayres) Born December 28, 1908, Minneapolis, Minnesota. Married Lola Lane; divorced 1933. Married Ginger Rogers (1933); divorced 1940. Married Diana Hall (1964).

Sound Feature Films: *The Sophomore* (Pathé, 1929), *All Quiet on the Western Front* (Univ., 1930), *Common Clay* (Fox, 1930), *Doorway to Hell* (WB, 1930), *East Is West* (Univ., 1930), *Iron Man* (Univ., 1931),

Lionel Barrymore and Lew Ayres in *Young Dr. Kildare.*

Up for Murder (Univ., 1931), *Many a Slip* (Univ., 1931), *Spirit of Notre Dame* (Univ., 1931), *Heaven on Earth* (Univ., 1931), *Impatient Maiden* (Univ., 1932), *Night World* (Univ., 1932), *Okay America!* (Univ., 1932), *State Fair* (Fox, 1933), *Don't Bet on Love* (Univ., 1933), *My Weakness* (Fox, 1933), *Cross Country Cruise* (Univ., 1934), *Let's Be Ritzy* (Univ., 1934), *She Learned About Sailors* (Fox, 1934), *Servants' Entrance* (Fox, 1934), *Lottery Lover* (Fox, 1935), *Silk Hat Kid* (Fox, 1935), *The Leathernecks Have Landed* (Rep., 1936), *Panic on the Air* (Col., 1936), *Shakedown* (Col., 1936), *Lady Be Careful* (Par., 1936), *Murder With Pictures* (Par., 1936), *The Crime Nobody Saw* (Par., 1937), *Last Train From Madrid* (Par., 1937), *Hold 'Em Navy* (Par., 1937), *King of the Newsboys* (Rep., 1938), *Scandal Street* (Par., 1938), *Holiday* (Col., 1938), *Rich Man—Poor Girl* (MGM, 1938), *Young Dr. Kildare* (MGM, 1938), *Spring Madness* (MGM, 1938), *Ice Follies of 1939* (MGM, 1939), *Broadway Serenade* (MGM, 1939), *Calling Dr. Kildare* (MGM, 1939), *These Glamour Girls* (MGM, 1939), *Remember?* (MGM, 1939), *Secret of Dr. Kildare* (MGM, 1939), *Dr. Kildare's Strange Case* (MGM, 1940), *The Golden Fleecing* (MGM, 1940), *Dr. Kildare Goes Home* (MGM, 1940), *Dr. Kildare's Crisis* (MGM, 1940), *Maisie Was a Lady* (MGM, 1941), *The People vs. Dr. Kildare* (MGM, 1941), *Dr. Kildare's Wedding Day* (MGM, 1942), *Dr. Kildare's Victory* (MGM, 1942), *Fingers at the Window* (MGM,1942), *The Dark Mirror* (Univ., 1946), *The Unfaithful* (WB, 1947), *Johnny Belinda* (WB, 1948), *The Capture* (RKO, 1950), *New Mexico* (UA, 1951), *No Escape* (UA, 1953), *Donovan's Brain* (UA, 1953), *Advise and Consent* (Col., 1962), *The Carpetbaggers* (Par., 1964).

Lauren Bacall and Humphrey Bogart in *Dark Passage.*

LAUREN BACALL (Betty Joan Perske) Born September 16, 1924, New York, New York. Married Humphrey Bogart (1945), children: Stephen, Leslie; widowed 1957. Married Jason Robards, Jr. (1961), child: Sam.

Feature Films: *To Have and Have Not* (WB, 1944), *Confidential Agent* (WB, 1945), *Two Guys From Milwaukee* (WB, 1946),* *The Big Sleep* (WB, 1946), *Dark Passage* (WB, 1947), *Key Largo* (WB, 1948), *Young Man With a Horn* (WB, 1950), *Bright Leaf* (WB, 1950), *How to Marry a Millionaire* (20th, 1953), *Woman's World* (20th, 1954), *The Cobweb* (MGM, 1955), *Blood Alley* (WB, 1955), *Written on the Wind* (Univ., 1956), *Designing Woman* (MGM, 1957), *The Gift of Love* (20th, 1958), *Flame Over India* (20th, 1960), *Shock Treatment* (20th, 1964), *Sex and the Single Girl* (WB, 1965), *Harper* (WB, 1966).

*Unbilled guest appearance

FAY BAINTER Born December 7, 1892, Los Angeles, California. Married Reginald Venable (1922), child: Reginald; widowed 1964. Died April 16, 1968.

Feature Films: *This Side of Heaven* (MGM, 1934), *Quality Street* (RKO, 1937), *The Soldier and the Lady* (RKO, 1937), *Make Way for Tomorrow* (Par., 1937), *Jezebel* (WB, 1938), *White Banners* (WB,

Judy Garland and Fay Bainter in *Presenting Lily Mars.*

LUCILLE BALL Born August 6, 1910, Butte, Montana. Married Desi Arnaz (1940), children: Lucie, Desi; divorced 1960. Married Gary Morton (1961).

Feature Films: *Roman Scandals* (UA, 1933), *Blood Money* (UA, 1933), *Moulin Rouge* (UA, 1934), *Nana* (UA, 1934), *Hold That Girl* (Fox, 1934), *Jealousy* (Col., 1934), *Fugitive Lady* (Col., 1934), *Men of the Night* (Col., 1934), *Bottoms Up* (Fox, 1934), *Broadway Bill* (Col., 1934), *Bulldog Drummond Strikes Back* (UA, 1934), *Kid Millions* (UA, 1934), *Affairs of Cellini* (UA, 1934), *Roberta* (RKO, 1935), *Old Man Rhythm* (RKO, 1935), *Carnival* (Col., 1935), *I Dream Too Much* (RKO, 1935), *Top Hat* (RKO, 1935), *Chatterbox* (RKO, 1936), *Winterset* (RKO, 1936), *Follow the Fleet* (RKO, 1936), *The Farmer in the Dell* (RKO, 1936), *Bunker Bean* (RKO, 1936), *That Girl From Paris* (RKO, 1936), *Don't Tell the Wife* (RKO, 1937), *Stage Door* (RKO, 1937), *Joy of Living* (RKO, 1938), *Go Chase Yourself* (RKO, 1938), *Having Wonderful Time* (RKO, 1938), *The Affairs of Annabel* (RKO, 1938), *Room Service* (RKO, 1938), *Next Time I Marry* (RKO, 1938), *Annabel Takes a Tour* (RKO, 1938), *Beauty for the Asking* (RKO, 1939), *Twelve Crowded Hours* (RKO, 1939), *Panama Lady* (RKO, 1939), *Five Came Back* (RKO, 1939), *That's Right, You're Wrong* (RKO, 1939), *The Marines Fly High* (RKO, 1940), *You Can't Fool Your Wife* (RKO, 1940), *Dance, Girl, Dance* (RKO, 1940), *Too Many Girls* (RKO, 1940), *A Girl, a Guy and a Gob* (RKO, 1941), *Look Who's Laughing* (RKO, 1941), *Valley of the Sun* (RKO, 1942), *The Big Street* (RKO, 1942), *Seven Days' Leave* (RKO, 1942), *Du Barry Was a Lady* (MGM, 1943), *Best Foot Forward* (MGM, 1943), *Thousands Cheer* (MGM, 1943), *Meet the People* (MGM, 1944), *Abbott and Costello in Hollywood* (MGM, 1945), *Without Love* (MGM, 1945), *Ziegfeld Follies of*

1938), *Mother Carey's Chickens* (RKO, 1938), *The Arkansas Traveler* (Par., 1938), *The Shining Hour* (MGM, 1938), *Yes, My Darling Daughter* (WB, 1939), *The Lady and the Mob* (Col., 1939), *Daughters Courageous* (WB, 1939), *Our Neighbors, the Carters* (Par., 1939), *Young Tom Edison* (MGM, 1940), *A Bill of Divorcement* (RKO, 1940), *Our Town* (UA, 1940), *Maryland* (20th, 1940), *Babes on Broadway* (MGM, 1941), *Woman of the Year* (MGM, 1942), *The War Against Mrs. Hadley* (MGM, 1942), *Mrs. Wiggs of the Cabbage Patch* (Par., 1942), *Journey for Margaret* (MGM, 1942), *The Human Comedy* (MGM, 1943), *Presenting Lily Mars* (MGM, 1943), *Salute to the Marines* (MGM, 1943), *Cry Havoc* (MGM, 1943), *The Heavenly Body* (MGM, 1943), *Dark Waters* (UA, 1944), *Three Is a Family* (UA, 1944), *State Fair* (20th, 1945), *The Kid From Brooklyn* (RKO, 1946), *The Virginian* (Par., 1946), *Deep Valley* (WB, 1947), *The Secret Life of Walter Mitty* (RKO, 1947), *Give My Regards to Broadway* (20th, 1948), *June Bride* (WB, 1948), *Close to My Heart* (WB, 1951), *The President's Lady* (20th, 1953), *The Children's Hour* (UA, 1962).

Carroll Baker, Hanna Landy and Red Buttons in *Harlow.*

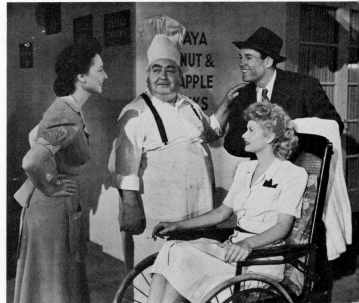

Agnes Moorehead, Eugene Pallette, Henry Fonda and Lucille Ball in *The Big Street.*

CARROLL BAKER Born May 28, 1931, Johnstown, Pennsylvania. Married Jack Garfein (1955), children: Blanche, Herschel.

Feature Films: *Easy to Love* (MGM, 1953), *Giant* (WB, 1956), *Baby Doll* (WB, 1956), *The Big Country* (UA, 1958), *The Miracle* (WB, 1959), *But Not for Me* (Par., 1959), *Something Wild* (UA, 1961), *Bridge to the Sun* (MGM, 1961), *How the West Was Won* (MGM, 1963), *Station Six—Sahara* (AA, 1964), *The Carpetbaggers* (Par., 1964), *Cheyenne Autumn* (WB, 1964), *The Greatest Story Ever Told* (UA, 1965), *Sylvia* (UA, 1965), *Mr. Moses* (UA, 1965), *Harlow* (Par., 1965), *Jack of Diamonds* (MGM, 1967), *Her Harem* (Sancro, 1968).

1946 (MGM, 1946), *The Dark Corner* (20th, 1946), *Lover Come Back* (Univ., 1946), *Easy to Wed* (MGM, 1946), *Two Smart People* (MGM, 1946), *Lured* (UA, 1947), *Her Husband's Affairs* (Col., 1947), *Miss Grant Takes Richmond* (Col., 1949), *Sorrowful Jones* (Par., 1949), *Easy Living* (RKO, 1949), *Fancy Pants* (Par., 1950), *A Woman of Distinction* (Col., 1950),* *The Fuller Brush Girl* (Col., 1950), *The Magic Carpet* (Col., 1951), *The Long, Long Trailer* (MGM, 1954), *Forever Darling* (MGM, 1956), *The Facts of Life* (UA, 1960), *Critic's Choice* (WB, 1963), *A Guide for the Married Man* (20th, 1967), *Yours, Mine and Ours* (UA, 1968).

*Unbilled guest appearance.

Martin Balsam and Paul Newman in *Hombre*.

Gordon Westcott, Gary Cooper, Tallulah Bankhead and Charles Laughton in *Devil and the Deep*.

MARTIN BALSAM (Martin Henry Balsam) Born November 4, 1919, New York, New York. Married Pearl Somner (1952); divorced 1954. Married Joyce Van Patten (1959), child: Talia; divorced 1962. Married Irene Miller (1963).

English-Language Feature Films: *On the Waterfront* (Col., 1954), *12 Angry Men* (UA, 1957), *Time Limit* (UA, 1957), *Marjorie Morningstar* (WB, 1958), *Al Capone* (AA, 1959), *Middle of the Night* (Col., 1959), *Psycho* (Par., 1960), *Ada* (MGM, 1961), *Breakfast at Tiffany's* (Par., 1961), *Cape Fear* (UA, 1962), *Who's Been Sleeping in My Bed?* (Par., 1963), *The Carpetbaggers* (Par., 1964), *Youngblood Hawke* (WB, 1964), *Seven Days in May* (Par., 1964), *Harlow* (Par., 1965), *The Bedford Incident* (Col., 1965), *A Thousand Clowns* (UA, 1965), *After the Fox* (UA, 1966), *Hombre* (20th, 1967), *2001: A Space Odyssey* (MGM, 1968).

Steven Hill and Anne Bancroft in *The Slender Thread*.

ANNE BANCROFT (Anna Maria Italiano) Born September 17, 1931, Bronx, New York. Married Martin May (1953); divorced 1957. Married Mel Brooks (1964).

Feature Films: *Don't Bother to Knock* (20th, 1952), *Tonight We Sing* (20th, 1953), *Treasure of the Golden Condor* (20th, 1953), *The Kid From Left Field* (20th, 1953), *Demetrius and the Gladiators* (20th, 1954), *The Raid* (20th, 1954), *Gorilla at Large* (20th, 1954), *A Life in the Balance* (20th, 1955), *New York Confidential* (WB, 1955), *The Naked Street* (UA, 1955), *The Last Frontier* (Col., 1955), *Walk the Proud Land* (Univ., 1956), *Nightfall* (Col., 1956), *The Restless Breed* (20th, 1957), *The Girl in Black Stockings* (UA, 1957), *The Miracle Worker* (UA, 1962), *The Pumpkin Eater* (UA, 1964), *The Slender Thread* (Par., 1965), *Seven Women* (MGM, 1965), *The Graduate* (Embassy, 1967).

TALLULAH BANKHEAD Born January 31, 1902, Huntsville, Alabama. Married John Emery (1937); divorced 1941.

Sound Feature Films: *Tarnished Lady* (Par., 1931), *My Sin* (Par., 1931), *The Cheat* (Par., 1931), *Thunder Below* (Par., 1932), *Make Me a Star* (Par., 1932),* *Devil and the Deep* (Par., 1932), *Faithless* (Par., 1932), *Stage Door Canteen* (UA, 1943), *Lifeboat* (20th, 1944), *A Royal Scandal* (20th, 1945), *Main Street to Broadway* (MGM, 1953), *Die! Die! My Darling!* (Col., 1965), *The Daydreamer* (voice only; Embassy, 1966).

*Unbilled guest appearance.

LYNN BARI (Marjorie Schuyler Fisher) Born December 18, 1917, Roanoke, Virginia. Married Walter Kane (1938), divorced 1943. Married Sid Luft (1943), child: John; divorced 1950. Married Nathan Rickles (1955).

Feature Films: *Dancing Lady* (MGM, 1933), *Meet the Baron* (MGM, 1933), *Coming Out Party* (Fox, 1934), *Stand Up and Cheer* (Fox, 1934), *Search for Beauty* (Par., 1934), *George White's Scandals* (Fox, 1935), *Caravan* (Fox, 1934), *Spring Tonic* (Fox, 1935), *My Marriage* (20th, 1935), *The Man Who Broke the Bank at Monte Carlo* (Fox, 1935), *Redheads on Parade* (Fox, 1935), *Thanks a Million* (Fox, 1935), *Music is Magic* (Fox, 1935), *Everybody's Old Man* (20th, 1936), *Ladies in Love* (20th, 1936), *The Song and Dance Man* (20th, 1936), *Crack-Up* (20th, 1936), *Pigskin Parade* (20th, 1936), *Sing, Baby, Sing* (20th, 1936), *36 Hours to Kill* (20th, 1936), *Wee Willie Winkie* (20th, 1937), *This Is My Affair* (20th, 1937), *Sing and Be Happy* (20th, 1937), *Love Is News* (20th, 1937), *Lancer Spy* (20th, 1937), *Wife, Doctor and Nurse* (20th, 1937), *On the Avenue* (20th, 1937), *I'll Give a Million* (20th, 1938), *Rebecca of Sunnybrook Farm* (20th, 1938), *Josette* (20th, 1938), *Speed to Burn* (20th, 1938), *The Baroness and the Butler* (20th, 1938), *Walking Down Broadway* (20th, 1938), *Mr. Moto's Gamble* (20th, 1938), *Battle of Broadway* (20th, 1938), *Always Goodbye* (20th, 1938), *Sharpshooters*

Lynn Bari and Edward G. Robinson in *Tampico*.

(20th, 1938), *Meet the Girls* (20th, 1938), *Return of the Cisco Kid* (20th, 1939), *Chasing Danger* (20th, 1939), *News Is Made at Night* (20th, 1939), *Pack Up Your Troubles* (20th, 1939), *Elsa Maxwell's Hotel for Women* (20th, 1939), *Charlie Chan in City in Darkness* (20th, 1939), *Hollywood Cavalcade* (20th, 1939), *Pardon Our Nerve* (20th, 1939), *City of Chance* (20th, 1940), *Free, Blonde and 21* (20th, 1940), *Lillian Russell* (20th, 1940), *Earthbound* (20th, 1940), *Pier 13* (20th, 1940), *Kit Carson* (UA, 1940), *Charter Pilot* (20th, 1940), *Sleepers West* (20th, 1941), *Blood and Sand* (20th, 1941), *We Go Fast* (20th, 1941), *Sun Valley Serenade* (20th, 1941), *Moon Over Her Shoulder* (20th, 1941), *The Perfect Snob* (20th, 1941), *Secret Agent of Japan* (20th, 1942), *Night Before the Divorce* (20th, 1942), *The Falcon Takes Over* (RKO, 1942), *The Magnificent Dope* (20th, 1942), *Orchestra Wives* (20th, 1942), *China Girl* (20th, 1942), *Hello, Frisco, Hello* (20th, 1943), *The Bridge of San Luis Rey* (UA, 1944), *Tampico* (20th, 1944), *Sweet and Lowdown* (20th, 1944), *Captain Eddie* (20th, 1945), *Shock* (20th, 1946), *Home Sweet Homicide* (20th, 1946), *Margie* (20th, 1946), *Nocturne* (RKO, 1946), *The Man From Texas* (EL, 1948), *The Spiritualist* (EL, 1948), *The Kid From Cleveland* (Rep., 1949), *I'd Climb the Highest Mountain* (20th, 1951), *On the Loose* (RKO, 1951), *Sunny Side of the Street* (Col., 1951), *Has Anybody Seen My Gal* (Univ., 1952), *I Dream of Jeannie* (Rep., 1952), *Francis Joins the WACs* (Univ., 1954), *Abbott and Costello Meet the Keystone Kops* (Univ., 1955), *The Women of Pitcairn Island* (20th, 1956), *Damn Citizen* (Univ., 1958), *Trauma* (Parade, 1964).

Brenda Joyce, Lex Barker and Evelyn Ankers in *Tarzan's Magic Fountain.*

LEX BARKER (Alexander Crichlow Barker) Born May 8, 1919, Rye, New York. Married Constance Thurlow (1942), children: Lynne Alexander; divorced 1951. Married Arlene Dahl (1951); divorced 1952. Married Lana Turner (1953); divorced 1957. Married Irene Labhart (1959), child: Christopher; widowed 1962. Married Maria Cervera (1965).

English-Language Feature Films: *Doll Face* (20th, 1945), *Do You Love Me?* (20th, 1946), *Two Guys From Milwaukee* (WB, 1946), *Farmer's Daughter* (RKO, 1947), *Dick Tracy Meets Gruesome* (RKO, 1947), *Crossfire* (RKO, 1947), *Under the Tonto Rim* (RKO, 1947), *Unconquered* (Par., 1947), *Mr. Blandings Builds His Dream House* (RKO, 1948), *Return of the Bad Men* (RKO, 1948), *The Velvet Touch* (RKO, 1948), *Tarzan's Magic Fountain* (RKO, 1949), *Tarzan and the Slave Girl* (RKO, 1950), *Tarzan's Peril* (RKO, 1951), *Tarzan's Savage Fury* (RKO, 1952), *Battles of Chief Pontiac* (Realart, 1952), *Tarzan and the She-Devil* (RKO, 1953), *Thunder Over the Plains* (WB, 1953), *The Yellow Mountain* (Univ., 1954), *The Man From Bitter Ridge* (Univ., 1955), *Duel on the Mississippi* (Col., 1955), *Mystery of the Black Jungle* (Rep., 1955), *The Price of Fear* (Univ., 1956), *Away All Boats* (Univ., 1956), *The Girl in the Kremlin* (Univ., 1957), *War Drums* (UA, 1957), *Jungle Heat* (UA, 1957), *The Deerslayer* (20th, 1957), *The Girl in Black Stockings* (UA, 1957), *Strange Awakening* (Merton Park Studios, 1958), *Mission in Morocco* (Venus Enterprises, 1959), *Code 7, Victim 5* (Col., 1964), *24 Hours to Kill* (7 Arts, 1966), *Woman Times Seven* (Embassy, 1967), *Devil May Care* (Feature Film Corp. of America, 1968).

BINNIE BARNES (Gitelle Enoyce Barnes) Born March 25, 1906, London, England. Married Samuel Joseph (1932); divorced 1936. Married Mike Frankovich (1940), children: Michael, Michelle, Peter.

Janet Blair, Joan Blondell and Binnie Barnes in *Three Girls About Town.*

Feature Films: *Night in Montmartre* (Gaumont-British, 1931), *Love Lies* (British International, 1931), *Dr. Josser, K. C.* (British International, 1931), *Out of the Blue* (British International, 1931), *Down Our Street* (Par., 1931), *Murder at Covent Garden* (Twickenham, 1931), *Strip Strip Hooray* (British International, 1932), *Partners, Please* (PDC, 1932), *The Last Coupon* (British International, 1932), *Old Spanish Customs* (British International, 1932), *Innocents in Chicago* (British International, 1932), *Council's Opinion* (London Films, 1933), *Heads We Go* (British International, 1933), *The Private Life of Henry VIII* (UA, 1933), *The Private Life of Don Juan* (UA, 1934), *The Lady Is Willing* (Col., 1934), *Gift of Gab* (Univ., 1934), *There's Always Tomorrow* (Univ., 1934), *One Exciting Adventure* (Univ., 1934), *No Escape* (British, 1934), *Diamond Jim* (Univ., 1935), *Rendezvous* (MGM, 1935), *Small Town Girl* (MGM, 1936), *Sutter's Gold* (Univ., 1936), *The Last of the Mohicans* (UA, 1936), *The Magnificent Brute* (Univ., 1936), *Breezing Home* (Univ., 1937), *Three Smart Girls* (Univ., 1937), *Broadway Melody of 1938* (MGM, 1937), *The First Hundred Years* (MGM, 1938), *The Adventures of Marco Polo* (UA, 1938), *Holiday* (Col., 1938), *Always Goodbye* (20th, 1938), *Gateway* (20th, 1938), *Tropic Holiday* (Par., 1938), *Three Blind Mice* (20th, 1938), *Thanks for Everything* (20th, 1938), *The Divorce of Lady X* (UA, 1939), *Wife, Husband and Friend* (20th, 1939), *The Three Musketeers* (20th, 1939), *Man About Town* (Par., 1939), *Frontier Marshal* (20th, 1939), *Day-Time Wife* (20th, 1939), *Till We Meet Again* (WB, 1940), *New Wine* (UA, 1941), *This Thing Called Love* (Col., 1941), *Angels With Broken Wings* (Rep., 1941), *Tight Shoes* (Univ., 1941), *Skylark* (Par., 1941), *Three Girls About Town* (Col., 1941), *Call Out the Marines* (RKO, 1942), *I Married an Angel* (MGM, 1942), *In Old California* (Rep., 1942), *The Man From Down Under* (MGM, 1943), *Barbary Coast Gent* (MGM, 1944), *The Hour Before the Dawn* (Par., 1944), *Up in Mabel's Room* (UA, 1944), *It's in the Bag* (UA, 1945), *The Spanish Main* (RKO, 1945), *Getting Gertie's Garter* (UA, 1945), *The Time of Their Lives* (Univ., 1946), *If Winter Comes* (MGM, 1947), *The Dude Goes West* (AA, 1948), *My Own True Love* (Par., 1948), *The Pirates of Capri* (Film Classics, 1949), *Fugitive Lady* (Rep., 1951), *Decameron Nights* (RKO, 1953), *Fire Over Africa* (Col., 1954), *Shadow of the Eagle* (UA, 1955), *The Trouble With Angels* (Col., 1966), *Where Angels Go . . . Trouble Follows* (Col., 1968).

ETHEL BARRYMORE (Ethel Mae Barrymore) Born August 15, 1879, Philadelphia, Pennsylvania. Married Russell Colt (1909), children: Samuel, John, Ethel; divorced 1923. Died June 18, 1959.

Sound Feature Films: *Rasputin and the Empress* (MGM, 1932), *None But the Lonely Heart* (RKO, 1944), *The Spiral Staircase* (RKO, 1946), *The Farmer's Daughter* (RKO, 1947), *Moss Rose* (20th, 1947), *Night Song* (RKO, 1947), *The Paradine Case* (Selznick, 1948), *Moonrise* (Rep., 1948), *Portrait of Jennie* (Selznick, 1948), *The Great Sinner* (MGM, 1949), *That Midnight Kiss* (MGM, 1949), *The Red Danube* (MGM, 1949), *Pinky* (20th, 1949), *Kind Lady* (MGM, 1951), *The Secret of Convict Lake* (20th, 1951), *It's a Big Country* (MGM, 1951), *Deadline, U.S.A.* (20th, 1952), *Just for You* (Par., 1952), *The Story of Three Loves* (MGM, 1953), *Main Street to Broadway* (MGM, 1953), *Young at Heart* (WB, 1954), *Johnny Trouble* (WB, 1957).

Maurice Evans, Betsy Blair, Ethel Barrymore, Keenan Wynn and Angela Lansbury in *Kind Lady*.

Peter Holden, John Barrymore, Virginia Weidler and Katharine Alexander in *The Great Man Votes*.

JOHN BARRYMORE Born Feb. 15, 1882, Philadelphia, Pennsylvania. Married Katherine Harris (1910); divorced 1917. Married Mrs. Leonard Thomas (1917), child: Diana; divorced 1928. Married Dolores Costello (1928); divorced 1935. Married Elaine Barrie (1936); divorced 1940. Died May 29, 1942.

Sound Feature Films: *Show of Shows* (WB, 1929), *General Crack* (WB, 1929), *The Man From Blankley's* (WB, 1930), *Moby Dick* (WB, 1930), *Svengali* (WB, 1931), *Mad Genius* (WB, 1931), *Arsene Lupin* (MGM, 1932), *Grand Hotel* (MGM, 1932), *State's Attorney* (RKO, 1932), *A Bill of Divorcement* (RKO, 1932), *Rasputin and the Empress* (MGM, 1932), *Topaze* (RKO, 1933), *Reunion in Vienna* (MGM, 1933), *Dinner at Eight* (MGM, 1933), *Night Flight* (MGM, 1933), *Counsellor at Law* (Univ., 1933), *Long Lost Father* (RKO, 1934), *Twentieth Century* (Col., 1934), *Romeo and Juliet* (MGM, 1936), *Maytime* (MGM, 1937), *Bulldog Drummond Comes Back* (Par., 1937), *Night Club Scandal* (Par., 1937), *True Confession* (Par., 1937), *Bulldog Drummond's Revenge* (Par., 1937), *Bulldog Drummond's Peril* (Par., 1938), *Romance in the Dark* (Par., 1938), *Spawn of the North* (Par., 1938), *Marie Antoinette* (MGM, 1938), *Hold That Co-ed* (20th, 1938), *The Great Man Votes* (RKO, 1939), *Midnight* (Par., 1939), *The Great Profile* (20th, 1940), *The Invisible Woman* (Univ., 1941), *World Premiere* (Par., 1941), *Playmates* (RKO, 1941).

LIONEL BARRYMORE Born April 28, 1878, Philadelphia, Pennsylvania. Married Doris Rankin (1904); divorced 1922. Married Irene Fenwick (1932); widowed 1936. Died November 15, 1954.

Sound Feature Films: *Alias Jimmy Valentine* (MGM, 1928), *Mysterious Island* (MGM, 1929), *Hollywood Revue of 1929* (MGM, 1929), *Free and Easy* (MGM, 1930), *A Free Soul* (MGM, 1931), *Guilty Hands* (MGM, 1931), *Yellow Ticket* (Fox, 1931), *Mata Hari* (MGM, 1931), *Broken Lullaby* (Par., 1932), *Arsene Lupin* (MGM, 1932), *Grand Hotel* (MGM, 1932), *Washington Masquerade* (MGM, 1932), *Rasputin and*

John Barrymore and Lionel Barrymore in *Arsene Lupin*.

the Empress (MGM, 1932), *Sweepings* (RKO, 1933), *Looking Forward* (MGM, 1933), *Dinner at Eight* (MGM, 1933), *Stranger's Return* (MGM, 1933), *Night Flight* (MGM, 1933), *One Man's Journey* (RKO, 1933), *Christopher Bean* (MGM, 1933), *Should Ladies Behave?* (MGM, 1933), *This Side of Heaven* (MGM, 1934), *Carolina* (Fox, 1934), *Treasure Island* (MGM, 1934), *Girl From Missouri* (MGM, 1934), *David Copperfield* (MGM, 1935), *Mark of the Vampire* (MGM, 1935), *Little Colonel* (Fox, 1935), *Public Hero Number One* (MGM, 1935), *The Return of Peter Grimm* (RKO, 1935), *Ah! Wilderness* (MGM, 1936), *The Voice of Bugle Ann* (MGM, 1936), *The Road to Glory* (20th, 1936), *The Devil Doll* (MGM, 1936), *The Gorgeous Hussy* (MGM, 1936), *Camille* (MGM, 1936), *Captains Courageous* (MGM, 1937), *A Family Affair* (MGM, 1937), *Saratoga* (MGM, 1937), *Navy Blue and Gold* (MGM, 1937), *Test Pilot* (MGM, 1938), *A Yank at Oxford* (MGM, 1938), *You Can't Take It With You* (Col., 1938), *Young Dr. Kildare* (MGM, 1938), *Let Freedom Ring* (MGM, 1939), *Calling Dr. Kildare* (MGM, 1939), *On Borrowed Time* (MGM, 1939), *Secret of Dr. Kildare* (MGM, 1939), *Dr. Kildare's Strange Case* (MGM, 1940), *Dr. Kildare Goes Home* (MGM, 1940), *Dr. Kildare's Crisis* (MGM, 1940), *The Bad Man* (MGM, 1941), *The Penalty* (MGM, 1941), *The People vs. Dr. Kildare* (MGM, 1941), *Lady Be Good* (MGM, 1941), *Dr. Kildare's Wedding Day* (MGM, 1941), *Dr. Kildare's Victory* (MGM, 1942), *Calling Dr. Gillespie* (MGM, 1942), *Dr. Gillespie's New Assistant* (MGM, 1942), *Tennessee Johnson* (MGM, 1942), *Thousands Cheer* (MGM, 1943), *Dr. Gillespie's Criminal Case* (MGM, 1943), *A Guy Named Joe* (MGM, 1943), *Three Men in White* (MGM, 1944), *Since You Went Away* (UA, 1944), *Valley of Decision* (MGM, 1945), *Between Two Women* (MGM, 1945), *Three Wise Fools* (MGM, 1946), *The Secret Heart* (MGM, 1946), *It's A Wonderful Life* (RKO, 1946), *Duel in the Sun* (Selznick, 1946), *Dark Delusion* (MGM, 1947), *Key Largo* (WB, 1948), *Down to the Sea in Ships* (20th, 1949), *Malaya* (MGM, 1949), *Right Cross* (MGM, 1950), *Bannerline* (MGM, 1951), *Lone Star* (MGM, 1952), *Main Street to Broadway* (MGM, 1953).

RICHARD BARTHELMESS (Richard Semler Barthelmess) Born May 9, 1895, New York, New York. Married Mary Hay (1920), child: Mary; divorced 1926. Married Jessica Sargeant (1928). Died August 17, 1963.

Richard Barthelmess, Clyde Cook, Douglas Fairbanks, Jr., and Edmund Breon in *Dawn Patrol*.

Sound Feature Films: *Weary River* (WB, 1929), *Drag* (WB, 1929), *Young Nowheres* (WB, 1929), *The Show of Shows* (WB, 1929), *Son of the Gods* (WB, 1930), *The Dawn Patrol* (WB, 1930), *The Lash* (WB, 1930), *The Finger Points* (WB, 1931), *The Last Flight* (WB, 1931), *Alias the Doctor* (WB, 1932), *Cabin in the Cotton* (WB, 1932), *Central Airport* (WB, 1933), *Heroes for Sale* (WB, 1933), *Massacre* (WB, 1934), *A Modern Hero* (WB, 1934), *Midnight Alibi* (WB, 1934), *Four Hours to Kill* (Par., 1935), *Spy of Napoleon* (Twickenham-Unity Prod., 1936), *Only Angels Have Wings* (Col., 1939), *The Man Who Talked Too Much* (WB, 1940), *The Mayor of 44th Street* (RKO, 1942), *The Spoilers* (Univ., 1942).

Freddie Bartholomew and Victor McLaglen in *Professional Soldier*.

FREDDIE BARTHOLOMEW (Frederick Llewellyn) Born March 28, 1924, London, England. Married Maely Daniele (1946); divorced 1953. Married Aileen Paul (1953), children: Kathleen, Frederick.

Feature Films: *David Copperfield* (MGM, 1935), *Anna Karenina* (MGM, 1935), *Professional Soldier* (MGM, 1935), *Little Lord Fauntleroy* (MGM, 1936), *The Devil Is a Sissy* (MGM, 1936), *Lloyds of London* (20th, 1936), *Captains Courageous* (MGM, 1937), *Kidnapped* (20th, 1938), *Lord Jeff* (MGM, 1938), *Listen, Darling* (MGM, 1938), *Spirit of Culver* (Univ., 1938), *Two Bright Boys* (Univ., 1939), *Swiss Family Robinson* (RKO, 1940), *Tom Brown's School Days* (RKO, 1940), *Naval Academy* (Col., 1941), *Cadets on Parade* (Col., 1942), *A Yank at Eton* (MGM, 1942), *The Town Went Wild* (PRC, 1944), *Sepia Cinderella* (Herald Pictures, 1947), *St. Benny the Dip* (UA, 1951).

FLORENCE BATES (Florence Rabe) Born April 15, 1888, San Antonio, Texas. Married 1909, child: Ann; divorced. Married Will Jacoby (1929); widowed 1951. Died January 31, 1954.

Feature Films: *The Man in Blue* (Univ., 1937), *Rebecca* (UA, 1940), *Calling All Husbands* (WB, 1940), *The Son of Monte Cristo* (UA, 1940), *Hudson's Bay* (20th, 1940), *Kitty Foyle* (RKO, 1940), *Road*

Raymond Hatton and Florence Bates in *County Fair.*

Show (UA, 1941), *Strange Alibi* (WB, 1941), *Love Crazy* (MGM, 1941), *The Devil and Miss Jones* (RKO, 1941), *The Chocolate Soldier* (MGM, 1941), *Mexican Spitfire at Sea* (RKO, 1942), *The Tuttles of Tahiti* (RKO, 1942), *We Were Dancing* (MGM, 1942), *The Moon and Sixpence* (UA, 1942), *My Heart Belongs to Daddy* (Par., 1942), *They Got Me Covered* (RKO, 1943), *Slightly Dangerous* (MGM, 1943), *Mister Big* (Univ., 1943), *Mr. Lucky* (RKO, 1943) *Heaven Can Wait* (20th, 1943), *His Butler's Sister* (Univ., 1943), *The Mask of Dimitrios* (WB, 1944), *Since You Went Away* (UA, 1944), *Kismet* (MGM, 1944), *The Belle of the Yukon* (RKO, 1944), *Tahiti Nights* (Col., 1945), *Tonight and Every Night* (Col., 1945), *Out of This World* (Par., 1945), *San Antonio* (WB, 1945), *Saratoga Trunk* (WB, 1945), *Whistle Stop* (UA, 1946), *The Diary of a Chambermaid* (UA, 1946), *Cluny Brown* (20th, 1946), *Claudia and David* (20th, 1946), *The Time, the Place and the Girl* (WB, 1946), *The Brasher Doubloon* (20th, 1947), *Love and Learn* (WB, 1947), *The Secret Life of Walter Mitty* (RKO, 1947), *Desire Me* (MGM, 1947), *The Inside Story* (Rep., 1948), *I Remember Mama* (RKO, 1948), *Winter Meeting* (WB, 1948), *River Lady* (Univ., 1948), *Texas, Brooklyn and Heaven* (UA, 1948), *My Dear Secretary* (UA, 1948), *Portrait of Jennie* (UA, 1948), *A Letter to Three Wives* (20th, 1949), *The Judge Steps Out* (RKO, 1949), *The Girl From Jones Beach* (WB, 1949), *On the Town* (MGM, 1949), *Belle of Old Mexico* (Rep., 1950), *County Fair* (Mon., 1950), *The Second Woman* (UA, 1951), *The Lullaby of Broadway* (WB, 1951), *Father Takes the Air* (Mon., 1951), *The Tall Target* (MGM, 1951), *Havana Rose* (Rep., 1951), *The San Francisco Story* (WB, 1952), *Les Miserables* (20th, 1952), *Main Street to Broadway* (MGM, 1953), *Paris Model* (Col., 1953).

Anne Baxter and Dana Andrews in *Swamp Water.*

ANNE BAXTER Born May 7, 1923, Michigan City, Indiana. Married John Hodiak (1946), child: Katrina; divorced 1953. Married Randolph Galt (1960), children: Maginal, Melissa; divorced 1968.

Feature Films: *Twenty Mule Team* (MGM, 1940), *The Great Profile* (20th, 1940), *Charley's Aunt* (20th, 1941), *Swamp Water* (20th, 1941), *The Magnificent Ambersons* (RKO, 1942), *The Pied Piper* (20th, 1942), *Crash Dive* (20th, 1943), *Five Graves to Cairo* (Par., 1943), *The North Star* (RKO, 1943), *The Sullivans* (20th, 1944), *The Eve of St. Mark* (20th, 1944), *Guest in the House* (UA, 1944), *Sunday Dinner for a Soldier* (20th, 1944), *A Royal Scandal* (20th, 1945), *Smoky* (20th, 1946), *Angel on My Shoulder* (UA, 1946), *The Razor's Edge* (20th, 1946), *Mother Wore Tights* (narrator; 20th, 1947), *Blaze of Noon* (Par., 1947), *Homecoming* (MGM, 1948), *The Luck of the Irish* (20th, 1948), *The Walls of Jericho* (20th, 1948), *Yellow Sky* (20th, 1949), *You're My Everything* (20th, 1949), *A Ticket to Tomahawk* (20th, 1950), *All About Eve* (20th, 1950), *Follow the Sun* (20th, 1951), *Outcasts of Poker Flat* (20th, 1952), *My Wife's Best Friend* (20th, 1952), *O. Henry's Full House* (20th, 1952), *I Confess* (WB, 1953), *The Blue Gardenia* (WB, 1953), *Carnival Story* (RKO, 1954), *Bedevilled* (MGM, 1955), *One Desire* (Univ., 1955), *The Spoilers* (Univ., 1955), *The Come-On* (AA, 1956), *The Ten Commandments* (Par., 1956), *Three Violent People*

(Par., 1957), *Chase a Crooked Shadow* (WB, 1958), *Cimarron* (MGM, 1960), *Mix Me a Person* (Blackton, 1961), *Season of Passion* (UA, 1961), *Walk on the Wild Side* (Col., 1962), *The Family Jewels* (Par., 1965),* *Tall Women* (AA, 1967), *The Busy Body* (Par., 1967).

*Unbilled guest appearance

J. Carroll Naish, Carlos De Valdez, Ann Loring and Warner Baxter in *Robin Hood of El Dorado*.

Louise Beavers, Betty Roadman and Evelyn Venable in *The Headleys at Home*.

WARNER BAXTER Born March 29, 1892, Columbus, Ohio. Married Winifred Bryson (1917). Died May 7, 1951.

Sound Feature Films: *In Old Arizona* (Fox, 1929), *Through Different Eyes* (Fox, 1929), *Behind That Curtain* (Fox, 1929), *Romance of the Rio Grande* (Fox, 1929), *Happy Days* (Fox, 1930), *Such Men Are Dangerous* (Fox, 1930), *Arizona Kid* (Fox, 1930), *Renegades* (Fox, 1930), *Doctor's Wives* (Fox, 1931), *Squaw Man* (MGM, 1931), *Daddy Long Legs* (Fox, 1931), *Their Mad Moment* (Fox, 1931), *Cisco Kid* (Fox, 1931), *Surrender* (Fox, 1931), *Amateur Daddy* (Fox, 1932), *Man About Town* (Fox, 1932), *Six Hours to Live* (Fox, 1932), *Dangerously Yours* (Fox, 1933), *42nd Street* (WB, 1933), *I Loved You Wednesday* (Fox, 1933), *Paddy the Next Best Thing* (Fox, 1933), *Penthouse* (MGM, 1933), *As Husbands Go* (Fox, 1934), *Stand Up and Cheer* (Fox, 1934), *Such Women Are Dangerous* (Fox, 1934), *Grand Canary* (Fox, 1934), *Broadway Bill* (Col., 1934), *Hell in the Heavens* (Fox, 1934), *One More Spring* (Fox, 1935), *Under the Pampas Moon* (Fox, 1936), *King of Burlesque* (Fox, 1935), *Robin Hood of El Dorado* (MGM, 1936), *The Prisoner of Shark Island* (20th, 1936), *The Road to Glory* (20th, 1936), *To Mary—With Love* (20th, 1936), *White Hunter* (20th, 1936), *Slave Ship* (20th, 1937), *Vogues of 1938* (UA, 1937), *Wife, Doctor and Nurse* (20th, 1938), *Kidnapped* (20th, 1938), *I'll Give a Million* (20th, 1938), *Wife, Husband and Friend* (20th, 1939), *Return of the Cisco Kid* (20th, 1939), *Barricade* (20th, 1939), *Earthbound* (20th, 1940), *Adam Had Four Sons* (Col., 1941), *Crime Doctor* (Col., 1943), *Crime Doctor's Strangest Case* (Col., 1943), *Lady in the Dark* (Par., 1944), *Shadows in the Night* (Col., 1944), *The Crime Doctor's Courage* (Col., 1945), *Just Before Dawn* (Col., 1946), *The Crime Doctor's Man Hunt* (Col., 1946), *The Millerson Case* (Col., 1947), *The Crime Doctor's Gamble* (Col., 1947), *A Gentleman From Nowhere* (Col., 1948), *Prison Warden* (Col., 1949), *The Devil's Henchman* (Col., 1949), *The Crime Doctor's Diary* (Col., 1949), *State Penitentiary* (Col., 1950).

LOUISE BEAVERS Born 1902, Cincinnati, Ohio. Married Le Roy Moore. Died October 26, 1962.

Sound Feature Films: *Coquette* (UA, 1929), *Barnum Was Right* (Univ., 1929), *Glad Rag Doll* (Univ., 1929), *Nix on Dames* (Fox, 1929), *Wall Street* (Col., 1929), *Wide Open* (WB, 1930), *She Couldn't Say No* (WB, 1930), *Back Pay* (WB, 1930), *Safety in Numbers* (Par., 1930), *Party Husbands* (WB, 1931), *Annabelle's Affairs* (Fox, 1931), *Girls About Town* (Par., 1931), *Sundown Trail* (RKO, 1931), *Good Sport* (Fox, 1931), *Six Cylinder Love* (Fox, 1931), *The Expert* (WB, 1932), *Freaks* (MGM, 1932), *Night World* (Univ., 1932), *Ladies of the Big House*

(Par. 1932), *It's Tough to be Famous* (WB, 1932), *Young America* (Fox, 1932), *Street of Women* (WB, 1932), *What Price Hollywood* (RKO, 1932), *Unashamed* (MGM, 1932), *Divorce in the Family* (MGM, 1932), *Wild Girl* Fox, (1932), *Too Busy to Work* (Fox, 1932), *Pick Up* (Par., 1933), *She Done Him Wrong* (Par., 1933), *Girl Missing* (WB, 1933), *What Price Innocence* (Col., 1933), *A Shriek in the Night* (Allied, 1933), *Her Bodyguard* (Par., 1933), *Notorious But Nice* (Chesterfield, 1933), *Bombshell* (MGM, 1933), *Her Splendid Folly* (Progressive, 1933), *Bedside* (WB, 1934), *In the Money* (Chesterfield, 1934), *I've Got Your Number* (WB, 1934), *Cheaters* (Liberty, 1934), *Glamour* (Univ., 1934), *The Merry Frinks* (WB, 1934), *Imitation of Life* (Univ., 1934), *West of the Pecos* (RKO, 1934), *I Believed in You* (Fox, 1934), *I Give My Love* (Univ., 1934), *Merry Wives of Reno* (WB, 1934), *A Modern Hero* (WB, 1934), *Registered Nurse* (WB, 1934), *Annapolis Farewell* (Par., 1935), *Bullets or Ballots* (WB, 1936), *Wives Never Know* (Par., 1936), *General Spanky* (MGM, 1936), *Rainbow on the River* (RKO, 1936), *Make Way for Tomorrow* (Par., 1937), *Wings Over Honolulu* (Univ., 1937), *Love in a Bungalow* (Univ., 1937), *The Last Gangster* (MGM, 1937), *Scandal Street* (Par., 1938), *Life Goes On* (Million Dollar Productions, 1938), *Brother Rat* (WB, 1938), *Reckless Living* (Univ., 1938), *The Headleys at Home* (Standard, 1938), *Peck's Bad Boy With the Circus* (RKO, 1938), *Made for Each Other* (UA, 1939), *The Lady's From Kentucky* (Par., 1939), *Reform School* (Million Dollar Productions, 1939), *Women Without Names* (Par., 1940), *Parole Fixer* (Par., 1940), *No Time for Comedy* (WB, 1940), *I Want a Divorce* (Par., 1940), *Virginia* (Par., 1941), *Belle Starr* (20th, 1941), *Sign of the Wolf* (Mon., 1941), *Shadow of the Thin Man* (MGM, 1941), *The Vanishing Virginian* (MGM, 1941), *Reap the Wild Wind* (Par., 1942), *Young America* (20th, 1942), *Holiday Inn* (Par., 1942), *The Big Street* (RKO, 1942), *Tennesse Johnson* (MGM, 1942), *Seven Sweethearts* (MGM, 1942), *Good Morning, Judge* (Univ., 1943), *Du Barry Was a Lady* (MGM, 1943), *Top Man* (Univ., 1943), *All by Myself* (Univ., 1943), *Jack London* (UA, 1943), *There's Something About a Soldier* (Col., 1943), *Follow the Boys* (Univ., 1944), *South of Dixie* (Univ., 1944), *Dixie Jamboree* (PRC, 1944), *Barbary Coast Gent* (MGM, 1944), *Delightfully Dangerous* (UA, 1945), *Lover Come Back* (Univ., 1946), *Banjo* (RKO, 1947), *Good Sam* (RKO, 1948), *Mr. Blandings Builds His Dream House* (RKO, 1948), *For the Love of Mary* (Univ., 1948), *Tell It to the Judge* (Col., 1949), *Girls' School* (Col., 1950), *The Jackie Robinson Story* (EL, 1950), *Colorado Sundown* (Rep., 1952), *I Dream of Jeannie* (Rep., 1952), *Never Wave at a WAC* (RKO, 1952), *Goodbye, My Lady* (WB, 1956), *You Can't Run Away From It* (Col., 1956), *Teenage Rebel* (20th, 1956), *Tammy and the Bachelor* (Univ., 1957), *The Goddess* (Col., 1958), *The Facts of Life* (UA, 1960), *All the Fine Young Cannibals* (MGM, 1960).

WALLACE BEERY Born April 1, 1889, Kansas City, Missouri. Married Gloria Swanson (1916); divorced 1918. Married Areta Gillman (1924), child: Carol. Died April 1, 1949.

Wallace Beery and Leo Carrillo in *Wyoming*.

Sound Feature Films: *Chinatown Nights* (Par., 1929), *River of Romance* (Par., 1929), *Big House* (MGM, 1930), *Way for a Sailor* (MGM, 1930), *Billy the Kid* (MGM, 1930), *A Lady's Morals* (MGM, 1930), *Min and Bill* (MGM, 1930), *Secret Six* (MGM, 1931), *Hell Divers* (MGM, 1931), *The Champ* (MGM, 1931), *Grand Hotel* (MGM, 1932), *Flesh* (MGM, 1932), *Dinner at Eight* (MGM, 1933), *Tugboat Annie* (MGM, 1933), *The Bowery* (UA, 1933), *Viva Villa!* (MGM, 1934), *Treasure Island* (MGM, 1934), *The Mighty Barnum* (UA, 1934), *West Point of the Air* (MGM, 1935), *China Seas* (MGM, 1935), *O'Shaughnessy's Boy* (MGM, 1935), *Ah! Wilderness* (MGM, 1936), *A Message to Garcia* (20th, 1936), *Old Hutch* (MGM, 1936), *Good Old Soak* (MGM, 1937), *Slave Ship* (20th, 1937), *The Bad Man of Brimstone* (MGM, 1938), *Port of Seven Seas* (MGM, 1938), *Stablemates* (MGM, 1938), *Stand Up and Fight* (MGM, 1939), *Sergeant Madden* (MGM, 1939), *Thunder Afloat* (MGM, 1939), *The Man From Dakota* (MGM, 1940), *20 Mule Team* (MGM, 1940), *Wyoming* (MGM, 1940), *Barnacle Bill* (MGM, 1941), *The Bugle Sounds* (MGM, 1941), *Jackass Mail* (MGM, 1942), *Salute to the Marines* (MGM, 1943), *Rationing* (MGM, 1944), *Barbary Coast Gent* (MGM, 1944), *This Man's Navy* (MGM, 1945), *Bad Bascomb* (MGM, 1946), *The Mighty McGurk* (MGM, 1946), *Alias a Gentleman* (MGM, 1948), *A Date With Judy* (MGM, 1948), *Big Jack* (MGM, 1949).

Susan Hayward, Ed Begley and Jimmy Conlin in *Tulsa*.

ED BEGLEY (Edward James Begley) Born March 25, 1901, Hartford, Connecticut. Married Amada Huff (1922), children: Allene, Edward; widowed 1957. Married Dorothy Reeves (1961); divorced 1963. Married Helen Jordan (1963), child: Maureen.

Feature Films: *Big Town* (Par., 1947), *Boomerang* (20th, 1947), *Deep Waters* (20th, 1948), *Sitting Pretty* (20th, 1948), *Street With No Name* (20th, 1948), *Sorry, Wrong Number* (Par., 1948), *Tulsa* (EL, 1949), *It Happens Every Spring* (20th, 1949), *The Great Gatsby* (Par., 1949), *Backfire* (WB, 1950), *Stars in My Crown* (MGM, 1950), *Wyoming Mail* (Univ., 1950), *Convicted* (Col., 1950), *Saddle Tramp* (Univ., 1950),

Dark City (Par., 1950), *Lady From Texas* (Univ., 1951), *On Dangerous Ground* (RKO, 1951), *You're in the Navy Now* (20th, 1951), *Deadline, U.S.A.* (20th, 1952), *Boots Malone* (Col., 1952), *Turning Point* (Par., 1952), *What Price Glory* (20th, 1952), *Lone Star* (MGM, 1952), *Patterns* (UA, 1956), *12 Angry Men* (UA, 1957), *Odds Against Tomorrow* (UA, 1959), *The Green Helmet* (MGM, 1961), *Sweet Bird of Youth* (MGM, 1962), *The Unsinkable Molly Brown* (MGM, 1964), *The Oscar* (Par., 1966), *Warning Shot* (Par., 1967), *A Time to Sing* (MGM, 1968), *Hang 'Em High* (UA, 1968), *Firecreek* (WB-7 Arts, 1968).

David Holt and Ralph Bellamy in *Straight From the Shoulder*.

RALPH BELLAMY Born June 17, 1904. Married Alice Delbridge (1922); divorced 1930. Married Catherine Willard (1931), children: Lynn, Willard; divorced 1945. Married Ethel Smith (1945); divorced 1947. Married Alice Murphy (1949).

Feature Films: *The Secret Six* (MGM, 1931), *Magnificent Lie* (Par., 1931), *Surrender* (Fox, 1931), *West of Broadway* (MGM, 1932), *Forbidden* (Col., 1932), *Disorderly Conduct* (Fox, 1932), *Young America* (Fox, 1932), *The Woman in Room 13* (Fox, 1932), *Rebecca of Sunnybrook Farm* (Fox, 1932), *Almost Married* (Fox, 1932), *Wild Girl* (Fox, 1932), *Air Mail* (Univ., 1932), *Second Hand Wife* (Fox, 1933), *Parole Girl* (Col., 1933), *Destination Unknown* (Univ., 1933), *Picture Snatchers* (WB, 1933), *Below the Sea* (Col., 1933), *Narrow Corner* (WB, 1933), *Flying Devils* (RKO, 1933), *Headline Shooters* (RKO, 1933), *Ever in My Heart* (WB, 1933), *Blind Adventure* (RKO, 1933), *Ace of Aces* (RKO, 1933), *Spitfire* (RKO, 1934), *This Man Is Mine* (RKO, 1934), *Once to Every Woman* (Col., 1934), *Before Midnight* (Col., 1934), *One Is Guilty* (Col., 1934), *Girl in Danger* (Col., 1934), *Crime of Helen Stanley* (Col., 1934), *Woman in the Dark* (RKO, 1935), *Helldorado* (Fox, 1935), *Wedding Night* (UA, 1935), *Rendezvous at Midnight* (Univ., 1935), *Eight Bells* (Col., 1935), *Air Hawks* (Col., 1935), *The Healer* (Mon., 1935), *Gigolette* (RKO, 1935), *Navy Wife* (Fox, 1935), *Hands Across the Table* (Par., 1935), *Dangerous Intrigue* (Col., 1936), *Roaming Lady* (Col., 1936), *Straight From the Shoulder* Par., 1936), *The Final Hours* (Col., 1936), *Wild Brian Kent* (RKO, 1936), *The Man Who Lived Twice* (Col., 1936), *Counterfeit Lady* (Col., 1937), *Let's Get Married* (Col., 1937), *The Awful Truth* (Col., 1937), *The Crime of Dr. Hallet* (Univ., 1938), *Fools for Scandal* (WB, 1938), *Boy Meets Girl* (WB, 1938), *Carefree* (RKO, 1938), *Girls' School* (Col., 1938), *Trade Winds* (UA, 1938), *Let Us Live* (Col., 1939), *Smashing the Spy Ring* (Col., 1939), *Blind Alley* (Col., 1939), *Coast Guard* (Col., 1939), *His Girl Friday* (Col., 1940), *Flight Angels* (WB, 1940), *Brother Orchid* (WB, 1940), *Queen of the Mob* (Par., 1940), *Dance, Girl, Dance* (RKO, 1940), *Public Deb No. 1* (20th, 1940), *Ellery Queen, Master Detective* (Col., 1940), *Meet the Wildcat* (Univ., 1940), *Ellery Queen's Penthouse Mystery* (Col., 1941), *Footsteps in the Dark* (WB, 1941), *Affectionately Yours* (WB, 1941), *Ellery Queen and the Perfect Crime* (Col., 1941), *Dive Bomber* (WB, 1941), *Ellery Queen and the Murder Ring* (Col., 1941), *The Wolf Man* (Univ., 1941), *The Ghost of Frankenstein* (Univ., 1942), *Lady in a Jam* (Univ., 1942), *Men of Texas* (Univ.,

1942), *The Great Impersonation* (Univ., 1942), *Stage Door Canteen* (UA, 1943), *Guest in the House* (UA, 1944), *Delightfully Dangerous* (UA, 1945), *Lady on a Train* (Univ., 1945), *The Court-Martial of Billy Mitchell* (WB, 1955), *Sunrise at Campobello* (WB, 1960), *The Professionals* (Col., 1966), *Rosemary's Baby* (Par., 1968).

Alan Ladd and William Bendix in *The Blue Dahlia*.

WILLIAM BENDIX Born January 4, 1906, New York, New York. Married Therese Stefanotti (1928), children: Lorraine, Stephanie. Died December 14, 1964.

Feature Films: *Woman of the Year* (MGM, 1942), *Brooklyn Orchid* (UA, 1942), *Wake Island* (Par., 1942), *The Glass Key* (Par., 1942), *Who Done It?* (Univ., 1942), *Star Spangled Rhythm* (Par., 1942), *The Crystal Ball* (UA, 1943), *Taxi, Mister* (UA, 1943), *China* (Par., 1943), *Hostages* (Par., 1943), *Guadalcanal Diary* (20th, 1943), *Lifeboat* (20th, 1944), *The Hairy Ape* (UA, 1944), *Abroad With Two Yanks* (UA, 1944), *Greenwich Village* (20th, 1944), *It's in the Bag* (UA, 1945), *Don Juan Quilligan* (20th, 1945), *A Bell for Adano* (20th, 1945), *Sentimental Journey* (20th, 1946), *The Blue Dahlia* (Par., 1946), *The Dark Corner* (20th, 1946), *Two Years Before the Mast* (Par., 1946), *White Tie and Tails* (Univ., 1946), *I'll Be Yours* (Univ., 1947), *Blaze of Noon* (Par., 1947), *Calcutta* (Par., 1947), *The Web* (Univ., 1947), *Where There's Life* (Par., 1947), *Variety Girl* (Par., 1947), *The Time of Your Life* (UA, 1948), *Race Street* (RKO, 1948), *The Babe Ruth Story* (AA, 1948), *The Life of Riley* (Univ., 1949), *A Connecticut Yankee in King Arthur's Court* (Par., 1949), *Streets of Laredo* (Par., 1949), *Cover Up* (UA, 1949), *The Big Steal* (RKO, 1949), *Johnny Holiday* (UA, 1949), *Kill the Umpire* (Col., 1950), *Gambling House* (RKO, 1950), *Submarine Command* (Par., 1951), *Detective Story* (Par., 1951), *Macao* (RKO, 1952), *A Girl in Every Port* (RKO, 1952), *Blackbeard the Pirate* (RKO, 1952), *Dangerous Mission* (RKO, 1954), *Crashout* (Filmakers, 1955), *Battle Stations* (Col., 1956), *The Deep Six* (WB, 1958), *Idle on Parade* (Col., 1959), *Portrait of a Sinner* (AIP, 1961), *Boys' Night Out* (MGM, 1962), *The Young and the Brave* (MGM, 1963), *For Love or Money* (Univ., 1963), *Law of the Lawless* (Par., 1964), *The Phony American* (Signal International, 1964), *Young Fury* (Par., 1965), *Johnny Nobody* (Medallion, 1965).

CONSTANCE BENNETT (Constance Campbell Bennett) Born October 22, 1905, New York, New York. Married Chester Moorhead (1921); divorced 1924. Married Philip Plant (1925), child: Peter; divorced 1930. Married Henri de la Falaise (1932); divorced 1940. Married Gilbert Roland (1941), children: Linda, Gyl Christina; divorced 1945. Married John Coulter (1946). Died July 24, 1965.

Sound Feature Films: *This Thing Called Love* (Pathé, 1929), *Son of the Gods* (WB, 1930), *Rich People* (Pathé, 1930), *Common Clay* (Fox, 1930), *Three Faces East* (WB, 1930), *Sin Takes a Holiday* (Pathé, 1930), *The Easiest Way* (MGM, 1931), *Born to Love* (RKO, 1931), *The Common Law* (RKO, 1931), *Bought* (WB, 1931), *Lady With a Past* (RKO, 1932), *What Price Hollywood* (RKO, 1932), *Two Against the*

Tullio Carminati, Franchot Tone and Constance Bennett in *Moulin Rouge*.

World (WB, 1932), *Rockabye* (RKO, 1932), *Our Betters* (RKO, 1933), *Bed of Roses* (RKO, 1933), *After Tonight* (RKO, 1933), *Moulin Rouge* (UA, 1934), *Affairs of Cellini* (UA, 1934), *Outcast Lady* (MGM, 1934), *After Office Hours* (MGM, 1935), *Everything Is Thunder* (Gaumont-British, 1936), *Ladies in Love* (20th, 1936), *Topper* (MGM, 1937), *Merrily We Live* (MGM, 1938), *Service De Luxe* (Univ., 1938), *Topper Takes a Trip* (UA, 1938), *Tail Spin* (20th, 1939), *Escape to Glory* (Col., 1940), *Law of the Tropics* (WB, 1941), *Two-Faced Woman* (MGM, 1941), *Wild Bill Hickok Rides* (WB, 1941), *Sin Town* (Univ., 1942), *Madame Spy* (Univ., 1942), *Paris Underground* (UA, 1945), *Centennial Summer* (20th, 1946), *The Unsuspected* (WB, 1947), *Smart Woman* (AA, 1948), *Angel on the Amazon* (Rep., 1949), *As Young as You Feel* (20th, 1951), *It Should Happen to You* (Col., 1953), *Madame X* (Univ., 1966).

Francis Lederer and Joan Bennett in *The Man I Married*.

JOAN BENNETT Born February 27, 1910, Palisades, New Jersey. Married John Fox (1926), child: Diana; divorced 1928. Married Gene Markey (1932), child: Melinda; divorced 1937. Married Walter Wanger (1940), children: Stephanie, Shelley; divorced 1962.

Feature Films: *Power* (Pathé, 1928), *Bulldog Drummond* (UA, 1929), *Three Live Ghosts* (UA, 1929), *Disraeli* (WB, 1929), *Mississippi Gambler* (Univ., 1929), *Puttin' on the Ritz* (UA, 1930), *Crazy That Way* (Fox, 1930), *Moby Dick* (WB, 1930), *Maybe It's Love* (WB, 1930), *Scotland Yard* (Fox, 1930), *Many a Slip* (Univ., 1931), *Doctors'*

Jack Benny and Marie Dressler in *Chasing Rainbows*.

Wives (Fox, 1931), *Hush Money* (Fox, 1931), *She Wanted a Millionaire* (Fox, 1932), *Careless Lady* (Fox, 1932), *The Trial of Vivienne Ware* (Fox, 1932), *Weekends Only* (Fox, 1932), *Wild Girl* (Fox, 1932), *Me and My Gal* (Fox, 1932), *Arizona to Broadway* (Fox, 1933), *Little Women* (RKO, 1933), *The Pursuit of Happiness* (Par., 1934), *The Man Who Reclaimed His Head* (Univ., 1935), *Private Worlds* (Par., 1935), *Mississippi* (Par., 1935), *Two for Tonight* (Par., 1935), *The Man Who Broke the Bank at Monte Carlo* (Fox, 1935), *She Couldn't Take It* (Col., 1935), *13 Hours by Air* (Par., 1936), *Big Brown Eyes* (Par., 1936), *Two in a Crowd* (Univ., 1936), *Wedding Present* (Par., 1936), *Vogues of 1938* (UA, 1937), *I Met My Love Again* (UA, 1938), *The Texans* (Par., 1938), *Artists and Models Abroad* (Par., 1938), *Trade Winds* (UA, 1939), *Man in the Iron Mask* (UA, 1939), *The Housekeeper's Daughter* (UA, 1939), *Green Hell* (Univ., 1940), *The House Across the Bay* (UA, 1940), *The Man I Married* (20th, 1940), *Son of Monte Cristo* (UA, 1940), *She Knew All the Answers* (Col., 1941), *Man Hunt* (20th, 1941), *Wild Geese Calling* (20th, 1941), *Confirm or Deny* (20th, 1941), *Twin Beds* (UA, 1942), *The Wife Takes a Flyer* (Col., 1942), *Girl Trouble* (20th, 1942), *Margin for Error* (20th, 1943), *Woman in the Window* (RKO, 1944), *Nob Hill* (20th, 1945), *Scarlet Street* (Univ., 1945), *Col. Effingham's Raid* (20th, 1946), *The Macomber Affair* (UA, 1947), *Secret Beyond the Door* (Univ., 1947), *Woman on the Beach* (RKO, 1947), *Hollow Triumph* ("The Scar"—EL, 1948), *The Reckless Moment* (Col., 1949), *Father of the Bride* (MGM, 1950), *For Heaven's Sake* (20th, 1950), *Father's Little Dividend* (MGM, 1951), *The Guy Who Came Back* (20th, 1951), *Highway Dragnet* (AA, 1954), *We're No Angels* (Par., 1955), *There's Always Tomorrow* (Univ., 1956), *Navy Wife* (AA, 1956), *Desire in the Dust* (20th, 1960).

JACK BENNY (Benjamin Kubelsky) Born February 14, 1894, Waukegan, Illinois. Married Mary Livingston (1927).

Feature Films: *Hollywood Revue of 1929* (MGM, 1929), *Chasing Rainbows* (MGM, 1930), *Medicine Man* (Tif., 1930), *Transatlantic Merry-Go-Round* (UA, 1934), *Broadway Melody of 1936* (MGM, 1935), *It's in the Air* (MGM, 1935), *The Big Broadcast of 1937* (Par., 1936), *College Holiday* (Par., 1936), *Artists and Models* (Par., 1937), *Artists and Models Abroad* (Par., 1938), *Man About Town* (Par., 1939), *Buck Benny Rides Again* (Par., 1940), *Love Thy Neighbor* (Par., 1940), *Charley's Aunt* (20th, 1941), *To Be or Not to Be* (UA, 1942), *George Washington Slept Here* (WB, 1942), *The Meanest Man in the World* (20th, 1943), *Hollywood Canteen* (WB, 1944), *It's in the Bag* (UA, 1945), *The Horn Blows at Midnight* (WB, 1945), *Without Reservations* (RKO, 1946),* *The Great Lover* (Par., 1949),* *Somebody Loves Me* (Par., 1952),* *Susan Slept Here* (RKO, 1954),* *Beau James* (Par., 1957),* *Gypsy* (WB, 1962),* *It's A Mad, Mad, Mad, Mad World* (UA, 1963),* *A Guide For the Married Man* (20th, 1967).

*Unbilled guest appearance.

INGRID BERGMAN Born August 29, 1915, Stockholm, Sweden. Married Petter Lindstrom (1937), child: Pia; divorced 1950. Married Roberto Rossellini (1950), children: Renato, Isotta Ingrid, Isabella; annulled 1958. Married Lars Schmidt (1958).

English-Language Feature Films: *Intermezzo* (UA, 1939), *Adam Had Four Sons* (Col., 1941), *Rage in Heaven* (MGM, 1941), *Dr. Jekyll and Mr. Hyde* (MGM, 1941), *Casablanca* (WB, 1942), *For Whom the Bell Tolls* (Par., 1943), *Gaslight* (MGM, 1944), *Spellbound* (UA, 1945), *Saratoga Trunk* (WB, 1945), *The Bells of St. Mary's* (RKO, 1946), *Notorious* (RKO, 1946), *Arch of Triumph* (UA, 1948), *Joan of Arc* (RKO, 1948), *Under Capricorn* (WB, 1949), *Strangers* (Fine Arts, 1955), *Anastasia* (20th, 1956), *Indiscreet* (WB, 1958), *The Inn of the Sixth Happiness* (20th, 1958), *Goodbye Again* (UA, 1961), *The Visit* (20th, 1964), *The Yellow Rolls-Royce* (MGM, 1965), *Stimulantia* (Swedish, 1967), *Fugitive in Vienna* (WB, 1968).

Ingrid Bergman and Warner Baxter in *Adam Had Four Sons*.

CHARLES BICKFORD Born January 1, 1889. Cambridge, Massachusetts. Married Beatrice Loring (1919), children: Doris, Rex. Died November 9, 1967.

Feature Films: *Dynamite* (Par., 1929), *South Sea Rose* (Fox, 1929), *Hell's Heroes* (Univ., 1929), *Anna Christie* (MGM, 1930), *Sea Bat* (MGM, 1930), *Passion Flower* (MGM, 1930), *River's End* (WB, 1931), *Squaw Man* (MGM, 1931), *East of Borneo* (Univ., 1931), *Pagan Lady* (Col., 1931), *Men in Her Life* (Col., 1931), *Panama Flo* (RKO, 1932), *Thunder Below* (Par., 1932), *Scandal for Sale* (Univ., 1932), *Last Man* (Col., 1932), *Vanity Street* (Col., 1932), *No Other Woman* (RKO, 1933), *Song of the Eagle* (Par., 1933), *This Day and Age* (Par., 1933), *White Woman* (Par., 1933), *Little Miss Marker* (Par., 1934), *A Wicked Woman* (MGM, 1934), *A Notorious Gentleman* (Univ., 1935), *Under Pressure* (Fox, 1935), *The Farmer Takes a Wife* (Fox, 1935), *East of Java* (Univ., 1935), *The Littlest Rebel* (Fox, 1935), *Rose of the Rancho* (Par., 1936), *Pride of the Marines* (Col., 1936), *The Plainsman* (Par., 1936), *Night Club Scandal* (Par., 1937), *Thunder Trail* (Par., 1937),

Claire Trevor and Charles Bickford in *Valley of the Giants*.

Daughter of Shanghai (Par., 1937), *High, Wide and Handsome* (Par., 1937), *Gangs of New York* (Rep., 1938), *Valley of The Giants* (WB, 1938), *The Storm* (Univ., 1938), *Thou Shalt Not Kill* (Rep., 1940), *Girl From God's Country* (Rep., 1940), *South to Karanga* (Univ., 1940), *Queen of the Yukon* (Mon., 1940), *Riders of Death Valley* (Univ. serial, 1941), *Burma Convoy* (Univ., 1941), *Reap the Wild Wind* (Par., 1942), *Tarzan's New York Adventure* (MGM, 1942), *Mr. Lucky* (RKO, 1943), *The Song of Bernadette* (20th, 1943), *Wing and a Prayer* (20th, 1944), *Captain Eddie* (20th, 1945), *Fallen Angel* (20th, 1945), *Duel in the Sun* (Selznick, 1946), *The Farmer's Daughter* (RKO, 1947), *The Woman on the Beach* (RKO, 1947), *Brute Force* (Univ., 1947), *Four Faces West* (UA, 1948), *The Babe Ruth Story* (AA, 1948), *Johnny Belinda* (WB, 1948), *Command Decision* (MGM, 1948), *Roseanna McCoy* (RKO, 1949), *Whirlpool* (20th, 1949), *Guilty of Treason* (EL, 1949), *Branded* (Par., 1950), *Riding High* (Par., 1950), *Jim Thorpe—All American* (WB, 1951), *The Raging Tide* (Univ., 1951), *Elopement* (20th, 1951), *A Star Is Born* (WB, 1954), *Prince of Players* (20th, 1955), *Not as a Stranger* (UA, 1955), *The Court-Martial Of Billy Mitchell* (WB, 1955), *You Can't Run Away From It* (Col., 1956), *Mister Cory* (Univ., 1957), *The Big Country* (UA, 1958), *The Unforgiven* (UA, 1960), *Days of Wine and Roses* (WB, 1962), *Big Hand for the Little Lady* (WB, 1966).

Kay Francis, Gloria Warren and Sidney Blackmer in *Always in My Heart.*

SIDNEY BLACKMER Born July 13, 1898, Salisbury, North Carolina. Married Leonore Ulric (1928); divorced 1939. Married Suzanne Kaaren (1942).

Sound Feature Films: *A Most Immoral Lady* (WB, 1929), *The Love Racket* (WB, 1930), *Sweethearts and Wives* (WB, 1930), *Strictly Modern* (WB, 1930), *Bad Man* (WB, 1930), *Kismet* (WB, 1930), *Mothers Cry* (WB, 1930), *Lady Who Dared* (WB, 1931), *Woman Hungry* (WB, 1931), *It's a Wise Child* (MGM, 1931), *Daybreak* (MGM, 1931), *Once a Sinner* (Fox, 1931), *From Hell to Heaven* (Par., 1933), *Cocktail Hour* (Col., 1933), *The Wrecker* (Col., 1933), *The Deluge* (RKO, 1933), *This Man Is Mine* (RKO, 1934), *Goodbye Love* (RKO, 1934), *Count of Monte Cristo* (UA, 1934), *Down to Their Last Yacht* (RKO, 1934), *Transatlantic Merry-Go-Round* (UA, 1934), *The President Vanishes* (Par., 1934), *A Notorious Gentleman* (Univ., 1935), *The Great God Gold* (Mon., 1935), *Behind Green Lights* (Mascot, 1935), *The Little Colonel* (Fox, 1935), *Smart Girl* (Par., 1935), *The Girl Who Came Back* (Chesterfield, 1935), *The Firetrap* (Empire, 1935), *False Pretenses* (Chesterfield, 1935), *Streamline Express* (Mascot, 1935), *Forced Landing* (Rep., 1935), *Woman Trap* (Par., 1936), *Florida Special* (Par., 1936), *Early to Bed* (Par., 1936), *Heart of the West* (Par., 1936), *The President's Mystery* (Rep., 1936), *Missing Girls* (Chesterfield, 1936), *Girl Overboard* (Univ., 1937), *John Meade's Woman* (Par., 1937), *A Doctor's Diary* (Par., 1937), *Michael O'Halloran* (Rep., 1937), *This Is My Affair* (20th, 1937), *Wife, Doctor and Nurse* (20th, 1937), *Heidi* (20th, 1937), *Shadows of the Orient* (Mon., 1937), *Charlie Chan at*

Monte Carlo (20th, 1937), *Thank You, Mr. Moto* (20th, 1937), *The Last Gangster* (MGM, 1937), *In Old Chicago* (20th, 1938), *Speed to Burn* (20th, 1938), *Straight, Place and Show* (20th, 1938), *Orphans of the Street* (Rep., 1938), *Sharpshooters* (20th, 1938), *Trade Winds* (UA, 1938), *Suez* (20th, 1938), *Fast and Loose* (MGM, 1939), *Trapped in the Sky* (Col., 1939), *Within the Law* (MGM, 1939), *It's a Wonderful World* (MGM, 1939), *Unmarried* (Par., 1939), *Hotel for Women* (20th, 1939), *Law of the Pampas* (Par., 1939), *Framed* (Univ., 1940), *Maryland* (20th, 1940), *Dance, Girl, Dance* (RKO, 1940), *I Want a Divorce* (Par., 1940), *Cheers for Miss Bishop* (UA, 1941), *Murder Among Friends* (20th, 1941), *Rookies on Parade* (Rep., 1941), *The Great Swindle* (Col., 1941), *Love Crazy* (MGM, 1941), *Angels With Broken Wings* (Rep., 1941), *Ellery Queen and the Perfect Crime* (Col., 1941), *Down Mexico Way* (Rep., 1941), *The Feminine Touch* (MGM, 1941), *The Officer and the Lady* (Col., 1941), *Obliging Young Lady* (RKO, 1941), *The Panther's Claw* (PRC, 1942), *Always in My Heart* (WB, 1942), *Nazi Agent* (MGM, 1942), *Sabotage Squad* (Col., 1942), *Prison Girls* (PRC, 1942), *Quiet Please—Murder* (20th, 1942), *I Escaped From the Gestapo* (Mon., 1943), *Murder in Times Square* (Col., 1943), *In Old Oklahoma* (Rep., 1943), *Broadway Rhythm* (MGM, 1944), *Duel in the Sun* (Selznick, 1946), *My Girl Tisa* (WB, 1948), *A Song Is Born* (RKO, 1948), *People Will Talk* (20th, 1951), *Saturday's Hero* (Col., 1951), *The San Francisco Story* (WB, 1952), *The Washington Story* (MGM, 1952), *Johnny Dark* (Univ., 1954), *The High and the Mighty* (WB, 1954), *The View From Pompey's Head* (20th, 1955), *Accused of Murder* (Rep., 1956), *High Society* (MGM, 1956), *Beyond a Reasonable Doubt* (RKO, 1956), *Tammy and the Bachelor* (Univ., 1957), *How to Murder Your Wife* (UA, 1965), *Joy in the Morning* (MGM, 1965), *A Covenant With Death* (WB, 1967), *Rosemary's Baby* (Par., 1968).

VIVIAN BLAINE (Vivian S. Stapleton) Born November 21, 1921, Newark, New Jersey. Married Manuel "Manny" Frank (1945); divorced 1956. Married Milton Rackmil (1959); divorced 1961.

Feature Films: *Through Different Eyes* (20th, 1942), *Girl Trouble* (20th, 1942), *He Hired the Boss* (20th, 1943), *Jitterbugs* (20th, 1943), *Greenwich Village* (20th, 1944), *Something for the Boys* (20th, 1944), *Nob Hill* (20th, 1945), *State Fair* (20th, 1945), *Doll Face* (20th, 1945), *If I'm Lucky* (20th, 1946), *Three Little Girls in Blue* (20th, 1946), *Skirts Ahoy* (MGM, 1952), *Main Street to Broadway* (MGM, 1953), *Guys and Dolls* (MGM, 1955), *Public Pigeon No. One* (RKO, 1957).

JANET BLAIR (Martha Janet Lafferty) Born April 23, 1921, Altoona, Pennsylvania. Married Lou Bush (1943); divorced 1950. Married Nick Mayo (1952), children: Amanda, Andrew.

Perry Como, Martha Stewart, Vivian Blaine, Reed Hadley, Carmen Miranda and Dennis O'Keefe in *Doll Face.*

William Lundigan and Janet Blair in *The Fabulous Dorseys.*

Feature Films: *Three Girls About Town* (Col., 1941), *Blondie Goes to College* (Col., 1942), *Two Yanks in Trinidad* (Col., 1942), *Broadway* (Univ., 1942), *My Sister Eileen* (Col., 1942), *Something to Shout About* (Col., 1943), *Once Upon a Time* (Col., 1944), *Tonight and Every Night* (Col., 1945), *Tars and Spars* (Col., 1946), *Gallant Journey* (Col., 1946), *The Fabulous Dorseys* (UA, 1947), *I Love Trouble* (Col., 1948), *The Black Arrow* (Col., 1948), *The Fuller Brush Man* (Col., 1948), *Public Pigeon No. One* (RKO, 1957), *Boys' Night Out* (MGM, 1962), *Burn, Witch, Burn* (AIP, 1962), *The One and Only Genuine, Original Family Band* (BV, 1968).

JOAN BLONDELL Born August 30, 1909, New York, New York. Married George Barnes (1932); divorced 1935. Married Dick Powell (1936), children: Ellen, Norman; divorced 1944. Married Mike Todd (1947), child: Michael; divorced 1950.

Feature Films: *Office Wife* (WB, 1930), *Sinners' Holiday* (WB, 1930), *Illicit* (WB, 1931), *Millie* (RKO, 1931), *My Past* (WB, 1931), *Big Business Girl* (WB, 1931), *Public Enemy* (WB, 1931), *God's Gift to Women* (WB, 1931), *Other Men's Women* (WB, 1931), *The Reckless Hour* (WB, 1931), *Night Nurse* (WB, 1931), *Blonde Crazy* (WB, 1931), *The Greeks Had a Word for Them* (UA, 1932), *Union Depot* (WB, 1932), *The Crowd Roars* (WB, 1932), *Famous Ferguson Case* (WB, 1932), *Make Me a Star* (Par., 1932), *Miss Pinkerton* (WB, 1932), *Big City Blues* (WB, 1932), *Three on a Match* (WB, 1932), *Central Park* (WB, 1932), *Lawyer Man* (WB, 1932), *Broadway Bad* (Fox, 1933), *Blondie Johnson* (WB, 1933), *Gold Diggers of 1933* (WB, 1933), *Goodbye Again* (WB, 1933), *Footlight Parade* (WB, 1933), *Havana Widows* (WB, 1933), *Convention City* (WB, 1933), *I've Got Your Number* (WB, 1934), *Smarty* (WB, 1934), *He Was Her Man* (WB, 1934), *Dames* (WB, 1934), *Kansas City Princess* (WB, 1934), *Traveling Saleslady* (WB, 1935), *Broadway Gondolier* (WB, 1935), *We're in the Money* (WB, 1935), *Miss Pacific Fleet* (WB, 1935), *Colleen* (WB, 1936), *Sons o' Guns* (WB, 1936), *Bullets or Ballots* (WB, 1936), *Stage Struck* (WB, 1936), *Three Men on a Horse* (WB, 1936), *Gold*

Joan Blondell and Dick Powell in *I Want a Divorce.*

Diggers of 1937 (WB, 1936), *The King and the Chorus Girl* (WB, 1937), *Back in Circulation* (WB, 1937), *Perfect Specimen* (WB, 1937), *Stand-In* (UA, 1937), *There's Always a Woman* (Col., 1938), *Off the Record* (WB, 1939), *East Side of Heaven* (Univ., 1939), *The Kid From Kokomo* (WB, 1939), *Good Girls Go to Paris* (Col., 1939), *The Amazing Mr. Williams* (Col., 1939), *Two Girls on Broadway* (MGM, 1940), *I Want a Divorce* (Par., 1940), *Topper Returns* (UA, 1941), *Model Wife* (Univ., 1941), *Three Girls About Town* (Col., 1941), *Lady for a Night* (Rep., 1941), *Cry Havoc* (MGM, 1943), *A Tree Grows in Brooklyn* (20th, 1945), *Don Juan Quilligan* (20th, 1945), *Adventure* (MGM, 1945), *The Corpse Came C.O.D.* (Col., 1947), *Nightmare Alley* (20th, 1947), *Christmas Eve* (UA, 1947), *For Heaven's Sake* (20th, 1950), *The Blue Veil* (RKO, 1951), *The Opposite Sex* (MGM, 1956), *Lizzie* (MGM, 1957), *This Could Be the Night* (MGM, 1957), *Desk Set* (20th, 1957), *Will Success Spoil Rock Hunter?* (20th, 1957), *Angel Baby* (AA, 1961), *Advance to the Rear* (MGM, 1964), *The Cincinnati Kid* (MGM, 1965), *Ride Beyond Vengeance* (Col., 1966), *Paradise Road* (Syzygy, 1966), *Waterhole No. 3* (Par., 1967), *Kona Coast* (WB-7 Arts, 1968), *Stay Away, Joe* (MGM, 1968).

Barbara Stanwyck and Eric Blore in *Breakfast for Two.*

ERIC BLORE Born December 23, 1887, London, England. Married Clara Machin (1926); widowed. Married Viola Winter. Died March 1, 1959.

Feature Films: *Laughter* (Par., 1930), *My Sin* (Par., 1931), *Tarnished Lady* (Par., 1931), *Flying Down to Rio* (RKO, 1933), *Gay Divorcee* (RKO, 1934), *Limehouse Blues* (Par., 1934), *Behold My Wife* (Par., 1935), *Folies Bergère* (UA, 1935), *Casino Murder Case* (MGM, 1935), *The Good Fairy* (Univ., 1935), *Diamond Jim* (Univ., 1935), *Old Man Rhythm* (RKO, 1935), *I Live My Life* (MGM, 1935), *Top Hat* (RKO, 1935), *I Dream Too Much* (RKO, 1935), *To Beat the Band* (RKO, 1935), *Seven Keys to Baldpate* (RKO, 1935), *Two in the Dark* (RKO, 1936), *The Ex-Mrs. Bradford* (RKO, 1936), *Sons o' Guns* (WB, 1936), *Piccadilly Jim* (MGM, 1936), *Swing Time* (RKO, 1936), *Smartest Girl in Town* (RKO, 1936), *Quality Street* (RKO, 1937), *The Soldier and the Lady* (RKO, 1937), *Shall We Dance* (RKO, 1937), *It's Love I'm After* (WB, 1937), *Breakfast for Two* (RKO, 1937), *Hitting a New High* (RKO, 1937), *The Joy of Living* (RKO, 1938), *Swiss Miss* (MGM, 1938), *A Desperate Adventure* (Rep., 1938), *$1,000 a Touchdown* (Par., 1939), *Island of Lost Men* (Par., 1939), *The Man Who Wouldn't Talk* (Univ., 1940), *The Lone Wolf Strikes* (Col., 1940), *Music in My Heart* (Col., 1940), *Till We Meet Again* (WB, 1940), *The Lone Wolf Meets a Lady* (Col., 1940), *The Boys From Syracuse* (Univ., 1940), *Earl of Puddlestone* (Rep., 1940), *South of Suez* (WB, 1940), *Road to Zanzibar* (Par., 1941), *The Lone Wolf Keeps a Date* (Col., 1941), *The Lady Eve* (Par., 1941), *The Lone Wolf Takes a Chance* (Col., 1941), *Red Head* (Mon., 1941), *New York Town* (Par., 1941), *Lady Scarface* (RKO, 1941), *Three Girls About Town* (Col., 1941), *Confirm or Deny* (20th, 1941), *Sullivan's Travels* (Par., 1941), *The Shanghai Gesture* (UA, 1941), *Secrets of the Lone Wolf* (Col., 1941), *The Moon and Sixpence*

(UA, 1942), *Forever and a Day* (RKO, 1943), *Submarine Base* (PRC, 1943), *Holy Matrimony* (20th, 1943), *One Dangerous Night* (Col., 1943), *Passport to Suez* (Col., 1943), *The Sky's the Limit* (RKO, 1943), *San Diego, I Love You* (Univ., 1944), *Penthouse Rhythm* (Univ., 1945), *Easy to Look At* (Univ., 1945), *Kitty* (Par., 1945), *Men in Her Diary* (Univ., 1946), *The Notorious Lone Wolf* (Col., 1946), *Abie's Irish Rose* (UA, 1946), *Winter Wonderland* (Rep., 1947), *The Lone Wolf in London* (Col., 1947), *Romance on the High Seas* (WB, 1948), *Love Happy* (UA, 1949), *Fancy Pants* (Par., 1950), *Bowery to Bagdad* (AA, 1955).

Randolph Scott, Humphrey Bogart and George Regas in *Virginia City*.

Ann Blyth, Edmund Purdom and Fred Essler in *The Student Prince*.

ANN BLYTH (Ann Marie Blyth) Born August 16, 1928, Mt. Kisco, New York. Married James McNulty (1953), children: Timothy, Maureen, Kathleen, Terrence.

Feature Films: *Chip Off the Old Block* (Univ., 1944), *The Merry Monahans* (Univ., 1944), *Babes on Swing Street* (Univ., 1944), *Bowery to Broadway* (Univ., 1944), *Mildred Pierce* (WB, 1945), *Swell Guy* (Univ., 1946), *Brute Force* (Univ., 1947), *Killer McCoy* (MGM, 1947), *A Woman's Vengeance* (Univ., 1947), *Another Part of the Forest* (Univ., 1948), *Mr. Peabody and the Mermaid* (Univ., 1948), *Red Canyon* (Univ., 1949), *Once More, My Darling* (Univ., 1949), *Top o' the Morning* (Par., 1949), *Free For All* (Univ., 1949), *Our Very Own* (RKO, 1950), *The Great Caruso* (MGM, 1951), *Katie Did It* (Univ., 1951), *Thunder on the Hill* (Univ., 1951), *I'll Never Forget You* (20th, 1951), *The Golden Horde* (Univ., 1951), *The World in His Arms* (Univ., 1952), *One Minute to Zero* (RKO, 1952), *Sally and Saint Anne* (Univ., 1952), *All the Brothers Were Valiant* (MGM, 1953), *Rose Marie* (MGM, 1954), *The Student Prince* (MGM, 1954), *The King's Thief* (MGM, 1955), *Kismet* (MGM, 1955), *Slander* (MGM, 1957), *The Buster Keaton Story* (Par., 1957), *The Helen Morgan Story* (WB, 1957).

HUMPHREY BOGART (Humphrey De Forest Bogart) Born January 23, 1899, New York, New York. Married Helen Mencken (1926); divorced 1928. Married Mary Phillips (1928); divorced 1938. Married Mayo Methot (1938); divorced 1945. Married Lauren Bacall (1945), children: Stephen, Leslie. Died January 14, 1957.

Feature Films: *A Devil With Women* (Fox, 1930), *Up the River* (Fox, 1930), *Body and Soul* (Fox, 1931), *Bad Sister* (Univ., 1931), *Women of All Nations* (Fox, 1931), *A Holy Terror* (Fox, 1931), *Love Affair* (Col., 1932), *Three on a Match* (WB, 1932), *Midnight* (Univ., 1934), *The Petrified Forest* (WB, 1936), *Two Against the World* (WB, 1936), *Bullets or Ballots* (WB, 1936), *China Clipper* (WB, 1936), *Isle of Fury* (WB, 1936), *The Great O'Malley* (WB, 1937), *Black Legion* (WB, 1937), *San Quentin* (WB, 1937), *Marked Woman* (WB, 1937), *Kid Galahad* (WB, 1937), *Dead End* (UA, 1937), *Stand-In* (UA, 1937), *Swing Your Lady* (WB, 1938), *Men Are Such Fools* (WB, 1938), *The Amazing Dr. Clitterhouse* (WB, 1938), *Racket Busters* (WB, 1938),

Angels With Dirty Faces (WB, 1938), *King of the Underworld* (WB, 1939), *The Oklahoma Kid* (WB, 1939), *Dark Victory* (WB, 1939), *You Can't Get Away With Murder* (WB, 1939), *The Roaring Twenties* (WB, 1939), *The Return of Dr. X* (WB, 1939), *Invisible Stripes* (WB, 1939), *Virginia City* (WB, 1940), *It All Came True* (WB, 1940), *Brother Orchid* (WB, 1940), *They Drive by Night* (WB, 1940), *High Sierra* (WB, 1941), *The Wagons Roll at Night* (WB, 1941), *The Maltese Falcon* (WB, 1941), *All Through the Night* (WB, 1942), *The Big Shot* (WB, 1942), *In This Our Life* (WB, 1942)*, *Across the Pacific* (WB, 1942), *Casablanca* (WB, 1942), *Action in the North Atlantic* (WB, 1943), *Thank Your Lucky Stars* (WB, 1943), *Sahara* (Col., 1943), *To Have and Have Not* (WB, 1944), *Passage to Marseille* (WB, 1944), *Conflict* (WB, 1945), *The Big Sleep* (WB, 1946), *Two Guys From Milwaukee* (WB, 1946),* *The Two Mrs. Carrolls* (WB, 1947), *Dead Reckoning* (Col., 1947), *Dark Passage* (WB, 1947), *Treasure of the Sierra Madre* (WB, 1948), *Key Largo* (WB, 1948), *It's a Great Feeling* (WB, 1949), *Knock on Any Door* (Col., 1949), *Tokyo Joe* (Col., 1949), *Chain Lightning* (WB, 1950), *In a Lonely Place* (Col., 1950), *The Enforcer* (WB, 1951), *Sirocco* (Col., 1951), *The African Queen* (UA, 1952), *Deadline—U.S.A.* (20th, 1952), *Battle Circus* (MGM, 1953), *Beat the Devil* (UA, 1954), *The Caine Mutiny* (Col., 1954), *Sabrina* (Par., 1954), *The Barefoot Contessa* (UA, 1954), *Love Lottery* (Rank, 1954),* *We're No Angels* (Par., 1955), *The Left Hand of God* (20th, 1955), *The Desperate Hours* (Par., 1955), *The Harder They Fall* (Col., 1956).

*Unbilled guest appearance

MARY BOLAND Born January 28, 1880, Philadelphia, Pennsylvania. Died June 23, 1965.

Sound Feature Films: *Personal Maid* (Par., 1931), *Secrets of a Secretary* (Par., 1931), *The Night of June 13th* (Par., 1932), *Trouble in Paradise* (Par., 1932), *Evenings for Sale* (Par., 1932), *If I Had a Million* (Par., 1932), *Mama Loves Papa* (Par., 1933), *Three-Cornered Moon* (Par., 1933), *The Solitaire Man* (MGM, 1933), *Four Frightened People* (Par., 1934), *Six of a Kind* (Par., 1934), *Melody in Spring* (Par., 1934), *Stingaree* (RKO, 1934), *Here Comes the Groom* (Par., 1934), *Down to Their Last Yacht* (RKO, 1934), *The Pursuit of Happiness* (Par., 1934),

Benny Bartlett, Mary Boland and Etienne Giradot in *Danger—Love at Work*.

John Boles and Loretta Young in *The White Parade.*

Ruggles of Red Gap (Par., 1935), *People Will Talk* (Par., 1935), *Two for Tonight* (Par., 1935), *The Big Broadcast of 1936* (Par., 1935), *Early to Bed* (Par., 1936), *Wives Never Know* (Par., 1936), *A Son Comes Home* (Par., 1936), *College Holiday* (Par., 1936), *Marry the Girl* (WB, 1937), *There Goes the Groom* (RKO, 1937), *Danger—Love at Work* (20th, 1937), *Mama Runs Wild* (Rep., 1937), *Little Tough Guys in Society* (Univ., 1938), *Artists and Models Abroad* (Par., 1938), *Boy Trouble* (Par., 1939), *The Magnificent Fraud* (Par., 1939), *Night Work* (Par., 1939), *The Women* (MGM, 1939), *He Married His Wife* (20th, 1940), *The New Moon* (MGM, 1940), *Pride and Prejudice* (MGM, 1940), *The Hit Parade of 1941* (Rep., 1940), *One Night in the Tropics* (Univ., 1940), *In Our Time* (WB, 1944), *Forever Yours* (Mon., 1944), *Nothing But Trouble* (MGM, 1944), *Julia Misbehaves* (MGM, 1948), *Guilty Bystander* (Film Classics, 1950).

JOHN BOLES Born October 27, 1899, Greenville, Texas. Married Marcellite Dobbs.

Sound Feature Films: *Desert Song* (WB, 1929), *Rio Rita* (RKO, 1929), *Song of the West* (WB, 1930), *King of Jazz* (Univ., 1930), *Captain of the Guard* (Univ., 1930), *Queen of Scandal* (UA, 1930), *One Heavenly Night* (UA, 1930), *Resurrection* (Univ., 1931), *Seed* (Univ., 1931), *Frankenstein* (Univ., 1931), *Good Sport* (Fox, 1931), *Careless Lady* (Fox, 1932), *Six Hours to Live* (Fox, 1932), *Back Street* (Univ., 1932), *Child of Manhattan* (Col., 1933), *My Lips Betray* (Fox, 1933), *Only Yesterday* (Univ., 1933), *I Believed in You* (Fox, 1934), *Beloved* (Univ., 1934), *Bottoms Up* (Fox, 1934), *Stand Up and Cheer* (Fox, 1934), *Life of Vergie Winters* (RKO, 1934), *Wild Gold* (Fox, 1934), *Age of Innocence* (RKO, 1934), *The White Parade* (Fox, 1934), *Orchids to You* (Fox, 1935), *Curly Top* (Fox, 1935), *Redheads on Parade* (Fox, 1935), *The Littlest Rebel* (Fox, 1935), *Rose of the Rancho* (Par., 1936), *A Message to Garcia* (20th, 1936), *Craig's Wife* (Col., 1936), *As Good as Married* (Univ., 1937), *Stella Dallas* (UA, 1937), *Fight for Your Lady* (RKO, 1937), *She Married an Artist* (Col., 1938), *Romance in the Dark* (Par., 1938), *Sinners in Paradise* (Univ., 1938), *Between Us Girls* (Univ., 1942), *Thousands Cheer* (MGM, 1943), *Babes in Bagdad* (UA, 1952).

Beulah Bondi and Burl Ives in *So Dear to My Heart.*

BEULAH BONDI (Beulah Bondy) Born May 3, 1892, Chicago, Illinois.

Feature Films: *Street Scene* (UA, 1931), *Arrowsmith* (UA, 1931), *Rain* (UA, 1932), *Stranger's Return* (MGM, 1933), *Christopher Bean* (MGM, 1933), *Finishing School* (RKO, 1934), *The Painted Veil* (MGM, 1934), *Two Alone* (RKO, 1934), *Registered Nurse* (WB, 1934), *Ready for Love* (Par., 1934), *Bad Boy* (Fox, 1935), *The Good Fairy* (Univ., 1935), *Invisible Ray* (Univ., 1936), *Trail of the Lonesome Pine* (Par., 1936), *The Moon's Our Home* (Par., 1936), *The Case Against Mrs. Ames* (Par., 1936), *Hearts Divided* (WB, 1936), *The Gorgeous Hussy* (MGM, 1936), *Maid of Salem* (Par., 1937), *Make Way for Tomorrow* (Par., 1937), *The Buccaneer* (Par., 1938), *Of Human Hearts* (MGM, 1938), *Vivacious Lady* (RKO, 1938), *The Sisters* (WB, 1938), *On Borrowed Time* (MGM, 1939), *Mr. Smith Goes to Washington* (Col., 1939), *The Under-Pup* (Univ., 1939), *Remember the Night* (Par., 1940), *Our Town* (UA, 1940), *The Captain Is a Lady* (MGM, 1940), *Penny Serenade* (Col., 1941), *Shepherd of the Hills* (Par., 1941), *One Foot in Heaven* (WB, 1941), *Tonight We Raid Calais* (20th, 1943), *Watch on the Rhine* (WB, 1943), *I Love a Soldier* (Par., 1944), *She's a Soldier, Too* (Col., 1944), *Our Hearts Were Young and Gay* (Par., 1944), *And Now Tomorrow* (Par., 1944), *The Very Thought of You* (WB, 1944), *The Southerner* (UA, 1945), *Back to Bataan* (RKO, 1945), *Breakfast in Hollywood* (UA, 1946), *Sister Kenny* (RKO, 1946), *It's a Wonderful Life* (RKO, 1946), *High Conquest* (Mon., 1947), *The Sainted Sisters* (Par., 1948), *The Snake Pit* (20th, 1948), *So Dear to My Heart* (RKO, 1948), *The Life of Riley* (Univ., 1949), *Reign of Terror* (EL, 1949), *Mr. Soft Touch* (Col., 1949), *The Baron of Arizona* (Lip., 1950), *The Furies* (Par., 1950), *Lone Star* (MGM, 1952), *Latin Lovers* (MGM, 1953), *Track of the Cat* (WB, 1954), *Back From Eternity* (RKO, 1956), *The Unholy Wife* (Univ., 1957), *The Big Fisherman* (BV, 1959), *A Summer Place* (WB, 1959), *Tammy, Tell Me True* (Univ., 1961), *The Wonderful World of the Brothers Grimm* (MGM, 1962), *Tammy and the Doctor* (Univ., 1963).

Shirley Booth and Shirley MacLaine in *Hot Spell.*

SHIRLEY BOOTH (Thelma Booth Ford) Born August 30, 1907, New York, New York. Married Ed Gardner (1929); divorced 1941. Married William Baker (1943); widowed 1951.

Feature Films: *Come Back, Little Sheba* (Par., 1952), *Main Street to Broadway* (MGM, 1953), *About Mrs. Leslie* (Par., 1954), *The Matchmaker* (Par., 1958), *Hot Spell* (Par., 1958).

VEDA ANN BORG Born January 11, 1915, Boston, Massachusetts. Married Paul Herrick (1942); divorced. Married Andrew McLaglen (1946), child: Andrew; divorced 1958.

Feature Films: *Three Cheers for Love* (Par., 1936), *Men in Exile* (WB, 1937), *Kid Galahad* (WB, 1937), *The Case of the Stuttering Bishop* (WB, 1937), *Public Wedding* (WB, 1937), *The Singing Marine* (WB, 1937), *Confession* (WB, 1937), *San Quentin* (WB, 1937), *Marry the*

Veda Ann Borg, Basil Rathbone, Kay Francis and Laura Hope Crews in *Confession.*

Ernest Borgnine, Lloyd Bridges and Lenore Lonergan in *The Whistle at Eaton Falls.*

Girl (WB, 1937), *It's Love I'm After* (WB, 1937), *Submarine D-1* (WB, 1937), *Varsity Show* (WB, 1937), *Alcatraz Island* (WB, 1937), *Missing Witness* (WB, 1937), *She Loved a Fireman* (WB, 1938), *Over the Wall* (WB, 1938), *Cafe Hostess* (Col., 1939), *The Law Comes to Texas* (Col., 1939), *A Miracle on Main Street* (Col., 1940), *The Shadow* (Col. serial, 1940), *I Take This Oath* (PRC, 1940), *Dr. Christian Meets the Women* (RKO, 1940), *Laughing at Danger* (Mon., 1940), *Glamour for Sale* (Col., 1940), *Bitter Sweet* (MGM, 1940), *Behind the News* (Rep., 1940), *The Arkansas Judge* (Rep., 1941), *The Penalty* (MGM, 1941), *The Get-Away* (MGM, 1941), *The Pittsburgh Kid* (Rep., 1941), *Honky Tonk* (MGM, 1941), *Down in San Diego* (MGM, 1941), *The Corsican Brothers* (UA, 1941), *Duke of the Navy* (PRC, 1942), *About Face* (UA, 1942), *She's in the Army* (Mon., 1942), *Two Yanks in Trinidad* (Col., 1942), *I Married an Angel* (MGM, 1942), *Lady in a Jam* (Univ., 1942), *Murder in Times Square* (Col., 1943), *The Isle of Forgotten Sins* (PRC, 1943), *Revenge of the Zombies* (Mon., 1943), *The Girl From Monterey* (PRC, 1943), *The Unknown Guest* (Mon., 1943), *False Faces* (Rep., 1943), *Something to Shout About* (Col., 1943), *Smart Guy* (Mon., 1944), *Standing Room Only* (Par., 1944), *Irish Eyes Are Smiling* (20th, 1944), *Detective Kitty O'Day* (Mon., 1944), *Marked Trails* (Mon., 1944), *The Girl Who Dared* (Rep., 1944), *The Big Noise* (20th, 1944), *The Falcon in Hollywood* (RKO, 1944), *Jungle Raiders* (Col., serial, 1945), *What a Blonde* (RKO, 1945), *Fog Island* (PRC, 1945), *Rough, Tough and Ready* (Col., 1945), *Bring On the Girls* (Par., 1945), *Don Juan Quilligan* (20th, 1945), *Scared Stiff* (Par., 1945), *Nob Hill* (20th, 1945), *Dangerous Intruder* (PRC, 1945), *Love, Honor and Goodbye* (Rep., 1945), *Mildred Pierce* (WB, 1945), *Life With Blondie* (Col., 1946), *Avalanche* (PRC, 1946), *Accomplice* (PRC, 1946), *Wife Wanted* (Mon., 1946), *The Fabulous Suzanne* (Rep., 1946), *The Pilgrim Lady* (Rep., 1947), *Big Town* (Par., 1947), *The Bachelor and the Bobby Soxer* (RKO, 1947), *Mother Wore Tights* (20th, 1947), *Blonde Savage* (EL, 1948), *Julia Misbehaves* (MGM, 1948), *Chicken Every Sunday* (20th, 1948), *Mississippi Rhythm* (Mon., 1949), *One Last Fling* (WB, 1949), *Forgotten Women* (Mon., 1949), *Rider From Tucson* (RKO, 1950), *The Kangaroo Kid* (Howard C. Brown Productions, 1950), *Aaron Slick From Punkin' Crick* (Par., 1952), *Big Jim McLain* (WB, 1952), *Hold That Line* (Mon., 1952), *A Perilous Journey* (Rep., 1953), *Mister Scoutmaster* (20th, 1953), *Hot News* (AA, 1953), *Three Sailors and a Girl* (WB, 1953), *Bitter Creek* (AA, 1954), *You're Never Too Young* (Par., 1955), *Guys and Dolls* (MGM, 1955), *Love Me or Leave Me* (MGM, 1955), *I'll Cry Tomorrow* (MGM, 1955), *Frontier Gambler* (Associated, 1956), *The Fearmakers* (UA, 1958), *Thunder in the Sun* (Par., 1959), *The Alamo* (UA, 1960).

ERNEST BORGNINE (Ermes Effron Borgnine) Born January 24, 1917, Hamden, Connecticut. Married Rhoda Kemins (1949), child: Nancy; divorced 1958. Married Katy Jurado (1959); divorced 1964. Married Ethel Merman (1964); divorced 1964. Married Donna Rancourt (1965), children: Sharon, Christopher.

Feature Films: *China Corsair* (Col., 1951), *Whistle at Eaton Falls* (Col., 1951), *The Mob* (Col., 1951), *From Here to Eternity* (Col., 1953), *The Stranger Wore a Gun* (Col., 1953), *Demetrius and the Gladiators* (20th, 1954), *The Bounty Hunter* (WB, 1954), *Johnny Guitar* (Rep.,

1954), *Vera Cruz* (UA, 1954), *Bad Day at Black Rock* (MGM, 1954), *Run for Cover* (Par., 1955), *Marty* (UA, 1955), *Violent Saturday* (20th, 1955), *The Last Command* (Rep., 1955), *The Square Jungle* (Univ., 1955), *Jubal* (Col., 1956), *The Catered Affair* (MGM, 1956), *The Best Things in Life Are Free* (20th, 1956), *Three Brave Men* (20th, 1957), *The Vikings* (UA, 1958), *The Badlanders* (MGM, 1958), *Torpedo Run* (MGM, 1958), *The Rabbit Trap* (UA, 1959), *Man on a String* (Col., 1960), *Pay or Die* (AA, 1960), *Go Naked in the World* (MGM, 1961), *Season of Passion* (UA, 1961), *Barabbas* (Col., 1962), *McHale's Navy* (Univ., 1964), *The Flight of the Phoenix* (20th, 1965), *The Oscar* (Par., 1966), *The Dirty Dozen* (MGM, 1967), *Chuka* (Par., 1967), *Ice Station Zebra* (MGM, 1968), *The Legend of Lylah Clare* (MGM, 1968).

STEPHEN BOYD Born July 4, 1928, Belfast, Ireland. Married Mariella de Sarzona (1958); divorced 1959.

English-Language Feature Films: *An Alligator Named Daisy* (Rank, 1955), *A Hill in Korea* (British Lion Films Ltd., 1956), *The Man Who Never Was* (20th, 1956), *Abandon Ship* (Col., 1957), *Island in the Sun* (20th, 1957), *Seven Thunders* (Rank, 1957), *The Night That Heaven Fell* (Kingsley-International, 1958), *The Bravados* (20th, 1958), *Ben-Hur* (MGM, 1959), *Woman Obsessed* (20th, 1959), *The Best of Everything* (20th, 1959), *The Big Gamble* (20th, 1961), *Lisa* (20th, 1962), *Billy Rose's Jumbo* (MGM, 1962), *Imperial Venus* (Rizzoli, 1963), *The Fall of the Roman Empire* (Par., 1964), *The Third Secret* (20th, 1964), *Genghis Khan* (Col., 1965), *The Oscar* (Par., 1966), *Fantastic Voyage* (20th,

Stephen Boyd and Gregory Ratoff in *The Big Gamble.*

1966), *The Bible* (20th, 1966), *The Caper of the Golden Bulls* (Embassy, 1967), *Assignment K* (Col., 1968).

WILLIAM BOYD Born June 5, 1898, Cambridge, Ohio. Married Ruth Miller (1921); divorced. Married Elinor Faire; divorced 1929. Married Dorothy Sebastian (1930); divorced 1936. Married Grace Bradley (1937).

William Boyd and Judith Allen in *Burning Gold*.

Sound Feature Films: *Flying Fool* (Pathé, 1929), *High Voltage* (Pathé, 1929), *Locked Door* (UA, 1929), *His First Command* (Pathé, 1930), *Officer O'Brien* (Pathé, 1930), *Painted Desert* (Pathé, 1931), *Beyond Victory* (Pathé, 1931), *Big Gamble* (Pathé, 1931), *Suicide Fleet* (Pathé, 1931), *Carnival Boat* (RKO, 1932), *Lucky Devils* (RKO, 1933), *Men of America* (RKO, 1933), *Emergency Call* (RKO, 1933), *Flaming Gold* (RKO, 1934), *Cheaters* (Bert Lubin, 1934), *Port of Lost Dreams* (Chesterfield, 1934), *Hop-A-Long Cassidy* (Par., 1935), *Racing Luck* (Rep., 1935), *Bar 20 Rides Again* (Par., 1935), *Eagle's Brood* (Par., 1935), *Call of the Prairie* (Par., 1936), *Three on the Trail* (Par., 1936), *Federal Agent* (Rep., 1936), *Burning Gold* (Rep., 1936), *Heart of the West* (Par., 1936), *Go Get 'Em Haines* (Rep., 1936), *Hopalong Cassidy Returns* (Par., 1936), *Trail Dust* (Par., 1936), *Borderland* (Par., 1937), *Hills of Old Wyoming* (Par., 1937), *North of the Rio Grande* (Par., 1937), *Rustler's Valley* (Par., 1937), *Hopalong Rides Again* (Par., 1937), *Texas Trail* (Par., 1937), *Partners of the Plains* (Par., 1937), *Cassidy of Bar 20* (Par., 1938), *Bar 20 Justice* (Par., 1938), *Heart of Arizona* (Par., 1938), *Pride of the West* (Par., 1938), *In Old Mexico* (Par., 1938), *The Frontiersman* (Par., 1938), *Sunset Trail* (Par., 1938), *Silver on the Sage* (Par., 1939), *Law of the Pampas* (Par., 1939), *Range War* (Par., 1939), *Renegade Trail* (Par., 1939), *Santa Fe Marshal* (Par., 1940), *Showdown* (Par., 1940), *Hidden Gold* (Par., 1940), *Stagecoach War* (Par., 1940), *Three Men From Texas* (Par., 1940), *Doomed Caravan* (Par., 1941), *In Old Colorado* (Par., 1941), *Pirates on Horseback* (Par., 1941), *Border Vigilantes* (Par., 1941), *Wide-Open Town* (Par., 1941), *Secrets of the Wasteland* (Par., 1941), *Stick to Your Guns* (Par., 1941), *Twilight on the Trail* (Par., 1941), *Outlaws of the Desert* (Par., 1941), *Riders of the Timberline* (Par., 1941), *Undercover Man* (UA, 1942), *Lost Canyon* (UA, 1943), *Leather Burners* (UA, 1943), *Hoppy Serves a Writ* (UA, 1943), *Border Patrol* (UA, 1943), *Colt Comrades* (UA, 1943), *Bar 20* (UA, 1943), *False Colors* (UA, 1943), *Riders of the Deadline* (UA, 1943), *Texas Masquerade* (UA, 1944), *Lumberjack* (UA, 1944), *Forty Thieves* (UA, 1944), *Mystery Man* (UA, 1944), *The Devil's Playground* (UA, 1946), *Fool's Gold* (UA, 1946), *Unexpected Guest* (UA, 1946), *Dangerous Venture* (UA, 1947), *Hoppy's Holiday* (UA, 1947), *The Marauders* (UA, 1947), *Silent Conflict*

Charles Boyer and Katharine Hepburn in *Break of Hearts*.

(UA, 1948), *The Dead Don't Dream* (UA, 1948), *Strange Gamble* (UA, 1948), *Sinister Journey* (UA, 1948), *False Paradise* (UA, 1948), *Borrowed Trouble* (UA, 1948), *The Greatest Show On Earth* (Par., 1952).*

*Unbilled guest appearance

CHARLES BOYER Born August 28, 1899, Figeac Lot, France. Married Pat Paterson (1934), child: Michael.

English-Language Sound Feature Films: *Red-Headed Woman* (MGM, 1932), *The Man From Yesterday* (Par., 1932), *The Only Girl* (Gaumont-British, 1933), *Caravan* (Fox, 1934), *Thunder in the East* (UA, 1934), *Private Worlds* (Par., 1935), *Shanghai* (Par., 1935), *Break of Hearts* (RKO, 1935), *The Garden of Allah* (UA, 1936), *Tovarich* (WB, 1937), *Conquest* (MGM, 1937), *History Is Made at Night* (UA, 1937), *Algiers* (UA, 1938), *Love Affair* (RKO, 1939), *When Tomorrow Comes* (Univ., 1939), *All This, and Heaven, Too* (WB, 1940), *Hold Back the Dawn* (Par., 1941), *Back Street* (Univ., 1941), *Appointment for Love* (Univ., 1941), *Tales of Manhattan* (20th, 1942), *The Heart of a Nation* (narrator; AFE, 1943), *The Constant Nymph* (WB, 1943), *Flesh and Fantasy* (Univ., 1943), *Gaslight* (MGM, 1944), *Together Again* (Col., 1944), *Confidential Agent* (WB, 1945), *Cluny Brown* (20th, 1946), *A Woman's Vengeance* (Univ., 1947), *Arch of Triumph* (UA, 1948), *The First Legion* (UA, 1951), *The Thirteenth Letter* (20th, 1951), *The Happy Time* (Col., 1952), *Thunder in the East* (Par., 1953), *The Cobweb* (MGM, 1955), *Around the World in 80 Days* (UA, 1956), *The Buccaneer* (Par., 1958), *Fanny* (WB, 1961), *The Four Horsemen of the Apocalypse* (MGM, 1962), *Love Is a Ball* (UA, 1963), *A Very Special Favor* (Univ., 1965), *How to Steal a Million* (20th, 1966), *Is Paris Burning?* (Par., 1966), *Casino Royale* (Col., 1967), *Barefoot in the Park* (Par., 1967), *The Day the Hot Line Got Hot* (AIP, 1968).

Eddie Bracken and June Preisser in *Sweater Girl*.

EDDIE BRACKEN (Edward Vincent Bracken) Born February 7, 1920, Astoria, New York. Married Connie Nickerson (1939), children: Judith, Caroline, Michael, Susan, David.

Feature Films: *Too Many Girls* (RKO, 1940), *Life With Henry* (Par., 1941), *Reaching for the Sun* (Par., 1941), *Caught in the Draft* (Par., 1941), *Sweater Girl* (Par., 1942), *The Fleet's In* (Par., 1942), *Star Spangled Rhythm* (Par., 1942), *Happy Go Lucky* (Par., 1943), *Young and Willing* (UA, 1943), *The Miracle of Morgan's Creek* (Par., 1944), *Hail the Conquering Hero* (Par., 1944), *Rainbow Island* (Par., 1944), *Out of This World* (Par., 1945), *Bring on the Girls* (Par., 1945), *Duffy's Tavern* (Par., 1945), *Hold That Blonde* (Par., 1945), *Ladies' Man* (Par., 1947), *Fun on a Weekend* (UA, 1947), *The Girl From Jones Beach* (WB, 1949), *Summer Stock* (MGM, 1950), *Two Tickets to Broadway* (RKO, 1951), *We're Not Married* (20th, 1952), *About Face* (WB, 1952), *A Slight Case of Larceny* (MGM, 1953).

Alice Brady and Conway Tearle in *Should Ladies Behave?*

ALICE BRADY Born November 2, 1892, New York, New York. Married James Crane (1919), child: Donald; divorced 1922. Died October 28, 1939.

Sound Feature Films: *When Ladies Meet* (MGM, 1933), *Broadway to Hollywood* (MGM, 1933), *Beauty for Sale* (MGM, 1933), *Stage Mother* (MGM, 1933), *Should Ladies Behave?* (MGM, 1933), *Miss Fane's Baby Is Stolen* (Par., 1934), *The Gay Divorcee* (RKO, 1934), *Let 'Em Have It* (UA, 1935), *Gold Diggers of 1935* (WB, 1935), *Lady Tubbs* (Univ., 1935), *Metropolitan* (20th, 1935), *The Harvester* (Rep., 1936), *My Man Godfrey* (Univ., 1936), *Go West, Young Man* (Par., 1936), *Mind Your Own Business* (Par., 1936), *Three Smart Girls* (Univ., 1937), *Call It a Day* (WB, 1937), *Mama Steps Out* (MGM, 1937), *Mr. Dodd Takes the Air* (WB, 1937), *100 Men and a Girl* (Univ., 1937), *Merry-Go-Round of 1938* (Univ., 1937), *In Old Chicago* (20th, 1937), *Joy of Living* (RKO, 1938), *Goodbye, Broadway* (Univ., 1938), *Zenobia* (UA, 1939), *Young Mr. Lincoln* (20th, 1939).

Marlon Brando, Pat Hingle, Sandra Church and Judson Pratt in *The Ugly American.*

MARLON BRANDO (Marlon Brando, Jr.) Born April 3, 1924, Omaha, Nebraska. Married Anna Kashfi (1957), children: Christian, Devi; divorced 1959. Married Movita Castenada (1960); divorced.

Feature Films: *The Men* (UA, 1950), *A Streetcar Named Desire* (WB, 1951), *Viva Zapata!* (20th, 1952), *Julius Caesar* (MGM, 1953), *The Wild One* (Col., 1954), *On the Waterfront* (Col., 1954), *Desiree* (20th, 1954), *Guys and Dolls* (MGM, 1955), *The Teahouse of the August Moon* (MGM, 1956), *Sayonara* (WB, 1957), *The Young Lions* (20th, 1958), *The Fugitive Kind* (UA, 1960), *One-Eyed Jacks* (Par., 1961), *Mutiny on the Bounty* (MGM, 1962), *The Ugly American* (Univ., 1962), *Bedtime Story* (Univ., 1964), *The Saboteur—Code Name Morituri* (20th, 1965), *The Chase* (Col., 1966), *The Appaloosa* (Univ., 1966), *The Countess From Hong Kong* (Univ., 1967), *Reflections in a Golden Eye* (WB, 1967), *The Night of the Following Day* (Univ., 1968), *Candy* (Cinerama, 1968).

Heather Sears, Joan Crawford and Rossano Brazzi in *The Story of Esther Costello.*

ROSSANO BRAZZI Born September 18, 1918, Bologna, Italy. Married Lydia Bertolina (1940).

English-Language Feature Films: *Little Women* (MGM, 1949), *Volcano* (UA, 1953), *The Barefoot Contessa* (UA, 1954), *Three Coins in the Fountain* (20th, 1954), *Angela* (20th, 1955), *Summertime* (UA, 1955), *Loser Takes All* (British Lion, 1956), *Interlude* (Univ., 1957), *The Story of Esther Costello* (Col., 1957), *Legend of the Lost* (UA, 1957), *South Pacific* (Magna, 1958), *A Certain Smile* (20th, 1958), *Count Your Blessings* (MGM, 1959), *Light in the Piazza* (MGM, 1962), *Rome Adventure* (WB, 1962), *Dark Purpose* (Univ., 1964), *The Battle of the Villa Fiorita* (WB, 1965), *The Christmas That Almost Wasn't* (Childhood Productions, 1966), *The Bobo* (WB, 1967), *Woman Times Seven* (Embassy, 1967), *East of Java* (Cinerama, 1968).

WALTER BRENNAN Born July 25, 1894, Swampscott, Massachusetts. Married Ruth Wells (1920), children: Arthur, Walter, Ruth.

Sound Feature Films: *The Long, Long Trail* (Univ., 1929) *The Shannons of Broadway* (Univ., 1929) *Smilin' Guns* (Univ., 1929) *King of Jazz* (Univ., 1930) *One Hysterical Night* (Univ., 1930) *Dancing Dynamite* (Capitol Film Exchange, 1931) *Neck and Neck* (Sono Art-World Wide, 1931), *Law and Order* (Univ., 1932), *Texas Cyclone* (Col., 1932) *Two-Fisted Law* (Col., 1932) *All American* (Univ., 1932) *Parachute Jumper* (WB, 1933), *Man of Action* (Col., 1933), *Fighting for Justice* (Col., 1933), *Sing, Sinner, Sing* (Majestic, 1933) *Strange People* (Chesterfield, 1933) *Silent Men* (Col., 1933), *One Year Later* (Alliance, 1933) *Good Dame* (Par., 1934), *Half a Sinner* (Univ., 1934), *Northern Frontier* (Ambassador, 1935), *The Wedding Night* (UA, 1935), *Law Beyond the Range* (Col., 1935), *Bride of Frankenstein* (Univ., 1935), *Lady Tubbs* (Univ., 1935), *Man on the Flying Trapeze* (Par., 1935) *Metropolitan* (Fox, 1935), *Barbary Coast* (UA, 1935), *Seven Keys to Baldpate* (RKO, 1935), *These Three* (UA, 1936), *The Three Godfathers* (MGM, 1936), *The Moon's Our Home* (Par., 1936), *Fury* (MGM, 1936), *The Prescott Kid* (Col., 1936), *Come and Get It* (UA, 1936), *Banjo on My Knee*

Jane Withers and Walter Brennan in *Wild and Wooly.*

(20th, 1936), *She's Dangerous* (Univ., 1937), *When Love Is Young* (Univ., 1937), *Affair of Cappy Ricks* (Rep., 1937), *Wild and Woolly* (20th, 1937), *The Adventures of Tom Sawyer* (UA, 1938), *The Buccaneer* (Par., 1938), *The Texans* (Par., 1938), *Mother Carey's Chickens* (RKO, 1938), *Kentucky* (20th, 1938), *The Cowboy and the Lady* (UA, 1938), *The Story of Vernon and Irene Castle* (RKO, 1939), *They Shall Have Music* (UA, 1939), *Stanley and Livingstone* (20th, 1939), *Joe and Ethel Turp Call on the President* (MGM, 1939), *Northwest Passage* (MGM, 1940), *Maryland* (20th, 1940), *The Westerner* (UA, 1940), *This Woman Is Mine* (Univ., 1941), *Nice Girl?* (Univ., 1941), *Meet John Doe* (WB, 1941), *Sergeant York* (WB, 1941), *Swamp Water* (20th, 1941), *Rise and Shine* (20th, 1941), *The Pride of the Yankees* (RKO, 1942), *Stand By for Action* (MGM, 1942), *Slightly Dangerous* (MGM, 1943), *Hangmen Also Die* (UA, 1943), *The North Star* (RKO, 1943), *Home in Indiana* (20th, 1944), *To Have and Have Not* (WB, 1944), *The Princess and the Pirate* (RKO, 1944), *Dakota* (Rep., 1945), *A Stolen Life* (WB, 1946), *Centennial Summer* (20th, 1946), *Nobody Lives Forever* (WB, 1946), *My Darling Clementine* (20th, 1946), *Driftwood* (Rep., 1947), *Scudda Hoo! Scudda Hay!* (20th, 1948), *Red River* (UA, 1948), *Blood on the Moon* (RKO, 1948), *The Green Promise* (RKO, 1949) *The Great Dan Patch* (UA, 1949), *Brimstone* (Rep., 1949), *Task Force* (WB, 1949), *Singing Guns* (Rep., 1950), *Ticket to Tomahawk* (20th, 1950), *Curtain Call at Cactus Creek* (Univ., 1950), *The Showdown* (Rep., 1950), *Surrender* (Rep., 1950), *Best of the Bad Men* (RKO, 1951), *Along the Great Divide* (RKO, 1951), *The Wild Blue Yonder* (Rep., 1951), *Return of the Texan* (20th, 1952), *Lure of the Wilderness* (20th, 1952), *Sea of Lost Ships* (Rep., 1953), *Drums Across the River* (Univ., 1954), *Four Guns to the Border* (Univ., 1954), *Bad Day at Black Rock* (MGM, 1954), *The Far Country* (Univ., 1955), *At Gunpoint* (AA, 1955), *Come Next Spring* (Rep., 1956), *Glory* (RKO, 1956), *Good-Bye, My Lady* (WB, 1956), *The Proud Ones* (20th, 1956), *Tammy and the Bachelor* (Univ., 1957), *Shoot-Out at Big Sag* (Parallel, 1962), *The Way to the Gold* (*20th*, 1957), *God Is My Partner* (20th, 1957), *Rio Bravo* (WB, 1959), *How the West Was Won* (MGM, 1962), *Those Calloways* (BV, 1964), *The Oscar* (Par., 1966), *Who's Minding the Mint?* (Col., 1967), *The Gnome-Mobile* (BV, 1967), *The One and Only Genuine, Original Family Band* (BV, 1968).

GEORGE BRENT (George B. Nolan.) Born March 15, 1904, Dublin, Ireland. Married Helen Campbell (1922); divorced 1922. Married Ruth Chatterton (1932); divorced 1934. Married Constance Worth (1939); divorced 1939. Married Ann Sheridan (1942); divorced 1943. Married Janet Michael (1947), children: Suzanne, Barry.

Sound Feature Films: *Under Suspicion* (Fox, 1930), *Lightning Warrior* (Mascot serial, 1931), *Once a Sinner* (Fox, 1931), *Fair Warning* (Fox, 1931), *Charlie Chan Carries On* (Fox, 1931), *Ex-Bad Boy* (Univ., 1931), *So Big* (WB, 1932), *The Rich Are Always With Us* (WB, 1932), *Week-End Marriage* (WB, 1932), *Miss Pinkerton* (WB, 1932), *Purchase Price*

Kay Francis and George Brent in *Living on Velvet*.

(WB, 1932), *The Crash* (WB, 1932), *They Call It Sin* (WB, 1932), *Luxury Liner* (Par., 1933), *42nd Street* (WB, 1933), *The Keyhole* (WB, 1933), *Lilly Turner* (WB, 1933), *Baby Face* (WB, 1933), *Female* (WB, 1933), *Stamboul Quest* (MGM, 1934), *Housewife* (WB, 1934), *Desirable* (WB, 1934), *The Painted Veil* (MGM, 1934), *Living on Velvet* (WB, 1935), *Stranded* (WB, 1935), *Front Page Woman* (WB, 1935), *The Goose and the Gander* (WB, 1935), *Special Agent* (WB, 1935), *In Person* (RKO, 1935), *The Right to Live* (WB, 1936), *Snowed Under* (WB, 1936), *The Golden Arrow* (WB, 1936), *The Case Against Mrs. Ames* (Par., 1936), *Give Me Your Heart* (WB, 1936), *More Than a Secretary* (Col., 1936), *God's Country and the Woman* (WB,1937), *The Go-Getter* (WB,1937), *Mountain Justice* (WB, 1937), *Submarine D-1* (WB, 1937), *Gold Is Where You Find It* (WB, 1938), *Jezebel* (WB, 1938), *Racket Busters* (WB, 1938), *Secrets of an Actress* (WB, 1938), *Wings of the Navy* (WB, 1939), *Dark Victory* (WB, 1939), *Old Maid* (WB, 1939), *The Rains Came* (20th, 1939), *The Man Who Talked Too Much* (WB, 1940), *South of Suez* (WB, 1940), *Honeymoon for Three* (WB, 1941), *The Great Lie* (WB, 1941), *They Dare Not Love* (Col., 1941), *International Lady* (UA, 1941), *In This Our Life* (WB, 1942), *Twin Beds* (UA, 1942), *The Gay Sisters* (WB, 1942), *You Can't Escape Forever* (WB, 1942), *Silver Queen* (UA, 1942), *The Affairs of Susan* (Par., 1945), *Experiment Perilous* (RKO, 1945), *My Reputation* (WB, 1946), *The Spiral Staircase* (RKO, 1946), *Tomorrow Is Forever* (RKO, 1946), *Lover Come Back* (Univ., 1946), *Temptation* (Univ., 1946), *Slave Girl* (Univ., 1947), *Out of the Blue* (EL, 1947), *The Corpse Came C.O.D.* (Col., 1947), *Christmas Eve* (UA, 1947), *Luxury Liner* (MGM, 1948), *Angel on the Amazon* (Rep., 1948), *Red Canyon* (Univ., 1949), *Illegal Entry* (Univ., 1949), *Kid From Cleveland* (Rep., 1949), *Bride for Sale* (RKO, 1949), *FBI Girl* (Lip., 1951), *Man Bait* (Lip., 1952), *Montana Belle* (RKO, 1952), *Tangier Incident* (AA, 1953), *Death of a Scoundrel* (RKO, 1956).

Francis McDonald, Lloyd Bridges and Lon Chaney, Jr., in *Strange Confession*.

LLOYD BRIDGES Born January 15, 1913, San Leandro, California. Married Dorothy Simpson (1938), children: Beau, Jeffrey.

Feature Films: *The Lone Wolf Takes a Chance* (Col., 1941), *Cadets on Parade* (Col., 1941), *Son of Davy Crockett* (Col., 1941), *Here Comes Mr. Jordan* (Col., 1941), *The Medico of Painted Springs* (Col., 1941), *Two Latins From Manhattan* (Col., 1941), *Harmon of Michigan* (Col., 1941), *Alias Boston Blackie* (Col., 1942), *Sing for Your Supper* (Col., 1942), *Stand By All Networks* (Col., 1942), *Blondie Goes to College* (Col., 1942), *Shut My Big Mouth* (Col., 1942), *Flight Lieutenant* (Col., 1942), *Atlantic Convoy* (Col., 1942), *Talk of the Town* (Col., 1942), *Riders of the Northland* (Col., 1942), *North of the Rockies* (Col., 1942), *The Spirit of Stanford* (Col., 1942), *Commandos Strike at Dawn* (Col., 1942), *Pardon My Gun* (Col., 1943), *Sahara* (Col., 1943), *Hail to the Rangers* (Col., 1943), *The Heat's On* (Col., 1943), *Passport to Suez* (Col., 1943), *Crime Doctor's Strangest Case* (Col., 1943), *She's a Soldier, Too* (Col., 1944), *Louisiana Hayride* (Col., 1944), *The Master Race*

Hillary Brooke and Robert Lowery in *Big Town*.

Cesar Romero and Phyllis Brooks in *Dangerously Yours*.

(RKO, 1944), *Saddle Leather Law* (Col., 1944), *A Walk in the Sun* (20th, 1945), *Miss Susie Slagle's* (Par., 1945), *Strange Confession* (Univ., 1945), *Abilene Town* (UA, 1946), *Canyon Passage* (Univ., 1946), *Ramrod* (UA, 1947), *The Trouble With Women* (Par., 1947), *Secret Service Investigator* (Rep., 1948), *16 Fathoms Deep* (Mon., 1948), *Red Canyon* (Univ., 1949), *Hide-Out* (Rep., 1949), *Home of the Brave* (UA, 1949), *Calamity Jane and Sam Bass* (Univ., 1949), *Trapped* (EL, 1949), *Colt .45* (WB, 1950), *Rocket Ship XM* (Lip., 1950), *The White Tower* (RKO, 1950), *The Sound of Fury* (UA, 1950), *Little Big Horn* (Lip., 1951), *Three Steps North* (UA, 1951), *The Whistle at Eaton Falls* (Col., 1951), *High Noon* (UA, 1952), *Plymouth Adventure* (MGM, 1952), *Last of the Comanches* (Col., 1952) *City of Bad Men* (20th, 1953) *The Kid From Left Field* (20th, 1953) *The Limping Man* (Lip., 1953) *Deadly Game* (Lip., 1954), *Pride of the Blue Grass* (AA, 1954), *Wichita* (AA, 1955), *Wetbacks* (Bob Banner Associates, 1956), *The Rainmaker* (Par., 1956), *Ride Out for Revenge* (UA, 1957), *The Goddess* (Col., 1958), *Around the World Under the Sea* (MGM, 1966), *Attack on the Iron Coast* (UA, 1968).

HILLARY BROOKE (Beatrice Peterson) Born Long Island, New York. Married Jack Vaughn; divorced. Married Raymond Klune, child: Donald.

Feature Films: *New Faces of 1937* (RKO, 1937), *Eternally Yours* (UA, 1939), *Florian* (MGM, 1940), *New Moon* (MGM, 1940), *The Philadelphia Story* (MGM, 1940), *Two Girls on Broadway* (MGM, 1940), *Dr. Jekyll and Mr. Hyde* (MGM, 1941), *Maisie was a Lady* (MGM, 1941), *Mr. and Mrs. North* (MGM, 1941), *Unfinished Business* (MGM, 1941), *Born to Sing* (MGM, 1942), *Ship Ahoy* (MGM, 1942), *Sleepytime Gal* (Rep., 1942), *To the Shores of Tripoli* (20th, 1942), *Wake Island* (Par., 1942), *Counter Espionage* (Col., 1942), *Sherlock Holmes and the Voice of Terror* (Univ., 1942), *Sherlock Holmes Faces Death* (Univ., 1943), *Lady in the Dark* (Par., 1944), *And the Angels Sing* (Par., 1944), *Practically Yours* (Par., 1944), *Jane Eyre* (20th, 1944), *Standing Room Only* (Par., 1944), *Ministry of Fear* (Par., 1944), *The Enchanted Cottage* (RKO, 1945), *The Crime Doctor's Courage* (Col., 1945), *The Woman in Green* (Univ., 1945), *Road to Utopia* (Par., 1945), *Up Goes Maisie* (MGM, 1946), *Strange Impersonation* (Rep., 1946), *Monsieur Beaucaire* (Par., 1946), *The Gentleman Misbehaves* (Col., 1946), *Earl Carroll's Sketchbook* (Rep., 1946), *Strange Journey* (20th, 1946), *The Strange Woman* (UA, 1946), *Big Town* (Par., 1947), *I Cover Big Town* (Par., 1947), *Big Town After Dark* (Par., 1947), *Big Town Scandal* (Par., 1948), *The Fuller Brush Man* (Col., 1948), *Let's Live Again* (20th, 1948), *Africa Screams* (UA, 1949), *Alimony* (EL, 1949), *Unmasked* (Rep., 1950), *The Admiral Was a Lady* (UA, 1950), *Beauty on Parade* (Col., 1950), *Bodyhold* (Col., 1950), *Vendetta* (RKO, 1950), *Lucky Losers* (Mon., 1950), *Insurance Investigator* (Rep., 1951), *Skipalong Rosenbloom* (UA, 1951), *The Lost Continent* (Lip., 1951), *Confidence Girl* (UA, 1952), *Abbott and Costello Meet Captain Kidd* (WB, 1952), *Never Wave at a WAC* (RKO, 1952), *Mexican Manhunt* (AA, 1953), *The Lady Wants Mink* (Rep., 1953), *Invaders From Mars* (20th, 1953), *The Maze* (AA, 1953), *Heat Wave* (Lip., 1954), *Dragon's Gold* (UA, 1954), *Bengazi* (RKO, 1955), *The Man Who Knew Too Much* (Par., 1956), *Spoilers of the Forest* (Rep., 1957).

PHYLLIS BROOKS (Phyllis Weiler) Born July 18, 1914, Boise, Idaho. Married Torbert MacDonald, child: Torbert.

Feature Films: *I've Been Around* (Univ., 1934), *McFadden's Flats* (Par., 1935), *Lady Tubbs* (Univ., 1935), *To Beat the Band* (RKO, 1935), *Another Face* (RKO, 1935), *You Can't Have Everything* (20th, 1937), *Dangerously Yours* (20th, 1937), *City Girl* (20th, 1937), *Rebecca of Sunnybrook Farm* (20th, 1938), *In Old Chicago* (20th, 1938), *Walking Down Broadway* (20th, 1938), *Straight, Place and Show* (20th, 1938), *Up the River* (20th, 1938), *Charlie Chan in Honolulu* (20th, 1938), *Charlie Chan in Reno* (20th, 1939), *Slightly Honorable* (UA, 1940), *The Flying Squad* (Associated British, 1940), *The Shanghai Gesture* (UA, 1941), *Silver Spurs* (Rep., 1943), *Hi'Ya, Sailor* (Univ., 1943), *No Place for a Lady* (Col., 1943), *Lady in the Dark* (Par., 1944), *The Unseen* (Par., 1945), *High Powered* (Par., 1945), *Dangerous Passage* (Par., 1945).

Judy Canova, John Hubbard, Joe E. Brown and Gus Schilling in *Chatterbox*.

JOE E. BROWN (Joseph Even Brown) Born July 28, 1892, Hogate, Ohio. Married Kathryn McGraw (1915), children: Don, Joe, Mary, Kathryn.

Sound Feature Films *On With the Show!* (WB, 1929), *Painted Faces* (Tif., 1930), *Song of the West* (WB, 1930), *Hold Everything* (WB, 1930), *Top Speed* (WB, 1930), *Lottery Bride* (UA, 1930), *Maybe It's Love* (WB, 1930), *Going Wild* (WB, 1931), *Sit Tight* (WB, 1931),

Broad-Minded (WB, 1931), *Local Boy Makes Good* (WB, 1931), *Fireman Save My Child* (WB, 1932), *The Tenderfoot* (WB, 1932), *You Said a Mouthful* (WB, 1932), *Elmer the Great* (WB, 1933), *Son of a Sailor* (WB, 1933), *A Very Honorable Guy* (WB, 1934), *Circus Clown* (WB, 1934), *Six Day Bike Rider* (WB, 1934), *Alibi Ike* (WB, 1935), *Bright Lights* (WB, 1935), *A Midsummer Night's Dream* (WB, 1935), *Sons o' Guns* (WB, 1936), *Earthworm Tractors* (WB, 1936), *Polo Joe* (WB, 1936), *When's Your Birthday?* (RKO, 1937), *Riding on Air* (RKO, 1937), *Fit for a King* (RKO, 1937), *Wide Open Faces* (Col., 1938), *The Gladiator* (Col., 1938), *Flirting With Fate* (MGM, 1938), *$1000 a Touchdown* (Par., 1939), *Beware Spooks!* (Col., 1939), *So You Won't Talk* (Col., 1940), *Shut My Big Mouth* (Col., 1942), *Joan of the Ozarks* (Rep., 1942), *Chatterbox* (Rep., 1943), *Casanova in Burlesque* (Rep., 1944), *Pin-Up Girl* (20th, 1944), *Hollywood Canteen* (WB, 1944), *The Tender Years* (20th, 1947), *Show Boat* (MGM, 1951), *Around the World in 80 Days* (UA, 1956), *Some Like It Hot* (UA, 1959), *The Comedy of Terrors* (AIP, 1963).

Nigel Bruce and Rosalind Ivan in *Pursuit to Algiers.*

NIGEL BRUCE (William Nigel Bruce) Born February 4, 1895, Ensenada, Mexico. Married Violet Shelton (1922), children: Jennifer, Pauline. Died October 8, 1953.

Sound Feature Films: *Red Aces* (British, 1929) *The Squeaker* (British Lion, 1931), *Escape* (ARP, 1931), *The Calendar* (British Lion-Gainsborough, 1931), *Lord Camber's Ladies* (BIP, 1932), *The Midshipmaid* (Gaumont-British, 1932), *Channel Crossing* (Gaumont-British, 1933), *I Was a Spy* (Gaumont-British, 1933), *Springtime for Henry* (Fox, 1934), *Stand Up and Cheer* (Fox, 1934), *Coming Out Party* (Fox, 1934), *Murder in Trinidad* (Fox, 1934), *The Lady Is Willing* (Col., 1934), *Treasure Island* (MGM, 1934), *The Scarlet Pimpernel* (UA, 1935), *Becky Sharp* (RKO, 1935), *Jalna* (RKO, 1935), *She* (RKO, 1935), *The Man Who Broke the Bank at Monte Carlo* (Fox, 1935), *The Trail of the Lonesome Pine* (Par., 1936), *Under Two Flags* (20th, 1936), *The White Angel* (WB, 1936), *The Charge of the Light Brigade* (WB, 1936), *Follow Your Heart* (Rep., 1936), *Make Way for a Lady* (RKO, 1936), *The Man I Marry* (Univ., 1936), *Thunder in the City* (Col., 1937), *The Last of Mrs. Cheyney* (MGM, 1937), *The Baroness and the Butler* (20th, 1938), *Kidnapped* (20th, 1938), *Suez* (20th, 1938), *The Hound of the Baskervilles* (20th, 1939), *The Adventures of Sherlock Holmes* (20th, 1939), *Rebecca* (UA, 1940), *Adventure in Diamonds* (Par., 1940), *The Bluebird* (20th, 1940), *Lillian Russell* (20th, 1940), *A Dispatch From Reuters* (WB, 1940), *Hudson's Bay* (20th, 1940), *Playgirl* (RKO, 1941), *Free and Easy* (MGM, 1941), *The Chocolate Soldier* (MGM, 1941), *This Woman Is Mine* (Univ., 1941), *Suspicion* (RKO, 1941), *Roxie Hart* (20th, 1942), *This Above All* (20th, 1942), *Eagle Squadron* (Univ., 1942), *Sherlock Holmes and the Voice of Terror* (Univ., 1942), *Journey For Margaret* (MGM, 1942), *Sherlock Holmes and the Secret Weapon* (Univ., 1942), *Sherlock Holmes in Washington* (Univ., 1943), *Forever and a Day* (RKO, 1943), *Sherlock Holmes Faces Death* (Univ., 1943), *Crazy House* (Univ., 1943),* *Follow the Boys* (Univ., 1944), *The Pearl of Death* (Univ., 1944), *Gypsy Wildcat* (Univ., 1944), *The Scarlet ·

Virginia Bruce, Edmund Lowe, Grant Mitchell and Nat Pendleton in *The Garden Murder Case.*

Claw (Univ., 1944), *Frenchman's Creek* (Par., 1944), *Son of Lassie* (MGM, 1945), *House of Fear* (Univ., 1945), *The Corn Is Green* (WB, 1945), *The Woman in Green* (Univ., 1945), *Pursuit to Algiers* (Univ., 1945), *Terror by Night* (Univ., 1946), *Dressed to Kill* (Univ., 1946), *The Two Mrs. Carrolls* (WB, 1947), *The Exile* (Univ., 1947), *Julia Misbehaves* (MGM, 1948), *Vendetta* (RKO, 1950), *Hong Kong* (Par., 1951), *Bwana Devil* (UA, 1952).

　　*Unbilled guest appearance

VIRGINIA BRUCE Born September 29, 1910, Minneapolis, Minnesota. Married John Gilbert (1932), child: Susan; divorced 1934. Married J. Walter Ruben, child: Christopher; widowed. Married Ali Apar; divorced 1940.

Feature Films: *Woman Trap* (Par., 1929), *Why Bring That Up?* (Par., 1929), *The Love Parade* (Par., 1929), *Lilies of the Field* (Par., 1930), *Only the Brave* (Par., 1930), *Slightly Scarlet* (Par., 1930), *Paramount on Parade* (Par., 1930), *Young Eagles* (Par., 1930), *The Love Parade* (Par., 1930), *Safety in Numbers* (Par., 1930), *Social Lion* (Par., 1930), *Hell Divers* (MGM, 1931), *Are You Listening?* (MGM, 1932), *The Wet Parade* (MGM, 1932), *The Miracle Man* (Par., 1932), *Sky Bride* (Par., 1932), *Winner Take All* (WB, 1932), *Downstairs* (MGM, 1932), *Kongo* (MGM, 1932), *A Scarlet Week-End* (MGM, 1932), *Jane Eyre* (Mon., 1934), *The Mighty Barnum* (UA, 1934), *Dangerous Corner* (RKO, 1934), *Times Square Lady* (MGM, 1935), *Society Doctor* (MGM, 1935), *Shadow of Doubt* (MGM, 1935), *Let 'Em Have It* (UA, 1935), *Escapade* (MGM, 1935), *Here Comes the Band* (MGM, 1935), *The Murder Man* (MGM, 1935), *Metropolitan* (20th, 1935), *The Garden Murder Case* (MGM, 1936), *The Great Ziegfeld* (MGM, 1936), *Born to Dance* (MGM, 1936), *Women of Glamour* (Col., 1937), *When Love Is Young* (Univ., 1937), *Between Two Women* (MGM, 1937), *Wife, Doctor and Nurse* (20th, 1937), *The First Hundred Years* (MGM, 1938), *Arsene Lupin Returns* (MGM, 1938), *Bad Man of Brimstone* (MGM, 1938), *Yellow Jack* (MGM, 1938), *Woman Against Woman* (MGM, 1938), *There's That Woman Again* (Col., 1938), *There Goes My Heart* (UA, 1938), *Let Freedom Ring* (MGM, 1939), *Society Lawyer* (MGM, 1939), *Stronger Than Desire* (MGM, 1939), *Flight Angels* (WB, 1940), *The Man Who Talked Too Much* (WB, 1940), *Hired Wife* (Univ., 1940), *The Invisible Woman* (Univ., 1941), *Adventure in Washington* (Col., 1941), *Butch Minds the Baby* (Univ., 1942), *Pardon My Sarong* (Univ., 1942), *Careful, Soft Shoulders* (20th, 1942), *Brazil* (Rep., 1944), *Action in Arabia* (RKO, 1944), *Love, Honor and Goodbye* (Rep., 1945), *The Night Has a Thousand Eyes* (Par., 1948), *State Dept. —File 649* (Film Classics, 1949), *The Reluctant Bride* (Gaumont-British, 1952), *Istanbul* (Turkish, 1953), *Three Grooms for a Bride* (20th, 1957), *Strangers When We Meet* (Col., 1960).

YUL BRYNNER Born July 11, 1915, Sakhalin, Russia. Married Virginia Gilmore (1944), child: Yul; divorced 1960. Married Doris Kleiner (1960), child: Victoria.

Feature Films: *Port of New York* (EL, 1949), *The King and I* (20th, 1956), *The Ten Commandments* (Par., 1956), *Anastasia* (20th, 1956), *The Brothers Karamazov* (MGM, 1958), *The Buccaneer* (Par., 1958),

Pat Hingle and Yul Brynner in *Invitation to a Gunfighter*.

The Journey (MGM, 1959), *The Sound and the Fury* (20th, 1959), *Solomon and Sheba* (UA, 1959), *Once More, With Feeling* (Col., 1960), *The Magnificent Seven* (UA, 1960), *Surprise Package* (Col., 1960), *Escape From Zahrain* (Par., 1962), *Taras Bulba* (UA, 1962), *Kings of the Sun* (UA, 1963), *Flight From Ashiya* (UA, 1964), *Invitation to a Gunfighter* (UA, 1964), *The Saboteur—Code Name Morituri* (20th, 1965), *Cast a Giant Shadow* (UA, 1966), *Is Paris Burning?* (Par., 1966), *Return of the Seven* (UA, 1966), *Triple Cross* (WB, 1967), *The Double Man* (WB-7 Arts., 1967), *The Long Duel* (Rank, 1967), *Villa Rides* (Par., 1968), *The Picasso Summer* (CBS Films, 1968).

Jane Darwell and Edgar Buchanan in *Red Canyon*.

EDGAR BUCHANAN Born March 21, 1903, Humansville, Missouri. Married Mildred Spence, child: Bucky.

Feature Films: *When the Daltons Rode* (Univ., 1940), *The Doctor Takes a Wife* (Col., 1940), *Too Many Husbands* (Col., 1940), *My Son Is Guilty* (Col., 1940), *Tear Gas Squad* (WB, 1940), *The Sea Hawk* (WB, 1940), *Arizona* (Col., 1940), *Three Cheers for the Irish* (WB, 1940), *Penny Serenade* (Col., 1941), *Submarine Zone* (Col., 1941), *Her First Beau* (Col., 1941), *Richest Man in Town* (Col., 1941), *Texas* (Col., 1941), *You Belong to Me* (Col., 1941), *Tombstone, the Town Too Tough To Die* (Par., 1942), *The Talk of the Town* (Col., 1942), *Destroyer* (Col., 1943), *City Without Men* (Col., 1943), *Good Luck, Mr. Yates* (Col., 1943), *Buffalo Bill* (20th, 1944), *Bride by Mistake* (RKO, 1944), *The Impatient Years* (Col., 1944), *Strange Affair* (Col., 1944), *The Fighting Guardsman* (Col., 1945), *Abilene Town* (UA, 1946), *The Bandit of Sherwood Forest* (Col., 1946), *Renegades* (Col., 1946), *Perilous Holiday* (Col., 1946), *The Walls Came Tumbling Down* (Col., 1946), *If I'm Lucky* (20th, 1946), *The Sea of Grass* (MGM, 1947), *Framed* (Col., 1947), *The Swordsman* (Col., 1947), *Coroner Creek* (Col., 1948), *The Black Arrow* (Col., 1948), *Adventures in Silverado* (Col., 1948), *Best Man Wins* (Col., 1948), *The Man From Colorado* (Col., 1948), *The Untamed Breed* (Col., 1948), *Red Canyon* (Univ., 1949), *The Wreck of the Hesperus* (Col., 1948), *The Walking Hills* (Col., 1949), *Any Number*

Can Play (MGM, 1949), *The Big Hangover* (MGM, 1950), *Cheaper by the Dozen* (20th, 1950), *Cargo to Capetown* (Col., 1950), *Devil's Doorway* (MGM, 1950), *The Great Missouri Raid* (Par., 1950), *Rawhide* (20th, 1951), *Silver City* (Par., 1951), *Cave of Outlaws* (Univ., 1951), *Flaming Feather* (Par., 1951), *The Big Trees* (WB, 1952), *Toughest Man in Arizona* (Rep., 1952), *Wild Stallion* (Mon., 1952), *Shane* (Par., 1953), *It Happens Every Thursday* (Par., 1953), *She Couldn't Say No* (RKO, 1954), *Make Haste to Live* (Rep., 1954), *Dawn at Socorro* (Univ., 1954), *Human Desire* (Col., 1954), *Destry* (Univ., 1954), *Rage at Dawn* (RKO, 1955), *Wichita* (AA, 1955), *Lonesome Trail* (Lip., 1955), *Come Next Spring* (Rep., 1956), *Spoilers of the Forest* (Rep., 1957), *Day of the Bad Man* (Univ., 1958), *The Sheepman* (MGM, 1958), *King of the Wild Stallions* (AA, 1959), *It Started With a Kiss* (MGM, 1959), *Hound-Dog Man* (20th, 1959), *Edge of Eternity* (Col., 1959), *Four Fast Guns* (Univ., 1959), *Chartroose Caboose* (Univ., 1960), *Cimarron* (MGM, 1960), *Tammy, Tell Me True* (Univ., 1961), *The Comancheros* (20th, 1961), *Ride the High Country* (MGM, 1962), *A Ticklish Affair* (MGM, 1963), *McLintock* (UA, 1963), *Move Over, Darling* (20th, 1963), *The Man From Button Willow* (voice only; United Screen Arts, 1965) *The Rounders* (MGM, 1965), *Gunpoint* (Univ., 1966), *Welcome to Hard Times* (MGM, 1967).

BILLIE BURKE (Ethelbert Appleton Burke) Born August 7, 1884, Washington, D.C. Married Florenz Ziegfeld (1914), child: Patricia; widowed 1932.

Sound Feature Films: *A Bill of Divorcement* (RKO, 1932), *Christopher Strong* (RKO, 1933), *Dinner at Eight* (MGM, 1933), *Only Yesterday* (Univ., 1933), *Finishing School* (RKO, 1934), *Where Sinners Meet* (RKO, 1934), *We're Rich Again* (RKO, 1934), *Forsaking All Others* (MGM, 1934), *Society Doctor* (MGM, 1935), *After Office Hours* (MGM, 1935), *Doubting Thomas* (Fox, 1935), *Becky Sharp* (RKO, 1935), *She Couldn't Take It* (Col., 1935), *Splendor* (UA, 1935), *A Feather in Her Hat* (Col., 1935), *Piccadilly Jim* (MGM, 1936), *My American Wife* (Par., 1936), *Craig's Wife* (Col., 1936), *Parnell* (MGM, 1937), *Topper* (MGM, 1937), *The Bride Wore Red* (MGM, 1937), *Navy Blue and Gold* (MGM, 1937), *Everybody Sing* (MGM, 1938), *Merrily We Live* (MGM, 1938), *The Young in Heart* (UA, 1938), *Topper Takes a Trip* (UA, 1939), *Zenobia* (UA, 1939), *Bridal Suite* (MGM, 1939), *The Wizard of Oz* (MGM, 1939), *Eternally Yours* (UA, 1939), *Remember?* (MGM, 1939), *Irene* (RKO, 1940), *And One Was Beautiful* (MGM, 1940), *The Captain Is a Lady* (MGM, 1940), *Dulcy* (MGM, 1940), *Hullabaloo* (MGM, 1940), *The Ghost Comes Home* (MGM, 1940), *Topper Returns* (UA, 1941), *The Wild Man of Borneo* (MGM, 1941), *One Night in Lisbon* (Par., 1941), *The Man Who Came to Dinner* (WB, 1941), *What's Cookin'?* (Univ., 1942), *In This Our Life* (WB, 1942), *They All Kissed the Bride* (Col., 1942), *Girl Trouble* (20th, 1942), *Hi Diddle Diddle* (UA, 1943), *Gildersleeve on Broadway* (RKO, 1943), *So's Your Uncle* (Univ., 1943), *You're a*

Frances Grant, Will Rogers and Billie Burke in *Doubting Thomas*.

George Burns, Gracie Allen and Wade Boteler in *Love in Bloom*.

Lucky Fellow, Mr. Smith (Univ., 1943), *Swing Out, Sister* (Univ., 1945), *The Cheaters* (Rep., 945), *Breakfast in Hollywood* (UA, 1946), *The Bachelor's Daughters* (UA, 1946), *The Barkleys of Broadway* (MGM, 1949), *And Baby Makes Three* (Col., 1950), *Father of the Bride* (MGM, 1950), *Boy From Indiana* (EL, 1950), *Three Husbands* (UA, 1950), *Father's Little Dividend* (MGM, 1951), *Small Town Girl* (MGM, 1953), *The Young Philadelphians* (WB, 1959), *Sergeant Rutledge* (WB, 1960), *Pepe* (Col., 1960).

BURNS AND ALLEN

GEORGE (Nathan Burnbaum) Born January 20, 1896, New York, New York. Married Gracie Allen (1926), children: Sandra, Ronald; widowed 1964.

GRACIE (Grace Ethel Cecile Rosalie Allen) Born July 26, 1902, San Francisco, California. Married George Burns (1926), children: Sandra, Ronald. Died August 28, 1964.

Feature Films: *The Big Broadcast* (Par., 1932), *International House* (Par., 1933), *College Humor* (Par., 1933), *Six of a Kind* (Par., 1934), *We're Not Dressing* (Par., 1934), *Many Happy Returns* (Par., 1934), *Love in Bloom* (Par., 1935), *Here Comes Cookie* (Par., 1935), *Big Broadcast Of 1936* (Par., 1935), *Big Broadcast Of 1937* (Par., 1936), *College Holiday* (Par., 1936), *A Damsel in Distress* (RKO, 1937), *College Swing* (Par., 1938), *Honolulu* (MGM, 1939), *The Gracie Allen Murder Case* (Par., 1939),* *Mr. and Mrs. North* (MGM, 1941),* *Two Girls and a Sailor* (MGM, 1944).

*Without George Burns

RICHARD BURTON (Richard Walter Jenkins, Jr.) Born November 10, 1925, Pontrhydyfen, South Wales. Married Sybil Williams (1949), children: Jessica, Kate; divorced 1963. Married Elizabeth Taylor (1964).

Feature Films: *The Last Days of Dolwyn* (London Films, 1948), *Now Barabbas Was a Robber* (WB, 1949), *Waterfront* (GFD, 1950), *The Woman With No Name* (Rank, 1952), *My Cousin Rachel* (20th, 1952), *The Desert Rats* (20th, 1953), *The Robe* (20th, 1953), *Prince of Players* (20th, 1955), *The Rains of Ranchipur* (20th, 1955), *Alexander*

Lana Turner and Richard Burton in *The Rains of Ranchipur*.

the Great (UA, 1956), *Sea Wife* (20th, 1957), *Bitter Victory* (Col., 1958), *Look Back in Anger* (WB, 1959), *Bramble Bush* (WB, 1960), *Ice Palace* (WB, 1960), *A Midsummer Night's Dream* (narrator; Czechoslovakian-British, 1961), *The Longest Day* (20th, 1962), *Cleopatra* (20th, 1963), *The V.I.P.'s* (MGM, 1963), *Becket* (Par., 1964), *Night of the Iguana* (MGM, 1964), *Hamlet* (WB, 1964), *The Sandpiper* (MGM, 1965), *What's New, Pussycat?* (UA, 1965),* *The Spy Who Came In From the Cold* (Par., 1966), *Who's Afraid Of Virginia Woolf?* (WB, 1966), *The Taming of the Shrew* (Col., 1967), *Dr. Faustus* (Col., 1968), *Boom* (Univ., 1968), *Candy* (Cinerama, 1968).

*Unbilled guest appearance

SPRING BYINGTON Born October 17, 1893, Colorado Springs, Colorado. Married Roy Chandler, children: Lois, Phyllis; divorced.

Feature Films: *Little Women* (RKO, 1933), *Werewolf of London* (Univ., 1935), *Orchids to You* (Fox, 1935), *Love Me Forever* (Col., 1935), *Mutiny on the Bounty* (MGM, 1935), *Way Down East* (20th, 1935), *Broadway Hostess* (WB, 1935), *Ah! Wilderness* (MGM, 1935), *The Great Impersonation* (Univ., 1935), *The Voice of Bugle Ann* (MGM, 1936), *Every Saturday Night* (20th, 1936), *Palm Springs* (Par., 1936), *Educating Father* (20th, 1936), *Stage Struck* (WB, 1936), *Back to Nature* (20th, 1936), *Dodsworth* (UA, 1936), *The Girl on the Front Page* (Univ., 1936), *Charge of the Light Brigade* (WB, 1936), *Theodora Goes Wild* (Col., 1936), *Clarence* (Par., 1937), *Green Light* (WB, 1937), *Off to the Races* (20th, 1937), *Penrod and Sam* (WB, 1937), *Big Business* (20th, 1937), *A Family Affair* (MGM, 1937), *The Road Back* (Univ., 1937), *Hotel Haywire* (Par., 1937), *It's Love I'm After* (WB, 1937), *Hot Water* (20th, 1937), *Borrowing Trouble* (20th, 1937), *Love on a Budget* (20th, 1938), *The Buccaneer* (Par., 1938), *Jezebel* (WB, 1938), *Penrod and His Twin Brother* (WB, 1938), *A Trip to Paris* (20th, 1938), *Safety in Numbers* (20th, 1938), *You Can't Take It With You* (Col., 1938), *The Jones Family in Hollywood* (20th, 1939), *The Story of Alexander Graham Bell* (20th, 1939), *Down on the Farm* (20th, 1939), *Everybody's Baby* (20th, 1939), *Chicken Wagon Family* (20th, 1939), *Quick Millions* (20th, 1939), *Too Busy to Work* (20th, 1939), *Young as You Feel* (20th, 1940), *The Blue Bird* (20th, 1940), *The Ghost Comes Home* (MGM, 1940), *A Child Is Born* (WB, 1940), *My Love Came Back* (WB, 1940), *On Their Own* (20th, 1940), *Lucky Partners* (RKO, 1940), *Laddie* (RKO, 1940), *Arkansas Judge* (Rep., 1941), *The Devil and Miss Jones* (RKO, 1941), *Meet John Doe* (WB, 1941), *Ellery Queen and the Perfect Crime* (Col., 1941), *When Ladies Meet* (MGM, 1941), *The Vanishing Virginian* (MGM, 1941), *Roxie Hart* (20th, 1942), *Rings on Her Fingers* (20th, 1942), *The Affairs of Martha* (MGM, 1942), *The War Against Mrs. Hadley* (MGM, 1942), *Presenting Lily Mars* (MGM, 1943), *Heaven Can Wait* (20th, 1943), *The Heavenly Body* (MGM, 1943), *I'll Be Seeing You* (UA, 1944), *Salty O'Rourke* (Par., 1945), *The Enchanted Cottage* (RKO, 1945), *Thrill of a Romance* (MGM, 1945), *Captain Eddie* (20th, 1945), *A Letter for Evie* (MGM, 1945), *Dragonwyck* (20th, 1946), *Meet Me on Broadway* (Col., 1946), *Little Mr. Jim* (MGM, 1946), *Faithful in My Fashion* (MGM, 1946), *My Brother Talks to Horses* (MGM, 1946), *Cynthia* (MGM, 1947), *Living in a Big Way* (MGM, 1947), *Singapore* (Univ., 1947), *It Had to Be You* (Col., 1947), *B. F.'s Daughter* (MGM, 1948), *In the Good Old Summertime* (MGM, 1949), *The Big Wheel* (UA, 1949), *Please Believe Me* (MGM, 1950), *Devil's Doorway* (MGM, 1950), *The Skipper Surprised His Wife* (MGM, 1950), *Louisa* (Univ., 1950), *Walk Softly, Stranger* (RKO, 1950), *The Reformer and the Redhead* (Voice only; MGM, 1950), *According to Mrs. Hoyle* (Mon., 1951), *Angels in the Outfield* (MGM, 1951), *Bannerline* (MGM, 1951), *No Room for the Groom* (Univ., 1952), *Because You're Mine* (MGM, 1952), *The Rocket Man* (20th, 1954), *Please Don't Eat the Daisies* (MGM, 1960).

JAMES CAGNEY (James Francis Cagney, Jr.) Born July 17, 1899, New York, New York. Married Frances Vernon (1920).

Feature Films: *Sinner's Holiday* (WB, 1930), *Doorway to Hell* (WB, 1930), *Other Men's Women* (WB, 1931), *The Millionaire* (WB, 1931), *Public Enemy* (WB, 1931), *Smart Money* (WB, 1931), *Blonde Crazy* (WB, 1931), *Taxi* (WB, 1932), *The Crowd Roars* (WB, 1932), *Winner Take All* (WB, 1932), *Hard to Handle* (WB, 1933), *Picture Snatcher*

Kenneth Howell, Florence Roberts, Jed Prouty, George Ernest and Spring Byington in *The Jones Family in Hollywood*.

Hobart Cavanaugh, Matt Willis, Minerva Urecal and Judy Canova in *Louisiana Hayride*.

(WB, 1933), *Mayor of Hell* (WB, 1933), *Footlight Parade* (WB, 1933), *Lady Killer* (WB, 1933), *Jimmy the Gent* (WB, 1934), *He Was Her Man* (WB, 1934), *Here Comes the Navy* (WB, 1934), *St. Louis Kid* (WB, 1934), *Devil Dogs of the Air* (WB, 1935), *G-Men* (WB, 1935), *The Irish in Us* (WB, 1935), *A Midsummer Night's Dream* (WB, 1935), *Frisco Kid* (WB, 1935), *Ceiling Zero* (WB, 1935), *Great Guy* (GN, 1936), *Something to Sing About* (GN, 1937), *Boy Meets Girl* (WB, 1938), *Angels With Dirty Faces* (WB, 1938), *Oklahoma Kid* (WB, 1939), *Each Dawn I Die* (WB, 1939), *The Roaring Twenties* (WB, 1939), *The Fighting 69th* (WB, 1940), *Torrid Zone* (WB, 1940), *City for Conquest* (WB, 1940), *Strawberry Blonde* (WB, 1941), *The Bride Came C.O.D.* (WB, 1941), *Captain of the Clouds* (WB, 1942), *Yankee Doodle Dandy* (WB, 1942), *Johnny Come Lately* (UA, 1943), *Blood on the Sun* (UA, 1945), *13 Rue Madeleine* (20th, 1946), *The Time of Your Life* (UA, 1948), *White Heat* (WB, 1949), *West Point Story* (WB, 1950), *Kiss Tomorrow Goodbye* (WB, 1950), *Come Fill the Cup* (WB, 1951), *Starlift* (WB, 1951), *What Price Glory* (20th, 1952), *A Lion Is in the Streets* (WB, 1953), *Run for Cover* (Par., 1955), *Love Me or Leave Me* (MGM, 1955), *Seven Little Foys* (Par., 1955), *Mister Roberts* (WB, 1955), *Tribute to a Bad Man* (MGM, 1956), *These Wilder Years* (MGM, 1956), *Man of a Thousand Faces* (Univ., 1957), *Never Steal Anything Small* (Univ., 1959), *Shake Hands With the Devil* (UA, 1959), *The Gallant Hours* (UA, 1960), *One, Two, Three!* (UA, 1961), *Arizona Bushwhackers* (narrator; Par., 1968).

Barton MacLane and James Cagney in *Frisco Kid*.

JUDY CANOVA (Juliet Canova) Born November 20, 1916, Jacksonville, Florida. Married William Burns (1936); divorced 1939. Married James Ripley (1941); annulled 1941. Married Chester England, child: Julietta; divorced 1949. Married Philip Rivero (1950), child: Diane.

Feature Films: *Going Highbrow* (WB, 1935), *In Caliente* (WB, 1935), *Artists and Models* (Par., 1937), *Thrill of a Lifetime* (Par., 1937),

Scatterbrain (Rep., 1940), *Sis Hopkins* (Rep., 1941), *Puddin' Head* (Rep., 1941), *Sleepytime Gal* (Rep., 1942), *True to the Army* (Par., 1942), *Joan of Ozark* (Rep., 1942), *Chatterbox* (Rep., 1943), *Sleepy Lagoon* (Rep. 1943), *Louisiana Hayride* (Col., 1944), *Hit the Hay* (Col., 1945), *Singin' in the Corn* (Col., 1946), *Honeychile* (Rep., 1951), *Oklahoma Annie* (Rep., 1952), *The WAC From Walla Walla* (Rep., 1952), *Untamed Heiress* (Rep., 1954), *Carolina Cannonball* (Rep., 1955), *Lay That Rifle Down* (Rep., 1955), *The Adventures of Huckleberry Finn* (MGM, 1960).

Louise Hovick (Gypsy Rose Lee) and Eddie Cantor in *Ali Baba Goes to Town*.

EDDIE CANTOR (Edward Israel Iskowitz) Born January 31, 1892, New York, New York. Married Ida Tobias (1914), children: Marjorie, Natalie, Edna, Marilyn, Janet; widowed 1962. Died October 10, 1964.

Sound Feature Films: *Glorifying the American Girl* (Par., 1929), *Whoopee* (UA, 1930), *Palmy Days* (UA, 1931), *The Kid From Spain* (UA, 1932), *Roman Scandals* (UA, 1933), *Kid Millions* (UA, 1934), *Strike Me Pink* (UA, 1936), *Ali Baba Goes to Town* (20th, 1937), *Forty Little Mothers* (MGM, 1940), *Thank Your Lucky Stars* (WB, 1943), *Hollywood Canteen* (WB, 1944), *Show Business* (RKO, 1944), *If You Knew Susie* (RKO, 1948), *The Story of Will Rogers* (WB, 1952), *The Eddie Cantor Story* (WB, 1953).

HARRY CAREY (Harry DeWitt Carey II) Born January 16, 1878, New York, New York. Married Olive Golden (1913), children: Harry, Jr., Ellen. Died September 21, 1947.

Sound Feature Films: *The Vanishing Legion* (Mascot serial, 1931), *Trader Horn* (MGM, 1931), *Bad Company* (Pathé, 1931), *Cavalier of*

Raymond Hatton and Harry Carey in *The Thundering Herd*.

the West (Artclass Pictures, 1931), *Devil Horse* (Mascot serial, 1932), *Last of the Mohicans* (Mascot serial, 1932), *Without Honor* (Artclass Pictures, 1932), *Law and Order* (Univ., 1932), *Border Devils* (Artclass Pictures, 1932), *Night Rider* (Artclass Pictures, 1932), *Sunset Pass* (Par., 1933), *Man of the Forest* (Par., 1933), *Thundering Herd* (Par., 1933), *Wagon Trail* (Ajax, 1935), *Barbary Coast* (UA, 1935), *Powdersmoke Range* (RKO, 1935), *Last of the Clintons* (Ajax, 1935), *Wild Mustang* (William Berke, 1935), *The Last Outpost* (Par., 1935), *The Man Behind the Mask* (British, 1936), *Ghost Town* (Commodore, 1936), *The Prisoner of Shark Island* (20th, 1936), *Sutter's Gold* (Univ., 1936), *Little Miss Nobody* (20th, 1936), *Valiant Is the Word for Carrie* (Par., 1936), *The Accusing Finger* (Par., 1936), *Souls at Sea* (Par., 1937), *Aces Wild* (Commodore, 1937), *Burn 'Em Up O'Connor* (MGM, 1939), *Street of Missing Men* (Rep., 1939), *Inside Information* (Univ., 1939), *Mr. Smith Goes to Washington* (Col., 1939), *My Son Is Guilty* (Col., 1940), *Outside the 3-Mile Limit* (Col., 1940), *Beyond Tomorrow* (RKO, 1940), *They Knew What They Wanted* (Col., 1940), *The Shepherd of the Hills* (Par., 1941), *Parachute Battalion* (RKO, 1941), *Among the Living* (Par., 1941), *Sundown* (UA, 1941), *The Spoilers* (Univ., 1942), *Air Force* (WB, 1943), *Happy Land* (20th, 1943), *The Great Moment* (Par., 1944), *China's Little Devils* (Mon., 1945), *Duel in the Sun* (Selznick, 1946), *Angel and the Badman* (Rep., 1947), *The Sea of Grass* (MGM, 1947), *Red River* (UA, 1948), *So Dear to My Heart* (RKO, 1948).

LESLIE CARON (Leslie Claire Margaret Caron) Born July 1, 1931, Paris, France. Married George Hormel (1951); divorced 1954. Married Peter Hall (1956), children: Christopher, Jennifer; divorced 1966.

English-Language Feature Films: *An American in Paris* (MGM, 1951), *The Man With a Cloak* (MGM, 1951), *Glory Alley* (MGM, 1952), *The Story of Three Loves* (MGM, 1953), *Lili* (MGM, 1953), *Daddy Long Legs* (20th, 1955), *The Glass Slipper* (MGM, 1955), *Gaby* (MGM, 1956), *Gigi* (MGM, 1958), *The Doctor's Dilemma* (MGM, 1958), *The Man Who Understood Women* (20th, 1959), *The Subterraneans*

Warren Beatty and Leslie Caron in *Promise Her Anything*.

(MGM, 1960), *Fanny* (WB, 1961), *Guns of Darkness* (WB, 1962), *The L-Shaped Room* (Col., 1963), *Father Goose* (Univ., 1964), *A Very Special Favor* (Univ., 1965), *Promise Her Anything* (Par., 1966), *Is Paris Burning?* (Par., 1966).

JOHN CARRADINE (Richmond Reed Carradine) Born February 5, 1906, New York, New York. Married Ardanelle Cosner, children: Bruce, David; divorced 1944. Married Sonia Sorel (1945), children: Christopher, John; divorced 1955.

English-Language Feature Films:
as John Peter Richmond *Tol'able David* (Col., 1930), *Heaven on Earth* (Univ., 1931), *Forgotten Commandments* (Par., 1932), *The Sign of the Cross* (Par., 1932), *The Invisible Man* (Univ., 1933), *This Day and Age* (Par., 1933), *Cleopatra* (Par., 1934), *The Black Cat* (Univ., 1934).

as John Carradine *Bride of Frankenstein* (Univ., 1935), *Les Miserables* (UA, 1935), *Clive of India* (UA, 1935), *The Crusades* (Par., 1935), *Cardinal Richelieu* (UA, 1935), *The Man Who Broke the Bank at Monte*

Amelita Ward, John Carradine, Charles Arnt and Margo in *Gangway for Tomorrow*.

Carlo (Fox, 1935), *She Gets Her Man* (Univ., 1935), *Dimples* (20th, 1936), *Anything Goes* (Par., 1936), *A Message to Garcia* (20th, 1936), *Under Two Flags* (20th, 1936), *Captain January* (20th, 1936), *The Prisoner of Shark Island* (20th, 1936), *Mary of Scotland* (RKO, 1936), *The Garden of Allah* (UA, 1936), *Daniel Boone* (RKO, 1936), *Ramona* (20th, 1936), *Winterset* (RKO, 1936), *Love Under Fire* (20th, 1937), *Nancy Steele Is Missing* (20th, 1937), *Captains Courageous* (MGM, 1937), *This Is My Affair* (20th, 1937), *The Last Gangster* (MGM, 1937), *Ali Baba Goes to Town* (20th, 1937), *Thank You, Mr. Moto* (20th, 1937), *The Hurricane* (UA, 1937), *Of Human Hearts* (MGM, 1938), *Four Men and a Prayer* (20th, 1938), *Gateway* (20th, 1938), *Alexander's Ragtime Band* (20th, 1938), *Kidnapped* (20th, 1938), *Submarine Patrol* (20th, 1938), *International Settlement* (20th, 1938), *Frontier Marshal* (20th, 1939), *Jesse James* (20th, 1939), *The Three Musketeers* (20th, 1939), *Captain Fury* (UA, 1939), *Drums Along the Mohawk* (20th, 1939), *Five Came Back* (RKO, 1939), *Stagecoach* (UA, 1939), *Chad Hanna* (20th, 1940), *The Return of Frank James* (20th, 1940), *Brigham Young—Frontiersman* (20th, 1940), *The Grapes of Wrath* (20th, 1940), *Western Union* (20th, 1941), *Blood and Sand* (20th, 1941), *Man Hunt* (20th, 1941), *Swamp Water* (20th, 1941), *Son of Fury* (20th, 1942), *Northwest Rangers* (MGM, 1942), *Whispering Ghosts* (20th, 1942), *Reunion in France* (MGM, 1942), *The Black Swan* (20th, 1942), *Hitler's Madman* (MGM, 1943), *I Escaped From the Gestapo* (Mon., 1943), *The Isle of Forgotten Sins* (PRC, 1943), *Silver Spurs* (Rep., 1943), *Gangway for Tomorrow* (RKO, 1943), *Voodoo Man* (Mon., 1944), *Adventures of Mark Twain* (WB, 1944), *Barbary Coast Gent* (MGM, 1944), *Alaska* (Mon., 1944), *Bluebeard* (PRC, 1944), *The Invisible Man's Revenge*) Univ., 1944), *It's in the Bag* (UA, 1945), *House of Frankenstein* (Univ., 1945), *Captain Kidd* (UA, 1945), *Fallen Angel* (20th, 1945), *House of Dracula* (Univ., 1945), *The Face of Marble* (Mon., 1946), *Down Missouri Way* (PRC, 1946), *The Private Affairs of Bel Ami* (UA, 1947), *C-Man* (Film Classics, 1949), *Casanova's Big Night* (Par., 1954), *Johnny Guitar* (Rep., 1954), *The Egyptian* (20th, 1954), *Thunder Pass* (Lip., 1954), *Stranger on Horseback* (UA, 1955), *The Kentuckian* (UA, 1955), *Desert Sands* (UA, 1955), *The Black Sleep* (UA, 1956), *Dark Venture* (WB, 1956), *Female Jungle* (AIP, 1956), *Around the World in 80 Days* (UA, 1956), *The Ten Commandments* (Par., 1956), *The Court Jester* (Par., 1956), *The True Story of Jesse James* (20th, 1957), *The Unearthly* (Rep., 1957), *The Story of Mankind* (WB, 1957), *Hell Ship Mutiny* (Rep., 1957), *Half Human* (DCA, 1957), *The Proud Rebel* (BV, 1958), *Showdown at Boot Hill* (20th, 1958), *The Last Hurrah* (Col., 1958), *The Cosmic Man* (AA, 1959), *Invisible Invaders* (UA, 1959), *The Oregon Trail* (20th, 1959), *The Adventures of Huckleberry Finn* (MGM, 1960), *Tarzan the Magnificent* (Par., 1960), *Sex Kittens Go to College* (AA, 1960), *The Incredible Petrified World* (Governor, 1960), *Invasion of the Animal People* (Jerry Warren Productions, 1962), *The Man Who Shot Liberty Valance* (Par., 1962), *The Patsy* (Par., 1964), *Cheyenne Autumn* (WB, 1964), *Wizard of Mars* (American Releasing Corp., 1964), *Billy the Kid vs. Dracula* (Embassy, 1966), *Munster Go Home* (Univ., 1966), *Hillbillies in a Haunted House* (Woolner, 1967), *The Hostage* (Crown International, 1967), *Dracula's Castle* (American Releasing, 1967), *Creatures of the Red Planet* (American Releasing, 1967), *Fiend With the Electronic Brain* (American Releasing, 1967), *Lonely Man* (American Releasing, 1967) *Dr. Terror's Gallery of Horrors* (Independent, 1967), *The Astro Zombies* (ATV Mikels Productions, 1968), *The Fakers* (East West International, 1968), *Genesis* (narrator; General Film Distributing Co., 1968).

LEO CARRILLO Born August 6, 1881, Los Angeles, California. Married Edith Haeselbarth (1940), child: Antoinette; widowed 1953. Died September 10, 1961.

Sound Feature Films: *Mr. Antonio* (Tif., 1929), *Hell Bound* (Tif., 1931), *Lasca of the Rio Grande* (Univ., 1931), *Homicide Squad* (Univ., 1931), *Guilty Generation* (Col., 1931), *Girl of the Rio* (RKO, 1932), *Broken Wing* (Par., 1932), *Parachute Jumper* (WB, 1933), *Deception* (Col., 1933), *Obey the Law* (Col., 1933), *Racetrack* (World Wide, 1933), *Men Are Such Fools* (RKO, 1933), *Moonlight and Pretzels* (Univ., 1933), *Before Morning* (Col., 1933), *Viva Villa!* (MGM, 1934), *Four Frightened People* (Par., 1934), *Manhattan Melodrama* (MGM, 1934), *Barretts of Wimpole Street* (MGM, 1934), *The Band Plays On* (MGM, 1934), *The Gay Bride* (MGM, 1934), *The Winning Ticket* (MGM, 1935), *In Caliente* (WB, 1935), *If You Could Only Cook* (Col., 1935), *Moonlight Murder* (MGM, 1936), *It Had to Happen* (20th, 1936), *The Gay Desperado* (UA, 1936), *History Is Made at Night* (UA, 1937), *I Promise to Pay* (Col., 1937), *Hotel Haywire* (Par., 1937), *52nd Street* (UA, 1937), *Manhattan Merry-Go-Round* (Rep., 1937), *The Barrier* (Par., 1937), *Girl of the Golden West* (MGM, 1938), *Little Miss Roughneck* (Col., 1938), *City Streets* (Col., 1938), *Too Hot to Handle* (MGM, 1938), *The Arizona Wildcat* (20th, 1938), *Flirting With Fate* MGM, 1938), *Fisherman's Wharf* (RKO, 1939), *Society Lawyer* (MGM, 1939), *Rio* (Univ., 1939), *Chicken Wagon Family* (20th, 1939), *20-Mule Team* (MGM, 1940), *Lillian Russell* (20th, 1940), *Captain Caution* (UA, 1940), *Wyoming* (MGM, 1940), *One Night in the Tropics* (Univ., 1940), *Horror Island* (Univ., 1941), *Riders of Death Valley* (Univ. serial, 1941), *Tight Shoes* (Univ., 1941), *Barnacle Bill* (MGM, 1941), *The Kid From Kansas* (Univ., 1941), *Road Agent* (Univ., 1941), *What's Cooking?* (Univ., 1942), *Unseen Enemy* (Univ., 1942), *Escape From Hong Kong* (Univ., 1942), *Men of Texas* (Univ., 1942), *Danger in the Pacific* (Univ., 1942), *Top Sergeant* (Univ., 1942), *Sin Town* (Univ., 1942), *American Empire* (UA., 1942), *Follow the Band* (Univ., 1943), *Larceny With Music* (Univ., 1943), *The Phantom of the Opera* (Univ., 1943), *Frontier Badmen* (Univ., 1943), *Crazy House* (Univ., 1943), *Ghost Catchers* (Univ., 1944), *Gypsy Wildcat* (Univ., 1944), *Bowery to Broadway* (Univ., 1944), *Moonlight and Cactus* (Univ., 1944), *Under Western Skies* (Univ., 1945), *Crime, Inc.* (PRC, 1945), *Mexicana* (Rep., 1945), *The Fugitive* (RKO, 1947), *The Valiant Hombre* (UA, 1948), *The Gay Amigo* (UA, 1949), *The Daring Caballero* (UA, 1949), *Satan's Cradle* (UA, 1949), *The Girl From San Lorenzo* (UA, 1950).

Armida, Duncan Renaldo and Leo Carrillo in *The Gay Amigo.*

MADELEINE CARROLL (Marie-Madeleine Bernadette O'Carroll) Born February 26, 1906, West Bromwich, England. Married Philip Astly (1931); divorced 1939. Married Sterling Hayden (1942) divorced 1946. Married Henri Lavorel (1946); divorced 1949. Married Andrew Heiskell (1950), child: Dianne; divorced 1965.

Feature Films: *Guns at Loos* (New Era, 1928), *What Money Can't Buy* (Par., 1929), *The American Prisoner* (British International, 1929), *Atlantic* (British International, 1930), *Young Woodley* (British International, 1930), *Escape* (ATP, 1930), *The "W" Plan* (Burlington, 1931), *Mme. Guillotine* (Fogwell, 1931), *Kissing Cup's Race* (Butchers, 1931), *French Leave* (Talking Picture Epics, 1931), *Fascination* (British International, 1932), *First Born* (Gainsborough, 1932), *School for Scandal* (Par., 1933), *Sleeping Car* (Gaumont-British, 1933), *I Was a Spy* (Fox, 1934), *The World Moves On* (Fox, 1934), *Loves of a Dictator* (Gaumont-British, 1935), *The 39 Steps* (Gaumont-British, 1935), *The Case Against Mrs. Ames* (Par., 1936), *Secret Agent* (Gaumont-British, 1936), *The General Died at Dawn* (Par., 1936), *Lloyds of London* (20th, 1936), *On the Avenue* (20th, 1937), *The Prisoner of Zenda* (UA, 1937), *It's All Yours* (Col., 1938), *Blockade* (UA, 1938), *Honeymoon in Bali* (Par., 1939), *Cafe Society* (Par., 1939), *My Son, My Son* (UA, 1940), *Safari* (Par., 1940), *North West Mounted Police* (Par., 1940), *Virginia* (Par., 1941), *One Night in Lisbon* (Par., 1941), *Bahama Passage* (Par., 1941), *My Favorite Blonde* (Par., 1942), *White Cradle Inn* ("High Fury"—UA, 1947), *An Innocent Affair* ("Don't Trust Your Husband"—UA, 1948), *The Fan* (Fox, 1949).

NANCY CARROLL (Ann Veronica LaHiff) Born November 19, 1906; New York, New York. Married Jack Kirkland (1924), child: Patricia; divorced 1931. Married Francis Bolton Mallory (1931); divorced 1935. Married C. H. J. Groen (1955). Died August 6, 1965.

Sound Feature Films: *The Shopworn Angel* (Par., 1929), *The Wolf of Wall Street* (Par., 1929), *Sin Sister* (Fox, 1929), *Close Harmony* (Par.,

Madeleine Carroll and Sterling Hayden in *Bahama Passage.*

Jack Benny, Nancy Carroll and Carlyle Moore, Jr., in *Transatlantic Merry-Go-Round*.

1929), *The Dance of Life* (Par., 1929), *Illusion* (Par., 1929), *Sweetie* (Par., 1929), *Dangerous Paradise* (Par., 1930), *Honey* (Par., 1930), *Paramount on Parade* (Par., 1930), *The Devil's Holiday* (Par., 1930), *Follow Through* (Par., 1930), *Laughter* (Par., 1930), *Stolen Heaven* (Par., 1931), *The Night Angel* (Par., 1931), *Personal Maid* (Par., 1931), *Broken Lullaby* (Par., 1932), *Wayward* (Par., 1932), *Scarlet Dawn* (WB, 1932), *Hot Saturday* (Par., 1932), *Under Cover Man* (Par., 1932), *Child of Manhattan* (Col., 1933), *The Woman Accused* (Par., 1933), *The Kiss Before the Mirror* (Univ., 1933), *I Love That Man* (Par., 1933), *Springtime for Henry* (Fox, 1934), *Transatlantic Merry-Go-Round* (UA, 1934), *Jealousy* (Col., 1934), *I'll Love You Always* (Col., 1935), *After the Dance* (Col., 1935), *Atlantic Adventure* (Col., 1935), *There Goes My Heart* (UA, 1938), *That Certain Age* (Univ., 1938).

JACK CARSON (John Elmer Carson) Born October 27, 1910, Carmen, Manitoba, Canada. Married Betty Lynn; divorced. Married Kay St. Germaine (1940), children: John, Germaine; divorced 1950. Married Lola Albright (1952); divorced 1958. Married Sandra Tucker (1961). Died January 3, 1963.

Fernando Lamas, Esther Williams and Jack Carson in *Dangerous When Wet*.

Feature Films: *You Only Live Once* (UA, 1937), *Too Many Wives* (RKO, 1937), *Music for Madame* (RKO, 1937), *It Could Happen To You* (Rep., 1937), *Stage Door* (RKO, 1937), *Stand-In* (UA, 1937), *High Flyers* (RKO, 1937), *Reported Missing* (Univ., 1937), *The Toast of New York* (RKO, 1937), *Crashing Hollywood* (RKO, 1938), *Bringing Up Baby* (RKO, 1938), *She's Got Everything* (RKO, 1938), *Quick Money* (RKO, 1938), *Everybody's Doing It* (RKO, 1938), *Night Spot*

(RKO, 1938), *Go Chase Yourself* (RKO, 1938), *Law of the Underworld* (RKO, 1938), *The Saint in New York* (RKO, 1938), *Vivacious Lady* (RKO, 1938), *This Marriage Business* (RKO, 1938), *Maid's Night Out* (RKO, 1938), *Having Wonderful Time* (RKO, 1938), *Carefree* (RKO, 1938), *The Kid From Texas* (MGM, 1939), *Mr. Smith Goes to Washington* (Col., 1939), *Legion of Lost Flyers* (Univ., 1939), *The Escape* (20th, 1939), *Destry Rides Again* (Univ., 1939), *The Honeymoon's Over* (20th, 1939), *I Take This Woman* (MGM, 1940), *Shooting High* (20th, 1940), *Young as You Feel* (20th, 1940), *Enemy Agent* (Univ., 1940), *Parole Fixer* (Par., 1940), *Typhoon* (Par., 1940), *Alias the Deacon* (Univ., 1940), *The Girl in 313* (20th, 1940), *Queen of the Mob* (Par., 1940), *Sandy Gets Her Man* (Univ., 1940), *Love Thy Neighbor* (Par., 1940), *Mr. and Mrs. Smith* (RKO, 1941), *The Strawberry Blonde* (WB, 1941), *Love Crazy* (MGM, 1941), *The Bride Came C.O.D.* (WB, 1941), *Navy Blues* (WB, 1941), *Blues in the Night* (WB, 1941), *Larceny, Inc.* (WB, 1942), *The Male Animal* (WB, 1942), *Wings for the Eagle* (WB, 1942), *The Hard Way* (WB, 1942), *Gentleman Jim* (WB, 1942), *Princess O'Rourke* (WB, 1943), *Thank Your Lucky Stars* (WB, 1943), *Arsenic and Old Lace* (WB, 1944), *The Doughgirls* (WB, 1944), *Hollywood Canteen* (WB, 1944), *Shine On, Harvest Moon* (WB, 1944), *Make Your Own Bed* (WB, 1944), *Roughly Speaking* (WB, 1945), *Mildred Pierce* (WB, 1945), *One More Tomorrow* (WB, 1946), *Two Guys From Milwaukee* (WB, 1946), *The Time, The Place and the Girl* (WB, 1946), *Love And Learn* (WB, 1947), *April Showers* (WB, 1948), *Romance on the High Seas* (WB, 1948), *Two Guys From Texas* (WB, 1948), *It's a Great Feeling* (WB, 1949), *My Dream Is Yours* (WB, 1949), *John Loves Mary* (WB, 1949), *Bright Leaf* (WB, 1950), *The Good Humor Man* (Col., 1950), *Mr. Universe* (EL, 1951), *The Groom Wore Spurs* (Univ., 1951), *Dangerous When Wet* (MGM, 1953), *Red Garters* (Par., 1954), *A Star Is Born* (WB, 1954), *Phffft* (Col., 1954), *Ain't Misbehavin'* (Univ., 1955), *The Bottom of the Bottle* (20th, 1956), *Magnificent Roughnecks* (AA, 1956), *The Tattered Dress* (Univ., 1957), *The Tarnished Angels* (Univ., 1957), *Cat on a Hot Tin Roof* (MGM, 1958), *Rally Round The Flag, Boys!* (20th, 1958), *The Bramble Bush* (WB, 1960), *King of the Roaring 20's—The Story of Arnold Rothstein* (AA, 1961).

JOAN CAULFIELD (Joan Beatrice Caulfield) Born June 1, 1922, Orange, New Jersey. Married Frank Ross (1950), child: Caulfield; divorced 1959. Married Robert Peterson (1960), child: John; divorced 1966.

Feature Films: *Miss Susie Slagle's* (Par., 1945), *Duffy's Tavern* (Par., 1945), *Blue Skies* (Par., 1946), *Monsieur Beaucaire* (Par., 1946), *Welcome Stranger* (Par., 1947), *Dear Ruth* (Par., 1947), *The Unsuspected* (WB, 1947), *Variety Girl* (Par., 1947), *The Sainted Sisters* (Par., 1948), *Larceny* (Univ., 1948), *Dear Wife* (Par., 1949), *The Petty Girl* (Col., 1950), *The Lady Says No* (UA, 1951), *The Rains of Ranchipur* (20th, 1955), *Cattle King* (MGM, 1963), *Red Tomahawk* (Par., 1967), *Buckskin* (Par., 1968).

George Reeves and Joan Caulfield in *The Sainted Sisters*.

Eugene Iglesias, Jeff Chandler, Earl Holliman and Charles Horvath in *East of Sumatra*.

JEFF CHANDLER (Ira Grossel) Born December 15, 1918, Brooklyn, New York. Married Marjorie Hoshelle (1946), children: Jamie, Dana; divorced 1959. Died June 17, 1961.

Feature Films: *Johnny O'Clock* (Col., 1947), *Invisible Wall* (20th, 1947), *Roses Are Red* (20th, 1947), *Mr. Belvedere Goes to College* (20th, 1949), *Sword in the Desert* (Univ., 1949), *Abandoned* (Univ., 1949), *Broken Arrow* (20th, 1950), *Two Flags West* (20th, 1950), *Deported* (Univ., 1950), *Bird of Paradise* (20th, 1951), *Smuggler's Island* (Univ., 1951), *Iron Man* (Univ., 1951), *Flame of Araby* (Univ., 1951), *Meet Danny Wilson* (Univ., 1952),* *Red Ball Express* (Univ., 1952), *Battle at Apache* Pass (Univ., 1952), *Yankee Buccaneer* (Univ., 1952), *Because of You* (Univ., 1952), *Great Sioux Uprising* (Univ., 1953), *East of Sumatra* (Univ., 1953), *War Arrow* (Univ., 1953), *Yankee Pasha* (Univ., 1954), *Taza, Son of Cochise* (Univ., 1954),* *Sign of the Pagan* (Univ., 1954), *Foxfire* (Univ., 1955), *Female on the Beach* (Univ., 1955), *The Spoilers* (Univ., 1956), *Toy Tiger* (Univ., 1956), *Away All Boats* (Univ., 1956), *Pillars of the Sky* (Univ., 1956), *Drango* (UA, 1957), *Jeanne Eagles* (Col., 1957), *Man in the Shadow* (Univ., 1958), *The Lady Takes a Flyer* (Univ., 1958), *Raw Wind in Eden* (Univ., 1958), *Stranger in my Arms* (Univ., 1959), *Thunder in the Sun* (Par., 1959), *Ten Seconds To Hell* (UA, 1959), *The Jayhawkers* (Par., 1959), *Story of David* (WB, 1960), *The Plunderers* (AA, 1960), *Return to Peyton Place* (20th, 1961), *Merrill's Marauders* (WB, 1961).

　　*Unbilled guest appearance

LON CHANEY, JR. (Creighton Chaney) Born 1907. Married, children: Lon, Ronald; divorced. Married Patsy Beck (1937).

English-Language Feature Films:

　　as Creighton Chaney *The Last Frontier* (RKO serial, 1932), *Girl Crazy* (RKO, 1932), *Bird of Paradise* (RKO, 1932), *Lucky Devils* (RKO, 1933), *Scarlet River* (RKO, 1933), *Son of the Border* (RKO, 1933), *Sixteen Fathoms Deep* (Mon., 1934), *The Life of Vergie Winters* (RKO, 1934), *Girl o' My Dreams* (Mon., 1934).

　　as Lon Chaney, Jr. *Captain Hurricane* (RKO, 1935), *Accent on Youth* (Par., 1935), *Hold 'Em Yale* (Par., 1935), *Shadow of Silk Lennox* (Commodore, 1935), *The Marriage Bargain* (Hollywood Exchange, 1935), *Scream in the Night* (Commodore, 1935), *Ace Drummond* (Univ. serial, 1936), *Undersea Kingdom* (Rep. serial, 1936), *The Singing Cowboy* (Rep., 1936), *Killer at Large* (Col., 1936), *The Old Corral* (Rep., 1936), *Secret Agent X-9* (Univ. serial, 1937), *Midnight Taxi* (20th, 1937), *Angel's Holiday* (20th, 1937), *Wild and Woolly* (20th, 1937), *Wife, Doctor and Nurse* (20th, 1937), *The Lady Escapes* (20th, 1937), *Love and Hisses* (20th, 1937), *One Mile From Heaven* (20th, 1937), *Second Honeymoon* (20th, 1937), *That I May Live* (20th, 1937), *City Girl* (20th, 1937), *Charlie Chan on Broadway* (20th, 1937), *Slave Ship* (20th, 1937), *Born Reckless* (20th, 1937), *Thin Ice* (20th, 1937), *Alexander's Ragtime Band* (20th, 1938), *Straight, Place and Show* (20th, 1938), *Walking Down Broadway* (20th, 1938), *Passport Husband* (20th, 1938), *Road Demon* (20th, 1938), *Submarine Patrol* (20th, 1938), *Mr. Moto's Gamble* (20th, 1938), *Speed to Burn* (20th, 1938), *Happy Landing* (20th, 1938), *Josette* (20th, 1938), *Jesse James* (20th, 1939), *Frontier Marshal* (20th, 1939), *Charlie Chan in City in Darkness* (20th,

1939), *Of Mice and Men* (UA, 1939), *Union Pacific* (Par., 1939), *One Million B.C.* (UA, 1940), *North West Mounted Police* (Par., 1940), *Riders of Death Valley* (Univ. serial, 1941), *Man-Made Monster* (Univ., 1941), *Billy the Kid* (MGM, 1941), *San Antonio Rose* (Univ., 1941), *Badlands of Dakota* (Univ., 1941), *Too Many Blondes* (Univ., 1941), *The Wolf Man* (Univ., 1941), *Overland Mail* (Univ. serial, 1942), *North to the Klondike* (Univ., 1942), *The Ghost of Frankenstein* (Univ., 1942), *The Mummy's Tomb* (Univ., 1942), *Frankenstein Meets the Wolf Man* (Univ., 1943), *Eyes of the Underworld* (Univ., 1943), *Frontier Badman* (Univ., 1943), *Son of Dracula* (Univ., 1943), *Crazy House* (Univ., 1943), *Calling Dr. Death* (Univ., 1943), *Follow the Boys* (Univ., 1944), *Ghost Catchers* (Univ., 1944), *Cobra Woman* (Univ., 1944), *The Mummy's Ghost* (Univ., 1944), *Weird Woman* (Univ., 1944), *Dead Man's Eyes* (Univ., 1944), *Here Come the Co-eds* (Univ., 1945), *House of Frankenstein* (Univ., 1945), *The Mummy's Curse* (Univ., 1945), *The Frozen Ghost* (Univ., 1945), *House of Dracula* (Univ., 1945), *The Daltons Ride Again* (Univ., 1945), *Pillow of Death* (Univ., 1945), *Strange Confession* (Univ., 1945), *My Favorite Brunette* (Par., 1947), *Albuquerque* (Par., 1948), *16 Fathoms Deep* (Mon. 1948), *Abbott and Costello Meet Frankenstein* (Univ., 1948), *The Counterfeiters* (20th, 1948), *There's a Girl in My Heart* (AA, 1949), *Captain China* (Par., 1949), *Once a Thief* (UA, 1950), *Inside Straight* (MGM, 1951), *Only the Valiant* (WB, 1951), *Behave Yourself* (RKO, 1951), *Flame of Araby* (Univ., 1951), *The Bushwhackers* (Realart, 1952), *High Noon* (UA, 1952), *Thief of Damascus* (Col., 1952), *Springfield Rifle* (WB, 1952), *The Black Castle* (Univ., 1952), *Raiders of the Seven Seas* (UA, 1953), *A Lion Is in the Streets* (WB, 1953), *Jivaro* (Par., 1954), *The Boy From Oklahoma* (WB, 1954), *Casanova's Big Night* (Par., 1954), *Passion* (RKO, 1954), *Silver Star* (Lip., 1955), *Big House, U.S.A.* (UA, 1955), *Not as a Stranger* (UA, 1955), *I Died a Thousand Times* (WB, 1955), *The Indian Fighter* (UA, 1955), *Manfish* (UA, 1956), *Pardners* (Par., 1956), *The Black Sleep* (UA, 1956), *The Indestructible Man* (AA, 1956), *Daniel Boone, Trail Blazer* (Rep., 1956), *Cyclops* (AA, 1957), *The Defiant Ones* (UA, 1958), *Money, Women and Guns* (Univ., 1958), *The Alligator People* (20th, 1959), *The Phantom* (American Releasing, 1961), *Rebellion in Cuba* (International, 1961), *The Haunted Palace* (AIP, 1963), *Law of the Lawless* (Par., 1964), *Stage to Thunder Rock* (Par., 1964), *Witchcraft* (20th, 1964), *Black Spurs* (Par., 1965), *Young Fury* (Par., 1965), *Town Tamer* (Par., 1965), *Apache Uprising* (Par., 1966), *Johnny Reno* (Par., 1966), *Welcome to Hard Times* (MGM, 1967), *Hillbillies in a Haunted House* (Woolner, 1967). *Dr. Terror's Gallery of Horrors* (Par., 1967), *The Frontiersman* (Par., 1968), *Buckskin* (Par., 1968).

Will Rogers, Jr., and Lon Chaney, Jr., in *The Boy From Oklahoma*.

CHARLES CHAPLIN (Charles Spencer Chaplin) Born April 16, 1889, London, England. Married Mildred Harris (1917); divorced 1920. Married Lita Grey (1924), children: Charles, Sydney; divorced 1927. Married Paulette Goddard (1936); divorced 1942. Married Oona O'Neill (1943), children: Geraldine, Michael, Josephine, Victoria, Jane, Annette, Eugene, Christopher.

Marlon Brando and Charles Chaplin in *A Countess From Hong Kong.*

Sound Feature Films: *The Great Dictator* (UA, 1940), *Monsieur Verdoux* (UA, 1947), *Limelight* (UA, 1952), *A King in New York* (UA, 1957), *A Countess From Hong Kong* (Univ., 1967).

CYD CHARISSE (Tula Ellice Finklea) Born March 8, 1921, Amarillo, Texas. Married Nico Charisse (1939), child: Nicky; divorced 1947. Married Tony Martin (1948), child: Tony.

Margaret O'Brien and Cyd Charisse in *The Unfinished Dance.*

Feature Films:

As Lily Norwood *Mission to Moscow* (WB, 1943), *Something to Shout About* (Col., 1943).

As Cyd Charisse *Ziegfeld Follies of 1946* (MGM, 1946), *The Harvey Girls* (MGM, 1946), *Three Wise Fools* (MGM, 1946), *Till the Clouds Roll By* (MGM, 1946), *Fiesta* (MGM, 1947), *The Unfinished Dance* (MGM, 1947), *On an Island With You* (MGM, 1948), *Words and Music* (MGM, 1948), *The Kissing Bandit* (MGM, 1949), *East Side, West Side* (MGM, 1949), *Tension* (MGM, 1949), *Mark of the Renegade* (Univ., 1951), *The Wild North* (MGM, 1952), *Singin' in the Rain* (MGM, 1952), *Sombrero* (MGM, 1953), *The Band Wagon* (MGM, 1953), *Easy to Love* (MGM, 1953),* *Brigadoon* (MGM, 1954), *Deep in My Heart* (MGM, 1954), *It's Always Fair Weather* (MGM, 1955), *Meet*

Me in Las Vegas (MGM, 1956), *Invitation to the Dance* (MGM, 1957), *Silk Stockings* (MGM, 1957), *Twilight for the Gods* (Univ., 1958), *Party Girl* (MGM, 1958), *Five Golden Hours* (Col., 1961), *Black Tights* (Magna, 1962), *Two Weeks in Another Town* (MGM, 1962), *The Silencers* (Col., 1966), *Maroc 7* (Univ., 1967), *Assassination in Rome* (Walter Manly, 1967).

*Unbilled guest appearance

RUTH CHATTERTON Born December 24, 1893, New York, New York. Married Ralph Forbes (1924); divorced 1932. Married George Brent (1932); divorced 1934. Married Barry Thomson (1942); widowed 1960. Died November 21, 1961.

Sound Feature Films: *The Doctor's Secret* (Par., 1929), *The Dummy* (Par., 1929), *Madame X* (MGM, 1929), *Charming Sinners* (Par., 1929), *The Laughing Lady* (Par., 1929), *Sarah and Son* (Par., 1930), *Paramount on Parade* (Par., 1930), *The Lady of Scandal* (MGM, 1930), *Anybody's Woman* (Par., 1930), *The Right to Love* (Par., 1930), *Unfaithful* (Par., 1931), *Magnificent Lie* (Par., 1931), *Once a Lady* (Par., 1931), *Tomorrow and Tomorrow* (Par., 1932), *The Rich Are Always With Us* (WB, 1932), *The Crash* (WB, 1932), *Frisco Jenny* (WB, 1933), *Lilly Turner* (WB, 1933), *Female* (WB, 1933), *Journal of a Crime* (WB, 1934), *Lady of Secrets* (Col., 1936), *Girls' Dormitory* (20th, 1936), *Dodsworth* (UA, 1936), *The Rat* (London Films, 1938), *The Royal Divorce* (Imperator, 1938).

Robert Allen and Ruth Chatterton in *Lady of Secrets.*

MAURICE CHEVALIER (Maurice Auguste Chevalier) Born September 12, 1888, Paris, France. Married Yvonne Vallee (1927); divorced 1935.

English-Language Sound Feature Films: *Innocents of Paris* (Par., 1929), *The Love Parade* (Par., 1929), *Paramount on Parade* (Par., 1930), *The Big Pond* (Par., 1930), *The Playboy of Paris* (Par., 1930), *The Smiling Lieutenant* (Par., 1931), *One Hour With You* (Par., 1932) *Make Me a Star* (Par., 1932),* *Love Me Tonight* (Par., 1932), *A Bedtime Story* (Par., 1933), *The Way to Love* (Par., 1933), *The Merry Widow* (MGM, 1934), *Folies Bergere* (UA, 1935), *The Beloved Vagabond* (Col., 1937), *Love in the Afternoon* (AA, 1957), *Gigi* (MGM, 1958), *Count Your Blessings* (MGM, 1959), *A Breath of Scandal* (Par., 1960), *Can-Can* (20th, 1960), *Pepe* (Col., 1960), *Fanny* (WB, 1961), *Jessica* (UA, 1962), *Black Tights* (Magna, 1962), *In Search of the Castaways* (BV, 1962), *A New Kind of Love* (Par., 1963), *Panic Button* (Gorton Associates, 1964), *I'd Rather Be Rich* (Univ., 1964), *Monkeys, Go Home* (BV, 1967).

*Unbilled guest appearance

Myrna Loy, Maurice Chevalier and Jeanette MacDonald in *Love Me Tonight*.

Ginger Rogers and Fred Clark in *Dream Boat*.

DANE CLARK (Bernard Zanville) Born February 18, 1915, New York, New York. Married Margo Yoder (1941).

Feature Films: *The Glass Key* (Par., 1942), *Sunday Punch* (MGM, 1942), *Pride of the Yankees* (RKO, 1942), *Wake Island* (Par., 1942), *Tennessee Johnson* (MGM, 1942), *Action in the North Atlantic* (WB, 1943), *Destination Tokyo* (WB, 1943), *The Very Thought of You* (WB, 1944), *Hollywood Canteen* (WB, 1944), *God Is My Co-Pilot* (WB, 1945), *Pride of the Marines* (WB, 1945), *Her Kind of Man* (WB, 1946), *A Stolen Life* (WB, 1946), *That Way With Women* (WB, 1947), *Deep Valley* (WB, 1947), *Moonrise* (Rep., 1948), *Embraceable You* (WB, 1948), *Whiplash* (WB, 1948), *Without Honor* (UA, 1949), *Barricade* (WB, 1950), *Backfire* (WB, 1950), *Time Running Out* (British, 1950), *Never Trust a Gambler* (Col., 1951), *Fort Defiance* (UA, 1951), *Highly Dangerous* (Lip., 1951), *Gambler and the Lady* (Lip., 1952), *Go, Man, Go!* (UA, 1954), *Paid to Kill* (Lip., 1954), *Blackout* (Lip., 1954), *Port of Hell* (AA, 1954), *Thunder Pass* (Lip., 1954), *Toughest Man Alive* (AA, 1955), *Massacre* (20th, 1956), *The Man Is Armed* (Rep., 1956), *Outlaw's Son* (UA, 1957), *Whistle* (MPO Videotronics-ASA Films, 1967).

Tony Martinez, Frank Marlowe, Dane Clark and Robert Douglas in *Barricade*.

FRED CLARK (Frederic Leonard Clark) Born March 9, 1914, Lincoln, California. Married Benay Venuta (1952); divorced 1963. Married Gloria Glaser (1966).

Feature Films: *The Unsuspected* (WB, 1947), *Ride the Pink Horse* (Univ., 1947), *Hazard* (Par., 1948), *Cry of the City* (20th, 1948), *Two Guys From Texas* (WB, 1948), *Alias Nick Beal* (Par., 1949), *Flamingo Road* (WB, 1949), *The Younger Brothers* (WB, 1949), *Task Force* (WB,

1949), *White Heat* (WB, 1949), *The Lady Takes a Sailor* (WB, 1949), *Sunset Boulevard* (Par., 1950), *The Eagle and the Hawk* (Par., 1950), *Return of the Frontiersman* (WB, 1950), *The Jackpot* (20th, 1950), *Mrs. O'Malley and Mr. Malone* (MGM, 1950), *The Lemon Drop Kid* (Par., 1951), *Hollywood Story* (Univ., 1951), *A Place in the Sun* (Par., 1951), *Meet Me After the Show* (20th, 1951), *Three for Bedroom C* (WB, 1952), *Dreamboat* (20th, 1952), *The Stars Are Singing* (Par., 1953), *The Caddy* (Par., 1953), *How to Marry a Millionaire* (20th, 1953), *Here Come the Girls* (Par., 1953), *Living It Up* (Par., 1954), *Abbott And Costello Meet the Keystone Kops* (Univ., 1955), *Daddy Long Legs* (20th, 1955), *How to Be Very, Very Popular* (20th, 1955), *The Court-Martial of Billy Mitchell* (WB, 1955), *Miracle in the Rain* (WB, 1956), *The Birds and the Bees* (Par., 1956), *The Solid Gold Cadillac* (Col., 1956), *Back From Eternity* (RKO, 1956), *Joe Butterfly* (Univ., 1957), *The Fuzzy Pink Nightgown* (UA, 1957), *Don't Go Near the Water* (MGM, 1957), *Mardi Gras* (20th, 1958), *Auntie Mame* (WB, 1958), *The Mating Game* (MGM, 1959), *It Started With a Kiss* (MGM, 1959), *Visit To a Small Planet* (Par., 1960), *Bells Are Ringing* (MGM, 1960), *Zotz!* (Col., 1962), *Boys' Night Out* (MGM, 1962), *Hemingway's Adventures of a Young Man* (20th, 1962), *Move Over, Darling* (20th, 1963), *John Goldfarb, Please Come Home* (20th, 1964), *The Curse of the Mummy's Tomb* (Col., 1965), *Sergeant Deadhead* (AIP, 1965), *Dr. Goldfoot and the Bikini Machine* (AIP, 1965), *When the Boys Meet the Girls* (MGM, 1965), *War Italian Style* (AIP, 1967), *Year of the Horse* (BV, 1968).

MAE CLARKE Born August 16, 1910, Philadelphia, Pennsylvania. Married Lew Brice (1928); divorced 1930. Married Stephen Bancroft (1937); divorced. Married Herbert Langdon; divorced.

Jack Holt and Mae Clarke in *Trouble in Morocco*.

Feature Films: *Big Time* (Fox, 1929), *Nix on Dames* (Fox, 1929), *Fall Guy* (WB, 1930), *Dancers* (Fox, 1930), *Front Page* (UA, 1931), *Men on Call* (Fox, 1931), *Public Enemy* (WB, 1931), *Good Bad Girl* (Col., 1931), *Waterloo Bridge* (Univ., 1931), *Reckless Living* (Col., 1931), *Frankenstein* (Univ., 1931), *Final Edition* (Col., 1932), *Three Wise Girls* (Col., 1932), *Impatient Maiden* (Col., 1932), *Night World* (Univ., 1932), *Breach of Promise* (World Wide, 1932), *Penguin Pool Murder* (RKO, 1932), *Fast Workers* (MGM, 1933), *Parole Girl* (Col., 1933), *Made on Broadway* (MGM, 1933), *Turn Back the Clock* (MGM, 1933), *As the Devil Commands* (Col., 1933), *Penthouse* (MGM, 1933), *Lady Killer* (WB, 1933), *Flaming Gold* (RKO, 1934), *This Side of Heaven* (MGM, 1934), *Nana* (UA, 1934), *Let's Talk It Over* (Univ., 1934), *Operator 13* (MGM, 1934), *Man With Two Faces* (WB, 1934), *The Daring Young Man* (Fox, 1935), *Silk Hat Kid* (Fox, 1935), *Hitch Hike Lady* (Rep., 1935), *The House of a Thousand Candles* (Rep., 1936), *Hearts in Bondage* (Rep., 1936), *Wild Brian Kent* (20th, 1936), *Great Guy* (GN, 1936), *Hats Off* (GN, 1936), *Trouble in Morocco* (Col., 1937), *Outlaws of the Orient* (Col., 1937), *Women in War* (Rep., 1940), *Sailors on Leave* (Rep., 1941), *Flying Tigers* (Rep., 1942), *Lady From Chungking* (PRC, 1942), *Here Come the Waves* (Par., 1944), *And Now Tomorrow* (Par., 1944), *Kitty* (Par., 1945), *Daredevils of the Clouds* (Rep., 1948), *King of the Rocket Men* (Rep. serial, 1949), *Streets of San Francisco* (Rep., 1949), *Gun Runner* (Mon., 1949), *Annie Get Your Gun* (MGM, 1950), *The Yellow Cab Man* (MGM, 1950), *The Great Caruso* (MGM, 1951), *Mr. Imperium* (MGM, 1951), *The People Against O'Hara* (MGM, 1951), *Callaway Went Thataway* (MGM, 1951), *The Unknown Man* (MGM, 1951), *Because of You* (MGM, 1952), *Horizons West* (Univ., 1952), *Singin' in the Rain* (MGM, 1952), *Thunderbirds* (Rep., 1952), *Pat and Mike* (MGM, 1952), *Magnificent Obsession* (Univ., 1954), *Women's Prison* (Col., 1955), *Not as a Stranger* (UA, 1955), *Wichita* (AA, 1955), *I Died a Thousand Times* (WB, 1955), *Come Next Spring* (Rep., 1956), *Mohawk* (20th, 1956), *The Desperadoes Are in Town* (20th, 1956), *Ride the High Iron* (Col., 1956), *Voice in the Mirror* (Univ., 1958), *Ask Any Girl* (MGM, 1959), *Big Hand for the Little Lady* (WB, 1966), *Thoroughly Modern Millie* (Univ., 1967).

Cornell Borchers and Montgomery Clift in *The Big Lift*.

MONTGOMERY CLIFT (Edward Montgomery Clift) Born October 17, 1920, Omaha, Nebraska. Died July 23, 1966.

Feature Films: *The Search* (MGM, 1948), *Red River* (UA, 1948), *The Heiress* (Par., 1949), *The Big Lift* (20th, 1950), *A Place in the Sun* (Par., 1951), *I Confess* (WB, 1953), *From Here to Eternity* (Col., 1953), *Indiscretion of an American Wife* (Col., 1954), *Raintree County* (MGM, 1957), *The Young Lions* (20th, 1958), *Lonelyhearts* (UA, 1959), *Suddenly, Last Summer* (Col., 1959), *Wild River* (20th, 1960), *The Misfits* (UA, 1961), *Judgment at Nuremberg* (UA, 1961), *Freud* (Univ., 1962), *The Defector* (7 Arts, 1966).

LEE J. COBB (Leo Jacob) Born December 8, 1911, New York, New York. Married Helen Beverly (1940), children: Vincent, Julie; divorced 1952. Married Mary Hirsch (1957), children: Tony, Jerry.

William Holden and Lee J. Cobb in *The Dark Past*.

Feature Films: *North of Rio Grande* (Par., 1937), *Ali Baba Goes to Town* (20th, 1937), *Rustler's Valley* (Par., 1937), *Danger on the Air*, (Univ., 1938), *The Phantom Creeps* (Univ. serial, 1939), *Golden Boy* (Col., 1939), *Men of Boys Town* (MGM, 1941), *This Thing Called Love* (Col., 1941), *Paris Calling* (Univ., 1941), *Tonight We Raid Calais* (20th, 1943), *Buckskin Frontier* (UA, 1943), *The Moon Is Down* (20th, 1943), *The Song of Bernadette* (20th, 1943), *Winged Victory* (20th, 1944), *Anna and the King of Siam* (20th, 1946), *Boomerang* (20th, 1947), *Johnny O'Clock* (Col., 1947), *Captain From Castile* (20th, 1947), *Call Northside 777* (20th, 1948), *The Miracle of the Bells* (RKO, 1948), *The Luck of the Irish* (20th, 1948), *The Dark Past* (Col., 1948), *Thieves' Highway* (20th, 1949), *The Man Who Cheated Himself* (20th, 1950), *Sirocco* (Col., 1951), *The Family Secret* (Col., 1951), *The Fighter* (UA, 1952), *The Tall Texan* (Lip., 1953), *Yankee Pasha* (Univ., 1954), *Gorilla at Large* (20th, 1954), *On the Waterfront* (Col., 1954), *Day of Triumph* (George J. Schaefer, 1954), *The Racers* (20th, 1955), *The Road to Denver* (Rep., 1955), *The Left Hand of God* (20th, 1955), *The Man in the Gray Flannel Suit* (20th, 1956), *Miami Exposé* (Col., 1956), *12 Angry Men* (UA, 1957), *The Garment Jungle* (Col., 1957), *The Three Faces of Eve* (20th, 1957), *The Brothers Karamazov* (MGM, 1958), *Man of the West* (UA, 1958), *Party Girl* (MGM, 1958), *The Trap* (Par., 1959), *Green Mansions* (MGM, 1959), *But Not for Me* (Par., 1959), *Exodus* (UA, 1960), *The Four Horsemen of the Apocalypse* (MGM, 1962), *How the West Was Won* (MGM, 1963), *Come Blow Your Horn* (Par., 1963), *Our Man Flint* (20th, 1966), *In Like Flint* (20th, 1967), *MacKenna's Gold* (Col., 1968), *Our Man From Las Vegas* (WB-7 Arts, 1968).

Charles Coburn and Spencer Tracy in *Edison the Man*.

CHARLES COBURN (Charles Douville Coburn) Born June 19, 1877, Savannah, Georgia. Married Ivah Wills (1906); widowed 1937. Married Winifred Natzka (1959). Died August 30, 1961.

Feature Films: *The People's Enemy* (RKO, 1935), *Of Human Hearts* (MGM, 1938), *Vivacious Lady* (RKO, 1938), *Yellow Jack* (MGM, 1938), *Lord Jeff* (MGM, 1938), *Idiot's Delight* (MGM, 1939), *The Story of Alexander Graham Bell* (20th, 1939), *Made for Each Other* (UA, 1939), *Bachelor Mother* (RKO, 1939), *Stanley and Livingstone* (20th, 1939), *In Name Only* (RKO, 1939), *Road to Singapore* (Par., 1940), *Florian* (MGM, 1940), *Edison, The Man* (MGM, 1940), *Three Faces West* (Rep., 1940), *The Captain Is a Lady* (MGM, 1940), *The Lady Eve* (Par., 1941), *The Devil and Miss Jones* (RKO, 1941), *Our Wife* (Col., 1941), *Unexpected Uncle* (RKO, 1941), *H. M. Pulham, Esq.* (MGM, 1941), *Kings Row* (WB, 1941), *In This Our Life* (WB, 1942), *George Washington Slept Here* (WB, 1942), *The More the Merrier* (Col., 1943), *The Constant Nymph* (WB, 1943), *Heaven Can Wait* (20th, 1943), *Princess O'Rourke* (WB, 1943), *My Kingdom for a Cook* (Col., 1943), *Knickerbocker Holiday* (UA, 1944), *Wilson* (20th, 1944), *The Impatient Years* (Col., 1944), *A Royal Scandal* (20th, 1945), *Rhapsody in Blue* (WB, 1945), *Over 21* (Col., 1945), *Colonel Effingham's Raid* (20th, 1945), *Shady Lady* (Univ., 1945), *The Green Years* (MGM, 1946), *Lured* (UA, 1947), *B. F.'s Daughter* (MGM, 1948), *The Paradine Case* (Selznick, 1948), *Green Grass of Wyoming* (20th, 1948), *Impact* (UA, 1949), *Yes Sir, That's My Baby* (Univ., 1949), *Everybody Does It* (20th, 1949), *The Doctor and the Girl* (MGM, 1949), *The Gal Who Took the West* (Univ., 1949), *Louisa* (Univ., 1950), *Peggy* (Univ., 1950), *Mr. Music* (Par., 1950), *The Highwayman* (AA, 1951), *Monkey Business* (20th, 1952), *Has Anybody Seen My Gal* (Univ., 1952), *Gentlemen Prefer Blondes* (20th, 1953), *Trouble Along the Way* (WB, 1953), *The Long Wait* (UA, 1954), *The Rocket Man* (20th, 1954), *How To Be Very, Very Popular* (20th, 1955), *The Power and the Prize* (MGM, 1956), *Around the World in 80 Days* (UA, 1956), *Town on Trial* (Col., 1957), *The Story of Mankind* (WB, 1957), *How to Murder a Rich Uncle* (Col., 1957), *Stranger in My Arms* (Univ., 1959), *The Remarkable Mr. Pennypacker* (20th, 1959), *John Paul Jones* (WB, 1959), *Pepe* (Col., 1960).

JAMES COBURN Born August 31, 1928, Laurel, Nebraska. Married Beverly Kelly (1958), children: Lisa, James.

Anthony Quinn and James Coburn in A *High Wind in Jamaica*.

Feature Films: *Ride Lonesome* (Col., 1959), *Face of a Fugitive* (Col., 1959), *The Magnificent Seven* (UA, 1960), *Hell Is for Heroes* (Par., 1962), *The Great Escape* (UA, 1963), *Charade* (Univ., 1963), *The Man From Galveston* (WB, 1964), *The Americanization of Emily* (MGM, 1964), *Major Dundee* (Col., 1965), *A High Wind in Jamaica* (20th, 1965), *The Loved One* (MGM, 1965), *Our Man Flint* (20th, 1966), *Dead Heat on a Merry-Go-Round* (Col., 1966), *In Like Flint* (20th, 1967), *Waterhole No. 3* (Par., 1967), *The President's Analyst* (Par., 1967), *Duffy* (Col., 1968).

Gene Nelson, Steve Cochran, Paul Picerni (on stage) and Paul Bryar in *She's Back on Broadway*.

STEVE COCHRAN (Robert A. Cochran) Born May 25, 1917, Eureka, California. Married Florence Lockwood, child: Xandra; divorced 1946. Married Fay McKenzie (1946); divorced 1948. Married Jonna Jensen (1961); divorced. Died June 15, 1965.

English-Language Feature Films: *Wonder Man* (RKO, 1945), *Boston Blackie Booked on Suspicion* (Col., 1945), *The Gay Senorita* (Col., 1945), *The Best Years of Our Lives* (RKO, 1946), *The Chase* (UA, 1946), *Copacabana* (UA, 1947), *The Kid From Brooklyn* (RKO, 1947), *A Song Is Born* (RKO, 1948), *White Heat* (WB, 1949), *The Damned Don't Cry* (WB, 1950), *Dallas* (WB, 1950), *Highway 301* (WB, 1950), *Storm Warning* (WB, 1950), *Raton Pass* (WB, 1951), *Inside the Walls of Folsom Prison* (WB, 1951), *Jim Thorpe—All American* (WB, 1951), *Tomorrow Is Another Day* (WB, 1951), *The Tanks Are Coming* (WB, 1951), *The Lion and the Horse* (WB, 1952), *Operation Secret* (WB, 1952), *She's Back on Broadway* (WB, 1953), *The Desert Song* (WB, 1953), *Back to God's Country* (Univ., 1953), *Shark River* (UA, 1953), *Carnival Story* (RKO, 1954), *Private Hell 36* (Filmakers, 1954), *Come Next Spring* (Rep., 1956), *Slander* (MGM, 1956), *The Weapon* (Rep., 1957), *Quantrill's Raiders* (AA, 1958), *I, Mobster* (20th, 1958), *The Big Operator* (MGM, 1959), *The Beat Generation* (MGM, 1959), *The Deadly Companions* (Pathé-American, 1961), *Of Love and Desire* (20th, 1963), *Mozambique* (7 Arts, 1965), *Tell Me in the Sunlight* (Movie-Rama Color Corp., 1967).

CLAUDETTE COLBERT (Lily Chauchoin) Born September 13, 1905, Paris, France. Married Norman Foster (1928); divorced 1935. Married Joel Pressman (1935); widowed 1968.

John Barrymore and Claudette Colbert in *Midnight*.

English-Language Sound Feature Films: *The Hole in the Wall* (Par., 1929), *The Lady Lies* (Par., 1929), *Manslaughter* (Par., 1930), *The Big Pond* (Par., 1930), *Young Man of Manhattan* (Par., 1930), *The Smiling Lieutenant* (Par., 1931), *Honor Among Lovers* (Par., 1931), *Secrets of a Secretary* (Par., 1931), *His Woman* (Par., 1931), *The Wiser Sex* (Par., 1932), *Make Me a Star* (Par., 1932),* *Misleading Lady* (Par., 1932), *Man From Yesterday* (Par., 1932), *Phantom President* (Par., 1932), *The Sign of the Cross* (Par., 1932), *Tonight Is Ours* (Par., 1933), *I Cover the Waterfront* (UA, 1933), *Three-Cornered Moon* (Par., 1933), *Torch Singer* (Par., 1933), *Four Frightened People* (Par., 1934), *It Happened One Night* (Col., 1934), *Cleopatra* (Par., 1934), *Imitation of Life* (Univ., 1934), *The Gilded Lily* (Par., 1935), *Private Worlds* (Par., 1935), *She Married Her Boss* (Col., 1935), *The Bride Comes Home* (Par., 1935), *Under Two Flags* (20th, 1936), *Maid of Salem* (Par., 1937), *I Met Him in Paris* (Par., 1937), *Tovarich* (WB, 1937), *Bluebeard's Eighth Wife* (Par., 1938), *Zaza* (Par., 1939), *Midnight* (Par., 1939), *It's a Wonderful World* (MGM, 1939), *Drums Along the Mohawk* (20th, 1939), *Boom Town* (MGM, 1940), *Arise, My Love* (Par., 1940), *Skylark* (Par., 1941), *The Palm Beach Story* (Par., 1942), *Remember the Day* (20th, 1942), *No Time for Love* (Par., 1943), *So Proudly We Hail* (Par., 1943), *Since You Went Away* (UA, 1944), *Practically Yours* (Par., 1944), *Guest Wife* (UA, 1945), *Without Reservations* (RKO, 1946), *Tomorrow Is Forever* (RKO, 1946), *The Secret Heart* (MGM, 1946), *The Egg and I* (Univ., 1947), *Sleep, My Love* (UA, 1948), *Family Honeymoon* (Univ., 1949), *Bride for Sale* (RKO, 1949), *Three Came Home* (20th, 1950), *The Secret Fury* (RKO, 1950), *Thunder on the Hill* (Univ., 1951), *Let's Make It Legal* (20th, 1951), *Outpost in Malaya* (UA, 1952), *Texas Lady* (RKO, 1955), *Parrish* (WB, 1961).

*Unbilled guest appearance

JOAN COLLINS Born May 23, 1933, London, England. Married Maxwell Reed (1952); divorced 1957. Married Anthony Newley (1963), children: Tara, Anthony.

Dolores Gray, Leslie Nielsen, June Allyson, Joan Collins, Sam Levene and Jonathan Hale in *The Opposite Sex*.

Feature Films: *Lady Godiva Rides Again* (Carroll Pictures, 1951), *Cosh Boy* ("The Slasher"—British Lion, 1952), *I Believe in You* (Univ., 1953), *Turn the Key Softly* (Rank, 1953), *The Square Ring* (Rep., 1953), *Decameron Nights* (RKO, 1953), *The Woman's Angle* (Associated British, 1954), *The Good Die Young* (UA, 1954), *Our Girl Friday* ("The Adventures of Sadie"—Associated British, 1954), *Judgement Deferred* (Eros, 1955), *Land of the Pharaohs* (WB, 1955), *The Virgin Queen* (20th, 1955), *The Girl in the Red Velvet Swing* (20th, 1955), *The Opposite Sex* (MGM, 1956), *The Wayward Bus* (20th, 1957), *Island in the Sun* (20th, 1957), *Sea Wife* (20th, 1957), *Stopover Tokyo* (20th, 1957), *The Bravados* (20th, 1958), *Rally 'Round the Flag, Boys!* (20th, 1958), *Seven Thieves* (20th, 1959), *Esther and the King* (20th, 1960), *Road to Hong Kong* (UA, 1962), *Warning Shot* (Par., 1967).

Ronald Colman (dual role) and Halliwell Hobbes in *The Masquerader*.

RONALD COLMAN Born February 9, 1891, Richmond, Surrey, England. Married Thelma Raye (1919); divorced 1934. Married Benita Hume (1938), child: Juliet. Died May 19, 1958.

Sound Feature Films: *Bulldog Drummond* (UA, 1929), *Condemned* (UA, 1929), *Raffles* (UA, 1930), *The Devil to Pay* (UA, 1930), *The Unholy Garden* (UA, 1931), *Arrowsmith* (UA, 1931), *Cynara* (UA, 1932), *The Masquerader* (UA, 1933), *Bulldog Drummond Strikes Back* (UA, 1934), *Clive of India* (UA, 1935), *The Man Who Broke the Bank at Monte Carlo* (Fox, 1935), *A Tale of Two Cities* (MGM, 1935), *Under Two Flags* (20th, 1936), *Lost Horizon* (Col., 1937), *The Prisoner of Zenda* (UA, 1937), *If I Were King* (Par., 1938), *The Light That Failed* (Par., 1939), *Lucky Partners* (RKO, 1940), *My Life With Caroline* (RKO, 1941), *The Talk of the Town* (Col., 1942), *Random Harvest* (MGM, 1942), *Kismet* (MGM, 1944), *The Late George Apley* (20th, 1947), *A Double Life* (Univ., 1948), *Champagne For Caesar* (UA, 1950), *Around the World in 80 Days* (UA, 1956), *The Story of Mankind* (WB, 1957).

SEAN CONNERY (Thomas Connery) Born August 25, 1930, Edinburgh, Scotland. Married Diana Cilento (1962), children: Giovanna, Jason.

Lana Turner and Sean Connery in *Another Time, Another Place*.

Feature Films: *Action of the Tiger* (MGM, 1957), *No Road Back* (RKO, 1957), *Timelock* (DCA, 1957), *Hell Drivers* (Rank, 1957), *Another Time, Another Place* (Par., 1958), *Darby O'Gill and the Little People* (BV, 1959), *Tarzan's Greatest Adventure* (Par., 1959), *On The Fiddle* ("Operation Snafu"—Anglo Amalgamated, 1961), *The Frightened City* (AA, 1961), *The Longest Day* (20th, 1962), *Dr. No* (UA, 1963), *From Russia With Love* (UA, 1964), *Marnie* (Univ., 1964), *Woman of*

Straw (UA, 1964), *Goldfinger* (UA, 1964), *The Hill* (UA, 1965), *Thunderball* (UA, 1965), *A Fine Madness* (WB, 1966), *You Only Live Twice* (UA, 1967).

WALTER CONNOLLY Born April 8, 1887, Cincinnati, Ohio. Married Hedda Harrington (1923), child: Anne. Died May 28, 1940.

Walter Connolly and Verree Teasdale in *First Lady*.

Sound Feature Films: *No More Orchids* (Col., 1932), *Washington Merry-Go-Round* (Col., 1932), *Man Against Woman* (Col., 1932), *Lady For a Day* (Col., 1933), *East of Fifth Avenue* (Col., 1933), *The Bitter Tea of General Yen* (Col., 1933), *Paddy the Next Best Thing* (Col., 1933), *Master of Men* (Col., 1933), *Man's Castle* (Col., 1933), *It Happened One Night* (Col., 1934), *Once to Every Woman* (Col., 1934), *Eight Girls in a Boat* (Par., 1934), *Twentieth Century* (Col., 1934), *Whom the Gods Destroy* (Col., 1934), *Servant's Entrance* (Fox, 1934), *Lady by Choice* (Col., 1934), *Broadway Bill* (Col., 1934), *The Captain Hates the Sea* (Col., 1934), *White Lies* (Col., 1934), *Father Brown, Detective* (Par., 1935), *She Couldn't Take It* (Col., 1935), *So Red the Rose* (Par., 1935), *One Way Ticket* (Col., 1935), *The Music Goes 'Round* (Col., 1936), *Soak the Rich* (Par., 1936), *The King Steps Out* (WB, 1936), *Libeled Lady* (MGM, 1936), *The Good Earth* (MGM, 1937), *Nancy Steele Is Missing* (20th, 1937), *Let's Get Married* (Col., 1937), *The League Of Frightened Men* (Col., 1937), *First Lady* (WB, 1937), *Nothing Sacred* (UA, 1937), *Penitentiary* (Col., 1938), *Start Cheering* (Col., 1938), *Four's a Crowd* (WB, 1938), *Too Hot to Handle* (MGM, 1938), *The Girl Downstairs* (MGM, 1939), *Adventures of Huckleberry Finn* (MGM, 1939), *Bridal Suite* (MGM, 1939), *Good Girls Go to Paris* (Col., 1939), *Coast Guard* (Col., 1939), *Those High Gray Walls* (Col., 1939), *Fifth Avenue Girl* (RKO, 1939), *The Great Victor Herbert* (Par., 1939).

GARY COOPER (Frank James Cooper) Born May 7, 1901, Helena, Montana. Married Veronica Balfe (1933), child: Marie. Died May 13, 1961.

Sound Feature Films: *The Virginian* (Par., 1929), *Only the Brave* (Par., 1930), *Paramount on Parade* (Par., 1930), *The Texan* (Par., 1930), *Seven Days Leave* (Par., 1930), *A Man From Wyoming* (Par., 1930), *The Spoilers* (Par., 1930), *Morocco* (Par., 1930), *Fighting Caravans* (Par., 1931), *City Streets* (Par., 1931), *I Take This Woman* (Par., 1931), *His Woman* (Par., 1931), *The Devil and the Deep* (Par., 1932), *Make Me a Star* (Par., 1932), *If I Had a Million* (Par., 1932), *Farewell To Arms* (Par., 1932), *Today We Live* (MGM, 1933), *One Sunday Afternoon* (Par., 1933), *Design For Living* (Par., 1933), *Alice in Wonderland* (Par., 1933), *Operator 13* (MGM, 1934), *Now and Forever* (Par., 1934), *The Wedding Night* (UA, 1935), *Lives of a Bengal Lancer* (Par., 1935), *Peter Ibbetson* (Par., 1935), *Desire* (Par., 1936), *Mr. Deeds Goes to Town* (Col., 1936), *The General Died at Dawn* (Par., 1936), *Hollywood Boulevard* (Par., 1936), *The Plainsman* (Par., 1936), *Souls at Sea* (Par., 1937), *Adventures of Marco Polo* (UA, 1938), *Bluebeard's Eighth Wife* (Par., 1938), *The Cowboy and the Lady* (UA, 1938), *Beau*

Sigrid Gurie and Gary Cooper in *The Adventures of Marco Polo.*

Geste (Par., 1939), *The Real Glory* (UA, 1939), *The Westerner* (UA, 1940), *North West Mounted Police* (Par., 1940), *Meet John Doe* (WB, 1941), *Sergeant York* (WB, 1941), *Ball of Fire* (RKO, 1941), *The Pride of the Yankees* (RKO, 1942), *For Whom The Bell Tolls* (Par., 1943), *The Story Of Dr. Wassell* (Par., 1944), *Casanova Brown* (RKO, 1944), *Along Came Jones* (RKO, 1945), *Saratoga Trunk* (WB, 1945), *Cloak and Dagger* (WB, 1946), *Unconquered* (Par., 1947), *Variety Girl* (Par., 1947), *Good Sam* (RKO, 1948), *The Fountainhead* (WB, 1949), *It's a Great Feeling* (WB, 1949), *Task Force* (WB, 1949), *Bright Leaf* (WB, 1950), *Dallas* (WB, 1950), *You're in the Navy Now* (20th, 1951), *Starlift* (WB, 1951), *It's a Big Country* (MGM, 1951), *Distant Drums* (WB, 1951), *High Noon* (UA, 1952), *Springfield Rifle* (WB, 1952), *Return To Paradise* (UA, 1953), *Blowing Wild* (WB, 1953), *Garden of Evil* (20th, 1954), *Vera Cruz* (UA, 1954), *The Court-Martial Of Billy Mitchell* (WB, 1955), *Friendly Persuasion* (AA, 1956), *Love in the Afternoon* (AA, 1957), *Ten North Frederick* (20th, 1958), *Man of the West* (UA, 1958), *The Hanging Tree* (WB, 1959), *They Came to Cordura* (Col., 1959), *The Wreck of the Mary Deare* (MGM, 1959), *Alias Jesse James* (UA, 1959),* *The Naked Edge* (UA, 1961).

*Unbilled guest appearance

GLADYS COOPER Born December 18, 1888, Lewisham, England. Married Herbert Buckmaster (1908) children: Joan, John; divorced 1922. Married Sir Neville Pearson (1928), child: Sally; divorced 1936. Married Philip Merivale (1937); widowed 1946.

Gladys Cooper, Claude Rains and Ilka Chase in *Now, Voyager.*

Sound Feature Films: *The Iron Duke* (Gaumont-British, 1935), *Rebecca* (UA, 1940), *Kitty Foyle* (RKO, 1940), *That Hamilton Woman* (UA, 1941), *The Black Cat* (Univ., 1941), *The Gay Falcon* (RKO, 1941), *This Above All* (20th, 1942), *Eagle Squadron* (Univ., 1942), *Now, Voyager* (WB, 1942), *Forever and a Day* (RKO, 1943), *Mr. Lucky* (RKO, 1943), *Princess O'Rourke* (WB, 1943), *The Song of Bernadette* (20th, 1943), *The White Cliffs of Dover* (MGM, 1944), *Mrs. Parkington* (Par., 1944), *Valley of Decision* (MGM, 1945), *Love Letters* (Par., 1945), *The Green Years* (MGM, 1946), *The Cockeyed Miracle* (MGM, 1946), *Green Dolphin Street* (MGM, 1947), *The Bishop's Wife* (RKO, 1947), *Beware of Pity* (Two Cities, 1947), *Homecoming* (MGM, 1948), *The Pirate* (MGM, 1948), *The Secret Garden* (MGM, 1949), *Madame Bovary* (MGM, 1949), *Thunder on the Hill* (Univ., 1951), *At Sword's Point* (RKO, 1952), *The Man Who Loved Redheads* (UA, 1955), *Separate Tables* (UA, 1958), *The List of Adrian Messenger* (Univ., 1963), *My Fair Lady* (WB, 1964), *The Happiest Millionaire* (BV, 1967).

JACKIE COOPER (John Cooper, Jr) Born September 15, 1922, Los Angeles, California. Married June Horne (1944), child: John; divorced 1945. Married Hildy Parks (1949); divorced 1950. Married Barbara Kraus (1954), children: Russell, Julie, Christina.

Ralph Graves, Jackie Cooper and Charles "Chic" Sale in *When a Feller Needs a Friend.*

Sound Feature Films: *Sunny Side Up* (Fox, 1929), *Skippy* (Par., 1931), *Young Donovan's Kid* (RKO, 1931), *The Champ* (MGM, 1931), *Sooky* (Par., 1931), *When a Feller Needs a Friend* (MGM, 1932), *Divorce in the Family* (MGM, 1932), *Broadway to Hollywood* (MGM, 1933), *The Bowery* (UA, 1933), *Lone Cowboy* (Par., 1934), *Treasure Island* (MGM, 1934), *Peck's Bad Boy* (Fox, 1934), *Dinky* (WB, 1935), *O'Shaughnessy's Boy* (MGM, 1935), *Tough Guy* (MGM, 1936), *The Devil Is a Sissy* (MGM, 1936), *Boy of the Streets* (Mon., 1937), *White Banners* (WB, 1938), *Gangster's Boy* (Mon., 1938), *That Certain Age* (Univ., 1938), *Newsboys' Home* (Univ., 1939), *Scouts to the Rescue* (Univ. serial, 1939), *Spirit of Culver* (Univ., 1939), *Streets of New York* (Mon., 1939), *What a Life!* (Par., 1939), *Two Bright Boys* (Univ., 1939), *The Big Guy* (Univ., 1940), *Seventeen* (Par., 1940), *The Return of Frank James* (20th, 1940), *Gallant Sons* (MGM, 1940), *Life With Henry* (Par., 1941), *Ziegfeld Girl* (MGM, 1941), *Her First Beau* (Col., 1941), *Glamour Boys* (Par., 1941), *Syncopation* (RKO, 1942), *Men of Texas* (Univ., 1942), *The Navy Comes Thru* (RKO, 1942), *Where Are Your Children?* (Mon., 1943), *Stork Bites Man* (UA, 1947), *Kilroy Was Here* (Mon., 1947), *French Leave* (Mon., 1948).

ELLEN CORBY (Ellen Hansen) Born June 3, 1913, Racine, Wisconsin.

Feature Films: *The Dark Corner* (20th, 1946), *Cornered* (RKO, 1945), *From This Day Forward* (RKO, 1946), *It's a Wonderful Life* (RKO, 1946), *Till the End of Time* (RKO, 1946), *Cuban Pete* (Univ., 1946), *Crack-Up* (RKO, 1946), *The Spiral Staircase* (RKO, 1946), *Sister Kenny* (RKO, 1946), *Lover Come Back* (Univ., 1946), *The Truth About Murder*

Ellen Corby and Philip Tonge in *Macabre.*

(RKO, 1946), *Beat the Band* (RKO, 1947), *Born to Kill* (RKO, 1947), *Forever Amber* (20th, 1947), *They Won't Believe Me* (RKO, 1947), *Driftwood* (Rep., 1947), *Fighting Father Dunne* (RKO, 1948), *Strike It Rich* (AA, 1948), *I Remember Mama* (RKO, 1948), *The Noose Hangs High* (EL, 1948), *If You Knew Susie* (RKO, 1948), *Little Women* (MGM, 1949), *Mighty Joe Young* (RKO, 1949), *The Dark Past* (Col., 1949), *Rusty Saves a Life* (Col., 1949), *A Woman's Secret* (RKO, 1949), *Madame Bovary* (MGM, 1949), *Captain China* (Par., 1949), *The Gunfighter* (20th, 1950), *Caged* (WB, 1950), *Peggy* (Univ., 1950), *Edge of Doom* (RKO, 1950), *Harriet Craig* (Col., 1950), *Goodbye, My Fancy* (WB, 1951), *The Mating Season* (Par., 1951), *Angels in the Outfield* (MGM, 1951), *The Sea Hornet* (Rep., 1951), *The Barefoot Mailman* (Col., 1951), *On Moonlight Bay* (WB, 1951), *The Big Trees* (WB, 1952,) *Fearless Fagan* (MGM, 1952), *Monsoon* (UA, 1952), *Shane* (Par., 1953), *The Woman They Almost Lynched* (Rep., 1953), *The Vanquished* (Par., 1953), *A Lion Is in the Streets* (WB, 1953), *Untamed Heiress* (Rep., 1954), *About Mrs. Leslie* (Par., 1954), *The Bowery Boys Meet the Monster* (AA, 1954), *Sabrina* (Par., 1954), *Susan Slept Here* (RKO, 1954), *Illegal* (WB, 1955), *Slightly Scarlet* (RKO, 1956), *Stagecoach to Fury* (20th, 1956), *Night Passage* (Univ., 1957), *The Seventh Sin* (MGM, 1957), *God is My Partner* (20th, 1957), *Rockabilly Baby* (20th, 1957), *All Mine to Give* (Univ., 1957), *Macabre* (AA, 1958), *Vertigo* (Par., 1958), *Visit to a Small Planet* (Par., 1960), *A Pocketful of Miracles* (UA, 1961), *Saintly Sinners* (UA, 1962), *The Caretaker* (UA, 1963), *The Strangler* (AA, 1964), *Hush . . . Hush, Sweet Charlotte* (20th, 1965), *The Family Jewels* (Par., 1965), *The Night of the Grizzly* (Par., 1966), *The Gnome-Mobile* (BV, 1967), *A Quiet Couple* (CBS Theatrical Films, 1968).

WENDELL COREY Born March 20, 1914, Dracut, Massachusetts. Married Alice Wiley (1939), children: Robin, Jonathan, Jennifer, Ronald.

Feature Films: *Desert Fury* (Par., 1947), *I Walk Alone* (Par., 1947), *The Search* (MGM, 1948), *Man-Eater of Kumaon* (Univ., 1948), *Sorry, Wrong Number* (Par., 1948), *The Accused* (Par., 1948), *Any Number Can Play* (MGM, 1949), *File on Thelma Jordan* (Par., 1949), *Holiday Affair* (RKO, 1949), *No Sad Songs for Me* (Col., 1950), *The Furies* (Par., 1950), *Harriet Craig* (Col., 1950), *The Great Missouri Raid* (Par., 1950), *Rich, Young and Pretty* (MGM, 1951), *The Wild Blue Yonder* (Rep., 1951), *The Wild North* (MGM, 1952), *Carbine Williams*

Mary Astor and Wendell Corey in *Any Number Can Play.*

(MGM, 1952), *My Man and I* (MGM, 1952), *Jamaica Run* (Par., 1953), *Hell's Half Acre* (Rep., 1954), *Rear Window* (Par., 1954), *The Big Knife* (UA, 1955), *The Bold and the Brave* (RKO, 1956), *The Killer Is Loose* (UA, 1956), *The Rack* (MGM, 1956), *The Rainmaker* (Par., 1956), *Loving You* (Par., 1957), *The Light in the Forest* (BV, 1958), *Alias Jesse James* (UA, 1959), *Blood on the Arrow* (AA, 1964), *Agent for H.A.R.M.* (Univ., 1965), *Waco* (Par., 1966), *Women of the Prehistoric Planet* (Realart, 1966), *Picture Mommy Dead* (Embassy, 1966), *Red Tomahawk* (Par., 1967), *Cyborg 2087* (PRO, 1967), *The Astro Zombies* (ATV Mikels Productions, 1968), *Buckskin* (Par., 1968).

RICARDO CORTEZ (Jake Krantz) Born September 19, 1899, Brooklyn, New York. Married Alma Rubens (1926); widowed 1931.

William Boyd, Ricardo Cortez and Kay Francis in *The House on 56th Street.*

Sound Feature Films: *The Phantom in The House* (Continental, 1929), *Lost Zeppelin* (Tif., 1930), *Montana Moon* (MGM, 1930), *Her Man* (Pathé, 1930), *Big Business Girl* (WB, 1931), *Illicit* (WB, 1931), *Ten Cents a Dance* (Col., 1931), *Behind Office Doors* (RKO, 1931), *The Maltese Falcon* (WB, 1931), *White Shoulders* (RKO, 1931), *Transgression* (RKO, 1931), *Bad Company* (Pathé, 1931), *Reckless Living* (Univ., 1931), *No One Man* (Par., 1932), *Men of Chance* (RKO, 1932), *Symphony of Six Million* (RKO, 1932), *Is My Face Red?* (RKO, 1932), *Thirteen Women* (RKO, 1932), *Phantom of Crestwood* (RKO, 1932), *Flesh* (MGM, 1932), *Broadway Bad* (Fox., 1933), *Midnight Mary* (MGM, 1933), *Big Executive* (Par., 1933), *Torch Singer* (Par., 1933), *House on 56th Street* (WB, 1933), *Big Shakedown* (WB, 1934), *Wonder Bar* (WB, 1934), *Mandalay* (WB, 1934), *Man With Two Faces* (WB, 1934), *Hat, Coat and Glove* (WB, 1934), *A Lost Lady* (WB, 1934), *The Firebird* (WB, 1934), *I Am a Thief* (WB, 1935), *Shadow of Doubt* (MGM, 1935), *White Cockatoo* (WB, 1935), *Manhattan Moon* (Univ., 1935), *Special Agent* (WB, 1935), *Frisco Kid* (WB, 1935), *Man Hunt* (WB, 1936), *The Murder of Dr. Harrigan* (WB, 1936), *The Walking

Dead (WB, 1936), *Postal Inspector* (Univ., 1936), *The Case of the Black Cat* (WB, 1936), *Her Husband Lies* (Par., 1937), *Talk of the Devil* (Gaumont-British, 1937), *The Californian* (20th, 1937), *West of Shanghai* (WB, 1937), *City Girl* (20th, 1937), *Mr. Moto's Last Warning* (20th, 1939), *Charlie Chan in Reno* (20th, 1939), *Murder Over New York* (20th, 1940), *Romance of the Rio Grande* (20th, 1941), *A Shot in the Dark* (WB, 1941), *World Premiere* (Par., 1941), *I Killed That Man* (Mon., 1941), *Who Is Hope Schuyler?* (20th, 1942), *Rubber Racketeers* (Mon., 1942), *Tomorrow We Live* (PRC, 1942), *Make Your Own Bed* (WB, 1944), *The Inner Circle* (Rep., 1946), *The Locket* (RKO, 1946), *Blackmail* (Rep., 1947), *Mystery In Mexico* (RKO, 1948), *Bunco Squad* (RKO, 1950), *The Last Hurrah* (Col., 1958).

JOSEPH COTTEN (Joseph Chesire Cotten) Born May 15, 1905, Petersburg, Virginia. Married Lenore Kipp (1931); widowed 1960. Married Patricia Medina (1960).

Jennifer Jones and Joseph Cotten in *Portrait of Jennie.*

English-Language Feature Films: *Citizen Kane* (RKO, 1941), *Lydia* (UA, 1941), *The Magnificent Ambersons* (RKO, 1942), *Journey into Fear* (RKO, 1942), *Shadow of a Doubt* (Univ., 1943), *Hers to Hold* (Univ., 1943), *Gaslight* (MGM, 1944), *Since You Went Away* (UA, 1944), *I'll Be Seeing You* (UA, 1944), *Love Letters* (Par., 1945); *Duel in the Sun* (Selznick, 1946), *The Farmer's Daughter* (RKO, 1947), *Portrait of Jennie* (Selznick, 1948), *Under Capricorn* (WB, 1949), *Beyond the Forest* (WB, 1949), *The Third Man* (Selznick, 1950), *Walk Softly, Stranger* (RKO, 1950), *Two Flags West* (20th, 1950), *September Affair* (Par., 1950), *Half Angel* (20th, 1951), *Peking Express* (Par., 1951), *The Man With a Cloak* (MGM, 1951), *Untamed Frontier* (Univ., 1952), *The Steel Trap* (20th, 1952), *Niagara* (20th, 1953), *Blueprint for Murder* (20th, 1953), *Special Delivery* (Col., 1955), *The Bottom of the Bottle* (20th, 1956), *The Killer Is Loose* (UA, 1956), *The Halliday Brand* (UA, 1957), *Touch of Evil* (Univ., 1958),* *From the Earth to the Moon* (WB, 1958), *The Angel Wore Red* (MGM, 1960), *The Last Sunset* (Univ., 1961), *Hush . . . Hush, Sweet Charlotte* (20th, 1965), *The Great Sioux Massacre* (Col., 1965), *The Oscar* (Par., 1966), *The Tramplers* (Embassy, 1966), *The Money Trap* (MGM, 1966), *Brighty of the Grand Canyon* (Feature Film Corp. of America, 1967), *The Diamond Spy* (Embassy, 1967), *Jack of Diamonds* (MGM, 1967), *Some May Live* (RKO, 1967), *The Hellbenders* (Embassy, 1967), *Days of Fire* (Italian, 1968).

*Unbilled guest appearance

JEROME COWAN (Jerome Palmer Cowan) Born October 6, 1897, New York, New York. Married, child: William; divorced. Married Helen Dodge (1938), child: Suzanne.

Sound Feature Flims: *Beloved Enemy* (UA, 1936), *You Only Live Once* (UA, 1937), *Shall We Dance* (RKO, 1937), *New Faces of 1937* (RKO, 1937), *Vogues of 1938* (UA, 1937), *The Hurricane* (UA, 1937), *The Goldwyn Follies* (UA, 1938), *There's Always a Woman* (Col., 1938),

Marie McDonald, Barry Sullivan, Dennis O'Keefe and Jerome Cowan in *Getting Gertie's Garter*.

The Saint Strikes Back (RKO, 1939,) *St. Louis Blues* (Par., 1939), *Exile Express* (GN, 1939), *East Side of Heaven* (Univ., 1939), *The Gracie Allen Murder Case* (Par., 1939), *She Married a Cop* (Rep., 1939), *The Old Maid* (WB, 1939), *The Great Victor Herbert* (Par., 1939), *Wolf of New York* (Rep., 1940), *Castle on the Hudson* (WB 1940), *Ma, He's Making Eyes at Me* (Univ., 1940), *Torrid Zone* (WB, 1940), *Framed* (Univ., 1940). *Street of Memories* (20th, 1940), *City for Conquest* (WB, 1940), *The Quarterback* (Par., 1940), *Meet the Wildcat* (Univ., 1940), *Melody Ranch* (Rep., 1940), *Victory* (Par., 1940), *High Sierra* (WB, 1941), *The Roundup* (Par., 1941), *The Great Lie* (WB, 1941), *Affectionately Yours* (WB, 1941), *Out of the Fog* (WB, 1941), *Rags to Riches* (Rep., 1941), *Too Many Blondes* (Univ., 1941), *The Maltese Falcon* (WB, 1941), *One Foot in Heaven* (WB, 1941), *Mr. and Mrs. North* (MGM, 1941), *A Gentleman at Heart* (20th, 1942), *Moontide* (20th, 1942), *The Girl From Alaska* (Rep., 1942), *Thru Different Eyes* (20th, 1942), *Joan of Ozark* (Rep., 1942), *Street of Chance* (Par., 1942), *Who Done It?* (Univ., 1942), *Frisco Lil* (Univ., 1942), *Ladies' Day* (RKO, 1943), *Mission to Moscow* (WB, 1943), *Silver Spurs* (Rep., 1943,) *Hi' Ya, Sailor* (Univ., 1943), *Find the Blackmailer* (WB, 1943), *The Song of Bernadette* (20th, 1943), *No Place for a Lady* (Col., 1943), *Crime Doctor's Strangest Case* (Col., 1943), *Sing a Jingle* (Univ., 1944), *Mr. Skeffington* (WB, 1944), *South of Dixie* (Univ., 1944), *Minstrel Man* (PRC, 1944), *Crime by Night* (WB, 1944), *Guest in the House* (UA, 1944), *Fog Island* (PRC, 1945), *G. I. Honeymoon* (Mon., 1945), *The Crime Doctor's Courage* (Col., 1945), *Divorce* (Mon., 1945), *Blonde Ransom* (Univ., 1945), *Jungle Captive* (Univ., 1945), *Behind City Lights* (Rep., 1945), *Getting Gertie's Garter* (UA, 1945), *My Reputation* (WB, 1946), *One Way to Love* (Col., 1946), *Murder in the Music Hall* (Rep., 1946), *The Kid From Brooklyn* (RKO, 1946), *Deadline at Dawn* (RKO, 1946,) *A Night in Paradise* (Univ., 1946), *One Exciting Week* (Rep., 1946), *Mr. Ace* (UA, 1946), *Claudia and David* (20th, 1946), *Blondie Knows Best* (Col., 1946), *The Perfect Marriage* (Par., 1946), *Blondie's Holiday* (Col., 1947), *The Miracle on 34th Street* (20th, 1947), *Riffraff* (RKO, 1947), *Cry Wolf* (WB, 1947), *Blondie in the Dough* (Col., 1947), *Blondie's Big Moment* (Col., 1947), *Driftwood* (Rep., 1947), *Dangerous Years* (20th, 1947), *Blondie's Anniversary* (Col., 1947), *Arthur Takes Over* (20th, 1948), *So This Is New York* (UA, 1948), *Wallflower* (WB, 1948), *The Night Has a Thousand Eyes* (Par., 1948), *June Bride* (WB, 1948), *Blondie's Reward* (Col., 1948), *Blondie's Big Deal* (Col., 1949), *The Fountainhead* (WB, 1949), *The Girl From Jones Beach* (WB, 1949), *Scene of the Crime* (MGM, 1949), *Always Leave Them Laughing* (WB, 1949), *Blondie Hits the Jackpot* (Col., 1949), *Young Man With a Horn* (WB, 1950), *Joe Palooka Meets Humphrey* (Mon., 1950), *Peggy* (Univ., 1950), *When You're Smiling* (Col., 1950), *The Fuller Brush Girl* (Col., 1950), *Dallas* (WB, 1950), *The West Point Story* (WB, 1950), *The Fat Man* (Univ., 1951), *Criminal Lawyer* (Col., 1951), *Disc Jockey* (AA, 1951), *The System* (WB, 1953), *Have Rocket, Will Travel* (Col., 1959), *Visit to a Small Planet* (Par., 1960), *Private Property* (Citation, 1960), *All in a Night's Work* (Par., 1961), *Pocketful of Miracles* (UA, 1961), *Critic's Choice* (WB, 1963), *Black Zoo* (AA, 1963), *The Patsy* (Par., 1964), *John Goldfarb, Please Come Home* (20th, 1964), *Frankie and Johnny* (UA, 1965), *Penelope* (MGM, 1966), *The Gnome-mobile* (BV, 1967).

BUSTER LARRY CRABBE (Clarence Linden Crabbe) Born February 7, 1908, Oakland, California. Married Adah Held (1933), children: Caren, Susan, Cullen.

Feature Films: *Most Dangerous Game* (RKO, 1932), *That's My Boy* (Col., 1932), *Tarzan the Fearless* (Principal serial, 1933), *King of the Jungle* (Par., 1933), *Man of the Forest* (Par., 1933), *To the Last Man* (Par., 1933), *The Sweetheart of Sigma Chi* (Mon., 1933), *Thundering Herd* (Par., 1933), *Search for Beauty* (Par., 1934), *You're Telling Me* (Par., 1934), *Badge of Honor* (Mayfair, 1934), *We're Rich Again* (RKO, 1934), *The Oil Raider* (Mayfair, 1934), *She Had to Choose* (Majestic, 1934), *Hold 'Em Yale* (Par., 1935), *Nevada* (Par., 1935), *The Wanderer of the Wasteland* (Par., 1935), *Flash Gordon* (Univ. serial, 1936), *Drift Fence* (Par., 1936), *Desert Gold* (Par., 1936), *Arizona Raiders* (Par., 1936), *Lady Be Careful* (Par., 1936), *Rose Bowl* (Par., 1936), *Arizona Mahoney* (Par., 1937), *Murder Goes to College* (Par., 1937), *King of Gamblers* (Par., 1937), *Forlorn River* (Par., 1937), *Sophie Lang Goes West* (Par., 1937), *Daughter of Shanghai* (Par., 1937), *Thrill of a Lifetime* (Par., 1937), *Red Barry* (Univ. serial, 1938), *Flash Gordon's Trip to Mars* (Univ. serial, 1938), *Tip-Off Girls* (Par., 1938), *Hunted*

Monte Blue, Richard Carle, Raymond Hatton, Buster Crabbe and Sid Saylor in *Nevada*.

Men (Par., 1938), *Illegal Traffic* (Par., 1938), *Buck Rogers* (Univ. serial, 1939), *Unmarried* (Par., 1939), *Million Dollar Legs* (Par., 1939), *Colorado Sunset* (Rep., 1939), *Call a Messenger* (Univ., 1939), *Sailor's Lady* (20th, 1940), *Flash Gordon Conquers the Universe* (Univ. serial, 1940), *Billy the Kid Wanted* (PRC, 1941), *Jungle Man* (PRC, 1941), *Billy the Kid's Roundup* (PRC, 1941), *Billy the Kid Trapped* (PRC, 1942), *Smoking Guns* (PRC, 1942), *Jungle Siren* (PRC, 1942), *Wildcat* (Par., 1942), *Law and Order* (PRC, 1942), *Mysterious Rider* (PRC, 1942), *Sheriff of Sage Valley* (PRC, 1942), *Queen of Broadway* (PRC, 1942), *The Kid Rides Again* (PRC, 1943), *Fugitive of the Plains* (PRC, 1943), *Western Cyclone* (PRC, 1943), *The Renegade* (PRC, 1943), *Cattle Stampede* (PRC, 1943), *Blazing Frontier* (PRC, 1943), *Devil Riders* (PRC, 1943), *The Drifter* (PRC, 1944), *Nabonga* (PRC, 1944), *Frontier Outlaws* (PRC, 1944), *Thundering Gun Slingers* (PRC, 1944), *Valley of Vengeance* (PRC, 1944), *The Contender* (PRC, 1944), *Fuzzy Settles Down* (PRC, 1944), *Code of the Plains* (PRC, 1944), *Rustlers' Hideout* (PRC, 1944), *Wild Horse Phantom* (PRC, 1944), *Oath of Vengeance* (PRC, 1944), *His Brother's Ghost* (PRC, 1945), *Shadows of Death* (PRC, 1945), *Gangster's Den* (PRC, 1945), *Stagecoach Outlaws* (PRC, 1945), *Border Badmen* (PRC, 1945), *Fighting Bill Carson* (PRC, 1945), *Prairie Rustlers* (PRC, 1945), *Lightning Raiders* (PRC, 1945), *Ghost of Hidden Valley* (PRC, 1946), *Gentlemen With Guns* (PRC, 1946), *Terrors on Horseback* (PRC, 1946), *Overland Raiders* (PRC, 1946), *Outlaws of the Plains* (PRC, 1946), *Swamp Fire* (Par., 1946), *Prairie Badmen* (PRC, 1946), *Last of the Redmen* (Col., 1947), *The Sea Hound* (Col. serial, 1947), *Caged Fury* (Par., 1948), *Captive Girl* (Col., 1950), *Pirates of the High Seas* (Col. serial, 1950), *King of the Congo* (Col. serial, 1952), *Gun Brothers* (UA, 1956), *The Lawless Eighties* (Rep., 1957), *Badman's Country* (WB, 1958), *Gunfighters of Abilene* (UA, 1960), *The Bounty Killer* (Embassy, 1965), *Arizona Raiders* (Col., 1965).

JEANNE CRAIN Born May 25, 1925, Barstow, California. Married Paul Brinkman (1945), children: Paul, Michael, Timothy, Jeanine, Lisabette, Maria, Christopher.

Jeanne Crain and Lynn Bari in *Margie*.

English-Language Feature Films: *The Gang's All Here* (20th, 1943), *Home in Indiana* (20th, 1944), *In the Meantime, Darling* (20th, 1944), *Winged Victory* (20th, 1944), *State Fair* (20th, 1945), *Leave Her to Heaven* (20th, 1945), *Centennial Summer* (20th, 1946), *Margie* (20th, 1946), *Apartment for Peggy* (20th, 1948), *You Were Meant for Me* (20th, 1948), *A Letter to Three Wives* (20th, 1949), *The Fan* (20th, 1949), *Pinky* (20th, 1949), *Cheaper by the Dozen* (20th, 1950), *I'll Get By* (20th, 1950),* *Take Care of My Little Girl* (20th, 1951), *People Will Talk* (20th, 1951), *The Model and the Marriage Broker* (20th, 1952), *Belles on Their Toes* (20th, 1952), *O. Henry's Full House* (20th, 1952), *Dangerous Crossing* (20th, 1953), *City of Badmen* (20th, 1953), *Vicki* (20th, 1953), *Duel in the Jungle* (WB, 1954), *Man Without a Star* (Univ., 1955), *Gentlemen Marry Brunettes* (UA, 1955), *The Second Greatest Sex* (Univ., 1955), *The Fastest Gun Alive* (MGM, 1956), *The Tattered Dress* (Univ., 1957), *The Joker Is Wild* (Par., 1957), *Guns of the Timberland* (WB, 1960), *Twenty Plus Two* (AA, 1961), *Madison Avenue* (20th, 1962), *52 Miles to Terror* (MGM, 1964), *Hot Rods to Hell* (MGM, 1967).

*Unbilled guest appearance

Broderick Crawford, Randolph Scott, Kay Francis and Mary Gordon in *When the Daltons Rode*.

BRODERICK CRAWFORD (William Broderick Crawford) Born December 9, 1911, Philadelphia, Pennsylvania. Married Kay Griffith (1940), children: Kim, Kelly; divorced. Married Joan Tabor (1962); divorced 1967.

English-Language Feature Films: *Woman Chases Man* (UA, 1937), *Submarine D-1* (WB, 1937), *Start Cheering* (Col., 1938), *Sudden Money* (Par., 1939), *Ambush* (Par., 1939), *Undercover Doctor* (Par., 1939), *Beau Geste* (Par., 1939), *Eternally Yours* (UA, 1939), *Island of Lost Men* (Par., 1939), *The Real Glory* (UA, 1939), *Slightly Honorable* (UA,

1940), *I Can't Give You Anything But Love, Baby* (Univ., 1940), *When the Daltons Rode* (Univ., 1940), *Seven Sinners* (Univ., 1940), *Trail of the Vigilantes* (Univ., 1940), *Texas Rangers Ride Again* (Par., 1940), *The Black Cat* (Univ., 1941), *Tight Shoes* (Univ., 1941), *Badlands of Dakota* (Univ., 1941), *South of Tahiti* (Univ., 1941), *North of the Klondike* (Univ., 1942), *Larceny, Inc.* (WB, 1942), *Butch Minds the Baby* (Univ., 1942), *Broadway* (Univ., 1942), *Men of Texas* (Univ., 1942), *Sin Town* (Univ., 1942), *The Runaround* (Univ., 1946), *Black Angel* (Univ., 1946)), *Slave Girl* (Univ., 1947), *The Flame* (Rep., 1947), *The Time of Your Life* (UA, 1948), *Sealed Verdict* (Par., 1948), *Bad Men of Tombstone* (AA, 1948), *A Kiss in the Dark* (WB, 1949), *Night Unto Night* (WB, 1949), *Anna Lucasta* (Col., 1949), *All The King's Men* (Col., 1949), *Cargo to Capetown* (Col., 1950), *Convicted* (Col., 1950), *Born Yesterday* (Col., 1950), *The Mob* (Col., 1951), *Scandal Sheet* (Col., 1952), *Lone Star* (MGM, 1952), *Stop, You're Killing Me* (WB, 1952), *Last of the Comanches* (Col., 1952), *Night People* (20th, 1954), *Down Three Dark Streets* (UA, 1954), *Human Desire* (Col., 1954), *New York Confidential* (WB, 1955), *Big House, U.S.A.* (UA, 1955), *Not as a Stranger* (UA, 1955), *The Fastest Gun Alive* (MGM, 1956), *Between Heaven and Hell* (20th, 1956), *The Decks Ran Red* (MGM, 1958), *Convicts 4* (AA, 1962), *The Castilian* (WB, 1963), *Square of Violence* (MGM, 1963), *A House Is Not a Home* (Embassy, 1964), *Up From the Beach* (20th, 1965), *The Oscar* (Par, 1966), *Kid Rodelo* (Par., 1966), *The Texican* (Col., 1966), *Red Tomahawk* (Par., 1967), *The Vulture* (Par., 1967), *The Fakers* (East West International, 1968).

JOAN CRAWFORD (Lucille Le Sueur) Born March 23, 1904, San Antonio, Texas. Married Douglas Fairbanks, Jr. (1929); divorced 1933. Married Franchot Tone (1935); divorced 1939. Married Philip Terry (1942), child: Christopher; divorced 1946. Married Alfred Steele (1956); widowed 1959. Children adopted while Miss Crawford was unmarried: Christina, Cathy, Cindy.

Sound Feature Films: *Hollywood Revue of 1929* (MGM, 1929), *Untamed* (MGM, 1929), *Montana Moon* (MGM, 1930), *Our Blushing Brides* (MGM, 1930), *Paid* (MGM, 1930), *Dance, Fools, Dance* (MGM, 1931), *Laughing Sinners* (MGM, 1931), *This Modern Age* (MGM, 1931), *Possessed* (MGM, 1931), *Grand Hotel* (MGM, 1932), *Letty Lynton* (MGM, 1932), *Rain* (UA, 1932), *Today We Live* (MGM, 1933), *Dancing Lady* (MGM, 1933), *Sadie McKee* (MGM, 1934), *Chained* (MGM, 1934), *Forsaking All Others* (MGM, 1934), *No More Ladies* (MGM,

Clark Gable and Joan Crawford in *Dancing Lady*.

1935), *I Live My Life* (MGM, 1935), *The Gorgeous Hussy* (MGM, 1936), *Love on the Run* (MGM, 1936), *The Last of Mrs. Cheyney* (MGM, 1937), *The Bride Wore Red* (MGM, 1937), *Mannequin* (MGM, 1938), *The Shining Hour* (MGM, 1938), *Ice Follies of 1939* (MGM, 1939), *The Women* (MGM, 1939), *Strange Cargo* (MGM, 1940), *Susan and God* (MGM, 1940), *A Woman's Face* (MGM, 1941), *When Ladies Meet* (MGM, 1941), *They All Kissed the Bride* (Col., 1942), *Reunion in France* (MGM, 1942), *Above Suspicion* (MGM, 1943), *Hollywood Canteen* (WB, 1944), *Mildred Pierce* (WB, 1945), *Humoresque* (WB, 1946), *Possessed* (WB, 1947), *Daisy Kenyon* (20th, 1947), *Flamingo Road* (WB, 1949), *The Damned Don't Cry* (WB, 1950), *Harriet Craig* (Col., 1950), *Goodbye, My Fancy* (WB, 1951), *This Man Is Dangerous* (WB, 1952), *Sudden Fear* (RKO, 1952), *Torch Song* (MGM, 1953), *Johnny Guitar* (Rep., 1954), *Female on the Beach* (Univ., 1955), *Queen Bee* (Col., 1955), *Autumn Leaves* (Col., 1956), *The Best of Everything* (20th, 1959), *What Ever Happened to Baby Jane?* (WB, 1962), *The Caretakers* (UA, 1963), *Strait-Jacket* (Col., 1964), *I Saw What You Did* (Univ., 1965), *Berserk!* (Col., 1967).

LAIRD CREGAR (Samuel Laird Cregar) Born July 28, 1916, Philadelphia, Pennsylvania. Died December 9, 1944.

Monty Woolley, Laird Cregar and Gracie Fields in *Holy Matrimony*.

Feature Films: *Granny Get Your Gun* (WB, 1940), *Hudson's Bay* (20th, 1940), *Oh Johnny, How You Can Love* (Univ., 1940), *Blood and Sand* (20th, 1941), *Charley's Aunt* (20th, 1941), *I Wake Up Screaming* (20th, 1941), *Joan of Paris* (RKO, 1942), *Rings on Her Fingers* (20th, 1942), *This Gun for Hire* (Par., 1942), *Ten Gentlemen From West Point* (20th, 1942), *The Black Swan* (20th, 1942), *Hello, Frisco, Hello* (20th, 1943), *Heaven Can Wait* (20th, 1943), *Holy Matrimony* (20th, 1943), *The Lodger* (20th, 1944), *Hangover Square* (20th, 1945).

DONALD CRISP Born 1880, Aberfeddy, Scotland. Married Marie Stark; divorced 1919. Married Jane Murphin (1932); divorced 1944.

Sound Feature Films: *The Return of Sherlock Holmes* (Par., 1929), *Scotland Yard* (Fox, 1930), *Svengali* (WB, 1931), *Kick In* (Par., 1931), *Passport to Hell* (Fox, 1932), *Red Dust* (MGM, 1932), *Broadway Bad* (Fox, 1933), *Crime Doctor* (RKO, 1934), *Life of Vergie Winters* (RKO, 1934), *What Every Woman Knows* (MGM, 1934), *The Little Minister* (RKO, 1934), *Vanessa—Her Love Story* (MGM, 1935), *Laddie* (RKO, 1935), *Oil for the Lamps of China* (WB, 1935), *Mutiny on the Bounty* (MGM, 1935), *The White Angel* (WB, 1936), *Mary of Scotland* (RKO, 1936), *Charge of the Light Brigade* (WB, 1936), *A Woman Rebels* (RKO, 1936), *Beloved Enemy* (UA, 1936), *The Great O'Malley* (WB, 1937), *Parnell* (MGM, 1937), *That Certain Woman* (WB, 1937), *The Life of Emile Zola* (WB, 1937), *Confession* (WB, 1937), *Jezebel* (WB, 1938), *Sergeant Murphy* (WB, 1938), *Beloved Brat* (WB, 1938), *The Amazing Dr. Clitterhouse* (WB, 1938), *Valley of the Giants* (WB, 1938), *The Dawn Patrol* (WB, 1938), *Comet Over Broadway* (WB, 1938), *The Sisters* (WB, 1938), *Wuthering Heights* (UA, 1939), *The Oklahoma Kid* (WB, 1939), *Juarez* (WB, 1939), *Daughters Courageous* (WB, 1939),

James Stephenson, Donald Crisp and Vera Lewis in *Shining Victory*.

The Old Maid (WB, 1939), *The Private Lives of Elizabeth and Essex* (WB, 1939), *The Story of Dr. Ehrlich's Magic Bullet* (WB, 1940), *Brother Orchid* (WB, 1940), *The Sea Hawk* (WB, 1940), *City for Conquest* (WB, 1940), *Knute Rockne—All American* (WB, 1940), *Shining Victory* (WB, 1941), *Dr. Jekyll and Mr. Hyde* (WB, 1941), *How Green Was My Valley* (20th, 1941), *The Gay Sisters* (WB, 1942), *Forever and a Day* (RKO, 1943), *Lassie Come Home* (MGM, 1943), *The Uninvited* (Par., 1944), *The Adventures of Mark Twain* (WB, 1944), *National Velvet* (MGM, 1944), *Son of Lassie* (MGM, 1945), *Valley of Decision* (MGM, 1945), *Ramrod* (UA, 1947), *Hills of Home* (MGM, 1948), *Whispering Smith* (Par., 1948), *Bright Leaf* (WB, 1950), *Home Town Story* (MGM, 1951), *Prince Valiant* (20th, 1954), *The Long Gray Line* (Col., 1955), *The Man From Laramie* (Col., 1955), *Drango* (UA, 1957), *Saddle the Wind* (MGM, 1958), *The Last Hurrah* (Col., 1958), *A Dog of Flanders* (20th, 1959), *Pollyanna* (BV, 1960), *Greyfriar's Bobby* (BV, 1961), *Spencer's Mountain* (WB, 1963).

HUME CRONYN (Hume Blake) Born July 18, 1911, London, Ontario, Canada. Married Jessica Tandy (1942), children: Christopher, Tandy.

Hume Cronyn and John Carroll in A *Letter for Evie*.

Feature Films: *Shadow of a Doubt* (Univ., 1943), *Phantom of the Opera* (Univ., 1943), *The Cross of Lorraine* (MGM, 1943), *The Seventh Cross* (MGM, 1944), *Main Street After Dark* (MGM, 1944), *Lifeboat* (20th, 1944), *A Letter for Evie* (MGM, 1945), *The Sailor Takes a Wife* (MGM, 1945), *The Green Years* (MGM, 1946), *The Postman Always Rings Twice* (MGM, 1946), *The Ziegfeld Follies* (MGM, 1946), *The Secret Heart* (voice only; MGM, 1946), *The Beginning of the End* (MGM, 1947), *Brute Force* (Univ., 1947), *The Bride Goes Wild* (MGM, 1948), *Top o' the Morning* (Par., 1949), *People Will Talk* (20th, 1951), *Crowded Paradise* (Tudor, 1956), *Sunrise at Campobello* (WB, 1960), *Cleopatra* (20th, 1963), *Hamlet* (WB, 1964).

BING CROSBY (Harry Lillis Crosby) Born May 2, 1904, Tacoma, Washington. Married Dixie Lee (1930), children: Gary, Dennis, Philip, Lindsay; widowed 1952. Married Kathryn Grant (1957), children: Harry, Nathaniel, Mary.

Ned Sparks, Louise Campbell and Bing Crosby in *The Star Maker.*

Feature Films: *King of Jazz* (Univ., 1930), *The Big Broadcast* (Par., 1932), *College Humor* (Par., 1933), *Too Much Harmony* (Par., 1933), *Going Hollywood* (MGM, 1933), *We're Not Dressing* (Par., 1934), *She Loves Me Not* (Par., 1934), *Here Is My Heart* (Par., 1934), *Mississippi* (Par., 1935), *Two for Tonight* (Par., 1935), *Big Broadcast of 1936* (Par., 1935), *Anything Goes* (Par., 1936), *Rhythm on the Range* (Par., 1936), *Pennies From Heaven* (Par., 1936), *Waikiki Wedding* (Par., 1937), *Double or Nothing* (Par., 1937), *Dr. Rhythm* (Par., 1938), *Sing You Sinners* (Par., 1938), *Paris Honeymoon* (Par., 1939), *East Side of Heaven* (Univ., 1939), *The Star Maker* (Par., 1939), *Road to Singapore* (Par., 1940), *If I Had My Way* (Univ., 1940), *Rhythm on the River* (Par., 1940), *Road to Zanzibar* (Par., 1941), *Birth of the Blues* (Par., 1941), *My Favorite Blonde* (Par., 1942),* *Holiday Inn* (Par., 1942), *Road to Morocco* (Par., 1942), *Star Spangled Rhythm* (Par., 1942), *Dixie* (Par., 1943), *Going My Way* (Par., 1944), *The Princess and the Pirate* (RKO, 1944),* *Here Come the Waves* (Par., 1945), *Duffy's Tavern* (Par., 1945), *Road to Utopia* (Par., 1945), *Out of This World* (voice only; Par., 1945), *The Bells of St. Mary's* (RKO, 1945), *Blue Skies* (Par., 1946), *Variety Girl* (Par., 1947), *Welcome Stranger* (Par., 1947), *My Favorite Brunette* (Par., 1947),* *Road to Rio* (Par., 1947), *The Emperor Waltz* (Par., 1948), *A Connecticut Yankee In King Arthur's Court* (Par., 1949), *The Adventures of Ichabod and Mr. Toad* (voice only; RKO, 1949), *Top o' the Morning* (Par., 1949), *Riding High* (Par., 1950), *Mr. Music* (Par., 1950), *Here Comes the Groom* (Par., 1951), *The Greatest Show on Earth* (Par., 1952),* *Just for You* (Par., 1952), *Son of Paleface* (Par., 1952),* *Road to Bali* (Par., 1952), *Scared Stiff* (Par., 1953),* *Little Boy Lost* (Par., 1953), *White Christmas* (Par., 1954), *The Country Girl* (Par., 1954), *Anything Goes* (Par., 1956), *High Society* (MGM, 1956), *Man on Fire* (MGM, 1957), *Say One for Me* (20th, 1959), *Alias Jesse James* (UA, 1959),* *High Time* (20th, 1960), *Pepe* (Col., 1960), *Road to Hong Kong* (UA, 1962), *Robin and the 7 Hoods* (WB, 1964), *Bing Crosby's Cinerama Adventures* (Cinerama, 1966), *Stagecoach* (20th, 1966).

*Unbilled guest appearance

ROBERT CUMMINGS (Clarence Robert Orville Cummings) Born June 10, 1910, Joplin, Missouri. Married Vivian Janis (1933); divorced 1943. Married Mary Elliot (1945), children: Robert, Mary, Melinda, Sharon, Patricia, Laurel, Anthony.

Feature Films: *The Virginia Judge* (Par., 1935), *So Red the Rose* (Par., 1935), *Millions in the Air* (Par., 1935), *Forgotten Faces* (Par., 1936), *Desert Gold* (Par., 1936), *Arizona Mahoney* (Par., 1936), *Border Flight* (Par., 1936), *Three Cheers for Love* (Par., 1936), *Hollywood Boulevard* (Par., 1936), *The Accusing Finger* (Par., 1936), *Hideaway Girl*

Nina Koshetz, Alexis Minotis, Bob Cummings and Alex Montoya in *The Chase.*

(Par., 1937), *Last Train From Madrid* (Par., 1937), *Souls at Sea* (Par., 1937), *Wells Fargo* (Par., 1937), *College Swing* (Par., 1938), *You and Me* (Par., 1938), *The Texans* (Par., 1938), *Touchdown Army* (Par., 1938), *I Stand Accused* (Rep., 1938), *Three Smart Girls Grow Up* (Univ., 1939), *The Under-Pup* (Univ., 1939), *Rio* (Univ., 1939), *Everything Happens at Night* (20th, 1939), *Charlie McCarthy, Detective* (Univ., 1939), *And One Was Beautiful* (MGM, 1940), *Private Affairs* (Univ., 1940), *Spring Parade* (Univ., 1940), *One Night in the Tropics* (Univ., 1941), *Free and Easy* (MGM, 1941), *The Devil and Miss Jones* (RKO,, 1941), *Moon Over Miami* (20th, 1941), *It Started With Eve* (Univ., 1941), *Kings Row* (WB, 1941), *Saboteur* (Univ., 1942), *Between Us Girls* (Univ., 1942), *Forever and a Day* (RKO, 1943), *Princess O'Rourke* (WB, 1943), *Flesh and Fantasy* (Univ., 1943), *You Came Along* (Par., 1945), *The Bride Wore Boots* (Par., 1946), *The Chase* (UA, 1946), *Heaven Only Knows* (UA, 1947), *The Lost Moment* (Univ., 1947), *Sleep, My Love* (UA, 1948), *Let's Live a Little* (EL, 1948), *The Accused* (Par., 1948), *Free for All* (Univ., 1949), *Tell it to the Judge* (Col., 1949), *Paid in Full* (Par., 1950), *The Petty Girl* (Col., 1950), *For Heaven's Sake* (20th, 1950), *The Barefoot Mailman* (Col., 1951), *The First Time* (Col., 1952), *Marry Me Again* (RKO, 1953), *Lucky Me* (WB, 1954), *Dial M for Murder* (WB, 1954), *How to Be Very, Very Popular* (20th, 1955), *My Geisha* (Par., 1962), *Beach Party* (AIP, 1963), *What a Way to Go!* (20th, 1964), *The Carpetbaggers* (Par., 1964), *Promise Her Anything* (Par., 1966), *Stagecoach* (20th, 1966).

TONY CURTIS (Bernard Schwartz) Born June 3, 1925, Bronx, New York. Married Janet Leigh (1951), children: Kelly, Jamie; divorced 1962. Married Christine Kaufmann (1963), children: Alexandria, Allegra; divorced 1967.

Feature Films: *Criss Cross* (Univ., 1949), *City Across the River* (Univ., 1949), *The Lady Gambles* (Univ., 1949), *Johnny Stool Pigeon* (Univ., 1949), *Francis* (Univ., 1949), *I Was a Shoplifter* (Univ., 1950), *Winchester '73* (Univ., 1950), *The Prince Who Was a Thief* (Univ., 1951), *Flesh*

Tony Curtis in *The Great Imposter.*

and Fury (Univ., 1952), *No Room for the Groom* (Univ., 1952), *Son of Ali Baba* (Univ., 1952), *Houdini* (Par., 1953), *The All American* (Univ., 1953), *Forbidden* (Univ., 1953), *Beachhead* (UA, 1954), *The Black Shield of Falworth* (Univ., 1954), *Johnny Dark* (Univ., 1954), *So This Is Paris* (Univ., 1954), *The Purple Mask* (Univ., 1954), *Six Bridges to Cross* (Univ., 1955), *The Square Jungle* (Univ., 1955), *Trapeze* (UA, 1956), *The Rawhide Years* (Univ., 1956), *Mister Cory* (Univ., 1957), *The Midnight Story* (Univ., 1957), *Sweet Smell of Success* (UA, 1957), *The Vikings* (UA, 1958), *Kings Go Forth* (UA, 1958), *The Defiant Ones* (UA, 1958), *The Perfect Furlough* (Univ., 1958), *Some Like It Hot* (UA, 1959), *Operation Petticoat* (Univ., 1959), *Pepe* (Col., 1960),* *Who Was That Lady?* (Col., 1960), *The Rat Race* (Par., 1960), *Spartacus* (Univ., 1960), *The Great Imposter* (Univ., 1960), *The Outsider* (Univ., 1961), *40 Pounds of Trouble* (Univ., 1962), *Taras Bulba* (UA, 1962), *The List of Adrian Messenger* (Univ., 1963), *Captain Newman, M.D.* (Univ., 1963), *Paris When It Sizzles* (Par., 1964), *Wild and Wonderful* (Univ., 1964), *Goodbye Charlie* (20th, 1964), *Sex and the Single Girl* (WB, 1964), *The Great Race* (WB, 1965), *Boeing-Boeing* (Par., 1965), *Not With My Wife You Don't* (WB, 1966), *Chamber of Horrors* (WB, 1966),* *Arrividerci, Baby* (Par., 1966), *Don't Make Waves* (MGM, 1967), *The Chastity Belt* (WB-7 Arts, 1968).

*Unbilled guest appearance

ARLENE DAHL (Arlene Carol Dahl) Born August 11, 1924, Minneapolis, Minnesota. Married Lex Barker (1951); divorced 1952. Married Fernando Lamas (1954), child: Lorenzo; divorced 1960. Married Christian Holmes (1960), child: Carol; divorced 1964. Married Alexi Lichine (1965); divorced 1967.

Tom Helmore, Van Johnson and Arlene Dahl in *Scene of the Crime.*

Feature Films: *Life with Father* (WB, 1947), *My Wild Irish Rose* (WB, 1947), *The Bride Goes Wild* (MGM, 1948), *A Southern Yankee* (MGM, 1948), *Reign of Terror* (EL, 1949), *Scene of the Crime* (MGM, 1949), *Ambush* (MGM, 1949), *The Outriders* (MGM, 1950), *Three Little Words* (MGM, 1950), *Watch the Birdie* (MGM, 1950), *Inside Straight* (MGM, 1951), *No Questions Asked* (MGM, 1951), *Caribbean* (Par., 1952), *Jamaica Run* (Par., 1953), *Desert Legion* (Univ., 1953), *Sangaree* (Par., 1953), *The Diamond Queen* (WB, 1953), *Here Come the Girls* (Par., 1953), *Woman's World* (20th, 1954), *Bengal Brigade* (Univ., 1954), *Slightly Scarlet* (RKO, 1956), *Wicked as They Come* (Col., 1957), *She Played With Fire* (Col., 1958), *Journey to the Center of the Earth* (20th, 1959), *Kisses for My President* (WB, 1964).

DAN DAILEY (Dan Dailey Jr.) Born December 14, 1917, New York, New York. Married Esther Rodier; divorced 1941. Married Elizabeth Hofert (1942), child: Dan; divorced 1951. Married Gwendolyn O'Connor (1955); divorced 1961.

Feature Films: *The Mortal Storm* (MGM, 1940), *The Captain Is a Lady* (MGM, 1940), *Hullabaloo* (MGM, 1940), *Susan and God* (MGM, 1940),

Dan Dailey and Lynn Bari in *Moon Over Her Shoulder.*

Ziegfeld Girl (MGM, 1941), *Washington Melodrama* (MGM, 1941), *The Wild Man of Borneo* (MGM, 1941), *The Get-Away* (MGM, 1941), *Lady Be Good* (MGM, 1941), *Down in San Diego* (MGM, 1941), *Moon Over Her Shoulder* (20th, 1941), *Mokey* (MGM, 1942), *Sunday Punch* (MGM, 1942), *Panama Hattie* (MGM, 1942), *Timber* (Univ., 1942), *Give Out, Sister* (Univ., 1942), *Mother Wore Tights* (20th, 1947), *You Were Meant for Me* (20th, 1948), *Give My Regards to Broadway* (20th, 1948), *Chicken Every Sunday* (20th, 1948), *When My Baby Smiles at Me* (20th, 1948), *You're My Everything* (20th, 1949), *When Willie Comes Marching Home* (20th, 1950), *I'll Get By* (20th, 1950), *Ticket to Tomahawk* (20th, 1950), *My Blue Heaven* (20th, 1950), *I Can Get It for You Wholesale* (20th, 1951), *Call Me Mister* (20th, 1951), *The Pride of St. Louis* (20th, 1952), *What Price Glory* (20th, 1952), *Meet Me at the Fair* (Univ., 1952), *Taxi* (20th, 1953), *The Girl Next Door* (20th, 1953), *The Kid From Left Field* (20th, 1953), *There's No Business Like Show Business* (20th, 1954), *It's Always Fair Weather* (MGM, 1955), *The Best Things in Life Are Free* (20th, 1956), *The Wings of Eagles* (MGM, 1957), *Oh, Men! Oh, Women!* (20th, 1957), *The Wayward Bus* (20th, 1957), *Underwater Warrior* (MGM, 1958), *Pepe* (Col., 1960), *Hemingway's Adventures of a Young Man* (20th, 1962).

LINDA DARNELL (Monetta Eloyse Darnell) Born October 16, 1923, Dallas, Texas. Married Peverell Marley (1943), child: Charlotte; divorced 1952. Married Philip Leibman (1954); divorced 1955. Married Merle Robertson (1957); Divorced 1963. Died April 10, 1965.

English-Language Feature Films: *Elsa Maxwell's Hotel for Women* (20th, 1939), *Daytime Wife* (20th, 1939), *Star Dust* (20th, 1940), *Brigham Young—Frontiersman* (20th, 1940), *The Mark of Zorro* (20th, 1940), *Chad Hanna* (20th, 1940), *Blood and Sand* (20th, 1941), *Rise and Shine* (20th, 1941), *Loves of Edgar Allan Poe* (20th, 1942), *City Without Men* (Col., 1943), *The Song of Bernadette* (20th, 1943),* *It Happened Tomorrow* (UA, 1944), *Buffalo Bill* (20th, 1944), *Summer Storm* (UA, 1944), *Sweet and Lowdown* (20th, 1944), *Hangover Square* (20th, 1945), *The Great John L.* (UA, 1945), *Fallen Angel* (20th, 1945), *Centennial Summer* (20th, 1946), *Anna and the King of Siam* (20th,

George Murphy and Linda Darnell in *Rise and Shine.*

Jane Darwell and Sally Blane in *The Great Hospital Mystery.*

1946), *My Darling Clementine* (20th, 1946), *Forever Amber* (20th, 1947), *The Walls of Jericho* (20th, 1948), *Unfaithfully Yours* (20th, 1948), *A Letter to Three Wives* (20th, 1949), *Slattery's Hurricane* (20th, 1949), *Everybody Does It* (20th, 1949), *No Way Out* (20th, 1950), *Two Flags West* (20th, 1950), *The Thirteenth Letter* (20th, 1951), *The Guy Who Came Back* (20th, 1951), *The Lady Pays Off* (Univ., 1951), *Island of Desire* (UA, 1952), *Night Without Sleep* (20th, 1952), *Blackbeard the Pirate* (RKO, 1952), *Second Chance* (RKO, 1953), *This Is My Love* (RKO, 1954), *Dakota Incident* (Rep., 1956), *Zero Hour!* (Par., 1957), *Black Spurs* (Par., 1965).

*Unbilled guest appearance

JANE DARWELL (Patti Woodward) Born October 15, 1884, Palmyra, Missouri. Died August 14, 1967.

Feature Films: *Tom Sawyer* (Par., 1930), *Fighting Caravans* (Par., 1931), *Huckleberry Finn* (Par., 1931), *Ladies of the Big House* (Par., 1932), *Hot Saturday* (Par., 1932), *Back Street* (Par., 1932), *No One Man* (Par., 1932), *Murders in the Zoo* (Par., 1933), *Air Hostess* (Par., 1933), *Child of Manhattan* (Par., 1933), *Women Won't Tell* (Par., 1933), *Bondage* (Fox, 1933), *Design for Living* (Par., 1933), *Jennie Gerhardt* (Par., 1933), *One Sunday Afternoon* (Par., 1933), *Before Dawn* (RKO, 1933), *Emergency Call* (RKO, 1933), *Only Yesterday* (Univ., 1933), *Roman Scandals* (UA, 1933), *He Couldn't Take It* (Mon., 1933), *Once to Every Woman* (Col., 1934), *Happiness Ahead* (WB, 1934), *Wonder Bar* (WB, 1934), *Fashions of 1934* (WB, 1934), *Desirable* (WB, 1934), *Wake Up and Dream* (Univ., 1934), *The Firebird* (WB, 1934), *Let's Talk It Over* (Univ., 1934), *David Harum* (Fox, 1934), *Heat Lightning* (WB, 1934), *Change of Heart* (Fox, 1934), *Most Precious Thing in Life* (Col., 1934), *The Scarlet Empress* (Par., 1934), *Blind Date* (Col., 1934), *Embarrassing Moments* (Univ., 1934), *The White Parade* (Fox, 1934), *Gentlemen Are Born* (WB, 1934), *Journal of a Crime* (WB, 1934), *One More Spring* (Fox, 1935), *Million Dollar Ransom* (Univ., 1934), *One Night of Love* (Col., 1934), *Tomorrow's Youth* (Mon., 1935), *McFadden's Flats* (Par., 1935), *Life Begins at Forty* (Fox, 1935), *Curly Top* (Fox, 1935), *Metropolitan* (Fox, 1935), *Navy Wife* (Fox, 1935), *Paddy O'Day* (Fox, 1935), *Bright Eyes* (Fox, 1935), *We're Only Human* (RKO, 1936), *The Country Doctor* (20th, 1936), *Little Miss Nobody* (20th, 1936), *Captain January* (20th, 1936), *The First Baby* (20th, 1936), *Poor Little Rich Girl* (20th, 1936), *Private Number* (20th, 1936), *Star for a Night* (20th, 1936), *White Fang* (20th, 1936), *Ramona* (20th, 1936), *Craig's Wife* (Col., 1936), *Love Is News* (20th, 1937), *Laughing at Trouble* (20th, 1937), *Nancy Steele Is Missing* (20th, 1937), *Fifty Roads to Town* (20th, 1937), *Slave Ship* (20th, 1937), *The Great Hospital Mystery* (20th, 1937), *Wife, Doctor and Nurse* (20th, 1937), *The Singing Marine* (WB, 1937), *Dangerously Yours* (20th, 1937), *The Jury's Secret* (Univ., 1938), *Change of Heart* (20th, 1938), *Battle of Broadway* (20th, 1938), *Three Blind Mice* (20th, 1938), *Little Miss Broadway* (20th, 1938), *Time Out for Murder* (20th, 1938), *Five of a Kind* (20th, 1938), *Up the River* (20th, 1938), *Inside Story* (20th, 1938), *Jesse James* (20th, 1939), *Zero Hour* (Rep., 1939), *Grand Jury Secrets* (Par., 1939), *Unexpected Father* (Univ., 1939), *The Rains Came* (20th, 1939), *20,000 Men a Year* (20th, 1939), *Gone With the Wind* (MGM, 1939), *A Miracle on Main Street* (Col., 1940), *The Grapes of Wrath* (20th, 1940), *Untamed*

(Par., 1940), *Youth Will Be Served* (20th, 1940), *Chad Hanna* (20th, 1940), *Brigham Young—Frontiersman* (20th, 1940), *Private Nurse* (20th, 1941), *All That Money Can Buy* (RKO, 1941), *Small Town Deb* (20th, 1941), *All Through the Night* (WB, 1942), *On the Sunny Side* (20th, 1942), *Young America* (20th, 1942), *It Happened in Flatbush* (20th, 1942), *The Loves of Edgar Allan Poe* (20th, 1942), *Men of Texas* (Univ., 1942), *Highways by Night* (RKO, 1942), *The Great Gildersleeve* (RKO, 1942), *Gildersleeve's Bad Day* (RKO, 1943), *The Ox-Bow Incident* (20th, 1943), *Government Girl* (RKO, 1943), *Stage Door Canteen* (UA, 1943), *Tender Comrade* (RKO, 1943), *Music in Manhattan* (RKO, 1944), *Reckless Age* (Univ., 1944), *The Impatient Years* (Col., 1944), *She's a Sweetheart* (Col., 1944), *Sunday Dinner for a Soldier* (20th, 1944), *Captain Tugboat Annie* (Rep., 1945), *Three Wise Fools* (MGM, 1946), *My Darling Clementine* (20th, 1946), *The Dark Horse* (Univ., 1946), *The Red Stallion* (EL, 1947), *Keeper of the Bees* (Col., 1947), *Train to Alcatraz* (Rep., 1948), *Three Godfathers* (MGM, 1948), *Red Canyon* (Univ., 1949), *Wagonmaster* (RKO, 1950), *Caged* (WB, 1950), *The Daughter of Rosie O'Grady* (WB, 1950), *Redwood Forest Trail* (Rep., 1950), *Surrender* (Rep., 1950), *Three Husbands* (UA, 1950), *The Second Face* (EL, 1950), *Father's Wild Game* (Mon., 1950), *The Lemon Drop Kid* (Par., 1951), *Excuse My Dust* (MGM, 1951), *Journey into Light* (20th, 1951), *We're Not Married* (20th, 1952), *It Happens Every Spring* (Univ., 1953), *Affair With a Stranger* (RKO, 1953), *The Sun Shines Bright* (Rep., 1953), *There's Always Tomorrow* (Univ., 1956), *The Last Hurrah* (Col., 1958), *Hound-Dog Man* (20th, 1959), *Mary Poppins* (BV, 1964).

MARION DAVIES (Marion Cecilia Douras) Born January 3, 1900, New York, New York. Married Horace Brown (1951). Died September 22, 1961.

Robert Greig, Onslow Stevens and Marion Davies in *Peg o' My Heart.*

Sound Feature Films: *Marianne* (MGM, 1929), *Hollywood Revue of 1929* (MGM, 1929), *Not So Dumb* (MGM, 1930), *Floradora Girl* (MGM, 1930), *Bachelor Father* (MGM, 1931), *It's a Wise Child* (MGM, 1931), *Five and Ten* (MGM, 1931), *Polly of the Circus* (MGM, 1932), *Blondie of the Follies* (MGM, 1932,) *Peg O'My Heart* (MGM, 1933), *Going Hollywood* (MGM, 1933), *Operator 13* (MGM, 1934), *Page Miss Glory* (WB, 1935), *Hearts Divided* (WB, 1936), *Cain and Mabel* (WB, 1936), *Ever Since Eve* (WB, 1937).

BETTE DAVIS (Ruth Elizabeth Davis) Born April 5, 1908, Lowell, Massachusetts. Married Harmon Nelson (1932); divorced 1938. Married Arthur Farnsworth (1940); widowed 1943. Married William Grant Sherry (1945), child: Barbara; divorced 1949. Married Gary Merrill (1950), children: Margo, Michael; divorced 1960.

Feature Films: *Bad Sister* (Univ., 1931), *Seed* (Univ., 1931), *Waterloo Bridge* (Univ., 1931), *Way Back Home* (RKO, 1932), *The Menace*

Bette Davis and Paul Muni in *Border Town*.

(Col., 1932), *Hell's House* (Capital Film Exchange, 1932), *Man Who Played God* (WB, 1932), *So Big* (WB, 1932), *The Rich Are Always With Us* (WB, 1932), *The Dark Horse* (WB, 1932), *Cabin in the Cotton* (WB, 1932), *Three on a Match* (WB, 1932), *20,000 Years in Sing Sing* (WB, 1933), *Parachute Jumper* (WB, 1933), *The Working Man* (WB, 1933), *Ex-Lady* (WB, 1933), *Bureau of Missing Persons* (WB, 1933), *Fashions of 1934* (WB, 1934), *The Big Shakedown* (WB, 1934), *Jimmy the Gent* (WB, 1934), *Fog Over Frisco* (WB, 1934), *Of Human Bondage* (RKO, 1934), *Housewife* (WB, 1934), *Bordertown* (WB, 1935), *The Girl From Tenth Avenue* (WB, 1935), *Front Page Woman* (WB, 1935), *Special Agent* (WB, 1935), *Dangerous* (WB, 1935), *The Petrified Forest* (WB, 1936), *The Golden Arrow* (WB, 1936), *Satan Met a Lady* (WB, 1936), *Marked Woman* (WB, 1937), *Kid Galahad* (WB, 1937), *That Certain Woman* (WB, 1937), *It's Love I'm After* (WB, 1937), *Jezebel* (WB, 1938), *The Sisters* (WB, 1938), *Dark Victory* (WB, 1939), *Juarez* (WB, 1939), *The Old Maid* (WB, 1939), *The Private Lives of Elizabeth and Essex* (WB, 1939), *All This, and Heaven Too* (WB, 1940), *The Letter* (WB, 1940), *The Bride Came C.O.D.* (WB, 1941), *The Little Foxes* (RKO, 1941), *The Man Who Came to Dinner* (WB, 1941), *In This Our Life* (WB, 1942), *Now, Voyager* (WB, 1942), *Watch on the Rhine* (WB, 1943), *Thank Your Lucky Stars* (WB, 1943), *Old Acquaintance* (WB, 1943), *Mr. Skeffington* (WB, 1944), *Hollywood Canteen* (WB, 1944), *The Corn Is Green* (WB, 1945), *A Stolen Life* (WB, 1946), *Deception* (WB, 1947), *Winter Meeting* (WB, 1948), *June Bride* (WB, 1948), *Beyond the Forest* (WB, 1949), *All About Eve* (20th, 1950), *Payment on Demand* (RKO, 1951), *Another Man's Poison* (UA, 1951), *Phone Call From a Stranger* (20th, 1952), *The Star* (20th, 1953), *The Virgin Queen* (20th, 1955), *Storm Center* (Col., 1956), *The Catered Affair* (MGM, 1956), *John Paul Jones* (WB, 1959), *The Scapegoat* (MGM, 1959), *A Pocketful of Miracles* (UA, 1961), *What Ever Happened to Baby Jane?* (WB, 1962), *Dead Ringer* (WB, 1964), *The Empty Canvas* (Embassy, 1964), *Where Love Has Gone* (Par., 1964), *Hush . . . Hush, Sweet Charlotte* (20th, 1965), *The Nanny* (20th, 1965), *The Anniversary* (20th, 1968).

JOAN DAVIS (Madonna Josephine Davis) Born June 29, 1907, St. Paul, Minnesota. Married Seranus Willis (1931), child: Beverly; divorced 1947. Died May 22, 1961.

Feature Films: *Millions in the Air* (Par., 1935), *The Holy Terror* (20th, 1937), *Time Out for Romance* (20th, 1937), *Nancy Steele Is Missing* (20th, 1937), *Wake Up and Live* (20th, 1937), *You Can't Have Everything* (20th, 1937), *Angel's Holiday* (20th, 1937), *The Great Hospital Mystery* (20th, 1937), *Thin Ice* (20th, 1937), *On the Avenue* (20th, 1937), *Life Begins in College* (20th, 1937), *Love and Hisses* (20th, 1937), *Sally, Irene and Mary* (20th, 1938), *Josette* (20th, 1938), *My Lucky Star* (20th, 1938), *Hold That Co-ed* (20th, 1938), *Just Around the Corner* (20th, 1938), *Tailspin* (20th, 1939), *Daytime Wife* (20th, 1939), *Too Busy to Work* (20th, 1939), *Free, Blonde and 21* (20th, 1940), *Manhattan Heartbeat* (20th, 1940), *Sailor's Lady* (20th, 1940), *For Beauty's Sake* (20th, 1941), *Sun Valley Serenade* (20th, 1941), *Hold That Ghost* (Univ., 1941), *Two Latins From Manhattan* (Col., 1941), *Yokel Boy*

(Rep., 1942), *Sweethearts of the Fleet* (Col., 1942), *He's My Guy* (Univ., 1943), *Two Senoritas From Chicago* (Col., 1943), *Around the World* (RKO, 1943), *Show Business* (RKO, 1944), *Beautiful But Broke* (Col., 1944), *Kansas City Kitty* (Col., 1944), *She Gets Her Man* (Univ., 1945), *George White's Scandals* (RKO, 1945), *She Wrote the Book* (Univ., 1946), *If You Knew Susie* (RKO, 1948), *Make Mine Laughs* (RKO, 1949), *Traveling Saleswoman* (Col., 1949), *Love That Brute* (20th, 1950), *The Groom Wore Spurs* (Univ., 1951), *Harem Girl* (Col., 1952).

Peggie Castle and Joan Davis in *Harem Girl*.

SAMMY DAVIS, JR. Born December 8, 1925, New York, New York. Married Loray White (1958); divorced 1959. Married May Britt (1960), children: Tracey, Mark, Jeff.

Feature Films: *Anna Lucasta* (UA, 1958), *Porgy and Bess* (Col., 1959), *Ocean's 11* (WB, 1960), *Pepe* (Col., 1960), *Sergeants 3* (UA, 1962), *Convicts 4* (AA, 1962), *Johnny Cool* (UA, 1963), *Robin and the 7 Hoods* (WB, 1964), *Nightmare in the Sun* (Zodiac, 1965), *A Man Called Adam* (Embassy, 1966), *Salt and Pepper* (UA, 1968), *Sweet Charity* (Univ., 1969).

Sammy Davis, Jr., in *Convicts Four*.

DORIS DAY (Doris von Kappelhoff) Born April 3, 1924, Cincinnati, Ohio. Married Al Jorden (1941), child: Terry; divorced 1943. Married George Weidler (1946); divorced 1949. Married Marty Melcher (1951).

Feature Films: *Romance on the High Seas* (WB, 1948), *My Dream Is Yours* (WB, 1949), *It's a Great Feeling* (WB, 1949), *Young Man With a Horn* (WB, 1950), *Tea for Two* (WB, 1950), *The West Point Story* (WB, 1950), *Storm Warning* (WB, 1950), *The Lullaby of Broadway* (WB, 1951), *On Moonlight Bay* (WB, 1951), *Starlift* (WB, 1951), *I'll See You in My Dreams* (WB, 1951), *April in Paris* (WB, 1952), *The Winning Team* (WB, 1952), *By the Light of the Silvery Moon* (WB, 1953), *Calamity Jane* (WB, 1953), *Lucky Me* (WB, 1954), *Young at*

Doris Day and Gordon MacRae in *By the Light of the Silvery Moon.*

Heart (WB, 1954), *Love Me or Leave Me* (MGM, 1955), *The Man Who Knew Too Much* (Par., 1956), *Julie* (MGM, 1956), *The Pajama Game* (WB, 1957), *Teacher's Pet* (Par., 1958), *The Tunnel of Love* (MGM, 1958), *It Happened to Jane* (Col., 1959), *Pillow Talk* (Univ., 1959), *Please Don't Eat the Daisies* (MGM, 1960), *Midnight Lace* (Univ., 1960), *Lover Come Back* (Univ., 1961), *That Touch of Mink* (Univ., 1962), *Billy Rose's Jumbo* (MGM, 1962), *The Thrill of It All* (Univ., 1963), *Move Over, Darling* (20th, 1963), *Send Me No Flowers* (Univ., 1964), *Do Not Disturb* (20th, 1965), *The Glass-Bottom Boat* (MGM, 1966), *Caprice* (20th, 1967), *The Ballad of Josie* (Univ., 1968), *Where Were You When the Lights Went Out?* (MGM, 1968).

LARAINE DAY (Loraine Johnson) Born October 13, 1919, Roosevelt, Utah. Married James Ray Hendricks (1942), children: Angela, Christopher, Melinda; divorced 1946. Married Leo Durocher (1947); divorced 1960. Married Michael Grilikhes (1961), children: Gigi, Dana.

Feature Films:
as Laraine Johnson *Stella Dallas* (UA, 1937), *Border G-Men* (RKO, 1938), *Scandal Street* (Par., 1938), *Painted Desert* (RKO, 1938), *The Arizona Legion* (RKO, 1939), *Sergeant Madden* (MGM, 1939).

Laraine Day and Kirk Douglas in *My Dear Secretary.*

as Laraine Day *Calling Dr. Kildare* (MGM, 1939), *Tarzan Finds a Son* (MGM, 1939), *Secret of Dr. Kildare* (MGM, 1939), *My Son, My Son* (UA, 1940), *I Take This Woman* (MGM, 1940), *And One Was Beautiful* (MGM, 1940), *Dr. Kildare's Strange Case* (MGM, 1940), *Foreign Correspondent* (UA, 1940), *Dr. Kildare Goes Home* (MGM, 1940), *Dr. Kildare's Crisis* (MGM, 1940), *The Bad Man* (MGM, 1941), *The Trial of Mary Dugan* (MGM, 1941), *The People vs. Dr. Kildare* (MGM, 1941), *Dr. Kildare's Wedding Day* (MGM, 1941), *Unholy Partners* (MGM, 1941), *Kathleen* (MGM, 1941), *Journey for Margaret* (MGM, 1942), *Fingers at the Window* (MGM, 1942), *A Yank on the Burma Road* (MGM, 1942), *Mr. Lucky* (RKO, 1943),

The Story of Dr. Wassell (Par., 1944), *Bride by Mistake* (RKO, 1944), *Those Endearing Young Charms* (RKO, 1945), *Keep Your Powder Dry* (MGM, 1945), *The Locket* (RKO, 1946), *Tycoon* (RKO, 1947), *My Dear Secretary* (UA, 1948), *I Married a Communist* ("The Woman On Pier 13—RKO, 1949), *Without Honor* (UA, 1949), *The High and the Mighty* (WB, 1954), *Toy Tiger* (Univ., 1956), *Three for Jamie Dawn* (AA, 1956), *The Third Voice* (20th, 1960).

JAMES DEAN (James Byron Dean) Born February 8, 1931, Marian, Nebraska. Died September 30, 1955.

Richard Davalos, James Dean and Jo Van Fleet in *East of Eden.*

Feature Films: *Sailor Beware* (Par., 1951), *Fixed Bayonets* (20th, 1951), *Has Anybody Seen My Gal* (Univ., 1952), *East of Eden* (WB, 1955), *Rebel Without a Cause* (WB, 1955), *Giant* (WB, 1956),

ROSEMARY DE CAMP Born November 14, 1914, Prescott, Arizona. Married John Shidler (1941) children: Margaret, Martha, Valerie, Nita.

Moroni Olsen, Dane Clark, Rosemary De Camp and John Garfield in *Pride of the Marines.*

Feature Films: *Cheers for Miss Bishop* (UA, 1941), *Hold Back the Dawn* (Par., 1941), *Jungle Book* (UA, 1942), *Yankee Doodle Dandy* (WB, 1942), *Eyes in the Night* (MGM, 1942), *Commandos Strike at Dawn* (Col., 1942), *Smith of Minnesota* (Col., 1942), *City Without Men* (Col., 1943), *This Is the Army* (WB, 1943), *The Merry Monahans* (Univ., 1944), *Bowery to Broadway* (Univ., 1944), *Blood on the Sun* (UA, 1945), *Practically Yours* (Par., 1945), *Weekend at the Waldorf* (MGM, 1945), *Rhapsody in Blue* (WB, 1945), *Pride of the Marines* (WB, 1945), *Danger Signal* (WB, 1945), *Too Young to Know* (WB, 1945), *From This Day*

Forward (RKO, 1946), *Two Guys From Milwaukee* (WB, 1946), *Nora Prentiss* (WB, 1947), *Night Unto Night* (WB, 1949), *The Life of Riley* (Univ., 1949), *Look for the Silver Lining* (WB, 1949), *The Story of Seabiscuit* (MGM, 1949), *The Big Hangover* (MGM, 1950), *Night into Morning* (MGM, 1951), *On Moonlight Bay* (WB, 1951), *Scandal Sheet* (Col., 1952), *The Treasure of Lost Canyon* (Univ., 1952), *By the Light of the Silvery Moon* (WB, 1953), *Main Street to Broadway* (MGM, 1953), *So This Is Love* (WB, 1953), *Strategic Air Command* (Par., 1955), *Many Rivers to Cross* (MGM, 1955), *13 Ghosts* (Col., 1960).

YVONNE DE CARLO (Peggy Yvonne Middleton) Born September 1, 1922, Vancouver, Canada. Married Robert Morgan (1955), children: Bruce, Michael.

English-Language Feature Films: *This Gun for Hire* (Par., 1942), *Har-*

Yvonne De Carlo and Alan Badel in *Magic Fire*.

vard, Here I Come (Col., 1942), *Road to Morocco* (Par., 1942), *Lucky Jordan* (Par., 1942), *Youth on Parade* (Col., 1942), *Let's Face It* (Par., 1943), *The Crystal Ball* (UA, 1943), *Salute for Three* (Par., 1943), *For Whom the Bell Tolls* (Par., 1943), *True to Life* (Par., 1943), *So Proudly We Hail!* (Par., 1943), *The Deerslayer* (Rep., 1943), *Practically Yours* (Par., 1944), *The Story of Dr. Wassell* (Par., 1944), *Standing Room Only* (Par., 1944), *Here Come the Waves* (Par., 1944), *Kismet* (MGM, 1944), *Salome, Where She Danced* (Univ., 1945), *Frontier Gal* (Univ., 1945), *Song of Scheherazade* (Univ., 1947), *Brute Force* (Univ., 1947), *Slave Girl* (Univ., 1947), *Black Bart* (Univ., 1948), *Casbah* (Univ., 1948), *River Lady* (Univ., 1948), *Criss Cross* (Univ., 1949), *Calamity Jane and Sam Bass* (Univ., 1949), *The Gal Who Took the West* (Univ., 1949), *Buccaneer's Girl* (Univ., 1950), *The Desert Hawk* (Univ., 1950), *Hotel Sahara* (UA, 1951), *Tomahawk* (Univ., 1951), *Silver City* (Par., 1951), *The San Francisco Story* (WB, 1952), *Scarlet Angel* (Univ., 1952), *Hurricane Smith* (Par., 1952), *Sombrero* (MGM, 1953), *Sea Devils* (RKO, 1953), *Fort Algiers* (UA, 1953), *The Captain's Paradise* (UA, 1953), *Border River* (Univ., 1954), *Passion* (RKO, 1954), *Tonight's the Night* (AA, 1954), *Shotgun* (AA, 1955), *Flame of the Islands* (Rep., 1955), *Magic Fire* (Rep., 1956), *Raw Edge* (Univ., 1956), *The Ten Commandments* (Par., 1956), *Death of a Scoundrel* (RKO, 1956), *Band of Angels* (WB, 1957), *Timbuctu* (UA, 1959), *McLintock* (UA, 1963), *A Global Affair* (MGM, 1964), *Law of the Lawless* (Par., 1964), *Munster, Go Home* (Univ., 1966), *Hostile Guns* (Par., 1967), *Arizona Bushwhackers* (Par., 1968), *The Power* (MGM, 1968).

SANDRA DEE (Alexandra Zuck) Born April 23, 1942, Bayonne, New Jersey. Married Bobby Darin (1960), child: Dodd; divorced 1967.

Feature Films: *Until They Sail* (MGM, 1957), *The Reluctant Debutante* (MGM, 1958), *The Restless Years* (Univ., 1958), *Stranger in My Arms* (Univ., 1959), *Imitation of Life* (Univ., 1959), *Snow Queen* (voice only, Univ., 1959), *The Wild and the Innocent* (Univ., 1959), *Gidget* (Col., 1959), *A Summer Place* (WB, 1959),

Teresa Wright and Sandra Dee in *The Restless Years*.

Portrait in Black (Univ., 1960), *Romanoff and Juliet* (Univ., 1961), *Tammy, Tell Me True* (Univ., 1961), *Come September* (Univ., 1961), *If a Man Answers* (Univ., 1962), *Tammy and the Doctor* (Univ., 1963), *Take Her, She's Mine* (20th, 1963), *I'd Rather Be Rich* (Univ., 1964), *That Funny Feeling* (Univ., 1965), *A Man Could Get Killed* (Univ., 1966), *Doctor, You've Got to Be Kidding!* (MGM, 1967), *Rosie!* (Univ., 1968).

GLORIA DE HAVEN (Gloria Mildred De Haven) Born July 23, 1924, Los Angeles, California. Married John Payne (1944), children: Kathleen, Thomas; divorced 1950. Married Martin Kimmel (1953); divorced 1954. Married Richard Fincher (1957), child: Harry; divorced 1963. Remarried 1964.

Feature Films: *The Great Dictator* (UA, 1940), *Susan and God* (MGM, 1940), *Keeping Company* (MGM, 1941), *Two-Faced Woman* (MGM, 1941), *The Penalty* (MGM, 1941), *Best Foot Forward* (MGM, 1943), *Thousands Cheer* (MGM, 1943), *Broadway Rhythm* (MGM, 1944), *Two Girls and a Sailor* (MGM, 1944), *Step Lively* (RKO, 1944), *The Thin Man Goes Home* (MGM, 1944), *Between Two Women* (MGM, 1945), *Summer Holiday* (MGM, 1948), *Scene of the Crime* (MGM, 1949), *The Doctor and the Girl* (MGM, 1949), *Yes Sir, That's My Baby* (Univ., 1949), *The Yellow Cab Man* (MGM, 1950), *Three Little Words* (MGM, 1950), *Summer Stock* (MGM, 1950), *I'll Get By* (20th, 1950), *Two Tickets to Broadway* (RKO, 1951), *Down Among the Sheltering Palms* (20th, 1953), *So This Is Paris* (Univ., 1955), *The Girl Rush* (Par., 1955).

William Lundigan, Gloria De Haven and Lyle Talbot in *Down Among the Sheltering Palms*.

OLIVIA DE HAVILLAND Born July 1, 1916, Tokyo, Japan. Married Marcus Goodrich (1946), child: Benjamin; divorced 1952. Married Pierre Paul Galante (1955), child: Giselle.

Great Commandment (20th, 1939), *Beau Geste* (Par., 1939), *Dr. Cyclops* (Par., 1940), *Strange Cargo* (MGM, 1940), *Rangers of Fortune* (Par., 1940), *Seven Sinners* (Univ., 1940), *You're the One* (Par., 1941), *Blonde Inspiration* (MGM, 1941), *Reaching for the Sun* (Par., 1941), *Buy Me That Town* (Par., 1941), *Among the Living* (Par., 1941), *Honky Tonk* (MGM, 1941), *The Lady Has Plans* (Par., 1942), *In Old California* (Rep., 1942), *Wake Island* (Par., 1942), *Night in New Orleans* (Par., 1942), *Yokel Boy* (Par., 1942), *Once Upon a Honeymoon* (RKO, 1942), *Star Spangled Rhythm* (Par., 1942), *Buckskin Frontier* (UA, 1943), *The Kansan* (UA, 1943), *In Old Oklahoma* (Rep., 1943), *The Woman of the Town* (UA, 1943), *The Hitler Gang* (narrator; Par., 1944), *Experiment Perilous* (RKO, 1944), *Salome, Where She Danced* (Univ., 1945), *Incendiary Blonde* (Par., 1945), *Hold That Blonde* (Par., 1945), *Suspense* (Mon., 1946), *The French Key* (Rep., 1946), *The Killers* (Univ., 1946), *Two Years Before the Mast* (Par., 1946), *California* (Par., 1946), *Wyoming* (Rep., 1947), *Slave Girl* (Univ., 1947), *The Pretender* (Rep., 1947), *The Fabulous Texan* (Rep., 1947), *Gentleman's Agreement* (20th, 1947), *Cass Timberlane* (MGM, 1947), *Fury at Furnace Creek* (20th, 1948), *Lulu Belle* (Col., 1948), *Bride of Vengeance* (Par., 1949), *Tarzan's Magic Fountain* (RKO, 1949), *Search for Danger* (Film Classics, 1949), *The Kid From Texas* (Univ., 1950), *Destination Murder* (RKO, 1950), *The Furies* (Par., 1950), *As Young As You Feel* (20th, 1951), *Wait Till the Sun Shines, Nellie* (20th, 1952), *The Silver Chalice* (WB, 1954), *Kiss Me Deadly* (UA, 1955), *Illegal* (WB, 1955), *East of Eden* (WB, 1955), *She Devil* (20th, 1957), *Machete* (UA, 1958), *These Thousand Hills* (20th, 1959), *The Sound and the Fury* (20th, 1959), *Middle of the Night* (Col., 1959), *The Wonderful Country* (UA, 1959), *Suddenly, Last Summer* (Col., 1959), *Come Spy With Me* (20th, 1967), *Gammera, the Invincible* (World Entertainment Corp., 1967).

DOLORES DEL RIO (Dolores Asunsolo) Born August 3, 1905, Durango, Mexico. Married Jaime Del Rio (1921); widowed 1928. Married Cedric Gibbons (1930); divorced 1941. Married Lewis Riley (1959).

James Leong, Dolores Del Rio, Dick Baldwin and June Lang in *International Settlement.*

English-language Feature Films: *Evangeline* (UA, 1929), *The Bad One* (UA, 1930), *Girl of the Rio* (RKO, 1932), *Bird of Paradise* (RKO, 1932), *Flying Down to Rio* (RKO, 1933), *Wonder Bar* (WB, 1934), *Madame Du Barry* (WB, 1934), *In Caliente* (WB, 1935), *I Live for Love* (WB, 1935), *Widow From Monte Carlo* (WB, 1935), *Accused* (UA, 1936), *Devil's Playground* (Col., 1937), *Lancer Spy* (20th, 1937), *International Settlement* (20th, 1938), *The Man From Dakota* (MGM, 1940), *Journey Into Fear* (RKO, 1942), *The Fugitive* (RKO, 1947), *Flaming Star* (20th, 1960), *Cheyenne Autumn* (WB, 1964), *More Than a Miracle* (MGM, 1967).

REGINALD DENNY (Reginald Leigh Dugmore Denny) Born November 20, 1891, Richmond, Surrey, England. Married Irene Haisman (1913), child: Barbara; divorced 1927. Married Isobel Steifeel (1928), children: Reginald, Joan. Died June 16, 1967.

Feature Films: *A Midsummer Night's Dream* (WB, 1935), *Alibi Ike* (WB, 1935), *The Irish in Us* (WB, 1935), *Captain Blood* (WB, 1935), *Anthony Adverse* (WB, 1936), *The Charge of the Light Brigade* (WB, 1936), *Call It a Day* (WB, 1937), *The Great Garrick* (WB, 1937), *It's Love I'm After* (WB, 1937), *Gold Is Where You Find It* (WB, 1938), *Hard to Get* (WB, 1938), *The Adventures of Robin Hood* (WB, 1938), *Four's a Crowd* (WB, 1938), *Wings of the Navy* (WB, 1939), *Dodge City* (WB, 1939), *The Private Lives of Elizabeth and Essex* (WB, 1939), *Gone With the Wind* (MGM, 1939), *Raffles* (UA, 1940), *My Love Came Back* (WB, 1940), *Santa Fe Trail* (WB, 1940), *Strawberry Blonde* (WB, 1941), *Hold Back the Dawn* (Par., 1941), *They Died With Their Boots On* (WB, 1941), *The Male Animal* (WB, 1942), *In This Our Life* (WB, 1942), *Thank Your Lucky Stars* (WB, 1943), *Princess O' Rourke* (WB, 1943), *Government Girl* (RKO, 1943), *Devotion* (WB, 1946), *The Well-Groomed Bride* (Par., 1946), *To Each His Own* (Par., 1946), *The Dark Mirror* (Univ., 1946), *The Snake Pit* (20th, 1948), *The Heiress* (Par., 1949), *My Cousin Rachel* (20th, 1953), *That Lady* (20th, 1955), *Not as a Stranger* (UA, 1955), *The Ambassador's Daughter* (UA, 1956), *Proud Rebel* (BV, 1958), *Libel* (MGM, 1959), *Light in the Piazza* (MGM, 1962), *Hush . . . Hush, Sweet Charlotte* (20th, 1964), *Lady in a Cage* (Par., 1964).

ALBERT DEKKER Born December 20, 1905, Brooklyn, New York. Married Esther Guerini (1929), children: Jan, John, Benjamin; divorced. Died May 5, 1968.

Feature Films: *The Great Garrick* (WB, 1937), *The Last Warning* (Univ., 1938), *She Married an Artist* (Col., 1938), *The Lone Wolf in Paris* (Col., 1938), *Extortion* (Col., 1938), *Marie Antoinette* (MGM, 1938), *Paris Honeymoon* (Par., 1939), *Never Say Die* (Par., 1939), *Hotel Imperial* (Par., 1939), *The Man in the Iron Mask* (UA, 1939), *The*

Albert Dekker, Porter Hall and Claire Trevor in *Woman of the Town.*

Mary Nolan and Reginald Denny in *Good Morning Judge*.

Sound Feature Films: *One Hysterical Night* (Univ., 1930), *What a Man!* (Sono Art-World Wide, 1930), *Embarrassing Moments* (Univ., 1930), *Those Three French Girls* (MGM, 1930), *A Lady's Morals* (MGM, 1930), *Madame Satan* (MGM, 1930), *Oh, For a Man!* (Fox, 1930), *Stepping Out* (MGM, 1931), *Kiki* (UA, 1931), *Parlor, Bedroom and Bath* (MGM, 1931), *Private Lives* (MGM, 1931), *Strange Justice* (RKO, 1932), *Iron Master* (Allied, 1933), *The Barbarian* (MGM, 1933), *Big Bluff* (Tower, 1933), *Only Yesterday* (Univ., 1933), *Fog* (Col., 1934), *Lost Patrol* (RKO, 1934), *We're Rich Again* (RKO, 1934), *The World Moves On* (Fox, 1934), *Dancing Man* (Pyramid, 1934), *Of Human Bondage* (RKO, 1934), *One More River* (Univ., 1934), *Richest Girl in the World* (RKO, 1934), *The Little Minister* (RKO, 1934), *Lottery Lover* (Fox, 1935), *Vagabond Lady* (MGM, 1935), *No More Ladies* (MGM, 1935), *Anna Karenina* (MGM, 1935), *Here's to Romance* (Fox, 1935), *Midnight Phantom* (Reliable, 1935), *Remember Last Night?* (Univ., 1935), *Lady in Scarlet* (Chesterfield, 1936), *Penthouse Party* (Liberty, 1936), *The Preview Murder Mystery* (Par., 1936), *Romeo and Juliet* (MGM, 1936), *It Couldn't Have Happened* (Invincible, 1936), *Two in a Crowd* (Univ., 1936), *More Than a Secretary* (Col., 1936), *Join the Marines* (Rep., 1937), *Women of Glamour* (Col., 1937), *Bulldog Drummond Escapes* (Par., 1937), *Let's Get Married* (Col., 1937), *The Great Gambini* (Par., 1937), *Bulldog Drummond Comes Back* (Par., 1937), *Beg, Borrow or Steal* (MGM, 1937), *Bulldog Drummond's Revenge* (Par., 1937), *Bulldog Drummond's Peril* (Par., 1938), *Four Men and a Prayer* (20th, 1938), *Blockade* (UA, 1938), *Bulldog Drummond in Africa* (Par., 1938), *Arrest Bulldog Drummond* (Par., 1939), *Bulldog Drummond's Secret Police* (Par., 1939), *Bulldog Drummond's Bride* (Par., 1939), *Rebecca* (UA, 1940), *Spring Parade* (Univ., 1940), *Seven Sinners* (Univ., 1940), *One Night in Lisbon* (Par., 1941), *International Squadron* (WB, 1941), *Appointment for Love* (Univ., 1941), *Sherlock Holmes and the Voice of Terror* (Univ., 1942), *Eyes in the Night* (MGM, 1942), *Thunder Birds* (20th, 1942), *Over My Dead Body* (20th, 1942), *Crime Doctor's Strangest Case* (Col., 1943), *Song of the Open Road* (UA, 1944), *Love Letters* (Par., 1945), *Tangier* (Univ., 1946), *The Locket* (RKO, 1946), *The Macomber Affair* (UA, 1947), *My Favorite Brunette* (Par., 1947), *The Secret Life of Walter Mitty* (RKO, 1947), *Escape Me Never* (WB, 1947), *Christmas Eve* (UA, 1947), *Mr. Blandings Builds His Dream House* (RKO, 1948), *The Iroquois Trail* (UA, 1950), *The Hindu* ("Sabaka"—Ferrin, 1953), *Abbott and Costello Meet Dr. Jekyll and Mr. Hyde* (Univ., 1953), *Fort Vengeance* (AA, 1953), *World for Ransom* (AA, 1954), *Escape to Burma* (RKO, 1955), *Around the World in 80 Days* (UA, 1956), *Cat Ballou* (Col., 1965), *Batman* (20th, 1966).

ANDY DEVINE Born October 7, 1905, Flagstaff, Arizona. Married Dorothy House (1933), children: Tad, Denny.

Sound Feature Films: *Spirit of Notre Dame* (Univ., 1931), *The Criminal Code* (Col., 1931), *Law and Order* (Univ., 1932), *Destry Rides Again* (Univ., 1932), *Three Wise Girls* (Col., 1932), *Impatient Maiden* (Univ., 1932), *Information Kid* (Univ., 1932), *Man Wanted* (WB, 1932), *Man From Yesterday* (Par., 1932), *Radio Patrol* (Univ., 1932), *Tom Brown of Culver* (Univ., 1932), *Fast Companions* (Univ., 1932), *All American* (Univ., 1932), *Cohens and Kellys in Trouble* (Univ., 1933), *Song of the Eagle* (Par., 1933), *The Big Cage* (Univ., 1933), *Midnight*

som (Univ., 1934), *Wake Up and Dream* (Un ... .), ... *Heavens* (Fox, 1934), *The President Vanishes* (Par., 1934), *Straight From the Heart* (Univ., 1935), *Hold 'Em Yale* (Par., 1935), *The Farmer Takes a Wife* (Fox, 1935), *Chinatown Squad* (Univ., 1935), *Fighting Youth* (Univ., 1935), *Way Down East* (Fox, 1935), *Coronado* (Par., 1935), *Small Town Girl* (MGM, 1936), *Romeo and Juliet* (MGM, 1936), *The Big Game* (RKO, 1936), *Yellowstone* (Univ., 1936), *Flying Hostess* (Univ., 1936), *Mysterious Crossing* (Univ., 1937), *A Star Is Born* (UA, 1937), *The Road Back* (Univ., 1937), *Double or Nothing* (Par., 1937), *You're a Sweetheart* (Univ., 1937), *In Old Chicago* (20th, 1938), *Dr. Rhythm* (Par., 1938), *Yellow Jack* (MGM, 1938), *The Storm* (Univ., 1938), *Personal Secretary* (Univ., 1938), *Men With Wings* (Par., 1938), *Strange Faces* (Univ., 1938), *Swing That Cheer* (Univ., 1938), *Stagecoach* (UA, 1939), *Never Say Die* (Par., 1939), *The Spirit of Culver* (Univ., 1939), *Geronimo* (Par., 1939), *Mutiny on the Blackhawk* (Univ., 1939), *Legion of Lost Flyers* (Par., 1939), *The Man From Montreal* (Univ., 1939), *Tropic Fury* (Univ., 1940), *Little Old New York* (20th, 1940), *Buck Benny Rides Again* (Par., 1940), *Danger on Wheels* (Univ., 1940), *Torrid Zone* (WB, 1940), *Hot Steel* (Univ., 1940), *When the Daltons Rode* (Univ., 1940), *The Leather Pushers* (Univ., 1940), *Black Diamonds* (Univ., 1940), *The Devil's Pipeline* (Univ., 1940), *Trail of the Vigilantes* (Univ., 1940), *A Dangerous Game* (Univ., 1941), *Lucky Devils* (Univ., 1941), *The Flame of New Orleans* (Univ., 1941), *Mutiny in the Arctic* (Univ., 1941), *Men of the Timberland* (Univ., 1941), *Badlands of Dakota* (Univ., 1941), *South of Tahiti* (Univ., 1941), *Road Agent* (Univ., 1941), *Raiders of the Desert* (Univ., 1941), *Unseen Enemy* (Univ., 1942), *North to the Klondike* (Univ., 1942), *Escape From Hong Kong* (Univ., 1942), *Danger in the Pacific* (Univ., 1942), *Between Us Girls* (Univ., 1942), *Sin Town* (Univ., 1942), *Top Sergeant* (Univ., 1942), *Rhythm of the Islands* (Univ., 1943), *Frontier Badmen* (Univ., 1943), *Corvette K-225* (Univ., 1943), *Crazy House* (Univ., 1943), *Ali Baba and the Forty Thieves* (Univ., 1944), *Follow the Boys* (Univ., 1944), *Ghost Catchers* (Univ., 1944), *Babes on Swing Street* (Univ., 1944), *Bowery to Broadway* (Univ., 1944), *Sudan* (Univ., 1945), *Frisco Sal* (Univ., 1945), *That's the Spirit* (Univ., 1945), *Frontier Gal* (Univ., 1945), *Canyon Passage* (Univ., 1946), *The Michigan Kid* (Univ., 1947), *Bells of San Angelo* (Rep., 1947), *Springtime in the Sierras* (Rep., 1947), *Slave Girl* (Univ., 1947), *The Marauders* (UA, 1947), *On the Old Spanish Trail* (Rep., 1947), *The Vigilantes Return* (Univ., 1947), *The Gay Ranchero* (Rep., 1948), *Old Los Angeles* (Rep., 1948), *Under California Skies* (Rep., 1948), *Eyes of Texas* (Rep., 1948), *Grand Canyon Trail* (Rep., 1948), *Nighttime in Nevada* (Rep., 1948), *The Far Frontier* (Rep., 1948), *The Last Bandit* (Rep., 1949), *Traveling Saleswoman* (Col., 1950), *Never a Dull Moment* (RKO 1950), *New Mexico* (UA, 1951), *The Red Badge of Courage* (MGM, 1951), *Slaughter Trail* (RKO, 1951), *Montana Belle* (RKO, 1952), *Island in the Sky* (WB, 1953), *Pete Kelly's Blues* (WB, 1955), *Around the World in 80 Days* (UA, 1956), *The Adventures of Huckleberry Finn* (MGM, 1960), *Two Rode Together* (Col., 1961), *The Man Who Shot Liberty Valance* (Par., 1962), *How the West Was Won* (MGM, 1963), *It's a Mad, Mad, Mad, Mad World* (UA, 1963), *Zebra in the Kitchen* (MGM, 1965), *The Ballad of Josie* (Univ., 1968).

Linda Evans, Brandon De Wilde and Walter Brennan in *Those Calloways*.

BRANDON DE WILDE (Andre Brandon de Wilde) Born April 9, 1942, Brooklyn, New York. Married Susan Maw (1963).

Feature Films: *The Member of the Wedding* (Col., 1952), *Shane* (Par., 1953), *Good-bye, My Lady* (WB, 1956), *Night Passage* (Univ., 1957). *The Missouri Traveler* (BV, 1958), *Blue Denim* (20th, 1959), *All Fall Down* (MGM, 1962), *Hud* (Par., 1963), *Those Calloways* (BV, 1964). *In Harm's Way* (Par., 1965).

BILLY DE WOLFE (William Andrew Jones) Born Wollaston, Massachusetts.

Billy De Wolfe, Gordon Jones, Edward Arnold, William Holden and Joan Caulfield in *Dear Wife*.

Feature Films: *Dixie* (Par., 1943), *Miss Susie Slagle's* (Par., 1945), *Our Hearts Were Growing Up* (Par., 1946), *Blue Skies* (Par., 1946), *Dear Ruth* (Par., 1947), *The Perils of Pauline* (Par., 1947), *Variety Girl* (Par., 1947), *Isn't It Romantic?* (Par., 1948), *Dear Wife* (Par., 1949), *Tea for Two* (WB, 1950), *Dear Brat* (Par., 1951), *Lullaby of Broadway* (WB, 1951), *Call Me Madam* (20th, 1953), *Billie* (UA, 1965).

ANGIE DICKINSON Born September 30, 1931, Kulm, North Dakota. Married Bert Bacharach (1965), child: Lea.

Angie Dickinson and Efram Zimbalist, Jr., in *A Fever in the Blood*.

Feature Films: *Lucky Me* (WB, 1954), *Man With the Gun* (UA, 1955), *Tennessee's Partner* (RKO, 1955), *The Return of Jack Slade* (AA, 1955), *Hidden Guns* (Rep., 1956), *Gun the Man Down* (UA, 1956), *Tension at Table Rock* (RKO, 1956), *The Black Whip* (20th, 1957), *Shoot-Out at Medicine Bend* (WB, 1957), *Calypso Joe* (AA, 1957), *China Gate* (20th, 1957), *Cry Terror* (MGM, 1958), *Rio Bravo* (WB, 1959), *The Bramble Bush* (WB, 1960), *Ocean's 11* (WB, 1960), *A Fever in the Blood* (WB, 1961), *The Sins of Rachel Cade* (WB, 1961), *Rome Adventure* (WB, 1962), *Jessica* (UA, 1962), *Captain Newman, M.D.* (Univ., 1963), *The Killers* (Univ., 1964), *The Art of Love* (Univ., 1965), *The Chase* (Col., 1966), *Cast a Giant Shadow* (UA, 1966), *Point Blank* (MGM, 1967), *The Last Challenge* (MGM, 1967).

MARLENE DIETRICH (Maria Magdalene von Lòsch) Born December 27, 1900, Schoenberg, Germany. Married Rudolf Sieber (1924), child: Maria.

Charles Boyer, Alan Marshall, Marlene Dietrich and Joseph Schildkraut in *The Garden of Allah*.

English-Language Feature Films: *The Blue Angel* (Par., 1930), *Morocco* (Par., 1930), *Dishonored* (Par., 1931), *Shanghai Express* (Par., 1932), *Blonde Venus* (Par., 1932), *The Song of Songs* (Par., 1933), *The Scarlet Empress* (Par., 1934), *The Devil Is a Woman* (Par., 1935), *Desire* (Par., 1936), *The Garden of Allah* (UA, 1936), *Knight Without Armour* (UA, 1937), *Angel* (Par., 1937), *Destry Rides Again* (Univ., 1939), *Seven Sinners* (Univ., 1940), *The Flame of New Orleans* (Univ., 1941), *Manpower* (WB, 1941), *The Lady Is Willing* (Col., 1942), *The Spoilers* (Univ., 1942), *Pittsburgh* (Univ., 1942), *Follow the Boys* (Univ., 1944), *Kismet* (MGM, 1944), *Golden Earrings* (Par., 1947), *A Foreign Affair* (Par., 1948), *Jigsaw* (UA, 1949),* *Stage Fright* (WB, 1950), *No Highway in the Sky* (20th, 1951), *Rancho Notorious* (RKO, 1952), *Around the World in 80 Days* (UA, 1956), *The Monte Carlo Story* (UA, 1957), *Witness for the Prosecution* (UA, 1957), *Touch of Evil* (Univ., 1958),* *Judgment at Nuremberg* (UA, 1961), *The Black Fox* (narrator; Capri 1963), *Paris When It Sizzles* (Par., 1964).*

*Unbilled guest appearance

RICHARD DIX (Ernest Carlton Brimmer) Born July 18, 1894, St. Paul, Minnesota. Married Winifred Coe (1931), child: Martha; divorced 1933. Married Virginia Webster (1934), children: Richard, Robert, Sara. Died September 20, 1949.

Sound Feature Films: *Nothing But the Truth* (Par., 1929), *The Wheel of Life* (Par., 1929), *The Love Doctor* (Par., 1929), *Seven Keys to Baldpate* (RKO, 1929), *Lovin' the Ladies* (RKO, 1930), *Shooting Straight* (RKO, 1930), *Cimarron* (RKO, 1931), *Young Donovan's Kid* (RKO, 1931), *Public Defender* (RKO, 1931), *Secret Service* (RKO, 1931), *The Lost Squadron* (RKO, 1932), *Roar of the Dragon* (RKO, 1932), *Hell's Highway* (RKO, 1932), *The Conquerors* (RKO, 1932), *The Great Jasper* (RKO, 1933), *No Marriage Ties* (RKO, 1933), *Day of Reckoning* (MGM, 1933), *The Ace of Aces* (RKO, 1933), *Stingaree* (RKO, 1934),

Boris Karloff, Richard Dix and Jackie Cooper in *Young Donovan's Kid.*

Barbara Stanwyck and Brian Donlevy in *The Great Man's Lady.*

His Greatest Gamble (RKO, 1934), *West of the Pecos* (RKO, 1934), *The Arizonian* (RKO, 1935), *Trans-Atlantic Tunnel* (Gaumont-British, 1935), *Yellow Dust* (RKO, 1936), *Special Investigator* (RKO, 1936), *Devil's Squadron* (Col., 1936), *The Devil's Playground* (Col., 1937), *The Devil Is Driving* (Col., 1937), *It Happened in Hollywood* (Col., 1937), *Blind Alibi* (RKO, 1938), *Sky Giant* (RKO, 1938), *Twelve Crowded Hours* (RKO, 1939), *Man of Conquest* (Rep., 1939), *Here I Am a Stranger* (20th, 1939), *Reno* (RKO, 1939), *The Marines Fly High* (RKO, 1940), *Men Against the Sky* (RKO, 1940), *Cherokee Strip* (Par., 1940), *The Roundup* (Par., 1941), *Badlands of Dakota* (Univ., 1941), *Tombstone, the Town Too Tough to Die* (Par., 1942), *American Empire* (UA, 1942), *Eyes of the Underworld* (Univ., 1943), *Buckskin Frontier* (UA, 1943), *The Kansan* (UA, 1943), *Top Man* (Univ, 1943), *The Ghost Ship* (RKO, 1943), *The Whistler* (Col., 1944), *The Mark of the Whistler* (Col., 1944), *The Power of the Whistler* (Col., 1945), *The Voice of the Whistler* (Col., 1946), *The Mysterious Intruder* (Col., 1946), *The Secret of the Whistler* (Col., 1946), *The 13th Hour* (Col., 1947).

TROY DONAHUE (Merle Johnson, Jr.) Born January 27, 1937, New York, New York. Married Suzanne Pleshette (1964); divorced 1964. Married Valerie Allen (1966).

Feature Films: *Man Afraid* (Univ., 1957), *Tarnished Angels* (Univ., 1958), *This Happy Feeling* (Univ., 1958), *Voice in the Mirror* (Univ., 1958), *Summer Love* (Univ., 1958), *Live Fast, Die Young* (Univ., 1958), *Wild Heritage* (Univ., 1958), *Monster on the Campus* (Univ., 1958), *The Perfect Furlough* (Univ., 1959), *Imitation of Life* (Univ., 1959), *A Summer Place* (WB, 1959), *The Crowded Sky* (WB, 1960), *Parrish* (WB, 1961), *Susan Slade* (WB, 1961), *Rome Adventure* (WB, 1962), *Palm Springs Weekend* (WB, 1963), *A Distant Trumpet* (WB, 1964), *My Blood Runs Cold* (WB, 1965), *Come Spy With Me* (20th, 1967), *Blast-off* (AIP, 1967).

Troy Donahue (right) in *The Crowded Sky.*

BRIAN DONLEVY Born February 9, 1903, Portadown County, Armagh, Eire. Married Marjorie Lane (1936), child: Judith; divorced 1947. Married Lillian Lugosi (1966).

Sound Feature Films: *Mother's Boy* (Pathé, 1929), *Gentlemen of the Press* (Par., 1929), *Barbary Coast* (UA, 1935), *Mary Burns, Fugitive* (Par., 1935), *Another Face* (RKO, 1935), *Strike Me Pink* (UA, 1936), *Human Cargo* (20th, 1936), *Half Angel* (20th, 1936), *High Tension* (20th, 1936), *36 Hours to Kill* (20th, 1936), *Crack-Up* (20th, 1936), *Midnight Taxi* (20th, 1937), *This Is My Affair* (20th, 1937), *Born Reckless* (20th, 1937), *In Old Chicago* (20th, 1938), *Battle of Broadway* (20th, 1938), *Sharpshooters* (20th, 1938), *Jesse James* (20th, 1939), *Union Pacific* (Par., 1939), *Allegheny Uprising* (RKO, 1939), *Behind Prison Gates* (Col., 1939), *Beau Geste* (Par., 1939), *Destry Rides Again* (Univ., 1939), *The Great McGinty* (Par., 1940), *When the Daltons Rode* (Univ., 1940), *Brigham Young—Frontiersman* (20th, 1940), *I Wanted Wings* (Par., 1941) *Hold Back the Dawn* (Par., 1941),* *Birth of the Blues* (Par., 1941), *South of Tahiti* (Univ., 1941), *Billy the Kid* (MGM, 1941), *The Great Man's Lady* (Par., 1942), *A Gentleman After Dark* (UA, 1942), *The Remarkable Andrew* (Par., 1942), *Two Yanks in Trinidad* (Col., 1942), *Wake Island* (Par., 1942), *The Glass Key* (Par., 1942), *Nightmare* (Univ., 1942), *Stand By for Action* (MGM, 1942), *Hangmen Also Die* (UA, 1943), *The Miracle of Morgan's Creek* (Par., 1944), *An American Romance* (MGM, 1944), *Duffy's Tavern* (Par., 1945), *The Virginian* (Par., 1946), *Our Hearts Were Growing Up* (Par., 1946), *Canyon Passage* (Univ., 1946), *Two Years Before the Mast* (Par., 1946), *Song of Scheherazade* (Univ., 1947), *The Beginning or the End* (MGM, 1947), *The Trouble With Women* (Par., 1947), *Kiss of Death* (20th, 1947), *Heaven Only Knows* (UA, 1947), *Killer McCoy* (MGM, 1947), *A Southern Yankee* (MGM, 1948), *Command Decision* (MGM, 1948), *Impact* (UA, 1949), *The Lucky Stiff* (UA, 1949), *Shakedown* (Univ., 1950), *Kansas Raiders* (Univ., 1950), *Fighting Coast Guards* (Rep., 1951), *Slaughter Trail* (RKO, 1951), *Hoodlum Empire* (Rep., 1952), *Ride the Man Down* (Rep., 1952), *The Woman They Almost Lynched* (Rep., 1953), *The Big Combo* (AA, 1955), *The Creeping Unknown* (UA, 1956), *A Cry in the Night* (WB, 1956), *Enemy From Space* (UA, 1957), *Escape From Red Rock* (20th, 1958), *Cowboy* (Col., 1958), *Juke Box Rhythm* (Col., 1959), *Never So Few* (MGM, 1959), *The Errand Boy* (Par., 1961), *The Pigeon That Took Rome* (Par., 1962), *The Curse of the Fly* (20th, 1965), *How to Stuff a Wild Bikini* (AIP, 1965), *The Fat Spy* (Magna, 1966), *Waco* (Par., 1966), *Gammera, the Invincible* (World Entertainment Corp., 1967), *Arizona Bushwhackers* (Par., 1968), *Hostile Guns* (Par., 1967), *Rogue's Gallery* (Par., 1968).

*Unbilled guest appearance

JEFF DONNELL (Jean Marie Donnell) Born July 10, 1921, South Windham, Maine. Married William Anderson (1940), children: Michael, Sally; divorced. Married Aldo Ray (1954); divorced 1956. Married John Bricker (1958).

John Gallaudet, Jeff Donnell and Roy Barcroft in *Outcasts of the Trail.*

Feature Films: *My Sister Eileen* (Col., 1942), *The Boogie Man Will Get You* (Col., 1942), *What's Buzzin' Cousin?* (Col., 1943), *A Night to Remember* (Col., 1943), *City Without Men* (Col., 1943), *She's a Soldier, Too* (Col., 1944), *Nine Girls* (Col., 1944), *Stars on Parade* (Col., 1944), *Three Is a Family* (UA, 1944), *Carolina Blues* (Col., 1944), *Mr. Winkle Goes to War* (Col., 1944), *Once Upon a Time* (Col., 1944), *Power of the Whistler* (Col., 1945), *Edie Was a Lady* (Col., 1945), *Dancing in Manhattan* (Col., 1945), *Over 21* (Col., 1945), *Tars and Spars* (Col., 1946), *Song of the Prairie* (Col., 1945), *Throw a Saddle on a Star* (Col., 1946), *The Phantom Thief* (Col., 1946), *Night Editor* (Col., 1946), *That Texas Jamboree* (Col., 1946), *The Unknown* (Col., 1946), *Singing on the Trail* (Col., 1946), *It's Great to Be Young* (Col., 1946), *Cowboy Blues* (Col., 1946), *Mr. District Attorney* (Col., 1947), *Roughshod* (RKO, 1949), *Stage Coach Kid* (RKO, 1949), *Easy Living* (RKO, 1949), *Post Office Investigator* (Rep., 1949), *Outcasts of the Trail* (Rep., 1949,) *In a Lonely Place* (Col., 1950), *Hoedown* (Col., 1950), *Walk Softly, Stranger* (RKO, 1950), *The Fuller Brush Girl* (Col., 1950), *Redwood Forest Trail* (Rep., 1950), *Tall Timber* (Mon., 1950), *Three Guys Named Mike* (MGM, 1951), *Skirts Ahoy* (MGM, 1952), *Thief of Damascus* (Col., 1952), *The First Time* (Col., 1952), *Because You're Mine* (MGM, 1952), *So This Is Love* (WB, 1953), *Flight Nurse* (Rep., 1953), *The Blue Gardenia* (WB, 1953), *Magnificent Roughnecks* (AA, 1956), *The Guns of Fort Petticoat* (Col., 1957), *Destination 60,000* (AA, 1957), *Sweet Smell of Success* (UA, 1957), *My Man Godfrey* (Univ., 1957), *Gidget Goes Hawaiian* (Col., 1961), *Gidget Goes to Rome* (Col., 1963), *The Swingin' Maiden* (Col., 1964).

RUTH DONNELLY Born May 17, 1896 Trenton, New Jersey. Married Basil de Guichard (1932); widowed 1958.

Feature Films: *Transatlantic* (Fox, 1931), *The Spider* (Fox, 1931), *Wicked* (Fox, 1931), *Rainbow Trail* (Fox, 1932), *Blessed Event* (WB, 1932), *Jewel Robbery* (WB, 1932), *Make Me a Star* (Par., 1932), *Hard to Handle* (WB, 1933), *Employees' Entrance* (WB, 1933), *The Ladies They Talk About* (WB, 1933), *Lilly Turner* (WB, 1933), *Goodbye*

Robert Allen, Ruth Donnelly and June Lang in *Meet the Girls.*

Again (WB, 1933), *Private Detective 62* (WB, 1933), *Sing Sinner Sing* (Majestic, 1933), *Bureau of Missing Persons* (WB, 1933), *Footlight Parade* (WB, 1933), *Ever in My Heart* (WB, 1933), *Female* (WB, 1933), *Havana Widows* (WB, 1933), *Convention City* (WB, 1933), *Wonder Bar* (WB, 1934), *Heat Lightning* (WB, 1934), *Mandalay* (WB, 1934), *Merry Wives of Reno* (WB, 1934), *Housewife* (WB, 1934), *Romance in the Rain* (Univ., 1934), *Happiness Ahead* (WB, 1934), *You Belong to Me* (Par., 1934), *The White Cockatoo* (WB, 1935), *Maybe It's Love* (WB, 1935), *Traveling Saleslady* (WB, 1935), *Alibi Ike* (WB, 1935), *Red Salute* (UA, 1935), *Metropolitan* (20th, 1935), *Personal Maid's Secret* (WB, 1935), *Hands Across the Table* (Par., 1935), *The Song and Dance Man* (20th, 1936), *13 Hours by Air* (Par., 1936), *Mr. Deeds Goes to Town* (Col., 1936), *Fatal Lady* (Par., 1936), *Cain and Mabel* (WB, 1936), *More Than a Secretary* (Col., 1936), *Roaring Timber* (Col., 1937), *Portia on Trial* (Rep., 1937), *A Slight Case of Murder* (WB, 1938), *Army Girl* (Rep., 1938), *Meet the Girls* (20th, 1938), *The Affairs of Annabel* (RKO, 1938), *Annabel Takes a Tour* (RKO, 1938), *Personal Secretary* (Univ., 1938), *The Family Next Door* (Univ., 1939), *The Amazing Mr. Williams* (Col., 1939), *Mr. Smith Goes to Washington* (Col., 1939), *My Little Chickadee* (Univ., 1940), *Scatterbrain* (Rep., 1940), *Meet the Missus* (Rep., 1940), *Model Wife* (Univ., 1941), *Petticoat Politics* (Rep., 1941), *The Roundup* (Par., 1941), *The Gay Vagabond* (Rep., 1941), *Sailors on Leave* (Rep., 1941), *Rise and Shine* (20th, 1941) *You Belong to Me* (Col., 1941), *Johnny Doughboy* (Rep., 1942), *This Is the Army* (WB, 1943), *Thank Your Lucky Stars* (WB, 1943), *Sleepy Lagoon* (Rep., 1943), *Pillow to Post* (WB, 1945), *The Bells of St. Mary's* (RKO, 1945), *Cinderella Jones* (WB, 1946), *In Old Sacramento* (Rep., 1946), *The Ghost Goes Wild* (Rep., 1947), *Little Miss Broadway* (Col., 1947), *The Fabulous Texan* (Rep., 1947), *Fighting Father Dunne* (RKO, 1948), *The Snake Pit* (20th, 1948), *Where the Sidewalk Ends* (20th, 1950), *I'd Climb the Highest Mountain* (20th, 1951), *The Secret of Convict Lake* (20th, 1951), *The Wild Blue Yonder* (Rep., 1951), *A Lawless Street* (Col., 1955), *The Spoilers* (Univ., 1955), *Autumn Leaves* (Col., 1956), *The Way to the Gold* (20th, 1957).

ANN DORAN Born July 28, 1913, Amarillo, Texas.

Beulah Bondi, Paulette Goddard and Ann Doran in *I Love a Soldier.*

Feature Films: *Charlie Chan in London* (Fox, 1934), *Servants' Entrance* (Fox, 1934), *One Exciting Adventure* (Univ., 1934), *Way Down East* (Fox, 1935), *Night Life of the Gods* (Univ., 1935), *Mary Burns, Fugitive* (Par., 1935), *Case of the Missing Man* (Col., 1935) *Dangerous Intrigue* (Col., 1936), *The Man Who Lived Twice* (Col., 1936), *Palm Springs* (Par., 1936), *Ring Around the Moon* (Chesterfield, 1936), *Let's Sing Again* (RKO, 1936), *The Little Red School House* (Chesterfield, 1936), *Missing Girls* (Chesterfield, 1936), *Devil's Playground* (Col., 1937), *The Shadow* (Col., 1937), *Paid to Dance* (Col., 1937), *Marry the Girl* (WB, 1937), *When You're in Love* (Col., 1937), *Red Lights Ahead* (Chesterfield, 1937), *City Streets* (Col., 1938), *Penitentiary* (Col., 1938), *Women in Prison* (Col., 1938), *Extortion* (Col., 1938), *Highway Patrol* (Col., 1938), *You Can't Take It With You* (Col., 1938), *The Lady*

Objects (Col., 1938), *Blondie* (Col., 1938), *The Spider's Web* (Col. serial, 1938), *Start Cheering* (Col., 1938), *The Main Event* (Col., 1938), *She Married an Artist* (Col., 1938), *Rio Grande* (Col., 1938), *The Green Hornet* (Univ. serial, 1939), *Smashing the Spy Ring* (Col., 1939), *Coast Guard* (Col, 1939), *Blind Alibi* (RKO, 1939), *The Man They Could Not Hang* (Col., 1939), *Mr. Smith Goes to Washington* (Col., 1939), *Flying G-Men* (Col. serial, 1939), *My Son Is a Criminal* (Col., 1939), *Romance of the Redwoods* (Col., 1939), *A Woman Is the Judge* (Col., 1939), *Manhattan Heartbeat* (20th, 1940), *Untamed* (Par., 1940), *Girls of the Road* (Col., 1940), *Five Little Peppers at Home* (Col., 1940), *Glamour For Sale* (Col., 1940), *Buy Me That Town* (Par., 1941), *Ellery Queen's Penthouse Mystery* (Col., 1941), *Dr. Kildare's Wedding Day* (MGM, 1941), *Penny Serenade* (Col., 1941), *The Kid From Kansas* (Univ., 1941), *Meet John Doe* (WB, 1941), *Blue, White and Perfect* (20th, 1941), *Sun Valley Serenade* (20th, 1941), *Murder Among Friends* (20th, 1941), *New York Town* (Par., 1941), *They All Kissed the Bride* (Col., 1942), *My Sister Eileen* (Col., 1942), *Mr. Wise Guy* (Mon., 1942), *Beyond the Blue Horizon* (Par., 1942), *The Hard Way* (WB, 1942), *Yankee Doodle Dandy* (WB, 1942), *Air Force* (WB, 1943), *So Proudly We Hail* (Par., 1943), *True to Life* (Par., 1943), *Old Acquaintance* (WB, 1943), *Gildersleeve on Broadway* (RKO, 1943), *The More the Merrier* (Col., 1943), *Slightly Dangerous* (MGM, 1943), *I Love a Soldier* (Par., 1944), *The Story of Dr. Wassell* (Par., 1944), *Henry Aldrich's Little Secret* (Par., 1944), *Mr. Skeffington* (WB, 1944), *Roughly Speaking* (WB, 1945), *Here Come the Waves* (Par., 1945), *Pride of the Marines* (WB, 1945), *The Strange Love of Martha Ivers* (Par., 1946), *Our Hearts Were Growing Up* (Par., 1946), *The Perfect Marriage* (Par., 1946), *Fear in the Night* (Par., 1947), *My Favorite Brunette* (Par., 1947), *Seven Were Saved* (Par., 1947), *The Crimson Key* (20th, 1947), *Second Chance* (20th, 1947), *Magic Town* (RKO, 1947), *Road to the Big House* (Screen Guild, 1947), *For the Love of Rusty* (Col., 1947), *The Son of Rusty* (Col., 1947), *Variety Girl* (Par., 1947), *The Babe Ruth Story* (AA, 1948), *My Dog Rusty* (Col., 1948), *The Return of the Whistler* (Col., 1948), *Pitfall* (UA, 1948), *No Minor Vices* (MGM, 1948), *The Snake Pit* (20th, 1948), *Rusty Leads the Way* (Col., 1948), *Sealed Verdict* (Par., 1948), *The Walls of Jericho* (20th, 1948), *Rusty Saves a Life* (Col., 1949), *The Clay Pigeon* (RKO, 1949), *Calamity Jane and Sam Bass* (Univ., 1949), *The Fountainhead* (WB, 1949), *One Last Fling* (WB, 1949), *The Kid From Cleveland* (Rep., 1949), *Beyond the Forest* (WB, 1949), *Air Hostess* (Col., 1949), *The Clay Pigeon* (Par., 1949), *Holiday in Havana* (Col., 1949), *Rusty's Birthday* (Col., 1949), *No Sad Songs for Me* (Col., 1950), *Lonely Hearts Bandits* (Rep., 1950), *Never a Dull Moment* (RKO, 1950), *Gambling House* (RKO, 1950), *Riding High* (Par., 1950), *Starlift* (WB, 1951), *Tomahawk* (Univ., 1951), *The Painted Hills* (MGM, 1951), *Her First Romance* (Col., 1952), *The People Against O'Hara* (MGM, 1951), *Rodeo* (Mon., 1951), *Here Come the Nelsons* (Univ., 1952), *Love Is Better Than Ever* (MGM, 1952), *The Rose Bowl Story* (Mon., 1952), *So This Is Love* (WB, 1953), *The Eddie Cantor Story* (WB, 1953), *The High and the Mighty* (WB, 1954), *The Bob Mathias Story* (AA, 1954), *Them* (WB, 1954), *The Desperate Hours* (Par., 1955), *Rebel Without a Cause* (WB, 1955), *The Man Who Turned to Stone* (Col., 1957), *Young and Dangerous* (20th, 1957), *Shoot-Out at Medicine Bend* (WB, 1957), *Step Down to Terror* (Univ., 1958), *The Badlanders* (MGM, 1958), *Day of the Bad Man* (Univ., 1958), *The Deep Six* (WB, 1958), *The Female Animal* (Univ., 1958), *Violent Road* (WB, 1958), *Voice in the Mirror* (Univ., 1958), *Life Begins at 17* (Col., 1958), *The Rawhide Trail* (AA, 1958), *It! The Terror From Beyond Space* (UA, 1958), *Joy Ride* (AA, 1958), *A Summer Place* (WB, 1959), *Riot in Juvenile Prison* (UA, 1959), *Cast a Long Shadow* (UA, 1959), *Warlock* (20th, 1959), *Captain Newman, M. D.* (Univ., 1963), *The Brass Bottle* (Univ., 1964), *Where Love Has Gone* (Par., 1964), *The Carpetbaggers* (Par., 1964), *Kitten With a Whip* (Univ., 1964), *Mirage* (Univ., 1965), *Not With My Wife You Don't* (WB, 1966), *The Hostage* (Heartland, 1966), *Rosie!* (Univ., 1968).

KIRK DOUGLAS (Issur Danielovitch) Born December 9, 1916, Amsterdam, New York. Married Diana Dill (1943), children: Michael, Joel; divorced 1951. Married Anne Buydens (1954), children: Peter, Vincent.

Beverly Washburn and Kirk Douglas in *The Juggler*.

Feature Films: *The Strange Love of Martha Ivers* (Par., 1946), *Mourning Becomes Electra* (RKO, 1947), *Out of the Past* (RKO, 1947), *I Walk Alone* (Par., 1947), *The Walls of Jericho* (20th, 1948), *My Dear Secretary* (UA, 1948), *A Letter to Three Wives* (20th, 1948), *Champion* (UA, 1949), *Young Man With a Horn* (WB, 1950), *The Glass Menagerie* (WB, 1950), *Along the Great Divide* (WB, 1951), *Ace in the Hole* ("The Big Carnival"—Par., 1951), *Detective Story* (Par., 1951), *The Big Trees* (WB, 1952), *The Big Sky* (RKO, 1952), *The Bad and the Beautiful* (MGM, 1952), *The Story of Three Loves* (MGM, 1953), *The Juggler* (Col., 1953), *Act of Love* (UA, 1953), *20,000 Leagues Under the Sea* (BV, 1954), *Man Without a Star* (Univ., 1955), *The Racers* (20th, 1955), *Ulysses* (Par., 1955), *The Indian Fighter* (UA, 1955), *Lust for Life* (MGM, 1956), *Top Secret Affair* (WB, 1957), *Gunfight at the O.K. Corral* (Par., 1957), *Paths of Glory* (UA, 1957), *The Vikings* (UA, 1958), *Last Train From Gun Hill* (Par., 1959), *The Devil's Disciple* (UA, 1959), *Strangers When We Meet* (Col., 1960), *Spartacus* (Univ., 1960), *The Last Sunset* (Univ., 1961), *Town Without Pity* (UA, 1961), *Lonely Are the Brave* (Univ., 1962), *Two Weeks in Another Town* (MGM, 1962), *The Hook* (MGM, 1963), *The List of Adrian Messenger* (Univ., 1963), *For Love or Money* (Univ., 1963), *Seven Days in May* (Par., 1964), *In Harm's Way* (Par., 1965), *The Heroes of Telemark* (Col., 1965), *Cast a Giant Shadow* (Par., 1966), *Is Paris Burning?* (Par., 1966), *The War Wagon* (Univ., 1967), *The Way West* (UA, 1967), *The Brotherhood* (Par., 1968), *A Lovely Way to Die* (Univ., 1968).

MELVYN DOUGLAS (Melvyn E. Hesselberg) Born April 5, 1901, Macon, Georgia. Married Helen Gahagan (1931), children: Gregory, Peter, Mary.

Feature Films: *Tonight or Never* (UA, 1931), *Prestige* (RKO, 1932), *The Wiser Sex* (Par., 1932), *Broken Wing* (Par., 1932), *As You Desire Me* (MGM, 1932), *The Old Dark House* (Univ., 1932), *Nagana* (Univ.,

Philip Friend, Melvyn Douglas and Phyllis Calvert in *My Own True Love.*

1933), *The Vampire Bat* (Majestic, 1933), *Counsellor-at-Law* (Univ., 1933), *Woman in the Dark* (RKO, 1934), *Dangerous Corner* (RKO, 1934), *People's Enemy* (RKO, 1935), *She Married Her Boss* (Col., 1935), *Mary Burns—Fugitive* (Par., 1935), *Annie Oakley* (RKO, 1935), *The Lone Wolf Returns* (Col., 1936), *And So They Were Married* (Col., 1936), *The Gorgeous Hussy* (MGM, 1936), *Theodora Goes Wild* (Col., 1936), *Women of Glamour* (Col., 1937), *Captains Courageous* (MGM, 1937), *I Met Him in Paris* (Par., 1937), *Angel* (Par., 1937), *I'll Take Romance* (Col., 1937), *There's Always a Woman* (Col., 1938), *Arsene Lupin Returns* (MGM, 1938), *The Toy Wife* (MGM, 1938), *Fast Company* (MGM, 1938), *That Certain Age* (Univ., 1938), *The Shining Hour* (MGM, 1938), *There's That Woman Again* (Col., 1938), *Tell No Tales* (MGM, 1939), *Good Girls Go to Paris* (Col., 1939), *The Amazing Mr. Williams* (Col., 1939), *Ninotchka* (MGM, 1939), *Too Many Husbands* (Col. 1940), *He Stayed for Breakfast* (Col., 1940), *Third Finger—Left Hand* (MGM, 1940), *This Thing Called Love* (Col., 1941), *That Uncertain Feeling* (Col., 1941), *A Woman's Face* (MGM, 1941), *Our Wife* (Col., 1941), *Two-Faced Woman* (MGM, 1941), *They All Kissed the Bride* (Col., 1942), *Three Hearts for Julia* (MGM, 1943), *The Sea of Grass* (MGM, 1947), *The Guilt of Janet Ames* (Col., 1947), *Mr. Blandings Builds His Dream House* (RKO, 1948), *My Own True Love* (Par., 1948), *A Woman's Secret* (RKO, 1949), *The Great Sinner* (MGM, 1949), *My Forbidden Past* (RKO, 1951), *On the Loose* (RKO, 1951), *Billy Budd* (AA, 1962), *Hud* (Par., 1963), *Advance to the Rear* (MGM, 1964), *The Americanization of Emily* (MGM, 1964), *Rapture* (International Classics, 1965), *Hotel* (WB, 1967).

PAUL DOUGLAS Born November 4, 1907, Philadelphia, Pennsylvania. Married Elizabeth Farnsworth; divorced. Married Sussie Welles; divorced. Married Geraldine Higgins; divorced. Married Virginia Field, child: Margaret; divorced 1946. Married Jan Sterling (1950), child: Adam. Died September 11, 1959.

Grace Kelly, Paul Douglas and Stewart Granger in *Green Fire*.

Feature Films: *A Letter to Three Wives* (20th, 1948), *It Happens Every Spring* (20th, 1949), *Everybody Does It* (20th, 1949), *The Big Lift* (20th, 1950), *Love That Brute* (20th, 1950), *Panic in the Streets* (20th, 1950), *14 Hours* (20th, 1951), *The Guy Who Came Back* (20th, 1951), *Rhubarb* (Par., 1951),* *When in Rome* (MGM, 1952), *Clash by Night* (RKO, 1952), *We're Not Married* (20th, 1952), *Never Wave at a WAC* (RKO, 1952), *Forever Female* (Par., 1953), *Executive Suite* (MGM, 1954), *The Maggie* ("High and Dry"—Univ., 1954), *Green Fire* (MGM, 1954), *Joe MacBeth* (Col. 1956), *The Leather Saint* (Par., 1956), *The Solid Gold Cadillac* (Col., 1956), *The Gamma People* (Col., 1956), *This Could Be the Night* (MGM, 1957), *Beau James* (Par., 1957), *The Mating Game* (MGM, 1959).

*Unbilled guest appearance

MARIE DRESSLER (Leila Von Koerber) Born November 9, 1869, Coburg, Canada. Died July 28, 1934.

Polly Moran (left) and Marie Dressler (right) in *Reducing*.

Sound Feature Films: *Hollywood Revue of 1929* (MGM, 1929), *The Vagabond Lover* (RKO, 1929), *Chasing Rainbows* (MGM, 1930), *The Girl Said No* (MGM, 1930), *Anna Christie* (MGM, 1930), *One Romantic Night* (UA, 1930), *Caught Short* (MGM, 1930), *Let Us Be Gay* (MGM, 1930), *Min and Bill* (MGM, 1930), *Reducing* (MGM, 1931), *Politics* (MGM, 1931), *Emma* (MGM, 1932), *Prosperity* (MGM, 1932), *Dinner at Eight* (MGM, 1933), *Christopher Bean* (MGM, 1933), *Tugboat Annie* (MGM, 1933).

ELLEN DREW (Terry Ray) Born November 23, 1915, Kansas City, Missouri. Married Fred Wallace, (1935) child: David; divorced 1940. Married Sy Bartlett (1941); divorced 1950. Married William Walker (1951).

Feature Films:

as **Terry Ray** *College Holiday* (Par., 1936), *Yours for the Asking* (Par., 1936), *The Return of Sophie Lang* (Par., 1936), *My American Wife* (Par., 1936), *Rhythm on the Range* (Par., 1936), *Hollywood Boulevard* (Par., 1936), *Big Broadcast of 1937* (Par., 1936), *Murder With Pictures* (Par., 1936), *Wives Never Know* (Par., 1936), *Rose Bowl* (Par., 1936), *Lady Be Careful* (Par., 1936), *The Crime Nobody Saw* (Par., 1937), *Night of Mystery* (Par., 1937), *Internes Can't Take Money* (Par., 1937), *Make Way for Tomorrow* (Par., 1937), *Turn Off the Moon* (Par., 1937), *Hotel Haywire* (Par., 1937), *Mountain Music* (Par., 1937), *This Way Please* (Par., 1937), *Murder Goes to College* (Par., 1937), *Cocoanut Grove* (Par., 1938), *The Buccaneer* (Par., 1938), *Dangerous to Know* (Par., 1938), *Bluebeard's Eighth Wife* (Par., 1938), *You and Me* (Par., 1938).

as **Ellen Drew** *Sing You Sinners* (Par., 1938), *If I Were King* (Par., 1938), *The Lady's From Kentucky* (Par., 1939), *The Gracie Allen Murder Case* (Par., 1939), *Geronimo* (Par., 1939), *Women Without*

Vincent Price and Ellen Drew in *The Baron of Arizona*.

Names (Par., 1940), *Buck Benny Rides Again* (Par., 1940), *French Without Tears* (Par., 1940), *Christmas in July* (Par., 1940), *The Monster and the Girl* (Par., 1941), *Texas Rangers Ride Again* (Par., 1941), *The Mad Doctor* (Par., 1941), *Reaching for the Sun* (Par., 1941), *The Parson of Panamint* (Par., 1941), *The Night of January 16th* (Par., 1941), *Our Wife* (Col., 1941), *Star Spangled Rhythm* (Par., 1942), *The Remarkable Andrew* (Par., 1942), *My Favorite Spy* (RKO, 1942), *Ice-Capades Revue* (Rep., 1942), *Night Plane From Chungking* (Par., 1943), *The Impostor* (Univ., 1944), *Dark Mountain* (Par., 1944), *That's My Baby!* (Rep., 1944), *China Sky* (RKO, 1945), *Isle of the Dead* (RKO, 1945), *Man Alive* (RKO, 1945), *Sing While You Dance* (Col., 1946), *Crime Doctor's Man Hunt* (Col., 1946), *Johnny O'Clock* (Col., 1947), *The Swordsman* (Col., 1947), *The Man From Colorado* (Col., 1948), *The Crooked Way* (UA, 1949), *The Baron of Arizona* (Lip., 1950), *Cargo to Capetown* (Col., 1950), *Davy Crockett, Indian Scout* (UA, 1950), *Stars in My Crown* (MGM, 1950), *The Great Missouri Raid* (Par., 1950), *Man in the Saddle* (Col., 1951), *Outlaw's Son* (UA, 1957).

JOANNE DRU (Joanne Laycock) Born January 31, 1923, Logan, West Virginia. Married Dick Haymes (1941), children: Dick, Helen, Barbara; divorced 1949. Married John Ireland (1949), children: Peter, John; divorced 1956. Married George Pierose (1963).

Joanne Dru and Gilbert Roland in *The Wild and the Innocent*.

Feature Films: *Abie's Irish Rose* (UA, 1946), *Red River* (UA, 1948), *She Wore a Yellow Ribbon* (RKO, 1949), *All the King's Men* (Col., 1949), *Wagonmaster* (RKO, 1950), *711 Ocean Drive* (Col., 1950), *Vengeance Valley* (MGM, 1951), *Mr. Belvedere Rings the Bell* (20th, 1951), *Return of the Texan* (20th, 1952), *The Pride of St. Louis* (20th, 1952), *My Pal Gus* (20th, 1952), *Thunder Bay* (Univ., 1953), *Forbidden* (Univ., 1953), *Outlaw Territory* (Realart, 1953), *Duffy of San Quentin* (WB, 1954), *The Siege at Red River* (20th, 1954), *Southwest Passage* (UA, 1954), *Three Ring Circus* (Par., 1954), *Day of Triumph* (Geo. J. Schaefer, 1954), *The Warriors* (AA, 1955), *Sincerely Yours* (WB, 1955), *Hell on Frisco Bay* (WB, 1955), *Drango* (UA, 1957), *The Light in the Forest* (BV, 1958), *The Wild and the Innocent* (Univ., 1959), *September Storm* (20th, 1960), *Sylvia* (Par., 1965).

MARGARET DUMONT Born 1889. Married John Moller; widowed. Died March 6, 1965.

Feature Films: *The Cocoanuts* (Par., 1929), *Animal Crackers* (Par., 1930), *Girl Habit* (Par., 1931), *Duck Soup* (Par., 1933), *Kentucky Kernels* (RKO, 1934), *Fifteen Wives* (Invincible, 1934), *Gridiron Flash* (RKO, 1934), *A Night at the Opera* (MGM, 1935), *Orchids to You* (Fox, 1935), *Rendezvous* (MGM, 1935), *The Song and Dance Man* (20th, 1936), *Anything Goes* (Par., 1936), *A Day at the Races* (MGM, 1937), *The Life of the Party* (RKO, 1937), *Youth on Parole* (Rep., 1937), *High Flyers* (RKO, 1937), *Wise Girl* (RKO, 1937), *Dramatic School* (MGM, 1938), *At the Circus* (MGM, 1939), *The Big Store* (MGM, 1941), *For Beauty's Sake* (20th, 1941), *Never Give a Sucker an Even*

Margaret Dumont and Groucho Marx in *The Big Store*.

Break (Univ., 1941), *About Face* (UA, 1942), *Born to Sing* (MGM, 1942), *Sing Your Worries Away* (RKO, 1942), *Rhythm Parade* (Mon., 1942), *The Dancing Masters* (20th, 1943), *Seven Days Ashore* (RKO, 1944), *Up in Arms* (RKO, 1944), *Bathing Beauty* (MGM, 1944), *The Horn Blows at Midnight* (WB, 1945), *Diamond Horseshoe* (20th, 1945), *Sunset in Eldorado* (Rep., 1945), *Little Giant* (Univ., 1946), *Susie Steps Out* (UA, 1946), *Stop, You're Killing Me* (WB, 1951), *Three for Bedroom C* (WB, 1952), *Shake, Rattle and Rock* (AIP, 1956), *Auntie Mame* (WB, 1958), *Zotz!* (Col., 1962), *What a Way to Go!* (20th, 1964).

JAMES DUNN (James Howard Dunn) Born November 2, 1906, New York, New York. Married Edna D'Olier; divorced. Married Frances Gifford; divorced. Married Edna Rush. Died September 3, 1967.

Johnny Hines, James Dunn and Vince Barnett in *The Girl in 419*.

Feature Films: *Bad Girl* (Fox, 1931), *Sob Sister* (Fox, 1931), *Over the Hill* (Fox, 1931), *Dance Team* (Fox, 1932), *Society Girl* (Fox, 1932), *Walking Down Broadway* (Fox, 1932), *Handle With Care* (Fox, 1932), *Sailor's Luck* (Fox, 1933), *Hello Sister* (Fox, 1933), *Hold Me Tight* (Fox, 1933), *Girl in 419* (Par., 1933), *Arizona to Broadway* (Fox, 1933), *Take a Chance* (Par., 1933), *Jimmy and Sally* (Fox, 1933), *Hold That Girl* (Fox, 1934), *Stand Up and Cheer* (Fox, 1934), *Change of Heart* (Fox, 1934), *365 Nights in Hollywood* (Fox, 1934), *Bright Eyes* (Fox, 1934), *George White's Scandals of 1935* (Fox, 1935), *The Daring Young Man* (Fox, 1935), *The Pay-Off* (WB, 1935), *Welcome Home* (Fox, 1935), *Bad Boy* (Fox, 1935), *Don't Get Personal* (Univ., 1936), *Hearts in Bondage* (Rep., 1936), *Two-Fisted Gentleman* (Col., 1936), *Come Closer Folks* (Col., 1936), *Mysterious Crossing* (Univ., 1937), *We Have Our Moments* (Univ., 1937), *Venus Makes Trouble* (Col., 1937), *Living on Love* (RKO, 1937), *Shadows Over Shanghai* (GN, 1938), *Pride of the Navy* (Rep., 1939), *Son of the Navy* (Mon., 1940), *A Fugitive From Justice* (WB, 1940), *Mercy Plane* (PRC, 1940), *Hold That Woman* (PRC, 1940), *The Living Ghost* (Mon., 1942), *The Ghost and the Guest* (PRC, 1943), *Government Girl* (RKO, 1943), *Leave It to the Irish*

(Mon, 1944), *A Tree Grows in Brooklyn* (20th, 1945), *The Caribbean Mystery* (20th, 1945), *That Brennan Girl* (Rep., 1946), *Killer McCoy* (MGM, 1947), *The Golden Gloves Story* (EL, 1950), *A Wonderful Life* (Protestant Film Co., 1951), *The Bramble Bush* (WB, 1960), *Hemingway's Adventures of a Young Man* (20th, 1962), *The Oscar* (Par., 1966).

Irene Dunne and Melvyn Douglas in *Theodora Goes Wild.*

IRENE DUNNE Born December 20, 1904, Louisville, Kentucky. Married Francis Griffin (1928), child: Mary; widowed 1965.

Feature Films: *Leathernecking* (RKO, 1930), *Bachelor Apartment* (RKO, 1931), *Cimarron* (RKO, 1931), *Great Lover* (MGM, 1931), *Consolation Marriage* (RKO, 1931), *Symphony of Six Million* (RKO, 1932), *Thirteen Women* (RKO, 1932), *Back Street* (Univ., 1932), *Secret of Madame Blanche* (MGM, 1933), *No Other Woman* (RKO, 1933), *Silver Cord* (RKO, 1933), *Ann Vickers* (RKO, 1933), *If I Were Free* (RKO, 1933), *This Man Is Mine* (RKO, 1934), *Stingaree* (RKO, 1934), *Age of Innocence* (RKO, 1934), *Roberta* (RKO, 1935), *Sweet Adeline* (WB, 1935), *Magnificent Obsession* (Univ., 1935), *Showboat* (Univ., 1936), *Theodora Goes Wild* (Col., 1936), *High, Wide and Handsome* (Par., 1937), *The Awful Truth* (Col., 1937), *Joy of Living* (RKO, 1938), *Love Affair* (RKO, 1939), *Everything's on Ice* (RKO, 1939), *Invitation to Happiness* (Par., 1939), *When Tomorrow Comes* (Univ., 1939), *My Favorite Wife* (RKO, 1940), *Penny Serenade* (Col., 1941), *Unfinished Business* (Univ., 1941), *Lady in a Jam* (Univ., 1942), *A Guy Named Joe* (MGM, 1943), *The White Cliffs of Dover* (MGM, 1944), *Together Again* (Col., 1944), *Over 21* (Col., 1945), *Anna and the King of Siam* (20th, 1946), *Life With Father* (WB, 1947), *I Remember Mama* (RKO, 1948), *Never a Dull Moment* (RKO, 1950), *The Mudlark* (20th, 1950), *It Grows on Trees* (Univ., 1952).

MILDRED DUNNOCK (Mildred Dorothy Dunnock) Born January 25, 1906, Baltimore, Maryland. Married Keith Urmy (1933), children: Linda, Mary.

Danny Thomas, Mildred Dunnock and Peggy Lee in *The Jazz Singer.*

Feature Films: *The Corn Is Green* (WB, 1945), *Kiss of Death* (20th, 1947), *I Want You* (RKO, 1951), *Death of a Salesman* (Col., 1951), *The Girl in White* (MGM, 1952), *Viva Zapata!* (20th, 1952), *The Jazz Singer* (WB, 1953), *Bad for Each Other* (Col., 1953), *Hansel and Gretel* (voice only; RKO, 1954), *The Trouble With Harry* (Par., 1955), *Love Me Tender* (20th, 1956), *Baby Doll* (WB, 1956), *Peyton Place* (20th, 1957), *The Nun's Story* (WB, 1959), *The Story on Page One* (20th, 1959), *Butterfield 8* (MGM, 1960), *Something Wild* (UA, 1961), *Sweet Bird of Youth* (MGM, 1962), *Behold a Pale Horse* (Col., 1964), *Youngblood Hawke* (WB, 1964), *Seven Women* (MGM, 1965).

DEANNA DURBIN (Edna Mae Durbin) Born December 4, 1921, Winnipeg, Canada. Married Vaughn Paul (1941); divorced 1943. Married Felix Jackson (1945), child: Jessica; divorced 1948. Married Charles David (1950), child: Peter.

Herbert Marshall, Arthur Treacher and Deanna Durbin in *Mad About Music.*

Feature Films: *Three Smart Girls* (Univ., 1936), *100 Men and a Girl* (Univ., 1937), *Mad About Music* (Univ., 1938), *That Certain Age* (Univ., 1938), *Three Smart Girls Grow Up* (Univ., 1939), *First Love* (Univ., 1939), *It's a Date* (Univ., 1940), *Spring Parade* (Univ., 1940), *Nice Girl?* (Univ., 1941), *It Started With Eve* (Univ., 1941), *The Amazing Mrs. Holliday* (Univ., 1943), *Hers to Hold* (Univ., 1943), *His Butler's Sister* (Univ., 1944), *Christmas Holiday* (Univ., 1944), *Can't Help Singing* (Univ., 1944), *Lady on a Train* (Univ., 1945), *Because of Him* (Univ., 1946), *I'll Be Yours* (Univ., 1947), *Something in the Wind* (Univ., 1947), *Up in Central Park* (Univ., 1948), *For the Love of Mary* (Univ., 1948).

DAN DURYEA Born January 23, 1907, White Plains, New York. Married Helen Bryan (1931), children: Peter, Richard; widowed 1967.

Dan Duryea and Deanna Durbin in *Lady on a Train.*

English-Language Feature Films: *The Little Foxes* (RKO, 1941), *Ball of Fire* (RKO, 1941), *The Pride of the Yankees* (RKO, 1942), *That Other Woman* (20th, 1942), *Sahara* (Col., 1943), *None But the Lonely Heart* (RKO, 1944), *Mrs. Parkington* (MGM, 1944), *Ministry of Fear* (Par., 1944), *Woman in the Window* (RKO, 1944), *Valley of Decision* (MGM, 1945), *The Great Flamarion* (Rep., 1945), *Along Came Jones* (RKO, 1945), *Lady on a Train* (Univ., 1945), *Scarlet Street* (Univ., 1945), *Black Angel* (Univ., 1946), *White Tie and Tails* (Univ., 1946), *Black Bart* (Univ., 1948), *Another Part of the Forest* (Univ., 1948), *River Lady* (Univ., 1948), *Larceny* (Univ., 1948), *Criss Cross* (Univ., 1949), *Too Late for Tears* (UA, 1949), *Johnny Stool Pigeon* (Univ., 1949), *Manhandled* (Par., 1949), *One Way Street* (Univ., 1950), *Underworld Story* (UA, 1950), *Winchester '73* (Univ., 1950), *Al Jennings of Oklahoma* (Col., 1951), *Chicago Calling* (UA, 1951), *Thunder Bay* (Univ., 1953), *Sky Commando* (Col., 1953), *World for Ransom* (AA, 1954), *Ride Clear of Diablo* (Univ., 1954), *This Is My Love* (RKO, 1954), *Silver Lode* (RKO, 1954), *Rails into Laramie* (Univ., 1954), *The Marauders* (MGM, 1955), *Foxfire* (Univ., 1955), *Storm Fear* (UA, 1955), *Battle Hymn* (Univ., 1956), *The Burglar* (Col., 1957), *Night Passage* (Univ., 1957), *Slaughter on Tenth Avenue* (Univ., 1957), *Kathy O'* (Univ., 1958), *Platinum High School* (MGM, 1960), *Six Black Horses* (Univ., 1962), *He Rides Tall* (Univ., 1964), *Walk a Tightrope* (Par., 1964), *Taggart* (Univ., 1964), *The Bounty Killer* (Embassy, 1965), *The Flight of the Phoenix* (20th, 1965), *Incident at Phantom Hill* (Univ., 1966), *Operation Bluebook* (Jerry Fairbanks Productions, 1967), *A River of Dollars* (UA, 1967), *The Bamboo Saucer* (Jerry Fairbanks Productions, 1967).

ANN DVORAK (Ann McKim) Born August 2, 1912, New York, New York. Married Leslie Fenton (1932); divorced 1945. Married Igo Dega (1947); divorced 1950.

Ann Dvorak and Richard Barthelmess in *Massacre*.

Feature Films: *The Hollywood Revue of 1929* (MGM, 1929), *Way Out West* (MGM, 1930), *Free and Easy* (MGM, 1930), *The Guardsman* (MGM, 1931), *This Modern Age* (MGM, 1931), *Sky Devils* (UA, 1932), *The Crowd Roars* (WB, 1932), *Scarface* (UA, 1932), *The Strange Love of Molly Louvain* (WB, 1932), *Love Is a Racket* (WB, 1932), *Stranger in Town* (WB, 1932), *Crooner* (WB, 1932), *Three on a Match* (WB, 1932), *The Way to Love* (Par., 1933), *College Coach* (WB, 1933), *Massacre* (WB, 1934), *Heat Lightning* (WB, 1934), *Midnight Alibi* (WB, 1934), *Friends of Mr. Sweeney* (WB, 1934), *Housewife* (WB, 1934), *Side Streets* (WB, 1934), *Gentlemen Are Born* (WB, 1934), *I Sell Anything* (WB, 1934), *Murder in the Clouds* (WB, 1934), *Sweet Music* (WB, 1935), *G-Men* (WB, 1935), *Folies Bergere* (UA, 1935), *Bright Lights* (WB, 1935), *Dr. Socrates* (WB, 1935), *Thanks a Million* (Fox, 1935), *We Who Are About to Die* (RKO, 1936), *Racing Lady* (RKO, 1937), *Midnight Court* (WB, 1937), *She's No Lady* (Par., 1937), *The Case of the Stuttering Bishop* (WB, 1937), *Manhattan Merry-Go-Round*

(Rep., 1937), *Merrily We Live* (MGM, 1938), *Gangs of New York* (Rep., 1938), *Blind Alley* (Col., 1939), *Stronger Than Desire* (MGM, 1939), *Cafe Hostess* (Col., 1940), *Girls of the Road* (Col., 1940), *This Was Paris* (WB, 1942), *Squadron Leader X* (RKO, 1943), *Escape to Danger* (RKO, 1944), *Flame of Barbary Coast* (Rep., 1945), *Masquerade in Mexico* (Par., 1945), *The Bachelor's Daughters* (UA, 1946), *Abilene Town* (UA, 1946), *The Private Affairs of Bel Ami* (UA, 1947), *The Long Night* (RKO, 1947), *Out of the Blue* (EL, 1947), *The Walls of Jericho* (20th, 1948), *A Life of Her Own* (MGM, 1950), *Our Very Own* (RKO, 1950), *The Return of Jesse James* (Lip., 1950), *Mrs. O'Malley and Mr. Malone* (MGM, 1950), *I Was an American Spy* (AA, 1951), *The Secret of Convict Lake* (20th, 1951).

NELSON EDDY Born June 29, 1901, Providence, Rhode Island. Married Anne Franklin (1939). Died March 6, 1967.

Nelson Eddy, Illona Massey and Roland Varno in *Balalaika*.

Feature Films: *Broadway to Hollywood* (MGM, 1933), *Dancing Lady* (MGM, 1933), *Student Tour* (MGM, 1934), *Naughty Marietta* (MGM, 1935), *Rose Marie* (MGM, 1936), *Maytime* (MGM, 1937), *Rosalie* (MGM, 1937), *Girl of the Golden West* (MGM, 1938), *Sweethearts* (MGM, 1938), *Let Freedom Ring* (MGM, 1939), *Balalaika* (MGM, 1939), *New Moon* (MGM, 1940), *Bitter Sweet* (MGM, 1940), *The Chocolate Soldier* (MGM, 1941), *I Married an Angel* (MGM, 1942), *The Phantom of the Opera* (Univ., 1943), *Knickerbocker Holiday* (UA, 1944), *Make Mine Music* (voice only; RKO, 1946), *Northwest Outpost* (Rep., 1947).

SALLY EILERS (Dorothea Sally Eilers) Born December 11, 1908, New York, New York. Married Hoot Gibson (1930); divorced 1933. Married Harry Brown (1933), child: Harry; divorced. Married Howard Barney; divorced. Married John Hollingsworth Morse (1949).

Ward Bond, Sally Eilers and Robert Armstrong in *Without Orders*.

Sound Feature Films: *Cradle Snatchers* (WB, 1928), *Dry Martini* (Fox, 1928), *Broadway Daddies* (Col., 1928), *Good-Bye Kiss* (WB, 1928), *Broadway Babies* (WB, 1929), *Trial Marriage* (WB, 1929), *Show of Shows* (WB, 1929), *The Long, Long Trail* (Univ., 1929), *Sailor's Holiday* (Pathé, 1929), *She Couldn't Say No* (WB, 1930), *Let Us Be Gay* (MGM, 1930), *Roaring Ranch* (Univ., 1930), *Trigger Tricks* (Univ., 1930), *Dough Boys* (MGM, 1930), *Reducing* (MGM, 1931), *Quick Millions* (Fox, 1931), *Clearing the Range* (Capitol Film Exchange, 1931), *Black Camel* (Fox, 1931), *Bad Girl* (Fox, 1931), *Holy Terror* (Fox, 1931), *Over the Hill* (Fox, 1931), *Dance Team* (Fox, 1931), *Disorderly Conduct* (Fox, 1932), *Hat Check Girl* (Fox, 1932), *State Fair* (Fox, 1933), *Second Hand Wife* (Fox, 1933), *Sailor's Luck* (Fox, 1933), *Made on Broadway* (MGM, 1933), *I Spy* (BIP, 1933), *Central Airport* (WB, 1933), *Hold Me Tight* (Fox, 1933), *Walls of Gold* (Fox, 1933), *She Made Her Bed* (Par., 1934), *Three on a Honeymoon* (Fox, (1934), *Morning After* (Majestic, 1934), *Carnival* (Col., 1935), *Alias Mary Dow* (Univ., 1935), *Pursuit* (MGM, 1935), *Remember Last Night?* (Univ., 1935), *Don't Get Personal* (Univ., 1936), *Strike Me Pink* (UA, 1936), *Florida Special* (Par., 1936), *Without Orders* (RKO, 1936), *We Have Our Moments* (Univ., 1937), *Talk of the Devil* (Gaumont-British, 1937), *Danger Patrol* (RKO, 1937), *Lady Behave* (Rep., 1937), *Nurse From Brooklyn* (Univ., 1938), *Everybody's Doing It* (RKO, 1938), *Condemned Women* (RKO, 1938), *Tarnished Angel* (RKO, 1938), *They Made Her a Spy* (RKO, 1939), *Full Confession* (RKO, 1939), *I Was a Prisoner on Devil's Island* (Col., 1941), *A Wave, a Wac and a Marine* (Mon., 1944), *Strange Illusion* (PRC, 1945), *Coroner Creek* (Col., 1948), *Stage to Tucson* (Col., 1950).

LEON ERROL Born July 3, 1881, Sydney, New South Wales, Australia. Married Stella Chatelaine (1906); widowed 1946. Died October 12, 1951.

Leon Errol, ZaSu Pitts and Mitzi Green in *Finn and Hattie.*

Sound Feature Films: *Paramount on Parade* (Par., 1930), *Queen of Scandal* (UA, 1930), *Only Saps Work* (Par., 1930), *One Heavenly Night* (UA, 1930), *Finn and Hattie* (Par., 1931), *Her Majesty Love* (WB, 1931), *Alice in Wonderland* (Par., 1933), *We're Not Dressing* (Par., 1934), *The Notorious Sophie Lang* (Par., 1934), *The Captain Hates the Sea* (Col., 1934), *Princess O'Hara* (Univ., 1935), *Coronado* (Par., 1935), *Make a Wish* (RKO, 1937), *Girl From Mexico* (RKO, 1939), *Dancing Co-ed* (MGM, 1939), *Mexican Spitfire* (RKO, 1939), *Pop Always Pays* (RKO, 1940), *Mexican Spitfire Out West* (RKO, 1940), *The Golden Fleecing* (MGM, 1940), *Six Lessons From Madame La-Zonga* (Univ., 1941), *Where Did You Get That Girl?* (Univ., 1941), *Hurry, Charlie, Hurry* (RKO, 1941), *Mexican Spitfire's Baby* (RKO, 1941), *Moonlight in Hawaii* (Univ., 1941), *Never Give a Sucker an Even Break* (Univ., 1941), *Melody Lane* (Univ., 1941), *Mexican Spitfire at Sea* (RKO, 1942), *Mexican Spitfire Sees a Ghost* (RKO, 1942), *Mexican Spitfire's Elephant* (RKO, 1942), *Strictly in the Groove* (Univ., 1943), *Cowboy in Manhattan* (Univ., 1943), *Follow The Band* (Univ., 1943), *Mexican Spitfire's Blessed Event* (RKO, 1943), *Gals, Inc.* (Univ., 1943), *Higher and Higher* (RKO, 1943), *Hat Check Honey* (Univ., 1944), *Slightly Terrific* (Univ., 1944), *Invisible Man's Revenge* (Univ., 1944), *Twilight on the Prairie* (Univ., 1944), *Babes on Swing Street* (Univ., 1944), *She Gets Her Man* (Univ., 1945), *Under Western Skies* (Univ., 1945), *What a Blonde* (RKO, 1945), *Mama Loves Papa* (RKO, 1945), *Riverboat Rhythm* (RKO, 1946), *Joe Palooka, Champ* (Mon., 1946), *Gentleman Joe Palooka* (Mon., 1946), *Joe Palooka in the Knockout* (Mon., 1947), *Fighting Mad* (Mon., 1948), *The Noose Hangs High* (EL, 1948), *Variety Time* (RKO, 1948), *Joe Palooka in the Big Fight* (Mon., 1949), *Joe Palooka in the Counterpunch* (Mon., 1949), *Joe Palooka in Humphrey Takes a Chance* (Mon., 1950), *Footlight Varieties* (RKO, 1951).

STUART ERWIN Born February 14, 1903, Squaw Valley, California. Married June Collyer (1931), children: Stuart, Judy. Died December 21, 1967.

Helen Kane and Stuart Erwin in *Sweetie.*

Sound Feature Films: *The Trespasser* (UA, 1929), *The Sophomore* (Pathé, 1929), *Speakeasy* (Fox, 1929), *Thru Different Eyes* (Fox, 1929), *Cock-Eyed World* (Fox, 1929), *Dangerous Curves* (Par., 1929), *Sweetie* (Par., 1929), *This Thing Called Love* (Pathé, 1929), *Men Without Women* (Fox, 1930), *Paramount on Parade* (Par., 1930), *Young Eagles* (Par., 1930), *Dangerous Nan McGrew* (Par., 1930), *Love Among the Millionaires* (Par., 1930), *Playboy of Paris* (Par., 1930), *Only Saps Work* (Par., 1930), *Along Came Youth* (Par., 1930), *No Limit* (Par., 1930), *Dude Ranch* (Par., 1931), *Up Pops the Devil* (Par., 1931), *The Magnificent Lie* (Par., 1931), *Working Girls* (Par., 1931), *Two Kinds of Women* (Par., 1932), *Strangers in Love* (Par., 1932), *Misleading Lady* (Par., 1932), *Make Me a Star* (Par., 1932), *Big Broadcast* (Par., 1932), *Face in the Sky* (Fox., 1933), *Crime of the Century* (Par., 1933), *He Learned About Women* (Par., 1933), *Under the Tonto Rim* (Par., 1933), *The Stranger's Return* (Par., 1933), *Hold Your Man* (MGM, 1933), *International House* (Par., 1933), *Before Dawn* (RKO, 1933), *Day of Reckoning* (MGM, 1933), *Going Hollywood* (MGM, 1933), *Palooka* (UA, 1934), *Viva Villa!* (MGM, 1934), *The Party's Over* (Col., 1934), *Bachelor Bait* (RKO, 1934), *Chained* (MGM, 1934), *The Band Plays On* (MGM, 1934), *After Office Hours* (MGM, 1935), *Ceiling Zero* (WB, 1935), *Exclusive Story* (MGM, 1936), *Absolute Quiet* (MGM, 1936), *Women Are Trouble* (MGM, 1936), *All American Chump* (MGM, 1936), *Pigskin Parade* (20th, 1936), *Dance, Charlie, Dance* (WB, 1937), *Small Town Boy* (GN, 1937), *Slim* (WB, 1937), *Second Honeymoon* (20th, 1937), *Checkers* (20th, 1937), *I'll Take Romance* (Col., 1937), *Mr. Boggs Steps Out* (GN, 1938), *Passport Husband* (20th, 1938), *Three Blind Mice* (20th, 1938), *Back Door to Heaven* (Par., 1939), *It Could Happen to You* (20th, 1939), *Hollywood Cavalcade* (20th, 1939), *The Honeymoon's Over* (20th, 1939), *Our Town* (UA, 1940), *When the Daltons Rode* (Univ., 1940), *A Little Bit of Heaven* (Univ., 1940), *Sandy Gets Her Man* (Univ., 1940), *Cracked Nuts* (Univ., 1941), *The Bride Came C.O.D.* (WB, 1941), *The Adventures* of *Martin Eden* (Col., 1942), *Drums of the Congo* (Col., 1942), *Blondie for Victory* (Col., 1942), *He Hired the Boss* (20th, 1943), *Great Mike* (PRC, 1944), *Pillow to Post* (WB, 1945), *Killer Dill* (EL, 1947), *Heading for Heaven* (EL, 1947), *Strike It Rich* (AA, 1948), *Father Is a Bachelor* (Col., 1950), *Main Street to Broadway* (MGM, 1953), *For the Love of Mike* (20th, 1960), *Son of Flubber* (BV, 1964), *The Misadventures of Merlin Jones* (BV, 1964).

DALE EVANS (Frances Octavia Smith) Born October 31, 1912, Uvalde, Texas. Married Thomas Fox, (1928), child: Thomas; widowed 1929. Married Robert Dale Butts; divorced 1945. Married Roy Rogers (1947), children: Robin, John, Mary Little Doe, Marion, Deborah.

Roy Rogers, Forrest Taylor, Dale Evans, John Eldredge and Ken Carson in *Song of Nevada*.

Feature Films: *Orchestra Wives* (20th, 1942), *Girl Trouble* (20th, 1942), *The West Side Kid* (Rep., 1943), *Swing Your Partner* (Rep., 1943), *Hoosier Holiday* (Rep., 1943), *In Old Oklahoma* (Rep., 1943), *Here Comes Elmer* (Rep., 1943), *Casanova in Burlesque* (Rep., 1944), *The Cowboy and the Senorita* (Rep., 1944), *The Yellow Rose of Texas* (Rep., 1944), *Song of Nevada* (Rep., 1944), *San Fernando Valley* (Rep., 1944), *Lights of Old Santa Fe* (Rep., 1944), *Hitchhike to Happiness* (Rep., 1945), *Utah* (Rep., 1945), *The Big Show-Off* (Rep., 1945), *Bells of Rosarita* (Rep., 1945), *The Man From Oklahoma* (Rep., 1945), *Sunset in Eldorado* (Rep., 1945), *Don't Fence Me In* (Rep., 1945), *Along the Navajo Trail* (Rep., 1945), *Song of Arizona* (Rep., 1946), *Rainbow Over Texas* (Rep., 1946), *My Pal Trigger* (Rep., 1946), *Roll On, Texas Moon* (Rep., 1946), *Out California Way* (Rep., 1946), *Under Nevada Skies* (Rep., 1946), *Home in Oklahoma* (Rep., 1946), *Helldorado* (Rep., 1946), *Apache Rose* (Rep., 1947), *Bells of San Angelo* (Rep., 1947), *The Trespasser* (Rep., 1947), *Slippy McGee* (Rep., 1948), *Susanna Pass* (Rep., 1949), *Down Dakota Way* (Rep., 1949), *The Golden Stallion* (Rep., 1949), *Twilight in the Sierras* (Rep., 1950), *Bells of Coronado* (Rep., 1950), *Trigger, Jr.* (Rep., 1950), *South of Caliente* (Rep., 1951), *Pals of the Golden West* (Rep., 1951).

MADGE EVANS Born July 1, 1909, New York, New York. Married Sidney Kingsley (1939).

Sound Feature Films: *Sporting Blood* (MGM, 1931), *Son of India* (MGM, 1931), *Guilty Hands* (MGM, 1931), *Heartbreak* (Fox, 1931), *West of Broadway* (MGM, 1932), *Are You Listening?* (MGM, 1932), *Lovers Courageous* (MGM, 1932), *The Greeks Had a Word for Them* (UA, 1932), *Huddle* (MGM, 1932), *Fast Life* (MGM, 1932), *Hell Below* (MGM, 1933), *Hallelujah, I'm a Bum* (UA, 1933), *Made on Broadway* (MGM, 1933), *Dinner at Eight* (MGM, 1933), *The Nuisance* (MGM, 1933), *Mayor of Hell* (WB, 1933), *Broadway to Hollywood* (MGM, 1933), *Beauty for Sale* (MGM, 1933), *Day of Reckoning* (MGM, 1933), *Fugitive Lovers* (MGM, 1934), *The Show-Off* (MGM, 1934), *Stand Up and Cheer* (Fox, 1934), *Death on the Diamond* (MGM,

Spencer Tracy and Madge Evans in *The Show-off*.

1934), *Grand Canary* (Fox, 1934), *Paris Interlude* (MGM, 1934), *What Every Woman Knows* (MGM, 1934), *Helldorado* (Fox, 1935), *David Copperfield* (MGM, 1935), *Age of Indiscretion* (MGM, 1935), *Transatlantic Tunnel* (Gaumont-British, 1935), *Calm Yourself* (MGM, 1935), *Men Without Names* (Par., 1935), *Moonlight Murder* (MGM, 1936), *Exclusive Story* (MGM, 1936), *Piccadilly Jim* (MGM, 1936), *Pennies From Heaven* (Col., 1936), *Espionage* (MGM, 1937), *The Thirteenth Chair* (MGM, 1937), *Sinners in Paradise* (Univ., 1938), *Army Girl* (Rep., 1938).

DOUGLAS FAIRBANKS, JR. (Douglas Elton Ullman, Jr.) Born December 9, 1909. Married Joan Crawford (1928); divorced 1933. Married Mary Hartford (1939), children: Daphne, Victoria, Melissa.

English-Language Sound Feature Films: *The Forward Pass* (WB, 1929), *The Careless Age* (WB, 1929), *Fast Life* (WB, 1929), *Show of Shows* (WB, 1929), *Party Girl* (Tif., 1930), *Loose Ankles* (WB, 1930), *The Dawn Patrol* (WB, 1930), *Little Accident* (Univ., 1930), *The Way of All Men* (WB, 1930), *Outward Bound* (WB, 1930), *Little Caesar* (WB, 1930), *One Night at Susie's* (WB, 1930), *Chances* (WB, 1931), *I Like Your Nerve* (WB, 1931), *Union Depot* (WB, 1932), *It's Tough to Be Famous* (WB, 1932), *Love Is a Racket* (WB, 1932), *Parachute Jumper* (WB, 1933), *The Narrow Corner* (WB, 1933), *Morning Glory* (RKO, 1933), *Captured* (WB, 1933), *Catherine the Great* (UA, 1934), *Success at Any Price* (RKO, 1934), *Mimi* (Alliance, 1935), *The Amateur Gentleman* (UA, 1936), *Accused* (UA, 1936), *When Thief Meets Thief* (Univ., 1937), *The Prisoner of Zenda* (UA, 1937), *The Joy of Living* (RKO, 1938), *The Rage of Paris* (Univ., 1938), *Having Wonderful Time* (RKO, 1938), *The Young in Heart* (UA, 1938), *Gunga Din* (RKO, 1939), *The Sun Never Sets* (Par., 1939), *Rulers of the Sea* (Par., 1939), *Green Hell* (Univ., 1940), *Safari* (Par., 1940), *Angels Over Broadway* (Col., 1940), *The Corsican Brothers* (UA, 1941), *Sinbad the Sailor* (RKO, 1947), *The Exile* (Univ., 1947), *That Lady In Ermine* (20th, 1948), *The Fighting O'Flynn* (Univ., 1949), *State Secret* (Col., 1950), *Mr. Drake's Duck* (UA, 1951).

Douglas Fairbanks, Jr., Billy Gilbert and Lynne Overman in *Safari*.

Frances Farmer in *Ride a Crooked Mile*.

FRANCES FARMER Born September 19, 1910, Seattle, Washington. Married Leif Erikson (1934); divorced 1942. Married Alfred Lobley, 1954; divorced 1958. Married Leland Mikesell (1958).

Feature Films: *Too Many Parents* (Par., 1936), *Border Flight* (Par., 1936), *Rhythm on the Range* (Par., 1936), *Come and Get It* (UA, 1936), *The Toast of New York* (RKO, 1937), *Exclusive* (Par., 1937), *Ebb Tide* (Par., 1937), *Ride a Crooked Mile* (Par., 1938), *South of Pago Pago* (UA, 1940), *Flowing Gold* (WB, 1940), *World Premiere* (Par., 1941), *Badlands of Dakota* (Univ., 1941), *Among the Living* (Par., 1941), *Son of Fury* (20th, 1942), *The Party Crashers* (Par., 1958).

GLENDA FARRELL Born June 30, 1904, Enid, Oklahoma. Married Thomas Richards, child: Thomas; divorced. Married Henry Ross (1941).

Willard Robertson, Glenda Farrell and Barton MacLane in *Torchy Gets Her Man*.

Feature Films: *Lucky Boy* (Tif., 1929), *Little Caesar* (WB, 1930), *Scandal for Sale* (Univ., 1932), *Life Begins* (WB, 1932), *I Am a Fugitive From a Chain Gang* (WB, 1932), *Three on a Match* (WB, 1932), *The Match King* (WB, 1932), *Grand Slam* (WB, 1933), *Mystery of the Wax Museum* (WB, 1933), *Girl Missing* (WB, 1933), *The Keyhole* (WB, 1933), *Gambling Ship* (Par., 1933), *Lady for a Day* (Col., 1933), *Mary Stevens, M.D.* (WB, 1933), *Bureau of Missing Persons* (WB, 1933), *Havana Widows* (WB, 1933), *Man's Castle* (Col., 1933), *Big Shakedown* (WB, 1934), *I've Got Your Number* (WB, 1934), *Heat Lightning* (WB, 1934), *Hi Nellie* (WB, 1934), *Dark Hazard* (WB, 1934), *Merry Wives of Reno* (WB, 1934), *Personality Kid* (WB, 1934), *Kansas City Princess* (WB, 1934), *Gold Diggers of 1935* (WB, 1935), *The Secret Bride* (WB, 1935), *Traveling Saleslady* (WB, 1935), *Go into Your Dance* (WB, 1935), *In Caliente* (WB, 1935), *We're in the Money*

(WB, 1935), *Little Big Shot* (WB, 1935), *Miss Pacific Fleet* (WB, 1935), *Snowed Under* (WB, 1936), *The Law in Her Hands* (WB, 1936), *Nobody's Fool* (Univ., 1936), *High Tension* (20th, 1936), *Gold Diggers of 1937* (WB, 1936), *Smart Blonde* (WB, 1936), *Here Comes Carter!* (WB, 1936), *Fly-Away Baby* (WB, 1937), *Dance, Charlie, Dance* (WB, 1937), *You Live and Learn* (WB, 1937), *Breakfast for Two* (RKO, 1937), *The Adventurous Blonde* (WB, 1937), *Hollywood Hotel* (WB, 1937), *Blondes at Work* (WB, 1938), *Stolen Heaven* (Par., 1938), *The Road to Reno* (Univ., 1938), *Prison Break* (Univ., 1938), *Torchy Gets Her Man* (WB, 1938), *Exposed* (Univ., 1938), *Torchy Blane in Chinatown* (WB, 1939), *Torchy Runs for Mayor* (WB, 1939), *Johnny Eager* (MGM, 1941), *Twin Beds* (UA, 1942), *The Talk of the Town* (Col., 1942), *A Night for Crime* (PRC, 1942), *Klondike Kate* (Col., 1943), *City Without Men* (Col., 1943), *Ever Since Venus* (Col., 1944), *Heading for Heaven* (EL, 1947), *Mary-Lou* (Col., 1947), *I Love Trouble* (Col., 1947), *Lulu Belle* (Col., 1948), *Apache War Smoke* (MGM, 1952), *Girls in the Night* (Univ., 1953), *Secret of the Incas* (Par., 1954), *Susan Slept Here* (RKO, 1954), *The Girl in the Red Velvet Swing* (20th, 1955), *Middle of the Night* (Col., 1959), *Kissin' Cousins* (MGM, 1964), *The Disorderly Orderly* (Par., 1964).

ALICE FAYE (Alice Jeanne Leppert) Born May 5, 1912, New York, New York. Married Tony Martin (1937); divorced 1940. Married Phil Harris (1941), children: Alice, Phyllis.

Warner Baxter and Alice Faye in *Barricade*.

Feature Films: *George White's Scandals* (Fox, 1934), *Now I'll Tell* (Fox, 1934), *She Learned About Sailors* (Fox, 1934), *365 Nights in Hollywood* (Fox, 1934), *George White's Scandals of 1935* (Fox, 1935), *Every Night at Eight* (Par., 1935), *Music Is Magic* (Fox, 1935), *King of Burlesque* (20th, 1936), *Poor Little Rich Girl* (20th, 1936), *Sing, Baby, Sing* (20th, 1936), *Stowaway* (20th, 1936), *On the Avenue* (20th, 1937), *Wake Up and Live* (20th, 1937), *You Can't Have Everything* (20th, 1937), *You're a Sweetheart* (Univ., 1937), *Sally, Irene and Mary* (20th, 1938), *In Old Chicago* (20th, 1938), *Alexander's Ragtime Band* (20th, 1938), *Tail Spin* (20th, 1939), *Rose of Washington Square* (20th, 1939), *Hollywood Cavalcade* (20th, 1939), *Barricade* (20th, 1939), *Little Old New York* (20th, 1940), *Lillian Russell* (20th, 1940), *Tin Pan Alley* (20th, 1940), *That Night in Rio* (20th, 1941), *The Great American Broadcast* (20th, 1941), *Weekend in Havana* (20th, 1941), *Hello, Frisco, Hello* (20th, 1943), *The Gang's All Here* (20th, 1943), *Four Jills in a Jeep* (20th, 1944),* *Fallen Angel* (20th, 1945), *State Fair* (20th, 1962).

*Unbilled guest appearance

JOSÉ FERRER (José Vincente Ferrery Centron) Born January 8, 1909, Santurce, Puerto Rico. Married Uta Hagen (1938), child: Leticia; divorced 1948. Married Phyllis Hill (1948); divorced 1953. Married Rosemary Clooney (1953), children: Maria, Miguel, Gabriel, Monsita, Raphael.

Gene Tierney and José Ferrer in *Whirlpool*.

Bing Crosby and W. C. Fields in *Mississippi*.

English-Language Feature Films: *Joan of Arc* (RKO, 1948), *Whirlpool* (20th, 1949), *Crisis* (MGM, 1950), *Cyrano de Bergerac* (UA, 1950), *Anything Can Happen* (Par., 1952), *Moulin Rouge* (UA, 1952), *Miss Sadie Thompson* (Col., 1953), *The Caine Mutiny* (Col., 1954), *Deep in My Heart* (MGM, 1954), *The Shrike* (Univ., 1955), *The Cockleshell Heroes* (Col., 1956), *The Great Man* (Univ., 1956), *I Accuse!* (MGM, 1958), *The High Cost of Loving* (MGM, 1958), *Lawrence of Arabia* (Col., 1962), *Nine Hours to Rama* (20th, 1963), *Stop Train 349* (AA, 1964), *The Greatest Story Ever Told* (UA, 1965), *Ship of Fools* (Col., 1965), *Enter Laughing* (Col., 1967), *Cervantes* (AIP, 1968).

BETTY FIELD Born February 8, 1918, Boston, Massachusetts. Married Elmer Rice (1943), children: John, Judith, Paul; divorced 1956. Married Edward Lukas (1956).

Alan Ladd and Betty Field in *The Great Gatsby*.

Feature Films: *What a Life!* (Par., 1939), *Of Mice and Men* (UA, 1940), *Seventeen* (Par., 1940), *Victory* (Par., 1941), *The Shepherd of the Hills* (Par., 1941), *Blues in the Night* (WB, 1941), *Kings Row* (WB, 1942), *Are Husbands Necessary?* (Par., 1942), *Flesh and Fantasy* (Univ., 1943), *The Great Moment* (Par., 1944), *Tomorrow the World* (UA, 1944), *The Southerner* (UA, 1945), *The Great Gatsby* (Par., 1949), *Picnic* (Col., 1955), *Bus Stop* (20th, 1956), *Peyton Place* (20th, 1957), *Hound-Dog Man* (20th, 1959), *Butterfield 8* (MGM, 1960), *Bird Man of Alcatraz* (UA, 1962), *Seven Women* (MGM, 1965), *How to Save a Marriage—and Ruin Your Life* (Col., 1968).

W. C. FIELDS (William Claude Dukinfield) Born February 10, 1879, Philadelphia, Pennsylvania. Married Harriet Hughes (1900), child: William. Died December 25, 1946.

Sound Feature Films: *Her Majesty Love* (WB, 1931), *Million Dollar Legs* (Par., 1932), *If I Had a Million* (Par., 1932), *International House* (Par., 1933), *Tillie and Gus* (Par., 1933), *Alice in Wonderland* (Par., 1933), *Six of a Kind* (Par., 1934), *You're Telling Me* (Par., 1934), *Old-Fashioned Way* (Par., 1934), *Mrs. Wiggs of the Cabbage Patch* (Par., 1934), *It's a Gift* (Par., 1934), *David Copperfield* (MGM, 1935), *Mississippi* (Par., 1935), *The Man on the Flying Trapeze* (Par., 1935), *Poppy* (Par., 1936), *Big Broadcast of 1938* (Par., 1938), *You Can't Cheat an Honest Man* (Univ., 1939), *My Little Chickadee* (Univ., 1940), *The Bank Dick* (Univ., 1940), *Never Give A Sucker an Even Break* (Univ., 1941), *Follow the Boys* (Univ., 1944), *Song of the Open Road* (UA, 1944), *Sensations of 1945* (UA, 1944).

BARRY FITZGERALD (William Joseph Shields) Born March 10, 1888, Dublin, Ireland. Died January 4, 1961.

George Sanders, Barry Fitzgerald and William Henry in *Four Men and a Prayer*.

Feature Films: *Juno and the Paycock* (Bluebeard, 1930), *When Knights Were Bold* (Capital Films, 1936), *The Plough and the Stars* (RKO, 1936), *Ebb Tide* (Par., 1937), *Bringing Up Baby* (RKO, 1938), *Marie Antoinette* (MGM, 1938), *Four Men and a Prayer* (20th, 1938), *The Dawn Patrol* (WB, 1938), *The Saint Strikes Back* (RKO, 1939), *Pacific Liner* (RKO, 1939), *Full Confession* (RKO, 1939), *The Long Voyage Home* (UA, 1940), *San Francisco Docks* (Univ., 1941), *The Sea Wolf* (WB, 1941), *How Green Was My Valley* (20th, 1941), *Tarzan's Secret Treasure* (MGM, 1941), *The Amazing Mrs. Holliday* (Univ., 1943), *Two Tickets to London* (Univ., 1943), *Corvette K-225* (Univ., 1943), *Going My Way* (Par., 1944), *I Love a Soldier* (Par., 1944), *None But the Lonely Heart* (RKO, 1944), *Incendiary Blonde* (Par., 1945), *And Then There Were None* (20th, 1945), *Duffy's Tavern* (Par., 1945), *Stork Club* (Par., 1945), *Two Years Before the Mast* (Par., 1946), *California* (Par., 1946), *Easy Come, Easy Go* (Par., 1947), *Welcome Stranger* (Par., 1947), *Variety Girl* (Par., 1947), *The Sainted Sisters* (Par., 1948), *The Naked City* (Univ., 1948), *Miss Tatlock's Millions* (Par., 1948), *Top o' the Morning* (Par., 1949), *The Story of Seabiscuit* (WB, 1949), *Union Station* (Par., 1950), *Silver City* (Par., 1951), *The Quiet Man* (Rep., 1952), *Tonight's the Night* (AA, 1954), *The Catered Affair* (MGM, 1956), *Rooney* (Rank, 1958), *Broth of a Boy* (Kingsley International, 1959).

Geraldine Fitzgerald and Jeffrey Lynn in *Flight From Destiny*.

GERALDINE FITZGERALD Born November 24, 1914, Dublin, Ireland. Married Edward Lindsay-Hogg (1936), child: Michael; divorced 1946. Married Stuart Scheftel (1946), child: Susan.

Feature Films: *The Turn of the Tide* (Gaumont-British, 1935), *Three Witnesses* (Universal-British, 1935), *Blind Justice* (British, 1935), *Radio Parade of 1935* (BIP, 1935), *Department Store* (RKO, 1935), *Mill on the Floss* (British Lion, 1936), *Wuthering Heights* (UA, 1939), *Dark Victory* (WB, 1939), *A Child Is Born* (WB, 1940), *Till We Meet Again* (WB, 1940), *Flight From Destiny* (WB, 1941), *Shining Victory* (WB, 1941), *The Gay Sisters* (WB, 1942), *Watch on the Rhine* (WB, 1943), *Ladies Courageous* (Univ., 1944), *Wilson* (20th, 1944), *The Strange Affair of Uncle Harry* (Univ., 1945), *Three Strangers* (WB, 1946), *O. S. S.* (Par., 1946), *Nobody Lives Forever* (WB, 1946), *So Evil, My Love* (Par., 1948), *The Late Edwina Black* ("The Obsessed"—UA, 1951), *10 North Frederick* (20th, 1958), *The Fiercest Heart* (20th, 1961), *The Pawnbroker* (Landau, 1965).

RHONDA FLEMING (Marilyn Louis) Born August 10, 1923, Los Angeles, California. Married Tom Lane (1940), child: Kent; divorced 1942. Married Lewis Morrill (1952); divorced 1958. Married Lang Jeffreys (1960); divorced 1962. Married Hall Bartlett (1966).

English-Language Feature Films: *In Old Oklahoma* (Rep., 1943), *Since You Went Away* (UA, 1944), *When Strangers Marry* ("Betrayed"—Mon., 1944), *Spellbound* (UA, 1945), *The Spiral Staircase* (RKO, 1945), *Abilene Town* (UA, 1946), *Adventure Island* (Par., 1947), *Out of the Past* (RKO, 1947), *A Connecticut Yankee in King Arthur's Court* (Par., 1949), *The Great Lover* (Par., 1949), *The Eagle and the Hawk* (Par., 1950), *The Redhead and the Cowboy* (Par., 1950), *Cry Danger* (RKO, 1951), *The Last Outpost* (Par., 1951), *Little Egypt* (Univ., 1951), *Crosswinds* (Par., 1951), *Hong Kong* (Par., 1951), *The Golden Hawk* (Col., 1953), *Tropic Zone* (Par., 1953), *Pony Express* (Par., 1953), *Serpent of the Nile* (Col., 1953), *Inferno* (20th, 1953), *Those Redheads From Seattle* (Par., 1953), *Jivaro* (Par., 1954), *Yankee Pasha* (Univ., 1954), *Tennessee's Partner* (RKO, 1955), *The Killer Is Loose* (UA, 1956), *Slightly Scarlet* (RKO, 1956), *While the City Sleeps* (RKO, 1956), *Odongo* (Col., 1956), *The Buster Keaton Story* (Par., 1957), *Gunfight at the O. K. Corral* (Par., 1957), *Gun Glory* (MGM, 1957), *Bullwhip* (AA, 1958), *Home Before Dark* (WB, 1958), *Alias Jesse*

Fernando Lamas, Rhonda Fleming and Brian Keith in *Jivaro*.

James (UA, 1959), *The Big Circus* (AA, 1959), *The Crowded Sky* (WB, 1960), *The Patsy* (Par., 1964),* *Run for Your Wife* (AA, 1966), *An American Wife* (AA, 1967).

   *Unbilled guest appearance

ERROL FLYNN (Erroll Leslie Flynn) Born June 20, 1909, Hobart, Tasmania. Married Lili Damita (1935), child: Sean; divorced 1943. Married Nora Eddington (1943), children: Deidre, Rory; divorced 1949. Married Patrice Wymore (1950). Died October 14, 1959.

Roman Bohnen, Errol Flynn and Ann Sheridan in *Edge of Darkness*.

Feature Films: *In the Wake of the Bounty* (Australian, 1933), *Murder in Monte Carlo* (WB, 1935), *The Case of the Curious Bride* (WB, 1935), *Don't Bet on Blondes* (WB, 1935), *Captain Blood* (WB, 1935), *I Found Stella Parish* (WB, 1935), *The Charge of the Light Brigade* (WB, 1936), *Green Light* (WB, 1937), *The Prince and the Pauper* (WB, 1937), *Another Dawn* (WB, 1937), *The Perfect Specimen* (WB, 1937), *The Adventures of Robin Hood* (WB, 1938), *Four's a Crowd* (WB, 1938), *The Sisters* (WB, 1938), *The Dawn Patrol* (WB, 1938), *Dodge City* (WB, 1939), *The Private Lives of Elizabeth and Essex* (WB, 1939), *Virginia City* (WB, 1940), *The Sea Hawk* (WB, 1940), *Santa Fe Trail* (WB, 1940), *Footsteps in the Dark* (WB, 1941), *Dive Bomber* (WB, 1941), *They Died With Their Boots On* (WB, 1941), *Desperate Journey* (WB, 1942), *Gentleman Jim* (WB, 1942), *Edge of Darkness* (WB, 1943), *Thank Your Lucky Stars* (WB, 1943), *Uncertain Glory* (WB, 1944), *Objective Burma* (WB, 1945), *San Antonio* (WB, 1945), *Never Say Goodbye* (WB, 1946), *Cry Wolf* (WB, 1947), *Escape Me Never* (WB, 1947), *Silver River* (WB, 1948), *The Adventures of Don Juan* (WB, 1948), *That Forsyte Woman* (MGM, 1949), *Hello God* (William Marshall, 1950), *Montana* (WB, 1950), *Rocky Mountain* (WB, 1950), *Kim* (MGM, 1950), *The Adventures of Captain Fabian* (Rep., 1951), *Mara Maru* (WB, 1952), *Against All Flags* (Univ., 1952), *The Master of Ballantrae* (WB, 1953), *Crossed Swords* (UA, 1953), *Lilacs in the Spring* (Rep., 1955), *The Warriors* (AA, 1955), *King's Rhapsody* (British Lion, 1955), *The Big Boodle* (UA, 1957), *Istanbul* (Univ., 1957), *The Sun Also Rises* (20th, 1957), *Too Much, Too Soon* (WB, 1958), *The Roots of Heaven* (20th, 1958), *Cuban Rebel Girls* (Joseph Brenner Associates, 1959).

NINA FOCH (Nina Consuelo Maud Fock) Born April 20, 1924, Leyden, Holland. Married James Lipton (1954); divorced 1958. Married Dennis Brite (1959); divorced 1963. Married Michael Dewell (1967).

Feature Films: *The Return of the Vampire* (Col., 1943), *Nine Girls* (Col., 1944), *Cry of the Werewolf* (Col., 1944), *She's a Soldier, Too* (Col., 1944), *Shadows in the Night* (Col., 1944), *She's a Sweetheart* (Col., 1944), *Strange Affair* (Col., 1944), *A Song to Remember* (Col., 1945), *I Love a Mystery* (Col., 1945), *Boston Blackie's Rendezvous* (Col., 1945), *My Name Is Julia Ross* (Col., 1945), *Prison Ship* (Col., 1945), *Johnny O'Clock* (Col., 1947), *The Guilt of Janet Ames* (Col., 1947), *The Dark Past* (Col., 1949), *The Undercover Man* (Col., 1949), *Johnny Allegro* (Col., 1949), *St. Benny the Dip* (UA, 1951), *An American*

Otto Kruger and Nina Foch in *Escape in the Fog*.

in Paris (MGM 1951), *Scaramouche* (MGM, 1952), *Young Man With Ideas* (MGM, 1952), *Sombrero* (MGM, 1953), *Fast Company* (MGM, 1953), *Executive Suite* (MGM, 1954), *Four Guns to the Border* (Univ., 1954), *You're Never Too Young* (Par., 1955), *Illegal* (WB, 1955), *The Ten Commandments* (Par., 1956), *Three Brave Men* (20th, 1957), *Cash McCall* (WB, 1959), *Spartacus* (Univ., 1960).

HENRY FONDA (Henry Jaynes Fonda) Born May 16, 1905, Grand Island, Nebraska. Married Margaret Sullavan (1931); divorced 1933. Married Frances Brokaw (1936), children: Jane, Peter; widowed 1950. Married Susan Blanchard (1950), child: Amy; divorced 1956. Married Alfreda Franchetti (1957); divorced 1962. Married Shirlee Adams (1965).

Feature Films: *The Farmer Takes a Wife* (Fox, 1935), *Way Down East* (Fox, 1935), *I Dream Too Much* (RKO, 1935), *Trail of the Lonesome Pine* (Par., 1936), *The Moon's Our Home* (Par., 1936), *Spendthrift* (Par., 1936), *Wings of the Morning* (20th, 1937), *You Only Live Once* (UA, 1937), *Slim* (WB, 1937), *That Certain Woman* (WB, 1937), *I Met My Love Again* (UA, 1938), *Jezebel* (WB, 1938), *Blockade* (UA, 1938), *Spawn of the North* (Par., 1938), *The Mad Miss Manton* (RKO, 1938), *Jesse James* (20th, 1939), *Let Us Live* (Col., 1939), *Story of Alexander Graham Bell* (20th, 1939), *Young Mr. Lincoln* (20th, 1939), *Drums Along the Mohawk* (20th, 1939), *The Grapes of Wrath* (20th, 1940), *Lillian Russell* (20th, 1940), *The Return of Frank James* (20th, 1940), *Chad Hanna* (20th, 1940), *The Lady Eve* (Par., 1941), *Wild Geese Calling* (20th, 1941), *You Belong to Me* (Col., 1941), *The Male Animal* (WB, 1942), *Rings on Her Fingers* (20th, 1942), *The Magnificent Dope* (20th, 1942), *Tales of Manhattan* (20th, 1942), *The Big Street* (RKO, 1942), *The Immortal Sergeant* (20th, 1943), *The Ox-Bow Incident* (20th, 1943), *My Darling Clementine* (20th, 1946), *The Long Night* (RKO, 1947), *The Fugitive* (RKO, 1947), *Daisy Kenyon* (20th, 1947), *On Our Merry Way* (UA, 1948), *Fort Apache* (RKO, 1948),

Henry Fonda and Janet Gaynor in *The Farmer Takes a Wife*.

Jigsaw (UA, 1949), *Mister Roberts* (WB, 1955), *War and Peace* (Par., 1956), *The Wrong Man* (WB, 1957), *12 Angry Men* (UA, 1957), *The Tin Star* (Par., 1957), *Stage Struck* (BV, 1958), *Warlock* (20th., 1959), *The Man Who Understood Women* (20th, 1959), *Advise and Consent* (Col., 1962), *The Longest Day* (20th, 1962), *How the West Was Won* (MGM, 1963), *Spencer's Mountain* (WB, 1963), *The Best Man* (UA, 1964), *Fail Safe* (Col., 1964), *Sex and the Single Girl* (WB, 1964), *The Rounders* (MGM, 1965), *In Harm's Way* (Par., 1965), *The Battle of the Bulge* (WB, 1965), *The Dirty Game* (AIP, 1966), *A Big Hand for the Little Lady* (WB, 1966), *Welcome to Hard Times* (MGM, 1967), *Firecreek* (WB-7 Arts, 1968), *Madigan* (Univ., 1968), *Yours, Mine and Ours* (UA, 1968).

JANE FONDA (Jane Seymour Fonda) Born December 21, 1937, New York, New York. Married Roger Vadim (1965).

Ken Lynch, Jane Fonda, Capucine, Laurence Harvey and Barbara Stanwyck in *Walk on the Wild Side*.

English-Language Feature Films: *Tall Story* (WB, 1960), *Walk on the Wild Side* (Col., 1962), *The Chapman Report* (WB, 1962), *Period of Adjustment* (MGM, 1962), *In the Cool of the Day* (MGM, 1963), *Sunday in New York* (MGM, 1963), *Joy House* (MGM, 1964), *Cat Ballou* (Col., 1965), *The Chase* (Col., 1966), *Any Wednesday* (WB, 1966), *Hurry Sundown* (Par., 1967), *Barefoot in the Park* (Par., 1967), *Barbarella* (Par., 1968).

JOAN FONTAINE (Joan de Beauvoir de Havilland) Born October 22, 1917, Tokyo, Japan. Married Brian Aherne (1939); divorced 1945. Married William Dozier (1946), child: Deborah; divorced 1951. Married Collier Young (1952); divorced 1961. Married Alfred Wright (1964). Child adopted while Miss Fontaine was unmarried: Martita Pareja Calderon.

Feature Films: *No More Ladies* (MGM, 1935), *Quality Street* (RKO, 1937), *You Can't Beat Love* (RKO, 1937), *Music for Madame* (RKO, 1937), *A Damsel in Distress* (RKO, 1937), *A Million to One* (Puritan, 1938), *Maid's Night Out* (RKO, 1938), *Blonde Cheat* (RKO, 1938), *The Man Who Found Himself* (RKO, 1938), *Sky Giant* (RKO, 1938), *The Duke of West Point* (UA, 1938), *Gunga Din* (RKO, 1939), *Man of Conquest* (Rep., 1939), *The Women* (MGM, 1939), *Rebecca* (UA, 1940), *Suspicion* (RKO, 1941), *This Above All* (20th, 1942), *The Constant Nymph* (WB, 1943), *Jane Eyre* (20th, 1944), *Frenchman's Creek* (Par., 1945), *The Affairs of Susan* (Par., 1945), *From This Day Forward* (RKO, 1946), *Ivy* (Univ., 1947), *The Emperor Waltz* (Par., 1948), *Kiss the Blood Off My Hands* (Univ., 1948), *Letter From an Unknown Woman* (Univ., 1948), *You Gotta Stay Happy* (Univ., 1948), *Born to Be Bad* (RKO, 1950), *September Affair* (Par., 1950), *Darling, How Could You!* (Par., 1951), *Something to Live For* (Par., 1952), *Ivanhoe* (MGM, 1952), *Decameron Nights* (RKO, 1953), *Flight to Tangier*

Nino Martini, Joan Fontaine and Lee Patrick in *Music for Madame*.

(Par., 1953), *The Bigamist* (Filmakers, 1953), *Casanova's Big Night* (Par., 1954), *Othello* (UA, 1955),* *Serenade* (WB, 1956), *Beyond a Reasonable Doubt* (RKO, 1956), *Island in the Sun* (20th, 1957), *Until They Sail* (MGM, 1957), *A Certain Smile* (20th, 1958), *Voyage to the Bottom of the Sea* (20th, 1961), *Tender Is the Night* (20th, 1961), *The Devil's Own* (20th, 1967).

*Unbilled guest appearance

GLENN FORD (Gwyllyn Ford) Born May 1, 1916, Quebec, Canada. Married Eleanor Powell (1943), child: Peter; divorced 1959. Married Kathryn Hays (1966).

Feature Films: *Heaven With a Barbed Wire Fence* (20th, 1940), *My Son Is Guilty* (Col., 1940), *Convicted Woman* (Col., 1940), *Men Without Souls* (Col., 1940), *Babies for Sale* (Col., 1940), *Blondie Plays Cupid* (Col., 1940), *Lady in Question* (Col., 1940), *So Ends Our Night* (UA, 1941), *Texas* (Col., 1941), *Go West, Young Lady* (Col., 1941), *The Adventures of Martin Eden* (Col., 1942), *Flight Lieutenant* (Col., 1942), *The Desperadoes* (Col., 1943), *Destroyer* (Col., 1943), *Gilda* (Col., 1946), *A Stolen Life* (WB, 1946), *Framed* (Col., 1947), *The Mating of Millie* (Col., 1948), *The Loves of Carmen* (Col., 1948), *The Return of October* (Col., 1948), *The Man From Colorado* (Col., 1948), *The Undercover Man* (Col., 1949), *Mr. Soft Touch* (Col., 1949), *Lust for Gold* (Col., 1949), *The Doctor and the Girl* (MGM, 1949), *The White Tower* (RKO, 1950), *Convicted* (Col., 1950), *The Redhead and the Cowboy* (Par., 1950), *The Flying Missile* (Col., 1950), *Follow the Sun* (20th, 1951), *The Secret of Convict Lake* (20th, 1951), *The Green Glove* (UA, 1952), *Affair in Trinidad* (Col., 1952), *Young Man With Ideas* (MGM, 1952), *Terror on a Train* (MGM, 1953), *The Man From the Alamo* (Univ., 1953), *Plunder of the Sun* (WB, 1953), *The Big Heat* (Col., 1953), *Appointment in Honduras* (RKO, 1953), *Human Desire* (Col., 1954), *The Americano* (RKO, 1955), *The Violent Men* (Col., 1955), *The Blackboard Jungle* (MGM, 1955), *Interrupted Melody* (MGM, 1955), *Trial* (MGM,

Harry Swoger and Glenn Ford in *Pocketful of Miracles*.

1955), *Ransom* (MGM, 1956), *Jubal* (Col., 1956), *The Fastest Gun Alive* (MGM, 1956), *The Teahouse of the August Moon* (MGM, 1956), *3:10 to Yuma* (Col., 1957), *Don't Go Near the Water* (MGM, 1957), *Cowboy* (Col., 1958), *The Sheepman* (MGM, 1958), *Imitation General* (MGM, 1958), *Torpedo Run* (MGM, 1958), *It Started With a Kiss* (MGM, 1959), *The Gazebo* (MGM, 1959), *Cimarron* (MGM, 1960), *Cry for Happy* (Col., 1961), *Pocketful of Miracles* (UA, 1961), *The Four Horsemen of the Apocalypse* (MGM, 1962), *Experiment in Terror* (Col., 1962), *Love Is a Ball* (UA, 1963), *The Courtship of Eddie's Father* (MGM, 1963), *Advance to the Rear* (MGM, 1964), *Fate Is the Hunter* (20th, 1964), *Dear Heart* (WB, 1964), *The Rounders* (MGM, 1965), *The Money Trap* (MGM, 1966), *Is Paris Burning?* (Par., 1966), *The Rage* (Col., 1967), *The Last Challenge* (MGM, 1967), *A Time for Killing* (Col., 1968), *Evil Gun* (MGM, 1968).

WALLACE FORD (Samuel Jones) Born February 12, 1898, Batton, Lancashire, England. Married Martha Harworth (1922), child: Patricia; widowed 1966. Died 1966.

Feature Films: *Swellhead* (Tif., 1930), *Possessed* (MGM, 1931), *Hypnotized* (World Wide, 1932), *The Beast of the City* (MGM, 1932), *Freaks* (MGM, 1932), *Goodbye Again* (WB, 1933), *Headline Shooter* (RKO, 1933), *Night of Terror* (Col., 1933), *My Woman* (Col., 1933), *She Had to Say Yes* (WB, 1933), *East of Fifth Avenue* (Col., 1933), *Three-Cornered Moon* (Par., 1933), *The Lost Patrol* (RKO, 1934), *A Woman's Man* (Mon., 1934), *Money Means Nothing* (Mon., 1934), *Men in White* (MGM, 1934), *I Hate Women* (Goldsmith, 1934), *The Informer* (RKO, 1935), *The Nut Farm* (Mon., 1935), *The Whole Town's Talking* (Col., 1935), *In Spite of Danger* (Col., 1935), *Man of the Hour* (Col., 1935), *She Couldn't Take It* (Col., 1935), *The Mysterious Mr. Wong* (Mon., 1935), *The Man Who Reclaimed His Head* (Univ., 1935), *Sanders of the River* (UA, 1935), *Get That Man* (Empire, 1935), *Mary Burns—Fugitive* (Par., 1935), *Another Face* (RKO, 1935), *Absolute Quiet* (MGM, 1936), *Two in the Dark* (RKO, 1936), *A Son Comes Home* (Par., 1936), *The Rogues' Tavern* (Puritan, 1936), *Swing It Sailor* (GN, 1937), *Exiled to Shanghai* (Rep., 1937), *Dark Sands* (Record, 1938), *Two Girls on Broadway* (MGM, 1940), *Isle of Destiny* (RKO, 1940), *Scatterbrain* (Rep., 1940), *The Mummy's Hand* (Univ., 1940), *Love, Honor and Oh, Baby!* (Univ., 1940), *Give Us Wings* (Univ., 1940), *A Man Betrayed* (Rep., 1941), *The Roar of the Press* (Mon., 1941), *You're in the Army Now* (WB, 1941), *Blues in the Night* (WB, 1941), *X Marks the Spot* (Rep., 1942), *The Mummy's Tomb* (Univ., 1942), *Shadow of a Doubt* (Univ., 1943), *The Ape Man* (Mon., 1943), *The Marines Come Through* (Astor, 1943), *The Cross of Lorraine* (MGM, 1943), *Secret Command* (Col., 1944), *Machine Gun Mama* (PRC, 1944), *Spellbound* (UA, 1945), *They Were Expendable* (MGM, 1945), *Blood on the Sun* (UA, 1945), *A Guy Could Change* (Rep., 1946), *The Green Years* (MGM, 1946), *Lover Come Back* (Univ., 1946), *Crack-Up* (RKO, 1946), *Black Angel* (Univ., 1946), *Rendezvous With Annie* (Rep., 1946), *Magic Town* (RKO, 1947), *Dead Reckoning* (Col., 1947), *T-Men* (EL, 1947), *Shed No Tears* (EL, 1948), *Coroner Creek* (Col., 1948), *The Man From Texas* (EL, 1948), *Embraceable*

Peter Brocco, John Garfield, Wallace Ford, Guy Thomajan and William Campbell in *The Breaking Point*.

You (WB, 1948), *Belle Starr's Daughter* (20th, 1948), *Red Stallion in the Rockies* (EL, 1949), *The Set-Up* (RKO, 1949), *The Breaking Point* (WB, 1950), *The Furies* (Par., 1950), *Dakota Lil* (20th, 1950), *Harvey* (Univ., 1950), *Painting the Clouds With Sunshine* (WB, 1951), *Warpath* (Par., 1951), *He Ran All the Way* (UA, 1951), *Rodeo* (Mon., 1952), *Flesh and Fury* (Univ., 1952), *The Nebraskan* (Col., 1953), *Destry* (Univ., 1954), *Three Ring Circus* (Par., 1954), *The Man From Laramie* (Col., 1955), *Wichita* (AA, 1955), *The Spoilers* (Univ., 1955), *A Lawless Street* (Col., 1955), *Lucy Gallant* (Par., 1955), *The Rainmaker* (Par., 1956), *Twilight for the Gods* (Univ., 1958), *The Matchmaker* (Par., 1958), *The Last Hurrah* (Col., 1958), *Warlock* (20th, 1959), *Tess of the Storm Country* (20th, 1961), *A Patch of Blue* (MGM, 1965).

PRESTON FOSTER (Preston S. Foster) Born August 24, 1902, Ocean City, New Jersey. Married Gertrude Warren, child: Stephanie; divorced 1946. Married Sheila Darcy (1946).

George E. Stone and Preston Foster in *The Last Mile*.

Feature Films: *Heads Up* (Par., 1930), *Two Seconds* (WB, 1932), *The Last Mile* (World-Wide, 1932), *Life Begins* (WB, 1932), *Doctor X* (WB, 1932), *I Am a Fugitive From a Chain Gang* (WB, 1932), *You Said a Mouthful* (WB, 1932), *The All American* (Univ., 1932), *Ladies They Talk About* (WB, 1933), *Elmer the Great* (WB, 1933), *Corruption* (Imperial, 1933), *The Man Who Dared* (Fox, 1933), *Devil's Mate* (Mon., 1933), *Hoopla* (Fox, 1933), *Sensation Hunters* (Mon., 1933), *Wharf Angel* (Par., 1934), *Heat Lightning* (WB, 1934), *Sleepers East* (Fox, 1934), *The Band Plays On* (MGM, 1934), *Strangers All* (RKO, 1935), *People's Enemy* (RKO, 1935), *The Informer* (RKO, 1935), *The Arizonian* (RKO, 1935), *Last Days of Pompeii* (RKO, 1935), *Annie Oakley* (RKO, 1935), *We're Only Human* (RKO, 1936), *Muss 'Em Up* (RKO, 1936), *Love Before Breakfast* (Univ., 1936), *We Who Are About to Die* (RKO, 1936), *The Plough and the Stars* (RKO, 1936), *Sea Devils* (RKO, 1937), *Outcasts of Poker Flat* (RKO, 1937), *You Can't Beat Love* (RKO, 1937), *First Lady* (WB, 1937), *The Westland Case* (Univ., 1937), *Double Danger* (RKO, 1938), *Everybody's Doing It* (RKO, 1938), *Lady in the Morgue* (Univ., 1938), *Army Girl* (Rep., 1938), *The Last Warning* (Univ., 1938), *Up the River* (20th, 1938), *The Storm* (Univ., 1938), *Submarine Patrol* (20th, 1938), *Society Smugglers* (Univ., 1939), *Chasing Danger* (20th, 1939), *News Is Made at Night* (20th, 1939), *Geronimo* (Par., 1939), *Missing Evidence* (Univ., 1939), *20,000 Men a Year* (20th, 1939), *Cafe Hostess* (Col., 1940), *North West Mounted Police* (Par., 1940), *Moon Over Burma* (Par., 1940), *The Round-up* (Par., 1941), *Unfinished Business* (Univ., 1941), *A Gentleman After Dark* (UA, 1942), *Secret Agent of Japan* (20th, 1942), *Night in New Orleans* (Par., 1942), *Little Tokyo, USA* (20th, 1942), *Thunder Birds*

(20th, 1942), *American Empire* (UA, 1942), *My Friend Flicka* (20th, 1943), *Guadalcanal Diary* (20th, 1943), *Bermuda Mystery* (20th, 1944), *Roger Touhy, Gangster* (20th, 1944), *Thunderhead, Son of Flicka* (20th, 1945), *Abbott and Costello in Hollywood* (MGM, 1945), *Valley of Decision* (MGM, 1945), *Twice Blessed* (MGM, 1945), *Tangier* (Univ., 1946), *The Harvey Girls* (MGM, 1946), *Inside Job* (Univ., 1946), *Strange Triangle* (20th, 1946), *Blonde From Brooklyn* (Col., 1946), *Ramrod* (UA, 1947), *King of the Wild Horses* (Col., 1947), *I Shot Jesse James* (Screen Guild, 1949), *The Big Cat* (EL, 1949), *The Tougher They Come* (Col., 1950), *Tomahawk* (Univ., 1951), *3 Desperate Men* (Lip., 1951), *The Big Gusher* (Col., 1951), *The Big Night* (UA, 1951), *Montana Territory* (Col., 1952), *Kansas City Confidential* (UA, 1952), *Law and Order* (Univ., 1953), *I, The Jury* (UA, 1953), *Destination 60,000* (AA, 1957), *Advance to the Rear* (MGM, 1964), *The Man From Galveston* (WB, 1964), *The Time Travelers* (AIP, 1964), *Chubasco* (WB, 1967), *You've Got to Be Smart* (PRO, 1968).

SUSANNA FOSTER (Susanna DeLee Flanders Larson) Born December 6, 1924, Chicago, Illinois. Married Wilbur Evans (1948), children: Michael, Philip; divorced 1956.

Allan Jones, Lynne Overman and Susanna Foster in *Hard-boiled Canary*.

Feature Films: *The Great Victor Herbert* (Par., 1939), *The Hard-Boiled Canary* (Par., 1941), *Glamour Boy* (Par., 1941), *Star Spangled Rhythm* (Par., 1942), *Top Man* (Univ., 1943), *The Phantom of the Opera* (Univ., 1943), *Follow the Boys* (Univ., 1944), *This Is the Life* (Univ., 1944), *The Climax* (Univ., 1944), *Bowery to Broadway* (Univ., 1944), *Frisco Sal* (Univ., 1945), *That Night With You* (Univ., 1945).

ANNE FRANCIS Born September 16, 1930, Ossining, New York. Married Bamblet Price (1952); divorced 1955. Married Robert Abeloff (1960), child: Jane; divorced 1964.

Adeline de Walt Reynolds and Anne Francis in *Lydia Bailey*.

Feature Films: *Summer Holiday* (MGM, 1948), *Portrait of Jennie* (Selznick, 1948), *So Young, So Bad* (UA, 1950), *The Whistle at Eaton Falls* (Col., 1951), *Elopement* (20th, 1951), *Lydia Bailey* (20th, 1952), *Dreamboat* (20th, 1952), *A Lion Is in the Streets* (WB, 1953), *The Rocket Man* (20th, 1954), *Susan Slept Here* (RKO, 1954), *Rogue Cop* (MGM, 1954), *Bad Day at Black Rock* (MGM, 1954), *Battle Cry* (WB, 1955), *The Blackboard Jungle* (MGM, 1955), *The Scarlet Coat* (MGM, 1955), *Forbidden Planet* (MGM, 1956), *The Rack* (MGM, 1956), *The Great American Pastime* (MGM, 1956), *The Hired Gun* (MGM, 1957), *Don't Go Near the Water* (MGM, 1957), *Girl of the Night* (WB, 1960), *The Crowded Sky* (WB, 1960), *The Satan Bug* (UA, 1965), *Brainstorm* (WB, 1965), *Funny Girl* (Col., 1968), *Star* (20th, 1968).

KAY FRANCIS (Katherine Edwina Gibbs) Born January 13, 1903, Oklahoma City, Oklahoma. Married James Francis (1922); divorced 1925. Married William Gaston (1926); divorced 1928. Married Kenneth MacKenna (1931); divorced 1933.

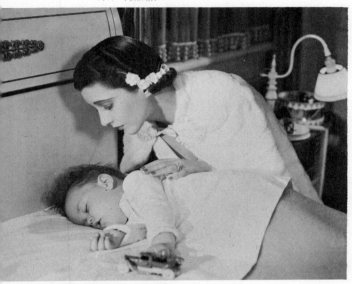

Kay Francis in *Give Me Your Heart.*

Feature Films: *Gentlemen of the Press* (Par., 1929), *The Cocoanuts* (Par., 1929), *Dangerous Curves* (Par., 1929), *Illusion* (Par., 1929), *The Marriage Playground* (Par., 1929), *Behind the Makeup* (Par., 1930), *The Street of Chance* (Par., 1930), *Paramount on Parade* (Par., 1930), *A Notorious Affair* (WB, 1930), *Raffles* (UA, 1930), *For the Defense* (Par., 1930), *Let's Go Native* (Par., 1930), *The Virtuous Sin* (Par., 1930), *Passion Flower* (MGM, 1930), *Scandal Sheet* (Par., 1931), *Ladies' Man* (Par., 1931), *The Vice Squad* (Par., 1931), *Transgression* (RKO, 1931), *Guilty Hands* (MGM, 1931), *24 Hours* (Par., 1931), *Girls About Town* (Par., 1931), *The False Madonna* (Par., 1932), *Strangers in Love* (Par., 1932), *Man Wanted* (WB, 1932), *Street of Women* (WB, 1932), *Jewel Robbery* (WB, 1932), *One Way Passage* (WB, 1932), *Trouble in Paradise* (Par., 1932), *Cynara* (UA, 1932), *The Keyhole* (WB, 1933), *Storm at Daybreak* (MGM, 1933), *Mary Stevens, M. D.* (WB, 1933), *I Loved a Woman* (WB, 1933), *House on 56th Street* (WB, 1933), *Mandalay* (WB, 1934), *Wonder Bar* (WB, 1934), *Doctor Monica* (WB, 1934), *British Agent* (WB, 1934), *Stranded* (WB, 1935), *The Goose and the Gander* (WB, 1935), *I Found Stella Parish* (WB, 1935), *The White Angel* (WB, 1936), *Give Me Your Heart* (WB, 1936), *Stolen Holiday* (WB, 1937), *Confession* (WB, 1937), *Another Dawn* (WB, 1937), *First Lady* (WB, 1937), *Women Are Like That* (WB, 1938), *My Bill* (WB, 1938), *Secrets of an Actress* (WB, 1938), *Comet Over Broadway* (WB, 1938), *King of the Underworld* (WB, 1939), *Women in the Wind* (WB, 1939), *In Name Only* (RKO, 1939), *It's a Date* (Univ., 1940), *Little Men* (RKO, 1940), *When the Daltons Rode* (Univ., 1940), *Play Girl* (RKO, 1940), *The Man Who Lost Himself* (Univ., 1941), *Charley's Aunt* (20th, 1941), *The Feminine Touch* (MGM, 1941), *Always in My Heart* (WB, 1942), *Between Us Girls* (Univ., 1942), *Four Jills in a Jeep* (20th, 1944), *Divorce* (Mon., 1945), *Allotment Wives* (Mon., 1945), *Wife Wanted* (Mon., 1946).

WILLIAM FRAWLEY Born February 26, 1887, Burlington, Iowa. Married 1914; divorced 1927. Died March 3, 1966.

Feature Films: *Moonlight and Pretzels* (Univ., 1933), *Hell and High Water* (Par., 1933), *Crime Doctor* (RKO, 1934), *Miss Fane's Baby Is Stolen* (Par., 1934), *Bolero* (Par., 1934), *The Witching Hour* (Par., 1934), *Shoot the Works* (Par., 1934), *The Lemon Drop Kid* (Par., 1934), *Here Is My Heart* (Par., 1934), *Car 99* (Par., 1935), *Hold 'Em Yale* (Par., 1935), *Alibi Ike* (WB, 1935), *College Scandal* (Par., 1935), *Welcome Home* (Fox, 1935), *Harmony Lane* (Mascot, 1935), *Ship Cafe* (Par., 1935), *Strike Me Pink* (UA, 1936), *F-Man* (Par., 1936), *Desire* (Par., 1936), *The Princess Comes Across* (Par., 1936), *Three Cheers for Love* (Par., 1936), *The General Died at Dawn* (Par., 1936), *Three Married Men* (Par., 1936), *Rose Bowl* (Par., 1936), *Something to Sing About* (GN, 1937), *Double or Nothing* (Par., 1937), *High, Wide and Handsome* (Par., 1937), *Blossoms on Broadway* (Par., 1937), *Mad About Music* (Univ., 1938), *Professor Beware* (Par., 1938), *Sons of the Legion* (Par., 1938), *Touchdown Army* (Par., 1938), *Ambush* (Par., 1939), *Adventures of Huckleberry Finn* (MGM, 1939), *St. Louis Blues* (Par., 1939), *Persons in Hiding* (Par., 1939), *Rose of Washington Square* (20th, 1939), *Ex-Champ* (Univ., 1939), *Grand Jury Secrets* (Par., 1939), *Stop, Look and Love* (20th, 1939), *Night Work* (Par., 1939), *The Farmer's Daughter* (Par., 1940), *Opened By Mistake* (Par., 1940), *Those Were the Days* (Par., 1940), *Untamed* (Par., 1940), *Golden Gloves* (Par., 1940), *Rhythm on the River* (Par., 1940), *The Quarterback* (Par., 1940), *One Night in the Tropics* (Univ., 1940), *Sandy Gets Her Man* (Univ., 1940), *Six Lessons From Madame La Zonga* (Univ., 1941), *Dancing on a Dime* (Par., 1941), *Footsteps in the Dark* (WB, 1941), *Cracked Nuts* (Univ., 1941), *The Bride Came C.O.D.* (WB, 1941), *Blondie in Society* (Col., 1941), *Public Enemies* (Rep., 1941), *Roxie Hart* (20th, 1942), *Treat 'Em Rough* (Univ., 1942), *It Happened in Flatbush* (20th, 1942), *Give Out, Sisters* (Univ., 1942), *Wildcat* (Par., 1942), *Gentleman Jim* (WB, 1942), *Moonlight in Havana* (Univ., 1942), *We've Never Been Licked* (Univ., 1943), *Whistling in Brooklyn* (MGM, 1943), *Larceny With Music* (Univ., 1943), *Fighting Seabees* (Rep., 1944), *Minstrel Man* (PRC, 1944), *Going My Way* (Par., 1944), *Lake Placid Serenade* (Rep., 1944), *Flame of Barbary Coast* (Rep., 1945), *Hitchhike to Happiness* (Rep., 1945), *Lady on a Train* (Univ., 1945), *The Ziegfeld Follies* (MGM, 1946), *The Virginian* (Par., 1946), *Rendezvous With Annie* (Rep., 1946), *The Inner Circle* (Rep., 1946), *The Crime Doctor's Manhunt* (Col., 1946), *Monsieur Verdoux* (UA, 1947), *The Miracle on 34th Street* (20th, 1947), *The Hit Parade of 1947* (Rep., 1947), *I Wonder Who's Kissing Her Now* (20th, 1947), *Mother Wore Tights* (20th, 1947), *Down to Earth* (Col., 1947), *Blondie's Anniversary* (Col., 1947), *My Wild Irish Rose* (WB, 1947), *The Babe Ruth Story* (AA, 1948), *Good Sam* (RKO, 1948), *Texas, Brooklyn and Heaven* (UA, 1948), *Joe Palooka in Winner Take All* (Mon., 1948), *Home in San Antone* (Col., 1949), *The Lady Takes a Sailor* (WB, 1949), *East Side, West Side* (MGM, 1949), *The Lone Wolf and His Lady* (Col., 1949), *Kill the Umpire!* (Col., 1950), *Pretty Baby* (WB, 1950), *Kiss Tomorrow Goodbye* (WB, 1950), *Blondie's Hero* (Col., 1950), *Abbott and Costello Meet the Invisible Man* (Univ., 1951), *The Lemon Drop Kid* (Par., 1951), *Rancho Notorious* (RKO, 1952), *Safe at Home!* (Col., 1962).

George Raft, Frances Drake and William Frawley in *Bolero.*

Scott Brady and Mona Freeman in *I Was a Shoplifter*.

MONA FREEMAN (Monica Freeman) Born June 9, 1926, Baltimore, Maryland. Married Patrick Nerney (1945), child: Mona; divorced 1952. Married Jack Ellis (1961).

Feature Films: *National Velvet* (MGM, 1944) *Our Hearts Were Young and Gay* (Par., 1944), *Till We Meet Again* (Par., 1944), *Here Come the Waves* (Par., 1944), *Together Again* (Col., 1944), *Roughly Speaking* (WB, 1945), *Junior Miss* (20th, 1945), *Danger Signal* (WB, 1945), *Black Beauty* (20th, 1946), *That Brennan Girl* (Rep., 1946), *Our Hearts Were Growing Up* (Par., 1946), *Variety Girl* (Par., 1947), *Dear Ruth* (Par., 1947), *Mother Wore Tights* (20th, 1947), *Isn't It Romantic?* (Par., 1948), *Streets of Laredo* (Par., 1949), *The Heiress* (Par., 1949), *Dear Wife* (Par., 1949), *Branded* (Par., 1950), *Copper Canyon* (Par., 1950), *I Was a Shoplifter* (Univ., 1950), *Dear Brat* (Par., 1951), *Darling, How Could You!* (Par., 1951), *The Lady From Texas* (Univ., 1951), *Flesh and Fury* (Univ., 1952), *Jumping Jacks* (Par., 1952), *The Greatest Show on Earth* (Par., 1952),* *Angel Face* (RKO, 1952), *Thunderbirds* (Rep., 1952), *Battle Cry* (WB, 1955), *The Road to Denver* (Rep., 1955), *The Way Out* (RKO, 1956), *Shadow of Fear* (UA, 1956), *Hold Back the Night* (AA, 1956), *Huk* (UA, 1956), *Dragoon Wells Massacre* (AA, 1957), *The World Was His Jury* (Col., 1958).

*Unbilled guest appearance

CLARK GABLE (William Clark Gable) Born Feb 1, 1901, Cadiz, Ohio. Married Josephine Dillon (1924); divorced 1930. Married Rhea Langham (1930); divorced 1939. Married Carole Lombard (1939); widowed 1942. Married Sylvia Hawkes (1949); divorced 1952. Married Kay Spreckels (1955), child: John. Died November 16, 1960.

Sound Feature Films: *The Painted Desert* (Pathé, 1931), *The Easiest Way* (MGM, 1931), *Dance Fools Dance* (MGM, 1931), *The Secret Six* (MGM, 1931), *Laughing Sinners* (MGM, 1931), *A Free Soul* (MGM, 1931), *Night Nurse* (WB, 1931), *Sporting Blood* (MGM, 1931),

Edgar Buchanan, Frank Morgan and Clark Gable in *Any Number Can Play*.

Susan Lennox—Her Fall and Rise (MGM, 1931), *Possessed* (MGM, 1931), *Hell Divers* (MGM, 1931), *Polly of the Circus* (MGM, 1932), *Strange Interlude* (MGM, 1932), *Red Dust* (MGM, 1932), *No Man of Her Own* (Par., 1932), *The White Sister* (MGM, 1933), *Hold Your Man* (MGM, 1933), *Night Flight* (MGM, 1933), *Dancing Lady* (MGM, 1933), *It Happened One Night* (Col., 1934), *Men in White* (MGM, 1934), *Manhattan Melodrama* (MGM, 1934), *Chained* (MGM, 1934), *Forsaking All Others* (MGM, 1934), *After Office Hours* (MGM, 1935), *Call of the Wild* (UA, 1935), *China Seas* (MGM, 1935), *Mutiny on the Bounty* (MGM, 1935), *Wife vs. Secretary* (MGM, 1936), *San Francisco* (MGM, 1936), *Cain and Mabel* (WB, 1936), *Love on the Run* (MGM, 1936), *Parnell* (MGM, 1937), *Saratoga* (MGM, 1937), *Test Pilot* (MGM, 1938), *Too Hot to Handle* (MGM, 1938), *Idiot's Delight* (MGM, 1939), *Gone With the Wind* (MGM, 1939), *Strange Cargo* (MGM, 1940), *Boom Town* (MGM, 1940), *Comrade X* (MGM, 1940), *They Met in Bombay* (MGM, 1941), *Honky Tonk* (MGM, 1941), *Somewhere I'll Find You* (MGM, 1942), *Adventure* (MGM, 1945), *The Hucksters* (MGM, 1947), *Homecoming* (MGM, 1948), *Command Decision* (MGM, 1948), *Any Number Can Play* (MGM, 1949), *Key to the City* (MGM, 1950), *To Please a Lady* (MGM, 1950), *Across the Wide Missouri* (MGM, 1951), *Callaway Went Thataway* (MGM, 1951), *Lone Star* (MGM, 1952), *Never Let Me Go* (MGM, 1953), *Mogambo* (MGM, 1953), *Betrayed* (MGM, 1954), *Soldier of Fortune* (20th, 1955), *The Tall Men* (20th, 1955), *The King and Four Queens* (UA, 1956), *Band of Angels* (WB, 1957), *Run Silent, Run Deep* (UA, 1958), *Teacher's Pet* (Par., 1958), *But Not for Me* (Par., 1959), *It Started in Naples* (Par., 1960), *The Misfits* (UA, 1961).

GRETA GARBO (Greta Lovisa Gustafsson) Born September 18, 1905, Stockholm, Sweden.

Clark Gable and Greta Garbo in *Susan Lennox, Her Rise and Fall*.

Sound Feature Films: *Anna Christie* (MGM, 1930), *Romance* (MGM, 1930), *Inspiration* (MGM, 1931), *Susan Lennox—Her Fall and Rise* (MGM, 1931), *Mata Hari* (MGM, 1931), *Grand Hotel* (MGM, 1932), *As You Desire Me* (MGM, 1932), *Queen Christina* (MGM, 1933), *The Painted Veil* (MGM, 1934), *Anna Karenina* (MGM, 1935), *Camille* (MGM, 1936), *Conquest* (MGM, 1937), *Ninotchka* (MGM, 1939), *Two-Faced Woman* (MGM, 1941).

REGINALD GARDINER (William Reginald Gardiner) Born February 27, 1903, Wimbelton, Surrey, England. Married Nayda Petrova (1942), children: Robert, Karen, Peter.

Feature Films: *Josser on the River* (British International, 1932), *The Lovelorn Lady* (British International, 1932), *Just Smith* (Gaumont-

Reginald Gardiner and Maureen O'Hara in *Do You Love Me?*

British, 1933), *Leave It to Smith* (Gaumont-British, 1933), *How's Chances?* (Fox, 1934), *Born to Dance* (MGM, 1936), *A Damsel in Distress* (RKO, 1937), *Everybody Sing* (MGM, 1938), *Marie Antoinette* (MGM, 1938), *Sweethearts* (MGM, 1938), *The Girl Downstairs* (MGM, 1939), *The Flying Deuces* (RKO, 1939), *The Night of Nights* (Par., 1939), *The Doctor Takes a Wife* (Col., 1940), *Dulcy* (MGM, 1940), *The Great Dictator* (UA, 1940), *My Life With Caroline* (RKO, 1941), *A Yank in the R. A. F.* (20th, 1941), *Sundown* (UA, 1941), *The Man Who Came to Dinner* (WB, 1941), *Captains of the Clouds* (WB, 1942), *The Immortal Sergeant* (20th, 1943), *Forever and a Day* (RKO, 1943), *Sweet Rosie O'Grady* (20th, 1943), *Claudia* (20th, 1943), *Molly and Me* (20th, 1945), *The Horn Blows at Midnight* (WB, 1945), *Christmas in Connecticut* (WB, 1945), *The Dolly Sisters* (20th, 1945), *Do You Love Me?* (20th, 1946), *Cluny Brown* (20th, 1946), *One More Tomorrow* (WB, 1946), *I Wonder Who's Kissing Her Now* (20th, 1947), *That Wonderful Urge* (20th, 1948), *Fury at Furnace Creek* (20th, 1948), *That Lady in Ermine* (20th, 1948), *Wabash Avenue* (20th, 1950), *Halls of Montezuma* (20th, 1950), *Elopement* (20th, 1951), *Androcles and the Lion* (RKO, 1952), *The Barefoot Contessa* (UA, 1954), *Black Widow* (20th, 1954), *Ain't Misbehavin'* (Univ., 1955), *Around the World in 80 Days* (UA, 1956), *The Birds and the Bees* (Par., 1956), *The Story of Mankind* (WB, 1957), *Rock-a-Bye Baby* (Par., 1958), *Back Street* (Univ., 1961), *Mr. Hobbs Takes a Vacation* (20th, 1962), *What a Way to Go!* (20th, 1964), *Do Not Disturb* (20th, 1965), *Sergeant Deadhead* (AIP, 1965).

AVA GARDNER (Ava Lavinia Gardner) Born December 24, 1922, Grabtown, North Carolina. Married Mickey Rooney (1942); divorced 1943. Married Artie Shaw (1945); divorced 1947. Married Frank Sinatra (1951); divorced 1957.

Feature Films: *We Were Dancing* (MGM, 1942), *Joe Smith, American* (MGM, 1942), *Sunday Punch* (MGM, 1942), *This Time for Keeps* (MGM, 1942), *Calling Dr. Gillespie* (MGM, 1942), *Kid Glove Killer* (MGM, 1942), *Pilot No. 5* (MGM, 1943), *Hitler's Madman* (MGM,

Gregory Peck and Ava Gardner in *The Great Sinner.*

1943), *Ghosts on the Loose* (Mon., 1943), *Reunion in France* (MGM, 1943), *Du Barry Was a Lady* (MGM, 1943), *Young Ideas* (MGM, 1943), *Lost Angel* (MGM, 1943), *Swing Fever* (MGM, 1944), *Music for Millions* (MGM, 1944), *Three Men in White* (MGM, 1944), *Blonde Fever* (MGM, 1944), *Maisie Goes to Reno* (MGM, 1944), *Two Girls and a Sailor* (MGM, 1944), *She Went to the Races* (MGM, 1945), *Whistle Stop* (UA, 1946), *The Killers* (Univ., 1946), *The Hucksters* (MGM, 1947), *Singapore* (Univ., 1947), *One Touch of Venus* (Univ., 1948), *The Great Sinner* (MGM, 1949), *East Side, West Side* (MGM, 1949), *The Bribe* (MGM, 1949), *My Forbidden Past* (RKO, 1951), *Show Boat* (MGM, 1951), *Pandora and the Flying Dutchman* (MGM, 1951), *Lone Star* (MGM, 1952), *The Snows of Kilimanjaro* (20th, 1952), *Ride Vaquero!* (MGM, 1953), *The Band Wagon* (MGM, 1953),* *Mogambo* (MGM, 1953), *Knights of the Round Table* (MGM, 1953), *The Barefoot Contessa* (UA, 1954), *Bhowani Junction* (MGM, 1956), *The Little Hut* (MGM, 1957), *The Sun Also Rises* (20th, 1957), *The Naked Maja* (UA, 1959), *On the Beach* (UA, 1959), *The Angel Wore Red* (MGM, 1960), *55 Days at Peking* (AA, 1963), *Seven Days in May* (Par., 1964), *The Night of the Iguana* (MGM, 1964), *The Bible* (20th, 1966), *Mayerling* (MGM, 1968).

*Unbilled guest appearance

JOHN GARFIELD (Julius Garfinkle) Born March 4, 1912, New York, New York. Married Roberta Mann (1933), children: David, Julie. Died May 20, 1952.

John Garfield and Claude Rains in *Daughters Courageous.*

Feature Films: *Footlight Parade* (WB, 1933), *Four Daughters* (WB, 1938), *They Made Me a Criminal* (WB, 1939), *Blackwell's Island* (WB, 1939), *Juarez* (WB, 1939), *Daughters Courageous* (WB, 1939), *Dust Be My Destiny* (WB, 1939), *Castle on the Hudson* (WB, 1940), *Saturday's Children* (WB, 1940), *Flowing Gold* (WB, 1940), *East of the River* (WB, 1940), *The Sea Wolf* (WB, 1941), *Out of the Fog* (WB, 1941), *Dangerously They Live* (WB, 1942), *Tortilla Flat* (MGM, 1942), *Air Force* (WB, 1943), *The Fallen Sparrow* (RKO, 1943), *Thank Your Lucky Stars* (WB, 1943), *Destination Tokyo* (WB, 1943), *Between Two Worlds* (WB, 1944), *Hollywood Canteen* (WB, 1944), *Pride of the Marines* (WB, 1945), *The Postman Always Rings Twice* (MGM, 1946), *Nobody Lives Forever* (WB, 1946), *Humoresque* (WB, 1946), *Body and Soul* (UA, 1947), *Gentleman's Agreement* (20th, 1947), *Force of Evil* (MGM, 1948), *We Were Strangers* (Col., 1949), *Jigsaw* (UA, 1949),* *Under My Skin* (20th, 1950), *The Breaking Point* (WB, 1950), *He Ran All the Way* (UA, 1951).

*Unbilled guest appearance

JUDY GARLAND (Frances Gumm) Born June 10, 1922, Grand Rapids, Minnesota. Married David Rose (1941); divorced 1943. Married Vincente Minnelli (1945), child: Liza; divorced 1950. Married

113

Gene Kelly and Judy Garland in *The Pirate*.

Sid Luft (1952), children: Lorna, Joseph; divorced 1965. Married Mark Herron (1965); divorced 1967.

Feature Films: *Pigskin Parade* (20th, 1936), *Broadway Melody of 1938* (MGM, 1937), *Thoroughbreds Don't Cry* (MGM, 1937), *Everybody Sing* (MGM, 1938), *Listen Darling* (MGM, 1938), *Love Finds Andy Hardy* (MGM, 1938), *The Wizard of Oz* (MGM, 1939), *Babes in Arms* (MGM, 1939), *Strike Up the Band* (MGM, 1940), *Little Nellie Kelly* (MGM, 1940), *Andy Hardy Meets Debutante* (MGM, 1940), *Ziegfeld Girl* (MGM, 1941), *Life Begins for Andy Hardy* (MGM, 1941), *Babes on Broadway* (MGM, 1941), *For Me and My Gal* (MGM, 1942), *Presenting Lily Mars* (MGM, 1943), *Girl Crazy* (MGM, 1943), *Thousands Cheer* (MGM, 1943), *Meet Me in St. Louis* (MGM, 1944), *The Clock* (MGM, 1945), *The Harvey Girls* (MGM, 1946), *Ziegfeld Follies* (MGM, 1946), *Till the Clouds Roll By* (MGM, 1946), *The Pirate* (MGM, 1948), *Easter Parade* (MGM, 1948), *Words and Music* (MGM, 1948), *In the Good Old Summertime* (MGM, 1949), *Summer Stock* (MGM, 1950), *A Star Is Born* (WB, 1954), *Pepe* (voice only; Col., 1960), *Judgment at Nuremberg* (UA, 1961), *Gay Purr-ee* (voice only; WB, 1962), *A Child Is Waiting* (UA, 1963), *I Could Go On Singing* (UA, 1963).

JAMES GARNER (James Baumgarner) Born April 7, 1928, Norman, Oklahoma. Married Lois Clarke (1956), children: Kimberly, Greta.

Andra Martin and James Garner in *Up Periscope*.

Feature Films: *Toward the Unknown* (WB, 1956), *The Girl He Left Behind* (WB, 1956), *Shoot-Out at Medicine Bend* (WB, 1957), *Sayonara* (WB, 1957), *Darby's Rangers* (WB, 1958), *Up Periscope* (WB, 1959),

Cash McCall (WB, 1959), *The Children's Hour* (UA, 1962), *Boys' Night Out* (MGM, 1962), *The Great Escape* (UA, 1963), *The Thrill of It All* (Univ., 1963), *The Wheeler Dealers* (MGM, 1963), *Move Over, Darling* (20th, 1963), *The Americanization of Emily* (MGM, 1964), *36 Hours* (MGM, 1964), *The Art of Love* (Univ., 1965), *Duel at Diablo* (UA, 1966), *A Man Could Get Killed* (Univ., 1966), *Mister Buddwing* (MGM, 1966), *Grand Prix* (MGM, 1966), *Hour of the Guns* (UA, 1967), *The Jolly Pink Jungle* (Univ., 1968), *How Sweet It Is* (National General, 1968).

PEGGY ANN GARNER Born February 3, 1931, Canton, Ohio. Married Richard Hayes (1951); divorced 1953. Married Albert Salmi (1956), child: Catherine; divorced 1963. Married Kenyon Brown (1964).

Peggy Ann Garner and Lon McCallister in *The Big Cat*.

Feature Films: *Little Miss Thoroughbred* (WB, 1938), *Blondie Brings Up Baby* (Col., 1939), *In Name Only* (RKO, 1939), *Abe Lincoln in Illinois* (RKO, 1940), *The Pied Piper* (20th, 1942), *Eagle Squadron* (Univ., 1942), *Jane Eyre* (20th, 1944), *A Tree Grows in Brooklyn* (20th, 1945), *Keys of the Kingdom* (20th, 1945), *Nob Hill* (20th, 1945), *Junior Miss* (20th, 1945), *Home Sweet Homicide* (20th, 1946), *Daisy Kenyon* (20th, 1947), *Thunder in the Valley* (20th, 1947), *The Sign of the Ram* (Col., 1948), *The Lovable Cheat* (Film Classics, 1949), *Bomba, the Jungle Boy* (Mon., 1949), *The Big Cat* (EL, 1949), *Teresa* (MGM, 1951), *Black Widow* (20th, 1954), *Eight Witnesses* (Vitapix, 1954), *The Black Forest* (Vitapix, 1954), *The Cat* (Embassy, 1967).

BETTY GARRETT Born May 23, 1919, St. Joseph, Missouri. Married Larry Parks (1944), children: Andrew, Gary.

Jack Lemmon and Betty Garrett in *My Sister Eileen*.

Feature Films: *Big City* (MGM, 1948), *Words and Music* (MGM, 1948), *Take Me Out to the Ball Game* (MGM, 1949), *Neptune's Daughter* (MGM, 1949), *On the Town* (MGM, 1949), *My Sister Eileen* (Col., 1955), *The Shadow on the Window* (Col., 1957).

GREER GARSON Born September 29, 1908, County Down, Ireland. Married Edwin Snelson (1933); divorced 1937. Married Richard Ney (1943); divorced 1947. Married Elijah (Buddy) Fogelson (1949).

Greer Garson and Richard Hart in *Desire Me*.

Feature Films: *Goodbye, Mr. Chips* (MGM, 1939), *Remember?* (MGM, 1939), *Pride and Prejudice* (MGM, 1940), *Blossoms in the Dust* (MGM, 1941), *When Ladies Meet* (MGM, 1941), *Mrs. Miniver* (MGM, 1942), *Random Harvest* (MGM, 1942), *The Youngest Profession* (MGM, 1943), *Madame Curie* (MGM, 1943), *Mrs. Parkington* (MGM, 1944), *Valley of Decision* (MGM, 1945), *Adventure* (MGM, 1945), *Desire Me* (MGM, 1947), *Julia Misbehaves* (MGM, 1948), *That Forsyte Woman* (MGM, 1949), *The Miniver Story* (MGM, 1950), *The Law and the Lady* (MGM, 1951), *Julius Caesar* (MGM, 1953), *Scandal at Scourie* (MGM, 1953), *Her Twelve Men* (MGM, 1954), *Strange Lady in Town* (WB, 1955), *Pepe* (Col., 1960), *Sunrise at Campobello* (WB, 1960), *The Singing Nun* (MGM, 1966), *The Happiest Millionaire* (BV, 1967).

JANET GAYNOR (Laura Gainor) Born October 6, 1906, Philadelphia, Pennsylvania. Married Lydell Peck (1929); divorced 1934. Married Gilbert Adrian (1939), child: Robin; widowed 1959. Married Paul Gregory (1964).

Henry Fonda and Janet Gaynor in *Way Down East*.

Sound Feature Films: *Sunny Side Up* (Fox, 1929), *Happy Days* (Fox, 1930), *High Society Blues* (Fox, 1930), *The Man Who Came Back* (Fox, 1930), *Daddy Long Legs* (Fox, 1931), *Merely Mary Ann* (Fox, 1931), *Delicious* (Fox, 1931), *The First Year* (Fox, 1932), *Tess of the Storm Country* (Fox, 1932), *State Fair* (Fox, 1933), *Adorable* (Fox, 1933), *Paddy The Next Best Thing* (Fox, 1933), *Carolina* (Fox, 1934), *Change of Heart* (Fox, 1934), *Servants' Entrance* (Fox, 1934), *One More Spring* (Fox, 1935), *The Farmer Takes a Wife* (Fox, 1935), *Small Town Girl* (MGM, 1936), *Ladies in Love* (20th, 1936), *A Star Is Born* (UA, 1937), *Three Loves Has Nancy* (MGM, 1938), *The Young in Heart* (UA, 1938), *Bernardine* (20th, 1957).

MITZI GAYNOR (Francesca Mitzi Gerber) Born September 4, 1930, Chicago, Illinois. Married Jack Bean (1954).

Mitzi Gaynor and Kirk Douglas in *For Love or Money*.

Feature Films: *My Blue Heaven* (20th, 1950), *Take Care of My Little Girl* (20th, 1951), *Golden Girl* (20th, 1951), *We're Not Married* (20th, 1952), *Bloodhounds of Broadway* (20th, 1952), *The I Don't Care Girl* (20th, 1953), *Down Among the Sheltering Palms* (20th, 1953), *Three Young Texans* (20th, 1954), *There's No Business Like Show Business* (20th, 1954), *Anything Goes* (Par., 1956), *The Birds and the Bees* (Par., 1956), *The Joker Is Wild* (Par., 1957), *Les Girls* (MGM, 1957), *South Pacific* (20th, 1958), *Happy Anniversary* (UA, 1959), *Surprise Package* (Col., 1960), *For Love or Money* (Univ., 1963).

GLADYS GEORGE (Gladys Anna Clare) Born September 13, 1900, Patten, Maine. Married Arthur Erway; divorced 1930. Married Edward Fowler (1933); divorced 1935. Married Leonard Penn (1935); divorced 1944. Married Kenneth Bradley (1946); divorced 1950. Died December 8, 1954.

Sound Feature Films: *Straight Is the Way* (MGM, 1934), *Valiant Is the*

Gladys George and Robert C. Fischer in *The Way of All Flesh*.

Word for Carrie (Par., 1936), *Madame X* (MGM, 1937), *They Gave Him a Gun* (MGM, 1937), *Love Is a Headache* (MGM, 1938), *Marie Antoinette* (MGM, 1938), *I'm From Missouri* (Par., 1939), *Here I Am a Stranger* (20th, 1939), *The Roaring Twenties* (WB, 1939), *A Child Is Born* (WB, 1940), *The House Across the Bay* (UA, 1940), *The Way of All Flesh* (Par., 1940), *Hit the Road* (Univ., 1941), *The Lady From Cheyenne* (Univ., 1941), *The Maltese Falcon* (WB, 1941), *The Hard Way* (WB, 1942), *Nobody's Darling* (Rep., 1943), *The Crystal Ball* (UA, 1943), *Christmas Holiday* (Univ., 1944), *Minstrel Man* (PRC, 1944), *Steppin' in Society* (Rep., 1945), *The Best Years of Our Lives* (RKO, 1946), *Millie's Daughter* (Col., 1947), *Alias a Gentleman* (MGM, 1948), *Flamingo Road* (WB, 1949), *Bright Leaf* (WB, 1950), *Undercover Girl* (Univ., 1950), *Lullaby of Broadway* (WB, 1951), *He Ran All the Way* (UA, 1951), *Silver City* (Par., 1951), *Detective Story* (Par., 1951), *It Happens Every Thursday* (Univ., 1953).

CONNIE GILCHRIST Born July 29, 1901, Brooklyn, New York. Married Edwin O'Hanlon (1928), child: Dorothy.

Connie Gilchrist and Leo Gorcey in *Sunday Punch*.

Feature Films: *Hullabaloo* (MGM, 1940), *Down in San Diego* (MGM, 1941), *Billy the Kid* (MGM, 1941), *Dr. Kildare's Wedding Day* (MGM, 1941), *The Wild Man of Borneo* (MGM, 1941), *A Woman's Face* (MGM, 1941), *H. M. Pulham, Esq.* (MGM, 1941), *Barnacle Bill* (MGM, 1941), *Johnny Eager* (MGM, 1941), *Whistling in the Dark* (MGM, 1941), *Two-Faced Woman* (MGM, 1941), *Married Bachelor* (MGM, 1941), *This Time for Keeps* (MGM, 1942), *Sunday Punch* (MGM, 1942), *Tortilla Flat* (MGM, 1942), *Grand Central Murder* (MGM, 1942), *Apache Trail* (MGM, 1942), *The War Against Mrs. Hadley* (MGM, 1942), *Thousands Cheer* (MGM, 1943), *Presenting Lily Mars* (MGM, 1943), *Swing Shift Maisie* (MGM, 1943), *Cry Havoc* (MGM, 1943), *The Heavenly Body* (MGM, 1943), *The Human Comedy* (MGM, 1943), *Rationing* (MGM, 1944), *See Here, Private Hargrove* (MGM, 1944), *Nothing But Trouble* (MGM, 1944), *Music for Millions* (MGM, 1944), *The Seventh Cross* (MGM, 1944), *The Thin Man Goes Home* (MGM, 1944), *Valley of Decision* (MGM, 1945), *Junior Miss* (20th, 1945), *Cloak and Dagger* (WB, 1946), *Bad Bascomb* (MGM, 1946), *Faithful in My Fashion* (MGM, 1946), *The Hucksters* (MGM, 1947), *Song of the Thin Man* (MGM, 1947), *Good News* (MGM, 1947), *Tenth Avenue Angel* (MGM, 1948), *The Big City* (MGM, 1948), *Luxury Liner* (MGM, 1948), *Act of Violence* (MGM, 1948), *A Letter to Three Wives* (20th, 1948), *Chicken Every Sunday* (20th, 1948), *Little Women* (MGM, 1949), *The Story of Molly X* (Univ., 1949), *Stars in My Crown* (MGM, 1950), *Buccaneer's Girl* (Univ., 1950), *A Ticket to Tomahawk* (20th, 1950), *Louisa* (Univ., 1950), *Peggy* (Univ., 1950), *Undercover Girl* (Univ., 1950), *Tripoli* (Par., 1950), *The Killer That Stalked New York* (Col., 1950), *Here Comes the Groom* (Par., 1951), *Thunder on the Hill* (Univ., 1951), *Chain of Circumstance* (Col., 1951), *One Big Affair* (UA, 1952), *The Half-Breed* (RKO, 1952), *Flesh and Fury* (Univ.,

1952), *Houdini* (Par., 1953), *The Great Diamond Robbery* (MGM, 1953), *It Should Happen to You* (Col., 1954), *Long John Silver* (DCA, 1955), *The Man in the Gray Flannel Suit* (20th, 1956), *Machine Gun Kelly* (AIP, 1958), *Auntie Mame* (WB, 1958), *Some Came Running* (MGM, 1958), *Say One for Me* (20th, 1959), *The Interns* (Col., 1962), *Swingin' Along* (20th, 1962), *A Tiger Walks* (BV, 1964), *The Misadventures of Merlin Jones* (BV, 1964), *A House Is Not a Home* (Embassy, 1964), *Two on a Guillotine* (WB, 1965), *Sylvia* (Par., 1965), *Fluffy* (Univ., 1965), *Tickle Me* (AA, 1965), *The Monkey's Uncle* (BV, 1965).

LILLIAN GISH (Lillian Diana Gish) Born October 14, 1896, Springfield, Ohio.

Lauren Bacall and Lillian Gish in *The Cobweb.*

Sound Feature Films: *One Romantic Night* (UA, 1930), *His Double Life* (Par., 1933), *The Commandos Strike at Dawn* (Col., 1942), *Top Man* (Univ., 1943), *Miss Susie Slagle's* (Par., 1945), *Duel in the Sun* (Selznick, 1946), *Portrait of Jennie* (Selznick, 1948), *The Cobweb* (MGM, 1955), *The Night of the Hunter* (UA, 1955), *Orders to Kill* (United Motion Picture Organization, 1958), *The Unforgiven* (UA, 1960), *Follow Me, Boys* (BV, 1966), *Warning Shot* (Par., 1967), *The Comedians* (MGM, 1967).

JAMES GLEASON Born May 23, 1886, New York, New York. Married Lucille Webster (1905), child: Russell; widowed 1947. Died April 12, 1959.

Feature Films: *The Shannons of Broadway* (Univ., 1929), *The Broadway Melody* (MGM, 1929), *Oh Yeah!* (Pathé, 1930), *Puttin' On the Ritz*

James Gleason, Gertrude Michael and Robert Armstrong in *Search for Beauty.*

116

(UA, 1930), *Swellhead* (Tif., 1930), *Dumbbells in Ermine* (WB, 1930), *Matrimonial Bed* (WB, 1930), *Her Man* (Pathé, 1930), *Big Money* (Pathé, 1930), *It's a Wise Child* (MGM, 1931), *Beyond Victory* (Pathé, 1931), *A Free Soul* (MGM, 1931), *Sweepstakes* (RKO, 1931), *Big Gamble* (Pathé, 1931), *Suicide Fleet* (Pathé, 1931), *Information Kid* (Univ., 1932), *Blondie of the Follies* (MGM, 1932), *Lady and Gent* (Par., 1932), *The Crooked Circle* (Sono Art-World Wide, 1932), *The Penguin Pool Murder* (RKO, 1932), *The All American* (Univ., 1932), *The Devil Is Driving* (Par., 1932), *Fast Companions* (Univ., 1932), *Orders Is Orders* (Gaumont-British, 1933), *Billion Dollar Scandal* (Par., 1933), *Clear All Wires* (MGM, 1933), *Hoopla* (Fox, 1933), *Search for Beauty* (Par., 1934), *Meanest Gal in Town* (RKO, 1934), *Murder on the Blackboard* (RKO, 1934), *West Point of the Air* (MGM, 1935), *Helldorado* (Fox, 1935), *Murder on a Honeymoon* (RKO, 1935), *Hot Tip* (RKO, 1935), *We're Only Human* (RKO, 1936), *The Ex-Mrs. Bradford* (RKO, 1936), *Murder on a Bridal Path* (RKO, 1936), *Yours for the Asking* (Par., 1936), *The Big Game* (RKO, 1936), *Don't Turn 'Em Loose* (RKO, 1936), *The Plot Thickens* (RKO, 1936), *Forty Naughty Girls* (RKO, 1937), *Manhattan Merry-Go-Round* (Rep., 1937), *Army Girl* (Rep., 1938), *The Higgins Family* (Rep., 1938), *My Wife's Relatives* (Rep., 1939), *On Your Toes* (WB, 1939), *Should Husbands Work?* (Rep., 1939), *The Covered Trailer* (Rep., 1939), *Money to Burn* (Rep., 1940), *Grandpa Goes to Town* (Rep., 1940), *Earl of Puddlestone* (Rep., 1940), *Meet John Doe* (WB, 1941), *Affectionately Yours* (WB, 1941), *Here Comes Mr. Jordan* (Col., 1941), *Tanks a Million* (UA, 1941), *Nine Lives Are Not Enough* (WB, 1941), *A Date With the Falcon* (RKO, 1941), *Babes on Broadway* (MGM, 1941), *Tramp, Tramp, Tramp* (Col., 1942), *Hay Foot* (UA, 1942), *My Gal Sal* (20th, 1942), *The Falcon Takes Over* (RKO, 1942), *Footlight Serenade* (20th, 1942), *Tales of Manhattan* (20th, 1942), *Manila Calling* (20th, 1942), *Crash Dive* (20th, 1943), *A Guy Named Joe* (MGM, 1943), *Once Upon a Time* (Col., 1944), *Arsenic and Old Lace* (WB, 1944), *A Tree Grows in Brooklyn* (20th, 1945), *This Man's Navy* (MGM, 1945), *Keys of the Kingdom* (20th, 1944), *The Clock* (MGM, 1945), *Captain Eddie* (20th, 1945), *The Hoodlum Saint* (MGM, 1946), *The Well-Groomed Bride* (Par., 1946), *Home Sweet Homicide* (20th, 1946), *Lady Luck* (RKO, 1946), *The Homestretch* (20th, 1947), *Down to Earth* (Col., 1947), *The Bishop's Wife* (RKO, 1947), *Tycoon* (RKO, 1947), *The Dude Goes West* (AA, 1948), *Smart Woman* (AA, 1948), *The Return of October* (Col., 1948), *When My Baby Smiles at Me* (20th, 1948), *The Life of Riley* (Univ., 1949), *Bad Boy* (AA, 1949), *Take One False Step* (Univ., 1949), *Miss Grant Takes Richmond* (Col., 1950), *Riding High* (Par., 1950), *Key to the City* (MGM, 1950), *The Jackpot* (20th, 1950), *Two Gals and a Guy* (UA, 1951), *Come Fill the Cup* (WB, 1951), *I'll See You in My Dreams* (WB, 1951), *Joe Palooka in Triple Cross* (Mon., 1951), *We're Not Married* (20th, 1952), *The Will Rogers Story* (WB, 1952), *What Price Glory* (20th, 1952), *Forever Female* (Par., 1953), *Suddenly* (UA, 1954), *The Night of the Hunter* (UA, 1955), *The Girl Rush* (Par., 1955), *Star in the Dust* (Univ., 1956), *Spring Reunion* (UA, 1957), *Loving You* (Par., 1957), *Man in the Shadow* (Univ., 1957), *The Female Animal* (Univ., 1958), *Man or Gun* (Rep., 1958), *Once Upon a Horse* (Univ., 1958), *Money, Women and Guns* (Univ., 1958), *Rock-a-Bye Baby* (Par., 1958), *The Last Hurrah* (Col., 1958).

PAULETTE GODDARD (Pauline Levy) Born June 3, 1911, Great Neck, New York. Married Edward James (1932); divorced 1932. Married Charles Chaplin (1936); divorced 1942. Married Burgess Meredith (1944); divorced (1950). Married Erich Maria Remarque (1958).

Feature Films: *The Girl Habit* (Par., 1931), *The Mouthpiece* (WB, 1932), *The Kid From Spain* (UA, 1932), *Modern Times* (UA, 1936), *The Young in Heart* (UA, 1938), *Dramatic School* (MGM, 1938), *The Women* (MGM, 1939), *The Cat and the Canary* (Par., 1939), *The Ghost Breakers* (Par., 1940), *The Great Dictator* (UA, 1940), *North West Mounted Police* (Par., 1940), *Second Chorus* (Par., 1940), *Pot o' Gold* (UA, 1941), *Nothing But the Truth* (Par., 1941), *Hold Back the Dawn* (Par., 1941), *The Lady Has Plans* (Par., 1942), *Reap the Wild Wind* (Par., 1942), *The Forest Rangers* (Par., 1942), *Star Spangled Rhythm* (Par., 1942), *The Crystal Ball* (UA, 1943), *So Proudly We Hail!* (Par., 1943), *Standing Room Only* (Par., 1944), *I Love a Soldier* (Par., 1944), *Duffy's Tavern* (Par., 1945), *Kitty* (Par., 1945), *The Diary of a*

Virginia Grey, Paulette Goddard, Lana Turner, Luise Rainer, Dorothy Granger and Ann Rutherford in *Dramatic School.*

Chambermaid (UA, 1946), *Suddenly It's Spring* (Par., 1947), *Variety Girl* (Par., 1947), *Unconquered* (Par., 1947), *An Ideal Husband* (20th, 1948), *On Our Merry Way* (UA, 1948), *Hazard* (Par., 1948), *Bride of Vengence* (Par., 1949), *Anna Lucasta* (Col., 1949), *The Torch* (EL, 1950), *Babes in Bagdad* (UA, 1952), *Vice Squad* (UA, 1953), *Paris Model* (Col., 1953), *Sins of Jezebel* (Lip., 1953), *Charge of the Lancers* (Col., 1954), *The Unholy Four* (Lip., 1954), *Time of Indifference* (Continental, 1966).

BETTY GRABLE (Elizabeth Grable) Born December 18, 1916, St. Louis, Missouri. Married Jackie Coogan (1937); divorced 1940. Married Harry James (1943), children: Victoria, Jessica; divorced 1965.

Betty Grable and Victor Mature in *Song of the Islands.*

Feature Films: *Let's Go Places* (Fox, 1930), *New Movietone Follies of 1930* (Fox, 1930), *Whoopee* (UA, 1930), *Kiki* (UA, 1931), *Palmy Days* (UA, 1931), *The Greeks Had a Word for Them* (UA, 1932), *The Kid From Spain* (UA, 1932), *Child of Manhattan* (Col., 1933), *Probation* (Chesterfield, 1932), *Hold 'Em Jail* (RKO, 1932), *Cavalcade* (Fox, 1933), *What Price Innocence* (Col., 1933), *Student Tour* (MGM, 1934), *The Gay Divorcee* (RKO, 1934), *The Nitwits* (RKO, 1935), *Old Man Rhythm* (RKO, 1935), *Collegiate* (Par., 1935), *Follow the Fleet* (RKO, 1936), *Pigskin Parade* (20th, 1936), *Don't Turn 'Em Loose* (RKO, 1936), *This Way Please* (Par., 1937), *Thrill of a Lifetime* (Par., 1937), *College Swing* (Par., 1938), *Give Me a Sailor* (Par., 1938), *Campus Confessions* (Par., 1938), *Man About Town* (Par., 1939), *Million Dollar*

Legs (Par., 1939), *The Day the Bookies Wept* (RKO, 1939), *Down Argentine Way* (20th, 1940), *Tin Pan Alley* (20th, 1940), *Moon Over Miami* (20th, 1941), *A Yank in the R.A.F.* (20th, 1941), *I Wake Up Screaming* (20th, 1941), *Footlight Serenade* (20th, 1942), *Song of the Islands* (20th, 1942), *Springtime in the Rockies* (20th, 1942), *Coney Island* (20th, 1943), *Sweet Rosie O'Grady* (20th, 1943), *Four Jills in a Jeep* (20th, 1944), *Pin-Up Girl* (20th, 1944), *Billy Rose's Diamond Horseshoe* (20th, 1945), *The Dolly Sisters* (20th, 1945), *Do You Love Me?* (20th, 1946),* *The Shocking Miss Pilgrim* (20th, 1947), *Mother Wore Tights* (20th, 1947), *That Lady in Ermine* (20th, 1948), *When My Baby Smiles at Me* (20th, 1948), *The Beautiful Blonde From Bashful Bend* (20th, 1949), *Wabash Avenue* (20th, 1950), *My Blue Heaven* (20th, 1950), *Call Me Mister* (20th, 1951), *Meet Me After the Show* (20th, 1951), *The Farmer Takes a Wife* (20th, 1953), *How To Marry a Millionaire* (20th, 1953), *Three for the Show* (Col., 1955), *How to Be Very, Very Popular* (20th, 1955).

*Unbilled guest appearance

GLORIA GRAHAME (Gloria Grahame Hallward) Born November 28, 1925, Los Angeles, California. Married Stanley Clements (1945); divorced 1948. Married Nicholas Ray (1948), child: Timothy; divorced 1952. Married Cy Howard (1954), child: Mariana; divorced 1957. Married Tony Ray (1961).

Humphrey Bogart and Gloria Grahame in *In a Lonely Place.*

Feature Films: *Blonde Fever* (MGM, 1944), *Without Love* (MGM, 1945), *It's a Wonderful Life* (RKO, 1946), *It Happened in Brooklyn* (MGM, 1947), *Merton of the Movies* (MGM, 1947), *Crossfire* (RKO, 1947), *Song of the Thin Man* (MGM, 1947), *A Woman's Secret* (RKO 1949), *Roughshod* (RKO, 1949), *In a Lonely Place* (Col., 1950), *Macao* (RKO, 1952), *The Greatest Show on Earth* (Par., 1952), *Sudden Fear* (RKO, 1952), *The Bad and the Beautiful* (MGM, 1952), *The Glass Wall* (Col., 1953), *Man on a Tightrope* (20th, 1953), *The Big Heat* (Col., 1953), *Prisoners of the Casbah* (Col., 1953), *Human Desire* (Col., 1954), *Naked Alibi* (Univ., 1954), *The Good Die Young* (UA, 1955), *Not as a Stranger* (UA, 1955), *The Cobweb* (MGM, 1955), *Oklahoma!* (Magna, 1955), *The Man Who Never Was* (20th, 1956), *Ride Out for Revenge* (UA, 1958), *Odds Against Tomorrow* (UA, 1959), *Ride Beyond Vengeance* (Col., 1966).

FARLEY GRANGER (Farley Earle Granger) Born July 1, 1925, San Jose, California.

English-Language Feature Films: *The North Star* (RKO, 1943), *The Purple Heart* (20th, 1944), *They Live by Night* (RKO, 1948), *Rope* (WB, 1948), *Enchantment* (RKO, 1948), *Side Street* (MGM, 1949), *Edge of Doom* (RKO, 1950), *Our Very Own* (RKO, 1950), *Strangers on a Train* (WB, 1951), *I Want You* (RKO, 1951), *Behave Yourself* (RKO, 1951), *O. Henry's Full House* (20th, 1952), *Hans Christian Andersen*

Farley Granger and Evelyn Keyes in *Enchantment.*

(RKO, 1952), *The Story of Three Loves* (MGM, 1953), *Small Town Girl* (MGM, 1953), *The Naked Street* (UA, 1955), *The Girl in the Red Velvet Swing* (20th, 1955), *Rogue's Gallery* (Par., 1968).

STEWART GRANGER (James Stewart) Born May 6, 1913, London, England. Married Elspeth March, children: Jamie, Lindsay; divorced 1950. Married Jean Simmons (1950), child: Tracey; divorced 1960. Married Caroline Lecerf (1964).

Jean Simmons and Stewart Granger in *Young Bess.*

English-Language Feature Films: *So This Is London* (20th, 1940), *Convoy* (Ealing, 1940), *Secret Mission* (Hellman, 1941), *Thursday's Child* (Associated British, 1943), *The Lamp Still Burns* (Two Cities, 1943), *The Man in Grey* (Gainsborough, 1943) *Fanny by Gaslight* (Gainsborough, 1944), *Love Story* (Gainsborough, 1944), *Waterloo Road* (Gainsborough, 1945), *Madonna of the Seven Moons* (Rank, 1945), *Caesar and Cleopatra* (UA, 1946), *Caravan* (Gainsborough, 1946), *Magic Bow* (Gainsborough, 1946), *Captain Boycott* (Individual, 1947), *Blanche Fury* (Cineguild, 1947), *Precious Bane* (Soskind, 1947), *Saraband for Dead Lovers* (Ealing, 1948), *Woman Hater* (Rank, 1949), *Adam and Evalyn* (Two Cities, 1950), *King Solomon's Mines* (MGM, 1950), *Soldiers Three* (MGM, 1951), *The Light Touch* (MGM, 1951), *Wild North* (MGM, 1952), *Scaramouche* (MGM, 1952), *The Prisoner of Zenda* (MGM, 1952), *Salome* (Col., 1953), *Young Bess* (MGM, 1953), *All the Brothers Were Valiant* (MGM, 1953), *Beau Brummel* (MGM, 1954), *Green Fire* (MGM, 1954), *Moonfleet* (MGM, 1955), *Footsteps in the Fog* (Col., 1955), *Bhowani Junction* (MGM, 1956), *The Last Hunt* (MGM, 1956), *The Little Hut* (MGM, 1957), *Gun Glory* (MGM, 1957), *North to Alaska* (20th, 1960), *The Secret Partner*

(MGM,, 1961), *Swordsman of Siena* (MGM, 1963), *Sodom and Gomorrah* (20th, 1963), *The Secret Invasion* (UA, 1964), *Commando* (AIP, 1964), *Crooked Road* (7 Arts, 1965), *Mission to Hong Kong* (Woolner, 1967), *The Last Safari* (Par., 1967), *Red Dragon* (Woolner, 1967), *The Trygon Factor* (7 Arts, 1967), *The Flaming Frontier* (WB-7 Arts, 1968).

CARY GRANT (Alexander Archibald Leach) Born January 18, 1904, Bristol, England. Married Virginia Cherrill (1933); divorced 1935. Married Barbara Hutton (1942); divorced (1945). Married Betsy Drake (1949); divorced. Married Dyan Cannon (1965), child: Jennifer; divorced 1968.

Sig Rumann, Allyn Joslyn, Jean Arthur, Noah Beery, Jr., and Cary Grant in *Only Angels Have Wings*.

Feature Films: *This Is the Night* (Par., 1932), *Sinners in the Sun* (Par., 1932), *Merrily We Go to Hell* (Par., 1932), *Devil and the Deep* (Par., 1932), *Blonde Venus* (Par., 1932), *Hot Saturday* (Par., 1932), *Madame Butterfly* (Par., 1932), *She Done Him Wrong* (Par., 1933), *Woman Accused* (Par., 1933), *The Eagle and the Hawk* (Par., 1933), *Gambling Ship* (Par., 1933), *I'm No Angel* (Par., 1933), *Alice in Wonderland* (Par., 1933), *Thirty-Day Princess* (Par., 1934), *Born to Be Bad* (UA, 1934), *Kiss and Make Up* (Par., 1934), *Ladies Should Listen* (Par., 1934), *Enter Madame* (Par., 1934), *Wings in the Dark* (Par., 1935), *Last Outpost* (Par., 1935), *Sylvia Scarlett* (RKO, 1935), *Big Brown Eyes* (Par., 1936), *Suzy* (MGM, 1936), *Wedding Present* (Par., 1936), *Amazing Quest* (GN, 1936), *When You're in Love* (Col., 1937), *Toast of New York* (RKO, 1937), *Topper* (MGM, 1937), *The Awful Truth* (Col., 1937), *Bringing Up Baby* (RKO, 1938), *Holiday* (Col., 1938), *Gunga Din* (RKO, 1939), *Only Angels Have Wings* (Col., 1939), *In Name Only* (RKO, 1939), *His Girl Friday* (Col., 1940), *My Favorite Wife* (RKO, 1940), *The Howards of Virginia* (Col., 1940), *The Philadelphia Story* (MGM, 1940), *Penny Serenade* (Col., 1941), *Suspicion* (RKO, 1941), *Talk of the Town* (Col., 1942), *Once Upon a Honeymoon* (RKO, 1942), *Mr. Lucky* (RKO, 1943), *Destination Tokyo* (WB, 1943), *Once Upon a Time* (Col., 1944), *Arsenic and Old Lace* (WB, 1944) *None But the Lonely Heart* (RKO, 1944), *Night and Day* (WB, 1946), *Without Reservations* (RKO, 1946),* *Notorious* (RKO, 1946), *The Bachelor and the Bobby-Soxer* (RKO, 1947), *The Bishop's Wife* (RKO, 1947), *Mr. Blandings Builds His Dream House* (RKO, 1948), *Every Girl Should Be Married* (RKO, 1948), *I Was a Male War Bride* (20th, 1949), *Crisis* (MGM, 1950), *People Will Talk* (20th, 1951), *Room for One More* (WB, 1952), *Monkey Business* (20th, 1952), *Dream Wife* (MGM, 1953), *To Catch a Thief* (Par., 1955), *The Pride and the Passion* (UA, 1957), *An Affair to Remember* (20th, 1957), *Kiss Them for Me* (20th, 1957), *Indiscreet* (WB, 1958), *Houseboat* (Par., 1958), *North by Northwest* (MGM, 1959), *Operation Petticoat* (Univ., 1959), *The Grass Is Greener* (Univ., 1960), *That Touch of Mink* (Univ., 1962), *Charade* (Univ., 1963), *Father Goose* (Univ., 1964), *Walk, Don't Run* (Col., 1966).

*Unbilled guest appearance

Kay Johnson, Claude Rains and Bonita Granville in *White Banners*.

BONITA GRANVILLE Born February 2, 1923, New York, New York. Married Jack Wrather (1947), children: Molly, Jack, Linda, Christopher.

Feature Films: *Westward Passage* (RKO, 1932), *Silver Dollar* (WB, 1932), *Cavalcade* (Fox, 1933), *Cradle Song* (Par., 1933), *Life of Virgie Winters* (RKO, 1934), *A Wicked Woman* (MGM, 1934), *Ah, Wilderness* (MGM, 1935), *These Three* (UA, 1936), *Song of the Saddle* (WB, 1936), *The Plough and the Stars* (RKO, 1936), *The Garden of Allah* (UA, 1936), *Maid of Salem* (Par., 1937), *Call It a Day* (WB, 1937), *Quality Street* (RKO, 1937), *The Life of Emile Zola* (WB, 1937), *It's Love I'm After* (WB, 1937), *Merrily We Live* (MGM, 1938), *Beloved Brat* (WB, 1938), *White Banners* (WB, 1938), *My Bill* (WB, 1938), *Hard to Get* (WB, 1938), *Nancy Drew, Detective* (WB, 1938), *Angels Wash Their Faces* (WB, 1939), *Nancy Drew, Reporter* (WB, 1939), *Nancy Drew, Troubleshooter* (WB, 1939), *Nancy Drew and the Hidden Staircase* (WB, 1939), *Forty Little Mothers* (MGM, 1940), *Those Were the Days* (Par., 1940), *The Mortal Storm* (MGM, 1940), *Third Finger, Left Hand* (MGM, 1940), *Escape* (MGM, 1940), *Gallant Sons* (MGM, 1940), *The People vs. Dr. Kildare* (MGM, 1941), *Wild Man of Borneo* (MGM, 1941), *Down in San Diego* (MGM, 1941), *H. M. Pulham, Esq.* (MGM, 1941), *Syncopation* (RKO, 1942), *The Glass Key* (Par., 1942), *Now, Voyager* (WB, 1942), *Seven Miles From Alcatraz* (RKO, 1943), *Hitler's Children* (RKO, 1943), *Song of the Open Road* (UA, 1944), *Andy Hardy's Blonde Trouble* (MGM, 1944), *Youth Runs Wild* (RKO, 1944), *The Beautiful Cheat* (Univ., 1945), *Senorita From the West* (Univ., 1945), *The Truth About Murder* (RKO, 1946), *Breakfast in Hollywood* (UA, 1946), *Suspense* (Mon., 1946), *Love Laughs at Andy Hardy* (MGM, 1946), *The Guilty* (Mon., 1947), *Strike It Rich* (AA, 1948), *Guilty of Treason* (EL, 1950), *The Lone Ranger* (WB, 1956).

KATHRYN GRAYSON (Zelma Kathryn Hedrick) Born February 9, 1922, Winston Salem, North Carolina. Married John Shelton (1940); divorced 1946. Married Johnny Johnston (1947), child: Patricia; divorced 1951.

Kathryn Grayson and Theresa Harris in *Grounds for Marriage*.

Feature Films: *Andy Hardy's Private Secretary* (MGM, 1941), *The Vanishing Virginian* (MGM, 1941), *Rio Rita* (MGM, 1942), *Seven Sweethearts* (MGM, 1942), *Thousands Cheer* (MGM, 1943), *Anchors Aweigh* (MGM, 1945), *Two Sisters From Boston* (MGM, 1946), *Ziegfeld Follies of 1946* (MGM, 1946), *Till the Clouds Roll By* (MGM, 1946), *It Happened in Brooklyn* (MGM, 1947), *The Kissing Bandit* (MGM, 1948), *That Midnight Kiss* (MGM, 1949), *Toast of New Orleans* (MGM, 1950), *Grounds for Marriage* (MGM, 1950), *Show Boat* (MGM, 1951), *Lovely to Look At* (MGM, 1952), *The Desert Song* (WB, 1953), *So This Is Love* (WB, 1953), *Kiss Me, Kate!* (MGM, 1953), *The Vagabond King* (Par., 1956).

CHARLOTTE GREENWOOD (Frances Charlotte Greenwood) Born June 25, 1893, Philadelphia, Pennsylvania. Married Martin Broones (1924).

Harry Stubbs (with girl on back), Charlotte Greenwood, Reginald Denny and Leila Hyams in *Stepping Out.*

Sound Feature Films: *Baby Mine* (MGM, 1928), *So Long, Letty* (WB, 1929), *Parlor, Bedroom and Bath* (MGM, 1931), *Stepping Out* (MGM, 1931), *The Man in Possession* (MGM, 1931), *Palmy Days* (UA, 1931), *Flying High* (MGM, 1931), *Cheaters at Play* (Fox, 1932), *Orders Is Orders* (Gaumont-British, 1933), *Star Dust* (20th, 1940), *Young People* (20th, 1940), *Down Argentine Way* (20th, 1940), *Tall, Dark and Handsome* (20th, 1941), *Moon Over Miami* (20th, 1941), *The Perfect Snob* (20th, 1941), *Springtime in the Rockies* (20th, 1942), *Dixie Dugan* (20th, 1943), *The Gang's All Here* (20th, 1943), *Up in Mabel's Room* (UA, 1944), *Home in Indiana* (20th, 1944), *Wake Up and Dream* (20th, 1946), *Driftwood* (Rep., 1947), *The Great Dan Patch* (UA, 1949), *Oh, You Beautiful Doll* (20th, 1949), *Peggy* (Univ., 1950), *Dangerous When Wet* (MGM, 1953), *Oklahoma!* (Magna, 1955), *Glory* (RKO, 1956), *The Opposite Sex* (MGM, 1956).

JANE GREER (Bettyjane Greer) Born September 9, 1924, Washington, D.C. Married Rudy Vallee (1943); divorced 1945. Married Edward Lasker (1947), children: Albert, Lawrence, Stephen.

Feature Films:
  as **Bettejane Greer** *Pan Americana* (RKO, 1945), *Two O'Clock Courage* (RKO, 1945), *George White's Scandals* (RKO, 1945).
  as **Jane Greer** *Dick Tracy* (RKO, 1945), *The Falcon's Alibi* (RKO, 1946), *The Bamboo Blonde* (RKO, 1946), *Sunset Pass* (RKO, 1946), *Sinbad the Sailor* (RKO, 1947), *They Won't Believe Me* (RKO, 1947), *Out of the Past* (RKO, 1947), *Station West* (RKO, 1948), *The Big Steal* (RKO, 1949), *You're in the Navy Now* (20th, 1951), *The Company She Keeps* (RKO, 1951), *The Prisoner of Zenda* (MGM, 1952), *Desperate Search* (MGM, 1952), *You for Me* (MGM, 1952), *The Clown* (MGM, 1953), *Down Among the Sheltering Palms* (20th, 1953), *Run*

Jane Greer and Robert Young in *They Won't Believe Me.*

for the Sun (UA, 1956), *Man of a Thousand Faces* (Univ., 1957), *Where Love Has Gone* (Par., 1964), *Billie* (UA, 1965).

VIRGINIA GREY Born March 22, 1917, Los Angeles, California.

Sound Feature Films: *Misbehaving Ladies* (WB, 1931), *Secrets* (UA, 1933), *The St. Louis Kid* (WB, 1934), *Dames* (WB, 1934), *The Firebird* (WB, 1934), *She Gets Her Man* (Univ., 1935), *Gold Diggers of 1935* (WB, 1935), *Old Hutch* (MGM, 1936), *Secret Alley* (20th, 1936), *The Great Ziegfeld* (MGM, 1936), *Bad Guy* (MGM, 1937), *Rosalie* (MGM, 1937), *Test Pilot* (MGM, 1938), *Rich Man, Poor Girl* (MGM, 1938), *Ladies in Distress* (Rep., 1938), *Youth Takes a Fling* (Univ., 1938), *Dramatic School* (MGM, 1938), *Shopworn Angel* (MGM, 1938), *Idiot's Delight* (MGM, 1939), *Broadway Serenade* (MGM, 1939), *The Hardys Ride High* (MGM, 1939), *Thunder Afloat* (MGM, 1939), *Another Thin Man* (MGM, 1939), *The Women* (MGM, 1939), *Three Cheers for the Irish* (WB, 1940), *The Captain Is a Lady* (MGM, 1940), *Hullabaloo* (MGM, 1940), *The Golden Fleecing* (MGM, 1940), *Keeping Company* (MGM, 1941), *Blonde Inspiration* (MGM, 1941), *Washington Melodrama* (MGM, 1941), *The Big Store* (MGM, 1941), *Whistling in the Dark* (MGM, 1941), *Mr. and Mrs. North* (MGM, 1941), *Tarzan's New York Adventure* (MGM, 1942), *Grand Central Murder* (MGM, 1942), *Tish* (MGM, 1942), *Bells of Capistrano* (Rep., 1942), *Secrets of the Underground* (Rep., 1943), *Idaho* (Rep., 1943), *Stage Door Canteen* (UA, 1943), *Sweet Rosie O'Grady* (20th, 1943), *Strangers in the Night* (Rep., 1944), *Grissly's Millions* (Rep., 1945), *Flame of Barbary Coast*

Frank Morgan, Donald Meek, Dan Dailey and Virginia Grey in *Hullabaloo.*

(Rep., 1945), *Blonde Ransom* (Univ., 1945), *The Men in Her Diary* (Univ., 1945), *Smooth as Silk* (Univ., 1946), *Swamp Fire* (Par., 1946), *House of Horrors* (Univ., 1946), *Wyoming* (Rep., 1947), *Unconquered* (Par., 1947), *Who Killed "Doc" Robbin?* (UA, 1948), *Glamour Girl* (Col., 1948), *So This Is New York* (UA, 1948), *Unknown Island* (Film Classics, 1948), *Miraculous Journey* (Film Classics, 1948), *Mexican Hayride* (Univ., 1948), *When My Baby Smiles at Me* (20th, 1948), *Leather Gloves* (Col., 1948), *Jungle Jim* (Col., 1949), *The Threat* (RKO, 1949), *Highway 301* (WB, 1950), *The Bullfighter and the Lady* (Rep., 1951), *Three Desperate Men* (Lip., 1951), *Slaughter Trail* (RKO, 1951), *Desert Pursuit* (Mon., 1952), *The Fighting Lawman* (AA, 1953), *A Perilous Journey* (Rep., 1953), *Captain Scarface* (Astor, 1953), *Hurricane at Pilgrim Hill* (Howco, 1953), *The Forty-Niners* (AA, 1954), *Target Earth* (AA, 1954), *The Eternal Sea* (Rep., 1955), *The Last Command* (Rep., 1955), *All That Heaven Allows* (Univ., 1955), *The Rose Tattoo* (Par., 1955), *Accused of Murder* (Rep., 1956), *Crime of Passion* (UA, 1957), *Jeanne Eagles* (Col., 1957), *The Restless Years* (Univ., 1958), *No Name on the Bullet* (Univ., 1959), *Portrait in Black* (Univ., 1960), *Tammy, Tell Me True* (Univ., 1961), *Flower Drum Song* (Univ., 1961), *Back Street* (Univ., 1961), *Bachelor in Paradise* (MGM, 1961), *Black Zoo* (AA, 1963), *The Naked Kiss* (AA, 1964), *Love Has Many Faces* (Col., 1965), *Madame X* (Univ., 1966), *Rosie!* (Univ., 1968).

EDMUND GWENN Born September 26, 1875, Glamorgan, Wales. Married Minnie Terry (1901). Died September 6, 1959.

Patricia Neal and Edmund Gwenn in *Something for the Birds.*

English-Language Sound Feature Films: *How He Lied to Her Husband* (British International, 1931), *Money for Nothing* (British International, 1932), *Condemned to Death* (Timely, 1931), *Frail Women* (British, 1931), *Hindle Wakes* (Gaumont-British, 1931), *Tell Me Tonight* (Gaumont-UFA, 1932), *The Admiral's Secret* (British, 1932), *Love on Wheels* (Gaumont-British, 1932), *The Skin Game* (Powers, 1932), *The Good Companions* (Gaumont-British, 1933), *I Was a Spy* (Gaumont-British, 1933), *Early to Bed* (Gaumont-British, 1933), *Cash* (Par., 1933), *Friday the 13th* (Gaumont-British, 1933), *Marooned* (Fox, 1933), *Java Head* (Associated British, 1934), *Spring in the Air* (Pathé, 1934), *Channel Crossing* (Gaumont-British, 1934), *Passing Shadows* (Fox, 1934), *Waltzes From Vienna* ("Strauss' Great Waltz"—Arnold, 1934), *Father and Son* (British, 1934), *Warn London* (British Lion, 1934), *The Bishop Misbehaves* (MGM, 1935), *Sylvia Scarlett* (RKO, 1935), *The Walking Dead* (WB, 1936), *Anthony Adverse* (WB, 1936), *All American Chump* (MGM, 1936), *Mad Holiday* (MGM, 1936), *Laburnham Grove* (ATP, 1936), *Parnell* (MGM, 1937), *A Yank at Oxford* (MGM, 1938), *South Riding* (UA, 1938), *Penny Paradise* (Academy, 1938), *An Englishman's Home* (UA, 1939), *Cheer Boys Cheer* (Academy, 1940), *The Earl of Chicago* (MGM, 1940), *Mad Men of Europe* (Col., 1940), *The Doctor Takes a Wife* (Col, 1940), *Pride and Prejudice* (MGM, 1940), *Foreign Correspondent* (UA, 1940), *Scotland Yard* (20th, 1941), *Cheers for Miss Bishop* (UA, 1941), *The Devil and Miss Jones* (RKO, 1941), *Charley's Aunt* (20th, 1941), *One Night in Lisbon* (Par., 1941), *The Meanest Man in the World* (20th, 1943), *Forever and a Day* (RKO, 1943), *Lassie Come Home* (MGM, 1943), *Between Two Worlds* (WB, 1944), *Keys of the Kingdom* (20th, 1945), *Bewitched* (MGM, 1945), *Dangerous Partners* (MGM, 1945), *She Went to the Races* (MGM, 1945), *Of Human Bondage* (WB, 1946), *Undercurrent* (MGM, 1946), *The Miracle on 34th Street* (20th, 1947), *Thunder in the Valley* (20th, 1947), *Life With Father* (WB, 1947), *Green Dolphin Street* (MGM, 1947), *Apartment for Peggy* (20th, 1948), *Hills of Home* (MGM, 1948), *Challenge to Lassie* (MGM, 1949), *A Woman of Distinction* (Col., 1950), *Louisa* (Univ., 1950), *Pretty Baby* (WB, 1950), *Mister 880* (20th, 1950), *For Heaven's Sake* (20th, 1950), *Peking Express* (Par., 1951), *Sally and Saint Anne* (Univ., 1952), *Bonzo Goes to College* (Univ., 1952), *Les Miserables* (20th, 1952), *Something for the Birds* (20th, 1952), *Mister Scoutmaster* (20th, 1953), *Them* (WB, 1954), *The Student Prince* (MGM, 1954), *The Trouble With Harry* (Par., 1955), *It's a Dog's Life* (MGM, 1955).

JEAN HAGEN (Jean Shirley Ver Hagen) Born Chicago, Illinois. Married Tom Seidel (1947), children: Christine, Aric.

Barry Sullivan and Jean Hagen in *No Questions Asked.*

Feature Films: *Side Street* (MGM, 1949), *Adam's Rib* (MGM, 1949), *Ambush* (MGM, 1950), *The Asphalt Jungle* (MGM, 1950), *A Life of Her Own* (MGM, 1950), *Night into Morning* (MGM, 1951), *No Questions Asked* (MGM, 1951), *Singin' in the Rain* (MGM, 1952), *Shadow in the Sky* (MGM, 1952), *Carbine Williams* (MGM, 1952), *Latin Lovers* (MGM, 1953), *Arena* (MGM, 1953), *Half a Hero* (MGM, 1953), *The Big Knife* (UA, 1955), *Spring Reunion* (UA, 1957), *The Shaggy Dog* (BV, 1959), *Sunrise at Campobello* (WB, 1960), *Panic in Year Zero* (AIP, 1962), *Dead Ringer* (WB, 1964).

ALAN HALE (Alan MacKahn) Born February 10, 1892, Washington, D.C. Married Gretchen Hartman (1914), children: Alan, Karen, Jeanne. Died January 22, 1950.

Alan Hale and Sonja Henie in *Thin Ice.*

121

Sound Feature Films: *The Leatherneck* (Pathé, 1929), *Sal of Singapore* (Pathé, 1929), *The Sap* (WB, 1929), *Red Hot Rhythm* (Pathé, 1929), *Sailor's Holiday* (Pathé, 1929), *She Got What She Wanted* (Tif., 1930), *Aloha* (Tif., 1931), *Night Angel* (Par., 1931), *Susan Lennox—Her Fall and Rise* (MGM, 1931), *The Sin of Madelon Claudet* (MGM, 1931), *Sea Ghost* (Peerless, 1931), *Union Depot* (WB, 1932), *So Big* (WB, 1932), *The Match King* (WB, 1932), *What Price Decency?* (Majestic, 1933), *Eleventh Commandment* (Allied Pictures, 1933), *Destination Unknown* (Univ., 1933), *Picture Brides* (Allied, 1933), *The Lost Patrol* (RKO, 1934), *It Happened One Night* (Col., 1934), *Miss Fane's Baby Is Stolen* (Par., 1934), *Fog Over Frisco* (WB, 1934), *Little Man, What Now?* (Univ., 1934), *Of Human Bondage* (RKO, 1934), *The Scarlet Letter* (Majestic, 1934), *There's Always Tomorrow* (Univ., 1934), *Imitation of Life* (Univ., 1934), *Babbitt* (WB, 1934), *Great Expectations* (Univ., 1934), *The Little Minister* (RKO, 1934), *The Good Fairy* (Univ., 1935), *Grand Old Girl* (RKO, 1935), *The Crusades* (Par., 1935), *Last Days of Pompeii* (RKO, 1935), *Another Face* (RKO, 1935), *Two in the Dark* (RKO, 1936), *The Country Beyond* (20th, 1936), *A Message to Garcia* (20th, 1936), *Parole!* (Univ., 1936), *Our Relations* (MGM, 1936), *Yellowstone* (Univ., 1936), *God's Country and the Woman* (WB, 1936), *The Prince and the Pauper* (WB, 1937), *Stella Dallas* (UA, 1937), *High, Wide and Handsome* (Par., 1937), *Thin Ice* (20th, 1937), *Music for Madame* (RKO, 1937), *The Adventures of Marco Polo* (UA, 1938), *Four Men and A Prayer* (20th, 1938), *The Adventures of Robin Hood* (WB, 1938), *Valley of the Giants* (WB, 1938), *Algiers* (UA, 1938), *Listen, Darling* (MGM, 1938), *The Sisters* (WB, 1938), *Pacific Liner* (RKO, 1939), *Dodge City* (WB, 1939), *The Man in the Iron Mask* (UA, 1939), *Dust Be My Destiny* (WB, 1939), *On Your Toes* (WB, 1939), *The Private Lives of Elizabeth and Essex* (WB, 1939), *Three Cheers for the Irish* (WB, 1940), *Green Hell* (Univ., 1940), *Virginia City* (WB, 1940), *The Fighting 69th* (WB, 1940), *They Drive by Night* (WB, 1940), *The Sea Hawk* (WB, 1940), *Tugboat Annie Sails Again* (WB, 1940), *Santa Fe Trail* (WB, 1940), *Strawberry Blonde* (WB, 1941), *Footsteps in the Dark* (WB, 1941), *Thieves Fall Out* (WB, 1941), *Manpower* (WB, 1941), *The Smiling Ghost* (WB, 1941), *The Great Mr. Nobody* (WB, 1941), *Captains of the Clouds* (WB, 1942), *Juke Girl* (WB, 1942), *Desperate Journey* (WB, 1942), *Gentleman Jim* (WB, 1942), *Action in the North Atlantic* (WB, 1943), *This is Your Army* (WB, 1943), *Thank Your Lucky Stars* (WB, 1943), *Destination Tokyo* (WB, 1943), *The Adventures of Mark Twain* (WB, 1944), *Make Your Own Bed* (WB, 1944), *Janie* (WB, 1944), *Hollywood Canteen* (WB, 1944), *Roughly Speaking* (WB, 1945), *God Is My Co-Pilot* (WB, 1945), *Hotel Berlin* (WB, 1945), *Escape in the Desert* (WB, 1945), *Perilous Holiday* (Col., 1946), *Night and Day* (WB, 1946), *The Time, the Place and the Girl* (WB, 1946), *The Man I Love* (WB, 1946), *That Way With Women* (WB, 1947), *Pursued* (WB, 1947), *Cheyenne* (WB, 1947), *My Wild Irish Rose* (WB, 1947), *My Girl Tisa* (WB, 1948), *Whiplash* (WB, 1948), *Adventures of Don Juan* (WB, 1948), *South of St. Louis* (WB, 1949), *The Younger Brothers* (WB, 1949), *The House Across the Street* (WB, 1949), *Always Leave Them Laughing* (WB, 1949), *The Inspector General* (WB, 1949), *Stars in My Crown* (MGM, 1950), *Colt. 45* (WB, 1950), *Rogues of Sherwood Forest* (Col., 1950).

BARBARA HALE Born April 18, 1922, DeKalb, Illinois. Married Bill Williams (1946), children: Barbara (Jody), William, Laura.

James Stewart and Barbara Hale in *The Jackpot*.

Feature Films: *Higher and Higher* (RKO, 1943), *Gildersleeve on Broadway* (RKO, 1943), *Government Girl* (RKO, 1943), *The Iron Major* (RKO, 1943), *Mexican Spitfire's Blessed Event* (RKO, 1943), *The Seventh Victim* (RKO, 1943), *Gildersleeve's Bad Day* (RKO, 1943), *The Falcon Out West* (RKO, 1944), *Belle of the Yukon* (RKO, 1944), *Heavenly Days* (RKO, 1944), *Goin' to Town* (RKO, 1944), *The Falcon in Hollywood* (RKO, 1944), *West of the Pecos* (RKO, 1945), *First Yank into Tokyo* (RKO, 1945), *Lady Luck* (RKO, 1946), *A Likely Story* (RKO, 1947), *The Boy With Green Hair* (RKO, 1948), *The Clay Pigeon* (RKO, 1949), *The Window* (RKO, 1949), *Jolson Sings Again* (Col., 1949), *And Baby Makes Three* (Col, 1950), *The Jackpot* (20th, 1950), *Emergency Wedding* (Col., 1950), *Lorna Doone* (Col., 1951), *The First Time* (Col., 1952), *Last of the Comanches* (Col., 1952), *Seminole* (Univ., 1953), *Lone Hand* (Univ., 1953), *A Lion Is in the Streets* (WB, 1953), *Unchained* (WB, 1955), *The Far Horizons* Par., 1955), *The Houston Story* (Col., 1956), *Seventh Cavalry* (Col., 1956), *The Oklahoman* (AA, 1957), *Slim Carter* (Univ., 1957), *Desert Hell* (20th, 1958), *Buckskin* (Par., 1968),, *The Frontiersman* (Par., 1968).

JON HALL (Charles Hall Locher) Born February 23, 1913, Fresno, California. Married Frances Langford (1938); divorced 1955. Married Racquel Ames (1959).

Douglass Dumbrille, Olympe Bradna, Jon Hall, Frances Farmer and Victor McLaglen in *South of Pago Pago*.

Feature Films:

as Charles Locher *Women Must Dress* (Mon., 1935), *Charlie Chan in Shanghai* (20th, 1935), *The Clutching Hand* (Stage and Screen serial, 1936), *The Lion Man* (Normandy Pictures, 1936), *The Mysterious Avenger* (Col., 1936).

as Lloyd Crane *Mind Your Own Business* (Par., 1936), *Girl From Scotland Yard* (Par., 1937).

as Jon Hall *The Hurricane* (UA, 1937), *Sailor's Lady* (20th, 1940), *Kit Carson* (UA, 1940), *Aloma of the South Seas* (Par., 1941), *Tuttles of Tahiti* (RKO, 1942), *Eagle Squadron* (Univ., 1942), *Invisible Agent* (Univ., 1942), *Arabian Nights* (Univ., 1942), *White Savage* (Univ., 1943), *Ali Baba and the Forty Thieves* (Univ., 1944), *Lady in the Dark* (Par., 1944), *Invisible Man's Revenge* (Univ., 1944), *Cobra Woman* (Univ., 1944), *Gypsy Wildcat* (Univ., 1944), *San Diego, I Love You* (Univ., 1944), *Sudan* (Univ., 1945), *Men in Her Diary* (Univ., 1945), *The Michigan Kid* (Univ., 1947), *Last of the Redmen* (Col., 1947), *The Vigilantes Return* (Univ., 1947), *The Prince of Thieves* (Col., 1948), *The Mutineers* (Col., 1949), *Zamba* (EL, 1949), *Deputy Marshal* (Screen Guild, 1949), *On the Isle of Samoa* (Col., 1950), *When the Redskins Rode* (Col., 1951), *China Corsair* (Col., 1951), *Hurricane Island* (Col., 1951), *Brave Warrior* (Col., 1952), *Last Train From Bombay* (Col., 1952), *Hell Ship Mutiny* (Rep., 1957), *Forbidden Island* (Col., 1959), *Beach Girls and the Monster* (United States Films, 1965).

GEORGE HAMILTON Born August 12, 1940, Memphis, Tennessee.

English-Language Feature Films: *Crime and Punishment, USA* (AA, 1959), *Home From the Hill* (MGM, 1960), *All the Fine Young Cannibals*

Mercedes McCambridge and George Hamilton in *Angel Baby*.

(MGM, 1960), *Where the Boys Are* (MGM, 1960), *Angel Baby* (AA, 1961), *By Love Possessed* (UA, 1961), *A Thunder of Drums* (MGM, 1961), *Light in the Piazza* (MGM, 1962), *Two Weeks in Another Town* (MGM, 1962), *The Victors* (Col., 1963), *Act One* (WB, 1963), *Looking for Love* (MGM, 1964),* *Your Cheatin' Heart* (MGM, 1964), *Doctor, You've Got to Be Kidding!* (MGM, 1967), *That Man George* (AA, 1967), *Jack of Diamonds* (MGM, 1967), *The Power* (MGM, 1968), *A Time for Killing* (Col., 1968).

*Billed guest appearance

MARGARET HAMILTON (Margaret Brainard Hamilton) Born December 9, 1902, Cleveland, Ohio. Married Paul Meserve (1931), child: Hamilton; divorced 1938.

Feature Films: *Another Language* (MGM, 1933), *Hat, Coat and Glove* (RKO, 1934), *By Your Leave* (RKO, 1934), *Broadway Bill* (Col., 1934), *There's Always Tomorrow* (Univ., 1934), *The Farmer Takes a Wife* (Fox, 1935), *Way Down East* (Fox, 1935), *Chatterbox* (RKO, 1936), *The Trail of the Lonesome Pine* (Par., 1936), *These Three* (UA, 1936), *The Moon's Our Home* (Par., 1936), *The Witness Chair* (RKO, 1936), *Laughing at Trouble* (20th, 1937), *You Only Live Once* (UA, 1937), *When's Your Birthday?* (RKO, 1937), *Good Old Soak* (MGM, 1937), *Mountain Justice* (WB, 1937), *Nothing Sacred* (UA, 1937), *Saratoga* (MGM, 1937), *I'll Take Romance* (Col., 1937), *A Slight Case of Murder* (WB, 1938), *Adventures of Tom Sawyer* (UA, 1938), *Mother Carey's Chickens* (RKO, 1938), *Four's a Crowd* (WB, 1938), *Breaking the Ice* (RKO, 1938), *Stablemates* (MGM, 1938), *King of the Turf* (UA, 1939), *The Wizard of Oz* (MGM, 1939), *Angels Wash Their Faces* (WB, 1939), *Babes in Arms* (MGM, 1939), *Main Street Lawyer* (Rep., 1939), *My*

Margaret Hamilton and Harold Lloyd in *Mad Wednesday*.

Little Chickadee (Univ., 1940), *The Villain Still Pursued Her* (RKO, 1940), *I'm Nobody's Sweetheart Now* (Univ., 1940), *The Invisible Woman* (Univ., 1941), *Play Girl* (RKO, 1941), *The Gay Vagabond* (Rep., 1941), *The Shepherd of the Hills* (Par., 1941), *Twin Beds* (UA, 1942), *Meet the Stewarts* (Col., 1942), *The Affairs of Martha* (MGM, 1942), *City Without Men* (Col., 1943), *The Ox-Bow Incident* (20th, 1943), *Johnny Come Lately* (UA, 1943), *Guest in the House* (UA, 1944), *George White's Scandals* (RKO, 1945), *Janie Gets Married* (WB, 1946), *Faithful in My Fashion* (MGM, 1946), *Mad Wednesday* (UA, 1947), *Dishonored Lady* (UA, 1947), *Driftwood* (Rep., 1947), *State of the Union* (MGM, 1948), *Texas, Brooklyn and Heaven* (UA, 1948), *Bungalow 13* (20th, 1948), *The Sun Comes Up* (MGM, 1949), *The Red Pony* (Rep., 1949), *The Beautiful Blonde From Bashful Bend* (20th, 1949), *Riding High* (Par., 1950), *The Great Plane Robbery* (UA, 1950), *Wabash Avenue* (20th, 1950), *People Will Talk* (20th, 1951), *Comin' Round the Mountain* (Univ., 1951), *Thirteen Ghosts* (Col., 1960), *Paradise Alley* (Sutton, 1962), *The Daydreamer* (Voice only; Embassy, 1966), *Rosie!* (Univ., 1968).

NEIL HAMILTON (James Neil Hamilton) Born September 9, 1899, Lynn, Massachusetts. Married Elsa Whitner (1922).

Fay Wray, Gary Cooper, Neil Hamilton, Frances Fuller and Jack Clifford in *One Sunday Afternoon*.

Sound Feature Films: *Dangerous Woman* (Par., 1929), *Studio Murder Mystery* (Par., 1929), *Mysterious Dr. Fu Manchu* (Par., 1929), *Darkened Rooms* (Par., 1929), *Kibitzer* (Par., 1929), *Anybody's Woman* (Par., 1930), *Return of Dr. Fu Manchu* (Par., 1930), *Dawn Patrol* (WB, 1930), *Ladies Must Play* (Col., 1930), *The Cat Creeps* (Univ., 1930), *Widow From Chicago* (WB, 1930), *The Spy* (Fox, 1931), *Strangers May Kiss* (MGM, 1931), *Command Performance* (Tif., 1931), *Ex-Flame* (Tif., 1931), *This Modern Age* (MGM, 1931), *Laughing Sinners* (MGM, 1931), *Great Lover* (MGM, 1931), *The Sin of Madelon Claudet* (MGM, 1931), *Tarzan the Ape Man* (MGM, 1932), *Are You Listening?* (MGM, 1932), *Wet Parade* (MGM, 1932), *The Woman in Room 13* (Fox, 1932), *What Price Hollywood* (RKO, 1932), *Two Against the World* (WB, 1932), *Payment Deferred* (MGM, 1932), *The Animal Kingdom* (RKO, 1932), *Terror Aboard* (Par., 1933), *World Gone Mad* (Majestic, 1933), *Silk Express* (WB, 1933), *One Sunday Afternoon* (Par., 1933), *As the Devil Commands* (Col., 1933), *Tarzan and His Mate* (MGM, 1934), *Here Comes the Groom* (Par., 1934), *Blind Date* (Col., 1934), *Once to Every Bachelor* (Liberty, 1934), *One Exciting Adventure* (Univ., 1934), *By Your Leave* (RKO, 1934), *Fugitive Lady* (Col., 1934), *The Daring Young Man* (Fox, 1935), *Keeper of the Bees* (Mon., 1935), *Honeymoon Limited* (Mon., 1935), *Mutiny Ahead* (Majestic, 1936), *Southern Roses* (Grafton Films, 1936), *Everything in Life* (British, 1936), *Portia on Trial*

(Rep., 1937), *Lady Behave* (Rep., 1937), *Hollywood Stadium Mystery* (Rep., 1938), *Army Girl* (Rep., 1938), *The Saint Strikes Back* (RKO, 1939), *Queen of the Mob* (Par., 1940), *King of the Texas Rangers* (Rep., serial, 1941), *Federal Fugitives* (PRC, 1941), *Father Takes a Wife* (RKO, 1941), *Dangerous Lady* (PRC, 1941), *Look Who's Laughing* (RKO, 1941), *Too Many Women* (PRC, 1942), *X Marks the Spot* (Rep., 1942), *Secrets of the Underground* (Rep., 1943), *All by Myself* (Univ., 1943), *The Sky's the Limit* (RKO, 1943), *When Strangers Marry* (Mon., 1944), *Brewster's Millions* (UA, 1945), *The Devil's Hand* (Crown International, 1962), *The Little Shepherd of Kingdom Come* (20th, 1962), *The Patsy* (Par., 1964), *Good Neighbor Sam* (Col., 1964), *The Family Jewels* (Par., 1965), *Madame X* (Univ., 1966), *Batman* (20th, 1966).

ANN HARDING (Dorothy Walton Gatley) Born August 7, 1902, Fort Sam Houston, San Antonio, Texas. Married Harry Bannister (1926), child: Jane; divorced 1932. Married Werner Janssen (1937); divorced 1963.

Cedric Hardwicke, Joseph Calleia and Gene Kelly in *The Cross of Lorraine*.

Clive Brook and Ann Harding in *Gallant Lady*.

Feature Films: *Paris Bound* (Pathé, 1929), *Her Private Affair* (Pathé, 1929), *Condemned* (UA, 1929), *Holiday* (Pathé, 1930), *Girl of the Golden West* (WB, 1930), *East Lynne* (Fox, 1931), *Devotion* (RKO, 1931), *Prestige* (RKO, 1932), *Westward Passage* (RKO, 1932), *The Conquerors* (RKO, 1932), *The Animal Kingdom* (RKO, 1932), *When Ladies Meet* (MGM, 1933), *Double Harness* (RKO, 1933), *Right to Romance* (RKO, 1933), *Gallant Lady* (UA, 1933), *Life of Vergie Winters* (RKO, 1934), *The Fountain* (RKO, 1934), *Biography of a Bachelor Girl* (MGM, 1935), *Enchanted April* (RKO, 1935), *The Flame Within* (MGM, 1935), *Peter Ibbetson* (Par., 1935), *The Lady Consents* (RKO, 1936), *The Witness Chair* (RKO, 1936), *Love From a Stranger* (UA, 1937), *Eyes in the Night* (MGM, 1942), *Mission to Moscow* (WB, 1943), *The North Star* (RKO, 1943), *Janie* (WB, 1944), *Nine Girls* (Col., 1944), *Those Endearing Young Charms* (RKO, 1945), *Janie Gets Married* (WB, 1946), *It Happened on Fifth Avenue* (AA, 1947), *Christmas Eve* (UA, 1947), *The Magnificent Yankee* (MGM, 1950), *Two Weeks With Love* (MGM, 1950), *The Unknown Man* (MGM, 1951), *The Man in the Gray Flannel Suit* (20th, 1956), *I've Lived Before* (Univ., 1956), *Strange Intruder* (AA, 1956).

SIR CEDRIC HARDWICKE (Cedric Webster Hardwicke) Born February 19, 1893; Lye, England. Married Helena Pickard (1928), child: Edward; divorced 1948. Married Mary Scott (1950); divorced 1961. Died August 6, 1964.

Sound Feature Films: *Dreyfus* (Col., 1931), *Rome Express* (Gaumont-British, 1932), *Orders Is Orders* (Gaumont-British, 1933), *The Ghoul* (Gaumont-British, 1933), *Nell Gwynne* (British and Dominion Productions, 1934), *The Lady Is Willing* (Col., 1934), *Jew Süss* (Gaumont-British, 1934), *King of Paris* (British and Dominion Productions, 1934), *Bella Donna* (Twickenham, 1935), *Les Miserables* (UA, 1935), *Peg of*

Old Drury (British and Dominion Productions, 1935), *Becky Sharp* (Pioneer-RKO, 1935), *Things to Come* (Korda-UA, 1936), *Tudor Rose* (Gaumont-British, 1936), *Laburnham Grove* (ATP, 1936), *Green Light* (WB, 1937), *King Solomon's Mines* (Gaumont-British, 1937), *On Borrowed Time* (MGM, 1939), *Stanley and Livingstone* (20th, 1939), *The Hunchback of Notre Dame* (RKO, 1939), *The Invisible Man Returns* (Univ., 1940), *Tom Brown's School Days* (RKO, 1940), *The Howards of Virginia* (Col., 1940), *Victory* (Par., 1940), *Suspicion* (RKO, 1941), *Sundown* (UA, 1941), *The Ghost of Frankenstein* (Univ., 1942), *Valley of the Sun* (RKO, 1942), *Invisible Agent* (Univ., 1942), *Commandos Strike at Dawn* (Col., 1942), *Forever and a Day* (RKO, 1943), *The Moon Is Down* (20th, 1943), *The Cross of Lorraine* (MGM, 1943), *The Lodger* (20th, 1944), *Wing and a Prayer* (20th, 1944), *Wilson* (20th, 1944), *The Keys of the Kingdom* (20th, 1945), *The Picture of Dorian Gray* (narrator; MGM, 1945), *Sentimental Journey* (20th, 1946), *The Imperfect Lady* (Par., 1947), *Ivy* (Univ., 1947), *Lured* (UA, 1947), *Song of My Heart* (AA, 1947), *Beware of Pity* (Univ., 1947), *Nicholas Nickleby* (Univ., 1947), *Tycoon* (RKO, 1947), *I Remember Mama* (RKO, 1948), *Rope* (WB-Univ., 1948), *A Connecticut Yankee in King Arthur's Court* (Par., 1949), *Now Barabbas Was a Robber* (WB, 1949), *The Winslow Boy* (EL, 1950), *The White Tower* (RKO, 1950), *Mr. Imperium* (MGM, 1951), *The Desert Fox* (20th, 1951), *The Green Glove* (UA, 1952), *Caribbean* (Par., 1952), *Salome* (Col., 1953), *Botany Bay* (Par., 1953), *The War of the Worlds* (narrator; Par., 1953), *Bait* (Col., 1954), *Richard III* (Lopert, 1955), *Helen of Troy* (WB, 1955), *Diane* (MGM, 1956), *Gaby* (MGM, 1956), *The Vagabond King* (Par., 1956), *The Power and the Prize* (MGM, 1956), *The Ten Commandments* (Par., 1956), *Around the World in 80 Days* (UA, 1956), *The Story of Mankind* (WB, 1957), *Baby Face Nelson* (UA, 1957), *Five Weeks in a Balloon* (20th, 1962), *The Pumpkin Eater* (Col., 1964), *The Magic Fountain* (Davis Distributing, 1964).

JEAN HARLOW (Harlean Carpentier) Born March 3, 1911, Kansas City, Kansas. Married Charles McGrew (1927); divorced 1930. Married

Spencer Tracy, Warren Hymer and Jean Harlow in *Goldie*.

Paul Bern (1932); widowed 1932. Married Hal Rossen (1933); divorced 1935. Died June 7, 1937.

Sound Feature Films: *The Love Parade* (Par., 1929), *The Saturday Night Kid* (Par., 1929), *Hell's Angels* (UA, 1930), *The Secret Six* (MGM, 1931), *Iron Man* (Univ., 1931), *Public Enemy* (WB, 1931), *Goldie* (Fox, 1931), *Platinum Blonde* (Col., 1931), *Three Wise Girls* (Col., 1932), *The Beast of the City* (MGM, 1932), *Red-Headed Woman* (MGM, 1932), *Red Dust* (MGM, 1932), *Dinner at Eight* (MGM, 1933), *Hold Your Man* (MGM, 1933), *Bombshell* (MGM, 1933), *The Girl From Missouri* (MGM, 1934), *Reckless* (MGM, 1935), *China Seas* (MGM, 1935), *Riffraff* (MGM, 1935), *Wife vs. Secretary* (MGM, 1936), *Suzy* (MGM, 1936), *Libeled Lady* (MGM, 1936), *Personal Property* (MGM, 1937), *Saratoga* (MGM, 1937).

JULIE HARRIS (Julia Ann Harris) Born December 2, 1925, Grosse Pointe, Michigan. Married Jay Julien (1946); divorced 1954. Married Manning Gurian (1954), child: Peter.

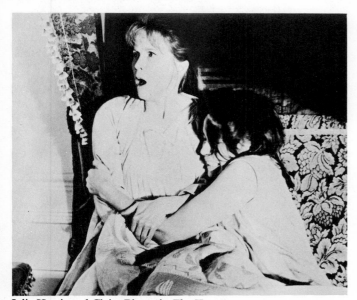

Julie Harris and Claire Bloom in *The Haunting*.

Feature Films: *The Member of the Wedding* (Col., 1953), *East of Eden* (WB, 1955), *I Am a Camera* (DCA, 1955), *The Truth About Women* (Continental, 1958), *Sally's Irish Rogue* ("The Poacher's Daughter"—Show Corp., 1960), *Requiem for a Heavyweight* (Col., 1962), *The Haunting* (MGM, 1963), *Harper* (WB, 1966), *You're a Big Boy Now* (7 Arts, 1966), *Reflections in a Golden Eye* (WB-7 Arts, 1967).

REX HARRISON (Reginald Carey Harrison) Born March 5, 1908, Huyton, Lancashire, England. Married Marjorie Thomas (1934), child: Noel; divorced 1942. Married Lilli Palmer (1943), child: Carey; divorced 1957. Married Kay Kendall (1957); widowed 1959. Married Rachel Roberts (1962).

Feature Films: *Get Your Man* (British, 1929), *All at Sea* (British, 1935), *The Great Game* (Gaumont-British, 1930), *School For Scandal* (Albion Films, 1930), *Men are Not Gods* (London Films, 1936), *Storm in a Teacup* (London Films, 1937), *School for Husbands* (Richard Wainwright, 1937), *St. Martin's Lane* (Par., 1938), *The Citadel* (MGM, 1938), *Over the Moon* (London Films, 1939), *Ten Days in Paris* (Col., 1939), *The Silent Battle* (Mon., 1939), *Night Train to Munich* (Gaumont-British, 1940), *Major Barbara* (UA, 1941), *Journey Together* (English Films, Inc., 1944), *I Live In Grosvenor Square* ("A Yank In London"—Associated British, 1945), *Blithe Spirit* (Two Cities, 1945), *The Rake's Progress* (Individual Pictures, 1945), *Anna and the King of Siam* (20th, 1946), *The Ghost and Mrs. Muir* (20th, 1947), *The Foxes of Harrow* (20th, 1947), *Escape* (20th, 1948), *Unfaithfully Yours* (20th, 1948), *The Long Dark Hall* (UA, 1951), *The Fourposter* (Col., 1952), *Main Street to Broadway* (MGM, 1953), *King Richard and the Crusaders*

Rex Harrison in *Doctor Dolittle*.

(WB, 1954), *The Constant Husband* (London Films, 1955), *The Reluctant Debutante* (MGM, 1958), *Midnight Lace* (Univ., 1960), *The Happy Thieves* (UA, 1962), *Cleopatra* (20th, 1963), *My Fair Lady* (WB, 1964), *The Yellow Rolls-Royce* (MGM, 1965), *The Agony and the Ecstasy* (20th, 1965), *The Honey Pot* (UA, 1967), *Doctor Dolittle* (20th, 1967), *A Flea in Her Ear* (20th, 1968).

LAURENCE HARVEY (Lauruska Mischa Skikne) Born October 1, 1928, Yonishkis, Lithuania. Married Margaret Leighton (1957); divorced 1961.

Feature Films: *House of Darkness* (Associated British Pictures Corp., 1948), *Man on the Run* (Associated British Pictures Corp., 1948), *Man From Yesterday* (Associated British Pictures Corp., 1949), *Cairo Road* (Associated British Picture Corp., 1949), *The Scarlet Thread* (Buraders, 1949), *The Black Rose* (20th, 1950), *There's Another Sun* (Butchers, 1951), *A Killer Walks* (Associated British Pictures Corp., 1952), *Women of Twilight* (Romulus, 1952), *Landfall* (Stratford, 1953), *I Believe in You* (Univ., 1953), *Romeo and Juliet* (UA, 1954), *King Richard and the Crusaders* (WB, 1954), *The Good Die Young* (UA, 1955), *Innocents in Paris* (Tudor, 1955), *I Am a Camera* (DCA, 1955), *Storm Over the Nile* (Col., 1956), *The Silent Enemy* (Univ., 1958),

Shirley MacLaine and Laurence Harvey in *Two Loves*.

125

The Truth About Women (Continental, 1958), *Three Men in a Boat* (Valiant, 1959), *Room at the Top* (Continental, 1959), *Butterfield 8* (MGM, 1960), *Expresso Bongo* (Continental, 1960), *The Long and the Short and the Tall* (Continental, 1961), *Summer and Smoke* (Par., 1961), *Two Loves* (MGM, 1961), *The Wonderful World of the Brothers Grimm* (MGM, 1962), *Walk on the Wild Side* (Col., 1962), *The Manchurian Candidate* (UA, 1962), *A Girl Named Tamiko* (Par., 1962), *The Running Man* (Col., 1963), *The Ceremony* (UA, 1964), *The Outrage* (MGM, 1964), *Of Human Bondage* (MGM, 1964), *Darling* (Embassy, 1965), *Life at the Top* (Royal Films International, 1965), *The Spy With a Cold Nose* (Embassy, 1966), *The Winter's Tale* (7 Arts, 1967), *A Dandy in Aspic* (Col., 1968), *Charge of the Light Brigade* (UA, 1969).

SIGNE HASSO (Signe Eleonora Cecilia Larsson) Born August 15, 1915, Stockholm, Sweden. Married Henry Hasso (1936), child: Henry; divorced 1941.

Signe Hasso and Jean-Pierre Aumont in *Assignment in Brittany*.

English-Language Feature Films: *Assignment in Brittany* (MGM, 1943), *Heaven Can Wait* (20th, 1943), *The Story of Dr. Wassell* (Par., 1944), *The Seventh Cross* (MGM, 1944), *Dangerous Partners* (MGM, 1945), *Johnny Angel* (RKO, 1945), *The House on 92nd Street* (20th, 1945), *Strange Triangle* (20th, 1946), *A Scandal in Paris* (UA, 1946), *Where There's Life* (Par., 1947), *To the Ends of the Earth* (Col., 1948), *A Double Life* (Univ., 1948), *Outside the Wall* (Univ., 1950), *Crisis* (MGM, 1950), *The True and the False* (Helene Davis, 1955), *Picture Mommy Dead* (Embassy, 1966).

JUNE HAVER (June Stovenour) Born June 10, 1926, Rock Island, Illinois. Married Jimmy Zito (1947); divorced 1948. Married Fred MacMurray (1955), children: Kathryn, Laurie.

Randy Stuart, S.Z. Sakall, Walter Catlett and June Haver in *Look for the Silver Lining*.

Feature Films: *The Gang's All Here* (20th, 1943), *Home in Indiana* (20th, 1944), *Irish Eyes Are Smiling* (20th, 1944), *Where Do We Go From Here?* (20th, 1945), *The Dolly Sisters* (20th, 1945), *Three Little Girls in Blue* (20th, 1946), *Wake Up and Dream* (20th, 1946), *I Wonder Who's Kissing Her Now* (20th, 1947), *Scudda Hoo! Scudda Hay!* (20th, 1948), *Oh, You Beautiful Doll!* (20th, 1949), *Look for the Silver Lining* (WB, 1949), *The Daughter of Rosie O'Grady* (WB, 1950), *I'll Get By* (20th, 1950), *Love Nest* (20th, 1951), *The Girl Next Door* (20th, 1953).

STERLING HAYDEN (John Hamilton) Born March 26, 1916, Montclair, New Jersey. Married Madeleine Carroll (1937); divorced 1946. Married Betty DeNoon (1947), children: Christian, Dana, Gretchen, Matthew; divorced 1955, Married Catherine McConnell (1960).

Sterling Hayden, Howard Petrie and Chill Wills in *Timberjack*.

Feature Films: *Virginia* (Par., 1941), *Bahama Passage* (Par., 1941), *Variety Girl* (Par., 1947), *Blaze of Noon* (Par., 1947), *El Paso* (Par., 1949), *Manhandled* (Par., 1949), *The Asphalt Jungle* (MGM, 1950), *Journey into Light* (20th, 1951), *Flaming Feather* (Par., 1952), *The Denver and Rio Grande* (Par., 1952), *The Golden Hawk* (Col., 1952), *Flat Top* (AA, 1952), *The Star* (20th, 1953), *Take Me to Town* (Univ., 1953), *Kansas Pacific* (AA, 1953), *Fighter Attack* (AA, 1953), *So Big* (WB, 1953), *Crime Wave* (WB, 1954), *Arrow in the Dust* (AA, 1954), *Prince Valiant* (20th, 1954), *Johnny Guitar* (Rep., 1954), *Naked Alibi* (Univ., 1954), *Suddenly* (UA, 1954), *Timberjack* (Rep., 1955), *The Eternal Sea* (Rep., 1955), *Shotgun* (AA, 1955), *Battle Taxi* (UA, 1955), *The Last Command* (Rep., 1955), *Top Gun* (UA, 1955), *The Come-On* (AA, 1956), *The Killing* (UA, 1956), *Five Steps to Danger* (UA, 1957), *Crime of Passion* (UA, 1957), *The Iron Sheriff* (UA, 1957), *Valerie* (UA, 1957), *Zero Hour!* (Par., 1957), *Gun Battle at Monterey* (AA, 1957), *Terror in a Texas Town* (UA, 1958), *Ten Days to Tulara* (UA, 1958), *Dr. Strangelove* (Col., 1964).

GEORGE "GABBY" HAYES (George F. Hayes) Born May 7, 1885, Wellsville, New York. Married Olive Ireland (1914); widowed.

Sound Feature Films: *Big News* (Pathé, 1929), *Rainbow Man* (Par., 1929), *Smiling Irish Eyes* (WB, 1929), *For the Defense* (Par., 1930), *Rose of the Rio Grande* (1931), *Big Business Girl* (WB, 1931), *God's Country and the Man* (Syndicate, 1931), *Nevada Buckaroo* (Tif., 1931), *Cavalier of the West* (Artclass Pictures, 1931), *Dragnet Patrol* (Artclass Pictures, 1931), *Riders of the Desert* (Sono Art-World Wide, 1932), *Without Honor* (Artclass Pictures, 1932), *From Broadway to Cheyenne* (Mon., 1932), *Klondike* (Mon., 1932), *Love Me Tonight* (Par., 1932), *Texas Buddies* (Sono Art-World Wide, 1932), *The Boiling Point* (Allied Pictures, 1932), *The Fighting Champ* (Mon., 1932), *Wild Horse Mesa* (Par., 1933), *Self Defense* (Mon., 1933), *Phantom Broadcast* (Mon., 1933), *Trailing North* (Mon., 1933), *Breed of the Border* (Mon., 1933), *Return of Casey Jones* (Mon., 1933), *The Sphinx* (Mon., 1933), *Gallant Fool* (Mon., 1933), *Fighting Texans* (Mon., 1933), *Skyway* (Mon., 1933), *Devil's Mate* (Mon., 1933), *Rangers' Code*

Bob Livingston, Richard Arlen and George "Gabby" Hayes in *The Big Bonanza.*

(Mon., 1933), *The Fugitive* (Mon., 1933), *Galloping Romeo* (Mon., 1933), *Riders of Destiny* (Mon., 1933), *The Lost Jungle* (Mascot serial, 1934), *House of Mystery* (Mon., 1934), *Lucky Texan* (Mon., 1934), *West of the Divide* (Mon., 1934), *Beggars in Ermine* (Mon, 1934), *Mystery Liner* (Mon., 1934), *City Limits* (Mon., 1934), *Monte Carlo Nights* (Mon., 1934), *Blue Steel* (Mon., 1934), *Man From Utah* (Mon., 1934), *Randy Rides Alone* (Mon., 1934), *The Star Packer* (Mon., 1934), *Brand of Hate* (William Steiner, 1934), *In Old Santa Fe* (Mascot, 1934), *'Neath Arizona Skies* (Mon., 1934), *The Lost City* (Sherman Krellberg serial, 1935), *Lawless Frontier* (Mon., 1935), *Death Flies East* (Col., 1935), *Rainbow Valley* (Mon., 1935), *Hoosier Schoolmaster* (Mon., 1935), *Justice of the Range* (Col., 1935), *Honeymoon Limited* (Mon., 1935), *Hop-A-Long Cassidy* (Par., 1935), *Smoky Smith* (William Steiner, 1935), *Thunder Mountain* (Fox, 1935), *Tumbling Tumbleweeds* (Rep., 1935), *Eagle's Brood* (Par., 1935), *Bar 20 Rides Again* (Par., 1935), *$1,000 a Minute* (Rep., 1935), *The Throwback* (Univ., 1935), *Hitch-Hike Lady* (Rep., 1935), *Swifty* (First Division, 1935), *Welcome Home* (Fox, 1935), *The Outlaw Tamer* (Empire, 1935), *Valley of the Lawless* (Supreme, 1936), *Call of the Prairie* (Par., 1936), *I Married a Doctor* (WB, 1936), *Mr. Deeds Goes to Town* (Col., 1936), *The Lawless Nineties* (Rep., 1936), *Three on the Trail* (Par., 1936), *Hearts in Bondage* (Rep., 1936), *Texas Rangers* (Par., 1936), *Heart of the West* (Par., 1936), *Hopalong Cassidy Returns* (Par., 1936), *Valiant Is the Word for Carrie* (Par., 1936), *Trail Dust* (Par., 1936), *Borderland* (Par., 1937), *Hills of Old Wyoming* (Par., 1937), *North of Rio Grande* (Par., 1937), *Mountain Music* (Par., 1937), *Hopalong Rides Again* (Par., 1937), *Rustler's Valley* (Par., 1937), *Texas Trail* (Par., 1937), *Heart of Arizona* (Par., 1938), *Gold Is Where You Find It* (WB, 1938), *Bar 20 Justice* (Par., 1938), *In Old Mexico* (Par., 1938), *Sunset Trail* (Par., 1938), *The Frontiersman* (Par., 1938), *Silver on the Sage* (Par., 1939), *Fighting Thoroughbreds* (Rep., 1939), *Let Freedom Ring* (MGM, 1939), *Man of Conquest* (Rep., 1939), *In Old Caliente* (Rep., 1939), *Saga of Death Valley* (Rep., 1939), *In Old Monterey* (Rep., 1939), *Renegade Trail* (Par., 1939), *Wall Street Cowboy* (Rep., 1939), *The Arizona Kid* (Rep., 1939), *Days of Jesse James* (Rep., 1939), *Dark Command* (Rep., 1940), *Young Buffalo Bill* (Rep., 1940), *Wagons Westward* (Rep., 1940), *The Carson City Kid* (Rep., 1940), *The Ranger and the Lady* (Rep., 1940), *Colorado* (Rep., 1940), *Young Bill Hickok* (Rep., 1940), *The Border Legion* (Rep., 1940), *Melody Ranch* (Rep., 1940), *Robin Hood of the Pecos* (Rep., 1941), *In Old Cheyenne* (Rep., 1941), *Sheriff of Tombstone* (Rep., 1941), *Nevada City* (Rep., 1941), *Jesse James at Bay* (Rep., 1941), *Bad Man of Deadwood* (Rep., 1941), *Red River Valley* (Rep., 1941), *South of Santa Fe* (Rep., 1942), *Sunset on the Desert* (Rep., 1942), *Man of Cheyenne* (Rep., 1942), *Romance on the Range* (Rep., 1942), *Sons of the Pioneers* (Rep., 1942), *Sunset Serenade* (Rep., 1942), *Heart of the Golden West* (Rep., 1942), *Ridin' Down the Canyon* (Rep., 1942), *Calling Wild Bill Elliott* (Rep., 1943), *Bordertown Gun Fighters* (Rep., 1943), *Wagon Tracks West* (Rep., 1943), *Death Valley Manhunt* (Rep., 1943), *In Old Oklahoma* (Rep., 1943), *Tucson Raiders* (Rep., 1944), *Hidden Valley Outlaws* (Rep., 1944), *Marshal of Reno* (Rep., 1944), *Mojave Firebrand* (Rep., 1944), *Tall in the Saddle* (RKO, 1944), *Lights*

of Old Santa Fe (Rep., 1944), *Utah* (Rep., 1945), *The Big Bonanza* (Rep., 1945), *Bells of Rosarita* (Rep., 1945), *The Man From Oklahoma* (Rep., 1945), *Sunset in Eldorado* (Rep., 1945), *Don't Fence Me In* (Rep., 1945), *Along the Navajo Trail* (Rep., 1945), *Song of Arizona* (Rep., 1946), *Badman's Territory* (RKO, 1946), *Rainbow Over Texas* (Rep., 1946), *My Pal Trigger* (Rep., 1946), *Roll on Texas Moon* (Rep., 1946), *Home in Oklahoma* (Rep., 1946), *Under Nevada Skies* (Rep., 1946), *Helldorado* (Rep., 1946), *Trail Street* (RKO, 1947), *Wyoming* (Rep., 1947), *Albuquerque* (Par., 1948), *The Untamed Breed* (Col., 1948), *El Paso* (Par., 1949), *The Cariboo Trail* (20th, 1950).

HELEN HAYES Born October 10, 1900, Washington, D.C. Married Charles MacArthur (1928), children: Mary, James; widowed 1956.

Brian Aherne and Helen Hayes in *What Every Woman Knows.*

Sound Feature Films: *The Sin of Madelon Claudet* (MGM, 1931), *Arrowsmith* (UA, 1931), *A Farewell to Arms* (Par., 1932), *The Son-Daughter* (MGM, 1933), *The White Sister* (MGM, 1933), *Another Language* (MGM, 1933), *Night Flight* (MGM, 1933), *What Every Woman Knows* (MGM, 1934), *Crime Without Passion* (Par., 1934),* *Vanessa* (MGM, 1935), *Stage Door Canteen* (UA, 1943), *My Son John* (Par., 1952), *Main Street to Broadway* (MGM, 1953), *Anastasia* (20th, 1956), *Third Man on The Mountain* (BV, 1959).*

*Unbilled guest appearance

LOUIS HAYWARD Born March 19, 1909, Johannesburg, South Africa. Married Ida Lupino (1939); divorced 1945. Married Peggy Morrow (1946); divorced 1950. Married June Blanchard (1950).

Feature Films: *Self-Made Lady* (UA, 1932), *Chelsea Life* (Par., 1933), *Sorrell and Son* (UA, 1934), *The Flame Within* (MGM, 1935), *A Feather in Her Hat* (Col., 1935), *Absolute Quiet* (MGM, 1936), *Trouble for Two* (MGM, 1936), *Anthony Adverse* (WB, 1936), *The Luckiest Girl in the World* (Univ., 1936), *The Woman I Love* (RKO, 1937), *Condemned Women* (RKO, 1938), *Midnight Intruder* (Univ., 1938), *The Saint in New York* (RKO, 1938), *The Rage of Paris* (Univ., 1938), *The Duke of West Point* (UA, 1938), *The Man in the Iron Mask* (UA, 1939), *My Son, My Son* (UA, 1940), *Dance, Girl, Dance* (RKO, 1940), *The Son of Monte Cristo* (UA, 1940), *Ladies in Retirement* (Col., 1941), *The Magnificent Ambersons* (RKO, 1942),* *And Then There Were None* (20th, 1945), *Young Widow* (UA, 1946), *The Strange Woman* (UA, 1946), *The Return of Monte Cristo* (Col., 1946), *Repeat Performance* (EL, 1947), *Ruthless* (EL, 1948), *The Black Arrow* (Col., 1948), *Walk a Crooked Mile* (Col., 1948), *The Pirates of Capri* (Film Classics, 1949), *House by the River* (Rep., 1950), *Fortunes of Captain Blood* (Col.,

Louis Hayward and Joan Bennett in *The Man in the Iron Mask*.

1950), *The Lady and the Bandit* (Col., 1951), *The Son of Dr. Jekyll* (Col., 1951), *Lady in the Iron Mask* (20th, 1952), *Captain Pirate* (Col., 1952), *The Royal African Rifles* (AA, 1953), *The Saint's Girl Friday* (RKO, 1954), *Duffy of San Quentin* (WB, 1954), *The Search for Bridey Murphy* (Par., 1956), *Chuka* (Par., 1967), *The Christmas Kid* (PRO, 1967), *Electric Man* (PRO, 1967).

*His major scenes were cut from the final print, although he appears amid the crowd in the ballroom sequence.

SUSAN HAYWARD (Edythe Marrener) Born June 30, 1918, Brooklyn, New York. Married Jess Barker (1944), children: Timothy, Gregory; divorced 1953. Married Floyd Eaton Chalkley (1957); widowed 1966.

Feature Films: *Hollywood Hotel* (WB, 1937), *The Sisters* (WB, 1938), *Comet Over Broadway* (WB, 1938), *Girls on Probation* (WB, 1938), *Beau Geste* (Par., 1939), *Our Leading Citizen* (Par., 1939), *$1,000 a Touchdown* (Par., 1939), *Adam Had Four Sons* (Col., 1941), *Sis Hopkins* (Rep., 1941), *Among the Living* (Par., 1941), *Reap the Wild Wind*

Joseph Allen, Jr., and Susan Hayward in *Our Leading Citizen*.

(Par., 1942), *Forest Rangers* (Par., 1942), *I Married a Witch* (UA, 1942), *Star Spangled Rhythm* (Par., 1942), *Hit Parade of 1943* (Rep., 1943), *Young and Willing* (UA, 1943), *Jack London* (UA, 1943), *The Fighting Seabees* (Rep., 1944), *The Hairy Ape* (UA, 1944), *And Now Tomorrow* (Par., 1944), *Deadline at Dawn* (RKO, 1946), *Canyon Passage* (Univ., 1946), *Smash-Up, The Story of a Woman* (Univ., 1947), *The Lost Moment* (Univ., 1947), *They Won't Believe Me* (RKO, 1947), *Tap Roots* (Univ., 1948), *The Saxon Charm* (Univ., 1948), *Tulsa* (EL, 1949), *House of Strangers* (20th, 1949), *My Foolish Heart* (RKO, 1949), *I'd Climb the Highest Mountain* (20th, 1951), *Rawhide* (20th, 1951), *I Can Get It for You Wholesale* (20th, 1951), *David and Bathsheba* (20th, 1951), *With a Song in My Heart* (20th, 1952), *The Snows of Kilimanjaro* (20th, 1952), *The Lusty Men* (RKO, 1952), *The President's Lady* (20th, 1953), *White Witch Doctor* (20th, 1953), *Demetrius and the Gladiators* (20th, 1954) *Garden of Evil* (20th, 1954), *Untamed* (20th, 1955), *Soldier of Fortune* (20th, 1955), *I'll Cry Tomorrow* (MGM, 1955), *The Conqueror* (RKO, 1956), *Top Secret Affair* (WB, 1957), *I Want to Live* (UA, 1958), *Woman Obsessed* (20th, 1959), *Thunder in the Sun* (Par., 1959), *The Marriage-Go-Round* (20th, 1960), *Ada* (MGM, 1961), *Back Street* (Univ., 1961), *I Thank a Fool* (MGM, 1962), *Stolen Hours* (UA, 1963), *Where Love Has Gone* (Par., 1964), *The Honey Pot* (UA, 1967), *Valley of the Dolls* (20th, 1967).

RITA HAYWORTH (Margarita Carmen Cansino) Born October 17, 1918, Brooklyn, New York. Married Edward Judson (1937); divorced 1943. Married Orson Welles (1943), child: Rebecca; divorced 1947. Married Aly Kahn (1949), child: Yasmin; divorced 1951. Married Dick Haymes (1953); divorced 1955. Married James Hill (1958); divorced 1961.

Larry Parks and Rita Hayworth in *Down to Earth*.

Feature Films:
   as Rita Cansino *Dante's Inferno* (Fox, 1935), *Under the Pampas Moon* (Fox, 1935), *Charlie Chan in Egypt* (Fox, 1935), *Paddy O'Day* (Fox, 1935), *Human Cargo* (20th, 1936), *A Message to Garcia* (20th, 1936), *Meet Nero Wolfe* (Col., 1936), *Rebellion* (Crescent, 1936), *Old Louisiana* (Crescent, 1937), *Hit the Saddle* (Rep., 1937), *Trouble in Texas* (GN, 1937).
   as Rita Hayworth *Criminals of the Air* (Col., 1937), *Girls Can Play* (Col., 1937), *The Game That Kills* (Col., 1937), *Paid to Dance* (Col., 1937), *The Shadow* (Col., 1937), *Who Killed Gail Preston?* (Col., 1938), *There's Always a Woman* (Col., 1938), *Convicted* (Col., 1938), *Juvenile Court* (Col., 1938), *Homicide Bureau* (Col., 1939), *The Lone Wolf Spy Hunt* (Col., 1939), *Renegade Ranger* (RKO, 1939), *Only Angels Have Wings* (Col., 1939), *Special Inspector* (Syndicate, 1939), *Music in My Heart* (Col., 1940), *Blondie on a Budget* (Col., 1940), *Susan and God* (MGM, 1940), *The Lady in Question* (Col., 1940), *Angels Over Broadway* (Col., 1940), *Strawberry Blonde* (WB, 1941), *Affectionately Yours* (WB, 1941), *Blood and Sand* (20th, 1941), *You'll Never Get Rich* (Col., 1941), *My Gal Sal* (20th, 1942), *Tales of Manhattan* (20th, 1942), *You Were Never Lovelier* (Col., 1942), *Cover Girl* (Col., 1944), *Tonight and Every*

Night (Col., 1945), *Gilda* (Col., 1946), *Down to Earth* (Col., 1947), *The Lady From Shanghai* (Col., 1948), *The Loves of Carmen* (Col., 1948), *Affair in Trinidad* (Col., 1952), *Salome* (Col., 1953), *Miss Sadie Thompson* (Col., 1953), *Fire Down Below* (Col., 1957), *Pal Joey* (Col., 1957), *Separate Tables* (UA, 1958), *They Came to Cordura* (Col., 1959), *The Story on Page One* (20th, 1959), *The Happy Thieves* (UA, 1962), *Circus World* (Par., 1965), *The Money Trap* (MGM, 1966), *The Rover* (ABC, 1968).

VAN HEFLIN (Emmett Evan Heflin) Born December 13, 1910, Walters, Oklahoma. Married Frances Neal (1942), children: Vana, Cathlee, Tracy; divorced 1968.

Peggy Moran and Van Heflin in *Seven Sweethearts*.

Feature Films: *A Woman Rebels* (RKO, 1936), *Outcasts of Poker Flat* (RKO, 1937), *Flight From Glory* (RKO, 1937), *Saturday's Heroes* (RKO, 1937), *Annapolis Salute* (RKO, 1937), *Back Door to Heaven* (Par., 1939), *Santa Fe Trail* (WB, 1940), *The Feminine Touch* (MGM, 1941), *Johnny Eager* (MGM, 1941), *H. M. Pulham, Esq.* (MGM, 1941), *Kid Glove Killer* (MGM, 1942), *Seven Sweethearts* (MGM, 1942), *Grand Central Murder* (MGM, 1942), *Tennessee Johnson* (MGM, 1942), *Presenting Lily Mars* (MGM, 1943), *The Strange Love of Martha Ivers* (Par., 1946), *Till the Clouds Roll By* (MGM, 1946), *Possessed* (WB, 1947), *Green Dolphin Street* (MGM, 1947), *Tap Roots* (Univ., 1948), *B.F.'s Daughter* (MGM, 1948), *The Three Musketeers* (MGM, 1948), *Act of Violence* (MGM, 1948), *Madame Bovary* (MGM, 1948), *The Secret Land* (narrator; MGM, 1948), *An Act of Violence* (MGM, 1948), *East Side, West Side* (MGM, 1949), *Tomahawk* (Univ., 1951), *The Prowler* (UA,, 1951), *Week-End With Father* (Univ., 1951), *My Son, John* (Par. 1952), *Wings of the Hawk* (Univ., 1953), *Shane* (Par., 1953), *Tanganyika* (Univ., 1954), *The Golden Mask* (UA, 1954), *The Raid* (20th, 1954), *A Woman's World* (20th, 1954), *Black Widow* (20th, 1954), *Count Three and Pray* (Col., 1955), *Battle Cry* (WB, 1955), *Patterns* (UA, 1956), *3:10 to Yuma* (Col., 1957), *Gunman's Walk* (Col., 1958), *They Came to Cordura* (Col., 1959), *Tempest* (Par., 1959), *Five Branded Women* (Par., 1960), *Under Ten Flags* (Par., 1960), *Cry of Battle* (AA, 1963), *To Be a Man* ("The Wastrel"—Medallion, 1964), *The Greatest Story Ever Told* (UA, 1965), *Once a Thief* (MGM, 1965), *Stagecoach* (20th, 1966), *The Man Outside* (Trio Films, 1967), *Each Man for Himself* (PCM, 1968).

WANDA HENDRIX (Dixie Wanda Hendrix) Born November 3, 1928, Jacksonville, Florida. Married Audie Murphy (1949); divorced 1950. Married James Stack; divorced.

Feature Films: *Confidential Agent* (WB, 1945), *Nora Prentiss* (WB, 1947), *Welcome Stranger* (Par., 1947), *Variety Girl* (Par., 1947), *Ride the Pink Horse* (Univ., 1947), *Miss Tatlock's Millions* (Par., 1948), *My Own True Love* (Par., 1948), *Prince of Foxes* (20th, 1949), *Song of Surrender* (Par., 1949), *Sierra* (Univ., 1950), *Captain Carey, U.S.A.* (Par., 1950), *The Admiral Was a Lady* (UA, 1950), *Saddle Tramp*

Henry Hull, Ray Bennett, Clancy Cooper, Georgia Bakus, Wanda Hendrix in *Song of Surrender.*

(Univ., 1950), *My Outlaw Brother* (EL, 1951), *The Highwayman* (AA, 1951), *Montana Territory* (Col., 1952), *The Last Posse* (Col., 1953), *Sea of Lost Ships* (Rep., 1953), *The Golden Mask* (UA, 1954), *Highway Dragnet* (AA, 1954), *The Black Dakotas* (Col., 1954), *Boy Who Caught a Crook* (UA, 1961), *Johnny Cool* (UA, 1963), *Stage to Thunder Rock* (Par., 1964).

SONJA HENIE Born April 8, 1912, Oslo, Norway. Married Dan Topping (1940); divorced 1946. Married Winthrop Gardiner (1949); divorced 1955. Married Niels Onsted (1956).

Sonja Henie and John Payne in *Iceland.*

Feature Films: *One in a Million* (20th, 1936), *Thin Ice* (20th, 1937), *Happy Landing* (20th, 1938), *My Lucky Star* (20th, 1938), *Second Fiddle* (20th, 1939), *Everything Happens at Night* (20th, 1939), *Sun Valley Serenade* (20th, 1941), *Iceland* (20th, 1942), *Wintertime* (20th, 1943), *It's a Pleasure* (RKO, 1945), *The Countess of Monte Cristo* (Univ., 1948).

PAUL HENREID (Paul George Julius Von Henreid) Born January 10, 1908, Trieste, Italy. Married Elisabeth Gluck (1936), children: Monica, Mimi.

English-Language Feature Films:

as **Paul Von Henreid** *Night Train* (Gaumont-British, 1939), *Goodbye, Mr. Chips* (MGM, 1939), *Under Your Hat* (British Lion, 1940).

as **Paul Henreid** *Joan of Paris* (RKO, 1942), *Now, Voyager* (WB, 1942), *Casablanca* (WB, 1942), *In Our Time* (WB, 1944), *Between Two Worlds* (WB, 1944), *The Conspirators* (WB, 1944), *Hollywood Canteen* (WB, 1944), *The Spanish Main* (RKO, 1945), *Devotion* (WB, 1946), *Of Human Bondage* (WB, 1946), *Deception* (WB, 1946), *Song of Love*

Ida Lupino, Nazimova and Paul Henreid in *In Our Time*.

(MGM, 1947), *Hollow Triumph* (EL, 1948), *Rope of Sand* (Par., 1949), *So Young, So Bad* (UA, 1950), *Last of the Buccaneers* (Col., 1950), *Pardon My French* (UA, 1951), *For Men Only* (Lip., 1952), *Thief of Damascus* (Col., 1952), *Siren of Bagdad* (Col., 1953), *Man in Hiding* (UA, 1953), *Deep in My Heart* (MGM, 1954), *Pirates of Tripoli* (Col., 1955), *Meet Me in Las Vegas* (MGM, 1956), *A Woman's Devotion* (Rep., 1956), *Ten Thousand Bedrooms* (MGM, 1957), *Holiday for Lovers* (20th, 1959), *The Four Horsemen of the Apocalypse* (MGM, 1962), *Operation Crossbow* (MGM, 1965), *Peking Remembered* (narrator; Butler-Hall, 1967).

AUDREY HEPBURN (Audry Hepburn-Ruston) Born May 4, 1929, Brussels, Belgium. Married Mel Ferrer (1954), child: Sean.

Anthony Perkins and Audrey Hepburn in *Green Mansions*.

English-Language Feature Films: *One Wild Oat* (Eros Films, 1951), *Young Wives' Tale* (AA, 1951), *Laughter in Paradise* (Stratford, 1951), *The Lavender Hill Mob* (Univ., 1951), *Monte Carlo Baby* (Mon, 1952), *The Secret People* (Lip., 1952), *Roman Holiday* (Par., 1953), *Sabrina* (Par., 1954), *War and Peace* (Par., 1956), *Funny Face* (Par., 1957), *Love in the Afternoon* (AA, 1957), *The Nun's Story* (WB, 1959), *Green Mansions* (MGM, 1959), *The Unforgiven* (UA, 1960), *Breakfast at Tiffany's* (Par., 1961), *The Children's Hour* (UA, 1962), *Charade* (Univ., 1963), *Paris When It Sizzles* (Par., 1964), *My Fair Lady* (WB, 1964), *How to Steal a Million* (20th, 1966), *Two For the Road* (20th, 1967), *Wait Until Dark* (WB, 1967).

KATHARINE HEPBURN (Katharine Houghton Hepburn) Born November 9, 1909, Hartford, Connecticut. Married Ludlow Ogden Smith (1928); divorced 1934.

John Beal and Katharine Hepburn in *The Little Minister*.

Feature Films: *A Bill of Divorcement* (RKO, 1932), *Christopher Strong* (RKO, 1933), *Morning Glory* (RKO, 1933), *Little Women* (RKO, 1933), *Spitfire* (RKO, 1934), *Break of Hearts* (RKO, 1935), *The Little Minister* (RKO, 1934), *Alice Adams* (RKO, 1935), *Sylvia Scarlett* (RKO, 1935), *Mary of Scotland* (RKO, 1936), *A Woman Rebels* (RKO, 1936), *Quality Street* (RKO, 1937), *Stage Door* (RKO, 1937), *Bringing Up Baby* (RKO, 1938), *Holiday* (Col., 1938), *The Philadelphia Story* (MGM, 1940), *Woman of the Year* (MGM, 1942), *Keeper of the Flame* (MGM, 1942), *Stage Door Canteen* (UA, 1943), *Dragon Seed* (MGM, 1944), *Without Love* (MGM, 1945), *Undercurrent* (MGM, 1946), *The Sea of Grass* (MGM, 1947), *Song of Love* (MGM, 1947), *State of the Union* (MGM, 1948), *Adam's Rib* (MGM, 1949), *The African Queen* (UA, 1951), *Pat and Mike* (MGM, 1952), *Summertime* (UA, 1955), *The Rainmaker* (Par., 1956), *The Iron Petticoat* (MGM, 1956), *Desk Set* (20th, 1957), *Suddenly, Last Summer* (Col., 1959), *Long Day's Journey into Night* (Embassy, 1962), *Guess Who's Coming to Dinner* (Col., 1967), *The Lion in Winter* (Embassy, 1968), *The Madwoman of Chaillot* (WB-7 Arts, 1968).

JEAN HERSHOLT Born July 12, 1886, Copenhagen, Denmark. Married Via Andersen (1914), child: Allan. Died June 2, 1956.

Sound Feature Films: *Hell Harbor* (UA, 1930), *Climax* (Univ., 1930), *The Case of Sergeant Grischa* (RKO, 1930), *Mamba* (Tif., 1930), *Viennese*

Jean Hersholt in *Mask of Fu Manchu*.

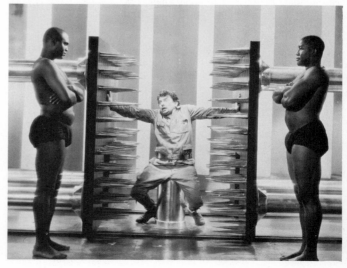

Nights (WB, 1930), *The Cat Creeps* (Univ., 1930), *East Is West* (Univ., 1930), *Third Alarm* (Tif., 1930), *Daybreak* (MGM, 1931), *Soldier's Plaything* (WB, 1931), *Susan Lennox—Her Fall and Rise* (MGM, 1931), *Phantom of Paris* (MGM, 1931), *Transatlantic* (Fox, 1931), *The Sin of Madelon Claudet* (MGM, 1931), *Private Lives* (MGM, 1931), *Beast of the City* (MGM, 1932), *Emma* (MGM, 1932), *Are You Listening?* (MGM, 1932), *Grand Hotel* (MGM, 1932), *Night Court* (MGM, 1932,) *New Morals for Old* (MGM, 1932), *Skyscraper Souls* (MGM, 1932), *Unashamed* (MGM, 1932), *Hearts of Humanity* (Majestic, 1932), *Flesh* (MGM, 1932), *The Mask of Fu Manchu* (MGM, 1932), *Crime of the Century* (Par., 1933), *Dinner at Eight* (MGM, 1933), *Song of the Eagle* (Par., 1933), *Christopher Bean* (MGM, 1933), *Cat and the Fiddle* (MGM, 1934), *Men in White* (MGM, 1934), *The Fountain* (RKO, 1934), *The Painted Veil* (MGM, 1934), *Mark of the Vampire* (MGM, 1935), *Murder in the Fleet* (MGM, 1935), *Break of Hearts* (RKO, 1935), *Tough Guy* (MGM, 1936), *The Country Doctor* (20th, 1936), *Sins of Man* (20th, 1936), *His Brother's Wife* (MGM, 1936), *Reunion* (20th, 1936), *One in a Million* (20th, 1936), *Seventh Heaven* (20th, 1937), *Heidi* (20th, 1937), *Happy Landing* (20th, 1938), *Alexander's Ragtime Band* (20th, 1938), *I'll Give a Million* (20th, 1938), *Five of a Kind* (20th, 1938), *Mr. Moto in Danger Island* (20th, 1939), *Meet Dr. Christian* (RKO, 1939), *Courageous Dr. Christian* (RKO, 1940), *Dr. Christian Meets the Women* (RKO, 1940), *Remedy for Riches* (RKO, 1940), *Melody for Three* (RKO, 1941), *Stage Door Canteen* (UA, 1943), *Dancing in the Dark* (20th, 1949), *Run for Cover* (Par., 1955).

CHARLTON HESTON Born October 4, 1924, Evanston, Illinois. Married Lydia Clark (1944), children: Fraser, Holly.

Lizabeth Scott and Charlton Heston in *Dark City*.

Feature Films: *Peer Gynt* (Brandon Films, 1942), *Julius Caesar* (Brandon Films, 1950), *Dark City* (Par., 1950), *The Greatest Show on Earth* (Par., 1952), *The Savage* (Par., 1952), *Ruby Gentry* (20th, 1952), *The President's Lady* (20th, 1953), *Pony Express* (Par., 1953), *Arrowhead* (Par., 1953), *Bad for Each Other* (Col., 1953), *The Naked Jungle* (Par., 1954), *Secret of the Incas* (Par., 1954), *The Far Horizons* (Par., 1955), *The Private War of Major Benson* (Univ., 1955), *Lucy Gallant* (Par., 1955), *The Ten Commandments* (Par., 1956), *Three Violent People* (Par., 1956), *Touch of Evil* (Univ., 1958), *The Big Country* (UA, 1958), *The Buccaneer* (Par., 1958), *The Wreck of the Mary Deare* (MGM, 1959), *Ben-Hur* (MGM, 1959), *El Cid* (UA, 1961), *The Pigeon That Took Rome* (Par., 1962), *Diamond Head* (Col., 1962), *55 Days at Peking* (AA, 1963), *The Greatest Story Ever Told* (UA, 1965), *Major Dundee* (Col., 1965), *The Agony and the Ecstasy* (20th, 1965), *The War Lord* (Univ., 1965), *Khartoum* (UA, 1966), *Counterpoint* (Univ., 1967), *Planet of the Apes* (20th, 1968), *Will Penny* (Par., 1968).

ROSE HOBART (Rose Kefer) Born May 1, 1906, New York, New York. Married Ben Webster (1924); divorced 1928. Married William Grosvenor (1932); divorced 1942. Married Barton Bosworth (1948).

Rose Hobart and Georges Renavent in *East of Borneo*.

Feature Films: *A Lady Surrenders* (Univ., 1930), *Liliom* (Fox, 1930), *Chances* (WB, 1931), *East of Borneo* (Univ., 1931), *Compromised* (British International, 1931), *Dr. Jekyll and Mr. Hyde* (Par., 1932), *Scandal for Sale* (Univ., 1932), *Shadow Laughs* (Invincible, 1933), *Convention Girl* (First Division, 1935), *The Tower of London* (Univ., 1939), *Wolf of New York* (Rep., 1940), *Susan and God* (MGM, 1940), *A Night at Earl Carroll's* (Par., 1940), *Ziegfeld Girl* (MGM, 1941), *Singapore Woman* (WB, 1941), *Lady Be Good* (MGM, 1941), *Nothing But the Truth* (Par., 1941), *I'll Sell My Life* (Select, 1941), *No Hands on the Clock* (Par., 1941), *Mr. and Mrs. North* (MGM, 1941), *Adventures of Smilin' Jack* (Univ. serial, 1942), *A Gentleman at Heart* (20th, 1942), *Who Is Hope Schuyler?* (20th, 1942), *Prison Girls* (PRC, 1942), *Dr. Gillespie's New Assistant* (MGM, 1942), *Salute to the Marines* (MGM, 1943), *Swing Shift Maisie* (MGM, 1943), *The Mad Ghoul* (Univ., 1943), *Crime Doctor's Strangest Case* (Col., 1943), *Song of the Open Road* (UA, 1944), *The Soul of a Monster* (Col., 1944), *Conflict* (WB, 1945), *The Brighton Strangler* (RKO, 1945), *The Cat Creeps* (Univ., 1946), *Canyon Passage* (Univ., 1946), *Claudia and David* (20th, 1946), *The Farmer's Daughter* (RKO, 1947), *The Trouble With Women* (Par., 1947), *Cass Timberlane* (MGM, 1947), *Mickey* (EL, 1948), *Bride of Vengeance* (Par., 1949).

JOHN HODIAK Born April 16, 1914, Pittsburgh, Pennsylvania. Married Anne Baxter (1946), child: Katrina; divorced 1953. Died October 19, 1955.

John Hodiak, Virginia Brissac and Lana Turner in *Marriage Is a Private Affair*.

Feature Films: *A Stranger in Town* (MGM, 1943), *Swing Shift Maisie* (MGM, 1943), *I Dood It* (MGM, 1943), *Song of Russia* (MGM, 1943), *Maisie Goes to Reno* (MGM, 1944) *Marriage Is a Private Affair* (MGM, 1944), *Lifeboat* (20th, 1944), *Sunday Dinner for a Soldier* (20th, 1944), *A Bell for Adano* (20th, 1945), *The Harvey Girls* (MGM,

1946), *Somewhere in the Night* (20th, 1946), *Two Smart People* (MGM, 1946), *The Arnelo Affair* (MGM, 1947), *Desert Fury* (Par., 1947), *Love From a Stranger* (EL, 1947), *Homecoming* (MGM, 1948), *Command Decision* (MGM, 1948), *The Bribe* (MGM, 1949), *Battleground* (MGM, 1949), *Malaya* (MGM, 1949), *Ambush* (MGM, 1949), *A Lady Without a Passport* (MGM, 1950), *The Miniver Story* (MGM, 1950), *Night into Morning* (MGM, 1951), *The People Against O'Hara* (MGM, 1951), *Across the Wide Missouri* (MGM, 1951), *The Sellout* (MGM, 1951), *Battle Zone* (AA, 1952), *Mission Over Korea* (Col., 1953), *Conquest of Cochise* (Col., 1953), *Ambush at Tomahawk Gap* (Col., 1953), *Dragonfly Squadron* (AA, 1954), *Trial* (MGM, 1955), *On the Threshold of Space* (20th, 1956).

WILLIAM HOLDEN (William Franklin Beedle) Born April 17, 1918, O'Fallon, Illinois. Married Brenda Marshall (1941), children: Virginia, Peter, Scott.

William Holden, Claire Trevor and Glenn Ford in *Texas*.

Feature Films: *Golden Boy* (Col., 1939), *Invisible Stripes* (WB, 1940), *Our Town* (UA, 1940), *Those Were the Days* (Par., 1940), *Arizona* (Col., 1940), *I Wanted Wings* (Par., 1941), *Texas* (Col., 1941), *The Fleet's In* (Par., 1942), *The Remarkable Andrew* (Par., 1942), *Meet the Stewarts* (Col., 1942), *Young and Willing* (UA, 1943), *Blaze of Noon* (Par., 1947), *Dear Ruth* (Par., 1947), *Variety Girl* (Par., 1947), *Rachel and the Stranger* (RKO, 1948), *Apartment for Peggy* (20th, 1948), *The Man From Colorado* (Col., 1948), *The Dark Past* (Col., 1949), *Streets of Laredo* (Par., 1949), *Miss Grant Takes Richmond* (Col., 1949), *Dear Wife* (Par., 1949), *Father Is a Bachelor* (Col., 1950), *Sunset Boulevard* (Par., 1950), *Union Station* (Par., 1950), *Born Yesterday* (Col., 1950), *Force of Arms* (WB, 1951), *Submarine Command* (Par., 1951), *Boots Malone* (Col., 1952), *The Turning Point* (Par., 1952), *Stalag 17* (Par., 1953), *The Moon Is Blue* (UA, 1953), *Forever Female* (Par., 1953), *Escape From Fort Bravo* (MGM, 1953), *Executive Suite* (MGM, 1954), *Sabrina* (Par., 1954), *The Country Girl* (Par., 1954), *The Bridges at Toko-Ri* (Par., 1954), *Love Is a Many-Splendored Thing* (20th, 1955), *Picnic* (Col., 1955), *The Proud and the Profane* (Par., 1956), *Toward the Unknown* (WB, 1956), *The Bridge on the River Kwai* (Col., 1957), *The Key* (Col., 1958), *The Horse Soldiers* (UA, 1959), *The World of Suzie Wong* (Par., 1960), *Satan Never Sleeps* (20th, 1962), *The Counterfeit Traitor* (Par., 1962), *The Lion* (20th, 1962), *Paris When It Sizzles* (Par., 1964), *The 7th Dawn* (UA, 1964), *Alvarez Kelly* (Col., 1966), *Casino Royale* (Col., 1967), *The Devil's Brigade* (UA, 1968).

JUDY HOLLIDAY (Judith Tuvim) Born June 21, 1922, New York, New York. Married David Oppenheim (1948), child: Jonathan; divorced 1958. Died June 7, 1965.

Judy Holliday in *Full of Life*.

Feature Films: *Greenwich Village* (20th, 1944), *Something for the Boys* (20th, 1944), *Winged Victory* (20th, 1944), *Adam's Rib* (MGM, 1949), *Born Yesterday* (Col., 1950), *The Marrying Kind* (Col., 1952), *It Should Happen to You* (Col., 1954), *Phffft* (Col., 1954), *The Solid Gold Cadillac* (Col., 1956), *Full of Life* (Col., 1956), *Bells Are Ringing* (MGM, 1960).

CELESTE HOLM Born April 29, 1919, New York, New York. Married Ralph Nelson, child: Theodore; divorced. Married Francis Davis (1940); divorced. Married Schuyler Dunning (1946), child: Daniel; divorced 1952.

Linda Darnell, Lucile Watson, Celeste Holm and Paul Douglas in *Everybody Does It*.

Feature Films: *Three Little Girls in Blue* (20th, 1946), *Carnival in Costa Rica* (20th, 1947), *Gentleman's Agreement* (20th, 1947), *Road House* (20th, 1948), *The Snake Pit* (20th, 1948), *Chicken Every Sunday* (20th 1948), *Come to the Stable* (20th, 1949), *Everybody Does It* (20th, 1949), *A Letter to Three Wives* (narrator; 20th, 1949), *All About Eve* (20th, 1950), *Champagne for Caesar* (UA, 1950), *The Tender Trap* (MGM, 1955), *High Society* (MGM, 1956), *Bachelor Flat* (20th, 1961), *Doctor, You've Got to Be Kidding!* (MGM, 1967).

BOB HOPE (Leslie Townes Hope) Born May 26, 1903, London, England. Married Dolores Reade (1933), children: Linda, Tony, Nora, Kelly.

Feature Films: *Big Broadcast of 1938* (Par., 1937), *College Swing* (Par., 1938), *Give Me a Sailor* (Par., 1938), *Thanks for the Memory* (Par., 1938), *Never Say Die* (Par., 1939), *Some Like It Hot* (Par., 1939), *The Cat and the Canary* (Par., 1939), *Road to Singapore* (Par., 1940), *The Ghost Breakers* (Par., 1940), *Road to Zanzibar* (Par., 1941), *Caught in the Draft* (Par., 1941), *Nothing But the Truth* (Par., 1941), *Louisiana Purchase* (Par., 1941), *My Favorite Blonde* (Par., 1942), *Road to Morocco* (RKO, 1942), *Star Spangled Rhythm* (Par., 1942), *They Got Me Cov-*

Jane Russell and Bob Hope in *Paleface*.

ered (Par., 1943), *Let's Face It* (Par., 1943), *The Princess and the Pirate* (Par., 1944), *Road to Utopia* (Par., 1945), *Monsieur Beaucaire* (Par., 1946), *My Favorite Brunette* (Par., 1947), *Where There's Life* (Par., 1947), *Variety Girl* (Par., 1947), *Road to Rio* (Par., 1948), *Paleface* (Par., 1948), *Sorrowful Jones* (Par., 1949), *The Great Lover* (Par., 1949), *Fancy Pants* (Par., 1950), *The Lemon Drop Kid* (Par., 1951), *My Favorite Spy* (Par., 1951), *The Greatest Show on Earth* (Par., 1952),* *Son of Paleface* (Par., 1952), *Road to Bali* (Par., 1952), *Off Limits* (Par., 1953), *Here Come the Girls* (Par., 1953), *Scared Stiff* (Par., 1953),* *Casanova's Big Night* (Par., 1954), *The Seven Little Foys* (Par., 1955), *That Certain Feeling* (Par., 1956), *The Iron Petticoat* (MGM, 1956), *Beau James* (Par., 1957), *Paris Holiday* (UA, 1958), *The Five Pennies* (Par., 1959),* *Alias Jesse James* (UA, 1959), *The Facts of Life* (UA, 1960), *Bachelor in Paradise* (MGM, 1961), *Road to Hong Kong* (UA, 1962), *Critic's Choice* (WB, 1963), *Call Me Bwana* (UA, 1963), *A Global Affair* (MGM, 1964), *I'll Take Sweden* (UA, 1965), *The Oscar* (Par., 1966),* *Boy, Did I Get a Wrong Number* (UA, 1966), *Eight on the Lam* (UA, 1967), *The Private Navy of Sgt. O'Farrell* (UA, 1968).

*Unbilled guest appearance

MIRIAM HOPKINS (Ellen Miriam Hopkins) Born October 18, 1902, Bainbridge, Georgia. Married Brandon Peters (1926); divorced 1931. Married Austin Parker (1931), child: Michael; divorced 1932. Married Anatole Litvak (1937); divorced 1939. Married Raymond Brock; divorced 1951.

Richard Ainley and Miriam Hopkins in *Lady With Red Hair*.

Feature Films: *Fast and Loose* (Par., 1930), *The Smiling Lieutenant* (Par., 1931), *24 Hours* (Par., 1931), *Dr. Jekyll and Mr. Hyde* (Par., 1932), *Two Kinds of Women* (Par., 1932), *Dancers in the Dark* (Par., 1932), *The World and the Flesh* (Par., 1932), *Trouble in Paradise* (Par., 1932), *The Story of Temple Drake* (Par., 1933), *Design for Living* (Par., 1933), *Stranger's Return* (MGM, 1933), *All of Me* (Par., 1934), *She Loves Me Not* (Par., 1934), *The Richest Girl in the World* (RKO, 1934), *Becky Sharp* (RKO, 1935), *Barbary Coast* (UA, 1935), *Splendor* (UA, 1935), *These Three* (UA, 1936), *Men Are Not Gods* (UA, 1937), *The Woman I Love* (RKO, 1937), *Woman Chases Man* (UA, 1937), *Wise Girl* (RKO, 1937), *The Old Maid* (WB, 1939), *Virginia City* (WB, 1940), *The Lady With Red Hair* (WB, 1940), *A Gentleman After Dark* (UA, 1942), *Old Acquaintance* (WB, 1943), *The Heiress* (Par., 1949), *The Mating Season* (Par., 1951), *Carrie* (Par., 1952), *Outcasts of Poker Flat* (20th, 1952), *The Children's Hour* (UA, 1962), *Fanny Hill: Memoirs of a Woman of Pleasure* (Favorite Films, 1965), *The Chase* (Col., 1966).

EDWARD EVERETT HORTON Born March 18, 1888, Brooklyn, New York.

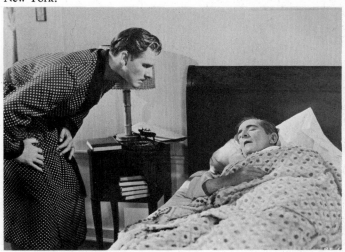

Errol Flynn and Edward Everett Horton in *The Perfect Specimen*.

Sound Feature Films: *The Hottentot* (WB, 1929), *Aviator* (WB, 1929), *Take the Heir* (Big Four, 1930), *Wide Open* (WB, 1930), *Holiday* (Pathé, 1930), *Once a Gentleman* (Sono Art-World Wide, 1930), *Kiss Me Again* (WB, 1931), *Reaching for the Moon* (UA, 1931), *Lonely Wives* (Pathé, 1931), *Front Page* (UA, 1931), *Six Cylinder Love* (Fox, 1931), *Smart Woman* (RKO, 1931), *Age for Love* (UA, 1931), *But the Flesh is Weak* (MGM, 1932), *Roar of the Dragon* (RKO, 1932), *Trouble in Paradise* (Par., 1932), *It's a Boy* (Gaumont-British, 1933), *A Bedtime Story* (Par., 1933), *The Way to Love* (Par., 1933), *Design for Living* (Par., 1933), *Alice in Wonderland* (Par., 1933), *A Woman in Command* (Gaumont-British, 1934), *Easy to Love* (WB, 1934), *Sing and Like It* (RKO, 1934), *Poor Rich* (Univ., 1934), *Smarty* (WB, 1934), *Success at Any Price* (RKO, 1934), *Uncertain Lady* (Univ., 1934), *Kiss and Make Up* (Par., 1934), *The Merry Widow* (MGM, 1934), *Ladies Should Listen* (Par., 1934), *The Gay Divorcee* (RKO, 1934), *The Private Secretary* (Twickenham-British, 1935,) *Biography of a Bachelor Girl* (MGM, 1935), *All the King's Horses* (Par., 1935), *The Night is Young* (MGM, 1935), *The Devil Is a Woman* (Par., 1935), *In Caliente* (WB, 1935), *$10 Raise* (Fox, 1935), *Going Highbrow* (WB, 1935), *Little Big Shot* (WB, 1935), *Top Hat* (RKO, 1935), *His Night Out* (Univ., 1935), *The Singing Kid* (WB, 1936), *Her Master's Voice* (Par., 1936), *Hearts Divided* (WB, 1936), *Nobody's Fool* (Univ., 1936), *The Man in the Mirror* (GN, 1937), *The King and the Chorus Girl* (WB, 1937), *Let's Make a Million* (Par., 1937), *Lost Horizon* (Col., 1937), *Shall We Dance* (RKO, 1937), *Oh Doctor!* (Univ., 1937), *Wild Money* (Par., 1937), *Angel* (Par., 1937), *The Perfect Specimen* (WB, 1937), *Danger—Love at Work* (20th, 1937), *The Great Garrick* (WB, 1937), *Hitting a New High* (RKO, 1937), *Bluebeard's Eighth Wife* (Par., 1938), *College Swing* (Par., 1938), *Holiday* (Col., 1938), *Little Tough Guys in Society* (Univ., 1938), *Paris Honeymoon* (Par., 1939), *That's Right—You're*

Wrong (RKO, 1939), *You're the One* (Par., 1941), *Ziegfeld Girl* (MGM, 1941), *Sunny* (RKO, 1941), *Bachelor Daddy* (Univ., 1941), *Here Comes Mr. Jordan* (Col., 1941), *Week-End for Three* (RKO, 1941), *Sandy Steps Out* (Univ., 1941), *I Married an Angel* (MGM, 1942), *The Magnificent Dope* (20th, 1942), *Springtime in the Rockies* (20th, 1942), *Forever and a Day* (RKO, 1943), *Thank Your Lucky Stars* (WB, 1943), *The Gang's All Here* (20th, 1943), *Summer Storm* (UA, 1944), *The Amazing Mr. Forrest* (PRC, 1944), *Her Primitive Man* (Univ., 1944), *San Diego, I Love You* (Univ., 1944), *Arsenic and Old Lace* (WB, 1944), *Brazil* (Rep., 1944), *The Town Went Wild* (PRC, 1944), *Steppin' in Society* (Rep., 1945), *Lady on a Train* (Univ., 1945), *Cinderella Jones* (WB, 1946), *Faithful in My Fashion* (MGM, 1946), *Earl Carroll's Sketchbook* (Rep., 1946), *The Ghost Goes Wild* (Rep., 1947), *Down to Earth* (Col., 1947), *Her Husband's Affair* (Col., 1947), *All My Sons* (Univ., 1948), *The Story of Mankind* (WB, 1957), *Pocketful of Miracles* (UA, 1961), *It's a Mad, Mad, Mad, Mad World* (UA, 1963), *Sex and the Single Girl* (WB, 1964), *The Perils of Pauline* (Univ., 1967).

LESLIE HOWARD (Leslie Howard Stainer) Born April 3, 1893; London, England. Married Ruth Martin (1916), children: Ronald, Leslie. Died June 1, 1943.

Spring Byington, Rochelle Hudson, Margaret Hamilton and Slim Summerville in *Way Down East*.

Kay Francis and Leslie Howard in *British Agent*.

Feature Films: *Outward Bound* (WB, 1930), *Never the Twain Shall Meet* (MGM, 1931), *A Free Soul* (MGM, 1931), *Five and Ten* (MGM, 1931), *Devotion* (RKO, 1931), *Reserved for Ladies* (Par., 1932), *Smilin' Through* (MGM, 1932), *The Animal Kingdom* (RKO, 1932), *Secrets* (UA, 1933), *Captured!* (WB, 1933), *Berkeley Square* (Fox, 1933), *The Lady Is Willing* (Col., 1934), *Of Human Bondage* (RKO, 1934), *British Agent* (WB, 1934), *The Scarlet Pimpernel* (UA, 1935), *The Petrified Forest* (WB, 1936), *Romeo and Juliet* (MGM, 1936), *It's Love I'm After* (WB, 1937), *Stand-In* (UA, 1937), *Pygmalion* (MGM, 1938), *Gone With the Wind* (MGM, 1939), *Intermezzo* (UA, 1939), *The First of the Few* ("Spitfire"—King, 1941), *Pimpernel Smith* (UA, 1942), *The Invaders* (Columbia, 1942).

ROCHELLE HUDSON Born March 6, 1914, Claremore, Oklahoma. Married Harold Thompson (1939); divorced 1947. Married Richard Hyland; divorced 1950.

Feature Films: *Are These Our Children?* (RKO, 1931), *Fanny Foley Herself* (RKO, 1931), *Beyond the Rockies* (RKO, 1932), *Hell's Highway* (RKO, 1932), *The Penguin Pool Murder* (RKO, 1932), *The Savage Girl* (Freuler, 1933), *She Done Him Wrong* (Par., 1933), *Love Is Dangerous* (Chesterfield, 1933), *Notorious But Nice* (Chesterfield, 1933), *Doctor Bull* (Fox, 1933), *Walls of Gold* (Fox, 1933), *Wild Boys of the Road* (WB, 1933), *Love Is Like That* (Chesterfield, 1933), *Mr. Skitch* (Fox, 1933), *Harold Teen* (WB, 1934), *Such Women Are Dangerous* (Fox,

1934), *Judge Priest* (Fox, 1934), *Bachelor Bait* (RKO, 1934), *Mighty Barnum* (UA, 1934), *Imitation of Life* (Univ., 1934), *I've Been Around* (Univ., 1935), *Life Begins at Forty* (Fox, 1935), *Les Miserables* (UA, 1935), *Way Down East* (Fox, 1935), *Curly Top* (Fox, 1935), *Show Them No Mercy* (20th, 1935), *The Music Goes Round* (Col., 1936), *Everybody's Old Man* (20th, 1936), *The Country Beyond* (20th, 1936), *Poppy* (Par., 1936), *Reunion* (20th, 1936), *Woman Wise* (20th, 1937), *That I May Live* (20th, 1937), *Born Reckless* (20th, 1937), *She Had to Eat* (20th, 1937), *Rascals* (20th, 1938), *Mr. Moto Takes a Chance* (20th, 1938), *Storm Over Bengal* (Rep., 1938), *Pride of the Navy* (Rep., 1939), *Missing Daughters* (Col., 1939), *A Woman Is the Judge* (Col., 1939), *Smuggled Cargo* (Rep., 1939), *Pirates of the Skies* (Univ., 1939), *Convicted Woman* (Col., 1940), *Konga, the Wild Stallion* (Col., 1940), *Men Without Souls* (Col., 1940), *Babies For Sale* (Col., 1940), *Island of Doomed Men* (Col., 1940), *Girls Under 21* (Col., 1940), *Meet Boston Blackie* (Col., 1941), *The Officer and the Lady* (Col., 1941), *The Stork Pays Off* (Col., 1941), *Rubber Racketeers* (Mon., 1942), *Queen of Broadway* (PRC, 1942), *Bush Pilot* (Screen Guild, 1947), *Devil's Cargo* (Film Classics, 1948), *Sky Liner* (Lip., 1949), *Rebel Without a Cause* (WB, 1955), *Strait-Jacket* (Col., 1964), *The Night Walker* (Univ., 1965), *Dr. Terror's Gallery of Horrors* (Par., 1967).

ROCK HUDSON (Roy Scherer, Jr.) Born November 17, 1927, Winnetka, Illinois. Married Phyllis Gates (1955); divorced 1958.

Doris Day and Rock Hudson in *Lover Come Back*.

Feature Films: *Fighter Squadron* (WB, 1948), *Undertow* (Univ., 1949), *I Was a Shoplifter* (Univ., 1950), *One Way Street* (Univ., 1950), *Winchester '73* (Univ., 1950), *Peggy* (Univ., 1950), *The Desert Hawk* (Univ., 1950), *The Fat Man* (Univ., 1951), *Air Cadet* (Univ., 1951), *Tomahawk* (Univ., 1951), *Iron Man* (Univ., 1951), *Bright Victory* (Univ., 1951), *Bend of the River* (Univ., 1952), *Here Come the Nelsons* (Univ., 1952)

Scarlet Angel (Univ., 1952), *Has Anybody Seen My Gal* (Univ., 1952), *Horizons West* (Univ., 1952), *The Lawless Breed* (Univ., 1952), *Seminole* (Univ., 1953), *Sea Devils* (RKO, 1953), *The Golden Blade* (Univ., 1953), *Back to God's Country* (Univ., 1953), *Taza, Son of Cochise* (Univ., 1954), *Magnificent Obsession* (Univ., 1954), *Bengal Brigade* (Univ., 1954), *Captain Lightfoot* (Univ., 1955), *One Desire* (Univ., 1955), *All That Heaven Allows* (Univ., 1955), *Never Say Goodbye* (Univ., 1956), *Giant* (WB, 1956), *Battle Hymn* (Univ., 1956), *Written on the Wind* (Univ., 1956), *Four Girls in Town* (Univ., 1956), *Something of Value* (MGM, 1957), *The Tarnished Angels* (Univ., 1957), *A Farewell to Arms* (20th, 1957), *Twilight for the Gods* (Univ., 1958), *This Earth Is Mine* (Univ., 1959), *Pillow Talk* (Univ., 1959), *The Last Sunset* (Univ., 1961), *Come September* (Univ., 1961), *Lover, Come Back* (Univ., 1961), *The Spiral Road* (Univ., 1962), *A Gathering of Eagles* (Univ., 1963), *Man's Favorite Sport?* (Univ., 1964), *Send Me No Flowers* (Univ., 1964), *Strange Bedfellows* (Univ., 1964), *A Very Special Favor* (Univ., 1965), *Blindfold* (Univ., 1966), *Seconds* (Par., 1966), *Tobruk* (Univ., 1967), *Ice Station Zebra* (MGM, 1968), *The Quiet Couple* (CBS Films, 1968).

MARSHA HUNT (Marcia Virginia Hunt) Born October 17, 1917, Chicago, Illinois. Married Jerry Hopper (1938); divorced 1943. Married Robert Presnell (1946).

Walter Fenner, Keenan Wynn, Sara Haden, Alan Napier, Philip Merivale, Howard Freeman, Kathleen Lockhart, Elisabeth Risdon, Marsha Hunt and Donald Meek in *Lost Angel*.

Feature Films: *The Virginia Judge* (Par., 1935), *The Accusing Finger* (Par., 1936), *Gentle Julia* (20th, 1936), *Desert Gold* (Par., 1936), *Arizona Raiders* (Par., 1936), *Hollywood Boulevard* (Par., 1936), *Easy to Take* (Par., 1936), *College Holiday* (Par., 1936), *Murder Goes to College* (Par., 1937), *Easy Living* (Par., 1937), *Thunder Trail* (Par., 1937), *Annapolis Salute* (RKO, 1937), *The Long Shot* (GN, 1938), *Born to the West* (Par., 1938), *Come On, Leathernecks* (Rep., 1938), *The Hardys Ride High* (MGM, 1939), *The Star Reporter* (Mon., 1939), *These Glamour Girls* (MGM, 1939), *Joe and Ethel Turp Call on the President* (MGM, 1939), *Winter Carnival* (UA, 1939), *Pride and Prejudice* (MGM, 1940), *Flight Command* (MGM, 1940), *Irene* (RKO, 1940), *Woman in Hiding* (Univ., 1940), *Ellery Queen, Master Detective* (Col., 1940), *Blossoms in the Dust* (MGM, 1941), *I'll Wait for You* (MGM, 1941), *The Trial of Mary Dugan* (MGM, 1941), *The Penalty* (MGM, 1941), *Cheers for Miss Bishop* (UA, 1941), *Unholy Partners* (MGM, 1941), *Kid Glove Killer* (MGM, 1942), *Joe Smith, American* (MGM, 1942), *The Affairs of Martha* (MGM, 1942), *Panama Hattie* (MGM, 1942), *Seven Sweethearts* (MGM, 1942), *Thousands Cheer* (MGM, 1943), *Pilot No. 5* (MGM, 1943), *The Human Comedy* (MGM, 1943), *Cry Havoc* (MGM, 1943), *Lost Angel* (MGM, 1943), *Bride by Mistake* (RKO, 1944), *None Shall Escape* (Col., 1944), *Music for Millions* (MGM, 1944), *Valley of Decision* (MGM, 1945), *A Letter for Evie* (MGM, 1945), *Smash-Up* (Univ., 1947), *Carnegie Hall* (UA,

1947), *The Inside Story* (Rep., 1948), *Raw Deal* (EL, 1948), *Jigsaw* (UA, 1949), *Take One False Step* (Univ., 1949), *Mary Ryan, Detective* (Col., 1950), *Actors and Sin* (UA, 1952), *The Happy Time* (Col., 1952), *Diplomatic Passport* (Eros, 1954), *No Place to Hide* (AA, 1956), *Bombers B-52* (WB, 1957), *Back From the Dead* (20th, 1957), *Blue Denim* (20th, 1959), *The Plunderers* (AA, 1960).

JEFFREY HUNTER (Henry Herman McKinnies, Jr.) Born November 25, 1927, New Orleans, Louisiana. Married Barbara Rush (1950), child: Christopher; divorced 1955. Married Dusty Bartlett (1957), child: Toddy; divorced 1967.

Jeffrey Hunter, John Larch, Chill Wills and Dean Stockwell in *Gun for a Coward*.

English-Language Feature Films: *Julius Caesar* (Brandon Films, 1950), *Fourteen Hours* (20th, 1951), *Call Me Mister* (20th, 1951), *Take Care of My Little Girl* (20th, 1951), *The Frogmen* (20th, 1951), *Red Skies of Montana* (20th, 1952), *Belles on their Toes* (20th, 1952), *Dreamboat* (20th, 1952), *Lure of the Wilderness* (20th, 1952), *Sailor of the King* (20th, 1953), *Three Young Texans* (20th, 1954), *Princess of the Nile* (20th, 1954), *Seven Angry Men* (AA, 1955), *White Feather* (20th, 1955), *Seven Cities of Gold* (20th, 1955), *The Searchers* (WB, 1956), *The Great Locomotive Chase* (BV, 1956), *The Proud Ones* (20th, 1956), *A Kiss Before Dying* (UA, 1956), *Four Girls in Town* (Univ, 1956), *Gun for a Coward* (Univ., 1957), *The True Story of Jesse James* (20th, 1957), *No Down Payment* (20th, 1957), *Count Five and Die* (20th, 1958), *The Last Hurrah* (Col., 1958), *In Love and War* (20th, 1958), *Mardi Gras* (20th, 1958), *Sergeant Rutledge* (WB, 1960), *Hell to Eternity* (AA, 1960), *Key Witness* (MGM, 1960), *Man-Trap* (Par., 1961), *King of Kings* (MGM, 1961), *No Man is an Island* (Univ., 1962), *The Longest Day* (20th, 1962), *The Man From Galveston* (WB, 1964), *Brainstorm* (WB, 1965), *Murieta* (WB, 1965), *Dimension 5* (Feature Film Corp. of America, 1966), *Frozen Alive* (PRO, 1967), *Witch Without a Broom* (PRO, 1967), *Custer of the West* (Cinerama, 1967), *A Guide for the Married Man* (20th, 1967), *The Christmas Kid* (PRO, 1967), *The Private Navy of Sgt. O'Farrell* (UA, 1968).

KIM HUNTER (Janet Cole) Born November 12, 1922, Detroit, Michigan. Married William Baldwin (1944), child: Kathryn; divorced 1946. Married Robert Emmett (1951), child: Sean.

Humphrey Bogart and Kim Hunter in *Deadline, U.S.A.*

Feature Films: *The Seventh Victim* (RKO, 1943), *Tender Comrade* (RKO, 1943), *When Strangers Marry* (Mon., 1944), *You Came Along* (Par., 1945), *Stairway to Heaven* (Univ., 1947), *A Canterbury Tale* (EL, 1949), *A Streetcar Named Desire* (WB, 1951), *Deadline U.S.A.* (20th, 1952), *Anything Can Happen* (Par., 1952), *Storm Center* (Col., 1956), *The Young Stranger* (Univ., 1957), *Bermuda Affair* (DCA, 1957), *Money, Women and Guns* (Univ., 1958), *Lilith* (Col., 1964), *Planet of the Apes* (20th, 1968).

TAB HUNTER (Arthur Gelien) Born July 1, 1931, New York, New York.

Tab Hunter and William Bishop in *Gun Belt*.

Feature Films: *The Lawless* (Par., 1950), *Island of Desire* (UA, 1952), *Gun Belt* (UA, 1953), *The Steel Lady* (UA, 1953), *Return to Treasure Island* (UA, 1954), *Track of the Cat* (WB, 1954), *Battle Cry* (WB, 1955), *The Sea Chase* (WB, 1955), *The Burning Hills* (WB, 1956), *The Girl He Left Behind* (WB, 1956), *Lafayette Escadrille* (WB, 1958), *Gunman's Walk* (Col., 1958), *Damn Yankees* (WB, 1958), *That Kind of Woman* (Par., 1959), *They Came to Cordura* (Col., 1959), *The Pleasure of His Company* (Par., 1961), *Operation Bikini* (AIP, 1963), *The Golden Arrow* (MGM, 1964), *Ride the Wild Surf* (Col., 1964), *The Loved One* (MGM, 1965), *War Gods of the Deep* (AIP, 1965), *Birds Do It* (Col., 1966), *Fickle Finger of Fate* (PRO, 1967), *Hostile Guns* (Par., 1967), *Cup of St. Sebastian* (PRO, 1967).

RUTH HUSSEY (Ruth Carol O'Rourke) Born October 30, 1914, Providence, Rhode Island. Married Robert Longenecker (1942), children: George, John, Mary.

Feature Films: *Madame X* (MGM, 1937), *Judge Hardy's Children* (MGM, 1938), *Man-Proof* (MGM, 1938), *Marie Antoinette* (MGM,

Ruth Hussey and John Howard in *I, Jane Doe*.

1938), *Hold That Kiss* (MGM, 1938), *Rich Man—Poor Girl* (MGM, 1938), *Time Out for Murder* (20th, 1938), *Spring Madness* (MGM, 1938), *Honolulu* (MGM, 1939), *Within the Law* (MGM, 1939), *Maisie* (MGM, 1939), *The Women* (MGM, 1939), *Another Thin Man* (MGM, 1939), *Blackmail* (MGM, 1939), *Fast and Furious* (MGM, 1939), *Northwest Passage* (MGM, 1940), *Susan and God* (MGM, 1940), *The Philadelphia Story* (MGM, 1940), *Flight Command* (MGM, 1940), *Free and Easy* (MGM, 1941), *Our Wife* (Col., 1941), *Married Bachelor* (MGM, 1941), *H. M. Pulham, Esq.* (MGM, 1941), *Pierre of the Plains* (MGM, 1942), *Tennessee Johnson* (MGM, 1942), *Tender Comrade* (RKO, 1943), *The Uninvited* (Par., 1944), *Marine Raiders* (RKO, 1944), *Bedside Manner* (UA, 1945), *I, Jane Doe* (Rep., 1948), *The Great Gatsby* (Par., 1949), *Louisa* (Univ., 1950), *Mr. Music* (Par., 1950), *That's My Boy* (Par., 1951), *Woman of the North Country* (Rep., 1952), *Stars and Stripes Forever* (20th, 1952), *The Lady Wants Mink* (Rep., 1953), *The Facts of Life* (UA, 1960).

WALTER HUSTON (Walter Houghston) Born April 6, 1884, Toronto, Canada. Married Rhea Gore (1905), child: John; divorced 1913. Married Bayonne Whipple (1914); divorced. Married Nanette Sunderland (1931). Died April 7, 1950.

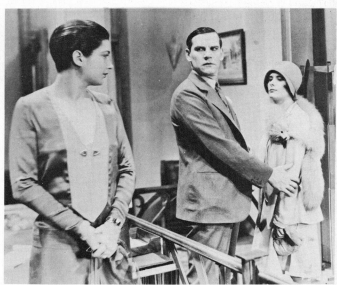

Kay Francis, Walter Huston and Betty Lawford in *Gentlemen of the Press*.

Feature Films: *Gentlemen of the Press* (Par., 1929), *The Lady Lies* (Par., 1929), *The Virginian* (Par., 1929), *The Bad Man* (WB, 1930), *The Virtuous Sin* (Par., 1930), *Abraham Lincoln* (UA, 1930), *The Criminal Code* (Col., 1931), *Star Witness* (WB, 1931), *The Ruling Voice* (WB, 1931), *A Woman From Monte Carlo* (WB, 1932), *A House Divided* (Univ., 1932), *Law and Order* (Univ., 1932), *The Beast of the City* (MGM, 1932), *The Wet Parade* (MGM, 1932), *Night Court* (MGM, 1932), *American Madness* (Col., 1932), *Kongo* (MGM, 1932), *Rain* (UA, 1932), *Hell Below* (MGM, 1933), *Gabriel Over the White House* (MGM, 1933), *The Prizefighter and the Lady* (MGM, 1933), *Storm at Daybreak* (MGM, 1933), *Ann Vickers* (RKO, 1933), *Keep 'Em Rolling!* (RKO, 1934), *Trans-Atlantic Tunnel* (Gaumont-British, 1935), *Rhodes of Africa* (Gaumont-British, 1936), *Dodsworth* (UA, 1936), *Of Human Hearts* (MGM, 1938), *The Light That Failed* (Par., 1940), *All That Money Can Buy* (RKO, 1941), *The Maltese Falcon* (WB, 1941),* *Swamp Water* (20th, 1941), *The Shanghai Gesture* (UA, 1941), *Always in My Heart* (WB, 1942), *In This Our Life* (WB, 1942),* *Yankee Doodle Dandy* (WB, 1942), *The Outlaw* (RKO, 1943), *Edge of Darkness* (WB, 1943), *Mission to Moscow* (WB, 1943), *The North Star* (RKO, 1943), *Dragon Seed* (MGM, 1944), *And Then There Were None* (20th, 1945), *Dragonwyck* (20th, 1946), *Duel in the Sun* (Selznick, 1946), *Treasure of the Sierra Madre* (WB, 1948), *Summer Holiday* (MGM, 1948), *The Great Sinner* (MGM, 1949), *The Furies* (Par., 1950).

*Unbilled guest appearance

BETTY HUTTON (Elizabeth June Thornburg) Born February 26, 1921, Battle Creek, Michigan. Married Ted Briskin (1945), children: Lindsay, Candice; divorced 1951. Married Charles O'Curran (1952); divorced 1955. Married Alan Livingston (1955); divorced 1958. Married Pete Candoli (1961), child: Carolyn; divorced 1966.

Diana Lynn, Dorothy Lamour, Raymond Walburn, Betty Hutton and Mimi Chandler in *And the Angels Sing*.

Feature Films: *The Fleet's In* (Par., 1942), *Star Spangled Rhythm* (Par., 1942), *Happy Go Lucky* (Par., 1943), *Let's Face It* (Par., 1943), *The Miracle of Morgan's Creek* (Par., 1944), *And the Angels Sing* (Par., 1944), *Here Come the Waves* (Par., 1944), *Incendiary Blonde* (Par., 1945), *Duffy's Tavern* (Par., 1945), *The Stork Club* (Par., 1945), *Cross My Heart* (Par., 1946), *The Perils of Pauline* (Par., 1947), *Dream Girl* (Par., 1948), *Red, Hot and Blue* (Par., 1949), *Annie Get Your Gun* (MGM, 1950), *Let's Dance* (Par., 1950), *Sailor Beware* (Par., 1951),* *Somebody Loves Me* (Par., 1952), *The Greatest Show on Earth* (Par., 1952), *Spring Reunion* (UA, 1957).

*Unbilled guest appearance

JIM HUTTON (James Hutton) Born Binghamton, New York. Married, children: Heidi, Timothy; divorced.

Lois Nettleton, Jim Hutton and Jane Fonda in *Period of Adjustment*.

Feature Films: *A Time to Love, and a Time to Die* (Univ., 1958), *Ten Seconds to Hell* (UA, 1959), *The Subterraneans* (MGM, 1960), *Where the Boys Are* (MGM, 1960), *The Honeymoon Machine* (MGM, 1961),

Bachelor in Paradise (MGM, 1961), *The Horizontal Lieutenant* (MGM, 1962), *Period of Adjustment* (MGM, 1962), *Looking for Love* (MGM, 1964),* *Major Dundee* (Col., 1965), *The Hallelujah Trail* (UA, 1965), *Never Too Late* (WB, 1965), *Walk, Don't Run* (Col., 1966), *The Trouble With Angels* (Col., 1966), *Who's Minding the Mint?* (Col., 1967), *The Green Berets* (WB-7 Arts, 1968).

*Unbilled guest appearance

MARTHA HYER Born August 10, 1924, Fort Worth, Texas. Married Ray Stahl (1951); divorced 1953. Married Hal Wallis (1966).

Martha Hyer, Van Johnson and Janet Leigh in *Wives and Lovers*.

English-Language Feature Films: *The Locket* (RKO, 1946), *Thunder Mountain* (RKO, 1947), *Born to Kill* (RKO, 1947), *Woman on the Beach* (RKO, 1947), *The Velvet Touch* (RKO, 1948), *Gun Smugglers* (RKO, 1948), *The Clay Pigeon* (RKO, 1949), *The Judge Steps Out* (RKO, 1949), *Roughshod* (RKO, 1949), *Rustlers* (RKO, 1949), *The Lawless* (Par., 1950), *Outcast of Black Mesa* (Col., 1950), *Salt Lake Raiders* (Rep., 1950), *Frisco Tornado* (Rep., 1950), *Wild Stallion* (Mon., 1952), *Yukon Gold* (Mon., 1952), *Geisha Girl* (Realart, 1952), *Abbott and Costello Go to Mars* (Univ., 1953), *So Big* (WB, 1953), *Riders to the Stars* (UA, 1954), *The Scarlet Spear* (UA, 1954), *Battle of Rogue River* (Col., 1954), *Lucky Me* (WB, 1954), *Down Three Dark Streets* (UA, 1954), *Sabrina* (Par., 1954), *Cry Vengeance* (AA, 1954), *Wyoming Renegades* (Col., 1955), *Francis in the Navy* (Univ., 1955), *Kiss of Fire* (Univ., 1955) *Paris Follies of 1956* (AA, 1955), *Red Sundown* (Univ., 1956), *Showdown at Abilene* (Univ., 1956), *Battle Hymn* (Univ., 1956), *Kelly and Me* (Univ., 1957), *Mister Cory* (Univ., 1957), *The Delicate Delinquent* (Par., 1957), *My Man Godfrey* (Univ., 1957), *Paris Holiday* (UA, 1958), *Once Upon a Horse* (Univ., 1958), *Houseboat* (Par., 1958), *Some Came Running* (MGM, 1958), *The Big Fisherman* (BV, 1959), *The Best of Everything* (20th, 1959), *Ice Palace* (WB, 1960), *Desire in the Dust* (20th, 1960), *The Right Approach* (20th, 1961), *The Last Time I Saw Archie* (UA, 1961), *A Girl Named Tamiko* (Par., 1962), *The Man From the Diners' Club* (Col., 1963), *Wives and Lovers* (Par., 1963), *The Carpetbaggers* (Par., 1964), *Pyro* (AIP, 1964), *Bikini Beach* (AIP, 1964), *First Men in the Moon* (Col., 1964), *Blood on the Arrow* (AA, 1964), *The Sons of Katie Elder* (Par., 1965), *The Chase* (Col., 1966), *The Night of the Grizzly* (Par., 1966), *Picture Mommy Dead* (Embassy, 1966), *The Happening* (Col., 1967), *Massacre at Fort Grant* (Butcher's, 1967), *Some May Live* (RKO, 1967), *War Italian Style* (AIP, 1967), *House of 1,000 Dolls* (AIP, 1968).

JOHN IRELAND (John Benjamin Ireland) Born January 30, 1914, Vancouver, British Columbia. Married Elaine Sheldon (1940); divorced 1948. Married Joanne Dru (1949), children: John, Peter; divorced 1956. Married Daphne Myrick (1962).

English-Language Feature Films: *A Walk in the Sun* (20th, 1945), *Behind Green Lights* (20th, 1946), *It Shouldn't Happen to a Dog* (20th,

John Ireland in *I Saw What You Did.*

1946), *My Darling Clementine* (20th, 1946), *Wake Up and Dream* (20th, 1946), *Railroaded* (EL, 1947), *The Gangster* (AA, 1947), *Open Secret* (EL, 1948), *Raw Deal* (EL, 1948), *I Love Trouble* (Col., 1948), *Red River* (UA, 1948), *A Southern Yankee* (MGM, 1948), *Joan of Arc* (RKO, 1948), *I Shot Jesse James* (Screen Guild, 1949), *Roughshod* (RKO, 1949), *The Walking Hills* (Col., 1949), *Anna Lucasta* (Col., 1949), *Mr. Soft Touch* (Col., 1949), *Doolins of Oklahoma* (Col., 1949), *All The King's Men* (Col., 1949), *Cargo to Capetown* (Col., 1950), *Return of Jesse James* (Lip., 1950), *The Scarf* (UA, 1951), *Little Big Horn* (Lip., 1951), *Vengeance Valley* (MGM, 1951), *The Basketball Fix* (Realart, 1951), *Red Mountain* (Par., 1951), *The Bushwhackers* (Realart, 1952), *Hurricane Smith* (Par., 1952), *Combat Squad* (Col., 1953), *The 49th Man* (Col., 1953), *Outlaw Territory* (Realart, 1953), *Security Risk* (AA, 1954), *Southwest Passage* (UA, 1954), *The Steel Cage* (UA, 1954), *The Fast and Furious* (American Releasing Corp., 1954), *Glass Tomb* (Lip., 1955), *The Good Die Young* (UA, 1955), *Queen Bee* (Col., 1955), *Hell's Horizon* (Col., 1955), *Gunfight at the O.K. Corral* (Par., 1957), *Stormy Crossing* ("Black Tide"—Eros, 1957), *Party Girl* (MGM, 1958), *No Place to Land* (Rep., 1958), *Spartacus* (Univ., 1960), *Return of a Stranger* (British, 1961), *Wild in the Country* (20th, 1961), *Brushfire!* (Par., 1962), *55 Days at Peking* (AA, 1963), *The Ceremony* (UA, 1963), *No Time to Kill* (Jerry Warren, 1963), *Faces in the Dark* (Pennington Eady, 1964), *The Fall of the Roman Empire* (Par., 1964), *I Saw What You Did* (Univ., 1965), *Day of the Nightmare* (Governor, 1966), *Fort Utah* (Par., 1967), *Flight of the Hawk* (C. B. Productions, 1967), *Arizona Bushwhackers* (Par., 1968).

DEAN JAGGER (Dean Jeffries) Born November 7, 1903, Lima, Ohio. Married Antoinette Lowrence (1935); divorced 1945. Married Gloria Ling (1947), child: Diane; divorced 1967.

Sound Feature Films: *Woman From Hell* (Fox, 1929), *Handcuffed* (Rayart 1929), *You Belong to Me* (Par., 1934), *College Rhythm* (Par., 1934), *Car 99* (Par., 1935), *Home on the Range* (Par., 1935), *Wings in*

the Dark (Par., 1935), *Behold My Wife* (Par., 1935), *People Will Talk* (Par., 1935), *Men Without Names* (Par., 1935), *Wanderer of the Wastelands* (Par., 1935), *Woman Trap* (Par., 1936), *13 Hours by Air* (Par., 1936), *Revolt of the Zombies* (Academy Pictures, 1936), *Pepper* (20th, 1936), *Star for a Night* (20th, 1936), *Dangerous Number* (MGM, 1937), *Under Cover of Night* (MGM, 1937), *Woman in Distress* (Col., 1937), *Escape by Night* (Rep., 1937), *Exiled to Shanghai* (Rep., 1937), *Brigham Young—Frontiersman* (20th, 1940), *Western Union* (Par., 1941), *The Men in Her Life* (Col., 1941), *Valley of the Sun* (RKO, 1942), *The Omaha Trail* (MGM, 1942), *I Escaped From the Gestapo* (Mon., 1943), *The North Star* (RKO, 1943), *When Strangers Marry* (Mon., 1944), *Alaska* (Mon., 1944), *I Live in Grosvenor Square* ("A Yank In London" —Associated British, 1945), *Sister Kenny* (RKO, 1946), *Pursued* (WB, 1947), *Driftwood* (Rep., 1947), *C-Man* (Film Classics, 1949), *Twelve O'Clock High* (20th, 1949), *Sierra* (Univ., 1950), *Dark City* (Par., 1950), *Rawhide* (20th, 1951), *Warpath* (Par., 1951), *The Denver and Rio Grande* (Par., 1952), *My Son, John* (Par., 1952), *It Grows on Trees* (Univ., 1952), *The Robe* (20th, 1953), *Executive Suite* (MGM, 1954), *Private Hell 36* (Filmakers, 1954) *White Christmas* (Par., 1954), *Bad Day at Black Rock* (MGM, 1954), *The Eternal Sea* (Rep., 1955), *It's a Dog's Life* (MGM, 1955), *On the Threshold of Space* (20th, 1956), *Red Sundown* (Univ., 1956), *The Great Man* (Univ., 1956), *Three Brave Men* (20th, 1957), *X The Unknown* (WB, 1957), *Bernardine* (20th, 1957), *Forty Guns* (20th, 1957), *The Proud Rebel* (BV, 1958), *King Creole* (Par., 1958), *The Nun's Story* (WB, 1959), *Cash McCall* (WB, 1959), *Elmer Gantry* (UA, 1960), *Parrish* (WB, 1961), *The Honeymoon Machine* (MGM, 1961), *Billy Rose's Jumbo* (MGM, 1962), *First to Fight* (WB, 1967), *Firecreek* (WB-7 Arts, 1968), *Evil Gun* (MGM, 1968).

GLORIA JEAN (Gloria Jean Schoonover) Born April 14, 1928, Buffalo, New York.

Bing Crosby, Gloria Jean and Moroni Olsen in *If I Had My Way.*

Feature Films: *The Under-Pup* (Univ., 1939), *If I Had My Way* (Par., 1940), *A Little Bit of Heaven* (Univ., 1940), *Never Give a Sucker an Even Break* (Univ., 1941), *What's Cooking?* (Univ., 1942), *Get Hep to Love* (Univ., 1942), *When Johnny Comes Marching Home* (Univ., 1943), *It Comes Up Love* (Univ., 1943), *Mister Big* (Univ., 1943), *Moonlight in Vermont* (Univ., 1943), *Follow the Boys* (Univ., 1944), *Pardon My Rhythm* (Univ., 1944), *Ghost Catchers* (Univ., 1944), *The Reckless Age* (Univ., 1944), *Destiny* (Univ., 1944), *I'll Remember April* (Univ., 1945), *Easy to Look at* (Univ., 1945), *River Gang* (Univ., 1945), *Copacabana* (UA, 1947), *An Old-Fashioned Girl* (EL, 1948), *I Surrender, Dear* (Col., 1948), *Manhattan Angel* (Col., 1949), *There's a Girl in My Heart* (AA, 1949), *Air Strike* (Lippert, 1955), *The Ladies' Man* (Par., 1961), *The Madcaps* (Boots and Saddles, 1963).

RITA JOHNSON Born August 13, 1913, Worcester, Massachusetts. Married L. Stanley Kahn (1940); divorced 1943. Died October 31, 1965.

Mary Astor and Dean Jagger in *Brigham Young, Frontiersman.*

Rita Johnson and John Carroll in *Congo Maisie*.

Feature Films: *London By Night* (MGM, 1937), *My Dear Miss Aldrich* (MGM, 1937), *Man-Proof* (MGM, 1938), *Rich Man—Poor Girl* (MGM, 1938), *Smashing the Rackets* (RKO, 1938), *Letter of Introduction* (Univ., 1938), *Honolulu* (MGM, 1939), *The Girl Downstairs* (MGM, 1939), *Broadway Serenade* (MGM, 1939), *Within the Law* (MGM, 1939), *6,000 Enemies* (MGM, 1939), *Stronger Than Desire* (MGM, 1939), *They All Come Out* (MGM, 1939), *Nick Carter, Master Detective* (MGM, 1939), *Congo Maisie* (MGM, 1940), *Forty Little Mothers* (MGM, 1940), *Edison the Man* (MGM, 1940), *The Golden Fleecing* (MGM, 1940), *Here Comes Mr. Jordan* (Col., 1941), *Appointment for Love* (Univ., 1941), *The Major and the Minor* (Par., 1942), *My Friend Flicka* (20th, 1943), *Thunderhead, Son of Flicka* (20th, 1945), *The Affairs of Susan* (Par., 1945), *The Naughty Nineties* (Univ., 1945), *Pardon My Past* (Col., 1946), *The Perfect Marriage* (Par., 1946), *The Michigan Kid* (Univ., 1947), *They Won't Believe Me* (RKO, 1947), *Sleep My Love* (UA, 1948), *The Big Clock* (Par., 1948), *An Innocent Affair* ("Don't Trust your Husband"—UA, 1948), *Family Honeymoon* (Univ., 1948), *The Second Face* (EL, 1950), *Susan Slept Here* (RKO, 1954), *Emergency Hospital* (UA, 1956), *All Mine to Give* (Univ., 1957).

VAN JOHNSON (Charles Van Johnson) Born August 25, 1916, Newport, Rhode Island. Married Eve Abbott (1947), child: Schuyler; divorced 1968.

Van Johnson, Lowell Gilmore, Noreen Corcoran, Dawn Addams and John Dehner in *Plymouth Adventure*.

Feature Films: *Too Many Girls* (RKO, 1940), *Somewhere I'll Find You* (MGM, 1942), *Murder in the Big House* (WB, 1942), *The War Against Mrs. Hadley* (MGM, 1942), *Dr. Gillespie's New Assistant* (MGM,

1942), *A Guy Named Joe* (MGM, 1943), *Dr. Gillespie's Criminal Case* (MGM, 1943), *The Human Comedy* (MGM, 1943), *Pilot No. 5* (MGM, 1943), *Madame Curie* (MGM, 1943), *White Cliffs of Dover* (MGM, 1944), *Three Men in White* (MGM, 1944), *Between Two Women* (MGM, 1944), *Thrill of a Romance* (MGM, 1945), *Ziegfeld Follies* (MGM, 1946), *Till the Clouds Roll By* (MGM, 1946), *No Leave, No Love* (MGM, 1946), *Easy to Wed* (MGM, 1946), *Command Decision* (MGM, 1948), *Battleground* (MGM, 1949), *Grounds for Marriage* (MGM, 1950), *Go for Broke* (MGM, 1951), *It's a Big Country* (MGM, 1951), *Three Guys Named Mike* (MGM, 1951), *Invitation* (MGM, 1952), *When in Rome* (MGM, 1952), *Washington Story* (MGM, 1952), *Plymouth Adventure* (MGM, 1952), *Confidentially Connie* (MGM, 1953), *Remains to Be Seen* (MGM, 1953), *Easy to Love* (MGM 1953), *The Caine Mutiny* (Col., 1954), *The Siege at Red River* (20th, 1954), *Men of the Fighting Lady* (MGM, 1954), *The Last Time I Saw Paris* (MGM, 1954), *Brigadoon* (MGM, 1954), *The End of the Affair* (Col., 1955), *Slander* (MGM, 1956), *Miracle in the Rain* (WB, 1956), *The Bottom of the Bottle* (20th, 1956), *23 Paces to Baker Street* (20th, 1956), *Kelly and Me* (Univ., 1957), *Action of the Tiger* (MGM, 1957), *The Last Blitzkrieg* (Col., 1958), *Web of Evidence* (AA, 1959), *Subway in the Sky* (UA, 1959), *Enemy General* (Col., 1960), *Wives and Lovers* (Par., 1963), *Divorce American Style* (Col., 1967), *Yours, Mine and Ours* (UA, 1968), *Where Angels Go...Trouble Follows* (Col., 1968).

AL JOLSON (Asa Yoelson) Born May 26, 1886, St. Petersburg, Russia. Married Henrietta Keller (1906); divorced 1919. Married Ethel Delmar (1922); divorced 1926. Married Ruby Keeler (1928), child; Al, Jr.; divorced 1939. Married Erle Galbraith (1945), child: Asa. Died October 23, 1950.

Beverly Roberts and A1 Jolson in *The Singing Kid*.

Feature Films:* *The Jazz Singer* (WB, 1927), *Singing Fool* (WB, 1928), *Sonny Boy* (WB, 1929), *Say It With Songs* (WB, 1929), *Mammy* (WB, 1930), *Big Boy* (WB, 1930), *Hallelujah, I'm a Bum* (UA, 1933), *Wonder Bar* (WB, 1934), *Go Into Your Dance* (WB, 1935), *The Singing Kid* (WB, 1936), *Rose of Washington Square* (20th, 1939), *Hollywood Cavalcade* (20th, 1939), *Swanee River* (20th, 1939), *Rhapsody in Blue* (WB, 1945), *The Jolson Story* (voice only; Col., 1946), *Jolson Sings Again* (voice only; Col., 1949).

    **Part-talking films included

CAROLYN JONES (Carolyn Sue Jones) Born April 28, 1929, Amarillo, Texas. Married Aaron Spelling (1953); divorced 1964.

Feature Films: *The Turning Point* (Par., 1952), *Road to Bali* (Par., 1952), *Off Limits* (Par., 1953), *The War of the Worlds* (Par., 1953), *House of Wax* (WB, 1953), *Geraldine* (Rep., 1953), *The Big Heat* (Col., 1953), *Make Haste to Live* (Rep., 1954), *The Saracen Blade* (Col., 1954), *Shield for Murder* (UA, 1954), *Three Hours to Kill* (Col., 1954), *Desirée* (20th, 1954), *The Seven-Year Itch* (20th, 1955), *East of Eden* (WB, 1955), *The Tender Trap* (MGM, 1955), *Invasion of the Body Snatchers*, AA, 1956), *The Man Who Knew Too Much* (Par., 1956), *The Opposite Sex*

Carolyn Jones in *Johnny Trouble*.

(MGM, 1956), *The Bachelor Party* (UA, 1957), *Johnny Trouble* (WB, 1957), *Baby Face Nelson* (UA, 1957), *Marjorie Morningstar* (WB, 1958), *King Creole* (Par., 1958), *Last Train From Gun Hill* (Par., 1959), *A Hole in the Head* (UA, 1959), *The Man in the Net* (UA, 1959), *Career* (Par., 1959), *Ice Palace* (WB, 1960), *Sail a Crooked Ship* (Col., 1961), *How the West Was Won* (MGM, 1963), *A Ticklish Affair* (MGM, 1963).

JENNIFER JONES (Phyllis Isley) Born March 2, 1919, Tulsa, Oklahoma. Married Robert Walker (1939), children: Robert, Michael; divorced 1945. Married David O. Selznick (1949), child: Mary; widowed 1965.

Laurence Olivier, Eddie Albert and Jennifer Jones in *Carrie*.

Feature Films:
as Phyllis Isley *New Frontier* (Rep., 1939), *Dick Tracy's G-Men* (Rep. serial, 1939).
as Jennifer Jones *The Song of Bernadette* (20th, 1943), *Since You Went Away* (UA, 1944), *Love Letters* (Par., 1945), *Cluny Brown* (20th, 1946), *Duel in the Sun* (Selznick, 1946), *Portrait of Jennie* (Selznick, 1948), *We Were Strangers* (Col., 1949), *Madame Bovary* (MGM, 1949), *Carrie* (Par., 1952), *The Wild Heart* (RKO, 1952), *Ruby Gentry* (20th, 1952), *Indiscretion of an American Wife* (Col., 1954), *Beat the Devil* (UA, 1954), *Love Is a Many-Splendored Thing* (20th, 1955), *Good Morning, Miss Dove* (20th, 1955), *The Man in the Gray Flannel Suit* (20th, 1956), *The Barretts of Wimpole Street* (MGM, 1957), *A Farewell to Arms* (20th, 1957), *Tender Is the Night* (20th, 1961), *The Idol* (Embassy, 1966).

SHIRLEY JONES (Shirley Mae Jones) Born March 31, 1933, Smithton, Pennsylvania. Married Jack Cassidy (1956), children: Shaun, David, Patrick, Ryan.

Shirley Jones, Ronny Howard and Glenn Ford in *The Courtship of Eddie's Father*.

Feature Films: *Oklahoma!* (Magna, 1955), *Carousel* (20th, 1956), *April Love* (20th, 1957), *Never Steal Anything Small* (Univ., 1959), *Bobbikins* (20th, 1960), *Elmer Gantry* (UA, 1960), *Pepe* (Col., 1960), *Two Rode Together* (Col., 1961), *The Music Man* (WB, 1962), *The Courtship of Eddie's Father* (MGM, 1963), *A Ticklish Affair* (MGM, 1963), *Dark Purpose* (Univ., 1964), *Bedtime Story* (Univ., 1964), *Fluffy* (Univ., 1965), *The Secret of My Success* (MGM, 1965).

VICTOR JORY Born November 23, 1902, Dawson City, Alaska. Married Jean Inness (1928), children: Jon, Jean.

Victor Jory, William Phipps, Sonny Tufts and Marie Windsor in *Cat Women of the Moon*.

Feature Films: *The Pride of the Legion* (Mascot, 1932), *Sailor's Luck* (Fox, 1933), *Infernal Machine* (Fox, 1933), *State Fair* (Fox, 1933), *Broadway Bad* (Fox, 1933), *Second Hand Wife* (Fox, 1933), *Trick for Trick* (Fox, 1933), *I Loved You Wednesday* (Fox, 1933), *Devil's in Love* (Fox, 1933), *My Woman* (Fox, 1933), *Smoky* (Fox, 1933), *I Believed in You* (Fox, 1934), *Murder in Trinidad* (Fox, 1934), *He Was Her Man* (WB, 1934), *Madame Du Barry* (WB, 1934), *Pursued* (Fox, 1934), *White Lies* (Col., 1934), *Mills of the Gods* (Col., 1935), *Party*

Wire (Col., 1935), *Streamline Express* (Mascot, 1935), *A Midsummer Night's Dream* (WB, 1935), *Escape From Devil's Island* (Col., 1935), *Too Tough to Kill* (Col., 1935), *Hell-Ship Morgan* (Col., 1936), *The King Steps Out* (WB, 1936), *Meet Nero Wolfe* (Col., 1936), *Glamorous Night* (Associated British Pictures, 1937), *First Lady* (WB, 1937), *Bulldog Drummond at Bay* (Rep., 1937), *The Adventures of Tom Sawyer* (UA, 1938), *Blackwell's Island* (WB, 1939), *Dodge City* (WB, 1939), *Wings of the Navy* (WB, 1939), *Man of Conquest* (Rep., 1939), *Women in the Wind* (WB, 1939), *Susannah of the Mounties* (20th, 1939), *Men With Whips* (Hoffberg, 1939), *Each Dawn I Die* (WB, 1939), *I Stole a Million* (Univ., 1939), *Call a Messenger* (Univ., 1939), *Gone With the Wind* (MGM, 1939), *The Shadow* (Col. serial, 1940), *The Green Archer* (Col. serial, 1940), *Knights of the Range* (Par., 1940), *The Light of Western Stars* (Par., 1940), *The Lone Wolf Meets a Lady* (Col., 1940), *River's End* (WB, 1940), *Girl From Havana* (Rep., 1940), *Cherokee Strip* (Par., 1940), *Lady With Red Hair* (WB, 1940), *Give Us Wings* (Univ., 1940), *Border Vigilantes* (Par., 1941), *Wide Open Town* (Par., 1941), *Bad Men of Missouri* (WB, 1941), *Charlie Chan in Rio* (20th, 1941), *Secrets of the Lone Wolf* (Col., 1941), *Riders of the Timberline* (Par., 1941), *The Stork Pays Off* (Col., 1941), *Shut My Big Mouth* (Col., 1942), *Tombstone, The Town Too Tough to Die* (Par., 1942), *Hoppy Serves a Writ* (UA, 1943), *Buckskin Frontier* (UA, 1943), *The Leather Burners* (UA, 1943), *The Kansan* (UA, 1943), *Bar 20* (UA, 1943), *Colt Comrades* (UA, 1943), *The Unknown Guest* (Mon., 1943), *Power of the Press* (Col., 1943), *The Loves of Carmen* (Col., 1948), *The Gallant Blade* (Col., 1948), *A Woman's Secret* (RKO, 1949), *South of St. Louis* (WB, 1949), *Canadian Pacific* (20th, 1949), *Fighting Man of the Plains* (20th, 1949), *The Capture* (RKO, 1950), *The Cariboo Trail* (20th, 1950), *The Highwayman* (AA, 1951), *Cave of Outlaws* (Univ., 1951), *Flaming Feather* (Par., 1951), *Son of Ali Baba* (Univ., 1952), *Toughest Man in Arizona* (Rep., 1952), *Cat Women of the Moon* (Astor, 1953), *The Hindu* ("Sabaka"—Ferrin, 1953), *The Man From the Alamo* (Univ., 1953), *Valley of the Kings* (MGM, 1954), *Manfish* (UA, 1956), *Blackjack Ketchum, Desperado* (Col., 1956), *Death of a Scoundrel* (RKO, 1956), *The Man Who Turned to Stone* (Col., 1957), *Last Stagecoach West* (Rep., 1957), *The Fugitive Kind* (UA, 1960), *The Miracle Worker* (UA, 1962), *Cheyenne Autumn* (WB, 1964).

BORIS KARLOFF (William Henry Pratt) Born November 23, 1887, Dulwich, England. Married Helen Soule (1923); divorced 1928. Married Dorothy Stine (1929), child: Sara; divorced 1946. Married Evelyn Helmore (1946).

Bela Lugosi and Boris Karloff in *The Raven.*

English-Language Sound Feature Films: *King of the Kongo* (Mascot serial, 1929), *The Unholy Night* (MGM, 1929), *Behind That Curtain* (Fox, 1929), *The Bad One* (UA, 1930), *The Sea Bat* (MGM, 1930), *The Utah Kid* (Tif., 1930), *Mothers Cry* (WB, 1930), *King of the Wild* (Mascot serial, 1931), *The Criminal Code* (Col., 1931), *Cracked Nuts* (RKO, 1931), *Young Donovan's Kid* (RKO, 1931), *Smart Money* (WB, 1931),

The Public Defender (RKO, 1931), *I Like Your Nerve* (WB, 1931), *Five Star Final* (WB, 1931), *The Mad Genius* (WB, 1931), *Guilty Generation* (Col., 1931), *The Yellow Ticket* (Fox, 1931), *Graft* (Univ., 1931), *Frankenstein* (Univ., 1931), *Tonight or Never* (UA, 1931), *Business and Pleasure* (Fox, 1932), *Alias the Doctor* (WB, 1932), *Scarface* (UA, 1932), *Cohens and Kellys in Hollywood* (Univ., 1932), *The Miracle Man* (Par., 1932), *Behind the Mask* (Col., 1932), *The Mummy* (Univ., 1932), *The Old Dark House* (Univ., 1932), *Night World* (Univ., 1932), *The Mask of Fu Manchu* (MGM, 1932), *The Ghoul* (Gaumont-British, 1933), *The House of Rothschild* (UA, 1934), *The Lost Patrol* (RKO, 1934), *The Black Cat* (Univ., 1934), *Gift of Gab* (Univ., 1934) *Mysterious Mr. Wong* (Mon., 1935), *Bride of Frankenstein* (Univ., 1935), *The Raven* (Univ., 1935), *The Black Room* (Col., 1935), *The Invisible Ray* (Univ., 1936), *The Walking Dead* (WB, 1936), *Charlie Chan at the Opera* (20th, 1936), *The Man Who Changed His Mind* (Gaumont-British, 1936), *Juggernaut* (GN, 1936), *Night Key* (Univ., 1937), *West of Shanghai* (WB, 1937), *The Invisible Menace* (WB, 1938), *Mr. Wong, Detective* (Mon., 1938), *The Man They Could Not Hang* (Col., 1939), *Mr. Wong in Chinatown* (Mon., 1939), *Son of Frankenstein* (Univ., 1939), *Tower of London* (Univ., 1939), *The Fatal Hour* (Mon., 1940), *British Intelligence* (WB, 1940), *Black Friday* (Univ., 1940), *The Man With Nine Lives* (Col., 1940), *Devil's Island* (WB, 1940), *Doomed to Die* (Mon., 1940), *Before I Hang* (Col., 1940), *The Ape* (Mon., 1940), *You'll Find Out* (RKO, 1940), *The Devil Commands* (Col., 1941), *The Boogie Man Will Get You* (Col., 1942), *The Climax* (Univ., 1944), *The House of Frankenstein* (Univ., 1944), *The Body Snatcher* (RKO, 1945), *Isle of the Dead* (RKO, 1945), *Bedlam* (RKO, 1946), *Lured* (UA, 1947), *The Secret Life of Walter Mitty* (RKO, 1947), *Dick Tracy Meets Gruesome* (RKO, 1947), *Unconquered* (Par., 1947), *Tap Roots* (Univ., 1948), *Abbott and Costello Meet the Killer* (Univ., 1949), *The Strange Door* (Univ., 1951), *The Black Castle* (Univ., 1952), *The Hindu* ("Sabaka"—Ferrin, 1953), *Abbott and Costello Meet Dr. Jekyll and Mr. Hyde* (Univ., 1953), *Voodoo Island* (UA, 1957), *Frankenstein—1970* (AA, 1958), *Grip of the Strangler* ("Haunted Strangler"—MGM, 1958), *The Terror* (AIP, 1963), *Corridors of Blood* (MGM, 1963), *The Raven* (AIP, 1963), *A Comedy of Terrors* (AIP, 1963), *Bikini Beach* (AIP, 1964), *Die, Monster, Die* (AIP, 1965), *The Daydreamer* (voice only; Embassy, 1966), *Ghost in the Invisible Bikini* (AIP, 1966), *The Venetian Affair* (MGM, 1967), *Mad Monster Party* (voice only; Embassy, 1967), *Mondo Balordo* (narrator; AIP, 1967), *The Sorcerer* (Tenser Films, 1968).

ROSCOE KARNS September 7, 1893, San Bernardino, California. Married, child: Todd.

Gary Cooper, Jack Oakie and Roscoe Karns in *If I Had a Million.*

Sound Feature Films; *This Thing Called Love* (Pathé, 1929), *New York Nights* (UA, 1930), *Troopers Three* (Tif., 1930), *Safety in Numbers*

(Par., 1930), *Man Trouble* (Fox, 1930), *Little Accident* (Univ., 1930), *Costello Case* (Sono Art-World Wide, 1930), *Dirigible* (Col., 1931), *Laughing Sinners* (MGM, 1931), *Leftover Ladies* (Tif., 1931), *Roadhouse Murder* (RKO, 1932), *Week-End Marriage* (WB, 1932), *Two Against the World* (WB, 1932), *The Crooked Circle* (Sono Art-World Wide, 1932), *I Am a Fugitive From a Chain Gang* (WB, 1932), *One Way Passage* (WB, 1932), *Night After Night* (Par., 1932), *Under-Cover Man* (Par., 1932), *If I Had a Million* (Par., 1932), *Today We Live* (Par., 1933), *A Lady's Profession* (Par., 1933), *Gambling Ship* (Par., 1933), *One Sunday Afternoon* (Par., 1933), *Alice in Wonderland* (Par., 1933), *Come On Marines* (Par., 1934), *Search for Beauty* (Par., 1934), *It Happened One Night* (Col., 1934), *Twentieth Century* (Col., 1934), *Elmer and Elsie* (Par., 1934), *Shoot the Works* (Par., 1934), *I Sell Anything* (WB, 1934), *Red Hot Tires* (WB, 1935), *Wings in the Dark* (Par., 1935), *Four Hours to Kill* (Par., 1935), *Alibi Ike* (WB, 1935), *Front Page Woman* (WB, 1935), *Woman Trap* (Par., 1936), *Border Flight* (Par., 1936), *Three Cheers for Love* (Par., 1936), *Three Married Men* (Par., 1936), *Cain and Mabel* (WB, 1936), *Clarence* (Par., 1937), *Murder Goes to College* (Par., 1937), *On Such a Night* (Par, 1937), *Partners in Crime* (Par., 1937), *Night of Mystery* (Par., 1937), *Scandal Street* (Par., 1938), *Tip-Off Girls* (Par., 1938), *Dangerous to Know* (Par., 1938), *You and Me* (Par., 1938), *Thanks for the Memory* (Par., 1938), *King of Chinatown* (Par., 1939), *Everything's on Ice* (RKO, 1939), *That's Right—You're Wrong* (RKO, 1939), *Dancing Co-ed* (MGM, 1939), *Double Alibi* (Univ., 1940), *His Girl Friday* (Col., 1940), *Saturday's Children* (WB, 1940), *They Drive by Night* (WB, 1940), *Ladies Must Live* (WB, 1940), *Meet the Missus* (Rep., 1940), *Petticoat Politics* (Rep., 1941), *Footsteps in the Dark* (WB, 1941), *The Gay Vagabond* (Rep., 1941), *A Tragedy at Midnight* (Rep., 1942), *Woman of the Year* (MGM, 1942), *Road to Happiness* (Mon., 1942), *Yokel Boy* (Rep., 1942), *You Can't Escape Forever* (WB, 1942), *Stage Door Canteen* (UA, 1943), *My Son, the Hero* (PRC, 1943), *Old Acquaintance* (WB, 1943), *The Navy Way* (Par., 1944), *Hi, Good Lookin'* (Univ., 1944), *Minstrel Man* (PRC, 1944), *I Ring Doorbells* (PRC, 1946), *One Way to Love* (Col., 1946), *Avalanche* (PRC, 1946), *It's a Wonderful Life* (RKO, 1946), *Vigilantes of Boomtown* (Rep., 1947), *That's My Man* (Rep., 1947), *Devil's Cargo* (Film Classics, 1948), *The Inside Story* (Rep., 1948), *Texas, Brooklyn and Heaven* (UA, 1948), *Speed to Spare* (Par., 1948), *Onionhead* (WB, 1958), *Man's Favorite Sport?* (Univ., 1964).

DANNY KAYE (David Kuminsky) Born January 18, 1913, Brooklyn, New York. Married Sylvia Fine (1940), child: Dena.

Elsa Lanchester and Danny Kaye in *The Inspector General.*

Feature Films: *Up in Arms* (RKO, 1944), *Wonder Man* (RKO, 1945), *The Kid From Brooklyn* (RKO, 1946), *The Secret Life of Walter Mitty* (RKO, 1947), *A Song Is Born* (RKO, 1948), *The Inspector General* (WB, 1949), *It's a Great Feeling* (WB, 1949), *On the Riviera* (20th, 1951), *Hans Christian Andersen* (RKO, 1952), *Knock on Wood* (Par., 1954), *White Christmas* (Par., 1954), *The Court Jester* (Par., 1956), *Merry Andrew* (MGM, 1958), *Me and the Colonel* (Col., 1958), *The*

Five Pennies (Par., 1959), *On the Double* (Par., 1961), *The Man From the Diners' Club* (Col., 1963).

BUSTER KEATON (Joseph Frank Keaton) Born October 4, 1895, Piqua, Kansas. Married Natalie Talmadge (1921), children: Robert, James; divorced 1932. Married Mae Scribbens (1933); divorced 1935. Married Eleanor Norris (1940). Died February 1, 1966.

Buster Keaton and Jimmy Durante in *What! No Beer?*

Sound Feature Films: *Hollywood Revue of 1929* (MGM, 1929), *Free and Easy* (MGM, 1930), *Dough Boys* (MGM, 1930), *Parlor, Bedroom and Bath* (MGM, 1931), *Sidewalks of New York* (MGM, 1931), *Passionate Plumber* (MGM, 1932), *Speak Easily* (MGM, 1932), *What, No Beer?* (MGM, 1933), *An Old Spanish Custom* (M.F. Hoffberg, 1936), *Hollywood Cavalcade* (20th, 1939), *The Villain Still Pursued Her* (RKO, 1940), *L'il Abner* (RKO, 1940), *Forever and a Day* (RKO, 1943), *Bathing Beauty* (MGM, 1944), *San Diego, I Love You* (Univ., 1944), *That's the Spirit* (Univ., 1945), *That Night With You* (Univ., 1945), *The Lovable Cheat* (Film Classics, 1949), *In The Good Old Summertime* (MGM, 1949), *You're My Everything* (20th, 1949), *Sunset Boulevard* (Par., 1950), *Limelight* (UA, 1952), *Around the World in 80 Days* (UA, 1956), *The Adventures of Huckleberry Finn* (MGM, 1960), *It's a Mad, Mad, Mad, Mad World* (UA, 1963), *Pajama Party* (AIP, 1964), *Beach Blanket Bingo* (AIP, 1965), *How to Stuff a Wild Bikini* (AIP, 1965), *Sergeant Deadhead* (AIP, 1965), *A Funny Thing Happened on the Way to the Forum* (UA, 1966), *War Italian Style* (AIP, 1967).

HOWARD KEEL (Harold Clifford Keel) Born April 13, 1917, Gillespie, Illinois. Married Rosemary Randall; divorced 1948. Married Helen Anderson (1949), children: Kaija, Gunnar, Kristine.

Ava Gardner and Howard Keel in *Ride, Vaquero.*

Feature Films: *The Small Voice* (British Lion, 1948), *Annie Get Your Gun* (MGM, 1950), *Pagan Love Song* (MGM, 1950), *Three Guys Named Mike* (MGM, 1951), *Show Boat* (MGM, 1951), *Texas Carnival* (MGM, 1951), *Callaway Went Thataway* (MGM, 1951), *Lovely to Look At* (MGM, 1952), *Desperate Search* (MGM, 1952), *I Love Melvin* (MGM, 1953),* *Fast Company* (MGM, 1953), *Ride, Vaquero* (MGM, 1953), *Calamity Jane* (WB, 1953), *Kiss Me, Kate!* (MGM, 1953), *Rose Marie* (MGM, 1954), *Seven Brides for Seven Brothers* (MGM, 1954), *Deep in My Heart* (MGM, 1954), *Jupiter's Darling* (MGM, 1955), *Kismet* (MGM, 1955), *Floods of Fear* (Univ., 1959), *The Big Fisherman* (BV, 1959), *Armored Command* (AA, 1962), *The Day of the Triffids* (AA, 1963), *The Man From Button Willow* (voice only; United Screen Arts, 1965), *Waco* (Par., 1966), *Red Tomahawk* (Par., 1967), *The War Wagon* (Univ., 1967), *Arizona Bushwhackers* (Par., 1968).

*Unbilled guest appearance

RUBY KEELER Born August 25, 1909, Halifax, Nova Scotia, Canada. Married Al Jolson (1928), child: Al, Jr.; divorced 1939. Married John Lowe (1941), children: Kathleen, Christine, Theresa, John.

Ruby Keeler and Lee Dixon in *Ready, Willing and Able.*

Feature Films: *42nd Street* (WB, 1933), *Gold Diggers of 1933* (WB, 1933), *Footlight Parade* (WB, 1933), *Dames* (WB, 1934), *Flirtation Walk* (WB, 1934), *Go into Your Dance* (WB, 1935), *Shipmates Forever* (WB, 1935), *Colleen* (WB, 1936), *Ready, Willing and Able* (WB, 1937), *Mother Carey's Chickens* (RKO, 1938), *Sweetheart of the Campus* (Col., 1941).

CECIL KELLAWAY Born August 22, 1893, Capetown, South Africa. Married, children: Peter, Brian.

Feature Films: *It Isn't Done* (British Empire, 1937), *Double Danger* (RKO, 1938), *Everybody's Doing it* (RKO, 1938), *Night Spot* (RKO, 1938), *This Marriage Business* (RKO, 1938), *Maid's Night Out* (RKO, 1938), *Tarnished Angel* (RKO, 1938), *Wuthering Heights* (UA, 1939), *The Sun Never Sets* (Univ., 1939), *We Are Not Alone* (WB, 1939), *Intermezzo* (UA, 1939), *Mexican Spitfire* (RKO, 1939), *The Under-Pup* (Univ., 1939), *The Invisible Man Returns* (Univ., 1940), *The House of the Seven Gables* (Univ., 1940), *Brother Orchid* (WB, 1940), *Phantom Raiders* (MGM, 1940), *Mexican Spitfire Out West* (RKO, 1940), *The Mummy's Hand* (Univ., 1940), *Diamond Frontier* (Univ., 1940), *The Letter* (WB, 1940), *Lady With Red Hair* (WB, 1940), *South of Suez* (WB, 1940), *A Very Young Lady* (20th, 1941), *West Point Widow* (Par., 1941), *New York Town* (Par., 1941), *Night of January 16th* (Par., 1941), *Burma Convoy* (Par., 1941), *Small Town Deb* (MGM,

Cecil Kellaway, Tim Ryan and Tyrone Power in *The Luck of the Irish.*

1941), *Appointment for Love* (Univ., 1941), *Bahama Passage* (Par., 1941), *The Lady Has Plans* (Par., 1942), *Take a Letter, Darling* (Par., 1942), *Night in New Orleans* (Par., 1942), *Are Husbands Necessary?* (Par., 1942), *I Married a Witch* (UA, 1942), *My Heart Belongs to Daddy* (Par., 1942), *Star Spangled Rhythm* (Par., 1942), *Forever and a Day* (RKO, 1943), *It Ain't Hay* (Univ., 1943), *The Good Fellows* (Par., 1943), *The Crystal Ball* (UA, 1943), *Frenchman's Creek* (Par., 1944), *Mrs. Parkington* (MGM, 1944), *And Now Tomorrow* (Par., 1944), *Practically Yours* (Par., 1945), *Bring on the Girls* (Par., 1945), *Love Letters* (Par., 1945), *Kitty* (Par., 1945), *The Postman Always Rings Twice* (MGM, 1946), *Easy to Wed* (MGM, 1946), *Monsieur Beaucaire* (Par., 1946), *The Cockeyed Miracle* (MGM, 1946), *Unconquered* (Par., 1947), *Always Together* (WB, 1947), *Variety Girl* (Par., 1947), *The Luck of the Irish* (20th, 1948), *Joan of Arc* (RKO, 1948), *The Decision of Christopher Blake* (WB, 1948), *Portrait of Jennie* (Selznick, 1948), *Down to the Sea in Ships* (20th, 1949), *The Reformer and the Redhead* (MGM, 1950), *Harvey* (Univ., 1950), *Kim* (MGM, 1950), *Francis Goes to the Races* (Univ., 1951), *Katie Did It* (Univ., 1951), *Half Angel* (20th, 1951), *The Highwayman* (AA, 1951), *Just Across the Street* (Univ., 1952), *My Wife's Best Friend* (20th, 1952), *Young Bess* (MGM, 1953), *The Beast From 20,000 Fathoms* (WB, 1953), *Cruisin' Down the River* (Col., 1953), *Paris Model* (Col., 1953), *Hurricane at Pilgrim Hill* (Howco, 1953), *Interrupted Melody* (MGM, 1955), *The Prodigal* (MGM, 1955), *Female on the Beach* (Univ., 1955), *Toy Tiger* (Univ., 1956), *Johnny Trouble* (WB, 1957), *The Proud Rebel* (BV, 1958), *The Shaggy Dog* (BV, 1959), *The Private Lives of Adam and Eve* (Univ., 1960), *Tammy, Tell Me True* (Univ., 1961), *Francis of Assisi* (20th, 1961), *Zotz!* (Col., 1962), *The Cardinal* (Col., 1963), *Hush . . . Hush, Sweet Charlotte* (20th, 1965), *Spinout* (MGM, 1966), *The Adventures of Bullwhip Griffin* (BV, 1967), *Fitzwilly* (UA, 1967), *Guess Who's Coming to Dinner* (Col., 1967).

GENE KELLY (Eugene Curran Kelly) Born August 23, 1912, Pittsburgh, Pennsylvania. Married Betsy Blair (1940), child: Kerry; divorced 1957. Married Jeanne Coyne (1960), child: Timothy.

George Murphy, Judy Garland and Gene Kelly in *For Me and My Gal.*

143

Feature Films: *For Me and My Gal* (MGM, 1942), *Pilot No. 5* (MGM, 1943), *Du Barry Was a Lady* (MGM, 1943), *Thousands Cheer* (MGM, 1943), *The Cross of Lorraine* (MGM, 1943), *Cover Girl* (Col., 1944), *Christmas Holiday* (Univ., 1944), *Anchors Aweigh* (MGM, 1945), *Ziegfeld Follies of 1946* (MGM, 1946), *Living in a Big Way* (MGM, 1947), *The Pirate* (MGM, 1948), *The Three Musketeers* (MGM, 1948), *Words and Music* (MGM, 1948), *Take Me Out to the Ball Game* (MGM, 1949), *On The Town* (MGM, 1949), *The Black Hand* (MGM, 1950), *Summer Stock* (MGM, 1950), *An American in Paris* (MGM, 1951), *It's a Big Country* (MGM, 1951), *Singin' in the Rain* (MGM, 1952), *The Devil Makes Three* (MGM, 1952), *Love Is Better Than Ever* (MGM, 1952), *Brigadoon* (MGM, 1954), *Crest of the Wave* (MGM, 1954), *Deep in My Heart* (MGM, 1954), *It's Always Fair Weather* (MGM, 1955), *Invitation to the Dance* (MGM, 1956), *The Happy Road* (MGM, 1957), *Les Girls* (MGM, 1957), *Marjorie Morningstar* (WB, 1958), *Inherit the Wind* (UA, 1960), *Let's Make Love* (20th, 1960), *What a Way to Go!* (20th, 1964), *The Young Girls of Rochefort* (WB-7 Arts, 1967).

GRACE KELLY Born November 12, 1928, Philadelphia, Pennsylvania. Married Prince Rainier (1956), children: Caroline, Albert, Stephanie.

Grace Kelly and Jessie Royce Landis in *The Swan*.

Feature Films: *Fourteen Hours* (20th, 1951), *High Noon* (UA, 1952), *Mogambo* (MGM, 1953), *Dial M for Murder* (WB, 1954), *Rear Window* (Par., 1954), *The Country Girl* (Par., 1954), *Green Fire* (MGM, 1954), *The Bridges at Toko-Ri* (Par., 1954), *To Catch a Thief* (Par., 1955), *The Swan* (MGM, 1956), *High Society* (MGM, 1956).

PATSY KELLY Born January 21, 1910, Brooklyn, New York.

Feature Films: *Going Hollywood* (MGM, 1933), *Countess of Monte Cristo* (Univ., 1934), *Party's Over* (Col., 1934), *The Girl From Missouri* (MGM, 1934), *Transatlantic Merry-Go-Round* (UA, 1934), *Go into Your Dance* (WB, 1935), *Every Night at Eight* (Par., 1935), *Page Miss Glory* (WB, 1935), *Thanks a Million* (20th, 1935), *Kelly the Second*

Ted Healy and Patsy Kelly in *Sing, Baby, Sing*.

(MGM, 1936), *Private Number* (20th, 1936), *Sing, Baby, Sing* (20th, 1936), *Pigskin Parade* (20th, 1936), *Nobody's Baby* (MGM, 1937), *Pick a Star* (MGM, 1937), *Wake Up and Live* (20th, 1937), *Ever Since Eve* (WB, 1937), *Merrily We Live* (MGM, 1938), *There Goes My Heart* (UA, 1938), *The Cowboy and the Lady* (UA, 1938), *The Gorilla* (20th, 1939), *The Hit Parade of 1941* (Rep., 1940), *Road Show* (UA, 1941), *Topper Returns* (UA, 1941), *Broadway Limited* (UA, 1941), *Playmates* (RKO, 1941), *Sing Your Worries Away* (RKO, 1942), *In Old California* (Rep., 1942), *My Son, the Hero* (PRC, 1943) *Ladies' Day* (RKO, 1943), *Danger! Women at Work* (PRC, 1943), *Please Don't Eat the Daisies* (MGM, 1960), *The Crowded Sky* (WB, 1960), *The Naked Kiss* (AA, 1964), *Ghost in the Invisible Bikini* (AIP, 1966), *C'mon, Let's Live a Little* (Par., 1967), *Rosemary's Baby* (Par., 1968).

PAUL KELLY (Paul Michael Kelly) Born August 9, 1899, Brooklyn, New York. Married Dorothy MacKaye (1931), children: Mimi, Mary; widowed 1940. Married Mardelle Zurcker (1941). Died November 6, 1956.

Paul Kelly and Chester Morris in *Public Hero Number One*.

Sound Feature Films: *Girl From Calgary* (Mon., 1932), *Broadway Through a Keyhole* (UA, 1933), *Love Captive* (Univ., 1934), *Side Streets* (WB, 1934), *Blind Date* (Col., 1934), *Death on the Diamond* (MGM, 1934), *School for Girls* (Liberty Productions, 1934), *The President Vanishes* (Par., 1934), *When a Man's a Man* (Fox, 1935), *Public Hero Number One* (MGM, 1935), *Star of Midnight* (RKO, 1935), *Silk Hat Kid* (Fox, 1935), *Speed Devils* (J.H. Hoffberg, 1935), *My Marriage* (20th, 1935), *It's a Great Life* (Par., 1936), *Here Comes Trouble* (20th,

1936), *The Song and Dance Man* (20th, 1936), *The Country Beyond* (20th, 1936), *Women Are Trouble* (MGM, 1936), *Murder With Pictures* (Par., 1936), *The Accusing Finger* (Par., 1936), *Parole Racket* (Col., 1937), *Join the Marines* (Rep., 1937), *It Happened Out West* (20th, 1937), *The Frame-up* (Col., 1937), *Fit for a King* (RKO, 1937), *Navy Blue and Gold* (MGM, 1937), *Nurse From Brooklyn* (Univ., 1938), *Torchy Blane in Panama* (WB, 1938), *Island in the Sky* (20th, 1938), *The Devil's Party* (Univ., 1938), *The Missing Guest* (Univ., 1938), *Juvenile Court* (Col., 1938), *Adventure in Sahara* (Col., 1938), *Forged Passport* (Rep., 1939), *The Flying Irishman* (RKO, 1939), *Within the Law* (MGM, 1939), *6,000 Enemies* (MGM, 1939), *The Roaring Twenties* (WB, 1939), *Invisible Stripes* (WB, 1940), *Queen of the Mob* (Par., 1940), *The Howards of Virginia* (Col., 1940), *Wyoming* (MGM, 1940), *Girls Under 21* (Col., 1940), *Flight Command* (MGM, 1940), *Ziegfeld Girl* (MGM, 1941), *I'll Wait for You* (MGM, 1941), *Parachute Battalion* (RKO, 1941), *Mystery Ship* (Col., 1941), *Mr. and Mrs. North* (MGM, 1941), *Gang Busters* (Univ. serial, 1942), *Call Out the Marines* (RKO, 1942), *Tarzan's New York Adventure* (RKO, 1942), *Tough as They Come* (Univ., 1942), *Flying Tigers* (Rep., 1942), *The Secret Code* (Col. serial, 1942), *The Man From Music Mountain* (Rep., 1943), *The Story of Dr. Wassell* (Par., 1944), *Dead Man's Eyes* (Univ., 1944), *Faces in the Fog* (Rep., 1944), *China's Little Devils* (Mon., 1945), *Grissly's Millions* (Rep., 1945), *Allotment Wives* (Mon., 1945), *San Antonio* (WB, 1945), *The Cat Creeps* (Univ., 1946), *The Glass Alibi* (Rep., 1946), *Deadline for Murder* (20th, 1946), *Strange Journey* (20th, 1946), *Fear in the Night* (Par., 1947), *Spoilers of the North* (Rep., 1947), *Crossfire* (RKO, 1947), *Adventure Island* (Par., 1947), *File on Thelma Jordan* (Par., 1949), *Side Street* (MGM, 1949), *Guilty of Treason* (EL, 1949), *The Secret Fury* (RKO, 1950), *Frenchie* (Univ., 1950), *The Painted Hills* (MGM, 1951), *Springfield Rifle* (WB, 1952), *Gunsmoke* (Univ., 1953), *Split Second* (RKO, 1953), *Duffy of San Quentin* (WB, 1954), *Johnny Dark* (Univ., 1954), *The High and the Mighty* (WB, 1954), *The Steel Cage* (UA, 1954), *The Square Jungle* (Univ., 1955), *Storm Center* (Col., 1956), *Bailout at 43,000* (UA, 1957).

ARTHUR KENNEDY

ARTHUR KENNEDY (John Arthur Kennedy) Born February 17, 1914, Worcester, Massachusetts. Married Marie Cheffey (1938); children: Terence, Laurie.

Marlene Dietrich and Arthur Kennedy in *Rancho Notorious*.

English-Language Feature Films: *City for Conquest* (WB, 1940), *High Sierra* (WB, 1941), *Strange Alibi* (WB, 1941), *Knockout* (WB, 1941), *Highway West* (WB, 1941), *Bad Men of Missouri* (WB, 1941), *They Died With Their Boots On* (WB, 1941), *Desperate Journey* (WB, 1942), *Air Force* (WB, 1943), *Devotion* (WB, 1946), *Boomerang* (20th, 1947), *Cheyenne* (WB, 1947), *Too Late for Tears* (UA, 1949), *Champion* (UA, 1949), *The Window* (RKO, 1949), *The Walking Hills* (Col., 1949), *Chicago Deadline* (Rep., 1949), *The Glass Menagerie* (WB, 1950), *Bright Victory* (Univ., 1951), *Red Mountain* (Par., 1951), *Rancho Notorious* (RKO, 1952), *The Girl in White* (MGM, 1952), *Bend of the River* (Univ., 1952), *The Lusty Men* (RKO, 1952), *The Man From Lara-*

mie (Col., 1955), *Trial* (MGM, 1955), *The Naked Dawn* (Univ., 1955), *The Desperate Hours* (Par., 1955), *Crashout* (Filmakers, 1955), *The Rawhide Years* (Univ., 1956), *Peyton Place* (20th, 1957), *Twilight for the Gods* (Univ., 1958), *Some Came Running* (MGM, 1958), *A Summer Place* (WB, 1959), *Elmer Gantry* (UA, 1960), *Home Is the Hero* (Showcorporation of America, 1961), *Claudelle Inglish* (WB, 1961), *Murder, She Said* (MGM, 1962), *Hemingway's Adventures of a Young Man* (20th, 1962), *Barabbas* (Col., 1962), *Lawrence of Arabia* (Col., 1962), *Cheyenne Autumn* (WB, 1964), *Joy in the Morning* (MGM, 1965), *Murieta* (WB, 1965), *Nevada Smith* (Embassy, 1966), *Monday's Child* (DuRona Productions, 1968), *The Prodigal Gun* (Cinerama, 1968), *Anzio* (Col., 1968), *Evil Gun* (MGM, 1968).

EDGAR KENNEDY

EDGAR KENNEDY Born April 26, 1890, Monterey County, California. Married Patricia Allwyn (1924), Children: Larry, Colleen. Died November 9, 1948

Edgar Kennedy, Cliff Edwards and Tom Conway in *The Falcon Strikes Back*.

Sound Feature Films: *They Had to See Paris* (Fox, 1929), *Bad Company* (Pathé, 1931), *Carnival Boat* (RKO, 1932), *Hold 'Em Jail* (RKO, 1932), *The Penguin Pool Murder* (RKO, 1932), *Little Orphan Annie* (RKO, 1932), *Scarlet River* (RKO, 1933), *Professional Sweetheart* (RKO, 1933), *Son of the Border* (RKO, 1933), *Crossfire* (RKO, 1933), *Tillie and Gus* (Par., 1933), *Duck Soup* (Par., 1933), *All of Me* (Par., 1934), *Heat Lightning* (WB, 1934), *Money Means Nothing* (Mon., 1934), *Twentieth Century* (Col., 1934), *Murder on the Blackboard* (RKO, 1934), *We're Rich Again* (RKO, 1934), *King Kelly of the U.S.A.* (Mon., 1934), *Kid Millions* (UA, 1934), *Silver Streak* (RKO, 1934), *Flirting With Danger* (Mon., 1934), *Gridiron Flash* (RKO, 1934), *The Marines Are Coming* (Mascot, 1934), *Living on Velvet* (WB, 1935), *Rendezvous at Midnight* (Univ., 1935), *Cowboy Millionaire* (20th, 1935), *The Little Big Shot* (WB, 1935), *Woman Wanted* (MGM, 1935), *$1,000 a Minute* (Rep., 1935), *In Person* (RKO, 1935), *The Bride Comes Home* (Par., 1935), *The Return of Jimmy Valentine* (Rep., 1936), *Robin Hood of El Dorado* (MGM, 1936), *Small Town Girl* (MGM, 1936), *Fatal Lady* (Par., 1936), *Yours for the Asking* (Par., 1936), *Mad Holiday* (MGM, 1936), *Three Men on a Horse* (WB, 1936), *San Francisco* (MGM, 1936), *When's Your Birthday?* (RKO, 1937), *A Star Is Born* (UA, 1937), *Super Sleuth* (RKO, 1937), *Double Wedding* (MGM, 1937), *True Confession* (Par., 1937), *Hollywood Hotel* (WB, 1937), *The Black Doll* (Univ., 1938), *Scandal Street* (Par., 1938), *Peck's Bad Boy at the Circus* (RKO, 1938), *It's a Wonderful World* (MGM, 1939), *Little Accident* (Univ., 1939), *Everything's on Ice* (RKO, 1939), *Charlie McCarthy, Detective* (Univ., 1939), *Laugh It Off* (Univ., 1939), *Li'l Abner* (RKO, 1940), *Frolics On Ice* (RKO, 1940), *Sandy Is a Lady* (Univ., 1940), *Dr. Christian Meets the Women* (RKO, 1940), *Margie* (Univ., 1940), *The Quarterback* (Par., 1940), *Who Killed Aunt Maggie?* (Rep., 1940), *Remedy for Riches* (RKO, 1940), *Sandy Gets Her Man* (RKO, 1940), *The Bride Wore Crutches* (20th, 1941), *Public Enemies* (Rep., 1941), *Blondie in Society* (Col., 1941), *Snuffy Smith, Yard Bird* (Mon., 1942).

Pardon My Stripes (Rep., 1942), *In Old California* (Rep., 1942), *Hillbilly Blitzkrieg* (Mon., 1942), *The Falcon Strikes Back* (RKO, 1943), *Cosmo Jones—Crime Smasher* (Mon., 1943), *Air Raid Wardens* (MGM, 1943), *Hitler's Madman* (MGM, 1943), *The Girl From Monterey* (PRC, 1943), *Crazy House* (Univ., 1943), *The Great Alaskan Mystery* (Univ. serial, 1944), *It Happened Tomorrow* (UA, 1944), *Anchors Aweigh* (MGM, 1945), *Captain Tugboat Annie* (Rep., 1945), *Mad Wednesday* (UA, 1947), *Heaven Only Knows* (UA, 1947), *Variety Time* (RKO, 1948), *Unfaithfully Yours* (20th, 1948), *My Dream Is Yours* (WB, 1949).

DEBORAH KERR (Deborah Kerr-Trimmer) Born September 30, 1921, Helensburgh, Scotland. Married Anthony Bartley (1945), children: Francesca, Melanie; divorced 1959. Married Peter Viertel (1960).

Deborah Kerr and Spencer Tracy in *Edward, My Son*.

Feature Films: *Contraband* (British National, 1939), *Major Barbara* (Rank, 1940), *Love on the Dole* (British National, 1941), *Hatter's Castle* (Par., 1941), *The Courageous Mr. Penn* ("Penn of Pennsylvania" —British National, 1942), *The Avengers* ("The Day Will Dawn"— Denham, 1942), *Colonel Blimp* ("The Life and Death of Colonel Blimp"—Rank, 1943), *Vacation From Marriage* ("Perfect Strangers"— MGM, 1945), *The Adventuress* ("I See a Dark Stranger"—Rank, 1946), *Black Narcissus* (Rank, 1946), *The Hucksters* (MGM, 1947), *If Winter Comes* (MGM, 1947), *Edward, My Son* (MGM, 1949), *Please Believe Me* (MGM, 1950), *King Solomon's Mines* (MGM, 1950), *Quo Vadis* (MGM, 1951), *The Prisoner of Zenda* (MGM, 1952), *Thunder in the East* (Par., 1953), *Dream Wife* (MGM, 1953), *Young Bess* (MGM, 1953), *Julius Caesar* (MGM, 1953), *From Here to Eternity* (Col., 1953), *The End of the Affair* (Col., 1955), *The Proud and Profane* (Par., 1956), *The King and I* (20th, 1956), *Tea and Sympathy* (MGM, 1956), *Heaven Knows, Mr. Allison* (20th, 1957), *An Affair to Remember* (20th, 1957), *Bonjour Tristesse* (Col., 1958), *Separate Tables* (UA, 1958), *The Journey* (MGM, 1959), *Count Your Blessings* (MGM, 1959), *Beloved Infidel* (20th, 1959), *The Sundowners* (WB, 1960), *The Grass Is Greener* (Univ., 1960), *The Naked Edge* (UA, 1961), *The Innocents* (20th, 1961), *The Chalk Garden* (Univ., 1964), *The Night of the Iguana* (MGM, 1964), *Marriage on the Rocks* (WB, 1965), *Casino Royale* (Col.,1967), *Eye of the Devil* (MGM, 1967), *Prudence and the Pill* (20th, 1968).

EVELYN KEYES (Evelyn Louise Keyes) Born November 20, 1919, Port Arthur, Texas. Married Barton Bainbridge; widowed 1940. Married Charles Vidor; divorced 1945. Married John Huston (1946), child: Pablo; divorced 1950. Married Artie Shaw (1957).

Feature Films: *The Buccaneer* (Par., 1938), *Sons of the Legion* (Par., 1938), *Men With Wings* (Par., 1938), *Artists and Models Abroad* (Par., 1938). *Dangerous to Know* (Par., 1938), *Gone With the Wind* (MGM, 1939), *Union Pacific* (Par., 1939), *Paris Honeymoon* (Par., 1939), *Sudden Money* (Par., 1939), *Slightly Honorable* (UA, 1940),

Evelyn Keyes and Keenan Wynn in *The Thrill of Brazil*.

Before I Hang (Col., 1940), *Lady in Question* (Col., 1940), *The Face Behind the Mask* (Col., 1941), *Beyond the Sacramento* (Col., 1941), *Here Comes Mr. Jordan* (Col., 1941), *Ladies in Retirement* (Col., 1941), *The Adventures of Martin Eden* (Col., 1942), *Flight Lieutenant* (Col., 1942), *The Desperadoes* (Col., 1943), *Dangerous Blondes* (Col., 1943), *There's Something About a Soldier* (Col., 1943), *Nine Girls* (Col., 1944), *Strange Affair* (Col., 1944), *A Thousand and One Nights* (Col., 1945), *Renegades* (Col., 1946), *The Thrill of Brazil* (Col., 1946), *The Jolson Story* (Col., 1946), *Johnny O'Clock* (Col., 1947), *The Mating of Millie* (Col., 1948), *Enchantment* (RKO, 1948), *Mr. Soft Touch* (Col., 1949), *Mrs. Mike* (UA, 1949), *The Killer That Stalked New York* (Col., 1950), *Smuggler's Island* (Univ., 1951), *The Prowler* (UA, 1951), *The Iron Man* (Univ., 1951), *One Big Affair* (UA, 1952), *Shoot First* (UA, 1953), *99 River Street* (UA, 1953), *Hell's Half Acre* (Rep., 1954), *Top of the World* (UA, 1955), *The Seven-Year Itch* (20th, 1955), *Around the World in 80 Days* (UA, 1957).

GUY KIBBEE (Guy Bridges Kibbee) Born March 6, 1886, El Paso, Texas. Married Helen Shea (1918), children: John, Robert; divorced. Married Esther Reed (1928), children: John, Guy, Shirley. Died May 24, 1956.

Guy Kibbee, Clem Bevans, Walter Huston, Beulah Bondi, Gene Reynolds and Arthur Aylesworth in *Of Human Hearts*.

Sound Feature Films: *Stolen Heaven* (Par., 1931), *Man of the World* (Par., 1931), *City Streets* (Par., 1931), *Laughing Sinners* (MGM, 1931), *Side Show* (WB, 1931), *New Adventures of Get Rich Quick Wallingford*

(MGM, 1931), *Flying High* (MGM, 1931), *Blonde Crazy* (WB, 1931), *Taxi* (WB, 1932), *Fireman Save My Child* (WB, 1932), *High Pressure* (WB, 1932), *Union Depot* (WB, 1932), *Play Girl* (WB, 1932), *The Crowd Roars* (WB, 1932), *Two Seconds* (WB, 1932), *Man Wanted* (WB, 1932), *Strange Love of Molly Louvain* (WB, 1932), *So Big* (WB, 1932), *Winner Takes All* (WB, 1932), *Dark Horse* (WB, 1932), *Crooner* (WB, 1932), *Big City Blues* (WB, 1932), *Rain* (UA, 1932), *Scarlet Dawn* (WB, 1932), *The Conquerors* (RKO, 1932), *Central Park* (WB, 1932), *They Just Had to Get Married* (Univ., 1932), *42nd Street* (WB, 1933), *Girl Missing* (WB, 1933), *Gold Diggers Of 1933* (WB, 1933), *Lilly Turner* (WB, 1933), *Life of Jimmy Dolan* (WB, 1933), *Silk Express* (WB, 1933), *Lady for a Day* (Col., 1933), *Footlight Parade* (WB, 1933), *The World Changes* (WB, 1933), *Havana Widows* (WB, 1933), *Convention City* (WB, 1933), *Easy to Love* (WB, 1934), *Harold Teen* (WB, 1934), *Wonder Bar* (WB, 1934), *Merry Wives of Reno* (WB, 1934), *Dames* (WB, 1934), *The Merry Frinks* (WB, 1934), *Big-Hearted Herbert* (WB, 1934), *Babbitt* (WB, 1934), *While the Patient Slept* (WB, 1935), *Mary Jane's Pa* (WB, 1935), *Going Highbrow* (WB, 1935), *Dont't Bet on Blondes* (WB, 1935), *I Live for Love* (WB, 1935), *Captain Blood* (WB, 1935), *Little Lord Fauntleroy* (UA, 1936), *Captain January* (20th, 1936), *The Big Noise* (WB, 1936), *I Married a Doctor* (WB, 1936), *Earthworm Tractors* (WB, 1936), *M'liss* (RKO, 1936), *Three Men on a Horse* (WB, 1936), *The Captain's Kid* (WB, 1936), *Don't Tell the Wife* (RKO, 1937), *Mama Steps Out* (MGM, 1937), *Mountain Justice* (WB, 1937), *Jim Hanvey, Detective* (Rep., 1937), *Riding on Air* (RKO, 1937), *The Big Shot* (RKO, 1937), *Of Human Hearts* (MGM, 1938), *Bad Man of Brimstone* (MGM, 1938), *Joy of Living* (RKO, 1938), *Three Comrades* (MGM, 1938), *Rich Man—Poor Girl* (MGM, 1938), *Let Freedom Ring* (MGM, 1939), *It's a Wonderful World* (MGM, 1939), *Mr. Smith Goes to Washington* (Col., 1939), *Babes in Arms* (MGM, 1939), *Bad Little Angels* (MGM, 1940), *Henry Goes Arizona* (MGM, 1940), *Our Town* (UA, 1940), *Street of Memories* (20th, 1940), *Scattergood Baines* (RKO, 1941), *Scattergood Pulls the Strings* (RKO, 1941), *Scattergood Meets Broadway* (RKO, 1941), *It Started With Eve* (Univ., 1941), *Design for Scandal* (MGM, 1941), *Scattergood Rides High* (RKO, 1942), *This Time for Keeps* (MGM, 1942), *Sunday Punch* (MGM, 1942), *Miss Annie Rooney* (UA, 1942), *Tish* (MGM, 1942), *Whistling in Dixie* (MGM, 1942), *Scattergood Survives a Murder* (RKO, 1942), *Cinderella Swings It* (RKO, 1943), *Girl Crazy* (MGM, 1943), *Dixie Jamboree* (PRC, 1944), *The Horn Blows at Midnight* (WB, 1945), *Gentleman Joe Palooka* (Mon., 1946), *Singing on the Trail* (Col., 1946), *Cowboy Blues* (Col., 1946), *Lone Star Moonlight* (Col., 1946), *Over the Santa Fe Trail* (Col., 1947), *The Red Stallion* (EL, 1947), *The Romance of Rosy Ridge* (MGM, 1947), *Fort Apache* (RKO, 1948).

OTTO KRUGER Born September 6, 1885, Toledo, Ohio. Married Sue MacManamy (1919), child: Ottilie.

Ralph Bellamy, Otto Kruger, Ronnie Crosby and Barbara Stanwyck in *Ever in My Heart*.

Sound Feature Films: *Turn Back the Clock* (MGM, 1933), *Beauty for*

Sale (MGM, 1933), *The Prizefighter and the Lady* (MGM, 1933), *Ever in My Heart* (WB, 1933), *Gallant Lady* (UA, 1933), *The Women in His Life* (MGM, 1933), *Treasure Island* (MGM, 1934), *Chained* (MGM, 1934), *Paris Interlude* (MGM, 1934), *Men in White* (MGM, 1934), *The Crime Doctor* (RKO, 1934), *Springtime for Henry* (Fox, 1934), *Vanessa, Her Love Story* (MGM, 1935), *Two Sinners* (Rep., 1935), *Living Dangerously* (Gaumont-British, 1936), *Dracula's Daughter* (Univ., 1936), *Glamorous Night* (Associated British Pictures, 1937), *They Won't Forget* (WB, 1937), *Counsel for Crime* (Col., 1937), *The Barrier* (Par., 1937), *Thanks for the Memory* (Par., 1938), *I Am the Law* (Col., 1938), *Exposed* (Univ., 1938), *Disbarred* (Par., 1939), *Housemaster* (Alliance, 1939), *The Zero Hour* (Rep., 1939), *A Woman Is the Judge* (Col., 1939), *Dr. Ehrlich's Magic Bullet* (WB, 1940), *A Dispatch From Reuters* (WB, 1940), *Seventeen* (Par., 1940), *The Hidden Menace* (Alliance, 1940), *The Man I Married* (20th, 1940), *The Big Boss* (Col., 1941), *The Man in Her Life* (Col., 1941), *Mercy Island* (Rep., 1941), *Saboteur* (Univ., 1942), *Friendly Enemies* (UA, 1942), *Secrets of a Co-ed* (PRC, 1942), *Corregidor* (PRC, 1943), *Night Plane From Chungking* (Par., 1943), *Hitler's Children* (RKO, 1943), *The Gang's All Here* (PRC, 1944), *Knickerbocker Holiday* (UA, 1944), *Murder, My Sweet* (RKO, 1944), *Cover Girl* (Col., 1944) *They Live in Fear* (Col., 1944), *Escape in the Fog* (Col., 1945), *Earl Carroll's Vanities* (Rep., 1945), *Wonder Man* (RKO, 1945), *The Great John L* (UA, 1945), *The Woman Who Came Back* (Rep., 1945), *On Stage Everybody* (Univ., 1945), *Jungle Captive* (Univ., 1945), *The Chicago Kid* (Rep., 1945), *Allotment Wives* (Mon., 1945), *The Fabulous Suzanne* (Rep., 1946), *Love and Learn* (WB, 1947), *Smart Woman* (AA, 1948), *Lulu Belle* (Col., 1948), *711 Ocean Drive* (Col., 1950), *Payment on Demand* (RKO, 1951), *High Noon* (UA, 1952), *Magnificent Obsession* (Univ., 1954), *Black Widow* (20th, 1954), *The Last Command* (Rep., 1955), *The Young Philadelphians* (WB, 1959), *Cash McCall* (WB, 1959), *The Wonderful World of the Brothers Grimm* (MGM, 1962), *Sex and the Single Girl* (WB, 1964).

ALAN LADD Born September 3, 1913, Hot Springs, Arkansas. Married Sue Carol (1942), children: David, Alana. Died January 3, 1964.

Ralph Moody, Francis McDonald and Alan Ladd in *Red Mountain*.

English-Language Feature Films: *Once in a Lifetime* (Univ., 1932), *Pigskin Parade* (20th, 1936), *Last Train From Madrid* (Par., 1937), *Souls at Sea* (Par., 1937), *Hold 'Em Navy* (Par., 1937), *The Goldwyn Follies* (UA, 1938), *Come On Leathernecks* (Rep., 1938), *The Green Hornet* (Univ. serial, 1939), *Rulers of the Sea* (Par., 1939), *Beast of Berlin* (PRC, 1939), *Light of Western Stars* (Par., 1940), *Gangs of Chicago* (Rep., 1940), *In Old Missouri* (Rep., 1940), *The Howards of Virginia* (Col., 1940), *Those Were the Days* (Par., 1940), *Captain Caution* (UA, 1940), *Wildcat Bus* (RKO, 1940), *Meet the Missus* (Rep., 1940), *Great Guns* (20th, 1941), *Citizen Kane* (RKO, 1941), *Cadet Girl* (20th, 1941), *Petticoat Politics* (Rep., 1941), *The Black Cat* (Univ., 1941), *The Reluctant Dragon* (RKO, 1941), *Paper Bullets* (PRC, 1941), *Joan of Paris* (RKO, 1942), *This Gun for Hire* (Par., 1942), *The Glass Key* (Par., 1942), *Lucky Jordan* (Par., 1942), *Star Spangled Rhythm* (Par.,

1942), *China* (Par., 1943), *And Now Tomorrow* (Par., 1944), *Salty O' Rourke* (Par., 1945), *Duffy's Tavern* (Par., 1945), *The Blue Dahlia* (Par., 1946), *O.S.S.* (Par., 1946), *Two Years Before the Mast* (Par., 1946), *Calcutta* (Par., 1947), *Variety Girl* (Par., 1947), *Wild Harvest* (Par., 1947), *My Favorite Brunette* (Par., 1947),* *Saigon* (Par., 1948), *Beyond Glory* (Par., 1948), *Whispering Smith* (Par., 1948), *The Great Gatsby* (Par., 1949), *Chicago Deadline* (Par., 1949), *Captain Carey, U.S.A.* (Par., 1950), *Branded* (Par., 1951), *Appointment With Danger* (Par., 1951), *Red Mountain* (Par., 1952), *The Iron Mistress* (WB, 1952), *Thunder in the East* (Par., 1953), *Desert Legion* (Univ, 1953), *Shane* (Par,. 1953), *Botany Bay* (Par., 1953), *Paratrooper* (Col., 1954), *Saskatchewan* (Univ, 1954), *Hell Below Zero* (Col., 1954), *The Black Knight* (Col., 1954), *Drum Beat* (WB, 1954), *The McConnell Story* (WB, 1955), *Hell on Frisco Bay* (WB, 1955), *Santiago* (WB, 1956), *The Big Land* (WB, 1957), *Boy on a Dolphin* (20th, 1957), *The Deep Six* (WB, 1958), *The Proud Rebel* (BV, 1958), *The Badlanders* (MGM, 1958), *The Man in the Net* (UA, 1959), *Guns of the Timberland* (WB, 1960), *All the Young Men* (Col., 1960), *One Foot in Hell* (20th, 1960), *13 West Street* (Col., 1962), *The Carpetbaggers* (Par., 1964).

*Unbilled guest appearance

ARTHUR LAKE (Arthur Silverlake) Born April 17, 1905, Corbin, Kentucky. Married Patricia Van Cleve (1937), children: Arthur, Marion.

Arthur Lake, Penny Singleton, Larry Simms and Dorothy Moore in *Blondie*.

Sound Feature Films: *On With the Show!* (WB, 1929), *Dance Hall* (RKO, 1929), *Tanned Legs* (RKO, 1929), *Cheer Up and Smile* (Fox, 1930), *She's My Weakness* (RKO, 1930), *Indiscreet* (UA, 1931), *Midshipman Jack* (RKO, 1933), *Girl o' My Dreams* (Mon., 1934), *Silver Streak* (RKO, 1934), *Women Must Dress* (Mon,. 1935), *Orchids to You* (Fox., 1935), *I Cover Chinatown* (Steiner, 1936), *23½ Hours Leave* (GN, 1937), *Topper* (MGM, 1937), *Annapolis Salute* (RKO, 1937), *Exiled to Shanghai* (Rep., 1937), *True Confession* (Par., 1937), *Double Danger* (RKO, 1938), *Everybody's Doing It* (RKO, 1938), *Blondie* (Col., 1938), *There Goes My Heart* (UA, 1938), *Blondie Meets the Boss* (Col., 1939), *Blondie Takes a Vacation* (Col., 1939), *Blondie Brings Up Baby* (Col., 1939), *Blondie on a Budget* (Col., 1940), *Blondie Has Servant Trouble* (Col., 1940), *Blondie Plays Cupid* (Col., 1940), *Blondie Goes Latin* (Col., 1941), *Blondie in Society* (Col., 1941), *Blondie Goes to College* (Col., 1942), *The Daring Young Man* (Col., 1942),* *Footlight Glamour* (Col., 1943), *It's a Great Life* (Col., 1943), *Sailor's Holiday* (Col., 1944), *The Ghost That Walks Alone* (Col., 1944), *Three Is a Family* (UA, 1944), *The Big Show-Off* (Rep., 1945), *Leave It to Blondie* (Col., 1946), *Life With Blondie* (Col., 1946), *Blondie's Lucky Day* (Col., 1946), *Blondie Knows Best* (Col., 1946), *Blondie's Holiday* (Col., 1947), *Blondie's Big Moment* (Col., 1947), *Blondie's in the Dough* (Col., 1947), *Blondie's Anniversary* (Col., 1947),

16 Fathoms Deep (Mon., 1948), *Blondie's Reward* (Col., 1948), *Blondie's Big Deal* (Col., 1949), *Blondie Hits the Jackpot* (Col., 1949), *Beware of Blondie* (Col., 1950), *Blondie's Hero* (Col., 1950).

*Unbilled guest appearance

VERONICA LAKE (Constance Frances Marie Ockelman) Born November 14, 1919. Brooklyn, New York, New York. Married John Detlie, children: Anthony, Elaine; divorced 1943. Married Andre de Toth (1944), children: Michael, Diane; divorced 1952. Married Joseph McCarthy (1955); divorced 1959. Married Ron House (1962).

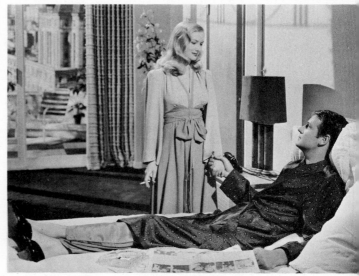

Veronica Lake and Joel McCrea in *Sullivan's Travels.*

Feature Films:

as **Constance Keane** *All Women Have Secrets* (Par., 1939), *Sorority House* (RKO, 1939), *Forty Little Mothers* (MGM, 1940).

as **Veronica Lake** *I Wanted Wings* (Par., 1941), *Sullivan's Travels* (Par., 1941), *Hold Back the Dawn* (Par., 1941),* *This Gun for Hire* (Par., 1942), *The Glass Key* (Par., 1942), *I Married a Witch* (UA, 1942), *Star Spangled Rhythm* (Par., 1942), *So Proudly We Hail* (Par., 1942), *The Hour Before the Dawn* (Par., 1944), *Bring On the Girls* (Par., 1945), *Out of This World* (Par., 1945), *Duffy's Tavern* (Par., 1945), *Hold That Blonde* (Par., 1945), *Miss Susie Slagle's* (Par., 1945), *The Blue Dahlia* (Par., 1946), *Ramrod* (UA, 1947), *Variety Girl* (Par., 1947), *The Sainted Sisters* (Par., 1948), *Saigon* (Par., 1948), *Isn't It Romantic?* (Par., 1948), *Slattery's Hurricane* (20th, 1949), *Stronghold* (Lip., 1952), *Footsteps in the Snow* (Evergreen Film, 1966).

*Unbilled guest appearance

HEDY LAMARR (Hedwig Eva Maria Kiesler) Born November 9, 1913, Vienna, Austria. Married Fritz Mandl (1933); divorced 1937. Married Gene Markey (1939); child: James; divorced 1940. Married John Loder (1943), children: Denise, Anthony; divorced 1947. Married Ernest Stauffer (1951); divorced 1952. Married W. Howard Lee (1953); divorced 1959. Married Lewis Bowles (1963); divorced 1965.

English-Language Feature Films: *Algiers* (UA, 1938), *Lady of the Tropics* (MGM, 1939), *I Take This Woman* (MGM, 1940), *Boom Town* (MGM, 1940), *Comrade X* (MGM, 1940), *Come Live With Me* (MGM, 1941), *Ziegfeld Girl* (MGM, 1941), *H. M. Pulham, Esq.* (MGM, 1941), *Tortilla Flat* (MGM, 1942), *Crossroads* (MGM, 1942), *White Cargo* (MGM, 1942), *The Heavenly Body* (MGM, 1943), *The Conspirators* (WB, 1944), *Experiment Perilous* (RKO, 1944), *Her Highness and the Bellboy* (MGM, 1945), *The Strange Woman* (UA, 1946), *Dishonored Lady* (UA, 1947), *Let's Live a Little* (EL, 1948), *Samson and Delilah* (Par., 1949), *A Lady Without Passport* (MGM, 1950), *Copper Canyon* (Par.,

Hedy Lamarr and Walter Pidgeon in *White Cargo.*

1950), *My Favorite Spy* (Par., 1951), *The Story of Mankind* (WB, 1957), *The Female Animal* (Univ., 1957).

DOROTHY LAMOUR (Dorothy Kaumeyer) Born December 10, 1914, New Orleans, Louisiana. Married Herbie Kaye (1935); divorced 1939. Married William Howard (1943), children: John, Richard.

Dorothy Lamour and Claire Trevor in *The Lucky Stiff.*

Feature Films: *The Jungle Princess* (Par., 1936), *Swing High, Swing Low* (Par., 1937), *Last Train From Madrid* (Par., 1937), *High, Wide and Handsome* (Par., 1937), *Thrill of a Lifetime* (Par., 1937), *The Hurricane* (UA, 1937), *Big Broadcast of 1938* (Par., 1938), *Her Jungle Love* (Par., 1938), *Spawn of the North* (Par., 1938), *Tropic Holiday* (Par., 1938), *St. Louis Blues* (Par., 1939), *Man About Town* (Par., 1939), *Disputed Passage* (Par., 1939), *Johnny Apollo* (20th, 1940), *Typhoon* (Par., 1940), *Road to Singapore* (Par., 1940), *Moon Over Burma* (Par., 1940), *Chad Hanna* (20th, 1940), *Road to Zanzibar* (Par., 1941), *Caught in the Draft* (Par., 1941), *Aloma of the South Seas* (Par., 1941), *The Fleet's In* (Par., 1942), *Beyond the Blue Horizon* (Par., 1942), *Road to Morocco* (Par., 1942), *Star Spangled Rhythm* (Par., 1942), *They Got Me Covered* (RKO, 1943), *Dixie* (Par., 1943), *Riding High* (Par., 1943), *And the Angels Sing* (Par., 1944), *Rainbow Island* (Par., 1944), *Road to Utopia* (Par., 1945), *A Medal for Benny* (Par., 1945), *Duffy's Tavern* (Par., 1945), *Masquerade in Mexico* (Par., 1945), *My Favorite Brunette* (Par., 1947), *Road to Rio* (Par., 1947), *Wild Harvest* (Par., 1947), *Variety Girl*

(Par., 1947), *On Our Merry Way* (UA, 1948), *Lulu Belle* (Col., 1948), *The Girl From Manhattan* (UA, 1948), *Slightly French* (Col., 1948), *Manhandled* (Par., 1948), *The Lucky Stiff* (UA, 1949), *Here Comes the Groom* (Par., 1951),* *The Greatest Show on Earth* (Par., 1952), *Road to Bali* (Par., 1952), *Road to Hong Kong* (UA, 1962), *Donovan's Reef* (Par., 1963), *Pajama Party* (AIP, 1964).

*Unbilled guest appearance

BURT LANCASTER (Burton Stephen Lancaster) Born November 2, 1913, New York, New York. Married Norma Anderson (1946), children: James, William, Susan, Joanne, Sighle.

Burt Lancaster and Barbara Stanwyck in *Sorry, Wrong Number.*

Feature Films: *The Killers* (Univ., 1946), *Variety Girl* (Par., 1947), *Brute Force* (Univ., 1947), *Desert Fury* (Par., 1947), *I Walk Alone* (Par., 1947), *All My Sons* (Univ., 1948), *Sorry, Wrong Number* (Par., 1948), *Kiss the Blood Off My Hands* (Univ., 1948), *Criss Cross* (Univ., 1949), *Rope of Sand* (Par., 1949), *The Flame and the Arrow* (WB, 1950), *Mister 880* (20th, 1950), *Vengeance Valley* (MGM, 1951), *Jim Thorpe —All American* (WB, 1951), *Ten Tall Men* (Col., 1951), *The Crimson Pirate* (WB, 1952), *Come Back, Little Sheba* (Par., 1952), *South Sea Woman* (WB, 1953), *From Here to Eternity* (Col., 1953), *His Majesty O'Keefe* (WB, 1953), *Three Sailors and a Girl* (WB, 1953),* *Apache* (UA, 1954), *Vera Cruz* (UA, 1954), *The Kentuckian* (UA, 1955), *The Rose Tattoo* (Par., 1955), *Trapeze* (UA, 1956), *The Rainmaker* (Par., 1956), *Gunfight at the O.K. Corral* (Par., 1957), *Sweet Smell of Success* (UA, 1957), *The Devil's Disciple* (UA, 1959), *The Unforgiven* (UA, 1960), *Elmer Gantry* (UA, 1960), *The Young Savages* (UA, 1961), *Judgment at Nuremberg* (UA, 1961), *Bird Man of Alcatraz* (UA, 1962), *A Child Is Waiting* (UA, 1963), *The List of Adrian Messenger* (Univ., 1963), *The Leopard* (20th, 1963), *Seven Days in May* (Par., 1964), *The Train* (UA, 1965), *The Hallelujah Trail* (UA, 1965), *The Professionals* (Col., 1966), *The Scalphunters* (UA, 1968), *Castle Keep* (Col., 1968), *The Swimmer* (Col., 1968).

*Unbilled guest appearance

ELSA LANCHESTER (Elizabeth Sullivan) Born October 28, 1902, Lewisham, England. Married Charles Laughton (1929); widowed 1962.

Sound Feature Films: *The Private Life of Henry VIII* (UA, 1933), *Bride of Frankenstein* (Univ., 1935), *Naughty Marietta* (MGM, 1935), *David Copperfield* (MGM, 1935), *Rembrandt* (UA, 1936), *The Ghost Goes West* (UA, 1936), *Ladies in Retirement* (Col., 1941), *Son of Fury* (20th, 1942), *Tales of Manhattan* (20th, 1942), *Forever and a Day* (RKO, 1943), *Thumbs Up* (Rep., 1943), *Lassie Come Home* (MGM, 1943), *Passport to Adventure* (RKO, 1944), *The Spiral Staircase* (RKO, 1946), *The Razor's Edge* (20th, 1946), *Northwest Outpost* (Rep., 1947),

Elsa Lanchester, Edith Barrett, Ida Lupino and Louis Hayward in *Ladies in Retirement*.

The Bishop's Wife (RKO, 1947), *The Big Clock* (Par., 1948), *The Secret Garden* (MGM, 1949), *Come to the Stable* (20th, 1949), *The Inspector General* (WB, 1949), *Buccaneer's Girl* (Univ., 1950), *Mystery Street* (MGM, 1950), *The Petty Girl* (Col., 1950), *Frenchie* (Univ., 1950), *Les Miserables* (20th, 1952), *Dreamboat* (20th, 1952), *Young Man With Ideas* (MGM, 1952), *Androcles and the Lion* (RKO, 1952), *The Girls of Pleasure Island* (Par., 1953), *Hell's Half Acre* (Rep., 1954), *Three Ring Circus* (Par., 1954), *The Glass Slipper* (MGM, 1955), *Witness for the Prosecution* (UA, 1957), *Bell, Book and Candle* (Col., 1958), *Honeymoon Hotel* (MGM, 1964), *Mary Poppins* (BV, 1964), *Pajama Party* (AIP, 1964), *That Darn Cat* (BV, 1965), *Easy Come, Easy Go* (Par., 1967), *Blackbeard's Ghost* (BV, 1968).

ELISSA LANDI (Elizabeth Marie Zanardi-Landi) Born December 6, 1904, Venice, Italy. Married John C. Lawrence (1928); divorced 1936. Married Curtiss Kinney (1943), child: Caroline. Died October 21, 1948.

Elissa Landi in *Enter Madame*.

English-Language Feature Films: *The Parisian* (Capitol Film Exchange, 1930), *Knowing Men* (Capitol Film Exchange, 1931), *The Price of Things* (Capitol Film Exchange, 1931), *The Inseparables* (Capitol Film Exchange, 1931), *Children of Chance* (British International, 1931), *Body and Soul* (Fox, 1931), *Always Goodbye* (Fox, 1931), *Wicked* (Fox, 1931), *The Yellow Ticket* (Fox, 1931), *The Devil's Lottery* (Fox, 1932), *Woman in Room 13* (Fox, 1932), *Passport to Hell* (Fox, 1932), *Sign of the Cross* (Par., 1932), *The Masquerader* (UA, 1933), *Warrior's Husband* (Fox, 1933), *I Loved You Wednesday* (Fox, 1933), *By Candlelight* (Univ., 1934), *Man of Two Worlds* (RKO, 1934), *Sisters Under the Skin* (Col., 1934), *Great Flirtation* (Par., 1934), *Count of Monte Cristo* (UA, 1934), *Enter Madame* (Par., 1935), *Without Regret* (Par., 1935), *The Amateur Gentleman* (UA, 1936), *Mad Holiday* (MGM,

1936), *After the Thin Man* (MGM, 1936), *The Thirteenth Chair* (MGM, 1937), *Corregidor* (PRC, 1943).

CAROLE LANDIS (Frances Lillian Mary Ridste) Born January 1, 1919, Fairchild, Wisconsin. Married Irving Wheeler (1934). divorced 1940. Married Willis Hunt (1940); divorced 1940. Married Thomas Wallace (1943); divorced 1945. Married W. Horace Schmidlapp (1945). Died July 5, 1948.

Phil Silvers, Kay Francis, Martha Raye, Carole Landis and Mitzi Mayfair in *Four Jills in a Jeep*.

Feature Films: *A Star Is Born* (UA, 1937), *A Day at the Races* (MGM, 1937), *Broadway Melody of 1938* (MGM, 1937), *The Emperor's Candlesticks* (MGM, 1937), *Varsity Show* (WB, 1937), *Adventurous Blonde* (WB, 1937), *Blondes at Work* (WB, 1937), *Hollywood Hotel* (WB, 1937), *Gold Diggers in Paris* (WB, 1938), *Boy Meets Girl* (WB, 1938), *Men Are Such Fools* (WB, 1938), *Over the Wall* (WB, 1938), *Four's a Crowd* (WB, 1938), *When Were You Born?* (WB, 1938), *Daredevils of the Red Circle* (Rep. serial, 1939), *Three Texas Steers* (Rep., 1939), *Cowboys From Texas* (Rep., 1939), *One Million B.C.* (UA, 1940), *Turnabout* (UA, 1940), *Mystery Sea Raider* (Par., 1940), *Road Show* (UA, 1941), *Topper Returns* (UA, 1941), *Dance Hall* (20th, 1941), *Moon Over Miami* (20th, 1941), *I Wake Up Screaming* (20th, 1941), *Cadet Girl* (20th, 1941), *A Gentleman at Heart* (20th, 1942), *It Happened in Flatbush* (20th, 1942), *My Gal Sal* (20th, 1942), *Orchestra Wives* (20th, 1942), *Manila Calling* (20th, 1942), *The Powers Girl* (UA, 1942), *Wintertime* (20th, 1943), *Secret Command* (Col., 1944), *Four Jills in a Jeep* (20th, 1944), *Having Wonderful Crime* (RKO, 1944), *Behind Green Lights* (20th, 1946), *It Shouldn't Happen to a Dog* (20th, 1946), *Scandal in Paris* (UA, 1946), *Out of the Blue* (EL, 1947), *The Brass Monkey* (UA, 1948), *The Silk Noose* (Mon., 1950).

JESSIE ROYCE LANDIS (Jessie Royse Medbury) Born November 25, 1904, Chicago, Illinois. Married Rex Smith (1937); divorced 1942. Married J.F.R. Seitz (1957).

Bob Hope, Jessie Royce Landis and Lucille Ball in *Critic's Choice*.

Feature Films: *Derelict* (Par., 1930), *Mr. Belvedere Goes to College* (20th, 1949), *It Happens Every Spring* (20th, 1949), *My Foolish Heart* (RKO, 1949), *Mother Didn't Tell Me* (20th, 1950), *Tonight at 8:30* (Continental, 1953), *To Catch a Thief* (Par., 1955), *The Swan* (MGM, 1956), *The Girl He Left Behind* (WB, 1956), *My Man Godfrey* (Univ., 1957), *I Married a Woman* (Univ., 1958), *North by Northwest* (MGM, 1959), *A Private Affair* (20th, 1959), *Goodbye Again* (UA, 1961), *Bon Voyage!* (BV, 1962), *Boys' Night Out* (MGM, 1962), *Critic's Choice* (WB, 1963), *Gidget Goes to Rome* (Col., 1963).

PRISCILLA LANE (Priscilla Mullican) Born June 12, 1917, Indianola, Iowa. Married Oren Haglund (1939); divorced 1940. Married Joseph Howard (1942), children: Larry, Hannah, Judith, James.

Priscilla Lane and May Robson in *Daughters Courageous.*

Feature Films: *Varsity Show* (WB, 1937), *Love, Honor and Behave* (WB, 1938), *Cowboy From Brooklyn* (WB, 1938), *Men Are Such Fools* (WB, 1938), *Four Daughters* (WB, 1938), *Brother Rat* (WB, 1938), *Yes, My Darling Daughter* (WB, 1939), *Daughters Courageous* (WB, 1939), *Dust Be My Destiny* (WB, 1939), *The Roaring Twenties* (WB, 1939), *Four Wives* (WB, 1939), *Three Cheers for the Irish* (WB, 1940), *Brother Rat and a Baby* (WB, 1940), *Ladies Must Live* (WB, 1940), *Four Mothers* (WB, 1941), *Million Dollar Baby* (WB, 1941), *Blues in the Night* (WB, 1941), *Saboteur* (Univ., 1942), *Silver Queen* (UA, 1942), *The Meanest Man in the World* (20th, 1943), *Arsenic and Old Lace* (WB, 1944), *Fun on a Weekend* (UA, 1947), *Bodyguard* (RKO, 1948).

HOPE LANGE Born November 28, 1935, Redding Ridge, Connecticut. Married Don Murray (1956), children: Christopher, Patricia; divorced 1961. Married Alan Pakula (1963).

Thomas Mitchell, Mickey Shaughnessy, Hope Lange, Glenn Ford and Peter Falk in *Pocketful of Miracles.*

Feature Films: *Bus Stop* (20th, 1956), *The True Story of Jesse James* (20th, 1957), *Peyton Place* (20th, 1957), *The Young Lions* (20th, 1958), *In Love and War* (20th, 1958), *The Best of Everything* (20th, 1959), *Wild in the Country* (20th, 1961), *Pocketful of Miracles* (UA, 1961), *Love Is a Ball* (UA, 1963).

ANGELA LANSBURY (Angela Brigid Lansbury) Born October 16, 1925, London, England. Married Richard Cromwell (1945); divorced 1946. Married Peter Shaw (1949), children: Anthony, Deirdre.

Angela Lansbury and Glenn Ford in *Dear Heart.*

Feature Films: *Gaslight* (MGM, 1944), *National Velvet* (MGM, 1944), *The Picture of Dorian Gray* (MGM, 1945), *The Harvey Girls* (MGM, 1946), *The Hoodlum Saint* (MGM, 1946), *Private Affairs of Bel Ami* (UA, 1947), *Till the Clouds Roll By* (MGM, 1946), *If Winter Comes* (MGM, 1947), *Tenth Avenue Angel* (MGM, 1948), *The Three Musketeers* (MGM, 1948), *State of the Union* (MGM, 1948), *The Red Danube* (MGM, 1949), *Samson and Delilah* (Par., 1949), *Kind Lady* (MGM, 1951), *Mutiny* (UA, 1952), *Remains to Be Seen* (MGM, 1953), *A Lawless Street* (Col., 1955), *The Purple Mask* (Univ., 1955), *Please Murder Me* (DCA, 1956), *The Court Jester* (Par., 1956), *The Reluctant Debutante* (MGM, 1958), *The Long Hot Summer* (20th, 1958), *The Dark at the Top of the Stairs* (WB, 1960), *A Breath of Scandal* (Par., 1960), *Blue Hawaii* (Par., 1961), *Season of Passion* (UA, 1961), *All Fall Down* (MGM, 1962), *The Four Horsemen of the Apocalypse* (voice only; MGM, 1962), *The Manchurian Candidate* (UA, 1962), *In the Cool of the Day* (MGM, 1963), *The World of Henry Orient* (UA, 1964), *Dear Heart* (WB, 1964), *The Greatest Story Ever Told* (UA, 1965), *Harlow* (Par., 1965), *The Amorous Adventures of Moll Flanders* (Par., 1965), *Mister Buddwing* (MGM, 1966).

MARIO LANZA (Alfred Arnold Cocozza) Born January 21, 1921, Philadelphia, Pennsylvania. Married Betty Hicks (1945), children: Colleen, Elisse, Damon. Died October 7, 1959.

Feature Films: *That Midnight Kiss* (MGM, 1949), *The Toast of New*

Mario Lanza and Johanna von Kocsian in *For the First Time.*

Orleans (MGM, 1950), *The Great Caruso* (MGM, 1951), *Because You're Mine* (MGM, 1952), *The Student Prince* (voice only; MGM, 1954), *Serenade* (WB, 1956), *The Seven Hills of Rome* (MGM, 1958), *For the First Time* (MGM, 1959).

CHARLES LAUGHTON Born July 1, 1899, Scarborough, England. Married Elsa Lanchester (1929). Died December 15, 1962.

Charles Laughton and Reginald Owen in *Captain Kidd*.

Sound Feature Films: *Piccadilly* (BIP, 1929), *Wolves* (British and Dominion Productions, 1930), *Down River* (Gaumont, 1931), *The Old Dark House* (Univ., 1932), *Devil and the Deep* (Par., 1932), *Payment Deferred* (MGM, 1932), *The Sign of the Cross* (Par., 1932), *If I Had a Million* (Par., 1932), *Island of Lost Souls* (Par., 1933), *The Private Life of Henry VIII* (UA, 1933), *White Woman* (Par., 1933), *The Barretts of Wimpole Street* (MGM, 1934), *Ruggles of Red Gap* (Par., 1935), *Les Miserables* (UA, 1935), *Mutiny on the Bounty* (MGM, 1935), *Rembrandt* (London Films, 1936), *Vessel of Wrath* (Par., 1938), *St. Martin's Lane* (Par., 1939), *Jamaica Inn* (Par., 1939), *The Hunchback of Notre Dame* (RKO, 1939), *They Knew What They Wanted* (RKO, 1940), *It Started With Eve* (Univ., 1941), *The Tuttles of Tahiti* (RKO, 1942), *Tales of Manhattan* (20th, 1942), *Stand by for Action* (MGM, 1942), *Forever and a Day* (RKO, 1943), *This Land Is Mine* (RKO, 1943), *The Man From Down Under* (MGM, 1943), *The Canterville Ghost* (MGM, 1944), *The Suspect* (Univ., 1944), *Captain Kidd* (UA, 1945), *Because of Him* (Univ., 1946), *The Paradine Case* (Selznick, 1948), *The Big Clock* (Par., 1948), *Arch of Triumph* (UA, 1948), *The Girl From Manhattan* (UA, 1948), *The Bribe* (MGM, 1949), *The Man on the Eiffel Tower* (RKO, 1949), *The Blue Veil* (RKO, 1951), *The Strange Door* (Univ., 1951), *O. Henry's Full House* (20th, 1952), *Abbott and Costello Meet Captain Kidd* (WB, 1952), *Salome* (Col., 1953), *Young Bess* (MGM, 1953), *Hobson's Choice* (UA, 1954), *Witness for the Prosecution* (UA, 1957), *Under Ten Flags* (Par., 1960), *Spartacus* (Univ., 1960), *Advise and Consent* (Col., 1962).

LAUREL AND HARDY
    STAN LAUREL (Arthur Stanley Jefferson) Born June 16, 1895, Ulverson, England. Married Lois Neilson, child: Lois; divorced 1934. Married Virginia Ruth (1934); divorced 1936. Remarried (1938); divorced 1939. Married Ida Kitaeva (1946). Died February 23, 1965.
    OLIVER HARDY (Oliver Norvell Hardy) Born January 18, 1892, Atlanta, Georgia. Married Myrtle Reeves (1921); divorced 1937. Married Lucille Jones (1940). Died August 7, 1957.

Sound Feature Films: *Hollywood Revue Of 1929* (MGM, 1929), *Rogue Song* (MGM, 1930), *Pardon Us* (MGM, 1931), *Pack Up Your Troubles* (MGM, 1932), *Devil's Brother* (MGM, 1933), *Sons of the Desert* (MGM, 1933), *Hollywood Party* (MGM, 1934), *Babes in Toyland* (MGM, 1934), *Bonnie Scotland* (MGM, 1935), *The Bohemian Girl* (MGM, 1936), *Our Relations* (MGM, 1936), *Way Out West* (MGM,

Oliver Hardy, Stan Laurel and Lupe Velez in *Hollywood Party*.

1936), *Swiss Miss* (MGM, 1938), *Blockheads* (MGM, 1938), *Zenobia* (UA, 1939),* *The Flying Deuces* (RKO, 1939), *A Chump at Oxford* (UA, 1940), *Saps at Sea* (UA, 1940), *Great Guns* (20th, 1941), *A-Haunting We Will Go* (20th, 1942), *Air Raid Wardens* (MGM, 1943), *Jitterbugs* (20th, 1943), *The Dancing Masters* (20th, 1943), *The Big Noise* (20th, 1944), *Nothing but Trouble* (MGM, 1944), *The Bull Fighters* (20th, 1945), *The Fighting Kentuckian* (Rep., 1949),* *Riding High* (Par., 1950),* *Atoll K* (Utopia-Fortezza Films, 1951).

    *Hardy appeared without Laurel

PIPER LAURIE (Rosetta Jacobs) Born January 22, 1932, Detroit, Michigan. Married Joe Morgenstern (1962).

Piper Laurie, Joan Fontaine, Jean Simmons and Sandra Dee in *Until They Sail*.

Feature Films: *Louisa* (Univ., 1950), *The Milkman* (Univ., 1950), *The Prince Who Was a Thief* (Univ., 1951), *Francis Goes to the Races* (Univ., 1951), *No Room for the Groom* (Univ., 1952), *Has Anybody Seen My Gal?* (Univ., 1952), *Son of Ali Baba* (Univ., 1952), *Mississippi Gambler* (Univ., 1953), *The Golden Blade* (Univ., 1953), *Dangerous Mission* (RKO, 1954), *Johnny Dark* (Univ., 1954), *Dawn at Socorro* (Univ., 1954), *Smoke Signal* (Univ., 1955), *Ain't Misbehavin'* (Univ., 1955), *Kelly and Me* (Univ., 1957), *Until They Sail* (MGM, 1957), *The Hustler* (20th, 1961).

PETER LAWFORD Born September 7, 1923, London, England. Married Patricia Kennedy (1954), children: Christopher, Sydney, Victoria, Robin; divorced 1966.

Feature Films: *Old Bill* (British, 1930), *Lord Jeff* (MGM, 1938), *Mrs.*

Reginald Owen, Helen Walker, Peter Lawford, Jennifer Jones and Margaret Bannerman in *Cluny Brown*.

Glenn Ford and Janet Leigh in *The Doctor and the Girl*.

Miniver (MGM, 1942), *Eagle Squadron* (Univ., 1942), *Thunder Birds* (20th, 1942), *A Yank at Eton* (MGM, 1942), *London Blackout Murders* (Rep., 1942), *Random Harvest* (MGM, 1942), *Girl Crazy* (MGM, 1943), *The Purple V* (Rep., 1943), *The Immortal Sergeant* (20th, 1943), *Pilot No. 5* (MGM, 1943), *Above Suspicion* (MGM, 1943), *Someone to Remember* (Rep., 1943), *The Man From Down Under* (MGM, 1943), *Sherlock Holmes Faces Death* (Univ., 1943), *The Sky's the Limit* (RKO, 1943), *Paris After Dark* (20th, 1943), *Flesh and Fantasy* (Univ., 1943), *Assignment in Brittany* (MGM, 1943), *Sahara* (Col., 1943), *West Side Kid* (Rep., 1943), *Corvette K-225* (Univ., 1943), *The White Cliffs of Dover* (MGM, 1944), *The Canterville Ghost* (MGM, 1944), *Mrs. Parkington* (MGM, 1944), *Son of Lassie* (MGM, 1945), *The Picture of Dorian Gray* (MGM, 1945), *Two Sisters From Boston* (MGM, 1946), *Cluny Brown* (20th, 1946), *My Brother Talks to Horses* (MGM, 1946), *It Happened in Brooklyn* (MGM, 1947), *Good News* (MGM, 1947), *On an Island With You* (MGM, 1948), *Easter Parade* (MGM, 1948), *Julia Misbehaves* (MGM, 1948), *Little Women* (MGM, 1949), *The Red Danube* (MGM, 1949), *Please Believe Me* (MGM, 1950), *Just This Once* (MGM, 1952), *Kangaroo* (20th, 1952), *You for Me* (MGM, 1952), *The Hour of 13* (MGM, 1952), *Rogue's March* (MGM, 1952), *It Should Happen to You* (Col., 1954), *Never So Few* (MGM, 1959), *Ocean's 11* (WB, 1960), *Exodus* (UA, 1960), *Pepe* (Col., 1960), *Sergeants 3* (UA, 1962), *Advise and Consent* (Col., 1962), *The Longest Day* (20th, 1962), *Dead Ringer* (WB, 1964), *Sylvia* (Par., 1965), *Harlow* (Par., 1965), *The Oscar* (Par., 1966), *A Man Called Adam* (Embassy, 1966), *Salt and Pepper* (UA, 1968), *Buona Sera, Mrs. Campbell* (UA, 1968).

JANET LEIGH (Jeanette Helen Morrison) Born July 6, 1927, Merced, California. Married Kenneth Carlisle (1942); annulled 1942. Married Stanley Reames (1945); divorced 1948. Married Tony Curtis (1951); children: Kelly, Jamie; divorced 1962. Married Robert Brandt (1962).

Feature Films: *The Romance of Rosy Ridge* (MGM, 1947), *If Winter Comes* (MGM, 1947), *Hills of Home* (MGM, 1948), *Words and Music* (MGM, 1948), *Act of Violence* (MGM, 1948), *Little Women* (MGM, 1949), *That Forsyte Woman* (MGM, 1949), *The Doctor and the Girl* (MGM, 1949), *The Red Danube* (MGM, 1949), *Holiday Affair* (RKO, 1949), *Strictly Dishonorable* (MGM, 1951), *Angels in the Outfield* (MGM, 1951), *Two Tickets to Broadway* (RKO, 1951), *It's a Big Country* (MGM, 1951), *Just This Once* (MGM, 1952), *Scaramouche* (MGM, 1952), *Fearless Fagan* (MGM, 1952), *The Naked Spur* (MGM, 1953), *Confidentially Connie* (MGM, 1953), *Houdini* (Par., 1953), *Walking My Baby Back Home* (Univ., 1953), *Prince Valiant* (20th, 1954), *Living It Up* (Par., 1954), *The Black Shield of Falworth* (Univ., 1954), *Rogue Cop* (MGM, 1954), *Pete Kelly's Blues* (WB, 1955), *My Sister Eileen* (Col.,

1955), *Safari* (Col., 1956), *Jet Pilot* (Univ., 1957), *Touch of Evil* (Univ., 1958), *The Vikings* (UA, 1958), *The Perfect Furlough* (Univ., 1958), *Who Was That Lady?* (Col., 1960), *Psycho* (Par., 1960), *Pepe* (Col., 1960), *The Manchurian Candidate* (UA, 1962), *Bye Bye Birdie* (Col., 1963), *Wives and Lovers* (Par., 1963), *Three on a Couch* (Col., 1966), *Harper* (WB, 1966), *Kid Rodelo* (Par., 1966), *An American Dream* (WB, 1966), *Hello Down There* (Par., 1968), *Grand Slam* (Par., 1968).

VIVIEN LEIGH (Vivian Mary Hartley) Born November 5, 1913, Darjeeling, India. Married Herbert Holman (1932), child: Suzanne; divorced 1940. Married Laurence Olivier (1940); divorced 1960. Died July 8, 1967.

Robert Taylor and Vivien Leigh in *Waterloo Bridge*.

Feature Films: *Things Are Looking Up* (Gainsborough, 1934), *The Village Squire* (British and Dominions, 1935), *Gentleman's Agreement* (British and Dominions, 1935), *Look Up and Laugh* (Associated Talking Pictures, 1935), *Fire Over England* (UA, 1937), *Dark Journey* (UA, 1937), *Storm in a Teacup* (UA, 1937), *A Yank at Oxford* (MGM, 1938), *St. Martin's Lane* ("The Sidewalks of London"—Par., 1938), *Gone With the Wind* (MGM, 1939), *Waterloo Bridge* (MGM, 1940), *Twenty-one Days Together* (Col., 1940), *That Hamilton Woman* (UA, 1941), *Caesar and Cleopatra* (UA, 1946), *Anna Karenina* (20th, 1948), *A Streetcar Named Desire* (WB, 1951), *The Deep Blue Sea* (20th, 1955), *The Roman Spring of Mrs. Stone* (WB, 1961), *Ship of Fools* (Col., 1965).

Jack Lemmon and Judy Holliday in *It Should Happen to You.*

JACK LEMMON (John Uhler Lemmon III) Born February 8, 1925, Boston, Massachusetts. Married Cynthia Stone (1950), child: Christopher; divorced 1956. Married Felicia Farr (1962).

Feature Films: *It Should Happen to You* (Col., 1954), *Phffft* (Col., 1954), *Three for the Show* (Col., 1955), *My Sister Eileen* (Col., 1955), *Mister Roberts* (WB, 1955), *You Can't Run Away From It* (Col., 1956), *Operation Mad Ball* (Col., 1957), *Fire Down Below* (Col., 1957), *Cowboy* (Col., 1958), *Bell, Book and Candle* (Col., 1959), *It Happened to Jane* (Col., 1959), *Some Like it Hot* (UA, 1959), *The Apartment* (UA, 1960), *The Wackiest Ship in the Army* (Col., 1960), *Pepe* (Col., 1960), *The Notorious Landlady* (Col., 1962), *Days of Wine and Roses* (WB, 1962), *Irma La Douce* (UA, 1963), *Under the Yum Yum Tree* (Col., 1963), *Good Neighbor Sam* (Col., 1964), *How to Murder Your Wife* (UA, 1964), *The Great Race* (WB, 1965), *The Fortune Cookie* (UA, 1966), *Luv* (Col., 1967), *The Odd Couple* (Par., 1968).

JOAN LESLIE (Joan Agnes Theresa Sadie Brodel) Born January 26, 1925, Detroit, Michigan. Married William Caldwell (1950), children: Patrice, Ellen.

Fred Astaire and Joan Leslie in *The Sky's the Limit.*

Feature Films:
    as Joan Brodel *Camille* (MGM, 1936), *Men With Wings* (Par., 1938), *Two Thoroughbreds* (RKO, 1939), *Nancy Drew, Reporter* (WB, 1939), *Winter Carnival* (UA, 1939), *Love Affair* (RKO, 1939), *Military Academy* (Col., 1940), *Star Dust* (20th, 1940), *Young as You Feel* (20th, 1940), *Susan and God* (MGM, 1940), *Laddie* (RKO, 1940), *Foreign Correspondent* (UA, 1940).
    as Joan Leslie *High Sierra* (WB, 1941), *Thieves Fall Out* (WB,

1941), *The Wagons Roll at Night* (WB, 1941), *Great Mr. Nobody* (WB, 1941), *Sergeant York* (WB, 1941), *The Hard Way* (WB, 1942), *Yankee Doodle Dandy* (WB, 1942), *The Male Animal* (WB, 1942), *This Is the Army* (WB, 1943), *Thank Your Lucky Stars* (WB, 1943), *The Sky's the Limit* (RKO, 1943), *Hollywood Canteen* (WB, 1944), *Rhapsody in Blue* (WB, 1945), *Where Do We Go From Here?* (20th, 1945), *Too Young To Know* (WB, 1945), *Cinderella Jones* (WB, 1946), *Janie Gets Married* (WB, 1946), *Two Guys From Milwaukee* (WB, 1946), *Repeat Performance* (EL, 1947), *Northwest Stampede* (EL, 1948), *Born to Be Bad* (RKO, 1950), *The Skipper Surprised His Wife* (MGM, 1950), *Man in the Saddle* (Col., 1951), *Hellgate* (Lip., 1952), *Toughest Man in Arizona* (Rep., 1952), *The Woman They Almost Lynched* (Rep., 1953), *Flight Nurse* (Rep., 1953), *Jubilee Trail* (Rep., 1953), *Hell's Outpost* (Rep., 1954), *The Revolt of Mamie Stover* (20th, 1956).

JERRY LEWIS (Joseph Levitch) Born March 16, 1926, Newark, New Jersey. Married Patti Palmer (1944), children: Gary, Ronald, Scott, Christopher, Anthony, Joseph.

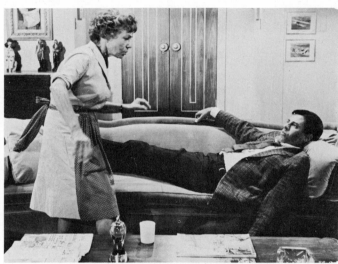

Thelma Ritter and Jerry Lewis in *Boeing-Boeing.*

Feature Films: *My Friend Irma* (Par., 1949), *My Friend Irma Goes West* (Par., 1950), *At War With the Army* (Par., 1951), *That's My Boy* (Par., 1951), *Sailor Beware* (Par., 1952), *Jumping Jacks* (Par., 1952), *Road to Bali* (Par., 1952),* *The Stooge* (Par., 1953), *Scared Stiff* (Par., 1953), *The Caddy* (Par., 1953), *Money From Home* (Par., 1954), *Living It Up* (Par., 1954), *Three Ring Circus* (Par., 1954), *You're Never Too Young* (Par., 1955), *Artists and Models* (Par., 1955), *Pardners* (Par., 1956), *Hollywood or Bust* (Par., 1956), *The Delicate Delinquent* (Par., 1957), *The Sad Sack* (Par., 1958), *Rock-a-Bye Baby* (Par., 1958), *The Geisha Boy* (Par., 1958), *Don't Give Up the Ship* (Par., 1959), *L'il Abner* (Par., 1959), *Visit to a Small Planet* (Par., 1960), *The Bellboy* (Par., 1960), *Cinderfella* (Par., 1960), *The Ladies' Man* (Par., 1961), *The Errand Boy* (Par., 1961), *It's Only Money* (Par., 1962), *It's a Mad, Mad, Mad, Mad World* (UA, 1963),* *The Nutty Professor* (Par., 1963), *Who's Minding the Store?* (Par., 1964), *The Patsy* (Par., 1964), *Disorderly Orderly* (Par., 1964), *Family Jewels* (Par., 1965), *Boeing-Boeing* (Par., 1965), *Three on a Couch* (Col., 1966), *Way, Way Out!* (20th, 1966), *The Big Mouth* (Col., 1967), *Don't Raise the Bridge, Lower the River* (Col., 1968).

        *Unbilled guest appearance

VIVECA LINDFORS (Elsa Viveca Torstens-Dotter Lindfors) Born December 29, 1920, Uppsala, Sweden. Married Folke Rogard (1941), children: Jan, Lena; divorced 1949. Married Donald Siegel (1949), child: Christopher; divorced 1953. Married George Tabori (1954).

English-Language Feature Films: *To the Victor* (WB, 1948), *Adventures of Don Juan* (WB, 1948), *Night Unto Night* (WB, 1949), *Backfire* (WB, 1950), *No Sad Songs for Me* (Col., 1950), *This Side of the Law* (WB, 1950), *Dark City* (Par., 1950), *Four in a Jeep* (UA, 1951), *Gypsy Fury*

Viveca Lindfors and Ronald Reagan in *Night Unto Night*.

(Mon., 1951), *The Flying Missile* (Col., 1951), *Journey into Light* (20th, 1951), *The Raiders* (Univ., 1952), *No Time for Flowers* (RKO, 1952), *Run for Cover* (Par., 1955), *Moonfleet* (MGM, 1955), *The Halliday Brand* (UA, 1957), *I Accuse!* (MGM, 1958), *The Tempest* (Par., 1959), *The Story of Ruth* (20th, 1960), *Weddings and Babies* (Zenith, 1960), *King of Kings* (MGM, 1962), *No Exit* (Zenith, 1962), *These Are the Damned* (Col., 1962), *An Affair of the Skin* (Zenith, 1964), *Brainstorm* (WB, 1965), *Sylvia* (Par., 1965), *The Witnesses* (voice only; Altura Films International, 1967).

MARGARET LINDSAY (Margaret Kies) Born September 19, 1910, Dubuque, Iowa.

James Burke, Charley Grapewin, Margaret Lindsay, Charles Lane and Anna May Wong in *Ellery Queen's Penthouse Mystery*.

Feature Films: *The All American* (Univ., 1932), *Okay America* (Univ., 1932), *The Fourth Horseman* (Univ., 1932), *Cavalcade* (Fox, 1933), *West of Singapore* (Mon., 1933), *Private Detective 62* (WB, 1933), *Voltaire* (WB, 1933), *Baby Face* (WB, 1933), *Captured* (WB, 1933), *Paddy the Next Best Thing* (Fox, 1933), *The World Changes* (WB, 1933), *From Headquarters* (WB, 1933), *House on 56th Street* (WB, 1933), *Lady Killer* (WB, 1933), *Gentlemen Are Born* (WB, 1934), *Fog Over Frisco* (WB, 1934), *Merry Wives of Reno* (WB, 1934), *The Dragon Murder Case* (WB, 1934), *The Florentine Dagger* (WB, 1935), *Devil Dogs of the Air* (WB, 1935), *Bordertown* (WB, 1935), *The Case of the Curious Bride* (WB, 1935), *G-Men* (WB, 1935), *Personal Maid's Secret* (WB, 1935), *Frisco Kid* (WB, 1935), *Dangerous* (WB, 1935), *The Lady Consents* (RKO, 1936), *The Law in Her Hands* (WB, 1936), *Public Enemy's Wife* (WB, 1936), *Isle of Fury* (WB, 1936), *Sinner Take All* (MGM, 1936), *Green Light* (WB, 1937), *Song of the City* (MGM,

1937), *Slim* (WB, 1937), *Back in Circulation* (WB, 1937), *Jezebel* (WB, 1938), *Gold Is Where You Find It* (WB, 1938), *When Were You Born?* (WB, 1938), *There's That Woman Again* (Col., 1938), *Broadway Musketeers* (WB, 1938), *Garden of the Moon* (WB, 1938), *On Trial* (WB, 1939), *Hell's Kitchen* (WB, 1939), *The Under-Pup* (20th, 1939), *20,000 Men a Year* (20th, 1939), *British Intelligence* (WB, 1940), *Double Alibi* (Univ., 1940), *Honeymoon Deferred* (Univ., 1940), *The House of Seven Gables* (Univ., 1940), *Meet the Wildcat* (Univ., 1940), *Ellery Queen, Master Detective* (Col., 1940), *Ellery Queen's Penthouse Mystery* (Col., 1941), *There's Magic in Music* (Par., 1941), *Ellery Queen and the Perfect Crime* (Col., 1941), *Ellery Queen and the Murder Ring* (Col., 1941), *A Close Call for Ellery Queen* (Col., 1942), *A Tragedy at Midnight* (Rep., 1942), *The Spoilers* (Univ., 1942), *Enemy Agents Meet Ellery Queen* (Col., 1942), *A Desperate Chance for Ellery Queen* (Col., 1942), *Crime Doctor* (Col., 1943), *Let's Have Fun* (Col., 1943), *No Place for a Lady* (Col., 1943), *Alaska* (Mon., 1944), *The Adventures of Rusty* (Col., 1945), *Scarlet Street* (Univ., 1945), *Club Havana* (PRC, 1946), *Her Sister's Secret* (PRC, 1946), *Seven Keys to Baldpate* (RKO, 1947), *Louisiana* (Mon., 1947), *Cass Timberlane* (MGM, 1947), *The Vigilantes Return* (Univ., 1947), *B. F.'s Daughter* (MGM, 1948), *Emergency Hospital* (UA, 1956), *The Bottom of the Bottle* (20th, 1956), *The Restless Years* (Univ., 1958), *Please Don't Eat the Daisies* (MGM, 1960), *Jet Over the Atlantic* (Inter-Continent, 1960), *Tammy and the Doctor* (Univ., 1963).

GENE LOCKHART (Eugene Lockhart) Born July 18, 1891, London, Ontario, Canada. Married Kathleen Arthur (1924), child: June. Died March 31, 1957.

Kathleen Lockhart and Gene Lockhart in *A Christmas Carol*.

Sound Feature Films: *By Your Leave* (RKO, 1934), *I've Been Around* (Univ., 1935), *Star of Midnight* (RKO, 1935), *Captain Hurricane* (RKO, 1935), *Thunder in the Night* (Fox, 1935), *Storm Over the Andes* (Univ., 1935), *Crime and Punishment* (Col., 1935), *The Garden Murder Case* (MGM, 1936), *Brides Are Like That* (WB, 1936), *The First Baby* (20th, 1936), *Times Square Playboy* (WB, 1936), *Earthworm Tractors* (WB, 1936), *The Gorgeous Hussy* (MGM, 1936), *The Devil Is a Sissy*

(MGM, 1936), *Wedding Present* (Par., 1936), *Mind Your Own Business* (Par., 1936), *Career Woman* (20th, 1936), *Come Closer Folks* (Col., 1936), *Too Many Wives* (RKO, 1937), *Mama Steps Out* (MGM, 1937), *Something to Sing About* (GN, 1937), *The Sheik Steps Out* (Rep., 1937), *Of Human Hearts* (MGM, 1938), *Sinners in Paradise* (Univ., 1938), *Men Are Such Fools* (WB, 1938), *Algiers* (UA, 1938), *Penrod's Double Trouble* (WB, 1938), *Sweethearts* (MGM, 1938), *A Christmas Carol* (MGM, 1938), *Blondie* (Col., 1938), *Meet the Girls* (20th, 1938), *Listen Darling* (MGM, 1938), *The Story of Alexander Graham Bell* (20th, 1939), *I'm From Missouri* (Par., 1939), *Hotel Imperial* (Par., 1939), *Tell No Tales* (MGM, 1939), *Bridal Suite* (MGM, 1939), *Our Leading Citizen* (Par., 1939), *Blackmail* (MGM, 1939), *Geronimo* (Par., 1939), *His Girl Friday* (Col., 1940), *Edison the Man* (MGM, 1940), *We Who Are Young* (MGM, 1940), *A Dispatch From Reuters* (WB, 1940), *Dr. Kildare Goes Home* (MGM, 1940), *Meet John Doe* (WB, 1941), *The Sea Wolf* (WB, 1941), *Billy The Kid* (MGM, 1941), *All That Money Can Buy* (RKO, 1941), *International Lady* (UA, 1941), *One Foot in Heaven* (WB, 1941), *They Died With Their Boots On* (WB, 1941), *Steel Against the Sky* (WB, 1941), *Juke Girl* (WB, 1942), *The Gay Sisters* (WB, 1942), *You Can't Escape Forever* (WB, 1942), *Forever and a Day* (RKO, 1943), *Hangmen Also Die* (UA, 1943), *Find the Black-mailer* (WB, 1943), *Northern Pursuit* (WB, 1943), *The Desert Song* (WB, 1943), *Action in Arabia* (RKO, 1944), *Going My Way* (Par., 1944), *Man From Frisco* (Rep., 1944), *That's the Spirit* (Univ., 1945), *The House on 92nd Street* (20th, 1945), *Leave Her to Heaven* (20th, 1945), *Meet Me on Broadway* (Col., 1946), *A Scandal in Paris* (UA, 1946), *The Strange Woman* (UA, 1946), *The Shocking Miss Pilgrim* (20th, 1947), *Honeymoon* (RKO, 1947), *The Miracle on 34th Street* (20th, 1947), *Cynthia* (MGM, 1947), *Her Husband's Affair* (Col., 1947), *The Foxes of Harrow* (20th, 1947), *I, Jane Doe* (Rep., 1948), *The Inside Story* (Rep., 1948), *Apartment for Peggy* (20th, 1948), *Joan of Arc* (RKO, 1948), *That Wonderful Urge* (20th, 1948), *Down to the Sea in Ships* (20th, 1949), *Madame Bovary* (MGM, 1949), *Red Light* (UA, 1949), *The Inspector General* (WB, 1949), *The Big Hangover* (MGM, 1950), *I'd Climb the Highest Mountain* (20th, 1951), *Rhubarb* (Par., 1951), *The Lady From Texas* (Univ., 1951), *Seeds of Destruction* (Astor, 1951), *A Girl in Every Port* (RKO, 1952), *Hoodlum Empire* (Rep., 1952), *Bonzo Goes to College* (Univ., 1952), *Apache War Smoke* (MGM, 1952), *Androcles and the Lion* (RKO, 1952), *Face to Face* (RKO, 1952), *Confidentially Connie* (MGM, 1953), *The Lady Wants Mink* (Rep., 1953), *Down Among the Sheltering Palms* (20th, 1953), *Francis Covers the Big Town* (Univ., 1953), *World for Ransom* (AA, 1954), *The Vanishing American* (Rep., 1955), *Carousel* (20th, 1956), *The Man in the Gray Flannel Suit* (20th, 1956), *Jeanne Eagles* (Col., 1957).

GINA LOLLOBRIGIDA Born July 4, 1927, Sibriaco, Italy. Married Milko Skofic (1949), child: Milko; divorced 1968.

Rock Hudson and Gina Lollobrigida in *Strange Bedfellows*.

English-Language Feature Films: *Beat the Devil* (UA, 1954), *Crossed Swords* (UA, 1954), *Trapeze* (UA, 1956), *The Hunchback of Notre Dame* (AA, 1957), *Solomon and Sheba* (UA, 1959), *Never So Few* (MGM, 1959), *Go Naked in the World* (MGM, 1961), *Come September* (Univ., 1961), *Woman of Straw* (UA, 1964), *Strange Bedfellows* (Univ., 1964), *Hotel Paradiso* (MGM, 1966), *Cervantes* (Aip, 1968), *Buona Sera, Mrs. Campbell* (Univ., 1968), *The Private Navy of Sgt. O'Farrell* (UA, 1968).

CAROLE LOMBARD (Jane Alice Peters) Born October 6, 1908, Fort Wayne, Indiana. Married William Powell (1931); divorced 1933. Married Clark Gable (1939). Died January 16, 1942.

Ray Milland and Carole Lombard in *Bolero*.

Sound Feature Films: *Show Folks* (Pathé, 1928), *Ned McCobb's Daughter* (Pathé, 1929), *High Voltage* (Pathé, 1929), *Big News* (Pathé, 1929), *Dynamite* (Pathé, 1929), *The Racketeer* (Pathé, 1929), *Arizona Kid* (Fox, 1930), *Safety in Numbers* (Par., 1930), *Fast and Loose* (Par., 1930), *It Pays to Advertise* (Par., 1931), *Man of the World* (Par., 1931), *Ladies' Man* (Par., 1931), *Up Pops the Devil* (Par., 1931), *I Take This Woman* (Par., 1931), *No One Man* (Par., 1932), *Sinners in the Sun* (Par., 1932), *Virtue* (Col., 1932), *No More Orchids* (Col., 1932), *No Man of Her Own* (Par., 1932), *From Hell to Heaven* (Par., 1933), *Supernatural* (Par., 1933), *The Eagle and the Hawk* (Par., 1933), *Brief Moment* (Col., 1933), *White Woman* (Par., 1933), *Bolero* (Par., 1934), *We're Not Dressing* (Par., 1934), *Twentieth Century* (Col., 1934), *Now and Forever* (Par., 1934), *Lady by Choice* (Col., 1934), *The Gay Bride* (MGM, 1934), *Rumba* (Par., 1935), *Hands Across the Table* (Par., 1935), *Love Before Breakfast* (Univ., 1936), *My Man Godfrey* (Univ., 1936), *The Princess Comes Across* (Par., 1936), *Swing High, Swing Low* (Par., 1937), *True Confession* (Par., 1937), *Nothing Sacred* (UA, 1937), *Fools for Scandal* (WB, 1938), *Made for Each Other* (UA, 1939), *In Name Only* (RKO, 1939), *Vigil in the Night* (RKO, 1940), *They Knew What They Wanted* (RKO, 1940), *Mr. and Mrs. Smith* (RKO, 1941), *To Be or Not to Be* (UA, 1942).

SOPHIA LOREN (Sofia Villani Scicolone) Born September 20, 1932, Rome, Italy. Married Carlo Ponti (1957).

English-Language Feature Films: *Quo Vadis* (MGM, 1951), *Boy on a Dolphin* (20th, 1957), *The Pride and the Passion* (UA, 1957), *Legend of the Lost* (UA, 1957), *Desire Under the Elms* (Par., 1958), *The Key* (Col., 1958), *Houseboat* (Par., 1958), *That Kind of Woman* (Par., 1959), *Black Orchid* (Par., 1959), *Heller in Pink Tights* (Par., 1960), *It Started in Naples* (Par., 1960), *A Breath of Scandal* (Par., 1960), *The Millionaires* (20th, 1960), *El Cid* (AA, 1961), *The Condemned of Altona* (20th, 1963), *Five Miles to Midnight* (UA, 1963), *The Fall of the Roman Empire*

Sophia Loren and Tab Hunter in *That Kind of Woman*.

(Par., 1964), *Operation Crossbow* (MGM, 1965), *Judith* (Par., 1966), *Arabesque* (Univ., 1966), *Lady L* (MGM, 1966), *The Countess From Hong Kong* (Univ., 1967). *More than a Miracle* (MGM, 1967), *Ghost Italian Style* (MGM, 1968), *Best House in Naples* (MGM, 1968).

PETER LORRE Born June 26, 1904, Rosenberg, Hungary. Married Cecilia Lovovsky (1933); divorced 1945. Married Kaaren Verne (1945); divorced. Married Anna Brenning (1952), child: Kathryn. Died March 23, 1965.

Frances Drake and Peter Lorre in *Mad Love*.

English-Language Sound Feature Films: *The Man Who Knew Too Much* (Gaumont-British, 1934), *Mad Love* (MGM, 1935), *Crime and Punishment* (Col., 1935), *Secret Agent* (Gaumont-British, 1936), *Crack-Up* (20th, 1936), *Nancy Steele Is Missing* (20th, 1937), *Lancer Spy* (20th, 1937), *Think Fast, Mr. Moto* (20th, 1937), *Thank You, Mr. Moto* (20th, 1937), *Mr. Moto's Gamble* (20th, 1938), *Mr. Moto Takes a Chance* (20th, 1938), *I'll Give a Million* (20th, 1938), *Mysterious Mr. Moto* (20th, 1938), *Mr. Moto's Last Warning* (20th, 1939), *Mr. Moto Takes a Vacation* (20th, 1939), *Mr. Moto in Danger Island* (20th, 1939), *Strange Cargo* (MGM, 1940), *Island of Doomed Men* (Col. 1940), *I Was an Adventuress* (20th, 1940), *Stranger on the Third Floor* (RKO, 1940), *You'll Find Out* (RKO, 1940), *The Face Behind the Mask* (Col., 1941), *Mr. District Attorney* (Rep., 1941), *They Met in Bombay* (MGM,

1941), *The Maltese Falcon* (WB, 1941), *All Through the Night* (WB, 1942), *The Boogie Man Will Get You* (Col., 1942), *Invisible Agent* (Univ., 1942), *In This Our Life* (WB, 1942),* *Casablanca* (WB, 1942), *The Constant Nymph* (WB, 1943), *Background to Danger* (WB, 1943), *Cross of Lorraine* (MGM, 1943), *Arsenic and Old Lace* (WB, 1944), *Passage to Marseille* (WB, 1944), *Hollywood Canteen* (WB, 1944), *The Mask of Dimitrios* (WB, 1944), *Conspirators* (WB, 1944), *Confidential Agent* (WB, 1945), *Hotel Berlin* (WB, 1945), *Three Strangers* (WB, 1946), *The Verdict* (WB, 1946), *Black Angel* (Univ., 1946), *The Beast With Five Fingers* (WB, 1946), *The Chase* (UA, 1946), *My Favorite Brunette* (Par., 1947), *Casbah* (Univ., 1948), *Rope of Sand* (Par., 1949), *Quicksand* (UA, 1950), *Double Confession* (Associated British Pictures, 1951), *Beat the Devil* (UA, 1954), *20,000 Leagues Under the Sea* (BV, 1954), *Meet Me in Las Vegas* (MGM, 1956),* *Congo Crossing* (Univ., 1956), *Around the World in 80 Days* (UA, 1956), *The Buster Keaton Story* (Par., 1957), *The Story of Mankind* (WB, 1957), *The Sad Sack* (Par., 1957), *Silk Stockings* (MGM, 1957), *Hell Ship Mutiny* (Rep., 1958), *The Big Circus* (AA, 1959), *Scent of Mystery* (Mike Todd, Jr., 1960), *Voyage to the Bottom of the Sea* (20th, 1961), *Five Weeks in a Balloon* (20th, 1962), *Tales of Terror* (AIP, 1962), *The Raven* (AIP, 1963), *Comedy of Terrors* (AIP, 1963), *The Patsy* (Par., 1964), *Muscle Beach Party* (AIP, 1964).*

*Unbilled guest appearance

ANITA LOUISE (Anita Louise Fremault) Born January 29, 1915, New York, New York. Married Buddy Adler (1940); widowed 1960. Married Henry Bergers (1962).

Anita Louise, Ross Alexander and Joseph Cawthorn in *Brides Are Like That*.

Sound Feature Films: *Wonder of Women* (MGM, 1929), *Square Shoulders* (Pathé, 1929), *The Marriage Playground* (Par., 1929), *What a Man!* (World Wide, 1930), *The Floradora Girl* (MGM, 1930), *Just Like Heaven* (Tiff., 1930), *The Third Alarm* (Tiff., 1930), *Millie* (RKO, 1931), *The Great Meadow* (MGM, 1931), *Woman Between* (RKO, 1931), *Everything's Rosie* (RKO, 1931), *Heaven on Earth* (Univ., 1931), *The Phantom of Crestwood* (RKO, 1932), *Our Betters* (RKO, 1933), *Most Precious Thing in Life* (Col., 1934), *Are We Civilized?* (Raspin Productions, 1934), *I Give My Love* (Univ., 1934), *Cross Streets* (Chesterfield, 1934), *Madame Du Barry* (WB, 1934), *Judge Priest* (Fox, 1934), *The Firebird* (WB, 1934), *Bachelor of Arts* (Fox, 1934), *Lady Tubbs* (Univ., 1935), *Here's to Romance* (Fox, 1935), *A Midsummer Night's Dream* (WB, 1935), *Personal Maid's Secret* (WB, 1935), *The Story of Louis Pasteur* (WB, 1935), *Brides Are Like That* (WB, 1936), *Anthony Adverse* (WB, 1936), *Call It a Day* (WB, 1937), *Green Light* (WB, 1937), *The Go-Getter* (WB, 1937), *First Lady* (WB, 1937), *That Certain Woman* (WB, 1937), *Tovarich* (WB, 1937), *My Bill* (WB, 1938), *Marie Antoinette* (MGM, 1938), *Going Places* (WB, 1938), *The Sisters* (WB, 1938), *The Gorilla* (20th, 1939), *Hero for a Day* (Univ., 1939), *Reno* (RKO, 1939), *These Glamour Girls* (MGM, 1939), *Main Street Lawyer* (Rep.,

1939), *The Little Princess* (20th, 1939), *Wagons Westward* (Rep., 1940), *The Villain Still Pursued Her* (RKO, 1940), *Glamour for Sale* (Col., 1940), *The Phantom Submarine* (Col., 1941), *Two in a Taxi* (Col., 1941), *Harmon of Michigan* (Col., 1941), *Dangerous Blondes* (Col., 1943), *Nine Girls* (Col., 1944), *Casanova Brown* (RKO, 1944), *Love Letters* (Par., 1945), *The Fighting Guardsman* (Col., 1945), *Shadowed* (Col., 1946), *The Bandit of Sherwood Forest* (Col., 1946), *The Devil's Mask* (Col., 1946), *Personality Kid* (Col., 1946), *Blondie's Big Moment* (Col., 1947), *Bulldog Drummond at Bay* (Col., 1947), *Retreat, Hell!* (WB, 1952).

FRANK LOVEJOY Born March 28, 1914, Bronx, New York. Married Joan Banks (1940), children: Judith, Stephen. Died October 2, 1962.

John Agar, Suzanne Dalbert and Frank Lovejoy in *Breakthrough*.

Feature Films: *Black Bart* (Univ., 1948), *Home of the Brave* (UA, 1949), *South Sea Sinner* (Univ., 1950), *In a Lonely Place* (Col., 1950), *Three Secrets* (WB, 1950), *Breakthrough* (WB, 1950), *The Sound of Fury* (UA, 1950), *Goodbye, My Fancy* (WB, 1951), *I Was a Communist for the FBI* (WB, 1951), *Force of Arms* (WB, 1951), *Starlift* (WB, 1951), *I'll See You in My Dreams* (WB, 1951), *Retreat, Hell!* (WB, 1952), *The Winning Team* (WB, 1952), *The Hitch Hiker* (RKO, 1953), *She's Back on Broadway* (WB, 1953), *The System* (WB, 1953), *House of Wax* (WB, 1953), *The Charge at Feather River* (WB, 1953), *Men of the Fighting Lady* (MGM, 1954), *Beachhead* (UA, 1954), *Strategic Air Command* (Par., 1955), *Mad at the World* (Filmakers, 1955), *Top of the World* (UA, 1955), *The Americano* (RKO, 1955), *Finger Man* (AA, 1955), *The Crooked Web* (Col., 1955), *Shack-Out on 101* (AA, 1955), *Julie* (MGM, 1956), *Three Brave Men* (20th, 1957), *Cole Younger, Gunfighter* (AA, 1958).

MYRNA LOY (Myrna Williams) Born August 2, 1905, Raidersburg, Montana. Married Arthur Hornblow, Jr. (1936); divorced 1942. Married John Hertz, Jr. (1942); divorced 1944. Married Gene Markey (1946); divorced 1950. Married Howland Sargeant (1951); divorced 1960.

Sound Feature Films: *The Jazz Singer* (WB, 1927), *The Desert Song* (WB, 1929), *Black Watch* (Fox, 1929), *The Squall* (WB, 1929), *Hardboiled Rose* (WB, 1929), *Evidence* (WB, 1929), *Show of Shows* (WB, 1929), *The Great Divide* (WB, 1930), *The Jazz Cinderella* (Chesterfield, 1930), *Cameo Kirby* (Fox, 1930), *Isle of Escape* (WB, 1930), *Under a Texas Moon* (WB, 1930), *Cock o' the Walk* (Sono Art-World Wide, 1930), *Bride of the Regiment* (WB, 1930), *Last of the Duanes* (Fox, 1930), *The Truth About Youth* (WB, 1930), *Renegades* (Fox, 1930), *Rogue of the Rio Grande* (Sono Art-World Wide, 1930), *The Devil to Pay* (UA, 1930), *Naughty Flirt* (WB, 1931), *Body and Soul* (Fox, 1931), *A Connecticut Yankee* (Fox, 1931), *Hush Money* (Fox, 1931), *Transatlantic* (Fox, 1931), *Rebound* (RKO, 1931), *Skyline* (Fox, 1931), *Consolation Marriage* (RKO, 1931), *Arrowsmith* (UA, 1931), *Emma* (MGM, 1932), *The Wet Parade*

William Powell and Myrna Loy in *Double Wedding*.

(MGM, 1932), *Vanity Fair* (Hollywood Exchange, 1932), *The Woman in Room 13* (Fox, 1932), *New Morals for Old* (MGM, 1932), *Love Me Tonight* (Par., 1932), *Thirteen Women* (RKO, 1932), *The Mask of Fu Manchu* (MGM, 1932), *The Animal Kingdom* (RKO, 1932), *Topaze* (RKO, 1933), *The Barbarian* (MGM, 1933), *The Prizefighter and the Lady* (MGM, 1933), *When Ladies Meet* (MGM, 1933), *Penthouse* (MGM, 1933), *Night Flight* (MGM, 1933), *Men in White* (MGM, 1934), *Manhattan Melodrama* (MGM, 1934), *The Thin Man* (MGM, 1934), *Stamboul Quest* (MGM, 1934), *Evelyn Prentice* (MGM, 1934), *Broadway Bill* (Col., 1934), *Wings in the Dark* (Par., 1935), *Whipsaw* (MGM, 1935), *Wife vs. Secretary* (MGM, 1936), *Petticoat Fever* (MGM, 1936), *The Great Ziegfeld* (MGM, 1936), *To Mary—With Love* (20th, 1936), *Libeled Lady* (MGM, 1936), *After the Thin Man* (MGM, 1936), *Parnell* (MGM, 1937), *Double Wedding* (MGM, 1937), *Man-Proof* (MGM, 1938), *Test Pilot* (MGM, 1938), *Too Hot to Handle* (MGM, 1938), *Lucky Night* (MGM, 1939), *The Rains Came* (20th, 1939), *Another Thin Man* (MGM, 1939), *I Love You Again* (MGM, 1940), *Third Finger, Left Hand* (MGM, 1940), *Love Crazy* (MGM, 1941), *Shadow of the Thin Man* (MGM, 1941), *The Thin Man Goes Home* (MGM, 1944), *So Goes My Love* (Univ., 1946), *The Best Years of Our Lives* (RKO, 1946), *The Bachelor and the Bobby-Soxer* (RKO, 1947), *Song of the Thin Man* (MGM, 1947), *The Senator Was Indiscreet* (Univ., 1947),* *Mr. Blandings Builds His Dream House* (RKO, 1948), *The Red Pony* (Rep., 1949), *Cheaper by the Dozen* (20th, 1950), *This Be Sin* (UA, 1950), *Belles on Their Toes* (20th, 1952), *The Ambassador's Daughter* (UA, 1956), *Lonelyhearts* (UA, 1958), *From the Terrace* (20th, 1960), *Midnight Lace* (Univ., 1960).

*Unbilled guest appearance

BELA LUGOSI (Bela Blasko) Born October 20, 1882, Lugos, Hungary. Married Beatrice Weeks (1924); divorced. Married Lillian Arch (1933), child: Bela; divorced 1953. Married Hope Lininger (1955). Died August 16, 1956.

Bela Lugosi and Minerva Urecal in *The Ape Man*.

English-Language Sound Feature Films: *Renegades* (Fox, 1930), *Wild Company* (Fox, 1930), *Such Men Are Dangerous* (Fox, 1930), *Oh, for a Man!* (Fox, 1930), *Women of All Nations* (Fox, 1931), *Dracula* (Univ., 1931), *Fifty Million Frenchmen* (WB, 1931), *Broad-Minded* (WB, 1931), *Black Camel* (Fox, 1931), *Murders in the Rue Morgue* (Univ., 1932), *White Zombie* (UA, 1932), *Chandu the Magician* (Fox, 1932), *Whispering Shadow* (Mascot serial, 1933), *Island of Lost Souls* (Par., 1933), *Death Kiss* (World Wide, 1933), *International House* (Par., 1933), *Night of Terror* (Col., 1933), *Return of Chandu* (Principal serial, 1934), *The Black Cat* (Univ., 1934), *The Gift of Gab* (Univ., 1934), *Best Man Wins* (Col., 1935), *Mysterious Mr. Wong* (Mon., 1935), *Mystery of the Marie Celeste* ("The Phantom Ship"—Guaranteed Pictures, 1935), *Murder by Television* (Imperial Pictures, 1935), *Mark of the Vampire* (MGM, 1935), *The Raven* (Univ., 1935), *Shadow of Chinatown* (Victory serial, 1936), *The Invisible Ray* (Univ., 1936), *Dracula's Daughter* (Univ., 1936), *Postal Inspector* (Univ., 1936), *S.O.S. Coast Guard* (Rep. serial, 1937), *The Phantom Creeps* (Univ. serial, 1939), *Son of Frankenstein* (Univ., 1939), *Ninotchka* (MGM, 1939), *Dark Eyes of London* ("The Human Monster"—Mon., 1939), *Saint's Double Trouble* (RKO, 1940), *Black Friday* (Univ., 1940), *You'll Find Out* (RKO, 1940), *Devil Bat* (PRC, 1940), *The Wolf Man* (Univ., 1941), *The Black Cat* (Univ., 1941), *The Invisible Ghost* (Mon., 1941), *Spooks Run Wild* (Mon., 1941), *Black Dragons* (Mon., 1942), *The Corpse Vanishes* (Mon., 1942), *Night Monster* (Univ., 1942), *The Ghost of Frankenstein* (Univ., 1942), *Bowery at Midnight* (Mon., 1942), *The Ape Man* (Mon., 1943), *Ghosts on the Loose* (Mon., 1943), *Frankenstein Meets the Wolf Man* (Univ., 1943), *Return of the Vampire* (Col., 1943), *Voodoo Man* (Mon., 1944), *Return of the Ape Man* (Mon., 1944), *One Body Too Many* (Par., 1944), *Zombies on Broadway* (RKO, 1945), *The Body Snatcher* (RKO, 1945), *Genius at Work* (RKO, 1946), *Scared to Death* (Screen Guild, 1947), *Abbott and Costello Meet Frankenstein* (Univ., 1948), *Bela Lugosi Meets a Brooklyn Gorilla* (Realart, 1952), *Old Mother Riley Meets the Vampire* ("Vampire Over London"—Gordon Films, 1952), *Bride of the Monster* (Banner Films, 1956), *Plan 9 From Outer Space* ("Grave Robbers From Outer Space"—DCA, 1959).

PAUL LUKAS (Paul Lugacs) Born May 26, 1894, Budapest, Hungary. Married Gizella Benes (1927); widowed 1962. Married Anna Driesens (1963).

Errol Flynn, Jean Sullivan and Paul Lukas in *Uncertain Glory.*

English-Language Sound Feature Films: *Illusion* (Par., 1929), *Half Way to Heaven* (Par., 1929), *Slightly Scarlet* (Par., 1930), *Benson Murder Case* (Par., 1930), *Young Eagles* (Par., 1930), *Devil's Holiday* (Par., 1930), *Anybody's Woman* (Par., 1930), *Grumpy* (Par., 1930), *Right to Love* (Par., 1930), *Unfaithful* (Par., 1931), *City Streets* (Par., 1931), *Vice Squad* (Par., 1931), *Women Who Love* (Univ., 1931), *Beloved Bachelor* (Par., 1931), *Strictly Dishonorable* (Par., 1931), *Working Girls* (Par., 1931), *Tomorrow and Tomorrow* (Par., 1932), *No One*

Man (Par., 1932), *Thunder Below* (Par., 1932), *Passport to Hell* (Fox, 1932), *Downstairs* (MGM, 1932), *Rockabye* (RKO, 1932), *Grand Slam* (WB, 1933), *Kiss Before the Mirror* (Univ., 1933), *Sing Sinner Sing* (Majestic, 1933), *Captured* (WB, 1933), *Secret of the Blue Room* (Univ., 1933), *Little Women* (RKO, 1933), *By Candlelight* (Univ., 1934), *Countess of Monte Cristo* (Univ., 1934), *Glamour* (Univ., 1934), *I Give My Love* (Univ., 1934), *Affairs of a Gentleman* (Univ., 1934), *The Fountain* (RKO, 1934), *The Gift of Gab* (Univ., 1934), *Father Brown—Detective* (Par., 1935), *Casino Murder Case* (MGM, 1935), *Age of Indiscretion* (MGM, 1935), *The Three Musketeers* (RKO, 1935), *I Found Stella Parish* (WB, 1935), *Dodsworth* (UA, 1936), *Ladies in Love* (20th, 1936), *Espionage* (MGM, 1937), *Dinner at the Ritz* (20th, 1937), *The Mutiny on the Elsinore* (Associated British Pictures, 1938), *The Lady Vanishes* (Gaumont-British, 1938), *Dangerous Secrets* (GN, 1938), *Confessions of a Nazi Spy* (WB, 1939), *Lady in Distress* (Times, 1939), *Captain Fury* (UA, 1939), *Strange Cargo* (MGM, 1940), *The Ghost Breakers* (Par., 1940), *The Monster and the Girl* (Par., 1941), *They Dare Not Love* (Col., 1941), *Chinese Den* (Film Alliance of the United States, 1941), *Watch on the Rhine* (WB, 1943), *Hostages* (Par., 1943), *Uncertain Glory* (WB, 1944), *Address Unknown* (Col., 1944), *Experiment Perilous* (RKO, 1944), *Deadline at Dawn* (RKO, 1946), *Temptation* (Univ., 1946), *Whispering City* (EL, 1947), *Berlin Express* (RKO, 1948), *Kim* (MGM, 1950), *20,000 Leagues Under the Sea* (BV, 1954), *The Roots of Heaven* (20th, 1958), *Scent of Mystery* (Mike Todd, Jr., 1960), *Tender Is the Night* (20th, 1960), *The Four Horsemen of the Apocalypse* (MGM, 1962), *55 Days At Peking* (AA, 1963), *Fun in Acapulco* (Par., 1963), *Lord Jim* (Col., 1965), *Sol Madrid* (MGM, 1968).

IDA LUPINO Born February 4, 1918, London, England. Married Louis Hayward (1938); divorced 1945. Married Collier Young (1948); divorced 1950. Married Howard Duff (1951), child: Bridget.

Ida Lupino and Ronald Colman in *The Light That Failed.*

Feature Films: *Her First Affaire* (Sterling, 1933), *Money for Speed* (UA, 1933), *High Finance* (WB, 1933), *The Ghost Camera* (Radio, 1933), *I Lived With You* (Gaumont-British, 1934), *Prince of Arcadia* (Gaumont-British, 1934), *Search for Beauty* (Par., 1934), *Come On Marines* (Par., 1934), *Ready for Love* (Par., 1934), *Paris in Spring* (Par., 1935), *Smart Girl* (Par., 1935), *Peter Ibbetson* (Par., 1935), *Anything Goes* (Par., 1936), *One Rainy Afternoon* (UA, 1936), *Yours for the Asking* (Par., 1936), *The Gay Desperado* (UA, 1936), *Sea Devils* (RKO, 1937), *Let's Get Married* (Col., 1937), *Artists and Models* (Par., 1937), *Fight for Your Lady* (RKO, 1937), *The Lone Wolf Spy Hunt* (Col., 1939), *The Lady and the Mob* (Col., 1939), *The Adventures of Sherlock Holmes* (20th, 1939), *The Light That Failed* (Par., 1940), *They Drive by Night* (WB, 1940), *High Sierra* (WB, 1941), *The Sea Wolf* (WB, 1941), *Out of the Fog* (WB, 1941), *Ladies in Retirement* (Col., 1941), *Moontide* (20th, 1942), *The Hard Way* (WB, 1942),

Life Begins at 8:30 (20th, 1942), *Forever and a Day* (RKO, 1943), *Thank Your Lucky Stars* (WB, 1943), *In Our Time* (WB, 1944), *Hollywood Canteen* (WB, 1944), *Pillow to Post* (WB, 1945), *Devotion* (WB, 1946), *The Man I Love* (WB, 1947), *Deep Valley* (WB, 1947), *Escape Me Never* (WB, 1947), *Road House* (20th, 1948), *Lust for Gold* (Col., 1949), *Woman in Hiding* (Univ., 1950), *On Dangerous Ground* (RKO, 1951), *Beware My Lovely* (RKO, 1952), *Jennifer* (AA, 1953), *The Bigamist* (Filmakers, 1953), *Private Hell 36* (Filmakers, 1954), *Women's Prison* (Col., 1955), *The Big Knife* (UA, 1955), *While the City Sleeps* (RKO, 1956), *Strange Intruder* (AA, 1956).

DIANA LYNN (Dolores Loehr) Born October 7, 1926, Los Angeles, California. Married John Lindsay (1948); divorced 1954. Married Mortimer Hall (1956), children: Mathew, Dorothy, Mary.

Feature Films:
   as Dolly Loehr *They Shall Have Music* (UA, 1939), *There's Magic in Music* (Par., 1941).
   as Diana Lynn *Star Spangled Rhythm* (Par., 1942), *The Major and the Minor* (Par., 1942), *Henry Aldrich Gets Glamour* (Par., 1943), *The Miracle of Morgan's Creek* (Par., 1944), *And the Angels Sing* (Par., 1944), *Henry Aldrich Plays Cupid* (Par., 1944), *Our Hearts Were Young and Gay* (Par., 1944), *Out of This World* (Par., 1945), *Duffy's Tavern* (Par., 1945), *Our Hearts Were Growing Up* (Par., 1946), *The Bride Wore Boots* (Par., 1946), *Easy Come, Easy Go* (Par., 1947), *Variety Girl* (Par., 1947), *Ruthless* (EL, 1948), *Texas, Brooklyn and Heaven* (UA, 1948), *Every Girl Should Be Married* (RKO, 1948), *My Friend Irma* (Par., 1949), *Paid in Full* (Par., 1950), *My Friend Irma Goes West* (Par., 1950), *Rogues of Sherwood Forest* (Col., 1950), *Peggy* (Univ., 1950), *Bedtime for Bonzo* (Univ., 1951), *The People Against O'Hara* (MGM, 1951), *Meet Me at the Fair* (Univ., 1952), *Plunder*

Diana Lynn, Charles Drake, Charles Coburn and Charlotte Greenwood in *Peggy.*

of the Sun (WB, 1953), *Track of the Cat* (WB, 1954), *An Annapolis Story* (AA, 1955), *The Kentuckian* (UA, 1955), *You're Never Too Young* (Par., 1955).

JEANETTE MacDONALD Born June 18, 1901, Philadelphia, Pennsylvania. Married Gene Raymond (1937). Died January 14, 1965.

Feature Films: *The Love Parade* (Par., 1929), *The Vagabond King* (Par., 1930), *Monte Carlo* (Par., 1930), *Let's Go Native* (Par., 1930), *The Lottery Bride* (UA, 1930), *Oh, for a Man* (Fox, 1930), *Don't Bet on Women* (Fox, 1931), *Annabelle's Affairs* (Fox, 1931), *One Hour With You* (Par., 1932), *Love Me Tonight* (Par., 1932), *The Cat and the Fiddle* (MGM, 1934), *The Merry Widow* (MGM, 1934), *Naughty Marietta* (MGM, 1935), *Rose Marie* (MGM, 1936), *San Francisco* (MGM, 1936), *Maytime* (MGM, 1937), *The Firefly* (MGM, 1937), *The Girl of the Golden West* (MGM, 1938), *Sweethearts* (MGM, 1938), *Broadway Serenade* (MGM, 1939), *New Moon* (MGM, 1940), *Bitter Sweet* (MGM, 1940), *Smilin' Through* (MGM, 1941), *I Married*

Ramon Novarro, Charles Butterworth, Jeanette MacDonald and Frank Morgan in *Cat and the Fiddle.*

an Angel (MGM, 1942), *Cairo* (MGM, 1942), *Follow the Boys* (Univ., 1944), *Three Daring Daughters* (MGM, 1948), *The Sun Comes Up* (MGM, 1948).

SHIRLEY MacLAINE (Shirley MacLean Beaty) Born April 24, 1934, Richmond, Virginia. Married Steve Parker (1954), child: Stephanie.

Shirley MacLaine and Mickey Shaughnessy in *The Sheepman.*

Feature Films: *The Trouble With Harry* (Par., 1955), *Artists and Models* (Par., 1955), *Around the World in 80 Days* (UA, 1956), *The Sheepman* (MGM, 1958), *The Matchmaker* (Par., 1958), *Hot Spell* (Par., 1958), *Some Came Running* (MGM, 1958), *Ask Any Girl* (MGM, 1959), *Career* (Par., 1959), *Ocean's 11* (WB, 1960,* *Can-Can* (20th, 1960), *The Apartment* (UA, 1960), *All in a Night's Work* (Par., 1961), *Two Loves* (MGM, 1961), *The Children's Hour* (UA, 1962), *My Geisha* (Par., 1962), *Two for the Seesaw* (UA, 1962), *Irma La Douce* (UA, 1963), *What a Way to Go!* (20th, 1964), *John Goldfarb, Please Come Home* (20th, 1964), *The Yellow Rolls-Royce* (MGM, 1965), *Gambit* (Univ., 1966), *Woman Times Seven* (Embassy, 1967), *The Bliss of Mr. Blossom* (Par., 1968), *Sweet Charity* (Univ., 1968).

ALINE MacMAHON (Aline Laveen MacMahon) Born May 3, 1899, McKeesport, Pennsylvania. Married Clarence Stein (1928).

Feature Films: *Five Star Final* (WB, 1931), *Heart of New York* (WB,

Aline MacMahon and Guy Kibbee in *Babbitt*.

1932), *The Mouthpiece* (WB, 1932), *Weekend Marriage* (WB, 1932), *One Way Passage* (WB, 1932), *Life Begins* (WB, 1932), *Silver Dollar* (WB, 1932), *Once in a Lifetime* (Univ., 1932), *Gold Diggers of 1933* (WB, 1933), *The Life of Jimmy Dolan* (WB, 1933), *Heroes for Sale* (WB, 1933), *The World Changes* (WB, 1933), *Heat Lightning* (WB, 1934), *Side Streets* (WB, 1934), *Big-Hearted Herbert* (WB, 1934), *Babbitt* (WB, 1934), *The Merry Frinks* (WB, 1934), *While the Patient Slept* (WB, 1935), *Mary Jane's Pa* (WB, 1935), *I Live My Life* (MGM, 1935), *Kind Lady* (MGM, 1935), *Ah, Wilderness* (MGM, 1935), *When You're in Love* (Col., 1937), *Back Door to Heaven* (Par., 1939), *Out of the Fog* (WB, 1941), *The Lady Is Willing* (Col., 1942), *Tish* (MGM, 1942), *Stage Door Canteen* (UA, 1943), *Seeds of Freedom* (narrator; Potemkin Productions, 1943), *Dragon Seed* (MGM, 1944), *Guest in the House* (UA, 1944), *The Mighty McGurk* (MGM, 1946), *The Search* (MGM, 1948), *Roseanna McCoy* (RKO, 1949), *The Flame and the Arrow* (WB, 1950), *The Eddie Cantor Story* (WB, 1953), *The Man From Laramie* (Col., 1955), *Cimarron* (MGM, 1960), *The Young Doctors* (UA, 1961), *I Could Go On Singing* (UA, 1963), *Diamond Head* (Col., 1963), *All the Way Home* (Par., 1963).

FRED MacMURRAY Born August 30, 1908, Kankakee, Illinois. Married Lillian Lamont (1936), children: Susan, Robert; widowed 1953. Married June Haver (1954), children: Kathryn, Laurie.

Feature Films: *Friends of Mr. Sweeney* (WB, 1934), *Grand Old Girl* (RKO, 1935), *The Gilded Lily* (Par., 1935), *Car 99* (Par., 1935), *Men Without Names* (Par., 1935), *Alice Adams* (RKO, 1935), *Hands Across the Table* (Par., 1935), *The Bride Comes Home* (Par., 1935), *The Trail of the Lonesome Pine* (Par., 1936), *13 Hours by Air* (Par., 1936), *The Princess Comes Across* (Par., 1936), *The Texas Rangers* (Par., 1936), *Maid of Salem* (Par., 1937), *Champagne Waltz* (Par., 1937), *Swing High—Swing Low* (Par., 1937), *Exclusive* (Par., 1937), *True Confession* (Par., 1937), *Cocoanut Grove* (Par., 1938), *Sing You Sinners* (Par.,

Fred MacMurray, Madeleine Carroll and Charles "Buddy" Rogers in *Don't Trust Your Husband*.

1938), *Men With Wings* (Par., 1938), *Cafe Society* (Par., 1939), *Invitation to Happiness* (Par., 1939), *Honeymoon in Bali* (Par., 1939), *Little Old New York* (20th, 1940), *Remember the Night* (Par., 1940), *Too Many Husbands* (Par., 1940), *Rangers of Fortune* (Par., 1940), *Virginia* (Par., 1941), *One Night in Lisbon* (Par., 1941), *New York Town* (Par., 1941), *Dive Bomber* (WB, 1941), *The Lady Is Willing* (Par., 1942), *Take a Letter, Darling* (Par., 1942), *The Forest Rangers* (Par., 1942), *Star Spangled Rhythm* (Par., 1942), *Flight for Freedom* (RKO, 1943), *Above Suspicion* (MGM, 1943), *No Time for Love* (Par., 1943), *Standing Room Only* (Par., 1944), *And the Angels Sing* (Par., 1944), *Double Indemnity* (Par., 1944), *Murder, He Says* (Par., 1945), *Practically Yours* (Par., 1945), *Where Do We Go From Here?* (20th, 1945), *Captain Eddie* (20th, 1945), *Pardon My Past* (Col., 1946), *Smoky* (20th, 1946), *Suddenly It's Spring* (Par., 1947), *The Egg and I* (Univ., 1947), *Singapore* (Univ., 1947), *The Miracle of the Bells* (RKO, 1948), *On Our Merry Way* (UA, 1948), *Don't Trust Your Husband* (UA, 1948), *Family Honeymoon* (Univ., 1948), *Father Was a Fullback* (20th, 1949), *Borderline* (Univ., 1950), *Never a Dull Moment* (RKO, 1950), *A Millionaire for Christy* (20th, 1951), *Callaway Went Thataway* (MGM, 1951), *Fair Wind to Java* (Rep., 1953), *The Moonlighter* (WB, 1953), *The Caine Mutiny* (Col., 1954), *Pushover* (Col., 1954), *Woman's World* (20th, 1954), *The Far Horizons* (Par., 1955), *The Rains of Ranchipur* (20th, 1955), *At Gunpoint* (AA, 1955), *There's Always Tomorrow* (Univ., 1956), *Gun For a Coward* (Univ., 1957), *Quantez* (Univ., 1957), *Day of the Bad Man* (Univ., 1958), *Good Day for a Hanging* (Col., 1958), *The Shaggy Dog* (BV, 1959), *Face of a Fugitive* (Col., 1959), *The Oregon Trail* (20th, 1959), *The Apartment* (UA, 1960), *The Absent-Minded Professor* (BV, 1961), *Bon Voyage* (BV, 1962), *Son of Flubber* (BV, 1963), *Kisses for My President* (WB, 1964), *Follow Me, Boys* (BV, 1966), *The Happiest Millionaire* (BV, 1967).

GEORGE MacCREADY Born August 29, 1909, Providence, Rhode Island. Married, children: Michael, Marcia. Elizabeth; widowed.

George MacCready, Nina Foch and George Raft in *Johnny Allegro*.

Feature Films: *Commandos Strike at Dawn* (Col., 1942), *The Story of Dr. Wassell* (Par., 1944), *Follow the Boys* (Univ., 1944), *The Seventh Cross* (MGM, 1944), *Soul of a Monster* (Col., 1944), *Wilson* (20th, 1944), *The Conspirators* (WB, 1944), *A Song to Remember* (Col., 1945), *The Monster and the Ape* (Col. serial, 1945), *The Missing Juror* (Col., 1945), *I Love a Mystery* (Col., 1945), *Counter-Attack* (Col., 1945), *Don Juan Quilligan* (20th, 1945), *My Name Is Julia Ross* (Col., 1945), *The Fighting Guardsman* (Col., 1945), *Gilda* (Col., 1946), *The Man Who Dared* (Col., 1946), *The Bandit Of Sherwood Forest* (Col., 1946), *The Walls Came Tumbling Down* (Col., 1946), *The Return of Monte Cristo* (Col., 1946), *Down to Earth* (Col., 1947), *The Swordsman* (Col., 1947), *The Big Clock* (Par., 1948), *Beyond Glory* (Par., 1948), *The Black Arrow* (Col., 1948), *Coroner Creek* (Col., 1948), *The Gallant Blade* (Col., 1948), *Alias Nick Beal* (Par., 1949), *Knock on Any Door* (Col., 1949), *Johnny Allegro* (Col., 1949), *The Doolins of Oklahoma* (Col., 1949), *The Nevadan* (Col., 1950), *The Fortunes of Captain Blood*

(Col., 1950), *The Rogues of Sherwood Forest* (Col., 1950), *A Lady Without a Passport* (MGM, 1950), *The Desert Hawk* (Univ., 1950), *Tarzan's Peril* (RKO, 1951), *The Desert Fox* (20th, 1951), *The Golden Horde* (Univ., 1951), *Detective Story* (Par., 1951), *The Green Glove* (UA, 1952), *Julius Caesar* (MGM, 1953), *Duffy of San Quentin* (WB, 1954), *Vera Cruz* (UA, 1954), *A Kiss Before Dying* (UA, 1956), *Thunder Over Arizona* (Rep., 1956), *The Abductors* (20th, 1957), *Paths of Glory* (UA, 1957), *Gunfire Over Indian Gap* (Rep., 1957), *Jet Across the Atlantic* (Intercontinent Releasing, 1959), *Plunderers of Painted Flats* (Rep., 1959), *The Alligator People* (20th, 1959), *Two Weeks in Another Town* (MGM, 1962), *Taras Bulba* (UA, 1962), *Dead Ringer* (WB, 1964), *Seven Days in May* (Par., 1964), *Where Love Has Gone* (Par., 1964), *The Great Race* (WB, 1965), *The Human Duplicators* (AA, 1965).

MERCEDES McCAMBRIDGE (Carlotta Mercedes Agnes McCambridge) Born March 17, 1918, Joliet, Illinois. Married William Fifield (1940), child: Jon; divorced 1946. Married Fletcher Markle (1950); divorced 1962.

Henry Hull, Virginia Mayo and Joel McCrea in *Colorado Territory*.

Broderick Crawford and Mercedes McCambridge in *All the King's Men.*

Feature Films: *All the King's Men* (Col., 1949), *Lightning Strikes Twice* (WB, 1951), *The Scarf* (UA, 1951), *Inside Straight* (MGM, 1951), *Johnny Guitar* (Rep., 1954), *Giant* (WB, 1956), *A Farewell to Arms* (20th, 1957), *Touch of Evil* (Univ., 1958),* *Suddenly, Last Summer* (Col., 1959), *Cimarron* (MGM, 1960), *Angel Baby* (AA, 1961), *Run Home Slow* (Emerson Film Distributors, 1965).

*Unbilled guest appearance

JOEL McCREA Born November 5, 1905, Los Angeles, California. Married Frances Dee (1933), children: Jody, David.

Sound Feature Films: *So This Is College* (MGM, 1929), *Dynamite* (Par., 1929), *Lightnin'* (Fox, 1930), *Silver Horde* (RKO, 1930), *Once a Sinner* (Fox, 1931), *Kept Husbands* (RKO, 1931), *Born to Love* (RKO, 1931), *Girls About Town* (Par., 1931), *Business and Pleasure* (Fox, 1932), *Lost Squadron* (RKO, 1932), *Bird of Paradise* (RKO, 1932), *Most Dangerous Game* (RKO, 1932), *Rockabye* (RKO, 1932), *The Sport Parade* (RKO, 1932), *The Silver Cord* (RKO, 1933), *Bed of Roses* (RKO, 1933), *One Man's Journey* (RKO, 1933), *Chance at Heaven* (RKO, 1933), *Gambling Lady* (WB, 1934), *Half a Sinner* (Univ., 1934), *Richest Girl in the World* (RKO, 1934), *Private Worlds* (Par., 1935), *Our Little Girl* (Fox, 1935), *Woman Wanted* (MGM, 1935), *Barbary Coast* (UA, 1935), *Splendor* (UA, 1935), *These Three* (UA, 1936),

Two in a Crowd (Univ., 1936), *Adventure in Manhattan* (Col., 1936), *Come and Get It* (UA, 1936), *Banjo on My Knee* (20th, 1936), *Internes Can't Take Money* (Par., 1937), *Wells Fargo* (Par., 1937), *Woman Chases Man* (Par., 1937), *Dead End* (UA, 1937), *Three Blind Mice* (20th, 1938), *Youth Takes a Fling* (Univ., 1938), *Union Pacific* (Par., 1939), *They Shall Have Music* (UA, 1939), *Espionage Agent* (WB, 1939), *He Married His Wife* (20th, 1940), *Primrose Path* (RKO, 1940), *Foreign Correspondent* (UA, 1940), *Reaching for the Sun* (Par., 1941), *Sullivan's Travels* (Par., 1941), *The Great Man's Lady* (Par., 1942), *The Palm Beach Story* (Par., 1942), *The More the Merrier* (Col., 1943), *Buffalo Bill* (20th, 1944), *Great Moment* (Par., 1944), *The Unseen* (Par., 1945), *The Virginian* (Par., 1946), *Ramrod* (UA, 1947), *Four Faces West* (UA, 1948), *South of St. Louis* (WB, 1949), *Colorado Territory* (WB, 1949), *Stars in My Crown* (MGM, 1950), *The Outriders* (MGM, 1950), *Saddle Tramp* (Univ., 1950), *Frenchie* (Univ., 1950), *The Hollywood Story* (Univ., 1951),* *Cattle Drive* (Univ., 1951), *The San Francisco Story* (WB, 1952), *Lone Hand* (Univ., 1953), *Shoot First* (UA, 1953), *Border River* (Univ., 1954), *Stranger on Horseback* (UA, 1955), *Wichita* (AA, 1955), *The First Texan* (AA, 1956), *The Oklahoman* (AA, 1957), *Trooper Hook* (UA, 1957), *Gunsight Ridge* (UA, 1957), *The Tall Stranger* (AA, 1957), *Cattle Empire* (20th, 1958), *Fort Massacre* (UA, 1958), *The Gunfight at Dodge City* (UA, 1959), *Ride the High Country* (MGM, 1962).

*Unbilled guest appearance

HATTIE McDANIEL Born June 10, 1895, Wichita, Kansas. Married James Crawford; divorced. Married Larry Williams; divorced 1950. Died October 26, 1952.

Feature Films: *The Golden West* (Fox, 1932), *Blonde Venus* (Par., 1932), *Hypnotized* (World Wide, 1932), *Washington Masquerade* (MGM, 1932), *I'm No Angel* (Par., 1933), *The Story of Temple Drake* (Par., 1933), *Operator 13* (MGM, 1934), *Judge Priest* (Fox, 1934), *Lost in the Stratosphere* (Mon., 1934), *Babbitt* (WB, 1934), *Little Men* (RKO, 1934), *Imitation of Life* (Univ., 1934), *The Little Colonel* (Fox, 1935), *Alice Adams* (RKO, 1935), *Music Is Magic* (20th, 1935), *Another Face* (RKO, 1935), *Traveling Saleslady* (WB, 1935), *Next Time We Love* (Univ., 1936), *Libeled Lady* (MGM, 1936), *Gentle Julia* (20th, 1936), *The First Baby* (20th, 1936), *Show Boat* (Univ., 1936), *Hearts Divided* (WB, 1936), *High Treason* (20th, 1936), *Star for a Night* (20th, 1936), *The Postal Inspector* (Univ., 1936), *The Bride Walks Out* (RKO, 1936), *The Singing Kid* (WB, 1936), *Valiant Is the Word for Carrie* (Par., 1936), *Reunion* (20th, 1936), *Can This Be Dixie?* (20th, 1936), *Racing Lady* (RKO, 1937), *Don't Tell the Wife* (RKO, 1937), *The Crime Nobody Saw* (Par., 1937), *Saratoga* (MGM, 1937), *Merry-Go-Round of 1938* (Univ., 1937), *True Confession* (Par., 1937), *The Wildcatter* (Univ., 1937), *45 Fathers* (20th, 1937), *Over the Goal* (WB, 1937), *Nothing Sacred* (UA, 1937), *Battle of Broad-*

Ben Carter, Hattie McDaniel and John Payne in *Maryland*.

way (20th, 1938), *The Shopworn Angel* (MGM, 1938), *Carefree* (RKO, 1938), *The Shining Hour* (MGM, 1938), *The Mad Miss Manton* (RKO, 1938), *Everybody's Baby* (20th, 1939), *Zenobia* (UA, 1939), *Gone With the Wind* (MGM, 1939), *Maryland* (20th, 1940), *The Great Lie* (WB, 1941), *Affectionately Yours* (WB, 1941), *They Died With Their Boots On* (WB, 1941), *The Male Animal* (WB, 1942), *In This Our Life* (WB, 1942), *George Washington Slept Here* (WB, 1942), *Reap the Wild Wind* (Par., 1942), *Johnny Come Lately* (UA, 1943), *Thank Your Lucky Stars* (WB, 1943), *Janie* (WB, 1944), *Since You Went Away* (UA, 1944), *Three Is a Family* (UA, 1944), *Hi, Beautiful* (Univ., 1945), *Janie Gets Married* (WB, 1946), *Margie* (20th, 1946), *Song of the South* (RKO, 1946), *Never Say Goodbye* (WB, 1946), *The Flame* (Rep., 1947), *Mickey* (EL, 1948), *Mr. Blandings Builds His Dream House* (RKO, 1948), *Family Honeymoon* (Univ., 1948).

RODDY McDOWALL (Roderick Andrew McDowall) Born September 17, 1928, London, England.

Feature Films: *Scruffy* (Independent, 1937), *Murder in the Family* (20th, 1937), *I See Ice* (Balcon, 1937), *John Halifax, Gentleman* (MGM, 1938), *Convict 99* (Gainsborough, 1938), *Hey! Hey! U.S.A.* (Gainsborough, 1938), *Sarah Siddons* (RKO, 1938), *The Outsider* (RKO, 1938), *Poison Pen* (Associated British Producing, 1938), *Dead Men's Shoes* (Associated British Producing, 1938), *Just William* (Associated British Producing, 1939), *His Brother's Keeper* (WB, 1939), *Dirt* (Balcon, 1939), *Saloon Bar* (Balcon, 1939), *You Will Remember* (British Lion, 1940), *This England* (British National, 1940), *Man Hunt* (20th, 1941), *How Green Was My Valley* (20th, 1941), *Confirm or Deny* (20th, 1941), *Son of Fury* (20th, 1942), *On the Sunny Side* (20th, 1942), *The Pied Piper* (20th, 1942), *My Friend Flicka* (20th, 1943),

Roddy McDowall and Jane Powell in *Holiday in Mexico*.

Lassie Come Home (MGM, 1943), *The White Cliffs of Dover* (MGM, 1944), *The Keys of the Kingdom* (20th, 1944), *Thunderhead, Son of Flicka* (20th, 1945), *Molly and Me* (20th, 1945), *Holiday in Mexico* (MGM, 1946), *Macbeth* (Rep., 1948), *Rocky* (Mon., 1948), *Kidnapped* (Mon., 1948), *Tuna Clipper* (Mon., 1949), *Black Midnight* (Mon., 1949) *Killer Shark* (Mon., 1949), *Big Timber* (Mon., 1950), *The Steel Fist* (Mon., 1952), *The Subterraneans* (MGM, 1960), *Midnight Lace* (Univ., 1960), *Cleopatra* (20th, 1963), *Shock Treatment* (20th, 1964), *The Greatest Story Ever Told* (UA, 1965), *The Third Day* (WB, 1965), *That Darn Cat* (BV, 1965), *The Loved One* (MGM, 1965), *Lord Love a Duck* (UA, 1966), *Inside Daisy Clover* (WB, 1966), *The Defector* (7 Arts, 1966), *Is Paris Burning?* (Par., 1966), *The Adventures of Bullwhip Griffin* (BV, 1967), *The Cool Ones* (WB, 1967), *It* (WB-7 Arts, 1967), *Hello Down There* (Par., 1968), *Planet of the Apes* (20th, 1968).

DOROTHY McGUIRE (Dorothy Hackett McGuire) Born June 14, 1918, Omaha, Nebraska. Married John Swope (1943), children: Mary, Mark.

Randy Stuart and Dorothy McGuire in *Mother Didn't Tell Me*.

Feature Films: *Claudia* (20th, 1943), *A Tree Grows in Brooklyn* (20th, 1945), *The Enchanted Cottage* (RKO, 1945), *The Spiral Staircase* (RKO, 1946), *Claudia and David* (20th, 1946), *Till the End of Time* (RKO, 1946), *Gentleman's Agreement* (20th, 1947), *Mother Didn't Tell Me* (20th, 1950), *Mister 880* (20th, 1950), *Callaway Went Thataway* (MGM, 1951), *I Want You* (RKO, 1951), *Invitation* (MGM, 1952), *Make Haste to Live* (Rep., 1954), *Three Coins in the Fountain* (20th, 1954), *Trial* (MGM, 1955), *Friendly Persuasion* (AA, 1956), *Old Yeller* (BV, 1957), *The Remarkable Mr. Pennypacker* (20th, 1959), *This Earth Is Mine* (Univ., 1959), *A Summer Place* (WB, 1959), *The Dark at the Top of the Stairs* (WB, 1960), *Swiss Family Robinson* (BV, 1960), *Susan Slade* (WB, 1961), *Summer Magic* (BV, 1963), *The Greatest Story Ever Told* (UA, 1965).

FRANK McHUGH (Francis Curray McHugh) Born May 23, 1898, Homestead, Pennsylvania. Married Dorothy Spencer (1933), children: Peter, Susan.

Sound Feature Films: *Top Speed* (WB, 1930), *Dawn Patrol* (WB, 1930), *College Lovers* (WB, 1930), *Bright Lights* (WB, 1931), *Widow From Chicago* (WB, 1931), *Front Page* (UA, 1931), *Millie* (RKO, 1931), *Kiss Me Again* (WB, 1931), *Going Wild* (WB, 1931), *Traveling Husbands* (RKO, 1931), *Up for Murder* (Univ., 1931), *Men of the Sky* (WB, 1931), *Corsair* (UA, 1931), *Bad Company* (Pathé, 1931), *Union Depot* (WB, 1932), *High Pressure* (WB, 1932), *The Crowd Roars* (WB, 1932), *The Strange Love of Molly Louvain* (WB, 1932), *Dark Horse* (WB, 1932), *Blessed Event* (WB, 1932), *One Way Passage* (WB, 1932), *Life Begins* (WB, 1932), *Mystery of the Wax Museum* (WB, 1933), *Parachute Jumper* (WB, 1933), *Grand Slam* (WB, 1933), *Private Jones* (Univ., 1933), *Telegraph Trail* (WB, 1933),

Jean Ames, Frank McHugh and Humphrey Bogart in *All Through the Night*.

Ex-Lady (WB, 1933), *Elmer the Great* (WB, 1933), *Professional Sweetheart* (WB, 1933), *Hold Me Tight* (WB, 1933), *Lilly Turner* (WB, 1933), *Tomorrow at Seven* (RKO, 1933), *Footlight Parade* (WB, 1933), *Havana Widows* (WB, 1933), *Son of a Sailor* (WB, 1933), *The House on 56th Street* (WB, 1933), *Convention City* (WB, 1933), *Fashions of 1934* (WB, 1934), *Heat Lightning* (WB, 1934), *Smarty* (WB, 1934), *Let's Be Ritzy* (WB, 1934), *Merry Wives of Reno* (WB, 1934), *Return of the Terror* (WB, 1934), *Here Comes the Navy* (WB, 1934), *Six Day Bike Rider* (WB, 1934), *Happiness Ahead* (WB, 1934), *Maybe It's Love* (WB, 1935), *Gold Diggers of 1935* (WB, 1935), *Devil Dogs of the Air* (WB, 1935), *Page Miss Glory* (WB, 1935), *The Irish in Us* (WB, 1935), *A Midsummer Night's Dream* (WB, 1935), *Stars Over Broadway* (WB, 1935), *Moonlight Murder* (MGM, 1936), *Snowed Under* (WB, 1936), *Freshman Love* (WB, 1936), *Bullets or Ballots* (WB, 1936), *Stage Struck* (WB, 1936), *Three Men on a Horse* (WB, 1936), *Ever Since Eve* (WB, 1937), *Mr. Dodd Takes the Air* (WB, 1937), *Marry the Girl* (WB, 1937), *Submarine D-1* (WB, 1937), *Swing Your Lady* (WB, 1938), *He Couldn't Say No* (WB, 1938), *Little Miss Thoroughbred* (WB, 1938), *Boy Meets Girl* (WB, 1938), *Valley of the Giants* (WB, 1938), *Four Daughters* (WB, 1938), *Dodge City* (WB, 1939), *Wings of the Navy* (WB, 1939), *Daughters Courageous* (WB, 1939), *Dust Be My Destiny* (WB, 1939), *The Roaring Twenties* (WB, 1939), *On Your Toes* (WB, 1939), *Indianapolis Speedway* (WB, 1939), *Four Wives* (WB, 1939), *Virginia City* (WB, 1940), *The Fighting 69th* (WB, 1940), *Till We Meet Again* (WB, 1940), *I Love You Again* (MGM, 1940), *City for Conquest* (WB, 1940), *Back Street* (Univ., 1941), *Four Mothers* (WB, 1941), *Manpower* (WB, 1941), *Her Cardboard Lover* (MGM, 1942), *All Through the Night* (WB, 1942), *Going My Way* (Par., 1944), *Marine Raiders* (RKO, 1944), *Bowery to Broadway* (Univ., 1944), *A Medal for Benny* (Par., 1945), *State Fair* (20th, 1945), *The Hoodlum Saint* (MGM, 1946), *The Runaround* (Univ., 1946), *Little Miss Big* (Univ., 1946), *Easy Come, Easy Go* (Par., 1947), *Carnegie Hall* (UA, 1947), *The Velvet Touch* (RKO, 1948), *Mighty Joe Young* (RKO, 1949), *Miss Grant Takes Richmond* (Col., 1949), *Paid in Full* (Par., 1950), *The Tougher They Come* (Col., 1950), *My Son, John* (Par., 1952), *The Pace That Thrills* (RKO, 1952), *It Happens Every Thursday* (Univ., 1953), *A Lion Is in the Streets* (WB, 1953), *There's No Business Like Show Business* (20th, 1954), *The Last Hurrah* (Col., 1958), *Say One for Me* (20th, 1959), *Career* (Par., 1959), *A Tiger Walks* (BV, 1964), *Easy Come, Easy Go* (Par., 1967).

VICTOR McLAGLEN Born December 10, 1886, Tunbridge Wells, England. Married Enid Lamont (1918), children: Sheila, Andrew; widowed 1942. Married Suzanne Brueggsman (1943); divorced 1948. Married Margaret Humphrey (1948). Died November 7, 1959.

Sound Feature Films: *Black Watch* (Fox, 1929), *Cock-Eyed World* (Fox, 1929), *Hot for Paris* (Fox, 1929), *Happy Days* (Fox, 1930), *On the Level* (Fox, 1930), *Devil With Women* (Fox, 1930), *Dishonored* (Par., 1931), *Not Exactly Gentlemen* (Fox, 1931), *Annabelle's Affairs* (Fox, 1931), *Women of All Nations* (Fox, 1931), *Wicked* (Fox, 1931), *The Gay Caballero* (Fox, 1932), *Devil's Lottery* (Fox, 1932), *While Paris Sleeps* (Fox, 1932), *Guilty as Hell* (Par., 1932), *Rackety Rax*

Victor McLaglen and Mae West in *Klondike Annie*.

(Fox, 1932), *Dick Turpin* (Gaumont-British, 1933), *Hot Pepper* (Fox, 1933), *Laughing at Life* (Mascot, 1933), *No More Women* (Par., 1934), *The Lost Patrol* (RKO, 1934), *Wharf Angel* (Par., 1934), *Murder at the Vanities* (Par., 1934), *The Captain Hates the Sea* (Col., 1934), *Under Pressure* (Fox, 1935), *Great Hotel Murder* (Fox, 1935), *The Informer* (RKO, 1935), *Professional Soldier* (Fox, 1935), *Klondike Annie* (Par., 1936), *Under Two Flags* (20th, 1936), *Mary of Scotland* (RKO, 1936), *The Magnificent Brute* (Univ., 1936), *Sea Devils* (RKO, 1937), *Nancy Steele Is Missing* (20th, 1937), *This Is My Affair* (20th, 1937), *Wee Willie Winkie* (20th, 1937), *Battle of Broadway* (20th, 1938), *The Devil's Party* (Univ., 1938), *We're Going to Be Rich* (20th, 1938), *Pacific Liner* (RKO, 1939), *Let Freedom Ring* (MGM, 1939), *Captain Fury* (UA, 1939), *Ex-Champ* (Univ., 1939), *Full Confession* (RKO, 1939), *Rio* (Univ., 1939), *The Big Guy* (Univ., 1939), *Diamond Frontier* (Univ., 1940), *Broadway Limited* (UA, 1941), *Call Out the Marines* (RKO, 1942), *Powder Town* (RKO, 1942), *China Girl* (20th, 1942), *Forever and a Day* (RKO, 1943), *Tampico* (20th, 1944), *Roger Tuohy, Gangster* (20th, 1944), *The Princess and the Pirate* (RKO, 1944), *Rough, Tough and Ready* (Col., 1945), *Love, Honor and Goodbye* (Rep., 1945), *Whistle Stop* (UA, 1946), *Calendar Girl* (Rep., 1947), *The Michigan Kid* (Univ., 1947), *The Foxes of Harrow* (20th, 1947), *Fort Apache* (RKO, 1948), *She Wore a Yellow Ribbon* (RKO, 1949), *Rio Grande* (Rep., 1950), *The Quiet Man* (Rep., 1952), *Fair Wind to Java* (Rep., 1953), *Prince Valiant* (20th, 1954), *Trouble in the Glen* (Rep., 1954), *Many Rivers to Cross* (MGM, 1955), *City of Shadows* (Rep., 1955), *Bengazi* (RKO, 1955), *Lady Godiva* (Univ., 1955), *The Abductors* (20th, 1957).

STEVE McQUEEN Born March 24, 1930, Slater, Missouri. Married Neile Adams (1955), children: Terry, Chadwick.

Aneta Corseaut, Steve McQueen, Olin Howland and Stephen Chase in *The Blob*.

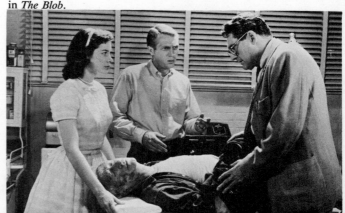

Feature Films: *Somebody Up There Likes Me* (MGM, 1956), *Never Love a Stranger* (AA, 1958), *The Blob* (Par., 1958), *Never So Few* (MGM, 1959), *The Great St. Louis Bank Robbery* (UA, 1959), *The Magnificent Seven* (UA, 1960), *The Honeymoon Machine* (MGM, 1961), *Hell Is for Heroes* (Par., 1961), *The War Lover* (Col., 1962), *The Great Escape* (UA, 1963), *Love With the Proper Stranger* (Par., 1963), *Soldier in the Rain* (AA, 1963), *Baby, the Rain Must Fall* (Col., 1965), *The Cincinnati Kid* (MGM, 1965), *Nevada Smith* (Par., 1966), *The Sand Pebbles* (20th, 1966), *Thomas Crown and Company* (UA, 1968).

MARJORIE MAIN (Mary Tomlinson) Born February 24, 1890, Acton, Indiana. Married Stanley Krebs (1921); widowed 1935.

Feature Films: *A House Divided* (Univ.; 1932), *Take a Chance* (Par., 1933), *Crime Without Passion* (Par., 1934), *Music in the Air* (Fox, 1934), *Naughty Marietta* (MGM, 1935), *Love in a Bungalow* (Univ., 1937), *Dead End* (UA, 1937), *Stella Dallas* (UA, 1937), *The Man Who Cried Wolf* (Univ., 1937), *The Wrong Road* (Rep., 1937), *The Shadow* (Col., 1937), *Boy of the Streets* (Mon., 1937), *Penitentiary* (Col., 1938), *King of the Newsboys* (Rep., 1938), *Test Pilot* (MGM, 1938), *Prison Farm* (Par., 1938), *Romance of the Limberlost* (Mon., 1938), *Little Tough Guy* (Univ., 1938), *Under the Big Top* (Mon., 1938), *Too Hot to Handle* (MGM, 1938), *Girls' School* (Col., 1938), *There Goes My Heart* (UA, 1938), *Three Comrades* (MGM, 1938), *City Girl* (20th, 1937), *Lucky Night* (MGM, 1939), *They Shall Have Music* (UA, 1939), *Angels Wash Their Faces* (WB, 1939), *The Women* (MGM, 1939), *Another Thin Man* (MGM, 1939), *Two Thoroughbreds* (RKO, 1939), *I Take This Woman* (MGM, 1940), *Women Without Names* (Par., 1940), *Dark Command* (Rep., 1940), *Turnabout* (UA, 1940), *Susan and God* (MGM, 1940), *The Captain Is a Lady* (MGM, 1940),

Marjorie Main and Wallace Beery in *Big Jack*.

Wyoming (MGM, 1940), *The Wild Man of Borneo* (MGM, 1941), *The Trial of Mary Dugan* (MGM, 1941), *A Woman's Face* (MGM, 1941), *Barnacle Bill* (MGM, 1941), *The Shepherd of the Hills* (Par., 1941), *Honky Tonk* (MGM, 1941), *The Bugle Sounds* (MGM, 1941), *We Were Dancing* (MGM, 1942), *The Affairs of Martha* (MGM, 1942), *Jackass Mail* (MGM, 1942), *Tish* (MGM, 1942), *Tennessee Johnson* (MGM, 1942), *Woman of the Town* (UA, 1943), *Heaven Can Wait* (20th, 1943), *Johnny Come Lately* (UA, 1943), *Rationing* (MGM, 1944), *Gentle Annie* (MGM, 1944), *Meet Me in St. Louis* (MGM, 1944), *Murder He Says* (Par., 1945), *The Harvey Girls* (MGM, 1946), *Bad Bascomb* (MGM, 1946), *Undercurrent* (MGM, 1946), *The Show-Off* (MGM, 1946), *The Egg and I* (Univ., 1947), *The Wistful Widow of Wagon Gap* (Univ., 1947), *Feudin', Fussin' and a-Fightin'* (Univ., 1948), *Ma and Pa Kettle* (Univ., 1949), *Big Jack* (MGM, 1949), *Ma and Pa Kettle Go to Town* (Univ., 1950), *Summer Stock* (MGM, 1950), *Mrs.*

O'Malley and Mr. Malone (MGM, 1950), *Ma and Pa Kettle Back on the Farm* (Univ., 1951), *The Law and the Lady* (MGM, 1951), *Mr. Imperium* (MGM, 1951), *It's a Big Country* (MGM, 1951), *The Belle of New York* (MGM, 1952), *Ma and Pa Kettle at the Fair* (Univ., 1952), *Ma and Pa Kettle on Vacation* (Univ., 1953), *Fast Company* (MGM, 1953), *The Long, Long Trailer* (MGM, 1954), *Rose Marie* (MGM, 1954), *Ma and Pa Kettle at Home* (Univ., 1954), *Ricochet Romance* (Univ., 1954), *Ma and Pa Kettle at Waikiki* (Univ., 1955), *The Kettles in the Ozarks* (Univ., 1956), *Friendly Persuasion* (AA, 1956), *The Kettles on Old MacDonald's Farm* (Univ., 1957).

KARL MALDEN (Malden Sukilovich) Born March 23, 1914, Gary, Indiana. Married Mona Graham (1938), children: Mila, Carla.

Karl Malden, Montgomery Clift and Brian Aherne in *I Confess*.

Feature Films: *They Knew What They Wanted* (RKO, 1940), *Winged Victory* (20th, 1944), *13 Rue Madeleine* (20th, 1946), *Boomerang* (20th, 1947), *The Gunfighter* (20th, 1950), *Where the Sidewalk Ends* (20th, 1950), *The Halls of Montezuma* (20th, 1950), *A Streetcar Named Desire* (WB, 1951), *Decision Before Dawn* (20th, 1952), *Diplomatic Courier* (20th, 1952), *Operation Secret* (WB, 1952), *Ruby Gentry* (20th, 1952), *I Confess* (WB, 1953), *Take the High Ground* (MGM, 1953), *Phantom of the Rue Morgue* (WB, 1954), *On the Waterfront* (Col., 1954), *Baby Doll* (WB, 1956), *Fear Strikes Out* (Par., 1957), *Bombers B-52* (WB, 1957), *The Hanging Tree* (WB, 1959), *Pollyanna* (BV, 1960), *The Great Imposter* (Univ., 1960), *Parrish* (WB, 1961), *One-Eyed Jacks* (Par., 1961), *Bird Man of Alcatraz* (UA, 1962), *Gypsy* (WB, 1962), *How the West Was Won* (MGM, 1963), *Come Fly With Me* (MGM, 1963), *Dead Ringer* (WB, 1964), *Cheyenne Autumn* (WB, 1964), *The Cincinnati Kid* (MGM, 1965), *Nevada Smith* (Par., 1966), *The Silencers* (Col., 1966), *Murderers' Row* (Col., 1966), *Hotel* (WB, 1967), *The Adventures of Bullwhip Griffin* (BV, 1967), *Billion Dollar Brain* (Par., 1967), *Blue* (Par., 1968).

DOROTHY MALONE (Dorothy Maloney) Born January 30, 1925, Chicago, Illinois. Married Jacques Bergerac (1959), children: Mimi, Diane; divorced 1964.

Dorothy Malone and Jack Carson in *Two Guys From Texas*.

Feature Films:

as **Dorothy Maloney** *Falcon and the Co-eds* (RKO, 1943), *One Mysterious Night* (Col., 1944), *Show Business* (RKO, 1944), *Seven Days Ashore* (RKO, 1944).

as **Dorothy Malone** *Hollywood Canteen* (WB, 1944), *Too Young to Know* (WB, 1945), *Janie Gets Married* (WB, 1946), *The Big Sleep* (WB, 1946), *Night and Day* (WB, 1946), *To the Victor* (WB, 1948), *Two Guys From Texas* (WB, 1948), *One Sunday Afternoon* (WB, 1948), *Flaxy Martin* (WB, 1949), *South of St. Louis* (WB, 1949), *Colorado Territory* (WB, 1949), *The Nevadan* (Col., 1950), *Convicted* (Col., 1950), *Mrs. O'Malley and Mr. Malone* (MGM, 1950), *The Killer That Stalked New York* (Col., 1950), *Saddle Legion* (RKO, 1951), *The Bushwhackers* (Realart, 1952), *Scared Stiff* (Par., 1953), *Torpedo Alley* (AA, 1953), *Law and Order* (Univ., 1953), *Jack Slade* (AA, 1953), *Loophole* (AA, 1954), *Pushover* (Col., 1954), *The Fast and Furious* (American Releasing Corp., 1954), *Security Risk* (AA, 1954), *Private Hell 36* (Filmakers, 1954), *Young at Heart* (WB, 1954), *The Lone Gun* (UA, 1954), *Five Guns West* (American Releasing Corp., 1955), *Battle Cry* (WB, 1955), *Tall Man Riding* (WB, 1955), *Sincerely Yours* (WB, 1955), *Artists and Models* (Par., 1955), *At Gunpoint* (AA, 1955), *Pillars of the Sky* (Univ., 1956), *Tension at Table Rock* (RKO, 1956), *Written on the Wind* (Univ., 1956), *Quantez* (Univ., 1957), *Man of a Thousand Faces* (Univ., 1957), *The Tarnished Angels* (Univ., 1957), *Tip on a Dead Jockey* (MGM, 1957), *Too Much, Too Soon* (WB, 1958), *Warlock* (20th, 1959), *The Last Voyage* (MGM, 1960), *The Last Sunset* (Univ., 1961), *Beach Party* (AIP, 1963), *Fate Is the Hunter* (20th, 1964).*

*Unbilled guest appearance

DAVID MANNERS (Rauff Acklon) Born April 30, 1902, Halifax, Nova Scotia.

David Manners and Jacqueline Wells (later Julie Bishop) in *The Black Cat.*

Feature Films: *Journey's End* (Tif., 1930), *He Knew Women* (RKO, 1930), *Sweet Mama* (WB, 1930), *Kismet* (WB, 1930), *Mother's Cry* (WB, 1930), *The Truth About Youth* (WB, 1930), *A Right to Love* (Par., 1930), *Dracula* (Univ., 1931), *The Millionaire* (WB, 1931), *The Miracle Woman* (Col., 1931), *Last Flight* (WB, 1931), *The Ruling Voice* (WB, 1931), *The Greeks Had a Word For Them* (UA, 1932), *Lady With a Past* (RKO, 1932), *Beauty and the Boss* (WB, 1932), *Man Wanted* (WB, 1932), *Stranger in Town* (WB, 1932), *Crooner* (WB, 1932), *A Bill of Divorcement* (RKO, 1932), *They Call It Sin* (WB, 1932), *The Mummy* (Univ., 1932), *The Death Kiss* (World Wide, 1933), *From Hell to Heaven* (Par., 1933), *The Warrior's Husband* (Fox, 1933), *The Girl in 419* (Par., 1933), *The Devil's in Love* (Fox, 1933), *Torch Singer* (Par., 1933), *Roman Scandals* (UA, 1933), *The Black Cat* (Univ., 1934), *The Great Flirtation* (Par., 1934), *The Moonstone* (Mon., 1934), *The Perfect Clue* (Majestic, 1935), *The Mystery of Edwin Drood* (Univ., 1935), *Jalna* (RKO, 1935), *Hearts in Bondage* (Rep., 1936), *A Woman Rebels* (RKO, 1936).

Leslie Brooks, Adolphe Menjou and Adele Mara in *You Were Never Lovelier.*

ADELE MARA (Adelaida Delgado) Born April 28, 1923, Highland Park, Michigan. Married Roy Huggins.

Feature Films: *Navy Blues* (WB, 1941), *Alias Boston Blackie* (Col., 1942), *Blondie Goes to College* (Col., 1942), *Shut My Big Mouth* (Col., 1942), *You Were Never Lovelier* (Col., 1942), *Vengeance of the West* (Col., 1942), *Lucky Legs* (Col., 1942), *Good Luck, Mr. Yates* (Col., 1943), *Redhead from Manhattan* (Col., 1943), *Reveille With Beverly* (Col., 1943), *Riders of the Northwest Mounted* (Col., 1943), *The Fighting Seabees* (Rep., 1944), *Atlantic City* (Rep., 1944), *Faces in the Fog* (Rep., 1944), *Thoroughbreds* (Rep., 1944), *The Vampire's Ghost* (Rep., 1945), *Grissly's Millions* (Rep., 1945), *Bells of Rosarita* (Rep., 1945), *Girls of the Big House* (Rep., 1945), *Song of Mexico* (Rep., 1945), *A Guy Could Change* (Rep., 1945), *The Tiger Woman* (Rep., 1945), *Passkey to Danger* (Rep., 1946), *The Catman of Paris* (Rep., 1946), *Flame of Barbary Coast* (Rep., 1945), *The Invisible Informer* (Rep., 1946), *The Last Crooked Mile* (Rep., 1946), *Night Train to Memphis* (Rep., 1946), *I've Always Loved You* (Rep., 1946), *The Inner Circle* (Rep., 1946), *The Magnificent Rogue* (Rep., 1946), *Traffic in Crime* (Rep., 1946), *Twilight on the Rio Grande* (Rep., 1947), *The Web of Danger* (Rep., 1947), *The Trespasser* (Rep., 1947), *Blackmail* (Rep., 1947), *Robin Hood of Texas* (Rep., 1947), *Exposed* (Rep., 1947), *The Gallant Legion* (Rep., 1948), *Campus Honeymoon* (Rep., 1948), *The Main Street Kid* (Rep., 1948), *Nighttime in Nevada* (Rep., 1948), *Wake of the Red Witch* (Rep., 1948), *Angel in Exile* (Rep., 1948), *I, Jane Doe* (Rep., 1948), *Sands of Iwo Jima* (Rep., 1949), *Rock Island Trail* (Rep., 1950), *The Avengers* (Rep., 1950), *California Passage* (Rep., 1950), *The Sea Hornet* (Rep., 1951), *Count the Hours* (RKO, 1953), *The Black Whip* (20th, 1956), *Back From Eternity* (RKO, 1956), *Curse of the Faceless Man* (UA, 1958), *The Big Circus* (AA, 1959).

FREDRIC MARCH (Ernest Frederick McIntyre Bickel) Born August 31, 1897, Racine, Wisconsin. Married Ellis Baker (1923); divorced. Married Florence Eldridge (1927), children: Penelope, Anthony.

Sound Feature Films: *The Dummy* (Par., 1929), *The Wild Party* (Par., 1929), *The Studio Murder Mystery* (Par., 1929), *Paris Bound* (Pathé, 1929), *Jealousy* (Par., 1929), *Footlights and Fools* (WB, 1929), *The Marriage Playground* (Par., 1929), *Sarah and Son* (Par., 1930), *Ladies Love Brutes* (Par., 1930), *Paramount on Parade* (Par., 1930), *True to the Navy* (Par., 1930), *Manslaughter* (Par., 1930), *Laughter* (Par., 1930), *The Royal Family of Broadway* (Par., 1930), *Honor Among Lovers* (Par., 1931), *The Night Angel* (Par., 1931), *My Sin* (Par., 1931), *Dr. Jekyll and Mr. Hyde* (Par., 1931), *Strangers in Love* (Par., 1932), *Merrily We Go to Hell* (Par., 1932), *Make Me a Star* (Par., 1932),* *Smilin' Through* (MGM, 1932), *The Sign of the Cross* (Par., 1932), *Tonight Is Ours* (Par., 1933), *The Eagle and the Hawk* (Par., 1933), *Design for Living* (Par., 1933), *All of Me* (Par., 1934), *Death Takes a Holiday* (Par., 1934), *Good Dame* (Par., 1934), *The Affairs of Cellini* (UA, 1934),

166

Miriam Hopkins, Fredric March and Gary Cooper in *Design for Living*.

The Barretts of Wimpole Street (MGM, 1934), *We Live Again* (UA, 1934), *Les Miserables* (UA, 1935), *Anna Karenina* (MGM, 1935), *The Dark Angel* (UA, 1935), *Anthony Adverse* (WB, 1936), *The Road to Glory* (20th, 1936), *Mary of Scotland* (RKO, 1936), *A Star Is Born* (UA, 1937), *Nothing Sacred* (UA, 1937), *The Buccaneer* (Par., 1938), *There Goes My Heart* (UA, 1938), *Trade Winds* (UA, 1938), *Susan and God* (MGM, 1940), *Victory* (Par., 1940), *So Ends Our Night* (UA, 1941), *One Foot in Heaven* (WB, 1941), *Bedtime Story* (Col., 1941), *I Married a Witch* (UA, 1942), *The Adventures of Mark Twain* (WB, 1944), *Tomorrow the World* (UA, 1944), *The Best Years of Our Lives* (RKO, 1946), *Another Part of the Forest* (Univ., 1948), *Live Today for Tomorrow* (Univ., 1948), *Christopher Columbus* (Rank, 1949), *It's a Big Country* (MGM, 1951), *Death of a Salesman* (Col., 1951), *Man on a Tightrope* (20th, 1953), *Executive Suite* (MGM, 1954), *The Bridges at Toko-Ri* (Par., 1954), *The Desperate Hours* (Par., 1955), *Alexander the Great* (UA, 1956), *The Man in the Gray Flannel Suit* (20th, 1956), *Albert Schweitzer* (narrator; DeRochemont, 1957), *Middle of the Night* (Col., 1959), *The Condemned of Altona* (20th, 1963), *Seven Days in May* (Par., 1964), *Hombre* (20th, 1967).

*Unbilled guest appearance

MARGO (Maria Margarita Guadalupe Bolado y Castilla) Born May 10, 1918, Mexico City, Mexico. Married Eddie Albert (1945), children: Edward, Marisa.

Margo and George Raft in *Rumba*.

Feature Films: *Crime Without Passion* (Par., 1934), *Rumba* (Par., 1935), *Robin Hood of El Dorado* (MGM, 1936), *Winterset* (RKO, 1936), *Lost Horizon* (Col., 1937), *A Miracle on Main Street* (Col., 1940), *The Leopard Man* (RKO, 1943), *Behind the Rising Sun* (RKO, 1943), *Gangway for Tomorrow* (RKO, 1943), *Viva Zapata!* (20th, 1952), *I'll Cry Tomorrow* (MGM, 1955), *From Hell to Texas* (20th, 1958), *Who's Got the Action?* (Par., 1962).

HERBERT MARSHALL Born May 23, 1890, London, England. Married Molly Maitland (1915); divorced 1928. Married Edna Best (1928), child: Sarah; divorced 1940. Married Lee Russell (1940), child: Anne; divorced 1946. Married Boots Mallory; widowed 1958. Married Dee Kahmann (1960). Died January 21, 1966.

Robert Montgomery, Herbert Marshall and Norma Shearer in *Riptide*.

Sound Feature Films: *The Letter* (Par., 1929), *Murder* (BIP, 1930), *Secrets of a Secretary* (Par., 1931), *Michael and Mary* (Univ., 1932), *Blonde Venus* (Par., 1932), *Trouble in Paradise* (Par., 1932), *Evenings for Sale* (Par., 1932), *Solitaire Man* (MGM, 1933), *Faithful Heart* (Helber Pictures, 1933), *I Was a Spy* (Fox, 1934), *Four Frightened People* (Par., 1934), *Riptide* (MGM, 1934), *Outcast Lady* (MGM, 1934), *The Painted Veil* (MGM, 1934), *The Good Fairy* (Univ., 1935), *The Flame Within* (MGM, 1935), *Accent on Youth* (Par., 1935), *The Dark Angel* (UA, 1935), *If You Could Only Cook* (Col., 1935), *The Lady Consents* (RKO, 1936), *Till We Meet Again* (Par., 1936), *Girls' Dormitory* (20th, 1936), *A Woman Rebels* (RKO, 1936), *Make Way for a Lady* (RKO, 1936), *Breakfast for Two* (RKO, 1937), *Angel* (Par., 1937), *Mad About Music* (Univ., 1938), *Always Goodbye* (20th, 1938), *Woman Against Woman* (MGM, 1938), *Zaza* (Par., 1939), *A Bill of Divorcement* (RKO, 1940), *Foreign Correspondent* (UA, 1940), *The Letter* (WB, 1940), *Adventure in Washington* (Col., 1941), *The Little Foxes* (RKO, 1941), *When Ladies Meet* (MGM, 1941), *Kathleen* (MGM, 1941), *The Moon and Sixpence* (UA, 1942), *Flight for Freedom* (RKO, 1943), *Forever and a Day* (RKO, 1943), *Young Ideas* (MGM, 1943), *Andy Hardy's Blonde Trouble* (MGM, 1944), *The Unseen* (Par., 1945), *The Enchanted Cottage* (RKO, 1945), *Crack-Up* (RKO, 1946), *The Razor's Edge* (20th, 1946), *Duel in the Sun* (Selznick, 1946), *Ivy* (Univ., 1947), *High Wall* (MGM, 1947), *The Secret Garden* (MGM, 1949), *The Underworld Story* (UA, 1950), *Anne of the Indies* (20th, 1951), *Angel Face* (RKO, 1952), *Captain Black Jack* (Classic, 1952), *Riders to the Stars* (UA, 1954), *Gog* (UA, 1954), *The Black Shield of Falworth* (Univ., 1954), *The Virgin Queen* (20th, 1955), *Wicked as They Come* (Col., 1957), *The Weapon* (Rep., 1957), *Stage Struck* (BV, 1958), *The Fly* (20th, 1958), *Midnight Lace* (Univ., 1960), *College Confidential* (Univ., 1960), *A Fever in the Blood* (WB, 1961), *Five Weeks in a Balloon* (20th, 1962), *The List of Adrian Messenger* (Univ., 1963), *The Caretaker* (UA, 1963), *The Third Day* (WB, 1965).

Martin Balsam, Dean Martin and Susan Hayward in *Ada*.

DEAN MARTIN (Dino Crocetti) Born June 17, 1917, Steubenville, Ohio. Married Betty McDonald (1940), children: Craig, Claudia, Gail, Dina; divorced 1949. Married Jean Bigger (1949), children: Dino, Ricci, Gina.

Feature Films: *My Friend Irma* (Par., 1949), *My Friend Irma Goes West* (Par., 1950), *At War With the Army* (Par., 1950), *That's My Boy* (Par., 1951), *Sailor Beware* (Par., 1951), *Jumping Jacks* (Par., 1952), *Road to Bali* (Par., 1952),* *The Stooge* (Par., 1952), *Scared Stiff* (Par., 1953), *The Caddy* (Par., 1953), *Money From Home* (Par., 1953), *Living it Up* (Par., 1954), *Three Ring Circus* (Par., 1954), *You're Never Too Young* (Par., 1955), *Artists and Models* (Par., 1955), *Pardners* (Par., 1956), *Hollywood or Bust* (Par., 1956), *Ten Thousand Bedrooms* (MGM, 1957), *The Young Lions* (20th, 1958), *Some Came Running* (MGM, 1958), *Rio Bravo* (WB, 1959), *Career* (Par., 1959), *Who Was That Lady?* (Col., 1960), *Bells Are Ringing* (MGM, 1960), *Ocean's 11* (WB, 1960), *Pepe* (Col., 1960),* *All in a Night's Work* (Par., 1961), *Ada* (MGM, 1961), *Sergeants 3* (UA, 1962), *Road to Hong Kong* (UA, 1962),* *Who's Got the Action?* (Par., 1962), *Come Blow Your Horn* (Par., 1963),* *Toys In The Attic* (UA, 1963), *Who's Been Sleeping in My Bed?* (Par., 1963), *4 for Texas* (WB, 1963), *What a Way to Go!* (20th, 1964), *Robin and the 7 Hoods* (WB, 1964), *Kiss Me, Stupid* (Lopert, 1964), *The Sons of Katie Elder* (Par., 1965), *The Silencers* (Col., 1966), *Texas Across the River* (Univ., 1966), *Murderers' Row* (Col., 1966), *Rough Night in Jericho* (Univ., 1967), *The Ambushers* (Col., 1967), *Bandolero* (20th, 1968), *How to Save a Marriage—And Ruin Your Life* (Col., 1968).

*Unbilled guest appearance

LEE MARVIN Born February 19, 1924, New York, New York. Married Betty Edeling (1951), children: Christopher, Courtenay, Cynthia, Claudia; divorced 1967.

Feature Films: *You're in the Navy Now* (20th, 1951), *Diplomatic Courier* (20th, 1952), *We're Not Married* (20th, 1952), *The Duel at*

Randolph Scott, Lee Marvin and Donna Reed in *Hangman's Knot*.

Silver Creek (Univ., 1952), *Eight Iron Men* (Col., 1952), *Hangman's Knot* (Col., 1952), *Seminole* (Univ., 1953), *Down Among the Sheltering Palms* (20th, 1953), *The Glory Brigade* (20th, 1953), *The Stranger Wore a Gun* (Col., 1953), *The Big Heat* (Col., 1953), *Gun Fury* (Col., 1953), *The Wild One* (Col., 1954), *Gorilla at Large* (20th, 1954), *The Caine Mutiny* (Col., 1954), *The Raid* (20th, 1954), *Bad Day at Black Rock* (MGM, 1954), *A Life in the Balance* (20th, 1955), *Violent Saturday* (20th, 1955), *Not as a Stranger* (UA, 1955), *Pete Kelly's Blues* (WB, 1955), *I Died a Thousand Times* (WB, 1955), *Shack-Out on 101* (AA, 1955), *The Rack* (MGM, 1956), *Seven Men From Now* (WB, 1956), *Pillars of the Sky* (Univ., 1956), *Attack!* (UA, 1956), *Raintree County* (MGM, 1957), *The Missouri Traveler* (BV, 1958), *The Comancheros* (20th, 1961), *The Man Who Shot Liberty Valance* (Par., 1962), *Donovan's Reef* (Par., 1963), *The Killers* (Univ., 1964), *Ship of Fools* (Col., 1965), *Cat Ballou* (Col., 1965), *The Professionals* (Col., 1966), *The Dirty Dozen* (MGM, 1967), *Point Blank* (MGM, 1967), *Tonite Let's Make Love in London* (documentary; Lorrimer, 1967), *Sergeant Ryker* (Univ., 1968).

MARX BROTHERS, THE

CHICO (Leonard Marx) Born March 22, 1891, New York, New York. Married Betty Carp, child: Maxine; divorced. Married Mary DiVithas (1958). Died October 11, 1961.

HARPO (Adolph Arthur Marx) Born November 23, 1893, New York, New York. Married Susan Fleming (1936), children: William, Alexander, Minny, James. Died September 28, 1964.

GROUCHO (Julius Henry Marx) Born October 2, 1895, New York, New York. Married Ruth Johnson (1920), children: Arthur, Miriam; divorced 1942. Married Catherine Gorcey (1945), child: Melinda; divorced 1951. Married Eden Hartford (1954).

ZEPPO (Herbert Marx) Born February 25, 1901, New York, New York. Married Marion Benda (1927), child: Tim; divorced.

Chico, Zeppo, Groucho and Harpo Marx in *Duck Soup*.

Sound Feature Films:

    with Chico, Harpo, Groucho, Zeppo *The Cocoanuts* (Par., 1929), *Animal Crackers* (Par., 1930), *Monkey Business* (Par., 1931), *Horse Feathers* (Par., 1932), *Duck Soup* (Par., 1933).

    with Chico, Harpo, Groucho *A Night at the Opera* (MGM, 1935), *A Day at the Races* (MGM, 1937), *Room Service* (RKO, 1938), *At the Circus* (MGM, 1939), *Go West* (MGM, 1940), *The Big Store* (MGM, 1941), *A Night in Casablanca* (UA, 1946), *Love Happy* (UA, 1950), *The Story of Mankind* (WB, 1957).

    with Harpo *Stage Door Canteen* (UA, 1943).

    with Groucho *Copacabana* (UA, 1947), *Mr. Music* (Par., 1950), *Double Dynamite* (RKO, 1951), *A Girl in Every Port* (RKO, 1952), *Will Success Spoil Rock Hunter?* (20th, 1957).*

    *Unbilled guest appearance

Angie Dickinson, James Mason and Jack Klugman in *Cry Terror*.

Illona Massey in *Rosalie*.

JAMES MASON (James Neville Mason) Born May 15, 1909, Huddersfield, England. Married Pamela Kellino (1939), children: Portland, Morgan; divorced 1964.

Feature Films: *Late Extra* (Fox, 1935), *Troubled Waters* (Fox, 1935), *Twice Branded* (George Smith, 1936), *The Prison Breakers* (George Smith, 1936), *Blind Man's Bluff* (20th, 1936), *The Secret of Stamboul* (Wainwright, 1936), *The Mill on the Floss* (John Klein, 1936), *The High Command* (Fanfare, 1937), *Catch as Catch Can* (20th, 1937), *Fire Over England* (London Films, 1937), *The Return of the Scarlet Pimpernel* (UA, 1937), *Deadwater* (KMK, 1937), *I Met a Murderer* (Gamma Films, 1939), *Hatter's Castle* (Par., 1941), *The Patient Vanishes* (Associated British Pictures, 1941), *This Man Is Dangerous* (Pathé, 1941), *Secret Mission* (Hellman, 1942), *Thunder Rock* (Charter, 1942), *Alibi* (British Lion, 1943), *The Bells Go Down* (Ealing, 1943), *Candlelight in Algeria* (King, 1943), *The Man in Grey* (Gainsborough, 1943), *They Met in the Dark* (Hellman, 1943), *Fanny by Gaslight* (Gainsborough, 1944), *Hotel Reserve* (RKO, 1944), *A Place of One's Own* (Gainsborough, 1945), *They Were Sisters* (Gainsborough, 1945), *The Wicked Lady* (Gainsborough, 1945), *The Seventh Veil* (Ortus, 1945), *Odd Man Out* (Rank, 1947), *The Upturned Glass* (Rank, 1947), *A Place of One's Own* (Rank, 1949), *Madame Bovary* (MGM, 1949), *The Reckless Moment* (Col., 1949), *East Side, West Side* (MGM, 1949), *One Way Street* (Univ., 1950), *The Desert Fox* (20th, 1951), *Pandora and the Flying Dutchman* (MGM, 1951), *Five Fingers* (20th, 1952), *Lady Possessed* (Rep., 1952), *The Prisoner of Zenda* (MGM, 1952), *Face to Face* (RKO, 1952), *The Story of Three Loves* (MGM, 1953), *The Desert Rats* (20th, 1953), *Julius Caesar* (MGM, 1953), *Botany Bay* (Par., 1953), *The Man Between* (UA, 1953), *Prince Valiant* (20th, 1954), *A Star Is Born* (WB, 1954), *20,000 Leagues Under the Sea* (BV, 1954), *Forever Darling* (MGM, 1956), *Bigger Than Life* (20th, 1956), *Island in the Sun* (20th, 1957), *Cry Terror* (MGM, 1958), *The Decks Ran Red* (MGM, 1958), *North by Northwest* (MGM, 1959), *Journey to the Center of the Earth* (20th, 1959), *A Touch of Larceny* (Par., 1960), *The Green Carnation* (Warwick, 1960), *The Marriage-Go-Round* (20th, 1960), *Escape From Zahrain* (Par., 1962), *Lolita* (MGM, 1962), *Hero's Island* (UA, 1962), *Tiara Tahiti* (Zenith International, 1963), *Torpedo Bay* (AIP, 1964), *The Fall of the Roman Empire* (Par., 1964), *The Pumpkin Eater* (Royal Film International, 1964), *Lord Jim* (Col., 1965), *Genghis Khan* (Col., 1966), *Georgy Girl* (Col., 1966), *The Deadly Affair* (Col., 1967), *Cop Out* (Cinerama, 1968), *Duffy* (Col., 1968), *Mayerling* (MGM, 1969).

ILONA MASSEY (Ilona Hajmassy) Born 1910, Budapest, Hungary. Married Nicholas Szavozd; divorced. Married Alan Curtis (1941); divorced 1942. Married Charles Walker (1952); divorced 1955. Married Donald Dawson (1955).

Feature Films: *Rosalie* (MGM, 1937), *Balalaika* (MGM, 1949), *New Wine* (UA, 1941), *International Lady* (UA, 1941), *Invisible Agent* (Univ., 1942), *Frankenstein Meets the Wolf Man* (Univ., 1943), *Holiday in Mexico* (MGM, 1946), *The Gentleman Misbehaves* (Col., 1946), *Northwest Outpost* (Rep., 1947), *The Plunderers* (Rep., 1948), *Love Happy* (UA, 1949), *Jet Over the Atlantic* (Inter-Continent, 1959).

RAYMOND MASSEY (Raymond Hart Massey) Born August 30, 1896, Toronto, Canada. Married Peggy Fremantle (1923), child: Geoffrey; divorced 1929. Married Adrianne Allen (1929), children: Daniel, Anna; divorced 1939. Married Dorothy Whitney (1939).

Moroni Olsen, Christian Rub, Ilka Gruning, Nancy Coleman, John Garfield and Raymond Massey in *Dangerously They Live*.

Feature Films: *The Speckled Band* (First Division, 1931), *The Old Dark House* (Univ., 1932), *The Scarlet Pimpernel* (UA, 1934), *Things to Come* (UA, 1936), *Fire Over England* (Korda, 1937), *Under the Red Robe* (20th, 1937), *The Prisoner of Zenda* (UA, 1937), *The Hurricane* (UA, 1937), *Drums* (UA, 1938), *Black Limelight* (Alliance Films, 1939), *Abe Lincoln in Illinois* (RKO, 1940), *Santa Fe Trail* (WB, 1940), *Dangerously They Live* (WB, 1941), *The Invaders* (Col., 1942), *Desperate Journey* (WB, 1942), *Reap the Wild Wind* (Par., 1942), *Action in the North Atlantic* (WB, 1943), *Arsenic and Old Lace* (WB, 1944), *The Woman in the Window* (RKO, 1944), *God Is My Co-Pilot* (WB, 1945), *Hotel Berlin* (WB, 1945), *Stairway to Heaven* (Rank, 1946), *Mourning Becomes Electra* (RKO, 1947), *Possessed* (WB, 1947), *The Fountainhead* (WB, 1949), *Roseanna McCoy* (RKO, 1949), *Chain Lightning* (WB, 1949), *Barricade* (WB, 1950), *Dallas* (WB, 1950), *Sugarfoot* (WB, 1951), *Come Fill the Cup* (WB, 1951), *David and Bathsheba* (20th, 1951), *Carson City* (WB, 1952), *The Desert Song* (WB, 1953), *Battle Cry* (WB, 1955), *Seven Angry Men* (AA, 1955), *Prince of Players* (20th, 1955), *East of Eden* (WB, 1955), *Omar Khayyam* (Par., 1957), *The Naked and the Dead* (WB, 1958), *The Great Impostor* (Univ.,

169

1960), *The Fiercest Heart* (20th, 1961), *The Queen's Guard* (Michael Powell Productions, 1961), *How the West Was Won* (MGM, 1963), *MacKenna's Gold* (Col., 1968).

WALTER MATTHAU (Walter Matthow) Born October 1, 1920, New York, New York. Married Grace Johnson (1948); divorced 1958. Married Carol Marcus (1959).

Walter Matthau, Jack Lemmon and Ned Glass in *The Fortune Cookie*.

Feature Films: *The Kentuckian* (UA, 1955), *The Indian Fighter* (UA, 1955), *Bigger Than Life* (20th, 1956), *A Face in the Crowd* (WB, 1957), *Slaughter on Tenth Avenue* (Univ., 1957), *Voice in the Mirror* (Univ., 1958), *King Creole* (Par., 1958), *Ride a Crooked Trail* (Univ., 1958), *Onionhead* (WB, 1958), *The Gangster Story* (Jonathan Daniels, 1960), *Strangers When We Meet* (Col., 1960), *Lonely Are the Brave* (Univ., 1962), *Who's Got the Action?* (Par., 1962), *Island of Love* (WB, 1963), *Charade* (Univ., 1963), *Ensign Pulver* (WB, 1964), *Fail Safe* (Col., 1964), *Goodbye Charlie* (20th, 1964), *Mirage* (Univ., 1965), *The Fortune Cookie* (UA, 1966), *A Guide for the Married Man* (20th, 1967), *The Odd Couple* (Par., 1968), *Guide for the Married Woman* (20th, 1968), *Candy* (Cinerama, 1968).

VICTOR MATURE Born January 29, 1916, Louisville, Kentucky. Married Frances Charles; divorced 1940. Married Martha Kemp; divorced 1943. Married Dorothy Berry (1948); divorced 1955. Married Adrianne Urwich (1959).

Robert Barrat, Louise Platt and Victor Mature in *Captain Caution*.

English-Language Feature Films: *The Housekeeper's Daughter* (UA, 1939), *One Million B.C.* (UA, 1940), *Captain Caution* (UA, 1940),

No, No, Nanette (RKO, 1940), *I Wake Up Screaming* (20th, 1941), *The Shanghai Gesture* (UA, 1941), *Song of the Islands* (20th, 1942), *My Gal Sal* (20th, 1942), *Footlight Serenade* (20th, 1942), *Seven Days' Leave* (RKO, 1942), *My Darling Clementine* (20th, 1946), *Moss Rose* (20th, 1947), *Kiss of Death* (20th, 1947), *Fury at Furnace Creek* (20th, 1948), *Cry of the City* (20th, 1948), *Red Hot and Blue* (Par., 1949), *Easy Living* (RKO, 1949), *Samson and Delilah* (Par., 1949), *Wabash Avenue* (20th, 1950), *I'll Get By* (20th, 1950),* *Stella* (20th, 1950), *Gambling House* (RKO, 1950), *The Las Vegas Story* (RKO, 1952), *Androcles and the Lion* (RKO, 1952), *Something for the Birds* (20th, 1952), *Million Dollar Mermaid* (MGM, 1952), *The Glory Brigade* (20th, 1953), *Affair With a Stranger* (RKO, 1953), *The Robe* (20th, 1953), *Veils of Bagdad* (Univ., 1953), *Dangerous Mission* (RKO, 1954), *Demetrius and the Gladiators* (20th, 1954), *Betrayed* (MGM, 1954), *The Egyptian* (20th, 1954), *Chief Crazy Horse* (Univ., 1955), *Violent Saturday* (20th, 1955), *The Last Frontier* (Col., 1955), *Safari* (Col., 1956), *The Sharkfighters* (UA, 1956), *Zarak* (Col., 1957), *Pickup Alley* (Col., 1957), *The Long Haul* (Col., 1957), *China Doll* (UA, 1958), *Tank Force* (Col., 1958), *Escort West* (UA, 1959), *The Bandit of Zhobe* (Col., 1959), *The Big Circus* (AA, 1959), *Timbuktu* (UA, 1959), *Hannibal* (WB, 1960), *After the Fox* (UA, 1966).

*Unbilled guest appearance

MARILYN MAXWELL (Marvel Marilyn Maxwell) Born August 3, 1921, Clarinda, Iowa. Married John Conte (1941); divorced 1946. Married Anders McIntyre (1950); divorced 1951. Married Jerry Davis (1954), child: Matthew; divorced 1960.

Mickey Rooney and Marilyn Maxwell in *Summer Holiday*.

Feature Films: *Stand By for Action* (MGM, 1942), *Du Barry Was a Lady* (MGM, 1943), *Presenting Lily Mars* (MGM, 1943), *Thousands Cheer* (MGM, 1943), *Dr. Gillespie's Criminal Case* (MGM, 1943), *Salute to the Marines* (MGM, 1943), *Swing Fever* (MGM, 1943), *Pilot No. 5* (MGM, 1943), *Best Foot Forward* (MGM, 1943), *Three Men in White* (MGM, 1944), *Lost in a Harem* (MGM, 1944), *Between Two Women* (MGM, 1945), *The Show-Off* (MGM, 1946), *High Barbaree* (MGM, 1947), *Summer Holiday* (MGM, 1948), *Race Street* (RKO, 1948), *Champion* (UA, 1949), *Key to the City* (MGM, 1950), *Outside the Wall* (Univ., 1950), *The Lemon Drop Kid* (Par., 1951), *New Mexico* (UA, 1951), *Off Limits* (Par., 1953), *East of Sumatra* (Univ., 1953), *Paris Model* (Col., 1953), *New York Confidential* (WB, 1955), *Forever, Darling* (MGM, 1956), *Rock-a-Bye Baby* (Par., 1958), *Critic's Choice* (WB, 1963), *Stage to Thunder Rock* (Par., 1964), *The Lively Set* (Univ., 1964), *Arizona Bushwhackers* (Par., 1968).

VIRGINIA MAYO (Virginia Jones) Born November 30, 1920, St. Louis, Missouri. Married Michael O'Shea (1947), child: Mary.

English-Language Feature Films: *The Adventures of Jack London* (UA,

Andrew Duggan and Virginia Mayo in *Westbound*.

1943), *Up in Arms* (RKO, 1944), *Seven Days Ashore* (RKO, 1944), *The Princess and the Pirate* (RKO, 1944), *Wonder Man* (RKO, 1945), *The Best Years of Our Lives* (RKO, 1946), *The Kid From Brooklyn* (RKO, 1947), *Out of the Blue* (EL, 1947), *The Secret Life of Walter Mitty* (RKO, 1947), *A Song Is Born* (RKO, 1948), *Smart Girls Don't Talk* (WB, 1948), *Flaxy Martin* (WB, 1949), *Colorado Territory* (WB, 1949), *The Girl From Jones Beach* (WB, 1949), *White Heat* (WB, 1949), *Red Light* (UA, 1949), *Always Leave Them Laughing* (WB, 1949), *Backfire* (WB, 1950), *The Flame and the Arrow* (WB, 1950), *The West Point Story* (WB, 1950), *Along the Great Divide* (WB, 1951), *Painting the Clouds With Sunshine* (WB, 1951), *Captain Horatio Hornblower* (WB, 1951), *Starlift* (WB, 1951), *She's Working Her Way Through College* (WB, 1952), *The Iron Mistress* (WB, 1952), *She's Back on Broadway* (WB, 1953), *South Sea Woman* (WB, 1953), *Devil's Canyon* (RKO, 1953), *King Richard and the Crusaders* (WB, 1954), *The Silver Chalice* (WB, 1954), *Pearl of the South Pacific* (RKO, 1955), *Great Day in the Morning* (RKO, 1956), *The Proud Ones* (20th, 1956), *Congo Crossing* (Univ., 1956), *The Big Land* (WB, 1957), *The Story of Mankind* (WB, 1957), *The Tall Stranger* (AA, 1957), *Fort Dobbs* (WB, 1958), *Westbound* (WB, 1959), *Jet Over the Atlantic* (Inter-Continent, 1959), *Young Fury* (Par., 1965), *Castle of Evil* (Feature Film Corp. of USA, 1966), *Fort Utah* (Par., 1967).

PATRICIA MEDINA Born July 19, 1923, London, England. Married Richard Greene (1941); divorced 1952. Married Joseph Cotten (1960).

Alan Ladd and Patricia Medina in *Botany Bay*.

English-Language Feature Films: *The Day Will Dawn* (Soskin, 1942), *They Met in the Dark* (Hellman, 1942), *Hotel Reserve* (RKO, 1944), *Don't Take It to Heart* (Two Cities, 1944), *Kiss the Boys Goodbye* (Butchers, 1944), *Waltz Time* (British International, 1945), *The Secret Heart* (MGM, 1946), *Moss Rose* (20th, 1947), *The Foxes of Harrow* (20th, 1947), *The Three Musketeers* (MGM, 1948), *O.K. Agostina* (Toeplitz, 1949), *The Fighting O'Flynn* (Univ., 1949), *Francis* (Univ., 1949), *Fortunes of Captain Blood* (Col., 1950), *Abbott and Costello in the Foreign Legion* (Univ., 1950), *The Jackpot* (20th, 1950), *Valentino*

(Col., 1951), *The Lady and the Bandit* (Col., 1951), *The Magic Carpet* (Col., 1951), *Aladdin and His Lamp* (Mon., 1952), *Lady in the Iron Mask* (20th, 1952), *Captain Pirate* (Col., 1952), *Desperate Search* (MGM, 1952), *Siren of Bagdad* (Col., 1953), *Sangaree* (Par., 1953), *Plunder of the Sun* (WB, 1953), *Botany Bay* (Par., 1953), *Phantom of the Rue Morgue* (WB, 1954), *Drums of Tahiti* (Col., 1954), *The Black Knight* (Col., 1954), *Pirates of Tripoli* (Col., 1955), *Duel on the Mississippi* (Col., 1955), *Mr. Arkadin* (WB, 1955), *Uranium Boom* (Col., 1956), *Stranger at My Door* (Rep., 1956), *Miami Exposé* (Col., 1956), *The Beast of Hollow Mountain* (UA, 1956), *The Buckskin Lady* (UA, 1957), *Missiles from Hell* (British, 1959), *Count Your Blessings* (MGM, 1959), *Snow White and the Three Stooges* (20th, 1961).

DONALD MEEK Born July 14, 1880, Glasgow, Scotland. Married Belle Walken (1909). Died November 18, 1946.

Shirley Temple and Donald Meek in *Little Miss Broadway*.

Sound Feature Films: *Hole in the Wall* (Par., 1929), *Love Kiss* (Celebrity Pictures, 1930), *Girl Habit* (Par., 1931), *Personal Maid* (Par., 1931), *Love, Honor and Oh-Baby!* (Univ., 1933), *College Coach* (WB, 1933), *Hi Nellie* (WB, 1934), *Bedside* (WB, 1934), *Last Gentleman* (UA, 1934), *Murder at the Vanities* (Par., 1934), *The Defense Rests* (Col., 1934), *The Merry Widow* (MGM, 1934), *Mrs. Wiggs of the Cabbage Patch* (Par., 1934), *The Captain Hates the Sea* (Col., 1934), *The Whole Town's Talking* (Col., 1935), *The Gilded Lily* (Par., 1935), *Mark of the Vampire* (MGM, 1935), *Baby Face Harrington* (MGM, 1935), *Society Doctor* (MGM, 1935), *Biography of a Bachelor Girl* (RKO, 1935), *Village Tale* (RKO, 1935), *The Informer* (RKO, 1935), *China Seas* (MGM, 1935), *Accent on Youth* (Par., 1935), *Old Man Rhythm* (RKO, 1935), *Return of Peter Grimm* (RKO, 1935), *She Couldn't Take It* (Col., 1935), *Barbary Coast* (UA, 1935), *Kind Lady* (MGM, 1935), *The Bride Comes Home* (Par., 1935), *Peter Ibbetson* (Par., 1935), *Captain Blood* (WB, 1935), *Happiness C.O.D.* (Chesterfield, 1935), *Everybody's Old Man* (20th, 1936), *Three Wise Guys* (MGM, 1936), *And So They Were Married* (Col., 1936), *One Rainy Afternoon* (UA, 1936), *Three Married Men* (Par., 1936), *Two in a Crowd* (Univ., 1936), *Old Hutch* (MGM, 1936), *Pennies From Heaven* (Col., 1936), *Maid of Salem* (Par., 1937), *The Three Legionnaires* (General Films, 1937), *Parnell* (MGM, 1937), *Behind the Headlines* (RKO, 1937), *Artists and Models* (Par., 1937), *Double Wedding* (MGM, 1937), *The Toast of New York* (RKO, 1937), *Make a Wish* (RKO, 1937), *Breakfast for Two* (RKO, 1937), *You're a Sweetheart* (Univ., 1937), *The Adventures of Tom Sawyer* (UA, 1938), *Double Danger* (RKO, 1938), *Goodbye Broadway* (Univ., 1938), *Little Miss Broadway* (20th, 1938), *Having Wonderful Time* (RKO, 1938), *You Can't Take It With You* (Col., 1938), *Hold That Co-ed* (20th, 1938), *Jesse James* (20th, 1939), *Stagecoach* (UA, 1939), *Young Mr. Lincoln* (20th, 1939), *The Housekeeper's Daughter* (UA, 1939), *Blondie Takes a Vacation*

(Col., 1939), *Nick Carter—Master Detective* (MGM, 1939), *My Little Chickadee* (Univ., 1940), *Oh Johnny, How You Can Love* (Univ., 1940), *Dr. Ehrlich's Magic Bullet* (WB, 1940), *The Man From Dakota* (MGM, 1940), *Turnabout* (UA, 1940), *Star Dust* (20th, 1940), *Phantom Raiders* (MGM, 1940), *The Return of Frank James* (20th, 1940), *Third Finger, Left Hand* (MGM, 1940), *Hullabaloo* (MGM, 1940), *Sky Murder* (MGM, 1940), *The Ghost Comes Home* (MGM, 1940), *Blonde Inspiration* (MGM, 1941), *Come Live With Me* (MGM, 1941), *A Woman's Face* (MGM, 1941), *The Wild Man of Borneo* (MGM, 1941), *Barnacle Bill* (MGM, 1941), *The Feminine Touch* (MGM, 1941), *Rise and Shine* (20th, 1941), *Babes on Broadway* (MGM, 1941), *Tortilla Flat* (MGM, 1942), *Maisie Gets Her Man* (MGM, 1942), *Seven Sweethearts* (MGM, 1942), *The Omaha Trail* (MGM, 1942), *Keeper of the Flame* (MGM, 1942), *They Got Me Covered* (RKO, 1943), *Air Raid Wardens* (20th, 1943), *Du Barry Was a Lady* (MGM, 1943), *Lost Angel* (MGM, 1943), *Rationing* (MGM, 1944), *Two Girls and a Sailor* (MGM, 1944), *Bathing Beauty* (MGM, 1944), *Barbary Coast Gent* (MGM, 1944), *Maisie Goes to Reno* (MGM, 1944), *The Thin Man Goes Home* (MGM, 1944), *State Fair* (20th, 1945), *Colonel Effingham's Raid* (20th, 1945), *Because of Him* (Univ., 1946), *Janie Gets Married* (WB, 1946), *Affairs of Geraldine* (Rep., 1946), *Magic Town* (RKO, 1947), *The Hal Roach Comedy Carnival* (UA, 1947).

ADOLPHE MENJOU (Adolph Jean Menjou) Born February 18, 1890, Pittsburgh, Pennsylvania. Married Katherine Tinsley (1919); divorced 1927. Married Kathryn Carver (1927); divorced 1933. Married Verree Teasdale (1934), child: Peter. Died October 29, 1963.

Christian Rub and Adolphe Menjou in *Cafe Metropole*.

English-Language Sound Feature Films: *Fashions in Love* (Par., 1929), *Morocco* (Par., 1930), *New Moon* (MGM, 1930), *Men Call it Love* (MGM, 1931), *The Easiest Way* (MGM, 1931), *The Front Page* (UA, 1931), *The Great Lover* (MGM, 1931), *Friends and Lovers* (RKO, 1931), *Prestige* (RKO, 1932), *Forbidden* (Univ., 1932), *Two White Arms* (MGM, 1932), *The Man From Yesterday* (Par., 1932), *Bachelor's Affairs* (Fox, 1932), *Night Club Lady* (Col., 1932), *A Farewell to Arms* (Par., 1932), *Blame the Woman* (Principal, 1932), *Circus Queen Murder* (Col., 1933), *Morning Glory* (RKO, 1933), *Worst Woman in Paris?* (Fox, 1933), *Convention City* (WB, 1933), *Journal of a Crime* (WB, 1934), *Easy to Love* (WB, 1934), *The Trumpet Blows* (Par., 1934), *Little Miss Marker* (Par., 1934), *Great Flirtation* (Par., 1934), *The Human Side* (Univ., 1934), *The Mighty Barnum* (UA, 1934), *Gold Diggers of 1935* (WB, 1935), *Broadway Gondolier* (WB, 1935), *The Milky Way* (Par., 1936), *Sing Baby, Sing* (20th, 1936), *Wives Never Know* (Par., 1936), *One in a Million* (20th, 1936), *A Star Is Born* (UA, 1937), *Cafe Metropole* (20th, 1937), *100 Men and a Girl* (Univ., 1937), *Stage Door* (RKO, 1937), *Goldwyn Follies* (UA, 1938), *Letter of Introduction* (Univ., 1938), *Thanks for Everything* (20th, 1938), *King of the Turf* (UA, 1939), *That's Right—You're Wrong* (RKO, 1939), *Golden Boy* (Col., 1939), *The Housekeeper's Daughter* (UA, 1939), *A Bill of Divorcement* (RKO, 1940), *Turnabout* (UA, 1940), *Road Show* (UA, 1941),

Father Takes a Wife (RKO, 1941), *Roxie Hart* (20th, 1942), *Syncopation* (RKO, 1942), *You Were Never Lovelier* (Col., 1942), *Hi Diddle Diddle* (UA, 1943), *Sweet Rosie O'Grady* (20th, 1943), *Step Lively* (RKO, 1944), *Man Alive* (RKO, 1945), *Heartbeat* (RKO, 1946), *The Bachelor's Daughters* (UA, 1946), *I'll Be Yours* (Univ., 1947), *Mr. District Attorney* (Col., 1947), *The Hucksters* (MGM, 1947), *State of the Union* (MGM, 1948), *My Dream Is Yours* (WB, 1949), *Dancing in the Dark* (20th, 1949), *To Please a Lady* (MGM, 1950), *The Tall Target* (MGM, 1951), *Across the Wide Missouri* (MGM, 1951), *The Sniper* (Col., 1952), *Man on a Tightrope* (20th, 1953), *Timberjack* (Rep., 1955), *The Ambassador's Daughter* (UA, 1956), *Bundle of Joy* (RKO, 1956), *The Fuzzy Pink Nightgown* (UA, 1957), *Paths of Glory* (UA, 1957), *I Married a Woman* (Univ., 1958), *Pollyanna* (BV, 1960).

BURGESS MEREDITH (Burgess George) Born November 16, 1908, Cleveland, Ohio. Married Helen Derby (1932); divorced 1935. Married Margaret Perry (1936); divorced 1938. Married Paulette Goddard (1944); divorced 1949. Married Kava Sundsten (1950), children: Jonathan, Tala.

Burgess Meredith, Paulette Goddard and Fred Astaire in *Second Chorus*.

Feature Films: *Winterset* (RKO, 1936), *There Goes the Groom* (RKO, 1937), *Spring Madness* (MGM, 1938), *Idiot's Delight* (MGM, 1939), *Of Mice and Men* (UA, 1939), *Castle on the Hudson* (WB, 1940), *Second Chorus* (Par., 1940), *San Francisco Docks* (Univ., 1941), *That Uncertain Feeling* (UA, 1941), *Tom, Dick and Harry* (RKO, 1941), *Street of Chance* (Par., 1942), *The Story of G.I. Joe* (UA, 1945), *The Diary of a Chambermaid* (UA, 1946), *Magnificent Doll* (Univ., 1946), *On Our Merry Way* (UA, 1948), *Mine Own Executioner* (20th, 1948), *Jigsaw* (UA, 1949),* *The Man on the Eiffel Tower* (RKO, 1949), *The Gay Adventure* (UA, 1953), *Joe Butterfly* (Univ., 1957), *Advise and Consent* (Col., 1962), *The Cardinal* (Col., 1963), *The Kidnappers* ("Man on the Run"—Manson, 1964), *In Harm's Way* (Par., 1965), *Crazy Quilt* (narrator; Walter Reade, 1966), *A Big Hand for the Little Lady* (WB, 1966), *Madame X* (Univ., 1966), *Batman* (20th, 1966), *Hurry Sundown* (Par., 1967), *The Torture Garden* (Col., 1968), *MacKenna's Gold* (Col., 1968), *Stay Away Joe* (MGM, 1968).

*Unbilled guest appearance

UNA MERKEL Born December 10, 1903, Covington, Kentucky. Married Ronald Burla (1932); divorced 1945.

Sound Feature Films: *Abraham Lincoln* (UA, 1930), *Eyes of the World* (UA, 1930), *The Bat Whispers* (UA, 1931), *Command Performance* (Tiff., 1931), *Don't Bet on Women* (Fox, 1931), *The Maltese Falcon* (WB, 1931), *Daddy Long Legs* (Fox, 1931), *Six Cylinder Love* (Fox, 1931), *The Bargain* (WB, 1931), *Secret Witness* ("Terror by Night"—Famous Attractions, 1931), *Private Lives* (MGM, 1931), *Secret Witness* (Col., 1931), *Huddle* (MGM, 1932), *She Wanted a Millionaire* (Fox,

Bob Burns and Una Merkel in *Comin' Round the Mountain*.

1932), *The Impatient Maiden* (Univ., 1932), *Man Wanted* (WB, 1932), *Red-Headed Woman* (MGM, 1932), *They Call It Sin* (WB, 1932), *42nd Street* (WB, 1933), *Clear All Wires* (MGM, 1933), *Secret of Madame Blanche* (MGM, 1933), *Whistling in the Dark* (MGM, 1933), *Men Are Such Fools* (RKO, 1933), *Reunion in Vienna* (MGM, 1933), *Midnight Mary* (MGM, 1933), *Broadway to Hollywood* (MGM, 1933), *Her First Mate* (Univ., 1933), *Beauty for Sale* (MGM, 1933), *Bombshell* (MGM, 1933), *Day of Reckoning* (MGM, 1933), *The Women in His Life* (MGM, 1933), *This Side of Heaven* (MGM, 1934), *Bulldog Drummond Strikes Back* (UA, 1934), *Have a Heart* (MGM, 1934), *The Cat's Paw* (Fox, 1934), *The Merry Widow* (MGM, 1934), *Paris Interlude* (MGM, 1934), *Murder in the Private Car* (MGM, 1934), *Biography of a Bachelor Girl* (MGM, 1934), *Evelyn Prentice* (MGM, 1934), *The Night Is Young* (MGM, 1934), *Baby Face Harrington* (MGM, 1935), *One New York Night* (MGM, 1935), *Murder in the Fleet* (MGM, 1935), *Broadway Melody of 1936* (MGM, 1935), *It's in the Air* (MGM, 1935), *Riffraff* (MGM, 1935), *Speed* (MGM, 1936), *Born to Dance* (MGM, 1936), *We Went to College* (MGM, 1936), *Don't Tell the Wife* (RKO, 1937), *Good Old Soak* (MGM, 1937), *Saratoga* (MGM, 1937), *True Confession* (Par., 1937), *Checkers* (20th, 1937), *Four Girls in White* (MGM, 1939), *Some Like It Hot* (Par., 1939), *On Borrowed Time* (MGM, 1939), *Destry Rides Again* (Univ., 1939), *Comin' 'Round the Mountain* (Par., 1940), *The Bank Dick* (Univ., 1940), *Sandy Gets Her Man* (Univ., 1940), *Road to Zanzibar* (Par., 1941), *Double Date* (Univ., 1941), *Cracked Nuts* (Univ., 1941), *Twin Beds* (UA, 1942), *The Mad Doctor of Market Street* (Univ., 1942), *The Silent Witness* (Mon., 1942), *This Is the Army* (WB, 1943), *Sweethearts of the U.S.A.* (Mon., 1944), *It's a Joke, Son* (EL, 1947), *The Bride Goes Wild* (MGM, 1948), *The Man From Texas* (EL, 1948), *Kill the Umpire* (Col., 1950), *My Blue Heaven* (20th, 1950), *Emergency Wedding* (Col., 1950), *Rich, Young and Pretty* (MGM, 1951), *A Millionaire for Christy* (20th, 1951), *Golden Girl* (20th, 1951), *With a Song in My Heart* (20th, 1952), *The Merry Widow* (MGM, 1952), *I Love Melvin* (MGM, 1953), *The Kentuckian* (UA, 1955), *The Kettles in the Ozarks* (Univ., 1956), *Bundle of Joy* (RKO, 1956), *The Fuzzy Pink Nightgown* (UA, 1957), *The Girl Most Likely* (Univ., 1957), *The Mating Game* (MGM, 1959), *The Parent Trap* (BV, 1961), *Summer and Smoke* (Par., 1961), *Summer Magic* (BV, 1963), *A Tiger Walks* (BV, 1964), *Spinout* (MGM, 1966).

ETHEL MERMAN (Ethel Zimmerman) Born January 16, 1909, Astoria, New York. Married William Smith (1940); divorced 1941. Married Robert Levitt (1941), children: Ethel, Robert; divorced 1952.

Bing Crosby and Ethel Merman in *Anything Goes*.

Married Robert Six (1953); divorced 1960. Married Ernest Borgnine (1964); divorced 1964.

Feature Films: *Follow the Leader* (Par., 1930), *We're Not Dressing* (Par., 1934), *Kid Millions* (UA, 1934), *Anything Goes* (Par., 1936), *Strike Me Pink* (UA, 1936), *Happy Landing* (20th, 1938), *Alexander's Ragtime Band* (20th, 1938), *Straight, Place and Show* (20th, 1938), *Stage Door Canteen* (UA, 1943), *Call Me Madam* (20th, 1953), *There's No Business Like Show Business* (20th, 1954), *Its a Mad, Mad, Mad, Mad World* (UA, 1963), *The Art of Love* (Univ., 1965).

GERTRUDE MICHAEL Born June 1, 1911, Talladega, Alabama. Died January 1, 1965.

Arthur Byron and Gertrude Michael in *The Notorious Sophie Lang*.

Feature Films: *Wayward* (Par., 1932), *Unashamed* (MGM, 1932), *Sailor Be Good* (RKO, 1933), *A Bedtime Story* (Par., 1933), *Night of Terror* (Col., 1933), *Ann Vickers* (RKO, 1933), *I'm No Angel* (Par., 1933), *Cradle Song* (Par., 1933), *Bolero* (Par., 1934), *I Believed in You* (Fox, 1934), *Search for Beauty* (Par., 1934), *Hold That Girl* (Fox, 1934), *Murder at the Vanities* (Par., 1934), *Murder on the Blackboard* (RKO, 1934), *Cleopatra* (Par., 1934), *Notorious Sophie Lang* (Par., 1934), *Menace* (Par., 1934), *George White's Scandals* (Fox, 1934), *The Witching Hour* (Par., 1934), *Father Brown, Detective* (Par., 1935), *It Happened in New York* (Univ., 1935), *Four Hours to Kill* (Par., 1935), *The Last Outpost* (Par., 1935), *Woman Trap* (Par., 1936), *Till We Meet Again* ("Forgotten Faces"—Par., 1936), *Return of Sophie Lang* (Par., 1936), *Second Wife* (RKO, 1936), *Make Way for a Lady* (RKO, 1936), *Mr. Dodd Takes the Air* (WB, 1937), *Sophie Lang Goes West* (Par., 1937), *Hidden Power* (Col., 1939), *Just Like a Woman* (Alliance, 1940), *The Hidden Menace* (Alliance, 1940), *The Farmer's Daughter* (Par., 1940), *Parole Fixer* (Par., 1940), *I Can't Give You Anything But Love, Baby* (Univ., 1940), *Slightly Tempted* (Univ., 1940), *Prisoner of Japan* (PRC, 1942), *Behind Prison Walls* (PRC, 1943), *Where Are Your Children?* (Mon., 1943), *Women in Bondage* (Mon., 1943), *Faces in the Fog* (Rep., 1944), *Three's a Crowd* (Rep., 1945), *Allotment Wives* (Mon., 1945), *Club Havana* (PRC, 1946), *Flamingo Road* (WB, 1949), *Caged* (WB, 1950), *Darling, How Could You!* (Par., 1951), *Bugles in the Afternoon* (WB, 1952), *No Escape* (UA, 1953), *Women's Prison* (Col., 1955), *The Outsider* (Univ., 1961), *Twist All Night* (AIP, 1962).

VERA MILES (Vera Ralston) Born August 23, 1930, Boise City, Idaho. Married Robert Miles (1948), children: Debra, Kelly; divorced 1954. Married Gordon Scott (1956), child: Michael; divorced. Married Keith Larsen (1960), child: Keith.

Feature Films: *Two Tickets to Broadway* (RKO, 1951), *For Men Only* (Lip., 1952), *The Rose Bowl Story* (Mon., 1952), *The Charge at Feather River* (WB, 1953), *So Big* (WB, 1953), *Pride of the Blue Grass* (AA, 1954), *Tarzan's Hidden Jungle* (RKO, 1955), *Wichita* (AA, 1955), *The Searchers* (WB, 1956), *Autumn Leaves* (Col., 1956), *23 Paces to*

Vera Miles and Van Johnson in *23 Paces to Baker Street*.

Baker Street (20th, 1956), *The Wrong Man* (WB, 1957), *Beau James* (Par., 1957), *The F.B.I. Story* (WB, 1959), *Web of Evidence* (AA, 1959), *A Touch of Larceny* (Par., 1960), *Five Branded Women* (Par., 1960), *Psycho* (Par., 1960), *Back Street* (Univ., 1961), *The Man Who Shot Liberty Valance* (Par., 1962), *A Tiger Walks* (BV, 1964), *Those Calloways* (BV, 1964), *Follow Me, Boys!* (BV, 1966), *The Spirit Is Willing* (Par., 1967), *Kona Coast* (WB-7 Arts, 1968), *Gentle Giant* (Par., 1967), *Sergeant Ryker* (WB, 1968).

RAY MILLAND (Reginald Truscott-Jones) Born January 3, 1907, Neath, Wales. Married Muriel Weber (1932), children: Daniel, Victoria.

Robert Preston, Gary Cooper and Ray Milland in *Beau Geste*.

Feature Films: *The Plaything* (British, 1930), *The Flying Scotsman* (British, 1930), *Bachelor Father* (WB, 1931), *Just a Gigolo* (MGM, 1931), *Bought* (WB, 1931), *Ambassador Bill* (Fox, 1931), *Blonde Crazy* (WB, 1931), *Polly of the Circus* (MGM, 1932), *The Man Who Played God* (WB, 1932), *Payment Deferred* (MGM, 1932), *This Is the Life* (British Lion, 1933), *Orders Is Orders* (Gaumont-British, 1933), *Bolero* (Par., 1934), *We're Not Dressing* (Par., 1934), *Many Happy Returns* (Par., 1934), *Menace* (Par., 1934), *Charlie Chan in London* (Fox, 1934), *The Gilded Lily* (Par., 1935), *One Hour Late* (Par., 1935), *Four Hours to Kill* (Par., 1935), *The Glass Key* (Par., 1935), *Alias Mary Dow* (Univ., 1935), *Next Time We Love* (Univ., 1936), *Return of Sophie Lang* (Par., 1936), *Big Broadcast of 1937* (Par., 1936), *The Jungle Prin-*

cess (Par., 1936), *Three Smart Girls* (Univ., 1937), *Wings Over Honolulu* (Univ., 1937), *Easy Living* (Par., 1937), *Ebb Tide* (Par., 1937), *Wise Girl* (RKO, 1937), *Bulldog Drummond Escapes* (Par., 1937), *Her Jungle Love* (Par., 1938), *Men With Wings* (Par., 1938), *Say it in French* (Par., 1938), *Hotel Imperial* (Par., 1939), *Beau Geste* (Par., 1939), *Everything Happens at Night* (20th, 1939), *French Without Tears* (Par., 1940), *Irene* (RKO, 1940), *The Doctor Takes a Wife* (Col., 1940), *Untamed* (Par., 1940), *Arise, My Love* (Par., 1941), *I Wanted Wings* (Par., 1941), *Skylark* (Par., 1941), *The Lady Has Plans* (Par., 1942), *Are Husbands Necessary?* (Par., 1942), *The Major and the Minor* (Par., 1942), *Reap the Wild Wind* (Par., 1942), *Star Spangled Rhythm* (Par., 1942), *Forever and a Day* (RKO, 1943), *The Crystal Ball* (UA, 1943), *The Uninvited* (Par., 1944), *Lady in the Dark* (Par., 1944), *Till We Meet Again* (Par., 1944), *Ministry of Fear* (Par., 1944), *The Lost Weekend* (Par., 1945), *Kitty* (Par., 1945), *The Well-Groomed Bride* (Par., 1946), *California* (Par., 1946), *The Imperfect Lady* (Par., 1947), *The Trouble With Women* (Par., 1947), *Golden Earrings* (Par., 1947), *Variety Girl* (Par., 1947), *The Big Clock* (Par., 1948), *So Evil My Love* (Par., 1948), *Sealed Verdict* (Par., 1948), *Alias Nick Beal* (Par., 1949), *It Happens Every Spring* (20th, 1949), *A Woman of Distinction* (Col., 1950), *A Life of Her Own* (MGM, 1950), *Copper Canyon* (Par., 1950), *Circle of Danger* (EL, 1951), *Night into Morning* (MGM, 1951), *Rhubarb* (Par., 1951), *Close to My Heart* (WB, 1951), *Bugles in the Afternoon* (WB, 1952), *Something to Live For* (Par., 1952), *The Thief* (UA, 1952), *Jamaica Run* (Par., 1953), *Let's Do it Again* (Col., 1953), *Dial M for Murder* (WB, 1954), *A Man Alone* (Rep., 1955), *The Girl in the Red Velvet Swing* (20th, 1955), *Lisbon* (Rep., 1956), *Three Brave Men* (20th, 1957), *The River's Edge* (20th, 1957), *The Safecracker* (MGM, 1958), *High Flight* (Col., 1958), *Premature Burial* (AIP, 1962), *Panic in Year Zero* (AIP, 1962), *"X" The Man with the X-Ray Eyes* (AIP, 1963).

ANN MILLER (Lucille Ann Collier) Born April 12, 1919, Chireno, Texas. Married Reese Milner (1946); divorced 1947. Married William Moss (1958); divorced 1961. Married Arthur Cameron (1961); annulled 1962.

John Hubbard, Ann Miller, Freddy Martin and his orchestra in *What's Buzzin' Cousin?*

Feature Films: *New Faces of 1937* (RKO, 1937), *Stage Door* (RKO, 1937), *Life of the Party* (RKO, 1937), *Radio City Revels* (RKO, 1938), *Room Service* (RKO, 1938), *You Can't Take It With You* (Col., 1938), *Tarnished Angel* (RKO, 1938), *Having Wonderful Time* (RKO, 1938), *Too Many Girls* (RKO, 1940), *The Hit Parade of 1941* (Rep., 1940), *Melody Ranch* (Rep., 1940), *Time Out for Rhythm* (Col., 1941), *Go West, Young Lady* (Col., 1941), *True to the Army* (Par., 1942), *Priorities on Parade* (Par., 1942), *Reveille With Beverly* (Col., 1943),

What's Buzzin', Cousin? (Col., 1943), *Jam Session* (Col., 1944), *Hey, Rookie* (Col., 1944), *Carolina Blues* (Col., 1944), *Eve Knew Her Apples* (Col., 1945), *Eadie Was a Lady* (Col., 1945), *Thrill of Brazil* (Col., 1946), *The Kissing Bandit* (MGM, 1948), *Easter Parade* (MGM, 1948), *On the Town* (MGM, 1949), *Watch the Birdie* (MGM, 1950), *Texas Carnival* (MGM, 1951), *Two Tickets to Broadway* (RKO, 1951), *Lovely To Look At* (MGM, 1952), *Kiss Me, Kate!* (MGM, 1953), *Small Town Girl* (MGM, 1953), *Deep in My Heart* (MGM, 1954), *Hit the Deck* (MGM, 1955), *The Opposite Sex* (MGM, 1956), *The Great American Pastime* (MGM, 1956).

HAYLEY MILLS (Hayley Catherine Rose Vivian Mills) Born April 18, 1946, London, England.

John Mills and Hayley Mills in *The Chalk Garden.*

Feature Films: *Tiger Bay* (Continental, 1959), *Pollyanna* (BV, 1960), *The Parent Trap* (BV, 1961), *Whistle Down the Wind* (Pathé-American, 1962), *In Search of the Castaways* (BV, 1962), *Summer Magic* (BV, 1963), *The Chalk Garden* (Univ., 1964), *The Moonspinners* (BV, 1964), *The Truth About Spring* (Univ., 1965), *That Darn Cat* (BV, 1965), *The Trouble With Angels* (Col., 1966), *The Daydreamer* (voice only; Embassy, 1966), *The Family Way* (WB, 1966), *Gypsy Girl* (Continental, 1967), *Pretty Polly* (Univ., 1968), *A Matter of Innocence* (Univ., 1968).

SAL MINEO (Salvadore Mineo) Born January 10, 1939, Bronx, New York.

Dolores Del Rio and Sal Mineo in *Cheyenne Autumn.*

Feature Films: *Six Bridges to Cross* (Univ., 1955), *The Private War of Major Benson* (Univ., 1955), *Rebel Without a Cause* (WB, 1955), *Crime in the Streets* (AA, 1956), *Somebody Up There Likes Me* (MGM,

1956), *Giant* (WB, 1956), *Rock, Pretty Baby* (Univ., 1956), *Dino* (AA, 1957), *The Young Don't Cry* (Col., 1957), *Tonka* (BV, 1958), *A Private's Affair* (20th, 1959), *The Gene Krupa Story* (Col., 1959), *Exodus* (UA, 1960), *Escape From Zahrain* (Par., 1962), *The Longest Day* (20th, 1962), *Cheyenne Autumn* (WB, 1964), *The Greatest Story Ever Told* (UA, 1965), *Who Killed Teddy Bear?* (Magna, 1966), *East of Java* (Cinerama, 1968).

CARMEN MIRANDA (Maria Do Carmo Miranda Da Cunha) Born February 9, 1914, Lisbon, Portugal. Married David Sebastian (1947). Died August 5, 1955.

John Payne and Carmen Miranda in *Week-End in Havana.*

English-Language Feature Films: *Down Argentine Way* (20th, 1940), *That Night in Rio* (20th, 1941), *Week-End in Havana* (20th, 1941), *Springtime in the Rockies* (20th, 1942), *The Gang's All Here* (20th, 1943), *Four Jills in a Jeep* (20th, 1944), *Greenwich Village* (20th, 1944), *Something for the Boys* (20th, 1944), *Doll Face* (20th, 1945), *If I'm Lucky* (20th, 1946), *Copacabana* (UA, 1947), *A Date With Judy* (MGM, 1948), *Nancy Goes to Rio* (MGM, 1950), *Scared Stiff* (Par., 1953).

THOMAS MITCHELL Born July 11, 1892, Elizabeth, New Jersey. Married, child: Anne. Died December 17, 1962.

Sound Feature Films: *Adventures in Manhattan* (Col., 1936), *Craig's Wife* (Col., 1936), *Theodora Goes Wild* (Col., 1936), *When You're in Love* (Col., 1937), *Man of the People* (MGM, 1937), *Lost Horizon* (Col., 1937), *I Promise to Pay* (Col., 1937), *Make Way For Tomorrow* (Par., 1937), *The Hurricane* (UA, 1937), *Love, Honor and Behave* (WB, 1938), *Trade Winds* (UA, 1938), *Stagecoach* (UA, 1939), *Only Angels Have Wings* (Col., 1939), *Mr. Smith Goes to Washington* (Col., 1939), *The Hunchback of Notre Dame* (RKO, 1939), *Gone With the Wind* (MGM, 1939), *Swiss Family Robinson* (RKO, 1940), *Three Cheers for the Irish* (WB, 1940), *Our Town* (UA, 1940), *The Long Voyage Home* (UA, 1940), *Angels Over Broadway* (Col., 1940), *Flight From Destiny* (WB, 1941), *Out of the Fog* (WB, 1941), *Joan of Paris* (RKO, 1942), *Song of the Islands* (20th, 1942), *Moontide* (20th, 1942), *This Above All* (20th, 1942), *Tales of Manhattan* (20th, 1942), *The Black Swan* (20th, 1942), *The Immortal Sergeant* (20th, 1943), *The Outlaw* (RKO, 1943), *Bataan* (MGM, 1943), *Flesh and Fantasy* (Univ., 1943), *The Sullivans* (20th, 1944), *Buffalo Bill* (20th, 1944), *Wilson* (20th, 1944), *Dark Waters* (UA, 1944), *Keys of the Kingdom* (20th, 1945), *Within These Walls* (20th, 1945), *Captain Eddie* (20th, 1945), *Adventure* (MGM, 1945), *Three Wise Fools* (MGM, 1946), *The Dark Mirror* (Univ., 1946), *High Barbaree* (MGM, 1947), *The Romance of Rosy Ridge* (MGM, 1947), *Silver River* (WB, 1948), *Alias Nick Beal* (Par., 1949), *The Big Wheel* (UA, 1949), *Journey into*

Roy Roberts and Thomas Mitchell in *Within These Walls.*

Light (20th, 1951), *High Noon* (UA, 1952), *Tumbleweed* (Univ., 1953), *Secret of the Incas* (Par., 1954), *Destry* (Univ., 1954), *While the City Sleeps* (RKO, 1956), *Handle With Care* (MGM, 1958), *Too Young to Love* (Go Pictures, 1961), *By Love Possessed* (UA, 1961), *Pocketful of Miracles* (UA, 1961).

ROBERT MITCHUM Born August 6, 1917, Bridgeport, Connecticut. Married Dorothy Spence (1940), children: James, Christopher, Petrine.

Robert Mitchum and Jane Greer in *Out of the Past.*

Feature Films: *Hoppy Serves a Writ* (UA, 1943), *The Leather Burners* (UA, 1943), *Border Patrol* (UA, 1943), *Follow the Band* (Univ., 1943), *Colt Comrades* (UA, 1943), *The Human Comedy* (MGM, 1943), *We've Never Been Licked* (Wanger-Univ., 1943), *Beyond the Last Frontier* (Rep., 1943), *Bar 20* (UA, 1943), *Doughboys in Ireland* (Col., 1943), *Corvette K-225* (Univ., 1943), *Aerial Gunner* (Par., 1943), *The Lone Star Trail* (Univ., 1943), *False Colors* (UA, 1943), *Dancing Masters* (20th, 1943), *Riders of the Deadline* (UA, 1943), *Cry Havoc* (MGM, 1943), *Gung Ho!* (Univ., 1943), *Johnny Doesn't Live Here Any More* (Mon., 1944), *When Strangers Marry* (Mon., 1944), *The Girl Rush* (RKO, 1944), *Thirty Seconds Over Tokyo* (MGM, 1944), *Nevada* (RKO, 1944), *West of the Pecos* (RKO, 1945), *The Story of G.I. Joe* (UA, 1945), *Till the End of Time* (RKO, 1946), *Undercurrent* (MGM, 1946), *The Locket* (RKO, 1946), *Pursued* (WB, 1947), *Crossfire* (RKO, 1947), *Desire Me* (MGM, 1947), *Out of the Past* (RKO,

1947), *Rachel and the Stranger* (RKO, 1948), *Blood on the Moon* (RKO, 1948), *The Red Pony* (Rep., 1949), *The Big Steal* (RKO, 1949), *Holiday Affair* (RKO, 1949), *Where Danger Lives* (RKO, 1950), *My Forbidden Past* (RKO, 1951), *His Kind of Woman* (RKO, 1951), *The Racket* (RKO, 1951), *Macao* (RKO, 1952), *One Minute to Zero* (RKO, 1952), *The Lusty Men* (RKO, 1952), *Angel Face* (RKO, 1952), *White Witch Doctor* (20th, 1953), *Second Chance* (RKO, 1953), *She Couldn't Say No* (RKO, 1954), *River of No Return* (20th, 1954), *Track of the Cat* (WB, 1954), *Not as a Stranger* (UA, 1955), *The Night of the Hunter* (UA, 1955), *Man With the Gun* (UA, 1955), *Foreign Intrigue* (UA, 1956), *Bandido* (UA, 1956), *Heaven Knows, Mr. Allison* (20th, 1957), *Fire Down Below* (Col., 1957), *The Enemy Below* (20th, 1957), *Thunder Road* (UA, 1958), *The Hunters* (20th, 1958), *The Angry Hills* (MGM, 1959), *The Wonderful Country* (UA, 1959), *Home From the Hill* (MGM, 1960), *The Night Fighters* (UA, 1960), *The Grass Is Greener* (Univ., 1960), *The Sundowners* (WB, 1960), *The Last Time I Saw Archie* (UA, 1961), *Cape Fear* (Univ., 1962), *The Longest Day* (20th, 1962), *Two for the Seesaw* (UA, 1962), *The List of Adrian Messenger* (Univ., 1963), *Rampage* (WB, 1963), *Man in the Middle* (20th, 1964), *What a Way To Go!* (20th, 1964), *Mr. Moses* (UA, 1965), *El Dorado* (Par., 1967), *Anzio* (Col., 1968), *Villa Rides* (Par., 1968).

MARILYN MONROE (Norma Jean Mortenson) Born June 1, 1926, Los Angeles, California. Married James Dougherty (1944); divorced 1946. Married Joe Di Maggio (1954); divorced 1954. Married Arthur Miller (1956); divorced 1961. Died August 5, 1962.

Yves Montand and Marilyn Monroe in *Let's Make Love.*

Feature Films: *Dangerous Years* (20th, 1947), *Ladies of the Chorus* (Col., 1948), *Love Happy* (UA, 1949), *A Ticket to Tomahawk* (20th, 1950), *The Asphalt Jungle* (MGM, 1950), *All About Eve* (20th, 1950), *Right Cross* (MGM, 1950), *The Fireball* (20th, 1950), *Hometown Story* (MGM, 1951), *As Young as You Feel* (20th, 1951), *Love Nest* (20th, 1951), *Let's Make It Legal* (20th, 1951), *Clash by Night* (RKO, 1952), *We're Not Married* (20th, 1952), *Don't Bother to Knock* (20th, 1952), *Monkey Business* (20th, 1952), *O. Henry's Full House* (20th, 1952), *Niagara* (20th, 1953), *Gentlemen Prefer Blondes* (20th, 1953), *How to Marry a Millionaire* (20th, 1953), *River of No Return* (20th, 1954), *There's No Business Like Show Business* (20th, 1954), *The Seven-Year Itch* (20th, 1955), *Bus Stop* (20th, 1956), *The Prince and the Showgirl* (WB, 1957), *Some Like It Hot* (UA, 1959), *Let's Make Love* (20th, 1960), *The Misfits* (UA, 1961).

RICARDO MONTALBAN Born November 25, 1920, Mexico City, Mexico. Married Georgiana Young (1944), children: Laura, Mark, Anita, Victor.

English-Language Feature Films: *Fiesta* (MGM, 1947), *On an Island With You* (MGM, 1948), *The Kissing Bandit* (MGM, 1948), *Neptune's Daughter* (MGM, 1949), *Border Incident* (MGM, 1949), *Battleground* (MGM, 1949), *Mystery Street* (MGM, 1950), *Right Cross* (MGM,

Cyd Charisse, Ricardo Montalban and Ann Miller in *The Kissing Bandit*.

1950), *Two Weeks With Love* (MGM, 1950), *Mark of the Renegade* (Univ., 1951), *Across the Wide Missouri* (MGM, 1951), *My Man and I* (MGM, 1952), *Sombrero* (MGM, 1953), *Latin Lovers* (MGM, 1953), *The Saracen Blade* (Col., 1954), *A Life in the Balance* (20th, 1955), *Three for Jamie Dawn* (AA, 1956), *Sayonara* (WB, 1957), *Let No Man Write My Epitaph* (Col., 1960), *Hemingway's Adventures of a Young Man* (20th, 1962), *The Reluctant Saint* (Davis-Royal Films International, 1962), *Love Is a Ball* (UA, 1963), *Cheyenne Autumn* (WB, 1964), *The Money Trap* (MGM, 1966), *Madame X* (Univ., 1966), *The Singing Nun* (MGM, 1966), *Sol Madrid* (MGM, 1968), *Blue* (Par., 1968).

MARIA MONTEZ (Maria Africa Vidal de Santo Silas) Born June 6, 1920, Barahona, Dominican Republic. Married Jean Pierre Aumont (1943), child: Maria Christina. Died September 7, 1951.

English-Language Feature Films: *Lucky Devils* (Univ., 1941), *The Invisible Woman* (Univ., 1941), *Boss of Bullion City* (Univ., 1941), *That Night in Rio* (20th, 1941), *Raiders of the Desert* (Univ., 1941), *Moonlight in Hawaii* (Univ., 1941), *South of Tahiti* (Univ., 1941), *Bombay*

Broderick Crawford, Maria Montez and Brian Donlevy in *South of Tahiti*.

Clipper (Univ., 1942), *Mystery of Marie Roget* (Univ., 1942), *Arabian Nights* (Univ., 1943), *Ali Baba and the Forty Thieves* (Univ., 1944), *Follow the Boys* (Univ., 1944), *Cobra Woman* (Univ., 1944), *Gypsy Wildcat* (Univ., 1944), *Bowery to Broadway* (Univ., 1944), *Sudan* (Univ., 1945), *Tangier* (Univ., 1946), *The Exile* (Univ., 1947), *Pirates of Monterey* (Univ., 1947), *Siren of Atlantis* (UA, 1948), *The Thief of Venice* (20th, 1952).

ROBERT MONTGOMERY (Henry Montgomery, Jr.) Born May 21, 1904, Beacon, New York. Married Elizabeth Allan (1928), children: Robert, Elizabeth; divorced 1950. Married Elizabeth Harkness (1950).

Robert Montgomery and Edward Arnold in *Earl of Chicago*.

Sound Feature Films: *So This Is College* (MGM, 1929), *Untamed* (MGM, 1929), *Three Live Ghosts* (MGM, 1929), *Single Standard* (MGM, 1929), *Their Own Desire* (MGM, 1930), *Free and Easy* (MGM, 1930), *The Divorcee* (MGM, 1930), *Big House* (MGM, 1930), *Our Blushing Brides* (MGM, 1930), *Sins of the Children* ("Richest Man in the World"—MGM, 1930), *Love in the Rough* (MGM, 1930), *War Nurse* (MGM, 1930), *The Easiest Way* (MGM, 1931), *Strangers May Kiss* (MGM, 1931), *Inspiration* (MGM, 1931), *Shipmates* (MGM, 1931), *Man in Possession* (MGM, 1931), *Private Lives* (MGM, 1931), *Lovers Courageous* (MGM, 1932), *But the Flesh Is Weak* (MGM, 1932), *Letty Lynton* (MGM, 1932), *Blondie of the Follies* (MGM, 1932), *Faithless* (MGM, 1932), *Hell Below* (MGM, 1933), *Made on Broadway* (MGM, 1933), *When Ladies Meet* (MGM, 1933), *Night Flight* (MGM, 1933), *Another Language* (MGM, 1933), *Fugitive Lovers* (MGM, 1934), *Riptide* (MGM, 1934), *Mystery of Mr. X* (MGM, 1934), *Hideout* (MGM, 1934), *Forsaking All Others* (MGM, 1935), *Vanessa, Her Love Story* (MGM, 1935), *Biography of a Bachelor Girl* (MGM, 1935), *No More Ladies* (MGM, 1935), *Petticoat Fever* (MGM, 1936), *Trouble for Two* (MGM, 1936), *Piccadilly Jim* (MGM, 1936), *The Last of Mrs. Cheyney* (MGM, 1937), *Night Must Fall* (MGM, 1937), *Ever Since Eve* (WB, 1937), *Live, Love and Learn* (MGM, 1937), *The First Hundred Years* (MGM, 1938), *Yellow Jack* (MGM, 1938), *Three Loves Has Nancy* (MGM, 1938), *Fast and Loose* (MGM, 1939), *The Earl of Chicago* (MGM, 1940), *Haunted Honeymoon* (MGM, 1940), *Rage in Heaven* (MGM, 1941), *Mr. and Mrs. Smith* (RKO, 1941), *Here Comes Mr. Jordan* (Col., 1941), *Unfinished Business* (Univ., 1941), *They Were Expendable* (MGM, 1945), *Lady in the Lake* (MGM, 1946), *Ride the Pink Horse* (Univ., 1947), *The Saxon Charm* (Univ., 1948), *The Secret Land* (narrator; MGM, 1948), *June Bride* (WB, 1948), *Once More, My Darling* (Univ., 1949), *Eye Witness* (EL, 1950).

IDA MOORE Born 1883, Altoona, Kansas.

Feature Films: *The Ghost That Walks Alone* (Col., 1944), *She's a Soldier, Too* (Col., 1944), *Riders of the Santa Fe* (Univ., 1944), *The Uninvited* (Par., 1944), *The Soul of a Monster* (Col., 1944), *Once Upon*

Barry Fitzgerald and Ida Moore in *Easy Come, Easy Go*.

a Time (Col., 1944), *Reckless Age* (Univ., 1944), *Rough, Tough and Ready* (Col., 1945), *Easy to Look At* (Univ., 1945), *Her Lucky Night* (Univ., 1945), *She Wouldn't Say Yes* (Col., 1945), *Girls of the Big House* (Rep., 1945), *From This Day Forward* (RKO, 1946), *To Each His Own* (Par., 1946), *The Bride Wore Boots* (Par., 1946), *The Dark Mirror* (Univ., 1946), *Cross My Heart* (Par., 1946), *The Show-Off* (MGM, 1946), *Talk About a Lady* (Col., 1946), *It's a Joke, Son* (EL, 1947), *Easy Come, Easy Go* (Par., 1947), *The Egg and I* (Univ., 1947), *Money Madness* (Film Classics, 1948), *Johnny Belinda* (WB, 1948), *Rusty Leads the Way* (Col., 1948), *Good Sam* (RKO, 1948), *Return of the Bad Men* (RKO, 1948), *Ma and Pa Kettle* (Univ., 1949), *Hold That Baby* (Mon., 1949), *Manhattan Angel* (Col., 1949), *Leave It to Henry* (Mon., 1949), *Dear Wife* (Par., 1949), *Roseanna McCoy* (RKO, 1949), *Rope of Sand* (Par., 1949), *The Sun Comes Up* (MGM, 1949), *Let's Dance* (Par., 1950), *Paid in Full* (Par., 1950), *Backfire* (WB, 1950), *Mr. Music* (Par., 1950), *Fancy Pants* (Par., 1950), *Harvey* (Univ., 1950), *Mother Didn't Tell Me* (20th, 1950), *Honeychile* (Rep., 1951), *Double Dynamite* (RKO, 1951), *The Lemon Drop Kid* (Par., 1951), *Comin' 'Round the Mountain* (Univ., 1951), *Leave It to the Marines* (Lip., 1951), *Showboat* (MGM, 1951), *Scandal Sheet* (Col., 1952), *The First Time* (Col., 1952), *Rainbow 'Round My Shoulder* (Col., 1952), *Carson City* (WB, 1952), *Just This Once* (MGM, 1952), *Something to Live For* (Par., 1952), *A Slight Case of Larceny* (MGM, 1953), *Scandal at Scourie* (MGM, 1953), *The Country Girl* (Par., 1954), *The Long, Long Trailer* (MGM, 1954), *Ma and Pa Kettle at Waikiki* (Univ., 1955), *Desk Set* (20th, 1957), *Rock-a-Bye Baby* (Par., 1958).

TERRY MOORE (Helen Koford) Born January 7, 1929, Los Angeles, California. Married Glenn Davis (1951); divorced 1952. Married Eugene McGrath (1956); divorced 1958. Married Stuart Cramer (1959), children: Stuart, Grant.

Feature Films:

as Helen Koford *Maryland* (20th, 1940), *The Howards of Virginia* (Col., 1940), *On the Sunny Side* (20th, 1942), *Sweet and Lowdown* (20th,

Terry Moore, Mickey Rooney and Ned Glass in *He's a Cockeyed Wonder*.

1944), *Since You Went Away* (UA, 1944), *Son of Lassie* (MGM, 1945), *Shadowed* (Col., 1946), *Summer Holiday* (MGM, 1948).

as Judy Ford *My Gal Sal* (20th, 1942), *True to Life* (Par., 1943), *Gaslight* (MGM, 1944).

as Jan Ford *The Devil on Wheels* (PRC, 1947).

as Terry Moore *The Return of October* (Col., 1948), *Mighty Joe Young* (RKO, 1949), *The Great Rupert* (EL, 1950), *He's a Cockeyed Wonder* (Col., 1950), *Gambling House* (RKO, 1950), *Two of a Kind* (Col., 1951), *On the Sunny Side of the Street* (Col., 1951), *The Barefoot Mailman* (Col., 1951), *Come Back, Little Sheba* (Par., 1952), *Man on a Tightrope* (20th, 1953), *Beneath the 12-Mile Reef* (20th, 1953), *King of the Khyber Rifles* (20th, 1953), *Daddy Long Legs* (20th, 1955), *Shack-Out on 101* (AA, 1955), *Postmark for Danger* (RKO, 1956), *Between Heaven and Hell* (20th, 1956), *Bernardine* (20th, 1957), *Peyton Place* (20th, 1957), *A Private Affair* (20th, 1959), *Cast a Long Shadow* (UA, 1959), *Platinum High School* (MGM, 1960), *Why Must I Die?* (AIP, 1960), *Black Spurs* (Par., 1965), *Town Tamer* (Par., 1965), *City of Fear* (AA, 1965), *Waco* (Par., 1966), *A Man Called Dagger* (MGM, 1968).

AGNES MOOREHEAD (Agnes Robertson Moorehead) Born December 6, 1906, Clinton, Massachusetts. Married John Lee (1930), child: Sean; divorced 1952. Married Robert Gist (1953); divorced 1958.

Eleanor Parker and Agnes Moorehead in *Caged*.

Feature Films: *Citizen Kane* (RKO, 1941), *The Magnificent Ambersons* (RKO, 1942), *Journey into Fear* (RKO, 1942), *The Big Street* (RKO, 1942), *The Youngest Profession* (MGM, 1943), *Government Girl* (RKO, 1943), *Jane Eyre* (20th, 1944), *Since You Went Away* (UA, 1944), *Dragon Seed* (MGM, 1944), *The Seventh Cross* (MGM, 1944), *Mrs. Parkington* (MGM, 1944), *Tomorrow the World* (UA, 1944), *Keep Your Powder Dry* (MGM, 1945), *Our Vines Have Tender Grapes* (MGM, 1945), *Her Highness and the Bellboy* (MGM, 1945), *The Beginning or the End* (MGM, 1947) (Her scenes were deleted from release print.), *Dark Passage* (WB, 1947), *The Lost Moment* (Univ., 1947), *Summer Holiday* (MGM, 1948), *The Woman in White* (WB, 1948), *Stations West* (RKO, 1948), *Johnny Belinda* (WB, 1948), *The Stratton Story* (MGM, 1949), *The Great Sinner* (MGM, 1949), *Without Honor* (UA, 1949), *Caged* (WB, 1950), *Fourteen Hours* (20th, 1951), *Show Boat* (MGM, 1951), *The Blue Veil* (RKO, 1951), *The Adventures of Captain Fabian* (Rep., 1951), *Captain Black Jack* (Classic, 1952), *The Blazing Forest* (Par., 1952), *The Story of Three Loves* (MGM, 1953), *Scandal at Scourie* (MGM, 1953), *Main Street to Broadway* (MGM, 1953), *Those Redheads From Seattle* (Par., 1953), *Magnificent Obsession* (Univ., 1954), *Untamed* (20th, 1955), *The Left Hand of God* (20th, 1955), *All That Heaven Allows* (Univ., 1956), *Meet Me in Las Vegas* (MGM, 1956), *The Conqueror* (RKO, 1956), *The Revolt of Mamie Stover* (20th, 1956), *The Swan* (MGM, 1956), *Pardners* (Par., 1956), *The Opposite Sex* (MGM, 1956), *Raintree County* (MGM, 1957), *The True Story of Jesse James* (20th, 1957), *Jeanne Eagles* (Col., 1957), *The Story of Mankind* (WB, 1957), *Night of the Quarter Moon* (MGM, 1959), *The Tempest* (Par., 1959), *The Bat* (AA, 1959), *Pollyanna* (BV, 1960), *Twenty Plus Two* (AA, 1961), *Bachelor in Paradise* (MGM,

1961), *Jessica* (UA, 1962), *How the West Was Won* (MGM, 1963), *Who's Minding the Store?* (Par., 1963), *Hush . . . Hush, Sweet Charlotte* (20th, 1964), *The Singing Nun* (MGM, 1966).

MANTAN MORELAND

Louis Armstrong, Rex Ingram and Mantan Moreland in *Cabin in the Sky.*

Feature Films: *Spirit of Youth* (GN, 1937), *Next Time I Marry* (RKO, 1938), *Frontier Scout* (GN, 1938), *There's That Woman Again* (Col., 1938) *Irish Luck* (Mon., 1939), *Tell No Tales* (MGM, 1939), *One Dark Night* (Sack Amusements, 1939), *Riders of the Frontier* (Mon., 1939), *Millionaire Playboy* (RKO, 1940), *Chasing Trouble* (Mon., 1940), *Pier 13* (20th, 1940), *The City of Chance* (20th, 1940), *The Man Who Wouldn't Talk* (20th, 1940), *Star Dust* (20th, 1940), *Maryland* (20th, 1940), *Viva Cisco Kid* (20th, 1940), *On the Spot* (Mon., 1940), *Laughing at Danger* (Mon., 1940), *Drums of the Desert* (Mon., 1940), *Ellery Queen's Penthouse Mystery* (Col., 1941), *Cracked Nuts* (Univ., 1941), *Up in the Air* (Mon., 1941), *King of the Zombies* (Mon., 1941), *The Gang's All Here* (Mon., 1941), *Hello Sucker* (Univ., 1941), *Dressed to Kill* (20th, 1941), *Four Jacks and a Jill* (RKO, 1941), *Footlight Fever* (RKO, 1941), *You're Out of Luck* (Mon., 1941), *Sign of the Wolf* (Mon., 1941), *Let's Go Collegiate* (Mon., 1941), *Sleepers West* (20th, 1941), *Marry the Boss's Daughter* (20th, 1941), *World Premiere* (Par., 1941), *Professor Creeps* (Dixie National, 1942), *Andy Hardy's Double Life* (MGM, 1942), *Strange Case of Dr. RX* (Univ., 1942), *Treat 'Em Rough* (Univ., 1942), *Mexican Spitfire Sees a Ghost* (RKO, 1942), *The Palm Beach Story* (Par., 1942), *Footlight Serenade* (20th, 1942), *Phantom Killer* (Mon., 1942), *Eyes in the Night* (MGM, 1942), *Girl Trouble* (20th, 1942), *Tarzan's New York Adventure* (MGM, 1942), *Hit the Ice* (Univ., 1943), *Cabin in the Sky* (MGM, 1943), *Cosmo Jones—Crime Smasher* (Mon., 1943), *Sarong Girl* (Mon., 1943), *Revenge of the Zombies* (Mon., 1943), *Melody Parade* (Mon., 1943), *She's for Me* (Univ., 1943), *My Kingdom for a Cook* (Col., 1943), *Slightly Dangerous* (MGM, 1943), *Swing Fever* (MGM, 1943), *You're a Lucky Fellow, Mr. Smith* (Univ., 1943), *We've Never Been Licked* (Univ., 1943), *This Is the Life* (Univ., 1944), *The Mystery of the River Boat* (Univ. serial, 1944), *The Chinese Cat* (Mon., 1944), *Moon Over Las Vegas* (Univ., 1944), *Chip off the Old Block* (Univ., 1944), *Pin-Up Girl* (20th, 1944), *South of Dixie* (Univ., 1944), *Black Magic* (Mon., 1944), *Bowery to Broadway* (Univ., 1944), *Charlie Chan in the Secret Service* (Mon., 1944), *See Here, Private Hargrove* (MGM, 1944), *She Wouldn't Say Yes* (Col., 1945), *The Scarlet Clue* (Mon., 1945), *The Jade Mask* (Mon., 1945), *The Shanghai Cobra* (Mon., 1945), *The Spider* (20th, 1945), *Captain Tugboat Annie* (Rep., 1945), *Mantan Messes Up* (Toddy Pictures, 1946), *Mantan Runs For Mayor* (Toddy Pictures, 1946), *Dark Alibi* (Mon., 1946), *Shadows Over Chinatown* (Mon., 1946), *The Trap* (Mon., 1947), *The Chinese Ring* (Mon., 1947), *Docks of New Orleans* (Mon., 1948), *The Mystery of the Golden Eye*

(Mon., 1948), *The Feathered Serpent* (Mon., 1948), *The Shanghai Chest* (Mon., 1948), *Best Man Wins* (Col., 1948), *Sky Dragon* (Mon., 1949), *Rockin' the Blues* (Fritz Pollard Assoc., 1956), *Rock 'n' Roll Revue* (Studio Films, 1956), *Rock 'n' Roll Jamboree* (Studio Films, 1957), *Enter Laughing* (Col., 1967).

RITA MORENO (Rosita Dolores Alverio) Born December 11, 1931, Humacao, Puerto Rico. Married Leonard Gordon (1965), child: Fernanda.

J. Carroll Naish, Mario Lanza and Rita Moreno in *Toast of New Orleans.*

Feature Films:
    as Rosita Moreno *So Young, So Bad* (UA, 1950).
    as Rita Moreno *Toast of New Orleans* (MGM, 1950), *Pagan Love Song* (MGM, 1950), *The Fabulous Señorita* (Rep., 1952), *Singin' in the Rain* (MGM, 1952), *The Ring* (UA, 1952), *Cattle Town* (WB, 1952), *Ma and Pa Kettle on Vacation* (Univ., 1953), *Latin Lovers* (MGM, 1953), *Fort Vengeance* (AA, 1953), *El Alamein* (Col., 1953), *Jivaro* (Par., 1954), *The Yellow Tomahawk* (UA, 1954), *Garden of Evil* (20th, 1954), *Untamed* (20th, 1955), *Seven Cities of Gold* (20th, 1955), *The Lieutenant Wore Skirts* (20th, 1956), *The King and I* (MGM, 1956), *The Vagabond King* (Par., 1956), *The Deerslayer* (20th, 1957), *This Rebel Breed* (WB, 1960), *Summer and Smoke* (Par., 1961), *West Side Story* (UA, 1961), *Samar* (WB, 1962), *Cry of Battle* (AA, 1963), *The Night of the Following Day* (Univ., 1968).

DENNIS MORGAN (Stanley Morner) Born December 30, 1910, Prentice, Wisconsin. Married Lillian Vedder (1933), children: Stanley, Kristine, James.

Alan Hale, Jr., Don De Fore, Dennis Morgan and Ben Blue in *One Sunday Afternoon.*

Feature Films:

    as Stanley Morner *I Conquer the Sea* (Academy Pictures, 1936), *Suzy* (MGM, 1936), *The Great Ziegfeld* (MGM, 1936), *Piccadilly Jim* (MGM, 1936), *Down the Stretch* (WB, 1936), *Old Hutch* (MGM, 1936), *Song of the City* (MGM, 1937), *Mama Steps Out* (MGM, 1937), *Navy Blue and Gold* (MGM, 1937), *Persons in Hiding* (Par., 1938), *Men With Wings* (Par., 1938), *King of Alcatraz* (Par., 1938).

    as Dennis Morgan *Waterfront* (WB, 1939), *Return of Dr. X* (WB, 1939), *No Place to Go* (WB, 1939), *Three Cheers for the Irish* (WB, 1940), *The Fighting 69th* (WB, 1940), *Tear Gas Squad* (WB, 1940), *Flight Angels* (WB, 1940), *River's End* (WB, 1940), *Kitty Foyle* (RKO, 1940), *Affectionately Yours* (WB, 1941), *Bad Men of Missouri* (WB, 1941), *Captains of the Clouds* (WB, 1942), *In This Our Life* (WB, 1942), *Wings for the Eagle* (WB, 1942), *The Hard Way* (WB, 1942), *Thank Your Lucky Stars* (WB, 1943), *The Desert Song* (WB, 1943), *The Very Thought of You* (WB, 1944), *Hollywood Canteen* (WB, 1944), *Shine on Harvest Moon* (WB, 1944), *God Is My Co-Pilot* (WB, 1945), *Christmas in Connecticut* (WB, 1945), *One More Tomorrow* (WB, 1946), *Two Guys From Milwaukee* (WB, 1946), *The Time, the Place and the Girl* (WB, 1946), *Cheyenne* (WB, 1947), *My Wild Irish Rose* (WB, 1947), *Always Together* (WB, 1947),* *To the Victor* (WB, 1948), *Two Guys From Texas* (WB, 1948), *One Sunday Afternoon* (WB, 1948), *It's a Great Feeling* (WB, 1949), *The Lady Takes a Sailor* (WB, 1949), *Perfect Strangers* (WB, 1950), *Pretty Baby* (WB, 1950), *Raton Pass* (WB, 1951), *Painting the Clouds With Sunshine* (WB, 1951), *This Woman Is Dangerous* (WB, 1952), *Cattle Town* (WB, 1952), *The Nebraskan* (Col., 1953), *Pearl of the South Pacific* (RKO, 1955), *The Gun That Won the West* (Col., 1955), *Uranium Boom* (Col., 1956), *Rogue's Gallery* (Par., 1968).

    *Unbilled guest appearance

FRANK MORGAN (Francis Philip Wuppermann) Born June 1, 1890, New York, New York. Married Alma Muller (1914). Died September 18, 1949.

Billie Burke, Cora Witherspoon and Frank Morgan in *Piccadilly Jim.*

Sound Feature Films: *Queen High* (Par., 1930), *Dangerous Nan McGrew* (Par., 1930), *Fast and Loose* (Par., 1930), *Laughter* (Par., 1930), *Secrets of the French Police* (RKO, 1932), *The Half-Naked Truth* (RKO, 1932), *Hallelujah, I'm a Bum* (UA, 1933), *Luxury Liner* (Par., 1933), *Billion Dollar Scandal* (Par., 1933), *Sailor's Luck* (Fox, 1933), *Reunion in Vienna* (MGM, 1933), *When Ladies Meet* (MGM, 1933), *Kiss Before the Mirror* (Univ., 1933), *The Nuisance* (MGM, 1933), *Best of Enemies* (Fox, 1933), *Broadway to Hollywood* (MGM, 1933), *Bombshell* (MGM, 1933), *The Cat and the Fiddle* (MGM, 1933), *Sisters Under the Skin* (Col., 1934), *Affairs of Cellini* (UA, 1934), *Success at Any Price* (RKO, 1934), *A Lost Lady* (WB, 1934), *There's Always Tomorrow* (Univ., 1934), *Naughty Marietta* (MGM, 1935), *Good Fairy* (Univ., 1935), *Enchanted April* (RKO, 1935), *Escapade* (MGM, 1935), *The Perfect Gentleman* (MGM, 1935), *I Live My Life*

(MGM, 1935), *The Great Ziegfeld* (MGM, 1936), *The Dancing Pirate* (RKO, 1936), *Trouble for Two* (MGM, 1936), *Piccadilly Jim* (MGM, 1936), *Dimples* (20th, 1936), *The Last of Mrs. Cheyney* (MGM, 1937), *The Emperor's Candlesticks* (MGM, 1937), *Saratoga* (MGM, 1937), *Beg, Borrow or Steal* (MGM, 1937), *Rosalie* (MGM, 1937), *Paradise for Three* (MGM, 1938), *The Crowd Roars* (MGM, 1938), *Port of Seven Seas* (MGM, 1938), *Sweethearts* (MGM, 1938), *Broadway Serenade* (MGM, 1939), *The Wizard of Oz* (MGM, 1939), *Balalaika* (MGM, 1939), *The Shop Around the Corner* (MGM, 1940), *Broadway Melody of 1940* (MGM, 1940), *Henry Goes Arizona* (MGM, 1940), *The Mortal Storm* (MGM, 1940), *Boom Town* (MGM, 1940), *Hullabaloo* (MGM, 1940), *The Ghost Comes Home* (MGM, 1940), *Honky Tonk* (MGM, 1941), *The Vanishing Virginian* (MGM, 1941), *Washington Melodrama* (MGM, 1941), *Wild Man of Borneo* (MGM, 1941), *Tortilla Flat* (MGM, 1942), *White Cargo* (MGM, 1942), *A Stranger in Town* (MGM, 1943), *The Human Comedy* (MGM, 1943), *Thousands Cheer* (MGM, 1943), *The Miracle of Morgan's Creek* (Par., 1944), *The White Cliffs of Dover* (MGM, 1944), *Hail the Conquering Hero* (Par., 1944), *Casanova Brown* (RKO, 1944), *Yolanda and the Thief* (MGM, 1945), *Pardon My Past* (Col., 1946), *Courage of Lassie* (MGM, 1946), *Lady Luck* (RKO, 1946), *The Cockeyed Miracle* (MGM, 1946), *Green Dolphin Street* (MGM, 1947), *Summer Holiday* (MGM, 1948), *The Three Musketeers* (MGM, 1948), *The Stratton Story* (MGM, 1949), *Any Number Can Play* (MGM, 1949), *The Great Sinner* (MGM, 1949), *Key to the City* (MGM, 1950).

RALPH MORGAN (Raphael Kuhner Wuppermann) Born July 6, 1883, New York, New York. Married Grace Arnold, child: Claudia; widowed. Died June 11, 1956.

Patricia Morison, Alan Curtin and Ralph Morgan in *Hitler's Madman.*

Sound Feature Films: *Honor Among Lovers* (Par., 1931), *Cheaters at Play* (Fox, 1932), *Charlie Chan's Chance* (Fox, 1932), *Dance Team* (Fox, 1932), *Disorderly Conduct* (Fox, 1932), *Devil's Lottery* (Fox, 1932), *Strange Interlude* (MGM, 1932), *Rasputin and the Empress* (MGM, 1932), *The Son-Daughter* (MGM, 1932), *Humanity* (Fox, 1933), *Trick for Trick* (Fox, 1933), *Shanghai Madness* (Fox, 1933), *Power and the Glory* (Fox, 1933), *Doctor Bull* (Fox, 1933), *Walls of Gold* (Fox, 1933), *Kennel Murder Case* (WB, 1933), *Mad Game* (Fox, 1933), *Orient Express* (Fox, 1934), *No Greater Glory* (Col., 1934), *Stand Up and Cheer* (Fox, 1934), *She Was a Lady* (Fox, 1934), *Their Big Moment* (RKO, 1934), *Girl of the Limberlost* (Mon., 1934), *Hell in the Heavens* (Fox, 1934), *Transatlantic Merry-Go-Round* (UA, 1934), *Little Men* (Mascot, 1934), *I've Been Around* (Univ., 1935), *Unwelcome Stranger* (Col., 1935), *Star of Midnight* (RKO, 1935), *Calm Yourself* (MGM, 1935), *Condemned to Live* (Chesterfield, 1935), *The Magnificent Obsession* (Univ., 1935), *Muss 'Em Up* (RKO, 1936), *Little Miss Nobody* (20th, 1936), *Human Cargo* (20th, 1936), *The Ex-Mrs. Bradford* (RKO, 1936), *Anthony Adverse* (WB, 1936), *Speed* (MGM, 1936), *Yellowstone* (Univ., 1936), *General Spanky* (MGM, 1936), *Crack-Up* (20th, 1936), *The Man in Blue* (Univ., 1937), *The Life of Emile Zola* (WB, 1937), *Behind Prison*

Bars (Mon., 1937), *Mannequin* (MGM, 1937), *Wells Fargo* (Par., 1937), *Love Is a Headache* (MGM, 1938), *That's My Story* (Univ., 1938), *Wives Under Suspicion* (Univ., 1938), *Army Girl* (Rep., 1938), *Mother Carey's Chickens* (RKO, 1938), *Barefoot Boy* (Mon., 1938), *Shadows Over Shanghai* (GN, 1938), *Orphans of the Street* (Rep., 1938), *Out West With the Hardys* (MGM, 1938), *Trapped in the Sky* (Col., 1939), *Fast and Loose* (MGM, 1939), *The Lone Wolf Spy Hunt* (Col., 1939), *Man of Conquest* (Rep., 1939), *Smuggled Cargo* (Rep., 1939), *Way Down South* (RKO, 1939), *Geronimo* (Par., 1939), *Forty Little Mothers* (RKO, 1940), *I'm Still Alive* (RKO, 1940), *Dick Tracy vs. Crime Inc.*, (Rep. serial, 1941), *Adventure in Washington* (Col., 1941), *Gang Busters* (Univ. serial, 1942), *The Mad Doctor* (Par., 1941), *Klondike Fury* (Mon., 1942), *Night Monster* (Univ., 1942), *The Traitor Within* (Rep., 1942), *Stage Door Canteen* (UA, 1943), *Hitler's Madman* (MGM, 1943), *Jack London* (UA, 1943), *Great Alaskan Mystery* (Univ. serial, 1944), *Weird Woman* (Univ., 1944), *Trocadero* (Rep., 1944), *Enemy of Women* (Mon., 1944), *The Impostor* (Univ., 1944), *The Monster Maker* (PRC, 1944), *The Monster and the Ape* (Col. serial, 1945), *This Love of Ours* (Univ., 1945), *Black Market Babies* (Mon., 1945), *Hollywood and Vine* (PRC, 1945), *Mr. District Attorney* (Col., 1947), *Song of the Thin Man* (MGM, 1947), *The Last Round-Up* (Col., 1947), *Sleep, My Love* (UA, 1948), *Sword of the Avenger* (EL, 1948), *Heart of the Rockies* (Rep., 1951), *Gold Fever* (Mon., 1952).

CHESTER MORRIS (John Chester Brooks Morris) Born February 16, 1901, New York, New York. Married Suzanne Kilborn (1927), children: Brooks, Cynthia; divorced 1938. Married Lillian Barker (1940).

Claire Rochelle and Chester Morris (right) in *Double Exposure*.

Sound Feature Films: *Alibi* (Univ., 1929), *Fast Life* (WB, 1929), *Woman Trap* (Par., 1929), *Show of Shows* (WB, 1929), *She Couldn't Say No* (WB, 1930), *Second Choice* (WB, 1930), *The Case of Sergeant Grischa* (RKO, 1930), *Playing Around* (WB, 1930), *The Divorcee* (MGM, 1930), *Big House* (MGM, 1930), *Bat Whispers* (UA, 1931), *Corsair* (UA, 1931), *The Miracle Man* (Par., 1932), *Cock of the Air* (UA, 1932), *Sinners in the Sun* (Par., 1932), *Red-Headed Woman* (MGM, 1932), *Breach of Promise* (Sono Art-World Wide, 1932), *Infernal Machine* (Fox, 1933), *Blondie Johnson* (WB, 1933), *Tomorrow at Seven* (RKO, 1933), *Golden Harvest* (Par., 1933), *King for a Night* (Univ., 1933), *Let's Talk it Over* (Univ., 1934), *Embarrassing Moments* (Univ., 1934), *The Gift of Gab* (Univ., 1934), *Gay Bride* (MGM, 1934), *I've Been Around* (Univ., 1935), *Public Hero Number One* (MGM, 1935), *Frankie and Johnnie* (RKO, 1935), *Society Doctor* (MGM, 1935), *Pursuit* (MGM, 1935), *Moonlight Murder* (MGM, 1936), *The Three Godfathers* (MGM, 1936), *Counterfeit* (Col., 1936), *They Met in a Taxi* (Col., 1936), *Devil's Playground* (Col., 1937), *I Promise to Pay* (Col., 1937), *Flight From Glory* (RKO, 1937), *Law of the Underworld* (RKO, 1938), *Sky Giant* (RKO, 1938), *Smashing the Rackets* (RKO, 1938), *Pacific Liner* (RKO, 1939), *Blind Alibi* (Col., 1939), *Five Came Back* (RKO, 1939), *Thunder*

Afloat (MGM, 1939), *The Marines Fly High* (RKO, 1940), *Wagons Westward* (Rep., 1940), *Girl From God's Country* (Rep., 1940), *No Hands on the Clock* (Par., 1941), *Confessions of Boston Blackie* (Col., 1941), *Meet Boston Blackie* (Col., 1941), *I Live on Danger* (Par., 1942), *Wrecking Crew* (Par., 1942), *Tornado* (Par., 1943), *The Chance of a Lifetime* (Col., 1943), *Aerial Gunner* (Par., 1943), *After Midnight With Boston Blackie* (Col., 1943), *High Explosive* (Par., 1943), *Gambler's Choice* (Par., 1944), *Secret Command* (Col., 1944), *One Mysterious Night* (Col., 1944), *Double Exposure* (Par., 1944), *Rough, Tough and Ready* (Col., 1945), *Boston Blackie Booked on Suspicion* (Col., 1945), *Boston Blackie's Rendezvous* (Col., 1945), *One Way to Love* (Col., 1946), *A Close Call for Boston Blackie* (Col., 1946), *The Phantom Thief* (Col., 1946), *Boston Blackie and the Law* (Col., 1946), *Blind Spot* (Col., 1947), *Trapped By Boston Blackie* (Col., 1948), *Boston Blackie's Chinese Venture* (Col., 1949), *Unchained* (WB, 1955).

WAYNE MORRIS (Bert de Wayne Morris) Born February 17, 1914, Oakland, California. Married Leonora Schinasi (1939), children: Bert, Patricia, Melinda; divorced 1940. Married Patricia O'Rourke (1942). Died September 14, 1959.

Ed Brophy, May Robson, Pat O'Brien, Joan Blondell and Wayne Morris in *The Kid From Kokomo*.

Feature Films: *China Clipper* (WB, 1936), *Here Comes Carter!* (WB, 1936), *King of Hockey* (WB, 1936), *Polo Joe* (WB, 1936), *Smart Blonde* (WB, 1936), *Once a Doctor* (WB, 1937), *Kid Galahad* (WB, 1937), *Submarine D-1* (WB, 1937), *Love, Honor and Behave* (WB, 1938), *The Kid Comes Back* (WB, 1938), *Men Are Such Fools* (WB, 1938), *Valley of the Giants* (WB, 1938), *Brother Rat* (WB, 1938), *The Kid From Kokomo* (WB, 1939), *The Return of Dr. X* (WB, 1939), *Brother Rat and a Baby* (WB, 1940), *Double Alibi* (WB, 1940), *An Angel From Texas* (WB, 1940), *Flight Angels* (WB, 1940), *Ladies Must Live* (WB, 1940), *The Quarterback* (Par., 1940), *Gambling on the High Seas* (WB, 1940), *Three Sons o' Guns* (WB, 1941), *I Wanted Wings* (Par., 1941), *Bad Men of Missouri* (WB, 1941), *The Smiling Ghost* (WB, 1941), *Deep Valley* (WB, 1947), *The Voice of the Turtle* (WB, 1947), *The Big Punch* (WB, 1948), *The Time of Your Life* (UA, 1948), *A Kiss in the Dark* (WB, 1949), *The Younger Brothers* (WB, 1949), *John Loves Mary* (WB, 1949), *The House Across the Street* (WB, 1949), *Task Force* (WB, 1949), *Johnny One-Eye* (UA, 1950), *The Tougher They Come* (Col., 1950), *Stage to Tucson* (Col., 1950), *Sierra Passage* (Mon., 1951), *The Big Gusher* (Col., 1951), *Yellow Fin* (Mon., 1951), *The Bushwhackers* (Realart, 1952), *Desert Pursuit* (Mon., 1952), *Arctic Flight* (Mon., 1952), *The Fighting Lawman* (AA, 1953), *The Marksman* (AA, 1953), *The Star of Texas* (AA, 1953), *Master Plan* (Astor, 1954), *Riding Shotgun* (WB, 1954), *The Desperado* (AA, 1954), *Two Guns and a Badge* (AA, 1954), *Port of Hell* (AA, 1954), *Lord of the Jungle* (AA, 1955), *The Green Buddha* (Rep., 1955), *Cross Channel* (Rep., 1955), *Lonesome Trail* (Lip., 1955), *Dynamiters* (Astor, 1956), *Paths of Glory* (UA, 1957), *Plunder Road* (20th, 1957), *The Crooked Sky* (Rank, 1959).

Paul Muni and John Sutton in *Hudson's Bay*.

PAUL MUNI (Muni Weisenfreund) Born September 22, 1895, Lwow (Lemberg) Poland. Married Bella Finkel (1921). Died August 25, 1967.

Feature Films: *The Valiant* (Fox, 1929), *Seven Faces* (Fox, 1929), *Scarface* (UA, 1932), *I Am a Fugitive From a Chain Gang* (WB, 1932), *The World Changes* (WB, 1933), *Hi Nellie* (WB, 1934), *Bordertown* (WB, 1935), *Black Fury* (WB, 1935), *Dr. Socrates* (WB, 1935), *The Story of Louis Pasteur* (WB, 1935), *The Good Earth* (MGM, 1937), *The Woman I Love* (RKO, 1937), *The Life of Emile Zola* (WB, 1937), *Juarez* (WB, 1939), *We Are Not Alone* (WB, 1939), *Hudson's Bay* (20th, 1940), *Commandos Strike at Dawn* (Col., 1942), *Stage Door Canteen* (UA, 1943), *A Song to Remember* (Col., 1945), *Counter-Attack* (Col., 1945), *Angel on My Shoulder* (UA, 1946), *Stranger on the Prowl* (UA, 1953), *The Last Angry Man* (Col., 1959).

AUDIE MURPHY Born June 20, 1924, Kingston, Texas. Married Wanda Hendrix (1949); divorced 1950. Married Pamela Archer (1951), children: Terry, James.

Hugh Corcoran and Audie Murphy in *No Name on the Bullet*.

Feature Films: *Beyond Glory* (Par., 1948), *Texas, Brooklyn and Heaven* (UA, 1948), *Bad Boy* (AA, 1949), *Sierra* (Univ., 1950), *The Kid From Texas* (Univ., 1950), *Kansas Raiders* (Univ., 1950), *The Red Badge of Courage* (MGM, 1951), *The Cimarron Kid* (Univ., 1951), *The Duel at Silver Creek* (Univ., 1952), *Gunsmoke* (Univ., 1953), *Column South* (Univ., 1953), *Tumbleweed* (Univ., 1953), *Ride Clear of Diablo* (Univ., 1954), *Drums Across the River* (Univ., 1954), *Destry* (Univ., 1954), *To Hell and Back* (Univ., 1955), *World in My Corner* (Univ., 1956), *Walk the Proud Land* (Univ., 1956), *The Guns of Fort Petticoat* (Col., 1957), *Joe Butterfly* (Univ., 1957), *Night Passage* (Univ., 1957), *The Quiet American* (UA, 1958), *Ride a Crooked Trail* (Univ., 1958), *The Gun Runners* (UA, 1958), *No Name on the Bullet* (Univ., 1959),

The Wild and the Innocent (Univ., 1959), *Cast a Long Shadow* (UA, 1959), *Hell Bent for Leather* (Univ., 1960), *The Unforgiven* (UA, 1960), *Seven Ways From Sundown* (Univ., 1960), *Posse From Hell* (Univ., 1961), *Battle at Bloody Beach* (20th, 1961), *Six Black Horses* (Univ., 1962), *Showdown* (Univ., 1963), *Gunfight at Comanche Creek* (AA, 1963), *The Quick Gun* (Col., 1964), *Bullet for a Badman* (Univ., 1964), *Apache Rifles* (20th, 1964), *Arizona Raiders* (Col., 1965), *Gunpoint* (Univ., 1966), *Trunk to Cairo* (AIP, 1966), *The Texican* (Col., 1966), *40 Guns to Apache Pass* (Col., 1967).

GEORGE MURPHY (George Lloyd Murphy) Born July 4, 1902, New Haven, Connecticut. Married Julie Johnson (1926), children: Dennis, Melissa.

Joan Davis, Eddie Cantor, Constance and George Murphy in *Show Business*.

Feature Films: *Kid Millions* (UA, 1934), *Jealousy* (Col., 1934), *I'll Love You Always* (Col., 1935), *After the Dance* (Col., 1935), *Public Menace* (Col., 1935), *Woman Trap* (Par., 1936), *Top of the Town* (Univ., 1937), *Women Men Marry* (MGM, 1937), *London by Night* (MGM, 1937), *Broadway Melody of 1938* (MGM, 1937), *You're a Sweetheart* (Univ., 1937), *Little Miss Broadway* (20th, 1938), *Letter of Introduction* (Univ., 1938), *Hold That Co-ed* (Univ., 1938), *Risky Business* (Univ., 1939), *Broadway Melody of 1940* (MGM, 1940), *Two Girls on Broadway* (MGM, 1940), *Public Deb No. 1* (20th, 1940), *Little Nellie Kelly* (MGM, 1940), *A Girl, a Guy, and a Gob* (RKO, 1941), *Tom, Dick and Harry* (RKO, 1941), *Ringside Maisie* (MGM, 1941), *Rise and Shine* (20th, 1941), *The Mayor of 44th Street* (RKO, 1942), *For Me and My Gal* (MGM, 1942), *The Navy Comes Through* (RKO, 1942), *The Powers Girl* (UA, 1942), *Bataan* (MGM, 1943), *This Is the Army* (WB, 1943), *Broadway Rhythm* (MGM, 1944), *Show Business* (RKO, 1944), *Step Lively* (RKO, 1944), *Having Wonderful Crime* (RKO, 1945), *Up Goes Maisie* (MGM, 1946), *The Arnelo Affair* (MGM, 1947), *Cynthia* (MGM, 1947), *Tenth Avenue Angel* (MGM, 1948), *The Big City* (MGM, 1948), *Border Incident* (MGM, 1949), *Battleground* (MGM, 1949), *No Questions Asked* (MGM, 1951), *It's a Big Country* (MGM, 1951), *Walk East on Beacon* (Col., 1952), *Talk About a Stranger* (MGM, 1952).

DON MURRAY Born July 31, 1929, Hollywood, California. Married Hope Lange (1956), child: Christopher; divorced 1961. Married Betty Johnson (1962).

Feature Films: *Bus Stop* (20th, 1956), *The Bachelor Party* (UA, 1957), *A Hatful of Rain* (20th, 1957), *From Hell to Texas* (20th, 1958), *These Thousand Hills* (20th, 1959), *Shake Hands With the Devil* (UA, 1959), *One Foot in Hell* (20th, 1960), *The Hoodlum Priest* (UA, 1961), *Advise and Consent* (Col., 1962), *Escape From East Berlin* (MGM, 1962), *One Man's Way* (UA, 1964), *Baby, the Rain Must Fall* (Col., 1965), *Kid Rodelo* (Par., 1966), *The Plainsman* (Univ., 1966), *Sweet Love,*

Dr. Norman Vincent Peale and Don Murray in *One Man's Way*.

Bitter (Film 2 Associates, 1967), *The Viking Queen* (20th, 1967), *Tale of the Cock* (Sinners Co., 1967).

J. CARROLL NAISH (Joseph Patrick Carrol Naish) Born January 21, 1901, New York, New York. Married Gladys Hearney (1928), child: Elaine.

J. Carroll Naish and Leo Carrillo in *Moonlight Murder*.

Feature Films: *Good Intentions* (Fox, 1930), *Scotland Yard* (Fox, 1930), *Royal Bed* (RKO, 1931), *Gun Smoke* (Par., 1931), *Kick In* (Par., 1931), *Homicide Squad* (Univ., 1931), *Hatchet Man* (WB, 1932), *Beast of the City* (MGM, 1932), *Two Seconds* (WB, 1932), *It's Tough to Be Famous* (WB, 1932), *Famous Ferguson Case* (WB, 1932), *Crooner* (WB, 1932), *Tiger Shark* (WB, 1932), *No Living Witness* (Mayfair, 1932), *The Kid From Spain* (UA, 1932), *The Conquerors* (RKO, 1932), *Cabin in the Cotton* (WB, 1932), *Mystery Squadron* (Mascot serial, 1933), *No Other Woman* (RKO, 1933), *Frisco Jenny* (WB, 1933), *Infernal Machine* (Fox, 1933), *Central Airport* (WB, 1933), *World Gone Mad* (Majestic, 1933), *The Past of Mary Holmes* (RKO, 1933), *Elmer the Great* (WB, 1933), *The Avenger* (Mon., 1933), *Arizona to Broadway* (Fox, 1933), *The Devil's in Love* (Fox, 1933), *The Whirlwind* (Col., 1933), *Captured* (WB, 1933), *The Big Chance* (Arthur Greenblatt, 1933), *Notorious But Nice* (Chesterfield, 1933), *Last Trail* (Fox, 1933), *Mad Game* (Fox, 1933), *Silent Men* (Col., 1933), *Sleepers East* (Fox, 1934), *What's Your Racket?* (Mayfair-Shallenberger, 1934), *Murder in Trinidad* (Fox, 1934), *One Is Guilty* (Col., 1934), *Upper World* (WB, 1934), *Return of the Terror* (WB, 1934), *Hell Cat* (Col., 1934), *Girl in Danger* (Col., 1934), *The Defense Rests* (Col., 1934), *Hell in the Heavens* (Fox, 1934), *The President Vanishes* (Par., 1934), *Marie Galante* (Fox, 1934), *Lives of a Bengal Lancer* (Par., 1935), *Behind the Green Lights* (Mascot, 1935), *Black Fury* (WB, 1935), *Under the Pampas Moon* (Fox, 1935), *Little Big Shot* (WB, 1935), *Front Page Woman* (WB, 1935), *The Crusades* (Par., 1935), *Special Agent* (WB, 1935), *Confidential* (Mascot, 1935), *Captain Blood* (WB, 1935), *The Leather-*

necks Have Landed (Rep., 1936), *Moonlight Murder* (MGM, 1936), *The Return of Jimmy Valentine* (Rep., 1936), *Exclusive Story* (MGM, 1936), *Robin Hood of El Dorado* (MGM, 1936), *Two in the Dark* (RKO, 1936), *Absolute Quiet* (MGM, 1936), *Charlie Chan at the Circus* (20th, 1936), *Special Investigator* (RKO, 1936), *Anthony Adverse* (WB, 1936), *Ramona* (20th, 1936), *We Who Are About to Die* (RKO, 1936), *Charge of the Light Brigade* (WB, 1936), *Crack-Up* (20th, 1936), *Think Fast, Mr. Moto* (20th, 1937), *Song of the City* (MGM, 1937), *Border Cafe* (RKO, 1937), *Hideaway* (RKO, 1937), *Bulldog Drummond Comes Back* (Par., 1937), *Sea Racketeers* (Rep., 1937), *Thunder Trail* (Par., 1937), *Night Club Scandal* (Par., 1937), *Daughter of Shanghai* (Par., 1937), *Her Jungle Love* (Par., 1938), *Tip-Off Girls* (Par., 1938), *Hunted Men* (Par., 1938), *Prison Farm* (Par., 1938), *Bulldog Drummond in Africa* (Par., 1938), *Illegal Traffic* (Par., 1938), *King of Alcatraz* (Par., 1938), *Persons in Hiding* (Par., 1939), *Hotel Imperial* (Par., 1939), *Undercover Doctor* (Par., 1939), *Beau Geste* (Par., 1939), *Island of Lost Men* (Par., 1939), *Typhoon* (Par., 1940), *Queen of the Mob* (Par., 1940), *Golden Gloves* (Par., 1940), *Down Argentine Way* (20th, 1940), *A Night at Earl Carroll's* (Par., 1940), *Mr. Dynamite* (Univ., 1941), *That Night in Rio* (20th, 1941), *Blood and Sand* (20th, 1941), *Forced Landing* (Par., 1941), *Accent on Love* (20th, 1941), *Birth of the Blues* (Par., 1941), *The Corsican Brothers* (UA, 1941), *Sunday Punch* (MGM, 1942), *Dr. Broadway* (Par., 1942), *Jackass Mail* (MGM, 1942), *The Pied Piper* (20th, 1942), *Tales of Manhattan* (20th, 1942), *The Man in the Trunk* (20th, 1942), *Dr. Renault's Secret* (20th, 1942), *Batman* (Col. serial, 1943), *Harrigan's Kid* (MGM, 1943), *Good Morning, Judge* (Univ., 1943), *Behind the Rising Sun* (RKO, 1943), *Sahara* (Col., 1943), *Gung Ho!* (Univ., 1943), *Calling Dr. Death* (Univ., 1943), *Voice in the Wind* (UA, 1944), *The Monster Maker* (PRC, 1944), *Two-Man Submarine* (Col., 1944), *Waterfront* (PRC, 1944), *The Whistler* (Col., 1944), *Jungle Woman* (Univ., 1944), *Dragon Seed* (MGM, 1944), *Enter Arsene Lupin* (Univ., 1944), *A Medal for Benny* (Par., 1945), *The Southerner* (UA, 1945), *House of Frankenstein* (Univ., 1945), *Getting Gertie's Garter* (UA, 1945), *Strange Confession* (Univ., 1945), *Bad Bascomb* (MGM, 1946), *The Beast With Five Fingers* (WB, 1946), *Humoresque* (WB, 1946), *Carnival in Costa Rica* (20th, 1947), *The Fugitive* (RKO, 1947), *Joan of Arc* (RKO, 1948), *The Kissing Bandit* (MGM, 1948), *Canadian Pacific* (20th, 1949), *That Midnight Kiss* (MGM, 1949), *Black Hand* (MGM, 1950), *Please Believe Me* (MGM, 1950), *Annie Get Your Gun* (MGM, 1950), *The Toast of New Orleans* (MGM, 1950), *Rio Grande* (Rep., 1950), *Mark of the Renegade* (Univ., 1951), *Bannerline* (MGM, 1951), *Across the Wide Missouri* (MGM, 1951), *The Denver and Rio Grande* (Par., 1952), *Clash by Night* (RKO, 1952), *Woman of the North Country* (Rep., 1952), *Ride the Man Down* (Rep., 1952), *Beneath the 12-Mile Reef* (20th, 1953), *Fighter Attack* (AA, 1953), *Saskatchewan* (Univ., 1954), *Sitting Bull* (UA, 1954), *Hit the Deck* (MGM, 1955), *Rage at Dawn* (RKO, 1955), *Violent Saturday* (20th, 1955), *New York Confidential* (WB, 1955), *The Last Command* (Rep., 1955), *Desert Sands* (UA, 1955), *Rebel in Town* (UA, 1956), *Yaqui Drums* (AA, 1956), *This Could Be the Night* (MGM, 1957), *The Young Don't Cry* (Col., 1957).

MILDRED NATWICK Born June 19, 1908, Baltimore, Maryland.

Mildred Natwick and Shirley MacLaine in *The Trouble With Harry*.

183

Feature Films: *The Long Voyage Home* (UA, 1940), *The Enchanted Cottage* (RKO, 1945), *Yolanda and the Thief* (MGM, 1945), *The Late George Apley* (20th, 1947), *A Woman's Vengeance* (Univ., 1947), *Three Godfathers* (MGM, 1948), *The Kissing Bandit* (MGM, 1948), *She Wore a Yellow Ribbon* (RKO, 1949), *Cheaper by the Dozen* (20th, 1950), *The Quiet Man* (Rep., 1952), *Against All Flags* (Univ., 1952), *The Trouble With Harry* (Par., 1955), *The Court Jester* (Par., 1956), *Teenage Rebel* (20th, 1956), *Tammy and the Bachelor* (Univ., 1957), *Barefoot in the Park* (Par., 1967).

PATRICIA NEAL (Patricia Louise Neal) Born January 20, 1926, Packard, Kentucky. Married Roald Dahl (1953), children: Olivia, Tessa, Theo, Lucy, Ophelia.

Ruth Roman and Patricia Neal in *Three Secrets*.

English-Language Feature Films: *John Loves Mary* (WB, 1949), *The Fountainhead* (WB, 1949), *It's a Great Feeling* (WB, 1949), *The Hasty Heart* (WB, 1950), *Bright Leaf* (WB, 1950), *Three Secrets* (WB, 1950), *The Breaking Point* (WB, 1950), *Operation Pacific* (WB, 1951), *Raton Pass* (WB, 1951), *Diplomatic Courier* (20th, 1951), *The Day the Earth Stood Still* (20th, 1951), *Weekend With Father* (Univ., 1951), *Washington Story* (MGM, 1952), *Something for the Birds* (20th, 1952), *Stranger From Venus* ("Immediate Disaster"—Princess Pictures, 1954), *A Face in the Crowd* (WB, 1957), *Breakfast at Tiffany's* (Par., 1961), *Hud* (Par., 1963), *Psyche 59* (Col., 1964), *In Harm's Way* (Par., 1965), *The Subject Was Roses* (MGM, 1968).

PAUL NEWMAN Born January 26, 1925, Shaker Heights, Ohio. Married Jacqueline Witte (1947), children: Scott, Susan, Stephanie; divorced 1956. Married Joanne Woodward (1958), children: Eleanor, Tessa, Cleo.

Feature Films: *The Silver Chalice* (WB, 1954), *Somebody Up There*

Paul Newman, John Dierkes and Colin Keith-Johnston in *The Left-Handed Gun.*

Likes Me (MGM, 1956), *The Rack* (MGM, 1956), *Until They Sail* (MGM, 1957), *The Helen Morgan Story* (WB, 1957), *The Long, Hot Summer* (20th, 1958), *The Left-Handed Gun* (WB, 1958), *Rally Round the Flag, Boys!* (20th, 1958), *Cat on a Hot Tin Roof* (MGM, 1958), *The Young Philadelphians* (WB, 1959), *From the Terrace* (20th, 1960), *Exodus* (UA, 1960), *The Hustler* (20th, 1961), *Paris Blues* (UA, 1961), *Sweet Bird of Youth* (MGM, 1962), *Hemingway's Adventures of a Young Man* (20th, 1962), *Hud* (Par., 1963), *A New Kind of Love* (Par., 1963), *The Prize* (MGM, 1963), *What a Way to Go!* (20th, 1964), *The Outrage* (MGM, 1964), *Lady L* (MGM, 1965), *Torn Curtain* (Univ., 1966), *Harper* (WB, 1966), *Hombre* (20th, 1967), *Cool Hand Luke* (WB, 1967), *The Private War of Harry Frigg* (Univ., 1968).

DAVID NIVEN (James David Graham Niven) Born March 1, 1911, Kirriemuir, Scotland. Married Primula Rollo (1940), children: David, Jamie; widowed 1946. Married Hjordis Tersmedes (1948), children: Kristina, Fiona.

Arthur Treacher, Virginia Field and David Niven in *Thank You, Jeeves.*

English-Language Feature Films: *Without Regret* (Par., 1935), *A Feather in Her Hat* (Col., 1935), *Splendor* (UA, 1935), *Rose Marie* (MGM, 1936), *Thank You, Jeeves* (20th, 1936), *Palm Springs* (Par., 1936), *Charge of the Light Brigade* (WB, 1936), *Dodsworth* (UA, 1936), *Beloved Enemy* (UA, 1936), *We Have Our Moments* (Univ., 1937), *Dinner at the Ritz* (20th, 1937), *The Prisoner of Zenda* (UA, 1937), *Four Men and a Prayer* (20th, 1938), *Bluebeard's Eighth Wife* (Par., 1938), *Three Blind Mice* (20th, 1938), *The Dawn Patrol* (WB, 1938), *Wuthering Heights* (UA, 1939), *Bachelor Mother* (RKO, 1939), *The Real Glory* (UA, 1939), *Eternally Yours* (UA, 1939), *Raffles* (UA, 1940), *The First of the Few* ("Spitfire"—King, 1941), *The Way Ahead* ("Immortal Battalion"—Rank, 1944), *The Perfect Marriage* (Par., 1946), *The Magnificent Doll* (Univ., 1946), *A Matter of Life and Death* ("Stairway to Heaven"—Rank, 1946), *The Other Love* (UA, 1947), *The Bishop's Wife* (RKO, 1947), *Bonnie Prince Charlie* (Korda, 1947), *Enchantment* (RKO, 1948), *The Elusive Pimpernel* ("The Scarlet Pimpernel"—Carrol Pictures, 1948), *A Kiss in the Dark* (WB, 1949), *A Kiss for Corliss* (UA, 1949), *The Toast of New Orleans* (MGM, 1950), *Soldiers Three* (MGM, 1951), *Happy Go Lovely* (MGM, 1951), *The Lady Says No* (UA, 1951), *Island Rescue* (Univ., 1952), *The Moon is Blue* (UA, 1953), *Love Lottery* (Continental Distributing, 1954), *Tonight's the Night* (AA, 1954), *The King's Thief* (MGM, 1955), *Court-Martial* (Kingsley International, 1955), *The Birds and the Bees* (Par., 1956), *Around the World in 80 Days* (UA, 1956), *Oh, Men! Oh, Women!* (20th, 1957), *The Little Hut* (MGM, 1957), *My Man Godfrey* (Univ., 1957), *The Silken Affair* (DCA, 1957), *Bonjour Tristesse* (Col., 1958), *Separate Tables* (UA, 1958), *Ask Any Girl* (MGM, 1959), *Happy Anniversary* (UA, 1959), *Please Don't Eat the Daisies* (MGM, 1960), *The Guns of Navarone* (Col., 1961), *Guns of Darkness* (WB, 1962), *Road to Hong Kong* (UA, 1962),* *The Best of Enemies* (Col., 1962), *55 Days at Peking* (AA, 1963), *Pink Panther* (UA, 1964), *Bedtime Story* (Univ., 1964),

Where the Spies Are (MGM, 1965), *Lady L* (MGM, 1966), *Casino Royale* (Col., 1967), *Eye of the Devil* (MGM, 1967), *The Extraordinary Seaman* (MGM, 1968), *Prudence and the Pill* (20th, 1968), *The Impossible Years* (MGM, 1968).

*Unbilled guest appearance

LLOYD NOLAN Born August 11, 1903, San Francisco, California. Married Mel Efird (1933), children: Melinda, Jay.

Lloyd Nolan, Alexis Smith and Craig Stevens in *Steel Against the Sky*.

Feature Films: *Stolen Harmony* (Par., 1935), *G-Men* (WB, 1935), *Atlantic Adventure* (Col., 1935), *She Couldn't Take It* (Col., 1935), *One Way Ticket* (Col., 1935), *You May Be Next* (Col., 1936), *Lady of Secrets* (Col., 1936), *Big Brown Eyes* (Par., 1936), *Devil's Squadron* (Col., 1936), *Counterfeit* (Col., 1936), *The Texas Rangers* (Par., 1936), *15 Maiden Lane* (20th, 1936), *Internes Can't Take Money* (Par., 1937), *King of Gamblers* (Par., 1937), *Exclusive* (Par., 1937), *Ebb Tide* (Par., 1937), *Wells Fargo* (Par., 1937), *Every Day's a Holiday* (Par., 1937), *Dangerous to Know* (Par., 1938), *Tip-Off Girls* (Par., 1938), *Hunted Men* (Par., 1938), *Prison Farm* (Par., 1938), *King of Alcatraz* (Par., 1938), *St. Louis Blues* (Par., 1939), *Ambush* (Par., 1939), *Undercover Doctor* (Par., 1939), *The Magnificent Fraud* (Par., 1939), *The Man Who Wouldn't Talk* (20th, 1940), *The House Across the Bay* (UA, 1940), *Johnny Apollo* (20th, 1940), *Gangs of Chicago* (Rep., 1940), *The Man I Married* (20th, 1940), *Pier 13* (20th, 1940), *Golden Fleecing* (MGM, 1940), *Michael Shayne, Private Detective* (20th, 1940), *Charter Pilot* (20th, 1940), *Behind the News* (Rep., 1940), *Sleepers West* (20th, 1941), *Mr. Dynamite* (Univ., 1941), *Dressed to Kill* (20th, 1941), *Buy Me That Town* (Par., 1941), *Blues in the Night* (WB, 1941), *Steel Against the Sky* (WB, 1941), *Blue, White and Perfect* (20th, 1941), *It Happened in Flatbush* (20th, 1942), *Apache Trail* (MGM, 1942), *Just Off Broadway* (20th, 1942), *Manila Calling* (20th, 1942), *Time to Kill* (20th, 1942), *Bataan* (MGM, 1943), *Guadalcanal Diary* (20th, 1943), *A Tree Grows in Brooklyn* (20th, 1945), *Circumstantial Evidence* (20th, 1945), *Captain Eddie* (20th, 1945), *The House on 92nd Street* (20th, 1945), *Somewhere in the Night* (20th, 1946), *Two Smart People* (MGM, 1946), *Lady in the Lake* (MGM, 1946), *Green Grass of Wyoming* (20th, 1948), *The Street With No Name* (20th, 1948), *Bad Boy* (AA, 1949), *The Sun Comes Up* (MGM, 1949), *Easy Living* (RKO, 1949), *The Lemon Drop Kid* (Par., 1951), *Island in the Sky* (WB, 1953), *Crazylegs* (Rep., 1953), *The Last Hunt* (MGM, 1956), *Santiago* (WB, 1956), *Toward the Unknown* (WB, 1956), *Abandon Ship!* (Col., 1957), *A Hatful of Rain* (20th, 1957), *Peyton Place* (20th, 1957), *Portrait in Black* (Univ., 1960), *Girl of the Night* (WB, 1960), *Susan Slade* (WB, 1961), *We Joined the Navy* (Dial, 1962), *The Girl Hunters* (Colorama Features, 1963), *Circus World* (Par., 1964), *Never Too Late* (WB, 1965), *An American Dream* (WB, 1966), *Double Man* (WB, 1967), *Ice Station Zebra* (MGM, 1968).

Kim Novak and James Stewart in *Vertigo*.

KIM NOVAK (Marilyn Pauline Novak) Born February 13, 1933, Chicago, Illinois. Married Richard Johnson 1965; divorced 1966.

Feature Films: *The French Line* (RKO, 1953), *Pushover* (Col., 1954), *Phffft* (Col., 1954), *Five Against the House* (Col., 1955), *Son of Sinbad* (RKO, 1955), *Picnic* (Col., 1955), *The Man With the Golden Arm* (UA, 1955), *The Eddy Duchin Story* (Col., 1954), *Jeanne Eagles* (Col., 1957), *Pal Joey* (Col., 1957), *Vertigo* (Par., 1958), *Bell, Book and Candle* (Col., 1958), *Middle of the Night* (Col., 1959), *Strangers When We Meet* (Col., 1960), *Pepe* (Col., 1960), *Boys' Night Out* (MGM, 1962), *The Notorious Landlady* (Col., 1962), *Of Human Bondage* (MGM, 1964), *Kiss Me, Stupid* (Lopert, 1964), *The Amorous Adventures of Moll Flanders* (Par., 1965), *The Legend of Lylah Clare* (MGM, 1968).

JACK OAKIE (Lewis Delaney Offield) Born November 12, 1903, Sedalia, Missouri. Married Venita Varden; divorced.

Jack Oakie, Bradley Page, Ruth Donnelly and Lucille Ball in *Annabel Takes a Tour*.

Sound Feature Films: *Chinatown Nights* (Par., 1929), *The Dummy* (Par., 1929), *Wild Party* (Par., 1929), *Close Harmony* (Par., 1929), *The Man I Love* (Par., 1929), *Fast Company* (Par., 1929), *Street Girl* (RKO, 1929), *Hard to Get* (WB, 1929), *Sweetie* (Par., 1929), *Paramount on Parade* (Par., 1930), *Hit the Deck* (RKO, 1930), *Social Lion* (Par., 1930), *Let's Go Native* (Par., 1930), *The Sap From Syracuse* (Par., 1930), *Sea Legs* (Par., 1930), *Gang Busters* (Par., 1931), *June Moon* (Par., 1931), *Dude Ranch* (Par., 1931), *Touchdown* (Par., 1931), *Dancers in the Dark* (Par., 1932), *Sky Bride* (Par., 1932), *Make Me a Star* (Par., 1932), *Million Dollar Legs* (Par., 1932), *Madison Square Garden* (Par., 1932), *If I Had a Million* (Par., 1932), *Once in a Lifetime* (Univ., 1932), *Uptown New York* (Sono Art-World Wide, 1932), *From Hell to Heaven* (Par., 1933), *Sailor Be Good* (Par., 1933), *Eagle and the Hawk* (Par., 1933), *College Humor* (Par., 1933), *Too Much*

Harmony (Par., 1933), *Sitting Pretty* (Par., 1933), *Alice in Wonderland* (Par., 1933), *Looking for Trouble* (UA, 1934), *Murder at the Vanities* (Par., 1934), *Shoot the Works* (Par., 1934), *College Rhythm* (Par., 1934), *Call of the Wild* (UA, 1935), *Big Broadcast of 1936* (Par., 1935), *King of Burlesque* (Fox, 1935), *Collegiate* (Par., 1936), *Colleen* (WB, 1936), *Florida Special* (Par., 1936), *The Texas Rangers* (Par., 1936), *That Girl From Paris* (RKO, 1936), *Champagne Waltz* (RKO, 1937), *Super Sleuth* (RKO, 1937), *The Toast of New York* (RKO, 1937), *Fight for Your Lady* (RKO, 1937), *Hitting a New High* (RKO, 1937), *Radio City Revels* (RKO, 1938), *The Affairs of Annabel* (RKO, 1938), *Annabel Takes a Tour* (RKO, 1938), *Thanks for Everything* (20th, 1938), *Young People* (20th, 1940), *The Great Dictator* (UA, 1940), *Tin Pan Alley* (20th, 1940), *Little Men* (RKO, 1940), *Rise and Shine* (20th, 1941), *Great American Broadcast* (20th, 1941), *Hello, Frisco, Hello* (20th, 1943), *Wintertime* (20th, 1943), *Something to Shout About* (Col., 1943), *It Happened Tomorrow* (UA, 1944), *The Merry Monahans* (Univ., 1944), *Sweet and Low Down* (20th, 1944), *Bowery to Broadway* (Univ., 1944), *That's the Spirit* (Univ., 1945), *On Stage Everybody* (Univ., 1945), *She Wrote the Book* (Univ., 1946), *Northwest Stampede* (EL, 1948), *When My Baby Smiles at Me* (20th, 1948), *Thieves' Highway* (20th, 1949), *Last of the Buccaneers* (Col., 1950), *Tomahawk* (Univ., 1951), *Around the World in 80 Days* (UA, 1956), *The Wonderful Country* (UA, 1959), *The Rat Race* (Par., 1960), *Lover Come Back* (Univ., 1961).

MERLE OBERON (Estelle Merle O'Brien Thompson) Born February 19, 1911, Tasmania, Australia. Married Alexander Korda (1939); divorced 1945. Married Lucien Ballard (1945); divorced 1949. Married Bruno Pagliai (1957), children: Bruno, Francesca.

Merle Oberon and Geraldine Fitzgerald in *Till We Meet Again.*

Feature Films: *Service For Ladies* ("Reserved For Ladies"—Par., 1932), *Dance of Witches* (London Film Productions, 1932), *Wedding Rehearsal* (London Film Productions., 1932), *The Private Life of Henry VIII* (UA, 1933), *The Private Life of Don Juan* (UA, 1934), *Thunder in the East* ("The Battle"—Leon Garganoff, 1934), *Broken Melody* (Olympic Pictures, 1934), *Men of Tomorrow* (Mundus, 1935), *The Scarlet Pimpernel* (UA, 1935), *Folies Bergere* (UA, 1935), *The Dark Angel* (UA, 1935), *These Three* (UA, 1936), *Beloved Enemy* (UA, 1936), *The Divorce of Lady X* (UA, 1938), *The Cowboy and the Lady* (UA, 1938), *Wuthering Heights* (UA, 1939), *The Lion Has Wings* (UA, 1940), *Over the Moon* (UA, 1940), *Till We Meet Again* (WB, 1940), *Affectionately Yours* (WB, 1941), *Lydia* (UA, 1941), *That Uncertain Feeling* (UA, 1941), *Forever and a Day* (RKO, 1943), *Stage Door Canteen* (UA, 1943), *First Comes Courage* (Col., 1943), *The Lodger* (20th, 1944), *Dark Waters* (UA, 1944), *A Song to Remember* (Col., 1945), *This Love of Ours* (Univ., 1945), *A Night in Paradise* (Univ., 1946), *Temptation* (Univ., 1946), *Night Song* (RKO, 1947), *Berlin Express* (RKO, 1948), *Pardon My French* (UA, 1951), *Affair in Monte Carlo* (AA, 1953), *Desirée* (20th, 1954), *Deep in My Heart* (MGM, 1954), *The Price of Fear* (Univ., 1956), *Of Love and Desire* (20th, 1963), *The Oscar* (Par., 1966), *Hotel* (WB, 1967).

EDMOND O'BRIEN Born September 10, 1915, New York, New York. Married Nancy Kelly (1941); divorced 1942. Married Olga San Juan (1948), children: Maria, Bridgette, Brenden.

Wendell Corey, Edmond O'Brien, Paul Newman, Anne Francis and Walter Pidgeon in *The Rack.*

Feature Films: *The Hunchback of Notre Dame* (RKO, 1939), *A Girl, a Guy and a Gob* (RKO, 1941), *Parachute Battalion* (RKO, 1941), *Obliging Young Lady* (RKO, 1941), *Powder Town* (RKO, 1942), *Amazing Mrs. Holliday* (Univ., 1943), *Winged Victory* (20th, 1944), *The Killers* (Univ., 1946), *The Web* (Univ., 1947), *Another Part of the Forest* (Univ., 1948), *A Double Life* (Univ., 1948), *An Act of Murder* (Univ., 1948), *For the Love of Mary* (Univ., 1948), *Fighter Squadron* (WB, 1948), *White Heat* (WB, 1949), *D.O.A.* (UA, 1949), *Backfire* (WB, 1950), *711 Ocean Drive* (Col., 1950), *The Admiral Was a Lady* (UA, 1950), *Between Midnight and Dawn* (Col., 1950), *The Redhead and the Cowboy* (Par., 1950), *Warpath* (Par., 1951), *Two of a Kind* (Col., 1951), *Silver City* (Par., 1951), *The Greatest Show on Earth* (Par., 1952),* *Denver and Rio Grande* (Par., 1952), *The Hitchhiker* (RKO, 1953), *Julius Caesar* (MGM, 1953), *Cow Country* (AA, 1953), *Man in the Dark* (Col., 1953), *China Venture* (Col., 1953), *The Bigamist* (Filmaker, 1953), *Shanghai Story* (Rep., 1954), *The Barefoot Contessa* (UA, 1954), *Shield for Murder* (UA, 1954), *Pete Kelly's Blues* (WB, 1955), *1984* (Col., 1956), *A Cry in the Night* (WB, 1956), *D-Day, the Sixth of June* (20th, 1956), *The Rack* (MGM, 1956), *The Girl Can't Help It* (20th, 1956), *The Big Land* (WB, 1957), *The World Was His Jury* (Col., 1958), *Sing Boy Sing* (20th, 1958), *Up Periscope* (WB, 1959), *The Last Voyage* (MGM, 1959), *The Third Voice* (20th, 1960), *The Great Impostor* (Univ., 1961), *Man Trap* (Par., 1961), *Bird Man of Alcatraz* (Col., 1962), *Moon Pilot* (BV, 1962), *The Man Who Shot Liberty Valance* (Par., 1962), *The Longest Day* (20th, 1962), *Seven Days in May* (20th, 1964), *The Climbers* (Robert Dorfman, 1964), *Rio Conchos* (20th, 1964), *Sylvia* (Par., 1965), *Synanon* (Col., 1965), *Fantastic Voyage* (20th, 1966), *The Viscount* (WB, 1967).

*Unbilled guest appearance

GEORGE O'BRIEN Born April 19, 1900, San Francisco, California. Married Marguerite Churchill (1933), children: Orin, Darcy; divorced 1948.

Sound Feature Films: *Salute* (Fox, 1929), *The Lone Star Ranger* (Fox, 1930), *Rough Romance* (Fox, 1930), *Last of the Duanes* (Fox, 1930), *Fair Warning* (Fox, 1931), *The Seas Beneath* (Fox, 1931), *A Holy Terror* (Fox, 1931), *Riders of the Purple Sage* (Fox, 1931), *The Rainbow*

Charles Middleton, Cecilia Parker, Noble Johnson, George O'Brien and Charlie Stevens in *Mystery Ranch*.

Trail (Fox, 1931), *The Gay Caballero* (Fox, 1932), *Mystery Ranch* (Fox, 1932), *The Golden West* (Fox, 1932), *Robber's Roost* (Fox, 1933), *Smoke Lightning* (Fox, 1933), *Life in the Raw* (Fox, 1933), *The Last Trail* (Fox, 1933), *Frontier Marshal* (Fox, 1934), *Ever Since Eve* (Fox, 1934), *The Dude Ranger* (Fox, 1934), *When a Man's a Man* (Fox, 1935), *The Cowboy Millionaire* (Fox, 1935), *Hard Rock Harrigan* (Fox, 1935), *Thunder Mountain* (20th, 1935), *Whispering Smith Speaks* (20th, 1935), *O'Malley of the Mounted* (20th, 1936), *The Border Patrolman* (20th, 1936), *Daniel Boone* (RKO, 1936), *Park Avenue Logger* (RKO, 1937), *Hollywood Cowboy* (RKO, 1937), *Windjammer* (RKO, 1937), *Gun Law* (RKO, 1938), *Border G-Man* (RKO, 1938), *Painted Desert* (RKO, 1938), *The Renegade Ranger* (RKO, 1938), *Lawless Valley* (RKO, 1938), *The Arizona Legion* (RKO, 1939), *Trouble in Sundown* (RKO, 1939), *Racketeers of the Range* (RKO, 1939), *Timber Stampede* (RKO, 1939), *The Fighting Gringo* (RKO, 1939), *The Marshal of Mesa City* (RKO, 1939), *Legion of the Lawless* (RKO, 1940), *Bullet Code* (RKO, 1940), *Prairie Law* (RKO, 1940), *Stage to Chino* (RKO, 1940), *Triple Justice* (RKO, 1940), *My Wild Irish Rose* (WB, 1947), *Fort Apache* (RKO, 1948), *She Wore a Yellow Ribbon* (RKO, 1949), *Gold Raiders* (UA, 1951), *Cheyenne Autumn* (WB, 1964).

MARGARET O'BRIEN (Angela Maxine O'Brien) Born January 15, 1937, Los Angeles, California. Married Harold Allen (1959).

Herbert Marshall, Brian Roper and Margaret O'Brien in *The Secret Garden*.

Feature Films: *Babes on Broadway* (MGM, 1941), *Journey for Margaret* (MGM, 1942), *Dr. Gillespie's Criminal Case* (MGM, 1943), *Thousands Cheer* (MGM, 1943), *Lost Angel* (MGM, 1943), *Madame Curie* (MGM, 1943), *Jane Eyre* (20th, 1944), *The Canterville Ghost* (MGM, 1944), *Meet Me in St. Louis* (MGM, 1944), *Music for Millions* (MGM, 1944),

Our Vines Have Tender Grapes (MGM, 1945), *Bad Bascomb* (MGM, 1946), *Three Wise Fools* (MGM, 1946), *The Unfinished Dance* (MGM, 1947), *Tenth Avenue Angel* (MGM, 1947), *Big City* (MGM, 1948), *Little Women* (MGM, 1949), *The Secret Garden* (MGM, 1949), *Her First Romance* (Col., 1951), *Glory* (RKO, 1956), *Heller in Pink Tights* (Par., 1960).

PAT O'BRIEN (William Joseph Patrick O'Brien) Born November 11, 1899, Milwaukee, Wisconsin. Married Eloise Taylor (1931), children: Mavourneen, Patrick, Terence, Kathleen.

Leon Ames and Pat O'Brien in *The Iron Major*.

Feature Films: *Front Page* (UA, 1931), *Honor Among Lovers* (Par., 1931), *Personal Maid* (Par., 1931), *Flying High* (MGM, 1931), *Consolation Marriage* (RKO, 1931), *Final Edition* (Col., 1932), *Hell's House* (Capitol Film Exchange, 1932), *Strange Case of Clara Deane* (Par., 1932), *Scandal for Sale* (Univ., 1932), *American Madness* (Col., 1932), *Hollywood Speaks* (Col., 1932), *Virtue* (Col., 1932), *Air Mail* (Univ., 1932), *Laughter in Hell* (Univ., 1932), *Destination Unknown* (Univ., 1933), *World Gone Mad* (Majestic, 1933), *Bureau of Missing Persons* (WB, 1933), *Bombshell* (MGM, 1933), *College Coach* (WB, 1933), *Flaming Gold* (RKO, 1934), *Gambling Lady* (WB, 1934), *I've Got Your Number* (WB, 1934), *20 Million Sweethearts* (WB, 1934), *Here Comes the Navy* (WB, 1934), *Personality Kid* (WB, 1934), *I Sell Anything* (WB, 1934), *Flirtation Walk* (WB, 1934), *Devil Dogs of the Air* (WB, 1935), *In Caliente* (WB, 1935), *Oil for the Lamps of China* (WB, 1935), *Page Miss Glory* (WB, 1935), *The Irish in Us* (WB, 1935), *Stars Over Broadway* (WB, 1935), *Ceiling Zero* (WB, 1935), *I Married a Doctor* (WB, 1936), *Public Enemy's Wife* (WB, 1936), *China Clipper* (WB, 1936), *The Great O'Malley* (WB, 1937), *Slim* (WB, 1937), *San Quentin* (WB, 1937), *Back in Circulation* (WB, 1937), *Submarine D-1* (WB, 1937), *Women Are Like That* (WB, 1938), *The Cowboy From Brooklyn* (WB, 1938), *Boy Meets Girl* (WB, 1938), *Garden of the Moon* (WB, 1938), *Angels With Dirty Faces* (WB, 1938), *Off the Record* (WB, 1939), *The Kid From Kokomo* (WB, 1939), *Indianapolis Speedway* (WB, 1939), *The Night of Nights* (Par., 1939), *The Fighting 69th* (WB, 1940), *Slightly Honorable* (UA, 1940), *Castle on the Hudson* (WB, 1940), *Till We Meet Again* (WB, 1940), *Torrid Zone* (WB, 1940), *Flowing Gold* (WB, 1940), *Knute Rockne—All American* (WB, 1940), *Submarine Zone* (Col., 1941), *Two Yanks in Trinidad* (Col., 1942), *Broadway* (Univ., 1942), *Flight Lieutenant* (Col., 1942), *The Navy Comes Through* (RKO, 1942), *Bombardier* (RKO, 1943), *The Iron Major* (RKO, 1943), *His Butler's Sister* (Univ., 1943), *Secret Command* (Col., 1944), *Marine Raiders* (RKO, 1944), *Having Wonderful Crime* (RKO, 1945), *Man Alive* (RKO, 1945), *Perilous Holiday* (Col., 1946), *Riffraff* (RKO, 1947), *Fighting Father Dunne* (RKO, 1948), *The Boy With Green Hair* (RKO, 1948), *A Dangerous Profession* (RKO, 1949), *Johnny One-Eye* (UA, 1950), *The Fireball* (20th, 1950), *The People Against O'Hara* (MGM, 1951), *Criminal Lawyer* (Col., 1951), *Okinawa* (Col., 1952), *Jubilee Trail* (Rep., 1954), *Ring of Fear* (WB, 1954), *Inside Detroit* (Col., 1955), *Kill Me Tomorrow* (Tudor Pictures, 1957), *The Last*

Hurrah (Col., 1958), *Some Like it Hot* (UA, 1959), *Town Tamer* (Par., 1965).

VIRGINIA O'BRIEN Born April 18, 1921, Los Angeles, California. Married Kirk Alyn (1942), child: Theresa; divorced 1955.

Bert Lahr and Virginia O'Brien (right) in *Meet the People*.

Feature Films: *Hullabaloo* (MGM, 1940), *Sky Murder* (MGM, 1940), *The Big Store* (MGM, 1941), *Ringside Maisie* (MGM, 1941), *Lady Be Good* (MGM, 1941), *Ship Ahoy* (MGM, 1942), *Panama Hattie* (MGM, 1942), *Du Barry Was a Lady* (MGM, 1943), *Thousands Cheer* (MGM, 1943), *Two Girls and a Sailor* (MGM, 1944), *Meet the People* (MGM, 1944), *Ziegfeld Follies* (MGM, 1946), *The Harvey Girls* (MGM, 1946), *The Show-Off* (MGM, 1946), *Till the Clouds Roll By* (MGM, 1946), *Merton of the Movies* (MGM, 1947), *Francis in the Navy* (Univ., 1955).

ARTHUR O'CONNELL Born March 29, 1908, New York, New York. Married Anne Hall (1962).

Arthur O'Connell and George Hamilton in *A Thunder of Drums*.

Feature Films: *Freshman Year* (Univ., 1938), *Dr. Kildare Goes Home* (MGM, 1940), *The Leather Pushers* (Univ., 1940), *And One Was Beautiful* (MGM, 1940), *Two Girls on Broadway* (MGM, 1940), *Citizen*

Kane (RKO, 1941), *Man From Headquarters* (Mon., 1942), *Canal Zone* (Col., 1942), *Fingers at the Window* (MGM, 1942), *Law of the Jungle* (Mon., 1942), *Shepherd of the Ozarks* (Rep., 1942), *Yokel Boy* (Rep., 1942), *It Happened Tomorrow* (UA, 1944), *One Touch of Venus* (Univ., 1948), *Open Secret* (EL, 1948), *State of the Union* (MGM, 1948), *Naked City* (Univ., 1948), *Homecoming* (MGM, 1948), *Countess of Monte Cristo* (Univ., 1948), *Force of Evil* (MGM, 1948), *Picnic* (Col., 1955), *The Solid Gold Cadillac* (Col., 1956), *The Man in the Gray Flannel Suit* (20th, 1956), *The Proud Ones* (20th, 1956), *Bus Stop* (20th, 1956), *The Monte Carlo Story* (UA, 1957), *Operation Mad Ball* (Col., 1957), *April Love* (20th, 1957), *The Violators* (Univ., 1957), *Voice in the Mirror* (Univ., 1958), *Man of the West* (UA, 1958), *Gidget* (Col., 1959), *Anatomy of a Murder* (Col., 1959), *Operation Petticoat* (Univ., 1959), *Hound-Dog Man* (20th, 1959), *The Great Impostor* (Univ., 1960), *Cimarron* (MGM, 1960), *Misty* (20th, 1961), *A Thunder of Drums* (MGM, 1961), *A Pocketful of Miracles* (UA, 1961), *Follow That Dream* (UA, 1962), *Seven Faces of Dr. Lao* (MGM, 1964), *Kissin' Cousins* (MGM, 1964), *The Third Secret* (20th, 1964), *Your Cheatin' Heart* (MGM, 1964), *Nightmare in the Sun* (Zodiac, 1965), *The Third Day* (WB, 1965), *The Monkey's Uncle* (BV, 1965), *Ride Beyond Vengeance* (Col., 1966), *The Silencers* (Col., 1966), *Fantastic Voyage* (20th, 1966), *A Covenant With Death* (WB, 1967), *The Reluctant Astronaut* (Univ., 1967), *The Power* (MGM, 1968).

DONALD O'CONNOR (Donald David Dixon Ronald O'Connor) Born August 30, 1925, Chicago, Illinois. Married Gwendolyn Carter (1944), child: Donna; divorced 1954. Married Gloria Noble (1957), child: Alicia.

Donald O'Connor, Mary Boland, Charlie Ruggles and Billy Lee in *Boy Trouble*.

Feature Films: *Sing You Sinners* (Par., 1938), *Sons of the Legion* (Par., 1938), *Men With Wings* (Par., 1938), *Tom Sawyer, Detective* (Par., 1938), *Unmarried* (Par., 1939), *Death of a Champion* (Par., 1939), *Million Dollar Legs* (Par., 1939), *Night Work* (Par., 1939), *On Your Toes* (WB, 1939), *Beau Geste* (Par., 1939), *Private Buckaroo* (Univ., 1942), *Give Out, Sisters* (Univ., 1942), *Get Hep to Love* (Univ., 1942), *When Johnny Comes Marching Home* (Univ., 1942), *Strictly in the Groove* (Univ., 1943), *It Comes Up Love* (Univ., 1943), *Mister Big* (Univ., 1943), *Top Man* (Univ., 1943), *Chip Off the Old Block* (Univ., 1944), *This Is the Life* (Univ., 1944), *Follow the Boys* (Univ., 1944), *The Merry Monahans* (Univ., 1944), *Bowery to Broadway* (Univ., 1944), *Patrick the Great* (Univ., 1945), *Something in the Wind* (Univ., 1947), *Are You With It?* (Univ., 1948), *Feudin', Fussin' and a-Fightin'* (Univ., 1948), *Yes Sir, That's My Baby* (Univ., 1949), *Francis* (Univ., 1949), *Curtain Call at Cactus Creek* (Univ., 1950), *The Milkman* (Univ., 1950), *Double Crossbones* (Univ., 1950), *Francis Goes to the Races* (Univ., 1951), *Singin' in the Rain* (MGM, 1952), *Francis Goes to West Point* (Univ., 1952), *Call Me Madam* (20th, 1953), *I Love Melvin* (MGM, 1953), *Francis Covers the Big Town* (Univ., 1953), *Walking My Baby Back Home* (Univ., 1953), *Francis Joins the WACs* (Univ., 1954), *There's No Business Like Show Business* (20th, 1954), *Francis in the Navy* (Univ., 1955), *Anything Goes* (Par., 1956), *The Buster Keaton*

Story (Par., 1957), *Cry for Happy* (Col., 1961), *The Wonders of Aladdin* (MGM, 1961), *That Funny Feeling* (Univ., 1965).

UNA O'CONNOR Born October 23, 1880, Belfast, Ireland. Died February 4, 1959.

Henry Stephenson and Una O'Connor in *The Perfect Gentleman*.

Feature Films: *Dark Red Roses* (British Sound Films, 1929), *Murder* (British International, 1930), *To Oblige a Lady* (British Lion, 1930), *Timbuctoo* (British Lion, 1930), *Cavalcade* (Fox, 1933), *Pleasure Cruise* (Fox, 1933), *Mary Stevens, M.D.* (WB, 1933), *The Invisible Man* (Univ., 1933), *Orient Express* (Fox, 1934), *The Poor Rich* (Univ., 1934), *All Men Are Enemies* (Fox, 1934), *Stingaree* (RKO, 1934), *The Barretts of Wimpole Street* (MGM, 1934), *Chained* (MGM, 1934), *David Copperfield* (MGM, 1935), *Father Brown, Detective* (Par., 1935), *Bride of Frankenstein* (Univ., 1935), *The Informer* (RKO, 1935), *Thunder in the Night* (Fox, 1935), *The Perfect Gentleman* (MGM, 1935), *Little Lord Fauntleroy* (UA, 1936), *Rose Marie* (MGM, 1936), *Suzy* (MGM, 1936), *Lloyds of London* (20th, 1936), *The Plough and the Stars* (RKO, 1936), *Personal Property* (MGM, 1937), *Call It a Day* (WB, 1937), *The Return of the Frog* (Imperator-British Lion, 1938), *The Adventures of Robin Hood* (WB, 1938), *We Are Not Alone* (WB, 1939), *All Women Have Secrets* (Par., 1939), *It All Came True* (WB, 1940), *Lillian Russell* (20th, 1940), *The Sea Hawk* (WB, 1940), *He Stayed for Breakfast* (Col., 1940), *Kisses for Breakfast* (WB, 1941), *Strawberry Blonde* (WB, 1941), *Her First Beau* (Col., 1941), *Three Girls About Town* (Col., 1941), *How Green Was My Valley* (20th, 1941), *Always in My Heart* (WB, 1942), *My Favorite Spy* (RKO, 1942), *Random Harvest* (MGM, 1942), *This Land Is Mine* (RKO, 1943), *Forever and a Day* (RKO, 1943), *Holy Matrimony* (20th, 1943), *Government Girl* (RKO, 1943), *The Canterville Ghost* (MGM, 1944), *My Pal Wolf* (RKO, 1944), *Christmas in Connecticut* (WB, 1945), *The Bells of St. Mary's* (RKO, 1945), *Cluny Brown* (20th, 1946), *Of Human Bondage* (WB, 1946), *Child of Divorce* (RKO, 1946), *Unexpected Guest* (UA, 1946), *The Return of Monte Cristo* (Col., 1946), *Lost Honeymoon* (EL, 1947), *Banjo* (RKO, 1947), *Ivy* (Univ., 1947), *The Corpse Came C.O.D.* (Col., 1947), *Fighting Father Dunne* (RKO, 1948), *Adventures of Don Juan* (WB, 1948), *Witness for the Prosecution* (UA, 1957).

MAUREEN O'HARA (Maureen FitzSimmons) Born August 17, 1920, Dublin, Ireland. Married George Brown (1938); annulled 1941. Married Will Price (1941), child: Bronwyn; divorced 1953. Married Charles Blair (1968).

Feature Films: *Jamaica Inn* (Par., 1939), *The Hunchback of Notre Dame* (RKO, 1939), *My Irish Molly* (Mon, 1939), *A Bill of Divorcement* (RKO, 1940), *Dance, Girl, Dance* (RKO, 1940), *They Met in Argentina* (RKO, 1941), *How Green Was My Valley* (20th, 1941), *To the Shores of Tripoli* (20th, 1942), *Ten Gentlemen From West Point* (20th, 1942), *The Black Swan* (20th, 1942), *The Immortal Sergeant* (20th, 1943), *This Land Is Mine* (RKO, 1943), *The Fallen Sparrow* (RKO, 1943), *Buffalo Bill* (20th, 1944), *The Spanish Main* (RKO,

Douglas Fairbanks, Jr., Anthony Quinn, Maureen O'Hara, John Dehner and Alan Napier in *Sinbad the Sailor*.

1945), *Sentimental Journey* (20th, 1946), *Do You Love Me?* (20th, 1946), *Sinbad the Sailor* (RKO, 1947), *The Homestretch* (20th, 1947), *The Miracle on 34th Street* (20th, 1947), *The Foxes of Harrow* (20th, 1947), *Sitting Pretty* (20th, 1948), *The Forbidden Street* (20th, 1949), *A Woman's Secret* (RKO, 1949), *Father Was a Fullback* (20th, 1949), *Bagdad* (Univ., 1949), *Comanche Territory* (Univ., 1950), *Tripoli* (Par., 1950), *Rio Grande* (Rep., 1950), *Flame of Araby* (Univ., 1951), *At Sword's Point* (RKO, 1952), *Kangaroo* (20th, 1952), *The Quiet Man* (Rep., 1952), *Against All Flags* (Univ., 1952), *The Redhead From Wyoming* (Univ., 1952), *War Arrow* (Univ., 1953), *Fire Over Africa* (Col., 1954), *The Long Gray Line* (Col., 1955), *The Magnificent Matador* (20th, 1955), *Lady Godiva* (Univ., 1955), *Lisbon* (Rep., 1956), *Everything But the Truth* (Univ., 1956), *The Wings of Eagles* (MGM, 1957), *Our Man in Havana* (Col., 1960), *The Parent Trap* (BV, 1961), *The Deadly Companions* (Pathé-American, 1961), *Mr. Hobbs Takes a Vacation* (20th, 1962), *Spencer's Mountain* (WB, 1963), *McLintock!* (UA, 1963), *The Battle of the Villa Fiorita* (WB, 1965), *The Rare Breed* (Univ., 1966).

DENNIS O'KEEFE (Edward James Flanagan) Born March 29, 1908, Fort Madison, Iowa. Married Louise Stanely; divorced. Married Steffi Duna (1940), child: Edward.

Wallace Ford and Dennis O'Keefe in *T-Men*.

Feature Films:
   as **Bud Flanagan** *Reaching for the Moon* (UA, 1931), *Cimarron* (RKO, 1931), *Crooner* (WB, 1932), *Two Against the World* (WB, 1932), *Cabin in the Cotton* (WB, 1932), *I Am a Fugitive From a Chain Gang* (WB, 1932), *Night After Night* (Par., 1932), *Central Park* (WB, 1932), *Hello Everybody!* (Par., 1933), *Girl Missing* (WB, 1933), *From Hell to Heaven* (Par., 1933), *The Eagle and the Hawk* (Par., 1933), *Gold Diggers of 1933* (WB, 1933), *Too Much Harmony* (Par., 1933), *I'm No Angel* (Par., 1933), *Duck Soup* (Par., 1933), *The House on 56th

Street (Par., 1933), Lady Killer (WB, 1933), Torch Singer (Par., 1933), Upperworld (WB, 1934), Wonder Bar (WB, 1934), Jimmy the Gent (WB, 1934), Smarty (WB, 1934), Registered Nurse (WB, 1934), Fog Over Frisco (WB, 1934), Man With Two Faces (WB, 1934), Madame Du Barry (WB, 1934), Lady By Choice (Col., 1934), College Rhythm (Par., 1934), Transatlantic Merry-Go-Round (UA, 1934), Imitation of Life (Univ., 1934), Devil Dogs of the Air (WB, 1935), Rumba (Par., 1935), Gold Diggers of 1935 (WB, 1935), Mississippi (Par., 1935), Let 'Em Have It (UA, 1935), Doubting Thomas (Fox, 1935), The Daring Young Man (Fox, 1935), Every Night at Eight (Par., 1935), Anna Karenina (MGM, 1935), Personal Maid's Secret (WB, 1935), It's in the Air (MGM, 1935), Shipmates Forever (WB, 1935), Broadway Hostess (WB, 1935), Anything Goes (Par., 1936), Hats Off (GN, 1936), Love Before Breakfast (Univ., 1936), Mr. Deeds Goes to Town (Col., 1936), 13 Hours By Air (Par., 1936), And So They Were Married (Col., 1936), Nobody's Fool (Univ., 1936), Sworn Enemy (MGM, 1936), Rhythm on the Range (Par., 1936), Yours for the Asking (Par., 1936), Libeled Lady (MGM, 1936), Theodora Goes Wild (Col., 1936), The Accusing Finger (Par., 1936), Born to Dance (MGM, 1936), The Plainsman (Par., 1936), Burning Gold (Rep., 1936), Great Guy (GN, 1936), Married Before Breakfast (MGM, 1937), Top of the Town (Univ., 1937), When's Your Birthday? (RKO, 1937), Parole Racket (Col., 1937), Swing High, Swing Low (Par., 1937), Captains Courageous (MGM, 1937), A Star Is Born (UA, 1937), Riding on Air (RKO, 1937), Girl From Scotland Yard (Par., 1937), Easy Living (Par., 1937), Saratoga (MGM, 1937), The Firefly (MGM, 1937), Blazing Barriers (Mon., 1937).

as **Dennis O'Keefe** Bad Man of Brimstone (MGM, 1938), Hold That Kiss (MGM, 1938), The Chaser (MGM, 1938), Vacation From Love (MGM, 1938), Burn 'Em Up O'Connor (MGM, 1939), The Kid From Texas (MGM, 1939), Unexpected Father (Univ., 1939), That's Right—You're Wrong (RKO, 1939), La Conga Nights (Univ., 1940), Alias the Deacon (Univ., 1940), Pop Always Pays (RKO, 1940), I'm Nobody's Sweetheart Now (Univ., 1940), Girl From Havana (Rep., 1940), Arise, My Love (Par., 1940), You'll Find Out (RKO, 1940), Mr. District Attorney (Rep., 1941), Bowery Boy (Rep., 1941), Topper Returns (UA, 1941), Broadway Limited (UA, 1941), Lady Scarface (RKO, 1941), Week-End for Three (RKO, 1941), The Affairs of Jimmy Valentine (Rep., 1942), Moonlight Masquerade (Rep., 1942), Hangmen Also Die (UA, 1943), Tahiti Honey (Rep., 1943), Good Morning, Judge (Univ., 1943), The Leopard Man (RKO, 1943), Hi Diddle Diddle (UA, 1943), The Fighting Seabees (Rep., 1944), Up in Mabel's Room (UA, 1944), The Story of Dr. Wassell (Par., 1944), Sensations of 1945 (UA, 1944), Abroad With Two Yanks (UA, 1944), Earl Carroll's Vanities (Rep., 1945), Brewster's Millions (UA, 1945), The Affairs of Susan (Par., 1945), Getting Gertie's Garter (UA, 1945), Doll Face (20th, 1945), Her Adventurous Night (Univ., 1946), Mr. District Attorney (Col., 1947), Dishonored Lady (UA, 1947), T-Men (EL, 1947), Raw Deal (EL, 1948), Walk a Crooked Mile (Col., 1948), Siren of Atlantis (UA, 1948), Cover Up (UA, 1949), The Great Dan Patch (UA, 1949), Abandoned (Univ., 1949), The Eagle and the Hawk (Par., 1950), Woman on the Run (Univ., 1950), The Company She Keeps (RKO, 1950), Follow the Sun (20th, 1951), Passage West (Par., 1951), One Big Affair (UA, 1952), Everything I Have Is Yours (MGM, 1952), The Lady Wants Mink (Rep., 1953), The Fake (UA, 1953), The Diamond Wizard (UA, 1953), Drums of Tahiti (Col., 1954), Angela (20th, 1955), Las Vegas Shakedown (AA, 1955), Chicago Syndicate (Col., 1955), Inside Detroit (Col., 1955), Dragoon Wells Massacre (AA, 1957), Sail into Danger (Patria, 1957), Lady of Vengeance (UA, 1957), All Hands on Deck (20th, 1961).

WARNER OLAND Born October 3, 1880, Ulmea, Sweden. Married Edith Shearn (1908). Died August 6, 1938.

Sound Feature Films: Chinatown Nights (Par., 1929), The Studio Murder Mystery (Par., 1929), The Mysterious Dr. Fu Manchu (Par., 1929), The Mighty (Par., 1929), The Vagabond King (Par., 1930), Dangerous Paradise (Par., 1930), Paramount on Parade (Par., 1930), The Return of Dr. Fu Manchu (Par., 1930), Drums of Jeopardy (Tif. 1931), Dishonored (Par., 1931), Charlie Chan Carries On (Fox, 1931), Black Camel (Fox, 1931), Daughter of the Dragon (Par., 1931), The Big Gamble (Pathé, 1931), Shanghai Express (Par., 1932), Charlie Chan's Chance

Virginia Field and Warner Oland in *Charlie Chan in Monte Carlo.*

(Fox, 1932), Passport to Hell (Fox, 1932), The Son-Daughter (MGM, 1932), Charlie Chan's Greatest Case (Fox, 1933), Before Dawn (RKO, 1933), As Husbands Go (Fox, 1934), Mandalay (WB, 1934), Bulldog Drummond Strikes Back (UA, 1934), Charlie Chan in London (Fox, 1934), Charlie Chan's Courage (Fox, 1934), The Painted Veil (MGM, 1934), Charlie Chan in Paris (Fox, 1935), Charlie Chan in Egypt (Fox, 1935), The Werewolf of London (Univ., 1935), Shanghai (Par., 1935), Charlie Chan in Shanghai (Fox, 1935), Charlie Chan's Secret (20th, 1936), Charlie Chan at the Circus (20th, 1936), Charlie Chan at the Race Track (20th, 1936), Charlie Chan at the Opera (20th, 1936), Charlie Chan at the Olympics (20th, 1937), Charlie Chan on Broadway (20th, 1937), Charlie Chan at Monte Carlo (20th, 1937).

EDNA MAY OLIVER (Edna May Cox-Oliver) Born November 9, 1883, Malden, Massachusetts. Married David Pratt (1928); divorced 1931. Died November 9, 1942.

Edna May Oliver and Joan Crawford in *No More Ladies.*

Sound Feature Films: The Saturday Night Kid (Par., 1929), Hook, Line and Sinker (RKO, 1930), Half Shot at Sunrise (RKO, 1930), Cimarron (RKO, 1931), Cracked Nuts (RKO, 1931), Laugh and Get Rich (RKO, 1931), Newly Rich (Par., 1931), Fanny Foley Herself (RKO, 1931), Ladies of the Jury (RKO, 1932), Hold 'Em Jail (RKO, 1932), The Conquerors (RKO, 1932), The Penguin Pool Murder (RKO,

1932), *Meet the Baron* (MGM, 1933), *The Great Jasper* (RKO, 1933), *It's Great to Be Alive* (Fox, 1933), *Ann Vickers* (RKO, 1933), *Only Yesterday* (Univ., 1933), *Little Women* (RKO, 1933), *Alice in Wonderland* (Par., 1933), *The Poor Rich* (Univ., 1934), *The Last Gentleman* (UA, 1934), *Murder on the Blackboard* (RKO, 1934), *We're Rich Again* (RKO, 1934), *David Copperfield* (MGM, 1935), *Murder on a Honeymoon* (RKO, 1935), *No More Ladies* (MGM, 1935), *A Tale of Two Cities* (MGM, 1935), *Romeo and Juliet* (MGM, 1936), *Parnell* (MGM, 1937), *My Dear Miss Aldrich* (MGM, 1937), *Rosalie* (MGM, 1937), *Paradise for Three* (MGM, 1938), *Little Miss Broadway* (20th, 1938), *Second Fiddle* (20th, 1938), *Nurse Edith Cavell* (RKO, 1939), *The Story of Vernon and Irene Castle* (RKO, 1939), *Drums Along the Mohawk* (20th, 1939), *Pride and Prejudice* (MGM, 1940), *Lydia* (UA, 1941).

SIR LAURENCE OLIVIER Born May 22, 1907, Dorking, Surrey, England. Married Jill Esmond (1930), child: Simon; divorced 1940. Married Vivien Leigh (1940); divorced 1960. Married Joan Plowright (1961), children: Richard, Tamsin.

Gloria Swanson and Laurence Olivier in *Perfect Understanding*.

Feature Films: *The Temporary Widow* (UFA, 1930), *Too Many Crooks* (Fox, 1930), *The Yellow Ticket* (Fox, 1931), *Friends and Lovers* (RKO, 1931), *Potiphar's Wife* (Elvey, 1931), *Westward Passage* (RKO, 1932), *The Perfect Understanding* (UA, 1933), *No Funny Business* (Principal, 1934), *Moscow Nights* (Lenauer, 1935), *As You Like It* (20th, 1936), *Fire Over England* (UA, 1937), *The Divorce of Lady X* (UA, 1938), *Conquest of the Air* (Shaw, 1938), *Twenty-One Days* (London, 1939), *Wuthering Heights* (UA, 1939), *Q Planes* (Col., 1939), *Rebecca* (UA, 1940), *Pride and Prejudice* (MGM, 1940), *The Invaders* ("The 49th Parallel"—Ortus, 1941), *Lady Hamilton* (Korda, 1941), *The Demi-Paradise* (Two Cities, 1942), *Henry V* (UA, 1946), *Hamlet* (Rank, 1948), *Carrie* (Par., 1952), *The Magic Box* (Rank, 1952), *The Beggar's Opera* (WB, 1953), *Richard III* (Lopert, 1955), *The Prince and the Showgirl* (WB, 1957), *The Devil's Disciple* (UA, 1959), *Spartacus* (Univ., 1960), *The Entertainer* (Continental Distributing, 1960), *Term of Trial* (WB, 1963), *Bunny Lake Is Missing* (Col., 1965), *Othello* (WB, 1965), *Khartoum* (UA, 1966).

MAUREEN O'SULLIVAN (Maureen Paula O'Sullivan) Born May 17, 1911, County Roscommon, Ireland. Married John Farrow (1936), children: Joseph, Maria (Mia), John, Prudence, Stephanie, Theresa, Michael; widowed 1963.

Feature Films: *Song o' My Heart* (Fox, 1930), *So This Is London* (Fox, 1930), *Just Imagine* (Fox, 1930), *Princess and the Plumber* (Fox, 1930), *A Connecticut Yankee* (Fox, 1931), *Skyline* (Fox, 1931), *Tarzan the Ape Man* (MGM, 1932), *The Silver Lining* (Patrician, 1932), *Big Shot* (RKO, 1932), *Information Kid* (Univ., 1932), *Strange Interlude* (MGM, 1932), *Skyscraper Souls* (MGM, 1932), *Payment Deferred* (MGM, 1932), *Okay America!* (Univ., 1932), *Fast Companions* (Univ., 1932), *Robber's Roost* (Fox, 1933), *Cohens and Kellys in Trouble* (Univ.,

Maureen O'Sullivan and Henry Fonda in *Let Us Live*.

1933), *Tugboat Annie* (MGM, 1933), *Stage Mother* (MGM, 1933), *Tarzan and His Mate* (MGM, 1934), *The Thin Man* (MGM, 1934), *The Barretts of Wimpole Street* (MGM, 1934), *Hideout* (MGM, 1934), *West Point of the Air* (MGM, 1935), *David Copperfield* (MGM, 1935), *Cardinal Richelieu* (UA, 1935), *The Flame Within* (MGM, 1935), *Anna Karenina* (MGM, 1935), *Woman Wanted* (MGM, 1935), *The Bishop Misbehaves* (MGM, 1935), *Tarzan Escapes* (MGM, 1936), *The Voice of Bugle Ann* (MGM, 1936), *The Devil-Doll* (MGM, 1936), *A Day at the Races* (MGM, 1937), *Between Two Women* (MGM, 1937), *The Emperor's Candlesticks* (MGM, 1937), *My Dear Miss Aldrich* (MGM, 1937), *A Yank at Oxford* (MGM, 1938), *Hold That Kiss* (MGM, 1938), *The Crowd Roars* (MGM, 1938), *Port of Seven Seas* (MGM, 1938), *Spring Madness* (MGM, 1938), *Let Us Live* (Col., 1939), *Tarzan Finds a Son* (MGM, 1939), *Pride and Prejudice* (MGM, 1940), *Sporting Blood* (MGM, 1940), *Maisie Was a Lady* (MGM, 1941), *Tarzan's Secret Treasure* (MGM, 1941), *Tarzan's New York Adventure* (MGM, 1942), *The Big Clock* (Par., 1948), *Where Danger Lives* (RKO, 1950), *Bonzo Goes to College* (Univ., 1952), *All I Desire* (Univ., 1953), *Mission Over Korea* (Col., 1953), *Duffy of San Quentin* (WB, 1954), *The Steel Cage* (UA, 1954), *The Tall T* (Col., 1957), *Wild Heritage* (Univ., 1958), *Never Too Late* (WB, 1965).

PETER O'TOOLE (Peter Seamus O'Toole) Born August 2, 1933, Connemara, County Galway, Ireland. Married Sian Phillips, child: Kate.

Hugh Miller, Donald Wolfit, Claude Rains and Peter O'Toole in *Lawrence of Arabia*.

Feature Films: *Kidnapped* (BV, 1960), *The Day They Robbed the Bank of England* (MGM, 1960), *The Savage Innocents* (Par., 1960), *Lawrence of Arabia* (Col., 1962), *Becket* (Par., 1964), *Lord Jim* (Col., 1965), *What's New, Pussycat?* (UA, 1965), *How to Steal a Million* (20th, 1966),

The Bible (20th, 1966), *The Night of the Generals* (Col., 1967), *Casino Royale* (Col., 1967),* *The Great Catherine* (WB-7 Arts, 1968), *The Lion in Winter* (Embassy, 1968).

*Unbilled guest appearance

MARIA OUSPENSKAYA Born July 29, 1867, Tula, Russia. Died December 3, 1949.

Catherine McLeod and Maria Ouspenskaya in *I've Always Loved You.*

Feature Films: *Dodsworth* (UA, 1936), *Conquest* (MGM, 1937), *Love Affair* (RKO, 1939), *The Rains Came* (20th, 1939), *Judge Hardy and Son* (MGM, 1939), *Dr. Ehrlich's Magic Bullet* (WB, 1940), *Waterloo Bridge* (MGM, 1940), *The Mortal Storm* (MGM, 1940), *The Man I Married* (20th, 1940), *Dance, Girl, Dance* (RKO, 1940), *Beyond Tomorrow* (RKO, 1940), *The Wolf Man* (Univ., 1941), *The Shanghai Gesture* (UA, 1941), *Kings Row* (WB, 1941), *The Mystery of Marie Roget* (Univ., 1942), *Frankenstein Meets the Wolf Man* (Univ., 1942), *Tarzan and the Amazons* (RKO, 1945), *I've Always Loved You* (Rep., 1946), *Wyoming* (Rep., 1947), *A Kiss in the Dark* (WB, 1949).

REGINALD OWEN (John Reginald Owen) Born August 5, 1887, Wheathampstead, England. Married Lydia Bilbrooke (1908); divorced 1923. Married Mrs. Harold Austin; widowed 1956. Married Barbara Haveman (1956).

Reginald Owen, James Gleason, Lynne Overman and Edgar Kennedy in *Yours for the Asking.*

Feature Films: *The Letter* (Par., 1929), *Platinum Blonde* (Col., 1931), *The Man in Possession* (MGM, 1931), *Sherlock Holmes* (Fox, 1932),

A Study in Scarlet (World Wide, 1933), *Double Harness* (RKO, 1933), *The Narrow Corner* (WB, 1933), *Voltaire* (WB, 1933), *Queen Christina* (MGM, 1933), *Nana* (UA, 1934), *The House of Rothschild* (UA, 1934), *Of Human Bondage* (RKO, 1934), *The Human Side* (Univ., 1934), *Countess of Monte Cristo* (Univ., 1934), *Here Is My Heart* (Par., 1934), *Fashions of 1934* (WB, 1934), *Mandalay* (WB, 1934), *Madame Du Barry* (WB, 1934), *Where Sinners Meet* (RKO, 1934), *Music in the Air* (Fox, 1934), *Enchanted April* (RKO, 1935), *Anna Karenina* (MGM, 1935), *The Bishop Misbehaves* (MGM, 1935), *Escapade* (MGM, 1935), *A Tale of Two Cities* (MGM, 1935), *The Good Fairy* (Univ., 1935), *Call of the Wild* (UA, 1935), *Petticoat Fever* (MGM, 1936), *Rose Marie* (MGM, 1936), *Trouble for Two* (MGM, 1936), *The Great Ziegfeld* (MGM, 1936), *Conquest* (MGM, 1937), *Rosalie* (MGM, 1937), *Personal Property* (MGM, 1937), *Dangerous Number* (MGM, 1937), *A Christmas Carol* (MGM, 1938), *Everybody Sing* (MGM, 1938), *Paradise for Three* (MGM, 1938), *Three Loves Has Nancy* (MGM, 1938), *Vacation From Love* (MGM, 1938), *Pride and Prejudice* (MGM, 1940), *The Earl of Chicago* (MGM, 1940), *Florian* (MGM, 1940), *Free and Easy* (MGM, 1941), *Blonde Inspiration* (MGM, 1941), *Tarzan's Secret Treasure* (MGM, 1941), *Charley's Aunt* (20th, 1941), *Random Harvest* (MGM, 1942), *Woman of the Year* (MGM, 1942), *Mrs. Miniver* (MGM, 1942), *Assignment in Britanny* (MGM, 1943), *Madame Curie* (MGM, 1943), *The Valley of Decision* (MGM, 1945), *The Sailor Takes a Wife* (MGM, 1945), *Kitty* (Par., 1945), *Monsieur Beaucaire* (Par., 1946), *Cluny Brown* (20th, 1946), *Thunder in the Valley* (20th, 1947), *Green Dolphin Street* (MGM, 1947), *If Winter Comes* (MGM, 1947), *Piccadilly Incident* (MGM, 1948), *The Three Musketeers* (MGM, 1948), *The Secret Garden* (MGM, 1949), *Challenge to Lassie* (MGM, 1949), *Kim* (MGM, 1950), *Grounds for Marriage* (MGM, 1950), *The Miniver Story* (MGM, 1950), *The Great Diamond Robbery* (MGM, 1953), *Red Garters* (Par., 1954), *Five Weeks in a Balloon* (20th, 1962), *Tammy and the Doctor* (Univ., 1963), *The Thrill of it All* (Univ., 1963), *Voice of the Hurricane* (Selected Pictures, 1964), *Mary Poppins* (BV, 1964).

GERALDINE PAGE (Geraldine Sue Page) Born November 22, 1924, Kirksville, Missouri. Married Alexander Schneider; divorced. Married Rip Torn (1963), child: Angelica.

Geraldine Page and Glenn Ford in *Dear Heart.*

Feature Films: *Out of the Night* (Moody Bible Institute, 1947), *Taxi* (20th, 1953), *Hondo* (WB, 1953), *Summer and Smoke* (Par., 1961), *Sweet Bird of Youth* (MGM, 1962), *Toys in the Attic* (UA, 1963), *Dear Heart* (WB, 1964), *You're a Big Boy Now* (7 Arts, 1966), *The Happiest Millionaire* (BV, 1967), *Monday's Child* (DuRoda Productions, 1968).

JANIS PAIGE (Donna Mae Tjaden) Born September 16, 1922, Tacoma, Washington. Married Frank Martinelli (1947); divorced 1950. Married Arthur Stander (1956); divorced 1957. Married Ray Gilbert (1962).

Feature Films: *Bathing Beauty* (MGM, 1944), *Hollywood Canteen*

Dennis Morgan and Janis Paige in *One Sunday Afternoon*.

Jed Prouty, Adrienne Ames and Eugene Pallette in *Black Sheep*.

(WB, 1944), *Her Kind of Man* (WB, 1946), *Of Human Bondage* (WB, 1946), *Two Guys From Milwaukee* (WB, 1946), *The Time, the Place and the Girl* (WB, 1946), *Love and Learn* (WB, 1947), *Cheyenne* (WB, 1947), *Always Together* (WB, 1947),* *Winter Meeting* (WB, 1948), *Wallflower* (WB, 1948), *Romance on the High Seas* (WB, 1948), *One Sunday Afternoon* (WB, 1948), *The Younger Brothers* (WB, 1949), *The House Across the Street* (WB, 1949), *This Side of the Law* (WB, 1950), *Mr. Universe* (EL, 1951), *Fugitive Lady* (Rep., 1951), *Two Gals and a Guy* (UA, 1951), *Silk Stockings* (MGM, 1957), *Please Don't Eat the Daisies* (MGM, 1960), *Bachelor in Paradise* (MGM, 1961), *Follow the Boys* (MGM, 1963), *The Caretakers* (UA, 1963), *Welcome to Hard Times* (MGM, 1967).

*Unbilled guest appearance

JACK PALANCE (Walter Jack Palance) Born February 18, 1920, Lattimer, Pennsylvania. Married Virginia Baker (1949), children: Holly, Brook.

Constance Smith and Jack Palance in *Man in the Attic*.

English-Language Feature Films: *Panic in the Streets* (20th, 1950), *Halls of Montezuma* (20th, 1950), *Sudden Fear* (RKO, 1952), *Shane* (Par., 1953), *Second Chance* (RKO, 1953), *Arrowhead* (Par., 1953), *Flight to Tangier* (Par., 1953), *Man in the Attic* (20th, 1953), *Sign of the Pagan* (Univ., 1954), *The Silver Chalice* (WB, 1954), *Kiss of Fire* (Univ., 1955), *The Big Knife* (UA, 1955), *I Died a Thousand Times* (WB, 1955), *Attack!* (UA, 1956), *The Lonely Man* (Par., 1957), *House of Numbers* (MGM, 1957), *The Man Inside* (Col., 1958), *Ten Seconds to Hell* (UA, 1959), *Beyond All Limits* (Sutton Picture Corp., 1961), *Barabbas* (Col., 1962), *The Mongols* (Colorama, 1962), *Once a Thief* (MGM, 1965), *The Professionals* (Col., 1966), *Kill a Dragon* (UA, 1967), *Torture Garden* (Col., 1968), *The Scalphunters* (UA, 1968), *Our Man From Las Vegas* (WB-7 Arts, 1968).

EUGENE PALLETTE Born July 8, 1889, Winfield, Kansas. Died September 3, 1954.

Sound Feature Films: *Lights of New York* (WB, 1928), *The Canary Murder Case* (Par., 1929), *The Dummy* (Par., 1929), *The Greene Murder Case* (Par., 1929), *Studio Murder Mystery* (Par., 1929), *The Virginian* (Par., 1929), *Pointed Heels* (Par., 1929), *Love Parade* (Par., 1929), *Slightly Scarlet* (Par., 1930), *The Benson Murder Case* (Par., 1930), *Paramount on Parade* (Par., 1930), *Kibitzer* (Par., 1930), *Men Are Like That* (Par., 1930), *Border Legion* (Par., 1930), *Follow Through* (Par., 1930), *Let's Go Native* (Par., 1930), *Sea God* (Par., 1930), *Santa Fe Trail* (Par., 1930), *Playboy of Paris* (Par., 1930), *Sea Legs* (Par., 1930), *Fighting Caravans* (Par., 1931), *It Pays to Advertise* (Par., 1931), *Gun Smoke* (Par., 1931), *Dude Ranch* (Par., 1931), *Huckleberry Finn* (Par., 1931), *Girls About Town* (Par., 1931), *Dancers in the Dark* (Par., 1932), *Shanghai Express* (Par., 1932), *Thunder Below* (Par., 1932), *Strangers of the Evening* (Tif., 1932), *Night Mayor* (Col., 1932), *Wild Girl* (Fox, 1932), *Half-Naked Truth* (RKO, 1932), *Hell Below* (MGM, 1933), *Made on Broadway* (MGM, 1933), *Storm at Daybreak* (MGM, 1933), *Shanghai Madness* (Fox, 1933), *The Kennel Murder Case* (WB, 1933), *From Headquarters* (WB, 1933), *Mr. Skitch* (Fox, 1933), *I've Got Your Number* (WB, 1934), *Cross Country Cruise* (Univ., 1934), *Friends of Mr. Sweeney* (WB, 1934), *Strictly Dynamite* (RKO, 1934), *The Dragon Murder Case* (WB, 1934), *Caravan* (Fox, 1934), *One Exciting Adventure* (Univ., 1934), *Bordertown* (WB, 1935), *Baby Face Harrington* (MGM, 1935), *All the King's Horses* (Par., 1935), *Black Sheep* (Fox, 1935), *Steamboat 'Round the Bend* (Fox, 1935), *The Ghost Goes West* (UA, 1936), *The Golden Arrow* (WB, 1936), *My Man Godfrey* (Col., 1936), *Easy to Take* (Par., 1936), *Luckiest Girl in the World* (Univ., 1936), *Stowaway* (20th, 1936), *Clarence* (Par., 1937), *The Crime Nobody Saw* (Par., 1937), *She Had to Eat* (20th, 1937), *100 Men and a Girl* (Univ., 1937), *Topper* (MGM, 1937), *The Adventures of Robin Hood* (WB, 1938), *There Goes My Heart* (UA, 1938), *Wife, Husband and Friend* (20th, 1939), *First Love* (Univ., 1939), *Mr. Smith Goes to Washington* (Col., 1939), *Young Tom Edison* (MGM, 1940), *It's a Date* (Univ., 1940), *Sandy Is a Lady* (Col., 1940), *He Stayed for Breakfast* (Col., 1940), *A Little Bit of Heaven* (Univ., 1940), *The Mark of Zorro* (20th, 1940), *Ride Kelly, Ride* (20th, 1941), *The Lady Eve* (Par., 1941), *The Bride Came C.O.D.* (WB, 1941), *Unfinished Business* (Univ., 1941), *World Premiere* (Par., 1941), *Appointment for Love* (Univ., 1941), *The Male Animal* (WB, 1941), *Are Husbands Necessary?* (Par., 1942), *Lady in a Jam* (Univ., 1942), *Almost Married* (Univ., 1942), *Tales of Manhattan* (20th, 1942), *The Big Street* (RKO, 1942), *The Forest Rangers* (Par., 1942), *Silver Queen* (UA, 1942), *Slightly Dangerous* (MGM, 1943), *It Ain't Hay* (Univ., 1943), *The Kansan* (UA, 1943), *Heaven Can Wait* (20th, 1943), *The Gang's All Here* (20th, 1943), *Pin-Up Girl* (20th, 1944), *Sensations of 1945* (UA, 1944), *Step Lively* (RKO, 1944), *Heavenly Days* (RKO, 1944), *In the Meantime, Darling* (20th, 1944), *Lake Placid Serenade* (Rep., 1945), *The Cheaters* (Rep., 1945), *Suspense* (Mon., 1946), *In Old Sacramento* (Rep., 1946).

LILLI PALMER (Maria Lilli Peiser) Born May 24, 1914, Posen, Germany. Married Rex Harrison (1943), child: Carey; divorced 1958. Married Carlos Thompson (1958).

Lilli Palmer, Dana Andrews and Louis Jourdan in *No Minor Vices*.

English-Language Feature Films: *Crime Unlimited* (1934), *Bad Blood* (1935), *First Offense* (Gainsborough, 1935), *Secret Agent* (Gaumont-British, 1936), *Wolf's Clothing* (1936), *The Great Barrier* (Gaumont-British, 1937), *Sunset in Vienna* (Wilcox, 1937), *Good Morning, Boys* ("Where There's a Will"—Gaumont-British, 1937), *Command Performance* (Grosvenor, 1937), *Crackerjack* (Gaumont-British, 1938), *Man With a Hundred Faces* (Gaumont-British, 1938), *A Girl Must Live* (Gainsborough, 1938), *Blind Folly* (1940), *The Door With Seven Locks* ("Chamber of Horrors"—Argyle, 1941), *Thunder Rock* (Charter, 1942), *The Gentle Sex* (Two Cities, 1943), *English Without Tears* (Two Cities, 1943), *Beware of Pity* (Two Cities, 1945), *The Rake's Progress* ("Notorious Gentleman"—Univ., 1946), *Cloak and Dagger* (WB, 1946), *Body and Soul* (UA, 1947), *My Girl Tisa* (WB, 1948), *No Minor Vices* (MGM, 1948), *Her Man Gilbey* (Univ., 1949), *The Wicked City* (UA, 1951), *The Long Dark Hall* (EL, 1951), *The Fourposter* (Col., 1952), *Main Street to Broadway* (MGM, 1953), *But Not for Me* (Par., 1959), *Conspiracy of Hearts* (Par., 1960), *The Pleasure of His Company* (Par., 1961), *The Counterfeit Traitor* (Par., 1962), *The Miracle of the White Stallions* (BV, 1963), *Torpedo Bay* (AIP, 1964), *Operation Crossbow* (MGM, 1965), *The Amorous Adventures of Moll Flanders* (Par., 1965), *Jack of Diamonds* (MGM, 1967), *Sebastian* (Par., 1968), *Nobody Runs Forever* (Rank, 1968), *The High Commissioner* (American Broadcasting Co., 1968), *Oedipus* (Univ., 1968).

FRANKLIN PANGBORN Born January 23, 1893, Newark, New Jersey. Died July 20, 1958.

Sound Feature Films: *Not So Dumb* (MGM, 1930), *Cheer Up and Smile* (Fox, 1930), *Her Man* (Pathé, 1930), *A Lady Surrenders* (Univ., 1930), *Woman of Experience* (Pathé, 1931), *International House* (Par., 1933), *Professional Sweetheart* (RKO, 1933), *Important Witness* (Tower, 1933), *Headline Shooter* (RKO, 1933), *Only Yesterday* (Univ.,

Franklin Pangborn, Edna Murphy, Patsy Ruth Miller and Alan Hale in *The Sap*.

1933), *Design for Living* (Par., 1933), *Flying Down to Rio* (RKO, 1933), *Manhattan Love Song* (Mon., 1934), *Unknown Blonde* (Majestic, 1934), *Many Happy Returns* (Par., 1934), *Strictly Dynamite* (RKO, 1934), *Young and Beautiful* (Mascot, 1934), *Imitation of Life* (Univ., 1934), *King Kelly of the U.S.A.* (Mon., 1934), *That's Gratitude* (Col., 1934), *College Rhythm* (Par., 1934), *Tomorrow's Youth* (Mon., 1935), *Eight Bells* (Col., 1935), *Headline Woman* (Mon., 1935), *She Couldn't Take It* (Col., 1935), *$1,000 a Minute* (Rep., 1935), *Tango* (Invincible, 1936), *Don't Gamble With Love* (Col., 1936), *Mr. Deeds Goes to Town* (Col., 1936), *Doughnuts and Society* (Mascot, 1936), *To Mary—With Love* (20th, 1936), *The Mandarin Mystery* (Rep., 1936), *Hats Off* (GN, 1936), *The Luckiest Girl in the World* (Univ., 1936), *Dangerous Number* (MGM, 1937), *She's Dangerous* (Univ., 1937), *Swing High—Swing Low* (Par., 1937), *Step Lively, Jeeves!* (20th, 1937), *Turn Off the Moon* (Par., 1937), *A Star Is Born* (UA, 1937), *Danger, Love at Work* (20th, 1937), *Hotel Haywire* (Par., 1937), *Dangerous Holiday* (Rep., 1937), *She Had to Eat* (20th, 1937), *Stage Door* (RKO, 1937), *Life of the Party* (RKO, 1937), *Thrill of a Lifetime* (Par., 1937), *Living on Love* (RKO, 1937), *When Love Is Young* (Univ., 1937), *High Hat* (Imperial, 1937), *Bluebeard's Eighth Wife* (Par., 1938), *Love on Toast* (Par., 1938), *Mad About Music* (Univ., 1938), *Joy of Living* (RKO, 1938), *Rebecca of Sunnybrook Farm* (20th, 1938), *She Married an Artist* (Col., 1938), *Vivacious Lady* (RKO, 1938), *Dr. Rhythm* (Par., 1938), *Four's a Crowd* (WB, 1938), *Three Blind Mice* (20th, 1938), *Carefree* (RKO, 1938), *Just Around the Corner* (20th, 1938), *Meet the Mayor* (Times Pictures, 1938), *Topper Takes a Trip* (UA, 1939), *The Girl Downstairs* (MGM, 1939), *Broadway Serenade* (MGM, 1939), *Fifth Avenue Girl* (RKO, 1939), *Turnabout* (UA, 1940), *Christmas in July* (Par., 1940), *Spring Parade* (Univ., 1940), *Public Deb No. 1* (20th, 1940), *The Bank Dick* (Univ., 1940), *Where Did You Get That Girl?* (Univ., 1941), *The Hit Parade of 1941* (Rep., 1941), *A Girl, a Guy and a Gob* (RKO, 1941), *The Flame of New Orleans* (Univ., 1941), *Bachelor Daddy* (Univ., 1941), *Tillie the Toiler* (Col., 1941), *Never Give a Sucker an Even Break* (Univ., 1941), *Week-End for Three* (RKO, 1941), *Obliging Young Lady* (RKO, 1941), *Sullivan's Travels* (Par., 1941), *Mr. District Attorney in The Carter Case* (Rep., 1941), *Sandy Steps Out* (Univ., 1941), *What's Cooking?* (Univ., 1942), *Call out the Marines* (RKO, 1942), *Moonlight Masquerade* (Rep., 1942), *Now, Voyager* (WB, 1942), *George Washington Slept Here* (WB, 1942), *Palm Beach Story* (Par., 1942), *Strictly in the Groove* (Univ., 1943), *Two Weeks to Live* (RKO, 1943), *Honeymoon Lodge* (Univ., 1943), *Holy Matrimony* (20th, 1943), *Crazy House* (Univ., 1943), *His Butler's Sister* (Univ., 1943), *Stage Door Canteen* (UA, 1943), *Reveille With Beverly* (Col., 1943), *My Best Gal* (Rep., 1944), *The Great Moment* (Par., 1944), *Hail the Conquering Hero* (Par., 1944), *Reckless Age* (Univ., 1944), *The Horn Blows at Midnight* (WB, 1945), *You Came Along* (Par., 1945), *Tell It to a Star* (Rep., 1945), *Two Guys From Milwaukee* (WB, 1946), *I'll Be Yours* (Univ., 1947), *Calendar Girl* (Rep., 1947), *Mad Wednesday* (UA, 1947), *Romance on the High Seas* (WB, 1949), *My Dream Is Yours* (WB, 1949), *Down Memory Lane* (EL, 1949), *The Story of Mankind* (WB, 1957), *Oh, Men! Oh, Women!* (20th, 1957).

ELEANOR PARKER Born June 26, 1922, Cedarville, Ohio. Married Fred Losee (1943); divorced 1944. Married Bert Friedlob (1946), children: Susan, Sharon, Richard; divorced 1953. Married Paul Clemens (1954), child: Paul, Jr.; divorced 1964. Married Raymond Hirsch (1966).

Feature Films: *Busses Roar* (WB, 1942), *Mysterious Doctor* (WB, 1943), *Mission to Moscow* (WB, 1943), *Between Two Worlds* (WB, 1944), *Crime by Night* (WB, 1944), *The Last Ride* (WB, 1944), *The Very Thought of You* (WB, 1944), *Hollywood Canteen* (WB, 1944), *Pride of the Marines* (WB, 1945), *Of Human Bondage* (WB, 1946), *Never Say Goodbye* (WB, 1946), *Escape Me Never* (WB, 1947), *Always Together* (WB, 1947),* *The Voice of the Turtle* (WB, 1947), *The Woman in White* (WB, 1948), *It's a Great Feeling* (WB, 1949), *Chain Lightning* (WB, 1950), *Caged* (WB, 1950), *Three Secrets* (WB, 1950), *Valentino* (Col., 1951), *A Millionaire for Christy* (20th, 1951), *Detective Story* (Par., 1951), *Scaramouche* (MGM, 1952), *Above and Beyond* (MGM, 1952), *Escape From Fort Bravo* (MGM, 1953), *The Naked Jungle* (Par., 1954), *Valley of the Kings* (MGM, 1954), *Many Rivers to Cross*

Agnes Moorehead, Eleanor Parker and Sheila Stevens (MacRae) in *Caged*.

(MGM, 1955), *Interrupted Melody* (MGM, 1955), *The Man With the Golden Arm* (UA, 1955), *The King and Four Queens* (UA, 1956), *Lizzie* (MGM, 1957), *The Seventh Sin* (MGM, 1957), *A Hole in the Head* (UA, 1959), *Home From the Hill* (MGM, 1960), *Return to Peyton Place* (20th, 1961), *Madison Avenue* (20th, 1962), *Panic Button* (Gorton Associates, 1964), *The Sound of Music* (20th, 1965), *The Oscar* (Par., 1966), *An American Dream* (WB, 1966), *Warning Shot* (Par., 1967), *The Tiger and the Pussycat* (Embassy, 1967).

   *Unbilled guest appearance

JEAN PARKER (Mae Green) Born August 11, 1912, Deer Lodge, Montana. Married George MacDonald (1936); divorced 1940. Married Douglas Dawson (1941); divorced. Married Curtis Grotter (1944); divorced 1949. Married Robert Lowery (1951); divorced 1957.

Jean Parker and Eric Linden in *Romance of the Limberlost*.

Feature Films: *Divorce in the Family* (MGM, 1932), *Rasputin and the Empress* (MGM, 1932), *Secret of Madame Blanche* (MGM, 1933), *Gabriel Over the White House* (MGM, 1933), *Made on Broadway* (MGM, 1933), *Storm at Daybreak* (MGM, 1933), *What Price Innocence* (Col., 1933), *Lady for a Day* (Col., 1933), *Little Women* (RKO, 1933), *Lazy River* (MGM, 1934), *You Can't Buy Everything* (MGM, 1934), *Two Alone* (RKO, 1934), *Operator 13* (MGM, 1934), *Caravan* (Fox, 1934), *Sequoia* (MGM, 1934), *A Wicked Woman* (MGM, 1934), *Limehouse Blues* (Par., 1934), *Have a Heart* (MGM, 1934), *Princess O'Hara* (Univ., 1935), *Murder in the Fleet* (MGM, 1935), *The Ghost Goes West* (UA, 1936), *The Farmer in the Dell* (RKO, 1936), *The Texas Rangers* (Par., 1936), *The Barrier* (Par., 1937), *Life Begins With Love* (Col., 1937), *Penitentiary* (Col., 1938), *Romance of the Limberlost* (Mon., 1938), *The Arkansas Traveler* (Par., 1938), *Zenobia* (UA, 1939), *Romance of the Redwoods* (Col., 1939), *She Married a Cop* (Rep., 1939), *Flight at Midnight* (Rep., 1939), *Parents on Trial* (Col., 1939),

The Flying Deuces (RKO, 1939), *Son of the Navy* (Mon., 1940), *Knights of the Range* (Par., 1940), *Beyond Tomorrow* (RKO, 1940), *The Roar of the Press* (Mon., 1941), *Power Dive* (Par., 1941), *Flying Blind* (Par., 1941), *The Pittsburgh Kid* (Rep., 1941), *No Hands on the Clock* (Par., 1941), *Torpedo Boat* (Par., 1942), *The Girl From Alaska* (Rep., 1942), *Hi, Neighbor* (Rep., 1942), *Hello, Annapolis* (Col., 1942), *I Live on Danger* (Par., 1942), *Tomorrow We Live* (PRC, 1942), *Wrecking Crew* (Par., 1942), *The Traitor Within* (Rep., 1942), *Alaska Highway* (Par., 1943), *Minesweeper* (Par., 1943), *The Deerslayer* (Rep., 1943), *High Explosive* (Par., 1943), *The Navy Way* (Par., 1944), *Detective Kitty O'Day* (Mon., 1944), *The Lady in the Death House* (PRC, 1944), *Oh, What a Night!* (Mon., 1944), *Dead Man's Eyes* (Univ., 1944), *Bluebeard* (PRC, 1944), *One Body Too Many* (Par., 1944), *The Adventures of Kitty O'Day* (Mon., 1945), *The Gunfighter* (20th, 1950), *Toughest Man in Arizona* (Rep., 1952), *Those Redheads From Seattle* (Par., 1953), *Black Tuesday* (UA, 1954), *A Lawless Street* (Col., 1955), *The Parson and the Outlaw* (Col., 1957), *Apache Uprising* (Par., 1966).

GAIL PATRICK (Margaret Fitzpatrick) Born June 20, 1916, Birmingham, Alabama. Married Robert Cobb (1936); divorced 1940. Married Arnold White (1944); divorced 1946. Married Cornwall Jackson (1947), children: Jennifer, Thomas.

Gail Patrick and Ricardo Cortez in *Her Husband Lies*.

Feature Films: *If I Had a Million* (Par., 1932), *Mysterious Rider* (Par., 1933), *Mama Loves Papa* (Par., 1933), *Pick-Up* (Par., 1933), *Murders in the Zoo* (Par., 1933), *Phantom Broadcast* (Mon., 1933), *To the Last Man* (Par., 1933), *Cradle Song* (Par., 1933), *Death Takes a Holiday* (Par., 1934), *Murder at the Vanities* (Par., 1934), *The Crime of Helen Stanley* (Col., 1934), *Wagon Wheels* (Par., 1934), *Take the Stand* (Liberty, 1934), *One Hour Late* (Par., 1935), *Rumba* (Par., 1935), *Mississippi* (Par., 1935), *Doubting Thomas* (Fox, 1935), *No More Ladies* (MGM, 1935), *Smart Girl* (Par., 1935), *The Big Broadcast of 1936* (Par., 1935), *Wanderer of the Wasteland* (Par., 1935), *Two Fisted* (Par., 1935), *Two in the Dark* (RKO, 1936), *The Lone Wolf Returns* (Col., 1936), *The Preview Murder Mystery* (Par., 1936), *Early to Bed* (Par., 1936), *My Man Godfrey* (Univ., 1936), *Murder With Pictures* (Par., 1936), *White Hunter* (20th, 1936), *John Meade's Woman* (Par., 1937), *Her Husband Lies* (Par., 1937), *Artists and Models* (Par., 1937), *Stage Door* (RKO, 1937), *Mad About Music* (Univ., 1938), *Dangerous to Know* (Par., 1938), *Wives Under Suspicion* (Univ., 1938), *King of Alcatraz* (Par., 1938), *Disbarred* (Par., 1939), *Man of Conquest* (Rep., 1939), *Grand Jury Secrets* (Par., 1939), *Reno* (RKO, 1939), *My Favorite Wife* (RKO, 1940), *The Doctor Takes a Wife* (Col., 1940), *Gallant Sons* (MGM, 1940), *Love Crazy* (MGM, 1941), *Kathleen* (MGM, 1941), *Tales of Manhattan* (20th, 1942), *Quiet Please—Murder* (20th, 1942), *We Were Dancing* (MGM, 1942), *The Hit Parade of 1943* (Rep., 1943), *Women in Bondage* (Mon., 1943), *Up in Mabel's Room* (UA, 1944), *Brewster's Millions* (UA, 1945), *Twice Blessed* (MGM, 1945), *The Madonna's Secret* (Rep., 1946), *Rendezvous With Annie*

(Rep., 1946), *Claudia and David* (20th, 1946), *The Plainsman and the Lady* (Rep., 1946), *Calendar Girl* (Rep., 1947), *King of the Wild Horses* (Col., 1947), *The Inside Story* (Rep., 1948).

LEE PATRICK (Lee Salome Patrick) Born November 22, 1911,. New York, New York. Married Thomas Wood (1937).

Lee Patrick, Dale Belding and Nana Bryant in *Inner Sanctum.*

Feature Films: *Strange Cargo* (Pathé, 1929), *Border Cafe* (RKO, 1937), *Music for Madame* (RKO, 1937), *Danger Patrol* (RKO, 1937), *Crashing Hollywood* (RKO, 1938), *Night Spot* (RKO, 1938), *Condemned Women* (RKO, 1938), *Law of the Underworld* (RKO, 1938), *The Sisters* (WB, 1938), *Fisherman's Wharf* (RKO, 1939), *Invisible Stripes* (WB, 1940), *Saturday's Children* (WB, 1940), *City for Conquest* (WB, 1940), *Ladies Must Live* (WB, 1940), *Money and the Woman* (WB, 1940), *South of Suez* (WB, 1940), *Father Is a Prince* (WB, 1940), *Footsteps in the Dark* (WB, 1941), *Honeymoon for Three* (WB, 1941), *Million Dollar Baby* (WB, 1941), *The Nurse's Secret* (WB, 1941), *The Smiling Ghost* (WB, 1941), *The Maltese Falcon* (WB, 1941), *Dangerously They Live* (WB, 1941), *In This Our Life* (WB, 1942), *Now, Voyager* (WB, 1942), *Somewhere I'll Find You* (MGM, 1942), *George Washington Slept Here* (WB, 1942), *A Night to Remember* (Col., 1943), *Jitterbugs* (20th, 1943), *Nobody's Darling* (Rep., 1943), *Larceny With Music* (Univ., 1943), *Moon Over Las Vegas* (Univ., 1944), *Gambler's Choice* (Par., 1944), *Mrs. Parkington* (MGM, 1944), *Faces in the Fog* (Rep., 1944), *See My Lawyer* (Univ., 1945), *Keep Your Powder Dry* (MGM, 1945), *Over 21* (Col., 1945), *Mildred Pierce* (WB, 1945), *The Walls Came Tumbling Down* (Col., 1946), *Strange Journey* (20th, 1946), *Wake Up and Dream* (20th, 1946), *Mother Wore Tights* (20th, 1947), *Inner Sanctum* (Film Classics, 1948), *The Snake Pit* (20th, 1948), *Singin' Spurs* (Col., 1948), *The Doolins of Oklahoma* (Col., 1949), *The Lawless* (Par., 1950), *The Fuller Brush Girl* (Col., 1950), *Caged* (WB, 1950), *Tomorrow Is Another Day* (WB, 1951), *Take Me to Town* (Univ., 1953), *There's No Business Like Show Business* (20th, 1954), *Vertigo* (Par., 1958), *Auntie Mame* (WB, 1958), *Pillow Talk* (Univ., 1959), *Visit to a Small Planet* (Par., 1960), *Goodbye Again* (UA, 1961), *Summer and Smoke* (Par., 1961), *A Girl Named Tamiko* (Par., 1962), *Wives and Lovers* (Par., 1963), *7 Faces of Dr. Lao* (MGM, 1964), *The New Interns* (Col., 1964).

ELIZABETH PATTERSON (Mary Elizabeth Patterson) Born November 22, 1874, Savannah, Tennessee. Died January 31, 1966.

Sound Feature Films: *Timothy's Quest* (Gotham Productions, 1929), *Words and Music* (Fox, 1929), *South Sea Rose* (Fox, 1929), *Lone Star Ranger* (Fox, 1930), *Harmony at Home* (Fox, 1930), *The Big Party* (Fox, 1930), *The Cat Creeps* (Univ., 1930), *Penrod and Sam* (WB, 1931), *Tarnished Lady* (Par., 1931), *The Smiling Lieutenant* (Par., 1931), *Daddy Long Legs* (Fox, 1931), *Heaven on Earth* (Univ., 1931), *Two Against the World* (WB, 1932), *Husband's Holiday* (Par., 1932), *The Expert* (WB, 1932), *Play Girl* (WB, 1932), *So Big* (WB, 1932), *New Morals for Old* (MGM, 1932), *Miss Pinkerton* (WB, 1932), *Love Me Tonight* (Par., 1932), *Life Begins* (WB, 1932), *Guilty as Hell* (Par., 1932), *A Bill of Divorcement* (RKO, 1932), *They Call It Sin*

Cecilia Parker and Elizabeth Patterson in *Old Hutch.*

(WB, 1932), *Breach of Promise* (World Wide, 1932), *No Man of Her Own* (Par., 1932), *The Conquerors* (RKO, 1932), *They Just Had to Get Married* (Univ., 1933), *Infernal Machine* (Fox, 1933), *The Story of Temple Drake* (Par., 1933), *Dinner at Eight* (MGM, 1933), *Hold Your Man* (MGM, 1933), *Doctor Bull* (Fox, 1933), *Secret of the Blue Room* (Univ., 1933), *Hideout* (MGM, 1934), *Golden Harvest* (Par., 1933), *Chasing Yesterday* (RKO, 1935), *So Red the Rose* (Par., 1935), *Men Without Names* (Par., 1935), *Her Master's Voice* (Par., 1936), *Small Town Girl* (MGM, 1936), *Timothy's Quest* (Par., 1936), *Three Cheers for Love* (Par., 1936), *The Return of Sophie Lang* (Par., 1936), *Old Hutch* (MGM, 1936), *Go West, Young Man* (Par., 1936), *High, Wide and Handsome* (Par., 1937), *Hold 'Em Navy* (Par., 1937), *Night Club Scandal* (Par., 1937), *Night of Mystery* (Par., 1937), *Scandal Street* (Par., 1938), *Bluebeard's Eighth Wife* (Par., 1938), *Bulldog Drummond's Peril* (Par., 1938), *Sing You Sinners* (Par., 1938), *Sons of the Legion* (Par., 1938), *The Story of Alexander Graham Bell* (20th, 1939), *Bulldog Drummond's Secret Police* (Par., 1939), *Bulldog Drummond's Bride* (Par., 1939), *The Cat and the Canary* (Par., 1939), *Our Leading Citizen* (Par., 1939), *Remember the Night* (Par., 1940), *Bad Little Angel* (MGM, 1940), *Adventure in Diamonds* (Par., 1940), *Anne of Windy Poplars* (RKO, 1940), *Earthbound* (20th, 1940), *Who Killed Aunt Maggie?* (Rep., 1940), *Michael Shayne, Private Detective* (20th, 1940), *Tobacco Road* (20th, 1940), *Kiss the Boys Goodbye* (Par., 1940), *Belle Starr* (20th, 1941), *Lucky Legs* (Col., 1942), *Her Cardboard Lover* (MGM, 1942), *Almost Married* (Univ., 1942), *My Sister Eileen* (Col., 1942), *I Married a Witch* (UA, 1942), *Beyond the Blue Horizon* (Par., 1942), *Lucky Legs* (Col., 1942), *The Sky's the Limit* (RKO, 1943), *Follow the Boys* (Univ., 1944), *Hail the Conquering Hero* (Par., 1944), *Together Again* (Col., 1944), *Lady on a Train* (Univ., 1945), *Colonel Effingham's Raid* (20th, 1945), *I've Always Loved You* (Rep., 1946), *The Secret Heart* (MGM, 1946), *The Shocking Miss Pilgrim* (20th, 1947), *Welcome Stranger* (Par., 1947), *Out of the Blue* (EL, 1947), *Miss Tatlock's Millions* (Par., 1948), *Little Women* (MGM, 1949), *Song of Surrender* (Par., 1949), *Intruder in the Dust* (MGM, 1949), *Bright Leaf* (WB, 1950), *Katie Did It* (Univ., 1951), *Washington Story* (MGM, 1952), *Las Vegas Shakedown* (AA, 1955), *Pal Joey* (Col., 1957), *The Oregon Trail* (20th, 1959), *Tall Story* (WB, 1960).

KATINA PAXINOU (Katina Konstantopoulou) Born 1900, Piraeus, Greece. Married Ivannis Paxinou (1916); divorced. Married Alexis Minotis (1940), child: Iliana.

Walter Slezak and Katina Paxinou in *The Miracle.*

English-Language Feature Films: *For Whom the Bell Tolls* (Par., 1943), *Hostages* (Par., 1943), *Confidential Agent* (WB, 1945), *Mourning Becomes Electra* (RKO, 1947), *The Inheritance* (Fine Arts, 1947), *Prince of Foxes* (20th, 1949), *Mr. Arkadin* (WB, 1955), *The Miracle* (WB, 1959), *The Trial* (Gibraltar, 1962).

JOHN PAYNE Born May 23, 1912, Roanoke, Virginia. Married Anne Shirley (1937), child: Julie; divorced 1943. Married Gloria DeHaven (1944), children: Kathy, Thomas; divorced 1950. Married Alexandra Curtis (1953).

Glenn Miller, Sonja Henie and John Payne in *Sun Valley Serenade*.

Feature Films: *Dodsworth* (UA, 1936), *Hats Off* (GN, 1936), *Fair Warning* (20th, 1937), *Love on Toast* (Par., 1938), *College Swing* (Par., 1938), *Garden of the Moon* (WB, 1938), *Wings of the Navy* (WB, 1939), *Indianapolis Speedway* (WB, 1939), *Kid Nightingale* (WB, 1939), *Star Dust* (20th, 1940), *Maryland* (20th, 1940), *The Great Profile* (20th, 1940), *King of the Lumberjacks* (WB, 1940), *Tear Gas Squad* (WB, 1940), *The Great American Broadcast* (20th, 1941), *Week-End in Havana* (20th, 1941), *Remember the Day* (20th, 1941), *Sun Valley Serenade* (20th, 1941), *To the Shores of Tripoli* (20th, 1942), *Iceland* (20th, 1942), *Springtime in the Rockies* (20th, 1942), *Hello, Frisco, Hello* (20th, 1943), *The Dolly Sisters* (20th, 1945), *Sentimental Journey* (20th, 1946), *The Razor's Edge* (20th, 1946), *Wake Up and Dream* (20th, 1946), *The Miracle on 34th Street* (20th, 1947), *Larceny* (Univ., 1948), *The Saxon Charm* (Univ., 1948), *El Paso* (Par., 1949), *The Crooked Way* (UA, 1949), *Captain China* (Par., 1949), *The Eagle and the Hawk* (Par., 1950), *Tripoli* (Par., 1950), *Passage West* (Par., 1951), *Crosswinds* (Par., 1951), *Caribbean* (Par., 1952), *The Blazing Forest* (Par., 1952), *Kansas City Confidential* (UA, 1952), *Raiders of the Seven Seas* (UA, 1953), *The Vanquished* (Par., 1953), *99 River Street* (UA, 1953), *Rails into Laramie* (Univ., 1954), *Silver Lode* (RKO, 1954), *Santa Fe Passage* (Rep., 1955), *Hell's Island* (Par., 1955), *The Road to Denver* (Rep., 1955), *Tennessee's Partner* (RKO, 1955), *Slightly Scarlet* (RKO, 1956), *Rebel in Town* (UA, 1956), *Hold Back the Night* (AA, 1956), *The Boss* (UA, 1956), *Bailout at 43,000* (UA, 1957), *Hidden Fear* (UA, 1957), *Gift of the Nile* (PRO, 1968), *They Ran for Their Lives* (Color Vision, 1968).

GREGORY PECK (Eldred Gregory Peck) Born April 5, 1916, La Jolla, California. Married Greta Rice (1942), children: Jonathan, Stephen, Carey; divorced 1954. Married Veronique Passani (1955), children: Anthony, Cecelia.

Feature Films: *Days of Glory* (RKO, 1944), *The Keys of the Kingdom* (20th, 1944), *The Valley of Decision* (MGM, 1945), *Spellbound* (UA, 1945), *The Yearling* (MGM, 1946), *Duel in the Sun* (Selznick, 1946), *The Macomber Affair* (UA, 1947), *Gentleman's Agreement* (20th, 1947), *The Paradine Case* (Selznick, 1948), *Yellow Sky* (20th, 1948), *The Great Sinner* (MGM, 1949), *The Gun Fighter* (20th, 1949), *12 O'Clock High* (20th, 1949), *Captain Horatio Hornblower* (WB, 1951), *Only the Valiant*

Tamara Toumanova, Gregory Peck and Lowell Gilmore in *Days of Glory*.

(WB, 1951), *David and Bathsheba* (20th, 1951), *The Snows of Kilimanjaro* (20th, 1952), *Roman Holiday* (Par., 1953), *Night People* (20th, 1953), *Man With a Million* (UA, 1954), *The Purple Plain* (UA, 1955), *The Man in the Gray Flannel Suit* (20th, 1956), *Moby Dick* (WB, 1956), *Designing Woman* (MGM, 1957), *The Big Country* (UA, 1958), *The Bravados* (20th, 1958), *Pork Chop Hill* (UA, 1959), *Beloved Infidel* (20th, 1959), *On the Beach* (UA, 1959), *The Guns of Navarone* (Col., 1961), *Cape Fear* (Univ., 1962), *To Kill a Mockingbird* (Univ., 1962), *How the West Was Won* (MGM, 1963), *Behold a Pale Horse* (Col., 1964), *Captain Newman, M.D.* (Univ., 1964), *Mirage* (Univ., 1965), *Arabesque* (Univ., 1966), *MacKenna's Gold* (Col., 1968), *The Stalking Moon* (National *General*, 1968).

GEORGE PEPPARD Born October 1, 1933, Detroit, Michigan. Married Helen Davies (1954), children: Bradford, Julie; divorced 1965. Married Elizabeth Ashley (1966), child: Christopher.

Janice Rule and George Peppard in *The Subterraneans*.

Feature Films: *The Strange One* (Col., 1957), *Pork Chop Hill* (UA, 1959), *Home From the Hill* (MGM, 1960), *The Subterraneans* (MGM, 1960), *Breakfast at Tiffany's* (Par., 1961), *How the West Was Won* (MGM, 1963), *The Victors* (Col., 1963), *The Carpetbaggers* (Par., 1964), *Operation Crossbow* (MGM, 1965), *The Third Day* (WB, 1965), *The Blue Max* (20th, 1966), *Tobruk* (Univ., 1967), *Rough Night in Jericho* (Univ., 1967), *P.J.* (Univ., 1968), *What's So Bad About Feeling Good* (Univ., 1968), *House of Cards* (Univ., 1968).

TONY PERKINS (Anthony Perkins) Born April 4, 1932, New York, New York.

English-Language Feature Films: *The Actress* (MGM, 1953), *Friendly*

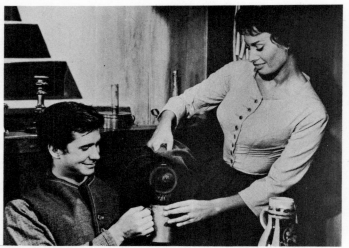

Tony Perkins and Sophia Loren in *Desire Under the Elms*.

Persuasion (AA, 1956), *The Lonely Man* (Par., 1957), *Fear Strikes Out* (Par., 1957), *The Tin Star* (Par., 1957), *This Angry Age* (Col., 1958), *The Matchmaker* (Par., 1958), *Green Mansions* (MGM, 1958), *On the Beach* (UA, 1959), *Tall Story* (WB, 1960), *Psycho* (Par., 1960), *Goodbye Again* (UA, 1961), *Phaedra* (Lopert, 1962), *Five Miles to Midnight* (UA, 1962), *The Trial* (Gibraltar, 1962), *Two Are Guilty* (MGM, 1964), *The Fool Killer* (Landau, 1965), *Is Paris Burning?* (Par., 1966), *The Champagne Murders* (Univ., 1968), *She Let Him Continue* (20th, 1968).

JEAN PETERS (Elizabeth Jean Peters) Born October 15, 1926, Canton, Ohio. Married Stuart Cramer (1954); divorced 1956. Married Howard Hughes (1957).

Joseph Cotten and Jean Peters in *A Blueprint for Murder*.

Feature Films: *Captain From Castile* (20th, 1947), *Deep Waters* (20th, 1948), *It Happens Every Spring* (20th, 1949), *Love That Brute* (20th, 1950), *Take Care of My Little Girl* (20th, 1951), *As Young as You Feel* (20th, 1951), *Anne of the Indies* (20th, 1951), *Viva Zapata!* (20th, 1952), *Wait Till the Sun Shines, Nellie* (20th, 1952), *Lure of the Wilderness* (20th, 1952), *O. Henry's Full House* (20th, 1952), *Niagara* (20th, 1953), *Pickup on South Street* (20th, 1953), *A Blueprint for Murder* (20th, 1953), *Vicki* (20th, 1953), *Three Coins in the Fountain* (20th, 1954), *Apache* (UA, 1954), *Broken Lance* (20th, 1954), *A Man Called Peter* (20th, 1955).

SUSAN PETERS (Suzanne Carnahan) Born July 3, 1921, Spokane, Washington. Married Richard Quine (1943), child: Timothy; divorced 1948. Died October 24, 1952.

Laraine Day, Susan Peters and Lana Turner in *Keep Your Powder Dry*.

Feature Films:
as **Suzanne Carnahan** *Santa Fe Trail* (WB, 1940), *Money and the Woman* (WB, 1940), *The Man Who Talked Too Much* (WB, 1940), *Susan and God* (MGM, 1940), *Strawberry Blonde* (WB, 1941), *Meet John Doe* (WB, 1941), *Here Comes Happiness* (WB, 1941).

as **Susan Peters** *Scattergood Pulls the Strings* (RKO, 1941), *Three Sons o' Guns* (WB, 1941), *Escape From Crime* (WB, 1942), *The Big Shot* (WB, 1942), *Tish* (MGM, 1942), *Random Harvest* (MGM, 1942), *Dr. Gillespie's New Assistant* (MGM, 1942), *Andy Hardy's Double Life* (MGM, 1942), *Assignment in Brittany* (MGM, 1943), *Young Ideas* (MGM, 1943), *Song of Russia* (MGM, 1943), *Keep Your Powder Dry* (MGM, 1945), *The Sign of the Ram* (Col., 1948).

WALTER PIDGEON Born September 23, 1897, East St. John, New Brunswick, Canada. Married Edna Pickles (1922), child: Edna; widowed 1924. Married Ruth Walker (1931).

Kay Francis, Eugene Pallette, Walter Pidgeon and Deanna Durbin in *It's a Date*.

Sound Feature Films: *Melody of Love* (Univ., 1928), *Her Private Life* (WB, 1929), *A Most Immoral Lady* (WB, 1929), *Bride of the Regiment* (WB, 1930), *Viennese Nights* (WB, 1930), *Sweet Kitty Bellaire* (WB, 1930), *Going Wild* (WB, 1931), *The Gorilla* (WB, 1931), *Kiss Me Again* (WB, 1931), *Hot Heiress* (WB, 1931), *Rockabye* (RKO, 1932), *The Kiss Before the Mirror* (Univ., 1933), *Journal of a Crime* (WB, 1934), *Fatal Lady* (Par., 1936), *Big Brown Eyes* (Par., 1936), *Girl Overboard* (Univ., 1937), *She's Dangerous* (Univ., 1937), *As Good as Married* (Univ., 1937), *Saratoga* (MGM, 1937), *My Dear Miss Aldrich* (MGM, 1937),

A Girl With Ideas (Univ., 1937), *Man-Proof* (MGM, 1938), *The Girl of the Golden West* (MGM, 1938), *The Shopworn Angel* (MGM, 1938), *Listen, Darling* (MGM, 1938), *Too Hot to Handle* (MGM, 1938), *Society Lawyer* (MGM, 1939), *6,000 Enemies* (MGM, 1939), *Stronger Than Desire* (MGM, 1939), *Nick Carter, Master Detective* (MGM, 1939), *It's a Date* (Univ., 1940), *Dark Command* (Rep., 1940), *The House Across the Bay* (UA, 1940), *Sky Murder* (MGM, 1940), *Flight Command* (MGM, 1940), *Man Hunt* (20th, 1941), *How Green Was My Valley* (20th, 1941), *Blossoms in the Dust* (MGM, 1941), *Design for Scandal* (MGM, 1941), *Mrs. Miniver* (MGM, 1942), *White Cargo* (MGM, 1942), *Madame Curie* (MGM, 1943), *The Youngest Profession* (MGM, 1943), *Mrs. Parkington* (MGM, 1944), *Weekend at the Waldorf* (MGM, 1945), *Holiday in Mexico* (MGM, 1946), *The Secret Heart* (MGM, 1946), *If Winter Comes* (MGM, 1947), *Cass Timberlane* (MGM, 1947)* *Julia Misbehaves* (MGM, 1948), *Command Decision* (MGM, 1948), *Red Danube* (MGM, 1949), *That Forsyte Woman* (MGM, 1949), *The Miniver Story* (MGM, 1950), *Soldiers Three* (MGM, 1951), *Calling Bulldog Drummond* (MGM, 1951), *The Unknown Man* (MGM, 1951), *The Sellout* (MGM, 1951), *Million Dollar Mermaid* (MGM, 1952), *The Bad and the Beautiful* (MGM, 1952), *Scandal at Scourie* (MGM, 1953), *Dream Wife* (MGM, 1953), *Executive Suite* (MGM, 1954), *Men of the Fighting Lady* (MGM, 1954), *The Last Time I Saw Paris* (MGM, 1954), *Deep in My Heart* (MGM, 1954), *Hit the Deck* (MGM, 1955), *Forbidden Planet* (MGM, 1956), *The Rack* (MGM, 1956), *Voyage to the Bottom of the Sea* (20th, 1961), *Big Red* (BV, 1962), *Advise and Consent* (Col., 1962), *Warning Shot* (Par., 1967), *Two Colonels* (Comet, 1967), *Funny Girl* (Col., 1968).

*Unbilled guest appearance

ZASU PITTS Born January 3, 1898, Parsons, Kansas. Married Tom Gallery (1921), child: Ann; divorced 1932. Married John Woodall (1934), child: Donald. Died June 7, 1963.

ZaSu Pitts, Helen Jerome Eddy and Marie Prevost in *War Nurse*.

Sound Feature Films: *The Dummy* (Par., 1929), *The Squall* (WB, 1929), *Twin Beds* (WB, 1929), *The Argyle Case* (WB, 1929), *This Thing Called Love* (Pathé, 1929), *Her Private Life* (WB, 1929), *The Locked Door* (UA, 1929), *Oh, Yeah!* (RKO, 1930), *No, No, Nanette* (WB, 1930), *Honey* (Par., 1930), *Devil's Holiday* (Par., 1930), *Monte Carlo* (Par., 1930), *Little Accident* (Univ., 1930), *Lottery Bride* (UA, 1930), *The Squealer* (Col., 1930), *Passion Flower* (MGM, 1930), *War Nurse* (MGM, 1930), *Sin Takes a Holiday* (RKO, 1930), *Finn and Hattie* (Par., 1931), *Bad Sister* (Univ., 1931), *River's End* (WB, 1931), *Beyond Victory* (RKO, 1931), *Seed* (Univ., 1931), *Woman of Experience* (RKO, 1931), *The Guardsman* (MGM, 1931), *Their Mad Moment* (Fox, 1931), *Big Gamble* (RKO, 1931), *Penrod and Sam* (WB, 1931), *Secret Witness* (Col., 1931), *Broken Lullaby* (Par., 1932), *Destry Rides Again* (Univ., 1932), *Unexpected Father* (Univ., 1932), *Steady Company* (Univ., 1932), *Shopworn* (Col., 1932), *The Trial of Vivienne Ware* (Fox, 1932), *Strangers of the Evening* (Tif., 1932), *Westward Passage* (RKO,

---

1932), *Is My Face Red?* (RKO, 1932), *Blondie of the Follies* (MGM, 1932), *Roar of the Dragon* (RKO, 1932), *Make Me a Star* (Par., 1932), *Vanishing Frontier* (Par., 1932), *The Crooked Circle* (Sono Art-World Wide, 1932), *Madison Square Garden* (Par., 1932), *Once in a Lifetime* (Univ., 1932), *Back Street* (Univ., 1932), *They Just Had to Get Married* (Univ., 1933), *Out All Night* (Univ., 1933), *Hello, Sister* (Fox, 1933), *Professional Sweetheart* (RKO, 1933), *Her First Mate* (Univ., 1933), *Aggie Appleby, Maker of Men* (RKO, 1933), *Meet the Baron* (MGM, 1933), *Love, Honor and Oh, Baby!* (Univ., 1933), *Mr. Skitch* (Par., 1933), *The Meanest Gal in Town* (RKO, 1934), *Sing and Like It* (RKO, 1934), *Two Alone* (RKO, 1934), *Love Birds* (Univ., 1934), *Three on a Honeymoon* (Fox, 1934), *Private Scandal* (Par., 1934), *Mrs. Wiggs of the Cabbage Patch* (Par., 1934), *The Gay Bride* (MGM, 1934), *Their Big Moment* (RKO, 1934), *Dames* (WB, 1934), *Ruggles of Red Gap* (Par., 1935), *Going Highbrow* (WB, 1935), *Hot Tip* (RKO, 1935), *She Gets Her Man* (Univ., 1935), *The Affairs of Susan* (Univ., 1935), *Spring Tonic* (Fox, 1935), *13 Hours By Air* (Par., 1936), *Mad Holiday* (MGM, 1936), *The Plot Thickens* (RKO, 1936), *Sing Me a Love Song* (WB, 1936), *Forty Naughty Girls* (RKO, 1937), *52nd Street* (UA, 1937), *Wanted* (British, 1937), *Merry Comes to Town* (Sound City, 1937), *The Lady's From Kentucky* (Par., 1939), *Mickey the Kid* (Rep., 1939), *Naughty but Nice* (WB, 1939), *Nurse Edith Cavell* (RKO, 1939), *Eternally Yours* (UA, 1939), *It All Came True* (WB, 1940), *No, No, Nanette* (RKO, 1940), *Broadway Limited* (UA, 1941), *Mexican Spitfire's Baby* (RKO, 1941), *Niagara Falls* (UA, 1941), *Weekend for Three* (RKO, 1941), *Miss Polly* (UA, 1941), *Mexican Spitfire at Sea* (RKO, 1942), *The Bashful Bachelor* (RKO, 1942), *Tish* (MGM, 1942), *Meet the Mob* (Mon., 1942), *So's Your Aunt Emma* (Mon., 1942), *Let's Face It* (Par., 1943), *Breakfast in Hollywood* (UA, 1946), *The Perfect Marriage* (Par., 1946), *Life With Father* (WB, 1947), *Francis* (Univ., 1949), *The Denver and Rio Grande* (Par., 1952), *Francis Joins the WACs* (Univ., 1954), *This Could Be the Night* (MGM, 1957), *The Gazebo* (MGM, 1959), *Teen-Age Millionaire* (UA, 1961), *The Thrill of It All* (Univ., 1963), *It's a Mad, Mad, Mad, Mad World* (UA, 1963).

SUZANNE PLESHETTE Born January 31, 1937, New York, New York. Married Troy Donahue (1964); divorced 1964.

Suzanne Pleshette and James Franciscus in *Youngblood Hawke*.

Feature Films: *The Geisha Boy* (Par., 1958), *Rome Adventure* (WB, 1962), *40 Pounds of Trouble* (Univ., 1962), *The Birds* (Univ., 1963), *Wall of Noise* (WB, 1963), *A Distant Trumpet* (WB, 1964), *Fate Is the Hunter* (20th, 1964), *Youngblood Hawke* (WB, 1964), *A Rage to Live* (UA, 1965), *The Ugly Dachshund* (BV, 1966), *Nevada Smith* (Par., 1966), *Mr. Buddwing* (MGM, 1966), *The Adventures of Bullwhip Griffin* (BV, 1967), *Blackbeard's Ghost* (BV, 1968), *What's in It for Harry?* (Palo-Alto-ABC, 1968).

SIDNEY POITIER Born February 20, 1927, Miami, Florida. Married Juanita Hardy, children: Beverly, Pamela, Sheri; divorced.

Feature Films: *From Whence Cometh Help* (U.S. Army, 1949), *No*

Elizabeth Hartman, Sidney Poitier and Shelley Winters in A *Patch of Blue*.

Way Out (20th, 1950), *Cry, the Beloved Country* (UA, 1952), *Red Ball Express* (Univ., 1952), *Go Man, Go!* (UA, 1954), *The Blackboard Jungle* (MGM, 1955), *Good-Bye, My Lady* (WB, 1956), *Edge of the City* (MGM, 1957), *Something of Value* (MGM, 1957), *Band of Angels* (WB, 1957), *The Mark of the Hawk* (Univ., 1958), *The Defiant Ones* (UA, 1958), *Porgy and Bess* (Col., 1959), *Virgin Island* (Films-Around-the-World, 1960), *All the Young Men* (Col, 1960), *A Raisin in the Sun* (Col., 1961), *Paris Blues* (UA, 1961), *Pressure Point* (UA, 1962), *Lilies of the Field* (UA, 1962), *The Long Ships* (Col., 1964), *The Greatest Story Ever Told* (UA, 1965), *The Bedford Incident* (Col., 1965), *A Patch of Blue* (MGM, 1965), *The Slender Thread* (Par., 1965), *Duel at Diablo* (UA, 1966), *In the Heat of the Night* (UA, 1967). *To Sir With Love* (Col., 1967), *Guess Who's Coming to Dinner* (Col., 1967), *For Love of Ivy* (Cinerama, 1968).

DICK POWELL (Richard E. Powell) Born November 14, 1904, Mountain View, Arkansas. Married Mildred Maund (1925); divorced 1932. Married Joan Blondell (1936), children: Norman, Ellen; divorced 1945. Married June Allyson (1945), children: Pamela, Richard. Died January 3, 1963.

Dick Powell and Anita Louise in *Going Places*.

Feature Films: *Blessed Event* (WB, 1932), *Too Busy to Work* (Fox,

1932), *The King's Vacation* (WB, 1933), *42nd Street* (WB, 1933), *Gold Diggers of 1933* (WB, 1933), *Footlight Parade* (WB, 1933), *College Coach* (WB, 1933), *Convention City* (WB, 1933), *Dames* (WB, 1934), *Wonder Bar* (WB, 1934), *Twenty Million Sweethearts* (WB, 1934), *Happiness Ahead* (WB, 1934), *Flirtation Walk* (WB, 1934), *Gold Diggers of 1935* (WB, 1935), *Page Miss Glory* (WB, 1935), *Broadway Gondolier* (WB, 1935), *A Midsummer Night's Dream* (WB, 1935), *Shipmates Forever* (WB, 1935), *Thanks a Million* (Fox, 1935), *Colleen* (WB, 1936), *Hearts Divided* (WB, 1936), *Stage Struck* (WB, 1936), *Gold Diggers of 1937* (WB, 1936), *On the Avenue* (20th, 1937), *The Singing Marine* (WB, 1937), *Varsity Show* (WB, 1937), *Hollywood Hotel* (WB, 1937), *Cowboy From Brooklyn* (WB, 1938), *Hard to Get* (WB, 1938), *Going Places* (WB, 1938), *Naughty but Nice* (WB, 1939), *Christmas in July* (Par., 1940), *I Want a Divorce* (Par., 1940), *Model Wife* (Univ., 1941), *In The Navy* (Univ., 1941), *Star Spangled Rhythm* (Par., 1942), *Happy Go Lucky* (Par., 1942), *True to Life* (Par., 1943), *Riding High* (Par., 1943), *It Happened Tomorrow* (UA, 1944), *Meet the People* (MGM, 1944), *Murder, My Sweet* (RKO, 1944), *Cornered* (RKO, 1945), *Johnny O'Clock* (Col., 1947), *To the Ends of the Earth* (Col., 1948), *Pitfall* (UA, 1948), *Station West* (RKO, 1948), *Rogue's Regiment* (Univ., 1948), *Mrs. Mike* (UA., 1949), *The Reformer and the Redhead* (MGM, 1950), *Right Cross* (MGM, 1950), *Callaway Went Thataway* (MGM, 1951), *Cry Danger* (RKO, 1951), *The Tall Target* (MGM, 1951), *You Never Can Tell* (Univ., 1951), *The Bad and the Beautiful* (MGM, 1952), *Susan Slept Here* (RKO, 1954).

ELEANOR POWELL (Eleanor Torrey Powell) Born November 21, 1912, Springfield, Massachusetts. Married Glenn Ford (1943), child: Peter; divorced 1959.

Eleanor Powell, Buddy Ebsen and George Murphy in *Broadway Melody of 1938*.

Feature Films: *George White's Scandals* (Fox, 1935), *Broadway Melody of 1936* (MGM, 1935), *Born to Dance* (MGM, 1936), *Broadway Melody of 1938* (MGM, 1937), *Rosalie* (MGM, 1937), *Honolulu* (MGM, 1939), *Broadway Melody of 1940* (MGM, 1940), *Lady Be Good* (MGM, 1941), *Ship Ahoy* (MGM, 1942), *I Dood It* (MGM, 1943), *Thousands Cheer* (MGM, 1943), *Sensations of 1945* (UA, 1944), *The Duchess of Idaho* (MGM, 1950).

JANE POWELL (Suzanne Burce) Born April 1, 1929, Portland, Oregon. Married Geary Steffen (1949), children: Geary, Suzanne; divorced 1953. Married Patrick Nerney (1954), child: Lindsey; divorced 1963. Married James Fitzgerald (1965).

Feature Films: *Song of the Open Road* (UA, 1944), *Delightfully Danger-*

Jane Powell in *The Girl Most Likely*.

ous (UA, 1945), *Holiday in Mexico* (MGM, 1946), *Three Daring Daughters* (MGM, 1948), *A Date With Judy* (MGM, 1948), *Luxury Liner* (MGM, 1948), *Nancy Goes to Rio* (MGM, 1950), *Two Weeks With Love* (MGM, 1950), *Royal Wedding* (MGM, 1951), *Rich, Young and Pretty* (MGM, 1951), *Small Town Girl* (MGM, 1953), *Three Sailors and a Girl* (WB, 1953), *Seven Brides for Seven Brothers* (MGM, 1954), *Athena* (MGM, 1954), *Deep in My Heart* (MGM, 1954), *Hit the Deck* (MGM, 1955), *The Girl Most Likely* (Univ., 1957), *The Female Animal* (Univ., 1958), *Enchanted Island* (WB, 1958).

WILLIAM POWELL (William Horatio Powell) Born July 29, 1892, Pittsburgh, Pennsylvania. Married Eileen Wilson, child: William; divorced 1931. Married Carole Lombard (1931); divorced 1933. Married Diana Lewis (1940).

William Powell, Ted Healy and Nat Pendleton in *Reckless*.

Sound Feature Films: *Interference* (Par., 1929), *The Canary Murder Case* (Par., 1929), *The Greene Murder Case* (Par., 1929), *Charming Sinners* (Par., 1929), *Four Feathers* (Par., 1929), *Pointed Heels* (Par., 1929), *The Benson Murder Case* (Par., 1930), *Paramount on Parade* (Par., 1930), *Shadow of the Law* (Par., 1930), *Behind the Makeup* (Par., 1930), *Street of Chance* (Par., 1930), *For the Defense* (Par., 1930), *Man of the World* (Par., 1931), *Ladies' Man* (Par., 1931), *Road to Singapore* (WB, 1931), *High Pressure* (WB, 1932), *Jewel Robbery* (WB, 1932), *One Way Passage* (WB, 1932), *Lawyer Man* (WB, 1932), *Double Harness* (RKO, 1933), *Private Detective 62* (WB, 1933), *The Kennel Murder Case* (WB, 1933), *Fashions of 1934* (WB, 1934), *The Key* (WB, 1934), *Manhattan Melodrama* (MGM, 1934), *The Thin Man* (MGM, 1934), *Evelyn Prentice* (MGM, 1934), *Reckless* (MGM, 1935), *Star of Midnight* (RKO, 1935), *Escapade* (MGM, 1935), *Rendezvous* (MGM, 1935), *The Great Ziegfeld* (MGM, 1936), *The Ex-Mrs. Bradford* (RKO,

1936), *My Man Godfrey* (Univ., 1936), *Libeled Lady* (MGM, 1936), *After the Thin Man* (MGM, 1936), *The Last of Mrs. Cheyney* (MGM, 1937), *The Emperor's Candlesticks* (MGM, 1937), *Double Wedding* (MGM, 1937), *The Baroness and the Butler* (20th, 1938), *Another Thin Man* (MGM, 1939), *I Love You Again* (MGM, 1940), *Love Crazy* (MGM, 1941), *Shadow of the Thin Man* (MGM, 1941), *Crossroads* (MGM, 1942), *The Youngest Profession* (MGM, 1943), *The Heavenly Body* (MGM, 1944), *The Thin Man Goes Home* (MGM, 1944), *Ziegfeld Follies* (MGM, 1946), *The Hoodlum Saint* (MGM, 1946), *Song of the Thin Man* (MGM, 1947), *Life With Father* (WB, 1947), *The Senator Was Indiscreet* (Univ., 1947), *Mr. Peabody and the Mermaid* (Univ., 1948), *Take One False Step* (Univ., 1949), *Dancing in the Dark* (20th, 1949), *The Treasure of Lost Canyon* (Univ., 1951), *It's a Big Country* (MGM, 1951), *The Girl Who Had Everything* (MGM, 1953), *How to Marry a Millionaire* (20th, 1953), *Mister Roberts* (WB, 1955).

TYRONE POWER (Tyrone Edmund Power) Born May 5, 1914, Cincinnati, Ohio. Married Annabella (1939); divorced 1948. Married Linda Christian (1949), children: Romina, Taryn; divorced 1955. Married Deborah Minardos (1958), child: Tyrone. Died November 15, 1958.

Tyrone Power and Joseph Schildkraut in *Suez*.

Feature Films: *Tom Brown of Culver* (Univ, 1932), *Flirtation Walk* (WB, 1934), *Girls' Dormitory* (20th, 1936), *Ladies in Love* (20th, 1936), *Lloyds of London* (20th, 1937), *Love Is News* (20th, 1937), *Cafe Metropole* (20th, 1937), *Thin Ice* (20th, 1937), *Second Honeymoon* (20th, 1937), *In Old Chicago* (20th, 1938), *Alexander's Ragtime Band* (20th, 1938), *Marie Antoinette* (MGM, 1938), *Suez* (20th, 1938), *Jesse James* (20th, 1939), *Rose of Washington Square* (20th, 1939), *Second Fiddle* (20th, 1939), *The Rains Came* (20th, 1939), *Daytime Wife* (20th, 1939), *Johnny Apollo* (20th, 1940), *Brigham Young—Frontiersman* (20th, 1940), *The Return of Frank James* (20th, 1940), *Mark of Zorro* (20th, 1940), *Blood and Sand* (20th, 1941), *A Yank in the R.A.F.* (20th, 1941), *Son of Fury* (20th, 1942), *This Above All* (20th, 1942), *The Black Swan* (20th, 1942), *Crash Dive* (20th, 1943), *The Razor's Edge* (20th, 1946), *Nightmare Alley* (20th, 1947), *Captain From Castile* (20th, 1947), *Luck of the Irish* (20th, 1948), *That Wonderful Urge* (20th, 1948), *Prince of Foxes* (20th, 1949), *The Black Rose* (20th, 1950), *An American Guerrilla in the Philippines* (20th, 1950), *Rawhide* (20th, 1951), *I'll Never Forget You* (20th, 1951), *Diplomatic Courier* (20th, 1952), *Pony Soldier* (20th, 1952), *Mississippi Gambler* (Univ., 1953), *King of the Khyber Rifles* (20th, 1953), *The Long Gray Line* (Col., 1955), *Untamed* (20th, 1955), *The Eddy Duchin Story* (Col., 1956), *Abandon Ship* (Col., 1957), *The Rising of the Moon* (WB, 1957), *The Sun Also Rises* (20th, 1957), *Witness for the Prosecution* (UA, 1957).

PAULA PRENTISS (Paula Ragusa) Born March 4, 1939, San Antonio, Texas. Married Richard Benjamin (1960).

Feature Films: *Where the Boys Are* (MGM, 1960), *The Honeymoon*

Steve McQueen, Brigid Bazlen, Paula Prentiss and Jim Hutton in *The Honeymoon Machine.*

Machine (MGM, 1961), *Bachelor in Paradise* (MGM, 1961), *The Horizontal Lieutenant* (MGM, 1962), *Follow the Boys* (MGM, 1963), *Man's Favorite Sport?* (Univ., 1964), *The World of Henry Orient* (UA, 1964), *Looking for Love* (MGM, 1964), *In Harm's Way* (Par., 1965), *What's New Pussycat?* (UA, 1965).

ELVIS PRESLEY Born January 8, 1935, Tupelo, Mississippi. Married Priscilla Beaulieu, (1967).

Dolores Del Rio and Elvis Presley in *Flaming Star.*

Feature Films: *Love Me Tender* (20th, 1956), *Loving You* (Par., 1957), *Jailhouse Rock* (MGM, 1957), *King Creole* (Par., 1958), *G.I. Blues* (Par., 1960), *Flaming Star* (20th, 1960), *Wild in the Country* (20th, 1961), *Blue Hawaii* (Par., 1961), *Kid Galahad* (UA, 1962), *Girls! Girls! Girls!* (Par., 1962), *Fun in Acapulco* (Par., 1963), *It Happened at the World's Fair* (MGM, 1963), *Kissin' Cousins* (MGM, 1964), *Viva Las Vegas* (MGM, 1964), *Roustabout* (Par., 1964), *Girl Happy* (MGM, 1965), *Tickle Me* (AA, 1965), *Harum Scarum* (MGM, 1965), *Frankie and Johnny* (UA, 1966), *Paradise—Hawaiian Style* (Par., 1966), *Spinout* (MGM, 1966), *Easy Come, Easy Go* (Par., 1967), *Double Trouble* (MGM, 1967), *Speedway* (MGM, 1968), *Stay Away, Joe* (MGM, 1968), *Clambake* (MGM, 1968).

ROBERT PRESTON (Robert Preston Meservey) Born June 8, 1918, Newton Highlands, Massachusetts. Married Catherine Craig (1940).

Feature Films: *King of Alcatraz* (Par., 1938), *Illegal Traffic* (Par., 1938), *Disbarred* (Par., 1939), *Union Pacific* (Par., 1939), *Beau Geste* (Par., 1939), *Typhoon* (Par., 1940), *North West Mounted Police* (Par., 1940), *Moon Over Burma* (Par., 1940), *The Lady From Cheyenne* (Univ., 1941), *Parachute Battalion* (RKO, 1941), *New York Town* (Par., 1941), *Night*

Robert Preston and Susan Hayward in *Tulsa.*

of January 16th (Par., 1941), *Star Spangled Rhythm* (Par., 1942), *Reap the Wild Wind* (Par., 1942), *This Gun for Hire* (Par., 1942), *Wake Island* (Par., 1942), *Pacific Blackout* (Par., 1942), *Night Plane From Chungking* (Par., 1943), *Wild Harvest* (Par., 1947), *The Macomber Affair* (UA, 1947), *Variety Girl* (Par., 1947), *Whispering Smith* (Par., 1948), *The Big City* (MGM, 1948), *Blood on the Moon* (RKO, 1948), *Tulsa* (EL, 1949), *The Lady Gambles* (Univ., 1949), *The Sundowners* (EL, 1950), *My Outlaw Brother* (EL, 1951), *When I Grow Up* (EL, 1951), *Best of the Bad Men* (RKO, 1951), *Cloudburst* (UA, 1952), *Face to Face* (RKO, 1952), *The Last Frontier* (Col., 1955), *The Dark at the Top of the Stairs* (WB, 1960), *The Music Man* (WB, 1962), *How the West Was Won* (MGM, 1962), *Island of Love* (WB, 1963), *All the Way Home* (Par., 1963).

VINCENT PRICE Born May 27, 1911, St. Louis, Missouri. Married Edith Barrett, child: Barrett; divorced 1948. Married Mary Grant (1949), child: Mary.

Lon Chaney, Jr., and Vincent Price in *The Haunted Palace.*

English-Language Feature Films: *Service DeLuxe* (Univ., 1938), *The Private Lives of Elizabeth and Essex* (WB, 1939), *Tower of London* (Univ., 1939), *Green Hell* (Univ., 1940), *The House of the Seven Gables* (Univ., 1940), *The Invisible Man Returns* (Univ., 1940), *Brigham Young —Frontiersman* (20th, 1940), *Hudson's Bay* (20th, 1940), *The Song of Bernadette* (20th, 1943), *The Eve of St. Mark* (20th, 1944), *Buffalo Bill* (20th, 1944), *Wilson* (20th, 1944), *Laura* (20th, 1944), *The Keys of the Kingdom* (20th, 1944), *Leave Her to Heaven* (20th, 1945), *A Royal Scandal* (20th, 1945), *Dragonwyck* (20th, 1946), *Shock* (20th, 1947), *The Long Night* (RKO, 1947), *Moss Rose* (20th, 1947), *The Web* (Univ., 1947), *Up in Central Park* (Univ., 1948), *Abbott and Costello Meet Frankenstein* (voice only; Univ., 1948), *The Three Musketeers* (MGM, 1948), *Rogue's Regiment* (Univ., 1948), *The Bribe* (MGM, 1949), *Bagdad* (Univ., 1949), *The Baron of Arizona* (Lip., 1950), *Champagne for*

Caesar (Univ., 1950), *Curtain Call at Cactus Creek* (Univ., 1950), *His Kind of Woman* (RKO, 1951), *Adventures of Captain Fabian* (Rep., 1951), *The Las Vegas Story* (RKO, 1952), *House of Wax* (WB, 1953), *Casanova's Big Night* (Par., 1954), *Dangerous Mission* (RKO, 1954), *The Mad Magician* (Col., 1954), *Son of Sinbad* (RKO, 1955), *Serenade* (WB, 1956), *While the City Sleeps* (RKO, 1956), *The Ten Commandments* (Par., 1956), *The Story of Mankind* (WB, 1957), *The Fly* (20th, 1958), *House on Haunted Hill* (AA, 1958), *The Return of the Fly* (20th, 1959), *The Bat* (AA, 1959), *The Big Circus* (AA, 1959), *The Tingler* (Col., 1959), *House of Usher* (AIP, 1960), *The Master of the World* (AIP, 1961), *The Pit and the Pendulum* (AIP, 1961), *Poe's Tales of Terror* (AIP, 1962), *Convicts 4* (AA, 1962), *Confessions of an Opium Eater* (AA, 1962), *Tower of London* (UA, 1962), *The Raven* (AIP, 1963), *The Haunted Palace* (AIP, 1963), *Twice Told Tales* (AIP, 1963), *Comedy of Terrors* (AIP, 1963), *Masque of the Red Death* (AIP, 1964), *Last Man on Earth* (AIP, 1964), *Tomb of Leigia* (AIP, 1965), *War Gods of the Deep* (AIP, 1965), *Taboos of the World* (narrator; AIP, 1965), *Dr. Goldfoot and the Bikini Machine* (AIP, 1965), *Dr. Goldfoot and the Girl Bombs* (AIP, 1966), *2165 A.D.—When the Sleeper Wakes* (AIP, 1967), *House of 1,000 Dolls* (AIP, 1968), *The Conquering Worm* (AIP, 1968), *Witchfinder General* (AIP, 1968).

ANTHONY QUINN Born April 21, 1915, Chihuahua, Mexico. Married Katherine DeMille (1937), children: Christina, Kathleen, Duncan Valentina; divorced. Married Yolanda Addolori (1966), child: Lawrence.

Barbara Stanwyck and Anthony Quinn in *Blowing Wild*.

English-Language Feature Films: *Parole!* (Univ., 1936), *Swing High—Swing Low* (Par., 1937), *Waikiki Wedding* (Par., 1937), *Last Train From Madrid* (Par., 1937), *Partners in Crime* (Par., 1937), *Daughter of Shanghai* (Par., 1937), *The Buccaneer* (Par., 1938), *Dangerous to Know* (Par., 1938), *Tip-Off Girls* (Par., 1938), *Hunted Men* (Par., 1938), *Bulldog Drummond In Africa* (Par., 1938), *King of Alcatraz* (Par., 1938), *King of Chinatown* (Par., 1939), *Union Pacific* (Par., 1939), *Island of Lost Men* (Par., 1939), *Television Spy* (Par., 1939), *Emergency Squad* (Par., 1940), *Road to Singapore* (Par., 1940), *Parole Fixer* (Par., 1940), *The Ghost Breakers* (Par., 1940), *City for Conquest* (WB, 1940), *Texas Rangers Ride Again* (Par., 1941), *Blood and Sand* (20th, 1941), *Thieves Fall Out* (WB, 1941), *Knockout* (WB, 1941), *Bullets for O'Hara* (WB, 1941), *Manpower* (WB, 1941), *The Perfect Snob* (20th, 1941), *They Died With Their Boots On* (WB, 1941), *Larceny, Inc.* (WB, 1942), *Road to Morocco* (Par., 1942), *The Black Swan* (20th, 1942), *The Ox-Bow Incident* (20th, 1943), *Guadalcanal Diary* (20th, 1943), *Buffalo Bill* (20th, 1944), *Ladies of Washington* (20th, 1944), *Roger Tuohy, Gangster* (20th, 1944), *Irish Eyes Are Smiling* (20th, 1944), *China Skies* (RKO, 1945), *Where Do We Go From Here?* (20th, 1945), *Back to Bataan* (RKO, 1945), *California* (Par., 1946), *Sinbad the Sailor* (RKO, 1947), *The Imperfect Lady* (Par., 1947), *Black Gold* (AA, 1947), *Tycoon* (RKO, 1947), *The Brave Bulls* (Col., 1951), *Mask of the Avenger* (Col., 1951),

Viva Zapata! (20th, 1952), *The World in his Arms* (Univ., 1952), *The Brigand* (Col., 1952), *Against All Flags* (Univ., 1952), *Seminole* (Univ., 1953), *City Beneath the Sea* (Univ., 1953), *Ride, Vaquero!* (MGM, 1953), *Blowing Wild* (WB, 1953), *The Long Wait* (UA, 1954), *The Magnificent Matador* (20th, 1955), *Ulysses* (Par., 1955), *The Naked Street* (UA, 1955), *Seven Cities of Gold* (20th, 1955), *Lust for Life* (MGM, 1956), *Man From Del Rio* (UA, 1956), *The Wild Party* (UA, 1956), *The River's Edge* (20th, 1957), *The Ride Back* (UA, 1957), *The Hunchback of Notre Dame* (AA, 1957), *Wild Is the Wind* (Par., 1957), *Hot Spell* (Par., 1958), *Warlock* (20th, 1959), *Last Train From Gun Hill* (Par., 1959), *Heller in Pink Tights* (Par., 1960), *Portrait in Black* (Univ., 1960), *The Savage Innocents* (Par., 1960), *The Guns of Navarone* (Col., 1961), *Barabbas* (Col., 1962), *Requiem for a Heavyweight* (Col., 1962), *Lawrence of Arabia* (Col., 1962), *Behold a Pale Horse* (Col., 1964), *The Visit* (20th, 1964), *Zorba the Greek* (International Classics, 1964), *A High Wind in Jamaica* (20th, 1965), *The Lost Command* (Col., 1966), *Marco the Magnificent* (MGM, 1966), *The 25th Hour* (MGM, 1967), *The Happening* (Col., 1967), *The Rover* (Cinerama, 1968), *The God Game* (20th, 1968), *Shoes of the Fisherman* (MGM, 1968), *Guns for San Sebastian* (MGM, 1968).

LUISE RAINER Born January 12, 1910, Vienna, Austria. Married Clifford Odets (1937); divorced 1940. Married Robert Knittel (1944), child: Franceska.

Luise Rainer in *The Toy Wife*.

Feature Films: *Escapade* (MGM, 1935), *The Great Ziegfeld* (MGM, 1936), *The Good Earth* (MGM, 1937), *The Big City* (MGM, 1937), *The Emperor's Candlesticks* (MGM, 1937), *The Great Waltz* (MGM, 1938), *The Toy Wife* (MGM, 1938), *Dramatic School* (MGM, 1938), *Hostages* (Par., 1943).

ELLA RAINES (Ella Wallace Raubes) Born August 6, 1921, Snoqualmie Falls, Washington. Married Kenneth Trout (1942); divorced 1945. Married Robin Olds (1947), children: Christina, Susan.

Ella Raines, Anna May Wong and Charles Coburn in *Impact*.

Feature Films: *Corvette K-225* (Univ., 1943), *Cry Havoc* (MGM, 1943), *Phantom Lady* (Univ., 1944), *Hail the Conquering Hero* (Par., 1944), *Tall in the Saddle* (RKO, 1944), *Enter Arsene Lupin* (Univ., 1944), *The Suspect* (Univ., 1945), *The Strange Affair of Uncle Harry* (Univ., 1945), *The Runaround* (Univ., 1946), *Time Out of Mind* (Univ., 1947), *The Web* (Univ., 1947), *Brute Force* (Univ., 1947), *The Senator Was Indiscreet* (Univ., 1947), *The Walking Hills* (Col., 1949), *Impact* (UA, 1949), *A Dangerous Profession* (RKO, 1949), *The Second Face* (EL, 1950), *Singing Guns* (Rep., 1950), *The Fighting Coast Guard* (Rep., 1951), *Ride the Man Down* (Rep., 1952), *Man in the Road* (Rep., 1957).

CLAUDE RAINS (William Claude Rains) Born November 10, 1889, London, England. Married Isabel Jeans (1913); divorced. Married Marie Hemingway (1920); divorced 1920. Married Beatrix Thomson (1924); divorced 1935. Married Frances Propper (1935), child: Jennifer; divorced 1959. Married Agi Jambor (1960). Died May 30, 1967.

Claude Rains and Billy Mauch in *The Prince and the Pauper.*

Feature Films: *The Invisible Man* (Univ., 1933), *Crime Without Passion* (Par., 1934), *The Man Who Reclaimed His Head* (Univ., 1935), *The Clairvoyant* (Gaumont-British, 1935), *The Mystery of Edwin Drood* (Univ., 1935), *The Last Outpost* (Par., 1935), *Anthony Adverse* (WB, 1936), *Hearts Divided* (WB, 1936), *Stolen Holiday* (WB, 1936), *The Prince and the Pauper* (WB, 1937), *They Won't Forget* (WB, 1937), *Gold Is Where You Find It* (WB, 1938), *The Adventures of Robin Hood* (WB, 1938), *White Banners* (WB, 1938), *Four Daughters* (WB, 1938), *They Made Me a Criminal* (WB, 1939), *Juarez* (WB, 1939), *Daughters Courageous* (WB, 1939), *Mr. Smith Goes to Washington* (Col., 1939), *Four Wives* (WB, 1939), *Saturday's Children* (WB, 1940), *The Sea Hawk* (WB, 1940), *The Lady With Red Hair* (WB, 1940), *Four Mothers* (WB, 1941), *Here Comes Mr. Jordan* (Col., 1941), *The Wolf Man* (Univ., 1941), *Kings Row* (WB, 1941), *Moontide* (20th, 1942), *Now, Voyager* (WB, 1942), *Casablanca* (WB, 1942), *The Phantom of the Opera* (Univ., 1943), *Forever and a Day* (RKO, 1943), *Passage to Marseilles* (WB, 1944), *Mr. Skeffington* (WB, 1944), *This Love of Ours* (Univ., 1945), *Angel on My Shoulder* (UA, 1946), *Caesar and Cleopatra* (UA, 1946), *Strange Holiday* (PRC, 1946), *Notorious* (RKO, 1946), *Deception* (WB, 1946), *The Unsuspected* (WB, 1947), *One Woman's Story* (Univ. 1949), *Rope of Sand* (Par., 1949), *Song of Surrender* (Par., 1949), *The White Tower* (RKO, 1950), *Where Danger Lives* (RKO, 1950), *Sealed Cargo* (RKO, 1951), *The Paris Express* (George J. Schaeffer, 1953), *Lisbon* (Rep., 1956), *This Earth Is Mine* (Univ., 1959), *The Lost World* (20th, 1960), *Lawrence of Arabia* (Col., 1962), *Twilight of Honor* (MGM, 1963), *The Greatest Story Ever Told* (UA, 1965).

GEORGE RAFT (George Ranft) Born September 24, 1903, New York, New York. Married Grace Mulrooney (1925).

English-Language Feature Films: *Queen of the Night Clubs* (WB, 1929),

Warren Hymer, George E. Stone, Robert Cummings, George Raft, Roscoe Karns, Joe Gray and Jack Pennick in *You and Me.*

Quick Millions (Fox, 1931), *Hush Money* (Fox, 1931), *Palmy Days* (UA, 1931), *Taxi* (WB, 1932), *Scarface* (UA, 1932), *Dancers in the Dark* (Par., 1932), *Madame Racketeer* (Par., 1932), *Night After Night* (Par., 1932), *If I Had a Million* (Par., 1932), *Undercover Man* (Par., 1932), *Pick-Up* (Par., 1933), *The Midnight Club* (Par., 1933), *The Bowery* (UA, 1933), *Bolero* (Par., 1934), *All of Me* (Par., 1934), *The Trumpet Blows* (Par., 1934), *Limehouse Blues* (Par., 1934), *Rumba* (Par., 1935), *Stolen Harmony* (Par., 1935), *The Glass Key* (Par., 1935), *Every Night at Eight* (Par., 1935), *She Couldn't Take It* (Col., 1935), *It Had to Happen* (20th, 1936), *Souls at Sea* (Par., 1937), *You and Me* (Par., 1938), *The Lady's From Kentucky* (Par., 1939), *Each Dawn I Die* (WB, 1939), *I Stole a Million* (Univ., 1939), *They Drive by Night* (WB, 1940), *Invisible Stripes* (WB, 1940), *House Across the Bay* (UA, 1940), *Manpower* (WB, 1941), *Broadway* (Univ., 1942), *Stage Door Canteen* (UA, 1943), *Background to Danger* (WB, 1943), *Follow the Boys* (Univ., 1944), *Johnny Angel* (RKO, 1945), *Nocturne* (RKO, 1946), *Mr. Ace* (UA, 1946), *Whistle Stop* (UA, 1946), *Christmas Eve* (UA, 1947), *Intrigue* (UA, 1947), *Race Street* (RKO, 1948), *Johnny Allegro* (Col., 1949), *A Dangerous Profession* (RKO, 1949), *Outpost in Morocco* (UA, 1949), *Red Light* (UA, 1949), *Lucky Nick Cain* (20th, 1951), *Loan Shark* (Lip., 1952), *I'll Get You* (Lip., 1953), *Man From Cairo* (Lip., 1953), *Rogue Cop* (MGM, 1954), *Black Widow* (20th, 1954), *A Bullet for Joey* (UA, 1955), *Around the World in 80 Days* (UA, 1956), *Jet Across the Atlantic* (Intercontinent Releasing, 1959), *Some Like It Hot* (UA, 1959), *Ocean's 11* (WB, 1960),* *Ladies' Man* (Par., 1961), *For Those Who Think Young* (UA, 1964), *The Patsy* (Par., 1964),* *Casino Royale* (Col., 1967),* *The Silent Treatment* (Ralph Andrew, 1968).

   *Unbilled guest appearance

VERA RALSTON (Vera Hruba) Born July 12, 1919, Prague, Czechoslovakia. Married Herbert Yates (1952); widowed 1966.

Feature Films:
   as Vera Hruba *Ice-Capades* (Rep., 1941), *Ice-Capades Revue* (Rep., 1942).

John Carroll and Vera Ralston in *Belle Le Grand.*

as Vera Hruba Ralston *The Lady and the Monster* (Rep., 1944), *Storm Over Lisbon* (Rep., 1944), *Lake Placid Serenade* (Rep., 1944), *Dakota* (Rep., 1945), *Murder in the Music Hall* (Rep., 1946).

as Vera Ralston *The Plainsman and the Lady* (Rep., 1946), *The Flame* (Rep., 1947), *Wyoming* (Rep., 1947), *I, Jane Doe* (Rep., 1948), *Angel on the Amazon* (Rep., 1948), *The Fighting Kentuckian* (Rep., 1949), *Surrender* (Rep., 1950), *Belle Le Grand* (Rep., 1951), *The Wild Blue Yonder* (Rep., 1951), *Hoodlum Empire* (Rep., 1952), *Fair Wind to Java* (Rep., 1953), *A Perilous Journey* (Rep., 1953), *Jubilee Trail* (Rep., 1954), *Timberjack* (Rep., 1955), *Accused of Murder* (Rep., 1956), *Spoilers of the Forest* (Rep., 1957), *Gunfire at Indian Gap* (Rep., 1957), *The Notorious Mr. Monks* (Rep., 1958), *The Man Who Died Twice* (Rep., 1958).

MARJORIE RAMBEAU Born July 15, 1889, San Francisco, California. Married Willard Mack (1912), divorced 1917. Married Hugh Dillman (1919); divorced 1923. Married Francis Gudger (1931).

Elizabeth Patterson and Marjorie Rambeau in *Tobacco Road.*

Sound Feature Films: *Her Man* (Pathé, 1930), *Min and Bill* (MGM, 1930), *The Easiest Way* (MGM, 1931), *Inspiration* (MGM, 1931), *A Tailor-Made Man* (MGM, 1931), *Strangers May Kiss* (MGM, 1931), *Secret Six* (MGM, 1931), *Laughing Sinners* (MGM, 1931), *This Modern Age* (MGM, 1931), *Son of India* (MGM, 1931), *Silence* (Par., 1931), *Hell Divers* (MGM, 1931), *Left Over Ladies* (Tiff., 1931), *Strictly Personal* (Par., 1933), *Warrior's Husband* (Fox, 1933), *Man's Castle* (Col., 1933), *Palooka* (UA-Reliance, 1934), *A Modern Hero* (WB, 1934), *Grand Canary* (Fox, 1934), *Ready for Love* (Par., 1934), *Under Pressure* (Fox, 1935), *Dizzy Dames* (Liberty, 1935), *First Lady* (WB, 1937), *Merrily We Live* (MGM, 1938), *Woman Against Woman* (MGM, 1938), *The Rains Came* (20th, 1939), *Laugh It Off* (Univ., 1939), *Sudden Money* (Par., 1939), *Primrose Path* (RKO, 1940), *Heaven With a Barbed Wire Fence* (20th, 1940), *Santa Fe Marshal* (Par., 1940), *Twenty Mule Team* (MGM, 1940), *East of the River* (WB, 1940), *Tugboat Annie Sails Again* (WB, 1940), *Tobacco Road* (20th, 1941), *Three Sons o' Guns* (WB, 1941), *Broadway* (Univ., 1942), *In Old Oklahoma* (Rep., 1943), *Army Wives* (Mon., 1944), *Oh, What a Night!* (Mon., 1944), *Salome, Where She Danced* (Univ., 1945), *The Walls of Jericho* (20th, 1948), *Any Number Can Play* (MGM, 1949), *The Lucky Stiff* (UA, 1949), *Abandoned* (Univ., 1949), *Torch Song* (MGM, 1953), *Forever Female* (Par., 1953), *Bad for Each Other* (Col., 1953), *A Man Called Peter* (20th, 1955), *The View From Pompey's Head* (20th, 1955), *Slander* (MGM, 1956), *Man of a Thousand Faces* (Univ., 1957).

TONY RANDALL (Anthony L. Randall) Born February 26, 1920, Tulsa, Oklahoma. Married Florence Mitchell (1942).

Feature Films: *Oh, Men! Oh, Women!* (20th, 1957), *Will Success*

Robert Preston and Tony Randall in *Island of Love.*

Spoil Rock Hunter? (20th, 1957), *No Down Payment* (20th, 1957), *The Mating Game* (MGM, 1959), *Pillow Talk* (Univ., 1959), *Adventures of Huckleberry Finn* (MGM, 1960), *Let's Make Love* (20th, 1960), *Lover Come Back* (Univ., 1961), *Boys' Night Out* (MGM, 1962), *Island of Love* (WB, 1963), *The Brass Bottle* (Univ., 1964), *The Seven Faces of Dr. Lao* (MGM, 1964), *Send Me No Flowers* (Univ., 1964), *Fluffy* (Univ., 1965), *The Alphabet Murders* (MGM, 1966), *Bang, Bang, You're Dead* (AIP, 1966).

BASIL RATHBONE (Philip St. John Basil Rathbone) Born June 13, 1892, Johannesburg, South Africa. Married Ethel Forman (1914), child: Rodion; divorced. Married Ouida Fitzmaurice (1926), child: Barbara. Died July 21, 1967.

Irving Bacon and Basil Rathbone in *Rio.*

English-Language Sound Feature Films: *The Last of Mrs. Cheyney* (MGM, 1929), *Barnum Was Right* (Univ., 1929), *This Mad World* (MGM, 1930), *Flirting Widow* (WB, 1930), *A Notorious Affair* (WB, 1930), *A Lady Surrenders* (Univ., 1930), *Sin Takes a Holiday* (Pathé, 1930), *The Bishop Murder Case* (MGM, 1930), *The Lady of Scandal* (MGM, 1930), *A Woman Commands* (RKO, 1932), *After the Ball* (Fox, 1933), *Loyalties* (Auten, 1934), *Captain Blood* (WB, 1935), *David Copperfield* (MGM, 1935), *Anna Karenina* (MGM, 1935), *The Last Days* of Pompeii (RKO, 1935), *A Tale of Two Cities* (MGM, 1935), *Kind Lady* (MGM, 1935), *A Feather in Her Hat* (Col., 1935), *Romeo and Juliet* (MGM, 1936), *The Garden of Allah* (UA, 1936), *Private Number* (20th, 1936), *Tovarich* (WB, 1937), *Love From a Stranger* (UA, 1937), *Confession* (WB, 1937), *Make a Wish* (RKO, 1937), *The Adventures of Robin Hood* (WB, 1938), *The Adventures of Marco Polo* (UA, 1938), *If I Were King* (Par., 1938), *Dawn Patrol* (WB, 1938), *The Son of Frankenstein* (Univ., 1939), *Tower of London* (Univ., 1939), *The Sun Never Sets* (Univ., 1939), *Rio* (Univ., 1939), *The Hound of the Baskervilles* (20th, 1939), *Adventures of Sherlock Holmes* (20th, 1939), *Rhythm on the River* (Par., 1940), *The Mark of Zorro* (20th, 1940), *The Mad Doctor* (Par., 1941), *The Black Cat* (Univ., 1941), *Paris Calling* (Univ, 1941), *International Lady* (UA, 1941), *Fingers at the Window* (MGM, 1942), *Crossroads* (MGM, 1942), *Sherlock Holmes and the Voice of Terror* (Univ., 1942), *Sherlock Holmes and the Secret Weapon* (Univ., 1942), *Sherlock Holmes in Washington* (Univ., 1943), *Sherlock Holmes Faces Death* (Univ., 1943) *Crazy House* (Univ., 1943),* *Above Suspicion* (MGM, 1943), *Frenchman's Creek* (Par., 1944), *Bathing Beauty* (MGM, 1944), *Sherlock Holmes and the Spider Woman* (Univ., 1944), *The Scarlet Claw* (Univ., 1944), *The Pearl of Death* (Univ., 1944), *The House of Fear* (Univ., 1945), *Pursuit to Algiers* (Univ., 1945), *The Woman Is Green* (Univ., 1945), *Terror by Night* (Univ., 1946), *Dressed to Kill* (Univ., 1946), *Heartbeat* (RKO, 1946), *The Adventures of Ichabod and Mr. Toad* (voice only; RKO, 1949), *Casanova's Big Night* (Par., 1954), *We're No Angels* (Par., 1955), *The Black Sleep* (UA, 1956), *The Court Jester* (Par., 1956), *The Last Hurrah* (Col., 1958), *The Magic Sword* (UA, 1962), *Tales of Terror* (AIP, 1962), *Comedy of Terrors* (AIP, 1963), *Queen of Blood* (AIP, 1966), *Ghost in the Invisible Bikini* (AIP, 1966), *Dr. Rock and Mr. Roll* (Blue Sky Productions, 1967), *Gill Women* (AIP, 1967), *Hillbillies in a Haunted House* (Woolner Bros., 1968),

*Unbilled guest appearance

MARTHA RAYE (Margaret Theresa Yvonne Reed) Born August 27, 1908, Butte, Montana. Married Bud Westmore (1937); divorced 1938. Married David Rose (1938); divorced 1941. Married Neil Lang (1941); divorced 1941. Married Nick Condos (1942), child: Melodye; divorced 1953. Married Edward Begley (1954); divorced 1956. Married Robert O'Shea (1958); divorced 1962.

Andy Devine, Martha Raye and Bob Hope in *Never Say Die*.

Feature Films: *Rhythm on the Range* (Par., 1936), *The Big Broadcast of 1937* (Par., 1936), *College Holiday* (Par., 1936), *Hideaway Girl* (Par., 1937), *Waikiki Wedding* (Par., 1937), *Mountain Music* (Par., 1937), *Double or Nothing* (Par., 1937), *Artists and Models* (Par., 1937), *The Big Broadcast of 1938* (Par., 1938), *College Swing* (Par., 1938), *Give Me a Sailor* (Par., 1938), *Tropic Holiday* (Par., 1938), *Never Say Die* (Par., 1939), *$1,000 a Touchdown* (Par., 1939), *The Farmer's Daughter* (Par., 1940), *The Boys From Syracuse* (Univ., 1940), *Navy Blues* (WB, 1941), *Keep 'Em Flying* (Univ., 1941), *Hellzapoppin'* (Univ., 1941), *Four Jills*

in a Jeep (20th, 1944), *Pin-Up Girl* (20th, 1944), *Monsieur Verdoux* (UA, 1947), *Billy Rose's Jumbo* (MGM, 1962).

RONALD REAGAN (Ronald Wilson Reagan) Born February 6, 1912, Tampico, Illinois. Married Jane Wyman (1940), children: Michael, Maureen; divorced 1948. Married Nancy Davis (1952), children: Patricia, Ronald.

Ronald Reagan and Shirley Temple in *That Hagen Girl*.

Feature Films: *Love Is on the Air* (WB, 1937), *Submarine D-1* (WB, 1937),* *Hollywood Hotel* (WB, 1937), *Sergeant Murphy* (WB, 1938), *Accidents Will Happen* (WB, 1938), *Cowboy From Brooklyn* (WB, 1938), *Boy Meets Girl* (WB, 1938), *Brother Rat* (WB, 1938), *Going Places* (WB, 1938), *Girls on Probation* (WB, 1938), *Dark Victory* (WB, 1939), *Secret Service of the Air* (WB, 1939), *Code of the Secret Service* (WB, 1939), *Naughty but Nice* (WB, 1939), *Hell's Kitchen* (WB, 1939), *Angels Wash Their Faces* (WB, 1939), *Smashing the Money Ring* (WB, 1939), *Brother Rat and a Baby* (WB, 1940), *An Angel From Texas* (WB, 1940), *Murder in the Air* (WB, 1940), *Knute Rockne, All American* (WB, 1940), *Tugboat Annie Sails Again* (WB, 1940), *Santa Fe Trail* (WB, 1940), *The Bad Man* (WB, 1941), *Million Dollar Baby* (WB, 1941), *Nine Lives Are Not Enough* (WB, 1941), *International Squadron* (WB, 1941), *Kings Row* (WB, 1941), *Juke Girl* (WB, 1942) *Desperate Journey* (WB, 1942), *This Is the Army* (WB, 1943), *Stallion Road* (WB, 1947), *That Hagen Girl* (WB, 1947), *The Voice of the Turtle* ("One for the Books"—WB, 1947), *John Loves Mary* (WB, 1949), *Night Unto Night* (WB, 1949), *The Girl From Jones Beach* (WB, 1949), *It's a Great Feeling* (WB, 1949), *The Hasty Heart* (WB, 1949), *Louisa* (Univ., 1950), *Storm Warning* (WB, 1950), *The Last Outpost* (Par., 1951), *Bedtime for Bonzo* (Univ., 1951), *Hong Kong* (Par., 1951), *She's Working Her Way Through College* (WB, 1952), *The Winning Team* (WB, 1952), *Tropic Zone* (Par., 1953), *Law and Order* (Univ., 1953), *Prisoner of War* (MGM, 1954), *Cattle Queen of Montana* (RKO, 1954), *Tennessee's Partner* (RKO, 1955), *Hellcat of the Navy* (Col., 1957), *The Young Doctors* (narrator; UA, 1961), *The Killers* (Univ., 1964).

*Scenes deleted from the final print

DONNA REED (Donna Mullenger) Born January 27, 1921, Denison, Iowa. Married William Tuttle (1943); divorced 1945. Married Tony Owen (1945), children: Penny, Tony, Timothy, Mary.

Feature Films:

as **Donna Adams** *Babes on Broadway* (MGM, 1941), *The Get-Away* (MGM, 1941).

as **Donna Reed** *The Shadow of the Thin Man* (MGM, 1941), *The Bugle Sounds* (MGM, 1941), *Calling Dr. Gillespie* (MGM, 1942), *The Courtship of Andy Hardy* (MGM, 1942), *Mokey* (MGM, 1942), *Eyes in the Night* (MGM, 1942), *Apache Trail* (MGM, 1942), *The Human Comedy* (MGM, 1943), *Dr. Gillespie's Criminal Case* (MGM, 1943), *Thousands Cheer* (MGM, 1943), *The Man From Down Under* (MGM, 1943), *See Here, Private Hargrove* (MGM, 1944), *Mrs.*

Donna Reed, George Dolenz and Van Johnson is *The Last Time I Saw Paris*.

Claudette Colbert and Anne Revere in *Remember the Day*.

Parkington (MGM, 1944), *Gentle Annie* (MGM, 1944), *The Picture of Dorian Gray* (MGM, 1945), *They Were Expendable* (MGM, 1945), *Faithful in My Fashion* (MGM, 1946), *It's a Wonderful Life* (RKO, 1946), *Green Dolphin Street* (MGM, 1947), *Beyond Glory* (Par., 1948), *Chicago Deadline* (Par., 1949), *Saturday's Hero* (Col., 1951), *Scandal Sheet* (Col., 1952), *Hangman's Knot* (Col., 1952), *Trouble Along the Way* (WB, 1953), *Raiders of the Seven Seas* (UA, 1953), *The Caddy* (Par, 1953), *From Here to Eternity* (Col., 1953), *Gun Fury* (Col., 1953), *Three Hours to Kill* (Col., 1954), *They Rode West* (Col., 1954), *The Last Time I Saw Paris* (MGM, 1954), *The Far Horizons* (Par., 1955), *Ransom* (MGM, 1956), *The Benny Goodman Story* (Univ., 1956), *Backlash* (Univ., 1956), *Beyond Mombasa* (Col., 1957), *The Whole Truth* (Col., 1958), *Pepe* (Col., 1960).

LEE REMICK (Lee Ann Remick) Born December 14, 1935, Quincy, Massachusetts. Married Bill Colleran (1957), children: Katherine, Matthew; divorced 1968.

Bradford Dillman and Lee Remick in *Sanctuary*.

Feature Films: *A Face in the Crowd* (WB, 1957), *The Long, Hot Summer* (20th, 1958), *These Thousand Hills* (20th, 1959), *Anatomy of a Murder* (Col., 1959), *Wild River* (20th, 1960), *Sanctuary* (20th, 1961), *Experiment in Terror* (Col., 1962), *Days of Wine and Roses* (WB, 1962), *The Running Man* (Col., 1963), *The Wheeler Dealers* (MGM, 1963), *Baby, the Rain Must Fall* (Col., 1965), *The Hallelujah Trail* (UA, 1965), *No Way to Treat a Lady* (Par., 1968), *The Detective* (20th, 1968).

ANNE REVERE Born June 25, 1903, New York, New York. Married Samuel Rosen (1935).

Feature Films: *Double Door* (Par., 1934), *One Crowded Hour* (RKO, 1940), *The Howards of Virginia* (Col., 1940), *Men of Boys Town* (MGM, 1941), *The Devil Commands* (Col., 1941), *H. M. Pulham, Esq.* (MGM, 1941), *Remember the Day* (20th, 1941), *The Falcon Takes Over* (RKO, 1942), *Meet the Stewarts* (Col., 1942), *The Gay Sisters* (WB, 1942), *Star Spangled Rhythm* (Par., 1942), *Shantytown* (Rep., 1943), *The Meanest Man in the World* (20th, 1943), *Old Acquaintance* (WB, 1943), *The Song of Bernadette* (20th, 1943), *Standing Room Only* (Par., 1944), *Rainbow Island* (Par., 1944), *The Thin Man Goes Home* (MGM, 1944), *Sunday Dinner for a Soldier* (20th, 1944), *National Velvet* (MGM, 1944), *The Keys of the Kingdom* (20th, 1944), *Don Juan Quilligan* (20th, 1945), *Fallen Angel* (20th, 1945), *Dragonwyck* (20th, 1946), *The Shocking Miss Pilgrim* (20th, 1947), *Carnival in Costa Rica* (20th, 1947), *Body and Soul* (UA, 1947), *Forever Amber* (20th, 1947), *Gentleman's Agreement* (20th, 1947), *Secret Beyond the Door* (Univ., 1948), *Scudda Hoo! Scudda Hay!* (20th, 1948), *Deep Waters* (20th, 1948), *You're My Everything* (20th, 1949), *The Great Missouri Raid* (Par., 1950), *A Place in the Sun* (Par., 1951).

DEBBIE REYNOLDS (Mary Frances Reynolds) Born April 1, 1932, El Paso, Texas. Married Eddie Fisher (1955), children: Carrie, Todd; divorced 1959. Married Harry Karl (1960).

Feature Films: *June Bride* (WB, 1948), *The Daughter of Rosie O'Grady* (WB, 1950), *Three Little Words* (MGM, 1950), *Two Weeks With Love* (MGM, 1950), *Mr. Imperium* (MGM, 1951), *Singin' in the Rain* (MGM,

Debbie Reynolds, Donald O'Connor and Noreen Corcoran in *I Love Melvin*.

1952), *Skirts Ahoy* (MGM, 1952),* *I Love Melvin* (MGM, 1953), *The Affairs of Dobie Gillis* (MGM, 1953), *Give the Girl a Break* (MGM, 1953), *Susan Slept Here* (RKO, 1954), *Athena* (MGM, 1954), *Hit the Deck* (MGM, 1955), *The Tender Trap* (MGM, 1955), *The Catered Affair* (MGM, 1956), *Bundle of Joy* (RKO, 1956), *Meet Me in Las Vegas* (MGM, 1956),* *Tammy and the Bachelor* (Univ., 1957), *This Happy Feeling* (Univ., 1958), *The Mating Game* (MGM, 1959), *Say One for Me* (20th, 1959), *It Started With a Kiss* (MGM, 1959), *The Gazebo* (MGM, 1959), *The Rat Race* (Par., 1960), *Pepe* (Col., 1960), *The Pleasure of His Company* (Par., 1961), *The Second Time Around* (20th, 1961), *How the West Was Won* (MGM, 1963), *My Six Loves* (Par., 1963), *Mary, Mary* (WB, 1963), *The Unsinkable Molly Brown* (MGM, 1964), *Goodbye Charlie* (20th, 1964), *The Singing Nun* (MGM, 1966), *Divorce American Style* (Col., 1967), *How Sweet It Is* (National General Pictures, 1968).

*Unbilled guest appearance

MARJORIE REYNOLDS (Marjorie Goodspeed) Born August 12, 1921, Buhl, Idaho. Married Jack Reynolds (1936), child: Linda.

Grant Withers, Marjorie Reynolds, James Flavin and Boris Karloff in *Mr. Wong in Chinatown.*

Sound Feature Films:

as Marjorie Moore *Collegiate* (Par., 1935).

as Marjorie Reynolds *Murder in Greenwich Village* (Col., 1937), *Tex Rides With the Boy Scouts* (GN, 1937), *The Overland Express* (Col., 1938), *Six Shootin' Sheriff* (GN, 1938), *Man's Country* (Mon., 1938), *Black Bandit* (Univ., 1938), *Rebellious Daughters* (Progressive Pictures, 1938), *Tailspin Tommy* (Mon., 1939), *Mystery Plane* (Mon., 1939), *Streets of New York* (Mon., 1939), *The Phantom Stage* (Univ., 1939), *Racketeers of the Range* (RKO, 1939), *Stunt Pilot* (Mon., 1939), *Mr. Wong in Chinatown* (Mon., 1939), *Danger Flight* (Mon., 1939), *Sky Patrol* (Mon., 1939), *Timber Stampede* (RKO, 1939), *Chasing Trouble* (Mon., 1940), *The Fatal Hour* (Mon., 1940), *Midnight Limited* (Mon., 1940), *Enemy Agent* (Univ., 1940), *Doomed to Die* (Mon., 1940), *Robin Hood of the Pecos* (Rep., 1941), *Up in the Air* (Mon., 1941), *Secret Evidence* (PRC, 1941), *The Great Swindle* (Col., 1941), *Dude Cowboy* (RKO, 1941), *Tillie the Toiler* (Col., 1941), *Cyclone on Horseback* (RKO, 1941), *Top Sergeant Mulligan* (Mon., 1941), *Holiday Inn* (Par., 1942), *Star Spangled Rhythm* (Par., 1942), *Dixie* (Par., 1943), *Up in Mabel's Room* (UA, 1944), *Ministry of Fear* (Par., 1944), *Three Is a Family* (UA, 1944), *Bring On the Girls* (Par., 1945), *Duffy's Tavern* (Par., 1945), *Meet Me on Broadway* (Col., 1946), *Monsieur Beaucaire* (Par., 1946), *The Time of Their Lives* (Univ., 1946), *Heaven Only Knows* (UA, 1947), *Bad Men of Tombstone* (AA, 1948), *That Midnight Kiss* (MGM, 1949), *Customs Agent* (Col., 1950), *The Great Jewel Robbery* (WB, 1950), *Rookie Fireman* (Col., 1950), *Home Town Story* (MGM, 1951), *His Kind of Woman* (RKO, 1951), *Models, Inc.* (Mutual Productions, 1952), *No Holds Barred* (Mon., 1952), *Mobs, Inc.* (Onyx Pictures, 1955), *Juke Box Rhythm* (Col., 1959), *The Silent Witness* (Emerson, Film Enterprises, 1964).

Luis Van Rooten, Thelma Ritter and Sharon McManus in *City Across the River.*

THELMA RITTER (Thelma Adele Ritter) Born February 14, 1905 Brooklyn, New York. Married Joseph Moran (1927), children: Joseph, Monica.

Feature Films: *The Miracle on 34th Street* (20th, 1947), *Call Northside 777* (20th, 1948), *A Letter to Three Wives* (20th, 1949), *City Across the River* (Univ., 1949), *Father Was a Fullback* (20th, 1949), *Perfect Strangers* (WB, 1950), *All About Eve* (20th, 1950), *I'll Get By* (20th, 1950), *The Mating Season* (Par., 1951), *As Young as You Feel* (20th, 1951), *The Model and the Marriage Broker* (20th, 1951), *With a Song in My Heart* (20th, 1952), *Titanic* (20th, 1953), *The Farmer Takes a Wife* (20th, 1953), *Pickup on South Street* (20th, 1953), *Rear Window* (Par., 1954), *Daddy Long Legs* (20th, 1955), *Lucy Gallant* (Par., 1955), *The Proud and Profane* (Par., 1956), *A Hole in the Head* (UA, 1959), *Pillow Talk* (Univ., 1959), *The Misfits* (UA, 1961), *The Second Time Around* (20th, 1961), *Bird Man of Alcatraz* (UA, 1962), *How the West Was Won* (MGM, 1963), *For Love or Money* (Univ., 1963), *A New Kind of Love* (Par., 1963), *Move Over, Darling* (20th, 1963), *Boeing-Boeing* (Par., 1965), *The Incident* (20th, 1967).

JASON ROBARDS, JR. (Jason Nelson Robards, Jr.) Born July 26, 1922, Chicago, Illinois. Married Eleanor Pitman (1946), children: Jason, Sarah, David; divorced 1958. Married Lauren Bacall (1961), child: Sam.

George Hamilton and Jason Robards, Jr., in *Act One.*

Feature Films: *The Journey* (MGM, 1959), *By Love Possessed* (UA, 1961), *Tender Is the Night* (20th, 1962), *Long Day's Journey into Night* (Embassy, 1962), *Act One* (WB, 1963), *A Thousand Clowns* (UA, 1965), *A Big Hand for the Little Lady* (WB, 1966), *Any Wednesday* (WB, 1966), *Divorce American Style* (Col., 1967), *Hour of the Guns* (UA, 1967), *St. Valentine's Day Massacre* (20th, 1967).

Lyda Roberti in *College Rhythm*.

LYDA ROBERTI Born May 20, 1909, Warsaw, Poland. Married Hugh Ernst (1935). Died March 12, 1938.

Feature Films: *Dancers in the Dark* (Par., 1932), *Million Dollar Legs* (Par., 1932), *The Kid From Spain* (UA, 1932), *Three-Cornered Moon* (Par., 1933), *Torch Singer* (Par., 1933), *College Rhythm* (Par., 1934), *George White's Scandals* (Fox, 1935), *The Big Broadcast of 1936* (Par., 1935), *Nobody's Baby* (MGM, 1937), *Pick a Star* (MGM, 1937), *Wide Open Faces* (Col., 1938).

CLIFF ROBERTSON (Clifford Parker Robertson III) Born September 9, 1925, La Jolla, California. Married Cynthia Stone (1957), child: Stephanie; divorced. Married Dina Merrill (1966).

Cliff Robertson and Robert Culp in *PT-109*.

Feature Films: *Picnic* (Col., 1955), *Autumn Leaves* (Col., 1956), *The Girl Most Likely* (Univ., 1957), *The Naked and the Dead* (WB, 1958), *Gidget* (Col., 1959), *Battle of the Coral Sea* (Col., 1959), *As the Sea Rages.* (Col., 1960), *All in a Night's Work* (Par., 1961), *The Big Show* (20th, 1961), *Underworld, U.S.A.* (Col., 1962), *The Interns* (Col., 1962), *My Six Loves* (Par., 1963), *PT-109* (WB, 1963), *Sunday in New York* (MGM, 1963), *The Best Man* (UA, 1964), *633 Squadron* (UA, 1964), *Up From the Beach* (20th, 1965), *Love Has Many Faces* (Col., 1965), *Masquerade* (UA, 1965), *The Honey Pot* (UA, 1967), *Charly* (Selmur, 1968), *The Devil's Brigade* (UA, 1968).

EDWARD G. ROBINSON (Emmanuel Goldenberg) Born December 12, 1893, Bucharest, Romania. Married Gladys Lloyd (1927), child: Emmanuel; divorced 1956.

Sound Feature Films: *The Hole in the Wall* (Par., 1929), *Night Ride*

Ed Brophy, Edward G. Robinson and John Carradine in *The Last Gangster*.

(Univ., 1930), *A Lady to Love* (MGM, 1930), *Outside the Law* (Univ., 1930), *East Is West* (Univ., 1930), *The Widow From Chicago* (WB, 1930), *Little Caesar* (WB, 1930), *Smart Money* (WB, 1931), *Five Star Final* (WB, 1931), *The Hatchet Man* (WB, 1932), *Two Seconds* (WB, 1932), *Tiger Shark* (WB, 1932), *Silver Dollar* (WB, 1932), *Little Giant* (WB, 1933), *I Loved a Woman* (WB, 1933), *Dark Hazard* (WB, 1934), *The Man With Two Faces* (WB, 1934), *The Whole Town's Talking* (Col., 1935), *Barbary Coast* (UA, 1935), *Bullets or Ballots* (WB, 1936), *Thunder in the City* (Col., 1937), *Kid Galahad* (WB, 1937), *The Last Gangster* (MGM, 1937), *A Slight Case of Murder* (WB, 1938), *The Amazing Dr. Clitterhouse* (WB, 1938), *I Am the Law* (Col., 1938), *Confessions of a Nazi Spy* (WB, 1939), *Blackmail* (MGM, 1939), *Dr. Ehrlich's Magic Bullet* (WB, 1940), *Brother Orchid* (WB, 1940), *A Dispatch From Reuters* (WB, 1940), *The Sea Wolf* (WB, 1941), *Manpower* (WB, 1941), *Larceny, Inc.* (WB, 1942), *Tales of Manhattan* (20th, 1942), *Destroyer* (Col., 1943), *Flesh and Fantasy* (Univ., 1943), *Tampico* (20th, 1944), *Double Indemnity* (Par., 1944), *Mr. Winkle Goes to War* (Col., 1944), *The Woman in the Window* (RKO, 1944), *Our Vines Have Tender Grapes* (MGM, 1945), *Scarlet Street* (Univ., 1945), *The Stranger* (RKO, 1946), *The Red House* (UA, 1947), *All My Sons* (Univ., 1948), *Key Largo* (WB, 1948), *The Night Has a Thousand Eyes* (Par., 1948), *House of Strangers* (20th, 1949), *It's a Great Feeling* (WB, 1949), *My Daughter Joy* (Col., 1950), *Actors and Sin* (UA, 1952), *Vice Squad* (UA, 1953), *The Big Leaguer* (MGM, 1953), *The Glass Web* (Univ., 1953), *Black Tuesday* (UA, 1954), *The Violent Men* (Col., 1955), *Tight Spot* (Col., 1955), *A Bullet for Joey* (UA, 1955), *Illegal* (WB, 1955), *Hell on Frisco Bay* (WB, 1955), *Nightmare* (UA, 1956), *The Ten Commandments* (Par., 1956), *A Hole in the Head* (UA, 1959), *Seven Thieves* (20th, 1960), *Pepe* (Col., 1960), *My Geisha* (Par., 1962), *Two Weeks in Another Town* (MGM, 1962), *Sammy Going South* (Bryanston, 1963), *The Prize* (MGM, 1963), *Good Neighbor Sam* (Col., 1964), *Robin and the 7 Hoods* (WB, 1964), *Cheyenne Autumn* (WB, 1964), *The Outrage* (MGM, 1964), *The Cincinnati Kid* (MGM, 1965) *The Biggest Bundle of Them All* (MGM, 1968), *Grand Slam* (Par., 1968), *MacKenna's Gold* (Col., 1968), *Operation St. Peter's* (Ultra-Marianne, 1968).

MAY ROBSON (Mary Robison) Born April 19, 1864, Melbourne, Australia. Married Edward Gore (1880) child: Edward; widowed 1883. Married A. H. Brown (1889); widowed 1922. Died October 20, 1942.

Sound Feature Films: *Mother's Millions* (Univ., 1931), *Strange Interlude* (MGM, 1932), *Letty Lynton* (MGM, 1932), *Red-Headed Woman* (MGM, 1932), *If I Had a Million* (Par., 1932), *Little Orphan Annie* (RKO, 1932), *The White Sister* (MGM, 1933), *Men Must Fight* (MGM, 1933), *Reunion in Vienna* (MGM, 1933), *Dinner at Eight* (MGM, 1933), *Lady for a Day* (Col., 1933), *Broadway to Hollywood* (MGM, 1933), *One Man's Journey* (RKO, 1933), *Beauty for Sale* (MGM, 1933), *The Solitaire Man* (MGM, 1933), *Dancing Lady* (MGM, 1933), *Alice in Wonderland* (Par., 1933), *You Can't Buy Everything* (MGM, 1934), *Straight Is the Way* (MGM, 1934), *Lady by Choice* (Col., 1934), *Grand Old Girl* (RKO, 1935), *Reckless* (MGM, 1935), *Mills of the Gods* (Col., 1935), *Vanessa—Her Love Story* (MGM, 1935), *Strangers All* (Radio, 1935), *Age of Indiscretion* (MGM, 1935), *Anna Karenina*

Ian Hunter, Roland Young, May Robson, Genevieve Tobin and Fay Bainter in *Yes, My Darling Daughter.*

(MGM, 1935), *Three Kids and a Queen* (Univ., 1935), *Wife vs. Secretary* (MGM, 1936), *Rainbow on the River* (RKO, 1936), *Woman in Distress* (Col., 1937), *A Star Is Born* (UA, 1937), *The Captain's Kid* (WB, 1937), *The Perfect Specimen* (WB, 1937), *Bringing Up Baby* (RKO, 1938), *The Adventures of Tom Sawyer* (UA, 1938), *The Texans* (Par., 1938), *Four Daughters* (WB, 1938), *Yes, My Darling Daughter* (WB, 1939), *They Made Me a Criminal* (WB, 1939), *The Kid From Kokomo* (WB, 1939), *Daughters Courageous* (WB, 1939), *That's Right—You're Wrong* (RKO, 1939), *Nurse Edith Cavell* (RKO, 1939), *Four Wives* (WB, 1939), *Granny, Get Your Gun* (WB, 1940), *Irene* (RKO, 1940), *Texas Rangers Ride Again* (Par., 1941), *Four Mothers* (WB, 1941), *Million Dollar Baby* (WB, 1941), *Playmates* (RKO, 1941), *Joan of Paris* (RKO, 1942).

GINGER ROGERS (Virginia Katherine McMath) Born July 16, 1911, Independence, Missouri. Married Jack Edward Culpepper (1929), divorced 1931. Married Lew Ayres (1934); divorced 1941. Married Jack Briggs (1943); divorced 1949. Married Jacques Bergerac (1953); divorced 1957. Married William Marshall (1961).

Ginger Rogers and Marjorie Rambeau in *The Primrose Path.*

Feature Films: *Young Man of Manhattan* (Par., 1930), *Queen High* (Par., 1930), *The Sap From Syracuse* (Par., 1930), *Follow the Leader* (Par., 1930), *Honor Among Lovers* (Par., 1931), *The Tip-Off* (Pathé, 1931), *Suicide Fleet* (Pathé, 1931), *Carnival Boat* (RKO, 1932), *The Tenderfoot* (WB, 1932), *The Thirteenth Guest* (Mon., 1932), *Hat Check Girl* (Fox, 1932), *You Said a Mouthful* (WB, 1932), *42nd Street* (WB,

1933), *Broadway Bad* (Fox, 1933), *Gold Diggers of 1933* (WB, 1933), *Professional Sweetheart* (RKO, 1933), *Shriek in the Night* (Allied, 1933), *Don't Bet on Love* (Univ., 1933), *Sitting Pretty* (Par., 1933), *Flying Down to Rio* (RKO, 1933), *Chance at Heaven* (RKO, 1933), *Rafter Romance* (RKO, 1934), *Finishing School* (RKO, 1934), *20 Million Sweethearts* (WB, 1934), *Change of Heart* (Fox, 1934), *Upper World* (WB, 1934), *The Gay Divorcee* (RKO, 1934), *Romance in Manhattan* (RKO, 1934), *Roberta* (RKO, 1935), *Star of Midnight* (RKO, 1935), *Top Hat* (RKO, 1935), *In Person* (RKO, 1935), *Follow the Fleet* (RKO, 1936), *Swing Time* (RKO, 1936), *Shall We Dance* (RKO, 1937), *Stage Door* (RKO, 1937), *Having Wonderful Time* (RKO, 1938), *Vivacious Lady* (RKO, 1938), *Carefree* (RKO, 1938), *The Story of Vernon and Irene Castle* (RKO, 1939), *Bachelor Mother* (RKO, 1939), *Fifth Avenue Girl* (RKO, 1939), *Primrose Path* (RKO, 1940), *Lucky Partners* (RKO, 1940), *Kitty Foyle* (RKO, 1940), *Tom, Dick and Harry* (RKO, 1941), *Roxie Hart* (20th, 1942), *Tales of Manhattan* (20th, 1942), *The Major and the Minor* (Par., 1942), *Once Upon a Honeymoon* (RKO, 1942), *Tender Comrade* (RKO, 1943), *Lady in the Dark* (Par., 1944), *I'll Be Seeing You* (Selznick-UA, 1944), *Weekend at the Waldorf* (MGM, 1945), *Heartbeat* (RKO, 1946), *Magnificent Doll* (Univ., 1946), *It Had to Be You* (Col., 1947), *The Barkleys of Broadway* (MGM, 1949), *Perfect Strangers* (WB, 1950), *Storm Warning* (WB, 1950), *The Groom Wore Spurs* (Univ., 1951), *We're Not Married* (20th, 1952), *Monkey Business* (20th, 1952), *Dreamboat* (20th, 1952), *Forever Female* (Par., 1953), *Black Widow* (20th, 1954), *Twist of Fate* (UA, 1954), *Tight Spot* (Col., 1955), *The First Traveling Saleslady* (RKO, 1956), *Teenage Rebel* (20th, 1956), *Oh, Men! Oh, Women!* (20th, 1957), *The Confession* (Wm. Marshall Prod., 1964, unreleased), *Harlow* (Magna, 1965),

ROY ROGERS (Leonard Slye) Born November 5, 1912, Cincinnati, Ohio. Married Arlene Wilkins (1936), children: Cheryl, Darlene, Linda, Roy, Marion; widowed 1946. Married Dale Evans (1947), children: Robin, John, Mary Little Doe, Deborah.

Claire Trevor and Roy Rogers in *Dark Command.*

Feature Films: *The Old Homestead* (Liberty, 1935), *The Big Show* (Rep., 1936), *Gallant Defender* (Col., 1935), *The Mysterious Avenger* (Col., 1936), *Rhythm on the Range* (Par., 1936), *The Old Corral* (Rep., 1936), *The Old Wyoming Trail* (Col, 1937), *Wild Horse Rodeo* (Rep., 1937), *The Old Barn Dance* (Rep., 1938), *Under Western Stars* (Rep., 1938), *Billy the Kid Returns* (Rep., 1938), *Come On Rangers* (Rep., 1938), *Shine On Harvest Moon* (Rep., 1938), *Rough Riders' Round-Up* (Rep., 1939), *Frontier Pony Express* (Rep., 1939), *Southward, Ho!* (Rep., 1939), *In Old Caliente* (Rep., 1939), *Wall Street Cowboy* (Rep., 1939), *The Arizona Kid* (Rep., 1939), *Jeepers Creepers* (Rep., 1939), *Saga of Death Valley* (Rep., 1939), *Days of Jesse James* (Rep., 1939), *Young Buffalo Bill* (Rep., 1940), *Dark Command* (Rep., 1940), *The Carson City Kid* (Rep., 1940), *The Ranger and the Lady* (Rep., 1940), *Colorado* (Rep., 1940), *Young Bill Hickok* (Rep., 1940), *The Border Legion*

(Rep., 1940), *Robin Hood of the Pecos* (Rep., 1941), *Arkansas Judge* (Rep., 1941), *In Old Cheyenne* (Rep., 1941), *Sheriff of Tombstone* (Rep., 1941), *Nevada City* (Rep., 1941), *Bad Man of Deadwood* (Rep., 1941), *Jesse James at Bay* (Rep., 1941), *Red River Valley* (Rep., 1941), *The Man From Cheyenne* (Rep., 1942), *South of Santa Fe* (Rep., 1942), *Sunset on the Desert* (Rep., 1942), *Romance on the Range* (Rep., 1942), *Sons of the Pioneers* (Rep., 1942), *Sunset Serenade* (Rep., 1942), *Heart of the Golden West* (Rep., 1942), *Ridin' Down the Canyon* (Rep., 1942), *Idaho* (Rep., 1943), *King of the Cowboys* (Rep., 1943), *Song of Texas* (Rep., 1943), *Silver Spurs* (Rep., 1943), *The Man From Music Mountain* (Rep., 1943), *Hands Across the Border* (Rep., 1943), *The Cowboy and the Senorita* (Rep., 1944), *The Yellow Rose of Texas* (Rep., 1944), *Song of Nevada* (Rep., 1944), *San Fernando Valley* (Rep., 1944), *Lights of Old Santa Fe* (Rep., 1944), *Brazil* (Rep., 1944)*, *Lake Placid Serenade* (Rep., 1944), *Hollywood Canteen* (WB, 1944), *Utah* (Rep., 1945), *Bells of Rosarita* (Rep., 1945), *The Man From Oklahoma* (Rep., 1945), *Sunset in El Dorado* (Rep., 1945), *Don't Fence Me In* (Rep., 1945), *Along the Navajo Trail* (Rep., 1945), *Song of Arizona* (Rep., 1946), *Rainbow Over Texas* (Rep., 1946), *My Pal Trigger* (Rep., 1946), *Under Nevada Skies* (Rep., 1946), *Roll on Texas Moon* (Rep., 1946), *Home in Oklahoma* (Rep., 1946), *Out California Way* (Rep., 1946), *Helldorado* (Rep., 1946), *Apache Rose* (Rep., 1947) *Hit Parade of 1947* (Rep., 1947), *Bells of San Angelo* (Rep., 1947), *Springtime in the Sierras* (Rep., 1947), *On the Old Spanish Trail* (Rep., 1947), *The Gay Ranchero* (Rep., 1948), *Under California Stars* (Rep., 1948), *Eyes of Texas* (Rep., 1948), *Melody Time* (RKO, 1948), *Night Time in Nevada* (Rep., 1948), *Grand Canyon Trail* (Rep., 1948), *The Far Frontier* (Rep., 1948), *Susanna Pass* (Rep., 1949), *Down Dakota Way* (Rep., 1949), *The Golden Stallion* (Rep., 1949), *Bells of Coronado* (Rep., 1950), *Twilight in the Sierras* (Rep., 1950), *Trigger, Jr.* (Rep., 1950), *Sunset in the West* (Rep., 1950), *North of the Great Divide* (Rep., 1950), *Trail of Robin Hood* (Rep., 1950), *Spoilers of the Plains* (Rep., 1951), *Heart of the Rockies* (Rep., 1951), *In Old Amarillo* (Rep., 1951), *South of Caliente* (Rep., 1951), *Pals of the Golden West* (Rep., 1951), *Son of Paleface* (Par., 1952), *Alias Jesse James* (UA, 1959).*

*Unbilled guest appearance

WILL ROGERS (William Penn Adair Rogers) Born November 4, 1879, Cologah, Indian Territory (Oklahoma). Married Betty Balke (1908), children: Will, Mary, James. Died August 15, 1935.

Will Rogers and Sterling Holloway in *Doubting Thomas*.

Sound Feature Films: *They Had to See Paris* (Fox, 1929), *Happy Days* (Fox, 1930), *So This Is London* (Fox, 1930), *Lightnin'* (Fox, 1930), *A Connecticut Yankee* (Fox, 1931), *Young As You Feel* (Fox, 1931), *Ambassador Bill* (Fox, 1931), *Business and Pleasure* (Fox, 1932), *Down to Earth* (Fox, 1932), *Too Busy to Work* (Fox, 1932), *State Fair* (Fox, 1933), *Doctor Bull* (Fox, 1933), *Mr. Skitch* (Fox, 1933), *David Harum* (Fox, 1934), *Handy Andy* (Fox, 1934), *Judge Priest* (Fox, 1934), *County Chairman* (Fox, 1935), *Life Begins at 40* (Fox, 1935), *Doubting Thomas* (Fox, 1935), *In Old Kentucky* (Fox, 1935), *Steamboat 'Round the Bend* (Fox, 1935).

Bill Neff, Gilbert Roland and Chris-Pin Martin in *King of the Bandits*.

GILBERT ROLAND (Louis Antonio Damaso Alonso) Born December 11, 1905, Chihuahua, Mexico. Married Constance Bennett (1941), children: Lynda, Gyl; divorced 1946. Married Guillermina Cantu (1954).

English-Language Sound Feature Films: *New York Nights* (UA, 1930), *Men of the North* (MGM, 1930), *The Passionate Plumber* (MGM, 1932), *Life Begins* (WB, 1932), *No Living Witness* (Mayfair, 1932), *Parisian Romance* (Allied, 1932), *Call Her Savage* (Fox, 1932), *She Done Him Wrong* (Par., 1933), *Our Betters* (RKO, 1933), *Gigolettes of Paris* (Equitable, 1933), *After Tonight* (RKO, 1933), *Elinor Norton* (Fox, 1934), *Mystery Woman* (Fox, 1935), *Ladies Love Danger* (Fox, 1935), *Midnight Taxi* (20th, 1937), *Last Train From Madrid* (Par, 1937), *Thunder Trail* (Par., 1937), *Gateway* (20th, 1938), *Juarez* (WB, 1939), *Isle of Destiny* (RKO, 1940), *The Sea Hawk* (WB, 1940), *Rangers of Fortune* (Par., 1940), *Gambling on the High Seas* (WB, 1940), *Angels With Broken Wings* (Rep., 1941), *My Life With Caroline* (RKO, 1941), *Isle of Missing Men* (Mon., 1942), *Enemy Agents Meet Ellery Queen* (Col., 1942), *The Desert Hawk* (Col. serial, 1944), *Captain Kidd* (UA, 1945), *The Gay Cavalier* (Mon., 1946), *Pirates of Monterey* (Univ., 1947), *King of the Bandits* (Mon., 1947), *Robin Hood of Monterey* (Mon., 1947), *Riding the California Trail* (Mon., 1947), *High Conquest* (Mon., 1947), *The Other Woman* (UA, 1947), *The Dude Goes West* (AA, 1948), *We Were Strangers* (Col., 1949), *Malaya* (MGM, 1949), *The Torch* (EL, 1950), *Crisis* (MGM, 1950), *The Furies* (Par., 1950), *Mark of the Renegade* (Univ., 1951), *Ten Tall Men* (Col., 1951), *The Bullfighter and the Lady* (Rep., 1951), *My Six Convicts* (Col., 1952), *Glory Alley* (MGM, 1952), *The Miracle of Our Lady of Fatima* (WB, 1952), *Apache War Smoke* (MGM, 1952), *The Bad and the Beautiful* (MGM, 1952), *Beneath the 12-Mile Reef* (20th, 1953), *The Diamond Queen* (WB, 1953), *Thunder Bay* (Univ., 1953), *The French Line* (RKO, 1954), *Underwater* (RKO, 1955), *The Racers* (20th, 1955), *That Lady* (20th, 1955), *The Treasure of Pancho Villa* (RKO, 1955), *Bandido* (UA, 1956), *Around the World in 80 Days* (UA, 1956), *Three Violent People* (Par., 1956), *The Midnight Story* (Univ., 1957), *The Last of the Fast Guns* (Univ., 1958), *The Wild and The Innocent* (Univ., 1959), *The Big Circus* (AA, 1959), *Guns of the Timberland* (WB, 1960), *Samar* (WB, 1962), *Cheyenne Autumn* (WB, 1964), *The Reward* (20th, 1965), *Each Man for Himself* (PCM, 1968).

RUTH ROMAN Born December 22, 1924, Boston, Massachusetts. Married Jack Flaxman (1940); divorced 1941. Married Mortimer Hall (1950), child: Richard; divorced 1955. Married Buddy Moss (1956).

Feature Films: *Stage Door Canteen* (UA, 1943), *Ladies Courageous* (Univ., 1944), *Since You Went Away* (UA, 1944), *Storm Over Lisbon* (Rep., 1944), *Jungle Queen* (Univ. serial, 1945), *The Affairs of Susan* (Par., 1945), *See My Lawyer* (Univ., 1945), *You Came Along* (Par., 1945), *Incendiary Blonde* (Par., 1945), *A Night in Casablanca* (UA, 1946), *White Stallion* (Astor, 1947), *The Big Clock* (Par., 1948), *The Night Has a Thousand Eyes* (Par., 1948), *Good Sam* (RKO, 1948), *Belle Starr's Daughter* (20th, 1948), *The Window* (RKO, 1949), *Champion* (UA, 1949), *Beyond the Forest* (WB, 1949), *Always Leave Them Laughing* (WB, 1949), *Barricade* (WB, 1950), *Colt .45* (WB, 1950),

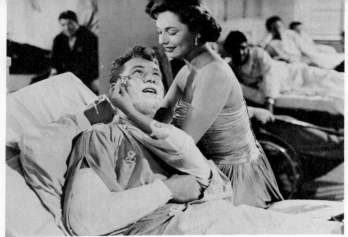

Ruth Roman in *Starlift*.

Three Secrets (WB, 1950), *Dallas* (WB, 1950), *Lightning Strikes Twice* (WB, 1951), *Strangers on a Train* (WB, 1951), *Starlift* (WB, 1951), *Tomorrow Is Another Day* (WB, 1951), *Invitation* (MGM, 1952), *Mara Maru* (WB, 1952), *Young Man With Ideas* (MGM, 1952), *Blowing Wild* (WB, 1953), *Tanganyika* (Univ., 1954), *Down Three Dark Streets* (UA, 1954), *The Shanghai Story* (Rep., 1954), *The Far Country* (Univ., 1955), *The Bottom of the Bottle* (20th, 1956), *Joe MacBeth* (Col., 1956), *Great Day in the Morning* (RKO, 1956), *Rebel in Town* (UA, 1956), *Five Steps to Danger* (UA, 1957), *Bitter Victory* (Col., 1958), *Desert Desperadoes* (RKO, 1959), *Look in Any Window* (AA 1961), *Love Has Many Faces* (Col., 1965).

CESAR ROMERO Born February 15, 1907, New York, New York.

Cesar Romero, George Montgomery and Jackie Gleason in *Orchestra Wives*.

Feature Films: *The Shadow Laughs* (Invincible, 1933), *The Thin Man* (MGM, 1934), *Cheating Cheaters* (Univ., 1934), *British Agent* (WB, 1934), *The Good Fairy* (Univ., 1935), *Strange Wives* (Univ., 1935), *Clive of India* (UA, 1935), *Cardinal Richelieu* (UA, 1935), *Hold 'Em Yale* (Par., 1935), *The Devil Is a Woman* (Par., 1935), *Diamond Jim* (Univ., 1935), *Metropolitan* (Fox, 1935), *Rendezvous* (MGM, 1935), *Show Them No Mercy* (Fox, 1935), *Love Before Breakfast* (Univ., 1936), *Nobody's Fool* (Univ., 1936), *Public Enemy's Wife* (WB, 1936), *15 Maiden Lane* (20th, 1936), *She's Dangerous* (Univ., 1937), *Armored Car* (Univ., 1937), *Wee Willie Winkie* (20th, 1937), *Dangerously Yours* (20th, 1937), *Happy Landing* (20th, 1938), *Always Goodbye* (20th, 1938), *My Lucky Star* (20th, 1938), *Five of a Kind* (20th, 1938), *Wife, Husband and Friend* (20th, 1939), *The Little Princess* (20th, 1939), *Return of the Cisco Kid* (20th, 1939), *Charlie Chan at Treasure Island* (20th, 1939), *Frontier Marshal* (20th, 1939), *Viva Cisco Kid* (20th, 1940), *He Married His Wife* (20th, 1940), *The Cisco Kid and the Lady* (20th, 1940), *The Gay Caballero* (20th, 1940), *Tall, Dark and Handsome*

(20th, 1941), *Romance of the Rio Grande* (20th, 1941), *Ride on, Vaquero* (20th, 1941), *The Great American Broadcast* (20th, 1941), *Dance Hall* (20th, 1941), *Week-End in Havana* (20th, 1941), *A Gentleman at Heart* (20th, 1942), *Tales of Manhattan* (20th, 1942), *Orchestra Wives* (20th, 1942), *Springtime in the Rockies* (20th, 1942), *Coney Island* (20th, 1943), *Wintertime* (20th, 1943), *Captain From Castile* (20th, 1947), *Carnival in Costa Rica* (20th, 1947), *Deep Waters* (20th, 1948), *That Lady in Ermine* (20th, 1948), *Julia Misbehaves* (MGM, 1948), *The Beautiful Blonde From Bashful Bend* (20th, 1949), *Love That Brute* (20th, 1950), *Once a Thief* (UA, 1950), *Happy Go Lovely* (RKO, 1951), *FBI Girl* (Lip., 1951), *The Lost Continent* (Lip., 1951), *Scotland Yard Inspector* (Lip., 1952), *The Jungle* (Lip., 1952), *Prisoners of the Casbah* (Col., 1953), *Shadow Man* (Lip., 1953), *Vera Cruz* (UA, 1954), *The Americano* (RKO, 1955), *The Racers* (20th, 1955), *Around the World in 80 Days* (UA, 1956), *The Sword of Granada* (Manson Dist. Co., 1956), *The Leather Saint* (Par., 1956), *The Story of Mankind* (WB, 1957), *Villa!* (20th, 1958), *Ocean's 11* (WB, 1960), *Pepe* (Col., 1960), *7 Women From Hell* (20th, 1961), *If a Man Answers* (Univ., 1962), *We Shall Return* (United International, 1963), *Donovan's Reef* (Par., 1963), *The Castilian* (WB, 1963), *A House Is Not a Home* (Embassy, 1964), *Two on a Guillotine* (WB, 1965), *Sergeant Deadhead* (AIP, 1965), *Marriage on the Rocks* (WB, 1965), *Batman* (20th, 1966).

MICKEY ROONEY (Joe Yule, Jr.) Born September 23, 1920, Brooklyn, New York. Married Ava Gardner (1942); divorced 1943. Married Betty Rase (1944), children: Mickey, Timothy; divorced 1947. Married Martha Vickers (1949), child: Ted; divorced 1951. Married Elaine Mahnken (1952); divorced 1959. Married Barbara Thomason (1959), children: Kelly, Kerry, Kimmy; widowed 1966. Married Margaret Lane (1966); divorced 1967.

Jeanne Cagney and Mickey Rooney in *Quicksand*.

Sound Feature Films: *Information Kid* (Univ., 1932), *Fast Companions* (Univ., 1932), *My Pal the King* (Univ., 1932), *Beast of the City* (MGM, 1932), *The Big Cage* (Univ., 1933), *The Life of Jimmy Dolan* (WB, 1933), *Broadway to Hollywood* (MGM, 1933), *The Big Chance* (Arthur Greenblatt, 1933), *The Chief* (MGM, 1933), *Lost Jungle* (Mascot serial, 1934), *Beloved* (Univ., 1934), *I Like It That Way* (Univ., 1934), *Love Birds* (Univ., 1934), *Manhattan Melodrama* (MGM, 1934), *Chained* (MGM, 1934), *Hide-Out* (MGM, 1934), *Upper World* (WB, 1934), *Half a Sinner* (Univ., 1934), *Blind Date* (Col., 1934), *Death on the Diamond* (MGM, 1934), *County Chairman* (Fox, 1935), *The Healer* (Mon., 1935), *A Midsummer Night's Dream* (WB, 1935), *Reckless* (MGM, 1935), *Ah, Wilderness* (MGM, 1935), *Riffraff* (MGM, 1935), *Little Lord Fauntleroy* (UA, 1936), *The Devil Is a Sissy* (MGM, 1936), *Down the Stretch* (WB, 1936), *Captains Courageous* (MGM, 1937), *A Family Affair* (MGM, 1937), *The Hoosier Schoolboy* (Mon., 1937), *Slave Ship* (20th, 1937), *Thoroughbreds Don't Cry* (MGM, 1937), *Live, Love and Learn* (MGM, 1937), *Love Is a Headache* (MGM, 1938), *Judge Hardy's Children* (MGM, 1938), *You're Only Young Once* (MGM,

1938), *Hold That Kiss* (MGM, 1938), *Lord Jeff* (MGM, 1938), *Love Finds Andy Hardy* (MGM, 1938), *Boys Town* (MGM, 1938), *Out West With the Hardys* (MGM, 1938), *Stablemates* (MGM, 1938), *Adventures of Huckleberry Finn* (MGM, 1939), *The Hardys Ride High* (MGM, 1939), *Andy Hardy Gets Spring Fever* (MGM, 1939), *Babes in Arms* (MGM, 1939), *Judge Hardy and Son* (MGM, 1939), *Young Tom Edison* (MGM, 1940), *Andy Hardy Meets Debutante* (MGM, 1940), *Strike Up the Band* (MGM, 1940), *Andy Hardy's Private Secretary* (MGM, 1941), *Men of Boys Town* (MGM, 1941), *Life Begins For Andy Hardy* (MGM, 1941), *Babes on Broadway* (MGM, 1941), *The Courtship of Andy Hardy* (MGM, 1942), *A Yank at Eton* (MGM, 1942), *Andy Hardy's Double Life* (MGM, 1942), *Andy Hardy Steps Out* (MGM, 1942), *The Human Comedy* (MGM, 1943), *Girl Crazy* (MGM, 1943), *Thousands Cheer* (MGM, 1943), *Andy Hardy's Blonde Trouble* (MGM, 1944), *National Velvet* (MGM, 1944), *Love Laughs at Andy Hardy* (MGM, 1946), *Killer McCoy* (MGM, 1947), *Summer Holiday* (MGM, 1948), *Words and Music* (MGM, 1948), *The Big Wheel* (UA, 1949), *Quicksand* (UA, 1950), *The Fireball* (20th, 1950), *He's a Cockeyed Wonder* (Col., 1950), *My Outlaw Brother*, (EL, 1951), *The Strip* (MGM, 1951), *Sound Off* (Col., 1952), *Off Limits* (Par., 1953), *A Slight Case of Larceny* (MGM, 1953), *Drive a Crooked Road* (Col., 1954), *The Atomic Kid* (Rep., 1954), *The Bridges at Toko-Ri* (Par., 1954), *The Twinkle in God's Eye* (Rep., 1955), *The Bold and the Brave* (RKO, 1956), *Francis in the Haunted House* (Univ., 1956), *Magnificent Roughnecks* (AA, 1956), *Operation Mad Ball* (Col., 1957), *Baby Face Nelson* (UA, 1957), *Andy Hardy Comes Home* (MGM, 1958), *A Nice Little Bank That Should Be Robbed* (20th, 1958), *The Last Mile* (UA, 1959), *The Big Operator* (MGM, 1959), *Platinum High School* (MGM, 1960), *The Private Lives of Adam And Eve* (Univ., 1960), *King of the Roaring 20's—The Story of Arnold Rothstein* (AA, 1961), *Breakfast at Tiffany's* (Par., 1961), *Everything's Ducky* (Col., 1961), *Requiem for a Heavyweight* (Col., 1962), *It's a Mad, Mad, Mad, Mad World* (UA, 1963), *The Secret Invasion* (UA, 1964), *How to Stuff a Wild Bikini* (AIP, 1965), *24 Hours to Kill* (7 Arts, 1965), *Ambush Bay* (UA, 1966), *The Extraordinary Seaman* (MGM, 1968), *The Devil in Love* (WB-7 Arts, 1968).

SHIRLEY ROSS (Bernice Gaunt) Born January 7, 1915, Omaha, Nebraska. Married Ken Dolan (1938), children: John, Ross; widowed 1951. Married Edward Blum, child: Victoria.

Edward Arnold and Shirley Ross in *Blossoms on Broadway*.

Feature Films: *Bombshell* (MGM, 1933), *Hollywood Party* (MGM, 1934), *Manhattan Melodrama* (MGM, 1934), *The Girl From Missouri* (MGM, 1934), *The Merry Widow* (MGM, 1934), *Age of Indiscretion* (MGM, 1935), *Calm Yourself* (MGM, 1935), *San Francisco* (MGM, 1936), *Devil's Squadron* (Col., 1936), *The Big Broadcast of 1937* (Par., 1936), *Hideaway Girl* (Par., 1937), *Waikiki Wedding* (Par., 1937), *Blossoms on Broadway* (Par., 1937), *Prison Farm* (Par., 1938), *Thanks for the Memory* (Par., 1938), *Paris Honeymoon* (Par., 1939), *Cafe Society* (Par., 1939), *Some Like It Hot* (Par., 1939), *Unexpected Father*

(Univ., 1939), *Sailors on Leave* (Rep., 1941), *Kisses for Breakfast* (WB, 1941), *A Song for Miss Julie* (Rep., 1945).

CHARLES RUGGLES (Charles Sherman Ruggles) Born February 8, 1892, Los Angeles, California. Married Adele Rowland (1914); divorced. Married Marion LaBarbe.

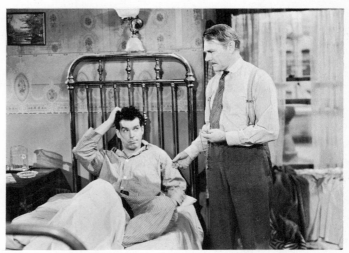

Fred MacMurray and Charles Ruggles in *Invitation to Happiness*.

Sound Feature Films: *Gentlemen of the Press* (Par., 1929), *The Lady Lies* (Par., 1929), *Battle of Paris* (Par., 1929), *Roadhouse Nights* (Par., 1930), *Young Man of Manhattan* (Par., 1930), *Queen High* (Par., 1930), *Her Wedding Night* (Par., 1930), *Charley's Aunt* (Col., 1930), *Honor Among Lovers* (Par., 1931), *The Smiling Lieutenant* (Par., 1931), *Girl Habit* (Par., 1931), *Beloved Bachelor* (Par., 1931), *Husband's Holiday* (Par., 1932), *This Reckless Age* (Par., 1932), *Make Me a Star* (Par., 1932), *Night of June 13* (Par., 1932), *One Hour With You* (Par., 1932), *This Is the Night* (Par., 1932), *70,000 Witnesses* (Par., 1932), *Trouble in Paradise* (Par., 1932), *Evenings for Sale* (Par., 1932), *If I Had a Million* (Par., 1932), *Madame Butterfly* (Par., 1932), *Love Me Tonight* (Par., 1932), *Murders in the Zoo* (Par., 1933), *Terror Aboard* (Par., 1933), *Mama Loves Papa* (Par., 1933), *Girl Without a Room* (Par., 1933), *Alice in Wonderland* (Par., 1933), *Goodbye Love* (RKO, 1933), *Melody Cruise* (RKO, 1933), *Melody in Spring* (Par., 1934), *Murder in the Private Car* (MGM, 1934), *Friends of Mr. Sweeney* (WB, 1934), *Six of a Kind* (Par., 1934), *Pursuit of Happiness* (Par., 1934), *Ruggles of Red Gap* (Par., 1935), *People Will Talk* (Par., 1935), *Big Broadcast of 1936* (Par., 1935), *No More Ladies* (MGM, 1935), *Anything Goes* (Par., 1936), *Early to Bed* (Par., 1936), *Wives Never Know* (Par., 1936), *Hearts Divided* (WB, 1936), *The Preview Murder Mystery* (Par., 1936), *Mind Your Own Business* (Par., 1936), *Turn Off the Moon* (Par., 1937), *Exclusive* (Par., 1937), *Bringing Up Baby* (RKO, 1938), *Breaking the Ice* (RKO, 1938), *Service DeLuxe* (Univ., 1938), *His Exciting Night* (Univ, 1938), *Yes, My Darling Daughter* (WB, 1939), *Boy Trouble* (Par., 1939), *Sudden Money* (Par., 1939), *Invitation to Happiness* (Par., 1939), *Night Work* (Par., 1939), *Balalaika* (MGM, 1939), *The Farmer's Daughter* (Par., 1940), *Opened by Mistake* (Par., 1940), *Maryland* (20th, 1940), *Public Deb No. 1* (20th, 1940), *No Time for Comedy* (WB, 1940), *The Invisible Woman* (Univ., 1941), *Go West, Young Lady* (Col., 1941), *Model Wife* (Univ., 1941), *The Perfect Snob* (20th, 1941), *The Parson of Panamint* (Par., 1941), *Friendly Enemies* (UA, 1942), *Dixie Dugan* (20th, 1943), *Our Hearts Were Young and Gay* (Par., 1944), *The Doughgirls* (WB, 1944), *Three Is a Family* (UA, 1944), *Incendiary Blonde* (Par., 1945), *Bedside Manner* (UA, 1945), *The Perfect Marriage* (Par., 1946), *Gallant Journey* (Col., 1946), *A Stolen Life* (WB, 1946), *My Brother Talks to Horses* (MGM, 1946), *It Happened on 5th Avenue* (AA, 1947), *Ramrod* (UA, 1947), *Give My Regards to Broadway* (20th, 1948), *Look for the Silver Lining* (WB, 1949), *The Lovable Cheat* (Film Classics, 1949), *All in a Night's Work* (Par., 1961), *The Pleasure of His Company* (Par., 1961), *The Parent Trap* (BV, 1961), *Son of Flubber* (BV, 1963), *Papa's Delicate Condition* (Par., 1963), *I'd Rather Be Rich* (Univ., 1964), *The Ugly Dacshund* (BV, 1965), *Follow Me, Boys* (BV, 1967).

Gale Sondergaard and Sig Rumann in *Seventh Heaven*.

Rhodes Reason, Barbara Rush and Rory Calhoun in *Flight to Hong Kong*.

SIG RUMANN (Siegfried Albon Ruman) Born c. 1890, Hamburg, Germany. Died February 14, 1967.

Feature Films: *The World Moves On* (Fox, 1934), *Servants' Entrance* (Fox, 1934), *Marie Galante* (Fox, 1934), *Under Pressure* (Fox, 1935), *The Wedding Night* (UA, 1935), *The Farmer Takes a Wife* (Fox, 1935), *A Night at the Opera* (MGM, 1935), *East of Java* (Univ., 1935), *The Princess Comes Across* (Par., 1936), *The Bold Caballero* (Rep., 1936), *On the Avenue* (20th, 1937), *Maytime* (MGM, 1937), *Midnight Taxi* (20th, 1937), *Think Fast, Mr. Moto* (20th, 1937), *This Is My Affair* (20th, 1937), *A Day at the Races* (MGM, 1937), *The Great Hospital Mystery* (20th, 1937), *Thin Ice* (20th, 1937), *Love Under Fire* (20th, 1937), *Lancer Spy* (20th, 1937), *Heidi* (20th, 1937), *Nothing Sacred* (UA, 1937), *Thank You, Mr. Moto* (20th, 1937), *Paradise for Three* (MGM, 1938), *The Saint in New York* (RKO, 1938), *I'll Give a Million* (20th, 1938), *Suez* (20th, 1938), *Girls on Probation* (WB, 1938), *The Great Waltz* (MGM, 1938), *Honolulu* (MGM, 1939), *Never Say Die* (Par., 1939), *Confessions of a Nazi Spy* (WB, 1939), *Only Angels Have Wings* (Col., 1939), *Ninotchka* (MGM, 1939), *Remember?* (MGM, 1939), *Dr. Ehrlich's Magic Bullet* (WB, 1940), *Outside the 3-Mile Limit* (Col., 1940), *I Was an Adventuress* (20th, 1940), *Four Sons* (20th, 1940), *Bitter Sweet* (MGM, 1940), *Comrade X* (MGM, 1940), *Victory* (Par., 1940), *So Ends Our Night* (UA, 1941), *That Uncertain Feeling* (UA, 1941), *The Man Who Lost Himself* (Univ., 1941), *The Wagons Roll at Night* (WB, 1941), *Love Crazy* (MGM, 1941), *Shining Victory* (WB, 1941), *World Premiere* (20th, 1941), *To Be or Not to Be* (UA, 1942), *Remember Pearl Harbor* (Rep., 1942), *Crossroads* (MGM, 1942), *Enemy Agents Meet Ellery Queen* (Col., 1942), *Desperate Journey* (WB, 1942), *Berlin Correspondent* (20th, 1942), *Tarzan Triumphs* (RKO, 1943), *They Came to Blow Up America* (20th, 1943), *Sweet Rosie O'Grady* (20th, 1943), *Government Girl* (RKO, 1943), *The Song of Bernadette* (20th, 1943), *It Happened Tomorrow* (UA, 1944), *The Hitler Gang* (Par., 1944), *Summer Storm* (UA, 1944), *House of Frankenstein* (Univ., 1944), *The Dolly Sisters* (20th, 1945), *A Royal Scandal* (20th, 1945), *The Men in Her Diary* (Univ., 1945), *She Went to the Races* (MGM, 1945), *A Night in Casablanca* (UA, 1946), *Faithful in My Fashion* (MGM, 1946), *Night and Day* (WB, 1946), *Mother Wore Tights* (20th, 1947), *If You Knew Susie* (RKO, 1948), *The Emperor Waltz* (Par., 1948), *Give My Regards to Broadway* (20th, 1948), *On The Riviera* (20th, 1951), *The World in His Arms* (Univ., 1952), *Ma and Pa Kettle on Vacation* (Univ., 1953), *Stalag 17* (Par., 1953), *Houdini* (Par., 1953), *The Glenn Miller Story* (Univ., 1954), *Living It Up* (Par., 1954), *Three Ring Circus* (Par., 1954), *Carolina Cannonball* (Rep., 1955), *Many Rivers to Cross* (MGM, 1955), *Spy Chasers* (AA, 1955), *The Wings of Eagles* (MGM, 1957), *The Errand Boy* (Par., 1961), *Robin and the 7 Hoods* (WB, 1964), *36 Hours* (MGM, 1964), *Last of the Secret Agents* (Par., 1966), *The Fortune Cookie* (UA, 1966).

BARBARA RUSH Born January 4, 1927, Denver, Colorado. Married Jeffrey Hunter (1950), child: Christopher; divorced 1955. Married Warren Cowan (1959), child: Claudia.

Feature Films: *The First Legion* (UA, 1951), *Molly* (Par., 1951), *Quebec* (Par., 1951), *Flaming Feather* (Par., 1951), *When Worlds Collide* (Par.,

1951), *It Came From Outer Space* (Univ., 1953), *Prince of Pirates* (Col., 1953), *Taza, Son of Cochise* (Univ., 1954), *Magnificent Obsession* (Univ., 1954), *The Black Shield of Falworth* (Univ., 1954), *Captain Lightfoot* (Univ., 1955), *Kiss of Fire* (Univ., 1955), *World in My Corner* (Univ., 1956), *Bigger Than Life* (20th, 1956), *Flight to Hong Kong* (UA, 1956), *Oh, Men! Oh, Women!* (20th, 1957), *No Down Payment* (20th, 1957), *The Young Lions* (20th, 1958), *Harry Black and the Tiger* (20th, 1958), *The Young Philadelphians* (WB, 1959), *The Bramble Bush* (WB, 1960), *Strangers When We Meet* (Col., 1960), *Come Blow Your Horn* (Par., 1963), *Robin and the 7 Hoods* (WB, 1964), *Hombre* (20th, 1967).

GAIL RUSSELL Born September 23, 1924, Chicago, Illinois. Married Guy Madison (1949); divorced 1954. Died August 26, 1961.

Gail Russell and Turhan Bey in *Song of India*.

Feature Films: *Henry Aldrich Gets Glamour* (Par., 1943), *Lady in the Dark* (Par., 1944), *The Uninvited* (Par., 1944), *Our Hearts Were Young and Gay* (Par., 1944), *Salty O'Rourke* (Par., 1945), *The Unseen* (Par., 1945), *Duffy's Tavern* (Par., 1945), *Our Hearts Were Growing Up* (Par., 1946), *The Bachelor's Daughters* (UA, 1946), *Calcutta* (Par., 1947), *Angel and the Badman* (Rep., 1947), *Variety Girl* (Par., 1947), *The Night Has a Thousand Eyes* (Par., 1948), *Moonrise* (Rep., 1948), *Wake of the Red Witch* (Rep., 1948), *El Paso* (Par., 1949), *Song of India* (Col., 1949), *The Great Dan Patch* (UA, 1949), *Captain China* (Par., 1949), *The Lawless* (Par., 1950), *Air Cadet* (Univ., 1951), *Seven Men From Now* (WB, 1956), *The Tattered Dress* (Univ., 1957), *No Place to Land* (Rep., 1958), *The Silent Call* (20th, 1961).

JANE RUSSELL (Ernestine Jane Geraldine Russell) Born June 21, 1921, Bemidji, Minnesota. Married Bob Waterfield (1943), children: Tracy, Thomas, Robert.

Feature Films: *The Outlaw* (RKO, 1943), *Young Widow* (UA, 1946), *The Paleface* (Par., 1948), *His Kind of Woman* (RKO, 1951), *Double*

Agnes Moorehead and Jane Russell in *The Revolt of Mamie Stover*.

Dynamite (RKO, 1951), *Las Vegas Story* (RKO, 1951), *Macao* (RKO, 1952), *Montana Belle* (RKO, 1952), *Son of Paleface* (Par., 1952), *Road to Bali* (Par., 1952)* *Gentlemen Prefer Blondes* (20th, 1953), *The French Line* (RKO, 1953), *Underwater* (RKO, 1955), *Foxfire* (Univ., 1955), *The Tall Men* (20th, 1955), *Gentlemen Marry Brunettes* (UA, 1955), *Hot Blood* (Col., 1956), *The Revolt of Mamie Stover* (20th, 1956), *The Fuzzy Pink Nightgown* (UA, 1957), *Fate Is the Hunter* (20th, 1964), *Johnny Reno* (Par., 1966), *Waco* (Par., 1966), *Born Losers* (AIP, 1967).

*Unbilled guest appearance

ROSALIND RUSSELL Born June 4, 1907, Waterbury, Connecticut. Married Fred Brisson (1941), child: Lance.

Ernest Truex, Roscoe Karns, Rosalind Russell and Frank Jenks in *His Girl Friday*.

Feature Films: *Evelyn Prentice* (MGM, 1934), *The President Vanishes* (Par., 1934), *West Point of the Air* (MGM, 1935), *Casino Murder Case* (MGM, 1935), *Reckless* (MGM, 1935), *China Seas* (MGM, 1935), *Rendezvous* (MGM, 1935), *Forsaking All Others* (MGM, 1935), *The Night Is Young* (MGM, 1935), *It Had to Happen* (20th, 1936), *Under Two Flags* (20th, 1936), *Trouble for Two* (MGM, 1936), *Craig's Wife* (Col., 1936), *Night Must Fall* (MGM, 1937), *Live, Love and Learn* (MGM, 1937), *Man-Proof* (MGM, 1938), *The Citadel* (MGM, 1938), *Four's a Crowd* (WB, 1938), *Fast and Loose* (MGM, 1939), *The Women* (MGM, 1939), *His Girl Friday* (Col., 1940), *No*

Time for Comedy (WB, 1940), *Hired Wife* (Univ., 1940), *This Thing Called Love* (Col., 1941), *They Met in Bombay* (MGM, 1941), *The Feminine Touch* (MGM, 1941), *Design For Scandal* (MGM, 1941), *Take a Letter, Darling* (Par., 1942), *My Sister Eileen* (Col., 1942), *Flight for Freedom* (RKO, 1943), *What a Woman* (Col., 1943), *Roughly Speaking* (WB, 1945), *She Wouldn't Say Yes* (Col., 1945), *Sister Kenny* (RKO, 1946), *The Guilt of Janet Ames* (Col., 1947), *Mourning Becomes Electra* (RKO, 1947), *The Velvet Touch* (RKO, 1948), *Tell It to the Judge* (Col., 1949), *A Woman of Distinction* (Col., 1950), *Never Wave at a WAC* (RKO, 1952), *The Girl Rush* (Par., 1955), *Picnic* (Col., 1955), *Auntie Mame* (WB, 1958), *A Majority of One* (WB, 1961), *Five Finger Exercise* (Col., 1962), *Gypsy* (WB, 1962), *The Trouble With Angels* (Col., 1966), *Oh Dad, Poor Dad, Mama's Hung You in the Closet and I'm Feeling So Sad* (Par., 1967), *Where Angels Go...Trouble Follows*, (Col., 1968), *Rosie!* (Univ., 1968).

ANN RUTHERFORD Born November 2, 1917, Toronto, Canada. Married David May (1942), child: Gloria; divorced 1953. Married William Dozier (1953).

Snowflake, Ann Rutherford, John Wayne and Rodney Hildebrand in *The Lonely Trail*.

Feature Films: *Waterfront Lady* (Mascot, 1935), *The Fighting Marines* (Mascot serial, 1935), *Melody Trail* (Rep., 1935), *The Singing Vagabond* (Rep., 1935), *The Lawless Nineties* (Rep., 1936), *Doughnuts and Society* (Mascot, 1936), *The Harvester* (Rep., 1936), *Comin' Round the Mountain* (Rep., 1936), *Down to the Sea* (Rep., 1936), *The Oregon Trail* (Rep., 1936), *The Lonely Trail* (Rep., 1936), *The Devil Is Driving* (Col., 1937), *The Bride Wore Red* (MGM, 1937), *Public Cowboy No. One* (Rep., 1937), *Espionage* (MGM, 1937), *Live, Love and Learn* (MGM, 1937), *Of Human Hearts* (MGM, 1938), *Judge Hardy's Children* (MGM, 1938), *You're Only Young Once* (MGM, 1938), *Love Finds Andy Hardy* (MGM, 1938), *A Christmas Carol* (MGM, 1938), *Dramatic School* (MGM, 1938), *Out West With the Hardys* (MGM, 1938), *Four Girls in White* (MGM, 1939), *The Hardys Ride High* (MGM, 1939), *Andy Hardy Gets Spring Fever* (MGM, 1939), *These Glamour Girls* (MGM, 1939), *Dancing Co-ed* (MGM, 1939), *Judge Hardy and Son* (MGM, 1939), *Gone With the Wind* (MGM, 1939), *Pride and Prejudice* (MGM, 1940), *Andy Hardy Meets Debutante* (MGM, 1940), *Wyoming* (MGM, 1940), *The Ghost Comes Home* (MGM, 1940), *Keeping Company* (MGM, 1941), *Andy Hardy's Private Secretary* (MGM, 1941), *Washington Melodrama* (MGM, 1941), *Whistling in the Dark* (MGM, 1941), *Life Begins for Andy Hardy* (MGM, 1941), *Badlands of Dakota* (Univ., 1941), *The Courtship of Andy Hardy* (MGM, 1942), *This Time for Keeps* (MGM, 1942), *Orchestra Wives* (20th, 1942), *Whistling in Dixie* (MGM, 1942), *Andy Hardy's Double Life* (MGM, 1942), *Whistling in Brooklyn* (MGM, 1943), *Happy Land* (20th, 1943), *Bermuda Mystery* (20th, 1944), *Two O'Clock Courage* (RKO, 1945), *Bedside Manner* (UA, 1945), *Murder in the Music Hall* (Rep., 1946), *The Madonna's Secret* (Rep., 1946), *Inside Job* (Univ., 1946), *The Secret Life of Walter Mitty* (RKO, 1947), *The Adventures of Don Juan* (WB, 1948), *Operation Haylift* (Lip., 1950).

Trudy Marshall, Tim Ryan and Peggy Ryan in *Shamrock Hill*.

PEGGY RYAN (Margaret Orene Ryan) Born August 28, 1924, Long Beach, California. Married James Cross (1947), child: James; divorced 1952. Married Ray McDonald, child: Kerry; divorced. Married Edward Sherman (1958).

Feature Films: *Top of the Town* (Univ., 1937), *The Women Men Marry* (MGM, 1937), *The Flying Irishman* (RKO, 1939), *She Married a Cop* (Rep., 1939), *The Grapes of Wrath* (20th, 1940), *Sailor's Lady* (20th, 1940), *Girls' Town* (PRC, 1942), *Miss Annie Rooney* (UA, 1942), *Private Buckaroo* (Univ., 1942), *Give Out, Sisters* (Univ., 1942), *Get Hep to Love* (Univ., 1942), *Mister Big* (Univ., 1943), *Top Man* (Univ., 1944), *When Johnny Comes Marching Home* (Univ., 1944), *Chip Off the Old Block* (Univ., 1944), *Follow the Boys* (Univ., 1944), *This Is the Life* (Univ., 1944), *The Merry Monahans* (Univ., 1944), *Babes on Swing Street* (Univ., 1944), *Bowery to Broadway* (Univ., 1944), *Patrick the Great* (Univ., 1945), *Here Come the Co-eds* (Univ., 1945), *That's the Spirit* (Univ., 1945), *On Stage Everybody* (Univ., 1945), *Men in Her Diary* (Univ., 1945), *Shamrock Hill* (EL, 1949), *There's a Girl in My Heart* (AA, 1949), *All Ashore* (Col., 1953).

ROBERT RYAN Born November 11, 1909, Chicago, Illinois. Married Jessica Cadwalader (1939), children: Timothy, Cheney, Lisa.

Feature Films: *Golden Gloves* (Par., 1940), *Queen of the Mob* (Par., 1940), *North West Mounted Police* (Par., 1940), *Bombardier* (RKO, 1943), *The Sky's the Limit* (RKO, 1943), *Behind the Rising Sun* (RKO, 1943), *Gangway for Tomorrow* (RKO, 1943), *The Iron Major* (RKO, 1943), *Tender Comrade* (RKO, 1943), *Marine Raiders* (RKO, 1944), *Trail Street* (RKO, 1947), *The Woman on the Beach* (RKO, 1947), *Crossfire* (RKO, 1947), *Berlin Express* (RKO, 1948), *Return of the Bad Men* (RKO, 1948), *Act of Violence* (MGM, 1948), *The Boy With Green Hair* (RKO, 1948), *Caught* (MGM, 1949), *The Set-Up* (RKO, 1949), *I Married a Communist* (RKO, 1949), *The Secret Fury* (RKO, 1950), *Born to Be Bad* (RKO, 1950), *Best of the Bad Men* (RKO, 1951), *Flying Leathernecks* (RKO, 1951), *The Racket* (RKO, 1951), *On Dangerous Ground* (RKO, 1951), *Clash by Night* (RKO, 1952), *Beware My Lovely* (RKO, 1952), *Horizons West* (Univ., 1952), *City Beneath the Sea* (Univ., 1953), *The Naked Spur* (MGM, 1953), *Inferno* (20th,

1953), *Alaska Seas* (Par., 1954), *About Mrs. Leslie* (Par., 1954), *Her 12 Men* (MGM, 1954), *Bad Day at Black Rock* (MGM, 1954), *Escape to Burma* (RKO, 1955), *House of Bamboo* (20th, 1955), *The Tall Men* (20th, 1955), *The Proud Ones* (20th, 1956), *Back From Eternity* (RKO, 1956), *Men in War* (UA, 1957), *God's Little Acre* (UA, 1958), *Lonelyhearts* (UA, 1958), *Day of the Outlaw* (UA, 1959), *Odds Against Tomorrow* (UA, 1959), *Ice Palace* (WB, 1960), *The Canadians* (20th, 1961), *King of Kings* (MGM, 1961), *Billy Budd* (AA, 1962), *The Longest Day* (20th, 1962), *The Inheritance* (narrator; Shochiku Films of America, 1964), *Battle of the Bulge* (WB, 1965), *Crooked Road* (7 Arts, 1965), *The Dirty Game* (AIP, 1965), *The Professionals* (Col., 1966), *The Busybody* (Par., 1967), *Custer of the West* (Cinerama, 1967), *Hour of the Guns* (UA, 1967), *The Prodigal Gun* (Cinerama, 1968), *Anzio* (Col., 1968).

SABU (Sabu Dastagir) Born March 15, 1924, Karapur, Mysore, India. Married Marilyn Cooper (1948), children: Paul, Jasmine. Died December 2, 1963.

Wendell Corey and Sabu in *Man-Eater of Kumaon*.

Feature Films: *Elephant Boy* (UA, 1937), *Drums* (UA, 1938), *The Thief of Bagdad* (UA, 1940), *The Jungle Book* (UA, 1942), *Arabian Nights* (Univ., 1942), *White Savage* (Univ., 1943), *Cobra Woman* (Univ., 1943), *Tangier* (Univ., 1946), *Black Narcissus* (Rank, 1947), *The End of the River* (Univ., 1948), *Man-Eater of Kumaon* (Univ., 1948), *Song of India* (Col., 1949), *Savage Drums* (Lip., 1951), *The Black Panther* (1955), *Jungle Hell* (Howco, 1956), *Jaguar* (Rep., 1956), *Sabu and the Magic Ring* (AA, 1957), *Rampage* (WB, 1963), *A Tiger Walks* (BV, 1964).

EVA MARIE SAINT Born September 4, 1924, Newark, New Jersey. Married Jeffrey Hayden (1951), children: Darrell, Laurette.

Feature Films: *On the Waterfront* (Col., 1954), *That Certain Feeling*

Angela Lansbury, Karl Malden, Eva Marie Saint and Brandon de Wilde in *All Fall Down*.

Robert Ryan and Ginger Rogers in *Tender Comrade*.

(Par., 1956), *A Hatful of Rain* (20th, 1957), *Raintree County* (MGM, 1957), *North by Northwest* (MGM, 1959), *Exodus* (UA, 1960), *All Fall Down* (MGM, 1962), *36 Hours* (MGM, 1964), *The Sandpiper* (MGM, 1965), *The Russians Are Coming, The Russians Are Coming* (UA, 1966), *Grand Prix* (MGM, 1966), *The Stalking Moon* (National General, 1968).

S. Z. "CUDDLES" SAKALL (Szoke Szakall) Born February 2, 1890, Budapest, Hungary. Died February 12, 1955.

Kathryn Grayson, S.Z. Sakall and Van Heflin in *Seven Sweethearts.*

English-Language Feature Films: *The Lilac Domino* (Select Attractions, Ltd., 1940), *It's a Date* (Univ., 1940), *Florian* (MGM, 1940), *My Love Came Back* (WB, 1940), *Spring Parade* (Univ., 1940), *The Man Who Lost Himself* (Univ., 1941), *That Night in Rio* (20th, 1941), *The Devil and Miss Jones* (RKO, 1941), *Ball of Fire* (RKO, 1941), *Broadway* (Univ., 1942), *Yankee Doodle Dandy* (WB, 1942), *Seven Sweethearts* (MGM, 1942), *Casablanca* (WB, 1942), *Thank Your Lucky Stars* (WB, 1943), *The Human Comedy* (MGM, 1943), *Wintertime* (20th, 1943), *Shine On, Harvest Moon* (WB, 1944), *Hollywood Canteen* (WB, 1944), *Wonder Man* (RKO, 1945), *Christmas in Connecticut* (WB, 1945), *The Dolly Sisters* (20th, 1945), *San Antonio* (WB, 1945), *Cinderella Jones* (WB, 1946), *Two Guys From Milwaukee* (WB, 1946), *Never Say Goodbye* (WB, 1946), *The Time, the Place and the Girl* (WB, 1946), *Cynthia* (MGM, 1947), *April Showers* (WB, 1948), *Romance on the High Seas* (WB, 1948), *Embraceable You* (WB, 1948), *Whiplash* (WB, 1948), *My Dream Is Yours* (WB, 1949), *In the Good Old Summertime* (MGM, 1949), *It's a Great Feeling* (WB, 1949), *Look for the Silver Lining* (WB, 1949), *Oh, You Beautiful Doll!* (20th, 1949), *Montana* (WB, 1950), *The Daughter of Rosie O'Grady* (WB, 1950), *Tea for Two* (WB, 1950), *The Lullaby of Broadway* (WB, 1951), *Sugarfoot* (WB, 1951), *Painting the Clouds With Sunshine* (WB, 1951), *It's a Big Country* (MGM, 1951), *Small Town Girl* (MGM, 1953), *The Student Prince* (MGM, 1954).

GEORGE SANDERS Born July 3, 1906, St. Petersburg, Russia. Married Susan Larsen (1940); divorced 1947. Married Zsa Zsa Gabor (1949); divorced 1957. Married Benita Hume (1958); widowed 1967.

Feature Films: *Strange Cargo* (British, 1936), *The Man Who Could Work Miracles* (UA, 1936), *Things to Come* (UA, 1936), *Lloyds of London* (20th, 1936), *Love Is News* (20th, 1937), *Slave Ship* (20th, 1937), *The Lady Escapes* (20th, 1937), *Lancer Spy* (20th, 1937), *International Settlement* (20th, 1938), *Four Men and a Prayer* (20th, 1938), *Mr. Moto's Last Warning* (20th, 1939), *The Saint Strikes Back* (RKO, 1939), *Confessions of a Nazi Spy* (WB, 1939), *The Saint in London* (RKO, 1939), *Allegheny Uprising* (RKO, 1939), *Nurse Edith Cavell* (RKO, 1939), *The Outsider* (Alliance, 1939), *Green Hell* (Univ., 1940), *Rebecca* (UA, 1940), *The Saint's Double Trouble* (RKO, 1940), *The House of Seven Gables* (Univ., 1940), *The Saint Takes Over* (RKO, 1940), *Foreign Correspondent* (UA, 1940), *Bitter Sweet* (MGM, 1940), *The Son of Monte Cristo* (UA, 1940), *Rage in Heaven* (MGM, 1941),

George Sanders and Norma Shearer in *Her Cardboard Lover.*

The Saint in Palm Springs (RKO, 1941), *Man Hunt* (20th, 1941), *The Gay Falcon* (RKO, 1941), *A Date With the Falcon* (RKO, 1941), *Sundown* (UA, 1941), *Son of Fury* (20th, 1942), *The Falcon Takes Over* (RKO, 1942), *Her Cardboard Lover* (MGM, 1942), *Tales of Manhattan* (20th, 1942), *The Moon and Sixpence* (UA, 1942), *The Falcon's Brother* (RKO, 1942), *The Black Swan* (20th, 1942), *Quiet Please—Murder* (20th, 1942), *This Land Is Mine* (RKO, 1943), *They Came to Blow Up America* (20th, 1943), *Appointment in Berlin* (Col., 1943), *Paris After Dark* (20th, 1943), *Action in Arabia* (RKO, 1944), *The Lodger* (20th, 1944), *Summer Storm* (UA, 1944), *The Picture of Dorian Gray* (MGM, 1945), *Hangover Square* (20th, 1945), *The Strange Affair of Uncle Harry* (Univ., 1945), *A Scandal in Paris* (UA, 1946), *The Strange Woman* (UA, 1946), *The Private Affairs of Bel Ami* (UA, 1947), *The Ghost and Mrs. Muir* (20th, 1947), *Lured* (UA, 1947), *Forever Amber* (20th, 1947), *The Fan* (20th, 1949), *Samson and Delilah* (Par., 1949), *All About Eve* (20th, 1950), *I Can Get It for You Wholesale* (20th, 1951), *The Light Touch* (MGM, 1951), *Ivanhoe* (MGM, 1952), *Captain Blackjack* (Classic, 1952), *Assignment Paris* (Col., 1952), *Call Me Madam* (20th, 1953), *Witness to Murder* (UA, 1954), *King Richard and the Crusaders* (WB, 1954), *Moonfleet* (MGM, 1955), *The Scarlet Coat* (MGM, 1955), *The King's Thief* (MGM, 1955), *Night Freight* (AA, 1955), *Never Say Goodbye* (Univ., 1956), *While the City Sleeps* (RKO, 1956), *That Certain Feeling* (Par., 1956), *Death of a Scoundrel* (RKO, 1956), *The Seventh Sin* (MGM, 1957), *The Whole Truth* (Col., 1958), *From the Earth to the Moon* (WB, 1958), *That Kind of Woman* (Par., 1959), *Solomon and Sheba* (UA, 1959), *A Touch of Larceny* (Par., 1960), *The Last Voyage* (MGM, 1960), *Bluebeard's Ten Honeymoons* (AA, 1960), *The Village of the Damned* (MGM, 1960), *Call Me Genius* (Continental Distributing, 1961), *Five Golden Hours* (Col., 1961), *Trouble in the Sky* (Univ., 1961), *Operation Snatch* (Continental Distributing, 1962), *In Search of the Castaways* (BV, 1962), *The Cracksman* (Associated British Pathé, 1963), *Cairo* (MGM, 1963), *Dark Purpose* (Univ., 1964), *A Shot in the Dark* (UA, 1964), *The Amorous Adventures of Moll Flanders* (Par., 1965), *Ecco* (narrator; Cresa Roma, 1965), *Trunk to Cairo* (AIP, 1966), *The Quiller Memorandum* (20th, 1966), *Warning Shot* (Par., 1967), *Good Times* (Par., 1967), *The Jungle Book* (voice only; BV, 1967), *King of Africa* (NTA, 1968).

LIZABETH SCOTT (Emma Matzo) Born September 29, 1922, Scranton, Pennsylvania.

Feature Films: *You Came Along* (Par., 1945), *The Strange Love of*

Lizabeth Scott, Wendell Corey and John Hodiak in *Desert Fury*.

Margaret Perry, Randolph Scott, Alice Brady and Elizabeth Patterson in *Go West, Young Man*.

Martha Ivers (Par., 1946), *Dead Reckoning* (Col., 1947), *Desert Fury* (Par., 1947), *I Walk Alone* (Par., 1947), *Variety Girl* (Par., 1947), *Pitfall* (UA, 1948), *Too Late for Tears* (UA, 1949), *Easy Living* (RKO, 1949), *Paid in Full* (Par., 1950), *Dark City* (Par., 1950), *The Racket* (RKO, 1951), *The Company She Keeps* (RKO, 1951), *Two of a Kind* (Col., 1951), *Red Mountain* (Par., 1951), *Stolen Face* (Lip., 1952), *Scared Stiff* (Par., 1953), *Bad for Each Other* (Col., 1954), *Silver Lode* (RKO, 1954), *Loving You* (Par., 1957), *The Weapon* (Rep., 1957).

MARTHA SCOTT (Martha Ellen Scott) Born September 22, 1914, Jamesport, Missouri. Married Carleton Alsop (1940), child: Carleton, divorced 1946. Married Mel Powell (1946), children: Mary, Scott.

Cary Grant, Martha Scott and Sir Cedric Hardwicke in *The Howards of Virginia*.

Feature Films: *Our Town* (UA, 1940), *The Howards of Virginia* (Col., 1940), *Cheers for Miss Bishop* (UA, 1941), *They Dare Not Love* (Col., 1941), *One Foot in Heaven* (WB, 1941), *Hi Diddle Diddle* (UA, 1943), *Stage Door Canteen* (UA, 1943), *In Old Oklahoma* (Rep., 1943), *So Well Remembered* (RKO, 1947), *Strange Bargain* (RKO, 1949), *When I Grow Up* (EL, 1951), *The Desperate Hours* (Par., 1955), *The Ten Commandments* (Par., 1956), *Sayonara* (WB, 1957), *Eighteen and Anxious* (Rep., 1957), *Ben-Hur* (MGM, 1959).

RANDOLPH SCOTT (Randolph Crane) Born January 23, 1903, Orange County, Virginia. Married Marion Somerville; divorced. Married Pat Stillman (1944).

Sound Feature Films: *The Women Men Marry* (Headline Pictures, 1931), *Sky Bride* (Par., 1932), *Hot Saturday* (Par., 1932), *Wild Horse Mesa* (Par., 1933), *Hello, Everybody!* (Par., 1933), *Murders in the Zoo*

(Par., 1933), *Heritage of the Desert* (Par., 1933), *Supernatural* (Par., 1933), *Sunset Pass* (Par., 1933), *Cocktail Hour* (Col., 1933), *Man of the Forest* (Par., 1933), *To the Last Man* (Par., 1933), *Broken Dreams* (Mon., 1933), *The Thundering Herd* (Par., 1933), *Last Round-Up* (Par., 1934), *The Lone Cowboy* (Par., 1934), *Wagon Wheels* (Par., 1934), *Rocky Mountain Mystery* (Par., 1935), *Roberta* (Par., 1935), *Home on the Range* (Par., 1935), *Village Tale* (RKO, 1935), *She* (RKO, 1935), *So Red the Rose* (Par., 1935), *Follow the Fleet* (RKO, 1936), *And Sudden Death* (Par., 1936), *The Last of the Mohicans* (UA, 1936), *Go West Young Man* (Par., 1936), *High, Wide and Handsome* (Par., 1937), *Rebecca of Sunnybrook Farm* (20th, 1938), *Road to Reno* (Univ., 1938), *The Texans* (Par., 1938), *Jesse James* (20th, 1939), *Susannah of the Mounties* (20th, 1939), *Coast Guard* (Col., 1939), *Frontier Marshal* (20th, 1939), *20,000 Men a Year* (20th, 1939), *Virginia City* (WB, 1940), *My Favorite Wife* (RKO, 1940), *When the Daltons Rode* (Univ., 1940), *Western Union* (20th, 1941), *Belle Starr* (20th, 1941), *Paris Calling* (Univ., 1941), *To the Shores of Tripoli* (20th, 1942), *The Spoilers* (Univ., 1942), *Pittsburgh* (Univ., 1942), *The Desperadoes* (Col., 1943), *Bombardier* (RKO, 1943), *Corvette K-225* (Univ., 1943), *Gung Ho!* (Univ., 1943), *Belle of the Yukon* (RKO, 1944), *Follow the Boys* (Univ., 1944), *China Sky* (RKO, 1945), *Captain Kidd* (UA, 1945), *Abilene Town* (UA, 1946), *Badman's Territory* (RKO, 1946), *Home Sweet Homicide* (20th, 1946), *Trail Street* (RKO, 1947), *Gunfighters* (Col., 1947), *Christmas Eve* (UA, 1947), *Albuquerque* (Par., 1948), *Return of the Bad Men* (RKO, 1948), *Coroner Creek* (Col., 1948), *Canadian Pacific* (20th, 1949), *The Walking Hills* (Col., 1949), *The Doolins of Oklahoma* (Col., 1949), *Fighting Man of the Plains* (20th, 1949), *The Nevadan* (Col., 1950), *Colt .45* (WB, 1950), *The Cariboo Trail* (20th, 1950), *Sugarfoot* (WB, 1951), *Starlift* (WB, 1951), *Santa Fe* (Col., 1951), *Fort Worth* (WB, 1951), *Man in the Saddle* (Col., 1951), *Carson City* (WB, 1952), *Hangman's Knot* (Col., 1952), *The Man Behind the Gun* (WB, 1952), *The Stranger Wore a Gun* (Col., 1953), *Thunder Over the Plains* (WB, 1953), *Riding Shotgun* (WB, 1954), *The Bounty Hunter* (WB, 1954), *Rage at Dawn* (RKO, 1955), *Ten Wanted Men* (Col., 1955), *Tall Man Riding* (WB, 1955), *A Lawless Street* (Col., 1955), *Seven Men From Now* (WB, 1956), *Seventh Cavalry* (Col., 1956), *The Tall T* (Col., 1957), *Shoot-Out at Medicine Bend* (WB, 1957), *Decision At Sundown* (Col., 1957), *Buchanan Rides Alone* (Col., 1958), *Ride Lonesome* (Col., 1959), *Westbound* (WB, 1959), *Comanche Station* (Col., 1960), *Ride the High Country* (MGM, 1962).

ZACHARY SCOTT (Zachary Thomson Scott) Born February 24, 1914, Austin, Texas. Married Elaine Anderson (1935), child: Waverly; divorced 1950. Married Ruth Ford (1952), child: Shelley. Died October 3, 1965.

Feature Films: *Mask of Dimitrios* (WB, 1944), *Hollywood Canteen* (WB, 1944), *The Southerner* (UA, 1945), *Mildred Pierce* (WB, 1945), *Danger Signal* (WB, 1945), *Her Kind of Man* (WB, 1946), *Stallion Road* (WB, 1947), *The Unfaithful* (WB, 1947), *Cass Timberlane* (MGM, 1947), *Ruthless* (EL, 1948), *Whiplash* (WB, 1948), *Flaxy Martin* (WB, 1949), *Colt .45* (WB, 1949), *South of St. Louis* (WB, 1949), *One Last Fling* (WB, 1949), *Guilty Bystander* (Film Classics, 1950),

218

Alexis Smith and Zachary Scott in *One Last Fling*.

Shadow on the Wall (MGM, 1950), *Pretty Baby* (WB, 1950), *Born to Be Bad* (RKO, 1950), *Lightning Strikes Twice* (WB, 1951), *The Secret of Convict Lake* (20th, 1951), *Let's Make It Legal* (20th, 1951), *Wings of Danger* (Lip., 1952), *Stronghold* (Lip., 1952), *Appointment in Honduras* (RKO, 1953), *Treasure of Ruby Hills* (AA, 1955), *Shotgun* (AA, 1955), *Flame of the Islands* (Rep., 1955), *Bandido* (UA, 1956), *The Counterfeit Plan* (WB, 1957), *Man in the Shadow* ("Violent Stranger" —Anglo Amalgamated, 1957), *Flight into Danger* (Anglo Amalgamated, 1957), *Natchez Trace* (Panorama, 1960), *The Young One* (Vitalite, 1961), *It's Only Money* (Par., 1962).

ANNE SEYMOUR (Anne Seymour Eckert) Born September 11, 1909, New York, New York.

Anne Seymour and Arthur O'Connell in *Misty*.

Feature Films: *All the King's Men* (Col., 1949), *The Whistle at Eaton Falls* (Col., 1951), *Four Boys and a Gun* (UA, 1957), *Man on Fire* (MGM, 1957), *The Gift of Love* (20th, 1958), *Desire Under the Elms* (Par., 1958), *Handle With Care* (MGM, 1958), *Home from the Hill* (MGM, 1960), *Pollyanna* (BV, 1960), *The Subterraneans* (MGM, 1960), *All the Fine Young Cannibals* (MGM, 1960), *Misty* (20th, 1961), *Stage to Thunder Rock* (Par., 1964), *Good Neighbor Sam* (Col., 1964), *Where Love Has Gone* (Par., 1964), *Mirage* (Univ., 1965), *Blindfold* (Univ., 1966), *Waco* (Par., 1966), *How to Succeed in Business Without Really Trying* (UA, 1967), *Fitzwilly* (UA, 1967), *Stay Away, Joe* (MGM, 1968).

WINIFRED "WINI" SHAW (Winifred Lei Momi) Born February 25, 1910, San Francisco, California. Married Leo Cummins (1925), children: Elizabeth, James, John; widowed 1929. Married William O'Malley (1955).

Wini Shaw, Patricia Ellis and James Melton in *Melody for Two*.

Feature Films:
as **Wini Shaw** *Wild Gold* (Fox, 1934), *Three on a Honeymoon* (Fox, 1934), *The Gift of Gab* (Univ., 1934), *Million Dollar Ransom* (Univ., 1934), *Wake Up and Dream* (Univ., 1934).
as **Winifred Shaw** *Sweet Adeline* (WB, 1934), *Front Page Woman* (WB, 1935), *The Case of the Curious Bride* (WB, 1935), *Gold Diggers of 1935* (WB, 1935), *In Caliente* (WB, 1935), *Broadway Hostess* (WB, 1935), *The Singing Kid* (WB, 1936), *Sons o' Guns* (WB, 1936), *The Case of the Velvet Claws* (WB, 1936), *Satan Met a Lady* (WB, 1936), *Smart Blonde* (WB, 1936), *Fugitive in the Sky* (WB, 1937), *Ready, Willing and Able* (WB, 1937), *Melody for Two* (WB, 1937).

NORMA SHEARER (Edith Norma Shearer) Born August 10, 1900, Montreal, Canada. Married Irving Thalberg (1927), children: Irving, Katherine; widowed 1936. Married Martin Arrouge (1942).

Conrad Veidt and Norma Shearer in *Escape*.

Sound Feature Films: *The Trial of Mary Dugan* (MGM, 1929), *The Last of Mrs. Cheyney* (MGM, 1929), *The Hollywood Revue* (MGM, 1929), *Their Own Desire* (MGM, 1930), *The Divorcee* (MGM, 1930), *Let Us Be Gay* (MGM, 1930), *Strangers May Kiss* (MGM, 1931), *A Free Soul* (MGM, 1931), *Private Lives* (MGM, 1931), *Strange Interlude* (MGM, 1932), *Smilin' Through* (MGM, 1932), *Riptide* (MGM, 1934), *The Barretts of Wimpole Street* (MGM, 1934), *Romeo and Juliet* (MGM, 1936), *Marie Antoinette* (MGM, 1938), *Idiot's Delight* (MGM, 1939), *The Women* (MGM, 1939), *Escape* (MGM, 1940), *We Were Dancing* (MGM, 1942), *Her Cardboard Lover* (MGM, 1942).

James Cagney, Joyce Compton, Frank McHugh, Anthony Quinn, Ann Sheridan and George Tobias in *City for Conquest.*

ANN SHERIDAN (Clara Lou Sheridan) Born February 21, 1915, Denton, Texas. Married Edward Norris (1936); divorced 1939. Married George Brent (1932); divorced 1943. Married Scott McKay (1966). Died January 21, 1967.

Feature Films:

as Clara Lou Sheridan *Search for Beauty* (Par., 1934), *Bolero* (Par., 1934), *Come On, Marines!* (Par., 1934), *Murder at the Vanities* (Par., 1934), *Kiss and Make Up* (Par., 1934), *Shoot the Works* (Par., 1934), *Notorious Sophie Lang* (Par., 1934), *Ladies Should Listen* (Par., 1934), *Wagon Wheels* (Par., 1934), *Mrs. Wiggs of the Cabbage Patch* (Par., 1934), *College Rhythm* (Par., 1934), *You Belong to Me* (Par., 1934), *Limehouse Blues* (Par., 1934), *Enter Madame* (Par., 1935), *Home on the Range* (Par., 1935), *Rumba* (Par., 1935).

as Ann Sheridan *Behold My Wife* (Par., 1935), *Car 99* (Par., 1935), *Rocky Mountain Mystery* (Par., 1935), *Mississippi* (Par., 1935), *The Glass Key* (Par., 1935), *The Crusades* (Par., 1935), *Red Blood of Courage* (Ambassador, 1935), *Fighting Youth* (Univ., 1935), *Sing Me a Love Song* (WB, 1936), *Black Legion* (WB, 1936), *The Great O'Malley* (WB, 1937), *San Quentin* (WB, 1937), *Wine, Women and Horses* (WB, 1937), *The Footloose Heiress* (WB, 1937), *Alcatraz Island* (WB, 1938), *She Loved a Fireman* (WB, 1938), *The Patient in Room 18* (WB, 1938), *Mystery House* (WB, 1938), *Cowboy From Brooklyn* (WB, 1938), *Little Miss Thoroughbred* (WB, 1938), *Letter of Introduction* (Univ., 1938), *Broadway Musketeers* (WB, 1938), *Angels With Dirty Faces* (WB, 1938), *They Made Me a Criminal* (WB, 1939), *Dodge City* (WB, 1939), *Naughty but Nice* (WB, 1939), *Winter Carnival* (UA, 1939), *Indianapolis Speedway* (WB, 1939), *Angels Wash Their Faces* (WB, 1939), *Castle on the Hudson* (WB, 1940), *It All Came True* (WB, 1940), *Torrid Zone* (WB, 1940), *They Drive by Night* (WB, 1940), *City for Conquest* (WB, 1940), *Honeymoon for Three* (WB, 1941), *Navy Blues* (WB, 1941), *Kings Row* (WB, 1941), *The Man Who Came to Dinner* (WB, 1941), *Juke Girl* (WB, 1942), *Wings for the Eagle* (WB, 1942), *George Washington Slept Here* (WB, 1942), *Edge of Darkness* (WB, 1943), *Thank Your Lucky Stars* (WB, 1943), *Shine On, Harvest Moon* (WB, 1944), *The Doughgirls* (WB, 1944), *One More Tomorrow* (WB, 1946), *Nora Prentiss* (WB, 1947), *The Unfaithful* (WB, 1947), *Treasure of the Sierra Madre* (WB, 1948),* *Silver River* (WB, 1948), *Good Sam* (RKO, 1948), *I Was a Male War Bride* (20th, 1949), *Stella* (20th, 1950), *Woman on the Run* (Univ., 1950), *Steel Town* (Univ., 1952), *Just Across the Street* (Univ., 1952), *Take Me to Town* (Univ., 1953), *Appointment in Honduras* (RKO, 1953), *Come Next Spring* (Rep., 1956), *The Opposite Sex* (MGM, 1956), *Woman and the Hunter* (Gross-Krasne-Phoenix, 1957).

*Unbilled guest appearance

ANNE SHIRLEY (Dawn Evelyeen Paris) Born April 17, 1918, New York, New York. Married John Payne (1937), child: Julie; divorced 1943. Married Adrian Scott (1945); divorced 1949. Married Charles Lederer (1949).

Barbara Stanwyck and Anne Shirley in *Stella Dallas.*

Feature Films:

as Dawn O'Day *Mother Knows Best* (Fox, 1928), *Four Devils* (Fox, 1929), *City Girl* (Fox, 1930), *Rich Man's Folly* (Par., 1931), *Young America* (Fox, 1932), *So Big* (WB, 1932), *The Purchase Price* (WB, 1932), *Three on a Match* (WB, 1932), *Rasputin and the Empress* (MGM, 1932), *Life of Jimmy Dolan* (WB, 1933), *Finishing School* (RKO, 1934), *This Side of Heaven* (MGM, 1934), *The Key* (WB, 1934), *School for Girls* (Liberty, 1934).

as Anne Shirley *Anne of Green Gables* (RKO, 1934), *Steamboat 'Round the Bend* (Fox, 1935), *Chasing Yesterday* (RKO, 1935), *Chatterbox* (RKO, 1936), *M'Liss* (RKO, 1936), *Make Way for a Lady* (RKO, 1936), *Too Many Wives* (RKO, 1937), *Meet the Missus* (RKO, 1937), *Stella Dallas* (UA, 1937), *Condemned Women* (RKO, 1938), *Law of the Underworld* (RKO, 1938), *Mother Carey's Chickens* (RKO, 1938), *A Man to Remember* (RKO, 1938), *Girls' School* (Col., 1938), *Boy Slaves* (RKO, 1939), *Sorority House* (RKO, 1939), *Career* (RKO, 1939), *Vigil in the Night* (RKO, 1940), *Saturday's Children* (WB, 1940), *Anne of Windy Poplars* (RKO, 1940), *West Point Widow* (Par., 1941), *Unexpected Uncle* (RKO, 1941), *Four Jacks and a Jill* (RKO, 1941), *All That Money Can Buy* (RKO, 1941), *The Mayor of 44th Street* (RKO, 1942), *The Powers Girl* (UA, 1942), *Lady Bodyguard* (Par., 1943), *Bombardier* (RKO, 1943), *Government Girl* (RKO, 1943), *Man From Frisco* (Rep., 1944), *Music in Manhattan* (RKO, 1944), *Murder, My Sweet* (RKO, 1944).

SYLVIA SIDNEY (Sophia Kosow) Born August 8, 1910, New York, New York. Married Bennett Cerf (1935); divorced 1936. Married Luther Adler (1938); child: Jody; divorced 1947. Married Carlton Alsop (1947); divorced 1950.

Feature Films: *Through Different Eyes* (Fox, 1929), *City Streets* (Par., 1931), *Confessions of a Co-ed* (Par., 1931), *An American Tragedy* (Par., 1931), *Street Scene* (UA, 1931), *Ladies of the Big House* (Par., 1932), *The Miracle Man* (Par., 1932), *Merrily We Go to Hell* (Par., 1932), *Make Me a Star* (Par., 1932),* *Madame Butterfly* (Par., 1932), *Pick-Up* (Par., 1933), *Jennie Gerhardt* (Par., 1933), *Good Dame* (Par., 1934), *Thirty Day Princess* (Par., 1934), *Behold My Wife* (Par., 1934), *Accent on Youth* (Par., 1935), *Mary Burns, Fugitive* (Par., 1935), *Trail of the Lonesome Pine* (Par., 1936), *Fury* (MGM, 1936), *A Woman Alone* (1936), *You Only Live Once* (UA, 1937), *Dead End* (UA, 1937), *You and Me* (Par., 1938), *. . . One Third of a Nation* (Par., 1939), *The Wagons Roll at Night* (WB, 1941), *Blood on the Sun* (UA, 1945), *The Searching Wind* (Par., 1946), *Mr. Ace* (UA, 1946), *Love From a*

Fred MacMurray, Sylvia Sidney and Henry Fonda in *The Trail of the Lonesome Pine.*

Stranger (EL, 1947), *Les Miserables* (20th, 1952), *Violent Saturday* (20th, 1955), *Behind the High Wall* (Univ., 1956).

*Unbilled guest appearance

JEAN SIMMONS (Jean Marilyn Simmons) Born January 31, 1929, London, England. Married Stewart Granger (1950), child: Tracy; divorced 1960. Married Richard Brooks (1960), child: Kate.

J. Carroll Naish and Jean Simmons in *This Could Be the Night.*

Feature Films: *Give Us the Moon* (Gainsborough, 1943), *Johnny in the Clouds* ("The Way to the Stars"—Anatol De Grunwold Productions, 1945), *Sports Day* (Two Cities, 1944), *Mr. Emmanuel* (Two Cities, 1945), *Meet Sexton Blake* (British National, 1945), *Kiss the Bride Goodbye* (Butchers PSI, 1945), *Caesar and Cleopatra* (Rank, 1946), *Great Expectations* (Rank, 1946), *Hungry Hill* (Two Cities, 1947), *Black Narcissus* (Rank, 1946), *The Inheritance* ("Uncle Silas"—Rank-Fine Arts, 1947), *The Woman in the Hall* (Wessex, 1947), *Hamlet* (Rank, 1948), *The Blue Lagoon* (Rank, 1949), *Adam and Evelyn* (Rank, 1949), *So Long at the Fair* (Rank, 1950), *Trio* (Par., 1950), *The Clouded Yellow* (Rank, 1950), *Cage of Gold* (Ealing, 1951), *Androcles and the Lion* (RKO, 1952), *Angel Face* (RKO, 1952), *Young Bess* (MGM, 1953), *Affair With a Stranger* (RKO, 1953), *The Robe* (20th, 1953), *The Actress* (MGM, 1953), *She Couldn't Say No* (RKO, 1954), *The Egyptian* (20th, 1954), *A Bullet Is Waiting* (Col., 1954), *Desirée* (20th, 1954), *Footsteps in the Fog* (Col., 1955), *Guys and Dolls* (MGM, 1955), *Hilda Crane* (20th, 1956), *This Could Be the Night* (MGM, 1957), *Until They Sail* (MGM, 1957), *The Big Country* (UA, 1958), *Home Before Dark* (WB, 1958), *This Earth Is Mine* (Univ., 1959), *Elmer Gantry* (UA,

1960), *Spartacus* (Univ., 1960), *The Grass Is Greener* (Univ., 1961), *All the Way Home* (Par., 1963), *Life at the Top* (Col., 1965), *Mr. Buddwing* (MGM, 1966), *Rough Night in Jericho* (Univ., 1967), *Divorce American Style* (Col., 1967).

FRANK SINATRA Born December 12, 1915, Hoboken, New Jersey. Married Nancy Barbato (1939), children: Nancy, Frank, Christina; divorced 1951. Married Ava Gardner (1951); divorced 1957. Married Mia Farrow (1966); divorced 1968.

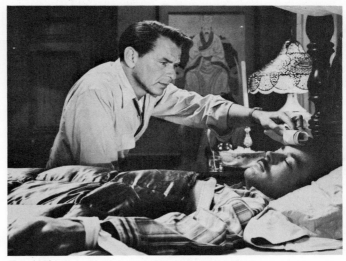

Frank Sinatra and Richard Johnson in *Never So Few.*

Feature Films: *Las Vegas Nights* (Par., 1941), *Ship Ahoy* (MGM, 1942), *Higher and Higher* (RKO, 1943), *Step Lively* (RKO, 1944), *Anchors Aweigh* (MGM, 1945), *Till the Clouds Roll By* (MGM, 1946), *It Happened in Brooklyn* (MGM, 1947), *Miracle of the Bells* (RKO, 1948), *The Kissing Bandit* (MGM, 1948), *Take Me Out to the Ball Game* (MGM, 1949), *On the Town* (MGM, 1949), *Double Dynamite* (RKO, 1951), *Meet Danny Wilson* (Univ., 1952), *From Here to Eternity* (Col., 1953), *Suddenly* (UA, 1954), *Young at Heart* (WB, 1954), *Not as a Stranger* (UA, 1955), *The Tender Trap* (MGM, 1955), *Guys and Dolls* (MGM, 1955), *The Man With the Golden Arm* (UA, 1955), *Meet Me in Las Vegas* (MGM, 1956),* *Johnny Concho* (UA, 1956), *Around the World in 80 Days* (UA, 1956), *High Society* (MGM, 1956), *The Pride and the Passion* (UA, 1957), *The Joker Is Wild* (Par., 1957), *Pal Joey* (Col., 1957), *Kings Go Forth* (UA, 1958), *Some Came Running* (MGM, 1958), *A Hole in the Head* (UA, 1959), *Never So Few* (MGM, 1959), *Can-Can* (20th, 1960), *Ocean's 11* (WB, 1960), *Pepe* (Col., 1960), *The Devil at 4 O'Clock* (Col., 1961), *Sergeants 3* (UA, 1962), *Road to Hong Kong* (UA, 1962),* *The Manchurian Candidate* (UA, 1962), *Come Blow Your Horn* (Par., 1963), *The List of Adrian Messenger* (Univ., 1963), *4 For Texas* (WB, 1963), *Robin and the 7 Hoods* (WB, 1964), *None But the Brave* (WB, 1965), *Von Ryan's Express* (20th, 1965), *Marriage on the Rocks* (WB, 1965), *The Oscar* (Par., 1966),* *Assault on a Queen* (Par., 1966), *Cast a Giant Shadow* (UA, 1966), *The Naked Runner* (WB, 1967), *Tony Rome* (20th, 1967), *The Detective* (20th, 1968).

*Unbilled guest appearance

PENNY SINGLETON (Mary Ann Dorothy McNulty) Born September 15, 1909, Philadelphia, Pennsylania. Married Lawrence Singleton (1937), child: Dorothy; divorced 1939. Married Robert Sparks (1941), child: Robin; widowed 1963.

Feature Films:
    as Dorothy McNulty *Good News* (MGM, 1930), *Love in the Rough* (MGM, 1930), *After the Thin Man* (MGM, 1936), *Vogues of 1938* (UA, 1937), *Sea Racketeers* (Rep., 1937).
    as Penny Singleton *Outside of Paradise* (Rep., 1938), *Swing Your Lady* (WB, 1938), *Men Are Such Fools* (WB, 1938), *Boy Meets Girl* (WB, 1938), *Mr. Chump* (WB, 1938), *The Mad Miss Manton* (RKO, 1938), *Garden of the Moon* (WB, 1938), *Secrets of an Actress* (WB,

Penny Singleton and Dick Wessel in *Blondie Hits the Jackpot.*

1938), *Hard to Get* (WB, 1938), *Blondie* (Col., 1938), *Racket Busters* (WB, 1938), *Blondie Meets the Boss* (Col., 1939), *Blondie Takes a Vacation* (Col., 1939), *Blondie Brings Up Baby* (Col., 1939), *Blondie on a Budget* (Col., 1940), *Blondie Has Servant Trouble* (Col., 1940), *Blondie Plays Cupid* (Col., 1940), *Blondie Goes Latin* (Col., 1941), *Blondie in Society* (Col., 1941), *Go West, Young Lady* (Col., 1941), *Blondie Goes to College* (Col., 1942), *Blondie's Blessed Event* (Col., 1942), *Blondie for Victory* (Col., 1942), *It's a Great Life* (Col., 1943), *Footlight Glamour* (Col., 1943), *Leave It to Blondie* (Col., 1945), *Life With Blondie* (Col., 1946), *Young Widow* (UA, 1946), *Blondie's Lucky Day* (Col., 1946), *Blondie Knows Best* (Col., 1946), *Blondie's Holiday* (Col., 1947), *Blondie's Big Moment* (Col., 1947), *Blondie in the Dough* (Col., 1947), *Blondie's Anniversary* (Col., 1947), *Blondie's Reward* (Col., 1948), *Blondie's Secret* (Col., 1948), *Blondie Hits the Jackpot* (Col., 1949), *Blondie's Big Deal* (Col., 1949), *Blondie's Hero* (Col., 1950), *Beware of Blondie* (Col., 1950), *The Best Man* (UA, 1964).

RED SKELTON (Richard Bernard Skelton) Born July 18, 1913, Vincennes, Indiana. Married Edna Stilwell (1938); divorced 1943. Married Georgia Morris (1945), children: Valentina, Richard.

Ann Codee (left) and Red Skelton in *Bathing Beauty.*

Feature Films: *Having a Wonderful Time* (RKO, 1938), *Flight Command* (MGM, 1940), *The People vs. Dr. Kildare* (MGM, 1941), *Lady Be Good* (MGM, 1941), *Whistling in the Dark* (MGM, 1941), *Dr. Kildare's Wedding Day* (MGM, 1941), *Ship Ahoy* (MGM, 1942), *Maisie Gets Her Man* (MGM, 1942), *Panama Hattie* (MGM, 1942), *Whistling in Dixie* (MGM, 1942), *Du Barry Was a Lady* (MGM, 1943), *I Dood It* (MGM, 1943), *Whistling in Brooklyn* (MGM, 1943), *Thousands Cheer* (MGM, 1943), *Bathing Beauty* (MGM, 1944), *Ziegfeld Follies of 1946* (MGM, 1946), *The Show-Off* (MGM, 1946), *Merton of the Movies* (MGM, 1947), *The Fuller Brush Man* (Col., 1948), *A*

Southern Yankee (MGM, 1948), *Neptune's Daughter* (MGM, 1949), *The Yellow Cab Man* (MGM, 1950), *Three Little Words* (MGM, 1950), *Watch the Birdie* (MGM, 1950), *Excuse My Dust* (MGM, 1951), *Texas Carnival* (MGM, 1951), *Lovely to Look At* (MGM, 1952), *The Clown* (MGM, 1953), *Half a Hero* (MGM, 1953), *The Great Diamond Robbery* (MGM, 1953), *Susan Slept Here* (RKO, 1954),* *Around the World in 80 Days* (UA, 1956), *Public Pigeon No. 1* (Univ., 1957), *Ocean's 11* (WB, 1960),* *Those Magnificent Men in Their Flying Machines* (20th, 1965).

*Unbilled guest appearance

ALISON SKIPWORTH (Alison Groom) Born July 25, 1883, London, England. Married Frank Markham Skipworth. Died July 5, 1952.

Dorothy Dell, Alison Skipworth and Victor McLaglen in *Wharf Angel.*

Sound Feature Films: *Strictly Unconventional* (MGM, 1930), *Raffles* (UA, 1930), *Oh, for a Man!* (Fox, 1930), *Outward Bound* (WB, 1930), *Du Barry* (UA, 1930), *Virtuous Husbands* (Univ., 1931), *Night Angel* (Par., 1931), *Road to Singapore* (WB, 1931), *Devotion* (Pathé, 1931), *Tonight or Never* (UA, 1931), *High Pressure* (WB, 1932), *Unexpected Father* (Univ., 1932), *Sinners in the Sun* (Par., 1932), *Madame Racketeer* (Par., 1932), *Night After Night* (Par., 1932), *If I Had a Million* (Par., 1932), *Tonight Is Ours* (Par., 1933), *A Lady's Profession* (Par., 1933), *He Learned About Women* (Par., 1933), *Midnight Club* (Par., 1933), *Song of Songs* (Par., 1933), *Tillie and Gus* (Par., 1933), *Alice in Wonderland* (Par., 1933), *Coming Out Party* (Fox, 1934), *Six of a Kind* (Par., 1934), *Wharf Angel* (Par., 1934), *Shoot the Works* (Par., 1934), *Notorious Sophie Lang* (Par., 1934), *Here Is My Heart* (Par., 1934), *The Captain Hates the Sea* (Col., 1934), *The Casino Murder Case* (MGM, 1935), *Doubting Thomas* (Fox, 1935), *The Devil Is a Woman* (Par., 1935), *Becky Sharp* (RKO, 1935), *The Girl From Tenth Avenue* (WB, 1935), *Shanghai* (Par., 1935), *Dangerous* (WB, 1935), *Hitch-Hike Lady* (Rep., 1935), *Stolen Holiday* (WB, 1936), *The Princess Comes Across* (Par., 1936), *Satan Met a Lady* (WB, 1936), *Two in a Crowd* (Univ., 1936), *The Gorgeous Hussy* (MGM, 1936), *White Hunter* (20th, 1936), *Two Wise Maids* (Rep., 1937), *King of the Newsboys* (Rep., 1938), *Wide Open Faces* (Col., 1938), *Ladies in Distress* (Rep., 1938).

WALTER SLEZAK Born May 3, 1902, Vienna, Austria. Married Johanna Van Ryn (1943), children: Erica, Ingrid, Leo.

English-Language Sound Feature Films: *Once Upon a Honeymoon* (RKO, 1942), *This Land Is Mine* (RKO, 1943), *The Fallen Sparrow* (RKO, 1943), *Lifeboat* (20th, 1944), *Till We Meet Again* (Par., 1944), *Step Lively* (RKO, 1944), *And Now Tomorrow* (Par., 1944), *The Princess and the Pirate* (RKO, 1944), *Salome, Where She Danced* (Univ., 1945),

Walter Slezak and Janet Leigh in *Confidentially Connie*.

The Spanish Main (RKO, 1945), *Cornered* (RKO, 1945), *Sinbad the Sailor* (RKO, 1947), *Born to Kill* (RKO, 1947), *Riffraff* (RKO, 1947), *The Pirate* (MGM, 1948), *The Inspector General* (WB, 1949), *The Yellow Cab Man* (MGM, 1950), *Spy Hunt* (Univ., 1950), *Abbott and Costello in the Foreign Legion* (Univ., 1951), *Bedtime for Bonzo* (Univ., 1951), *People Will Talk* (20th, 1951), *Call Me Madam* (20th, 1953), *Confidentially Connie* (MGM, 1953), *White Witch Doctor* (20th, 1953), *The Steel Cage* (UA, 1954), *Ten Thousand Bedrooms* (MGM, 1957), *Deadlier Than the Male* (Continental, 1957), *The Miracle* (WB, 1959), *Come September* (Univ., 1961), *The Wonderful World of the Brothers Grimm* (MGM, 1962), *Emil and the Detectives* (BV, 1964), *Wonderful Life* ("Swingers' Paradise"—Elstree, 1964), *A Very Special Favor* (Univ., 1965), *24 Hours to Kill* (7 Arts, 1965), *The Caper of the Golden Bulls* (Embassy, 1967), *Coppelia* (BHE, 1968).

EVERETT SLOANE Born October 1, 1909, New York, New York. Married Luba Herman (1933), children: Nathaniel, Erika. Died August 6, 1965.

Everett Sloane and Van Heflin in *Patterns*.

Feature Films: *Citizen Kane* (RKO, 1941), *Journey into Fear* (RKO, 1942), *The Lady From Shanghai* (Col., 1948), *Prince of Foxes* (20th, 1949), *The Men* (UA, 1950), *Bird of Paradise* (20th, 1951), *The Enforcer* (WB, 1951), *Sirocco* (Col., 1951), *The Prince Who Was a Thief* (Univ., 1951), *The Blue Veil* (RKO, 1951), *The Desert Fox* (20th, 1951), *The Sellout* (MGM, 1951), *Way of a Gaucho* (20th, 1952), *The Big Knife* (UA, 1955), *Patterns* (UA, 1956), *Somebody Up There Likes Me* (MGM, 1956), *Lust for Life* (MGM, 1956), *Marjorie Morningstar* (WB, 1958), *The Gun Runners* (UA, 1958), *Home From the Hill* (MGM, 1960), *By Love Possessed* (UA, 1961), *Brushfire!* (Par., 1962), *The Man From the Diners' Club* (Col., 1963), *The Patsy* (Par., 1964), *Ready for the People* (WB, 1964), *The Disorderly Orderly* (Par., 1964).

Alexis Smith and Philo McCullough (right) in *Whiplash*.

ALEXIS SMITH (Gladys Smith) Born June 8, 1921, Penticton, Canada. Married Craig Stevens (1944).

Feature Films: *Lady With Red Hair* (WB, 1940), *Affectionately Yours* (WB, 1941), *Singapore Woman* (WB, 1941), *Three Sons o' Guns* (WB, 1941), *She Couldn't Say No* (WB, 1941), *Passage From Hong Kong* (WB, 1941), *Flight From Destiny* (WB, 1941), *Steel Against the Sky* (WB, 1941), *The Smiling Ghost* (WB, 1941), *Dive Bomber* (WB, 1941), *Gentleman Jim* (WB, 1942), *Thank Your Lucky Stars* (WB, 1943), *The Constant Nymph* (WB, 1943), *Hollywood Canteen* (WB, 1944), *The Adventures of Mark Twain* (WB, 1944), *The Doughgirls* (WB, 1944), *Rhapsody in Blue* (WB, 1945), *Conflict* (WB, 1945), *San Antonio* (WB, 1945), *The Horn Blows at Midnight* (WB, 1945), *Night and Day* (WB, 1946), *One More Tomorrow* (WB, 1946), *Of Human Bondage* (WB, 1946), *The Two Mrs. Carrolls* (WB, 1947), *Stallion Road* (WB, 1947), *Always Together* (WB, 1947),* *Woman in White* (WB, 1948), *The Decision of Christopher Blake* (WB, 1948), *Whiplash* (WB, 1948), *South of St. Louis* (WB, 1949), *Any Number Can Play* (MGM, 1949), *One Last Fling* (WB, 1949), *Montana* (WB, 1950), *Wyoming Mail* (Univ., 1950), *Undercover Girl* (Univ., 1950), *Here Comes the Groom* (Par., 1951), *Cave of Outlaws* (Univ., 1951), *The Turning Point* (Par., 1952), *Split Second* (RKO, 1953), *The Sleeping Tiger* (Astor, 1954), *The Eternal Sea* (Rep., 1955), *Beau James* (Par., 1957), *This Happy Feeling* (Univ., 1958), *The Young Philadelphians* (WB, 1959).

*Unbilled guest appearance

SIR C. AUBREY SMITH (Charles Aubrey Smith) Born July 21, 1863, Brighton, England. Married Isabel Wood (1896), child: Honor. Died December 20, 1948.

Billie Burke, C. Aubrey Smith, Broderick Crawford and Loretta Young in *Eternally Yours*.

Sound Feature Films: *Trader Horn* (MGM, 1931), *Never the Twain Shall Meet* (MGM, 1931), *Bachelor Father* (MGM, 1931), *Daybreak*

(MGM, 1931), *Just a Gigolo* (MGM, 1931), *Son of India* (MGM, 1931), *Man in Possession* (MGM, 1931), *Phantom of Paris* (MGM, 1931), *Guilty Hands* (MGM, 1931), *Surrender* (Fox, 1931), *Polly of the Circus* (MGM, 1932), *Tarzan the Ape Man* (MGM, 1932), *But the Flesh Is Weak* (MGM, 1932), *Love Me Tonight* (Par., 1932), *Trouble in Paradise* (Par., 1932), *No More Orchids* (Col., 1932), *They Just Had to Get Married* (Univ., 1932), *Luxury Liner* (Par., 1933), *Secrets* (UA, 1933), *The Barbarian* (MGM, 1933), *Adorable* (Fox, 1933), *Monkey's Paw* (RKO, 1933), *Morning Glory* (RKO, 1933), *Bombshell* (MGM, 1933), *Queen Christina* (MGM, 1933), *House of Rothschild* (UA, 1934), *Gambling Lady* (WB, 1934), *Curtain at Eight* (Majestic, 1934), *Bulldog Drummond Strikes Back* (UA, 1934), *Cleopatra* (Par., 1934), *Madame Du Barry* (WB, 1934), *One More River* (Univ., 1934), *Caravan* (Fox, 1934), *The Firebird* (WB, 1934), *The Right to Live* (WB, 1935), *Lives of a Bengal Lancer* (Par., 1935), *Florentine Dagger* (WB, 1935), *The Gilded Lily* (Par., 1935), *Clive of India* (UA, 1935), *China Seas* (MGM, 1935), *Jalna* (RKO, 1935), *The Crusades* (Par., 1935), *Little Lord Fauntleroy* (UA, 1936), *Romeo and Juliet* (MGM, 1936), *The Garden of Allah* (UA, 1936), *Lloyds of London* (20th, 1936), *Wee Willie Winkie* (20th, 1937), *The Prisoner of Zenda* (UA, 1937), *Thoroughbreds Don't Cry* (MGM, 1937), *The Hurricane* (UA, 1937), *Four Men and a Prayer* (20th, 1938), *Kidnapped* (20th, 1938), *Sixty Glorious Years* (RKO, 1938), *East Side of Heaven* (Univ., 1939), *Five Came Back* (RKO, 1939), *The Sun Never Sets* (Univ., 1939), *Eternally Yours* (UA, 1939), *Another Thin Man* (MGM, 1939), *The Under-Pup* (Univ., 1939), *Balalaika* (MGM, 1939), *Rebecca* (UA, 1940), *City of Chance* (20th, 1940), *A Bill of Divorcement* (RKO, 1940), *Waterloo Bridge* (MGM, 1940), *Beyond Tomorrow* (RKO, 1940), *A Little Bit of Heaven* (Univ., 1940), *Free and Easy* (MGM, 1941), *Maisie Was a Lady* (MGM, 1941), *Dr. Jekyll and Mr. Hyde* (MGM, 1941), *Forever and a Day* (RKO, 1943), *Two Tickets to London* (Univ., 1943), *Flesh and Fantasy* (Univ., 1943), *Madame Curie* (MGM, 1943), *The White Cliffs of Dover* (MGM, 1944), *The Adventures of Mark Twain* (WB, 1944), *Secrets of Scotland Yard* (Rep., 1944), *Sensations of 1945* (UA, 1944), *They Shall Have Faith* (Mon., 1945), *And Then There Were None* (20th, 1945), *Scotland Yard Investigator* (Rep., 1945), *Cluny Brown* (20th, 1946), *Rendezvous With Annie* (Rep., 1946), *High Conquest* (Mon., 1947), *Unconquered* (Par., 1947), *Little Women* (MGM, 1949).

KENT SMITH (Frank Kent Smith) Born March 19, 1907, New York, New York. Married Elizabeth Gillette (1937), child: Elizabeth; divorced 1954. Married Edith Atwater (1962).

Dorothy McGuire, Troy Donahue, Kent Smith, Connie Stevens, Brian Aherne, Bert Convoy and Natalie Schafer in *Susan Slade*.

Feature Films: *Cat People* (RKO, 1942), *Forever and a Day* (RKO, 1943), *Hitler's Children* (RKO, 1943), *This Land Is Mine* (RKO, 1943), *Three Russian Girls* (UA, 1943), *The Curse of the Cat People* (RKO, 1944), *Youth Runs Wild* (RKO, 1944), *The Spiral Staircase* (RKO, 1946), *Magic Town* (RKO, 1947), *Nora Prentiss* (WB, 1947), *The Voice of the Turtle* (WB, 1947), *Design for Death* (narrator; RKO, 1948), *The Decision of Christopher Blake,* (WB, 1948), *The Fountain-*

head (WB, 1949), *My Foolish Heart* (RKO, 1949), *The Damned Don't Cry* (WB, 1950), *This Side of the Law* (WB, 1950), *Paula* (Col., 1952), *Comanche* (UA, 1956), *Sayonara* (WB, 1957), *The Imitation General* (MGM, 1958), *The Badlanders* (MGM, 1958), *The Mugger* (UA, 1958), *Party Girl* (MGM, 1958), *This Earth Is Mine* (Univ., 1959), *Strangers When We Meet* (Col., 1960), *Susan Slade* (WB, 1961), *Moon Pilot* (BV, 1962), *The Balcony* (Continental Distributing, 1963), *A Distant Trumpet* (WB, 1964), *The Young Lovers* (MGM, 1964), *Youngblood Hawke* (WB, 1964), *Trouble With Angels* (Col., 1966), *A Covenant With Death* (WB, 1967), *Assignment to Kill* (WB, 1968), *Games* (Univ., 1967).

GALE SONDERGAARD (Edith Holm Sondergaard) Born February 15, 1900, Litchfield, Minnesota. Married Neill O'Malley (1922); divorced 1930. Married Herbert Biberman (1930), children: Daniel, Joan.

Rondo Hatton and Gale Sondergaard in *The Spider Woman Strikes Back.*

Feature Films: *Anthony Adverse* (WB, 1936), *Maid of Salem* (Par., 1937), *Seventh Heaven* (20th, 1937), *The Life of Emile Zola* (WB, 1937), *Lord Jeff* (MGM, 1938), *Dramatic School* (MGM, 1938), *Never Say Die* (Par., 1939), *Juarez* (WB, 1939), *The Cat and the Canary* (Par., 1939), *The Llano Kid* (Par., 1940), *The Blue Bird* (20th, 1940), *The Mark of Zorro* (20th, 1940), *The Letter* (WB, 1940), *The Black Cat* (Univ., 1941), *Paris Calling* (Univ., 1941), *My Favorite Blonde* (Par., 1942), *Enemy Agent Meets Ellery Queen* (Col., 1942), *A Night to Remember* (Col., 1943), *Appointment in Berlin* (Col., 1943), *Isle of Forgotten Sins* (PRC, 1943), *The Strange Death of Adolf Hitler* (Univ., 1943), *The Spider Woman* (Univ., 1944), *Follow the Boys* (Univ., 1944), *Christmas Holiday* (Univ., 1944), *Invisible Man's Revenge* (Univ., 1944), *Gypsy Wildcat* (Univ., 1944), *The Climax* (Univ., 1944), *Enter Arsene Lupin* (Univ., 1944), *The Spider Woman Strikes Back* (Univ., 1946), *A Night in Paradise* (Univ., 1946), *Anna and the King of Siam* (20th, 1946), *The Time of Their Lives* (Univ., 1946), *Road to Rio* (Par., 1947), *The Pirates of Monterey* (Univ., 1947), *East Side, West Side* (MGM, 1949).

ANN SOTHERN (Harriette Lake) Born January 22, 1909, Valley City, North Dakota. Married Roger Pryor (1936); divorced 1942. Married Robert Sterling (1943), child: Patricia; divorced 1949.

Feature Films:

    as Harriet Lake *Show of Shows* (WB, 1929), *Dough Boys* (MGM, 1930).

    as Ann Sothern *Let's Fall in Love* (Col., 1934), *Melody in Spring* (Par., 1934), *Party's Over* (Col., 1934), *Hell Cat* (Col., 1934), *Blind Date* (Col., 1934), *Kid Millions* (UA, 1934), *Folies Bergere* (UA, 1935),

Virginia Weidler, Ann Sothern and Mary Nash in *Gold Rush Maisie*.

Eight Bells (Col., 1935), *Hooray for Love* (RKO, 1935), *The Girl Friend* (Col., 1935), *Grand Exit* (Col., 1935), *You May Be Next* (Col., 1936), *Hellship Morgan* (Col., 1936), *Don't Gamble With Love* (Col., 1936), *Walking on Air* (RKO, 1936), *My American Wife* (Par., 1936), *The Smartest Girl in Town* (RKO, 1936), *Dangerous Number* (MGM, 1937), *50 Roads to Town* (20th, 1937), *There Goes My Girl* (RKO, 1937), *Super Sleuth* (RKO, 1937), *Danger—Love At Work* (20th, 1937), *There Goes the Groom* (RKO, 1937), *She's Got Everything* (RKO, 1938), *Trade Winds* (UA, 1938), *Maisie* (MGM, 1939), *Fast and Furious* (MGM, 1939), *Elsa Maxwell's Hotel for Women* (20th, 1939), *Joe and Ethel Turp Call on the President* (MGM, 1939), *Congo Maisie* (MGM, 1940), *Brother Orchid* (WB, 1940), *Gold Rush Maisie* (MGM, 1940), *Dulcy* (MGM, 1940), *Maisie Was a Lady* (MGM, 1941), *Ringside Maisie* (MGM, 1941), *Lady Be Good* (MGM, 1941), *Maisie Gets Her Man* (MGM, 1942), *Panama Hattie* (MGM, 1942), *Three Hearts for Julia* (MGM, 1943), *Swing Shift Maisie* (MGM, 1943), *Thousands Cheer* (MGM, 1943), *Cry Havoc* (MGM, 1943), *Maisie Goes to Reno* (MGM, 1944), *Up Goes Maisie* (MGM, 1946), *Undercover Maisie* (MGM, 1947), *April Showers* (WB, 1948), *Words and Music* (MGM, 1948), *A Letter to Three Wives* (20th, 1948), *The Judge Steps Out* (RKO, 1949), *Nancy Goes to Rio* (MGM, 1950), *Shadow on the Wall* (MGM, 1950), *The Blue Gardenia* (WB, 1953), *Lady in a Cage* (Par., 1964), *The Best Man* (UA, 1964), *Sylvia* (Par., 1965), *Chubasco* (WB-7 Arts, 1968).

ROBERT STACK Born January 13, 1919, Los Angeles, California. Married Rosemarie Bowe (1956), children: Elizabeth, Charles.

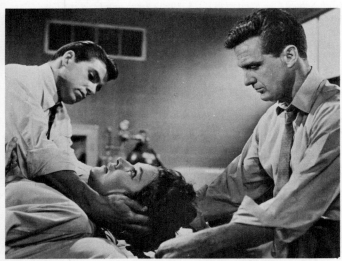

Van Williams, Polly Bergen and Robert Stack in *The Caretakers*.

Feature Films: *First Love* (Univ., 1939), *The Mortal Storm* (MGM, 1940), *A Little Bit of Heaven* (Univ., 1940), *Nice Girl?* (Univ., 1941), *Badlands of Dakota* (Univ., 1941), *To Be or Not to Be* (UA, 1942), *Eagle Squadron* (Univ., 1942), *Men of Texas* (Univ., 1942), *A Date With Judy* (MGM, 1948), *Miss Tatlock's Millions* (Par., 1948), *Fighter*

Squadron (WB, 1948), *Mr. Music* (Par., 1950), *My Outlaw Brother* (EL, 1951), *Bwana Devil* (UA, 1952), *War Paint* (UA, 1953), *Conquest of Cochise* (Col., 1953), *Sabre Jet* (UA, 1953), *The High and the Mighty* (WB, 1954), *The Iron Glove* (Col., 1954), *House of Bamboo* (20th, 1955), *Good Morning, Miss Dove* (20th, 1955), *Great Day in the Morning* (RKO, 1956), *Written on the Wind* (Univ., 1956), *The Tarnished Angels* (Univ., 1957), *The Gift of Love* (20th, 1958), *John Paul Jones* (WB, 1959), *The Last Voyage* (MGM, 1960), *The Caretakers* (UA, 1963), *Is Paris Burning?* (Par., 1966), *The Corrupt Ones* (WB-7 Arts, 1967), *Action Man* (Les Films Copernic, 1968).

BARBARA STANWYCK (Ruby Stevens) Born July 16, 1907, Brooklyn, New York. Married Frank Fay (1928), child: Dion; divorced 1935. Married Robert Taylor (1939); divorced 1952.

Gilbert Roland and Barbara Stanwyck in *The Other Love*.

Sound Feature Films: *Mexicali Rose* (Col., 1929), *Ladies of Leisure* (Col., 1930), *Ten Cents a Dance* (Col., 1931), *Illicit* (WB, 1931), *Miracle Woman* (Col., 1931), *Night Nurse* (WB, 1931), *Forbidden* (Col., 1932), *Shopworn* (Col., 1932), *So Big* (WB, 1932), *The Purchase Price* (WB, 1932), *The Bitter Tea of General Yen* (Col., 1933), *Ladies They Talk About* (WB, 1933), *Baby Face* (WB, 1933), *Ever in My Heart* (WB, 1933), *A Lost Lady* (WB, 1934), *Gambling Lady* (WB, 1934), *The Secret Bride* (WB, 1935), *The Woman in Red* (WB, 1935), *Red Salute* (UA, 1935), *Annie Oakley* (RKO, 1935), *A Message to Garcia* (20th, 1936), *The Bride Walks Out* (RKO, 1936), *His Brother's Wife* (MGM, 1936), *Banjo on My Knee* (20th, 1936), *The Plough and the Stars* (RKO, 1936), *Internes Can't Take Money* (Par., 1937), *This Is My Affair* (20th, 1937), *Stella Dallas* (UA, 1937), *Breakfast for Two* (RKO, 1937), *The Mad Miss Manton* (RKO, 1938), *Always Goodbye* (20th, 1938), *Union Pacific* (Par., 1939), *Golden Boy* (Col., 1939), *Remember the Night* (Par., 1940), *The Lady Eve* (Par., 1941), *Meet John Doe* (WB, 1941), *You Belong to Me* (Col., 1941), *Ball of Fire* (RKO, 1941), *The Great Man's Lady* (Par., 1942), *The Gay Sisters* (WB, 1942), *Lady of Burlesque* (UA, 1943), *Flesh and Fantasy* (Univ., 1943), *Double Indemnity* (Par., 1944), *Hollywood Canteen* (WB, 1944), *Christmas in Connecticut* (WB, 1945), *My Reputation* (WB, 1946), *The Bride Wore Boots* (Par., 1946), *The Strange Love of Martha Ivers* (Par., 1946), *California* (Par., 1946), *Variety Girl* (Par., 1947), *The Other Love* (UA, 1947), *The Two Mrs. Carrolls* (WB, 1947), *Cry Wolf* (WB, 1947), *B. F.'s Daughter* (MGM, 1948), *Sorry, Wrong Number* (Par., 1948), *The Lady Gambles* (Univ., 1949), *East Side, West Side* (MGM, 1949), *Thelma Jordan* (Par., 1949), *No Man of Her Own* (Par., 1950), *The Furies* (Par., 1950), *To Please a Lady* (MGM, 1950), *The Man With a Cloak* (MGM, 1951), *Clash by Night* (RKO, 1952), *Jeopardy* (MGM, 1953), *Titanic* (20th, 1953), *All I Desire* (Univ., 1953), *The Moonlighter* (WB, 1953), *Blowing Wild* (WB, 1953), *Executive Suite* (MGM, 1954), *Witness to Murder* (UA, 1954), *Cattle Queen of Montana* (RKO, 1954), *The Violent Men* (Col.,

1955), *Escape to Burma* (RKO, 1955), *There's Always Tomorrow* (Univ., 1956), *The Maverick Queen* (Rep., 1956), *These Wilder Years* (MGM, 1956), *Crime of Passion* (UA, 1957), *Trooper Hook* (UA, 1957), *Forty Guns* (20th, 1957), *Walk on the Wild Side* (Col., 1962), *Roustabout* (Par., 1964), *The Night Walker* (Univ., 1965).

ROD STEIGER (Rodney Stephen Steiger) Born April 14, 1925, Westhampton, Long Island, New York. Married Sally Gracie (1952); divorced 1954. Married Claire Bloom (1959), child: Anna.

Rod Steiger and Ayllene Gibbons in *The Loved One*.

Feature Films: *On the Waterfront* (Col., 1954), *Oklahoma!* (Magna, 1955), *The Big Knife* (UA, 1955), *The Court-Martial of Billy Mitchell* (WB, 1955), *The Harder They Fall* (Col., 1956), *Jubal* (Col., 1956), *Back From Eternity* (RKO, 1956), *Run of the Arrow* (Univ., 1957), *Across the Bridge* (Rank, 1957), *The Unholy Wife* (Univ., 1957), *Cry Terror* (MGM, 1958), *Al Capone* (AA, 1959), *Seven Thieves* (20th, 1960), *The Mark* (Continental Distributing, 1961), *On Friday at Eleven* ("World in My Pocket"—British Lion, 1961), *13 West Street* (Col., 1962), *Convicts 4* (AA, 1962), *The Longest Day* (20th, 1962), *The Pawnbroker* (Landau, 1965), *The Loved One* (MGM, 1965), *Doctor Zhivago* (MGM, 1965), *Time of Indifference* (Continental, 1966), *In the Heat of the Night* (UA, 1967), *The Girl and the General* (MGM, 1967) *The Sergeant* (WB-7 Arts, 1968), *No Way to Treat a Lady* (Par., 1968).

ANNA STEN (Anjuschka Stenski) Born December 3, 1910, Kiev, Russia. Married Eugene Frenke.

English-Language Feature Films: *Nana* (UA, 1934), *We Live Again* (UA, 1934), *The Wedding Night* (UA, 1935), *Two Who Dared* ("A Woman Alone"—GN, 1937), *Exile Express* (GN, 1939), *The Man I*

Lionel Atwill and Anna Sten in *Nana*.

Married (20th, 1940), *So Ends Our Night* (UA, 1941), *Chetniks* (20th, 1943), *They Came to Blow Up America* (20th, 1943), *Three Russian Girls* (UA, 1943), *Let's Live a Little* (EL, 1948), *Soldier of Fortune* (20th, 1955), *The Nun and the Sergeant* (UA, 1962).

JAN STERLING (Jane Sterling Adriance) Born April 3, 1923, New York, New York. Married Jack Merivale (1941); divorced 1948. Married Paul Douglas (1950), child: Adam; widowed 1959.

Jan Sterling and Carleton Carpenter in *Sky Full of Moon*.

Feature Films: *Johnny Belinda* (WB, 1948), *The Skipper Surprised His Wife* (MGM, 1950), *Mystery Street* (MGM, 1950), *Caged* (WB, 1950), *Union Station* (Par., 1950), *Appointment With Danger* (Par., 1951), *The Mating Season* (Par., 1951), *The Big Carnival* (Par., 1951), *Rhubarb* (Par., 1951), *Flesh and Fury* (Univ., 1952), *Sky Full of Moon* (MGM, 1952), *Split Second* (RKO, 1953), *The Vanquished* (Par., 1953), *Pony Express* (Par., 1953), *Alaska Seas* (Par., 1954), *The High and the Mighty* (WB, 1954), *Return From the Sea* (AA, 1954), *The Human Jungle* (AA, 1954), *Women's Prison* (Col., 1955), *Female on the Beach* (Univ., 1955), *Man With the Gun* (UA, 1955), *The Harder They Fall* (Col., 1956), *1984* (Col., 1956), *Slaughter on Tenth Avenue* (Univ., 1957), *The Female Animal* (Univ., 1958), *Kathy O'* (Univ., 1958), *High School Confidential* (MGM, 1958), *Love in a Goldfish Bowl* (Par., 1961), *The Incident* (20th, 1967).

JAMES STEWART (James Maitland Stewart) Born May 20, 1908, Indiana, Pennsylvania. Married Gloria McLean (1949), children: Judy, Kelly.

Feature Films: *Murder Man* (MGM, 1935), *Rose Marie* (MGM, 1936), *Next Time We Love* (Univ., 1936), *Wife vs. Secretary* (MGM, 1936), *Small Town Girl* (MGM, 1936), *Speed* (MGM, 1936), *The Gorgeous Hussy* (MGM, 1936), *Born to Dance* (MGM, 1936), *After the Thin Man*

James Stewart in *Navy Blue and Gold*.

(MGM, 1936), *Seventh Heaven* (20th, 1937), *The Last Gangster* (MGM, 1937), *Navy Blue and Gold* (MGM, 1937), *Of Human Hearts* (MGM, 1938), *Vivacious Lady* (RKO, 1938), *Shopworn Angel* (MGM, 1938), *You Can't Take It With You* (Col., 1938), *Made for Each Other* (UA, 1939), *Ice Follies of 1939* (MGM, 1939), *It's a Wonderful World* (MGM, 1939), *Mr. Smith Goes to Washington* (Col., 1939), *Destry Rides Again* (Univ., 1939), *The Shop Around the Corner* (MGM, 1940), *The Mortal Storm* (MGM, 1940), *No Time for Comedy* (WB, 1940), *The Philadelphia Story* (MGM, 1940), *Come Live With Me* (MGM, 1941), *Pot o' Gold* (UA, 1941), *Ziegfeld Girl* (MGM, 1941), *It's a Wonderful Life* (RKO, 1946), *Magic Town* (RKO, 1947), *Call Northside 777* (20th, 1948), *On Our Merry Way* (UA, 1948), *Rope* (WB, 1948), *You Gotta Stay Happy* (Univ., 1948), *The Stratton Story* (MGM, 1949), *Malaya* (MGM, 1949), *Winchester '73* (Univ., 1950), *Broken Arrow* (20th, 1950), *The Jackpot* (20th, 1950), *Harvey* (Univ., 1950), *No Highway in the Sky* (20th, 1951), *The Greatest Show on Earth* (Par., 1952), *Bend of the River* (Univ., 1952), *Carbine Williams* (MGM, 1952), *The Naked Spur* (MGM, 1953), *Thunder Bay* (Univ., 1953), *The Glenn Miller Story* (Univ., 1954), *Rear Window* (Par., 1954), *The Far Country* (Univ., 1955), *Strategic Air Command* (Par., 1955), *The Man From Laramie* (Col., 1955), *The Man Who Knew Too Much* (Par., 1956), *The Spirit of St. Louis* (WB, 1957), *Night Passage* (Univ., 1957), *Vertigo* (Par., 1958), *Bell, Book and Candle* (Col., 1958), *Anatomy of a Murder* (Col., 1959), *The FBI Story* (WB, 1959), *The Mountain Road* (Col., 1960), *Two Rode Together* (Col., 1961), *X-15* (narrator; UA, 1961), *The Man Who Shot Liberty Valance* (Par., 1962), *Mr. Hobbs Takes a Vacation* (20th, 1962), *How the West Was Won* (MGM, 1963), *Take Her, She's Mine* (20th, 1963), *Cheyenne Autumn* (WB, 1964), *Dear Brigitte* (20th, 1965), *Shenandoah* (Univ., 1965), *Flight of the Phoenix* (20th, 1966), *The Rare Breed* (Univ., 1966), *Firecreek* (WB- Arts, 1968), *Bandolero* (20th, 1968).

DEAN STOCKWELL Born March 5, 1936, Los Angeles, California. Married Millie Perkins (1960); divorced 1964.

Richard Widmark (left) and Dean Stockwell (center) in *Down to the Sea in Ships*.

Feature Films: *Valley of Decision* (MGM, 1945), *Anchors Aweigh* (MGM, 1945), *Bud Abbott and Lou Costello in Hollywood* (MGM, 1945), *The Green Years* (MGM, 1946), *Home Sweet Homicide* (20th, 1946), *The Mighty McGurk* (MGM, 1947), *The Arnelo Affair* (MGM, 1947), *Song of the Thin Man* (MGM, 1947), *The Romance of Rosy Ridge* (MGM, 1947), *Gentleman's Agreement* (20th, 1947), *The Boy With Green Hair* (RKO, 1948), *Deep Waters* (20th, 1948), *Down to the Sea in Ships* (20th, 1949), *The Secret Garden* (MGM, 1949), *Stars in My Crown* (MGM, 1950), *The Happy Years* (MGM, 1950), *Kim* (MGM, 1950), *Cattle Drive* (Univ., 1951), *Gun for a Coward* (Univ., 1957), *The Careless Years* (UA, 1957), *Compulsion* (20th, 1959), *Sons and Lovers* (20th, 1960), *Long Day's Journey into Night* (Embassy, 1962), *Rapture* (International Classics, 1965), *Psych-Out* (AIP, 1968).

Lewis Stone and Jackie Cooper in *Treasure Island*.

LEWIS STONE Born November 15, 1879, Worcester, Massachusetts. Married Margaret Langham, widowed. Married Florence Oakley, children: Virginia, Barbara; divorced. Married Hazel Wolf (1930). Died September 12, 1953.

Sound Feature Films: *Trial of Mary Dugan* (MGM, 1929), *Madame X* (MGM, 1929), *Their Own Desire* (MGM, 1930), *Strictly Unconventional* (MGM, 1930), *Big House* (MGM, 1930), *Romance* (MGM, 1930), *Father's Son* (WB, 1930), *Office Wife* (WB, 1930), *Passion Flower* (MGM, 1930), *My Past* (WB, 1931), *Inspiration* (MGM, 1931), *Secret Six* (MGM, 1931), *Always Goodbye* (Fox, 1931), *Phantom of Paris* (MGM, 1931), *The Bargain* (WB, 1931), *The Sin of Madelon Claudet* (MGM, 1931), *Mata Hari* (MGM, 1931), *Grand Hotel* (MGM, 1932), *Wet Parade* (MGM, 1932), *Night Court* (MGM, 1932), *Letty Lynton* (MGM, 1932), *New Morals for Old* (MGM, 1932), *Unashamed* (MGM, 1932), *Divorce in the Family* (MGM, 1932), *Red-Headed Woman* (MGM, 1932), *Mask of Fu Manchu* (MGM, 1932), *The Son-Daughter* (MGM, 1932), *The White Sister* (MGM, 1933), *Men Must Fight* (MGM, 1933), *Looking Forward* (MGM, 1933), *Bureau of Missing Persons* (WB, 1933), *Queen Christina* (MGM, 1933), *You Can't Buy Everything* (MGM, 1934), *Mystery of Mr. X* (MGM, 1934), *Treasure Island* (MGM, 1934), *Girl From Missouri* (MGM, 1934), *Vanessa—Her Love Story* (MGM, 1935), *West Point of the Air* (MGM, 1935), *David Copperfield* (MGM, 1935), *Public Hero Number One* (MGM, 1935), *China Seas* (MGM, 1935), *Woman Wanted* (MGM, 1935), *Shipmates Forever* (WB, 1935), *Small Town Girl* (MGM, 1936), *The Three Godfathers* (MGM, 1936), *The Unguarded Hour* (MGM, 1936), *Sworn Enemy* (MGM, 1936), *Suzy* (MGM, 1936), *Don't Turn 'Em Loose* (RKO, 1936), *Outcast* (Par., 1937), *The Thirteenth Chair* (MGM, 1937), *The Man Who Cried Wolf* (Univ., 1937), *You're Only Young Once* (MGM, 1937), *Bad Man of Brimstone* (MGM, 1938), *Judge Hardy's Children* (MGM, 1938), *Stolen Heaven* (Par., 1938), *Yellow Jack* (MGM, 1938), *The Chaser* (MGM, 1938), *Love Finds Andy Hardy* (MGM, 1938), *Out West With the Hardys* (MGM, 1938), *Ice Follies of 1939* (MGM, 1939), *The Hardys Ride High* (MGM, 1939), *Andy Hardy Gets Spring Fever* (MGM, 1939), *Judge Hardy and Son* (MGM, 1939), *Joe and Ethel Turp Call on the President* (MGM, 1939), *Andy Hardy Meets Debutante* (MGM, 1940), *Sporting Blood* (MGM, 1940), *Andy Hardy's Private Secretary* (MGM, 1941), *Life Begins for Andy Hardy* (MGM, 1941), *The Bugle Sounds* (MGM, 1941), *The Courtship of Andy Hardy* (MGM, 1942), *Andy Hardy's Double Life* (MGM, 1942), *Andy Hardy's Blonde Trouble* (MGM, 1944), *The Hoodlum Saint* (MGM, 1946), *Three Wise Fools* (MGM, 1946), *Love Laughs at Andy Hardy* (MGM, 1946), *State of the Union* (MGM, 1948), *The Sun Comes Up* (MGM, 1949), *Any Number Can Play* (MGM, 1949), *Stars in My Crown* (MGM, 1950), *Key to the City* (MGM, 1950), *Grounds for Marriage* (MGM, 1950), *Night into Morning* (MGM, 1951), *Angels in the Outfield* (MGM, 1951), *Bannerline* (MGM, 1951), *It's a Big Country* (MGM, 1951), *The Unknown Man* (MGM, 1951), *Just This Once* (MGM, 1952), *Scaramouche* (MGM, 1952), *Talk About a Stranger* (MGM, 1952), *The Prisoner of Zenda* (MGM, 1952), *All the Brothers Were Valiant* (MGM, 1953).

Margaret Sullavan and James Stewart in *The Shop Around the Corner.*

MARGARET SULLAVAN (Margaret Brooke Sullavan) Born May 16, 1911, Norfolk, Virginia. Married Henry Fonda (1931); divorced 1932. Married William Wyler (1934); divorced 1936. Married Leland Hayward (1936), children: Brooke, Bridget, William; divorced 1947. Married Kenneth Wagg (1950). Died January 1, 1960.

Feature Films: *Only Yesterday* (Univ., 1933), *Little Man, What Now?* (Univ., 1934), *The Good Fairy* (Univ., 1935), *So Red the Rose* (Par., 1935), *Next Time We Love* (Univ., 1936), *The Moon's Our Home* (Par., 1936), *Three Comrades* (MGM, 1938), *The Shopworn Angel* (MGM, 1938), *The Shining Hour* (MGM, 1938), *The Shop Around the Corner* (MGM, 1940), *The Mortal Storm* (MGM, 1940), *So Ends Our Night* (UA, 1941), *Back Street* (Univ., 1941), *Appointment for Love* (Univ., 1941), *Cry Havoc* (MGM, 1943), *No Sad Songs for Me* (Col., 1950).

GLORIA SWANSON (Gloria Josephine May Swanson) Born March 27, 1898, Chicago, Illinois. Married Wallace Beery (1916); divorced 1919. Married Herbert Somborn (1919), child: Gloria; divorced 1923. Married Henri de la Falaise (1925); divorced 1930). Married Michael Farmer (1931), child: Michelle; divorced 1934. Married William Davey (1945); divorced 1946. Child adopted while Miss Swanson was unmarried: Joseph Swanson.

Gloria Swanson (center) in *What a Widow!*

English-Language Sound Feature Films: *The Trespasser* (UA, 1929),

What a Widow! (UA, 1930), *Indiscreet* (UA, 1931), *Tonight or Never* (UA, 1931), *Perfect Understanding* (UA, 1933), *Music in the Air* (Fox, 1934), *Father Takes a Wife* (RKO, 1941), *Sunset Boulevard* (Par., 1950), *Three for Bedroom C* (WB, 1952).

AKIM TAMIROFF Born October 29, 1899, Tiflis, Russia. Married Tamara Shayne.

Arthur Hoyt, Akim Tamiroff, Brian Donlevy and William Demarest in *The Great McGinty.*

English-Language Feature Films: *Gabriel Over the White House* (MGM, 1933), *Storm at Daybreak* (MGM, 1933), *Queen Christina* (MGM, 1933), *Fugitive Lovers* (MGM, 1934), *Sadie McKee* (MGM, 1934), *Great Flirtation* (Par., 1934), *Chained* (MGM, 1934), *Scarlet Empress* (Par., 1934), *Now and Forever* (Par., 1934), *The Merry Widow* (MGM, 1934), *Whom the Gods Destroy* (Col., 1934), *The Captain Hates the Sea* (Col., 1934), *Here Is My Heart* (Par., 1934), *Murder in the Private Car* (MGM, 1934), *Naughty Marietta* (MGM, 1935), *The Winning Ticket* (MGM, 1935), *Rumba* (Par., 1935), *Lives of a Bengal Lancer* (Par., 1935), *Go into Your Dance* (WB, 1935), *Two Fisted* (Par., 1935), *Black Fury* (WB, 1935), *Paris in Spring* (Par., 1935), *China Seas* (MGM, 1935), *Big Broadcast of 1936* (Par., 1935), *The Last Outpost* (Par., 1935), *The Story of Louis Pasteur* (WB, 1935), *Gay Deception* (Fox, 1935), *Woman Trap* (Par., 1936), *Desire* (Par., 1936), *Anthony Adverse* (WB, 1936), *The General Died at Dawn* (Par., 1936), *The Jungle Princess* (Par., 1936), *Her Husband Lies* (Par., 1937), *The Soldier and the Lady* (RKO, 1937), *King of Gamblers* (Par., 1937), *High, Wide and Handsome* (Par., 1937), *The Buccaneer* (Par., 1938), *Dangerous to Know* (Par., 1938), *Spawn of the North* (Par., 1938), *Ride a Crooked Mile* (Par., 1938), *King of Chinatown* (Par., 1939), *Paris Honeymoon* (Par., 1939), *Union Pacific* (Par., 1939), *The Magnificent Fraud* (Par., 1939), *Disputed Passage* (Par., 1939), *Honeymoon in Bali* (Par., 1939), *The Way of All Flesh* (Par., 1940), *Untamed* (Par., 1940), *The Great McGinty* (Par., 1940), *North West Mounted Police* (Par., 1940), *Texas Rangers Ride Again* (Par., 1941), *New York Town* (Par., 1941), *The Corsican Brothers* (UA, 1941), *Tortilla Flat* (MGM, 1942), *Five Graves to Cairo* (Par., 1943), *For Whom the Bell Tolls* (Par., 1943), *His Butler's Sister* (Univ., 1943), *The Miracle of Morgan's Creek* (Par., 1944), *Dragon Seed* (MGM, 1944), *The Bridge of San Luis Rey* (UA, 1944), *Can't Help Singing* (Univ., 1944), *Pardon My Past* (Col., 1946), *A Scandal in Paris* (UA, 1946), *Fiesta* (MGM, 1947), *The Gangster* (AA, 1947), *My Girl Tisa* (WB, 1948), *Relentless* (Col., 1948), *Outpost in Morocco* (UA, 1949), *Black Magic* (UA, 1949), *Desert Legion* (Univ., 1953), *You Know What Sailors Are* (UA, 1954), *They Who Dare* (British Lion, 1954), *Mr. Arkadin* (WB, 1955), *The Black Sleep* (UA, 1956), *Anastasia* (20th, 1956), *Battle Hell* (DCA, 1957), *Cartouche* (RKO, 1957), *Touch of Evil* (Univ., 1958), *Me and the Colonel* (Col., 1958), *Desert Desperadoes* (RKO, 1959), *Ocean's 11* (WB, 1960), *Romanoff And Juliet* (Univ., 1961), *The Reluctant Saint* (Davis Royal, 1962), *The Trial* (Gibraltar, 1962), *Panic Button* (Gorton

Associates, 1964), *Topkapi* (UA, 1964), *Lord Jim* (Col., 1965), *Chimes at Midnight* (Counor, 1965), *Lt. Robinson Crusoe, USN* (BV, 1966), *Marco the Magnificent* (MGM, 1966), *Hotel Paradiso* (MGM, 1966), *After the Fox* (UA, 1966), *The Liquidator* (MGM, 1966), *The Happening* (Col., 1967), *The Vulture* (Par., 1967), *Catherine the Great* (WB-7 Arts, 1968.).

ELIZABETH TAYLOR (Elizabeth Rosemond Taylor) Born February 27, 1932, Hampstead Heath, England. Married Nicky Hilton (1949); divorced 1951. Married Michael Wilding (1952), children: Michael, Christopher; divorced 1957. Married Michael Todd (1957), child: Elizabeth; widowed 1958. Married Eddie Fisher (1959), child: Maria; divorced 1964. Married Richard Burton (1964).

Elizabeth Taylor and Honor Blackman in *Conspirator.*

Feature Films: *There's One Born Every Minute* (Univ., 1942), *Lassie Come Home* (MGM, 1943), *Jane Eyre* (20th, 1944), *The White Cliffs of Dover* (MGM, 1944), *National Velvet* (MGM, 1944), *Courage of Lassie* (MGM, 1946), *Cynthia* (MGM, 1947), *Life With Father* (WB, 1947), *A Date With Judy* (MGM, 1948), *Julia Misbehaves* (MGM, 1948), *Little Women* (MGM, 1949), *Conspirator* (MGM, 1950), *The Big Hangover* (MGM, 1950), *Father of the Bride* (MGM, 1950), *Father's Little Dividend* (MGM, 1951), *A Place in the Sun* (Par., 1951), *Quo Vadis* (MGM, 1951),* *Ivanhoe* (MGM, 1952), *The Girl Who Had Everything* (MGM, 1953), *Rhapsody* (MGM, 1954), *Elephant Walk* (Par., 1954), *Beau Brummel* (MGM, 1954), *The Last Time I Saw Paris* (MGM, 1954), *Giant* (WB, 1956), *Raintree County* (MGM, 1957), *Cat on a Hot Tin Roof* (MGM, 1958), *Suddenly, Last Summer* (Col., 1959), *Scent of Mystery* (Michael Todd, Jr., 1960),* *Butterfield 8* (MGM, 1960), *Cleopatra* (20th, 1963), *The V.I.P.'s* (MGM, 1963), *The Sandpiper* (MGM, 1965), *Who's Afraid of Virginia Woolf?* (WB, 1966), *The Taming of the Shrew* (Col., 1967), *Reflections in a Golden Eye* (WB-7 Arts, 1967), *The Comedians* (MGM, 1967), *Dr. Faustus* (Col., 1968), *Boom* (Univ., 1968).

*Unbilled guest appearance

ROBERT TAYLOR (Spangler Arlington Brough) Born August 5, 1911, Finley, Nebraska. Married Barbara Stanwyck (1939); divorced 1952. Married Ursula Thiess (1954), children: Terence, Tessa.

Feature Films: *Handy Andy* (Fox, 1934), *There's Always Tomorrow* (Univ., 1934), *Wicked Woman* (MGM, 1934), *Society Doctor* (MGM, 1935), *West Point of the Air* (MGM, 1935), *Times Square Lady* (MGM, 1935), *Murder in the Fleet* (MGM, 1935), *Broadway Melody of 1936* (MGM, 1935), *Magnificent Obsession* (Univ., 1935), *Small Town Girl* (MGM, 1936), *Private Number* (20th, 1936), *His Brother's Wife* (MGM, 1936), *The Gorgeous Hussy* (MGM, 1936), *Camille* (MGM, 1936), *Personal Property* (MGM, 1937), *This Is My Affair* (20th, 1937), *Broadway Melody of 1938* (MGM, 1937), *A Yank at Oxford* (MGM, 1938), *Three Comrades* (MGM, 1938), *The Crowd*

Robert Taylor, Nat Pendleton and Ted Healy in *Murder in the Fleet.*

Roars (MGM, 1938), *Stand Up and Fight* (MGM, 1939), *Lucky Night* (MGM, 1939), *Lady of the Tropics* (MGM, 1939), *Remember?* (MGM, 1939), *Waterloo Bridge* (MGM, 1940), *Escape* (MGM, 1940), *Flight Command* (MGM, 1940), *Billy the Kid* (MGM, 1941), *When Ladies Meet* (MGM, 1941), *Johnny Eager* (MGM, 1942), *Her Cardboard Lover* (MGM, 1942), *Stand by for Action* (MGM, 1943), *The Youngest Profession* (MGM, 1943),* *Bataan* (MGM, 1943), *Song of Russia* (MGM, 1944), *Undercurrent* (MGM, 1946), *The High Wall* (MGM, 1947), *The Secret Land* (narrator; MGM, 1948), *The Bribe* (MGM, 1949), *Ambush* (MGM, 1949), *Devil's Doorway* (MGM, 1950), *Conspirator* (MGM, 1950), *Quo Vadis* (MGM, 1951), *Westward the Women* (MGM, 1951), *Ivanhoe* (MGM, 1952), *Above and Beyond* (MGM, 1952), *I Love Melvin* (MGM, 1953),* *Ride, Vaquero!* (MGM, 1953), *All the Brothers Were Valiant* (MGM, 1953), *Knights of the Round Table* (MGM, 1953), *Valley of the Kings* (MGM, 1954), *Rogue Cop* (MGM, 1954), *Many Rivers to Cross* (MGM, 1955), *Quentin Durward* (MGM, 1955), *The Last Hunt* (MGM, 1956), *D-Day, the Sixth of June* (20th, 1956), *The Power and the Prize* (MGM, 1956), *Tip on a Dead Jockey* (MGM, 1957), *Saddle the Wind* (MGM, 1958), *The Law and Jake Wade* (MGM, 1958), *Party Girl* (MGM, 1958), *The Hangman* (Par., 1959), *The House of the Seven Hawks* (MGM, 1959), *Killers of Kilimanjaro* (Col., 1960), *The Miracle of the White Stallions* (BV, 1963), *Cattle King* (MGM, 1963), *A House Is Not a Home* (Embassy, 1964), *The Night Walker* (Univ., 1965), *Savage Pampas* (Daca, 1966), *Johnny Tiger* (Univ., 1966), *Where Angels Go...Trouble Follows* (Col., 1968), *The Day the Hot Line Got Hot* (AIP, 1968), *Devil May Care* (Feature Film Corp. of America, 1968), *The Glass Sphinx* (AIP, 1968).

*Unbilled guest appearance

ROD TAYLOR (Rodney Taylor) Born June 11, 1930, Sydney, Australia. Married Mary Hilem (1954), child: Felicia.

English-Language Feature Films: *Long John Silver* (DCA, 1955), *The Virgin Queen* (20th, 1955), *Top Gun* (UA, 1955), *Hell on Frisco Bay* (WB, 1955), *World Without End* (AA, 1956), *The Rack* (MGM,

Richard Anderson, Rock Hudson, Rod Taylor and Henry Silva in *A Gathering of Eagles.*

229

1956), *The Catered Affair* (MGM, 1956), *King of the Coral Sea* (AA, 1956), *Giant* (WB, 1956), *Raintree County* (MGM, 1957), *Step Down to Terror* (Univ., 1958), *Separate Tables* (UA, 1958), *Ask Any Girl* (MGM, 1959), *The Time Machine* (MGM, 1960), *One Hundred and One Dalmatians* (voice only; BV, 1961), *Seven Seas to Calais* (MGM, 1963), *The Birds* (Univ., 1963), *A Gathering of Eagles* (Univ., 1963), *The V.I.P.'s* (MGM, 1963), *Sunday in New York* (MGM, 1963), *Fate Is the Hunter* (20th, 1964), *36 Hours* (MGM, 1964), *Young Cassidy* (MGM, 1965), *Do Not Disturb* (20th, 1965), *The Glass-Bottom Boat* (MGM, 1966), *The Liquidator* (MGM, 1966), *Hotel* (WB, 1967), *Chuka* (Par., 1967), *Dark of the Sun* (MGM, 1968), *A Time for Heroes* (Univ., 1968), *The High Commissioner* (Selmur, 1968), *Nobody Runs Forever* (Rank, 1968).

SHIRLEY TEMPLE (Shirley Jane Temple) Born April 23, 1928, Santa Monica, California. Married John Agar (1945), child: Linda Susan; divorced 1949. Married Charles Black (1950), child: Lori.

Claire Trevor and Shirley Temple in *Baby Take a Bow*.

Feature Films: *The Red-Haired Alibi* (Capitol Film Exchange, 1932), *To the Last Man* (Par., 1933), *Out All Night* (Univ., 1933), *Carolina* (Fox, 1934), *Mandalay* (WB, 1934), *Stand Up and Cheer* (Fox, 1934), *Now I'll Tell* (Fox, 1934), *Change of Heart* (Fox, 1934), *Little Miss Marker* (Par., 1934), *Baby Take a Bow* (Fox, 1934), *Now and Forever* (Par., 1934), *Bright Eyes* (Fox, 1934), *The Little Colonel* (Fox, 1935), *Our Little Girl* (Fox, 1935), *Curly Top* (Fox, 1935), *The Littlest Rebel* (Fox, 1935), *Captain January* (20th, 1936), *Poor Little Rich Girl* (20th, 1936), *Dimples* (20th, 1936), *Stowaway* (20th, 1936), *Wee Willie Winkie* (20th, 1937), *Heidi* (20th, 1937), *Rebecca of Sunnybrook Farm* (20th, 1938), *Little Miss Broadway* (20th, 1938), *Just Around the Corner* (20th, 1938), *The Little Princess* (20th, 1939), *Susannah of the Mounties* (20th, 1939), *The Blue Bird* (20th, 1940), *Young People* (20th, 1940), *Kathleen* (MGM, 1941), *Miss Annie Rooney* (UA, 1942), *Since You Went Away* (UA, 1944), *I'll Be Seeing You* (UA, 1944), *Kiss and Tell* (Col., 1945), *Honeymoon* (RKO, 1947), *The Bachelor and the Bobby-Soxer* (RKO, 1947), *That Hagen Girl* (WB, 1947), *Fort Apache* (RKO, 1948), *Mr. Belvedere Goes to College* (20th, 1949), *Adventure in Baltimore* (RKO, 1949), *Story of Seabiscuit* (WB, 1949), *A Kiss for Corliss* (UA, 1949).

PHYLLIS THAXTER (Phyllis St. Felix Thaxter) Born November 20, 1920, Portland, Maine. Married James Aubrey (1944), children: Susan, James; divorced 1962. Married Gilbert Lea (1962).

Hank Daniels, Phyllis Thaxter and Sharon McManus in *Bewitched*.

Feature Films: *Thirty Seconds Over Tokyo* (MGM, 1944), *Bewitched* (MGM, 1945), *Weekend at the Waldorf* (MGM, 1945), *The Sea of Grass* (MGM, 1947), *Living in a Big Way* (MGM, 1947), *The Sign of the Ram* (Col., 1948), *Tenth Avenue Angel* (MGM, 1948), *Blood on the Moon* (RKO, 1948), *Act of Violence* (MGM, 1948), *No Man of Her Own* (Par., 1950), *The Breaking Point* (WB, 1950), *Fort Worth* (WB, 1951), *Jim Thorpe—All American* (WB, 1951), *Come Fill the Cup* (WB, 1951), *She's Working Her Way Through College* (WB, 1952), *Springfield Rifle* (WB, 1952), *Operation Secret* (WB, 1952), *Women's Prison* (Col., 1955), *Man Afraid* (Univ., 1957), *The World of Henry Orient* (UA, 1964).

GENE TIERNEY (Gene Eliza Taylor Tierney) Born November 20, 1920, Brooklyn, New York. Married Oleg Cassini (1941), children: Daria, Christina; divorced 1952. Married W. Howard Lee (1960).

Gene Tierney, Tyrone Power and Isabel Randolph in *That Wonderful Urge*.

Feature Films: *Return of Frank James* (20th, 1940), *Hudson's Bay* (20th, 1940), *Tobacco Road* (20th, 1941), *Belle Starr* (20th, 1941), *Sundown* (UA, 1941), *The Shanghai Gesture* (UA, 1941), *Son of Fury* (20th, 1942), *Rings on Her Fingers* (20th, 1942), *Thunder Birds* (20th, 1942), *China Girl* (20th, 1942), *Heaven Can Wait* (20th, 1943), *Laura* (20th, 1944), *A Bell for Adano* (20th, 1945), *Leave Her to Heaven* (20th, 1945), *Dragonwyck* (20th, 1946), *The Razor's Edge* (20th, 1946), *The Ghost and Mrs. Muir* (20th, 1947), *The Iron Curtain* (20th, 1948), *That Wonderful Urge* (20th, 1948), *Whirlpool* (20th, 1949), *Night and the City* (20th, 1950), *Where the Sidewalk Ends* (20th, 1950), *The Mating Season* (Par., 1951), *On the Riviera* (20th, 1951), *The Secret of Convict Lake* (20th, 1951), *Close to My Heart* (WB, 1951), *Way of a Gaucho* (20th, 1952), *Plymouth Adventure* (MGM, 1952), *Never Let Me Go* (MGM, 1953), *Personal Affair* (UA, 1954), *Black Widow* (20th, 1954),

The Egyptian (20th, 1954), *The Left Hand of God* (20th, 1955), *Advise and Consent* (Col., 1962), *Toys in the Attic* (UA, 1963), *The Pleasure Seekers* (20th, 1964).

GENEVIEVE TOBIN Born November 29, 1904, New York, New York. Married William Keighley (1938).

Adolphe Menjou, Genevieve Tobin and Mary Astor in *Easy to Love.*

Feature Films: *A Lady Surrenders* (Univ., 1930), *Free Love* (Univ., 1930), *Seed* (Univ., 1931), *Up for Murder* (Univ., 1931), *Woman Pursued* (RKO, 1931), *The Gay Diplomat* (RKO, 1931), *One Hour With You* (Par., 1932), *Hollywood Speaks* (Col., 1932), *Cohens and Kellys in Hollywood* (Univ., 1932), *Infernal Machine* (Fox, 1933), *Perfect Understanding* (UA, 1933), *Pleasure Cruise* (Fox, 1933), *The Wrecker* (Col., 1933), *Goodbye Again* (WB, 1933), *I Loved a Woman* (WB, 1933), *Golden Harvest* (Par., 1933), *The Ninth Guest* (Col., 1934), *Easy to Love* (WB, 1934), *Dark Hazard* (WB, 1934), *Uncertain Lady* (Univ., 1934), *Success at Any Price* (RKO, 1934), *Kiss and Make Up* (Par., 1934), *By Your Leave* (RKO, 1934), *The Woman in Red* (WB, 1935), *The Goose and the Gander* (WB, 1935), *The Case of the Lucky Legs* (WB, 1935), *Here's to Romance* (Fox, 1935), *Broadway Hostess* (WB, 1935), *The Petrified Forest* (WB, 1936), *Snowed Under* (WB, 1936), *The Great Gambini* (Par., 1937), *The Duke Comes Back* (Rep., 1937), *The Man in the Mirror* (Twickenham, 1937), *Kate Plus Ten* (Wainwright-GFD, 1938), *Dramatic School* (MGM, 1938), *Zaza* (Par., 1939), *Yes, My Darling Daughter* (WB, 1939), *Our Neighbors the Carters* (Par., 1939), *No Time for Comedy* (WB, 1940).

THELMA TODD Born July 29, 1905, Lawrence, Massachusetts. Married Pasquale Di Cicco (1932); divorced 1934. Died December 16, 1935.

Sound Feature Films: *The Haunted House* (WB, 1928), *Naughty Baby* (WB, 1929), *Seven Footprints to Satan* (WB, 1929), *Bachelor Girl* (Col., 1929), *Careers* (WB, 1929), *House of Horror* (WB, 1929), *Her Private Life* (WB, 1929), *Follow Through* (Par., 1930), *Her Man* (Pathé, 1930), *Command Performance* (Tif., 1930), *Aloha* (Tif., 1930), *Swanee River* (World Wide, 1930), *No Limit* (Par., 1930), *The Hot Heiress* (WB, 1931), *Corsair* (UA, 1931),* *Broad-Minded* (WB, 1931), *Monkey Business* (Par., 1931), *The Maltese Falcon* (WB, 1931), *Beyond Victory* (Pathé, 1931), *This Is the Night* (Par., 1932), *Speak Easily* (MGM, 1932), *Horse Feathers* (Par., 1932), *Klondike* (Mon., 1932), *Big Timer* (Col., 1932), *Call Her Savage* (Fox, 1932), *Air Hostess* (Col., 1933), *Deception* (Col., 1933), *Devil's Brother* (MGM, 1933), *Cheating Blondes* (Capitol Film Exchange, 1933), *Mary Stevens, M.D.* (WB, 1933), *Counsellor at Law* (Univ., 1933), *Sitting Pretty* (Par., 1933), *Son of a Sailor* (WB, 1933), *Palooka* (UA, 1934), *Hips, Hips, Hooray* (RKO, 1934),

Thelma Todd, Chico and Groucho Marx in *Horse Feathers.*

Bottoms Up (Fox, 1934), *The Poor Rich* (Univ., 1934), *Cockeyed Cavaliers* (RKO, 1934), *Take the Stand* (Liberty, 1934), *Lightning Strikes Twice* (RKO, 1935), *After the Dance* (Col., 1935), *Two for Tonight* (Par., 1935), *The Bohemian Girl* (MGM, 1936).

　　*Billed as Alison Lloyd

SIDNEY TOLER Born April 28, 1874, Warrenburg, Missouri. Married Viva Tattersal. Died February 12, 1947.

Feature Films: *Madame X* (MGM, 1929), *White Shoulders* (RKO, 1931), *Strictly Dishonorable* (Univ., 1931), *Strangers in Love* (Par., 1932), *Is My Face Red?* (RKO, 1932), *Radio Patrol* (Univ., 1932), *Speak Easily* (MGM, 1932), *Blondie of the Follies* (MGM, 1932), *Blonde Venus* (Par., 1932), *Phantom President* (Par., 1932), *Tom Brown of Culver* (Univ., 1932), *Billion Dollar Scandal* (Par., 1933), *King of the Jungle* (Par., 1933), *He Learned About Women* (Par., 1933), *The Narrow Corner* (WB, 1933), *Way to Love* (Par., 1933), *Dark Hazard* (WB, 1934), *Massacre* (WB, 1934), *Spitfire* (RKO, 1934), *The Trumpet Blows* (Par., 1934), *Here Comes the Groom* (Par., 1934), *Operator 13* (MGM, 1934), *Registered Nurse* (WB, 1934), *Upper World* (WB, 1934), *The Daring Young Man* (Fox, 1935), *Call of the Wild* (UA, 1935), *Orchids to You* (Fox, 1935), *Champagne for Breakfast* (Col., 1935), *This Is the Life* (Fox, 1935), *The Three Godfathers* (MGM, 1936), *Give Us This Night* (Par., 1936), *The Longest Night* (MGM, 1936), *The Gorgeous Hussy* (MGM, 1936), *Our Relations* (MGM, 1936), *That Certain Woman* (WB, 1937), *Double Wedding* (MGM, 1937), *Gold Is Where You Find It* (WB, 1938), *Wide Open Faces* (Col., 1938), *One Wild Night* (20th, 1938), *Charlie Chan in Honolulu* (20th, 1938), *Up the River* (20th, 1938), *Mysterious Rider* (Par., 1938), *If I Were King* (Par., 1938), *King of Chinatown* (Par., 1939), *Disbarred* (Par., 1939), *Heritage of the Desert* (Par., 1939), *The Kid From Kokomo* (WB, 1939), *Charlie Chan in Reno* (20th, 1939), *Charlie Chan at Treasure Island* (20th, 1939), *Law of the Pampas* (Par., 1939), *Charlie Chan in City in Darkness*

Sidney Toler, Joseph Crehan and Gloria Warren in *Dangerous Money.*

Franchot Tone, Joan Crawford and Robert Young in *Today We Live*.

(20th, 1939), *Charlie Chan in Panama* (20th, 1940), *Charlie Chan's Murder Cruise* (20th, 1940), *Charlie Chan at the Wax Museum* (20th, 1940), *Murder Over New York* (20th, 1940), *Dead Men Tell* (20th, 1941), *Charlie Chan in Rio* (20th, 1941), *Castle in the Desert* (20th, 1942), *A Night to Remember* (Col., 1943), *White Savage* (Univ., 1943), *Isle of Forgotten Sins* (PRC, 1943), *Charlie Chan in the Secret Service* (Mon., 1944), *The Chinese Cat* (Mon., 1944), *Black Magic* (Mon., 1944), *The Scarlet Clue* (Mon., 1945), *It's in the Bag* (UA, 1945), *The Jade Mask* (Mon., 1945), *The Shanghai Cobra* (Mon., 1945), *The Red Dragon* (Mon., 1945), *Dark Alibi* (Mon., 1946), *The Trap* (Mon., 1947).

FRANCHOT TONE (Stanislas Pascal Franchot Tone) Born February 27, 1905, Niagara Falls, New York. Married Joan Crawford (1935); divorced 1939. Married Jean Wallace (1941); divorced 1948. Married Barbara Payton (1951); divorced 1952. Married Dolores Dorn-Heft (1956); divorced 1959.

Feature Films: *The Wiser Sex* (Par., 1932), *Gabriel Over the White House* (MGM, 1933), *Dancing Lady* (MGM, 1933), *Today We Live* (MGM, 1933), *Stage Mother* (MGM, 1933), *Bombshell* (MGM, 1933), *The Stranger's Return* (MGM, 1933), *Midnight Mary* (MGM, 1933), *Moulin Rouge* (UA, 1934), *The World Moves On* (Fox, 1934), *Straight Is the Way* (MGM, 1934), *Gentlemen Are Born* (WB, 1934), *The Girl From Missouri* (MGM, 1934), *Sadie McKee* (MGM, 1934), *Lives of a Bengal Lancer* (Par., 1935), *Mutiny on the Bounty* (MGM, 1935), *Reckless* (MGM, 1935), *No More Ladies* (MGM, 1935), *Dangerous* (WB, 1935), *One New York Night* (MGM, 1935), *Exclusive Story* (MGM, 1936), *The King Steps Out* (Col., 1936), *The Unguarded Hour* (MGM, 1936), *The Gorgeous Hussy* (MGM, 1936), *Between Two Women* (MGM, 1937), *The Bride Wore Red* (MGM, 1937), *They Gave Him a Gun* (MGM, 1937), *Quality Street* (RKO, 1937), *Three Comrades* (MGM, 1938), *Love Is a Headache* (MGM, 1938), *Man-Proof* (MGM, 1938), *Three Loves Has Nancy* (MGM, 1938), *Thunder Afloat* (MGM, 1939), *Fast and Furious* (MGM, 1939), *Trail of the Vigilantes* (Univ., 1940), *Nice Girl?* (Univ., 1941), *Highly Irregular* (Col., 1941), *She Knew All the Answers* (Col., 1941), *Virginia* (Par., 1941), *Star Spangled Rhythm* (Par., 1942), *His Butler's Sister* (Univ., 1943), *This Woman Is Mine* (Univ., 1943), *Five Graves to Cairo* (Par., 1943), *The Hour Before Dawn* (Par., 1944), *Phantom Lady* (Univ., 1944), *Dark Waters* (UA, 1944), *Her Husband's Affair* (Col., 1947), *Every Girl Should Be Married* (RKO, 1948), *I Love Trouble* (Col., 1948), *Jigsaw* (UA, 1949), *The Man on the Eiffel Tower* (RKO, 1949), *Without Honor* (UA, 1949), *Here Comes the Groom* (Par., 1951), *Uncle Vanya* (Continental Distributing, 1958), *Advise and Consent* (Col., 1962), *In Harm's Way* (Par., 1965), *Mickey One* (Col., 1965).

AUDREY TOTTER Born December 20, 1918, Joliet, Illinois. Married Leo Fred (1952), child: Mea.

Feature Films: *Main Street After Dark* (MGM, 1944), *Dangerous*

Brian Donlevy and Audrey Totter in *The Beginning or the End*.

Partners (MGM, 1945), *Her Highness and the Bellboy* (MGM, 1945), *The Sailor Takes a Wife* (MGM, 1945), *Adventure* (MGM, 1945), *The Hidden Eye* (MGM, 1945), *The Secret Heart* MGM, 1946), *The Postman Always Rings Twice* (MGM, 1946), *The Cockeyed Miracle* (MGM, 1946), *Lady in the Lake* (MGM, 1946), *The Beginning or the End* (MGM, 1947), *The Unsuspected* (WB, 1947), *High Wall* (MGM, 1947), *Tenth Avenue Angel* (MGM, 1948), *The Saxon Charm* (Univ., 1948), *The Set-Up* (RKO, 1949), *Alias Nick Beal* (Par., 1949), *Any Number Can Play* (MGM, 1949), *Tension* (MGM, 1949), *Under the Gun* (Univ., 1950), *The Blue Veil* (RKO, 1951), *FBI Girl* (Lip., 1951), *The Sellout* (MGM, 1951), *Assignment—Paris* (Col., 1952), *My Pal Gus* (20th, 1952), *The Woman They Almost Lynched* (Rep., 1953), *Man in the Dark* (Col., 1953), *Cruisin' Down the River* (Col., 1953), *Mission Over Korea* (Col., 1953), *Champ for a Day* (Rep., 1953), *Massacre Canyon* (Col., 1954), *A Bullet for Joey* (UA, 1955), *Women's Prison* (Col., 1955), *The Vanishing American* (Rep., 1955), *Ghost Diver* (20th, 1957), *Jet Attack* (AIP, 1958), *Man or Gun* (Rep., 1958), *The Carpetbaggers* (Par., 1964), *Harlow* (Magna, 1965), *Chubasco* (WB-7 Arts, 1968).).

LEE TRACY Born April 14, 1898, Atlanta, Georgia. Married Helen Thomas (1938).

Feature Films: *Big Time* (Fox, 1929), *Born Reckless* (Fox, 1930), *Liliom* (Fox, 1930), *She Got What She Wanted* (Tif. 1930), *The Strange Love of Molly Louvain* (WB, 1932), *Love Is a Racket* (WB, 1932), *Doctor X* (WB, 1932), *Blessed Event* (WB, 1932), *Washington Merry-Go-Round* (Col., 1932), *Night Mayor* (Col., 1932), *Half-Naked Truth* (RKO, 1932), *Clear All Wires* (MGM, 1933), *Private Jones* (Univ., 1933), *The Nuisance* (MGM, 1933), *Dinner at Eight* (MGM, 1933), *Turn Back the Clock* (MGM, 1933), *Bombshell* (MGM, 1933), *Advice to the Lovelorn* (UA, 1933), *I'll Tell the World* (Univ., 1934), *You Belong to Me* (Par., 1934), *Lemon Drop Kid* (Par., 1934), *Carnival* (Col., 1935), *Two Fisted* (Par., 1935), *Sutter's Gold* (Univ., 1936), *Wanted—Jane Turner* (RKO, 1936), *Criminal Lawyer* (RKO, 1937), *Behind the Headlines* (RKO, 1937), *Crashing Hollywood* (RKO, 1938), *Fixer Dugan* (RKO, 1939), *Spellbinder* (RKO, 1939), *Millionaires in*

Benita Hume and Lee Tracy in *Clear All Wires*.

Spencer Tracy and Gladys George in *They Gave Him a Gun*.

Prison (RKO, 1940), *The Payoff* (PRC, 1942), *Power of the Press* (Col., 1943), *Betrayal from the East* (RKO, 1945), *I'll Tell the World* (Univ., 1945), *High Tide* (Mon., 1947), *The Best Man* (UA, 1964).

SPENCER TRACY Born April 5, 1900, Milwaukee, Wisconsin. Married Louise Treadwell (1928), children: John, Susan. Died June 10, 1967.

Feature Films: *Up the River* (Fox, 1930), *Quick Millions* (Fox, 1931), *Six Cylinder Love* (Fox, 1931), *Goldie* (Fox, 1931), *She Wanted a Millionaire* (Fox, 1932), *Sky Devils* (UA, 1932), *Disorderly Conduct* (Fox, 1932), *Young America* (Fox, 1932), *Society Girl* (Fox, 1932), *Painted Woman* (Fox, 1932), *Me and My Gal* (Fox, 1932), *20,000 Years in Sing Sing* (WB, 1933), *Face in the Sky* (Fox, 1933), *The Power and the Glory* (Fox, 1933), *Shanghai Madness* (Fox, 1933), *The Mad Game* (Fox, 1933), *Man's Castle* (Col., 1933), *Looking for Trouble* (UA, 1934), *The Show-Off* (MGM, 1934), *Bottoms Up* (Fox, 1934), *Now I'll Tell* (Fox, 1934), *Marie Galante* (Fox, 1934), *It's a Small World* (Fox, 1935), *Murder Man* (MGM, 1935), *Dante's Inferno* (Fox, 1935), *Whipsaw* (MGM, 1935), *Riffraff* (MGM, 1936), *Fury* (MGM, 1936), *San Francisco* (MGM, 1936), *Libeled Lady* (MGM, 1936), *Captains Courageous* (MGM, 1937), *They Gave Him a Gun* (MGM, 1937), *The Big City* (MGM, 1937), *Mannequin* (MGM, 1938), *Test Pilot* (MGM, 1938), *Boys Town* (MGM, 1938), *Stanley and Livingstone* (20th, 1939), *I Take This Woman* (MGM, 1940), *Northwest Passage* (MGM, 1940), *Edison the Man* (MGM, 1940), *Boom Town* (MGM, 1940), *Men of Boys Town* (MGM, 1941), *Dr. Jekyll and Mr. Hyde* (MGM, 1941), *Woman of the Year* (MGM, 1942), *Tortilla Flat* (MGM, 1942), *Keeper of the Flame* (MGM, 1942), *A Guy Named Joe* (MGM, 1943), *The Seventh Cross* (MGM, 1944), *Thirty Seconds Over Tokyo* (MGM, 1944), *Without Love* (MGM, 1945), *The Sea of Grass* (MGM, 1947), *Cass Timberlane* (MGM, 1947), *State of the Union* (MGM, 1948), *Edward, My Son* (MGM, 1949), *Adam's Rib* (MGM, 1949), *Malaya* (MGM, 1949), *Father of the Bride* (MGM, 1950), *Father's Little Dividend* (MGM, 1951), *The People Against O'Hara* (MGM, 1951), *Pat and Mike* (MGM, 1952), *Plymouth Adventure* (MGM, 1952), *The Actress* (MGM, 1954), *Broken Lance* (20th, 1954), *Bad Day at Black Rock* (MGM, 1955), *The Mountain* (Par., 1956), *The Desk Set* (20th, 1957), *The Old Man and the Sea* (WB, 1958), *The Last Hurrah* (Col., 1958), *Inherit the Wind* (UA, 1960), *The Devil at 4 O'Clock* (Col., 1961), *Judgment at Nuremberg* (UA, 1961), *How the West Was Won* (MGM, 1963), *It's a Mad, Mad, Mad, Mad World* (UA, 1963), *Guess Who's Coming to Dinner* (Col., 1967).

ARTHUR TREACHER (Arthur Veary) Born July 23, 1894, Brighton, England. Married Virginia Taylor (1940).

Feature Films: *Battle of Paris* (Par., 1929), *Alice in Wonderland* (Par., 1933), *Fashions of 1934* (WB, 1934), *Desirable* (WB, 1934), *Viva Villa!* (MGM, 1934), *Madame Du Barry* (WB, 1934), *The Captain Hates the Sea* (Col., 1934), *Here Comes the Groom* (Par., 1934), *Holly-*

Eugene Pallette and Arthur Treacher in *She Had to Eat*.

wood Party (MGM, 1934), *Forsaking All Others* (MGM, 1934), *Bordertown* (WB, 1935), *No More Ladies* (MGM, 1935), *David Copperfield* (MGM, 1935), *Cardinal Richelieu* (UA, 1935), *I Live My Life* (MGM, 1935), *Personal Maid's Secret* (WB, 1935), *Bright Lights* (WB, 1935), *Curly Top* (Fox, 1935), *Remember Last Night?* (Univ., 1935), *Let's Live Tonight* (Col., 1935), *The Daring Young Man* (Fox, 1935), *Splendor* (UA, 1935), *Hitch-Hike Lady* (Rep., 1935), *A Midsummer Night's Dream* (WB, 1935), *Go Into Your Dance* (WB, 1935), *The Winning Ticket* (MGM, 1935), *Stowaway* (20th, 1936), *Anything Goes* (Par., 1936), *Thank You, Jeeves* (20th, 1936), *Heidi* (20th, 1937), *Mad About Music* (Univ., 1938), *The Little Princess* (20th, 1939), *Brother Rat and a Baby* (WB, 1940), *Star Spangled Rhythm* (Par., 1942), *The Amazing Mrs. Holliday* (Univ., 1943), *Forever and a Day* (RKO, 1943), *Chip Off the Old Block* (Univ., 1944), *National Velvet* (MGM, 1944), *Delightfully Dangerous* (UA, 1945), *The Countess of Monte Cristo* (Univ., 1948), *That Midnight Kiss* (MGM, 1949), *Mary Poppins* (BV, 1964).

CLAIRE TREVOR (Claire Wemlinger) Born March 8, 1912, Bensonhurst, New York. Married Clark Andrews (1938); divorced 1942. Married Cylos Dunsmoore (1943), child: Charles; divorced 1947. Married Milton Bren (1948).

Feature Films: *Life in the Raw* (Fox, 1933), *The Last Trail* (Fox, 1933), *The Mad Game* (Fox, 1933), *Jimmy and Sally* (Fox, 1933), *Hold That Girl* (Fox, 1934), *Wild Gold* (Fox, 1934), *Baby Take a Bow* (Fox, 1934), *Elinor Norton* (Fox, 1934), *Spring Tonic* (Fox, 1935), *Black Sheep* (Fox, 1935), *Dante's Inferno* (Fox, 1935), *Navy Wife* (Fox, 1935), *My Marriage* (20th, 1936), *The Song and Dance Man* (20th, 1936), *Human Cargo* (20th, 1936), *To Mary—With Love* (20th, 1936), *Star for a Night* (20th, 1936), *15 Maiden Lane* (20th, 1936), *Career Woman* (20th, 1936), *Time Out for Romance* (20th, 1937), *King of Gamblers* (Par., 1937), *One Mile From Heaven* (20th, 1937), *Dead End* (UA, 1937), *Second Honeymoon* (20th, 1937), *Big Town Girl* (20th, 1937), *Walking Down Broadway* (20th, 1938), *Two of a Kind* (20th, 1938), *The Amazing Dr. Clitterhouse* (WB, 1938), *Valley of the Giants* (WB, 1938), *Stagecoach* (UA, 1939), *I Stole a Million* (Univ., 1939), *Alle-*

Claire Trevor and Fred MacMurray in *Borderline*.

gheny Uprising (RKO, 1939), *Dark Command* (Rep., 1940), *Texas* (Col., 1941), *Honky Tonk* (MGM, 1941), *The Adventures of Martin Eden* (Col., 1942), *Crossroads* (MGM, 1942), *Street of Chance* (Par., 1942), *The Desperadoes* (Col., 1943), *Good Luck, Mr. Yates* (Col., 1943), *Woman of the Town* (UA, 1943), *Murder, My Sweet* (RKO, 1944), *Johnny Angel* (RKO, 1945), *Crack-Up* (RKO, 1946), *The Bachelor's Daughters* (UA, 1946), *Born to Kill* (RKO, 1947), *Raw Deal* (EL, 1948), *Key Largo* (WB, 1948), *The Velvet Touch* (RKO, 1948), *The Babe Ruth Story* (AA, 1948), *The Lucky Stiff* (UA, 1949), *Borderline* (Univ., 1950), *Best of the Badmen* (RKO, 1951), *Hard, Fast and Beautiful* (RKO, 1951), *Hoodlum Empire* (Rep., 1952), *My Man and I* (MGM, 1952), *Stop, You're Killing Me* (WB, 1952), *The Stranger Wore a Gun* (Col., 1953), *The High and the Mighty* (WB, 1954), *Man Without a Star* (Univ., 1955), *Lucy Gallant* (Par., 1955), *The Mountain* (Par., 1956), *Marjorie Morningstar* (WB, 1958), *Two Weeks in Another Town* (MGM, 1962), *The Stripper* (20th, 1963), *How to Murder Your Wife* (UA, 1965).

SONNY TUFTS (Bowen Charleston Tufts III) Born July 16, 1912, Boston, Massachusetts. Married Barbara Dare (1937); divorced.

Olivia De Havilland and Sonny Tufts in *Government Girl.*

Feature Films: *So Proudly We Hail!* (Par., 1943), *Government Girl* (RKO, 1943), *I Love a Soldier* (Par., 1944), *In the Meantime, Darling* (20th, 1944), *Here Come the Waves* (Par., 1944), *Bring on the Girls* (Par., 1945), *Duffy's Tavern* (Par., 1945), *Miss Susie Slagle's* (Par., 1945), *The Well-Groomed Bride* (Par., 1946), *The Virginian* (Par., 1946), *Cross My Heart* (Par., 1946), *Swell Guy* (Univ., 1946), *Easy Come, Easy Go* (Par., 1947), *Blaze of Noon* (Par., 1947), *Variety Girl* (Par., 1947), *The Untamed Breed* (Col., 1948), *The Crooked Way* (UA, 1949), *Easy Living* (RKO, 1949), *The Gift Horse* ("Glory at Sea"— Compton Bennett, 1952), *Run for the Hills* (Jack Broder, 1953), *No Escape* (UA, 1953), *Cat Women of the Moon* (Astor, 1953), *Serpent Island* (Astor, 1954), *The Seven Year Itch* (20th, 1955), *Come Next Spring* (Rep., 1956), *The Parson and the Outlaw* (Col., 1957), *Town Tamer* (Par., 1965), *Cottonpickin' Chickenpickers* (Southeastern Pictures, 1967).

LANA TURNER (Julia Jean Mildred Frances Turner) Born February 8, 1920, Wallace, Idaho. Married Artie Shaw (1940); divorced 1941. Married Stephen Crane (1942), child: Cheryl; divorced 1944. Married Bob Topping (1948); divorced 1952. Married Lex Barker (1953); divorced 1957. Married Fred May (1960); divorced 1962. Married Robert Eaton (1965).

Feature Films: *A Star Is Born* (UA, 1937), *They Won't Forget* (WB, 1937), *The Great Garrick* (WB, 1937), *The Adventures of Marco Polo* (UA, 1938), *Four's a Crowd* (WB, 1938), *Love Finds Andy Hardy* (MGM, 1938), *Rich Man, Poor Girl* (MGM, 1938), *Dramatic School* (MGM, 1938), *Calling Dr. Kildare* (MGM, 1939), *These Glamour

Richard Carlson, Lana Turner and Monty Woolley in *Dancing Co-Ed.*

Girls (MGM, 1939), *Dancing Co-ed* (MGM, 1939), *Two Girls on Broadway* (MGM, 1940), *We Who Are Young* (MGM, 1940), *Ziegfeld Girl* (MGM, 1941), *Dr. Jekyll and Mr. Hyde* (MGM, 1941), *Honky Tonk* (MGM, 1941), *Johnny Eager* (MGM, 1941), *Somewhere I'll Find You* (MGM, 1942), *The Youngest Profession* (MGM, 1943), *Slightly Dangerous* (MGM, 1943), *Du Barry Was a Lady* (MGM, 1943),* *Marriage Is a Private Affair* (MGM, 1944), *Keep Your Powder Dry* (MGM, 1945), *Weekend at the Waldorf* (MGM, 1945), *The Postman Always Ring Twice* (MGM, 1946), *Green Dolphin Street* (MGM, 1947), *Cass Timberlane* (MGM, 1947), *Homecoming* (MGM, 1948), *The Three Musketeers* (MGM, 1948), *A Life of Her Own* (MGM, 1950), *Mr. Imperium* (MGM, 1951), *The Merry Widow* (MGM, 1952), *The Bad and the Beautiful* (MGM, 1952), *Latin Lovers* (MGM, 1953), *Flame and the Flesh* (MGM, 1954), *Betrayed* (MGM, 1954), *The Prodigal* (MGM, 1955), *The Sea Chase* (WB, 1955), *The Rains of Ranchipur* (20th, 1955), *Diane* (MGM, 1955), *Peyton Place* (20th, 1957), *The Lady Takes a Flyer* (Univ., 1958), *Another Time, Another Place* (Par., 1958), *Imitation of Life* (Univ., 1959), *Portrait in Black* (Univ., 1960), *By Love Possessed* (UA, 1961), *Bachelor in Paradise* (MGM, 1961), *Who's Got the Action?* (Par., 1962), *Love Has Many Faces* (Col., 1965), *Madame X* (Univ., 1966).

*Unbilled guest appearance

JO VAN FLEET Born December 30, 1919, Oakland, California. Married William Bales (1946), child: Michael.

James Dean and Jo Van Fleet in *East of Eden.*

Feature Films: *East of Eden* (WB, 1955), *The Rose Tattoo* (Par., 1955), *I'll Cry Tomorrow* (MGM, 1955), *The King and Four Queens* (UA, 1956), *Gunfight at the O. K. Corral* (Par., 1957), *This Angry Age* (Col., 1958), *Wild River* (20th, 1960), *Cool Hand Luke* (WB-7 Arts), *I Love You, Alice B. Toklas* (WB-7 Arts, 1968).

LUPE VELEZ (Guadeloupe Velez de Villalobos) Born July 18, 1908, San Luis de Potosí, Mexico. Married Johnny Weissmuller (1933); divorced 1938. Died December 14, 1944.

Lupe Velez and Leon Errol in *The Girl From Mexico*.

Sound Feature Films: *Lady of the Pavements* (UA, 1929), *Tiger Rose* (WB, 1929), *Wolf Song* (Par., 1929), *Where East Is East* (MGM, 1929), *The Storm* (Univ., 1930), *Hell Harbor* (UA, 1930), *East Is West* (Univ., 1930), *Resurrection* (Univ., 1931), *The Squaw Man* (MGM, 1931), *Cuban Love Song* (MGM, 1931), *The Broken Wing* (Par., 1932), *Kongo* (MGM, 1932), *The Half-Naked Truth* (RKO, 1932), *Hot Pepper* (Fox, 1933), *Mr. Broadway* (Broadway-Hollywood Productions, 1933), *Laughing Boy* (MGM, 1934), *Palooka* (UA, 1934), *Hollywood Party* (MGM, 1934), *Strictly Dynamite* (RKO, 1934), *The Morals of Marcus* (Twickenham, 1936), *Gypsy Melody* (Associated British Pathé, 1936), *High Flyers* (RKO, 1937), *Mad About Money* ("He Loved an Actress" —British Lion, 1938), *Girl From Mexico* (RKO, 1939), *Mexican Spitfire* (RKO, 1939), *Mexican Spitfire Out West* (RKO, 1940), *Six Lessons From Madame La Zonga* (Univ., 1941), *Mexican Spitfire's Baby* (RKO, 1941), *Playmates* (RKO, 1941), *Honolulu Lu* (Col., 1941), *Mexican Spitfire at Sea* (RKO, 1942), *Mexican Spitfire Sees a Ghost* (RKO, 1942), *Mexican Spitfire's Elephant* (RKO, 1942), *Ladies' Day* (RKO, 1943), *Mexican Spitfire's Blessed Event* (RKO, 1943), *Redhead From Manhattan* (Col., 1943).

VERA-ELLEN (Vera-Ellen Westmeyr Rohe) Born February 16, 1926, Cincinnati, Ohio. Married Robert Hightower (1945); divorced 1946. Married Victor Rothschild (1954).

Feature Films: *Wonder Man* (RKO, 1945), *The Kid From Brooklyn* (RKO, 1946), *Three Little Girls in Blue* (20th, 1946), *Carnival in Costa Rica* (20th, 1947), *Words and Music* (MGM, 1948), *Love Happy* (UA, 1949), *On the Town* (MGM, 1949), *Three Little Words* (MGM, 1950),

Tony Martin and Vera-Ellen in *Let's Be Happy*.

Happy Go Lovely (RKO, 1951), *The Belle of New York* (MGM, 1952), *Call Me Madam* (20th, 1953), *The Big Leaguer* (MGM, 1953), *White Christmas* (Par., 1954), *Let's Be Happy* (AA, 1957).

ROBERT WAGNER Born February 10, 1930, Detroit, Michigan. Married Natalie Wood (1957); divorced 1963. Married Marion Donen (1963), child: Katherine.

Robert Wagner and Steve McQueen in *The War Lover*.

Feature Films: *The Happy Years* (MGM, 1950), *Halls of Montezuma* (20th, 1950), *The Frogmen* (20th, 1951), *Let's Make It Legal* (20th, 1951), *With a Song in My Heart* (20th, 1952), *Stars and Stripes Forever* (20th, 1952), *What Price Glory* (20th, 1952), *The Silver Whip* (20th, 1953), *Titanic* (20th, 1953), *Beneath the 12-Mile Reef* (20th, 1953), *Prince Valiant* (20th, 1954), *Broken Lance* (20th, 1954), *White Feather* (20th, 1955), *A Kiss Before Dying* (UA, 1956), *The Mountain* (Par., 1956), *Between Heaven and Hell* (20th, 1956), *The True Story of Jesse James* (20th, 1957), *Stopover Tokyo* (20th, 1957), *The Hunters* (20th, 1958), *Mardi Gras* (20th, 1958), *In Love and War* (20th, 1958), *Say One for Me* (20th, 1959), *All the Fine Young Cannibals* (MGM, 1960), *Sail a Crooked Ship* (Col., 1961), *The Longest Day* (20th, 1962), *The War Lover* (Col., 1962), *The Condemned of Altona* (20th, 1963), *The Pink Panther* (UA, 1964), *Harper* (WB, 1966), *Banning* (Univ., 1967), *The Biggest Bundle of Them All* (MGM, 1968), *Don't Just Stand There* (Univ., 1968).

ROBERT WALKER (Robert Hudson Walker) Born October 13, 1914, Salt Lake City, Utah. Married Jennifer Jones (1939), children: Robert, Michael; divorced 1945. Married Barbara Ford (1948). Died August 28, 1951.

Feature Films: *Winter Carnival* (UA, 1939), *Bataan* (MGM, 1943), *Madame Curie* (MGM, 1943), *See Here, Private Hargrove* (MGM, 1944), *Since You Went Away* (UA, 1944), *Thirty Seconds Over Tokyo*

Henry Daniell and Robert Walker in *Song of Love*.

(MGM, 1944), *The Clock* (MGM, 1945), *Her Highness and the Bellboy* (MGM, 1945), *What Next, Corporal Hargrove?* (MGM, 1945), *The Sailor Takes a Wife* (MGM, 1945), *Till the Clouds Roll By* (MGM, 1946), *The Sea of Grass* (MGM, 1947), *The Beginning or the End* (MGM, 1947), *Song of Love* (MGM, 1947), *One Touch of Venus* (Univ., 1948), *Please Believe Me* (MGM, 1950), *The Skipper Surprised His Wife* (MGM, 1950), *Vengeance Valley* (MGM, 1951), *Strangers on a Train* (WB, 1951), *My Son, John* (Par., 1952).

Maurice Manson, Eli Wallach and Edward G. Robinson in *Seven Thieves*.

ELI WALLACH Born December 7, 1915, Brooklyn, New York. Married Anne Jackson (1948), children: Peter, Roberta, Katherine.

Feature Films: *Baby Doll* (WB, 1956), *The Lineup* (Col., 1958), *Seven Thieves* (20th, 1960), *The Magnificent Seven* (UA, 1960), *The Misfits* (UA, 1961), *Hemingway's Adventures of a Young Man* (20th, 1962), *How the West Was Won* (MGM, 1963), *The Victors* (Col., 1963), *Act One* (WB, 1963), *The Moon Spinners* (BV, 1964), *Kisses for My President* (WB, 1964), *Lord Jim* (Col., 1965), *Genghis Khan* (Col., 1965), *How to Steal a Million* (20th, 1966), *The Tiger Makes Out* (Col., 1967), *The Good, the Bad and the Ugly* (UA, 1967), *MacKenna's Gold* (Col., 1968), *A Lovely Way to Die* (Univ., 1968), *How to Save a Marriage—And Ruin Your Life* (Col., 1968).

LUCILE WATSON Born May 27, 1879, Ottawa, Canada. Married Rockcliffe Fellowes; divorced. Married Louis E. Shipman (1928); widowed 1933. Died June 24, 1962.

Feature Films: *What Every Woman Knows* (MGM, 1934), *The Bishop Misbehaves* (MGM, 1935), *A Woman Rebels* (RKO, 1936), *The Garden of Allah* (UA, 1936), *Three Smart Girls* (Univ., 1936), *The Young in Heart* (UA, 1938), *Sweethearts* (MGM, 1938), *Made for Each Other* (UA, 1939), *The Women* (MGM, 1939), *Florian* (MGM, 1940), *Waterloo Bridge* (MGM, 1940), *Mr. and Mrs. Smith* (RKO, 1941), *The Great Lie* (WB, 1941), *Rage in Heaven* (MGM, 1941), *Footsteps in the Dark*

Brian Aherne, Madge Evans and Lucile Watson in *What Every Woman Knows*.

(WB, 1941), *Model Wife* (Univ., 1941), *Watch on the Rhine* (WB, 1943), *Uncertain Glory* (WB, 1944), *Till We Meet Again* (Par., 1944), *The Thin Man Goes Home* (MGM, 1944), *My Reputation* (WB, 1946), *Tomorrow Is Forever* (RKO, 1946), *Song of the South* (RKO, 1946), *Never Say Goodbye* (WB, 1946), *The Razor's Edge* (20th, 1946), *Ivy* (Univ., 1947), *The Emperor Waltz* (Par., 1948), *Julia Misbehaves* (MGM, 1948), *That Wonderful Urge* (20th, 1948), *Little Women* (MGM, 1949), *Everybody Does It* (20th, 1949), *Let's Dance* (Par., 1950), *Harriet Craig* (Col., 1950), *My Forbidden Past* (RKO, 1951).

JOHN WAYNE (Marion Michael Morrison) Born May 26, 1907, Winterset, Iowa. Married Josephine Saenz (1933), children: Antonio, Melinda, Michael, Patrick; divorced 1944. Married Esperanza Baur (1946); divorced 1953. Married Pilar Pallette (1954), children: Aissa, Marisa, Ethan.

Barbara Stanwyck and John Wayne in *Baby Face*.

Sound Feature Films: *Salute* (Fox, 1929), *Men Without Women* (Fox, 1930), *Rough Romance* (Fox, 1930), *The Big Trail* (Fox, 1930), *Girls Demand Excitement* (Fox, 1931), *Three Girls Lost* (Fox, 1931), *Men Are Like That* (Col., 1931), *Range Feud* (Col., 1931), *Hurricane Express* (Mascot serial, 1932), *Shadow of the Eagle* (Mascot serial, 1932), *Maker of Men* (Col., 1932), *Two Fisted Law* (Col., 1932), *Texas Cyclone* (Col., 1932), *Lady and Gent* (Par., 1932), *Ride Him Cowboy* (WB, 1932), *The Big Stampede* (WB, 1932), *The Three Musketeers* (Mascot serial, 1933), *Haunted Gold* (WB, 1933), *Telegraph Trail* (WB, 1933), *His Private Secretary* (Showman's Pictures, 1933), *Central Airport* (WB, 1933), *Somewhere in Sonora* (WB, 1933), *The Life of Jimmy Dolan* (WB, 1933), *Baby Face* (WB, 1933), *The Man From Monterey* (WB, 1933), *Riders of Destiny* (Mon., 1933), *College Coach* (WB, 1933), *West of the Divide* (Mon., 1934), *Blue Steel* (Mon., 1934), *Lucky Texan* (Mon., 1934), *The Man From Utah* (Mon., 1934), *Randy Rides Alone* (Mon., 1934), *The Star Packer* (Mon., 1934), *The Trail Beyond* (Mon., 1934), *'Neath Arizona Skies* (Mon., 1934), *Texas Terror* (Mon., 1934), *The Lawless Frontier* (Mon., 1935), *Rainbow Valley* (Mon., 1935), *Paradise Canyon* (Mon., 1935), *The Dawn Rider* (Mon., 1935), *Westward Ho!* (Rep., 1935), *Desert Trail* (Mon., 1935), *The Lawless 90's* (Rep., 1936), *King of the Pecos* (Rep., 1936), *The Oregon Trail* (Rep., 1936), *Winds of the Wasteland* (Rep., 1936), *The Sea Spoilers* (Univ., 1936), *The Lonely Trail* (Rep., 1936), *Conflict* (Univ., 1936), *California Straight Ahead* (Univ., 1937), *I Cover the War* (Univ., 1937), *Idol of the Crowds* (Univ., 1937), *Adventure's End* (Univ., 1937), *Born to the West* (Par., 1938), *Pals of the Saddle* (Rep., 1938), *Overland Stage Raiders* (Rep., 1938), *Santa Fe Stampede* (Rep., 1938), *Red River Range* (Rep., 1938), *Stagecoach* (UA, 1939), *Night Riders* (Rep., 1939), *Three Texas Steers* (Rep., 1939), *Wyoming Outlaw* (Rep., 1939), *New Frontier* (Rep., 1939), *Allegheny Uprising* (RKO, 1939), *Dark Command* (Rep., 1940), *Three Faces West* (Rep., 1940), *The Long Voyage Home* (UA, 1940), *Seven Sinners* (Univ., 1940), *A Man Betrayed* (Rep., 1941), *The Lady From Louisiana* (Rep., 1941),

The Shepherd of the Hills (Par., 1941), *Lady for a Night* (Rep., 1941), *Reap the Wild Wind* (Par., 1942), *The Spoilers* (Univ., 1942), *In Old California* (Rep., 1942), *The Flying Tigers* (Rep., 1942), *Reunion* (MGM 1942), *Pittsburgh* (Univ., 1942), *A Lady Takes a Chance* (RKO, 1943), *In Old Oklahoma* (Rep., 1943), *The Fighting Seabees* (Rep., 1944), *Tall in the Saddle* (RKO, 1944), *Back to Bataan* (RKO, 1945), *Flame of Barbary Coast* (Rep., 1945), *Dakota* (Rep., 1945), *They Were Expendable* (MGM, 1945), *Without Reservations* (RKO, 1946), *Angel and the Badman* (Rep., 1947), *Tycoon* (RKO, 1947), *Fort Apache* (RKO, 1948), *Red River* (UA, 1948), *Three Godfathers* (MGM, 1948), *Wake of the Red Witch* (Rep., 1948), *The Fighting Kentuckian* (Rep., 1949), *She Wore a Yellow Ribbon* (RKO, 1949), *Sands of Iwo Jima* (Rep., 1949), *Rio Grande* (Rep., 1950), *Operation Pacific* (WB, 1951), *Flying Leathernecks* (RKO, 1951), *Big Jim McLain* (WB, 1952), *The Quiet Man* (Rep., 1952), *Trouble Along the Way* (WB, 1953), *Island in the Sky* (WB, 1953), *Hondo* (WB, 1953), *The High and the Mighty* (WB, 1954), *The Sea Chase* (WB, 1955), *Blood Alley* (WB, 1955), *The Conqueror* (RKO, 1956), *The Searchers* (WB, 1956), *Wings of Eagles* (MGM, 1957), *Jet Pilot* (Univ., 1957), *Legend of the Lost* (UA, 1957), *The Barbarian and the Geisha* (20th, 1958), *Rio Bravo* (WB, 1959), *The Horse Soldiers* (UA, 1959), *North to Alaska* (20th, 1960), *The Alamo* (UA, 1960), *The Comancheros* (20th, 1961), *The Man Who Shot Liberty Valance* (Par., 1962), *Hatari* (Par., 1962), *The Longest Day* (20th, 1962), *How the West Was Won* (MGM, 1963), *Donovan's Reef* (Par., 1963), *McLintock* (UA, 1963), *Circus World* (UA, 1964), *The Greatest Story Ever Told* (UA, 1965), *In Harm's Way* (Par., 1965), *The Sons of Katie Elder* (Par., 1965), *Cast a Giant Shadow* (UA, 1966), *El Dorado* (Par., 1967), *The War Wagon* (Univ., 1967), *The Green Berets* (WB-7 Arts, 1968).

MARJORIE WEAVER Born March 2, 1913, Grossville, Tennessee.

Marjorie Weaver, Jean Hersholt and Warner Baxter in *I'll Give a Million*.

Feature Films: *Transatlantic Merry-Go-Round* (UA, 1934), *China Clipper* (WB, 1936), *Big Business* (20th, 1937), *This is My Affair* (20th, 1937), *The Californian* (20th, 1937), *Life Begins in College* (20th, 1937), *Hot Water* (20th, 1937), *Second Honeymoon* (20th, 1937), *Sally, Irene and Mary* (20th, 1938), *Kentucky Moonshine* (20th, 1938), *I'll Give a Million* (20th, 1938), *Three Blind Mice* (20th, 1938), *Hold That Co-ed* (20th, 1938), *Young Mr. Lincoln* (20th, 1939), *Chicken Wagon Family* (20th, 1939), *The Honeymoon's Over* (20th, 1939), *The Cisco Kid and the Lady* (20th, 1940), *Shooting High* (20th, 1940), *Charlie Chan's Murder Cruise* (20th, 1940), *Maryland* (20th, 1940), *Murder Over New York* (20th, 1940), *Michael Shayne, Private Detective* (20th, 1940), *Murder Among Friends* (20th, 1941), *For Beauty's Sake* (20th, 1941), *Men At Large* (20th, 1941), *The Man*

Who Wouldn't Die (20th, 1942), *Just Off Broadway* (20th, 1942), *The Mad Martindales* (20th, 1942), *Let's Face It* (Par., 1943), *You Can't Ration Love* (Par., 1944), *Pardon My Rhythm* (Univ., 1944), *Shadow of Suspicion* (Mon., 1944), *The Great Alaskan Mystery* (Univ. serial, 1944), *Fashion Model* (Mon., 1945), *Leave It to Blondie* (Col., 1945).

CLIFTON WEBB (Webb Parmallee Hollenbeck) Born November 19, 1891, Indianapolis, Indiana. Died October 13, 1966.

Edmund Gwenn and Clifton Webb in *For Heaven's Sake*.

Sound Feature Films: *Laura* (20th, 1944), *The Dark Corner* (20th, 1946), *The Razor's Edge* (20th, 1946), *Sitting Pretty* (20th, 1948), *Mr. Belvedere Goes to College* (20th, 1949), *Cheaper by the Dozen* (20th, 1959), *For Heaven's Sake* (20th, 1950), *Mr. Belvedere Rings the Bell* (20th, 1951), *Elopement* (20th, 1951), *Dreamboat* (20th, 1952), *Stars and Stripes Forever* (20th, 1952), *Titanic* (20th, 1953), *Mister Scoutmaster* (20th, 1953), *Woman's World* (20th, 1954), *Three Coins in the Fountain* (20th, 1954), *The Man Who Never Was* (20th, 1956), *Boy on a Dolphin* (20th, 1957), *The Remarkable Mr. Pennypacker* (20th, 1959), *Holiday for Lovers* (20th, 1959), *Satan Never Sleeps* (20th, 1962).

JOHNNY WEISSMULLER Born June 2, 1907, Chicago, Illinois. Married Camille Louier; divorced. Married Bobbe Arnst; divorced 1932. Married Lupe Velez (1933); divorced 1938. Married Beryle Scott; divorced 1943. Married Allene Gates (1948), children: Wendy, John, Heidi; divorced 1962.

Feature Films: *Tarzan, the Ape Man* (MGM, 1932), *Tarzan and His*

Johnny Weissmuller, Maureen O'Sullivan, Paul Cavanagh and Neil Hamilton in *Tarzan and His Mate*.

Mate (MGM, 1934), *Tarzan Escapes* (MGM, 1936), *Tarzan Finds a Son* (MGM, 1939), *Tarzan's Secret Treasure* (MGM, 1941), *Tarzan's New York Adventure* (MGM, 1942), *Tarzan Triumphs* (RKO, 1943), *Stage Door Canteen* (UA, 1943), *Tarzan's Desert Mystery* (RKO, 1943), *Tarzan and the Amazons* (RKO, 1945), *Tarzan and the Leopard Women* (RKO, 1946), *Swamp Fire* (Par., 1946), *Tarzan and the Huntress* (RKO, 1947), *Tarzan and the Mermaids* (RKO, 1948), *Jungle Jim* (Col., 1948), *The Lost Tribe* (Col., 1949), *Captive Girl* (Col., 1950), *Mark of the Gorilla* (Col., 1950), *Pygmy Island* (Col., 1950), *Fury of the Congo* (Col., 1951), *Jungle Manhunt* (Col., 1951), *Jungle Jim and the Forbidden Land* (Col., 1952), *Voodoo Tiger* (Col., 1952), *Savage Mutiny* (Col., 1953), *Valley of the Headhunters* (Col., 1953), *Killer Ape* (Col., 1953), *Jungle Man-Eaters* (Col., 1954), *Cannibal Attack* (Col., 1954), *Jungle Moon Men* (Col., 1955), *Devil Goddess* (Col., 1955).

TUESDAY WELD (Susan Ker Weld) Born August 27, 1943, New York, New York. Married Claude Harz (1965).

Tuesday Weld and Mary Astor in *Return to Peyton Place*.

Feature Films: *Rock, Rock, Rock* (Vanguard, 1956), *The Wrong Man* (WB, 1956), *Rally 'Round the Flag, Boys!* (20th, 1958), *The Five Pennies* (Par., 1959), *Because They're Young* (Col., 1960), *High Time* (20th, 1960), *Sex Kittens Go to College* (AA, 1960), *The Private Lives of Adam and Eve* (Univ., 1960), *Return to Peyton Place* (20th, 1961), *Wild in the Country* (20th, 1961), *Bachelor Flat* (20th, 1961), *Soldier in the Rain* (AA, 1963), *I'll Take Sweden* (UA, 1965), *The Cincinnati Kid* (MGM, 1965), *Lord Love a Duck* (UA, 1966). *Pretty Poison* (20th, 1968), *She Let Him Continue* (20th, 1968).

ORSON WELLES (George Orson Welles) Born May 6, 1915, Kenosha, Wisconsin. Married Virginia Nicholson (1934), child: Christopher; divorced 1940. Married Rita Hayworth (1943), child: Rebecca; divorced 1947. Married Paola Mori (1956).

English-Language Feature Films: *Swiss Family Robinson* (narrator; RKO, 1940), *Citizen Kane* (RKO, 1941), *The Magnificent Ambersons*

Stephen Bekassy and Orson Welles in *Black Magic*.

(narrator; RKO, 1942), *Journey into Fear* (RKO, 1942), *Jane Eyre* (20th, 1944), *Follow the Boys* (Univ., 1944), *Tomorrow Is Forever* (RKO, 1946), *The Stranger* (RKO, 1946), *Duel in the Sun* (narrator; Selznick, 1946), *The Lady From Shanghai* (Col., 1948), *Macbeth* (Rep., 1948), *The Third Man* (Selznick, 1949), *Black Magic* (UA, 1949), *Prince of Foxes* (20th, 1949), *The Black Rose* (20th, 1950), *Return to Glennascaul* (British, 1951), *Trent's Last Case* (Rep., 1953), *Trouble in the Glen* (Rep., 1954), *Mr. Arkadin* ("Confidential Report"—WB, 1955), *Three Cases of Murder* (Associated Artists, 1955), *Othello* (UA, 1955), *Moby Dick* (WB, 1956), *Man in the Shadow* (Univ., 1957), *Touch of Evil* (Univ., 1958), *The Long, Hot Summer* (20th, 1958), *The Roots of Heaven* (20th, 1958), *High Journey* (narrator; Baylis, 1959), *South Seas Adventure* (narrator; Dudley, 1959), *Ferry to Hong Kong* (20th, 1959), *Compulsion* (20th, 1959), *A Crack in the Mirror* (20th, 1960), *Masters of the Congo Jungle* (narrator; 20th, 1960), *King of Kings* (narrator; MGM, 1961) *The Trial* (Gibraltar, 1962), *The V.I.P.'s* (MGM, 1963), *The Finest Hours* (narrator; Col., 1964), *Chimes at Midnight* ("Falstaff"—Counor, 1965), *Is Paris Burning?* (Par., 1966), *A Man for All Seasons* (Col., 1966), *Marco the Magnificent* (MGM, 1966), *Casino Royale* (Col., 1967), *The Sailor From Gibraltar* (Lopert, 1967), *I'll Never Forget What's 'is Name* (Rank, 1968), *House of Cards* (Univ., 1968). *Oedipus* (Univ., 1968).

MAE WEST Born August 17, 1892, Brooklyn, New York. Married Frank Wallace (1911); divorced 1943.

Mae West and Paul Cavanagh in *Goin' to Town*.

Feature Films: *Night After Night* (Par., 1932), *She Done Him Wrong* (Par., 1933), *I'm No Angel* (Par., 1933), *Belle of the Nineties* (Par., 1934), *Goin' to Town* (Par., 1935), *Klondike Annie* (Par., 1936), *Go West, Young Man* (Par., 1936), *Every Day's a Holiday* (Par., 1938), *My Little Chickadee* (Univ., 1940), *The Heat's On* (Col., 1943).

STUART WHITMAN (Stuart Maxwell Whitman) Born February 1, 1929, San Francisco, California. Married Patricia LaLonde (1952), children: Anthony, Michael, Linda, Scott; divorced 1966. Married Caroline Boubis (1966).

Feature Films: *When Worlds Collide* (Par., 1951), *The Day the Earth Stood Still* (20th, 1951), *Barbed Wire* (Col., 1952), *Appointment in Honduras* (RKO, 1953), *The All American* (Univ., 1953), *Rhapsody* (MGM, 1954), *Silver Lode* (RKO, 1954), *Brigadoon* (MGM, 1954), *Passion* (RKO, 1954), *King of the Carnival* (Rep. serial, 1955), *Diane* (MGM, 1955), *Seven Men From Now* (WB, 1956), *Crime of Passion* (UA, 1957), *War Drums* (UA, 1957), *Johnny Trouble* (WB, 1957), *Hell Bound* (UA, 1957), *The Girl in Black Stockings* (UA, 1957), *Bomb-*

Dennis Holmes, Stuart Whitman and Fabian in *Hound-Dog Man*.

ers *B-52* (WB, 1957), *Darby's Rangers* (WB, 1958), *10 North Frederick* (20th, 1958), *China Doll* (UA, 1958), *The Decks Ran Red* (MGM, 1958), *These Thousand Hills* (20th, 1959), *The Sound and the Fury* (20th, 1959), *Hound-Dog Man* (20th, 1959), *The Story of Ruth* (20th, 1960), *Murder, Inc.* (20th, 1960), *The Fiercest Heart* (20th, 1961), *Francis of Assisi* (20th, 1961), *The Mark* (Continental Distributing, 1961), *The Comancheros* (20th, 1961), *Convicts 4* (AA, 1962), *The Longest Day* (20th, 1962), *Shock Treatment* (20th, 1964), *The Day and the Hour* (MGM, 1964), *Rio Conchos* (20th, 1964), *Signpost to Murder* (MGM, 1964), *Those Magnificent Men in Their Flying Machines* (20th, 1965), *Sands of the Kalahari* (Par., 1965), *An American Dream* (WB, 1966).

DAME MAY WHITTY Born June 19, 1865, London, England. Married Ben Webster (1891), child: Margaret; widowed 1946. Died May 29, 1948.

Dame May Whitty and Edward G. Robinson in *Flesh and Fantasy*.

Feature Films: *Night Must Fall* (MGM, 1937), *The Thirteenth Chair* (MGM, 1937), *Conquest* (MGM, 1937), *I Met My Love Again* (UA, 1938), *The Lady Vanishes* (Gaumont-British, 1938), *Raffles* (UA, 1940), *A Bill of Divorcement* (RKO, 1940), *One Night in Lisbon* (Par., 1941), *Suspicion* (RKO, 1941), *Mrs. Miniver* (MGM, 1942), *Thunder Birds* (20th, 1942), *Slightly Dangerous* (MGM, 1943), *Forever and a Day* (RKO, 1943), *Crash Dive* (20th, 1943), *The Constant Nymph* (WB, 1943), *Lassie, Come Home* (MGM, 1943), *Flesh and Fantasy* (Univ., 1943), *Madame Curie* (MGM, 1943), *Stage Door Canteen* (UA, 1943), *The White Cliffs of Dover* (MGM, 1944), *Gaslight* (MGM, 1944), *My Name Is Julia Ross* (Col., 1945), *Devotion* (WB, 1946), *This Time for Keeps* (MGM, 1947), *Green Dolphin Street* (MGM, 1947), *If Winter Comes* (MGM, 1947), *The Sign of the Ram* (Col., 1948).

Whit Bissell, Lisa Golm, Mary Wickes, Broderick Crawford and Gale Page in *Anna Lucasta*.

MARY WICKES (Mary Isabelle Wickenhauser) Born St. Louis, Missouri.

Feature Films: *The Man Who Came to Dinner* (WB, 1941), *The Mayor of 44th Street* (RKO, 1942), *Private Buckaroo* (Univ., 1942), *Now, Voyager* (WB, 1942), *Who Done It?* (Univ., 1942), *How's About It?* (Univ., 1943), *Rhythm of the Islands* (Univ., 1943), *Happy Land* (20th, 1943), *My Kingdom for a Cook* (Col., 1943), *Higher and Higher* (RKO, 1943), *June Bride* (WB, 1948), *The Decision of Christopher Blake* (WB, 1948), *Anna Lucasta* (Col., 1949), *The Petty Girl* (Col., 1950), *On Moonlight Bay* (WB, 1951), *I'll See You in My Dreams* (WB, 1951), *The Will Rogers Story* (WB, 1952), *Young Man With Ideas* (MGM, 1952), *By the Light of the Silvery Moon* (WB, 1953), *The Actress* (MGM, 1953), *Half a Hero* (MGM, 1953), *Destry* (Univ., 1954), *Good Morning, Miss Dove* (20th, 1955), *Dance With Me, Henry* (UA, 1956), *Don't Go Near the Water* (MGM, 1957), *It Happened to Jane* (Col., 1959), *Cimarron* (MGM, 1960), *The Sins of Rachel Cade* (WB, 1961), *The Music Man* (WB, 1962), *Who's Minding the Store?* (Par., 1963), *Fate Is the Hunter* (20th, 1964), *Dear Heart* (WB, 1964), *How to Murder Your Wife* (UA, 1965), *The Trouble With Angels* (Col., 1966), *Where Angels Go . . . Trouble Follows* (Col., 1968).

RICHARD WIDMARK Born December 26, 1914, Sunrise, Minnesota. Married Jean Hazelwood (1942), child: Anne.

Cecil Kellaway and Richard Widmark in *Down to the Sea in Ships*.

Feature Films: *Kiss of Death* (20th, 1947), *Road House* (20th, 1948), *Street With No Name* (20th, 1948), *Yellow Sky* (20th, 1949), *Down to the Sea in Ships* (20th, 1949), *Slattery's Hurricane* (20th, 1949), *Night and the City* (20th, 1950), *Panic in the Streets* (20th, 1950), *No Way Out*

(20th, 1950), *Halls of Montezuma* (20th, 1950), *The Frogmen* (20th, 1951), *O. Henry's Full House* (20th, 1952), *Don't Bother to Knock* (20th, 1952), *Red Skies of Montana* (20th, 1952), *My Pal Gus* (20th, 1952), *Destination Gobi* (20th, 1953), *Hell and High Water* (20th, 1954), *Broken Lance* (20th, 1954), *Garden of Evil* (20th, 1954), *A Prize of Gold* (Col., 1955), *The Cobweb* (MGM, 1955), *Backlash* (Univ., 1956), *Run for the Sun* (UA, 1956), *The Last Wagon* (20th, 1956), *Saint Joan* (UA, 1957), *Time Limit!* (UA, 1957), *The Law and Jake Wade* (MGM, 1958), *The Tunnel of Love* (MGM, 1958), *The Trap* (Par., 1959), *Warlock* (20th, 1959), *The Alamo* (UA, 1960), *The Secret Ways* (Univ., 1961), *Two Rode Together* (Col., 1961), *Judgment at Nuremberg* (UA, 1961), *How the West Was Won* (MGM, 1963), *Flight From Ashiya* (UA, 1964), *The Long Ships* (Col., 1964), *Cheyenne Autumn* (WB, 1964), *The Bedford Incident* (Col., 1965), *Alvarez Kelly* (Col., 1966), *The Way West* (UA, 1967), *Madigan* (Univ., 1968).

CORNEL WILDE Born October 13, 1915, New York, New York. Married Patricia Knight (1937), child: Wendy; divorced 1951. Married Jean Wallace (1951).

Cornel Wilde and Finlay Currie in *Treasure of the Golden Condor.*

Feature Films: *The Lady With Red Hair* (WB, 1940), *Kisses for Breakfast* (WB, 1941), *High Sierra* (WB, 1941), *Right to the Heart* (WB, 1941), *The Perfect Snob* (20th, 1942), *Life Begins at 8:30* (20th, 1942), *Manila Calling* (20th, 1942), *Wintertime* (20th, 1943), *Guest in the House* (UA, 1944), *A Thousand and One Nights* (Col., 1945), *A Song to Remember* (Col., 1945), *Leave Her to Heaven* (20th, 1945), *The Bandit of Sherwood Forest* (Col., 1946), *Centennial Summer* (20th, 1946), *The Homestretch* (20th, 1947), *Forever Amber* (20th, 1947), *It Had to Be You* (Col., 1947), *Roadhouse* (20th, 1948), *The Walls of Jericho* (20th, 1948), *Four Days Leave* (Film Classics, 1950), *Two Flags West* (20th, 1950), *At Sword's Point* (RKO, 1952), *The Greatest Show on Earth* (Par., 1952), *California Conquest* (Col., 1952), *The Treasure of The Golden Condor* (20th, 1953), *Main Street To Broadway* (MGM, 1953), *Saadia* (MGM, 1953), *Passion* (RKO, 1954), *Woman's World* (20th, 1954), *The Scarlet Coat* (MGM, 1955), *Storm Fear* (UA, 1955), *The Big Combo* (AA, 1955), *Star of India* (UA, 1956), *Hot Blood* (Col., 1956), *The Devil's Hairpin* (Par., 1957), *Omar Khayyam* (Par., 1957), *Beyond Mombasa* (Col., 1957), *Maracaibo* (Par., 1958), *The Edge of Eternity* (Col., 1959), *Constantine and the Cross* (Embassy, 1962), *The Sword of Lancelot* (Univ., 1963), *The Naked Prey* (Par., 1966), *Beach Red* (UA, 1967).

WARREN WILLIAM (Warren Krech) Born December 2, 1895, Aitkin, Minnesota. Died September 24, 1948.

Feature Films: *Expensive Women* (WB, 1931), *Honor of the Family* (WB, 1931), *Woman From Monte Carlo* (WB, 1932), *Under Eighteen* (WB, 1932), *The Mouthpiece* (WB, 1932), *Beauty and the Boss* (WB, 1932), *Dark Horse* (WB, 1932), *Skyscraper Souls* (WB, 1932), *Three on a Match* (WB, 1932), *The Match King* (WB, 1932),

Kay Francis and Warren William in *Dr. Monica.*

Employees' Entrance (WB, 1933), *Mind Reader* (WB, 1933), *Gold Diggers of 1933* (WB, 1933), *Lady for a Day* (Col., 1933), *Goodbye Again* (WB, 1933), *Bedside* (WB, 1934), *Smarty* (WB, 1934), *Dr. Monica* (WB, 1934), *Upper World* (WB, 1934), *Dragon Murder Case* (WB, 1934), *Cleopatra* (Par., 1934), *Case of the Howling Dog* (WB, 1934), *Imitation of Life* (Univ., 1934), *Outcast* (Par., 1937), *Midnight Madonna* (Par., 1937), *The Firefly* (MGM, 1937), *Madame X* (MGM, 1937), *Arsene Lupin Returns* (MGM, 1938), *The First Hundred Years* (MGM, 1938), *Wives Under Suspicion* (Univ., 1938), *The Lone Wolf Spy Hunt* (Col., 1939), *Gracie Allen Murder Case* (Par., 1939), *The Man in the Iron Mask* (UA, 1939), *Daytime Wife* (20th, 1939), *The Lone Wolf Strikes* (Col., 1940), *Lillian Russell* (20th, 1940), *The Lone Wolf Meets a Lady* (Col., 1940), *Arizona* (Col., 1940), *Trail of the Vigilantes* (Univ., 1940), *The Lone Wolf Takes a Chance* (Col., 1941), *The Lone Wolf Keeps a Date* (Col., 1941), *Wild Geese Calling* (20th, 1941), *The Wolf Man* (Univ., 1941), *One Dangerous Night* (Col., 1943), *Passport to Suez* (Col., 1943), *Strange Illusion* (PRC, 1945), *Fear* (Mon., 1946), *The Private Affairs of Bel Ami* (UA, 1947).

ESTHER WILLIAMS Born August 8, 1923, Los Angeles, California. Married Leonard Kovner (1940); divorced 1944. Married Benjamin Gage (1945), children: Benjamin, Kimball, Susan; divorced 1957. Married Fernando Lamas (1963).

Feature Films: *Andy Hardy's Double Life* (MGM, 1942), *A Guy Named*

Cliff Robertson and Esther Williams in *The Big Show.*

240

Joe (MGM, 1943), *Bathing Beauty* (MGM, 1944), *Thrill of a Romance* (MGM, 1945), *The Hoodlum Saint* (MGM, 1946), *Ziegfeld Follies of 1946* (MGM, 1946), *Easy to Wed* (MGM, 1946), *Till the Clouds Roll By* (MGM, 1946), *Fiesta* (MGM, 1947), *This Time for Keeps* (MGM, 1947), *On an Island With You* (MGM, 1948), *Take Me Out to the Ball Game* (MGM, 1949), *Neptune's Daughter* (MGM, 1949), *Duchess of Idaho* (MGM, 1950), *Pagan Love Song* (MGM, 1950), *Texas Carnival* (MGM, 1951), *Callaway Went Thataway* (MGM, 1951),* *Skirts Ahoy* (MGM, 1952), *Million Dollar Mermaid* (MGM, 1952), *Dangerous When Wet* (MGM, 1953), *Easy to Love* (MGM, 1953), *Jupiter's Darling* (MGM, 1955), *The Unguarded Moment* (Univ., 1956), *Raw Wind in Eden* (Univ., 1958), *The Big Show* (20th, 1961), *The Magic Fountain* (Agiula Films, 1961).

*Unbilled guest appearance

MARIE WINDSOR (Emily Marie Bertelson) Born December 11, 1922, Marysvale, Utah. Married Ted Steele (1947), annulled 1947. Married Jack Hupp (1954), child: Richard.

Forrest Tucker and Marie Windsor in *Hellfire*.

Feature Films: *All American Co-ed* (UA, 1941), *Call Out the Marines* (RKO, 1942), *Smart Alecks* (Mon., 1942), *Parachute Nurse* (Col., 1942), *The Big Street* (RKO, 1942), *George Washington Slept Here* (WB, 1942), *Three Hearts for Julia* (MGM, 1943), *Pilot No. 5* (MGM, 1943), *Let's Face It* (Par., 1943), *The Hucksters* (MGM, 1947), *Romance of Rosy Ridge* (MGM, 1947), *The Song of the Thin Man* (MGM, 1947), *The Unfinished Dance* (MGM, 1947), *On an Island With You* (MGM, 1948), *The Three Musketeers* (MGM, 1948), *The Kissing Bandit* (MGM, 1948), *Force of Evil* (MGM, 1949), *Outpost in Morocco* (UA, 1949), *The Beautiful Blonde From Bashful Bend* (20th, 1949), *The Fighting Kentuckian* (Rep., 1949), *Hellfire* (Rep., 1949), *Dakota Lil* (20th, 1950), *The Showdown* (Rep., 1950), *Frenchie* (Univ., 1950), *Double Deal* (RKO, 1950), *Little Big Horn* (Lip., 1951), *Hurricane Island* (Col., 1951), *Two Dollar Bettor* (Realart, 1951), *Japanese War Bride* (20th, 1952), *The Sniper* (Col., 1952), *The Narrow Margin* (RKO, 1952), *Outlaw Woman* (Lip., 1952), *The Jungle* (Lip., 1952), *The Tall Texan* (Lip., 1953), *Trouble Along the Way* (WB, 1953), *The City That Never Sleeps* (Rep., 1953), *So This Is Love* (WB, 1953), *The Eddie Cantor Story* (WB, 1953), *Cat Women of the Moon* (Astor, 1953), *Hell's Half Acre* (Rep., 1954), *The Bounty Hunter* (WB, 1954), *Silver Star* (Lip., 1954), *Abbott and Costello Meet the Mummy* (Univ., 1955), *No Man's Woman* (Rep., 1955), *Two Gun Lady* (Associated, 1955), *The Killing* (UA, 1956), *Swamp Women* (Woolner Bros., 1956), *The Unholy Wife* (Univ., 1957), *The Girl in Black Stockings* (UA, 1957), *The Story of Mankind* (WB, 1957), *The Parson and the Outlaw* (Col., 1957), *The Day of the Bad Man* (Univ., 1958), *Island Women* (UA, 1958), *Paradise Alley* (Sutton, 1962), *Critic's Choice* (WB, 1963), *The Day Mars Invaded Earth* (20th, 1963), *Mail Order Bride* (MGM, 1964), *Bedtime Story* (Univ., 1964), *Chamber of Horrors* (WB, 1966).

Farley Granger and Shelley Winters in *Behave Yourself!*

SHELLEY WINTERS (Shirley Schrift) Born August 18, 1922, St. Louis, Missouri. Married Mack Meyer (1943); divorced 1948. Married Vittorio Gassman (1952), child: Vittoria; divorced 1954. Married Anthony Franciosa (1957); divorced 1960.

English-Language Feature Films: *What a Woman!* (Col., 1943), *Nine Girls* (Col., 1944), *She's a Soldier, Too* (Col., 1944), *Sailor's Holiday* (Col., 1944), *Racket Man* (Col., 1944), *Knickerbocker Holiday* (UA, 1944), *Two Man Submarine* (Col., 1944), *Cover Girl* (Col., 1944), *Tonight and Every Night* (Col., 1945), *A Thousand and One Nights* (Col., 1945), *The Gangster* (AA, 1947), *Living in a Big Way* (MGM, 1947), *A Double Life* (Univ., 1948), *Larceny* (Univ., 1948), *Red River* (UA, 1948), *Cry of the City* (20th, 1948), *Take One False Step* (Univ., 1949), *The Great Gatsby* (Par., 1949), *Johnny Stool Pigeon* (Univ., 1949), *South Sea Sinner* (Univ., 1950), *Winchester '73* (Univ., 1950), *Frenchie* (Univ., 1950), *A Place in the Sun* (Par., 1951), *He Ran All the Way* (UA, 1951), *Behave Yourslf* (RKO, 1951), *The Raging Tide* (Univ., 1951), *Meet Danny Wilson* (Univ., 1951), *Phone Call From a Stranger* (20th, 1952), *Untamed Frontier* (Univ., 1952), *My Man and I* (MGM, 1952), *Saskatchewan* (Univ., 1954), *Tennessee Champ* (MGM, 1954), *Executive Suite* (MGM, 1954), *Playgirl* (Univ., 1954), *Mambo* (Par., 1955), *I Am a Camera* (DCA, 1955), *The Night of the Hunter* (UA, 1955), *The Big Knife* (UA, 1955), *I Died a Thousand Times* (WB, 1955), *The Treasure of Pancho Villa* (RKO, 1955), *Cash on Delivery* (RKO, 1956), *The Diary of Anne Frank* (20th, 1959), *Odds Against Tomorrow* (UA, 1959), *Let No Man Write My Epitaph* (Col., 1960), *The Young Savages* (UA, 1961), *Lolita* (MGM, 1962), *The Chapman Report* (WB, 1962), *The Balcony* (Continental, 1963), *Wives and Lovers* (Par., 1963), *A House Is Not a Home* (Embassy, 1964), *The Greatest Story Ever Told* (UA, 1965), *A Patch of Blue* (MGM, 1965), *Harper* (WB, 1966), *Alfie* (Par., 1966), *A Time of Indifference* (Continental, 1966), *Enter Laughing* (Col., 1967), *The Scalphunters* (UA, 1968), *Buona Sera, Mrs. Campbell* (Univ., 1968), *Wild in the Streets* (AIP, 1968).

JANE WITHERS Born April 12, 1926, Atlanta, Georgia. Married William Moss (1947), children: William, Wendy, Randy. divorced 1954. Married Kenneth Errair (1955), children: Kenneth, Kendall.

Jane Withers and Andrew Tombes in *The Holy Terror*.

Feature Films: *Handle With Care* (Fox, 1932), *Bright Eyes* (Fox, 1934), *Ginger* (Fox, 1935), *The Farmer Takes a Wife* (Fox, 1935), *This Is the Life* (Fox, 1935), *Paddy O'Day* (Fox, 1935), *Gentle Julia* (20th, 1936), *Little Miss Nobody* (20th, 1936), *Pepper* (20th, 1936), *Can This Be Dixie?* (20th, 1936), *The Holy Terror* (20th, 1937), *Angel's Holiday* (20th, 1937), *Wild and Woolly* (20th, 1937), *45 Fathers* (20th, 1937), *Checkers* (20th, 1937), *Rascals* (20th, 1938), *Keep Smiling* (20th, 1938), *Always in Trouble* (20th, 1938), *The Arizona Wildcat* (20th, 1938), *Boy Friend* (20th, 1939), *Pack Up Your Troubles* (20th, 1939), *Chicken Wagon Family* (20th, 1939), *Shooting High* (20th, 1940), *High School* (20th, 1940), *Youth Will Be Served* (20th, 1940), *Girl From Avenue A* (20th, 1940), *Golden Hoofs* (20th, 1941), *A Very Young Lady* (20th, 1941), *Her First Beau* (Col., 1941), *Small Town Deb* (20th, 1941), *Young America* (20th, 1942), *Johnny Doughboy* (Rep., 1942), *The Mad Martindales* (20th, 1942), *The North Star* (RKO, 1943), *My Best Gal* (Rep., 1944), *Faces in the Fog* (Rep., 1944), *Affairs of Geraldine* (Rep., 1946), *Danger Street* (Par., 1947), *Giant* (WB, 1956), *The Right Approach* (20th, 1961), *Captain Newman, M.D.* (Univ., 1963).

ANNA MAY WONG Born January 3, 1907, Los Angeles, California. Died February 3, 1961.

Eric Blore and Anna May Wong in *Island of Lost Men*.

English-Language Sound Feature Films: *Crimson City* (WB, 1928), *Piccadilly* (World Wide, 1929), *The Flame of Love* (British International 1930), *Daughter of the Dragon* (Par., 1931), *Shanghai Express* (Par., 1932), *A Study in Scarlet* (Fox-World Wide, 1933), *Tiger Bay* (Wyndham, 1933), *Limehouse Blues* (Par., 1934), *Chu Chin Chow* (Gaumont-British, 1934), *Java Head* (First Division, 1935), *Daughter of Shanghai* (Par., 1937), *Dangerous to Know* (Par., 1938), *When Were You Born?* (WB, 1938), *King of Chinatown* (Par., 1939), *Island of Lost Men* (Par., 1939), *Ellery Queen's Penthouse Mystery* (Col., 1941), *Bombs Over Burma* (PRC, 1942), *Lady From Chungking* (PRC, 1942), *Impact* (UA, 1949), *Portrait in Black* (Univ., 1960).

NATALIE WOOD (Natasha Gurdin) Born July 20, 1938, San Francisco, California. Married Robert Wagner (1957); divorced 1963.

Feature Films:
    as Natasha Gurdin *Happy Land* (20th, 1943).
    as Natalie Wood *Tomorrow Is Forever* (RKO, 1946), *The Bride Wore Boots* (Par., 1946), *The Miracle on 34th Street* (20th, 1947), *The Ghost and Mrs. Muir* (20th, 1947), *Driftwood* (Rep., 1947), *Scudda Hoo! Scudda Hay!* (20th, 1948), *Chicken Every Sunday* (20th, 1948), *The Green Promise* (RKO, 1949), *Father Was a Fullback* (20th, 1949), *Our Very Own* (RKO, 1950), *No Sad Songs for Me* (Col., 1950), *The Jackpot* (20th, 1950), *Never a Dull Moment* (RKO, 1950), *Dear Brat* (Par., 1951), *The Blue Veil* (RKO, 1951), *Just for You* (Par., 1952), *The Rose Bowl Story* (Mon., 1952), *The Star* (20th, 1953), *The Silver*

Robert Redford and Natalie Wood in *This Property is Condemned*.

Chalice (WB, 1954), *One Desire* (Univ., 1955), *Rebel Without a Cause* (WB, 1955), *The Searchers* (WB, 1956), *The Burning Hills* (WB, 1956), *A Cry in the Night* (WB, 1956), *The Girl He Left Behind* (WB, 1956), *Bombers B-52* (WB, 1957), *Marjorie Morningstar* (WB, 1958), *Kings Go Forth* (UA, 1958), *Cash McCall* (WB, 1959), *All the Fine Young Cannibals* (MGM, 1960), *Splendor in the Grass* (WB, 1961), *West Side Story* (UA, 1961), *Gypsy* (WB, 1962), *Love With the Proper Stranger* (Par., 1963), *Sex and the Single Girl* (WB, 1964), *The Great Race* (WB, 1965), *Inside Daisy Clover* (WB, 1965), *This Property Is Condemned* (Par., 1966), *Penelope* (MGM, 1966).

JOANNE WOODWARD (Joanne Gignilliat Woodward) Born February 27, 1930, Thomasville, Georgia. Married Paul Newman (1958), children: Elinore, Tessa, Cleo.

Claire Trevor and Joanne Woodward in *The Stripper*.

Feature Films: *Count Three and Pray* (Col., 1955), *A Kiss Before Dying* (UA, 1956), *The Three Faces of Eve* (20th, 1957), *No Down Payment* (20th, 1957), *The Long, Hot Summer* (20th, 1958), *Rally 'Round the Flag, Boys* (20th, 1958), *The Sound and the Fury* (20th, 1959), *The Fugitive Kind* (UA, 1959), *From the Terrace* (20th, 1960), *Paris Blues* (UA, 1961), *The Stripper* (20th, 1963), *A New Kind of Love* (Par., 1963), *Signpost to Murder* (MGM, 1964), *A Big Hand for the Little Lady* (WB, 1966), *A Fine Madness* (WB, 1966), *The Jest of God* (WB-7 Arts, 1968), *Rachel, Rachel* (WB-7 Arts, 1968).

MONTY WOOLLEY (Edgar Montillion Woolley) Born August 17, 1888, New York, New York. Died May 6, 1963.

Feature Films: *Live, Love and Learn* (MGM, 1937), *Nothing Sacred* (UA, 1937), *Arsene Lupin Returns* (MGM, 1938), *Girl of the Golden West* (MGM, 1938), *Everybody Sing* (MGM, 1938), *Three Comrades*

Monty Woolley, Ida Lupino and Cornel Wilde in *Life Begins at 8:30*.

(MGM, 1938), *Lord Jeff* (MGM, 1938), *Artists and Models Abroad* (Par., 1938), *Young Dr. Kildare* (MGM, 1938), *Vacation From Love* (MGM, 1938), *Never Say Die* (Par., 1939), *Midnight* (Par., 1939), *Zaza* (Par., 1939), *Man About Town* (Par., 1939), *Dancing Co-ed* (MGM, 1939), *The Man Who Came to Dinner* (WB, 1941), *The Pied Piper* (20th, 1942), *Life Begins at 8:30* (20th, 1942), *Holy Matrimony* (20th, 1943), *Since You Went Away* (UA, 1944), *Irish Eyes Are Smiling* (20th, 1944), *Molly and Me* (20th, 1945), *Night and Day* (WB, 1946), *The Bishop's Wife* (RKO, 1947), *Miss Tatlock's Millions* (Par., 1948), *As Young as You Feel* (20th, 1951), *Kismet* (MGM, 1955).

FAY WRAY Born September 10, 1907, Alberta, Canada. Married John Monk Saunders (1928), child: Susan; divorced 1939. Married Robert Riskin (1942), children: Robert, Vicky; widowed 1955.

Fay Wray and Robert Allen in *White Lies*.

Sound Feature Films: *Four Feathers* (Par., 1929), *Thunderbolt* (Par., 1929), *Pointed Heels* (Par., 1929), *Behind the Makeup* (Par., 1930), *Paramount on Parade* (Par., 1930), *The Texan* (Par., 1930), *The Border Legion* (Par., 1930), *The Sea God* (Par., 1930), *The Finger Points* (WB, 1931), *The Conquering Horde* (Par., 1931), *Not Exactly Gentlemen* (Fox, 1931), *Dirigible* (Col., 1931), *Captain Thunder* (WB, 1931), *The Lawyer's Secret* (Par., 1931), *The Unholy Garden* (UA, 1931), *Stowaway* (Univ., 1932), *Doctor X* (WB, 1932), *The Most Dangerous Game* (RKO, 1932), *Vampire Bat* (Majestic, 1933), *Mystery of the Wax Museum* (WB, 1933), *King Kong* (RKO, 1933), *Below the Sea* (Col., 1933), *Ann Carver's Profession* (Col., 1933), *The Woman I Stole* (Col., 1933), *The Big Brain* (RKO, 1933), *One Sunday Afternoon* (Par., 1933), *Shanghai Madness* (Fox, 1933), *The Bowery* (UA, 1933), *Master of Men* (Col., 1933), *Madame Spy* (Univ., 1943), *Once to Every Woman* (Col., 1934), *The Countess of Monte Cristo* (Univ., 1934), *Viva Villa!* (MGM, 1934), *The Affairs of Cellini* (UA, 1934), *Black Moon* (Col., 1934), *The Richest*

Girl in the World (RKO, 1934), *The Captain Hates the Sea* (Col., 1934), *Cheating Cheaters* (Univ., 1934), *Woman in the Dark* (RKO, 1934), *White Lies* (Col., 1934), *Bulldog Jack* (Gaumont-British, 1935), *Come Out of the Pantry* (UA, 1935), *Mills of the Gods* (Col., 1935), *The Clairvoyant* (Gaumont-British, 1935), *Roaming Lady* (Col., 1936), *When Knights Were Bold* (General Film Distributors, 1936), *They Met in a Taxi* (Col., 1936), *It Happened in Hollywood* (Col., 1937), *Once a Hero* (Col., 1937), *Murder in Greenwich Village* (Col., 1937), *The Jury's Secret* (Univ., 1938), *Smashing the Spy Ring* (Col., 1938), *Navy Secrets* (Mon., 1939), *Wildcat Bus* (RKO, 1940), *Adam Had Four Sons* (Col., 1941), *Melody for Three* (RKO, 1941), *Not a Ladies' Man* (Col., 1942), *Treasure of the Golden Condor* (20th, 1953), *Small Town Girl* (MGM, 1953), *The Cobweb* (MGM, 1955), *Queen Bee* (Col., 1955), *Hell on Frisco Bay* (WB, 1955), *Rock Pretty Baby* (Univ., 1957), *Crime of Passion* (UA, 1957), *Tammy and the Bachelor* (Univ., 1957), *Summer Love* (Univ., 1958), *Dragstrip Riot* (AIP, 1958).

TERESA WRIGHT (Muriel Teresa Wright) Born October 27, 1918, New York, New York. Married Niven Busch (1942), children: Niven, Mary; divorced 1952. Married Robert Anderson (1959).

Teresa Wright and David Niven in *Enchantment*.

Feature Films: *The Little Foxes* (RKO, 1941), *Mrs. Miniver* (MGM, 1942), *The Pride of the Yankees* (RKO, 1942), *Shadow of a Doubt* (Univ., 1943), *Casanova Brown* (RKO, 1944), *The Best Years of Our Lives* (RKO, 1946), *Pursued* (WB, 1947), *The Imperfect Lady* (Par., 1947), *The Trouble with Women* (Par., 1947), *Enchantment* (RKO, 1948), *The Capture* (RKO, 1950), *The Men* (UA, 1950), *Something to Live For* (Par., 1952), *California Conquest* (Col., 1952), *The Steel Trap* (20th, 1952), *Count the Hours* (RKO, 1953), *The Actress* (MGM, 1953), *Track of the Cat* (WB, 1954), *The Search for Bridey Murphy* (Par., 1956), *Escapade in Japan* (Univ., 1957), *The Restless Years* (Univ., 1958).

JANE WYATT Born August 10, 1911, Campgaw, New Jersey. Married Edgar Ward (1935), children: Christopher, Michael.

Ronald Colman and Jane Wyatt in *Lost Horizon*.

Feature Films: *One More River* (Univ., 1934), *Great Expectations* (Univ., 1934), *We're Only Human* (RKO, 1936), *Luckiest Girl in the World* (Univ., 1936), *Lost Horizon* (Col., 1937), *Girl From God's Country* (Rep., 1940), *Hurricane Smith* (Rep., 1941), *Weekend for Three* (RKO, 1941), *Kisses for Breakfast* (WB, 1941), *The Navy Comes Through* (RKO, 1942), *Army Surgeon* (RKO, 1942), *Buckskin Frontier* (UA, 1943), *The Kansan* (UA, 1943), *None But the Lonely Heart* (RKO, 1944), *Strange Conquest* (Univ., 1946), *The Bachelor's Daughters* (UA, 1946), *Boomerang* (20th. 1947), *Gentleman's Agreement* (20th, 1947), *Pitfall* (UA, 1948), *No Minor Vices* (MGM, 1948), *Bad Boy* (AA, 1949), *Canadian Pacific* (20th, 1949), *Task Force* (WB, 1949), *Our Very Own* (RKO, 1950), *House by the River* (Rep., 1950), *My Blue Heaven* (20th, 1950), *The Man Who Cheated Himself* (20th, 1950), *Criminal Lawyer* (Col., 1951), *Interlude* (Univ., 1957), *The Two Little Bears* (20th, 1961), *Never Too Late* (WB, 1965).

JANE WYMAN (Sarah Jane Fulks) Born January 4, 1914, St. Joseph, Missouri. Married Myron Futterman (1937); divorced 1938. Married Ronald Reagan (1940), children: Michael, Maureen; divorced 1948. Married Fred Karger (1952); divorced 1954. Remarried 1961.

Jane Wyman and Jack Carson in *Make Your Own Bed*.

Feature Films: *Gold Diggers of 1937* (WB, 1936), *My Man Godfrey* (Univ., 1936), *King of Burlesque* (20th, 1936), *Smart Blonde* (WB, 1936), *Stage Struck* (WB, 1936), *The King and the Chorus Girl* (WB, 1937), *Ready, Willing and Able* (WB, 1937), *Slim* (WB, 1937), *The Singing Marine* (WB, 1937), *Public Wedding* (WB, 1937), *Mr. Dodd Takes the Air* (WB, 1937), *The Spy Ring* (Univ., 1938), *He Couldn't Say No* (WB, 1938), *Wide Open Faces* (Col., 1938), *The Crowd Roars* (MGM, 1938), *Brother Rat* (WB, 1938), *Fools For Scandal* (WB, 1938), *Tailspin* (20th, 1939), *Private Detective* (WB, 1939), *The Kid From Kokomo* (WB, 1939), *Torchy Plays With Dynamite* (WB, 1939), *Kid Nightingale* (WB, 1939), *Brother Rat and a Baby* (WB, 1940), *An Angel From Texas* (WB, 1940), *Flight Angels* (WB, 1940), *My Love Came Back* (WB, 1940), *Tugboat Annie Sails Again* (WB, 1940), *Gambling on the High Seas* (WB, 1940), *Honeymoon for Three* (WB, 1941), *Bad Men of Missouri* (WB, 1941), *You're in the Army Now* (WB, 1941), *The Body Disappears* (WB, 1941) *Larceny, Inc.* (WB, 1942), *My Favorite Spy* (RKO, 1942), *Footlight Serenade* (20th, 1942), *Princess O'Rourke* (WB, 1943), *Make Your Own Bed* (WB, 1944), *Crime By Night* (WB, 1944), *The Doughgirls* (WB, 1944), *Hollywood Canteen* (WB, 1944), *The Lost Weekend* (Par., 1945), *One More Tomorrow* (WB, 1946), *Night and Day* (WB, 1946), *The Yearling* (MGM, 1946), *Cheyenne* (WB, 1947), *Magic Town* (RKO, 1947), *Johnny Belinda* (WB, 1948), *A Kiss in the Dark* (WB, 1949), *The Lady Takes a Sailor* (WB, 1949), *It's a Great Feeling* (WB, 1949), *Stage Fright* (WB, 1950), *The Glass Menagerie* (WB, 1950), *Three Guys Named Mike* (MGM, 1951), *Here Comes the Groom* (Par., 1951), *The Blue Veil* (RKO, 1951), *Starlift* (WB, 1951), *The Will Rogers Story* (WB, 1952), *Just for You* (Par., 1952), *Let's Do It Again* (WB, 1953), *So Big* (WB, 1953), *Magnificent*

Obsession (Univ., 1954), *Lucy Gallant* (Par., 1955), *All That Heaven Allows* (Univ., 1955), *Miracle in the Rain* (WB, 1956), *Holiday for Lovers* (20th, 1959), *Pollyanna* (BV, 1960), *Bon Voyage* (BV, 1962).

ED WYNN (Isaiah Edwin Leopold) Born November 9, 1886, Philadelphia, Pennsylvania. Married Hilda Keenan (1914), child: Keenan; divorced 1937. Married Frieda Mierse (1937); divorced 1939. Died June 19, 1966.

Effie Ellsler, Ed Wynn and Dorothy Mackill in *The Chief*.

Sound Feature Films: *Follow the Leader* (Par., 1930), *The Chief* (MGM, 1933), *Alice in Wonderland* (voice only; RKO, 1951), *The Great Man* (Univ., 1956), *Marjorie Morningstar* (WB, 1958), *The Diary of Anne Frank* (20th, 1959), *Cinderfella* (Par., 1960), *The Absent-Minded Professor* (BV, 1961), *Babes in Toyland* (BV, 1961), *Son of Flubber* (BV, 1963), *The Patsy* (Par., 1964), *Mary Poppins* (BV, 1965), *The Greatest Story Ever Told* (UA, 1965), *Dear Brigitte* (20th, 1965), *Those Calloways* (BV, 1965), *The Daydreamer* (voice only; Embassy, 1966), *The Gnome-Mobile* (BV, 1967).

KEENAN WYNN (Francis Xavier Aloysius Keenan Wynn) Born July 27, 1916, New York, New York. Married Eve Abbott (1939), children: Edmond, Tracy; divorced 1946. Married Betty Butler (1949); divorced 1953. Married Sharley Hudson (1954), children: Wynnie, Hilda.

Feature Films: *Somewhere I'll Find You* (MGM, 1942), *Northwest Rangers* (MGM, 1942), *For Me and My Gal* (MGM, 1942), *Lost Angel* (MGM, 1943), *See Here, Private Hargrove* (MGM, 1944), *Since You Went Away* (UA, 1944), *Marriage Is a Private Affair* (MGM, 1944), *Without Love* (MGM, 1945), *The Clock* (MGM, 1945), *Between Two Women* (MGM, 1945), *Weekend at the Waldorf* (MGM, 1945), *What Next, Corporal Hargrove?* (MGM, 1945), *Ziegfeld Follies of 1946* (MGM, 1946), *Easy to Wed* (MGM, 1946), *The Thrill of Brazil* (Col., 1946),

Keenan Wynn and Fred Essler in *What Next, Corporal Hargrove?*

No Leave, No Love (MGM, 1946), The Cockeyed Miracle (MGM, 1946), The Hucksters (MGM, 1947), Song of the Thin Man (MGM, 1947), B.F.'s Daughter (MGM, 1948), The Three Musketeers (MGM, 1948), My Dear Secretary (UA, 1948), Neptune's Daughter (MGM, 1949), That Midnight Kiss (MGM, 1949), Love That Brute (20th, 1950), Annie Get Your Gun (MGM, 1950), Three Little Words (MGM, 1950), Royal Wedding (MGM, 1951), Angels in the Outfield (MGM, 1951), Texas Carnival (MGM, 1951), It's a Big Country (MGM, 1951), Phone Call From a Stranger (20th, 1952), The Belle of New York (MGM, 1952), Fearless Fagan (MGM, 1952), Sky Full of Moon (MGM, 1952), Desperate Search (MGM, 1952), Holiday for Sinners (MGM, 1952), Battle Circus (MGM, 1953), Code Two (MGM, 1953), All the Brothers Were Valiant (MGM, 1953), Kiss Me, Kate! (MGM, 1953), The Long, Long Trailer (MGM, 1954), Men of the Fighting Lady (MGM, 1954), Tennessee Champ (MGM, 1954), The Marauders (MGM, 1955), The Glass Slipper (MGM, 1955), Running Wild (Univ., 1955), Shack-out on 101 (AA, 1955), The Man in the Gray Flannel Suit (20th, 1956), Johnny Concho (UA, 1956), The Naked Hills (AA, 1956), The Great Man (Univ., 1956), Joe Butterfly (Univ., 1957), The Fuzzy Pink Nightgown (UA, 1957), Don't Go Near the Water (MGM, 1957), The Deep Six (WB, 1958), A Time to Love and a Time to Die (Univ., 1958), The Perfect Furlough (Univ., 1958), A Hole in the Head (UA, 1959), That Kind of Woman (Par., 1959), The Crowded Sky (WB, 1960), The Absent-Minded Professor (BV, 1961), King of the Roaring 20's—The Story of Arnold Rothstein (AA, 1961), Pattern For Plunder ("Operation Mermaid"—Herts Lion International, 1963), Son of Flubber (BV, 1963), Man in the Middle (20th, 1964), Dr. Strangelove (Col., 1964), Honeymoon Hotel (MGM, 1964), Stage to Thunder Rock (Par., 1964), The Patsy (Par., 1964), Bikini Beach (AIP, 1964), The Americanization of Emily (MGM, 1964), Nightmare in the Sun (Zodiac, 1965), The Great Race (WB, 1965), Promise Her Anything (Par., 1966), Stagecoach (20th, 1966), Around the World Under the Sea (MGM, 1966), Night of the Grizzly (Par., 1966), Warning Shot (Par., 1967), Run Like a Thief (Feature Film Corporation of America, 1967), Welcome to Hard Times (MGM, 1967), The War Wagon (Univ., 1967), MacKenna's Gold (Col., 1968), Finian's Rainbow (WB-7 Arts, 1968), Blood Holiday (Cinegai-Jolly, 1968).

Rock Hudson and Gig Young in Strange Bedfellows.

GIG YOUNG (Byron Ellsworth Barr) Born November 4, 1917, St. Cloud, Minnesota. Married Sheila Stapler; divorced. Married Sophie Rosenstein; widowed 1952. Married Elizabeth Montgomery (1956); divorced. Married Elaine Whitman (1963), child: Jennifer.

Feature Films:

as Byron Barr: Misbehaving Husbands (PRC, 1940), Navy Blues (WB, 1941), One Foot in Heaven (WB, 1941), They Died With Their Boots On (WB, 1941), Sergeant York (WB, 1941), You're in the Army Now (WB, 1941), The Male Animal (WB, 1942), The Affairs of Susan (Par., 1945).

as Gig Young: Captains of the Clouds (WB, 1942), The Gay Sisters (WB, 1942), Air Force (WB, 1943), Old Acquaintance (WB, 1943), Escape Me Never (WB, 1947), The Woman in White (WB, 1948), Wake of the Red Witch (Rep., 1948), Lust for Gold (Col., 1949), Tell It to the Judge (Col., 1949)., Hunt the Man Down (RKO, 1950), Target Unknown (Univ., 1951), Only the Valiant (WB, 1951), Come Fill the Cup (WB, 1951), Slaughter Trail (RKO, 1951), Too Young to Kiss (MGM, 1951), Holiday for Sinners (MGM, 1952), You for Me (MGM, 1952), The Girl Who Had Everything (MGM, 1953), Arena (MGM, 1953), Torch Song (MGM, 1953), Young at Heart (WB, 1954), The Desperate Hours (Par., 1955), Desk Set (20th, 1957), Teacher's Pet (Par., 1958), The Tunnel of Love (MGM, 1958), Ask Any Girl (MGM, 1959), The Story on Page One (20th, 1959), That Touch of Mink (Univ., 1962), Kid Galahad (UA, 1962), Five Miles to Midnight (UA, 1963), For Love or Money (Univ., 1963), A Ticklish Affair (MGM, 1964), Strange Bedfellows (Univ., 1964), The Shuttered Room (WB-7 Arts 1967).

LORETTA YOUNG (Gretchen Young) Born January 6, 1913, Salt Lake City, Utah. Married Grant Withers (1930); annulled 1931. Married Thomas Lewis (1940), children: Judy, Christopher, Peter.

Spencer Tracy, Loretta Young and Walter Connolly in Man's Castle.

Sound Feature Films: The Forward Pass (WB, 1929), The Squall (WB, 1929), The Careless Age (WB, 1929), Fast Life (WB, 1929), Show of Shows (WB, 1929), Loose Ankles (WB, 1930), The Man From Blankley's (WB, 1930), The Second Floor Mystery (WB, 1930), Road to Paradise (WB, 1930), Kismet (WB, 1930), Truth About Youth (WB, 1930), The Devil to Pay (UA, 1930), Beau Ideal (RKO, 1931), Right of Way (WB, 1931), Three Girls Lost (Fox, 1931), Too Young to Marry (WB, 1931), Big Business Girl (WB, 1931), I Like Your Nerve (WB, 1931), Platinum Blonde (Col., 1931), The Ruling Voice (WB, 1931), Taxi (WB, 1932), The Hatchet Man (WB, 1932), Three Wise Girls (Col., 1932), Play Girl (WB, 1932), Zoo in Budapest (Fox, 1933), Week-End Marriage (WB, 1932), Life Begins (WB, 1932), They Call It Sin (WB, 1932), Employees' Entrance (WB, 1933), Grand Slam (WB, 1933), The Life of Jimmy Dolan (WB, 1933), Midnight Mary (MGM, 1933), Heroes for Sale (WB, 1933), The Devil's in Love (Fox, 1933), She Had to Say Yes (WB, 1933), Man's Castle (Col., 1933), House of Rothschild (UA, 1934), Bulldog Drummond Strikes Back (UA, 1934), Born to Be Bad (UA, 1934), Caravan (Fox, 1934), The White Parade (Fox, 1934), Clive of India (UA, 1935), Call of the Wild (UA, 1935), Shanghai (Par., 1935), The Crusades (Par., 1935), The Unguarded Hour (MGM, 1936), Private Number (20th, 1936), Ramona (20th, 1936), Ladies in Love (20th, 1936), Love Is News (20th, 1937), Cafe Metropole (20th, 1937), Love Under Fire (20th, 1937), Wife, Doctor and Nurse (20th, 1937), Second Honeymoon (20th, 1937), Four Men and a Prayer (20th, 1938), Three Blind Mice (20th, 1938), Suez (20th, 1938), Kentucky (20th,

1938), *Wife, Husband and Friend* (20th, 1939), *The Story of Alexander Graham Bell* (20th, 1939), *Eternally Yours* (UA, 1939), *The Doctor Takes a Wife* (Col., 1940), *He Stayed for Breakfast* (Col., 1940), *The Lady From Cheyenne* (Univ., 1941), *The Men in Her Life* (Col., 1941), *Bedtime Story* (Col., 1941), *A Night to Remember* (Col., 1942), *China* (Par., 1943), *Ladies Courageous* (Univ., 1944), *And Now Tomorrow* (Par., 1944), *Along Came Jones* (RKO, 1945), *The Stranger* (RKO, 1946), *The Perfect Marriage* (Par., 1946), *The Farmer's Daughter* (RKO, 1947), *The Bishop's Wife* (RKO, 1947), *Rachel and the Stranger* (RKO, 1948), *The Accused* (Par., 1948), *Mother Is a Freshman* (20th, 1949), *Come to the Stable* (20th, 1949), *Key to the City* (MGM, 1950), *Cause for Alarm* (MGM, 1951), *Half Angel* (20th, 1951), *Paula* (Col., 1952), *Because of You* (Univ., 1952), *It Happens Every Thursday* (Univ., 1953).

Robert Young, Barbara Stanwyck and Hardie Albright in *Red Salute*.

ROBERT YOUNG Born February 22, 1907, Chicago, Illinois. Married Elizabeth Henderson (1933), children: Carol, Barbara, Elizabeth, Kathleen.

Feature Films: *Black Camel* (Fox, 1931), *The Sin of Madel on Claudet* (MGM, 1931), *Guilty Generation* (Col., 1931), *Hell Divers* (MGM, 1931), *Wet Parade* (MGM, 1932), *Strange Interlude* (MGM, 1932), *New Morals for Old* (MGM, 1932), *Unashamed* (MGM, 1932), *The Kid From Spain* (UA, 1932), *Today We Live* (MGM, 1933), *Hell Below* (MGM, 1933), *Men Must Fight* (MGM, 1933), *Tugboat Annie* (MGM, 1933), *Saturday's Millions* (Univ., 1933), *Right to Romance* (RKO, 1933), *House of Rothschild* (UA, 1934), *Carolina* (Fox, 1934), *Lazy River* (MGM, 1934), *Spitfire* (RKO, 1934), *Whom the Gods Destroy* (Col., 1934), *Paris Interlude* (MGM, 1934), *Death on the Diamond* (MGM, 1934), *The Band Plays On* (MGM, 1934), *West Point of the Air* (MGM, 1935), *Vagabond Lady* (MGM, 1935), *Calm Yourself* (MGM, 1935), *Red Salute* (UA, 1935), *The Bride Comes Home* (Par., 1935), *Remember Last Night?* (Univ., 1935), *Secret Agent* (Gaumont-British, 1936), *It's Love Again* (Gaumont-British, 1936), *Three Wise Guys* (MGM, 1936), *Sworn Enemy* (MGM, 1936), *The Bride Walks Out* (RKO, 1936), *The Longest Night* (MGM, 1936), *Stowaway* (20th, 1936), *Dangerous Number* (MGM, 1937), *I Met Him in Paris* (Par., 1937), *The Emperor's Candlesticks* (MGM, 193d), *Married Before Breakfast* (MGM, 1937), *The Bride Wore Red* (MGM, 1937), *Navy Blue and Gold* (MGM, 1937), *Paradise for Three* (MGM, 1938), *Josette* (20th, 1938), *The Toy Wife* (MGM, 1938), *Three Comrades* (MGM, 1938), *Rich Man—Poor Girl* (MGM, 1938), *The Shining Hour* (MGM, 1938), *Honolulu* (MGM, 1939), *Bridal Suite* (MGM, 1939), *Maisie* (MGM, 1939), *Miracles For Sale* (Col., 1939), *Florian* (MGM, 1940), *Northwest Passage* (MGM, 1940), *The Mortal Storm* (MGM, 1940), *Sporting Blood* (MGM, 1940), *Dr. Kildare's Crisis* (MGM, 1940), *The Trial of Mary Dugan* (MGM, 1941), *Western Union* (20th, 1941), *Lady Be Good* (MGM, 1941), *Married Bachelor* (MGM, 1941),

H.M. Pulham, Esq. (MGM, 1941), *Joe Smith, American* (MGM, 1942), *Cairo* (MGM, 1942), *Journey for Margaret* (MGM, 1942), *Slightly Dangerous* (MGM, 1943), *Claudia* (20th, 1943), *Sweet Rosie O'Grady* (20th, 1943), *The Canterville Ghost* (MGM, 1944), *Those Endearing Young Charms* (RKO, 1945), *The Enchanted Cottage* (RKO, 1945), *The Searching Wind* (Par., 1946), *Lady Luck* (RKO, 1946), *Claudia and David* (20th, 1946), *They Won't Believe Me* (RKO, 1947), *Crossfire* (RKO, 1947), *Relentless* (Col., 1948), *Sitting Pretty* (20th, 1948), *Adventure in Baltimore* (RKO, 1949), *Bride for Sale* (RKO, 1949), *That Forsyte Woman* (MGM, 1950), *And Baby Makes Three* (Col., 1950), *Goodbye, My Fancy* (WB, 1951), *The Second Woman* (UA, 1951), *On The Loose* (RKO, 1951), *The Half-Breed* (RKO, 1952), *Secret of the Incas* (Par., 1954).

ROLAND YOUNG Born November 11, 1887, London, England. Married Marjorie Kummer (1921); divorced 1940. Married Patience DuCroz (1948). Died June 5, 1953.

Roland Young and Joan Blondell in *Topper Returns*.

Feature Films: *Unholy Night* (MGM, 1929), *Her Private Life* (WB, 1929), *Wise Girl* (MGM, 1930), *The Bishop Murder Case* (MGM, 1930), *Madam Satan* (MGM, 1930), *New Moon* (MGM, 1930), *The Prodigal* (MGM, 1931), *Don't Bet on Women* (Fox, 1931), *Squaw Man* (MGM, 1931), *Annabelle's Affairs* (Fox, 1931), *The Guardsman* (MGM, 1931), *Pagan Lady* (Col., 1931), *Wedding Rehearsal* (London, 1932), *Lovers Courageous* (MGM, 1932), *A Woman Commands* (RKO, 1932), *One Hour With You* (Par., 1932), *This Is the Night* (Par., 1932), *Street of Women* (WB, 1932), *They Just Had to Get Married* (Univ., 1933), *A Lady's Profession* (Par., 1933), *Pleasure Cruise* (Fox, 1933), *Blind Adventure* (RKO, 1933), *His Double Life* (Par., 1933), *Here Is My Heart* (Par., 1934), *Ruggles of Red Gap* (MGM, 1935), *David Copperfield* (MGM, 1935), *The Unguarded Hour* (MGM, 1936), *One Rainy Afternoon* (UA, 1936), *Give Me Your Heart* (WB, 1936), *Call It a Day* (WB, 1937), *The Man Who Could Work Miracles* (UA, 1937), *Topper* (MGM, 1937), *Ali Baba Goes to Town* (20th, 1937), *Sailing Along* (Gaumont-British, 1938), *The Young in Heart* (UA, 1938), *Topper Takes a Trip* (UA, 1939), *Yes, My Darling Daughter* (WB, 1939), *The Night of Nights* (Par., 1939), *Here I Am, a Stranger* (20th, 1939), *He Married His Wife* (20th, 1940), *Irene* (RKO, 1940), *Star Dust* (20th, 1940), *Private Affairs* (Univ., 1940), *Dulcy* (MGM, 1940), *No, No, Nanette* (RKO, 1940), *The Philadelphia Story* (MGM, 1940), *Topper Returns* (UA, 1941), *The Flame of New Orleans* (Univ., 1941), *Two-Faced Woman* (MGM, 1941), *The Lady Has Plans* (Par., 1942), *They All Kissed the Bride* (Col., 1942), *Tales of Manhattan* (20th, 1942), *Forever and a Day* (RKO, 1943), *Standing Room Only* (Par., 1944), *And Then There Were None* (20th, 1945), *You Gotta Stay Happy* (Univ., 1948), *The Great Lover* (Par., 1949), *Bond Street* (Stratford, 1950), *Let's Dance* (Par., 1950), *St. Benny the Dip* (UA, 1951), *That Man From Tangier* (UA, 1953).

CHAPTER III

THE FILMS

Abbott and Costello Meet Frankenstein with Glenn Strange, Lou Costello and Bud Abbott.

ABBOTT AND COSTELLO MEET FRANKENSTEIN (1948) Univ. Producer, Robert Arthur. Director, Charles T. Barton. Original Screenplay, Robert Lees, Frederic I. Rinaldo, John Grant. Art Directors, Bernard Herzbrun, Hilyard Brown. Music, Frank Skinner. Photography, Charles Van Enger. Editor, Frank Gross. 92 minutes

Chick: Bud Abbott, *Wilbur:* Lou Costello, *Lawrence Talbot:* Lon Chaney, *Dracula:* Bela Lugosi, *Monster:* Glenn Strange, *Sandra Mornay:* Lenore Aubert, *Joan Raymond:* Jane Randolph, *Mr. McDougal:* Frank Ferguson, *Dr. Stevens:* Charles Bradstreet, *Mr. Harris:* Howard Negley, *Man:* Joe Kirk, *Man in Armor:* Clarence Straight, *Photographer:* Harry Brown, *Woman at Baggage Counter:* Helen Spring, *Sergeant:* Paul Stader, *Voice of the Invisible Man:* Vincent Price.

ABE LINCOLN IN ILLINOIS (1940) RKO. Presented by Max Gordon Plays and Pictures Corp. Produced by Max Gordon. Directed by John Cromwell. Based on the play by Robert E. Sherwood. Screenplay, Robert E. Sherwood, Grover Jones. Music, Roy Webb. Dance Director, David Robel. Cameraman, James Wong Howe. Special Effects, Vernon Walker. Montage, Douglas Travers. 110 minutes

Abraham Lincoln: Raymond Massey, *Stephen Douglas:* Gene Lockhart, *Mary Todd Lincoln:* Ruth Gordon, *Ann Rutledge:* Mary Howard, *Elizabeth Edwards:* Dorothy Tree, *Ninian Edwards:* Harvey Stephens, *Joshua Speed:* Minor Watson, *Billy Herndon:* Alan Baxter, *Jack Armstrong:* Howard da Silva, *Judge Bowling Green:* Aldrich Bowker, *John McNeil:* Maurice Murphy, *Mentor Graham:* Louis Jean Heydt, *Ben Mattling:* Clem Bevans, *Denton Offut:* Harlan Briggs, *Sarah Lincoln:* Elisabeth Risdon, *Tom Lincoln:* Charles Middleton, *Seth Gale:* Herbert Rudley, *Mr. Crimmin:* Roger Imhof, *Stage Driver:* Andy Clyde, *Mr. Rutledge:* Edmund Elton, *Mrs. Rutledge:* Leona Roberts, *Mrs. Bowling Green:* Florence Roberts, *Dr. Chandler:*

Abe Lincoln in Illinois with Raymond Massey and Mary Howard.

Above and Beyond with Eleanor Parker and Robert Taylor.

George Rosener, *Mrs. Gale:* Fay Helm, *John Hanks:* Trevor Bardette, *John Johnston:* Sid Saylor, *Gobey:* Napoleon Simpson, *Trem Cogdall:* Alec Craig, *Little Girl:* Peggy Ann Garner.

ABOVE AND BEYOND (1952) MGM. Producers, Melvin Frank, Norman Panama. Directors, Melvin Frank, Norman Panama. Author, Beirne Lay, Jr. Screenplay, Melvin Frank, Norman Panama, Beirne Lay, Jr. Music, Hugo Friedhofer. Art Directors, Cedric Gibbons, Malcolm Brown. Sound, Douglas Shearer. Sets, Edwin B. Willis, Ralph Hurst. Cinematographer, Ray June. Editor, Cotton Warburton. Music conducted by Andre Previn. Montage Sequences, Peter Ballbusch. Special Effects, A. Arnold Gillespie, Warren Newcombe. 122 minutes

Colonel Paul Tibbets: Robert Taylor, *Lucey Tibbets:* Eleanor Parker, *Major Uanna:* James Whitmore, *Major Gen. Vernon C. Brent:* Larry Keating, *Captain Parsons:* Larry Gates, *Marge Bratton:* Marilyn Erskine, *Major Harry Bratton:* Stephen Dunne, *General Samuel E. Roberts:* Robert Burton, *Dr. Ramsey:* Hayden Rorke, *Dr. Van Dyke:* Larry Dobkin, *Dr. Fiske:* Jack Raine, *Dutch Van Kirk:* Jonathan Cott, *Thomas Ferebee:* Jeff Richards, *Bob Lewis:* Dick Simmons, *Wyatt Duzenbury:* John McKee, *Radio Operator:* Patrick Conway, *Paul Tibbets, Jr.:* Christie Olsen, *Driver:* William Lester, *Mary Malone:* Barbara Ruick, *General LeMay:* Jim Backus, *Major Gen. Creston:* G. Pat Collins, *Chaplain Downey:* Harlan Warde, *General Corlane:* Crane Whitley, *Dexter:* Don Gibson, *Captain:* John W. Baer, *Co-Pilot:* John Close, *General Roberts' Aide:* Lee MacGregor, *General Wolfe:* Ewing Mitchell, *General Irvine:* Mack Williams, *Captain:* Sam McKim, *M. P. Officer:* Robert Forrest, *Haddock:* Dabbs Greer, *Nurse:* Dorothy Kennedy, *Lieut. Malone:* John Hedloe, *Sergeant Wilson:* Frank Gerstle, *Miller:* John Pickard, *Burns:* Gregory Walcott, *Johnson:* Roger McGee, *Extra:* Robert Fuller.

ABRAHAM LINCOLN (1930) UA. Produced and directed by D. W. Griffith. Adapted for the screen by Stephen Vincent Benét. Screenplay, Stephen Vincent Benét, Gerrit Lloyd. Art Director, William Cameron Menzies. Costumes, Walter Israel, Dialogue Director. Harry Stubbs. Photography, Karl Struss. Editors, James Smith, Hal C. Kern. Sound, Harold Witt. A Feature Production. Griffith's first sound film. 97 minutes

Abraham Lincoln: Walter Huston, *Ann Rutledge:* Una Merkel, *Mary Todd Lincoln:* Kay Hammond, *John Wilkes Booth:* Ian Keith, *D.*

Abraham Lincoln with Kay Hammond and Walter Huston.

Offut: Otto Hoffman, *General Lee:* Hobart Bosworth, *Colonel Marshall:* Henry B. Walthall, *Nancy Hanks Lincoln:* Helen Freeman, *Tom Lincoln:* W. L. Thorne, *Midwife:* Lucille La Verne, *Armstrong:* Edgar Dearing, *Stephen A. Douglas:* E. Alyn Warren, *Lincoln's Employer:* Russell Simpson, *Sheriff:* Charles Crockett, *Mrs. Edwards:* Helen Ware, *Billy Herndon:* Jason Robards, *Tad Lincoln:* Gordon Thorpe, *John Hay:* Cameron Prudhomme, *General Scott:* James Bradbury, Sr., *Young Soldier:* Jimmie Eagles, *General Grant:* Fred Warren, *Secretary of War Stanton:* Oscar Apfel, *General Philip Sheridan:* Frank Campeau, *New Englander:* Henry Kolker, *Bit:* Mary Forbes, *Man:* Robert E. Homans.

THE ABSENT-MINDED PROFESSOR (1961) BV. Producer, Walt Disney. Director, Robert Stevenson. Screenplay, Bill Walsh. Based on a story by Samuel W. Taylor. Photography, Edward Colman. Music, George Bruns. Art Direction, Carroll Clark. Editor, Cotton Warburton. Special Effects, Peter Ellenshaw and Eustace Lycett. Sound, Dean Thomas. Associate Producer, Bill Walsh. Assistant Director, Robert G. Shannon. Film debuts of Keenan Wynn's son Ned, and Steve Allen's mother Belle Montrose. 97 minutes

Ned Brainard: Fred MacMurray, *Betsy Carlisle:* Nancy Olson, *Alonzo Hawk:* Keenan Wynn, *Bill Hawk:* Tommy Kirk, *Fire Chief:* Ed Wynn, *President Rufus Daggett:* Leon Ames, *Coach Elkins:* Wally Brown, *First Referee:* Alan Carney, *Shelby Ashton:* Elliott Reid, *Defense Secretary:* Edward Andrews, *General Singer:* David Lewis, *Air Force Captain:* Jack Mullaney, *Mrs. Chatsworth:* Belle Montrose, *Officer Kelly:* Forrest Lewis, *Officer Hanson:* James Westerfield, *Youth:* Ned Wynn, *Reverend Bosworth:* Gage Clarke, *General Hotchkiss:* Alan Hewitt, *Admiral Olmstead:* Raymond Bailey, *General Poynter:* Wendell Holmes, *Lenny:* Don Ross, *Sig:* Charlie Briggs, *TV Newsman:* Wally Boag, *Basketball Player (#18):* Leon Tyler.

The Absent-Minded Professor with Fred MacMurray and Nancy Olson.

248

ADAM'S RIB (1949) MGM. Producer, Lawrence Weingarten. Director, George Cukor. Screenplay, Garson Kanin, Ruth Gordon. Music, Miklos Rozsa. Art Directors, Cedric Gibbons, William Ferrari. Photography, George J. Folsey. Editor, George Boemler. Song by Cole Porter: "Farewell Amanda." 101 minutes

Adam Bonner: Spencer Tracy, *Amanda Bonner:* Katharine Hepburn, *Doris Attinger:* Judy Holliday, *Warren Attinger:* Tom Ewell, *Kip Lurie:* David Wayne, *Beryl Caighn:* Jean Hagen, *Olympia La Pere:* Hope Emerson, *Grace:* Eve March, *Judge Reiser:* Clarence Kolb, *Jules Frikke:* Emerson Treacy, *Mrs. McGrath:* Polly Moran, *Judge Marcasson:* Will Wright, *Dr. Margaret Brodeigh:* Elizabeth Flournoy, *Mary (Maid):* Janna da Loos, *Dave:* James Nolan, *Roy:* David Clarke, *Court Clerk:* John Maxwell, *Court Stenographer:* Marvin Kaplan, *Police Matron:* Gracille LaVinder, *Benjamin Klausner:* William Self, *Emerald:* Paula Raymond, *Photographer:* Ray Walker, *Reporter:* Tommy Noonan, *Adam's Assistants:* De Forrest Lawrence, John Fell, *Amanda's Assistant:* Sid Dubin, *Mr. Bonner:* Joe Bernard, *Mrs. Bonner:* Madge Blake, *Mrs. Marcasson:* Marjorie Wood, *Judge Poynter:* Lester Luther, *Mrs. Poynter:* Anna Q. Nilsson, *Hurlock:* Roger David, *Elderly Elevator Operator:* Louis Mason, *Fat Man:* Rex Evans, *Young District Attorney:* Charles Bastin.

Adventure with Greer Garson, Clark Gable and Joan Blondell.

THE ADVENTURES OF ROBIN HOOD (1938) WB. Producer, Hal B. Wallis. Associate Producer, Henry Blanke. Directors, Michael Curtiz, William Keighley. Color by Technicolor. Authors and Screenplay, Norman Reilly Raine, Seton I. Miller. Art Director, Carl Jules Weyl. Music, Erich Wolfgang Kornold. Musical Director, Leo F. Forbstein. Cameramen, Tony Gaudio, Sol Polito, W. Howard Green. Editor, Ralph Dawson. 105 minutes

Robin Hood: Errol Flynn, *Maid Marian:* Olivia De Havilland, *Prince John:* Claude Rains, *Sir Guy:* Basil Rathbone, *King Richard:* Ian Hunter, *Friar Tuck:* Eugene Pallette, *Little John:* Alan Hale, *High Sheriff:* Melville Cooper, *Will Scarlett:* Patric Knowles, *Much, the Miller:* Herbert Mundin, *Bess, the Maid:* Una O'Connor, *Bishop of Black Canon:* Montagu Love, *Dicken Malbott:* Harry Cording, *Sir Geoffrey:* Robert Warwick, *Sir Ralfe:* Robert Noble, *Sir Mortimer:* Kenneth Hunter, *Essex:* Leonard Willey, *Sir Ivor:* Lester Matthews, *Sir Baldwin:* Colin Kenny, *Captain of Archers:* Howard Hill, *Proprietor of Kent Road Tavern:* Ivan F. Simpson, *Crippen:* Charles McNaughton, *Humility Prin:* Lionel Belmore, *Humility's Daughter:* Janet Shaw, *Sir Nigel:* Austin Fairman, *Sir Norbett:* Craufurd Kent, *Robin's Outlaws:* Val Stanton, Ernie Stanton, Olaf Hytten, Alec Harford, Peter Hobbes, Edward Dew, *Richard's Knight:* John Sutton, *Sir Guy's Squire:* Marten Lamont, *High Sheriff's Squire:* Hal Brazeale, *Seneschal:* Herbert Evans, *Referee:* Holmes Herbert, *Norman Officer:* Leyland Hodgson.

Adam's Rib with Spencer Tracy, David Wayne, Judy Holliday and Katharine Hepburn.

ADVENTURE (1945) MGM. Producer, Sam Zimbalist. Director, Victor Fleming. Author, Clyde Brion Davis. Screenplay, Frederick Hazlitt Brennan, Vincent Lawrence. Adaptation, Anthony Veiller, William H. Wright. Musical Score, Herbert Stothart. Art Directors, Cedric Gibbons and Urie McCleary. Cameraman, Joseph Ruttenberg. Special Effects, Warren Newcombe. Editor, Frank Sullivan. 125 minutes

Harry Patterson: Clark Gable, *Emily Sears:* Greer Garson, *Helen Melohn:* Joan Blondell, *Mudgin:* Thomas Mitchell, *Gus:* Tom Tully, *Model T:* John Qualen, *Limo:* Richard Haydn, *Maria:* Lina Romay, *Old Ramon:* Philip Merivale, *Dr. Ashlon:* Harry Davenport, *Young Ramon:* Tito Renaldo, *Felipe:* Pedro de Cordoba, *Jabbo:* Gary Owen, *Joe:* Ralph Peters, *Ed:* Joseph Crehan, *Rico:* Ray Teal, *Littelton:* Byron Foulger, *Ethel:* Audrey Totter, *Adele:* Marta Linden, *Doctor:* Harry Tyler, *Modiste:* Bess Flowers, *Red:* Kay Medford, *Preacher:* Rex Ingram, *Model:* Joan Thorsen, *Bits in Library:* Max Davidson, Claire McDowell, *Rudolfo:* Chef Joseph Milani, *Nick the Bartender:* Martin Garralaga, *Captain:* Jack Young, *Cashier:* Dorothy Granger, *First Dame:* Elizabeth Russell, *Blister:* Esther Howard, *Landlady:* Florence Auer, *Big Mug:* Harry Wilson, *Mrs. Buckley:* Betty Blythe, *Mr. Buckley:* Pierre Watkin, *Tony:* Charles La Torre, *Mrs. Ludlow:* Dorothy Vaughan, *Mr. Ludlow:* Morris Ankrum.

The Adventures of Robin Hood with Basil Rathbone and Errol Flynn.

THE ADVENTURES OF TOM SAWYER (1938) UA. Produced by David O. Selznick. Directed by Norman Taurog. Color by Technicolor. Based on the story by Mark Twain. Screenplay, John V. A. Weaver. Assistant to the Producer, William H. Wright. Music, Lou Forbes. Art Directors, Lyle Wheeler, William Cameron Menzies,

The Adventures of Tom Sawyer with Philip Hurlic and Tommy Kelly.

Casey Roberts. Special Effects, Jack Cosgrove. Continuity, Barbara Keon. Assistant Director, Eric Stacey. Research, Lillian K. Deighton. Color Supervisor, Natalie Kalmus. Photography, James Wong Howe and Wilfred M. Cline. Editors, Hal C. Kern and Margaret Clancey. Filmed at Lake Malibu. 93 minutes

Tom Sawyer: Tommy Kelly, *Aunt Polly:* May Robson, *Huck Finn:* Jackie Moran, *Muff Potter:* Walter Brennan, *Injun Joe:* Victor Jory, *Mary Sawyer:* Marcia Mae Jones, *Sheriff:* Victor Kilian, *Mrs. Thatcher:* Nana Bryant, *Becky Thatcher:* Ann Gillis, *Joe Harper:* Mickey Rentschler, *Amy Lawrence:* Cora Sue Collins, *Judge Thatcher:* Charles Richman, *Widow Douglas:* Spring Byington, *Mrs. Harper:* Margaret Hamilton, *Little Jim:* Philip Hurlic, *Sid Sawyer:* David Holt, *Ben Rogers:* Georgie Billings, *Billy Fisher:* Byron Armstrong, *Schoolmaster:* Olin Howland, *Sunday School Superintendent:* Donald Meek, *Churchgoer:* Harry C. Myers.

Affair in Trinidad with Rita Hayworth (in poster) and Glenn Ford.

AFFAIR IN TRINIDAD (1952) Col. Producer and Director, Vincent Sherman. Authors, Virginia Van Upp, Berne Giler. Screenplay, Oscar Saul, James Gunn. Art Director, Walter Holscher. Sets, William Kiernam. Music, Morris Stoloff, George Duning. Cinematographer, Joseph Walker. Editor, Viola Lawrence. Songs by Lester Lee and Bob Russell: "I've Been Kissed Before" and "Trinidad Lady." 98 minutes

Chris Emery: Rita Hayworth, *Steve Emery:* Glenn Ford, *Max Fabian:* Alexander Scourby, *Veronica:* Valerie Bettis, *Inspector Smythe:* Torin Thatcher, *Anderson:* Howard Wendell, *Walters:* Karel Ste-

panek, *Dr. Franz Huebling:* George Voskovec, *Wittol:* Steven Geray, *Peter Bronec:* Walter Kohler, *Dominique:* Juanita Moore, *Olaf:* Gregg Martell, *Martin:* Mort Mills, *Pilot:* Robert Boon, *Coroner:* Ralph Moody, *Neal:* Ross Elliott, *Refugee:* Franz Roehn, *Mr. Peters (Reporter):* Don Kohler, *Englishman:* John Sherman, *Fisherman:* Joel Fluellen, *Airport Clerk:* Fred Baker, *Stewardess:* Kathleen O'Malley, *Refugee:* Leonidas Ossetynski, *Bobby:* Don Blackman, *Fisherman:* Ivan Browning, *Fisherman:* Roy Glenn.

The Affairs of Susan with Joan Fontaine and George Brent.

THE AFFAIRS OF SUSAN (1945) Par. Producer, Hal B. Wallis. Director, William A. Seiter. Authors, Thomas Monroe, Laszlo Gorog. Screenplay, Thomas Monroe, Laszlo Gorog, Richard Flournoy. Score, Frederick Hollander. Art Directors, Hans Dreier, Franz Bachelin. Cameraman, David Abel. Process Photography, Farciot Edouart. Editor, Eda Warren. Song by E. Y. Harburg and Franz Waxman: "Something in My Heart." 110 minutes

Susan Darell: Joan Fontaine, *Roger Berton:* George Brent, *Bill Anthony:* Dennis O'Keefe, *Richard Aiken:* Walter Abel, *Mike Ward:* Don De Fore, *Mona Kent:* Rita Johnson, *Nancy:* Mary Field, *Chick:* Byron Barr, *Uncle Jemmy:* Francis Pierlot, *Mr. Cusp:* Lewis Russell, *Brooklyn Girl:* Vera Marshe, *Brooklyn Boy:* Frank Faylen, *Major:* James Millican, *Lieutenant:* Robert Sully, *First Captain:* John Whitney, *Second Captain:* Jerry James, *Colonel:* Crane Whitley, *Waiter:* Bill Meader, *Waiter:* Warren Hymer, *Messenger Boy:* Ralph Brooke, *First Girl at the Bright Dollar:* Natalie Draper, *Dowager:* Alice Fleming, *Mrs. Oakleaf:* Almeda Fowler, *Bartender at the Bright Dollar:* Eddie Laughton, *Whortle:* Milton Kibbee, *Fisherman:* Howard Mitchell, *Evie:* Kitty O'Neil, *Mr. Giddon:* Gordon Richards, *Mr. Hughes:* Cyril Ring, *Second Girl at the Bright Dollar:* Ruth Roman, *Grumpy Man at the Bright Dollar:* Eddy C. Waller, *Actress at First Party:* Mira McKinney, *Taxi Driver:* Douglas Carter, *Girl:* Teala Loring, *Boy:* Joel Friend, *Secretary:* Renee Dupuis, *Secretary:* Grace Gillern.

AN AFFAIR TO REMEMBER (1957) 20th. Produced by Jerry Wald. Directed by Leo McCarey. Stereophonic Sound. In CinemaScope and De Luxe Color. Screenplay, Delmer Daves and Leo McCarey. Story, Leo McCarey and Mildred Cram. Art Directors, Lyle R. Wheeler and Jack Martin Smith. Music, Hugo Friedhofer. Conducted by Lionel Newman. Orchestrations, Edward B. Powell and Peter King. Title song by Harry Warren, lyrics by Leo McCarey and Harold Adamson. Sung by Vic Damone. Wardrobe Designer, Charles LeMaire. Assistant Director, Gilbert Mandelik. Cinematography, Milton Krasner. Special Photographic Effects, L. B. Abbott. Editor, James B. Clark. A remake of *Love Affair* (RKO, 1939). 119 minutes

Nickie Ferrante: Cary Grant, *Terry McKay:* Deborah Kerr, *Kenneth:* Richard Denning, *Lois:* Neva Patterson, *Grandmother:* Cathleen Nesbitt, *Announcer:* Robert Q. Lewis, *Hathaway:* Charles Watts, *Courbet:* Fortunio Bonanova, *Doctor:* Walter Woolf King, *French Commentator:* Roger Til, *English TV Commentator:* Jack Raine, *Italian Commen-*

An Affair to Remember with Deborah Kerr, Cary Grant and Cathleen Nesbitt.

After the Thin Man with Myrna Loy, William Powell and Sam Levene.

tator: Dino Bolognese, *Painter:* Jack Lomas, *Mother:* Dorothy Adams, *Doctor:* Robert Lynn, *Blonde:* Patricia Powell, *Airline Stewardess:* Alena Murray, *Ship Passenger:* Minta Durfee, *Father McGrath:* Matt Moore, *Marius:* Louis Mercier, *Miss Webb:* Geraldine Wall, *Miss Lane:* Sarah Selby, *Gladys:* Nora Marlowe, *Bartender:* Alberto Morin, *Gabrielle:* Genevieve Aumont, *Landlady:* Jesslyn Fax, *Red-Head:* Tommy Nolan, *Orphans:* Theresa Emerson, Richard Allen, Tina Thompson, Scotty Morrow, Kathleen Charney, Terry Ross Kelman, Norman Champion, III, *Teachers:* Mary Carroll, Suzanne Ellers, Juney Ellis, *Page Boy:* Don Pietro, *Bit Man:* Paul Bradley, *Waiter:* Tony De Mario, *Waiter on Ship:* Michka Egan, *Maitre D':* Bert Stevens, *Boy, age 5:* Brian Corcoran, *French Child:* Priscilla Garcia, *Ship's Photographer:* Marc Snow, *Page Boy:* Anthony Mazzola, *Nurse:* Helen Mayon.

THE AFRICAN QUEEN (1951) UA. Producer, S. P. Eagle. Director, John Huston. Color by Technicolor. Screenplay, James Agee and John Huston. Based on the novel by C. S. Forester. Music, Allan Gray. 106 minutes

Charlie Allnut: Humphrey Bogart, *Rose Sayer:* Katherine Hepburn, *Reverend Samuel Sayer:* Robert Morley, *Captain of* LOUISA: Peter Bull, *First Officer:* Theodore Bikel, *Second Officer:* Walter Gotell, *Petty Officer:* Gerald Onn, *First Officer of* SHONA: Peter Swanick, *Second Officer of* SHONA: Richard Marner.

The African Queen with Peter Bull, Katharine Hepburn and Humphrey Bogart.

AFTER THE THIN MAN (1936) MGM. Produced by Hunt Stromberg. Directed by W. S. Van Dyke. Author, Dashiell Hammett. Screenplay by Francis Goodrich, Albert Hackett. Musical Score, Herbert Stothart, Edward Ward. Cameraman, Oliver T. Marsh. Editor, Robert J. Kern. Songs: "Smoke Dreams" by Arthur Freed and Nacio Herb Brown; "Blow That Horn" by Walter Donaldson, Bob Wright, and Chet Forrest. Second in the series of six pictures. 110 minutes

Nora Charles: Myrna Loy, *Nick Charles:* William Powell, *David Graham:* James Stewart, *Dancer:* Joseph Calleia, *Salma Landis:* Elissa Landi, *Aunt Katherine Forrest:* Jessie Ralph, *Robert Landis:* Alan Marshall, *Lt. Abrams:* Sam Levene, *Polly Byrnes:* Dorothy McNulty (later Penny Singleton), *Charlotte:* Dorothy Vaughn, *Helen:* Maude Turner Gordon, *Floyd Casper:* Teddy Hart, *Lum Kee:* William Law, *Lucius:* William Burress, *William:* Thomas Pogue, *Dr. Adolph Kammer:* George Zucco, *Henry (the Butler):* Tom Ricketts, *Phil Byrnes:* Paul Fix, *Joe:* Joe Caits, *Willie:* Joe Phillips, *Hattie:* Edith Kingdon, *Jerry:* John T. Murray, *Harold:* John Kelly, *Lucius:* Clarence Kolb, *Lucy:* Zeffie Tilbury, *S. F. Police Captain:* George Guhl, *Chief of Detectives:* Guy Usher, *Bill, S. F. Policeman:* Ed Dearing, *Reporter:* Jack Norton, *S. F. Detective:* Dick Rush, *Rose (the Cook):* Mary Gordon, *Emily:* Alice H. Smith, *Eddie:* George Taylor, *Burton Forrest:* Harlan Briggs, *Kid:* Murray Alper, *Headwaiter:* Richard Loo, *Peter (Butler):* Eric Wilton, *Wrestler's Manager:* Vince Barnett, *Fingers:* Harry Tyler, *Leader of Late Crowd:* Bobby Watson.

The Agony and the Ecstasy with Charlton Heston and Rex Harrison.

THE AGONY AND THE ECSTASY (1965) 20th. Director, Carol Reed. Screen story and screenplay, Philip Dunne. Based on the novel by Irving Stone. Music, Alex North. Director of Photography, Leon Shamroy. Assistant Director, Gus Agosti. Costumes, Vittorio Nino Novarese. In Todd-AO and De Luxe Color. 140 minutes

Michelangelo: Charlton Heston, *Pope Julius II:* Rex Harrison, *Contessina de' Medici:* Diane Cilento, *Bramante:* Harry Andrews, *Duke of Urbino:* Alberto Lupo, *Giovanni de' Medici:* Adolfo Celi, *Paris De-Grassis:* Venantino Venantini, *Sangallo:* John Stacy, *Foreman:* Fausto Tozzi, *Woman:* Maxine Audley, *Raphael:* Tomas Milian.

Air Force with John Garfield, Harry Carey, Ray Montgomery (on ground) and Charles Drake.

AIR FORCE (1943) WB. Produced by Hal B. Wallis. Directed by Howard Hawks. Original Screenplay, Dudley Nichols. Music, Franz Waxman. Music Director, Leo F. Forbstein. Chief Pilot, Paul Mantz. Editor, George Amy. 124 minutes

Captain Mike (Irish) Quincannon, Pilot: John Ridgely, *Lt. Bill Williams, Copilot:* Gig Young, *Lt. Tommy McMartin, Bombardier:* Arthur Kennedy, *Lt. Munchauser, Navigator:* Charles Drake, *Sgt. Robby White, Crew Chief:* Harry Carey, *Corp. Weinberg, Assistant Crew Chief:* George Tobias, *Corp. Peterson, Radio Operator:* Ward Wood, *Pvt. Chester, Assistant Radio Operator:* Ray Montgomery, *Sgt. Joe Winocki, Aerial Gunner:* John Garfield, *Lt. Tex Rader, Pursuit Pilot:* James Brown, *Major Mallory:* Stanley Ridges, *Colonel:* Willard Robertson, *Colonel Blake, C. O.:* Moroni Olsen, *Sgt. J. J. Callahan:* Edward S. Brophy, *Major W. G. Roberts:* Richard Lane, *Lt. P. T. Moran:* Bill Crago, *Susan McMartin:* Faye Emerson, *Major Daniels:* Addison Richards, *Major A. M. Bagley:* James Flavin, *Mary Quincannon:* Ann Doran, *Mrs. Chester:* Dorothy Peterson, *Marine with Dog:* James Millican, *Group Cmdr. Jack Harper:* William Forrest, *Corporal, Demolition Squad:* Murray Alper, *Officer at Hickam Field:* George Neise, *Marine:* Tom Neal, *Quincannon's Son:* Henry Blair, *Control Officer:* Warren Douglas, *Nurse:* Ruth Ford, *Second Nurse:* Leah Baird, *Sergeants:* Bill Hopper and Sol Gorss, *Control Officer:* James Bush, *Ground Crew Man:* George Offerman, Jr., *Joe (Sergeant):*

The Alamo with Chill Wills and John Wayne.

Walter Sande, *Nurses:* Lynne Baggett and Marjorie Hoshelle, *First Lieutenant:* Theodore von Eltz, *Second Lieutenant:* Ross Ford, *Copilot:* Rand Brooks.

THE ALAMO (1960) UA. Producer-Director, John Wayne. Todd-AO and Technicolor. Screenplay, James Edward Grant. Music, Dimitri Tiomkin. Songs, Dimitri Tiomkin and Paul Francis Webster. A Batjac Production. Second Unit Director, Cliff Lyons. Photography, William Clothier. Editor, Stuart Gilmore. Art Director, Alfred Ybarra. Sets, Victor A. Gangelin. Technical Supervision, Frank Beetson and Jack Pennick. Assistant Directors, Robert E. Relyea, Robert Saunders, John Ford. Costumes, Frank Beetson and Ann Peck. Special Effects, Lee Zavitz. Make-up, Web Overlander. Production Manager, Nate Edwards. Assistant to the Producer, Michael Wayne. Songs, "The Green Leaves of Summer" and "Lisa." Bit player Le Jeane Guye, 27, was killed October 11, 1959. Filmed in Texas. 192 minutes

Col. David Crockett: John Wayne, *Col. James Bowie:* Richard Widmark, *Col. William Travis:* Laurence Harvey, *Gen. Sam Houston:* Richard Boone, *Lt. Reyes:* Carlos Arruza, *Smitty:* Frankie Avalon, *James Bonham:* Pat Wayne, *Flaca:* Linda Cristal, *Mrs. Dickinson:* Joan O'Brien, *Beekeeper:* Chill Wills, *Juan Seguin:* Joseph Calleia, *Capt. Dickinson:* Ken Curtis, *Parson:* Hank Worden, *Gambler Thimblerig:* Denver Pyle, *Angelina:* Aissa Wayne, *Silverio Sequin:* Julian Trevino, *Jethro:* Jester Hairston, *Blind Nell:* Veda Ann Borg, *Mrs. Dennison:* Olive Carey, *Emil:* Wesley Lau, *Bull:* Tom Hennesy, *Dr. Sutherland:* Bill Henry, *Pete:* Cy Malis, *Jocko Robertson:* John Dierkes, *Lieutenant Finn:* Guinn "Big Boy" Williams, *Sgt. Lightfoot:* Jack Pennick, *Bearded Volunteer:* Fred Graham, *Colonel Neill:* Bill Daniel, *Tennessean:* Chuck Roberson, *Woman:* Le Jeane Guye.

Alexander's Ragtime Band with Alice Faye, Tyrone Power, Jack Haley and Don Ameche.

ALEXANDER'S RAGTIME BAND (1938) 20th. Producer, Darryl F. Zanuck. Associate Producer, Harry Joe Brown. Director, Henry King. Screenplay, Kathryn Scola, Lamar Trotti, Richard Sherman. Art Directors, Bernard Herzbrun, Boris Leven. Cameraman, Peverell Marley. Editor, Barbara McLean. Songs by Irving Berlin: "Now It Can Be Told", "My Walking Stick", "Alexander's Ragtime Band", "I'm Marching Along With Time." Dances staged by Seymour Felix. 105 minutes

Alexander (Roger Grant): Tyrone Power, *Stella Kirby:* Alice Faye, *Charlie Dwyer:* Don Ameche, *Jerry Allen:* Ethel Merman, *Davey Lane:* Jack Haley, *Professor Heinrich:* Jean Hersholt, *Aunt Sophie:* Helen Westley, *Taxi Driver:* John Carradine, *Bill:* Paul Hurst, *Wally Vernon:* Himself, *Ruby:* Ruth Terry, *Snapper:* Douglas Fowley, *Louie:* Chick Chandler, *Corporal Collins:* Eddie Collins, *Dillingham's Stage Manager:* Joseph Crehan, *Dirty Eddie:* Robert Gleckler, *Specialty:* Dixie Dunbar, *Charles Dillingham:* Joe King, *Babe:* Grady Sutton, *Singer:* Donald Douglas, *Headwaiter:* Charles Coleman, *Captain:* Stanley Andrews, *Agent:* Charles Williams, *Trio:* Jane Jones,

Mel Kalish, Otto Fries, *Drill Sergeant:* Jack Pennick, *Member of Band:* Cully Richards, *Manager of Radio Station:* Selmer Jackson, *Dillingham's Secretary:* Charles Tannen, *Photographer:* Lon Chaney, Jr., *Assistant Stage Manager:* Arthur Rankin, *Stage Manager:* Paul McVey, *Quartette:* King's Men, *Major:* Edward Keane, *Captain:* James Flavin, *Assistant Stage Manager:* Tyler Brooke, *Captain:* Ralph Dunn, *Martha:* Eleanor Wesselhoeft, *Reporter:* Robert Lowery.

Alibi with Chester Morris (right).

ALIBI (1929) UA. Produced and directed by Roland West. From the play *Nightstick* by John Wray, J. C. Nugent, and Elaine Sterne Carrington. Story and dialogue, Roland West and C. Gardner Sullivan. Music, Hugo Risenfeld. Photography, Ray June. Editor, Hal Kern. Titles for silent version, Roland West and C. Gardner Sullivan. Shot originally as a silent, this was refilmed with sound on the *Coquette* set, at night. 90 minutes

Chick Williams (No. 1065): Chester Morris, *Danny McGann:* Regis Toomey, *Daisy Thomas:* Mae Busch, *Joan Manning:* Eleanor Griffith, *Buck Bachman:* Harry Stubbs, *Toots:* Irma Harrison, *Brown:* Al Hill, *Blake:* James Bradbury, Jr., *Soft Malone:* Elmer Ballard, *Trask:* Kernan Cripps, *Pete Manning:* Purnell B. Pratt, *Tommy Glennon:* Pat O'Malley, *O'Brien:* DeWitt Jennings, *George Stanislaus David:* Edward Brady, *Singers in Theater:* Virginia Flohri, Edward Jardon.

ALICE ADAMS (1935) RKO. Produced by Pandro S. Berman. Directed by George Stevens. From Booth Tarkington's 1921 Pulitzer Prize novel. Screenplay, Dorothy Yost and Mortimer Offner. Adaptation, Jane Murfin. Photography, Robert de Grasse. Song: "I Can't Waltz Alone" by Dorothy Fields and Max Steiner. 99 minutes

Alice Adams with Katharine Hepburn and Fred Stone.

Alice Adams: Katharine Hepburn, *Arthur Russell:* Fred MacMurray, *Mr. Adams:* Fred Stone, *Mildred Palmer:* Evelyn Venable, *Walter Adams:* Frank Albertson, *Mrs. Adams:* Ann Shoemaker, *Mr. Lamb:* Charles Grapewin, *Frank Dowling:* Grady Sutton, *Mrs. Palmer:* Hedda Hopper, *Mr. Palmer:* Jonathan Hale, *Henrietta Lamb:* Janet McLeod, *Mrs. Dowling:* Virginia Howell, *Mrs. Dresser:* Zeffie Tilbury, *Ella Dowling:* Ella McKenzie, *Malena:* Hattie McDaniel.

ALL ABOUT EVE (1950) 20th. Producer, Darryl F. Zanuck. Director-Screenplay, Joseph Mankiewicz. Author, Mary Orr from *The Wisdom of Eve.* Music, Alfred Newman. Art Directors, Lyle Wheeler, George W. Davis. Photography, Milton Krasner. Editor, Barbara McLean. Scenes filmed at the Curran Theatre, San Francisco. 138 minutes

Margo Channing: Bette Davis, *Eve Harrington:* Anne Baxter, *Addison De Witt (Narrator):* George Sanders, *Karen Richards:* Celeste Holm, *Bill Sampson:* Gary Merrill, *Lloyd Richards:* Hugh Marlowe, *Birdie:* Thelma Ritter, *Miss Caswell:* Marilyn Monroe, *Max Fabian:* Gregory Ratoff, *Phoebe:* Barbara Bates, *Speaker at Dinner:* Walter Hampden, *Girl:* Randy Stuart, *Leading Man:* Craig Hill, *Doorman:* Leland Harris, *Autograph Seeker:* Barbara White, *Stage Manager:* Eddie Fisher, *Clerk:* William Pullen, *Pianist:* Claude Stroud, *Frenchman:* Eugene Borden, *Reporter:* Helen Mowery, *Captain of Waiters:* Steven Geray, *Well-Wisher:* Bess Flowers.

All About Eve with Celeste Holm, Hugh Marlowe, Bette Davis and Anne Baxter.

ALL QUIET ON THE WESTERN FRONT (1930) Univ. Directed by Lewis Milestone. Based on the novel by Erich Maria Remarque. Screenplay, Dell Andrews, Maxwell Anderson and George Abbott. Art Directors, Charles D. Hall and W. R. Schmitt. Synchronization and Score, David Broekman. Assistant Director, Nate Watt. Photography, Arthur Edeson. Editors, Edgar Adams and Milton Carruth. Sound, C. Roy Hunter. Titles (Silent Version), Walter Anthony. Filmed at Universal City, Balboa, the Irving Ranch. The European version featured ZaSu Pitts as Mrs. Baumer (she was in the original film, before being replaced by Beryl Mercer). Reissued in 1939 with a narrator telling of the horrors of war. 140 minutes

Paul Baumer: Lew Ayres, *Katczinsky:* Louis Wolheim, *Himmelstoss:* John Wray, *Gerard Duval:* Raymond Griffith, *Tjaden:* George (Slim) Summerville, *Muller:* Russell Gleason, *Albert:* William Bakewell, *Leer:* Scott Kolk, *Behm:* Walter Browne Rogers, *Kemmerick:* Ben Alexander, *Peter:* Owen Davis, Jr., *Mrs. Baumer:* Beryl Mercer, *Mr. Baumer:* Edwin Maxwell, *Detering:* Harold Goodwin, *Miss Baumer:* Marion Clayton, *Westhus:* Richard Alexander, *Lieutenant Bertinck:* G. Pat Collins, *Suzanne:* Yola D'Avril, *French Girls:* Renée Damonde, Poupée Androit, *Kantorek:* Arnold Lucy, *Ginger:*

All Quiet on the Western Front with Lew Ayres and Raymond Griffith.

Bill Irving, *Herr Meyer:* Edmund Breese, *Hammacher:* Heinie Conklin, *Sister Libertine:* Bertha Mann, *Watcher:* Bodil Rosing, *Poster Girl:* Joan Marsh, *Orderly:* Tom London, *Cook:* Vince Barnett, *Man:* Fred Zinnemann. Lewis Milestone's hand was used for Ayres' at the end when Paul reaches for a butterfly.

ALL THE KING'S MEN (1949) Col. Producer, Robert Rossen. Director, Robert Rossen. Based on the novel by Robert Penn Warren. Screenplay, Robert Rossen. Musical Director, Morris Stoloff. Art Director, Sturges Carne. Photography, Burnett Guffey. Editor, Al Clark. 109 minutes

All the King's Men with Mercedes McCambridge, John Ireland, Broderick Crawford and Walter Burke.

Willie Stark: Broderick Crawford, *Tom Stark:* John Derek, *Anne Stanton:* Joanne Dru, *Jack Burden:* John Ireland, *Sadie Burke:* Mercedes McCambridge, *Adam Stanton:* Shepperd Strudwick, *Tiny Duffy:* Ralph Dumke, *Lucy Stark:* Ann Seymour, *Mrs. Burden:* Katharine Warren, *Judge Stanton:* Raymond Greenleaf, *Sugar Boy:* Walter Burke, *Dolph Pillsbury:* Will Wright, *Floyd McEvoy:* Grandon Rhodes, *Pa Stark:* H. C. Miller, *Hale:* Richard Hale, *Commissioner:* William Bruce, *Sheriff:* A. C. Tillman, *Madison:* Houseley Stevenson, *Minister:* Truett Myers, *Football Coach:* Phil Tully, *Helene Hale:* Helene Stanley, *Politician:* Judd Holdren, *Receptionist:* Reba Watterson, *Man:* Paul Ford, *Dance Caller:* Ted French, *Local Chairman:*

Paul Maxey, *Doctor:* Frank McLure, *Man:* Frank Wilcox, *Butler:* Irving Smith, *Minister:* Louis Mason, *Drunk:* John Skins Miller, *Radio Announcer:* Edwin Chandler, *Reporter:* King Donovan, *Politician:* Pat O'Malley.

All the Way Home with Georgia Simmons, Ronnie Claire Edwards, Jean Simmons, Edwin Wolfe, Pat Hingle, Michael Kearney and Robert Preston.

ALL THE WAY HOME (1963) Par. Producer, David Susskind. Director, Alex Segal. Screenplay, Philip Reisman, Jr.. Based on play by Tad Mosel, adapted from novel by James Agee, *A Death in the Family.* Music, Alec Wilder. Associate Producer, Jack Grosseberg. Assistant Directors, Larry Sturhahn, Michael Hertzberg. Cinematographer, Boris Kaufman. Editor, Carl Lerner. 103 minutes

Mary: Jean Simmons, *Jay:* Robert Preston, *Ralph:* Pat Hingle, *Aunt Hannah:* Aline MacMahon, *Joel:* Thomas Chalmers, *Andrew:* John Cullum, *Sally:* Ronnie Claire Edwards, *Rufus:* Michael Kearney, *Walter Starr:* John Henry Faulk, *Great-Great-Granmaw:* Lylah Tiffany, *Grand-Aunt Sadie:* Mary Perry, *Jessie:* Georgia Simmons, *John Henry:* Edwin Wolfe, *Father Jackson:* Ferdie Hoffman.

ALL THIS, AND HEAVEN TOO (1940) WB. Vice President in Charge of Production, Jack Warner. Executive Producer, Hal B. Wallis. Associate Producer, David Lewis. Directed by Anatole Litvak. Based on the novel by Rachel Field. Screenplay, Casey Robinson. Art Director, Jules Weyl. Photography, Ernest Haller. Sound, Robert

All This, and Heaven Too with Janet Beecher, Bette Davis and Jeffrey Lynn.

E. Lee. Editor, Warren Low. Costumes, Orry-Kelly. Make-up, Perc Westmore. Music, Max Steiner. Orchestral Arrangements, Hugo Friedhofer. Assistant Director, Sherry Shourds. Songs by Jack Scholl and M. K. Jerome: "Lotus Song" and "The War of Roses." 143 minutes

Henriette: Bette Davis, *Duc De Praslin:* Charles Boyer, *Reverend Henry Field:* Jeffrey Lynn, *Duchess De Praslin:* Barbara O'Neil, *Louise:* Virginia Weidler, *Pasquier:* Walter Hampden, *Pierre:* Harry Davenport, *Abbé:* Fritz Leiber, *Madame Le Maire:* Helen Westley, *Mlle. Maillard:* Sibyl Harris, *Miss Haines:* Janet Beecher, *Marechal Sebastiani:* Montagu Love, *Charpentier:* George Couatouris, *Broussais:* Henry Daniell, *Delangle:* Ian Keith, *Isabelle:* June Lockhart, *Berthe:* Ann Todd, *Raynald:* Richard Nichols, *Madame Gauthier:* Mrs. Gardner Crane (Madge Terry), *Gendarme:* Victor Kilian, *Dr. Louis:* Edward Fielding, *Emily Schuyler:* Ann Gillis, *Rebecca Jay:* Mary Anderson, *Helen Lexington:* Peggy Stewart, *Loti:* Christian Rub, *Police Official:* Frank Reicher, *Doctor:* Egon Brecher, *Elizabeth Ward:* Betty-Jean Hainey, *Louise de Rham:* Cora Sue Collins, *Clara Parker:* Betty Jane Graham, *Agnes Brevoort:* Doris Bren, *Marianna Van Horn:* Marilyn Knowlden, *Isabelle Loullard:* Ann Howard, *Kate Delancey:* Gloria Fisher, *Mary Simpson:* Jeanne Wells, *Dora Vanderbilt:* Susanne Ransom, *Officer:* Creighton Hale, *Maxine:* Carmen Bretta.

Along Came Jones with Dan Duryea and Gary Cooper.

ALONG CAME JONES (1945) RKO. Producer, Gary Cooper. Director, Stuart Heisler. Author, Alan LeMay. Screenplay, Nunnally Johnson. Production Designer, Wiard B. Ihnen. Music Score, Arthur Lange. Cameraman, Milton Krasner. Editor, Thomas Neff. Song by Arthur Lange and Al Stewart: "Round and Round." 90 minutes

Melody Jones: Gary Cooper, *Cherrie:* Loretta Young, *George Fury:* William Demarest, *Monte:* Dan Duryea, *Avery de Longpre:* Frank Sully, *Ira Waggoner:* Walter Sande, *Leo Gledhill:* Don Costello, *Luke Packard:* Willard Robertson, *Pop de Longpre:* Russell Simpson,

Sheriff: Arthur Loft, *Boone:* Lane Chandler, *Kriendler:* Ray Teal, *Guard on Coach:* Frank Cordell, *Bartender:* Erville Alderson, *Man at Bar:* Paul Sutton, *Town Character:* Lane Watson, *Small Man:* Paul E. Burns, *Store Proprietor:* Chris-Pin Martin, *Rancher on Street:* Jack Baxley, *Rifleman:* Doug Morrow, *Cotton:* Ralph Dunn, *Card Player:* Charles Morton, *Deputy:* Lee Phelps, *Wagon Driver:* Billy Engle, *Posse:* Bob Kortman, Frank McCarroll, Hank Bell, Chalky Williams

AMERICA AMERICA (1963) WB. Produced, directed and written by Elia Kazan. From his book. Costumes, Anna Hill Johnstone. Associate Producer, Charles H. Maguire. Music, Manos Hadjidakis.

America America with Stathis Giallelis.

Lyrics, Nikos Gatsos. Production Assistant, Burtt Harris. Cinematographer, Haskell Wexler. Editor, Dede Allen. 174 minutes

Stavros Topouzoglou: Stathis Giallelis, *Vartan Damadian:* Frank Wolff, *Isaac Topouzoglou:* Harry Davis, *Vasso Topouzoglou:* Elena Karam, *Grandmother Topouzoglou:* Estelle Hemsley, *Hohanness Gardashian:* Gregory Rozakis, *Abdul:* Lou Antonio, *Odysseus Topouzoglou:* Salem Ludwig, *Garabet:* John Marley, *Vartuhi:* Johanna Frank, *Aleko Sinnkoglou:* Paul Mann, *Thomna Sinnikoglou:* Linda Marsh, *Aratoon Kebabian:* Robert H. Harris, *Sophia Kebabian:* Katherine Balfour.

AN AMERICAN IN PARIS (1951) MGM. Producer, Arthur Freed. Director, Vincente Minnelli. Color by Technicolor. Art Directors, Cedric Gibbons, Preston Ames. Musical Directors, Johnny Green and Saul Chapell. Author, Alan Jay Lerner. Screenplay, Alan Lin. Photography, Alfred Gilks, John Alton. Editor, Adrienne Fazan. Songs by Ira and George Gershwin: "I Got Rhythm," "Embraceable You," "'s' Wonderful," "By Strauss," "Tra-La-La-La," "Our Love Is Here to Stay," "I'll Build a Stairway to Paradise" (lyrics by E. Ray Goetz and B. G. DeSylva), "Concerto in F" and "An American in Paris" (both instrumental numbers). 113 minutes

Jerry Mulligan: Gene Kelly, *Lise Bourvier:* Leslie Caron, *Adam Cook:* Oscar Levant, *Henri Baurel:* Georges Guetary, *Milo Roberts:* Nina Foch, *Georges Mattieu:* Eugene Borden, *Mathilde Mattieu:* Martha Bamattre, *Old Woman Dancer:* Mary Young, *Therese:* Ann Codee, *Francois:* George Davis, *Tommy Baldwin:* Hayden Rorke, *John McDowd:* Paul Maxey, *Ben Macrow:* Dick Wessel, *Honeymoon Couple:* Don Quinn, Adele Coray, *Boys with Bubble Gum:* Lucian Planzoles, Christian Pasques, Anthony Mazola, *Nuns:* Jeanne Lafayette, Louise Laureau, *Postman:* Alfred Paix, *American Girl:* Noel Neill, *Maid:* Nan Boardman, *Jack Jansen:* John Eldredge, *Kay Jansen:* Anna Q. Nilsson, *Edna Mae Bestram (Customer):* Madge Blake, *Driver:* Art Dupuis, *Artist:* Greg McClure *Dancing Partner:* Andre Charisse, *News Vendor:* Marie Antoinette Andrews.

An American in Paris with Gene Kelly and Leslie Caron.

The Americanization of Emily with James Garner, Julie Andrews and Joyce Grenfell.

THE AMERICANIZATION OF EMILY (1964) MGM. Producer, Martin Ransohoff. Director, Arthur Hiller. Screenplay, Paddy Chayefsky. Based on novel by William Bradford Huie. Director of Photography, Philip Lathrop. Music, Johnny Mandel. Song, Johnny Mercer. Associate Producer, John Calley. Costumes, Bill Thomas. Assistant Director, Al Shenberg. A Filmways Picture. Reissued as *Emily* in 1967. 117 minutes

Lt. Comdr. Charles Madison: James Garner, *Emily Barham:* Julie Andrews, *Admiral William Jessup:* Melvyn Douglas, *Lt. Cmdr. "Bus" Cummings:* James Coburn, *Mrs. Barham:* Joyce Grenfell, *Admiral Thomas Healy:* Edward Binns, *Sheila:* Liz Fraser, *Old Sailor:* Keenan Wynn, *Capt. Harry Spaulding:* William Windom, *Chief Petty Officer Paul Adams:* John Crawford, *Capt. Marvin Ellender:* Douglas Henderson, *Admiral Hoyle:* Edmond Ryan, *Young Sailor:* Steve Franken, *Gen. William Hallerton:* Paul Newlan, *Lt. Victor Wade:* Gary Cockrell, *Enright:* Alan Sues, *Port Commander:* Bill Fraser, *Nurse Captain:* Lou Byrne, *Port Ensign:* Alan Howard, *Pat:* Linda Marlow, *Nameless Broads:* Janine Gray, Judy Carne, Kathy Kersh.

Anastasia with Ingrid Bergman and Helen Hayes.

ANASTASIA (1956) 20th. Producer, Buddy Adler. Director, Anatole Litvak. CinemaScope, De Luxe Color. From the play by Marcelle Maurette as adapted by Guy Bolton. Screenplay, Arthur Laurents. Art Directors, Andrei Andrejew, Bill Andrews. Music, Alfred Newman. Orchestration, Edward B. Powell. Cinematographer, Jack Hildyard. Editor, Bert Bates. 105 minutes.

Anastasia: Ingrid Bergman, *Prince:* Yul Brynner, *Dowager Empress:* Helen Hayes, *Chernov:* Akim Tamiroff, *Livenbaum:* Martita Hunt, *Chamberlain:* Felix Aylmer, *Petrovin:* Sacha Piteoff, *Prince Paul:* Ivan Desny, *Lissemskaia:* Natalie Schafer, *Stepan:* Gregoire Gromoff, *Vlados:* Karel Stepanek, *Marusia:* Ina De La Haye, *Maxime:* Katherine Kath, *Zhadanov:* Olaf Pooley, *Older Man:* Andre Mickhelson, *Countess Baranova:* Olga Valery, *Von Drivnitz:* Eric Pohlman, *Bechmetieff:* Alexis Bobrinskoy, *Footman:* Edward Forsyth, *Empress' Cossack:* Stanley Zevick, *Kasbek Dancers:* Tutte Lemkow and Anatole Smirnoff, *Grischa:* Peter Sallis, *Zenia:* Tamara Shane, *Blonde Man:* Alan Cuthbertson, *Prince Bolkonoski:* Henry Vidon, *Blonde Lady:* Hy Hazell, *Schiskin:* Mr. Pavlov, *Jean:* Paula Catton, *Marguerite:* Marguerite Brennan.

Anatomy of a Murder with James Stewart, Joseph N. Welch, Lee Remick and George C. Scott.

ANATOMY OF A MURDER (1959) Col. Producer-Director, Otto Preminger. Screenplay, Wendell Mayes. Music by Duke Ellington, Assistant Director, David Silver. Art Director, Boris Leven. Cinematographer, Sam Leavitt. Editor, Louis R. Loeffler. A Carlyle Production. Based on the novel by Robert Traver (Michigan Supreme Court Justice John D. Voelker). Filmed in Ishpeming, Michigan. Film debut of Boston lawyer Joseph N. Welch. 160 minutes

Paul Biegler: James Stewart, *Laura Manion:* Lee Remick, *Lt. Manion:* Ben Gazzara, *Parnell McCarthy:* Arthur O'Connell, *Maida:* Eve Arden, *Mary Pilant:* Kathryn Grant, *Claude Dancer:* George C. Scott, *Dr. Smith:* Orson Bean, *Mr. Lemon:* Russ Brown, *Paquette:* Murray Hamilton, *Mitch Lodwick:* Brooks West, *Sgt. Durgo:* Ken Lynch, *Sulo:* John Qualen, *Pie Eye:* Duke Ellington, *Judge Weaver:* Joseph N. Welch, *Sheriff Battisfore:* Royal Beal, *Dr. Dompierre:* Howard McNear, *Dr. Raschid:* Ned Wever, *Madigan:* Jimmy Conlin, *Mr. Burke:* Joseph Kearns, *Duane Miller:* Don Russ, *Court Clerk:* Lloyd LeVasseur, *An Army Sergeant:* James Waters, *Dr. Harcourt:* Alexander Campbell, *Distinguished Gentleman:* Irv Kupcinet, *Juror:* Mrs. Joseph Welch.

ANCHORS AWEIGH (1945) MGM. Producer, Joe Pasternak. Director, George Sidney. Color by Technicolor. Author, Natalie Marcin. Screenplay, Isobel Lennart. Musical Director, Georgie Stoll. Art Directors, Cedric Gibbons, Randall Duell. Cameramen, Robert Planck, Charles Boyle. Editor, Adrienne Fazan. Songs: "We Hate to Leave," "What Makes the Sun Set?", "The Charm of You," "I Begged Her" and "I Fall in Love Too Easily" by Sammy Cahn and Jule Styne; "The Worry Song" by Ralph Freed and Sammy Fain. 140 minutes

Anchors Aweigh with William "Bill" Phillips, Gene Kelly, Frank Sinatra, Douglas Cowan and Henry Armetta.

Joseph Brady: Gene Kelly, *Clarence Doolittle:* Frank Sinatra, *Susan Abbott:* Kathryn Grayson, *Jose Iturbi:* Himself, *Donald Martin:* Dean Stockwell, *Carlos:* Carlos Ramirez, *Admiral Hammond:* Henry O'Neill, *Commander:* Leon Ames, *Police Sergeant:* Rags Ragland, *Police Captain:* Edgar Kennedy, *Girl from Brooklyn:* Pamela Britton, *Hamburger Man:* Henry Armetta, *Cafe Manager:* Billy Gilbert, *Little Girl Beggar:* Sharon McManus, *Studio Cop:* James Burke, *Radio Cop:* James Flavin, *Iturbi's Assistant:* Chester Clute, *Bertram Kramer:* Grady Sutton, *Specialty (cartoon):* Tom and Jerry, *Lana Turner Double:* Peggy Maley, *Iturbi Secretary:* Sondra Rodgers, *Soldiers:* Garry Owen, Steve Brodie, *Butler:* Charles Coleman, *Bearded Man:* Milton Parsons, *Waitress:* Renie Riano, *Commander:* Alex Callam. *Sailors:* Harry Barris, John James, Wally Cassell, Douglas Cowan, Henry Daniels, Jr., Phil Hanna, William "Bill" Phillips, Tom Trout, *Hamburger Woman:* Esther Michelson, *Movie Director:* William Forrest, *Asst. Movie Director:* Ray Teal, *Bartender:* Milton Kibbee.

ANGELS WITH DIRTY FACES (1938) WB. Producer, Sam Bischoff. Director, Michael Curtiz. Original Story, Rowland Brown. Screenplay, John Wexley, Warren Duff. Cameraman, Sol Polito. Editor, Owen Marks. Song by Fred Fisher and Maurice Spitalny: "Angels With Dirty Faces." 97 minutes

Rocky Sullivan: James Cagney, *Jerry Connelly:* Pat O'Brien, *James*

Angels With Dirty Faces with Humphrey Bogart and James Cagney

Frazier: Humphrey Bogart, *Laury Ferguson:* Ann Sheridan, *Mac Keefer:* George Bancroft, *Soapy:* Billy Halop, *Swing:* Bobby Jordan, *Bim:* Leo Gorcey, *Hunky:* Bernard Punsley, *Pasty:* Gabriel Dell, *Crab:* Huntz Hall, *Rocky (as a boy):* Frankie Burke, *Jerry (as a boy):* William Tracy, *Laury (as a girl):* Marilyn Knowlden, *Steve:* Joe Downing, *Blackie:* Adrian Morris, *Guard Kennedy:* Oscar O'Shea, *Guard Edwards:* Edward Pawley, *Bugs, Gunman:* William Pawley, *Police Captain:* John Hamilton, *Priest:* Earl Dwire, *Death Row Guard:* Jack Perrin, *Mrs. Patrick:* Mary Gordon, *Soapy's Mother:* Vera Lewis, *Warden:* William Worthington, *R. R. Yard Watchman:* James Farley, *Red:* Chuck Stubbs, *Maggione Boy:* Eddie Syracuse, *Policeman:* Robert Homans, *Basketball Captain:* Harris Berger, *Pharmacist:* Harry Hayden, *Gangsters:* Dick Rich, Stevan Darrell, Joe A. Devlin, *Italian:* William Edmunds, *Buckley:* Charles Wilson, *Boys:* Frank Coghlan Jr., David Durand.

Animal Crackers with Chico Marx, Robert Greig and Harpo Marx.

ANIMAL CRACKERS (1930) Par. Directed by Victor Heerman. Based on the Marx Brothers musical by George S. Kaufman, Bert Kalmar, Morrie Ryskind, and Harry Ruby. Screenplay, Morrie Ryskind and Pierre Collings. Photography, George Folsey. Sound, Ernest F. Zatorsky. Songs: "Why Am I So Romantic?", "Hooray for Captain Spaulding" by Kalmar and Ruby; "Collegiate" by Moe Jaffe and Nat Bonx; "Some of These Days" by Shelton Brooks. Filmed in Long Island, N. Y. Studios. Ann Roth is Lillian Roth's sister. 100 minutes

Captain Geoffrey T. Spaulding: Groucho Marx, *The Professor:* Harpo Marx, *Emanuel Ravelli:* Chico Marx, *Horatio W. Jamison:* Zeppo Marx, *Arabella Rittenhouse:* Lillian Roth, *Mrs. Rittenhouse:* Margaret Dumont, *Roscoe Chandler:* Louis Sorin, *John Parker:* Hal Thompson, *Mrs. Whitehead:* Margaret Irving, *Grace Carpenter:* Kathryn Reece, *Hives:* Robert Greig, *Hennessey:* Edward Metcalf, *Footmen:* The Music Masters, *Girl:* Ann Roth.

The Animal Kingdom with Leslie Howard and Myrna Loy.

THE ANIMAL KINGDOM (1932) RKO. Directed by Edward H. Griffith. Based on the play by Philip Barry. Adaptation, Horace Jackson. Photography, George Folsey. Editor, Daniel Mandell. Sound, Daniel Cutler. The first feature to play the Roxy Theatre, New York. Remade as *One More Tomorrow* (WB, 1946). 90 minutes

Daisy Sage: Ann Harding, *Tom Collier:* Leslie Howard, *Cecelia Henry:* Myrna Loy, *Owen:* Neil Hamilton, *Regan:* William Gargan, *Rufus Collier:* Henry Stephenson, *Grace:* Ilka Chase, *Franc:* Leni Stengel, *Joe:* Donald Dillaway.

Anna and the King of Siam with Irene Dunne and Rex Harrison.

ANNA AND THE KING OF SIAM (1946) 20th. Producer, Louis D. Lighton. Director, John Cromwell. Based on the book by Margaret Landon. Screenplay, Talbot Jennings, Sally Benson. Musical Score, Bernard Herrman. Art Directors, Lyle Wheeler, William Darling. Cameraman, Arthur Miller. Special Effects, Fred Sersen. Editor, Harmon Jones. Remade as *The King and I* (20th, 1956). 128 minutes

Anna: Irene Dunne, *The King:* Rex Harrison, *Tuptim:* Linda Darnell, *Kralahome:* Lee Cobb, *Lady Thiang:* Gale Sondergaard, *Alak:* Mikhail Rasumny, *Sir Edward:* Dennis Hoey, *Prince (grown up):* Tito Renaldo, *Louis Owens:* Richard Lyon, *Moonshee:* William Edmunds, *Phya Phrom:* John Abbott, *Interpreter:* Leonard Strong, *Prince:* Mickey Roth, *Beebe:* Connie Leon, *Princess Fa-Ying:* Diana Van den Ecker, *Dancer:* Si-lan Chen, *Miss MacFarlane:* Marjorie Eaton, *Mrs. Cortwright:* Helena Grant, *Mr. Cortwright:* Stanley Mann, *Captain Orton:* Addison Richards, *Phra Palat:* Neyle Morrow, *Government Clerk:* Julian Rivero, *Lady Sno Klin:* Yvonne Rob, *Wives of King:* Loretta Luiz, Chabing, Marianne Quon, Lillian Molieri, Buff Cobb, Sydney Logan, *Old Woman:* Oie Chan, *Judge:* Ted Hecht, *Third Judge:*

Anna Christie with Charles Bickford and Greta Garbo.

Ben Welden, *Guard:* Aram Katcher, *Guide:* Pedro Regas, *Guard:* Rico DeMontes, *Slave:* Hazel Shon.

ANNA CHRISTIE (1930) MGM. Directed by Clarence Brown. Based on the play by Eugene O'Neill. Screenplay, Frances Marion. Art Director, Cedric Gibbons. Photography, William Daniels. Editor, Hugh Wynn. Sound, Douglas Shearer. Titles (silent version), Madeleine Ruthven. Garbo's first talkie; she also starred in a German version for MGM. Remake of 1923 First National film, in which George Marion also played Chris. 86 minutes

Anna Gustafson (Anna Christie): Greta Garbo, *Matt Burke:* Charles Bickford, *Chris Gustafson:* George F. Marion, *Marthy Owens:* Marie Dressler, *Larry, the Bartender:* Lee Phelps, *Johnny the Harp:* James T. Mack.

ANNA KARENINA (1935) MGM. Produced by David O. Selznick. Directed by Clarence Brown. From Count Leo Tolstoy's novel. Screenplay, Clemence Dane, Salka Viertel. Adaptation and Dialogue, S. N. Behrman. Collaborator, Erich von Stroheim. Art Director, Cedric Gibbons. Costumes, Adrian. Music, Herbert Stothart. Ballet staged by Margarete Wallmann. Mazurka staged by Chester Hale. Consultant, Count Andrey Tolstoy. Associate Art Directors, Fredric Hope and Edwin B. Willis, Technical Adviser, Erich von Stroheim. Assistant Director, Charlie Dorian. Photography, William Daniels. Sound, Douglas Shearer. Editor, Robert J. Kern. Vocal and choral effects by Russian Symphony Choir. Other versions: *Love* (MGM, 1927), *Anna Karenina* (20th Century-Fox [British], 1948). 95 minutes

Anna Karenina with Basil Rathbone, Greta Garbo, Ethel Griffies, Fredric March and Constance Collier.

Anna Karenina: Greta Garbo, *Count Alexei Vronsky* Fredric March, *Kitty:* Maureen O'Sullivan, *Countess Vronsky:* May Robson, *Countess Lidia:* Constance Collier, *Stiva:* Reginald Owen, *Sergei Karenin:* Freddie Bartholomew, *Alexei Karenin:* Basil Rathbone, *Dolly:* Phoebe Foster, *Capt. Nicki Yashvin:* Reginald Denny, *Levin:* Gyles Isham, *Grisha:* Buster Phelps, *Anna's Maid:* Ella Ethridge, *Vronsky's Valet:* Sidney Bracy, *Tania:* Cora Sue Collins, *Butler:* Olaf Hytten, *Butler:* Joseph E. Tozer, *Tutor, Ivanovich:* Guy D'Ennery, *Cord:* Harry Allen, *Princess Sorokino:* Mary Forbes, *Barbara:* Helen Preeman, *Mme. Kartasoff:* Ethel Griffies, *Matve:* Harry Beresford, *Governess:* Sarah Padden, *Lily:* Joan Marsh, *Best Man:* Dennis O'Keefe, *Mahotin:* Mischa Auer, *Woman:* Betty Blythe, *Colonel:* Robert Warwick, *Mr. Kartasoff:* Keith Kenneth, *Colonel:* Mahlon Hamilton, *Officer:* Pat Somerset, *Officers at Banquet:* Harry Cording, Francis McDonald, Larry Steers, *Waiter:* Gino Corrado.

Annie Get Your Gun with J. Carrol Naish and Betty Hutton.

ANNIE GET YOUR GUN (1950) MGM. Producer, Arthur Freed. Director, George Sidney. Color by Technicolor. Based on the musical by Dorothy Fields and Herbert Fields. Screenplay, Sidney Sheldon. Musical Director, Adolph Deutsch. Art Directors, Cedric Gibbons, Paul Groesse. Photography, Charles Rosher. Editor, James E. Newcom. Songs by Irving Berlin: "Colonel Buffalo Bill," "Doin' What Comes Naturally," "The Girl That I Marry," "You Can't Get a Man With a Gun," "There's No Business Like Show Business," "My Defenses Are Down," "I'm an Indian Too," "I Got the Sun in the Morning," "Anything You Can Do," and "They Say It's Wonderful." 107 minutes

Annie Oakley: Betty Hutton, *Frank Butler:* Howard Keel, *Buffalo Bill:* Louis Calhern, *Sitting Bull:* J. Carrol Naish, *Pawnee Bill:* Edward Arnold, *Charlie Davenport:* Keenan Wynn, *Dolly Tate:* Benoy Venuta, *Foster Wilson:* Clinton Sundberg, *Mac:* James H. Harrison, *Little Jake:* Bradley Mora, *Nellie:* Diana Dick, *Jessie:* Susan Odin, *Minnie:* Eleanor Brown, *Little Horse:* Chief Yowlachie, *Conductor:* Robert Malcolm, *Waiter:* Lee Tung Foo, *Barker:* William Tannen, *Miss Willoughby:* Anne O'Neal, *Queen Victoria:* Evelyn Beresford, *Ship Captain:* John Hamilton, *Tall Man:* William Bill Hall, *Footman:* Edward Earle, *Constance:* Marjorie Wood, *Helen:* Elizabeth Flournoy, *Mrs. Adams:* Mae Clarke Langdon, *Mr. Clay:* Frank Wilcox, *President Loubet of France:* Andre Charlot, *King Victor Emmanuel:* Nino Pipitone, *Kaiser Wilhelm II:* John Mylong, *Cowboys:* Carl Sepulveda, Carol Henry, Fred Gilman.

ANOTHER THIN MAN (1939) MGM. Producer, Hunt Stromberg. Director, W. S. Van Dyke II. Author, Dashiell Hammett. Art Director, Cedric Gibbons. Musical Score, Edward Ward. Cameramen, Oliver T. Marsh, William Daniels. Editor, Frederick Y. Smith. 105 minutes

Another Thin Man with William Powell, William Anthony Poulson, Myrna Loy and Asta.

MRS. NICK CHARLES

Nick Charles: William Powell, *Nora Charles:* Myrna Loy, *Col. Burr MacFay:* C. Aubrey Smith, *Van Slack:* Otto Kruger, *Lieut. Guild:* Nat Pendleton, *Lois MacFay:* Virginia Grey, *Freddie Coleman:* Tom Neal, *Smitty:* Muriel Hutchison, *Dorothy Waters:* Ruth Hussey, *Sam Church:* Sheldon Leonard, *Mrs. Bellam:* Phyllis Gordon, *"Diamond Back" Vogel:* Don Costello, *Dudley Horn:* Patric Knowles, *"Creeps" Binder:* Harry Bellaver, *Dum-Dum:* Abner Biberman, *Mrs. Dolley:* Marjorie Main, *Pedro:* Martin Garralaga, *South American:* Alex D'Arcy, *Pete:* Frank Sully, *MacFay's Chauffeur:* Horace MacMahon, *Maid:* Nell Craig, *Nicky:* William Anthony Poulsen, *Deputy (Les):* Milton Kibbee, *Detective:* Thomas Jackson, *Quinn:* Edward Gargan, *First Thug:* Joseph Downing, *Thug:* Matty Fain, *Cookie:* Bert Roach, *Wacky:* Shemp Howard, *Mrs. Wacky:* Nellie V. Nichols, *Telephone Operator:* Claire Rochelle, *Guard:* Winstead "Doodles" Weaver, *Slim (Guard):* Roy Barcroft, *Barney:* Joe Devlin, *Medical Examiner:* Milton Parsons, *Investigator:* Dick Elliott, *Cuban Proprietor:* Nestor Paiva, *Fingerprint Man:* Gladden James, *Trooper:* Edwin Parker, *Larry:* Murray Alper.

Anthony Adverse with Fredric March and Gale Sondergaard.

ANTHONY ADVERSE (1936) WB. Produced by Jack L. Warner. Associate Executive in charge of Production, Hal B. Wallis. Directed by Mervyn LeRoy. Supervisor, Henry Blanke. From the novel by Hervey Allen. Screenplay by Sheridan Gibney. Cinematographer, Tony Gaudio. Director of Recording, Major Nathan Levinson. Film Editor, Ralph Dawson. Art Director, Anton Grot. Costumer, Milo Anderson. Original Musical Score, Erich Wolfgang Korngold. Operatic Sequences, Aldo Franchetti. Assistant Director, Bill Cannon. Film debut of Gale Sondergaard. 136 minutes

Anthony Adverse: Fredric March, *Angela Guisseppi:* Olivia De Havilland, *Maria:* Anita Louise, *John Bonnyfeather:* Edmund Gwenn, *Don Luis:* Claude Rains, *Vincente Nolte:* Donald Woods, *Dennis Moore:* Louis Hayward, *Faith:* Gale Sondergaard, *Carlo Cibo:* Akim Tamiroff, *Neleta:* Steffi Duna, *Anthony (age 10):* Billy Mauch, *Father Xavier:* Henry O'Neill, *De Bruille:* Ralph Morgan, *Ouvrard:* Fritz Leiber, *Tony Guisseppi:* Luis Alberni, *Florence Udney (age 10):* Marilyn Knowlden, *Angela (as a child):* Ann Howard, *Napoleon Bonaparte:* Rollo Lloyd, *Sancho:* George E. Stone, *Captain Elisha Jorham:* Joseph Crehan, *Mrs. Jorham:* Clara Blandick, *Little Boy Anthony:* Scotty Beckett, *Captain Matanze:* Addison Richards, *Major Doumet:* J. Carrol Naish, *Brother Francois:* Pedro de Cordoba, *Lucia:* Grace Stafford, *Captain, Boat to America:* Joseph King, *Mother Superior:* Eily Malyon, *De Bourrienne:* Leonard Mudie, *Senora Bovina:* Rafaela Ottiano, *Cook Guisseppi:* Mathilde Comont, *Driver, Coach to Paris:* Frank Reicher, *Ferdinando:* Paul Sotoff, *Half-caste Dancer:* Joan Woodbury, *Arabs:* Frank Lackteen, Martin Garralaga, *Old Woman at Chalet:* Zeffie Tilbury, *Sister Ursula:* Tola Nesmith, *Second Nun:* Myra Marsh, *Third Nun:* Bess Flowers.

APACHE (1954) UA. Producer, Harold Hecht. Director, Robert Aldrich. Assistant Director, Sid Sidman. Screenplay by James R.

Apache with Burt Lancaster and Jean Peters.

Webb. Based on novel by Paul I. Wellman. Music by David Raksin. Cinematographer, Ernest Laszlo. Editor, Alan Crosland, Jr. 91 minutes

Massai: Burt Lancaster, *Nalinle:* Jean Peters, *Al Sieber:* John McIntire, *Hondo:* Charles Buchinsky (Charles Bronson), *Weddle:* John Dehner, *Santos:* Paul Guilfoyle, *Glagg:* Ian MacDonald, *Lt. Col. Beck:* Walter Sande, *Dawson:* Morris Ankrum, *Geronimo:* Monte Blue.

The Apartment with Jack Lemmon and Shirley MacLaine.

THE APARTMENT (1960) UA. Producer-Director, Billy Wilder. Screenplay, Billy Wilder and I. A. L. Diamond. Associate Producers, Doane Harrison and I. A. L. Diamond. Music, Adolph Deutsch. Assistant Director, Hal Polaire. A Mirisch Company Production in Panavision. Art Director, Alexander Trauner. Sets, Edward G. Boyle. Sound, Gordon E. Sawyer. Background Music, Adolph Deutsch. Cinematography, Joseph LaShelle. Editor, Daniel Mandell. Songs: "Lonely Room" (Theme from the Apartment) by Adolph Deutsch, "Jealous Lover" by Charles Williams. Locations filmed in New York. Intruder scenes from *Stagecoach* (UA, 1939). Film debut of Edie Adams. 125 minutes

C. C. (Bud) Baxter: Jack Lemmon, *Fran Kubelik:* Shirley MacLaine, *Jeff D. Sheldrake:* Fred MacMurray, *Joe Dobisch:* Ray Walston, *Al Kirkeby:* David Lewis, *Dr. Dreyfuss:* Jack Kruschen, *Sylvia:* Joan Shawlee, *Miss Olsen:* Edie Adams, *Margie MacDougall:* Hope Holiday, *Karl Matuschka:* Johnny Seven, *Mrs. Dreyfuss:* Naomi Stevens, *Mrs. Lieberman:* Frances Weintraub Lax, *The Blonde:* Joyce Jameson, *Mr. Vanderhof:* Willard Waterman, *Mr. Eichelberger:* David White, *Bartender:* Benny Burt, *Santa Claus:* Hal Smith, *Office Worker:* Dorothy Abbott.

APARTMENT FOR PEGGY (1948) 20th. Producer, William Perlberg. Directors, Henry Koster, George Seaton. Color by Technicolor. From a story by Faith Baldwin. Screenplay, George Seaton. Art Directors, Lyle Wheeler, Richard Irvine. Musical Director, Lionel Newman. Photography, Harry Jackson. Editor, Robert Simpson. Technicolor Director, Natalie Kalmus. Associate, Clemens Finley. 98 minutes

Peggy: Jeanne Crain, *Jason:* William Holden, *Prof. Henry Barnes:* Edmund Gwenn, *Prof. Edward Bell:* Gene Lockhart, *Dr. Conway:* Griff Barnett, *Dorothy:* Randy Stuart, *Ruth:* Marion Marshall, *Jeanne:* Pati Behrs, *Prof. Roland Pavin:* Henri Letondal, *Prof. T. J. Beck:* Houseley Stevenson, *Della:* Helen Ford, *Mrs. Landon:* Almira Sessions, *Prof. Collins:* Charles Lane, *Delivery Boy:* Ronnald Burns, *Jerry:* Gene Nelson, *Student:* Bob Patten, *Wife:* Betty Lynn, *Nurse:* Theresa Lyon, *Nurse:* Ann Staunton, *Salesmen:* Hal K. Dawson, Robert Williams, *Mailman:* Robert Adler.

Apartment for Peggy with Edmund Gwenn, Jeanne Crain and William Holden.

APPLAUSE (1929) Par. Directed by Rouben Mamoulian. From the novel by Beth Brown. Adaptation, Garrett Fort. Photography, George Folsey. Editor, John Bassler. Filmed at Paramount's Astoria, Long Island, Studios and in New York City: Grand Central Station, the Battery, Brooklyn Bridge. Songs: "What Wouldn't I Do for That Man" by E. Y. Harburg and Jay Gorney; "Everybody's Doing It," "Doing the New Raccoon," "Give Your Little Baby Lots of Lovin'" by Dolly Morse and Joe Burke. Also silent version. First film directed by Mamoulian. Film debut of Helen Morgan. 87 minutes

Kitty Darling: Helen Morgan, *April Darling:* Joan Peers, *Hitch Nelson:* Fuller Melish, Jr., *Tony:* Henry Wadsworth, *Joe King:* Jack Cameron, *Mother Superior:* Dorothy Cumming, *Producer:* Jack Singer, *Slim Lamont:* Paul Barrett.

Applause with Joan Peers and Fuller Mellish, Jr.

Arabesque with Gregory Peck and Sophia Loren.

ARABESQUE (1966) Univ. Screenplay by Julian Mitchell, Stanley Price and Pierre Malton. Based on the novel *The Cipher* by Gordon Cotler. Produced and directed by Stanley Donen. A Stanley Donen Enterprises production. 104 minutes

David Pollock: Gregory Peck, *Yasmin Azir:* Sophia Loren, *Beshraavi:* Alan Badel, *Yussef:* Kieron Moore, *Hassan Jena:* Carl Duering, *Sloane:* John Merivale, *Webster:* Duncan Lamont, *Rasheb:* George Coulouris, *Beauchamp:* Ernest Clark, *Mohammed Lufti:* Harold Kasket.

Around the World in 80 Days with Shirley MacLaine, David Niven, Cantinflas and Buster Keaton.

AROUND THE WORLD IN 80 DAYS (1956) UA. Producer, Michael Todd. Associate Producer, William Cameron Menzies. Director, Michael Anderson. Screenplay by S. J. Perelman. Based on Jules Vernes' novel. Music by Victor Young. Costumes by Miles White. Choreography by Paul Godkin. In Todd-AO Process and Eastman Color. Locations: London; Southern France; on the Mediterranean; India; Hong Kong; Pakistan; Siam; Yokohama, Japan; Durango, Colorado; San Francisco; Mexico; Spain; Egypt; Chatsworth, California. Prologue includes the Melies version of Verne's "A Trip to the Moon," 1902. 168 minutes

Phileas Fogg: David Niven, *Passepartout:* Cantinflas, *Mr. Fix:* Robert Newton, *Aouda:* Shirley MacLaine, *Monsieur Gasse:* Charles Boyer, *Stationmaster:* Joe E. Brown, *Tourist:* Martine Carol, *Colonel Proctor Stamp:* John Carradine, *Clerk:* Charles Coburn, *Official of Railway:* Ronald Colman, *Steward:* Melville Cooper, *Hesketh-Baggott:* Noel

Coward, *Whist Partner:* Finlay Currie, *Police Chief:* Reginald Denny, *First Mate:* Andy Devine, *Hostess:* Marlene Dietrich, *Bullfighter:* Luis Miguel Dominguin, *Coachman:* Fernandel, *Foster:* Sir John Gielgud, *Sportin' Lady:* Hermione Gingold, *Dancer:* Jose Greco, *Sir Francis Gromarty:* Sir Cedric Hardwicke, *Fallentin:* Trevor Howard, *Companion:* Glynis Johns, *Conductor:* Buster Keaton, *Flirt:* Evelyn Keyes, *Revivalist:* Beatrice Lillie, *Steward:* Peter Lorre, *Engineer:* Edmund Lowe, *Helmsman:* Victor McLaglen, *Commander:* Colonel Tim McCoy, *Club Member:* A. E. Mathews, *Character:* Mike Mazurki, *Cabby:* John Mills, *Consul:* Alan Mowbray, *Ralph:* Robert Morley, *Narrator:* Edward R. Murrow, *Captain:* Jack Oakie, *Bouncer:* George Raft, *Achmed Abdullah:* Gilbert Roland, *Henchman:* Cesar Romero, *Pianist:* Frank Sinatra, *Drunk:* Red Skelton, *Member:* Ronald Squire, *Member:* Basil Sydney, *Hinshaw:* Harcourt Williams, *Spectator:* Ava Gardner.

Arrowsmith with Alec B. Francis, Myrna Loy and Ronald Colman.

ARROWSMITH (1931) UA. Produced by Samuel Goldwyn. Directed by John Ford. Based on the novel by Sinclair Lewis. Scenario and Dialogue, Sidney Howard. Photography, Ray June. Editor, Hugh Bennett. Sound, Jack Noyes. Music Score, Alfred Newman. Settings, Richard Day. 108 minutes

Martin Arrowsmith: Ronald Colman, *Leora Tozer:* Helen Hayes, *Dr. Gustav, Sondelius:* Richard Bennett, *Professor Max Gottlieb:* A. E. Anson, *Doctor Tubbs:* Cluaude King, *Terry Wickett:* Russell Hopton, *Joyce Lanyon:* Myrna Loy, *Bert Tozer:* Bert Roach, *The Pioneer Girl:* Charlotte Henry, *The Old Doctor:* James Marcus, *Mr. Tozer:* DeWitt Jennings, *Mrs. Tozer:* Beulah Bondi, *Henry Novak:* John M. Qualen, *Mrs. Novak:* Adele Watson, *Doctor Hesselink:* Sidney DeGrey, *State Veterinary:* David Landau, *Twyford:* Alec B. Francis, *Miss Twyford:* Florence Britton, *Sir Robert Fairland:* Lumsden Hare, *Oliver Marchand:* Clarence Brooks, *Cop:* Ward Bond, *Ship's Officers:* Pat Somerset, Eric Wilton, *Pioneer:* Erville Alderson, *Italian Uncle:* George Humbert, *Drunk:* Raymond Hatton, *Native Mother:* Theresa Harris.

Arsenic and Old Lace with Cary Grant, Leo White and Priscilla Lane.

ARSENIC AND OLD LACE (1944) WB. Produced by Howard Lindsay and Russell Crouse. Directed by Frank Capra. Based on the play by Joseph Kesselring, which closed in 1944 after a 3½-year run. Screenplay, Julius J. and Philip G. Epstein. Music, Max Steiner. Music Director, Leo F. Forbstein. Orchestral Arrangements, Hugo Friedhofer. Editor, Daniel Mandell. Josephine Hull, Jean Adair, John Alexander repeat their Broadway roles. 118 minutes

Mortimer Brewster: Cary Grant, *Elaine Harper:* Priscilla Lane, *Jonathan Brewster:* Raymond Massey, *O'Hara:* Jack Carson, *Mr. Witherspoon:* Edward Everett Horton, *Doctor Einstein:* Peter Lorre, *Lieutenant Rooney:* James Gleason, *Abby Brewster:* Josephine Hull, *Martha Brewster:* Jean Adair, *Teddy "Roosevelt" Brewster:* John Alexander, *Reverend Harper:* Grant Mitchell, *Brophy:* Edward McNamara, *Taxi Driver:* Garry Owen, *Saunders:* John Ridgely, *Judge Cullman:* Vaughan Glaser, *Doctor Gilchrist:* Chester Clute, *Reporter:* Charles Lane, *Gibbs:* Edward McWade, *Man in Phone Booth:* Leo White, *Marriage License Clerk:* Spencer Charters, *Photographer:* Hank Mann, *Umpire:* Lee Phelps.

Artists and Models with Gail Patrick and Jack Benny.

ARTISTS AND MODELS (1937) Par. Produced by Lewis E. Gensler. Directed by Raoul Walsh. Screenplay by Walter DeLeon and Francis Martin. Based on an adaptation by Eve Greene and Harlan Ware of a story by Sig Herzig and Gene Thackrey. Photography, Victor Milner. Editor, Ellsworth Hoagland. Musical Arrangements, Victor Young. Songs: "Mister Esquire," by Ted Koehler and Victor Young; "I Have Eyes" by Leo Robin and Ralph Rainger; "Pop Goes the Bubble," "Public Enemy No. 1," "Stop You're Breaking My Heart" by Ted Koehler and Burton Lane; "Whispers in the Dark," "Moonlight and Shadows" by Frederick Hollander and Leo Robin. Remade by Paramount in 1955. 97 minutes.

Mac Brewster: Jack Benny, *Paula:* Ida Lupino, *Alan Townsend:* Richard Arlen, *Cynthia:* Gail Patrick, *Jupiter Pluvius:* Ben Blue, *Toots:* Judy Canova, *Stella:* Cecil Cunningham, *Dr. Zimmer:* Donald Meek, *Mrs. Townsend:* Hedda Hopper, *Specialties:* Martha Raye, Andre Kostelanetz and his Orchestra, Russell Patterson's Personettos, Louis Armstrong and Orchestra, Judy, Anne and Zeke (The Canovas), The Yacht Club Boys, Connee Boswell, *Artists:* Peter Arno, McClelland Barclay, Arthur William Brown, Rube Goldberg, John La Gatta, Russell Patterson, *Model:* Sandra Storme, *Marjorie:* Madelon Grey, *Craig Sheldon:* Alan Birmingham, *Lois:* Kathryn Kay, *Bartender:* Jerry Bergen, *Water Waltzers:* Mary Shepherd and Gloria Wheeden, *Lord:* Dell Henderson, *Seamstress:* Virginia Brissac, *Jugglers:* Henry and Harry C. Johnson, *Cycling Star:* Jack Stary, *Sharpshooter:* Harvey Poirier, *Tumbler:* Pat Moran, *Romeo:* David Newell, *Flunkey:* Edward

Earle, *King:* Little Billy, *Miss Gordon:* Jane Weir, *Mr. Currie:* Howard Hickman.

THE ASPHALT JUNGLE (1950) MGM. Producer, Arthur Hornblow, Jr. Director, John Huston. Author, W. R. Burnett. Screenplay, Ben Maddow, John Huston. Art Directors, Cedric Gibbons, Randal Duell. Photography, Harold Rosson. Editor, George Boemer. Sound, Douglas Shearer. Make-up, Sydney Guilarott. Remade as *Cairo* (MGM-British, 1963). 112 minutes

The Asphalt Jungle with Sterling Hayden, Brad Dexter, Louis Calhern and Sam Jaffe.

Dix Handley: Sterling Hayden, *Alonzo D. Emmerich:* Louis Calhern, *Doll Conovan:* Jean Hagen, *Gus Minissi:* James Whitmore, *Doc Erwin Riedenschneider:* Sam Jaffe, *Police Commissioner Hardy:* John McIntire, *Cobby:* Marc Lawrence, *Lieut. Ditrich:* Barry Kelley, *Louis Ciavelli:* Anthony Caruso, *Maria Ciavelli:* Teresa Celli, *Angela Phinlay:* Marilyn Monroe, *Timmons:* William Davis, *May Emmerich:* Dorothy Tree, *Bob Brannon:* Brad Dexter, *Maxwell:* Alex Gerry, *James X. Connery:* Thomas Browne Henry, *Janocek:* James Seay, *Andrews:* Don Haggerty, *Franz Schurz:* Henry Rowland, *Jeannie:* Helene Stanley, *Tallboy:* Raymond Roe, *Red:* Charles (Chuck) Courtney, *Woman:* Jean Carter, *Older Officer:* Ralph Dunn, *Younger Officer:* Pat Flaherty, *Jack (Police Clerk):* Tim Ryan, *Karl Anton Smith:* Strother Martin, *William Doldy:* Henry Corden, *Night Clerk:* Frank Cady, *Driver:* Benny Burt, *Truck Driver:* Fred Graham, *Evans:* David Hydes, *Private Policeman:* Saul Gorss, *Man:* Wilson Wood, *Suspect:* William Washington, *Vivian:* Eloise Hardt, *Eddie Donato:* Albert Morin.

AS YOU DESIRE ME (1932) MGM. Directed by George Fitzmaurice. Adapted from Luigi Pirandello's play. Adaptation and Dialogue, Gene Markey. Photography, William Daniels. Editor, George Hively. 71 minutes

As You Desire Me with Erich Von Stroheim, Melvyn Douglas and Greta Garbo.

Zara: Greta Garbo, *Bruno:* Melvyn Douglas, *Salter:* Erich Von Stroheim, *Tony:* Owen Moore, *Madame Mantari:* Hedda Hopper, *Lena:* Rafaela Ottiano, *Baron:* Warburton Gamble, *Captain:* Albert Conti, *Pietro:* William Ricciardi, *Albert:* Roland Varno.

At War With the Army with Jerry Lewis and Dean Martin.

AT WAR WITH THE ARMY (1950) Par. Produced by Fred F. Finklehoffe. Executive Producer, Abner J. Greshler. Directed by Hal Walker. Based on a play by James B. Allardice. Screenplay, Fred F. Finklehoffe. A York Pictures Corporation and Screen Associates Production. Songs by Mack David and Jerry Livingston: "The Navy Gets the Gravy But the Army Gets the Beans," "Tonda Wanda Hoy," "You and Your Beautiful Eyes." Martin and Lewis' first starring film. 93 minutes

Sergeant Vic Puccinelli: Dean Martin, *Pfc. Korwin:* Jerry Lewis, *Sergeant McVey:* Mike Kellin, *Eddie:* Jimmy Dundee, *Pokey:* Dick Stabile, *Corporal Clark:* Tommy Farrell, *Corporal Shaughnessy:* Frank Hyers, *Sergeant Miller:* Dan Dayton, *Captain Caldwell:* William Mendrek, *Lieutenant Davenport:* Kenneth Forbes, *Private Edwards:* Paul Livermore, *Lieutenant Terray:* Ty Perry, *Millie:* Jean Ruth, *Mrs. Caldwell:* Angela Greene, *Helen Palmer:* Polly Bergen, *Colonel:* Douglas Evans, *Doctor:* Steven Roberts, *Orderly:* Al Negbo, *Bartender:* Dewey Robinson, *Soldier:* Lee Bennett.

Auntie Mame with Peggy Cass and Rosalind Russell.

AUNTIE MAME (1958) WB. Directed by Morton DaCosta. In Technirama and Technicolor. Screenplay, Betty Comden and Adolph Green. From the novel by Patrick Dennis, and the play as adapted by Jerome Lawrence and Robert E. Lee, which evolved into the musical "Mame." Music, Bronislau Kaper. Costumes, Orry-Kelly. Assistant

Director, Don Page. Art Director, Malcolm Bert. Musical Director, Ray Heindorf. Cinematographer, Harry Stradling. Editor, William Ziegler. Sound, M. A. Merrick. Russell, Smith, Cass, Handzlik, Shimoda and Alexander repeat their original stage roles. Film debut of Jan Handzlik, 11. 143 minutes

Auntie Mame Dennis: Rosalind Russell, *Beauregard Burnside:* Forrest Tucker, *Vera Charles:* Coral Browne, *Mr. Babcock:* Fred Clark, *Patrick Dennis:* Roger Smith, *Lindsay Woolsey:* Patric Knowles, *Agnes Gooch:* Peggy Cass, *Patrick as a boy:* Jan Handzlik, *Gloria Upson:* Joanna Barnes, *Pegeen Ryan:* Pippa Scott, *Mrs. Upson:* Lee Patrick, *Mr. Upson:* Willard Waterman, *Brian O'Bannion:* Robin Hughes, *Norah Muldoon:* Connie Gilchrist, *Ito:* Yuki Shimoda, *Sally Cato:* Brook Byron, *Mrs. Burnside:* Carol Veazie, *Acacius Page:* Henry Brandon, *Emory:* Butch Hengen, *Veterinarian:* Dub Taylor, *Woman in White:* Evelyn Ceder, *Cousin Jeff:* Doye O'Dell, *Michael:* Terry Kelman, *Edwin Dennis:* Morton DaCosta, *Pianist:* Rand Harper, *Vladimir Klinkoff:* Gregory Gay, *Mrs. Klinkoff:* Gladys Roach, *Perry:* Booth Colman, *Dr. Feuchtwanger:* Charles Heard, *Stage Manager:* Paul Davis, *Dowager-type Lady:* Olive Blakeney, *Noblewoman:* Margaret Dumont, *Man with Monocle:* Owen McGiveney, *Lord Dudley:* Robert Gates, *Reginald:* Mark Dana, *Mr. Krantz:* Dick Reeves, *Mrs. Krantz:* Barbara Pepper, *Mr. Loomis:* Chris Alexander, *Mrs. Jennings:* Ruth Warren.

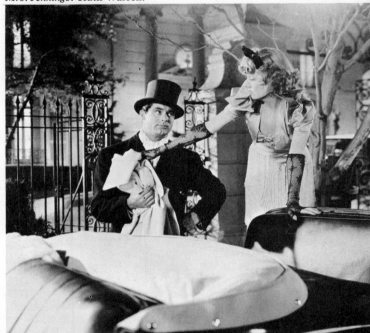

The Awful Truth with Cary Grant and Irene Dunne.

THE AWFUL TRUTH (1937) Col. Produced by Leo McCarey. Associate Producer, Everett Riskin. Directed by Leo McCarey. Based on the 1922 play by Arthur Richman. Screenplay, Viña Delmar. Assistant Director, William Mull. Art Directors, Stephen Goosson and Lionel Banks. Music Director, Morris Stoloff. Interior Decorations, Babs Johnstone. Gowns, Kalloch. Photography, Joseph Walker. Editor, Al Clark. Sound, Edward Bernds. Songs by Ben Oakland and Milton Drake: "My Dreams Have Gone With the Wind" and "I Don't Like Music." Remade by Columbia as *Let's Do It Again*, 1953. 90 minutes

Lucy Warriner: Irene Dunne, *Jerry Warriner:* Cary Grant, *Daniel Leeson:* Ralph Bellamy, *Armand Duvalle:* Alexander D'Arcy, *Aunt Patsy:* Cecil Cunningham, *Barbara Vance:* Molly Lament, *Mrs. Leeson:* Esther Dale, *Dixie Belle Lee (Toots Binswanger):* Joyce Compton, *Frank Randall:* Robert Allen, *Mr. Vance:* Robert Warwick, *Mrs. Vance:* Mary Forbes, *Lord Fabian:* Claud Allister, *Lady Fabian:* Zita Moulton, *Motor Cop:* Edgar Dearing, *Mr. Barnsley:* Scott Colton, *Mrs. Barnsley:* Wyn Cahoon, *Judge:* Paul Stanton, *Jerry's Attorney:* Mitchell Harris, *Motor Cop:* Alan Bridge, *Butler:* Leonard Carey,

Japanese Servant: Miki Morita, *M.C.:* Frank Wilson, *Police Sergeant:* Vernon Dent, *Caretaker:* George C. Pearce, *Hotel Clerk:* Bobby Watson, *Secretary:* Byron Foulger, *Celeste:* Kathryn Curry, *Bailiff:* Edward Peil, Sr., *Viola Heath:* Bess Flowers, *Hank:* John Tyrrell, *Lucy's Attorney:* Edward Mortimer.

Babes in Arms with Mickey Rooney and Judy Garland.

BABES IN ARMS (1939) MGM. Produced by Arthur Freed. Directed by Busby Berkeley. Based on the musical by Richard Rodgers and Lorenz Hart. Screenplay by Jack MacGowan and Kay Van Riper. Art Director, Cedric Gibbons. Associate, Merrill Pye. Wardrobe, Dolly Tree. Photography, Ray June. Editor, Frank Sullivan. Songs: "Babes in Arms," "Where or When," "The Lady Is a Tramp" by Rodgers and Hart; "You Are My Lucky Star," "Good Morning" by Arthur Freed and Nacio Herb Brown; "I Cried for You" by Arthur Freed, Gus Arnheim, and Abe Lyman; "God's Country" by E. Y. Harburg and Harold Arlen. Music Director, George Stoll. 97 minutes.

Mickey Moran: Mickey Rooney, *Patsy Barton:* Judy Garland, *Joe Moran:* Charles Winninger, *Judge Black:* Guy Kibbee, *Rosalie Essex:* June Preisser, *Florrie Moran:* Grace Hayes, *Molly Moran:* Betty Jaynes, *Don Brice:* Douglas McPhail, *Jeff Steele:* Rand Brooks, *Dody Martini:* Leni Lynn, *Bobs:* John Sheffield, *Madox:* Henry Hull, *William:* Barnett Parker, *Mrs. Barton:* Ann Shoemaker, *Martha Steele:* Margaret Hamilton, *Mr. Essex:* Joseph Crehan, *Brice:* George McKay, *Shaw:* Henry Roquemore, *Mrs. Brice:* Lelah Tyler, *Boy:* Lon McCallister.

The Bachelor and the Bobby-Soxer with Myrna Loy, Cary Grant, Harry Davenport, Shirley Temple and Ray Collins.

THE BACHELOR AND THE BOBBY-SOXER (1947) RKO. Producer, Dore Schary. Director, Irving Reis. Author, I. Sidney Sheldon. Screenplay, I. Sidney Sheldon. Art Directors, Albert D'Agostino, Carroll Clark. Music, Leigh Harline. Music Director, C. Bakaleinikoff. Cameraman, Robert De Grasse. Editor, Frederick Knudtson. 95 minutes

Dick: Cary Grant, *Margaret:* Myrna Loy, *Susan:* Shirley Temple, *Tommy:* Rudy Vallee, *Beemish:* Ray Collins, *Thaddeus:* Harry Davenport, *Jerry:* Johnny Sands, *Tony:* Don Beddoe, *Bessie:* Lillian Randolph, *Agnes Prescott:* Veda Ann Borg, *Walters:* Dan Tobin, *Judge Treadwell:* Ransom Sherman, *Winters:* William Bakewell, *Melvin:* Irving Bacon, *Perry:* Ian Bernard, *Florence:* Carol Hughes, *Anthony Herman:* William Hall, *Maitre d'Hotel:* Gregory Gay, *Mr. Mittwick:* Charles Halton, *Miss Wells:* Myra Marsh, *Mr. Roberts:* Charles Marsh, *Bailiff:* J. Farrell MacDonald, *Woman:* Ellen Corby, *Cops in Courtroom:* Jack Gargan, Mickey Simpson, *Mrs. Baldwin:* Elena Warren, *Mr. Baldwin:* William Forrest, *Doris Baldwin:* Carlotta Jelm, *Cab Driver:* Ned Roberts, *Coach:* Pat Flaherty, *Man at Gate:* Robert Bray.

The Bachelor Party with E. G. Marshall, Philip Abbott, Jack Warden, Don Murray and Larry Blyden.

THE BACHELOR PARTY (1957) UA. Producer, Harold Hecht. Director, Delbert Mann. Associate Producer, Paddy Chayefsky. Story and screenplay by Paddy Chayefsky. Costumes by Mary Grant. Music by Paul Madeira. Assistant Directors, Richard Mayberry and Edward Denault. A Norma Production. 93 minutes

Charlie Samson: Don Murray, *Walter:* E. G. Marshall, *Eddie:* Jack Warden, *Arnold:* Philip Abbott, *Kenneth:* Larry Blyden, *Helen Samson:* Patricia Smith, *Existentialist:* Carolyn Jones, *Julie:* Nancy Marchand, *Hostess:* Karen Norris, *Girl on Stoop:* Barbara Ames, *Stripteaser:* Norma Arden Campbell.

BACK STREET (1932) Univ. Produced by Carl Laemmle, Jr. Associate Producer, E. M. Asher. Directed by John M. Stahl. From the novel by Fannie Hurst. Screenplay and Continuity, Gladys Lehman. Dialogue, Lynn Starling. Art Director, Charles D. Hall. Costumes, Vera. Assistant Director, Scott R. Beal. Photography, Karl Freund. Editor, Milton Carruth. Sound, C. Roy Hunter. Remade by Universal in 1941 and 1961. 93 minutes.

Ray Schmidt: Irene Dunne, *Walter Saxel:* John Boles, *Freda Schmidt:* June Clyde, *Kurt Shendler:* George Meeker, *Mrs. Dole:* ZaSu Pitts, *Francine:* Shirley Grey, *Mrs. Saxel:* Doris Lloyd, *Richard:* William Bakewell, *Beth:* Arletta Duncan, *Mrs. Saxel, Sr.:* Maude Turner Gordon, *Bakeless:* Walter Catlett, *Profhero:* James Donlan, *Mr. Schmidt:* Paul Weigel, *Mrs. Schmidt:* Jane Darwell, *Hugo:* Paul Fix, *Uncle Felix:* Robert McWade.

Back Street with George Meeker and Irene Dunne.

The Bad and the Beautiful with Kirk Douglas, Paul Stewart and Barry Sullivan.

THE BAD AND THE BEAUTIFUL (1952) MGM. Producer, John Houseman. Director, Vincente Minelli. Author, George Bradshaw. Screenplay, Charles Schnee. Music, David Raskin. Art Directors, Cedric Gibbons, Edward Carfagno. Sound, Douglas Shearer. Sets, Edwin B. Willis, Keough Gleason. Cinematographer, Robert Surtees. Editor, Conrad A. Nervig. 118 minutes

Georgia Lorrison: Lana Turner, *Jonathan Shields:* Kirk Douglas, *Harry Pebbel:* Walter Pidgeon, *James Lee Bartlow:* Dick Powell, *Fred Amiel:* Barry Sullivan, *Rosemary Bartlow:* Gloria Grahame, *Victor "Gaucho"*

Ribera: Gilbert Roland, *Henry Whitfield:* Leo G. Carroll, *Kay Amiel:* Vanessa Brown, *Syd Murphy:* Paul Stewart, *Gus:* Sammy White, *Lila:* Elaine Stewart, *Assistant Director:* Jonathan Cott, *Von Ellstein:* Ivan Triesault, *Miss March:* Kathleen Freeman, *Ida:* Marietta Canty, *Blonde:* Lucille Knoch, *Leading Man:* Steve Forrest, *Secretary:* Perry Sheehan, *McDill:* Robert Burton, *Eulogist:* Francis X. Bushman, *Wardrobe Man:* Ned Glass, *Little Girl:* Sandy Descher, *Lionel Donovan:* George Lewis, *Linda Ronley:* Dee Turnell, *Casting Director:* Bob Carson, *Lucien:* Barbara Billingsley, *Priest:* Alex Davidoff, *Mrs. Rosser:* Madge Blake, *Amiel's Boy:* Chris Olsen, *Rosa:* Karen Verne, *Joe:* Ben Astar, *Arlene:* Dorothy Patrick, *Mr. Z:* Jay Adler, *Joe's Friend:* Bess Flowers, *Singer:* Peggy King, *Sheriff:* Stanley Andrews, *Ferraday:* John Bishop, *Hugo Shields:* William E. Green, *Assistant Director:* William "Bill" Phillips.

BAD DAY AT BLACK ROCK (1954) MGM. Producer, Dore Schary. Associate Producer, Herman Hoffman. Director, John Sturges. Screenplay, Millard Kaufman. Art Directors, Cedric Gibbons, Malcolm Brown. Editor, Newell P. Kimlin. CinemaScope-Eastman Color. Adaptation, Don McGuire. Based on a story by Howard Breslin. Music, Andre Previn. Assistant Director, Joel Freeman. Photography, William C. Mellor. 81 minutes

John J. MacReedy: Spencer Tracy, *Reno Smith:* Robert Ryan, *Liz Wirth:* Anne Francis, *Tim Horn:* Dean Jagger, *Doc Velie:* Walter Brennan, *Pete Wirth:* John Ericson, *Coley Trimble:* Ernest Borgnine, *Hector David:* Lee Marvin, *Mr. Hastings:* Russell Collins, *Sam:* Walter Sande.

Bad Day at Black Rock with Anne Francis and Spencer Tracy.

THE BAD SEED (1956) WB. Director, Mervyn LeRoy. Screenplay by John Lee Mahin. Based on play by Maxwell Anderson, and novel by William March. Music by Alex North. Costumes by Moss Mabry. Assistant Director, Mel Mellar. 129 minutes

Christine: Nancy Kelly, *Rhoda:* Patty McCormack, *LeRoy:* Henry Jones, *Mrs. Daigle:* Eileen Heckart, *Monica:* Evelyn Varden, *Kenneth:*

The Bad Seed with Nancy Kelly and Joan Croydon.

265

Ball of Fire with Gary Cooper, Barbara Stanwyck and Dan Duryea.

William Hopper, *Bravo:* Paul Fix, *Emory:* Jesse White, *Tasker:* Gage Clarke, *Miss Fern:* Joan Croydon, *Mr. Daigle:* Frank Cady.

BALL OF FIRE (1941) RKO. Producer, Samuel Goldwyn. Director, Howard Hawks. Authors, Billy Wilder, Thomas Monroe. Screenplay, Charles Brackett, Billy Wilder. Music, Alfred Newman. Art Director, Perry Ferguson. Cameraman, Gregg Toland. Editor, Daniel Mandell. Film debut of Richard Haydn. Remade as *A Song Is Born* (RKO, 1948). 111 minutes

Prof. Bertram Potts: Gary Cooper, *Sugarpuss O'Shea:* Barbara Stanwyck, *Prof. Gurkakoff:* Oscar Homolka, *Prof. Jerome:* Henry Travers, *Prof. Magenbruch:* S. Z. Sakall, *Prof. Robinson:* Tully Marshall, *Prof. Quintana:* Leonid Kinskey, *Prof. Oddly:* Richard Haydn, *Prof. Peagram:* Aubrey Mather, *Garbageman:* Allen Jenkins, *Joe Lilac:* Dana Andrews, *Duke Pastrami:* Dan Duryea, *Asthma Anderson:* Ralph Peters, *Miss Bragg:* Kathleen Howard, *Miss Totten:* Mary Field, *Larsen:* Charles Lane, *McNeary:* Charles Arnt, *Waiter:* Elisha Cook, *Horseface:* Alan Rhein, *Pinstripe:* Eddie Foster, *Justice of the Peace:* Aldrich Bowker, *District Attorney:* Addison Richards, *Bum:* Pat West, *College Boy:* Kenneth Howell, *Newsboy:* Tommy Ryan, *Motor Cop:* Tim Ryan, *Benny, the Creep:* Will Lee, Gene Krupa and his Orchestra, *Stage Doorman:* Otto Hoffmann, *Deputy:* Pat Flaherty, *Deputy:* George Sherwood, *Hula Dancer:* Geraldine Fissette.

THE BANDIT OF SHERWOOD FOREST (1946) Col. Producers, Leonard S. Picker, Clifford Sanforth. Directors, George Sherman, Henry Levin. Color by Technicolor. Authors, Paul A. Castleton,

The Bandit of Sherwood Forest with Cornel Wilde and Lloyd Corrigan.

William H. Pettitt (from *Son of Robin Hood* by Paul A. Castleton). Screenplay, Wilfred H. Pettitt, Melvin Levy. Art Directors, Stephen Goosson, Rudolph Sternard. Musical Score, Hugo Friedhofer. Musical Director, M. W. Stoloff. Cameramen, Tony Gaudio, William Snyder, George B. Meehan, Jr. Editor, Richard Fantl. 86 minutes

Robert of Nottingham (Son of Robin Hood): Cornel Wilde, *Lady Catherine Maitland:* Anita Louise, *Queen Mother:* Jill Esmond, *Friar Tuck:* Edgar Buchanan, *The Regent:* Henry Daniell, *Fitz-Herbert:* George MacCready, *Robin Hood:* Russell Hicks, *Will Scarlet:* John Abbott, *Sheriff of Nottingham:* Lloyd Corrigan, *Mother Meg:* Eva Moore, *Little John:* Ray Teal, *Allan-A-Dale:* Leslie Denison, *Lord Mortimer:* Ian Wolfe, *The King:* Maurice R. Tauzin, *Men-at-Arms:* Mauritz Hugo, Philip Van Zandt, Robert Williams, Harry Cording, Ralph Dunn, Dick Curtis, *Robin Hood Men:* Nelson Leigh, Ben Corbett, George Eldredge, Francis McDonald, Robert Scott, Ross Hunter, *Innkeeper:* Ferdinand Munier, *Outlaws:* Dan Stowell, Lane Chandler, *Baron:* Holmes Herbert, *Crossbowman:* Jimmy Lloyd, *Jailor:* Gene Stutenroth, *Captain of the Watch:* Ted Allan.

The Barefoot Contessa with Ava Gardner and Humphrey Bogart.

THE BAREFOOT CONTESSA (1954) UA. Written and directed by Joseph L. Mankiewicz. Assistant Director, Pietro Mussetta. Music by Mario Nascimbene. Color by Technicolor. 128 minutes

Harry Dawes: Humphrey Bogart, *Maria Vargas:* Ava Gardner, *Oscar Muldoon:* Edmond O'Brien, *Alberto Bravano:* Marius Goring, *Eleanora Torlato-Favrini:* Valentina Cortesa, *Vincenzo Torlato-Favrini:* Rossano Brazzi, *Jerry:* Elizabeth Sellars, *Kirk Edwards:* Warren Stevens, *Pedro:* Franco Interlenghi, *Myrna:* Mari Aldon, *Nightclub Proprietor:* Alberto Rabagliati, *The Pretender:* Tonio Selwart, *The Pretender's Wife:* Margaret Anderson, *Mrs. Eubanks:* Bessie Love, *Busboy:* Enzo Staiola, *Maria's Mother:* Maria Zanoli, *Maria's Father:* Renato Chiantoni, *J. Montague Brown:* Bill Fraser, *Mr. Black:* John Parrish, *Mr. Blue:* Jim Gerald, *Drunken Blonde:* Diana Decker, *Gypsy Dancer:* Riccardi Rioli, *Lulu McGee:* Gertrude Flynn, *Hector Eubanks:* John Horne, *Eddie Blake:* Robert Christopher.

BAREFOOT IN THE PARK (1967) Par. Produced by Hal Wallis. Directed by Gene Saks. Color by Technicolor. Based on the play by Neil Simon. Screenplay by Neil Simon. Produced in association with Nancy Productions. Associate Producers, Paul Nathan and Neil Simon. Assistant Director, Bud Grace. Music by Neal Hefti. Title song by Neal Hefti and Johnny Mercer. Costumes by Edith Head. Art Direction, Hal Pereira and Walter Tyler. Sets, Arthur Krams. Production Manager, Frank Caffey. Photography, Joseph La Shelle. Editor, William A. Lyon. Sound, Harold Lewis. Backgrounds filmed in New York. Redford and Natwick repeat their stage roles. 104 minutes

Barefoot in the Park with Jane Fonda and Robert Redford.

Paul Bratter: Robert Redford, *Corie Bratter:* Jane Fonda, *Victor Velasco:* Charles Boyer, *Ethel Banks:* Mildred Natwick, *Harry Pepper:* Herbert Edelman, *Aunt Harriet:* Mabel Albertson, *Restaurant Owner:* Fritz Feld, *Delivery Man:* James Stone, *Frank:* Ted Hartley, *Cop:* John Indrisano, *Bum in Park:* Paul E. Burns.

THE BARKLEYS OF BROADWAY (1949) MGM. Produced by Arthur Freed. Directed by Charles Walters. Color by Technicolor. Original screenplay by Betty Comden and Adolph Green. Art Directors, Cedric Gibbons and Edward Carfagno. Photography, Harry Stradling. Editor, Albert Akst. Music, Harry Warren. Music Director, Lennie Hayton. Songs: "You'd Be Hard to Replace," "Week-End in the Country," "Manhattan Downbeat," "Shoes With Wings On," "My One and Only Highland Fling" by Ira Gershwin and Harry Warren; "They Can't Take That Away From Me" by Ira and George Gershwin (from *Shall We Dance*, 1937). The last Astaire-Rogers film (and the first since *The Story of Vernon and Irene Castle* in 1939) and the only one in color. 109 minutes

The Barkleys of Broadway with Fred Astaire and Ginger Rogers.

Josh Barkely: Fred Astaire, *Dinah Barkley:* Ginger Rogers, *Ezra Miller:* Oscar Levant, *Mrs. Belney:* Billie Burke, *Shirlene May:* Gale Robbins, *Jacques Barredout:* Jacques Francois, *The Judge:* George Zucco, *Bert Felsher:* Clinton Sundberg, *Pamela Driscoll:* Inez Cooper, *Gloria Amboy:* Carol Brewster, *Larry:* Wilson Wood, *First Woman:* Jean Andren, *Second Woman:* Laura Treadwell, *Mary (Maid):* Margaret Bert, *Taxi Driver:* Allen Wood, *Guests in Theater Lobby:* Forbes Murray, Bess Flowers, Lois Austin, Betty Blythe, *Doorman at Theater:* Bill Tannen, *Apartment Doorman:* Mahlon Hamilton, *Cleo Fernby:* Lorraine Crawford, *Blonde:* Dee Turnell, *Husband:* Reginald Simpson, *Ladislaus Ladi:* Hans Conried, *Chauffeur:* Sherry Hall, *Mr. Perkins:* Frank Ferguson, *Stage Doorman:* Nolan Leary, *Duke de Morny:* Joe Granby, *Sarah's Mother:* Esther Somers, *Sarah's Aunt:* Helen Eby-Rock, *Genevieve:* Joyce Mathews, *Henrietta:* Roberta Johnson, *Clementine:* Mary Jo Ellis, *Ticket Man:* Jack Rice.

The Barretts of Wimpole Street with Fredric March and Norma Shearer.

THE BARRETTS OF WIMPOLE STREET (1934) MGM. Produced by Irving G. Thalberg. Directed by Sidney Franklin. Author, Rudolf Besier. Screenplay by Ernst Vajda, Claudine West, Donald Ogden Stewart. Film Editor, Margaret Booth. Photographer, William Daniels. Recording Engineer, Douglas Shearer. Assistant Director, Hugh Boswell. Art Director, Cedric Gibbons. Associate Art Directors, Harry McAffe, Edwin B. Willis. Costumes, Adrian. Musical Numbers, Herbert Stothart. TV title: *Forbidden Alliance*. Remade by MGM, 1959. 110 minutes

Elizabeth Barrett: Norma Shearer, *Robert Browning:* Fredric March, *Barrett:* Charles Laughton, *Henrietta Barrett:* Maureen O'Sullivan, *Arabel:* Katharine Alexander, *Captain Cook:* Ralph Forbes, *Wilson:* Una O'Connor, *Bella:* Marion Clayton, *Bevan:* Ian Wolfe, *Dr. Chambers:* Ferdinand Munier, *Dr. Waterloo:* Leo G. Carroll *Brothers:* Alan Conrad, Neville Clark, Peter Hobbes, Mathew Smith, *Octavius.* Vernon P. Downing, *Butler:* Lowden Adams, *Clergyman:* Winter Hall, *Coachman:* George Kirby, *Brother:* Robert Carleton.

Bataan with Robert Walker, Robert Taylor, Kenneth Spencer and Phillip Terry.

BATAAN (1943) MGM. Producer, Irving Starr. Director, Tay Garnett. Screenplay, Robert D. Andrews. Musical Score, Bronislau Kaper. Art Director, Cedric Gibbons. Cameraman, Sidney Wagner. Special Effects, Arnold Gillespie, Warren Newcombe. Editor, George White. "Unofficial" remake of *The Lost Patrol* (RKO, 1934). 114 minutes

Sergeant Bill Dane: Robert Taylor, *Lt. Steve Bentley:* George Murphy, *Corp. Jake Feingold:* Thomas Mitchell, *Corp. Barney Todd:* Lloyd Nolan, *Capt. Lassiter:* Lee Bowman, *Leonard Purckett:* Robert Walker, *Felix Ramirez:* Desi Arnaz, *F. X. Matowski:* Barry Nelson, *Gilbert Hardy:* Phillip Terry, *Corp. Jesus Katigbay:* Roque Espiritu, *Wesley Epps:* Kenneth Spencer, *Yankee Salazar:* J. Alex Havier, *Sam Malloy:* Tom Dugan, *Lieutenant:* Donald Curtis, *Nurses:* Lynne Carver, Mary McLeod, Dorothy Morris, *Infantry Officer:* Bud Geary, *Wounded Soldier:* Ernie Alexander, *Machine Gunner:* Phil Schumacher.

Battle Cry with Tab Hunter, Aldo Ray and William Campbell.

BATTLE CRY (1955) WB. Director, Raoul Walsh. CinemaScope, WarnerColor. Based on Leon Uris' novel. Screenplay, Leon M. Uris. Art Director, John Beckman. Musical Director, Max Steiner. Cinematographer, Sid Hickox. Editor, William Ziegler. 149 minutes

Colonel Huxley: Van Heflin, *Andy:* Aldo Ray, *Kathy:* Mona Freeman, *Pat:* Nancy Olson, *Mac:* James Whitmore, *General Snipes:* Raymond Massey, *Danny:* Tab Hunter, *Elaine Yarborough:* Dorothy Malone, *Rae:* Anne Francis, *Ski:* Bill Campbell, *Marion:* John Lupton, *L. Q.:* Justus Mc Queen (L. Q. Jones), *Spanish Joe:* Perry Lopez, *Speedy:* Fess Parker, *Lightower:* Jonas Applegarth, *Ziltch:* Tommy Cook,

Battleground with Ricardo Montalban, John Hodiak and Van Johnson.

Indian Marine: Felix Noriego, *Susan:* Susan Morrow, *Major Wellman:* Carleton Young, *Pedro:* Victor Millan, *Seabags:* Glenn Denning, *Sgt. Beller:* Gregory Walcott, *Enoch Rogers:* Rhys Williams, *Chaplain Petersen:* Chick Chandler, *Mr. Forrest:* Willis Bouchey, *Mrs. Forrester:* Sarah Selby, *Bud Forrester:* Harold Knudsen, *Mr. Walker:* Frank Ferguson, *Mrs. Walker:* Kay Stewart, *Waitress:* Allyn McLerie, *First New Zealander:* Lumsden Hare, *Second New Zealander:* Carl Harbaugh, *Mrs. Rogers:* Hilda Plowright, *Old Man:* George Selk (Budd Buster).

BATTLEGROUND (1949) MGM. Producer, Dore Schary. Director, William Wellman. Author-Screenplay, Robert Pirosh. Art Directors, Cedric Gibbons, Hans Peters. Music Score, Lennie Hayton. Photography, Paul C. Vogel. Editor, John Dunning. 118 minutes

Holley: Van Johnson, *Jarvess:* John Hodiak, *Roderiguez:* Ricardo Montalban, *"Pop" Ernest. Stazak:* George Murphy, *Jim Layton:* Marshall Thompson, *Abner Spudler:* Jerome Courtland, *Standiferd:* Don Taylor, *Wolowicz:* Bruce Cowling, *Kinnie:* James Whitmore, *"Kipp" Kippton:* Douglas Fowley, *Chaplain:* Leon Ames, *Hansan:* Guy Anderson, *Doc "Medic":* Thomas E. Breen, *Denise:* Denise Darcel, *Bettis:* Richard Jaeckel, *Garby:* Jim Arness, *William J. Hooper:* Scotty Beckett, *Lt. Teiss:* Brett King, *German Lieutenant:* Roland Varno, *Major:* Edmon Ryan, *Levenstein:* Michael Browne, *Supply Sergeant:* Jim Drum, *G. I. Stragglers:* Dewey Martin, Tom Noonan, David Holt, *G.I.'s:* George Offerman, Jr., William Self, *Sergeant:* Steve Pendleton, *German Sergeant:* Jerry Paris, *Runner:* Tommy Bond, *Belgian Woman Volunteer:* Nan Boardman, *German Captain:* Ivan Triesault, *German:* Henry Rowland, *German Major:* John Mylong, *American Colonel:* Ian MacDonald, *Tank Destroyer Man:* William Leicester (Lester), *Mess Sergeant:* George Chandler, *Tanker:* Dick Jones, *Medic Private:* Chris Drake, *Casualty:* Tommy Kelly.

Battle of the Bulge with Henry Fonda and Robert Ryan.

BATTLE OF THE BULGE (1965) WB. Producers, Milton Sperling, Philip Yordan. Director, Ken Annakin. Screenplay, Philip Yordan, Milton Sperling, John Melson. Director of Photography, Jack Hildyard. Costumes, Laure De Zarate. Music, Benjamin Frankel. Assistant Directors, Jose Lopez Rodero, Martin Sacristan, Luis Garcia. A Sidney Harmon, in association with United States Pictures, Inc., Production. In Ultra Panavision and Technicolor. Lyrics "Panzerlied" by Kurt Wiehle. 162 minutes

Lt. Col. Kiley: Henry Fonda, *Col. Hessler:* Robert Shaw, *Gen. Grey:* Robert Ryan, *Col. Pritchard:* Dana Andrews, *Sgt. Duquesne:* George Montgomery, *Schumacher:* Ty Hardin, *Louise:* Pier Angeli, *Elena:* Barbara Werle, *Wolenski:* Charles Bronson, *Gen. Kohler:* Werner Peters, *Conrad:* Hans Christian Blech, *Lt. Weaver:* James McArthur, *Guffy:* Telly Savalas.

BEAT THE DEVIL (1954) UA. A Santana-Romulus Production. Director, John Huston. Screenplay by John Huston and Truman

Beat the Devil with Humphrey Bogart and Jennifer Jones.

Capote. Based on novel by James Helvick. Art Director, Wilfred Shingleton. Cinematographers, Oswald Morris, Freddie Francis. Editor, Ralph Kemplen. 92 minutes

Billy Dannreuther: Humphrey Bogart, *Gwendolen Chelm:* Jennifer Jones, *Maria Dannreuther:* Gina Lollobrigida, *Petersen:* Robert Morley, *O'Hara:* Peter Lorre, *Harry Chelm:* Edward Underdown, *Major Ross:* Ivor Barnard, *C.I.D. Inspector:* Bernard Lee, *Ravello:* Marco Tulli, *Purser:* Marrio Perroni, *Hotel Manager:* Alex Pochet, *Charles:* Aldo Silvani.

Becket with Richard Burton and Peter O'Toole.

BECKET (1964) Par. Producer, Hal Wallis. Director, Peter Glenville. Panavision, Technicolor. Screenplay, Edward Anhalt. Based on play of same name by Jean Anouilh. Music, Laurence Rosenthal. Cinematographer, Geoffrey Unsworth. Costumes, Margaret Furse. Assistant Director, Colin Brewe. Production Design, John Bryan. Art Direction, Maurice Carter. Sound, Buster Ambler. Filmed in England. 148 minutes

Thomas Becket: Richard Burton, *King Henry II:* Peter O'Toole, *Bishop Folliot:* Sir Donald Wolfit, *King Louis VII:* Sir John Gielgud, *Queen Matilda:* Martita Hunt, *Queen Eleanor:* Pamela Brown, *Gwendolen:* Sian Phillips, *Pope Alexander III:* Paolo Stoppa, *Cardinal Zambelli:* Gino Cervi, *Brother John:* David Weston, *Archbishop of Canterbury:* Felix Aylmer, *Barons:* Niall MacGinnis, Percy Herbert, Christopher Rhodes, Peter Jeffrey, *Duke of Leicester:* Inigo Jackson, *French Girl:* Veronique Vendell, *Bishop of Winchester:* John Phillips, *Bishop of York:* Frank Pettingell, *Bishop of Chichester:* Hamilton Dyce, *William of Corbeil:* Patrick Newall, *Prince Henry:* Riggs O'Hara, *Brother Philip:* Geoffrey Bayldon.

Behind the Rising Sun with J. Carroll Naish, Adeline de Walt Reynolds and Margo.

BEHIND THE RISING SUN (1943) RKO. Director, Edward Dmytryk. Based on the book by James R. Young. Screenplay, Emmett Lavery. Musical Director, C. Bakaleinkoff. Art Directors, Albert S. D'Agostino, Al Herman. Cameraman, Russell Metty. Special Effects, Vernon L. Walker. Editor, Joseph Noriega. 89 minutes

Tama: Margo, *Taro:* Tom Neal, *Publisher:* J. Carrol Naish, *Lefty:* Robert Ryan, *Sara:* Gloria Holden, *O'Hara:* Don Douglas, *Boris:* George Givot, *Grandmother:* Adeline deWalt Reynolds, *Tama's Father:* Leonard Strong, *Woman Secretary:* Iris Wong, *Max:* Wolfgang Zilzer, *Servant:* Shirley Lew, *Japanese Officer:* Benson Fong, *Dinner Guest:* Lee Tung Foo, *Japanese Wrestler:* Mike Mazurki, *Japanese Officer:* William Yip, *Policeman:* H. T. Tsiang, *Officer:* Luke Chan, *First Agent:* Bruce Wong, *Japanese Guard:* Leon Lontoc, *Geisha Girl:* Mei Lee Foo, *Capt. Matsuda:* Allan Jung, *Inspector:* Abner Biberman, *Tama's Mother:* Connie Leon, *Sister:* Nancy Gates, *Takahashi:* Fred Essler, *Japanese Officer:* Philip Ahn, *Takahashi's Servant:* Daisy Lee, *Japanese Officer:* Richard Loo, *Girl Given Dope:* Barbara Jean Wong, *Japanese Major:* Beal, Wong, *Broker:* Charles Lung, *Prof. Namachi:* Robert Katcher.

BELL, BOOK AND CANDLE (1958) Col. Producer, Julian Blaustein. Director, Richard Quine. Technicolor. Based on the play by John Van Druten. Screenplay, Daniel Taradash. Music composed by George Duning. Cinematographer, James Wong Howe. Editor, Charles Nelson. A Phoenix Production. Native primitive art by Carlebach Gallery, New York. Backgrounds filmed in New York. 106 minutes

Shepherd Henderson: James Stewart, *Gillian Holroyd:* Kim Novak, *Nicky Holroyd:* Jack Lemmon, *Sidney Redlitch:* Ernie Kovacs, *Bianca De Pass:* Hermione Gingold, *Queenie:* Elsa Lancaster, *Merle Kittridge:* Janice Rule, *French Singer:* Philippe Clay, *Secretary:* Bek Nelson, *Andy White:* Howard McNear, *Musicians:* The Brothers Candoli, *Proprietor:* Wolfe Barzell, *Exterminator:* Joe Barry, *Merle's Maid:* Gail Bonney, *Herb Store Owner:* Monty Ash, *Pyewacket, the Cat:* Himself, *Elevator Operator,* Ollie O'Toole, *Cab Driver:* Don Brodie, *Ad-Lib Bit:* Dick Crockett, *Man:* Ted Mapes, *Waldo:* James Lanphier.

Bell, Book and Candle with Elsa Lanchester, Kim Novak and Jack Lemmon.

The Bellboy with Jerry Lewis.

THE BELLBOY (1960) Par. Produced, directed and written by Jerry Lewis. Associated Producer, Ernest D. Glucksman. Assistant Director, Ralph Axness. Music, Walter Scharf. Musical numbers staged by Nick Castle. Art Directors, Hal Pereira and Henry Bumstead. Cinematography, Haskell Boggs. Special Effects, John P. Fulton. Editor, Stanley Johnson. 72 minutes

Stanley: Jerry Lewis, *Manager:* Alex Gerry, *Bell Captain:* Bob Clayton, *Bellboys:* Sonnie Sands, Eddie Shaeffer, Herkie Styles, David Landfield, *Man in Black as Stan Laurel:* Bill Richmond, *Apple Man:* Larry Best, *Guest Stars:* Milton Berle, Gary Middlecoff, The Novelties, Joe Levitch, *Fighting Couple:* Jimmy and Tilly Gerard.

BELLE OF THE NINETIES (1934) Par. Produced by William Le Baron. Director Leo McCarey. Author, Mae West. Music and Lyrics, Arthur Johnston, Sam Coslow. Cameraman, Karl Struss. Editor, LeRoy Stone. New songs by Arthur Johnston and Sam Coslow: "When a St. Louis Woman Goes Down to New Orleans," "My Old Flame," "My American Beauty," "Troubled Waters." 75 minutes

Ruby Carter: Mae West, *Tiger Kid:* Roger Pryor, *Brooks Claybourne:* John Mack Brown, *Molly Brant:* Katherine De Mille, *Ace Lamont:* John Miljan, *Kirby:* James Donlan, *Gilbert:* Tom Herbert, *Dirk:* Stuart Holmes, *Slade:* Harry Woods, *Stogie:* Edward Gargan, *Jasmine:* Libby Taylor, *Colonel Claybourne:* Frederick Burton, *Mrs. Claybourne:* Augusta Anderson, *Blackie:* Benny Baker, *Butch:* Morrie Cohan, *St. Louis Fighter:* Warren Hymer: *Editor:* Wade Boteler, *Leading Man:* George Walsh, *Comedians:* Eddie Borden, Fuzzy Knight, Tyler Brooke, *Beef Trust Chorus Girl:* Kay Deslys, *Extra:* Mike Mazurki. Duke Ellington and Orchestra.

Belle of the Nineties with John Miljan and Mae West.

The Bells of St. Mary's with Ingrid Bergman and Bing Crosby.

THE BELLS OF ST. MARY'S (1945) RKO. Producer and Director, Leo McCarey. Author, Leo McCarey. Screenplay, Dudley Nichols. Musical Score, Robert Emmett Dolan. Art Director, William Flannery. Cameraman, George Barnes. Special Effects, Vernon L. Walker. Editor, Harry Marker. Songs: "Aren't You Glad You're You?" by Johnny Burke and Jimmy Van Heusen; "In the Land of Beginning Again" by Grant Clarke and George W. Meyer; "The Bells of St. Mary's" by Douglas Furber and A. Emmett Adams; "Ave Maria." A Rainbow Production. 126 minutes

Father O'Malley: Bing Crosby, *Sister Benedict:* Ingrid Bergman, *Bogardus:* Henry Travers, *Patsy's Father:* William Gargan, *Sister Michael:* Ruth Donnelly, *Patsy:* Joan Carroll, *Patsy's Mother:* Martha Sleeper, *Dr. McKay:* Rhys Williams, *Eddie:* Dickie Tyler, *Mrs. Breen:* Una O'Connor, *Tommy:* Bobby Frasco, *Nuns:* Aina Constant, Gwen Crawford, Eva Novak, *Clerk in Store:* Matt McHugh, *Delphine:* Edna Wonacott, *Luther:* Jimmy Crane, *Truck Driver:* Dewey Robinson, *Taxi Driver:* Jimmy Dundee, *Workman:* Joseph Palma, *Landlady:* Minerva Urecal, *Blind Man:* Peter Sasso, *Old Lady:* Cora Shannon.

BEND OF THE RIVER (1952) Univ. Producer, Aaron Rosenberg. Director, Anthony Mann. Color by Technicolor. From William Gulick's *Bend of the Snake*. Screenplay, Borden Chase. Art Directors, Bernard Herzbrun, Nathan Juran. Music, Hans J. Salter. Cinematographer, Irving Glassberg. Editor, Russell Schoengarth. 91 minutes

Glyn McLyntock: James Stewart, *Cole Garett:* J. Arthur Kennedy, *Laura Baile:* Julia Adams, *Trey Wilson:* Rock Hudson, *Marjie Baile:* Lori Nelson, *Jeremy Baile:* Jay C. Flippen, *Shorty:* Henry Morgan, *Captain Mello:* Chubby Johnson, *Long Tom:* Royal Dano, *Tom Hendricks:* Howard Petrie, *Adam:* Stepin' Fetchit, *Red:* Jack Lambert, *Don Grundy:* Frank Ferguson, *Mrs. Prentiss:* Frances Bavier, *Wullie:* Cliff Lyons, *Lock:* Jennings Miles, *Wasco:* Frank Chase, *Aunt Tildy:* Lillian Randolph, *Roustabout:* Britt Wood, *Miner:* Gregg Barton, *Johnson:* Hugh Prosser, *Barkers:* Donald Kerr, Harry Arnie.

Bend of the River with Rock Hudson, Jay C. Flippen, Julie Adams and James Stewart.

Ben-Hur with Charlton Heston.

BEN-HUR (1959) MGM. Producer, Sam Zimbalist. Director, William Wyler. Screenplay, Karl Tunberg. Based on novel by Lew Wallace. Music by Miklos Rozsa. Associated Directors, Andrew Marton, Yakima Canutt and Mario Soldati. Assistant Directors, Gus Agosti and Alberto Cardone. Costumes by Elizabeth Haffenden. Art Directors, William A. Horning, Edward Carfagno. Cinematographer, Robert L. Surtees. Additional Photography, Harold E. Wellman, Pietro Portalupi. Editors, Ralph E. Winters, John D. Dunning. Technicolor, Camera 65. Produced in Italy. Photographed in Panavision. 217 minutes

Judah Ben-Hur: Charlton Heston, *Quintus Arrius:* Jack Hawkins, *Messala:* Stephen Boyd, *Ester:* Haya Harareet, *Skeik Ilderim:* Hugh Griffith, *Miriam:* Martha Scott, *Simonides:* Sam Jaffe, *Tirzah:* Cathy O'Donnell, *Balthasar:* Finlay Currie, *Pontius Pilate:* Frank Thring, *Drusus:* Terence Longden, *Sextus:* Andre Morell, *Flavia:* Marina Berti, *Tiberius:* George Relph, *Malluch:* Adi Berber, *Amrah:* Stella Vitelleschi, *Mary:* Jose Greci, *Joseph:* Laurence Payne, *Spintho:* John Horsley, *Metellus:* Richard Coleman, *Marius:* Duncan Lamont, *Aide to Tiberius:* Ralph Truman, *Gaspar:* Richard Hale, *Melchior:* Reginald Lal Singh, *Quaestor:* David Davies, *Jailer:* Dervis Ward, *The Christ:* Claude Heater, *Gratus:* Mino Doro, *Chief of Rowers:* Robert Brown, *Leper:* Tutte Lemkow, *Hortator:* Howard Lang, *Captain, Rescue Ship:* Ferdy Mayne, *Doctor:* John Le Mesurier, *Blind Man:* Stevenson Lang, *Barca:* Aldo Mozele, *Marcello:* Dino Fazio, *Raimondo:* Michael Cosmo, *Decurian:* Remington Olmstead, *Mario:* Hugh Billingsley, *Man in Nazareth:* Aldo Silvani, *The Lubian:* Cliff Lyons, *The Egyptian:* Joe Yrigoyrn, *Sportsman:* Joe Canutt.

BERKELEY SQUARE (1933) Fox. Produced by Jesse L. Lasky. Directed by Frank Lloyd. From the play by John L. Balderston. Adaptation, Sonya Levien and John L. Balderston. Sets and Costumes, William Carling. Music Director, Louis De Francesco. Photography, Ernest Palmer. Editor, Howard Schuster. Sound, Joseph Aiken. Leslie

Berkeley Square with Leslie Howard and Valerie Taylor.

Howard produced and starred in the play. Remade as *I'll Never Forget You* (20th Century-Fox, 1951). 87 minutes

Peter Standish: Leslie Howard, *Helen Pettigrew:* Heather Angel, *Kate Pettigrew:* Valerie Taylor, *Lady Ann Pettigrew:* Irene Browne, *Mrs. Barwick:* Berly Mercer, *Tom Pettigrew:* Colin Keith-Johnston, *Major Clinton:* Alan Mowbray, *Duchess of Devonshire:* Juliette Compton, *Marjorie Frant:* Betty Lawford, *Mr. Throstle:* Ferdinand Gottschalk, *American Ambassador:* Samuel Hinds, *Sir Joshua Reynolds:* Olaf Hytten, *Lord Stanley:* David Torrence.

The Best of Everything with Stephen Boyd and Hope Lange.

THE BEST OF EVERYTHING (1959) 20th. Producer, Jerry Wald. Director, Jean Negulesco. Screenplay by Edith Sommer and Mann Rubin. Based on novel by Rona Jaffe. Music by Alfred Newman. Title song by Sammy Cahn and Alfred Newman, sung by Johnny Mathis. Costumes by Adele Palmer. Assistant Director, Eli Dunn. In CinemaScope and De Luxe Color. Art Directors, Lyle R. Wheeler, Jack Martin Smith, Mark-Lee Kirk. Orchestration, Herbert Spencer and Earle Hagen. Photography, William C. Mellor. Editor, Robert Simpson. Locations filmed in New York City. Film debut of Donald Harron, stage actor. 127 minutes

Caroline Bender: Hope Lange, *Mike Rice:* Stephen Boyd, *Gregg Adams:* Suzy Parker, *Barbara Lemont:* Martha Hyer, *April Morrison:* Diane Baker, *Fred Shalimar:* Brian Aherne, *Dexter Key:* Robert Evans, *Eddie Harris:* Brett Halsey, *Sidney Carter:* Donald Harron, *Mary Agnes:* Sue Carson, *Jane:* Linda Hutchings, *Paul Landis:* Lionel Kane, *Dr. Ronnie Wood:* Ted Otis, *David Savage:* Louis Jourdan, *Amanda Farrow:* Joan Crawford, *Brenda:* June Blair, *Judy Masson:* Myrna Hansen, *Scrubwoman:* Nora O'Mahoney, *Joe:* David Hoffman, *Margo Stewart:* Theodora Davitt, *Girls in Typing Pool:* Alena Murray, Rachel Stephens, Julie Payne, *Drunk:* Wally Brown, *Man:* Al Austin.

THE BEST YEARS OF OUR LIVES (1946) RKO. Producer, Samuel Goldwyn. Director, William Wyler. From the novel *Glory For Me* by MacKinlay Kanter. Screenplay, Robert E. Sherwood. Art Directors, George Jenkins, Perry Ferguson. Cameraman, Gregg Toland. Editor, Daniel Mandell. Song by Sidney Arodin and Hoagy Carmichael, "Lazy River." Only film of amputee Harold Russell. 172 minutes

Milly Stephenson: Myrna Loy, *Al Stephenson:* Fredric March, *Fred Derry:* Dana Andrews, *Peggy Stephenson:* Teresa Wright, *Marie Derry:* Virginia Mayo, *Wilma Cameron:* Cathy O'Donnell, *Butch Engle:* Hoagy Carmichael, *Homer Parrish:* Harold Russell, *Hortense Derry:* Gladys George, *Pat Derry:* Roman Bohnen, *Mr. Milton:* Ray Collins, *Mrs. Parrish:* Minna Gombell, *Mr. Parrish:* Walter Baldwin, *Cliff:* Steve Cochran, *Mrs. Cameron:* Dorothy Adams, *Mr. Cameron;* Don Beddoe, *Woody:* Victor Cutler, *Luella Parrish:* Marlene Aames, *Prew:* Charles Halton, *Mr. Mollett:* Ray Teal, *Thorpe:* Howland Chamberlin, *Novak:* Dean White, *Bullard:* Erskine Sanford,

The Best Years of Our Lives with Dana Andrews, Myrna Loy, Donald Kerr (bartender), Fredric March, Hoagy Carmichael and Harold Russell.

Rob Stephenson: Michael Hall, *Merkle:* Norman Phillips, *Dexter:* Teddy Infuhr, *Taxi Driver:* Clancy Cooper, *Mr. Gibbons:* Ralph Sanford, *Tech. Sergeant:* Robert Karnes, *ATC Sergeant:* Bert Conway, *Corporal:* Blake Edwards, *Gus (Waiter):* John Tyrrell, *Steve (Bartender):* Donald Kerr, *Desk Clerk:* Jack Rice, *Miss Garrett:* Ruth Sanderson, *Latham:* Ben Erway, *Mrs. Talburt:* Claire Dubrey, *Minister:* Harry Cheshire, *Karney:* Pat Flaherty, *Jackie:* James Ames.

THE BIBLE (1966) 20th (In association with Seven Arts). Produced by Dino De Laurentiis. Directed by John Huston. 70mm, De Luxe Color. Associate Producer, Luigi Luraschi. Screenplay, Christopher Fry. Camera, Guiseppe Rotunno. Editor, Ralph Kemplen. Music, Toshiro Mayuzumi. Assistants on Screenplay, Jonathan Griffin, Ivo Perilli, Vittorio Bonicelli. Art Director, Mario Chiari. Sets, Enzo Eusepi and Bruno Avesani. Special Effects, Augie Lohman. Choreography, Katherine Dunham. Costumes, Mario De Matteis. Make-up, Alberto De Rossi. Assistant Directors, Vana Caruso and Ottavio Oppo. Filmed in Rome, Sicily, Sardinia, North Africa. 174 minutes

Adam: Michael Parks, *Eve:* Ulla Bergryd, *Cain:* Richard Harris, *Noah:* John Huston, *Nimrod:* Stephen Boyd, *Abraham:* George C. Scott, *Sarah:* Ava Gardner, *The Three Angels:* Peter O'Toole, *Hagar:* Zoe Sallis, *Lot:* Gabriele Ferzetti, *Lot's Wife:* Eleonora Rossi Drago, *Abel:* Franco Nero, *Isaac:* Alberto Lucantoni, *Ishmael:* Luciano Conversi, *Abraham's Steward:* Robert Rietty, *Lot's Daughters:* Adriana Ambesi, Grazia Maria Spina, *Narrator:* John Huston.

The Bible with Michael Parks and Ulla Bergryd.

BIG BROADCAST OF 1937 (1936) Par. Produced by Lewis E. Gensler. Directed by Mitchell Leisen. Authors, Erwin Gelsey, Arthur Kober, Barry Trivers. Screenplay, Walter DeLeon, Francis Martin. Art Directors, Hans Dreier, Robert Usher. Cameraman, Theodore Sparkuhl. Editor, Stuart Heisler. Dance Ensembles, LeRoy Prinz. Songs by Leo Robin and Ralph Rainger: "Vote for Mr. Rhythm," "La Bomba,"

The Big Broadcast of 1937 with George Burns, Martha Raye and Gracie Allen.

"Night in Manhattan," "I'm Talking Through My Heart," "You Came to My Rescue," "Here's Love in Your Eye." Third "Big Broadcast" film. 100 minutes

Jack Carson: Jack Benny, *Mr. and Mrs. Platt:* George Burns and Gracie Allen, *Bob Black:* Bob Burns, *Patsy:* Martha Raye, *Gwen Holmes:* Shirley Ross, *Bob Miller:* Raymond Milland, *Frank Rossman:* Frank Forest, *Benny Fields:* Benny Fields, *Schlepperman:* Sam Hearn, *Kavvy:* Stan Kavanaugh, *Themselves:* Benny Goodman and his Orchestra, *Flower Girl:* Virginia Weidler, *Train Bearers:* David Holt, Billy Lee, *Themselves:* Leopold Stokowski and his Symphony Orchestra, *Specialties:* Louis Da Pron, Eleanore Whitney, Larry Adler, *Property Man:* Irving Bacon, *Page Boy:* Don Hulbert, *The Uncle:* Ernest Cossart, *Mrs. Peters:* Billie Bellport, *Property Man:* Bill Bletcher, *Assistant Stage Manager:* Harry Depp, *Stage Manager:* Pat West, *Penelope:* Cupid Ainsworth, *Trombone Player:* Frank Jenks, *Woman Singer:* Avril Cameron, *Home Economics Woman:* Nora Cecil, *Violinsky:* Harrison Greene, *Russian:* Leonid Kinskey, *Violinist:* Gino Corrado, *Tap Dancer:* Henry Arthur, *Minister:* Edward J. Le Saint, *Clerk:* Jack Mulhall, *Telephone Girl:* Terry Ray (Ellen Drew), *Taxi Driver:* Murray Alper, *Jones:* Billy Arnold, *Suzie:* Gertrude Short.

The Big Country with Charlton Heston and Gregory Peck.

THE BIG COUNTRY (1958) UA. Producers, William Wyler and Gregory Peck. Director, William Wyler. Screenplay by James R. Webb, Sy Bartlett and Robert Wilder. Adaptation by Jessamyn West and Robert Wyler. From the novel by Donald Hamilton. Costumes by Emile Santiago and Yvonne Wood. Assistant Directors, Ivan Volkman, Ray Gosnell and Henry Hartman. Music by Jerome Moross. An Anthony-Worldwide Production in Technirama and Technicolor. Gregory Peck's three sons make their film debuts. Filmed on the Drais Ranch, near Stockton, California. 165 minutes

James McKay: Gregory Peck, *Julie Maragon:* Jean Simmons, *Patricia Terrill:* Carroll Baker, *Steve Leech:* Charlton Heston, *Rufus Hannassey:* Burl Ives, *Major Henry Terrill:* Charles Bickford, *Ramon:* Alfonso Bedoya, *Buck Hannassey:* Chuck Connors, *Rafe Hannassey:* Chuck Hayward, *Dude Hannassey:* Buff Brady, *Blackie Hannassey:* Jim Burk, *Hannassey Woman:* Dorothy Adams, *Terrill Cowboys:* Chuck Rober son, Bob Morgan, John McKee, Jay Slim Talbot, *Liveryman:* Donald Kerr, *Guests:* Ralph Sanford, Harry V. Cheshire, Dick Alexander, *Boys:* Jonathan, Stephen, Carey Paul Peck.

THE BIG HOUSE (1930) MGM. Directed by George Hill. Story, Frances Marion. Screenplay, Frances Marion, Joe Farnham, and Martin Flavin. Art Director, Cedric Gibbons. Photography, Harold Wenstrom. Editor, Blanche Sewell. Sound, Douglas Shearer. Jute mill scenes filmed at the Pacific Woolen and Blanket Works, Long Beach. A Cosmopolitan Production. Also French, German, Italian and Spanish versions. 88 minutes

The Big House with Chester Morris and Wallace Beery.

John Morgan: Chester Morris, *Butch Schmidt:* Wallace Beery, *Warden James Adams:* Lewis Stone, *Kent Marlowe:* Robert Montgomery, *Anne Marlowe:* Leila Hyams, *Pop Riker:* George F. Marion, *Mr. Marlowe:* J. C. Nugent, *Olsen:* Karl Dane, *Captain Wallace:* DeWitt Jennings, *Gopher:* Mathew Betz, *Mrs. Marlowe:* Claire McDowell, *Sergeant Donlin:* Robert Emett O'Connor, *Uncle Jed:* Tom Kennedy, *Sandy, a Guard:* Tom Wilson, *Dopey:* Eddie Foyer, *Putnam:* Rosco Ates, *Oliver:* Fletcher Norton, *Prison Barber:* Adolph Seidel, *Bits:* Eddie Lambert, Michael Vavitch.

THE BIG SLEEP (1946) WB. Producer and Director, Howard Hawks. From the novel by Raymond Chandler. Screenplay, William Faulkner, Leigh Brackett, Jules Furthman. Art Director, Carl Jules Weyl. Music, Leo F. Forbstein. Cameraman, Sid Hickox. Special Effects, E. Roy Davidson. Editor, Christian Nyby. Song, "Her Tears Flowed Like Wine." Footage from *Case of the Stuttering Bishop* (WB, 1937). 114 minutes

The Big Sleep with Humphrey Bogart and Lauren Bacall.

Phil Marlowe: Humphrey Bogart, *Vivian Sterwood Rutledge:* Lauren Bacall, *Eddie Mars:* John Ridgely, *Carmen Sternwood:* Martha Vickers, *Proprietress:* Dorothy Malone, *Mona Mars:* Peggy Knudsen, *Bernie Ohls:* Regis Toomey, *General Sternwood:* Charles Waldron, *Norris, the Butler:* Charles D. Brown, *Canino:* Bob Steele, *Harry Jones:* Elisha Cook, Jr., *Joe Brody:* Louis Jean Heydt, *Agnes Lowzier:* Sonia Darrin, *Captain Cronjager:* James Flavin, *Medical Examiner:* Joseph Crehan, *Carol Lundgren:* Tom Rafferty, *Arthur Gwynne Geiger:* Theodore Von Eltz, *Taxicab Driver:* Joy Barlowe, *Sidney:* Tom Fadden, *Pete:* Ben Welden, *Art Huck:* Trevor Bardette, *Ed, Deputy:* Emmett Vogan, *Furtive Man:* Forbes Murray, *Motorcycle Officer:* Pete Kooy, *Librarian:* Carole Douglas, *Croupier:* Jack Chefe, *Mars' Thugs:* Paul Weber, Jack Perry, Wally Walker, *Hatcheck Girl:* Lorraine Miller, *Cigarette Girl:* Shelby Payne, *Waitresses:* Janis Chandler, Deannie Bert. Cut are: Thomas Jackson as District Attorney Wilde, Dan Wallace as Owen Taylor.

A Bill of Divorcement with Katharine Hepburn, Billie Burke and John Barrymore.

A BILL OF DIVORCEMENT (1932) RKO. Executive Producer, David O. Selznick. Directed by George Cukor. Assistant Director, Dewey Starkey. From the play by Clemence Dane. Screenplay, Howard Estabrook and Harry Wagstaff Gribble. Art Director, Carroll Clark. Costume Design, Josette De Lima. Photography, Sid Hickox. Editor, Arthur Roberts. Sound, George Ells. Film debut of Katharine Hepburn. Remade by RKO in 1940. 76 minutes

Hillary Fairfield: John Barrymore, *Sydney Fairfield:* Katharine Hepburn, *Margeret Fairfield:* Billie Burke, *Kit Humphrey:* David Manners, *Gray Meredith:* Paul Cavanagh, *Doctor Alliot:* Henry Stephenson, *Aunt Hester:* Elizabeth Patterson, *Bassett:* Gayle Evers.

Billy Budd with John Neville, Peter Ustinov and Paul Rogers.

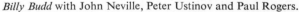

BILLY BUDD (1962) AA. Executive Producer, A. Ronald Lubin. Producer-Director, Peter Ustinov. Based on the novel by Herman Melville (*Billy Budd, Foretopman*) and the play by Robert Chapman and Louis O. Coxe. Screenplay, Peter Ustinov, DeWitt Bodeen. Art Director, Peter Murton. Musical Director, Anthony Hopkins. Cinematographer, Robert Krasker. Editor, Jack Harris. Costumes, Anthony Mendelson. Assistant Director, Michael Birkett. 112 minutes

Master-at-Arms Claggart: Robert Ryan, *Capt. Edward Fairfax Vere:* Peter Ustinov, *The Dansker:* Melvyn Douglas, *Billy Budd:* Terence Stamp, *Lt. Wyatt:* David McCallum, *Lt. John Ratcliffe:* John Neville, *Jenkins:* Ronald Lewis, *Squeak:* Lee Montague, *Lt. Seymour:* Paul Rogers, *Capt. Graveling:* Niall MacGinnis, *Kincaid:* John Meillon, *O'Daniel:* Ray McAnally, *Talbot:* Robert Brown.

Billy Rose's Diamond Horseshoe with Betty Grable, Phil Silvers, Beatrice Kay and William Gaxton (in photo).

BILLY ROSE'S DIAMOND HORSESHOE (1945) 20th. Producer, William Perlberg. Director, George Seaton. Color by Technicolor. Screenplay, George Seaton. Dance Director, Hermes Pan. Musical Directors, Alfred Newman, Charles Henderson. Art Directors, Lyle Wheeler, Joseph C. Wright. Cameraman, Ernest Palmer. Special Effects, Fred Sersen. Editor, Robert Simpson. Technicolor Director, Natalie Kalmus. Associate, Richard Mueller. Suggested by a play by John Kenyon Nicholson. Songs by Mack Gordon and Harry Warren: "The More I See You," "Welcome to the Diamond Horseshoe," "I Wish I Knew," "In Acapulco," "A Nickel's Worth of Jive," "Moody," "Cooking Up a Show," "Play Me an Old-Fashioned Melody." 104 minutes

Bonnie Collins: Betty Grable, *Joe Davis, Jr.:* Dick Haymes, *Blinky Walker:* Phil Silvers, *Joe Davis, Sr.:* William Gaxton, *Claire Williams:* Beatrice Kay, *Specialty:* Carmen Cavallaro, *Specialty:* Willie Solar, *Mrs. Standish:* Margaret Dumont, *Harper:* Roy Benson, *Pop (Stage Doorman):* George Melford, *Carter:* Hal K. Dawson, *Dance Director:* Kenny Williams, *Interne:* Reed Hadley, *Clarinet Player:* Eddie Acuff, *Stagehand:* Edward Gargan, *Wardrobe Woman:* Ruth Rickaby, *Stagehand:* Milton Kibbee, *Dorothy:* Dorothy Day, *Waiter:* Dick Elliott, *Man:* Bruce Warren, *Girl:* Julie London, *Waiter:* Harry Seymour, *Men:* Frank Penny, Bud Jamison, Ray Teal, *Boy:* Donald Hayden, *Girl:* Barbara Sears (Bobo Rockefeller), *Major Catastrophe:* Alex Melesh, *Marquis of Queensbury:* Arthur Foster, *Lady Be Good:* Jean Fenwick, *Duke of Duchess:* Evan Thomas, *Prince Too Much Belly:* Ferdinand Munier, *Sir How Dare You:* Eric Wilton, *King Otto IV:* Paul Bakanas, *Major Domo:* Charles Coleman, *Duchess of Duke:* Bess Flowers.

BILLY THE KID (1941) MGM. Produced by Irving Asher. Directed by David Miller. Color by Technicolor. Suggested by the book *The Saga of Billy The Kid* by Walter Noble Burns. Screenplay, Gene Fowler.

Story, Howard Emmett Rogers and Bradbury Foote. Music, David Snell. Photography, Leonard Smith and William V. Skall. Editor, Robert J. Kern. Remake of the 1930 MGM film. 95 minutes

Billy Bonney: Robert Taylor, *Jim Sherwood:* Brian Donlevy, *Eric Keating:* Ian Hunter, *Edith Keating:* Mary Howard, *Dan Hickey:* Gene Lockhart, *Tim Ward:* Henry O'Neill, *Pedro Gonzales:* Frank Puglia, *Cass McAndrews (Sheriff):* Cy Kendall, *Mildred:* Connie Gilchrist, *Mrs. Hanky:* Ethel Griffies, *Tom Patterson:* Chill Wills, *Ed Bronson:* Guinn Williams, *Mrs. Patterson:* Olive Blakeney, *Spike Hudson:* Lon Chaney, Jr., *Judge Blake:* Frank Conlan, *Bart Hodges:* Mitchell Lewis, *Kirby Claxton:* Dick Curtis, *Bill Cobb:* Ted Adams, *Jesse Martin:* Earl Gunn, *Pat Shanahan:* Eddie Dunn, *Ed Shanahan:* Grant Withers, *Milton:* Joe Yule, *"Bat" Smithers:* Carl Pitti, *Drunk:* Arthur Housman, *The Duke:* Lew Harvey, *Bessie:* Priscilla Lawson, *Thad Decker:* Kermit Maynard, *Butch:* Slim Whitaker, *Axel:* Ray Teal, *Bud:* Wesley White, *Hickey Gang Members:* Ben Pitti, George Chesebro, Jack L. King, *Vagrant #1:* Jules Cowles, *Vagrant #2:* Edwin J. Brady, *Man in Saloon:* Frank Hagney, *Gambler:* Buck Mack, *Leader:* Tom London.

Billy the Kid with Brian Donlevy and Robert Taylor.

BIRD MAN OF ALCATRAZ (1962) UA. Executive Producer, Harold Hecht. Producers, Stuart Millar, Guy Trosper. Director, John Frankenheimer. Screenplay, Guy Trosper. Based on the book by Thomas E. Gaddis. Art Director, Ferdie Carrere. Music, Elmer Bernstein. Cinematographer, Burnett Guffey. Editor, Edward Mann. A Norma Production. 147 minutes

Bird Man of Alcatraz with Burt Lancaster and Neville Brand.

274

Robert Stroud: Burt Lancaster, *Harvey Shoemaker:* Karl Malden, *Elizabeth Stroud:* Thelma Ritter, *Stella Johnson:* Betty Field, *Bull Ransom:* Neville Brand, *Tom Gaddis:* Edmond O'Brien, *Roy Comstock:* Hugh Marlowe, *Feto Gomez:* Telly Savalas, *Kramer:* Crahan Denton, *Jess Younger:* James Westerfield, *Logue:* Chris Robinson, *Dr. Ellis:* Whit Bissell, *Eddie Kassellis:* Leo Penn, *Chaplain Wentzel:* Lewis Charles, *Guard Captain:* Art Stewart, *Judge:* Raymond Greenleaf, *Crazed Prisoner:* Nick Dennis, *Fred Daw:* William Hansen, *City Editor:* Harry Holcombe, *Senator Ham Lewis:* Robert Burton, *Burns:* Len Lesser, *Father Matthieu:* George Mitchell, *John Clary:* Ed Mallory, *Mrs. Woodrow Wilson:* Adrienne Marden, *Reporter:* Harry Jackson.

The Birds with Rod Taylor, Jessica Tandy, Tippi Hedren and Angela Cartwright.

THE BIRDS (1963) Univ. Producer-Director, Alfred Hitchcock. Screenplay, Evan Hunter. From the story by Daphne du Maurier. Assistant Director, James H. Brown. Costumes, Edith Head. In Technicolor. Backgrounds filmed in San Francisco. Cinematographer, Robbert Burks. Editor, George Tomasini. 120 minutes

Mitch Brenner: Rod Taylor, *Melanie Daniels:* Tippi Hedren, *Lydia Brenner:* Jessica Tandy, *Annie Hayworth:* Suzanne Pleshette, *Cathy Brenner:* Veronica Cartwright, *Mrs. Bundy:* Ethel Griffies, *Sebastian Sholes:* Charles McGraw, *Mrs. MacGruder:* Ruth McDevitt, *Travelling Salesman:* Joe Mantell, *Deputy Al Malone:* Malcolm Atterbury, *Drunk:* Karl Swenson, *Helen Carter:* Elizabeth Wilson, *Deke Carter:* Lonny Chapman, *Fisherman:* Doodles Weaver, *Postal Clerk:* John McGovern, *Man in Elevator:* Richard Deacon, *Man:* William Quinn, *Man Leaving Pet Shop with White Poodles:* Alfred Hitchcock, *Hysterical Woman:* Doreen Lang.

THE BISHOP'S WIFE (1947) RKO. Producer, Samuel Goldwyn. Director, Henry Koster. From the novel by Robert Nathan. Screenplay, Robert E. Sherwood, Leonardo Bercovici. Music, Hugo Friedhofer. Musical Director, Emil Newman. Art Directors, George Jenkins,

The Bishop's Wife with David Niven and Cary Grant.

Perry Ferguson. Cameraman, Gregg Toland. Editor, Monica Collingswood. Song by Edgar DeLange, Emile Newman and Herbert Spencer: "Lost April." 108 minutes

Dudley: Cary Grant, *Julia Brougham:* Loretta Young, *Henry Brougham:* David Niven, *Professor Wutheridge:* Monty Woolley, *Sylvester:* James Gleason, *Mrs. Hamilton:* Gladys Cooper, *Matilda:* Elsa Lanchester, *Mildred Cassaway:* Sara Haden, *Debby Brougham:* Karolyn Grimes, *Maggenti:* Tito Vuolo, *Mr. Miller:* Regis Toomey, *Mrs. Duffy:* Sara Edwards, *Miss Trumbull:* Margaret McWade, *Mrs. Ward:* Ann O'Neal, *Mr. Perry:* Ben Erway, *Stevens:* Erville Alderson, *Defense Captain:* Bobby Anderson, *Attack Captain:* Teddy Infuhr, *Michel:* Eugene Borden, *First Lady in Michel's:* Almira Sessions, *Second Lady:* Claire DuBrey, *Third Lady:* Florence Auer, *Hat Shop Proprietress:* Margaret Wells, *Hat Shop Customer:* Kitty O'Neill, *Hysterical Mother:* Isable Jewell, *Blind Man:* David Leonard, *Delia:* Dorothy Vaughan, *Cop:* Edgar Dearing, *Saleslady:* Edythe Elliott, *Santa Claus:* Joseph J. Greene.

The Blackboard Jungle with Paul Mazursky, Chris Randall, John Erman, Vic Morrow, Sidney Poitier and Glenn Ford.

THE BLACKBOARD JUNGLE (1955) MGM. Producer, Pandro Berman. Director, Richard Brooks. Screenplay, Richard Brooks. Art Directors, Cedric Gibbons, Randall Duell. Musical Adaptation, Charles Wolcott. Cinematographer, Russell Harlan. Editor, Ferris Webster. Music, Bill Haley and the Comets. Includes "Rock Around the Clock." 101 minutes

Richard Dadier: Glenn Ford, *Anne Dadier:* Anne Francis, *Jim Murdock:* Louis Calhern, *Lois Judby Hammond:* Margaret Hayes, *Mr. Warneke:* John Hoyt, *Joshua Edwards:* Richard Kiley, *Mr. Halloran:* Emile Meyer, *Dr. Bradley:* Warner Anderson, *Prof. A. R. Kraal:* Basil Ruysdael, *Gregory Miller:* Sidney Poitier, *Artie West:* Vic Morrow, *Belazi:* Dan Terranova, *Pete V. Morales:* Rafeal Campos, *Emmanuel Stoker:* Paul Mazursky, *Detective:* Horace McMahon, *Santini:* Jameel Farah, *De Lica:* Danny Dennis, *Lou Savoldi:* David Alpert, *Levy:* Christ Randall, *Tomita:* Yoshi Tomita, *Carter:* Gerald Phillips, *Miss Panucci:* Dorothy Neumann, *Miss Brady:* Henny Backus, *Mr. Lefkowitz:* Paul Hoffman, *Manners:* Tom McKee, *Mr. Katz:* Robert Foulk, *Italian Proprietor:* Manuel Paris.

BLACK LEGION (1936) WB. Directed by Archie Mayo. Original Story, Robert Lord. Screenplay by William Wister Haines, Abem Finkel. Cameraman, George Barnes. Editor, Owen Marks. 83 minutes

Frank Taylor: Humphrey Bogart, *Ed Jackson:* Richard (Dick) Foran, *Betty Grogan:* Ann Sheridan, *Ruth Taylor:* Erin O'Brien Moore, *Pearl Davis:* Helen Flint, *Billings:* Paul Harvey, *Osgood:* Charles Halton, *Cliff Moore:* Joseph Sawyer, *Judge:* Samuel S. Hinds, *Prosecuting Attorney:* Addison Richards, *Alexander Hargrave:* Alonzo Price, *Mike Grogan:* Clifford Soubier, *Mrs. Grogan:* Dorothy Vaughan,

Black Legion with Humphrey Bogart, Robert E. Homans, Eddy Chandler and Billy Wayne.

Bud Taylor: Dickie Jones, *Sam Dombrowsky:* Henry Brandon, *Old Man Dombrowsky:* Egon Brecher, *Nick Strumpas:* Pat C. Flick, *Tommy Smith:* John Litel, *Metcalf:* Eddie Acuff, *Dr. Barkham:* Paul Stanton, *Jones:* Harry Hayden; *Charlie:* Francis Sayles, *Drunken Member:* Don Barclay, *News Commentator:* Emmett Vogan, *Counterman:* Billy Wayne, *Helper:* Frank Sully, *First Cop:* Eddy Chandler, *Second Cop:* Robert E. Homans, *Truck Driver:* Max Wagner, *March of Time Voice:* Fredrich Lindsley, *Reporters:* Carlyle Moore, Jr., Dennis Moore, Milt Kibbee, *Guard:* Lee Phelps, *Bailiff:* Wilfred Lucas, *County Clerk:* Jack Hower.

THE BLACK ROSE (1950) 20th. Producer, Louis D. Lighton. Director, Henry Hathaway. Color by Technicolor. Based on the novel by Thomas B. Costain. Screenplay, Talbot Jennings. Music, Muir Mathieson. Composer, Richard Addinsell. Art Directors, Paul Sherrif, W. Andrews. Photography, Jack Cardiff. Editor, Manuel Del Campo. Technicolor Consultant, Joan Bridge. 120 minutes

Walter of Gurnie: Tyrone Power, *Bayan:* Orsen Welles, *Miriam:* Cecile Aubry, *Tristram:* Jack Hawkins, *King Edward:* Michael Rennie, *Alfgar:* Finlay Curray, *Anemus:* Herbert Lom, *Countess of Lessford:* Mary Clare, *Mahmoud:* Bobby Blake, *Lu Chung:* Alfonso Bedoya, *Wilderkin:* Gibb McLaughlin, *Simeon Beautrie:* James Robertson, *Justice, Friar Roger Bacon:* Henry Oscar, *Edmond:* Laurence Harvey, *Harry:* Torin Thatcher, *Hal, the Miller:* Hilary Pritchard, *Empress of China:* Madame Phang, *Chinese Captain:* Ley On, *Chinese Minister:* Valery Inkijinoff, *Warder:* George Woodbridge, *Guard:* Ben Williams, *Dickon:* Rufus Cruishank, *Young Man:* Peter Drury, *Mongolian Officer:* Carl Jaffe.

BLOOD AND SAND (1941) 20th. Producer, Darryl F. Zanuck. Associated Producer, Robert T. Kane. Director, Rouben Mamoulian. Color by Technicolor. Based on the novel by Vicente Blasco Ibañez. Screenplay, Jo Swerling. Technicolor Director, Natalie Kalmus. Musical Director, Alfred Newman. Art Directors, Richard Day, Joseph C. Wright. Cameramen, Ernest Palmer, Ray Rennahan.

The Black Rose with Jack Hawkins and Tyrone Power.

Editor, Robert Bischoff. Remake of the 1922 Paramount film. 123 minutes

Juan: Tyrone Power, *Carmen Espinosa:* Linda Darnell, *Doña Sol:* Rita Hayworth, *Señora Augustias:* Nazimova, *Manola de Palma:* Anthony Quinn, *Garabato:* J. Carrol Naish, *Nacional:* John Carradine, *Encarnacion:* Lynn Bari, *Natalio Curro:* Laird Cregar, *Antonio:* William Montague (Monty Banks), *Captain Pierre Laurel:* George Reeves, *Guitarist:* Vicente Gomez, *Don Jose:* Pedro de Cordoba, *Pedro Espinosa:* Fortunio Bonanova, *Priest:* Victor Kilian, *La Pulga:* Michael Morris (Adrian Morris), *Pablo:* Charles Stevens, *Carmen as a child:* Ann Todd, *Encarnacion as a child:* Cora Sue Collins, *Marquis:* Russell Hicks, *Juan as a Boy:* Rex Downing, *El Milquetoast:* Maurice Cass, *Francisco:* John Wallace, *Gachi:* Jacqueline Dalya, *Manola as a boy:* Cullen Johnson, *La Pulga as a boy:* Ted Frye, *Pablo as a boy:* Larry Harris, *Nacional as a boy:* Schuyler Standish, *Specialty Dancers:* Elena Verdugo, Mariquita Flores, *Singer:* Rosita Granada, *Woman:* Kay Linaker, *Friend:* Francis McDonald, *Ortega:* Paul Ellis.

Blood and Sand with Rita Hayworth and Tyrone Power.

Blossoms in the Dust with Greer Garson, Walter Pidgeon and Charles Arnt.

276

BLOSSOMS IN THE DUST (1941) MGM. Produced by Irving Asher. Directed by Mervyn LeRoy. Color by Technicolor. Based on a story by Ralph Wheelwright. Art Director, Cedric Gibbons. Associate, Urie McCleary. Gowns, Adrian. Men's Costumes, Gile Steele. Screenplay, Anita Loos. Hair Styles, Sydney Guilaroff. Photography, Karl Freund, W. Howard Green. Color Director, Natalie Kalmus. Color Associate, Henri Jaffa. Score, Herbert Stothart. Sound, Douglas Shearer. Sets, Edwin B. Willis. Special Effects, Warren Newcombe. Editor, George Boemler. Make-up, Jack Dawn. 100 minutes

Edna Gladney: Greer Garson, *Sam Gladney:* Walter Pidgeon, *Dr. Max Breslar:* Felix Bressart, *Charlotte:* Marsha Hunt, *Mrs. Kahly:* Fay Holden, *Mr. Kahly:* Samuel S. Hinds, *Mrs. Keats:* Kathleen Howard, *Mr. Keats:* George Lessey, *Allan Keats:* William Henry, *Judge:* Henry O'Neill, *Damon:* John Eldredge, *Zeke:* Clinton Rosemond, *Cleo:* Theresa Harris, *G. Harrington Hedger:* Charlie Arnt, *Mrs. Gilworth:* Cecil Cunningham, *Mrs. Loring:* Ann Morriss, *Sammy:* Richard Nichols, *Tony:* Pat Barker, *Helen:* Mary Taylor, *La Verne:* Marc Lawrence.

Blue Denim with Brandon de Wilde and Carol Lynley.

BLUE DENIM (1959) 20th. Produced by Charles Brackett. Directed by Philip Dunne. Stereophonic Sound and CinemaScope. Screenplay by Edith Sommer and Philip Dunne. Based on the play by James Leo Herlihy and William Noble. Art Directors, Lyle R. Wheeler and Leland Fuller. Music, Bernard Hermann. Cinematography, Leo Tover. Editor, William Reynolds. 89 minutes

Arthur Bartley: Brandon De Wilde, *Janet Willard:* Carol Lynley, *Major Malcolm Bartley:* Macdonald Carey, *Jessie Bartley:* Marsha Hunt, *Lillian Bartley:* Nina Shipman, *Ernie:* Warren Berlinger, *Axel Sorensòn:* Buck Class, *Professor Willard:* Vaughn Taylor, *Cherie:* Roberta Shore, *Aunt Bidda:* Mary Young, *Vice President:* William Schallert, *Hobie:* Michael Gainey, *Marion:* Jenny Maxwell, *Woman in Car:* Juney Ellis, *Bank Teller:* Harry Carter, *Junk Man:* Mike Ross, *Aunt Margaret:* Jesslyn Fax, *Wedding Guest:* Hal Rand, *Caterer's Man:* Joe Brooks, *Marriage License Clerk:* Malcolm Atterbury, *Young Boy:* Jimmy Murphy, *Blonde's Boy Friend:* Page Slattery, *Bit Woman:* Billie Bird, *Bit Girl:* Gerrie Bender, *Chief Petty Officer:* Gregg Martell, *Young Girl:* Dion O'Hara, *Blonde Girl:* Miranda Jones, *Girl with Orchid:* Sandra Gould, *Woman at Doctor's House:* Grace Field, *Doctor:* Sam Buffington, *Soda Jerk:* Anthony J. Corso.

BLUE HAWAII (1961) Par. Producer, Hal Wallis. Director, Norman Taurog. Panavision and Technicolor. Screenplay, Hal Kanter. Associate

Blue Hawaii with Elvis Presley.

Producer, Paul Nathan. Assistant Director, Mickey Moore. Based on Allan Weiss' story "Beach Boy." Photography, Charles Lang, Jr. Art Direction, Hal Pereira and Walter Tyler. Sets, Sam Comer and Frank McKelvy. Editors, Warren Low and Terry Morse. Technical Advisor, Colonel Tom Parker. Costumes, Edith Head. Make-up, Wally Westmore. Color Consultant, Richard Mueller. Sound, Philip Mitchell, Charles Grenzbach. Music, Joseph J. Lilley. Numbers staged by Charles O'Curran. Songs. "Blue Hawaii," "Aloha Oe," "Rock-a-Hula Blues," "Can't Help Falling in Love," "Almost Always True," "Hawaiian Wedding Song," "Calypso Chant," "Slicin' Sand," "Moonlight Swim," "You're Stepping Out of Line." "Island Of Love," "I Love You More Today," "Ito Eat," "Please Come Back to My Heart," "Sleep, Hawaii Sleep." Locations filmed in Hawaii. 101 minutes

Chad Gates: Elvis Presley, *Maile Duval:* Joan Blackman, *Abigail Prentace:* Nancy Walters, *Fred Gates:* Roland Winters, *Sarah Lee Gates:* Angela Lansbury, *Jack Kelman:* John Archer, *Mr. Chapman:* Howard McNear, *Mrs. Manaka:* Flora Hayes, *Mr. Duval:* Gregory Gay, *Tucker Garvey:* Steve Brodie, *Enid Garvey:* Iris Adrian, *Patsy:* Darlene Tompkins, *Sandy:* Pamela Akert, *Beverly:* Christian Kay, *Ellie Corbett:* Jenny Maxwell, *Ito O'Hara:* Frank Atienza, *Carl:* Lani Kai, *Ernie:* Jose De Varga, *Wes:* Ralph Hanalie, *Waihila:* Hilo Hattie, *Accompanists:* The Jordanaires, *Bit:* Tiki Hanalie, *Harmonica-Playing Convict:* Richard Reeves, *Lt. Grey:* Michael Ross.

THE BLUE MAX (1966) 20th. Executive Producer, Elmo Williams. Producer, Christian Ferry. Director, John Guillermin. Adaptation by Ben Barzman and Basilio Franchina. Screenplay, David Pursall, Jack Seddon, Gerald Hanley. Based on the novel by Jack Hunter. Director of Photography, Doughlas Slocombe. Music composed and conducted by Jerry Goldsmith. Color by De Luxe. 156 minutes

Bruno Stachel: George Peppard, *Count Von Klugermann:* James Mason, *Countess Kaeti:* Ursula Andress, *Willi Von Klugermann:* Jeremy Kemp,

The Blue Max with Ursula Andress and George Peppard.

Body and Soul with John Garfield, Joseph Pevney, Anne Revere and Lilli Palmer.

Heidemann: Karl Michael Vogler, *Elfi Heidemann:* Loni Von Friedl, *Holbach:* Anton Diffring, *Rupp:* Peter Woodthorpe, *Fabian:* Derren Nesbitt, *Von Richthofen:* Carl Schell, *Ziegel:* Derek Newark, *Kettering:* Harry Towb, *Field Marshal Von Lenndorf:* Friedrich Ledebur, *Crown Prince:* Roger Ostime, *Hans:* Hugo Schuster, *Pilots:* Tim Parkes, Ian Kingsley, Ray Browne.

BODY AND SOUL (1947) UA. Enterprise. Producer, Bob Roberts. Director, Robert Rossen. Screenplay, Abraham Polansky. Art Director, Nathan Juran. Musical Director, Rudolph Polk. Cameraman, James Wong Howe. Editor, Francis Lyon. 104 minutes

Charlie Davis: John Garfield, *Peg Born:* Lilli Palmer, *Alice:* Hazel Brooks, *Anna Davis:* Anne Revere, *Quinn:* William Conrad, *Shorty Polaski:* Joseph Pevney, *Ben Chaplin:* Canada Lee, *Roberts:* Lloyd Goff, *David Davis:* Art Smith, *Arnold:* James Burke, *Irma:* Virginia Gregg, *Drummer:* Peter Virgo, *Prince:* Joe Devlin, *Grocer:* Shimen Ruskin, *Miss Tedder:* Mary Currier, *Dan:* Milton Kibbee, *Shelton:* Tim Ryan, *Jack Marlowe:* Artie Dorrell, *Victor:* Cy Ring, *Marine:* Glen Lee, *Referee:* John Indrisano, *Fight Announcer:* Dan Tobey, *Doctor:* Wheaton Chambers.

BONNIE AND CLYDE (1967) WB-7 Arts Produced by Warren Beatty. Associate Producer, Elaine Michael. Directed by Arthur Penn. Color by Technicolor. A Tatira-Hiller Production. Original screenplay by David Newman and Robert Benton. Music by Charles Strouse includes Flatt and Scruggs' "Foggy Mountain Breakdown." Assistant Director, Jack N. Reddish. Production Mana-

Bonnie and Clyde with Warren Beatty and Faye Dunaway.

ger, Russ Saunders. Costumes, Theadora Van Runkle. Art Director, Dean Tavoularis. Sets, Raymond Paul. Special Effects, Danny Lee. Photography, Burnett Guffey. Editor, Dede Allen. Sound, Francis E. Stahl. Includes a scene from *Gold Diggers of 1933* with Charles C. Wilson, Ned Sparks, and with Ginger Rogers singing "We're in the Money." Other songs heard include: "Night Wind," "The Shadow Waltz," "One Hour With You." Filmed mainly in Dallas, Texas. 111 minutes

Clyde Barrow: Warren Beatty, *Bonnie Parker:* Faye Dunaway, *C. W. Moss:* Michael J. Pollard, *Buck Barrow:* Gene Hackman, *Blanche Barrow:* Estelle Parsons, *Malcolm Moss:* Dub Taylor, *Captain Frank Hamer:* Denver Pyle, *Velma Davis:* Evans Evans, *Eugene Grizzard:* Gene Wilder, *Grocery Owner:* James Stiver.

BON VOYAGE (1962) BV. Producer, Walt Disney. Associate Producers, Bill Walsh. Ron Miller. Director, James Neilson. Screenplay, Bill Walsh. Based on the novel by Marrijane and Joseph Hayes. Music, Paul Smith. Title Song, Richard M. and Robert B. Sherman.

Bon Voyage with Fred MacMurray and Jane Wyman.

Costumes, Bill Thomas. Assistant Director, Joseph L. McEveety. In Technicolor. French Production Supervisor, Sacha Kamenka. Filmed in New York, Paris, Cannes. Cinematographer, William Snyder. Editor, Cotton Warburton. 133 minutes

Harry Willard: Fred MacMurray, *Katie Willard:* Jane Wyman, *Nick O'Mara:* Michael Callen, *Amy Willard:* Deborah Walley, *Countessa DuFresne:* Jessie Royce Landis, *Elliott Willard:* Tommy Kirk, *Skipper Willard:* Kevin Corcoran, *Rudolph Hunschak:* Ivan Desny, *The Girl:* Francoise Prevost, *Madame Clebert:* Georgette Anys, *Judge Henderson:* Howard I. Smith, *Passport Clerk:* Philip Coolidge, *Penelope Walthorne:* Carol White, *Florelle Clebert:* Marie Sirago, *Horace Bidwell:* Alex Gerry, *The Tight Suit:* Casey Adams, *Ship's Librarian:* James Milhollin, *Sewer Guide:* Marcel Hillaire, *Englishman:* Richard Wattis, *Mrs. Henderson:* Doris Packer, *Shamra:* Ana Maria Majalca, *Shamra's Father:* Hassan Khayyam.

BOOMERANG (1947) 20th. Producer, Louis de Rochemont. Director, Elia Kazan. Based on a *Reader's Digest* article by Anthony Abbott. Screenplay, Richard Murphy. Art Directors, Richard Day, Chester Gore. Music, David Buttolph. Music Director, Alfred Newman. Cameraman, Norbert Brodine. Editor, Harmon Jones. Filmed in Connecticut. 88 minutes

Boomerang with Dana Andrews.

Henry L. Harvey: Dana Andrews, *Mrs. Harvey:* Jane Wyatt, *Chief Robinson:* Lee J. Cobb, *Irene Nelson:* Cara Williams, *John Waldron:* Arthur Kennedy, *Woods:* Sam Levene, *Wade:* Taylor Holmes, *Mc-Creery:* Robert Keith, *Harris:* Ed Begley, *Crossman:* Philip Coolidge, *Whitney:* Lewis Leverett, *Sgt. Dugan:* Barry Kelley, *Mr. Rogers:* Richard Garrick, *Lieut. White:* Karl Malden, *James:* Ben Lackland, *Annie:* Helen Carew, *Father Lambert:* Wyrley Birch, *Rev. Gardiner:* Johnny Stearns, *Dr. Rainsford:* Dudley Sadler, *Mayor Swayze:* Walter Greaza, *Miss Manion:* Helen Hatch, *Cartucci:* Guy Thomajan, *Mrs. Lukash:* Lucin Sager, *Mr. Lukash:* Joe Kazan, *Miss Roberts:* Ida Mc-Guire, *Callahan:* John Carmody, *Cary:* Lester Lonergan, *Mr. Rogers:* Richard Garrick, *O'Shea:* George Petrie, *Judge Tate:* Clay Clement, *McDonald:* E. G. Ballantine, *Stone:* William Challee, *Coroner:* Edgar Stehli, *Bill (Reporter):* Jimmy Dobson, *Man:* Robert Keith, Jr. (Brian Keith), *Mrs. Crossman:* Leona Robarts, *Tom:* Bernard Hoffman, *Graham:* Fred Stewart, *Warren:* Anthony Ross, *Man:* Bert Freed.

BOOM TOWN (1940) MGM. Produced by Sam Zimbalist. Directed by Jack Conway. Based on the short story "A Lady Comes to Burknurnet" by James Edward Grant. Screenplay by John Lee Mahin. Art Director, Cedric Gibbons. Musical Score, Franz Waxman. Cameraman, Elwood Bredell. Special Effects, Arnold Gillespie. Montage, John Hoffman. Editor, Paul Landers. 116 minutes

Big John McMasters: Clark Gable, *Square John Sand:* Spencer Tracy, *Betsy Bartlett:* Claudette Colbert, *Karen Vanmeer:* Hedy Lamarr, *Luther Aldrich:* Frank Morgan, *Harry Compton:* Lionel Atwill, *Harmony Jones:* Chill Wills, *Whitey:* Marion Martin, *Spanish Eva:* Minna Gombell, *Ed Murphy:* Joe Yule, *Tom Murphy:* Horace Murphy, *McCreery:* Roy Gordon, *Assistant District Attorney:* Richard Lane, *Little Jack:* Casey Johnson, *Baby Jack:* Bady Quintanilla, *Judge:* George Lessey, *Miss Barnes:* Sara Haden, *Barber:* Frank Orth, *Deacon:* Frank McGlynn, Jr., *Ferdie:* Curt Bois, *Hiring Boss:* Dick Curtis.

BORN TO DANCE (1936) MGM. Assistant Producer, Jack Cummings. Directed by Roy Del Ruth. Authors, Jack McGowan, Sid Silvers, B. G. DeSylva. Screenplay by Jack McGowan, Sid Silvers. Musical Director, Alfred Newman. Musical Arrangements, Roger Edens. Dances, Dave Gould. Cameraman, Ray June. Editor, Blanche Sewell.

Boom Town with Hedy Lamarr and Clark Gable.

Born to Dance with Frances Langford, Buddy Ebsen, Eleanor Powell, James Stewart, Una Merkel and Sid Silvers.

Songs by Cole Porter: "I've Got You Under My Skin," "Easy to Love," "Love Me, Love My Pekinese," "I'm Nuts About You," "Rap-Tap on Wood," "Swingin' the Jinx Away," "Rolling Home," "Hey, Babe, Hey." American debut of Reginald Gardiner. 108 minutes

Nora Paige: Eleanor Powell, *Ted Barker:* James Stewart, *Lucy James:* Virginia Bruce, *Jenny Saks:* Una Merkel, *Gunny Saks:* Sid Silvers, *Peggy Turner:* Frances Langford, *Captain Dingby:* Raymond Walburn, *McKay:* Alan Dinehart, *Mush Tracy:* Buddy Ebsen, *Sally Saks:* Juanita Quigley, *Georges & Jalna:* Themselves, *Policeman:* Reginald Gardiner, *Floorwalker:* Barnett Parker, *The Foursome:* J. Marshall Smith, L. Dwight Snyder, Jay Johnson, Del Porter, *Girl:* Mary Dees, *Recruiter:* John Kelly, *Telephone Operator:* Helen Troy, *Acrobats:* William and Joe Mandel, *Maid:* Anita Brown, *Acrobats:* Leona and Naomi Keene, *Stage Manager:* Charles (Levison) Lane, *Assistant Stage Manager:* Bobby Watson, *Waiter:* Charles Coleman, *Ship's Officer:* James Flavin, *Hector:* Jonathan Hale, *Newsboy:* Billy Watson, *Pianist:* Fuzzy Knight, *Cameraman:* Sherry Hall, *Extra:* Dennis O'Keefe, *Man:* David Horsley.

BORN YESTERDAY (1950) Col. Producer, S. Sylvan Simon. Director, George Cukor. Based on the play by Garson Kanin. Screenplay, Albert Mannheimer. Art Director, Harry Horner. Musical Director, Morris Stoloff. Photography, Joseph Walker. Editor, Charles Nelson. 103 minutes

Billie Dawn: Judy Holliday, *Harry Brook:* Broderick Crawford, *Paul Verrall:* William Holden, *Jim Devery:* Howard St. John, *Eddie:* Frank Otto, *Norval Hedges:* Larry Oliver, *Mrs. Hedges:* Barbara Brown,

Born Yesterday with Judy Holliday and William Holden.

Boys' Night Out with Kim Novak and James Garner.

Sanborn: Grandon Rhodes, *Helen:* Claire Carleton, *Bootblack:* Smoki Whitfield, *Manicurist:* Helyn Eby Rock, *Bellboy:* William Mays, *Barber:* David Pardoll, *Elevator Operator:* Mike Mahoney, *Interpreter:* Paul Marion, *Native:* John L. Morley, *Native:* Ram Singh, *Policeman:* Charles Cane.

BOYS' NIGHT OUT (1962) MGM. Producer, Martin Ransohoff. Director, Michael Gordon. Screenplay. Ira Wallach. Adaptation, Marion Hargrove. Based on story by Marvin Worth and Arne Sultan. Associated Producer, James Pratt. Assistant Director, Ivan Volkman. Musical Score, Frank DeVol. A KimcoFilmways Picture in Cinema Scope and MetroColor. A Joseph E. Levine Presentation. Songs: "Boys' Night Out" and "Cathy" by James Van Heusen and Sammy Cahn. 115 minutes *Cathy:* Kim Novak, *Fred Williams:* James Garner, *George Drayton:* Tony Randall, *Doug Jackson:* Howard Duff, *Marge Drayton:* Janet Blair, *Joanne McIllenny:* Patti Page, *Ethel Williams:* Jessie Royce Landis, *D. Prokosch:* Oscar Homolka, *Howard McIllenny:* Howard Morris, *Toni Jackson:* Anne Jeffreys, *Boss' Girl Friend:* Zsa Zsa Gabor, *Mr. Bohannon:* Fred Clark, *Slattery:* William Bendix, *Peter Bowers:* Jim Backus, *Mr. Bingham:* Larry Keating, *Beulah Partridge:* Ruth McDevitt.

BOYS TOWN (1938) Loew's, Inc. Producer, John W. Considine, Jr. Director, Norman Taurog. Authors, Dore Schary, Eleanor Griffin. Screenplay, John Meehan, Dore Schary. Cameraman, Sidney Wagner. Editor, Elmo Vernon. Sequel was *Men of Boys Town*, 1941. 90 minutes

Father Flanagan: Spencer Tracy, *Whitey Marsh:* Mickey Rooney, *Davie Morris:* Henry Hull: *Tony Ponessa:* Gene Reynolds, *Mo Kahn:* Sidney Miller, *Freddie Fuller:* Frankie Thomas, *Pee Wee:* Bobs Watson, *Hillbilly:* Murray Harris, *Paul Ferguson:* Jimmy Butler, *Red:* Tom Noonan, *Apples:* Al Hill, Jr., *Butch:* Wesley Giraud, *Dan Farrow:* Leslie Fenton, *Hargraves:* Jonathan Hale, *Judge:* Addison Richards,

Boys Town with Frankie Thomas, Spencer Tracy and Mickey Rooney.

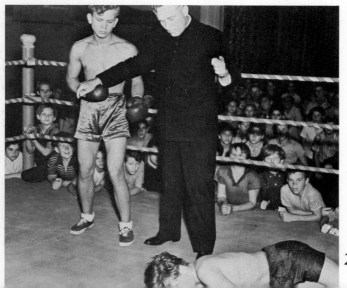

Alabama: Donald Haines, *Young Thunder:* Bennie Chorre, *Weasel:* John Wray, *Warden:* John Hamilton, *Bishop:* Minor Watson, *Jimmy:* Ronald Paige, *Tommy Anderson:* Mickey Rentschler, *Skinny:* Martin Spellman, *Mr. Reynolds:* Robert Glockler, *Warden:* Orville Caldwell, *Burton:* Robert Emmett Keane, *Sheriff:* Victor Killian, *Tim:* Arthur Aylsworth, *Rod:* Al Hill, *Lane (Reporter):* Roger Converse, *Judge:* Walter Young, *Governor:* William Worthington, *Joe Marsh:* Edward Norris, *Calateri:* George Humbert, *Jackson (Reporter):* Kane Richmond *Sister (Nun):* Barbara Bedford, *Doctor:* Gladden James, *Reporter:* Phillip Terry, *Gangster (with Marsh):* Jay Novello, *Charley Haines:* Johnny Walsh.

BRANDED (1950) Par. Producer, Mel Epstein. Director, Rudolph Mate. Color by Technicolor. Based on novel *Montana Rides* by Evan Evans. Screenplay, Sydney Boehm, Cyril Hume. Art Directors, Hans Dreier, Roland Anderson. Music, Roy Webb. Photography, Charles B. Lang, Jr. Editor, Alma Macrorie. Filmed in Arizona. 104 minutes

Choya: Alan Ladd, *Ruth Lavery:* Mona Freeman, *Mr. Lavery:* Charles Bickford, *Leffingwell:* Robert Keith, *Rubriz:* Joseph Calleia, *Tonio:* Peter Hansen, *Mrs. Lavery:* Selena Royle, *Ransome:* Tom Tully, *Andy:* George Lewis, *Hank:* Robert Kortman, *Tatto:* John Berkes, *Jake:* Pat Lane, *Peon,* Natividad Vacio, *Hernandez:* Martin Garralaga,

Branded with Charles Bickford and Alan Ladd.

Dad Travis: Edward Clark, *Joe's Wife:* Julia Montoya, *Spig (Lavery Cook):* John Butler, *Link:* Jimmie Dundee, *Roberto:* Salvador Baguez, *Burly Fellow:* Frank McCarroll, *Second Man:* Len Hendry, *Dawson:* Milburn Stone, *Tully:* Ed Peil, *Bank Clerk:* Olan Soule.

BREAKFAST AT TIFFANY'S (1961) Par. Producers, Martin Jurow, Richard Shepherd. Director, Blake Edwards. Technicolor. Based on the novel by Truman Capote. Screenplay, George Axelrod. Art Directors, Hal Pereira, Roland Anderson. Music, Henry Mancini. Song, "Moon River" by Johnny Mercer, Henry Mancini. Cinematographer, Franz Planer. Process Photography, Farciot Edouart. Special Photographic Effects, John P. Fulton. Editor, Howard Smith. 115 minutes

Holly Golightly: Audrey Hepburn, *Paul Varjak:* George Peppard, *2-E:* Patricia Neal, *Doc Golightly:* Buddy Ebsen, *O.J. Berman:* Martin Balsam, *José:* Villalonga, *Tiffany's Salesman:* John McGiver, *Sally Tomato:* Alan Reed, *Mag Wildwood:* Dorothy Whitney, *Stripper:* Miss Beverly Hills, *Rusty Trawler:* Stanley Adams, *Sid Arbuck:* Claude Stroud, *Librarian:* Elvia Allman, *Mr. Yunioshi:* Mickey Rooney, *Girl in Low-cut Dress:* Joan Staley, *Taxi Driver:* Dick Crockett, *The Cousin:* James Lanphier, *Man at Party:* Gil Lamb, *Chinese Girl at Party:* Annabella Soong, *Man at Party:* Wilson Wood, *Hindu at Party:* William Benegal Rav, *Man at Party:* Tommy Farrell, *Delivery Boy:* Kip King, *Woman at Party:* Hanna Landy, *Woman at Party:* Fay McKenzie, *Woman at Party:* Helen Spring.

Breakfast at Tiffany's with Audrey Hepburn.

The Bride Comes Home with Robert Young and Fred MacMurray.

THE BRIDE COMES HOME (1935) Par. Produced and directed by Wesley Ruggles. Story, Elizabeth Sanxay Holding. Screenplay, Claude Binyon. Photography, Leo Tover. 82 minutes

Jeannette Desmereau: Claudette Colbert, *Cyrus Anderson:* Fred MacMurray, *Jack Bristow:* Robert Young, *Alfred Desmereau:* William Collier, Sr., *The Judge:* Donald Meek, *Frank (Butler):* Richard Carle, *Henry:* Edgar Kennedy, *Otto:* Johnny Arthur, *Emma:* Kate MacKenna, *Len Noble:* James Conlin, *Elevator Starter:* William R. (Billy) Arnold, *Helene, the Maid:* Belle Mitchell, *Husky:* Tom Kennedy, *Cab Driver:* Edward Gargan, *Painter:* Robert McKenzie, *Girl (Elevated):* Ruth Warren, *Conductor (Elevated):* Frank Mills, *Conductor:* Tom Dugan, *Elevator Operator:* Eddie Dunn, *Bystander:* Charles West, *Office Clerk:* Charles Sylber, *Cop in Chicago Park:* A. S. "Pop" Byron, *Bartender:* C. L. Sherwood.

BRIDE OF FRANKENSTEIN (1935) Univ. Produced by Carl Laemmle, Jr. Directed by James Whale. Story and Screenplay, John L. Balderston and William Hurlbut. Music, Franz Waxman. Photography, John Mescall. Editor, Ted Kent. A sequel to 1931's *Frankenstein*, based on Mary Shelley's book. 80 minutes

The Monster: Boris Karloff, *Henry Frankenstein:* Colin Clive, *Elizabeth:* Valerie Hobson, *The Bride/Mary Shelley:* Elsa Lanchester, *Doctor Pretorious:* Ernest Thesiger, *The Hermit:* O. P. Heggie, *Karl:* Dwight Frye, *Ludwig:* Ted Billings, *Burgomaster:* E. E. Clive, *Minnie:* Una O'Connor, *Shepherdess:* Anne Darling, *Percy Shelley:* Douglas Walton, *Lord Byron:* Gavin Gordon, *Rudy:* Neil Fitzgerald, *Hans:* Reginald

Barlow, *Hans' Wife:* Mary Gordon, *Uncle Glutz:* Gunnis Davis, *Aunt Glutz:* Tempe Pigott, *Albert the Butler:* Lucien Prival, *A Hunter:* John Carradine, *Neighbor:* Rollo Lloyd, *Baby:* Billy Barty, *Neighbor:* Walter Brennan, *A Hunter:* Robert Adair, *Priest:* Lucio Villegas, *A Mother:* Brenda Fowler, *The Coroner:* Edwin Mordant, *Marta:* Sarah Schwartz, *A Hunter:* John Curtis, *A Neighbor:* Mary Stewart, *Little Archbishop:* Norman Ainsley, *Little Queen:* Joan Woodbury, *Henry VIII (Little King):* Arthur S. Byron, *Communion Girl:* Helen Parrish, *A Hunter:* Frank Terry, *Mermaid:* Josephine McKim, *Ballerina:* Kensas DeForrest, *Villagers:* Ed Peil, Sr., Anders Van Haden, John George.

Bride of Frankenstein with Elsa Lanchester and Boris Karloff.

THE BRIDGE ON THE RIVER KWAI (1957) Col. Producer, Sam Spiegel. Director, David Lean. Screenplay by Pierre Boulle based on his novel. Assistant Directors, Gus Agosti and Ted Sturgis. Music by Malcolm Arnold. In CinemaScope and Technicolor. A Horizon Picture. Filmed in Ceylon. 161 minutes

Shears: William Hoden, *Colonel Nicholson:* Alec Guinness, *Major Warden:* Jack Hawkins, *Colonel Saito:* Sessue Hayakawa, *Major Clipton:* James Donald, *Lieutenant Joyce:* Geoffrey Horne, *Colonel Green:* Andre Morell, *Major Reeves:* Peter Williams, *Major Hughes:* John Boxer, *Grogan:* Percy Herbert, *Baker:* Harold Goodwin, *Nurse:* Ann Sears, *Captain Kanematsu:* Henry Okawa, *Lieutenant Miura:* Keiichiro Katsumoto, *Yai:* M. R. B. Chakrabandhu, *Siamese Girls:* Vilaiwan Seeboonreaung, Ngamta Suphaphongs, Javanart Punychoti, Kannikar Bowklee.

The Bridge on the River Kwai with Sessue Hayakawa and Alec Guinness.

281

The Bridges at Toko-Ri with Mickey Rooney and William Holden.

THE BRIDGES AT TOKO-RI (1954) Par.

Producers, William Perlberg, George Seaton. Director, Mark Robson. Technicolor, VistaVision. Based on the novel by James Michener. Screenplay, Valentine Davies. Art Directors, Hal Pereira, Henry Bumstead. Cameramen, Loyal Griggs, Charles G. Clarke. Editor, Alma Macorie. 103 minutes.

Lt. Harry Brubaker (USNR): William Holden, *Nancy Brubaker:* Grace Kelly, *Rear Admiral George Tarrant:* Fredric March, *Mike Forney:* Mickey Rooney, *Beer Barrel:* Robert Strauss, *Commander Wayne Lee:* Charles McGraw, *Kimiko:* Kelko Awaji, *Nestor Gamidge:* Earl Holliman, *Lt. (S. G.) Olds:* Richard Shannon, *Capt. Evans:* Willis B. Bouchey, *Kathey Brubaker:* Nadene Ashdown, *Susie:* Cheryl Lynn Callaway, *Asst. C. I. C. Officer:* James Jenkins, *Pilot:* Marshall V. Beebe, *M.P. Major:* Charles Tannen, *Japanese Father:* Teru Shimada, *Air Intelligence Officer:* Dennis Weaver, *C.I.C. Officer:* Gene Reynolds, *Officer of the Day:* James Hyland, *Flight Surgeon:* Robert A Sherry, *C.P.O. 2nd Class:* Gene Hardy, *Quartermaster:* Jack Roberts, *Bellboy:* Rollin Moriyama, *Bartender:* Robert Kino, *Captain Parker:* Paul Kruger.

BRIGADOON (1954) MGM.

Producer, Arthur Freed. Director, Vincente Minnelli. CinemaScope, Ansco Color. Based on the musical by Alan Jay Lerner. Screenplay by Lerner. Art Directors, Cedric Gibbons, Preston Ames. Musical Director, Johnny Green. Cinematographer, Joseph Ruttenberg. Editor, Albert Akst. Choreography, Gene Kelly. Songs: "The Heather on the Hill," "From This Day On," "The Gathering of the Clans," "The Wedding Dance," "I'll Go Home with Bonnie Jean," "It's Almost Like Being in Love," "Brigadoon," "The Chase," "Prologue," "Waiting for My Dearie," by Frederick Loewe and Alan Jay Lerner. 108 minutes

Tommy Albright: Gene Kelly, *Jeff Douglas:* Van Johnson, *Fiona Cambpell:* Cyd Charisse, *Jane Ashton:* Elaine Stewart, *Mr. Lundie:* Barry Jones, *Harry Beaton:* Hugh Laing, *Andrew Campbell:* Albert Sharpe, *Jean Campbell:* Virginia Bosler, *Charlie Chisholm Dalrymple:* Jimmy Thompson, *Archie Beaton:* Tudor Owen, *Angus:* Owen McGiveney, *Ann:* Dee Turnell, *Meg Brockie:* Dody Heath, *Sandy:* Eddie Quillan, *Mrs. McIntosh:* Madge Blake, *Mr. McIntosh:* Hugh Boswell, *Tinker:* Warren Macgregor, *Toy Booth:* Hank Mann, *Bar-*

Brigadoon with Van Johnson, Cyd Charisse and Gene Kelly.

tender: Oliver Blake, *Waiter:* Paul Bryan, *Patrons:* Dick Simmons, Stuart Whitman, *Dancer:* George Chakiris.

BRIGHT VICTORY (1951) Univ.

Producer, Robert Buckner. Director, Mark Robson. Based on a novel by Baynard Kendrick (*Lights Out*). Screenplay, Robert Buckner. Art Directors, Bernard Herzbrun, Nathan Juran. Music, Frank Skinner. Photography, William Daniels. Editor, Russell Schoengarth. 97 minutes

Larry Nevins: Arthur Kennedy, *Judy Greene:* Peggy Dow, *Chris Paterson:* Julia Adams, *Joe Morgan:* James Edwards, *Mr. Nevins:* Will Geer, *Mr. Paterson:* Minor Watson, *Bill Grayson:* Jim Backus, *Janet Grayson:* Joan Banks, *Mrs. Nevins:* Nana Bryant, *Mrs. Paterson:* Marjorie Crossland, *Sergeant John Masterson:* Richard Egan, *Private Fred Tyler:* Russell Dennis, *Corporal John Flagg:* John Hudson, *Pete Hamilton:* Murray Hamilton, *"Moose" Garvey:* Donald Miele, *Jess Coe:* Larry Keating, *Captain Phelan:* Hugh Reilly, *Nurse Bailey:* Mary Cooper, *Dudek:* Rock Hudson, *Scanlon:* Ken Harvey, *Lt. Atkins:* Phil Faversshim, *Psychiatrist:* Robert F. Simon, *Reynolds:* Jerry Paris, *Nurse:* Ruth Esherick, *Negro Soldier:* Bernard Hamilton, *M. P.:* Robert Anderson, *Nurse at Oran:* June Whitley, *Dr. Bannerman:* Sydney Mason, *Bartenders:* Richard Karlan, Billy Newell, *Mrs. Coe:* Virginia Mullen, *Lt. Conklin:* Glen Charles Gordon.

Bright Victory with Peggy Dow and Arthur Kennedy.

THE BROADWAY MELODY (1929) MGM.

Directed by Harry Beaumont. Scenes in Technicolor. Story, Edmund Goulding. Continuity, Sarah Y. Mason. Dialogue, Norman Houston and James Gleason. Photography, John Arnold. Musical Director, Nacio Herb Brown. Titles, Earl Baldwin. Art Director, Cedric Gibbons. Costumes, David Cox. Songs by Arthur Freed and Nacio Herb Brown: "The Broadway Melody," "You Were Meant For Me," "Wedding of the Painted Doll," "Boy Friend," "Love Boat," "Harmony Babies From Melody Lane," "Give My Regards to Broadway" by George M. Cohan; "Truthful Deacon Brown" by Willard Robison. Sound, Douglas Shearer. Editors, Sam S. Zimbalist (sound), William Levanway (silent version). The first of a series of "Broadway Melody" films; other editions: 1936, 1938, and 1940. Remade by MGM as *Two Girls On Broadway*, 1940. 110 minutes

Hank Mahoney: Bessie Love, *Queenie Mahoney:* Anita Page, *Eddie Kearns:* Charles King, *Uncle Jed:* Jed Prouty, *Jack Warriner:* Kenneth Thomson, *Flo:* Mary Doran, *Francis Zanfield:* Eddie Kane, *Dillon, Stage Manager:* Edward Dillon, *Babe Hatrick:* J. Emmett Beck, *Stew:* Marshall Ruth, *Turpe:* Drew Demarest, *Singer:* James Burrows,

The Broadway Melody with Mary Doran, Anita Page, Bessie Love and Charles King.

Jimmy Gleason, Music Publisher: James Gleason, *Bellhop:* Ray Cooke, *Pianist at Gleason's:* Nacio Herb Brown.

BROADWAY MELODY OF 1936 (1935) MGM. Produced by John W. Considine, Jr. Directed by Roy Del Ruth. Original Story, Moss Hart. Screenplay, Jack McGowan, Sid Silvers. Art Director, Cedric Gibbons. Costumes, Adrian. Dances created and staged by Dave Gould. "Lucky Star" ballet staged by Albertina Rasch. Assistant Director, Bill Scully. Photography, Charles Rosher. Sound, Douglas Shearer. Editor, Blanche Sewell. Songs by Nacio Herb Brown and Arthur Freed: "Broadway Rhythm," "You Are My Lucky Star," "I Gotta Feelin' You're Foolin'," "On a Sunday Afternoon," "Sing Before Breakfast." Additional Dialogue, Harry Conn. 103 minutes.

Bert Keeler: Jack Benny, *George Brown:* Robert Taylor, *Kitty Corbett:* Una Merkel, *Irene (Mlle. Arlette):* Eleanor Powell, *Lillian:* June Knight, *Sally:* Vilma Ebsen, *Buddy Burke:* Buddy Ebsen, *Basil Newcombe:* Nick Long, Jr., *Hornblow:* Robert Wildhack, *Snoop Blue:* Sid Silvers, *Singers:* Frances Langford, Harry Stockwell, *Show Girls:* Irene Coleman, Beatrice Coleman, Georgina Gray, Mary Jane Halsey, Lucille Lund, Ada Ford, *Managing Editor:* Paul Harvey, *Maid:* Theresa Harris, *Headwaiter:* Max Barwyn, *Waitresses:* Bernadene Hayes, Treva Lawler, *Pullman Porter:* Bud Williams, *Conductor:* Lee Phelps, *Hotel Manager:* Andre Cheron, *Assistant Hotel Manager:* Rolfe Sedan, *Bellhop:* Eddie Tamblyn, *Hotel Clerk:* Bert Moorhouse,

Broadway Melody of 1936 with June Knight and Robert Taylor.

Character Man: Neely Edwards, *Copy Boy:* Bobby Gordon, *Chorus Girls:* Anya Teranda, Luana Walters, Patricia Gregory.

BROKEN ARROW (1950) 20th. Produced by Julian Blaustein. Directed by Delmer Daves. Color by Technicolor. Based on the novel *Blood Brother* by Elliott Arnold. Screenplay, Michael Blankfort. Music Director, Alfred Newman. Art Directors, Lyle Wheeler and Arthur Hogsett. Photography, Ernest Palmer. Editor, J. Watson Webb, Jr. Later the basis for a TV series, the initial episode (in 1956) being an adaptation of the feature. 93 minutes

Tom Jeffords: James Stewart, *Cochise:* Jeff Chandler, *Sonseeahray:* Debra Paget, *General Howard:* Basil Ruysdael, *Ben Slade:* Will Geer, *Terry:* Joyce MacKenzie, *Duffield:* Arthur Hunnicutt, *Colonel Bernall:* Raymond Bramley, *Goklia:* Jay Silverheels, *Nalikadeya:* Argentina Brunetti, *Boucher:* Jack Lee, *Lonergan:* Robert Adler, *Miner:* Harry Carter, *Lowrie:* Robert Griffin, *Juan:* Billy Wilkerson, *Chip Slade:* Mickey Kuhn, *Nochalo:* Chris Willow Bird, *Pionsenay:* J. W. Cody, *Nahilzay:* John War Eagle, *Skinyea:* Charles Soldani, *Teese:* Iron Eyes Cody, *Machogee:* Robert Foster Dover, *Maury:* John Marston, *Sergeant:* Edward Rand, *Mule Driver:* John Docuette, *Adjutant:* Richard Van Opel, *Barber:* Nacho Galindo, *Stage Passenger:* Trevor Bardette.

Broken Arrow with Jeff Chandler and James Stewart.

THE BROTHERS KARAMAZOV (1958) MGM. Producer, Pandro S. Berman. Associate Producer, Kathryn Hereford. Director, Richard Brooks. MetroColor. Adaptation by Julius J. and Philip G. Epstein from the novel by Fyodor Dostoyevsky in its English translation by Constance Garnett. Screenplay, Richard Brooks. Art Directors, William A. Horning, Paul Groesse. Music, Bronislau Kaper. Cinematographer, John Alton. Editor, John Dunning. 146 minutes

Dmitri Karamazov: Yul Brynner, *Grushenka:* Maria Schell, *Katya:* Claire Bloom, *Fyodor Karamazov:* Lee J. Cobb, *Ivan Karamazov:* Richard Basehart, *Smerdyakov:* Albert Salmi, *Alexey Karamazov:* William Shatner, *Mme. Anna Hohlakov:* Judith Evelyn, *Grigory:* Edgar Stehli, *Ippolit Kirillov:* Harry Townes, *Illusha Snegiryov:* Miko Oscard, *Capt. Snegiryov:* David Opatoshu, *Mavrayek:* Simon Oakland, *Pawnbroker:* Jay Adler, *Captain Vrublevski:* Frank de Kova, *Defense Counsel:* Gage Clarke, *Marya:* Ann Morrison, *Trifon Borissovitch:* Mel Welles, *Polish Officer:* Charles Horvath, *Tipsy Merchant:* Sam Buffington, *Chief Judge:* Frederic Ledebur, *Party Girl:* Giselle D'Arc, *Girl:* Gloria Pall, *Waiter:* Than Wyenn, *Peter:* Shepard Menken, *Second Officer:* Jerry Riggio, *Third Officer:* Leonard Graves, *Innkeeper:* Stafford Repp, *M.P.:* George Barrows, *Waiter:* Hal Norman, *Skate Sharpener:* Michael Mark, *Gypsy Singer:* Ziva Rodann, *Friend:* Guy Prescott, *Puppeteers:* John W. Zweers, John Warren Leland, *Old Crone:* Dorothy Neumann, *Father Zossima:* William Vedder, *Michael:* Stephen Roberts, *Mother:* Molly Glessing, *Young Girl:* Mary Ann Bernard, *Guard:* Len Lesser, *Moronic Prisoner:* Harry Hines, *Juror:* Gregg Martell.

The Brothers Karamazov with Lee J. Cobb and Maria Schell.

THE BUCCANEER (1938) Par. Producer, Cecil B. De Mille. Associate Producer, William H. Pine. Director, Cecil B. De Mille. Author, Lyle Saxon (from *Lafitte, the Pirate*). Screenplay, Jeanie MacPherson, Edwin Justus Mayer, Harold Lamb, C. Gardner Sullivan. Musical Director, Boris Morros. Cameraman, Victor Milner. Editor, Anne Bauchens. Technical Assistance, Louisiana State Museum. Remade by De Mille in 1958. 90 minutes

Jean Lafitte: Fredric March, *Gretchen:* Franciska Gaal, *Dominique You:* Akim Tamiroff, *Annette de Remy:* Margot Grahame, *Ezra Peavey:* Walter Brennan, *Crawford:* Ian Keith, *Dolly Madison:* Spring Byington, *Governor Claiborne:* Douglass Dumbrille, *Captain Brown:* Robert Barrat, *Andrew Jackson:* Hugh Sothern, *Aunt Charlotte:* Beulah Bondi, *Beluche:* Anthony Quinn, *Marie de Remy:* Louise Campbell, *Admiral Cockburn:* Montagu Love, *General Ross:* Eric Stanley, *Gramby:* Fred Kohler, *Captain Lockyer:* Gilbert Emery, *Captain McWilliams:* Holmes Herbert, *Mouse:* John Rogers, *Tarsus:* Hans Steinke, *Collector of Port:* Stanley Andrews, *Sir Harry Smith:* Evan Thomas, *John Freeman:* Thaddeus Jones, *Ship's Surgeon:* Reginald Sheffield, *James Smith:* Eugene Jackson, *Colonel Butler:* Davison Clark, *Creole:* James Craig, *Lieutenant Reed:* Richard Denning, *Dying Pirate:* Paul Fix, *Charles:* Jack Hubbard, *Madeleine:* Evelyn Keyes, *Roxanne:* Lina Basquette, *Suzette:* Luana Walters, *Jailer:* J. P. McGowan, *Villere:* Barry Norton, *Daniel Carrol:* Charles Trowbridge, *Scipio:* Alex Hill, *Girl:* Terry Ray (Ellen Drew), *Vincent Nolte:* Charles Brokaw, *Major Latour:* Alphonse Martell, *Woman:* Mae Busch.

The Buccaneer with Fredric March and Franciska Gaal.

BULLDOG DRUMMOND (1929) UA. Produced by Samuel Goldwyn. Directed by F. Richard Jones. Based on the British play by Sapper (Herman Cyril McNeile). Dialogue, Sidney Howard. Photography, George Barnes and Gregg Toland. Editors, Frank and Viola Lawrence. Song by Jack Yellen and Harry Akst, "(I Says to Myself Says I) There's the One for Me." Art Director, William Cameron Menzies. Assistant Director, Paul Jones. Scenario, Wallace Smith and Sidney Howard. Talkie debuts of Ronald Colman and Joan Bennett. 90 minutes

Bulldog Drummond: Ronald Colman, *Phyllis Clavering:* Joan Bennett, *Erma:* Lilyan Tashman, *Peterson:* Montagu Love, *Doctor Lakington:* Lawrence Grant, *Danny:* Wilson Benge, *Algy Longworth:* Claude Allister, *Marcovitch:* Adolph Milar, *Travers:* Charles Sellon, *Chong:* Tetsu Komai.

Bulldog Drummond with Ronald Colman and Joan Bennett.

BULLETS OR BALLOTS (1936) WB. Produced by Lou Edelman. Directed by William Keighley. Authors, Martin Mooney, Seton I. Miller. Screenplay by Seton I. Miller. Cameraman, Hal Mohr. Editor, Jack Killifer. 77 minutes

Johnny Blake: Edward G. Robinson, *Lee Morgan:* Joan Blondell, *Al Kruger:* Barton MacLane, *"Bugs" Fenner:* Humphrey Bogart, *Herman:* Frank McHugh, *Captain Dan MacLaren:* Joseph King, *Ed Driscoll:* Richard Purcell, *Wires:* George K. Stone, *Nellie LaFleur:* Louise Beavers, *Grand Jury Spokesman:* Joseph Crehan, *Bryant:* Henry O' Neill, *Thorndyke:* Gilbert Emery, *Hollister:* Henry Kolker, *Caldwell:* Herbert Rawlinson, *Specialty:* Rosalind Marquis, *Vinci:* Norman Willis, *Gatley:* Frank Faylen, *Announcer's Voice:* Addison Richards, *Proprietor:* Ray Brown, *Actor Impersonating Kruger:* Max Wagner, *Judge:* Ed Stanley, *Jury Foreman:* Milton Kibbee, *Chauffeur:* Frank Marlowe, *Eddie:* Joe Connors, *Mary:* Virginia Dabney, *Crail:*

Bullets or Ballots with Humphrey Bogart, Barton MacLane and Edward G. Robinson.

Bus Stop with Marilyn Monroe and Eileen Heckart.

William Pawley, *Kruger's Secretary:* Carlyle Moore, Jr. *Bank Secretaries:* Gordon Elliott, Ann Nagel, *Garber:* Ed Butler, *Kelly:* Ralph M. Ramley, *Rose (Maid):* Edna Mae Harris, *Lambert:* Wallace Gregory, *Ben:* Chic Bruno, *Jail Keeper:* Tom Wilson, *Timothy:* John Lester Johnson, *Police Captain:* Tom Brower, *Policeman:* Ralph Dunn.

BUS STOP (1956) 20th. Producer, Buddy Adler. Director, Joshua Logan. CinemaScope, De Luxe Color. Based on the play by William Inge. Screenplay, George Axelrod. Art Directors, Lyle R. Wheeler, Mark-Lee Kirk. Musical Director, Alfred Newman. Music, Alfred Newman, Cyril J. Mockridge. Orchestration, Edward B. Powell. Song, Ken Darby. Cinematographer, Milton Krasner. Editor, William Reynolds. Later a TV series. 96 minutes

Cherie: Marilyn Monroe, *Bo:* Don Murray, *Virgil:* Arthur O'Connell, *Grace:* Betty Field, *Vera:* Eileen Heckart, *Carl:* Robert Bray, *Elma:* Hope Lange, LIFE *Photographer:* Hans Conreid, LIFE *Reporter:* Casey Adams, *Manager of Nightclub:* Henry Slate, *Gerald:* Terry Kelman, *Landlady:* Helen Mayon, *Blonde on Street:* Lucille Knox, *Elderly Passengers:* Kate Mac Kenna, George Selk (Budd Buster), *Cashier:* Mary Carroll, *Preacher:* Phil J. Munch, *Usher:* Fay L. Ivor, *Announcer:* G. E. "Pete" Logan, *Orville:* J. M. Dunlap, *Japanese Cook:* Jim Katugi Noda.

BUTTERFIELD 8 (1960) MGM. Produced by Pandro S. Berman. Directed by Daniel Mann. CinemaScope and MetroColor. Based on the novel by John O'Hara. Screenplay, Charles Schnee and John Michael Hayes. Music, Bronislau Kaper. Costumes, Helen Rose. Associate Producer, Kathryn Hereford. Assistant Directors, Hank Moonjean and John Clarke Bowman. Art Directors, George W. Davis and Urie McCleary. Cinematography, Joseph Ruttenberg, Charles Harten. Editor, Ralph E. Winters. An Afton-Lindbrook Production. 109 minutes

Gloria Wandrous: Elizabeth Taylor, *Weston Liggett:* Laurence Harvey, *Steve Carpenter:* Eddie Fisher, *Emily Liggett:* Dina Merrill, *Mrs. Wandrous:* Mildred Dunnock, *Mrs. Fanny Thurber:* Betty Field, *Bingham Smith:* Jeffrey Lynn, *Happy:* Kay Medford, *Norma:* Susan Oliver, *Dr. Tredman:* George Voskovec, *Clerk:* Virginia Downing,

Butterfield 8 with Elizabeth Taylor and Eddie Fisher.

Mrs. Jescott: Carmen Matthews, *Anderson:* Whitfield Connor, *Elevator Man:* Dan Bergin, *Cabbie:* Vernon Dowling, *Doorman:* Samuel Schwartz, *Tipsy Man:* Robert Pastene, *Doorman:* John Armstrong, *Policeman:* Leon B. Stevens, *Bartender:* Tom Ahearne, *Big Man:* Rudy Bond, *Irate Man:* Victor Harrison, *Chauffeur:* Beau Tilden, *Irate Woman:* Marion Leeds, *Gossip:* Helen Stevens, *Photographer:* Don Burns, *Man:* Philip Faversham, Messenger: Joseph Boley, *State Trooper:* Richard X. Slattery.

Bwana Devil with Nigel Bruce and Robert Stack.

BWANA DEVIL (1952) UA. Producer and Director, Arch Oboler. Ansco Color, 3-Dimension. Screenplay, Arch Oboler. Natural Vision Supervision, M.L. Gunzberg. Music composed and directed by Gordon Jenkins. Orchestrations, Fred Neff. Three Dimension Technician, O. S. Bryhn. Sound, Con McKay. Technical Consultants, Major Ramsay Hill, Bhogwam Singh. Special Effects, Russell Shearman, Henry Maak. Cinematographer, Joseph F. Biroc. Editor, John Hoffman. 79 minutes

Bob Hayward: Robert Stack, *Alice Hayward:* Barbara Britton, *Dr. Ross:* Nigel Bruce, *Major Parkhurst:* Ramsay Hill, *Commissioner:* Paul McVey, *Portuguese Girl:* Hope Miller, *Drayton:* John Dodsworth, *Indian Dancer:* Bhupesh Guha.

BYE BYE BIRDIE (1963) Col. Producer, Fred Kohlmar. Director, George Sidney. Panavision, Technicolor. Based on the musical by Michael Stewart. Screenplay, Irving Brecher. Music supervised, arranged and conducted by Johnny Green. Orchestration, Johnny Green, Al Woodbury. Cinematographer, Joseph Biroc. Editor, Charles Nelson. Songs by Charles Strouse and Lee Adams: "Bye Bye Birdie," "Kids," "Honestly Sincere," "Put on a Happy Face," "Telephone Hour," "A Lot of Living to Do," "Rosie," "One Last Kiss," "One Boy,"

Bye Bye Birdie with Ann-Margret, Trudi Ames, Jesse Pearson, Janet Leigh, Dick Van Dyke, Frank Albertson and Beverly Yates.

285

"Hymn for a Sunday Evening," "How Lovely to Be a Woman," "The Shriners Ballet." Dick Van Dyke and Paul Lynde repeat their 1960 stage roles. 111 minutes

Rosie DeLeon: Janet Leigh, *Albert Peterson:* Dick Van Dyke, *Kim McAfee:* Ann-Margret, *Mama Peterson:* Maureen Stapleton, *Hugo Peabody:* Bobby Rydell, *Conrad Birdie:* Jesse Pearson, *Ed Sullivan:* Ed Sullivan, *Mr. McAfee:* Paul Lynde, *Mrs. McAfee:* Mary LaRoche, *Claude Paisley:* Michael Evans, *Bob Precht:* Robert Paige, *Borov:* Gregory Morton, *Randolph:* Bryan Russell, *Mr. Maude:* Milton Frome, *Ballet Manager:* Ben Astar, *Ursula:* Trudi Ames, *Mr. Nebbitt:* Cyril Delevanti, *Mayor:* Frank Albertson, *Mayor's Wife:* Beverly Yates, *Bartender:* Frank Sully, *Ursula's Mother:* Bo Peep Karlin, *Teenager:* Melinda Marx, *Shriner:* Mell Turner, *Shriner:* Gil Lamb, *Leader:* Lee Aaker, *Prima Ballerina:* Karel Shimoff, *Russian Consul:* Donald Lawton, *Telephone Operator:* Yvonne White, *Debbie:* Debbie Stern, *Sheila:* Sheila Denner, *Harvey:* Pete Menefee, *Tommy:* George Spicer, *Leader, Fireman's Band:* Dick Winslow, *Marge, Birdie's Secretary:* Hazel Shermet.

California with George Coulouris, Barbara Stanwyck and Anthony Quinn.

The Caine Mutiny with Joe Haworth, Guy Anderson, Van Johnson, Humphrey Bogart, Fred MacMurray, Arthur Franz and Jerry Paris.

THE CAINE MUTINY (1954) Col. Producer, Stanley Kramer. Director, Edward Dmytryk. Technicolor. Based on the novel by Herman Wouk. Screenplay, Stanley Roberts. Art Director, Cary Odell. Cinematographer, Frank Planer. Editor, William A. Lyon. 125 minutes

Captain Queeg: Humphrey Bogart, *Lt. Barney Greenwald:* José Ferrer, *Lt. Steve Maryk:* Van Johnson, *Lt. Tom Keefer:* Fred MacMurray, *Ensign Willie Keith:* Robert Francis, *May Wynn:* May Wynn, *Captain DeVriess:* Tom Tully, *Lt. Cdr. Challee:* E. G. Marshall, *Lt. Paynter:* Arthur Franz, *Meatball:* Lee Marvin, *Captain Blakely:* Warner Anderson, *Horrible:* Claude Akins, *Mrs. Keith:* Katharine Warren, *Ensign Harding:* Jerry Paris, *Chief Budge:* Steve Brodie, *Stilwell:* Todd Karns, *Lt. Cdr. Dickson:* Whit Bissell, *Lt. Jorgensen:* James Best, *Ensign Carmody:* Joe Haworth, *Ensign Rabbit:* Guy Anderson, *Whittaker:* James Edwards, *Urban:* Don Dubbins, *Engstrand:* David Alpert, *Uncle Lloyd:* Dayton Lummis, *Commodore Kelvey:* James Todd, *Court Stenographer:* Don Keefer, *Movie Operator:* Patrick Miller, *Sgt.-at-Arms:* Ted Cooper, *Chauffeur:* Don Dillaway, *Winston:* Eddie Laguna.

CALIFORNIA (1946) Par. Producer, Seton I, Miller. Director, John Farrow. Color by Technicolor. Based on a story by Boris Ingster. Screenplay, Frank Butler, Theodore Strauss. Music, Victor Young. Art Directors, Hans Dreier, Roland Anderson. Cameraman, Ray Rennahan. Editor, Eda Warren. Songs by E. Y. Harburg and Earl Robinson: "Said I to My Heart Said I," "California or Bust," "California," "I Shoulda Stood in Pennsylvania" and "Lily-I-Lay-De-O." Technicolor Directors, Natalie Kalmus, Robert Brower. 97 minutes

Jonathan Trumbo: Ray Milland, *Lily Bishop:* Barbara Stanwyck, *Michael Fabian:* Barry Fitzgerald, *Pharaoh Coffin:* George Coulouris, *Mr. Pike:* Albert Dekker, *Don Luis Rivera y Hernandez:* Anthony Quinn, *Whitey:* Frank Faylen, *Booth Pennock:* Gavin Muir, *Pokey:* James Burke, *Padre:* Eduardo Ciannelli, *Colonel Stuart:* Roman Bohnen, *Elvira:* Argentina Brunetti, *Senator Creel:* Howard Freeman, *Wagon Woman:* Julia Faye, *Town Marshal:* Alan Bridge, *Blacksmith:* Bud Geary, *Piano Player:* Pepito Perez, *Abe Clinton:* Crane Whitley, *Pennock's Partner:* Joey Ray, *Elwyn Smith:* Tommy Tucker, *Elwyn's Mother:* Frances Morris, *Emma (Town Matron)* Minerva Urecal, *Second Town Matron:* Virginia Farmer, *Higgins:* Sam Flint, *Willoughby:* Stanley Andrews, *Stark:* Don Beddoe, *Barrett:* Harry Hayden, *President Polk:* Ian Wolfe, *Eddie (Cashier):* Phil Tead, *Reb:* Ethan Laidlaw, *Old Woman:* Gertrude Hoffman, *Mike, Dealer:* Lester Vorr, *Jessie:* Francis Ford, *Stranger:* Rex Lease.

CALL ME MADAM (1953) 20th. Producer, Sol C. Siegel. Director, Walter Lang. Color by Technicolor. Based on the musical by Howard Lindsay and Russel Crouse. Screenplay, Arthur Sheekman. Art Directors, Lyle Wheeler, John De Cuir. Cinematographer, Leon Shamroy. Editor, Robert Simpson. Technicolor Consultant, Leonard Doss. Choreography, Robert Alton. Songs by Irving Berlin: "The Hostess With the Mostes'," "You're Just in Love," "The Best Thing for Me Would Be You," "It's a Lovely Day Today," "What Chance Have I With Love," "International Rag," "The Ocarina." Ethel Merman repeats her stage role. 117 minutes

Mrs. Sally Adams: Ethel Merman, *Kenneth:* Donald O'Connor, *Princess Maria:* Vera-Ellen, *Cosmo Constantine:* George Sanders, *Pemberton Maxwell:* Billy De Wolfe, *Prince Hugo:* Helmut Dantine, *Tantinnin:* Walter Slezak, *Sebastian:* Steven Geray, *Grand Duke:* Ludwig Stossel, *Grand Duchess:* Lilia Skala, *Senator Brockway:* Charles Dingle, *Senator Gallagher:* Emory Parnell, *Senator Wilkins:* Percy Helton, *Leader:*

Call Me Madam with Ethel Merman, Walter Slezak and George Sanders.

Leon Belasco, *Chamberlain:* Oscar Beregi, *Miccoli:* Nester Paiva, *Proprietor:* Sidney Marion, *Supreme Court Justice:* Richard Garrick, *Secretary of State:* Walter Woolf King, *Clerk:* Olan Soule, *Ronchin:* John Wengraf, *Hat Clerk:* Fritz Feld, *Music Clerk:* Erno Verebes, *Switchboard Operator:* Hannelore Axman, *Minister from Magrador:* Lal Chand Mehra, *Reporters:* Charles Conrad, Don Dillaway, Frank Gerstle, *Cameramen:* Allen Wood, Johnny Downs, *Reporter:* Rennie McEvoy, *Equerry:* Gene Roth.

CALL NORTHSIDE 777 (1948) 20th. Producer, Otto Lang. Director, Henry Hathaway. Based on articles by James P. McGuire. Screenplay, Jerome Cady, Jay Dratler. Art Directors, Lyle Wheeler, Mark-Lee Kirk. Photography, Joe MacDonald. Editor, J. Watson Webb, Jr. Adaptation, Leonard Hoffman and Quentin Reynolds. Narrator, Truman Bradley. Filmed at Statesville Prison and in Chicago. 111 minutes

McNeal: James Stewart, *Frank Wiecek:* Richard Conte, *Brian Kelly:* Lee J. Cobb, *Laura McNeal:* Helen Walker, *Wanda Skutnik:* Betty Garde, *Tillie:* Kasia Orzazewski, *Helen Wiecek-Rayska:* Joanne de Bergh, *Palmer:* Howard Smith, *Parole Board Chairman:* Moroni Olsen, *Sam Faxon:* John McIntire, *Martin Burns:* Paul Harvey, *Tomek Zaleska:* George Tyne, *Warden:* Richard Bishop, *Boris:* Otto Waldis, *Frank, Jr.:* Michael Chapin, *Rayska:* E. G. Marshall, *Sullivan (Bailiff):* J. M. Kerrigan, *Judge Charles Moulton:* Samuel S. Hinds, *Bartenders:* Henry Kulky, Cy Kendall, *Jan Gruska:* John Bleifer, *John Albertson:* Addison Richards, *Larson:* Richard Rober, *Patrolman:* Eddie Dunn, *William Decker (Mailman):* Percy Helton, *Prosecuting Attorney:* Charles Lane, *Detective:* Norman McKay, *Detective:* Walter Greaza, *Police Sergeant:* William Post, Jr., *Corrigan:* Lionel Stander, *Robert Winston:* Jonathan Hale, *Policeman:* Lew Eckles, *Holdup Men:* Freddie Steele, George Turner, *Anna Felczak:* Jane Crowley, *Spitzer:* Robert Karnes, *Secretary:* Helen Foster.

Call Northside 777 with Robert Karnes, James Stewart, E. G. Marshall, Michael Chapin and Joanne de Bergh.

CAMELOT (1967) WB-7 Arts. Produced by Jack L. Warner. Directed by Joshua Logan. Panavision and Technicolor. Based on the musical by Frederick Loewe, Alan Jay Lerner, and Moss Hart, from the novel *The Once and Future King* by T. H. White. Screenplay, Alan Jay Lerner. Music by Frederick Loewe. Music supervised and conducted by Alfred Newman. Associate musical supervision by Ken Darby. Costumes, scenery and production design by John Truscott. Art direction and sets by Edward Carrere. Assistant Producer, Joel Freeman. Assistant Director, Arthur Jacobson. Second Unit directed by Tap and Joe Canutt. Photography, Richard H. Kline. Editor, Folmer Blangsted. Sound, M. A. Merrick and Dan Wallin. Songs Alan Jay Lerner and Frederick Loewe: "I Wonder What the King Is Doing Tonight," "The Simple Joys of Maidenhood," "Camelot," "C'est Moi," "The Lusty Month of May," "Follow Me," "How to Handle a Woman," "Take Me to the Fair," "If Ever I Would Leave You," "What Do the Simple Folk Do?", "I Loved You Once in Silence," "Guinevere." 179 minutes

Camelot with Franco Nero, Richard Harris and Vanessa Redgrave.

King Arthur: Richard Harris, *Guinevere:* Vanessa Redgrave, *Lancelot du Lac:* Franco Nero, *Mordred:* David Hemmings, *King Pellinore:* Lionel Jeffries, *Merlin:* Laurence Naismith, *Dap:* Pierre Olaf, *Lady Clarinda:* Estelle Winwood, *Sir Lionel:* Gary Marshal, *Sir Dinadan:* Anthony Rogers, *Sir Sagramore:* Peter Bromilow, *Lady Sybil:* Sue Casey, *Tom:* Gary Marsh, *Arthur as a boy:* Nicholas Beauvy.

CAMILLE (1936) MGM. Directed by George Cukor. Author, Alexandre Dumas. Screenplay by Joe Akins, Frances Marion, James Hilton. Musical Score, Herbert Stothart. Dances, Val Raset. Cameraman, William Daniels, Editor, Margaret Booth. 108 minutes

Marguerite Gautier: Greta Garbo, *Armand:* Robert Taylor, *General Duval:* Lionel Barrymore, *Baron de Varville:* Henry Daniell, *Nichette:* Elizabeth Allan, *Olympe:* Lenore Ulric, *Prudence:* Laura Hope Crews, *Nanine:* Jessie Ralph, *Gaston:* Rex O'Malley, *Gustave:* Russell Hardie, *St. Gadeau:* E. E. Clive, *Henri:* Douglas Walton, *Corinne:* Marion Ballou, *Marie Jeanette:* Joan Brodel (Joan Leslie), *Louise:* June Wilkins, *Madame Duval:* Elsie Esmond, *Valentine:* Fritz Leiber, Jr, *Doctor:* Edwin Maxwell, *Therese:* Eily Malyon, *Friend of Camille:* Mariska Aldrich, *DeMusset:* John Bryan, *Companion:* Rex Evans, *Gypsy Leader:* Eugene King, *Singer:* Adrienne Matzenauer, *Streetwalker:* Georgia Caine, *Madame Barjon:* Mabel Colcord, *Priest:* Chappel Dossett, *Attendant:* Elspeth Dudgeon, *Grandma Duval:* Effie Ellsler, *Georges Sand:* Sibyl Harris, *Aunt Henriette:* Maude Hume, *Croupier:* Olaf Hytten, *Governess:* Gwendolyn Logan, *Priest:* Ferdinand Munier, *Emille:* Barry Norton, *Orchestra Leader:* John Picorri, *Auctioneer:* Guy Bates Post, *Old Duchess:* Zeffie Tilbury.

Camille with Robert Taylor, Greta Garbo, Laura Hope Crews and Rex O'Malley.

Can-Can with Frank Sinatra and Shirley MacLaine.

CAN-CAN (1960) 20th. Produced by Jack Cummings. Directed by Walter Lang. De Luxe Color, Todd-AO. Associate Producer, Saul Chaplin. Based on the musical comedy of 1953 by Abe Burrows. Screenplay, Dorothy Kingsley and Charles Lederer. Choreography, Hermes Pan. Art Directors, Lyle Wheeler and Jack Martin Smith. Music arranged and conducted by Nelson Riddle. Cinematography, William H. Daniels. Editor, Robert Simpson. Songs by Cole Porter: "Let's Do It," "Just One of Those Things," "You Do Something to Me," "I Love Paris," "It's All Right with Me," "C'est Magnifique," "Come Along with Me," "Maidens Typical of France," "Live and Let Live," "Montmart." A Suffolk-Cummings Production. 131 minutes

Francois Durnais: Frank Sinatra, *Simone Pistache:* Shirley MacLaine, *Paul Barriere:* Maurice Chevalier, *Philippe Forrestier:* Louis Jourdan, *Claudine:* Juliet Prowse, *Andre (Headwaiter):* Marcel Dalio, *Orchestra Leader, Arturo:* Leon Belasco, *Bailiff:* Nestor Paiva, *Photographer:* John A. Neris, *Judge Merceaux:* Jean Del Val, *League President:* Ann Codee, *Chevrolet:* Eugene Borden, *Recorder:* Jonathan Kidd, *Adam:* Marc Wilder, *Policeman Dupont:* Peter Coe, *Plainclothesman:* Marcel de la Broesse, *Dowagers:* Rene Godfrey, Lili Valenty, *Knife Thrower:* Charles Carman, *Gigi:* Carole Bryan, *Camille:* Barbara Carter, *Renee:* Jane Earl, *Julie:* Ruth Earl, *Germine:* Laura Fraser, *Gabrielle:* Vera Lee, *Fifi:* Lisa Mitchell, *Maxine:* Wanda Shannon, *Gisele:* Darlene Tittle, *Lili:* Wilda Taylor, *Apache Dancer:* Ambrogio Malerba, *Butler:* Alphonse Martell, *Secretary:* Genevieve Aumont, *Judge:* Edward Le Veque, *Bailiff:* Maurice Marsac.

CAPTAIN BLOOD (1935) WB. Produced by Harry Joe Brown. Directed by Michael Curtiz. From the novel by Rafael Sabatini. Screenplay, Casey Robinson. Photography, Hal Mohr. Editor, George Amy. Locations: Corona, Laguna Beach, Palm Canyon near Palm Springs, California. A Cosmopolitan Production. 119 minutes

Dr. Peter Blood: Errol Flynn, *Arabella Bishop:* Olivia De Havilland, *Colonel Bishop:* Lionel Atwill, *Captain Levasseur:* Basil Rathbone, *Jeremy Pitt:* Ross Alexander, *Hagthorpe:* Guy Kibbee, *Lord Willoughby:* Henry Stephenson, *Governor Steed:* George Hassell, *Honesty Nuthall:* Forrester Harvey, *Wolverstone:* Robert Barrat, *Dr. Bronson:* Hobart Cavanaugh, *Dr. Whacker:* Donald Meek, *Reverend Ogle:* Frank McGlynn, Sr., *Andrew Baynes:* David Torrence, *Cahusac:* J. Carrol Naish, *Don Diego:* Pedro de Cordoba, *Lord Jeffries:* Leonard Mudie, *Mrs. Barlowe:* Jessie Ralph, *Captain Hobart:* Stuart Casey, *Lord Sunderland:* Halliwell Hobbes, *Lord Chester Dyke:* Colin Kenny, *Court Clerk:* E. E. Clive, *Captain Gardiner:* Holmes Herbert, *Mrs. Steed:* Mary Forbes, *Dixon:* Reginald Barlowe, *Prosecutor:* Ivan F. Simpson, *Lord Gildoy:* Denis d'Auburn, *King James II:* Vernon Steele, *French Captain:* Georges Renavent, *Clerk in Governor Steed's Court:* Murray Kinnell, *Kent:* Harry Cording, *Baynes' Wife:* Maude Leslie, *Governor's Attendant:* Stymie Beard, *Judge Advocate:* Ivan F. Simpson, *Slave:* Gardner James, *Gunner:* Sam Appel, *Sentry:* Chris-Pin Martin, *Girls in Tavern:* Yola D'Avril, Tina Menard, *French Officer:* Frank Puglia, *Pirates:* Artie Ortego, Gene Alsace, Kansas Moehring, Tom Steele, Blackie Whiteford, Jim Thorpe, William Yetter, Buddy Roosevelt, Jimmy Mason.

CAPTAIN FROM CASTILE (1947) 20th. Producer, Lamar Trotti. Director, Henry King. Color by Technicolor. From the novel by Samuel Shellabargar, Screenplay, Lamar Trotti. Musical Director, Alfred Newman. Art Directors, Richard Day, James Basevi. Cameraman, Charles Clarke, Arthur E. Arling. Editor, Barbara McLean. Technicolor Director, Natalie Kalmus. Associate, Richard Mueller. Film debut of Jean Peters. 140 minutes

Pedro De Vargas: Tyrone Power, *Catana:* Jean Peters, *Cortez:* Cesar Romero, *Juan Garcia:* Lee J. Cobb, *Diego De Silva:* John Sutton, *Don Francisco:* Antonio Moreno, *Father Bartolomé:* Thomas Gomez, *Botello:* Alen Mowbray, *Luiza:* Barbara Lawrence, *Marquis De Caravajal:* George Zucco, *Captain Alvarado:* Roy Roberts, *Corio:* Marc Lawrence, *Manuel:* Robert Karnes, *Soler:* Fred Libby, *Dona Maria:* Virginia Brissac, *Coatl:* Jay Silverheels, *Cermeno:* John Laurenz, *Mercedes:* Dolly Arriaga, *Escudero:* Reed Hadley, *Donna Marino:* Stella Inda, *Sancho Lopez:* Chris-Pin Martin, *Crier:* Edward Mundy, *Reyes:* Robert Adler, *Aztec Ambassador:* Gilberto Gonzales, *Aztec:* Ramon Sanchez, *Captain Sandoval:* Harry Carter, *Hernandez:* Mimi Aguglia, *Sailor:* Bud Wolfe, *Singer:* David Cato.

Captain From Castile with Jean Peters and Thomas Gomez.

Captain Blood with Guy Kibbee, Robert Barrat, Frank McGlynn, Sr., and Errol Flynn.

Captain Newman, M.D. with Robert F. Simon, Gregory Peck and Angie Dickinson.

CAPTAIN NEWMAN, M.D. (1963) Univ. Produced by Robert Arthur. Directed by David Miller. In Eastman Color by Pathé. A Brentwood-Reynard Production. Screenplay, Richard L. Breen and Phoebe and Henry Ephron. From the novel by Leo Rosten. Photography, Russell Metty. Music, Frank Skinner. Costumes, Rosemary Odell. Assistant Director, Phil Bowles. Art Directors, Alexander Golitzen and Alfred Sweeney. Music Supervisor, Joseph Gershenson. Editor, Alma Macrorie. 126 minutes

Captain Josiah Newman: Gregory Peck, *Corporal Jackson Laibowitz:* Tony Curtis, *Lt. Francie Corum:* Angie Dickinson, *Col. Norval Algate Bliss:* Eddie Albert, *Corporal Jim Tompkins:* Bobby Darin, *Col. Edgar Pyser:* James Gregory, *Lt. Grace Blodgett:* Jane Withers, *Helene Winston:* Bethel Leslie, *Capt. Paul Cabot Winston:* Robert Duvall, *Lt. Alderson:* Dick Sargent, *Corporal Gavoni:* Larry Storch, *Lt. Colonel Larrabee:* Robert F. Simon, *Major General Snowden:* Crahan Denton, *Captain Howard:* Gregory Walcott, *Patient:* Martin West, *Master Sgt. Arkie Kopp:* Syl Lamont, *Major Alfredo Fortuno:* Vito Scottl, *Waitress at Blue Grotto:* Penny Santon, *Kathie:* Amzie Strickland, *Major Dawes:* Barry Atwater, *Mrs. Pyser:* Ann Doran, *Maccarades:* Joey Walsh, *Patient:* David Winters, *Hollingshead:* Byron Morrow, *Corporal:* David Landfield, *Chaplain (Priest):* Ron Brogan, *Chaplain (Rabbi):* Robert Strong, *Officer:* John Hart, *Gorkow:* Charles Briggs, *Arthur Werbel:* Paul Carr, *Haskell:* Sam Reese, *Carrozzo:* Ted Bessell, *Patients:* Marc Cavell, Seamon Glass, Jack Grinnage.

CAPTAINS COURAGEOUS (1937) MGM. Produced by Louis D. Lighton. Directed by Victor Fleming. Based on the novel by Rudyard Kipling. Screenplay, John Lee Mahin, Marc Connelly, Dale Van Every. Music Score, Franz Waxman. Marine Director, James Havens. Art Director, Cedric Gibbons. Associate Art Directors, Arnold Gillespie and Edwin B. Willis. Photography, Harold Rosson. Editor, Elmo Vernon. Sound, Douglas Shearer. Songs, "Don't Cry Little Fish" and "Ooh, What a Terrible Man!" by Franz Waxman and Gus Kahn. 116 minutes

Harvey: Freddie Bartholomew, *Manuel:* Spencer Tracy, *Disko:* Lionel Barrymore, *Father:* Melvyn Douglas, *Dan:* Mickey Rooney,

Captains Courageous with Spencer Tracy, Freddie Bartholomew and Lionel Barrymore.

Uncle Salters: Charley Grapewin, *Old Clemant:* Christian Rub, *Dr. Finley:* Walter Kingsford, *Tyler:* Donald Briggs, *Doc:* Sam McDaniel, *Tom:* Dave Thursby, *Long Jack:* John Carradine, *Elliott:* William Stack, *Burns:* Leo G. Carroll, *Dr. Walsh:* Charles Trowbridge, *First Steward:* Richard Powell, *Charles:* Billy Burrud, *Pogey:* Jay Ward, *Alvin:* Kenneth Wilson, *Nate Rogers:* Roger Gray, *Priest:* Jack La Rue, *Cushman:* Oscar O'Shea, *Reporter:* Bobby Watson, *Soda Steward:* Billy Gilbert, *Robbins:* Norman Ainsley, *Secretary Cobb:* Gladden James, *Boys:* Tommy Bupp, Wally Albright, *Mrs. Disko:* Katherine Kenworthy, *Lars:* Dave Wengren, *Ministers:* Murray Kinnell, *Appleton's Wife:* Dora Early, *Nate's Wife:* Gertrude Sutton.

The Cardinal with Tom Tryon.

THE CARDINAL (1963) Col. Producer-Director, Otto Preminger. Screenplay, Robert Dozier. Based on novel by Henry Morton Robinson. Music, Jerome Moross. Associate Producer, Martin C. Schute. Costumes, Donald Brooks. Choreography, Buddy Schwab. Assistant Directors, Gerry O'Hara, Bob Vietro, Bryan Coates, Hermann Leitner, Robert Fiz, Erich Von Stroheim, Jr. In Panavision and Technicolor. Cinematographer, Leon Shamroy. Editor, Louis R. Loeffler. 175 minutes

Stephen Fermoyle: Tom Tryon, *Mona:* Carol Lynley, *Celia:* Dorothy Gish, *Florrie:* Maggie McNamara, *Frank:* Bill Hayes, *Din:* Cameron Prud'Homme, *Monsignor Monaghan:* Cecil Kellaway, *Cornelius J. Deegan:* Loring Smith, *Benny Rampell:* John Saxon, *Cardinal Glennon:* John Huston, *Ramon Gongaro:* José Duval, *Father Callahan:* Peter MacLean, *Bobby:* Robert Morse, *Father Lyons:* James Hickman, *Mrs. Rampell:* Berenice Gahm, *Master of Ceremonies:* Billy Reed, *Hercule Menton:* Pat Henning, *Father Ned Halley:* Burgess Meredith, *Lalage Menton:* Jill Haworth, *Dr. Heller:* Russ Brown, *Cardinal Quarenghi:* Raf Vallone, *Cardinal Giacobbi:* Tullio Carminati, *Father Gillis:* Ossie Davis, *Ordination Master of Ceremonies:* Don Francesco Mancini, *Italian Monsignor:* Dino Di Luca, *Liturgical Chants:* Monks of Abbey at Casamari, *Regina Fermoyle:* Carol Lynley, *Father Eberling:* Donald Hayne, *Monsignor Whittle:* Chill Wills, *Sheriff Dubrow:* Arthur Hunnicutt, *Woman Picket:* Doro Merande, *Cecil Turner:* Patrick O'Neal, *Lafe:* Murray Hamilton, *Annemarie:* Romy Schneider, *Kurt Von Hartman:* Peter Weck, *Drinking Man at Ball:* Rudolph Forster, *Cardinal Innitzer:* Josef Meinrad, *Madame Walter:* Dagmar Schmedes, *Seyss-Inquart:* Eric Frey, *Von Hartman Butler:* Josef Krastel, *Father Neidermoser:* Mathias Fuchs, *Sister Wilhelmina:* Vilma Degischer, *S. S. Major:* Wolfgang Preiss, *Army Lieutenant:* Jurgen Wilke, *Soloist:* Wilma Lipp, and the Wiener Jeunesse Choir.

CARMEN JONES (1954) 20th. Producer-Director, Otto Preminger. Assistant Director, David Silver. Book and lyrics by Oscar Hammerstein II. Screenplay by Harry Kleiner. Music by Georges Bizet. Art Director, Edward L. Ilou. Cinematographer, Sam Leavitt. A CinemaScope Production in De Luxe Color. Stereophonic sound. Songs by Oscar Hammerstein II, based on the music of Georges Bizet: "Stand Up and Fight," "Beat Out That Rhythm on a Drum," "Dere's a Cafe on de

Carmen Jones with Harry Belafonte and Dorothy Dandridge.

Corner," "Lift 'em Up and Put 'em Down," "Dat's love (I Go For You, But You're Taboo)," "You Talk Just Like My Maw," "Dis Flower," "De Cards Don't Lie," "My Joe," "Dat's Our Man," "Whiz-zin' Away Along de Track." 105 minutes

Carmen: Dorothy Dandridge, *Joe:* Harry Belafonte, *Cindy Lou:* Olga James, *Frankie:* Pearl Bailey, *Myrt:* Diahann Carroll, *Rum:* Roy Glenn, *Dink:* Nick Stewart, *Husky:* Joe Adams, *Sgt. Brown:* Broc Peters, *T-Bone:* Sandy Lewis, *Sally:* Mauri Lynn, *Trainer:* De-Forest Covan. Marilyn Horne sings for Dorothy Dandridge, LeVern Hutcherson for Harry Belafonte, and Marvin Hayes for Joe Adams.

CAROUSEL (1956) 20th. Producer, Henry Ephron. Director, Henry King. Screenplay by Phoebe and Henry Ephron from Rodgers and Hammerstein's musical play based on Ferenc Molnar's *Liliom* as adapted by Benjamin F. Glazer. Music by Richard Rodgers. Book and lyrics by Oscar Hammerstein II. Choreography by Rod Alexander. Louise's ballet by Agnes De Mille. Costumes by Mary Wills. In CinemaScope and De Luxe Color. 128 minutes

Billy: Gordon MacRae, *Julie:* Shirley Jones, *Jigger:* Cameron Mitchell, *Carrie:* Barbara Ruick, *Cousin Nettie:* Claramae Turner, *Mr. Snow:* Robert Rounseville, *Starkeeper:* Gene Lockhart, *Mrs. Mullin:* Audrey Christie, *Louise:* Susan Lucket, *Heavenly Friend:* William Le Massena, *Mr. Bascombe:* John Dehner, *Louise's Dancing Partner:* Jacques D'Amboise, *Captain Watson:* Frank Tweddell, *Policeman:* Richard Deacon, *Enoch Snow, Jr.:* Dee Pollock.

Carousel with Gordon MacRae, Shirley Jones and Barbara Ruick.

The Carpetbaggers with Carroll Baker and George Peppard.

THE CARPETBAGGERS (1964) Par. Producer, Joseph E. Levine. Director, Edward Dmytryk. Technicolor. Based on the novel by Harold Robbins. Screenplay, John Michael Hayes. Art Directors, Hal Pereira, Walter Tyler. Music, Elmer Bernstein. Cinematographer, Joseph MacDonald. Special Photographic Effects, Paul K. Lerpae. Editor, Frank Bracht. Last film of Alan Ladd. Sequel was *Nevada Smith* (1966). 150 minutes

Jonas Cord: George Peppard, *Nevada Smith:* Alan Ladd, *Dan Pierce:* Bob Cummings, *Jennie Denton:* Martha Hyer, *Monica:* Elizabeth Ashley, *McAllister:* Lew Ayres, *Bernard Norman:* Martin Balsam, *Buzz Dalton:* Ralph Taeger, *Jedediah:* Archie Moore, *Jonas Cord, Sr.:* Leif Erickson, *Rina Marlowe Cord:* Carroll Baker, *Morrissey:* Arthur Franz, *Amos Winthrop:* Tom Tully, *Woman:* Audrey Totter, *Moroni:* Anthony Warde, *Denby:* Charles Lane, *David Woolf:* Tom Lowell, *Ed Ellis:* John Conte, *Doctor:* Vaughn Taylor, *Cynthia Randall:* Francesca Bellini, *Jo-Ann Cord:* Victoria Jean, *Bellboy:* Frankie Darro, *Moroni's Secretary:* Lisa Seagram, *Woman Reporter:* Ann Doran, *Reporter:* Joseph Turkel, *Sound Man:* Donald Barry, *Asst. Director:* Peter Duryea.

CASABLANCA (1942) WB. Produced by Hal B. Wallis. Directed by Michael Curtiz. Based on *Everybody Comes to Rick's*, an unproduced play by Murray Burnett and Joan Alison. Screenplay, Julius J. Epstein, Philip G. Epstein, Howard Koch. Music, Max Steiner. Music Director, Leo F. Forbstein. Orchestral Arrangements, Hugo Friedhofer. Editor, Owen Marks. Photography, Arthur Edeson. Sound, Francis J. Scheid. Art Director, Carl Jules Weyl. Sets, George James Hopkins. Special Effects, Lawrence Butler. Songs by M. K. Jerome and Jack Scholl: "Knock on Wood," "That's What Noah Done," "Muse's Call"; "As Time Goes By" by Herman Hupfeld. Montages, Don Siegel and James Leicester. Special Effects Director, Willard Van Enger. Gowns, Orry-Kelly. Assistant Director, Lee Katz. Make-up, Perc Westmore. Dialogue Director, Hugh MacMullan. Technical Advisor, Robert Aisner. Filmed near Palm Springs. Originally named for the leads were Ann Sheridan, Ronald Reagan, and Dennis Morgan. Elliott Carpenter played the piano for Dooley Wilson, who, in his film debut, sang "As Time Goes By" and "It Had to Be You." 102 minutes

Rick Blaine: Humphrey Bogart, *Ilsa Lund Laszlo:* Ingrid Bergman, *Victor Laszlo:* Paul Henreid, *Captain Louis Renault:* Claude Rains, *Maj. Heinrich Strasser:* Conrad Veidt, *Senor Ferrari:* Sydney Greenstreet, *Ugarte:* Peter Lorre, *Carl:* S. Z. Sakall, *Yvonne:* Madeleine LeBeau, *Sam:* Dooley Wilson, *Annina Brandel:* Joy Page, *Berger:* John Qualen, *Sascha:* Leonid Kinskey, *Jan Brandel:* Helmut Dantine, *Dark European:* Curt Bois, *Croupier:* Marcel Dalio, *Singer:* Corinna Mura, *Mr. Leuchtag:* Ludwig Stossel, *Mrs. Leuchtag:* Ilka Gruning, *Senor Martinez:* Charles La Torre, *Arab Vendor:* Frank Puglia, *Abdul:* Dan Seymour, *Blue Parrot Waiter:* Oliver Prickett (Oliver Blake), *German Banker:* Gregory Gay, *Friend:* George Meeker, *Contact:* William Edmunds, *Banker:* Torben Meyer, *Waiter:* Gino Corrado, *Casselle:* George Dee, *Englishwoman:* Norma Varden, *Fydor:* Leo

Casablanca with Dooley Wilson, Humphrey Bogart and Ingrid Bergman.

Cass Timberlane with Spencer Tracy, Cameron Mitchell and Lana Turner.

Mostovoy, *Heinz:* Richard Ryen, *Headwaiter:* Martin Garralaga, *Prosperous Man:* Olaf Hytten, *American:* Monte Blue, *Vendor:* Michael Mark, *Dealer:* Leon Belasco, *Native:* Paul Porcasi, *German Officer:* Hans Twardowski, *French Officer:* Albert Morin, *Customer:* Creighton Hale, *German Officer:* Henry Rowland.

CASANOVA BROWN (1944) RKO. Producer, Nunnally Johnson. Director, Sam Wood. Screenplay, Nunnally Johnson. Musical Score, Arthur Lange. Art Director, Perry Ferguson. Cameraman, John Seitz. Editor, Thomas Neff. From the play *Bachelor Father* by Floyd Dell and Thomas Mitchell. An International Pictures-Christie Production. 94 minutes

Casanova Brown: Gary Cooper, *Isabel Drury:* Teresa Wright, *Mr. Ferris:* Frank Morgan, *Madge Ferris:* Anita Louise, *Mrs. Drury:* Patricia Collinge, *Mr. Drury:* Edmond Breon, *Dr. Zernerke:* Jill Esmond, *Frank:* Emory Parnell, *Mrs. Ferris:* Isabel Elsom, *Monica:* Mary Treen, *Butler:* Halliwell Hobbes, *Chauffeur:* Gerald Oliver Smith, *English Maid:* Hilda Plowright, *Fire Chief:* John Brown, *Junior:* Larry Joe Olsen, *Organist:* Cecil Stewart, *Soloist:* Helen St. Rayner, *Fletcher:* Byron Foulger, *Florist's Assistant:* Walter Tetley, *Landlady:* Sarah Padden, *Mrs. Dean:* Mary Young, *Doris Ferris:* Eloise Hardt, *Tod:* Grady Sutton, *Rev. Dean:* Frederick Burton, *Marriage Clerk:* Robert Dudley, *Clerk's Wife:* Isabel LaMal, *Nurse Phillips:* Florence Lake, *Hicks:* Charles Cane, *Spano:* Charles LaTorre, *Orderly:* Lane Chandler, *Woman Patient:* Kay Deslys, *X-Ray Nurse:* Julia Faye, *Nurse Clark:* Dorothy Tree, *Doctor:* Edward Earle, *Hotel Manager:* Irving Bacon, *Yokes:* Robert Emmett Keane, *O'Leary:* James Burke.

CASS TIMBERLANE (1947) MGM. Producer, Arthur Hornblow, Jr. Director, George Sidney. Based on the novel by Sinclair Lewis. Screenplay, Donald Ogden Stewart. Art Directors, Cedric Gibbons, Daniel B. Cathcart. Music Score, Roy Webb. Musical Director, Constantin Bakaleinikoff. Cameraman, Robert Planck. Editor, John Dunning. Locations: Minnesota, Idaho, Florida, Los Angeles. 119 minutes

Cass Timberlane: Spencer Tracy, *Virginia Marshland:* Lana Turner, *Brad Criley:* Zachary Scott, *Jamie Wargate:* Tom Drake, *Queenie Havock:* Mary Astor, *Boone Havock:* Albert Dekker, *Louise Wargate:* Selena Royle, *Lillian Drover:* Josephine Hutchinson, *Chris Grace:* Margaret Lindsay, *Diantha Marl:* Rose Hobart, *Webb Wargate:* John Litel, *Mrs. Avis Elderman:* Mona Barrie, *Roy Drover:* John Alexander, *Gregg Marl:* Frank Wilcox, *Alice:* Pat Clark, *Dennis Thayne:* Richard Gaines, *John Prutt:* Willis Claire, *Henrietta Prutt:* Winnona Walthal, *Eino Rochinan:* Cameron Mitchell, *Mrs. Higbie:* Jessie Grayson, *Herman:* Griff Barnett, *Harvey Plint:* Howard Freeman, *George Hame:* Guy Beach, *Humbert Bellile:* Cliff Clark, *Himself:* Walter Pidgeon, *Sheriff Alex Carlson:* Ken Christy, *Dr. Leskett:* Selmer Jackson, *Court Clerk:* Frank Ferguson, *Nestor Purdwin:* Milburn Stone, *Zilda Hatter:* Almira Sessions, *Vincent Osprey:* Jack Rice, *Ellen Olliford:* Mimi Doyle, *Arthur Olliford:* Bill Conselman, *Charles Sayward:* Sam Flint, *Dagmar:* Greta Granstedt, *Policeman:* Robert Williams, *Chauffeur:* William Tannen, *Charlie Ellis:* Tim Ryan, *Mary Ann Milligan:* Bess Flowers, *Raveau:* William Trenk.

CAT BALLOU (1965) Col. Producer, Harold Hecht. Associate Producer, Mitch Lindemann. Director, Elliott Silverstein. Technicolor.

Casanova Brown with Gary Cooper and Teresa Wright.

Cat Ballou with Lee Marvin (dual role).

Based on the novel by Roy Chanslor. Screenplay, Walter Newman, Frank R. Pierson. Art Director, Malcolm Brown. Music, De Vol. Songs, Mack David, Jerry Livingston. Cinematographer, Jack Marta. Editor, Charles Nelson. 96 minutes

Cat Ballou: Jane Fonda, *Kid Shelleen/Strawn:* Lee Marvin, *Clay Boone:* Michael Callan, *Jed:* Dwayne Hickman, *Shouter:* Nat King Cole, *Shouter:* Stubby Kaye, *Jackson Two-Bears:* Tom Nardini, *Frankie Ballou:* John Marley, *Sir Harry Percival:* Reginald Denny, *Sheriff Cardigan:* Jay C. Flippen, *Butch Cassidy:* Arthur Hunnicutt, *Sheriff Maledon:* Bruce Cabot, *Accouser:* Burt Mustin, *Train Messenger:* Paul Gilbert, *Klem:* Robert Phillips, *James:* Charles Wagenheim, *Homer:* Duke Hobbie, *Hedda:* Ayllene Gibbons, *Train Engineer:* Everett L. Rohrer, *Train Conductor:* Harry Harvey, Sr., *Honey Girl:* Hallene Hill, *Mabel Bentley:* Gail Bonney, *Frenchie:* Joseph Hamilton, *Singing Tart:* Dorothy Claire, *Hardcase:* Charles Horvath, *Armed Guard:* Chuck Roberson, *Ad-Lib:* Nick Cravat, *Gunslinger:* Ted White, *Valet:* Erik Sorensen, *Train Fireman:* Ivan L. Middleton, *Mrs. Parker:* Carol Veazie.

The Catered Affair with Bette Davis, Ernest Borgnine and Debbie Reynolds.

THE CATERED AFFAIR (1956) MGM. Producer, Sam Zimbalist. Director, Richard Brooks. Based on the TV play by Paddy Chayefsky. Screenplay, Gore Vidal. Art Directors, Cedric Gibbons, Paul Groesse. Musical Director, Andre Previn. Cinematographer, John Alton. Editors, Gene Ruggiero, Frank Santillo. 93 minutes

Mrs. Tom Hurley: Bette Davis, *Tom Hurley:* Ernest Borgnine, *Jane Hurley:* Debbie Reynolds, *Uncle Jack Conlon:* Barry Fitzgerald, *Ralph Halloran:* Rod Taylor, *Mr. Halloran:* Robert Simon, *Mrs. Halloran:* Madge Kennedy, *Mrs. Rafferty:* Dorothy Stickney, *Mrs. Casey:* Carol Veazie, *Alice:* Joan Camden, *Eddie Hurley:* Ray Stricklyn, *Sam Leiter:* Jay Adler, *Hotel Caterer:* Dan Tobin, *Bill:* Paul Denton, *Mrs. Musso:* Augusta Merighi, *Joe, Mechanic:* Howard Graham, *Young Woman:* Janice Carroll, *Girl on Phone:* Joan Bradshaw, *Counterman:* Harry Hines, *Saleswoman:* Mae Clarke, *Tailor:* Jimmie Fox, *Bartender:* John Costello, *Father Murphy:* Thomas Dillon.

CAT ON A HOT TIN ROOF (1958) MGM. An Avon Production. Producer, Lawrence Weingarten. Director, Richard Brooks. Color by MetroColor. Screenplay by Richard Brooks and James Poe. Based on the play by Tennessee Williams. Assistant Director, William Shanks. Wardrobe by Helen Rose. Art Directors, William A. Horning and Urie McCleary. Film Editor, Ferris Webster. Cinematography by William Daniels. 108 minutes

Maggie: Elizabeth Taylor, *Brick:* Paul Newman, *Big Daddy:* Burl Ives, *Gooper:* Jack Carson, *Big Mama:* Judith Anderson, *Mae:* Madeleine Sherwood, *Dr. Baugh:* Larry Gates, *Deacon Davis:* Vaughn Taylor, *Lacy:* Vince Townsend, Jr., *Sookey:* Zelda Cleaver, *Boy:* Brian Corcoran, *Buster:* Hugh Corcoran, *Sonny:* Rusty Stevens,

Cat on a Hot Tin Roof with Paul Newman and Elizabeth Taylor.

Dixie: Patty Ann Gerrity, *Trixie:* Deborah Miller, *Party Guests:* Tony Merrill, Jeane Wood, *Groom:* Bobby Johnson.

CAT PEOPLE (1942) RKO. Producer, Val Lewton. Director, Jacques Tourneur. Screenplay, DeWitt Bodeen. Musical Director, C. Bakaleinikoff. Score, Roy Webb. Art Directors, Albert d'Agostino, Walter E. Keller. Cameraman, Nicholas Musuraca. Editor, Mark Robson. Sequel was *The Curse of the Cat People* (RKO, 1944). 73 minutes

Irena Dubrovna: Simone Simon, *Oliver Reed:* Kent Smith, *Doctor Judd:* Tom Conway, *Alice Moore:* Jane Randolph, *The Commodore:* Jack Holt, *Carver:* Alan Napier, *Miss Plunkett:* Elizabeth Dunne, *The Cat Woman:* Elizabeth Russell, *Blondie:* Mary Halsey, *Zookeeper:* Alec Craig, *Minnie:* Theresa Harris, *The Organ Grinder:* Steve Soldi, *Bus Driver:* Charles Jordan, *Whistling Cop:* George Ford, *Mrs. Hansen:* Betty Roadmon, *Mrs. Agnew:* Dot Farley, *Taxi Driver:* Don Kerr, *Woman:* Connie Leon, Henrietta Burnside, *Patient:* Leda Nicova, *Cafe Proprietor:* John Piffle, *Sheep Caretaker:* Murdoc MacQuarrie, *Mounted Cop:* Bud Geary, *Street Cop:* Eddie Dew.

The Cat People with Elizabeth Dunne, Kent Smith, Jane Randolph and Mary Halsey.

CAUGHT IN THE DRAFT (1941) Par. Producer, B. G. DeSylva. Director, David Butler. Original Story and Screenplay, Harry Tugend. Art Directors, Hans Dreier, Haldane Douglas. Musical Score, Victor Young. Cameraman, Karl Struss. Editor, Irene Morra. Additional Dialogue, Wilkie C. Mahoney. Song by Frank Loesser and Louis Alter: "Love Me as I Am." 82 minutes

Don Gilbert: Bob Hope, *Tony Fairbanks:* Dorothy Lamour, *Steve:* Lynne Overman, *Bert:* Eddie Bracken, *Colonel Peter Fairbanks:* Clarence Kolb, *Sergeant Burns:* Paul Hurst, *Yetta:* Ferike Boros,

Caught in the Draft with Lynne Overman, Bob Hope and Dorothy Lamour.

Margie: Phyllis Ruth, *Cogswell:* Irving Bacon, *Director:* Arthur Loft, *Recruiting Sergeant:* Edgar Dearing, *Make-up Man:* Murray Alper, *Colonel's Orderly:* Dave Willock, *Twitchell:* Frank Marlowe, *Sign Hanger:* Heinie Conklin, *Susan:* Phyllis Kennedy, *Medical Examiner:* Edwin Stanley, *Fat Girl:* June Bryde, *Sergeant at Examining Depot:* Weldon Heyburn, *Quartermaster Sergeant:* George McKay, *Pilot:* Peter Lynn, *Justice of the Peace:* Andrew Tombes, *Operation Manager (Captain):* Edward Hearn.

CAVALCADE (1933) Fox. Produced by Winfield Sheehan. Directed by Frank Lloyd. Based on the play by Noel Coward. Adaptation and Dialogue, Reginald Berkeley. Continuity Editor, Sonya Levien. Art Director, William Darling. Ladies' Costumes, Earl Luick. Men's Costumes, A. McDonald. War Scenes, William Cameron Menzies. Technical Advisor, Lance Baxter. Dialogue Director, George Hadden. Unit Manager, Charles Woolstenhulme. Assistant Director, William Tummel. Photography, Ernest Palmer. Editor, Margaret Clancy. Sound, Joseph E. Aiken. Dances, Sammy Lee. Filmed entirely at Movietone City, Westwood, Cal. Song by Noel Coward: "Twentieth Century Blues." 109 minutes

Robert Marryot: Clive Brook, *Jane Marryot:* Diana Wynyard, *Fanny Bridges:* Ursula Jeans, *Alfred Bridges:* Herbert Mundin, *Ellen Bridges:* Una O'Connor, *Annie:* Merle Tottenham, *Margaret Harris:*

Cavalcade with Herbert Mundin, Diana Wynyard, Clive Brook and Una O'Connor.

Irene Browne, *Cook:* Beryl Mercer, *Joe Marryot:* Frank Lawton, *Edward Marryot:* John Warburton, *Edith Harris:* Margaret Lindsay, *Mrs. Snapper:* Tempe Piggott, *George Grainger:* Billy Bevan, *Ronnie James:* Desmond Roberts, *Uncle Dick:* Frank Atkinson, *Mirabelle:* Ann Shaw, *Ada:* Adele Crane, *Tommy Jolly:* Will Stanton, *Lieutenant Edgar:* Stuart Hall, *Duchess of Churt:* Mary Forbes, *Major Domo:* C. Montague Shaw, *Uncle George:* Lionel Belmore, *Edward, age 12:* Dick Henderson, Jr., *Joey, age 8:* Douglas Scott, *Edith, age 10:* Sheila MacGill, *Fanny at 7-12:* Bonita Granville, *Agitator:* Howard Davies, *Man at Disarmament Conference:* David Torrence, *Man at Microphone:* Lawrence Grant, *Minister:* Winter Hall, *Speaker (Officer):* Claude King, *Ringsider:* Pat Somerset, *Soldier (Friend):* Douglas Walton, *Waiter:* Tom Ricketts, *Girl on Couch:* Betty Grable, *Buskers:* Harry Allen, John Rogers, *Gilbert & Sullivan Actor:* Brandon Hurst.

Ceiling Zero with James Cagney, June Travis and Pat O'Brien.

CEILING ZERO (1935) WB. Produced by Harry Joe Brown. Directed by Howard Hawks. Based on the play by Frank Wead. Screenplay, Frank Wead. Photography, Arthur Edeson. Editor, William Holmes. A Cosmopolitan Production. 95 minutes

Dizzy Davis: James Cagney, *Jake Lee:* Pat O'Brien, *Tommy Thomas:* June Travis, *Texas Clark:* Stuart Erwin, *Tay Lawson:* Henry Wadsworth, *Lou Clark:* Isabel Jewell, *Al Stone:* Barton MacLane, *Mary Lee:* Martha Tibbetts, *Joe Allen:* Craig Reynolds, *Buzz Gordon:* James H. Bush, *Les Bogan:* Robert Light, *Fred Adams:* Addison Richards, *Eddie Payson:* Carlyle Moore, Jr., *Smiley Johnson:* Richard Purcell, *Transportation Agent:* (Bill) Gordon Elliott, *Baldy Wright:* Pat West, *Doc Wilson:* Edward Gargan, *Mike Owens:* Garry Owen, *Mama Gini:* Mathilde Comont, *Birdie:* Carol Hughes, *Stunt Fliers:* Frank Tomick, Paul Mantz.

CHAINED (1934) MGM. Produced by Hunt Stromberg. Directed by Clarence Brown. Original story, Edgar Selwyn. Screenplay by John Lee Mahin. Cameraman, George Folsey. Editor, Robert J. Kern. Music, Herbert Stothart. 71 minutes

Chained with Clark Gable, Stuart Erwin and Joan Crawford.

Diana: Joan Crawford, *Mike:* Clark Gable, *Mr. Field:* Otto Kruger, *Johnny:* Stuart Erwin, *Ann:* Una O'Connor, *Mrs. Field:* Marjorie Gateson, *Secretary:* Theresa Maxwell Conover, *Chef:* Adrian Rosley, *Stewart:* Louis Natheaux, *Bartender:* Lee Phelps, *Sailor:* Ward Bond, *Deck Steward:* Ernie Alexander, *Spinsters:* Grace Hayle, Nora Cecil, *Boy Swimmer:* Mickey Rooney, *Hotel Manager:* Paul Porcasi, *Chef on Ranch:* Akim Tamiroff, *Peon:* Chris-Pin Martin, *Cafe Manager:* George Humbert, *Waiter:* Gino Corrado, *Clerk:* Sam Flint, *Butler:* William Stack, *Boy:* Kendall McComas, *Mechanic:* Wade Boteler.

The Champ with Wallace Beery, Ed Brophy, Jackie Cooper and Roscoe Ates.

THE CHAMP (1931) MGM. Directed by King Vidor. Original story by Frances Marion. Scenario and Dialogue, Leonard Praskins. Photography, Gordon Avil. Editor, Hugh Wynn. Scenes filmed in Mexico and at the Caliente race track. Remade as *The Clown* (MGM, 1953) with Red Skelton. 86 minutes

Champ: Wallace Beery, *Dink:* Jackie Cooper, *Linda Carson:* Irene Rich, *Sponge:* Rosco Ates, *Tim:* Edward Brophy, *Tony:* Hale Hamilton, *Jonah:* Jesse Scott, *Mary Lou:* Marcia Mae Jones, *Louie (Bartender):* Lee Phelps, *Manuel:* Frank Hagney.

CHAMPION (1949) UA. Producer, Stanley Kramer. Associate Producer, Robert Stillman. Director, Mark Robson. From the story by Ring Lardner. Screenplay, Carl Foreman. Art Director, Rudolph Sternad. Musical Director, Dimitri Tiomkin. Photography, Frank Planer. Editor, Harry Gerstad. A Screen Plays Corporation Production. Polly Bergen's voice is heard on a juke box. 99 minutes

Midge Kelly: Kirk Douglas, *Grace Diamond:* Marilyn Maxwell, *Connie Kelly:* Arthur Kennedy, *Tommy Haley:* Paul Stewart, *Emma Bryce:* Ruth Roman, *Mrs. Harris:* Lola Albright, *Jerome Harris:* Luis Van Rooten, *Johnny Dunne:* John Day, *Lew Bryce:* Harry Shannon.

Champion with Kirk Douglas and Arthur Kennedy.

The Chapman Report with Glynis Johns and Andrew Duggan.

THE CHAPMAN REPORT (1962) WB. Producer, Richard D. Zanuck. Director, George Cukor. Technicolor. Based on the novel by Irving Wallace. Screenplay, Wyatt Cooper, Don M. Mankiewicz. Adaptation, Grant Stuart, Gene Allen. Music, Leonard Rosenman. Cinematographer, Harold Lipstein. Editor, Robert Simpson. A Darryl F. Zanuck Production. 125 minutes

Paul Radford: Efrem Zimbalist, Jr., *Sarah Garnell:* Shelley Winters, *Kathleen Barclay:* Jane Fonda, *Naomi Shields:* Claire Bloom, *Teresa Harnish:* Glynis Johns, *Fred Linden:* Ray Danton, *Dr. George C. Chapman:* Andrew Duggan, *Geoffrey Harnish:* John Dehner, *Ed Kraski:* Ty Hardin, *Frank Garnell:* Harold J. Stone, *Wash Dillon:* Corey Allen, *Grace Waterton:* Jennifer Howard, *Miss Selby:* Cloris Leachman, *Dr. Jonas:* Henry Daniell, *Ruth Linden:* Hope Cameron, *Cass Kelly:* Evan Thompson, *Ted Dyson:* Jack Cassidy, *Alan Roby:* Roy Roberts, *Boy Barclay:* John Baer, *Water Boy:* Chad Everett, *Simon:* Grady Sutton, *Bardelli:* Alex Viespi, *Musicians:* Jack Littlefield, Ray Foster, *Teenage Girl:* Pamela Austin, *Johnny Dillon:* William Hummer, *Cook:* Fern Barry.

CHARADE (1963) Univ. Producer, Stanley Donen. Associate Producer, James Ware. Director, Stanley Donen. Technicolor. Authors, Peter Stone, Marc Behm. Screenplay, Peter Stone. Art Director, Jean D'Eaubonne. Music, Henry Mancini. "Charade," lyric, Johnny Mercer; music, Henry Mancini. Cinematographer, Charles Lang, Jr., Editor, James Clark. Filmed in Paris, Megcve, the French Alps. 114 minutes

Alexander Dyle, or Adam Canfield, or Peter Joshua, or Bryan Cruikshank: Cary Grant, *Reggie Lampert (Vass):* Audrey Hepburn, *Hamilton*

Charade with Cary Grant and Audrey Hepburn.

Bartholomew: Walter Matthau, *Tex:* James Coburn, *Herman Scobie:* George Kennedy, *Leopold Gideon:* Ned Glass, *Insp. Grandpierre:* Jacques Marin, *Felix:* Paul Bonifas, *Sylvie:* Dominique Minot, *Jean-Louis:* Thomas Chelimsky.

The Charge at Feather River with Henry Kulky, Vera Miles, Lane Chandler, Neville Brand and Guy Madison.

THE CHARGE AT FEATHER RIVER (1953) WB. Producer, David Weisbart. Director, Gordon Douglas. 3-Dimension and Warner-Color. Author, James R. Webb. Screenplay, James R. Webb. Art Director, Stanley Fleischer. Cinematographer, Peverell Marley. Editor, Folmar Blangsted. 96 minutes

Miles Archer: Guy Madison, *Sgt. Baker:* Frank Lovejoy, *Anne McKeever:* Helen Westcott, *Jennie McKeever:* Vera Miles, *Cullen:* Dick Wesson, *Grover Johnson:* Onslow Stevens, *Johnny McKeever:* Ron Hagerthy, *Ryan:* Steve Brodie, *Morgan:* Neville Brand, *Smiley:* Henry Kulky, *Lieutenant Colonel Kilrain:* Fay Roope, *Poinsett:* Lane Chandler, *Conner:* James Brown, *Adams:* Rand Brooks, *Carver:* Ben Corbett, *Dabney:* John Damler, *Curry:* Louis Tomei, *Hudkins:* Carl Andre, *Leech:* Fred Kennedy, *Danowicz:* Dub Taylor, *Wilhelm:* Ralph Brooke, *Griffin:* David Alpert, *Chief Thunder Hawk:* Fred Carson, *Signal Private:* Wayne Taylor, *Sentry:* Richard Bartlett, *Quartermaster Sergeant:* Joe Bassett, *Ordinance Sergeant:* Dennis Dengate, *Mamie:* Vivian Mason, *Officer:* John Pickard.

The Charge of the Light Brigade with Errol Flynn.

THE CHARGE OF THE LIGHT BRIGADE (1936) WB. Produced by Hal B. Wallis. Directed by Michael Jacoby. Assistant Producer, Sam Bischoff. Based on the poem by Alfred Tennyson. Story, Michael Jacoby. Screenplay by Michel Jacoby and Rowland Leigh. Musical Director, Leo F. Forbstein. Music, Max Steiner. Art Director, Jack Hughes. Cameramen, Sol Polito, Fred Jackman. Editor, George Amy. Photographic Effects, Fred Jackman. Technical Advisor, Captain E. Rochfort-John. Tactical and Military Drills, Major Sam Harris. 116 minutes

Captain Geoffrey Vickers: Errol Flynn, *Elsa Campbell:* Olivia De Havilland, *Captain Perry Vickers:* Patric Knowles, *Colonel Campbell:* Donald Crisp, *Sir Charles Macefield:* Henry Stephenson, *Sir Benjamin Warrenton:* Nigel Bruce, *Captain James Randall:* David Niven, *Major Jowett:* G. P. Huntley, Jr., *Lady Octavia Warrenton:* Spring Byington, *Surat Khan:* C. Henry Gordon, *Sir Humphrey Harcourt:* E. E. Clive, *Colonel Woodward:* Lumsden Hare, *Count Igor Volonoff:* Robert Barrat, *Cornet Barclay:* Walter Holbrook, *Cornet Pearson:* Charles Sedgwick, *Subahdar Major Puran Singh:* J. Carrol Naish, *Prema Singh:* Scotty Beckett, *Prema's Mother:* Princess Beigum, *Wazir:* George Regas, *Mrs. Jowett:* Helen Sanborn, *Captain Brown:* Crauford Kent, *Suristani:* George David, *Court Interpreter:* Carlos San Martin, *Orderly:* Jimmy Aubrey, *Major Domo:* Herbert Evans, *Sepoy Chief:* Harry Semels, *Russian General:* Michael Visaroff, *Panjari:* Frank Lackteen, *Panjari:* Martin Garralaga, *Bentham:* Reginald Sheffield, *General Canrobert:* Georges Renevent, *Lord Cardigan:* Charles Croker King, *Lord Raglan:* Brandon Hurst, *Captain:* Wilfred Lucas, *General Dunbar:* Boyd Irwin, *Colonel Coventry:* Gorden Hart, *General O'Neill:* Holmes Herbert.

Charley's Aunt with Kay Francis and Jack Benny.

CHARLEY'S AUNT (1941) 20th. Producer, William Perlberg. Director, Archie Mayo. Based on the play by Brandon Thomas. Screenplay, George Seaton. Music, Alfred Newman. Art Directors, Richard Day, Nathan Juran. Costumes, Travis Banton. Cameraman, Peverell Marley. Editor, Robert Bischoff. Sets, Thomas Little. Other versions: PDC, 1925; Columbia, 1930. Musical version: *Where's Charley?* (Warners, 1952). 81 minutes

Babbs: Jack Benny, *Donna Lucia:* Kay Francis, *Jack Chesney:* James Ellison, *Amy:* Anne Baxter, *Stephen Spettigue:* Edmund Gwenn, *Redcliff:* Reginald Owen, *Sir Francis Chesney:* Laird Cregar, *Kitty Verdun:* Arleen Whelan, *Charley Wyckham:* Richard Haydn, *Brassett:* Ernest Cossart, *Harley Stafford:* Morton Lowry, *Babberly:* Lionel Pape, *Spectators:* Claude Allister, William Austin, *Messenger:* Will Stanton, *Elderly Man:* C. Montague Shaw, *Octogenarian:* Maurice Cass, *Umpire:* Stanley Mann, *Coach:* Brandon Hurst, *Teammates:* Russell Burroughs, Gilchrist Stuart, John Meredith.

Cheaper by the Dozen with Clifton Webb, Myrna Loy, Jimmy Hunt, Jeanne Crain, Betty Lynn and Carole Nugent (second from right).

CHEAPER BY THE DOZEN (1950) 20th. Producer, Lamar Trotti. Director, Walter Lang. Color by Technicolor. Based on the novel by Frank B. Gilbreth, Jr. and Ernestine Gilbreth Carey. Screenplay, Lamar Trotti. Musical Director, Lionel Newman. Art Directors, Lyle Wheeler, Leland Fuller. Photography, Leon Shamroy. Editor, J. Watson Webb, Jr. Sequel was *Belles on Their Toes*, 20th, 1952. 85 minutes

Frank Bunker Gilbreth: Clifton Webb, *Ann Gilbreth:* Jeanne Crain, *Mrs. Lillian Gilbreth:* Myrna Loy, *Libby Lancaster:* Betty Lynn, *Dr. Burton:* Edgar Buchanan, *Ernestine:* Barbara Bates, *Mrs. Mebane:* Mildred Natwick, *Mrs. Monahan:* Sara Allgood, *Fred Gilbreth:* Anthony Sydes, *Jack Gilbreth:* Roddy McCaskill, *Frank Gilbreth, Jr.:* Norman Ollestad, *Martha Gilbreth:* Patti Brady, *Lillie Gilbreth:* Carole Nugent, *William Gilbreth:* Jimmy Hunt, *Dan Gilbreth:* Teddy Driver, *Mary Gilbreth:* Betty Barker, *School Principal:* Evelyn Varden, *Mr. Higgins:* Frank Orth, *Tom Black:* Craig Hill, *Mrs. Benson:* Virginia Brissac, *Jim Bracken:* Walter Baldwin, *Joe Scales:* Bennie Bartlett, *Plumber:* Syd Saylor, *Mailman:* Ken Christy, *Music Teacher:* Mary Field, *Jane, age 1:* Denise Courtemarche, *Jane, age 2:* Tina Thompson, *Messenger Boy:* Vincent Graeff, *Assistant Principal:* Anita Gegna, *Baby Denise:* Judy Ann Whaley.

CHECK AND DOUBLE CHECK (1930) RKO. Directed by Melville Brown. Story, Bert Kalmar and Harry Ruby. Adapted by J. Walter Ruben. Assistant Director, Frederick Tyler. Sound, George E. Ellis. Photography, William Marshall, Songs: "Three Little Words" and "Ring Dem Bells" by Bert Kalmar and Harry Ruby; "Old Man Blues" by Irving Mills and Duke Ellington. Film debuts of radio's Amos 'n' Andy. 71 minutes

Amos: Freeman F. Gosden, *Andy:* Charles V. Correll, *Jean Blair:* Sue Carol, *Richard Williams:* Charles Morton, *Ralph Crawford:* Ralf Harolde, *John Blair:* Edward Martindel, *Mrs. Blair:* Irene Rich, *Elinor Crawford:* Rita La Roy, *Kingfish:* Russell Powell. Duke Ellington and his Orchestra.

Check and Double Check with Freeman F. Gosden and Charles V. Correll.

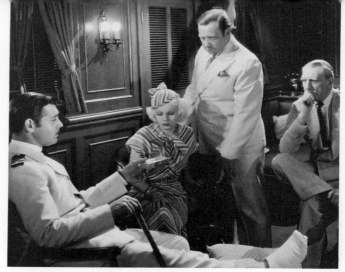

China Seas with Clark Gable, Jean Harlow, Wallace Beery and C. Aubrey Smith.

CHINA SEAS (1935) MGM. Produced by Albert Lewin. Directed by Tay Garnett. Based on the 1931 novel by the late Crosbie Garstin. Screenplay, Jules Furthman and James Keven McGuinness. Photography, Ray June. Editor, William Levanway. Song: "China Seas" by Arthur Freed and Nacio Herb Brown. 89 minutes

Captain Alan Gaskell: Clark Gable, *China Doll (Dolly Portland):* Jean Harlow, *Jamesy MacArdle:* Wallace Beery, *Tom Davids:* Lewis Stone, *Sybil Barclay:* Rosalind Russell, *Dawson:* Dudley Digges, *Sir Guy Wilmerding:* C. Aubrey Smith, *Charlie McCaleb:* Robert Benchley, *Rockwell:* William Henry, *Mrs. Vollberg:* Live Demaigret, *Mrs. Timmons:* Lillian Bond, *Wilbur Timmons:* Edward Brophy, *Yu-Lan:* Soo Yong, *Carol Ann:* Carol Ann Beery, *Romanoff:* Akim Tamiroff, *Ngah:* Ivan Lebedeff, *Isabel McCarthy:* Hattie McDaniel, *Chess Player:* Donald Meek, *Lady:* Emily Fitzroy, *Second Officer Kingston:* Pat Flaherty, *Ship's Officer:* Tom Gubbins, *Steward:* Forrester Harvey, *Purser, Bertie:* Charles Irwin, *Cabin Boy:* Willie Fung, *Police Superintendent:* Ferdinand Munier, *Rickshaw Boy:* Chester Gan, *Pilot:* John Ince.

CHRISTMAS IN CONNECTICUT (1945) WB. Producer, William Jacobs. Director, Peter Godfrey. Author, Aileen Hamilton. Screenplay, Lionel Houser, Adele Commandini. Art Director, Stanley Fleischer. Musical Score, Frederick Hollander. Musical Director, Leo F. Forbstein. Cameraman, Carl Guthrie. Editor, Frank Magee. Song by Jack Scholl and M. K. Jerome: "The Wish That I Wish Tonight." 101 minutes

Christmas in Connecticut with Robert Shayne, Reginald Gardiner, S.Z. Sakall and Barbara Stanwyck.

Elisabeth Lane: Barbara Stanwyck, *Jefferson Jones:* Dennis Morgan, *Alexander Yardley:* Sydney Greenstreet, *John Sloan:* Reginald Gardiner, *Felix Bassenak:* S. Z. Sakall, *Dudley Beecham:* Robert Shayne, *Norah:* Una O'Connor, *Sinkewicz:* Frank Jenks, *Mary Lee:* Joyce Compton, *Judge Crothers:* Dick Elliott, *Nurse Smith:* Betty Alexander, *Postman:* Allen Fox, *Prim Secretary:* Lillian Bronson, *Bartender:* Charles Sherlock, *Sam:* Emmett Smith, *Sleigh Driver:* Arthur Aylesworth, *Mrs. Gerseg:* Jody Gilbert, *Mr. Higgenbottom:* Charles Arnt, *Harper:* Fred Kelsey, *Potter:* Walter Baldwin, *First State Trooper:* Jack Mewar, *Second State Trooper:* John Dehner, *Mrs. Wright:* Marie Blake, *Elkins:* Olaf Hytten.

Cimarron with Richard Dix, Douglas Scott and Irene Dunne.

CIMARRON (1931) RKO. Associate Producer, Louis Sarecky. Directed by Wesley Ruggles. Based on the novel by Edna Ferber. Scenario and Dialogue, Howard Estabrook. Assistant Directors, Doran Cox and Dewey Starkey. Art Director and Costumes, Max Ree. Photography, Edward Cronjager. Editor, William Hamilton. Sound, Clem Portman. Remade by MGM in 1961. 130 minutes

Yancey Cravat: Richard Dix, *Sabra Cravat:* Irene Dunne, *Dixie Lee:* Estelle Taylor, *Felice Venable:* Nance O'Neil, *The Kid:* William Collier, Jr., *Jess Rickey:* Rosco Ates, *Sol Levy:* George E. Stone, *Lon Yountis:* Stanley Fields, *Louie Heffner:* Robert McWade, *Mrs. Tracy Wyatt:* Edna May Oliver, *Mr. Bixley:* Frank Darien, *Isaiah:* Eugene Jackson, *Ruby Big Elk (elder):* Dolores Brown, *Ruby (younger):* Gloria Vonic, *Murch Rankin:* Otto Hoffman, *Grat Gotch:* William Orlamond, *Louis Venable:* Frank Beal, *Donna Cravat (elder):* Nancy Dover, *Donna (younger):* Helen Parrish, *Cim (elder):* Donald Dillaway, *Cim (younger):* Junior Johnson, *Cim (youngest):* Douglas Scott, *Yancey, Jr.:* Reginald Streeter, *Felice, Jr.:* Lois Jane Campbell, *Aunt Cassandra:* Ann Lee, *Sabney Venable:* Tyrone Brereton, *Cousin Bella:* Lillian Lane, *Jouett Goforth:* Henry Roquemore, *Arminta Greenwood:* Nell Craig, *Pat Leary:* Robert McKenzie, *Indian Girl:* Clara Hunt, *Bits:* Bob Kortman, Dennis O'Keefe.

THE CINCINNATI KID (1965) MGM. Producer, Martin Ransohoff. Associate Producer, John Calley. Director, Norman Jewison. Metro-Color. Based on the novel by Richard Jessup. Screenplay, Ring Lardner, Jr., Terry Southern. Art Directors, George W. Davis, Edward Carfagno. Music, Lalo Schifrin. Music composed by Robert Armbruster. Song: "The Cincinnati Kid," lyrics by Dorcas Cochran, sung by Ray Charles. Cinematographer, Philip H. Lathrop. Editor, Hal Ashby. 113 minutes

The Cincinnati Kid: Steve McQueen, *Lancey Howard:* Edward G. Robinson, *Melba:* Ann-Margret, *Shooter:* Karl Malden, *Christian Rudd:* Tuesday Weld, *Lady Fingers:* Joan Blondell, *Slade:* Rip Torn, *Pig:* Jack Weston, *Yeller:* Cab Calloway, *Hoban:* Jeff Corey, *Felix:* Theo Marcuse, *Sokal:* Milton Selzer, *Mr. Rudd:* Karl Swenson, *Cajun:* Emile Genest, *Danny:* Ron Soble, *Mrs. Rudd:* Irene Tedrow, *Mrs. Slade:* Midge Ware, *Dealer:* Dub Taylor, *Mrs. Hoban:* Joyce Perry, *Desk Clerk:* Olan Soule, *Eddie:* Barry O'Hara, *Poker Players:*

The Cincinnati Kid with Steve McQueen and Edward G. Robinson.

Pat McCaffrie, John Hart, *Charlie, Poker Player:* Howard Wendell, *Slade's Girl Friend:* Mimi Dillard, *Danny's Henchman:* Gregg Martell, *Old Men:* Harry Hines, Burt Mustin, William Challee, Charles Wagenheim, *Employee:* Virginia Harrison, *Cajun's Woman:* Breena Howard, *Tillie:* Robert Do Qui.

CITIZEN KANE (1941) RKO. Produced and directed by Orson Welles. A Mercury Theatre Production. Original Screenplay, Herman J. Mankiewicz and Orson Welles. Photography, Gregg Toland. Music composed and conducted by Bernard Herrmann. Art Director, Van Nest Polglase. Associate, Perry Ferguson. Sets, Darrell Silvera. Special Effects, Vernon L. Walker. Costumes, Edward Stevenson. Sound, Bailey Fesler and James G. Stewart. Editor, Robert Wise. Film debuts of Orson Welles, Joseph Cotten, Agnes Moorehead, Ruth Warrick, Paul Stewart, Ray Collins; Dorothy Comingore formerly acted as Linda Winters. 119 minutes

Charles Foster Kane: Orson Welles, *Susan Alexander:* Dorothy Comingore, *Jedediah Leland:* Joseph Cotten, *Bernstein:* Everett Sloane, *Walter Parks Thatcher:* George Coulouris, *James W. Gettys:* Ray Collins, *Emily Norton:* Ruth Warrick, *Herbert Carter:* Erskine Sanford, *Thompson (Narrator):* William Alland, *Mrs. Kane:* Agnes Moorehead, *Hillman:* Richard Baer, *Raymond:* Paul Stewart, *Matiste:* Fortunio Bonanova, *Georgia:* Joan Blair, *Kane at 8:* Buddy Swan, *Kane, Sr.:* Harry Shannon, *Bertha:* Georgia Backus, *Mike:* Al Eben, *Entertainer:* Charles Bennett, *Rawlston:* Philip Van Zandt, *Reporter:*

Citizen Kane with Ray Collins, Dorothy Comingore, Orson Welles and Ruth Warrick.

Milt Kibbee, *Teddy Roosevelt:* Tom Curran, *Kane III:* Sonny Bupp, *Dr. Corey:* Irving Mitchell, *Nurse:* Edith Evanson, *Orchestra Leader:* Arthur Kay, *Chorus Master:* Tudor Williams, *City Editor:* Herbert Corthell, *Reporters:* Alan Ladd, Louise Currie, Eddie Coke, Walter Sande, Arthur O'Connell, Richard Wilson, Katherine Trosper, *Smather:* Benny Rubin, ENQUIRER *Reporter:* Edmund Cobb, *Ethel:* Frances Neal, *Photographer:* Robert Dudley, *Miss Townsend:* Ellen Lowe, *Headwaiter:* Gus Schilling, *Gino, Waiter:* Gino Corrado.

Clash by Night with Paul Douglas, Barbara Stanwyck and Robert Ryan.

City Streets with Gary Cooper and Sylvia Sidney.

CITY STREETS (1931) Par. Directed by Rouben Mamoulian. Story, Dashiell Hammett. Screenplay, Max Marcin and Oliver H. P. Garrett. Photography, Lee Garmes. Sound, J. A. Goodrich and M. M. Paggi. Terry Carroll is Nancy's sister. Clara Bow was replaced by Sylvia Sidney as Nan. 82 minutes

The Kid: Gary Cooper, *Nan:* Sylvia Sidney, *Big Fellow Maskal:* Paul Lukas, *McCoy:* William (Stage) Boyd, *Pop Cooley:* Guy Kibbee, *Blackie:* Stanley Fields, *Aggie:* Wynne Gibson, *Pansy:* Betty Sinclair, *Woman:* Barbara Leonard, *Esther March:* Terry Carroll, *Inspector:* Robert E. Homans, *Detective:* Willard Robertson, *Cop:* Allan Cavan, *Baldy, a Henchman:* Bert Hanlon, *Man Who's Stabbed with a Fork:* Matty Kemp, *Shooting Gallery Patrons:* Edward Le Saint, Hal Price, *Killer at Prison:* Ethan Laidlaw, *Machine-Gunner:* George Regas, *Servant:* Bob Kortman, *Henchman:* Leo Willis, *Dance Extra:* Bill Elliott.

CLASH BY NIGHT (1952) RKO. Producer, Harriet Parsons. Director, Fritz Lang. Based on the play by Clifford Odets. Screenplay, Alfred Hayes. Art Directors: Albert S. D'Agostino, Carroll Clark. Music Director, C. Bakaleinikoff. Cinematographer, Nicholas Musuraca. Editor, George J. Amy. Song by Dick Gasparre, Jack Baker and George Fragos: "I Hear a Rhapsody." A Wald-Krasna Production. 105 minutes

Mae: Barbara Stanwick, *Jerry:* Paul Douglas, *Earl:* Robert Ryan, *Peggy:* Marilyn Monroe, *Uncle Vince:* J. Carrol Naish, *Joe Doyle:* Keith Andes, *Papa:* Silvio Minciotti, *Twin Baby:* Diane Stewart,

Twin Baby: Deborah Stewart, *Sad-eyed Waiter:* Julius Tannen, *Bartender:* Bert Stevans, *Waiter:* William Bailey, *Bartender:* Mario Siletti, *Customer:* Bill Slack, *Customer:* Art Dupuis, *Art:* Frank Kreig, *Fisherman at Pier:* Tony Dante.

CLAUDIA (1943) 20th. Producer, William Perlberg. Director, Edmund Goulding. Based on the play by Rose Franken. Screenplay, Morrie Ryskind. Musical Score, Alfred Newman. Art Directors, James Basevi, Albert Hogsett. Cameraman, Leon Shamroy. Special Effects, Fred Sersen. Editor, Robert Simpson. Song by Alfred Newman and Charles Henderson: "From Yesterday to Tomorrow." Film debut of Dorothy McGuire, 24, repeating her stage role. 91 minutes

Claudia Naughton: Dorothy McGuire, *David Naughton:* Robert Young, *Mrs. Brown:* Ina Claire, *Jerry Seymour:* Reginald Gardiner, *Madame Daruschka:* Olga Baclanova, *Julia:* Jean Howard, *Fritz:* Frank Tweddell, *Bertha:* Elsa Janssen, *Carl:* John Royce.

Claudia with Robert Young, Ina Claire and Dorothy McGuire.

CLEOPATRA (1934) Par. Produced and directed by Cecil B. De Mille, Screenplay, Waldemar Young and Vincent Lawrence. Adaptation. Bartlett Cormack. Music, Rudolph Kopp. Photography, Victor Milner. U. S. film debut of Henry Wilcoxon. Other versions of *Cleopatra:* Helen Gardner Pictures, 1912; Fox, 1917; MGM, 1928 short; 20th Century-Fox, 1963. 101 minutes

Cleopatra: Claudette Colbert, *Julius Caesar:* Warren William, *Marc Antony:* Henry Wilcoxon, *Calpurnia:* Gertrude Michael, *Herod:* Joseph Schildkraut, *Octavian:* Ian Keith, *Enobarbus:* C. Aubrey Smith, *Cassius:* Ian Maclaren, *Brutus:* Arthur Hohl, *Pothinos:* Leonard Mudie, *Apollodorus:* Irving Pichel, *Octavia:* Claudia Dold, *Charmian:* Eleanor Phelps, *Drussus:* John Rutherford, *Iras:* Grace Durkin, *Achillas:* Robert Warwick, *Casca:* Edwin Maxwell, *Cicero:* Charles Morris, *The Soothsayer:* Harry Beresford, *Slave Girl:* Olga Celeste, *Leopard:* Ecki, *Glabrio:* Ferdinand Gottschalk, *Senator:* William Farnum, *Flora:* Florence Roberts, *Scribes:* Kenneth Gibson, Wedgwood Nowell, *Romans:* John Peter Richmond (John Carradine),

Cleopatra with Henry Wilcoxon and Claudette Colbert.

The Clock with Robert Walker and Judy Garland.

Jane Regan, Celia Rylan, Robert Manning, *Party Guest:* Lionel Belmore, *Egyptian Messenger:* Dick Alexander, *Romans Greeting Antony:* Jack Mulhall, Wilfred Lucas, *Onlooker at Procession:* Hal Price, *Murderer:* Edgar Dearing.

CLEOPATRA (1963) 20th. Producer, Walter Wanger. Director, Joseph L. Mankiewicz. Based upon histories by Plutarch, Suetonius, Appian, other ancient sources and *The Life and Times of Cleopatra* by C. M. Franzero. Screenplay, Joseph L. Mankiewicz, Ranald Mac-Dougall, Sidney Buchman. Art Directors, John De Cuir, Jack Martin Smith, Hilyard Brown, Herman Blumenthal, Elven Webb, Maurice Pelling, Boris Juraga. Music composed and conducted by Alex North. Associate Music Conductor, Lionel Newman. Cinematographer, Leon Shamroy. Special Photographic Effects, L. B. Abbott, Emil Kosa, Jr. Editor, Dorothy Spencer. 243 minutes

Cleopatra: Elizabeth Taylor, *Mark Antony:* Richard Burton, *Julius Caesar:* Rex Harrison, *High Priestess:* Pamela Brown, *Flavius:* George Cole, *Sosigenes:* Hume Cronyn, *Apollodorus:* Cesare Danova, *Brutus:* Kenneth Haigh, *Agrippa:* Andrew Keir, *Rufio:* Martin Landau, *Octavio:* Roddy McDowall, *Germanicus:* Robert Stephens, *Eiras:* Francesca Annis, *Pothinus:* Gregoire Aslan, *Ramos:* Martin Benson, *Theodotus:* Herbert Berghof, *Phoebus:* John Cairney, *Lotus:* Jacqui Chan, *Charmian:* Isabelle Cooley, *Achillas:* John Doucette, *Canidius:* Andrew Faulds, *Metullus Cimber:* Michael Gwynne, *Cicero:* Michael Hordern, *Cassius:* John Hoyt, *Euphranor:* Marne Maitland, *Casca:* Carroll O'Connor, *Ptolemy:* Richard O'Sullivan, *Calpurnia:* Gwen Watford, *Decimus:* Douglas Wilmer, *Titus:* Finlay Currie, *Queen at Tarsus:* Marina Berti, *High Priest:* John Carlson, *Caesarion at 4:* Loris Loddy, *Caesarion at 7:* Del Russell, *Caesarion at 12:* Kenneth Nash, *Octavia:* Jean Marsh, *Marcellus:* Gin Mart, *Mithridates:* Furio Meniconi, *Vallus:* John Valva, *Archesilaus:* Laurence Naismith, *First Officer:* John Alderson, *Second Officer:* Peter Forster.

Cleopatra with Rex Harrison and Elizabeth Taylor.

THE CLOCK (1945) MGM. Producer, Arthur Freed. Director, Vincente Minnelli. Based on a story by Paul and Pauline Gallico. Screenplay, Robert Nathan, Joseph Schrank. Score, George Bassman. Art Directors, Cedric Gibbons, William Ferrari. Cameraman, George Folsey. Special Effects, A. Arnold Gillespie. Editor, George White. 90 minutes

Alice Mayberry: Judy Garland, *Corporal Joe Allen:* Robert Walker, *Al Henry:* James Gleason, *The Drunk:* Keenan Wynn, *Bill:* Marshall Thompson, *Mrs. Al Henry:* Lucile Gleason, *Helen:* Ruth Brady, *Michael Henry:* Chester Clute, *Friendly Man:* Dick Elliott, *Official:* Robert E. Homans, *Blood Tester:* Arthur Space, *Cop:* Ray Teal, *Bartender:* Paul E. Burns, *Extra:* Major Sam Harris.

THE COCK-EYED WORLD (1929) Fox. Directed by Raoul Walsh. Story, Laurence Stallings, Maxwell Anderson, Wilson Mizner, Tom Barry. Dialogue, William K. Wells. Photography, Arthur Edeson. Assistant Director, Archie Buchanan. Technical Advisers, Captain Ross Adams and Lt. Commander Cheadle of U. S. S. *Henderson;* Colonel Rhea, Marine Commander at Mare Island; Captain Kearney, Mare Island Commandant. Filmed at Mare Island Navy Yard, Vallejo, Cal.: U. S. Marine Base at San Diego; aboard U. S. S. *Henderson* in San Francisco Bay; Fox Hollywood Studios and Fox-Movietone City, Westwood Hills, Cal. Songs by Con Conrad, Sidney Mitchell, and Archie Gottler: "So Long," "Elenita," and "So Dear to Me." Scenario, Raoul Walsh. Chief Sound Man, Edmund H. Hansen. Titles (silent version), Wilbur Morse Jr. Editor, Jack Dennis. Sequel to *What Price Glory* (Fox, 1927). 115 minutes

Top Sergeant Flagg: Victor McLaglen, *Sergeant Harry Quirt:* Edmund Lowe, *Mariana Elenita:* Lily Damita, *Olga:* Lelia Karnelly, *Olson:*

The Cock-eyed World with Victor McLaglen and Edmund Lowe.

El Brendel, *Connors:* Bobby Burns, *Fanny:* Jean Bary, *Brownie:* Joe Brown, *Buckley:* Stuart Erwin, *Sanovich:* Ivan Linow, *Innkeeper:* Solidad Jiminez, *O'Sullivan:* Albert "Curley" Dresden, *Jacobs:* Joe Rochay, *Katinka:* Jeanette Dagna, *Scout:* Warren Hymer, *Conductor:* Con Conrad, *Bit:* William K. Wells, *Brawlers:* "Sugar" Willie Keeler, Joe Herrick, Leo Houck, Charlie Sullivan. Navy Bands from Mare Island and San Diego Marine Base. Mexican Marimba Band of Agua Caliente. Jose Arias Spanish String Band Serenaders. Kamerko Balalaika Orchestra.

The Collector with Samantha Eggar and Terence Stamp.

THE COLLECTOR (1965) Col. Producers, Jud Kinberg, John Kohn. Director, William Wyler. Based on the novel by John Fowles. Screenplay, Stanley Mann, John Kohn. Art Director, John Stoll. Music, Maurice Jarre. Cinematographers, Robert L. Surtees, Robert Krasker. Editors, Robert Swink, David Hawkins. 119 minutes

Freddie Clegg: Terence Stamp, *Miranda Grey:* Samantha Eggar, *Aunt Annie:* Mona Washbourne, *Neighbor:* Maurice Dallimore, *Crutchley:* William Beckley, *Clerk:* Gordon Barclay, *Clerk:* David Haviland.

COLLEGE HOLIDAY (1936) Par. Produced by Harlan Thompson. Directed by Frank Tuttle. Screenplay, J. P. McEvoy, Harlan Ware, Jay Gorney, Henry Myers. Cameraman, Theodor Sparkuhl. Costumes, Edith Head. Dances, LeRoy Prinz. Songs: "A Rhyme For Love," "I Adore You," "So What?" by Leo Robin and Ralph Rainger; "The Sweetheart Waltz," "Who's That Knocking at My Heart" by Ralph Freed and Burton Lane; "Love in Bloom" (from *She Loves Me Not*, 1934) by Leo Robin and Ralph Rainger. 87 minutes

College Holiday with Mary Boland, Leif Erikson and Marsha Hunt.

J. Davis Bowster: Jack Benny, *George Hymen and (Gracie) Calliope Dove:* George Burns and Gracie Allen, *Carola Gaye:* Mary Boland, *Daisy Schloggenheimer:* Martha Raye, *Professor Hercules Dove:* Etienne Girardot, *Sylvia Smith:* Marsha Hunt, *Dick Winters:* Leif Erikson, *Eleanore Wayne:* Eleanore Whitney, *Johnny Jones:* Johnny Downs, *Felice L'Hommedieu:* Olympe Bradna, *Barry Taylor:* Louis DaPron, *Stagehand:* Ben Blue, *Sheriff John J. Trimble:* Jed Prouty, *Judge Bent:* Richard Carle, *Mrs. Schloggenheimer:* Margaret Seddon, *Wisconsin:* Nick Lukats, *Lafayette:* Spec O'Donnell, *Colgate:* Jack Chapin, The California Collegians, *Rahma:* Lal Chand Mehra, *Miss Elkins:* Nora Cecil, *Students:* Kay Griffith, Priscilla Lawson, Terry Ray (Ellen Drew), Gail Sheridan, *Porter:* Fred (Snowflake) Toones, *Sour Puss:* Barlowe Borland, *Ticket Clerk:* Charlie Arnt, *Doctor:* Edward J. LeSaint, *Mr. Smith:* Harry Hayden, *Minstrel:* Buddy Messinger, *Dancer:* Eddie Foy.

Colt .45 with Randolph Scott, Chief Thundercloud and Ruth Roman.

COLT .45 (1950) WB. Producer, Saul Elkins. Director, Edward L. Marin. Author-Screenplay, Thomas Blackburn. Art Director, Douglas Bacon. Music, William Lava. Photography, Wilfred M. Cline. Editor, Frank Magee. Later the basis for a Warner Brothers TV series. 74 minutes

Steve Farrell: Randolph Scott, *Beth Donovan:* Ruth Roman, *Jason Brett:* Zachary Scott, *Paul Donovan:* Lloyd Bridges, *Sheriff Harris:* Alan Hale, *Miller:* Ian MacDonald, *Walking Bear:* Chief Thundercloud, *Judge Tucker:* Lute Crockett, *Carl:* Walter Coy, *Redrock Sheriff:* Charles Evans, *Driver:* Stanley Andrews, *Guard:* Buddy Roosevelt, *Driver:* Hal Taliaferro, *First Bystander:* Art Miles, *Second Bystander:* Barry Reagan, *Squaw:* Aurora Navarro, *Townsmen:* Paul Newland, Franklyn Farnum, Ed Peil, Sr., *Posseman:* Jack Watt, *Henchmen:* Ben Corbett, Kansas Moehring.

Come and Get It with Walter Brennan, Edward Arnold, Mady Christians and Frances Farmer.

COME AND GET IT (1936) UA. A Samuel Goldwyn Production. Produced by Merritt Hulburd. Directed by Howard Hawks and William Wyler. Logging scenes by Richard Rosson. From Edna Ferber's novel. Adapted by Jules Furthman and Jane Murfin. Editor, Edward Curtiss. Camera, Gregg Toland and Rudolph Mate. Film debuts of Robert Lowery and tennis player Frank Shields. Reissued as *Roaring Timber*. 99 minutes

Barney Glasgow: Edward Arnold, *Richard Glasgow:* Joel McCrea, *Lotta Morgan/Lotta Bostrom:* Frances Farmer, *Swan Bostrom:* Walter Brennan, *Evvie Glasgow:* Andrea Leeds, *Tony Schwerke:* Frank Shields, *Karie:* Mady Christians, *Emma Louise Glasgow:* Mary Nash, *Gunnar Gallagher:* Clem Bevans, *Sid Le Maire:* Edwin Maxwell, *Josie:* Cecil Cunningham, *Gubbins:* Harry Bradley, *Steward:* Rollo Lloyd, *Hewitt:* Charles Halton, *Chore Boy:* Phillip Cooper, *Goodnow:* Al K. Hall, *Young Man:* Robert Lowery.

Come Back, *Little Sheba* with Burt Lancaster and Shirley Booth.

COME BACK, LITTLE SHEBA (1952) Par. Producer, Hal B. Wallis. Director, Daniel Mann. Based on the play by William Inge. Screenplay, Ketti Frings. Art Directors, Hal Pereira, Henry Bumstead. Sets, Sam Comer, Russ Dowd. Sound, Walter Oberst, Don McKay. Musical Score, Franz Waxman. Cinematographer, James Wong Howe. Editor, Warren Low. Film debut of Shirley Booth. 99 minutes

Doc Delaney: Burt Lancaster, *Lola Delaney:* Shirley Booth, *Marie Loring:* Terry Moore, *Turk Fisher:* Richard Jaeckel, *Ed Anderson:* Philip Ober, *Elmo Huston:* Edwin Max, *Mrs. Coffman:* Lisa Golm, *Bruce:* Walter Kelley, *Postman:* Paul McVey, *Milkman:* Peter Leeds, *Mr. Cruthers:* Anthony Jochim, *Pearl Stinson:* Kitty McHugh, *Parent: Henrietta:* Virginia Mullen, *Blonde:* Virginia Hall, *Judy Coffman:* Beverly Mook, *Interne:* William Haade.

COME BLOW YOUR HORN (1963) Par. Executive Producer, Howard W. Koch. Producers, Norman Lea, Bud Yorkin. Director, Bud Yorkin. Panavision, Technicolor. From the play by Neil Simon.

Come Blow Your Horn with Frank Sinatra and Tony Bill.

Screenplay, Norman Lear. Art Directors, Hal Pereira, Roland Anderson. Music, Nelson Riddle. "Come Blow Your Horn": lyrics, Sammy Cahn, music, James Van Heusen, orchestration, Gil Grau. Cinematographer, William H. Daniels. Special Photographic Effects, Paul K. Lerpae. Editor, Frank P. Keller. An Essex-Tandem Production. Film debut of Tony Bill. 112 minutes

Alan: Frank Sinatra, *Father:* Lee J. Cobb, *Mother:* Molly Picon, *Connie:* Barbara Rush, *Peggy:* Jill St. John, *Buddy:* Tony Bill, *Mr. Eckman:* Dan Blocker, *Mrs. Eckman:* Phyllis McGuire, *Waiter:* Herbie Faye, *Manager:* Grady Sutton, *Elevator Boy:* Eddie Quillan, *Rudy, the Barber:* Romo Vincent, *Hansom Cab Driver:* George Davis, *Max:* Vinnie De Carlo, *Manicurist:* Charlotte Fletcher, *Desk Clerk:* Jack Nestle, *William (Dry Cleaner):* Warren Cathcart, *Snow Eskanazi:* Joyce Nizzari, *Eunice:* Carole Wells, *Man:* George Sawaya, *Man:* Frank Hagney, *Tailor:* Phil Arnold, *Shoe Salesman:* James Cavanaugh, *Cab Driver:* John Indrisano, *Wino:* Dean Martin.

Come September with Rock Hudson and Walter Slezak.

COME SEPTEMBER (1961) Univ. Producer, Robert Arthur. Associate Producer, Henry Wilson. Director, Robert Mulligan. Technicolor. Screenplay, Stanley Shapiro, Maurice Richlin. Art Director, Henry Bumstead. Music Supervision, Joseph Gershenson. Music, Hans J. Salter. Songs: "Multiplication," words and music by Bobby Darin; "Come September," music by Bobby Darin. Cinematographer, William Daniels. Editor, Russell F. Schoengarth. Filmed in Italy. 112 minutes

Robert Talbot: Rock Hudson, *Lisa:* Gina Lollobrigida, *Sandy:* Sandra Dee, *Tony:* Bobby Darin, *Maurice:* Walter Slezak, *Margaret:* Brenda De Banzie, *Spencer:* Ronald Howard, *Anna:* Rosanna Rory, *Beagle:* Joel Grey, *Sparrow:* Ronnie Haran, *Larry:* Chris Seitz, *Julia:* Cindy Conroy, *Linda:* Joan Freeman, *Patricia:* Nancy Anderson, *Ron:* Michael Eden, *Carol:* Claudia Brack, *Marie, Maid:* Anna Maestri, *Teresa, Maid:* Stella Vitelleschi, *Melina, Maid:* Melina Vukotic, *Warren:* Charles Fawcett, *Douglas:* John Stacy, *Claire:* Katherine Guildford, *Lisa's Maid:* Edy Nogara, *Seamstress:* Liliana Celli, *Robert's Secretary:* Franco Tensi, *Elena:* Betty Foa, *Mother Superior:* Liliana Del Balzo, *Katherine:* Helen Stirling.

COME TO THE STABLE (1949) 20th. Producer, Samuel G. Engel. Director, Henry Koster. Based on a story by Clare Booth Luce. Screenplay, Oscar Millard, Sally Benson. Musical Director, Lionel Newman. Art Directors, Lyle Wheeler, Joseph C. Wright. Photography, Joseph La Shelle. Editor, William Reynolds. Songs: "My Bolero" by James Kennedy and Nat Simon; "Through a Long and Sleepless Night" by Mack Gordon and Alfred Newman. 94 minutes

Sister Margaret: Loretta Young, *Sister Scholastica:* Celeste Holm, *Robert Mason:* Hugh Marlowe, *Miss Potts:* Elsa Lanchester, *Luigi Rossi:* Thomas Gomez, *Kitty:* Dorothy Patrick, *Bishop:* Basil Ruysdael, *Anthony James:* Dooley Wilson, *Monsignor:* Regis Toomey, *Father Barraud:* Henri Letondal, *Jarman:* Walter Baldwin, *Heavy Man:*

Come to the Stable with Celeste Holm and Loretta Young.

Mike Mazurki, *Mr. Thompson:* Tim Huntley, *Mrs. Thompson:* Virginia Keiley, *Mr. Newman:* Louis Jean Heydt, *Nuns:* Pati Behrs, Nan Boardman, Louise Colombet, Georgette Duane, Yvette Reynard, Loulette Sablon, *Mr. Matthews:* Ian MacDonald, *Mrs. Matthews:* Jean Prescott, *Willie:* Gordon Gebert, *Johnnie:* Gary Pagett, *Station Master:* Nolan Leary, *Sheldon:* Wallace Brown, *George:* Danny Jackson, *Whitey:* Edwin Max, *Policeman:* Russ Clark, *Policeman:* Robert Foulk, *Manicurist:* Marion Martin.

COMMAND DECISION (1948) MGM. Producer, Sidney Franklin. Director, Sam Wood. Based on the play by William Wister Haines. Screenplay, William R. Laidlaw, George Froeschel. Art Directors, Cedric Gibbons, Urie McCleary. Music Score, Miklos Rozsa. Photography, Harold Rosson. Editor, Harold F. Kress. 112 minutes

Brigadier General K.C. "Casey" Dennis: Clark Gable, *Major General Roland Goodlow Kane:* Walter Pidgeon, *Technical Sergeant Immanuel T. Evans:* Van Johnson, *Brigadier General Clifton I. Garnet:* Brian Donlevy, *Colonel Edward Rayton Martin:* John Hodiak, *Elmer Brockhurst:* Charles Bickford, *Congressman Arthur Malcolm:* Edward Arnold, *Captain George Washington Bellpepper Lee:* Marshall Thompson, *Major George Rockton:* Richard Quine, *Lieutenant Ansel Goldberg:* Cameron Mitchell, *Major Homer V. Prescott:* Clinton Sundberg, *Major Desmond Lansing:* Ray Collins, *Colonel Earnest Haley:* Warner Anderson, *Major Belding Davis:* John McIntire, *Captain Incius Malcolm Jenks:* Michael Steele, *Lieutenant Colonel Virgil Jackson:* Mack Williams, *Congressman Stone:* Moroni Olsen, *James Carwood:* John Ridgely, *Congressman Watson:* Edward Earle, *Major Garrett Davenport:* James Millican, *Parker, the Chauffeur:* William Leicester (William Lester), *Congressmen:* Henry Hall, Sam Flint, *R.A.F. Officer:* Martin Lamont, *Chairman:* Holmes Herbert, *Jeep Driver:* William "Bill" Phillips, *Sergeant:* Gregg Barton, *Sergeant Cahill:* Alvin Hammer, *Command Officer:* Don Haggerty, *Operations Officer:* Bruce Cowling, *Loudspeaker Voice:* Barry Nelson, *G. I. Waiter:* George Offerman, Jr., *Officer:* John James, *Command Sgt.:* Pete Martin.

Command Decision with Clark Gable and John Hodiak.

Commandos Strike at Dawn with Paul Muni and Robert Coote.

COMMANDOS STRIKE AT DAWN (1942) Col. Produced by Lester Cowan. Directed by John Farrow. Based on the *Cosmopolitan* magazine story by C. S. Forester. Screenplay, Irwin Shaw. Art Direction, Edward Jewell. Music Score, Louis Gruenberg. Music Director, M. W. Stoloff. Photography, William C. Mellor. Sound, John Goodrich. Editor, Anne Bauchens. Songs: "Commandos March" by Ann Ronell and Louis Gruenberg; "Out to Pick the Berries" by Ann Ronell. 98 minutes

Erik Toresen: Paul Muni, *Judith Bowen:* Anna Lee, *Mrs. Bergesen:* Lillian Gish, *Admiral Bowen:* Sir Cedric Hardwicke, *Robert Bowen:* Robert Coote, *Bergesen:* Ray Collins, *Hilma Arnesen:* Rosemary De Camp, *Gunner Korstad:* Richard Derr, *German Captain:* Alexander Knox, *Pastor:* Rod Cameron, *Lars Arnesen:* Louis Jean Heydt, *Anna Korstad:* Elizabeth Fraser, *Johan Garmo:* Erville Alderson, *Schoolteacher:* George MacCready, *Mrs. Olav:* Barbara Everest, *German Colonel:* Arthur Margetson, *Solveig Toresen:* Ann Carter, *Mrs. Korstad:* Elsa Janssen, *Mr. Korstad:* Ferdinand Munier, *Alfred Korstad:* John Arthur Stockton, *Young Soldier:* Lloyd Bridges, *Otto:* Walter Sande, *Thirsty Soldier:* Philip Van Zandt.

COMPULSION (1959) 20th. Producer, Richard D. Zanuck. Director, Richard Fleischer. Screenplay by Richard Murphy. Based on the novel and play by Meyer Levin. Music by Lionel Newman. Wardrobe, Charles LeMaire. Assistant Director, Ben Kadish. Art Directors, Lyle R. Wheeler, Mark-Lee Kirk. Orchestration, Earle Hagen. Cinematographer, William C. Mellor. Editor, William Reynolds. A Darryl F. Zanuck Production in CinemaScope and High Fidelity Stereophonic Sound. Straus and Steiner are based on the real-life Leopold and Loeb, who murdered young Bobby Franks in Chicago in 1924 and were defended by Clarence Darrow. Dean Stockwell repeats his role from the 1957 play. 103 minutes

Compulsion with Dean Stockwell, Bradford Dillman and Orson Welles.

Jonathan Wilk: Orson Welles, *Ruth Evans:* Diane Varsi, *Judd Steiner:* Dean Stockwell, *Artie Straus:* Bradford Dillman, *D. A. Horn:* E. G. Marshall, *Sid Brooks:* Martin Milner, *Max Steiner:* Richard Anderson, *Lieutenant Johnson:* Robert Simon, *Tom Daly:* Edward Binns, *Mr. Straus:* Robert Burton, *Mrs. Straus:* Louise Lorimer, *Mr. Steiner:* Wilton Graff, *Padua:* Gavin MacLeod, *Benson:* Terry Becker, *Edgar Llewellyn:* Russ Bender, *Emma:* Gerry Lock, *Detective Davis:* Harry Carter, *Detective Brown:* Simon Scott, *Judge:* Voltaire Perkins, *Albert:* Peter Brocco, *Coroner:* Jack Lomas, *Jonas Kessler:* Wendell Holmes, *Waiter:* Henry Kulky, *Doctor:* Dayton Lummis.

Coney Island with Betty Grable.

CONEY ISLAND (1943) 20th. Producer, William Perlberg. Director, Walter Lang. Color by Technicolor. Screenplay, George Seaton. Dance Director, Hermes Pan. Musical Director, Alfred Newman. Art Directors, Richard Day, Joseph C. Wright. Cameraman, Ernest Palmer. Editor, Robert Simpson. Songs by Leo Robin and Ralph Rainger: "Take It From There," "Beautiful Coney Island," "Miss Lulu From Louisville," "Get the Money," "There's Danger in a Dance" and "Old Demon Rum." Technicolor Director, Natalie Kalmus. Associate, Henri Jaffa. Remade by 20th with Grable as *Wabash Avenue* (1950). 96 minutes

Kate Farley: Betty Grable, *Eddie Johnson:* George Montgomery, *Joe Rocco:* Cesar Romero, *Finnegan:* Charles Winninger, *Frankie:* Phil Silvers, *Hammerstein:* Matt Briggs, *Louie:* Paul Hurst, *Bartender:* Frank Orth, *Dolly:* Phyllis Kennedy, *Dancer:* Carmen D'Antonio, *Carter:* Andrew Tombes, *Cashier:* Hal K. Dawson, *Singing Waiter:* Bud Williams, *Man:* Alec Craig, *Policeman:* Ed McNamara, *Policeman:* William Halligan, *Headwaiter:* Alphonse Martell, *Fitch:* Tom Dugan, *Stiltwalker:* Harold DeGarro, *Man Outside Harem:* Dewey Robinson, *Maid:* Libby Taylor, *Bartender:* Bud Jamison, *Girl Friends:* Trudy Marshall, Clairo James, *Quartette ("Irish" Number):* Delos Jewkes, Harry Masters, Frank Orth, Joe Niemeyer, *Quartette (Singing Waiters):* Tene Ramey, Gus Reed, Delos Jewkos, George Gramlich, *Horse Routine:* Harry Maestrs, George Boyeo.

CONFESSIONS OF A NAZI SPY (1939) WB. Directed by Anatole Litvak. Screenplay, Milton Krims and John Wexley. Based on materials gathered by Leon G. Turrou, former FBI agent. Camera, Sol Polito. 102 minutes

Ed Renard: Edward G. Robinson, *Schneider:* Francis Lederer, *Schlager:* George Sanders, *Dr. Kassel:* Paul Lukas, *D. A. Kellogg:* Henry O'Neill, *Erika Wolff:* Lya Lys, *Mrs. Schneider:* Grace Stafford, *Scotland Yard Man:* James Stephenson, *Krogman:* Sig Rumann, *Phillips:* Fred Tozere, *Hilda:* Dorothy Tree, *Mrs. Kassel:* Celia Sibelius, *Renz:* Joe Sawyer, *Hintze:* Lionel Royce, *Wildebrandt:* Hans von Twardowsky, *Helldorf:* Henry Victor, *Captain Richter:* Frederick Vogeding, *Klauber:* George Rosener, *Straubel:* Robert Davis, *Westphal:* John Voigt, *Gruetz-*

Confessions of a Nazi Spy with Edward G. Robinson and Francis Lederer.

wald: Willy Kaufman, *Captain Von Eichen:* William Vaughn (Von Brincken), *McDonald:* Jack Mower, *Harrison:* Robert Emmett Keane, *Mrs. MacLaughlin:* Eily Malyon, *Staunton:* Frank Mayo, *Postman:* Alec Craig, *Kassel's Nurse:* Jean Brook, *Kranz:* Lucien Prival, *A Man:* Niccolai Yoshkin, *Anna:* Bodil Rosing, *Young:* Charles Sherlock, *U.S. District Court Judge:* Frederick Burton, *Narrator:* John Deering, *American Legionnaire:* Ward Bond, *Goebbels:* Martin Kosleck.

A CONNECTICUT YANKEE (1931) Fox. Directed by David Butler. Based on Mark Twain's story *A Connecticut Yankee at King Arthur's Court.* Adaptation and Dialogue, William Conselman. Photography, Ernest Palmer. Editor, Irene Morra. Sound, Joseph E. Aiken. Other versions of *A Connecticut Yankee at King Arthur's Court:* Fox, 1921; Paramount, 1949. 96 minutes

Hank (Sir Boss): Will Rogers, *Alisande:* Maureen O'Sullivan, *Queen Morgan Le Fay:* Myrna Loy, *Clarence:* Frank Albertson, *King Arthur:* William Farnum, *Merlin:* Mitchell Harris, *Sagramor:* Brandon Hurst.

A Connecticut Yankee with Will Rogers and Myrna Loy.

The Conqueror with John Wayne and Susan Hayward.

THE CONQUEROR (1956) RKO. Produced and directed by Dick Powell. Technicolor and CinemaScope. Screenplay, Oscar Millard. Music, Victor Young. Music Director, Constantin Bakaleinikoff. Art Directors, Albert D'Agostino and Carroll Clark. Photography, Joseph La Shelle, Leo Tover, Harry J. Wild, William Snyder. Editor, Stuart Gilmore. Associate Editors, Robert Ford and Kennie Marstella. Sound, Bernard Freericks and Terry Kellum. A Howard Hughes Presentation. Costumes, Michael Woulfe and Yvonne Wood. Assistant Director, Edward Killy. Choreography, Robert Sidney. Associate Producer, Richard Sokolove. 111 minutes

Temujin: John Wayne, *Bortai:* Susan Hayward, *Jamuga:* Pedro Armendariz, *Hunlun:* Agnes Moorehead, *Wang Khan:* Thomas Gomez, *Shaman:* John Hoyt, *Kasar:* William Conrad, *Kumlek:* Ted de Corsia, *Targutai:* Leslie Bradley, *Chepei:* Lee Van Cleef, *Bogurchi:* Peter Mamakos, *Tartar Captain:* Leo Gordon, *Captain of Wang's Guard:* Richard Loo, *Guard:* Ray Spiker, *Solo Dancer:* Sylvia Lewis, *Girl in Bath:* Jarma Lewis, *Girl in Bath:* Pat McMahon, *Sibilant Sam:* George E. Stone, *Honest John:* Phil Arnold, *Scribe:* Torben Meyer, *Wang Khan's Wife:* Pat Lawler, *Wang Khan's Wife:* Pat Tiernan, *Drummer Boy:* John George, *Mongol:* Weaver Levy, *First Chieftain:* Michael Granger, *Second Chieftain:* Fred Aldrich, *Third Chieftain:* Paul Hoffman, *Fourth Chieftain:* Lane Bradford, *Merkit Captain:* Carl Vernell, *Subaya:* Fred Graham, *Jalair:* Gregg Barton, *Sorgan:* Ken Terrell, *Hochin:* Jeanne Gerson, *Mongolian Warriors:* Chivwit Indian tribe.

COOL HAND LUKE (1967) WB. Produced by Gordon Carroll. Directed by Stuart Rosenberg. Panavision and Technicolor. A Jalem Production. Based on the novel by Donn Pearce. Screenplay, Donn Pearce and Frank R. Pierson. Music, Lalo Schifrin. Assistant Director, Hank Moonjean. Associate Producer, Carter DeHaven, Jr. Photography, Conrad Hall. Editor, Sam O'Steen. Filmed near Stockton, California. 126 minutes

Cool Hand Luke with Paul Newman and Robert Drivas.

Luke: Paul Newman, *Dragline:* George Kennedy, *Society Red:* J. D. Cannon, *Koko:* Lou Antonio, *Loudmouth Steve:* Robert Drivas, *The Captain:* Strother Martin, *Arletta:* Jo Van Fleet, *Carr:* Clifton James, *Boss Godfrey:* Morgan Woodward, *Boss Paul:* Luke Askew, *Rabbitt:* Marc Cavell, *Tattoo:* Warren Finnerty, *Babalugats:* Dennis Hopper, *Boss Kean:* John McLiam, *Gambler:* Wayne Rogers, *Boss Higgins:* Charles Tyner, *Alibi:* Ralph Waite, *Dog Boy:* Anthony Zerbe, *Dynamite:* Buck Kartalian, *The Girl:* Joy Harmon, *Sleepy:* Jim Gammon, *Fixer:* Joe Don Baker, *Sailor:* Donn Pearce, *Stupid Blondie:* Norman Goodwins, *Chief:* Chuck Hicks, *John, Sr.* John Pearce, *John, Jr.* Eddie Rosson, *Patrolman:* Rush Williams, *Wickerman:* James Jeter, *Jabo:* Robert Luster, *Negro Boys:* James Bradley, Jr., Cyril "Chips" Robinson, *Sheriff:* Rance Howard, *Tramp:* Dean Stanton, *Blind Dick:* Richard Davalos, *Boss Shorty:* Robert Donner.

The Corn is Green with Bette Davis.

THE CORN IS GREEN (1945) WB. Producer, Jack Chertok. Director, Irving Rapper. Screenplay, Casey Robinson and Frank Cavett. Based on the play by Emlyn Williams. Score, Max Steiner. Art Director, Carl Jules Weyl. Musical Director, Leo F. Forbstein. Cameraman, Sol Polito. Editor, Frederick Richards. Film debut of John Dall. 114 minutes

Miss Moffat: Bette Davis, *Morgan Evans:* John Dall, *Bessie Watty:* Joan Lorring, *The Squire:* Nigel Bruce, *Mr. Jones:* Rhys Williams, *Mrs. Watty:* Rosalind Ivan, *Miss Ronberry:* Mildred Dunnock, *Sarah Pugh:* Gwyneth Hughes, *Idwal Morris:* Billy Roy, *Old Tom:* Thomas Louden, *William Davis:* Arthur Shields, *John Owen:* Leslie Vincent, *Rhys Norman:* Robert Regent, *Will Hughes:* Tony Ellis, *Glyn Thomas:* Elliott Dare, *Dai Evans:* Robert Cherry, *Gwilym Jones:* Gene Ross, *Trap Driver:* George Mathews, *Squire's Groom:* Jock Watt, *Tudor:* Jack Owen, *Welshman:* John Dehner, *Lewellyn Powell:* Brandon Hurst, *Wylodine:* Rhoda Williams, *Old Woman Reading:* Adeline De Walt Reynolds, *Militant Corps Woman:* Margaret Hoffman, *Mrs. Watty's Friend:* Sarah Edwards, *Station Master:* Leonard Mudie.

THE COUNT OF MONTE CRISTO (1934) UA. A Reliance Pictures Production. Supervision, Edward Small. Director, Rowland V. Lee. Based on the novel by Alexandre Dumas. Screenplay, Philip Dunne, Dan Totheroh, Rowland V. Lee. Cameraman, Peverell Marley. Editor, Grant Whytock. Music Director, Alfred Newman. Song, "The World Is Mine" by E. Y. Harburg and Johnny Green. 113 minutes

Edmond Dantes: Robert Donat, *Mercedes de Rosas:* Elissa Landi, *Raymond De Villefort, Jr.:* Louis Calhern, *Fernand de Mondego:* Sidney Blackmer, *Danglars:* Raymond Walburn, *Abbe Faria:* O. P. Heggie, *Captain Leclere:* William Farnum, *Madame de Rosas:* Georgia

The Count of Monte Cristo with Luis Alberni, Robert Donat and Clarence Muse.

Caine, *Morrel:* Walter Walker, *De Villefort, Sr.:* Lawrence Grant, *Jacopo:* Luis Alberni, *Valentine De Villefort:* Irene Hervey, *Albert de Mondego:* Douglas Walton, *Clothilde:* Juliette Compton, *Fouquet:* Clarence Wilson, *Haydee:* Eleanor Phelps, *Louis XVIII:* Ferdinand Munier, *Judge:* Holmes Herbert, *Napoleon:* Paul Irving, *Captain Vampa:* Mitchell Lewis, *Ali:* Clarence Muse, *Prison Governor:* Lionel Belmore, *Detective:* Wilfred Lucas, *Cockeye:* Tom Ricketts, *Bertrand:* Edward Keane, *Ali Pasha:* Sydney Jarvis, *Blacas:* Desmond Roberts, *Pellerin:* John Marsden, *Batistino:* Alphonse Martell, *Manouse:* Russell Powell, *Albert, age 8:* Wallace Albright, *Beauchamp:* Leon Waycoff (Ames), *Angry Man:* Paul Fix, *Fencing Master:* Fred Cavens.

THE COUNTRY DOCTOR (1936) 20th. Produced by Darryl F. Zanuck. Directed by Henry King. Author, Charles E. Blake. Screenplay, Sonya Levien. Cameramen, John Seitz, Daniel B. Clark. Editor, Barbara McLean. 110 minutes

Quintuplets: The Dionne Quintuplets, *Dr. Roy Luke:* Jean Hersholt, *Nurse Andrews:* Dorothy Peterson, *Mary:* June Lang, *Ogden:* Slim Summerville, *Tony:* Michael Whalen, *Mac Kenzie:* Robert Barrat, *Mike:* J. Anthony Hughes, *Asa Wyatt:* John M. Qualen, *Greasy:* George Chandler, *Sir Basil:* Montagu Love, *Dr. Paul Luke:* Frank Reicher, *Dr. Wilson:* George Meeker, *Nurse:* Jane Darwell, *Governor General:* David Torrence, *Peg-leg Walter:* William Conlon, *Gawker:* William Benedict, *Joe:* Joseph Sawyer, *Lumberjack:* Harry Cording, *Editor:* Edward McWade, *Mrs. Ogden:* Helen Jerome Eddy, *Young Logger:* Kane Richmond, *Jerry:* Carry Ovon, *Mack:* Paul McVey, *Minister:* Harry C. Bradley, *Women:* Mary Carr, Cecil Weston, *Proprietor:* Wilfred Lucas, *Piano Player:* Dillon Ober, *Mrs. Wyatt:* Aileen Carlyle, *Bishop:* Richard Carlyle, *Secretary:* Margaret Fielding, *Toastmaster:* Claude King, *City Editor:* John Dilson, *Grandmother:* Florence Roberts.

The Country Doctor with Delmar Watson, Jean Hersnolt and Dorothy Peterson.

The Country Girl with Bing Crosby and William Holden.

THE COUNTRY GIRL (1954) Par. Producers, William Perlberg, George Seaton. Director-Screenplay, George Seaton. Based on the play by Clifford Odets. Art Director, Hal Pereira. Cameraman, John F. Warren. Editor, Ellsworth Hoagland. Musical numbers staged by Robert Alton. Songs by Ira Gershwin and Harold Arlen: "Live and Learn," "The Pitchman," "The Search Is Through." 104 minutes

Frank Elgin: Bing Crosby, *Georgie Elgin:* Grace Kelly, *Bernie Dodd:* William Holden, *Phil Cook:* Anthony Ross, *Larry:* Gene Reynolds, *Singer-Actress:* Jacqueline Fontaine, *Ed:* Eddie Ryder, *Paul Unger:* Robert Kent, *Henry Johnson:* John W. Reynolds, *First Woman:* Ida Moore, *Bartender:* Frank Scanell, *Second Woman:* Ruth Rickaby, *Actor:* Hal K. Dawson, *Actor:* Howard Joslin, *Photographer:* Charles Tannen, *Jimmie:* Jonathan Provost, *Bellboy:* Bob Alden, *Ralph (Dresser):* Chester Jones.

COVER GIRL (1944) Col. Directed by Charles Vidor. Color by Technicolor. Story, Erwin Gelsey. Screenplay, Virginia Van Upp. Adaptation, Marion Parsonnet and Paul Gangelin. Music Director, M. W. Stoloff. Orchestrations, Carmen Dragon. Editor, Viola Lawrence. Songs by Jerome Kern and Ira Gershwin: "Long Ago and Far Away," "Cover Girl," "Sure Thing," "The Show Must Go On," "Who's Complaining?", "Put Me to the Test," "Make Way for Tomorrow." Gene Kelly dances the Alter Ego ballet. Film debut of Shelley Winters, 20, although released after several succeeding films. 107 minutes

Rusty Parker/Maribelle Hicks: Rita Hayworth, *Danny McGuire:* Gene Kelly, *Noel Wheaton:* Lee Bowman, *Genius:* Phil Silvers, *Jinx:* Jinx Falkenburg, *Maurine Martin:* Leslie Brooks, *Cornelia (Stonewall) Jackson:* Eve Arden, *John Coudair:* Otto Kruger, *Coudair as a young man:* Jess Barker, *Anita:* Anita Colby, *Chem:* Curt Bois, *Joe:* Ed Brophy, *Tony Pastor:* Thurston Hall, *Harry (Drunk):* Jack Norton, *Pop: (Doorman):* Robert Homans, *Mac (Cop):* Eddie Dunn, *Autograph*

Cover Girl with Leslie Brooks (second left), Rita Hayworth and Gene Kelly.

Hound: Ilene (Betty) Brewer, *Pianist:* Johnny Mitchell, *"Who's Complaining?" Dancer:* Virginia Wilson (Virginia de Luce), *Girl:* Shelley Winters, *Cover Girls:* AMERICAN MAGAZINE: Jean Colleran, AMERICAN HOME: Francine Counihan, COLLIER'S MAGAZINE: Helen Mueller, CORONET: Cecilia Meagher, COSMOPOLITAN: Betty Jane Hess, FARM JOURNAL: Dusty Anderson, GLAMOUR: Eileen McClory, HARPER'S BAZAAR: Cornelia B. Von Hessert, LIBERTY: Karen X. Gaylord, LOOK: Cheryl Archer, MADEMOISELLE: Peggy Lloyd, MC CALLS: Betty Jane Graham, REDBOOK: Martha Outlaw, VOGUE: Susann Shaw, WOMEN'S HOME COMPANION: Rose May Robson, *Chorus Girl:* Barbara Pepper, *Elevator Boy:* Stanley Clements, *Receptionist:* Constance Worth, *Coudair's Secretary:* Frances Morris, *Naval Officer:* William Sloan, *Florist Boy:* Billy Benedict.

Crossfire with Robert Ryan and Sam Levene.

THE CRUSADES (1935) Par. Produced and directed by Cecil B. De Mille. Story and Screenplay, Harold Lamb, Waldemar Young, and Dudley Nichols. Camera, Victor Milner. "Song of the Crusades" by Leo Robin, Richard Whiting, and Rudolph Kopp. Technical Effects, Gordon Jennings. 123 minutes

Berengaria, Princess of Navarre: Loretta Young, *King Richard:* Henry Wilcoxon, *Saladin, Sultan of Islam:* Ian Keith, *The Hermit:* C. Aubrey Smith, *Princess Alice:* Katharine De Mille, *Conrad, Marquis of Montferrat:* Joseph Schildkraut, *Blondel:* Alan Hale, *King Philip II:* C. Henry Gordon, *Sancho, King of Navarre:* George Barbier, *The Blacksmith:* Montagu Love, *Robert, Earl of Leicester:* Lumsden Hare, *Duke Hugo of Burgundy:* William Farnum, *Duke Frederick:* Hobart Bosworth, *Karakush:* Pedro de Cordoba, *Prince John:* Ramsay Hill, *Monk:* Mischa Auer, *Alan:* Maurice Murphy, *Duke Leopold of Austria:* Albert Conti, *Sverre, the Norse King:* Sven-Hugo Borg, *Prince Michael of Russia:* Paul Satoff, *King William of Sicily:* Fred W. Malatesta, *Count Nicholas of Hungary:* Hans Von Twardowski, *Duenna:* Anna Demetrio, *Soldier:* Perry Askam, *Ship's Master:* Edwin Maxwell, *Archbishop:* Winter Hall, *Alan's Mother:* Emma Dunn, *Amir/Slave in Saladin's Garden:* Jason Robards, *Nun:* Georgia Caine, *Arab Slave Dealer:* J. Carrol Naish, *Christian Girl:* Ann Sheridan, *Buyer:* Josef Swickard, *Christian Girl:* Jean Fenwick, *Priest:* Alphonz Ethier, *Knight:* Jack Rutherford, *Stranger (Messenger):* Colin Tapley, *Amir:* Harry Cording, *Amir:* Stanley Andrews, *Sentry:* Addison Richards, *Amir:* Maurice Black, *Amir:* William B. Davidson, *Greybeard/Templar:* Guy Usher, *Templar:* Boyd Irwin, Sr., *Templar:* Gordon Griffith, *Captain of Hospitalers:* Sam Flint, *King/Wise Man:* John Carradine, *Whipping Master:* Dewey Robinson.

The Crusades with Loretta Young and Ian Keith.

Crime Without Passion with Claude Rains and Margo.

CRIME WITHOUT PASSION (1934) Par. Directors, Ben Hecht and Charles MacArthur. From *Caballero of The Law* by Ben Hecht and Charles MacArthur, who also adapted it. Special Effects, Slavko Vorkapich. Photography, Lee Garmes. Filmed in Paramount's Astoria, Long Island, Studios. Film debuts of Esther Dale and Margo. 80 minutes

Lee Gentry: Claude Rains, *Carmen Brown:* Margo, *Katy Costello:* Whitney Bourne, *Eddie White:* Stanley Ridges, *Buster Malloy:* Paula Trueman, *O'Brien:* Leslie Adams, *Della:* Greta Granstedt, *Miss Keeley:* Esther Dale, *Lieutenant Norton:* Charles Kennedy, *Judge:* Fuller Mellish, *Reporters:* Charles MacArthur, Ben Hecht, *Extra in Hotel Lobby:* Helen Hayes.

CROSSFIRE (1947) RKO. Producer, Adrian Scott. Director, Edward Dmytryk. From a novel by Richard Brooks (*The Brick Foxhole*). Screenplay, John Paxton. Art Directors, Albert S. D'Agostino, Alfred Herman. Musical Director, C. Bakaleinikoff. Cameraman, J. Roy Hunt. Editor, Harry Gerstad. 86 minutes

Captain Finlay: Robert Young, *Sgt. Peter Keeley:* Robert Mitchum, *Montgomery:* Robert Ryan, *Ginny Tremaine:* Gloria Grahame, *The Man:* Paul Kelly, *Joseph Samuels:* Sam Levene, *Mary Mitchell:* Jacqueline White, *Floyd Bowers:* Steve Brodie, *Arthur Mitchell:* George Cooper, *Bill Williams:* Richard Benedict, *Detective:* Richard Powers (Tom Keene), *Leroy:* William Phipps, *Harry:* Lex Barker, *Miss Lewis:* Marlo Dwyer, *Tenant:* Harry Harvey, *Deputy:* Carl Faulkner, *M. P.:* Jay Norris, *M. P.:* Robert Bray, *Police Sergeant:* Philip Morris, *Major:* Kenneth McDonald, *M. P.:* George Turner, *Soldier:* Allen Ray, *M. P.:* Don Cadell, *Waiter:* Bill Nind, *Police Surgeon:* George Meader.

Daddy Long Legs with Fred Astaire and Leslie Caron.

Cyrano De Bergerac with Mala Powers and José Ferrer.

CYRANO DE BERGERAC (1950) UA. Produced by Stanley Kramer. Directed by Michael Gordon. Filmed with the Garutso Lens. From the Brian Hooker translation of the play by Edmond Rostand. Screenplay, Carl Foreman. Music composed and directed by Dimitri Tiomkin. Production Design, Rudolph Sternad. Photography, Frank Planer. Editor, Harry Gerstad. Fencing Máster, Fred Cavens. 112 minutes

Cyrano: José Ferrer, *Roxane Robin:* Mala Powers, *Baron Christian de Neuvillette:* William Prince, *Captain Le Bret:* Morris Carnovsky, *Count Antoine de Guiche:* Ralph Clanton, *Ragueneau:* Lloyd Corrigan, *Duenna:* Virginia Farmer, *Cardinal:* Edgar Barrier, *Orange Girl:* Elena Verdugo, *Viscount Valvert:* Albert Cavens, *Montfleury:* Arthur Blake, *The Meddler:* Don Beddoe, *Bellerose:* Percy Helton, *Sister Marthe:* Virginia Christine, *Doctor:* Gil Warren, *Man with Gazette:* Philip Van Zandt, *Guardsman:* Eric Sinclair, *Marquis:* Richard Avonde, *Cadets:* Paul Dubov, John Crawford, Jerry Paris, Robin Hughes, *Monk:* Francis Pierlot, *Lackey (Assassin):* John Harmon.

DADDY LONG LEGS (1931) Fox. Directed by Alfred Santell. From the play and novel by Jean Webster. Scenario, Sonya Levien. Dialogue, Sonya Levien and S. N. Behrman. Photography, Lucien Andriot. Editor, Ralph Dietrich. Other versions: First National, 1919; 20th Century-Fox, 1955. 73 minutes

Judy Abbott: Janet Gaynor, *Jervis Pendleton:* Warner Baxter, *Sally McBride:* Una Merkel, *Jimmy McBride:* John Arledge, *Riggs:* Claude Gillingwater, Sr., *Mrs. Pendleton:* Kathlyn Williams, *Miss Pritchard:* Louise Closser Hale, *Mrs. Lippett:* Elizabeth Patterson, *Freddie Perkins:* Kendall McComas, *Gloria Pendleton:* Sheila Mannors, *Wykoff:* Edwin Maxwell, *Mrs. Semple:* Effie Ellsler, *Katie:* Martha Lee Sparks, *Billy:* Billy Barty.

Daddy Long Legs with Una Merkel, Janet Gaynor, John Arledge, Sheila Mannors, Warner Baxter and Kathlyn Williams.

DADDY LONG LEGS (1955) 20th. Producer, Samuel G. Engel. Director, Jean Negulesco. CinemaScope. Technicolor. Screenplay by Phoebe and Henry Ephron. Based on novel and play by Jean Webster. Music by Johnny Mercer and Alex North. Choreography by Fred Astaire, David Robel, and Roland Petit. Art Directors, Lyle Wheeler and John De Cuir. Music Director, Alfred Newman. Photography, Leon Shamroy. Editor, William Reynolds. Songs by Johnny Mercer: "Dream," "Sluefoot," "Something's Gotta Give," "History of the Beat," "Welcome Egghead," "C-A-T Spells Cat." Earlier versions: First National, 1919; Fox, 1931. 126 minutes

Jervis Pendleton: Fred Astaire, *Julie:* Leslie Caron, *Linda:* Terry Moore, *Miss Pritchard:* Thelma Ritter, *Griggs:* Fred Clark, *Sally:* Charlotte Austin, *Alexander Williamson:* Larry Keating, *Gertrude:* Kathryn Givney, *Jimmy McBride:* Kelly Brown, *Pat:* Sara Shane, *Jean:* Numa Lapeyre, *Madame Sevanne:* Ann Codee, *Emile:* Steven Geray, *Professor:* Percival Vivian, *College Dean:* Helen Van Tuyl, *Larry Hamilton:* Damian O'Flynn, *Mr. Bronson:* Ralph Dumke, *Themselves:* Ray Anthony and his Orchestra, *Guide:* Joseph Kearns, *Butler:* Larry Kent, *Hotel Manager:* Charles Anthony Hughes, *Miss Carrington:* Kathryn Card, *Cab Driver:* Harry Seymour, *Deliveryman:* J. Anthony Hughes, *Chauffeur:* George Dunn, *Athletic Girl Dancer:* Janice Carroll, *Woman:* Gertrude Astor, *Jeweler:* David Hoffman, *Second Jeweler:* Paul Bradley, *French Lieutenant:* Guy Des Rochers, *Commission Members:* Carleton Young and Paul Power, *Army Sergeant:* William Hines, *French Farmer:* Frank Kreig, *Deliveryman:* Bob Adler, *College Girls:* Diane Jergens, Marjorie Hellen (Leslie Parrish).

DANGEROUS (1935) WB. Produced by Harry Joe Brown. Directed by Alfred E. Green. Original Story and Screenplay, Laird Doyle. Photography, Ernest Haller. Assistant Director, Russ Saunders. Art Director, Hugo Reticker. Editor, Thomas Richards. Unit Manager, Lee Huginin. Remade by WB as *Singapore Woman* (WB, 1941). 78 minutes

Dangerous with Alison Skipworth and Bette Davis.

Joyce Heath: Bette Davis, *Don Bellows*: Franchot Tone, *Gail Armitage*: Margaret Lindsay, *Mrs. Williams*: Alison Skipworth, *Gordon Heath*: John Eldredge, *Teddy*: Richard (Dick) Foran, *George Sheffield*: Pierre Watkin, *Roger Farnsworth*: Walter Walker, *Charles Melton*: George Irving, *Reed Walsh*: William B. Davidson, *Elmont*: Douglas Wood, *Pitt Hanly*: Richard Carle, *Roger's Chauffeur, Williams*: Milton Kibbee, *Waiter*: George Andre Beranger, *Bartender*: Frank O'Connor, *Cato*: Miki Morita, *Waiter*: Larry McGrath, *Foreman*: Eddie Shubert, *Secretary*: Florence Fair, *Gail's Maid, Betty*: Pauline Garon, *Male Lead*: (Bill) Gordon Elliott, *Beulah*: Libby Taylor, *Reporter*: Craig Reynolds, *Huree*: Mary Treen, *Doctor*: Edward Keane, *Passerby (Extra)*: Eddie Foster, *Teddy's Chauffeur*: Billy Wayne.

The Dark at the Top of the Stairs with Dorothy McGuire, Robert Preston and Robert Eyer.

THE DARK AT THE TOP OF THE STAIRS (1960) WB. Produced by Michael Garrison. Directed by Delbert Mann. In Technicolor. Based on the play by William Inge. Screenplay, Harriet Frank, Jr. and Irving Ravetch. Music, Max Steiner. Art Director, Leo K. Kuter. Costumes, Marjorie Best. Assistant Director, Russell Llewellyn. Orchestration, Murray Cutter. Cinematography, Harry Stradling, Sr. Editor, Folmer Blangsted. 123 minutes

Rubin Flood: Robert Preston, *Cora Flood*: Dorothy McGuire, *Lottie*: Eve Arden, *Mavis Pruitt*: Angela Lansbury, *Reenie Flood*: Shirley Knight, *Morris*: Frank Overton, *Sammy Golden*: Lee Kinsolving, *Sonny Flood*: Robert Eyer, *Flirt Conroy*: Penney Parker, *Punky Givens*: Dennis Whitcomb, *Harry Ralston*: Ken Lynch, *Ed Peabody*: Nelson Leigh, *George Williams*: Emerson Treacy, *Joseph Moody*: Ben Erway, *Mrs. Haycox*: Helen Brown, *Mr. Delman*: Jean Paul King, *Lydia Harper*: Helen Wallace, *Edna Harper*: Peg LaCentra, *Jonah Mills*: Paul Birch, *Mrs. Ralston*: Mary Patton, *Jenkins*: Paul Comi, *Harris*: Addison Richards, *Harold*: Robin Warga, *Percy Weems*: Charles Seel, *Cadet*: Stoddard Kirby.

Dark Victory with Bette Davis, Dorothy Peterson and George Brent.

DARK VICTORY (1939) WB. Associate Producer, David Lewis. Director, Edmund Goulding. From the play by George Brewer, Jr. and Bertram Bloch. Screenplay, Casey Robinson. Cameraman, Ernest Haller. Editor, William Holmes. Song by Elsie Janis and Edmund Goulding: "Oh Give Me Time for Tenderness." Remade as *Stolen Hours* (UA, 1963). 106 minutes

Judith Traherne: Bette Davis, *Dr. Frederick Steele*: George Brent, *Michael O'Leary*: Humphrey Bogart, *Ann King*: Geraldine Fitzgerald, *Alec Hamin*: Ronald Reagan, *Dr. Parsons*: Henry Travers, *Carrie Spottswood*: Cora Witherspoon, *Martha*: Virginia Brissac, *Miss Wainwright*: Dorothy Peterson, *Colonel Mantle*: Charles Richman, *Dr. Carter*: Herbert Rawlinson, *Dr. Driscoll*: Leonard Mudie, *Miss Dodd*: Fay Helm, *Lucy*: Lottie Williams, *Agatha*: Diane Bernard, *Veterinarian*: Jack Mower, *First Specialist*: William Worthington, *Second Specialist*: Alexander Leftwich, *Secretary*: Ila Rhodes, *Doctor*: Stuart Holmes, *Anxious Little Man*: Frank Darien, *First Man*: John Harron, *Second Man*: John Ridgely, *Bartender*: Sidney Bracy, *Girl in Box*: Rosella Towne, *Trainer*: Edgar Edwards.

A Date With Judy with Carmen Miranda, Xavier Cugat, Jane Powell and Elizabeth Taylor.

A DATE WITH JUDY (1948) MGM. Producer, Joe Pasternak. Director, Richard Thorpe. Color by Technicolor. Screenplay, Dorothy Cooper, Dorothy Kingsley. Musical Director, Georgie Stoll. Art Directors, Cedric Gibbons, Paul Groesse. Photography, Robert Surtees. Editor, Harold F. Kress. Based on the characters created by Aleen Leslie. Songs: "Judaline" by Don Raye and Gene DePaul; "It's a Most Unusual Day" by Harold Adamson and Jimmy McHugh; "I'm Strictly on the Corny Side" by Stella Unger and Alec Templeton; "I've Got a Date With Judy" and "I'm Gonna Meet My Mary" by Bill Katz and Calvin Jackson. 113 minutes

Melvin R. Foster: Wallace Beery, *Judy Foster*: Jane Powell, *Carol Foster*: Elizabeth Taylor, *Rosita Conchellas*: Carmen Miranda, *Cugat*: Xavier Cugat, *Stephen Andrews*: Robert Stack, *Mrs. Foster*: Selena Royle, *Ogden "Oogie" Pringle*: Scotty Beckett, *Mr. Lucien T. Pringle*: Leon Ames, *Gramps*: George Cleveland, *Pop Scully*: Lloyd Corrigan, *Jameson*: Clinton Sundberg, *Mitzie*: Jean McLaren, *Randolph Foster*: Jerry Hunter, *Jo-Jo Hoffenpepper*: Buddy Howard, *Nightingale*: Lillian Yarbo, *Miss Clarke*: Eula Guy, *Prof. Green*: Francis Pierlot, *Olga*: Rena Lenart, *Little Girl in Drugstore*: Sheila Stein, *Girl*: Alice Kelley, *Elderly Woman*: Polly Bailey, *Miss Sampson*: Fern Eggen, *Headwaiter*: Paul Bradley.

DAVID AND BATHSHEBA (1951) 20th. Producer, Darryl F. Zanuck. Director, Henry King. Color by Technicolor. Screenplay, Philip Dunne. Music, Alfred Newman. Art Directors, Lyle Wheeler, George Davis. Photography, Leon Shamroy. Editor, Barbara McLean.

David and Bathsheba with Jayne Meadows, Gregory Peck, Susan Hayward and James Robertson Justice.

Technicolor Consultant, Leonard Doss. Filmed in Arizona. 116 minutes

David: Gregory Peck, *Bathsheba:* Susan Hayward, *Nathan:* Raymond Massey, *Uriah:* Kieron Moore, *Abishai:* James Robertson Justice, *Michal:* Jayne Meadows, *Ira:* John Sutton, *Joab:* Dennis Hoey, *Goliath:* Walter Talun, *Adultress:* Paula Morgan, *King Saul:* Francis X. Bushman, *Jonathan:* Teddy Infuhr, *David as a boy:* Leo Pessin, *Specialty Dancer:* Gwyneth (Gwen) Verdon, *Absalom:* Gilbert Barnett, *Priest:* John Burton, *Old Shepherd:* Lumsden Hare, *Egyptian Ambassador:* George Zucco, *Amnon:* Allan Stone, *Samuel:* Paul Newlan, *Jesse:* Holmes Herbert, *Executioners:* Robert Stephenson, Harry Carter, *Jesse's First Son:* Richard Mickelson, *Jesse's Second Son:* Dick Winters, *Jesse's Third Son:* John Duncan, *Court Announcer:* James Craven, *Police Guard:* Shepard Menken, *Ahithoplel:* John Dodsworth.

DAVID AND LISA (1963) Continental. Producer, Paul M. Heller. Director, Frank Perry. Screenplay, Eleanor Perry. Based on book by Theodore Isaac Rubin. Music, Mark Lawrence. Costumes, Anna Hill Johnstone. Associate Producer, Vision Associates. Art Director, Paul M. Heller. Music arranged and conducted by Norman Paris. Cinematographer, Leonard Hirschfield. Editor, Irving Oshman. 94 minutes

David: Keir Dullea, *Lisa:* Janet Margolin, *Dr. Swinford:* Howard Da Silva, *Mrs. Clemens:* Neva Patterson, *John:* Clifton James, *Mr. Clemens:* Richard McMurray, *Maureen:* Nancy Nutter, *Simon:* Mathew Anden, *Kate:* Coni Hudak, *Carlos:* Jaime Sanchez, *Sandra:* Janet Lee Parker, *Josette:* Karen Gorney.

David and Lisa with Janet Margolin and Keir Dullea.

David Copperfield with Frank Lawton, W.C. Fields and Roland Young.

DAVID COPPERFIELD (1935) MGM. Produced by David O. Selznick. Directed by George Cukor. Based on the novel by Charles Dickens. Adaptation, Hugh Walpole. Screenplay, Howard Estabrook. Special Effects, Slavko Vorkapich. Art Director, Cedric Gibbons. Costumes, Dolly Tree. Musical Numbers, Herbert Stothart. Assistant Director, Joe Newman. Photography, Oliver T. Marsh. Editor, Robert J. Kern. Sound, Douglas Shearer. American film debut of Freddie Bartholomew. Other version: Associated Exhibitors, 1923. 133 minutes

Mr. Micawber: W. C. Fields, *Dan Peggotty:* Lionel Barrymore, *Dora:* Maureen O'Sullivan, *Agnes:* Madge Evans, *Aunt Betsey:* Edna May Oliver, *Mr. Wickfield:* Lewis Stone, *David, the man:* Frank Lawton, *David, the child:* Freddie Bartholomew, *Mrs. Copperfield:* Elizabeth Allan, *Uriah Heep:* Roland Young, *Mr. Murdstone:* Basil Rathbone, *Clickett:* Elsa Lanchester, *Mrs. Micawber:* Jean Cadell, *Nurse Peggotty:* Jessie Ralph, *Mr. Dick:* Lennox Pawle, *Jane Murdstone:* Violet Kemble-Cooper, *Mrs. Gummidge:* Una O'Connor, *Ham:* John Buckler, *Steerforth:* Hugh Williams, *Limmiter:* Ivan Simpson, *Barkis:* Herbert Mundin, *Little Em'ly, the child:* Fay Chaldecott, *Little Em'ly, the woman:* Florine McKinney, *Agnes, the child:* Marilyn Knowlden, *Dr. Chillip:* Harry Beresford, *Mary Ann:* Mabel Colcord, *The Vicar:* Hugh Walpole, *Janet:* Renee Gadd, *Donkey Man:* Arthur Treacher.

A DAY AT THE RACES (1937) MGM. Associate Producer, Max Siegel. Directed by Sam Wood. Story, Robert Pirosh and George Seaton. Screenplay, Robert Pirosh, George Seaton, George Oppenheimer. Art Director, Cedric Gibbons. Music Director, Franz Wax-

A Day at the Races with Maureen O'Sullivan, Allan Jones, Groucho, Chico and Harpo Marx.

man. Dances, Dave Gould. Choral, Leo Arnaud. Photography, Joseph Ruttenberg. Editor, Frank E. Hull. Songs by Bronislau Kaper, Walter Jurmann, and Gus Kahn: "A Message From the Man in the Moon," "On Blue Venetian Waters," "Tomorrow Is Another Day," "All God's Chillun Got Rhythm." 111 minutes

Dr. Hugo Z. Hackenbush: Groucho Marx, *Tony:* Chico Marx, *Stuffy:* Harpo Marx, *Gil Stewart:* Allan Jones, *Judy Standish:* Maureen O'Sullivan, *Emily Upjohn:* Margaret Dumont, *Whitmore:* Leonard Ceeley, *Morgan:* Douglass Dumbrille, *Flo Marlowe:* Esther Muir, *Dr. Leopold X. Steinberg:* Sig Rumann, *Sheriff:* Robert Middlemass, *Solo Dancer:* Vivien Fay, *Dr. Wilmerding:* Charles Trowbridge, *Doctors:* Frank Dawson, Max Lucke, *Morgan's Jockey:* Frankie Darro, *Detective:* Pat Flaherty, *Messenger:* Si Jenks, *Race Judge:* Hooper Atchley, *Judges:* John Hyams, Wilbur Mack, *Nurse:* Mary MacLaren, *Doctor:* Edward LeSaint, *Drunk:* Jack Norton, *Extra:* Carole Landis. And Ivie Anderson and the Crinoline Choir.

Days of Wine and Roses with Lee Remick, Charles Bickford and Debbie Megowan.

DAYS OF WINE AND ROSES (1962) WB. Producer, Martin Manulis. Director, Blake Edwards. Screenplay, J. P. Miller. Art Director, Joseph Wright. Music, Henry Mancini. "Days of Wine and Roses": lyric, Johnny Mercer, music, Henry Mancini. Cinematographer, Phil Lathrop. Editor, Patrick McCormack. Martin Manulis-Salem Production. 117 minutes

Joe Clay: Jack Lemmon, *Kirsten Arnesen:* Lee Remick, *Ellis Arnesen:* Charles Bickford, *Jim Hungerford:* Jack Klugman, *Radford Leland:* Alan Hewitt, *Debbie Clay:* Debbie Megowan, *Mrs. Nolan:* Katherine Squire, *Dottie:* Maxine Stuart, *Trayner:* Jack Albertson, *Proprietor, Liquor Store:* Ken Lynch, *Ballefoy:* Tom Palmer, *Gladys:* Gail Bonney, *Tenants:* Mary Benoit, Ella Ethridge, Rita Kenaston, Pat O'Malley, Robert "Buddy" Shaw, Al Paige, *Boors:* Doc Stortt, Russ Bennett, Dick Crockett, *Abe:* Roger Barrett, *Waiter:* Jack Railey, *Belly Dancer:* Lisa Guiraut, *Loud Man:* Carl Arnold, *Bettor:* Tom Rosqui, *Guests:* Barbara Hines, Charlene Holt.

DEAD END (1937) UA. Produced by Samuel Goldwyn. Associate Producer, Merritt Hulburd. Directed by William Wyler. Based on the play by Sidney Kingsley. Screenplay, Lillian Hellman. Cinematography, Gregg Toland. Art Director, Richard Day. Musical Director, Alfred Newman. Editor, Daniel Mandell. Costumes, Omar Khayyam. Assistant Director, Eddie Bernoudy. Set Decorator, Julie Heron. Sound, Frank Maher. 93 minutes

Drina: Sylvia Sidney, *Dave:* Joel McCrea, *Baby Face Martin:* Humphrey Bogart, *Kay:* Wendy Barrie, *Francie:* Claire Trevor, *Hunk:* Allen Jenkins, *Mrs. Martin:* Marjorie Main, *Tommy:* Billy Halop, *Dippy:* Huntz Hall, *Angel:* Bobby Jordan, *Spit:* Leo Gorcey, *T.B.:* Gabriel Dell, *Milty:* Bernard Punsley, *Philip Griswold:* Charles Peck,

Dead End with Billy Halop, Leo Gorcey and Joel McCrea.

Mr. Griswold: Minor Watson, *Mulligan:* James Burke, *Doorman:* Ward Bond, *Mrs. Connell:* Elizabeth Risdon, *Janitress, Mrs. Fenner:* Esther Dale, *Pascagli:* George Humbert, *Governess:* Marcelle Corday, *Whitey:* Charles Halton, *Cop:* Robert E. Homans, *Drunk:* Bill Dagwell, *Milty's Brother:* Jerry Cooper, *Milty's Sister:* Kath Ann Lujan, *Old Lady:* Gertrude Valerie, *Old Man:* Tom Ricketts, *Women with Poodle:* Charlotte Treadway, Maude Lambert, *Kay's Chauffeur:* Bud Geary, *Well-dressed Couple:* Frank Shields, Lucille Brown, *Tough Boys:* Micky Martin, Wesley Girard, *Woman with Coarse Voice:* Esther Howard, *Man with Weak Voice:* Gilbert Clayton, *Griswold Chauffeur:* Earl Askam, *Nurse:* Mona Monet, *Interne:* Don Barry.

DEAR RUTH (1947) Par. Producer, Paul Jones. Director, William D. Russell. Based on the play by Norman Krasna. Screenplay, Arthur Sheekman. Art Directors, Hans Dreier, Earl Hedrick. Musical Score, Robert Emmet Dolan. Cameraman, Ernest Laszlo. Editor, Archie Marshek. Song by Johnny Mercer and Robert Emmett Dolan: "Fine Things." Sequels: *Dear Wife* (1949), *Dear Brat* (1951) 95 minutes

Ruth Wilkins: Joan Caulfield, *Lieut. William Seacroft:* William Holden, *Miriam Wilkins:* Mona Freeman, *Judge Harry Wilkins:* Edward Arnold, *Albert Kummer:* Billy De Wolfe, *Mrs. Wilkins:* Mary Philips, *Martha Seacroft:* Virginia Welles, *Sergeant Chuck Vincent:* Kenny O'Morrison, *Dora, the Maid:* Marietta Canty, *Delivery Man:* Irving Bacon, *Harold Klobbermeyer:* Jimmie Dundee, *Cab Driver:* Jay Gerard, *Woman:* Isabel Randolph, *Headwaiter:* Erno Verebes.

Dear Ruth with William Holden, Joan Caulfield and Edward Arnold.

Death of a Salesman with Fredric March.

DEATH OF A SALESMAN (1951) Col. Producer, Stanley Kramer. Director, Laslo Benedek. From the play by Arthur Miller. Screenplay, Stanley Roberts. Musical Director, Morris Stoloff. Art Director, Cary Odell. Photography, Frank F. Planer. Editor, William Lyon. 115 minutes

Willy Loman: Fredric March, *Linda Loman:* Mildred Dunnock, *Biff:* Kevin McCarthy, *Happy:* Cameron Mitchell, *Charley:* Howard Smith, *Ben:* Royal Beal, *Bernard:* Don Keefer, *Stanley:* Jesse White, *Miss Francis:* Claire Carleton, *Howard Wagner:* David Alpert, *Miss Forsythe:* Elizabeth Fraser, *Letta:* Patricia Walker, *Mother:* Gail Bonney, *Boy:* Roger Broaddus, *Girl:* Beverly Aadland, *Girl:* Wanda Perry, *Girl:* Christa Gail Walker, *Mother:* Jeanne Bates, *Subway Guard:* Paul Bryar.

THE DEFIANT ONES (1958) UA. Producer-Director, Stanley Kramer. Screenplay by Nathan E. Douglas and Harold Jacob Smith. Music by Ernest Gold. Assistant Director, Paul Helmick. Song "Long Gone" by W. C. Handy and Chris Smith. A Lomitas-Curtleigh Production. Filmed in Georgia. Last film of Carl "Alfalfa" Switzer, one of Our Gang. 97 minutes

John "Joker" Jackson: Tony Curtis, *Noah Cullen:* Sidney Poitier, *Sheriff Max Muller:* Theodore Bikel, *Captain Frank Gibbons:* Charles McGraw, *Big Sam:* Lon Chaney, Jr., *Solly:* King Donovan, *Mac:* Claude Akins, *Editor:* Lawrence Dobkin, *Lou Gans:* Whit Bissell, *Angus:* Carl Switzer, *The Kid:* Kevin Coughlin, *The Woman:* Cara Williams, *Joe:* Boyd (Red) Morgan, *Wilson, Posseman:* Robert Hoy, *State Trooper:* Don Brodie.

The Defiant Ones with Tony Curtis and Sidney Poitier.

DELICIOUS (1931) Fox. Directed by David Butler. Based on a story by Guy Bolton. Scenario and Dialogue, Guy Bolton and Sonya Levien. Photography, Ernest Palmer. Editor, Irene Morra. Sound, Joseph E. Aiken. Songs by George and Ira Gershwin: "You Started It," "New York Rhapsody," "Somebody From Somewhere," "Delicious." 106 minutes

Heather Gordon: Janet Gaynor, *Larry Beaumont:* Charles Farrell, *Jansen:* El Brendel, *O'Flynn:* Lawrence O'Sullivan, *Diana Van Bergh:* Virginia Cherrill, *Mrs. Van Bergh:* Olive Tell, *Sascha:* Raul Roulien, *Olga:* Manya Roberti, *Mischa:* Mischa Auer, *Momotschka:* Jeanette Gegna, *Tosha:* Marvine Maazel.

Delicious with Charles Farrell and Virginia Cherrill.

Demetrius and the Gladiators with Michael Rennie and Victor Mature.

DEMETRIUS AND THE GLADIATORS (1954) 20th. Producer, Frank Ross. Director, Delmer Daves. CinemaScope, Technicolor. From the novel *The Robe* by Lloyd C. Douglas. Screenplay, Philip Dunne. Art Directors, Lyle Wheeler, George W. Davis. Cinematographer, Milton Krasner. Editors, Dorothy Spencer, Robert Fritch, Franz Waxman, Alfred Newman. Music, Frank Waxman. Music Director, Alfred Newman. Sequel to *The Robe* (20th, 1953). 101 minutes

Demetrius: Victor Mature, *Messalina:* Susan Hayward, *Peter:* Michael Rennie, *Lucia:* Debra Paget, *Paula:* Anne Bancroft, *Caligula:* Jay Robinson, *Claudius:* Barry Jones, *Glydon:* William Marshall, *Dardanius:* Richard Egan, *Strabo:* Ernest Borgnine, *Cassius Chaerea:* Charles Evans, *Kaeso:* Everett Glass, *Macro:* Karl Davis, *Albus:* Jeff York, *Slave Girl:* Carmen de Lavallade, *Varus:* John Cliff, *Specialty Dancers:* Barbara James, Willetta Smith, *Senator:* Selmar Jackson, *Cousin:* Douglas Brooks, *Decurion:* Fred Graham, *Magistrate:* Dayton Lummis, *Chamberlain:* George Eldredge, *Prisoner:* Paul Richards.

Destination Tokyo with Cary Grant, William Prince, Peter Whitney, Maurice Murphy, Bob Hutton, John Garfield, Alan Hale, Warner Anderson, John Ridgely and Bill Kennedy.

DESTINATION TOKYO (1943) WB. Producer, Jerry Wald. Director, Delmer Daves. Author, Steve Fisher. Screenplay, Delmer Daves, Albert Maltz. Musical Score, Franz Waxman. Art Director, Leo K. Kuter. Musical Director, Leo F. Forbstein. Cameraman, Bert Glennon. Special Effects, Lawrence Butler, Willard Van Enger. Editor, Chris Nyby. Narrated by Lou Marcelle. 135 minutes

Captain Cassidy: Cary Grant, *Wolf:* John Garfield, *Cookie:* Alan Hale, *Reserve:* John Ridgely, *Tin Can:* Dane Clark, *Executive:* Warner Anderson, *Pills:* William Prince, *Tommy:* Bob Hutton, *Mike:* Tom Tully, *Mrs. Cassidy:* Faye Emerson, *Dakota:* Peter Whitney, *English Officer:* Warren Douglas, *Sparks:* John Forsythe, *Sound Man:* John Alvin, *Torpedo Officer:* Bill Kennedy, *Commanding Officer:* John Whitney, *Quartermaster:* William Challee, *Yo Yo:* Whitner Bissell, *Chief of Boat:* George Lloyd, *Toscanini:* Maurice Murphy, *Admiral:* Pierre Watkin, *Admiral's Aide:* Stephen Richards (Mark Stevens), HORNET's *Admiral:* Cliff Clark, *Debby Cassidy:* Deborah Daves, *Michael Cassidy:* Michael Daves, *Admiral's Aide:* Jack Mower, *Tin Can's Girl:* Mary Landa, *Man on Phone:* Carlyle Blackwell, *Captain:* Kirby Grant, *C.P.O.:* Lane Chandler, *Wolf's Girl:* Joy Barlowe, *Market St. "Commando":* Bill Hunter, *Crewmen:* George Robotham, Dan Borzage, William Hudson, Charles Sullivan, Duke York, Harry Bartell, Jay Ward, Paul Langton.

DESTRY RIDES AGAIN (1939) Univ. Producer, Joseph Pasternak. Director, George Marshall. Based on the novel by Max Brand. Screenplay, Felix Jackson, Gertrude Purcell, Henry Myers. Cameraman, Hal Mohr. Editor, Milton Carruth. Songs by Frank Loesser and

Destry Rides Again with Marlene Dietrich and Lillian Yarbo.

Frederick Hollander: "Little Joe, The Wrangler," "You've Got That Look That Leaves Me Weak" and "(See What) The Boys In the Back Room (Will Have)." Assistant Director, Vernon Keays. Other Universal versions: *Destry Rides Again* (1932); *Frenchie* (1950); *Destry* (1954). 94 minutes

Tom Destry: James Stewart, *Frenchy:* Marlene Dietrich, *Boris Callahan:* Mischa Auer, *"Wash" Dimsdale:* Charles Winninger, *Kent:* Brian Donlevy, *Gyp Watson:* Allen Jenkins, *Bugs Watson:* Warren Hymer, *Janice Tyndall:* Irene Hervey, *Lily Belle Callahan:* Una Merkel, *Lem Claggett:* Tom Fadden, *Judge Slade:* Samuel S. Hinds, *Clara:* Lillian Yarbo, *Rockwell:* Edmund MacDonald, *Bartender, Loupgerou:* Billy Gilbert, *Sophie Claggett:* Virginia Brissac, *Claggett Girl:* Ann Todd, *Eli Whitney Claggett:* Dickie Jones, *Jack Tyndall:* Jack Carson, *Dancer:* Carmen D'Antonio, *Sheriff Keogh:* Joe King, *Rowdy:* Harry Cording, *Cowboy:* Dick Alexander, *Mrs. DeWitt:* Minerva Urecal, *Doctor:* Bob McKenzie, *Pianist:* Billy Bletcher, *Turner, Express Agent:* Lloyd Ingraham, *Small Boy:* Bill Cody, Jr., *Jugglers:* Loren Brown, Harold DeGarro, *Cowboy:* Bill Steele Gettinger, *Stage Rider:* Harry Tenbrook, *Stage Driver:* Bud McClure, *Asst. Bartender:* Alex Voloshin, *Indian:* Chief John Big Tree.

Detective Story with Luis Van Rooten, Kirk Douglas and William Bendix.

DETECTIVE STORY (1951) Par. Producer-Director, William Wyler. Based on the play by Sidney Kingsley. Screenplay, Philip Yordan, Robert Wyler. Art Directors, Hal Pereira, Earl Hedrick. Photography, Lee Garmes. Editor, Robert Swink. 103 minutes

Jim McLeod: Kirk Douglas, *Mary McLeod:* Eleanor Parker, *Lou Brody:* William Bendix, *Susan:* Cathy O'Donnell, *Karl Schneider:* George MacCready, *Lieutenant Monahan:* Horace McMahon, *Miss Hatch:* Gladys George, *First Burglar:* Joseph Wiseman, *Shoplifter:* Lee Grant, *Tami Giacoppetti:* Gerald Mohr, *Gallagher:* Frank Faylen, *Arthur:* Craig Hill, *Lewis Abbott:* Michael Strong, *Joe Feinson:* Luis Van Rooten, *Dakis:* Bert Freed, *Sims:* Warner Anderson, *O'Brien:* Grandon Rhodes, *Callahan:* William (Bill) Phillips, *Barnes:* Russell Evens, *Detective Ed:* Edmund F. Cobb, *Willie (Janitor):* Burt Mustin, *Mr. Pritchett:* James Maloney, *Gus Keogh:* Howard Joslin, *Coleman:* Mike Mahoney, *Mrs. Farragut:* Catherine Doucet, *Frenchwoman:* Ann Codee, *Finney:* Ralph Montgomery, *Desk Sgt.:* Pat Flaherty, *Mulvey:* Bob Scott, *Gallants:* Harper Goff, *Taxi Driver:* Donald Kerr.

THE DEVIL AT 4 O'CLOCK (1961) Col. Producer, Fred Kohlmar. Director, Mervyn LeRoy. Eastman Color. Based on the novel by Max Catto. Screenplay, Liam O'Brien. Art Director, John Beckman. Music, George Duning. Orchestration, Arthur Morton. Cinematographer, Joseph Biroc. Editor, Charles Nelson. 126 minutes

Father Matthew Doonan: Spencer Tracy, *Harry:* Frank Sinatra, *Father Joseph Perreau:* Kerwin Mathews, *Jacques:* Jean Pierre Aumont,

The Devil at Four O'Clock with Martin Brandt, Spencer Tracy, Bernie Hamilton, Cathy Lewis and Frank Sinatra.

Marcel: Gregoire Aslan, *The Governor:* Alexander Scourby, *Camille:* Barbara Luna, *Matron:* Cathy Lewis, *Charlie:* Bernie Hamilton, *Dr. Wexler:* Martin Brandt, *Aristide:* Lou Merrill, *Gaston:* Marcel Dalio, *Paul:* Tom Middleton, *Clarisse:* Ann Duggan, *Corporal:* Louis Mercier, *Margot:* Michele Montau, *Fleur:* Nanette Tanaka, *Antoine:* Tony Maxwell, *Louis:* Jean Del Val, *Sonia:* Moki Hana, *Napoleon:* Warren Hsieh, *Constable:* William Keaulani, *Captain Olsen:* "Lucky" Luck, *Fouquette:* Norman Josef Wright, *Marianne:* Robin Shimatsu, *Grellou:* Max Dommar, *Citizen:* Eugene Borden, *French Woman:* Janine Grandel, *Tavi:* Guy Lee, *Radio Operator:* Earl D'Eon.

DEVIL IS A SISSY (1936) MGM.

Produced by Frank Davis. Directed by W. S. Van Dyke. Author, Roland Brown. Screenplay by John Lee Mahin, Richard Schayer. Musical Score, Herbert Stothart. Music and Lyrics, Arthur Freed, Nacio Herb Brown. Cameramen, Harold Rosson, George Schneiderman. Editor, Tom Held. Song, "Say Ah!" by Arthur Freed and Nacio Herb Brown. 92 minutes

Claude: Freddie Bartholomew, *Buck Murphy:* Jackie Cooper, *Gig Stevens:* Mickey Rooney, *Mr. Pierce:* Ian Hunter, *Rose:* Peggy Conklin, *Mrs. Pierce:* Katharine Alexander, *Mr. Murphy:* Gene Lockhart, *Mrs. Stevens:* Dorothy Peterson, *Mrs. Murphy:* Kathleen Lockhart, *Judge:* Jonathan Hale, *Principal:* Etienne Girardot, *Mrs. Robbins:* Mary Doran, *Bugs:* Sherwood Bailey, *Six Toes:* Buster Flavin, *Roy:* John Kelly, *Pawnbroker:* Rollo Lloyd, *Priest:* John Wray, *Mr. Muldoon:* Andrew Tombes, *Willie:* Harold Huber, *Kraus:* Jason Robards, *Krump:* Grant Mitchell, *Joe:* Stanley Fields, *Doorman:* Charles Coleman, *Doctor:* Stanley Andrews, *Plainclothesman:* George Guhl, *Joe's Mother:* Myre Marsh, *Toy Vender:* Harry Tyler, *Stone Cutter:* Christian Rub, *Pawnbroker:* Ian Wolfe.

The Devil Is a Sissy with Mickey Rooney, Freddie Bartholomew and Jackie Cooper.

Dial "M" for Murder with John Williams, Grace Kelly and Ray Milland.

DIAL M FOR MURDER (1954) WB.

Producer and Director, Alfred Hitchcock. Assistant Director, Mel Dellar. Screenplay by Frederick Knott as adapted from his play. Music by Dimitri Tiomkin. Art Director, Edward Carrere. Cinematographer, Robert Burks. Editor, Rudi Fehr. Color by WarnerColor, 3-Dimension. 105 minutes

Tony: Ray Milland, *Margot:* Grace Kelly, *Mark:* Robert Cummings, *Inspector Hubbard:* John Williams, *Captain Lesgate:* Anthony Dawson, *The Storyteller:* Leo Britt, *Pearson:* Patrick Allen, *Williams:* George Leigh, *First Detective:* George Alderson, *Police Sergeant:* Robin Hughes, *Man in Photo:* Alfred Hitchcock, *Detectives:* Guy Doleman, Thayer Roberts, Sanders Clark, *Police Photographer:* Robert Dobson, *Man in Phone Booth:* Major Sam Harris, *Bobby:* Jack Cunningham.

DIAMOND HEAD (1962) Col.

Producer, Jerry Bresler. Director, Guy Green. Panavision, Eastman Color. Based on the novel by Peter Gilman. Screenplay, Marguerite Roberts. Art Director, Malcolm Brown. Music, Johnny Williams. *Diamond Head* theme, Hugo Winterhalter. Orchestration, Arthur Morton. Cinematographer, Sam Leavitt. Editor, William A. Lyon. 107 minutes

Richard Howland: Charlton Heston, *Sloan Howland:* Yvette Mimieux, *Dr. Dean Kahana:* George Chakiris, *Mei Chen:* France Nuyen, *Paul Kahana:* James Darren, *Kapiolani Kahana:* Aline MacMahon, *Laura Beckett:* Elizabeth Allen, *Judge James Blanding:* Vaughn Taylor, *Yamagata:* Richard Loo, *Bobbie Chen:* Marc Marno, *Emekona:* Philip Ahn, *Coyama:* Harold Fong, *Robert Parsons:* Edward Mallory, *Mario:* Lou Gonsalves, *Felipe:* Frank Morris, *Sammy:* Clarence Kim, *Loe Kim Lee:* Kam Fong Chun, *Pianist:* Leo Ezell, *Heckler:* Al Lebuse, *Nurse:* R. Ramos, *Blue Goose:* Seagai Faumunina.

Diamond Head with Yvette Mimieux and Charlton Heston.

313

The Diary of Anne Frank with Millie Perkins and Joseph Schildkraut.

THE DIARY OF ANNE FRANK (1959) 20th. Producer, George Stevens. Associate Producer, George Stevens, Jr. Director, George Stevens. CinemaScope. Authors, Frances Goodrich, Albert Hackett (from *Anne Frank: The Diary of a Young Girl*). Screenplay, Frances Goodrich, Albert Hackett. Art Directors, Lyle R. Wheeler, George W. Davis. Music, Alfred Newman. Orchestration, Edward B. Powell. Cinematographer, William C. Mellor. Special Photographic Effects, L. B. Abbott. Editors, Robert Swink, David Brotherton, William Mace. Film debut of Millie Perkins. 170 minutes

Anne Frank: Millie Perkins, *Otto Frank:* Joseph Schildkraut, *Mrs. Van Daan:* Shelley Winters, *Mr. Dussell:* Ed Wynn, *Peter Van Daan:* Richard Beymer, *Mrs. Frank:* Gusti Huber, *Mr. Van Daan:* Lou Jacobi, *Margot Frank:* Diane Baker, *Kraler:* Douglas Spencer, *Miep:* Dody Heath, *Sneak Thief:* Charles Wagenheim, *Night Watchman:* Frank Tweddell, *SS Men:* Delmar Erickson, Robert Boon, *Dutch Girl:* Gretchen Goertz, *Workman in Shop:* William Kirschner.

DINNER AT EIGHT (1933) MGM. Directed by George Cukor. Based on the 1932 play by George S. Kaufman and Edna Ferber. Adaptation, Frances Marion and Herman J. Mankiewicz. Photography, William Daniels. Editor, Ben Lewis. 113 minutes

Carlotta Vance: Marie Dressler, *Larry Renault:* John Barrymore, *Dan Packard:* Wallace Beery, *Kitty Packard:* Jean Harlow, *Oliver Jordan:* Lionel Barrymore, *Max Kane:* Lee Tracy, *Dr. Wayne Talbot:* Edmund Lowe, *Millicent Jordan:* Billie Burke, *Paula Jordan:* Madge Evans, *Jo Stengel:* Jean Hersholt, *Lucy Talbot:* Karen Morley, *Hattie Loomis:* Louise Closser Hale, *Ernest De Graff:* Phillips Holmes, *Mrs. Wendel, the Cook:* May Robson, *Ed Loomis:* Grant Mitchell, *Miss Alden:* Phoebe Foster, *Miss Copeland:* Elizabeth Patterson,

Dinner at Eight with Madge Evans and John Barrymore.

Tina, Kitty's Maid: Hilda Vaughn, *Fosdick:* Harry Beresford, *Mr. Fitch, Hotel Manager:* Edwin Maxwell, *Mr. Hatfield, Assistant Manager:* John Davidson, *Eddie:* Edward Woods, *Gustave, the Butler:* George Baxter, *The Waiter:* Herman Bing, *Dora, Maid:* Anna Duncan.

The Dirty Dozen with John Cassavetes, Lee Marvin and Richard Jaeckel.

THE DIRTY DOZEN (1967) MGM. Produced by Kenneth Hyman. Directed by Robert Aldrich. 70mm and MetroColor. An M. K. H. Production. Associate Producer, Raymond Anzarut. Based on the novel by E. M. Nathanson. Screenplay, Nunnally Johnson and Lukas Heller. Music by Frank DeVol. Assistant Director, Bart Batt. Production Manager, Julian Mackintosh. Art Director, W. E. Hutchinson. Photography, Edward Scaife. Editor, Michael Luciano. Special Effects, Cliff Richardson. Sound, Franklin Milton and Claude Hitchcock. Songs: "The Bramble Bush" by Frank DeVol and Mack David; "Einsam" by Frank DeVol and Sibylle Siegfried. Filmed in England. 149 minutes

Major Reisman: Lee Marvin, *General Worden:* Ernest Borgnine, *Joseph Wladislaw:* Charles Bronson, *Robert Jefferson:* Jim Brown, *Victor Franko:* John Cassavetes, *Sergeant Bowren:* Richard Jaeckel, *Major Max Armbruster:* George Kennedy, *Pedro Jiminez:* Trini Lopez, *Captain Stuart Kinder:* Ralph Meeker, *Colonel Everett Dasher-Breed:* Robert Ryan, *Archer Maggott:* Telly Savalas, *Samson Posey:* Clint Walker, *General Denton:* Robert Webber, *Vernon Pinkley:* Donald Sutherland, *Milo Vladek:* Tom Busby, *Glenn Gilpin:* Ben Carruthers, *Roscoe Lever:* Stuart Cooper, *Corporal Morgan:* Robert Phillips, *Seth Sawyer:* Colin Maitland, *Tassos Bravos:* Al Mancini, *Private Gardner:* George Roubicek, *Worden's Aide:* Thick Wilson, *German Girl:* Dora Reisser.

DISHONORED (1931) Par. Directed and written by Josef von Sternberg. Scenario, Daniel N. Rubin. Photography, Lee Garmes.

Dishonored with Barry Norton and Marlene Dietrich.

Sound, Harry D. Mills. Technical Adviser, Alexis Davidoff. 91 minutes

X27 (*Marie Kolverer*): Marlene Dietrich, *Colonel Kranau:* Victor McLaglen, *Colonel Kovrin:* Lew Cody, *Secret Service Head:* Gustav von Seyffertitz, *Colonel Von Hindau:* Warner Oland, *Young Lieutenant:* Barry Norton, *Court Officer:* Davison Clark, *General Dymov:* Wilfred Lucas, *Manager:* Bill Powell, *Accident Victim:* Ruth Mayhew, *Officer:* Alexis Davidoff, *Firing Squad Officer:* William B. Davidson, *Russian Corporal:* Ethan Laidlaw, *Russian Officer:* Joseph Girard, *Contact at Cafe:* George Irving.

Disraeli with Joan Bennett, Anthony Bushnell and George Arliss.

DISRAELI

DISRAELI (1929) WB. Directed by Alfred E. Green. From the play by Louis N. Parker. Adaptation, Julian Josephson. Orchestra Conductor, Louis Silvers. Hughenden (Disraeli's estate) scenes filmed at Busch Gardens, Pasadena. Photography, Lee Garmes. Editor, Owen Marks. Titles (silent version), DeLeon Anthony. Other versions of *Disraeli:* Paul Cromelin, 1917; United Artists, 1921 (also starring George Arliss). Film debut of Anthony Bushell. 89 minutes

Disraeli: George Arliss, *Lady Clarissa Pevensey of Glastonbury:* Joan Bennett, *Lady Mary Beaconsfield:* Florence Arliss, *Charles, Lord Deeford:* Anthony Bushell, *Sir Michael, Lord Probert:* David Torrence, *Hugh Myers:* Ivan Simpson, *Mrs. Agatha Travers:* Doris Lloyd, *Duchess of Glastonbury:* Gwendolen Logan, *Duke of Glastonbury:* Henry Carvill, *Potter:* Charles E. Evans, *Mr. Terle:* Kyrle Bellew, *Bascot:* Jack Deery, *Count Bosrinov:* Michael Visaroff, *Foljambe:* Norman Cannon, *Dr. Williams:* Shayle Gardner, *Flookes:* Powell York, *Queen Victoria:* Margaret Mann, *Bit:* George Atkinson.

DIVE BOMBER

DIVE BOMBER (1941) WB. Producer, Hal B. Wallis. Associate Producer, Robert Lord. Technicolor. Director, Michael Curtiz. Author, Frank Wead. Screenplay, Frank Wead, Robert Buckner. Art Director, Robert Haas. Musical Director, Leo F. Forbstein. Cameramen, Bert Glennon, Winton C. Hoch. Aerial Photography, Elmer Dyer, Charles Marshall. Editor, George Amy. 133 minutes

Dive Bomber with Errol Flynn and Fred MacMurray.

Doug Lee: Errol Flynn, *Joe Blake:* Fred MacMurray, *Dr. Lance Rogers:* Ralph Bellamy, *Linda Fisher:* Alexis Smith, *Tim Griffin:* Regis Toomey, *Art Lyons:* Robert Armstrong, *Lucky Dice:* Allen Jenkins, *John Thomas Anthony:* Craig Stevens, *Chubby:* Herbert Anderson, *Senior Flight Surgeon:* Moroni Olson, *Swede:* Louis Jean Heydt, *Mrs. James:* Dennie Moore, *Corps Man:* Cliff Nazarro, *Helen:* Ann Doran, *Senior Flight Surgeon:* Addison Richards, *Admiral:* Russell Hicks, *Admiral:* Howard Hickman, *Pilot:* De Wolfe Hopper (William Hopper), *Pilot:* Charles Drake, *Pilot:* Byron Barr (Gig Young), *Squadron Commander:* Alexander Lockwood, *Commander:* George Meeker, *General:* Wedgwood Nowell, *Hospital Attendant:* Creighton Hale, *Hostess:* Charlotte Wynters, *Singer:* Jane Randolph, *Cigarette Girl:* Juanita Stark, *Girl at Newsstand:* Alice Talton, *Squadron C.O.:* Max Hoffman, Jr., *Pilot:* Alan Hale, Jr., *Pilot:* Sol Gorss, *Blue Jacket:* Walter Sande, *Telephone Man:* Michael Ames (Tod Andrews), *Flag Man:* Harry Lewis.

The Divorcee with Chester Morris and Norma Shearer.

THE DIVORCEE

THE DIVORCEE (1930) MGM. Directed by Robert Z. Leonard. Based on Ursula Parrott's novel *Ex-Wife.* Adapted by Nick Grinde and Zelda Sears. Continuity and Dialogue, John Meehan. Costumes, Adrian. Art Director, Cedric Gibbons. Photography, Norbert Brodine. Editors, Hugh Wynn and Truman K. Wood. Sound, Douglas Shearer. 80 minutes

Jerry: Norma Shearer, *Ted:* Chester Morris, *Paul:* Conrad Nagel, *Don:* Robert Montgomery, *Helen:* Florence Eldredge, *Mary:* Helene Millard, *Bill:* Robert Elliott, *Janice:* Mary Doran, *Hank:* Tyler Brooke, *Hannah:* Zelda Sears, *Dr. Bernard:* George Irving, *Dorothy:* Helen Johnson.

DIXIE

DIXIE (1943) Par. Associate Producer, Paul Jones. Directed by A. Edward Sutherland. Color by Technicolor. From a story by William Rankin. Screenplay, Karl Tunberg and Darrell Ware. Adaptation, Claude Binyon. Music Director, Robert Emmett Dolan. Vocal Arrangements, Joseph J. Lilley. Photography, William C. Mellor. Editor, William Shea. Songs by Johnny Burke and Jimmy Van Heusen: "Sunday, Monday and Always," "She's From Missouri," "Miss Jemima Walks By," "If You Please," "Kinda Peculiar Brown" and "A Horse That Knows His Way Back Home." 89 minutes

Dan Emmett: Bing Crosby, *Millie Cook:* Dorothy Lamour, *Jean Mason:* Marjorie Reynolds, *Mr. Bones:* Billy De Wolfe, *Mr. Whitlock:* Lynne Overman, *Mr. Cook:* Raymond Walburn, *Mr. Felham:* Eddie Foy, Jr., *Mr. Mason:* Grant Mitchell, *Minstrel Dancer:* Louis Da Pron, *Mrs. Mason:* Clara Blandick, *Homer:* Tom Herbert, *Mr. Devereaux:* Olin Howlin, *Mr. La Plant:* Robert Warwick, *Mr. Masters:* Stanley Andrews, *Mrs. La Plant:* Norma Varden, *Mrs. Masters:*

Dixie with Bing Crosby, Dorothy Lamour and Billy De Wolfe.

Hope Landin, *Riverboat Captain:* James Burke, *Lucius:* George H. Reed, *Drummer:* Harry Barris, *Publishers:* Jimmy Conlin, George Anderson, Harry C. Bradley, William Halligan, *Assistant to Publishers:* Wilbur Mack, *Southern Colonel:* Sam Flint, *Stage Manager:* Dell Henderson, *Waiter:* Fortunio Bonanova, *Steward:* Willie Best, *Barkeeper:* Tom Kennedy, *Blind Man:* Harry Tyler, *Woman:* Ethel Clayton, *Boy:* Carl "Alfalfa" Switzer, *Members of Minstrel Show:* John "Skins" Miller, Donald Kerr, Fred Santley, Warren Jackson, Jimmy Ray, Hal Rand, Charles Mayon, Allen Ray, Jerry James, Jimmy Clemons.

DOCTOR DOLITTLE (1967) 20th. Produced by Arthur P. Jacobs. Directed by Richard Fleischer. 70mm. Todd-AO and De Luxe Color. An Apjac Production. Based on the Doctor Dolittle stories by Hugh Lofting. Screenplay by Leslie Bricusse. Music scored and conducted by Lionel Newman and Alexander Courage. Production Design, Mario Chiari. Animals and birds from Jungleland. Assistant Director, Richard Lang. Special Effects, L. B. Abbott, Art Cruickshank, Emil Kosa Jr., and Howard Lydecker. Photography, Robert Surtees. Editors, Samuel E. Beetley and Marjorie Fowler. Sound, James Corcoran, Murray Spivack, Douglas Williams, Bernard Freericks, and John Myers. Songs by Leslie Bricusse: "My Friend the Doctor," "The Reluctant

Doctor Dolittle with Samantha Eggar and Rex Harrison.

Vegetarian," "If I Could Talk to the Animals," "At the Crossroads," "I've Never Seen Anything Like It," "Beautiful," "When I Look In Your Eyes," "Like Animals," "After Today," "Fabulous Places," "I Think I Like You," "This Is the World of Doctor Dolittle." 152 minutes

Doctor John Dolittle: Rex Harrison, *Emma Fairfax:* Samantha Eggar, *Matthew Mugg:* Anthony Newley, *Albert Blossom:* Richard Attenborough, *General Bellowes:* Peter Bull, *Mrs. Blossom:* Muriel Landers, *Tommy Stubbins:* William Dix, *Willie Shakespeare:* Geoffrey Holder, *Sarah Dolittle:* Portia Nelson, *Lady Petherington:* Norma Varden.

Dr. Jekyll and Mr. Hyde with Fredric March and Miriam Hopkins.

DR. JEKYLL AND MR. HYDE (1932) Par. Directed by Rouben Mamoulian. Based on Robert Louis Stevenson's story. Adaptation and Dialogue, Samuel Hoffenstein and Percy Heath. Assistant Director, Bob Lee. Art Director, Hans Dreier. Costume Design, Travis Banton. Photography, Karl Struss. Editor, William Shea. Sound, Martin Paggi. The book was published in London in 1885; the first stage version starred Richard Mansfield at the Boston Museum in 1887. Other film versions: Paramount, 1920; Pioneer Film Corp., 1920; MGM, 1941; *Two Faces of Dr. Jekyll* ("House of Fright"—British, 1961). Robert Louis Stevenson, a nephew of the author, has a bit. Miriam Hopkins sings "Champagne Ivy Is My Name." 90 minutes

Dr. Henry Jekyll/Mr. Hyde: Fredric March, *Ivy Pearson:* Miriam Hopkins, *Muriel Carew:* Rose Hobart, *Dr. Lanyan:* Holmes Herbert, *Brig. Gen. Sir Danvers Carew:* Halliwell Hobbes, *Poole, Jekyll's Butler:* Edgar Norton, *Utterson:* Arnold Lucy, *Hobson, Carew's Butler:* Colonel MacDonnell, *Mrs. Hawkins:* Tempe Pigott, *Briggs, Lanyan's Butler:* Eric Wilton, *Student:* Douglas Walton, *Waiter:* John Rogers, *Doctor:* Murdock MacQuarrie, *Dance Extra:* Major Sam Harris.

DR. NO (1963) UA. Producers, Harry Saltzman, Albert R. Broccoli. Director, Terence Young. Screenplay, Richard Maibaum, Johanna Harwood, Berkley Mather. Based on novel by Ian Fleming. Music, Monty Norman. Art Director, Syd Cain. Editor, Peter Hunt. 111 minutes

Doctor No with Sean Connery and Ursula Andress.

James Bond: Sean Connery, *Felix Leiter:* Jack Lord, *Dr. No:* Joseph Wiseman, *Honey Ryder:* Ursula Andress, *Miss Taro:* Zena Marshall, *Sylvia:* Eunice Gayson, *Moneypenny:* Lois Maxwell, *Photographer:* Margaret LeWars, *Quarrel:* John Kitzmiller, *"M":* Bernard Lee, *Professor Dent:* Anthony Dawson, *Puss Feller:* Lester Prendergast, *Strangways:* Tim Moxon, *Jones:* Reggie Carter, *Major Boothroyd:* Peter Burton, *Duff:* William Foster-Davis, *Playdell-Smith:* Louis Blaazer, *Sister Rose:* Michele Mok, *Mary:* Dolores Keator.

DR. STRANGELOVE: OR HOW I LEARNED TO STOP WORRYING AND LOVE THE BOMB (1964) Col. Producer-Director, Stanley Kubrick. Screenplay, Stanley Kubrick, Terry Southern, Peter George. Based on book *Red Alert* by Peter George. Associate Producer, Victor Lyndon. Director of Photography, Gilbert Taylor. Music, Laurie Johnson. Assistant Director, Eric Rattray. 93 minutes

Group Captain Lionel Mandrake/President Muffley/Dr. Strangelove: Peter Sellers, *General "Buck" Turgidson:* George C. Scott, *General Jack D. Ripper:* Sterling Hayden, *Colonel "Bat" Guano:* Keenan Wynn, *Major T. J. "King" Kong:* Slim Pickens, *Ambassador de Sadesky:* Peter Bull, *Miss Scott:* Tracy Reed, *Lt. Lothar Zogg:* James Earl Jones, *Mr. Staines:* Jack Creley, *Lt. H. R. Dietrich:* Frank Berry, *Lt. W. D. Kivel:* Glenn Beck, *Capt. G. A. "Ace" Owens:* Shane Rimmer, *Lt. B. Goldberg:* Paul Tamarin, *General Faceman:* Gordon Tanner, *Admiral Randolph:* Robert O'Neil, *Frank:* Roy Stephens, *Members of Defense Team:* Laurence Herder, John McCarthy, Hal Galili.

Dr. Strangelove with George C. Scott, Peter Bull and Peter Sellers.

Doctor Zhivago with Tom Courtenay and Julie Christie.

DOCTOR ZHIVAGO (1965) MGM. Producer, Carlo Ponti. Director, David Lean. Screenplay, Robert Bolt. From the novel by Boris Pasternak. Director of Photography, Fred A. Young. Music, Maurice Jarre. Executive Producer, Arvid L. Griffen. Assistant Directors, Roy Stevens, Pedro Vidal, Jose Maria Ochoa. Costumes, Phyllis Dalton. In Panavision and Color. 197 minutes

Tonya: Geraldine Chaplin, *Lara:* Julie Christie, *Pasha:* Tom Courtenay, *Yevgraf:* Alec Guinness, *Anna:* Siobhan McKenna, *Alexander:* Ralph Richardson, *Yuri:* Omar Sharif, *Komarovsky:* Rod Steiger, *The Girl:* Rita Tushingham, *Amelia:* Adrienne Corri, *Prof. Kurt:* Geoffrey Keen, *Sasha:* Jeffrey Rockland, *Katya:* Lucy Westmore, *Razin:* Noel Willman, *Liberius:* Gerard Tichy, *Kostoyed:* Klaus Kinski, *Petya:* Jack MacGowran, *Gentlewoman:* Maria Martin, *Yuri (at 8):* Tarek Sharif, *Tonya (at 7):* Mercedes Ruiz, *Colonel:* Roger Maxwell, *Major:* Inigo Jackson, *Captain:* Virgilio Texeira, *Bolshevik:* Bernard Kay, *Old Soldier:* Eric Chitty, *Priest:* Jose Nieto, *Young Engineer:* Mark Eden, *Mr. Sventytski:* Emilio Carrer, *David:* Gerhard Jersch, *Comrade Yelkin:* Wolf Frees, *Comrade Kaprugina:* Gwen Nelson, *Militiaman:* Jose Caffarel, *Streetwalker:* Brigitte Trace, *Mrs. Sventytski:* Luana Alcaniz, *Raddled Woman:* Lili Murati, *Raped Woman:* Catherine Ellison, *Demented Woman:* Maria Vico, *Dragoon Colonel:* Dodo Assad Bahador.

DODGE CITY (1939) WB. Produced by Robert Lord. Directed by Michael Curtiz. Original Screenplay, Robert Buckner. Color by Technicolor. Music, Max Steiner. Photography, Sol Polito. Technicolor Cameraman, Ray Rennahan. Editor, George Amy. Georgia Caine replaced Elisabeth Risdon. 105 minutes

Dodge City with Alan Hale and Errol Flynn.

Wade Hatton: Errol Flynn, *Abbie Irving:* Olivia De Havilland, *Ruby Gilman:* Ann Sheridan, *Jeff Surrett:* Bruce Cabot, *Joe Clemens:* Frank McHugh, *Rusty Hart:* Alan Hale, *Matt Cole:* John Litel, *Yancy:* Victor Jory, *Lee Irving:* William Lundigan, *Dr. Irving:* Henry Travers, *Colonel Dodge:* Henry O'Neill, *Tex Baird:* Guinn "Big Boy" Williams, *Mrs. Cole:* Gloria Holden, *Munger:* Douglas Fowley, *Mrs. Irving:* Georgia Caine, *Surrett's Lawyer:* Charles Halton, *Bud Taylor:* Ward Bond, *Harry Cole:* Bobs Watson, *Crocker:* Nat Carr, *Orth:* Russell Simpson, *Charlie, Barber:* Clem Bevans, *Mrs. McCoy:* Cora Witherspoon, *Hammond:* Joseph Crehan, *Twitchell:* Thurston Hall, *Coggins:* Chester Clute, *Barlow, Indian Agent:* Monte Blue, *Cattle Auctioneer:* James Burke, *Mail Clerk:* Robert Homans, *Marshal Jason:* George Guhl, *Minister:* Spencer Charters, *Stagecoach Driver/Waiter:* Bud Osborne, *Bartender:* Wilfred Lucas, *Clerk:* Richard Cramer, *Printer:* Milton Kibbee, *Woman:* Vera Lewis, *Spieler:* Earle Hodgins, *Al:* Fred Graham, *Passenger:* Tom Chatterton, *Conductor:* Pat O'Malley, *Cowhand:* Pat Flaherty.

Dodsworth with Ruth Chatterton and Walter Huston.

DODSWORTH (1936) UA. Produced by Samuel Goldwyn. Directed by William Wyler. Based on the novel by Sinclair Lewis. Screenplay by Sidney Howard. Associate Producer, Merritt Hulburd. Art Director, Richard Day. Music, Alfred Newman. Costumes, Omar Khayyam. Photography, Rudolph Mate. Editor, Daniel Mandell. Assistant Director, Eddie Bernoudy. Sound, Oscar Lagerstrom. Special Effects, Ray Binger. Film debut of John Payne. 90 minutes

Sam Dodsworth: Walter Huston, *Fran Dodsworth:* Ruth Chatterton, *Arnold Iselin:* Paul Lukas, *Edith Cortright:* Mary Astor, *Lockert:* David Niven, *Kurt von Obersdorf:* Gregory Gaye, *Baroness von Obersdorf:* Maria Ouspenskaya, *Madame de Penable:* Odette Myrtil, *Emily:* Kathryn Marlowe, *Harry:* John Payne, *Matey Pearson:* Spring Byington, *Tubby Pearson:* Harlan Briggs.

The Dolly Sisters with Betty Grable, June Haver and S.Z. Sakall.

THE DOLLY SISTERS (1945) 20th. Producer, George Jessel. Director, Irving Cummings. Color by Technicolor. Screenplay, John Larkin, Marian Spitzer. Dance Director, Seymour Felix. Musical Directors, Alfred Newman, Charles Henderson. Art Directors, Lyle Wheeler, Leland Fuller. Cameraman, Ernest Palmer. Special Effects, Fred Sersen. Editor, Barbara McLean. Technicolor Director, Natalie Kalmus. Associate, Richard Mueller. Songs: "I Can't Begin to Tell You" and "Don't Be Too Old-Fashioned (Old-Fashioned Girl)" by Mack Gordon and Jimmy Monaco; "Give Me the Moonlight, Give Me the Girl" by Lew Brown and Albert Von Tilzer; "We Have Been Around" by Mack Gordon and Charles Henderson; "Carolina in the Morning" by Walter Donaldson; "Powder, Lipstick and Rouge" by Mack Gordon and Harry Revel; "Darktown Strutters' Ball" by Shelton Brooks; "Smiles" by Lee Roberts; "Arrah Go on I'm Gonna Go Back to Oregon" by Joe Yound, Sam Lewis and Bert Grant; "Oh, Frenchie" by Sam Ehrlich and Con Conrad; "I'm Always Chasing Rainbows" by Joseph McCarthy and Harry Carroll; "On the Mississippi" by Ballard MacDonald, Buddy Fields and Harry Carroll. 114 minutes

Jenny Dolly: Betty Grable, *Harry Fox:* John Payne, *Rosie Dolly:* June Haver, *Uncle Latsie:* S. Z. Sakall, *Duke:* Reginald Gardiner, *Irving Netcher:* Frank Latimore, *Professor Winnup:* Gene Sheldon, *Tsimmis:* Sig Rumann, *Lenore:* Trudy Marshall, *Flo Daly:* Collette Lyons, *Jenny, as a child:* Evon Thomas, *Rosie, as a child:* Donna Jo Gribble, *Hammerstein:* Robert Middlemass, *Dowling:* Paul Hurst, *Morrie Keno:* Lester Allen, *Stage Manager:* Frank Orth, *Will Rogers:* Sam Garrett, *Al Smith:* J. C. Fowler, *Mrs. Al Smith:* Betty Farrington, *Nun:* Virginia Brissac, *Man:* Charles Evans, *Frank Tinny:* George O'Hara, *Madame Polaire:* Ricki Van Dusen, *Doorman:* J. Farrell MacDonald, *Fields (Weber & Fields):* Herbert Ashley, *Bartender:* William Nye, *Man:* Julius Tannen, *Conductor:* Walter Soderling, *Pianist:* Harry Seymour, *French Juggler:* George Davis, *German Actress:* Trudy Berliner, *Russian Actor:* Igor Lolgoruki, *French Actor:* Nino Bellini, *Ellabelle:* Theresa Harris, *Hammerstein's Secretary:* Mary Currier, *Phillipe:* Andre Charlot, *Harris:* Edward Kano, *Flower Lady:* Mae Marsh, *Kathi:* Else Janssen.

Don't Go Near the Water with Fred Clark, Russ Tamblyn and Glenn Ford.

DON'T GO NEAR THE WATER (1957) MGM. Producer, Lawrence Weingarten. Director, Charles Walters. CinemaScope, MetroColor. Screenplay by Dorothy Kingsley and George Wells. Based on novel by William Brinkley. Music by Bronislau Kaper. Lyrics for song by Sammy Cahn, sung by the Lancers. Assistant Director, Al Jennings. Costumes by Helen Rose. An Avon Production. Photography, Robert Bronner. 107 minutes

Lt. Max Siegel: Glenn Ford, *Melora:* Gia Scala, *Adam Garrett:* Earl Holliman, *Lt. Alice Tomlen:* Anne Francis, *Gordon Ripwell:* Keenan Wynn, *Lt. Comdr. Clinton Nash:* Fred Clark, *Deborah Aldrich:* Eva Gabor, *Ensign Tyson:* Russ Tamblyn, *Lt. Ross Pendleton:* Jeff

Richards, *Farragut Jones:* Mickey Shaughnessy, *Admiral Boatwright:* Howard Smith, *Mr. Alba:* Romney Brent, *Janie:* Mary Wickes, *Lt. Comdr. Gladstone:* Jack Straw, *Lt. Comdr. Hereford:* Robert Nichols, *Lt. Comdr. Diplock:* John Alderson, *Rep. George Jansen:* Jack Albertson, *Rep. Arthur Smithfield:* Charles Watts, *Mr. Seguro:* Julian Rivero, *Lt. Comdr. Pratt:* Ike Gibson, *Lt. Hepburn:* Don Burnett, *Jerry Wakely:* Hugh Boswell, *Yeoman:* Wilson Wood, *Corp. Donohue:* John Dennis, *Seaman Flaherty:* Steve Warren, *Lt. Boone:* William Ogden Joyce, *Boatswain:* Gregg Martell, *Seabee Metkoff:* John L. Cason, *Lt. Comdr. Flaherty:* Paul Bryar.

Double Indemnity with Richard Gaines, Bess Flowers, Edward G. Robinson and Fred MacMurray.

DOUBLE INDEMNITY (1944) Par. Produced by Joseph Sistrom. Directed by Billy Wilder. From the novel by James M. Cain, also presented in *Liberty* magazine. Screenplay, Billy Wilder and Raymond Chandler. Musical Score, Miklos Rozsa. Art Directors, Hans Dreier and Hal Pereira. Camera, John Seitz. Process Photography, Farciot Edouart. Editor, Doane Harrison. Based on the 1927 slaying of Albert Snyder in Queens Village, New York, by his wife Ruth and her lover Judd Gray, for his insurance. Cut from the release print were scenes dealing with MacMurray's execution. Bits in these sequences included: Alan Bridge (Execution Chamber Guard), Edward Hearn (Warden's Secretary), George Anderson (Warden), Boyd Irwin and George Melford (Doctors), Lee Shumway (Door Guard), and William O'Leary (Chaplain). 106 minutes

Walter Neff: Fred MacMurray, *Phyllis Dietrichson:* Barbara Stanwyck, *Barton Keyes:* Edward G. Robinson, *Mr. Jackson:* Porter Hall, *Lola Dietrichson:* Jean Heather, *Mr. Dietrichson:* Tom Powers, *Nino Zachetti:* Byron Barr, *Edward S. Norton:* Richard Gaines, *Sam Gorlopis:* Fortunio Bonanova, *Joe Peters:* John Philliber, *Bit:* George Magrill, *Norton's Secretary:* Bess Flowers, *Conductor:* Kernan Cripps, *Redcap:* Harold Garrison, *Pullman Porter:* Oscar Smith, *Nettie, the Maid:* Betty Farrington, *Woman:* Constance Purdy, *Pullman Conductor:* Dick Rush, *Pullman Porter:* Frank Billy Mitchell, *Train Conductor:* Edmund Cobb, *Pullman Porter:* Floyd Shackelford, *Pullman Porter:* James Adamson, *Garage Attendant, Charlie:* Sam McDaniel, *Man:* Clarence Muse, *Telephone Operator:* Judith Gibson, *Keyes' Secretary:* Miriam Franklin, *Lou Schwartz:* Douglas Spencer.

DRACULA (1931) Univ. Directed by Tod Browning. From the novel by Bram Stoker and the play by Hamilton Deane and John Balderston. Scenario, Garrett Fort. Photography, Karl Freund. Editor, Milton Carruth. Sound, C. Roy Hunter. Bela Lugosi repeats his 1927 stage role, which was to have been played in the film by Lon Chaney, Sr. 84 minutes

Count Dracula: Bela Lugosi, *Mina Seward:* Helen Chandler, *John Harker:* David Manners, *Renfield:* Dwight Frye, *Professor Van Helsing:* Edward Van Sloan, *Doctor Seward:* Herbert Bunston, *Lucy Weston:* Frances Dade, *Martin:* Charles Gerrard, *Maid:* Joan Standing, *Briggs:* Moon Carroll, *English Nurse:* Josephine Velez, *Innkeeper:* Michael Visaroff.

Dracula with Bela Lugosi and Helen Chandler.

DRAGNET (1954) WB. Producer, Stanley Meyer. Director, Jack Webb. Color by WarnerColor. A Mark VII Production. Art Director, Field Gray. Cinematographer, Edward Colman. Editor, Robert M. Leeds. 89 minutes

Joe Friday: Jack Webb, *Frank Smith:* Ben Alexander, *Captain Hamilton:* Richard Boone, *Max Troy:* Stacy Harris, *Grace Downey:* Ann Robinson, *Mrs. Starkie:* Virginia Gregg, *Miller Starkie:* Dub Taylor, *Belle Davitt:* Georgia Ellis, *Chester Davitt:* Willard Sage, *Jesse Quinn:* Jim Griffith, *Adolph Alexander:* Vic Perrin, *Lee Reinhard:* Malcolm Atterbury, *Charlie Weaver:* Cliff Arquette, *Captain Lohrman:* Dennis Weaver, *Fred Kemp:* James Anderson, *Fabian Gerard:* Monte Masters, *Ray Pinker:* Olan Soule, *Roy Cleaver:* Dick Cathcart, *Cuban Singer:* Meg Myles, *Mrs. Caldwell:* Virginia Christine, *Mr. Archer:* Herb Vigran, *Officer Tilden:* Fred Dale, *Sergeant McCreadie:* Roy Whaley, *Ken, Stenotypist:* Charles Hibbs, *Walker Scott:* Guy Hamilton, *McQueen:* George Sawaya, *Eddy King:* Eddy King, *Pat, Script Secretary:* Jean Dean, *Lieutenant Stevens:* Harry Bartell, *Booking Sergeant:* Herb Ellis, *Jailer:* Mauritz Hugo, *Hank Wild:* Bill Brundidge, *Doctor:* Art Gilmore, *Hotel Clerk:* Dick Paxton, *Intelligence Officer:* Ross Elliott, *Wesley Cannon:* Ramsay Williams, *Interne:* Harlan Warde, *Officer Keeler:* Gayle Kellogg, *Officer Gene James:* Ken Peters, *Officer Greeley:* Harry Lauter.

Dragnet with Ben Alexander, Jack Webb and Georgia Ellis.

DRAGON SEED (1944) MGM. Produced by Pandro S. Berman. Directed by Jack Conway and Harold S. Bucquet. Based on the novel by Pearl S. Buck. Screenplay, Marguerite Roberts and Jane Murfin. Music, Herbert Stothart. Photography, Sidney Wagner. Editor, Harold F. Kress. 145 minutes

319

Dragon Seed with Katharine Hepburn and Turhan Bey.

Jade: Katharine Hepburn, *Ling Tan:* Walter Huston, *Mrs. Ling Tan:* Aline MacMahon, *Wu Lien:* Akim Tamiroff, *Lao Er:* Turhan Bey, *Lao San:* Hurd Hatfield, *Orchid:* Frances Rafferty, *Third Cousin's Wife:* Agnes Moorehead, *Third Cousin:* Henry Travers, *Captain Sato:* Robert Lewis, *Japanese Kitchen Overseer:* J. Carroll Naish, *Lao Ta:* Robert Bice, *Mrs. Wu Lien:* Jacqueline de Wit, *Fourth Cousin:* Clarence Lung, *Neighbor Shen:* Paul E. Burns, *Wu Sao:* Anna Demetrio, *Major Yohagi:* Ted Hecht, *Captain Yasuda:* Abner Biberman, *Old Peddler:* Leonard Mudie, *Japanese Diplomat:* Charles Lung, *Student:* Benson Fong, *Japanese Guard:* Philip Van Zandt, *Japanese Officer:* Al Hill, *Japanese Soldier:* J. Alex Havier, *Leader of City People:* Phillip Ahn, *Speaker with Movies:* Roland Got, *Young Farmer:* Robert Lee, *Old Clerk:* Frank Puglia, *Hysterical Woman:* Claire DuBrey, *Innkeeper:* Lee Tung Foo, *Japanese Soldier:* Jay Novello, *Japanese Official:* Leonard Strong, *Narrator:* Lionel Barrymore.

DRAGONWYCK (1946) 20th. Producer, Darryl F. Zanuck. Director, Joseph L. Mankiewicz. Based on the novel by Anya Seton. Screenplay, Joseph L. Mankiewicz. Musical Score, Alfred Newman. Art Directors, Lyle Wheeler, J. Russell Spencer. Dance Director, Arthur Appel. Cameraman, Arthur Miller. Special Effects, Fred Sersen. Editor, Dorothy Spencer. 103 minutes

Miranda: Gene Tierney, *Ephraim Wells:* Walter Huston, *Nicholas Van Ryn:* Vincent Price, *Dr. Jeff Turner:* Glenn Langan, *Abigail:* Anne Revere, *Magda:* Spring Byington, *Katrine:* Connie Marshall, *Bleecker:* Henry Morgan, *Johanna:* Vivienne Osborne, *Peggy O'Malley:* Jessica Tandy, *Elizabeth Van Bordon:* Trudy Marshall, *Count De Grenier:* Reinhold Schunzel, *Tabitha:* Jane Nigh, *Cornelia Van Borden:* Ruth Ford, *Mrs. McNab:* Betty Faifax, *Zack Wilson:* Michael Garrison, *Hotel Clark:* Grady Sutton, *Tom Wells:* Scott Elliott, *Tompkins:* Boyd Irwin, *Mr. McNab:* Keith Hitchcock, *Countess De Grenier:* Maya Van Horn, *Dr. Brown:* Francis Pierlot, *French Count:* John Chellot, *French Countess:* Nanette Vallon, *Helena:* Virginia Lindley, *Nathaniel:* Mickey Roth, *Seth:* Jaime Dana, *Messenger Boy:* Robert (Buzz) Henry, *Mayor:* Douglas Wood.

Dragonwyck with Glenn Langan, Vincent Price and Gene Tierney.

DRUMS ALONG THE MOHAWK (1939) 20th. Associate Producer, Raymond Griffith. Directed by John Ford. Color by Technicolor. Based on the novel by Walter D. Edmonds. Screenplay, Lamar Trotti and Sonya Levien. Director of Photography, Bert Glennon. Technicolor Director of Photography, Ray Rennahan. Technicolor Director, Natalie Kalmus. Associate, Henri Jaffa. Editor, Robert Simpson. 103 minutes

Lana (Magdelana) Martin: Claudette Colbert, *Gil Martin:* Henry Fonda, *Sarah McKlennar:* Edna May Oliver, *Christian Reall:* Eddie Collins, *Caldwell:* John Carradine, *Mary Reall:* Dorris Bowdon, *Mrs. Weaver:* Jessie Ralph, *Reverend Rosenkrantz:* Arthur Shields, *John Weaver:* Robert Lowery, *General Nicholas Herkimer:* Roger Imhof, *Joe Boleo:* Francis Ford, *Adam Helmer:* Ward Bond, *Mrs. Demooth:* Kay Linaker, *Dr. Petry:* Russell Simpson, *Landlord:* Spencer Charters, *Jacob Small:* Si Jenks, *Amos Hartman:* Jack Pennick, *George Weaver:* Arthur Aylesworth, *Blue Back:* Chief Big Tree, *Dr. Robert Johnson:* Charles Tannen, *Captain Mark Demooth:* Paul McVey, *Mrs. Reall:* Elizabeth (Tiny) Jones, *Daisy:* Beulah Hall Jones, *Reverend Daniel Gros:* Edwin Maxwell, *Mr. Borst:* Robert Greig, *Mrs. Borst:* Clara Blandick, *Morgan:* Tom Tyler, *General:* Lionel Pape, *Indian:* Noble Johnson, *Paymaster:* Clarence H. Wilson, *Pioneer Woman:* Mae Marsh.

Drums Along the Mohawk with Henry Fonda and Claudette Colbert.

DUEL IN THE SUN (1946) Selznick Releasing Organization. Produced by David O. Selznick. Directed by King Vidor. Second Units directed by Otto Brower and Reaves Eason. Color by Technicolor. A Vanguard Production. Suggested by the novel by Niven Busch. Screenplay, David O. Selznick. Adaptation, Oliver H. P. Garrett. Art Director, James Basevi. Associate, John Ewing. Production Design, J. McMillan Johnson. Technical Director, Natalie Kalmus. Solo Dances, Tilly Losch. Group Dances, Lloyd Shaw. Music, Dimitri Tiomkin. Song, "Gotta Get Me Somebody to Love" by Allie Wrubel. Narrated by Orson Welles. Costumes, Walter Plunkett. Photography, Lee Garmes, Hal Rosson, Ray Rennahan. Special Effects, Clarence Lifer and Jack Cosgrove. Supervising Editor, Hal C. Kern. Editors, William Ziegler, John Saure. Film debut of Joan Tetzel, 22. 138 minutes

Pearl Chavez: Jennifer Jones, *Jesse McCanles:* Joseph Cotten, *Lewt McCanles:* Gregory Peck, *Senator McCanles:* Lionel Barrymore, *Laura Belle McCanles:* Lillian Gish, *The Sinkiller:* Walter Huston, *Scott Chavez:* Herbert Marshall, *Sam Pierce:* Charles Bickford, *Helen Langford:* Joan Tetzel, *Lem Smoot:* Harry Carey, *Mr. Langford:* Otto Kruger, *The Lover:* Sidney Blackmer, *Mrs. Chavez:* Tilly Losch, *Sid:* Scott McKay, *Vashti:* Butterfly McQueen, *Gambler:* Francis McDonald, *Gambler:* Victor Kilian, *The Jailer:* Griff Barnett, *Ken:* Frank Cordell, *Ed:* Dan White, *Jake:* Steve Dunhill, *Captain of U.S.*

Duel in the Sun with Jennifer Jones and Lionel Barrymore.

Cavalry: Lane Chandler, *Caller at Barbecue:* Lloyd Shaw, *Engineer:* Thomas Dillon, *Bartender:* Robert McKenzie, *Sheriff Thomson:* Charles Dingle, *Barfly, Presidio Bar:* Kermit Maynard, *Ranch Hand:* Hank Bell, *Hand at Barbecue:* Johnny Bond, *An Eater:* Bert Roach, *Dancers at Barbecue:* Si Jenks, Hank Worden, Rose Plummer, *Barfly:* Guy Wilkerson, *Engineer:* Lee Phelps.

DUFFY'S TAVERN (1945) Par. Associate Producer, Danny Dare. Directed by Hal Walker. Based on characters created by Ed Gardner. Original Screenplay, Melvin Frank and Norman Panama. Sketches, Norman Panama and Melvin Frank, Abram S. Burrows, Barney Dean, George White, Eddie Davis and Matt Brooks. Music Director, Robert Emmett Dolan. Photography, Lionel Lindon. Songs: "The Hard Way" by Johnny Burke and Jimmy Van Heusen; "You Can't Blame a Girl for Tryin'" by Ben Raleigh and Bernie Wayne. Bing's sons Gary, 11, Dennis and Phillip, 10, and Lindsay, 6, make their film debuts. 97 minutes

Themselves: Bing Crosby, Betty Hutton, Paulette Goddard, Alan Ladd, Dorothy Lamour, Eddie Bracken, Brian Donlevy, Sonny Tufts, Veronica Lake, Arturo De Cordova, William Bendix, Joan Caulfield, Gail Russell, *Bing's Father:* Barry Fitzgerald, *Archie:* Ed Gardner, *Michael O'Malley:* Victor Moore, *Peggy O'Malley:* Marjorie Reynolds, *Danny Murphy:* Barry Sullivan, *Finnegan:* Charles Cantor, *Eddie, the Waiter:* Eddie Green, *Miss Duffy:* Ann Thomas, *Heavy:* Howard da Silva, *Doctor:* Billy De Wolfe, *Director:* Walter Abel, *Dancer-Waiter:* Johnny Coy, *Ronald:* Charles Quigley, *Gloria:* Olga San Juan, *Dancer:* Miriam Franklin, *Piano Specialty:* Maurice Rocco, *Themselves:* Cass Daley, Diana Lynn, Robert Benchley, William Demarest, James

Duffy's Tavern with Jean Heather, Bing Crosby, Helen Walker and Gail Russell.

Brown, Helen Walker, Gary, Phillip, Dennis, and Lin Crosby, Jean Heather, Barney Dean, *Masseur:* Bobby Watson, *Customer:* Frank Faylen, *Mr. Richardson:* George M. Carleton, *Mr. Smith:* Addison Richards, *Regan:* George McKay, *Assistant Director:* James Millican, *Make-up Man:* Emmett Vogan, *Nurse:* Catherine Craig, *School Kid:* Noel Neill.

EAGLE SQUADRON (1942) Univ. Produced by Walter Wanger. Directed by Arthur Lubin. From the *Cosmopolitan* magazine story by C. S. Forrester. Screenplay, Norman Reilly Raine. Art Directors, Jack Otterson and Alexander Golitzen. Score, Frank Skinner. Music Director, Charles Previn. Camera, Stanley Cortez. Special Effects, John Fulton. Editor, Philip Cahn. 109 minutes

Eagle Squadron with Diana Barrymore, John Loder, Jon Hall, Leif Erikson, Robert Stack and Edgar Barrier.

Chuck Brewer: Robert Stack, *Anne Partridge:* Diana Barrymore, *Paddy Carson:* John Loder, *Leckie:* Eddie Albert, *McKinnon:* Nigel Bruce, *Johnny Coe:* Leif Erikson, *Wadislaw Borowsky:* Edgar Barrier, *Hank Starr:* Jon Hall, *Nancy Mitchell:* Evelyn Ankers, *Dame Elizabeth Whitby:* Isobel Elsom, *Olesen:* Alan Hale, Jr., *Ramsey:* Don Porter, *Grenfall:* Frederick Worlock, *Air Minister:* Stanley Ridges, *The Kid:* Gene Reynolds, *Bullock:* Robert Warwick, *Chandler:* Clarence Straight, *Meeker:* Edmund Glover, *Aunt Emmeline:* Gladys Cooper, *Sergeant Johns:* Rhys Williams, *Sir John:* Paul Cavanagh, *Severn:* Gavin Muir, *Lieutenant Jefferys:* Richard Fraser, *Griffith:* Richard Crane, *Barker:* Howard Banks, *Welch:* Harold Landon, *Meyers:* Todd Karns, *Chubby:* Charles King, Jr., *Phyllis:* Jill Esmond, *Sir Charles Porter:* Ian Wolfe, *Black Watch Officer:* Alan Napier, *Private Owen:* Harold deBecker, *Hoskins:* Donald Stuart, *Lubbock:* Carl Harbord, *Sir Benjamin Trask:* Charles Irwin, *Day Controller:* Olaf Hytten, *R. A. F. Flyers:* Stanley Smith, Richard Davies, *Lankershire Blonde:* Queenie Leonard, *Simms:* Ivan Simpson, *Wing Commander:* John Burton, *King:* Bruce Lester, *Allison:* Tom Stevenson, *Blind Patient:* James Eagles, *Medical Officer:* James Seay, *Nurse:* Audrey Long, *Mother:* Mary Carr, *Pilot:* Peter Lawford, *German Soldier:* Rex Lease, *Children:* Tarquin Olivier, William Severn, Linda Bieber, Peggy Ann Garner.

EASTER PARADE (1948) MGM. Producer, Arthur Freed. Director, Charles Walters. Color by Technicolor. Original Story, Frances Goodrich, Albert Hackett. Screenplay, Sidney Sheldon, Frances Goodrich, Albert Hackett. Art Directors, Cedric Gibbons, Jack Martin Smith. Musical Director, Johnny Green. Orchestration, Conrad Salinger, Van Cleave, Leo Arnaud. Editor, Albert Akst. Photography by Harry Stradling. Songs by Irving Berlin: "Happy Easter," "Drum Crazy," "It Only Happens When I Dance With You," "Everybody's Doing It," "I Wanna Go Back to Michigan," "A Fella With an Umbrella," "I Love a Piano," "Snooky Ookums," "Ragtime Violin", "When the Midnight Choo Choo Leaves for Alabam," "Shaking the Blues

Easter Parade with Peter Lawford, Judy Garland and Fred Astaire.

Away," "Stepping Out With My Baby," "A Couple of Swells," "Beautiful Faces Need Beautiful Clothes," "The Girl on the Magazine Cover," "Better Luck Next Time," "Easter Parade." 103 minutes

Don Hewes: Fred Astaire, *Hannah Brown:* Judy Garland, *Jonathan Harrow III:* Peter Lawford, *Nadine Hale:* Ann Miller, *Mike, the Bartender:* Clinton Sundberg, *Francois:* Jules Munshin, *Essie:* Jeni LeGon, *Singer:* Richard Beavers, *Al, Stage Manager for Ziegfeld:* Dick Simmons, *Boy in "Drum Crazy":* Jimmy Bates, *Cabby:* Jimmy Dodd, *Cop Who Gives Johnny a Ticket:* Robert Emmett O'Connor, *Specialty Dancers:* Patricia Jackson, Bobbie Priest, Dee Turnell, *Hat Models:* Lola Albright, Joi Lansing, *"Delineator" Twins:* Lynn and Jean Romer, *Modiste:* Helene Heigh, *Marty:* Wilson Wood, *Dog Act:* Hector and His Pals (Carmi Tryon), *Sam, Valet:* Peter Chong, *Drug Clerk:* Nolan Leary, *Mary:* Doris Kemper, *Headwaiter:* Frank Mayo, *Bar Patron:* Benay Venuta.

EAST OF EDEN (1955) WB. Producer, Elia Kazan. Director, Elia Kazan. CinemaScope and WarnerColor. Screenplay, Paul Osborn. Art Directors, James Basevi, Malcolm Bert. Musical Director, Leonard Rosenman. Cinematographer, Ted McCord. Editor, Owen Marks. 115 minutes

Cal: James Dean, *Abra:* Julie Harris, *Adam:* Raymond Massey, *Sam:* Burl Ives, *Kate:* Jo Van Fleet, *Aron:* Richard Davalos, *Will:* Albert Dekker, *Anne:* Lois Smith, *Mr. Albecht:* Harold Gordon, *Dr. Edwards:* Richard Garrick, *Joe:* Timothy Carey, *Rantini:* Nick Dennis, *Roy:* Lonnie Chapman, *Nurse:* Barbara Baxley, *Madame:* Bette Treadville, *Bartender:* Tex Mooney, *Bouncer:* Harry Cording, *Card Dealer:* Loretta Rush, *Coalman:* Bill Phillips, *Piscora:* Mario Siletti, *Piscora's Son:* Jonathan Haze, *Carnival People:* Jack Carr, Roger Creed, Effie

East of Eden with Jo Van Fleet and James Dean.

Laird, Wheaton Chambers, Ed Clark, Al Ferguson, Franklyn Farnum, Rose Plummer, *Photographer:* John George, *Shooting Gallery Attendant:* Earle Hodgins, *English Officer:* C. Ramsay Hill, *Soldier:* Edward McNally.

Easy to Wed with Lucille Ball and Keenan Wynn.

EASY TO WED (1946) MGM. Producer, Jack Cummings. Director, Edward Buzzell. Color by Technicolor. Authors, Maurine Watkins, Howard Emmett Rogers, George Oppenheimer (from *Libeled Lady*). Screenplay, Dorothy Kingsley. Musical Score Supervision and Direction, Johnny Green. Technicolor Director, Natalie Kalmus. Art Director, Cedric Gibbons. Photography, Harry Stradling, Editor, Blanche Sewell. Songs: "Easy to Wed" by Ted Duncan and Johnny Green; "Goosey-Lucy" and "It Shouldn't Happen to a Duck" by Robert Franklin and Johnny Green; "Continental Polka" and "(Tell You What I'm Gonna Do) Gonna Fall in Love With You" by Ralph Blane and Johnny Green; "Come Closer to Me" by Osvaldo Farres. Remake of MGM's *Libeled Lady*, 1936. 110 minutes

Bill Chandler: Van Johnson, *Connie Allenbury:* Esther Williams, *Gladys Benton:* Lucille Ball, *Warren Haggerty:* Keenan Wynn, *J. B. Allenbury:* Cecil Kellaway, *Carlos:* Carlos Ramirez, *Spike Dolan:* Ben Blue, *Ethel:* Ethel Smith, *Babs Norvell:* June Lockhart, *Homer Henshaw:* Grant Mitchell, *Mrs. Burns Norvell:* Josephine Whittell, *Frances:* Jean Porter, *Farwood:* Paul Harvey, *Boswell:* Jonathan Hale, *Joe:* James Flavin, *Farwood's Secretary:* Celia Travers, *Taxi Driver:* Robert Emmett O'Connor, *Truck Drivers:* Charles Sullivan, Frank Hagney, *Receptionist:* Sybil Merritt, *Orchestra Leader:* Dick Winslow, *Justice of the Peace:* Joel Friedkin, *Private Detective:* Milton Kibbee, *Waiter:* Tom Dugan, *Masseuse:* Katherine Black, *Butler:* Guy Bates Post, *Mr. Dibson:* Walter Soderling, *Mrs. Dibson:* Sarah Edwards, *Lifeguard:* Jack Shea.

THE EDDY DUCHIN STORY (1956) Col. Producer, Jerry Wald. Associate Producer, Jonie Taps. Director, George Sidney. CinemaScope, Technicolor. Author, Leo Katcher. Screenplay, Samuel Taylor. Art Director, Walter Holscher. Music supervised and conducted by Morris Stoloff. Piano recordings by Carmen Cavallaro. Incidental music, George Duning. Cinematographer, Harry Stradling. Editors, Viola Lawrence, Jack W. Ogilvie. 123 minutes

Eddy Duchin: Tyrone Power, *Marjorie Oelrichs:* Kim Novak, *Chiquita:* Victoria Shaw, *Lou Sherwood:* James Whitmore, *Peter Duchin at 12:* Rex Thompson, *Peter at 5:* Mickey Maga, *Mr. Wadsworth:* Shepperd Strudwick, *Mrs. Wadsworth:* Frieda Inescort, *Mrs. Duchin:* Gloria Holden, *Leo Reisman:* Larry Keating, *Mr. Duchin:* John Mylong, *Philip:* Gregory Gay, *Native Boy:* Warren Hsieh, *Piano Tuner:* Jack Albertson, *Doctor:* Carlyle Mitchell, *Nurse:* Lois Kimbrell, *Mayor Walker:* Ralph Gamble, *Captain:* Richard Cutting, *Seaman:* Richard Crane, *Seaman:* Brad Trumbull, *Mrs. Rutledge:* Gloria Ann Simpson, *Bit Man:* Rick Person, *Bit Man:* Michael Legend, *Girl:* Betsy Jones Moreland, *Young Man:* Kirk Alyn.

The Eddy Duchin Story with Kim Novak, James Whitmore and Tyrone Power.

The Egyptian with Richard Allan, Tyler McDuff, Victor Mature and Edmund Purdom.

THE EGYPTIAN (1954) 20th. Producer, Darryl F. Zanuck. Director, Michael Curtiz. CinemaScope, De Luxe Color. Based on the novel by Mika Waltari. Screenplay, Philip Dunne, Casey Robinson. Art Directors, Lyle Wheeler, George W. Davis. Cinematographer, Leon Shamroy. Editor, Barbara McLean. 140 minutes

Sinuhe: Edmund Purdom, *Merit:* Jean Simmons, *Horemheb:* Victor Mature, *Baketamon:* Gene Tierney, *Akhanton:* Michael Wilding, *Nefer:* Bella Darvi, *Kaptah:* Peter Ustinov, *Taia:* Judith Evelyn, *Mikera:* Henry Daniell, *Grave Robber:* John Carradine, *Senmut:* Carl Benton Reid, *Thoth:* Tommy Rettig, *Nefertiti:* Anitra Stevens, *Egyptian Dancer:* Carmen de Lavallade, *Lady in Waiting:* Donna Martell, *Little Princess:* Mimi Gibson, *Nubian Leopard Attendant:* Harry Thompson, *Libyan Guards:* Tiger Joe Marsh, Karl Davis, *Ship's Captain:* Ian MacDonald, *Sinuhe, age 10:* Peter Raynolds, *Governess:* Joan Winfield, *Foreman of Death House:* Mike Mazurki, *Cadets:* Richard Allan, Tyler McDuff, *Kipa:* Angela Clarke, *Patient in Dispensary:* Edmund Cobb, *Hittite Commander:* Michael Ansara.

EL CID (1961) AA. Producer, Samuel Bronston. Director, Anthony Mann. Associate Producers, Michael Waszynski, Jaime Prades. Screenplay, Fredric M. Frank, Philip Yordan. Music, Miklos Rozsa. Assistant Directors, Yakima Canutt, Luciano Sacripanti, Jose Maria Ochoa, Jose Lopez Rodero. Produced in association with Dear Film Productions in 70-mm Super Technirama and Technicolor. 184 minutes

El Cid (Rodrigo Diaz): Charlton Heston, *Chimene:* Sophia Loren, *Ordonez:* Raf Vallone, *Urraca:* Genevieve Page, *Alfonso:* John Fraser, *Sancho:* Gary Raymond, *Arias:* Hurd Hatfield, *Fanez:* Massimo Serato, *Ben Yussuf:* Herbert Lom, *Gormaz:* Andrew Cruickshank, *Don Martin:*

El Cid with Raf Vallone, Charlton Heston and Douglas Wilmer.

Christopher Rhodes, *Don Diego:* Michael Hordern, *King Ferdinand:* Ralph Truman, *Don Pedro:* Tullio Carminati, *King Ramiro:* Gerard Tichy, *Bermudez:* Carlo Giustini, *Moutamin:* Douglas Wilmer, *Al Kadir:* Frank Thring.

ELMER GANTRY (1960) UA. Producer, Bernard Smith. Director, Richard Brooks. Assistant Directors, Tom Shaw, Rowe Wallerstein, Carl Beringer. Costumes, Dorothy Jeakins. Screenplay, Richard Brooks. Based on the novel by Sinclair Lewis. Art Director, Ed Carrere. Music, Andre Previn. Cinematography, John Alton. Editor, Marge Fowler. Color by Eastman Color. 146 minutes

Elmer Gantry: Burt Lancaster, *Sister Sharon Falconer:* Jean Simmons, *Jim Lefferts:* Arthur Kennedy, *Lulu Bains:* Shirley Jones, *William L. Morgan:* Dean Jagger, *Sister Rachel:* Patti Page, *George Babbitt:* Edward Andrews, *Rev. Pengilly:* John McIntire, *Pete:* Joe Maross, *Rev. Brown:* Everett Glass, *Rev. Phillips:* Michael Whalen, *Rev. Garrison:* Hugh Marlowe, *Rev. Planck:* Philip Ober, *Rev. Ulrich:* Wendell Holmes, *Captain Holt:* Barry Kelley, *Preacher:* Rex Ingram, *Publisher Eddington:* Dayton Lummis, *Friends:* Ray Walker, Ralph Dumke, George Cisar, Norman Leavitt, *Mac, Bartender:* Larry J. Blake, *Sam, Storekeeper:* John Qualen, *Valet:* George Selk (Budd Buster), *Clean-up Man:* Guy Wilkerson, *Revivalist:* Milton Parsons, *Speaker:* Dan Riss, *Prostitutes:* Jean Willes and Sally Fraser, *Benny, Photographer:* Peter Brocco, *Deaf Man:* Casey Adams, *Cheerleader:* George (Buck) Flower.

Elmer Gantry with Burt Lancaster.

Emma with Marie Dressler and Myrna Loy.

EMMA (1932) MGM. Directed by Clarence Brown. Story, Frances Marion. Adaptation and Dialogue, Leonard Praskins. Additional Dialogue, Zelda Sears. Art Director, Cedric Gibbons. Gowns, Adrian. Photography, Oliver T. Marsh. Assistant Director, Charles Dorian. Editor, William Levanway. Recording Engineer, A. MacDonald. 73 minutes

Emma: Marie Dressler, *Ronnie Smith:* Richard Cromwell, *Mr. Smith:* Jean Hersholt, *Isabelle:* Myrna Loy, *District Attorney:* John Miljan, *Haskins:* Purnell B. Pratt, *Matilda:* Leila Bennett, *Gypsy:* Barbara Kent, *Sue:* Kathryn Crawford, *Bill:* George Meeker, *Maid:* Dale Fuller, *Drake:* Wilfred Noy, *Count Pierre:* Andre Cheron.

THE EMPEROR WALTZ (1948) Par. Producer, Charles Brackett. Director, Billy Wilder. Color by Technicolor. Screenplay, Charles Brackett, Billy Wilder. Art Directors, Hans Dreier, Franz Bachelin. Musical Score, Victor Young. Photography, George Barnes. Editor, Doane Harrison. Technicolor Director, Natalie Kalmus. Associate, Robert Brower. Musical numbers: "Get Yourself a Phonograph" by Johnny Burke and Jimmy Van Heusen; "Friendly Mountains" (melody based on Swiss airs with lyrics by Johnny Burke); "A Kiss in Your Eyes" by Richard Heuberger and Johnny Burke; "I Kiss Your Hand, Madame" by Ralph Erwin and Fritz Rotter; "Whistler and His Dog" by Arthur Pryor; "The Emperor Waltz" (melody based on music by Johann Strauss with lyrics by Johnny Burke). 106 minutes

Virgil Smith: Bing Crosby, *Johanna Augusta Franziska:* Joan Fontaine, *Baron Holenia:* Roland Culver, *Princess Bitotska:* Lucile Watson, *Emperor Franz Joseph:* Richard Haydn, *Chamberlain:* Harold Vermilyea, *Dr. Zwieback:* Sig Rumann, *Archduchess Stephanie:* Julia

The Emperor Waltz with Sig Rumann, Joan Fontaine and Roland Culver.

Dean, *Chauffeur:* Bert Prival, *Proprietress of the Inn:* Alma Macrorie, *Chambermaid:* Roberta Jonay, *Obersthofmeister:* John Goldsworthy, *Tyrolean Girl:* Doris Dowling, *Abbé:* James Vincent, *Gamekeeper:* Harry Allen, *Tennis Player:* Eleanor Tennant, *Butler:* Vesey O'Davoren, *Dr. Zwieback's Assistant:* Norbert Schiller, *Von Usedon:* Frank Elliott, *Hungarian Officer:* Paul de Corday, *Master of Ceremonies:* Jack Gargan, *Diplomat:* Cyril Delevanti, *Parliamentary Politician:* Frank Mayo, *Spanish Marquess:* Franco Corsaro.

THE ENEMY BELOW (1957) 20th. Producer-Director, Dick Powell. CinemaScope, De Luxe Color. Based on the novel by Commander D. A. Rayner. Screenplay, Wendell Mayes. Art Directors, Lyle R. Wheeler, Albert Hogsett. Music, Leigh Harline, conducted by Lionel Newman. Orchestration, Edward B. Powell. Cinematographer, Harold Rosson. Special Photographic Effects, L. B. Abbott. Editor, Stuart Gilmore. 98 minutes

The Enemy Below with A1 Hedison, Robert Mitchum and Doug McClure.

Captain Murrell: Robert Mitchum, *Von Stolberg:* Curt Jurgens, *Lieutenant Ware:* (David) Al Hedison, *Schwaffer:* Theodore Bikel, *Doctor:* Russell Collins, *Von Holem:* Kurt Krueger, *C.P.O. Crain:* Frank Albertson, *Quartermaster:* Biff Elliott, *Mackeson:* Alan Dexter, *Ensign Merry:* Doug McClure, *Corky:* Jeff Daley, *Ellis:* David Bair, *Robbins:* Joe Di Reda, *Lieutenant Bonelli:* Ralph Manza, *Messenger:* Ted Perritt, *Quiroga:* Jimmy Bayes, *Kunz:* Arthur La Ral, *Braun:* Frank Obershall, *Chief Engineer:* Robert Boon, *Mueller:* Werner Reichow, *Andrews:* Peter Dane, *American Sailor:* Ronnie Rondell, *Striker:* Lee J. Winters, *Lewis:* David Post, *Fireman:* Ralph Reed, *Cook:* Maurice Doner, *Albert, a German Sailor:* Jack Kramer, *Torpedo Petty Officer:* Robert Whiteside.

EXECUTIVE SUITE (1954) MGM. Producer, John Houseman. Director, Robert Wise. Author, Cameron Hawley. Screenplay, Ernest Lehman. Art Directors, Cedric Gibbons, Edward Carfango. Cinematographer, George Folsey. Editor, Ralph E. Winters. 104 minutes

McDonald Walling: William Holden, *Mary Blemond Walling:* June Allyson, *Julia O. Tredway:* Barbara Stanwyck, *Loren Phineas Shaw:* Fredric March, *Frederick Alderson:* Walter Pidgeon, *Eva Bardeman:* Shelley Winters, *Josiah Dudley:* Paul Douglas, *George Nyle Caswell:* Louis Calhern, *Jesse Grimm:* Dean Jagger, *Erica Martin:* Nina Foch,

324

Executive Suite with Nina Foch, Barbara Stanwyck, Walter Pidgeon, William Holden, Dean Jagger, Louis Calhern and Fredric March.

Mike Walling: Tim Considine, *Bill Lundeen:* William Phipps, *Mrs. Caswell:* Lucille Knoch, *Sara Grimm:* Mary Adams, *Edith Alderson:* Virginia Brissac, *Julius Steigel:* Edgar Stehli, *Ed Benedeck:* Harry Shannon, *Grimm's Secretary:* May McAvoy, *Luigi Cassoni:* Charles Wagenheim, *Cop:* Jonathan Cott, *Morgue Officials:* Willis Bouchey, John Doucette, *News Dealers:* Esther Michelson, Gus Schilling, *Stork Club Waiter:* Paul Bryar, *Enrique, Waiter Captain at Stork Club:* John Banner, *Jimmy Farrell:* Roy Engel, *Wailing Housekeeper:* Maidie Norman, *City Editor:* Dan Riss, *Avery Bullard:* Raoul Freeman, *Lee Ormond:* Bob Carson, *Shaw's Secretary:* Ann Tyrrell, *Alderson's Secretary:* Ray Mansfield, *Liz:* Kazia Orzazewski, *Sam Teal:* Burt Mustin, *Miss Clark:* Helen Brown, *Airport Clerk:* Wilson Wood, *Servant:* Matt Moore.

EXODUS (1960) UA. Producer-Director, Otto Preminger. Screenplay, Dalton Trumbo. From the novel by Leon Uris. Music, Ernest Gold. Costumes, Rudi Gernreich, Hope Bryce. Assistant Directors, Otto Plaschkes, Gerry O'Hara, Yoel Silberg, Larry Frisch, Christopher Trumbo. In Super-Panavision 70 and Technicolor. Art Director, Richard Day. Cinematography, Sam Leavitt. Editor, Louis R. Loeffler. Produced in Israel. 213 minutes

Ari Ben Canaan: Paul Newman, *Kitty Fremont:* Eva Marie Saint, *General Sutherland:* Ralph Richardson, *Major Caldwell:* Peter Lawford, *Barak Ben Canaan:* Lee J. Cobb, *Dov Landau:* Sal Mineo, *Taha:* John Derek, *Mandria:* Hugh Griffith, *Lakavitch:* Gregory Ratoff, *Dr. Lieberman:* Felix Aylmer, *Akiva:* David Opatoshu, *Karen:* Jill Haworth, *Von Storch:* Marius Goring, *Jordana:* Alexandra Stewart, *David:* Michael Wager, *Mordekai:* Martin Benson, *Reuben:* Paul Stevens, *Sarah:* Betty Walker, *Dr. Odenheim:* Martin Miller, *Sergeant:* Victor Maddern, *Yaov:* George Maharis, *Hank:* John Crawford, *Proprietor:* Samuel Segal, *Uzi:* Dahn Ben Amotz, *Colonel:* Ralph Truman, *Dr. Clement:* Peter Madden, *Avidan:* Joseph Furst, *Driver:* Paul Stassino, *Lieutenant O'Hara:* Marc Burns, *Mrs. Hirshberg:* Esther Reichstadt, *Mrs. Frankel:* Zeporah Peled, *Novak:* Philo Hauser.

Exodus with Sal Mineo and Paul Newman.

Fanny with Georgette Anys, Charles Boyer, Horst Buchholz and Leslie Caron.

FANNY (1961) WB. Associate Producer, Ben Kadish. Director, Joshua Logan. Screenplay, Julius J. Epstein. Based on play *Fanny* and the trilogy by Marcel Pagnol. Music and Lyrics, Harold Rome. Adapted by Harry Sukman. Assistant Director, Michel Romanoff. Costumes, Anne-Marie Marchand. A Mansfield Production in Technicolor. Based on three French films by Marcel Pagnol, *Cesar*, *Marius*, and *Fanny*. Filmed in France on the Marseilles waterfront, the Chateau d'If, Notre Dame de la Garde. 133 minutes

Fanny: Leslie Caron, *Panisse:* Maurice Chevalier, *César:* Charles Boyer, *Marius:* Horst Buchholz, *Escartifique:* Baccaloni, *Monsieur Brun:* Lionel Jeffries, *Admiral:* Raymond Bussieres, *Louis Panisse:* Victor Francen, *Honorine:* Georgette Anys, *Cesario:* Joel Flateau.

A FACE IN THE CROWD (1957) WB. A Newton Production. Director, Elia Kazan. Story and screenplay by Budd Schulberg. Score by Tom Glazer. Songs by Tom Glazer and Budd Schulberg. Costumes by Anna Hill Johnstone. Wardrobe by Florence Transfield. Assistant Director, Charles H. Maguire. From the short story "Your Arkansas Traveler" by Budd Schulberg. James G. McGhee plays the guitar for Andy Griffith. Songs: "Mama Git-tar," "Free Man in the Morning." Film debuts of Andy Griffith, 30 and Lee Remick, 21. 125 minutes

Lonesome Rhodes: Andy Griffith, *Marcia Jeffries:* Patricia Neal, *Joey Kiely:* Anthony Franciosa, *Mel Miller:* Walter Matthau, *Betty Lou Fleckum:* Lee Remick, *Col. Hollister:* Percy Waram, *Beanie:* Rod Brasfield, *Mr. Luffler:* Charles Irving, *J. B. Jeffries:* Howard Smith, *Macey:* Paul McGrath, *First Mrs. Rhodes:* Kay Medford, *Jim Collier:* Alexander Kirkland, *Senator Fuller:* Marshall Nielan, *Sheriff Hosmer:*

A Face in the Crowd with Walter Matthau, Patricia Neal and Andy Griffith.

Big Jeff Bess, *Abe Steiner:* Henry Sharp, *Themselves:* Bennett Cerf, Faye Emerson, Betty Furness, Virginia Graham, Burl Ives, Sam Levenson, John Cameron Swayze, Mike Wallace, Earl Wilson, Walter Winchell.

Fancy Pants with Bob Hope and Lucille Ball.

FANCY PANTS (1950) Par. Produced by Robert Welch. Directed by George Marshall. Color by Technicolor. Based on the story *Ruggles of Red Gap* by Harry Leon Wilson. Screenplay, Edmund Hartman and Robert O'Brien. Art Directors, Hans Dreier and Earl Hedrick. Music, Van Cleave. Photography, Charles B. Lang, Jr. Editor, Archie Marshek. Songs by Ray Evans and Jay Livingston: "Fancy Pants," "Home Cookin'" and "Yes, M'Lord." Remake of *Ruggles of Red Gap* (Paramount, 1935) 92 minutes

Humphrey: Bob Hope, *Aggie Floud:* Lucille Ball, *Cart Belknap:* Bruce Cabot, *Mike Floud:* Jack Kirkwood, *Effie Floud:* Lea Penman, *George Van Basingwell:* Hugh French, *Sir Wimbley:* Eric Blore, *Wampum:* Joseph Vitale, *Teddy Roosevelt:* John Alexander, *Lady Maude:* Norma Varden, *Rosalind:* Virginia Kelley, *Twombley:* Colin Keith-Johnston, *Wong:* Joe Wong, *Cyril:* Robin Hughes, *Mayor Fogarty:* Percy Helton, *Millie:* Hope Sansberry, *Dolly:* Grace Gillern Albertson, *Mr. Andrews:* Oliver Blake, *Guest:* Chester Conklin, *Mr. Jones:* Edgar Dearing, *Daisy:* Alva Marie Lacy, *Betsy and Bessie:* Ida Moore, *Mrs. Wilkins:* Ethel Wales, *Miss Wilkins:* Jean Ruth, *First Henchman:* Jimmie Dundee, *Second Henchman:* Bob Kortman, *Umpire:* Major Sam Harris, *Wicket Keeper:* Gilchrist Stuart, *Man:* Charley Cooley, *Stage Manager:* Olaf Hytten, *Stagehand:* Alex Frazer, *First Secret Service Man:* Howard Petrie, *Second Secret Service Man:* Ray Bennett, *Belle:* Almira Sessions.

FANTASIA (1940) Walt Disney-RKO. Produced by Walt Disney. Production Supervisor, Ben Sharpsteen. In Wide Screen, Multiplane Technicolor, and Fantasound (later Stereoponic Sound). Story Directors, Joe Grant and Dick Huemer. Directors of individual numbers: Samuel Armstrong, James Algar, Bill Roberts, Paul Satterfield, Hamilton Luske, Jim Handley, Ford Beebe, T. Hee, Norm Ferguson, Wilfred Jackson. Music Director, Edward H. Plumb. Music Film Editor,

Fantasia.

Stephen Csillag. Fantasound recorded by RCA, developed in collaboration with Walt Disney Studio. Recording, William E. Garity, C. O. Slyfield, J. N. A. Hawkins. Selections: "Toccata and Fugue in D Minor" by Bach, "The Nutcracker Suite" by Tchaikovsky, "The Sorcerer's Apprentice" by Dukas, "The Pastoral Symphony" by Beethoven, "Rite of Spring" by Stravinsky, "Dance of the Hours" by Ponchielli, "Night on Bald Mountain" by Moussorgsky, "Ave Maria" by Franz Schubert. 135 minutes

Leopold Stokowski conducts the Philadelphia Orchestra. Deems Taylor does the narrative introductions. Mickey Mouse is featured in "The Sorcerer's Apprentice." Bela Lugosi was the model for Tchernabog.

FANTASTIC VOYAGE (1966) 20th. Saul David Production. Directed by Richard Fleischer. CinemaScope and De Luxe Color. Screenplay, Harry Kleiner. Based on a story by Otto Klement and Jay Lewis Bixby, as adapted by David Duncan. Camera, Ernest Laszlo. Editor, William B. Murphy. Music, Leonard Rosenman. Assistant Director, Ad Schaumer. 100 minutes

Grant: Stephen Boyd, *Cora:* Raquel Welch, *Gen. Carter:* Edmond O'Brien, *Dr. Michaels:* Donald Pleasance, *Colonel Reid:* Arthur O'Connell, *Captain Owens:* William Redfield, *Dr. Duval:* Arthur Kennedy, *Jan Benes:* Jean Del Val, *Communications Aide:* Barry Coe, *Secret Service:* Ken Scott, *Nurse:* Shelby Grant, *Technician:* James Brolin, *Wireless Operator:* Brendan Fitzgerald.

Fantastic Voyage with Raquel Welch, Arthur Kennedy, William Redfield, Donald Pleasance and Stephen Boyd.

THE FAR COUNTRY (1955) Univ. Produced by Aaron Rosenberg. Directed by Anthony Mann. In Technicolor. Story and screenplay by Borden Chase. Assistant Directors, John Sherwood, Ronnie Rondell, Terry Nelson. Costumes, Jay A. Morley, Jr. Art Directors, Bernard Herzbrun and Alexander Golitzen. Musical Director, Joseph Gershenson. Cinematographer, William Daniels. Editor, Russell Schoengarth. Filmed in Canada. 97 minutes

Jeff Webster: James Stewart, *Ronda Castle:* Ruth Roman, *Renee Vallon:* Corinne Calvet, *Ben Tatem:* Walter Brennan, *Mr. Gannon:* John McIntire, *Rube:* Jay C. Flippen, *Ketchum:* Henry Morgan, *Ives:* Steve Brodie, *Luke:* Royal Dano, *Hominy:* Connie Gilchrist, *Madden:* Bob Wilke, *Dusty:* Chubby Johnson, *Newberry:* Jack Elam, *Grits:* Kathleen Freeman, *Yukon Sam:* Eddy Waller, *Kingman:* Robert Foulk, *Doc Vallon:* Eugene Borden, *Bosun:* Allan Ray, *Rounds:* Gregg Barton, *Molasses:* Connie Van, *Tanana Pete:* Guy Wilkerson, *Captain Benson:* Stuart Randall, *Latigo:* Chuck Roberson, *Shep:* Jack Williams, *Gant:* William J. Williams, *Miner:* John Doucette, *Sheriff:* Paul Bryar, *Second Mate:* Damian O'Flynn, *Joe Merin:* Terry Frost, *Carson:* Edwin Parker, *Tom Kane:* Don C. Harvey, *Bartender:* John Halloran, *Miner:* Robert Bice, *Girls:* Marjorie Stapp, Gina Holland, *Man:* Andy Brennan, *Sourdough:* Carl Harbaugh, *Miners:* Paul

The Far Country with James Stewart and Walter Brennan.

Savage, James W. Horan, Gerard Baril, Ted Kemp, John Mackin, Dick Taylor, Dick Dickinson, *Deputies:* Ted Mapes, Len McDonald, Jack Dixon, *Mrs. Kingman:* Angeline Engler, *Porcupine Smith:* Charles Sweetlove.

A FAREWELL TO ARMS (1932) Par. Directed by Frank Borzage. Assistant Directors, Lou Borzage and Art Jacobson. Based on the novel by Ernest Hemingway. Adapted by Benjamin Glazer, Oliver H. P. Garrett. Photography, Charles Lang. Sound, Harold C. Lewis. Art Director, Roland Anderson. Costumes, Travis Banton. Technical Director of war sequences, Charles Griffin. Technical Director of hospital sequences, Dr. Jardini. Editor, Otho Lovering. Remade as *Force of Arms* (Warners, 1951), *A Farewell to Arms* (20th Century-Fox, 1957). 78 minutes

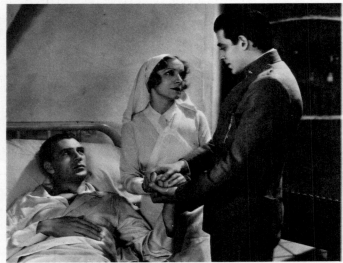

A Farewell to Arms with Gary Cooper, Helen Hayes and Jack La Rue.

Catherine Barkley: Helen Hayes, *Frederic Henry:* Gary Cooper, *Major Rinaldi:* Adolphe Menjou, *Helen Ferguson:* Mary Philips, *The Priest:* Jack La Rue, *Head Nurse:* Blanche Frederici, *Bonello:* Henry Armetta, *Piani:* George Humbert, *Manera:* Fred Malatesta, *Miss Van Campen:* Mary Forbes, *Count Greffi:* Tom Ricketts, *Gordoni:* Robert Cauterio, *British Major:* Gilbert Emery.

A FAREWELL TO ARMS (1957) 20th. Producer, David O. Selznick. Director, Charles Vidor. Screenplay by Ben Hecht. Based on the novel by Ernest Hemingway. Music by Mario Nascimbene. In CinemaScope and De Luxe Color. Filmed in Italy. Remake of *A Farewell to Arms* (Paramount, 1932), *Force of Arms* (WB, 1951). 150 minutes

Lieutenant Frederic Henry: Rock Hudson, *Nurse Catherine Berkley:* Jennifer Jones, *Major Alessandro Rinaldi:* Vittorio De Sica, *Father*

A Farewell to Arms with Rock Hudson.

Galli: Alberto Sordi, *Bonello:* Kurt Kasznar, *Miss Van Campen:* Mercedes McCambridge, *Dr. Emerich:* Oscar Homolka, *Helen Ferguson:* Elaine Stritch, *Passini:* Leopoldo Trieste, *Aymo:* Franco Interlenghi, *Major Stampi:* Jose Nieto, *Captain Bassi:* Georges Brehat, *Nino:* Memmo Carotenuto, *Colonel Valentini:* Victor Francen, *Nurse:* Joan Shawlee.

THE FARMER'S DAUGHTER (1947) RKO. Producer, Dore Schary. Director, H.C. Potter. Suggested by a play by Juhni Tervataa. Screenplay, Allen Rivkin, Laura Kerr. Art Directors, Albert S. D'Agostino, Field Gray. Music, Leigh Harline. Musical Director, C. Bakaleinikoff. Cameraman, Milton Krasner. Editor, Harry Marker. Song by Frank Loesser and Frederick Hollander, "Jungle Jingle." Later the basis for a TV series. 97 minutes

Katrin Holstrom: Loretta Young, *Glenn Morley:* Joseph Cotten, *Mrs. Morley:* Ethel Barrymore, *Clancy:* Charles Bickford, *Virginia Thatcher:* Rose Hobart, *Adolph:* Rhys Williams, *Dr. Matthew Sutven:* Harry Davenport, *Hy Nordick:* Tom Powers, *Ward Hughes:* William Harrigan, *Olaf Holstrom:* Lex Barker, *Mr. Holstrom:* Harry Shannon, *Sven Holstrom:* Keith Andes, *Wilbur Johnson:* Thurston Hall, *A. J. Finley:* Art Baker, *Einar:* Don Beddoe, *Peter Holstrom:* James Aurness (Arness), *Mrs. Holstrom:* Anna Q. Nilsson, *Dr. Mattsen:* Sven Hugo Borg, *Van:* John Gallaudet, *Eckers:* William B. Davidson, *Fisher:* Charles McGraw, *Night Editor:* Jason Robards, *Sweeney:* Cy Kendall, *Matternack:* Frank Ferguson, *Windor:* William Bakewell, *Jackson, Reporter:* Charles Lane, *Silbey, Politician:* Douglas Evans, *Assistant Announcer:* Robert Clarke, *Woman:* Bess Flowers.

The Farmer's Daughter with Joseph Cotten, Loretta Young, Charles Bickford and Ethel Barrymore.

Father Goose with Cary Grant and Leslie Caron.

FATHER GOOSE (1964) Univ. Producer, Robert Arthur. Director, Ralph Nelson. Technicolor. Author, S. H. Barnett. Screenplay, Peter Stone, Frank Tarloff. Art Directors, Alexander Golitzen, Henry Bumstead. Music, Cy Coleman. Music Supervisor, Joseph Gershenson. "Pass Me By," music, Cy Coleman; lyrics, Caroline Leigh. Cinematographer, Charles Lang, Jr. Editor, Ted J. Kent. 115 minutes

Walter Eckland: Cary Grant, *Catherine Freneau:* Leslie Caron, *Commander Frank Houghton:* Trevor Howard, *Lieutenant Stebbins:* Jack Good, *Christine:* Verina Greenlaw, *Anne:* Pip Sparke, *Harriet:* Jennifer Berrington, *Elizabeth:* Stephanie Berrington, *Angelique:* Laurelle Felsette, *Dominique:* Nicole Felsette, *Jenny:* Sharyl Locke, *Submarine Captain:* Simon Scott, *Submarine Executive:* John Napier, *Radioman:* Richard Lupino, *Doctor:* Alex Finlayson, *Chaplain:* Peter Forster, *Navigator:* Don Spruance, *Helmsman:* Ken Swofford.

FATHER OF THE BRIDE (1950) MGM. Producer, Pandro S. Berman. Director, Vincente Minnelli. Author, Edward Streeter. Screenplay, Frances Goodrich, Albert Hackett. Art Directors, Cedric Gibbons, Leonid Vasian. Music, Adolph Deutsch. Photography, John Alton. Editor, Ferris Webster. Sequel was *Father's Little Dividend* (1951). 93 minutes

Stanley T. Banks: Spencer Tracy, *Ellie Banks:* Joan Bennett, *Kay Banks:* Elizabeth Taylor, *Buckley Dunstan:* Don Taylor, *Mrs. Doris Dunstan:* Billie Burke, *Mr. Massoula:* Leo G. Carroll, *Herbert Dunstan:* Moroni Olsen, *Mr. Tringle:* Melville Cooper, *Warner:* Taylor Holmes, *Rev. A. I. Galsworthy:* Paul Harvey, *Joe:* Frank Orth, *Tommy Banks:* Rusty Tamblyn, *Ben Banks:* Tom Irish, *Delilah:* Marietta Canty, *Dixon:* Willard Waterman, *Fliss:* Nancy Valentine, *Effie:* Mary Jane Smith, *Peg:* Jacqueline Duval, *Miss Bellamy:* Fay Baker, *Duffy:* Frank Hyers, *Usher:* Chris Drake, *Organist:* Douglas Spencer,

Father of the Bride with Spencer Tracy and Elizabeth Taylor.

Fat Man: Paul Maxey, *Young Man* (*Usher*): Peter Thompson, *Young Man With Coke* (*Usher*): Carleton Carpenter, *Timid Guest:* Frank Cady, *Teacher:* Lillian Bronson, *Stranger:* Thomas Browne Henry, *Movers:* Dewey Robinson, Ed Gargon, Ralph Peters, Dick Wessel, Dick Alexander, Joe Brown, Jr., Jim Hayward, Gil Perkins, *Foreman of Movers:* William "Bill" Phillips.

Father's Little Dividend with Spencer Tracy and Elizabeth Taylor.

FATHER'S LITTLE DIVIDEND (1951) MGM. Producer, Pandro S. Berman. Director, Vincente Minnelli. Screenplay, Albert Hackett, Frances Goodrich. Art Directors, Cedric Gibbons, Leonid Vasian. Musical Director, Georgie Stoll. Photography, John Alton. Editor, Ferris Webster. Sequel to *Father of the Bride* (MGM, 1950). 82 minutes

Stanley Banks: Spencer Tracy, *Ellie Banks:* Joan Bennett, *Kay Dunstan:* Elizabeth Taylor, *Buckley Dunstan:* Don Taylor, *Doris Dunstan:* Billie Burke, *Herbert Dunstan:* Moroni Olsen, *Policeman:* Frank Faylen, *Delilah:* Marietta Canty, *Tommy Banks:* Rusty Tamblyn, *Ben Banks:* Tom Irish, *Dr. Andrew Nordell:* Hayden Rorke, *Reverend Galsworthy:* Paul Harvey, *Nurse:* Beverly Thompson, *Taxi Driver:* Dabbs Greer, *Officer:* Robert B. Williams, *Diaper Man:* Frank Sully, *Mike:* James Menzies, *Red:* Thomas Menzies, *Old Man:* Harry Hines, *Bridesmaids:* Nancy Valentine, Wendy Waldron, *Elderly Man on Porch:* Lon Poff, *Gym Instructor:* George Bruggeman, *The Dividend:* Donald Clark.

THE FBI STORY (1959) WB. Producer-Director, Mervyn LeRoy. Screenplay by Robert L. Breen and John Twist. Based on the book by Don Whitehead. Music by Max Steiner. Costumes by Adele Palmer. Assistant Directors, David Silver, Gil Kissel. In Technicolor. Art Director, John Beckman. Orchestration, Murray Cutter. Photography, Joseph Biroc. Editor, Philip W. Anderson. Locations filmed in Washington, D. C., and New York City. 149 minutes

FBI Story with Murray Hamilton and James Stewart.

Chip Hardesty (Narrator): James Stewart, *Lucy Hardesty:* Vera Miles, *Sam Crandall:* Murray Hamilton, *George Crandall:* Larry Pennell, *Jack Graham:* Nick Adams, *Jennie (adult):* Diane Jergens, *Anna Sage (The Lady In Red):* Jean Willes, *Anne (adult):* Joyce Taylor, *Mario:* Victor Millan, *Harry Dakins:* Parley Baer, *Dwight MacCutcheon:* Fay Roope, *U.S. Marshal/Radio Announcer:* Ed Prentiss, *Medicine Salesman:* Robert Gist, *Mike (adult):* Buzz Martin, *Casket Salesman:* Kenneth Mayer, *Whitey (Suspect):* Paul Genge, *Wedding Minister:* Forrest Taylor, *Mrs. Ballard:* Ann Doran, *John Dillinger:* Scott Peters, *Baby Face Nelson:* William Phipps, *Interrogator:* John Damler, *Taylor:* Paul Smith, *Mrs. Graham:* Eleanor Audley, *Neighbor:* Harry Harvey, *Doctor:* Sam Flint, *Schneider:* Burt Mustin, *Cliff:* Guy Wilkerson, *Minister:* Grandon Rhodes, *Sandy:* Nesdon Booth, *Cabby:* Ray Montgomery, *Girl:* Lori Martin, *Himself:* J. Edgar Hoover.

55 Days at Peking with Robert Helpmann, David Niven and Charlton Heston.

55 DAYS AT PEKING (1963) AA. Producer, Samuel Bronston. Director, Nicholas Ray. Super Technirama 70 and Technicolor. Executive Producer, Michael Waszynski. Screenplay, Philip Yordan. Bernard Gordon. Music, Dimitri Tiomkin. Costumes, Veniero Colasanti, John Moore. Associate Producer, Alan Brown. Assistant Directors, Jose Lopez Rodero, Jose Maria Ochoa. Second unit directed by Andrew Marton. Title art by Dong Kingman. Music, Dimitri Tiomkin. "So Little Time,": lyrics, Paul Francis Webster. Cinematographer, Jack Hildyard. Editor, Robert Lawrence. Filmed in Spain. 150 minutes

Maj. Matt Lewis: Charlton Heston, *Baroness Natalie Ivanoff:* Ava Gardner, *Sir Arthur Robertson:* David Niven, *Dowager Empress Tzu Hsi:* Flora Robson, *Sergeant Harry:* John Ireland, *Father de Bearn:* Harry Andrews, *General Jung-Lu:* Leo Genn, *Prince Tuan:* Robert Helpmann, *Colonel Shiba:* Ichizo Itami, *Baron Sergei Ivanoff:* Kurt Kasznar, *Julliard:* Philippe LeRoy, *Dr. Steinfeldt:* Paul Lukas, *Teresa:* Lynne Sue Moon, *Lady Sarah Robertson:* Elizabeth Sellars, *Garibaldi:* Massimo Serato, *Maj. Bobrinski:* Jacques Sernas, *Lt. Andy Marshall:* Jerome Thor, *Smythe:* Geoffrey Bayldon, *Capt. Hanselman:* Joseph Furst, *Capt. Hoffman:* Walter Gotell, *Gerald:* Alfred Lynch, *Hugo Bergmann:* Martin Miller, *Baron Von Meck:* Eric Pohlmann, *Spanish Minister:* Alfredo Mayo, *Madame Baumaire:* Conchita Montes, *Italian Minister:* Jose Nieto, *Baumaire:* Aram Stepham, *Captain Hanley:* Robert Urquhart, *Dutch Minister:* Felix Defauce, *Austrian Minister:* Andre Esterhazy, *Japanese Minister:* Carlos Casaravilla, *Belgian Minister:* Fernando Sancho, *Chiang:* Michael Chow, *U.S.Marine:* Mitchell Kowal, *Sergeant Britten:* Ex-RSM Brittain.

THE FIGHTING 69TH (1940) In Charge of Production, Jack L. Warner. Executive Producer, Hal B. Wallis. Associate Producer, Louis F. Edelman. Directed by William Keighley. Original Screenplay, Norman Reilly Raine, Fred Niblo, Jr., and Dean Franklin. Photography, Tony Gaudio. Special Effects, Byron Haskin and Rex Wimpy. Editor, Owen Marks. Technical Advisors, Captain John T. Prout and Mark White. Battlefield scenes filmed at the Calabasas ranch. 89 minutes

The Fighting 69th with George Reeves and James Cagney.

Jerry Plunkett: James Cagney, *Father Duffy:* Pat O'Brien, *Wild Bill Donovan:* George Brent, *Joyce Kilmer:* Jeffrey Lynn, *Sergeant Big Mike Wynn:* Alan Hale, *"Crepe Hanger" Burke:* Frank McHugh, *Lieutenant Ames:* Dennis Morgan, *Lt. Long John Wynn:* Dick Foran, *Timmy Wynn:* William Lundigan, *Paddy Dolan:* Guinn "Big Boy" Williams, *The Colonel:* Henry O'Neill, *Captain Mangan:* John Litel, *Mike Murphy:* Sammy Cohen, *Major Anderson:* Harvey Stephens, *Private Turner:* DeWolfe (William) Hopper, *Private McManus:* Tom Dugan, *Jack O'Keefe:* George Reeves, *Moran:* John Ridgely, *Chaplain Holmes:* Charles Trowbridge, *Lt. Norman:* Frank Wilcox, *Casey:* Herbert Anderson, *Healey:* J. Anthony Hughes, *Captain Bootz:* Frank Mayo, *Carroll:* John Harron, *Ryan:* George Kilgen, *Tierney:* Richard Clayton, *Regan:* Edward Dew, *Doctors:* Wilfred Lucas, Emmett Vogan, *Sergeant:* Frank Sully, *Doctor:* Joseph Crehan, *Supply Sergeant:* James Flavin, *Jimmy:* Frank Coghlan, Jr., *Eddie:* George O'Hanlon, *Major:* Jack Perrin, *Alabama Men:* Trevor Bardette, John Arledge, Frank Melton, Edmund Glover, *Soldier:* Johnny Day, *Engineer Sergeant:* Frank Faylen, *Engineer Officer:* Edgar Edwards, *Soldier:* Sol Gorss, *Medical Captain:* Ralph Dunn.

THE FIREFLY (1937) MGM. Produced by Hunt Stromberg. Directed by Robert Z. Leonard. Based on the 1912 musical *The Firefly*, book and lyrics by Otto A. Harbach, music by Rudolf Friml. Screenplay, Frances Goodrich and Albert Hackett. Adaptation, Ogden Nash. Music Director, Herbert Stothart. Editor, Robert J. Kern. Filmed in Sepia. Photography, Oliver Marsh. Dances, Albertina Rasch. Pyrenees Mountains scenes shot at Lone Pine at the foot of the Sierras.

The Firefly with Warren William and Jeanette MacDonald.

Art Director, Cedric Gibbons. Song. "Donkey Serenade" by Bob Wright, Chet Forrest, and Rudolf Friml (written for the film); songs by Rudolf Friml and Otto Harbach: "Love Is Like a Firefly," "When a Maid Comes Knocking at Your Heart," "A Woman's Kiss," "Giannina Mia," "Sympathy," "When the Wine Is Full of Fire," "He Who Loves and Runs Away." Film debut of Leonard Penn, Gladys George's husband. 138 minutes

Nina Maria Azara: Jeanette MacDonald, *Don Diego Manrique de Lara/ Captain Francois DeCoucourt:* Allan Jones, *Colonel DeRougemont:* Warren William, *Innkeeper:* Billy Gilbert, *General Savary:* Henry Daniell, *Marquis DeMelito:* Douglass Dumbrille, *Etienne:* Leonard Penn, *King Ferdinand:* Tom Rutherfurd, *Lola:* Belle Mitchell, *St. Clair, Chief of French Secret Service:* George Zucco, *Duval:* Corbett Morris, *Duke of Wellington:* Matthew Boulton, *Juan:* Robert Spindola, *Izquierdo, Minister:* Ian Wolfe, *Pedro:* Manuel Alvarez Maciste, *Pablo:* Frank Puglia, *Cafe Proprietor:* John Picorri, *Smiling Waiter:* James B. Carson, *Spanish Patriot:* Jason Robards, *French Soldier:* Alan Curtis, *French Lieutenant:* Ralph Byrd, *French Soldier-Admirer:* Dennis O'Keefe, *Strawberry Vendor:* Maurice Cass, *Fruit Vendor:* Sam Appel, *Pigeon Vendor:* Maurice Black, *Hat Vendor:* Rolfe Sedan, *Flower Woman:* Inez Palange, *Secret Service Adjutant:* Harry Worth, *French Officer:* John Merton, *French Officer:* Hooper Atchley, *Joseph Bonaparte:* Stanley Price, *English General:* Brandon Hurst, *Spanish General:* Pedro de Cordoba, *Captain Pierlot:* Theodore von Eltz, *Captain of the Guard:* Lane Chandler, *Colonel (Chief of Staff):* Edward Keane, *Secretary:* Sidney Bracy, *Captain:* Eddie Phillips, *Stablehand:* Russ Powell, *Peasant:* Agostino Borgato, *Cafe Extras:* Robert Z. Leonard, Albertina Rasch.

Five Fingers with James Mason and Oscar Karlweis.

FIVE FINGERS (1952) 20th. Producer, Otto Lang. Director, Joseph L. Mankiewicz. From a novel by L. C. Mayzisch, *Operation Cicero.* Screenplay, Michael Wilson. Art Directors, Lyle Wheeler, George W. Davis. Music, Bernard Herrmann. Cinematographer, Norbert Brodine. Editor, James B. Clark. Filmed in Ankara and Istanbul. Narrator, John Sutton. Later a TV series. 108 minutes

Cicero: James Mason, *Anna:* Danielle Darrieux, *George Travers:* Michael Rennie, *Sir Frederic:* Walter Hampden, *Mayzisch:* Oscar Karlweis, *Col. Von Richter.* Herbert Berghof, *Von Papen:* John Wengraf, *Siebert:* Ben Astar, *Macfadden:* Roger Plowden, *Morrison:* Michael Pate, *Steuben:* Ivan Trlesault, *Van Papen's Secretary:* Hannelore Axman, *Da Costa:* David Wolfe, *Santos:* Larry Dobkin, *Turkish Ambassador:* Nestor Paiva, *Japanese Ambassador:* Richard Loo, *Johnson:* Keith McConnell, *Charwoman:* Jeroma Moshan, *British Military Attaché:* Stuart Hall, *Butler:* Albert Morin, *Kaltenbrunner:* Alfred Zeisler, *Pullman Porter:* Otto Waldis, *Proprietor:* Konstantin Shayne, *Turk:* Aram Katcher, *Butler:* Martin Garralaga, *Banker:* Marc Snow, *Undersecretary:* Lester Matthews, *Ship's Captain:* Salvador Baguez, *German Singer:* Faith Kruger, *Italian Ambassador:* Antonio Filauri.

The Five Pennies with Danny Kaye and Susan Gordon.

THE FIVE PENNIES (1959) Par. Produced by Jack Rose. Directed by Melville Shavelson. VistaVision and Technicolor. Screenplay, Rose and Shavelson. Choreography, Earl Barton. New songs by Sylvia Fine: "The Five Pennies," "Lullaby in Ragtime," "Follow the Leader," "Good Night, Sleep Tight," "Five Pennies Saints" (special lyrics for "When the Saints Come Marching In"). A Dena Production. Red Nichols plays the trumpet for Danny Kaye. 117 minutes

Red (Ernest Loring) Nichols: Danny Kaye, *Bobbie Meredith (Willa Stutzmeyer):* Barbara Bel Geddes, *Himself:* Louis Armstrong, *Tony Valani:* Harry Guardino, *Wil Paradise:* Bob Crosby, *Artie Shutt:* Bobby Troup, *Dorothy Nichols, ages 6 to 8:* Susan Gordon, *Dorothy Nichols at 12 to 14:* Tuesday Weld, *Jimmy Dorsey:* Ray Anthony, *Dave Tough:* Shelly Manne, *Glenn Miller:* Ray Daley, *Tommye Eden:* Valerie Allen, *Choreographer:* Earl Barton, *Murray:* Ned Glass, *Hawaiian Announcer:* Peter Potter, *Headmistress:* Blanche Sweet, *Barber:* Tito Vuolo, *Taxi Driver:* Joe McTurk, *Richard:* Paul Sullivan, *Girls at Party:* Carol Sydes (Cindy Carol), Susan Seaforth, *Boy at Party:* Richard Shavelson, *Patient:* Charles Herbert, *Rehabilitation Patient:* Babbette Bain, *Specialty Dancer:* Frank C. Radcliffe, *Himself:* Bob Hope.

FIVE STAR FINAL (1931) WB. Directed by Mervyn LeRoy. From the play by Louis Weitzenkorn. Art Director, Jack Okey. Scenario, Robert Lord. Dialogue, Byron Morgan. Assistant Director, G. Hollingshead. Photography, Sol Polito. Editor, Frank Ware. Gowns, Earl Luick. Vitaphone orchestra conducted by Leo Forbstein. Remade as *Two Against the World* (Warners, 1936). 89 minutes

Five Star Final with Oscar Apfel, Edward G. Robinson, Anthony Bushnell, Marian Marsh and Boris Karloff.

Joseph Randall: Edward G. Robinson, *Michael Townsend:* H. B. Warner, *Jenny Townsend:* Marian Marsh, *Phillip Weeks:* Anthony Bushell, *Ziggie Feinstein:* George E. Stone, *Nancy (Vorhees) Townsend:* Frances Starr, *Kitty Carmody:* Ona Munson, *Telephone Operator:* Polly Walters, *Brannegan:* Robert Elliott, *Miss Taylor:* Aline MacMahon, *Miss Edwards:* Gladys Lloyd, *T. Vernon Isopod:* Boris Karloff, *Mrs. Weeks:* Evelyn Hall, *Mr. Weeks:* David Torrence, *Arthur Goldberg:* Harold Waldridge, *Bernard Hinchecliffe:* Oscar Apfel, *Robert French:* Purnell Pratt, *Reporter:* James Donlan, *Schwartz, Assistant Undertaker:* Frank Darien.

The Flame and the Arrow with Nick Cravat, Virginia Mayo, Robert Douglas and Burt Lancaster.

THE FLAME AND THE ARROW (1950) WB. Produced by Harold Hecht and Frank Ross. Directed by Jacques Tourneur. Color by Technicolor. A Norma Production. Original Screenplay, Waldo Salt. Art Director, Edward Carrere. Music, Max Steiner. Photographer, Ernest Haller. Editor, Alan Crosland, Jr. 88 minutes

Dardo: Burt Lancaster, *Anne:* Virginia Mayo, *Alessandro:* Robert Douglas, *Nonna Bartoli:* Aline MacMahon, *Ulrich:* Frank Allenby, *Piccolo:* Nick Cravat, *Francesca:* Lynn Baggett, *Rudi:* Gordon Gebert, *Troubadour:* Norman Lloyd, *Apothecary:* Victor Kilian, *Papa Pietro:* Francis Pierlot, *Skinner:* Robin Hughes.

FLAMINGO ROAD (1949) WB. Producer, Jerry Wald. Director, Michael Curtiz. Based on a play by Robert Wilder and Sally Wilder. Screenplay, Robert Wilder. Musical Director, Ray Heindorf. Art Director, Leo K. Kuter. Photography, Ted McCord. Editor, Folmer Blangsted. Additional Dialogue, Edmund H. North. Song, "If I Could Be With You" by Henry Creamer and Jimmy Johnson. Film debut of David Brian. 94 minutes

Lane Bellamy: Joan Crawford, *Fielding Carlisle:* Zachary Scott, *Titus Semple:* Sydney Greenstreet, *Dan Reynolds:* David Brian, *Lute-Mae Sanders:* Gladys George, *Annabelle Weldon:* Virginia

Flamingo Road with Sydney Greenstreet and Joan Crawford.

Huston, *Doc Waterson:* Fred Clark, *Millie:* Gertrude Michael, *Gracie:* Alice White, *Boatright:* Sam McDaniel, *Pete Ladas:* Tito Vuolo, *Barker:* Dick Ryan, *Barker:* Pat Gleason, *Fire-Eater:* Louis J. Manley, *Juggler:* Duke Johnson, *Harem Girls:* Dolores Castle, Bridget Brown, *Strong Man:* Mike Carillo, *Todd:* Walter Baldwin, *Tom Coyne:* Dick Elliott, *Angry Man:* James Flavin, *Willie Weaver:* Ken Britton, *John Shelton:* William Bailey: *Ed Parker:* Tristram Coffin, *Leo Mitchell:* Frank Cady, *Tom Hill:* John Gallaudet, *Niles:* Morgan Farley, *Johnny Simms:* Merwyn Bogue, *Tunis Simms:* Dale Robertson, *Postman:* Gary Owen, *Blanche:* Iris Adrian, *Specialty:* Raquel Flores, *Burr Lassen:* William Haade, *Bellboy:* Sam McKim, *Peterson:* Robert Strange, *Martin:* Larry Blake, *Sarah:* Jan Kayne, *Senators:* Pierre Watkin, Roy Gordon.

FLIRTATION WALK (1934) WB. Produced and directed by Frank Borzage. Story, Delmer Daves, Lou Edelman. Dances directed by Bobby Connolly. Photography, Sol Polito and George Barnes. Editor, William Holmes. Screenplay, Delmer Daves. Songs by Allie Wrubel and Mort Dixon: "Flirtation Walk," "Mr. and Mrs. Is the Name," "No Horse, No Wife, No Mustache," "I See Two Lovers," "Smoking in the Dark," and "When Do We Eat?" Hawaiian dances, the Luau, Hula-Kui, and Pi-ulu are performed. Scenes filmed at West Point. 97 minutes

Flirtation Walk with Ross Alexander, Ruby Keeler, Dick Powell and John Arledge.

Dick "Canary" Dorcy: Dick Powell, *Kathleen (Kit) Fitts:* Ruby Keeler, *Sergeant Scrapper Thornhill:* Pat O'Brien, *Oskie:* Ross Alexander, *Spike:* John Arledge, *Lieutenant Robert Biddle:* John Eldredge, *General John Brent Fitts:* Henry O'Neill, *Sleepy:* Guinn (Big Boy) Williams, *General Paul Landacre:* Frederick Burton, *Chase:* John Darrow, *Eight Ball:* Glen Boles, *Superintendent:* Colonel Tim Lonergan, *Dancer:* Gertrude Keeler, *Extra:* Tyrone Power, *Cadet:* Lieutenant Joe Cummins, *Soldiers:* Cliff Saum and Paul Fix, *Native Leader:* Sol Bright, *Civilian:* William J. Worthington, *Officer:* Emmett Vogan, *Dowager:* Maude Turner Gordon, *Butler:* Frank Dawson, *Blonde:* Frances Lee, *Redhead:* Avis Johnson, *Girl:* Mary Russell, *Cadets:* Carlyle Blackwell Jr., Dick Winslow. Sol Hoopii's Native Orchestra, University of Southern California and Army polo teams.

FLOWER DRUM SONG (1961) Univ. Producer, Ross Hunter. Director, Henry Koster. Panavision, Eastman Color. Author, C.Y. Lee. Screenplay, Joseph Fields. Art Directors, Alexander Golitzen, Joseph Wright. Music supervised and conducted by Alfred Newman. Music, Richard Rodgers. Lyrics, Oscar Hammerstein II. Songs: "You Are Beautiful," "A Hundred Million Miracles," "I Enjoy Being a Girl," "I Am Going to Like It Here," "Chop Suey," "Don't Marry Me," "Grant Avenue," "Love, Look Away," "Fan Tan Fanny," "Gliding Through My Memory," "The Other Generation," "Sunday." Editor, Milton Carruth. Choreography, Hermes Pan. Based on the musical by Rodgers and Hammerstein and Joseph Fields. 133 minutes

Flower Drum Song with Kam Tong, Miyoshi Umeki, James Shigeta, Nancy Kwan and Victor Sen Yung.

Linda Low: Nancy Kwan, *Wang Ta:* James Shigeta, *Mei Li:* Miyoshi Umeki, *Madame Liang:* Juanita Hall, *Sammy Fong:* Jack Soo, *Wang:* Benson Fong, *Wang San:* Patrick Adiarte, *Helen Chao:* Reiko Sato, *Doctor Li:* Kam Tong, *Frankie Wing:* Victor Sen Yung, *Madame Fong:* Soo Yong, *Doctor Chon:* Spencer Chan, *Doctor Fong:* Arthur Song, *Professor:* Ching Wah Lee, *Policeman:* Weaver Levy, *Holdup Man:* Herman Rudin, *Headwaiter:* James Hong, *San's Girl Friends:* Cherylene Lee, Virginia Lee, *TV Heroine:* Virginia Grey, *TV Sheriff:* Paul Sorensen, *Great White Hunter (TV):* Ward Ramsey, *Mexican Girl (TV):* Laurette Luez, *Bank Manager:* Robert Kino, *Tailor:* Beal Wong, *Square Dance Caller:* Jon Fong, *Tradesmen:* Willard Lee, Frank Kumagai.

THE FLY (1958) 20th. Producer, Kurt Neumann. Director, Kurt Neumann. CinemaScope, De Luxe Color. Story, George Langelaan. Screenplay, James Clavell. Art Directors, Lyle R. Wheeler, Theobold Holsopple. Music, Paul Sawtell. Cinematographer, Karl Struss. Editor, Merrill G. White. Sequel was *Return of the Fly* (1959). 94 minutes

Andre: (David) Al Hedison, *Helene:* Patricia Owens, *Francois:* Vincent Price, *Inspector Chares:* Herbert Marshall, *Emma:* Kathleen Freeman, *Nurse Andersone:* Betty Lou Gerson, *Philippe:* Charles Herbert, *Dr. Ejoute:* Eugene Borden, *Gaston:* Torben Meyer, *Orderly:* Harry Carter, *Doctor:* Charles Tannen, *Police Doctor:* Franz Roehn. *French Waiter:* Arthur Dulac.

The Fly with Vincent Price and Herbert Marshall.

FLYING DOWN TO RIO (1933) RKO. Directed by Thornton Freeland. From a play by Anne Caldwell. Screenplay, Louis Brock. Dances, Dave Gould. Photography, J. J. Faulkner. Editor, Jack Kitchin. Scenes filmed over Malibu Beach; backgrounds shot in Rio de Janeiro. Songs by Vincent Youmans, Edward Eliscu, Gus Kahn: "Flying Down to Rio," "The Carioca," "Orchids in the Moonlight," "Music Makes Me." First film pairing Astaire and Rogers. 89 minutes

Belinha de Rezende: Dolores Del Rio, *Roger Bond:* Gene Raymond, *Julio Rubeiro:* Raul Roulien, *Honey Hale:* Ginger Rogers, *Fred Ayres:* Fred Astaire, *Dona Elena:* Blanche Frederici, *Senor de Rezende:* Walter Walker, *Negro Singer:* Etta Moten, *Greeks:* Roy D'Arcy, Maurice Black, Armand Kaliz, *Mayor:* Paul Porcasi, *Banker, Alfredo:* Reginald Barlow, *Concert Singer:* Alice Gentle, *Hammerstein, Hotel Manager:* Franklin Pangborn, *Assistant Manager:* Eric Blore, *Rio Casino Manager:* Luis Alberni, *Banjo Player:* Ray Cooke, *Pilot:* Wallace MacDonald, *Messenger:* Gino Corrado, *Blonde Friend:* Mary Kornman, *Caddy:* Clarence Muse, *Sign Poster:* Harry Semels, *Musician:* Jack Rice, *Musician:* Eddie Borden, *Bits:* Betty Furness, Lucile Browne, Julian Rivero, Pedro Regas, Movita Castaneda, *Dancer:* Martha La Venture, *Bands:* The Brazilian Turunas, The American Clippers Band, *Rodriguez, Chauffeur:* Sidney Bracey.

Flying Down to Rio with Gene Raymond, Fred Astaire and Ginger Rogers.

FOLLOW ME, BOYS (1966) BV. Producers, Walt Disney and Winston Hibler. Technicolor. Director, Norman Tokar. Screenplay, Louis Pelletier. Based on book *God and My Country* by MacKinlay Kantor. Camera, Clifford Stine. Music, George Bruns. Editor, Robert Stafford. 131 minutes

Lemuel Siddons: Fred MacMurray, *Vida Downey:* Vera Miles, *Hetty Seibert:* Lillian Gish, *John Everett Hughes:* Charlie Ruggles, *Ralph Hastings:* Elliot Reid, *Whitey:* Kurt Russell, *Nora White:* Luana Patten, *Melody Murphy:* Ken Murray, *Edward White, Jr.:* Donald May, *Edward White, Sr.:* Sean McClory, *P.O.W. Lieutenant:* Steve Franken, *Mayor Hi Plommer:* Parley Baer, *Hoodoo Henderson (as a man):* William Reynolds, *Leo (as a man):* Craig Hill, *Doctor Ferris:* Tol Avery, *Judge:* Willis Bouchey, *Ralph's Lawyer:* John Zaremba,

Follow Me, Boys! with Fred MacMurray.

Cora Anderson: Madge Blake, *Tank Captain*: Carl Reindel, *Frankie Martin (as a man)*: Hank Brandt, *Umpire*: Richard Bakalyan, *Corporal*: Tim McIntire, *Huong Lee (as a man)*: Willie Soo Hoo, *Hetty's Lawyer*: Tony Regan, *Artie*: Robert B. Williams, *First P.O.W. Soldier*: Jimmy Murphy, *Hoodoo Henderson*: Dean Moray, *P.O.W. Sergeant*: Adam Williams, *Leo*: Bill Booth, *Beefy Smith*: Keith Taylor, *Frankie Martin*: Rickey Kelman, *Mickey Doyle*: Gregg Shank, *Red*: Donnie Carter, *Oliver*: Kit Lloyd, *Tiger*: Ronnie Dapo, *Jimmy*: Dennis Rush, *Eggy*: Kevin Burchett, *Duke*: David Bailey, *Harry*: Eddie Sallia, *David*: Bill "Wahoo" Mills.

Follow the Fleet with Fred Astaire, Ginger Rogers and Jack Randall.

FOLLOW THE FLEET

FOLLOW THE FLEET (1936) RKO. Produced by Pandro S. Berman. Directed by Mark Sandrich. Founded upon the play *Shore Leave* by Hubert Osborne and Allan Scott. Screenplay, Dwight Taylor. Music Director, Max Steiner. Cameraman, David Abel. Editor, Henry Berman. Ensembles staged by Hermes Pan. Songs by Irving Berlin: "Let Yourself Go," "Let's Face the Music and Dance," "I'm Putting All My Eggs in One Basket," "We Saw the Sea," "Here Am I, But Where Are You?" "Get Thee Behind Me, Satan," "I'd Rather Lead a Band." Film debut of Tony Martin, 20. Other versions: *Shore Leave* (First National, 1925), *Hit the Deck* (RKO, 1930). 110 minutes

Baker: Fred Astaire, *Sherry Martin*: Ginger Rogers, *Bilge Smith*: Randolph Scott, *Connie Martin*: Harriet Hilliard, *Iris Manning*: Astrid Allwyn, *Dopey*: Ray Mayer, *Captain Hickey*: Harry Beresford, *Lieutenant Williams*: Addison (Jack) Randall, *Jim Nolan*: Russell Hicks, *Sullivan*: Brooks Benedict, *Kitty Collins*: Lucille Ball, *Trio*: Betty Grable, Joy Hodges, Jennie Gray, *Sailor*: Tony Martin, *Hostess*: Maxine Jennings, *Sailor*: Edward Burns, *Waitress*: Jane Hamilton, *Sailor*: Frank Mills, *Sailor*: Frank Jenks, *Webber*: Herbert Rawlinson.

FOOTLIGHT PARADE

FOOTLIGHT PARADE (1933) WB. Directed by Lloyd Bacon. Dances by Busby Berkeley. Story, Manuel Seff and James Seymour. Photography, George Barnes. Editor, George Amy. Songs: "By a Waterfall," "Ah the Moon Is Here," "Sittin' on a Backyard Fence" by Sammy Fain and Irving Kahal; "Shanghai Lil" and "Honeymoon Hotel" by Harry Warren and Al Dubin. John Wayne, Frank McHugh, and Marceline Day in final scene from *Telegraph Trail* (WB, 1933). 102 minutes

Chester Kent: James Cagney, *Nan Prescott*: Joan Blondell, *Bea Thorn*: Ruby Keeler, *Scotty Blair*: Dick Powell, *Silas Gould*: Guy Kibbee, *Harriet Bowers Gould*: Ruth Donnelly, *Vivian Rich*: Claire Dodd, *Charlie Bowers*: Hugh Herbert, *Francis*: Frank McHugh, *Al Frazer*: Arthur Hohl, *Harry Thompson*: Gordon Westcott, *Cynthia Kent*: Renee Whitney, *Joe Farrington*: Philip Faversham, *Miss Smythe*:

Footlight Parade with Guy Kibbee, Joan Blondell, James Cagney, Arthur Hohl and Paul Porcasi.

Juliet Ware, *Fralick, Music Director*: Herman Bing, *George Appolinaris*: Paul Porcasi, *Doorman*: William Granger, *Cop*: Charles C. Wilson, *Gracie*: Barbara Rogers, *Specialty Dancer*: Billy Taft, *Chorus Girls*: Marjean Rogers, Pat Wing, Donna Mae Roberts, *Chorus Boy*: Dave O'Brien, *Drugstore Attendant*: George Chandler, *Title-Thinker-Upper*: Hobart Cavanaugh, *Auditor*: William V. Mong, *Mac, Dance Director*: Lee Moran, "*Sittin' on a Backyard Fence" Mouse*: Billy Barty, "*Honeymoon Hotel" Desk Clerk*: Harry Seymour, *Porter*: Sam MacDaniel, *Little Boy*: Billy Barty, *House Detective*: Fred Kelsey, *Uncle*: Jimmy Conlin, "*Shanghai Lil" Sailor-pal*: Roger Gray, *Sailor*: John Garfield, *Seaman on Table*: Duke York, *Girl*: Renee Whitney, *Joe, Assistant Dance Director*: Harry Seymour, *Chorus Girl*: Donna LaBarr.

A FOREIGN AFFAIR

A FOREIGN AFFAIR (1948) Par. Producer, Charles Brackett. Director, Billy Wilder. Author, David Shaw. Screenplay, Charles Brackett, Billy Wilder, Richard Breen. Art Directors, Hans Dreier, Walter Tyler. Photography, Charles B. Lang, Jr., Editor, Doane Harrison. Songs by Frederik Hollander: "Black Market," "Illusions," "Ruins of Berlin." Theme song, "Isn't It Romantic?" Backgrounds filmed in Berlin: Templehof Airfield, the Reichstag, Brandenburg Gate. 116 minutes

Phoebe Frost: Jean Arthur, *Erika Von Schluetow*: Marlene Dietrich, *Captain John Pringle*: John Lund, *Col. Rufus John Plummer*: Millard Mitchell, *Hans Otto Birgel*: Peter Von Zerneck, *Mike*: Stanley Prager, *Joe*: Bill Murphy, *First M.P.*: Gordon Jones, *Second M.P.*: Freddie Steele, *Pennecott*: Raymond Bond, *Giffin*: Boyd Davis, *Kraus*: Robert Malcolm, *Yandell*: Charles Meredith, *Salvatore*: Michael Raffetto, *Lt. Hornby*: James Larmore, *Lt. Colonel*: Damian O'Flynn, *Lt. Lee Thompson*: William Neff, *Major Matthews*: Frank Fenton, *Hitler*: Bobby Watson, *Russian Sergeant*: Henry Kulky, *File Room Guard*: Norman Leavitt, *General McAndrew*: Harland Tucker, *General Finney*:

A Foreign Affair with Marlene Dietrich.

George Carleton, *Staff Sergeant:* Len Hendry, *German Man:* Edward Van Sloan, *German Woman:* Lisa Golm, *German Wife:* Ilka Gruning, *German Husband:* Paul Panzer, *Maier:* Richard Ryen, *Wac Tech. Sgt.:* Phyllis Kennedy, *Gerhardt (Maier, Jr.):* Ted Cottle, *Inspector:* Otto Waldis, *Accordion Player:* Frank Yaconelli, *German Policeman:* Otto Reichow, *Corporal:* Harry Lauter, *M.P. Lieutenant,* Rex Lease.

Foreign Correspondent with Eduardo Ciannelli, Herbert Marshall, Laraine Day and Joel McCrea.

FOREIGN CORRESPONDENT (1940) UA. Produced by Walter Wanger. Directed by Alfred Hitchcock. Based on *Personal History* by Vincent Sheean. Screenplay, Charles Bennett and Joan Harrison. Dialogue, James Hilton and Robert Benchley. Music, Alfred Newman. Art Director, Alexander Golitzen. Assistant Director, Edmond Bernoudy. Special Effects, Lee Zavitz. Art Associate, Richard Irvine. Photography, Rudy Mate. Editor, Otho Lovering. 119 minutes

Johnny Jones (later Huntley Haverstock): Joel McCrea, *Carol Fisher:* Laraine Day, *Stephen Fisher:* Herbert Marshall, *Scott ffolliott:* George Sanders, *Van Meer:* Albert Bassermann, *Stebbins:* Robert Benchley, *Rowley:* Edmund Gwenn, *Krug:* Eduardo Ciannelli, *Tramp:* Martin Koslock, *Mr. Powers:* Harry Davenport, *Doreen:* Barbara Popper, *Latvian Diplomat:* Eddie Conrad, *Assassin:* Charles Wagenheim, *Toastmaster:* Craufurd Kent, *Mrs. Sprague:* Frances Carson, *Valet:* Alexander Granach, *Jones' Mother:* Dorothy Vaughan, *Donald:* Jack Rice, *Sophie:* (Becky) Rebecca Bohannen, *Clipper Captain:* Marten Lamont, *Miss Pimm:* Hilda Plowright, *Mrs. Benson:* Gertrude W. Hoffman, *Miss Benson:* Jane Novak, *Mr. Brood:* Roy Gordon, *Inspector McKenna:* Leonard Mudie, *Commissioner ffolliott:* Holmes Herbert, *John Martin,* "MOHICAN" *Captain:* Emory Parnell, *Dutch Peasant:* James finlayson, *Bradley:* Charles Halton, *Jones' Sister:* Joan Brodel (Joan Leslie), *Dr. Williamson:* Paul Irving, *Jones' Father:* Ferris Taylor, *Clark:* John T. Murray, *Stiles, the Butler:* Ian Wolfe, *Captain Lanson:* Louis Borrell, *Italian Waiter:* Gino Corrado, *English Cashier:* Eily Malyon, *English Radio Announcer:* John Burton, *Mr. Naismith:* E. E. Clive, *Man with Newspaper:* Alfred Hitchcock.

FOREVER AMBER (1947) 20th. Producer, William Perlberg. Director, Otto Preminger. Color by Technicolor. From the novel by Kathleen Winsor. Screenplay, Philip Dunne, Ring Lardner, Jr. Musical Director, Alfred Newman. Art Director, Lyle Wheeler. Cameraman, Leon Shamroy. Editor, Charles Loeffler. Adaptation, Jerome Cady. Technicolor Director, Natalie Kalmus. Associate, Richard Mueller. 138 minutes

Amber: Linda Darnell, *Bruce Carlton:* Cornel Wilde, *Almsbury:* Richard Greene, *King Charles II:* George Sanders, *Rex Morgan:* Glenn Langan, *Earl of Radcliffe:* Richard Haydn, *Nan Britton:* Jessica Tandy, *Mother Red Cap:* Anne Revere, *Black Jack Mallard:* John Russell, *Corina:* Jane Ball, *Sir Thomas Dudley:* Robert Coote, *Matt Goodgroome:* Leo G. Carroll, *Countess of Castelmaine:* Natalie Draper, *Mrs. Spong:* Margaret Wycherly, *Lady Redmond:* Alma Kruger, *Lord Redmond:* Edmond Breon, *Landale:* Alan Napier, *Little Bruce:* Perry (Bill) Ward, *Mrs. Chiverton:* Ottola Nesmith, *Lord Rossmore:*

Boyd Irwin, *Bob Starling:* Richard Bailey, *Mr. Starling:* Houseley Stevenson, *Queen Catherine:* Lillian Molieri, *Beck Marshall:* Susan Blanchard, *Ivers:* Tim Huntley, *Benvolio:* Robin Hughes, *Mrs. Abbott:* Norma Varden, *Killigrew:* Tom Moore, *Sarah:* Edith Evanson, *Marge:* Ellen Corby, *Bruce at 3:* Jimmy Lagano, *Jack (Wounded Cavalier):* Marten Lamont, *Blueskin:* Skelton Knaggs, *Nicks:* John Rogers, *Deacon:* Peter Shaw, *Moss Gumble:* Arthur E. Gould-Porter, *Galeazzo:* Jimmy Ames.

Forever Amber with Linda Darnell, George Sanders and Jane Ball.

FORSAKING ALL OTHERS (1934) MGM. Directed by W. S. Van Dyke. Adapted from the 1933 play by Edward Barry Roberts and Frank Morgan Cavett. Adaptation, Joseph L. Mankiewicz. Photography, Gregg Toland and George Folsey. Editor, Tom Held. Title song by Gus Kahn and Walter Donaldson. 84 minutes

Mary: Joan Crawford, *Jeff:* Clark Gable, *Dill:* Robert Montgomery, *Shep:* Charles Butterworth, *Paula:* Billie Burke, *Connie:* Frances Drake, *Eleanor:* Rosalind Russell, *Wiffens:* Tom Ricketts, *Johnson:* Arthur Treacher, *Bella:* Greta Meyer.

Forsaking All Others with Joan Crawford and Clark Gable.

FORT APACHE (1948) RKO. Producers John Ford, Merian C. Cooper. Director, John Ford. Suggested by the story "Massacre" by James Warner Bellah. Screenplay, Frank S. Nugent. Art Director, James Basevi. Photography, Archie Stout. Editor, Jack Murray. Music, Richard Hageman. An Argosy Pictures Production. Filmed in Monument Valley, Utah, and Chatsworth, California. Film debut of John Agar, 26. 127 minutes

Capt. Kirby York: John Wayne, *Col. Owen Thursday:* Henry Fonda, *Philadelphia Thursday:* Shirley Temple, *Lt. Mickey O'Rourke:* John Agar, *Sgt. Beaufort:* Pedro Armendariz, *Sgt. Major Michael O'Rourke:* Ward Bond, *Mary O'Rourke:* Irene Rich, *Capt. Sam Collingwood:*

Fort Apache with Henry Fonda, John Wayne, George O'Brien and Ward Bond.

George O'Brien, *Emily Collingwood:* Anna Lee, *Sgt. Mulcahy:* Victor McLaglen, *Sgt. Quincannon:* Dick Foran, *Sgt. Shattuck:* Jack Pennick, *Doctor Wilkins:* Guy Kibbee, *Silas Meacham:* Grant Withers, *Cochise:* Miguel Inclan, *Martha:* Mae Marsh, *Ma (Barmaid):* Mary Gordon, *Guadalupe:* Movita, *Southern Rercuit:* Hank Worden, *Recruit:* Ray Hyke, *Fen (Stage Guard)* Francis Ford, *Stage Driver:* Cliff Clark, *Cavalryman:* Fred Graham, *Noncommissioned Officer:* Mickey Simpson, *Reporters:* Frank Ferguson, William Forrest, *Man:* Philip Keiffer.

FOR WHOM THE BELL TOLLS (1943) Par. Producer, Sam Wood. Director, Sam Wood. Color by Technicolor. Based on the novel by Ernest Hemingway. Screenplay, Dudley Nichols. Music Score, Victor Young. Technicolor Director, Natalie Kalmus. Art Directors, Hans Dreier, Haldane Douglas. Production Designer, William Cameron Menzies. Cameraman, Ray Rennahan. Special Effects, Gordon Jennings. Process Photography, Farciot Edouart. Editor, Sherman Todd. Songs: "A Love Like This" by Ned Washington and Victor Young; "For Whom the Bell Tolls" by Milton Drake and Walter Kent. U.S. film debut of Katina Paxinou. 170 minutes

Robert Jordan: Gary Cooper, *Maria:* Ingrid Bergman, *Pablo:* Akim Tamiroff, *Agustin:* Arturo de Cordova, *Anselmo:* Vladimir Sokoloff, *Rafael:* Mikhail Rasumny, *Fernando:* Fortunio Bonanova, *Andres:* Eric Feldary, *Primitivo:* Victor Varconi, *Pilar:* Katina Paxinou, *El Sordo:* Joseph Calleia, *Joaquin:* Lilo Yarson, *Paco:* Alexander

For Whom the Bell Tolls with Akim Tamiroff, Eric Feldary, Mikhail Rasumny, Katina Paxinou, Ingrid Bergman, Gary Cooper and Arturo de Cordova.

Granach, *Gustavo:* Adia Kuznetzoff, *Ignacio:* Leonid Snegoff, *General Golz:* Leo Bulgakov, *Lieutenant Berrendo:* Duncan Renaldo, *Andre Massart:* George Coulouris, *Captain Gomez:* Frank Puglia, *Colonel Miranda:* Pedro de Cordoba, *Staff Officer:* Michael Visaroff, *Karkov:* Konstantin Shayne, *Captain Mora:* Martin Garralaga, *Sniper:* Jean Del Val, *Colonel Duval:* Jack Mylong, *Kashkin:* Feodor Chaliapin, *Don Frederico Gonzales:* Pedro de Cordoba, *Don Richardo:* Mayo Newhall, *Don Benito Garcia, The Mayor:* Michael Dalmatoff, *Don Guillermo:* Antonio Vidal, *Don Faustino Rivero:* Robert Tafur, *Julian:* Armand Roland, *Drunkard:* Luis Rojas, *Spanish Singer:* Trini Varela, *Sergeant (Eilas Man):* Dick Botiller, *Don Guillermo's Wife:* Soledad Jiminez, *Young Cavalry Man:* Yakima Canutt, *First Sentry:* Tito Renaldo, *Girl in Cafe:* Yvonne De Carlo.

42nd Street with George Brent, Bebe Daniels, Ruby Keeler, Warner Baxter and George Irving.

42ND STREET (1933) WB. Directed by Lloyd Bacon. Dances by Busby Berkeley. From the novel of the same name by Bradford Ropes. Adaptation and Dialogue, James Seymour and Rian James. Art Director, Jack Okey. Assistant Director, Gordon Hollingshead. Costumes, Orry-Kelly. Photography, Sol Polito. Editor, Thomas Pratt. Songs by Al Dubin and Harry Warren: "42nd Street," "Shuffle off to Buffalo," "You're Getting to Be a Habit With Me," "Young and Healthy," "It Must Be June." Editor, Frank Ware. In her first leading role, Ruby Keeler appears with sisters Gertrude and Helen. Guy Kibbee's brother Milton has a bit. 98 minutes

Julian Marsh: Warner Baxter, *Dorothy Brock:* Bebe Daniels, *Pat Denning:* George Brent, *Lorraine Fleming:* Una Merkel, *Peggy Sawyer:* Ruby Keeler, *Abner Dillon:* Guy Kibbee, *Billy Lawler:* Dick Powell, *Ann Lowell (Anytime Annie):* Ginger Rogers, *Andy Lee:* George E. Stone, *Al Jones:* Robert McWade, *Thomas Barry:* Ned Sparks, *Terry Neil:* Eddie Nugent, *MacElory:* Allen Jenkins, *Jerry:* Harry Akst, *Groom, "Shuffle off to Buffalo":* Clarence Nordstrom, *The Actor:* Henry B. Walthall, *Songwriters:* Al Dubin, Harry Warren, *"Young and Healthy" Girl:* Toby Wing, *Chorus Girl:* Pat Wing, *Slim Murphy:* Tom Kennedy, *Dr. Chadwick:* Wallis Clark, *A Mug:* Jack La Rue, *Pansy:* Louise Beavers, *Chorus Boy:* Dave O'Brien, *Secretary:* Patricia Ellis, *House Doctor:* George Irving, *An Author:* Charles Lane, *News Spreader:* Milton Kibbee, *Stage Aide:* Rolfe Sedan, *Geoffrey Waring:* Lyle Talbot, *Chorus Girls:* Gertrude and Helen Keeler, Geraine Grear (Joan Barclay), Ann Hovey, Renee Whitney, Dorothy Coonan, Barbara Rogers, June Glory, Jayne Shadduck, Adele Lacy, Loretta Andrews, Margaret La Marr, Mary Jane Halsey, Ruth Eddings, Edna Callaghan, Patsy Farnum, Maxine Cantway, Lynn Browning, Donna Mae Roberts, Lorena Layson, Alice Jans.

FOUR DAUGHTERS (1938) WB. Producer, Hal B. Wallis. Associate Producer, Benjamin Glazer. Director, Michael Curtiz. Author, Fannie

Four Daughters with Eddie Acuff, Donald Kerr, Tom Dugan, John Garfield, Priscilla Lane.

Hurst, from *Sister Act* in *Cosmopolitan* magazine. Screenplay, Julius Epstein, Lenore Coffee. Art Director, John Hughes. Musical Score, Max Steiner. Cameraman, Ernest Haller. Editor, Ralph Dawson. Assistant Director, Sherry Shourds. Dialogue Director, Irving Rapper. Unit Manager, Al Alleborn. Remade as *Young at Heart* (WB, 1954). 90 minutes

Adam Lemp: Claude Rains, *Ann Lemp:* Priscilla Lane, *Felix Deitz:* Jeffrey Lynn, *Mickey Borden:* John Garfield, *Emma Lemp:* Gale Page, *Kay Lemp:* Rosemary Lane, *Thea Lemp:* Lola Lane, *Ben Crowley:* Frank McHugh, *Aunt Etta:* May Robson, *Ernest Talbot:* Dick Foran, *Mrs. Ridgefield:* Vera Lewis, *Jake:* Tom Dugan, *Sam:* Eddie Acuff, *Earl:* Donald Kerr, *Waiter:* Joe Cunningham, *Man:* Jerry Mandy, *Doctor:* Wilfred Lucas.

FOURTEEN HOURS (1951) 20th. Producer, Sol C. Siegel. Director, Henry Hathaway. From a story by Joel Sayre, "The Man on the Ledge." Screenplay, John Paxton. Art Directors, Lyle Wheeler, Leland Fuller. Music. Alfred Newman. Photography, Joe MacDonald. Editor, Dorothy Spencer. Film debut of Grace Kelly. 92 minutes

Dunnigan: Paul Douglas, *Robert Cosick:* Richard Basehart, *Virginia:* Barbara Bel Geddes, *Ruth:* Debra Paget, *Mrs. Cosick:* Agnes Moore-

Fourteen Hours with Richard Basehart and Barbara Bel Geddes.

head, *Mr. Cosick:* Robert Keith, *Lieut. Moksar:* Howard da Silva, *Danny:* Jeffrey Hunter, *Dr. Strauss:* Martin Gabel, *Mrs. Fuller:* Grace Kelly, *Waiter:* Frank Faylen, *Sgt. Farley:* Jeff Corey, *Sgt. Boyle:* James Millican, *Dr. Benson:* Donald Randolph, *Mr. Harris:* Willard Waterman, *Police Operator:* Kenneth Harvey, *Evangelist:* George MacQuarrie, *Mrs. Dunnigan:* Ann Morrison, *Police Commissioner:* Forbes Murray, *Radio Announcer:* George Putnam, *TV Announcer:* Michael Fitzmaurice, *Regan:* Russell Hicks, *Cab Drivers:* David Burns, Ossie Davis, Henry Slate, Harvey Lembeck, *Reporters:* Brad Dexter, Shep Menken, Dan Riss, *Barbara:* Joyce Van Patten, *Radio Man:* Rennie McEvoy, *Operator:* Sandra Gould, *Frantic Guest:* Frank Nelson, *Hotel Clerk:* William Welsh, Jr., *Secretary:* Alice Talton, *Kemper:* Robert Pitkin, *Dunnigan Boy:* Gordon Gebert, *Mr. Fuller:* James Warren.

The Foxes of Harrow with Maureen O'Hara, Rex Harrison and Richard Haydn.

THE FOXES OF HARROW (1947) 20th. Producer, William A. Bacher. Director, John M. Stahl. Based on the novel by Frank Yerby. Screenplay, Wanda Tuchock. Musical Director, Alfred Newman. Art Directors, Lyle Wheeler, Maurice Ransford. Cameraman, Joe LaShelle. Editor, James B. Clark. 117 minutes

Stephen Fox: Rex Harrison, *Odalie D'Arceneaux:* Maureen O'Hara, *Andre LeBlanc:* Richard Haydn, *Mike Farrell:* Victor McLaglen, *Aurore D'Arceneaux:* Vanessa Brown, *Desiree:* Patricia Medina, *The Vicomte:* Gene Lockhart, *Sean Fox:* Charles Irwin, *Hugo Ludenbach.* Hugo Hass, *Master Of Harrow:* Dennis Hoey, *Tom Warren:* Roy Roberts, *St.-Ange:* Marcel Journet, *Achille:* Kenneth Washington, *Zorline:* Helen Crozier, *Josh:* Sam McDaniel, *Angelina:* Libby Taylor, *Little Inch:* Renee Beard, *Tante Caleen:* A. C. Bilbrew, *Belle:* Suzette Harbin, *Etienne Fox, age 6:* Perry Wm. (Bill) Ward, *Ty Demon:* William (Bill) Walker, *Mrs. Warren:* Mary Currier, *Little Inch, age 3:* Clear Nelson, Jr., *Etienne, age 3:* James Lagano, *Maspero:* Henri Letondal, *Dr. Le Fevre:* Jean Del Val, *Mrs. Fox:* Dorothy Adams, *Dr. Terrebone:* Andre Charlot, *Priest:* Georges Renavent, *Jode:* Jaspar Weldon, *Minna Ludenbach:* Celia Lovsky, *Georges:* Napoleon Simpson, *French Auctioneer:* Eugene Borden, *Captain:* Joseph Crehan, *Fencing Instructor:* Ralph Faulkner, *Auctioneer:* Robert Emmett Keane, *Stephen's Mother:* Randy Stuart.

FRANCIS (1949) Univ. Producer, Robert Arthur. Director, Arthur Lubin. Based on the novel by David Stern. Screenplay, David Stern. Art directors, Bernard Herzbrun, Richard H. Fields. Music, Frank Skinner. Photography, Irving Glassberg. Editor, Milton Carruth. First of the series of seven films, ending with *Francis in the Haunted House* (1956). 91 minutes

Peter Stirling: Donald O'Connor, *Maureen Gelder:* Patricia Medina, *Valerie Humpert:* ZaSu Pitts, *Colonel Hooker:* Ray Collins, *General Stevens:* John McIntire, *Colonel Plepper:* Eduard Franz, *Major Nadel:* Howland Chamberlin, *Colonel Saunders:* James Todd, *Carmichael:*

Francis with Francis and Donald O'Connor.

Robert Warwick, *Sgt. Chillingbacker:* Frank Faylen, *Captain Jones:* Anthony Curtis, *Major Garber:* Mikel Conrad, *Major Richards:* Loren Tindall, *Banker Munroe:* Charles Meredith, *First Correspondent:* Harry Harvey, *Second Correspondent:* Howard Negley, *Sergeant Poor:* Duke York, *Third Correspondent:* Peter Prouse, *Japanese Lieutenant:* Joseph Kim, *Captain Grant:* Robert Anderson, *Sergeant Miller:* Jack Shutta, *First Ambulance Man:* Judd Holdren, *Lt. Bremm:* Tim Graham, *Second Ambulance Man:* Robert Blunt, *Captain Norman:* Jim Hayward, *Captain Dean:* Al Ferguson, *First M.C. Lt.:* Marvin Kaplan, *Japanese Soldier:* Harold Fong, *Captain Addison:* Mickey McCardle, and FRANCIS, The Talking Army Mule (voice of Chill Wills).

Francis Goes to the Races with Piper Laurie, Donald O'Connor and Cecil Kellaway.

FRANCIS GOES TO THE RACES (1951) Univ. Producer, Leonard Goldstein. Director, Arthur Lubin. Author, Robert Arthur. Screenplay, Oscar Brodney, David Stern. Art Directors, Bernard Herzbrun, Emrich Nicholson. Music, Frank Skinner. Photography, Irving Glassberg. Editor, Milton Carruth. Based on the character created by David Stern. Second "Francis" film. 88 minutes

Peter Sterling: Donald O'Connor, *Frances Travers:* Piper Laurie, *Col. Travers:* Cecil Kellaway, *Frank Daner:* Jesse White, *Mallory:* Barry Kelly, *Rogers:* Hayden Rorke, *Harrington:* Vaughn Taylor, *Head Steward:* Larry Keating, *Dr. Marberry:* Peter Brocco, *Dr. Quimby:* Don Beddoe, *First Mug:* Ed Max, *Second Mug:* Jack Wilson, *Sam:* Bill Walker, *Jockey:* George Webster, *Voice of Francis:* Chill Wills, *Banker Munroe:* Charles Meredith, *Chuck:* Dick Wessell, *Proprietor:* Bernard Szold, *Driver:* Nolan Leary, *Steward:* Kenneth MacDonald, *Wong:* Peter Chong, *Smith:* Ewing Mitchell, *Jones:* Sam Flint, *Sheriff:* William Gould, *Exerciser:* Willard Willingham, *Guard:* Mike Pat Donovan.

FRANKENSTEIN (1931) Univ. Directed by James Whale. Based on the novel by Mary Wollstonecraft Shelley. Scenario and Dialogue, Garrett Fort and Francis Edward Faragoh. Special Electrical Effects, Frank Graves, Kenneth Strickfadden, Raymond Lindsay. Technical Assistant, Dr. Cecil Reynolds. Photography, Arthur Edeson. Editor, Clarence Kolster. Sound, C. Roy Hunter. In a prologue, Edward Van Sloan warns the audience about what they are to see, on behalf of Mr. Carl Laemmle. 71 minutes

Henry Frankenstein: Colin Clive, *Elizabeth:* Mae Clarke, *Victor Moritz:* John Boles, *The Monster:* Boris Karloff, *Baron Frankenstein:* Frederick Kerr, *Doctor Waldman:* Edward Van Sloan, *Fritz:* Dwight Frye, *Vogel, the Burgomaster:* Lionel Belmore, *Little Maria:* Marilyn Harris, *Ludwig, Peasant Father:* Michael Mark, *Bridesmaids:* Arletta Duncan, Pauline Moore, *Extra at Lecture/Wounded Villager on the Hill:* Francis Ford.

Frankenstein with Boris Karloff and Colin Clive.

FREAKS (1932) MGM. Directed by Tod Browning. Based on "Spurs" by Tod Robbins. Screenplay, Willis Goldbeck and Leon Gordon. Dialogue, Edgar Allan Woolf and Al Boasberg. Photography, Merritt B. Gerstad. Editor, Basil Wrangell. Sound, Gavin Burns. The short story "Spurs" appeared in *Munsey's* magazine, February, 1923. Harry and Daisy Earles are brother and sister. 64 minutes

Phroso: Wallace Ford, *Venus:* Leila Hyams, *Cleopatra:* Olga Baclanova, *Roscoe:* Rosco Ates, *Hercules:* Henry Victor, *Hans:* Harry Earles, *Frieda:* Daisy Earles, *Madame Tetrallini:* Rose Dione, *Siamese Twins:* Daisy and Violet Hilton, *Rollo Brothers:* Edward Brophy, Matt McHugh, *Bearded Lady:* Olga Roderick, *Boy with Half a Torso* Johnny Eck, *Hindu Living Torso:* Randian, *White Pin Heads:* Schlitzie, Elvira and Jennie Lee Snow, *Living Skeleton:* Pete Robinson, *Bird Girl:* Koo Coo, *Half-Woman Half-Man:* Josephine-Joseph, *Armless Wonder:* Martha Morris, *Turtle Girl:* Frances O'Connor, *Midget:* Angelo Rossito, *Specialties:* Zip and Pip, Elizabeth Green, *Landowner:* Albert Conti, *Jean, the Caretaker:* Michael Visaroff, *Sideshow Patron:* Ernie S. Adams, *Maid:* Louise Beavers.

Freaks with Rose Dione, Harry Earles, child and Olga Baclanova.

A Free Soul with Norma Shearer, Lionel Barrymore and Clark Gable.

A FREE SOUL (1931) MGM. Directed by Clarence Brown. Based on the book and magazine serial by Adela Rogers St. John, and the play, dramatized by Willard Mack. Adapted by John Meehan. Art Director, Cedric Gibbons. Photography, William Daniels. Editor, Hugh Wynn. Sound, Anstruther MacDonald. Remade by MGM as *The Girl Who Had Everything*, 1953. 91 minutes

Jan Ashe: Norma Shearer, *Steve Ashe:* Lionel Barrymore, *Ace Wilfong:* Clark Gable, *Dwight Winthrop:* Leslie Howard, *Eddie:* James Gleason, *Grandmother Ashe:* Lucy Beaumont, *Aunt Helen:* Claire Whitney, *Prosecuting Attorney:* Frank Sheridan, *Bottomley, Ace's Chinese Boy:* E. Alyn Warren, *Johnson, Defense Attorney:* George Irving, *Slouch:* Edward Brophy, *Dick:* William Stacy, *Reporter:* James Donlin, *Valet:* Sam MacDaniel, *Court Clerk:* Lee Phelps, *Men's Room Patron:* Roscoe Ates, *Casino Proprietor:* Larry Steers, *Detective:* Henry Hall, *Skid Row Drunk:* Francis Ford.

FRENCHMAN'S CREEK (1944) Par. Producer, B.G. DeSylva. Associate Producer, David Lewis. Director, Mitchell Leisen. Color by Technicolor. Screenplay, Talbot Jennings. Musical Score, Victor Young. Art Directors, Hans Dreier, Ernest Fegte. Process Photography, Farciot Edouart. From Daphne du Maurier's novel. Cameraman, George Barnes. Special Effects, Gordon Jennings. Editor, Alma Macrorie. Technicolor Director, Natalie Kalmus. Associate, Robert Brower. 113 minutes

Dona St. Columb: Joan Fontaine, *The Frenchman, Jean Benoit Aubery:* Arturo de Cordova, *Lord Rockingham:* Basil Rathbone, *Lord Godolphin:* Nigel Bruce, *William:* Cecil Kellaway, *Harry St. Columb:* Ralph Forbes, *Edmond:* Harald Ramond, *Pierre Blanc:* Billy Daniels, *Lady Godolphin:* Moyna Macgill, *Henrietta:* Patricia Barker, *James:* David James, *Prue:* Mary Field, *Martin (the Coachman):* David Clyde, *Thomas (the Footman):* Charles Coleman, *Luc:* Paul Oman, *Thomas*

Frenchman's Creek with Basil Rathbone, Nigel Bruce and Joan Fontaine.

Eustick: Arthur Gould-Porter, *Robert Penrose:* Evan Thomas, *John Nankervis:* Leslie Denison, *Philip Rashleigh:* Denis Green, *Doctor Williams:* George Kirby, *Pirate:* Fred Kohler, Jr., *Jailer:* Charles Irwin, *Women in Gaming House:* Constance Worth and Phyllis Barry, *Ostler:* David Thursby, *Alice:* Lauri Beatty.

Friendly Persuasion with Anthony Perkins, Dorothy McGuire and Gary Cooper.

FRIENDLY PERSUASION (1956) AA. Produced and directed by William Wyler. Associate Producer, Robert Wyler. Color by De Luxe. Based on the book by Jessamyn West. Assistant Director, Austen Jewell. Costumes, Dorothy Jeakins and Bert Henrikson. A B-M Production. Songs by Paul Francis Webster and Dimitri Tiomkin: "Friendly Persuasion," sung by Pat Boone, "Mocking Bird in a Willow Tree," "Marry Me, Marry Me," "Indiana Holiday," "Coax Me a Little." 139 minutes

Jess Birdwell: Gary Cooper, *Eliza Birdwell:* Dorothy McGuire, *Widow Hudspeth:* Marjorie Main, *Josh Birdwell:* Anthony Perkins, *Little Jess:* Richard Eyer, *Sam Jordan:* Robert Middleton, *Mattie Birdwell:* Phyllis Love, *Gard Jordan:* Mark Richman, *Professor Quigley:* Walter Catlett, *Elder Purdy:* Richard Hale, *Enoch:* Joel Fluellen, *Army Major:* Theodore Newton, *Caleb:* John Smith, *Opal, Pearl, Ruby Hudspeth:* Edna Skinner, Marjorie Durant, Frances Farwell, *Elders:* Russell Simpson, Charles Halton, Everett Glass, *The Goose:* Samantha, *Shell Game Operator:* Frank Jenks, *Poor Losers:* Joe Turkel, James Anderson, *Mrs. Purdy:* Jean Inness, *Minister:* Nelson Leigh, *Old Lady:* Helen Kleeb, *Quaker Woman (Emma):* Mary Carr, *Quaker Girl (Elizabeth):* Diane Jergens, *Leader:* John Craven, *Barker:* Harry Hines, *O'Hara:* Henry Rowland, *Billy Goat:* Ivan Rasputin, *Manager:* Donald Kerr, *Haskell:* Steve Warren, *Shooting Gallery Operator:* Earle Hodgins, *Farmer:* Tom London, *Ex-Sergeant:* John Pickard, *Bushwhacker:* Richard Garland, *Clem:* Norman Leavitt, *Buster:* Don Kennedy.

FROM HERE TO ETERNITY (1953) Col. Producer, Buddy Adler. Director, Fred Zinneman. From the novel by James Jones. Screenplay, Daniel Taradash. Art Director, Cary Odell. Cinematographer, Burnett Guffey. Editor, William Lyon. 118 minutes

Sgt. Milton Warden: Burt Lancaster, *Robert E. Lee Prewitt:* Montgomery Clift, *Karen Holmes:* Deborah Kerr, *Lorene:* Donna Reed, *Angelo Maggio:* Frank Sinatra, *Capt. Dana Holmes:* Philip Ober, *Sgt. Leva:* Mickey Shaughnessy, *Mazzioli:* Harry Bellaver, *Sgt. "Fatso" Judson:* Ernest Borgnine, *Corp. Buckley:* Jack Warden, *Sgt. Ike Galovitch:* John Dennis, *Sal Anderson:* Merle Travis, *Sgt. Pete Karelsen:* Tim Ryan, *Treadwell:* Arthur Keegan, *Mrs. Kipfer:* Barbara Morrison, *Annette:* Jean Willes, *Sgt. Baldy Dhom:* Claude Akins, *Sgt. Turp Thornhill:* Robert Karnes, *Sgt. Henderson:* Robert Wilke, *Corp. Champ Wilson:* Douglas Henderson, *Sgt. Maylon Stark:* George Reeves, *Friday Clark:* Don Dubbins, *Corp. Paluso:* John Cason, *Georgette:* Kristine Miller, *Capt. Ross:* John Bryant, *Sandra:* Joan Shawlee, *Jean:* Angela Stevens, *Nancy:* Mary Carver, *Suzanne:* Vicki Bakken, *Roxanne:* Margaret Barstow, *Billie:*

From Here to Eternity with Montgomery Clift, Frank Sinatra and Burt Lancaster.

Delia Salvi, *Lt. Col.:* Willis Bouchey, *Nair:* Al Sargent, *Bill:* William Lundmark, *Bartender:* Weaver Levy, *Major Stern:* Tyler McVey.

FROM RUSSIA WITH LOVE (1964) UA. Producers, Harry Saltzman, Albert R. Broccoli. Director, Terence Young. Screenplay, Richard Maibaum. Adaptation, Johanna Harwood. Based on the novel by Ian Fleming. Music, John Barry. Title song, Lionel Bart, sung by Matt Munro. Theme music, Monty Norman. Assistant Director, David Anderson. Director of Photography, Ted Moore. Costumes, Jocelyn Rickards. Eon Production in Technicolor. 118 minutes

From Russia With Love with Sean Connery, Daniela Bianchi and Robert Shaw.

James Bond: Sean Connery, *Tatiana Romanova:* Daniela Bianchi, *Kerim Bey:* Pedro Armendariz, *Rosa Klebb:* Lotte Lenya, *Red Grant:* Robert Shaw, *"M":* Bernard Lee, *Sylvia:* Eunice Gayson, *Morzeny:* Walter Gotell, *Vavra:* Francis de Wolff, *Train Conductor:* George Pastell, *Kerim's Girl:* Nadja Regin, *Miss Moneypenny:* Lois Maxwell, *Vida:* Aliza Gur, *Zora:* Martine Beswick, *Kronsteen:* Vladek Sheybal, *Belly Dancer:* Leila, *Foreign Agent:* Hasan Ceylan, *Krilencu:* Fred Haggerty, *Chauffeur:* Neville Jason, *Benz:* Peter Bayliss, *Tempo:* Nushet Atear, *McAdams:* Peter Madden.

FROM THE TERRACE (1960) 20th. Produced and directed by Mark Robson. CinemaScope and De Luxe Color. Based on the novel by John O'Hara. Screenplay, Ernest Lehman. Music, Elmer Bernstein. Orchestration, Edward B. Powell. Gowns, Travilla. Assistant Director, Hal Herman. Art Directors, Lyle R. Wheeler, Maurice Ransford, Howard Richman. Cinematography, Leo Tover. Special Effects, L.

From the Terrace with Leon Ames, Myrna Loy and Paul Newman.

B. Abbott and James B. Gordon. Editor, Dorothy Spencer. 144 minutes

Alfred Eaton: Paul Newman, *Mary St. John:* Joanne Woodward, *Martha Eaton:* Myrna Loy, *Natalie:* Ina Balin, *Samuel Eaton:* Leon Ames, *Sage Rimmington:* Elizabeth Allen, *Clemmie:* Barbara Eden, *Lex Porter:* George Grizzard, *Dr. Jim Roper:* Patrick O' Neal, *Mac-Hardie:* Felix Aylmer, *Fritz Thornton:* Raymond Greenleaf, *George Fry:* Malcolm Attenbury, *Mr. St. John:* Raymond Bailey, *Mr. Benziger:* Ted de Corsia, *Duffy:* Howard Caine, *Mrs. St. John:* Kathryn Givney, *Secretary:* Cyril Delevanti, *Trimmingham:* Rachel Stephens, *Mrs. Benziger:* Dorothy Adams, *Frolick:* Lauren Gilbert, *Nellie:* Blossom Rock, *Josephine:* Cecil Elliott, *Steve Rimmington:* Rory Harrity, *Lady Servringham:* Ottola Nesmith, *Lord Sevringham:* Clive L. Halliday, *Governess:* Mae Marsh, *Weinkoop:* Gordon B. Clarke, *Jones:* Ralph Dunn, *Jean Duffy:* Felippa Rock, *Sandy:* Jimmy Martin, *Von·Elm:* William Quinn, *Kelly:* Stuart Randall, *Newton Orchid:* John Harding, *Mrs. Pearson:* Sally Winn, *Mrs. Ripley:* Elektra Rozanska, *Doctor:* Truman Smith, *Frolick's Woman:* Elizabeth Russell, *Partners:* John Warburton, Douglas Evans, Robert Shayne, Harry Cheshire, Johnstone White, Alexander Campbell, Henry Hunter.

THE FRONT PAGE (1931) UA. Produced by Howard Hughes. Directed by Lewis Milestone. Based on the 1928 play by Ben Hecht and Charles MacArthur. Scenario, Bartlett Cormack. Dialogue, Bartlett Cormack and Charles Lederer. Art Director, Richard Day. Assistant Director, Nate Watt. Photography, Glen MacWilliams. Editor, Duncan Mansfield. Sound, Frank Grenzbach. A Caddo Company Production. Remade as *His Girl Friday* (Columbia, 1940). 101 minutes

Walter Burns: Adolphe Menjou, *Hildy Johnson:* Pat O'Brien, *Peggy Grant:* Mary Brian, *Bensinger:* Edward Everett Horton, *Murphy:* Walter Catlett, *Earl Williams:* George E. Stone, *Molly:* Mae Clarke,

The Front Page with Adolphe Menjou, Pat O'Brien and Maurice Black.

339

Pincus: Slim Summerville, *Kruger:* Matt Moore, *McCue:* Frank Mc-Hugh, *Sheriff Hartman:* Clarence H. Wilson, *Schwartz:* Fred Howard, *Wilson:* Phil Tead, *Endicott:* Eugene Strong, *Woodenshoe:* Spencer Charters, *Diamond Louie:* Maurice Black, *Mrs. Grant:* Effie Ellsler, *Jenny:* Dorothea Wolbert, *The Mayor:* James Gordon, *Jacobi:* Dick Alexander, *Bit:* Herman J. Mankiewicz, *Bit:* Lewis Milestone, *Reporter:* James Donlan.

THE FULLER BRUSH MAN (1948) Col. Producer and Director, S. Sylvan Simon. Based on a story by Roy Huggins. Screenplay, Frank Tashlin, Devery Freeman. Art Directors, Stephen Goosson, Carl Anderson. Musical Score, Franz Roemhold. Photography, Lester White. Editor, Al Clark. An Edward Small Production. 93 minutes

The Fuller Brush Man with Don McGuire and Red Skelton.

Red Jones: Red Skelton, *Ann Elliot:* Janet Blair, *Keenan Wallick:* Don McGuire, *Mrs. Trist:* Hillary Brooke, *Miss Sharmley:* Adele Jergens, *Freddie Trist:* Ross Ford, *Sara Franzen:* Trudy Marshall, *Commissioner Trist:* Nicholas Joy, *Gregory Cruckston:* Donald Curtis, *Lieutenant Quint:* Arthur Space, *Henry Seward:* Selmer Jackson, *Detective Foster:* Roger Moore, *Detective Ferguson:* Stanley Andrews, *Jiggers:* Bud Wolfe, *Skitch:* David Sharpe, *Blackie:* Chick Collins, *Herman:* Billy Jones, *Chauffeur:* Jimmy Lloyd, *Butler:* Jimmy Logan, *Junior:* Jimmy Hunt, *Maid:* Ann Staunton, *Bartender:* Fred Sears, *Junior's Mother:* Verna Felton, *Milkman:* Garry Owen, *Officer #1:* Cliff Clark, *Girl:* Susan Simon, *Ranger Leader:* Mary Field, *Police Doctor:* Emmett Vogan, *Photographer:* Charles Jordan, *Plainclothesman:* Virgil Johansen, *District Attorney:* Rod O'Connor, *Policeman:* Jack Perrin, *Police Sergeant:* Dick Wessel, *Police Announcer:* William Newell.

FUNNY FACE (1957) Par. Producer, Roger Edens. Director, Stanley Donen. VistaVision, Technicolor. Screenplay, Leonard Gershe. Art Directors, Hal Pereira, George W. Davis. Music adapted and conducted by Adolph Deutsch. Orchestral Arrangements, Conrad Salinger, Van Cleave, Alexander Courage, Skip Martin. Cinematographer, Ray June. Special Photographic Effects, John P. Fulton. Process Photography, Farciot Edouart. Editor, Frank Bracht. Songs by George and Ira Gershwin: "Funny Face," "'S Wonderful," "How Long Has This Been Going On," "Let's Kiss and Make Up," "He Loves and She Loves" and "Clap Yo' Hands"; by Roger Edens and Leonard Gershe: "Think Pink," "Bonjour Paris," "Basal Metabolism," "On How to Be Lovely" and "Marche Funebre." Dance Routines, Eugene Loring and Fred Astaire. Filmed in Paris, New York, and Hollywood. 103 minutes

Jo Stockton: Audrey Hepburn, *Dick Avery:* Fred Astaire, *Maggie Prescott:* Kay Thompson, *Professor Emile Flostre:* Michel Auclair, *Paul Duval:* Robert Flemyng, *Marion:* Dovima, *Babs:* Virginia Gibson, *Specialty Dancer (Pink Number):* Suzy Parker, *Laura:* Sue England, *Specialty Dancer (Pink Number):* Sunny Harnett, *Lettie:* Ruta Lee, *Hairdresser:* Jean Del Val, *Dovitch:* Alex Gerry, *Armande:* Iphigenie

Funny Face with Audrey Hepburn and Fred Astaire.

Castiglioni, *Beautician:* Albert D'Arno, *Assistant Hairdresser:* Nina Borget, *Receptionist:* Marilyn White, *Junior Editor:* Louise Glenn, *Junior Editor:* Heather Hopper, *Junior Editor:* Cecile Rogers, *Melissa:* Nancy Kilgas, *Assistant Beautician:* Emilie Stevens, *Specialty Dancer:* Don Powell, *Assistant Dance Director:* Bruce Hoy, *Specialty Dancer:* Carole Eastman, *Steve:* Paul Smith, *Mimi:* Diane Du Bois, *Gigi:* Karen Scott, *Madame La Farge:* Elizabeth "Lizz" Slifer, *Southern Man:* Nesdon Booth.

A FUNNY THING HAPPENED ON THE WAY TO THE FORUM (1966) UA. A Quadrangle (Melvin Frank) Production. Director, Richard Lester. De Luxe Color. Screenplay, Melvin Frank and Michael Pertwee. Musical Comedy Book, Burt Shevelove and Larry Gelbart. Camera, Nicholas Roeg. Production and Costume Design, Tony Walton. Music Director, Irwin Kostal. Editor, John Victor Smith. Choreography, Ethel and George Martin. Filmed at Bronston Studios, Spain. Songs by Stephen Sondheim: "Comedy Tonight," "Everybody Ought to Have a Maid," "Free," "Lovely," "Bring Me My Bride." Incidental Music, Ken Thorne. Assistant Director, Jos Lopez Rodero. Art Director, Syd Cain. Second Unit Director, Bob Simmons. Special Effects, Cliff Richardson. 99 minutes

Pseudolus: Zero Mostel, *Lycus:* Phil Silvers, *Erronius:* Buster Keaton, *Hysterium:* Jack Gilford, *Hero:* Michael Crawford, *Philia:* Annette Andre, *Domina:* Patricia Jessel, *Senex:* Michael Hordern, *Gymnasia:*

A Funny Thing Happened on the Way to the Forum with Zero Mostel and Jack Gilford.

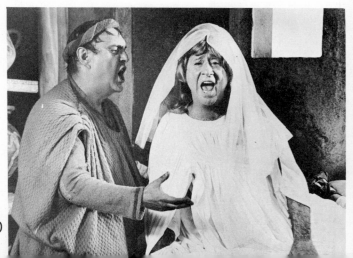

340

Inga Neilsen, *Miles Gloriosus:* Leon Greene, *Vibrata:* Myrna White, *Panacea:* Lucienne Bridou, *Tintinabula:* Helen Funai, *Geminae:* Jennifer and Susan Baker, *Fertilla:* Janet Webb, *High Priestress:* Pamela Brown, *Coliseum Guard:* Alfie Bass, *Bit.* Roy Kinnear.

FURY (1936) MGM. Produced by Joseph L. Mankiewicz. Directed by Fritz Lang. Based on a story by Norman Krasna. Screenplay, Bartlett Cormack, Fritz Lang. Cameraman, Joseph Ruttenberg. Editor, Frank Sullivan. 90 minutes.

Fury with Esther Muir and Spencer Tracy.

Joe Wilson: Spencer Tracy, *Katherine Grant:* Sylvia Sidney, *District Attorney:* Walter Abel, *Sheriff Hummel:* Edward Ellis, *Bugs Meyers:* Walter Brennan, *Kirby Dawson:* Bruce Cabot, *Tom Wilson:* George Walcott, *Charlie Wilson:* Frank Albertson, *Durkin:* Arthur Stone, *Fred Garrett:* Morgan Wallace, *Milton Jackson:* George Chandler, *Stranger:* Roger Gray, *Vickery:* Edwin Maxwell, *Governor:* Howard C. Hickman, *Defense Attorney:* Jonathan Hale, *Edna Hooper:* Leila Bennett, *Mrs. Whipple:* Esther Dale, *Franchette:* Helen Flint, *Judge Hopkins:* Frederick Burton, *Donelli:* Carlos Martin, *Girl in Nightclub:* Esther Muir, *Doctor:* Edward Le Saint, *Goofy:* Ben Hall, *Defendant:* George Offerman, Jr., *Hysterical Woman:* Mira McKinney, *Dynamiter:* Frank Sully, *Assistant Defense Attorney:* Guy Usher, *Waiter:* Bert Roach, *Hector:* Raymond Hatton, *Jorgeson:* Victor Potel, *Objector:* Ward Bond, *Pippin:* Clarence Kolb, *Mrs. Tuttle:* Gertrude Sutton, *Taxi Driver:* Daniel Haynes, *Bessie:* Minerva Urecal, *Counterman:* William Newell, *Anderson:* Harry Harvey, *Peanut Vendor:* Eddie Quillan, *Uncle Billy:* Si Jenks, *Baggage Clerk:* Sid Saylor.

GAMBIT (1966) Univ. Produced by Leo L. Fuchs. Directed by Ronald Neame. Technicolor and TechniScope. Based on a story by Sidney

Gambit with Shirley MacLaine and Michael Caine.

Carroll. Screenplay, Jack Davies and Alvin Sargent. Photography, Clifford Stine. Assistant Director, Joseph Kenny. Editor, Alma Macrorie. Music, Maurice Jarre. Song, Paul Godkin and Harper McKay. Make-up, Bud Westmore. Music Supervision, Joseph Gershenson. Gowns, Jean Louis. Hair Styles, Sidney Guilaroff. Filmed in Hollywood. 108 minutes

Nicole Chang: Shirley MacLaine, *Harry Dean:* Michael Caine, *Ahmad Shahbandar:* Herbert Lom, *Emile Fournier:* John Abbott, *Abdul:* Arnold Moss, *Ram:* Roger C. Carmel, *Colonel Salim:* Richard Angarola, *Hotel Clerk:* Maurice Marsac, *Cafe Extra:* Paul Bradley.

THE GANG'S ALL HERE (1943) 20th. Producer, William Le Baron. Director, Busby Berkeley. Color by Technicolor. Authors, Nancy Wintner, George Root, Jr., Tom Bridges. Screenplay, Walter Bullock. Dances, Busby Berkeley. Art Directors, James Basevi, Joseph C. Wright. Musical Directors, Alfred Newman, Charles Henderson. Cameraman, Edward Cronjager. Editor, Ray Curtiss. Songs by Leo Robin and Harry Warren: "No Love No Nothing," "Journey to a Star," "The Lady in the Tutti-Frutti Hat," "The Polka-Dot Polka," "You Discover You're in New York," "Paducah," "Minnie's in the Money," "Pickin' on Your Mama," Sleepy Moon" and "Drums and Dreams." Technicolor Director, Natalie Kalmus. 103 minutes

Eadie: Alice Faye, *Rosita:* Carmen Miranda, *Phil Baker:* Himself, *Benny Goodman & Band:* Themselves, *Mr. Mason, Sr.:* Eugene Pallette, *Mrs. Peyton Potter:* Charlotte Greenwood, *Peyton Potter:* Edward Everett Horton, *Tony DeMarco:* Himself, *Andy Mason:* James Ellison, *Vivian:* Sheila Ryan, *Sergeant Casey:* Dave Willock, *Specialty Dancer:* Miriam Lavelle, *Jitterbug Dancer:* Charles Saggau, *Jitterbug Dancer:* Deidre Gale, *Benson:* George Dobbs, *Waiter:* Leon Belasco, *Maybelle:* June Haver, *Marine:* Frank Faylen, *Sailor:* Russell Hoyt, *Secretary:* Virginia Sale, *Bulter:* Leyland Hodgson, *Bit Man:* Lee Bennett, *Girl:* Jeanne Crain, *Maid:* Lillian Yarbo, *Doorman:* Frank Darien, *Stage Manager:* Al Murphy, *Old Lady:* Hallene Hill, *Organ Grinder:* Gabriel Canzona, *Newsboy:* Fred Walburn, *Dancing Partner:* Virginia Wilson (Virginia de Luce).

The Gang's All Here with Alice Faye, Frank Faylen and James Ellison.

GASLIGHT (1944) MGM. Producer, Arthur Hornblow, Jr. Director, George Cukor. From the play by Patrick Hamilton. Screenplay, John Van Druten, Walter Reisch, John L. Balderston. Musical Score, Bronislau Kaper. Art Director, Cedric Gibbons. Cameraman, Joseph Ruttenberg. Special Effects, Warren Newcombe. Editor, Ralph E. Winters. Remake of the 1940 British film. 114 minutes

Gregory Anton: Charles Boyer, *Paula:* Ingrid Bergman, *Brian Cameron:* Joseph Cotten, *Miss Thwaites:* Dame May Whitty, *Elizabeth Tompkins:* Barbara Everest, *Nancy Oliver:* Angela Lansbury, *Budge:* Eustace Wyatt, *Mario Guardi:* Emil Rameau, *General Huddelston:* Edmund

Gaslight with Charles Boyer and Ingrid Bergman.

Breon, *Mr. Mufflin:* Halliwell Hobbes, *Paula (age 14):* Judy Ford (Terry Moore), *Williams:* Tom Stevenson, *Lady Dalroy:* Heather Thatcher, *Lord Dalroy:* Lawrence Grossmith, *Wilkins:* Charles McNaughton, *Policeman:* Harry Adams, *Lamplighter:* Bobby Hale, *Young Girl:* Phyllis Yuse, *Turnkey:* Alec Craig, *Guide:* Leonard Carey, *Boy in Museum:* Simon Oliver, *Girl of 10:* Alix Terry, *Footman:* Ronald Bennett, *Butler:* Arthur Blake, *Miss Pritchard:* Joy Harington, *Lady:* Lillian Bronson, *Valet:* Eric Wilton, *Boy:* George Nokes, *Policeman:* Pat Malone, *Lamplighter:* Frank Eldridge.

THE GAY DIVORCEE (1934) RKO. Produced by Pandro S. Berman. Directed by Mark Sandrich. Based on the novel and the 1932 musical, *The Gay Divorce* by Dwight Taylor. Screenplay, George Marion Jr., Dorothy Yost, Edward Kaufman. Music adaptation, Kenneth Webb and Samuel Hoffenstein. Music Director, Max Steiner. Dances, Dave Gould. Songs: "Night and Day" by Cole Porter; "The Continental" and "Looking for a Needle in a Haystack" by Con Conrad and Herb Magidson; "Don't Let It Bother You" and "Let's Knock K-neez" by Mack Gordon and Harry Revel. Photography, David Abel. Editor, William Hamilton. Astaire, Rhodes and Blore repeat their stage roles. 107 minutes

The Gay Divorcee with Ginger Rogers and Fred Astaire.

Guy Holden: Fred Astaire, *Mimi Glossop:* Ginger Rogers, *Aunt Hortense:* Alice Brady, *Egbert Fitzgerald:* Edward Everett Horton, *Rodolfo Tonetti:* Erik Rhodes, *Waiter:* Eric Blore, *Dancer:* Betty Grable, *Guy's Valet:* Charles Coleman, *Cyril Glossop:* William Austin, *Guest:* Lillian Miles, *French Waiters:* George Davis, Alphonse Martell, *French Headwaiter:* Paul Porcasi, *Call Boy at Dock:* Charles Hall, *Chief Customs Inspector:* E. E. Clive.

GENTLEMAN'S AGREEMENT (1947) 20th. Producer, Darryl F. Zanuck. Director, Elia Kazan. From the novel by Laura Z. Hobson. Screenplay, Moss Hart. Music, Alfred Newman. Art Directors, Lyle Wheeler, Mark-Lee Kirk. Cameraman, Arthur Miller. Editor, Harman Jones. 118 minutes

Phil Green: Gregory Peck, *Kathy:* Dorothy McGuire, *Dave:* John Garfield, *Anne:* Celeste Holm, *Mrs. Green:* Anne Revere, *Miss Wales:* June Havoc, *John Minify:* Albert Dekker, *Jane:* Jane Wyatt, *Tommy:* Dean Stockwell, *Dr. Craigie:* Nicholas Joy, *Professor Lieberman:* Sam Jaffe, *Jordan:* Harold Vermilyea, *Bill Payson:* Ransom M. Sherman, *Mr. Calkins:* Roy Roberts, *Mrs. Minify:* Kathleen Lockhart, *Bert McAnny:* Curt Conway, *Bill:* John Newland, *Weisman:* Robert Warwick, *Ex-G.I.'s in Restaurant:* Robert Karnes, Gene Nelson, *Guest:* Marion Marshall, *Miss Miller:* Louise Lorimer, *Tingler:* Howard Negley, *Olsen:* Victor Kilian, *Harry:* Frank Wilcox, *Receptionist:* Marilyn Monk, *Maitre D':* Wilton Graff, *Clerk:* Morgan Farley, *Columnist:* Mauritz Hugo, *Women:* Olive Deering, Jane Green, Virginia Gregg, *Elevator Starter:* Jesse White.

Gentleman's Agreement with Gregory Peck, Celeste Holm, John Garfield, Gene Nelson and Robert Karnes.

GENTLEMEN PREFER BLONDES (1953) 20th. Producer, Sol C. Siegel. Director, Howard Hawks. Technicolor. Based on the musical by Anita Loos and Joseph Fields. Screenplay, Charles Lederer. Art Directors, Lyle Wheeler, Joseph C. Wright. Cinematographer, Harry J. Wild. Editor, Hugh S. Fowler. Music Director, Lionel Newman. Costumes, Travilla. Choreography, Jack Cole. Songs: "When Love Goes Wrong" and "Anyone Here for Love?" by Hoagy Carmichael and Harold Adamson. Songs by Jule Styne and Leo Robin: "Two Little Girls From Little Rock," "Diamonds Are a Girl's Best Friend," "Bye, Bye, Baby." Remake of 1928 Warners film. 91 minutes

Dorothy: Jane Russell, *Loreli:* Marilyn Monroe, *Sir Francis Beekman:* Charles Coburn, *Malone:* Elliott Reid, *Gus Esmond:* Tommy Noonan, *Henry Spofford III:* George Winslow, *Magistrate:* Marcel Dalio, *Esmond, Sr.:* Taylor Holmes, *Lady Beekman:* Norma Varden, *Watson:* Howard Wendell, *Hotel Manager:* Steven Geray, *Grotier:* Henri Letondal, *Pritchard:* Alex Frazer, *Dancer:* George Chakiris, *Bit:* Robert Fuller, *Phillipe:* Leo Mostovoy, *Cab Driver:* George Davis,

Gentlemen Prefer Blondes with Marilyn Monroe.

Headwaiter: Alphonse Martell, *Boy Dancers:* Jimmie Moultrie, Freddie Moultrie, *Winslow:* Harry Carey, Jr., *Ship's Captain:* Jean Del Val, *Peters:* Ray Montgomery, *Anderson:* Alvy Moore, *Evans:* Robert Nichols, *Ed:* Charles Tannen, *Stevens:* Jimmy Young, *Purser:* Charles De Ravenne, *Coach:* John Close, *Sims:* William Cabanne, *Steward:* Philip Sylvestre, *Pierre:* Alfred Paix, *Court Clerk:* Max Willenz, *Waiter:* Rolfe Sedan, *Passport Officials:* Robert Foulk, Ralph Peters, *Captain of Waiters:* Harry Seymour.

GIANT (1956) WB. Producers, George Stevens, Henry Ginsberg. Director, George Stevens. WarnerColor. Based on the novel by Edna Ferber. Screenplay, Fred Guiol, Ivan Moffat. Music composed and directed by Dimitri Tiomkin. Cinematographer, William C. Mellor. Editor, William Hornbeck. Film editor, Fred Bohanan, Phil Anderson. James Dean's last film. 198 minutes

Leslie Lynnton Benedict: Elizabeth Taylor, *Bick Benedict:* Rock Hudson, *Jett Rink:* James Dean, *Luz Benedict:* Mercedes McCambridge, *Uncle Bawley:* Chill Wills, *Vashti Snythe:* Jane Withers, *Pinky Snythe:*

Giant with Rock Hudson, Elizabeth Taylor and Mercedes McCambridge.

Robert Nichols, *Jordan Benedict III:* Dennis Hopper, *Juana:* Elsa Cardenas, *Judy Benedict:* Fran Bennett, *Luz Benedict II:* Carroll Baker, *Bob Dace:* Earl Holliman, *Dr. Horace Lynnton:* Paul Fix, *Mrs Horace Lynnton:* Judith Evelyn, *Lacey Lynnton:* Carolyn Craig, *Sir David Karfrey:* Rodney Taylor, *Old Polo:* Alexander Scourby, *Angel Obregon II:* Sal Mineo, *Bale Clinch:* Monte Hale, *Adarene Clinch:* Mary Ann Edwards, *Swazey:* Napoleon Whiting, *Whiteside:* Charles Watts, *Dr. Guerra:* Maurice Jara, *Angel Obregon I:* Victor Millan, *Mrs. Obregon:* Pilar Del Rey, *Gomez:* Felipe Turich, *Gabe Target:* Sheb Wooley, *Mexican Priest:* Francisco Villalobos, *Watts:* Ray Whitley, *Lupe:* Tina Menard, *Petra:* Ana Maria Majalca, *Sarge:* Mickey Simpson, *Lona Lane:* Noreen Nash, *Harper:* Guy Teague, *Eusubio:* Natividad Vacio, *Dr. Walker:* Max Terhune, *Dr. Borneholm:* Ray Bennett, *Mary Lou Decker:* Barbara Barie, *Vern Decker:* George Dunne, *Clay Hodgins:* Slim Talbot, *Clay Hodgins, Sr.:* Tex Driscoll, *Essie Lou Hodgins:* Juney Ellis.

G. I. BLUES (1960) Par. Producer, Hal Wallis. Associate Producer, Paul Nathan. Director, Norman Taurog. Technicolor. Screenplay, Edmund Beloin, Henry Garson. Art Director, Walter Tyler. Music scored and conducted by Joseph J. Lilley. Cinematographer, Loyal Griggs. Supervising Film Editor, Warren Low. Songs: "G. I. Blues," "Tonight Is So Right for Love," "Wooden Heart," "Big Boots," "Doin' the Best I Can," "Frankfurt Special," "Pocketful of Rainbows," "Shoppin' Around," "Didja Ever?" "What's She Really Like?" Locations filmed in Germany. 104 minutes

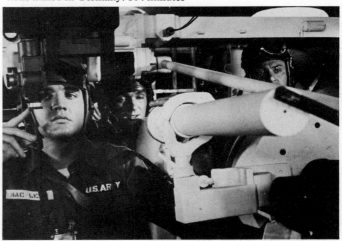

G.I. Blues with Elvis Presley, Mickey Knox and James Douglas.

Tulsa: Elvis Presley, *Lili:* Juliet Prowse, *Cookie:* Robert Ivers, *Tina:* Leticia Roman, *Rick:* James Douglas, *Marla:* Sigrid Maier, *Sergeant McGraw:* Arch Johnson, *Jeeter:* Mickey Knox, *Captain Hobart:* John Hudson, *Mac:* Ken Becker, *Turk:* Jeremy Slate, *Warren:* Beach Dickerson, *Mickey:* Trent Dolan, *Walt:* Carl Crow, *Papa Mueller:* Fred Essler, *Harvey:* Ronald Starr, *Trudy:* Erika Peters, *Owner of Puppet Show:* Ludwig Stossel, *Guitarist-Leader:* Robert Boon, *Mrs. Hagermann:* Edit Angold, *Orchestra Leader:* Dick Winslow, *Red:* Ed Faulkner, *Band Leader:* Edward Coch, *Herr Klugmann:* Fred Kruger, *Headwaiter:* Torben Meyer, *Businessmen:* Gene Roth, Roy C. Wright, *M.P.s:* Harper Carter, Tip McClure, *Chaplain:* Walter Conrad, *Dynamite:* Edward Stroll, *Kaffeehouse Manager:* William Kaufmann, *Strolling Girl Singer:* Hannerl Melcher, *Sergeant:* Elisha Matthew (Bitsy) Mott, Jr., *Fritzie:* Judith Rawlins, *Bargirl:* Marianne Gaba.

GIGI (1958) MGM. Producer, Arthur Freed. Director, Vincente Minnelli. CinemaScope, Technicolor. Based on the novel by Colette. Screenplay, Alan Jay Lerner. Art Directors, William A. Horning, Preston Ames. Musical Director, Andre Previn. Lyrics, Alan Jay Lerner. Music, Frederick Loewe. Orchestration, Conrad Salinger. Cinematographer, Joseph Ruttenberg. Editor, Adrienne Fazan. Other versions: a French film with Danielle Delorme, and a play with Audrey Hepburn. Filmed in Hollywood, exteriors made in Paris and at Maxim's. Betty Wand sings for Leslie Caron. Songs by Alan Jay Lerner and Fe-

Gigi with Hermione Gingold, Louis Jourdan, and Leslie Caron.

Gilda with Rita Hayworth and Steven Geray.

derick Loewe: "It's a Bore," "Gigi," "The Parisians," "The Night They Invented Champagne," "Say a Prayer for Me Tonight," "Thank Heaven for Little Girls," "I Remember It Well," "I'm Glad I'm Not Young Any More," "Gossip," "Waltz at Maxim's (She's Not Thinking of Me)." 116 minutes

Gigi: Leslie Caron, *Honoré Lachaille:* Maurice Chevalier, *Gaston Lachaille:* Louis Jourdan, *Mme. Alvarez:* Hermione Gingold, *Liane d'Exelmans:* Eva Gabor, *Sandomir:* Jacques Bergerac, *Aunt Alicia:* Isabel Jeans, *Manuel:* John Abbott, *Charles (Butler):* Edwin Jerome, *Simone:* Lydia Stevens, *Prince Berensky:* Maurice Marsac, *Showgirl:* Monique Van Vooren, *Designer:* Dorothy Neuman, *Mannequin:* Maruja Plose, *Red head:* Marilyn Sims, *Harlequin:* Richard Bean, *Blonde:* Pat Sheahan.

GIGOT (1962) 20th. Producer, Kenneth Hyman. Director, Gene Kelly. Screenplay, John Patrick. Based on the story by Jackie Gleason. Music, Jackie Gleason. Assistant Director, Paul Feyder. A Seven Arts Production in De Luxe Color. 104 minutes

Gigot: Jackie Gleason, *Colette:* Katherine Kath, *Madame Brigitte:* Gabrielle Dorziat, *Gaston:* Jean Lefebvre, *Jean:* Jacques Marin, *Alphonse:* Albert Remy, *Lucille Duval:* Yvonne Constant, *Madame Greuze:* Germaine Delbat, *Bistro Proprietor:* Albert Dinan, *Nicole:* Diane Gardner, *The Priest:* Camille Guerini, *Albert:* Rene Havard *Monsieur Duval:* Louis Falavigna, *The Gendarme:* Jean Michaud, *The Baker:* Richard Francoeur, *Baker's Wife:* Paula Dehelly, *Blade:* Jacques Ary, *Pierre:* Frank Villard.

GILDA (1946) Col. Producer, Virginia Van Upp. Director, Charles Vidor. Story, E. A. Ellington. Screenplay, Marion Parsonnet. Art

Gigot with Jackie Gleason.

Directors, Stephen Goosson, Van Nest Polglase. Musical Directors, M.W. Stoloff, Marin Skiles. Cameraman, Rudolph Mate. Editor, Charles Nelson. Adaptation, Jo Eisinger. Songs by Doris Fisher and Allan Roberts: "Amada Mio" and "Put the Blame on Mame." 110 minutes

Gilda: Rita Hayworth, *Johnny Farrell:* Glenn Ford, *Ballin Mundson:* George MacCready, *Obregon:* Joseph Calleia, *Uncle Pio:* Steven Geray, *Casey:* Joe Sawyer, *Captain Delgado:* Gerald Mohr, *Gabe Evans:* Robert Scott, *German:* Ludwig Donath, *Thomas Langford:* Don Douglas, *German:* Lionel Royce, *Little Man:* S. Z. Martel; *Huerta:* George J. Lewis, *Maria:* Rosa Rey, *Girl:* Ruth Roman, *Social Citizen:* Ted Hecht, *Woman:* Argentina Brunetti, *Doorman:* Jerry DeCastro, *Man:* Robert Stevens (Robert Kellard), *Bendolin's Wife:* Fernanda Eliscu, *Argentine:* Frank Leyva, *American:* Forbes Murray, *Frenchman:* Oscar Lorraine, *American:* Sam Flint, *Italian:* George Humbert, *Englishman:* Herbert Evans, *Man:* Rodolfo Hoyos, *Bendolin:* Edvardo Cianelli, *Clerk:* Ropert Tafur, *Escort:* Russ Vincent, *Frenchman:* Jean DeBriac.

GIRL CRAZY (1943) MGM. Producer, Arthur Freed. Director, Norman Taurog. Authors, Guy Bolton, Jack McGowan. Screenplay, Fred F. Finklehoffe. Musical Adaptation, Roger Edens. Musical Director, Georgie Stoll. Dance Director, Charles Walters. Art Director, Cedric Gibbons. Cameramen, William Daniels, Robert Planck. Editor, Albert Akst. Songs by Ira and George Gershwin: "Treat Me Rough," "Sam and Delilah," "Bidin' My Time," "Embraceable You," "Fascinating Rhythm," "I Got Rhythm," "But Not for Me," "Barbary Coast" and "Cactus Time in Arizona." Remade by MGM as *When the Girls Meet the Boys* (1965). 99 minutes

Girl Crazy with Henry O'Neill, Mickey Rooney, Judy Garland and Guy Kibbee.

Danny Churchill, Jr.: Mickey Rooney, *Ginger Gray:* Judy Garland, *Bud Livermore:* Gil Stratton, *Henry Lathrop:* Robert E. Strickland, *"Rags":* Rags Ragland, *Specialty:* June Allyson, *Polly Williams:* Nancy Walker, *Dean Phineas Armour:* Guy Kibbee, *Tommy Dorsey & His Band:* Themselves, *Marjorie Tait:* Frances Rafferty, *Governor Tait:* Howard Freeman, *Mr. Churchill, Sr.:* Henry O'Neill, *Ed:* Sidney Miller, *Governor's Secretary:* Sarah Edwards, *Radio Man:* William Bishop, *Brunette:* Eve Whitney, *Blonde:* Carol Gallagher, *Buckets:* Jess Lee Brooks, *Maitre d'Hotel:* Charles Coleman, *Nervous Man:* Harry Depp, *Dignified Man:* Richard Kipling, *Fat Man:* Henry Roquemore, *Waiter:* Alphonse Martel, *Churchill's Secretary:* Barbara Bedford, *Station Master:* Victor Potel, *Tom:* William Beaudine, Jr., *Reception Clerk:* Irving Bacon, *Messenger:* George Offerman, Jr., *Blonde:* Kathleen Williams, *Southern Girl:* Mary Elliott, *Girl:* Katharine Booth, *Boy:* Don Taylor, *Showgirls:* Georgia Carroll, Noreen Roth (Noreen Nash), Hazel Brooks Inez Cooper, *Roly-poly Man:* Frank Jaquet, *Boy:* Peter Lawford, *Committee Woman:* Bess Flowers.

Girl of the Golden West with Leo Carrillo, Nelson Eddy and Jeanette MacDonald.

THE GIRL OF THE GOLDEN WEST (1938) MGM. Produced by William Anthony McGuire. Directed by Robert Z. Leonard. Based on the play by David Belasco. Screenplay, Isabel Dawn and Boyce DeGaw. Music Director, Herbert Stothart. Filmed in Sepia. Photography, Oliver Marsh. Editor, W. Donn Hayes. Dances, Albertina Rasch. Montage, Slavko Vorkapich. Songs by Sigmund Romberg and Gus Kahn: "Mariachi," "There's a Brand New Song in Town," "The Golden West," "The West Ain't Wild Anymore," "Señorita," "Soldiers of Fortune," "Who Are We to Say?," "From Sun-Up to Sundown." The fourth MacDonald-Eddy film. Previous versions of *The Girl of the Golden West:* Paramount, 1914; Warner Brothers, 1923; Warner Brothers, 1930. Cut from the release print were Ray Bolger as Happy Moore and Carol Tevis as Trixie LaVerne. 120 minutes

Mary Robbins: Jeanette MacDonald, *Ramerez (Lt. Johnson):* Nelson Eddy, *Sheriff Jack Rance:* Walter Pidgeon, *Mosquito:* Leo Carrillo, *Alabama:* Buddy Ebsen, *Pedro:* Leonard Penn, *Nina Martinez:* Priscilla Lawson, *Sonora Slim:* Bob Murphy, *Trinidad Joe:* Olin Howland, *Minstrel Joe:* Cliff Edwards, *Nick:* Billy Bevan, *The Professor:* Brandon Tynan, *Father Sienna:* H. B. Warner, *Governor:* Monty Woolley, *Uncle Davy:* Charley Grapewin, *The General:* Noah Beery, Sr., *Gringo:* Bill Cody, Jr., *The Girl Mary:* Jeanne Ellis, *Wowkle:* Ynez Seabury, *Stage Driver:* Victor Potel, *Billy Jack Rabbit:* Nick Thompson, *Handsome Charlie:* Tom Mahoney, *Long Face:* Phillip Armenta, *Indian Chief:* Chief Big Tree, *Pioneer:* Russell Simpson, *First Renegade:* Armand "Curley" Wright, *Second Renegade:* Pedro Regas, *Manuel:* Gene Coogan, *Jose:* Sergei Arabeloff, *Juan:* Alberto Morin, *Felipe:* Joe Dominguez, *Pete, a Gambler:* Frank McClynn, *Hank, a Gambler:*

Cy Kendall, First Miner: E. Alyn Warren, *Second Miner:* Francis Ford, *Deputy:* Hank Bell, *Lieutenant Johnson:* Walter Bonn, *Colonel:* Richard Tucker, *Governor's Wife:* Virginia Howell.

The Glenn Miller Story with The Modernaires, Frances Langford and James Stewart.

THE GLENN MILLER STORY (1954) Univ. Producer, Aaron Rosenberg. Director, Anthony Mann. Technicolor. Screenplay, Valentine Davies. Art Directors, Bernard Herzbrun, Alexander Golitzen. Cinematographer, William Daniels. Editor, Russell Schoengarth. 116 minutes

Glenn Miller: James Stewart, *Helen Burger:* June Allyson, *Don Haynes:* Charles Drake, *Chummy:* Henry Morgan, *Si Schribman:* George Tobias, *Herself:* Frances Langford, *Himself:* Louis Armstrong, *Himself:* Gene Krupa, *Himself:* Ben Pollack, *General Arnold:* Barton MacLane, *Kranz:* Sig Rumann, *Mr. Miller:* Irving Bacon, *Mr. Burger:* James Bell, *Mrs. Miller:* Kathleen Lockhart, *Mrs. Burger:* Katharine Warren, *Colonel Spaulding:* Dayton Lummis, *Polly Haynes:* Marion Ross, *Joe Becker:* Phil Garris, *Jonnie Dee:* Deborah Sydes, *Themselves:* The Modernaires, *Themselves:* The Archie Savage Dancers, *Girl Singer:* Ruth Hampton, *Colonel Baker:* Damian O'Flynn, *Adjutant General:* Carleton Young, *Sergeant:* William Challee, *Lieutenant Colonel Baessell:* Steve Pendleton, *Doctor:* Harry Harvey, Sr., *Schillinger:* Leo Mostovoy, *Garage Man:* Dick Ryan, *Used Car Salesman:* Hal K. Dawson, *Singing Foursome:* The Mello-Men, *Skating Act:* The Rolling Robinsons, *Boy:* Robert A. Davis, *Bobby-soxer:* Lisa Gaye, *Wilbur Schwartz:* Nino Tempo, *Himself:* Babe Russin, *Music Cutter:* Carl Vernell, *Irene:* Bonnie Eddy, *Herbert:* Anthony Sydes.

"G" MEN (1935) WB. Directed by William Keighley. From "Public Enemy No. 1" by Seton I. Miller. Screenplay, Seton I. Miller. Camera-

"G" Men with Russell Hopton, James Cagney, Edward Pawley and Barton MacLane.

man, Sol Polito. Editor, Jack Killifer. Music Director, Leo Forbstein. Song, "You Bother Me an Awful Lot" by Sammy Fain and Irving Kahal. Technical Director, Frank Gompert. Gowns, Orry-Kelly. Dance Director, Bobby Connolly. Art Director, John J. Hughes. Reissued in 1949, on the FBI's 25th anniversary, with a prologue featuring David Brian as The Chief and Douglas Kennedy as an agent. 85 minutes

James (Brick) Davis: James Cagney, *Jean Morgan:* Ann Dvorak, *Kay McCord:* Margaret Lindsay, *Jeff McCord:* Robert Armstrong, *Brad Collins:* Barton MacLane, *Hugh Farrell:* Lloyd Nolan, *McKay:* William Harrigan, *Danny Leggett:* Edward Pawley, *Gerard:* Russell Hopton, *Durfee:* Noel Madison, *Eddie Buchanan:* Regis Toomey, *Bruce J. Gregory:* Addison Richards, *Venke:* Harold Huber, *The Man:* Raymond Hatton, *Analyst:* Monte Blue, *Gregory's Secretary:* Mary Treen, *Accomplice:* Adrian Morris, *Joseph Kratz:* Edwin Maxwell, *Bill, Ballistics Expert:* Emmett Vogan, *Agent:* James Flavin, *Bank Cashier:* Ed Keane, *Cops:* Stanley Blystone, Pat Flaherty, *Agent:* James T. Mack, *Congressman:* Jonathan Hale, *Short Man:* Charles Sherlock, *Henchman at Lodge:* Wheeler Oakman, *Police Broadcaster:* Eddie Dunn, *Interne:* Gordon (Bill) Elliott, *Doctor at Store:* Perry Ivins, *Hood Shot at Lodge:* Frank Marlowe, *Collins' Moll:* Gertrude Short, *Gerard's Moll:* Marie Astaire, *Durfee's Moll:* Florence Dudley, *Moll:* Frances Morris, *Hood:* Al Hill, *Gangster:* Huey White, *Headwaiter:* Glen Cavender, *Italian, Tony:* John Impilito, *Sergeant:* Bruce Mitchell, *Deputy Sheriff:* Monte Vandergrift, *Chief:* Frank Shannon, *Announcer:* Frank Bull, *Nurse:* Martha Merrill, *Lounger:* Gene Morgan, *J. E. Blattner, Florist:* Joseph DeStefani, *Machine Gunner:* George Daly, *Machine Gunner:* Ward Bond, *Prison Guard:* Tom Wilson, *Police Driver:* Henry Hall, *McCord's Aide:* Lee Phelps, *Hood at Lodge:* Marc Lawrence, *Man:* Brooks Benedict.

The Goddess with Kim Stanley (hysterical).

THE GODDESS (1958) Col. Producer, Milton Perlman. Director, John Cromwell. Written by Paddy Chayefsky. Music by Virgil Thomson. Costumes by Frank Thompson. Assistant Director, Charles H. Maguire. Photography, Arthur J. Ornitz. Art Director, Edward Haworth. Costumes, Frank L. Thompson. Editor, Carl Lerner. Special Supervision, George Justin. Presented in three acts: Portrait of a Child, Portrait of a Girl, Portrait of a Goddess. Film debut of Kim Stanley. 105 minutes

Emily Ann Faulkner: Kim Stanley, *The Mother:* Betty Lou Holland, *The Aunt:* Joan Copeland, *The Uncle:* Gerald Hiken, *The Boy:* Burt Brinckerhoff, *John Tower:* Steve Hill, *The Minister:* Gerald Petrarca, *Bridesmaid:* Linda Soma, *The Writer:* Curt Conway, *Joanna:* Joan Linville, *Hillary:* Joyce Van Patten, *Dutch Seymour:* Lloyd Bridges, *Lester Brackman:* Bert Freed, *R. M. Lucas:* Donald McKee, *The Cook:* Louise Beavers, *Secretary:* Elizabeth Wilson, *Burt Harris:* David White,

First G.I.: Roy Shuman, *Second G.I.:* John Lawrence, *Emily Ann, age 4:* Chris Flanagan, *Emily Ann, age 8:* Patty Duke, *First Man:* Mike O'Dowd, *Second Man:* Sid Raymond, *Mrs. Woolsy:* Margaret Brayton, *Mr. Woolsy:* Werner Klemperer, *The Elder:* Fred Herrick, *Emily's Daughter:* Gail Haworth.

God Is My Co-pilot with Stanley Ridges, Raymond Massey, Minor Watson and Dennis Morgan.

GOD IS MY CO-PILOT (1945) WB. Producer, Robert Buckner. Director, Robert Florey. Based on the novel by Colonel Robert L. Scott. Art Director, John Hughes. Cameraman, Sid Hickox. Editor, Folmer Blangsted. Screenplay, Peter Milne and Abem Finkel. 90 minutes

Colonel Robert L. Scott: Dennis Morgan, *Johnny Petach:* Dane Clark, *Major General Claire L. Chennault:* Raymond Massey, *"Big Mike" Harrigan:* Alan Hale, *Catherine Scott:* Andrea King, *Tex Hill:* John Ridgely, *Colonel Meriam Cooper:* Stanley Ridges, *Ed Rector:* Craig Stevens, *Bob Neale:* Warren Douglas, *Sergeant Baldridge:* Stephen Richards (Mark Stevens), *Private Motley:* Charles Smith, *Colonel Caleb V. Haynes:* Minor Watson, *"Tokyo Joe":* Richard Loo, *Sergeant Aaltonen:* Murray Alper, *Gil Bright:* Bernie Sell, *Lieutenant Doug Sharp:* Joel Allen, *Lieutenant "Alabama" Wilson:* John Miles, *Lieutenant Jack Horner:* Paul Brooke, *"Prank":* Clarence Muse, *Doctor Reynolds:* William Forrest, *Chinese Captain:* Frank Tang, *Japanese Announcer at Hong Kong:* Philip Ahn, *Frank Schiel:* Dan Dowling, *General Kitcheburo:* Paul Fung, *Specialty Dancer:* Frances Chan, *British Officer-Prisoner:* Sanders Clark, *American Girl Prisoner:* Phyllis Adair, *American Pilots:* Dale Van Sickle, Tom Steele, Art Foster, *Scott as a boy:* Buddy Burroughs, *Catherine's Father:* George Cleveland, *Robin Lee:* Ghislaine (Gigi) Perreau, *A.V.G. Groundmen:* Don McGuire, William Challee, *Newspaper Editor:* Joel Friedkin, *Major:* James Flavin.

GOD'S LITTLE ACRE (1958) UA. Producer, Sidney Harmon. Director, Anthony Mann. Screenplay by Philip Yordan. Based on the

God's Little Acre with Fay Spain, Buddy Hackett and Robert Ryan.

novel by Erskine Caldwell. Music, by Elmer Bernstein. Assistant Director, Louis Brandt. Costumes by Sophia Stutz. A Security Pictures Production. 110 minutes

Ty Ty Walden: Robert Ryan, *Bill Thompson:* Aldo Ray, *Griselda:* Tina Louise, *Pluto:* Buddy Hackett, *Buck Walden:* Jack Lord, *Darlin' Jill:* Fay Spain, *Shaw Walden:* Vic Morrow, *Rosamund:* Helen Westcott, *Jim Leslie:* Lance Fuller, *Uncle Felix:* Rex Ingram, *Dave Dawson:* Michael Landon.

Go for Broke! with Don Haggerty and Van Johnson.

GO FOR BROKE! (1951) MGM. Producer, Dore Schary. Director-Author-Screenplay, Robert Pirosh. Art Directors, Cedric Gibbons, Eddie Imazu. Music, Alberto Colombo. Photography, Paul C. Vogel. Editor, James E. Newcom. Song by Robert Pirosh, Alberto Colombo and Ken Okamoto: "The Meaning of Love." 92 minutes

Lieutenant Michael Grayson: Van Johnson, *Sam:* Lane Nakano, *"Chick":* George Miki, *Frank:* Akira Fukunaga, *"Kaz":* Ken K. Okamoto, *Ohhara:* Henry Oyasato, *Masami:* Harry Hamada, *Tommy:* Henry Nakamura, *Colonel Charles W. Pence:* Warner Anderson, *Sergeant Wilson I. Culley:* Don Haggerty, *Rosina:* Gianna Canale, *Captain Solari:* Dan Riss, *Ohhara's Brother:* George Tanaguchi, *Platoon Leader:* Frank Okada, *Captain:* Walter Reed, *Chaplain:* Hugh Beaumont, *General:* Frank Wilcox, *Sergeant Major:* Tsutomu Paul Nakamura, *First General:* Edward Earle, *Second General:* Freeman Lusk, *Officer:* Richard Anderson, *German Officer:* Henry Guttman, *Italian Farmer:* Mario Siletti, *German Officer:* John Banner, *Pianist:* Ann Codee, *Texan:* Jack Reilly, *French Farmer:* Louis Mercier, *German Prisoner:* Tony Christian, *Interpreter:* Toru Iura.

GOING MY WAY (1944) Par. Producer and director, Leo McCarey. Author, Leo McCarey. Screenplay, Frank Bulter, Frank Cavett. Art

Going My Way with Barry Fitzgerald and Bing Crosby.

Directors, Hans Dreier, William Flannery. Musical Director, Robert Emmett Dolan. Cameraman, Lionel Lindon. Special Effects, Gordon Jennings. Editor, LeRoy Stone. Songs: "Swinging on a Star," "Day After Forever" and "Going My Way" by Johnny Burke and Jimmy Van Heusen; "Too-Ra-Lo-Too-Roo-La" by J. R. Shannon. 130 minutes

Father O'Malley: Bing Crosby, *Genevieve Linden:* Risë Stevens, *Father Fitzgibbon:* Barry Fitzgerald, *Father Timothy O'Dowd:* Frank McHugh, *Ted Haines:* James Brown, *Haines, Sr.:* Gene Lockhart, *Carol James:* Jean Heather, *Mr. Belknap:* Porter Hall, *Tomaso Bozanni:* Fortunio Bonanova, *Mrs. Carmody:* Eily Malyon, *Robert Mitchell Boychoir:* Themselves, *Pee-Wee Belknap:* George Nokes, *Officer Patrick McCarthy:* Tom Dillon, *Tony Scaponi:* Stanley Clements, *Herman Langerhanke:* Carl "Alfalfa" Switzer, *Interne:* Bill Henry, *Pitch Pipe:* Hugh Maguire, *Don Jose:* Robert Tafur, *Zuniga:* Martin Garralaga, *Maid at Metropolitan Opera House:* Sybyl Lewis, *Mr. Van Heusen:* George McKay, *Max:* William Frawley, *Mr. Lilley:* Jack Norton, *Mrs. Quimp:* Anita Bolster, *Fireman:* Jimmie Dundee, *Taxi Driver:* Julie Gibson, *Mrs. Molly Fitzgibbon:* Adeline DeWalt Reynolds, *Churchgoer:* Gibson Gowland.

Gold Diggers of Broadway with Neely Edwards and Lee Moran.

GOLD DIGGERS OF BROADWAY (1929) WB. Directed by Roy Del Ruth. Color by Technicolor. Story, Robert Lord. From the play *The Gold Diggers* by Avery Hopwood. Numbers staged by Larry Ceballos. Sound, Western Electric Vitaphone. Songs by Al Dubin and Joe Burke: "Painting the Clouds With Sunshine," "Tip-Toe Through the Tulips," "And They Still Fall in Love," "Go to Bed," "What Will I Do Without You?", "In a Kitchenette." Editor, William Holmes. Titles, De Leon Anthony. Costumes, Earl Luick. Assistant Director, Ross Lederman. Orchestra conducted by Louis Silvers. Technicians, L. Geib, M. Parker, F. N. Murphy, and V. Vance. Photography, Barney McGill and Ray Rennahan. Also silent version. Other versions by Warner Brothers: *Gold Diggers* (1923), *Gold Diggers of 1933, Painting the Clouds With Sunshine* (1951). Other editions of *Gold Diggers* series 1933, 1935 and *Gold Diggers in Paris* (1938). 98 minutes

Jerry: Nancy Welford, *Stephen Lee:* Conway Tearle, *Mabel:* Winnie Lightner, *Ann Collins:* Ann Pennington, *Eleanor:* Lilyan Tashman, *Wally:* William Bakewell, *Nick:* Nick Lucas, *Violet:* Helen Foster, *Blake:* Albert Gran, *Topsy:* Gertrude Short, *Stage Manager:* Neely Edwards, *Cissy Gray:* Julia Swayne Gordon, *Dance Director:* Lee Moran, *Barney Barnett:* Armand Kaliz.

GOLD DIGGERS OF 1933 (1933) WB. Directed by Mervyn LeRoy. Based on the play *Gold Diggers* by Avery Hopwood. Adaptation, Erwin Gelsey and James Seymour. Dialogue, David Boehm and Ben Markson. Photography, Sol Polito. Editor, George Amy. Dances by

Gold Diggers of 1933 with Aline MacMahon, Guy Kibbee, Dick Powell, Tammany Young and Joan Blondell.

Busby Berkeley. Songs by Harry Warren and Al Dubin: "The Gold Diggers' Song (We're in the Money)," "I've Got to Sing a Torch Song," "Pettin' in the Park," "The Shadow Waltz," "Remember My Forgotten Man." Remake of *Gold Diggers of Broadway*, 1929. 96 minutes

J. Lawrence Bradford: Warren William, *Carol:* Joan Blondell, *Trixie Lorraine:* Aline MacMahon, *Polly Parker:* Ruby Keeler, *Brad Roberts (Robert Treat Bradford):* Dick Powell, *Thaniel H. Peabody:* Guy Kibbee, *Barney Hopkins:* Ned Sparks, *Fay Fortune:* Ginger Rogers, *Gordon:* Clarence Nordstrom, *Dance Director:* Robert Agnew, *Gigolo Eddie:* Tammany Young, *Messenger Boy:* Sterling Holloway, *Clubman:* Ferdinand Gottschalk, *Gold Digger Girl:* Lynn Browning, *Deputy:* Charles C. Wilson, *"Pettin' in the Park" Baby:* Billy Barty, *Negro Couple:* Snowflake (Fred Toones), Theresa Harris, *Chorus Girl:* Joan Barclay, *Stage Manager:* Wallace MacDonald, *Society Reporters:* Wilbur Mack, Grace Hayle, Charles Lane, *Dog Salesman:* Hobart Cavanaugh, *Dance Extra:* Bill Elliott, *Extra during Intermission:* Dennis O'Keefe, *Call Boy:* Busby Berkeley, *"Detective Jones":* Fred Kelsey, *First Forgotten Man:* Frank Mills.

GOLD DIGGERS OF 1935 (1935) WB. Directed by Busby Berkeley. Story, Robert Lord and Peter Milne. Screenplay, Manuel Seff and Peter Milne. Dances created by Busby Berkeley. Photography, George Barnes. Editor, George Amy. Songs by Harry Warren and Al Dubin: "Lullaby of Broadway," "I'm Going Shopping With You," "The Words Are in My Heart." Film debut of Jack La Rue's sister Emily, 18. Cut from the film: Harry Holman as Mr. Higpy, Marjorie Nichols as Letitia Fry, Grace Hayle as Mrs. Fry. 95 minutes

Dick Curtis: Dick Powell, *Nikolai Nicoleff:* Adolphe Menjou, *Ann Prentiss:* Gloria Stuart, *Matilda Prentiss:* Alice Brady, *Betty Hawes:* Glenda Farrell, *Humbolt Prentiss:* Frank McHugh, *T. Mosley Thorpe:*

Gold Diggers of 1935 with Alice Brady, Adolphe Menjou and Joseph Cawthorn.

Hugh Herbert, *August Schultz:* Joseph Cawthorn, *Louis Lampson:* Grant Mitchell, *Arline Davis:* Dorothy Dare, *Wini Shaw:* Winifred Shaw, *Haggarty:* Thomas Jackson, *Singer, "The Words Are in My Heart":* Virginia Grey, *Girl:* Emily La Rue, *Dancers:* Ramon and Rosita, *Tap Dancer:* Matty King, *Head Bellhop:* Phil Tead, *Maitre D'Hotel:* Eddie Kane, *Housekeeper:* Nora Cecil, *Head Barman:* Arthur Aylesworth, *Martin (Clerk):* Gordon (Bill) Elliott, *Bellhop:* John Quillan, *Photographer:* Don Brodie, *Reporters:* Eddie Fetherstone, Billy Newell, George Riley, Harry Seymour, *Bellhop:* Ray Cooke, *Bartender:* Franklyn Farnum, *Manders, Doorman:* Charles Coleman, *Westbrook, Chauffeur:* E. E. Clive, *Perfume Clerk:* Leo White.

Goldfinger with Gert Frobe and Sean Connery.

GOLDFINGER (1964) UA. Producers, Harry Saltzman, Albert R. Broccoli. Director, Guy Hamilton. Screenplay, Richard Maibaum, Paul Dehn. Based on the novel by Ian Fleming. Director of Photography, Ted Moore. Title song, Leslie Bricusse, Anthony Newley; sung by Shirley Bassey. Music, John Barry. Assistant Director, Frank Ernest. An Eon Production in Technicolor. 108 minutes

James Bond: Sean Connery, *Goldfinger:* Gert Frobe, *Pussy Galore:* Honor Blackman, *Jill Masterson:* Shirley Eaton, *Tilly Masterson:* Tania Mallett, *Oddjob:* Harold Sakata, *"M":* Bernard Lee, *Solo:* Martin Benson, *Felix Lieter:* Cec Linder, *Simmons:* Austin Willis, *Miss Moneypenny:* Lois Maxwell, *Midnight:* Bill Nagy, *Capungo:* Alf Joint, *Old Lady:* Varley Thomas, *Bonita:* Nadja Regin, *Sierra:* Raymond Young, *Smithers:* Richard Vernon, *Brunskill:* Denis Cowles, *Kisch:* Michael Mellinger, *Mr. Ling:* Bert Kwouk, *Strap:* Hal Galili, *Henchman:* Lenny Rabin.

The Goldwyn Follies with Vera Zorina, Charlie McCarthy and Edgar Bergen.

THE GOLDWYN FOLLIES (1938) UA. Produced by Samuel Goldwyn. Directed by George Marshall. Color by Technicolor. Story and Screenplay, Ben Hecht, Associate Producer, Georgie Haight. Additional comedy sequences by Sam Perrin and Arthur Phillips. Art Director, Richard Day. Music Director, Alfred Newman. Orchestrations, Edward Powell. Ballets, George Balanchine. Photography, Gregg Toland. Editor, Sherman Todd. Assistant Director, Eddie Bernoudy. Ballet Music, Vernon Duke. Songs: "Love Walked In," "Love Is Here to Stay," "I Was Doing All Right," and "I Love to Rhyme" by George and Ira Gershwin; "Spring Again" and "I'm Not Complaining" by Ira Gershwin and Kurt Weill; "Here Pussy Pussy" by Ray Golden and Sid Kuller; arias from *La Traviata*. Film debut of Helen Jepson. Andrea Leeds replaced Virginia Verrill, who dubbed the songs for her. New York newsman Harry Selby (pseudonym) was to do the original story. Cut were dancers Olga Phillips and John Kohl. 115 minutes

Oliver Merlin: Adolphe Menjou, *Themselves:* The Ritz Brothers, *Themselves:* Edgar Bergen and Charlie McCarthy, *Olga Samara:* Vera Zorina, *Danny Beecher:* Kenny Baker, *Hazel Dawes:* Andrea Leeds, *Leona Jerome:* Helen Jepson, *Michael Day:* Phil Baker, *Glory Wood:* Ella Logan, *A. Basil Crane, Jr.:* Bobby Clark, *Director Lawrence:* Jerome Cowan, *Ada:* Nydia Westman, *Alfredo in* LA TRAVIATA: Charles Kullman, *Assistant Director:* Frank Shields, *Theater Manager:* Joseph Crehan, *Roland* (Igor in "Forgotten Dance"): Roland Drew, *Prop Man:* Frank Mills, *Auditioning Singer:* Alan Ladd, *Westinghouse, a Singer:* Walter Sande. The American Ballet of the Metropolitan Opera, under the direction of George Balanchine.

Gone With the Wind with Vivien Leigh and Clark Gable.

GONE WITH THE WIND (1939) MGM. A Selznick International Picture. Producer, David O. Selznick. Director, Victor Fleming. Technicolor. From the novel by Margaret Mitchell. Screenplay, Sidney Howard. Art Director, Lyle Wheeler. Musical Score, Max Steiner. Dance Directors, Frank Floyd, Eddie Prinz. Cameraman, Ernest Haller. Special Effects, Jack Cosgrove, Lee Zavitz. Editors, Hal C. Kern, James E. Newcom. Costumes, Walter Plunkett. Production Designer, William Cameron Menzies. Interiors, Joseph B. Platt. Interior Decoration, Edward G. Boyle. Make-up and Hair Styling, Mouty Westmore, Hazel Rogers, Ben Nye. Historian, Wilbur G. Kurtz. Technical Advisors, Susan Myrick and Will Price. Research, Lillian K. Deighton. Production Manager, Raymond A. Klune. Technicolor Supervision, Natalie Kalmus and Henri Jaffa. Assistant Directors, Eric G. Stacey and Ridgeway Callow. Reissued in 1967 with Stereophonic Sound, and in 70mm Wide Screen. 219 minutes

AT TARA *Brent Tarleton:* Fred Crane, *Stuart Tarleton:* George Reeves, *Scarlett O'Hara:* Vivien Leigh, *Mammy:* Hattie McDaniel, *Big Sam:* Everett Brown, *Elijah:* Zack Williams, *Gerald O'Hara:* Thomas Mitchell, *Pork:* Oscar Polk, *Ellen O'Hara:* Barbara O'Neill, *Jonas*

Wilkerson: Victor Jory, *Suellen O'Hara:* Evelyn Keyes, *Careen O'Hara:* Ann Rutherford, *Prissy:* Butterfly McQueen.

AT TWELVE OAKS *John Wilkes:* Howard Hickman, *India Wilkes:* Alicia Rhett, *Ashley Wilkes:* Leslie Howard, *Melanie Hamilton:* Olivia De Havilland, *Charles Hamilton:* Rand Brooks, *Frank Kennedy:* Carroll Nye, *Cathleen Calvert:* Marcella Martin, *Rhett Butler:* Clark Gable, *Gentleman:* James Bush.

AT THE BAZAAR IN ATLANTA *Aunt Pittypat Hamilton:* Laura Hope Crews, *Doctor Meade:* Harry Davenport, *Caroline Meade:* Leona Roberts, *Dolly Merriwether:* Jane Darwell, *Rene Picard:* Albert Morin, *Maybelle Merriwether:* Mary Anderson, *Fanny Elsing:* Terry Shero, *Old Levi:* William McClain.

OUTSIDE THE *EXAMINER* OFFICE *Uncle Peter:* Eddie Anderson, *Phil Meade:* Jackie Moran.

AT THE HOSPITAL *Reminiscent Soldier:* Cliff Edwards, *Belle Watling:* Ona Munson, *The Sergeant:* Ed Chandler, *Wounded Soldier in Pain:* George Hackathorne, *A Convalescent Soldier:* Roscoe Ates, *A Dying Soldier:* John Arledge, *An Amputation Case:* Eric Linden, *Card player* (*Wounded*): Guy Wilkerson.

DURING THE EVACUATION *A Commanding Officer:* Tom Tyler, *Soldier Aiding Doctor Meade:* Frank Faylen.

DURING THE SIEGE *A Mounted Officer:* William Bakewell, *Bartender:* Lee Phelps.

GEORGIA AFTER SHERMAN *A Yankee Deserter:* Paul Hurst, *Carpetbagger's Friend:* Ernest Whitman, *A Returning Veteran:* William Stelling, *A Hungry Soldier:* Louis Jean Heydt, *Emmy Slattery:* Isabel Jewell.

DURING RECONSTRUCTION *A Yankee Major:* Robert Elliott, *His Poker-Playing Captains:* George Meeker, Wallis Clark, *The Corporal:* Irving Bacon, *A Carpetbagger Orator:* Adrian Morris, *Johnny Gallegher:* J. M. Kerrigan, *A Yankee Businessman:* Olin Howland, *A Renegade:* Yakima Canutt, *His Companion:* Blue Washington, *Tom, a Yankee Captain:* Ward Bond, *Bonnie Blue Butler:* Cammie King, *Beau Wilkes:* Mickey Kuhn, *Bonnie's Nurse:* Lillian Kemble Cooper, *Yankee on Street:* Si Jenks, *Tom's Aide:* Harry Strang.

GOODBYE, MR. CHIPS (1939) MGM. Producer, Victor Saville. Director, Sam Wood. From the novel by James Hilton. Screenplay, R.C. Sherriff, Claudine West, Eric Maschwitz. Cameraman, F.A. Young. Editor, Charles Frend. 114 minutes

Mr. Chipping: Robert Donat, *Katherine Chipping:* Greer Garson, *John Colley: Peter Colley II Peter Colley III Peter Colley III:* Terry Kilburn, *Peter Colley as a young man:* John Mills, *Staefel:* Paul Von Hernried (Henried), *Flora:* Judith Furse, *Wetherby:* Lyn Harding, *Chatteris:* Milton Rosmer, *Marsham:* Frederick Leister, *Mrs. Wickett:* Louise Hampton, *Ralston:* Austin Trevor, *Jackson:* David Tree,

Goodbye, Mr. Chips with Robert Donat and Greer Garson.

Colonel Morgan: Edmond Breon, *Helen Colley:* Jill Furse, *Sir John Colley:* Scott Sunderland.

THE GOOD EARTH (1937) MGM. Produced by Irving G. Thalberg. Associate Producer, Albert Lewin. Directed by Sidney Franklin. Based on the novel by Pearl S. Buck. Adapted for the stage by Owen and Donald Davis. Screenplay, Talbot Jennings, Tess Schlesinger, Claudine West. Music Score, Herbert Stothart. Art Director, Cedric Gibbons. Associate Art Directors, Harry Oliver, Arnold Gillespie, Edwin B. Willis. Wardrobe, Dolly Tree. Montage, Slavko Vorkapich. Photography, Karl Freund. Editor, Basil Wrangell. Photographed in Sepia. Backgrounds filmed in China. The voice of Lotus Lui used in place of Tilly Losch's. Dedicated to Irving Grant Thalberg, his last production. 138 minutes

The Good Earth with Paul Muni and Luise Rainer.

Wang: Paul Muni, *O-lan:* Luise Rainer, *Uncle:* Walter Connolly, *Lotus:* Tillie Losch, *Cuckoo:* Jessie Ralph, *Old Father:* Charley Grapewin, *Elder Son:* Keye Luke, *Cousin:* Harold Huber, *Younger Son:* Roland Got (Roland Lui), *Old Mistress Aunt:* Soo Young, *Ching:* Chingwah Lee, *Gateman:* William Law, *Little Bride:* Mary Wong, *Banker:* Charles Middleton, *Little Fool:* Suzanna Kim, *Dancer:* Caroline Chew, *Singer In Tea House:* Chester Gan, *Grain Merchant, Liu:* Olaf Hytten, *House Guest of Wang:* Miki Morita, *Captain:* Philip Ahn, *Chinaman:* Sammee Tong, *Farmer/Rabble-rouser/Peach Seller:* Richard Loo.

GOOD NEIGHBOR SAM (1964) Col. Producer, David Swift. Associate Producer, Marvin Miller. Director, David Swift. Eastman Color. Based on the novel by Jack Finney. Screenplay, James Fritzell, Everett Greenbaum, David Swift. Music, Frank DeVol. Cinematographer, Burnett Guffey. Editor, Charles Nelson Costumes, Micheline and Jacqueline. 130 minutes

Good Neighbor Sam with Edward Andrews, κomy Schneider, Edward G. Robinson and Jack Lemmon.

Sam Bissel: Jack Lemmon, *Janet Lagerlof:* Romy Schneider, *Minerva Bissel:* Dorothy Provine, *Howard Ebbets:* Michael Connors, *Mr. Burke:* Edward Andrews, *Reinhold Shiffner:* Louis Nye, *Earl:* Robert Q. Lewis, *Girl:* Joyce Jameson, *Irene:* Anne Seymour, *Jack Bailey:* Charles Lane, *Edna:* Linda Watkins, *Phil Reisner:* Peter Hobbs, *Sonny Blatchford:* Tris Coffin, *Larry Boling:* Neil Hamilton, *Miss Halverson:* Riza Royce, *Millard Mellner:* William Forrest, *The Hi-Lo's:* The Hi-Lo's, *Simon Nurdlinger:* Edward G. Robinson, *Receptionist:* Barbara Bouchet, *Taragon:* Bernie Kopell, *Wyeth:* Patrick Waltz, *Hausner:* William Bryant, *Jenna:* Vickie Cos, *Ardis:* Kym Karath, *Marsha:* Quinn O'Hara, *McVale:* Hal Taggart, *Gloria:* Jan Brooks, *Mrs. Burke:* Bess Flowers, *Hertz Com'l Man:* Dave Ketchum, *Fran:* Aneta Corsaut, *Director:* David Swift, *Drunk:* Gil Lamb, *Cop:* Jim Bannon.

THE GORGEOUS HUSSY (1936) MGM. Produced by Joseph Mankiewicz. Directed by Clarence Brown. From the book by Samuel Hopkins Adams. Screenplay, Ainsworth Morgan and Stephen Morehouse Avery. Music Score, Herbert Stothart. Art Director, Cedric Gibbons. Dance staged by Val Raset. Photography, George Folsey. Editor, Blanche Sewell. 102 minutes

The Gorgeous Hussy with Robert Taylor, Gene Lockhart and Joan Crawford.

Peggy O'Neal Eaton: Joan Crawford, *Bow Timberlake:* Robert Taylor, *Andrew Jackson:* Lionel Barrymore, *John Randolph:* Melvyn Douglas, *Rowdy (Roderick) Dow:* James Stewart, *John Eaton:* Franchot Tone, *Sunderland:* Louis Calhern, *Mrs. Beall:* Alison, Skipworth, *Rachel Jackson:* Beulah Bondi, *Cuthbert:* Melville Cooper, *Lady Vaughn:* Edith Atwater, *Daniel Webster:* Sidney Toler, *Major O'Neal:* Gene Lockhart, *Emily Donaldson:* Phoebe Foster, *Louisa Abbott:* Clara Blandick, *John C. Calhoun:* Frank Conroy, *Maybelle:* Nydia Westman, *Aunt Sukey:* Louise Beavers, *Martin Van Buren:* Charles Trowbridge. *Secretary Ingham:* Willard Robertson, *Mrs. Oxenrider:* Greta Meyer, *Horatius:* Fred (Snowflake) Toone, *Herr Oxenrider:* William Orlamond, *Bartender:* Lee Phelps, *Mrs. Bellamy:* Rubye de Remer, *Mrs. Wainwright:* Betty Blythe, *Braxton:* George Reed, *Major Domo:* Bert Roach, *Tompkins:* Oscar Apfel, *Leader of Mob:* Franklin Parker, *Mrs. Daniel Beall:* Zeffie Tilbury, *Auctioneer:* Harry Holman, *Slave Buyer:* Morgan Wallace, *W. R. Earle:* William Stack, *President's Secretary:* Harry C. Bradley, *Officer:* Ward Bond, *Butler:* Sam McDaniel, *Commander:* Samuel S. Hinds.

THE GRADUATE (1967) Embassy. Produced by Lawrence Turman. Directed by Mike Nichols. Panavision and Technicolor. Based on the novel by Charles Wobb. Screenplay, Calder, Willingham and Buck Henry. Songs by Paul Simon, sung by Simon and Garfunkel: "Mrs. Robinson," "The Sounds of Silence." Music by Dave Grusin. Production Design, Richard Sylbert. Assistant Director, Don Kranze. Photography, Robert Surtees. Editor, Sam O'Steen. Sound, Jack Soloman. 105 minutes

The Graduate with Anne Bancroft and Dustin Hoffman.

Mrs. Robinson: Anne Bancroft, *Ben Braddock:* Dustin Hoffman, *Elaine Robinson:* Katharine Ross, *Mr. Braddock:* William Daniels, *Mr. Robinson:* Murray Hamilton, *Mrs. Braddock:* Elizabeth Wilson, *Carl Smith:* Brian Avery, *Mr. Maguire:* Walter Brooke, *Mr. McCleery:* Norman Fell, *Second Lady:* Elizabeth Fraser, *Mrs. Singleman:* Alice Ghostley, *Room Clerk:* Buck Henry, *Miss De Witt:* Marion Lorne.

GRAND HOTEL (1932) MGM. Directed by Edmund Goulding. From the play *Menschen im Hotel* by Vicki Baum. American version by William A. Drake. Art Director, Cedric Gibbons. Gowns, Adrian. Assistant Director, Charles Dorian. Photography, William Daniels. Editor, Blanche Sewell. Sound, Douglas Shearer. MGM financed the 1930 Broadway version. Unofficially remade many times; officially remade by MGM as *Weekend at the Waldorf,* 1945. 115 minutes

Grusinskaya: Greta Garbo, *Baron Felix von Geigern:* John Barrymore, *Flaemmchen:* Joan Crawford, *Preysing:* Wallace Beery, *Otto Kringelein:* Lionel Barrymore, *Dr. Otternschlag:* Lewis Stone, *Senf:* Jean Hersholt, *Meierheim:* Robert McWade, *Zinnowitz:* Purnell B. Pratt, *Pimenov:* Ferdinand Gottschalk, *Suzette:* Rafaela Ottiano, *Chauffeur:* Morgan Wallace, *Gerstenkorn:* Tully Marshall, *Rohna:* Frank Conroy, *Schweimann:* Murray Kinnell, *Dr. Waitz:* Edwin Maxwell, *Honeymooner:* Mary Carlisle, *Hotel Manager:* John Davidson, *Bartender:* Sam MacDaniel, *Clerk:* Rolfe Sedan, *Clerk:* Herbert Evans, *Extra in Lobby:* Lee Phelps.

Grand Hotel with Frank Conroy, Ferdinand Gottschalk, John Davidson, Greta Garbo, Robert McWade and Rafaela Ottiano.

GRAND PRIX (1966) MGM. Produced by Edward Lewis. Directed by John Frankenheimer. Cinerama and Super Panavision and Metro-Color. Screen story and screenplay, Robert Alan Arthur. Music composed and conducted by Maurice Jarre. Director of Photography, Lionel Linde. A.S.C. Production Designer, Richard Sylbert. Editors, Henry German, Stewart Linder, Frank Santillo. A Joel-JFP-Cherekee Co-Production. Story and Screenplay, Robert Alan Aurthur. Music

Grand Prix with Enzo Fiermonte and Yves Montand.

composed and conducted by Maurice Jarre. Production Design, Richard Sylbert. Costumes, Make-up and Hair Supervision, Sydney Guilaroff. Assistant Director, Enrice Issace. Photography, Lionel Linden. Editors, Fredric Steinkamp, Henry Berman, Stewart Linder, Frank Santille. Special Effects, Milt Rice. Filmed in Europe and United States. 179 minutes

Pete Aron: James Garner, *Louise Frederickson:* Eva Marie Saint, *Jean-Pierre Sarti:* Yves Montand, *Izo Yamura:* Toshiro Mifune, *Scott Stoddard:* Brian Bedford, *Pat Stoddard:* Jessica Walter, *Nino Barlini:* Antonio Sabato, *Lisa:* Francoise Hardy, *Agostini Manetta:* Adolfo Celi, *Hugo Simon:* Claude Dauphin, *Monique Delvaux Sarti:* Genevieve Page, *Guido:* Enzo Fiermonte, *Jeff Jordan:* Jack Watson, *Wallace Bennett:* Donal O'Brien, *Mrs. Stoddard:* Rachel Kempson, *Mr. Stoddard:* Ralph Michael, *Mrs. Randolph:* Evans Evans, *Claude:* Arthur Howard, *Photographer, David:* John Bryson, *John Hogarth:* Richie Giuther, *Douglas McClendon:* Bruce McLaren, *Children's Father:* Jean Michaud, *Tim Randolph:* Phil Hill, *Bob Turner:* Graham Hill, *Victor, Journalist:* Bernard Cahier, *Sportscasters:* Alan Fordney, Anthony Marsh, Tommy Franklin, *Grand Prix Drivers:* Lorenzo Bandini, Bob Bondurant, Jack Brabham, *American Boy:* Alain Gerard, *Doctor at Monza:* Tiziano Feroldi, *Rafael:* Gilberto Mazzi, *BBC Interviewer:* Raymond Baxter, *Ferrari Official:* Eugenio Dragoni, *Japanese Interpreter:* Maasaki Asukai, *Monte Carlo Doctor:* Albert Remy.

THE GRAPES OF WRATH (1940) 20th. Produced by Darryl F. Zanuck. Associate Producer, Nunnally Johnson. Directed by John Ford. Based on the novel by John Steinbeck. Screenplay, Nunnally Johnson. Music Director, Alfred Newman. Art Directors, Richard Day and Mark-Lee Kirk. Photography, Gregg Toland. Sound, George Leverett and Roger Heman. Editor, Robert Simpson. Assistant Director, Eddie O'Fearna. Theme, "Red River Valley." 128 minutes

Tom Joad: Henry Fonda, *Ma Joad:* Jane Darwell, *Casey:* John Carradine, *Grampa:* Charley Grapewin, *Rosasharn/Joad Rivers:* Doris Bowdon, *Old Tom (Pa) Joad:* Russell Simpson, *Al:* O. Z. Whitehead,

The Grapes of Wrath with Henry Fonda, John Carradine, Frank Darien, Russell Simpson, Norman Willis (with gun), Adrian Morris and Paul Guilfoyle.

Muley: John Qualen, *Connie Rivers:* Eddie Quillan, *Granma:* Zeffie Tilbury, *Noah:* Frank Sully, *Uncle John:* Frank Darien, *Winfield Joad:* Darryl Hickman, *Ruth Joad:* Shirley Mills, *Thomas:* Roger Imhof, *Caretaker:* Grant Mitchell, *Wilkie:* Charles D. Brown, *Davis:* John Arledge, *Policeman:* Ward Bond, *Bert:* Harry Tyler, *Bill:* William Pawley, *Father:* Arthur Aylesworth, *Joe:* Charles Tannen, *Inspection Officer:* Selmer Jackson, *Leader:* Charles Middleton, *Proprietor:* Eddy Waller, *Floyd:* Paul Guilfoyle, *Frank:* David Hughes, *City Man:* Cliff Clark, *Bookkeeper:* Joseph Sawyer, *Agent:* Adrian Morris, *Muley's Son:* Hollis Jewell, *Spencer:* Robert Homans, *Roy (a Driver):* Irving Bacon, *Mae:* Kitty McHugh, *Tim Wallace:* Frank Faylen, *Sheriff:* Tom Tyler, *Floyd's Wife:* Mae Marsh, *Joe (Deputy):* Norman Willis, *Hungry Girl:* Peggy Ryan, *Boy who Ate:* Wally Albright, *Arkansas Storekeeper:* Erville Alderson, *Fred (Truck Driver):* Harry Strang, *Cop:* Rex Lease, *Woman in Camp:* Inez Palange, *Man at Camp:* Louis Mason, *Deputy/Troublemaker:* Harry Tenbrook, *Deputy:* Frank O'Connor, *Bit Woman:* Georgia Simmons, *Deputy:* Ralph Dunn, *Gas Station Man:* Herbert Heywood, *New Mexico Border Guard:* Walter Miller, *Gas Station Attendants:* Gaylord (Steve) Pendleton, Robert Shaw, *First Deputy:* Lee Shumway, *Second Deputy:* Dick Rich, *Guard:* James Flavin, *Clerk:* George O'Hara, *Motor Cop:* Thornton Edwards, *Jule:* Trevor Bardette, *Committeeman:* Jack Pennick, *Leader of Gang:* Walter McGrail, *Boy:* George Breakstone, *Deputy Driver:* William Haade, *State Policeman:* Ted Oliver, *Gas Station Attendant:* Ben Hall, *Waitress:* Gloria Roy.

The Great Caruso with Carl Milletaire, Vincent Renne, Shepard Menken, Mario Lanza, Ann Blyth and Ludwig Donath.

THE GREAT CARUSO (1951) MGM. Producer, Joe Pasternack. Director, Richard Thorpe. Color by Technicolor. Author, Dorothy Caruso. Screenplay, Sonia Levien, William Ludwig. Art Directors, Cedric Gibbons, Gabriel Scognamillo. Musical Supervision, Johnny Green. Photography, Joseph Ruttenberg. Editor, Gene Ruggiero. Song based on the melody of the Vienese waltz "Over the Waves" with lyrics by Paul Francis Webster: "The Loveliest Night of the Year." 109 minutes

Enrico Caruso: Mario Lanza, *Dorothy Benjamin:* Ann Blyth, *Louise Heggar:* Dorothy Kirsten, *Maria Selka:* Jarmila Novotna, *Carlo Santi:* Richard Hageman, *Park Benjamin:* Carl Benton Reid, *Guilio Gatti-Casazza:* Eduard Franz, *Alfredo Brazzi:* Ludwig Donath, *Jean de Reszke:* Alan Napier, *Antonio Scotti:* Paul Javor, *Gino:* Carl Milletaire, *Fucito:* Shepard Menken, *Tullio:* Vincent Renno, *Egisto Barretto:* Nestor Paiva, *Caruso as a boy:* Peter Edward Price, *Papa Caruso:* Mario Siletti, *Mrs. Caruso:* Angela Clarke, *Hutchins:* Ian Wolfe, *Musetta:* Yvette Duguay, *Mrs. Barretto:* Argentina Brunetti, *Papa Gino:* Maurice Samuels, *Blanche Thebom:* Lucine Amara, *Teresa Celli:* Robert E. Bright, *Nicolo Moscona:* Marina Koshetz, *Guiseppe Valdengo:* Gilbert Russell, *Hilda:* Edit Angold, *Papa Riccardo:* Antonio Filauri, *Father Bronzetti:* Peter Brocco, *Father Angelico:* David Bond,

Finch: Charles Evans, *Max:* Matt Moore, *Musetta as a child:* Sherry Jackson, *Ottello Carmini:* Mario DeLaval, *Fucito (at 8 years):* Anthony Mazola, *Woman:* Mae Clarke.

THE GREAT DICTATOR (1940) UA. Produced, directed and written by Charles Chaplin. Music Director, Meredith Willson. Assistant Directors, Dan James, Wheeler Dryden and Bob Meltzer. Photography by Karl Struss and Roland Totheroh. Art Director, J. Russell Spencer. Editor, Willard Nico. Sound, Percy Townsend and Glen Rominger. 129 minutes

The Great Dictator with Henry Daniell, Charlie Chaplin and Jack Oakie.

Hynkel (Dictator of Tomania)/A Jewish Barber: Charles Chaplin, *Hannah:* Paulette Goddard, *Napaloni (Dictator of Bacteria):* Jack Oakie, *Schultz:* Reginald Gardiner, *Garbitsch:* Henry Daniell, *Herring:* Billy Gilbert, *Mr. Jaeckel:* Maurice Moscovich, *Mrs. Jaeckel:* Emma Dunn, *Madame Napaloni:* Grace Hayle, *Bacterian Ambassador:* Carter de Haven, *Mr. Mann:* Bernard Gorcey, *Mr. Agar:* Paul Weigel, *Bits:* Chester Conklin, Hank Mann, Esther Michelson, Florence Wright, Eddie Gribbon, Robert O. Davis, Eddie Dunn, Nita Pike, Peter Lynn.

THE GREAT ESCAPE (1963) UA. Producer-Director, John Sturges. Screenplay, James Clavell, W. R. Burnett. Based on a book by Paul Brickhill. Assistant Director, Jack Reddish. Music, Elmer Bernstein. A Mirisch-Alpha Picture in Panavision and De Luxe Color. Art Director, Fernando Carrere. Cinematographer, Daniel Fapp. Editor, Ferris Webster. Remake of *Danger Within* ("*Breakout*") British, 1958. 168 minutes

"Cooler King" Hilts: Steve McQueen, *"The Scrounger" Hendley:* James Garner, *"Big X" Bartlett:* Richard Attenborough, *Senior Officer Ramsey:* James Donald, *Danny Velinski:* Charles Bronson, *"The Forger" Blythe:* Donald Pleasence, *"The Manufacturer" Sedg-*

The Great Escape with Richard Attenborough, Donald Pleasance and James Garner.

wick: James Coburn, *Ashley-Pitt:* David McCallum, *MacDonald:* Gordon Jackson, *Willie:* John Leyton, *"The Mole" Ives:* Angus Lennie, *Cavendish:* Nigel Stock, *Goff:* Jud Taylor, *Sorren:* William Russell, *"The Tailor" Griffith:* Robert Desmond, *Nimmo:* Tom Adams, *Haynes:* Lawrence Montaigne, *Von Luger:* Hannes Messemer, *Werner:* Robert Graf, *Strachwitz:* Harry Riebauer, *Kuhn:* Hans Reiser, *Posen:* Robert Freitag, *Kramer:* Heinz Weiss, *Frick:* Til Kiwe, *Preissen:* Ulrich Beiger.

The Greatest Show on Earth with Henry Wilcoxon, James Stewart and Betty Hutton.

THE GREATEST SHOW ON EARTH (1952) Par. Producer, Cecil B. De Mille. Associate Producer, Henry Wilcoxon. Director, Cecil B. De Mille. Color by Technicolor. Authors, Fredric M. Frank, Theodore St. John, Frank Cavett. Screenplay, Fredric M. Frank, Barre Lyndon, Theodore St. John. Art Directors, Hal Pereira, Walter Tyler. Music Score, Victor Young. Cinematographers, George Barnes, J. Peverell Marley, Wallace Kelley. Editor, Anne Bauchens. Songs: "Be a Jumping Jack" and "The Greatest Show on Earth" by Ned Washington and Victor Young; "Popcorn and Lemonade," "Sing a Happy Song" and "A Picnic in the Park" by John Murray Anderson and Henry Sullivan; "Lovely Luawana Lady" by E. Ray Goetz and John Ringling North. Assistant Director, Edward Salven. Unit Director, Arthur Rosson. Costumes, Edith Head and Dorothy Jeakins. Circus Costumes, Miles White (by Brooks Costume Company, New York). Special Effects, Gordon Jennings, Devereaux Jennings, Paul Lerpae. Sets, Sam Comer and Ray Moyer. Numbers staged by John Murray Anderson. Choreography, Richard Barstow. Make-up, Wally Westmore. Sound, Harry Lindgren and John Cope. Produced with the cooperation of Ringling Brothers-Barnum & Bailey Circus. Filmed in Sarasota, Florida. 153 minutes

Holly: Betty Hutton, *Sebastian:* Cornel Wilde, *Brad:* Charlton Heston, *Phyllis:* Dorothy Lamour, *Angel:* Gloria Grahame, *Buttons:* James Stewart, *Detective:* Henry Wilcoxon, *Himself:* Emmett Kelly, *Klaus:* Lyle Bettger, *Henderson:* Lawrence Tierney, *Harry:* John Kellogg, *Jack Steelman:* John Ridgely, *Circus Doctor:* Frank Wilcox, *Ringmaster:* Bob Carson, *Buttons' Mother:* Lillian Albertson, *Birdie:* Julia Faye, *Himself:* John Ringling North, *Tuffy:* Tuffy Genders, *Jack Lawson:* John Parrish, *Keith:* Keith Richards, *Reporter:* Brad Johnson, *Mable:* Adele Cook Johnson, *Circus Girl:* Lydia Clarke, *Chuck:* John Merton, *Dave:* Lane Chandler, *Osborne:* Bradford Hatton, *Foreman:* Herbert Lytton, *Truesdale:* Norman Field, *Board Member:* Everett Glass, *Boy:* Lee Aaker, *Hank:* Ethan Laidlaw, *Spectators:* Bing Crosby, Bob Hope, Mona Freeman, Nancy Gates, Clarence Nash, Bess Flowers, *Midway Barker:* Edmond O'Brien, *Hopalong Cassidy:* William Boyd, *Circus Acts:* Lou Jacobs, Felix Adler, Liberty Horses, The Flying Concellos, Paul Jung, The Maxellos.

THE GREATEST STORY EVER TOLD (1965) UA. Producer-Director, George Stevens. Ultra Panavision 70, Technicolor. Screenplay, James Lee Barrett, George Stevens, in Creative Association with Carl Sandburg. Music, Alfred Newman. Executive Producer, Frank I. Davis.

Associate Producers, George Stevens, Jr., Antonio Vellani. Costumes, Vittorio Nino Novarese. Screenplay based on the Bible, other ancient writings, *The Greatest Story Ever Told* by Fulton Oursler, and writings by Henry Denker. Directors of Photography, William C. Mellor, Loyal Griggs. Assistant Directors, Ridgeway Callow, John Veitch. Filmed in Utah. Choral Supervision, Ken Darby. 195 minutes

The Greatest Story Ever Told with Max von Sydow.

Jesus: Max Von Sydow, *Mary:* Dorothy McGuire, *Joseph:* Robert Loggia, *John the Baptist:* Charlton Heston, *James the Younger:* Michael Anderson, Jr., *Simon the Zealot:* Robert Blake, *Andrew:* Burt Brinckerhoff, *John:* John Considine, *Thaddaeus:* Jamie Farr, *Philip:* David Hedison, *Nathanael:* Peter Mann, *Judas Iscariot:* David McCallum, *Matthew:* Roddy McDowall, *Peter:* Gary Raymond, *Thomas:* Tom Reese, *James the Elder:* David Sheiner, *Martha of Bethany:* Ina Balin, *Mary of Bethany:* Janet Margolin, *Lazarus:* Michael Tolan, *Simon of Cyrene:* Sidney Poitier, *Mary Magdalene:* Joanna Dunham, *Veronica:* Carroll Baker, *Young Man at the Tomb:* Pat Boone, *Bar Amand:* Van Heflin, *Uriah:* Sal Mineo, *Woman of No Name:* Shelley Winters, *Old Aram:* Ed Wynn, *The Centurion:* John Wayne, *Pontius Pilate:* Telly Savalas, *Claudia:* Angela Lansbury, *Pilate's Aide:* Johnny Seven, *Questor:* Paul Stewart, *General Varus:* Harold J. Stone, *Caiaphas:* Martin Landau, *Shemiah:* Nehemiah Persoff, *Nicodemus:* Joseph Schildkraut, *Sorak:* Victor Buono, *Emissary:* Robert Busch, *Alexander:* John Crawford, *Scribe:* Russell Johnson, *Speaker of Capernaum:* John Lupton, *Joseph of Arimathaea:* Abraham Sofaer, *Theophilus:* Chet Stratton, *Annas:* Ron Whelan, *Herod Antipas:* José Ferrer, *Herod the Great:* Claude Rains, *Aben:* John Abbott, *Captain of Lancers:* Rodolfo Acosta, *Herod's Commander:* Michael Ansara, *Chuza:* Philip Coolidge, *Philip:* Dal Jenkins, *Archelaus:* Joe Perry, *Herodias:* Marian Seldes, *Dark Hermit:* Donald Pleasence, *Barabbas:* Richard Conte, *The Tormentor:* Frank DeKova, *Dumah:* Joseph Sirola, *Melchior:* Cyril Delevanti, *Balthazar:* Mark Lenard, *Caspar:* Frank Silvera. And members of the Inbal Dance Theatre of Israel.

THE GREAT RACE (1965) WB. Producer, Martin Jurow. Associate Producer, Dick Crockett. Director, Blake Edwards. Panavision, Technicolor. Authors, Blake Edwards, Arthur Ross. Screenplay,

The Great Race with Tony Curtis, Natalie Wood and Keenan Wynn.

Arthur Ross. Art Director, Fernando Carrere. Music, Henry Mancini. Songs: "The Sweetheart Tree," "He Shouldn't-a Hadn't-a, Oughtn't-a Swang on Me," words, Johnny Mercer, music, Henry Mancini. Cinematographer, Russell Harlan. Editor, Ralph E. Winters. 150 minutes

Leslie Gallant III: Tony Curtis, *Professor Fate:* Jack Lemmon, *Maggie DuBois:* Natalie Wood, *Maximillian Meen:* Peter Falk, *Hezekiah Sturdy:* Keenan Wynn, *Henry Goodbody:* Arthur O'Connell, *Hester Goodbody:* Vivian Vance, *Lilly Olay:* Dorothy Provine, *Texas Jack:* Larry Storch, *Baron Rolfe Von Stuppe:* Ross Martin, *General Kuhster:* George MacCready, *Frisbee:* Marvin Kaplan, *Chairman:* J. Edward McKinley, *Vice-Chairman:* Robert Carson, *First Employee:* Paul Smith, *Starter:* Frank Kreig, *Mayor:* Hal Smith, *Sheriff:* Denver Pyle, *M.C.:* Charles Fredericks, *Man:* Clegg Hoyt, *Freight Agent:* Charles Seel, *Conductor:* Joe Palma, *Policeman:* Paul Bryar, *Man in Bear Suit:* Chester Hayes, *Soldiers:* Chuck Hayward, Greg Benedict, *First Palace Guard:* Ken Wales, *Second Palace Guard:* Robert Herron, *Guard:* Wm. Bryant, *Prison Guard:* John Truax, *Bakers:* Johnny Silver, Hal Riddle, Stunt Double: Dave Sharpe.

The Great Ziegfeld with Luise Rainer, William Powell and Marcelle Corday.

THE GREAT ZIEGFELD (1936) MGM. Produced by Hunt Stromberg. Directed by Robert Z. Leonard. Story and Screenplay by William Anthony McGuire. Cinematographers, Oliver T. Marsh, Ray June, George Folsey, Merritt B. Gerstad. Recording Engineer, Douglas Shearer. Film Editor, William S. Gray. Art Director, Cedric Gibbons. Costumer, Adrian. Musical Director, Arthur Lange. Harriet Hoctor Ballet. Lyrics, Herb Magidson. Ballet Music, Con Conrad. Dances and Ensembles staged by Seymour Felix. Songs by Walter Donaldson and Harold Adamson: "I Wish You'd Come and Play With Me," "It's Delightful to Be Married," "A Circus Must Be Different in a Ziegfeld Show," "It's Been So Long," "You Gotta Pull Strings," "You," "Queen of the Jungle," "She's a Follies Girl," "You Never Looked So Beautiful," and "A Pretty Girl Is Like a Melody" by Irving Berlin. Orchestrations, Frank Skinner. Allan Jones' singing voice dubbed for Dennis Morgan. 184 minutes

Flo Ziegfeld: William Powell, *Anna Held:* Luise Rainer, *Billie Burke:* Myrna Loy, *Billings:* Frank Morgan, *Sampston:* Reginald Owen, *Sandow:* Nat Pendleton, *Audrey Lane:* Virginia Bruce, *Sidney:* Ernest Cossart, *Joe:* Robert Greig, *Sage:* Raymond Walburn. *Fannie Brice:* Fannie Brice, *Mary Lou:* Jean Chatburn, *Ann Pennington:* Ann Pennington, *Ray Bolger:* Ray Bolger, *Harriett Hoctor:* Harriett Hoctor, *Julian Mitchell:* Charles Trowbridge, *Dr. Ziegfeld:* Joseph Cawthorn, *Gilda Gray:* Gilda Gray, *Will Rogers:* A. A. Trimble, *Patricia*

Ziegfeld: Jean Holland, *Eddie Cantor:* Buddy Doyle, *Pierre:* Charles Judels, *Leon Errol:* Leon Error, *Marie:* Marcelle Corday, *Prima Donna:* Esther Muir, *Customer:* Herman Bing, *Erlanger:* Paul Irving, *Gene Buck:* William Demarest, *Little Egypt:* Miss Morocco, *Miss Blair:* Suzanne Kaaren, *Telegraph Boy:* Mickey Daniels, *Customers:* Richard Tucker, Clay Clement, *Customer:* Selmer Jackson, *Alice:* Alice Keating, *Marilyn Miller:* Rosina Lawrence, *Girl with Sage:* Susan Fleming, *Charles Froman:* Edwin Maxwell, *Lillian Russell:* Ruth Gillette, *Dave Stamper:* John Hyams, *Wille Zimmerman:* Boothe Howard, *"Pretty Girl" Singer:* Stanley Morner (Dennis Morgan), *Chorus Girl:* Virginia Grey.

Green Dolphin Street with Lana Turner and Van Heflin.

GREEN DOLPHIN STREET (1947) MGM. Producer, Carey Wilson, Director, Victor Saville. Based on Elizabeth Goudge's novel. Screenplay, Samson Raphaelson. Music, Bronislau Kaper. Editor, George White. Song by Ned Washington and Bronislau Kaper: "On Green Dolphin Street." 141 minutes

Marianne Patourel: Lana Turner, *Timothy Haslam:* Van Heflin, *Marguerite Patourel:* Donna Reed, *William Ozanne:* Richard Hart, *Dr. Edmund Ozanne:* Frank Morgan, *Octavius Patourel:* Edmund Gwenn, *Mother Superior:* Dame May Whitty, *Captain O'Hara:* Reginald Owen, *Sophie Patourel:* Gladys Cooper, *Mrs. Metivier:* Moyna Macgill, *Hing-Moa:* Linda Christian, *Jacky-Pato:* Bernie Gozier, *Kapua-Manga:* Pat Aherne, *Native:* Al Kikume, *Sister Angelique:* Edith Leslie, *Veronica (4 years):* Gigi Perreau, *Sir Charles Maloney:* Douglas Walton, *Captain Hartley:* Leslie Dennison, *Anderson:* Lumsden Hare, *Nat:* William Fawcett, *Priest:* Pedro De Cordoba, *Eurasian Girl:* Lila Leeds, *Emily:* Rhea Mitchell, *Corinne:* Ramsey Ames, *Brother:* Franco Corsaro, *Young Fisherman:* Guy Kingsford, *Government General:* Wyndham Standing, *Wife:* Florence Wix, *Commodore Hartley:* Leslie Dennison, *Niece:* Patricia Emery, *Chinaman:* Tetsu Kamei, *Brown:* Michael Kirby, *Chinese Longshoreman:* James B. Leong, *Mr. Samuel Kelly:* Murray Yeats, *Mrs. Samuel Kelly:* Lucille Curtis, *Maori Chieftain:* George Bennett, *Young Priest:* Richard Abbott, *Veronica (7 years):* Carol Nugent.

Green Pastures with Rex Ingram.

THE GREEN PASTURES (1936) WB. Produced by Jack L. Warner. Associate Executive in Charge of Production, Hal B. Wallis. Supervisor, Henry Blanke. Directed by Marc Connelly and William Keighley. Based on the play by Marc Connelly. Suggested by Roark Bradford's Southern sketches, *Ol' Man Adam An' His Chillun*. Screenplay, Marc Connelly and Sheridan Gibney. Cinematography, Hal Mohr. Sound, Major Nathan Levinson. Editor, George Amy. Art Directors, Allen Saalburg and Stanley Fleischer. Costumes, Milo Anderson. Assistant Director, Sherry Shourds. Choral music arranged and conducted by Hall Johnson. 93 minutes

De Lawd/Adam/Hezdrel: Rex Ingram, *Gabriel:* Oscar Polk, *Moses/Sexton:* Frank Wilson, *Pharaoh:* Ernest Whitman, *Noah:* Eddie Anderson, *Deshee/Isaac:* George Reed, *High Priest:* George Randol, *Abraham/King of Babylon/Head Magician:* Billy Cumby, *Zeba:* Edna M. Harris, *Master of Ceremonies/Man on Ground:* Slim Thomson, *Mrs. Noah:* Ida Forsyne, *Cain:* Al Stokes, *Eve:* Myrtle Anderson, *Joshua:* Reginald Fenderson, *Aaron:* David Bethea, *Cain the Sixth:* Jimmy Fuller, *Archangel:* Abraham Gleaves, *Dancer #1:* John Alexander, *Prophet:* Clinton Rosemond, *Zipporah:* Rosena Weston, *Mr. Randall:* William Broadus, *Mrs. Randall:* Amanda Drayton, *Zubo:* Fred (Snowflake) Toone, *Flatfoot/Gambler:* Charles Andrews, *Ham:* Dudley Dickerson, *Shem:* Ray Martin, *Japheth:* James Burruss, *Mrs. Ham:* Minnie Gray, *Mrs. Shem:* Bessie Guy, *Mrs. Japheth:* Dorothy Bishop, *Gambler:* Ben Carter, *Jacob:* Ivory Williams, *General:* Jesse Graves, *Abel/Dancer #2:* Duke Upshaw, *Mrs. Prohack:* Bessie Lyle, *Viney Prohack:* Lillian Davis, *Carlotta Prohack:* Charlotte Sneed, *Henry (Angel):* Willie Best, *Angel:* Johnny Lee, *Carlisle (Lucky)* Hurlick, *Angel Chorus:* The Hall Johnson Choir.

The Green Years with Dean Stockwell and Charles Coburn.

THE GREEN YEARS (1946) MGM. Producer, Leon Gordon. Director, Victor Saville. Based on the novel by A. J. Cronin. Screenplay, Robert Ardrey, Sonya Levien. Musical Score, Herbert Stothart. Art Directors, Cedric Gibbons, Hans Peters. Cameraman, George Folsey. Special Effects, A. Arnold Gillespie, Donald Jahraus. Editor, Robert J. Kern. 127 minutes

Alexander (Dandy) Gow: Charles Coburn, *Robert Shannon:* Tom Drake, *Alison Keith:* Beverly Tyler, *Papa Leckie:* Hume Cronyn, *Grandma Leckie:* Gladys Cooper, *Robert Shannon (8 years):* Dean Stockwell, *Mama Leckie:* Selena Royle, *Kate Leckie:* Jessica Tandy, *Jason Reid:* Richard Haydn, *Saddler Boag:* Andy Clyde, *Adam Leckie:* Norman Lloyd, *Murdoch Leckie:* Robert North, *James Nigg:* Wallace Ford, *Alison Keith (7 years):* Eileen Janssen, *Gavin Blair (19 years):* Hank Daniels, *Gavin Blair (9 years):* Richard Lyon, *Canon Roche:* Henry O'Neill, *Professor Rattray Blakely:* Henry Stephenson, *Mrs. Bosomley:* Norma Varden, *McEwen:* Ashley Cowan, *Peter Dickie:* Forrester Harvey, *Lawyer McKellar:* Lumsden Hare, *Dr. Gailbraith:* Morris Ankrum, *Rector:* Herbert Evans, *Louisa:* Peggy Miller, *Smithy:* Mitchell Lewis, *Purser:* Harry Allen, *Miss Glennie:* Sylvia Andrew, *Organ Grinder:* Gabriel Ganzona, *Boy:* Guy Stockwell, *Mr. McTavish:*

Bill O'Leary, Mrs. McTavish: Kathryn Batos, *Angus:* Charles Sadler, *Bertie Jamieson:* George McDonald, *Bookseller:* Brandon Hurst, *Angelo Friscalli:* Charles Bates, *Father Friscalli:* Pete Cusanelli, *Mother Friscalli:* Carmela Restivo, *Daughter Friscalli:* Dorothy Reisner.

Guadalcanal Diary with William Bendix, Anthony Quinn and Eddie Acuff.

GUADALCANAL DIARY (1943) 20th. Producer, Byron Foy. Associate Producer, Islin Auster. Director, Lewis Seiler. Adapted by Jerry Cady from the book by Richard Tregaskis. Screenplay, Lamar Trotti. Art Directors, James Basevi, Leland Fuller. Musical Score, David Buttolph. Musical Director, Emil Newman. Cameraman, Charles Clarke. Special Effects, Fred Sersen. Editor, Fred Allen. Film debut of Richard Jaeckel. 93 minutes

Father Donnelly: Preston Foster, *Gunner O'Hara:* Lloyd Nolan, *Taxi Potts:* William Bendix, *Captain Davis:* Richard Conte, *Soose:* Anthony Quinn, *Private Johnny Anderson:* Richard Jaeckel, *Captain Cross:* Roy Roberts, *Colonel Grayson:* Minor Watson, *Ned Rowman:* Ralph Byrd, *Butch:* Lionel Stander, *Correspondent:* Reed Hadley, *Lieutenant Thurmond:* John Archer, *Tex:* Eddie Acuff, *Sammy:* Robert Rose, *Weatherby:* Miles Mander, *Dispatch Officer:* Harry Carter, *Major:* Jack Luden, *Lieutenant:* Louis Hart, *Captain:* Tom Dawson, *Colonel Thompson:* Selmer Jackson, *Japanese Officer:* Allen Jung, *Japanese Prisoner:* Paul Fung.

THE GUARDSMAN (1931) MGM. Directed by Sidney Franklin. Based on Ferenc Molnar's play. Adaptation, Ernest Vajda and Claudine West. Photography, Norbert Brodine. Editor, Conrad A. Nervig. *Elizabeth, the Queen* scene by permission of Maxwell Anderson. Lunt and Fontanne's talkie debut, repeating the roles they created on Broadway in 1924. 83 minutes

The Guardsman with Alfred Lunt and Lynn Fontanne.

The Actor: Alfred Lunt, *The Actress:* Lynn Fontanne, *The Critic:* Roland Young, *Liesl, the Maid:* ZaSu Pitts, *Mama:* Maude Eburne, *A Creditor:* Herman Bing, *A Fan:* Ann Dvorak.

Guess Who's Coming to Dinner with Sidney Poitier, Katharine Houghton, Katharine Hepburn and Spencer Tracy.

GUESS WHO'S COMING TO DINNER (1967) Col. Produced and directed by Stanley Kramer. Associate Producer, George Glass. Color by Technicolor. Original screenplay by William Rose. Assistant Director, Ray Gosnell. Music by Frank DeVol. Title song by Billy Hill. Production Design, Robert Clatworthy. Photography, Sam Leavitt. Editor, Robert C. Jones. Sound, Charles J. Rice and Robert Martin. Last film of Spencer Tracy (released posthumously) and film debut of Katharine Houghton, 22, Hepburn's niece. 112 minutes

Matt Drayton: Spencer Tracy, *Christina Drayton:* Katharine Hepburn, *John Prentice:* Sidney Poitier, *Joey Drayton:* Katharine Houghton, *Monignor Ryan:* Cecil Kellaway, *Mr. Prentice:* Roy E. Glenn, Sr., *Mrs. Prentice:* Beah Richards, *Tillie:* Isabell Sanford, *Hilary St. George:* Virginia Christine, *Car Hop:* Alexandra Hay, *Dorothy:* Barbara Randolph, *Frankie:* D'Urville Martin, *Peter:* Tom Heaton, *Judith:* Grace Gaynor, *Delivery Boy:* Skip Martin, *Cab Driver:* John Hudkins.

GUNFIGHT AT THE O.K. CORRAL (1957) Par. Produced by Hal B. Wallis. Directed by John Sturges. A Wallis-Hazen Production. In VistaVision and Technicolor. Screenplay, Leon Uris. Suggested by the article, "The Killer," by George Scullin. Assistant Director, Michael D. Moore. Costumes, Edith Head. Associate Producer, Paul Nathan. Music composed and conducted by Dimitri Tiomkin. Title song by Dimitri Timokin and Ned Washington, sung by Frankie Laine. Art Directors, Hal Pereira and Walter Tyler. Cinematographer, Charles Lang, Jr. Special Photographic Effects, John P. Fulton. Editor, Warren Low. Filmed in Arizona. 122 minutes

Gunfight at the O.K. Corral with Kirk Douglas and Jo Van Fleet.

Wyatt Earp: Burt Lancaster, *John H. "Doc" Holliday:* Kirk Douglas, *Laura Denbow:* Rhonda Fleming, *Kate Fisher:* Jo Van Fleet, *Johnny Ringo:* John Ireland, *Ike Clanton:* Lyle Bettger, *Cotton Wilson:* Frank Faylen, *Charles Bassett:* Earl Holliman *Shanghai Pierce:* Ted de Corsia, *Billy Clanton:* Dennis Hopper, *John P. Clum:* Whit Bissell, *John Shanssey:* George Mathews, *Virgil Earp:* John Hudson, *Morgan Earp:* DeForest Kelley, *James Earp:* Martin Milner, *Bat Masterson:* Kenneth Tobey, *Barber:* Tony Merrill, *Cockeyed Frank Loving:* Harry B. Mendoza, *Deputy/Killer/Townsman:* Roger Creed, *Tommy Earp:* Charles Herbert, *Old Timer:* Tony Jochim, *Card Player:* James Davies, *Card Player:* Joe Forte, *Cowboy:* Gregg Martell, *Cowboy:* Dennis Moore, *Card Player:* Max Power, *Card Player:* Courtland Shepard, *Killer:* Morgan Lane, *Killer:* Paul Gary, *Ed Bailey:* Lee Van Cleef, *Betty Earp:* Joan Camden, *Mrs. Clanton:* Olive Carey, *Rick:* Brian Hutton, *Mayor Kelley:* Nelson Leigh, *Tom McLowery:* Jack Elam, *Drunken Cowboy:* Don Castle, *Stuntman:* Bill Williams, *Finn Clanton:* Lee Roberts, *Frank McLowery:* Mickey Simpson, *Hotel Clerk:* Frank Carter, *Deputy:* Edward Ingram, *Bartender:* Bing Russell, *Girl:* Dorothy Abbott, *Alby:* Henry Wills, *Wayne:* William S. Meigs, *Bartender:* Ethan Laidlaw, *Rig Driver:* John Benson, *Foreman:* Richard J. Reeves, *Bartender:* Frank Hagney, *Shaughnessy Man:* Robert C. Swan, *Bit Cowboy:* Len Hendry, *Social Hall Guest:* Trude Wyler, *Merchant:* John Maxwell.

Gunga Din with Douglas Fairbanks, Jr., Sam Jaffe and Victor McLaglen.

GUNGA DIN (1939) RKO. Pandro S. Berman in charge of production. Producer and Director, George Stevens. Based on the poem by Rudyard Kipling. Story, Ben Hecht, Charles MacArthur. Screenplay, Joel Sayre, Fred Guiol. Art Director, Van Nest Polglase. Musical Director, Alfred Newman. Cameraman, Joseph H. August. Special Effects, Vernon L. Walker. Editors, Henry Berman, John Lockert. Art Associate, Perry Ferguson. Sets, Darrell Silvera. Gowns, Edward Stevenson. Assistant Directors, Edward Killy and Dewey Starkey. Technical Advisers, Captain Clive Morgan, William Briers and Sir Robert Erskine Holland. Sound, John E. Tribby, James Stewart. 117 minutes

Cutter: Cary Grant, *MacChesney:* Victor McLaglen, *Ballantine:* Douglas Fairbanks, Jr., *Gunga Din:* Sam Jaffe, *Gura:* Eduardo Ciannelli, *Emmy:* Joan Fontaine, *Colonel Weed:* Montagu Love, *Higginbotham:* Robert Coote, *Chota:* Abner Biberman, *Major Mitchell:* Lumsden Hare, *Mr. Stebbins:* Cecil Kellaway, *Journalist:* Reginald Sheffield, *Girls at Party:* Ann Evers, Audrey Manners, Fay McKenzie, *Telegraph Operator:* Charles Bennett, *Corporal:* Les Sketchley, *Native Merchant:* Frank Levya, *Fulad:* Olin Francis, *Thug Chieftains:* George Ducount, Jamiel Hasson, George Regas, *Scotch Sergeant:* Bryant Fryer, *Jadoo:* Lal Chard Mehra, *Lieutenant Markham:* Roland Varno, *Lancer Captain:* Clive Morgan.

The Guns of Navarone with Anthony Quinn and Gregory Peck.

THE GUNS OF NAVARONE (1961) Col. Produced and written by Carl Foreman. Based on the novel by Alistair MacLean. Director, J. Lee Thompson. Music, Dimitri Tiomkin. Associate Producers, Cecil F. Ford, Leon Becker. Assistant Director, Peter Yates. Costumes, Monty Berman. A Highroad Presentation in Eastman Color by Pathé and CinemaScope. Lyrics by Paul Francis Webster. Music played by Sinfonia of London. Filmed on the Island of Rhodes, Greece. Songs sung by Elga Anderson. 159 minutes

Captain Keith Mallory: Gregory Peck, *Corporal Miller:* David Niven, *Colonel Andrea Stavros:* Anthony Quinn, *CPO Brown:* Stanley Baker, *Major Roy Franklin:* Anthony Quayle, *Maria Pappadimos:* Irene Papas, *Anna:* Gia Scala, *Private Spyros Pappadimos:* James Darren, *Commander Jensen/Narrator:* James Robertson Justice, *Barnsby, Squadron Leader:* Richard Harris, *Cohn:* Bryan Forbes, *Baker:* Allan Cuthbertson, *Weaver:* Michael Trubshawe, *Sergeant Grogan:* Percy Herbert, *Sessler:* George Mikell, *Muesel:* Walter Gotell, *Nikolai:* Tutte Lemkow, *Commandant, Captain Muesel:* Albert Lieven, *Group Captain:* Norman Wooland, *Bride:* Cleo Scouloudi, *Patrol Boat Captain:* Nicholas Papakonstantinou, *German Gunnery Officer:* Christopher Rhodes.

A GUY NAMED JOE (1943) MGM. Producer, Everett Riskin. Director, Victor Fleming. Authors, Chandler Sprague, David Boehm. Screenplay, Dalton Trumbo. Musical Score, Herbert Stothart. Art Director, Cedric Gibbons. Special Effects, Arnold Gillespie, Donald Jahraus, Warren Newcombe. Cameramen, George Folsey, Karl Freund. Editor, Frank Sullivan. Song by Roy Turk and Fred Ahlert: "I'll Get By (As Long as I Have You)". 118 minutes

Pete Sandidge: Spencer Tracy, *Dorinda Durston:* Irene Dunne, *Ted Randall:* Van Johnson, *Al Yackey:* Ward Bond, *"Nails" Kilpatrick:*

A Guy Named Joe with Van Johnson, Spencer Tracy, James Gleason and Ward Bond.

James Gleason, *The General:* Lionel Barrymore, *Dick Rumney:* Barry Nelson, *"Powerhouse" O'Rourke:* Don DeFore, *Colonel Hendricks:* Henry O'Neill, *Major Corbett:* Addison Richards, *Sanderson:* Charles Smith, *Dance Hall Girl:* Mary Elliott, *Colonel Sykes:* Earl Schenck, *Captain Robertson:* Maurice Murphy, *Old Woman:* Gertrude Hoffmann, *Lieutenant:* Mark Daniels, *Ray:* William Bishop, *Powerhouse Girl:* Eve Whitney, *Ellen Bright:* Esther Williams, *Girl At Bar:* Kay Williams, *Mess Sergeant:* Walter Sande, *Bartender:* Gibson Gowland, *Officers in Heaven:* John Whitney, Kirk Alyn, *Orderly:* James Millican, *Davy:* Ernest Severn, *George:* Edward Hardwicke, *Cyril:* Raymond Severn, *Elizabeth:* Yvonne Severn, *Peter:* Christopher Severn, *Lieutenant Ridley:* John Frederick, *Majors:* Frank Faylen, Phil Van Zandt, *Fliers:* Marshall Reed, Blake Edwards, *Corporal:* Irving Bacon, *Sergeant Hanson:* Peter Cookson, *Lieutenant Hunter:* Matt Willis, *Helen:* Jacqueline White.

GUYS AND DOLLS (1955) MGM. Produced by Samuel Goldwyn. Directed by Joseph L. Mankiewicz. CinemaScope and Eastman Color. Based on the 1950 musical by Jo Swerling and Abe Burrows, from a story by Damon Runyon. Screenplay, Joseph L. Mankiewicz. Dances and musical numbers staged by Michael Kidd. Costumes, Irene Sharaff. Art Director, Joseph Wright. Music Director, Jay Blackton. Orchestrations, Skip Martin, Nelson Riddle, Alexander Courage, Al Sendrey. Cinematography, Harry Stradling. Editor, Daniel Mandell. Make-up, Ben Lane. Production Design, Oliver Smith. Songs by Frank Loesser: "Fugue for Tinhorns," "Follow the Fold," "The Oldest Established (Permanent Floating Crap Game in New York)," "I'll Know," "Adelaide's Lament," "Guys and Dolls," "If I Were a Bell," "Take Back Your Mink," "Luck Be a Lady," "Sit Down, You're Rockin' the Boat," and "Sue Me." "Pet Me, Papa" and "A Woman in Love" were written for the film. Blaine, Kaye, Silver, Pully, repeat their original stage roles. 138 minutes

Guys and Dolls with Renee Renor, Marlon Brando and Jean Simmons.

Sky Masterson: Marlon Brando, *Sarah Brown:* Jean Simmons, *Nathan Detroit:* Frank Sinatra, *Miss Adelaide:* Vivian Blaine, *Lieutenant Brannigan:* Robert Keith, *Nicely-Nicely Johnson:* Stubby Kaye, *Big Jule:* B. S. Pully, *Benny Southstreet:* Johnny Silver, *Harry the Horse:* Sheldon Leonard, *Rusty Charlie:* Danny Dayton, *Society Max:* George E. Stone, *Arvide Abernathy:* Regis Toomey, *General Cartwright:* Kathryn Givney, *Laverne:* Veda Ann Borg, *Agatha:* Mary Alan Hokanson, *Angie the Ox:* Joe McTurk, *Calvin:* Kay Kuter, *Mission Member:* Stapleton Kent, *Cuban Singer:* Renee Renor, *The Champ:* Matt Murphy, *Mug in Barber Shop:* Harry Wilson, *Pitchman:* Earle Hodgins, *Max, a Waiter:* Harry Tyler, *Ringsiders ("Pet Me, Papa" number):* Major Sam Harris, Franklyn Farnum, *Man with Packages ("Guys and Dolls" number):* Frank Richards, *Liverlips Louie:* Johnny Indrisano, *Havana Waiter:* Julian Rivero, *The Goldwyn Girls:* Larri Thomas, Jann Darlyn, June Kirby, Madelyn Darrow, Barbara Brent. Ed Sullivan appears in the trailer.

GYPSY (1962) WB. Producer, Mervyn LeRoy. Director, Mervyn LeRoy. Technirama, Technicolor. Based on Gypsy Rose Lee's memoirs

Gypsy with Karl Malden, Natalie Wood, Rosalind Russell and Ann Jilliann.

and the musical by Arthur Laurents. Screenplay, Leonard Spigelglass. Art Director, John Beckman. Music, Jule Styne. Lyrics, Stephen Sondheim. Songs: "Let Me Entertain You," "Small World," "Baby June and Her Newsboys," "Some People," "Mr. Goldstone," "Little Lamb," "You'll Never Get Away From Me," "If Momma Was Married," "All I Need is the Girl," "Wherever We Go," "You Gotta Get a Gimmick," "Rose's Turn." Music composed and conducted by Frank Perkins. Orchestration, Frank Perkins, Carl Brandt. Cinematographer, Harry Stradling, Sr. Editor, Philip W. Anderson. 149 minutes

Rose: Rosalind Russell, *Louise:* Natalie Wood, *Herbie Sommers:* Karl Malden, *Tulsa:* Paul Wallace, *Tessie Tura:* Betty Bruce, *Mr. Kringelein:* Parley Baer, *Grandpa:* Harry Shannon, *"Baby" June:* Suzanne Cupito, *"Dainty" June:* Ann Jilliann, *"Baby" Louise:* Diane Pace, *Mazeppa:* Faith Dane, *Electra:* Roxanne Arlen, *George:* George Petrie, *Mr. Beckman:* James Millhollin, *Mr. Willis:* William Fawcett, *Mervyn Goldstone:* Ben Lessy, *Pastey:* Guy Raymond, *Cigar:* Louis Quinn, *Yonkers:* Danny Lockin, *Angie:* Ian Tucker, *Farmboy:* Bert Michaels, *Agnes:* Lois Roberts, *Dolores:* Dina Claire, *Phil·* Harvery Korman, *Betty Cratchitt:* Jean Willes.

HAIL THE CONQUERING HERO (1944) Par. Director, Preston Sturges. Screenplay, Preston Sturges. Art Directors, Hans Dreier, Haldane Douglas. Musical Score, Werner Heymann. Musical Director, Sigmund Krumgold. Cameraman, John Seitz. Editor, Stuart Gilmore. Song: "Home to the Arms of Mother" by Preston Sturges. 101 minutes

Woodrow: Eddie Bracken, *Libby:* Ella Raines, *Mr. Noble:* Raymond Walburn, *Sergeant:* William Demarest, *Chairman of Reception Committee:* Franklin Pangborn, *Libby's Aunt:* Elizabeth Patterson, *Mrs. Truesmith:* Georgia Caine, *Bugsy:* Freddie Steele, *Forrest Noble:*

Hail the Conquering Hero with Franklin Pangborn, Eddie Bracken and William Demarest.

Bill Edwards, *Doc Bissell:* Harry Hayden, *Judge Dennis:* Jimmy Conlin, *Corporal:* Jimmy Dundee, *Political Boss:* Alan Bridge, *Mrs. Noble:* Esther Howard, *Marine Colonel:* Robert Warwick, *Juke:* Len Hendry, *Jonesy:* James Damore, *Bill:* Stephen Gregory, *Progressive Band-Leader:* Victor Potel, *Alfie, Junior Bandleader:* Merrill Rodin, *Regular Band Leader:* Jack Norton, *American Legion Bandleader:* Johnny Sinclair, *Mr. Schultz:* Torben Meyer, *Western Union Man:* Chester Conklin, *Reverend Upperman:* Arthur Hoyt, *Sheriff:* George Melford, *Town Painter:* Frank Moran, *Town Councilmen:* Tom McGuire, Philo McCullough, Franklyn Farnum, Kenneth Gibson, *Manager of Cafe:* Paul Porcasi, *Bartender:* George Anderson, *Singer:* Julie Gibson, *Marine Colonel's Wife:* Mildred Harris, *Mamie's Mother:* Dot Farley, *Mamie:* Marjean Neville, *Colonel's Daughter:* Maxine Fife, *Telephone Operator:* Pauline Drake.

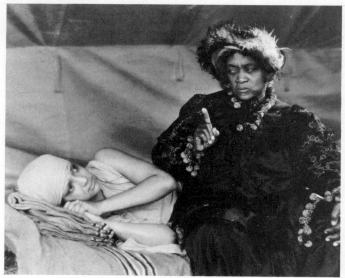

Hallelujah with Nina Mae McKinney and Fannie Belle de Knight.

HALLELUJAH! (1929) MGM. Produced and directed by King Vidor. Story, King Vidor. Scenario, Wanda Tuchock. Dialogue, Ransom Rideout. Photography, Gordon Avil. Editor, Hugh Wynn. Sound, Western Electric Sound (on disk). Titles for silent version, Marian Ainslee. Editor of silent version, Anson Stevenson. Adaptation, Richard Schayer. Music Supervision, Eva Jessye. Wardrobe, Henriette Frazer. Assistant Director, Robert A. Golden. Second Assistant Director, William Allen Garrison. Filmed in Memphis, along the Mississippi, and in Culver City, Hollywood. Songs by Irving Berlin: "The End of the Road," "Swanee Shuffle." The first all-Negro talkie. Nina Mae McKinney, 17. in her film debut, replaced Honey Brown. Ex-slave Harry Gray, 86, also made his film debut. 109 minutes

Zeke: Daniel L. Haynes, *Chick:* Nina Mae McKinney, *Hot Shot:* William Fountaine, *Parson:* Harry Gray, *Mammy:* Fannie Belle de Knight, *Spunk:* Everett McGarrity, *Missy Rose:* Victoria Spivey, *Johnson Kids:* Milton Dickerson, Robert Couch, Walter Tait, *Singer:* Evelyn Pope Burwell, *Singer and Bit:* Eddie Connors, *Heavy:* William Allen Garrison ("Slickem"); and The Dixie Jubilee Singers, directed by Eva Jessye.

HALLS OF MONTEZUMA (1950) 20th. Producer, Robert Bassler. Director, Lewis Milestone. Color by Technicolor. Author-Screenplay, Michael Blankfort. Art Directors, Lyle Wheeler and Albert Hogstett. Music, Lionel Newman. Photography, Winton C. Hoch, Harry Jackson. Editor, Charles LeMaire. Technicolor Consultant, Leonard Doss. 113 minutes

Lieutenant Anderson: Richard Widmark, *Pidgeon Lane:* Walter (Jack) Palance, *Sergeant Johnson:* Reginald Gardiner, *Coffman:* Robert Wagner, *Doc:* Karl Malden, *Corporal Conroy:* Richard Hylton, *Lieutenant Colonel Gilfillan:* Richard Boone, *Pretty Boy:* Skip Homeier, *Lieutenant Butterfield:* Don Hicks, *Correspondent Dickerman:* Jack Webb, *Slattery:* Bert Freed, *Sergeant Zelenko:* Neville Brand, *Private Whitney:*

Halls of Montezuma with Richard Widmark, Richard Boone and Reginald Gardiner.

Martin Milner, *Nomura:* Philip Ahn, *Captain Makino:* Howard Chuman, *Romeo:* Frank Kumagai, *Captain McCreavy:* Fred Coby, *Captain Seaman:* Paul Lees, *Pharmacist's Mate:* Fred Dale, *Frank:* Chris Drake, *Corpsman:* George Conrad, *Radioman:* Harry McKim, *Paskowicz:* William Hawes, *Davis:* Roger McGee, *Aunt Emma:* Helen Hatch, *Ship's Captain:* Michael Road, *Fukado:* Rollin Moriyama, *Willie:* Ralph Nagai, *Nurse:* Marion Marshall, *Bos'n Mate:* Harry Carter, *Private Stewart:* Richard Allan.

HANS CHRISTIAN ANDERSEN (1952) RKO. Producer, Samuel Goldwyn. Director, Charles Vidor. Color by Technicolor. Screenplay, Moss Hart. Based on a story by Myles Connolly. Words and music by Frank Loesser. Choreography by Roland Petit. 120 minutes

Hans Christian Andersen: Danny Kaye, *Niels:* Farley Granger, *Doro:* Jeanmaire, *Peter:* Joey Walsh, *Otto:* Philip Tonge, *The Hussar:* Erik Bruhn, *The Prince in the Ballet:* Roland Petit, *Schoolmaster:* John Brown, *Burgomaster:* Jehn Qualen, *Celine:* Jeanne Lafayette, *Stage Doorman:* Robert Malcolm, *Farmer:* George Chandler, *First Gendarme:* Fred Kelsey, *Second Gendarme:* Gil Perkins, *Lars:* Peter Votrian.

Hans Christian Andersen with Jeanmaire, Farley Granger and Danny Kaye.

HAPPY LANDING (1938) 20th. Associate Producer, David Hempstead. Director, Roy Del Ruth. Authors, Milton Sperling, Boris Ingster. Screenplay, Milton Sperling, Boris Ingster. Cameraman, John Mescal. Editor, Louis Loeffler. Songs by Jack Yellen and Samuel Pokrass: "Hot and Happy," "Yonny and His Oompah," "You Are The Words to the Music in My Heart" and "A Gypsy Told Me." "You Appeal to Me" by Walter Bullock and Harold Spina. Dances, Harry Losee. Assistant Director, Booth McCracken. Music Director, Louis Silvers. 102 minutes

Trudy Erickson: Sonja Henie, *Jimmy Hall:* Don Ameche, *Flo Kelly:* Ethel Merman, *Sargent:* Cesar Romero, *Herr Erickson:* Jean Herscholt,

Happy Landing with Sonja Henie, Cesar Romero and Don Ameche.

Counter Man: Billy Gilbert, *Specialty:* Raymond Scott and His Quintet, *Al Mahoney:* Wally Vernon, *Specialty Song with Orchestra:* Leah Ray, *Specialty:* Condos Brothers, *Yonnie:* El Brendel, *Agent:* Joseph Crehan, *Count:* Alex Novinsky, *Manager:* William B. Davidson, *Rajah:* Marcel de Labrosse, *Justice of the Peace:* William Wagner, *Manager, Madison Square Garden:* Ben Welden, *Tuba Player:* Sid Saylor, *Hecklers:* Harvey Parry, Matt McHugh, *Olaf:* Louis Adlon, Jr. *Gypsy:* Marcelle Corday, *Waiter:* Eddy Conrad, *Turnkey:* Fred Kelsey, *Stewardess:* June Storey, *Reporters:* Robert Lowery and Lon Chaney, Jr., *Specialty:* The Peters Sisters.

THE HARD WAY (1942) WB. Producer, Jerry Wald. Director, Vincent Sherman. Screenplay, Daniel Fuchs, Peter Viertel. Art Director, Max Parker. Dance Director, LeRoy Prinz. Musical Director, Leo F. Forbstein. Cameraman, James Wong Howe. Special Effects, Willard Van Enger. Editor, Thomas Pratt. Songs: "Am I Blue" by Grant Clarke and Harry Akst; "Youth Must Have Its Fling," "Good Night Oh My Darling" by Jack Scholl and M. K. Jerome. 109 minutes

The Hard Way with Jack Carson, Ida Lupino, Thurston Hall and Joan Leslie.

Helen Chernen: Ida Lupino, *Paul Collins:* Dennis Morgan, *Katherine Chernen:* Joan Leslie, *Albert Runkel:* Jack Carson, *Lily Emery:* Gladys George, *Blonde Waitress:* Faye Emerson, *John Shagrue:* Paul Cavanagh, *Laura Bithorn:* Leona Maricle, *Sam Chernen:* Roman Bohnen, *Johnny Gilpin:* Ray Montgomery, *Chorine:* Julie Bishop, *Max Wade:* Nestor Paiva, *Maria:* Joan Woodbury, *Dorshka:* Ann Doran, *Motion Picture Executive:* Thurston Hall, *Frenchy:* Lou Lubin, *Anderson:* Jody Gilbert, *Duglatz:* Murray Alper, *Policemen:* Frank Faylen, Emory Parnell, Edgar Dearing, *Interne:* Bill Edwards, *Police Officer:* Eddy Chandler, *Bum:* Wallace Scott, *Pudgy Girl:* Jean Ames, *Serious Young Man:* Harry Lewis, *Second Young Girl:* Dolores Moran, *Janitor:* Hank Mann, *Midget:* Mary Curtis, *Midget:* Billy Curtis, *Radio Announcer:* Bill Kennedy, *Stage Manager:* Philip Van Zandt, *Essie:* Libby Taylor, *Call Boy:* Bud (Lon) McCallister, *Flora Ames:* Jean Inness, *Jimmy at 6:* Joel Davis.

Harper with Paul Newman.

HARPER (1966) WB. Release of a Jerry Gershwin-Elliott Kastner production. Director, Jack Smight. Technicolor. Screenplay, William Goldman. Based on Ross MacDonald's novel, *The Moving Target*. Camera, Conrad Hall. Editor, Stefan Arnsten. Music, Johnny Mandel. Song, Dory and Andre Previn. 121 minutes

Lew Harper: Paul Newman, *Mrs. Simpson:* Lauren Bacall, *Betty Fraley:* Julie Harris, *Albert Graves:* Arthur Hill, *Susan Harper:* Janet Leigh, *Miranda Sampson:* Pamela Tiffin, *Alan Traggert:* Robert Wagner, *Dwight Troy:* Robert Webber, *Fay Estabrook:* Shelley Winters, *Sheriff:* Harold Gould, *Claude:* Strother Martin, *Puddler:* Roy Jensen, *Deputy:* Martin West, *Mrs. Kronberg:* Jacqueline de Wit, *Felix:* Eugene Iglesias, *Fred Platt:* Richard Carlyle, *Eddie Fraley:* Tom Steele, *Telephone Operator:* Kathryn Janssen, *Albino Waiter:* Herbert Sullivan, Jr., *Bunny Dancer:* China Lee.

HARVEY (1950) Univ. Producer, John Beck. Director, Henry Koster. From the play by Mary C. Chase. Screenplay, Mary C. Chase, Oscar Brodney. Art Directors, Bernard Herzbrun, Nathan Juran. Music, Frank Skinner. Photography, William Daniels. Editor, Ralph Dawson. 104 minutes

Elwood P. Dowd: James Stewart, *Veta Louise Simmons:* Josephine Hull, *Miss Kelly:* Peggy Dow, *Doctor Sanderson:* Charles Drake, *Doctor Chumley:* Cecil Kellaway, *Myrtle Mae:* Victoria Horne, *Wilson:* Jesse White, *Judge Gaffney:* William Lynn, *Lofgren:* Wallace Ford, *Mrs. Chumley:* Nana Bryant, *Mrs. Chauvenet:* Grace Mills, *Herman:* Clem Bevans, *Mrs. McGiff:* Ida Moore, *Cracker:* Richard Wessel, *Policeman:* Pat Flaherty, *Cab Driver:* Norman Leavitt, *Elvira:* Maudie Prickett, *Salesman:* Ed Max, *Mrs. Strickleberger:* Grace Hampton, *Nurse Dunphy:* Minerva Urecal, *Miss LaFay:* Ruth Elma

Harvey with Peggy Dow, Charles Drake and James Stewart.

Stevens, *Mrs. Halsey:* Almira Sessions, *Nurse:* Anne O'Neal, *Mrs. Johnson:* Eula Guy, *Minninger:* Sam Wolfe, *Chauffeur:* William Val, *Eccentric Man:* Gino Corrado, *Mrs. Krausmeyer:* Polly Bailey, *Mailman:* Don Brodie, *Meegles:* Harry Hines, *Mrs. Tewksbury:* Aileen Carlyle, *Mrs. Cummings:* Sally Corner.

The Harvey Girls with Virginia O'Brien, Judy Garland and Cyd Charisse.

THE HARVEY GIRLS (1946) MGM. Producer, Arthur Freed. Associate Producer, Roger Edens. Director, George Sidney. Color by Technicolor. Based on the book by Samuel Hopkins Adams. Original Story, Eleanore Griffin, William Rankin. Screenplay, Edmund Beloin, Nathaniel Curtis. Musical Director, Lennie Hayton. Art Directors, Cedric Gibbons, William Ferrari. Cameraman, George Folsey. Special Effects, Warren Newcombe. Editor, Albert Akst. Songs by Johnny Mercer and Harry Warren: "On the Atchinson, Topeka and the Santa Fe," "In the Valley When the Evening Sun Goes Down," "Wait and See," "Swing Your Partner Round and Round," "The Wild Wild West" and "It's a Great Big World." 104 minutes

Susan Bradley: Judy Garland, *Ned Trent:* John Hodiak, *Chris Maule:* Ray Bolger, *Judge Sam Purvis:* Preston Foster, *Alma:* Virginia O'Brien, *Em:* Angela Lansbury, *Sonora Cassidy:* Marjorie Main, *H. H. Hartsey:* Chill Wills, *Terry O'Halloran:* Kenny Baker, *Miss Bliss:* Selena Royle, *Deborah:* Cyd Charisse, *Ethel:* Ruth Brady, *Louise:* Catherine McLeod, *Marty Peters:* Jack Lambert, *Jed Adams:* Edward Earle, *Jane:* Virginia Hunter, *First Cowboy:* William "Bill" Phillips, *Second Cowboy:* Norman Leavitt, *Reverend Claggett:* Morris Ankrum, *John Henry:* Ben Carter, *Sandy:* Mitchell Lewis, *Goldust McClean:* Horace McNally (Stephen McNally), *Big Joe:* Bill Hall, *Conductor:* Ray Teal, *Mule Skinner:* Jim Toney, *Fireman:* Jack Clifford, *Engineer:* Vernon Dent, *Conductor:* Robert Emmett O'Connor, *Station Agent:* Paul Newlan, *Trick Roper:* Sam Garrett.

Hatari! with Red Buttons and Elsa Martinelli.

HATARI! (1962) Par. Producer, Howard Hawks. Associate Producer, Paul Helmick. Director, Howard Hawks. Technicolor. Author, Harry Kurnitz. Screenplay, Leigh Brackett. Art Directors, Hal Pereira, Carl Anderson. Music Score, Henry Mancini. "Just for Tonight," lyrics, Johnny Mercer; music, Hoagy Carmichael. Cinematographer, Russell Harlan. Special Photographic Effects, John P. Fulton. Editor, Stuart Gilmore. A Malabar Production. Assistant Directors, Tom Connors and Russ Saunders. 159 minutes

Sean: John Wayne, *Kurt:* Hardy Kruger, *Dallas:* Elsa Martinelli, *Pockets:* Red Buttons, *Chips:* Gererd Blain, *Indian:* Bruce Cabot, *Brandy:* Michele Girardon, *Luis:* Valentine de Vargas, *Doctor:* Eduard Franz, *Joseph:* Jon Chevron, *Nurse:* Queenie Leonard, *Bartender:* Emmett E. Smith, *Man:* Jack Williams, *Sikh Clerk:* Henry Scott, *Masai Warrior:* Jack Williams, *Native Boy:* Jack Williams.

A Hatful of Rain with Don Murray and Lloyd Nolan.

A HATFUL OF RAIN (1957) 20th. Producer, Buddy Adler. Director, Fred Zinnemann. CinemaScope. Based on the play by Michael Vincente Gazzo. Screenplay, Michael Vincente Gazzo, Alfred Hayes. Art Directors, Lyle R. Wheeler, Leland Fuller. Music, Bernard Herrmann. Cinematographer, Joe MacDonald. Editor, Dorothy Spencer. 109 minutes

Celia Pope: Eva Marie Saint, *Johnny Pope:* Don Murray, *Polo:* Anthony Franciosa, *John Pope, Sr.:* Lloyd Nolan, *Mother:* Henry Silva, *Chuch:* Gerald O'Loughlin, *Apples:* William Hickey, *Cab Driver:* Michael Vale, *Mounted Cop:* Art Fleming, *Bartender:* Tom Ahearne, *Middle-aged Man:* Gordon B. Clark, *John:* Norman Willis, *Boss:* Jason Johnson, *Bartender:* Paul Kruger, *Man:* Rex Lease, *Man:* William Bailey, *Wiry Man:* Herb Vigran, *Doctor:* Jay Jostyn, *Spectator:* Ralph Montgomery, *Executive:* William Tannen, *Office Manager:* Emerson Treacy.

HAWAII (1966) UA. Release of a Mirisch Corp. presentation. Produced by Walter Mirisch. Director, George Roy Hill. Panavision,

Hawaii with Max Von Sydow and Julie Andrews.

De Luxe Color. Screenplay, Dalton Trumbo, Daniel Taradash. Based on James A. Michener's novel. Camera, Russell Harlan. Choreography, Miriam Nelson, Costumes, Dorothy Jeakins. Editor, Stuart Gilmore, Music, Elmer Bernstein. Song, "My Wishing Doll," Bernstein, Mack David. 186 minutes

Jerusha Bromley: Julie Andrews, *Abner Hale:* Max Von Sydow, *Rafer Hoxworth:* Richard Harris, *Charles Bromley:* Carroll O'Connor, *Abigail Bromley:* Elizabeth Cole, *Charity Bromley:* Diane Sherry, *Mercy Bromley:* Heather Menzies, *Reverend Thorn:* Torin Thatcher, *Reverend John Whipple:* Gene Hackman, *Reverend Immanuel Quigley:* John Cullum, *Reverend Abraham Hewlett:* Lou Antonio, *Malama:* Jocelyne La Garde, *Keoki:* Manu Tupou, *Kelolo:* Ted Nobriga, *Noelani:* Elizabeth Logue, *Iliki:* Lokelani S. Chicarell, *Gideon Hale:* Malcolm Atterbury, *Hepzibah Hale:* Dorothy Jeakins, *Captain Janders:* George Rose, *Mason:* Michael Constantine, *Collins:* John Harding, *Cridland:* Robert Crawford, *Micah (18):* Bertil Werjefelt, *Micah (4):* Robert Oakley, *Micah (7):* Henrik Von Sydow, *Micah (12):* Clas Von Sydow.

HEAVEN CAN WAIT (1943) 20th. Produced and directed by Ernest Lubitsch. Color by Technicolor. Based on the play *Birthday* by Lazlo Bush-Fekete. Screenplay, Samson Raphaelson. Score, Alfred Newman. Art Directors, James Basevi and Leland Fuller. Technicolor Director, Natalie Kalmus. Photography, Edward Cronjager. Editor, Dorothy Spencer. 113 minutes

Martha: Gene Tierney, *Henry Van Cleve:* Don Ameche, *Grandfather (Hugo Van Cleve):* Charles Coburn, *Mrs. Strabel:* Marjorie Main, *His Excellency:* Laird Cregar, *Bertha Van Cleve:* Spring Byington, *Albert Van Cleve:* Allyn Joslyn, *Mr. Strabel:* Eugene Pallette, *Mademoiselle:* Signe Hasso, *Randolph Van Cleve:* Louis Calhern, *Peggy Nash:* Helene Reynolds, *James:* Aubrey Mather, *Jack Van Cleve:* Michael Ames (Tod Andrews), *Flogdell:* Leonard Carey, *Jasper:* Clarence Muse, *Henry (age 15):* Dickie Moore, *Albert (age 15):* Dickie Jones, *Jane:* Trudy Marshall, *Mrs. Craig:* Florence Bates, *Grandmother:* Clara Blandick, *Mrs. Cooper-Cooper:* Anita Bolster, *Albert's Father:* Alfred Hall, *Albert's Mother:* Grayce Hampton *Smith:* Gerald Oliver Smith, *Jack as a child:* Nino Pipitone, Jr., *Miss Ralston:* Claire DuBrey, *Clerk in Britano's:* Charles Halton, *Policeman:* James Flavin, *Henry age 15 months:* Michael McLean, *Doctor:* Edwin Maxwell, *Henry age 9:* Scotty Beckett, *Mary:* Marlene Mains, *Nurse:* Doris Merrick.

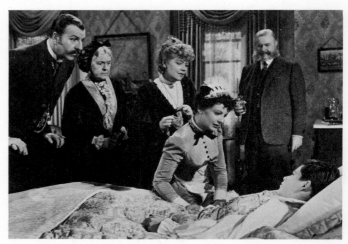

Heaven Can Wait with Louis Calhern, Clara Blandick, Spring Byington, Signe Hasso, Charles Coburn and Dickie Moore.

HEAVEN KNOWS, MR. ALLISON (1957) 20th. Producers, Buddy Adler and Eugene Frenke. Director, John Huston. Screenplay by John Lee Mahin and John Huston. Based on the novel by Charles Shaw. Music by Georges Auric. Costumes by Elizabeth Haffenden. Assistant Director, Adrian Pryco-Jones. In CinemaScope and De Luxe Color. Filmed on the Island of Tobago, British West Indies. 107 minutes

Heaven Knows, Mr. Allison with Deborah Kerr and Robert Mitchum.

Sister Angela: Deborah Kerr, *Corporal Allison, USMC:* Robert Mitchum.

THE HEIRESS (1949) Par. Produced and directed by William Wyler. Screenplay, Ruth and Augustus Goetz. Based on the play *The Heiress* by the Goetzes. Suggested by the novel *Washington Square* by Henry James. Art Director, John Meehan. Music, Aaron Copland. Photography, Leo Tover. Editor, William Hornbeck. Song by Ray Evans and Jay Livingston, "My Love Loves Me." 115 minutes

Catherine Sloper: Olivia De Havilland, *Morris Townsend:* Montgomery Clift, *Doctor Austin Sloper:* Ralph Richardson, *Lavinia Penniman:* Miriam Hopkins, *Maria:* Vanessa Brown, *Marian Almond:* Mona Freeman, *Jefferson Almond:* Ray Collins, *Mrs. Montgomery:* Betty Linley, *Elizabeth Almond:* Selena Royle, *Arthur Townsend:* Paul Lees, *Mr. Abeel:* Harry Antrim, *Quintus:* Russ Conway, *Geier:* David Thursby.

The Heiress with Olivia De Havilland and Montgomery Clift.

HELL DIVERS (1931) MGM. Directed by George Hill. Story by Lieutenant Commander Frank Wead. Adaptation, Harvey Gates and Malcolm Stuart Boylan. Photography, Harold Wenstrom. Editor, Blanche Sewell. Filmed at North Island, Panama, aboard the aircraft carrier *Saratoga*, during naval maneuvers. 113 minutes

Windy: Wallace Beery, *Steve:* Clark Gable, *Duke:* Conrad Nagel, *Ann:* Dorothy Jordan, *Mame Kelsey:* Marjorie Rambeau, *Lulu:* Marie Prevost, *Baldy:* Cliff Edwards, *Griffin:* John Miljan, *Admiral:* Landers Stevens, *Lieutenant Fisher:* Reed Howes, *Captain:* Alan Roscoe, *Chaplain:* Frank Conroy, *Young Officer:* Robert Young, *Trainee:* Jack Pennick, *Sailor:* John Kelly.

Hell Divers with John Kelly (rear), Clark Gable and Wallace Beery.

HELLO, FRISCO, HELLO (1943) 20th. Producer, Milton Sperling. Director, Bruce Humberstone. Color by Technicolor. Screenplay, Robert Ellis, Helen Logan, Richard Macauley. Dance Directors, Hermes Pan, Val Raset. Art Directors, James Basevi, Boris Leven. Musical Directors, Charles Henderson, Emil Newman. Cameramen, Charles Clarke, Allen Davey. Editor, Barbara McLean. Technical Director, Natalie Kalmus. Songs: "You'll Never Know" and "I Gotta Have You" by Mack Gordon and Harry Warren; "Ragtime Cowboy Joe" by Grant Clarke, Maurice Abrahams and Lewis E. Muir. 98 minutes

Trudy Evans: Alice Faye, *Johnnie Cornell:* John Payne, *Dan Daley:* Jack Oakie, *Bernice:* Lynn Bari, *Sam Weaver:* Laird Creger, *Beulah:* June Havoc, *Sharkey:* Ward Bond, *Cochran:* Aubrey Mather, *Colonel Weatherby:* George Barbier, *Ned:* John Archer, *Lou, the Bartender:* Frank Orth, *Proprietor:* George Lloyd, *Missionary:* Frank Darien, *Burkham:* Harry Hayden, *Foreman:* Eddie Dunn, *O'Reilly:* Charles Cane, *Auctioneer:* Frank Thomas, *Cockney Maid:* Mary Field, *Bit:* Ted (Michael) North, *Roller Skating Specialty:* James Sills and Marie Brown, *Specialty Singer:* Kirby Grant, *Waiter:* Ralph Dunn, *Aunt Harriet:* Esther Dale, *Doorman:* Edward Clark, *Opera Singers:* Gino Corrado, Adia Kuznetzoff, Fortunio Bonanova, *Singer:* Lorraine Elliott, *Stage Manager:* Edward Earle, *Heawaiters:* Ken Christy, James Flavin, *Child Dancers:* Jackie Averill, Jimmie Clemens, Jr., *Singer:* Ruth Gillette.

Hello, Frisco, Hello with John Payne and Alice Faye.

HELL'S ANGELS (1930) UA. Directed by Howard Hughes. Red tints, ball sequence in Technicolor. Story, Marshall Neilan and Joseph Moncure March. Dialogue Director, James Whale. Scenario, Howard Estabrook and Harry Behn. Photography, Tony Gaudio, Harry Perry, E. Burton Steene. Art Directors, J. Boone Fleming and Carroll Clarke.

Hell's Angels with Jean Harlow and Ben Lyon.

Orchestra conducted by Hugo Riesenfeld. Assistant Directors, Reginald Callow, William J. Scully, Fred A. Fleck. Editors, Frank Lawrence, Douglas Biggs, Perry Hollingsworth. Sound, Lodge Cunningham. A Caddo Company Production, filmed at Metropolitan Studios, Caddo Field in Van Nuys, Inglewood, Chatsworth, Santa Cruz, Encino, Ryan Field in San Diego, March Field in Riverside, Oakland Airport. Started in 1927 as a silent; Jean Harlow replaced Greta Nissen when the sound version was made. Shot silent, the air scenes were later dubbed. Wide screen was used twice during the film. 87 planes and 137 pilots were used on the production; killed were fliers Al Johnson and Phil Jones; cameraman Steene died of a stroke. English titles translate the German dialogue. 135 minutes

Monte Rutledge: Ben Lyon, *Roy Rutledge:* James Hall, *Helen:* Jean Harlow, *Karl Arnstedt:* John Darrow, *Baron von Kranz:* Lucien Prival, *Lieutenant von Bruen:* Frank Clarke, *Baldy Maloney:* Roy Wilson, *Captain Redfield:* Douglas Gilmore, *Baroness von Kranz:* Jane Winton, *Lady Randolph:* Evelyn Hall, *Staff Major:* William B. Davidson, *Squadron Commander, Royal Flying Corps:* Wyndham Standing, *Zeppelin Commander:* Carl Von Haartman, *First Officer of Zeppelin:* F. Schumann-Heink, *Elliott:* Stephen Carr, *Marryat:* Pat Somerset, *Von Richthofen:* William Von Brincken, *Von Schlieben:* Hans Joby, *Gretchen, German Waitress:* Lena Malena, *Anarchist:* Harry Semels, *Girl Selling Kisses:* Marilyn Morgan (Marian Marsh), *Pilots:* Stewart Murphy, Ira Reed, Maurice "Loop the Loop" Murphy, Leo Nomis, Frank Tomick, Al Wilson, Roscoe Turner.

HERE COMES MR. JORDAN (1941) Col. Producer, Everett Riskin. Director, Alexander Hall. Based on a play by Harry Segall. Screenplay, Seton I. Miller, Sidney Buchman. Art Director, Lionel Banks. Music, M. W. Stoloff. Cameraman. Joseph Walker. Editor, Viola Lawrence. Sequel was *Down to Earth* (1947). 93 minutes

Here Comes Mr. Jordan with Robert Montgomery and James Gleason.

Joe Pendleton: Robert Montgomery, *Bette Logan:* Evelyn Keyes, *Mr. Jordan:* Claude Rains, *Julia Farnsworth:* Rita Johnson, *Messenger 7013:* Edward Everett Horton, *Max Corkle:* James Gleason, *Tony Abbott:* John Emery, *Inspector Williams:* Donald MacBride, *Lefty:* Don Costello, *Sisk:* Halliwell Hobbes, *Bugs:* Benny Rubin, *Plainclothesman:* Ken Christy, *Doctor:* Joseph Crehan, *Handler:* Billy Newell, *Announcer:* Tom Hanlon, *Gilbert:* Joe Hickey, *Charlie:* Warren Ashe, *Johnny:* Billy Dawson, *Chips:* Bobby Larson, *Sparring Partner:* John Kerns, *Secretary:* Mary Currier, *Newsboy:* Chester Conklin, *Copilot:* Lloyd Bridges, *Elderly Man:* Edmund Elton.

HERE COMES THE GROOM (1951) Par. Producer-Director, Frank Capra. Story, Robert Riskin, Liam O'Brien. Screenplay, Virginia Van Upp, Liam O'Brien, Myles Connolly. Art Directors, Hal Pereira, Earl Hedrick. Musical Director, Joseph J. Lilley. Photography, George Barnes. Editor, Ellsworth Hoagland. Songs: "Misto Christofo Columbo," "Bonne Nuit" and "Your Own Little House" by Ray Evans and Jay Livingston; "In the Cool, Cool, Cool of the Evening" by Johnny Mercer and Hoagy Carmichael. 113 minutes

Pete: Bing Crosby, *Emmadel Jones:* Jane Wyman, *Winifred Stanley:* Alexis Smith, *Wilbur Stanley:* Franchot Tone, *Pa Jones:* James Barton, *George Degnan:* Robert Keith, *Bobby:* Jacky Gencel, *Suzi:* Beverly Washburn, *Ma Jones:* Connie Gilchrist, *McGonigle:* Walter Catlett, *Mr. Godfrey:* Alan Reed, *Mrs. Godfrey:* Minna Gombell, *Governor:* Howard Freeman, *Aunt Abby:* Maidel Turner, *Uncle Elihu:* H. B. Warner, *Uncle Prentiss:* Nicholas Joy, *Uncle Adam:* Ian Wolfe, *Mrs. McGonigle:* Ellen Corby, *Policeman:* James Burke, *Baines:* Irving Bacon, *Paul Pippitt:* Ted Thorpe, *Radio Announcer:* Art Baker, *Therese:* Anna Maria Alberghetti, *Maid:* Laura Elliot, *Herself:* Dorothy Lamour, *Himself:* Frank Fontaine, *Himself:* Louis Armstrong, *Himself:* Phil Harris, *Herself:* Cass Daley, *Marcel:* Chris Appel, *Gray Lady:* Odette Myrtil, *Cusick:* Charles Halton, *Priest:* Rev. Neal Dodd, *Burchard, FBI:* Charles Lane, *Aunt Amy:* Adeline de Walt Reynolds, *Mayor:* Charles Evans, *Man:* J. Farrell MacDonald, *Messenger:* Carl Switzer, *Newsreel Director:* Walter McGrail, *Newsreel Cameraman:* Howard Joslin.

Here Comes the Groom with Neal Dodd (reverend), Charles Lane, Bing Crosby, Beverly Washburn, Jane Wyman and Jacky Gencel.

HERE COMES THE NAVY (1934) WB. Directed by Lloyd Bacon. Story, Ben Markson. Screenplay by Ben Markson, Earl Baldwin. Cameraman, Arthur Edeson. Editor, George Amy. Song, "Hey, Sailor!" by Irving Kahal and Sammy Fain. 86 minutes

Chesty: James Cagney, *Biff:* Pat O'Brien, *Dorothy:* Gloria Stuart, *Droopy:* Frank McHugh, *Gladys:* Dorothy Tree, *Commander Denny:* Robert Barrat, *Lieutenant Commander:* Willard Robertson, *Floor Manager:* Guinn Williams, *Droopy's Ma:* Maude Eburne, *First Girl:* Martha Merrill, *Second Girl:* Lorena Layson, *Aunt:* Ida Darling, *Riveter:* Henry Otho, *Hatcheck Girl:* Pauline True, *Porter:* Sam McDaniels, *Foreman:* Frank La Rue, *Recruiting Officer:* Joseph Crehan, *C.P.O.:* James Burtis, *Supply Sergeant:* Edward Chandler, *Professor:* Leo White, *Officer:* Niles Welch, *Sailor:* Fred "Snowflake" Toone,

Here Comes the Navy with Dorothy Tree and James Cagney.

Skipper: Eddie Shubert, *Admiral:* George Irving, *Captain:* Howard Hickman, *Navy Chaplain:* Edward Earle, *Lieutenant:* Emmett Vogan, *Bit:* Bill Elliott.

HERE COME THE WAVES (1944) Par. Producer and Director, Mark Sandrich. Original Screenplay, Allan Scott, Ken Englund, Zion Myers. Musical Director, Robert Emmett Dolan. Art Directors, Hans Dreier, Roland Anderson. Process Photography, Farciot Edouart. Special Effects, Gordon Jennings, Paul Lerpae. Cameraman, Charles Lang. Editor, Ellsworth Hoagland. Songs by Johnny Mercer and Harold Arlen: "I Promise You," "There's a Fellow Waiting in Pough-keepsie," "My Mama Thinks I'm a Star," "Let's Take the Long Way Home," "Here Come the Waves" and "Accent-Chu-Ate the Positive." 99 minutes

Johnny Cabot: Bing Crosby, *Susie and Rosemary Allison:* Betty Hutton, *Windy:* Sonny Tufts, *Ruth:* Ann Doran, *Tex:* Gwen Crawford, *Dorothy:* Noel Neill, *Lieutenant Townsend:* Catherine Craig, *Isabel:* Marjorie Henshaw, *Bandleader:* Harry Barris, *Ensign Kirk:* Mae Clarke, *High-Ranking Officer:* Minor Watson, *Specialty Dancers:* Dorothy Jarnac and Joel Friend, *The Commodore:* Oscar O'Shea, *Miles & Kover Trio:* Don Kramer, Eddie Kover, Ruth Miles, *Specialty Dancers:* Roberta Jonay, Guy Zanett, *First Fainting Girl:* Mona Freeman, *Second Fainting Girl:* Carlotta Jelm, *Waiter* (Cabana Club): Jack Norton, *Chief Petty Officer:* Jimmie Dundee, *Cabot Fan:* Lillian Bronson, *Girl:* Jean Willes, *Waiter:* Alex Havier, *Shore Patrolman:* James Flavin, *First Civilian:* Weldon Heyburn, *Second Civilian:* Edward Emerson, *Yellow Cab Driver:* Kit Guard, *First Pretty Girl:* Kay Linaker, *Second Pretty Girl:* Terry Adams, *Girl Window Washer:* Babe London, *Wave Control Tower Operator:* Greta Granstedt, *Girl:* Yvonne De Carlo, *Recruit:* George Turner, *C.P.O.:* William Haade, *Lieutenant Commander:* William Forrest, *Lieutenant Colonel:* Cyril Ring, *Captain Johnson:* Charles D. Brown.

Here Come the Waves with Bing Crosby, Betty Hutton (dual role) and Sonny Tufts.

Hers to Hold with Deanna Durbin and Joseph Cotten.

HERS TO HOLD (1943) Univ. Produced by Felix Jackson. Associate Producer, Frank Shaw. Directed by Frank Ryan. Based on a story by John D. Klorer. Screenplay, Lewis R. Foster. Music Director, Charles Previn. Art Director, John B. Goodman. Photography, Woody Bredell. Editor, Ted Kent. Songs: "Begin the Beguine" by Cole Porter; "Say A Prayer for the Boys Over There" by Jimmy McHugh and Herb Magidson; "Seguidilla" aria from Georges Bizet's *Carmen*, "Kashmiri Song." Filmed at Vega Aircraft in Burbank and at Lockheed Air Terminal. Sequel to *Three Smart Girls*, 1936, *Three Smart Girls Grow Up*, 1939, incorporating scenes from them and from *Mad About Music*, 1938. 94 minutes

Penny Craig: Deanna Durbin, *Bill Morley:* Joseph Cotten, *Judson Craig:* Charles Winninger, *Dorothy Craig:* Nella Walker, *Rosey Blake:* Gus Schilling, *Binns:* Ludwig Stossel, *Doctor Bacon:* Irving Bacon, *Nurse Willing:* Nydia Westman, *Smiley, Foreman:* Murray Alper, *Doctor Crane:* Samuel S. Hinds, *Arlene:* Iris Adrian, *Hannah Gordon:* Fay Helm, *Peter Cartwright:* Douglas Wood, *Mrs. Cartwright:* Minna Phillips, *Flo Simpson:* Evelyn Ankers, *Reporters:* Eddie Acuff, Eddie Dunn, *Doctor:* Harry Holman, *Guests:* Henry Roquemore, Brooks Benedict, *Al, a Guest:* William B. Davidson, *Aircraft Worker at Inn:* Billy Nelson, *Joe, Coast Guardsman:* Billy Wayne, *Coast Guardsman with Tommy Gun:* George O'Hanlon, *Orchestra Leader:* Leon Belasco, *Miss Crawford:* Ruth Lee, *Babe:* Jody Gilbert, *Guest Eating Sandwich:* Eddie Borden, *Flier's Father:* Ernie S. Adams, *Enlisted Man:* George Chandler, *Hazel:* Alice Talton, *Ella Mae:* Marie Harmon, *Personnel Woman:* Virginia Sale, *Bomber Captain:* James Bush, *Jeanne:* Evelyn Wahle, *William Morley:* Spec O'Donnell, *Joey:* Teddy Infuhr, *Girl:* Jennifer Holt.

THE HIGH AND THE MIGHTY (1954) WB. A Wayne-Fellows Production. Director, William A. Wellman. Screenplay by Ernest K. Gann from his novel. Music by Dimitri Tiomkin. Assistant Director, Andrew McLaglen. Art Director, Al Ybarra. Cinematographer, Archie Stout. Editor, Ralph Dawson. a CinemaScope and Warner-Color. 147 minutes

The High and the Mighty with John Qualen, Sidney Blackmer, Robert Newton, John Wayne, Laraine Day and Jan Sterling.

Dan Roman: John Wayne, *May Holst:* Claire Trevor, *Lydia Rice:* Laraine Day, *Sullivan:* Robert Stack, *Sally McKee:* Jan Sterling, *Ed Joseph:* Phil Harris, *Gustave Pardee:* Robert Newton, *Ken Childs:* David Brian, *Flaherty:* Paul Kelly, *Humphrey Agnew:* Sidney Blackmer, *Spalding:* Doe Avedon, *Nell Buck:* Karen Sharpe, *Milo Buck:* John Smith, *Lillian Pardee:* Julie Bishop, *Gonzalez:* Gonzalez-Gonzalez, *Howard Rice:* John Howard, *Wilby:* Wally Brown, *Hobie Wheeler:* William Campbell, *Mrs. Joseph:* Ann Doran, *Jose Locota:* John Qualen, *Frank Briscoe:* Paul Fix, *Ben Sneed:* George Chandler, *Dorothy Chen:* Joy Kim, *Toby Field:* Michael Wellman, *Alsop:* Douglas Fowley, *Garfield:* Regis Toomey, *Ensign Keim:* Carl Switzer, *Lieutenant Mowbray:* Robert Keys, *Roy:* William DeWolf Hopper, *Dispatcher:* William Schallert.

HIGH NOON (1952) UA. Producer, Stanley Kramer. Director, Fred Zinnemann. Music by Dimitri Tiomkin. Screenplay, Carl Foreman. Based on story "The Tin Star" by John W. Cunningham. A Stanley Foreman production. Title Song "High Noon (Do Not Forsake Me, Oh My Darlin)" by Johnny Mercer and Dimitri Tiomkin, sung by Tex Ritter. 85 minutes

Will Kane: Gary Cooper, *Jonas Henderson:* Thomas Mitchell, *Harvey Pell:* Lloyd Bridges, *Helen Ramirez:* Katy Jurado, *Amy Kane:* Grace Kelly, *Percy Mettrick:* Otto Kruger, *Martin Howe:* Lon Chaney, *William Fuller:* Henry Morgan, *Frank Fuller:* Ian MacDonald, *Mildred Fuller:* Eve McVeagh, *Cooper:* Harry Shannon, *Jack Colby:* Lee Van Cleef, *James Pierce:* Bob Wilke, *Ben Miller:* Sheb Woolley, *Sam:* Tom London.

High Noon with Lon Chaney, Jr., Thomas Mitchell, Henry Morgan, Eve McVeagh, Otto Kruger, Grace Kelly and Gary Cooper.

HIGH SIERRA (1941) WB. Producers, Jack L. Warner, Hal B. Wallis. Associate Producer, Mark Hellinger. Director, Raoul Walsh. Screenplay, John Huston, W. R. Burnett. Cameraman, Tony Gaudio. Editor, Jack Killifer. From the novel by W. R. Burnett. Remade by Warner Brothers as *Colorado Territory*, 1949; *I Died a Thousand Times*, 1955. 100 minutes

Roy Earle: Humphrey Bogart, *Marie:* Ida Lupino, *Babe:* Alan Curtis, *Red:* Arthur Kennedy, *Velma:* Joan Leslie, *"Doc" Banton:* Henry Hull, *Jake Krammer:* Barton MacLane, *Pa:* Henry Travers, *Ma:* Elisabeth Risdon, *Louis Mendoza:* Cornel Wilde, *Mrs. Baugham:* Minna Gombell, *Mr. Baugham:* Paul Harvey, *Big Mac:* Donald MacBride, *Healy:* Jerome Cowan, *Lou Preiser:* John Eldredge, *Blonde:* Isabel Jewell, *Algernon:* Willie Best, *Auto Court Owner:* Arthur Aylesworth, *Art:* Robert Strange, *Sheriff:* Wade Boteler, *Radio Commentater:* Sam Hayes, *Gangster:* George Lloyd, *Farmer:* Erville Alderson, *Ed:* Spencer Charters, *Fisherman:* Carl Harbaugh, *Shaw:* Cliff Saum, *Pfiffer:* George Meeker, *Policeman:* Eddy Chandler, *Woman:* Charlette Wynters, *Man:* Louis Jean Heydt, *Watchman:* William Gould, *Blonde:* Maris Wrixon, *Brunette:* Lucia Carroll, *Margie:* Dorothy Appleby, *Joe:* Garry Owen, *Bus Driver:* Eddie Acuff, *Druggist:* Harry Hayden.

High Sierra with Humphrey Bogart and Ida Lupino.

HIGH SOCIETY (1956) MGM. Producer, Sol C. Siegel. Director, Charles Walters. VistaVision, Technicolor. Based on the play *The Philadelphia Story* by Philip Barry. Screenplay, John Patrick. Art Directors, Cedric Gibbons, Hans Peters. Music supervised and adapted by Johnny Green, Saul Chaplin. Music, Lyrics, Cole Porter. Orchestration, Conrad Salinger, Nelson Riddle. Cinematographer, Paul A. Vogel. Editor, Ralph E. Winters. Remake of *The Philadelphia Story* (MGM, 1940). Locations filmed in Newport, Rhode Island. Last film of Louis Calhern, whe died at 61 on May 12, 1956. Songs by Cole Porter: "True Love," "High Society," "Well, Did You Evah?," "You're Sensational," "Who Wants to Be a Millionaire," "Little One," "New You Has Jazz," "Mind If I Make Love to You," "I Love You, Samantha." 107 minutes

High Society with Frank Sinatra and Grace Kelly.

C. K. Dexter-Haven: Bing Crosby, *Tracy Lord:* Grace Kelly, *Mike Connor:* Frank Sinatra, *Liz Imbrie:* Celeste Holm, *George Kittredge:* John Lund, *Uncle Willie:* Louis Calhern, *Seth Lord:* Sidney Blackmer, *Himself:* Louis Armstrong, *Mrs. Seth Lord:* Margalo Gillmore, *Caroline Lord:* Lydia Reed, *Dexter-Haven's Butler:* Gordon Richards, *Lord's Butler:* Richard Garrick, *Mac:* Richard Keene, *Matrons:* Ruth Lee, Helen Spring, *Editor:* Paul Keast, *Uncle Willie's Butler:* Reginald Simpson, *Parson:* Hugh Boswell.

HITLER'S CHILDREN (1943) RKO. Produced by Edward A. Golden. Directed by Edward Dmytryk. Based on the book *Education For Death* by Gregor Ziemer. Screenplay, Emmet Lavery. Music, Roy Webb. Music Director, C. Bakaleinikoff. Editor, Joseph Noriega. Film debut of Orley Lindgren, 3. 83 minutes

Karl Bruner: Tim Holt, *Anna Muller:* Bonita Granville, *Professor Nichols (Narrator):* Kent Smith, *Colonel Henkel:* Otto Kruger, *The*

Hitler's Children with Bonita Granville, Kent Smith and Tim Holt.

Bishop: H. B. Warner, *Franz Erhart:* Lloyd Corrigan, *Doctor Schmidt:* Erford Gage, *Doctor Graf:* Hans Conreid, *Brenda:* Nancy Gates, *Nazi Major:* Gavin Muir, *Murph:* Bill Burrud, *Irwin:* Jimmy Zaner, *Gestapo Man:* Richard Martin, *Arresting Sergeant:* Goetz Van Eyck (Peter Van Eyck), *Gestapo Officer:* John Merton, *Plane Dispatcher:* Max Lucke, *N.S.V. Worker:* Anna Loos, *Mother:* Bessie Wade, *Boys:* Orley Lindgren, Billy Brow, Chris Wren, *Mr. Muller:* Egon Brecher, *Mrs. Muller:* Elsa Janssen, *American Vice Consul:* William Forrest, *Young Matrons:* Ariel Heath and Rita Corday, *Bit:* Mary Stuart, *Lieutenant S.A.:* Roland Varno, *Whipping Sergeant:* Crane Whitley, *Chief Trial Judge:* Edward Van Sloan, *Radio Announcer:* Douglas Evans, *Magda:* Carla Boehm, *Storm Trooper:* Bruce Cameron, *First Matron:* Betty Roadman, *Chief Matron:* Kathleen Wilson, *Bit (Labor Camp):* Joey Ray, *Bit Boy:* Harry McKim, *Gestapo Officer:* John Stockton.

HOLD BACK THE DAWN (1941) Par. Producer, Arthur Hornblow. Director, Michael Leison. Author, Ketti Frings. Screenplay, Charles Brackett, Billy Wilder. Art Directors, Hans Dreier, Robert Usher. Cameraman, Leo Tover. Editor, Doane Harrison. Song, "My Boy, My Boy" by Frank Loesser, Jimmy Berg, Fred Spielman and Fred Jacobson. 115 minutes

Georges Iscoveseu: Charles Boyer, *Emmy Brown:* Olivia De Havilland, *Anita Dixon:* Paulette Goddard, *Van Den Luecken:* Victor Francen, *Inspector Hammock:* Walter Abel, *Bonbois:* Curt Bois, *Berta Kurz:* Rosemary De Camp, *Josef Kurz:* Eric Feldary, *Flores:* Nestor Paiva, *Lupita:* Eva Puig, *Christine:* Micheline Cheirel, *Anni:* Madeleine LeBeau, *Tony:* Billy Lee, *Mechanic:* Mikhail Rasumny, *Mr. Saxon:* Mitchell Leisen, *Actor:* Brian Donlevy, *Actor:* Richard Webb, *Actress:* Veronica Lake, *Mac:* John Hamilton, *Mr. Spitzer:* Leon Belasco, *Vivienne Worthington:* June Wilkins, *Sam:* Sonny Boy Williams, *American Consul:* Edward Fielding, *Joe:* Don Douglas, *Young Woman at Climax Bar:* Gertrude Astor, *Mexican Doctor:* Francisco Maran,

Hold Back The Dawn with Charles Boyer and Olivia De Havilland.

Mexican Judge: Carlos Villarlas, *Hollander Planter (Mr. Flvestad):* Arthur Loft, *Mr. MacAdams:* Charles Arnt, *American Immigration Official:* Harry T. Shannon, *Assistant Director:* William Faralla, *Bride:* Ella Neal, *Mexican Priest:* Antonio Filauri, *Old Peon:* Placido Sigueiros, *Mexican Bridegroom:* Ray Mala, *Old Peon's Wife:* Soledad Jimenez.

Hold That Ghost with Joan Davis, Evelyn Ankers, Bud Abbott, Richard Carlson and Lou Costello.

HOLD THAT GHOST (1941) Univ. Associate Producers, Burt Kelly, Glenn Tryon. Director, Arthur Lubin. Authors, Robert Lees, Fred Rinaldo. Screenplay, Robert Lees, Fred Rinaldo, John Grant. Art Director, Jack Otterson. Musical Director, H. J. Salter. Musical Numbers, Nick Castle. Cameramen, Elwood Bredell, Joseph Valentine. Editor, Philip Cahn. Songs: "Sleepy Serenade" by Mort Greene and Lou Singer; "Aurora" by Harold Adamson, Maria Logo and Roberto Roberti, "When My Baby Smiles at Me," "Me and My Shadow." 86 minutes

Chuck Murray: Bud Abbott, *Ferdinand Jones:* Lou Costello, *Doctor Jackson:* Richard Carlson, *Norma Lind:* Evelyn Ankers, *Camille Brewster:* Joan Davis, *Charlie Smith:* Marc Lawrence, *Harry Hoskins:* Milton Parsons, *Snake-Eyes:* Frank Penny, *Irondome:* Edgar Dearing, *Strangler:* Don Terry, *High Collar:* Edward Pawley, *Glum:* Nestor Paiva, *Gregory:* Mischa Auer, *Soda Jerk:* Shemp Howard, *Lawyer Bannister:* Russell Hicks, *Moose Matson:* William Davidson *Jenkins:* Harry Hayden; The Andrews Sisters, Ted Lewis and Band; *Alderman:* Thurston Hall, *Alderman's Girl:* Janet Shaw, *Gunman:* Frank Richards, *Customer:* William Ruhl.

A HOLE IN THE HEAD (1959) UA. Producer-Director, Frank Capra. Panavision, De Luxe Color. Screenplay by Arnold Shulman. Based on the TV play *The Heart's a Lonely Hotel*, and the 1957 stage play by

A Hole in the Head with Carolyn Jones and Frank Sinatra.

Arnold Shulman. Filmed in Cypress Gardens, Florida. Film debut of Eddie Hodges, 11. Main titles on a banner carried by Goodyear blimp. Music by Nelson Riddle. Costumes by Edith Head. Assistant Directors, Arthur S. Black, Jr. and Jack R. Berne. Art Director, Eddie Imazu. Cinematographer, William H. Daniels. Editor, William Hornbeck. A SinCap Production. Songs by Sammy Cahn and Jimmy Van Heusen: "High Hopes" and "All My Tomorrows." 120 minutes

Tony Manetta (Narrator): Frank Sinatra, *Mario Manetta:* Edward G. Robinson, *Eloise Rogers:* Eleanor Parker, *Ally Manetta:* Eddie Hodges, *Shirl:* Carolyn Jones, *Sophie Manetta:* Thelma Ritter, *Jerry Marks:* Keenan Wynn, *Dorine:* Joi Lansing, *Mendy:* George DeWitt, *Julius Manetta:* Jimmy Komack, *Fred:* Dub Taylor, *Miss Wexler:* Connie Sawyer, *Abe Diamond:* Benny Rubin, *Sally:* Ruby Dandridge, *Hood No. 1:* B. S. Pully, *Alice:* Joyce Nizzari, *Master of Ceremonies:* Pupi Campo, *Cabby:* Robert B. Williams, *Sheriff:* Emory Parnell, *Andy:* Bill Walker.

Holiday with Katharine Hepburn, Cary Grant and Henry Kolker.

Planer. Editors, Otto Meyer, Al Clark. Remake of the 1930 Pathé film. 93 minutes

Linda Seton: Katharine Hepburn, *Johnny Case:* Cary Grant, *Julia Seton:* Doris Nolan, *Ned Seton:* Lew Ayres, *Nick Potter:* Edward Everett Horton, *Edward Seton:* Henry Kolker, *Laura Cram:* Binnie Barnes, *Susan Potter:* Jean Dixon, *Seton Cram:* Henry Daniell, *Banker:* Charles Trowbridge, *Henry:* George Pauncefort, *Thayer:* Charles Richman, *Jennings:* Mitchell Harris, *Edgar:* Neil Fitzgerald, *Grandmother:* Marion Ballou, *Man in Church:* Howard Hickman, *Woman in Church:* Hilda Plowright, *Cook:* Mabel Colcord, *Countess:* Bess Flowers *Scotchmen:* Harry Allen, Edward Cooper, *Farmer's Wife:* Margaret McWade, *Farmer:* Frank Shannon, *Farm Girl:* Aileen Carlyle, *Taxi Driver:* Matt McHugh, *Steward:* Maurice Brierre, *Mrs. Jennings:* Esther Peck, *Mrs. Thayer:* Lillian West, *Grandfather:* Luke Cosgrave.

HOLIDAY INN (1942) Par. Producer and Director, Mark Sandrich. Screenplay, Claude Binyon. Musical Director, Robert Emmett Dolan. Adapted by Elmer Rice from an original idea by Irving Berlin. Dance Director, Danny Dare. Art Directors, Hans Dreier, Roland Anderson. Cameraman, David Abel. Editor, Ellsworth Hoagland. Songs by Irving Berlin: "Be Careful It's My Heart," "White Christmas," "Abraham," "You're Easy to Dance With," "Let's Start the New Year Right," "Plenty to Be Thankful For," "I'll Capture Your Heart Singing" and "Happy Holiday." 101 minutes.

Jim Hardy: Bing Crosby, *Ted Hanover:* Fred Astaire, *Linda Mason:* Marjorie Reynolds, *Lila Dixon:* Virginia Dale, *Danny Reed:* Walter Abel, *Mamie:* Louise Beavers, *Gus:* Irving Bacon, *Francois:* Marek Windheim, *Dunbar:* James Bell, *Parker:* John Gallaudet, *Vanderbilt:* Shelby Bacon, *Daphne:* Joan Arnold, *Specialty Dancer:* June Ealey, *Specialty Dancer:* David Tihmar, *Man at Holiday Inn:* Edward Emerson, *Proprietor in Flower Shop:* Leon Belasco, *Orchestra Leader:* Harry Barris, *Assistant Headwaiter:* Jacques Vanaire, *Orchestra Leader:* Ronnie Rondell, *Assistant Director:* Keith Richards, *Assistant*

Holiday Inn With Bing Crosby and Marjorie Reynolds.

Holiday with Ann Harding and Mary Astor.

HOLIDAY (1930) RKO-Pathé. Produced by E. B. Derr. Directed by Edward H. Griffith. Based on the play by Philip Barry. Scenario, Horace Jackson. Art Director, Carroll Clark. Assistant Director, Paul Jones. Orchestra conducted by Josiah Zuro. Costumes, Gwen Wakeling. Photography, Norbert Brodine. Editor, Daniel Mandell. Sound, D. A. Cutler and Harold Stine. Remade by Columbia in 1938. The William Holden is not the same Holden of today. 89 minutes

Linda Seton: Ann Harding, *Julia Seton:* Mary Astor, *Nick Potter:* Edward Everett Horton, *John Case:* Robert Ames, *Susan Potter:* Hedda Hopper, *Ned Seton:* Monroe Owsley, *Edward Seton:* William Holden, *Seton Cram:* Hallam Cooley, *Mary Jessup:* Mabel Forrest, *Laura:* Elizabeth Forrester, *Pete Hedges:* Creighton Hale, *Mrs. Pritchard Ames:* Mary Elizabeth Forbes.

HOLIDAY (1938) Col. Associate Producer, Everett Riskin. Director, George Cukor. From the play by Philip Barry. Screenplay, Donald Ogden Stewart, Sidney Buchman. Art Directors, Stephen Goosson, Lionel Banks. Musical Director, Morris Stoloff. Cameraman, Franz

367

Director: Reed Porter, *Doorman:* Oscar G. Hendrian, *Doorman:* Bob Homans, *Hatcheck Girl:* Katharine Booth, *Cigarette Girl:* Judith Gibson, *Dancing Girl:* Lynda Grey, *Woman:* Kitty Kelly, *Man:* Edward Arnold, Jr., *Man:* Mel Ruick, *Santa Claus:* Bud Jamison.

Hollywood Canteen with Joan Crawford, Dane Clark and Robert Hutton.

HOLLYWOOD CANTEEN (1944) WB. Producer, Alex Gottlieb. Director, Delmer Daves. Original Screenplay, Delmer Daves. Musical Numbers, LeRoy Prinz. Art Director, Leo Kuter. Musical Director, Leo F. Forbstein. Music Adaptation, Ray Heindorf. Cameraman, Bert Glennon. Editor, Christian Nyby. Musical numbers: "Don't Fence Me In" by Cole Porter; "You Can Always Tell a Yank" by E. Y. Harburg and Burton Lane; "What Are You Doin' the Rest of Your Life?" by Ted Koehler and Burton Lane; "We're Having a Baby (My Baby and Me)" by Harold Adamson and Vernon Duke; "Sweet Dreams Sweetheart" by Ted Koehler and M. K. Jerome; "Voodoo Moon" by Marian Sunshine, Julio Blanco and Obdulio Morales; "The General Jumped at Dawn" by Larry Neal and Jimmy Mundy; "Tumblin' Tumbleweeds" by Bob Nolan; "Ballet In Jive" by Ray Heindorf; "Hollywood Canteen" by Ted Koehler, Ray Heindorf and M. K. Jerome; "Gettin' Corns for My Country" by Jean Barry, Leah Worth, Dick Charles; "Once to Every Heart"; violin numbers, "The Bee" and "Slavonic Dance." Sets, Casey Roberts. Assistant Director, Art Lueker. Make-up, Perc Westmore. Wardrobe, Milo Anderson. Unit Manager, Chuck Hansen. Sound, Oliver S. Garretson and Charles David Forrest. 124 minutes.

Joan Leslie: Joan Leslie, *Slim:* Robert Hutton, *Sergeant:* Dane Clark, *Angela:* Janis Paige, *Themselves:* Andrews Sisters, Jack Benny, Joe E. Brown, Eddie Cantor, Kitty Carlisle, Jack Carson, Joan Crawford, Helmut Dantine, Bette Davis, Faye Emerson, Victor Francen, John Garfield, Sydney Greenstreet, Alan Hale, Paul Henreid, Andrea King, Peter Lorre, Ida Lupino, Irene Manning, Nora Martin, Joan McCracken, Dolores Moran, Dennis Morgan, Eleanor Parker, William Prince, Joyce Reynolds, John, Ridgely, Roy Rogers and Trigger, S. Z. Sakall, Alexis Smith, Zachary Scott, Barbara Stanwyck, Craig Stevens, Joseph Szigeti, Donald Woods, Jane Wyman, Jimmy Dorsey and his Band, Carmen Cavallaro and his Orchestra, Golden Gate Quartet, Rosario and Antonio, Sons of the Pioneers, Virginia Patton, Lynne Baggett, Betty Alexander, Julie Bishop, Robert Shayne, Johnny Mitchell, John Sheridan, Colleen Townsend, Angela Green, Paul Brooke, Marianne O'Brien, Dorothy Malone, Bill Kennedy, Mary Gordon, Chef Joseph Milani, *Mr. Brodel:* Jonathan Hale, *Mrs. Brodel:* Barbara Brown, *Betty Brodel:* Betty Brodel, *Soldiers on Deck:* Steve Richards (Mark Stevens), Dick Erdman, *Marine Sergeant:* James Flavin, *Dance Director:* Eddie Marr, *Director:* Theodore von Eltz, *Captain:* Ray Teal, *Orchestra Leader:* Rudolph Friml, Jr., *Dance Specialty:* Betty Bryson, Willard Van Simons, William Alcorn, Jack Mattis, Jack Coffey, *Tough Marine:* George Turner.

368

HOLLYWOOD CAVALCADE (1939) 20th. Executive Producer, Darryl F. Zanuck. Directed by Irving Cummings. Associate Producer, Harry Joe Brown. Color by Technicolor. Authors, Hilary Lynn, Brown Holmes. Screenplay, Ernest Pascal. Art Directors, Richard Day, Wiard B. Ihnen. Musical Director, Louis Silvers. Cameramen, Allen M. Davey, Ernest Palmer. Editor, Walter Thompson. 96 minutes.

Molly Adair: Alice Faye, *Michael Linnett Connors:* Don Ameche, *Dave Spingold:* J. Edward Bromberg, *Nicky Hayden:* Alan Curtis, *Pete Tinney:* Stuart Erwin, *Chief of Police:* Jed Prouty, *Buster Keaton:* Himself, *Lyle P. Stout:* Donald Meek, *Claude (Actor):* George Givot, *Keystone Cops:* Eddie Collins, Hank Mann, Heinie Conklin, James Finlayson, *Assistant Director, Chick:* Chick Chandler, *Henry Potter:* Robert Lowery, *Roberts:* Russell Hicks, *Agent:* Ben Welden, *Willie:* Willie Fung, *Lawyer:* Paul Stanton, *Mrs. Gaynes:* Mary Forbes, *Attorney, Bill:* Joseph Crehan, *Clerk:* Irving Bacon, *Bartender:* Ben Turpin, *Sheriff:* Chester Conklin, *Telephone Operator:* Marjorie Beebe, *Thomas:* Frederick Burton, *Themselves:* Lee Duncan, Mack Sennett, Al Jolson, *Rin-Tin-Tin:* Rin-Tin-Tin, Jr., *Porter:* Snowflake, *Prop Boy:* Harold Goodwin, *Slim, Counterman:* Victor Potel, *Actor:* Edward Earle, *Court Officer:* John Ince, *Well-Wisher:* Franklyn Farnum, *Motorcycle Cop:* J. Anthony Hughes, *Actress in The Man Who Came Back:* Lynn Bari.

Hollywood Cavalcade with Don Ameche and Donald Meek.

THE HOLLYWOOD REVUE OF 1929 MGM. Produced by Harry Rapf. Directed by Charles F. Reisner. Dialogue, Al Boasberg and Robert E. Hopkins. Dances and Ensembles, Sammy Lee, assisted by George Cunningham. Orchestral Arrangements, Arthur Lange. Skit, Joe Farnham. Photography, John Arnold, Irving G. Ries, and Maximilian Fabian. Settings, Cedric Gibbons and Richard Day. Costumes, David Cox. Editor, William Gray. Sound, Douglas Shearer. With Technicolor sequences. Songs: "Singin' In the Rain," "You Were Meant for Me," and "Tommy Atkins on Parade" by Arthur Freed and Nacio Herb Brown; "Low-Down Rhythm" by Raymond Klages and Jesse Greer; "For I'm the Queen" by Andy Rice and Martin Broones; "Gotta Feelin' For You," by Jo Trent and Louis Alter; "Bones and Tambourines," "Strike Up the Band," "Tableaux of

Hollywood Revue of 1929 with The Brox Sisters.

Jewels" by Fred Fisher; "Lon Chaney Will Get You If You Don't Watch Out," "Strolling Through the Park One Day," "Your Mother and Mine," "Orange Blossom Time," "Minstrel Days," "Nobody But You," "I Never Knew I Could Do a Thing Like That" by Joe Goodwin and Gus Edwards.

Specialties: Jack Benny (M.C.), Buster Keaton, Joan Crawford, John Gilbert, Norma Shearer, Laurel and Hardy, Marion Davies, Marie Dressler, William Haines, Lionel Barrymore, Anita Page, Conrad Nagel (M.C.), Polly Moran, Bessie Love, Charles King, Cliff Edwards, Gus Edwards, Karl Dane, George K. Arthur, Nils Asther, The Brox Sisters, Albertina Rasch, Gwen Lee, Natacha Natova and Company, The Rounders, The Biltmore Quartet, Ernest Belcher's Dancing Tots, *Chorus Girl:* Ann Dvorak.

Homecoming with Lana Turner and Clark Gable.

HOMECOMING (1948) MGM. Producer, Sidney Franklin. Associate Producer, Gottfried Reinhardt. Director, Mervyn LeRoy. Author, Sidney Kingsley. Screenplay, Paul Osborn. Art Directors, Cedric Gibbons, Randall Duell. Musical Director, Charles Previn. Photography, Harold Rosson. Editor, John Dunning. 113 minutes.

Ulysses Delby Johnson: Clark Gable, *Lt. Jane "Snapshot" McCall:* Lana Turner, *Penny Johnson:* Anne Baxter, *Dr. Robert Sunday:* John Hodiak, *Lt. Colonel Avery Silver:* Ray Collins, *Mrs. Kirby:* Gladys Cooper, *Monkevickz:* Cameron Mitchell, *Williams:* Art Baker, *Miss Stoker:* Lurene Tuttle, *Sarah:* Jessie Grayson, *Sol:* J. Louis Johnson, *Mac:* Marshall Thompson, *Jr. Lieutenant:* Bill Self, *Cigarette Smoker:* Jeff Corey, *Young Man:* Thomas E. Breen, *Mrs. Lovette:* Kay Mansfield, *Miss Simpson:* Peggy Badey, *Guests:* William Forrest, Dorothy Christy, Anne Nagel, *Instructor:* James Bush, *Sergeant:* David Clark, *Col. Morgan, C. O.:* Joseph Crehan, *Lieutenant:* Johnny James, *Colonel Norton:* Arthur Space, *Patient:* Wally Cassell, *Officer:* Jay Norris, *Anna:* Lisa Golm, *Head Nurse:* Geraldine Wall, *M. P.:* Alan Hale, Jr., *Driver:* Arthur O'Connell, *Corpsman:* Michael Kirby.

Home From the Hill with George Peppard and Luana Patten.

HOME FROM THE HILL (1960) MGM. Produced by Edmund Grainger. Directed by Vincente Minnelli. CinemaScope and Metro-Color. Based on the novel by William Humphrey. Screenplay, Harriet Frank Jr. and Irving Ravetch. Music, Bronislau Kaper. Costumes, Walter Plunkett. Art Directors, George W. Davis and Preston Ames. Music conducted by Charles Wolcott. Assistant Director, William McGarry. Cinematography, Milton Krasner. Editor, Harold F. Kress. A Sol C. Siegel Production. 150 minutes.

Capt. Wade Hunnicutt: Robert Mitchum, *Hannah Hunnicutt:* Eleanor Parker, *Rafe Copley:* George Peppard, *Theron Hunnicutt:* George Hamilton, *Albert Halstead:* Everett Sloane, *Libby Halstead:* Luana Patten, *Sarah Halstead:* Anne Seymour, *Opal Bixby:* Constance Ford, *Chauncey:* Ken Renard, *Dr. Reuben Carson:* Ray Teal, *Melba:* Hilda Haynes, *Dick Gibbons:* Charlie Briggs, *Hugh Macauley:* Guinn "Big Boy" Williams, *Marshall Bradley:* Denver Pyle, *Peyton Stiles:* Dan Sheridan, *Ed Dinwoodie:* Orville Sherman, *Bob Skaggs:* Dub Taylor, *Ramsey:* Stuart Randall, *John Ellis:* Tom Gilson, *Minister:* Rev. Duncan Gray, Jr., *Foreman:* Joe Ed Russell, *Gas Station Attendant:* Burt Mustin.

Home of the Brave with Lloyd Bridges and Steve Brodie.

HOME OF THE BRAVE (1949) UA. Produced by Stanley Kramer. Directed by Mark Robson. A Screen Plays Corporation Production. Screenplay, Carl Foreman. Based on the play by Arthur Laurents. Music, Dimitri Tiomkin. Art Director, Rudolph Sternad. Photography, Robert De Grasse. Editor, Harry Gerstad. Film debut of James Edwards. 85 minutes.

Major Robinson: Douglas Dick, *T. J.:* Steve Brodie, *The Doctor:* Jeff Corey, *Finch:* Lloyd Bridges, *Mingo:* Frank Lovejoy, *Moss:* James Edwards, *Colonel:* Cliff Clark.

HONDO (1953) WB. Produced by Robert Fellows. Directed by John Farrow. In 3-Dimension and WarnerColor. A Wayne-Fellows Production. From the *Collier's* magazine story by Louis L'Amour. Screenplay, James Edward Grant. Music, Emil Newman and Hugo Friedhofer. Art Director, Al Yberra. Cinematographers, Robert Burks, Archie Stout. Filmed in Camargo, Mexico. 93 minutes.

Hondo with John Wayne and Geraldine Page.

Hondo: John Wayne, *Angie Lowe:* Geraldine Page, *Buffalo:* Ward Bond, *Vittorio:* Michael Pate, *Lennie:* James Arness, *Silva:* Rodolfo Acosta, *Ed Lowe:* Leo Gordon, *Lieutenant McKay:* Tom Irish, *Johnny:* Lee Aaker, *Major Sherry:* Paul Fix, *Pete:* Rayford Barnes.

HONKY TONK (1941) MGM. Producer, Pandro S. Berman. Director, Jack Conway. Screenplay, Marguerite Roberts, John Sanford. Music Score, Franz Waxman. Art Director, Cedric Gibbons. Cameraman, Harold Rosson. Editor, Blanche Sewell. Songs by Jack Yellen and Milton Ager: "I'm the Last of the Red-Hot Mamas," "I'm Doin' What I'm Doin' for Love," "He's a Good Man to Have Around," "I'm Feathering a Nest (For A Little Bluebird)" and "I Don't Want to Get Thin." 105 minutes.

Candy Brown: Clark Gable, *Elizabeth Cotton:* Lana Turner, *Judge Cotton:* Frank Morgan, *"Gold Dust" Nelson:* Claire Trevor, *Reverend Mrs. Varner:* Marjorie Main, *Brazos Hearn:* Albert Dekker, *The Sniper:* Chill Wills, *Daniel Wells:* Henry O'Neill, *Kendall:* John Maxwell, *Adams:* Morgan Wallace, *Governor Wilson:* Douglas Wood, *Mrs. Wilson:* Betty Blythe, *Senator Ford:* Hooper Atchley, *Harry Gates:* Harry Worth, *Eleanore:* Veda Ann Borg, *Pearl:* Dorothy Granger, *Louise:* Sheila Darcy, *Man With Tar:* Cy Kendall, *Man with Rail:* Erville Alderson, *Man with Feathers:* John Farrell, *Man with Gun:* Don Barclay, *Poker Player:* Ray Teal, *Prostitute:* Esther Muir, *Dealer:* Ralph Bushman (Francis X. Bushman Jr.), *Dealer:* Art Miles, *Tug:* Demetrius Alexis, *Nurse:* Anne O'Neal, *Dr. Otis:* Russell Hicks, *Butcher:* Henry Roquemore, *Blackie:* Lew Harvey, *Brazos' Henchman:* John (Jack) Carr.

Honky Tonk with Clark Gable, Chill Wills, Lana Turner and Frank Morgan.

THE HOODLUM PRIEST (1961) UA. Producers, Don Murray and Walter Wood. Director, Irvin Kershner. Screenplay, Don Deer and Joseph Landon. Music, Richard Markowitz. Assistant Directors, George Batcheller and Eddie Bernoudy. Art director, Jack Poplin. Cinematographer, Haskell Wexler. Editor, Maurice Wright. 101 minutes.

Rev. Charles Dismas Clark: Don Murray, *Louis Rosen:* Larry Gates, *Ellen Henley:* Cindi Wood, *Billy Lee Jackson:* Keir Dullea, *George Hale:* Logan Ramsey, *Pio Gentile:* Don Joslyn, *Mario Mazziotti:* Sam Capuano, *Asst. District Attorney:* Vince O'Brien, *Judge Garrity:* Al Mack, *Angelo Mazziotti:* Lou Martini, *Father Dunne:* Norman KacKaye, *Hector Sterne:* Joseph Cusanelli, *Weasel:* Bill Atwood, *Detective Shattuck:* Roger Ray, *Genny:* Kelley Stephens, *Governor:* Ralph Petersen, *Prisoner:* Jack Eigen, *Father David Michaels:* Walter L. Wiedmer, *Warden:* Warren Parker, *Prison Chaplain:* Joseph Hamilton.

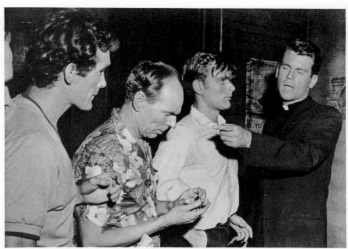

The Hoodlum Priest with Keir Dullea (third from left) and Don Murray.

THE HORSE SOLDIERS (1959) UA. Produced by John Lee Mahin and Martin Rackin. Directed by John Ford. Color by De Luxe. Screenplay by John Lee Mahin and Martin Rackin. Based on the novel by Harold Sinclair. Art Director, Frank Hotaling. Assistant Directors, Wingate Smith and Ray Gosnell Jr. Music, David Buttolph. Song, "I Left My Love," by Stan Jones. Cinematography, William Clothier. Editor, Jack Murray. A Mirisch Production. Special Effects, Augie Lohman. Make-up, Webb Overlander. Filmed in Louisiana and Mississippi. Based on the Civil War exploits of Union Col. Benjamin Grierson, who destroyed Confederacy's supply route in Tennessee. Film debut of tennis star Althea Gibson. Stuntman Fred Kennedy died as the result of a horse fall. Production Manager, Allen K. Wood. Sound, Jack Solomon. Editor, Jack Murray. Wardrobe, Frank Bretson and Ann Peck. 119 minutes

Colonel John Marlowe: John Wayne, *Major Henry Kendall:* William Holden, *Hannah Hunter:* Constance Towers, *Lukey:* Althea Gibson, *Brown:* Hoot Gibson, *Mrs. Buford:* Anna Lee, *Sheriff:* Russell Simpson, *General Ulysses S. Grant:* Stan Jones, *Colonel Jonathan Miles:* Carleton Young, *Commandant:* Basil Ruysdael, *Sergeant Kirby:* Judson Pratt, *Colonel Phil Seacord:* Willis Bouchey, *Major Richard Gray:* William Leslie, *Wilkie:* Ken Curtis, *Dunker:* Bing Russell, *Union Officer:* Walter Reed, *Deacon:* Hank Worden, *Bugler:* Ron Hagerthy, *Dr. Marvin:* Donald Foster, *Bartender:* Charles Seel, *Confederate Lieutenant:* Bill Henry, *Sergeant-Major Mitchell:* Jack Pennick, *General Sherman:* Richard Cutting, *Hopkins:* O. Z. Whitehead, *General Steve Hurlburt:* William Forrest, *Woodward:* Chuck Hayward, *Virgil:* Strother Martin, *Joe:* Denver Pyle, *Union Scout:* Fred Graham, *Southern Major:* Major Sam Harris, *Sergeant:* Cliff Lyons, *Cavalryman:* Fred Kennedy, *Bugler:* William Wellman, Jr., *Dying Man:* Jan Stine.

The Horse Soldiers with Cliff Lyons, John Wayne, Donald Foster, Constance Towers, O.Z. Whitehead and William Holden.

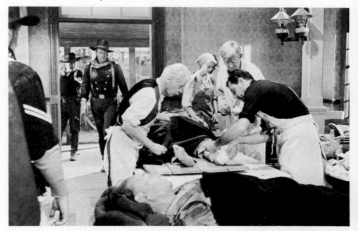

Houseboat with Mimi Gibson, Charles Herbert, Sophia Loren and Cary Grant.

HOUSEBOAT (1958) Par. Produced by Jack Rose. Directed by Mel Shavelson. VistaVision and Technicolor. Screenplay, Jack Rose and Mel Shavelson. A Scribe Production. Songs by Jay Livingston and Ray Evans: "Almost in Your Arms," sung by Sam Cooke; and "Bing! Bang! Bong!" Scenes filmed in Washington, D.C. 110 minutes.

Tom Winters: Cary Grant, *Cinzia Zaccardi:* Sophia Loren, *Carolyn Gibson:* Martha Hyer, *Angelo Donatello:* Harry Guardino, *Arturo Zaccardi:* Eduardo Ciannelli, *Alan Wilson:* Murray Hamilton, *Elizabeth Winters:* Mimi Gibson, *David Winters:* Paul Petersen, *Robert Winters:* Charles Herbert, *Mrs. Farnsworth:* Madge Kennedy, *Mr. Farnsworth:* John Litel, *Harold Messner:* Werner Klemperer, *Elizabeth Wilson:* Peggy Connelly, *Women in Laundromat:* Kathleen Freeman, Helen Brown, *Laundromat Attendant:* Florence MacAfee, *Spanish Diplomat:* Julian Rivero, *French Diplomat:* Ernst Brengk, *British Society Woman:* Mary Forbes, *Justice of the Peace:* William R. Remick, *Pitchmen:* Wally Walker, Brooks Benedict, Joe McTurk, *Pizza Saleswoman:* Gilda Oliva, *Clown:* Pat Moran, *Specialty Dancer:* Marc Wilder.

THE HOUSE OF ROTHSCHILD (1934) UA. A 20th Century Picture. Produced by Darryl F. Zanuck. Associate Producers, William Goetz and Raymond Griffith. Presented by Joseph M. Schenck. Directed by Alfred Werker. From an unproduced play by George Hembert Westley. Last sequence in Technicolor. Screenplay, Nunnally Johnson. Music, Alfred Newman. Photography, Peverell Marley. Editors, Alan McNeil and Barbara McLean. 86 minutes.

Mayer Rothschild/Nathan Rothschild: George Arliss, *Count Ledrantz:* Boris Karloff, *Julie Rothschild:* Loretta Young, *Captain Fitzroy:* Robert Young, *Duke of Wellington:* C. Aubrey Smith, *Baring:* Arthur

The House of Rothschild with Florence Arliss, George Arliss, Loretta Young, Robert Young and C. Aubrey Smith.

Byron, *Gudula Rothschild:* Helen Westley, *Herries:* Reginald Owen, *Hannah Rothschild:* Florence Arliss, *Metternich:* Alan Mowbray, *Rowerth:* Holmes Herbert, *Solomon Rothschild:* Paul Harvey, *Amschel Rothschild:* Ivan Simpson, *Carl Rothschild:* Noel Madison, *James Rothschild:* Murray Kinnell, *Talleyrand:* Georges Renavent, *Prussian Officer:* Oscar Apfel, *Prince Regent:* Lumsden Hare, *Amschel's Secretary:* Leo McCabe, *Prime Minister:* Gilbert Emery, *Nesselrode:* Charles Evans, *Guest at Hall of Reception:* Desmond Roberts, *Messenger in Stock Exchange:* Earl McDonald, *Woman Guest at Hall of Reception:* Ethel Griffies, *Doctor:* Lee Kohlmar, *Messenger:* William Strauss, *Prussian Guard:* Matthew Betz, *Stock Traders:* Reginald Sheffield, Brandon Hurst, Harold Minjir, Horace Claude Cooper, Craufurd Kent, *Rothschild Children:* Gerald Pierce, Milton Kahn, George Offerman, Jr., Cullen Johnson, Bobbie La Manche, *Tax Collector:* Leonard Mudie, *Prussian Soldier:* Walter Long, *Page:* Wilfred Lucas.

HOUSE OF WAX (1953) WB. Producer, Bryan Foy. Director, Andre de Toth. 3-Dimension, WarnerColor. Author, Charles Belden. Screenplay, Crane Wilbur. Art Director, Stanley Fleischer. Cinematographer, Bert Glennon. Editor, Rudi Fehr. Remake of Warners' *Mystery of the Wax Museum* (1933). 88 minutes.

House of Wax with Paul Cavanagh, Phyllis Kirk, Paul Picerni and Vincent Price.

Professor Henry Jarrod: Vincent Price, *Matthew Burke:* Roy Roberts, *Sidney Wallace:* Paul Cavanagh, *Cathy Gray:* Carolyn Jones, *Sue Allen:* Phyllis Kirk, *Scott Andrews:* Paul Picerni, *Mrs. Andrews:* Angela Clarke, *Lieutenant Tom Brennan:* Frank Lovejoy, *Sergeant Jim Shane:* Dabbs Greer, *Igor:* Charles Buchinsky (Charles Bronson), *Leon Averill:* Ned Young, *Barker:* Reggie Rymal, *Bruce Alison:* Philip Tonge, *Ma Flanagan:* Riza Royce, *Scrubwoman:* Ruth Warren, *First Detective:* Richard Benjamin, *Second Detective:* Jack Mower, *Surgeon:* Grandon Rhodes, *Medical Examiner:* Frank Ferguson, *Pompous Man:* Oliver Blake, *Portly Man:* Leo Curley, *Millie:* Mary Lou Holloway, *Ticket Taker:* Merry Townsend, *Waiter:* Lyle Latell.

THE HOUSE ON 92ND STREET (1945) 20th. Produced by Louis de Rochemont. Directed by Henry Hathaway. Story by Charles G. Booth. Screenplay, Barre Lyndon, Charles G. Booth, and John Monks, Jr. Art Directors, Lyle Wheeler and Lewis Creber. Score, David Buttolph. Music Director, Emil Newman. Cameraman, Norbert Brodine. Special Effects, Fred Sersen. Editor, Harmon Jones. Filmed with the cooperation of the Federal Bureau of Investigation, and comprised, in part, of prewar and wartime footage taken by the FBI. Shot on location in Washington, D.C., and New York City. 88 minutes.

Bill Dietrich: William Eythe, *Inspector George A. Briggs:* Lloyd Nolan, *Elsa Gebhardt:* Signe Hasso, *Charles Ogden Roper:* Gene Lockhart, *Colonel Hammersohn:* Leo G. Carroll, *Johanna Schmedt:* Lydia St. Clair, *Walker:* William Post, Jr., *Max Cobura:* Harry Bellaver, *Adolphe Lange:* Bruno Wick, *Conrad Arnulf:* Harro Meller, *Gus Huzmann:* Charles Wagenheim, *Klaen:* Alfred Linder, *Luise Vadja:* Renee Carson,

The House on 92nd Street with William Eythe and Leo G. Carroll.

Dr. Arthur C. Appleton: John McKee, *Major General:* Edwin Jerome, *Freda Kassel:* Elisabeth Neumann, *Frank Jackson:* George Shelton, *Colonel Strassen:* Alfred Zeisler, *Admiral:* Rusty Lane, *Franz Von Wirt:* Salo Douday, *Sergeant:* Paul Ford, *Customs Officer:* William Adams, *Policeman:* Lew Eckles, *Interne:* Tom Brown, *Narrator:* Reed Hadley, *F. B. I. Man:* Bruce Fernald, *Aide:* Benjamin Burroughs, *Colonel:* Douglas Rutherford, *Customer:* Sheila Bromley, *Toll Guard:* Victor Sutherland, *Instructor:* Stanley Tackney, *Trainees:* Vincent Gardenia, Frank Richards, *Policeman:* Fred Hillebrand, *Attendant at Morgue:* Edward (E.G.) Marshall, *Travel Agent:* Frank Kreig.

How Green Was My Valley with Walter Pidgeon and Roddy McDowall.

HOW GREEN WAS MY VALLEY (1941) 20th. Producer, Darryl F. Zanuck. Director, John Ford. Based on the novel by Richard Llewellyn. Screenplay, Philip Dunne. Cameraman, Arthur Miller. Editor, James B. Clark. Song by Alfred Newman: "How Green Was My Valley." 118 minutes.

Mr. Gruffydd: Walter Pidgeon, *Angharad:* Maureen O'Hara, *Mr. Morgan:* Donald Crisp, *Bronwyn:* Anna Lee, *Huw:* Roddy McDowall, *Ianto:* John Loder, *Mrs. Morgan:* Sara Allgood, *Cyfartha:* Barry Fitzgerald, *Ivor:* Patric Knowles, *Mr. Jonas:* Morton Lowry, *Mr. Parry:* Arthur Shields, *Cienwen:* Ann Todd, *Dr. Richards:* Frederic Worlock, *Davy:* Richard Fraser, *Gwilym:* Evan S. Evans, *Owen:* James Monks, *Dai Bando:* Rhys Williams, *Mervyn:* Clifford Severn, *Mr. Evans:* Lionel Pape, *Mrs. Nicholas:* Ethel Griffies, *Meillyn Lewis:* Eve March, *Iestyn Evans:* Marten Lamont, *Narrator:* Irving Pichel, *Welsh Singers:* Themselves, *Ensemble Singer:* Tudor Williams, *Postman:* Herbert Evans, *Eve:* Mary Field, *Woman:* Mae Marsh.

HOW THE WEST WAS WON (1962)* MGM. Producer, Bernard Smith. Directors, John Ford, Henry Hathaway, George Marshall.

How the West Was Won with James Stewart, Barry Harvey, Carroll Baker, Kim Charney, Brian Russell and Karl Malden.

Cinerama and Technicolor. Screenplay, James R. Webb. Art Directors, George W. Davis, William Ferrari, Addison Hehr. Music, Alfred Newman. "How the West Was Won," music by Alfred Newman, lyrics by Ken Darby; "Home in the Meadow," lyrics by Sammy Cahn; "Raise a Ruckus," "Wait for the Hoedown," "What Was Your Name in the States," lyrics by Johnny Mercer. Cinematographers, William H. Daniels, Milton Krasner, Charles Lang, Jr., Joseph LaShelle. Editor, Harold F. Kress. 165 minutes.

Eve Prescott: Carroll Baker, *Marshal:* Lee J. Cobb, *Jethro Stuart:* Henry Fonda, *Julie Rawlings:* Carolyn Jones, *Zebulon Prescott:* Karl Malden, *Cleve Van Valen:* Gregory Peck, *Zeb Rawlings:* George Peppard, *Roger Morgan:* Robert Preston, *Lilith Prescott:* Debbie Reynolds, *Linus Rawlings:* James Stewart, *Charlie Gant:* Eli Wallach, *General Sherman:* John Wayne, *Mike King:* Richard Widmark, *Dora:* Brigid Bazlen, *Colonel Hawkins:* Walter Brennan, *Attorney:* David Brian, *Peterson:* Andy Devine, *Abraham Lincoln:* Raymond Massey, *Rebecca Prescott:* Agnes Moorehead, *General Grant:* Henry (Harry) Morgan, *Agatha Clegg:* Thelma Ritter, *Deputy:* Mickey Shaughnessy, *Reb Soldier:* Russ Tamblyn, *Narrator:* Spencer Tracy, *Sam Prescott:* Kim Charney, *Zeke Prescott:* Bryan Russell, *Harvey:* Tudor Owen, *Angus:* Barry Harvey, *Bruce:* Jamie Ross, *Colin:* Mark Allen, *Marty:* Lee Van Cleef, *Barker:* Charles Briggs, *Huggins:* Jay C. Flippen, *Hylan Seabury:* Clinton Sundberg, *Gamblers:* James Griffith, Walter Burke, *Ship's Officer:* Joe Sawyer, *Grimes:* John Larch, *Corporal Murphy:* Jack Pennick, *James Marshall:* Craig Duncan, *Jeremiah:* Claude Johnson, *Henchman:* Rodolfo Acosta.

*U.S. release: 1963

HOW TO MARRY A MILLIONAIRE (1953) 20th. Producer, Nunnally Johnson. Director, Jean Negulesco. CinemaScope, Technicolor.

How to Marry a Millionaire with Marilyn Monroe, William Powell and Lauren Bacall.

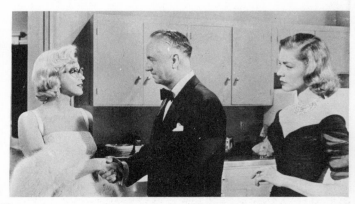

Based on plays by Zoe Akins, Dale Eunson, Katherine Albert. Screenplay, Nunnally Johnson. Art Directors, Lyle Wheeler, Leland Fuller. Cinematographer, Joe MacDonald. Editor, Louis Loeffler. "Street Scene" composed and conducted by Alfred Newman. 95 minutes.

Loco: Betty Grable, *Pola:* Marilyn Monroe, *Schatze Page:* Lauren Bacall, *Freddie Denmark:* David Wayne, *Eben:* Rory Calhoun, *Tom Brookman:* Cameron Mitchell, *J. Stewart Merrill:* Alex D'Arcy, *Waldo Brewster:* Fred Clark, *J. D. Hanley:* William Powell, *Mike (Elevator Man):* George Dunn, *Elevator Operator:* Harry Carter, *Cab Driver:* Robert Adler, *Mr. Otis:* Tudor Owen, *Antoine:* Maurice Marsac, *Man at Bridge:* Emmett Vogan, *Madame:* Hermene Sterler, *Secretary:* Abney Mott, *Bennett:* Rankin Mansfield, *Jewelry Salesman:* Ralph Reid, *Tony:* Jan Arvan, *Maid:* Ivis Goulding, *Justice:* Dayton Lummis, *Butler:* Eric Wilton, *Captain of Waiters:* Ivan Triesault, *Emir:* George Saurel, *Mrs. Salem:* Hope Landin, *Motorcycle Cop:* Tom Greenway, *Models:* Charlotte Austin, Merry Anders.

How to Murder Your Wife with Jack Lemmon and Eddie Mayehoff.

HOW TO MURDER YOUR WIFE (1965) UA. Produced and written by George Axelrod. Executive Producer, Gordon Carroll. Director, Richard Quine. Music, Neal Hefti. Director of Photography, Harry Stradling. Assistant Director, Carter De Haven. Choreographer, Robert Sidney. In Technicolor. 118 minutes.

Stanley Ford: Jack Lemmon, *Mrs. Ford:* Virna Lisi, *Charles:* Terry-Thomas, *Harold Lampson:* Eddie Mayehoff, *Edna:* Claire Trevor, *Judge Blackstone:* Sidney Blackmer, *Tobey Rowlins:* Max Showalter (Casey Adams), *Dr. Bentley:* Jack Albertson, *District Attorney:* Alan Hewitt, *Harold's Secretary:* Mary Wickes.

How to Steal a Million with Roger Treville and Audrey Hepburn.

HOW TO STEAL A MILLION (1966) 20th. Produced by Fred Kohlmar. Directed by William Wyler. Panavision and De Luxe Color. Screenplay by Harry Kurnitz, based on a story by George Bradshaw. Photography, Charles Lang. Music, Johnny Williams. Production Design, Alexander Trauner. Assistant Director, Paul Feyder. Second Unit Director and Editor, Robert Swink. Filmed in Paris. 127 minutes.

Nicole Bonnet: Audrey Hepburn, *Simon Demmott:* Peter O'Toole, *David Leland:* Eli Wallach, *Charles Bonnet:* Hugh Griffith, *De Solnay:* Charles Boyer, *Grammont:* Fernand Gravey, *Senor Paravideo:* Marcel Dalio, *Chief Guard:* Jacques Marin, *Guard:* Moustache, *Auctioneer:* Roger Treville, *Insurance Clerk:* Eddie Malin, *Marcel:* Bert Bertram.

HOW TO SUCCEED IN BUSINESS WITHOUT REALLY TRYING (1967) UA. Produced and directed by David Swift. Panavision and De Luxe Color. A Mirisch Corporation Presentation. Based on the musical by Abe Burrows, Jack Weinstock, and Willie Gilbert, and the novel by Shepherd Mead. Screenplay by David Swift. Art Director, Robert Boyle. Sets, Edward G. Boyle. Music directed by Nelson Riddle. Choreography by Dale Moreda, based on Bob Fosse's staging. Costumes by Micheline. Associate Producer, Irving Temaner. Assistant Directors, John D. Bloss and Michael J. Dmytryk. Production Manager, Nate Edwards. Photography, Burnett Guffey. Visual gags by Virgil Partch. Editors, Ralph Winters and Allan Jacobs. Sound, Robert Martin. Songs by Frank Loesser: "How To," "The Company Way," "A Secretary Is Not a Toy," "Been a Long Day," "I Believe in You." "Grand Old Ivy," "Rosemary," "Brotherhood of Man." A Frank Production. Locations filmed in New York. Most of the Broadway cast repeat their roles. 121 minutes

How to Succeed in Business Without Really Trying with Murray Matheson and Robert Morse.

J. Pierpont Finch: Robert Morse, *Japser B. Biggley:* Rudy Vallee, *Rosemary Pilkington:* Michele Lee, *Bud Frump:* Anthony (Scooter) Teague, *Hedy LaRue:* Maureen Arthur, *Benjamin Ovington:* Murray Matheson, *Smitty:* Kay Reynolds, *Mr. Twimble:* Sammy Smith, *Wally Womper:* Sammy Smith, *Bert O. Bratt:* John Myhers, *Mattews:* John Holland, *Johnson:* Dan Tobin, *Tackaberry:* Robert Q. Lewis, *Toynbee:* Paul Hartman, *Jenkins:* Justin Smith, *Gatch:* Jeff De Benning, *Miss Jones:* Ruth Kobart, *Lucille Krumholtz:* Carol Worthington, *Brenda:* Janice Carroll, *TV Announcer (Himself):* George Fenneman, *Gertrude Biggley:* Anne Seymour, *Mrs. Frump:* Erin O'Brien Moore, *Receptionist:* Lory Patrick, *Media Man #1:* Patrick O'Moore, *Media Man #2:* Wally Strauss, *Taxi Driver:* Joey Faye, *Finch's Landlady:* Ellen Verbit, *Cleaning Woman:* Virginia Sale, *News Seller:* Al Nesor, *Elevator Operator:* David Swift, *The President of the U.S.:* Ivan Volkman, *The Voice:* Carl Princi, *First Executive:* Carl Princi, *Second Executive:* Hy Averback, *Third Executive:* Bob Sweeney, *First Girl:* Sheila Rodgers, *TV Board Member:* Paul Bradley, *Junior Executive (Dancer):* Tucker Smith, *Passerby:* Don Koll.

THE HUCKSTERS (1947) MGM. Producer, Arthur Hornblow, Jr. Director, Jack Conway. Based on the novel by Frederic Wakeman.

The Hucksters with Clark Gable and Sydney Greenstreet.

Screenplay, Luther Davis. Art Directors, Cedric Gibbons, Urie Mc-Cleary. Musical Score, Lennie Hayton. Cameraman, Harold Rosson. Editor, Frank Sullivan. Song by Buddy Pepper: "Don't Tell Me." 115 minutes.

Victor Albee Norman: Clark Gable, *Kay Dorrance:* Deborah Kerr, *Evan Llewellyn Evans:* Sydney Greenstreet, *Mr. Kimberly:* Adolph Menjou, *Jean Ogilvie:* Ava Gardner, *Buddy Hare:* Keenan Wynn, *Dave Lash:* Edward Arnold, *Valet:* Aubrey Mather, *Cooke:* Richard Gaines, *Max Herman:* Frank Albertson, *Michael Michaelson:* Clinton Sundberg, *Georgie Gaver:* Douglas Fowley, *Mrs. Kimberly:* Gloria Holden, *Betty:* Connie Gilchrist, *Regina Kennedy:* Kathryn Card, *Miss Hammer:* Lillian Bronson, *Secretary:* Vera Marshe, *Allison:* Ralph Bunker, *Kimberly Receptionist:* Virginia Dale, *Blake:* Jimmy Conlin, *Freddie Callahan:* George O'Hanlon, *George Rockton:* Ransom Sherman, *Paul Evans:* Tom Stevenson, *Teletypist:* Anne Nagel, *Radio Announcer:* John Hiestand, *Clerk:* Jack Rice, *Doorman:* Robert Emmett O'Connor, *Ellen Dorrance:* Dianne Perine, *Cab Driver:* Johnny Day, *Hal Dorrance:* Eugene Baxtor Day, *Secretary:* Florence Stephens, *Kimberly Butler:* Gordon Richards, *Taxi Driver:* Fred Sherman, *First Girl:* Marie Windsor, *Western Union Messenger:* Sammy McKim, *Indian:* Chief Yowlachie, *Harry Spooner:* Edwin Cooper, *Joe Lorrison:* Harry V. Cheshire, *Bellboy:* Billy Benedict, *Businessman:* Mahlon Hamilton.

HUD (1963) Par. Producers, Martin Ritt, Irving Ravetch. Director, Martin Ritt. Based on the novel *Horseman, Pass By* by Larry McMurtry. Screenplay, Irving Ravetch, Harriet Frank, Jr. Art Directors, Hal Pereira, Tambi Larsen. Music Score, Elmer Bernstein. Cinematographer, James Wong Howe. Special Photographic Effects, Paul K. Lerpae. Editor, Frank Bracht. A Salem-Dover Production. 112 minutes.

Hud with Paul Newman, Melvyn Douglas and Brandon de Wilde.

Hud Bannon: Paul Newman, *Homer Bannon:* Melvyn Douglas, *Alma Brown:* Patricia Neal, *Lon Bannon:* Brandon de Wilde, *Burris:* Whit Bissell, *Hermy:* John Ashley, *Joe Scanlon:* George Petrie, *Thompson:* Sheldon Allman, *Kirby:* Carl Low, *Charlie Tucker:* Don Kennedy, *Jesse:* Crahan Denton, *Jose:* Val Avery, *Truman Peters:* Curt Conway, *Larker:* Pitt Herbert, *Announcer:* Robert Hinkle, *Myra:* Sharyn Hillyer, *Lilly Peters:* Yvette Vickers, *Cowboy:* John Indrisano, *Proprietor:* Carl Saxe, *Cowboy:* Monty Montana, *George:* Peter Brooks, *Donald:* David Kent, *Dumb Billy:* Frank Killmond.

The Human Comedy with John Craven and Van Johnson.

THE HUMAN COMEDY (1943) MGM. Producer and Director, Clarence Brown. From the novel by William Saroyan. Screenplay, Howard Estabrook. Dance Director, Ernst Matray. Musical Score, Herbert Stothart. Art Director, Cedric Gibbons. Cameraman, Harry Stradling. Editor, Conrad A. Nervig. 118 minutes.

Homer Macauley: Mickey Rooney, *Tom Spangler:* James Craig, *Willie Grogan:* Frank Morgan, *Mrs. Macauley:* Fay Bainter, *Diana Steed:* Marsha Hunt, *Marcus Macauley:* Van Johnson, *Bess Macauley:* Donne Reed, *Tobey George:* John Craven, *Mary Arena:* Dorothy Morris, *Ulysses Macauley:* Jackie (Butch) Jenkins, *Miss Hicks:* Mary Nash, *Mrs. Steed:* Katharine Alexander, *Matthew:* Ray Collins, *Charles Steed:* Henry O'Neill, *Lionel:* Darryl Hickman, *Mr. Ara:* S. Z. Sakall, *Brad Stickman:* Alan Baxter, *Fat:* Barry Nelson, *Texas:* Don DeFore, *Horse:* Bob Mitchum, *Mrs. Sandoval:* Ann Ayars, *Negro:* Ernest Whitman, *Soldier:* Mark Daniels, *Librarian:* Adeline de Walt Reynolds, *Helen Elliott:* Rita Quigley, *Hubert Ackley:* David Holt, *Dolly:* Connie Gilchrist, *Mr. Mechano:* Howard J. Stevenson, *Larry:* Frank Jenks, *Rev. Holly:* Howard Freeman, *Felix:* Jay Ward, *Leonine Type Man:* Gibson Gowland, *Soldier:* Don Taylor, *Blenton:* Byron Foulger, *Principal:* Wallis Clark, *Mrs. Beaufrere:* Mary Servoss, *Mr. Beaufrere:* Morris Ankrum, *Daughter:* Lynne Carver, *Auggie:* Carl "Alfalfa" Switzer, *Henderson:* Clem Bevans.

The Hunchback of Notre Dame with Charles Laughton and Maureen O'Hara.

THE HUNCHBACK OF NOTRE DAME (1939) RKO. Producer, Pandro S. Berman. Director, William Dieterle. From the novel by Victor Hugo. Screenplay, Sonya Levien, Bruno Frank. Musical Adaptor, Alfred Newman. Art Director, Van Nest Polglase. Dance Director, Ernst Matray. Cameraman, Joseph H. August. Special Effects, Vernon L. Walker. Editors, William Hamilton, Robert Wise. American film debut of Maureen O'Hara. Film debut of Edmond O'Brien, 23. 117 minutes.

Quasimodo: Charles Laughton, *Frollo:* Sir Cedric Hardwicke, *Clopin:* Thomas Mitchell, *Esmeralda:* Maureen O'Hara, *Gringoire:* Edmond O'Brien, *Phoebus:* Alan Marshal, *Archbishop:* Walter Hampden, *King Louis XI:* Harry Davenport, *Fleur's Mother:* Katharine Alexander, *Procurator:* George Zucco, *Fleur:* Helene Whitney, *Queen of Beggars:* Minna Gombell, *Old Nobleman:* Fritz Leiber, *Doctor:* Etienne Girardot, *Olivier:* Arthur Hohl, *Beggar:* George Tobias, *Phillipo:* Rod La Rocque, *Court Clerk:* Spencer Charters.

The Hurricane with Dorothy Lamour and Jon Hall.

THE HURRICANE (1937) UA. Produced by Samuel Goldwyn. Directed by John Ford and Stuart Heisler. From the novel by Charles Nordhoff and James Norman Hall. Adaptation, Dudley Nichols and Oliver H. P. Garrett. Score, Alfred Newman. Associate Producer, Merritt Hulburd. Photography, Bert Glennon. Editor, Lloyd Nosler. Sound, Jack Noyes. Song by Frank Loesser and Alfred Newman, "Moon of Manakoora." 110 minutes.

Marama: Dorothy Lamour, *Terangi:* Jon Hall, *Madame De Laage:* Mary Astor, *Father Paul:* C. Aubrey Smith, *Doctor Kersaint:* Thomas Mitchell, *Governor De Laage:* Raymond Massey, *Warden:* John Carradine, *Captain Nagle:* Jerome Cowan, *Chief Mehevi:* Al Kikume, *Tita:* Kuulei De Clercq, *Mako:* Layne Tom, Jr., *Hitia:* Mamo Clark, *Aral:* Movita Castenada, *Reri:* Reri, *Tavi:* Francis Kaai, *Mata:* Pauline Steele, *Mama Rua:* Flora Hayes, *Marunga:* Mary Shaw, *Judge:* Spencer Charters, *Captain of Guards:* Roger Drake, *Girl On Ship:* Inez Courtney, *Stuntman:* Paul Stader.

HURRY SUNDOWN (1967) Par. Produced and directed by Otto Preminger. Panavision and Technicolor. Based on the novel by K. B.

Hurry Sundown with Jane Fonda and Michael Caine.

Gilden (Katya and Bert Gilden). Screenplay, Thomas C. Ryan and Horton Foote. Music, Hugo Montenegro. Production Design, Gene Callahan. Assistant Directors, Burtt Harris, Howard Joslin, John Avildsen. Assistant to Producer, Nat Rudich. Production Managers, Stephen F. Kesten and Eva Monley. Photography, Milton Krasner and Loyal Griggs. Sets, John Godfrey. Costumes, Estevez. Special Effects, Willis Cook. Editors, Louis R. Loeffler and James D. Wells. Sound, Harold Lewis, Franklin Milton, Bertil Hallberg, Glenn Anderson. A Sigma Production. 146 minutes

Henry Warren: Michael Caine, *Julie Ann Warren:* Jane Fonda, *Rad McDowell:* John Philip Law, *Vivian Thurlow:* Diahann Carroll, *Reeve Scott:* Robert Hooks, *Lou McDowell:* Faye Dunaway, *Judge Purcell:* Burgess Meredith, *Lars Finchley:* Robert Reed, *Sheriff Coombs:* George Kennedy, *Reverend Clem De Lavery:* Frank Converse, *Thomas Elwell:* Loring Smith, *Rose Scott:* Beah Richards, *Eula Purcell:* Madeleine Sherwood, *Sukie Purcell:* Donna Danton, *Professor Thurlow:* Rex Ingram, *Colie Warren:* John Mark, *Ada Hemmings:* Doro Merande, *Dolph Higginson:* Luke Askew, *Carter Sillens:* Jim Backus, *Charles McDowell:* Steve Sanders, *Ruby McDowell:* Dawn Barcelona, *Wyatt McDowell:* David Sanders, *Timmy McDowell:* Michael Henry Roth, *Lipscomb:* Peter Goff, *Bishop:* William Elder, *Mrs. Coombs:* Gladys Newman, *Kissie:* Joan Parks, *Ozzie Higginson:* Robert C. Bloodwell, *Kenny:* Charles Keel, *Dottie:* Kelly Ross, *Clara:* Ada Hall Covington, *Hunt Club Members:* Gene Rutherford, Bill Hart, Dean Smith.

Hush . . . Hush, Sweet Charlotte with Olivia De Havilland and Bette Davis.

HUSH...HUSH, SWEET CHARLOTTE (1965) 20th. Producer-Director, Robert Aldrich. Screenplay, Henry Farrell, Lukas Heller. Story by Henry Farrell. Associate Producer, Walter Blake. Director of Photography, Joseph Biroc. Music, Frank DeVol. Title Song Lyrics, Mack David. Assistant Directors, William McGarry, Sam Strangis. Costumes, Norma Koch. Choreography, Alex Ruiz. An Associates and Aldrich Production. Art Director, William Glasgow. Editor, Michael Luciano. Sound, Bernard Freericks. Production Supervisor, Jack R. Berne. 133 minutes.

Charlotte Hollis: Bette Davis, *Miriam Deering:* Olivia De Havilland, *Dr. Drew Bayliss:* Joseph Cotten, *Velma Cruther:* Agnes Moorehead, *Harry Willis:* Cecil Kellaway, *Big Sam Hollis:* Victor Buono, *Mrs. Jewel Mayhew:* Mary Astor, *Paul Marchand:* William Campbell, *Sheriff Luke Standish:* Wesley Addy, *John Mayhew:* Bruce Dern, *Foreman:* George Kennedy, *Taxi Driver:* Dave Willock, *Boy:* John Megna, *Gossips:* Ellen Corby, Helen Kleeb, Marianne Stewart, *Newspaper Editor:* Frank Ferguson.

The Hustler with Paul Newman and Myron McCormick.

THE HUSTLER (1961) 20th. Producer, Robert Rossen. Director, Robert Rossen. CinemaScope. Based on the novel by Walter Tevis. Screenplay, Robert Rossen, Sidney Carroll. Art Directors, Harry Horner, Albert Brenner. Cinematographer, Gene Shufton. Editor, Deedee Allan. Filmed in New York City. 135 minutes.

Eddie Felson: Paul Newman, *Sarah Packard:* Piper Laurie, *Bert Gordon:* George C. Scott, *Minnesota Fats:* Jackie Gleason, *Charlie Burns:* Myron McCormick, *Oames Findley:* Murray Hamilton, *Big John:* Michael Constantine, *Preacher:* Stefan Gierasch, *Bartender:* Jack LaMotte, *Cashier-Bennington's:* Gordon B. Clarke, *Scorekeeper:* Alexander Rose, *Waitress:* Carolyn Coates, *Young Man:* Carl York, *Bartender:* Vincent Gardenia, *Willie:* Willie Mosconi, *Old Man Attendant:* Art Smith, *Another Player:* Don De Leo, *Bartender:* Tom Aherne, *Player:* Brendan Fay, *Turk:* Cliff Pellow, *Waiter:* Charles Andre, *First Man:* Sid Raymond, *Second Man:* Charles Mosconi, *Old Doctor:* Wm. P. Adams, *Reservation Clerk:* Charles McDaniel, *Hotel Proprietor:* Jack Healy, *Racetrack Ticket Clerk:* Don Koll.

I AM A FUGITIVE FROM A CHAIN GANG (1932) WB. Directed by Mervyn LeRoy. Based on a story by Robert E. Burns, "I Am a Fugitive From a Georgia Chain Gang." Screenplay, Howard J. Green and Brown Holmes. Art Director, Jack Okey. Photography, Sol Polito. Editor, William Holmes. Gowns, Orry-Kelly. Technical

I Am a Fugitive From a Chain Gang with Glenda Farrell and Paul Muni.

Advisers, S. H. Sullivan and Jack Miller. Cut from existing prints: Spencer Charters (C. K. Hobb), Roscoe Karns (Steve), William Janney (Sheriff's Son), Harry Holman (Sheriff of Monroe). Actors replaced during production: Oscar Apfel by Edward Le Saint, C. Henry Gordon by Douglass Dumbrille, John Marston by Willard Robertson, Russell Simpson by Erville Alderson, Sam Baker by Everett Brown, Dewey Robinson by Walter Long, Edward Arnold by Wallis Clark, Morgan Wallace by Robert McWade. 93 minutes.

James Allen: Paul Muni, *Marie Woods:* Glenda Farrell, *Helen:* Helen Vinson, *Pete:* Preston Foster, *Barney Sykes:* Allen Jenkins, *Bomber Wells:* Edward Ellis, *Nordine:* John Wray, *Reverend Robert Clinton Allen:* Hale Hamilton, *Guard:* Harry Woods, *Warden:* David Landau, *Second Warden:* Edward J. McNamara, *Ramsey:* Robert McWade, *Prison Commissioner:* Willard Robertson, *Linda:* Noel Francis, *Mrs. Allen:* Louise Carter, *The Judge:* Berton Churchill, *Allen's Secretary:* Sheila Terry, *Alice:* Sally Blane, *Red:* James Bell, *Chairman of Chamber of Commerce:* Edward Le Saint, *District Attorney:* Douglass Dumbrille, *Fuller:* Robert Warwick, *Train Conductor:* Charles Middleton, *Parker:* Reginald Barlow, *Ackerman:* Jack La Rue, *Owner of Hot Dog Stand:* Charles Sellon, *Chief of Police:* Erville Alderson, *Wilson:* George Pat Collins, *Doggy:* William Pawley, *Mike, Proprietor of Diner:* Lew Kelly, *Sebastian T. Yale:* Everett Brown, *Texas:* William LeMaire, *Vaudevillian:* George Cooper, *Lawyer:* Wallis Clark, *Blacksmith:* Walter Long, *Georgia Prison Official:* Frederick Burton, *Barber, Bill:* Irving Bacon, *Arresting Officers:* Lee Shumway, J. Frank Glendon, *Dance Extra:* Dennis O'Keefe.

I'LL BE SEEING YOU (1944) UA. Producer, Dore Schary. Director, William Dieterle. Author, Charles Martin. Screenplay, Marion Parsonnet. Musical Score, Daniele Amfitheatrof. Art Director, Mark-Lee Kirk. Cameraman, Tony Gaudio. Editor, William H. Ziegler.

I'll Be Seeing You with Chill Wills, Joseph Cotten and Ginger Rogers.

Song by Irving Kahal and Sammy Fain: "I'll Be Seeing You." 85 minutes.

Mary Marshall: Ginger Rogers, *Zachary Morgan:* Joseph Cotten, *Barbara Marshall:* Shirley Temple, *Mrs. Marshall:* Spring Byington, *Mr. Marshall:* Tom Tully, *Swanson:* Chill Wills, *Lieutenant Bruce:* Dare Harris (John Derek), *Sailor on Train:* Kenny Bowers.

I'll Cry Tomorrow with Richard Conte and Susan Hayward.

I'LL CRY TOMORROW (1955) MGM. Producer, Lawrence Weingarten. Director, Daniel Mann. Based on the book by Lillian Roth, Mike Connolly and Gerold Frank. Screenplay, Helen Deutsch, Jay Richard Kennedy. Art Directors, Cedric Gibbons, Malcolm Brown. Musical Director, Charles Henderson. Music. Alex North. Cinematographer, Arthur E. Arlings Editor, Harold F. Kress. 117 minutes.

Lillian Roth: Susan Hayward, *Tony Bardeman:* Richard Conte, *Burt McGuire:* Eddie Albert, *Katie:* Jo Van Fleet, *Wallie:* Don Taylor, *David Tredman:* Ray Danton, *Selma:* Margo, *Ellen:* Virginia Gregg, *Jerry:* Don Barry, *David as a child:* David Kasday, *Lillian as a child:* Carole Ann Campbell, *Richard:* Peter Leeds, *Fat Man:* Tol Avery, *Man:* Guy Wilkerson, *Derelict:* Tim Carey, *Stage Manager:* Charles Tannen, *Director:* Ken Patterson, *Mr. Byrd:* Voltaire Perkins, *Messenger:* George Lloyd, *Nurse:* Nora Marlowe, *Director:* Stanley Farrar, *Stage Manager:* Harlan Warde, *Doctor:* Peter Brocco, *Henry:* Bob Dix, *Paul, the Butler:* Anthony Jochim, *Dress Designer:* Kay English, *Ethel:* Eve McVeagh, *Waitress:* Veda Ann Borg, *Lillian (age 15):* Gail Ganley, *Stagehand:* Robert B. Williams, *M. C.:* Bob Hopkins, *Club Manager:* Vernon Rich, *Conductor:* Herbert C. Lytton, *Switchman:* George Selk (Budd Buster), *Elderly Lady:* Cheerio Meredith.

I MET HIM IN PARIS (1937) Par. Produced and directed by Wesley Ruggles. Based on a story by Helen Meinardi. Screenplay, Claude Binyon. Art Directors, Hans Dreier and Ernst Fegte. Musical Direc-

I Met Him in Paris with Melvyn Douglas, Claudette Colbert and Robert Young.

tor, Boris Morros. Special Effects, Farciot Edouart. Camera, Leo Tover. Editor, Otho Lovering. Interior Decorator, A. E. Freudeman. Technical Adviser, D'Arcy Rutherford. Title song, Helen Meinardi and Hoagy Carmichael. Costumes, Travis Banton. Sound, Earl Hayman and Don Johnson. 86 minutes.

Kay Denham: Claudette Colbert, *George Potter:* Melvyn Douglas, *Gene Anders:* Robert Young, *Berk Sutter:* Lee Bowman, *Helen Anders:* Mona Barrie, *Cutter Driver:* George Davis, *Swiss Hotel Clerk:* Fritz Feld, *Romantic Waiter:* Rudolph Amendt (Rudolph Anders), *John Hadley:* Alexander Cross, *Hotel Clerk:* George Sorel, *Bartender:* Louis La Bey, *Upper Tower Man (Emile):* Egon Brecher, *Lower Tower Man:* Hans Joby, *Frenchman (Flirt):* Jacques Vanaire, *Double Talk Waiter:* Gennaro Curci, *Headwaiter:* Eugene Borden, *Elevator Operator:* Captain Fernando Garcia, *Headwaiter:* Albert Morin, *Hotel Clerk:* Arthur Hurni, *Conductor:* Albert Pollet, *Bartender:* Jacques Lory, *Couple in Apartment:* Francesco Maran, Yola d'Avril, *Steward:* Jean De Briec, *Waiters:* Charles Haas, Otto Jehly, Paco Moreno, Roman Novins, *Bartender:* Joe Ploski, *Porter:* Alexander Schonberg, *Assistant Bartender:* Joe Thoben, *Women:* Gloria Williams, Priscilla Moran.

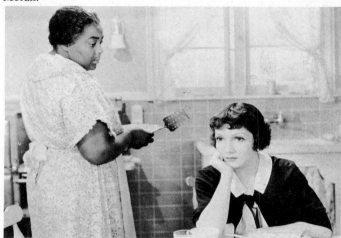
Imitation of Life with Louise Beavers and Claudette Colbert.

IMITATION OF LIFE (1934) Univ. Directed by John Stahl. Based on the novel by Fannie Hurst. Screenplay, William Hurlbut. Cameraman, Merritt Gerstad. Editor, Phil Cahn. Remade by Universal, 1959. 106 minutes.

Beatrice (Bea) Pullman: Claudette Colbert, *Stephen Archer:* Warren William, *Elmer:* Ned Sparks, *Delilah Johnson:* Louise Beavers, *Jessie Pullman at 3:* Baby Jane, *Jessie at 8:* Marilyn Knowlden, *Jessie at 18:* Rochelle Hudson, *Peola Johnson at 4:* Sebie Hendricks, *Peola at 9:* Dorothy Black, *Peola at 19:* Fredi Washington, *Martin (Furniture Man):* Alan Hale, *Landlord:* Clarence Hummel Wilson, *Painter:* Henry Armetta, *Dr. Preston:* Henry Kolker, *Butler:* Wyndham Standing, *French Maid:* Alice Ardell, *Restaurant Manager:* Paul Porcasi, *Man:* William B. Davidson, *Man at Party:* G. P. Huntley, Jr., *Hugh:* Walter Walker, *Mrs. Eden:* Noel Francis, *Mr. Carven:* Franklin Pangborn, *Tipsy Man:* Tyler Brooke, *Englishman:* William Austin, *Butler:* Edgar Norton, *Maid:* Hazel Washington, *Mrs. Carven:* Alma Tell, *Mrs. Dale:* Lenita Lane, *Young Man:* Barry Norton, *Woman:* Joyce Compton, *Minister:* Reverend Gregg, *Chauffeur:* Curry Lee, *Teacher:* Claire McDowell, *Cook:* Madame Sul-Te-Wan, *Undertaker:* Stuart Johnston, *Bits at Funeral:* Fred (Snowflake) Toone, Hattie McDaniel, *Dance Extra:* Dennis O'Keefe.

I'M NO ANGEL (1933) Par. Directed by Wesley Ruggles. Story, Mae West and Lowell Brentano. Adaptation, Harlan Thompson. Dialogue, Mae West. Photography, Leo Tover. Editor, Otho Lovering. Sound, Phil S. Wisdon and F. E. Dine. Songs by Harvey Brooks, Gladys du Bois, Ben Ellison: "They Call Me Sister Honky Tonk," "No One Loves Me Like That Dallas Man," "I Found a New Way to Go to Town," "I Want You, I Need You," "I'm No Angel." Mae dances the Mid-way. 87 minutes

I'm No Angel with Mae West.

Tira: Mae West, *Jack Clayton:* Cary Grant, *Bill Barton:* Edward Arnold, *Slick Wiley:* Ralf Harolde, *Flea Madigan:* Russell Hopton, *Alicia Hatton:* Gertrude Michael, *Kirk Lawrence:* Kent Taylor, *Thelma:* Dorothy Peterson, *Benny Pinkowitz:* Gregory Ratoff, *Beulah Thorndyke:* Gertrude Howard, *The Chump (Ernest Brown):* William Davidson, *Rajah:* Nigel de Brulier, *Bob, the Attorney:* Irving Pichel, *Omnes:* George Bruggeman, *Harry:* Nat Pendleton, *Chauffeur:* Morrie Cohen, *Judge:* Walter Walker, *Sailor:* Monte Collins, *Sailor:* Ray Cooke, *Maid:* Hattie McDaniel, *Libby (Maid):* Libby Taylor, *Reporter:* Dennis O'Keefe.

INCENDIARY BLONDE (1945) Par. Director, George Marshall. Screenplay, Claude Binyon, Frank Butler. Musical Director, Robert Emmett Dolan. Dance Director, Danny Dare. Art Directors, Hans Dreier, William Flannery. Cameraman, Ray Rennahan. Special Effects, Farciot Edouart. Editor, Archie Marshek. Authors, Thomas and W. D. Guinan (from *Life of Texas Guinan*). Songs: "Ragtime Cowboy Joe" by Maurice Abrahams and Lewis F. Muir; "Ida" by Eddie Leonard; "Oh By Jingo Oh By Gee" by Lew Brown and Albert Von Tilzer; "What Do You Want to Make Those Eyes at Me For?" by Howard Johnson, Joseph McCarthy and Jimmy Monaco; "Row, Row, Row" by William Jerome and Jimmy Monaco; "Darktown Strutters' Ball" by Shelton Brooks; "It Had to Be You" by Gus Kahn and Isham Jones; "Sweet Genevieve" by Henry Tucker and George Cooper. 113 minutes

Texas Guinan: Betty Hutton, *Bill Kilgannon:* Arturo de Cordova, *Cherokee Jim:* Charlie Ruggles, *Cadden:* Albert Dekker, *Mike Guinan:* Barry Fitzgerald, *Bessie Guinan:* Mary Phillips, *Tim Callahan:* Bill

Incendiary Blonde with Betty Hutton.

Goodwin, *Nick, The Greek:* Eduardo Ciannelli, *The Maxellos:* Themselves, *Maurice Rocco:* Himself, *Waco Smith:* Ted Mapes, *Mr. Ballinger:* Charles C. Wilson, *Pearl Guinan, 21 years:* Maxine Fife, *Pearl Guinan, 17 years:* Carlotta Jelm, *Pearl Guinan, 7 years:* Ann Carter, *Tommy Guinan, 19 years:* Billy Lechner, *Tommy Guinan, 15 years:* Eddie Nichols, *Tommy Guinan, 5 years:* George Nokes, *Willie Guinan:* Robert Winkler, *Texas Guinan, 9 years:* Patricia Prest, *Baby Joe:* Billy Curtis, *Charley Rinaldo:* Edmund MacDonald, *Gus Rinaldo:* Don Costello, *Louella Parsons:* Catherine Craig, *Singer:* Johnnie Johnston, *Specialty Singer:* Jane Jones, *Woman:* Ruth Roman, *Hatcheck Girl:* Betty Walker, *Master of Ceremonies:* George McKay, *George, a cop:* Harry Shannon, *O'Keefe:* Matt McHugh, *Jenkins:* Russell Simpson, *McKee:* Arthur Loft, *Hadley:* Andrew Tombes, *Otto Hammel:* Pierre Watkin, *Hector:* James Millican, *Mr. Zweigler:* Edwin Stanley, *Gus, Stage Manager:* Ray Walker, *Horace Biggs:* Harry Hayden, *Hotel Clerk:* Frank Faylen.

In Cold Blood with Robert Blake and Scott Wilson.

IN COLD BLOOD (1967) Col. Produced and directed by Richard Brooks. Panavision. Based on the book by Truman Capote. Adapted by Richard Brooks. Assistant Director, Tom Shaw. Music, Quincy Jones. Art Direction, Robert Boyle. Sets, Jack Ahern. Photography, Conrad Hall. Sound, William Randall Jr., Jack Haynes, A. Piantadosi, Richard Tyler. Editor, Peter Zinner. Filmed in Kansas, Missouri, Nevada, Colorado, Texas, Mexico. 134 minutes

Perry Smith: Robert Blake,* *Dick Hickock:* Scott Wilson, *Alvin Dewey:* John Forsythe, *Reporter:* Paul Stewart, *Harold Nye:* Gerald S. O'Loughlin, *Mr. Hickock:* Jeff Corey, *Roy Church:* John Gallaudet, *Clarence Duntz:* James Flavin, *Mr. Smith:* Charles McGraw, *Officer Rohleder:* James Lantz, *Prosecutor:* Will Geer, *Herbert Clutter:* John McLiam, *Bonnie Clutter:* Ruth Storey, *Nancy Clutter:* Brenda C. Currin, *Kenyon Clutter:* Paul Hough, *Good Samaritan:* Vaughn Taylor, *Young Reporter:* Duke Hobbie, *Reverend Post:* Sheldon Allman, *Mrs. Smith:* Sammy Thurman, *Herself:* Mrs. Sadie Truitt, *Herself:* Myrtle Clare, *Young Hitchhiker:* Teddy Eccles, *Old Hitchhiker:* Raymond Hatton, *Susan Kidwell:* Mary-Linda Rapelye, *Nancy's Friend:* Ronda Fultz, *Sheriff:* Al Christy, *Salesman:* Don Sollars, *Mrs. Hartman:* Harriet Levitt, *Insurance Man:* Stan Levitt.

*Inasmuch as most of the critics identified Robert Blake as a newcomer, the following footnote is in order: Far from being a newcomer, Robert Blake started out with Our Gang at MGM in 1939 under his real name, Michael Gubitosi. Later, as Bobby Blake, he played Little Beaver in all the Red Ryder Western features at Republic. As an adult, he co-starred in "Revolt in the Big House" (1958) and "The Purple Gang" (1960), and was one of Richard Boone's repertory company on his TV series.

Indiscreet with Cary Grant and Ingrid Bergman.

INDISCREET (1958) WB. Producer-Director, Stanley Donen. Screenplay by Norman Krasna, from his play *Kind Sir*. Associate Producer, Sydney Streeter. Music by Richard Bennett and Ken Jones. Song by Sammy Cahn and James Van Heusen. Assistant Director, Tom Pevsner. A Grandon Production in Technicolor. 100 minutes

Philip Adams: Cary Grant, *Ann Kalman:* Ingrid Bergman, *Alfred Munson:* Cecil Parker, *Margaret Munson:* Phyllis Calvert, *Carl Banks:* David Kossoff, *Doris Banks:* Megs Jenkins, *Finleigh:* Oliver Johnston, *Finleigh's Clerk:* Middleton Woods.

THE INFORMER (1935) RKO. Produced by Cliff Reid. Directed by John Ford. From the book by Liam O'Flaherty, first published in London in 1925. Screenplay, Dudley Nichols. Music, Max Steiner. Art Director, Van Nest Polglase. Art Associate, Charles Kirk. Photography, Joseph H. August. Editor, George Hively. Sound, Hugh McDowell, Jr. American film debut of English actress Margot Grahame. 91 minutes

Gypo Nolan: Victor McLaglen, *Mary McPhillip:* Heather Angel, *Dan Gallagher:* Preston Foster, *Katie Madden:* Margot Grahame, *Frankie McPhillip:* Wallace Ford, *Mrs. McPhillip:* Una O'Connor, *Terry:* J. M. Kerrigan, *Bartly Mulholland:* Joseph Sauers (Joe Sawyer), *Tommy Connor:* Neil Fitzgerald, *Peter Mulligan:* Donald Meek, *The Blind Man:* D'Arcy Corrigan, *Donahue:* Leo McCabe, *Dennis Daly:* Gaylord (Steve) Pendleton, *Flynn:* Francis Ford, "*Aunt*" *Betty:* May Boley, *The Lady:* Grizelda Harvey, *Street Singer:* Dennis O'Dea, *Man at Wake:* Jack Mulhall, *Young Soldier:* Bob Parrish, *Singer:* Anne O'Neal, *McCabe, Bouncer in House:* Frank Moran, *House Patrons:* Cornelius Keefe, Eddy Chandler, *Admirers:* Pat Moriarity, Frank Marlowe, Harry Tenbrook, *Detractor:* Robert E. Homans, *Policeman:* Frank Hagney, *Bartender:* Bob Perry, *British Officer:* Pat Somerset.

The Informer with Clyde Cook, Victor McLaglen and J.M. Kerrigan.

In Harm's Way with Henry Fonda and John Wayne.

IN HARM'S WAY (1965) Par. Producer-Director, Otto Preminger. In Panavision. Screenplay, Wendell Mayes. Based on the novel by James Bassett. Music, Jerry Goldsmith. Director of Photography, Loyal Griggs. Special Photography, Farciot Edouart. Assistant Directors, Daniel McCauley, Howard Joslin, Michael Daves. 165 minutes

Capt. Rockwell Torrey: John Wayne, *Comdr. Paul Eddington:* Kirk Douglas, *Lt. Maggie Haynes:* Patricia Neal, *Lt. J.G. William McConnel:* Tom Tryon, *Bev. McConnel:* Paula Prentiss, *Ens. Jeremiah Torrey:* Brandon de Wilde, *Ens. Annalee Dorne:* Jill Haworth, *Admiral 'Blackjack' Broderick:* Dana Andrews, *Clayton Canfil:* Stanley Holloway, *Comdr. Egan Powell:* Burgess Meredith, *Admiral:* Franchot Tone, *Comdr. Neal O'Wynn:* Patrick O'Neal, *Lt. Comdr. Vurke:* Carroll O'Connor, *C.P.O. Culpepper:* Slim Pickens, *Liz Eddington:* Barbara Bouchet, *Air-Force Major:* Hugh O'Brian, CINCPAC *Admiral:* Henry Fonda, *Ensign Griggs:* James Mitchum, *Colonel Gregory:* George Kennedy, *Quartermaster Quoddy:* Bruce Cabot, *Captain Tuthill:* Tod Andrews, *Lt. (J.G.) Cline:* Larry Hagman, *Ensign Balch:* Stewart Moss, *Lt. (J.G.) Tom Agar:* Richard Le Pore, *Ship's Doctor:* Chet Stratton, *Tearful Woman:* Soo Young, *Boston:* Dort Clark, *PT Boat Skipper:* Phil Mattingly.

INHERIT THE WIND (1960) UA. Producer-Director, Stanley Kramer. Screenplay, Nathan E. Douglas and Harold Jacob Smith. Based on the play by Jerome Lawrence and Robert E. Lee. Music, Ernest Gold. Assistant Director, Ivan Volkman. Wardrobe, Joe King. Cinematography, Ernest Laszlo. Editor, Frederic Knudtson. 127 minutes

Inherit the Wind with Fredric March and Spencer Tracy.

Henry Drummond: Spencer Tracy, *Matthew Harrison Brady:* Fredric March, *E. K. Hornbeck:* Gene Kelly, *Mrs. Brady:* Florence Eldridge, *Bertram T. Cates:* Dick York, *Rachel Brown:* Donna Anderson, *Judge:* Harry Morgan, *Davenport:* Elliott Reid, *Mayor:* Philip Coolidge, *Rev. Brown:* Claude Akins, *Meeker:* Paul Hartman, *Howard:* Jimmy Boyd, *Stebbins:* Noah Beery, Jr., *Sillers:* Gordon Polk, *Dunlap:* Ray Teal, *Radio Announcer:* Norman Fell, *Mrs. Krebs:* Hope Summers, *Mrs. Stebbins:* Renee Godfrey.

The Inn of the Sixth Happiness with Robert Donat, Ingrid Bergman and Curt Jurgens.

INN OF THE SIXTH HAPPINESS (1958) 20th. Producer, Buddy Adler. Director, Mark Robson. CinemaScope and De Luxe Color. Screenplay by Isobel Lennart. Based on the novel *The Small Woman* by Alan Burgess. Music by Malcolm Arnold. Costumes by Margaret Furse. Assistant Director, David Middlemas. Photography, F. A. Young. 158 minutes

Gladys: Ingrid Bergman, *Linnan:* Curt Jurgens, *The Mandarin:* Robert Donat, *Hok-A:* Michael David, *Mrs. Lawson:* Athene Seyler, *Sir Francis:* Ronald Squire, *Dr. Robinson:* Moultrie Kelsall, *Mr. Murfin:* Richard Wattis, *Yang:* Peter Chong, *Sui Lan:* Tsai Chin, *Secretary:* Edith Sharpe, *Cook:* Joan Young, *Miss Thompson:* Noel Hood, *Li:* Burt Kwouk, *Woman with Baby:* Lian Shin Yang, *Young Lin:* Ronald Kyaing, *Bai Boa:* Ye Min, *Mai Da:* Louise Lin, *Sixpense:* Judith Lai, *Timothy:* Frank Goh, *Russian Commissar:* Andre Mikhelson, *Russian Conductor:* Stanislaw Mikula, *Innkeeper's Wife:* Lin Chen, *Chief Muleteer:* Ronald Lee, *Mandarin's Aide:* Michael Wee, *Tax Collector:* Christopher Chen, *Buddhist Priest:* Aung Min, *Madman:* Frank Blaine.

IN OLD ARIZONA (1929) Fox. Directed by Raoul Walsh and Irving Cummings. Based on the character created by O. Henry. Scenario, adaptation, and dialogue, Tom Barry. Photography, Arthur Edeson. Sound, Edmund H. Hansen. Editor, Louis Loeffler. Assistant Directors, Archie Buchanan and Charles Woolstenhulme. The first Fox Movietone feature. Filmed in Zion National Park and Bryce Canyon, Utah; the Mohave Desert at Victorville, Cal.; San Fernando's old

In Old Arizona with Warner Baxter and Dorothy Burgess.

mission; Cedar City, Utah; San Juan Capistrano mission. Theme, "My Tonia," by DeSylva, Brown, and Henderson. Film debut of Dorothy Burgess. Talkie debuts of Warner Baxter, Roy Stewart. 95 minutes

Sergeant Mickey Dunn: Edmund Lowe, *The Cisco Kid:* Warner Baxter, *Tonia Maria:* Dorothy Burgess, *Tad:* J. Farrell MacDonald, *Russian Immigrant:* Ivan Linow, *Cook:* Soledad Jiminez, *Piano Player:* Fred Warren, *Barber:* Henry Armetta, *Cowpunchers:* Frank Campeau, Frank Nelson, Tom Santschi, Duke Martin, Pat Hartigan, *Blacksmith:* James Marcus, *Commandant:* Roy Stewart, *Sheriff:* Alphonse Ethier, *Soldier:* James Bradbury, Jr., *Second Soldier:* John Dillon, *Bartender:* Joe Brown, *Italian Girl:* Lola Salvi, *Man:* Edward Piel, Sr., *Woman:* Helen Lynch.

In Old Chicago with Alice Faye and Tyrone Power.

IN OLD CHICAGO (1938) 20th. Produced by Darryl F. Zanuck. Associate Producer, Kenneth Macgowan. Directed by Henry King. Screenplay, Lamar Trotti and Sonya Levien. Research, Chicago Historical Society. Editor, Barbara McLean. Based on the story "We the O'Learys" by Niven Busch. Photography, Peverell Marley. Art Director, William Darling. Associate, Rudolph Sternad. Sets, Thomas Little. Unit Manager, Booth McCracken. Assistant Director, Robert Webb. Costumes, Royer. Music Direction, Louis Silvers. Songs: "In Old Chicago" by Mack Gordon and Harry Revel; "I've Taken a Fancy to You," "I'll Never Let You Cry," "Take a Dip in the Sea" by Sidney Mitchell and Lew Pollack; "Carry Me Back to Old Virginny." Special Effects Director, H. Bruce Humberstone. Special Effects Photography, Daniel B. Clark. Special Effects Staged by Fred Sersen, Ralph Hammeras, Louis J. Witte. Sound, Eugene Grossman. 110 minutes

Dion O'Leary: Tyrone Power, *Belle Fawcett:* Alice Faye, *Jack O'Leary:* Don Ameche, *Molly O'Leary:* Alice Brady, *Pickle Bixby:* Andy Devine, *Gil Warren:* Brian Donlevy, *Ann Colby:* Phyllis Brooks, *Bob O'Leary:* Tom Brown, *General Phil Sheridan:* Sidney Blackmer, *Senator Colby:* Berton Churchill, *Gretchen O'Leary:* June Storey, *Mitch:* Paul Hurst, *Specialty Singer:* Tyler Brooke, *Patrick O'Leary:* J. Anthony Hughes, *Dion as a boy:* Gene Reynolds, *Bob as a boy:* Bobs Watson, *Jack as a boy:* Billy Watson, *Hattie:* Madame Sul-Te-Wan, *Beavers:* Spencer Charters, *Rondo, Bodyguard:* Rondo Hatton, *Carrie Donahue:* Thelma Manning, *Miss Lou:* Ruth Gillette, *Drunk:* Eddie Collins, *Beef King:* Scotty Mattraw, *Stuttering Clerk:* Joe Twerp, *Booking Agent:* Charles Lane, *Lawyer:* Clarence Hummel Wilson, *Judge:* Frank Dae, *Fire Commissioner:* Harry Stubbs, *Ship's Captain:* Joe King, *Driver:* Francis Ford, *Police Officers:* Robert Murphy, Wade Boteler, *Men in Jack's Office:* Gustav von Seyffertitz, Russell Hicks, *Specialty:* Rice and Cady, *Johnson, Secretary:* Harry Hayden, *Witness:*

Vera Lewis, *Wagon Driver:* Ed Brady, *Frantic Mother:* Minerva Urecal.

IN OLD KENTUCKY (1935) Fox. Produced by Edward Butcher. Directed by George Marshall. Story, Charles T. Dazey. Screenplay, Sam Hellman and Gladys Lehman. Photography, L. W. O'Connell. 86 minutes

In Old Kentucky with Will Rogers and Bill Robinson.

Steve Tapley: Will Rogers, *Nancy Martingale:* Dorothy Wilson, *Lee Andrews:* Russell Hardie, *Wash Jackson:* Bill Robinson, *Arlene Shattuck:* Louise Henry, *Slick Doherty:* Alan Dinehart, *Ezra Martingale:* Charles Sellon, *Pole Shattuck:* Charles Richman, *Dolly Breckenridge:* Esther Dale, *The Rain Maker:* Etienne Girardot, *The Sheriff:* John Ince, *Jockey:* Fritz Johannet, *Jailer:* Everett Sullivan, *Deputy Officer:* G. Raymond (Bill) Nye, *Bit:* William J. Worthington, *Steward:* Edward Le Saint, *Jockey:* Bobby Rose, *Saleslady:* Dora Clemant, *Bookie:* Ned Norton, *Jockey:* Eddie Tamblyn, *Stewards:* Allen Cavan, Stanley Andrews.

THE INTERNS (1962) Col. Producer, Robert Cohn. Director, David Swift. Based on the novel by Richard Frede. Screenplay, Walter Newman, David Swift. Art Director, Don Ament. Music, Leith Stevens. Cinematographer, Russell L. Metty. Editors, Al Clark, Jerome Thoms. Sequel: *The New Interns* (1964). 120 minutes

Dr. Considine: Michael Callan, *Dr. John Paul Otis:* Cliff Robertson, *Dr. Lew Worship:* James MacArthur, *Dr. Sid Lackland:* Nick Adams, *Lisa Cardigan:* Suzy Parker, *Mado:* Haya Hararit, *Mildred:* Anne Helm, *Gloria:* Stefanie Powers, *Dr. Sidney Wohl:* Buddy Ebsen, *Dr. Riccio:* Telly Savalas, *Nurse Flynn:* Katharine Bard, *Didi Loomis:* Kay Stevens, *Dr. Hugo Granchard:* Gregory Morton, *Mrs. Auer:* Angela Clarke, *Nurse Connie Dean:* Connie Gilchrist, *Loara:* Ellen Davalos, *Dr. Dave Simon:* Charles Robinson, *Olga:* Carroll Harrison,

The Interns with Cliff Robertson, Baruch Lumet and James MacArthur.

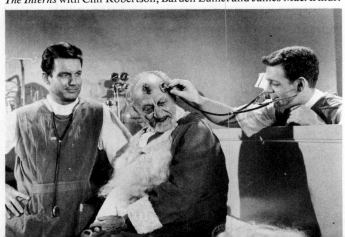

Dr. Duane: John Banner, *Samantha:* Mari Lynn, *Dr. Joe Parelli:* Brian Hutton, *Dr. Bonny:* J. Edward McKinley, *Gwen:* Bobo Lewis, *First Intern:* Ira Barmak, *Rosco:* Bill Gunn, *Dr. Apschult:* William O. Douglas, *Dr. Petchek:* Don Edmonds, *Mrs. Lawrence:* Mavis Neal, *Dr. Baker:* Brent Sargent, *Samantha's Son:* Mark Kantor, *Dr. Greenberg:* Michael Fox, *Byrd:* Baruch Lumet, *Van Wyck:* Jud Taylor, *Mr. Auer:* Peter Brocco, *Slattery:* Harry Hines, *Betay (Model):* Jackie Stoloff.

INTERRUPTED MELODY (1955) MGM. Producer, Jack Cummings. Director, Curtis Bernhardt. CinemaScope, Eastman Color. Based on her life story by Marjorie Lawrence. Screenplay, William Ludwig, Sonya Levien. Art Directors, Cedric Gibbons, Daniel B. Cathcart. Operatic recordings supervised and conducted by Walter Du Cloux. Musical Supervision, Saul Chaplin. Music Adviser, Harold Gelman. Dramatic music score adapted and conducted by Adolph Deutsch. Cinematographers, Joseph Ruttenberg, Paul C. Vogel. Editor, John Dunning. Eileen Farrell sings for Eleanor Parker. 106 minutes

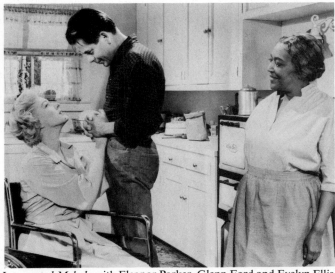

Interrupted Melody with Eleanor Parker, Glenn Ford and Evelyn Ellis.

Dr. Thomas King: Glenn Ford, *Marjorie Lawrence:* Eleanor Parker, *Cyril Lawrence:* Roger Moore, *Bill Lawrence:* Cecil Kellaway, *Dr. Ed Ryson:* Peter Leeds, *Clara:* Evelyn Ellis, *Jim Owens:* Walter Baldwin, *Madame Gilly:* Ann Codee, *Himself:* Leopold Sachse, *Comte Claude des Vigneux:* Stephen Bekassy, *Ted Lawrence:* Charles R. Keane, *Eileen Lawrence:* Fiona Hale, *Tenors:* Rudolf Petrak, William Olvis, *Volunteer Worker:* Doris Lloyd, *Adjudicator:* Alex Frazer, *Gilly Secretary:* Penny Santon, *Louise:* Phyllis Altivo, *Tenor's Manager:* Gabor Curtiz, *Tenor:* Claude Stroud, *Monsieur Bertrand:* Andre Charlot, *Metropolitan Cashier:* Paul McGuire, *Nurse:* Doris Merrick, *Suzie:* Sandra Descher, *Mr. Norson:* Jack Raine, *Accompanist:* Freda Stoll, *Mrs. Schultz:* Gloria Rhods, *Man on Beach:* Stuart Whitman, *Vocal Student:* Eileen Farrell.

IN THE HEAT OF THE NIGHT (1967) UA. Produced by Walter Mirisch. Directed by Norman Jewison. A Mirisch Corporation Presentation. In De Luxe Color. Based on the novel by John Ball. Screenplay, Stirling Silliphant. Supervision, Allan K. Wood. Production Manager, James E. Henderling. Art Director, Paul Groesse. Sets, Bob Priestley. Music, Quincy Jones. Title song by Quincy Jones, Marilyn and Alan Bergman, sung by The Ray Charles Singers. Assistant Directors, Newton Arnold and Terry Morse, Jr. Titles, Murray Naidich. Photography, Haskell Wexler. Editor, Hal Ashby. Sound, Walter Goss. Filmed in Sparta, Ill. 109 minutes

Virgil Tibbs: Sidney Poitier, *Police Chief Bill Gillespie:* Rod Steiger, *Deputy Sam Wood:* Warren Oates, *Mrs. Leslie Colbert:* Lee Grant, *Purdy:* James Patterson, *Delores Purdy:* Quentin Dean, *Eric Endicott:* Larry Gates, *Webb Schubert:* William Schallert, *Mama Caleba (Mrs. Bellamy):* Beah Richards, *Harvey Oberst:* Scott Wilson, *Philip Col-*

In the Heat of the Night with Sidney Poitier and Rod Steiger.

bert: Jack Teter, *Packy Harrison:* Matt Clark, *Ralph Henshaw:* Anthony James, *H. E. Henderson:* Kermit Murdock, *Jess:* Khalil Bezaleel, *George Courtney:* Peter Whitney, *Harold Courtney:* William Watson, *Shagbag Martin:* Timothy Scott, *City Council:* Michael LeGlaire, Larry D. Mann, Stewart Nisbet, *Charlie Hawthorne:* Eldon Quick, *Dr. Stuart:* Fred Stewart, *Ted Ulam:* Arthur Malet, *Arnold Fryer:* Peter Masterson, *Engineers:* Alan Oppenheimer, Philip Garris, *Henry:* Jester Hairston, *Deputy:* Clegg Hoyt, *Young Toughs:* Phil Adams Nikita Knatz, *Baggage Master:* David Stinehart, *Conductor:* Buzz Barton.

IN THIS OUR LIFE (1942) WB. Producer, Hal B. Wallis. Associate Producer, David Lewis. Director, John Huston. Screenplay, Howard Koch. Based on Ellen Glasgows' novel. Art Director, Robert Haas. Musical Director, Leo F. Forbstein. Music, Max Steiner. Cameraman, Ernie Haller. Special Effects, Byron Haskin, Robert Burks. Editor, William Holmes. 97 minutes

Stanley Timberlake: Bette Davis, *Roy Timberlake:* Olivia De Havilland, *Craig Fleming:* George Brent, *Peter Kingsmill:* Dennis Morgan, *William Fitzroy:* Charles Coburn, *Asa Timberlake:* Frank Craven, *Lavinia Timberlake:* Billie Burke, *Minerva Clay:* Hattie McDaniel, *Betty Wilmoth:* Lee Patrick, *Charlotte Fitzroy:* Mary Servoss, *Parry Clay:* Ernest Anderson, *Jim Purdy:* William Davidson, *Dr. Buchanan:* Edward Fielding, *Inspector:* John Hamilton, *Ranger:* William Forrest, *Workers:* Elliott Sullivan, Eddie Acuff, Walter Baldwin, Herbert Heywood, Alan Bridge, *Butler:* George Reed, *Waiter:* Dudley Dickerson, *Cab Driver:* Walter Brooke, *Young Mother:* Ruth Ford, *Customer:* Billy Wayne, *Bartender:* Walter Huston, *Negro:* Ira Buck Wood, *Negro:* Sam McDaniel, *Negro:* Billy Mitchell, *Negro:* Napoleon Simpson, *Negro:* Sunshine Sammy Morrison, *Announcer:* Reid Kilpatrick, *Roadhouse Customers (Extras):* Humphrey Bogart, Mary Astor, Peter Lorre, Sydney Greenstreet, Ward Bond, Barton MacLane, Elisha Cook, Jr.

In This Our Life with George Brent, Ernest Anderson and Bette Davis.

Intruder in the Dust with Elizabeth Patterson, Elzie Emanuel and Claude Jarman, Jr.

INTRUDER IN THE DUST (1949) MGM. Producer, Clarence Brown. Director, Clarence Brown. Based on the novel by William Faulkner. Screenplay, Ben Maddow. Music Score, Adolph Deutsch. Art Directors, Cedric Gibbons, Randell Duell. Photography, Robert Surtees. Editor, Robert J. Kren. 89 minutes

John Gavin Stevens: David Brian, *Chick Mallison:* Claude Jarman Jr., *Lucas Beauchamp:* Juano Hernandez, *Nub Gowrie:* Porter Hall, *Miss Habersham:* Elizabeth Patterson, *Crawford Gowrie:* Charles Kemper, *Sheriff Hampton:* Will Geer, *Vinson Gowrie:* David Clarke, *Aleck:* Elzie Emanuel, *Mrs. Mallison:* Lela Bliss, *Mr. Mallison:* Harry Hayden, *Mr. Tubbs:* Harry Antrim, *Will Legate:* Dan White, *Paralee:* Alberta Dishmon, *Mr. Lilley:* R. X. Williams, *Gowrie Twins:* Ephraim Lowe, Edmund Lowe, *Molly Beauchamp:* Julia S. Marshbanks, *Truck Driver:* Jack Odom, *Barber:* Freddie B. Patton, *Deputy:* W. G. Kimmons, *Fraser's Son:* Eugene Roper, *Negro Convicts:* John Morgan, James Kirkwood, *Girl:* Ann Hartsfield, *Attendant:* Ben H. Hilbun.

I REMEMBER MAMA (1948) RKO. Producers, George Stevens, Harriet Parsons. Director, George Stevens. Based on the 1944 play by John Van Druten and Kathryn Forbes' novel, *Mama's Bank Account.* Screenplay, DeWitt Bodeen. Art Directors, Albert S. D'Agostino, Carroll Clark. Music, Roy Webb. Music Director, C. Bakaleinikoff. Photography, Nick Musuraca. Editor, Robert Swink. Later the basis for a TV series. 134 minutes

Mama: Irene Dunne, *Katrin:* Barbara Bel Geddes, *Uncle Chris:* Oscar Homolka, *Papa:* Philip Dorn, *Mr. Hyde:* Sir Cedric Hardwicke, *Peter Thorkelsen:* Edgar Bergen, *Dr. Johnson:* Rudy Vallee, *Jessie Brown:* Barbara O'Neil, *Florence Dana Moorehead:* Florence Bates, *Christine:* Peggy McIntyre, *Dagmar:* June Hedin, *Nels:* Steve Brown, *Aunt Trina:* Ellen Corby, *Aunt Jenny:* Hope Landin, *Aunt Sigrid:* Edith Evanson, *Cousin Arne:* Tommy Ivo, *Nurse:* Lela Bliss, *Nurse:* Constance Purdy, *Minister:* Stanley Andrews, *Man:* Franklyn Farnum, *Schoolteacher:* Cleo Ridgley, *Postman:* George Atkinson.

I Remember Mama with Philip Dorn, Irene Dunne, Barbara Bel Geddes, Steve Brown and June Hedin.

Irish Eyes Are Smiling with Michael Dalmatoff, Monty Woolley, Dick Haymes, June Haver and Beverly Whitney.

IRISH EYES ARE SMILING (1944) 20th. Producer, Damon Runyon. Director, Gregory Ratoff. Color by Technicolor. Story, A. E. Ellingham. Screenplay, Earl Baldwin, John Tucker Battle. Dance Director, Hermes Pan. Art Directors, Lyle Wheeler, Joseph C. Wright. Musical Directors, Alfred Newman, Charles Henderson. Cameraman, Harry Jackson. Special Effects, Fred Sersen. Editor, Harmon Jones. Technicolor Director, Natalie Kalmus. Associate, Richard Mueller. Songs by Mack Gordon and Jimmy Monaco: "Bessie in a Bustle" and "I Don't Want a Million Dollars." 90 minutes

Edgar Brawley: Monty Woolley, *Mary "Irish" O'Brien:* June Haver, *Ernest R. Ball:* Dick Haymes, *Al Jackson:* Anthony Quinn, *Lucille Lacey:* Beverly Whitney, *Stanley Ketchel:* Maxie Rosenbloom, *Belle La Tour:* Veda Ann Borg, *Betz:* Clarence Kolb, *Metropolitan Opera Singers:* Leonard Warren, Blanche Thebom, *Stage Manager:* Chick Chandler, *Specialty Dancer:* Kenny Williams, *Headwaiter:* Michael Dalmatoff, *Prima Donna:* Marian Martin, *Song Plugger:* Charles Williams, *Sportsmen's Quartette:* Max Smith, Martin Sperzel, John Rarig, Gurney Bell, *Sparring Partner:* Art Foster, *Referee/Stage Manager:* John Sheehan, *Phoebe (Maid):* Marietta Canty, *Electrician:* Joey Ray, *Electrician:* George Chandler, *Piano Player:* Sam Wren, *Acrobats:* Mary Adams Hayes, Ray Spiker, *Pawnbroker:* Leo Mostovoy, *Irish Woman:* Mary Gordon, *Purser:* Emmett Vogan, *Hoofers:* Frank Marlowe, Ray Walker, *Detective:* Charles Wilson, *Dr. Medford:* Maurice Cass, *Barker:* Arthur Hohl, *Pianist:* Harry Seymour, *Doorman:* J. Farrell MacDonald, *Policeman:* Robert Homans, *Harry:* Eddie Acuff.

IRMA LA DOUCE (1963) UA. Producer-Director. Billy Wilder. Screenplay, Billy Wilder, I. A. L. Diamond. Based on a play by Alexandre Breffort. Music, Marguerite Monnot. Assistant Director, Hal Polaire. Costumes, Orry-Kelly. Presented by the Mirisch Company and Edward L. Alperson. Music Score, Andre Previn. Presented in

Irma La Douce with Jack Lemmon and Shirley MacLaine.

association with Phalanx Productions. In Panavision and Technicolor. Associate Producers, I. A. L. Diamond, Doane Harrison. Art Director, Alexander Trauner. Cinematographer, Joseph La Shelle. 142 minutes

Nestor Patou: Jack Lemmon, *Irma La Douce:* Shirley MacLaine, *Moustache:* Lou Jacobi, *Hippolyte:* Bruce Yarnell, *Inspector Lefevre:* Herschel Bernardi, *Lolita:* Hope Holiday, *Amazon Annie:* Joan Shawlee, *Kiki the Cossack:* Grace Lee Whitney, *Andre:* Paul Dubov, *Concierge:* Howard McNear, *Police Sergeant:* Cliff Osmond, *Jojo:* Diki Lerner, *Casablanca Charlie:* Herb Jones, *Zebra Twins:* Ruth and Jane Earl, *Suzette Wong:* Tura Santana, *Texan Customer:* James Brown, *Tattooed Sailor:* Bill Bixby, *Mimi the MauMau:* Harriette Young, *Carmen:* Sheryl Deauville, *Customers:* Lou Krugman, John Alvin, *Poule with Balcony:* Susan Woods, *Officer DuPont:* Billy Beck, *Jack:* Jack Sahakian, *Man with Samples:* Don Diamond, *General Lafayette:* Edgar Barrier, *Englishman:* Richard Peel, *Prison Guard:* Joe Palma.

Island in the Sun with Harry Belafonte and Dorothy Dandridge.

ISLAND IN THE SUN (1957) 20th. Producer, Darryl F. Zanuck. Director, Robert Rossen. Screenplay by Alfred Hayes. Based on the novel by Alec Waugh. Music by Malcolm Arnold. Assistant Director, Gerry O'Hara. Costumes by David Ffolkes. In CinemaScope and De Luxe Color. 119 minutes

Maxwell Fleury: James Mason, *Mavis:* Joan Fontaine, *Margot Seaton:* Dorothy Dandridge, *Jocelyn:* Joan Collins, *Hilary Carson:* Michael Rennie, *Mrs. Fleury:* Diana Wynward, *Col. Whittingham:* John Williams, *Euan Templeton:* Stephen Boyd, *Sylvia:* Patricia Owens, *Julian Fleury:* Basil Sydney, *David Archer:* John Justin, *The Governor:* Ronald Squire, *Bradshaw:* Hartley Power, *David Boyeur:* Harry Belafonte.

IS PARIS BURNING? (1966) Par. French Title, *Paris Brule-t-Il?* In 70 mm. Panavision. Last scene, Technicolor. Seven Arts Presentation. A Transcontinental-Marianne production. Produced by Paul Graetz. Director, Rene Clement. Screenplay, Gore Vidal and Francis Ford Coppola with Jean Aurenche, Pierre Bost and Claude Brule. From the book by Larry Colls and Dominique Lapierre. Photographed by Marcel Grignon. Musical score by Maurice Jarre. Film Editor, Robert Lawrence. 173 minutes

Morandot: Jean-Paul Belmondo, *Monod:* Charles Boyer, *Francoise Labe:* Leslie Caron, *Henri Karcher:* Jean-Pierre Cassel, *G. I. in Tank:* George Chakiris, *Lebel:* Claude Dauphin, *Jacques Chaban-Delmas:* Alain Delon, *General Patton:* Kirk Douglas, *General Bradley:* Glenn Ford, *Gen. Von Choltitz:* Gert Frobe, *Bayet:* Daniel Gelin, *Bizien:* Yves Montand, *Warren:* Anthony Perkins, *Pisani:* Michel Piccoli, *General Leclerc:* Claude Rich, *Cafe Proprietress:* Simone Signoret, *General Sibert:* Robert Stack, *Serge:* Jean-Louis Trintignant, *Gallois:* Pierre Vaneck, *G. I. with Warren:* Skip Ward, *Nordling:* Orson Welles, *Colonel Rol:* Bruno Cremer, *Parodi:* Pierre Dux, *Hitler:* Billy Frick, *Joliot-Curie:* Sacha Pitoeff, *Ebernach:* Wolfgang Preiss, *Claire:*

Is Paris Burning? with Orson Welles and Leslie Caron.

Marie Versini, *A Parisienne:* Suzy Delair, *Von Arnim:* Harry Meyen, *Landrieux:* Georges Poujouly, *Jodl:* Hannes Messemer, *Commander Huhm:* Klaus Holm, *Old Woman:* Germaine de France, *Commandant:* George Georges Geret, *Chief of Explosives:* Michel Berger, *General Burgdorff:* Peter Jakob, *Bernard Labe:* Toni Taffin.

IT HAPPENED ONE NIGHT (1934) Col. Produced by Harry Cohn. Directed by Frank Capra. Based on the *Cosmopolitan* magazine sharp story "Night Bus" by Samuel Hopkins Adams. Screenplay, Robert Riskin. Art Director, Stephen Goosson. Assistant Director, C.C. Coleman. Photography, Joseph Walker. Editor, Gene Havlick. Sound, E. E. Bernds. Costumes, Robert Kalloch. Music Director, Louis Silvers. Remade as *You Can't Run Away From It* (Columbia, 1956), *Eve Knew Her Apples* (Columbia, 1945). 105 minutes

Peter Warne: Clark Gable, *Ellie Andrews:* Claudette Colbert, *Oscar Shapeley:* Roscoe Karns, *Alexander Andrews:* Walter Connolly, *Danker:* Alan Hale, *Bus Driver:* Ward Bond, *Bus Driver:* Eddy Chandler, *King Westley:* Jameson Thomas, *Lovington:* Wallis Clark, *Zeke:* Arthur Hoyt, *Zeke's Wife:* Blanche Frederici, *Joe Gordon:* Charles C. Wilson, *Reporter:* Charles D. Brown, *Henderson:* Harry C. Bradley, *Auto Camp Manager:* Harry Holman, *Manager's Wife:* Maidel Turner, *Station Attendant:* Irving Bacon, *Flag Man:* Harry Todd, *Tony:* Frank Yaconelli, *Drunken Boy:* Henry Wadsworth, *Mother:* Claire McDowell, *Detectives:* Ky Robinson, Frank Holliday, James Burke, Joseph Crehan, *Drunk:* Milton Kibbee, *Vender:* Mickey Daniel, *Dykes:* Oliver Eckhardt, *Boy:* George Breakston, *Secretary:* Bess Flowers, *Minister:* Father Dodds, *Best Man:* Edmund Burns, *Maid of Honor:* Ethel Sykes, *Old Man:* Tom Ricketts, *Radio Announcer:* Eddie Kane, *Bus Passengers:* Ernie Adams, Kit Guard, Billy Engle, Allen Fox, Marvin Loback, Dave Wengren, Bert Starkey, Rita Ross, *Reporter:* Hal Price.

It Happened One Night with Clark Gable and Claudette Colbert.

IT'S A MAD, MAD, MAD, MAD WORLD (1963) UA. Producer-Director, Stanley Kramer. Screenplay, William and Tania Rose. Music, Ernest Gold. In Ultra Panavision and Technicolor. A Casey Production. Title song by Ernest Gold and Mack David. Cinematography, Ernest Laszlo. Editors, Frederic Knudson, Robert C. Jones, and Gene Fowler Jr. Sound Director, Gordon E. Sawyer. Sound Effects, Walter G. Elliott. Stunt Supervisor, Carey Loftin. Dance sequence played by The Shirelles, sung by The Four Mads. Filmed at Santa Rosita Beach State Park. 190 minutes (cut to 153 minutes)

Captain C. G. Culpeper: Spencer Tracy, *J. Russell Finch:* Milton Berle, *Melville Crump:* Sid Caesar, *Benjy Benjamin:* Buddy Hackett, *Mrs. Marcus:* Ethel Merman, *Ding Bell:* Mickey Rooney, *Sylvester Marcus:* Dick Shawn, *Otto Meyer:* Phil Silvers, *Lientenant Colonel J. Algernon Hawthorne:* Terry-Thomas, *Lennie Pike:* Jonathan Winters, *Monica Crump:* Edie Adams, *Emmeline Finch:* Dorothy Provine, *First Cab Driver:* Eddie "Rochester" Anderson, *Tyler Fitzgerald:* Jim Backus, *Airplane Pilot:* Ben Blue, *Police Sergeant:* Alan Carney, *Mrs. Halliburton:* Barrie Chase, *Chief of Police:* William Demarest, *Second Cab Driver:* Peter Falk, *Col. Wilberforce:* Paul Ford, *Third Cab Driver:* Leo Gorcey, *Dinckler:* Edward Everett Horton, *Jimmy, the Crook:* Buster Keaton, *Nervous Man:* Don Knotts, *Tower Control:* Carl Reiner, *Firemen:* Moe Howard, Larry Fine, Joe DeRita (The Three Stooges), *Union Official:* Joe E. Brown, *Sheriff Mason:* Andy Devine, *Fire Chief:* Sterling Holloway, *Irwin:* Marvin Kaplan, *Airport Manager:* Charles Lane, *Lieutenant Matthews:* Charles McGraw, *Switchboard Operator:* ZaSu Pitts, *Police Secretary Schwartz:* Madlyn Rhue, *Ray:* Arnold Stang, *Radio Tower Operator:* Jesse White, *Mayor:* Lloyd Corrigan, *Culpeper's Wife:* Voice of Selma Diamond, *Deputy Sheriff:* Stan Freberg, *Billie Sue:* Voice of Louise Glenn, *George, the Steward:* Ben Lessy, *Pilot's Wife:* Bobo Lewis, *Miner:* Mike Mazurki, *Truck Driver:* Nick Stewart, *Chinese Laundryman:* Sammee Tong, *Detectives:* Norman Fell, Nicholas Georgiade, *Smiler Grogan:* Jimmy Durante, *Police Officer:* Allen Jenkins, *Detective:* Stanley Clements, *Radio Operator:* Harry Lauter, *Salesman:* Doodles Weaver, *Traffic Cop:* Tom Kennedy, *Bits:* Chick Chandler, Barbara Pepper, Cliff Norton, Roy Roberts, *Tower Radioman:* Eddie Ryder, *Helicopter Observer:* Don C. Harvey, *Patrolmen:* Roy Engel, Paul Birch, *Stuntman:* Dale Van Sickel, *Man on Road:* Jack Benny, *Mad Driver:* Jerry Lewis.

It's a Mad, Mad, Mad, Mad World with Sid Caesar and Edie Adams.

IT'S A WONDERFUL LIFE (1946) RKO. Produced and directed by Frank Capra. A Liberty Films Production. Based on the short story "The Greatest Gift" by Philip Van Doren Stern. Screenplay, Frances Goodrich, Albert Hackett, and Frank Capra. Additional Scenes, Jo Swerling. Music composed and directed by Dimitri Tiomkin. Art Director, Jack Okey. Photography, Joseph Walker and Joseph Biroc. Editor, William Hornbeck. 129 minutes

George Bailey: James Stewart, *Mary Hatch:* Donna Reed, *Mr. Potter:* Lionel Barrymore, *Uncle Billy:* Thomas Mitchell, *Clarence:* Henry Travers, *Mrs. Bailey:* Beulah Bondi, *Ernie:* Frank Faylen, *Bert:*

It's a Wonderful Life with William Edmunds, James Stewart and Stanley Andrews.

Ward Bond, *Violet Bick:* Gloria Grahame, *Mr. Gower:* H. B. Warner, *Sam Wainwright:* Frank Albertson, *Harry Bailey:* Todd Karns, *Pa Bailey:* Samuel S. Hinds, *Cousin Tilly:* Mary Treen, *Ruth Dakin:* Virginia Patton, *Cousin Eustace:* Charles Williams, *Mrs. Hatch:* Sara Edwards, *Mr. Martini:* Bill Edmunds, *Annie:* Lillian Randolph, *Mrs. Martini:* Argentina Brunetti, *Little George:* Bobby Anderson, *Little Sam:* Ronnie Ralph, *Little Mary:* Jean Gale, *Little Violet:* Jeanine Anne Roose, *Little Marty Hatch:* Danny Mummert, *Little Harry Bailey:* Georgie Nokes, *Nick:* Sheldon Leonard, *Potter's Bodyguard:* Frank Hagney, *Joe (Luggage Shop):* Ray Walker, *Real Estate Salesman:* Charlie Lane, *The Bailey Children: Janie:* Carol Coomes, *Zuzu:* Karolyn Grimes, *Pete:* Larry Sims, *Tommy:* Jimmy Hawkins, *High School Principal:* Harry Holman, *Marty Hatch:* Hal Landon, *Freddie:* Alfalfa Switzer, *Mickey:* Bobby Scott, *Dr. Campbell:* Harry Cheshire, *Bit:* Ellen Corby.

IVANHOE (1952) MGM. Producer, Pandro S. Berman. Director, Richard Thorpe. Technicolor. Screenplay, Noel Langley. Adaptation by Aeneas MacKenzie. Based on the novel by Sir Walter Scott. Music, Miklos Rozsa. Filmed in England. 106 minutes

Ivanhoe: Robert Taylor, *Rebecca:* Elizabeth Taylor, *Rowena:* Joan Fontaine, *De Bois-Guilbert:* George Sanders, *Wamba:* Emlyn Williams, *Sir Hugh De Bracy:* Robert Douglas, *Cedric:* Finlay Currie, *Isaac:* Felix Aylmer, *Font De Boeuf:* Francis DeWolff, *Prince John:* Guy Rolfe, *King Richard:* Norman Wooland, *Waldemar Fitzurse:* Basil Sydney, *Locksley:* Harold Warrender.

Ivanhoe with Elizabeth Taylor, Robert Taylor, Joan Fontaine and Emlyn Williams.

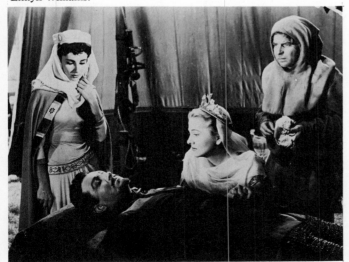

I Wake Up Screaming with Alan Mowbray, Carole Landis, Allyn Joslyn and Victor Mature.

I WAKE UP SCREAMING (1941) 20th. Produced by Milton Sperling. Directed by H. Bruce Humberstone. Based on the novel by Steve Fisher. Screenplay, Dwight Taylor. Photography, Edward Cronjager. Music Director, Cyril J. Mockridge. Editor, Robert Simpson. Song, "The Things I Love" by Harold Barlow and Lewis Harris. Themes, "Street Scene Theme" and "Over the Rainbow." Locations filmed in New York. 81 minutes

Jill Lynn: Betty Grable, *Frankie Christopher (Botticelli):* Victor Mature, *Vicky Lynn:* Carole Landis, *Ed Cornell:* Laird Cregar, *Jerry McDonald:* William Gargan, *Robin Ray:* Alan Mowbray, *Larry Evans:* Allyn Joslyn, *Harry Williams:* Elisha Cook, Jr., *Reporter:* Chick Chandler, *Assistant D. A.:* Morris Ankrum, *Mrs. Handel:* May Beatty, *Reporter:* Cyril Ring, *Florist Keating:* Charles Lane, *Caretaker:* Frank Orth, *Headwaiter:* Gregory Gaye, *Newsboy:* Stanley Clements, *Detectives:* Dick Rich, James Flavin, Tim Ryan, *Detective-partners:* Ralph Dunn, Wade Boteler, *Police Matron:* Cecil Weston, *Cop:* Stanley Blystone, *Officer Murphy:* Harry Strang, *Old Man:* Edward McWade, *Bartender:* Harry Seymour, *Newsman:* Pat McKee, *Waiter:* Albert Pollet, *Girl at Table:* Dorothy Dearing, *Mr. Handel:* Forbes Murray, *Extra:* Brooks Benedict.

I WANTED WINGS (1941) Par. Produced by Arthur Hornblow, Sr. Directed by Mitchell Leisen. Screenplay by Richard Maibaum, Lieut. Beirne Lay, Jr. and Sig Herzig. Based on a story by Eleanore Griffin and Frank Wead. From the book *I Wanted Wings* by Lieut. Beirne Lay, Jr. Art Directors, Hans Dreier and Robert Usher. Editor, Hugh Bennett. Director of Photography: Leo Tover. Aerial photography by Elmer Dyer. Song, "Born to Love," by Ned Washington and Victor Young. 131 minutes

Jeff Young: Ray Milland, *Al Ludlow:* William Holden, *Tom Cassidy:* Wayne Morris, *Capt. Mercer:* Brian Donlevy, *Carolyn Bartlett:*

I Wanted Wings with Wayne Morris, William Holden and Brian Donlevy.

Constance Moore, *Sally Vaughn:* Veronica Lake, *"Sandbags" Riley:* Harry Davenport, *Jimmy Masters:* Phil Brown, *President of the Court:* Edward Fielding, *Judge Advocate:* Willard Robertson, *Flight Commander:* Richard Lane, *Flight Surgeon:* Addison Richards, *Mickey:* Hobart Cavanaugh, *Lieut. Hopkins:* Douglas Aylesworth, *Lieut. Ronson:* John Trent, *Lieut. Clankton:* Archie Twitchell, *Cadet Captain:* Richard Webb, *Radio Announcer:* John Hiestand, *Montgomery (co-pilot):* Harlan Warde, *Ranger:* Lane Chandler, *Cadet:* Charles Drake, *Cadet:* Alan Hale, Jr., *Cadet:* Renny McEvoy, *Detective:* Ed Peil, Sr., *Detective:* Frank O'Connor, *Corporal:* James Millican, *Sergeant:* Emory Johnson, *Supply Sergeant:* Russ Clark, *Private:* George Turner, *Private:* Hal Brazeale, *Cadet Adjutant:* Warren Ashe, *Meteorology Instructor:* Charles A. Hughes, *Buzzer Class Instructor:* George Lollier, *Mrs. Young:* Hedda Hopper, *Mr. Young:* Herbert Rawlinson.

I WANT TO LIVE! (1958) UA. Producer, Walter Wanger. Director, Robert Wise. Screenplay, Nelson Gidding and Don Mankiewicz. Based on newspaper articles by Ed Montgomery and letters of Barbara Graham. Music by John Mandel. Assistant Director, George Vieira. A Figaro Production. Jazz played by Gerry Mulligan, Shelly Manne, Art Farmer, Bud Shank, Red Mitchell, Frank Rosolino, Pete Jolly. 120 minutes

I Want to Live! with Susan Hayward.

Barbara Graham: Susan Hayward, *Ed Montgomery:* Simon Oakland, *Peg:* Virginia Vincent, *Carl Palmberg:* Theodore Bikel, *Henry Graham:* Wesley Lau, *Emmett Perkins:* Philip Coolidge, *Jack Santo:* Lou Krugman, *Bruce King:* James Philbrook, *District Attorney:* Bartlett Robinson, *Richard Tibrow:* Gage Clark, *Al Matthews:* Joe De Santis, *Father Devers:* John Marley, *San Quentin Captain:* Dabbs Greer, *Warden:* Raymond Bailey, *Nurse:* Alice Backes, *Matron:* Gertrude Flynn, *San Quentin Sergeant:* Russell Thorson, *Detective Sergeant:* Stafford Repp, *Lieutenant:* Gavin MacLeod, *Ben Miranda:* Peter Breck, *Rita:* Marion Marshall, *Corona Warden:* Olive Blakeney, *Corona Guard:* Lorna Thayer, *Personal Effects Clerk:* Evelyn Scott, *NCO:* Jack Weston, *San Francisco Hood:* Leonard Bell, *Himself:* George Putnam, *Newsman:* Bill Stout, *Bixel:* Jason Johnson, *Judge:* Rusty Lane, *San Quentin Officer:* S. John Launer, *Police Broadcaster:* Dan Sheridan, *Detective:* Wendell Holmes.

I WAS A MALE WAR BRIDE (1949) 20th. Producer, Sol C. Siegel. Director, Howard Hawks. From a story by Henri Rochard. Screenplay, Charles Lederer, Leonard Spigelglass, Hagar Wilde. Musical Director,

I Was a Male War Bride with Ann Sheridan and Cary Grant.

Lionel Newman. Art Directors, Thomas Little, Walter M. Scott. Photography, Norbert Brodine, O. Borrodaile. Editor, James B. Clark. 105 minutes

Henri Rochard: Cary Grant, *Lieutenant Catherine Gates:* Ann Sheridan, *WACS:* Marion Marshall, Randy Stuart, *Captain Jack Rumsey:* William Neff, *Tony Jewitt:* Eugene Gericke, *Innkeeper's Assistant:* Ruben Wendorf, *Waiter:* Lester Sharpe, *Trumble:* John Whitney, *Seaman:* Ken Tobey, *Shore Patrol:* Joe Haworth, *Sergeants:* William Pullen, William Self, *Sergeant:* Bill Murphy, *Lieutenant:* Robert Stevenson, *Bartender:* Alfred Linder, *Chaplain:* David McMahon, *First German Policeman:* Otto Reichow, *Second German Policeman:* William Yetter, *French Minister:* Andre Charlot, *Waiter:* Alex Gerry, *Commander Willis:* Russ Conway, *Lieutenant:* Harry Lauter, *Major Prendergast:* Kay Young, *Innkeeper's Wife:* Lillie Kann, *Jail Officer:* Carl Jaffe, *Schindler:* Martin Miller, *Burgermeister:* Paul Hardmuth, *French Notary:* John Serrett.

I WONDER WHO'S KISSING HER NOW (1947) 20th. Producer, George Jessel. Director, Lloyd Bacon. Color by Technicolor. Original Screenplay, Lewis R. Foster. Musical Director, Alfred Newman. Art Directors, Richard Day, Boris Leven. Cameraman, Ernest Palmer. Editor, Louis Loeffler. Additional Dialogue, Marion Turk. Songs by Frank Adams, Will Hough and Joe Howard: "Honeymoon," "What's the Use of Dreaming?" "Hello My Baby," "Oh Gee Be Sweet to Me Kid," "How'd You Like to Be the Umpire?" and "I Wonder Who's Kissing Her Now." Dances, Hermes Pan. Special Songs, George Jessel and Charles Henderson. Technicolor Director, Natalie Kalmus. Associate, Leonard Doss. 108 minutes

Katie: June Haver, *Joe Howard:* Mark Stevens, *Lulu Madison:* Martha Stewart, *Will Hough:* Reginald Gardiner, *Fritzi Barrington:* Lenore Aubert, *Jim Mason:* William Frawley, *Tommy Yale:* Gene Nelson, *Martin Webb:* Truman Bradley, *John McCullem:* George Cleveland, *Charley:* Harry Seymour, *T. J. Milford:* Lewis L. Russell, *Kassel:* John "Skins" Miller, *Karl:* Lew Hearn, *Anita:* Eve Miller, *Marie:*

I Wonder Who's Kissing Her Now with Mark Stevens, June Haver, William Frawley and Martha Stewart.

Florence O'Brien, *Singer:* Alice Mock, *Harris:* Emmett Vogan, *Herman Bartholdy:* Charles Judels, *Mr. Fennabeck:* Milton Parsons, *King Louis:* Dewey Robinson, *President Theodore Roosevelt:* John Merton, *Mr. Kurlinger:* Robert Emmett Keane, *Stage Doorman:* John Sheehan, *Waiter:* Sam McDaniel, *Clerk:* John Arledge, *Song Plugger:* Steve Olsen, *Stage Managers:* Frank Scannell, Harry Cheshire, *Bartender:* Joe Whitehead, *Critic:* Perry Ivins, *Doorman:* Herbert Heywood, *Italian Barber:* Antonio Filauri, *Miss Claybourne:* Almira Sessions, *"Willie":* Merrill Rodin, *Stagehands:* Eddie Dunn, Ralph Dunn.

JAILHOUSE ROCK (1957) MGM. Produced by Pandro S. Berman. Directed by Richard Thorpe. Panavision. Associate Producer, Kathryn Hereford. Based on a story by Ned Young. Screenplay, Guy Trosper. Assistant Director, Robert E. Relyea. An Avon Production. Songs by Mike Stoller and Jerry Leiber, and Roy C. Bennett, Aaron Schroeder, Abner Silver, Sid Tepper, Ben Weisman: "One More Day," "Young and Beautiful," "I Wanna Be Free," "Don't Leave Me Now," "Treat Me Nice," "Jailhouse Rock," "Baby, I Don't Care." Last film of Judy Tyler, 24, who was killed July 3, 1957. 96 minutes

Jailhouse Rock with Elvis Presley.

Vince Everett: Elvis Presley, *Peggy Van Alden:* Judy Tyler, *Hunk Houghton:* Mickey Shaughnessy, *Mr. Shores (Narrator):* Vaughn Taylor, *Sherry Wilson:* Jennifer Holden, *Teddy Talbot:* Dean Jones, *Laury Jackson:* Anne Neyland, *Prof. August Van Alden:* Grandon Rhodes, *Mrs. Van Alden:* Katharine Warren, *Mickey Alba:* Don Burnett, *Musicians:* The Jordanaires, *Jake, Bartender:* George Cisar, *Simpson, Convict:* Glenn Strange, *Convict:* John Indrisano, *Extra in Cafe:* Dorothy Abbott, *Bardeman, TV Studio Manager:* Robert Bice, *Warden:* Hugh Sanders, *Sam Brewster:* Percy Helton, *Jack Lease:* Peter Adams, *Studio Head:* William Forrest, *Paymaster:* Dan White, *Dotty:* Robin Raymond, *Ken:* John Day, *Judge:* S. John Launer, *Guard:* Dick Rich, *Cleaning Woman:* Elizabeth Slifer, *Striptease:* Gloria Pall, *Bartender:* Fred Coby, *Shorty:* Walter Johnson, *Drunk:* Frank Kreig, *Record Distributor:* William Tannen, *Record Engineer:* Wilson Wood, TV *Director:* Tom McKee, *Photographer:* Donald Kerr, *Drummond:* Carl Milletaire, *Surgeon:* Francis DeSales, *Hotel Clerk:* Harry Hines.

THE JAZZ SINGER (1927) WB. Directed by Alan Crosland. Based on the 1925 play by Samson Raphaelson. Adaptation, Alfred A. Cohn. Titles, Jack Jarmuth. Songs: "Blue Skies" by Irving Berlin; "Mammy" by Sam Lewis, Joe Young, Walter Donaldson; "Toot Toot Tootsie, Goodbye" by Gus Kahn, Ernie Erdman, Dan Russo; "Dirty Hands, Dirty Face" by Edgar Leslie, Grant Clarke, Al Jolson, Jimmy Monaco; "Mother I Still Have You" by Al Jolson and Louis Silvers; "Kol Nidre," "Yahrzeit." A part-talking film, considered the first sound movie. Film debut of Al Jolson, 44. Remade by Warners in 1952. 88 minutes

Jakie Rabinowitz (Jack Robin): Al Jolson, *Mary Dale:* May McAvoy, *Cantor Rabinowitz:* Warner Oland, *Sara Rabinowitz:* Eugenie Besserer,

The Jazz Singer with Al Jolson.

Moisha Yudleson: Otto Lederer, *Jakie at 13:* Bobbie Gordon, *Harry Lee:* Richard Tucker, *Himself:* Cantor Josef Rosenblatt, *Levi:* Nat Carr, *Buster Billings:* William Demarest, *Dillings:* Anders Randolf, *Doctor:* Will Walling, *The Agent:* Roscoe Karns, *Chorus Girl:* Myrna Loy.

JESSE JAMES (1939) 20th. Producer, Darryl F. Zanuck. Associate Producer, Nunnally Johnson. Director, Henry King. Technicolor. Original Screenplay, Nunnally Johnson. Technicolor Director, Natalie Kalmus. Art Directors, William Darling, George Dudley. Musical Director, Louis Silvers. Cameraman, George Barnes. Technicolor Photography, W. H. Greene. Editor, Barbara McLean. 105 minutes

Jesse James: Tyrone Power, *Frank James:* Henry Fonda, *Zee:* Nancy Kelly, *Will Wright:* Randolph Scott, *Major:* Henry Hull, *Jailer:* Slim Summerville, *Runyon, Pinkerton Man:* J. Edward Bromberg, *Barshee:* Brian Donlevy, *The Killer:* John Carradine, *Mc Coy:* Donald Meek, *Jesse James, Jr.:* John Russell, *Mrs. Samuels:* Jane Darwell, *Charles Ford:* Charles Tannen, *Mrs. Ford:* Claire Du Brey, *Clark:* Willard Robertson, *Lynch:* Paul Sutton, *Pinky:* Ernest Whitman, *Bill:* Paul Burns, *Preacher:* Spencer Charters, *Tom:* Arthur Aylsworth, *Heywood:* Charles Halton, *Roy:* George Chandler, *Old Marshall:* Erville Alderson, *Farmer:* Harry Tyler, *Farmer Boy:* George Breakston, *Boy's Mother:* Virginia Brissac, *Judge Rankin:* Edward J. Le Saint, *Judge Matthews:* John Elliott, *One of Jesse's Gang:* Lon Chaney, Jr., *Engineer:* Harry Holman, *Barshee's Henchmen:* Wylie Grant, Ethan Laidlaw, *Infantry Captain:* Don Douglas, *Cavalry Captain:* James Flavin, *Teller:* George O'Hara, *Doctor:* Charles Middleton.

Jesse James with Tyrone Power and Nancy Kelly.

Jezebel with Bette Davis, Henry Fonda and Jac George.

JEZEBEL (1938) WB. Associate Producer, Henry Blanke. Directed by William Wyler. From the play by Owen Davis, Sr. Screenplay, Clements Ripley, Abem Finkel, and John Huston. Art Director, Robert Haas. Music Score, Max Steiner. Camera, Ernest Haller. Editor, Warren Low. Songs, "Jezebel," by Johnny Mercer and Harry Warren; "Raise a Ruckus" by Warren and Dubin. 104 minutes

Julie Morrison: Bette Davis, *Preston Dillard:* Henry Fonda, *Buck Cantrell:* George Brent, *Amy Bradford Dillard:* Margaret Lindsay, *Aunt BelleMassey:* Fay Bainter, *Ted Dillard:* Richard Cromwell, *Dr. Livingstone:* Donald Crisp, *General Bogardus:* Henry O'Neill, *Jean La Cour:* John Litel, *Dick Allen:* Gordon Oliver, *Molly Allen:* Janet Shaw, *Mrs. Kendrick:* Spring Byington, *Stephanie Kendrick:* Margaret Early, *Huger:* Irving Pichel, *De Lautrec:* Georges Renavent, *Uncle Cato:* Lew Payton, *Gros Bat:* Eddie Anderson, *Zette:* Theresa Harris, *Ti Bat:* Stymie Beard, *Mrs. Petion:* Georgia Caine, *Bob:* Fred Lawrence, *Madame Poulard, Dressmaker:* Ann Codee, *Durette:* Jacques Vanaire, *Negro Flower Girl:* Daisy Bufford, *Negro Servant:* Jesse A. Graves, *First Director:* Frederick Burton, *Second Director:* Edward McWade, *Bookkeeper:* Frank Darien, *Midinette:* Suzanne Dulier, *Jenkins:* John Harron, *Erronens:* Phillip "Lucky" Hurlic, *Errata:* Dolores Hurlic, *Deputy Sheriff:* Davison Clark, *Sheriff at Plantation:* Trevor Bardette, *Fugitive Planter:* George Guhl, *Drunk:* Jack Norton, *Bar Companion:* Louis Mercier, *New Orleans Sheriff:* Alan Bridge, *Customer:* Charles Wagenheim, *Orchestra Leader:* Jac George.

JOAN OF ARC (1948) RKO-Sierra. Producer, Walter Wanger. Director, Victor Fleming. Color by Technicolor. Adapted from Maxwell Anderson's play *Joan of Lorraine*. Screenplay, Maxwell Anderson, Andrew Solt. Musical Director, Emil Newman. Art Director, Richard Day. Photography, Joe Valentine. Editor, Frank Sullivan. 145 minutes

Joan of Arc: Ingrid Bergman, *Dauphin:* José Ferrer, *Robert De Baudricourt:* George Coulouris, *Jean De Metz:* Richard Derr, *Bertrand De Poulengy:* Ray Teal, *Durand Laxart:* Roman Bohnen, *Jacques D'Arc:* Robert Barrat, *Pierre D'Arc:* Jimmie Lydon, *Jean D'Arc:* Rand Brooks, *Isabelle D'Arc:* Selena Royle, *Pierre Cauchon:* Francis Sullivan, *Catherine Le Royer:* Irene Rich, *Henry Le Royer:* Nestor Paiva, *George De La Tremoille:* Gene Lockhart, *Archbishop of Theims:* Nicholas Joy, *Duke of Bedford:* Frederic Worlock, *Raoul De Gaucourt:* Tom Brown Henry, *Duke of Burgundy:* Colin Keith Johnson, *Alain Chartier:* Vincent Donahue, *Duke of Claremont:* Richard Ney, *Jean Dunois:* Leif Erickson, *Duke of Alencon:* John Emery, *La Hire:* Ward Bond, *St. Severe:* John Ireland, *Giles De Raiz:* Henry Brandon, *Admiral De Culan:* Gregg Barton, *John of Luxembourg:* J. Carrol Naish, *William Glasdale:* Dennis Hoey, *Jean D'Aulon:* Ethan Laidlaw, *Father Pasquerel:* Hurd Hatfield, *Jean Le Maistre:* Cecil Kellaway, *Poton De Xantrailles:* Morris Ankrum, *Jean D'Estivet:* Philip Bourneuf, *Jean Massieu:* Sheppard Strudwick, *Thomas De Courcelles:* Stephen Roberts, *Avranches:* Taylor Holmes, *Nicholas De Houppeville:* Frank Puglia, *Winchester:* Houseley Stevenson, *Nicholas Midi:* Victor Wood,

Joan of Arc with Herbert Rudley, Sheppard Strudwick, Ingrid Bergman and Aubrey Mather.

Earl of Warwick: Alan Napier, *Thirache (Executioner):* Bill Kennedy, *Jean Fournier:* David Bond, *Constable of Clervaux:* George Zucco, *Isombard De La Pierre:* Herbert Rudley, *La Fontaine:* Aubrey Mather, *Judge Mortemer:* James Kirkwood, *Judge Marguerie:* Herbert Rawlinson, *Judge Courneille:* Matt Moore.

JOHNNY BELINDA (1948) WB. Producer, Jerry Wald. Director, Jean Negulesco. Based on the play by Elmer Harris. Screenplay, Irmgard Von Cube, Allen Vincent. Art Director, Robert Haas. Musical Director, Leo F. Forbstein. Photography, Ted McCord. Editor, David Weisbart. Film debut of Jan Sterling. 102 minutes

Belinda McDonald: Jane Wyman, *Dr. Robert Richardson:* Lew Ayres, *Black McDonald:* Charles Bickford, *Aggie McDonald:* Agnes Moorehead, *Locky McCormick:* Stephen McNally, *Stella Maguire:* Jan Sterling, *Mrs. Poggety:* Rosalind Ivan, *Pacquet:* Dan Seymour, *Mrs. Lutz:* Mabel Paige, *Mrs. McKee:* Ida Moore, *Defense Attorney:* Alan Napier, *Ben:* Monte Blue, *Mountie:* Douglas Kennedy, *Interpreter:* James Craven, *Floyd McQuiggen:* Richard Taylor (Jeff Richards), *Fergus McQuiggen:* Richard Walsh, *Mrs. Tim Moore:* Joan Winfield, *Rector:* Ian Wolfe, *Judge:* Holmes Herbert, *Dr. Gray:* Jonathan Hale, *Tim Moore:* Ray Montgomery, *Dan'l:* Blayney Lewis, *Gracie Anderson:* Barbara Bates, *Prosecutor:* Fred Worlock, *Bailiff:* Creighton Hale.

Johnny Belinda with Charles Bickford, Jane Wyman and Lew Ayres.

JOHNNY EAGER (1941) MGM. Producer, John W. Considine, Jr. Director, Mervyn LeRoy. Author, James Edward Grant. Screenplay, John Lee Mahin, James Edward Grant. Cameraman, Harold Rosson. Editor, Albert Akst. 107 minutes

Johnny Eager: Robert Taylor, *Lisbeth Bard:* Lana Turner, *John Benson Farrell:* Edward Arnold, *Jeff Hartnett:* Van Heflin, *Jimmy Courtney:*

Robert Sterling, *Garnet:* Patricia Dane, *Mae Blythe:* Glenda Farrell, *Mr. Verne:* Henry O'Neill, *Judy Janford:* Diana Lewis, *Lew Rankin:* Barry Nelson, *Marco:* Charles Dingle, *Julio:* Paul Stewart, *Halligan:* Cy Kendall, *Billiken:* Don Costello, *Benjy:* Lou Lubin, *Ryan:* Joseph Downing, *Peg:* Connie Gilchrist, *Matilda:* Robin Raymond, *Miss Mines:* Leona Maricle, *Officer No. 711:* Byron Shores.

Johnny Eager with Joseph Downing, Robert Taylor and Cy Kendall.

JOHNNY GUITAR (1954) Rep. Director, Nicholas Ray. Trucolor. Based on Roy Chanslor's novel. Screenplay, Philip Yordan. Art Director, James Sullivan. Cinematographer, Harry Stradling. Editor, Richard L. Van Enger. 110 minutes

Vienna: Joan Crawford, *Johnny Guitar:* Sterling Hayden, *Emma Small:* Mercedes McCambridge, *Dancin' Kid:* Scott Brady, *John McIvers* Ward Bond, *Turkey Ralston:* Ben Cooper, *Bart Lonergan:* Ernest Borgnine, *Old Tom:* John Carradine, *Corey:* Royal Dano, *Marshall Williams:* Frank Ferguson, *Eddie:* Paul Fix, *Mr. Andrews:* Rhys Williams, *Pete:* Ian MacDonald, *Ned:* Will Wright, *Jake:* John Maxwell, *Sam:* Robert Osterloh, *Frank:* Frank Marlowe, *Jenks:* Trevor Bardette, *Possemen:* Sumner Williams, Sheb Wooley, Denver Pyle, Clem Harvey.

Johnny Guitar with Ben Cooper, Joan Crawford, Frank Marlowe, Sterling Hayden and Scott Brady.

THE JOKER IS WILD (1957) Par. Produced by Samuel J. Briskin. Directed by Charles Vidor. In VistaVision. From the book by Art Cohn, based on the life of Joe E. Lewis. Screenplay, Oscar Saul. Art Directors, Hal Pereira and Roland Anderson. Music scored and conducted by Walter Scharf. Assistant Director, C. C. Coleman, Jr. Costumes, Edith Head. Dances staged by Josephine Earl. Photography, Daniel L. Fapp. Special Effects, John P. Fulton. Editor, Everett

The Joker Is Wild with Eddie Albert and Frank Sinatra.

Douglas. An A. M. B. L. Production. Song by Sammy Cahn and James Van Heusen, "All the Way." Reissued as *All the Way*, 1966. 126 minutes

Joe E. Lewis: Frank Sinatra, *Letty Page:* Jeanne Crain, *Martha Stewart:* Mitzi Gaynor, *Austin Mack:* Eddie Albert, *Cassie Mack:* Beverly Garland, *Swifty Morgan:* Jackie Coogan, *Captain Hugh McCarthy:* Barry Kelley, *Georgie Parker:* Ted de Corsia, *Tim Coogan:* Leonard Graves, *Flora:* Valerie Allen, *Burlesque Comedian:* Hank Henry, *Photographer:* Dennis McMullen, *Heckler:* Wally Brown, *Harry Bliss:* Harold Huber, *Johnson:* Ned Glass, *Dr. Pierson:* Ned (Ed H.) Wever, *Mr. Page:* Walter Woolf King, *Hecklers:* Don Beddoe, Mary Treen, Paul Bryar, *Runner:* Sid Melton, *Man Shaving:* Dick Elliott, *Allen:* John Harding, *Girl:* Lucy Knoch, *Letty's Husband:* William Pullen, *Judge:* F. Oliver McGowan, *Burlesque Straight Man:* James J. Cavanaugh, *Burlesque Girls:* Harriette Tarler, Paula Hill, *Elevator Starter:* George Offerman, *Jack:* James Cross, *Butler:* Eric Wilton, *Doorman of The Valencia:* Kit Guard, *Mugs:* Paul T. Salata, Bill Hickman, John D. Benson.

Jolson Sings Again with Larry Parks.

JOLSON SINGS AGAIN (1949) Col. Produced by Sidney Buchman. Directed by Henry Levin. Color by Technicolor. Story, Sidney Buchman. Music, George Duning. Music Director, Morris Stoloff. Art Director, Walter Holscher. Photography, William Snyder. Editor, William Lyon. A sequel to 1946's *The Jolson Story*, this was based on the later life and career of Al Jolson, and featured many of his songs. Evelyn Keyes as Julie Benson (based on Ruby Keeler) was seen only in a newspaper photograph. Songs: "I Only Have Eyes For You" by Al Dubin and Harry Warren; "I'm Just Wild About Harry" by Noble Sissle and Eubie Blake; "Ma Blushin' Rosie" by Edgar Smith and John Stromberg; "April Showers" by B. G. DeSylva, and Louis Silvers; "Swanee" by Irving Caesar and George Gershwin; "I'm Looking Over a Four-Leaf Clover" by Mort Dixon and Harry M. Woods; "California Here I Come" by B. G. DeSylva, Al Jolson and Joseph Meyer; "Chinatown My Chinatown" by Joe Young, Sam Lewis and Jean Schwartz; "Carolina In the Morning" by Gus Kahn and Walter Donaldson; "Pretty Baby" by Gus Kahn, Tony Jackson and Egbert Van Alstyne; "Baby Face" by Benny Davis and Harry Akst. 96 minutes

Al Jolson: Larry Parks, The singing voice of Al Jolson, *Larry Parks:* Larry Parks, *Ellen Clark:* Barbara Hale, *Steve Martin:* William Demarest, *Cantor Yoelson:* Ludwig Donath, *Tom Baron:* Bill Goodwin, *Ralph Bryant:* Myron McCormick, *Mama Yoelson:* Tamara Shayne, *Henry:* Eric Wilton, *Charlie:* Robert Emmett Keane, *Man:* Jock O'Mahoney (Jock Mahoney), *Woman:* Gertrude Astor, *Captain of Waiters:* Peter Brocco, *Soldier:* Dick Cogan, *Mr. Estrada:* Martin Garralaga, *Writer:* Michael Cisney, *Writer:* Ben Erway, *Script Girl:* Helen Mowery, *Orchestra Leader:* Morris Stoloff, *Sound Mixer:* Philip Faulkner, Jr., *Theater Manager:* Nelson Leigh, *Mrs. Bryant:* Virginia Mullen, *Nurse:* Margie Stapp.

THE JOLSON STORY (1946) Col. Produced by Sidney Skolsky. Associate Producer, Gordon Griffith. Directed by Alfred E. Green. Color by Technicolor. Assistant Director, Wilbur McGaugh. Montage Director, Lawrence W. Butler. Screenplay, Stephen Longstreet. Adaptation, Harry Chandlee and Andrew Solt. Dances, Jack Cole. Production Numbers, Joseph H. Lewis. Gowns, Jean Louis. Musical Director, M. W. Stoloff. Photography, Joseph Walker. Technicolor Color Director, Natalie Kalmus. Associate, Morgan Padelford. Editor, William Lyon. Art Directors, Stephen Goosson and Walter Holscher. Sets, William Kiernan and Louis Diage. Make-up, Clay Campbell. Hair Styles, Helen Hunt. Sound, Hugh McDowell. Vocal Arrangements, Saul Chaplin. Orchestral Arrangements, Martin Fried. Music Recording, Edwin Wetzel. Re-recording, Richard Olson. Songs: "By the Light of the Silvery Moon" by Edward Madden and Gus Edwards; "You Made Me Love You" by Joseph McCarthy and Jimmy Monaco; "I'm Sitting on Top of the World" by Sam Lewis, Joe Young and Ray Henderson; "There's a Rainbow 'Round My Shoulder" by Al Jolson, Billy Rose and Dave Dreyer; "My Mammy" by Sam Lewis, Joe Young and Walter Donaldson; "Rock-a-bye Your Baby to a Dixie Melody" by Sam Lewis, Joe Young and Jean Schwartz; "Liza" by Ira and George Gershwin; "Waiting for the Robert E. Lee" by L. Wolfe Gilbert and Lewis E. Muir; "April Showers" by B. G. DeSylva and Louis Silvers; "About a Quarter to Nine" by Al Dubin

The Jolson Story with John Alexander, Larry Parks and William Demarest.

and Harry Warren; "I Want a Girl Just Like the Girl That Married Dear Old Dad" by Will Dillon and Harry Von Tilzer; "Anniversary Song" by Al Jolson; "The Spaniard Who Blighted My Life" by Billy Merson. Based on the career of Al Jolson, and featuring his songs. A sequel, *Jolson Sings Again* (1949), traced Jolson's later life. Julie Benson is based on Ruby Keeler. 128 minutes

Songs sung by Al Jolson. *Al Jolson:* Larry Parks, *Julie Benson:* Evelyn Keyes, *Steve Martin:* William Demarest, *Tom Baron:* Bill Goodwin, *Cantor Yoelson:* Ludwig Donath, *Mrs. Yoelson:* Tamara Shayne, *Lew Dockstader:* John Alexander, *Ann Murray:* Jo-Carroll Dennison, *Father McGee:* Ernest Cossart, *Al as a boy:* Scotty Beckett, *Dick Glenn:* William Forrest, *Ann as a girl:* Ann E. Todd, *Oscar Hammerstein:* Edwin Maxwell, *Jonsey:* Emmett Vogan, *Ziegfeld:* Eddie Kane, *Roy Anderson:* Jimmy Lloyd, *Young Priest:* Coulter Irwin, *Ingenue:* Adele Roberts, *Henry:* Bob Stevens, *Policeman, Riley:* Harry Shannon, *Call Boy:* Bud Gorman, *Assistant Stage Manager:* Charles Jordan, *Architect:* Pierre Watkin, *Woman:* Lillian Bond, *Headwaiter:* Eugene Borden, *Master of Ceremonies:* Eddie Rio, *Sourpuss Movie Patron:* Will Wright, *Stage Manager:* Arthur Loft, *Director:* Edward Keane, *Assistant Stage Manager:* Eddie Fetherstone, *Orchestra Leader:* Bill Brandt, *Cameraman:* Pat Lane, *Lab Manager:* Mike Lally, *Gaffer:* George Magrill, *Dancer-Actress:* Helen O'Hara, *Wardrobe Woman:* Jessie Arnold, *Girl Publicist:* Donna Dax, *Cutter:* Fred Sears, *Harry, the Butler:* Eric Wilton, *Choir:* The Robert Mitchell Boy Choir, *Extra in Audience:* Franklyn Farnum, *Nightclubber:* Major Sam Harris.

Journey for Margaret with Laraine Day, Billy Severn, Robert Young and Margaret O'Brien.

JOURNEY FOR MARGARET (1942) MGM. Producer, B. P. Fineman. Director, Major W. S. Van Dyke. Author, William L. White. Screenplay, David Hertz, William Ludwig. Art Director, Cedric Gibbons. Cameraman, Ray June. Editor, George White. 81 minutes

John Davis: Robert Young, *Nora Davis:* Laraine Day, *Trudy Strauss:* Fay Bainter, *Anya:* Signe Hasso, *Margaret:* Margaret O'Brien, *Herbert V. Allison:* Nigel Bruce, *Peter Humphreys:* William Severn, *Rugged:* G. P. Huntley, Jr., *Mrs. Barrie:* Doris Lloyd, *Mr. Barrie:* Halliwell Hobbes, *Susan Fleming:* Jill Esmond, *Fairoaks:* Charles Irwin, *Mrs. Bailey:* Elisabeth Risdon, *Frau Weber:* Lisa Golm, *Man:* Herbert Evans, *Child:* Clare Sandars, *Censor:* Leyland Hodgson, *Woman:* Anita Bolster, *Warden:* Matthew Boulton, *Nurse:* Lilyan Irene, *Manager:* Olaf Hytten, *Nurse:* Ottola Nesmith, *Surgeon:* John Burton, *Steward:* Colin Kenny, *Porter:* Jimmy Aubrey, *Mrs. Harris:* Heather Thatcher, *Isabel:* Joan Kemp, *Hans:* Norbert Muller, *Policeman:* Al Ferguson, *Nora's Mother:* Bea Nigro, *Stage Manager:* Cyril Delevanti, *Mme. Bornholm:* Jody Gilbert, *Everton:* Craufurd Kent, *Japanese Statesman:* Keye Luke, *Air Raid Warden:* David Thursby, *Polish Captain:* Henry Guttman.

JOURNEY'S END (1930) Tiff. Directed by James Whale. Supervised by George Pearson. Based on the play by R. C. Sheriff. Scenario, Joseph Moncure March. Art Director, Hervey Libbert. Photography,

Journey's End with Billy Bevan and David Manners.

Benjamin Kline. Editor, Claude Berkeley. Sound, Bud Myers. A Gainsborough Production. Colin Clive repeats his role from the London stage. 130 minutes

Captain Stanhope: Colin Clive, *Lieutenant Osborne:* Ian MacLaren, *Second Lieutenant Raleigh:* David Manners, *Second Lieutenant Hibbert:* Anthony Bushell, *Second Lieutenant Trotter:* Billy Bevan, *Private Mason:* Charles Gerrard, *Captain Hardy:* Robert A'Dair, *Company Sergeant Major:* Thomas Whiteley, *The Colonel:* Jack Pitcairn, *German Soldier:* Werner Klinger.

JOURNEY TO THE CENTER OF THE EARTH (1959) 20th. Producer, Charles Brackett. Director, Henry Levin. CinemaScope, De Luxe Color. Based on the novel by Jules Verne. Screenplay, Walter Reisch, Charles Brackett. Art Directors, Lyle R. Wheeler, Franz Bachelin, Herman A. Blumenthal. Music, Bernard Herrmann. Cinematographer, Leo Tover. Special Photographic Effects, L. B. Abbott, James B. Gordon, Emil Kosa, Jr. Editors, Stuart Gilmore, Jack W. Holmes. 132 minutes

Alec McEwen: Pat Boone, *Professor Oliver Lindenbrook:* James Mason, *Carla:* Arlene Dahl, *Jenny:* Diane Baker, *Count Saknussemm:* Thayer David, *Hans:* Peter Ronson, *Groom:* Bob Adler, *Dean:* Alan Napier, *Chancellor:* Frederick Halliday, *Rector:* Alan Caillou, *Goetaborg:* Ivan Triesault, *Groom:* John Epper, *Laird:* Peter Wright, *Housekeeper:*

Journey to the Center of the Earth with Pat Boone, Peter Ronson, James Mason and Arlene Dahl.

Molly Roden, *Icelandic Proprietress:* Edith Evanson, *Shopkeeper,* Owen McGiveney: *Scotch Newsman:* Kendrik Huxham, *Woman News Vendor:* Molly Giessing, *Professor Bayle:* Alex Finlayson, *Paisley:* Ben Wright, *Kirsty:* Mary Brady.

Juarez with Paul Muni.

JUAREZ (1939) WB. Produced by Hal B. Wallis. Directed by William Dieterle. Based on the play *Maximilian and Carlotta* by Franz Werfel and the novel *The Phantom Crown* by Bertita Harding. Associate Producer, Henry Blanke. Screenplay, John Huston, Wolfgang Reinhardt, Aeneas MacKenzie. Art Director, Anton Grot. Music, Erich Wolfgang Korngold. Musical Director, Leo F. Forbstein. Cameraman, Tony Gaudio. Editor, Warren Low. Bette Davis recites an English translation of the Mexican love song "La Paloma." Mexico City sequences filmed at Calabasas, Cal. 132 minutes

Benito Pablo Juarez: Paul Muni, *Empress Carlota von Habsburg:* Bette Davis, *Emperor Maximilian von Habsburg:* Brian Aherne, *Louis Napoleon:* Claude Rains, *Porfirio Diaz:* John Garfield, *Marechal Bazaine:* Donald Crisp, *Empress Eugenie:* Gale Sondergaard, *Alejandro Uradi:* Joseph Calleia, *Colonel Miguel Lopez:* Gilbert Roland, *Miguel Miramon:* Henry O'Neill, *Riva Palacio:* Pedro de Cordoba, *Jose de Montares:* Montagu Love, *Dr. Samuel Basch:* Harry Davenport, *Achille Fould:* Walter Fenner, *Drouyn de Lhuys:* Alex Leftwich, *Countess Battenberg:* Georgia Caine, *Major DuPont:* Robert Warwick, *Senor de Leon:* Gennaro Curci, *Tomás Mejía:* Bill Wilkerson, *Mariano Escobedo:* John Miljan, *John Bigelow:* Hugh Sothern, *Senor Salas:* Fred Malatesta, *Tailor:* Carlos de Valdez, *Carbajal:* Irving Pichel, *Coachman:* Frank Lackteen, *Senator del Valle:* Walter O. Stahl, *Duc de Morny:* Frank Reicher, *Marshall Randon:* Holmes Herbert, *Prince Metternich:* Walter Kingsford, *Baron von Magnus:* Egon Brecher, *Lerdo de Tejada:* Monte Blue, *LeMarc:* Louis Calhern, *Pepe:* Manuel Diaz, *Augustin Iturbide:* Mickey Kuhn, *Josefa Iturbide:* Lillian Nicholson, *Regules:* Noble Johnson, *Negroni:* Martin Garralaga, *Camilo:* Vladimir Sokoloff, *Mr. Harris:* Grant Mitchell, *Mr. Roberts:* Charles Halton.

JUDGMENT AT NUREMBERG (1961) UA. Producer-Director, Stanley Kramer. Associate Producer, Philip Langner. Screenplay, Abby Mann. Music, Ernest Gold. A Roxlom Production. Production Designer, Rudolph Sternad. Cinematographer, Ernest Laszlo. Editor, Fred Knudtson. 178 minutes

Judge Dan Haywood: Spencer Tracy, *Ernst Janning:* Burt Lancaster, *Colonel Tad Lawson:* Richard Widmark, *Mme. Bertholt:* Marlene Dietrich, *Hans Rolfe:* Maximilian Schell, *Irene Hoffman:* Judy Garland, *Rudolph Petersen:* Montgomery Clift, *Captain Byers:* William Shatner, *Senator Burkette:* Edward Binns, *Judge Kenneth Norris:* Kenneth MacKenna, *Emil Hahn:* Werner Klemperer, *General Merrin:* Alan Baxter, *Werner Lammpe:* Torben Meyer, *Judge Curtiss Ives:* Ray Teal, *Freidrich Hofstetter:* Martin Brandt, *Mrs. Halbestadt:* Virginia Christine, *Major Abe Radnitz:* Joseph Bernard, *Halbestadt:* Ben Wright, *Dr. Wieck:* John Wengraf, *Dr. Geuter:* Karl Swenson,

Judgment at Nuremberg with Spencer Tracy and Marlene Dietrich.

Wallner: Howard Caine, *Pohl:* Otto Waldis, *Mrs. Lindnow:* Olga Fabian, *Mrs. Ives:* Sheilia Bromley, *Perkins:* Bernard Kates, *Elsa Scheffler:* Jana Taylor, *Schmidt:* Paul Busch, *Spectator:* Joseph Crehan.

JULIA MISBEHAVES (1948) MGM. Producer, Everett Riskin. Director, Jack Conway. Author, Margery Sharp. Screenplay, William Ludwig, Harry Ruskin, Arthur Wimperis. Adaptation, Gina Kaus, Monckton Hoffe. Art Directors, Cedric Gibbons, Daniel B. Cathcart. Music Score, Adolph Deutsch. Photography, Joseph Ruttenberg. Editor, John Dunning. Song by Jerry Seelen and Hal Borne: "When You're Playing with Fire." 99 minutes

Julia Packett: Greer Garson, *William Packett:* Walter Pidgeon, *Ritchie:* Peter Lawford, *Fred:* Cesar Romero, *Susan Packett:* Elizabeth Taylor, *Mrs. Packett:* Lucile Watson, *Col. Willowbrook:* Nigel Bruce, *Mrs. Gennochio:* Mary Boland, *Bennie Hawkins:* Reginald Owen, *Hobson:* Ian Wolfe, *Daisy:* Phyllis Morris, *Jamie:* Edmond Breon, *Pepito:* Fritz Feld, *Gabby:* Marcelle Corday, *Louise:* Veda Ann Borg, *Vicar:* Aubrey Mather, *Lord Pennystone:* Henry Stephenson, *Lady Pennystone:* Winifred Harris, *Woman in Pawn Shop:* Elspeth Dudgeon, *Pawn Shop Clerk:* Stanley Fraser, *Bill Collector:* James Finlayson, *Postman:* Victor Wood, *Piano Player in Pub:* Herbert Wyndham, *Waiter in Pub:* Sid D'Albrook, *Drunk:* Jimmy Aubrey, *French Messenger:* Roland Dupre, *Bellhop:* Alex Goudavich, *Stage Doorman:* Andre Charlot, *The Head:* Joanee Wayne, *Train Official:* Mitchell Lewis, *Mannequins:* Joi Lansing, Lola Albright, *Commissar:* Torben Meyer.

Julia Misbehaves with Walter Pidgeon, Greer Garson and Elizabeth Taylor.

Julius Caesar with Louis Calhern and James Mason.

JULIUS CAESAR (1953) MGM. Producer, John Houseman. Director, Joseph Mankiewicz. Based on the play by William Shakespeare. Art Directors, Cedric Gibbons, Edward Carfagno. Cinematographer, Joseph Ruttenberg. Editor, John Dunning. 120 minutes

Mark Antony: Marlon Brando, *Brutus:* James Mason, *Cassius:* John Gielgud, *Julius Caesar:* Louis Calhern, *Casca:* Edmond O'Brien, *Calpurnia:* Greer Garson, *Portia:* Deborah Kerr, *Marullus:* George MacCready, *Flavius:* Michael Pate, *Soothsayer:* Richard Hale, *Cicero:* Alan Napier, *Decius Brutus:* John Hoyt, *Metellus Cimber:* Tom Powers, *Cinna:* William Cottrell, *Trebonius:* Jack Raine, *Casius Ligarius:* Ian Wolfe, *Lucius:* John Hardy, *Artemidorus:* Morgan Farley, *Antony's Servant:* Bill Phipps, *Octavius Caesar:* Douglas Watson, *Lepidus:* Douglass Dumbrille, *Lucillus:* Rhys Williams, *Pindarus:* Michael Ansara, *Messala:* Dayton Lummis, *Volumnius:* Thomas Browne Henry, *Strato:* Edmund Purdom, *Citizens of Rome:* Paul Guilfoyle, John Doucette, Lawrence Dobkin, *Caesar's Servant:* Chester Stratton, *Publius:* Lumsden Hare, *Popilius Lena:* Victor Perry, *Officer:* Michael Tolan, *Varro:* John Lupton, *Claudius:* Preston Hanson, *Titinius:* John Parrish, *Clitus:* Joe Waring, *Dardanius:* Stephen Roberts, *Cinna, Poet:* O. Z. Whitehead, *Cobbler:* Ned Glass.

KEEPER OF THE FLAME (1942) MGM. Produced by Victor Saville. Associate Producer, Leon Gordon. Directed by George Cukor. Based on the novel by I. A. R. Wylie. Screenplay, Donald Ogden Stewart. Art Director, Cedric Gibbons. Score, Bronislau Kaper. Camera, William Daniels. Editor, James E. Newcom. 100 minutes

Steven O'Malley: Spencer Tracy, *Christine Forrest:* Katharine Hepburn, *Clive Spencer:* Richard Whorf, *Mrs. Forrest:* Margaret Wycherly, *Mr. Arbuthnot:* Donald Meek, *Freddie Ridges:* Horace (Stephen) McNally, *Jane Harding:* Audrey Christie, *Dr. Fielding:* Frank Craven, *Geoffrey Midford:* Forrest Tucker, *Orion:* Percy Kilbride, *Jason Rickards:* Howard da Silva, *Jeb Rickards:* Darryl Hickman, *Piggot:* William Newell, *John:* Rex Evans, *Anna:* Blanche Yurka, *Janet:*

Keeper of the Flame with Spencer Tracy, Darryl Hickman and Katharine Hepburn.

Mary McLeod, *William:* Clifford Brooke, *Ambassador:* Craufurd Kent, *Messenger Boy:* Mickey Martin, *Reporters:* Manart Kippen, Donald Gallaher, Cliff Danielson, *Men:* Major Sam Harris, Art Howard, Harold Miller, *Pete:* Jay Ward, *Susan:* Rita Quigley, *Auctioneer:* Dick Elliott, *Lawyer:* Edward McWade, *Boy Reporter:* Irvin Lee, *Girls:* Diana Dill (Diana Douglas), Gloria Tucker, *Minister's Voice:* Dr. Charles Frederick Lindsley, *Tim:* Robert Pittard, *Gardener:* Louis Mason.

Key Largo with Humphrey Bogart, Claire Trevor and Lauren Bacall.

KEY LARGO (1948) WB. Producer, Jerry Wald. Director, John Huston. Based on the play by Maxwell Anderson. Screenplay, Richard Brooks, John Huston. Art Director, Leo K. Kuter. Music, Max Steiner. Photography, Karl Freund. Editor, Rudi Fehr. Song by Howard Dietz and Ralph Rainger: "Moanin' Low." 101 minutes

Frank McCloud: Humphrey Bogart, *Johnny Rocco:* Edward G. Robinson, *Nora Temple:* Lauren Bacall, *James Temple:* Lionel Barrymore, *Gaye:* Claire Trevor, *Curley:* Thomas Gomez, *Toots:* Harry Lewis, *Deputy Sawyer:* John Rodney, *Ziggy:* Marc Lawrence, *Angel:* Dan Seymour, *Ben Wade:* Monte Blue, *Osceola Brothers:* Jay Silverheels, Rodric Redwing, *Bus Driver:* Joe P. Smith, *Skipper:* Albert Marin, *Man:* Pat Flaherty, *Ziggy's Henchmen:* Jerry Jerome, John Phillips, Lute Crockett, *Old Indian Woman:* Felipa Gomez.

KEYS OF THE KINGDOM (1944) 20th. Producer, Joseph L. Mankiewicz. Director, John M. Stahl. Based on the novel by A. J. Cronin. Screenplay, Joseph L. Mankiewicz, Nunnally Johnson. Musical Score, Alfred Newman. Art Directors, James Basevi, William Darling. Cameraman, Arthur Miller. Special Effects, Fred Sersen. Editor, James B. Clark. 137 minutes

The Keys of the Kingdom with Arthur Shields, Vincent Price and Gregory Peck.

Father Francis Chisholm: Gregory Peck, *Dr. Willie Tullock:* Thomas Mitchell, *Rev. Angus Mealy:* Vincent Price, *Mother Maria Veronica:* Rose Stradner, *Francis as a boy:* Roddy McDowall, *Rev. Hamish MacNabb:* Edmund Gwenn, *Monsignor Sleeth:* Sir Cedric Hardwicke, *Nora as a child:* Peggy Ann Garner, *Nora:* Jane Ball, *Dr. Wilbur Fiske:* James Gleason, *Agnes Fiske:* Anne Revere, *Lisbeth Chisholm:* Ruth Nelson, *Joseph:* Benson Fong, *Mr. Chia:* Leonard Strong, *Mr. Pao:* Philip Ahn, *Father Tarrant:* Arthur Shields, *Aunt Polly:* Edith Barrett, *Sister Martha:* Sara Allgood, *Lieutenant Shon:* Richard Loo, *Sister Clotilde:* Ruth Ford, *Father Craig:* Kevin O'Shea, *Hosannah Wang:* H. T. Tsiang, *Philomena Wang:* Si-Lan Chen, *Anna:* Eunice Soo Hoo, *Alex Chisholm:* Dennis Hoey, *Bandit Captain:* Abner Biberman, *Ned Bannon:* J. Anthony Hughes, *Andrew:* George Nokes, *Chia-Yu:* Hayward Soo Hoo, *Taoist Priest:* James Leong, *Chinese Physician:* Moy Ming, *Father Chou:* Frank Eng, *Grandmother:* Oie Chan, *Captain:* Beal Wong, *Joshua:* Eugene Louie, *Sister Mercy Mary:* Ruth Clifford.

THE KID FROM BROOKLYN (1946) RKO. Producer, Samuel Goldwyn. Director, Norman Z. McLeod. Color by Technicolor. Based on a play by Lynn Root and Harry Clork (*The Milky Way*). Screenplay, Grover Jones, Frank Butler, Richard Connell. Adaptation, Don Hartman, Melville Shavelson. Art Directors, Peggy Ferguson, Stewart Chaney. Musical Director, Carmen Dragon. Musical Supervisor, Louis Forbes. Cameraman, Gregg Toland. Editor, Daniel Mandell. Songs: "I Love an Old-Fashioned Song," "You're the Cause of It All," "Hey, What's Your Name?", "Josie" and "Sunflower Song" by Sammy Cahn and Jule Styne. "Pavlova" by Sylvia Fine. Dorothy Ellers sings for Vera-Ellen, Betty Russell for Virginia Mayo. Remake of *The Milky Way* (Paramount, 1936). 114 minutes

The Kid From Brooklyn with Ralph Dunn, Danny Kaye, Clarence Kolb and Billy Nelson.

Burleigh Sullivan: Danny Kaye, *Polly Pringle:* Virginia Mayo, *Susie Sullivan:* Vera-Ellen, *Speed McFarlane:* Steve Cochran, *Ann Westley:* Eve Arden, *Gabby Sloan:* Walter Abel, *Spider Schultz:* Lionel Stander, *Mrs. E. Winthrop LeMoyne:* Fay Bainter, *Mr. Austin:* Clarence Kolb, *Photographer:* Victor Cutler, *Willard:* Charles Cane, *Fight Announcer:* Jerome Cowan, *Radio Announcer:* Don Wilson, *Radio Announcer:* Knox Manning, *Matron:* Kay Thompson, *Master of Ceremonies:* Johnny Downs, *Guests:* Torben Meyer, Jack Norton, William Forrest, *Seconds:* Ralph Dunn, Billy Nelson, *The Goldwyn Girls:* Karen X. Gaylord, Ruth Valmy, Shirley Ballard, Virginia Belmont, Betty Cargyle, Jean Cronin, Vonne Lester, Diana Mumby, Mary Simpson, Virginia Thorpe, Tyra Vaughn, Kismi Stefan, Betty Alexander, Martha Montgomery, Joyce MacKenzie, Helen Kimball, Donna Hamilton, Jan Bryant, *Specialty Dancer in "What's Your Name":* Jimmy Kelly, *Specialty Dancers in "Old Fashioned":* Eddie Cutler, Harvey Karels, Al Ruiz, *Technical Man and Boxing Instructor:* John Indrisano.

THE KID FROM SPAIN (1932) UA. Produced by Samuel Goldwyn. Directed by Leo McCarey. Dances by Busby Berkeley. Story and

The Kid From Spain with John Miljan, Eddie Cantor and J. Carroll Naish.

Screenplay, William Anthony McGuire, Bert Kalmar, Harry Ruby. Photography, Gregg Toland. Editor, Stuart Heisler. Sound, Vinton Vernon. Songs by Bert Kalmar and Harry Ruby: "Look What You've Done," "In the Moonlight," and "What a Perfect Combination" by Kalmar, Ruby and Harry Akst. 90 minutes

Eddie Williams: Eddie Cantor, *Rosalie:* Lyda Roberti, *Ricardo:* Robert Young, *Anita Gomez:* Ruth Hall, *Pancho:* John Miljan, *Alonza Gomez:* Noah Beery, *Pedro:* J. Carroll Naish, *Crawford:* Robert Emmett O'Connor, *Jose:* Stanley Fields, *Gonzales, Border Guard:* Paul Porcasi, *Dalmores:* Julian Rivero, *Martha Oliver:* Theresa Maxwell Conover, *The Dean:* Walter Walker, *Red:* Ben Hendricks, Jr., *The American Matador (Himself):* Sidney Franklin, *Goldwyn Girls:* Betty Grable, Paulette Goddard, Toby Wing, *Negro Bull Handler:* Edgar Connor, *Robber:* Leo Willis, *Traffic Cop:* Harry Gribbon, *Patron:* Eddie Foster, *Man on Line:* Harry C. Bradley.

THE KILLERS (1946) Univ. Producer, Mark Hellinger. Director, Robert Siodmak. From the short story by Ernest Hemingway. Screenplay by Anthony Veiller. Music by Miklos Rosza. Film Editor, Arthur Hilton. Photographed by Woody Bredell. Film debuts of Burt Lancaster, 32, and William Conrad. Song, "The More I Know of Love," music by Miklos Rosza, lyrics by Jack Brooks. Art directors, Jack Otterson and Martin Obzina. Remade by Universal, 1964. 105 minutes

Jim Reardon: Edmond O'Brien, *Kitty Collins:* Ava Gardner, *Big Jim Colfax:* Albert Dekker, *Lt. Sam Lubinsky:* Sam Levene, *Jake:* John Miljan, *Lilly:* Virginia Christine, *Charleston:* Vince Barnett, *Swede (Pete Lunn/Ole Anderson):* Burt Lancaster, *Packy Robinson:* Charles D. Brown, *Kenyon:* Donald MacBride, *Nick Adams:* Phil Brown, *Al:* Charles McGraw, *Max:* William Conrad, *Queenie:* Queenie Smith, *Joe:* Garry Owen, *George:* Harry Hayden, *Sam:* Bill Walker, *Dum Dum:* Jack Lambert, *Blinky:* Jeff Corey, *Charlie:* Wally Scott, *Ginny:* Gabrielle Windsor, *Man:* Rex Dale, *Paymaster:* Harry Brown, *Nurse:* Beatrice Roberts, *Police Chief:* Howard Freeman, *Plunther:* John Berkes, *Doctor:* John Sheehan, *Farmer Brown:* Charles

The Killers with Ava Gardner and Burt Lancaster.

Middleton, *Customer:* Al Hill, *Lou Tingle:* Noel Cravat, *Minister:* Rev. Neal Dodd, *Doctor:* George Anderson, *Mrs. Hirsch:* Vera Lewis, *Policeman:* Howard Negley, *Waiter:* Milton Wallace, *Stella:* Ann Staunton, *Motorman:* William Ruhl, *Housekeeper:* Therese Lyon, *Policeman:* Perc Launders, *Gimp:* Ernie Adams, *Police Driver:* Jack Cheatham, *Conductor:* Ethan Laidlaw, *Policeman:* Geoffrey Ingham, *Pete:* Michael Hale, *Bartender:* Wally Rose, *Waiter:* Nolan Leary, John Trebach, *Assistant Paymaster:* Audley Anderson, *Timekeeper:* Mike Donovan.

KIM (1950) MGM. Produced by Leon Gordon. Directed by Victor Saville. Color by Technicolor. Based on the novel by Rudyard Kipling. Screenplay, Leon Gordon, Helen Deutsch, and Richard Schayer. Art Directors, Cedric Gibbons and Hans Peters. Music, André Previn. Photography, William Skall. Editor, George Boemler. Filmed in India. 113 minutes

Mahbub Ali, the Red Beard: Errol Flynn, *Kim:* Dean Stockwell, *Lama:* Paul Lukas, *Colonel Creighton:* Robert Douglas, *Emissary:* Thomas Gomez, *Hurree Chunder:* Cecil Kellaway, *Lurgan Sahib:* Arnold Moss, *Father Victor:* Reginald Owen, *Laluli:* Laurette Luez, *Hassan Bey:* Richard Hale, *The Russians:* Roman Toporow, Ivan Triesault, *Major Ainsley:* Hayden Rorke, *Dr. Bronson:* Walter Kingsford, *Wanna:* Henry Mirelez, *Shadow:* Frank Lackteen, *Abul:* Frank Richards, *Conspirators:* Henry Corden, Peter Mamakos, *Haiku:* Donna Martell, *Foster Mother:* Jeanette Nolan, *Servant:* Rod Redwing, *Guard:* Michael Ansara, *Policeman:* Lal Chand Mehra, *Water Carrier:* Stanley Price, *Woman with Baby:* Movita Castenada, *British General:* Wallis Clark, *Guard:* Lou Krugman, *Old Maharanee:* Adeline DeWalt Reynolds, *Letter Writer:* Francis McDonald, *Biggs:* Danny Rees, *Thorpe:* Robin Camp, *Master:* Keith McConnell, *Miss Manners:* Betty Daniels, *Gerald:* Wilson Wood, *Mr. Fairlee:* Olaf Hytten, *Car Driver:* Bobby Barber, *Farmer:* Mitchell Lewis.

Kim with Paul Lukas and Dean Stockwell.

THE KING AND I (1956) 20th. Producer, Charles Brackett. Director, Walter Lang. CinemaScope, De Luxe Color. From Margaret Landon's book *Anna and the King of Siam.* Screenplay, Ernest Lehman. Book and Lyrics, Oscar Hammerstein II. Music, Richard Rodgers. Music supervised and conducted by Alfred Newman. Orchestration, Edward B. Powell, Gus Levene, Bernard Mayers, Robert Russell Bennett. Art Directors, Lyle R. Wheeler, John De Cuir. Cinematographer, Leon Shamroy. Editor, Robert Simpson. Choreography by Jerome Robbins. Marni Nixon sings for Deborah Kerr. Songs by Richard Rodgers and Oscar Hammerstein II: "The Small House of Uncle Thomas," "March of the Siamese Children," "Getting to Know You," "Whistle a Happy Tune," "Hello, Young Lovers," "I Have Dreamed," "Shall We Dance?" "Something Wonderful," "Is a Puzzlement," "Shall I Tell You What I Think of You?" "We Kiss in a Shadow." Remake of 20th's *Anna and the King of Siam* (1946). 133 minutes

394

The King and I with Deborah Kerr and Yul Brynner.

Anna: Deborah Kerr, *The King:* Yul Brynner, *Tuptim:* Rita Moreno, *Kralahome:* Martin Benson, *Lady Thiang:* Terry Saunders, *Louis Leonowens:* Rex Thompson, *Lun Tha:* Carlos Rivas, *Prince Chulalongkorn:* Patrick Adiarte, *British Ambassador:* Alan Mowbray, *Ramsey:* Geoffrey Toone, *Eliza (in Ballet):* Yuriko, *Simon Legree (in Ballet):* Marion Jim, *Keeper of the Dogs:* Robert Banas, *Uncle Thomas (in Ballet):* Dusty Worrall, *Specialty Dancer:* Gemze de Lappe, *Twins:* Thomas Bonilla, Dennis Bonilla, *Angel (in Ballet):* Michiki Iseri, *Ship's Captain:* Charles Irwin, *Interpreter:* Leonard Strong, *Whipping Guards:* Fuji, Weaver Levy, *High Priest:* William Yip, *Messenger:* Eddie Luke, *Princess Ying Yoowalak:* Jocelyn Lew.

KING KONG (1933) RKO. Executive Producer, David O. Selznick. Directed by Merian C. Cooper and Ernest B. Schoedsack. Story, Edgar Wallace and Merian C. Cooper. Adaptation, James Creelman and Ruth Rose. Chief Technician, Willis O'Brien. Editor, Ted Cheeseman. Sound, E. A. Wolcott. Music, Max Steiner. Idea created by Merian C. Cooper. Technical Staff, E. B. Gibson, Marcel Delgado, Fred Reefe, Orville Goldner, Carol Shepphird. Art Directors, Carroll Clark and Al Herman. Photography, Edward Linden, Verne Walker, J. O. Taylor. Sound Effects, Murray Spivak. Production Assistants, Archie S. Marshek and Walter Daniels. Art Technicians, Mario Larrinaga and Byron L. Crabbe. Sets also used in RKO's *The Most Dangerous Game*, 1932. 100 minutes

Ann Redman: Fay Wray, *Carl Denham:* Robert Armstrong, *John Driscoll:* Bruce Cabot, *Captain Englehorn:* Frank Reicher, *Weston:* Sam Hardy, *Native Chief:* Noble Johnson, *Briggs, Second Mate:* James Flavin, *Witch King:* Steve Clemento, *Lumpy:* Victor Long, *Mate:* Ethan Laidlaw, *Sailor:* Dick Curtis, *Sailor:* Charlie Sullivan, *Theater Patron:* Vera Lewis, *Theater Patron:* LeRoy Mason, *Apple Vendor:* Paul Porcasi, *Reporters:* Lynton Brent, Frank Mills, and King Kong, the Eighth Wonder of the World.

King Kong with Fay Wray.

King of Kings with Jeffrey Hunter and Siobhan McKenna.

KING OF KINGS (1961) MGM. Producer, Samuel Bronston. Director, Nicholas Ray. Screenplay, Philip Yordan. Music, Miklos Rozsa. Costumes, George Wakhevitch. Filmed in Technirama 70 and Technicolor. Associate Producers, Alan Brown, Jaime Prades. Cinematographers, Franz F. Planer, Milton Krasner, Manuel Berenguer. Special Photographic Effects, Lee LeBlanc. Editors, Harold Kress, Renee Lichtig. 168 minutes

Jesus Christ: Jeffrey Hunter, *Mary:* Siobhan McKenna, *Pontius Pilate:* Hurd Hatfield, *Lucius:* Ron Randell, *Claudia:* Viveca Lindfors, *Herodias:* Rita Gam, *Mary Magdalene:* Carmen Sevilla, *Salome:* Brigid Bazlen, *Barabbas:* Harry Guardino, *Judas:* Rip Torn, *Herod Antipas:* Frank Thring, *Caiphas:* Guy Rolfe, *Nicodemus:* Maurice Marsac, *Herod:* Gregoire Aslan, *Peter:* Royal Dano, *Balthazar:* Edric Connor, *John The Baptist:* Robert Ryan, *Camel Driver:* George Coulouris, *General Pompey:* Conrado San Martin, *Joseph:* Gerard Tichy, *Young John:* Jose Antonio, *Good Thief:* Luis Prendes, *Burly Man:* David Davies, *Caspar:* Jose Nicto, *Matthew:* Ruben Rojo, *Madman:* Fernando Sancho, *Thomas:* Michael Wager, *Joseph of Arimathea:* Felix de Powes, *Melchior:* Adriano Rimoldi, *Bad Thief:* Barry Keegan, *Simon of Cyrene:* Rafael Luis Calvo, *Andrew:* Tino Barrero, *Blind Man:* Fransico Moran.

KING SOLOMON'S MINES (1950) MGM. Produced by Sam Zimbalist. Directed by Compton Bennett and Andrew Marton. Color by Technicolor. Based on the novel by H. Rider Haggard. Screenplay, Helen Deutsch. Art Directors, Cedric Gibbons and Conrad A. Nervig. Photography, Robert Surtees. Editors, Ralph E. Winters and Conrad A. Nervig. Produced in Africa: Belgian Congo, Tanganyika, Uganda, Kenya. Songs by Eric Maschwitz and Mischa Spoliansky: "Climbing Up, Climbing Up" and "Ho! Ho!" Other versions: *King Solomon's Mines* (Gaumont-British, 1937), *Watusi* (MGM, 1959). 102 minutes

Elizabeth Curtis: Deborah Kerr, *Allan Quartermain:* Stewart Granger, *John Goode:* Richard Carlson, *Van Brun:* Hugo Haas, *Eric Masters:* Lowell Gilmore, *Khiva:* Kimursi, *Umbopa:* Siriaque, *Chief Gagool:* Sekaryongo, *King Twala:* Baziga, *Chief Bilu:* Corp. Munto Anampio, *Kafa:* Gutare, *Blue Star:* Ivargwema, *Black Circle:* Benempinga, *Austin:* John Banner, *Traum:* Henry Rowland, *Double for "Umbopa":* Gutare.

King Solomon's Mines with Stewart Granger, Deborah Kerr and Richard Carlson.

Kings Row with Ronald Reagan and Ann Sheridan.

KINGS ROW (1941) WB. Producer, Hal B. Wallis. Associate Producer, David Lewis. Director, Sam Wood. Based on the novel by Henry Bellamann. Screenplay by Casey Robinson. Film Editor, Ralph Dawson. Photographed by James Wong Howe. Music by Erich Wolfgang Korngold. Art Director, Carl Jules Weyl. 127 minutes

Randy Monoghan: Ann Sheridan, *Parris Mitchell:* Robert Cummings, *Drake McHugh:* Ronald Reagan, *Cassandra Tower:* Betty Field, *Dr. Henry Gordon:* Charles Coburn, *Dr. Alexander Tower:* Claude Rains, *Mrs. Harriet Gordon:* Judith Anderson, *Louise Gordon:* Nancy Coleman, *Elise Sandor:* Karen Verne, *Madame Von Eln:* Maria Ouspenskaya, *Colonel Skeffington:* Harry Davenport, *Pa Monoghan:* Ernest Cossart, *Tom Monoghan:* Pat Moriarty, *Ann, the Maid:* Ilka Gruning, *Sam Winters:* Minor Watson, *Dr. Berdoff:* Ludwig Stossel, *Mr. Sandor:* Erwin Kalser, *Dr. Candell:* Egon Brecher, *Randy, as child:* Ann Todd, *Parris, as child:* Scotty Beckett, *Drake, as child:* Douglas Croft, *Cassandra, as child:* Mary Thomas, *Louise, as child:* Joan Du Valle, *Benny Singer:* Danny Jackson, *Willie:* Henry Blair, *Aunt Mamie:* Leah Baird, *Mrs. Tower:* Eden Gray, *Poppy Ross:* Julie Warren, *Ginny Ross:* Mary Scott, *Esther:* Bertha Powell, *Deputy Constable:* Walter Baldwin, *Conductor:* Frank Mayo, *Freight Conductor:* Jack Mower, *Patterson Lawes:* Thomas W. Ross, *Teller:* Frank Milan, *Livery Stable Keeper:* Hank Mann, *Bill Hockinson:* Fred Kelsey, *Arnold Kelly:* Herbert Heywood, *Harley Davis:* Emory Parnell, *Nurse:* Elizabeth Valentine, *Porter:* Ludwig Hardt, *Secretary:* Hermine Sterler, *Gordons' Maid:* Hattie Noel.

KITTY (1945) Par. Produced by Karl Tunberg. Directed by Mitchell Leisen. Based on the novel by Rosamond Marshall. Screenplay, Darrell Ware and Karl Tunberg. Music, Victor Young. Art Directors, Hans Dreier and Walter Tyler. Dance Director, Billy Daniels. Process Photography, Farciot Edouart. Special Effects, Gordon Jennings. Photography, Daniel L. Fapp. Editor, Alma Macrorie. 103 minutes

Kitty with Paulette Goddard and Eric Blore.

Kitty: Paulette Goddard, *Sir Hugh Marcy:* Ray Milland, *Brett Hardwood, Earl of Carstairs:* Patric Knowles, *Duke of Malmunster:* Reginald Owen, *Thomas Gainsborough:* Cecil Kellaway, *Lady Susan Dowitt:* Constance Collier, *Jonathan Selby:* Dennis Hoey, *Old Meg:* Sara Allgood, *Dobson:* Eric Blore, *Sir Joshua Reynolds:* Gordon Richards, *The Prince of Wales:* Michael Dyne, *Earl of Campton:* Edgar Norton, *Elaine Carlisle:* Patricia Cameron, *Doctor Holt:* Percival Vivian, *Nanny:* Mary Gordon, *Nullens:* Anita Bolster, *Lil:* Heather Wilde, *Majordomo:* Charles Coleman, *Molly:* Mae Clarke, *Madame Aurelie:* Ann Codee, *Philip:* Douglas Walton, *McNab:* Alec Craig, *Sir Harbord Harbord:* Edward Cooper, *Duchess of Gloucester:* Anne Curson, *Sir Joshua's Friend:* Craufurd Kent, *Mr. Thickness:* Colin Kenny, *Mrs. Thickness:* Hilda Plowright, *Barrows:* Charles Irwin, *Duke's Maid:* Jean Ransome, *Duke's Maid:* Mary MacLaren, *Rupert:* George Porter, *Undertaker:* Paul Scardon, *Duchess:* Ruth St. Denis, *Chaplain:* Evan Thomas, *Mr. Sheridan:* Leslie Denison, *Mrs. Sheridan:* Mary McLeod, *Cripplegate:* Anthony Marsh, *Sir Geoffrey Tennant:* Sydney Lawford, *"All Hot" Hawker:* Cyril Delevanti, *Prison Guard:* Gibson Gowland, *Earl of Barrymore:* John Deauville, *Colonel St. Leger:* Byron Poindexter.

KITTY FOYLE (1940) RKO. Produced by Harry E. Edington and David Hempstead. Directed by Sam Wood. From the novel by Christopher Morley. Screenplay, Dalton Trumbo. Additional Dialogue, Donald Ogden Stewart. Art Director, Van Nest Polglase. Music, Roy Webb. Photography, Robert De Grasse. Editor, Henry Berman. Special Effects, Vernon L. Walker. Art Director's Associate, Mark-Lee Kirk. Gowns, Renie. Sets, Darrell Silvera. Sound, John L. Cass. Assistant Director, Argyle Nelson. 108 minutes

Kitty Foyle with Ginger Rogers, Dennis Morgan, Eduardo Ciannelli and Gino Corrado.

Kitty Foyle: Ginger Rogers, *Wyn Strafford:* Dennis Morgan, *Mark:* James Craig, *Giono:* Eduardo Ciannelli, *Pop:* Ernest Cossart, *Mrs. Strafford:* Gladys Cooper, *Delphine Detaille:* Odette Myrtil, *Pat:* Mary Treen, *Molly:* Katharine Stevens, *Mr. Kennett:* Walter Kingsford, *Grandmother:* Cecil Cunningham, *Aunt Jessica:* Nella Walker, *Uncle Edgar:* Edward Fielding, *Wyn's Wife:* Kay Linaker, *Wyn's Boy:* Richard Nichols, *Customer:* Florence Bates, *Girl in Prologue:* Heather Angel, *Boy in Prologue:* Tyler Brooke, *Negro Woman:* Hattie Noel, *Parry:* Frank Milan, *Bill:* Charles Quigley, *Miss Bala:* Harriett Brandon, *Butler:* Howard Entwistle, *Neway:* Billy Elmer, *Trumpeter:* Walter Sande, *Saxaphonist:* Ray Teal, *Drummer:* Joey Ray, *Violinist-Leader:* Mel Ruick, *Pianist:* Doodles Weaver, *Hotel Clerk:* Theodore Von Eltz, *Flower Man:* Max Davidson, *Doctor:* Charles Miller, *Charwoman:* Mary Gordon, *Prim Girl:* Fay Helm, *Girl in Elevator:* Helen Lynd, *Charwoman:* Dorothy Vaughan, *Jane:* Mimi Doyle, *Nurse:* Hilda Plowright, *Father:* Spencer Charters, *Guest:* Gino Corrado.

KNOCK ON WOOD (1954) Par. Produced, directed, and written by Norman Panama and Melvin Frank. Color by Technicolor. Assistant

Knock on Wood with Danny Kaye and Mai Zetterling.

Director, Francisco Day. Dances and musical numbers staged by Michael Kidd. Art Directors, Hal Pereira and Henry Bumstead. Cinematography, Daniel Fapp. Editor, Alma Macrorie. Songs by Sylvia Fine. 103 minutes

Jerry: Danny Kaye, *Ilse Nordstrom:* Mai Zetterling, *Langston:* Torin Thatcher, *Marty Brown:* David Burns, *Gromek:* Leon Askin, *Papinek:* Abner Biberman, *Car Salesman:* Gavin Gordon, *Brodnik:* Otto Waldis, *Dr. Kreuger:* Steven Geray, *Princess:* Diana Adams, *Mama Morgan:* Patricia Denise, *Audrey:* Virginia Huston, *Customer:* Rex Evans, *First Trenchcoat Man:* Carl Milletaire, *Second Trenchcoat Man:* Henry Brandon, *Chief Inspector Wilton:* Paul England, *Langston's Secretary:* Johnstone White, *Inspector Cranford:* Lewis Martin, *Brutchik:* Philip Van Zandt, *English Woman:* Winifred Harris, *Old Man:* Kenneth Hunter, *Little Man:* Noel Drayton, *Irishman:* Phil Tully, *French Stage Manager:* Donald Lawton, *Airline Hostess:* Genevieve Aumont, *Hotel Clerk:* Tony Christian, *Bobby:* John Alderson, *Doorman:* Eric Wilton, *Police Officer:* Alphonse Martell, *French Diplomat:* Larry Arnold, *Woman in Shower:* Helen Dickson, *Zelda:* Helen Chapman, *Danny, Jr.:* Christopher Olsen.

THE LADY EVE (1941) Par. Produced by Paul Jones. Directed by Preston Sturges. Based on a story by Monckton Hoffe. Screenplay, Preston Sturges. Photography, Victor Milner. Editor, Stuart Gilmore. Remade as *The Birds and the Bees* (Paramount, 1956). 97 minutes

The Lady Eve with Charles Coburn, Barbara Stanwyck and Henry Fonda.

Jean: Barbara Stanwyck, *Charles:* Henry Fonda, *"Colonel" Harrington:* Charles Coburn, *Mr. Pike:* Eugene Pallette, *Muggsy:* William Demarest, *Sir Alfred McGlennan Keith:* Eric Blore, *Gerald:* Melville Cooper, *Martha:* Martha O'Driscoll, *Mrs. Pike:* Janet Beecher, *Burrows:* Robert Greig, *Gertrude:* Dora Clemant, *Pike's Chef:* Luis Alberni, *Stewards:* Jimmy Conlin, Alan Bridge, Victor Potel, *Bartender at Party:* Frank C. Moran, *Social Secretary:* Pauline Drake, *Piano Tuner:* Harry Rosenthal, *Man with Potted Palm:* Abdullah Abbas, *Sir Alfred's Servant:* Norman Ainsley, *Lawyers:* Julius Tannen, J. W. Johnston, Ray Flynn, Harry A. Bailey, Arthur Hoyt, *Sparky:* Wally Walker, *Purser:* Torben Meyer, *Bank Manager:* Robert Warwick, *Mac:* Ambrose Barker, *Professor Jones:* Reginald Sheffield, *Sweetie:* Jean Phillips, *Bartender:* Pat West, *Daughters on Boat:* Ella Neal, Wanda McKay, Marcelle Christopher, *Young Man on Boat:* John Hartley, *Husbands on Boat:* Cyril Ring, Sam Ash, Robert Dudley.

LADY FOR A DAY (1933) Col. Directed by Frank Capra. Based on the story "Madame La Gimp" by Damon Runyon. Adaptation, Robert Riskin. Art Director, Stephen Goosson. Costumes, Robert Kalloch. Assistant Director, Charles C. Coleman. Photography, Joseph Walker. Editor, Gene Havlick. Sound, E. L. Bernds. A blind man, Dad Mills, portrays a blind man in the film. Remade as *Pocketful of Miracles* (United Artists, 1961). 95 minutes

Dave the Dude: Warren William, *Apple Annie:* May Robson, *Judge Blake:* Guy Kibbee, *Missouri Martin:* Glenda Farrell, *Happy:* Ned Sparks, *Louise:* Jean Parker, *Count Romero:* Walter Connolly, *Shakespeare:* Nat Pendleton, *Inspector:* Robert Emmett O'Connor, *Commissioner:* Wallis Clark, *Governor:* Hobart Bosworth, *Blind Man:* Dad Mills, *Carlos:* Barry Norton.

Lady for a Day with Hobart Bosworth, Jean Parker, May Robson, Barry Norton, Walter Connolly, Samuel S. Hinds.

LADY IN THE DARK (1944) Par. Associate Producer, Richard Blumenthal. Directed by Mitchell Leisen. Color by Technicolor. Based on the play by Moss Hart with music by Kurt Weill and lyrics by Ira Gershwin. Screenplay, Frances Goodrich and Albert Hackett. Music scored and directed by Robert Emmett Dolan. Orchestral Arrangements, Robert Russell Bennett. Art Director, Hans Dreier. Photography, Ray Rennahan. Editor, Alma Macrorie. Special Effects, Gordon Jennings. Songs: "One Life to Live," "Girl of the Moment," "It Looks Like Liza," "This Is New," "My Ship," and "Jenny" by Ira Gershwin and Kurt Weill; "Artist's Waltz" by Robert Emmett Dolan; "Suddenly It's Spring" by Johnny Burke and Jimmy Van Heusen; and "Dream Lover" by Clifford Grey and Victor Schertzinger. 100 minutes

Liza Elliott: Ginger Rogers, *Charley Johnson:* Ray Milland, *Kendall Nesbitt:* Warner Baxter, *Randy Curtis:* Jon Hall, *Doctor Brooks:* Barry Sullivan, *Russell Paxton:* Mischa Auer, *Allison DuBois:* Phyllis Brooks, *Maggie Grant:* Mary Phillips, *Doctor Carlton:* Edward Fielding, *Adams:* Don Loper, *Miss Parker:* Mary Parker, *Miss Foster:*

Lady in the Dark with Ray Milland and Ginger Rogers.

Catherine Craig, *Martha:* Marietta Canty, *Miss Edwards:* Virginia Farmer, *Miss Bowers:* Fay Helm, *Barbara:* Gail Russell, *Miss Stevens:* Marian Hall, *Liza's Mother:* Kay Linaker, *Liza's Father:* Harvey Stephens, *Office Boy:* Billy Daniels, *Miss Sullivan:* Georgia Backus, *Ben:* Rand Brooks, *Clown:* Pepito Perez, *Barbara's Boy Friend:* Charles Smith, *Librarian:* Mary MacLaren, *Jack Goddard:* Paul McVey, *Specialty Dancers:* Paul Pierce, George Mayon, *Men:* Tristram Coffin, Dennis Moore, Jack Luden, *Captain of Waiters:* George Calliga, *Girl with Randy:* Frances Robinson, *Miss Shawn:* Jan Buckingham, *Photographer:* Jack Mulhall, *Miss Barr:* Hillary Brooke, *Dancer:* Miriam Franklin, *Autograph Hunter:* Dorothy Granger, *Butler:* Charles Coleman, *Pianist:* Lester Sharpe, *Charley as a boy:* Bobby Beers, *Barbara at 7:* Phyllis M. Brooks, *Liza at 5 and 7:* Marjean Neville, *David:* Charles Bates.

LASSIE COME HOME (1943) MGM. Producer, Samuel Marx. Director, Fred M. Wilcox. From the novel by Eric Knight. Screenplay, Hugo Butler. Musical Score, Daniele Amfitheatrof. Art Director, Cedric Gibbons. Cameraman, Leonard Smith. Special Effects, Warren Newcombe. Editor, Ben Lewis. 88 minutes

Joe Carraclough: Roddy McDowall, *Sam Carraclough:* Donald Crisp, *Rowlie:* Edmund Gwenn, *Dolly:* Dame May Whitty, *Duke of Rudling:* Nigel Bruce, *Mrs. Carraclough:* Elsa Lanchester, *Priscilla:* Elizabeth Taylor, *Hynes:* J. Patrick O'Malley, *Dan'l Fadden:* Ben Webster, *Snickers:* Alec Craig, *Buckles:* John Rogers, *Jock:* Arthur Shields, *Andrew:* Alan Napier, *Butcher:* Roy Parry, *Allen:* George Broughton, *Cobbler:* Howard Davies, *Miner:* John Power, *Teacher:* Nelson Leigh, *Fat Woman:* May Beatty, *Tom:* Charles Irwin, *Teacher:* Hugh Harrison.

Lassie Come Home with Elsa Lanchester, Roddy McDowall, Lassie and Donald Crisp.

The Last Hurrah with Spencer Tracy and Jeffrey Hunter.

THE LAST HURRAH (1958) Col. Produced and directed by John Ford. Based on the novel by Edwin O'Connor. Screenplay, Frank Nugent. Assistant Directors, Wingate Smith and Sam Nelson. Art Director, Robert Peterson. Photography, Charles Lawton, Jr. Editor, Jack Murray. Cut from release print was Edmund Lowe as Johnny Byrne. Last film of Ed Brophy, who died at 65, May 27, 1960. 121 minutes

Frank Skeffington: Spencer Tracy, *Adam Caulfield:* Jeffrey Hunter, *Maeve Caulfield:* Dianne Foster, *John Gorman:* Pat O'Brien, *Norman Cass, Sr.:* Basil Rathbone, *The Cardinal:* Donald Crisp, *Cuke Gillen:* James Gleason, *Ditto Boland:* Edward Brophy, *Amos Force:* John Carradine, *Roger Sugrue:* Willis Bouchey, *Bishop Gardner:* Basil Ruysdael, *Sam Weinberg:* Ricardo Cortez, *Hennessey:* Wallace Ford, *Festus Garvey:* Frank McHugh, *Mr. Winslow:* Carleton Young, *Jack Mangan:* Frank Albertson, *Degnan:* Bob Sweeney, *Dan Herlihy:* William Leslie, *Gert:* Anna Lee, *Monsignor Killian:* Ken Curtis, *Delia:* Jane Darwell, *Norman Cass, Jr.:* O. Z. Whitehead, *Frank Skeffington, Jr.:* Arthur Walsh, *Ellen Davin:* Ruth Warren, *Kevin McCluskey:* Charles Fitzsimons, *Mrs. McCluskey:* Helen Westcott, *Mamie Burns:* Mimi Doyle, *Pete:* Dan Borzage, *Police Captain:* James Flavin, *Doctor:* William Forrest, *Fire Captain:* Frank Sully, *Chauffeur:* Charlie Sullivan, *Young Politicians:* Bill Henry, Rand Brooks. Harry Lauter, *Riley:* Jack Pennick, *Nurse:* Ruth Clifford, *Club Secretary:* Richard Deacon, *Retainer:* Harry Tyler, *Jules Kowalsky:* Robert Levin, *Mr. Kowalsky:* Julius Tannen, *Managing Editor:* Hal K. Dawson, *Footsie:* Harry Tenbrook, *News Commentator:* Clete Roberts, *Man:* Edmund Cobb, *Man:* Charles Trowbridge, *Gregory McClusky:* Tommy Earwood, *Man:* Tommy Jackson.

THE LAST OF MRS. CHENEY (1929) MGM. Supervised by Irving Thalberg. Directed by Sidney Franklin. From the play by Frederick Lonsdale. Continuity, Hans Kraly and Claudine West. Photography, William Daniels. Editor, Conrad A. Nervig. Also silent version. Remakes: *The Last of Mrs. Cheyney* (MGM, 1937), *The Law and the Lady* (MGM, 1951), *Frau Cheney's Ende* (German, 1962). 94 minutes

The Last of Mrs. Cheney with Basil Rathbone and Norma Shearer.

Mrs. Cheney: Norma Shearer, *Lord Arthur Dilling:* Basil Rathbone, *Charles:* George Barraud, *Lady Marie:* Hedda Hopper, *Mrs. Webley:* Maude Turner Gordon, *Lord Elton:* Herbert Bunston, *Joan:* Moon Carroll, *Mrs. Winton:* Madeline Seymour, *Willie Winton:* Cyril Chadwick, *William:* Finch Smiles, *George:* George K. Arthur.

Laura with Vincent Price, Judith Anderson, Gene Tierney and Clifton Webb.

LAURA (1944) 20th. Producer and Director, Otto Preminger. From the novel by Vera Caspary. Screenplay, Jay Dratler, Samuel Hoffenstein, Betty Reinhardt. Art Directors, Lyle Wheeler, Leland Fuller. Musical Score, David Raskin. Musical Director, Emil Newman. Cameraman, Joseph La Shelle. Editor, Louis Loeffler. Song by Johnny Mercer and David Raskin, "Laura." 88 minutes

Laura: Gene Tierney, *Mark McPherson:* Dana Andrews, *Waldo Lydecker:* Clifton Webb, *Shelby Carpenter:* Vincent Price, *Ann Treadwell:* Judith Anderson, *Bessie Clary:* Dorothy Adams, *McAvity:* James Flavin, *Bullitt:* Clyde Fillmore, *Fred Callahan:* Ralph Dunn, *Corey:* Grant Mitchell, *Louise:* Kathleen Howard, *Detectives:* Harold Schlickenmayer, Harry Strang, Lane Chandler, *Hairdresser:* Frank La Rue, *Bits:* Dorothy Christy, Aileen Pringle, Forbes Murray, Cyril Ring, *Girls:* Kay Linaker, Cara Williams, *Office Boy:* Buster Miles, *Secretary:* Jane Nigh, *Man:* William Forrest, *Jacoby:* John Dexter.

LAWRENCE OF ARABIA (1962) Col. Producer, Sam Spiegel. Director, David Lean. Screenplay, Robert Bolt. Music, Maurice Jarre. Filmed in Super Panavision 70 and Technicolor. Music played by the London Symphony Orchestra. A Horizon Pictures Production. Art Director, John Box. Cinematographer, F.A. Young. 221 minutes

T. E. Lawrence: Peter O'Toole, *Prince Feisal:* Alec Guinness, *Auda abu Tayi:* Anthony Quinn, *General Allenby:* Jack Hawkins, *Dryden:* Claude Rains, *Colonel Harry Brighton:* Anthony Quayle, *Jackson Bentley:* Arthur Kennedy, *The Bey:* José Ferrer, *Sherif Ali ibn el*

Lawrence of Arabia with Anthony Quayle, Omar Sharif and Peter O'Toole.

Kharish: Omar Sharif, *Farraj:* Michel Ray, *Daud:* John Dimech, *Gasim:* I. S. Johar, *General Murray:* Donald Wolfit, *Majid:* Gamil Ratib, *Tafas:* Zia Mohyeddin, *Corporal Jenkins:* Norman Rossington, *Elder Harith:* John Ruddock, *Medical Officer:* Howard Marion Crawford, *Club Secretary:* Jack Gwillim, *R.A.M.C. Colonel:* Hugh Miller, *Allenby's Aide:* Kenneth Fortescue, *Regimental Sergeant Major:* Stuart Saunders, *Turkish Sergeant:* Fernando Sancho, *Reciter:* Henry Oscar.

Leave Her to Heaven with Vincent Price, Gene Tierney and Cornel Wilde.

LEAVE HER TO HEAVEN (1945) 20th. Producer, William A. Bacher. Director, John M. Stahl. Color by Technicolor. Based on the novel by Ben Ames Williams. Screenplay, Jo Swerling. Musical Score, Alfred Newman. Art Directors, Lyle Wheeler, Maurice Ransford. Cameraman, Leon Shamroy. Special Effects, Fred Sersen. Editor, James B. Clark. Technicolor Director, Natalie Kalmus. Associate, Richard Mueller. Locations filmed in Wyoming. 111 minutes

Ellen Berent: Gene Tierney, *Richard Harland:* Cornel Wilde, *Ruth Berent:* Jeanne Crain, *Russell Quinton:* Vincent Price, *Mrs. Berent:* Mary Phillips, *Glen Robie:* Ray Collins, *Dr. Saunders:* Gene Lockhart, *Dr. Mason:* Reed Hadley, *Danny Harland:* Darryl Hickman, *Leick Thorne:* Chill Wills, *Judge:* Paul Everton, *Mrs. Robie:* Olive Blakeney, *Bedford:* Addison Richards, *Catterson:* Harry Depp, *Carlson:* Grant Mitchell, *Medcraft (Mortician):* Milton Parsons, *Norton:* Earl Schenck, *Lin Robie:* Hugh Maguire, *Tess Robie:* Betty Hannon, *Nurse:* Kay Riley, *Sheriff:* Guy Beach, *Cook at Robie's Ranch:* Audrey Betz, *Conductor:* Jim Farley, *Man:* Charles Tannen, *Fisherwoman:* Mae Marsh.

The Left Hand of God with Humphrey Bogart and Richard Cutting.

THE LEFT HAND OF GOD (1955) 20th. Producer, Buddy Adler. Director, Edward Dmytryk. CinemaScope, De Luxe Color. Based on the novel by William E. Barrett. Screenplay, Alfred Hayes. Art Directors, Lyle R. Wheeler, Maurice Ransford. Music, Victor Young. Orchestration, Edward Powell. Cinematographer, Franz Planer. Editor, Dorothy Spencer. 87 minutes

Jim Carmody: Humphrey Bogart, *Anne Scott:* Gene Tierney, *Mieh Yang:* Lee J. Cobb, *Beryl Sigman:* Agnes Moorehead, *Dr. Sigman:* E. G. Marshall, *Mary Yin:* Jean Porter, *Rev. Cornelius:* Carl Benton Reid, *John Wong:* Victor Sen Yung, *Jan Teng:* Philip Ahn, *Chun Tien:* Benson Fong, *Father O'Shea:* Richard Cutting, *Pao-Ching:* Leon Lontok, *Father Keller:* Don Forbes, *Woman in Sarong:* Noel Toy, *Feng Merchant:* Peter Chong, *Woman in Kimona:* Marie Tsien, *The Boy:* Stephen Wong, *Li Kwan:* George Chan, *Nurse:* Doris Chung, *Old Man:* Moy Ming, *Pao Chu:* Stella Lynn, *Rev. Marvin:* Robert Burton, *Midwife:* Soo Yong, *Girl:* Candace Lee, *Moslem:* Kam Tong, *Servant:* Sammee Tong.

THE LEMON DROP KID (1951) Par. Producer, Robert L. Welch. Director, Sidney Lanfield. Based on the story by Damon Runyon. Screenplay, Edmund Hartmann, Robert O'Brien. Story, Edmund Beloin. Additional Dialogue, Irving Ellinson. Art Directors, Hal Pereira, Franz Bachelin. Photography, Daniel L. Fapp. Songs by Ray Evans and Jay Livingston: "Silver Bells," "It Doesn't Cost a Dime to Dream" and "They Obviously Want Me to Sing." Remake of *The Lemon Drop Kid* (Paramount, 1934). 91 minutes

Lemon Drop Kid: Bob Hope, *Brainy Baxter:* Marilyn Maxwell, *Charley:* Lloyd Nolan, *Nellie Thursday:* Jane Darwell, *Stella:* Andrea King, *Moose Moran:* Fred Clark, *Straight Flush:* Jay C. Flippen, *Gloomy Willie:* William Frawley, *Sam The Surgeon:* Harry Bellaver, *Little Louie:* Sid Melton, *Singin' Solly:* Ben Walden, *Bird Lady:* Ida Moore, *Goomba:* Charles Cooley, *Society Kid Hogan:* Society Kid Hogan, *Policeman John:* Harry Shannon, *Honest Harry:* Bernard Szold, *Judges:* Roy Gordon, Stanley Andrews, *Maxie:* Richard Karlan, *Wrestlers:* Tor Johnson, Bill Varga, *Mrs. Santoro:* Almira Sessions, *Henry Regan:* Francis Pierlot, *Girl:* Mary Murphy, *Benny Southstreet:* Fred Zendar, *Professor Murdock:* Slim Gaut, *Brainy's Girl Friend:* Jean Whitney, *Boy Scout:* Tommy Ivo, *Ellen:* Helen Brown, *Pimlico Pete:* Fred Graff, *Groom:* Sid Tomack, *George:* Jim Hayward, *Muscleman:* Jack Kruschen, *Muscleman:* John Doucette, *Thin Santa Claus:* Douglas Spencer, *Santa Claus:* Harry O. Tyler, *Dance Director:* Bill Sheehan, *Willie:* Ray Cooke.

The Lemon Drop Kid with Bob Hope and Harry Bellaver.

LES GIRLS (1957) MGM. Producer, Sol C. Siegel. Associate Producer, Saul Chaplin. Director, George Cukor. CinemaScope, MetroColor. Author, Vera Caspary. Screenplay, John Patrick. Art Directors, William A. Horning, Gene Allen. Music adapted and conducted by Adolph Deutsch. Orchestration, Alexander Courage, Skip Martin. Songs by Cole Porter: "Ladies in Waiting," "Les Girls," "Flower Song," "Ça,

Les Girls with Kay Kendall, Mitzi Gaynor, Gene Kelly and Taina Elg.

C'est L'Amour," "You're Just Too, Too," "Why Am I So Gone About That Gal?" Cinematographer, Robert Surtees. Editor, Ferris Webster. Choreography, Jack Cole. 114 minutes

Barry Nichols: Gene Kelly, *Joy Henderson:* Mitzi Gaynor, *Lady Wren:* Kay Kendall, *Angele Ducros:* Taina Elg, *Pierre Ducros:* Jacques Bergerac, *Sir Gerald Wren:* Leslie Phillips, *Judge:* Henry Daniell, *Sir Percy:* Patrick Macnee, *Mr. Outward:* Stephen Vercoe, *Associate Judge:* Philip Tonge, *Court Usher:* Owen McGiveney, *French Stage Manager:* Francis Ravel, *Wardrobe Woman:* Adrienne d'Ambricaut, *French House Manager:* Maurice Marsac, *English Photographer:* Gil Stuart, *Fanatic:* Cyril Delevanti, *Waiter:* George Navarro, *Headwaiter:* Marcel de la Brosse, *Spanish Peasant Man:* Nestor Paiva, *Stage Manager:* Alberto Morin, *Stout French Woman:* Maya van Horn, *Sleepy Frenchman:* George Davis, *Flamenco Dancer:* Louisa Triana, *Shopkeeper:* Genevieve Pasques, *Dancer:* Lilyan Chauvin, *Stagehand:* Dick Alexander.

LES MISERABLES (1935) UA. A 20th Century Pictures Production. Produced by Darryl F. Zanuck. Associate Producers, William Goetz and Raymond Griffith. Directed by Richard Boleslawski. Based on the novel by Victor Hugo. Screenplay, W. P. Lipscomb. Art Director, Richard Day. Costumes, Omar Khayyam. Musical Numbers, Alfred Newman. Assistant Director, Eric Stacey. Cinematography, Gregg Toland. Editor, Barbara McLean. Sound, Frank Maher and Roger Heman. 108 minutes

Jean Valjean: Fredric March, *Inspector Javert:* Charles Laughton, *Cosette:* Rochelle Hudson, *Little Cosette:* Marilyn Knowlden, *Eponine Thernardier:* Frances Drake, *Marius:* John Beal, *Bishop Bienvenu:* Sir Cedric Hardwicke, *Madame Magloire:* Jessie Ralph, *Mlle. Baptieme:* Mary Forbes, *Fantine:* Florence Eldridge, *M. Thernardier:* Ferdinand Gottschalk, *Madame Thernardier:* Jane Kerr, *Mother Superior:* Eily Malyon, *Brissac:* Vernon Downing, *LeMarque:* Lyons Wickland, *Enjolras:* John Carradine, *Brevet:* Charles Jockey Haefeli, *Genflou:* Leonid Kinskey, *Chenildieu:* John M. Bleifer, *Cochepaille:* Harry Semels, *Toussaint:* Florence Roberts, *Valsin (Dog Fancier):* Lorin Raker, *Inspector Devereury:* Perry Ivins, *Francois:* Pat Somer-

Les Miserables with Frances Drake, John Beal and Rochelle Hudson.

set, *Judge at Favorelles:* Herbert Bunston *Senior Prefect:* Keith Kenneth *Jacques:* G. Raymond (Bill) Nye, *Prison Governor:* Robert Greig, *Old Beggarwoman:* Virginia Howell, *Beam Warder:* Harry Cording, *Innkeeper:* Paul Irving, *Duval:* Lowell Drew, *L'Estrange:* Thomas R. Mills, *Marcin:* Davison Clark, *Factory Foreman:* Montague Shaw, *Factory Forewoman:* Margaret Bloodgood, *Mayor's Clerk:* Sidney Bracy, *Lodging Housekeeper:* Cecil Weston, *Head Gardener at Convent:* Ian Maclaren, *Duchaine:* Gilbert Clayton, *Priest:* Leonard Mudie, *Pierre:* Olaf Hytten.

The Letter with Gale Sondergaard, Bette Davis and Tetsu Komai.

THE LETTER (1940) WB. In Charge of Production, Jack L. Warner. Executive Producer, Hal G. Wallis. Producers, Jack L. Warner, Hal B. Wallis. Associate Producer, Robert Lord. Director, William Wyler. From the story by W. Somerset Maugham. Screenplay, Howard Koch. Cameraman, Tony Gaudio. Editor, George Amy. Orchestral Arrangements, Hugo Friedhofer. Technical Advisers, Louis Vincenot and John Vallasin. Other versions: *The Letter* (Paramount, 1929), *The Unfaithful* (WB, 1947). 97 minutes

Leslie Crosbie: Bette Davis, *Robert Crosbie:* Herbert Marshall, *Howard Joyce:* James Stephenson, *Dorothy Joyce:* Frieda Inescort, *Mrs. Hammond:* Gale Sondergaard, *John Withers:* Bruce Lester, *Adele Ainsworth:* Elizabeth Earl, *Prescott:* Cecil Kellaway, *Ong Chi Seng:* (Victor) Sen Yung, *Mrs. Cooper:* Doris Lloyd, *Chung Hi:* Willie Fung, *Head Boy:* Tetsu Komai, *Fred:* Leonard Mudie, *Driver:* John Ridgely, *Bob's Friends:* Charles Irwin, Holmes Herbert, *Well-Wisher:* Douglas Walton.

A Letter to Three Wives with Ann Sothern, Linda Darnell and Jeanne Crain.

A LETTER TO THREE WIVES (1948) 20th. Producer, Sol C. Siegel. Director-Screenplay, Joseph L. Mankiewicz. Adapted by Vera Cospary, from a *Cosmopolitan* magazine novel by John Klempner. Art Directors, Lyle Wheeler, J. Russell Spencer. Music, Alfred Newman. Photography, Arthur Miller. Editor, J. Watson Webb, Jr. 103 minutes

Deborah Bishop: Jeanne Crain, *Lora May Hollingsway:* Linda Darnell, *Rita Phipps:* Ann Sothern, *George Phipps:* Kirk Douglas, *Porter Hollingsway:* Paul Douglas, *Babe:* Barbara Lawrence, *Brad Bishop:* Jeffrey Lynn, *Mrs. Finney:* Connie Gilchrist, *Mrs. Manleigh:* Florence Bates, *Mr. Manleigh:* Hobart Cavanaugh, *Kathleen:* Patti Brady, *Miss Hawkins:* Ruth Vivian, *Sadie:* Thelma Ritter, *Old Man:* Stuart Holmes, *Nick:* George Offerman, Jr., *Character:* Ralph Brooks, *Thomasino:* Joe Bautista, *Butler:* James Adamson, *Waiter:* John Davidson, *Messengers:* Carl Switzer, John Venn, *Waiter:* Sammy Finn.

LIBELED LADY (1936) MGM. Produced by Lawrence Weingarten. Directed by Jack Conway. Story, Wallace Sullivan. Screenplay, Maurine Watkins, Howard Emmett Rogers, and George Oppenheimer. Camera, Norbert Brodine. Editor, Frederick Y. Smith. Score, William Axt. Remade as *Easy to Wed* (MGM, 1946). 98 minutes

Bill Chandler: William Powell, *Gladys:* Jean Harlow, *Connie Allenbury:* Myrna Loy, *Haggerty:* Spencer Tracy, *Mr. Allenbury:* Walter Connolly, *Mr. Bane:* Charley Grapewin, *Mrs. Burns-Norvell:* Cora Witherspoon, *Fishing Instructor:* E. E. Clive, *Babs:* Bunny Lauri Beatty, *Ching:* Otto Yamaoka, *Graham:* Charles Trowbridge, *Magistrate:* Spencer Charters, *Bellhop:* George Chandler, *Connie's Maid:* Greta Meyer, *Johnny:* Billy Benedict, *Harvey Allen:* Hal K. Dawson, *Divorce Detective:* William Newell, *Taxi Driver:* Duke York, *Jacques:* Harry Allen, *Detective:* Pat West, *Clerk:* Edwin Stanley, *Photographer:* Wally Maher, *Alex:* Tom Mahoney, *Photographer:* Pat Somerset, *Barker:* Richard Tucker, *Maid:* Libby Taylor, *Dickson:* Jed Prouty, *Barker:* Jack Mulhall, *Steward:* Charles Irwin, *Moe:* Eddie Shubert, *Waiter:* George Davis, *Minister:* Thomas Pogue, *Maid in Hall:* Hattie McDaniel, *Cable Editor:* Howard C. Hickman, *Barker:* Charles King, *Archibald:* Charles Croker King, *Fortune Teller:* Ines Palange, *Justice of the Peace:* Harry C. Bradley, *Justice's Wife:* Bodil Ann Rosing, *Butler:* Barnett Parker, *Palmer:* Robin Adair, *Ragamuffins:* Buster Phelps, Bobby (Bobs) Watson, Tommy Bond.

Libeled Lady with Jean Harlow, William Powell and Spencer Tracy.

LIFE BEGINS FOR ANDY HARDY (1941) MGM. Directed by George Seitz. Based on the characters created by Aurania Rouverol. Screenplay, Agnes Christine Johnston. Art Director, Cedric Gibbons. Music Director, Georgie Stoll. Photography, Lester White. Editor, Elmo Veron. 100 minutes

Andy Hardy: Mickey Rooney, *Judge Hardy:* Lewis Stone, *Betsy Booth:* Judy Garland, *Mrs. Hardy:* Fay Holden, *Polly Benedict:* Ann Ruther-

Life Begins for Andy Hardy with Judy Garland and Lewis Stone.

ford, *Aunt Milly:* Sara Haden, *Jennitt Hicks:* Patricia Dane, *Jimmy Frobisher:* Ray McDonald, *Beezy:* George Breakston, *Father Gallagher:* Ralph Byrd, *Rabbi Strauss:* Manart Kippen, *Dr. Griffin:* William J. Holmes, *Dr. Storfen:* Purnell Pratt, *Dr. Waggoner:* Pierre Watkin, *Operator:* Frances Morris, *Chuck:* Tommy Kelly, *Private:* Robert Winkler, *Commandant:* William Forrest, *Jackson:* Byron Shores, *Ted:* Hollis Jewell, *Boys:* Sidney Miller, Roger Daniel, *Policemen:* Arthur Loft, James Flavin, *Elizabeth Norton:* Charlotte Wynters, *Delivery Boy:* Bob Pittard, *Mr. Maddox:* Lester Matthews, *Clerk:* Don Brodie, *Taxi Driver:* John Harmon, *Stationer:* Frank Ferguson, *Boy "Kelly":* Leonard Sues, *Florist:* George Carleton, *Janitor:* George Ovey, *Watchman:* Robert Homans, *Miss Dean:* Ann Morriss, *Miss Gomez:* Mira McKinney, *Miss Howard:* Nora Lane, *Paul McWilliams:* John Eldredge, *Peter Dugan:* Joseph Crehan, *Secretary:* Bess Flowers, *Truckmen:* Paul Newlan, Duke York.

LIFEBOAT (1944) 20th. Producer, Kenneth Macgowan. Director, Alfred Hitchcock. Author, John Steinbeck. Screenplay, Jo Swerling. Art Directors, James Basevi, Maurice Ransford. Musical Score, Hugo W. Friedhofer. Musical Director, Emil Newman. Cameraman, Glen MacWilliams. Special Effects, Fred Sersen. Editor, Dorothy Spencer. 96 minutes

Connie Porter: Tallulah Bankhead, *Gus:* William Bendix, *The German:* Walter Slezak, *Alice:* Mary Anderson, *Kovak:* John Hodiak, *Rittenhouse:* Henry Hull, *Mrs. Higgins:* Heather Angel, *Stanley Garrett:* Hume Cronyn, *Joe:* Canada Lee, *German Sailor:* William Yetter, Jr., *Man in Before and After Ad:* Alfred Hitchcock.

Lifeboat with Hume Cronyn, Henry Hull, Tallulah Bankhead, John Hodiak, Mary Anderson and Canada Lee.

THE LIFE OF EMILE ZOLA (1937) WB. Vice-President in Charge of Production, Jack L. Warner. Associate Executive in Charge of Production, Hal B. Wallis. Supervisor, Henry Blanke. Directed by William Dieterle. Story, Heinz Herald and Geza Herczeg. Screenplay, Heinz Herald, Geza Herczeg, and Norman Reilly Raine. Music, Max Steiner. Orchestra Direction, Leo Forbstein. Assistant Director, Russ Saunders. Cinematography, Tony Gaudio. Editor, Warren Lowe. Art Director, Anton Grot. Make-up, Perc Westmore. Dialogue Director, Irving Rapper. Gowns, Milo Anderson and Ali Hubert. Interior Decorator, Albert C. Wilson. 116 minutes

Emile Zola: Paul Muni, *Lucie Dreyfus:* Gale Sondergaard, *Captain Alfred Dreyfus:* Joseph Schildkraut, *Alexandrine Zola:* Gloria Holden, *Maitre Labori:* Donald Crisp, *Nana:* Erin O'Brien-Moore, *Charpentier:* John Litel, *Colonel Picquart:* Henry O'Neill, *Anatole France:* Morris Carnovsky, *Major Dort:* Louis Calhern, *Commander of Paris:* Ralph Morgan, *Major Walsin-Esterhazy:* Robert Barrat, *Paul Cezanne:* Vladimir Sokoloff, *Chief of Staff:* Harry Davenport, *Major Henry:* Robert Warwick, *M. Delagorgue:* Charles Richman, *Pierre Dreyfus:* Dickie Moore, *Jeanne Dreyfus:* Rolla Gourvitch, *Minister of War:* Gilbert Emery, *Colonel Sandherr:* Walter Kingsford, *Assistant Chief of Staff:* Paul Everton, *Cavaignac:* Montagu Love, *Van Cassell:* Frank Sheridan, *Mr. Richards:* Lumsden Hare, *Helen Richards:* Marcia Mae Jones, *Madame Zola:* Florence Roberts, *Georges Clemenceau:* Grant Mitchell, *Captain Guignet:* Moroni Olsen, *Brucker:* Egon Brecher, *M. Perrenx:* Frank Reicher, *Senator Scheurer-Kestner:* Walter O. Stahl, *Albert:* Frank Darien, *Madame Charpentier:* Countess Iphigenie Castiglioni, *Chief Censor:* Arthur Aylesworth, *Mathieu Dreyfus:* Frank Mayo, *Major D'Aboville:* Alexander Leftwich, *La Rue:* Paul Irving, *Prefect of Police:* Pierre Watkin, *Commander of Paris:* Holmes Herbert, *General Gillian:* Robert Cummings, Sr., *Lieutenant:* Harry Worth, *Swartzkoppen:* William von Brincken.

Life of Emile Zola with Vladimir Sokoloff, Paul Muni and Josephine Hutchinson.

LIFE WITH FATHER (1947) WB. Produced by Robert Buckner. Directed by Michael Curtiz. Color by Technicolor. From Oscar Serlin's stage production of the play by Howard Lindsay and Russell Crouse. Screenplay, Donald Ogden Stewart. Art Director, Robert Hass. Technicolor Color Director, Natalie Kalmus. Associate, Monroe W. Burbank. Photography, Peverell Marley and William V. Skall. Music Director, Leo F. Forbstein. Assistant Director, Robert Vreeland. Editor, George Amy. Sound, C. A. Riggs. Dialogue Director, Herschel Daugherty. Montages, James Leicester. Special Effects, William McGann. Special Effects Director, Ray Foster. Technical Advisor, Mrs. Clarence Day. Sets, George James Hopkins. Wardrobe, Milo Anderson. Make-up, Perc Westmore. Music, Max Steiner. Orchestral Arrangements, Murray Cutter. The play ran from 1939 to 1947, inspiring a sequel, *Life With Mother* (1948-9), and a TV series (1955). 118 minutes

Father Clarence: William Powell, *Vinnie:* Irene Dunne, *Mary:* Elizabeth Taylor, *Reverend Dr. Lloyd:* Edmund Gwenn, *Cora:* ZaSu

Life With Father with William Powell, Irene Dunne, Derek Scott, James Lydon, Johnny Calkins and Martin Milner.

Pitts, Clarence: Jimmy Lydon, *Margaret:* Emma Dunn, *Dr. Humphries:* Moroni Olsen, *Mrs. Whitehead:* Elisabeth Risdon, *Harlan:* Derek Scott, *Whitney:* Johnny Calkins, *John:* Martin Milner, *Annie:* Heather Wilde, *The Policeman:* Monte Blue, *Nora:* Mary Field, *Maggie:* Queenie Leonard, *Delia:* Nancy Evans, *Miss Wiggins:* Clara Blandick, *Dr. Somers:* Frank Elliott, *Scrub Woman:* Clara Reid, *Milk Man:* Philo McCullough, *Corsetierre:* Loie Bridge, *Salesman:* George Meader, *Mr. Morley:* Douglas Kennedy, *Clerk:* Phil Van Zandt, *Stock Quotation Operator:* Russell Arms, *Hilda:* Faith Kruger, *Francois:* Jean Del Val, *Twins:* Michael and Ralph Mineo, *Father of Twins:* Creighton Hale, *Mother of Twins:* Jean Andren, *Ellen:* Elaine Lange, *Perkins (Clerk):* John Beck, *Chef:* Jack Martin, *Girl in Delmonico's:* Arlene Dahl.

LIGHTS OF NEW YORK (1928) WB. Directed by Bryan Foy. Story and Scenario, F. Hugh Herbert and Murray Roth. Cameraman, E. B. Dupar. Editor, Jack Killiger. The first all-talking film, this also had titles in the silent tradition. 57 minutes

Kitty Lewis: Helene Costello, *Eddie Morgan:* Cullen Landis, *Hawk Miller:* Wheeler Oakman, *Gene:* Eugene Pallette, *Molly Thompson:* Gladys Brockwell, *Mrs. Morgan:* Mary Carr, *Detective Crosby:* Robert Elliott, *Sam:* Tom Dugan, *Police Chief Collins:* Tom McQuire, *Tommy:* Guy D'Ennery, *Jake Jackson:* Walter Percival, *Dan Dickson:* Jere Delaney.

Lights of New York with Cullen Landis and Helene Costello.

LILI (1953) MGM. Producer, Edwin H. Knopf. Director, Charles Walters. Technicolor. From a story by Paul Gallico. Screenplay, Helen Deutsch. Art Directors, Cedric Gibbons, Paul Groesse. Cinematographer, Robert Planck. Editor, Ferris Webster. Choreography, Charles Walters and Dorothy Jarnac. Song, "Hi-Lili, Hi-Lo" by Helen Deutsch and Bronislau Kaper. 81 minutes

Lili with Leslie Caron.

Lili Daurier: Leslie Caron, *Paul Berthalet:* Mel Ferrer, *Marc:* Jean Pierre Aumont, *Rosalie:* Zsa Zsa Gabor, *Jacquot:* Kurt Kasznar, *Peach Lips:* Amanda Blake, *Proprietor:* Alex Gerry, *Monsieur Corvier:* Ralph Dumke, *Monsieur Tonit:* Wilton Graff, *Monsieur Erique:* George Baxter, *Fruit Peddler:* Eda Reiss Merin, *Workman:* George Davis, *Second Workman:* Reginald Simpson, *Concessionaire:* Mitchell Lewis, *Whistler:* Fred Walton, *Flirting Vendor:* Richard Grayson, *Specialty Dancer:* Dorothy Jarnac, *Specialty Dancers:* Arthur Mendez, Dick Lerner, Frank Radcliffe, Lars Hensen.

LILIES OF THE FIELD (1963) UA. Producer-Director, Ralph Nelson. Screenplay, James Poe. Based on a novel by William E. Barrett. Associate Producer, J. Paul Popkin. Music, Jerry Goldsmith. A Rainbow Production. Cinematographer, Ernest Haller. Editor, John McCafferty. 94 minutes

Homer Smith: Sidney Poitier, *Mother Maria:* Lilia Skala, *Sister Gertrude:* Lisa Mann, *Sister Agnes:* Isa Crino, *Sister Albertine:* Francesca Jarvis, *Sister Elizabeth:* Pamela Branch, *Juan Acalito:* Stanley Adams, *Father Murphy:* Dan Frazer, *Ashton, the Contractor:* Ralph Nelson.

Lilies of the Field with Isa Crino, Pamela Branch, Lilia Skala, Francesca Jarvis, Lisa Mann and Sidney Poitier.

Lillian Russell with Alice Faye, Don Ameche and Edward Arnold.

LILLIAN RUSSELL (1940) 20th. Producer, Darryl F. Zanuck. Associate Producer, Gene Markey. Director, Irving Cummings. Screenplay, William Anthony McGuire. Cameraman, Leon Shamroy. Editor, Walter Thompson. Songs: "Blue Love Bird" by Gus Kahn and Bronislau Kaper; "Adored One" by Mack Gordon and Alfred Newman; "Waltz Is King" by Mack Gordon and Charles Henderson; "Back in the Days of Old Broadway" by Charles Henderson and Alfred Newman. 127 minutes

Lillian Russell: Alice Faye, *Edward Solomon:* Don Ameche, *Alexander Moore:* Henry Fonda, *Diamond Jim Brady:* Edward Arnold, *Jesse Lewisohn:* Warren William, *Tony Pastor:* Leo Carrillo, *Grandma Leonard:* Helen Westley, *Cynthia Leonard:* Dorothy Peterson, *Charles Leonard:* Ernest Truex, *William Gilbert:* Nigel Bruce, *Edna McCauley:* Lynn Bari, *Sullivan:* Claud Allister, *Weber and Fields:* Joe Weber and Lew Fields, *Eddie Foy, Sr.:* Eddie Foy, Jr., *Marie:* Una O'Connor, *Leopold Damrosch:* Joseph Cawthorn, *Dorothy:* Diane Fisher, *President Cleveland:* William B. Davidson, *Dr. Dobbins:* Charles Halton, *Mrs. Rose:* Ferike Boros, *Official:* Frank Thomas, *Mrs. Hobbs:* Cecil Cunningham, *Lillian's Sisters:* Elyse Knox, Joan Valerie, Alice Armand, *Chauffeur:* Hal K. Dawson, *Jeweler:* Robert Emmett Keane, *Coachman:* Frank Darien, *Hank:* Frank Sully, *Miss Smyth:* Ottola Nesmith, *Stage Doorman:* Bob Homans, *First Soldier:* William Haade, *Second Soldier:* Irving Bacon, *Third Soldier:* Paul Burns, *First Reporter:* Milburn Stone, *Tenor:* Philip Winter, *Hotel Clerk:* Leyland Hodgson, *Moso:* Thaddeus Jones, *Manager:* Harry Hayden, *Drunk:* Dave Morris, *Owen:* Bob Ryan, *Frank:* Tom London, *Stage Manager:* Paul McVey, *Man:* Robert Shaw.

LIMELIGHT (1952) UA. Producer-Director, Charles Chaplin. Screenplay by Charles Chaplin. Music by Charles Chaplin. Assistant Director, Robert Aldrich. 114 minutes

Limelight with Claire Bloom and Charlie Chaplin.

Calvero: Charles Chaplin, *Terry:* Claire Bloom, *Neville:* Sydney Chaplin, *Harlequin:* Andre Eglevsky, *Columbine:* Melissa Hayden, *Clowns:* Charles Chaplin, Jr. Wheeler Dryden, *Cast:* Nigel Bruce, Norman Lloyd, Buster Keaton, Marjorie Bennett, *Children:* Geraldine, Michael and Victoria Chaplin.

LITTLE BOY LOST (1953) Par. Producer, William Perlberg. Director, George Seaton. Based on the story by Marghanita Laski. Screenplay, George Seaton. Art Directors, Hal Pereira, Henry Blumstead. Cinematographer, George Barnes. Editor, Alma Macrorie. Filmed in Paris. 95 minutes

Bill Wainwright: Bing Crosby, *Pierre Verdier:* Claude Dauphin, *Jean:* Christian Fourcade, *Mother Superior:* Gabrielle Dorziat, *Lisa Garret:* Nicole Maurey, *Nelly:* Colette Dereal, *Madame Quilleboeuf:* Georgette Anys, *Tracing Service Clerk:* Henri Letondal, *Attaché:* Michael Moore, *Lt. Walker:* Peter Baldwin, *Helene:* Gladys de Segonzac, *Madame Le Blanc:* Yola d'Avril, *Ronnie:* Bruce Payne, *Dr. Biroux:* Jean Del Val, *Nurse:* Adele St. Maur, *Suzanne Pitou:* Ninon Straty, *Pitchman:* Paul Magranville, *Maid:* Christiane Fourcade, *Paul:* Jacques Gallo, *Stewardess:* Karin Vengay, *Sister Therese:* Tina Blagoi, *Waiter:* Arthur Dulac.

Little Boy Lost with Claude Dauphin and Bing Crosby.

LITTLE CAESAR (1930) WB. Directed by Mervyn LeRoy. Based on the novel by W. R. Burnett. Scenario and Dialogue, Francis Faragoh. Photography, Tony Gaudio. Vitaphone. 77 minutes

Caesar Enrico Bandello: Edward G. Robinson, *Joe Massara:* Douglas Fairbanks, Jr., *Olga Strassoff:* Glenda Farrell, *Tony Passa:* William Collier, Jr., *Diamond Pete Montana:* Ralph Ince, *Otero:* George E. Stone, *Lt. Tom Flaherty:* Thomas Jackson, *Sam Vettori:* Stanley Fields, *DeVoss:* Armand Kaliz, *The Big Boy:* Sidney Black-

Little Caesar with Edward G. Robinson and Douglas Fairbanks, Jr.

mer, *Gabby:* Landers Stevens, *Little Arnie Lorch:* Maurice Black, *Peppi:* Noel Madison, *Ritz Colonna:* Nick Bela, *Ma Magdalena:* Lucille La Verne, *Kid Bean:* Ben Hendricks, Jr., *Waiter:* Al Hill, *Cashier:* Ernie S. Adams, *Cafe Guest:* Larry Steers, *Machine Gunner:* George Daly.

Little Miss Marker with Dorothy Dell, John Kelly, Adolphe Menjou and Shirley Temple.

Memphis: Sleep 'n Eat (Willie Best), *Eddie:* Puggy White, *Buggs:* Tammany Young, *Bennie The Gouge:* Sam Hardy, *Marky's Father:* Edward Earle, *Sore Toe:* Warren Hymer, *Canvas Back:* John Kelly, *Doctor Ingalls:* Frank Conroy, *Detective Reardon:* James Burke, *Bookie:* Stanley Price, *Bettors:* Ernie Adams, Don Brodie.

THE LITTLEST REBEL (1935) 20th. Produced by Darryl F. Zanuck. Associate Producer, B. G. DeSylva. Directed by David Butler. Screenplay, Edwin Burke. Musical Arrangement, Cyril Mockridge. Photography, John Seitz. Editor, Irene Morra. From the play by Edward Peple. Assistant Director, Booth McCracken. Art Director, William Darling. Settings, Thomas K. Little. Costumes, Gwen Wakeling. Sound, S. C. Chapman and Roger Heman. 70 minutes

Virgie Cary: Shirley Temple, *Captain Herbert Cary:* John Boles, *Colonel Morrison:* Jack Holt, *Mrs. Cary:* Karen Morely, *Uncle Billy:* Bill Robinson, *Sergeant Dudley:* Guinn (Big Boy) Williams, *James Henry:* Willie Best, *Abraham Lincoln:* Frank McGlynn, Sr., *Mammy:* Bessie Lyle, *Sally Ann:* Hannah Washington, *Guard:* James Flavin.

The Little Foxes with Herbert Marshall and Bette Davis.

THE LITTLE FOXES (1941) RKO. Produced by Samuel Goldwyn. Directed by William Wyler. Based on the play by Lillian Hellman. Music, Meredith Willson. Screenplay, Lillian Hellman. Art Director, Stephen Goosson. Assistant Director, William Tummel. Costumes, Orry-Kelly. Sets, Howard Bristol. Miss Davis' make-up, Perc Westmore. Photography, Gregg Toland. Editor, Daniel Mandell. Sound, Frank Maher. Sequel was *Another Part of the Forest* (Univ., 1948), which was set 20 years earlier. 116 minutes

Regina Hubbard Giddens: Bette Davis, *Horace Giddens:* Herbert Marshall, *Alexandra Giddens:* Teresa Wright, *David Hewitt:* Richard Carlson, *Birdie Hubbard:* Patricia Collinge, *Leo Hubbard:* Dan Duryea, *Ben Hubbard:* Charles Dingle, *Oscar Hubbard:* Carl Benton Reid, *Addie:* Jessica Grayson, *Cal:* John Marriott, *William Marshall:* Russell Hicks, *Sam Manders:* Lucien Littlefield, *Lucy Hewitt:* Virginia Brissac, *Julia:* Terry Nibert, *Dawson, Hotel Manager:* Alan Bridge, *Simon:* Charles R. Moore, *Servant:* Kenny Washington, *Bit:* Henry "Hot Shot" Thomas, *Train Companion:* Lew Kelly, *Guest:* Hooper Atchely, *Depositor:* Henry Roquemore.

LITTLE MISS MARKER (1934) Par. Produced by B. P. Schulberg. Directed by Alexander Hall. From a story by Damon Runyon. Screenplay, William R. Lipman, Sam Hellman, Gladys Lehman. Photography, Alfred Gilks. Editor, William Shea. Songs by Ralph Rainger and Leo Robin: "I'm a Black Sheep Who Is Blue," "Low Down Lullaby," "Laugh You Son-of-a-Gun." Remade as *Sorrowful Jones* (Paramount, 1949). 80 minutes

Sorrowful Jones: Adolphe Menjou, *Bangles Carson:* Dorothy Dell, *Big Steve Halloway:* Charles Bickford, *Marthy Jane, Miss Marker:* Shirley Temple, *Regret:* Lynne Overman, *Doc Chesley:* Frank McGlynn, Sr., *Sun Rise:* Jack Sheehan, *Grinder:* Gary Owen, *Dizzy*

The Littlest Rebel with James Flavin, John Boles and Shirley Temple.

LITTLE WOMEN (1933) RKO. Executive Producer, Merian C. Cooper. Supervised by Kenneth MacGowan. Directed by George Cukor. From the novel by Louisa May Alcott. Screenplay, Sarah Y. Mason and Victor Heerman. Music, Max Steiner. Photography, Henry Gerrard. Editor, Jack Kitchin. Sound, Frank H. Harris. Remade by MGM, 1949. 107 minutes (originally 115 mins.)

Jo: Katharine Hepburn, *Amy:* Joan Bennett, *Fritz Bhaor:* Paul Lukas, *Meg:* Frances Dee, *Beth:* Jean Parker, *Aunt March:* Edna May Oliver, *Laurie:* Douglass Montgomery, *Mr. Laurence:* Henry Stephenson, *Marmee:* Spring Byington, *Mr. March:* Samuel Hinds, *Hannah:* Mabel Colcord, *Brooks:* John Davis Lodge, *Mamie:* Nydia Westman.

Little Women with Katharine Hepburn and Edna May Oliver.

THE LIVES OF A BENGAL LANCER (1935) Par. Produced by Louis D. Lighton. Directed by Henry Hathaway. From the book by Francis Yeats-Brown. Screenplay, Waldemar Young, John L. Balderston, Achmed Abdullah, Grover Jones, William Slavens McNutt. Assistant Directors, Paul Wing and Clem Beauchamp. Editor, Ellsworth Hoagland. Cinematography, Charles Lang. Recording Engineer, Harold Lewis. Art Directors, Hans Dreier and Roland Anderson. Costumes, Travis Banton. 109 minutes

Captain McGregor: Gary Cooper, *Lieutenant Fortesque:* Franchot Tone, *Lieutenant Stone:* Richard Cromwell, *Colonel Stone:* Sir Guy Standing, *Major Hamilton:* C. Aubrey Smith, *Hamzulla Kahn:* Monte Blue, *Tania Volkanskaya:* Kathleen Burke, *Lieutenant Barrett:* Colin Tapley, *Mohammed Khan:* Douglass R. Dumbrille, *Emir:* Akim Tamiroff, *Hendrickson:* Jameson Thomas, *Ram Singh:* Noble Johnson, *Major General Woodley:* Lumsden Hare, *Grand Vizier:* J. Carrol Naish, *The Ghazi:* Rollo Lloyd, *McGregor's Servant:* Charles Stevens, *Afridi:* Mischa Auer, *Solo Dancer:* Myra Kinch, *Shah:* Boghwan Singh, *Ali Hamdi:* Abdul Hassan, *Lieutenant Norton:* Clive Morgan, *Servant:* Eddie Das, *Snake Charmer:* Leonid Kinskey, *Muezzin:* Hussain Nasri, *Lieutenant Gilhooley:* James Warwick, *Kushal Khan:* George Regas, *British Officer:* Major Sam Harris, *Indian Officers:* Ram Singh, Jamiel Hasson, James Bell, General Ikonnikoff, F. A. Armenta, *Experienced Clerk:* Claude King, *Novice:* Reginald Sheffield, *Girl on Train:* Lya Lys.

Lives of a Bengal Lancer with Franchot Tone and Gary Cooper.

Living It Up with Dean Martin and Jerry Lewis.

LIVING IT UP (1954) Par. Producer, Paul Jones. Director, Norman Taurog. Technicolor. Story, Ben Hecht (from the musical comedy *Hazel Flagg* based on a story by James Street). Screenplay, Jack Rose, Melville Shavelson. Art Directors, Hal Pereira, Albert Nozaki. Cinematographer, Daniel Fapp. Editor, Archie Marshek. Remake of *Nothing Sacred* (UA, 1937) 95 minutes

Steve: Dean Martin, *Homer:* Jerry Lewis, *Wally Cook:* Janet Leigh, *The Mayor:* Edward Arnold, *Oliver Stone:* Fred Clark, *Jitterbug Dancer:* Sheree North, *Waiter:* Sammy White, *Master of Ceremonies:* Sid Tomack, *Dr. Egelhofer:* Sig Rumann, *Dr. Lee:* Richard Loo, *Conductor:* Raymond Greenleaf, *Isaiah:* Walter Baldwin, *First Manicurist:* Marla English, *Manicurist:* Kathryn Grandstaff (Grant), *Station Attendant:* Emmett Lynn, *Head Ranger:* Dabbs Greer, *Slugger:* Clancy Cooper, *Catcher:* John Alderson, *Fernandez:* Booth Colman, *Engineer:* Stanley Blystone, *Barber:* Fritz Feld, *Chef:* Torben Meyer, *Radio Announcer:* Art Baker, *Gift Shop Proprietor:* Grady Sutton, *Photographer:* Norman Leavitt, *Bellboy Captain:* Frankie Darro, *French Chef:* Jean Del Val, *Cop:* Lane Chandler, *Shoe Specialist:* Gino Corrado, *Martin:* Donald Kerr, *Slugger:* Al Hill, *Bus Boy:* Hank Mann, *Specialty Dancer:* Gretchen Houser.

LLOYDS OF LONDON (1936) 20th. Associate Producer, Kenneth Macgowan. Directed by Henry King. Author, Curtis Kenyon. Screenplay by Ernest Pascal, Walter Ferris. Musical Director, Louis Silvers. Cameraman, Bert Glennon. Editor, Barbara McLean. 115 minutes.

Young Jonathan: Freddie Bartholomew, *Clementine:* Madeleine Carroll, *Angerstein:* Sir Guy Standing, *Jonathan:* Tyrone Power, *Old "Q":* C. Aubrey Smith, *Polly:* Virginia Field, *Hawkins:* Montagu Love, *Gavin Gore:* Gavin Muir, *First Captain:* Arthur Hohl, *Watson:* J. M. Kerrigan, *Young Nelson:* Douglas Scott, *Captain Suckling:* Lumsden Hare, *Waiter at Lloyd's:* Charles Coleman, *Waiter at Lloyd's:* Charles McNaughton, *Jukes:* Miles Mander, *Waiter at Lloyd's:* Leonard Mudie, *Reverend Nelson:* Murray Kinnell, *Widow Blake:* Una O'Connor, *Smutt:* Will Stanton, *Potts:* Forrester Harvey, *Lord Stacy:* George Sanders, *Magistrate:* E. E. Clive, *Lord Drayton:* Robert Greig, *Lord*

Lloyds of London with Tyrone Power and Madeleine Carroll.

Nelson: John Burton, *Old Man:* Ivan F. Simpson, *Spokesman:* Holmes Herbert, *Lady Masham:* May Beatty, *Prince of Wales:* Hugh Huntley, *Willoughby:* Charles Croker-King, *French Lieutenant:* Georges Renavent, *Captain Hardy:* Lester Matthews, *Joshua Lamb:* Barlowe Borand, *Sir Thomas Lawrence:* Vernon Steele, *Dr. Beatty:* Winter Hall, *Catherine:* Ann Howard, *Susannah:* Fay Chaldecott, *Ann:* Yvonne Severn, *Benjamin Franklin:* Thomas Pogue, *Dr. Johnson:* Yorke Sherwood, *Boswell:* William Wagner, *Singer:* Constance Purdy.

LONG DAY'S JOURNEY INTO NIGHT (1962) Embassy. Producer, Ely Landau. Director, Sidney Lumet. Based on the play by Eugene O'Neill. Music, Andre Previn. Costumes, Motley. Cinematographer, Boris Kaufman. 180 minutes

Mary Tyrone: Katharine Hepburn, *James Tyrone, Sr.:* Ralph Richardson, *James Tyrone, J.:* Jason Robards, Jr., *Edmund Tyrone:* Dean Stockwell, *Cathleen:* Jeanne Barr.

Long Day's Journey Into Night with Jason Robards, Jr., Dean Stockwell, Katharine Hepburn and Sir Ralph Richardson.

THE LONGEST DAY (1962) 20th. Produced by Darryl F. Zanuck. Associate Producer, Elmo Williams. Directors, (American episodes) Andrew Marton, (British episodes) Ken Annakin, (German episodes) Bernhard Wicki. Based on the book by Cornelius Ryan, who also did the screenplay. Additional episodes written by Romain Gary, James Jones, David Pursall, Jack Seddon. Art Directors, Ted Aworth, Leon Barsacq, Vincent Korda. Thematic music by Paul Anka. Music composed and conducted by Maurice Jarre. Arrangements, Mitch Miller. Assistant Directors, Bernard Farrel, Louis Pitzele, Gerard Renateau, Henri Sokal. Cinematography, Henri Persin, Walter Wottitz, Pierre Levent, Jean Bourgoin. Editor, Samuel E. Beetley. Filmed in France. 180 minutes

Lt. Colonel Benjamin Vandervoort: John Wayne, *Brig. General Norman Cota:* Robert Mitchum, *Brig. General Theodore Roosevelt:* Henry Fonda, *Brig. General James M. Gavin:* Robert Ryan, *Destroyer Commander:* Rod Steiger, *U.S. Rangers:* Robert Wagner, Paul Anka, Fabian, Tommy Sands, *Private Dutch Schultz:* Richard Beymer, *Major General Robert Haines:* Mel Ferrer, *Sergeant Fuller:* Jeffrey Hunter, *Private Martini:* Sal Mineo, *Private Morris:* Roddy McDowall, *Lieutenant Sheen:* Stuart Whitman, *Captain Harding:* Steve Forrest, *Colonel Tom Newton:* Eddie Albert, *General Raymond O. Barton:* Edmond O'Brien, *Private John Steele:* Red Buttons, *Lieutenant Wilson:* Tom Tryon, *Major Gen. Walter Bedell Smith:* Alexander Knox, *Captain Frank:* Ray Danton, *General Dwight D. Eisenhower:* Henry Grace, *Private Harris:* Mark Damon, *Private Wilder:* Dewey Martin, *Colonel Caffey:* John Crawford, *Joe Williams:* Ron Randell, *Lt. General Omar N. Bradley:* Nicholas Stuart, *Rear-Admiral Alan G. Kirk:* John Meillon, *Major of the Rangers:* Fred Dur, *R.A.F. Pilots:* Richard Burton, Donald Houston, *Captain Colin Maud:* Kenneth

The Longest Day with Steve Forrest and John Wayne.

More, *Lord Lovat:* Peter Lawford, *Major John Howard:* Richard Todd, *Brig. General Parker:* Leo Genn, *British Padre:* John Gregson, *Private Flanagan:* Sean Connery, *Private Watney:* Michael Medwin, *R.A.F. Officer:* Leslie Phillips, *Janine Boitard:* Irina Demich, *Mayor of Colleville:* Bourvil, *Father Roulland:* Jean-Louis Barrault, *Commander Philippe Kieffer:* Christian Marquand, *Madame Barrault:* Arletty, *Maj. General Gunther Blumentritt:* Curt Jurgens, *Field Marshal Erwin Rommel:* Werner Hinz, *Field Marshal Gerd von Rundstedt:* Paul Hartmann, *Sergeant Kaffeeklatsch:* Gerd Froebe, *Major General Max Pemsel:* Wolfgang Preiss, *Lt. Colonel Ocker:* Peter Van Eyck, *Col. General Alfred Jodl:* Wolfgang Luckschy, *Several Bits:* Christopher Lee, *General Sir Bernard L. Montgomery:* Trevor Reid, *Nazi Soldier:* Eugene Deckers, *British Soldier:* Richard Wattis.

THE LONG GRAY LINE (1955) Col. Produced by Robert Arthur. Directed by John Ford. In CinemaScope and Technicolor. Based on *Bringing Up the Brass* by Marty Maher and Nardi Reeder Campion. Screenplay, Edward Hope. Art Director, Robert Peterson, Music Director, Morris Stoloff. Musical Adaptation, George Duning. Gowns, Jean Louis. Assistant Directors, Wingate Smith and Jack Corrick. Cinematography, Charles Lawton, Jr., Editor, William Lyon. 138 minutes

Marty Maher: Tyrone Power, *Mary O'Donnell:* Maureen O'Hara, *James Sundstrom, Jr.:* Robert Francis, *Old Martin:* Donald Crisp, *Captain Herman J. Koehler:* Ward Bond, *Kitty Carter:* Betsy Palmer, *Charles Dotson:* Phil Carey, *Red Sundstrom:* William Leslie, *Dwight Eisenhower:* Harry Carey, Jr., *Cherub Overton:* Patrick Wayne, *Dinny Maher:* Sean McClory, *Corporal Rudolph Heinz:* Peter Graves, *Captain John Pershing:* Milburn Stone, *Mike Shannon:* Walter D. Ehlers, *Major Thomas:* Willis Bouchey, *McDonald:* Don Barclay, *Jim O'Carberry:* Martin Milner, *Whitey Larson:* Chuck Courtney, *Superintendent:* Major Philip Kieffer, *Gus Dorais:* Norman Van Brocklin, *The President:* Elbert Steele, *Nurse:* Diane DeLaire, *Army Captain:* Donald Murphy, *Eleanor:* Lisa Davis, *Girl:* Jean Moorhead, *Peggy:* Dona Cole, *Priest:* Pat O'Malley, *Priest:* Harry Denny, *Lieutenant:* Robert

The Long Gray Line with Tyrone Power and Peter Graves.

Knapp, *Cadet Pirelli:* Robert Roark, *Cadet Kennedy:* Robert Hoy, *Cadet Short:* Robert Ellis, *Cadet Curly Stern:* Mickey Roth, *Peter Dotson:* Tom Hennesy, *Cadet Ramsey:* John Herrin, *Cadet Thorne:* James Lilburn, *Specialty:* Ken Curtis, *Recruiting Sergeant:* Jack Pennick, *Knute Rockne:* James Sears, *New York Policeman:* Mickey Simpson, *Mrs. Koehler:* Erin O'Brien-Moore.

THE LONG HOT SUMMER (1958) 20th. Produced by Jerry Wald. Directed by Martin Ritt. Based on William Faulkner's novel *The Hamlet* and his short stories "Barn Burning" and "The Spotted Horses." Screenplay, Irving Ravetch and Harriet Frank, Jr. CinemaScope, De Luxe Color and Stereophonic Sound. Song, "The Long Hot Summer" by Sammy Cahn and Alex North, sung by Jimmie Rodgers. Photography, Joseph La Shelle. Film debut of Sarah Marshall. Filmed in Baton Rouge, Louisiana. Later the basis for a TV series. 115 minutes

Ben Quick: Paul Newman, *Clara Varner:* Joanne Woodward, *Jody Varner:* Anthony Franciosa, *Will Varner:* Orson Welles, *Eula Varner:* Lee Remick, *Minnie Littlejohn:* Angela Lansbury, *Agnes Stewart:* Sarah Marshall, *Alan Stewart:* Richard Anderson, *Mrs. Stewart:* Mabel Albertson, *Ratliff:* J. Pat O'Malley, *Lucius:* William Walker, *Peabody:* George Dunn, *Armistead:* Jess Kirkpatrick, *Wilk:* Val Avery, *Houstin:* I. Stanford Jolley, *Mrs. Houstin:* Helen Wallace, *Harris:* Byron Foulger, *Justice of the Peace:* Victor Rodman, *Pete Armistead:* Terry Rangno, *Ambulance Driver:* Bob Adler, *Negro Girl:* Pat Rosemond, *John Fisher:* Nicholas King, *Tom Shortly:* Lee Erickson, *J.V. Bookright:* Ralph Reed, *Buddy Peabody:* Steve Widders, *Linus Olds:* Jim Brandt, *Harry Peabody:* Brian Corcoran, *Waiter:* Eugene Jackson.

The Long Hot Summer with Anthony Franciosa, Lee Remick, Paul Newman and Orson Welles.

THE LONG, LONG TRAILER (1954) MGM. Produced by Pandro S. Berman. Directed by Vincente Minnelli. Based on a novel by Clinton Twiss. Screenplay, Albert Hackett and Frances Goodrich. Art Directors, Cedric Gibbons and Edward Carfagno. Music, Adolph Deutsch. Cinematography, Robert Surtees. Editor, Ferris Webster. Photographed in Ansco Color, print by Technicolor. Theme, "Breezin' Along With the Breeze" by Haven Gillespie, Seymour Simmons, and Richard A. Whiting. 96 minutes

Tacy Collini: Lucille Ball, *Nicky Collini:* Desi Arnaz, *Mrs. Hittaway:* Marjorie Main, *Policeman:* Keenan Wynn, *Mrs. Bolton:* Gladys Hurlbut, *Mr. Tewitt:* Moroni Olsen, *Foreman:* Bert Freed, *Aunt Anastacia:* Madge Blake, *Uncle Edgar:* Walter Baldwin, *Mr. Judlow:* Oliver Blake, *Bridesmaid:* Perry Sheehan, *Little Boy:* Charles Herbert, *Trailer Salesman:* Herb Vigran, *Mr. Bolton:* Emmett Vogan, *Manager:* Edgar Dearing, *Inspector:* Karl Lukas, *Mr. Hittaway:* Howard McNear, *Mechanic:* Jack Kruschen, *Girl Friends:* Geraldine Carr, Sarah Spencer, *Minister:* Dallas Boyd, *Mrs. Dudley:* Ruth Warren, *Mrs. Barrett:* Edna Skinner, *Mr. Elliott:* Alan Lee, *Carl Barrett:* Robert Anderson, *Mr. Dudley:* Phil Rich, *Shorty:* John Call, *Garage Owner:* Wilson Wood,

The Long, Long Trailer with Frank Gerstle, Desi Arnaz and Lucille Ball.

Aunt Ellen: Dorothy Neumann, *Uncle Bill:* Howard Wright, *Grace:* Connie Van, *Jody:* Dennis Ross, *Tom:* Christopher Olsen, *Candy Store Clerk:* Ida Moore, *Officer:* Emory Parnell, *Judge:* Fay Roope, *Garage Manager:* Peter Leeds, *Mrs. Tewitt:* Ruth Lee, *Father:* Dick Alexander, *Bettie:* Judy Sackett, *Kay:* Janet Sackett, *Driver:* Norman Leavitt, *Waitress:* Juney Ellis, *Attendant:* Frank Gerstle.

THE LONG VOYAGE HOME (1940) UA. Produced by Walter Wanger. Directed by John Ford. An Argosy Production. Based on four one-act plays by Eugene O'Neill: *The Moon of the Caribbees, Bound East for Cardiff, In the Zone* and *The Long Voyage Home,* performed under the unifying title, *S. S. Glencairn.* Screenplay, Dudley Nichols. Music, Richard Hageman. Music Director, Edward Paul. Art Director, James Basevi. Photography, Gregg Toland. Editor, Sherman Todd. Special Effects, R. T. Layton and R. O. Binger. Interior Decorations, Julia Heron. Film debut of Baltimore stage actress Mildred Natwick. 104 minutes

Ole Olson: John Wayne, *Driscoll:* Thomas Mitchell, *Smitty:* Ian Hunter, *Cocky:* Barry Fitzgerald, *The Captain:* Wilfred Lawson, *Freda:* Mildred Natwick, *Axel Swanson:* John Qualen, *Yank:* Ward Bond, *Donkey Man:* Arthur Shields, *Davis:* Joseph Sawyer, *Crimp (Nick):* J. M. Kerrigan, *Tropical Woman:* Rafaela Ottiano, *Bumboat Girls:* Carmen Morales, Carmen D'Antonio, Tina Menard, Judith Linden, Elena Martinez, Lita Cortez, Soledad Gonzales, *Scotty:* David Hughes, *Joe, Proprietor:* Billy Bevan, *First Mate:* Cyril McLaglen, *Second Mate:* Douglas Walton, *Frank:* Constantine Romanoff, *Cook:* Edgar "Blue" Washington, *Mr. Clifton:* Lionel Pape, *Kate:* Jane Crowley, *Mag:* Maureen Roden-Ryan, *Paddy:* Bob Perry, *Norway:* Constant Franke, *Max:* Harry Tenbrook, *Tim:* Dan Borzage, *Captain of the* AMINDRA: Arthur Miles, *First Mate of* AMINDRA: Harry Woods, *Dock Policemen:* James Flavin, Lee Shumway, *British Naval Officer:* Wyndham Standing, *Bald Man:* Lowell Drew, *Seaman:* Sammy Stein, *Bergman:* Jack Pennick.

The Long Voyage Home with Ward Bond and Thomas Mitchell.

Lord Jim with Peter O'Toole.

LORD JIM (1965) Col. Director, Richard Brooks. Screenplay, Richard Brooks. Technicolor. Art Directors, Bill Hutchinson, Ernest Archer. Music, Bronislau Kaper. Music conducted by Muir Mathieson. Cinematographer, Frederick A. Young. Editor, Alan Osbiston. Based on the novel by Joseph Conrad. 154 minutes

Lord Jim: Peter O'Toole, *Gentleman Brown:* James Mason, *Cornelius:* Curt Jurgens, *The General:* Eli Wallach, *Marlow:* Jack Hawkins, *Stein:* Paul Lukas, *The Girl:* Daliah Lavi, *Schomberg:* Akim Tamiroff, *Waris:* Ichizo Itami, *Du-Ramin:* Tatsuo Saito, *Brierly:* Andrew Keir, *Robinson:* Jack MacGowran, *Malay:* Eric Young, *Captain Chester:* Noel Purcell, *Captain of* PATNA: Walter Gotell, *Moslem Leader:* Rafik Anwar, *Elder:* Marne Maitland, *Doctor:* Newton Blick, *Magistrate:* A. J. Brown, *French Officer:* Christian Marquand.

LOST HORIZON (1937) Col. Produced and directed by Frank Capra. Based on the novel by James Hilton. Screenplay, Robert Riskin. Art Director, Stephen Goosson. Musical Score, Dimitri Tiomkin. Musical Director, Max Steiner. Assistant Director, C. C. Coleman. Cinematography, Joseph Walker. Aerial Photography, Elmer Dyer. Editors, Gene Havlick and Gene Milford. Costumes, Ernst Dryden. Technical Advisor, Harrison Forman. Special Camera Effects, E. Roy Davidson and Ganahl Carson. Interior Decorations, Babs Johnstone. Voices, Hall Johnson Choir. Henry B. Walthall and Walter Connolly were replaced by Sam Jaffe in the part of the High Lama. 118 minutes

Robert Conway: Ronald Colman, *Sondra:* Jane Wyatt, *Alexander P. Lovett:* Edward Everett Horton, *George Conway:* John Howard, *Henry Barnard:* Thomas Mitchell, *Maria:* Margo, *Gloria Stone:* Isabel Jewell, *Chang:* H. B. Warner, *High Lama:* Sam Jaffe, *Lord Gainsford:* Hugh Buckler, *Carstairs:* John Miltern, *First Man:* Lawrence Grant, *Wynant:* John Burton, *Meeker:* John T. Murray, *Seiveking:* Max Rabinowitz, *Bandit Leader:* Willie Fung, *Missionary:*

Lost Horizon with John Howard, Edward Everett Horton and Ronald Colman.

Wyrley Birch, *Montaigne:* John Tettener, *Assistant Foreign Secretary:* Boyd Irwin, Sr. *Foreign Secretary:* Leonard Mudie, *Steward:* David Clyde, *Radio Operator:* Neil Fitzgerald, *Talu:* Val Durand, *Missionaries:* Ruth Robinson, Margaret McWade, *Leader of Porters:* Noble Johnson, *Aviator:* Dennis D'Auburn, *Fenner:* Milton Owen, *Bandit Leader:* Victor Wong, *Missionary:* Carl Stockdale, *Passengers:* Beatrice Curtis, Mary Lou Dix, Beatrice Blinn, Arthur Rankin, *Radio Operator:* Darby Clark, *Chinese Priest:* George Chan, *Englishman:* Eric Wilton, *Porter:* Chief Big Tree, *Shanghai Airport Official:* Richard Loo.

THE LOST PATROL (1934) RKO. Associate Producer, Cliff Reid. Directed by John Ford. From the story "Patrol" by Philip MacDonald. Screenplay, Dudley Nichols. Adaptation, Garrett Fort. Music, Max Steiner. Photography, Harold Wenstrom. Editor, Paul Weatherwax. Remakes: *Bad Lands* (RKO, 1939), *Bataan* (MGM, 1943) (Partial remake). 74 minutes

Sergeant: Victor McLaglen, *Sanders:* Boris Karloff, *Morelli:* Wallace Ford, *Brown:* Reginald Denny, *Quincannon:* J. M. Kerrigan, *Hale:* Billy Bevan, *Abelson:* Sammy Stein, *Cook:* Alan Hale, *Pearson:* Douglas Walton, *Corporal Bell:* Brandon Hurst, *Mackay:* Paul Hanson, *Lieutenant Hawkins:* Neville Clark, *Aviator:* Howard Wilson.

The Lost Patrol with Brandon Hurst and Victor McLaglen.

THE LOST WEEKEND (1945) Par. Produced by Charles Brackett. Directed by Billy Wilder. From the novel by Charles R. Jackson. Screenplay, Charles Brackett and Billy Wilder. Art Direction, Hans Dreier and Earl Hedrick. Music, Miklos Rozsa. Photography, John F. Seitz. Editor, Doane Harrison. Special Effects, Gordon Jennings. Process Photography, Farciot Edouart. Costumes, Edith Head. Makeup, Wally Westmore. Sound, Stanley Cooley and Joel Moss. Sets,

The Lost Weekend with Ray Milland and Pat Moriarity.

Bertram Granger. Film debut of Lilian Fontaine, mother of Joan Fontaine and Olivia De Havilland. Filmed in New York City, including Bellevue's alcoholic ward. 101 minutes

Don Birnam: Ray Milland, *Helen St. James:* Jane Wyman, *Wick Birnam:* Phillip Terry, *Nat:* Howard da Silva, *Gloria:* Doris Dowling, *Bim:* Frank Faylen, *Mrs. Deveridge:* Mary Young, *Mrs. Foley:* Anita Bolster, *Mrs. St. James:* Lilian Fontaine, *Mr. St. James:* Lewis L. Russell, *Attendant at Opera:* Frank Orth, *Mrs. Wertheim:* Gisela Werbisek, *Mr. Brophy:* Eddie Laughton, *Piano Player:* Harry Barris, *M.M.:* Jayne Hazard, *M.M.'s Escort:* Craig Reynolds, *Dave (Janitor):* David Clyde, *Hardware Man:* William Meader, *Albany:* Walter Baldwin, *Waiter:* Crane Whitley, *Mike (Bouncer):* Max Wagner, *Little Girl:* Bunny Sunshine, *Washroom Attendants:* Fred "Snowflake" Toones, Clarence Muse, *Fruit Clerk:* Stanley Price, *Mrs. Frink:* Helen Dickson, *Mrs. Wertheim's Assistant:* Willa Pearl Curtis, *Man with Ear in Bandage:* Ted Hecht, *Mattress Man:* Al Stewart, *Shaky and Sweaty:* Peter Potter, *Beetle:* Douglas Spencer, *Doctor:* Emmett Vogan, *Male Nurse:* James Millican, *Negro Man Talking to Himself:* Ernest Whitman, *Guard:* Lee Shumway, *Liquor Store Proprietor:* William Newell, *Irishman:* Pat Moriarity.

LOUISIANA PURCHASE (1941) Par.

Associate Producer, Harold Wilson. Directed by Irving Cummings. Color by Technicolor. Based on the musical comedy by Morrie Ryskind, from a story by B. G. De-Sylva. Screenplay, Jerome Chodorov and Joseph Fields. Art Directors, Hans Dreier and Robert Usher. Camera, Harry Hallenberger. Color Camera, Ray Rennahan. Color Director, Natalie Kalmus. Associate, Morgan Padelford. Editor, LeRoy Stone. Songs by Irving Berlin: "You're Lonely and I'm Lonely," "Louisiana Purchase," "It's a Lovely Day Tomorrow," "Dance With Me at the Mardi Gras." 98 minutes

Jim Taylor: Bob Hope, *Marina Von Minden:* Vera Zorina, *Senator Oliver P. Loganberry:* Victor Moore, *Madame Bordelaise:* Irene Bordoni, *Beatrice:* Dona Drake, *Colonel Davis, Sr.:* Raymond Walburn, *The Shadow:* Maxie Rosenbloom, *Emmy Lou:* Phyllis Ruth, *Davis, Jr.:* Frank Albertson, *Captain Whitfield:* Donald MacBride, *Dean Manning:* Andrew Tombes, *Speaker of the House:* Robert Warwick, *Gaston:* Charles LaTorre, *Danseur:* Charles Laskey, *Lawyer:* Emory Parnell, *Lawyer's Secretary:* Iris Meredith, *Saleslady:* Catherine Craig, *Jester:* Jack Norton, *Sam:* Sam McDaniel, *Louisiana Belles:* Kay Aldridge, Katharine Booth, Alaine Brandes, Barbara Britton, Brooke Evans, Blanche Grady, Lynda Grey, Margaret Hayes, Louise LaPlanche, Barbara Slater, Eleanor Stewart, Jean Wallace, *House Detective:* Edgar Dearing, *Ambulance Driver:* William Wright, *Cabby:* Tom Patricola, *Bellhop:* Dave Willock, *Jester:* Donald Kerr, *Girl Jesters:* Joy Barlowe, Patsy Mace, *Fuchsia Man:* Douglas Dean, *Radio Commentator:* John Hiestand, *Club Doorman:* Floyd Shackelford.

Louisiana Purchase with Victor Moore and Irene Bordoni.

Love Affair with Irene Dunne, Maria Ouspenskaya and Charles Boyer.

LOVE AFFAIR (1939) RKO.

Produced and directed by Leo Mc-Carey. Screenplay, Delmer Daves and Donald Ogden Stewart. Story by Mildred Cram and Leo McCarey. Camera, Rudolph Mate. Editors, Edward Dmytryk and George Hiveley, Special Effects, Vernon Walker. Assistant Director, James Anderson. Montage, Douglas Travers. Songs: "Wishing" by B. G. DeSylva; "Sing My Heart" by Harold Arlen and Ted Koehler. Remade as *An Affair to Remember* (20th, 1957). 87 minutes

Terry McKay: Irene Dunne, *Michel Marnet:* Charles Boyer, *Grandmother:* Maria Ouspenskaya, *Ken Bradley:* Lee Bowman, *Lois Clarke:* Astrid Allwyn, *Maurice Cobert:* Maurice Moscovich, *Boy on Ship:* Scotty Beckett, *Couple on Deck:* Bess Flowers, and Harold Miller, *Autograph Seeker:* Joan Brodel (Joan Leslie), *Cafe Manager:* Dell Henderson, *Nightclub patron:* Carol Hughes, *Doctor:* Leyland Hodgson, *Boarding House Keeper:* Ferike Boros, *Orphanage Superintendent "Picklepuss":* Frank McGlynn, Sr., *Priest:* Oscar O'Shea, *Drunk with Christmas Tree:* Tom Dugan, *Doctor:* Lloyd Ingraham, *Maid:* Phyllis Kennedy, *Extra:* Gerald Mohr.

LOVE FINDS ANDY HARDY (1938) MGM.

Directed by George B. Seitz. From the stories by Vivien R. Bretherton, based on the characters created by Aurania Rouverol. Screenplay, William Ludwig. Music, David Snell. Photography, Lester White. Editor, Ben Lewis. Songs: "In Between" by Roger Edens; "What Do You Know About Love?" "Meet the Beat of My Heart" and "It Never Rains But It Pours" by Mack Gordon and Harry Revel. 90 minutes

Judge James Hardy: Lewis Stone, *Andy Hardy:* Mickey Rooney, *Betsy Booth:* Judy Garland, *Marian Hardy:* Cecilia Parker, *Mrs. Hardy:* Fay Holden, *Polly Benedict:* Ann Rutherford, *Aunt Milly:* Betty Ross Clarke, *Cynthia Potter:* Lana Turner, *Augusta:* Marie Blake, *Dennis Hunt:* Don Castle, *Jimmy MacMahon:* Gene Reynolds, *Mrs. Tompkins:* Mary Howard, *Beezy:* George Breakston, *Peter Dugan:*

Love Finds Andy Hardy with Cecilia Parker, Lewis Stone, Fay Holden, Mickey Rooney and Judy Garland.

Raymond Hatton, *Bill Collector:* Frank Darien, *Judge:* Rand Brooks, *Court Attendant:* Erville Alderson.

LOVE IS A MANY SPLENDORED THING (1955) 20th. Producer, Buddy Adler. Director, Henry King. CinemaScope, De Luxe Color. Author, Han Suyin (from *A Many Splendored Thing*). Screenplay, John Patrick. Art Directors, Lyle R. Wheeler, George W. Davis. Music, Alfred Newman. Orchestration, Edward B. Powell. Cinematographer, Leon Shamroy. Editor, William Reynolds. 102 minutes

Love Is a Many Splendored Thing with Jennifer Jones and William Holden.

Mark Elliott: William Holden, *Han Suyin:* Jennifer Jones, *Mr. Palmer-Jones:* Torin Thatcher, *Adeline Palmer-Jones:* Isobel Elsom, *Dr. Tam:* Murray Matheson, *Ann Richards:* Virginia Gregg, *Robert Hung:* Richard Loo, *Nora Hing:* Soo Yong, *Third Uncle:* Philip Ahn, *Suzanne:* Jorja Curtright, *Suchen:* Donna Martell, *Oh-No:* Candace Lee, *Dr. Sen:* Kam Tong, *Fifth Brother:* James Hong, *Father Low:* Herbert Heyes, *Mei Loo:* Angela Loo, *Rosie Wu:* Marie Tsien, *British Sailor:* Ashley Cowan, *Nurse:* Jean Wong, *General Song:* Joseph Kim, *Wine Steward:* Marc Krah, *Hotel Manager:* Salvador Baguez, *Dining Room Captain:* Edward Colmans, *Fortune Teller:* Leonard Strong, *Second Brother:* Howard Soo Hoo, *Third Brother:* Walter Soo Hoo, *Elder Brother:* Keye Luke, *Old Loo:* Lee Tung Foo.

Love Letters with Jennifer Jones and Joseph Cotten.

LOVE LETTERS (1945) Par. Produced by Hal Wallis. Directed by William Dieterle. From the novel by Chris Massie. Screenplay, Ayn Rand. Art Directors, Hans Dreier and Roland Anderson. Music, Victor Young. Special Effects, Gordon Jennings. Process Photography, Farciot Edouart. Photography, Lee Garmes. Editor, Anne Bauchens. Song, "Love Letters," by Victor Young. 101 minutes

Singleton: Jennifer Jones, *Alan Quinton:* Joseph Cotten, *Dilly Carson:* Ann Richards, *Helen Wentworth:* Anita Louise, *Mack:* Cecil Kellaway, *Beatrice Remington:* Gladys Cooper, *Derek Quinton:* Byron Barr, *Roger Morland:* Robert Sully, *Defense Attorney:* Reginald Denny, *Bishop:* Ernest Cossart, *Jim Connings:* James Millican, *Mr. Quinton:* Lumsden Hare, *Mrs. Quinton:* Winifred Harris, *Bishop's Wife:* Ethel May Halls, *Judge:* Matthew Boulton, *Postman:* David Clyde, *Vicar:* Ian Wolfe, *Dodd:* Alec Craig, *Jupp:* Arthur Hohl, *Boy in Library:* Conrad Binyon, *Barmaid in Italian Inn:* Nina Borget, *Nurse:* Mary Field, *Proprietor of Italian Inn:* George Humbert, *Old Hag:* Constance Purdy, *Elderly Nurse:* Ottola Nesmith, *Farmer:* Harry Allen, *Young Man at Party:* Anthony Marsh, *Clare Foley:* Louise Currie, *Jeanette Campbell:* Catherine Craig.

Love Me or Leave Me with Dale Van Sickel, James Cagney and Johnny Day.

LOVE ME OR LEAVE ME (1955) MGM. Producer, Joe Pasternak. Director, Charles Vidor. CinemaScope, Eastman Color. Author, Daniel Fuchs. Screenplay, Daniel Fuchs, Isobel Lennart. Art Directors, Cedric Gibbons, Urie McCleary. Musical Director, George Stoll. Cinematographer, Arthur E. Arling. Editor, Ralph E. Winters. Dances, Alex Romero. 122 minutes

Ruth Etting: Doris Day, *Martin Snyder:* James Cagney, *Johnny Alderman:* Cameron Mitchell, *Bernard V. Loomis:* Robert Keith, *Frobisher:* Tom Tully, *Georgie:* Harry Bellaver, *Paul Hunter:* Richard Gaines, *Fred Taylor:* Peter Leeds, *Eddie Fulton:* Claude Stroud, *Jingle Girl:* Audrey Young, *Greg Trent:* John Harding, *Dancer:* Dorothy Abbott, *Bouncer:* Phil Schumacher, *Bouncer:* Henry Kulky, *Second Bouncer:* Otto Reichow, *Orry:* Jay Adler, *Irate Customer:* Mauritz Hugo, *Hostess:* Veda Ann Borg, *Claire:* Claire Carleton, *Stage Manager:* Benny Burt, *Mr. Brelston: Radio Station Manager:* Robert B. Carson, *Assistant Director:* James Drury, *Dance Director:* Richard Simmons,

Assistant Director: Michael Kostrick, *First Reporter:* Roy Engel, *Second Reporter:* John Damler, *Woman:* Genevieve Aumont, *Prop Man:* Roy Engel, *Stagehands:* Dale Van Sickel, Johnny Day.

LOVE ME TENDER (1956) 20th. Producer, David Weisbart. Director, Robert D. Webb. CinemaScope. Based on a story by Maurice Geraghty. Screenplay, Robert Buckner. Art Directors, Lyle R. Wheeler, Maurice Ransford. Music, Lionel Newman. Songs, Elvis Presley, Vera Matson. Orchestration, Edward B. Powell. Cinematographer, Leo Tover. Special Photographic Effects, Ray Kellogg. Editor, Hugh S. Fowler. Film debut of Elvis Presley, 21. 89 minutes

Love Me Tender with Richard Egan, Debra Paget and Elvis Presley.

Vance: Richard Egan, *Cathy:* Debra Paget, *Clint:* Elvis Presley, *Siringo:* Robert Middleton, *Brett Reno:* William Campbell, *Mike Gavin:* Neville Brand, *The Mother:* Mildred Dunnock, *Major Kincaid:* Bruce Bennett, *Ray Reno:* James Drury, *Ed Galt:* Russ Conway, *Kelso:* Ken Clark, *Davis:* Barry Coe, *Fleming:* L. Q. Jones, *Jethro:* Paul Burns, *Train Conductor:* Jerry Sheldon, *Storekeeper:* James Stone, *Auctioneer:* Ed Mundy, *First Soldier:* Joe Di Reda, *Station Agent:* Bobby Rose, *Paymaster:* Tom Greenway, *Major Harris:* Jay Jostyn, *Train Conductor:* Steve Darrell.

LOVE ME TONIGHT (1932) Par. Produced and directed by Rouben Mamoulian. Story, Leopold Marchand and Paul Arment. Screenplay, Samuel Hoffenstein, Waldemar Young, George Marion, Jr. Photography, Victor Milner. Songs by Richard Rodgers and Lorenz Hart: "The Song of Paree," "How Are You?", "Isn't It Romantic?", "Lover," "Mimi," "Poor Apache," "Love Me Tonight," "A Woman Needs Something Like That," "The Son of a Gun Is Nothing But a Tailor." 104 minutes

Love Me Tonight with Myrna Loy and Maurice Chevalier.

Maurice Courtelin: Maurice Chevalier, *Princess Jeanette:* Jeanette MacDonald, *Vicomte Gilbert de Vareze:* Charlie Ruggles, *Count de Savignac:* Charles Butterworth, *Countess Valentine:* Myrna Loy, *The Duke:* C. Aubrey Smith, *First Aunt:* Elizabeth Patterson, *Second Aunt:* Ethel Griffies, *Third Aunt:* Blanche Frederici, *Bridge Player:* Major Sam Harris, *The Doctor:* Joseph Cawthorn, *Major-Domo:* Flamond: Robert Greig, *Madame Dutoit, Dressmaker:* Ethel Wales, *Bakery Girl:* Marion "Peanuts" Byron, *Madame Dupont:* Mary Doran, *Emile:* Bert Roach, *Laundress:* Cecil Cunningham, *Composer:* Tyler Brooke, *Valet:* Edgar Norton, *Groom:* Herbert Mundin, *Chambermaid:* Rita Owin, *Shirtmaker:* Clarence Wilson, *Collector:* Gordon Westcott, *Pierre Dupont:* George Davis, *Taxi Driver:* Rolfe Sedan, *Hat Maker:* Tony Merlo, *Boot Maker:* William H. Turner, *Grocer:* George (Gabby) Hayes, *Bit:* Tom Ricketts, *Chef:* George Humbert,

THE LOVE PARADE (1929) Par. Produced and directed by Ernst Lubitsch. From the play *The Prince Consort* by Leon Xanrof and Jules Chancel. Story, Ernest Vajda and Guy Bolton. Editor, Merrill White. Photography, Victor Milner. Songs by Victor Schertzinger and Clifford Grey: "My Love Parade," "Dream Lover," "Let's Be Common," "Anything to Please the Queen," "March of the Grenadiers," "Paris Stays the Same," "Nobody's Using It Now," "Oo La La La," "The Queen Is Always Right." Film debut of Jeanette MacDonald. 110 minutes

Count Alfred Renard: Maurice Chevalier, *Queen Louise:* Jeanette MacDonald, *Jacques:* Lupino Lane, *Lulu:* Lillian Roth, *Master of Ceremonies:* Edgar Norton, *Prime Minister:* Lionel Belmore, *Foreign Minister:* Albert Roccardi, *Admiral:* Carl Stockdale, *Minister of War:* Eugene Pallette, *Sylvanian Ambassador:* E. H. Calvert, *Afghan Ambassador:* Russell Powell, *First Lady-in-Waiting:* Margaret Fealy, *Second Lady-in-Waiting:* Virginia Bruce, *Paulette:* Yola D'Avril, *Paulette's Husband:* Andre Cheron, *Priest:* Winter Hall, *Cross-eyed Lackey:* Ben Turpin, *Extra in Theater Audience Theatre Box: and to the Left of* Jean Harlow.

The Love Parade with Jeanette MacDonald and Maurice Chevalier.

LOVE WITH THE PROPER STRANGER (1963) Par. Produced by Alan J. Pakula. Directed by Robert Mulligan. A Pakula-Mulligan and Rona Production. Screenplay, Arnold Schulman. Music, Elmer Bernstein. Costumes, Edith Head. Art Directors, Hal Pereira and Roland Anderson. Cinematography, Milt Krasner. Editor, Aaron Stell. Title song by Johnny Mercer and Elmer Bernstein, sung by Jack Jones. Scenes filmed in New York City. 100 minutes

Angie Rossini: Natalie Wood, *Rocky Papasano:* Steve McQueen, *Barbie (Barbara of Seville):* Edie Adams, *Dominick Rossini:* Herschel Bernardi, *Anthony Columbo:* Tom Bosley, *Julio Rossini:* Harvey Lembeck, *Mama Rossini:* Penny Santon, *Anna:* Virginia Vincent, *Guido Rossini:* Nick Alexander, *Mrs. Papasano:* Augusta Ciolli, *Beetie:* Anne Hegira, *Lou:* Henry Howard, *Elio Papasano:* Mario Badolati,

Love With the Proper Stranger with Steve McQueen and Natalie Wood.

Lust for Life with Kirk Douglas and Anthony Quinn.

Woman Doctor: Elena Karam, *Mrs. Columbo:* Nina Varela, *Gina:* Marilyn Chris, *Priest:* Wolfe Barzell, *Little Boy:* Keith Worthey, *Carlos:* Frank Marth, *Flower Vendor:* Richard Bowler, *Truck Driver:* Lennie Bremen, *Yuki:* Nobu McCarthy, *Charlene:* Jean Shulman, *Harold:* Lou Herbert, *Moish:* M. Enserro, *Sidney:* Barney Martin, *Flooey:* Louis Guss, *Fat:* Tony Mordente, *Stein:* Val Avery, *Louie:* Dick Mulligan, *Klepp:* Paul Price, *Marge:* Arlene Golonka, *Accountant:* Richard Dysart, *Maria:* Loraine Abate, *Call Boy:* Vincent Deadrick, *Cye:* Victor Tayback.

LUCKY JORDAN (1942) Par. Associate Producer, Fred Kohlmar. Directed by Frank Tuttle. From a story by Charles Leonard. Screenplay, Darrell Ware and Karl Tunberg. Art Directors, Hans Dreier and Ernest Fegte. Cameraman, John Seitz. Editor, Archie Marshek. 84 minutes

Lucky Jordan: Alan Ladd, *Jill Evans:* Helen Walker, *Slip Moran:* Sheldon Leonard, *Annie:* Mabel Paige, *Pearl:* Marie McDonald, *Ernest Higgins:* Lloyd Corrigan, *Eddie:* Russell Hoyt, *Angelo Palacio:* Dave Willock, *Kesselman:* John Wengraf, *Kilpatrick:* Miles Mander, *Sergeant:* Charles Cane, *Little Man:* George F. Meader, *Woman with Little Man:* Virginia Brissac, *First Killer:* Al M. Hill, *Second Killer:* Fred Kohler, Jr., *Johnny:* Jack Roberts, *Gas Station Attendant:* Clem Bevans, *Charles* (Servant): Olaf Hytten, *Miller* (Gateman): William Halligan, *Mrs. Maggotti:* Kitty Kelly, *Joe Maggotti:* George Humbert, *Maid at Hollyhock School:* Dorothy Dandridge, *Harrison:* Joseph Downing, *Girl in Back Room:* Carol Hughes, *Army Guard:* Ralph Dunn, *Man:* Edward Earle, *Army Guard:* Lyle Latell, *Private Secretary:* Edythe Elliott, *Big-Ears:* John Harmon, *Colonel:* John Hamilton, *Colonel:* Roy Gordon, *Pearl's Boy Friend:* Kirk Alyn, *Hearndon:* Arthur Loft, *Florist:* Ronnie Rondell, *Sentry:* Terry Ray, *Helen:* Sara Berner, *Commanding Officer:* William Forrest, *Woman:* Ethel Clayton, *Gunman:* Anthony L. Caruso, *Saleslady in Toy Shop:* Georgia Backus, *Girl:* Yvonne De Carlo.

Lucky Jordan with Helen Walker and Alan Ladd.

LUST FOR LIFE (1956) MGM. Producer, John Houseman. Associated Producer, Jud Kinberg. Director, Vincente Minnelli. Cinema-Scope, MetroColor. Based on the novel by Irving Stone. Screenplay, Norman Corwin. Art Directors, Cedric Gibbons, Hans Peters, Preston Ames. Musical Director, Miklos Rozsa. Cinematographers, F. A. Young, Russell Harlan. Editor, Adrienne Fazan. 122 minutes

Vincent Van Gogh: Kirk Douglas, *Paul Gauguin:* Anthony Quinn, *Theo Van Gogh:* James Donald, *Christine:* Pamela Brown, *Dr. Gachet:* Everett Sloane, *Roulin:* Niall MacGinnis, *Anton Mauve:* Noel Purcell, *Theodorus Van Gogh:* Henry Daniell, *Anna Cornelia Van Gogh:* Madge Kennedy, *Willemien:* Jill Bennett, *Dr. Peyron:* Lionel Jeffries, *Dr. Bosman:* Laurence Naismith, *Colbert:* Eric Pohlmann, *Kay:* Jeanette Sterke, *Johanna:* Toni Gerry, *Rev. Stricker:* Wilton Graff, *Mrs. Stricker:* Isobel Elsom, *Rev. Peeters:* Davis Horne, *Commissioner Van Den Berghe:* Noel Howlett, *Commissioner De Smet:* Ronald Adam, *Ducrucq:* John Ruddock, *Rachel:* Julie Robinson, *Camille Pissarro:* David Leonard, *Emile Bernard:* William Phipps, *Seurat:* David Bond, *Pere Tanguy:* Frank Perls, *Waiter:* Jay Adler, *Adeline Ravoux:* Laurence Badie, *Durand-Ruel:* Rex Evans, *Sister Clothilde:* Marion Ross, *Elizabeth:* Mitzi Blake, *Cor:* Anthony Sydes, *Tersteeg:* Anthony Eustrel, *Jet:* Ernestine Barrier, *Lautrec:* Jerry Bergen, *Mme. Tanguy:* Belle Mitchell, *Dr. Rey:* Alec Mango, *Cordan:* Fred Johnson, *Pier:* Norman MacCowan, *Jan:* Mickey Maga.

MADAME CURIE (1943) MGM. Produced by Sidney Franklin. Directed by Mervyn LeRoy. Based on the book by Eve Curie. Screenplay, Paul Osborn and Paul H. Rameau. Art Director, Cedric Gibbons. Associate, Paul Groesse. Set Decorations, Edwin B. Willis. Associate, Hugh Hunt. Music, Herbert Stothart. Photography, Joseph Ruttenberg. Special Effects, Warren Newcombe. Costume Supervision, Irene Sharaff. Men's Costumes, Giles Steele. Make-up, Jack Dawn. Editor, Harold F. Kress. Sound, Douglas Shearer. Narrated by James Hilton. Film debut of Gigi Perreau, 2. 124 minutes

Madame Curie with Greer Garson and Walter Pidgeon.

Madame Marie Curie: Greer Garson, *Pierre Curie:* Walter Pidgeon, *Eugene Curie:* Henry Travers, *Professor Perot:* Albert Basserman, *David LeGros:* Robert Walker, *Lord Kelvin:* C. Aubrey Smith, *Madame Eugene Curie:* Dame May Whitty, *University President:* Victor Francen, *Madame Perot:* Elsa Basserman, *Doctor Becquerel:* Reginald Owen, *Reporter:* Van Johnson, *Irene, age 5:* Margaret O'Brien, *Eve, 18 months:* Ghislaine (Gigi) Perreau, *Professor Roget:* Lumsden Hare, *President of Businessmen's Board:* Moroni Olsen, *Businessmen:* Miles Mander, Arthur Shields, Frederic Worlock, *Doctor:* Eustace Wyatt, *Jewelry Salesman:* Marek Windheim, *Lucille:* Lisa Golm, *Doctor Bladh:* Alan Napier, *Lecturer's Voice:* Ray Collins, *Professor Constant's Voice:* Howard Freeman, *Monsieur Michaud:* Francis Pierlot, *Madame Michaud:* Almira Sessions, *Master Michaud:* Dickie Meyers, *Photographer:* Leo Mostovoy, *Singing Professor:* George Meader, *King Oscar:* Wyndham Standing, *Swedish Queen:* Ruty Cherrington, *Driver:* Ray Teal, *Seamstress:* Ilka Gruning.

Madame X with Ruth Chatterton and Mary Gordon.

MADAME X (1929) MGM. Directed by Lionel Barrymore. From the play by Alexandre Bisson. Scenario and Dialogue, Willard Mack. Photography, Arthur Reed. Editor, William S. Gray. Sound, Western Electric Movietone (Fox-Case) Process. Recording Engineer, Douglas Shearer. Art Director, Cedric Gibbons. Wardrobe, David Cox. Other versions of *Madame X:* Pathé, 1915; Goldwyn, 1920; MGM, 1937; Universal, 1966; *The Trial of Madame X* (British, 1955). 95 minutes

Floriot: Lewis Stone, *Jacqueline:* Ruth Chatterton, *Raymond:* Raymond Hackett, *Noel:* Holmes Herbert, *Rose:* Eugenie Besserer, *Doctor:* John P. Edington, *Colonel Hamby:* Mitchell Lewis, *Larocque:* Ullrich Haupt, *Merivel:* Sidney Toler, *Perissard:* Richard Carle, *Darrell:* Carroll Nye, *Valmorin:* Claude King, *Judge:* Chappell Dossett, *Baby's Nurse:* Mary Gordon.

THE MAGNIFICENT AMBERSONS (1942) RKO. Produced and directed by Orson Welles. A Mercury Production. Based on the novel

The Magnificent Ambersons with Tim Holt and Dolores Costello.

by Booth Tarkington. Screenplay, Orson Welles. Art Director, Mark-Lee Kirk. Music, Bernard Herrmann. Cameraman, Stanley Cortez. Special Effects, Vernon L. Walker. Editor, Robert Wise. Remake of *Pampered Youth* (Vitagraph, 1925). 88 minutes

Eugene: Joseph Cotten, *Isabel:* Dolores Costello, *Lucy:* Anne Baxter, *George:* Tim Holt, *Fanny:* Agnes Moorehead, *Jack:* Ray Collins, *Major Amberson:* Richard Bennett, *Benson:* Erskine Sanford, *Wilbur Minafer:* Don Dillaway, *Sam, the Butler:* J. Louis Johnson, *Uncle John:* Charles Phipps, *Spectators at Funeral:* Dorothy Vaughan, Elmer Jerome, *Mary:* Olive Ball, *Guests:* Nina Guilbert, John Elliott, *Mrs. Foster:* Anne O'Neal, *Matrons:* Kathryn Sheldon, Georgia Backus, *Hardware Man:* Henry Roquemore, *Nurse:* Hilda Plowright, *Fred Kinney:* Mel Ford, *Charles Johnson:* Bob Pittard, *Landlady:* Lillian Nicholson, *House Servant:* Billy Elmer, *Citizens:* Lew Kelly, Maynard Holmes, *Drug Clerk:* Gus Schilling, *George as a boy:* Bobby Cooper, *Elijah:* Drew Roddy, *Reverend Smith:* Jack Baxley, *Laborer:* Heenan Elliott, *Girl:* Nancy Gates, *Young Man:* John Maguire, *Chauffeur/Citizen:* Ed Howard, *Youth at Accident:* William Blees, *Cop at Accident:* James Westerfield, *Cop:* Philip Morris, *Barber:* Jack Santoro, *Ballroom Extra (cut from featured role):* Louis Hayward.

MAGNIFICENT OBSESSION (1954) Univ. Producer, Ross Hunter. Director, Douglas Sirk. Technicolor. Based on the novel by Lloyd C. Douglas and screenplay by Sarah Y. Mason, Victor Heerman. Adaptation, Wells Root. Screenplay, Robert Blees. Art Directors, Bernard Herzbrun, Emrich Nicolson. Cinematographer, Russell Metty. Editor, Milton Carruth. Remake of Universal's 1935 film. 108 minutes

Magnificent Obsession with Jane Wyman and Rock Hudson.

Helen Phillips: Jane Wyman, *Bob Merrick:* Rock Hudson, *Nancy Ashford:* Agnes Moorehead, *Joyce Phillips:* Barbara Rush, *Tom Masterson:* Gregg Palmer, *Randolph:* Otto Kruger, *Dr. Giraud:* Paul Cavanagh, *Valerie:* Sara Shane, *Dr. Dodge:* Richard H. Cutting, *Judy:* Judy Nugent, *Mrs. Eden:* Helen Kleeb, *Sgt. Burnham:* Robert B. Williams, *Sgt. Ames:* Will White, *Williams:* George Lynn, *First Mechanic:* Jack Kelly, *Switchboard Girl:* Lisa Gaye, *Customers:* William Leslie, Lance Fuller, Brad Jackson, Myrna Hansen, *Dr. Allan:* Alexander Campbell, *Dr. Fuss:* Rudolph Anders, *Dr. Laradetti:* Fred Nurney, *Dr. Hofer:* John Mylong, *Dan:* Joe Mell, *Mr. Jouvet:* Harold Dyrenforth, *Mr. Long:* Norbert Schiller, *Mrs. Miller:* Mae Clarke, *Switchboard Girl:* Kathleen O'Malley, *Maid:* Joy Hallward, *Second Mechanic:* Lee Roberts, *Chris:* Harvey Grant.

THE MAJOR AND THE MINOR (1942) Par. Produced by Arthur Hornblow, Jr. Directed by Billy Wilder. Suggested by the play *Connie Goes Home* by Edward Childs Carpenter, and the *Saturday Evening Post* story "Sunny Goes Home" by Fannie Kilbourne. Screenplay, Charles Brackett and Billy Wilder. Art Directors, Hans Dreier and Roland Anderson. Music Score, Robert Emmett Dolan. Cameraman, Leo Tover. Editor, Doane Harrison. Remade as *You're Never Too Young* (Paramount, 1955) with Martin and Lewis. 100 minutes

The Major and the Minor with Ray Milland, Ginger Rogers, Edward Fielding and Rita Johnson.

Susan Applegate: Ginger Rogers, *Major Kirby:* Ray Milland, *Pamela Hill:* Rita Johnson, *Mr. Osborne:* Robert Benchley, *Lucy Hill:* Diana Lynn, *Colonel Hill:* Edward Fielding, *Cadet Osborne:* Frankie Thomas, Jr., *Cadet Wigton:* Raymond Roe, *Cadet Korner:* Charles Smith, *Cadet Babcock:* Larry Nunn, *Cadet Miller:* Billy Dawson, *Cadet Summerville:* Billy Ray, *Shumaker:* Stanley Desmond, *Bertha:* Marie Blake, *Mrs. Applegate:* Lela Rogers, *Mrs. Osborne:* Norma Varden, *Mrs. Shackleford:* Gretl Sherk, *Mother in Railroad Station:* Mary Field, *Reverend Doyle:* Aldrich Bowker, *Major Griscom:* Boyd Irwin, *Captain Durand:* Byron Shores, *Will Duffy:* Richard Fiske, *Doorman:* Dell Henderson, *Station Master:* Ed Peil, Sr., *Elevator Boy:* Ken Lundy.

MAKE WAY FOR TOMORROW (1937) Par. Produced and directed by Leo McCarey. Based on the novel *The Years Are So Long* by Josephine Lawrence, and a play by Helen and Nolan Leary. Screenplay, Vina Delmar. Art Directors, Hans Dreier and Bernard Herzbrun. Music, George Antheil. Arrangements, Victor Young. Musical Director, Boris Morros. Title song by Leo Robin, Sam Coslow, and Jean Schwartz. Camera, William C. Mellor. Editor, LeRoy Stone. Special Effects, Gordon Jennings. Assistant Director, Harry Scott, Sound, Walter Oberst and Don Johnson. Minna Gombell and Ray Mayer replaced Margaret Hamilton and Charles Arnt. 92 minutes

Barkley Cooper: Victor Moore, *Lucy Cooper:* Beulah Bondi, *Anita Cooper:* Fay Bainter, *George Cooper:* Thomas Mitchell, *Harvey Chase:* Porter Hall, *Rhoda Cooper:* Barbara Read, *Max Rubens:* Maurice Moscovitch, *Cora Payne:* Elisabeth Risdon, *Mr. Henning:* Gene Lockhart, *Bill Payne:* Ralph M. Remley, *Mamie:* Louise Beavers, *Doctor:* Louis Jean Heydt, *Carlton Gorman:* Gene Morgan, *Auto Salesman:* Dell Henderson, *Nellie Chase:* Minna Gombell, *Robert Cooper:* Ray Mayer, *Secretary:* Ruth Warren, *Hotel Manager:* Paul Stanton, *Richard Payne:* George Offerman, Jr., *Jack Payne:* Tommy Bupp, *Mrs. Rubens:* Ferike Boros, *Mr. Hunter:* Granville Bates, *Mr. Dale:* Byron Foulger, *Mrs. McKenzie:* Averil Cameron, *Boy Friend:* Nick Lukats, *Head Usherette:* Kitty McHugh, *Usherette:* Terry Ray (Ellen Drew), *Doorman:* Ralph Brooks, *Woman Customer:* Ethel Clayton, *Businessmen:* Ralph Lewis, Phillips Smalley, *Letter* Howard Mitchell, *Man:* Don Brodie, *Ticket Seller:* William Newell, *Carrier: Woman:* Rosemary Theby, *Man:* Richard R. Neill, *Bridge*

Make Way for Tomorrow with Thomas Mitchell, Beulah Bondi and Victor Moore.

Player: Helen Dickson, *Passerby/Man in Overcoat/Carpet Sweeper:* Leo McCarey.

THE MALE ANIMAL (1942) WB. Producer, Hal B. Wallis. Associate Producer, Wolfgang Reinhardt. Directed by Elliott Nugent. From the play by James Thurber and Elliott Nugent. Screenplay, Julius J. and Philip G. Epstein and Stephen Morehouse Avery. Photography, Arthur Edeson. Editor, Thomas Richards. Remade as *She's Working Her Way Through College* (WB, 1952), which also featured Don DeFore. 101 minutes

Tommy Turner: Henry Fonda, *Ellen Turner:* Olivia De Havilland, *Joe Ferguson:* Jack Carson, *Patricia Stanley:* Joan Leslie, *Ed Keller:* Eugene Pallette, *Michael Barnes:* Herbert Anderson, *Cleota:* Hattie McDaniel, *Dr. Damon:* Ivan Simpson, *Wally:* Don DeFore, *Hot Garters Garner:* Jean Ames, *Blanche Damon:* Minna Phillips, *Myrtle Keller:* Regina Wallace, *Coach Sprague:* Frank Mayo, *Alumnus:* William B. Davidson, *Nutsy Miller:* Bobby Barnes, *Boy:* Albert Faulkner, *Secretary:* Jane Randolph, *Faculty Member:* Howard Hickman, *Editor:* John Maxwell, *News Dealer:* Edward Clark, *Newspapermen:* George Meeker, Will Morgan, Raymond Bailey, *Trustee:* Arthur Loft, *Trustee's Wife:* Leah Baird, *Students:* Spec O'Donnell, Ray Montgomery, David Willock, Byron Barr (Gig Young), Michael Ames (Tod Andrews), Audrey Long, Charles Drake, Joan Winfield, *Reporters:* Walter Brooke, Hank Mann, De Wolfe Hopper (William Hopper), Creighton Hale.

The Male Animal with Henry Fonda and Olivia De Havilland.

THE MALTESE FALCON (1941) WB. Executive Producer, Hal B. Wallis. Associate Producer, Henry Blanke. Directed by John Huston. Based on the novel by Dashiell Hammett. Screenplay, John Huston. Art Director, Robert Haas. Music, Adolph Deutsch. Photography, Arthur Edeson. Editor, Thomas Richards. Assistant Director, Claude

The Maltese Falcon with Humphrey Bogart, Mary Astor and Jerome Cowan.

Archer. Dialogue Director, Robert Foulk. Sound, Oliver S. Garretson. Orchestrations, Arthur Lange. Make-up, Perc Westmore. Gowns, Orry-Kelly. Film debut of Sydney Greenstreet, 61; John Huston's first film as a director. Previous Warner Brothers versions: *The Maltese Falcon* (also, *Dangerous Female*, 1931), and *Satan Met a Lady* (1936). 100 minutes

Sam Spade: Humphrey Bogart, *Brigid O'Shaughnessy:* Mary Astor, *Iva Archer:* Gladys George, *Joel Cairo:* Peter Lorre, *Detective Lt. Dundy:* Barton MacLane, *Effie Perine:* Lee Patrick, *Kasper Gutman:* Sydney Greenstreet, *Detective Tom Polhaus:* Ward Bond, *Miles Archer:* Jerome Cowan, *Wilmer Cook:* Elisha Cook, Jr., *Luke:* James Burke, *Frank Richman:* Murray Alper, *District Attorney Bryan:* John Hamilton, *Mate of the* LA PALOMA *Emory* Parnell, *Policeman:* Robert E. Homans, *Stenographer:* Creighton Hale, *Reporters:* Charles Drake, William Hopper, Hank Mann, *Announcer:* Jack Mower, *Captain Jacobi:* Walter Huston.

A MAN CALLED PETER (1955) 20th. Producer, Samuel G. Engel. Director, Henry Koster. CinemaScope, De Luxe Color. Based on the novel by Catherine Marshall. Screenplay, Eleanore Griffin. Art Directors, Lyle Wheeler, Maurice Ransford. Musical Director, Alfred Newman. Cinematographer, Harold Lipstein. Special Photographic Effects, Ray Kellogg. Editor, Robert Simpson. 119 minutes

A Man Called Peter with Jean Peters and Richard Todd.

Peter Marshall: Richard Todd, *Catherine Marshall:* Jean Peters, *Mrs. Fowler:* Marjorie Rambeau, *Mrs. Findlay:* Jill Esmond, *Senator Harvey:* Les Tremaine, *Mr. Peyton:* Robert Burton, *Mrs. Peyton:* Gladys Hurlbut, *Col. Tremaine:* Richard Garrick, *Barbara Tremaine:* Gloria Gordon, *Peter John Marshall:* Billy Chapin, *Mrs. Tremaine:* Sally Corner, *Senator Wiley:* Voltaire Perkins, *Emma:* Marietta Canty, *Senator Prescott:* Edward Earle, *Peter Marshall (ages 7 and 14):* Peter Votrian, *Maitre 'D:* Sam McDaniel, *Miss Crilly:* Dorothy Neumann, *Miss Hopkins:* Doris Lloyd, *President:* William Forrest, *Miss Standish:* Barbara Morrison, *Dr. Black:* Carlyle Mitchell, *Willie:* Amanda Randolph, *Mr. Briscoe:* Emmett Lynn, *Butler:* William Walker, *President of Senate:* Charles Evans, *Chaplain Thomas:* Larry Kent, *Holden:* Roy Glenn, Sr., *Nurse:* Ruth Clifford, *Mr. Findlay:* Ben Wright, *Mrs. Ferguson:* Florence MacAfee.

THE MANCHURIAN CANDIDATE (1962) UA. Producers, George Axelrod, John Frankenheimer. Director, John Frankenheimer. Screenplay, George Axelrod. Based on the novel by Richard Condon. Executive Producer, Howard W. Koch. Music, David Amram. Assistant Director, Joseph Behm. Costumes, Moss Mabry. An M. C. Production. Executive Producer, Howard W. Koch. Art Director, Richard Sylbert. Cinematographer, Lionel Lindon. Editor, Ferris Webster. 126 minutes

Bennett Marco: Frank Sinatra, *Raymond Shaw:* Laurence Harvey, *Rosie:* Janet Leigh, *Raymond's mother:* Angela Lansbury, *Chunjin:*

The Manchurian Candidate with Frank Sinatra and Janet Leigh.

Henry Silva, *Senator John Iselin:* James Gregory, *Jocie Jordon:* Leslie Parrish, *Senator Thomas Jordon:* John McGiver, *Yen Lo:* Knigh Dhiegh, *Cpl. Melvin:* James Edwards, *Colonel:* Douglas Henderson, *Zilkov:* Albert Paulsen, *Secretary of Defense:* Barry Kelley, *Holborn Gaines:* Lloyd Corrigan, *Berezovo:* Madame Spivy.

THE MAN FROM LARAMIE (1955) Col. Producer, William Goetz. Director, Anthony Mann. CinemaScope, Technicolor. Based on a story by Thomas T. Flynn. Screenplay, Philip Yordan, Frank Burt. Art Director, Cary Odell. Musical Director, Morris Stoloff. Cinematographer, Charles Lang, Jr. Editor, William Lyon. 104 minutes

Will Lockhart: James Stewart, *Vic Hansbro:* Arthur Kennedy, *Alec Waggoman:* Donald Crisp, *Barbara Waggoman:* Cathy O'Donnell, *Dave Waggoman:* Alex Nicol, *Kate Canaday:* Aline MacMahon, *Charley O'Leary:* Wallace Ford, *Chris Boldt:* Jack Elam, *Frank Darrah:* John War Eagle, *Tom Quigby:* James Millican, *Fritz:* Gregg Barton, *Spud Oxton:* Boyd Stockman, *Padre:* Frank de Kova, *Dr. Selden:* Eddy Waller.

The Man From Laramie with Aline MacMahon and James Stewart.

MANHATTAN MELODRAMA (1934) MGM. Produced by David O. Selznick. Directed by W. S. Van Dyke. Original Story, Arthur Caesar. A Cosmopolitan Production. Screenplay, Oliver H. P. Garrett and Joseph L. Mankiewicz. Photography, James Wong Howe. Editor, Ben Lewis. Song by Richard Rodgers and Lorenz Hart, "The Bad in Every Man," later became "Blue Moon." 93 minutes

(Edward) Blackie Gallagher: Clark Gable, *Jim Wade:* William Powell, *Eleanor Packer:* Myrna Loy, *Father Joe:* Leo Carrillo, *Spud:* Nat Pendleton, *Poppa Rosen:* George Sidney, *Annabelle:* Isabel Jewell, *Tootsie Malone:* Muriel Evans, *Richard Snow:* Thomas Jackson, *Miss Adams:* Claudelle Kaye, *Blackie's Attorney:* Frank Conroy, *Mannie Arnold:* Noel Madison, *Blackie at 12:* Mickey Rooney, *Jim at 12:* Jimmy Butler, *Dancer on Boat:* Vernon Dent, *Heckler:* Pat

Manhattan Melodrama with Clark Gable, Nat Pendleton and John Marston.

Moriarity, *Trotskyite:* Leonid Kinskey, *Yacht Captain Swenson:* Edward Van Sloan, *Politician:* George Irving, *Assistant Prosecutor:* Emmett Vogan, *Bailiff (Extra):* Lee Phelps, *Negro Con:* Sam McDaniel, *Warden:* Samuel S. Hinds, *Guard:* Wade Boteler, *Cotton Club Singer:* Shirley Ross, *Coates:* John Marston.

THE MAN IN THE GRAY FLANNEL SUIT (1956) 20th. Producer, Darryl F. Zanuck. Director, Nunnally Johnson. CinemaScope, De Luxe Color. Based on the novel by Sloan Wilson. Screenplay, Nunnally Johnson. Art Directors, Lyle R. Wheeler, Jack Martin Smith. Music, Bernard Herrmann. Cinematographer, Charles G. Clarke. Editor, Dorothy Spender. 153 minutes

The Man in the Gray Flannel Suit with Sandy Descher, Jennifer Jones, Gregory Peck, Portland Mason.

Tom Rath: Gregory Peck, *Betsy Rath:* Jennifer Jones, *Hopkins:* Fredric March, *Maria:* Marisa Pavan, *Judge Bernstein:* Lee J. Cobb, *Mrs. Hopkins:* Ann Harding, *Caesar Gardella:* Keenan Wynn, *Hawthorne:* Gene Lockhart, *Susan Hopkins:* Gigi Perreau, *Janie:* Portland Mason, *Walker:* Arthur O'Connell, *Bill Ogden:* Henry Daniell, *Mrs. Manter:* Connie Gilchrist, *Edward Schultz:* Joseph Sweeney, *Barbara:* Sandy Descher, *Pete:* Mickey Maga, *Mahoney:* Kenneth Tobey, *Miriam:* Geraldine Wall, *Police Sergeant:* Jack Mather, *Dr. Pearce:* Frank Wilcox, *Miss Lawrence:* Nan Martin, *Gina:* Phyllis Graffeo, *Mrs. Hopkins' Maid:* Dorothy Adams, *Maid:* Dorothy Phillips, *Waiter:* John Breen, *Carriage Driver:* Mario Siletti, *Master Sergeant Mathews:* Roy Glenn, *First German Soldier:* Robert Boon, *Second German Soldier:* Jim Brandt, *Third German Soldier:* Otto Reichow, *Soldier:* Harry Lauter, *Soldier:* William Phipps, *Medic:* De Forrest Kelley.

THE MAN WHO CAME TO DINNER (1941) WB. Vice-president in Charge of Production, Jack L. Warner Executive Producer, Hal B. Wallis. Associate Producers, Jack Saper and Jerry Wald. Directed by William Keighley. Based on the play by George S. Kaufman and Moss

The Man Who Came to Dinner with Junior Coghlan, Bette Davis and Monty Woolley.

Hart (which evolved into the musical *Sherry,* 1967). Screenplay, Julius J. and Philip G. Epstein. Art Director, Robert Haas. Music, Frederick Hollander. Music Director, Leo F. Forbstein. Photography, Tony Gaudio. Editor, Jack Killifer. Assistant Director, Dick Mayberry. Sound, Charles Long. Gowns, Orry-Kelly. Make-up, Perc Westmore. Monty Woolley repeats his stage role, a caricature of Alexander Woollcott. 112 minutes

Sheridan Whiteside: Monty Woolley, *Maggie Cutler:* Bette Davis, *Lorraine Sheldon:* Ann Sheridan, *Bert Jefferson:* Richard Travis, *Banjo:* Jimmy Durante, *Beverly Carlton:* Reginald Gardiner, *Mrs. Stanley:* Billie Burke, *June Stanley:* Elisabeth Fraser, *Ernest Stanley:* Grant Mitchell, *Dr. Bradley:* George Barbier, *Miss Preen:* Mary Wickes, *Richard Stanley:* Russell Arms, *Harriett Stanley:* Ruth Vivian, *John:* Edwin Stanley, *Sarah:* Betty Roadman, *Mrs. Gibbons:* Laura Hope Crews, *Mr. Gibbons:* Chester Clute, *Sandy:* Charles Drake, *Cosette:* Nanette Vallon, *Radio Man:* John Ridgely, *Harry:* Pat McVey, *Telegraph Boy:* Frank Coghlan, Jr., *Newspaperman:* Roland Drew, *Announcer:* Sam Hayes, *Guard:* Eddy Chandler, *Michaelson:* Frank Moran, *Haggerty:* Ernie Adams, *Expressmen:* Hank Mann, Cliff Saum, *Vendor:* Billy Wayne, *Porter:* Dudley Dickerson, *Radio Men:* Herbert Gunn, Creighton Hale, *Plainclothesmen:* Jack Mower, Frank Mayo, *Man:* Fred Kelsey, *Girls:* Georgia Carroll, Lorraine Gettman (Leslie Brooks), Peggy Diggins, Alix Talton.

THE MAN WHO KNEW TOO MUCH (1956) Par. Producer, Alfred Hitchcock. Associate Producer, Herbert Coleman. Director, Alfred Hitchcock. VistaVision, Technicolor. Authors, Charles Bennett, D. B. Wyndham-Lewis. Screenplay, John Michael Hayes, Angus MacPhail. Art Directors, Hal Pereira, Henry Bumstead. Musical Director, Bernard Herrman. Cinematographer, Robert Burks. Editor, George Tomasini. Songs: "Que Sera Sera" by Livingston and Evans; "Storm

The Man Who Knew Too Much with Doris Day and James Stewart.

Cloud Cantata" by Arthur Benjamin and D. B. Wyndham-Lewis. Remake of the 1934 Gaumont-British Hitchcock film. 120 minutes

Ben McKenna: James Stewart, *Jo McKenna:* Doris Day, *Mrs. Drayton:* Brenda de Banzie, *Mr. Drayton:* Bernard Miles, *Buchanan:* Ralph Truman, *Louis Bernard:* Daniel Gelin, *Ambassador:* Magens Wieth, *Val Parnell:* Alan Mowbray, *Jan Peterson:* Hillary Brooke, *Hank McKenna:* Christopher Olsen, *Rien-Assassin:* Reggie Nalder, *Asst. Mgr.:* Richard Wattis, *Woburn:* Noel Willman, *Helen Parnell:* Alix Talton, *Police Inspector:* Yves Brainville, *Cindy Fontaine:* Carolyn Jones, *Foreign Prime Minister:* Alexi Bobrinskoy, *Arab:* Abdelhaq Chraibi, *Edna:* Betty Baskcomb, *Chauffeur:* Leo Gordon, *English Handyman:* Patrick Aherne, *French Police:* Louis Mercier, Anthony Warde, *Detective:* Lewis Martin, *Bernard's Girl Friend:* Gladys Holland, *Headwaiter:* Peter Camlin, *Henchman:* Ralph Neff, *Butler:* John Marshall, *Special Branch Officer:* Eric Snowden, *Arab:* Lou Krugman, *Guard:* Milton Frome.

THE MAN WHO PLAYED GOD (1932) WB. Directed by John G. Adolfi. Based on the short story by Gouverneur Morris, and the play *The Silent Voice* by Jules Eckert Goodman. Scenario and Dialogue, Julian Josephson and Maude Howell. Photography, James Van Trees. Editor, William Holmes. George Arliss starred in the play and the 1922 silent version. Other versions: *The Man Who Played God* (United Artists, 1922), *Sincerely Yours* (Warners, 1955) with Liberace. 81 minutes

Montgomery Royle: George Arliss, *Mildred Miller:* Violet Heming, *Battle:* Ivan Simpson, *Florence Royle:* Louise Closser Hale, *Grace Blair:* Bette Davis, *The King:* Andre Luguet, *Harold Van Adam:* Donald Cook, *Doctor:* Charles E. Evans, *Lip Reader:* Oscar Apfel, *French Concert Manager:* Paul Porcasi, *Eddie:* Ray Milland, *Jenny:* Dorothy LeBaire, *First Boy:* William Janney, *First Girl:* Grace Durkin, *Reporter:* Russell Hopton, *King's Aide:* Murray Kinnell, *Chittendon:* Harry Stubbs, *Alice Chittendon:* Hedda Hopper, *Detective:* Wade Boteler, *Russian Officers:* Alex Ikonikoff, Michael Visaroff, Paul Panzer, *Man:* Fred Howard.

The Man Who Played God with Bette Davis and George Arliss.

THE MAN WITH THE GOLDEN ARM (1955) UA. Produced and directed by Otto Preminger. From the novel by Nelson Algren. Screenplay, Walter Newman and Lewis Meltzer. Music, Elmer Bernstein. Jazz by Shorty Rogers and his Giants with Shelly Manne. Assistant to the Producer, Maximilian Slater. Designed by Joe Wright. Assistant Directors, Horace Hough and James Engle. Costume Superviser, Mary Ann Nyberg. Music Editor, Leon Birnbaum. Photography, Sam Leavitt. Editor, Louis R. Loeffler. 119 minutes

Frankie: Frank Sinatra, *Zosh:* Eleanor Parker, *Molly:* Kim Novak, *Sparrow:* Arnold Stang, *Louie:* Darren McGavin, *Schwiefka:* Robert Strauss, *Drunky:* John Conte, *Vi:* Doro Merande, *Markette:* George E. Stone, *Williams:* George Mathews, *Dominowski:* Leonid Kinskey,

Man With the Golden Arm with Frank Sinatra and Kim Novak.

Bednar: Emile Meyer, *Shorty Rogers:* Himself, *Shelly Manne:* Himself, *Piggy:* Frank Richards, *Lane:* Will Wright, *Kvorka:* Tommy Hart, *Antek:* Frank Marlowe, *Chester:* Ralph Neff, *Vangie:* Martha Wentworth.

MARIE ANTOINETTE (1938) MGM. Producer, Hunt Stromberg. Director, W. S. Van Dyke. Based on the book by Stephan Zweig. Screenplay, Claudine West, Donald Ogden Stewart, Ernest Vajda. Art Director, Cedric Gibbons. Montage, Slavko Vorkapich. Score, Herbert Stothart. Dances, Albertina Rasch. Cameraman, William Daniels, Editor, Robert J. Kern. Song by Bob Wright, Chet Forrest and Herbert Stothart: "Amour Eternal Amour." 160 minutes

Marie Antoinette: Norma Shearer, *Count Axel de Fersen:* Tyrone Power, *King Louis XV:* John Barrymore, *Mme. DuBarry:* Gladys George, *King Louis XVI:* Robert Morley, *Princess DeLamballe:* Anita Louise, *Duke of Orleans:* Joseph Schildkraut, *Count Mercy:* Henry Stephenson, *Artois:* Reginald Gardiner, *Gamin:* Peter Bull, *Provence:* Albert Van Dekker, *Prince DeRohan:* Barnett Parker, *Mme. De-Noailles:* Cora Witherspoon, *Drouet:* Joseph Calleia, *Court Aide:* Henry Kolker, *Rabblerouser:* Horace MacMahon, *Citizen-Officer:* Robert Barrat, *Sauce:* Ivan F. Simpson, *Robespierre:* George Meeker, *Princess Theresa:* Marilyn Knowlden, *Dauphin:* Scotty Beckett, *La Motte:* Henry Daniell, *Empress Marie Theresa:* Alma Kruger, *Toulan:* Leonard Penn, *Gov. of Conciergerie:* George Zucco, *Herbert (Jailer):* Ian Wolfe, *LaFayette:* John Burton, *Mme. La Motte:* Mae Busch, *Mme. DeLerchenfeld:* Cecil Cunningham, *Mme. LePolignac:* Ruth Hussey, *Benjamin Franklin:* Walter Walker, *Choisell:* Claude King, *Goguelot:* Herbert Rawlinson, *Danton:* Wade Crosby, *Marquis De St. Priest:* George Houston, *Bearded Man, a Leader of the People:* Morini Olsen, *Peddler:* Barry Fitzgerald, *M. de Cosse:* Harry Davenport, *Boehmer (Jeweler):* Olaf Hytten, *Marat:* Anthony Warde, *Louise:* Rafaela Ottiano.

Marie Antoinette with Mae Busch, Anita Louise, Olaf Hytten and Norma Shearer.

Marjorie Morningstar with Everett Sloane, Natalie Wood and Ed Wynn.

MARJORIE MORNINGSTAR (1958) WB. Producer, Milton Sperling. Director, Irving Rapper. WarnerColor. Screenplay by Everett Freeman. Based on novel by Herman Wouk. Costumes by Howard Shoup. Assistant Director, Don Page. Music by Max Steiner. "A Very Precious Love," song by Sammy Fain and Paul Francis Webster. Dances and musical numbers staged by Jack Baker. A Beachwold Picture. Photography, Harry Stradling. 123 minutes

Noel Airman: Gene Kelly, *Marjorie Morgenstern:* Natalie Wood, *Uncle Samson:* Ed Wynn, *Rose Morgenstern:* Claire Trevor, *Arnold Morgenstern:* Everett Sloane, *Wally:* Marty Milner, *Marsha Zelenko:* Carolyn Jones, *Greech:* George Tobias, *Lou Michaelson:* Jesse White, *Doctor David Harris:* Martin Balsam, *Puddles Podell:* Alan Reed, *Sandy Lamm:* Edward Byrnes, *Seth:* Howard Bert, *Philip Berman:* Paul Picerni, *Imogene:* Ruta Lee, *Karen:* Patricia Denise, *Elevator Operator:* Lester Dorr, *Leon Lamm:* Carl Sklover, *Mary Lamm:* Jean Vachon, *Miss Kimble:* Elizabeth Harrower, *Mr. Klabber:* Guy Raymond, *Carlos:* Edward (Eddie) Foster, *Blair:* Leslie Bradley, *Tonia Zelenko:* Maida Severn, *Helen Harris:* Fay Nuell, *Nate:* Fred Rapport, *Frank:* Harry Seymour, *Seth's Girl Friend:* Shelly Fabares, *Mr. Zelenko:* Walter Clinton, *Civil Official:* Pierre Watkin, *Clerk:* Reginald Sheffield, *Betsy:* Sandy Livingston, *Alec:* Peter Brown, *Wally's Girl Friend:* Gail Ganley, *Harry Morgenstern:* Russell Ash, *Romeo:* Rad Fulton.

MARKED WOMAN (1937) WB. Executive Producer, Hal B. Wallis. Associate Producer, Lou Edelman. Directed by Lloyd Bacon. Original Screenplay, Robert Rossen and Abem Finkel. Art Director, Max Parker. Music Director, Leo F. Forbstein. Photography, George Barnes. Editor, Jack Killifer. Song by Harry Warren and Al Dubin, "My Silver Dollar Man." 96 minutes

Mary Dwight (Strauber): Bette Davis, *David Graham:* Humphrey Bogart, *Betty Strauber:* Jane Bryan, *Johnny Vanning:* Eduardo Ciannelli, *Emmy Lou Egan:* Isabel Jewell, *Louie:* Allen Jenkins, *Estelle Porter:* Mayo Methot, *Gabby Marvin:* Lola Lane, *Charley Delaney:* Ben Welden, *D. A. Arthur Sheldon:* Henry O'Neill, *Florrie Liggett:*

Marked Woman with Ralph Dunn, Humphrey Bogart, Gordon Hart and Bette Davis.

Rosalind Marquis, *Gordon:* John Litel, *Ralph Krawford:* Damian O'Flynn, *George Beler:* Robert Strange, *Bell Captain:* James (Archie) Robbins, *Bob Crandall:* William B. Davidson, *Vincent, Sugar Daddy:* John Sheehan, *Mac:* Sam Wren, *Eddie, Sugar Daddy:* Kenneth Harlan, *Lawyer at Jail:* Raymond Hatton, *Henchmen:* Alan Davis, Allen Matthews, *Taxi Driver:* John Harron, *Taxi Driver:* Frank Faylen, *Mug:* Norman Willis, *Detectives: Ferguson,* Guy Usher, *Casey,* Ed Stanley, *Judge:* Gordon Hart, *Sheriff John Truble:* Arthur Aylesworth, *Court Clerk:* Ralph Dunn, *Foreman of Jury:* Wilfred Lucas, *Drunk:* Jack Norton, *Elevator Boy:* Carlyle Moore, Jr., *Court Clerk:* Emmett Vogan, *Foreman:* Jack Mower, *Judge:* Pierre Watkin, *Little Joe:* Herman Marks.

THE MARK OF ZORRO (1940) 20th. Director, Rouben Mamoulian. Based on the story "The Curse of Capistrano" by Johnston McCulley. Adaptation, Garret Ford, Bess Meredith. Cameraman. Arthur Miller. Editor, Robert Bischoff. Remake of 1920 UA film. 93 minutes

Diego Vega: Tyrone Power, *Lolita Quintero:* Linda Darnell, *Captain Esteban Pasquale:* Basil Rathbone, *Inez Quintero:* Gale Sondergaard, *Fray Felipe:* Eugene Pallette, *Don Luis Quintero:* J. Edward Bromberg, *Don Alejandro Vega:* Montagu Love, *Senora Isabella Vega:* Janet Beecher, *Rodrigo:* Robert Lowery, *Turnkey:* Chris-Pin Martin, *Sgt. Gonzales:* George Regas, *Maria:* Belle Mitchell, *Pedro:* John Bleifer, *Proprietor:* Frank Puglia, *Don Miguel:* Pedro de Cordoba, *Don Jose:* Guy D'Ennery, *Officer of Day:* Eugene Borden, *First Sentry:* Fred Malatesta, *Sentry:* Fortunio Bonanova, *Caballeros:* Harry Worth, Lucio Villegas, *Soldier:* Paul Sutton, *Officer-Student:* Ralph Byrd, *Bit:* (Michael) Ted North, *Manservant:* Rafael Corio, *Orderly:* Franco Corsaro, *Peon Selling Cocks:* William Edmunds, *Peon at Inn:* Hector Sarno, *Jose, a Peon:* Charles Stevens, *Commanding Officer:* Stanley Andreuh, *Boatman:* Victor Kilian, *Caballero:* Gino Corrado.

The Mark of Zorro with Tyrone Power and Basil Rathbone.

419

Marty with Ernest Borgnine and Betsy Blair.

MARTY (1955) UA. Producer, Harold Hecht. Director, Delbert Mann. Story and screenplay by Paddy Chayefsky. Costumes by Norma. Music by Roy Webb. Assistant Directors, Paul Helmick and Mark Sandrich, Jr. A Hecht-Lancaster-Steven Production. Title song by Harry Warren. Originally presented as a drama on TV Playhouse. Filmed in the Bronx. Ed Sullivan is seen in a TV kinescope. 99 minutes

Marty Pilletti: Ernest Borgnine, *Clara Snyder:* Betsy Blair, *Mrs. Pilletti:* Esther Minciotti, *Catherine:* Augusta Ciolli, *Angie:* Joe Mantell, *Virginia:* Karen Steele, *Thomas:* Jerry Paris, *Ralph:* Frank Sutton, *The Kid:* Walter Kelley, *Joe:* Robin Morse, *Lou, Bartender:* Charles Cane, *A Bachelor:* Nick Brkich, *Herb:* Alan Wells, *Mrs. Rosari:* Minerva Urecal, *Mr. Snyder,* James Bell.

MARY POPPINS (1964) BV. Producer, Walt Disney. Directed by Robert Stevenson. Technicolor. Co-produced and written by Bill Walsh. Based on Mary Poppins books by P. L. Travers. Music, Irwin Kostal. Songs by Richard M. and Robert B. Sherman: "Chim-Chim-Cheree," "Spoonful of Sugar," "Jolly Holiday," "Supercalifragilisticexpialidocious," "The Life I Lead," "Sister Suffragette," "Step in Time," "Stay Awake," "A Man Has Dreams," "Feed the Birds (Tuppence a Bag)," "I Love to Laugh." Choreography, Marc Breaux and Dee Dee Wood. Costume and Design Consultant, Tony Walton. Photography, Edward Colman. Art Directors, Carroll Clark and William H. Tuntke. Editor, Cotton Warburton. Sets, Emile Kuri and Hal Gausman. Costumes, Bill Thomas. Sound, Robert O. Cook. Costumes, Chuck Keehne and Gertrude Casey. Assistant Directors, Joseph L. McEveety and Paul Feiner. Animation Director, Hamilton Luske. 140 minutes

Mary Poppins: Julie Andrews, *Bert/Old Dawes:* Dick Van Dyke, *Mr. Banks:* David Tomlinson, *Mrs. Banks:* Glynis Johns, *Ellen:* Hermione Baddeley, *Jane Banks:* Karen Dotrice, *Michael Banks:* Matthew Garber, *Katie Nanna:* Elsa Lanchester, *Uncle Albert:* Ed Wynn, *Bird Woman:* Jane Darwell, *Constable Jones:* Arthur Treacher, *Admiral Boom:* Reginald Owen, *Mrs. Brill:* Reta Shaw, *Mr. Dawes, Jr.:* Arthur Malet, *Mr. Binnacle:* Don Barclay, *Miss Lark:* Marjorie Bennett, *Miss Persimmon:* Marjorie Eaton, *Citizen:* Major Sam Harris, *Depositor:* Doris Lloyd, *Bank Directors: Mr. Grubbs,* Cyril

Mary Poppins with Dick Van Dyke, Julie Andrews, Matthew Garber and Karen Dotrice.

Delevanti, *Mr. Tomes,* Lester Mathews, *Mr. Mousley,* Clive L. Halliday, *Mrs. Corry:* Alma Lawton.

MATA HARI (1931) MGM. Directed by George Fitzmaurice. Story by Benjamin Glazer and Leo Birinski. Dialogue, Doris Anderson and Gilbert Emery. Photography, William Daniels. Editor, Frank Sullivan. Sound, J. K. Brock. 91 minutes

Mata Hari: Greta Garbo, *Lieutenant Alexis Rosanoff:* Ramon Novarro, *General Serge Shubin:* Lionel Barrymore, *Andriani:* Lewis Stone, *Dubois:* C. Henry Gordon, *Carlotta:* Karen Morley, *Major Caron:* Alec B. Francis, *Sister Angelica:* Blanche Frederici, *Warden:* Edmund Breese, *Sister Genevieve:* Helen Jerome Eddy, *The Cook-Spy:* Frank Reicher, *Sister Teresa:* Sarah Padden, *Ivan:* Harry Cording, *Aide:* Gordon De Main, *Condemned Man:* Mischa Auer, *Gambler:* Cecil Cunningham, *Orderly:* Michael Visaroff.

Mata Hari with Greta Garbo and Ramon Novarro.

MAYTIME (1937) MGM. Produced by Hunt Stromberg. Directed by Robert Z. Leonard. Based on the 1917 operetta; book and lyrics by Rida Johnson Young, score by Sigmund Romberg. Screenplay, Noel Langley. Music adapted and directed by Herbert Stothart. Photography, Oliver T. Marsh. Editor, Conrad A. Nervig. Songs: "Sweetheart (Will You Remember?)," "Maytime Finale" by Romberg and Young; "Virginia Ham and Eggs," "Vive L'Opera" by Herbert Stothart, Bob Wright, and Chet Forrest: "Student Drinking Song" by Stothart; "Carry Me Back to Old Virginny" by James A. Bland; "Czaritza," based on Tchaikovsky's Fifth Symphony, libretto by Wright and Forrest; "Reverie," based on Romberg airs. "Jump Jim Crow," "Road to Paradise" and "Dancing Will Keep You Young" by Rida Johnson Young, Cyrus Wood and Sigmund Romberg; "Maypole" by Ed Ward. "Street Singer" by Bob Wright, Chet Forrest and Herbert Stothart. Adaptation of French libretto, Gilles Guilbert. Vocal arrangements, Leo Arnaud. Opera sequences, William Von Wymetal. Associate Art Directors, Fredric Hope and Edwin B. Willis. Gowns, Adrian. Sound, Douglas Shearer. Film debuts of Lynne Carver, 19, and Joan Crawford's niece Joan Le Sueur, 3. 132 minutes

Marcia Mornay (Miss Morrison): Jeanette MacDonald, *Paul Allison:* Nelson Eddy, *Nicolai Nazaroff:* John Barrymore, *August Archipenko:* Herman Bing, *Kip:* Tom Brown, *Barbara Roberts:* Lynne Carver, *Ellen:* Rafaela Ottiano, *Cabby:* Charles Judels, *Composer Trentini:* Paul Porcasi, *Fonchon:* Sig Rumann, *Rudyard:* Walter Kingsford, *Secretary:* Edgar Norton, *Emperor Louis Napoleon:* Guy Bates Post, *Empress Eugenie:* Iphigenie Castiglioni, *Madame Fanchon:* Anna Demetrio, *Orchestra Conductor:* Frank Puglia, *Dubrovsky, Czaritza's Minister/Student at Cafe:* Adia Kuznetzoff, *Maypole Dancer:* Joan Le Sueur, *M. Bulliet, Voice Coach:* Russell Hicks, *Opera Directors:* Harry Davenport Harry Hayden, Howard Hickman, Robert C. Fischer, *Bearded Director:* Harlan Briggs, *O'Brien, a Director:* Frank

Maytime with Nelson Eddy and Jeanette MacDonald.

Sheridan, *Drunk:* Billy Gilbert, *Empress' Dinner Companion:* Ivan Lebedeff, *Student in Bar:* Leonid Kinskey, *Waiter:* Clarence Wilson, *Opera House Manager:* Maurice Cass, *Massilon, Hotel Manager:* Douglas Wood, *Assistant Manager:* Bernard Suss, *Publicity Man:* Henry Roquemore, *French Proprietor:* Alexander Schonberg, *Opera Singer:* Mariska Aldrich, *Singers:* The Don Cossack Chorus.

MEET JOHN DOE (1941) WB. Produced and directed by Frank Capra. Based on a story by Richard Connell and Robert Presnell. Screenplay, Robert Riskin. Art Director, Stephen Goosson. Music, Dimitri Tiomkin. Choral Arrangements, Hall Johnson. Music Director, Leo F. Forbstein. Assistant Director, Arthur S. Black. Photography, George Barnes. Sound, C. A. Riggs. Editor, Daniel Mandell. Gowns, Natalie Visart. Special Effects, Jack Cosgrove. Montage Effects, Slavko Vorkapich. 135 minutes

Long John Willoughby (John Doe): Gary Cooper, *Ann Mitchell:* Barbara Stanwyck, *D. B. Norton:* Edward Arnold, *The Colonel:* Walter Brennan, *Mrs. Mitchell:* Spring Byington, *Henry Connell:* James Gleason, *Mayor Lovett:* Gene Lockhart, *Ted Sheldon:* Rod La Rocque, *Beany:* Irving Bacon, *Bert Hansen:* Regis Toomey, *Mrs. Hansen:* Ann Doran, *Sourpuss Smithers:* J. Farrell MacDonald, *Angelface:* Warren Hymer, *Mayor Hawkins:* Andrew Tombes, *Hammett:* Pierre Watkin, *Weston:* Stanley Andrews, *Bennett:* Mitchell Lewis, *Charlie Dawson:* Charles C. Wilson, *Governor:* Vaughan Glaser, *Dan:* Sterling Holloway, *Radio Announcer:* Mike

Meet John Doe with Barbara Stanwyck, Gary Cooper and James Gleason.

Frankovich, *Radio Announcers at Convention:* Knox Manning, Selmer Jackson, John B. Hughes, *Pop Dwyer:* Aldrich Bowker, *Mrs. Brewster:* Mrs. Gardner Crane, *Mike:* Pat Flaherty, *Ann's Sisters:* Carlotta Jelm, Tina Thayer, *Red, Office Boy:* Bennie Bartlett, *Mrs. Hawkins:* Sarah Edwards, *Radio M.C.:* Edward Earle, *Sheriff:* James McNamara, *Mrs. Delaney:* Emma Tansey, *Grubbel:* Frank Austin, *Relief Administrator:* Edward Keane, *Mr. Delaney:* Lafe McKee, *Joe, Newsman:* Edward McWade, *Bixler:* Guy Usher, *Barrington:* Walter Soderling, *Policeman:* Edmund Cobb, *Midget:* Billy Curtis, *Lady Midget:* Johnny Fern, *Jim, Governor's Associate:* John Hamilton, *Governor's Associate:* William Forrest, *Fired Reporter:* Charles K. French, *Mayor's Secretary:* Edward Hearn, *Newspaper Secretary:* Bess Flowers, *Ed, a Photographer:* Hank Mann, *Photographer:* James Millican. And The Hall Johnson Choir.

Meet Me in St. Louis with Leon Ames, Judy Garland, Harry Davenport, Lucille Bremer, Hank Daniels, Margaret O'Brien and Mary Astor.

MEET ME IN ST. LOUIS (1944) MGM. Producer, Arthur Freed. Director, Vincente Minnelli. Color by Technicolor. Screenplay by Irving Brecher and Fred F. Finklehoffe. Based on the *New Yorker* stories and the novel by Sally Benson. Title song by Andrew B. Sterling and Kerry Mills. New songs by Hugh Martin and Ralph Blane: "The Boy Next Door," "The Trolley Song," "Have Yourself a Merry Little Christmas," "Skip to My Lou." Dances by Paul Jones. Music adapted by Roger Edens. Music Director, Georgie Stoll. Orchestrations by Conrad Salinger. Film Editor, Albert Akst. Photographed by George Folsey. Dance Director, Charles Walters. Art Directors, Cedric Gibbons and Lemuel Ayers. 113 minutes

Esther Smith: Judy Garland, *"Tootie" Smith:* Margaret O'Brien, *Mrs. Anne Smith:* Mary Astor, *Rose Smith:* Lucille Bremer, *Lucille Ballard:* June Lockhart, *John Truett:* Tom Drake, *Katie (Maid):* Marjorie Main, *Grandpa:* Harry Davenport, *Mr. Alonzo Smith:* Leon Ames, *Lon Smith, Jr.:* Henry H. Daniels, Jr. (Hank Daniels), *Agnes Smith:* Joan Carroll, *Colonel Darly:* Hugh Marlowe, *Warren Sheffield:* Robert Sully, *Mr. Neely:* Chill Wills, *Doctor Terry:* Donald Curtis, *Ida Boothby:* Mary Jo Ellis, *Quentin:* Ken Wilson, *Motorman:* Robert Emmet O'Connor, *Johnny Tevis:* Darryl Hickman, *Conductor:* Leonard Walker, *Baggage Man:* Victor Kilian, *Mailman:* John Phipps, *Mr. March:* Major Sam Harris, *Mr. Braukoff:* Mayo Newhall, *Mrs. Braukoff:* Belle Mitchell, *Hugo Borvis:* Sidney Barnes, *George:* Myron Tobias, *Driver:* Victor Cox, *Clinton Badgers:* Kenneth Donner, Buddy Gorman, Joe Cobb, *Girl on Trolley:* Helen Gilbert,

THE MEN (1950) UA. Produced by Stanley Kramer. Directed by Fred Zinnemann. Story and Screenplay, Carl Foreman. Music composed and directed by Dimitri Tiomkin. Photography, Robert De Grasse. Editor, Harry Gerstad. Filmed at Birmingham Veterans Administration Hospital. Film debut of Marlon Brando, 25. Reissued as *Battle Stripe* (NTA, 1957). 86 minutes

The Men with Marlon Brando and Teresa Wright.

Ken: Marlon Brando, *Ellen:* Teresa Wright, *Doctor Brock:* Everett Sloane, *Norm:* Jack Webb, *Leo:* Richard Erdman, *Angel:* Arthur Jurado, *Nurse Robbins:* Virginia Farmer, *Ellen's Mother:* Dorothy Tree, *Ellen's Father:* Howard St. John, *Dolores:* Nita Hunter, *Laverne:* Patricia Joiner, *Mr. Doolin:* John Miller, *Dr. Kameran:* Cliff Clark, *Man at Bar:* Ray Teal, *Angel's Mother:* Marguerita Martin, *The Lookout:* Obie Parker, *Thompson:* Ray Mitchell, *Mullin:* Pete Simon, *Hopkins:* Paul Peltz, *Fine:* Tom Gillick, *Baker:* Randall Updyke III, *Romano:* Marshall Ball, *Gunderson:* Carlo Lewis, *Walter:* William Lea, Jr.

MIDDLE OF THE NIGHT (1959) Col. Producer, George Justin. Director, Delbert Mann. Screenplay by Paddy Chayefsky, originally a TV play. Music by George Bassman. Gowns by Jean Louis. Costumes by Frank L. Thompson. Assistant Director, Charles H. Maguire. Art Director, Edward S. Haworth. Cinematographer, Joseph Brun. Editor, Carl Lerner. A Sudan Production. Filmed in New York City. 118 minutes

Jerry Kingsley: Fredric March, *Betty Preisser:* Kim Novak, *Mrs. Mueller:* Glenda Farrell, *Alice:* Jan Norris, *Marilyn:* Lee Grant, *The Neighbor, Mrs. Herbert:* Effie Afton, *George:* Lee Philips, *Evelyn Kingsley:* Edith Meiser, *Lillian:* Joan Copeland, *Jack:* Martin Balsam, *Paul Kingsley:* David Ford, *Elizabeth Kingsley:* Audrey Peters, *The Widow, Rosalind Neiman:* Betty Walker, *Walter Lockman:* Albert Dekker, *Gould:* Rudy Bond, *Sherman:* Lou Gilbert, *Lucy Lockman:* Dora Weissman, *Joey Lockman:* Lee Richardson, *Caroline:* Anna Berger, *Ellman:* Alfred Leberfeld, *Erskine:* Nelson Olmsted.

Middle of the Night with Fredric March and Kim Novak.

MIDNIGHT LACE (1960) Univ. Produced by Ross Hunter and Martin Melcher. Directed by David Miller. In Eastman Color. Based on the play *Matilda Shouted Fire* by Janet Green. Screenplay, Ivan Goff and Ben Roberts. Music, Frank Skinner. Music Director, Joseph Ger-

Midnight Lace with Doris Day and Anthony Dawson.

shenson. Art Directors, Alexander Golitzen and Robert Clatworthy. Gowns, Irene. Assistant Directors, Phil Bowles and Carl Beringer. Photography, Russell Metty. Editors, Russell F. Schoengarth and Leon Barsha. A Hunter-Arwin Production. Songs: "Midnight Lace" by Joe Lubin and Jerome Howard; "What Does a Woman Do?" by Allie Wrubel and Maxwell Anderson. 108 minutes

Kit Preston: Doris Day, *Tony Preston:* Rex Harrison, *Brian Younger:* John Gavin, *Aunt Bea:* Myrna Loy, *Malcolm:* Roddy McDowall, *Charles Manning:* Herbert Marshall, *Peggy Thompson:* Natasha Parry, *Inspector Byrnes:* John Williams, *Dora Hammer:* Hermione Baddeley, *Daniel Graham:* Richard Ney, *Victor Elliott:* Rhys Williams, *Ash:* Anthony Dawson, *Simon Foster:* Richard Lupino, *Nora:* Doris Lloyd, *Doctor Garver:* Hayden Rorke, *Basil Stafford:* Rex Evans, *Woman:* Elspeth March, *Policeman:* Keith McConnell, *Tim:* Terence De Marney, *Salesman in Gun Shop:* Gage Clarke, *Bus Driver:* Jimmy Fairfax, *Salesman:* Anthony Eustrel, *M. P.:* Jack Livesey, *Beautician:* Pamela Light, *Harry:* Roy Dean, *Kevin:* Paul Collins, *Tommy:* Richard Peel, *Workman:* Peter Fontaine, *Attaché:* Peter Adams, *Dancers:* Anna Cheselka, Vladimir Oukhtomsky, *Blonde:* Joan Staley, *Attendant:* John Sheffield, *Blind Man:* Ramsey Hill.

A MIDSUMMER NIGHT'S DREAM (1935) WB. Produced by Max Reinhardt. Directed by Max Reinhardt and William Dieterle. From William Shakespeare's play, with Felix Mendelssohn's *A Midsummer Night's Dream* music. Screenplay, Charles Kenyon and Mary McCall, Jr. Musical Arrangement, Erich Wolfgang Korngold. Dance Ensembles, Bronislawa Nijinska. Photography, Hal Mohr, Fred Jackman, Byron Haskin, H. F. Koenekamp. Editor, Ralph Dawson. Film debut of Olivia De Havilland. 132 minutes

A Midsummer Night's Dream with Hugh Herbert, Frank McHugh, Arthur Treacher, Otis Harlan, Dewey Robinson, James Cagney and Joe E. Brown.

Bottom: James Cagney, *Lysander:* Dick Powell, *Flute:* Joe E. Brown, *Helena:* Jean Muir, *Snout:* Hugh Herbert, *Theseus:* Ian Hunter, *Quince:* Frank McHugh, *Oberon:* Victor Jory, *Hermia:* Olivia De Havilland, *Demetrius:* Ross Alexander, *Egeus:* Grant Mitchell, *First Fairy:* Nini Theilade, *Hippolyta, Queen of Amazons:* Verree Teasdale, *Titania:* Anita Louise, *Puck:* Mickey Rooney, *Snug:* Dewey Robinson, *Philostrate:* Hobart Cavanaugh, *Starveling:* Otis Harlan, *Ninny's Tomb:* Arthur Treacher, *Mustardseed:* Billy Barty.

MILDRED PIERCE (1945) WB. Producer, Jerry Wald. Director, Michael Curtiz. From a novel by James M. Cain. Screenplay, Ranald MacDougall, Catherine Turney. Musical Score, Max Steiner. Art Director, Anton Grot. Cameraman, Ernest Haller. Special Effects, Willard Van Enger. Editor, David Weisbart. 113 minutes

Mildred Pierce: Joan Crawford, *Wally Fay:* Jack Carson, *Monte Beragon:* Zachary Scott, *Ida:* Eve Arden, *Veda Pierce:* Ann Blyth, *Bert Pierce:* Bruce Bennett, *Mr. Chris:* George Tobias, *Maggie Binderhof:* Lee Patrick, *Inspector Peterson:* Moroni Olsen, *Kay Pierce:* Jo Ann Marlowe, *Mrs. Forrester:* Barbara Brown, *Mr. Williams:* Charles Trowbridge, *Ted Forrester:* John Compton, *Lottie:* Butterfly McQueen, *Policeman on Pier:* Garry Owen, *Policemen:* Clancy Cooper, Tom Dillon, *Two Detectives:* James Flavin, Jack O'Connor, *Policeman:* Charles Jordan, *High School Boy:* Robert Arthur, *Waitresses:* Joyce Compton, Lynne Baggett, *Party Guest:* Ramsay Ames, *Police Matron:* Leah Baird, *Singing Teacher:* John Christian, *Piano Teacher:* Joan Winfield, *Houseboy:* Jimmy Lono, *Nurse:* Mary Servoss, *Doctor Gale:* Manart Kippen, *Pancho:* David Cota, *Mr. Jones:* Chester Clute, *Wally's Lawyer:* Wallis Clark.

Mildred Pierce with Garry Owen and Joan Crawford.

MILLION DOLLAR MERMAID (1952) MGM. Producer, Arthur Hornblow, Jr. Director, Mervyn LeRoy. Technicolor, partly in Wide Screen. Screenplay, Everett Freeman. Sound, Douglas Shearer. Musical

Million Dollar Mermaid with Victor Mature, Esther Williams and Jesse White.

Director, Adolph Deutsch. Orchestrations, Alexander Courage. Production numbers staged by Busby Berkeley. Art Director, Cedric Gibbons. Sets, Edwin R. Willis, Richard Pefferie. Cinematographer, George J. Folsey. Editor, John McSweeney, Jr. 115 minutes

Annette Kellerman: Esther Williams, *James Sullivan:* Victor Mature, *Frederick Kellerman:* Walter Pidgeon, *Alfred Harper:* David Brian, *Annette, 10 years:* Donna Corcoran, *Doc Cronnol:* Jesse White, *Pavlova* Maria Tallchief, *Aldrich:* Howard Freeman, *Policeman:* Charles Watts, *Garvey:* Wilton Graff, *Prosecutor:* Frank Ferguson, *Judge:* James Bell, *Conductor:* James Flavin, *Director:* Willis Bouchey, *Marie, Housekeeper:* Adrienne D'Ambricourt, *Judge:* Clive Morgan, *Mrs Craves:* Queenie Leonard, *Son:* Stuart Torres, *Pawnbroker:* James Aubrey, *Master of Ceremonies:* Patrick O'Moore, *Soprano:* Elizabeth Slifer, *Casey:* Gordon Richards, *London Bobby:* Al Ferguson, *Bum:* Benny Burt, *Marcellino, the Clown:* Rod Rogers, *Bud Williams:* George Wallace, *Watchman:* Harry Hines, *Newsboy:* Clarence Hennecke, *Maid:* Genevive Pasques, *Policeman:* Pat Flaherty, *Second Policeman:* James L. "Tiny" Kelly, *Process Server:* Thomas Dillon, *Band Leader:* Paul Frees, *Nurse:* Louise Lorimer, *Robbie, Prop Man:* Mack Chandler, *Bit:* Rosemarie Bowe.

MIN AND BILL (1930) MGM. Directed by George Hill. From the book *Dark Star* by Lorna Moon. Scenario and Dialogue, Frances Marion and Marion Jackson. Photography, Harold Wenstrom. Editor, Basil Wrangell. Sound, Douglas Shearer. Art Director, Cedric Gibbons. Film debut of Don Dillaway. 69 minutes

Min Divot: Marie Dressler, *Bill:* Wallace Beery, *Nancy Smith:* Dorothy Jordan, *Bella Pringle:* Marjorie Rambeau, *Dick Cameron:* Donald Dillaway, *Groot:* DeWitt Jennings, *Alec Johnson:* Russell Hopton, *Mr. Southard:* Frank McGlynn, *Mrs. Southard:* Gretta Gould, *Woman:* Miss Vanessi, *Merchant Seaman:* Jack Pennick, *Bella's Stateroom Lover:* Henry Roquemore, *Sailor:* Hank Bell.

Min and Bill with Wallace Beery and Marie Dressler.

THE MIRACLE OF MORGAN'S CREEK (1944) Par. Directed by Preston Sturges. Screenplay, Preston Sturges. Music, Leo Shuken and Charles Bradshaw. Art Directors, Hans Dreier and Ernest Fegte. Photography, John Seitz. Editor, Stuart Gilmore. Remade as *Rock-A-Bye Baby* (Paramount, 1958). 99 minutes

Norval Jones: Eddie Bracken, *Trudy Kockenlocker:* Betty Hutton, *Emmy Kockenlocker:* Diana Lynn, *McGinty:* Brian Donlevy, *The Boss:* Akim Tamiroff, *Justice of the Peace:* Porter Hall, *Mr. Tuerck:* Emory Parnell, *Mr. Johnson:* Alan Bridge, *Mr. Rafferty:* Julius Tannen, *Newspaper Editor:* Victor Potel, *Justice's Wife:* Almira Sessions, *Sally:* Esther Howard, *Sheriff:* J. Farrell MacDonald, *Cecilia:* Connie Tompkins, *Mrs. Johnson:* Georgia Caine, *Doctor:* Torben Meyer, *U.S. Marshal:* George Melford, *The Mayor:* Jimmy Conlin, *Mr. Schwartz:* Harry Rosenthal, *Pete:* Chester Conklin, *First M. P.:* Frank Moran, *Second M. P.:* Budd Fine, *McGinty's Secretary:* Byron Foulger, *McGinty's Secretary:* Arthur Hoyt, *Head Nurse:* Nora Cecil, *Man Opening Champagne:* Jack Norton, *Mussolini:* Joe Devlin, *Hitler:* Bobby Watson, *Officer Kockenlocker:* William Demarest.

The Miracle of Morgan's Creek with Betty Hutton, William Demarest and Diana Lynn.

MIRACLE ON 34th STREET (1947) 20th.

Producer, William Perlberg. Director, George Seaton. Story, Valentine Davies. Screenplay, George Seaton. Art Directors, Richard Day, Richard Irvine. Musical Director, Alfred Newman. Music, Cyril Mockridge. Cameramen, Charles Clarke, Lloyd Ahern. Editor, Robert Simpson. Filmed in New York City. Film debut of Thelma Ritter. 96 minutes

Doris Walker: Maureen O'Hara, *Fred Gailey:* John Payne, *Kris Kringle:* Edmund Gwenn, *Judge Henry X. Harper:* Gene Lockhart, *Susan Walker:* Natalie Wood, *Mr. Sawyer:* Porter Hall, *Charles Halloran:* William Frawley, *D. A. Thomas Mara:* Jerome Cowan, *Mr. Shellhammer:* Philip Tonge, *Doctor Pierce:* James Seay, *Mr. Macy:* Harry Antrim, *Peter's Mother:* Thelma Ritter, *Girl's Mother:* Mary Field, *Cleo:* Theresa Harris, *Alfred:* Alvin Greenman, *Mrs. Mara:* Anne Staunton, *Thomas Mara, Jr.:* Robert Hyatt, *Reporters:* Richard Irving, Jeff Corey, *Sawyer's Secretary:* Anne O'Neal, *Mrs. Shellhammer:* Lela Bliss, *Peter:* Anthony Sydes, *Dr. Rogers:* William Forrest, *Mara's Assistant:* Alvin Hammer, *Bailiff:* Joseph McInerney, *Drum Majorette:* Ida McGuire, *Santa Claus:* Percy Helton, *Mrs. Harper:* Jane Green, *Dutch Girl:* Marlene Lyden, *Post Office Employees:* Guy Thomajan, Jack Albertson, *Mr. Gimbel:* Herbert H. Heyes, *Guard:* Stephen Roberts, *Salesman (Macy's):* Robert Lynn, *Window Dresser:* Robert Gist, *Terry:* Teddy Driver, *Alice:* Patty Smith, *Interne:* Robert Karnes, *Mail-bearing Court Officer:* Snub Pollard.

Miracle on 34th Street with Natalie Wood and Edmund Gwenn.

The Miracle Worker with Patty Duke and Anne Bancroft.

THE MIRACLE WORKER (1962) UA.

Producer, Fred Coe. Director, Arthur Penn. Screenplay, William Gibson. Music, Laurence Rosenthal. Costumes, Ruth Morley. A Playfilms' Production. Based on Helen Keller's *The Story of My Life.* William Gibson's "The Miracle Worker" was originally an unproduced ballet in 1953, then a Playhouse 90 TV presentation in 1957, and a play in 1959, in which Anne Bancroft and Patty Duke originated their roles. Exteriors filmed in New Jersey, interiors in New York City. 106 minutes

Annie Sullivan: Anne Bancroft, *Helen Keller:* Patty Duke, *Captain Keller:* Victor Jory, *Kate Keller:* Inga Swenson, *James Keller:* Andrew Prine, *Aunt Ev:* Kathleen Comegys, *Viney:* Beah Richards, *Mr. Anagnos:* Jack Hollander, *Percy (10 years):* Michael Darden, *Helen at 7:* Peggy Burke, *Martha at 10:* Dale Ellen Bethea, *Percy at 8:* Walter Wright, Jr., *Martha at 7:* Donna Bryan, *Helen at 5:* Mindy Sherwood, *Martha at 5:* Diane Bryan, *Percy at 6:* Keith Moore, *Young Annie:* Michele Farr, *Young Jimmie:* Allan Howard, *Crones:* Judith Lowry, William F. Haddock, Helen Ludlum.

THE MISFITS (1961) UA.

Producer, Frank E. Taylor. Director, John Huston. Screenplay, Arthur Miller. Music, Alex North. Assistant Director, Carl Beringer. A Seven Arts Production. Art Directors, Stephen Grimes, William Newberry. Music composed and conducted by Alex North. Cinematographer, Russell Metty. Editor, George Tomasini. 124 minutes

Gay Langland: Clark Gable, *Roslyn Taber:* Marilyn Monroe, *Perce Howland:* Montgomery Clift, *Isabelle Steers:* Thelma Ritter, *Guido:* Eli Wallach, *Old Man in Bar:* James Barton, *Church Lady:* Estelle Winwood, *Raymond Taber:* Kevin McCarthy, *Young Boy in Bar:* Dennis Shaw, *Charles Steers:* Philip Mitchell, *Old Groom:* Walter Ramage, *Young Bride:* Peggy Barton, *Fresh Cowboy in Bar:* J. Lewis Smith, *Susan:* Marietta Tree, *Bartender:* Bobby La Salle, *Man in Bar:* Ryall Bowker, *Ambulance Driver:* Ralph Roberts.

The Misfits with Eli Wallach, Thelma Ritter, Clark Gable and Marilyn Monroe.

Miss Susie Slagle's with Joan Caulfield and Sonny Tufts.

MISS SUSIE SLAGLE'S (1945) Par. Associate Producer, John Houseman. Directed by John Berry. From a novel by Augusta Tucker. Screenplay, Anne Froelick and Hugo Butler. Adaptation, Anne Froelick and Adrian Scott. Additional Dialogue, Theodore Strauss. Art Directors, Hans Dreier and Earl Hedrick. Music, Daniele Amfitheatrof. Photography, Charles Lang, Jr. Process Photography, Farciot Edouart. Editor, Archie Marshek. Song, "Little Eliza," by Ben Raleigh and Bernie Wayne. 88 minutes

Miss Susie Slagle: Lillian Gish, *Nan Rogers:* Veronica Lake, *Pug Prentiss:* Sonny Tufts, *Margaretta Howe:* Joan Caulfield, *Dr. Elijah Howe:* Ray Collins, *Ben Mead:* Billy De Wolfe, *Elijah Howe, Jr.:* Bill Edwards, *Elbert Riggs:* Pat Phelan, *Dean Wingate:* Roman Bohnen, *Dr. Fletcher:* Morris Carnovsky, *Clayton Abernathy:* Renny McEvoy, *Silas Holmes:* Lloyd Bridges, *Irving Asron:* Michael Sage, *Mrs. Johnson:* Dorothy Adams, *Dr. Metz:* E. J. Ballantine, *Dr. Boyd:* Theodore Newton, *Hizer:* J. Lewis Johnson, *Otto:* Ludwig Stossel, *Mr. Johnson:* Charles E. Arnt, *Mrs. Howe:* Isabel Randolph, *Miss Wingate:* Kathleen Howard, *Dr. Bowen:* Frederick Burton, *Doctor:* Hal Taliaferro, *Dark-haired Boy:* John Kellogg, *Instrument Man:* Cyril Ring, *Thomas:* William Moss, *Boy with Wounded Dog:* Bobby Driscoll, *Davies:* Buddy Yarus, *Dr. Benton:* Damian O'Flynn, *O'Connor:* Shimen Ruskin, *Dr. Rice:* Walter Fenner, *Superintendent:* Pierre Watkin, *Woman:* Laura Bowman, *Paul:* Chester (Chet) Morrison.

MISTER ROBERTS (1955) WB. Producer, Leland Hayward. Directors, John Ford, Mervyn LeRoy. Screenplay by Frank Nugent and Joshua Logan. Based on the play by Thomas Heggen and Joshua Logan, from the novel by Thomas Heggen. Music by Franz Waxman. Assistant Director, Wingate Smith. An Orange Production in Cinema-Scope and WarnerColor, Stereophonic Sound. Filmed in Hawaii. 123 minutes

Lieutenant (jg) Doug Roberts: Henry Fonda, *The Captain:* James Cagney, *Doc:* William Powell, *Ensign Pulver:* Jack Lemmon, *Lieutenant Ann Girard:* Betsy Palmer, *C.P.O. Dowdy:* Ward Bond, *Mannion:*

Mr. Roberts with William Powell, Jack Lemmon and Henry Fonda.

Phil Carey, *Shore Patrol Officer:* Martin Milner, *Shore Patrolman:* Gregory Walcott, *Military Policeman:* James Flavin, *Marine Sergeant:* Jack Pennick, *Native Chief:* Duke Kahanamoko, *Reber:* Nick Adams, *Dolan:* Ken Curtis, *Stefanowski:* Harry Carey, Jr., *Gerhart:* Frank Aletter, *Lindstrom:* Fritz Ford, *Mason:* Buck Kartalian, *Lieutenant Billings:* William Henry, *Olson:* William Hudson, *Schlemmer:* Stubby Kruger, *Cookie:* Harry Tenbrook, *Rodrigues:* Perry Lopez, *Insigna:* Robert Roark, *Bookser:* Pat Wayne, *Wiley:* Tiger Andrews, *Kennedy:* Jim Moloney, *Gilbert:* Denny Niles, *Cochran:* Francis Connor, *Johnson:* Shug Fisher, *Jonesy:* Danny Borzage, *Taylor:* Jim Murphy, *Nurses:* Kathleen O'Malley, Jeanne Murray, Maura Murphy, Lonnie Pierce, Mimi Doyle.

MOBY DICK (1956) WB. Producer, John Huston. Associate Producer, Lehman Katz. Director, John Huston. Technicolor. Based on the novel by Herman Melville. Screenplay, Ray Bradbury, John Huston. Art Director, Ralph Brinton. Music composed by Philip Stainton. Musical Director, Louis Levy. Cinematographer, Oswald Morris. Editor, Russell Lloyd. A Moulin Picture. Filmed in Youghal, Ireland, in Wales, and off the coasts of Madeira and the Canary Islands. The vessel *Pequod* was actually a ship called the *Hispanola*. Narrated by Richard Basehart. Remake of *The Sea Beast* (1926), *Moby Dick* (1930). 116 minutes

Captain Ahab: Gregory Peck, *Ishmael:* Richard Basehart, *Starbuck.* Leo Genn, *Father Mapple:* Orson Welles, *Captain Boomer:* James Robertson Justice, *Stubb:* Harry Andrews, *Manxman:* Bernard Miles, *Carpenter:* Noel Purcell, *Daggoo:* Edric Connor, *Peleg:* Mervyn Johns, *Peter Coffin:* Joseph Tomelty, *Captain Gardiner:* Francis De Wolff, *Bildad:* Philip Stainton, *Elijah:* Royal Dano, *Flask:* Seamus Kelly, *Queequeg:* Friedrich Ledebur, *Blacksmith:* Ted Howard, *Pip:* Tamba Alleney, *Tashtego:* Tom Clegg, *Lady with Bibles:* Iris Tree, *Blacksmith:* Ted Howard.

Moby Dick with Gregory Peck.

MOGAMBO (1953) MGM. Produced by Sam Zimbalist. Directed by John Ford. Based on a play by Wilson Collison. Color by Technicolor. Screenplay, John Lee Mahin. Art Director, Alfred Junge. Cinematographers, Robert Surtees, F. A. Young. Editor, Frank

Mogambo with Ava Gardner, Grace Kelly and Clark Gable.

Clarke. Filmed in Africa. Remake of MGM's *Red Dust*, 1932; and *Congo Maisie*, 1940. 115 minutes

Victor Marswell: Clark Gable, *Eloise Kelly:* Ava Gardner, *Linda Nordley:* Grace Kelly, *Donald Nordley:* Donald Sinden, *John Brown-Pryce:* Philip Stainton, *Leon Boltchak:* Eric Pohlmann, *Skipper:* Laurence Naismith, *Father Josef:* Denis O'Dea.

MONEY FROM HOME (1953) Par. Producer, Hal B. Wallis. Director, George Marshall. 3-Dimension, Technicolor. Based on a story by Damon Runyon. Screenplay, Hal Kanter. Art Directors, Hal Pereira, Henry Bumstead, Cinematographer, Daniel L. Fapp. Adaptation, James Allardice and Hal Kanter. 100 minutes

Honey Talk Nelson: Dean Martin, *Virgil Yokum:* Jerry Lewis, *Phyllis Leigh:* Marjie Millar, *Autumn Claypool:* Pat Crowley, *Bertie Searles:* Richard Haydn, *Seldom Seen Kid:* Robert Strauss, *Marshall Preston:* Gerald Mohr, *Jumbo Schneider:* Sheldon Leonard, *The Poojah:* Romo Vincent, *Short Boy:* Jack Kruschen, *Henchman:* Charles Frank Horvath, *Henchman:* Richard J. Reeves, *Sam:* Lou Lubin, *Driver:* Frank Richards, *First Judge:* Harry Hayden, *Second Judge:* Henry McLemore, *Third Judge:* Mortie Dutra, *Announcer:* Wendell Niles, *Hard Top Harry:* Joe McTurk, *Lead Pipe Louie:* Frank F. Mitchell, *Society Kid (Himself):* Sam Hogan, *Crossfire:* Phil Arnold, *Hot Horse Herbie:* Louis Nicoletti, *Dr. Capulet:* Edward Clark, *Mrs. Cheshire:* Grace Hayle, *First Reporter:* Al Hill, *Manservant:* Ben Astar, *Bankfair:* Robin Hughes, *Waitress:* Mara Corday, *Grogan the Growler:* Sidney Marion, *Poojah's Wife:* Carolyn Phillips, *Mattie:* Maidie Norman, *Conductor:* Rex Lease.

Money From Home with Jerry Lewis, Marjie Millar and Dean Martin.

THE MONKEY'S UNCLE (1965) BV. Producer, Walt Disney. Co-producer, Ron Miller. Director, Robert Stevenson. Technicolor. Screenplay, Tom and Helen August. Music, Buddy Baker. Title Song, Richard M. Sherman, Robert B. Sherman. Sung by The Beach Boys.

The Monkey's Uncle with Annette Funicello and Tommy Kirk.

Director of Photography, Edward Colman. Assistant Director, Joseph L. McEveety. Costumes, Chuck Keehne, Gertrude Casey. 87 minutes

Merlin Jones: Tommy Kirk, *Jennifer:* Annette Funicello, *Judge Holmsby:* Leon Ames, *Mr. Dearborne:* Frank Faylen, *Darius Green III:* Arthur O'Connell, *Leon:* Leon Tyler, *Norman:* Norman Grabowski, *Prof. Shattuck:* Alan Hewitt, *Housekeeper:* Connie Gilchrist, *Lisa:* Cheryl Miller, *College President:* Gage Clarke, *Haywood:* Mark Goddard, *Board of Regents:* Harry Holcombe, Alexander Lockwood, Harry Antrim.

THE MOON IS BLUE (1953) UA. Produced and directed by Otto Preminger. Screenplay by F. Hugh Herbert, from his play. Song by Herschel Burke Gilbert and Sylvia Fine: "The Moon Is Blue." Cinematographer, Ernest Laszlo. Editor, Otto Ludwig. Film debut of Maggie McNamara. 99 minutes

Donald Gresham: William Holden, *David Slater:* David Niven, *Patty O'Neill:* Maggie McNamara, *Michael O'Neill:* Tom Tully, *Cynthia Slater:* Dawn Addams, *Television Announcer:* Fortunio Bonanova.

The Moon Is Blue with William Holden and Maggie McNamara.

THE MORE THE MERRIER (1943) Col. Produced and directed by George Stevens. Associate Producer, Fred Guiol. Story, Robert Russell and Frank Ross. Screenplay, Robert Russell, Frank Ross, Richard Flournoy, Lewis R. Foster. Art Directors, Lionel Banks and Rudolph Sternad. Music, Leigh Harline. Music Director, Morris W. Stoloff. Photography, Ted Tetzlaff. Editor, Otto Meyer. Song, "Damn the Torpedos (Full Speed Ahead)" by Henry Meyers, Edward Eliscu and Jay Gorney. Remade by Columbia as *Walk, Don't Run* (1966). 104 minutes

Connie Milligan: Jean Arthur, *Joe Carter:* Joel McCrea, *Benjamin Dingle:* Charles Coburn, *Charles J. Pendergast:* Richard Gaines, *Evans:* Bruce Bennett, *Pike:* Frank Sully, *Senator Noonan:* Clyde Fill-

The More the Merrier with Jean Arthur, Joel McCrea and Charles Coburn.

more, *Morton Rodakiewicz:* Stanley Clements, *Harding:* Don Douglas, *Miss Dalton:* Ann Savage, *Waiter:* Grady Sutton, *Dancer:* Sugar Geise, *Drunk:* Don Barclay, *Drunk:* Frank Sully, *Girl:* Shirley Patterson, *Miss Bilby:* Ann Doran, *Waitress:* Mary Treen, *Barmaid:* Gladys Blake, *Miss Allen:* Kay Linaker, *Miss Chasen:* Nancy Gay, *Air Corps Captain:* Byron Shores, *Miss Finch:* Betzi Beaton, *Texan:* Harrison Greene, *Southerner:* Robert McKenzie, *Cattleman:* Vic Potel, *Character:* Lon Poff, *Senator:* Frank La Rue, *Senator:* Douglas Wood, *Minister:* Harry Bradley, *Miss Geeskin:* Betty McMahan, *Dumpy Woman:* Helen Holmes, *Fat Statistician:* Marshall Ruth, *Second Statistician:* Hal Gerard, *Reporter:* Henry Roquemore, *Taxi Driver:* Jack Carr, *Hotel Clerk:* Chester Clute, *Head Waiter:* Robert F. Hill, *Police Captain:* Eddy Chandler, *Dancer:* Peggy Carroll, *Caretaker:* George Reed, *Taxi Driver:* Kitty McHugh.

MORNING GLORY (1933) RKO. Directed by Lowell Sherman. Story, Zoe Akins. Adaptation, Howard J. Green. Photography, Bert Glennon. Editor, George Nicholls, Jr. Sound, Hugh McDowell. Remade as *Stage Struck* (Buena Vista, 1958). 74 minutes

Eva Lovelace (Ada Love): Katharine Hepburn, *Joseph Sheridan:* Douglas Fairbanks, Jr., *Louis Easton:* Adolphe Menjou, *Rita Vernon:* Mary Duncan, *Robert Harley Hedges:* C. Aubrey Smith, *Pepe Velez:* Don Alvarado, *Will Seymour:* Frederic Santley, *Henry Lawrence:* Richard Carle, *Charles Van Dusen:* Tyler Brooke, *Gwendolyn Hall:* Geneva Mitchell.

Morning Glory with Katharine Hepburn, Douglas Fairbanks, Jr., Frederic Santley and Adolphe Menjou.

MOROCCO (1930) Par. Directed by Josef von Sternberg. From the play *Amy Jolly* by Benno Vigny. Scenario and Dialogue, Jules Furthman. Photography, Lee Garmes. Editor, Sam Winston. 90 minutes

Tom Brown: Gary Cooper, *Amy Jolly:* Marlene Dietrich, *Labessier:* Adolphe Menjou, *Adjutant Caesar:* Ulrich Haupt, *Anna Dolores:* Juliette Compton, *Sergeant Barney Latoche:* Francis McDonald,

Morocco with Gary Cooper, Marlene Dietrich and Adolphe Menjou.

Colonel Quinnovieres: Albert Conti, *Madame Caesar:* Eve Southern, *Barrative:* Michael Visaroff, *Lo Tinto:* Paul Porcasi, *Camp Follower:* Theresa Harris.

THE MORTAL STORM (1940) MGM. Directed by Frank Borzage. Based on the novel by Phyllis Bottome. Screenplay, Claudine West, Andersen Ellis and George Froeschel. Art Director, Cedric Gibbons. Associate, Wade Rubottom. Music, Edward Kane. Assistant Director, Lew Borzage. Photography, William Daniels. Sound, Douglas Shearer. Editor, Elmo Veron. Gowns, Adrian. Men's Wardrobe, Giles Steele. Make-up, Jack Dawn. Hair Styles, Sidney Guilaroff. 100 minutes

Freya Roth: Margaret Sullavan, *Martin Brietner:* James Stewart, *Fritz Marberg:* Robert Young, *Professor Roth:* Frank Morgan, *Otto Von Rohn:* Robert Stack, *Elsa:* Bonita Granville, *Mrs. Roth:* Irene Rich, *Erich Von Rohn:* William T. Orr, *Mrs. Brietner:* Maria Ouspenskaya, *Rudi:* Gene Reynolds, *Rector:* Russell Hicks, *Lehman:* William Edmunds, *Marta:* Esther Dale, *Holl:* Dan Dailey, Jr., *Berg:* Granville Bates, *Professor Werner:* Thomas Ross, *Franz:* Ward Bond, *Theresa:* Sue Moore, *Second Colleague:* Harry Depp, *Third Colleague:* Julius Tannen, *Fourth Colleague:* Gus Glassmire, *Guard:* Dick Rich, *Guard:* Ted Oliver, *Man:* Howard Lang, *Woman:* Bodil Rosing, *Passport Officials:* Lucien Prival, Dick Elliott, *Gestapo Official:* Henry Victor, *Waiter:* William Irving, *Fat Man in Cafe:* Bert Roach, *Gestapo Guard:* Bob Stevenson, *Old Man:* Max Davidson, *Gestapo Official:* John Stark, *Oppenheim:* Fritz Leiber, *Hartman:* Robert O. Davis.

The Mortal Storm with Margaret Sullavan, William Edmunds and Irene Rich.

MOTHER WORE TIGHTS (1947) 20th. Produced by Lamar Trotti. Directed by Walter Lang. Color by Technicolor. Based on the book by Miriam Young. Screenplay, Lamar Trotti. Art Directors, Richard

Mother Wore Tights with Betty Grable and Dan Dailey.

Day and Joseph C. Wright. Dances staged by Seymour Felix and Kenny Williams. Music Direction, Alfred Newman. Vocal Arrangements, Charles Henderson. Orchestral Arrangements, Gene Rose. Photography, Harry Jackson. Technicolor Director, Natalie Kalmus. Associate, Leonard Doss. Sets, Thomas Little. Editor, J. Watson Webb Jr. Songs: "Tra-La-La-La" by Mack Gordon and Harry Warren; "Kokomo, Indiana," "You Do," "There's Nothing Like a Song," "This Is My Favorite City," "Fare-Thee-Well Dear Alma Mater," "On a Little Two-Seat Tandem," and "Rolling Down to Bowling Green" by Mack Gordon and Josef Myrow. Filmed partly in San Francisco. 107 minutes

Myrtle McKinley Burt: Betty Grable, *Frank Burt:* Dan Dailey, *Iris Burt:* Mona Freeman, *Mikie Burt:* Connie Marshall, *Bessie:* Vanessa Brown, *Bob Clarkman:* Robert Arthur, *Grandmother McKinley:* Sara Allgood, *Mr. Schneider:* William Frawley, *Miss Ridgeway:* Ruth Nelson, *Alice Flemmerhammer:* Anabel Shaw, *Roy Bivins:* Michael (Stephen) Dunne, *Grandfather McKinley:* George Cleveland, *Rosemary Olcott:* Veda Ann Borg, *Papa:* Sig Rumann, *Lil:* Lee Patrick, *Specialty:* Señor Wences with Johnny, *Mrs. Muggins:* Maude Eburne, *Papa Capucci:* Antonio Filauri, *Stage Doorman:* Frank Orth, *Mama:* Lotte Stein, *Mr. Clarkman:* William Forrest, *Mrs. Clarkman:* Kathleen Lockhart, *Ed:* Chick Chandler, *Dance Director:* Kenny Williams, *Withers:* Will Wright, *Opera Singer:* Eula Morgan, *Man:* Tom Moore, *Man:* Harry Seymour, *Boy:* Lee MacGregor, *Myrtle's Dancing Partner:* Stephen Kirchner, *Clarence:* Alvin Hammer, *Minister:* Harry Cheshire, *Sailor:* Brad Slaven, *Sailor:* Ted Jordan, *Waiter:* George Davis, *Mikie at 3:* Ann Gowland, *Iris at 6:* Karolyn Grimes, *Narrator:* Anne Baxter.

MOULIN ROUGE (1952) UA. Produced and directed by John Huston. Associate Producer, Jack Clayton. A Romulus Films Production. Color by Technicolor. From the novel by Pierre LaMure. Screenplay, Anthony Veiller and John Huston. Music composed by Georges

Moulin Rouge with Suzanne Flon and José Ferrer.

Auric. Production Manager, Leigh Aman. Art Director, Paul Sheriff. Photography, Ossie Morris. Editor, Ralph Kemplin. Costumes, Marcel Vértés. Filmed in France. 123 minutes

Toulouse-Lautrec and The Comte de Toulouse-Lautrec: José Ferrer, *Marie Charlet:* Colette Marchand, *Myriamme:* Suzanne Flon, *Jane Avril:* Zsa Zsa Gabor, *La Goulue:* Katherine Kath, *Countess de Toulouse-Lautrec:* Claude Nollier, *Aicha:* Muriel Smith, *Patou:* Georges Lannes, *Aicha's Partner:* Tutte Lemkow, *Chocolat:* Rupert John, *Bar Proprietor:* Eric Pohlmann, *Valentin Dessosse:* Walter Crisham, *Madame Loubet:* Mary Clare, *Maurice Joyant:* Lee Montague, *Denise:* Maureen Swanson, *Pere Cotelle:* Jim Gerald, *Zidler:* Harold Gasket, *Sarah:* Jill Bennett, *Racing Fan:* Peter Cushing.

MOVE OVER, DARLING (1963) 20th. Produced by Aaron Rosenberg and Martin Melcher. Directed by Michael Gordon. Cinema-Scope and De Luxe Color. Based on the screenplay *My Favorite Wife* by Bella and Samuel Spewack. Story by the Spewacks and Leo Mc-Carey. Screenplay, Hal Kanter and Jack Sher. Music, Lionel Newman. Art Directors, Jack Martin Smith and Hilyard Brown. Orchestration, Arthur Morton and Warren Barker. Gowns, Moss Mabry. Assistant Director, Ad Schaumer. Cinematography, Daniel L. Fapp. Special Effects, L.B. Abbott and Emil Kosa, Jr. Editor, Robert Simpson. Songs: "Move Over, Darling" by Joe Lubin, Hal Kanter, and Terry Melcher; "Twinkle Lullaby" by Joe Lubin. A remake of *My Favorite Wife* (RKO, 1940) this was begun in 1962 as the ill-fated *Something's Got to Give* with Marilyn Monroe and Dean Martin. 103 minutes

Ellen Wagstaff Arden: Doris Day, *Nick Arden:* James Garner, *Bianca Steele Arden:* Polly Bergen, *Stephen Burkett (Adam):* Chuck Connors, *Grace Arden:* Thelma Ritter, *Mr. Codd:* Fred Clark, *Shoe Salesman:* Don Knotts, *Dr. Herman Schlick:* Elliott Reid, *Judge Bryson:* Edgar Buchanan, *Clyde Prokey:* John Astin, *District Attorney:* Pat Harrington, Jr., *Bellboy:* Eddie Quillan, *Desk Clerk:* Max Showalter (Casey Adams), *Waiter:* Alvy Moore, *Jenny Arden:* Pami Lee, *Didi Arden:* Leslie Farrell, *Maria:* Rosa Turich, *Bailiff:* Herold Goodwin, *Court Clerk:* Alan Sues, *The Drunk:* Pat Moran, *Woman:* Bess Flowers, *Injured Man's Wife:* Rachel Roman, *Bartender:* Jack Orrison, *Ambulance Attendants:* Kelton Garwood, Joel Collins, *Waiter at Pool:* Sid Gould, *Commander:* Ed McNally, *Skipper:* James Patridge, *Executive Seaman:* Christopher Connelly, *Seamen:* Billy Halop, Mel Flory, *Process Servers:* Emile Meyer, Brad Trumble, *Floorwalker:* Michael Romanoff, *Cab Driver:* John Harmon.

Move Over, Darling with Thelma Ritter, Doris Day, James Garner and Polly Bergen.

MR. BELVEDERE GOES TO COLLEGE (1949) 20th. Producer, Samuel G. Engel. Director, Elliott Nugent. Authors, Richard Sale, Mary Loos, Mary McCall, Jr. Music, Alfred Newman. Art Directors, Lyle Wheeler, Richard Irvine. Photography, Lloyd Ahern. Based on a character created by Gwen Davenport. Sequel to *Sitting Pretty* (1948). Second sequel was *Mr. Belvedere Rings the Bell* (1951). 83 minutes

Lynn Belvedere: Clifton Webb, *Ellen Baker:* Shirley Temple, *Bill Chase:* Tom Drake, *Avery Brubaker:* Alan Young, *Mrs. Chase:* Jessie

Mr. Belvedere Goes to College with Alan Young and Clifton Webb.

Royce Landis, *Kay Nelson:* Kathleen Hughes, *Dr. Gibbs:* Taylor Holmes, *Corny Whittaker:* Alvin Greenman, *Dr. Keating:* Paul Harvey, *Griggs:* Barry Kelly, *Joe Fisher:* Bob Patten, *Pratt:* Jeff Chandler, *McCarthy:* Clancy Cooper, *Marta:* Lotte Stein, *Sally:* Eevlynn Eaton, *Barbara:* Judy Brubaker, *Babe:* Kathleen Freeman, *Jean Auchincloss:* Peggy Call, *Nancy:* Ruth Tobey, *Peggy:* Elaine Ryan, *Isabelle:* Pattee Chapman, *Fluffy:* Joyce Otis, *Davy:* Lonnie Thomas, *Professor Ives:* Reginald Sheffield, *Miss Cadwaller:* Katherine Lang, *Mrs. Myrtle:* Isabel Withers, *Instructor:* Arthur Space, *Beanie:* Gil Stratton, Jr., *Girls:* Carol Brannon, Sally Feeney (Sally Forrest), Geneva Gray, *Drunk:* Frank Mills.

MR. BLANDINGS BUILDS HIS DREAM HOUSE (1948) RKO. Selznick Releasing Organization. Producers, Norman Panama, Melvin Frank. Director, H. C. Potter. Based on the novel by Eric Hodgins. Screenplay, Norman Panama, Melvin Frank. Art Directors, Albert D'Agostino, Carroll Clark. Music, C. Bakaleinikoff. Photography, James Wong Howe. Editor, Harry Marker. 94 minutes

Jim Blandings: Cary Grant, *Muriel Blandings:* Myrna Loy, *Bill Cole:* Melvyn Douglas, *Henry Simms:* Reginald Denny, *Joan Blandings:* Sharyn Moffett, *Betsy Blandings:* Connie Marshall, *Gussie:* Louise Beavers, *Smith:* Ian Wolfe, *W. D. Tesander:* Harry Shannon, *Mr. Zucca:* Tito Vuolo, *Joe Appollonio:* Nestor Paiva, *John Retch:* Jason Robards, *Mary:* Lurene Tuttle, *Carpenter Foreman:* Lex Barker, *Mr. Pe Delford:* Emory Parnell, *Bunny Funkhauser:* Dan Tobin, *Eph Hackett:* Will Wright, *Judge Quarles:* Frank Darien, *Murphy:* Stanley Andrews, *Jones:* Cliff Clark, *Simpson:* Franklin Parker, *Wrecker:* Charles Middleton, *Workman:* Robert Bray, *Workman:* Frederick Ledebur, *Charlie:* Don Brodie, *Mr. Selby:* Hal K. Dawson, *Cop:* Kernan Cripps, *Customer:* Bud Wiser.

Mr. Blandings Builds His Dream House with Cary Grant, Myrna Loy, Sharyn Moffett and Connie Marshall.

MR. DEEDS GOES TO TOWN (1936) Col. Produced and directed by Frank Capra. Author, Clarence Buddington Kelland (from "Opera Hat"). Cinematographer, Robert Riskin. Recording Engineer, Edward Bernds. Film Editor, Gene Havlick. Art Director, Stephen Goosson. Costumer, Samuel Lange. Musical Director, Howard Jackson. Assistant Director, C. C. Coleman. 115 minutes.

Mr. Deeds Goes to Town with Walter Catlett, Gary Cooper and Jean Arthur.

Longfellow Deeds: Gary Cooper, *Babe Bennett:* Jean Arthur, *MacWade:* George Bancroft, *Cornelius Cobb:* Lionel Stander, *John Cedar:* Douglass Dumbrille, *Walter:* Raymond Walburn, *Madame Pomponi:* Margaret Matzenauer, *Judge Walker:* H. B. Warner, *Bodyguard:* Warren Hymer, *Theresa:* Muriel Evans, *Mabel Dawson:* Ruth Donnelly *Mal:* Spencer Charters, *Mrs. Meredith:* Emma Dunn, *Psychiatrist:* Wryley Birch, *Budington:* Arthur Hoyt, *James Cedar:* Stanley Andrews, *Arthur Cedar:* Pierre Watkin, *Farmer:* John Wray, *Swenson:* Christian Rub, *Mr. Semple:* Jameson Thomas, *Mrs. Semple:* Mayo Methot, *Doctor Malcolm:* Russell Hicks, *Dr. Frazier:* Gustav Von Seyffertitz, *Dr. Fosdick:* Edward Le Saint, *Hallor:* Charles (Levison) Lane, *Frank:* Irving Bacon, *Bob:* George Cooper, *Waiter:* Gene Morgan, *Morrow:* Walter Catlett, *The Butler:* Barnett Parker, *Jane Faulkner:* Margaret Seddon, *Amy Faulkner:* Margaret McWade, *Anderson:* Harry C. Bradley, *Second Bodyguard:* Edward Gargan, *Douglas:* Edwin Maxwell, *First Deputy:* Paul Hurst, *Italian:* Paul Porcasi, *Tailor:* Franklin Pangborn, *Farmers' Spokesman:* George F. Hayes, *Cabby:* Billy Bevan, *Reporter:* Dennis O'Keefe, *Brookfield:* George Meeker, *Lawyer:* Dale Van Sickel.

MR. LUCKY (1943) RKO. Produced by David Hempstead. Directed by H. C. Potter. Based on the story *Bundles for Freedom* by Milton Holmes. Screenplay, Milton Holmes and Adrian Scott. Music, Roy Webb, Music Director, C. Bakaleinikoff. Art Directors, Albert S. D'Agostino and Mark-Lee Kirk. Photography, George Barnes. Special Effects, Vernon L. Walker. Editor, Theron Warth. Remade by RKO as *Gambling House* (1950). 98 minutes

Joe Adams: Cary Grant, *Dorothy Bryant:* Laraine Day, *Swede:* Charles Bickford, *Captain Steadman:* Gladys Cooper, *Crunk:* Alan Carney, *Mr. Bryant:* Henry Stephenson, *Zepp:* Paul Stewart, *Mrs. Ostrander:* Kay Johnson, *Gaffer:* Erford Gage, *Commissioner Hargraves:* Walter Kingsford, *McDougal:* J. M. Kerrigan, *Foster:* Edward Fielding, *Greek Priest:* Vladimir Sokoloff, *Siga:* John Bleifer, *Joe*

Mr. Lucky with Cary Grant.

Bascopolus: Juan Varro, *Dealer (Gaffer):* Don Brodie, *Workman at Slot Machine:* Frank Mills, *Dowager:* Mary Forbes, *Girls:* Mary Stuart, Rita Corday, Ariel Heath, *Plainclothesman:* Joseph Crehan, *Plainclothesman:* Kernan Cripps, *Draft Board Director:* Hal K. Dawson, *Captain Costello:* Robert Strange, *Reporter on Street:* Frank Henry, *Comstock:* Charles Cane, *Stevedore:* Budd Fine, *Maid:* Hilda Plowright, *Taxi Driver:* Lloyd Ingraham, *Dock Watchman:* Emory Parnell, *Gambler (Extra):* Major Sam Harris, *Mrs. Van Every:* Florence Bates.

MR. SKEFFINGTON (1944) WB. Produced by Philip G. and Julius J. Epstein. Directed by Vincent Sherman. Based on the story by "Elizabeth." Screenplay, Philip G. and Julius J. Epstein. Photography, Ernest Haller. Score, Franz Waxman. Music Direction, Leo F. Forbstein. Orchestral Arrangements, Leonid Raab. Art Director, Robert Haas. Editor, Ralph Dawson. Costumes, Orry-Kelly. 146 minutes

Fanny Trellis Skeffington: Bette Davis, *Job Skeffington:* Claude Rains, *George Trellis:* Walter Abel, *Trippy Trellis:* Richard Waring, *Doctor Byles:* George Coulouris, *Young Fanny:* Marjorie Riordan, *MacMahon:* Robert Shayne, *Jim Conderley:* John Alexander, *Edward Morrison:* Jerome Cowan, *Johnny Mitchell:* Johnny Mitchell, *Manby:* Dorothy Peterson, *Chester Forbish:* Peter Whitney, *Thatcher:* Bill Kennedy, *Reverend Hyslup:* Tom Stevenson, *Soames:* Halliwell Hobbes, *Doctor Melton:* Walter Kingsford, *Young Fanny at 2.5:* Gigi Perreau, *Young Fanny at 5:* Bunny Sunshine, *Singer:* Dolores Gray, *Miss Morris:* Molly Lamont, *Young Fanny at 10:* Sylvia Arslan, *The Rector:* Harry Bradley, *Casey, Employee:* Creighton Hale, *Nursemaid:* Ann Doran, *Mrs. Newton:* Georgia Caine, *Mrs. Forbish:* Lelah Tyler, *Mrs. Hyslup:* Mary Field, *Mrs. Conderley:* Regina Wallace, *Mrs. Thatcher:* Bess Flowers, *Justice of the Peace:* Edward Fielding, *Justice's Wife:* Vera Lewis, *Doctor Fawcette:* Erskine Sanford, *Perry Lanks:* Cyril Ring, *"Louie":* Crane Whitley, *Drunks:* Matt McHugh, Will Stanton, *Plainclothesman:* Saul Gorss, *French Modiste:* Ann Codee, *Henri:* Jack George, *Woman:* Dagmar Oakland, *Clinton:* William Forrest.

Mr. Skeffington with Walter Abel, Richard Waring, Bette Davis and Claude Rains.

MRS. MINIVER (1942) MGM. Produced by Sidney Franklin. Directed by William Wyler. Based on the novel by Jan Struther. Screenplay, Arthur Wimperis, George Froeschel, James Hilton, Claudine West. Music Score, Herbert Stothart. Photography, Joseph Ruttenberg. Sound, Douglas Shearer. Art Director, Cedric Gibbons. Associate, Urie McCleary. Set Decorations, Edwin B. Willis. Special Effects, Arnold Gillespie and Warren Newcombe. Gowns, Kalloch. Men's Wardrobe, Gile Steele. Miss Garson's Hair Styles, Sydney Guilaroff. Editor, Harold F. Kress. Song, "Midsummer's Day" by Gene Lockhart. The sequel was *The Miniver Story* (1950). 134 minutes

Kay Miniver: Greer Garson, *Clem Miniver:* Walter Pidgeon, *Carol Beldon:* Teresa Wright, *Lady Beldon:* Dame May Whitty, *Mr. Ballard:* Henry Travers, *Foley:* Reginald Owen, *Vicar:* Henry Wilcoxon, *Vin Miniver:* Richard Ney, *Toby Miniver:* Christopher Severn, *Gladys:*

Mrs. Miniver with Teresa Wright, Walter Pidgeon, Greer Garson and Richard Ney.

Brenda Forbes, *Judy Miniver:* Clare Sandars, *Horace:* Rhys Williams, *Ada:* Marie De Becker, *German Flyer:* Helmut Dantine, *Miss Spriggins:* Mary Field, *Nobby:* Paul Scardon, *Ginger:* Ben Webster, *George (Innkeeper):* Aubrey Mather, *Huggins:* Forrester Harvey, *Fred (Porter):* John Abbott, *Simpson:* Connie Leon, *Conductor:* Billy Bevan, *Saleslady:* Ottola Nesmith, *Car Dealer:* Gerald Oliver Smith, *Joe:* Alec Craig, *Mrs. Huggins:* Clara Reid, *William:* Harry Allen, *Halliday:* John Burton, *Beldon's Butler:* Leonard Carey, *Marston:* Eric Lonsdale, *Mac:* Charles Irwin, *Dentist:* Ian Wolfe, *Sir Henry:* Arthur Wimperis, *Carruthers:* David Clyde, *Bickles:* Colin Campbell, *Doctor:* Herbert Clifton, *Man in Tavern:* Walter Byron, *Mr. Verger:* Thomas Louden, *Pilot:* Peter Lawford, *German Agent's Voice:* Miles Mander. St. Luke's Choristers.

MR. SMITH GOES TO WASHINGTON (1939) Col. Producer and Director, Frank Capra. Author, Lewis R. Foster. Screenplay, Sidney Buchman. Art Director, Lionel Banks. Musical Director, H. W. Stoloff. Score, Dimitri Tiomkin. Cameraman, Joseph Walker. Montage Effects, Slavko Vorkapich. Editors, Gene Havlick, Al Clark. 125 minutes

Saunders: Jean Arthur, *Jefferson Smith:* James Stewart, *Senator Joseph Paine:* Claude Rains, *Jim Taylor:* Edward Arnold, *Governor Hubert Hopper:* Guy Kibbee, *Diz Moore:* Thomas Mitchell, *Chick McCann:* Eugene Pallette, *Ma Smith:* Beulah Bondi, *Senator Fuller:* H. B. Warner, *President of the Senate:* Harry Carey, *Susan Paine:* Astrid Allwyn, *Emma Hopper:* Ruth Donnelly, *Senator MacPherson:* Grant Mitchell, *Senator Monroe:* Porter Hall, *Senator Barnes:* Pierre Watkin, *Nosey:* Charles Lane, *Bill Griffith:* William Demarest, *Carl Cook:* Dick Elliott. *The Hopper Boys:* Billy and Delmar Watson, John Russell, Harry and Garry Watson, Baby Dumpling (Larry Simms), *Broadcaster:* H. V. Kaltenborn, *Announcer:* Kenneth Carpenter, *Sweeney:* Jack Carson, *Summers:* Joe King, *Flood:* Paul Stanton, *Allen:* Russell Simpson, *Senator Hodges:* Stanley Andrews, *Senator Pickett:* Walter Soderling, *Senator Byron:* Frank Jaquet, *Senator Carlisle:* Ferris Taylor, *Senator Burdette:* Carl Stockdale, *Senator Dwight:* Alan Bridge, *Senator Gower:* Edmund Cobb, *Senator Dearhorn:* Frederick Burton, *Mrs. Edwards:* Vera Lewis, *Mrs. McGann:* Dora Clemant, *Mrs. Taylor:* Laura Treadwell, *Paine's Secretary:* Ann Doran,

Mr. Smith Goes to Washington with Eugene Pallette, James Stewart, Edward Arnold, Allan Cavan, Maurice Costello and Lloyd Whitlock.

Francis Scott Key: Douglas Evans, *Ragner:* Allan Cavan, *Diggs:* Maurice Costello, *Schultz:* Lloyd Whitlock, *Jane Hopper:* Myonne Walsh, *Bit Girls:* Frances Gifford, Lorna Gray, Adrian Booth, Linda Winters (Dorothy Comingore).

MRS. PARKINGTON (1944) MGM. Produced by Leon Gordon. Directed by Tay Garnett. Based on the novel by Louis Bromfie!d. Screenplay, Robert Thoeren and Polly James. Art Directors, Cedric Gibbons and Randall Duell. Music, Bronislau Kaper. Photography, Joseph Ruttenberg. Editor, George Boemler. In the European version, Hugo Haas as the King was substituted for the part of the Prince of Wales, and Tala Birell's character was changed to a Countess. 124 minutes

Susie Parkington: Greer Garson, *Major Augustus Parkington:* Walter Pidgeon, *Amory Stilham:* Edward Arnold, *Aspasia Conti:* Agnes Moorehead, *Edward, Prince of Wales:* Cecil Kellaway, *Alice, Duchess De Brancourt:* Gladys Cooper, *Jane Stilham:* Frances Rafferty, *Ned Talbot:* Tom Drake, *Thornley:* Peter Lawford, *Jack Stilham:* Dan Duryea, *John Marbey:* Hugh Marlowe, *Mattie Trounsen:* Selena Royle, *Signor Cellini:* Fortunio Bonanova, *Madeleine:* Lee Patrick, *Humphrey:* Harry Cording, *Belle:* Celia Travers, *Mrs. Graham:* Mary Servoss, *Al Swann:* Rod Cameron, *Lady Nora Ebbsworth:* Tala Birell, *Helen Stilham:* Helen Freeman, *Taylor:* Gerald Oliver Smith, *Bridgett:* Ruthe Brady, *Vance:* Byron Foulger, *Captain McTavish:* Wallis Clark, *Madame Dupont:* Ann Codee, *French Doctor:* Frank Reicher, *Minnie:* Kay Medford, *Mr. Ernst:* Hans Conried, *Reverend Pilbridge:* Edward Fielding, *Mrs. Jacob Livingstone:* Alma Kruger, *Mrs. Humphrey:* Rhea Mitchell, *Albert:* Ivo Henderson, *Sam:* Lee Tung Foo, *Gaston:* Marek Windheim, *Madame De Thebes:* Marcelle Corday, *Mr. Orlando:* Robert Greig, *James (Butler):* Gordon Richards, *Doctor Herrick:* Howard Hickman, *Herbert Parkington:* Warren Farlan, *Caterer:* Doodles Weaver, *Fat Man:* Rex Evans.

Mrs. Parkington with Greer Garson and Walter Pidgeon.

THE MUSIC MAN (1962) WB. Producer, Morton DaCosta. Director, Morton DaCosta. Technirama, Technicolor. Based on the musical by Meredith Willson. Screenplay, Marion Hargrove. Art Director, Paul Groesse. Music Supervisor and Conductor, Ray Heindorf. Orchestration, Ray Heindorf, Frank Comstock, Gus Levene. Cinematographer, Robert Burks. Editor, William Ziegler. Songs by Meredith Willson: "Rock Island," "Iowa Stubborn," "Trouble," "Piano Lesson," "Goodnight My Someone," "76 Trombones," "Sincere," "The Sadder-But-Wiser Girl," "Pickilittle," "Goodnight My Ladies," "Marian the Librarian," "Being in Love," "Wells Fargo Wagon," "It's You," "Shipoopi," "Lida Rose," "Will I Ever Tell You," "Gary, Indiana," "Till There Was You." Choreography, Onna White, Tom Panko. 151 minutes

Harold Hill: Robert Preston, *Marian Paroo:* Shirley Jones, *Mayor Shinn:* Paul Ford, *Marcellus Washburn:* Buddy Hackett, *Eulalie Mackechnie Shinn:* Hermione Gingold, *Amaryllis:* Monique Vermont, *Winthrop Paroo:* Ronny Howard, *Mrs. Paroo:* Pert Kelton, *Norbert Smith:* Ronnie Dapo, *Jacey Squires Olin Britt, Ewart Dunlop, Oliver*

The Music Man with Buddy Hackett and Robert Preston.

Hix: The Buffalo Bills, *Constable Locke:* Charles Lane, *Tommy Djilas:* Timmy Everett, *Zaneeta Shinn:* Susan Luckey, *Charlie Cowell:* Harry Hickox, *Mrs. Squires:* Mary Wickes, *Avis Grubb:* Jesslyn Fax, *Gracie Shinn:* Patty Lee Hilka, *Dewey:* Garry Potter, *Harley MacCauley:* J. Delos Jewkes, *Harry Joseph:* Ray Kellogg, *Lester Lonnergan:* William Fawcett, *Oscar Jackson:* Rance Howard, *Gilbert Hawthorne:* Roy Dean, *Chet Glanville:* David Swain, *Herbert Malthouse:* Arthur Mills, *Duncan Shyball:* Rand Barker, *Jessie Shyball:* Jeannine Burnier, *Amy Dakin:* Shirley Claire, *Truthful Smith:* Natalie Core, *Dolly Higgins:* Therese Lyon, *Lila O'Brink:* Penelope Martin, *Feril Hawkes:* Barbara Pepper, *Stella Jackson:* Anne Loos, *Ada Nutting:* Peggy Wynne, *Undertaker:* Hank Worden, *Farmer:* Milton Parsons, *Farmer's Wife:* Natalie Masters.

MUTINY ON THE BOUNTY (1935) MGM. Produced by Irving Thalberg. Associate Producer, Albert Lewin. Directed by Frank Lloyd. Based on the novel by Charles Nordhoff and James Norman Hall. Art Director, Cedric Gibbons. Musical Score, Herbert Stothart. Cinematographer, Arthur Edeson. Recording Engineer, Douglas Shearer. Editor, Margaret Booth. Screenplay by Talbot Jennings, Jules Furthman, Carey Wilson. Song, "Love Song of Tahiti," by Gus Kahn, Bronislau Kaper, and Walter Jurmann. Remade by MGM in 1962. 132 minutes

Fletcher Christian: Clark Gable, *Captain Bligh:* Charles Laughton, *Byam:* Franchot Tone, *Bachus:* Dudley Digges, *Sir Joseph Banks:* Henry Stephenson, *Burkitt:* Donald Crisp, *Ellison:* Eddie Quillan, *Captain Nelson:* Francis Lister, *Mrs. Byam:* Spring Byington, *Tehani:* Maria Castaneda (Movita), *Maimiti:* Mamo Clark, *Young:* Robert Livingston, *Stewart:* Douglas Walton, *Samuel:* Ian Wolfe, *Fryer:* DeWitt C. Jennings, *Morgan:* Ivan Simpson, *Hayward:* Vernon Downing, *Muspratt:* Stanley Fields, *Morrison:* Wallis Clark, *Tinkler:* Dick Winslow, *Quintal:* Byron Russell, *Coleman:* Percy Waram, *Lord Hood:* David Torrence, *Mr. Purcell:* John Harrington, *Mary Ellison:* Marion Clayton, *Millard:* Hal LeSueur, *Hitihiti:* William Bainbridge, *McIntosh:* David Thursby, *Lieutenant Edwards:* Craufurd Kent, *Churchill:*

Mutiny on the Bounty with Franchot Tone and Charles Laughton.

Pat Flaherty, *McCoy:* Alec Craig, *Byrne:* Charles Irwin, *Hillebrandt:* John Powers, *Richard Skinner:* King Mojave, *Cockney Moll:* Doris Lloyd, *Judge Advocate:* William Stack, *Captain Colpoys:* Harold Entwhistle, *Portsmouth Joe:* Will Stanton, *Innkeeper:* Lionel Belmore, *Soldier:* Harry Cording, *Peddler:* Mary Gordon, *Smith:* Herbert Mundin, *Captain of Board:* Eric Wilton.

Mutiny on the Bounty with Marlon Brando and Trevor Howard.

MUTINY ON THE BOUNTY (1962) MGM. Producer, Aaron Rosenberg. Director, Lewis Milestone. Screenplay, Charles Lederer. Based on the novel by Charles Nordhoff and James Norman Hall. Music, Bronislau Kaper. Assistant Director, Ridgeway Callow. Costumes, Moss Mabry. Choreographer, Hamil Petroff. An Arcola Picture in Ultra Panavision and Technicolor. Art Directors, George W. Davis, J. McMillan Johnson. Cinematographer, Robert L. Surtees. Editor, John McSweeney, Jr. Previous versions: *In the Wake of the Bounty* (Australian, 1933), *Mutiny on the Bounty* (MGM. 1935). 179 minutes

Fletcher Christian: Marlon Brando, *Captain Bligh:* Trevor Howard, *John Mills:* Richard Harris, *Smith:* Hugh Griffith, *Brown:* Richard Haydn, *Maimiti:* Tarita, *Quintal:* Percy Herbert, *Williams:* Duncan Lamont, *Birkett:* Gordon Jackson, *Byrne:* Chips Rafferty, *McCoy:* Noel Purcell, *Mack:* Ashley Cowan, *Fryer:* Eddie Byrne, *Minarii:* Frank Silvera, *Young:* Tim Seely, *Morrison:* Keith McConnell.

MY DARLING CLEMENTINE (1946) 20th. Producer, Samuel G. Engel. Director, John Ford. Authors, Sam Hellman, Stuart N. Lake (from *Wyatt Earp, Frontier Marshall*). Screenplay, Samuel G. Engel, Winston Miller. Music, Alfred Newman. Art Directors, James Basevi,

My Darling Clementine with Henry Fonda and Cathy Downes.

Lyle Wheeler. Cameraman, Joe MacDonald. Editor, Dorothy Spencer. Remake of *Frontier Marshal* (Fox, 1939). 97 minutes

Wyatt Earp: Henry Fonda, *Chihuahua:* Linda Darnell, *Doc Holliday:* Victor Mature, *Old Man Clanton:* Walter Brennan, *Virgil Earp:* Tim Holt, *Clementine:* Cathy Downs, *Morgan Earp:* Ward Bond, *Thorndyke:* Alan Mowbray, *Billy Clanton:* John Ireland, *Mayor:* Roy Roberts, *Kate:* Jane Darwell, *Ike Clanton:* Grant Withers, *Bartender:* J. Farrell Macdonald, *John Simpson:* Russell Simpson, *James Earp:* Don Garner, *Town Drunk:* Francis Ford, *Barber:* Ben Hall, *Hotel Clerk:* Arthur Walsh, *Francois:* Louis Mercier, *Sam Clanton:* Mickey Simpson, *Phin Clanton:* Fred Libby, *Owner of Oriental Saloon:* William B. Davidson, *Gambler:* Earle Foxe, *Townsman and Guitar Player:* Aleth (Speed) Hansen, *Townsman and Accordian Player:* Dan Borzage, *Opera House Owner:* Don Barclay, *Marshal:* Harry Woods, *Indian Charlie:* Charles Stevens, *Piano Player:* Frank Conlan, *Stagecoach Driver:* Robert Adler.

MY FAIR LADY (1964) WB. Produced by Jack L. Warner. Directed by George Cukor. Technicolor and Super Panavision 70. Based on the musical play *My Fair Lady* by Alan Jay Lerner and Frederick Loewe, and the play *Pygmalion* by George Bernard Shaw. Screenplay, Alan Jay Lerner. Art Director, Gene Allen. Music supervised and conducted by Andre Previn. Orchestration, Alexander Courage, Robert Franklyn, Al Woodbury. Choreography, Hermes Pan. Costumes, Cecil Beaton. Assistant Director, David Hall. Photography, Harry Stradling. Editor, William Ziegler. Songs by Lerner and Loewe: "Why Can't the English," "Wouldn't It Be Loverly?" "I'm an Ordinary Man," "With a Little Bit of Luck," "Just You Wait," "The Servants' Chorus," "The Rain in Spain," "I Could Have Danced All Night," "Ascot Gavotte," "On the Street Where You Live," "The Embassy Waltz," "You Did It," "Show Me," "The Flower Market," "Get Me to the Church on Time," "A Hymn to Him," "Without You," "I've Grown Accustomed to Her Face." Remake of *Pygmalion* (MGM, 1938). The musical, *My Fair Lady*, ran on Broadway from 1956 to 1962, and was originally called *Lady Liza*. Rex Harrison, Wilfrid Hyde-White, and Olive Reeves-Smith repeated their original roles in the film. Last film of Henry Daniell, 69, who died October 31, 1963. 170 minutes

My Fair Lady with Rex Harrison, Audrey Hepburn and Wilfrid Hyde-White.

Professor Henry Higgins: Rex Harrison, *Eliza Doolittle:* Audrey Hepburn, *Alfred P. Doolittle:* Stanley Holloway, *Colonel Hugh Pickering:* Wilfrid Hyde-White, *Mrs. Higgins:* Gladys Cooper, *Freddy Eynsford-Hill:* Jeremy Brett, *Zoltan Karpathy:* Theodore Bikel, *Mrs. Eynsford-Hill:* Isobel Elsom, *Mrs. Pearce:* Mona Washbourne, *Butler:* John Holland, *Jamie:* John Alderson, *Harry:* John McLiam, *Bystander (Warns Eliza):* Walter Burke, *Man at Coffee Stand:* Owen McGiveney, *Cockney with Pipe:* Marjorie Bennett, *George:* Jack Greening, *Algernon/Bartender:* Ron Whelan, *First Maid:* Dinah Anne Rogers, *Second Maid:* Lois Battle, *Parlor Maid:* Jacqueline Squire, *Cook:* Gwen Watts, *King:* Charles Fredericks, *Lady Ambassador:* Lily Kemble-Cooper, *Lady Boxington:* Moyna MacGill, *Prince Gregor of Transyl-*

vania: Henry Daniell, *Queen of Transylvania:* Baroness Rothschild, *Footman at Ball:* Ben Wright, *Greek Ambassador:* Oscar Beregi, *Ad-lib at Ball:* Betty Blythe, *Prince:* Buddy Bryan, *Dancer:* Nick Navarro, *Ambassador:* Alan Napier, *Mrs. Higgins' Maid:* Jennifer Crier, *Mrs. Hopkins:* Olive Reeves-Smith, *Landlady:* Miriam Schiller, *Fat Woman at Pub:* Ayllene Gibbons, *Doolittle's Dance Partner:* Barbara Pepper, *Ascot Extra/Guest at Ball:* Grady Sutton, *Guest at Ball:* Major Sam Harris.

MY FAVORITE BLONDE (1942) Par. Associate Producer, Paul Jones. Directed by Sidney Lanfield. Story, Melvin Frank and Norman Panama. Screenplay, Don Hartman and Frank Butler. Art Directors, Hans Dreier and Robert Usher. Music Score, David Buttolph. Photography, William Mellor. Editor, William Shea. 78 minutes

Larry Haines: Bob Hope, *Karen Bentley:* Madeleine Carroll, *Madame Stephanie Runick:* Gale Sondergaard, *Dr. Hugo Streger:* George Zucco, *Karl:* Lionel Royce, *Dr. Faber:* Walter Kingsford, *Miller:* Victor Varconi, *Lanz:* Otto Reichow, *Turk O'Flaherty:* Charles Cane, *Ulrich:* Crane Whitley, *Sheriff:* Erville Alderson, *Mrs. Topley:* Esther Howard, *Mulrooney:* Ed Gargan, *Union Secretary:* James Burke, *Porter:* Dooley Wilson, *Mortician:* Milton Parsons, *Tom Douglas:* Tom Fadden, *Sam:* Fred Kelsey, *Joe:* Edgar Dearing, *Elvan:* Leslie Dennison, *Burton:* Robert Emmett Keane, *Herbert Wilson:* Addison Richards, *Colonel Ashmont:* Matthew Boulton, *Conductor:* Wade Boteler, *Colonel Raeburn:* William Forrest, *Frederick:* Carl "Alfalfa" Switzer, *Frederick's Mother:* Isabel Randolph, *Train Official:* Edward Hearn, *English Driver:* Leyland Hodgson, *Spectator:* Jack Luden, *Cop at Union Hall:* Monte Blue, *Backstage Doorman:* Dick Elliott, *Male Nurse:* Arno Frey, *Apartment Manager:* Lloyd Whitlock, *Ole, Bartender:* Vernon Dent, *Mrs. Weatherwax:* Sarah Edwards, *Dr. Higby:* Paul Scardon, *Telegraph Operator:* Bill Lally, *Frozen-faced Woman:* Minerva Urecal, *Truck Driver:* James Millican, *Yard Man:* Edmund Cobb, *Stuttering Boy:* Jimmy Dodd, *Pilots:* Eddie Dew, George Turner, Kirby Grant, William Cabanne.

My Favorite Blonde with Isabel Randolph, Carl "Alfalfa" Switzer, Bob Hope and Madeleine Carroll.

MY FAVORITE BRUNETTE (1947) Par. Producer, Daniel Dare. Director, Elliott Nugent. Screenplay, Edward Beloin, Jack Rose. Art Directors, Hans Dreier, Earl Hedrick. Musical Score, Robert Emmet Dolan. Cameraman, Lionel Lindon. Editor, Ellsworth Hoagland. Songs by Ray Evans and Jay Livingston: "Beside You" and "My Favorite Brunette." 87 minutes

Ronnie Jackson: Bob Hope, *Carlotta Montay:* Dorothy Lamour, *Kismet:* Peter Lorre, *Willie:* Lon Chaney, Jr., *Dr. Lundau:* John Hoyt, *Major Simon Montague:* Charles Dingle, *James Collins:* Reginald Denny, *Baron Montay:* Frank Puglia, *Miss Rogers:* Ann Doran, *Prison Warden:* Willard Robertson, *Tony:* Jack La Rue, *Crawford:* Charles Arnt, *Reporter:* Garry Owen, *Reporter:* Richard Keene,

"Raft" Character: Tony Caruso, *"Cagney" Character:* Matt McHugh, *Prison Guard:* George Lloyd, *Prison Guard:* Jack Clifford, *State Trooper:* Ray Teal, *State Trooper:* Al Hill, *Caddie:* Eddie Johnson, *Mr. Dawsen:* Boyd Davis, *Man in Condemned Row:* Clarence Muse, *Mabel:* Helena Evans, *Baby Fong:* Roland Soo Hoo, *Doctor:* John Westley, *Waiter:* Charley Cooley, *Mrs. Fong:* Jean Wong, *Matron:* Betty Farrington, *Butler:* Brandon Hurst, *Henri (Waiter):* Jack Chefe, *Asst. Manager:* Reginald Simpson, *Mac (Detective):* James Flavin, *Second Detective:* Jim Pierce, *Third Detective:* Budd Fine, *Guest Star:* Bing Crosby.

My Favorite Brunette with Bob Hope and Dorothy Lamour.

MY FAVORITE WIFE (1940) RKO. Producer, Leo McCarey. Director, Garson Kanin. Authors, Sam and Bella Spewack, Leo McCarey. Screenplay, Sam and Bella Spewack. Cameraman, Rudolph Mate. Editor, Robert Wise. Remade as *Move Over, Darling* (Fox, 1963). 88 minutes

Ellen: Irene Dunne, *Nick:* Cary Grant, *Burkett:* Randolph Scott, *Bianca:* Gail Patrick, *Ma:* Ann Shoemaker, *Tim:* Scotty Beckett, *Chinch:* Mary Lou Harrington, *Hotel Clerk:* Donald MacBride, *Johnson:* Hugh O'Connell, *Judge:* Granville Bates, *Dr. Kohlmar:* Pedro de Cordoba, *Dr. Manning:* Brandon Tynan, *Henri:* Leon Belasco, *Assistant Clerk:* Harold Gerard, *Bartender:* Murray Alper, *Clerk of Court:* Earl Hodgins, *Lawyer:* Clive Morgan, *Witness:* Florence Dudley, *Contestant:* Cy Ring, *Witness:* Jean Acker, *Lawyer:* Bert Moorhouse, *Phillip:* Joe Cabrillas, *Photographer:* Frank Marlowe, *Miss Rosenthal:* Thelma Joel, *Truck Driver:* Horace MacMahon, *Little Man:* Chester Clute, *Janitor:* Eli Schmudkler, *Waiter:* Franco Corsaro, *Caretaker:* Pat West, *Detective:* Cy Kendall.

My Favorite Wife with Gail Patrick, Ann Shoemaker, Irene Dunne, Cary Grant, Scotty Beckett and Mary Lou Harrington.

My Friend Irma with Marie Wilson and John Lund.

MY FRIEND IRMA (1949) Par. Produced by Hal B. Wallis. Directed by George Marshall. Based on the C.B.S. radio program created by Cy Howard. Screenplay, Cy Howard and Parke Levy. Music, Roy Webb. Art Directors, Hans Dreier and Henry Bumstead. Photography, Leo Tover. Editor, LeRoy Stone. A Wallis-Hazen Production. Songs by Jay Livingston and Ray Evans: "My Friend Irma," "Here's to Love," "Just for Fun," "My One, My Only, My All." Feature film debut of the team of Martin and Lewis. A sequel, *My Friend Irma Goes West* (1950), had the same stars. 103 minutes

Irma Peterson: Marie Wilson, *Al:* John Lund, *Jane Stacy:* Diana Lynn, *Richard Rhinelander:* Don DeFore, *Steve Laird:* Dean Martin, *Seymour:* Jerry Lewis, *Professor Kropotkin:* Hans Conried, *Mrs. Rhinelander:* Kathryn Givney, *Mr. Clyde:* Percy Helton, *Mr. Ubang and His Brother:* Erno Verebes, *Mrs. O'Reilly:* Gloria Gordon, *Alice:* Margaret Field, *Interior Decorator:* Douglas Spencer, *Truck Driver:* Dewey Robinson, *Photographer:* Jack Mulhall, *Income Tax Man:* Francis Pierlot, *Mushie:* Nick Cravat, *Sam, Pet Shop Man:* Joey Ray, *Burcher:* Billy Snyder, *Indian:* Chief Yowlachie, *Announcer:* Ken Niles, *Wallpaper Man:* Jimmie Dundee, *Newspaperman:* Tony Merrill, *Customer:* Bill Meader, *Man in Parking Lot:* Howard M. Mitchell, *Orchestra Leader:* Leonard B. Ingoldest, *Butler:* Charles Coleman.

MY GAL SAL (1942) 20th. Directed by Irving Cummings. Produced by Robert Basler. Color by Technicolor. Screenplay by Seton I. Miller, Darrell Ware and Karl Iunberg. Based on Theodore Dreiser's *My Brother Paul.* Songs: "Come Tell Me What's Your Answer, Yes or No," "I'se Your Honey If You Wants Me, Liza Jane," "On the Banks of the Wabash," "The Convict and the Bird," "My Gal Sal," "Mr. Volunteer" (or "You Don't Belong to the Regulars, You're Just a Volunteer"), by Paul Dreiser. Additional songs: "Me and My Fella and a Big Umbrella," "On the Gay White Way," "Oh the Pity of It All," "Here You Are," "Midnight at the Masquerade," by Leo Robin and Ralph Rainger. Dances staged by Hermes Pan and Val Raset. Director of Photography, Ernest Palmer. Technicolor Director, Natalie Kalmus. Associate, Henri Jaffa. Musical Direction, Alfred Newman. Art Direction, Richard Day. Set Decorations, Thomas Little. Film Editor, Robert Simpson. Costumes, Gwen Wakeling. Make-up Artist, Guy Pearce. Sound, Alfred Bruzlin, Roger Heman. 103 minutes

My Gal Sal with John Sutton, Phil Silvers and Rita Hayworth.

Sally Elliott: Rita Hayworth, *Paul Dreiser:* Victor Mature, *Fred Haviland:* John Sutton, *Mae Collins:* Carole Landis, *Pat Hawley:* James Gleason, *Wiley:* Phil Silvers, *Colonel Truckee:* Walter Catlett, *Countess Rossini:* Mona Maris, *McGuinness:* Frank Orth, *Mr. Dreiser:* Stanley Andrews, *Mrs. Dreiser:* Margaret Moffat, *Ida:* Libby Taylor, *John L. Sullivan:* John Kelly, *De Rochement:* Curt Bois, *Garnier:* Gregory Gaye, *Corbin:* Andrew Tombes, *Henri:* Albert Conti, *Tailor:* Charles Arnt, *Quartette:* Clarence Badger, Kenneth Rundquist, Gene Ramey, Delos Jewkes, *Murphy:* Chief Thundercloud, *Specialty Dancer:* Hermes Pan, *Sally's Friends:* Robert Lowery, Dorothy Dearing, (Michael) Ted North, Roseanne Murray, *Carrie:* Judy Ford (Terry Moore), *Theodore:* Barry Downing, *Usher:* Tommy Seide, *Men:* Gus Glassmire, Tom O'Grady, Frank Ferguson, John "Skins" Miller, Cyril Ring, *Midget Driver:* Billy Curtis, *Midget Footman:* Tommy Cotton.

MY MAN GODFREY (1936) Univ. Produced and directed by Gregory LaCava. Author, Eric Hatch. Screenplay by Morrie Ryskind, Eric Hatch, Gregory LaCava. Cameraman, Ted Tetzlaff. Editor, Ted Kent. Film debut of Jane Wyman, 22. Remade by Universal, 1957. 95 minutes

Godfrey: William Powell, *Irene Bullock:* Carole Lombard, *Angelica Bullock:* Alice Brady, *Alexander Bullock:* Eugene Pallette, *Cornelia Bullock:* Gail Patrick, *Tommy Gray:* Alan Mowbray, *Molly:* Jean Dixon, *Carlo:* Mischa Auer, *George:* Robert Light, *Mike:* Pat Flaherty, *Hobo:* Robert Perry, *Scorekeeper:* Franklyn Pangborn, *Guest (Blake):* Selmer Jackson, *Forgotten Man:* Ernie Adams, *Party Guest:* Phyllis Crane, *Von Ronkel:* Grady Sutton, *Headwaiter:* Jack Chefe, *Process Server:* Eddie Fetherston, *Detectives:* Edward Gargan, James Flavin, *Chauffeur:* Art Singley, *Mayor:* Reginald Mason, *Girl at Party:* Jane Wyman, *Guest:* Bess Flowers.

My Man Godfrey with Carole Lombard and William Powell.

MY REPUTATION (1946) WB. Producer, Henry Blanke. Director, Curtis Bernhardt. From a novel by Clare Jaynes (*Instruct My Sorrows*). Screenplay, Catherine Turney. Musical Score, Max Steiner. Art Director, Anton Grot. Musical Director, Leo F. Forbstein. Cameraman, James Wong Howe. Special Effects, Roy Davidson. Editor, David Weisbart. Song by Stanley Adams and Max Steiner, "While You're Away." 96 minutes

Jessica Drummond: Barbara Stanwyck, *Scott Landis:* George Brent, *Frank Everett:* Warner Anderson, *Mrs. Kimball:* Lucile Watson, *Cary Abbott:* John Ridgely, *Ginna Abbott:* Eve Arden, *George Van Orman:* Jerome Cowan, *Anna:* Esther Dale, *Kim Drummond:* Scotty Beckett, *Keith Drummond:* Bobby Cooper, *Riette Van Orman:* Leona Maricle, *Mary:* Mary Servoss, *Mrs. Thompson:* Cecil Cunningham, *Penny Boardman:* Janice Wilson, *Gretchen Van Orman:* Ann Todd, *Baby Hawks:* Nancy Evans, *Dave:* Oliver Prickett (Oliver Blake),

My Reputation with George Brent and Barbara Stanwyck.

Butcher: Charles Jordan, *Bill "Droopy" Hawks:* Darwood Kaye, *Conductor:* Fred Kelsey, *Phyllis:* Marjorie Hoshelle, *Man in Bar:* Bruce Warren, *Hotel Desk Clerk:* Harry Seymour, *Elevator Operator:* Frank Darien, *Woman:* Leah Baird, *Les Hanson:* Hugh Prosser, *Mrs. Hanson:* Helen Eby-Rock, *Johnson:* (Sam) Deacon McDaniel, *Orchestra leader:* Dick Winslow, *Tipsy Man:* Dick Elliott.

MY SON JOHN (1952) Par. Producer, Leo McCarey. Director, Leo McCarey. Story, Leo McCarey. Screenplay, Myles Connolly, Leo McCarey. Art Directors, Hal Pereira, William Flannery. Music Score, Robert Emmett Dolan. Cinematographer, Henry Stradling. Editor, Marvin Coil. Adaptation, John Lee Mahin. Used Robert Walker's out-takes from *Strangers on a Train.* 122 minutes

Lucille Jefferson: Helen Hayes, *Stedman:* Van Heflin, *John Jefferson:* Robert Walker, *Dan Jefferson:* Dean Jagger, *Dr. Carver:* Minor Watson, *Father O'Dowd:* Frank McHugh, *Chuck Jefferson:* Richard Jaeckel, *Ben Jefferson:* James Young, *Nurse:* Nancy Hale, *Bedford:* Todd Karns, *Secretary:* Frances Morris, *Parcel Post Man:* William McLean, *Cleaner:* Fred Sweeney, *FBI Agent:* Russell Conway, *Boy:* Lee William Aaker, *Secretary:* Vera Stokes, *Government Employee:* Douglas Evans, *Jail Matron:* Gail Bonney, *Ruth Carlin:* Irene Winston, *FBI Agent:* David Newell, *Professor:* Erskine Sanford, *Nurse:* Margaret Wells, *College Professor:* David Bond, *College Professor:* Eghiche Harout, *Taxi Driver:* Jimmie Dundee.

My Son John with Robert Walker, Helen Hayes and Dean Jagger.

MY WILD IRISH ROSE (1947) WB. Produced by William Jacobs. Directed by David Butler. Color by Technicolor. Based on the book *Song in His Heart* by Rita Olcott. Screenplay, Peter Milne. Additional Dialogue, Edwin Gilbert and Sidney Fields. Art Director, Ed Carrere. Music Director, Leo F. Forbstein. Photography, Arthur Edeson and William V. Skall. Editor, Irene Morra. Dances, LeRoy and Eddie Prinz. Based on the life of Chauncey Olcott, and featuring traditional songs in addition to: "Wee Rose of Killarney," "The Natchez and the Robert E. Lee," "Miss Lindy Lou," and "There's Room in My Heart for Them All," by M. K. Jerome and Ted Koehler; "Come Down Ma Evenin' Star" by Robert B. Smith and John Stromberg; "My Nellie's Blue Eyes" by William J. Scanlon; "One Little Sweet Little Girl" by

My Wild Irish Rose with George O'Brien, Ben Blue, Dennis Morgan and Eddie Parker.

Dan Sullivan; "My Wild Irish Rose" by Chauncey Olcott; "A Little Bit of Heaven" by J. K. Brennan and Ernest Ball. Music composed and adapted by Max Steiner. Orchestral Arrangements, Murray Cutter. 101 minutes

Chauncey Olcott (Jack Chancellor): Dennis Morgan, *Lillian Russell:* Andrea King, *Rose Donovan:* Arlene Dahl, *John Donovan:* Alan Hale, *Nick Popolis:* George Tobias, *William "Duke" Muldoon:* George O'Brien, *Mrs. Brennan:* Sara Allgood, *Hopper:* Ben Blue, *William Scanlan:* William Frawley, *Terry O'Rourke:* Don McGuire, *Foote:* Charles Irwin, *Joe Brennan:* Clifton Young, *Augustus Pitou:* Paul Stanton, *Captain Brennan:* George Cleveland, *Pat Daly:* Oscar O'Shea, *Della:* Ruby Dandridge, *Brown:* Grady Sutton, *Brewster:* William B. Davidson, *Rawson:* Douglas Wood, *Stone:* Charles Marsh, *Herman:* Andrew Tombes, *Tenor:* Robert Lowell, *Theatre Manager:* Philo McCullough, *Maitre 'D:* Gino Corrado, *Bruiser:* Eddie Parker, *Office Boy:* Ross Ford, *Joe Webb:* Eddie Kane, *Lee:* Tom Stevenson, *Eileen, Leading Lady:* Peggy Knudsen, *Barman:* Monte Blue, *Drummer:* Wally Ruth, *Doctor:* Emmett Vogan, *Justice of the Peace:* Edward Clark, *Mr. O'Rourke:* William Gould, *Michael, Gardener:* Brandon Hurst, *Stage Father:* Forbes Murray, *Stage Mother:* Winifred Harris, *Riverboat Captain:* Billy Greene, *Specialties:* Igor Dega, Pierre Andre, The Three Dunhills, Lou Wills, Jr, *Singer:* Penny Edwards, *Pat:* Rodney Bell.

THE NAKED CITY (1948) Univ. Producer, Mark Hellinger. Director, Jules Dassin. Author, Malvin Wald. Screenplay, Albert Maltz, Malvin Wald. Art Director, John F. De Cuir. Musical Supervisor, Milton Schwartzwald. Photography, William Daniels. Editor, Paul Weatherwax. Associate Producer, Jules Buck. Filmed in New York City. 96 minutes

Lieutenant Dan Muldoon: Barry Fitzgerald, *Frank Niles:* Howard Duff, *Ruth Morrison:* Dorothy Hart, *Jimmy Halloran:* Don Taylor, *Garzah:* Ted DeCorsia, *Little Old Lady:* Jean Adair, *McCormick:* Nicholas Joy, *Dr. Stoneman:* House Jameson, *Mrs. Halloran:*

The Naked City with Barry Fitzgerald, Dorothy Hart, Enid Markey and Don Taylor.

Anne Sargent, *Mrs. Batory:* Adelaide Klein, *Mr. Batory:* Grover Burgess, *Detective Perelli:* Tom Pedi, *Mrs. Hylton:* Enid Markey, *Captain Donahue:* Frank Conroy, *Backalis:* Walter Burke, *Ben Miller:* David Opatoshu, *Constentino:* John McQuade, *Nurse:* Hester Sondergaard, *Henry Fowler:* Paul Ford, *Dr. Hoffman:* Ralph Bunker, *Nick:* Curt Conway, *Qualen:* Kermit Kegley, *Fredericks:* George Lynn, *Shaeffer:* Arthur O'Connell, *Martha:* Virginia Mullen, *Mrs. Stoneman:* Beverly Bayne, *Proprietress:* Celia Adler, *Miss Livingston:* Grace Coppin, *Druggist:* Robert Harris, *Hicks:* James Gregory, *Publisher:* Edwin Jerome, *Ed Garzah:* Anthony Rivers, *Wrestler:* Bernard Hoffman, *Freed:* G. Pat Collins, *Ned Harvey:* Joe Kerr, *Mr. Stillman:* Johnny Dale, *Publisher:* Judson Laire, *Stout Girl:* Kathleen Freeman, *City Editor:* Raymond Greenleaf.

THE NAKED SPUR (1953) MGM. Produced by William H. Wright. Directed by Anthony Mann. Color by Technicolor. Screenplay, Sam Rolfe and Harold Jack Bloom. Music, Bronislau Kaper. Art Director, Cedric Gibbons, Malcolm Brown. Cinematographer, William Mellor. Editor, George White. Filmed in Durango, Colorado. 91 minutes

Howard Kemp: James Stewart, *Lina Patch:* Janet Leigh, *Ben Vandergroat:* Robert Ryan, *Roy Anderson:* Ralph Meeker, *Jesse Tate:* Millard Mitchell.

The Naked Spur with Millard Mitchell, Robert Ryan, Janet Leigh, Ralph Meeker and James Stewart.

NATIONAL VELVET (1944) MGM. Producer, Pandro S. Berman. Director, Clarence Brown. Color by Technicolor. Based on the novel by Enid Bagnold. Screenplay by Theodore Reeves and Helen Deutsch. Music score by Herbert Stothart. Film Editor, Robert J. Kern. Photographed by Leonard Smith. Art Directors, Cedric Gibbons and Urie McCleary. Special effects by Warren Newcombe. 125 minutes

Mi Taylor: Mickey Rooney, *Mr. Brown:* Donald Crisp, *Velvet Brown:* Elizabeth Taylor, *Mrs. Brown:* Anne Revere, *Edwina Brown:* Angela Lansbury, *Malvolia Brown:* Juanita Quigley, *Donald Brown:* Jack

National Velvet with Mickey Rooney and Elizabeth Taylor.

(Butch) Jenkins, *Farmer Ede:* Reginald Owen, *Ted:* Terry Kilburn, *Tim:* Alec Craig, *Mr. Taski:* Eugene Loring, *Miss Sims:* Norma Varden, *Mr. Hallam:* Arthur Shields, *Mr. Greenford:* Dennis Hoey, *Entry Official:* Aubrey Mather, *Stewart:* Frederic Worlock, *Man with Umbrella:* Arthur Treacher, *Van Driver:* Harry Allen, *Constable:* Billy Bevan, *Townsman:* Barry Macollum, *Entry Clerk:* Matthew Boulton, *First Pressman:* Leyland Hodgson, *Second Pressman:* Leonard Carey, *Cockney:* Colin Campbell, *Englishman:* Frank Benson, *Jockey:* Wally Cassell, *Valet:* Alec Harford, *Reporter:* William Austin, *Cameraman:* Gerald Oliver Smith, *First Villager:* Olaf Hytten, *Second Villager:* George Kirby, *Woman:* Moyna MacGill, *American:* Donald Curtis, *Schoolboy:* Howard Taylor.

NAUGHTY MARIETTA (1935) MGM. Produced by Hunt Stromberg. Directed by W. S. Van Dyke. Based on the 1910 operetta by Victor Herbert, book by Rida Johnson Young. Screenplay, John Lee Mahin, Frances Goodrich, Albert Hackett. Musical Adaptation, Herbert Stothart. Art Director, Cedric Gibbons. Sound, Douglas Shearer. Costumes, Adrian. Assistant Director, Eddie Woehler. Photography, William Daniels. Editor, Blanche Sewell. Violin obligato by Jan Rubini. Songs by Victor Herbert, Rida Johnson Young, Gus Kahn: "I'm Falling in Love With Some One," "Chansonette," "The Owl and the Polecat," "Antoinette and Anatole," "Live for Today," "Tramp, Tramp, Tramp Along the Highway," "Dance of the Marionettes," "Italian Street Song," "Neath the Southern Moon," "Ah Sweet Mystery of Life," "Students' Song." Dr. Lippe is Nelson Eddy's coach. The first MacDonald-Eddy musical. 106 minutes

Princess Marie (Marietta): Jeanette MacDonald, *Captain Warrington:* Nelson Eddy, *Governor d'Annard:* Frank Morgan, *Madame d'Annard:* Elsa Lanchester, *Uncle:* Douglass Dumbrille, *Herr Schuman:* Joseph Cawthorn, *Julie:* Cecelia Parker, *Don Carlos:* Walter Kingsford, *Frau Schuman:* Greta Meyer, *Rudolpho:* Akim Tamiroff, *Abe:* Harold Huber, *Zeke:* Edward Brophy, *Casquette Girls:* Marjorie Main, Mary Doran, Jean Chatburn, Pat Farley, Jane Barnes, Kay English, Linda Parker, Jane Mercer, *Bit:* Dr. Edouard Lippe, *Pirate Leader:* Walter Long, *Madame Renavant:* Olive Carey, *Gendarme Chief:* William Desmond, *Felice:* Cora Sue Collins, *Ship's Captain:* Guy Usher, *Duelist:* Louis Mercier, *Town Crier:* Robert McKenzie, *Mama's Boy:* Ben Hall, *Prospective Groom:* Harry Tenbrook, *Major Bonnell:* Edward Keane, *Suitors:* Edward Norris, Ralph Brooks, *Messenger:* Richard Powell, *Announcer:* Wilfred Lucas, *Scouts:* Arthur Belasco, Tex Driscoll, Edward Hearn, Edmund Cobb, Charles Dunbar, Frank Hagney, Ed Brady.

Naughty Marietta with Jeanette MacDonald, Cecelia Parker and Douglass Dumbrille.

NEPTUNE'S DAUGHTER (1949) MGM. Producer, Jack Cummings. Director, Edward Buzzell. Color by Technicolor. Screenplay, Dorothy Kingsley. Musical Director, Georgie Stoll. Art Directors, Cedric Gibbons, Edward Carfagno. Photography, Charles Rosher. Editor, Irvine Warburton. **Songs** by Frank Loesser: "My Heart Beats Faster," "Baby, It's Cold Outside" and "I Love Those Men." 93 minutes

Neptune's Daughter with Keenan Wynn, Esther Williams and Ricardo Montalban.

Eve Barrett: Esther Williams, *Jack Spratt:* Red Skelton, *Jose O'Rourke:* Ricardo Montalban, *Betty Barrett:* Betty Garrett, *Joe Beckett:* Keenan Wynn, *Xavier Cugat and His Orchestra:* Themselves, *Lukie Luzette:* Ted de Corsia, *Mac Mazolla:* Mike Mazurki, *Julio:* Mel Blanc, *Second Groom:* Juan Duval, *Tall Wrangler:* George Mann, *Little Wrangler:* Frank Mitchell, *Coach:* Harold S. Kruger, *Official:* Matt Moore, *Linda:* Joy Lansing, *Announcer:* Carl Saxe, *Matilda:* Theresa Harris, *Voice of Record:* Juan Duval, *Miss Pratt:* Elaine Sterling, *Headwaiter:* Henry Sylvester, *Cigarette Girl:* Lillian Molieri, *First Henchman:* Dewey Robinson, *Second Henchman:* Michael Jordon, *Mr. Magoo:* Dick Simmons, *Models:* Bette Arlen, Jonnie Pierce, Dorothy Abbott, *Mr. Canford:* Pierre Watkin, *Man:* Dell Henderson, *Woman:* Kay Mansfield, *Gardner:* Clarence Hennecke, *Groom:* Heinie Conklin.

NIAGARA (1953) 20th. Produced by Charles Brackett. Directed by Henry Hathaway. Color by Technicolor. Story by Charles Brackett, Walter Reisch, Richard Breen. Music, Sol Kaplan. Art Directors, Lyle Wheeler and Maurice Ransford. Photography, Joe MacDonald. Editor, Barbara McLean. Filmed at Niagara Falls. 89 minutes

Rose Loomis: Marilyn Monroe, *George Loomis:* Joseph Cotten, *Polly Cutler:* Jean Peters, *Ray Cutler:* Casey Adams, *Inspector Starkey:* Denis O'Dea, *Patrick:* Richard Allan, *Mr. Kettering:* Don Wilson, *Mrs. Kettering:* Lurene Tuttle, *Mr. Qua:* Russell Collins, *Boatman:* Will Wright, *Doctor:* Lester Matthews, *Policeman:* Carleton Young, *Sam:* Sean McClory, *Landlady:* Minerva Urecal, *Wife:* Nina Varela, *Husband:* Tom Reynolds, *Straw Boss:* Winfield Hoeny, *Canadian Customs Officer:* Neil Fitzgerald, *Morris:* Norman McKay, *American Guide:* Gene (Baxter) Wesson, *Carillon Tower Guide:* George Ives, *Detective:* Patrick O'Moore, *Cab Driver:* Arch Johnson, *Motorcycle Cops:* Henry Beckman and Willard Sage, *Young Men:* Bill Foster and Robert Ellis, *Cab Driver:* Harry Carey, Jr., *Dancer:* Gloria Gordon.

Niagara with Marilyn Monroe.

Night and Day with Cary Grant and Alexis Smith.

NIGHT AND DAY (1946) WB. Produced by Arthur Schwartz. Directed by Michael Curtiz. Based on the career and featuring the songs of Cole Porter (1891–1964). Color by Technicolor. Screenplay, Charles Hoffman, Leo Townsend, and William Bowers. Adaptation, Jack Moffitt. Art Director, John Hughes. Music Director, Leo F. Forbstein. Orchestral Arrangements, Ray Heindorf. Photography, Peverell Marley and William V. Skall. Technicolor Director, Natalie Kalmus. Production numbers orchestrated and conducted by Ray Heindorf. Dance Numbers, LeRoy Prinz. Additional Music, Max Steiner. Vocal Arrangements, Dudley Chambers. Montages, James Leicester. Sets, Armor Marlowe. Special Effects, Robert Burks. Editor, David Weisbart. Sound, Everett A. Brown and David Forrest. Songs by Cole Porter: "In the Still of the Night," "Old-Fashioned Garden," "Let's Do It," "You Do Something to Me," "Miss Otis Regrets," "What Is This Thing Called Love?", "I've Got You Under My Skin," "Just One of Those Things," "You're the Top," "I Get a Kick Out of You," "Easy to Love", "My Heart Belongs to Daddy," "Begin the Beguine" and "Night and Day." Film debut of Joe Kirkwood, Jr., later "Joe Palooka." 128 minutes

Cole Porter: Cary Grant, *Linda Lee Porter:* Alexis Smith, *Monty Woolley:* Monty Woolley, *Carole Hill:* Ginny Simms, *Gracie Harris:* Jane Wyman, *Gabrielle:* Eve Arden, *Anatole Giron:* Victor Francen, *Leon Dowling:* Alan Hale, *Nancy:* Dorothy Malone, *Bernie:* Tom D'Andrea, *Kate Porter:* Selena Royle, *Ward Blackburn:* Donald Woods, *Omer Cole:* Henry Stephenson, *Bart McClelland:* Paul Cavanagh, *Willowsky:* Sig Rumann, *Specialty Singer:* Carlos Ramirez, *Specialty Dancer:* Milada Mladova, *Specialty Dancer:* George Zoritch, *Specialty Team:* Adam and Jayne DeGatano, *Specialty Dancer:* Estelle Sloan, *Mary Martin:* Mary Martin, *Petey:* John Alvin, *Caleb:* Clarence Muse, *O'Halloran:* George Riley, *Producer:* Howard Freeman, *Director:* Bobby Watson, *First "Peaches":* John "Red" Pierson, *Second "Peaches":* Herman Bing, *Classmate:* Joe Kirkwood, Jr., *Dean:* Boyd Davis, *Clarence, Piano Player:* Harry Seymour, *Tina:* JoAnn Marlowe, *Tina's Mother:* Regina Wallace, *Tina's Father:* Frank Ferguson, *Sexboat:* Lynne Baggett, *Chorus Girl:* Rebel Randall, *Red:* James Dodd, *Orchestra Leader:* Emile Hilb, *Customer:* Richard Erdman, *Customer:* Robert Arthur, *Wayne Blackburn as a boy:* George Nokes, *Cochran:* Gordon Richards, *Librettist:* Philip Van Zandt, *Chorine:* Joyce Compton, *Headwaiter:* Eddie Kane.

A NIGHT AT THE OPERA (1935) MGM. Produced by Irving Thalberg. Directed by Sam Wood. Story, James Kevin McGuinness. Screenplay, George S. Kaufman and Morrie Ryskind. Music Score, Herbert Stothart. Editor, William Levanway. Dances, Chester Hale. Photography, Merritt B. Gerstad. Songs: "Alone" by Nacio Herb Brown and Arthur Freed; "Cosi-Cosa" by Bronislau Kaper, Walter Jurmann, Ned Washington. The show was tested on the stage before filming. The first Marx Brothers film without Zeppo. 96 minutes

Otis B. Driftwood: Groucho Marx, *Fiorello:* Chico Marx, *Tomasso:* Harpo Marx, *Rosa Castaldi:* Kitty Carlisle, *Riccardo Baroni:* Allan Jones, *Rodolfo Lassparri:* Walter Woolf King, *Herman Gottlieb:* Sig Rumann, *Mrs. Claypool:* Margaret Dumont, *Captain:* Edward Keane,

A Night At the Opera with Allan Jones, Sig Rumann, Harpo, Chico and Groucho Marx.

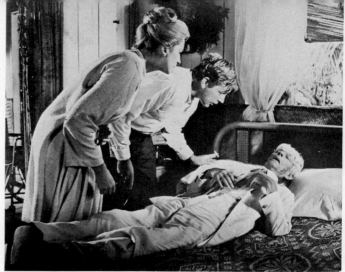

The Night of the Iguana with Deborah Kerr, Richard Burton and Cyril Delevanti.

Detective Henderson: Robert Emmett O'Connor, *Steward:* Gino Corrado, *Mayor:* Purnell Pratt, *Engineer:* Frank Yaconelli, *Engineer's Assistant/Peasant:* Billy Gilbert, *Extra on Ship and at Dock:* Sam Marx, *Police Captain:* Claude Peyton, *Dancers:* Rita and Rubin, *Ruiz:* Luther Hoobyar, *Count di Luna:* Rodolfo Hoyos, *Azucena:* Olga Dane, *Ferrando:* James J. Wolf, *Maid:* Ines Palange, *Stage Manager:* Jonathan Hale, *Elevator Man:* Otto Fries, *Captain of Police:* William Gould, *Aviators:* Leo White, Jay Eaton, Rolfe Sedan, *Committee:* Wilbur Mack, George Irving, *Policeman:* George Guhl, *Sign Painter:* Harry Tyler, *Committee:* Phillips Smalley, Selmer Jackson, *Immigration Inspector:* Alan Bridge, *Doorman:* Harry Allen, *Louisa:* Lorraine Bridges.

NIGHT MUST FALL (1937) MGM. Produced by Hunt Stromberg. Directed by Richard Thorpe. From the play by Emlyn Williams. Screenplay, John Van Druten. Art Director, Cedric Gibbons. Music, Edward Ward. Photography, Ray June. Editor, Robert J. Kern. Remade by MGM as a British film in 1964. 117 minutes.

Danny: Robert Montgomery, *Olivia:* Rosalind Russell, *Mrs. Bramson:* Dame May Whitty, *Justin:* Alan Marshal, *Dora:* Merle Tottenham, *Mrs. Terence:* Kathleen Harrison, *Belsize:* Matthew Boulton, *Nurse:* Eily Malyon, *Guide:* E. E. Clive, *Saleslady:* Beryl Mercer, *Mrs. Laurie:* Winifred Harris.

Night Must Fall with Robert Montgomery, Dame May Whitty and Rosalind Russell.

THE NIGHT OF THE IGUANA (1964) MGM. Producer, Ray Stark. Director, John Huston. Screenplay, Anthony Veiller, John Huston. Based on the play by Tennessee Williams. Director of Photography, Gabriel Figueroa. Music, Benjamin Frankel. An MGM Seven Arts Presentation. Assistant Director, Tom Shaw. 125 minutes

Reverend T. Lawrence Shannon: Richard Burton, *Maxine Faulk:* Ava Gardner, *Hannah Jelkes:* Deborah Kerr, *Charlotte Goodall:* Sue Lyon, *Hank Prosner:* James Ward, *Judith Fellowes:* Grayson Hall, *Nonno:* Cyril Delevanti, *Miss Peebles:* Mary Boylan, *Miss Dexter:* Gladys Hill, *Miss Throxton:* Billie Matticks, *Pepe:* Fidelmar Duran, *Pedro:* Roberto Leyva, *Chang:* C. G. Kim, *Teachers:* Eloise Hardt, Thelda Victor, Betty Proctor, Dorothy Vance, Liz Rubey, Bernice Starr, Barbara Joyce.

NINOTCHKA (1939) MGM. Produced and directed by Ernst Lubitsch. Based on an original story by Melchior Lengyel. Screenplay, Charles Brackett, Billy Wilder, and Walter Reisch. Art Director, Cedric Gibbons. Associate, Randall Duell. Music, Werner R. Heymann. Photography, William Daniels. Editor, Gene Ruggiero. Sound, Douglas Shearer. Make-up, Jack Dawn. Assistant Director, Horace Hough. Remade by MGM as *The Iron Petticoat* (1956) and *Silk Stockings* (1957). 110 minutes

Ninotchka (Lena Yakushova): Greta Garbo, *Count Leon Dalga:* Melvyn Douglas, *Grand Duchess Swana:* Ina Claire, *Michael Iranoff:* Sig Rumann, *Buljanoff:* Felix Bressart, *Kopalski:* Alexander Granach, *Commissar Razinin:* Bela Lugosi, *Count Alexis Rakonin:* Gregory Gaye, *Gaston:* Richard Carle, *Mercier:* Edwin Maxwell, *Hotel Manager:* Rolfe Sedan, *Russian Visa Official:* George Tobias, *Swana's Maid, Jacqueline:* Dorothy Adams, *General Savitsky:* Lawrence Grant, *Pere Mathieu, Cafe Owner:* Charles Judels, *Lawyer:* Frank Reicher, *Lawyer:* Edwin Stanley, *French Maid:* Peggy Moran, *Manager:* Marek Windheim, *Lady Lavenham:* Mary Forbes, *Bearded Man:* Alexander Schonberg, *Porter:* George Davis, *Louis (Headwaiter):* Armand Kaliz, *Taxi Driver:* Wolfgang Zilzer, *Anna:* Tamara Shayne, *Bartender:* William Irving, *Gossip:* Bess Flowers, *Indignant Woman:* Elizabeth Williams, *Vladimir:* Paul Weigel, *Neighbor-Spy:* Harry Semels, *Streetcar Conductress:* Jody Gilbert, *Marianne:* Florence Shirley.

Ninotchka with Greta Garbo and Melvyn Douglas.

Nob Hill with George Raft, Peggy Ann Garner and Joan Bennett.

NOB HILL (1945) 20th. Producer, Andre Daven. Director, Henry Hathaway. Color by Technicolor. Author, Eleanore Griffin. Screenplay, Wanda Tuchock, Norman Reilly Raine. Dance Director, Nick Castle. Musical Directors, Emil Newman, Charles Henderson. Technicolor Director, Natalie Kalmus. Art Directors, Lyle Wheeler, Russell Spencer. Cameraman, Edward Cronjager. Special Effects, Fred Sersen. Editor, Harmon Jones. Songs by Harold Adamson and Jimmy McHugh: "I Don't Care Who Knows It" and "I Walked Right in With My Eyes Wide Open." 95 minutes

Johnny Angelo: George Raft, *Harriet Carruthers:* Joan Bennett, *Sally Templeton:* Vivian Blaine, *Katie Flanagan:* Peggy Ann Garner, *Dapper Jack Harrigan:* Alan Reed, *Joe, the Bartender:* B. S. Pully, *At the Piano:* Emil Coleman, *Lash Carruthers:* Edgar Barrier, *Rafferty:* George Anderson, *Fighting Bartender:* Don Costello, *Headwaiter:* Joseph J. Greene, *Cabby:* J. Farrell Macdonald, *Specialty:* The Three Swifts, *Big Tim:* William Haade, *Rafferty's Fighter:* Mike Mazurki, *Chinese Servants:* Beal Wong, George T. Lee, *Jose:* Frank McCown (Rory Calhoun), *Butler:* Robert Greig, *Chips Conlon:* Charles Cane, *Turner:* Arthur Loft, *Luigi:* Nestor Paiva, *Ruby:* Jane Jones, *Mr. Devereaux:* Grandon Rhodes, *Mrs. Devereaux:* Barbara Sears (Bobo Rockefeller), *Mayor:* Forbes Murray, *Indian Chief:* Chief Thundercloud, *Housekeeper:* Olive Blakeney, *Swedish Sailor:* Otto Reichow, *Guide:* Chick Chandler, *Policeman:* Harry Shannon, *Men:* Frank Orth, Harry Harvey, Sr., Julius Tannen, Syd Saylor, *Doorman:* Paul Hurst, *Chinese Boy:* Benson Fong, *Usher:* Byron Foulger, *Dance Team:* Lillian and Mario Salvaneschi, *Bouncer:* Fred Graham.

NO LEAVE, NO LOVE (1946) MGM. Producer, Joe Pasternak. Director, Charles Martin. Screenplay, Charles Martin, Leslie Karkos. Musical Director, Georgie Stoll. Art Director, Cedric Gibbons. Cameramen, Harold Rosson, Robert Surtees. Editor, Conrad A. Nervig. Orchestration, Calvin Jackson and Dewey Bergman. Songs: "Love on a Greyhound Bus" by Kay Thompson, Ralph Blane and George Stoll: "All the Time" by Ralph Freed and Sammy Fain; "Isn't It Wonderful" by Kay Thompson; "It'll Be Great to Be Back

No Leave, No Love with Van Johnson, Edward Arnold and Pat Kirkwood.

Home" by Charles Martin; "Old Sad Eyes" by Irving Kahal and Sammy Fain; "When It's Love" by Edgar DeLange and Nicholas Kharito. 119 minutes

Sergeant Michael Hanlon: Van Johnson, *Slinky:* Keenan Wynn, *Guy Lombardo and His Orchestra:* Themselves, *Susan Malby Duncan:* Pat Kirkwood, *Hobart Canford Stiles:* Edward Arnold, *Rosalind:* Marie Wilson, *Colonel Elliott:* Leon Ames, *Countess Strogoff:* Marina Koshetz, *Mrs. Hanlon:* Selena Royle, *Mr. Crawley:* Wilson Wood, *Ben:* Vince Barnett, *Boy Piano Player:* Frank "Sugarchile" Robinson, *Xavier Cugat and His Orchestra:* Themselves, *Dance Specialty:* The Garcios, *Sledgehammer:* Walter Sande, *Nick:* Arthur Walsh, *Boy Drum Specialty:* Joey Preston, *Hat Salesman:* Grady Sutton, *Hotel Clerk:* Bert Roach, *Mr. Tansey:* Chester Clute, *Lonely Little Man:* Hobart Cavanaugh, *Gruff Father:* Pat McVey, *Marine on Transport:* Sid Mercer, *Board of Directors:* Major Sam Harris, Herschel Graham, Reginald Simpson, Howard Mitchell, Larry Steers, Harry Denny, Tom Leffingwell, Nolan Leary, Frank McLure, Wedgewood Nowell, *Drunk:* Jack Norton, *Gardener:* Eddie Borden.

NONE BUT THE LONELY HEART (1944) RKO. Producer, David Hempstead. Associate Producer, Sherman Todd. Director, Clifford Odets. From the novel by Richard Llewellyn. Screenplay, Clifford Odets. Art Directors, Albert S. D'Agostino, Jack Okey. Musical Score, Hanns Eisler. Musical Director, C. Bakaleinikoff. Cameraman, George Barnes. Special Effects, Vernon L. Walker. Editor, Roland Gross. 113 minutes

Ernie Mott: Cary Grant, *Ma Mott:* Ethel Barrymore, *Twite:* Barry Fitzgerald, *Ada:* June Duprez, *Aggie Hunter:* Jane Wyatt, *Jim Mordinoy:* George Coulouris, *Lew Tate:* Dan Duryea, *Ike Weber:* Konstantin Shayne, *Ma Chalmers:* Eva Leonard Boyne, *Taz:* Morton Lowry, *Sister Nurse:* Helene Thimig, *Knocker:* William Challee, *Blake:* Forrester Harvey, *Rossi:* Chef Milani, *Madam La Vaka:* Marie De Becker, *Cash:* Joseph Vitale, *Dad Pettyjohn:* Roman Bohnen, *Flo:* Renie Riano, *Percy:* Marcel Dill, *Lame Girl:* Amelia Romano, *Ma Snowden:* Queenie Vassar, *Mrs. Tate:* Rosalind Ivan, *Marjoriebanks:* Art Smith, *Barmaid:* Claire Verdera, *Millie Wilson:* Katherine Allen, *Defeated Man:* Charles Thompson, *Miss Tate:* Diedra Vale, *Dad Fitchitt:* Herbert Heywood, *Ma Segwiss:* Virginia Farmer, *Pa Floom:* Walter Soderling, *Ma Floom:* Polly Bailey, *Blind Man:* Bill Wolfe, *Dancer:* Barry Regan, *Ike Lesser:* Milton Wallace, *Dancer:* Rosemary Blong, *Dancer:* Jack Jackson, *Dancer:* Rosemary La Planche, *Slush:* Skelton Knaggs.

None But the Lonely Heart with Cary Grant and Ethel Barrymore.

Nora Prentiss with Robert Alda, Kent Smith and Ann Sheridan.

NORA PRENTISS (1947) WB. Produced by William Jacobs. Directed by Vincent Sherman. From a story by Paul Webster and Jack Sobell. Screenplay, N. Richard Nash. Music, Franz Waxman. Music Director, Leo F. Forbstein. Orchestral Arrangements, Leonid Raab. Art Director, Anton Grot. Photography, James Wong Howe. Editor, Owen Marks. Songs by Jack Scholl, Eddie Cherkose, M. K. Jerome: "Who Cares What People Say?" and "Would You Like a Souvenir?" 111 minutes

Nora Prentiss: Ann Sheridan, Dr. Richard Talbot: Kent Smith, Dr. Joel Merriam: Bruce Bennett, Phil McDade: Robert Alda, Lucy Talbot: Rosemary De Camp, Walter Bailey: John Ridgely, Gregory Talbot: Robert Arthur, Bonita Talbot: Wanda Hendrix, Miss Judson: Helen Brown, Fleming: Rory Mallinson, Police Lieutenant: Harry Shannon, District Attorney: James Flavin, Doctor: Douglas Kennedy, Truck Driver: Don McGuire, Policeman: Clifton Young, Sheriff: Jack Mower, Reporters: John Newland, John Compton, Ramon Ros, Warden: Philo McCullough, Turnkey: Fred Kelsey, Judge: Louis Quince, Agnes: Lottie Williams, Mrs. Dobie: Gertrude Carr, Bystander: Richard Walsh, Flower Woman: Tiny Jones, Mrs. Sterritt: Georgia Caine, Rod, Piano Player: Dean Cameron, Oberlin: Roy Gordon, Newsboy: David Fresco, Captain of Waiters: Creighton Hale, Doorman: Lee Phelps, Billy, Chauffeur: Ross Ford, Policemen: Clancy Cooper, Alan Bridge, Detectives: Ralph Dunn, Eddy Chandler, Drunks: Matt McHugh, Wallace Scott, Court Clerk: Charles Jordan, Chaplain: John Elliott.

NORTH BY NORTHWEST (1959) MGM. Produced and directed by Alfred Hitchcock. Associate Producer, Herbert Coleman. Technicolor and VistaVision. Screenplay, Ernest Lehman. Music, Bernard Herrmann. Art Directors, William A. Horning and Merrill Pye. Assistant Director, Robert Saunders. Photography, Robert Burks. Editor, George Tomasini. Filmed on location: Plaza Hotel Oak Room, N.Y.C.; UN Building; Grand Central Station; Long Island; Chicago's Ambassador East; Indiana plains; Mount Rushmore, South Dakota. 136 minutes

Roger Thornhill: Cary Grant, Eve Kendall: Eva Marie Saint, Phillip Vandamm: James Mason, Clara Thornhill: Jessie Royce Landis, Professor: Leo G. Carroll, Lester Townsend: Philip Ober, Handsome Woman: Josephine Hutchinson, Leonard: Martin Landau, Valerian: Adam Williams, Victor Larrabee: Edward Platt, Licht: Robert Ellenstein, Auctioneer: Les Tremayne, Dr. Cross: Philip Coolidge, Captain Junket: Edward Binns, Chicago Policemen: Pat McVey, Ken Lynch, Sergeant Emile Klinger: John Beradino, Housekeeper, Anna: Nora Marlowe, Maggie: Doreen Lang, Judge Anson B. Flynn: Alexander Lockwood, Lieutenant Harding: Stanley Adams, Cartoonist: Larry Dobkin, Stock Broker: Harvey Stephens, Reporter: Walter Coy, Housewife: Madge Kennedy, Elevator Starter: Tommy Farrell, Captain of Waiters: Harry Seymour, Weltner: Frank Wilcox, Larry Wade: Robert Shayne, Fanning Nelson: Carleton Young, Lieutenant Hagerman: Paul Genge, Patrolman Waggoner: Robert B. Williams, Maid, Elsie: Maudie Prickett, Valet: James McCallion, Taxi Driver: Baynes Barron, Indian Girl: Doris Singh, Girl Attendants: Sally Fraser, Susan

North by Northwest with Cary Grant and Philip Ober.

Whitney, Maura McGiveney, Ticket Agent: Ned Glass, Conductor: Howard Negley, Woman: Jesslyn Fax, Steward: Jack Daly, Man on Road: Malcolm Atterbury, Assistant Auctioneer: Olan Soule, Woman Bidder: Helen Spring, Bit: Patricia Cutts, Ranger: Dale Van Sickel, Cab Driver, Dakota: Frank Marlowe, Assistant Conductor: Harry Strang, Telephone Operator: Sara Berner, Man Who Misses Bus: Alfred Hitchcock.

NORTH TO ALASKA (1960) 20th. Produced and directed by Henry Hathaway. CinemaScope and De Luxe Color. Based on the play Birthday Gift by Laszlo Fodor, from an idea by John Kafka. Screenplay, John Lee Mahin, Martin Rackin, and Claude Binyon. Music, Lionel Newman. Orchestration, Urban Thielmann and Bernard Mayers. Costumes, Bill Thomas. Choreography, Josephine Earl. Assistant Director, Stanley Hough. Art Directors, Duncan Cramer and Jack Martin Smith. Cinematography, Leon Shamroy. Special Effects, L. B. Abbott and Emil Kosa, Jr. Editor, Dorothy Spencer. Song by Russell Faith, Robert P. Marcucci and Peter DeAngelis: "If You Knew." 122 minutes

North to Alaska with Capucine, Fabian, Stewart Granger, John Wayne and Mickey Shaughnessy.

Sam McCord: John Wayne, *George Pratt:* Stewart Granger, *Frankie Canon:* Ernie Kovacs, *Billy Pratt:* Fabian, *Michelle:* Capucine, *Boggs:* Mickey Shaughnessy, *Lars:* Karl Swenson, *Commissioner:* Joe Sawyer, *Lena:* Kathleen Freeman, *Lumberjack:* John Qualen, *Breezy:* Stanley Adams, *Duggan:* Stephen Courtleigh, *Lieutenant:* Douglas Dick, *Sergeant:* Jerry O'Sullivan, *Mack:* Ollie O'Toole, *Arnie:* Frank Faylen, *Ole:* Fred Graham, *Bartender:* Alan Carney, *Olaf:* Peter Bourne, *Gold Buyers:* Charles Seel, Rayford Barnes, *Lumberjacks:* Fortune Gordien, Roy Jensen, *Sourdough:* Joey Faye, *Woman at Picnic:* Esther Dale, *Captain:* Oscar Beregi, *Skinny Sourdough:* Richard Collier, *Desk Clerk:* Richard Deacon, *Bish, the Waiter:* Max Mellinger, *Queen Lil:* Arlene Harris, *Pony Dancer:* Pamela Raymond, *Butler:* Marcel Hillaire, *Jenny:* Lilyan Chauvin, *Bartender:* Maurice Delamore, *Specialty Dancer:* Patty Wharton, *Coachman:* Johnny Lee, *Barber:* Tom Dillon, *Speaker:* James Griffith, *Purser:* Tudor Owen, *Townsman (Extra):* Kermit Maynard.

NORTH WEST MOUNTED POLICE (1940) Par. Producer, Cecil B. De Mille. Associate Producer, William H. Pine. Director, Cecil B. De Mille. Author, R. C. Fetherstonhaugh (from *Royal Canadian Mounted Police*). Screenplay, Alan Le May, Jesse Lasky, Jr., C. Gardner Sullivan. Cameramen, Victor Milner, Duke Green. Song by Frank Loesser and Victor Young: "Does the Moon Shine Through the Tall Pine?" Associate Director, Arthur Rosson. Assistant Director, Eric Stacey. Second Unit Camera, Dewey Wrigley. 125 minutes

Dusty Rivers: Gary Cooper, *April Logan:* Madeleine Carroll, *Louvette Corbeau:* Paulette Goddard, *Sergeant Jim Brett:* Preston Foster, *Ronnie Logan:* Robert Preston, *Jacques Corbeau:* George Bancroft, *Tod McDuff:* Lynne Overman, *Dan Duroc:* Akim Tamiroff, *Big Bear:* Walter Hampden, *Shorty:* Lon Chaney, Jr., *Inspector Cabot:* Montagu Love, *Louis Riel:* Francis McDonald, *Johnny Pelang:* George E. Stone, *Supt. Harrington:* Willard Robertson, *Constable Jerry Moore:* Regis Toomey, *Constable Thornton:* Richard Denning, *Constable Carter:* Douglas Kennedy, *Constable Dumont:* Robert Ryan, *Constable Fenton:* James Seay, *Constable Fyffe:* Lane Chandler, *Constable Ackroyd:* Ralph Byrd, *Constable Kent:* Eric Alden, *Constable Rankin:* Wallace Reid, Jr., *Constable Herrick:* Bud Geary, *Captain Gower:* Evan Thomas, *Sergeant Field:* Jack Pennick, *Corporal Underhill:* Rod Cameron, *Surgeon Roberts:* Davison Clark, *Bugler:* Jack Chapin, *Wandering Spirit:* Chief Thundercloud, *The Crow:* Harry Burns, *Lesur:* Lou Merrill, *Mrs. Burns:* Clara Blandick, *Mrs. Shorty:* Ynez Seabury, *Ekawo:* Eva Puig, *Wapiskau:* Julia Faye, *Freddie:* George Regas, *Niska:* Norma Nelson, *Corporal:* John Laird, *Constable Grove:* James Dundee, *Constable Cameron:* Weldon Heyburn, *Constable Judson:* Phillip Terry, *Constable Porter:* Kermit Maynard, *George Higgins:* Emory Parnell.

North West Mounted Police with Preston Foster, Gary Cooper and Lynne Overman.

NORTHWEST PASSAGE (1940) MGM. Produced by Hunt Stromberg. Directed by King Vidor. Color by Technicolor. Based on the novel *Northwest Passage*, Book I, "Rogers' Rangers," by Kenneth

Northwest Passage with Truman Bradley, Spencer Tracy and Robert Young.

Roberts. Screenplay, Laurence Stallings and Talbot Jennings. Technicolor Director, Natalie Kalmus. Art Director, Cedric Gibbons. Associate, Malcolm Brown. Music, Herbert Stothart. Photography, Sidney Wagner and William V. Skall. Sound, Douglas Shearer. Editor, Conrad A. Nervig. Make-up, Jack Dawn. Assistant Director, Robert Golden. Later the basis for a TV series. 126 minutes

Major Robert Rogers: Spencer Tracy, *Langdon Towne:* Robert Young, *Hunk Marriner:* Walter Brennan, *Elizabeth Browne:* Ruth Hussey, *Cap Huff:* Nat Pendleton, *Reverend Browne:* Louis Hector, *Humphrey Towne:* Robert Barrat, *General Amherst:* Lumsden Hare, *Sergeant McNott:* Donald MacBride, *Jennie Coit:* Isabel Jewell, *Lieutenant Avery:* Douglas Walton, *Lieutenant Crofton:* Addison Richards, *Jesse Beacham:* Hugh Sothern, *Webster:* Regis Toomey, *Wiseman Clagett:* Montagu Love, *Sam Livermore:* Lester Matthews, *Captain Ogden:* Truman Bradley, *Konkapot:* Andrew Pena, *A Ranger:* Tom London, *A Ranger:* Eddie Parker, *Richard Towne:* Don Castle, *Eben Towne:* Rand Brooks, *Odiorne Towne:* Kent Rogers, *Mrs. Towne:* Verna Felton, *Sheriff Packer:* Richard Cramer, *Bradley McNeil:* Ray Teal, *Captain Butterfield:* Edward Gargan, *Lieutenant Dunbar:* John Merton, *MacPherson:* Gibson Gowland, *Captain Grant:* Frank Hagney, *Mrs. Brown:* Gwendolen Logan, *Jane Browne:* Addie McPhail, *Sarah Hadden:* Helen MacKellar, *Flint, Innkeeper:* Arthur Aylesworth, *Farrington:* Ted Oliver, *Billy, Indian Boy:* Lawrence Porter, *Captain Jacobs:* Tony Guerrero, *Stoodley:* Ferdinand Munier, *McMullen:* George Eldredge, *Solomon:* Robert St. Angelo, *Captain Williams:* Denis Green, *Turner:* Peter George Lynn, *Sir William Johnson:* Frederic Worlock, *A Ranger:* Hank Worden.

NOT AS A STRANGER (1955) UA. Producer-Director, Stanley Kramer. Screenplay by Edna and Edward Anhalt. Based on the novel by Morton Thompson. Music by George Antheil. Song by Jimmy Van Heusen and Buddy Kaye. Assistant Director, Carter DeHaven, Jr. Gowns by Don Loper. 135 minutes

Kristina Hedvigson: Olivia De Havilland, *Lucas Marsh:* Robert Mitchum, *Alfred Boone:* Frank Sinatra, *Harriet Lang:* Gloria Grahame, *Dr. Aarons:* Broderick Crawford, *Dr. Runkleman:* Charles Bickford,

Not as a Stranger with Myron McCormick and Robert Mitchum.

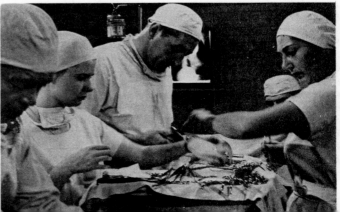

Dr. Snider: Myron McCormick, Job Marsh: Lon Chaney, Ben Cosgrove: Jesse White, Oley: Harry Morgan, Brundage: Lee Marvin, Bruni: Virginia Christine, Dr. Dietrich: Whit Bissell, Dr. Lettering: Jack Raine, Miss O'Dell: Mae Clarke.

NO TIME FOR SERGEANTS (1958) WB. Produced and directed by Mervyn LeRoy. From the TV and Broadway play by Ira Levin, based on the novel by Mac Hyman. Screenplay, John Lee Mahin. Music, Ray Heindorf. Assistant Director, Dick Moder. Photography, Harold Rosson. Art Director, Malcolm Brown. Editor, William Ziegler. Sound, Stanley Jones. Sammy Jackson starred as Will on the 1964–65 TV series of the same name. Griffith starred in the stage and TV versions; McCormick repeats his stage role. Film debut of Don Knotts. 111 minutes.

Will Stockdale (Narrator): Andy Griffith, Sergeant King: Myron McCormick, Ben Whitledge: Nick Adams, Irvin Blanchard: Murray Hamilton, General Bush: Howard Smith, Lieutenant Bridges: Will Hutchins, General Pollard: Sydney Smith, Psychiatrist: James Milhollin, Corporal Brown: Don Knotts, W. A. F. Captain: Jean Willes, Captain: Bartlett Robinson, Lieutenant Cover: Henry McCann, Draft Board Man: Dub Taylor, Pa Stockdale: William Fawcett, Colonel: Raymond Bailey, Lieutenant Gardella: Jameel Farah (Jamie Farr), Lieutenant Kendall: Bob Stratton, Sheriff: Jack Mower, Man with Applications: Malcolm Atterbury, Rosabelle: Peggy Hallack, Inductees: Sammy Jackson, Rad Fulton, Tiger: Dan Barton, Supervising Sergeant: Francis De Sales, Oculist: Robert Sherman, Infantryman: Dick Wessel, Senator: Tom Browne Henry, Charles, Aide: Tom McKee, Baker: George Neise, Abel: Benny Baker, Sentry: Fred Coby, M.P.: John Close, Announcer's Voice: Verne Smith.

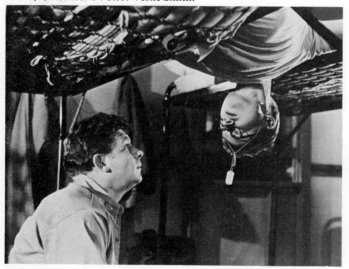

No Time for Sergeants with Andy Griffith and Nick Adams.

NOTORIOUS (1946) RKO. Producer-Director, Alfred Hitchcock. Screenplay, Ben Hecht. Art Directors, Albert S. D'Agostino, Carroll Clark. Musical Score, Roy Webb. Musical Director, C. Bakaleinikoff. Cameraman, Ted Tetzlaff. Special Effects, Vernon L. Walker, Paul Eagler. Editor, Theron Warth. 103 minutes

Devlin: Cary Grant, Alicia Huberman: Ingrid Bergman, Alexander Sebastian: Claude Rains, Paul Prescott: Louis Calhern, Mme. Sebastian: Madame Konstantin, "Dr. Anderson": Reinhold Schunzel, Walter Beardsley: Moroni Olsen, Eric Mathis: Ivan Triesault, Joseph: Alex Minotis, Mr. Hopkins: Wally Brown, Ernest Weylin: Gavin Gordon, Commodore: Sir Charles Mendl, Dr. Barbosa: Ricardo Costa, Hupka: Eberhard Krumschmidt, Ethel: Fay Baker, Señor Ortiza: Antonio Moreno, Knerr: Frederick Ledebur, Dr. Silva: Luis Serrano, Adams: William Gordon, Judge: Charles D. Brown, Dr. Silva: Ramon Nomar, Rossner: Peter Von Zerneck, Huberman: Fred Nurney, Mr. Cook: Herbert Wyndham, Defense Council: Harry Hayden, Clerk of Court: Dink Trout, District Attorney: Warren Jackson, Bailiff: Howard Mitchell, Motor Cop: Garry Owen, Mrs.

Notorious with Ingrid Bergman and Cary Grant.

Jackson: Patricia Smart, Motor Cop: Lester Dorr, Maid: Tina Menard, Ribero: Alfredo DeSa, File Clerks: Bea Benaderet, Virginia Gregg, Bernice Barrett.

NO WAY OUT (1950) 20th. Producer, Darryl F. Zanuck. Director, Joseph Mankiewicz. Authors-Screenplay, Joseph Mankiewicz, Lesser Samuels. Music, Alfred Newman. Art Directors, Lyle Wheeler, George W. Davis. Photography, Milton Krasner. Editor, Barbara McLean. Film debut of Sidney Poitier. 106 minutes

Ray Biddle: Richard Widmark, Edie: Linda Darnell, Dr. Wharton: Stephen McNally, Dr. Luther Brooks: Sidney Poitier, Cora: Mildred Joanne Smith, George Biddle: Harry Bellaver, Dr. Moreland: Stanley Ridges, Lefty: Dots Johnson, Gladys: Amanda Randolph, Connie: Ruby Dee, John: Ossie Davis, Whitey: George Tyne, Rocky: Bert Freed, Luther's Mother: Maude Simmons, Kowalsky: Ken Christy, Mac: Frank Richards, Assistant Deputy: Robert Adler, Deputy Sheriff: Jim Toney, Day Deputy: Ray Teal, Dr. Cheney: Will Wright, Jonah: Wade Dumas, Ambulance Driver: Fred Graham, Ambulance Doctor: William Pullen, Henry: Jasper Weldon, Polish Husband: Ruben Wendorf, Polish Wife: Laiola Wendorf, Johnny Biddle: Dick Paxton, Internes: Stan Johnson, Frank Overton, Landlady: Kitty O'Neil, Joe: Emmett Smith, Terry: Ralph Hodges, Priest: Thomas Ingersoll, Man: Jack Kruschen.

No Way Out with Sidney Poitier and Richard Widmark.

NOW, VOYAGER (1942) WB. Producer, Hal B. Wallis. Director, Irving Rapper. From the novel by Olive Higgins Prouty. Screenplay, Casey Robinson. Art Director, Robert Haas. Cameraman, Sol Polito. Editor, Warren Low. Song: "It Can't Be Wrong" by Kim Gannon and Max Steiner. 117 minutes

Charlotte Vale: Bette Davis, Jerry (J. D.) Durrence: Paul Henreid, Dr. Jaquith: Claude Rains, Mrs. Vale: Gladys Cooper, June Vale: Bonita Granville, Elliott Livingston: John Loder, Lisa Vale: Ilka

Now, Voyager with Bette Davis, Ilka Chase and John Loder.

The Nutty Professor with Jerry Lewis.

Chase, *"Deb" McIntyre:* Lee Patrick, *Frank McIntyre:* James Rennie, *Leslie Trotter:* Charles Drake, *Miss Trask:* Katharine Alexander, *Tina:* Janis Wilson, *Dora Pickford:* Mary Wickes, *Dr. Dan Regan:* Michael Ames (Tod Andrews), *Mr. Thompson:* Franklin Pangborn, *William:* David Clyde, *Hilda:* Claire du Brey, *George Weston:* Don Douglas, *Grace Weston:* Charlotte Wynters, *Manoel:* Frank Puglia, *Captain:* Lester Matthews, *Katie:* Sheila Hayward, *Passenger:* Mary Field, *Celestine:* Yola d'Avril, *M. Henri:* Georges Renavent, *Hamilton Hunneker:* Bill Kennedy, *Henry Montague:* Reed Hadley, *Woman:* Dorothy Vaughan, *Aunt Hester:* Elspeth Dudgeon, *Uncle Herbert:* George Lessey, *Lloyd:* Ian Wolfe, *Rosa:* Constance Purdy, *Hilary:* Corbett Morris, *Justine:* Hilda Plowright, *Mrs. Smith:* Tempe Pigott.

THE NUN'S STORY (1959) WB. Producer, Henry Blanke. Director, Fred Zinnemann. Technicolor. From the book by Kathryn C. Hulme. Screenplay, Robert Anderson. Art Director, Alexander Trauner. Music composed and conducted by Franz Waxman. Cinematographer, Franz Planer. Editor, Walter Thompson. 149 minutes

Sister Luke: Audrey Hepburn, *Dr. Fortunati:* Peter Finch, *Mother Emmanuel:* Edith Evans, *Mother Mathilde:* Peggy Ashcroft, *Dr. Van Der Mal:* Dean Jagger, *Sister Margharita:* Mildred Dunnock, *Mother Christophe:* Beatrice Straight, *Sister William:* Patricia Collinge, *Simone:* Patricia Bosworth, *Mother Marcella:* Ruth White, *Mother Katherine:* Barbara O'Neil, *Sister Pauline:* Margaret Phillips, *Archangel:* Colleen Dewhurst, *Sister Augustine:* Molly Urquhart, *Sister Aurelie:* Dorothy Alison, *Father Vermeuhlen:* Niall MacGinnis, *Sister Eleanor:* Rosalie Crutchley, *Kalulu:* Orlando Martins, *Sister Marie:* Eva Kotthaus, *Illunga:* Errol John, *Louise:* Jeannette Sterke, *Pierre:* Richard O'Sullivan, *Marie:* Marina Wolkonsky, *Jeannette Milonet:* Penelope Horner, *Pascin:* Charles Lamb, *Sister Bernard:* Ave Ninchi, *Bishop:* Ludovice Bonhomme, *Doctor Coovaerts:* Lionel Jeffries, *Sister Ellen:* Dara Gavin, *Sister Timothy:* Elfrida Simbari.

The Nun's Story with Audrey Hepburn.

THE NUTTY PROFESSOR (1963) Par. Producer, Ernest D. Glucksman. Associate Producer, Arthur P. Schmidt. Director, Jerry Lewis. Technicolor. Screenplay, Jerry Lewis, Bill Richmond. Art Directors, Hal Pereira, Walter Tyler. Music scored and conducted by Walter Scharf. "We've Got a World That Swings," lyrics, Lil Mattis, music, Yule Brown. Cinematographer, Wallace Kelley. Special Photographic Effects, Paul K. Lerpae. Editor, John Woodcock. 107 minutes

Professor Julius Ferris Kelp/Buddy Love: Jerry Lewis, *Stella Purdy:* Stella Stevens, *Dr. Warfield:* Del Moore, *Millie Lemmon:* Kathleen Freeman, *College Student:* Med Flory, *College Student:* Norman Alden, *Kelp's Father:* Howard Morris, *Kelp's Mother:* Elvia Allman, *Dr. Leevee:* Milton Frome, *Bartender:* Buddy Lester, *English Boy:* Marvin Kaplan, *College Student:* David Landfield, *College Student:* Skip Ward, *College Student:* Julie Parrish, *College Student:* Henry Gibson, *Boy:* Gary Lewis, *Bartender:* Dave Willock, *Rube:* Doodles Weaver, *Cab Driver:* Mushy Callahan, *Salesman Clothier:* Gavin Gordon, *College Student:* Celeste Yarnall, *Girl Student:* Francine York, *Faculty Member:* Joe Forte, *Cigarette Girl:* Terry Higgins, *Judo Instructor:* Murray Alper.

OCEAN'S 11 (1960) WB. Produced and directed by Lewis Milestone. Associate Producers, Henry W. Sanicola and Milton Ebbins. Assistant Director, Ray Gosnell, Jr. In Technicolor and Panavision. Screenplay, Harry Brown and Charles Lederer. Story, George Clayton Johnson and Jack Golden Russell. Music composed and conducted by Nelson Riddle. Orchestration, Arthur Morton. Art Director, Nicolai Remisoff. Costumes, H. Shoup. Cinematography, William H. Daniels. Editor, Philip W. Anderson. A Dorchester Production. Songs by Sammy Cahn and James Van Heusen: "Ain't That a Kick in the Head," "Ee-O-Leven." 127 minutes

Danny Ocean: Frank Sinatra, *Sam Harmon:* Dean Martin, *Josh Howard:* Sammy Davis, Jr., *Jimmy Foster:* Peter Lawford, *Beatrice Ocean:* Angie Dickinson, *Anthony Bergdorf:* Richard Conte, *Duke Santos:* Cesar Romero, *Adele Ekstrom:* Patrice Wymore, *Mushy O'Conners:* Joey Bishop, *Spyros Acebos:* Akim Tamiroff, *Roger Corneal:* Henry Silva, *Mrs. Restes:* Ilka Chase, *Vincent Massler:* Buddy Lester, *Curly Steffens:* Richard Benedict, *Mrs. Bergdorf:* Jean Willes, *Peter*

Ocean's 11 with Frank Sinatra, Peter Lawford and Richard Conte.

Rheimer: Norman Fell, *Louis Jackson:* Clem Harvey, *Mr. Kelly:* Hank Henry, *Mr. Cohen:* Charles Meredith, *Delores:* Anne Neyland, *Helen:* Joan Staley, *Proprietor:* George E. Stone, *Customer:* Marjorie Bennett, *De Wolfe:* Louis Quinn, *Sugarface:* Laura Cornell, *Texan:* John Indrisano, *Snake Dancer:* Shiva, *Major Taylor:* Steve Pendleton, *Timmy:* Ronnie Dapo, *Hungry Girl:* Carmen Phillips, *Police Officer:* Paul Bryar, *Client:* Red Skelton, *Cashier:* John Craven, *Jealous Young Man:* Lew Gallo, *Man:* John Holland, *First Girl:* Shirley MacLaine, *Second Girl:* Barbara Sterling, *Deputy:* Murray Alper, *TV Newscaster:* Tom Middleton, *Roadblock Deputy:* Hoot Gibson, *Riviera Manager:* Sparky Kaye, *Sands Manager:* Forrest Lederer, *Jack Strager:* George Raft, *Castleman:* Rummy Bishop, *Freeman:* Gregory Gay, *McCoy:* Don "Red" Barry, *Parelli:* William Justine.

OF HUMAN BONDAGE (1934) RKO. Directed by John Cromwell. Based on the novel by Somerset Maugham. Screenplay, Lester Cohen. Photography, Henry W. Gerrard. Editor, William Morgan. Remakes: Warner Brothers, 1946; MGM, 1964. 83 minutes

Philip Carey: Leslie Howard, *Mildred Rogers:* Bette Davis, *Sally Athelny:* Frances Dee, *Athelny:* Reginald Owen, *Harry Griffiths:* Reginald Denny, *Norah:* Kay Johnson, *Emil:* Alan Hale, *Dunsford:* Reginald Sheffield, *Dr. Jacobs:* Desmond Roberts, *Landlady:* Tempe Pigott.

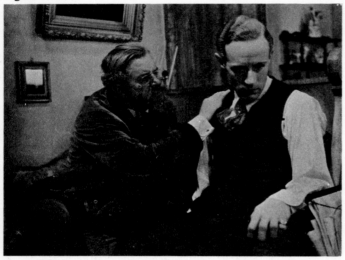

Of Human Bondage with Reginald Owen and Leslie Howard.

OF MICE AND MEN (1939) UA. Producer, Lewis Milestone. Associate Producer, Frank Ross. Director, Lewis Milestone. Based on the novel by John Steinbeck. Screenplay, Eugene Solow. Art Director, Nicolai Remisoff. Musical Score, Aaron Copland. Cameraman, Norbert Brodine. Photographic Effects, Roy Seawright. Editor, Bert Jordan. Also produced on the stage by Sam H. Harris, staged by George S. Kaufman. 107 minutes

Of Mice and Men with Burgess Meredith and Lon Chaney, Jr.

George: Burgess Meredith, *Mae:* Betty Field, *Lennie:* Lon Chaney, Jr., *Slim:* Charles Bickford, *Candy:* Roman Bohnen, *Curley:* Bob Steele, *Whit:* Noah Beery, Jr., *Jackson:* Oscar O'Shea, *Carlson:* Granville Bates, *Crooks:* Leigh Whipper, *Aunt Clara:* Leona Roberts, *Susie:* Helen Lynd, *Second Girl:* Barbara Pepper, *Third Girl:* Henriette Kaye, *Bus Driver:* Eddie Dunn, *Sheriff:* Howard Mitchell, *Ranch Hands:* Whitney de Rhan, Baldy Cooke, Charles Watt, Jack Lawrence, Carl Pitti, John Beach.

Oklahoma! with Gordon MacRae and Shirley Jones.

OKLAHOMA! (1955) Magna. Producer, Arthur Hornblow, Jr. Director, Fred Zinnemann. Music by Richard Rodgers. Book and lyrics by Oscar Hammerstein II. Screenplay by Sonya Levien and William Ludwig. Choreography by Agnes De Mille. Costumes by Orry-Kelly and Motley. Adapted from Rodgers and Hammerstein's musical which was based on a play, *Green Grow the Lilacs,* by Lynn Riggs. Assistant Director, Arthur Black, Jr. Production designed by Oliver Smith. Music conducted and supervised by Jay Blackton. Editor, Gene Ruggiero. Songs: "Oklahoma!" "Oh What a Beautiful Mornin;" "The Surrey With the Fringe on Top," "Everything's Up-to-Date in Kansas City," "Many a New Day," "People Will Say Were in Love," "The Farmer and the Cowman," "I Can't Say No," "All Er Nuthin," "Pore Jud." A Rodgers and Hammerstein Production filmed in Eastman Color and Todd-AO. 145 minutes

Curly: Gordon MacRae, *Ado Annie:* Gloria Grahame, *Will Parker:* Gene Nelson, *Aunt Eller:* Charlotte Greenwood, *Laurey:* Shirley Jones, *Ali Hakim:* Eddie Albert, *Carnes:* James Whitmore, *Jud Fry:* Rod Steiger, *Gertie:* Barbara Lawrence, *Skidmore:* J. C. Flippen, *Marshal:* Roy Barcroft, *Dream Curly:* James Mitchell, *Dream Laurey:* Bambi Linn, *Dancers:* James Mitchell, Bambi Linn, Jennie Workman, Kelly Brown, Marc Platt, Lizanne Truex, Virginia Bosler, Evelyn Taylor, Jane Fischer.

The Old Maid with Bette Davis and Miriam Hopkins.

THE OLD MAID (1939) WB. Producer, Hal B. Wallis. Associate Producer, Henry Blanke. Director, Edmund Goulding. Authors, Zoe Akins, Edith Wharton. Screenplay, Casey Robinson. Art Director, Robert Haas. Music, Max Steiner. Orchestral Arrangements, Hugo Freidhofer. Musical Director, Leo F. Forbstein. Cameraman, Tony Gaudio. Editor, George Amy. 95 minutes

Charlotte Lovell: Bette Davis, *Delia Lovell:* Miriam Hopkins, *Clem Spender:* George Brent, *Tina:* Jane Bryan, *Doctor Lanskell:* Donald Crisp, *Dora:* Louise Fazenda, *Jim Ralston:* James Stephenson, *Joe Ralston:* Jerome Cowan, *Lanning Halsey:* William Lundigan, *Grandmother Lovell:* Cecilia Loftus, *Jim:* Rand Brooks, *Dee:* Janet Shaw, *John:* DeWolf Hopper, *Tina as a child:* Marlene Burnett, *Man:* Rod Cameron, *Aristocratic Maid:* Doris Lloyd, *Mr. Halsey:* Frederick Burton.

The Old Man and the Sea with Spencer Tracy.

THE OLD MAN AND THE SEA (1958) WB. Producer, Leland Hayward. Director, John Sturges. WarnerColor. Screenplay, Peter Viertel. Based on the novel by Ernest Hemingway. Art Directors, Art Loel, Edward Carrere. Music composed and conducted by Dimitri Tiomkin. Cinematographer, James Wong Howe. Additional Photography, Floyd Crosby, Tom Tutwiler. Underwater Photography, Lamar Boren. Editor, Arthur P. Schmidt. Locations: Nassau, Bahamas; Cojimar Bay near Havana, and Boca de Jaruco, Cuba; Colombia; in the waters off Peru, Ecuador, Panama, the Galapagos Islands, and Kona, Hawaii. 86 minutes

Old Man (Narrator): Spencer Tracy, *Boy:* Felipe Pazos, *Martin:* Harry Bellaver, *Cafe Proprietor:* Don Diamond, *Hand Wrestler:* Don Blackman, *Professional Gambler:* Joey Ray, *Other Gamblers:* Richard Alameda, Tony Rosa, Carlos Rivera, Robert Alderette, Mauritz Hugo, *Tourist:* Mary Hemingway. Scenes of the marlin are of a prize catch made by Alfred Glassell, Jr.

Old Yeller with Kevin Corcoran and Spike.

OLD YELLER (1957) BV. Producer, Walt Disney. Director, Robert Stevenson. Screenplay by Fred Gipson and William Tunberg. Based on the novel by Fred Gipson. Associate Producer, William H. Anderson. Music by Oliver Wallace. Songs by Gil George and Oliver Wallace. Assistant Director, Robert G. Shannon. Costumes by Chuck Keehne and Gertrude Casey. In Technicolor. Animal fights directed by Yakima Canutt. 83 minutes

Katie Coates: Dorothy McGuire, *Jim Coates:* Fess Parker, *Travis Coates:* Tommy Kirk, *Arliss Coates:* Kevin Corcoran, *Bud Searcy:* Jeff York, *Burn Sanderson:* Chuck Connors, *Lisbeth Searcy:* Beverly Washburn, *Old Yeller:* Spike.

ONE-EYED JACKS (1961) Par. Producer, Frank P. Rosenberg. Executive Producers, George Glass and Walter Seltzer. Directed by Marlon Brando. In VistaVision and Technicolor. Based on the novel *The Authentic Death of Hendry Jones* by Charles Neider. Screenplay, Guy Trosper, Calder Willingham. Art Directors, Hal Pereira and J. McMillan Johnson. Music, Hugo Friedhofer. Assistant Directors, Francisco Day and Harry Caplan. Costumes, Yvonne Wood. Dances, Josephine Earl. Cinematography, Charles Lang, Jr. Special Effects, John P. Fulton. Editor, Archie Marshek. A Pennebaker Production. Stanley Kubrick was replaced as the director by Brando (his first effort) before filming began at Monterey Beach in 1958. More than a million feet were shot, and the film was cut from an original running time of 4 hours, 42 minutes. Brando's stand-in (since *Viva Zapata!*) Larry Duran made his acting debut. The only American film of Pina Pellicer, who killed herself at 24, on December 10, 1964, after a brief Mexican career. 141 minutes

One-Eyed Jacks with Mickey Finn, Karl Malden, Marlon Brando and Slim Pickens.

Rio: Marlon Brando, *Dad Longworth:* Karl Malden, *Maria:* Katy Jurado, *Louisa:* Pina Pellicer, *Lon:* Slim Pickens, *Bob Amory:* Ben Johnson, *Harvey:* Sam Gilman, *Modesto:* Larry Duran, *Howard Tetley:* Timothy Carey, *Redhead:* Miriam Colon, *Bank Teller:* Elisha Cook, Jr., *Rurales Officer:* Rudolph Acosta, *Bartender:* Ray Teal, *Barber-Photographer:* John Dierkes, *Nika, Flamenco Dancer:* Margarita Cordova, *Doc:* Hank Worden, *Margarita, Castilian Girl:* Nina Martinez, *Uncle:* Philip Ahn, *Tim:* Clem Harvey, *Banker:* William Forrest, *Owner of Cantina:* Shichizo Takeda, *Posseman:* Henry Wills, *Blacksmith:* Mickey Finn, *Squaredance Caller:* Fenton Jones, *Corral Keeper:* Joe Dominguez, *Mexican Vendor:* Margarita Martin, *Rurales Sergeant:* John Michael Quijada, *Cantina Girl:* Francy Scott, *Card Sharp:* Felipe Turich, *Townsman:* Nesdon Booth, *Mexican Townsman:* Nacho Galindo, *Bouncer in Shack:* Jorge Moreno.

ONE FOOT IN HEAVEN (1941) WB. Producers, Jack L. Warner, Hal B. Wallis. Associate Producers, Robert Lord, Irving Rapper. Directed by Irving Rapper. Screenplay, Casey Robinson. Cameraman, Charles Rosher. Editor, Warren Low. From the novel by Hartzell

One Foot in Heaven with Nana Bryant, Martha Scott and Ernest Cossart.

Spence. Scenes from William S. Hart's *The Silent Man*, 1916. 108 minutes

William Spence: Fredric March, *Mother:* Martha Scott, *Mrs. Lydia Sandow:* Beulah Bondi, *Preston Thurston:* Gene Lockhart, *Clayton Potter:* Grant Mitchell, *Dr. John Romer:* Moroni Olsen, *Samson:* Harry Davenport, *Eileen (18 years old):* Elisabeth Fraser, *Hartzell (17 years old):* Frankie Thomas, *Mrs. Thurston:* Laura Hope Crews, *Dr. Horrigan:* Jerome Cowan, *John E. Morris:* Ernest Cossart, *Mrs. Morris:* Nana Bryant, *Louella Digby:* Mary Field, *Case:* Hobart Bosworth, *George Reynolds:* Roscoe Ates, *Mrs. Watkins:* Clara Blandick, *Haskins:* Charles Halton, *Miss Peabody:* Paula Trueman, *Mrs. Jellison:* Virginia Brissac, *Fraser Spence:* Casey Johnson, *Eileen (11 years old):* Carlotta Jelm, *Hartzell (10 years old):* Peter Caldwell, *Alf McAfee:* Milt Kibbee, *Druggist MacFarlan:* Harlan Briggs, *Zeke:* Olin Howland, *Drummer:* Frank Mayo, *Conductor:* Fred Kelsey, *Mrs. Simpson:* Vera Lewis, *Mrs. Ehrlich:* Dorothy Vaughan, *Mrs. Dibble:* Tempe Pigott, *Mrs. Spicer:* Sarah Edwards, *Storekeeper:* Herbert Heywood, *Casper Cullenbaugh:* Dick Elliott, *Ella Hodges:* Charlotte Treadway *Bride:* Ann Edmonds, *Groom:* Byron Barr (Gig Young).

ONE HOUR WITH YOU (1932) Par. Produced by Ernst Lubitsch. Directed by George Cukor. From the play *Only a Dream* by Lothar Schmidt. Screenplay, Samson Raphaelson. Photography, Victor Milner. Songs by Leo Robin, Oscar Straus, Richard Whiting: "One Hour With You," "Oh, That Mitzi," "We Will Always Be Sweethearts," "Three Times a Day," "What Would You Do?" Film debut of Florine McKinney. Remake of *The Marriage Circle* (Warners, 1924). 80 minutes

Dr. Andre Bertier: Maurice Chevalier, *Colette Bertier:* Jeanette MacDonald, *Mitzi Olivier:* Genevieve Tobin, *Adolph:* Charles Ruggles, *Professor Olivier:* Roland Young, *Police Commissioner:* George Barbier, *Mademoiselle Martel:* Josephine Dunn, *Detective:* Richard Carle, *Policeman:* Charles Judels, *Mitzi's Maid:* Barbara Leonard, *Girl:* Florine McKinney, *Singer:* Donald Novis, *Marcel, Butler:* Charles Coleman, *Butler:* Eric Wilton, *Cabby:* George Davis, *Dance Extra:* Bill Elliott.

One Hour With You with Genevieve Tobin and Maurice Chevalier.

100 Men and a Girl with Mischa Auer and Deanna Durbin.

100 MEN AND A GIRL (1937) Univ. Produced by Charles R. Rogers. Associate Producer, Joseph Pasternak. Directed by Henry Koster. Screenplay, Bruce Manning, Charles Kenyon, and Hans Kraly. Photography, Joseph Valentine. Editor, Bernard W. Burton. Songs: "It's Raining Sunbeams" by Frederick Hollander and Sam Coslow; "A Heart That's Free" by Alfred G. Robyn and Thomas T. Railey. 84 minutes

Patricia Cardwell: Deanna Durbin, *Leopold Stokowski:* Leopold Stokowski, *John Cardwell:* Adolphe Menjou, *Mrs. Frost:* Alice Brady, *John R. Frost:* Eugene Pallette, *Michael Borodoff:* Mischa Auer, *Garage Owner:* Billy Gilbert, *Mrs. Tyler:* Alma Kruger, *Doorman, Marshall:* Jack (J. Scott) Smart, *Tommy Bitters:* Jed Prouty, *Russell:* Jameson Thomas, *Johnson:* Howard Hickman, *Taxi Driver:* Frank Jenks, *Gustave Brandstetter:* Christian Rub, *Stevens, Butler:* Gerald Oliver Smith, *Rudolph, a Bearded Musician/A Boarder:* Jack Mulhall, *Music Lover:* James Bush, *Manager:* John Hamilton, *Butler:* Eric Wilton, *Theater Patron:* Mary Forbes, *Guests:* Rolfe Sedan, Charles Coleman, Hooper Atchley, *Pianist:* Leonid Kinskey, *Ira Westing, Music Editor:* Edwin Maxwell.

ONE IN A MILLION (1936) 20th. Produced by Darryl F. Zanuck. Directed by Sidney Lanfield. Associate Producer, Raymond Griffith.

One in a Million with Jean Hersholt and Sonja Henie.

Authors, Leonare Praskins, Mark Kelly. Musical Director, Louis Silvers. Skating Ensembles, Jack Haskell. Cameraman, Edward Cronjager. Editor, Robert Simpson. Songs by Sidney D. Mitchell and Lew Pollack: "One in a Million," "Who's Afraid of Love?", "The Moonlight Waltz," "Lovely Lady in White," "We're Back in Circulation Again." 95 minutes

Greta Muller: Sonja Henie, *Tad:* Adolphe Menjou, *Heinrich Muller:* Jean Hersholt, *Photographer:* Ned Sparks, *Ritz Brothers:* Themselves, *Billie:* Arline Judge, *Goldie:* Dixie Dunbar, *Bob:* Don Ameche, *Adolph:* Borrah Minevitch, *Ratoffsky:* Montagu Love, *Leah:* Leah Ray, *Members of Girls' Band:* Shirley Deane, June Gale, Lillian Porter, Diana Cook, Bonnie Bannon, June Wilkins, Clarice Sherry, Pauline Craig, *Manager of St. Moritz Hotel:* Albert Conti, *Chapelle:* Julius Tannen, *French Skater:* Margo Webster, *German Announcer:* Frederic Gierman, *Woman in Box:* Bess Flowers, *Chairman:* Egon Brecher, *Announcer, Madison Square Garden:* Paul McVey.

ONE NIGHT OF LOVE (1934) Col. Produced by Harry Cohn. Directed by Victor Schertzinger. Story, Dorothy Speare and Charles Beahan. Screenplay, S. K. Lauren, James Gow, and Edmund North. Art Director, Stephen Goosson. Photography, Joseph Walker. Editor, Gene Milford. Sound, Paul Neal. Assistant Director, Arthur Balch. Costumes, Robert Kalloch. Music Director, Dr. Pietro Cimini. Special Effects, John Hoffman. Song, "One Night of Love," by Gus Kahn and Victor Schertzinger. Music, Louis Silvers. 82 minutes

One Night of Love with Lyle Talbot and Grace Moore.

Mary: Grace Moore, *Monteverdi:* Tullio Carminati, *Bill Houston:* Lyle Talbot, *Lally:* Mona Barrie, *Muriel:* Nydia Westman, *Angelina:* Jessie Ralph, *Giovanni:* Luis Alberni, *Frappazini:* Rosemary Glosz, *Mary's Mother:* Jane Darwell, *Mary's Father:* William Burress, *Impresario:* Frederick Burton, *Cafe Proprietor:* Henry Armetta, *Caluppi:* Andres De Segurola, *Radio Announcer:* Sam.Hayes, *Stage Manager:* Reginald Barlow, *First Doctor:* Fredrik Vogeding, *Second Doctor:* Arno Johnson, *Viennese Valet:* Olaf Hytten, *Florist:* Leo White, *Vegetable Man:* Herman Bing, *Stage Director:* Edward Keane, *Opera Director:* Reginald Le Borg, *Men:* Wilfred Lucas, Edmund Burns, *Pinkerton:* Paul Ellis, *Captain of Italian Yacht:* Joseph Mack, *German Girl:* Marion Lessing, *Taxi Driver:* Hans Joby, *Man:* Rafael Storm, *Cora Florida:* Victoria Stuart, *Radio Judge:* John Ardizoni, *Viennese Stage Manager:* Kurt Furberg, *Call Boy:* Spec O'Donnell, *Flower Store Man:* Michael Mark, *Steward:* Richard La Marr, *Judge:* Wadsworth Harris, *Sugar Daddy:* Arthur Stuart Hull.

ONE, TWO, THREE (1961) UA. Producer-Director, Billy Wilder. Screenplay, Billy Wilder, I. A. L. Diamond. Based on play by Ferenc Molnar. Music, Andre Previn. Associate Producers, I. A. L. Diamond, Doane Harrison. Assistant Director, Tom Pevsner. Presented by Mirisch Company in association with Pyramid Productions. Filmed in Panavision. Second Unit Director, Andre Smagghe. Art Director, Alex Trauner. Cinematographer, Daniel Fapp. Editor, Daniel Mandell. 108 minutes

One, Two, Three with Arlene Francis, James Cagney and Pamela Tiffin.

MacNamara: James Cagney, *Otto:* Horst Buchholz, *Scarlett:* Pamela Tiffin, *Phylis:* Arlene Francis, *Ingeborg:* Lilo Pulver, *Hazeltine:* Howard St. John, *Schlemmer:* Hanns Lothar, *Mrs. Hazeltine:* Lois Bolton, *Peripetchikoff:* Leon Askin, *Mishkin:* Peter Capell, *Borodenko:* Ralf Wolter, *Fritz:* Karl Lieffen, *Dr. Bauer:* Henning Schluter, *M. P. Sergeant:* Red Buttons, *Tommy MacNamara:* John Allen, *Cindy MacNamara:* Christine Allen, *Count von Droste-Schattenburg:* Hubert Von Meyerinck, *Newspaperman:* Tile Kiwe, *Zeidlitz:* Karl Ludwig Lindt, *Bertha:* Rose Renee Roth, *M. P. Corporal:* Ivan Arnold, *Pierre:* Jacques Chevalier, *Krause:* Paul Bos.

ONE WAY PASSAGE (1932) WB. Directed by Tay Garnett. Original Story, Robert Lord. Screenplay, Wilson Mizner and Joseph Jackson. Editor, Ralph Dawson. Camera, Robert Kurrle. Filmed aboard the Pacific liner S. S. *Calawaii.* Theme, "Where Was I." Remade as *Till We Meet Again* (1940). 69 minutes

Dan Hardesty: William Powell, *Joan Ames:* Kay Francis, *Skippy:* Frank McHugh, *Countess Barilhaus (Barrel House Betty):* Aline MacMahon, *Steve Burke:* Warren Hymer, *Doctor:* Frederick Burton, *Sir Harold:* Douglas Gerrard, *Steward:* Herbert Mundin, *Ship's Bartender:* Roscoe Karns, *Singing Drunk:* Wilson Mizner, *Singer ("If I Had My Way"):* Heinie Conklin, *Hong Kong Bartender:* Mike Donlin, *Honolulu Contact:* Dewey Robinson, *Agua Caliente Bartender:* William Halligan, *Captain:* Stanley Fields, *Curio Dealer:* Willie Fung, *Ship's Officer:* Harry Seymour, *Joan's Friends:* Ruth Hall, Allan Lane.

One Way Passage with William Powell and Kay Francis.

On Moonlight Bay with Doris Day, Gordon MacRae and Jack Smith.

ON MOONLIGHT BAY (1951) WB. Producer, William Jacobs. Director, Roy Del Ruth. Color by Technicolor. From the Penrod stories by Booth Tarkington. Screenplay, Jack Rose, Melville Shavelson. Art Director, Douglas Bacon. Music, Max Steiner. Photography, Ernest Haller. Editor, Thomas Reilly. Dances, LeRoy Prinz. Songs: "Love Ya" by Charles Tobias and Peter De Rose; "Christmas Story" by Pauline Walsh; "On Moonlight Bay" by Edward Madden and Percy Wenrich; "Cuddle Up a Little Closer" by Otto Harbach and Karl Hoschna; "Tell Me Why Nights Are Lonely" by W. J. Callahan and Max Kortlander; "I'm Forever Blowing Bubbles" by Jean Kenbrovin and John W. Kellette; "Every Little Movement Has a Meaning All Its Own" by Otto Harbach and Karl Hoschna; "Till We Meet Again" by Ray Egan and Richard Whiting; "Pack Up Your Troubles in Your Old Kit Bag" by Felix Powell and George Asaf; "Love Your Honey" and "Yoo Hoo." Film debut of Jack Smith. 98 minutes

Marjorie Winfield: Doris Day, *William Sherman:* Gordon MacRae, *Hubert Wakley:* Jack Smith; *George Winfield:* Leon Ames, *Mrs. Winfield:* Rosemary De Camp, *Stella:* Mary Wickes, *Miss Stevens:* Ellen Corby, *Wesley Winfield:* Billy Gray, *Jim Sherman:* Jeffrey Stevens, *Aunt Martha:* Esther Dale, *Cora:* Suzanne Whitney, *Barker:* Eddie Marr, *Dancing Instructor:* Sig Arno, *Soldier:* Jimmy Dobson, *Sleeping Soldier:* Rolland Morris, *Cast of the Silent Movie: Mother:* Lois Austin, *Father:* Creighton Hale, *Daughter:* Ann Kimball, *Bartender:* Ray Spiker, *Salesman:* Hank Mann, *Salesman:* Jack Mower, *Salesman:* Ralph Montgomery.

ON THE AVENUE (1937) 20th. Associate Producer, Gene Markey. Directed by Roy Del Ruth. Screenplay, Gene Markey and William Conselman. Music Director, Arthur Lange. Dance Director, Seymour Felix. Orchestrations, Herbert Spencer. Art Director, Mark-Lee Kirk. Associate Art Director, Haldane Douglas. Set Decoration, Thomas Little. Assistant Director, William J. Scully. Costumes, Gwen Wakeling. Photography, Lucien Andriot. Editor, Allen McNeil. Sound, Joseph Aiken and Roger Heman. Songs by Irving Berlin: "Slumming on Park Avenue," "I've Got My Love to Keep Me Warm," "This Year's Kisses," "You're Laughing at Me," "He Ain't Got Rhythm," "The Girl on the Police Gazette." 89 minutes

On the Avenue with Dick Powell (in photo) and Madeleine Carroll.

Gary Blake: Dick Powell, *Mimi Caraway:* Madeleine Carroll, *Mona Merrick:* Alice Faye, *Themselves:* The Ritz Brothers, *Commodore Caraway:* George Barbier, *Frederick Sims:* Alan Mowbray, *Aunt Fritz Peters:* Cora Witherspoon, *Jake Dibble:* Walter Catlett, *Eddie Eads:* Douglas Fowley, *Miss Katz:* Joan Davis, *Step:* Stepin Fetchit, *Herr Hanfstangel:* Sig Rumann, *Joe Papaloupas:* Billy Gilbert, *Vince, the Cabby:* E. E. Clive, *Mr. Trivet:* Douglas Wood, *Stage Manager:* John Sheehan, *Harry Morris:* Paul Irving, *Kelly:* Harry Stubbs, *Luigi:* Ricardo Mandia, *Chorus Girl ("I've Got My Love to Keep Me Warm"):* Lynn Bari, *Chorine:* Geneva Sawyer, *Footman in Sketch:* Hank Mann.

ON THE BEACH (1959) UA. Producer-Director, Stanley Kramer. A Lomitas Production. Screenplay by John Paxton and James Lee Barrett. Based on the novel by Nevil Shute. Music by Ernest Gold. Song by Marie Cowan and A. B. Patterson, "Waltzing Matilda." Costumes, Joe King. Assistant Director, Ivan Volkman. Art Director, Fernando Carrere. Cinematographer, Giuseppe Rotunno. Auto Race Photography, Daniel Fapp. Editor, Frederic Knudtson. Produced in Australia. Production Design, Rudolph Sternad. Production Manager, Clem Beauchamp. Special Effects, Lee Zavitz. Sound, Hans Wetzel. Make-up, John O'Gorman and Frank Prehoda. Hairstyles, Jane Shugrue. Technical Advisor, Admiral Charles A. Lockwood. Film debut of Donna Anderson, 19. 133 minutes

Dwight Towers: Gregory Peck, *Moira Davidson:* Ava Gardner, *Julian Osborn:* Fred Astaire, *Peter Holmes:* Anthony Perkins, *Mary Holmes:* Donna Anderson, *Admiral Bridie:* John Tate, *Lieutenant Hosgood:* Lola Brooks, *Davidson:* Lou Vernon, *Farrel:* Guy Doleman, *Benson:* Ken Wayne, *Swain:* John Meillon, *Davis:* Richard Meikle, *Sundstrom:* Harp McGuire, *Chrysler:* Jim Barrett, *Sir Douglas Froude:* Basil Buller Murphy, *Dr. Fletcher:* Keith Eden, *Senior Officer:* John Royle, *Radio Officer:* Frank Gatcliff, *Port Man:* Paddy Moran, *Salvation Army Captain:* John Casson, *Dr. King:* Kevin Brennan, *Dykers:* C. Harding Brown, *Morgan:* Grant Taylor, *Professor Jorgenson:* Peter Williams, *Sykes:* Harvey Adams, *Jones:* Stuart Finch, *Ackerman:* Joe McCormick, *Betty:* Audine Leith, *Fogarty, Sonar Operator:* Jerry Ian Seals, *Boy:* Carey Paul Peck, *Jennifer Holmes:* Katherine Hill.

On the Beach with Ava Gardner and Gregory Peck.

ON THE TOWN (1949) MGM. Produced by Arthur Freed. Directed by Gene Kelly and Stanley Donen. Color by Technicolor. Screenplay, Adolph Green and Betty Comden. Based on the musical; book and lyrics by Comden and Green, music by Leonard Bernstein, from an idea by Jerome Robbins. New songs by Roger Edens, Comden and Green. Songs: "New York, New York," "Miss Turnstiles," "Prehistoric Man," "Come Up to My Place," "Main Street," "You're Awful," "On the Town," "Count on Me," "A Day in New York." Score, Roger Edens and Lennie Hayton. Musical Director, Lennie Hayton.

On the Town with Jules Munshin, Ann Miller, Gene Kelly, Betty Garrett and Frank Sinatra.

Art Directors, Cedric Gibbons and Jack Martin Smith. Photography, Harold Rosson. Editor, Ralph E. Winters. Filmed in New York City. Alice Pearce repeats her role from the 1944 musical. 98 minutes

Gabey: Gene Kelly, *Chip:* Frank Sinatra, *Brunhilde Esterhazy:* Betty Garrett, *Claire Huddesen:* Ann Miller, *Ozzie:* Jules Munshin, *Ivy Smith:* Vera-Ellen, *Madame Dilyovska:* Florence Bates, *Lucy Shmeeler:* Alice Pearce, *Professor:* George Meader, *Worker ("New York, New York"):* Bern Hoffman, *Subway Passenger:* Lester Dorr, *Working Girl:* Bea Benaderet, *Sign Poster:* Walter Baldwin, *Photo Layout Man:* Don Brodie, *Spud:* Sid Melton, *Officer, Car 44:* Robert B. Williams, *Officer Tracy, Car 44:* Tom Dugan, *Cab Company Owner:* Murray Alper, *François, Headwaiter:* Hans Conreid, *Redhead:* Claire Carleton, *Sailor Simpkins:* Dick Wessel, *Sailor:* William "Bill" Phillips, *Cop:* Frank Hagney, *Dancer in Green ("A Day in New York"):* Carol Haney.

ON THE RIVIERA (1951) 20th. Producer, Sol C. Siegel. Director, Walter Lang. Color by Technicolor. Screenplay, Phoebe and Henry Ephron. Based on a play by Rudolph Lothar and Hans Adler. Adapted by Jessie Ernst. Songs: "On the Riviera," "Popo the Puppet," "Rhythm of a New Romance," "Happy Ending," by Sylvia Fine. "Ballin' the Jack" by Chris Smith. Technicolor Consultant, Leonard Doss. Musical Direction, Alfred Newman. Photography, Leon Shamroy. Art Direction, Lyle Wheeler, Leland Fuller. Musical Settings, Joseph C. Wright. Set Decorations, Thomas Little, Walter M. Scott. Editor, J. Watson Webb, Jr. Wardrobe, Charles Le Maire. Costumes designed by Travilla. Costumes for Miss Tierney designed by Oleg Cassini. Dances staged by Jack Cole. Vocal Direction, Jeff Alexander. Orchestration, Earle Hagon, Edward Powell. Make-up, Ben Nye. Photographic Effects, Fred Sersen. Sound, E. Clayton Ward, Roger Heman. Remake of *Folies Bergere* (UA, 1935), and *That Night in Rio* (20th, 1941). 89 minutes

On the Riviera with Jean Murat, Danny Kaye, Gene Tierney and Ann Codee.

Henri Duran and Jack Martin: Danny Kaye, *Lilli:* Gene Tierney, *Colette:* Corinne Calvet, *Philippe Lebrix:* Marcel Dalio, *Periton:* Jean Murat, *Louis Forel:* Henri Letondal, *Antoine:* Clinton Sundberg, *Gapeaux:* Sig Rumann, *Mimi:* Joyce MacKenzie, *Minette:* Monique Chantal, *Mme. Cornet:* Marina Koshetz, *Mme. Periton:* Ann Codee, *Eugenie:* Mari Blanchard, *Dance Team:* Ethel Martin, George Martin, Vernal "Buzz" Miller, *Specialty Dancers:* Ellen Ray, Gwyneth Verdon (Gwen Verdon), *Spanish Dancer:* Rosario Imperio, *Chef:* Antonio Filauri, *Andre:* Charles Andre, *Elna Petrovna:* Franchesca Di Scaffa, *Marilyn Turner:* Joi Lansing, *Announcer:* Eugene Borden, *Airport Official:* Albert Pollet, *Leon:* George Davis.

ON THE WATERFRONT (1954) Col. Producer, Sam Spiegel. Director, Elia Kazan. Screenplay, Budd Schulberg, from his story based on articles by Malcolm Johnson. Music by Leonard Bernstein. Filmed in New York City and Hoboken, New Jersey. Eva Marie Saint's film debut. 108 minutes

Terry Malloy: Marlon Brando, *Father Barry:* Karl Malden, *Johnny Friendly:* Lee J. Cobb, *Charles Malloy:* Rod Steiger, *"Kayo" Dugan:* Pat Henning, *Edie Doyle:* Eva Marie Saint, *Glover:* Leif Erickson, *Big Mac:* James Westerfield, *Truck:* Tony Galento, *Tillio:* Tami Mauriello, *"Pop" Doyle:* John Hamilton, *Mott:* John Heldabrand, *Moose:* Rudy Bond, *Luke:* Don Blackman, *Jimmy:* Arthur Keegan, *Barney:* Abe Simon, *J. P.:* Barry Macollum, *Specs:* Mike O'Dowd, *Gillette:* Marty Balsam, *Slim:* Fred Gwynne, *Tommy:* Thomas Handley, *Mrs. Collins:* Anne Hegira, *Cab Driver:* Nehemiah Persoff.

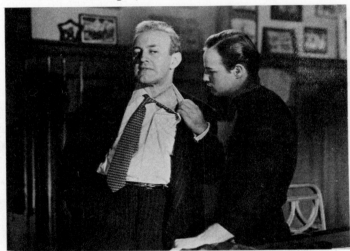

On the Waterfront with Lee J. Cobb and Marlon Brando.

OPERATION CROSSBOW (1965) MGM. Producer, Carlo Ponti. Director, Michael Anderson. Panavision, MetroColor. Screenplay, Richard Imrie, Derry Quinn, Ray Rigby. Music, Ron Goodwin. Director of Photography, Erwin Hillier. Assistant Director, Basil Rayburn. Subtitles, Bernard Doret. Subsequently called *The Great Spy Manhunt*. 116 minutes

Operation Crossbow with Sophia Loren and George Peppard.

Nora: Sophia Loren, *John Curtis:* George Peppard, *Professor Linde-mann:* Trevor Howard, *Boyd of M. I. 6:* John Mills, *Duncan Sandys:* Richard Johnson, *Robert Hendshaw:* Tom Courtenay, *Phil Bradley:* Jeremy Kemp, *Bamford:* Anthony Quayle, *Frieda:* Lilli Palmer, *Zie-mann:* Paul Henreid, *Linz:* Helmut Dantine, *Hanna Reitsch:* Barbara Rueting, *Wing Comdr. Kendall:* Richard Todd, *Constance Babington Smith:* Sylvia Syms, *Flight Lieutenant Kenny:* John Fraser, *R. A. F. Officer:* Maurice Denham, *Winston Churchill:* Patrick Wymark, *Professor Hoffer:* Karl Stepanek, *Colonel Kenneth Post:* Moray Watson, *Sir Charles Sims:* Richard Wattis, *German Technical Examiner:* Allan Cuthbertson, *Air Commodore:* Robert Brown.

OPERATION PACIFIC (1951) WB. Produced by Louis F. Edelman. Director, George Waggner. Story and Screenplay, George Waggner. Art Director, Leo K. Kuter. Music, Max Steiner. Photography, Bert Glennon. Editor, Alan Crosland, Jr. Filmed partly in Honolulu. Cary Grant is seen in a clip from *Destination Tokyo* (1943). 111 minutes

Commander Duke Gifford: John Wayne, *Mary Stuart:* Patricia Neal, *Captain Pop Perry:* Ward Bond, *Larry:* Scott Forbes, *Bob Perry:* Philip Carey, *Jonesy:* Paul Picerni, *The Talker:* Bill Campbell, *Commander Steele:* Kathryn Givney, *Caldwell:* Martin Milner, *Comsubpac:* Cliff Clark, *The Chief:* Jack Pennick, *Sister Anna:* Virginia Brissac, *Soundman:* Vincent Fotre, *Squad Commander:* Lewis Martin, *Junior:* Sam Edwards, *Radarman:* Louis Mosconi, *Herbie:* Gayle Kellogg, *Rafferty:* Steve Wayne, *Quartermaster:* Bob Nash, *Helmsman:* William Self, *Shore Patrolman:* Carl Saxe, *Shore Patrol Chief, Mick:* James Flavin, *Hawaiian:* Al Kikume, *Torpedo Officer:* Bob Carson, *Talker:* Ray Hyke, *Radioman, Sparks:* Chris Drake, *Sub Commander, Freddie:* Harry Lauter, *Briefing Officer, USAF:* Carleton Young, *Commander:* Harlan Warde, *Fighter Pilot:* John Baer, *Japanese Flyer:* Richard Loo.

Operation Pacific with John Wayne and Ward Bond.

OPERATION PETTICOAT (1959) Univ. Produced by Robert Arthur. Directed by Blake Edwards. In Eastman Color. Story, Paul

Operation Petticoat with Tony Curtis and Dina Merrill.

King and Joseph Stone. Screenplay, Stanley Shapiro and Maurice Richlin. Music, David Rose. Art Directors, Alexander Golitzen and Robert E. Smith. Gowns, Bill Thomas. Assistant Directors, Frank Shaw, Wilson Shyer, and Charles Scott. Photography, Russell Harlan. Special Photography, Clifford Stine. Editors, Ted J. Kent and Frank Gross. A Granart Production. Filmed at Key West, Florida and on the submarine *Balboa*. 124 minutes

Admiral Matt Sherman: Cary Grant, *Lieutenant Nick Holden:* Tony Curtis, *Lieutenant Dolores Crandall:* Joan O'Brien, *Lieutenant Barbara Duran:* Dina Merrill, *Sam Tostin:* Arthur O'Connell, *Molumphrey:* Gene Evans, *Stovall:* Richard Sargent, *Major Edna Hayward:* Virginia Gregg, *Captain J. B. Henderson:* Robert F. Simon, *Watson:* Robert Gist, *Ernest Hunkle:* Gavin MacLeod, *The Prophet:* George Dunn, *Harmon:* Dick Crockett, *Lieutenant Claire Reid:* Madlyn Rhue, *Lieutenant Ruth Colfax:* Marion Ross, *Ramon:* Clarence E. Lung, *Dooley:* Frankie Darro, *Fox:* Tony Pastor, Jr., *Kraus:* Nicky Blair, *Williams:* John Morley, *Reiner:* Robert Hoy, *Control Talker:* Glenn Jacobson, *Crewman:* Nino Tempo, *Filipino Farmer:* Leon Lontoc, *Lieutenant Commander Daly:* James F. Lanphier, *Navy Chief:* Alan Dexter, *Admiral Koenig:* Nelson Leigh, *Captain Kress:* Francis De Sales, *Lieutenant Colonel Simpson:* Preston Hanson, *M.P. Sergeant:* Hal Baylor, *Marine Lieutenant:* Bob Stratton, *Soldier:* Harry Harvey, Jr., *Pregnant Filipino Woman:* Vi Ingraham, *Chief of Demolition Crew:* Alan Scott, *Third Class Petty Officer:* Francis L. Ward, *Lieutenant Morrison:* William R. Callinan, *Colonel Higginson:* Gordon Casell, *Witch Doctor:* Tusi Faiivae.

OUR MAN FLINT (1966) 20th. Saul David production. Director, Daniel Mann. CinemaScope, De Luxe Color. Screenplay, Hal Fimberg, Ben Starr. Based on story by Fimberg. Camera, Daniel L. Fapp. Music, Jerry Goldsmith. Editor, William Reynolds. Art Direction, Jack Martin Smith and Ed Graves. Special action scenes by Buzz Henry. 107 minutes

Derek Flint: James Coburn, *Cramden:* Lee J. Cobb, *Gila:* Gila Golan, *Malcolm Rodney:* Rodney Mulhare, *Dr. Wu:* Benson Fong, *Leslie:* Shelby Grant, *Anna:* Sigrid Valdis, *Gina:* Gianna Serra, *Sakito:* Helen Funai, *Gruber:* Michael St. Clair, *Dr. Krupov:* Rhys Williams, *American General:* Russ Conway, *Wac:* Ena Hartman, *American Diplomat:* William Walker, *Dr. Schneider:* Peter Brocco.

Our Man Flint with Lee J. Cobb and James Coburn.

OUR TOWN (1940) UA. Produced by Sol Lesser. Directed by Sam Wood. A Principal Artists Production. From the Pulitzer Prize play by Thornton Wilder. Screenplay, Thornton Wilder, Frank Craven, and Harry Chandlee. Music, Aaron Copland. Orchestra Director, Irvin Talbot. Production Designer, William Cameron Menzies. Associate, Harry Horner. Photography, Bert Glennon. Editor, Sherman Todd. Craven and Scott repeat their stage roles. Scott in film debut. 90 minutes

Our Town with Martha Scott and William Holden.

Mr. Morgan, The Narrator: Frank Craven, George Gibbs: William Holden, Emily Webb: Martha Scott, Dr. Gibbs: Thomas Mitchell, Mrs. Gibbs: Fay Bainter, Editor Webb: Guy Kibbee, Mrs. Webb: Beulah Bondi, Howie Newsome: Stuart Erwin, Simon Stimson: Phillip Wood, Rebecca Gibbs: Ruth Toby, Wally Webb: Douglas Gardiner, Constable: Spencer Charters, Mrs. Soames: Doro Merande, Professor Willett: Arthur Allen, Reverend: Charles Trowbridge, Joe Crowell: Tim Davis, Si Crowell: Dix Davis, Wedding Guest: Dan White.

OUR VERY OWN (1950) RKO. Producer, Samuel Goldwyn. Director, Dave Miller. Author-Screenplay, F. Hugh Herbert. Music, Victor Young. Art Director, Richard Day. Photography, Lee Garmes. Editor, Sherman Todd. 93 minutes

Gail: Ann Blyth, Chuck: Farley Granger, Joan: Joan Evans, Lois Macaulay: Jane Wyatt, Mrs. Lynch: Ann Dvorak, Fred Macaulay: Donald Cook, Penny: Natalie Wood, Frank: Gus Schilling, Zaza: Phyllis Kirk, Violet: Jessie Grayson, Bert: Martin Milner, Gwendolyn: Rita Hamilton, Mr. Lynch: Ray Teal.

Our Very Own with Jane Wyatt and Ann Blyth.

THE OUTLAW (1943) RKO. Produced and directed by Howard Hughes. Screenplay, Jules Furthman. Music Director, Victor Young. Photography, Gregg Toland. Editor, Wallace Grissell. Photographic Effects, Roy Davidson. Originally scheduled for United Artists release in 1941, this was officially distributed in 1950. Film debuts of Jane Russell and Jack Buetel. 123 minutes

Rio: Jane Russell, Billy the Kid: Jack Buetel, Pat Garrett: Thomas Mitchell, Doc Holliday: Walter Huston, Aunt Guadalupe: Mimi Aguglia, Woodruff: Joe Sawyer, Dolan: Emory Parnell, Waiter: Martin Garralaga, Pablo: Julian Rivero.

The Outlaw with Thomas Mitchell, Walter Huston, Jane Russell and Jack Beutel.

OUTWARD BOUND (1930) WB. Directed by Robert Milton. Based on the play by Sutton Vane, first produced in London in 1923. Scenario, J. Grubb Alexander. Photography, Hal Mohr. Editor, Ralph Dawson. Film debut of Leslie Howard, who was Henry in the play. Remade as *Between Two Worlds* (Warners, 1944), *The Flight That Disappeared* (United Artists, 1961). 82 minutes

Outward Bound with Alec B. Francis, Helen Chandler and Douglas Fairbanks, Jr.

Tom Prior: Leslie Howard, Henry: Douglas Fairbanks, Jr., Ann: Helen Chandler, Mrs. Midget: Beryl Mercer, Scrubby: Alec B. Francis, Mrs. Cliveden-Banks: Alison Skipworth, Reverend William Duke: Lyonel Watts, Mr. Lingley: Montagu Love, Thompson, The Examiner: Dudley Digges, The Policeman: Walter Kingsford, Dog: Laddie.

THE OX-BOW INCIDENT (1943) 20th. Produced by Lamar Trotti. Directed by William A. Wellman. Based on the novel by Walter Van Tilburg Clark. Screenplay, Lamar Trotti. Art Directors, Richard Day and James Basevi. Photography, Arthur Miller. Music, Cyril J. Mockridge. Editor, Allen McNeil. Adapted for TV's 20th Century-Fox Hour in 1956. 75 minutes

Gil Carter: Henry Fonda, Martin: Dana Andrews, Rose Mapen: Mary Beth Hughes, Mexican: Anthony Quinn, Gerald: William Eythe, Art Croft: Henry Morgan, Ma Grier: Jane Darwell, Judge Tyler: Matt Briggs, Davies: Harry Davenport, Major Tetley: Frank Conroy, Farnley: Marc Lawrence, Darby: Victor Kilian, Monty Smith: Paul Hurst, Poncho: Chris-Pin Martin, Joyce: Ted (Michael) North, Mr. Swanson: George Meeker, Mrs. Swanson: Almira Sessions, Mrs. Larch: Margaret Hamilton, Mapes: Dick Rich, Old Man: Francis Ford, Bartlett: Stanley Andrews, Greene: Billy Benedict, Hart: Rondo Hatton, Winder: Paul Burns, Sparks: Leigh Whipper, Moore: George Lloyd, Jimmy Cairnes: George Chandler, Red: Hank Bell, Mark: Forrest Dillon, Alec Small: George Plues, Sheriff: Willard Robertson, Deputy: Tom London.

The Ox-Bow Incident with Anthony Quinn, Dick Rich, Francis Ford, Dana Andrews, George Lloyd, Henry Fonda, Rondo Hatton, Frank Conroy and Jane Darwell.

THE PAJAMA GAME (1957) WB.

Produced by George Abbott and Stanley Donen. Associate Producers, Frederick Brisson, Robert E. Griffith, and Harold S. Prince. Directed by George Abbott and Stanley Donen. WarnerColor. Screenplay by George Abbott and Richard Bissell, from their musical based on Richard Bissell's novel *7.5 Cents.* Choreography, Bob Fosse. Art Director, Malcolm Bert. Orchestral Arrangements, Nelson Riddle and Buddy Bregman. Photography, Harry Stradling. Editor, William Ziegler. Costumes, William and Jean Eckart, assisted by Frank Thompson. Assistant Director, Russ Llewellyn. Sound, M. A. Merrick and Dolph Thomas. Songs by Richard Adler and Jerry Ross: "The Pajama Game," "I'm Not at All in Love," "Hey There," "Once-a-Year-Day," "Small Talk," "There Once Was a Man," "Steam Heat," "Hernando's Hideaway," "Seven and a Half Cents," "Her Is," "Racing With the Clock," "I'll Never Be Jealous Again." Technical Adviser, Weldon Pajama Company. Filmed in part at Hollenbeck Park, L. A. Repeating their roles from the 1954 musical: Raitt, Foy, Haney, Shaw, Dunn, Chambers, Miller, Pelish, Waldron, Gennaro, LeRoy. 101 minutes

(Katie) Babe Williams: Doris Day, *Sid Sorokin:* John Raitt, *Gladys Hotchkiss:* Carol Haney, *Vernon Hines:* Eddie Foy, Jr., *Mabel:* Reta Shaw, *Poopsie:* Barbara Nichols, *Mae:* Thelma Pelish, *Prez:* Jack Straw, *Hasler:* Ralph Dunn, *Max:* Owen Martin, *First Helper:* Jackie Kelk, *Charlie:* Ralph Chambers, *Brenda:* Mary Stanton, *Dancers:* Buzz Miller, Kenneth LeRoy, *Salesman:* Jack Waldron, *Second Helper:* Ralph Volkie, *Pop Williams:* Franklyn Fox, *Joe:* William A. Forester, *Dancer:* Peter Gennaro, *Waiter:* Elmore Henderson, *Tony,* *Headwaiter:* Fred Villani, *Holly:* Kathy Marlowe, *Otis:* Otis Griffith.

The Pajama Game with John Raitt and Doris Day.

The Paleface with George Chandler, Bob Hope and Nestor Paiva.

THE PALEFACE (1948) Par.

Produced by Robert L. Welch. Directed by Norman Z. McLeod. Color by Technicolor. Original Screenplay, Edmund Hartmann and Frank Tashlin. Additional Dialogue, Jack Rose. Art Directors, Hans Dreier and Earl Hedrick. Music, Victor Young. Dances, Billy Daniel. Photography, Ray Rennahan. Technicolor Director, Natalie Kalmus. Editor, Ellsworth Hoagland. Songs: "Buttons and Bows" and "Meetcha 'Round the Corner" by Jay Livingston and Ray Evans, and "Get a Man" by Joseph J. Lilley. The sequel was *Son of Paleface* (1952). 91 minutes

Painless Peter Potter: Bob Hope, *Calamity Jane:* Jane Russell, *Terris:* Robert Armstrong, *Pepper:* Iris Adrian, *Toby Preston:* Robert (Bobby) Watson, *Jasper Martin:* Jackie Searl, *Indian Scout:* Joseph Vitale, *Wapato, Medicine Man:* Henry Brandon, *Governor Johnson:* Charles Trowbridge, *Hank Billings:* Clem Bevans, *Joe:* Jeff York, *Commissioner Emerson:* Stanley Andrews, *Jeb:* Wade Crosby, *Chief Yellow Feather:* Chief Yowlachie, *Chief Iron Eyes:* Iron Eyes Cody, *Village Gossip:* John Maxwell, *Bartender:* Tom Kennedy, *Lance:* Francis J. McDonald, *Greg:* Frank Hagney, *Pete:* Skelton Knaggs, *Undertaker:* Olin Howlin, *First Patient:* George Chandler, *Second Patient:* Nestor Paiva, *Clem:* Earl Hodgins, *Zach:* Arthur Space, *Sheriff:* Edgar Dearing, *Mr. X:* Charles Cooley, *Bath House Attendant:* Dorothy Granger, *Bob:* Eric Alden, *Woman in Bath House:* Jody Gilbert, *Pioneer:* Al M. Hill, *Justice of the Peace:* Harry Harvey, *Handsome Cowboy:* Hall Bartlett, *Onlooker:* Stanley Blystone, *Onlooker:* Bob Kortman, *Character:* Oliver Blake, *Tough Galoot:* Lane Chandler, *Cowboy:* Syd Saylor, *Justice of the Peace:* Paul E. Burns, *The Mayor:* Dick Elliott, *Child:* Sharon McManus.

PAL JOEY (1957) Col.

Produced by Fred Kohlmar. Directed by George Sidney. Color by Technicolor. From the musical play and book by John O'Hara. Screenplay, Dorothy Kingsley. Music Adaptation, George Duning and Nelson Riddle. Choreography, Hermes Pan. Gowns, Jean Louis. Assistant Director, Art Black. Music supervised and conducted by Morris Stoloff. Art Director, Walter Holscher. Orchestration, Arthur Morton. Photography, Harold Lipstein. Editors, Viola Lawrence and Jerome Thoms. An Essex-George Sidney Production. Songs by Richard Rodgers and Lorenz Hart: "The Lady Is a Tramp," "I Didn't Know What Time It Was," "There's a Small

Pal Joey with Frank Sinatra and Kim Novak.

Hotel," "My Funny Valentine," "Bewitched, Bothered and Bewildered," "Zip," "What Do I Care for a Dame?", "I Could Write a Book," "Do It the Hard Way," "Big Town," "What Is a Man?" The 1941 play and 1952 revival had Joey as a dancer; the film changes him into a singer. 111 minutes

Joey Evans: Frank Sinatra, *Vera Simpson:* Rita Hayworth, *Linda English:* Kim Novak, *Gladys:* Barbara Nichols, *Ned Galvin:* Bobby Sherwood, *Mike Miggins:* Hank Henry, *Mrs. Casey:* Elizabeth Patterson, *Bartender:* Robin Morse, *Colonel Langley:* Frank Wilcox, *Mr. Forsythe:* Pierre Watkin, *Anderson:* Barry Bernard, *Carol:* Ellie Kent, *Sabrina:* Mara McAfee, *Patsy:* Betty Utey, *Lola:* Bek Nelson, *Specialty Dance Double:* Jean Corbett, *Detective:* Tol Avery, *Stanley:* John Hubbard, *Livingstone:* James Seay, *Policeman:* Robert Anderson, *Pet Store Owner:* Everett Glass, *Barker:* Frank Sully, *Shorty:* Henry McCann, *Chef Tony:* Ernesto Molinari, *Headwaiter:* George Nardelli, *Vera's Maid:* Giselle D'Arc, *Bit:* Bess Flowers, *Bit:* Franklyn Farnum, *Choreographer:* Hermes Pan.

PANIC IN THE STREETS (1950) 20th. Producer, Sol C. Siegel. Director, Elia Kazan. Authors, Edna Anhalt, Edward Anhalt (from *Quarantine, and Some Like 'em Cold*). Screenplay, Richard Murphy. Adaptation, Daniel Fuchs. Music, Alfred Newman. Art Directors, Lyle Wheeler, Maurice Ransford. Photography, Joe MacDonald. Editor, Harmon Jones. Filmed entirely in New Orleans. 93 minutes

Panic in the Streets with Richard Widmark and Paul Douglas.

Clinton Reed: Richard Widmark, *Police Captain Tom Warren:* Paul Douglas, *Nancy Reed:* Barbara Bel Geddes, *Blackie:* Walter (Jack) Palance, *Raymond Fitch:* Zero Mostel, *Neff:* Dan Riss, *John Mefaris:* Alexis Minotis, *Poldi:* Guy Thomajan, *Vince Poldi:* Tommy Cook, *Jordan:* Edward Kennedy, *Cook:* H. T. Tsiang, *Kochak:* Lewis Charles, *Dubin:* Raymond Muller, *Tommy Reed:* Tommy Rettig, *Jeanette:* Lonka Peterson, *Pat:* Pat Walshe, *Dr. Paul Gafney:* Paul Hostetler, *Kleber:* George Ehmig, *Lee:* John Schilleci, *Ben:* Waldo Pitkin, *Sergeant Phelps:* Leo Zinser, *Dr. Mackey:* Beverly C. Brown, *Cortelyou:* William Dean, *Murray:* H. Waller Fowler, Jr., *Wynant:* Rex Moad, *Johnston:* Irvine Vidacovich, *Commissioner Dan Quinn:* Val Winter, *Charlie:* Wilson Bourg, Jr., *Angie Fitch:* Mary Liswood, *Rita Mefaris:* Aline Stevens, *Redfield:* Stanley J. Reyes, *Violet:* Darwin Greenfield, *Captain Beauclyde:* Emile Meyer, *Scott:* Herman Cottman, *Al:* Al Theriot, *Hotel Proprietor:* Juan Villasana, *Coast Guard Lieutenant:* Robert Dorsen, *Anson:* Henry Mamet, *Bosun:* Tiger Joe Marsh, *Lascar Boy:* Arthur Tong.

THE PARADINE CASE (1948) Selznick Releasing Organization. Produced by David O. Selznick. Directed by Alfred Hitchcock. A Vanguard Films Production. Based on the novel by Robert Hichens. Screenplay, David O. Selznick. Adaptation, Alma Reville and James Bridie. Music, Franz Waxman. Production Design, J. McMillan Johnson. Art Director, Thomas Morahan. Photography, Lee Garmes.

The Paradine Case with Ann Todd, Charles Coburn and Gregory Peck.

Editor, Hal C. Kern. Associate, John Faure. American film debuts of Louis Jourdan and Alida Valli. 131 minutes

Anthony Keane: Gregory Peck, *Lord Horfield:* Charles Laughton, *Sir Simon Flaquer:* Charles Coburn, *Gay Keane:* Ann Todd, *Lady Horfield:* Ethel Barrymore, *Andre Latour:* Louis Jourdan, *Mrs. Paradine:* Valli, *Sir Joseph Farrell:* Leo G. Carroll, *Judy Flaquer:* Joan Tetzel, *Keeper at Inn:* Isobel Elsom, *Man Carrying a Cello:* Alfred Hitchcock.

PARAMOUNT ON PARADE (1930) Par. Supervision, Elsie Janis. Directors, Dorothy Arzner, Otto Brower, Edmund Goulding, Victor Heerman, Edwin H. Knopf, Rowland V. Lee, Ernst Lubitsch, Lothar Mendes, Victor Schertzinger, Edward Sutherland, Frank Tuttle. With Technicolor sequences. Photography, Harry Fischbeck and Victor Milner. Songs: "Paramount on Parade," "I'm True to the Navy Now" and "Anytime Is the Time to Fall in Love" by Elsie Janis and Jack King; "Sweeping the Clouds Away" by Sam Coslow; "All I Want Is Just One Girl" by Leo Robin and Richard Whiting; "Dancing to Save Your Soul," "I'm in Training for You" and "Drink to the Girl of My Dreams" by L. Wolfe Gilbert and Abel Baer; "Come Back to Sorrento" by Leo Robin and Ernesto De Curtis; "My Marine" by Ray Egan and Richard Whiting, "What Did Cleopatra Say?" by Janis and King; "We're the Masters of Ceremony" by Ballard MacDonald and Dave Dreyer; "I'm Isadore the Toreador" by David Franklin. Dances directed by David Bennett. 102 minutes

Specialties: Richard Arlen, Jean Arthur, William Austin, George Bancroft, Clara Bow, Evelyn Brent, Mary Brian, Virginia Bruce, Nancy Carroll, Ruth Chatterton, Maurice Chevalier, Gary Cooper, Leon Errol, Stuart Erwin, Kay Francis, Skeets Gallagher, Harry Green, Mitzi Green, James Hall, Phillips Holmes, Helen Kane, Dennis King, Abe Lyman and his Band, Fredric March, Nino Martini, Mitzi Mayfair, David Newell, Jack Oakie, Zelma O'Neal, Joan Peers, Charles "Buddy" Rogers, Lillian Roth, Stanley Smith, Fay Wray, *Sherlock Holmes:* Clive Brook, *Dr. Fu Manchu:* Warner Oland, *Sergeant*

Paramount on Parade with Maurice Chevalier and Evelyn Brent.

Heath: Eugene Pallette, *Philo Vance:* William Powell, *Chorus Girl (Chevalier Number):* Iris Adrian, *Bench Sitter:* Rolfe Sedan, *Guest:* Henry Fink, The Marion Morgan Dancers, *Soldier:* Jack Pennick, *Guest:* Mischa Auer, *Egyptian:* Robert Greig, *Hostess:* Cecil Cunningham, *Himself:* Edmund Goulding.

PARIS HOLIDAY (1958) UA. Producer, Robert Hope. Director, Gerd Oswald. Screenplay by Edmund Beloin and Dean Riesner. Based on story by Robert Hope. Music by Joseph J. Lilley. Associate Producer, Cecil Foster Kemp. Costumes by Pierre Balmain. Assistant Director, Paul Feyder. A Tolda Production in Technirama and Technicolor. Filmed in Paris and Hollywood. 100 minutes

Robert Leslie Hunter: Bob Hope, *Fernydel:* Fernandel, *Zara:* Anita Ekberg, *Ann McCall:* Martha Hyer, *Serge Vitry:* Preston Sturges, *American Ambassador:* Andre Morell, *Bits:* Alan Gifford, Maurice Teynac, Yves Brainville, Jean Murat.

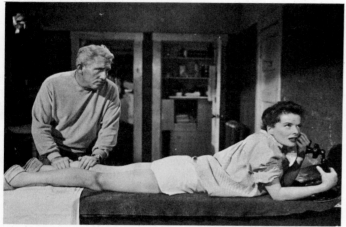

Paris Holiday with Anita Ekberg and Bob Hope.

PARRISH (1961) WB. Producer and Director, Delmer Daves. Technicolor. From the novel by Mildred Savage. Screenplay, Delmer Daves. Art Director, Leo K. Kuter. Music, Max Steiner. Songs, John Barracudo, Alfonso Marshall, Terry Carter. Orchestration, Murray Cutter. Cinematographer, Harry Stradling, Sr. Editor, Owen Marks. Locations filmed in Connecticut. 137 minutes

Parrish McLean: Troy Donahue, *Ellen McLean:* Claudette Colbert, *Judd Raike:* Karl Malden, *Sala Post:* Dean Jagger, *Alison Post:* Diane McBain, *Lucy:* Connie Stevens, *Paige Raike:* Sharon Hugueny, *Teet Howie:* Dub Taylor, *Edgar Raile:* Hampton Fancher, *Evaline:* Saundra Edwards, *Mary Howie:* Hope Summers, *Rosie:* Bibi Osterwald, *Addie:* Madeleine Sherwood, *Eileen:* Sylvia Miles, *Gladstone:* Alfonso Marshall, *Willis:* John Barracudo, *Cartwright:* Terry Carter, *John Donati:* Ford Rainey, *Tully:* Edgar Stehli, *Gramma:* Sara Taft, *Maples:* Wade Dumas, *Skipper:* John McGovern, *Tom Weldon:*

Parrish with Dean Jagger, Troy Donahue and Diane McBain.

Hayden Rorke, *Maizie Weldon:* Irene Windust, *Max Maine:* Don Dillaway, *Miss Daly:* Gertrude Flynn, *Oermeyer:* House Jameson, *Lemmie:* Ken Allen, *Operator:* Karen Norris, *Foreman:* Frank Campanella, *Firechief:* Carroll O'Connor, *Gas Station Attendant:* Vincent Gardenia, *Bandleader:* Bernie Richards, *Mr. Gilliam:* Martin Eric.

Pat and Mike with Spencer Tracy and Katharine Hepburn.

PAT AND MIKE (1952) MGM. Producer, Lawrence Weingarten. Director, George Cukor. Story and Screenplay, Ruth Gordon, Garson Kanin. Music, David Raskin. Art Directors, Cedric Gibbons, Urie McCleary. Cinematographer, William Daniels. Editor, George Boemler. 94 minutes

Mike Conovan: Spencer Tracy, *Pat Pemberton:* Katharine Hepburn, *Davie Hucko:* Aldo Ray, *Collier Weld:* William Ching, *Barney Grau:* Sammy White, *Spec Cauley:* George Mathews, *Mr. Beminger:* Loring Smith, *Mrs. Beminger:* Phyllis Povah, *Hank Tasling:* Charles Buchinski (Bronson), *Sam Garsell:* Frank Richards, *Charles Barry:* Jim Backus, *Police Captain:* Chuck Connors, *Gibby:* Joseph E. Bernard, *Harry MacWade:* Owen McGiveney, *Waiter:* Lou Lubin, *Bus Boy:* Carl Switzer, *Pat's Caddy:* William Self, *Caddies:* Billy McLean, Frankie Darro, Paul Brinegar, "Tiny" Jimmie Kelly, *Women Golfers:* Mae Clarke, Helen Eby-Rock, Elizabeth Holmes, *Commentator:* Hank Weaver, *Sportscaster:* Tom Harmon, *Themselves:* Gussie Moran, Babe Didrikson Zaharias, Don Budge, Alice Marble, Frank Parker, Betty Hicks, Beverly Hanson, Helen Dettweiler.

The Pawnbroker with Rod Steiger and Brock Peters.

THE PAWNBROKER (1965) Landau-Unger. Executive Producer, Worthington Miner. Director, Sidney Lumet. Screenplay, David Friedkin, Morton Fine. Based on novel by Edward Lewis Wallant. Producers, Roger H. Lewis, Philip Langer. Director of Photography, Boris Kaufman. Music, Quincy Jones. Associate Producer, Joseph Manduke. Costumes, Anna Hill Johnstone. Assistant Director, Dan Eriksen. 110 minutes

Sol Nazerman: Rod Steiger, *Marilyn Birchfield:* Geraldine Fitzgerald, *Rodriguez:* Brock Peters, *Jesus Ortiz:* Jaime Sanchez, *Ortiz' Girl:* Thelma Oliver, *Tessie:* Marketa Kimbrell, *Mendel:* Baruch Lumet, *Mr. Smith:* Juano Hernandez, *Ruth:* Linda Geiser, *Bertha:* Nancy R. Pollock, *Tangee:* Raymond St. Jacques, *Buck:* John McCurry, *Robinson:* Ed Morehouse, *Mrs. Ortiz:* Eusebia Cosme, *Savarese:* Warren Finnerty, *Morton:* Jack Ader, *Papa:* E. M. Margolese, *Joan:* Marianne Kanter.

PEPE (1960) Col. Produced and directed by George Sidney. Associate Producer, Jacques Gelman. A George Sidney-Posa Films International Production. In CinemaScope and Eastman Color by Pathé. Based on a play by L. Bush-Fekete, *Broadway Zauber* (also called *Broadway Magic*). Screenplay, Dorothy Kingsley and Claude Binyon. Story, Leonard Spigelgass and Sonya Levien. Choreography, Eugene Loring and Alex Romero. Gowns, Edith Head. Assistant Director, David Silver. Art Director, Ted Haworth. Photography, Joe MacDonald. Editors, Viola Lawrence and Al Clark. Songs: "Pepe" by Hans Wittstatt and Dory Langdon; "The Faraway Part of Town" and "That's How It Went, All Right" by Andre Previn and Dory Langdon; "The Rumble" by Andre Previn; "Lovely Day" by Augustin Lara, Spanish lyrics by Maria Teresa Lara. Special English lyrics by Dory Langdon. Music Supervision and Background Score, Johnny Green. 195 minutes

Pepe: Cantinflas, *Ted Holt:* Dan Dailey, *Suzie Murphy:* Shirley Jones, *Rodriguez, the Auctioneer:* Carlos Montalban, *Lupita:* Vicki Trickett, *Dancer:* Matt Mattox, *Immigration Inspector:* Ernie Kovacs, *Dennis The Menace:* Jay North, *Studio Gateman:* William Demarest, *Manager:* Hank Henry, *Carmen:* Suzanne Lloyd, *Dancer:* Michael Callan, *Jewelry Salesman:* Stephen Bekassy, *Waitress:* Carol Douglas, *Charro:* Joe Hyams, *Second Immigration Officer:* Robert B. Williams, *Dowager:* Lela Bliss, *Assistant Director:* Ray Walker, *Priest:* Francisco Reguerra, *Girl:* Dorothy Abbott, *Senorita Dancer:* Shirley DeBurgh, *Dancer:* Bonnie Green, *Guest Stars:* Maurice Chevalier, Bing Crosby, Richard Conte, Bobby Darin, Sammy Davis, Jr., Jimmy Durante, Zsa Zsa Gabor, The Voice of Judy Garland, Greer Garson, Hedda Hopper, Joey Bishop, Peter Lawford, Janet Leigh, Jack Lemmon, Kim Novak, Andre Previn, Donna Reed, Debbie Reynolds, Edward G. Robinson, Cesar Romero, Frank Sinatra, Billie Burke, Ann B. "Schultzy" Davis, Tony Curtis, Dean Martin, Jack Entratter, Colonel E. E. Fogelson, Jane Robinson, Bunny Waters, Charles Coburn, Don Juan, Carlos Rivas.

Pepe with Cantinflas and Jack Lemmon.

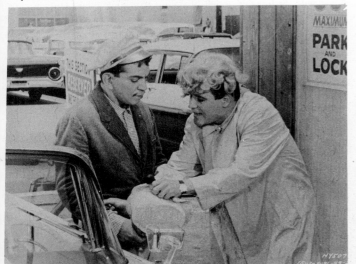

Pete Kelly's Blues with Jack Webb and Peggy Lee.

PETE KELLY'S BLUES (1955) WB. Director, Jack Webb. Assistant Director, Harry D'Arcy. Screenplay by Richard L. Breen. Costumes by Howard Shoup. Music by Ray Heindorf, Sammy Cahn and Arthur Hamilton. A Mark VII Production in CinemaScope and WarnerColor. Kelly's Big 7 arrangements by Matty Matlock. Cornet solo by Ted Buckner. Plantation scene filmed in Flemming, Louisiana. 95 minutes

Pete Kelly (Narrator): Jack Webb, *Ivy Conrad:* Janet Leigh, *Fran McCarg:* Edmond O'Brien, *Rose Hopkins:* Peggy Lee, *George Tenell:* Andy Devine, *Al Gannaway:* Lee Marvin, *Maggie Jackson:* Ella Fitzgerald, *Joey Firestone:* Martin Milner, *Cigarette Girl:* Jayne Mansfield, *Rudy:* Than Wyenn, *Bedido:* Herb Ellis, *Guy Bettenhouser:* John Dennis, *Cootie Jacobs:* Mort Marshall, *Squat Henchman:* Nesdon Booth, *Dako:* William Lazerus, *Cornetist:* Dick Cathcart, *Clarinetist:* Matty Matlock, *Trombonist:* Moe Schneider, *Saxophonist:* Eddie Miller, *Guitarist:* George Van Eps, *Drummer:* Nick Fatool, *Pianist:* Ray Sherman, *Bass Player:* Jud de Naut, *Waiter in Rudy's:* Snub Pollard. The Israelite Spiritual Church Choir of New Orleans.

THE PETRIFIED FOREST (1936) WB. Directed by Archie L. Mayo. Based on the play by Robert Sherwood. Screenplay, Charles Kenyon and Delmer Daves. Camera, Sol Polito. Editor, Owen Marks. 83 minutes

Alan Squier: Leslie Howard, *Gabrielle Maple:* Bette Davis, *Mrs. Chisholm:* Genevieve Tobin, *Boze Hertzlinger:* Dick Foran, *Duke Mantee:* Humphrey Bogart, *Jackie:* Joseph Sawyer, *Jason Maple:* Porter Hall, *Gramp Maple:* Charley Grapewin, *Mr. Chisholm:* Paul Harvey, *Lineman:* Eddie Acuff, *Ruby:* Adrian Morris, *Paula:* Nina Campana, *Slim:* Slim Thompson, *Joseph, the Chauffeur:* John Alexander, *Commander of Black Horse Troopers:* Arthur Aylesworth, *Trooper:* George Guhl, *Mantee's Girl:* Constance Bergen, *Second Lineman:* Francis Shide, *Postman:* Gus Leonard, *Sheriff:* James Farley, *Deputy:* Jack Cheatham.

The Petrified Forest with Humphrey Bogart, Leslie Howard and Bette Davis.

Peyton Place with Lana Turner and Diane Varsi.

PEYTON PLACE (1957) 20th. Producer, Jerry Wald. Director, Mark Robson. CinemaScope, De Luxe Color. Based on the novel by Grace Metalious. Screenplay, John Michael Hayes. Art Directors, Lyle R. Wheeler, Jack Martin Smith. Music, Franz Waxman. Orchestration, Edward B. Powell. Cinematographer, William Mellor. Special Photographic Effects, L. B. Abbott. Editor, David Brotherton. Later a TV series. 162 minutes

Constance MacKenzie: Lana Turner, *Selena Cross:* Hope Lange, *Michael Rossi:* Lee Philips, *Dr. Swain:* Lloyd Nolan, *Allison:* Diane Varsi, *Lucas Cross:* Arthur Kennedy, *Norman Page:* Russ Tamblyn, *Betty Anderson:* Terry Moore, *Rodney Harrington:* Barry Coe, *Ted Carter:* David Nelson, *Nellie Cross:* Betty Field, *Mrs. Thornton:* Mildred Dunnock, *Harrington:* Leon Ames, *Prosecutor:* Lorne Greene, *Seth Bushwell:* Robert H. Harris, *Margie:* Tami Connor, *Charles Partridge:* Staats Cotsworth, *Marion Partridge:* Peg Hillias, *Mrs. Page:* Erin O'Brien-Moore, *Joey Cross:* Scotty Morrow, *Paul Cross:* Bill Lundmark, *Matt:* Alan Reed, Jr., *Pee Wee:* Kip King, *Kathy:* Steffi Sidney, *Judge:* Tom Greenway, *Naval Officer:* Ray Montgomery, *Messenger:* Jim Brandt, *Miss Colton:* Edith Claire, *Army Sergeant:* John Doucette, *Bailiff:* Alfred Tonkel, *Cory Hyde:* Edwin Jerome, *Jury Foreman:* Bob Adler, *Court Clerk:* Harry Carter.

THE PHILADELPHIA STORY (1940) MGM. Produced by Joseph L. Mankiewicz. Directed by George Cukor. Based on the play by Philip Barry. Screenplay, Donald Ogden Stewart. Art Director, Cedric Gibbons. Associate, Wade B. Rubottom. Music, Franz Waxman. Photography, Joseph Ruttenberg. Editor, Frank Sullivan. Sound, Douglas Shearer. Set Decorations, Edwin B. Willis. Gowns, Adrian. Hair Styles, Sidney Guilaroff. Remade as a musical, *High Society* (MGM, 1956). 112 minutes

The Philadelphia Story with Katharine Hepburn, Ruth Hussey and James Stewart.

Dexter Haven: Cary Grant, *Tracy Lord:* Katharine Hepburn, *Mike Connor:* James Stewart, *Liz Imbrie:* Ruth Hussey, *George Kittredge:* John Howard, *Uncle Willie:* Roland Young, *Seth Lord:* John Halliday, *Dinah Lord:* Virginia Weidler, *Margaret Lord:* Mary Nash, *Sidney Kidd:* Henry Daniell, *Edward:* Lionel Pape, *Thomas:* Rex Evans, *John:* Russ Clark, *Librarian:* Hilda Plowright, *Manicurist:* Lita Chevret, *Bartender:* Lee Phelps, *Mac:* David Clyde, *Willie's Butler:* Claude King, *Dr. Parsons:* Robert de Bruce, *Elsie:* Veda Buckland, *First Mainliner:* Dorothy Fay, *Second Mainliner:* Florine McKinney, *Third Mainliner:* Helene Whitney, *Fourth Mainliner:* Hillary Brooke.

PICNIC (1955) Col. Producer, Fred Kohlmar. Director, Joshua Logan. CinemaScope, Technicolor. Based on the play by William Inge. Screenplay, Daniel Taradash. Art Director, William Flannery. Musical Director, Morris Stoloff. Music, George Duning. Orchestration, Arthur Morton. Cinematographer, James Wong Howe. Editors, Charles Nelson, William A. Lyon. Film debut of Susan Strasberg. 113 minutes

Hal Carter: William Holden, *Rosemary Sydney:* Rosalind Russell, *Madge Owens:* Kim Novak, *Flo Owens:* Betty Field, *Millie Owens:* Susan Strasberg, *Alan:* Cliff Robertson, *Howard Bevans:* Arthur O'Connell, *Mrs. Helen Potts:* Verna Felton, *Linde Sue Breckenridge:* Reta Shaw, *Bomber:* Nick Adams, *Mr. Benson:* Raymond Bailey, *Christine Schoenwalder:* Elizabeth W. Wilson, *Juanita Badger:* Phyllis Newman, *First Policeman:* Don C. Harvey, *Second Policeman:* Steve Benton, *President of Chamber of Commerce:* Henry P. Watson, *Trainman:* Abraham Weinlood, *Foreman:* Wayne R. Sullivan, *Stranger:* Warren Frederick Adams, *Grain Elevator Worker:* Carle E. Baker, *Mayor:* Henry Pegueo, *Committee Woman:* Flomanita Jackson, *Neighbor:* George E. Bemis.

Picnic with Arthur O'Connell, Rosalind Russell, William Holden and Susan Strasberg.

THE PIED PIPER (1942) 20th. Produced by Nunnally Johnson. Directed by Irving Pichel. Based on the novel, which appeared in *Collier's* magazine, by Nevil Shute. Screenplay, Nunnally Johnson. Art Directors, Richard Day and Maurice Ransford. Set Decorations, Thomas Little. Costumes, Dolly Tree. Score, Alfred Newman. Photography, Edward Cronjager. Editor, Allen McNeil. Sound, E. Clayton Ward and Roger Heman. 87 minutes

Howard: Monty Woolley, *Ronnie Cavanaugh:* Roddy McDowall, *Nicole Rougeron:* Anne Baxter, *Major Diessen:* Otto Preminger, *Aristide Rougeron:* J. Carrol Naish, *Mr. Cavanaugh:* Lester Matthews, *Mrs. Cavanaugh:* Jill Esmond, *Madame:* Ferike Boros, *Sheila Cavanaugh:* Peggy Ann Garner, *Willem:* Merrill Rodin, *Pierre:* Maurice Tauzin, *Rose:* Fleurette Zama, *Frenchman:* William Edmunds, *Foquet:* Marcel Dalio, *Madame Bonne:* Marcelle Corday, *Charendon:* Edward Ashley, *Roger Dickinson:* Morton Lowry, *Madame Rougeron:* Odette Myrtil, *Railroad Official:* Jean Del Val, *Barman:* George Davis, *Lieutenant:* Robert O. Davis, *Military Policeman:* Henry Rowland,

The Pied Piper with Roddy McDowall, Merrill Rodin, Fleurette Zama, Peggy Ann Garner, Monty Woolley, Ann Baxter and Maurice Tauzin.

Aide: Helmut Dantine, *German Soldiers:* Otto Reichow, Henry Guttman, *Sergeants:* Hans Von Morhart, Hans Von Twardowsky, *Officer at Road:* William Yetter, *Servant:* Adrienne d'Ambricourt, *Proprietress:* Mici Gory, *Fisherman:* Jean De Briac, *Soldier:* Ernst Hausman, *Anna:* Julika, *Waiter:* Wilson Benge, *Major Domo:* Brandon Hurst, *Medford:* Thomas Louden.

PIGSKIN PARADE (1936) 20th. Associate Producer, Bogart Rogers. Directed by David Butler. Story, Arthur Sheekman, Nat Perrin, and Mark Kelly. Screenplay, Harry Tugend, Jack Yellen, and William Conselman. Music Director, David Buttolph. Camera, Arthur Miller. Editor, Irene Morra. Songs by Sidney Mitchell and Lew Pollack: "It's Love I'm After," "The Balboa," "You're Slightly Terrific," "You Do the Darndest Things, Baby," "T. S. U. Alma Mater," "Hold That Bulldog," "The Texas Tornado." By Yacht Club Boys: "We'd Rather Be in College," "Down With Everything." Feature film debut of Judy Garland, 93 minutes

Amos Dodd: Stuart Erwin, *Bessie Winters:* Patsy Kelly, *Slug (Winston) Winters:* Jack Haley, *Chip Carson:* Johnny Downs, *Laura Watson:* Betty Grable, *Sally Saxon:* Arline Judge, *Ginger Jones:* Dixie Dunbar, *Sairy Dodd:* Judy Garland, *Tommy Barker:* Tony Martin, *Biff Bentley:* Fred Kohler, Jr., *Herbert Terwilliger Van Dyck:* Elisha Cook, Jr., *Sparks:* Eddie Nugent, *Mortimer Higgins:* Grady Sutton, *Doctor Burke:* Julius Tannen, *The Yacht Club Boys:* Themselves, *Radio Announcer (Himself):* Sam Hayes, *Country Boy:* Robert McClung, *Professor:* George Herbert, *Usher:* Jack Murphy, *Referee:* Pat Flaherty, *Messenger Boy:* Dave Sharpe, *Baggage Master:* Si Jenks, *Doctor:* John Dilson, *Policeman:* Jack Stoney, *Brakeman:* George Y. Harvey, *Boy in Stadium:* Ben Hall, *Girl in Stadium:* Lynn Bari, *Yale Coach:* Charles Wilson, *Freddy, Yale Reporter:* George Offerman, Jr., *Professor Tutweiler:* Maurice Cass, *Professor McCormick:* Jack Best, *Professor Dutton:* Douglas Wood, *Professor Pillsbury:* Charles Croker King, *Student:* Alan Ladd, *Judge:* Edward Le Saint.

Pigskin Parade with Judy Garland, Patsy Kelly, Johnny Downes and Betty Grable.

PILLOW TALK (1959) Univ. Producers, Ross Hunter and Martin Melcher. Director, Michael Gordon. Screenplay by Stanley Shapiro and Maurice Richlin. Based on story by Russell Rouse and Clarence Greene. Music by Frank DeVol. Gowns by Jean Louis. Assistant Director, Phil Bowles. Art Directors, Alexander Golitzen, Richard H. Riedel. Musical Director, Joseph Gershenson. Cinematographer, Arthur E. Arling. Special Photography, Clifford Stine, Roswell Hoffman. Editor, Milton Carruth. An Arwin Production in CinemaScope and Eastman Color. Songs: "Pillow Talk" by Buddy Pepper and Inez James; "I Need No Atmosphere," "You Lied," "Possess Me" and "Inspiration" by Joe Lubin and I. J. Roth; "Roly Poly" by Elsa Doran and Sol Lake. Locations filmed in New York City. 110 minutes

Brad Allen: Rock Hudson, *Jan Morrow:* Doris Day, *Jonathan Forbes:* Tony Randall, *Alma:* Thelma Ritter, *Tony Walters:* Nick Adams, *Marie:* Julia Meade, *Harry:* Allen Jenkins, *Pierot:* Marcel Dalio, *Mrs. Walters:* Lee Patrick, *Nurse Resnick:* Mary McCarty, *Dr. Maxwell:* Alex Gerry, *Mr. Conrad:* Hayden Rorke, *Eileen:* Valerie Allen, *Yvette:* Jacqueline Beer, *Tilda:* Arlen Stuart, *Singer:* Perry Blackwell, *Mr. Walters:* Don Beddoe, *Mr. Graham:* Robert B. Williams, *Fat Girl:* Muriel Landers, *Hotel Clerk:* William Schallert, *Miss Dickenson:* Karen Norris, *Jonathan's Secretary:* Lois Rayman, *Hansom Cabby:* Harry Tyler, *Dry Goods Man:* Joe Mell, *A Trucker:* Boyd (Red) Morgan, *A Singer:* Dorothy Abbott.

Pillow Talk with Doris Day and Tony Randall.

THE PINK PANTHER (1964) UA. Producer, Martin Jurow. Director, Blake Edwards. Technirama, Technicolor. Screenplay, Maurice Richlin, Blake Edwards. Associate Producer, Dick Crockett. Music, Henry Mancini. Director of Photography, Philip Lathrop. Assistant Director, Ottavio Oppo. Wardrobe principally by Yves St. Laurent. Presented by Mirisch Company. Song, "It Had Better Be Tonight" (Meglio Stasera) by Henry Mancini, Johnny Mercer, Franco Misliacci. 113 minutes

The Pink Panther with Capucine, Peter Sellers and Robert Wagner.

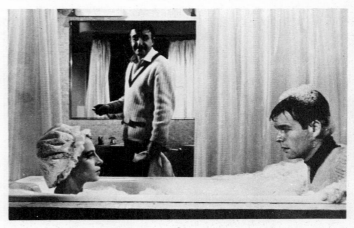

457

Sir Charles: David Niven, *Inspector Jacques Clouseau:* Peter Sellers, *George:* Robert Wagner, *Simone Clouseau:* Capucine, *Princess Dala:* Claudia Cardinale, *Angela Dunning:* Brenda De Banzie, *Greek "Cousin":* Fran Jeffries, *Tucker:* Colin Gordon, *Defense Attorney:* John LeMesurier, *Saloud:* James Lanphier, *Artoff:* Guy Thomajan, *Novelist:* Michael Trubshawe, *Greek Shipowner:* Riccardo Billi, *Hollywood Starlet:* Meri Wells, *Photographer:* Martin Miller.

PINKY (1949) 20th. Producer, Darryl F. Zanuck. Director, Elia Kazan. From a novel by Cid Ricketts Summer, *Quality.* Screenplay, Philip Dunne, Dudley Nichols. Art Directors, Lyle Wheeler, J. Russell Spencer. Photography, Joe MacDonald. Editor, Harmon Jones. Song by Harry Ruby and Alfred Newman: "Blue (With You or Without You)." 102 minutes

Pinky: Jeanne Crain, *Miss Em:* Ethel Barrymore, *Granny:* Ethel Waters, *Dr. Thomas Adams:* William Lundigan, *Judge Walker:* Basil Ruysdael, *Dr. Canady:* Kenny Washington, *Rozelia:* Nina Mae McKinney, *Dr. Joe:* Griff Barnett, *Jake Walters:* Frederick O'Neal, *Melba Wooley:* Evelyn Varden, *Judge Shoreham:* Raymond Greenleaf, *Stanley:* Dan Riss, *Mr. Goolby:* William Hansen, *Police Chief:* Arthur Hunnicutt, *Police Officer:* Robert Osterloh, *Saleslady:* Jean Inness, *Boy:* Shelby Bacon, *Mr. Wooley:* Everett Glass, *Teejore:* Rene Beard, *Nurses:* Tonya Overstreet, Juanita Moore.

Pinky with Arthur Hunnicutt, Jeanne Crain, Robert Osterloh, Frederick O'Neal and Nina Mae McKinney.

A PLACE IN THE SUN (1951) Par. Producer-Director, George Stevens. From a novel by Theodore Dreiser (*An American Tragedy*). Screenplay, Michael Wilson, Harry Brown. Art Directors, Hans Dreier, Walter Tyler. Music Score, Franz Waxman. Photography, William C. Mellor. Editor, William Hornbeck. Filmed at Lake Tahoe in High Sierras. Remake of Paramount's *An American Tragedy* (1931). 122 minutes

A Place in the Sun with Montgomery Clift and Shelley Winters.

George Eastman: Montgomery Clift, *Angela Vickers:* Elizabeth Taylor, *Alice Tripp:* Shelley Winters, *Hannah Eastman:* Anne Revere, *Earl Eastman:* Keefe Brasselle, *Bellows:* Fred Clark, *Marlowe:* Raymond Burr, *Charles Eastman:* Herbert Heyes, *Anthony Vickers:* Shepperd Strudwick, *Mrs. Vickers:* Frieda Inescort, *Mrs. Louise Eastman:* Kathryn Givney, *Jansen:* Walter Sande, *Judge:* Ted de Corsia, *Coroner:* John Ridgely, *Marsha:* Lois Chartrand, *Mr. Whiting:* William R. Murphy, *Boatkeeper:* Douglas Spencer, *Kelly:* Charles Dayton, *Morrison:* Paul Frees, *Joe Parker:* John Reed, *Frances Brand:* Marilyn Dialon, *Dr. Wyeland:* Ian Wolfe, *Secy. to Charles Eastman:* Josephine Whittell, *Truck Driver:* Frank Yaconelli, *Policeman:* Ralph A. Dunn, *Eagle Scout:* Bob Anderson, *Maid:* Lisa Golm, *Mrs. Roberts (Landlady):* Mary Kent, *A Warden:* Ken Christy, *Martha:* Kathleen Freeman, *Butler at Eastman Home:* Hans Moebus, *Butler:* Eric Wilton, *Motorcycle Officer:* Mike Mahoney, *Bailiff:* Al Ferguson, *Tom Tipton:* James W. Horne, *Miss Harper:* Laura Elliot, *Miss Newton:* Pearl Miller, *Jailer:* Major Philip Kieffer, *Man:* Major Sam Harris.

THE PLAINSMAN (1936) Par. Produced and directed by Cecil B. De Mille. Based on data from stories by Courtney Ryley Cooper and *Wild Bill Hickok* by Frank Wilstach. Screenplay, Waldemar Young, Lynn Riggs, and Harold Lamb. Data compiled by Jeanie Macpherson. Associate Director, Richard Harlan. Camera, Victor Milner and George Robinson. Editor, Anne Bauchens. Special Effects, Farciot Edouart and Gordon Jennings. Music Director, Boris Morros, Special Score, George Antheil. Dialogue Supervision, Edwin Maxwell. Remade by Universal, 1966. 113 minutes

Wild Bill Hickok: Gary Cooper, *Calamity Jane:* Jean Arthur, *Buffalo Bill Cody:* James Ellison, *John Lattimer:* Charles Bickford, *Louisa Cody:* Helen Burgess, *Jack McCall:* Porter Hall, *Yellow Hand:* Paul Harvey, *Painted Horse:* Victor Varconi, *General George A. Custer:* John Miljan, *Abraham Lincoln:* Frank McGlynn, Sr., *Van Ellyn:* Granville Bates, *Young Trooper of the Seventh Cavalry:* Frank Albertson, *Captain Wood:* Purnell Pratt, *Jake, a Teamster:* Fred Kohler, Sr., *Breezy:* George Hayes, *Sergeant McGinnis:* Patrick Moriarity, *Tony, the Barber:* Charles Judels, *Quartermaster Sergeant:* Harry Woods, *Northern Cheyenne Indian:* Anthony Quinn, *A River Gambler:* Francis McDonald, *Boy on the Dock:* George Ernest, *General Merritt:* George MacQuarrie, *Schuyler Colfax:* John Hyams, *Stanton, Secretary of War:* Edwin Maxwell, *Purser of the Lizzie Gill:* Bruce Warren, *Injun Charley:* Charlie Stevens, *Van Ellyn's Associates:* Arthur Aylesworth, Douglas Wood, George Cleveland, *Southern Girl:* Lona Andre, *Hysterical Trooper:* Irving Bacon, *Old Veteran:* Francis Ford, *Corporal Brannigan:* William Royle, *Dave, a Miner:* Fuzzy Knight, *Mary Todd Lincoln:* Leila McIntyre, *John F. Usher:* Harry Stubbs, *James Speed:* Davison Clark, *William H. Seward:* Charies W. Herzinger, *Hugh McCulloch:* William Humphries, *Giddeon Wells:* Sidney Jarvis, *Extra:* Hank Worden, *Bit Man:* Bud Flanagan (Dennis O'Keefe), *Indian:* Noble Johnson, *William Dennison:* Wadsworth Harris, *Major:* Jonathan Hale.

The Plainsman with Gary Cooper, Anthony Quinn and James Ellison.

Please Don't Eat the Daisies with Flip Mark, Stanley Livingston, Hobo, David Niven, Charles Herbert, Spring Byington, Doris Day, Patsy Kelly and Baby Gellert.

PLEASE DON'T EAT THE DAISIES (1960) MGM. Produced by Joe Pasternak. Associate Producer, Martin Melcher. Directed by Charles Walters. In Panavision and MetroColor. Based on the book by Jean Kerr. Screenplay, Isobel Lennart. Music, David Rose. Art Directors, George W. Davis and Hans Peters. Costumes, Morton Haack. Assistant Director, Al Jennings. Cinematography, Robert Bronner. Editor, John McSweeney, Jr. A Euterpe Production. Songs: "Please Don't Eat the Daisies" by Jay Lubin; "Any Way the Wind Blows" by Marilyn and Joe Hooven and By Dunham. Scene filmed in New York. Later a TV series. 111 minutes

Kate Mackay: Doris Day, *Larry Mackay:* David Niven, *Deborah Vaughn:* Janis Paige, *Suzie Robinson:* Spring Byington, *Alfred North:* Richard Haydn, *Maggie:* Patsy Kelly, *Joe Positano:* Jack Weston, *Reverend Dr. McQuarry:* John Harding, *Mona James:* Margaret Lindsay, *Mary Smith:* Carmen Phillips, *Mrs. Hunter:* Mary Patton, *David Mackay:* Charles Herbert, *Gabriel Mackay:* Stanley Livingston, *George Mackay:* Flip Mark, *Adam Mackay:* Baby Gellert, *Dog:* Hobo, *Jane March:* Marina Koshetz, *Dr. Sprouk:* Geraldine Wall, *Miss Yule (Principal):* Kathryn Card, *Justin Withers:* Donald Foster, *Mrs. Greenfield:* Irene Tedrow, *Paul Foster:* Anatole Winogradoff, *Young Men:* Burt Douglas, John Brennan, Guy Stockwell, *Girl:* Marianne Gaba, *Pete:* Benny Rubin, *Mrs. Kilkinny:* Madge Blake, *Waiter:* Len Lesser, *Photographer:* Wilson Wood, *Larry's Secretary:* Peter Leeds, *Pianist:* Joe Cronin, *Martha:* Amy Douglass, *Woman:* Gail Bonney, *Salesman:* Richard Collier, *Upholstery Man:* Charles Seel, *Interviewer:* Frank Wilcox, *Gus, Waiter:* Milton Frome, *Man:* Robert Darin, *Actress:* Jhean Burton.

PORGY AND BESS (1959) Col. Producer, Samuel Goldwyn. Director, Otto Preminger. Screenplay by N. Richard Nash. Music by George Gershwin. Libretto by DuBose Heyward. Lyrics by DuBose Heyward and Ira Gershwin. Based on the play *Porgy* by DuBose and Dorothy Heyward. Costumes by Irene Sharaff. Choreographer, Hermes Pan. Art Directors, Serge Krizman, Joseph Wright. Musical Director,

Porgy and Bess with Sidney Poitier.

Andre Previn. Cinematographer, Leon Shamroy. Editor, Daniel Mandell. In Todd-AO and Technicolor. 138 minutes

Porgy: Sidney Poitier, *Bess:* Dorothy Dandridge, *Sportin' Life:* Sammy Davis, Jr., *Maria:* Pearl Bailey, *Crown:* Brock Peters, *Jake:* Leslie Scott, *Clara:* Diahann Carroll, *Serena:* Ruth Attaway, *Peter:* Clarence Muse, *Annie:* Everdinne Wilson, *Robbins:* Joel Fluellen, *Mingo:* Earl Jackson, *Nelson:* Moses LaMarr, *Lily:* Margaret Hairston, *Jim:* Ivan Dixon, *Scipio:* Antoine Durousseau, *Strawberry Woman:* Helen Thigpen, *Elderly Man:* Vince Townsend, Jr., *Undertaker:* William Walker, *Frazier:* Roy Glenn, *Coroner:* Maurice Manson, *Detective:* Claude Atkins.

POSSESSED (1947) WB. Producer, Jerry Wald. Director, Curtis Bernhardt. Based on the story *One Man's Secret* by Rita Weiman. Screenplay, Silvia Richards, Ranald MacDougall. Art Director, Anton Grot. Cameraman, Joseph Valentine. Editor, Rudi Fehr. Song by Max Leif and Joseph Meyer: "How Long Will It Last?" 108 minutes

Louise Howell: Joan Crawford, *David Sutton:* Van Heflin, *Dean Graham:* Raymond Massey, *Carol Graham:* Geraldine Brooks, *Dr. Harvey Williard:* Stanley Ridges, *Harker:* John Ridgely, *Dr. Ames:* Moroni Olsen, *Dr. Max Sherman:* Erskine Sanford, *Wynn Graham:* Gerald Perreau (Peter Miles), *Nurse Rosen:* Isabel Withers, *Elsie:* Lisa Golm, *Assistant D. A.:* Douglas Kennedy, *Norris:* Monte Blue, *Dr. Craig:* Don McGuire, *Coroner's Assistant:* Rory Mallinson, *Interne:* Clifton Young, *Coroner:* Griff Barnett, *Motorman:* Ralph Dunn, *Proprietor:* Frank Marlowe, *Foreman:* James Conaty, *Secretary:* Creighton Hale, *Man at Concert:* Tristram Coffin, *Walter Sveldon:* Jacob Gimpel, *Nurse:* Nell Craig, *Dean's Secretary:* Henry Sylvester, *Caretaker's Wife:* Sarah Padden, *Waiter:* Wheaton Chambers, *Bartender:* Eddie Hart, *Nurse:* Bunty Cutler, *Butler:* Philo McCullough.

Possessed with Joan Crawford and Raymond Massey.

THE POSTMAN ALWAYS RINGS TWICE (1946) MGM. Producer, Carey Wilson. Director, Tay Garnett. Based on the novel by James M. Cain. Screenplay, Harry Ruskin, Niven Busch. Musical Score, George Basserman. Art Directors, Cedric Gibbons, Randall Duell. Cameraman, Sidney Wagner. Editor, George White. Song by Neil Moret and Richard Whiting: "(I Got a Woman Crazy 'Bout Me) She's Funny That Way." 113 minutes

Cora Smith: Lana Turner, *Frank Chambers:* John Garfield, *Nick Smith:* Cecil Kellaway, *Arthur Keats:* Hume Cronyn, *D. A. Kyle Sackett:* Leon Ames, *Madge Gorland:* Audrey Totter, *Ezra Liam Kennedy:* Alan Reed, *Blair:* Jeff York, *Doctor:* Charles Williams, *Willie:* Cameron Grant, *Ben:* Wally Cassell, *Judge:* William Halligan, *Judge:* Morris Ankrum, *Truck Driver:* Garry Owen, *Nurse:* Dorothy Phillips, *Doctor:* Edward Earle, *Picnic Manager:* Byron Foulger,

The Postman Always Rings Twice with John Garfield, Lana Turner and Alan Reed.

Matron: Sondra Morgan, *Reporter:* Dick Crockett, *Bailiff:* Frank Mayo, *Customer:* Betty Blythe, *John X. McHugh:* Joel Friedkin, *Headwaiter:* Jack Chefe, *Telegraph Messenger:* George Noisom, *Snooty Woman:* Virginia Randolph, *Father McConnell:* Tom Dillon, *Warden:* James Farley, *Man:* Paul Bradley.

THE PRIDE AND THE PASSION (1957) UA. Producer-Director, Stanley Kramer. Story and screenplay by Edna and Edward Anhalt. Based on the novel *The Gun* by C. S. Forester. Music by George Antheil. Assistant Director, Carter DeHaven, Jr. Costumes, Joe King. Choreography, Paco Reyes. Song by Peggy Lee. In VistaVision and Technicolor. Filmed in Spain. 132 minutes

Captain Anthony Trumbull: Cary Grant, *Miguel:* Frank Sinatra, *Juana:* Sophia Loren, *General Jouvet:* Theodore Bikel, *Sermaine:* John Wengraf, *Ballinger:* Jay Novello, *Carlos:* Jose Nieto, *Vidal:* Philip Van Zandt, *Manolo:* Paco el Laberinto, *Jose:* Carlos Larranaga.

The Pride and the Passion with Jose Nieto and Cary Grant.

THE PRIDE OF THE YANKEES (1942) RKO. Produced by Samuel Goldwyn. Directed by Sam Wood. Assistant Director, John Sherwood. Original Story, Paul Gallico. Screenplay, Jo Swerling and Herman J. Mankiewicz. Production Design, William Cameron Menzies. Art Director, Perry Ferguson. Associate Art Director, McClure Capps. Set Decorations, Howard Bristol. Costumes, Rene Hubert. Music, Leigh Harline. Photography, Rudolph Mate. Editor, Daniel Mandell. Sound, Frank Maher. Special Effects, Jack Cosgrove. Song, "Always," by Irving Berlin. Lou Gehrig died June 2, 1941. 128 minutes

Lou Gehrig: Gary Cooper, *Eleanor Gehrig:* Teresa Wright, *Babe Ruth:* Himself, *Sam Blake:* Walter Brennan, *Hank Hanneman:* Dan Duryea, *Mom Gehrig:* Elsa Janssen, *Pop Gehrig:* Ludwig Stossel, *Myra:* Virginia Gilmore, *Bill Dickey:* Himself, *Miller Huggins:* Ernie Adams,

The Pride of the Yankees with Gary Cooper.

Mr. Twitchell: Pierre Watkin, *Joe McCarthy:* Harry Harvey, *Robert W. Meusel:* Himself, *Mark Koenig:* Himself, *Bill Stern:* Himself, *Coach:* Addison Richards, *Van Tuyl:* Hardie Albright, *Clinic Doctor:* Edward Fielding, *Mayor of New Rochelle:* George Lessey, *Lou as a boy:* Douglas Croft, *Laddie:* Rip Russell, *Third Base Coach:* Frank Faylen, *Hammond:* Jack Shea, *Wally Pip:* George McDonald, *Billy:* Gene Collins, *Billy at 17:* David Holt, *Mayor La Guardia:* David Manley, *Colletti:* Max Willenz, *Sasha:* Jimmy Valentine, *Sasha's Mother:* Anita Bolster, *Murphy:* Robert Winkler, *Mr. Larsen:* Spencer Charters, *Mrs. Fabini:* Rosina Galli, *Joe Fabini:* Billy Roy, *Mrs. Robert:* Sarah Padden, *Tessie:* Janet Chapman, *Mrs. Worthington:* Eva Dennison, *Mr. Worthington:* Montague Shaw, *Ed Barrow:* Jack Stewart, *Christy Mathewson:* Fay Thomas, *Fraternity Boys:* Jack Arnold, John Kellogg, Dane Clark, Tom Neal. Veloz and Yolanda. Ray Noble and his Orchestra.

THE PRINCESS AND THE PIRATE (1944) RKO. Producer, Sam Goldwyn. Associate Producer, Don Hartman. Director, David Butler. Technicolor. Suggested by a story by Sy Burtlett. Screenplay, Don Hartman, Melville Shavelson, Everett Freeman. Musical Score, David Rose. Art Director, Ernst Fegte. Cameramen, Victor Milner, William Snyder. Special Effects, R. O. Binger, Clarence Slifer. Editor, Daniel Mandell. Song by Harold Adamson and Jimmy McHugh, "How Would You Like to Kiss Me in the Moonlight?" Adaptation, Allen Boretz and Curtis Kenyon. A Regent Pictures Production. 94 minutes

Sylvester: Bob Hope, *Margaret:* Virginia Mayo, *Featherhead:* Walter Brennan, *Gov. La Roche:* Walter Slezak, *The Hook:* Victor McLaglen, *Pedro:* Marc Lawrence, *Proprietor, "Bucket of Blood":* Hugo Haas, *Landlady:* Maude Eburne, *Don Jose:* Adia Kuznetzoff, *Mr. Pelly:* Brandon Hurst, *Alonzo:* Tom Kennedy, *Captain, MARY ANN:* Stanley Andrews, *The King:* Robert Warwick, *Lieutenant:* Tom Tyler, *Gorilla Man:* Rondo Hatton, *Holdup Man:* Dick Alexander, *Citizen:* Ernie Adams, *Murderous Pirate:* Ralph Dunn, *Drunken Pirate's Companion:* Bert Roach, *Drunken Pirate:* Francis Ford, *Captain, King's Ship:* Edwin Stanley, *Guard:* Ray Teal, *Palace Guard:* Weldon Heyburn,

The Princess and the Pirate with Walter Slezak and Bob Hope.

Palace Guard: Edward Peil, *Soldier:* Crane Whitley, *Naval Officer:* James Flavin, *Pirate:* Alan Bridge, *Pirate:* Al Hill, *Pirate:* Dick Rich, *Pirate:* Mike Mazurki, *Bartender:* Jack Carr, *First Mate* MARY ANN: Colin Kenny, *Guest Star:* Bing Crosby.

THE PRISONER OF SHARK ISLAND (1936) 20th. Produced by Darryl F. Zanuck. Directed by John Ford. Screenplay by Nunnally Johnson. Musical Director, Louis Silvers. Cameraman, Bert Glennon. Editor, Jack Murray. 95 minutes

Dr. Samuel Mudd: Warner Baxter, *Peggy Mudd:* Gloria Stuart, *Marth Mudd:* Joyce Kay, *Colonel Dyer:* Claude Gillingwater, Sr., *General Ewing:* Douglas Wood, *Sergeant Cooper:* Fred Kohler, Jr., *Commandant:* Harry Carey, *David Herold:* Paul Fix, *Sergeant Rankin:* John Carradine, *John Wilkes Booth:* Francis McDonald, *Erickson:* Arthur Byron, *Dr. McIntire:* O. P. Heggie, *Lovett:* John McGuire, *Hunter:* Paul McVey, *O'Toole:* Francis Ford, *Buck:* Ernest Whitman, *Judge Advocate Holt:* Frank Shannon, *Lincoln:* Frank McGlynn, Sr., *Carpetbagger:* Arthur Loft, *Orderly:* Maurice Murphy, *Orator:* Paul Stanton, *Signal Man:* Ronald (Jack) Pennick, *Commandant's Aide:* Merrill McCormick, *Blacksmith:* James Marcus, *Actress:* Jan Duggan, *Major Rathbone:* Lloyd Whitlock, *Mrs. Lincoln:* Leila McIntyre, *Actor:* Dick Elliott, *Spangler:* Murdock MacQuarrie, *Sergeant:* Duke Lee, *Druggist:* Robert Dudley, *Colonel:* Wilfred Lucas, *Mrs. Surratt:* Cecil Weston, *Maurice O'Laughlin:* Cyril Thornton, *Sergeant:* Robert E. Homans, *Blanche:* Beulah Hall Jones, *Judge Maiben:* J. M. Kerrigan, *Sergeant:* Bud Geary, *Rosabelle:* Etta McDaniels, *Ship's Captain:* J. P. McGowan, *Mate:* Harry Strang.

The Prisoner of Shark Island with Gloria Stuart and Warner Baxter.

THE PRISONER OF ZENDA (1937) UA. Produced by David O. Selznick. Assistant to the Producer, William H. Wright. Directed by John Cromwell and W. S. Van Dyke. Partly in Sepiatone. Based on the novel by Anthony J. Hope and the play by Edward Rose. Screenplay, John Ballderston, Wills Root, Donald Ogden Stewart. Art Director, Lyle Wheeler. Music, Alfred Newman. Costumes, Ernest Dryden. Interior Decoration, Casey Roberts. Photography, James Wong Howe. Special Effects, Jack Cosgrove. Editors, Hal C. Kern and James E. Newcom. Assistant Director, Frederick A. Spencer. Sepia Processing, John M. Nicholaus. Recorder (Sound), Oscar Lagerlof. Technical Advisors, Prince Sigvard Bernadotte and Colonel Ivar Enhorning. Other versions made by MGM in 1922 and 1952. 101 minutes

Rudolph Rassendyl/King Rudolf V: Ronald Colman, *Princess Flavia:* Madeleine Carroll, *Rupert of Hentzau:* Douglas Fairbanks, Jr., *Antoinette De Mauban:* Mary Astor, *Colonel Zapt:* C. Aubrey Smith, *Black Michael:* Raymond Massey, *Captain Fritz von Tarlenheim:* David Niven, *Cook:* Eleanor Wesselhoeft, *Johann:* Byron Foulger, *Detchard:* Montagu Love, *Kraftstein:* William Von Brincken, *Lauengram:* Phillip Sleeman, *Bersonin:* Ralph Faulkner, *De Gauiet:* Alexander D'Arcy, *Michael's Butler:* Torben Meyer, *Cardinal:* Ian MacLaren, *Marshal Strakencz:* Lawrence Grant, *Josef:* Howard Lang, *British*

The Prisoner of Zenda with C. Aubrey Smith, David Niven and Ronald Colman.

Ambassador: Ben Webster, *British Ambassador's Wife:* Evelyn Beresford, *Master of Ceremonies:* Boyd Irwin, *Von Haugwitz, Lord High Chamberlain:* Emmett King, *Bishop:* Charles K. French, *Orchestra Leader:* Al Shean, *Passport Officer:* Charles Halton, *Luggage Officer:* Otto Fries, *Duenna:* Florence Roberts, *Porter:* Spencer Charters, *Travelers:* Russ Powell, D'Arcy Corrigan, *Man:* Francis Ford.

THE PROFESSIONALS (1966) Col. Produced and directed by Richard Brooks. Color by Technicolor. Based on the novel *A Mule for the Marquesa* by Frank O'Rourke. Camera, Conrad Hall. Editor, Peter Zinner, Music, Maurice Jarre. Assistant Director, Tom Shaw. Second Unit Director, Lee Lukather. Filmed in Death Valley, Nevada; along the Mexican Border. 116 minutes

Bill Dolworth: Burt Lancaster, *Rico (Henry Fardan):* Lee Marvin, *Hans Ehrengard:* Robert Ryan, *Jesus Raza:* Jack Palance, *Maria Grant:* Claudia Cardinale, *Grant:* Ralph Bellamy, *Jake Sharp:* Woody Strode, *Pascual Ortega:* Joe De Santis, *Fierro:* Rafael Bertrand, *Eduardo Padillia:* Jorge Martinez De Hoyos, *Chiquita:* Marie Gomez, *Revolutionaries:* Jose Chavez, Carlos Romero, *Banker:* Vaughn Taylor.

The Professionals with Woody Strode, Lee Marvin and Burt Lancaster.

PSYCHO (1960) Par. Producer-Director, Alfred Hitchcock. Screenplay, Joseph Stefano. From a novel by Robert Bloch. Music, Bernard Herrmann. Art Directors, Joseph Hurley and Robert Clatworthy. Cinematography, John L. Russell. A Shamley Production. Locations: Phoenix, Arizona; Route 99 of the Fresno-Bakersfield Highway; the San Fernando Valley; a Hollywood thoroughfare. Interiors filmed at Revue Studios. 109 minutes

Psycho with Anthony Perkins and Janet Leigh.

Norman Bates: Anthony Perkins, *Marion Crane:* Janet Leigh, *Lila Crane:* Vera Miles, *Sam Loomis:* John Gavin, *Milton Arbogast:* Martin Balsam, *Sheriff Chambers:* John McIntire, *Dr. Richmond:* Simon Oakland, *Tom Cassidy:* Frank Albertson, *Caroline:* Pat Hitchcock, *George Lowery:* Vaughn Taylor, *Mrs. Chambers:* Lurene Tuttle, *Car Salesman:* John Anderson, *Policeman:* Mort Mills, *Officials:* Sam Flint, Francis De Sales, George Eldredge, *Man Outside Office in Cowboy Hat:* Alfred Hitchcock.

THE PUBLIC ENEMY (1931) WB. Directed by William A. Wellman. Story by Kubec Glasmon and John Bright. Adaptation by Harvey Thew. Photography, Dev Jennings. Editor, Ed McCormick. Theme, "I'm Forever Blowing Bubbles." Although billed as Bess, Louise Brooks does not appear in the film. 83 minutes

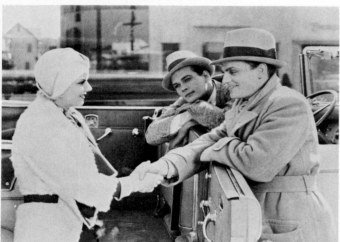

The Public Enemy with Jean Harlow, Eddie Woods and James Cagney.

Tom Powers: James Cagney, *Gwen Allen:* Jean Harlow, *Matt Doyle:* Edward Woods, *Mame:* Joan Blondell, *Ma Powers:* Beryl Mercer, *Mike Powers:* Donald Cook, *Kitty:* Mae Clarke, *(Samuel) Nails Nathan:* Leslie Fenton, *Paddy Ryan:* Robert Emmett O'Connor, *Putty Nose:* Murray Kinnell, *Molly Doyle:* Rita Flynn, *Hack:* Snitz Edwards, *Bugs Moran:* Ben Hendricks, Jr., *Tommy as a boy:* Frank Coghlan, Jr., *Matt as a boy:* Frankie Darro, *Officer Pat Burke:* Robert E. Homans, *Nails' Girl:* Dorothy Gee, *Officer Powers:* Purnell Pratt, *Steve, Bartender:* Lee Phelps, *Jane:* Mia Marvin, *Dutch:* Clark Burroughs, *Mrs. Doyle:* Adele Watson, *Little Girls:* Helen Parrish, Dorothy Gray, Nancie Price, *Bugs as a boy:* Ben Hendricks III, *Machine-Gunner:* George Daly, *Joe, Headwaiter:* Eddie Kane, *Mug:* Charles Sullivan, *Assistant Tailor:* Douglas Gerrard, *Negro Headwaiter:* Sam MacDaniel, *Pawnbroker:* William H. Strauss.

QUICK MILLIONS (1931) Fox. Directed by Rowland Brown. Story by Courtney Terrett and Rowland Brown. Dialogue by Terrett, Brown, and John Wray. Photography, Joseph August. Editor, Duncan Cramer. Sound, W. W. Lindsay, Jr. The first film directed by ex-writer Rowland Brown. 69 minutes

Quick Millions with Spencer Tracy and Sally Eilers.

Bugs Raymond: Spencer Tracy, *Dorothy Stone:* Marguerite Churchill, *Daisy de Lisle:* Sally Eilers, *Arkansas Smith:* Robert Burns, *Kenneth Stone:* John Wray, *Nails Markey:* Warner Richmond, *Jimmy Kirk:* George Raft, *Contractor:* John Swor.

THE QUIET MAN (1952) Republic. Produced by Merian C. Cooper. Directed by John Ford. Color by Technicolor. An Argosy Production. Based on a story by Maurice Walsh. Screenplay, Frank S. Nugent. Music, Victor Young. Photography, Winton C. Hoch and Archie Stout. Songs: "Galway Bay" by Dr. Edward Colahan and three traditional Irish songs, "The Wild Colonial Boy," "The Humour Is on Me Now" and "Mush Mush (Tread on the Tail of Me Coat)." Filmed in Ireland. 129 minutes

Sean Thornton: John Wayne, *Mary Kate Danaher:* Maureen O'Hara, *Red Will Danaher:* Victor McLaglen, *Michaeleen Flynn:* Barry Fitzgerald, *Father Peter Lonergan, Narrator:* Ward Bond, *Sarah Tillane:* Mildred Natwick, *Dan Tobin:* Francis Ford, *Reverend Cyril "Snuffy" Playfair:* Arthur Shields, *Elizabeth Playfair:* Eileen Crowe, *The Woman:* May Craig, *Forbes:* Charles FitzSimons, *Father Paul:* James Lilburn, *Owen Glynn:* Sean McClory, *Feeney:* Jack McGowran, *Maloney, Guard:* Joseph O'Dea, *Costello, Castletown Engineer:* Eric Gorman, *Fireman:* Kevin Lawless, *Porter:* Paddy O'Donnell, *Bailey, Stationmaster:* Web Overlander, *Dermot Fahy:* Ken Curtis, *Pat Cohan:* Harry Tyler, *Father Paul's Mother:* Mae Marsh, *Second:* Bob Perry, *General:* Major Sam Harris, *Children at Race:* Melinda and Pat Wayne, *Teenagers at Race:* Mike and Toni Wayne, *Guppy:* Don Hatswell, *Sergeant Hanan:* Harry Tenbrook, *Ring Physician:* Douglas Evans, *Constable:* David H. Hughes, *Boxer:* Jack Roper, *Referee:* Al Murphy, *Man:* Pat O'Malley.

The Quiet Man with Maureen O'Hara and John Wayne.

QUO VADIS (1951) MGM. Produced by Sam Zimbalist. Directed by Mervyn LeRoy. Color by Technicolor. Based on the novel by Henryk Sienkiewicz. Screenplay, John Lee Mahin, S. N. Behrman, Sonya Levien. Art Directors, William A. Horning, Cedric Gibbons, Edward Carfagno. Photography, Robert Surtees, William V. Skall. Editor, Ralph E. Winters. Filmed in Italy. 171 minutes

Quo Vadis with Patricia Laffan and Peter Ustinov.

Marcus Vinicius: Robert Taylor, *Lygia:* Deborah Kerr, *Petronius:* Leo Genn, *Nero:* Peter Ustinov, *Poppaea:* Patricia Laffan, *Peter:* Finlay Currie, *Paul:* Abraham Sofaer, *Eunice:* Marina Berti, *Ursus:* Buddy Baer, *Plautius:* Felix Aylmer, *Pomponia:* Nora Swinburne, *Tigellinus:* Ralph Truman, *Nerva:* Norman Wooland, *Nazarius:* Peter Miles, *Terpnos:* Geoffrey Dunn, *Seneca:* Nicholas Hannen, *Phaon:* D. A. Clarke-Smith, *Acte:* Rosalie Crutchley, *Chilo:* John Ruddock, *Croton:* Arthur Walge, *Miriam:* Elspeth March, *Rufia:* Strelsa Brown, *Lucan:* Alfredo Varelli, *Flavius:* Roberto Ottaviano, *Anaxander:* William Tubbs, *Galba:* Pietro Tordi, *Pedicurist:* Lia De Leo, *Extra:* Sophia Loren, *Extra (Guest):* Elizabeth Taylor.

Rainbow on the River with Charles Butterworth, May Robson and Bobby Breen.

RAINBOW ON THE RIVER (1936) RKO. Produced by Sol Lesser. Directed by Kurt Neumann. Associate Producer, Edward Gross. Author, Mrs. C. V. Jamison (from *Toinette's Philip*). Screenplay by Earle Snell, Harry Chandlee, William Hurlbut. Musical Settings, Hugo Riesenfeld, Abe Meyer. Cameraman, Charles Schoenbaum. Editor, Robert Crandall. Songs, "Rainbow on the River," "A Thousand Dreams of You," "You Only Live Once" by Paul Francis Webster and Louis Alter; "Waiting for the Sun to Rise" by Arthur Swanstrom and Karl Hajos. 87 minutes.

Philip: Bobby Breen, *Mrs. Ainsworth:* May Robson, *Barrett:* Charles Butterworth, *Ralph Layton:* Alan Mowbray, *Julia Layton:* Benita Hume, *Father Josef:* Henry O'Neill, *Toinette:* Louise Beavers, *Lucille Layton:* Marilyn Knowlden, *Seline:* Lillian Yarbo, *Lilybell:* Stymie Beard, *Doctor:* Eddie Anderson, *Flower Buyer:* Betty Blythe, *Mrs. Logan:* Theresa Maxwell Conover, *Pedestrian:* Clarence H. Wilson, *Cabman:* Lew Kelly, *Superintendent:* Lillian Harmer, *Hall Johnson Singers:* St. Luke's Choristers.

THE RAINS CAME (1939) 20th. Produced by Darryl F. Zanuck. Associate Producer, Harry Joe Brown. Directed by Clarence Brown. Based on the novel by Louis Bromfield. Screenplay, Philip Dunne and

The Rains Came with Maria Ouspenskaya, George Brent and Myrna Loy.

Julien Josephson. Music, Alfred Newman. Photography, Arthur Miller. Editor, Barbara McLean. Special effects scenes staged by Fred Sersen. Sets, Thomas Little. Costumes, Gwen Wakeling. Sound, Alfred Bruzlin and Roger Heman. Songs: "The Rains Came" by Mack Gordon and Harry Revel; and "Hindoo Song of Love" by Lal Chand Mehra. Remade by 20th as *The Rains of Ranchipur* (1955). 103 minutes

Lady Edwina Esketh: Myrna Loy, *Major Rama Safti:* Tyrone Power, *Tom Ransome:* George Brent, *Fern Simon:* Brenda Joyce, *Lord Albert Esketh:* Nigel Bruce, *Maharani:* Maria Ouspenskaya, *Mr. Bannerjee:* Joseph Schildkraut, *Miss MacDaid:* Mary Nash, *Aunt Phoebe Smiley:* Jane Darwell, *Mrs. Simon:* Marjorie Rambeau, *Reverend Homer Smiley:* Henry Travers, *Maharajah:* H. B. Warner, *Lily Hoggett-Egbury:* Laura Hope Crews, *Raschid Ali Khan:* William Royle, *General Keith:* Montague Shaw, *Reverend Elmer Simon:* Harry Hayden, *Bates:* Herbert Evans, *John the Baptist:* Abner Biberman, *Mrs. Bannerjee:* Mara Alexander, *Mr. Das:* William Edmunds, *Princesses:* Adele Labansat, Sonia Charsky, *Maid:* Rita Page, *Nurse:* Rosina Galli, *Nurse:* Connie Leon, *Official:* Pedro Regas, *Bit:* Lal Chand Mehra, *Engineer:* Frank Lackteen, *Rajput:* George Regas, *Doctor:* Leyland Hodgson, *Hindu Woman:* Fern Emmett, *Mr. Durga:* Guy D'Enery, *Aide-de-camp:* Jamiel Hasson.

RAINTREE COUNTY (1957) MGM. Produced by David Lewis. Directed by Edward Dmytryk. Technicolor and Panavision, Perspecta Sound. Based on the 1948 novel *Raintree County* by Ross Lockridge, Jr. Screenplay, Millard Kaufman. Art Direction, William A. Horning and Urie McCleary. Set Decoration, Edwin B. Willis and Hugh Hunt. Costume Design, Walter Plunkett. Score, Johnny Green. Songs by Johnny Green and Paul Francis Webster: "Never Till Now" and "Song of Raintree," the latter sung by Nat King Cole during the credits. Photography, Robert Surtees. First film made with MGM Camera 65 process, in which a 65 mm negative is reduced to 35 mm for release prints. Filmed in Danville, Kentucky; Natchez and Port Gibson, Mississippi; swamp scenes filmed at Reelfoot Lake, Tiptonville, Tennessee. Film debut of Gardner McKay, 24. 168 minutes

John Wickliff Shawnessy: Montgomery Clift, *Susanna Drake:* Elizabeth Taylor, *Nell Gaither:* Eva Marie Saint, *Professor Jerusalem Webster Stiles:* Nigel Patrick, *Orville "Flash" Perkins:* Lee Marvin, *Garwood B. Jones:* Rod Taylor, *Ellen Shawnessy:* Agnes Moorehead, *T. D. Shawnessy:* Walter Abel, *Barbara Drake:* Jarma Lewis, *Bobby Drake:* Tom Drake, *Ezra Gray:* Rhys Williams, *Niles Foster:* Russell Collins, *Southern Officer:* DeForrest Kelley, *Lydia Gray:* Myrna Hansen, *Jake, Bartender:* Oliver Blake, *Cousin Sam:* John Eldredge, *Soona:* Isabelle Cooley, *Parthenia:* Ruth Attaway, *Miss Roman:* Eileene Stevens, *Bessie:* Rosalind Hayes, *Tom Conway:* Don Burnett, *Nat Franklin:* Michael Dugan, *Jesse Gardner:* Ralph Vitti (Michael Dante), *Starter:* Phil Chambers, *Man with Gun:* James Griffith, *Granpa Peters:* Burt Mustin, *Madam Gaubert:* Dorothy Granger, *Blind Man:* Owen McGiveney, *Party Guest:* Charles Watts, *Union Lieutenant:* Stacey Harris, *Jim Shawnessy (age 2.5 Yrs):* Donald Losby,

Raintree County with Montgomery Clift and Elizabeth Taylor.

Jim Shawnessy (age 4 Yrs.): Mickey Maga, *Pantomimist in Blackface:* Robert Foulk, *Photographer:* Jack Daly, *Old Negro Man:* Bill Walker, *Bearded Soldier:* Gardner McKay.

RALLY 'ROUND THE FLAG, BOYS! (1958) 20th. Produced and directed by Leo McCarey. CinemaScope and De Luxe Color. Based on the novel by Max Shulman. Screenplay, Claude Binyon and Leo McCarey. Music, Cyril J. Mockridge. Art Directors, Lyle R. Wheeler and Leland Fuller. Music Director, Lionel Newman. Photographer, Leon Shamroy. Assistant Director, Jack Gertsman. Wardrobe, Charles LeMaire. Special Effects, L. B. Abbott. Orchestration, Edward B. Powell. Editor, Louis R. Loeffler. Song by Leo McCarey, "Seein' as How You're Mah Boojum." 106 minutes

Harry Bannerman: Paul Newman, *Grace Bannerman:* Joanne Woodward, *Angela Hoffa:* Joan Collins, *Captain Hoxie:* Jack Carson, *Grady Metcalf:* Dwayne Hickman, *Comfort Goodpasture:* Tuesday Weld, *Colonel Thorwald:* Gale Gordon, *Opie:* Tom Gilson, *Isaac Goodpasture:* O. Z. Whitehead, *Oscar Hoffa:* Murvyn Vye, *Danny Bannerman:* Ralph Osborn III, *Peter:* Stanley Livingston, *George Melvin:* Jon Lormer, *Manning Thaw:* Joseph Holland, *Milton Evans:* Burt Mustin, *Waldo Pike:* Percy Helton, *Betty O'Shiel:* Nora O'Mahoney, *Zack Crummitt:* Richard Collier, *Delinquents:* LeRoy Prinz, Jr., Nick Venet, *Conductor:* Jesse Kirkpatrick, *Air Force General:* John Roy, *Hotel Clerk:* Richard Cutting, *Bellboy:* Billy Benedict, *Delinquent:* Sammy Ogg, *Hoxie's Driver:* Jack Ging, *TV Director:* Charles Tannen, *Soldier:* Edward "Tap" Canutt.

Rally 'Round the Flag, Boys! with Joan Collins and Paul Newman.

Random Harvest with Greer Garson and Ronald Colman.

RANDOM HARVEST (1942) MGM. Producer, Sidney Franklin. Director, Mervyn LeRoy. From the novel by James Hilton. Screenplay, Claudine West, George Froeschel, Arthur Wimperis. Score, Herbert Stothart. Art Director, Cedric Gibbons. Cameraman, Joseph Ruttenberg. Editor, Harold F. Kress. 124 minutes

Charles Ranier: Ronald Colman, *Paula:* Greer Garson, *Dr. Jonathan Benet:* Philip Dorn, *Kitty:* Susan Peters, *"Biffer":* Reginald Owen, *Prime Minister:* Edmund Gwenn, *Dr. Sims:* Henry Travers, *Mrs. Deventer:* Margaret Wycherly, *Harrison:* Bramwell Fletcher, *Chetwynd:* Arthur Margetson, *Lydis (Chet's Wife):* Jill Esmond, *Jill (Kitty's Mother):* Marta Linden, *George:* Melville Cooper, *Julian:* Alan Napier, *Sheila:* Pax Walker, *Beddoes:* Clement May, *Chemist:* Arthur Shields, *Henry Chilcotte:* David Cavendish, *Julia:* Norma Varden, *Bridget:* Ann Richards, *Mrs. Lloyd:* Elisabeth Risdon, *Mr. Lloyd:* Charles Waldron, *The Vicar:* Ivan Simpson, *Pearson:* John Burton, *Sam:* Rhys Williams, *Comedian:* Alec Craig, *Heavy Man:* Henry Daniell, *Vicar's Wife:* Marie De Becker, *Mrs. Sims:* Mrs. Gardner Crane, *Sheldon:* Aubrey Mather, *Julia's Husband:* Montague Shaw, *Sir John:* Lumsden Hare, *Paula's Lawyer:* Frederic Worlock, *Jones:* Wallis Clark, *Badgeley:* Harry T. Shannon, *Trempitt:* Arthur Space, *Tobacconist:* Una O'Connor, *Registrar:* Ian Wolfe, *Woman:* Olive Blakeney, *Soldier:* Peter Lawford.

RASPUTIN AND THE EMPRESS (1932) MGM. Directed by Richard Boleslavsky. Story and Screenplay, Charles MacArthur. Photography, William Daniels. Editor, Tom Held. Music, Herbert Stothart. Art Directors, Cedric Gibbons and Alexander Toluboff. Costumes, Adrian. Assistant Director, Cullen Tate. Sound, Douglas Shearer. Only film of the three Barrymores. 133 minutes

Prince Paul Chegodieff: John Barrymore, *Empress Alexandra:* Ethel Barrymore, *Rasputin:* Lionel Barrymore, *Emperor Nikolai:* Ralph

Rasputin and the Empress with John Barrymore, Ethel Barrymore, Tad Alexander and Lionel Barrymore.

Morgan, *Natasha:* Diana Wynyard, *Alexis:* Tad Alexander, *Grand Duke Igor:* C. Henry Gordon, *Doctor:* Edward Arnold, *Doctor Wolfe:* Gustav von Seyffertitz, *Anastasia:* Dawn O'Day (Anne Shirley), *Maria:* Jean Parker, *Landlady:* Sarah Padden, *Chief of Secret Police:* Henry Kolker, *Professor Propotkin:* Frank Shannon, *German Language Teacher:* Frank Reicher, *Policeman:* Hooper Atchley, *Revelers:* Lucien Littlefield, Leo White, *Soldier:* Maurice Black, *Soldier (Extra):* Dave O'Brien, *Butler:* Mischa Auer, *Girl:* Charlotte Henry.

THE RAT RACE (1960) Par. Produced by William Perlberg and George Seaton. Directed by Robert Mulligan. Color by Technicolor. Based on the play by Garson Kanin. Screenplay, Garson Kanin. Music, Elmer Bernstein. Art Direction, Tambi Larsen. Costumes, Edith Head. Assistant Director, Richard Caffey. Cinematography, Robert Burks. Editor, Alma Macrorie. A Perlsea Production. 105 minutes

Pete Hammond, Jr.: Tony Curtis, *Peggy Brown:* Debbie Reynolds, *Mac:* Jack Oakie, *Soda:* Kay Medford, *Nellie:* Don Rickles, *Edie:* Marjorie Bennett, *Bo:* Hal K. Dawson, *Telephone Man:* Norman Fell, *Toni:* Lisa Drake, *Frankie:* Joe Bushkin, *Carl (Tip):* Sam Butera, *Gerry:* Gerry Mulligan, *Mickey:* Jack (Tipp) McClure, *Tip:* Dick Winslow, *Hotel Clerk:* Wally Cassell, *Tod:* David Joseph Landfield, *French Sailor:* Jacques Gailo, *Sergeant Marcus Karp:* Joseph G. Sullivan, *Cab Driver:* Stanley Adams, *Boy:* Louis M. Lettieri, *Janitor:* Johnny Lee, *Eddie:* Richard Keene, *Norm:* Donald Lamont, *Trumpet Player:* Bob Kenaston, *Sailor:* Mark Russell, *Good Humor Man:* Frank Mitchell.

The Rat Race with Tony Curtis.

THE RAZOR'S EDGE (1946) 20th. Produced by Darryl F. Zanuck. Directed by Edmund Goulding. Based on the novel by W. Somerset Maugham. Screenplay, Lamar Trotti. Art Directors, Richard Day and Nathan Juran. Music, Alfred Newman. Photography, Arthur Miller. Editor, J. Watson Webb. Dances staged by Harry Pilcer. Gene Tierney's costumes designed by Oleg Cassini. Song, "Mam'-selle," by Mack Gordon and Edmund Goulding. Herbert Marshall repeats his Maugham characterization from *The Moon and Sixpence* (United Artists, 1942). 146 minutes

Larry Darrell: Tyrone Power, *Isabel Bradley:* Gene Tierney, *Gray Maturin:* John Payne, *Sophie:* Anne Baxter, *Elliott Templeton:* Clifton Webb, *Somerset Maugham:* Herbert Marshall, *Louisa Bradley:* Lucile Watson, *Bob MacDonald:* Frank Latimore, *Miss Keith:* Elsa Lanchester, *Kosti:* Fritz Kortner, *Joseph:* John Wengraf, *Holy Man:* Cecil Humphreys, *Specialty Dancer:* Harry Pilcer, *Princess Novemali:* Cobina Wright, Sr., *Maid:* Isabelle Lamore, *Bishop:* Andre Charlot, *Albert:* Albert Petit, *Police Inspector:* Henri Letondal, *Russian Singer:* Noel Cravat, *Specialty Dancer:* Laura Stevens, *Sea Captain:* Eugene Borden, *Abbe:* Demetrius Alexis, *Mr. Maturin:* Forbes Murray, *Singer:* Robert Laurent, *Matron:* Bess Flowers, *Coco:* Roger Valmy, *Princess' Escort:* Barry Norton, *Sophie's Daughter:* Gale Entrekin,

The Razor's Edge with Tyrone Power, Gene Tierney, Louise Colombet and George Davis.

Concierge: George Davis, *Concierge's Wife:* Louise Colombet, *Show Girl:* Dorothy Abbott, *Hospital Telephone Operator:* Greta Granstedt, *Isabel's Daughters:* Susan Hartmann, Suzanne O'Connor, *Waiter:* Marek Windheim, *Guest:* Pati Behrs, *Corsican:* Bud Wolfe, *Adagio Dancers:* Ruth Miles and Edward Kover, *Adagio Dancers:* Don and Dolores Graham, *Drunk:* Saul Gorss.

REAP THE WILD WIND (1942) Par. Producer, Cecil B. De Mille. Associate Producer, William Pine. Director, Cecil B. De Mille. Color by Technicolor. Screenplay, Alan LeMay, Charles Bennett, Jesse Lasky, Jr. Score, Victor Young. Art Directors, Hans Dreier, Roland Anderson. Color Cameraman, William V. Skall. Process Photography, Farciot Edouart. Special Effects, Gordon Jennings. Cameraman, Victor Milner. Editor, Anna Bauchens. Songs: "Sea Chantey" by Frank Loesser and Victor Young; "'Tis But a Little Faded Flower" by J. R. Thomas and Troy Sanders. Based on a *Saturday Evening Post* story by Thelma Strabel. Underwater Photography, Dewey Wrigley. 124 minutes

Stephen Tolliver: Ray Milland, *Captain Jack Stuart:* John Wayne, *Loxi Claiborne:* Paulette Goddard, *King Cutler:* Raymond Massey, *Dan Cutler:* Robert Preston, *Captain Phillip Philpott:* Lynne Overman, *Drusilla Alston:* Susan Hayward, *Mate of the TYFIB:* Charles Bickford, *Commodore Devereaux:* Walter Hampden, *Maum Maria:* Louise Beavers, *Ivy Devereaux:* Martha O'Driscoll, *Mrs. Claiborne:* Elisabeth Risdon, *Aunt Henrietta:* Hedda Hopper, *Widgeon:* Victor Kilian, *Salt Meat:* Oscar Polk, *Mrs. Mottram:* Janet Beecher, *Chinkapin:* Ben Carter, *The Lamb:* Wee Willie (William) Davis, *Sam:* Lane Chandler, *Judge Marvin:* Davison Clark, *Captain of the PELICAN:* Lou Merrill, *Doctor Jepson:* Frank M. Thomas, *Captain Carruthers:* Keith Richards, *Lubbock:* Victor Varconi, *Port Captain:* J. Farrell Macdonald, *Mace:* Harry Woods, *Master Shipwright:* Raymond Hatton, *Lieutenant Farragut:* Milburn Stone, *Charleston Ladies:* Barbara Britton, Julia Faye, *Pete:* Constantine Romanoff, *Jake:* Fred Graham, *Stoker Boss:* Dick Alexander, *Dancing Lady:* Mildred Harris, *Devereaux Agent:* John Saint Polis, *Dr. Jepson's Boy:* Eugene Jackson, *Girl's Father:* James Flavin, *Officer at Tea:* Monte Blue, *Ettie:* Claire McDowell, *Devereaux Secretary:* Stanhope Wheatcroft.

Reap the Wild Wind with Martha O'Driscoll, Ray Milland and Paulette Goddard.

Rear Window with Thelma Ritter, Grace Kelly and James Stewart.

REAR WINDOW (1954) Par. Director, Alfred Hitchcock. Technicolor. Based on Cornell Woolrich's short story. Screenplay, John Michael Hayes. Art Director, Hal Pereira. Cinematographer, Robert Burks. Editor, George Tomasini. 112 minutes

Jeff: James Stewart, *Lisa Fremont:* Grace Kelly, *Thomas J. Doyle:* Wendell Corey, *Stella:* Thelma Ritter, *Lars Thorwald:* Raymond Burr, *Miss Lonely Hearts:* Judith Evelyn, *Song Writer:* Ross Bagdasarian, *Miss Torso:* Georgine Darcy, *Woman on Fire Escape:* Sara Berner, *Fire Escape Man:* Frank Cady, *Miss Hearing Aid:* Jesslyn Fax, *Honeymooner:* Rand Harper, *Mrs. Thorwald:* Irene Winston, *Newlywed:* Harris Davenport, *Party Girl:* Marla English, *Party Girl:* Kathryn Grandstaff (Kathryn Grant), *Landlord:* Alan Lee, *Detective:* Anthony Warde, *Miss Torso's Friend:* Benny Bartlett, *Stunt Detective:* Fred Graham, *Young Man:* Harry Landers, *Man:* Dick Simmons, *Bird Woman:* Iphigenie Castiglioni, *Waiter (Carl):* Ralph Smiley, *Stunt Detective:* Edwin Parker, *Woman with Poodle:* Bess Flowers, *Dancer:* Jerry Antes, *Choreographer:* Barbara Bailey, *A Butler:* Alfred Hitchcock.

REBECCA (1940) UA. Selznick International Pictures. Produced by David O. Selznick. Directed by Alfred Hitchcock. From Daphne du Maurier's novel. Screenplay by Robert E. Sherwood and Joan Harrison. Adapted by Philip MacDonald and Michael Hogan. Music by Franz Waxman. Photography by George Barnes. Hitchcock's first American film. 130 minutes.

Maxim de Winter: Laurence Olivier, *Mrs. de Winter:* Joan Fontaine, *Jack Favell:* George Sanders, *Mrs. Danvers:* Judith Anderson, *Major Giles Lacy:* Nigel Bruce, *Colonel Julyan:* C. Aubrey Smith, *Frank Crawley:* Reginald Denny, *Beatrice Lacy:* Gladys George, *Robert:* Philip Winter, *Frith:* Edward Fielding, *Mrs. Van Hopper:* Florence Bates, *Coroner:* Melville Cooper, *Dr. Baker:* Leo G. Carroll, *Chalcroft:* Forrester Harvey, *Tabbs:* Lumsden Hare, *Ben:* Leonard Carey, *Man Outside Phone Booth:* Alfred Hitchcock.

Rebecca with Joan Fontaine and Laurence Olivier.

Rebel Without a Cause with Ann Doran, James Dean and Jim Backus.

REBEL WITHOUT A CAUSE (1955) WB. Produced by David Weisbart. Directed by Nicholas Ray. CinemaScope and WarnerColor. From a story by Nicholas Ray. Adaptation, Irving Shulman. Screenplay, Stewart Stern. Assistant Directors, Don Page and Robert Farfan. Music, Leonard Rosenman. Costumes, Moss Mabry. Art Director, Malcolm Bert. Cinematography, Ernest Haller. Editor, William Ziegler. Sound, Stanley Jones. 111 minutes

Jim: James Dean, *Judy:* Natalie Wood, *Plato:* Sal Mineo, *Jim's Father:* Jim Backus, *Jim's Mother:* Ann Doran, *Buzz:* Corey Allen, *Judy's Father:* William Hopper, *Judy's Mother:* Rochelle Hudson, *Jim's Grandma:* Virginia Brissac, *Moose:* Nick Adams, *Cookie:* Jack Simmons, *Goon:* Dennis Hopper, *Plato's Maid:* Marietta Canty, *Chick:* Jack Grinnage, *Helen:* Beverly Long, *Mil:* Steffi Sidney, *Crunch:* Frank Mazzola, *Harry:* Tom Bernard, *Cliff:* Clifford Morris, *Lecturer:* Ian Wolfe, *Ray:* Edward Platt, *Gene:* Robert Foulk, *Beau:* Jimmy Baird, *Guide:* Dick Wessel, *Sergeant:* Nelson Leigh, *Nurse:* Dorothy Abbott, *Woman Officer:* Louise Lane, *Officer:* House Peters, *Attendant:* Gus Schilling, *Monitor:* Bruce Noonan, *Old Lady Teacher:* Almira Sessions, *Hoodlum:* Peter Miller, *Desk Sergeant:* Paul Bryar, *Police Chief:* Paul Birch, *Moose's Father, Ed:* Robert B. Williams, *Crunch's Father:* David McMahon.

THE RED BADGE OF COURAGE (1951) MGM. Producer, Gottfried Reinhardt. Director-Screenplay, John Huston. Adaptation, Albert Band. Art Directors, Cedric Gibbons, Hans Peter. Photography, Harold Rosson. Editor, Ben Lewis. 69 minutes

Youth: Audie Murphy, *Loud Soldier:* Bill Mauldin, *Lieutenant:* Douglas Dick, *Tattered Man:* Royal Dano, *Tall Soldier:* John Dierkes, *Bill Porter:* Arthur Hunnicutt, *Thompson:* Robert Easton Burke, *Captain:* Smith Ballew, *Colonel:* Glenn Strange, *Sergeant:* Dan White, *Captain:* Frank McGraw, *General:* Tim Durant, *Veterans:* Emmett Lynn, Stanford Jolley, William "Bill" Phillips, House Peters, Jr., Frank Sully, *Union Soldiers:* George Offerman, Jr., Joel Marston, Robert Nichols, *Veterans:* Lou Nova, Fred Kohler, Jr., Dick Curtis,

The Red Badge of Courage with Bill Mauldin and Audie Murphy.

Guy Wilkerson, Buddy Roosevelt, *Soldier:* Jim Hayward, *Southern Girl:* Gloria Eaton, *Soldier Who Sings:* Robert Cherry, *Wounded Officer:* Whit Bissell, *Officer:* William Phipps, *Corporal:* Ed Hinton, *Confederate:* Lynn Farr.

RED DUST (1932) MGM. Directed by Victor Fleming. Based on the play by Wilson Collison. Screenplay, John Mahin. Photography, Harold Rosson. Editor, Blanche Sewell. Remade as *Congo Maisie* (MGM, 1940), and *Mogambo* (MGM, 1953), also with Clark Gable. 83 minutes

Dennis Carson: Clark Gable, *Vantine:* Jean Harlow, *Gary Willis:* Gene Raymond, *Barbara Willis:* Mary Astor, *Guidon:* Donald Crisp, *McQuarg:* Tully Marshall, *Limey:* Forrester Harvey, *Hoy:* Willie Fung.

Red Dust with Mary Astor, Gene Raymond, Jean Harlow and Clark Gable.

RED RIVER (1948) United Artists-Monterey. Producer-Director, Howard Hawks. Author, Borden Chase. Screenplay, Borden Chase, Charles Schnee. Music, Dimitri Tiomkin. Art Director, John Datu Arensma. Photography, Russell Harlan. Editor, Christian Nyby. Film debut of Montgomery Clift, although his second film *The Search* was released first. 125 minutes

Tom Dunson: John Wayne, *Matthew Garth:* Montgomery Clift, *Tess Millay:* Joanne Dru, *Groot Nadine:* Walter Brennan, *Fen:* Coleen Gray, *Cherry Valance:* John Ireland, *Buster McGee:* Noah Beery, Jr., *Mr. Melville:* Harry Carey, Sr., *Dan Latimer:* Harry Carey, Jr., *Teeler Yacey:* Paul Fix, *Matt as a boy:* Mickey Kuhn, *Quo:* Chief Yowlachie,

Red River with John Ireland, John Wayne and Montgomery Clift.

Bunk Kenneally: Ivan Parry, *Walt Jergens:* Ray Hyke, *Simms:* Hank Worden, *Laredo:* Dan White, *Fernandez:* Paul Fiero, *Wounded Wrangler:* William Self, *Old Leather:* Hal Taliaferro, *A Quitter:* Tom Tyler, *Colonel:* Lane Chandler, *Naylor:* Glenn Strange, *Dancehall Girl:* Shelley Winters.

REQUIEM FOR A HEAVYWEIGHT (1962) Col. Producer, David Susskind. Director, Ralph Nelson. Associate Producer, Jack Grossberg. Screenplay, Rod Serling. Music, Laurence Rosenthal. Assistant Directors, Anthony LaMarca. Michael Hertzberg. Art Director, Burr Smidt. Cinematographer, Arthur J. Ornitz. Editor, Carl Lerner. 87 minutes

Mountain Rivera: Anthony Quinn, *Maish Rennick:* Jackie Gleason, *Army:* Mickey Rooney, *Grace Miller:* Julie Harris, *Perelli:* Stan Adams, *Ma Greeny:* Madame Spivy, *Bartender:* Herbie Faye, *Jack Dempsey:* Himself, *Ring Opponent:* Cassius Clay, *Hotel Desk Clerk:* Steve Belloise, *Ring Doctor:* Lou Gilbert, *Referee:* Arthur Mercante.

Requiem for a Heavyweight with Mickey Rooney and Anthony Quinn.

RHAPSODY IN BLUE (1945) WB. Produced by Jesse L. Lasky. Directed by Irving Rapper. Based on an original story by Sonya Levien. Screenplay, Howard Koch and Elliot Paul. Art Directors, John Hughes and Anton Grot. Dance Director, LeRoy Prinz. Music Director, Leo F. Forbstein. Photography, Sol Polito. Special Effects, Roy Davidson and Willard Van Enger. Editor, Folmer Blangsted. Orchestral Arrangements, Ray Heindorf and Ferde Grofe. Vocal Arrangements, Dudley Chambers. Piano Solo Recordings, Oscar Levant and Ray Turner. Based on the life of George Gershwin, and featuring his music, with lyrics by Ira Gershwin, Irving Caesar, B. G. DeSylva, Arthur Frances. Musical numbers by George Gershwin with lyrics by Ira Gershwin or those listed: "Swanee" (Irving Caesar), "'S Wonderful," "Somebody Loves Me," "The Man I Love," "Embraceable You," "Summertime," "It Ain't Necessarily So," "Oh Lady Be Good", "I Got Rhythm," "Love Walked In," "Clap Yo' Hands," "Do It Again," "I'll Build a Stairway to Paradise" (Arthur Frances and B.G. DeSylva), "Liza," "Someone to Watch Over Me," "Bidin' My Time," "Delicious," "I Got Plenty of Nuttin," and "Rhapsody in Blue" and "An American in Paris." Film debut of Robert Alda. 139 minutes

George Gershwin: Robert Alda, *Julie Adams:* Joan Leslie, *Christine Gilbert:* Alexis Smith, *Max Dreyfus:* Charles Coburn, *Lee Gershwin:* Julie Bishop, *Professor Frank:* Albert Basserman, *Papa Gershwin:* Morris Carnovsky, *Mama Gershwin:* Rosemary De Camp, *Ira Gershwin:* Herbert Rudley, *Themselves:* Al Jolson, Paul Whiteman and his Orchestra, Oscar Levant, George White, Hazel Scott, Tom Patricola, *Bess:* Anne Brown, *George as a boy:* Mickey Roth, *Ira as a boy:* Darryl Hickman, *Hubert Stone:* Bill Kennedy, *Buddy De Sylva:* Eddie Marr, *Otto Kahn:* Ernest Golm, *Jascha Heifitz:* Martin Noble, *Walter Damrosch:* Hugo Kirchhoffer, *Rachmaninoff:* Will Wright, *Dancer:* Johnny Downs, *Christine's Escort:* Robert Shayne, *Mr. Million:* Andrew Tombes, *Muscatel:* Walter Soderling, *Kast:* Charles Halton, *Mr. Katzman:* Gregory Golubeff, *Commentator:* John B.

Rhapsody in Blue with Paul Whiteman, Charles Coburn, Robert Alda, Albert Basserman and Herbert Rudley.

Hughes, *William Foley:* Theodore Von Eltz, *Ravel:* Oscar Lorraine, *Guest in Nightclub:* Ivan Lebedeff, *Comic:* George Riley, *Cashier:* Virginia Sale, *Prima Donna:* Yola d'Avril, *Receptionist:* Claire DuBrey, *Swedish Janitor:* Christian Rub, *Madame DeBreteuil:* Odette Myrtil, *Orchestra Leader:* Jay Novello, *Sport:* Robert Johnson, *Porgy:* William Gillespie, *Singer:* Mark Stevens.

RHYTHM ON THE RANGE (1936) Par. Produced by Benjamin Glazer. Directed by Norman Taurog. Based on a story by Mervin J. Houser. Screenplay, John C. Moffett, Sidney Salkow, Walter DeLeon, Francis Martin. Musical Director, Boris Morros. Camera, Karl Struss. Editor, Ellsworth Hoagland. Songs: "I Can't Escape From You" (Leo Robin, Richard Whiting), "I'm an Old Cowhand" (Johnny Mercer), "If You Can't Sing It You'll Have to Swing It (Mr. Paganini)" (Sam Coslow), "The House Jack Built for Jill" (Leo Robin, Frederick Hollander), "Drink It Down" (Leo Robin, Ralph Rainger), "Hang Up My Saddle" and "Rhythm on the Range" (Walter Bullock, Richard Whiting), "Memories" (Richard Whiting, Frederick Hollander), "Roundup Lullaby" (Bager Clark, Gertrude Ross), and "Empty Saddles" (Billy Hill, J. Keirn Brennan). Remade as *Pardners* (Paramount, 1956) with Martin and Lewis. Film debut of Martha Raye, 27. 87 minutes

Jeff Larrabee: Bing Crosby, *Doris Halliday:* Frances Farmer, *Buck Burns:* Bob Burns, *Emma:* Martha Raye, *Robert Halliday:* Samuel S. Hinds, *Big Brain:* Warren Hymer, *Penelope Ryland:* Lucille Webster Gleason, *Shorty:* George E. Stone, *Wabash:* James Burke, *Constance:* Martha Sleeper, *Gila Bend:* Clem Bevans, *Mischa:* Leonid Kinskey, *Gopher:* Charles Williams, *Cuddles:* Beau Baldwin, *Clerk:* Emmett Vogan, *Shorty:* Billy Bletcher, *Field Judge:* Eddy Waller, *Heckler:* Bud Flanagan (Dennis O'Keefe), *Officer:* Duke York, *Conductor:* James Blaine, *Brakeman:* Herbert Ashley, *Porter:* James "Slim" Thompson, *Conductor:* Robert E. Homans, *Oil Station Proprietor:* Jim Toney, *Conductor:* Edward LeSaint, *Porter:* Sam McDaniel, *Gus:* Sid Saylor, *Waiter:* Oscar Smith, *Steward:* Charles E. Arnt, *Minister:* Harry C. Bradley, *Chinese Houseboy:* Otto Yamaoka, *Farmer:* Bob McKenzie, *Announcer:* Irving Bacon, *Driver:* Heinie Conklin, *Butler:* Frank Dawson, *Singers:* Sons of the Pioneers, including Roy Rogers.

Rhythm on the Range with Martha Raye, James "Slim" Thompson, Bob Burns and Lucille Webster Gleason.

RIO BRAVO (1959) WB. Producer-Director, Howard Hawks. Screenplay by Jules Furthman and Leigh Brackett. From a story by B. H. McCampbell. Music by Dimitri Tiomkin. Songs by Dimitri Tiomkin and Paul Francis Webster. Costumes by Marjorie Best. Assistant Director, Paul Helmick. Art Director, Leo K. Kuter. Cinematographer, Russell Harlan. Editor, Folmer Blangsted. An Armada Production in Technicolor. Songs by Dimitri Tiomkin and Paul Francis Webster: "Rio Bravo," "My Rifle, My Pony and Me." 141 minutes

John T. Chance: John Wayne, *Dude:* Dean Martin, *Colorado Ryan:* Ricky Nelson, *Feathers:* Angie Dickinson, *Stumpy:* Walter Brennan, *Pat Wheeler:* Ward Bond, *Nathan Burdette:* John Russell, *Carlos:* Pedro Gonzalez-Gonzalez, *Joe Burdette:* Claude Akins, *Jake:* Malcolm Atterbury, *Harold:* Harry Carey, Jr., *Matt Harris:* Bob Steele, *Barfly:* Myron Healey, *Gunman:* Fred Graham, *Messenger:* Riley Hill, *Henchman:* Tom Monroe, *Consuela:* Estelita Rodriguez.

Rio Bravo with Claude Akins and John Wayne.

RIO RITA (1929) RKO. Produced by William Le Baron. Directed by Luther Reed. Ballroom Scene in Technicolor. Based on the Florenz Ziegfeld musical by Guy Bolton and Fred Thompson. Adapted by Luther Reed. Dances staged by Pearl Eaton. Dialogue, Russell Mack. Sound, RCA Photophone. Songs by Harry Tierney and Joe McCarthy: "The Ranger Song," "Rio Rita," "Sweetheart, We Need Each Other," "If You're in Love You'll Waltz," "The Kinkajou," "Following the Sun Around" and "You're Always in My Arms" (But Only in My Dreams); by E. Y. Harburg and Harold Arlen: "Long Before You Came Along." Photography, Robert Kurle and Lloyd Knetchel. Editor, William Hamilton. Art Director, Max Ree. Musical Director, Victor Daravalle. Chorus Master, Pietro Cimini. Film debut of the team of Wheeler and Woolsey. Remade by MGM in 1942. 135 minutes

Chick Bean: Bert Wheeler, *Lovett:* Robert Woolsey, *Rita Ferguson:* Bebe Daniels, *Captain Jim Stewart:* John Boles, *Dolly:* Dorothy Lee,

Rio Rita with Fred Burns, George Renavent, Bebe Daniels, John Boles and Benny Corbett.

Roberto Ferguson: Don Alvarado, *General Ravenoff:* Georges Renavent, *Carmen:* Eva Rosita, *McGinn:* Sam Nelson, *Wilkins:* Fred Burns, *Cafe Owner:* Sam Blum, *Padrone:* Nick De Ruiz, *Davalos:* Tiny Sandford, *Mrs. Bean:* Helen Kaiser.

ROAD TO BALI (1952) Par. Producer, Harry Tugend. Director, Hal Walker. Color by Technicolor. Screenplay, Frank Butler, Hal Kanter, William Morrow. Art Directors, Hal Pereira, Joseph McMillan Johnson. Sets, Sam Comer, Russ Dowd. Sound, Gene Merritt, John Cope. Musical Direction, Joseph J. Lilley. Musical numbers staged by Charles O'Curran. Orchestral Arrangements, Van Cleave. Cinematographer, George Barnes. Editor, Archie Marshek. Story, Frank Butler and Harry Tugend. Songs by Johnny Burke and James Van Heusen: "Chicago Style," "Moonflowers," "Hoot Mon," "To See You," "The Merry Go Runaround." Sixth "Road" film, last was *Road to Hong Kong* (1962). 91 minutes

Harold Gridley: Bob Hope, *George Cochran:* Bing Crosby, *Lalah:* Dorothy Lamour, *Ken Arok:* Murvyn Vye, *Gung:* Peter Coe, *Bhoma Da:* Ralph Moody, *Ramayana:* Leon Askin, *Guest Stars:* Jane Russell, Dean Martin, Jerry Lewis, *Specialty Dancer:* Jack Claus, *Bo Kassar:* Bernie Gozier, *Priest:* Herman Cantor, *Himself:* Bob Crosby, *Guard:* Michael Ansara, *Lalah at seven:* Bunny Lewbel, *Employment Agency Clerk:* Donald Lawton, *Attendant:* Larry Chance, *Verna's Father:* Harry Cording, *Eunice's Father:* Roy Gordon, *Conductor:* Richard Keene, *Eunice:* Carolyn Jones, *Verna:* Jan Kayne, *Eunice's Brother:* Allan Nixon, *Verna's Brother:* Douglas Yorke.

Road to Bali with Bing Crosby, Dorothy Lamour and Bob Hope.

ROAD TO MOROCCO (1942) Par. Associate Producer, Paul Jones. Directed by David Butler. Original Screenplay, Frank Butler and Don Hartman. Musical Director, Victor Young. Art Directors, Hans Dreier and Robert Usher. Camera, William C. Mellor. Editor, Irene Morra. Songs by Johnny Burke and Jimmy Van Heusen: "Moonlight Becomes You," "Ain't Got a Dime to My Name," "Aladdin's Daughter," "Constantly," and "Road to Morocco" Third of the "Road" pictures. 83 minutes

Road to Morocco with Bing Crosby and Bob Hope.

Jeff Peters: Bing Crosby, *Turkey Jackson/Aunt Lucy:* Bob Hope, *Princess Shalmar:* Dorothy Lamour, *Mullay Kasim:* Anthony Quinn, *Mihirmah:* Dona Drake, *Ahmed Fey:* Mikhail Rasumny, *Hyder Khan:* Vladimir Sokoloff, *Neb Jolla:* George Givot, *Oso Bucco:* Andrew Tombes, *Yusef:* Leon Belasco, *First Aide to Mullay Kasim:* Jamiel Hasson, *Second Aid to Mullay Kasin:* Monte Blue, *Handmaidens:* Louise LaPlanche, Theo de Voe, Brooke Evans, Suzanne Ridgway, Patsy Mace, Yvonne De Carlo, Poppy Wilde, *First Guard:* George Lloyd, *Second Guard:* Sammy Stein, *Arabian Waiter:* Ralph Penney, *Arabian Buyer:* Dan Seymour, *Philippine Announcer:* Pete G. Katchenaro, *English Announcer:* Brandon Hurst, *Chinese Announcer:* Richard Loo, *Russian Announcer:* Leo Mostovoy, *Knife Dancer:* Vic Groves, *Knife Dancer:* Joe Jewett, *Arab Pottery Vendor:* Michael Mark, *Arab Sausage Vendor:* Nestor Paiva, *Idiot:* Stanley Price, *Specialty Dancer:* Rita Christiani, *Gigantic Bearded Arab:* Robert Barron, *Proprietor of Fruit Stand:* Cy Kendall, *Voice for Lady Camel:* Sara Berner, *Voice for Man Camel:* Kent Rogers, *Warrior:* Harry Cording, *Warrior:* Dick Botiller, *Bystander:* Edward Emerson, *Dancer:* Sylvia Opert.

Road to Rio with LaVerne and Maxine Andrews, Bing Crosby and Patti Andrews.

ROAD TO RIO (1947) Par. Producer, Daniel Dare. Director, Norman Z. McLeod. Authors-Screenplay, Edmund Beloin, Jack Rose. Musical Director, Robert Emmett Dolan. Art Directors, Hans Dreier, Earl Hendrick. Cameraman, Ernest Laszlo. Editor, Ellsworth Hoagland. Dances, Bernard Pearce and Billy Daniel. Songs by Johnny Burke and Jimmy Van Heusen: "But Beautiful," "Experience," "You Don't Have to Know the Language," "Apalachicola, Florida," "For What?" Fifth "Road" picture. 100 minutes

Scat Sweeney: Bing Crosby, *Hot Lips Barton:* Bob Hope, *Lucia Maria De Andrade:* Dorothy Lamour, *Catherine Vail:* Gale Sondergaard, *Trigger:* Frank Faylen, *Tony:* Joseph Vitale, *Rodrigues:* Frank Puglia, *Cardoso:* Nestor Paiva, *Johnson:* Robert Barrat; The Stone-Barton Puppeteers, The Carioca Boys; *Cavalry Captain:* Jerry Colonna, *Three Musicians:* The Wiere Brothers, *The Andrews Sisters:* Themselves, *Pilot:* Tad Van Brunt, *Cavalry Officer:* Raul Roulien, *Farmer:* Charles Middleton, *Sherman Malley:* George Meeker, *Captain Harmon:* Stanley Andrews, *Ship's Purser:* Harry Woods, *Samson:* Tor Johnson, *Specialty Dancer:* Albert Ruiz, *Specialty Dancer:* Laura Corbay, *Steward:* Donald Kerr, *Assistant Purser:* Stanley Blystone, *The Prefeito:* George Sorel, *Dancer:* John "Skins" Miller, *Ship's Officer:* Alan Bridge, *Foreman:* Ralph Dunn, *Valet:* George Chandler, *Barber:* Gino Corrado, *Mr. Stanton:* Arthur Q. Bryan, *Buck:* Ray Teal.

Road to Singapore with Claire James, Bob Hope and Bing Crosby.

ROAD TO SINGAPORE (1940) Par. Produced by Harlan Thompson. Directed by Victor Schertzinger. Based on a story by Harry Hervey. Screenplay, Don Hartman and Frank Butler. Art Directors, Hans Dreier and Robert Odell. Music Director, Victor Young. Dances, LeRoy Prinz. Photography, William C. Mellor. Editor, Paul Weatherwax. Songs: "The Moon and the Willow Tree" and "Captain Custard" by Johnny Burke and Victor Schertzinger; "Sweet Potato Piper," "Too Romantic," and "Kaigoon" by Johnny Burke and James Monaco. The first "Road" picture (of seven). 84 minutes

Josh Mallon: Bing Crosby, *Mima:* Dorothy Lamour, *Ace Lannigan:* Bob Hope, *Joshua Mallon IV:* Charles Coburn, *Gloria Wycott:* Judith Barrett, *Caesar:* Anthony Quinn, *Achilles Bombanassa:* Jerry Colonna, *Timothy Willow:* Johnny Arthur, *Morgan Wycott:* Pierre Watkin, *Gordon Wycott:* Gaylord (Steve) Pendleton, *Sir Malcolm Drake:* Miles Mander, *Zato:* Pedro Regas, *Babe:* Greta Granstedt, *Bill:* Edward Gargan, *Sailor:* John Kelly, *Sailor's Wife:* Kitty Kelly, *Father:* Roger Gray, *Native Boy:* Benny Inocencio, *Ninky Poo:* Gloria Franklin, *Native Dancing Girl:* Carmen D'Antonio, *Fred:* Don Brodie, *Secretary:* Harry C. Bradley, *Cameraman:* Richard Keene, *Columnist:* Jack Pepper, *Native Shopkeeper:* Belle Mitchell, *Native Policemen:* Fred Malatesta, Bob St. Angelo, *High Priest:* Monte Blue, *Immigration Officer:* Robert Emmett O'Connor, *Ship's Officer:* Cyril Ring, *Proprietress:* Margarita Padula, *Chaperon:* Grace Hayle, *Ship's Officer:* Richard Tucker, *Homely Girl:* Elvia Allman, *Bartender:* Arthur Q. Bryan, *Dumb-Looking Little Man:* Bobby Barber, *Society Girl:* Helen Lynd.

ROAD TO UTOPIA (1945) Par. Produced by Paul Jones. Directed by Hal Walker. Original Screenplay, Norman Panama and Melvin Frank. Music, Leigh Harline. Music Director, Robert Emmett Dolan. Dance Director, Danny Dare. Art Directors, Hans Dreier and Roland Anderson. Animations, Jerry Fairbanks. Photography, Lionel Lindon. Process Photography, Farciot Edouart. Editor, Stuart Gilmore. Songs by Johnny Burke and Jimmy Van Heusen: "Personality," "Put It There, Pal," "Good Time Charlie," "Welcome to My Dream," "It's Anybody's Spring," "Would You?" The fourth "Road" picture. 89 minutes

Duke Johnson/Junior Hooton: Bing Crosby, *Chester Hooton:* Bob Hope, *Sal Van Hoyden:* Dorothy Lamour, *Kate:* Hillary Brooke, *Ace Larson:* Douglass Dumbrille, *Le Bec:* Jack La Rue, *Sperry:* Robert Barrat, *McGurk:* Nestor Paiva, *Narrator:* Robert Benchley, *Mr. Latimer:* Will Wright, *Ringleader of Henchmen:* Jimmy Dundee, *Newsboy:* Billy Benedict, *Purser:* Arthur Loft, *Official at Boat:* Stanley Andrews, *Boat Captain:* Alan Bridge, *Top Hat:* Romaine Callender, *Ship's Purser:* Paul Newlan, *First Man:* Jack Rutherford, *Second Man:* Al Hill, *Master of Ceremonies:* Edward Emerson, *Hotel Manager:* Ronnie Rondell, *Henchmen:* Allen Pomeroy, Jack Stoney, *Waiter:* George McKay, *Ringleader:* Larry Daniels, *Bear:* Charles Gemora, *Girls:* Claire James, Maxine Fife, *Santa Claus:* Ferdinand Munier, *Officials:* Edgar Dearing, Charles C. Wilson, *Passenger:* Jim Thorpe.

Road to Utopia with Bob Hope, Dorothy Lamour and Bing Crosby.

ROAD TO ZANZIBAR (1941) Par. Produced by Paul Jones. Directed by Victor Schertzinger. Based on the story *Find Colonel Fawcett* by Don Hartman and Sy Bartlett. Screenplay, Frank Butler and Don Hartman. Camera, Ted Tetzlaff. Editor, Alma Macrorie. Songs by Johnny Burke and Jimmy Van Heusen: "Birds of a Feather," "It's Always You," "You're Dangerous," "You Lucky People You," "African Etude," "Road to Zanzibar." Dances, LeRoy Prinz. The second "Road" film. 92 minutes

Chuck Reardon: Bing Crosby, *Fearless (Hubert) Frazier:* Bob Hope, *Donna Latour:* Dorothy Lamour, *Julia Quimby:* Una Merkel, *Charles Kimble:* Eric Blore, *Proprietor of Native Booth:* Luis Alberni, *Dimples:* Joan Marsh, *Fat Lady:* Ethel Loreen Greer, *French Soubrette:* Iris Adrian, *Saunders:* Georges Renavent, *Slave Trader:* Douglass Dumbrille, *Monsieur Lebec:* Lionel Royce, *Thonga:* Buck Woods, *Scarface:* Leigh Whipper, *Whiteface:* Ernest Whitman, *Chief:* Noble Johnson, *Boy:* Leo Gorcey, *Police Inspector:* Robert Middlemass, *Clara Kimble:* Norma Varden, *Turk at Slave Mart:* Paul Porcasi, *Solomon:* Jules Strongbow, *Curzon Sisters:* Priscilla White, LaVerne Vess, *Acrobats:* Harry C. Johnson, Harry C. Johnson, Jr., *Policeman:* Alan Bridge, *Cafe Proprietor:* Henry Roquemore, *Waiter:* James B. Carson, *Barber:* Eddy Conrad, *Clerk:* Richard Keene, *Commentator:* Ken Carpenter, *Gorilla:* Charlie Gemora.

Road to Zanzibar with Una Merkel, Bob Hope, Dorothy Lamour and Bing Crosby.

THE ROARING TWENTIES (1939) WB. Producer, Hal B. Wallis. Directed by Raoul Walsh and Anatole Litvak. Associate Producer, Samuel Bischoff. Author, Mark Hellinger. Screenplay, Jerry Wald, Richard Macaulay, Robert Rossen. Art Director: Max Parker. Musical Director, Leo F. Forbstein. Orchestral Arrangements, Ray Heindorf. Cameraman, Ernie Heindorf. Cameraman, Ernie Haller. Special

The Roaring Twenties with Gladys George, James Cagney and Humphrey Bogart.

Effects, Byron Haskin, Edwin A. DuPar. Editor, Jack Killifer. Sound, E. A. Brunn. Narrator, John Deering. Themes, "Melancholy Baby" and "It Had to Be You." 104 minutes

Eddie Bartlett: James Cagney, *Jean Sherman:* Priscilla Lane, *George Hally:* Humphrey Bogart, *Lloyd Hart:* Jeffrey Lynn, *Panama Smith:* Gladys George, *Danny Green:* Frank McHugh, *Nick Brown:* Paul Kelly, *Mrs. Sherman:* Elisabeth Risdon, *Pete Henderson:* Ed Keane, *Sergeant Pete Jones:* Joseph Sawyer, *Lefty:* Abner Biberman, *Luigi, Proprietor:* George Humbert, *Bramfield, Broker:* Clay Clement, *Bobby Hart:* Don Thaddeus Kerr, *Orderly:* Ray Cooke, *Mrs. Gray:* Vera Lewis, *First Mechanic:* Murray Alper, *Second Mechanic:* Dick Wessel, *Fletcher, Foreman:* Joseph Crehan, *Bootlegger:* Norman Willis, *First Officer:* Robert Elliott, *Second Officer:* Eddy Chandler, *Judge:* John Hamilton, *Man in Jail:* Elliott Sullivan, *Jailer* Pat O'Malley, *Proprietor of Still:* Arthur Loft, *Ex-Cons: First Man:* Al Hill, *Second Man:* Raymond Bailey, *Third Man:* Lew Harvey, *Order-takers:* Joe Devlin, Jeffrey Sayre, *Mike:* Paul Phillips, *Masters:* George Meeker, *Piano Player:* Bert Hanlon, *Drunk:* Jack Norton, *Captain:* Alan Bridge, *Henchman:* Fred Graham, *Doorman:* James Blaine, *Couple:* Harry C. Bradley, Lottie Williams.

THE ROBE (1953) 20th. Producer, Frank Ross. Director, Henry Koster. CinemaScope, Technicolor. Based on the novel by Lloyd C. Douglas. Screenplay, Philip Dunne. Adaptation, Gina Kaus. Art Directors, Lyle Wheeler, George W. Davis. Cinematographer, Leon Shamroy. Editor, Barbara McLean. The first CinemaScope film. 135 minutes

Marcellus Gallio: Richard Burton, *Diana:* Jean Simmons, *Demetrius:* Victor Mature, *Peter:* Michael Rennie, *Caligula:* Jay Robinson, *Justus:* Dean Jagger, *Senator Gallio:* Torin Thatcher, *Pilate:* Richard Boone, *Miriam:* Betta St. John, *Paulus:* Jeff Morrow, *Emperor Tiberius:* Ernest Thesiger, *Junia:* Dawn Addams, *Abidor:* Leon Askin,

The Robe with Emmett Lynn (second left), Richard Burton, Victor Mature, Dean Jagger and Michael Rennie.

Quintus: Frank Pulaski, *Marcipor:* David Leonard, *Judas:* Michael Ansara, *Jonathan:* Nicholas Koster, *Dodinius:* Francis Pierlot, *Marius:* Thomas Browne Henry, *Sarpedon:* Anthony Eustrel, *Lucia:* Pamela Robinson, *Voice of Christ:* Cameron Mitchell, *Ship's Captain:* Ford Rainey, *Woman:* Mae Marsh, *Rebecca:* Helen Beverly, *Tiro:* Jay Novello, *David:* Harry Shearer, *Nathan:* Emmett Lynn, *Cornelia:* Sally Corner, *Julia:* Rosalind Ivan, *Lucius:* Peter Reynolds, *Specialty Dancer:* Virginia Lee, *Shalum:* Leo Curley, *Slave Girls:* Joan & Jean Corbett, *Slave Girl:* Gloria Saunders, *Caleb:* Percy Helton, *Chamberlain:* Roy Gordon, *Gracchus:* George E. Stone, *Cleander:* Ben Astar, *Auctioneer:* Marc Snow.

ROBERTA (1935) RKO. Produced by Pandro S. Berman. Directed by William A. Seiter. Based on the novel by Alice Duer Miller, and the 1933 musical *Gowns by Roberta* by Jerome Kern and Otto Harbach. Adaptation, Jane Murfin and Sam Mintz. Additional Dialogue, Glenn Tryon and Allan Scott. Dances, Fred Astaire. Director of Ensembles, Hermes Pan. Music director, Max Steiner. Production Associate, Zion Myers. Art Directors, Van Nest Polglase and Carroll Clark. Costumes, Bernard Newman. Photography, Edward Cronjager. Editor, William Hamilton. Sound, John Tribby. Songs by Jerome Kern, Otto Harbach, Dorothy Fields, Jimmy McHugh, Oscar Hammerstein II: "Lovely to Look At," "I Won't Dance," "Yesterdays," "I'll Be Hard to Handle," "The Touch of Your Hand," "Let's Begin," "Smoke Gets in Your Eyes." Remade as *Lovely to Look At* (MGM, 1952). 105 minutes

Roberta with Fred Astaire, Ginger Rogers and Candy Candido (on bass).

Stephanie: Irene Dunne, *Huck:* Fred Astaire, *Countess Scharwenka (Lizzie Gatz):* Ginger Rogers, *John Kent:* Randolph Scott, *Roberta (Aunt Minnie):* Helen Westley, *Ladislaw:* Victor Varconi, *Sophie:* Claire Dodd, *Voyda:* Luis Alberni, *Lord Delves:* Ferdinand Munier, *Albert:* Torben Meyer, *Professor:* Adrian Rosley, *Fernando:* Bodil Rosing, *Girl:* Lucille Ball, *Cossacks:* Mike Tellegen, Sam Savitsky, *Woman:* Zena Savine, *Orchestra:* Johnny "Candy" Candido, Muzzy Marcellino, Gene Sheldon, Howard Lally, William Carey, Paul McLarind, Hal Bown, Charles Sharpe, Ivan Dow, Phil Cuthbert, Delmon Davis, William Dunn, *Mannequins:* Jane Hamilton, Margaret McChrystal, Kay Sutton, Maxine Jennings, Virginia Reid, Lorna Low, Lorraine DeSart, Wanda Perry, Diane Cook, Virginia Carroll, Betty Dumbries, Donna Roberts, *Bits:* Mary Forbes, William B. Davidson, Judith Vosselli, Rita Gould.

ROBIN AND THE 7 HOODS (1964) WB. Produced by Frank Sinatra. Directed by Gordon Douglas Panavision and Technicolor. Screenplay, David Schwartz. A P-C Production. Photography, William H. Daniels. Executive Producer, Howard W. Koch. Associate Producer, William H. Daniels. Art Director, LeRoy Deane. Music scored and conducted by Nelson Riddle. Songs by Sammy Cahn and James Van Heusen: "My Kind of Town," "Style," "Mr. Booze," "All for One and One for All," "Charlotte Couldn't Charleston," "Any Man Who Loves His Mother," "Don't Be a Do-Badder," "Bang-Bang." Orchestration, Gil C. Grau. Editor, Sam O'Steen. 103 minutes

Robin and the 7 Hoods with Hank Henry, Dean Martin, Sammy Davis, Jr., Frank Sinatra, Richard Bakalyan, Bing Crosby and Phil Crosby.

Robbo: Frank Sinatra, *John:* Dean Martin, *Will:* Sammy Davis, Jr., *Allen A. Dale:* Bing Crosby, *Guy Gisborne:* Peter Falk, *Marian:* Barbara Rush, *Big Jim:* Edward G. Robinson, *Crocker:* Victor Buono, *Police Chief:* Barry Kelley, *Six Second:* Hank Henry, *Blue Jaw:* Robert Carricart, *Vermin:* Alle Jenkins, *Tomatoes:* Jack La Rue, *Mr. Ricks:* Hans Conreid, *Hammacher:* Sig Rumann, *Sheriff Glick:* Robert Foulk, *Robbo's Hoods:* Sonny King, Phil Crosby, Richard Bakalyan, *Gimp:* Phil Arnold, *Soup Meat:* Harry Swoger, *Tick:* Joseph Ruskin, *Liver Jackson:* Bernard Fein, *Cocktail Waitress:* Caryl Lee Hill, *"Booze" Witness:* Diane Sayer, *Prosecutor:* Bill Zuckert, *Judge:* Milton Rudin, *Dignitary:* Maurice Manson, *Jud:* Chris Hughes, *Hood:* Harry Wilson.

ROMAN HOLIDAY (1953) Par. Produced and directed by William Wyler. Story, Ian McLellan Hunter. Screenplay, Ian McLellan Hunter and John Dighton. Music, Georges Auric. Art Directors, Hal Pereira and Walter Tyler. Photography, Frank F. Planer and Henri Alekan. Editor, Robert Swink. Filmed in Rome and at Cinecittà Studios. American film debut of Audrey Hepburn. 119 minutes

Joe Bradley: Gregory Peck, *Princess Anne:* Audrey Hepburn, *Irving Radovich:* Eddie Albert, *Mr. Hennessy:* Hartley Power, *Hennessy's Secretary:* Laura Solari, *Ambassador:* Harcourt Williams, *Countess Vereberg:* Margaret Rawlings, *General Provno:* Tullio Carminati, *Mario Delani:* Paolo Carlini, *Giovanni:* Claudio Ermelli, *Charwoman:* Paola Borboni, *Dr. Bonnachoven:* Heinz Hindrich, *Shoe Seller:* Gorella Gori, *Taxi Driver:* Alfredo Rizzo.

Roman Holiday with Audrey Hepburn, Gregory Peck and Eddie Albert.

ROMAN SCANDALS (1933) UA. Produced by Samuel Goldwyn. Directed by Frank Tuttle. Original Story, George S. Kaufman and Robert E. Sherwood. Adaptation, William Anthony McGuire. Additional Dialogue, George Oppenheimer, Arthur Sheekman, Nat Perrin. Photography, Gregg Toland. Editor, Stuart Heisler. Sound,

Roman Scandals with Gloria Stuart and Eddie Cantor.

Vinton Vernon. Songs: "Rome Wasn't Built in a Day", "Build a Little Home," "Keep Young and Beautiful," and "No More Love" by Al Dubin and Harry Warren; "Tax on Love" by L. Wolfe Gilbert and Harry Warren. Dances, Busby Berkeley. Chariot Sequence Director, Ralph Cedar. 93 minutes

Eddie: Eddie Cantor, *Olga:* Ruth Etting, *Princess Sylvia:* Gloria Stuart, *Josephus:* David Manners, *Empress Agrippa:* Veree Teasdale, *Emperor Valerius:* Edward Arnold, *Majordomo:* Alan Mowbray, *Manius:* Jack Rutherford, *Slave Dancer:* Grace Poggi, *Warren F. Cooper:* Willard Robertson, *Mayor of West Rome:* Harry Holman, *Storekeeper:* Lee Kohlmar, *Slave Auctioneer:* Stanley Fields, *Slave Market Soloists:* The Abbottiers (Florence Wilson, Rose Kirsner, Genevieve Irwin, Dolly Bell), *Police Chief Charles Pratt:* Charles C. Wilson, *Buggs, Museum Keeper:* Clarence Wilson, *Official:* Stanley Andrews, *Cop/ Roman Jailer:* Stanley Blystone, *Soldier:* Harry Cording, *Soldier:* Lane Chandler, *Slave Buyer:* William Wagner, *Lady Slave Bidder:* Louise Carver, *Citizen:* Francis Ford, *Caius, Food Tester:* Charles Arnt, *Torturer:* Leo Willis, *Soldier:* Duke York, *Lucius, Aide:* Frank Hagney, *Assistant Cook:* Michael Mark, *Guard:* Dick Alexander, *Chef:* Paul Porcasi, *Senator:* John Ince, *Manager of Beauty Salon:* Jane Darwell, *Little Eddie:* Billy Barty, *Girl:* Iris Shunn, *Slave Dancer:* Aileen Riggin, *Slave Girls:* Katharine Mauk, Rosalie Fromson, Mary Lange, Vivian Keefer, Barbara Pepper, Theo Plane, Lucille Ball.

ROMEO AND JULIET (1936) MGM. Produced by Irving Thalberg. Directed by George Cukor. Based on the play by William Shakespeare. Arranged for the screen by Talbot Jennings. Musical Score, Herbert Stothart. Art Director, Cedric Gibbons. Dance Director, Agnes De Mille. Camera, William Daniels. Editor, Margaret Booth. Settings, Cedric Gibbons and Oliver Messel. Associates, Fredric Hope and Edwin B. Willis. Costumes, Oliver Messel and Adrian. Artistic Consultant, Oliver Messel. Literary Consultant, Prof. William Strunk, Jr. Other versions: Biograph 1914; Metro, 1916; Fox, 1916; British-made, 1954; Russian ballet film, 1955; British ballet film, 1966; British, 1968. 127 minutes

Romeo and Juliet with Norma Shearer and Ralph Forbes.

472

Juliet: Norma Shearer, *Romeo:* Leslie Howard, *Nurse:* Edna May Oliver, *Mercutio:* John Barrymore, *Lord Capulet:* C. Aubrey Smith, *Tybalt:* Basil Rathbone, *Peter:* Andy Devine, *Friar Lawrence:* Henry Kolker, *Lady Capulet:* Violet Kemble-Cooper, *Paris:* Ralph Forbes, *Benvolio:* Reginald Denny, *Balthasar:* Maurice Murphy, *Prince of Vernona:* Conway Tearle, *Lady Montague:* Virginia Hammond, *Lord Montague:* Robert Warwick, *Samson Capulet:* Vernon Downing, *Apothecary:* Ian Wolfe, *Gregory Capulet:* Anthony Kemble-Cooper, *Mercutio's Page:* Anthony March, *Abraham Montague:* Howard Wilson, *Tybalt's Page:* Carlyle Blackwell, Jr., *Friar John:* John Bryan, *Rosalind:* Katherine De Mille, *Town Watch:* Wallis Clark, *Bits:* Dean Richmond Bentor, Lita Chevret, Jeanne Hart, Dorothy Granger, *Noblemen:* Harold Entwistle, Charles Bancroft, Jose Rubio.

ROSE MARIE (1936) MGM. Produced by Hunt Stromberg. Directed by W. S. Van Dyke. Based on Arthur Hammerstein's production of the musical by Otto A. Harbach and Oscar Hammerstein II. Screenplay, Frances Goodrich, Albert Hackett, Alice Duer Miller. Music Director, Herbert Stothart. Camera, William Daniels. Editor, Blanche Sewell. Songs: "Rose Marie," "Song of the Mounties," "Lak Jeem," "Indian Love Call," "Totem Tom Tom" by Otto Harbach, Oscar Hammerstein II, and Rudolf Friml; "Just for You" by Gus Kahn, Herbert Stothart, and Rudolf Friml; "Pardon Me Madame" by Gus Kahn and Herbert Stothart; "Dinah" by Sam Lewis, Joe Young, and Harry Akst; "Some of These Days" by Shelton Brooks. Totem pole dance staged by Chester Hale. Operatic episodes staged by William von Wymetal. Sound, Douglas Shearer. Art Director's Associates, Joseph Wright and Edwin B. Willis. Gowns, Adrian. TV Title: *Indian Love Call.* Other versions made by MGM as a 1928 silent and in 1954. 113 minutes

Rose Marie with Jeanette MacDonald and Nelson Eddy.

Marie de Flor: Jeanette MacDonald, *Sergeant Bruce:* Nelson Eddy, *John Flower:* James Stewart, *Meyerson:* Reginald Owen, *Romeo:* Allan Jones, *Bella:* Gilda Gray, *Boniface:* George Regas, *Cafe Manager:* Robert Greig, *Anna:* Una O'Connor, *Storekeeper:* Lucien Littlefield, *Premier:* Alan Mowbray, *Teddy:* David Niven, *Mr. Daniels:* Herman Bing, *Joe:* James Conlin, *Edith:* Dorothy Gray, *Corn Queen:* Mary Anita Loos, *Susan:* Aileen Carlyle, *Mr. Gordon:* Halliwell Hobbes, *Emil:* Paul Porcasi, *Mounted Policeman:* Ed Dearing, *Traveling Salesman:* Pat West, *Stage Manager:* Milton Owen, *Doorman:* David Clyde, *Commandant:* Russell Hicks, *Men:* Rolfe Sedan, Jack Pennick, *Louis:* Leonard Carey, *Dancers:* David Robel, Rinaldo Alacorn, *Trapper:* Bert Lindley.

The Rose Tattoo with Anna Magnani.

THE ROSE TATTOO (1955) Par. Producer, Hal B. Wallis. Director, Daniel Mann. VistaVision. Based on the play *The Rose Tattoo* by Tennessee Williams. Screenplay, Tennessee Williams. Adaptation, Hal Kanter. Art Director, Hal Pereira, Tambi Larsen. Musical Director, Alex North. Cinematographer, James Wong Howe. Editor, Warren Low. 117 minutes

Serafina Delle Rose: Anna Magnani, *Alvaro Mangiacavallo:* Burt Lancaster, *Rosa Delle Rose:* Marisa Pavan, *Jack Hunter:* Ben Cooper, *Estelle Hohnegarten:* Virginia Grey, *Bessie:* Jo Van Fleet, *Assunta:* Mimi Aguglia, *Flora:* Florence Sundstrom, *Schoolteacher:* Dorrit Kelton, *Peppina:* Rossana San Marco, *Guiseppina:* Augueta Merighi, *Mariella:* Rosa Rey, *The Strega:* Georgia Simmons, *Miss Mangiacavallo:* Zolya Talma, *Pop Mangiacavallo:* George Humbert, *Grandma Mangiacavallo:* Margherita Pasquero, *Mamma Shigura (Tattoo Artist):* May Lee, *Taxi Driver:* Lewis Charles, *Rosario Delle Rose:* Larry Chance, *Violetta:* Jean Hart, *Doctor:* Roger Gunderson, *Salvatore:* Roland Vildo, *Taxi Driver:* Virgil Osborne, *Mario:* Albert Atkins.

ROYAL WEDDING (1951) MGM. Producer, Arthur Freed. Director, Stanley Donen. Color by Technicolor. Screenplay, Alan Jay Lerner. Art Directors, Cedric Gibbons, Jack Martin Smith. Musical Director, Johnny Green. Photography, Robert Planck. Editor, Albert Akst. Songs by Alan Jay Lerner and Burton Lane: "You're All the World to Me," "How Could You Believe Me," "Sunday Jumps," "Every Night at Seven," "Open Your Eyes," "The Happiest Day of My Life," "I Left My Hat in Haiti," "Too Late Now," "What a Lovely Day For a Wedding" and "I Got Me a Baby." Dances, Nick Castle. 93 minutes

Tom Bowen: Fred Astaire, *Ellen Bowen:* Jane Powell, *Lord John Brindale:* Peter Lawford, *Anne Ashmond:* Sarah Churchill, *Irving Klinger/Edgar Klinger:* Keenan Wynn, *James Ashmond:* Albert Sharpe, *Sarah Ashmond:* Viola Roache, *Purser:* Henri Letondal, *Cabby:* James Finlayson, *Chester:* Alex Frazer, *Pete Cumberly:* Jack Reilly, *Dick:* William Cabanne, *Billy:* John Hedloe, *Charles Gordon:* Francis Bethancourt, *Pop:* Jack Daley, *Young Man:* James Horne, *Bartender:* Jack Gargan, *Linda:* Kerry O'Day, *Barbara:* Pat Williams, *Harry:* Jimmy Fairfax, *Phone Operator:* Mae Clarke, *Chorus Girl:* Wendy Howard, *Man:* Eric Wilton, *Phone Operator:* Helen Winston, *Stage Door Man:* Wilson Benge, *Ellen's Maid:* Margaret Bert, *Man:* Leonard

Royal Wedding with Jane Powell and Fred Astaire.

Mudie, *Woman:* Phyllis Morris, *Bobby:* David Thursby, *Man in Bar:* Wilson Wood, *Woman Guest:* Bess Flowers, *Man Guest:* Oliver Cross.

RUGGLES OF RED GAP (1935) Par. Produced by Arthur Hornblow, Jr. Directed by Leo McCarey. Adapted from the play and novel by Harry Leon Wilson. Screenplay, Walter De Leon, Harlan Thomson, Humphrey Pearson. Editor, Edward Dmytryk. Cinematographer, Alfred Gilks. Recording Engineer, P. G. Wisdom. Assistant Director, A. F. Erickson. Art Directors, Hans Dreier and Robert Odell. Costumes, Travis Banton. Musical numbers by Ralph Rainger and Sam Coslow. Previous versions produced by Essanay, 1918, and Paramount, 1923. Remade as *Fancy Pants* (Paramount, 1950). 90 minutes

Ruggles: Charles Laughton, *Effie Froud:* Mary Boland, *Egbert Froud:* Charlie Ruggles, *Mrs. Judson:* ZaSu Pitts, *George Vane Bassingwell:* Roland Young, *Nell Kenner:* Leila Hyams, *Ma Pettingill:* Maude Eburne, *Charles Belknap-Jackson:* Lucien Littlefield, *Mrs. Belknap-Jackson:* Leota Lorraine, *Jeff Tuttle:* James Burke, *Sam:* Dell Henderson, *Baby Judson:* Baby Ricardo Lord Cezon, *Judy Ballard:* Brenda Fowler, *Mrs. Wallaby:* Augusta Anderson, *Mrs. Myron Carey:* Sarah Edwards, *Jake Henshaw:* Clarence Hummel Wilson, *Clothing Salesman:* Rafael Storm, *Hank:* George Burton, *Cowboy:* Victor Potel, *Buck:* Frank Rice, *Eddie:* William J. Welsh, *Red Gap Jailer:* Lee Kohlmar, *Cowboy:* Harry Bernard, *Lisette:* Alice Ardell, *Barber:* Rolfe Sedan, *Barfly:* Jack Norton, *Bit in Saloon:* Jim Welch, *Chinese Servant:* Willie Fung, *Negro Servant:* Libby Taylor, *Clothing Servant:* Armand Kaliz, *Photographer:* Harry Bowen, *Wedding Guests:* Henry Roquemore, Heinie Conklin, Edward Le Saint, *Waiter in Paris Cafe:* Charles Fallon, *Frank, Cabman:* Genaro Spagnoli, *Waiter at Carousel:* Albert Petit, *Effie's Guests in Paris:* Carrie Daumery, Isabelle La Mal, *Dishwasher:* Ernest S. (Ernie) Adams, *Station Agent:* Frank O'Connor.

Ruggles of Red Gap with Charlie Ruggles, Charles Laughton and James Burke.

The Russians Are Coming, The Russians Are Coming with Carl Reiner, Eva Marie Saint, Sheldon Golomb, John Philip Law and Alan Arkin.

THE RUSSIANS ARE COMING THE RUSSIANS ARE COMING (1966) UA. Produced and directed by Norman Jewison. A Mirisch Corporation Presentation. Panavision and De Luxe Color. Based on the novel *The Off-Islanders* by Nathaniel Benchley. Screenplay, William Rose. Photography, Joseph Biroc. Music, Johnny Mandel. Art Director, Robert F. Boyle. Assistant Director, Kurt Neuman, Jr. Editors, Hal Ashby and J. Terry Williams. Production Supervisor, Allen K. Wood. Production Manager, James E. Henderling. Unit Manager, Fred Lemoine. Assistant to the Producer, Peter Nelson. Sound, Alfred J. Overton and John Romness. Wardrobe, Wesley Jeffries. Music Editor, Richard Carruth. Second Assistant Director, Les Gorall. Set Decorator, Darrell Silvera. Set Designers, James F. McGuire and Lewis E. Hurst, Jr. Script Supervisor, Betty Levin. Dialogue Director, Leon Belasco. Special Effects, Daniel W. Hays. Make-up, Del Armstrong. Sound Editor, Sidney E. Sutherland. Hair Stylist, Sydney Guilaroff. Hairdresser, Naomi Cavin. Property, Anthony N. Bavero. Sketch Artist, Thomas J. Wright, Jr. Casting, Lynn Stalmaster. Titles, Pablo Ferro, Inc. Filmed in Northern California. Film debut of Alan Arkin. U.S. debut of John Phillip Law. 126 minutes

Walt Whittaker: Carl Reiner, *Elspeth Whittaker:* Eva Marie Saint, *Rozanov:* Alan Arkin, *Link Mattocks:* Brian Keith, *Norman Jonas:* Jonathan Winters, *The Captain:* Theodore Bikel, *Fendall Hawkins:* Paul Ford, *Alice Foss:* Tessie O'Shea, *Alexei Kolchin:* John Phillip Law, *Alison Palmer:* Andrea Dromm, *Luther Grilk:* Ben Blue, *Pete Whittaker:* Sheldon Golomb, *Annie Whittaker:* Cindy Putnam, *Lester Tilly:* Guy Raymond, *Charlie Hinkson:* Cliff Norton, *Oscar Maxwell:* Dick Schaal, *Isaac Porter:* Philip Coolidge, *Irving Christiansen:* Don Keefer, *Mr. Everett:* Parker Fennelly, *Muriel Everett:* Doro Merande, *Mr. Bell:* Vaughn Taylor, *Jerry Maxwell:* Johnnie Whittaker, *Polsky:* Danny Klega, *Brodsky:* Ray Baxter, *Maliavin:* Paul Verdier, *Gromolsky:* Nikita Knatz, *Vasilov:* Constantine Baksheef, *Hrushevsky:* Alex Hassilev, *Lysenko:* Milos Milos, *Kregitkin:* Gino Gottarelli, *Stanley, Airport Worker:* Michael J. Pollard, *Reverend Hawthorne:* Peter Brocco.

Sabrina with Humphrey Bogart and Audrey Hepburn.

SABRINA (1954) Par. Producer, Billy Wilder. Director, Billy Wilder. From Samuel Taylor's play *Sabrina Fair*. Screenplay, Billy Wilder. Art Directors, Hal Pereira, Walter Tyler. Cinematographer, Charles Lang, Jr. Editor, Doane Harrison. Filmed in Rye, New York; New York City; Glen Cove, Long Island; on the estate of Barney Balaban (President of Paramount Pictures). 113 minutes

Linus Larrabee: Humphrey Bogart, *Sabrina Fairchild:* Audrey Hepburn, *David Larrabee:* William Holden, *Oliver Larrabee:* Walter Hampden, *Thomas Fairchild:* John Williams, *Elizabeth Tyson:* Martha Hyer, *Gretchen Van Horn:* Joan Vohs, *Baron:* Marcel Dalio, *The Professor:* Marcel Hillaire, *Maude Larrabee:* Nella Walker, *Mr. Tyson:* Francis X. Bushman, *Miss McCardle:* Ellen Corby, *Margaret (Cook):* Marjorie Bennett, *Charles (Butler):* Emory Parnell, *Mrs. Tyson:* Kay Riehl, *Jenny (Maid):* Nancy Kulp, *Houseman:* Kay Kuter, *Doctor:* Paul Harvey, *Board Members:* Emmett Vogan, Colin Campbell, *Man (with Tray):* Harvey Dunn, *Spiller's Girl Friend:* Marion Ross, *Spiller:* Charles Harvey.

THE SAD SACK (1957) Par. Producer, Hal B. Wallis, Associate Producer, Paul Nathan. Director, George Marshall. VistaVision Based on the cartoon character created by George Baker. Screenplay, Edmund Beloin, Nate Monaster. Art Directors, Hal Pereira, John Goodman. Music scored and conducted by Walter Scharf. Cinematographer, Loyal Griggs. Editor, Archie Marshek. Costumes, Edith Head. Assistant Director, C.C. Coleman, Jr. Numbers staged by Charles O'Curran. Title Song by Hal David and Burt Bacharach. 98 minutes

Bixby: Jerry Lewis, *Dolan:* David Wayne, *Major Shelton:* Phyllis Kirk, *Abdul:* Peter Lorre, *Pvt. Stan Wenaslawsky:* Joe Mantell, *Sgt. Pulley:* Gene Evans, *Ali Mustapha:* George Dolenz, *Zita:* Liliane Montevecchi, *Gen. Vanderlip:* Shepperd Strudwick, *Hassim:* Abraham Sofaer, *Sgt. Hansen:* Mary Treen, *Lt. Wilson:* Drew Cahill, *Moki:* Michael G. Ansara, *Captain Ward:* Don Haggerty, *French General:* Jean Del Val, *Arab Chieftain:* Dan Seymour, *Hazel (Wac):* Yvette Vickers, *Cpt. Schultz:* Danny Davenport, *Foreign Legion Lt.:* Jacques Gallo, *Company Clerk:* Leon Tyler, *Sexy Girl:* Marilyn Hanold, *Brunette:* Isabella Rye, *Gloria:* Anitea Stevens, *Lorraine:* Jacqueline Park, *Donnelly:* Barbara Knudson, *Conductor:* Tony Merrill.

The Sad Sack with Jerry Lewis and David Wayne.

SAILOR BEWARE (1951) Par. Produced by Hal B. Wallis. Directed by Hal Walker. From the play *Sailor Beware* by Kenyon Nicholson and Charles Robinson. Screenplay, James Allardice and Martin Rackin. Additional Dialogue, John Grant. Adaptation, Elwood Ullman. Art Directors, Hal Pereira and Henry Bumstead. Music Director, Joseph J. Lilley. Photography, Daniel L. Fapp. Editor, Warren Low. Songs by Mack David and Jerry Livingston: "Sailors' Polka," "Never Before," "Merci Beaucoup," "The Old Calliope," and "Today, Tomorrow, Forever." Previous versions by Paramount: *Lady, Be Careful* (1936), *The Fleet's In* (1942). Bit player Duke Mitchell teamed with Sammy Petrillo to do a Martin & Lewis takeoff called *Bela Lugosi Meets a Brooklyn Gorilla* (Realart, 1952). 108 minutes

Sailor Beware with Dean Martin and Jerry Lewis.

Al Crowthers: Dean Martin, *Melvin Jones:* Jerry Lewis, *Guest Star:* Corinne Calvet, *Hilda Jones:* Marion Marshall, *Lardoski:* Robert Strauss, *Commander Lane:* Leif Erickson, *Mr. Chubby:* Don Wilson, *Blayden:* Vincent Edwards, *Mac:* Skip Homeier, *'Bama:* Dan Barton, *Tiger:* Mike Mahoney, *Ginger:* Mary Treen, *Turk:* Danny Arnold, *Navy Doctor:* Louis Jean Heydt, *Lieutenant Saunders:* Elaine Stewart, *Bull:* Drew Cahill, *Petty Officer:* James Flavin, *Lt. Connors:* Don Haggerty, *Pretty Girl:* Mary Murphy, *Corpsman:* Jerry Hausner, *Jeff Spencer:* Darr Smith, *Mayo Brothers:* Bobby and Eddie Mayo, *Guard:* Richard Karlan, *Killer Jackson:* Eddie Simms, *McDurk:* Stephen Gregory, *Navy Captain:* Robert Carson, *Petty Officer:* Richard Emory, *Hospital Corpsman:* Marshall Reed, *Hospital Corpsman:* John V. Close, *Female Commentator:* Elaine Riley, *Referee:* Larry McGrath, *Second:* Duke Mitchell, *Sailor:* James Dean, *Themselves:* The Marimba Merry Makers, *Chief Bos'n Mate:* Donald MacBride, *Bandleader:* Dick Stabile, *Betty:* Betty Hutton.

SALOME (1953) Col. Producer, Buddy Adler. Director, William Dieterle. Technicolor. Author, Jesse Lasky, Jr. Screenplay, Harry Kleiner. Art Director, John Meehan. Cinematographer, Charles Lang. Editor, Viola Lawrence. 103 minutes

Princess Salome: Rita Hayworth, *Commander Claudius:* Stewart Granger, *King Herod:* Charles Laughton, *Queen Herodias:* Judith Anderson, *Caesar Tiberius:* Sir Cedric Hardwicke, *John the Baptist:* Alan Badel, *Pontius Pilate:* Basil Sydney, *Ezra:* Maurice Schwartz, *Marcellus Fabius:* Rex Reason, *Micha:* Arnold Moss, *Oriental Dance Team:* Sujata and Asoka, *Courier:* Robert Warwick, *Salome's Servant:* Carmen D'Antonio, *Captain Quintus:* Michael Granger, *Slave Master:* Karl "Killer" Davis, *Simon:* Charles Wagenheim, *Guard:* Tris Coffin, *Sailor:* Rick Vallin, *Herod's Captain of the Guards:* Mickey Simpson, *Roman Guard:* Eduard Cansino, *Executioner:* Lou Nova, *Sword Dancer:* Fred Letuli, *Sword Dancer:* John Woodd, *Fire Eater:* William Spaeth, *Juggling Specialty:* Duke Johnson, *Galilean Soldier:* Earl Brown.

Salome with Charles Laughton and Rita Hayworth.

Samson and Delilah with Victor Mature and Hedy Lamarr.

SAMSON AND DELILAH (1949) Par. Producer-Director, Cecil B. De Mille. Color by Technicolor. Screenplay, Jesse Lasky, Jr., Frederick M. Frank. Music, Victor Young. Art Directors, Hans Dreier, Walter Tyler. Photography, George Barnes. Editor, Anne Bauchens. Song by Ray Evans, Jay Livingston and Victor Young: "Song of Delilah." From original treatments by Harold Lamb and Vladimir Jabotinsky. Based upon the history of Samson and Delilah in the Holy Bible, Judges 13-16. Choreography, Theodore Kosloff. Doubles for Victor Mature: fight sequences, Ed Hinton, lion-fighting sequence, Mel Koontz. 128 minutes

Delilah: Hedy Lamarr, *Samson:* Victor Mature, *The Saran of Gaza:* George Sanders, *Semadar:* Angela Lansbury, *Ahtur:* Henry Wilcoxon, *Miriam:* Olive Deering, *Hazel:* Fay Holden, *Hisham:* Julia Faye, *Saul:* Rusty Tamblyn, *Tubal:* William Farnum, *Teresh:* Lane Chandler, *Targil:* Moroni Olsen, *Story Teller:* Francis J. McDonald, *Garmiskar:* William Davis, *Lesh Lakish:* John Miljan, *Fat Philistine Merchant:* Arthur Q. Bryan, *Spectators:* Laura Elliot and Jeff York, *Lord of Ashdod:* Victor Varconi, *Lord of Gath:* John Parrish, *Lord of Ekron:* Frank Wilcox, *Lord of Ashkelon:* Russell Hicks, *First Priest:* Boyd Davis, *Lord Sharif:* Fritz Leiber, *Leader of Philistine Soldiers:* Mike Mazurki, *Merchant Prince:* Davison Clark, *Wounded Messenger:* George Reeves, *Bar Simon:* Pedro de Cordoba, *Village Barber:* Frank Reicher, *Princes:* Colin Tapley, Nils Asther, *Priests:* Pierre Watkin, Fred Graham, *Woman:* Karen Morley, *Danite Merchant:* Charles Judels, *Manoah, Samson's Father:* Charles Evans, *Prince:* James Craven, *Chief Scribe:* Lloyd Whitlock, *Court Astrologer:* Crauford Kent, *Gammad:* Harry Woods, *Bergam:* Stephen Roberts, *Makon:* Ed Hinton, *Gristmill Captain:* Tom Tyler, *Overseer at Gristmill:* Ray Bennett, *Spectators:* Margaret Field and John Kellogg, *Spectator:* Dorothy Adams, *Saran's Chariot Driver:* Henry Wills.

SAN ANTONIO (1945) WB. Produced by Robert Buckner. Directed by Robert Florey and David Butler. Color by Technicolor. Original Screenplay, Alan LeMay and W. R. Burnett. Art Director, Ted Smith. Music, Max Steiner. Music Director, Leo F. Forbstein. Orchestral Arrangements, Hugo Friedhofer. Photography, Bert Glennon. Editor, Irene Morra. Special Effects, Willard Van Enger. Songs: "Somewhere in Monterey" by Jack Scholl and Charles Kisco; "Put Your Little Foot Right Out" by Larry Spier; and "Some Sunday Morning" by Ted Koehler, M. K. Jerome, and Ray Heindorf. 111 minutes

Clay Hardin: Errol Flynn, *Jeanne Starr:* Alexis Smith, *Sacha Bozic:* S. Z. Sakall, *Legare:* Victor Francen, *Henrietta:* Florence Bates, *Charlie Bell:* John Litel, *Roy Stuart:* Paul Kelly, *Pony Smith:* John

San Antonio with Florence Bates, S.Z. Sakall, Alexis Smith and Errol Flynn.

Alvin, *Cleve Andrews:* Monte Blue, *Captain Morgan:* Robert Shayne, *Colonel Johnson:* Robert Barrat, *Ricardo Torreon:* Pedro de Cordoba, *Lafe McWilliams:* Tom Tyler, *Hymie Rosas:* Chris-Pin Martin, *Sojer Harris:* Charles Stevens, *San Antonio Stage Driver:* Poodles Hanneford, *Entertainer:* Doodles Weaver, *Joey Sims:* Dan White, *Rebel White:* Ray Spiker, *Hap Winters:* Al Hill, *Tip Brice:* Wallis Clark, *Hawker:* Harry Cording, *Poker Player:* Chalky Williams, *Roper:* Bill Steele, *Clay's Henchmen:* Howard Hill, Allen E. Smith, *Dancer:* Arnold Kent, *Head Customs Officer:* Dan Seymour, *Cowboys:* John Compton, Don McGuire, Brad King, Johnny Miles, Francis Ford, Lane Chandler, Hal Taliaferro, Jack Mower, William Gould, *Bartender:* Harry Seymour, *Jay Witherspoon:* Norman Willis, *Cattlemen:* Eddy Waller, Henry Hall, James Flavin.

THE SAND PEBBLES (1966) 20th. Produced and directed by Robert Wise. An Argyle-Solar Production. Panavision and De Luxe Color. Stereophonic Sound. Screenplay, Robert Anderson. Based on the novel by Richard McKenna. Camera, Joseph McDonald. Editor, William Reynolds. Special Effects, Jerry Endler. Sound, Bernard Freericks, Douglas O. Williams and Murray Spivack. Associate Producer and Second Unit Director, Charles Maguire. Music, Jerry Goldsmith. Conductor, Lionel Newman. Production Design, Boris Leven. Production Associate, Maurice Zuberano. Unit Production Manager, Saul Wurtzel. Assistant Director, Ridgeway Callow. Second Unit Photography, Richard Johnson. Photographic Effects, L. B. Abbott and Emil Kosa, Jr. Costumes, Renie. Technical adviser, Harley Misiner, MMC, USN (Ret.). Set Decorations, Walter M. Scott, John Sturtevent, William Kiernan. Make-up, Ben Nye, Bill Turner and Del Acevedo. Wardrobe, Ed Wynigear. Orchestrations, David Tamkin and Arthur Morton. Filmed in Taiwan and Hong Kong. 191 minutes

Jake Holman: Steve McQueen, *Frenchy Burgoyne:* Richard Attenborough, *Lt. Collins:* Richard Crenna, *Shirley Eckert:* Candice Bergen, *Maily:* Marayat Andriane, *Po-Han:* Mako, *Jameson:* Larry

The Sand Pebbles with Richard Attenborough and Steve McQueen.

Gates, *Ensign Bordelles:* Charles Robinson, *Stawski:* Simon Oakland, *Harris:* Ford Rainey, *Bronson:* Joe Turkel, *Crosley:* Gavin MacLeod, *Shanahan:* Joseph di Reda, *Major Chin:* Richard Loo, *Restorff:* Gus Trikonis, *Mama Chunk:* Beulah Quo, *Victor Shu:* James Hong, *Chief Franks:* Barney Phillips, *Perna:* Shepherd Sanders, *Farren:* James Jeter, *Jennings:* Tom Middleton, *Cho-Jen:* Paul Chinpae, *Chien:* Tommy Lee, *Haythorn:* Stephen Jahn, *Wilsey:* Jay Allan Hopkins, *Waldron:* Glenn Wilder, *Lamb:* Steve Ferry, *CPO Wellbeck:* Ted Fish, *Coleman:* Loren Janes, *Lop-eye Shing:* Henry Wang, *Englishman:* Ben Wright, *Bidder:* Walter Reed, *Customer:* Gil Perkins.

The Sandpiper with Elizabeth Taylor and Richard Burton.

THE SANDPIPER (1965) MGM. Producer, Martin Ransohoff. Director, Vincente Minnelli. MetroColor, Panavision. Adapted by Irene and Louis Kamp from an original by Martin Ransohoff. Screenplay, Dalton Trumbo, Michael Wilson. Art Directors, George W. Davis, Urie McCleary. Music, Johnny Mandel. Cinematographer, Milton Krasner. Editor, David Bretherton. 116 minutes

Laura Reynolds: Elizabeth Taylor, *Dr. Edward Hewitt:* Richard Burton, *Claire Hewitt:* Eva Marie Saint, *Cos Erickson:* Charles Bronson, *Ward Hendricks:* Robert Webber, *Larry Brant:* James Edwards, *Judge Thompson:* Torin Thatcher, *Walter Robinson:* Tom Drake, *Phil Suteliff:* Doug Henderson, *Danny Reynolds:* Morgan Mason, *Troopers:* Dusty Cadis, John Hart, *Trustee:* Jan Arvan, *Trustee's Wife:* Mary Beneit, *Trustee:* Tom Curtis, *Architect:* Paul Genge, *Celebrant #1:* Rex Holman, *Celebrant #2:* Kelton Garwood, *Celebrant #3:* Jimmy Murphy, *Celebrant #4:* Mel Gallagher, *Poet Celebrant #5:* Ron Whelan, *Celebrant #6:* Diane Sayer, *Celebrant #7:* Joan Connors, *Celebrant #8:* Peggy Adams Laird, *Celebrant #9:* Shirley Bonne, *Voice:* Peter O'Toole

SANDS OF IWO JIMA (1949) Rep. Associate Producer, Edmund Grainger. Director, Alan Dwan. Author, Harry Brown. Screenplay, Harry Brown, James Edward Grant. Music, Victor Young. Art Director, James Sullivan. Photography, Reggie Lanning. Editor, Richard L. Van Enger. 110 minutes

Sergeant John M. Stryker: John Wayne, *Pfc. Peter Conway:* John Agar, *Allison Bromley:* Adele Mara, *Pfc. Al Thomas:* Forrest Tucker, *Pfc.*

Sands of Iwo Jima with Forrest Tucker and John Wayne.

Benny Regazzi: Wally Cassell, *Pfc. Charlie Bass:* James Brown, *Pfc. Shipley:* Richard Webb, *Corporal Robert Dunne/Narrator:* Arthur Franz, *Mary:* Julie Bishop, *Pfc. Soames:* James Holden, *Pfc. Hellenpolis:* Peter Coe, *Pfc. Frank Flynn:* Richard Jaeckel, *Pfc. Eddie Flynn:* Bill Murphy, *Pfc. Harris:* George Tyne, *Private "Ski" Choynski:* Hal Fieberling (Hal Baylor), *Captain Joyce:* John McGuire, *Private Mike McHugh:* Martin Milner, *Private Sid Stein:* Leonard Gumley, *Private L. D. Fowler, Jr.* William Self, *Grenade Instructor:* Dick Wessel, *Forrestal:* I. Stanford Jolley, *Wounded Marine:* David Clarke, *Lieutenant Baker:* Gil Herman, *Scared Marine:* Dick Jones, *Colonel:* Don Haggerty, *Marine:* Bruce Edwards, *Tall Girl:* Dorothy Ford, *Lieutenant Thompson:* John Whitney, *Themslves:* Colonel D. M. Shoup, U.S.M.C., Lieutenant Colonel H. P. Crowe U.S.M.C., Captain Harold G. Schrier, U.S.M.C., and the three living survivors of the historic flag raising on Mount Suribachi: Pfc. Rene A. Gagnon, Pfc. Ira H. Hayes, PM 3/C John H. Bradley.

SAN FRANCISCO (1936) MGM. Produced by John Emerson, Bernard H. Hyman. Directed by W. S. Van Dyke. Story, Robert Hopkins. Screenplay by Anita Loos. Cinematographer, Oliver T. Marsh. Recording Engineer, Douglas Shearer. Film Editor, Tom Held. Art Director, Cedric Gibbons. Costumer, Adrian. Musical Director, Herbert Stothart. Songs: "San Francisco" by Gus Kahn and Bronislau Kaper; "Would You?" by Arthur Freed and Nacio Herb Brown; "The One Love" by Gus Kahn, Bronislau Kaper, and Walter Jurmann. Dances, Val Raset. 115 minutes

Blackie: Clark Gable, *Mary:* Jeanette MacDonald, *Tim:* Spencer Tracy, *Mr. Talbot:* Jack Holt, *Mat:* Ted Healy, *Della:* Margaret Irving, *Mrs. Talbot:* Jessie Ralph, *Babe:* Harold Huber, *Professor:* Al Shean, *Baldini:* William Ricciardi, *Chick:* Kenneth Harlan, *Alaska:* Roger Imhof, *Dealer:* Frank Mayo, *Drunk:* Tom Dugan, *Tony:* Charles Judels, *Red Kelly:* Russell Simpson, *Duane:* Bert Roach, *Hazelton:* Warren Hymer, *Sheriff:* Edgar Kennedy, *Madame Albani:* Adrienne d'Ambricourt, *Old Man:* Nigel de Brulier, *Dancer:* Mae Digges, *Singers:* Tudor Williams, Tandy MacKenzie, *Dancer:* Nyas Berry, *Captain of Police:* Tom Mahoney, *Drunk's Girl:* Gertrude Astor, *Father:* Jason Robards, *Fat Man:* Vernon Dent, *Kinko:* Jack

San Francisco with Al Shean. Jeanette MacDonald and Clark Gable.

477

Baxley, *Society Man:* Anthony Jowitt, *Salvation Man:* Carl Stockdale, *Members of Founder's Club:* Richard Carle, Oscar Apfel, Frank Sheridan, Ralph Lewis, *Jowl Lee:* Chester Gan, *Old Irishman:* Jack Kennedy, *Headwaiter:* Cy Kendall, *Coast Type:* Don Rowan.

SARATOGA (1937) MGM. Produced by Bernard H. Hyman. Associate Producer, John Emerson. Directed by Jack Conway. Original Story and Screenplay, Anita Loos and Robert Hopkins. Art Director, Cedric Gibbons. Music Score, Edward Ward. Camera, Ray June. Editor, Elmo Vernon. Songs: "The Horse With the Dreamy Eyes" and "Saratoga," music by Walter Donaldson, lyrics by Bob Wright and Chet Forrest. The last film of Jean Harlow, who died during its production, on June 7, 1937, at 26. Mary Dees replaced her and Paula Winslowe dubbed her voice. Seen are races at Tropical Park, Miami, and at Churchill Downs, Louisville, on Derby Day. 94 minutes

Saratoga Trunk with John Warburton, Jerry Austin, Gary Cooper and Ingrid Bergman.

Saratoga with Lionel Barrymore, Clark Gable and Cliff Edwards.

Duke Bradley: Clark Gable, *Carol Clayton:* Jean Harlow, *Grandpa Clayton:* Lionel Barrymore, *Hartley Madison:* Walter Pidgeon, *Jesse Kiffmeyer:* Frank Morgan, *Fritzi O'Malley:* Una Merkel, *Tip O'Brien:* Cliff Edwards, *Dr. Beard:* George Zucco, *Frank Clayton:* Jonathan Hale, *Rosetta:* Hattie McDaniel, *Dixie Gordon:* Frankie Darro, *Hard Riding Hurley:* Henry Stone, *Boswell:* Carl Stockdale, *Mrs. Hurley:* Ruth Gillette, *Valet:* Charley Foy, *Auctioneer:* Robert Emmett Keane, *Medbury, Trainer:* Edgar Dearing, *Kenyon:* Frank McGlynn, Sr., *Maizie:* Margaret Hamilton, *Judge:* Sam Flint, *Limpy:* Walter Robbins, *Horse Owner:* Pat West, *Clipper:* Harrison Greene, *Pullman Steward:* Forbes Murray, *Gardener:* Si Jenks, *Bartender:* Herbert Ashley, *Cameraman:* George Chandler, *Tout:* Mel Ruick, *Hurley's Kid:* Patsy O'Connor, *Bartender:* Charles R. Moore, *Porter:* Fred (Snowflake) Toones, *Bidder:* Hooper Atchley, *Steve, a Bidder:* Edward (Bud) Flanagan (Dennis O'Keefe), *Cameraman:* Drew Demarest, *Train Passengers:* Irene Franklin, Ernie Stanton, John (Skins) Miller, Hank Mann, Bert Roach.

SARATOGA TRUNK (1945) WB. Executive Producer, Jack L. Warner. Produced by Hal B. Wallis. Directed by Sam Wood. From the novel by Edna Ferber. Screenplay, Casey Robinson. Music, Max Steiner. Music Director, Leo F. Forbstein. Art Director, Carl Jules Weyl. Photography, Ernie Haller. Editor, Ralph Dawson. Sound, Robert B. Lee. Technical Advisor, Dalton S. Reymond. Special Effects, Lawrence Butler. Set Decorations, Fred MacLean. Production Design, Joseph St. Amaad. Make-up, Perc Westmore. Gowns, Leah Rhodes. Assistant Director, Phil Quinn. Unit Manager, Eric Stacey. Songs by Charles Tobias and Max Steiner, "As Long as I Live" and "Goin' Home." 135 minutes

Clint Maroon: Gary Cooper, *Clio Dulane:* Ingrid Bergman, *Angelique:* Flora Robson, *Cupidon:* Jerry Austin, *Sophie Bellop:* Florence Bates, *Bart Van Steed:* John Warburton, *Roscoe Bean:* John Abbott, *Augustin Haussy:* Curt Bois, *Clarissa Van Steed:* Ethel Griffies, *Raymond*

Soule: Louis Payne, *Monsieur Begue:* Fred Essler, *Mrs. Porcelain:* Marla Shelton, *Grandmother Dulane:* Adrienne D'Ambricourt, *Madame Dulane:* Helen Freeman, *Charlotte Dulane:* Sophie Huxley, *J. P. Reynolds:* Minor Watson, *Guilia Forosini:* Jacqueline de Wit, *Miss Diggs:* Sarah Edwards, *Turbaned Seller:* Ruby Dandridge, *Madame Begue:* Amelia Liggett, *Leon, the Headwaiter:* George Beranger, *McIntyre:* Edmund Breon, *Mr. Stone:* William B. Davidson, *Mr. Bowers:* Edward Fielding, *Mr. Pound:* Thurston Hall, *Woman on Piazza* Alice Fleming, *Engineer:* Ralph Dunn, *Al:* Lane Chandler, *Politician:* Dick Elliott, *Cowboy:* Glenn Strange, *Leader of Soule's Gang:* Frank Hagney, *Hotel Clerk:* Chester Clute, *Hotel Manager:* Theodore Von Eltz, *Engineer of Soule's Gang:* Alan Bridge, *Fireman on Train:* Monte Blue, *Ship's Captain:* Georges Renavent, *Officer:* Robert Barron, *First Mate:* Louis Mercier, *Diner:* Gino Corrado, *Soule Bodyguard:* Bob Reeves, *Gamblers:* Franklyn Farnum, Major Sam Harris.

SAYONARA (1957) WB. Produced by William Goetz. Directed by Joshua Logan. Technirama and Technicolor. Based on the novel by James A. Michener. Screenplay, Paul Osborn. Art Direction, Ted Haworth. Sets, Robert Priestly. Music, Franz Waxman. Costumes, Norma Koch. Revue numbers staged by LeRoy Prinz. Assistant Director, Ad Schaumer. Photography, Ellsworth Fredericks. Editing, Arthur P. Schmidt and Philip W. Anderson. Sound, William H. Mueller. Song, "Sayonara" by Irving Berlin. Filmed mostly in Kobe, Japan. Film debuts of Miiko Taka and Miyoshi Umeki. A Goetz Pictures-Pennebaker Production. 147 minutes

Major Lloyd Gruver: Marlon Brando, *Joe Kelly:* Red Buttons, *Nakamura:* Ricardo Montalban, *Hana-ogi:* Miiko Taka, *Katsumi:* Miyoshi Umeki, *Eileen Webster:* Patricia Owens, *Captain Mike Bailey:* James Garner, *Mrs. Webster:* Martha Scott, *General Webster:* Kent Smith, *Colonel Craford:* Douglas Watson, *Fumiko-san:* Reiko Kuba, *Teruko-san:* Soo Yong, *Consul:* Harlan Warde. The Shochuku Kagekidan Girls Revue.

Sayonara with James Garner, Reiko Kuba, Marlon Brando, Miyoshi Umeki and Red Buttons.

Scarface with Paul Muni and Ann Dvorak.

SCARFACE (1932) UA. Produced and supervised by Howard Hughes. Directed by Howard Hawks. Assistant Director, Richard Rosson. Based on the novel by Armitage Trail. Screenplay, Ben Hecht, Seton I. Miller, John Lee Mahin, W. R. Burnett, Fred Pasley. Photography, Lee Garmes and L. W. O'Connell. Editor, Edward Curtiss. Sound, William Snyder. 99 minutes

Tony Camonte: Paul Muni, *Cesca Camonte:* Ann Dvorak, *Poppy:* Karen Morley, *Johnny Lovo:* Osgood Perkins, *Guido Rinaldo:* George Raft, *Ben Guarino:* C. Henry Gordon, *Angelo:* Vince Barnett, *Pietro:* Henry Armetta, *Mrs. Camonte:* Inez Palange, *Louie Costillo:* Harry J. Vejar, *Chief of Detectives:* Edwin Maxwell, *Managing Editor:* Tully Marshall, *Gaffney:* Boris Karloff, *Epstein:* Bert Starkey, *Garston:* Purnell Pratt, *Gaffney Hood:* Paul Fix, *Worker:* Hank Mann, *Bootleggers:* Charles Sullivan, Harry Tenbrook, *Hood:* Maurice Black.

THE SEARCH (1948) MGM. Produced by Lazar Wechsler. Directed by Fred Zinnemann. A Praesens-Film, Zurich, Production. Original Screenplay, Richard Schweizer in collaboration with David Wechsler. Additional Dialogue, Paul Jarrico. Music, Robert Blum. Photography, Emil Berna. Editor, Hermann Haller. Produced in Switzerland and in the U. S. Occupied Zone of Germany, through the permission of the U. S. Army and the cooperation of I. R. O. The first postwar film to be shot in the Occupied Zone. Film debut of Ivan Jandl. 105 minutes

The Search with Aline MacMahon, Ivan Jandl and Montgomery Clift.

Ralph Stevenson: Montgomery Clift, *Mrs. Murray:* Aline MacMahon, *Mrs. Malik:* Jarmila Novotna, *Jerry Fisher:* Wendell Corey, *Karel Malik:* Ivan Jandl, *Mrs. Fisher:* Mary Patton, *Mr. Crookes:* Ewart G. Morrison, *Tom Fisher:* William Rogers, *Joel Makowksy:* Leopold Borkowski, *Raoul Dubois:* Claude Gambier.

The Searchers with Ward Bond, John Wayne and Pat Wayne.

THE SEARCHERS (1956) WB. Executive Producer, Merian C. Cooper. Associate Producer, Patrick Ford. Directed by John Ford. In VistaVision and Technicolor. Based on the novel by Alan LeMay. Screenplay, Frank S. Nugent. Music, Max Steiner. Wardrobe, Frank Beetson and Ann Peck. Assistant Director, Wingate Smith. Title Song, Stan Jones. A.C.V. Whitney Pictures, Inc. Production. Art Directors, Frank Hotaling and James Basevi. Orchestration, Murray Cutter. Photography, Winton C. Hoch. Editor, Jack Murray. Locations: Monument Valley, Utah-Arizona; Gunnison, Colorado; Alberta, Canada. 119 minutes

Ethan Edwards: John Wayne, *Martin Pawley:* Jeffrey Hunter, *Laurie Jorgensen:* Vera Miles, *Captain Rev. Clayton:* Ward Bond, *Debbie Edwards:* Natalie Wood, *Lars Jorgensen:* John Qualen, *Mrs. Jorgensen:* Olive Carey, *Chief Scar:* Henry Brandon, *Charlie McCorry:* Ken Curtis, *Brad Jorgensen:* Harry Carey, Jr., *Emilio Figueroa:* Antonio Moreno, *Lieutenant Greenhill:* Pat Wayne, *Mose Harper:* Hank Worden, *Debbie as a child:* Lana Wood, *Aaron Edwards:* Walter Coy, *Martha Edwards:* Dorothy Jordan, *Lucy Edwards:* Pippa Scott, *Look:* Beulah Archuleta, *Ranger Nesbitt:* Bill Steele, *Colonel Greenhill:* Cliff Lyons, *Texas Ranger:* Chuck Roberson, *Stuntmen:* Billy Cartledge, Chuck Hayward, Slim Hightower, Fred Kennedy, Frank McGrath, Dale Van Sickle, Henry Wills, Terry Wilson, *Comanches:* Navajo tribe, including Away Luna, Billy Yellow, Bob Many Mules, Exactley Sonnie Betsuie, Feather Hat, Jr., Harry Black Horse, Jack Tin Horn, Many Mules Son, Percy Shooting Star, Pete Gray Eyes, Pipe Line Begishe, Smile White Sheep.

THE SEA WOLF (1941) WB. Vice-president in Charge of Production, Jack L. Warner. Executive Producer, Hal B. Wallis. Directed by Michael Curtiz. Based on the novel by Jack London. Screenplay, Robert Rossen. Photography, Sol Polito. Music, Erich Wolfgang Korngold. Editor, George Amy. Associate Producer, Henry Blanke. Previous versions of *The Sea Wolf* made by: Bosworth, 1913; Paramount, 1920; PDC, 1925; and Fox, 1930. Remade as: *Barricade* (Warners, 1950); and *Wolf Larsen* (Allied Artists, 1958). 100 minutes

The Sea Wolf with Ida Lupino and John Garfield.

Wolf Larsen: Edward G. Robinson, *George Leach:* John Garfield, *Ruth Webster:* Ida Lupino, *Humphrey Van Weyden:* Alexander Knox, *Dr. Louie Prescott:* Gene Lockhart, *Cooky:* Barry Fitzgerald, *Johnson:* Stanley Ridges, *Svenson:* Francis McDonald, *Young Sailor:* David Bruce, *Harrison:* Howard da Silva, *Smoke:* Frank Lackteen, *Agent:* Ralf Harolde, *Crewman:* Louis Mason, *Crewman:* Dutch Hendrian, *First Detective:* Cliff Clark, *Second Detective:* William Gould, *First Mate:* Charles Sullivan, *Pickpocket:* Ernie Adams, *Singer:* Jeane Cowan, *Helmsman:* Wilfred Lucas.

THE SECRET LIFE OF WALTER MITTY (1947) RKO. Producer, Samuel Goldwyn. Director, Norman Z. McLeod. Color by Technicolor. From a story by James Thurber. Screenplay, Ken England, Everett Freeman. Art Directors, George Jenkins, Perry Ferguson. Music, David Raksin. Musical Director, Emil Newman. Cameraman, Lee Garmes. Editor, Monica Collingwood. Songs by Sylvia Fine: "Anatole of Paris" and "Symphony for Unstrung Tongues." 105 minutes

Walter Mitty: Danny Kaye, *Rosalind Van Hoorn:* Virginia Mayo, *Doctor Hugo Hollingshead:* Boris Karloff, *Mrs. Mitty:* Fay Bainter, *Gertrude Griswold:* Ann Rutherford, *Bruce Pierce:* Thurston Hall, *Tubby Wadsworth:* Gordon Jones, *Mrs. Griswold:* Florence Bates, *Peter Van Hoorn:* Konstantin Shayne, *R.A.F. Colonel:* Reginald Denny, *Hendrick:* Henry Gordon, *Mrs. Follinsbee:* Doris Lloyd, *Anatole:* Fritz Feld, *Maasdam:* Frank Reicher, *Butler:* Milton Parsons, *Goldwyn Girls:* Mary Brewer, Betty Cargyle, Sue Casey, Lorraine DeRome, Karen X. Gaylord, Mary Ellen Gleason, Jackie Jordan, Georgia Lange, Michael Mauree, Martha Montgomery, Pat Patrick, Irene Vernon, Lynn Walker, *Wolf Man:* George Magrill, *Mr. Grimsby:* Joel Friedkin, *Office Boy:* Harry Harvey, Jr. *Business Manager:* Warren Jackson, *Illustrator:* Bess Flowers, *Art Editor:* Sam Ash, *Dr. Remington:* John Hamilton, *Dr. Renshaw:* Charles Trowbridge, *Vincent:* Jack Overman, *Mrs. Pierce:* Mary Forbes, *Minister:* Pierre Watkin, *Western Character:* Hank Worden, *Dr. Benbow:* Henry Kolker, *Dr. Pritchard-Mitford:* Lumsden Hare.

The Secret Life of Walter Mitty with Danny Kaye.

SEE HERE, PRIVATE HARGROVE (1944) MGM. Producer, George Haight. Director, Wesley Ruggles. Based on the book by Marion Hargrove. Screenplay, Harry Kurnitz. Musical Score, David Snell. Art Director, Cedric Gibbons. Cameraman, Charles Lawton. Editor, Frank E. Hull. Song by Frank Loesser and Ted Grouya: "In My Arms." Sequel was *What Next, Corporal Hargrove?* (MGM, 1945). 101 minutes

Marion Hargrove: Robert Walker, *Carol Halliday:* Donna Reed, *Mr. Halliday:* Robert Benchley, *Private Mulvehill:* Keenan Wynn, *Bob:* Bob Crosby, *Brody S. Griffith:* Ray Collins, *Sergt. Cramp:* Chill Wills, *Mrs. Halliday:* Marta Linden, *Uncle George:* Grant Mitchell, *Private Orrin Esty:* George Offerman, Jr., *General Dillon:* Edward Fielding, *Sgt. Heldon:* Donald Curtis, *Private Bill Burk:*

See Here, Private Hargrove with Stephen Barclay, Robert Walker and Donna Reed.

William "Bill" Phillips, *Captain Manville:* Douglas Fowley, *Colonel Forbes:* Morris Ankrum, *Sergeant:* Mickey Rentschler, *M.P.:* Frank Faylen, *Doctor:* Jack Luden, *Lieutenant:* Maurice Murphy, *Capt. Hamilton:* Clarence Straight, *Mr. Smith:* William Newell, *Captain:* Louis Jean Heydt, *Corporal:* Ken Scott, *Officer of Day:* Michael Owen, *Corporal:* Stephen Barclay, *Exercise Sgt.:* John Kelly, *Mess Sgt.:* Joe Devlin, *Executive Officer:* Dennis Moore, *Field Operator:* Rod Bacon, *Farmer:* Louis Mason, *Farmer's Wife:* Connie Gilchrist, *Captain:* Harry Strang, *Old Man:* Harry Tyler, *Porter:* Mantan Moreland, *Lieutenant:* Myron Healey, *Girl Clerk:* Mary McLeod, *Captain Hammond:* Eddie Acuff, *Lieutenant:* Fred Kohler, Jr., *Executive Officer:* James Warren, *Field Operator:* Blake Edward.

SEPARATE TABLES (1958) UA. Producer, Harold Hecht. Director, Delbart Mann. Screenplay by Terence Rattigan and John Gay. Based on the play by Terence Rattigan. Music by David Raksin. Gowns by Edith Head. Song by Harry Warren and Harold Adamson, sung by Vic Damone. Assistant Director, Thomas F. Shaw. Costumes, Mary Grant. A Clifton Production for Hecht-Hill-Lancaster. 98 minutes

Separate Tables with Deborah Kerr and David Niven.

Ann Shankland: Rita Hayworth, *Sibyl Railton-Bell:* Deborah Kerr, *Major Pollock:* David Niven, *Pat Cooper:* Wendy Hiller, *John Malcolm:* Burt Lancaster, *Mrs. Railton-Bell:* Gladys Cooper, *Lady Matheson:* Cathleen Nesbitt, *Mr. Fowler:* Felix Aylmer, *Charles:* Rod Taylor, *Jean:* Audrey Dalton, *Miss Meacham:* May Hallatt, *Doreen:* Priscilla Morgan, *Mabel:* Hilda Plowright.

SERGEANTS 3 (1962) UA. Producer, Frank Sinatra. Director, John Sturges. Executive Producer, Howard W. Koch. Screenplay, W. R. Burnett. Music, Billy May. Song, Johnny Rotella. Franz Steininger. Assistant Director, Jack Reddish. An Essex-Claude Production in Panavision and Technicolor. Art Director, Frank Hotaling. Music,

Billy May. "And the Night Wind Song," music, Johnny Rotella, lyrics, Franz Steininger. Cinematographer, Winton Hoch. Editor, Ferris Webster. Remake of *Gunga Din* (RKO, 1939). 112 minutes

First Sergeant Mike Merry: Frank Sinatra, *Sergeant Chip Deal:* Dean Martin, *Jonah Williams:* Sammy Davis, Jr., *Sergeant Larry Barrett:* Peter Lawford, *Sergeant Major Roger Boswell:* Joey Bishop, *Mountain Hawk:* Henry Silva, *Willie Sharpknife:* Buddy Lester, *Amelia Parent:* Ruta Lee, *Corporal Ellis:* Philip Crosby, *Private Page:* Dennis Crosby, *Private Wills:* Lindsay Crosby, *Blacksmith:* Hank Henry, *Colonel William Collingwood:* Richard Simmons, *Watanka:* Michael Pate, *Caleb:* Armand Alzamora, *White Eagle:* Richard Hale, *Morton:* Mickey Finn, *Corporal:* Sonny King, *Mrs. Parent:* Madge Blake, *Mrs. Collingwood:* Dorothy Abbott.

Sergeants Three with Lindsay Crosby, Phil Crosby, Sammy Davis, Jr. and Dean Martin.

SERGEANT YORK (1941) WB. Producers, Jesse L. Lasky, Hal B. Wallis. Director, Howard Hawks. Screenplay, Aben Finkel, Harry Chandlee, Howard Koch, John Huston (from *War Diary of Sergeant York*, by Sam K. Cowan, *Sergeant York and His People* by Cowan, and *Sergeant York—Last of the Long Hunters* by Tom Skeyhill). Music, Max Steiner. Cameraman, Sol Polito. 134 minutes

Alvin York: Gary Cooper, *Pastor Rosier Pile:* Walter Brennan, *Gracie Williams:* Joan Leslie, *Pusher (Michael T. Ross):* George Tobias, *Bert Thomas:* David Bruce, *Major Buxton:* Stanley Ridges, *Ma York:* Margaret Wycherly, *George York:* Dickie Moore, *Ike Botkin:* Ward Bond, *Buck Lipscomb:* Noah Beery, Jr., *Captain Danforth:* Harvey Stephens, *Cordell Hull:* Charles Trowbridge, *German Major:* (Carl) Charles Esmond, *Zeb Andrews:* Robert Porterfield, *Lem:* Howard da Silva, *Zeke:* Clem Bevans, *Sergeant Early:* Joseph Sawyer, *Sergeant:* Frank Wilcox, *Captain Tillman:* Donald Douglas, *Sergeant Harry Parsons:* Pat Flaherty, *Corporal Savage:* Lane Chandler, *Beardsley:* Frank Marlowe, *Corporal Cutting:* Jack Pennick, *Eb:* James Anderson, *Tom:* Guy Wilkerson, *Rosie York:* June Lockhart, *Uncle Lige:*

Sergeant York with Gary Cooper and Joan Leslie.

Tully Marshall, *Luke (Target Keeper):* Lee "Lasses" White, *Nate Tompkins:* Erville Alderson, *Mountaineer:* Charles Middleton, *Andrews:* Victor Kilian, *Prison Camp Commander:* Theodore Von Eltz, *Gracie's Sister:* Jane Isbell, *Drummer:* Frank Orth, *Marter, Bartender:* Arthur Aylesworth, *Piano Player:* Elisha Cook, Jr., *Card Player:* William Haade, *General Pershing:* Joseph Girard, *Marshal Foch:* Jean Del Val, *Mayor Hylan:* Douglas Wood, *Oscar of the Waldorf:* Ed Keane.

SEVEN BRIDES FOR SEVEN BROTHERS (1954) MGM. Producer, Jack Cummings. Director, Stanley Donen. CinemaScope, Ansco Color. Screenplay, Albert Hackett, Francis Goodrich, Dorothy Kingsley. Art Director, Cedric Gibbons. Cinematographer, George Folsey. Editor, Ralph E. Winters. From Stephen Vincent Bent's story *The Sobbin' Women*. Dances, Michael Kidd. Songs by Johnny Mercer and Gene de Paul: "Bless Your Beautiful Hide," "Wonderful, Wonderful Day," "When You're in Love," "Sobbin' Women," "Goin' Courtin'," "Lament," "June Bride," "Spring, Spring, Spring." 102 minutes

Seven Brides for Seven Brothers with Marc Platt, Jacques D'Amboise, Matt Mattox, Jane Powell, Tommy Rall, Russ Tamblyn and Jeff Richards.

Milly: Jane Powell, *Adam:* Howard Keel, *Benjamin:* Jeff Richards, *Gideon:* Russ Tamblyn, *Frank:* Tommy Rall, *Pete Perkins:* Howard Petrie, *Liza:* Virginia Gibson, *Rev. Elcott:* Ian Wolfe, *Daniel:* Marc Platt, *Caleb:* Matt Mattox, *Ephraim:* Jacques d'Amboise, *Dorcas:* Julie Newmeyer, *Alice:* Nancy Kilgas, *Sarah:* Betty Carr, *Ruth:* Ruta Kilmonis, *Martha:* Norma Doggett, *Harry:* Earl Barton, *Matt:* Dante DiPaolo, *Carl:* Kelly Brown, *Ruth's Uncle:* Matt Moore, *Dorcas' Father:* Dick Rich, *Mrs. Bixby:* Marjorie Wood, *Mr. Bixby:* Russell Simpson, *Mrs. Elcott:* Anna Q. Nilsson, *Drunk:* Larry Blake, *Prospector:* Phil Rich, *Girl:* Lois Hall, *Swains:* Russ Saunders, Terry Wilson, George Robothom, *Lem:* Walter Beaver, *Lem's Girl Friend:* Jarma Lewis, *Dorcas' Sister:* Sheila James, *Fathers:* Stan Jolley, Tim Graham.

SEVEN DAYS IN MAY (1964) Par. Producer, Edward Lewis. Director, John Frankenheimer. Screenplay, Rod Serling. Based on a novel of the same name by Fletcher Knebel and Charles W. Bailey II. Music, Jerry Goldsmith. Cinematographer, Ellsworth Fredricks. A Seven Arts-Joel Productions, Inc. Production. 120 minutes

General James M. Scott: Burt Lancaster, *Colonel Martin (Jiggs) Casey:* Kirk Douglas, *President Jordan Lyman:* Fredric March, *Eleanor Holbrook:* Ava Gardner, *Senator Raymond Clark:* Edmond O'Brien, *Paul Girard:* Martin Balsam, *Christopher Todd:* George Macready, *Senator Prentice:* Whit Bissell, *Harold McPherson:* Hugh Marlowe, *Arthur Corwin:* Bart Burns, *Colonel Murdock:* Richard Anderson,

Seven Days in May with Burt Lancaster and Fredric March (on TV).

Lieutenant Hough: Jack Mullaney, *Colonel "Mutt" Henderson:* Andrew Duggan, *Colonel Broderick:* John Larkin.

THE SEVEN LITTLE FOYS (1955) Par. Producer, Jack Rose. Director, Melville Shavelson. VistaVision, Technicolor. Screenplay, Melville Shavelson, Jack Rose. Art Directors, Hal Pereira, John Goodman. Musical Director, Joseph J. Lilley. Cinematographer, John F. Warren. Editor, Ellsworth Hoagland. Choreography, Nick Castle. 95 minutes

Eddie Foy: Bob Hope, *Madeliene Morando:* Milly Vitale, *Barney Green:* George Tobias, *Clara:* Angela Clarke, *Judge:* Herbert Heyes, *Stage Manager:* Richard Shannon, *Brynie:* Billy Gray, *Charley:* Lee Erickson, *Richard Foy:* Paul De Rolf, *Mary Foy:* Lydia Reed, *Madeleine Foy:* Linda Bennett, *Eddie, Jr.,:* Jimmy Baird, *George M. Cohan:* James Cagney, *Irving:* Tommy Duran, *Father O'Casey:* Lester Mathews, *Elephant Act:* Joe Evans, *Elephant Act:* George Boyce, *Santa Claus:* Oliver Blake, *Driscoll:* Milton Frome, *Harrison:* King Donovan, *Stage Doorman:* Jimmy Conlin, *Soubrette:* Marian Carr, *Stage Doorman at Iroquois:* Harry Cheshire, *Italian Ballerina Mistress:* Renata Vanni, *Dance Specialty Double:* Betty Uitti, *Priest:* Noel Drayton, *Theater Manager:* Jack Pepper, *Tutor:* Dabbs Greer, *Customs Inspector:* Billy Nelson, *Second Priest:* Joe Flynn, *Brynie (5 years):* Jerry Mathers, *Presbyterian Minister:* Lewis Martin.

The Seven Little Foys with Bob Hope, Billy Gray, Lee Erickson, Paul De Rolf, Lydia Reed, Linda Bennett, Jimmy Baird and Tommy Duran.

THE SEVENTH VOYAGE OF SINBAD (1958) Col. Producer, Charles H. Schneer. Director, Nathan Juran. Screenplay by Kenneth Kolb. Visual effects by Ray Harryhausen. Music by Bernard Harrmann. Assistant Directors, Eugenio Martin and Pedro de Juan. A Morningside Production in Dynamation and Technicolor. 89 minutes

Captain Sinbad: Kerwin Mathews, *Princess Parisa:* Kathryn Grant, *The Genie, Baronni:* Richard Eyer, *Sokurah:* Torin Thatcher, *Caliph:* Alec Mango, *Karim:* Danny Green, *Sultan:* Harold Kasket, *Harufa:*

Seventh Voyage of Sinbad with Alec Mange, Harold Kasket, Kathryn Grant and Kerwin Mathews.

Alfred Brown, *Sadi:* Nana de Herrera, *Gaunt Sailor:* Nino Falanga, *Crewman:* Luis Guedes, *Ali:* Virgilio Teixeira.

THE SEVEN YEAR ITCH (1955) 20th. Producers, Charles K. Feldman, Billy Wilder. Director, Billy Wilder. CinemaScope, De Luxe Color. Based on the play by George Axelrod. Screenplay, Billy Wilder, George Axelrod. Art Directors, Lyle Wheeler, George W. Davis. Musical Director, Alfred Newman. Cinematographer, Milton Krasner. Editor, Hugh S. Fowler. 105 minutes

The Girl: Marilyn Monroe, *Richard Sherman:* Tom Ewell, *Helen Sherman:* Evelyn Keyes, *Tom MacKenzie:* Sonny Tufts, *Kruhulik:* Robert Strauss, *Dr. Brubaker:* Oscar Homolka, *Miss Morris (Secretary):* Marguerite Chapman, *Plumber:* Victor Moore, *Elaine:* Roxanne, *Brady:* Donald McBride, *Miss Finch (Night Nurse):* Carolyn Jones, *Ricky:* Butch Bernard, *Waitress:* Doro Merande, *Indian Girl:* Dorothy Ford, *Woman in R. R. Station:* Mary Young, *R. R. Station Gateman:* Ralph Sanford.

The Seven Year Itch with Marilyn Monroe and Tom Ewell.

THE SHAGGY DOG (1959) BV. Producer, Walt Disney. Director, Charles Barton. Associate Producer, Bill Walsh. Screenplay by Bill Walsh and Lillie Hayward. Suggested by *The Hound of Florence* by Felix Salten. Music by Paul Smith. Song by Gil George and Paul Smith. Assistant Director, Arthur Vitarelli. Art Director, Carroll Clark. Cinematographer, Edward Colman. Editor, James D. Ballas. Costumes by Chuck Keehne and Gertrude Casey. 104 minutes

Wilson Daniels: Fred MacMurray, *Frieda Daniels:* Jean Hagen, *Wilby Daniels:* Tommy Kirk, *Allison D'Allessio:* Annette Funicello, *Buzz Miller:* Tom Considine, *"Moochie" Daniels:* Kevin Corcoran, *Prof. Plumcutt:* Cecil Kellaway, *Dr. Mikhail Andrassy:* Alexander Scourby, *Franceska Andrassy:* Roberta Shore, *Officer Hanson:* James Westerfield, *Stefano:* Jacques Aubuchon, *Thurm:* Strother Martin, *Officer Kelly:* Forrest Lewis, and Shaggy,

The Shaggy Dog with Fred MacMurray and Jean Hagen.

Shane with Jean Arthur, Brandon De Wilde, Van Heflin and Alan Ladd.

SHALL WE DANCE (1937) RKO. Produced by Pandro S. Berman. Directed by Mark Sandrich. Suggested by the story *Watch Your Step* by Lee Loeb and Harold Buchman. Screenplay, Alan Scott, Ernest Pagano, P. J. Wolfson. Music Director, Nathaniel Shilkret. Ensembles staged by Hermes Pan. Ballets directed by Larry Losee. Art Director, Van Nest Polglase. Photography, David Abel. Special Effects, Vernon L. Walker. Editor, William Hamilton. Songs by George and Ira Gershwin: "Shall We Dance," "They Can't Take That Away From Me," "Let's Call the Whole Thing Off," "I've Got Beginner's Luck," "Slap That Bass," "They All Laughed," "Wake Up Brother and Dance." The seventh Astaire-Rogers teaming. 116 minutes

Shane: Alan Ladd, *Mrs. Starrett:* Jean Arthur, *Mr. Starrett:* Van Heflin, *Joey Starrett:* Brandon De Wilde, *Wilson:* Jack Palance, *Chris:* Ben Johnson, *Lewis:* Edgar Buchanan, *Ryker:* Emile Meyer, *Torrey:* Elisha Cook, Jr, *Mr. Shipstead:* Douglas Spencer, *Morgan:* John Dierkes, *Mrs. Torrey:* Ellen Corby, *Grafton:* Paul McVey, *Atkey:* John Miller, *Mrs. Shipstead:* Edith Evanson, *Wright:* Leonard Strong, *Johnson:* Ray Spiker, *Susan Lewis:* Janice Carroll, *Howells:* Martin Mason, *Mrs. Lewis:* Helen Brown, *Mrs. Howells:* Nancy Kulp, *Pete:* Howard J. Negley, *Ruth Lewis:* Beverly Washburn, *Ryker Man:* George Lewis, *Clerk:* Charles Quirk, *Ryker Men:* Jack Sterling, Henry Wills, Rex Moore, Ewing Brown.

SHANGHAI EXPRESS (1932) Par. Directed by Josef von Sternberg. Based on the story by Harry Hervey. Screenplay, Jules Furthman. Photography, Lee Garmes. Remade by Paramount as *Peking Express*, 1951. 80 minutes

Shall We Dance with Jerome Cowan, Edward Everett Horton and Fred Astaire.

Petrov (Pete Peters): Fred Astaire, *Linda Keene:* Ginger Rogers, *Jeffrey Baird:* Edward Everett Horton, *Cecil Flintridge:* Eric Blore, *Arthur Miller:* Jerome Cowan, *Lady Tarrington:* Ketti Gallian, *Jim Montgomery:* William Brisbane, *Harriet Hoctor:* Harriet Hoctor, *Mrs. Fitzgerald:* Ann Shoemaker, *Bandleader:* Ben Alexander, *Tai:* Emma Young, *Newsboy:* Sherwood Bailey, *Dancing Partner:* Pete Theodore, *Ballet Masters:* Marek Windheim, Rolfe Sedan, *Cop in Park:* Charles Coleman, *Big Man:* Frank Moran.

SHANE (1953) Par. Producer, George Stevens. Associate Producer, Ivan Moffat. Director, George Stevens. Associate Director, Fred Guiol. Technicolor. Based on the novel by Jack Schaefer. Screenplay, A. B. Guthrie, Jr. Additional Dialogue, Jack Sher. Art Directors Hal Pereira, Walter Tyler. Cinematographer, Loyal Griggs. Editor, William Hornbeck, Tom McAdoo. Technicolor Consultant, Richard, Mueller. 118 minutes

Shanghai Express with Clive Brook and Marlene Dietrich.

Shanghai Lilly (Madeline): Marlene Dietrich, *Captain Donald Harvey:* Clive Brook, *Hui Fei:* Anna May Wong, *Henry Chang:* Warner Oland, *Sam Salt:* Eugene Pallette, *Reverend Carmichael:* Lawrence Grant, *Mrs. Haggerty:* Louise Closser Hale, *Eric Baum:* Gustav von Seyffertitz, *Major Lenard:* Emile Chautard, *Albright:* Claude King, *Chinese Spy:* Neshida Minoru, *A Rebel:* James Leong, *Engineer:* Willie Fung, *Minister:* Leonard Carey, *Ticket Agent:* Forrester Harvey, *Officer:* Miki Morita.

SHE DONE HIM WRONG (1933) Par. Directed by Lowell Sherman. Based on the 1928 play *Diamond Lil* by Mae West. Adaptation and Dialogue, Harvey Thew and John Bright. Assistant Director, James

She Done Him Wrong with Mae West.

Dugan. Costumes, Edith Head. Art Director, Bob Usher. Photography, Charles Lang. Editor, Alexander Hall. Sound, Harry M. Lindgren. Songs by Ralph Rainger: "I Wonder Where My Easy Rider's Gone," "I Like a Man Who Takes His Time." 66 minutes

Lady Lou: Mae West, *Captain Cummings:* Cary Grant, *Serge Stanieff:* Gilbert Roland, *Gus Jordan:* Noah Beery, *Russian Rita:* Rafaela Ottiano, *Dan Flynn:* David Landau, *Sally Glynn:* Rochelle Hudson, *Chick Clark:* Owen Moore, *Rag Time Kelly:* Fuzzy Knight, *Chuck Connors:* Tammany Young, *Spider Kane:* Dewey Robinson, *Frances:* Grace La Rue, *Steak McGarry:* Harry Wallace, *Pete:* James C. Eagles, *Officer Doheney:* Robert E. Homans, *Big Bill:* Tom Kennedy, *Barfly:* Arthur Housman, *Pal:* Wade Boteler, *Mrs. Flaherty:* Aggie Herring, *Pearl:* Louise Beavers, *Jacobson:* Lee Kohlmar, *Mike:* Tom McGuire, *Janitor:* Michael Mark, *Cleaning Woman:* Mary Gordon, *Barfly:* Al Hill, *Man in Audience:* Ernie S. Adams, *Street Cleaner:* Heinie Conklin, *Patron Who Hits His Girl:* Jack Carr, *"Framed" Convict:* Frank Moran.

SHE LOVES ME NOT (1934), Par. Produced by Benjamin Glazer. Directed by Elliott Nugent. From the novel by Edward Hope and the play by Howard Lindsay. Screenplay by Benjamin Glazer. Cameraman, Charles Lang. Editor, Hugh Bennett. Songs: "Love In Bloom" by Leo Robin and Ralph Rainger; "After All You're All I'm After" by Edward Heyman and Arthur Schwartz; "Straight From the Shoulder (Right From the Heart)," "I'm Hummin', I'm Whistlin', I'm Singin'," and "Put a Little Rhythm in Everything You Do" by Mack Gordon and Harry Revel. Remade as *How to Be Very, Very Popular* (20th Century-Fox, 1955). 83 minutes

Paul Lanton: Bing Crosby, *Curly Flagg:* Miriam Hopkins, *Midge Mercer:* Kitty Carlisle, *Buzz Jones:* Edward Nugent, *Dean Mercer:* Henry Stephenson, *Mugg Schnitzel:* Warren Hymer, *Gus McNeal:* Lynne Overman, *Frances Arbuthnot:* Judith Allen, *J. Teorval Jones:* George Barbier, *Charles M. Lanton:* Henry Kolker, *Mrs. Arbuthnot:* Maude Turner Gordon, *Martha:* Margaret Armstrong, *J. B.:* Ralf

She Loves Me Not with Miriam Hopkins and Bing Crosby.

Harolde, *Andy:* Matt McHugh, *Arkle:* Franklyn Ardell, *Baldy O'Hara:* Vince Barnett.

SHENANDOAH (1965) Univ. Producer, Robert Arthur. Director, Andrew V. McLaglen. Technirama and Technicolor. Screenplay by James Lee Barrett. Director of Photography, William H. Clothier. Music by Frank Skinner. Costumes by Rosemary Odell. Assistant Director, Terence Nelson. Art Directors, Alexander Golitzen and Alfred Sweeney. Music supervised by Joseph Gershenson. Film Editor, Otho Lovering. 105 minutes

Shenandoah with Pat Wayne, Tim McIntire, James McMullan, Glenn Corbett, James Stewart and Charles Robinson.

Charlie Anderson: James Stewart, *Sam:* Doug McClure, *Jacob Anderson:* Glenn Corbett, *James Anderson:* Patrick Wayne, *Jennie Anderson:* Rosemary Forsyth, *Boy Anderson:* Phillip Alford, *Ann Anderson:* Katharine Ross, *Nathan Anderson:* Charles Robinson, *Dr. Tom Witherspoon:* Paul Fix, *Pastor Bjoerling:* Denver Pyle, *Colonel Fairchild:* George Kennedy, *Henry Anderson:* Tim McIntire, *John Anderson:* James McMullan, *Carter:* James Best, *Billy Packer:* Warren Oates, *Engineer:* Strother Martin, *Abernathy:* Dabbs Greer, *Jenkins:* Harry Carey, Jr., *Mule:* Kevin Hagen, *Lt. Johnson:* Tom Simcox, *Captain Richards:* Berkeley Harris, *Union Sergeant:* Edward Faulkner, *Confederate Corporal:* Peter Wayne, *Union Guard:* Gregg Palmer, *Union Guard with beard:* Bob Steele, *First Picket:* James Heneghan, Jr., *Gabriel:* Eugene Jackson, Jr., *Negro Woman:* Pae Miller, *Horace, a Marauder:* Rayford Barnes, *Ray:* Dave Cass, *Crying Prisoner:* Hoke Howell, *Carroll:* Kelly Thordsen, *Tinkham:* Lane Bradford, *Confederate Soldier:* Shug Fisher, *Osborne:* John Daheim, *Marshall:* Joe Yrigoyen, *Rider #1:* Henry Wills, *Rider #2:* Buzz Henry, *Rider #3:* James Carter, *Rider #4:* Leroy Johnson.

SHE WORE A YELLOW RIBBON (1949) RKO. Directed by John Ford. Color by Technicolor. An Argosy Pictures Production. From the *Saturday Evening Post* story by James Warner Bellah. Screenplay, Frank Nugent and Laurence Stallings. Score, Richard Hageman. Photography, Winton Hoch. Technical Advisers, Major Philip Kieffer, retired, and Cliff Lyons. Filmed in Monument Valley, Utah. 103 minutes

Captain Nathan Cutting Brittles: John Wayne, *Olivia Dandridge:* Joanne Dru, *Lieutenant Flint Cohill:* John Agar, *Sergeant Tyree:* Ben Johnson, *Lieutenant Ross Pennell:* Harry Carey, Jr., *Sergeant Quincannon:* Victor McLaglen, *Abby Allshard:* Mildred Natwick, *Major Mack Allshard:* George O'Brien, *Dr. O'Laughlin:* Arthur Shields, *Karl Rynders:* Harry Woods, *Pony-That-Walks:* Chief John Big Tree, *Red Shirt:* Noble Johnson, *Trooper Cliff:* Cliff Lyons, *Corp. Mike Quayne:* Tom Tyler, *Sergeant Hochbauer:* Michael Dugan, *Wagner:* Mickey Simpson, *Bugler/Indian:* Frank McGrath, *Jenkin:* Don Sommer, *Corporal Krumrein:* Fred Libbey, *Sergeant Major:* Jack Pennick, *Courier:* Billy Jones, *NCO:* Bill Goettinger, *Hench:* Fred Graham, *Badger:* Fred Kennedy, *Private Smith:* Rudy Bowman,

She Wore a Yellow Ribbon with Harry Carey, Jr., Joanne Dru, John Wayne, John Agar and Ben Johnson.

NCO: Post Parks, *McCarthy:* Ray Hyke, *Interpreter:* Lee Bradley, *Indian:* Chief Sky Eagle, *Gun-runner:* Paul Fix, *Bartender:* Francis Ford, *Narrator:* Irving Pichel.

SHIP OF FOOLS (1965) Col. Producer, Stanley Kramer. Director, Stanley Kramer. Based on the novel by Katherine Ann Porter. Screenplay, Abby Mann. Art Director, Robert Clatworthy. Music, Ernest Gold. Songs: "Heute Abend," "Geh'n Wir Bummelin Auf Der Reeperbahn," "Irgendwie, Irgendwo, Irgenwanh"; music, Ernest Gold, lyrics, Jack Lloyd. Cinematographer, Ernest Lazlo. Special Photographic Effects, Albert Whitlock. Editor, Robert C. Jones. 149 minutes

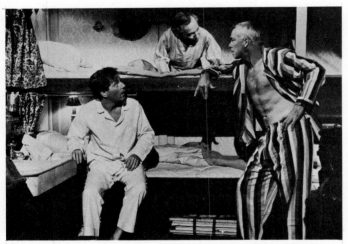

Ship of Fools with George Segal, Michael Dunn and Lee Marvin.

Mary Treadwell: Vivien Leigh, *La Condesa:* Simone Signoret, *Rieber:* José Ferrer, *Tenny:* Lee Marvin, *Dr. Schumann:* Oskar Werner, *Jenny:* Elizabeth Ashley, *David:* George Segal, *Pepe:* Jose Greco, *Glocken:* Michael Dunn, *Capt. Thiele:* Charles Korvin, *Lowenthal* Heinz Ruehmann, *Frau Hutten:* Lilia Skala, *Amparo:* Barbara Luna, *Lizzi:* Christiane Schmidtmer, *Freytag:* Alf Kjellin, *Lt. Huebner:* Werner Klemperer, *Graf:* John Wengraf, *Frau Schmitt:* Olga Fabian, *Elsa:* Gila Golan, *Lutz:* Oscar Beregi, *Hutten:* Stanley Adams, *Frau Lutz:* Karen Verne, *Johann:* Charles de Vries, *Pastora:* Lydia Torea, *Fat Man:* Henry Calvin, *Carlos:* Paul Daniel, *Woodcarver:* David Renard, *Ric:* Rudy Carrella, *Rac:* Silvia Marino, *Guitarist:* Anthony Brand, *Religious Man #1:* Peter Mamakos, *Waiter:* Walter Friedel, *Second Officer:* Bert Rumsey, *Student:* Jon Alvar, *Head-waiter:* Charles Hradilac, *Steward:* Steven Geray.

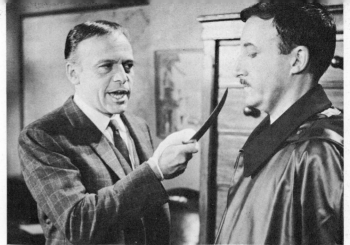

A Shot in the Dark with Herbert Lom and Peter Sellers.

A SHOT IN THE DARK (1964) UA. Producer-Director, Blake Edwards. Screenplay, Blake Edwards, William Peter Blatty. Based on plays by Harry Kurnitz and Marcel Achard. Music, Henry Mancini. Song, Henry Mancini, Robert Wells. Director of Photography, Chris Challis. Associate Producer, Cecil Fors. Assistant Director, Derek Cracknell. Costumes, Margaret Furse. A Mirsch-Geoffrey Production in Panavision and De Luxe Color. 101 minutes

Inspector Jacques Clouseau: Peter Sellers, *Maria Gambrelli:* Elke Sommer, *Benjamin Ballon:* George Sanders, *Chief Inspector Charles Dreyfus:* Herbert Lom, *Dominique Ballon:* Tracy Reed, *Hercule Lajoy:* Graham Stark, *Francois:* Andre Maranne, *Henri Lafarge:* Douglas Wilmer, *Madame Lafarge:* Vanda Godsell, *Pierre:* Maurice Kaufman, *Dudu:* Ann Lynn, *Georges:* David Lodge, *Simone:* Moira Redmond, *Maurice:* Martin Benson, *Kato:* Burt Kwouk, *Receptionist at Camp:* Reginald Beckwith, *Charlie:* Turk Thrust, *Doctor:* John Herrington, *Psychoanalyst:* Jack Melford.

SHOW BOAT (1936) Univ. Produced by Carl Laemmle, Jr. Directed by James Whale. From the novel by Edna Ferber and the musical by Oscar Hammerstein II and Jerome Kern. Music Director, Victor Baravelle. Photography, John Mescall. Editors, Ted Kent and Bernard W. Burton. Screenplay and Songs, Oscar Hammerstein II and Jerome Kern. Songs: "Ol' Man River," "Bill," "Make Believe," "Can't Help Lovin' Dat Man," "Ah Still Suits Me," "Gallivantin' Around," "I Have the Room Above," "You Are Love." Dance Director, LeRoy J. Prinz. Other versions: Universal, 1929; MGM, 1951. 110 minutes

Magnolia Hawks: Irene Dunne, *Gaylord Ravenal:* Allan Jones, *Captain Andy Hawks:* Charles Winninger, *Parthy Hawks:* Helen Westley, *Joe:* Paul Robeson, *Julie:* Helen Morgan, *Steve:* Donald Cook, *Frank:* Sammy White, *Ellie:* Queenie Smith, *Windy:* J. Farrell MacDonald, *Pete:* Arthur Hohl, *Vallon:* Charles Middleton, *Queenie:* Hattie McDaniel, *Rubberface:* Francis X. Mahoney, *Kim (elder):* Sunnie O'Dea,

Show Boat with Irene Dunne and Allan Jones.

Kim (younger): Marilyn Knowlden, *Kim as a baby:* Patricia Barry, *Chorus Girls:* Dorothy Granger, Barbara Pepper, Renee Whitney, *Jake:* Harry Barris, *Jim Green:* Charles Wilson, *Sam:* Clarence Muse, *Jeb:* Stanley Fields, *Backwoodsman:* (Tiny) Stanley J. Sandford, *Landlady:* May Beatty, *Lost Child:* Bobby Watson, *Mrs. Ewing:* Jane Keckley, *Englishman:* E. E. Clive, *Reporter:* Helen Jerome Eddy, *Press Agent:* Donald Briggs, *Dance Director:* LeRoy Prinz, *Young Negro:* Eddie Anderson, *Banjo Player:* Patti Patterson, *Simon Legree:* Theodore Lorch, *Woman:* Flora Finch, *Mrs. Brencenbridge:* Helen Hayward, *Drunk:* Arthur Housman, *Mother Superior:* Elspeth Dudgeon.

SHOW BOAT (1951) MGM. Producer, Arthur Freed. Director, George Sidney. Color by Technicolor. Based on the novel by Edna Ferber and the musical play by Jerome Kern and Oscar Hammerstein II. Screenplay, John Lee Mahin. Musical Director, Adolph Deutsch. Art Directors, Cedric Gibbons, Jack Martin Smith. Photography, Charles Rosher. Editor, John Dunning. Songs by Oscar Hammerstein II and Jerome Kern: "Why Do I Love You?", "Make Believe," "Old Man River," "Can't Help Lovin' That Man," "Bill"; with P. G. Wodehouse: "You Are Love," "Ballyhoo," "Gambler's Song," "I Fall Back on You," "After the Ball," "Life Upon the Wicked Stage." Dances, Robert Alton. Annette Warren sings for Ava Gardner. Remake of 1929 and 1936 Universal Films. 108 minutes

Show Boat with Emory Parnell, Marge Champion, Kathryn Grayson and Gower Champion.

Magnolia Hawks: Kathryn Grayson, *Julie Laverne:* Ava Gardner, *Gaylord Ravenal:* Howard Keel, *Captain Andy Hawks:* Joe E. Brown, *Ellie May Shipley:* Marge Champion, *Frank Schultz:* Gower Champion, *Stephen Baker:* Robert Sterling, *Parthy Hawks:* Agnes Moorehead, *Cameo McQueen:* Adele Jergens, *Joe:* William Warfield, *Pete:* Leif Erickson, *Windy McClain:* Owen McGiveney, *Queenie:* Frances Williams, *Sheriff (Ike Vallon):* Regis Toomey, *Mark Hallson:* Frank Wilcox, *Herman:* Chick Chandler, *Jake Green:* Emory Parnell, *Kim:* Sheila Clark, *Drunk Sport:* Ian MacDonald, *Troc Piano Player:* Fuzzy Knight, *George (Calliope Player):* Norman Leavitt, *Showboat Chorus Girls:* Lyn Wilde, Joyce Jameson, *Dabney:* Louis Mercier, *Renee:* Lisa Ferraday, *Hotel Manager:* Edward Keane, *Bellboy:* Tom Irish, *Doorman:* Jim Pierce, *Landlady:* Marjorie Wood, *Man with Julie:* William Tannen, *Seamstress:* Anna Q. Nilsson, *Drunk:* Bert Roach, *Doctor:* Frank Dae, *Piano Player:* Harry Seymour, *Bouncer:* William Hall, *Bartender:* Earle Hodgins, *Little Old Lady:* Ida Moore, *Headwaiter:* Alphonse Martell.

THE SHOW OF SHOWS (1929) WB. Supervising Director, Darryl F. Zanuck. Directed by John G. Adolfi. Color by Technicolor. Photography, Bernard McGill. Songs: "Military March," "What's Become of the Floradora Boys?", "Lady Luck" by Ray Perkins; "Motion Picture Pirates" by M. K. Jerome; "If I Could Learn to Love" by Herman Ruby and M. K. Jerome; "Ping Pongo" by Al Dubin and Joe

The Show of Shows with Louise Fazenda, Frank Fay, Beatrice Lillie and Lloyd Hamilton.

Burke; "Dear Little Pup," "The Only Song I Know" by J. Kiern Brennan and Ray Perkins; "Your Mother and Mine" by Joe Goodwin and Gus Edwards; "Meet My Sister" by Brennan and Perkins; "Singin' in the Bath-Tub" by Ned Washington, Herb Magidson, Michael Cleary; "Believe Me" by Eddie Ward; "Just an Hour Of Love" by Al Bryan and Eddie Ward; "Li-Po-Li" by Bryan and Ward; "Rockabye Your Baby With a Dixie Melody" by Joe Young, Sam Lewis, Jean Schwartz; "If Your Best Friend Won't Tell You" by Dubin and Burke; "Jumping Jack" by Herman Ruby and Rube Bloom; "Your Love Is All That I Crave" by Al Dubin, Perry Bradford, Jimmy Johnson; "Stars," "You Were Meant for Me" by Arthur Freed and Nacio Herb Brown. 127 minutes

PROLOGUE UNIQUE *M. C.:* Frank Fay, *The Minister:* William Courtenay, *The Victim:* H. B. Warner, *The Executioner:* Hobart Bosworth.

MILITARY PARADE Monte Blue, 300 dancing girls, Pasadena's American Legion Fife and Drum Corps.

FLORADORA *Floradora Sextette:* Marian Nixon, Sally O'Neil, Myrna Loy, Patsy Ruth Miller, Lila Lee, Alice Day, *Floradora Boys: Waiter,* Ben Turpin, *Ice Man,* Heinie Conklin, *Street Cleaner,* Lupino Lane, *Plumber,* Lee Moran, *Father,* Bert Roach, *Hansom Cabby,* Lloyd Hamilton.

SKULL AND CROSSBONES Introduced by Frank Fay, Jack Mulhall, Chester Morris, Sojin. Ted Lewis and his Band, Ted Williams Adagio Dancers. *Pirates:* Noah Beery, Tully Marshall, Wheeler Oakman, Bull Montana, Kalla Pasha, Anders Randolf, Philo McCullough, Otto Matiesen, Jack Curtis, *The Hero:* Johnny Arthur, *Ladies:* Carmel Myers, Ruth Clifford, Sally Eilers, Viola Dana, Shirley Mason, Ethlyne Claire, France Lee, Julanne Johnston, *Dancer:* Marcelle.

EIFFEL TOWER Georges Carpentier, Patsy Ruth Miller, Alice White, chorus of 75.

RECITATIONS Beatrice Lillie, Louise Fazenda, Lloyd Hamilton, Frank Fay.

EIGHT SISTER ACTS Introduced by Richard Barthelmess: Dolores and Helene Costello, Sally O'Neil and Molly O'Day, Alice and Marceline Day, Sally Blane and Loretta Young, Lola and Armida, Marion Byron and Harriet Lake (Ann Sothern), Ada Mae and Alberta Vaughan, Shirley Mason and Viola Dana.

SINGIN' IN THE BATH-TUB Winnie Lightner, Bull Montana, male chorus of 50.

IRENE BORDONI Assisted by Eddie Ward, Lou Silvers, Ray Perkins, Harry Akst, Michael Cleary, Norman Spencer, Dave Silverman, Joe Burke, M. K. Jerome, Lester Stevens.

CHINESE FANTASY Introduced by Rin-Tin-Tin. Nick Lucas, Myrna Loy, the Jack Haskell Girls.

BICYCLE BUILT FOR TWO Introduced by Frank Fay and Sid Silvers. *Ambrose:* Douglas Fairbanks, Jr., *Traffic Cop:* Chester Conklin, *Boys:* Grant Withers, William Collier Jr., Jack Mulhall, Chester Morris, William Bakewell, *Girls:* Lois Wilson, Gertrude Olmsted, Pauline Garon, Sally Eilers, Edna Murphy, Jacqueline Logan.

BLACK AND WHITE Frank Fay, Sid Silvers, Louise Fazenda, 75 dancing girls.

YOUR LOVE IS ALL THAT I CRAVE Frank Fay, Accompanied by Harry Akst.

KING RICHARD III John Barrymore, Anthony Bushell, E. J. Ratcliffe, Reginald Sharland.

MEXICAN MOONSHINE *The General:* Frank Fay, *Condemned Man:* Monte Blue, *Soldiers:* Albert Gran, Noah Beery, Lloyd Hamilton, Tully Marshall, Kalla Pasha, Lee Moran.

LADY LUCK Betty Compson, Alexander Gray, Chorus.

STARS Members of the cast.

The Sign of the Cross with Elissa Landi and Fredric March.

THE SIGN OF THE CROSS (1932) Par. Produced and directed by Cecil B. De Mille. From the play by Wilson Barrett. Screenplay, Waldemar Young and Sidney Buchman. Photography, Karl Struss. Editor, Anne Bauchens. Sound, Harry M. Lindgren. Reissued in 1944 with a prologue written by Dudley Nichols. 123 minutes

Marcus Superbus: Fredric March, *Mercia:* Elissa Landi, *Poppaea:* Claudette Colbert, *Nero:* Charles Laughton, *Tigellinus:* Ian Keith, *Dacia:* Vivian Tobin, *Flavius:* Harry Beresford, *Glabrio:* Ferdinand Gottschalk, *Titus:* Arthur Hohl, *Ancaria:* Joyzelle Joyner, *Stephan:* Tommy Conlon, *Strabo:* Nat Pendleton, *Servillus:* Clarence Burton, *Licinius:* William V. Mong, *Tibul:* Harold Healy, *Viturius:* Richard

Alexander, *Philodemus:* Robert Manning, *Tyros:* Charles Middleton, *The Mute Giant:* Joe Bonomo, *A Lover:* Kent Taylor, *Leader of Gladiators/Christian:* John Carradine, *Christian in Chains:* Lane Chandler, *Complaining Wife:* Ethel Wales, *Bettor:* Lionel Belmore, *Pygmy:* Angelo Rossitto.

1944 PROLOGUE *Chaplain James Costello:* Arthur Shields, *Chaplain Thomas Lloyd:* Stanley Ridges, *Captain Kevin Driscoll:* James Millican, *Hoboken:* Tom Tully, *Lieutenant Robert Hammond:* Oliver Thorndike, *Colonel Hugh Mason:* William Forrest, *Lieutenant Herb Hanson:* John James, *Bombardier:* Joel Allen.

SINCE YOU WENT AWAY (1944) UA. Produced by David O. Selznick. Directed by John Cromwell. Assistant Directors, Lowell J. Farrell, Edward F. Mull. A Selznick International Picture-Vanguard Films Production. Based on an adaptation of the book by Margaret Buell Wilder. Screenplay, David O. Selznick. Production Design, William L. Pereira. Music, Max Steiner. Associate, Louis Forbes. Settings, Mark-Lee Kirk. Special Effects, Jack Cosgrove. Associate, Clarence Slifer. Interior Decorations, Victor A. Gangelin. Technical Advisor, Lt. Colonel J. G. Taylor, USA. Dance Director, Charles Walters. Make-up, Robert Stephanoff. Wardrobe Director, Elmer Ellsworth. Associate, Adele Sadler. Photography, Stanley Cortez and Lee Garmes. Editor, Hal C. Kern. Sound, Charles L. Freeman. Recorder, Percy Townsend. Theme, "Together," by B. G. DeSylva, Lew Brown, Ray Henderson. Other songs: "Since You Went Away" by Kermit Goell and Ted Grouya; "The Dipsy Doodle" by Larry Clinton. Neil Hamilton's photo is used for the part of Tim Hilton. 172 minutes

Since You Went Away with Shirley Temple, Jennifer Jones, Robert Walker, Claudette Colbert and Agnes Moorehead.

Anne Hilton: Claudette Colbert, *Jane Hilton:* Jennifer Jones, *Lieutenant Tony Willett:* Joseph Cotten, *Bridget "Brig" Hilton:* Shirley Temple, *Colonel Smollett:* Monty Woolley, *The Clergyman:* Lionel Barrymore, *William G. Smollett II:* Robert Walker, *Fidelia:* Hattie McDaniel, *Emily Hawkins:* Agnes Moorehead, *Harold Smith:* Guy Madison, *Danny Williams:* Craig Stevens, *Lieutenant Solomon:* Keenan Wynn, *Dr. Sigmund Gottlieb Golden:* Albert Basserman, *Zosia Koslowska, a Welder:* Nazimova, *Mr. Mahoney:* Lloyd Corrigan, *Johnny Mahoney:* Jackie Moran, *A Marine Officer:* Gordon Oliver, *Gladys Brown:* Jane Devlin, *Becky Anderson:* Ann Gillis, *Sugar:* Dorothy (Cindy) Garner, *Former Plowboy:* Andrew McLaglen, *Waitress:* Jill Warren, *Refugee Child:* Helen Koford (Terry Moore), *Negro Officer:* Robert Johnson, *Negro Officer's Wife:* Dorothy Dandridge, *AWOL:* Johnny Bond, *Bartender:* Irving Bacon, *Cabby:* George Chandler, *Major Sam Atkins:* Addison Richards, *Pin Girl:* Barbara Pepper, *Principal:* Byron Foulger, *Businessman:* Edwin Maxwell, *Hungry Woman:* Florence

Bates, *Desk Clerk:* Theodore Von Eltz, *Elderly Woman:* Adeline de Walt Reynolds, *Convalescents:* Doodles Weaver, Warren Hymer, *Conductor:* Jonathan Hale, *Sergeant's Child:* Eilene Janssen, *Taxpayer:* William B. Davidson, *An Envious Girl:* Ruth Roman, *Girl:* Rhonda Fleming.

THE SINGING FOOL (1928) WB. Directed by Lloyd Bacon. From the play by Leslie S. Barrows. Scenario, C. Graham Baker. Cameraman, Byron Haskin. Editors, Ralph Dawson and Harold McCord. Dialogue and titles, Joseph Jackson. Songs: "Sonny Boy," "I'm Sittin' on Top of the World," "It All Depends on You" by Lew Brown, B. G. DeSylva, Ray Henderson; "There's A Rainbow Round My Shoulder" by Billy Rose, Al Jolson, Dave Dreyer. 110 minutes

Al: Al Jolson, *Grace:* Betty Bronson, *Molly:* Josephine Dunn, *John Perry:* Reed Howes, *Marcus:* Edward Martindel, *Blackie Joe:* Arthur Housman, *Sonny Boy:* Davy Lee, *Cafe Manager:* Robert Emmett O'Connor.

The Singing Fool with Josephine Dunn and Al Jolson.

THE SINGING NUN (1966) Metro release of Jon Beck (Hayes Goetz) production. Director, Henry Koster. Panavision and MetroColor. Screenplay, Sally Benson, John Furia, Jr. Story, John Furia. Camera, Milton Krasner. Music, Harry Sukman. Editor, Rita Roland. Songs by Soeur Sourire, English lyrics by Randy Sparks: "Dominique," "Sister Adele," "It's a Miracle," "Beyond the Stars," "A Pied Piper's Song," "Je Voudrais," "Mets Ton Joli Jupon," "Avec Toi," "Alleluia," "Raindrops," "Brother John" and "Lovely" by Randy Sparks. 98 minutes

Sister Ann: Debbie Reynolds, *Father Clementi:* Ricardo Montalban, *Mother Prioress:* Greer Garson, *Sister Cluny:* Agnes Moorehead, *Robert Gerade:* Chad Everett, *Nicole Arlien:* Katharine Ross, *Himself:*

The Singing Nun with Ricardo Montalban, Debbie Reynolds, Chad Everett, Juanita Moore and Monique Montaigne.

Ed Sullivan, *Sister Mary:* Juanita Moore, *Dominic Arlien:* Ricky Cordell, *Mr. Arlien:* Michael Pate, *Fitzpatrick:* Tom Drake, *Mr. Duvries:* Larry D. Mann, *Marauder:* Charles Robinson, *Sister Michele:* Monique Montaigne, *Sister Elise:* Joyce Vanderveen, *Sister Brigitte:* Anne Wakefield, *Sister Gertude:* Pam Peterson, *Sister Marthe:* Marina Koshetz, *Sister Therese:* Nancy Walters, *Sister Elizabeth:* Violet Rensing, *Sister Consuella:* Inez Petroza.

SINGIN' IN THE RAIN (1952) MGM. Producer, Arthur Freed. Directors, Gene Kelly, Stanley Donen. Color by Technicolor. Story and screenplay, Adolph Green, Betty Comden. Musical Director, Lennie Hayton. Art Directors, Cedric Gibbons, Randall Duell. Cinematographer, Harold Rosson. Editor, Adrienne Fazan. Songs: "Would You?", "Singin' in the Rain," "All I Do Is Dream of You," "I've Got a Feeling You're Fooling," "Wedding of the Painted Doll," "Should I?", "Make 'Em Laugh," "You Were Meant For Me," "You Are My Lucky Star," "Fit As A Fiddle and Ready For Love" and "Good Morning" by Arthur Freed and Nacio Herb Brown; "Moses" by Betty Comden, Adolph Green and Roger Edens; "Beautiful Girl," "Broadway Rhythm." Russ Saunders doubles for Gene Kelly. Footage from 1948's, *The Three Musketeers* (MGM). 103 minutes

Don Lockwood: Gene Kelly, *Cosmo Brown:* Donald O'Connor, *Kathy Selden:* Debbie Reynolds, *Lina Lamont:* Jean Hagen, *R. F. Simpson:* Millard Mitchell, *Zelda Zanders:* Rita Moreno, *Roscoe Dexter:* Douglas Fowley, *Dancer:* Cyd Charisse, *Dora Bailey:* Madge Blake, *Rod:* King Donovan, *Phoebe Dinsmore, Diction Coach:* Kathleen Freeman, *Diction Coach:* Bobby Watson, *Sid Phillips, Assistant Director:* Tommy Farrell, *Male Lead in "Beautiful Girl" Number:* Jimmie Thompson, *Assistant Director:* Dan Foster, *Wardrobe Woman:* Margaret Bert, *Hairdresser:* Mae Clarke, *Olga Mara:* Judy Landon, *Baron de la May de la Toulon:* John Dodsworth, *J. C. Spendrill III:* Stuart Holmes, *Don as a boy:* Dennis Ross, *Villain in Western, Bert:* Bill Lewin, *"Phil," Cowboy Hero:* Richard Emory, *Man on Screen:* Julius Tannen, *Ladies in Waiting:* Dawn Addams, Elaine Stewart, *Villain, "Dueling Cavalier" and "Broadway Rhythm":* Carl Milletaire, *Orchestra Leader:* Jac George, *Vallee Impersonator:* Wilson Wood, *Audience:* Dorothy Patrick, William Lester, Charles Evans, Joi Lansing, *Fencers:* Dave Sharpe, Russ Saunders.

Singin' in the Rain with Donald O'Connor and Gene Kelly.

SING YOU SINNERS (1938) Par. Produced and directed by Wesley Ruggles. Story and Screenplay, Claude Binyon. Music Director, Boris Morros. Vocal Arrangements, Max Terr. Assistant Director, Arthur Jacobson. Editor, Alma Ruth Macrorie. Photography, Karl Struss. Art Directors, Hans Dreier and Ernest Fegte. Songs: "Small Fry" by Frank Loesser and Hoagy Carmichael; "I've Got a Pocketful of Dreams," "Laugh and Call It Love," "Don't Let the Moon Get Away," "Where Is Central Park?", by Johnny Burke and Jimmy Monaco. 88 minutes

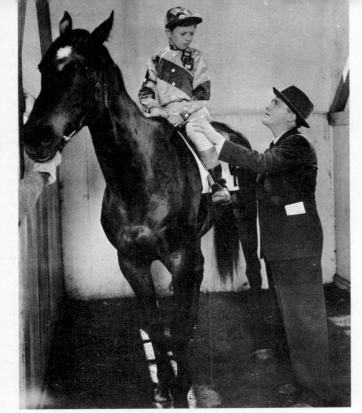

Sing You Sinners with Donald O'Connor and Bing Crosby.

Joe Beebe: Bing Crosby, *David Beebe:* Fred MacMurray, *Mike Beebe:* Donald O'Connor, *Mrs. Beebe:* Elizabeth Patterson, *Martha:* Ellen Drew, *Harry Ringmer:* John Gallaudet, *Pete:* William Haade, *Filter:* Paul White, *Lecturer:* Irving Bacon, *Race Fan:* Tom Dugan, *Nightclub Manager:* Herbert Corthell.

THE SIN OF MADELON CLAUDET (1931) MGM. Directed by
Edgar Selwyn. From the play *The Lullaby* by Edward Knoblock. Adaptation and Dialogue, Charles MacArthur. Art Director, Cedric Gibbons. Photography, Oliver T. Marsh. Editor, Tom Held. Talkie feature debut of Helen Hayes. 74 minutes

Smiling Lieutenant with Miriam Hopkins, Maurice Chevalier and George Barbier.

THE SMILING LIEUTENANT (1931) Par. Produced and directed by
Ernst Lubitsch. Based on Hans Muller's novel *Nux Der Prinzgemahl* and on *The Waltz Dream* by Leopold Jacobson and Felix Dormann. Adaptation and Screenplay, Ernest Vajda, Samson Raphaelson, Ernst Lubitsch. Photography, George Folsey. Editor, Merrill White. Sound, Ernest Zatorsky. Filmed at Paramount's Astoria, Long Island, Studios. Songs by Oscar Straus and Clifford Grey: "One More Hour of Love," "Breakfast Table Love," "Toujours L'Amour in the Army," "While Hearts Are Singing," "Jazz Up Your Lingerie." 102 minutes

Lieutenant Niki: Maurice Chevalier, *Franzi:* Claudette Colbert, *Princess Anna:* Miriam Hopkins, *Max:* Charles Ruggles, *King Adolf:* George Barbier, *Orderly:* Hugh O'Connell, *Adjutant von Rockoff:* Robert Strange, *Lily:* Janet Reade, *Emperor:* Con MacSunday, *Baroness von Schwedel:* Elizabeth Patterson, *Count von Halden:* Harry C. Bradley, *Joseph:* Werner Saxtorph, *Master of Ceremonies:* Karl Stall, *Bill Collector:* Granville Bates.

The Sin of Madelon Claudet with Helen Hayes and Neil Hamilton.

Madelon Claudet: Helen Hayes, *Carlo Boretti:* Lewis Stone, *Larry:* Neil Hamilton, *Jacques:* Robert Young, *Victor:* Cliff Edwards, *Doctor Dulac:* Jean Hersholt, *Rosalie:* Marie Prevost, *Alice:* Karen Morley, *The Photographer:* Charles Winninger, *Hubert:* Alan Hale, *Roget:* Halliwell Hobbes, *St. Jacques:* Lennox Pawle, *Claudet:* Russ Powell, *Jacques as a boy:* Frankie Darro.

Smilin' Through with Norma Shearer and Leslie Howard.

SMILIN' THROUGH (1932) MGM. Directed by Sidney Franklin.
Based on the play by Jane Cowl and Jane Murfin. Screenplay, Ernest Vajda and Claudine West. Dialogue, Donald Ogden Stewart and James Bernard Fagan. Assistant Director, Harry Bucquet. Art Director, Cedric Gibbons. Gowns. Adrian. Photography, Lee Garmes. Editor, Margaret Booth. Sound, Douglas Shearer. Other versions: First National, 1922; MGM, 1941. 97 minutes

Kathleen: Norma Shearer, *Kenneth Wayne:* Fredric March, *John Carteret:* Leslie Howard, *Doctor Owen:* O. P. Heggie, *Willie Ainley:* Ralph Forbes, *Mrs. Crouch:* Beryl Mercer, *Ellen:* Margaret Seddon, *Orderly:* Forrester Harvey, *Kathleen as a child:* Cora Sue Collins.

The Snake Pit with Olivia De Havilland and Leo Genn.

THE SNAKE PIT (1948) 20th. Producers, Anatole Litvak, Robert Bassler. Director, Anatole Litvak. From the novel by Mary Jane Ward. Screenplay, Frank Partos, Millen Brand. Music, Alfred Newman. Art Directors, Lyle Wheeler, Joseph C. Wright. Photography, Leo Tover. Editor, Dorothy Spencer. 108 minutes

Virginia Stuart Cunningham: Olivia De Havilland, *Robert Cunningham:* Mark Stevens, *Dr, Mark Kik:* Leo Genn, *Grace:* Celeste Holm, *Doctor Terry:* Glenn Langan, *Miss Davis:* Helen Craig, *Gordon:* Leif Erickson, *Mrs. Greer:* Beulah Bondi, *Asylum Inmate:* Lee Patrick, *Doctor Curtis:* Howard Freeman, *Mrs. Stuart:* Natalie Schafer, *Ruth:* Ruth Donnelly, *Margaret:* Katherine Locke, *Doctor Gifford:* Frank Conroy, *Miss Hart:* Minna Gombell, *Miss Bixby:* June Storey, *Virginia at 6:* Lora Lee Michel, *Mr. Stuart:* Damian O'Flynn, *Valerie:* Ann Doran, *Nurse Vance:* Esther Somers, *Celia Sommerville:* Jacqueline de Wit, *Hester:* Betsy Blair, *Miss Greene:* Lela Bliss, *Lola:* Queenie Smith, *Miss Seiffert:* Virginia Brissac, *Countess:* Grayce Hampton, *Miss Neumann:* Dorothy Neumann, *Singing Inmate:* Jan Clayton, *Asylum Inmate:* Isabel Jewell, *Visor:* Syd Saylor, *Tommy's Mother:* Mae Marsh, *Young Girl:* Marion Marshall, *Tommy:* Ashley Cowan, *Patient:* Minerva Urecal, *Miss Servis:* Helen Servis, *Gertrude:* Celia Lovsky, *Doctor Somer:* Lester Sharpe, *Nurse:* Mary Treen, *Patient:* Barbara Pepper, *Virginia at 2:* Victoria Albright.

The Snows of Kilimanjaro with Lisa Ferraday, Hildegarde Neff and Gregory Peck.

THE SNOWS OF KILIMANJARO (1952) 20th. Producer, Darryl F. Zanuck. Director, Henry King. Color by Technicolor. From the short story by Ernest Hemingway. Screenplay, Casey Robinson. Music, Bernard Herrmann. Art Direction, Lyle Wheeler, John De Cuir. Sets, Thomas Little, Paul S. Fox. Choreography, Antonio Triana. Cinematographer, Leon Shamroy. Special Photo-effects, Ray Kellogg. Editor, Barbara McLean. 117 minutes

Harry: Gregory Peck, *Helen:* Susan Hayward, *Cynthia:* Ava Gardner, *Countess Liz:* Hildegarde Neff, *Uncle Bill:* Leo G. Carroll, *Johnson:* Torin Thatcher, *Beatrice:* Ava Norring, *Connie:* Helene Stanley, *Emile:* Marcel Dalio, *Guitarist:* Vincent Gomez, *Spanish Dancer:* Richard Allan, *Dr. Simmons:* Leonard Carey, *Witch Doctor:* Paul Thompson, *Molo:* Emmett Smith, *Charles:* Victor Wood, *American Soldier:* Bert Freed, *Margot:* Agnes Laury, *Georgette:* Monique Chantel, *Annette:* Janine Grandel, *Compton:* John Dodsworth, *Harry (age 17):* Charles Bates, *Venduse:* Lisa Ferraday, *Princess:* Maya Van Horn, *Marquis:* Ivan Lebedeff, *Spanish Officer:* Martin Garralaga, *Servant:* George Davis, *Old Waiter:* Julian Rivero, *Clerk:* Edward Colmans, *Accordian Players:* Ernest Brunner, Arthur Brunner.

SNOW WHITE AND THE SEVEN DWARFS (1937) RKO. Produced by Walt Disney. Supervising Director, David Hand. Color by Technicolor. Based on the Grimm's fairy tale. Story Adaptation, Ted Sears, Otto Englander, Earl Hurd, Dorothy Ann Blank, Richard Creedon, Dick Richard, Merrill de Maris, Webb Smith. Sequence Directors, Perce Pearce, Larry Morey, William Cottrell, Wilfred Jackson, Ben Sharpsteen. Art Directors, Charles Philippi, High Hennesy, Terrell Stapp, McLaren Stewart, Harold Miles, Tom Codrick, Gustaf Tenggren, Kenneth Anderson, Kendall O'Connor, Hazel Sewell. Art Backgrounds, Samuel Armstrong, Mique Nelson, Merle Cox, Claude Coats, Phil Dike, Ray Lockrem, Maurice Nible. Supervising Animators, Hamilton Luske, Vladimir Tytla, Fred Moore, Herman Ferguson. Music, Frank Churchill, Leigh Harline, Paul Smith. Character Designers, Albert Hurter and Jose Grant. Animators, Frank Thomas, Duck Lundy, Arthur Babbitt, Eric Larson, Milton Kahl, Robert Stokes, James Algar, Al Eugster, Cy Young, Joshua Meader, Ugo D'Orsi, George Rowley, Les Clark, Fred Spencer, Bill Roberts, Bernard Garbutt, Grim Natwick, Jack Campbell, Marvin Woodward, James Culhane, Stan Quackenbush, Ward Kimball, Woolie Reitherman, Robert Martsch. Songs by Larry Morey and Frank Churchill: "Heigh Ho," "Just Whistle While You Work," "Some Day My Prince Will Come," "I'm Wishing," "One Song," "With a Smile and a Song," "The Washing Song," "Isn't This a Silly Song?", "Buddle-Uddle-Um-Dum," "Music in Your Soup" and "You're Never Too Old to Be Young." Adrienne Casillotti as the voice of Snow White. Margery Belcher (later Marge Champion) modeled for Snow White. 82 minutes

Snow White and the Seven Dwarfs.

490

The Solid Gold Cadillac with Judy Holliday and Neva Patterson.

THE SOLID GOLD CADILLAC (1956) Col. Producer, Fred Kohlmar. Director, Richard Quine. Based on the play by George S. Kaufman and Howard Teichmann. Screenplay, Abe Burrows. Art Director, Ross Bellah. Musical Director, Lionel Newman. Music composed by Cyril J. Mockridge. Orchestration, Bernard Mayers. Cinematographer, Charles Lang. Editor, Charles Nelson. 99 minutes

Laura Partridge: Judy Holliday, *Edward L. McKeever:* Paul Douglas, *Clifford Snell:* Fred Clark, *John T. Blessington:* John Williams, *Harry Harkness:* Hiram Sherman, *Amelia Shotgraven:* Neva Patterson, *Warren Gillie:* Ralph Dumke, *Alfred Metcalfe:* Ray Collins, *Jenkins:* Arthur O'Connell, *Williams:* Richard Deacon, *Miss L'Arriere:* Marilyn Hanold, *Blessington's Secretary:* Anne Loos, *Snell's Secretary:* Audrey Swanson, *Chauffeur:* Larry Hudson, *Receptionist:* Sandra White, *Senator Simpkins:* Harry Antrim, *Elevator Man:* Paul Weber, *Elderly Lady:* Emily Getchell, *First Lawyer:* Maurice Manson, *Model:* Suzanne Alexander, *Advertising Man:* Oliver Cliff, *Judge:* Voltaire Perkins, *Second Lawyer:* Joe Hamilton, *Farm Woman:* Jean G. Harvey, *Spanish-American War Veteran:* Bud Osborne, *Dowager:* Lulu Mae Bohrman, *Lady Commentator:* Madge Blake, *Bill Parker:* Jack Latham.

SOLOMON AND SHEBA (1959) UA. An Edward Small Presentation. Producer, Ted Richmond. Director, King Vidor. Screenplay by Anthony Veillier, Paul Dudley and George Bruce. From a story by Crane Wilbur. Music by Mario Nascimbene. Art Directors, Richard Day, Alfred Sweeney. Cinematographer, Freddie Young. Editor, John

Solomon and Sheba with Gina Lollobrigida and Yul Brynner.

Ludwig. In Technicolor and Technirama. Produced in Spain. Choreography, Jaroslav Berger. Special Effects, Alex Weldon. Sound, F. C. Hughesdon, Aubrey Lewis, and David Hildyard. Brynner replaced Tyrone Power, who died during production and is in the battle scenes. 139 minutes

Solomon: Yul Brynner, *Sheba:* Gina Lollobrigida, *Adonijah:* George Sanders, *Pharoah:* David Farrar, *Abishag:* Marisa Pavan, *Joab:* John Crawford, *Hezrai:* Laurence Naismith, *Ahab:* Jose Nieto, *Sittar:* Alejandro Rey, *Baltor:* Harry Andrews, *Zadok:* Julio Pena, *Bathsheba:* Maruchi Fresno, *Nathan:* William Devlin, *Egyptian General:* Felix De Pomes, *Takyan:* Jean Anderson, *Josiah:* Jack Gwillim, *King David:* Finlay Currie.

SOMEBODY UP THERE LIKES ME (1956) MGM. Produced by Charles Schnee. Directed by Robert Wise. Associate Producer, James E. Newcom. Based on the autobiography of Rocky Graziano as written by Rowland Barber. Screenplay, Ernest Lehman. Music, Bronislau Kaper. Title song by Sammy Cahn, sung by Perry Como. Assistant Director, Robert Saunders.

Somebody Up There Likes Me with Courtland Shepard and Paul Newman.

Rocky: Paul Newman, *Norma:* Pier Angeli, *Irving Cohen:* Everett Sloane, *Ma Barbella:* Eileen Heckart, *Romolo:* Sal Mineo, *Nick Barbella:* Harold J. Stone, *Benny:* Joseph Buloff, *Whitey Bimstein:* Sammy White, *Heldon:* Arch Johnson, *Questioner:* Robert Lieb, *Commissioner Eagan:* Theodore Newton, *Fidel:* Steve McQueen, *Corporal:* Robert Easton, *Ring Announcer:* Ray Walker, *Commissioner:* Billy Nelson, *Frankie Peppo:* Robert Loggia, *Lou Stillman:* Matt Crowley, *Johnny Hyland:* Judson Pratt, *Yolanda Barbella:* Donna Jo Gribble, *Colonel:* James Todd, *George:* Jack Kelk, *Captain Grifton:* Russ Conway, *Harry Wismen:* Himself, *Tony Zale:* Courtland Shepard, *Radio Announcer:* Sam Taub, *Rocky at 8:* Terry Rangno, *Yolanda at 12:* Jan Gillum, *Shorty:* Ralph Vitti (Michael Dante), *Polack:* Walter Cartier, *Warden Niles:* John Eldredge, *Captain Lancheck:* Clancy Cooper, *Private:* Dean Jones, *Bryson:* Ray Stricklyn, *Sam:* Caswell Adams, *Curtis Hughtower:* Charles Green, *Audrey at 3:* Angela Cartwright, *Mr. Mueller:* David Leonard.

SOME CAME RUNNING (1958) MGM. Producer, Sol C. Siegel. Director, Vincente Minnelli. CinemaScope, MetroColor. Based on the novel by James Jones. Screenplay, John Patrick, Arthur Sheekman. Art Directors, William A. Horning, Urie McCleary. Musical Director, Elmer Bernstein. Cinematographer, William H. Daniels. Editor, Adrienne Fazan. 127 minutes

Dave Hirsh: Frank Sinatra, *Bama Dillert:* Dean Martin, *Ginny Moorhead:* Shirley MacLaine, *Gwen French:* Martha Hyer, *Frank Hirsh:*

Some Came Running with Carmen Phillips, Dean Martin and Frank Sinatra.

Arthur Kennedy, *Edith Barclay:* Nancy Gates, *Agnes Hirsh:* Leora Dana, *Dawn Hirsh:* Betty Lou Keim, *Prof. Robert Haven French:* Larry Gates, *Raymond Lanchak:* Steven Peck, *Jane Barclay:* Connie Gilchrist, *Smitty:* Ned Wever, *Rosalie:* Carmen Phillips, *Wally Dennis:* John Brennan, *Al:* William Schallert, *Sheriff:* Roy Engel, *Sister Mary Joseph:* Marion Ross, *Dewey Cole:* Denny Miller, *Hotel Clerk:* Chuck Courtney, *George Huff:* Paul Jones, *Mrs. Stevens:* Geraldine Wall, *Virginia Stevens:* Janelle Richards, *Ned Deacon:* George Brengel, *Hubie Nelson:* George Cisar, *Doc Henderson:* Donald Kerr, *Club Manager:* Jan Arvan, *Ted Harperspoon:* Don Haggerty, *Waiter:* Frank Mitchell, *Bus Driver:* Dave White, *Dealer:* Len Lesser, *Joe:* Ric Roman, *Slim:* George E. Stone, *Judge Baskin:* Anthony Jochim.

SOME LIKE IT HOT (1959) UA. Producer-Director, Billy Wilder. Screenplay by Billy Wilder and I. A. L. Diamond. Suggested by a story by R. Thoeren and M. Logan. Associate Producers, Doane Harrison, I. A. L. Diamond. Score by Adolph Deutsch. Assistant Director, Sam Nelson. Gowns by Orry-Kelly. Art Director, Ted Haworth. Background Score, Adolph Deutsch. Cinematographer, Charles Lang, Jr. Editor, Arthur Schmidt. An Ashton Picture and Mirisch Company Presentation Song: "Runnin' Wild." 120 minutes

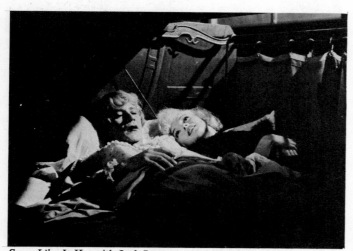

Some Like It Hot with Jack Lemmon and Marilyn Monroe.

Sugar Kane (Kumulchek): Marilyn Monroe, *Joe (Josephine):* Tony Curtis, *Jerry (Daphne):* Jack Lemmon, *Spats Columbo:* George Raft, *Mulligan:* Pat O'Brien, *Osgood Fielding III:* Joe E. Brown, *Bonaparte:* Nehemiah Persoff, *Sweet Sue:* Joan Shawlee, *Sig Poliakoff:* Billy Gray, *Toothpick:* George E. Stone, *Beinstock:* Dave Barry, *Spats' Henchmen:* Mike Mazurki, Harry Wilson, *Dolores:* Beverly Wills, *Nellie:* Barbara Drew, *Paradise:* Edward G. Robinson, Jr., *Bouncer:* Tom Kennedy, *Waiter:* John Indrisano.

SOMEWHERE I'LL FIND YOU (1942) MGM. Producer, Pandro S. Berman. Director, Wesley Ruggles. Author, Charles Hoffman. Screen-

Somewhere I'll Find You with Lee Patrick, Robert Sterling and Lana Turner.

play, Marguerite Roberts. Art Director, Cedric Gibbons. Musical Score, Bronislau Kaper. Cameraman, Harold Rosson. 108 minutes

Jonathon Davis: Clark Gable, *Paula Lane:* Lana Turner, *Kirk Davis:* Robert Sterling, *Willie Manning:* Reginald Owen, *Eve Manning:* Lee Patrick, *George L. Stafford:* Charles Dingle, *Mama Lugovska:* Tamara Shayne, *Dorloff:* Leonid Kinskey, *Penny:* Diana Lewis, *Nurse Winifred:* Molly Lamont, *Crystal Jones:* Patricia Dane, *Miss Coulter:* Sara Haden, *Prof. Anatole:* Richard Kean, *Pearcley:* Francis Sayles, *Bartender:* Tom O'Grady, *Waiter:* Donald Kerr, *Penny's Companion:* Gayne Whitman, *Boy:* Grady Sutton, *Girl:* Dorothy Morris, *Thomas Chang:* Keye Luke, *Fred Kirsten:* Miles Mander, *Ming:* Eleanor Soohoo, *Sam Porto:* Allen Jung, *Captain:* Douglas Fowley, *Felipe Morel:* Benny Inocencio, *Lieut. Hall:* Van Johnson, *Manuel Ortega:* Angel Cruz, *Sgt. Purdy:* Keenan Wynn, *Slim:* Frank Faylen, *Pete Brady:* J. Lewis Smith, *Chinese Doctor:* Lee Tung-Foo.

THE SONG OF BERNADETTE (1943) 20th. Producer, William Perlberg. Director, Henry King. From the novel by Franz Werfel. Screenplay, George Seaton. Art Directors, James Basevi, William Darling. Music, Alfred Newman. Orchestral Arrangements, Edward Powell. Cameraman, Arthur Miller. Special Effects, Fred Sersen. Editor, Barbara McLean. 156 minutes

Bernadette: Jennifer Jones, *Antoine:* William Eythe, *Peyremaie:* Charles Bickford, *Dutour:* Vincent Price, *Dr. Dozous:* Lee Cobb, *Sister Vauzous:* Gladys Cooper, *Louise Soubirous:* Anne Revere, *Francois Soubirous:* Roman Bohnen, *Jeanne Abadie:* Mary Anderson, *Empress Eugenie:* Patricia Morison, *Lacade:* Aubrey Mather, *Jacomet:* Charles Dingle, *Croisine:* Edith Barrett, *Louis Bouriette:* Sig Rumann, *Bernarde Casterot:* Blanche Yurka, *Marie Soubirous:* Ermadean Walters, *Callet:* Marcel Dalio, *Le Crampe:* Pedro de Cordoba, *Emperor Napoleon:* Jerome Cowan, *Bishop of Tarbes:* Charles Waldron, *Chaplain:* Moroni Olsen, *Convent Mother Superior:* Nana Bryant, *Charles*

Song of Bernadette with Jennifer Jones.

Bouhouhorts: Manart Kippen, *Jean Soubirous:* Merrill Rodin, *Justin Soubirous:* Nino Pipitone, Jr., *Father Pomian:* John Maxwell Hayes, *Estrade:* Jean Del Val, *Mme. Bruat:* Tala Birell, *Mme. Nicolau:* Eula Morgan, *Dr. St. Cyr:* Frank Reicher, *Duran:* Charles La Torre, *Blessed Virgin:* Linda Darnell, *Woman:* Mae Marsh, *Adolar:* Dickie Moore, *Mother Superior:* Dorothy Shearer, *Bishop:* Andre Charlot, *Psychiatrist:* Alan Napier, *Monks:* Fritz Leiber and Arthur Hohl, *Doctor:* Edward Van Sloan.

A SONG TO REMEMBER (1945) Col. Producer, Louis F. Edelman. Director, Charles Vidor. Color by Technicolor. From the story by Ernst Marischka. Screenplay, Sidney Buchman. Art Directors, Lionel Banks, Van Nest Polglase. Musical Supervisor, Mario Silva. Musical Director, M. W. Stoloff. Cameraman, Tony Gaudio. Allen M. Davey. Editor, Charles Nelson. Technicolor Director, Natalie Kalmus. 113 minutes

A Song to Remember with Cornel Wilde, Merle Oberon and Paul Muni.

Professor Joseph Elsner: Paul Muni, *George Sand:* Merle Oberon, *Frederick Chopin:* Cornel Wilde, *Franz Liszt:* Stephen Bekassy, *Constantia:* Nina Foch, *Louis Pleyel:* George Coulouris, *Henri Dupont:* Sig Arno, *Kalbrenner:* Howard Freeman, *Alfred DeMusset:* George MacCready, *Madame Mercier:* Claire Dubrey, *Monsieur Jollet:* Frank Puglia, *Madame Lambert:* Fern Emmett, *Isabelle Chopin:* Sybil Merritt, *Monsieur Chopin:* Ivan Triesault, *Madame Chopin:* Fay Helm, *Isabelle Chopin (age 9):* Dawn Bender, *Chopin (age 10):* Maurice Tauzin, *Paganini:* Roxy Roth, *Balzac:* Peter Cusanelli, *Titus:* William Challee, *Jan:* William Richardson, *Postman:* Charles LaTorre, *Albert:* Earl Easton, *Young Russian:* Gregory Gaye, *Major Domo:* Walter Bonn, *Russian Count:* Henry Sharp, *Countess:* Zoia Karabanova, *Russian Governor:* Michael Visaroff, *Servant:* John George, *Pleyel's Clerk:* Ian Wolfe, *Duchess of Orleans:* Norma Drury, *Duke of Orleans:* Eugene Borden, *De La Croux:* Al Luttringer.

SON OF FLUBBER (1963) BV. A Walt Disney presentation. Associate Producers, Bill Walsh, Ron Miller. Director, Robert Stevenson. Based on a story by Samuel W. Taylor and on the Danny Dunn books. Screenplay, Bill Walsh and Don Dagradi. Sequel to *The Absent-Minded Professor* (1959). Art Directors, Carroll Clark, Bill Tuntke. Music, George Bruns. Orchestration, Franklyn Marks. Cinematographer, Edward Colman. Editor, Cotton Warburton. 100 minutes

Ned Brainard: Fred MacMurray, *Betsy Brainard:* Nancy Olson, *Alonzo Hawk:* Keenan Wynn, *Biff Hawk:* Tommy Kirk, *A. J. Allen:* Ed Wynn, *President Rufus Daggett:* Leon Ames, *Mr. Hurley:* Ken Murray, *Mr. Hummel:* William Demarest, *Judge Murdock:* Charlie Ruggles, *Radio Announcer:* Paul Lynde, *Mr. Harker:* Bob Sweeney, *Shelby Ashton:* Elliott Reid, *Defense Secretary:* Edward Andrews, *Desiree delaRoche:* Joanna Moore, *First Referee:* Alan Carney, *Of-*

Son of Flubber with Fred MacMurray, Nancy Olson and Bob Sweeney.

ficer Kelly: Forrest Lewis, *Officer Hanson:* James Westerfield, *Prosecutor:* Alan Hewitt, *Coach Wilson:* Stuart Erwin, *Barley:* Jack Albertson, *Osbourne:* Eddie Ryder, *Mrs. Edna Daggett:* Harriet MacGibbon, *Humphrey Hacker:* Leon Tyler, *Assistant to Defense Secretary:* Robert Shayne, *TV Commercial Woman:* Beverly Wills, *Admiral:* Henry Hunter, *Bartender:* Hal Smith, *Sign Painter:* J. Pat O'Malley, *Rutland Football Player #33:* Norman Grabowski, *Rutland Coach:* Gordon Jones, *Newsboy (Joey Marriano):* Lindy Davis, *Secretary:* Hope Sansberry, *Proprietor:* Byron Foulger, *Second Juror:* Jack Rice, *First Juror:* Dal McKennon, *#1 Bailiff:* Burt Mustin, *Rutland Student Manager:* Ned Wynn.

SON OF KONG (1933) RKO. Directed by Ernest B. Schoedsack. Story, Ruth Rose. Cameramen, Eddie Linden, Vernon Walker, J. O. Taylor. Editor, Ted Cheeseman. Sound, Earl Colcott. Sequel to *King Kong*, and one of the rare instances that a sequel was released the same year as the original film. Locations filmed on **Catalina Island**. Repeating their original roles are Armstrong, Reicher, Johnson, Clemento. 70 minutes

Son of Kong with Helen Mack and Robert Armstrong.

Carl Denham: Robert Armstrong, *Hilda Peterson:* Helen Mack, *Captain Englehorn:* Frank Reicher, *Helstrom:* John Marston, *Charlie, Cook:* Victor Wong, *Mickey:* Lee Kohlmar, *Red:* Ed Brady, *Peterson:* Clarence Wilson, *Mrs. Hudson:* Katharine Ward, *Girl Reporter:* Gertrude Short, *Servant Girl:* Gertrude Sutton, *Chinese Trader:* James L. Leong, *Native Chief:* Noble Johnson, *Witch King:* Steve Clemento, *Process Server:* Frank O'Connor.

SON OF PALEFACE (1952) Par. Producer, Robert L. Welch. Director, Frank Tashlin. Color by Technicolor. Screenplay, Frank Tashlin, Robert L. Welch, Joseph Quillan. Cinematographer, Harry J. Wild. Special Photography, Gordon Jennings, Paul Lerpae. Process Photography, Farciot Edouart. Art, Hal Pereira, Poland Anderson. Editor,

Son of Paleface with Jane Russell, Bob Hope and Bill Williams.

Eda Warren. Music, Lyn Murray. Dances, Josephine Earl. Songs: "Buttons and Bows" (new version), "Wing Ding Tonight," "California Rose" and "What a Dirty Shame" by Ray Evans and Jay Livingston; "Am I in Love?" and "Four-Legged Friend" by Jack Brooks; "There's a Cloud in My Valley of Sunshine" by Jack Hope and Lyle Moraine. Sequel to *The Paleface* (1948). 95 minutes

Junior: Bob Hope, *Mike:* Jane Russell, *Roy Rogers:* Roy Rogers, *Kirk:* Bill Williams, *Doc Lovejoy:* Lloyd Corrigan, *Ebeneezer Hawkins:* Paul E. Burns, *Sheriff McIntyre:* Douglass Dumbrille, *Pre. Stoner:* Harry Von Zell, *Indian Chief:* Iron Eyes Cody, *Blacksmith:* Wee Willie Davis, *Charley:* Charley Cooley, *Guests:* Cecil B. De Mille, Bing Crosby, Robert L. Welch, *Ned:* Charles Morton, *Wally:* Don Dunning, *Crag:* Leo J. McMahon, *Genevieve:* Felice Richmond, *Bessie:* Charmienne Harker, *Isabel:* Isabel Cushin, *Clara:* Jane Easton, *Townsman:* Homer Dickinson, *Bank Clerk "Weaverly":* Lyle Moraine, *First Bartender:* Hank Mann, *Second Bartender "Micky":* Michael A. Cirillo, *"Becky":* Isabel Cushin, *Townsman "Chester":* Chester Conklin, *Townswoman "Flo":* Flo Stanton, *Townsman "Johnny":* John George, *Zeke:* Charles Quirk, *Dade:* Frank Cordell, *Jeb:* Willard Willingham, *Trav:* Warren Fiske, *Penelope:* Jean Willes, *Governor:* Jonathan Hale.

THE SONS OF KATIE ELDER (1965) Par. Producer, Hal Wallis. Associate Producer, Paul Nathan. Director, Henry Hathaway. Technicolor. Author, Talbot Jennings. Screenplay, William H. Wright, Allan Weiss, Harry Essex. Art Directors, Hal Pereira, Walter Tyler. Music, Elmer Bernstein. Cinematographer, Lucien Ballard. Editor, Warren Low. 122 minutes

John Elder: John Wayne, *Tom Elder:* Dean Martin, *Mary Glenney:* Martha Hyer, *Bud Elder:* Michael Anderson, Jr., *Matt Elder:* Earl Holliman, *Ben Latta:* Jeremy Slate, *Morgan Hastings:* James Gregory, *Sheriff Billy Wilson:* Paul Fix, *Curley:* George Kennedy, *Dave Hastings:* Dennis Hopper, *Deputy Harry Evers:* Sheldon Allman, *Preacher:* John Litel, *Hyselman:* John Doucette, *Banker Vennar:* James Westerfield, *Charlie Striker:* Rhys Williams, *Charlie:* John Qualen, *Bondie Adams:* Rodolfo Acosta, *Jeb Ross:* Strother Martin, *Doc Isdell/ Bartender:* Karl Swenson, *Mr. Peevey:* Percy Heiton, *Jeb (Blacksmith's*

The Sons of Katie Elder with John Wayne and Martha Hyer.

Son): Harvey Grant, *Amboy:* Jerry Gatlin, *Ned Reese:* Loren Janes, *Burr Sandeman:* Red Morgan, *Townsman:* Charles Roberson, *Bit Man:* Ralph Volkie, *Andy Sharp:* Jack Williams, *Gus Dolly:* Henry Wills, *Buck Mason:* Joseph Yrigoyen.

SONS OF THE DESERT (1933) MGM. Produced by Hal Roach. Original story and continuity by Frank Craven and Byron Morgan. Directed by William A. Seiter. Photography, Kenneth Peach. Editor, Bert Jordan. Remake of *Ambrose's First Falsehood* (Keystone, 1914); and *We Faw Down* (MGM, 1928). 68 minutes

Stan: Stan Laurel, *Oliver:* Oliver Hardy, *Mrs. Laurel:* Dorothy Christy, *Mrs. Hardy:* Mae Busch, *Charley:* Charley Chase, *Doc:* Lucien Littlefield, *Extra:* Hal Roach, *Bits:* John Elliott, Charles Hall, Stanley Blystone, *A Son:* John Merton.

Sons of the Desert with Stan Laurel and Oliver Hardy.

SO PROUDLY WE HAIL! (1943) Par. Producer and Director, Mark Sandrich. Author, Allan Scott. Art Directors, Hans Dreier, Earl Hedrick. Cameraman, Charles Lang. Song by Edward Heyman and Miklos Rozsa, "Loved One." Film debut of Sonny Tufts. 126 minutes

Lieutenant Janet Davidson: Claudette Colbert, *Lieutenant Joan O'Doul:* Paulette Goddard, *Lieutenant Olivia D'Arcy:* Veronica Lake, *Lieutenant John Sumners:* George Reeves, *Lieutenant Rosemary Larson:* Barbara Britton, *Chaplain:* Walter Abel, *Kansas:* Sonny Tufts, *Captain "Ma" McGregor:* Mary Servoss, *Dr. Jose Bardia:* Ted Hecht,

So Proudly We Hail! with Paulette Goddard, Mary Treen and Claudette Colbert.

Dr. Harrison: John Litel, *Ling Chee:* Dr. Hugh Ho Chang, *Lieutenant Sadie Schwartz:* Mary Treen, *Lieutenant Ethel Armstrong:* Kitty Kelly, *Lieutenant Elsie Bollenbacher:* Helen Lynd, *Lieutenant Toni Dacolli:* Lorna Gray, *Lieutenant Irma Emerson:* Dorothy Adams, *Lieutenant Betty Peterson:* Ann Doran, *Lieutenant Carol Johnson:* Jean Willes, *Lieutenant Fay Leonard:* Lynn Walker, *Lieutenant Margaret Stevenson:* Joan Tours, *Lieutenant Lynne Hopkins:* Jan Wiley, *Nurse:* Mimi Doyle, *Colonel White:* James Bell, *Flight Lieutenant Archie McGregor:* Dick Hogan, *Captain O'Rourke:* Bill Goodwin, *Captain O'Brien:* James Flavin, *Mr. Larson:* Byron Foulger, *Mrs. Larson:* Elsa Janssen, *Georgie Larson:* Richard Crane, *Colonel Mason:* Boyd Davis, *Colonel Clark:* Will Wright, *Nurse:* Frances Morris, *Young Ensign:* James Millican, *First Young Doctor:* Damian O'Flynn, *Ship's Captain:* Roy Gordon, *Nurse:* Julia Faye, *Steward:* Jack Luden, *Major Arthur:* Harry Strung, *Captain Lawrence:* Edward Dow, *Girl:* Yvonne De Carlo.

SORROWFUL JONES (1949) Par. Producer, Robert L. Welch. Director, Sidney Lanfield. Author, Damon Runyon. Screenplay, Melville Shavelson, Edmund Hartman, Jack Rose. Art Directors, Hans Dreier, Albert Nozake. Music Score, Robert Emmett Dolan. Photography, Daniel L. Fapp. Editor, Mary Kay Dodson. Songs by Ray Evans and Jay Livingston: "Having a Wonderful Wish" and "Rock-a-Bye Bangtail." Remake of Paramount's *Little Miss Marker,* 1934. 88 minutes

Sorrowful Jones: Bob Hope, *Gladys O'Neill:* Lucille Ball, *Regret:* William Demarest, *Big Steve Holloway:* Bruce Cabot, *Reardon:* Thomas Gomez, *Once Over Sam:* Tom Pedi, *Orville Smith:* Paul Lees, *Doc Chesley:* Houseley Stevenson, *Martha Jane Smith:* Mary Jayne Saunders, *Agnes "Happy Hips" Noonan:* Claire Carleton, *Blinky:* Harry Tyler, *Big Steve's Bodyguard:* Ben Welden, *Psychiatrist:* Maurice Cass, *Doctor:* John Shay, *Head Phone Man:* John "Skins" Miller, *Horseplayer:* Bob Kortman, *Horseplayer:* James Davies, *Shorty:* Charley Cooley, *Barber:* Marc Krah, *Waiter (Steve's Place):* Sid Tomack, *Charwoman:* Patsy O'Byrne, *Cab Driver:* Ralph Peters, *Police Lieutenant Mitchell:* Ed Dearing, *Plainclothesman:* Arthur Space, *Nurse:* Sally Rawlinson, *Psychiatrist:* Emmett Vogan, *Doctor:* Selmer Jackson.

Sorrowful Jones with Bob Hope, Mary Jane Saunders and William Demarest.

THE SOUND OF MUSIC (1965) 20th. Producer-Director, Robert Wise. Todd-AO and De Luxe Color. Associate Producer, Saul Chaplin. Director of Photography, Ted McCord. Screenplay, Ernest Lehman. From the musical play by Richard Rodgers and Oscar Hammerstein II. Lyrics, Oscar Hammerstein II. Music and Additional Lyrics, Richard Rodgers. Songs: "The Sound of Music," "Overture and Preludium," "Morning Hymn," "Maria," "I Have Confidence," "Sixteen Going On Seventeen," "My Favorite Things," "Climb Every Mountain," "The Lonely Goatherd," "Do-Re-Mi," "Something Good." "Edelweiss," "So Long, Farewell." Choreography, Marc Breaux and

The Sound of Music with Julie Andrews and children (Charmian Carr, Heather Menzies, Nicolas Hammond, Duane Chase, Angela Cartwright, Debbie Turner, Kym Karath).

Dee Dee Wood. Costumes, Dorothy Jeakins. Puppeteers, Bill and Cora Baird. Assistant Director, Ridgeway Callow. 171 minutes

Maria: Julie Andrews, *Captain Von Trapp:* Christopher Plummer, *The Baroness:* Eleanor Parker, *Max Detweiler:* Richard Haydn, *Mother Abbess:* Peggy Wood, *Liesl:* Charmian Carr, *Louisa:* Heather Menzies, *Friedrich:* Nicolas Hammond, *Kurt:* Duane Chase, *Brigitta:* Angela Cartwright, *Marta:* Debbie Turner, *Gretl:* Kym Karath, *Sister Margaretta:* Anna Lee, *Sister Berthe:* Portia Nelson, *Herr Zeller:* Ben Wright, *Rolfe:* Daniel Truhitte, *Frau Schmidt:* Norma Varden, *Franz:* Gil Stuart, *Sister Sophia:* Marni Nixon, *Sister Bernice:* Evadne Baker, *Baroness Ebberfeld:* Doris Lloyd.

THE SOUTHERNER (1945) UA. Produced by David Loew and Robert Hakim. Directed by Jean Renoir. Screenplay by Jean Renoir. From the novel *Hold Autumn in Your Hand* by George Sessions Perry. Music by Werner Janssen. Cameraman, Lucien Andriot. Editor, Gregg Tallas. Presented by Producing Artists, Inc. Assistant Director, Robert Aldrich. Narrated by Charles Kemper. 91 minutes

The Southerner with Zachary Scott and J. Carroll Naish.

Sam Tucker: Zachary Scott, *Nona Tucker:* Betty Field, *Granny Tucker:* Beulah Bondi, *Daisy Tucker:* Bunny Sunshine (Jean Vanderbuilt), *Jot Tucker:* Jay Gilpin, *Harmie:* Percy Kilbride, *Ma Tucker:* Blanche Yurka, *Tim:* Charles Kemper, *Devers:* J. Carroll Naish, *Finlay:* Norman Lloyd, *Doc White:* Jack Norworth, *Bartender:* Nestor Paiva, *Lizzie:* Estelle Taylor, *Party Girl:* Dorothy Granger, *Becky:* Noreen Roth (Noreen Nash), *Ruston:* Paul Harvey, *Uncle Pete Tucker:* Paul E. Burns, *Wedding Guest:* Earle Hodgins.

South Pacific with Mitzi Gaynor and Rossano Brazzi.

SOUTH PACIFIC (1958) Magna Theatre Corp. Producer, Buddy Adler. Director, Joshua Logan. Todd-AO and Technicolor. Adapted from the play *South Pacific* by Oscar Hammerstein II, Richard Rodgers, Joshua Logan, based on *Tales of the South Pacific* by James A. Michener. Book and lyrics by Oscar Hammerstein II. Music, Richard Rodgers. Screenplay, Paul Osborn. Art Directors, Lyle R. Wheeler, John De Cuir, Walter M. Scott, Paul S. Fox. Musical Director, Alfred Newman. Orchestratio.., Edward B. Powell, Pete King, Bernard Mayers, Robert Russell Bennett. Cinematographer, Leon Shamroy. Special Photographic Effects, L. B. Abbott. Editor, Robert Simpson. Songs by Richard Rodgers and Oscar Hammerstein II: "Some Enchanted Evening," "Younger Than Springtime," "Bali Ha'i," "Happy Talk," "A Cockeyed Optimist," "You've Got to Be Taught," "Dites-Moi Pourquoi," "Bloody Mary Is the Girl I Love," "I'm Gonna Wash That Man Right Out of My Hair," "I'm In Love With a Wonderful Guy," "Honey Bun," "Loneliness at Evening," "There Is Nothing Like a Dame," "This Nearly Was Mine," "Soliloquies," "My Girl Back Home." Giorgio Tozzi sings for Brazzi; Bill Lee for Kerr; Muriel Smith for Juanita Hall. Filmed in Kauai, Hawaii. Film debut of France Nuyen, 18. 171 minutes

Emile De Becque: Rossano Brazzi, *Nellie Forbush:* Mitzi Gaynor, *Lieutenant Cable:* John Kerr, *Luther Billis:* Ray Walston, *Bloody Mary:* Juanita Hall, *Liat:* France Nuyen, *Capt. Brackett:* Russ Brown, *Professor:* Jack Mullaney, *Stewpot:* Ken Clark, *Harbison:* Floyd Simmons, *Ngana, Emile's Daughter:* Candace Lee, *Jerome, His Son:* Warren Haieh, *Buzz Adams:* Tom Laughlin, *Dancer:* Beverly Aadland, *Sub Chief:* Galvan De Leon, *Copilot:* Ron Ely, *Communications Man:* Robert Jacobs, *Native Chief:* Archie Savage, *Nurse:* Darleen Engle, *Admiral Kester:* Richard Cutting, *Radio Man:* John Gabriel, *Nurse:* Evelyn Ford, *U. S. Commander:* Joe Bailey, *Pilots:* Doug McClure, Stephen Ferry.

SPARTACUS (1960) Univ. Produced by Edward Lewis. Executive Producer, Kirk Douglas. Directed by Stanley Kubrick. In Super Technirama 70 and Technicolor. Based on the novel by Howard Fast. Screenplay, Dalton Trumbo. Music composed and conducted by Alex North. Music co-conducted by Joseph Gershenson. Costumes, Bill Thomas and J. Arlington Valles. Assistant Directors, Marshall Green, Foster Phinney, Jim Welch, Joe Kenny, Charles Scott. Art Director, Eric Orbom. Cinematography, Russell Metty. Additional scenes photographed by Clifford Stine. Editor, Robert Lawrence. A Bryna Production. 196 minutes.

Spartacus: Kirk Douglas, *Marcus Crassus:* Laurence Olivier, *Antoninus:* Tony Curtis, *Varinia:* Jean Simmons, *Gracchus:* Charles Laughton, *Batiatus:* Peter Ustinov, *Julius Caesar:* John Gavin, *Helena Glabrus:* Nina Foch, *Tigranes:* Herbert Lom, *Crixus:* John Ireland, *Glabrus:* John Dall, *Marcellus:* Charles McGraw, *Claudia Marius:* Joanna Barnes, *Draba:* Woody Strode, *David:* Harold J. Stone, *Ramon:* Peter Brocco, *Gannicus:* Paul Lambert, *Guard Captain:* Bob Wilke, *Dionysius:* Nick Dennis, *Roman Officer, Caius:* John Hoyt, *Laelius:* Frederick Worlock, *Symmachus:* Dayton Lummis, *Old Crone:* Lili Valenty, *Julia:* Jill Jarmyn, *Slave Girl:* Jo Summers, *Otho:* James Griffith, *Marius:* Joe Haworth, *Trainer:* Dale Van Sickel,

Spartacus with Kirk Douglas and Woody Strode.

Metallius: Vinton Hayworth, *Herald:* Carleton Young, *Beggar Woman:* Hallene Hill, *Fimbria:* Paul Burns, *Garrison Officer:* Leonard Penn, *Slaves:* Harry Harvey, Jr., Eddie Parker, Herold Goodwin, Chuck Roberson, *Slave Leaders:* Saul Gorss, Charles Horvath, Gil Perkins, *Gladiators:* Bob Morgan, Reg Parton, Tom Steele, *Ad-Libs:* Ken Terrell, Boyd Red Morgan, *Guards:* Dick Crockett, Harvey Parry, Carey Loftin, *Pirates:* Bob Burns, Seaman Glass, George Robotham, Stubby Kruger, *Soldiers:* Chuck Courtney, Russ Saunders, Valley Keene, Tap Canutt, Joe Canutt, Chuck Hayward, Buff Brady, Cliff Lyons, Rube Schaffer, *Legionaires:* Ted de Corsia, Arthur Batanides, Robert Stevenson, *Majordomo:* Terence De Marney.

SPELLBOUND (1945) UA. Produced by David O. Selznick. Directed by Alfred Hitchcock. Based on the novel *The House of Dr. Edwardes* by Francis Beeding (pseudonym of Hilary St. John Saunders and Leslie Palmer). A Selznick International Pictures-Vanguard Films Production. Screenplay, Ben Hecht. Adaptation, Angus MacPhail. Music, Miklos Rozsa. Designer of Dream Sequence, Salvador Dali. Art Director, John Ewing. Production Designer, James Basevi. Unit Manager, Fred Aherne. Miss Bergman's Gowns, Howard Greer. Photography, George Barnes. Editor, William Ziegler. Assistant, Lowell Farrell. Sound, Richard De Weese. 111 minutes.

Dr. Constance Peterson: Ingrid Bergman, *J. B.:* Gregory Peck, *Matron:* Jean Acker, *Harry·* Donald Curtis, *Miss Carmichael·* Rhonda Fleming, *Dr. Fleurot:* John Emery, *Dr. Murchison:* Leo G. Carroll, *Garmes:* Norman Lloyd, *Dr. Graff:* Steven Geray, *Dr. Hanish:* Paul Harvey, *Dr. Galt:* Erskine Sanford, *Norma;* Janet Scott, *Sheriff:* Victor Kilian, *Stranger in Hotel Lobby:* Wallace Ford, *House Detective:* Bill Goodwin, *Bellboy:* Dave Willock, *Railroad Clerk:* George Meader, *Policeman at Railroad Station:* Matt Moore, *Gateman:* Harry Brown, *Lieutenant Cooley:* Art Baker, *Sergeant Gillespie:* Regis Toomey, *Dr. Alex Brulov:* Michael Chekhov, *Secretary at Police Station:* Clarence Straight, *J. B. as a boy:* Joel Davis, *J. B.'s Brother:* Teddy Infuhr, *Police Captain:* Addison Richards, *Ticket Taker:* Richard Bartell, *Dr. Edwardes:* Edward Fielding, *Man Carrying Violin:* Alfred Hitchcock.

Spellbound with Ingrid Bergman and Gregory Peck.

The Spirit of St. Louis with James Stewart.

THE SPIRIT OF ST. LOUIS (1957) WB. Producer, Leland Hayward. Director, Billy Wilder. CinemaScope, WarnerColor. Based on the 1953 Pulitzer Prize book by Charles A. Lindbergh. Screenplay, Billy Wilder, Wendell Mayes. Adaptation, Charles Lederer. Art Director, Art Loel. Music composed and conducted by Franz Waxman. Orchestration, Leonid Raab. Cinematographers, Robert Burks, J. Peverell Marley. Aerial Photography, Thomas Tutwiler. Editor, Arthur P. Schmidt. 138 minutes.

Charles Lindbergh: James Stewart, *Bud Gurney:* Murray Hamilton, *Mirror Girl:* Patricia Smith, *B. F. Mahoney:* Bartlett Robinson, *Knight:* Robert Cornthwaite, *Model-Dancer:* Sheila Bond, *Father Hussman:* Marc Connelly, *Donald Hall:* Arthur Space, *Boedecker:* Harlan Warde, *Goldsborough:* Dabbs Greer, *Blythe:* Paul Birch, *Harold Bixby:* David Orrick, *Major Lambert:* Robert Burton, *William Robertson:* James L. Robertson. Jr., *E. Lansing Ray:* Maurice Manson, *Earl Thompson:* James O'Rear, *Lane:* David McMahon, *Dad (Farmer):* Griff Barnett, *Jess, The Cook:* John Lee, *Casey Jones:* Herb Lytton, *Associate Producer:* Roy Gordon, *Director:* Nelson Leigh, *Louie:* Jack Daly, *Captain:* Carleton Young, *French Gendarme:* Eugene Borden, *Burt:* Erville Alderson, *Surplus Dealer:* Olin Howlin, *Mr. Fearless:* Aaron Spelling, *O. W. Schultz:* Charles Watts, *Secretary:* Virginia Christine, *Photographer:* Sid Saylor, *Barker:* Ray Walker, *Photographer:* Lee Roberts, *Editor, San Diego:* Robert B. Williams, *Levine:* Richard Deacon, *Mrs. Fearless:* Ann Morrison, *Professor:* Percival Vivian, *Mechanic:* George Selk (Budd Buster), *Oakie:* Paul Brinegar, *Indian:* Chief Yowlachie.

SPLENDOR IN THE GRASS (1961) WB. Director, Elia Kazan. Screenplay, William Inge. Associate Producers, William Inge, Charles H. Maguire. Assistant Director, Don Kranze. Music, David Amram. Choreographer, George Tapps. Costumes, Anna Hill Johnstone. An NBI Picture in Technicolor. Art Director, Richard Sylbert. Cinematographer, Boris Kaufman. Editor, Gene Milford. 124 minutes.

Splendor in the Grass with Pat Hingle and Warren Beatty.

Wilma Dean Loomis: Natalie Wood, *Bud Stamper:* Warren Beatty, *Ace Stamper:* Pat Hingle, *Mrs. Loomis:* Audrey Christie, *Ginny Stamper:* Barbara Loden, *Angelina:* Zohra Lampert, *Del Loomis:* Fred Stewart, *Mrs. Stamper:* Joanna Roos, *Juanita Howard:* Jan Norris, *Toots:* Gary Lockwood, *Kay:* Sandy Dennis, *Hazel:* Crystal Field, *June:* Marla Adams, *Carolyn:* Lynn Loring, *Doc Smiley:* John McGovern, *Miss Metcalf:* Martine Bartlett, *Glenn:* Sean Garrison, *Minister:* William Inge.

STAGECOACH (1939) UA. Produced by Walter Wanger. Directed by John Ford. From the story, *Stage to Lordsburg* by Ernest Haycox. Screenplay by Dudley Nichols. Music Director, Boris Morros. Horsemen, Yakima Canutt, John Eckert, Jack Mohr. Photography, Bert Glennon and Ray Binger. Editors, Dorothy Spencer and Walter Reynolds. Produced with the cooperation of the Navajo-Apache Indian agencies and the U. S. Department of the Interior. Locations: Kernville, Dry Lake, Fremont Pass, Victorville, Calabasas, Chatsworth, California; Kayenta, Mesa, Monument Valley, Arizona. Remade by 20th Century-Fox in 1966. Themes, "Bury Me Not On The Lone Prairie" and "I Dream of Jeannie." Music Adaptation, Richard Hageman, Franke Harling, Louis Gruenberg. 96 minutes.

Stagecoach with Andy Devine, George Bancroft, John Carradine, Donald Meek, Louise Platt, Claire Trevor and John Wayne.

The Ringo Kid: John Wayne, *Dallas:* Claire Trevor, *Dr. Josiah Boone:* Thomas Mitchell, *Curley Wilcox:* George Bancroft, *Buck:* Andy Devine, *Hatfield:* John Carradine, *Lucy Mallory:* Louise Platt, *Mr. Peacock:* Donald Meek, *Gatewood:* Berton Churchill, *Lieutenant Blanchard:* Tim Holt, *Chris:* Chris-Pin Martin, *Yakeema:* Elvira Rios, *Sergeant Billy Pickett:* Francis Ford, *Mrs. Pickett:* Marga Ann Daighton, *Nancy Whitney:* Florence Lake, *Captain Sickle:* Walter McGrail, *Express Agent:* Paul McVey, *Mrs. Gatewood:* Brenda Fowler, *Cheyenne Scout:* Chief Big Tree, *Cavalry Scout:* Yakima Canutt, *Indian Leader:* Chief White Horse, *Captain Simmons:* Bryant Washburn, *Lordsburg Sheriff:* Duke Lee, *Luke Plummer:* Tom Tyler, *Ike Plummer:* Joe Rickson, *Captain Whitney:* Cornelius Keefe, *Telegrapher:* Harry Tenbrook, *Doc's Landlady:* Nora Cecil, *Jerry, Bartender:* Jack Pennick, *Sheriff:* Lou Mason, *Lucy's Baby (2.½ days old):* Mary Kathleen Walker, *Billy, Jr.:* Kent Odell, *Cavalry Sergeant:* William Hopper, *Saloonkeeper:* Ed Brady, *Hank Plummer:* Vester Pegg, *Ranchers:* Buddy Roosevelt, Bill Cody, *Ed (Editor):* Robert Homans, *Bartender:* Si Jenks, *Jim (Expressman):* Jim Mason, *Deputy:* Franklyn Farnum, *Ogler:* Merrill McCormick, *Barfly, Lordsburg:* Artie Ortega, *Lordsburg Express Agent:* Theodore Lorch.

STAGE DOOR (1937) RKO. Associate Producer, Pandro S. Berman. Directed by Gregory La Cava. Based on the play by Edna Ferber and

Stage Door with Katharine Hepburn and Adolphe Menjou.

George S. Kaufman. Screenplay, Morrie Ryskind and Anthony Veiller. Art Director, Van Nest Polglase. Art Associate, Carroll Clark. Interior Decorations, Darrell Silvers. Music Director, Roy Webb. Costumes, Muriel King. Photography, Robert de Grasse. Editor, William Hamilton. Sound, John L. Cass. Assistant Director, James Anderson. 93 minutes.

Terry Randall (Sims): Katharine Hepburn, *Jean Maitland:* Ginger Rogers, *Anthony Powell:* Adolphe Menjou, *Linda Shaw:* Gail Patrick, *Catherine Luther:* Constance Collier, *Kaye Hamilton:* Andrea Leeds, *Henry Sims:* Samuel S. Hinds, *Judy Canfield:* Lucille Ball, *Milbank:* Jack Carson, *Bill:* William Corson, *Harcourt:* Franklin Pangborn, *Richard Carmichael:* Pierre Watkin, *Butcher:* Grady Sutton, *Stage Director:* Frank Reicher, *Hattie:* Phyllis Kennedy, *Eve:* Eve Arden, *Annie:* Ann Miller, *Ann Braddock:* Jane Rhodes, *Mary:* Margaret Early, *Dizzy:* Jean Rouverol, *Mrs. Orcutt:* Elizabeth Dunne, *Olga Brent:* Norma Drury, *Susan:* Peggy O'Donnell, *Madeline:* Harriett Brandon, *Cast of Play:* Katherine Alexander, Ralph Forbes, Mary Forbes, Huntley Gordon, *Aide:* Lynton Brent, *Elsworth, Critic:* Theodore Von Eltz, *Playwright:* Jack Rice, *Chauffeur:* Harry Strang, *Baggageman:* Bob Perry, *Theater Patron:* Larry Steers.

STAGE DOOR CANTEEN (1943) UA. Produced by Sol Lesser. Associate Producer, Barnett Briskin. Directed by Frank Borzage. Original Screenplay, Delmer Daves. Music Score, Freddie Rich. Music Director, C. Bakaleinikoff. Assistant Directors, Lew Borzage and Virgil Hart. Talent Co-ordinator, Radie Harris. Production Design, Harry Horner. Assistant, Clem Beauchamp. Art Director, Hans Peters. Interior Decorator, Victor Gangelin. Costumes, Albert Deano. Photography, Harry Wild. Sound, Hugh McDowell. Editor, Hal Kern. Songs: "She's A Bombshell From Brooklyn" by Sol Lesser, Al Dubin, Jimmy Monaco; "The Girl I Love to Leave Behind" by Lorenz Hart and Richard Rodgers; "We Mustn't Say Goodbye," "The Machine Gun Song," "American Boy," "Don't Worry Island," "Quick Sands," "A Rookie and His Rhythm," "Sleep Baby Sleep," "We Meet In The Funniest Places," and "You're Pretty Terrific Yourself" by Al Dubin and Jimmy Monaco; "Why Don't You Do Right?" Film debut of Sunset Carson. 132 minutes.

Stage Door Canteen with Otto Kruger and Ralph Morgan.

Eileen: Cheryl Walker, *Dakota:* William Terry, *Jean:* Marjorie Riordan, *California:* Lon McCallister, *Ella Sue:* Margaret Early, *Texas:* Michael Harrison (Sunset Carson), *Mamie:* Dorothea Kent, *Jersey:* Fred Brady, *Lillian:* Marion Shockley, *The Australian:* Patrick O'Moore, *Girl:* Ruth Roman, *Stars of the Stage Door Canteen:* Judith Anderson, Tallulah Bankhead, Ray Bolger, Katharine Cornell, Jane Darwell, Dorothy Fields, Arlene Francis, Lucile Gleason, Helen Hayes, Jean Hersholt, George Jessel, Tom Kennedy, Betty Lawford, Alfred Lunt, Harpo Marx, Yehudi Menuhin, Ralph Morgan, Elliott Nugent, Helen Parrish, Lanny Ross, Cornelia Otis Skinner, Ethel Waters, Dame May Whitty, Henry Armetta, Ralph Bellamy, Helen Broderick, Lloyd Corrigan, William Demarest, Gracie Fields, Vinton Freedley, Vera Gordon, Katharine Hepburn, Sam Jaffe, Roscoe Karns, Otto Kruger, Gertrude Lawrence, Bert Lytell, Elsa Maxwell, Ethel Merman, Alan Mowbray, Merle Oberon, Brock Pemberton, Selena Royle, Ned Sparks, Johnny Weissmuller, Ed Wynn, Kenny Baker, Edgar Bergen, Ina Claire, Jane Cowl, Virginia Field, Lynn Fontanne, Billy Gilbert, Virginia Grey, Hugh Herbert, Allen Jenkins, Virginia Kaye, June Lang, Gypsy Rose Lee, Aline MacMahon, Helen Menken, Paul Muni, Franklin Pangborn, George Raft, Martha Scott, Bill Stern, Arleen Whelan, Count Basie and his Band, Xavier Cugat and his Orchestra, with Lina Romay, Benny Goodman and his Orchestra, with Peggy Lee, Kay Kyser and his Band, Freddy Martin and his Orchestra, Guy Lombardo and his Orchestra.

STAGE FRIGHT (1950) WB. Director, Alfred Hitchcock. Author, Selwyn Jepson (from *Man Running; Outrun the Constable*). Screenplay, Whitfield Cook. Art Director, Terence Verity. Sound, Harold King. Music, Leighton Lucas. Musical Director, Louis Levy. Photography, Wilkie Cooper. Editor, Edward Jarins. Song by Cole Porter: "The Laziest Gal In Town." 110 minutes.

Stage Fright with Marlene Dietrich and Jane Wyman.

Charlotte Inwood: Marlene Dietrich, *Eve Gill:* Jane Wyman, *Smith:* Michael Wilding, *Jonathan Cooper:* Richard Todd, *Commodore Gill:* Alastair Sim, *Mrs. Gill:* Dame Sybil Thorndike, *Nellie:* Kay Walsh, *Bibulous Gent:* Miles Malleson, *Freddie:* Hector MacGregor, *Shooting Gallery Attendant:* Joyce Grenfell, *Inspector Byard:* Andre Morell, *Chubby:* Patricia Hitchcock.

STALAG 17 (1953) Par. Producer and Director, Billy Wilder. Based on the play by Donald Bevan and Edmund Trzinski. Screenplay, Billy Wilder, Edwin Blum. Cinematographer, Ernest Laszlo. Editor, Doane Harrison. 120 minutes.

Sefton: William Holden, *Lieutenant Dunbar:* Don Taylor, *Oberst Von Scherbach:* Otto Preminger, *Stosh:* Robert Strauss, *Harry:* Harvey Lembeck, *Hoffy:* Richard Erdman, *Price:* Peter Graves, *Duke:* Neville Brand, *Schulz:* Sig Rumann, *Manfredi:* Michael Moore, *Johnson:* Peter Baldwin, *Joey:* Robinson Stone, *Blondie:* Robert Shawley, *Marko:* William Pierson, *Cookie:* Gil Stratton, Jr., *Bagradian:* Jay

Stalag 17 with William Holden, Robert Strauss and Harvey Lembeck.

Lawrence, *Geneva Man:* Erwin Kalser, *Triz:* Edmund Trzcinski, *P.O.Ws:* Ross Bagdasarian, Robin Morse, Tommy Cook, *Barracks 1 P.O.W.:* Peter Leeds, *German Lieutenant:* Harold D. Maresh, *German Lieutenant:* Carl Forcht, *Prisoner with Beard:* Alex J. Wells, *Prisoner with Beard:* Bob Templeton, *Prisoner with Beard:* Paul T. Salata, *The Crutch:* Jerry Singer, *German Lieutenant Supervisor:* Max Willenz.

STANLEY AND LIVINGSTONE (1939) 20th. Associate Producer, Kenneth Macgowan. Directed by Henry King. Historical research and story outline by Hal Long and Sam Hellman. Screenplay, Philip Dunne and Julien Josephson. Sets, Thomas Little. Costumes, Royer. Photography, George Barnes. Sound, Alfred Bruzlin and Roger Heman. 101 minutes.

Stanley and Livingston with Walter Brennan and Spencer Tracy.

Stanley: Spencer Tracy, *Eve:* Nancy Kelly, *Gareth Tyce:* Richard Greene, *Jeff Slocum:* Walter Brennan, *Lord Tyce:* Charles Coburn, *Dr. Livingstone:* Sir Cedric Hardwicke, *Bennett:* Henry Hull, *John Kingsley:* Henry Travers, *John Gresham:* Miles Mander, *Mr. Cranston:* David Torrence, *Frederick Holcomb:* Holmes Herbert, *Sir Oliver French:* Montague Shaw, *Sir Henry Forrester:* Brandon Hurst, *Hasson:* Hasson Said, *Col. Grimes:* Paul Harvey, *Commissioner:* Russell Hicks, *Commissioner:* Frank Dae, *Sir Francis Vane:* Clarence Derwent, *Morehead:* Joseph Crehan, *Carmichael:* Robert Middlemass, *Senator:* Frank Jaquet, *Mace:* William Williams, *Zucco:* Ernest Baskett, *Bennett's Secretary:* Emmett Vogan, *Committeeman:* James McNamara, *Chuma:* William Dunn, *Susi:* Emmett Smith, *Mombay:* Jack Clisby, *Lieutenant:* Dick Stanley, *Corporal:* Thos. A. Coleman, *Sergeant:* William E. "Red" Blair, *Man with Pills:* Frank Orth, *Copy Boy:* Billy Watson, *Man:* Harry Harvey, *Newspaperman:* Vernon Dent, *Bongo:* Everett Brown.

A STAR IS BORN (1937) UA. Produced by David O. Selznick. Directed by William A. Wellman. Color by Technicolor. A Selznick

International Production. Story, William A. Wellman and Robert Carson. Screenplay, Dorothy Parker, Alan Campbell, Robert Carson. Color Design, Lansing C. Holden. Technicolor Adviser, Mrs. Natalie Kalmus. Music, Max Steiner. Settings, Lyle Wheeler. Associate, Edward Boyle. Costumes, Omar Khayyam. Assistant Director, Eric Stacey. Interior Decorations, Edward G. Boyle. Special Effects, Jack Cosgrove. Property Man, Robert Lander. Construction Superintendent, Harold Fenton. Location Manager, Mason Litson. Head Grip, Fred Williams. Head Electrician, James Potevin. Photography, W. Howard Greene. Editors, Hal C. Kern and Anson Stevenson. Sound, Oscar Lagerstrom. Film debut of Lana Turner, as an extra. Remade as a musical drama by Warner Brothers, 1954. Inspired by RKO's *What Price Hollywood* (1932) and the lives of John Bowers and Marguerite De La Motte. 111 minutes.

A Star is Born with Adolphe Menjou, Lionel Stander, Fredric March and Janet Gaynor.

Esther Blodgett, later Vicki Lester: Janet Gaynor, *Norman Maine (Alfred Hinkel):* Fredric March, *Oliver Niles:* Adolphe Menjou, *Danny McGuire:* Andy Devine, *Granny:* May Robson, *Libby:* Lionel Stander, *Casey Burke:* Owen Moore, *Anita Regis:* Elizabeth Jenns, *Theodore Blodgett:* J. C. Nugent, *Aunt Mattie:* Clara Blandick, *Alex:* A. W. Sweatt, *Central Casting Receptionist:* Peggy Wood, *Justice of the Peace:* Clarence Wilson, *Billy Moon:* Franklin Pangborn, *Night Court Judge:* Jonathan Hale, *Pop Randall:* Edgar Kennedy, *Cuddles:* Pat Flaherty, *Make-up Men:* Harris, Adrian Rosley, *Ward:* Arthur Hoyt, *Orchestra Leader in Hollywood Bowl:* Dr. Leonard Walker, *Voice Coach:* Edwin Maxwell, *Bert (Director):* Marshall Neilan, *Posture Coach:* Guinn Williams, *Artie Carver:* Jed Prouty, *Bernie (Photographer):* Vince Barnett, *Waitress:* Trixie Friganza, *Academy Award Speaker:* Paul Stanton, *Assistant Cameraman:* Charles Williams, *Bartender at Santa Anita:* Robert Emmett O'Connor, *Rustic (Jud Baker):* Olin Howland, *Cameraman:* Carleton Griffin, *Party Guests:* Claude King, Eddie Kane and Dennis O'Keefe, *Prisoners:* Francis Ford, Kenneth Howell, Chris-Pin Martin, *Extras in Santa Anita Bar:* Carole Landis and Lana Turner, *Witness:* Snowflake.

A STAR IS BORN (1954) WB. Producer, Sidney Luft. Associate Producer, Vern Alves. Director, George Cukor. Authors, William A. Wellman, Robert Carson. Screenplay, Moss Hart. Art Director, Malcolm Bert. Cinematographer, Sam Leavitt. Editor, Folmer Blangsted. CinemaScope and Technicolor. Assistant Directors, Earl Bellamy, Edward Graham, and Russell Llewellyn. Dances by Richard Barstow. Songs: "Born in a Trunk," by Leonard Gershe; "The Man That Got Away," "Gotta Have Me Go With You," "It's a New World," "Here's What I'm Here For," "Someone at Last," "Lose That Long Face," by Harold Arlen and Ira Gershwin. Remake of the 1937 UA film, inspired by *What Price Hollywood* (RKO, 1932). 181 minutes.

A Star Is Born with Judy Garland.

Esther Blodgett (*Vicki Lester*): Judy Garland, *Norman Maine:* James Mason, *Oliver Niles:* Charles Bickford, *Libby:* Jack Carson, *Danny McGuire:* Tommy Noonar., *Lola Lavery:* Lucy Marlow, *Susan Ettinger:* Amanda Blake, *Graves:* Irving Bacon, *Libby's Secretary:* Hazel Shermet, *Glenn Williams:* James Brown, *Miss Markham:* Lotus Robb, *Announcer:* Joan Shawlee, *Driver:* Dub Taylor, *Director:* Louis Jean Heydt, *Eddie:* Bob Jellison, *Man in Car:* Chick Chandler, *Landlady:* Kathryn Card, *Miss Fusselow:* Blythe Daly, *Director:* Leonard Penn, *Cameraman:* Eddie Dew, *Charley:* Olin Howland, *Justice of the Peace:* Emerson Treacy, *Director McBride:* Willis Bouchey, *Party Guest:* Mae Marsh, *Carver:* Grady Sutton, *M.C.:* Rex Evans, *Wallace:* Richard Webb, *Nigel Peters:* Steve Wyman, *Cuddles:* Henry Kulky, *Director:* Tristram Coffin, *Judge:* Frank Ferguson, *Gregory:* Percy Helton, *Reporter:* Dale Van Sickel, *Esther at 6:* Nadene Ashdown, *Esther at 3:* Heidi Meadows.

STAR SPANGLED RHYTHM (1942) Par. Associate Producer, Joseph Sistrom. Director, George Marshall. Original screenplay by Harry Tugend. Score written and directed by Robert Emmett Dolan. Editor, Paul Weatherwax. Directors of Photography, Leo Tover and Theodor Sparkuhl. Art Directors, Hans Dreier and Ernest Fegte. Songs by Johnny Mercer and Harold Arlen: "That Old Black Magic," "Hit the Road to Dreamland," "Old Glory," "A Sweater, a Sarong and a Peekaboo Bang," "I'm Doing It for Defense," "Sharp as a Tack," "On the Swing Shift," "He Loved Me Till the All-Clear Came." 99 minutes.

Old Glory Number: Bing Crosby, *Master of Ceremonies:* Bob Hope, *Men Playing Cards Skit:* Fred MacMurray, *Men Playing Cards Skit:* Franchot Tone, *Men Playing Cards Skit:* Ray Milland, *Pop Webster:* Victor Moore, *Sweater, Sarong and Peekaboo Bang Number:* Dorothy Lamour, *Sweater, Sarong and Peekaboo Bang Number:* Paulette Goddard, *Black Magic Number:* Vera Zorina, *Dreamland Number:* Mary Martin, *Dreamland Number:* Dick Powell, *Polly Judson:* Betty Hutton, *Jimmy Webster:* Eddie Bracken, *Sweater, Sarong and Peekaboo Bang Number:* Veronica Lake, *Scarface:* Alan Ladd, *Smart as a Tack Number:* Rochester, *Husband in Bob Hope Skit:* William Bendix, *Introduces Bob Hope Skit:* Jerry Colonna, *Louie the Lug:* Macdonald Carey, *Frisbee:* Walter Abel, *Genevieve in Priorities Number:* Susan Hayward, *Swing Shift Number:* Marjorie Reynolds, *Swing Shift Number:* Betty Rhodes, *Swing Shift Number:* Dona Drake, Don Castle, *Men Playing Cards Skit:* Lynne Overman, *Himself:* Gary Crosby, *Black Magic Number:* Johnnie Johnston, *Hi-Pockets:* Gil Lamb, *Mimi:* Cass Daley, *Murgatroyd in Priorities Number:* Ernest Truex, *Smart as a Tack Number Dancers:* Katherine Dunham, Slim and Slam, *Comic in Sweater, Sarong and Peekaboo Bang Number:* Arthur Treacher, *Comic in Sweater, Sarong and Peekaboo Bang Number:* Walter Catlett, *Comic in Sweater, Sarong and Peekaboo Bang Number:* Sterling Holloway, *Sweater, Sarong and Peekaboo Bang Hitler:* Tom Dugan, *Mussolini:* Paul Porcasi, *Hirohito:* Richard Loo, *Dreamland Number:* Golden Gate Quartette, *Specialty Act:* Walter Dare Wahl and Company, *Themselves:* Cecil B. De Mille, Preston Sturges, Ralph Murphy, Barney Dean, Jack Hope, *Finale:* Veronica Lake, Dorothy Lamour, Paulette Goddard, Albert Dekker, Marjorie Reynolds, Cecil Kellaway, Lynne Overman, Alan Ladd, Ellen Drew, Jimmy Lydon, Charles Smith, Frances Gifford, Susanna Foster, Robert Preston, Louise LaPlanche, Donivee Lee, Christopher King, Alice Kirby, Marcella Phillips, *Sarah:* Anne Revere, *Mr. Freemont:* Edward Fielding, *Mac:* Edgar Dearing, *Bit Soldier in Black Magic Number:* Frank Faylen, *Duffy:* William Haade, *Sailor:* Maynard Holmes, *Sailor:* James Millican, *Tommy:* Eddie Johnson, *Casey:* Arthur Loft, *Motorcycle Chauffeur for Rochester:* Woodrow W. Strode, *Wife in Bob Hope Skit:* Marion Martin, *Air Raid Warden in Bob Hope Skit:* Chester Clute, *Captain Kingsley:* Boyd Davis, *Petty Officers:* Eddie Dew, Rod Cameron.

STATE FAIR (1933) Fox. Produced by Winfield Sheehan. Directed by Henry King. From the novel by Phil Stong. Screenplay, Paul Green and Sonya Levien. Assistant Director, Ray Flynn. Costume Director, Rita Kaufman. Art Director, Duncan Cramer. Photography, Hal Mohr. Editor, L. W. Bischoff. Sound, A. L. Von Kirbach. Song by Val Burton and Will Jason: "Romantic." Music Director, Louis De Francesco. Remade by 20th Century-Fox in 1945 and 1962, as musicals. 80 minutes.

Abel Frake: Will Rogers, *Margy Frake:* Janet Gaynor, *Pat Gilbert:* Lew Ayres, *Emily Joyce:* Sally Eilers, *Wayne Frake:* Norman Foster, *Melissa Frake:* Louise Dresser, *The Storekeeper:* Frank Craven, *The Barker:* Victor Jory, *Harry Ware:* Frank Melton, *Barker at Aerial Act:* John Sheehan, *Lady at Food Contest:* Doro Merande, *Hog Owner:* Erville Alderson, *Hog Judge:* Harry Holman, *Hog Judge:* Hobart Cavanaugh.

State Fair with Norman Foster, Janet Gaynor, Louise Dresser and Will Rogers.

Star Spangled Rhythm with Betty Hutton, James Millican (background), Victor Moore, Gil Lamb, Eddie Bracken and Maynard Holmes.

State of the Union with Van Johnson, Katharine Hepburn, Irving Bacon, Angela Lansbury and Adolphe Menjou.

STATE OF THE UNION (1948) MGM. Producer-Director, Frank Capra. Associate Producer, Anthony Veiller. Based on the play by Howard Lindsay and Russell Crouse. Screenplay, Anthony Veiler, Myles Connolly. Musical Score, Victor Young. Art Directors, Cedric Gibbons, Urie McCleary. Photography, George J. Folsey. Editor, William Hornbeck. A Liberty Film Production. 124 minutes.

Grant Matthews: Spencer Tracy, *Mary Matthews:* Katharine Hepburn, *Spike McManus:* Van Johnson, *Kay Thorndyke:* Angela Lansbury, *Jim Conover:* Adolphe Menjou, *Sam Thorndyke:* Lewis Stone, *Sam Parrish:* Howard Smith, *Lulubelle Alexander:* Maidel Turner, *Judge Alexander:* Raymond Walburn, *Bill Hardy:* Charles Dingel, *Grace Draper:* Florence Auer, *Sen. Lauterbach:* Pierre Watkin, *Norah:* Margaret Hamilton, *Buck:* Irving Bacon, *Joyce:* Patti Brady, *Grant, Jr.:* George Nokes, *Bellboy:* Carl Switzer, *Barber:* Tom Pedi, *Waiter:* Tom Fadden, *Blink Moran:* Charles Lane, *Leith, Radio Announcer:* Art Baker, *Jenny:* Rhea Mitchell, *First Reporter:* Arthur O'Connell, *Blonde Girl:* Marion Martin, *Wrestler:* Tor Johnson, *Senator:* Stanley Andrews, *Pilot:* Dave Willock, *Politician:* Russell Meeker, *Joe Crandall:* Frank L. Clarke, *Rusty Miller:* David Clarke, *Broder:* Dell Henderson, *Bradbury:* Edwin Cooper, *Crump:* Davison Clark, *Josephs:* Francis Pierlot, *Editor:* Brandon Beach.

STEAMBOAT 'ROUND THE BEND (1935) Fox Films. Produced by Sol M. Wurtzel. Directed by John Ford. From the novel by Ben Lucien Burman. Screenplay, Dudley Nichols and Lamar Trotti. Music, Samuel Kaylin. Photography, George Schneiderman. Editor, Al De Gaetano. The last film of Will Rogers, released posthumously. 96 minutes.

Dr. John Pearly: Will Rogers, *Fleety Belle:* Anne Shirley, *Captain Eli:* Irvin S. Cobb, *Sheriff Rufe Jetters:* Eugene Pallette, *Duke:* John McGuire, *New Moses:* Berton Churchill, *Efe:* Francis Ford, *Pappy:* Roger Imhof, *Matt Abel:* Raymond Hatton, *Chaplain:* Hobart Bosworth, *Jonah:* Stepin Fetchit, *Popkins, Fleety Belle's Suitor:* Fred Kohler, Jr., *A Listener:* Hobart Cavanaugh, *Breck:* William Benedict, *Addie May:* Lois Verner, *Uncle Jeff:* John Lester Johnson, *New Elijah:*

Steamboat 'Round The Bend with Will Rogers and Irvin S. Cobb.

Pardner Jones, Fleety Belle's Father: Charles Middleton, *Fleety Belle's Brother:* Ben Hall, *Farmer:* Si Jenks, *Race Officials:* Louis Mason, Robert E. Homans, *Character Bit:* John Wallace, *Salesman:* Dell Henderson, *Prisoner:* Otto Richards, *River Man:* Jack Pennick, *Jailer:* Captain Anderson, *Sheriff's Wife:* Grace Goodall, *Governor:* Ferdinand Munier, *Hangman:* D'Arcy Corrigan, *Warden:* James Marcus, *Labor Boss:* Luke Cosgrave, *Jailbird:* Heinie Conklin.

THE STORY OF DR. WASSELL (1944) Par. Producer, Cecil B. De Mille. Associate Producer, Sidney Biddell. Director, Cecil B. De Mille. Color by Technicolor. Screenplay, Alan LeMay, Charles Bennett. Technicolor Director, Natalie Kalmus. Musical Score, Victor Young. Art Directors, Hans Dreier, Roland Anderson. Cameramen, Victor Milner, William Snyder. Process Photography, Farciot Edouart, Wallace Kelley. Based on the story of Commander Corydon M. Wassell, USN (MC), and the story by James Hilton. 140 minutes.

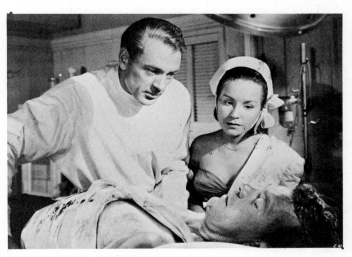

The Story of Dr. Wassell with Gary Cooper, Carol Thurston and Dennis O'Keefe.

Dr. Corydon M. Wassell: Gary Cooper, *Madeline:* Laraine Day, *Bettina:* Signe Hasso, *Hopkins (Hoppy):* Dennis O'Keefe, *Tremartini:* Carol Thurston, *Lieutenant Dirk van Daal:* Carl Esmond, *Murdock:* Paul Kelly, *Anderson (Andy):* Elliott Reid, *Commander Bill Goggins:* Stanley Ridges, *Johnny:* Renny McEvoy, *Alabam:* Oliver Thorndike, *Ping:* Philip Ahn, *Ruth:* Barbara Britton, *Francis:* Melvin Francis, *Kraus:* Joel Allen, *Whaley:* James Millican, *Borghetti:* Mike Kilian, *Hunter:* Doodles Weaver, *Dr. Ralph Wayne:* Lester Matthews, *Dr. Vranken:* Ludwig Donath, *Dr. Wei:* Richard Loo, *Dr. Holmes:* Davison Clark, *Captain Carruthers:* Richard Nugent, *Lieutenant Bainbridge:* Morton Lowry, *Captain Balen:* George Macready, *Captain Ryk:* Victor Varconi, *Admiral Hart:* Edward Fielding, *Captain in Charge of Evacuation:* Harvey Stephens, *Rear Admiral (Australia):* Minor Watson, *Little English Boy:* William Severn, *Mother of Little English Boy:* Edith Barrett, *Mrs. Wayne:* Catherine Craig, *Javanese Temple Guide:* Frank Puglia, *Missionary:* Irving Bacon, *Missionary's Wife:* Ottola Nesmith, *Admiral Hart's Aide:* Hugh Beaumont, *Lieutenant Smith:* George Lynn, *Fashta:* Linda Brent, *Praying Woman:* Ann Doran, *Anne, Dutch Nurse:* Julia Faye, *Girl:* Yvonne De Carlo.

THE STORY OF G. I. JOE (1945) UA. Producer, Lester Cowan. Associate Producer, David Hall. Director, William A. Wellman. Author, Ernie Pyle. Screenplay, Leopold Atlas, Guy Endore, Philip Stevenson. Musical Score, Ann Ronell, Louise Applebaum. Art Director, James Sullivan. Musical Director, Louis Forbes. Cameraman, Russell Metty. Editor, Otho Lovering. Musical numbers: "Linda" by Jack Lawrence and Ann Ronell; "I'm Coming Back" and "Infantry March" by Ann Ronell. 109 minutes.

Ernie Pyle: Burgess Meredith, *Lieutenant Walker:* Robert Mitchum, *Sergeant Warnicki:* Freddie Steele, *Private Dondaro:* Wally Cassell, *Private Spencer:* Jimmy Lloyd, *Private Murphy:* Jack Reilly, *Private Mew:* Bill Murphy, *Cookie:* William Self, *Sergeant at Showers:*

The Story of G.I. Joe with Robert Mitchum and Burgess Meredith.

Dick Rich, *Whitey:* Billy Benedict, *Themselves:* Combat veterans of the Campaigns of Africa, Sicily, Italy.

THE STORY OF LOUIS PASTEUR (1935) WB. Directed by William Dieterle. Story, Sheridan Gibney and Pierre Collins. Screenplay, Sheridan Gibney and Pierre Collins. Photography, Tony Gaudio. Editor, Ralph Dawson. 85 minutes.

Pasteur: Paul Muni, *Madame Pasteur:* Josephine Hutchinson, *Annette Pasteur:* Anita Louise, *Jean Martel:* Donald Woods, *Dr. Charbonnet:* Fritz Leiber, Sr., *Roux:* Henry O'Neill, *Dr. Rosignol:* Porter Hall, *Dr. Radisse:* Ray Brown, *Dr. Zaranoff:* Akim Tamiroff, *Napoleon III:* Walter Kingsford, *Empress Eugenie:* Iphigenie Castiglioni, *Boncourt:* Herbert Heywood, *Dr. Pheiffer:* Frank Reicher, *Dr. Lister:* Halliwell Hobbes, *Phillip Meister:* Dickie Moore, *Mrs. Meister:* Ruth Robinson, *President Thiers:* Herbert Corthell, *President Carnot:* Frank Mayo, *Doctor:* William Burress, *Magistrate:* Robert Strange, *A Lady:* Mabel Colcord, *Courier:* Niles Welch, *Coachman:* Leonard Mudie, *Midwife:* Brenda Fowler, *Lord Chamberlain:* Eric Mayne, *Finance Minister:* Alphonze Ethier, *Chairman:* Edward Van Sloan, *Assistant:* George Andre Beranger, *British Reporter:* Montague Shaw, *Farmer:* Otto Hoffman, *Woman:* Tempe Pigott, *Burly Farmer:* Richard Alexander, *Cecile:* Lottie Williams, *Fat Doctor:* Baron Hesse, *Alsatian:* Wheaton Chambers, *Russian Ambassador:* Leonid Snegoff, *Government Inspector:* Fred Walton, *Reporters:* Wilfred Lucas, Gordon (Bill) Elliott, Jack Santoro, Ferdinand Schumann-Heink.

The Story of Louis Pasteur with Donald Woods and Paul Muni.

STRANGERS ON A TRAIN (1951) WB. Produced and directed by Alfred Hitchcock. Based on the novel by Patricia Highsmith. Screenplay, Raymond Chandler and Czenzi Ormonde. Adaptation, Whitfield Cook. Art Director, Ted Haworth. Musical Director, Ray Heindorf. Photography, Robert Burks. Editor, William H. Ziegler. 101 minutes.

Strangers on a Train with Farley Granger and Robert Walker.

Guy Haines: Farley Granger, *Anne Morton:* Ruth Roman, *Bruno Antony:* Robert Walker, *Senator Morton:* Leo G. Carroll, *Barbara Morton:* Patricia Hitchcock, *Miriam Joyce Haines:* Laura Elliott, *Mrs. Antony:* Marion Lorne, *Mr. Antony:* Jonathan Hale, *Captain Turley:* Howard St. John, *Professor Collins:* John Brown, *Mrs. Cunnigham:* Norma Varden, *Det. Leslie Hennessy:* Robert Gist, *Det. Hammond:* John Doucette, *Tennis Player, Fred Reynolds:* Jack Cushingham, *Bill, Cabby:* Dick Wessel, *Miller, Owner of Music Store:* Ed Clark, *"Ring-the-Gong" Concessionaire:* Al Hill, *Minister:* Dick Ryan, *Judge Donahue:* Charles Meredith, *Man Asking for a Light:* Sam Flint, *Antony's Butler:* Leonard Carey, *Mrs. Joyce:* Edna Holland, *Miriam's Boy Friends:* Tommy Farrell, Rolland Morris, *Boy:* Louis Lettieri, *Boat Man:* Murray Alper, *Blind Man:* John Butler, *Lieutenant Campbell:* Eddie Hearn, *Secretary:* Mary Alan Hokanson, *M. Darville:* George Renevant, *Mme. Darville:* Odette Myrtil, *Dowager:* Moyna Andre, *Mrs. Anderson:* Laura Treadwell, *Mortons' Butler:* J. Louis Johnson, *Dowager:* Minna Phillips, *Soda Jerk:* Joe Warfield, *Seedy Man:* Ralph Moody, *Man under Merry-Go-Round:* Harry Hines, *Man Boarding Train with Bass Fiddle:* Alfred Hitchcock.

STRANGERS WHEN WE MEET (1960) Col. Produced and directed by Richard Quine. In CinemaScope and Eastman Color. Based on the novel by Evan Hunter. Screenplay, Evan Hunter. Music, George Duning. Music Supervision, Morris Stoloff. Orchestration, Arthur Morton. Gowns, Jean Louis. Assistant Director, Carter De Haven, Jr. Editor, Charles Nelson. A Bryna-Quine Production. Photography, Charles Lang, Jr. Art Direction, Ross Bellah. 117 minutes.

Strangers When We Meet with Kirk Douglas and Walter Matthau.

Larry Coe: Kirk Douglas, *Maggie Gault:* Kim Novak, *Roger Altar:* Ernie Kovacs, *Eve Coe:* Barbara Rush, *Felix Anders:* Walter Matthau, *Mrs. Wagner:* Virginia Bruce, *Stanley Baxter:* Kent Smith, *Betty Anders:* Helen Gallagher, *Ken Gault:* John Bryant, *Linda Harder:* Roberta Shore, *Marcia:* Nancy Kovak, *Honey Blonde:* Carol Douglas,

Gerandi: Paul Picerni, *Di Labbia:* Ernest Sarracino, *Bud Ramsey:* Harry Jackson, *Hank:* Bart Patton, *Bucky:* Robert Sampson, *David Coe:* Ray Ferrell, *Peter Coe:* Douglas Holmes, *Patrick Gault:* Timmy Molina, *Mrs. Gerandi:* Betsy Jones Moreland, *Mrs. Baxter:* Audrey Swanson, *Mrs. Ramsey:* Cynthia Leighton, *Daphne:* Sue Ane Langdon, *Waitress:* Ruth Batchelor, *Charlie:* Dick Crockett, *Redhead:* Lorraine Crawford.

Strategic Air Command with Barry Sullivan and James Stewart.

STRATEGIC AIR COMMAND (1955) Par. Producer, Samuel J. Briskin. Director, Anthony Mann. VistaVision, Technicolor. Screenplay, Valentine Davies, Beirne Lay, Jr. Art Directors, Hal Pereira, Earl Hedrick. Musical Director, Victor Young. Cinematographer, William Daniels. Special Photographic Effects, John P. Fulton. Aerial Photography, Thomas Tutwiler. Process Photography, Farciot Edouart. Editor, Eda Warren. 114 minutes.

Lieutenant Colonel Robert "Dutch" Holland: James Stewart, *Sally Holland:* June Allyson, *General Ennis C. Hawkes:* Frank Lovejoy, *Lieutenant Colonel Rocky Samford:* Barry Sullivan, *Ike Knowland:* Alex Nicol, *General Espy:* Bruce Bennett, *Doyle:* Jay C. Flippen, *General Castle:* James Millican, *Rev. Thorne:* James Bell, *Mrs. Thorne:* Rosemary De Camp, *Aircraft Commander:* Richard Shannon, *Captain Symington:* John R. McKee, *Sergeant Bible:* Henry Morgan, *Major Patrol Commander:* Don Haggerty, *Radio Operator:* Glenn Denning, *Colonel:* Anthony Warde, *Airman:* Strother Martin, *Nurse:* Helen Brown, *Forecaster:* Wm. Hudson, *Captain Brown:* David Vaile, *Captain Johnson:* Vernon Rich, *Duty Officer:* Harlan Warde, *Air Force Captain:* Robert House Peters, Jr.

THE STRATTON STORY (1949) MGM. Producer, Jack Cummings. Director, Sam Wood. Author, Douglas Morrow. Screenplay, Douglas Morrow, Guy Trosper. Musical Director, Adolph Deutsch. Art Directors, Cedric Gibbons, Paul Groesse. Photography, Harold Rosson. Editor, Ben Lewis. 106 minutes.

The Stratton Story with Frank Morgan, June Allyson and James Stewart.

Monty Stratton: James Stewart, *Ethel:* June Allyson, *Barney Wile:* Frank Morgan, *Ma Stratton:* Agnes Moorehead, *Gene Watson:* Bill Williams, *Ted Lyons:* Bruce Cowling, *Western All-Stars Pitcher:* Eugene Bearden, *Bill Dickey:* Himself, *Jimmy Dykes:* Himself, *Higgins:* Cliff Clark, *Dot:* Mary Lawrence, *Luke Appling:* Dean White, *Larnie:* Robert Gist, *White Sox Catcher:* Mervyn Shea, *Western Manager:* Pat Flaherty, *Giants Manager:* Captain F. G. Somers, *Conductor:* Mitchell Lewis, *Pitcher:* Michael Ross, *Mrs. Appling:* Florence Lake, *Mrs. Piet:* Anne Nagel, *Mrs. Shea:* Barbara Wooddell, *Headwaiter:* Alphonse Martel, *Doctor:* Holmes Herbert, *Waiter:* Lee Tung Foo, *Theater Usher:* Charles B. Smith, *Detroit Player:* Kenneth Tobey, *Western Pitcher:* Roy Partee.

THE STRAWBERRY BLONDE (1941) WB. Producers, Jack L. Warner, Hal B. Wallis. Associate Producer, William Cagney. Director, Raoul Walsh. From a play by James Hagan (*One Sunday Afternoon*). Screenplay, Julius J. and Philip G. Epstein. Cameraman, James Wong Howe. Editor, William Holmes. Remade as *One Sunday Afternoon* (WB, 1948). Earlier version: *One Sunday Afternoon* (Par., 1933). 97 minutes.

The Strawberry Blonde with Rita Hayworth, Jack Carson, Olivia De Havilland and James Cagney.

Biff Grimes: James Cagney, *Amy Lind:* Olivia De Havilland, *Virginia Brush:* Rita Hayworth, *Old Man Grimes:* Alan Hale, *Nick Pappalas:* George Tobias, *Hugo Barnstead:* Jack Carson, *Mrs. Mulcahey:* Una O'Connor, *Harold:* George Reeves, *Harold's Girl Friend:* Lucile Fairbanks, *Big Joe:* Edward McNamara, *Toby:* Herbert Heywood, *Josephine:* Helen Lynd, *Bank President:* Roy Gordon, *Street Cleaner Foreman:* Tim Ryan, *Official:* Addison Richards, *Policeman:* Frank Mayo, *Bartender:* Jack Daley, *Girl:* Suzanne Carnahan (Susan Peters), *Boy:* Herbert Anderson, *Baxter:* Frank Orth, *Inspector:* James Flavin, *Sailor:* George Campeau, *Singer:* Abe Dinovitch, *Guiseppi:* George Humbert, *Secretary:* Creighton Hale, *Treadway:* Russell Hicks, *Warden:* Wade Boteler.

A STREETCAR NAMED DESIRE (1951) WB. Producer, Charles K. Feldman. Director-Screenplay, Elia Kazan. Based on the play by Tennessee Williams. Adaptation, Oscar Saul. Musical Director, Ray Heindorf. Art Director, Richard Day. Photography, Harry Stradling. Editor, David Weisbart. 125 minutes.

Blanche DuBois: Vivien Leigh, *Stanley Kowalski:* Marlon Brando, *Stella Kowalski:* Kim Hunter, *Mitch:* Karl Malden, *Steve:* Rudy Bond, *Eunice:* Peg Hillias, *Pablo:* Nick Dennis, *Young Collector:* Wright King, *Mexican Woman:* Edna Thomas, *Strange Woman:* Ann Dere, *Strange Man:* Richard Garrick, *Sailor:* Mickey Kuhn, *Street Vendor:* Chester Jones, *Negro Woman:* Marietta Canty, *First Passerby:* Charles Wagenheim, *Second Passerby:* Maxie Thrower, *Policeman:* Lyle Latell, *Foreman:* Mel Archer.

503

A Streetcar Named Desire with Vivien Leigh and Karl Malden.

STREET SCENE (1931) UA. Produced by Samuel Goldwyn. Directed by King Vidor. Based on the play by Elmer Rice. Adaptation, Elmer Rice. Assistant Director, Lucky (Bruce) Humberstone. Art Director, Richard Day. Photography, George Barnes. Editor, Hugh Bennett. Sound, Charles Noyes. A Feature Production. Film debuts of Beulah Bondi and Eleanor Wesselhoeft. The play ran over two years, winning Elmer Rice the 1928-29 Pulitzer Prize. Repeating their stage roles: Bondi, Montor, Landau, Manning, McHugh, Wesselhoeft, Humbert, Qualen, Kostant, Washburne. 80 minutes.

Rose Maurrant: Sylvia Sidney, *Sam Kaplan:* William Collier, Jr., *Anna Maurrant:* Estelle Taylor, *Emma Jones:* Beulah Bondi, *Abe Kaplan:* Max Montor, *Frank Maurrant:* David Landau, *Vincent Jones:* Matt McHugh, *Steve Sankey:* Russell Hopton, *Mae Jones:* Greta Grandstedt, *George Jones:* Tom H. Manning, *Olga Olsen:* Adele Watson, *Karl Olsen:* John M. Qualen, *Shirley Kaplan:* Anna Kostant, *Filippo Fiorentino:* George Humbert, *Dick McGann:* Allan Fox, *Greta Fiorentino:* Eleanor Wesselhoeft, *Alice Simpson:* Nora Cecil, *Harry Easter:* Louis Natheaux, *Willie Maurrant:* Lambert Rogers, *Mary Hildebrand:* Virginia Davis, *Laura Hildebrand:* Helen Lovett, *Charlie Hildebrand:* Kenneth Selling, *Dan Buchanan:* Conway Washburne, *Dr. John Wilson:* Howard Russell, *Officer Harry Murphy:* Richard Powell, *Marshall James Henry:* Walter James, *Fred Cullen:* Harry Wallace, *Bits:* Monti Carter, Jane Mercer, Margaret Robertson, Walter Miller.

Street Scene with Sylvia Sidney and William Collier, Jr.

SUDDEN FEAR (1952) RKO. Producer, Joseph Kaufman. Director, David Miller. Screenplay by Lenore Coffee and Robert Smith. Based on a story by Edna Sherry. Music by Elmer Bernstein. Song by Jack Brooks and Elmer Bernstein: "Afraid." 110 minutes.

Sudden Fear with Joan Crawford and Jack Palance.

Myra Hudson: Joan Crawford, *Lester Blaine:* Jack Palance, *Irene Neves:* Gloria Grahame, *Steve Kearney:* Bruce Bennett, *Ann Taylor:* Virginia Huston, *Junior Kearney:* Touch (Michael) Connors.

SUDDENLY, LAST SUMMER (1959) Col. Producer, Sam Spiegel. Director, Joseph L. Mankiewicz. Screenplay by Gore Vidal and Tennessee Williams. Adapted from Tennessee Williams play of the same name. Music by Buxton Orr and Malcolm Arnold. Assistant Director, Bluey Hill. Art Director, William Kellner. Cinematographer, Jack Hildyard. Photographic Effects, Tom Howard. Editor, Thomas G. Stanford. A Horizon Limited Production in association with Academy Pictures and Camp Films. 114 minutes.

Catherine Holly: Elizabeth Taylor, *Mrs. Venable:* Katharine Hepburn, *Dr. Cukrowicz:* Montgomery Clift, *Dr. Hockstader:* Albert Dekker, *Mrs. Holly:* Mercedes McCambridge, *George Holly:* Gary Raymond, *Miss Foxhill:* Mavis Villiers, *Nurse Benson:* Patricia Marmont, *Sister Felicity:* Joan Young, *Lucy:* Maria Britneva, *Dr. Hockstader's Secretary:* Sheila Robbins, *Young Blonde Interne:* David Cameron.

Suddenly, Last Summer with Montgomery Clift and Elizabeth Taylor.

SUMMER AND SMOKE (1961) Par. Producer, Hal B. Wallis. Director, Peter Glenville. VistaVision, Technicolor. Screenplay, James Poe, Meade Roberts. Art Director, Walter Tyler. Music, Elmer Bernstein. Cinematographer, Charles Lang, Jr. Editor, Warren Low. From Tennessee Williams' play. 118 minutes.

John Buchanan: Laurence Harvey, *Alma Winemiller:* Geraldine Page, *Rosa:* Rita Moreno, *Mrs. Winemiller:* Una Merkel, *Dr. Buchanan:* John McIntire, *Papa Zacharias:* Thomas Gomez, *Nellie:* Pamela Tiffin, *Rev. Winemiller:* Malcolm Atterbury, *Mrs. Ewell:* Lee Patrick, *Roger:* Casey Adams, *Archie Kramer:* Earl Holliman, *Dr. Burke:* Harry Shannon, *Cynthia:* Pattee Chapman, *Thomas:* Jester Hairston, *Nico:* Pepe Hern, *Mrs. Anderson:* Elektra Rozanska, *Dr. Hodges:*

Dick Ryan, *Mrs. Bassett:* Winnie Chandler, *Twyla:* Linda Knutson, *John:* Robert Slade, *Knife Thrower:* Rico Alaniz, *Mr. Gilliam:* John Frank, *Saleslady:* Marjorie Bennett, *Betty Lou:* Susan Roberts, *Pearl:* Pamela Duncan, *Dusty:* Margaret Jane Blye, *Dignitary-Bandleader:* Charles Watts, *Alma as a girl:* Cheryl Anderson, *Woman:* Almira Sessions.

Summer and Smoke with Geraldine Page and Laurence Harvey.

A SUMMER PLACE (1959) WB. Producer and Director, Delmer Daves. Technicolor. Based on the novel by Sloan Wilson. Screenplay, Delmer Daves. Art Director, Leo K. Kuter. Music, Max Steiner. Orchestration, Murray Cutter. Cinematographer, Harry Stradling. Editor, Owen Marks. 130 minutes.

A Summer Place with Dorothy McGuire and Richard Egan.

Ken Jorgenson: Richard Egan, *Sylvia Hunter:* Dorothy McGuire, *Molly Jorgenson:* Sandra Dee, *Bart Hunter:* Arthur Kennedy, *John Hunter:* Troy Donahue, *Helen Jorgenson:* Constance Ford, *Mrs. Hamilton Hamble:* Beulah Bondi, *Claude Andrews:* Jack Richardson, *Todd Hasper:* Martin Eric, *Captain:* Peter Constanti, *Mr. Hamble:* Junius Matthews, *Mrs. Carter:* Gertrude Flynn, *Dr. Matthias:* Marshall Bradford, *Sheriff:* Phil Chambers, *Englehardt:* Robert Griffin, *Ken's Attorney:* Arthur Space, *Bart's Attorney:* George Taylor, *Anne Talbert:* Roberta Shore, *Mrs. Talbert:* Ann Doran, *Minister:* Dale J. Nicholson, *Doctor:* Lewis Martin, *Wife:* Helen Wallace, *Dean:* Everett Glass, *Mrs. Harrington:* Eleanor Audley, *Pawnbroker:* Richard Deacon, *Alvin Frost* (*Justice of the Peace*): Howard Hoffman, *Young Girls in Dormitory:* Nancy Matthews, Susan Odin, Cheryl Holdridge, Bonnie Franklin.

Summer Stock with Judy Garland, Gene Kelly and Gloria De Haven.

SUMMER STOCK (1950) MGM. Producer, Joe Pasternak. Director, Charles Walters. Color by Technicolor. Author, Sy Gomberg. Screenplay, George Wells, Sy Gomberg. Musical Director, Johnny Green. Art Directors, Cedric Gibbons, Jack Martin Smith. Photography, Robert Planck. Editor, Albert Akst. Songs by Mack Gordon and Harry Warren: "Friendly Star," "Mem'ry Island," "Dig-Dig-Dig for Your Dinner," "If You Feel Like Singing, Sing," "Happy Harvest," "Blue Jean Polka" and "You Wonderful You" (lyrics by Jack Brooks and Saul Chaplin). 109 minutes.

Jane Falbury: Judy Garland, *Joe D. Ross:* Gene Kelly, *Orville Wingait:* Eddie Bracken, *Abigail Falbury:* Gloria De Haven, *Esme:* Marjorie Main, *Herb Blake:* Phil Silvers, *Jasper G. Wingait:* Ray Collins, *Artie:* Carleton Carpenter, *Sarah Higgins:* Nita Bieber, *Harrison I. Keath:* Hans Conreid, *Frank:* Paul E. Burns, *Members of Stock Company:* Carole Haney, Arthur Loew, Jr., Jimmy Thompson, *Zeb:* Erville Alderson, *Show Girls:* Bette Arlen, Bunny Waters, *Clerk:* Jack Gargan, *Constance Fliggerton:* Almira Sessions, *Amy Fliggerton:* Kathryn Sheldon, *Boys:* Michael Chapin, Teddy Infuhr, *Producers:* Cameron Grant, Jack Daley, Reginald Simpson, *Sheriff:* Eddie Dunn.

SUMMERTIME (1955) UA. Producer, Ilya Lopert. Director, David Lean. Screenplay by David Lean and H. E. Bates. Based on the play *The Time of the Cuckoo* by Arthur Laurents. Music by Sandro Cicognini. Assistant Directors, Adrian Pryce-Jones and Alberto Cardone. Filmed in Venice in Eastman Color. An Alexander Korda Production for Lopert Films. 99 minutes.

Jane Hudson: Katharine Hepburn, *Renato Di Rossi:* Rossano Brazzi, *Signora Fiorini:* Isa Miranda, *Eddie Yaeger:* Darren McGavin, *Phyl Yaeger:* Mari Aldon, *Mrs. McIlhenny:* Jane Rose, *Mr. McIlhenny:*

Summertime with Katharine Hepburn, Isa Miranda, Mari Aldon and Darren McGavin.

MacDonald Parke, *Mauro:* Gaitano Audiero, *Englishman:* Andre Morell, *Vito Di Rossi:* Jeremy Spenser, *Giovanna:* Virginia Simeon.

THE SUN ALSO RISES (1957) 20th. Producer, Darryl F. Zanuck. Director, Henry King. CinemaScope, De Luxe Color. Based on the novel by Ernest Hemingway. Screenplay, Peter Viertel. Art Directors, Lyle R. Wheeler, Mark-Lee Kirk. Music, Hugo Friedhofer, conducted by Lionel Newman. Orchestration, Edward B. Powell. Cinematographer, Leo Tover. Editor, William Mace. 129 minutes.

Jake Barnes: Tyrone Power, *Lady Brett Ashley:* Ava Gardner, *Robert Cohn:* Mel Ferrer, *Mike Campbell:* Errol Flynn, *Bill Gorton:* Eddie Albert, *Count Mippipopolous:* Gregory Ratoff, *Georgette:* Juliette Greco, *Zizi:* Marcel Dalio, *Doctor:* Henry Daniell, *Harris:* Bob Cummingham, *The Girl:* Danik Patisson, *Pedro Romero:* Robert J. Evans, *Frances Cohn:* Rebecca Iturbi, *Mr. Braddock:* Eduardo Noreiga, *Mrs. Braddock:* Jacqueline Evans, *Montoya:* Carlos Muzquiz, *Manager of Romero:* Carlos David Ortigos, *English Girl:* Lilia Guizar, *American at Bullfight:* Lee Morgan.

The Sun Also Rises with Eddie Albert, Tyrone Power, Mel Ferrer and Errol Flynn.

THE SUNDOWNERS (1960) WB. Producer-Director, Fred Zinnemann. Screenplay, Isobel Lennart. Based on a novel by Jon Cleary. Music, Dimitri Tiomkin. Assistant Directors, Peter Bolton, Roy Stevens. Costumes, Elizabeth Haffenden. In Technicolor. Art Direction, Michael Stringer. Cinematography, Jack Hildyard. Editor, Jack Harris. Filmed in Australia. 133 minutes.

Ida Carmody: Deborah Kerr, *Paddy Carmody:* Robert Mitchum, *Venneker:* Peter Ustinov, *Mrs. Firth:* Glynis Johns, *Jean Halstead:*

The Sundowners with Dina Merrill and Deborah Kerr.

Dina Merrill, *Quinlan:* Chips Rafferty, *Sean:* Michael Anderson, Jr., *Liz:* Lola Brooks, *Herb Johnson:* Wylie Watson, *Bluey:* John Meillon, *Ocker:* Ronald Fraser, *Jack Patchogue:* Mervyn Johns, *Mrs. Bateman:* Molly Urquhart, *Halstead:* Ewen Solon.

SUNRISE AT CAMPOBELLO (1960) WB. Produced by Dore Schary. Associate Producer, Walter Reilly. Directed by Vincent J. Donehue. In Technicolor. Screenplay by Dore Schary, based on his play *Sunrise at Campobello.* Costumes, Marjorie Best. Music, Franz Waxman. Art Director, Edward Carrere. Assistant Director, Russell Saunders. Cinematography, Russell Harlan. Editor, George Boemler. 143 minutes.

Franklin D. Roosevelt: Ralph Bellamy, *Eleanor Roosevelt:* Greer Garson, *Louis Howe:* Hume Cronyn, *Missy Le Hand:* Jean Hagen, *Sara Roosevelt:* Ann Shoemaker, *Al Smith:* Alan Bunce, *James Roosevelt:* Tim Considine, *Anna Roosevelt:* Zina Bethune, *Elliot Roosevelt:* Pat Close, *Franklin, Jr.:* Robin Warga, *Johnny Roosevelt:* Tommy Carty, *Mr. Brimmer:* Lyle Talbot, *Mr. Lassiter:* David White, *Daley:* Herb Anderson, *Dr. Bennett:* Frank Ferguson, *Captain Skinner:* Walter Sande, *Marie:* Janine Grandel, *Edward:* Otis Greene, *Charles:* Ivan Browning, *Senator Walsh:* Al McGranary, *Speaker:* Jerry Crews, *Mr. Owens:* William Haddock, *Mailman:* Floyd Curtis, *Joe:* Jack Henderson, *Miss Garroway:* Ruth March, *Barker:* Ed Prentiss, *Riley:* Francis DeSales, *Newsboy:* Craig Curtis, *Sloan:* Don Dillaway, *Campaign Workers:* Fern Barry, Mary Benoit, Jack Perrin.

Sunrise at Campobello with Ralph Bellamy.

SUNSET BOULEVARD (1950) Par. Produced by Charles Brackett. Directed by Billy Wilder. Based on the story *A Can of Beans* by Charles Brackett and Billy Wilder. Screenplay, Charles Brackett, Billy Wilder and D. M. Marshman, Jr. Art Directors, Hans Dreier and John Meehan. Sets, Sam Comer and Ray Moyer. Music, Franz Waxman. Photography, John F. Seitz. Editors, Doane Harrison and Arthur Schmidt. Swanson is seen in a bit from 1929's *Queen Kelly* (largely unreleased); she also does a Sennett bathing beauty routine and a takeoff on Chaplin. Among the cut footage is the song, "Paramount-Don't-Want-Me Blues" by Ray Evans and Jay Livingston: and the framing story of the coroner. De Mille is seen on the set of *Samson and Delilah.* 110 minutes.

Joe Gillis: William Holden, *Norma Desmond:* Gloria Swanson, *Max Von Mayerling:* Erich Von Stroheim, *Betty Schaefer:* Nancy Olson, *Sheldrake:* Fred Clark, *Artie Green:* Jack Webb, *Morino:* Lloyd Gough, *Themselves:* Cecil B. De Mille, Hedda Hopper, Buster Keaton, Anna Q. Nilsson, H. B. Warner, Ray Evans, Jay Livingston, Sidney Skolsky, *Undertaker:* Franklyn Farnum, *First Finance Man:* Larry Blake, *Second Finance Man:* Charles Dayton, *Assistant Coroner:* Eddie Dew, *Salesman:* Michael Brandon (Archie Twitchell), *Sheldrake's Secretary:* Ruth Clifford, *Gordon Cole:* Bert Moorhouse, *Doctor/Courtier:* E. Mason Hopper, *Courtier:* Virginia Randolph, *First Assistant Director:* Stan Johnson, *Second Assistant Director:* William Sheehan, *Hisham:* Julia Faye, *Courtiers:* Gertrude Astor and Frank O'Connor, *Courtier:* Eva Novak, *Herself:* Berenice Mosk, *Hairdresser:*

Sunset Boulevard with Gloria Swanson and William Holden.

Gertie Messinger, *Electrician (Hog Eye)*: John Skins Miller, *Jonesy (Old Policeman)*: Robert E. O'Connor, *Connie*: Gerry Ganzer, *Boy*: Tommy Ivo, *Man*: Emmett Smith, *Woman*: Ottola Nesmith, *Captain of Police*: Howard Negley, *Captain of Homicide*: Ken Christy, *Police Sergeant*: Len Hendry.

SUSPICION (1941) RKO. Director, Alfred Hitchcock. Screenplay, Samson Raphaelson, Joan Harrison, Alma Reville. Music, Franz Waxman. Art Director, Van Nest Polglase. Cameraman, Harry Stradling. Special Effects, Vernon L. Walker. Editor, William Hamilton. From the novel *Before the Fact* by Francis Iles. 99 minutes

Johnnie: Cary Grant, *Lina*: Joan Fontaine, *Gen. McLaidlaw*: Sir Cedric Hardwicke, *Beaky*: Nigel Bruce, *Mrs. McLaidlaw*: Dame May Whitty, *Mrs. Newsham*: Isabel Jeans, *Ethel (Maid)*: Heather Angel, *Isobel Sedbusk*: Auriol Lee, *Reggie Wetherby*: Reginald Sheffield, *Capt. Melbeck*: Leo G. Carroll, *Winnie (Maid)*: Maureen Roden-Ryan, *Mrs. Fitzpatrick*: Constance Worth, *Mrs. Barham*: Violet Shelton, *Jessie Barham*: Carol Curtis-Brown, *Alice Barham*: Faith Brook, *Phoebe (Maid)*: Pax Walker, *Jenner (Butler)*: Leonard Carey, *Photographer*: Clyde Cook, *Sir Gerald*: Kenneth Hunter, *Mrs. Wetherby*: Gertrude Hoffmann, *Miss Wetherby*: Dorothy Lloyd, *Miss Wetherby*: Elsie Weller, *Mr. Webster*: Aubrey Mather, *Mr. Bailey*: Rex Evans, *Antique Shop Proprietor*: Edward Fielding, *Postmistress*: Hilda Plowright, *Registrar*: Ben Webster, *Bertram Sedbusk*: Gavin Gorden, *Phyllis Swinghurst*: Nondas Metcalf, *Inspector Hodgson*: Lumsden Hare, *Benson*: Vernon Downing, *Mrs. Craddock*: Clara Reid, *Ticket Taker*: Billy Bevan.

Suspicion with Joan Fontaine, Cary Grant, Nigel Bruce and Heather Angel.

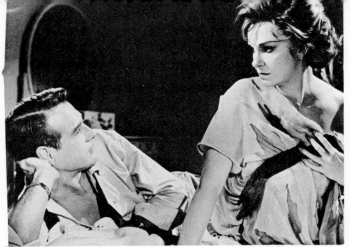

Sweet Bird of Youth with Paul Newman and Geraldine Page.

SWEET BIRD OF YOUTH (1962) MGM. Producer, Pandro S. Berman. Associate Producer, Kathryn Hereford. Director, Richard Brooks. CinemaScope, MetroColor. Based on the play by Tennessee Williams. Screenplay, Richard Brooks. Art Directors, George W. Davis, Urie McCleary. Music conducted by Robert Armbruster. Music Supervisor, Harold Gelman. Cinematographer, Milton Krasner. Editor, Henry Berman. A Roxbury Production. 120 minutes

Chance Wayne: Paul Newman, *Alexandra Del Lago*: Geraldine Page, *Heavenly Finley*: Shirley Knight, *"Boss" Finley*: Ed Begley, *Thomas J. Finley, Jr.*: Rip Torn, *Aunt Nonnie*: Mildred Dunnock, *Miss Lucy*: Madeleine Sherwood, *Dr. George Scudder*: Phillip Abbott, *Scotty*: Corey Allen, *Bud*: Barry Cahill, *Dan Hatcher*: Dub Taylor, *Leroy*: James Douglas, *Ben Jackson*: Barry Atwater, *Mayor Henricks*: Charles Arnt, *Mrs. Maribelle Norris*: Dorothy Konrad, *Professor Burtus Haven Smith*: James Chandler, *Deputy*: Mike Steen, *Sheriff Clark*: Kelly Thordsen, *Benny Taubman*: William Forrest, *Charles*: Roy Glenn, *Jackie*: Eddy Samuels, *Fly*: Davis Roberts, *Director*: Robert Burton.

SWEETHEARTS (1938) MGM. Producer, Hunt Stromberg. Director, W. S. Van Dyke. Color by Technicolor. Authors, Fred De Gresac, Harry D. Smith, Robert B. Smith. Screenplay, Dorothy Parker, Alan Campbell. Music, Victor Herbert. Cameramen, Oliver March, Allen Davey. Editor, Robert J. Kern. Songs by Chet Forrest, Bob Wright and Victor Herbert: "Angelus," "Every Lover Must Meet His Fate," "The Game of Love," "Grandmother," "Iron, Iron, Iron," "Mademoiselle on Parade," "Pretty as a Picture," "Summer Serenade," "Sweetheart," "Waiting for the Bride" and "Wooden Shoes." 120 minutes

Gwen Arden: Jeanette MacDonald, *Ernest Lane*: Nelson Eddy, *Felix Lehman*: Frank Morgan, *Fred*: Ray Bolger, *Kay Jordan*: Florence Rice, *Leo Kronk*: Mischa Auer, *Hannah*: Fay Holden, *Gwen's Brother*: Terry Kilburn, *Una Wilson*: Betty Jaynes, *Harvey Horton*: Douglas McPhail, *Norman Trumpett*: Reginald Gardiner, *Oscar Engel*: Herman Bing, *Dink Rogers*: Allyn Joslyn, *Orlando Lane*: Raymond

Sweethearts with Douglas McPhail and Jeanette MacDonald.

Walburn, *Mrs. Merrill*: Lucile Watson, *Samuel Silver*: Philip Loeb, *Aunt Amelia*: Kathleen Lockhart, *Augustus*: Gene Lockhart, *Sheridan Lane*: Berton Churchill, *Appleby*: Olin Howland, *Harry*: Gerald Hamer, *Boy*: Marvin Jones, *Girl*: Dorothy Gray, *Fire Inspector*: Emory Parnell, *Dowager*: Maude Turner Gordon, *Violinist*: Jac George, *Tommy (Fighter)*: Charles Sullivan, *Telephone Operators*: Mira McKinney, Grace Hayle, Barbara Pepper, *Assistant Director*: Irving Bacon, *Dance Director*: Lester Dorr, *Pianist*: Dalies Frantz.

SWEET ROSIE O'GRADY (1943) 20th. Producer, William Perlberg. Director, Irving Cummings. Color by Technicolor. Authors, William R. Lipman, Frederick Stephani, Edward Van Every. Screenplay, Ken Englund. Dance Director, Hermes Pan. Art Directors, James Basevi, Joseph C. Wright. Musical Directors, Alfred Newman, Charles Henderson. Cameraman, Ernest Palmer. Editor, Robert Simpson. Songs by Mack Gordon and Harry Warren: "My Heart Tells Me," "The Wishing Waltz," "Get Your Police Gazette," "My Sam," "Going to the County Fair" and "Where Oh Where Oh Where Is the Groom?" Technicolor Director, Natalie Kalmus. 74 minutes

Madeleine Marlowe: Betty Grable, *Sam Mackeever*: Robert Young, *Morgan*: Adolphe Menjou, *Duke Charles*: Reginald Gardiner, *Edna Van Dyke*: Virginia Grey, *Composer*: Phil Regan, *Joe Flugelman*: Sig Rumann, *Arthur Skinner*: Alan Dinehart, *Clark*: Hobart Cavanaugh, *Cabby*: Frank Orth, *Mr. Fox*: Jonathan Hale, *Little*: Edward Keane, *Singer*: Dorothy Granger, *Danny*: Stanley Clements, *Rimplemayer*: Byron Foulger, *Gracie*: Lilyan Irene, *Madison*: Milton Parsons, *Poindexter*: Hal K. Dawson, *Kelly*: George Chandler, *Husband*: Charles Trowbridge, *St. Brendan's Choir*: Themselves, *Leo Diamond and His Solidaires*: Themselves, *Andrews*: John Kelly, *Weston*: Billy Wayne, *Farmers*: Louis Mason, Paul Burns, *Storekeeper*: Eddy Waller, *Benny*: Ken Lundy, *Barney*: Robert Homans, *Mailman*: Walter Baldwin, *Editor Ellis*: Al Hill, *Editor Brooks*: Walter Fenner, *Editor Rogers*: Gus Glassmire, *Artist White*: Oliver Prickett (Oliver Blake), *Morley*: Bert Hicks.

Sweet Rosie O'Grady with Betty Grable, Reginald Gardiner, and Robert Young.

SWING HIGH, SWING LOW (1937) Par. Produced by Arthur Hornblow, Jr. Directed by Mitchell Leisen. Based on the play *Burlesque* by George Manker Watters and Arthur Hopkins. Screenplay, Virginia Van Upp and Oscar Hammerstein II. Art Directors, Hans Dreier and Ernst Fegte. Music Director, Boris Morros. Arrangements, Victor Young and Phil Boutelje. Photography, Ted Tetzlaff. Special Effects, Farciot Edouart. Editor, Eda Warren. Songs: "I Hear a Call to Arms" by Sam Coslow and Al Siegel; "Panamania" by Burton Lane and Ralph Freed; "If It Isn't Pain, Then It Isn't Love," by Ralph Rainger and Leo Robin. "Swing High, Swing Low" by Ralph Freed and Burton Lane, "Spring Is in the Air" by Ralph Freed and Charles Kisco. Other versions: *Dance of Life* (Paramount, 1929), *When My Baby Smiles at Me* (20th Century-Fox, 1948). 97 minutes

Maggie King: Carole Lombard, *Skid Johnson*: Fred MacMurray, *Harry*: Charles Butterworth, *Ella*: Jean Dixon, *Anita Alvarez*: Dorothy Lamour, *Harvey Dexter*: Harvey Stephens, *Murphy*: Cecil Cunningham, *Georgie*: Charlie Arnt, *Henri*: Franklin Pangborn, *The Don*: Anthony Quinn, *The Purser*: Bud Flannigan (Dennis O'Keefe), *Tony*: Charles Judels, *Chief of Police*: Harry Semels, *Interpreter*: Ricardo Mandia, *Judge*: Enrique DeRosas, *Sleepy Servant*: Chris-Pin Martin, *Panamanian at Cockfight*: Charles Stevens, *Musselwhite*: Ralph Remley, *Men in Nightclub*: Nick Lukats, Lee Bowman, *Negro Santa Claus*: Darby Jones, *Interpreter*: Eumenio Blanco, *Justice of Peace*: George W. Jimenez, *Manager*: George Sorel, *Italian*: Gino Corrado, *Army Surgeon*: Richard Kipling, *Customer*: Esther Howard, *Cook*: Spencer Chan, *Radio Technician*: Donald Kerr, *Army Lieutenant*: P. E. (Tiny) Newland, *Attendant*: William Wright.

Swing High, Swing Low with Fred MacMurray, Carole Lombard and Anthony Quinn.

SWING TIME (1936) RKO. Producer, Pandro S. Berman. Director, George Stevens. Author, Erwin Gelsey. Screenplay, Howard Lindsay, Allan Scott. Musical Director, Nathaniel Shilkret. Cameraman, David Abel. Editor, Henry Berman. Ensembles staged by Hermes Pan. Songs by Jerome Kern and Dorothy Fields: "The Way You Look Tonight," "A Fine Romance," "The Waltz in Swing Time," "Never Gonna Dance," "Pick Yourself Up," "Bojangles of Harlem." 103 minutes

Swing Time with Ginger Rogers and Fred Astaire.

John (Lucky) Garnett: Fred Astaire, *Penelope (Penny) Carrol:* Ginger Rogers, *Pop (Ed):* Victor Moore, *Mabel Anderson:* Helen Broderick, *Gordon:* Eric Blore, *Margaret Watson:* Betty Furness, *Ricardo Romero:* Georges Metaxa, *Judge Watson:* Landers Stevens, *Dice Raymond:* John Harrington, *Al Simpson:* Pierre Watkin, *Schmidt:* Abe Reynolds, *Eric:* Gerald Hamer, *Policeman:* Edgar Dearing, *Stagehands:* Harry Bowen, Harry Bernard, *Dancers:* Donald Kerr, Ted O'Shea, Frank Edmunds, Bill Brand, *Red:* Frank Jenks, *Hotel Clerk:* Ralph Byrd, *Taxi Driver:* Charles Hall, *Roulette Dealer:* Jean Perry, *Muggsy:* Olin Francis, *Romero's Butler:* Floyd Shackleford, *Minister:* Ferdinand Munier, *Announcer:* Joey Ray, *Wedding Guest:* Jack Rice, *Dancer:* Jack Good.

SWISS FAMILY ROBINSON (1960) BV. Producers, Walt Disney, Bill Anderson. Director, Ken Annakin. Screenplay, Lowell S. Hawley. Based on the novel by Johann Wyss. Music, William Alwyn. Associate Producer, Basil Keys. Assistant Director, Rene Dupont. Costumes, Julie Harris. In Panavision and Technicolor. Art Director, John Howell. Music Director, Muir Mathieson. Cinematography, Harry Waxman. Editor, Peter Boita. Song, "My Heart Was an Island," by Terry Gilkyson. Produced in England. Previous version: RKO, 1940. 126 minutes

Father: John Mills, *Mother:* Dorothy McGuire, *Fritz:* James MacArthur, *Ernst:* Tommy Kirk, *Francis:* Kevin Corcoran, *Capt. Moreland:* Cecil Parker, *Bertie:* Janet Munro, *Kuala:* Sessue Hayakawa.

Swiss Family Robinson with Kevin Corcoran, John Mills, Tommy Kirk, Dorothy McGuire and James MacArthur.

TAKE ME OUT TO THE BALL GAME (1949) MGM. Producer, Arthur Freed. Director, Busby Berkeley. Color by Technicolor. Authors, Gene Kelly, Stanley Donen. Screenplay, Harry Tugend, George Wells. Art Directors, Cedric Gibbons, Daniel B. Cathcart. Musical Director, Adolph Deutsch. Photography, George Folsey. Editor, Blanche Sewell. Songs by Betty Comden, Adolph Green and Roger Edens:

Take Me Out to the Ball Game with Esther Williams, Gene Kelly, Jules Munshin, Frank Sinatra, Murray Alper, Richard Lane and Tom Dugan.

"The Right Girl For Me," "It's Fate Baby It's Fate," "O'Brien to Ryan to Goldberg," "Strictly U.S.A." and "Yes Indeedy." 93 minutes

Dennis Ryan: Frank Sinatra, *K. C. Higgins:* Esther Williams, *Eddie O'Brien:* Gene Kelly, *Shirley Delwyn:* Betty Garrett, *Joe Lorgan:* Edward Arnold, *Nat Goldberg:* Jules Munshin, *Michael Gilhuly:* Richard Lane, *Slappy Burke:* Tom Dugan, *Zalinka:* Murray Alper, *Nick Donford:* Wilton Graff, *Two Henchmen:* Mack Gray, Charles Regan, *Steve:* Saul Gorss, *Karl:* Douglas Fowley, *Dr. Winston:* Eddie Parkes, *Cop in Park:* James Burke, *Specialty:* The Blackburn Twins, *Senator Catcher:* Gordon Jones, *Reporter:* Frank Scannell, *Burly Acrobat:* Henry Kulky, *Girl Dancer:* Dorothy Abbott, *Two Girls on Train:* Virginia Bates, Joy Lansing, *Kid:* Jackie Jackson, *Sam:* Si Jenks, *Room Clerk:* Jack Rice, *Teddy Roosevelt:* Ed Cassidy, *Umpire:* Dick Wessel, *Dancer:* Sally Forrest.

A TALE OF TWO CITIES (1935) MGM. Produced by David O. Selznick. Directed by Jack Conway. Based on the novel by Charles Dickens. Screenplay, W. P. Lipscomb and S. N. Behrman. Music, Herbert Stothart. Revolutionary sequences by Val Lewton and Jacques Tourneur. Photography, Oliver T. Marsh. Editor, Conrad A. Nervig. Christmas carols sung by Father Finn's Paulist Choristers. Other versions: *A Tale of Two Cities* (Fox, 1917), *The Only Way* (United Artists, 1926), *A Tale of Two Cities* (British: Rank, 1958). 121 minutes

A Tale of Two Cities with Ronald Colman, Elizabeth Allan, Edna May Oliver, Fay Chaldecott and Claude Gillingwater.

Sydney Carton: Ronald Colman, *Lucie Manette:* Elizabeth Allan, *Miss Pross:* Edna May Oliver, *Madame DeFarge:* Blanche Yurka, *Stryver:* Reginald Owen, *Marquis St. Evremonde:* Basil Rathbone, *Dr. Manotte:* Henry B. Walthall, *Charles Darnay:* Donald Woods, *Barsad:* Walter Catlett, *Gaspard:* Fritz Leiber, Sr., *Gabelle:* H. B. Warner, *Ernest DeFarge:* Mitchell Lewis, *Jarvis Lorry:* Claude Gillingwater, *Jerry Cruncher:* Billy Bevan, *Seamstress:* Isabel Jewell, *LaVengeance:* Lucille LaVerne, *Woodcutter:* Tully Marshall, *Lucie the Daughter:* Fay Chaldecott, *Mrs. Cruncher:* Eily Malyon, *Judge in Old Bailey:* E. E. Clive, *Prosecuting Attorney in Old Bailey:* Lawrence Grant, *Morveau:* John Davidson, *Tellson, Jr.:* Tom Ricketts, *Jerry Cruncher, Jr.:* Donald Haines, *Prosecutor:* Ralf Harolde, *Aristocrat:* Boyd Irwin, Sr., *Cartwright:* Ed Peil, Sr., *Leader:* Edward Hearn, *Executioner:* Richard Alexander, *Headsman:* Cyril McLaglen, *Jailer:* Frank Mayo, *Jacques #116:* Barlowe Borland, *Aristocrat:* Nigel DeBrulier, *Jailer, Victor:* Walter Kingsford, *Dandy Who's Condemned:* Rolfe Sedan, *Tribunal Judge:* Robert Warwick, *Old Hag:* Dale Fuller, *Chief Registrar:* Montague Shaw, *English Priest:* Chappell Dossett, *Old Hag:* Tempe Pigott, *Joe, Coach Guard:* Forrester Harvey, *Innkeeper:* Jimmy Aubrey, *Border Guard:* Billy House.

THE TALK OF THE TOWN (1942) Col. Producer, George Stevens. Associate Producer, Fred Guiol. Director, George Stevens. Author,

Talk of the Town with Cary Grant, George Watts, Ronald Colman and Tom Tyler.

Sidney Harmon. Screenplay, Irwin Shaw, Sidney Buchman. Art Director, Lionel Banks. Score, Frederick Hollander. Musical Director, M. W. Stoloff. Cameraman, Ted Tetzlaff. Editor, Otto Meyer. Adaptation, Dale Van Every. 118 minutes

Leopold Dilg: Cary Grant, *Nora Shelley:* Jean Arthur, *Michael Lightcap:* Ronald Colman, *Sam Yates:* Edgar Buchanan, *Regina Bush:* Glenda Farrell, *Andrew Holmes:* Charles Dingle, *Mrs. Shelley:* Emma Dunn, *Tilney:* Rex Ingram, *Jan Pulaski:* Leonid Kinskey, *Clyde Bracken:* Tom Tyler, *Chief of Police:* Don Beddoe, *Judge Grunstadt:* George Watts, *Senator James Boyd:* Clyde Fillmore, *District Attorney:* Frank W. Thomas, *Forrester:* Lloyd Bridges, *Second Moving Man:* Max Wagner, *First Cop:* Pat McVey, *First Moving Man:* Ralph Peters, *Henry:* Eddie Laughton, *Western Union Boy:* Billy Benedict, *Ball Player:* Harold "Stubby" Kruger, *Hound Keeper:* Lee "Lasses" White, *Sheriff:* William Gould, *Sergeant:* Edward Hearn, *Mrs. Pulaski:* Ferike Boros, *Jake:* Dewey Robinson, *Operator:* Mabel Todd, *Headwaiter:* Dan Seymour, *Waiter:* Gino Corrado, *Road Cop:* Frank Sully, *Sgt. at Arms:* Lee Prather, *Doorkeeper:* Clarence Muse, *Secretary:* Leslie Brooks, *Desk Sergeant:* Alan Bridge, *McGuire:* Joe Cunningham.

TARZAN THE APE MAN (1932) MGM. Directed by W. S. Van Dyke. Based on the character created by Edgar Rice Burroughs. Scenario, Cyril Hume. Dialogue, Ivor Novello. Cameramen, Harold Rosson and Clyde DeVinna. Editors, Ben Lewis and Tom Held. The first sound Tarzan film. 99 minutes.

Tarzan: Johnny Weissmuller, *Harry Holt:* Neil Hamilton, *Jane Parker:* Maureen O'Sullivan, *James Parker:* C. Aubrey Smith, *Mrs. Cutten:* Doris Lloyd, *Beamish:* Forrester Harvey, *Riano:* Ivory Williams.

Tarzan the Ape Man with Johnny Weissmuller and Maureen O'Sullivan.

Task Force with Stanley Ridges, Jane Wyatt and Gary Cooper.

TASK FORCE (1949) WB. Producer, Jerry Wald. Director-Author-Screenplay, Delmer Daves. Art Director, Leo K. Kuter. Music, Franz Waxman. Photography, Robert Burks, Wilfrid M. Cline. Editor, Alan Crosland, Jr. Last half in Technicolor. 116 minutes

Jonathon L. Scott: Gary Cooper, *Mary Morgan:* Jane Wyatt, *McKinney:* Wayne Morris, *Pete Richard:* Walter Brennan, *Barbara McKinney:* Julie London, *McClusky:* Bruce Bennett, *Reeves:* Jack Holt, *Bently:* Stanley Ridges, *Dixie Rankin:* John Ridgely, *Jack Southern:* Richard Rober, *Senator Vincent:* Art Baker, *Ames:* Moroni Olsen, *Timmy:* Harlan Warde, *Tom Cooper:* James Holden, *Winston:* Warren Douglas, *Jennings:* John Gallaudet, *Jerry Morgan:* Rory Mallinson, *Pilot:* Ray Montgomery, *Aide:* Charles Waldron, Jr., *Lt. Kelley:* Robert Rockwell, *Mr. Secretary:* William Gould, *Mrs. Secretary:* Sally Corner, *Capt. Williamson:* Kenneth Tobey, *Japanese Representative:* Tetsu Komai, *Japanese Naval Attaché:* Beal Wong, *Mrs. Ames:* Laura Treadwell, *Ames Attache:* Roscoe J. Behan, *Admiral:* Basil Ruysdael, *Commander Price:* Edwin Fowler, *Lt. Leenhouts:* William Hudson, *Ruth Rankin:* Mary Lawrence, *Supply Officer:* John McGuire, *Capt. Wren:* Charles Sherlock, *Officer:* Reed Howes, *Jones:* Mal Merrihue, *Lindsay:* Mickey McCardell, *Harrison:* Paul McWilliams, *Chairman:* Alex Gerry, *Presidential Representative:* Joe Forte.

TEA AND SYMPATHY (1956) MGM. Producer, Pandro S. Berman. Director, Vincente Minnelli. CinemaScope, MetroColor. Based on the play by Robert Anderson. Screenplay, Robert Anderson. Art Directors, William A. Horning, Edward Carfagno. Music, Adolph Deutsch. Cinematographer, John Alton. Editor, Ferris Webster. 122 minutes

Laura Reynolds: Deborah Kerr, *Tom Robinson Lee:* John Kerr, *Bill Reynolds:* Leif Erickson, *Herb Lee:* Edward Andrews, *Al:* Darryl Hickman, *Ellie Martin:* Norma Crane, *Ollie:* Dean Jones, *Lilly Sears:* Jacqueline de Wit, *Ralph:* Tom Laughlin, *Steve:* Ralph Votrian, *Phil:* Steven Terrell, *Ted:* Kip King, *Henry:* Jimmy Hayes, *Roger:* Richard Tyler, *Vic:* Don Burnett, *Mary Williams:* Mary Alan Hokanson, *Dick:* Ron Kennedy, *Pete:* Peter Miller, *Pat:* Bob Alexander, *Earl:*

Tea and Sympathy with Deborah Kerr and John Kerr.

Michael Monroe, *Umpire:* Byron Kane, *Alex:* Paul Bryar, *First Boy:* Harry Harvey, Jr., *Second Boy:* Bobby Ellis, *Burly Men:* Saul Gorss, Dale Van Sickel, *Headmaster at Bonfire:* Peter Leeds, *Ferdie:* Del Erickson.

TEA FOR TWO (1950) WB. Producer, William Jacobs. Director, David Butler. Color by Technicolor. Authors, Frank Mandel, Otto Harbach, Vincent Youmans, Emil Nyitray from the 1929 musical *No, No, Nanette.* Screenplay, Harry Clork. Art Director, Douglas Bacon. Musical Director, Ray Heindorf. Photography, Wilfrid M. Cline. Editor, Irene Morra. Songs: "I Know That You Know" by Anne Caldwell and Vincent Youmans; "Crazy Rhythm" by Irving Caesar, Roger Wolfe Kahn and Joseph Meyer; "I Only Have Eyes for You" by Al Dubin and Harry Warren; "Tea for Two" and "I Want to Be Happy" by Irving Caesar and Vincent Youmans; "Do Do Do" by Ira and George Gershwin; "Oh Me Oh My" by Arthur Francis and Vincent Youmans. Earlier versions of *No, No, Nanette:* First National (Warners), 1930; RKO, 1940. 98 minutes

Tea for Two with George Baxter, Bill Goodwin, Harry Harvey, Billy De Wolfe, Doris Day and Eve Arden.

Nanette Carter: Doris Day, *Jimmy Smith:* Gordon MacRae, *Tommy Trainor:* Gene Nelson, *Beatrice Darcy:* Patrice Wymore, *Pauline Hastings:* Eve Arden, *Larry Blair:* Billy De Wolfe, *J. Maxwell Bloomhaus:* S. Z. Sakall, *William Early:* Bill Goodwin, *Mabel Wiley:* Virginia Gibson, *Stevens:* Craufurd Kent, *Lynne:* Mary Eleanor Donahue, *Richard:* Johnny McGovern, *Crochety Man:* Harry Harvey, *Backer:* George Baxter, *Theater Manager:* Herschel Dougherty, *Taxi Driver:* Abe Dinovitch, *Secretary:* Elizabeth Flournoy, *Piano Mover:* Buddy Shaw, *Chorus Boy:* John Hedloe, *Truck Driver:* Jack Daley, *Radio Announcer:* Art Gilmore.

THE TEAHOUSE OF THE AUGUST MOON (1956) MGM. Producer, Jack Cummings. Director, Daniel Mann. CinemaScope, Metro-Color. Based on a book by Vern J. Sneider and the play by John Patrick.

The Teahouse of the August Moon with Glenn Ford, Philip Ahn and Marlon Brando.

Screenplay, John Patrick. Art Directors, William A. Horning, Eddie Imazu. Musical Director, Saul Chaplin. Cinematographer, John Alton. Editor, Harold F. Kress. 123 minutes.

Sakini: Marlon Brando, *Captain Fisby:* Glenn Ford, *Lotus Blossom:* Machiko Kyo, *Captain McLean:* Eddie Albert, *Colonel Purdy:* Paul Ford, *Mr. Seiko:* Jun Negami, *Miss Higa Jiga:* Nijiko Kiyokawa, *Little Girl:* Mitsuko Sawamura, *Sergeant Gregovich:* Henry (Harry) Morgan, *Ancient Man:* Shichizo Takeda, *Mr. Hokaida:* Kichizaemon Saramaru, *Mr. Omura:* Frank Tokunaga, *Mr. Oshira:* Raynum K. Tsukamoto, *Mr. Sumata:* Nishida, *Sumata's Father:* Dansho Miyazaki, *Old Woman on Jeep:* Miyoshi Jingu, *Daughter on Jeep:* Aya Oyama, *Judge:* Tsuruta Yozan, *Soldiers:* John Grayson, Roger McGee, Harry Harvey, Jr., Carl Fior.

THE TEN COMMANDMENTS (1956) Par. Producer, Cecil B. De Mille. Associate Producer, Henry Wilcoxon. Director, Cecil B. De Mille. VistaVision, Technicolor. Authors, Dorothy Clarke Wilson (from *Prince of Egypt*); Rev. J. H. Ingraham (from *Pillar of Fire*); Rev. A. E. Southon (from *On Eagle's Wings*). Screenplay, Aeneas MacKenzie, Jesse L. Lasky, Jr., Jack Gariss, Fredric M. Frank. Art Directors, Hal Pereira, Walter Tyler, Albert Nozaki. Cinematographer, Loyal Griggs. Additional Photography, J. Peverell Marley, John Warren, Wallace Kelley. Editor, Anna Bauchens. Remake of De Mille's 1923 film. 219 minutes

Moses: Charlton Heston, *Rameses:* Yul Brynner, *Nefretiri:* Anne Baxter, *Dathan:* Edward G. Robinson, *Sephora:* Yvonne De Carlo, *Lilia:* Debra Paget, *Joshua:* John Derek, *Sethi:* Sir Cedric Hardwicke, *Bithiah:* Nina Foch, *Yochabel:* Martha Scott, *Memnet:* Judith Anderson, *Baka:* Vincent Price, *Aaron:* John Carradine, *Jethro:* Eduard Franz, *Miriam:* Olive Deering, *Mered:* Donald Curtis, *Jannes:* Douglas Dumbrille, *Hur Ben Caleb:* Lawrence Dobkin, *Abiram:* Frank DeKova, *Amminadab:* H. B. Warner, *Pentaur:* Henry Wilcoxon, *Elisheba:* Julia Faye, *Jethro's Daughter:* Lisa Mitchell, Noelle Williams, Joanna Merlin, Pat Richard, Joyce Vanderveen, Diane Hall, *Rameses' Charioteer:* Abbas El Boughdadly, *The Infant Moses:* Fraser Heston, *The Blind One:* John Miljan, *Gershom:* Tommy Duran, *Simon:* Francis J. McDonald, *Rameses' Son:* Eugene Mazzola, *Rameses I:* Ian Keith, *Korah:* Ramsay Hill, *Eleazar:* Paul De Rolf, *Korah's Wife:* Joan Woodbury, *King of Ethiopia:* Woodrow Strode, *Princess Tharbis:* Esther Brown, Rushti Abaza, *Amalekite Herder:* Touch (Michael) Connors, *Sardinian Captain:* Clint Walker, *Old Hebrew:* Luis Alberni, *Taskmaster:* Michael Ansara, *Slave:* Frankie Darro, *Herald:* Walter Woolf King, *Spearman Hebrew:* Robert Vaughn.

The Ten Commandments with John Derek, Debra Paget, Olive Deering, Yvonne De Carlo and Charlton Heston.

Ten North Frederick with Geraldine Fitzgerald and Gary Cooper.

TEN NORTH FREDERICK (1958) 20th. Producer, Charles Brackett. Director, Philip Dunne. CinemaScope. From the novel by John O'Hara. Screenplay, Philip Dunne. Art Directors, Lyle R. Wheeler, Addison Hehr. Music, Leigh Harline. Music conducted by Lionel Newman. Orchestration, Edward B. Powell. Cinematographer, Joe MacDonald. Special Photographic Effects., L. B. Abbott. Editor, David Brotherton. 102 minutes

Joe Chapin: Gary Cooper, *Ann Chapin:* Diane Varsi, *Kate Drummond:* Suzy Parker, *Edith Chapin:* Geraldine Fitzgerald, *Slattery:* Tom Tully, *Joby:* Ray Stricklyn, *Lloyd Williams:* Philip Ober, *Paul Donaldson:* John Emery, *Charley Bongiorno:* Stuart Whitman, *Peg Slattery:* Linda Watkins, *Stella:* Barbara Nichols, *Dr. English:* Joe McGuinn, *Arthur McHenry:* Jess Kirkpatrick, *Harry Jackson:* Nolan Leary, *Marian Jackson:* Helen Wallace, *Waitress:* Beverly Jo Morrow, *Bill:* Buck Class, *Salesgirl:* Rachel Stephens, *Farmer:* Bob Adler, *Peter:* Linc Foster, *Robert Hooker:* John Harding, *Ted Wallace:* Dudley Manlove, *General Coates:* Mack Williams, *Board Chairman:* Vernon Rich, *Nurse:* Mary Carroll, *Waiter:* George Davis, *Taxi Driver:* Joey Faye, *Hoffman:* Fred Essler, *Wife:* Irene Seidner, *Hope:* Melinda Byron, *Sax Player:* Sean Meaney.

TEST PILOT (1938) MGM. Producer, Louis D. Lighton. Director, Victor Fleming. Author, Frank Wead. Screenplay, Vincent Lawrence, Waldemar Young. Cameraman, Ray June. Editor, Tom Held. 118 minutes.

Jim Lane: Clark Gable, *Ann Barton:* Myrna Loy, *Gunner Sloane:* Spencer Tracy, *Howard B. Drake:* Lionel Barrymore, *General Ross:* Samuel S. Hinds, *Frank Barton:* Arthur Aylesworth, *Mrs. Barton:* Claudia Coleman, *Mrs. Benson:* Gloria Holden, *Benson:* Louis Jean Heydt, *Joe:* Ted Pearson, *Landlady:* Marjorie Main, *Grant:* Gregory Gaye, *Sarah:* Virginia Grey, *Mabel:* Priscilla Lawson, *Mr. Brown:* Dudley Clements, *Fat Man:* Henry Roquemore, *Designer:* Byron Foulger, *Motor Expert:* Frank Jaquet, *Advertising Man:* Roger Converse, *Photographer:* Phillip Terry, *Attendant:* Robert Fiske, *Pilot:* Garry Owen, *Fat Woman:* Dorothy Vaughan, *Little Man:* Billy Engle, *Movie Leading Man:* Brent Sargent, *Movie Leading Woman:* Mary

Test Pilot with Clark Gable, Myrna Loy and Spencer Tracy.

Howard, *Interne:* Gladden James, *Singing Pilot in Café:* Douglas McPhail, *Pilots in Cafe:* Forbes Murray, Richard Tucker, Don Douglas, James Flavin, Hooper Atchley, Dick Winslow, Ray Walker and Frank Sully, *Saleslady:* Fay Holden, *Bartender:* Tom O'Grady, *Boss Loader:* Syd Saylor.

THANKS A MILLION (1935) 20th. Produced by Darryl F. Zanuck. Directed by Roy Del Ruth. Story, Nunnally Johnson. Photography, Peverell Marley. Editor, William Lambert. Songs by Arthur Johnston and Gus Kahn: "Thanks a Million," "Sing Brother Sing," "New O'leans," "Sugar Plum," "Sittin' on a Hilltop," "A Pocketful of Sunshine." Song by Bert Kalmar and Harry Ruby: "What a Beautiful Night." 87 minutes

Eric Land: Dick Powell, *Ned Allen:* Fred Allen, *Sally Mason:* Ann Dvorak, *Phoebe Mason:* Patsy Kelly, *Sequence with Beetle and Bottle:* Phil Baker, *Orchestra Leader:* David Rubinoff, *Band:* Paul Whiteman and Band, *Yacht Club Boys:* Charles Adler, James V. Kern, Billy Mann, George Kelly, *Tammany:* Benny Baker, *Governor (Opposition Party):* Charles Richman, *Mrs. Kruger:* Margaret Irving, *Mr. Kruger:* Alan Dinehart, *Mr. Grass:* Andrew Tombes, *Judge Culliman:* Raymond Walburn, *Maxwell:* Paul Harvey, *Casey:* Edwin Maxwell, *Mr. Bradley:* Russell Hicks, *Specialty:* Ramona, *Bus Driver:* Herbert Ashley, *Bit Politicians:* Harry Dunkinson, Walter Downing, Ralph Lewis, Ricca K. Allen, Frank Darien, *Father:* Si Jenks, *Hotel Clerk:* Wally Maher, *Mr. Hartford:* Yorke Sherwood, *Campaign Manager:* Harry Stubbs, *Butler:* Olaf Hytten, *Chairman:* Walter Walker, *Bit:* Stanhope Wheatcroft, *Sergeant of Motor Policemen:* Charles Wilson, *Father:* Harry C. Bradley, *Telephone Operator:* Lynn Bari.

Thanks a Million with Patsy Kelly, Ann Dvorak and David Rubinoff (orchestra leader).

THANK YOUR LUCKY STARS (1943) WB. Producer, Mark Hellinger. Director, David Butler. Original Story, Everett Freeman, Arthur Schwartz. Screenplay, Norman Panama, Melvin Frank, James V. Kern. Dance Director, LeRoy Prinz. Art Directors, Anton Grot, Leo E. Kuter. Musical Director, Leo F. Forbstein. Cameraman, Arthur Edeson. Special Effects, H. F. Koenekamp. Editor, Irene Morra. Songs by Frank Loesser and Arthur Schwartz: "They're Either Too Young or Too Old," "How Sweet You Are," "The Dreamer," "I'm Riding for A Fall," "Good Night Good Neighbor," "Love Isn't Born It's Made", "Ice Cold Katy," "Thank Your Lucky Stars," "We're Staying Home Tonight," "I'm Going North," "That's What You Jolly Well Get." 127 minutes.

Assistant Photographer: Hank Mann, *Fan:* Mary Treen, *Bill:* James Burke, *Dr. Kirby:* Paul Harvey, *Patient:* Bert Gordon, *Drunk:* (Bette

Thank Your Lucky Stars with Dennis Morgan, Joan Leslie and Eddie Cantor.

Davis Number): Jack Norton, *Jitterbug:* (*Davis Number*): Conrad Wiedell, *Fireman:* Matt McHugh, *Sailor:* Frank Faylen, *Charlie, the Indian:* Noble Johnson, *Olaf:* Mike Mazurki, *Joe Sampson:* Eddie Cantor, *Pat Dixon:* Joan Leslie, *Tommy Randolph:* Dennis Morgan, *Dinah Shore:* Herself, *Dr. Schlenna:* S. Z. Sakall, *Farnsworth:* Edward Everett Horton, *Nurse Hamilton:* Ruth Donnelly, *Girl with Book:* Joyce Reynolds, *Barney Jackson:* Richard Lane, *Don Wilson:* Himself, *Angelo:* Henry Armetta, *Specialities:* Humphrey Bogart, Jack Carson, Bette Davis, Olivia De Havilland, Errol Flynn, John Garfield, Alan Hale, Ida Lupino, Ann Sheridan, George Tobias, and Spike Jones and His City Slickers, *Themselves:* David Butler, Mark Hellinger, *Finchley, Butler:* Don Barclay, *Boy:* Stanley Clements, *Ice Cold Katie Number: Gossip,* Hattie McDaniel, *Soldier,* Willie Best, *Ice Cold Katie,* Rita Christiani, *The Justice,* Jess Lee Brooks, *The Trio:* Ford, Harris and Jones, *Good Night, Good Neighbor Number Dancer,* Alexis Smith, *Dancer:* Igor DeNavrotsky, *Dancer:* Arnold Kent, *Cab Driver:* Brandon Hurst, *Miss Latin America:* Lynne Baggett, *Miss Spain:* Mary Landa.

THAT HAMILTON WOMAN (1941) UA. Produced and directed by Alexander Korda. Original Screenplay, Walter Reisch and R. C. Sherriff. Music, Miklos Rosza. Photography, Rudolph Mate. Editor, William Hornbeck. Produced in Hollywood. British title: *Lady Hamilton.* Previous version: *Nelson* (British, 1927). 128 minutes

That Hamilton Woman with Laurence Olivier and Vivien Leigh.

Emma Hart, Lady Hamilton: Vivien Leigh, *Lord Horatio Nelson:* Laurence Olivier, *Sir William Hamilton:* Alan Mowbray, *Mrs. Cadogan-Lyon:* Sara Allgood, *Lady Frances Nelson:* Gladys Cooper, *Captain Hardy:* Henry Wilcoxon, *Mary Smith, a Street Girl:* Heather Angel, *Reverend Nelson:* Halliwell Hobbes, *Lord Spencer:* Gilbert Emery, *Lord Keith:* Miles Mander, *Josiah:* Ronald Sinclair, *King of*

Naples: Luis Alberni, *Queen of Naples:* Norma Drury, *French Ambassador:* George Renavent, *Hotel Manager:* Leonard Carey, *Orderly:* Alec Craig, *Gendarme:* George Davis.

THAT TOUCH OF MINK (1962) Univ. Executive Producer, Robert Arthur. Producers, Stanley Shapiro, Martin Melcher. Director, Delbert Mann. Eastman Color, Panavision. Screenplay, Stanley Shapiro, Nate Monaster. Art Directors, Alexander Golitzen, Robert Clatworthy. Cinematographer, Russell Metty. Editor, Ted Kent. A Granley-Arwin-Nob Hill Production. 99 minutes

Philip Shayne: Cary Grant, *Cathy Timberlake:* Doris Day, *Roger:* Gig Young, *Connie:* Audrey Meadows, *Dr. Gruber:* Alan Hewitt, *Beasley:* John Astin, *Young Man:* Richard Sargent, *Short Man:* Joey Faye, *Mr. Smith:* John Fiedler, *Hadges:* Willard Sage, *Dr. Richardson:* Jack Livesey, *Collins (Chauffeur):* John McKee, *Showgirl:* Laurie Mitchell, *Millie:* June Ericson, *Mrs. Golden:* Laiola Wendorff, *Roger Maris:* Roger Maris, *Mickey Mantle:* Mickey Mantle, *Yogi Berra:* Yogi Berra, *Umpire:* Art Passarella, *Stewardess:* Dorothy Abbott, *Taxi Driver:* Ralph Manza, *Leonard:* William Lanteau, *Mrs. Haskell:* Kathryn Givney, *Miriam:* Alice Backes, *Mr. Miller:* Richard Deacon, *Mr. Golden:* Fred Essler, *Mrs. Farnum:* Helen Brown, *Mr. Hackett:* Nelson Olmsted, *Truck Driver:* Clegg Hoyt, *Lisa:* Isabella Albonico, *Al:* Billy Greene, *Miss Farrell:* Melora Conway, *Fashion Consultant:* Yvonne Peattie, *Williams:* Russ Bender, *Mario:* Jon Silo, *Doorman:* Tyler McVey.

That Touch of Mink with Cary Grant and Billy M. Greene.

THERE'S NO BUSINESS LIKE SHOW BUSINESS (1954) 20th. Producer, Sol C. Siegel. Director, Walter Lang. CinemaScope, De Luxe Color. Author, Lamar Trotti. Screenplay, Phoebe and Henry Ephron. Musical Supervisors, Alfred Newman, Lionel Newman. Art Directors, Lyle Wheeler, John De Cuir. Cameraman, Leon Shamroy. Editor, Robert Simpson. Songs by Irving Berlin: "You'd Be Surprised," "After You Get What You Want, You Don't Want It," "Remember," "If You Believe," "Heat Wave," "A Man Chases a Girl," "Lazy," "A Sailor's Not a Sailor Till a Sailor's Been Tattooed," "There's No Business Like Show Business," "When That Midnight Choo Choo Leaves For Alabam," "Play a Simple Melody," "A Pretty Girl," "Let's Have Another Cup of Coffee," "Alexander's Ragtime Band." 117 minutes

Molly Donahue: Ethel Merman, *Tim Donahue:* Donald O'Connor, *Vicky:* Marilyn Monroe, *Terrance Donahue:* Dan Dailey, *Steve Donahue:* Johnny Ray, *Katy Donahue:* Mitzi Gaynor, *Lew Harris:* Richard Eastham, *Charles Biggs:* Hugh O'Brian, *Eddie Duggan:* Frank McHugh, *Father Dineen:* Rhys Williams, *Marge:* Lee Patrick, *Harry:* Chick Chandler, *Hatcheck Girl:* Eve Miller, *Lillian Sawyer:* Robin Raymond, *Stage Manager:* Lyle Talbot, *Kelly, Stage Door Man:* George Melford, *Katy's Boy Friend:* Alvy Moore, *Dance Director:* Henry Slate, *Geoffrey:* Gavin Gordon, *Katy, age 4:* Mimi Gibson,

There's No Business Like Show Business with Ethel Merman, Johnny Ray, Dan Dailey, Donald O'Connor and Mitzi Gaynor.

Katy, age 8: Linda Lowell, *Steve, age 2:* John Potter, *Steve, age 6:* Jimmy Baird, *Steve, age 10:* Billy Chapin, *Tim, age 2:* Neal Mc-Caskill, *Tim, age 6:* Donald Gamble, *Lorna:* Charlotte Austin, *Stage Manager:* John Doucette, *Sophie Tucker:* Isabelle Dwan, *Bobby Clark:* Donald Kerr.

THESE THREE (1936) UA. A Samuel Goldwyn Production. Producer, Samuel Goldwyn. Director, William Wyler. From the play *The Children's Hour* by Lillian Hellman. Screenplay, Lillian Hellman. Cameraman, Gregg Toland. Editor, Daniel Mandell. 93 minutes

Martha Dobie: Miriam Hopkins, *Karen Wright:* Merle Oberon, *Doctor Joseph Cardin:* Joel McCrea, *Mrs. Mortar:* Catherine Doucet, *Mrs. Tilford:* Alma Kruger, *Mary Tilford:* Bonita Granville, *Rosalie:* Marcia Mae Jones, *Evelyn:* Carmencita Johnson, *Lois:* Mary Ann Durkin, *Agatha:* Margaret Hamilton, *Helen Burton:* Mary Louise Cooper, *Taxi Driver:* Walter Brennan.

These Three with Miriam Hopkins and Merle Oberon.

THEY DRIVE BY NIGHT (1940) WB. Producer, Hal B. Wallis. Associate Producer, Mark Hellinger. Director, Raoul Walsh. From the novel *Long Haul* by A. I. Bezzerides. Screenplay, Jerry Wald and Richard Macaulay. Musical Director, Adolph Deutsch. Art Director, John Hughes. Cameraman, Arthur Edeson. Special Effects, Byron Haskins, H. F. Koenekamp. Editor, Oliver S. Garretson. Partial remake of *Bordertown* (Warners, 1935). 93 minutes

Joe Fabrini: George Raft, *Cassie Hartley:* Ann Sheridan, *Lana Carlsen:* Ida Lupino, *Paul Fabrini:* Humphrey Bogart, *Pearl Fabrini:* Gale Page, *Ed. Carlsen:* Alan Hale, *Irish McGurn:* Roscoe Karns, *Harry McNamara:* John Litel, *District Attorney:* Henry O'Neill, *George Rondolos:* George Tobias, *Farnsworth:* Charles Halton, *Sue Carter:* Joyce Compton, *Hank Dawson:* John Ridgely, *Pete Haig:*

Paul Hurst, *Mike Williams:* Charles Wilson, *Neves:* Norman Willis, *Barney:* George Lloyd, *Chloe:* Lillian Yarbo, *Truck Driver:* Eddy Chandler, *Mexican Helper:* Pedro Regas, *Driver:* Frank Faylen, *Driver:* Ralph Sanford, *Drivers:* Sol Gorss, Eddie Fetherston, Dick Wessel, Al Hill, Charles Sullivan, Eddie Acuff, Pat Flaherty, *Landlady:* Vera Lewis, *Fatso:* Joe Devlin, *Tough Driver:* William Haade, *Mike:* Mack Gray, *Sweeney (Driver):* Max Wagner, *Bailiff:* Wilfred Lucas, *Defense Attorney:* John Hamilton, *Judge:* Howard Hickman.

They Drive by Night with Humphrey Bogart, George Raft and Ann Sheridan.

THEY WERE EXPENDABLE (1945) MGM. Producer, John Ford. Associate Producer, Cliff Reid. Director, John Ford. Author, William L. White. Screenplay, Lieutenant Commander Frank Wead. Musical Score, Herbert Stothart. Art Directors, Cedric Gibbons and Malcolm Browne. Cameraman, Joseph H. August. Special Effects, A. Arnold Gillespie. Editors, Frank E. Hull, Douglass Biggs. Song by Earl Brent and Herbert Stothart: "To the End of the End of the World." 135 minutes

They Were Expendable with John Wayne and Jack Holt.

Lieutenant John Brickley: Robert Montgomery, *Lieutenant (jg) "Rusty" Ryan:* John Wayne, *Lieutenant Sandy Davyss:* Donna Reed, *General Martin:* Jack Holt, *"Boats" Mulcahey:* Ward Bond, *Ensign Snake Gardner:* Marshall Thompson, *Ensign "Andy" Andrews:* Paul Langton, *Major James Morton:* Leon Ames, *Seaman Jones:* Arthur Walsh,

Lieutenant (jg) "Shorty" Long: Donald Curtis, *Ensign George Cross:* Cameron Mitchell, *Ensign Tony Aiken:* Jeff York, *"Slug" Mahan:* Murray Alper, *"Squarehead" Larsen:* Harry Tenbrook, *"Doc" (Storekeeper):* Jack Pennick, *Benny Lecoco:* Alex Havier, *Admiral Blackwell:* Charles Trowbridge, *The General:* Robert Barrat, *Elder Tompkins:* Bruce Kellogg, *Engsign Brown:* Tim Murdock, *Ohio:* Louis Jean Heydt, *Dad Knowland:* Russell Simpson, *The Priest:* Pedro de Cordoba, *Army Doctor (at Corregidor):* Vernon Steele, *Captain at Airport:* Tom Tyler, *Gardner's Girl Friend:* Trina Lowe, *Boat Crew:* Stubby Kruger, Sammy Stein, Blake Edwards, Michael Kirby, *Bartender, Silver Dollar:* Robert Emmett O'Connor, *Army Orderly:* Phillip Ahn, *Filipino Girl Singer:* Pacita Tod-Tod, *Hotel Manager:* William B. Davidson, *Mayor of Cebu:* Max Ong, *Sergeant Smith:* Bill Wilkerson, *Lieutenant James:* John Carlyle, *Officer's Wife:* Betty Blythe, *Officer at Airport:* Kermit Maynard.

THEY WON'T FORGET (1937) WB. Produced and directed by Mervyn LeRoy. Based on the novel *Death in the Deep South* by Ward Greene. Screenplay, Robert Rossen and Aben Kandel. Music and Arrangements, Adolph Deutsch. Music Director, Leo F. Forbstein. Art Director, Robert Haas. Photography, Arthur Edeson and Warren Lynch. Film debuts of Allyn Joslyn and Gloria Dickson. 90 minutes

They Won't Forget with John Ridgely, Elisha Cook, Jr., William Moore (Peter Potter), Jerry Fletcher and Eddie Foster.

Andrew J. Griffin: Claude Rains, *Sybil Hale:* Gloria Dickson, *Robert Hale:* Edward Norris, *Gleason:* Otto Kruger, *Bill Brock:* Allyn Joslyn, *Mary Clay:* Lana Turner, *Imogene Mayfield:* Linda Perry, *Joe Turner:* Elisha Cook, Jr., *Det. Laneart:* Cy Kendall, *Tump Redwine:* Clinton Rosemond, *Carlisle P. Buxton:* E. Alyn Warren, *Mrs. Hale:* Elisabeth Risdon, *Jim Timberlake:* Clifford Soubier, *Det. Pindar:* Granville Bates, *Mrs. Mountford:* Ann Shoemaker, *Governor Mountford:* Paul Everton, *Harmon Drake:* Donald Briggs, *Mrs. Clay:* Sybil Harris, *Fred, Drug Clerk:* Eddie Acuff, *Bill Price:* Frank Faylen, *Foster:* Raymond Brown, *Judge Moore:* Leonard Mudie, *Shattuck Clay:* Trevor Bardette, *Luther Clay:* Eliott Sullivan, *Ransome Clay:* Wilmer Hines, *Briggs:* John Dilson, *Tucker:* Frank Rasmussen, *First Veteran:* Harry Davenport, *Second Veteran:* Harry Beresford, *Third Veteran:* Edward McWade, *Mrs. Timberlake:* Adele St. Maur, *First Detective:* Thomas Jackson, *Second Detective:* George Lloyd, *Dolly Holly:* Claudia Coleman, *Flannigan:* Owen King, *Stout Lady:* Maidel Turner, *Harrison (Young Juror):* Robert Porterfield, *Hazel:* Psyche Nibert, *Police Captain:* Howard Mitchell, *Pool Players:* John Ridgely, Bill Moore (Peter Potter), Jerry Fletcher, Eddie Foster.

THE THIEF (1952) UA. Producer, Clarence Greene. Director, Russell Rouse. Screenplay by Clarence Greene and Russell Rouse. Music by Herschel Gilbert. Filmed without dialogue. 85 minutes

Allan Fields: Ray Milland, *Mr. Bleek:* Martin Gabel, *The Girl:* Rita Gam, *Harris:* Harry Bronson, *Dr. Linstrum:* John McKutcheon, *Miss Philips:* Rita Vale, *Beal:* Rex O'Malley, *Walters:* Joe Conlin.

The Thief with Ray Milland.

THE THIN MAN (1934) MGM. Produced by Hunt Stromberg. Directed by W. S. Van Dyke. From the novel by Dashiell Hammett. Screenplay by Albert Hackett, Frances Goodrich. Film Editor, Robert J. Kern. Photographer, James Wong Howe. Recording Engineer, Douglas Shearer. Assistant Director, Les Selander. Art Director, Cedric Gibbons. Associate Art Directors, David Townesend, Edwin B. Willis. Costumes, Dolly Tree. Musical Numbers, Dr. William Axt. 93 minutes

The Thin Man with Myrna Loy, William Powell, Porter Hall and Minna Gombell.

Nick: William Powell, *Nora:* Myrna Loy, *Dorothy Wynant:* Maureen O'Sullivan, *Guild:* Nat Pendleton, *Mimi:* Minna Gombell, *McCauley:* Porter Hall, *Andrew:* Henry Wodsworth, *Gilbert:* William Henry, *Nunheim:* Harold Huber, *Chris:* Cesar Romero, *Julia:* Natalie Moorhead, *Morelli:* Edward Brophy, *First Reporter:* Thomas Jackson, *Mrs. Jorgenson:* Ruth Channing, *Wynant:* Edward Ellis, *Marion:* Gertrude Short, *Quinn:* Clay Clement, *Tanner:* Cyril Thornton, *Bill:* Robert E. Homans, *Dr. Walton:* Raymond Brown, *Taxi Driver:* Douglas Fowley, *Taxi Driver:* Sherry Hall, *Headwaiter:* Fred Malatesta, *Waiters:* Rolfe Sedan, Leo White, *Stutsy:* Walter Long, *Apartment Clerk:* Kenneth Gibson, *Stenographer:* Tui Lorraine, *Foster:* Bert Roach, *Tefler:* Huey White, *Reporter:* Creighton Hale, *Police Captain:* Ben Taggart, *Fight Manager:* Charles Williams, *Detective:* Garry Owen.

THIRTY SECONDS OVER TOKYO (1944) MGM. Produced by Sam Zimbalist. Directed by Mervyn LeRoy. Based on the book and story by Ted W. Lawson and Robert Considine. Screenplay, Dalton Trumbo. Music, Herbert Stothart. Editor, Frank Sullivan. Song by Art and Kay Fitch and Bert Lowe: "Sweetheart of All My Dreams." Film debut of Steve Brodie, 24. 138 minutes

Thirty Seconds Over Tokyo with Douglas Cowan, Don DeFore, Van Johnson, John R. Reilly and Robert Mitchum.

Lieutenant Colonel James H. Doolittle: Spencer Tracy, *Ted Lawson:* Van Johnson, *David Thatcher:* Robert Walker, *Ellen Jones Lawson:* Phyllis Thaxter, *Dean Davenport:* Tim Murdock, *Davey Jones:* Scott McKay, *Bob Clever:* Gordon McDonald, *Charles McClure:* Don DeFore, *Bob Gray:* Robert Mitchum, *Shorty Manch:* John R. Reilly, *Doc White:* Horace (Stephen) McNally, *Lieutenant Randall:* Donald Curtis, *Lieutenant Miller:* Louis Jean Heydt, *Don Smith:* William "Bill" Phillips, *Brick Holstrom:* Douglas Cowan, *Captain Ski York:* Paul Langton, *Lieutenant Jurika:* Leon Ames, *General:* Moroni Olsen, *Young Chung:* Benson Fong, *Old Chung:* Dr. Hsin Kung Chuan Chi, *Girls in Officer's Club:* Myrna Dell, Peggy Maley, Hazel Brooks, Elaine Shepard, Kay Williams, *Jane:* Dorothy Ruth Morris, *Mrs. Parker:* Ann Shoemaker, *Mr. Parker:* Alan Napier, *Foo Ling:* Wah Lee, *Guerrilla Charlie:* Ching Wah Lee, *Emmy York:* Jacqueline White, *Dick Joyce:* Jack McClendon, *Pilot:* John Kellogg, *Spike Henderson:* Peter Varney, *M. P.:* Steve Brodie, *Captain Halsey:* Morris Ankrum, *Mrs. Jones:* Selena Royle, *Judge:* Harry Hayden, *Second Officer:* Blake Edwards, *Hoss Wyler:* Will Walls, *Hallmark:* Jay Norris, *Jig White:* Robert Bice, *Bud Felton:* Bill Williams, *Sailor:* Wally Cassell.

THIS ABOVE ALL (1942) 20th. Producer, Darryl F. Zanuck. Director, Anatole Litvak. Based on the novel by Eric Knight. Screenplay, R. C. Sheriff. Art Director, Thomas Little. Cameraman, Arthur Miller. Editor, Walter Thompson. 110 minutes

This Above All with Philip Merivale, Joan Fontaine, Tyrone Power, Thomas Mitchell.

Clive: Tyrone Power, *Prudence:* Joan Fontaine, *Monty:* Thomas Mitchell, *General Cathaway:* Henry Stephenson, *Ramsbottom:* Nigel Bruce, *Iris:* Gladys Cooper, *Roger:* Philip Merivale, *Waitress in Tea Room:* Sara Allgood, *Rector:* Alexander Knox, *Violet:* Queenie Leonard, *Wilbur:* Melville Cooper, *Nurse Emily:* Jill Esmond, *Chaplain:* Arthur Shields, *Parsons:* Dennis Hoey, *Major:* Miles Mander, *Sergeant:* Rhys Williams, *Joe:* John Abbott, *Maid:* Carol Curtis-

Brown, *Maid:* Mary Field, *Rosie:* Lilyan Irene, *Dr. Mathias:* Holmes Herbert, *Dr. Ferris:* Denis Green, *Vicar:* Thomas Louden, *Vicar's Wife:* Mary Forbes, *Proprietor:* Forrester Harvey, *Conductor:* Harold de Becker, *Matron:* Jessica Newcombe, *Farmer:* Billy Bevan, *Mae (Singer):* Brenda Forbes, *Sergeant:* Doris Lloyd, *Porter:* Alan Edmiston, *Soldier:* Morton Lowry, *Proprietor:* Olaf Hytten.

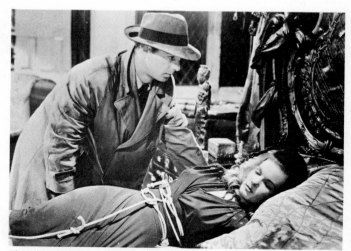

This Gun for Hire with Alan Ladd and Veronica Lake.

THIS GUN FOR HIRE (1942) Par. Produced by Richard M. Blumenthal. Directed by Frank Tuttle. Based on the novel by Graham Greene. Screenplay, Albert Maltz and W. R. Burnett. Photography, John Seitz. Editor, Archie Marshek. Songs by Frank Loesser and Jacques Press: "I've Got You" and "Now You See It." Cut was a dream sequence in which Dickie Jones played Raven as a boy and Hermine Sterler played his aunt. Remade by Paramount as *Short Cut to Hell*, 1957. 80 minutes

Ellen Graham: Veronica Lake, *Michael Crane:* Robert Preston, *Willard Gates:* Laird Cregar, *Raven:* Alan Ladd, *Alvin Brewster:* Tully Marshall, *Sluky:* Mikhail Rasumny, *Tommy:* Marc Lawrence, *Annie:* Pamela Blake, *Steve Finnerty:* Harry Shannon, *Albert Baker:* Frank Ferguson, *Baker's Secretary:* Bernadene Hayes, *Blair Fletcher:* Olin Howland, *Senator Burnett:* Roger Imhof, *Ruby:* Patricia Farr, *Night Watchman:* James Farley, *Crippled Girl:* Virita Campbell, *Brewster's Secretary:* Victor Kilian, *Police Captain:* Charles C. Wilson, *Salesgirl:* Mary Davenport, *Mr. Collins:* Earle Dewey, *Gates' Secretary:* Lynda Grey, *Charlie, Cop:* Emmett Vogan, *Mr. Stewart, Rooming House Manager:* Chester Clute, *Will Gates, Dressmaker:* Charles Arnt, *Lieutenant Clark:* Dick Rush, *Scissor Grinder:* Clem Bevans, *Restaurant Manager:* Harry Hayden, *Weems, Guard:* Tim Ryan, *Police Captain:* Edwin Stanley, *Officer Glennon:* Elliott Sullivan, *Mrs. Mason:* Sarah Padden, *Piano Player:* Don Barclay, *Young Man:* Richard Webb, *Keever:* John Sheehan, *Frog:* Alan Speer, *Waiter:* Cyril Ring, *Walt:* Fred Walburn, *Jimmie:* Robert Winkler, *Special Dancer at Neptune Club:* Yvonne De Carlo.

This Is the Army with George Murphy.

THIS IS THE ARMY (1943) WB. Warner. Producers, Jack L. Warner, Hal B. Wallis. Director, Michael Curtiz. Color by Technicolor. Author, Irving Berlin. Screenplay, Casey Robinson, Captain Claude Binyon. Technicolor Director, Natalie Kalmus. Art Directors, Lieutenant John Loenig, John Hughes. Musical Director, Leo F. Forbstein. Cameramen, Bert Glennon, Sol Polito. Special Effects, Jack Cosgrove. Editor, George Amy. Songs by Irving Berlin: "This Is the Army, Mr. Jones," "The Army's Made a Man Out of Me," "Mandy," "I'm Getting Tired So I Can Sleep," "What the Well-Dressed Man in Harlem Will Wear," "Give a Cheer for the Navy," "I Left My Heart at the Stage Door Canteen," "American Eagles," "Oh, How I Hate to Get Up in the Morning," "Poor Little Me I'm on K. P." and "God Bless America." 121 minutes

Himself: Irving Berlin, *Jerry Jones:* George Murphy, *Eileen Dibble:* Joan Leslie, *Maxie Stoloff:* George Tobias, *Sergeant McGee:* Alan Hale, *Eddie Dibble:* Charles Butterworth, *Ethel:* Rosemary De Camp, *Mrs. Davidson:* Dolores Costello, *Rose Dibble:* Una Merkel, *Major Davidson:* Stanley Ridges, *Mrs. O'Brien:* Ruth Donnelly, *Mrs. Nelson:* Dorothy Peterson, *Kate Smith:* Herself, *Cafe Singer:* Frances Langford, *Singer:* Gertrude Niesen, *Johnny Jones:* Lieutenant Ronald Reagan, *Joe Louis:* Sergeant Joe Louis, *Soldiers:* 1st Sergeant Allan Anderson, M/Sergeant Ezra Stone, *Tommy:* T/Sergeant Tom D'Andrea, *Soldier:* Sergeant Ross Elliott, *Ollie:* Sergeant Julie Oshins, *Ted Nelson:* Sergeant Robert Shanley, *Soldier:* Sergeant Philip Truex, *Danny Davidson:* Corporal Herbert Anderson, *Blake Nelson:* Sergeant Fisher, *Soldiers:* The Allon Trio, Corporal James MacColl, *Mrs. Twardofsky:* Ika Gruning, *Soldier on Cot:* Doodles Weaver, *Waiter:* Irving Bacon, *Old Timer's Wife:* Leah Baird, *Sports Announcer:* Warner Anderson, *Franklin D. Roosevelt:* Captain Jack Young, *Camp Cook Soldiers:* Frank Coghlan Jr. John Daheim, *Father of Soldier:* Victor Moore, *Father of Soldier:* Ernest Truex, *Mike Nelson:* Jackie Brown, *Marie Twardofsky:* Patsy Moran, *Doorman:* James Conlin.

THOROUGHLY MODERN MILLIE (1967) Univ. Produced by Ross Hunter. Directed by George Roy Hill. Color by Technicolor. Original Screenplay by Richard Morris. Music composed and directed by Elmer Bernstein. Musical number arranged and conducted by Andre Previn, supervised by Joseph Gershenson. Choreography by Joe Layton. Costumes, Jean Louis. Art Directors, Alexander Golitzen and George Webb. Sets, Howard Bristol. Assistant Director, Douglas Green. Production Manager, Ernest B. Wehmeyer. Photography, Russell Metty. Editor, Stuart Gilmore. Sound, Waldon O. Watson, William Russell, and Ronald Pierce. Songs: "Thoroughly Modern Millie" and "Tapioca" by James Van Heusen and Sammy Cahn; "Jimmy" by Jay Thompson; "The Jewish Wedding Song" (Trinkt Le Chaim) by Sylvia Neufeld; Standards: "Baby Face," "Do It Again," "Poor Butterfly," "Stumbling," "Japanese Sandman," "Jazz Baby," "Rose of Washington Square." 138 minutes

Millie Dillmount: Julie Andrews, *Dorothy Brown:* Mary Tyler Moore, *Muzzy Van Hossmere:* Carol Channing, *Jimmy Smith:* James Fox, *Trevor Graydon:* John Gavin, *Mrs. Meers:* Beatrice Lillie, *Number*

Thoroughly Modern Millie with Julie Andrews, James Fox and Carol Channing.

One: Jack Soo, *Number Two:* Pat Morita, *Tea:* Philip Ahn, *Miss Flannery:* Cavada Humphrey, *Juarez:* Anthony Dexter, *Cruncher:* Lou Nova, *Baron Richter:* Michael St. Clair, *Adrian:* Albert Carrier, *Gregory Huntley:* Victor Rogers, *Judith Tremaine:* Lizabeth Hush, *Taxi Driver:* Herbie Faye, *Singer:* Ann Dee, *Waiter:* Benny Rubin, *Woman in Office:* Mae Clarke.

THOSE MAGNIFICENT MEN IN THEIR FLYING MACHINES OR HOW I FLEW FROM LONDON TO PARIS IN 25 HOURS AND 11 MINUTES (1965) 20th. Producer, Stan Margulies. Associate Producer, Jack Davies. Director, Ken Annakin. Screenplay, Jack Davies, Ken Annakin. Music, Ron Goodwin. Director of Photography, Christopher Challis. Costumes, Osbert Lancaster. Assistant Director, Clive Reed. In Todd-AO and De Luxe Color. 152 minutes

Those Magnificent Men in Their Flying Machines with Karl Michael Vogler and Gert Frobe.

Orvil Newton: Stuart Whitman, *Patricia Rawnsley:* Sarah Miles, *Richard Mays:* James Fox, *Count Emilio Ponticelli:* Alberto Sordi, *Lord Rawnsley:* Robert Morley, *Col. Manfried Von Holstein:* Gert Frobe, *Pierre Dubois:* Jean-Pierre Cassel, *Courtney:* Eric Sykes, *Sir Percy Ware-Armitage:* Terry-Thomas, *Brigitte, Ingrid, Marlene, François, Yvette, Betty:* Irina Demich, *Fire Chief Perkins:* Benny Hill, *Yamamoto:* Yujiro Ishihara, *Mother Superior:* Flora Robson, *Capt. Rumpelstrosse:* Karl Michael Vogler, *George Gruber:* Sam Wanamaker, *Neanderthal Man:* Red Skelton, *French Postman:* Eric Barker, *Elderly Colonel:* Fred Emney, *McDougal:* Gordon Jackson, *Jean:* Davy Kaye, *French Painter:* John LeMesurier, *Lieutenant Parsons:* Jeremy Lloyd, *Sophia Ponticelli:* Zena Marshall, *Airline Hostess:* Millicent Martin, *Italian Mayor:* Eric Pohlman, *Waitress in Old Mill:* Marjorie Rhodes, *Tremayne Gascoyne:* William Rushton, *Niven:* Michael Trubshawe, *Popperwell:* Tony Hancock.

Thousands Cheer with Gene Kelly, John Boles and Kathryn Grayson.

THOUSANDS CHEER (1943) MGM. Producer, Joseph Pasternak. Director, George Sidney. Technicolor. Based on the story "Private Miss Jones" by Paul Jarrico, Richard Collins. Screenplay, Paul Jarrico, Richard Collins. Musical Director, Herbert Stothart. Art Director, Cedric Gibbons. Songs by Ferde Grofe, Harold Adamson, Lew Brown, Ralph Freed, Burton Lane, Walter Jurmann, Paul Francis Webster, Earl Brent, E. Y. Harburg, Dmitri Shostakovitch, Harold Rome. Cameraman, George Folsey. Editor, George Boemler. Musical numbers: "The Joint Is Really Jumping" by Ralph Blane and Hugh Martin; "I Dug a Ditch in Wichita" by Ralph Freed and Burton Lane; "Three Letters in the Mailbox" by Paul Francis Webster and Walter Jurmann; "Let There Be Music" by E. Y. Harburg and Earl Brent; "Daybreak" by Harold Adamson and Ferde Grofe; "Honeysuckle Rose" by Andy Razaf and Fats Waller; "United Nations on the March" by E. Y. Harburg, Harold Rome and Herbert Stothart; "Carnegie Hall" by Ralph Blane, Hugh Martin and Roger Edens; "Just as Long as I Know Katie's Waitin'" by George R. Brown and Lew Brown; "I'm Lost You're Lost" and "Why Don't We Try?" by Walter Ruick. 126 minutes

Kathryn Jones: Kathryn Grayson, *Eddie Marsh:* Gene Kelly, *Hyllary Jones:* Mary Astor, *José:* José Iturbi, *Colonel Jones:* John Boles, *Captain Avery:* Dick Simmons, *Chuck:* Ben Blue, *Sergeant Koslack:* Frank Jenks, *Alan:* Frank Sully, *Jack:* Wally Cassell, *Silent Monk:* Ben Lessy, *Marie:* Frances Rafferty, *Helen:* Mary Elliott, *Mama Corbino:* Odette Myrtil, *Papa Corbino:* Will Kaufman, *Themselves:* Kay Kyser Orchestra, *Announcer:* Lionel Barrymore, *Girl at Station:* Betty Jaynes, *Uncle Algy:* Sig Arno, *Taxicab Driver:* Connie Gilchrist, *Woman:* Bea Nigro, *Maid:* Daisy Buford, *Alex:* Pierre Watkin, *Specialty Dancer:* Paul Speer, *Soldiers:* Myron Healey, Don Taylor, *Ringmaster:* Ray Teal, *Sergeant Major:* Carl Saxe, *Lieutenant Colonel Brand:* Bryant Washburn, Jr., *Capt. Haines:* Harry Strang, *Mother at Station:* Florence Turner, *Guests:* Donna Reed, Marilyn Maxwell, Margaret O'Brien, June Allyson, Gloria DeHaven, Mickey Rooney, Judy Garland, Red Skelton, Eleanor Powell, Virginia O'Brien, José Iturbi and the MGM Orchestra and the Chorus of United Nations, Bob Crosby and His Orchestra, Lena Horne with Benny Carter and His Orchestra, and Don Loper and Maxine Barrat and *Frank Morgan Sketch: The Barber,* Frank Morgan, *First Girl,* Ann Sothern, *Second Girl,* Lucille Ball, *Third Girl,* Connie Gilchrist, *Fourth Girl,* Marsha Hunt, *New Nurse,* Sara Haden, *First Nurse,* Marta Linden, *Doctor,* John Conte.

THREE COINS IN THE FOUNTAIN (1954) 20th. Producer, Sol C. Siegel. Director, Jean Negulesco. CinemaScope, De Luxe Color. From a novel by John H. Secondari. Screenplay, John Patrick. Art Directors, Lyle Wheeler, John De Cuir. Cinematographer, Milton Krasner. Editor, William Reynolds, Remade as *The Pleasure Seekers* (20th, 1964). 102 minutes

Shadwell: Clifton Webb, *Miss Francis:* Dorothy McGuire, *Anita:* Jean Peters, *Prince Dino Di Cessi:* Louis Jourdan, *Maria:* Maggie McNamara, *Georgio:* Rossano Brazzi, *Burgoyne:* Howard St. John, *Mrs. Burgoyne:* Kathryn Givney, *Principessa:* Cathleen Nesbitt, *Dr. Martinelli:* Vincent Padula, *Bartender:* Mario Siletti, *Waiter:*

Three Coins in the Fountain with Maggie McNamara, Louis Jourdan and Cathleen Nesbitt.

Alberto Morin, *Headwaiter:* Dino Bolognese, *Venice Waiter:* Tony De Mario, *Consulate Clerk:* Jack Mattis, *Mr. Hoyt:* Willard Waterman, *Ticket Agent (Theatrical):* Zachary Yaconelli, *Baroness:* Celia Lovsky, *Waiter (Select Restaurant):* Larry Arnold, *Anna:* Renata Vanni, *Maid (Louisa):* Grazia Narcisso, *Butler:* Gino Corrado, *Women:* Iphigenie Castiglioni, Norma Varden, *Girl:* Merry Anders, *Chauffeur:* Charles La Toree.

THREE COMRADES (1938) MGM. Producer, Joseph L. Mankiewicz. Director, Frank Borzage. From the novel by Erich Maria Remarque. Screenplay, F. Scott Fitzgerald, Edward E. Paramore. Montage, Slavko Vorkapich. Art Director, Cedric Gibbons. Cameraman, Joseph Ruttenberg. Editor, Frank Sullivan. Songs by Chet Forrest, Bob Wright and Franz Waxman: "Yankee Ragtime College Jazz," "Comrade Song," "How Can I Leave Thee" and "Mighty Forest." 100 minutes

Three Comrades with Robert Young, Robert Taylor, Margaret Sullavan and Franchot Tone.

Erich Lohkamp: Robert Taylor, *Pat Hollmann:* Margaret Sullavan, *Otto Koster:* Franchot Tone, *Gottfried Lenz:* Robert Young, *Alfons:* Guy Kibbee, *Franz Freuer:* Lionel Atwill, *Dr. Heinrich Becker:* Henry Hull, *Dr. Plauten:* George Zucco, *Local Doctor:* Charley Grapewin, *Dr. Jaffe:* Monty Woolley, *Herr Schultz:* Spencer Charters, *Frau Schultz:* Sarah Padden, *Burgomaster:* Ferdinand Munier, *Owner of Wrecked Car:* Morgan Wallace, *Adolph:* George Offerman, Jr., *Tony:* Leonard Penn, *Frau Brunner:* Priscilla Lawson, *Frau Schmidt:* Esther Muir, *Adjutant:* Walter Bonn, *Major Domo:* Edward McWade, *Man with Patch:* Henry Brandon, *Bald-headed Man:* Harvey Clark, *Singer:* Alva Kellogg, *First Comic:* George Chandler, *Second Comic:* Ralph Bushman (Francis X. Bushman, Jr.) *Kid:* Donald Haines, *Eldest Vogt Man:* Norman Willis, *Younger Vogt Man:* William Haade, *Frau Zalewska:* Claire McDowell, *Rita:* Barbara Bedford, *Boris:* Mitchell Lewis, *Old Woman:* Marjorie Main, *Nurse:* Jessie Arnold, *Becker's Assistant:* Roger Converse, *Housekeeper:* Ricca Allen, *Bookstore Owner:* E. Alyn Warren.

THREE LITTLE WORDS (1950) MGM. Producer, Jack Cummings. Director, Richard Thorpe. Color by Technicolor. Screenplay, George Wells. Musical Director, Andre Previn. Art Directors, Cedric Gibbons, Urie McCleary. Photography, Harry Jackson. Editor, Ben Lewis. Songs by Kalmar and Ruby and collaborators: "Where Did You Get That Girl?" (With Harry Puck); "Come On Papa" (Edgar Leslie); "Thinking of You"; "Nevertheless"; "She's Mine All Mine"; "My Sunny Tennessee" (with Herman Ruby); "Three Little Words"; "So Long Oo-Long"; "Who's Sorry Now?" (with Ted Snyder); "All Alone Monday"; "I Wanna Be Loved by You"; "Hooray for Captain Spaulding"; and "I Love You So Much." Choreography, Hermes Pan. Anita Ellis sings for Vera-Ellen. 102 minutes

Bert Kalmar: Fred Astaire, *Harry Ruby:* Red Skelton, *Jessie Brown Kalmar:* Vera-Ellen, *Eileen Percy:* Arlene Dahl, *Charlie Kope:* Keenan

Three Little Words with Red Skelton, Fred Astaire and Vera-Ellen.

Wynn, *Terry Lordel:* Gale Robbins, *Mrs. Carter De Haven:* Gloria De Haven, *Phil Regan:* Himself, *Clanahan:* Harry Shannon, *Helen Kane:* Debbie Reynolds, *Al Masters:* Paul Harvey, *Dan Healy:* Carleton Carpenter, *Al Schacht:* George Metkovich, *Mendoza the Great:* Harry Mendoza, *Boy:* Billy Gray, *Coach:* Pat Flaherty, *Philip Goodman:* Pierre Watkin, *Barker:* Syd Saylor, *Negro Boy:* Elzie Emanuel, *Pianist:* Sherry Hall, *Assistant:* Pat Williams, *Waiter:* Charles Wagenheim, *Kid:* Tony Taylor, *Mother:* Phyllis Kennedy, *Stage Manager:* Donald Kerr, *Francesca Ladovan:* Beverly Michaels, *Photographers:* Bert Davidson, William Tannen, *Director:* George Sherwood, *Guest Piano Player:* Harry Barris, *Marty Collister:* Alex Gerry.

THE THREE MUSKETEERS (1948) MGM. Producer, Pandro S. Berman. Director, George Sidney. Color by Technicolor. Based on Alexandre Dumas' novel. Screenplay, Robert Ardrey. Musical Director, Herbert Stothart. Art Directors, Cedric Gibbons, Malcolm Brown. Photography, Robert Planck. Editor, Robert J. Kern. Songs by Walter Bullock and Samuel Pokrass: "Viola," "My Lady" and "Song of the Musketeers." 125 minutes

The Three Musketeers with Vincent Price and Gene Kelly.

Milady Countess DeWinter: Lana Turner, *D'Artagnan:* Gene Kelly, *Constance Bonacieux:* June Allyson, *Athos:* Van Heflin, *Queen Anne:* Angela Lansbury, *Louis XIII:* Frank Morgan, *Richelieu:* Vincent Price, *Planchet:* Keenan Wynn, *Duke of Buckingham:* John Sutton, *Porthos:* Gig Young, *Aramis:* Robert Coote, *Treville:* Reginald Owen, *Rochefort:* Ian Keith, *Kitty:* Patricia Medina, *Albert:* Richard Stapley, *Bonacieux:* Byron Foulger, *Jussac:* Sol Gorss, *Count DeWardes:* Richard Simmons, *D'Artagnan, Sr.:* Robert Warwick, *Grimaud:* Wm. "Bill" Phillips, *Bazin:* Albert Morin, *Mousqueton:* Norman Leavitt, *Dark-eyed Girl:* Marie Windsor, *Mother:* Ruth Robinson, *First Traveler:* Tom Tyler, *First Friend:* Kirk Alyn, *Second Friend:* John Holland, *Subaltern:* Reginald Sheffield, *Landlord:* William Ed-

munds, *Landlord's Wife:* Irene Seidner, *Fisherman:* Francis McDonald, *Major Domo:* Paul Maxey, *Dragon Rouge Host:* Arthur Hohl, *Guard:* Gil Perkins, *Executioner:* Mickey Simpson.

THREE SMART GIRLS (1936) Univ. Produced by Joseph Pasternak. Executive Producer, Charles R. Rogers. Directed by Henry Koster. Story by Adele Comandini. Camera, Joseph Valentine. Music Director, Charles Previn. Screenplay, Adele Comandini and Austin Parker. Editor, Ted Kent. Songs by Gus Kahn, Walter Jurmann, Bronislau Kaper: "My Heart Is Singing," "Someone to Care for Me." Feature debut of Deanna Durbin. 86 minutes

Three Smart Girls with Deanna Durbin, Barbara Read, Charles Winninger and Nan Grey.

Donna Lyons: Binnie Barnes, *Mrs. Lyons:* Alice Brady, *Lord Michael Stuart:* Ray Milland, *Judson Craig:* Charles Winninger, *Count Arisztid:* Mischa Auer, *Joan Craig:* Nan Grey, *Kay Craig:* Barbara Read, *Penny Craig:* Deanna Durbin, *Binns:* Ernest Cossart, *Wilbur Lamb:* Hobart Cavanaugh, *Bill Evans:* John King, *Trudel:* Lucile Watson, *Dorothy Craig:* Nella Walker.

THREE SMART GIRLS GROW UP (1939) Univ. Produced by Joe Pasternak. Directed by Henry Koster. Screenplay by Bruce Manning and Felix Jackson. Camera, Joe Valentine. Editor, Ted Kent. Sequel to *Three Smart Girls*, 1936. 87 minutes

Penny Craig: Deanna Durbin, *Judson Craig:* Charles Winninger, *Joan Craig:* Nan Grey, *Kay Craig:* Helen Parrish, *Harry Loren:* Robert Cummings, *Richard Watkins:* William Lundigan, *Binns:* Ernest Cossart, *Dorothy Craig:* Nella Walker.

THRILL OF A ROMANCE (1945) MGM. Producer, Joe Pasternak. Director, Richard Thorpe. Technicolor. Original Screenplay, Richard

Three Smart Girls Grow Up with Helen Parrish, Robert Cummings, Deanna Durbin and Nan Grey.

Thrill of Romance with Ray Goulding, Lauritz Melchior, Esther Williams, Van Johnson and Ethel Griffies.

Connell, Gladys Lehman. Musical Adaptation-Direction, Georgie Stoll. Art Directors, Cedric Gibbons, Hans Peters. Cameraman, Harry Stradling. Editor, George Boemler. Songs: "Please Don't Say No (Say Maybe)" by Ralph Freed and Sammy Fain; "I Should Care" by Sammy Cahn, Alex Stordahl and Paul Weston; "Lonely Night" by George Stoll and Richard Connell; "Vive L'Amour" by George Stoll, Ralph Blane and Kay Thompson; "Serenade" by Jack Meskill and Earl Brent. Orchestrations, Calvin Jackson, Joseph Nussbaum, Ted Duncan, Hugo Winterhalter, Fred Norman. 105 minutes

Cynthia Glenn: Esther Williams, *Major Thomas Milvaine:* Van Johnson, *Maude Bancroft:* Frances Gifford, *Hobart Glenn:* Henry Travers, *Nona Glemn:* Spring Byington, *Nils Knudsen:* Lauritz Melchior, *Orchestra Leader:* Tommy Dorsey, *Robert G. Delbar:* Carleton Young, *Susan:* Helene Stanley, *K. O. Karny:* Donald Curtis, *Lyonel:* Jerry Scott, *Dr. Tove:* Billy House, *Mrs. Fenway:* Ethel Griffies, *Oscar:* Vince Barnett, *Julio:* Fernando Alvarado, *Betty:* Joan Fay Macoboy, *Gypsy Orchestra Leader:* Carli Elinor, *J. P. Bancroft:* Thurston Hall, *Specialty:* King Sisters, *Chess Player:* Alex Novinsky, Stuart Holmes, *Tycoon:* Pierre Watkin, *Hotel Clerk:* Frank Ferguson, *Naval Ensign:* Tim Murdock, *Ga-Ga Bride:* Jean Porter, *Canadian Fliers:* Douglas Cowan, Henry Daniels, Jr. *Hotel Clerk:* Selmer Jackson, *Mr. Vemmering:* Robert Emmet O'Connor, *Guest at Reception:* Dagmar Oakland, *Johnny:* Tom Brannigan, *Headwaiter:* Arno Frey, *Mr. Carter:* Dick Earle, *Secretary:* Virginia Brissac, *Detective:* Jack Baxley, *Dance Extra:* Ray Goulding.

THUNDERBALL (1965) UA. Producer, Kevin McClory. Director, Terence Young. Director of Photography, Ted Moore. Screenplay, Richard Maibaum, John Hopkins. Based on story by Kevin McClory, Jack Whittingham, Ian Fleming. Assistant Director, Gus Agosti. Costumes. Anthony Mendleson. Music, John Barry. Title song lyrics by Don Black. Sung by Tom Jones. Presented by Albert R. Broccoli, Harry Saltzman. In Panavision and Technicolor. 132 minutes

Thunderball with Sean Connery and Claudine Auger.

James Bond: Sean Connery, *Domino:* Claudine Auger, *Emilio Largo:* Adolfo Celi, *Fiona:* Luciana Paluzzi, *Felix Leiter:* Rik Van Nutter, "*M*": Bernard Lee, *Paula:* Martine Beswick, *Count Lippe:* Guy Doleman, *Patricia:* Molly Peters, "*Q*": Desmond Llewelyn, *Moneypenny:* Lois Maxwell, *Foreign Secretary:* Roland Culver, *Pinder:* Earl Cameron, *Major Derval:* Paul Stassino, *Madame Boitier:* Rose Alba, *Vargas:* Philip Locke, *Kutze:* George Pravda, *Janni:* Michael Brennan, *Group Captain:* Leonard Sachs, *Air Vice Marshal:* Edward Underdown, *Kenniston:* Reginald Beckwith, *Quist:* Bill Cummings, *Mlle. La Porte:* Maryse Guy Mitsouko, *Jacques Boiter:* Bob Simmons.

THUNDERHEAD, SON OF FLICKA (1945) 20th. Producer, Robert Bassler. Director, Louis King. Color by Technicolor. Based on a novel by Mary O'Hara. Screenplay, Dwight Cummins, Dorothy Yost. Art Directors, Lyle Little, Fred J. Rode. Musical Score, Cyril J. Mockridge. Musical Director, Emil Newman. Cameraman, Charles Clarke. Editor, Nick De Maggio. Technicolor Director, Natalie Kalmus. 78 minutes

Thunderhead, Son of Flicka with Roddy McDowall and Preston Foster.

Ken McLaughlin: Roddy McDowall, *Rob McLaughlin:* Preston Foster, *Nelle:* Rita Johnson, *Gus:* James Bell, *Hildy:* Diana Hale, *Major Harris:* Carleton Young, *Mr. Sargent:* Ralph Sanford, *Tim:* Robert Filmer, *Dr. Hicks:* Alan Bridge.

TILL THE CLOUDS ROLL BY (1946) MGM. Producer, Arthur Freed. Director, Richard Whorf. Color by Technicolor. Author, Guy Bolton, Screenplay, Myles Connolly, Jean Halloway. Adaptation, George Wells. Musical Director, Lennie Hayton. Orchestration, Conrad Salinger. Art Director, Cedric Gibbons. Cameramen, Harry Stradling, George J. Folsey. Editor, Albert Akst. Vocal Arrangements, Kay Thompson. Musical numbers staged and directed by Robert Alton. Songs by Jerome Kern (lyricists' names in parentheses): "Make

Till the Clouds Roll By with Dorothy Patrick, Paul Langton and Robert Walker.

Believe" (Oscar Hammerstein II); "Can't Help Lovin' That Man" (Oscar Hammerstein II); "Ol' Man River" (Oscar Hammerstein II); "Till the Clouds Roll By" (P.G. Wodehouse); "How'd You Like to Spoon With Me?" (Edward Laska); "They Didn't Believe Me" (Herbert Reynolds); "The Last Time I Saw Paris" (Oscar Hammerstein II); "I Won't Dance" (Otto Harbach and Oscar Hammerstein II); "Why Was I Born?" (Oscar Hammerstein II); "Smoke Gets in Your Eyes" (Otto Harbach); "Who?" (Otto Harbach and Oscar Hammerstein II); "Look for the Silver Lining" (B.G. DeSylva); "Sunny" (Otto Harbach and Oscar Hammerstein II); "Cleopatterer" (P. G. Wodehouse); "Leave It to Jane" (P.G. Wodehouse); "Go Little Boat" (P.G. Wodehouse); "One More Dance" (Oscar Hammerstein II); "Land Where the Good Songs Go" (P.G. Wodehouse); "Yesterdays" (Otto Harbach); "Long Ago and Far Away" (Ira Gershwin); "A Fine Romance" (Dorothy Fields); "All the Things You Are" (Oscar Hammerstein II); "She Didn't Say Yes (She Didn't Say No)"; (Otto Harbach); and the Polka from the Mark Twain Suite. Judy Garland Numbers directed by Vincente Minnelli. Film debuts of Gower Champion and Sally Forrest. 137 minutes

Jerome Kern: Robert Walker, *Marilyn Miller:* Judy Garland, *Sally:* Lucille Bremer, *Sally as a girl:* Joan Wells, *James I. Hessler:* Van Heflin, *Oscar Hammerstein:* Paul Langton, *Mrs. Jerome Kern:* Dorothy Patrick, *Mrs. Muller:* Mary Nash, *Charles Frohman:* Harry Hayden, *Victor Herbert:* Paul Maxey, *Cecil Keller:* Rex Evans, *Hennessey:* William "Bill" Phillips, *Julie Sanderson:* Dinah Shore, *Bandleader:* Van Johnson, *Guest Stars:* June Allyson, Angela Lansbury, Ray McDonald, *Dance Specialties:* Maurice Kelly, Cyd Charisse, Gower Champion, *Orchestra Conductor:* Ray Teal, *Specialty:* Wilde Twins, *Frohman's Secretary:* Byron Foulger, *Miss Laroche:* Ann Codee, *Producer:* Russell, Hicks, *Director:* William Forest, *Dancer:* Sally Forrest.

SHOWBOAT NUMBER *Captain Andy:* William Halligan, *Ravenal:* Tony Martin, *Magnolia:* Kathryn Grayson, *Ellie:* Virginia O'Brien, *Julie:* Lena Horne, *Joe:* Caleb Peterson, *Steve:* Bruce Cowling.

FINALE Kathryn Grayson, Johnny Johnston, Lucille Bremer, Frank Sinatra, Virginia O'Brien, Lena Horne, Tony Martin.

THE TIME, THE PLACE AND THE GIRL (1946) WB. Producer, Alex Gottlieb. Director, David Butler. Color by Technicolor. Screenplay, Francis Swann, Agnes Christine Johnston and Lynn Starling. Original Story, Leonard Lee. Music, Arthur Schwartz. Orchestral Arrangements, Ray Heindorf. Art Director, Hugh Reticker. Musical Director, Leo F. Forbstein. Cameraman, William V. Skall. Editor, Irene Morra. Songs by Leo Robin and Arthur Schwartz: "A Gal in Calico," "Oh But I Do," "On A Rainy Night in Rio," "Through a Thousand Dreams," "A Solid Citizen of the Solid South" and "I Happened to Walk Down First Street." 105 minutes

Steven Ross: Dennis Morgan, *Jeff Howard:* Jack Carson, *Sue Jackson:* Janis Paige, *Victoria Cassell:* Martha Vickers, *Ladislaus Cassell:* S.Z. "Cuddles" Sakall, *John Braden:* Alan Hale, *Elaine Winters:* Angela Greene, *Martin Drew:* Donald Woods, *Mme. Lucia Cassell:* Florence Bates, and Carmen Cavallaro and Orchestra. *Inez:* Mimi Aguglia

The Time, The Place and the Girl with Dennis Morgan, Jack Carson and Martha Vickers.

Hurst, *Nurse:* Lynne Baggett, *Simpkins (Butler):* Brandon Hurst, *Apartment Manager:* Chester Clute, *First Piano Mover:* George Lloyd, *Second Piano Mover:* Robert Wilbur, *Stage Manager:* Monte Blue, *Elaine's Maid:* Lillian Yarbo, *Tough Urchin:* Donald Davis, *Scrub Woman:* Vera Lewis, *Process Server:* Bert Roach, *Elevator Operator:* Edward Kelly, *Wardrobe Designer:* Sada Brown, *Set Designer:* Richard Kipling, *Bar Patrons:* Jane Harker, Ramsay Ames, *Photographer:* Tom Wells.

TITANIC (1953). 20th. Producer, Charles Brackett. Director, Jean Negulesco. Author, Charles Brackett, Walter Reisch, Richard Breen. Screenplay, Charles Brackett, Walter Reisch, Richard Breen. Art Directors, Lyle Wheeler, Maurice Ransford. Cinematographer, Joe McDonald. Editor, Louis Loeffler. Other versions: *Titanic* (German, 1943); *A Night to Remember* (British, 1958). 98 minutes

Titanic with Clifton Webb and Barbara Stanwyck.

Richard Sturgess: Clifton Webb, *Mrs. Sturgess:* Barbara Stanwyck, *Giff Rogers:* Robert Wagner, *Annette:* Audrey Dalton, *Mrs. Young:* Thelma Ritter, *Captain Smith:* Brian Aherne, *Healey:* Richard Basehart, *Earl Meeker:* Allyn Joslyn, *Sandy Comstock:* James Todd, *John Jacob Astor:* William Johnstone, *Chief Officer Wilde:* Charles FitzSimons, *First Officer Murdock:* Barry Bernard, *Norman:* Harper Carter, *Officer Lightoller:* Edmund Purdon, *Mr. Guggenheim:* Camillo Guercio, *Sanderson:* Antony Eustrel, *Quartermaster:* Alan Marston, *Devlin:* James Lilburn, *Mrs. John Jacob Astor:* Frances Westcott, *Widener:* Guy Standing, Jr., *Mrs. Straus:* Hellen Van Tuyl, *Mr. Isidor Straus:* Roy Gordon, *Mrs. Uzcadum:* Marta Mitrovich, *Emma:* Ivis Goulding, *Bride:* Dennis Fraser, *Phillips:* Ashley Cowan, *Symons:* Lehmer Graham, *College Girls:* Merry Anders, Gloria Gordon, Melinda Markey, *College Boys:* Ronald F. Hagerthy, Conrad Feia, Richard West, *Woman:* Mae Marsh, *Ship Steward:* William Cottrell, *Tailor:* David Hoffman, *Manager:* Gordon Richards, *Steward:* Owen McGiveney, *Junior Officer:* Robin Hughes.

TO CATCH A THIEF (1955) Par. Producer, Alfred Hitchcock. Director, Alfred Hitchcock. VistaVision, Technicolor. Author, David Dodge.

To Catch a Thief with Grace Kelly and Cary Grant.

Screenplay, John Michael Hayes. Art Directors, Hal Pereira, Joseph MacMillan Johnson. Musical Director, Lyn Murray. Cinematographer, Robert Burks. Editor, George Tomasini. Filmed on the Riviera. 97 minutes

John Robie: Cary Grant, *Frances Stevens:* Grace Kelly, *Mrs. Stevens:* Jessie Royce Landis, *H.H. Hughson:* John Williams, *Bertani:* Charles Vanel, *Danielle:* Brigitte Auber, *Foussard:* Jean Martinelli, *Germaine:* Georgette Anys, *Claude:* Roland Lesaffre, *Mercier:* Jean Hebey, *Lepic:* Rene Blancard, *Big Man in Kitchen:* Wee Willie Davis, *Antoinette:* Dominique Davray, *Kitchen Help:* Edward Manouk, *Mr. Sanford:* Russell Gaige, *Mrs. Sanford:* Marie Stoddard, *Vegetable Man in Kitchen:* Paul "Tiny" Newlan, *Man with Milk in Kitchen:* Lewis Charles, *Woman in Kitchen:* Aimee Torriani, *Chef:* Frank Chelland, *Detective:* Don Megowan, *Detective:* John Alderson, *Chef:* Otto F. Schulze, *Monaco Policeman:* Leonard Penn, *Monaco Policeman:* Michael Hadlow, *Jewelry Clerk:* Philip Van Zandt, *Desk Clerk:* Steven Geray, *Elegant French Woman:* Gladys Holland, *Croupier:* Louis Mercier.

TO HAVE AND HAVE NOT (1944) WB. Produced and directed by Howard Hawks. Based on the novel by Ernest Hemingway. Screenplay, Jules Furthman and William Faulkner. Art Director, Charles Novi. Music Director, Leo F. Forbstein. Special Effects, Roy Davidson and Rex Wimpy. Photography, Sid Hickox. Editor, Christian Nyby. Songs by Hoagy Carmichael and Johnny Mercer: "How Little We Know" and "Hong Kong Blues"; also, "Am I Blue?" and "Limehouse Blues." Film debut of Lauren Bacall, 19. Remakes: *The Breaking Point* (WB, 1950), *The Gun Runners* (UA, 1958). 100 minutes

To Have and Have Not with Humphrey Bogart and Walter Brennan.

Harry Morgan: Humphrey Bogart, *Eddie:* Walter Brennan, *Marie Browning:* Lauren Bacall, *Hellene De Bursac:* Dolores Moran, *Cricket:* Hoagy Carmichael, *Paul De Dursac:* Walter Molnar, *Lieut. Coyo:* Sheldon Leonard, *Gerard:* Marcel Dalio, *Johnson:* Walter Sande, *Capt. Renard:* Dan Seymour, *Bodyguard:* Aldo Nadi, *Beauclerc:* Paul Marion, *Mrs. Beauclerc:* Patricia Shay, *Rosalie:* Janette Grae, *Bartender:* Pat West, *Horatio:* Sir Lancelot, *Quartermaster:* Eugene Borden, *Negro Urchins:* Elzie Emanuel, Harold Garrison, *Civilian:* Pedro Regas, *Headwaiter:* Maj. Fred Farrell, *Cashier:* Adrienne d'Ambricourt, *Emil:* Emmett Smith, *DeGaullists:* Maurice Marsao, Fred Dosch, George Suzanne, Louis Mercier, Crane Whitley, *Detective:* Hal Kelly, *Chef:* Chef Joseph Milani, *Naval Ensign:* Ron Randell, *Dancer:* Audrey Armstrong, *Cashier:* Marguerita Sylva.

TO HELL AND BACK (1955) Univ. Produced by Aaron Rosenberg. Directed by Jesse Hibbs. CinemaScope and Technicolor. Based on Audie Murphy's autobiography, *To Hell and Back*. Screenplay, Gil Doud. Music Director, Joseph Gershenson. Art Directors, Alexander Golitzen and Robert Clatworthy. Photography, Maury Gertsman. Editor, Edward Curtiss. 106 minutes

To Hell and Back with Audie Murphy, Paul Langton and Bruce Cowling.

Audie Murphy: Audie Murphy, *Johnson:* Marshall Thompson, *Kerrigan:* Jack Kelly, *Brandon:* Charles Drake, *Valentino:* Paul Picerni, *Lieutenant Manning:* Gregg Palmer, *Lieutenant Lee:* David Janssen, *Kovak:* Richard Castle, *Colonel Howe:* Paul Langton, *Captain Marks:* Bruce Cowling, *Steiner:* Julian Upton, *Thompson:* Denver Pyle, *Swope:* Felix Noriego, *Sanchez:* Art Aragon, *Saunders:* Brett Halsey, *Klasky:* Tommy Hart, *Lieutenant Burns:* Anthony Garcen, *Audie Murphy as a boy:* Gordon Gebert, *Mrs. Murphy:* Mary Field, *Mr. Huston:* Howard Wright, *Mrs. Huston:* Edna Holland, *Helen:* Anabel Shaw, *Maria:* Susan Kohner, *Julia:* Maria Costi, *Carla:* Didi Ramati, *Cleopatra:* Barbara James, *Vincenti:* Joey Costarella, *Lieutenant Harris:* Rand Brooks, *Maria's Mother:* Nan Boardman, *Stack:* Henry Kulky, *M.P.:* John Pickard, *Scottish Soldier:* Ashley Cowan, *Marine Recruit Sergeant:* Don Kennedy, *Chief Petty Officer:* Ralph Sanford, *Truck Driver:* Howard Price, *Rector:* Alexander Campbell, *Dr. Snyder:* Rankin Mansfield, *Corinne:* Madge Meredith, *Soldier:* Mort Mills, *Jim:* John Brayant.

TO KILL A MOCKINGBIRD (1962) Univ. Producer, Alan Pakula. Director, Robert Mulligan. Screenplay, Horton Foote. Based on the novel by Harper Lee. Music, Elmer Bernstein. Costumes, Rosemary Odell. Assistant Director, Joseph Kenny. A Brentwood Productions Picture. Art Directors, Alexander Golitzen and Henry Bumstead. Photography, Russell Harlan. Editor, Aaron Stell. 129 minutes

Atticus Finch: Gregory Peck, *Scout Finch:* Mary Badham, *Jem Finch:* Philip Alford, *Dill Harris:* John Megna, *Sheriff Heck Tate:* Frank Overton, *Miss Maudie Atkinson:* Rosemary Murphy, *Mrs. Dubose:* Ruth White, *Tom Robinson:* Brock Peters, *Calpurnia:* Estelle Evans, *Judge Taylor:* Paul Fix, *Mayella Ewell:* Collin Wilcox, *Bob Ewell:* James Anderson, *Stephanie Crawford:* Alice Ghostley, *Boo Radley:* Robert Duvall, *Gilmer:* William Windom, *Walter Cunningham:* Crahan Denton, *Mr. Radley:* Richard Hale, *Walter Cunningham, Jr.:* Steve Condit, *Rev. Sykes:* Bill Walker, *Dr. Reynolds:* Hugh Sanders, *Jessie:* Pauline Myers, *Spence Robinson:* Jester Hairston, *Hiram Townsend:* Jamie Forster, *School Teacher:* Nancy Marshall, *Helen Robinson:* Kim Hamilton, *Burly Man:* Kelly Thordsen, *Men:* Dan White, Tex Armstrong, *Cecil Jacobs:* Kim Hector, *Tom Robinson, Jr.,*: David Crawford, *School Boy:* Barry Seltzer, *Jury Foreman:* Guy Wilkerson, *Court Clerk:* Charles Fredericks, *Court Reporter:* Jay Sullivan.

To Kill a Mockingbird with Gregory Peck, Collin Wilcox, Paul Fix and Jay Sullivan.

Tom, Dick and Harry with Burgess Meredith, Ginger Rogers and Phil Silvers.

TOM, DICK AND HARRY (1941) RKO. Producer, Robert Sisk. Director, Garson Kanin. Story and Screenplay, Paul Jarrico. Cameraman, Merrit Gerstad. Special Effects, Vernon Walker. Editor, John Sturges. Song by Gene Rose and Roy Webb: "Tom Collins." Remade by RKO as *The Girl Most Likely*, 1957. 86 minutes

Janie: Ginger Rogers, *Tom:* George Murphy, *Dick Hamilton:* Alan Marshal, *Harry:* Burgess Meredith, *Pop:* Joe Cunningham, *Ma:* Jane Seymour, *Babs:* Lenore Lonergan, *Paula:* Vicki Lester, *Ice Cream Man:* Phil Silvers, *Gertrude:* Betty Breckenridge, *Announcer:* Sid Skolsky, *Miss Schlom:* Edna Holland, *Music Store Proprietor:* Gus Glassmire, *Sales Clerk:* Netta Packer, *Mrs. Burton:* Sarah Edwards, *Matron:* Ellen Lowe, *Mr. Burton:* William Halligan, *Judge:* Joe Bernard, *Bridge Matron:* Gertrude Short, *Stalled Car Driver:* Edward Colebrook, *Brenda:* Gayle Mellott, *Gypsy Oracle:* Dorothy Lloyd, *Boy Lead:* Berry Kroeger, *Girl Lead:* Lurene Tuttle, *Radio Announcer:* Knox Manning, *Newsreel Announcer:* William Alland, *Boy:* Jack Briggs.

TOMORROW IS FOREVER (1946) RKO-International. Producer, David Lewis. Director, Irving Pichel. Original, Gwen Bristow. Screenplay, Lenore Coffee. Art Director, Wiard B. Ihnen. Musical Score, Max Steiner. Associate Musical Director, Lou Forbes. Cameraman, Joseph Valentine. Editor, Ernest Nims. Song by Charles Tobias and Max Steiner: "Tomorrow Is Forever." 105 minutes

Tomorrow Is Forever with Lucile Watson, Sonny Howe, Orson Welles, Natalie Wood, George Brent, Richard Long and Claudette Colbert.

Elizabeth (MacDonald) Hamilton: Claudette Colbert, *John MacDonald (Kessler):* Orson Welles, *Larry Hamilton:* George Brent, *Aunt Jessie:* Lucile Watson, *Drew:* Richard Long, *Margaret:* Natalie Wood, *Brian:* Sonny Howe, *Dr. Ludwig:* John Wengraf, *Norton:* Ian Wolfe, *Charles Hamilton:* Douglas Wood, *Cherry:* Joyce MacKenzie, *Pudge:* Tom Wirick, *Butler:* Henry Hastings, *Hamilton's Secretary:* Lane Watson, *Baby Drew:* Michael Ward, *Servant:* Jesse

Graves, *Receptionist:* Lois Austin, *Freckle-faced Nurse:* Anne Loos, *Commentator's Voice:* Irving Pichel, *Englishman on Ship:* Thomas Louden, *Ship's Doctor:* Evan Thomas, *Immigration Officer:* Charles D. Brown, *Postman:* Milton Kibbee, *Maid:* Libby Taylor, *Technician:* Lane Chandler, *Dr. Callan:* Boyd Irwin.

TONY ROME (1967) 20th. Produced by Aaron Rosenberg. Directed by Gordon Douglas. Panavision and De Luxe Color. An Arcola-Millfield Production. Based on the novel *"Miami Mayhem"* by Marvin H. Albert. Screenplay by Richard L. Breen. Music by Billy May. Art Direction, Jack Martin Smith and James Roth. Assistant Director, Richard Lang. Stunt Director, Buzz Henry. Photography, Joseph Biroc. Editor, Robert Simpson. Sound, Howard Warren and David Dockendorf. Song, "Tony Rome" by Lee Hazlewood, sung by Nancy Sinatra. Songs, "Something Here Inside Me" and "Hard Times" by Billy May and Randy Newman. Filmed in Miami. 109 minutes

Tony Rome with Frank Sinatra and Jill St. John.

Tony Rome: Frank Sinatra, *Ann Archer:* Jill St. John, *Lt. Dave Santini:* Richard Conte, *Diana Kosterman Pines:* Sue Lyon, *Rita Neilson Kosterman:* Gena Rowlands, *Rudy Kosterman:* Simon Oakland, *Adam Boyd:* Jeffrey Lynn, *Vic Rood:* Lloyd Bochner, *Ralph Turpin:* Robert J. Wilke, *Georgia MacKay:* Deanna Lund, *Irma:* Elizabeth Fraser, *Fat Candy:* Joan Shawlee, *Donald Pines:* Richard Krisher, *Jules Langley:* Lloyd Gough, *Oscar:* Babe Hart, *Sam Boyd:* Stanley Ross, *Sally Bullock:* Virginia Vincent, *Packy:* Rocky Graziano, *Sal, Maitre D'.* Mike Romanoff, *Catleg:* Shecky Greene, *Lorna:* Jeanne Cooper, *Ruyter:* Harry Davis, *Mrs. Schuyler:* Templeton Fox, *Bartender:* Joe E. Ross, *Card Player:* Jilly Rizzo, *Girl:* Tiffany Bolling.

TOP HAT (1935) RKO. Produced by Pandro S. Berman. Directed by Mark Sandrich. Based on the musical *The Gay Divorcee* by Dwight Taylor, and on a play by Alexander Farago and Aladar Laszlo. Screenplay, Dwight Taylor and Allan Scott. Dances, Fred Astaire. Director of Ensembles, Hermes Pan. Art Directors, Van Nest Polglase and

Top Hat with Ginger Rogers and Fred Astaire.

Carroll Clark. Costumes, Bernard Newman. Photography, David Abel and Vernon Walker. Editor, William Hamilton. Sound, Hugh McDowell, Jr. Songs by Irving Berlin: "Top Hat," "Cheek to Cheek," "The Piccolino," "Isn't It a Lovely Day," "No Strings", "Get Thee Behind Me, Satan." Music Director, Max Steiner. 101 minutes

Jerry Travers: Fred Astaire, *Dale Tremont:* Ginger Rogers, *Horace Hardwick:* Edward Everett Horton, *Madge Hardwick:* Helen Broderick, *Alberto Beddini:* Erik Rhodes, *Bates:* Eric Blore, *Bits:* Ben Holmes, Nick Thompson, Tom Costello, John Impolite, Genaro Spagnoli, Rita Rozelle, Phyllis Coghlan, Charles Hall, *Flower Clerk:* Lucille Ball, *Flower Salesman:* Leonard Mudie, *Curate:* Donald Meek, *Curate's Wife:* Florence Roberts, *Hotel Manager, London:* Edgar Norton, *Hotel Manager, Venice:* Gino Corrado, *Call Boy:* Peter Hobbes.

TOPKAPI (1964) UA. Producer-Director, Jules Dassin. Technicolor. Screenplay, Monja Danischewsky. Based on *The Light of Day* by Eric Ambler. Music, Mano Hadjidakis. Photography, Henri Alekan. Costumes, Denny Vachlioti. Assistant Directors, Tom Pevsner, Joseph Dassin. A Filmways Presentation. Filmed in Istanbul. 120 minutes

Topkapi with Maximilian Schell, Melina Mercouri, Gilles Segal, Peter Ustinov, Jess Hahn and Robert Morley.

Elizabeth Lipp: Melina Mercouri, *Arthur Simpson:* Peter Ustinov, *Walter:* Maximilian Schell, *Cedric Page:* Robert Morley, *Geven:* Akim Tamiroff, *Giulio:* Gilles Segal, *Fischer:* Jess Hahn, *Harback:* Titos Wandis, *Major Tufan:* Ege Ernart, *First Shadow:* Senih Orkan, *Second Shadow:* Ahmet Danyal Topatan, *Josef:* Joseph Dassin, *Nanny:* Amy Dalby, *Voula:* Despo Diamantidou.

TO THE SHORES OF TRIPOLI (1942) 20th. Producer, Darryl F. Zanuck. Associate Producer, Milton Sperling. Director, Bruce Humberstone. Color by Technicolor. Author, Steve Fisher. Screenplay, Lamar Trotti. Cameramen, Edward Cronjager, William Skall, Harry Jackson. Editor, Allen McNeil. Technicolor Director, Natalie Kalmus. 86 minutes

Chris Winters: John Payne, *Second Lieutenant Mary Carter:* Maureen O'Hara, *Dixie Smith:* Randolph Scott, *Helene:* Nancy Kelly, *Johnny:*

To the Shores of Tripoli with Maureen O'Hara, John Payne and Randolph Scott.

William Tracy, *Okay:* Maxie Rosenbloom, *Mouthy:* Henry Morgan, *Butch:* Edmund Mac Donald, *Major Wilson:* Russell Hicks, *Captain Winter:* Minor Watson, *Bill Grady:* Ted North (Michael North), *Barber:* Frank Orth, *Blonde:* Iris Adrian, *Tom Hall:* Alan Hale, Jr., *Joe:* Basil Walker, *Swifty:* Charles Tannen, *Doctor:* Stanley Andrews, *Lieutenant:* Richard Lane, *Corporal:* Gordon Jones, *Corporal:* Gaylord (Steve) Pendleton, *Ensign:* Robert Conway, *Dancer Specialty:* Elena Verdugo, *Bartender:* James C. Morton, *Spanish Girls:* Esther Estrella, Marissa Flores, *Bellboy:* Frank Coghlan, Jr., *Truck Driver:* William Haade, *Pharmacist's Mate:* Walter Sande, *Warden:* James Flavin, *Orderly:* Hugh Beaumont, *Girl:* Hillary Brooke, *Captain:* Byron Shores, *Newscaster:* Knox Manning, *Officer:* Charles Brokaw, *C. P. O.:* Harry Strang, *Chinaman:* Chester Gan, *Radio Operator:* Pat McVey, *Truck Driver:* Frank Sully, *Officer:* Jack Anold.

TOYS IN THE ATTIC (1963) UA. Producer, Walter Mirisch. Director, George Roy Hill. Screenplay, James Poe. Based on the play by Lillian Hellman. Assistant Director, Emmett Emerson. Music, George Duning. Costumes, Bill Thomas. A Mirisch-Claude Production in Panavision. Art Director, Cary Odell. Cinematographer, Joseph F. Biroc. Editor, Stuart Gilmore. 90 minutes

Toys in the Attic with Geraldine Page, Dean Martin and Wendy Hiller.

Julian Berniers: Dean Martin, *Carrie Berniers:* Geraldine Page, *Lily Prine Berniers:* Yvette Mimieux, *Anna Berniers:* Wendy Hiller, *Albertine Prine:* Gene Tierney, *Charlotte Warkins:* Nan Martin, *Cyrus Warkins:* Larry Gates, *Henry:* Frank Silvera, *Gus:* Charles Lampkin.

TRADER HORN (1931) MGM. Directed by W. S. Van Dyke. Based on the 1927 novel by Alfred Aloysius Horn and Ethelreda Lewis. Adaptation, Dale Van Every and John Thomas Neville. Screenplay, Richard Schayer. Dialogue, Cyril Hume. Production Assistant, James McKay. Camera, Clyde De Vinna, assisted by Robert Roberts and George Nogel. Sound, Andrew Anderson. African locations: Nairobi, Lake Victoria, Tanganyika, Uganda, Belgian Congo, Masdini, Butabia, Panyamur, Murchison Falls at Lake Albert, and Kenya. Completed in Hollywood. Made with the cooperation of white hunters Major W. V. D. Dickinson, A. J. Waller, J. H. Barnes, H. R. Stanton. Editor, Ben Lewis. Property Man, Harry Albiez. 123 minutes

Trader Horn with Edwina Booth, Duncan Renaldo and Harry Carey.

Trader Horn: Harry Carey, *Nina Trend:* Edwina Booth, *Peru:* Duncan Renaldo, *Rencharo:* Mutia Omoolu, *Edith Trend:* Olive Fuller Golden (Olive Carey), *Trader:* C. Aubrey Smith.

THE TRAIN (1965) UA. Producer, Jules Bricken. Director, John Frankenheimer. Screen Story and Screenplay, Franklin Coen, Frank Davis. Based on *Le Front de l'Art* by Rose Valland. Directors of Photography, Jean Tournier, Walter Wottitz. Associate Producer, Bernard Farrel. Music, Maurice Jarre. A co-production of Productions Artists Associes, Films Ariane, Dear Films. 133 minutes

Labiche: Burt Lancaster, *Colonel Von Waldheim:* Paul Scofield, *Christine:* Jeanne Moreau, *Papa Boule:* Michel Simon, *Miss Villard:* Suzanne Flon, *Herren:* Wolfgang Preiss, *Von Lubitz:* Richard Munch, *Didont:* Albert Remy, *Pesquet:* Charles Millot, *Jacques:* Jacques Marin, *Spinet:* Paul Bonifas, *Schmidt:* Jean Bouchaud, *Schwartz:* Donal O'Brien, *Octave:* Jean-Pierre Zola, *Pilzer:* Art Brauss, *Major:* Jean-Claude Bercq, *Dietrich:* Howard Vernon, *Bernard:* Bernard La Jarrige, *Priest:* Damiel Lecourtois, *Grote:* Richard Bailey, *Robert:* Christian Fuin, *Gestapo Chief:* Max From, *Tauber:* Christian Remy.

The Train with Michel Simon and Burt Lancaster.

TRAPEZE (1956) UA. Producer, James Hill. Director, Carol Reed. CinemaScope, De Luxe Color. Screenplay by James R. Webb. Adaptation by Liam O'Brien. Assistant Directors, Dick McWhorter, Michel Romanoff and Robert Gendre. Music by Malcolm Arnold. Wardrobe by Frank Salvi and Gladys De Segonzac. A Susan Production. From *The Killing Frost* by Max Catto. Art Director, Rino Mondellini. Photography, Robert Krasker. Editor, Bert Bates. 105 minutes

Mike Ribble: Burt Lancaster, *Tino Orsini:* Tony Curtis, *Lola:* Gina Lollobrigida, *Rosa:* Katy Jurado, *Bouglione:* Thomas Gomez, *Max, The Dwarf:* Johnny Puleo, *John Ringling North:* Minor Watson, *Chikki:* Gerard Landry, *Otto:* J. P. Kerrien, *Snake Man:* Sidney James, *Old Woman:* Gabrielle Fontan, *Paul:* Pierre Tabard, *Stefan:* Gamil Ratab, *Ringmaster:* Michel Thomas.

Trapeze with Gina Lollobrigida, Gerard Landry, Tony Curtis, Katy Jurado, Burt Lancaster and Sidney James.

The Treasure of the Sierra Madre with Alfonso Bedoya and Humphrey Bogart.

THE TREASURE OF THE SIERRA MADRE (1948) WB. Producer, Henry Blanke. Director-Screenplay, John Huston. Based on the novel by B. Traven. Art Director, John Hughes. Musical Director, Leo F. Forbstein. Music, Max Steiner. Photography, Ted McCord. Editor, Owen Marks. Dave Sharpe doubles for Bogart. Filmed in Central Mexico and California's Mojave Desert. 126 minutes

Dobbs: Humphrey Bogart, *Howard:* Walter Huston, *Curtin:* Tim Holt, *Cody:* Bruce Bennett, *McCormick:* Barton MacLane, *Gold Hat:* Alfonso Bedoya, *Presidente:* A. Soto Rangel, *El Jefe:* Manuel Donde, *Pablo:* Jose Torvay, *Pancho:* Margarito Luna, *Flashy Girl:* Jacqueline Dalya, *Mexican Boy:* Bobby Blake, *Proprietor:* Spencer Chan, *Barber:* Julian Rivero, *White Suit:* John Huston, *Bartender:* Harry Vejar, *Customer:* Pat Flaherty, *Men:* Clifton Young, Jack Holt, Ralph Dunn, *Mexican Storekeeper:* Guillermo Calleo, *Mexican Lieutenant:* Roberto Canedo, *First Mexican Bandit:* Ernesto Escoto, *Second Mexican Bandit:* Ignacio Villalbajo, *Railroad Conductor:* Martin Garralaga, *Streetwalker:* Ann Sheridan.

A TREE GROWS IN BROOKLYN (1945) 20th. Producer, Louis D. Lighton. Director, Elia Kazan. Adapted from the novel by Betty Smith. Screenplay, Tess Slesinger, Frank Davis. Musical Score, Alfred Newman. Art Director, Lyle Wheeler. Cameraman, Leon Shamroy. Special Effects, Fred Sersen. Editor, Dorothy Spencer. 128 minutes

Katie: Dorothy McGuire, *Aunt Sissy:* Joan Blondell, *Johnny Nolan:* James Dunn, *McShane:* Lloyd Nolan, *Francie Nolan:* Peggy Ann Garner, *Neeley Nolan:* Ted Donaldson, *McGarrity:* James Gleason, *Miss McDonough:* Ruth Nelson, *Steve:* John Alexander, *Christmas Tree Vendor:* B. S. Pulley, *Grandma Rommely:* Ferike Boros, *Mr. Barker:* Charles Halton, *Sheila:* Patricia McFadden, *Doctor:* Robert Strange, *Street Singer:* Robert Tait, *Boys:* Teddy Infuhr, Mickey Kuhn, *Woman:* Constance Purdy, *Carney (Junk Man):* J. Farrell Macdonald, *Mrs. Waters:* Adeline DeWalt Reynolds, *Mr. Spencer:* George Melford, *Tynmore Sisters:* Mae Marsh, Edna Jackson, *Henny Gaddis:* Vincent Graeff, *Flossie Gaddis:* Susan Lester, *Mr. Crackenbox:* Johnnie Berkes, *Librarian:* Lillian Bronson, *Werner:* Alec Craig, *Cheap Charlie:* Al Bridge, *Hassler:* Joseph J. Greene, *Miss Tilford:* Virginia Brissac, *Herschel:* Harry Harvey, Jr., *Augie:* Robert Anderson, *Ice Man:* Art Smith, *Undertaker:* Erskine Sanford, *Mother:* Martha Wentworth, *Priest:* Francis Pierlot, *Union Representative:* Al Eben, *Floorwalker, 5 and 10:* Harry Seymour.

A Tree Grows in Brooklyn with Adeline de Walt Reynolds and Dorothy McGuire.

Trial with John Hodiak, Glenn Ford, Elisha Cook, Jr., Robert Middleton, Rafael Campos, John Hoyt, Paul Guilfoyle and Dorothy McGuire.

TRIAL (1955) MGM. Producer, Charles Schnee. Associate Producer, James E. Newcom. Director, Mark Robson. Screenplay, Don M. Mankiewicz, from his novel. Art Directors, Cedric Gibbons, Randall Duell. Musical Director, Daniele Amfitheatrof. Cinematographer, Robert Surtees. Editor, Albert Akst. 105 minutes

David Blake: Glenn Ford, *Abbe Nyle:* Dorothy McGuire, *Barney Castle:* Arthur Kennedy, *John J. Armstrong:* John Hodiak, *Consuela Chavez:* Katy Jurado, *Angel Chavez:* Rafael Campos, *Judge Theodore Motley:* Juano Hernandez, *A.S. "Fats" Sanders:* Robert Middleton, *Ralph Castillo:* John Hoyt, *Cap Grant:* Paul Guilfoyle, *Finn:* Elisha Cook, Jr., *Gail Wiltse:* Ann Lee, *Sam Wiltse:* Whit Bissell, *Dr. Schacter:* Richard Gaines, *Jim Backett:* Barry Kelley, *Canford:* Frank Cady, *Bailiff:* Charles Tannen, *County Clerk:* David Leonard, *Assistant District Attorney:* John Rosser, *Minister:* James Todd, *Butteridge:* Sheb Wooley, *Mrs. Webson:* Charlotte Lawrence, *Youval:* Percy Helton, *Mrs. Ackerman:* Dorothy Green, *Dean:* Everett Glass, *Terry Bliss:* Grandon Rhodes, *Lawyer #1:* Charles Evans, *Lawyer #2:* Frank Wilcox, *Checker:* Wilson Wood, *Abbott:* Robert Bice, *Benedict:* John Maxwell, *Pine:* Michael Dugan, *Dr. Abraham Tenfold:* Vince Townsend, *Kiley:* Frank Ferguson, *Reporters:* Robert Forrest, Mort Mills, *Lew Bardman:* Rodney Bell, *Johnson:* Richard Tyler, *Jury Foreman:* Mitchell Lewis.

Trouble in Paradise with Kay Francis, Herbert Marshall and Miriam Hopkins.

TROUBLE IN PARADISE (1932) Par. Produced and directed by Ernst Lubitsch. From the play *The Honest Finder* by Laszlo Aladar. Screenplay, Grover Jones and Samson Raphaelson. Photography, Victor Milner. Songs by W. Franke Harling and Leo Robin: "Trouble in Paradise," "Colet and Company." 83 minutes

Lily Vautier: Miriam Hopkins, *Mariette Colet:* Kay Francis, *Gaston Monescu (LaValle):* Herbert Marshall, *The Major:* Charlie Ruggles, *Francois Filiba:* Edward Everett Horton, *Adolph Giron:* C. Aubrey Smith, *Jacques, the Butler:* Robert Greig, *Waiter:* George Humbert, *Purse Salesman:* Rolfe Sedan, *Annoyed Opera Fan:* Luis Alberni, *Radical:* Leonid Kinsky, *Insurance Agent:* Hooper Atchley, *Madame Bouchet, Francois' Friend:* Nella Walker, *Radio Commentator:* Perry Ivins, *Singer:* Tyler Brooke, *Guest (Extra):* Larry Steers.

Tugboat Annie with Wallace Beery, Marie Dressler and Robert Young.

TUGBOAT ANNIE (1933) MGM. Directed by Mervyn LeRoy. From the *Saturday Evening Post* stories by Norman Reilly Raine. Adaptation, Zelda Sears and Eve Greene. Photography, Gregg Toland. Editor, Blanche Sewell. Other versions: *Tugboat Annie Sails Again* (Warners, 1940), *Captain Tugboat Annie* (Republic, 1945). 88 minutes

Annie Brennan: Marie Dressler, *Terry Brennan:* Wallace Beery, *Alec Brennan:* Robert Young, *Pat Severn:* Maureen O'Sullivan, *Red Severn:* Willard Robertson, *Shif'less:* Tammany Young, *Alec as a boy:* Frankie Darro, *Pete:* Jack Pennick, *Sam:* Paul Hurst, *Reynolds:* Oscar Apfel, *Mayor of Secoma:* Robert McWade, *First Mate:* Robert Barrat, *Cabby:* Vince Barnett, *Old Salt:* Robert E. Homans, *Auctioneer:* Guy Usher, *Chow, the Cook:* Willie Fung, *Mate:* Hal Price, *Sailor (Extra):* Christian Rub, *Onlooker:* Major Sam Harris.

Twelve Angry Men with Henry Fonda, Edward Binns, E. G. Marshall, Jack Klugman, Jack Warden, John Fiedler, Lee J. Cobb, Ed Begley, George Voscovec and Martin Balsam.

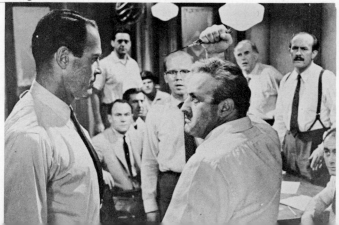

TWELVE ANGRY MEN (1957) UA. Produced by Henry Fonda and Reginald Rose. Associate Producer, George Justin. Directed by Sidney Lumet. Screenplay by Reginald Rose, based on his TV play. An Orion-Nova Production. 95 minutes

Juror 8: Henry Fonda, *Juror 1:* Martin Balsam, *Juror 2:* John Fielder, *Juror 3:* Lee J. Cobb, *Juror 4:* E. G. Marshall, *Juror 5:* Jack Klugman, *Juror 6:* Edward Binns, *Juror 7:* Jack Warden, *Juror 9:* Joseph Sweeney, *Juror 10:* Ed Begley, *Juror 11:* George Voskovec, *Juror 12:* Robert Webber, *Judge:* Rudy Bond, *Guard:* James A. Kelly, *Court Clerk:* Bill Nelson, *Defendant:* John Savoca.

Twelve O'Clock High with Dean Jagger, John Kellogg and Gregory Peck.

TWELVE O'CLOCK HIGH (1949) 20th. Producer, Darryl F. Zanuck. Director, Henry King. Based on the novel and screenplay by Cy Bartlett and Beirne Lay, Jr. Art Directors, Lyle Wheeler, Maurice Ransford. Music, Alfred Newman. Photography, Leon Shamroy. Editor, Barbara McLean. Later a TV series. 132 minutes

General Savage: Gregory Peck, *Lieutenant Colonel Ben Gately:* Hugh Marlowe, *Colonel Davenport:* Gary Merrill, *General Pritchard:* Millard Mitchell, *Major Stovall:* Dean Jagger, *Sergeant McIllhenny:* Robert Arthur, *Captain "Doc" Kaiser:* Paul Stewart, *Major Cobb:* John Kellogg, *Lieutenant Bishop:* Robert Patten, *Lieutenant Zimmerman:* Lee MacGregor, *Birdwell:* Sam Edwards, *Interrogation Officer:* Roger Anderson, *Sergeant Ernie:* John Zilly, *Lieutenant Pettinghill:* William Short, *Lieutenant McKessen:* Richard Anderson, *Captain Twombley:* Lawrence Dobkin, *Sentry:* Kenneth Tobey, *Operations Officer:* John McKee, *Mr. Britton:* Campbell Copelin, *Dwight:* Don Guadagno, *Weather Observer:* Peter Ortiz, *Clerk in Antique Shop:* Steve Clark, *Nurse:* Joyce MacKenzie, *Lieutenant Wilson:* Don Hicks, *Corporal (Bartender):* Ray Hyke, *Radio Officer:* Harry Lauter, *R.A.F. Officer:* Leslie Denison, *Operations Officer:* Russ Conway.

Twentieth Century with Carole Lombard and John Barryomore.

TWENTIETH CENTURY (1934) Col. Directed by Howard Hawks. Based on the play by Ben Hecht and Charles MacArthur, which was adapted from the play *Napoleon of Broadway* by Charles Bruce Milholland. Screenplay, Ben Hecht and Charles MacArthur. Photography, Joseph August. Editor, Gene Havlick. Remade as *Streamline Express* (Mascot, 1935). 91 minutes

Oscar Jaffe: John Barrymore, *Lilly Garland (Mildred Plotka):* Carole Lombard, *Owen O'Malley:* Roscoe Karns, *Oliver Webb:* Walter Connolly, *George Smith:* Ralph Forbes, *Sadie:* Dale Fuller, *Matthew J. Clark:* Etienne Girardot, *First Beard:* Herman Bing, *Second Beard:* Lee Kohlmar, *Train Conductor:* James P. Burtis, *Anita:* Billie Seward, *Max Jacobs (Mandelbaum):* Charles Levison (Lane), *Emmy Lou:* Mary Jo Mathews, *Sheriff:* Ed Gargan, *McGonigle:* Edgar Kennedy, *Schultz:* Gigi Parrish, *Detective On Train:* Fred Kelsey, *Flannigan:* Pat Flaherty, *Detective:* Ky Robinson, *Lockwood:* Cliff Thompson, *Treasurer:* Nick Copeland, *Doctor Johnson:* Howard Hickman, *Stage Actor:* Arnold Gray, *Chicago Detective:* James Burke, *Uncle Remus:* George Reed, *Stage Show Girl:* Anita Brown, *Stage Actress:* Irene Thompson, *Stage Actor:* Buddy Williams, *Southern Colonel:* Clarence Geldert, *Charwoman:* Lillian West, *Porter:* Snowflake, *Brother in play:* (Steve) Gaylord Pendleton, *Page Boy:* George Offerman, Jr., *Stage Carpenter:* Frank Marlowe, *Train Secretary:* Lynton Brent, *Artist:* Harry Semels, *McGonigle's Assistant:* King Mojave.

20,000 Leagues Under the Sea with Kirk Douglas and Peter Lorre.

20,000 LEAGUES UNDER THE SEA (1954) BV. Produced by Walt Disney. Directed by Richard Fleischer. CinemaScope and Technicolor. Based on the novel by Jules Verne. Screenplay, Earl Felton. Art Director, John Meehan. Camera, Franz Lehy, Ralph Hammeras, and Till Gabbani. Editor, Elmo Williams. Song, "A Whale of a Tale," by The Shermans, sung by Kirk Douglas. Filmed in New Providence, Bahamas; Long Bay, Jamaica; Disney Studios, Burbank, Cal. Stereophonic Sound. Remake of the 1916 Universal film. 122 minutes

Ned Land: Kirk Douglas, *Captain Nemo:* James Mason, *Professor Aronnax, Narrator:* Paul Lukas, *Conseil:* Peter Lorre, *First Mate of* NAUTILUS: Robert J. Wilke, *John Howard:* Carleton Young, *Captain Farragut:* Ted de Corsia, *Diver:* Percy Helton, *Mate of* LINCOLN: Ted Cooper, *Shipping Agent:* Edward Marr, *Casey Moore:* Fred Graham, *Billy:* J. M. Kerrigan, *Shipping Clerk:* Harry Harvey, *Nemo's Seal:* Esmeralda.

TWO YEARS BEFORE THE MAST (1946) Par. Associate Producer, Seton I. Miller. Director, John Farrow. Based on the book by Richard Henry Dana, Jr. Screenplay, Seton I. Miller, George Bruce. Art Directors, Hans Dreier, Franz Bechelin. Musical Score, Victor Young. Cameraman, Ernest Laszlo. Special Effects, Gordon and J.D. Jennings. 98 minutes

Charles Stewart: Alan Ladd, *Richard Henry Dana:* Brian Donlevy, *Amazeen:* William Bendix, *Terence O'Feenaghty:* Barry Fitzgerald, *Captain Francis Thompson:* Howard da Silva, *Maria Dominguez:*

Esther Fernandez, *Brown:* Albert Dekker, *Foster:* Luis Van Rooten, *Sam Hooper:* Darryl Hickman, *Macklin:* Roman Bohnen, *Mr. Gordon Stewart:* Ray Collins, *Hayes:* Theodore Newton, *Bellamer:* Tom Powers, *Carrick:* James Burke, *Hansen:* Frank Faylen, *Mexican Captain:* Duncan Renaldo, *Mrs. Gordon Stewart:* Kathleen Lockhart, *Mercedes (Maria's Maid):* Rosa Rey, *Don Sebastian:* Pedro de Cordoba, *Sailor #1:* John Roy, *Sailor #2:* Bink Hedberg, *Clark (Sailor #3):* Ethan Laidlaw, *Sailor #4:* George Bruggeman, *Sailor #5:* Clint Dorrington, *Bobson (Sailor #6):* Robert F. Kortman, *Sailor #7:* Carl Voss, *Sailor #8:* John "Blackie" Whiteford, *Sailor #9:* Mike Lally, *Sailor #10:* Joe Palma, *Sailor #11:* Dave Kashner, *Rider:* Rex Lease, *Chief Clerk:* Barry Macollum, *Blake:* Edwin Stanley, *Broker:* Crane Whitley, *Hallet:* George M. Carleton, *Crabtree:* Arthur Loft, *Staunton:* Pierre Watkin, *Crimp With Amazeen:* James Flavin, *Butler:* David Clyde, *Policeman:* Stanley Andrews.

Two Years Before the Mast with Barry Fitzgerald, Brian Donlevy and Alan Ladd.

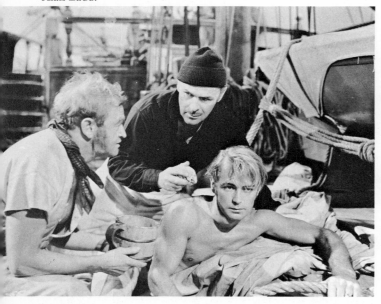

UNCONQUERED (1947) Par. Producer-Director, Cecil B. De Mille. Color by Technicolor. Based on the novel by Neil H. Swanson. Screenplay, Charles Bennett, Frederick M. Frank, Jesse Lasky, Jr. Art Directors, Hans Dreier, Walter Tyler. Cameraman, Ray Rennahan. Editor, Anne Bauchens. 146 minutes

Captain Christopher Holden: Gary Cooper, *Abby:* Paulette Goddard, *Garth:* Howard da Silva, *Guyasuta, Chief of the Senecas:* Boris Karloff, *Jeremy Love:* Cecil Kellaway, *John Fraser:* Ward Bond, *Hannah:* Katherine DeMille, *Captain Steele:* Henry Wilcoxon, *Lord Chief Justice:* Sir C. Aubrey Smith, *Captain Simeon Ecuyer:* Victor Varconi, *Diana:* Virginia Grey, *Leach:* Porter Hall, *Bone:* Mike Mazurki, *Colonel George Washington:* Richard Gaines, *Mrs. John Fraser:* Virginia Campbell, *Lieutenant Fergus McKenzie:* Gavin Muir, *Sir*

Unconquered with Howard da Silva, Paulette Goddard, Victor Varconi and Gary Cooper.

William Johnson: Alan Napier, *Mrs. Pruitt:* Nan Sunderland, *Sioto (Medicine Man):* Marc Lawrence, *Evelyn:* Jane Nigh, *Pontiac, Chief of the Ottawas:* Robert Warwick, *Lieutenant Hutchins:* Lloyd Bridges, *Lieutenant Baillie:* Oliver Thorndike, *Mamaultee:* Rus Conklin, *Colonel Henry Bouquet:* John Mylong, *Charles Mason:* George Kirby, *Jeremiah Dixon:* Leonard Carey, *Richard Henry Lee:* Frank R. Wilcox, *Mr. Carroll:* Davison Clark, *Brother Andrews:* Griff Barnett, *Venango Scout:* Raymond Hatton, *Widow Swivens:* Julia Faye, *Don McCoy:* Paul E. Burns, *Maggie:* Mary Field, *Jason:* Clarence Muse, *Captain Brooks:* Matthew Boulton, *Chief Killbuck:* Chief Thundercloud, *Joe Lovat:* Jack Pennick, *Royal American Officer:* Lex Barker, *Mulligan:* Charles Middleton.

Under the Yum Yum Tree with Edie Adams and Jack Lemmon.

UNDER THE YUM YUM TREE (1963) Col. Producer, Frederick Brisson. Director, David Swift. Eastman Color. Based on the play by Lawrence Roman. Screenplay, Lawrence Roman, David Swift. Music, Frank DeVol. "Under the Yum Yum Tree" by Sammy Cahn and James Van Heusen. Cinematographer, Joseph Biroc. Editor, Charles Nelson. A Sonnis-Swift Production. 110 minutes

Hogan: Jack Lemmon, *Robin:* Carol Lynley, *David:* Dean Jones, *Irene:* Edie Adams, *Dorkus:* Imogene Coca, *Murphy:* Paul Lynde, *Charles:* Robert Lansing, *Thin Man:* James Millhollin, *Dolores:* Pamela Curran, *Cheryl:* Asa Maynor, *Liz:* Jane Wald, *Boy Track Team:* Bill Bixby, *Girl in Class:* Vera Stough, *Teacher:* Bill Erwin, *Woman in Bus:* Maryesther Denver, *Writers:* Erskine Johnson, Army Archard, *Peggy:* Lyn Edginton, *Ardice:* Patty Joy Harmon, *Deliveryman:* Phil Arnold, *Woman:* Almira Sessions, *Josh:* Gary Waynesmith, *Suzy:* Irene Tsu, *Sandy:* Gloria Calomee, *Athletic Instructor:* Cliff Carnell, *Maitre D':* Matty Jordan, *Boxing Instructor:* John Indrisano, *Eve:* Laurie Sibbald, *Adam:* Jerry Antes.

UNION PACIFIC (1939) Par. Producer and Director, Cecil B. De Mille. Screenplay, Walter DeLeon, C. Gardner Sullivan, Jesse Lasky, Jr. Art Directors, Hans Dreier, Roland Anderson. Musical Score, George Antheil. Cameramen, Victor Milner, Dewey Wrigley. Editor, Anne Bauchens. Based on an adaptation by Jack Cunningham of a story by Ernest Haycox. Location Director, Arthur Rosson. 133 minutes

Mollie Monahan: Barbara Stanwyck, *Jeff Butler:* Joel McCrea, *Fiesta:* Akim Tamiroff, *Dick Allen:* Robert Preston, *Leach Overmile:* Lynn Overman, *Sid Campeau:* Brian Donlevy, *Duke Ring:* Robert Barrat, *Cordray:* Anthony Quinn, *Casement:* Stanley Ridges, *Asa M. Barrows:* Henry Kolker, *Grenville M. Dodge:* Francis McDonald, *Oakes Ames:* Willard Robertson, *Calvin:* Harold Goodwin, *Mrs. Calvin:* Evelyn Keyes, *Sam Reed:* Richard Lane, *Dusky Clayton:* William Haade, *Paddy O'Rourke:* Regis Toomey, *Monahan:* J. M. Kerrigan, *Cookie:* Fuzzy Knight, *Al Brett:* Harry Woods, *Dollarhide:*

Union Pacific with Joel McCrea and Barbara Stanwyck.

Lon Chaney, Jr., *General U.S. Grant:* Joseph Crehan, *Mame:* Julia Faye, *Rose:* Shella Darcy, *Shamus:* Joseph Sawyer, *Bluett:* Earl Askam, *Dr. Durant:* John Marston, *Andrew Whipple:* Byron Foulger, *Jerome:* Selmer Jackson, *Senator Smith:* Morgan Wallace, *Sargent:* Russell Hicks, *Mrs. Hogan:* May Beatty, *General Sheridan:* Ernie Adams, *Oliver Ames:* William J. Worthington, *Governor Stanford:* Guy Usher, *Mr. Mills:* James McNamara, *Governor Safford:* Gus Glassmire, *Dr. Harkness:* Stanley Andrews, *Rev. Dr. Tadd:* Paul Everton, *Harmonica Player:* Jack Pennick.

The Unsinkable Molly Brown with Vassili Lambrinos, Hayden Rorke, Audrey Christie and Debbie Reynolds.

THE UNSINKABLE MOLLY BROWN (1964) MGM. Producer, Lawrence Weingarten. Associate Producer, Roger Edens. Director, Charles Walters. Panavision, MetroColor. Based on the musical by Richard Morris. Screenplay, Helen Deutsch. Art Directors, George W. Davis, Preston Ames. Music supervised and conducted by Robert Armbruster. Songs, "Colorado is My Home," "I'll Never Say No," "Soliloquy," "He's My Friend," "Belly Up to the Bar, Boys," "I Ain't Down Yet." Music and Lyrics, Meredith Willson. Orchestration, Calvin Jackson, Leo Arnaud, Jack Elliott, Alexander Courage. Cinematographer, Daniel L. Fapp. Editor, Fredric Steinkamp. 128 minutes

Molly Brown: Debbie Reynolds, *Johnny Brown:* Harve Presnell, *Shamus Tobin:* Ed Begley, *Christmas Morgan:* Jack Kruschen, *Mrs Grogan:* Hermione Baddeley, *Prince Louis de Laniere:* Vassili Lambrinos, *Baron Karl Ludwig von Ettenburg:* Fred Essler, *Poluk:* Harvey Lembeck, *Mr. Fitzgerald:* Lauren Gilbert, *Mrs. Wadlington:* Kathryn Card,

Broderick: Hayden Rorke, *Mr. Wadlington:* Harry Holcombe, *Mrs. Fitzgerald:* Amy Douglass, *Monsignor Ryan:* George Mitchell, *Grand Duchess Elise Lupovinova:* Martita Hunt, *Mr. Cartwright:* Vaughn Taylor, *Roberts:* Anthony Eustrel, *Mrs. McGraw:* Audrey Christie, *Jam:* Grover Dale, *Murphy:* Brendan Dillon, *Daphne:* Maria Karnilova, *Joe:* Gus Trikonis, *Passenger:* Anna Lee, *Hotchkiss:* George Nicholson, *Lord Simon Primdale:* C. Ramsey Hill. *Lady Primdale:* Moyna Macgill, *Count Feranti:* Pat Benedetto, *Countess Feranti:* Mary Andre, *Vicar:* Pat Moran, *Spieler:* Herbert Vigran, *Mrs. Cartwright:* Eleanor Audley.

Up the Down Staircase with Roy Poole and Sandy Dennis.

UP THE DOWN STAIRCASE (1967) WB. A Pakula-Mulligan Production. Produced by Alan J. Pakula. Directed by Robert Mulligan. Color by Technicolor. Based on the novel by Bel Kaufman. Screenplay, Tad Mosel. Music, Fred Karlin. Art Director, George Jenkins. Assistant Director, Don Kranze. Photography, Joseph Coffey. Editor, Folmer Blangsted. Sound, Dennis Maitland. Filmed in New York City. 123 minutes

Sylvia Barrett: Sandy Dennis, *Paul Barringer:* Patrick Bedford, *Henrietta Pastorfield:* Eileen Heckart, *Beatrice Schachter:* Ruth White, *Sadie Finch:* Jean Stapleton, *Doctor Bester:* Sorrell Brooke, *McHabe:* Roy Poole, *Ella Friedenberg:* Florence Stanley, *Joe Ferone:* Jeff Howard, *Alice Blake:* Ellen O'Mara, *Jose Rodriguez:* Jose Rodriguez, *Ed Williams:* John Fantauzzi, *The Mother:* Vinnette Carroll, *Miss Gordon:* Janice Mars, *Social Studies Teacher:* Loretta Leversee, *Mr. Osborne:* Robert Levine, *Nurse Eagen:* Elena Karam, *Charlotte Wolf:* Frances Sternhagen, *Linda Rosen:* Candace Culkin, *Harry A. Kagan:* Salvatore Rosa, *Lou Martin:* Lew Wallach.

The Valley of Decision with Greer Garson and Gregory Peck.

THE VALLEY OF DECISION (1945) MGM. Producer, Edwin H. Knopf. Director, Tay Garnett. From the novel by Marcia Davenport. Screenplay, John Meehan, Sonya Levien. Score, Herbert Stothart. Art Directors, Cedric Gibbons, Paul Groesse. Cameraman, Joseph Ruttenberg. Special Effects, A. Arnold Gillespie. Editor, Blanche Sewell. 111 minutes

Mary Rafferty: Greer Garson, *Paul Scott:* Gregory Peck, *William Scott:* Donald Crisp, *Pat Rafferty:* Lionel Barrymore, *Jim Brennan:* Preston Foster, *Clarissa Scott:* Gladys Cooper, *Constance Scott:* Marsha Hunt, *McCready:* Reginald Owen, *William Scott, Jr.:* Dan Duryea, *Louise Kane:* Jessica Tandy, *.Delia:* Barbara Everest, *Ted Scott:* Marshall Thompson, *Julia Gaylord:* Mary Lord, *Giles, Earl of Moulton:* John Warburton, *Mrs. Gaylord:* Mary Currier, *Callahan:* Arthur Shields, *Mr. Gaylord:* Russell Hicks, *Kate Shannon:* Geraldine Wall, *Callahan's Son:* Norman Ollstead, *Mrs. Callahan:* Evelyn Dockson, *The Cook:* Connie Gilchrist, *Maid:* Willa Pearl Curtis, *O'Brien:* William O'Leary, *Minister:* Richard Abbott, *Paulie:* Dean Stockwell, *Stella:* Joy Harrington, *Dr. McClintock:* Lumsden Hare, *Nurse:* Anna Q. Nillson, *Clarrie:* Sherlee Collier, *Timmie (7 yrs):* Mike Ryan.

Valley of the Dolls with Barbara Parkins and Susan Hayward.

VALLEY OF THE DOLLS (1967) 20th. Produced by David Weisbart. Directed by Mark Robson. Panavision and De Luxe Color. A Red Lion Production. Based on the novel by Jacqueline Susann. Screenplay by Helen Deutsch and Dorothy Kingsley. Music by John Williams. Assistant Director, Eli Dunn. Art Direction, Jack Martin Smith and Richard Day. Sets, Walter M. Scott and Raphael G. Bretton. Photography, William Daniels. Editor, Dorothy Spencer. Sound, Don J. Bassman and David Dockendorf. Choreography, Robert Sidney. Gowns, Travilla. Production Manager, Francisco Day. Photographic Effects, L. B. Abbott, Art Cruickshank, and Emil Kosa, Jr. Orchestration, Herbert Spencer. Make-up, Ben Nye. Hair Styles, Kay Pownall. Supervised by Edith Lindon. Parkins' hair styles designed by Kenneth. Songs by Andre and Dory Previn: "Valley of the Dolls," sung by Dionne Warwick; "It's Impossible," "Come Live With Me," "Give a Little More," "I'll Plant My Own Tree." 123 minutes

Helen Lawson: Susan Hayward, *Neely O'Hara:* Patty Duke, *Anne Welles:* Barbara Parkins, *Jennifer North:* Sharon Tate, *Lyon Burke:* Paul Burke, *Tony Polar:* Tony Scotti, *Mel Anderson:* Martin Milner, *Kevin Gillmore:* Charles Drake, *Ted Casablanca:* Alex Davion, *Miriam Polar:* Lee Grant, *Miss Steinberg:* Naomi Stevens, *Henry Bellamy:* Robert H. Harris, *First Reporter:* Jacqueline Susann, *Director:* Robert Viharo, *Telethon Host:* Joey Bishop, *Host at Grammy Awards:* George Jessel, *Man:* Richard Angarola.

Variety Girl with Gary Cooper.

VARIETY GIRL (1947) Par. Producer, Daniel Dare. Director, George Marshall. Screenplay, Edmund Harmann, Frank Tashin, Robert Welch, Monte Brice. Musical Directors, Joseph J. Liley, Troy Sanders. Art Directors, Hans Dreier, Robert Clatworthy. Cameramen, Lionel Lindon, Stuart Thompson. Editor, LeRoy Stone. Puppetoon sequence by Thornton Hee and William Cottrell. Songs by Frank Loesser: "Tallahassee," "He Can Waltz," "Your Heart Calling Mine," "I Must Have Been Madly in Love," "I Want My Money Back," "Impossible Things" and "The French." 83 minutes

Catherine Brown: Mary Hatcher, *Amber La Vonne:* Olga San Juan, *Bob Kirby:* De Forest Kelly, *Bill Farris:* Glen Tyron, *Mrs. Webster:* Nella Walker, *Andre:* Torben Meyer, *Busboy:* Jack Norton, *Themselves:* Bing Crosby, Bob Hope, Gary Cooper, Ray Milland, Alan Ladd, Barbara Stanwyck, Paulette Goddard, Dorothy Lamour, Veronica Lake, Sonny Tufts, Joan Caulfield, William Holden, Lizabeth Scott, Burt Lancaster, Gail Russell, Diana Lynn, Sterling Hayden, Robert Preston, John Lund, William Bendix, Barry Fitzgerald, Cass Daley, Howard da Silva, Billy De Wolfe, MacDonald Carey, Arleen Whelan, Patrick Knowles, *Barker:* William Demarest, *Themselves:* Mona Freeman, Cecil Kellaway, Johnny Coy, Virginia Field, Richard Webb, Stanley Clements, *Stage Manager:* Frank Faylen, *J. R. O'Connell:* Frank Ferguson, *and* Cecil B. De Mille, Mitchell Leisen, Frank Butler, George Marshall, Roger Dann, Pearl Bailey, Jim and Mildred Mulcay, Spike Jones and his City Slickers, Mikhail Rasumny, Sally Rawlinson, Barney Dean, Mary Edwards, Virginia Welles, George Reeves, Patricia White, Wanda Hendrix, Nanette Parks.

VERA CRUZ (1954) UA. Producer, James Hill. Director, Robert Aldrich, Screenplay by Roland Kibbee and James R. Webb. Story by Borden Chase. Presented by Harold Hecht. Music by Hugo Friedhofer

Vera Cruz with Gary Cooper, Burt Lancaster and Cesar Romero.

and Sammy Cahn. Color by Technicolor. Filmed in Mexico. The first film in SuperScope. 94 minutes

Benjamin Trane: Gary Cooper, *Joe Erin:* Burt Lancaster, *Countess Marie Duvarre:* Denise Darcel, *Marquis De Labordere:* Cesar Romero, *Nina:* Sarita Montiel, *Emperor Maximilian:* George Macready, *Donnegan:* Ernest Borgnine, *General Aguilar:* Morris Ankrum, *Little-Bit:* James McCallion, *Charles:* Jack Lambert, *Danette:* Henry Brandon, *Pittsburgh:* Charles (Bronson) Buchinsky, *Tex:* Jack Elam, *Abilene:* James Seay, *Ballard:* Archie Savage, *Reno:* Charles Horvath, *Pedro:* Juan Garcia.

The Victors with George Hamilton and Peter Fonda.

THE VICTORS (1963) Col. Producer-Director-Writer, Carl Foreman. Based on a book by Alexander Baron. Music, Sol Kaplan. Associate Producer, Harold Buck. Assistant Director, Eric Rattray. A Highroad Production in Panavision. 175 minutes

Trower: George Hamilton, *Chase:* George Peppard, *Craig:* Eli Wallach, *Baker:* Vincent Edwards, *Maria:* Rosanna Schiaffino, *Grogan:* Jim Mitchum, *Sikh Soldier:* Tutte Lemkow, *French Lieutenant:* Maurice Ronet, *Jean-Pierre:* Joel Flateau, *French Woman:* Jeanne Moreau, *Regine:* Romy Schneider, *Eldridge:* Michael Callan, *Weaver:* Peter Fonda, *Madga:* Melina Mercouri, *Young British Soldier:* John Rogers, *Young French Girl:* Elizabeth Ercy, *Dennis:* Mervyn Johns, *Herr Metzger:* Albert Leiven, *Frau Metzger:* Marianne Deeming, *Trudi:* Senta Berger, *Helga:* Elke Sommer, *Russian Soldier:* Albert Finney.

THE VIKINGS (1958) UA. Producer, Jerry Bresler. Director, Richard Fleischer. Screenplay by Calder Willingham. Adaptation by Dale Wasserman. Based on a novel by Edison Marshall. Music by Mario Nascimbene. Assistant Director, Andre Smagghe. A Kirk Douglas Production in Technirama and Technicolor. 114 minutes

Einar: Kirk Douglas, *Eric:* Tony Curtis, *Ragnar:* Ernest Borgnine, *Morgana:* Janet Leigh, *Egbert:* James Donald, *Father Godwin:* Alexander Knox, *Aella:* Frank Thring, *Enid:* Maxine Audley, *Kitala:* Eileen Way, *Sandpiper:* Edric Connor, *Bridget:* Dandy Nichols, *Bjorm:* Per Buckhoj, *Pigtails:* Almut Berg.

The Vikings with Tony Curtis and Kirk Douglas.

THE V.I.P.'S (1963) MGM. Producer, Anatole de Grunwald. Director, Anthony Asquith. Screenplay, Terence Rattigan. Music, Miklos Rozsa. Associate Producer, Roy Parkinson. Assistant Director, Kip Gowans. Gowns, Hubert de Givenchy, Pierre Cardin. In Panavision and Metro-Color. 119 minutes

Francis Andros: Elizabeth Taylor, *Paul Andros:* Richard Burton, *Marc Champselle:* Louis Jourdan, *Gloria Gritti:* Elsa Martinelli, *Duchess of Brighton:* Margaret Rutherford, *Miss Mead:* Maggie Smith, *Les Mangam:* Rod Taylor, *Miriam Marshall:* Linda Christian, *Max Buda:* Orson Welles, *Coburn:* Robert Coote, *Sanders:* Richard Wattis, *Commander Millbank:* Dennis Price, *Joslin:* Ronald Fraser, *Mr. Damer:* Peter Illing, *Airport Director:* Michael Hordern, *Waiter:* Stringer Davis, *Miss Potter:* Joan Benham, *Doctor:* Peter Sallis, *Mrs. Damer:* Joyce Carey.

The V.I.P.'s with Elsa Martinelli, Orson Welles, Margaret Rutherford and Martin Miller.

VIVA LAS VEGAS (1964) MGM. Producers, Jack Cummings, George Sidney. Director, George Sidney. MetroColor. Screenplay, Sally Benson. Art Directors, George W. Davis, Edward Carfagno. Music,

George Stoll. Cinematographer, Joseph Biroc. Editor, John Mc-Sweeney, Jr. 86 minutes

Lucky Jackson: Elvis Presley, *Rusty Martin:* Ann-Margret, *Count Elmo Mancini:* Cesare Danova, *Mr. Martin:* William Demarest, *Shorty Farnsworth:* Nicky Blair, *Himself:* Jack Carter, *Swanson:* Robert B. Williams, *Big Gus Olson:* Bob Nash, *Baker:* Roy Engel, *Mechanic:* Barnaby Hale, *Driver:* Ford Dunhill, *M.C.:* Eddie Quillan, *Manager:* George Cisar, *Head Captain:* Ivan Triesault, *Francois:* Francis Raval, *Man:* Mike Ragan (Holly Bane).

Viva Las Vegas with Elvis Presley and Ann-Margret.

VIVA VILLA ! (1934) MGM. Produced by David O. Selznick. Directed by Jack Conway. Suggested by the book by Edgcumb Pinchon and O.B. Stade. Screenplay by Ben Hecht. Film Editor, Robert J. Kern. Photographers, James Wong Howe, Charles G. Clarke. Assistant Directors, Art Rosson, Johnny Walters. Musical Consultant, Juan Aguilar. Interior Decoration, Edwin B. Willis. Technical Advisor, Carlos Novarro. Technical Associate, Matias Santoyo. Recording Engineer, Douglas Shearer. Art Director, Harry Oliver. Costumes, Dolly Tree. Musical Numbers, Herbert Stothart. 115 minutes.

Pancho Villa: Wallace Beery, *Teresa:* Fay Wray, *Diego:* Leo Carrillo, *Don Felipe:* Donald Cook, *Johnny:* Stuart Erwin, *Chavito:* George E. Stone, *Pascal:* Joseph Schildkraut, *Madero:* Henry B. Walthall, *Rosita:* Katherine DeMille, *Bugle Boy:* David Durand, *Villa as a boy:* Phillip Cooper, *Father:* Frank Puglia, *Pascal's Aide:* John Merkel, *Staff:* Charles Stevens, Steve Clemento, Pedro Regas, *Old Man:* Carlos De Valdez, *Staff:* George Regas, *Majordomo:* Harry Cording, *Prosecuting Attorney:* Sam Godfrey, *Political Judge:* Nigel De Brulier, *Grandees:* Charles Requa, Tom Ricketts, *Jail Official:* Clarence Hummel Wilson, *Mexican Officer:* James Martin, *Dancer:* Anita Gordiana, *Villa's Man:* Francis McDonald, *Soldier:* Harry Semels, *Telegraph*

Viva Villa! with Wallace Beery, Henry B. Walthall and Joseph Schildkraut.

Operator: Julian Rivero, *Bartender:* Bob McKenzie, *Drunkard:* Dan Dix, *Newspaper Man:* Paul Stanton, *Military Attaché:* Mischa Auer, *Spanish Wife:* Belle Mitchell, *Statesmen:* John Davidson, Brandon Hurst, Leonard Moody, *Generals:* Herbert Prior, Emil Chautard, *Mendoza Brothers:* Adrian Rosley, Hector Sarno, Henry Armetta, *Calloway:* Ralph Bushman (Francis X. Bushman, Jr.) *English Reporter:* Arthur Treacher, *German Reporter:* William Von Brincken, *French Reporter:* Andre Cheron, *Russian Reporter:* Michael Visaroff, *Wrong Girl:* Shirley Chambers, *Butcher:* Arthur Thalasso, *Peons:* Chris-Pin Martin, Nick De Ruiz.

Viva Zapata! with Anthony Quinn (left) and Marlon Brando (right).

VIVA ZAPATA ! (1952) 20th. Produced by Darryl F. Zanuck. Directed by Elia Kazan. Written by John Steinbeck. Music Director, Alfred Newman. Art Directors, Lyle Wheeler and Leland Fuller. Photography, Joe MacDonald. Editor, Barbara McLean. Music, Alex North. 113 minutes

Zapata: Marlon Brando, *Josefa:* Jean Peters, *Eufemio:* Anthony Quinn, *Fernando:* Joseph Wiseman, *Don Nacio:* Arnold Moss, *Pancho Villa:* Alan Reed, *Soldadera:* Margo, *Pablo:* Lou Gilbert, *Madero:* Harold Gordon, *Senora Espejo:* Mildred Dunnock, *Huerta:* Frank Silvera, *Aunt:* Nina Varela, *Senor Espejo:* Florenz Ames, *Diaz:* Fay Roope, *Lazaro:* Will Kuluva, *Zapatista:* Bernie Gozier, *Col. Guajardo:* Frank De Kova, *Innocente:* Pedro Regas, *Old General:* Richard Garrick, *Officer:* Ross Bagdasarian, *Husband:* Leonard George, *Captain:* Abner Biberman, *C.O.:* Phil Van Zandt, *Soldier:* Henry Silva, *Eduardo:* Guy Thomajan, *Rurale:* George J. Lewis, *Soldiers:* Salvador Baquez, Peter Mamakos, *Manager:* Ric Roman, *Senior Officer:* Henry Corden, *New General:* Nester Paiva, *Captain of Rurales:* Robert Filmer, *Wife:* Julia Montoya.

Von Ryan's Express with Frank Sinatra, Vito Scotto, Sergio Fantoni and Trevor Howard.

VON RYAN'S EXPRESS (1965) 20th. Producer, Saul David. Director, Mark Robson. CinemaScope, De Luxe Color. Based on the novel by David Westheimer. Screenplay, Weldell Mayes, Joseph Landon. Art Directors, Jack Martin Smith, Hilyard Brown. Music, Jerry Goldsmith. Orchestration, Arthur Morton. Cinematographer, William A. Daniels. Special Photographic Effects, L. B. Abbott, Emil Kosa, Jr. Editor, Dorothy Spencer. 117 minutes

Colonel Joseph Ryan: Frank Sinatra, *Major Eric Fincham:* Trevor Howard, *Gabriella:* Raffaella Carra, *Sergeant Bostick:* Brad Dexter, *Captain Oriani:* Sergio Fantoni, *Orde:* John Leyton, *Constanzo:* Edward Mulhare, *Major Von Klemment:* Wolfgang Preiss, *Ames:* James Brolin, *Colonel Gortz:* John van Dreelen, *Battaglia:* Adolfo Celi, *Italian Train Engineer:* Vito Scotti, *Corporal Giannini:* Richard Bakalyan, *Captain Stein:* Michael Goodliffe, *Sergeant Dunbar:* Michael St. Clair, *Von Kleist:* Ivan Triesault, *Gortz's Aide:* Jacques Stanislavski, *American Soldiers:* Al Wyatt, Buzz Henry, John Day, James Sikking, *Ransom:* Eric Micklewood, *Oriani's Aide:* John Mitory, *Italian Corporal:* Benito Prezia, *Italian Soldier:* Dominick Delgarde, *Ransom's Batman:* Barry Ford, *Gortz's Aide #2:* Gino Gottarelli, *Pilot:* Peter Hellman, *Italian Nobleman:* Mike Romanoff, *German Captain:* Walter Linden, *German Sgt:* Bard Stevens, *Italian Tailor:* Ernesto Melinari, *POW Who Opens Sweat Box:* Bob Rosen, *Extra:* Don Grant (Don Glut).

Waikiki Wedding with Bing Crosby and Shirley Ross.

WAIKIKI WEDDING (1937) Par. Produced by Arthur Hornblow, Jr. Directed by Frank Tuttle. Based on a story by Frank Butler and Don Hartman. Screenplay, Frank Butler, Don Hartman, Walter DeLeon, Francis Martin. Music Director, Boris Morros. Orchestrations, Victor Young. Arrangements, Al Siegel and Arthur Franklin. Dance Director, LeRoy Prinz. Photography, Karl Struss. Editor, Paul Weatherwax. Hawaiian lyrics, Jimmy Lovell. Costumes, Edith Head. Special Effects, Farciot Eduoart. Hawaiian Exterior, Robert C. Bruce. Sound, Gene Merritt and Louis Mesenkop. Interior Decorations, A. E. Freudeman. Songs: "Sweet Leilani" by Harry Owens; "Blue Hawaii," "In a Little Hula Heaven," "Sweet Is the Word for You," "Nani Ona Pua," "Okolehao" by Ralph Rainger and Leo Robin. 89 minutes

Tony Marvin: Bing Crosby, *Shad Buggle:* Bob Burns, *Myrtle Finch:* Martha Raye, *Georgia Smith:* Shirley Ross, *J. P. Todhunter:* George Barbier, *Dr. Victor Quimby:* Leif Erikson, *Everett Todhunter:* Grady Sutton, *Uncle Herman:* Granville Bates, *Kimo:* Anthony Quinn, *Koalani:* Mitchell Lewis, *Muamua:* George Regas, *Assistant Purser:* Nick Lukats, *Priest:* Prince Lei Lani, *Kaiaka:* Maurice Liu, *Mahina:* Raquel Echeverria, *Maile:* Nalani De Clercq, *Lani:* Kuulei De Clercq, *Specialty Dancer:* Miri Rei, *Frame:* Spencer Charters, *Harrison:* Alexander Leftwich, *Tomlin:* Ralph Remley, *Specialty Dancer:* Augie Goupil, *Keith:* Harry Stubbs, *John Durkin:* Pierre Watkin, *Secretary:* Iris Yamaoka, *Photographer:* Jack Chapin, *Cab Driver:* Pedro Regas, *Suki:* Lotus Liu, *Radio Operator:* David Newell, *Tony's Mother:*

Emma Dunn, Singer: Ray Kinney, *First Policeman:* Robert Emmett O'Connor, *Second Policeman:* Lalo Encinas, *Bellboy:* Sojin, Jr.

Wait Until Dark with Richard Crenna and Audrey Hepburn.

WAIT UNTIL DARK (1967) WB-7 Arts. Produced by Mel Ferrer. Directed by Terence Young. Color by Technicolor. Based on the 1966 play by Frederick Knott. Screenplay, Robert and Jane-Howard Carrington. Music, Henry Mancini. Assistant Director, Jack Aldworth. Photography, Charles Lang. Editor, Gene Milford. Title song by Henry Mancini, Jay Livingston, and Ray Evans. Film debut of New York fashion model Samantha Jones. 108 minutes

Susy Hendrix: Audrey Hepburn, *Roat:* Alan Arkin, *Mike Talman:* Richard Crenna, *Carlino:* Jack Weston, *Sam Hendrix:* Efrem Zimbalist, Jr., *Lisa:* Samantha Jones, *Gloria:* Julie Herrod, *Shatner:* Frank O'Brien, *Boy:* Gary Morgan,

Wake Island with Macdonald Carey and Brian Donlevy.

WAKE ISLAND (1942) Par. Associate Producer, Joseph Sistrom. Director, John Farrow. Screenplay, W. R. Burnett, Frank Butler. Art Directors, Hans Dreier, Earl Hedrick. Cameraman, Theodore Sparkuhl. Editor, LeRoy Stone. Associate Cameraman, William C. Mellor. Filmed on the desert off Salton Sea, California. 78 minutes

Major Caton: Brian Donlevy, *Lieutenant Cameron:* Macdonald Carey, *Joe Doyle:* Robert Preston, *Smacksie Randall:* William Bendix, *Shad McCloskey:*, Albert Dekker, *Commander Roberts:* Walter Abel, *Probenzki:* Mikhail Rasumny, *Private Cunkel:* Don Castle, *Captain Lewis:* Rod Cameron, *Sergeant:* Bill Goodwin, *Sally Cameron:* Barbara Britton, *Captain Patrick:* Damian O'Flynn, *Johnny Rudd:* Frank

Albertson, *Private Warren:* Phillip Terry, *Corp. Goebbels:* Phillip Van Zandt, *Sparks Wilcox:* Keith Richards, *Colonel Cameron:* Willard Robertson, *Tommy:* Marvin Jones, *Squeaky Simpkins:* Jack Chapin, *Triunfo:* Rudy Robles, *Pete Hogan:* John Sheehan, *George Nielson:* Charles Trowbridge, *Cynthia Caton:* Mary Thomas, *Miss Pringle:* Mary Field, *Mr. Saburo Kurusu:* Richard Loo, *Tex Hannigan:* Earle Tex Harris, *Girl at Inn:* Hillary Brooke, *Girl at Inn:* Patti McCarty, *Major Johnson:* William Forrest, *Dr. Parkman:* Jack Mulhall, *Colonel:* Ivan Miller, *Captain:* Hugh Beaumont, *Commander:* Edward Earle, *Wounded Marine, First Lieutenant:* James Brown, *Rodrigo:* Angel Cruz, *Gordon:* Anthony Nace, *First Lieutenant:* Hollis Bane (Mike Ragan), *Wounded Marine:* Frank Faylen, *Marine:* Dane Clark, *Sight Setter:* Alan Hale, Jr.

Wake of the Red Witch with Kuda Tuitama, John Wayne, Henry Brandon, Gail Russell and Duke Kahanamoku.

WAKE OF THE RED WITCH (1948) Rep. Associate Producer, Edmund Grainger. Director, Edward Ludwig. Based on the novel by Garland Roark. Screenplay, Harry Brown, Kenneth Gamet. Art Director, James Sullivan. Music, Nathan Scott. Photography, Reggie Lanning. Editor, Richard L. Van Enger. 106 minutes

Captain Ralls: John Wayne, *Angelique Desaix:* Gail Russell, *Sam Rosen:* Gig Young, *Teleia Van Schreeven:* Adele Mara, *Mayrant Ruysdaal Sidneye:* Luther Adler, *Harmenszoon Van Schreeven:* Eduard Franz, *Captain Wilde Younguer:* Grant Withers, *Jacques Desaix:* Henry Daniell, *"Ripper" Arrezo:* Paul Fix, *Captain Munsey:* Dennis Hoey, *Mr. Loring:* Jeff Corey, *Dokter Van Arken:* Erskine Sanford, *Ua Nuka:* Duke Kahanamoku, *Kurinua:* Henry Brandon, *Maru:* Fernando Alvarado, *Prosecuting Attorney:* John Wengraf, *Taluna:* Jose Alvarado, *Hekkim (Cabin Boy):* Carl Thompson, *Sailor:* Wallace Scott, *Young Crew Member:* Myron Healey, *Second Officer:* Mickey Simpson, *Young Sailor:* Robert Wood, *Dirk:* Grant Means, *Seaman Lookout:* Fred Libby, *Sailor (Fight Bit):* Fred Graham, *First Diver:* Jim Nolan, *Second Diver:* John Pickard, *Officer:* Rory Mallinson, *Diver's Assistant:* Harlan Warde, *Jarma:* Harry Vejar, *Lawyer:* Norman Rainey, *Mullins:* David Clarke, *Ship Surgeon:* Fred Fox, *Native Servant:* Al Kikume, *Native:* Kuka Tuitama, *Native Priest:* Leo C. Richmond, *Native:* George Piltz, *Kharma:* Harold Lishman.

WAKE UP AND LIVE (1937) 20th. Produced by Darryl F. Zanuck. Associated Producer, Kenneth MacGowan. Directed by Sidney Lanfield. From a story by Curtis Kenyon, based on the book *Wake Up and Live* by Dorothea Brande. Screenplay, Harry Tugend and Jack Yellen. Music Director, Louis Silvers. Dance Director, Jack Haskell. Art Director, Mark-Lee Kirk. Art Associate, Haldane Douglas. Set Decoration, Thomas Little. Assistant Director, A.F. Erickson. Costumes, Gwen Wakeling. Photography, Edward Cronjager. Editor, Robert Simpson. Sound, W. D. Flick and Roger Heman. Songs by Mack Gordon and Harry Revel: "Wake Up and Live," "There's a

Wake Up and Live with Walter Winchell and Patsy Kelly.

Lull in My Life," "It's Swell Of You," "Oh, But I'm Happy," "I'm Bubbling Over," "Never in a Million Years," "I Love You Too Much, Muchacha," "Red Seal Malt," "Bernie's Love Song." Buddy Clark sings for Jack Haley. 91 minutes

Himself: Walter Winchell, *Themselves:* Ben Bernie and his Band, *Alice Huntley:* Alice Faye, *Patsy Kane:* Patsy Kelly, *Steve Cluskey:* Ned Sparks, *Eddie Kane:* Jack Haley, *Jean Roberts:* Grace Bradley, *Gus Avery:* Walter Catlett, *Cafe Singer:* Leah Ray, *Spanish Dancer:* Joan Davis, *Herman:* Douglas Fowley, *James Stratton:* Miles Mander, *Themselves:* The Condos Brothers, *Themselves:* The Brewster Twins, *Waldo Peebles:* Etienne Girardot, *McCabe:* Paul Hurst, *Manager:* George Givot, *Foster:* Barnett Parker, *Alberts:* Charles Williams, *First Gunman:* Warren Hymer, *Murphy:* Ed Gargan, *Attendants:* William Demarest, John Sheehan, *Chauffeur:* Robert Lowery, *Janitor:* George Chandler, *Announcer:* Gary Breckner, *Singer:* Rosemary Glosz, *Ford Driver:* Si Jenks, *Buick Driver:* Harry Tyler, *Accompanist:* Andre Beranger, *Girl:* Ellen Prescott, *Nurse:* Elyse Knox.

A Walk in the Sun with Chris Drake and Richard Conte.

A WALK IN THE SUN (1945) 20th. Producer, Lewis Milestone. Production Manager, Joseph H. Nadel. Director, Lewis Milestone. From the novel by Harry Brown. Screenplay, Robert Rossen. Art Director, Max Bertisch. Musical Score, Fredric Efrem Rich. Ballads, Millard Lampell, Earl Robinson. Cameraman, Russell Harlan. Editor, Duncan Mansfield. Film debut of John Ireland. 111 minutes

Sgt. Tyne: Dana Andrews, *Rivera:* Richard Conte, *Windy:* John Ireland, *Friedman:* George Tyne, *Sgt. Ward:* Lloyd Bridges, *McWilliams:* Sterling Holloway, *Sgt. Porter:* Herbert Rudley,

Archimbeau: Norman Lloyd, *Judson:* Steve Brodie, *Carraway:* Huntz Hall, *Sgt. Hoskins:* James Cardwell, *Rankin:* Chris Drake, *Tranella:* Richard Benedict, *Tinker:* George Offerman, Jr., *Trasker:* Danny Desmond, *Cousins:* Victor Cutler, *Giorgio:* Anthony Dante, *Cpl. Kramer:* Harry Cline, *James:* Jay Norris, *Johnson:* Al Hammer, *Dugan:* Don Summers, *Phelps:* Malcolm O'Guinn, *Smith:* Grant Maiben, *Riddle:* John Kellogg, *Long:* Dick Daniels, *Sgt.:* Matt Willis, *Reconnaissance:* George Turner.

Watch on the Rhine with Paul Lukas, Bette Davis and George Coulouris.

WATCH ON THE RHINE (1943) WB. Producer, Hal B. Wallis. Director, Herman Schumlin. From the play by Lillian Hellman. Screenplay, Dashiell Hammett. Musical Score, Max Steiner. Art Director, Carl Jules Weyl. Musical Director, Leo F. Forbstein. Cameramen, Merritt Gerstad, Hal Mohr. Special Effects, Jack Holden, Edwin B. DuPar. Editor, Rudi Fehr. 114 minutes

Sara Muller: Bette Davis, *Kurt Muller:* Paul Lukas, *Marthe DeBrancovis:* Geraldine Fitzgerald, *Fanny Farrelly:* Lucile Watson, *Anise:* Beulah Bondi, *Teck DeBrancovis:* George Coulouris, *David Farrelly:* Donald Woods, *Phili Von Ramme:* Henry Daniell, *Joshua Muller:* Donald Buka, *Bodo Muller:* Eric Roberts, *Babette Muller:* Janis Wilson, *Young Man:* Helmut Dantine, *Mrs. Mellie Sewell:* Mary Young, *Herr Blecher:* Kurt Katch, *Dr. Klauber:* Erwin Kalser, *Overdorff:* Robert O. Davis, *Sam Chandler:* Clyde Fillmore, *Joseph:* Frank Wilson, *Horace:* Clarence Muse, *Belle:* Violett McDowell, *Chauffeur:* Creighton Hale, *Doc:* William Washington, *Italian Woman:* Elvira Curci, *Italian Man:* Anthony Caruso, *Mr. Chabeuf:* Jean DeBriac, *Miss Drake:* Leah Baird, *Cyrus Penfield:* Howard Hickman, *Admiral:* Frank Reicher, *German Ambassador:* Robert O. Fischer, *Boy:* Alan Hale, Jr., *Trainman:* Jack Mower, *Taxi Driver:* Garry Owen.

WAR AND PEACE (1956) Par. Producer, Dino De Laurentiis. Director, King Vidor. VistaVision, Technicolor. From the novel by Leo Tolstoy. Screenplay, Bridget Boland, Robert Westerby, King Vidor, Mario Camerini, Ennio De Concini, Ivo Perilli. Art Director, Mario Chiari. Musical Director, Franco Ferrara. Music Score, Nino Rota. Cinematographers, Jack Cardiff, Aldo Tonti. Supervising Editor, Stuart Gilmore. Editor, Leo Cattozzo. Assistant Directors, Piero Musetta and Guidarino Guidi. Costumes by Maria De Matteis. A Ponti-DeLaurentiis Production. Filmed in Rome. 208 minutes

Natasha: Audrey Hepburn, *Pierre:* Henry Fonda, *Andrey:* Mel Ferrer, *Anatole:* Vittorio Gassman, *Platon:* John Mills, *Napoleon:* Herbert Lom, *General Kutuzov:* Oscar Homolka, *Helene:* Anita Ekberg, *Dolokhov:* Helmut Dantine, *Count Rostov:* Barry Jones, *Mary Bolkonsky:* Anna Maria Ferrero, *Lise:* Milly Vitale, *Nicholas Rostov:* Jeremy Brett, *Countess Rostov:* Lea Seidl, *Prince Bolkonsky:* Wilfred Lawson, *Petya Rostov:* Sean Barrett, *Kuragine:* Tullio Carminati, *Sonya:* May Britt, *Denisov:* Patrick Crean, *Peronskava:* Gertrude Flynn.

War and Peace with Lea Seidl, Barry Jones, Audrey Hepburn, Jeremy Brett, May Britt and Henry Fonda.

THE WAR OF THE WORLDS (1953) Par. Producer, George Pal. Director, Byron Haskin. Technicolor. Based on the novel by H. G. Wells. Screenplay, Barre Lyndon. Art Directors, Hal Pereira, Albert Nozaki. Cinematographer, George Barnes. Editor, Everett Douglas. Technicolor Consultant, Monroe Burbank. 85 minutes

Clayton Forrester: Gene Barry, *Sylvia Van Buren:* Ann Robinson, *General Mann:* Les Tremayne, *Dr. Pryor:* Bob Cornthwaite, *Dr. Bilderbeck:* Sandro Giglio, *Pastor Matthew Collins:* Lewis Martin, *Aide to General Mann:* Houseley Stevenson, Jr., *Radio Announcer:* Paul Frees, *Wash Perry:* Bill Phipps, *Col. Ralph Heffner:* Vernon Rich, *Cop:* Henry Brandon, *Salvatore:* Jack Kruschen, *Commentary by:* Sir Cedric Hardwicke, *Introductory Narration:* Paul Frees, *Prof. McPherson:* Edgar Barrier, *Buck Monahan:* Ralph Dumke, *Bird-Brained Blonde:* Carolyn Jones, *Man:* Pierre Cressoy, *Martian:* Charles Gemora, *Sheriff:* Walter Sande, *Dr. James:* Alex Frazer, *Dr. DuPrey:* Ann Codee, *Dr. Gratzman:* Ivan Lebedeff, *Ranger:* Robert Rockwell, *Zippy:* Alvy Moore, *Alonzo Hogue:* Paul Birch, *Fiddler Hawkins:* Frank Kreig, *Well-Dressed Man During Looting:* Ned Glass, *M. P. Driver:* Anthony Warde, *Woman News Vendor:* Gertrude Hoffman, *Secretary of Defense:* Freeman Lusk, *Fire Chief:* Sydney Mason, *Lookout:* Peter Adams, *Reporter:* Ted Hecht, *Japanese Diplomat:* Teru Shimada, *Chief of Staff, U.S.A.:* Herbert Lytton, *Staff Sergeant:* Douglas Henderson, *Looters:* Dave Sharpe, Dale Van Sickel, Fred Graham.

The War of the Worlds.

WEEKEND AT THE WALDORF (1945) MGM. Producer, Arthur Hornblow, Jr., Director, Robert Z. Leonard. Author, Vicki Baum. Screenplay, Sam and Bella Spewack. Adaptation, Guy Bolton. Musical Director, Johnny Green. Dance Director, Charles Walters. Art Directors, Cedric Gibbons, Daniel B. Cathcart. Cameraman, Robert Planck. Special Effects, Warren Newcombe. Editor, Robert J. Kern. Musical numbers by Sammy Fain: "And There You Are" (lyrics by Ted Koehler) and "Guadalajara." Remake of *Grand Hotel* (MGM, 1932). 130 minutes

Weekend at the Waldorf wtih Walter Pidgeon and Lana Turner.

Irene Malvern: Ginger Rogers, *Chip Collyer:* Walter Pidgeon, *Captain James Hollis:* Van Johnson, *Bunny Smith:* Lana Turner, *Randy Morton:* Robert Benchley, *Martin X. Edley:* Edward Arnold, *Mme. Jaleska:* Constance Collier, *Henry Burton:* Leon Ames, *Dr. Campbell:* Warner Anderson, *Cynthia Drew:* Phyllis Thaxter, *Oliver Webson:* Keenan Wynn, *Stevens:* Porter Hall, *Mr. Jessup:* Samuel S. Hinds, *Bey of Aribajan:* George Zucco, *Xavier Cugat:* Himself, *Juanita:* Lina Romay, *Singer:* Bob Graham, *Lieutenant John Rand:* Michael Kirby, *Jane Rand:* Cora Sue Collins, *Anna:* Rosemary De Camp, *Kate Douglas:* Jacqueline DeWit, *Emile:* Frank Puglia, *Hi Johns:* Charles Wilson, *Sam Skelly:* Irving Bacon, *British Secretary:* Miles Mander, *Mrs. H. Davenport Drew:* Nana Bryant, *McPherson:* Russell Hicks, *Irma:* Ludmilla Pitoeff, *Night Maid:* Naomi Childers, *House Detective Blake:* Moroni Olsen, *Chief Jennings:* William Halligan, *Alix:* John Wengraf, *The Woman:* Ruth Lee, *Cassidy (Doorman):* William Hall, *Pianist:* Rex Evans, *Literary Type:* Wyndham Standing, *Anna's Boy Friend:* Harry Barris, *Barber:* Byron Foulger, *Assistant Manager:* Gladden James, *Orchestra Leader:* Carli Elinor, *Bell Captain:* Dick Crockett.

Wee Willie Winkie with Shirley Temple and C. Aubrey Smith.

WEE WILLIE WINKIE (1937) 20th. Associate Producer, Gene Markey. Directed by John Ford. Based on the story by Rudyard Kipling. Screenplay, Ernest Pascal and Julien Josephson. Photography, Arthur Miller. Editor, Walter Thompson. 99 minutes

Priscilla Williams: Shirley Temple, *Sergeant McDuff:* Victor McLaglen, *Captain Williams:* C. Aubrey Smith, *Joyce:* June Lang, *Coppy (Lieutenant Brandes):* Michael Whalen, *Khoda Khan:* Cesar Romero, *Mrs. Allardyce:* Constance Collier, *Mott:* Douglas Scott, *Captain Bibberbeigh:* Gavin Muir, *Mohammed Dihn:* Willie Fung, *Major Allardyce:* Lionel Pape, *Bagby:* Brandon Hurst, *Pipe Major:* Clyde Cook, *Elsie Allardyce:* Lauri Beatty, *Mrs. MacMonachie:* Mary Forbes, *MacMonachie:* George Hassell, *Gen. Hammond:* Lionel Braham, *Tummel:* Cyril McLaglen, *English Soldier:* Pat Somerset, *Driver:* Hector V. Sarno, *Soldier:* Jack Pennick, *Sikh Policeman:* Noble Johnson, *Merchant:* Scotty Mattraw, *African Chieftain:* Louis Vincenot.

Welcome Stranger with Elizabeth Patterson, Percy Kilbride, Charles Dingle, Barry Fitzgerald, Lillian Bronson, Clarence Nordstrom, Robert Shayne, John Westley and John "Skins" Miller.

WELCOME STRANGER (1947) Par. Producer, Sol C. Siegel. Director, Elliott Nugent. Author, Frank Butler. Screenplay, Arthur Sheekman. Art Directors, Hans Dreier, Franz Bachelin. Musical Score, Robert Emmett Dolan. Cameraman, Lionel Lindon. Editor, Everett Douglas. Songs by Johnny Burke and Jimmy Van Heusen: "As Long as I'm Dreaming," "My Heart Is a Hobo," "Country Style," "Smile Right Back at the Sun" and "Smack in the Middle of Maine." 107 minutes

Dr. Jim Pearson: Bing Crosby, *Trudy Mason:* Joan Caulfield, *Dr. Joseph McRory:* Barry Fitzgerald, *Emily Walters:* Wanda Hendrix, *Bill Walters:* Frank Faylen, *Mrs. Gilley:* Elizabeth Patterson, *Roy Chesley:* Robert Shayne, *Dr. Ronnie Jenks:* Larry Young, *Nat Dorkas:* Percy Kilbride, *Charlie Chesley:* Charles Dingle, *Mort Elkins:* Don Beddoe, *Congressman Beeker:* Thurston Hall, *Miss Lennek:* Lillian Bronson, *Secretary, Boston:* Mary Field, *Mr. Daniels:* Paul Stanton, *Ed Chanock:* Pat McVey, *Ben, Bus Driver:* Milton Kibbee, *Clarence, Steward:* Clarence Muse, *Farmer Pinkett:* Charles Middleton, *Cousin Hattie (Photo):* Margaret Field (Maggie Mahoney), *Friends:* John Ince, Franklyn Farnum, *Train Companion:* Erville Alderson, *Mr. Cartwright:* John Westley, *Mr. Weaver:* Edward Clark, *Man:* Clarence Nordstrom, *Man:* Brandon Hurst, *Mrs. Sims:* Ethel Wales, *Mr. Crane:* Frank Ferguson, *Dr. White:* Elliott Nugent, *Telephone Operator:* Bea Allen, *Woman:* Julia Faye, *Miss Wendy:* Gertrude Hoffman, *Principal, Mr. Tilson:* Douglas Wood, *Al:* Fred Datig, Jr., *Citizen:* John "Skins" Miller.

WELLS FARGO (1937) Par. Produced and directed by Frank Lloyd. Associate Producer, Howard Estabrook. Assistant Director, William Tommel. Staff Director, John Boland. Based on a story by Stuart N. Lake. Screenplay, Paul Schofield, Gerald Geraghty, and Frederick Jackson. Music Score, Victor Young. Music Director, Boris Morros. Art Directors, Hans Dreier and John Goodman. Special Effects, Gordon Jennings. Photography, Theodor Sparkuhl. Editor, Hugh

Wells Fargo with Bob Burns, Joel McCrea and Robert Cummings.

Bennett. Song by Burton Lane and Ralph Freed, "Where I Ain't Been Before." 115 minutes

Ramsay MacKay: Joel McCrea, *Hank York, a Wanderer:* Bob Burns, *Justine Pryor:* Frances Dee, *Dal Slade:* Lloyd Nolan, *Henry Wells:* Henry O'Neill, *Mrs. Pryor:* Mary Nash, *Nicholas Pryor:* Ralph Morgan, *Talbot Carter:* John Mack Brown, *James Oliver:* Porter Hall, *William Fargo:* Jack Clark, *John Butterfield:* Clarence Kalb, *Dan Trimball, Prospector:* Robert Cummings, Sr., *Bradford, Banker:* Granville Bates, *Ingalls, Banker:* Harry Davenport, *Ward, Banker:* Frank Conroy, *Edwards, Newspaper Publisher:* Brandon Tynan, *Alice MacKay:* Peggy Stewart, *Pawnee:* Bernard Siegel, *Abe:* Stanley Fields, *Lucy Dorsett Trimball:* Jane Dewey, *Lincoln:* Frank McGlynn, *Young Alex Trimball:* David Durand, *Young Nick:* Scotty Beckett, *Nick, Jr.:* Jimmy Butler, *Mrs. Ward:* Dorothy Tennant, *Mrs. Edwards:* Clare Verdera, *Padden:* Edward Earle, *Larry:* Henry Brandon, *Dinsmore:* Harry B. Stafford, *Postmaster, San Francisco:* Lucien Littlefield, *Mother of Boy:* Helen Dickson, *Boy:* Jerry Tucker, *Alice at 6:* Babs Nelson, *Lola Montez:* Rebecca Wassem, *Ramsay, Jr.:* Ronnie Cosbey, *Marshal:* Erville Alderson, *Jonathan, Proprietor:* Louis Natheaux, *Zeke Martin:* Paul Newlan, *Alice at 10:* Shirley Coates.

The Westerner with Gary Cooper and Walter Brennan.

THE WESTERNER (1940) UA. Producer, Samuel Goldwyn. Director, William Wyler. Author, Stuart Lake. Screenplay, Jo Swerling, Niven Busch. Cameraman, Gregg Toland. Editor, Daniel Mandell. Film debuts of Forrest Tucker, 25, and Dana Andrews, 29. 99 minutes

Cole Hardin: Gary Cooper, *Judge Roy Bean:* Walter Brennan, *Jane-Ellen Mathews:* Doris Davenport, *Caliphet Mathews:* Fred Stone, *Chickenfoot:* Paul Hurst, *Southeast:* Chill Wills, *Mort Borrow:* Charles

Halton, *Wade Harper:* Forrest Tucker, *King Evans:* Tom Tyler, *Mr. Dixon:* Arthur Aylsworth, *Teresita:* Lupita Tovar, *Juan Gomez:* Julian Rivero, *Lily Langtry:* Lilian Bond, *Bart Cobble:* Dana Andrews, *Eph Stringer:* Roger Gray, *Bantry:* Jack Pennick, *Seth Tucker:* Arthur Mix, *Janice:* Helen Foster, *Shad Wilkins:* Trevor Bardette, *Langtry Maid:* Connie Leon, *Langtry Manager:* Charles Coleman, *Ticket Man:* Lew Kelly, *Man at Window:* Heinie Conklin, *A Stranger:* Lucien Littlefield, *Orchestra Leader:* Corbet Morris, *Sheriff:* Stanley Andrews, *Stage Manager:* Henry Roquemore, *Deputy:* Hank Bell.

WEST SIDE STORY (1961) UA. Producer, Robert Wise. Directors, Robert Wise, Jerome Robbins. Panavision 70, Technicolor. Screenplay, Ernest Lehman. Based on stage play by Arthur Laurents, based on an idea by Jerome Robbins. Music, Leonard Bernstein. Lyrics, Stephen Sondheim. Associate Producer, Saul Chaplin. Choreography,

West Side Story with Russ Tamblyn (left) and George Chakiris (right)

Jerome Robbins. Assistant Director, Robert Relyea. Costumes, Irene Sharaff. Assistant Choreographers, Howard Jeffrey, Margaret Banks. A Mirisch Pictures and Seven Arts Production. Locations filmed in New York. Songs by Leonard Bernstein and Stephen Sondheim: "Jet Song," "Something's Coming," "Dance at the Gym," "Tonight," "Maria," "In America," "One Hand, One Heart," "Officer Krupke," "The Rumble," "Cool," "I Feel Pretty," "Somewhere," "A Boy Like That," "I Have a Love," "There's a Place For Us." Marni Nixon sings for Wood, Jimmy Bryant sings for Beymer. 155 minutes

Maria: Natalie Wood, *Tony:* Richard Beymer, *Riff:* Russ Tamblyn, *Anita:* Rita Moreno, *Bernardo:* George Chakiris, *The Jets: Ice,* Tucker Smith, *Action,* Tony Mordente, *Baby John,* Eliot Feld, *A-Rab,* David Winters, *Snowboy,* Burt Michaels, *Joyboy,* Robert Banas, *Big Deal,* Scooter (Anthony) Teague, *Gee-Tar,* Tommy Abbott, *Mouthpiece,* Harvey Hohnecker, *Tiger,* David Bean, *Anybodys,* Sue Oakes, *Graziella:* Gina Trikonis, *Velma:* Carole D'Andrea, *The Sharks: Chino,* Joe De Vega, *Pepe,* Jay Norman, *Indio,* Gus Trikonis, *Luis,* Robert Thompson, *Rocco,* Larry Roquemore, *Loco,* Jaime Rogers, *Juano,* Eddie Verso, *Chile,* Andre Tayir, *Toro,* Nick Covvacevich, *Del Camp,* Rudy Del Campo, *Rosalia,* Suzie Kaye, *Consuelo,* Yvonne Othon, *Francisca,* Joanne Miya, *Lieutenant Schrank:* Simon Oakland, *Officer Krupke:* Bill Bramley, *Doc:* Ned Glass, *Glad Hand, Social Worker:* John Astin, *Madame Lucia:* Penny Santon.

WHAT A WAY TO GO! (1964) 20th. Producer, Arthur P. Jacobs. Director, J. Lee Thompson. CinemaScope, De Luxe Color. Author, Gwen Davis. Screenplay, Betty Comden, Adolph Green. Art Directors, Jack Martin Smith, Ted Haworth. Music, Nelson Riddle. "I Think That You and I Should Get Acquainted," "Musical Extravaganza," lyrics, Betty Comden, Adolph Green. Music, Jule Styne. Orchestration, Arthur Morton. Cinematographer, Leon Shamroy. Special Photographic Effects, L. B. Abbott, Emil Kosa, Jr. Editor, Marjorie Fowler. 111 minutes

Louisa Foster: Shirley MacLaine, *Larry Flint:* Paul Newman, *Rod Anderson:* Robert Mitchum, *Leonard Crawley:* Dean Martin, *Jerry Benson:* Gene Kelly, *Dr. Steffanson:* Bob Cummings, *Edgar Hopper:* Dick Van Dyke, *Painter:* Reginald Gardiner, *Mrs. Foster:* Margaret Dumont, *Trentino:* Lou Nova, *Baroness:* Fifi D'Orsay, *Rene:* Maurice Marsac, *Agent:* Wally Vernon, *Polly:* Jane Wald, *Hollywood Lawyer:* Lenny Kent, *Mrs. Freeman:* Marjorie Bennett, *Ned:* Christopher Connelly, *Girl on Plane:* Barbara Bouchet, *Lord Kensington:* Tom Conway, *Lady Kensington:* Queenie Leonard, *Willard:* Anthony Eustrel, *Publicity and Press Agent:* Phil Arnold, *Driscoll:* Richard Wilson, *Movie Executive:* Sid Gould, *Movie Executive's Girl:* Paula Lane, *TV Announcer:* (Army) Armand Archerd, *Movie Star:* Tracy Butler, *Mr. Foster:* Anton Arnold, *Minister:* Roy Gordon, *Crawleyville Lawyer:* Burt Mustin, *Leonard Crawley (age 7):* Billy Corcoran, *Jonathan Crawley (age 5):* Jeff Fithian, *Geraldine Crawley (age 4):* Pamelyn Ferdin, *Doris:* Helene F. Winston, *Chester:* Jack Greening.

What a Way to Go! with Shirley MacLaine and Robert Mitchum.

What Ever Happened to Baby Jane with Joan Crawford and Bette Davis.

What's New Pussycat? with Peter Sellers and Capucine.

Fritz Fassbender: Peter Sellers, *Michael James:* Peter O'Toole, *Carol Werner:* Romy Schneider, *Renee Lefebvre:* Capucine, *Liz:* Paula Prentiss, *Victor Shakapopolis:* Woody Allen, *Rita:* Ursula Andress, *Anna Fassbender:* Edra Gale, *Jacqueline:* Catherine Schaake, *Mr. Werner:* Jess Hahn, *Mrs. Werner:* Eleanor Hirt, *Tempest O'Brien:* Nicole Karen, *Marcel:* Jean Paredes, *Philippe:* Michel Subor, *Charlotte:* Jacqueline Fogt, *Car Renter:* Robert Rollis, *Gas Station Operator:* Daniel Emilfork, *Jean:* Louis Falavigna, *Etienne:* Jacques Balutin, *Emma:* Annette Poivre, *Man in Bar:* Richard Burton.

WHAT EVER HAPPENED TO BABY JANE (1962) WB. Producer-Director, Robert Aldrich. Screenplay, Lukas Heller. Based on a novel by Henry Farrell. Executive Producer, Kenneth Hyman. Costumes, Norma Koch. Assistant Director, Tom Connors. Choreography, Alex Romero. A Seven Arts Production. Art Director, William Glasgow. Music, Frank DeVol. Cinematographer, Ernest Haller. Editor, Michael Luciano. Scenes from *Parachute Jumper* (WB, 1933), Davis; *Sadie McKee* (MGM, 1934), Crawford. 132 minutes

Blanche Hudson: Joan Crawford, *Jane Hudson:* Bette Davis, *Edwin Flagg:* Victor Buono, *Della Flagg:* Marjorie Bennett, *Elvira Stitt:* Maidie Norman, *Mrs. Bates:* Anna Lee, *Liza Bates:* Barbara Merrill, *Baby Jane:* Julie Allred, *Blanche as a child:* Gina Gillespie, *Ray Hudson:* Dave Willock, *Cora Hudson:* Ann Barton.

WHAT'S NEW PUSSYCAT? (1965) UA. Producer, Charles K. Feldman. Executive Producer, John C. Shepridge. Director, Clive Donner. Associate Producer, Richard Sylbert. Screenplay, Woody Allen. Music, Burt Bacharach. Lyrics, Hal David. Director of Photography, Jean Badal. Assistant Director, Enrico Isacco. Costumes, Mia Fonssagrives, Vicki Tiel. In Technicolor. A Production of Famous Artists Productions and Famartists Productions. 108 minutes

WHEN MY BABY SMILES AT ME (1948) 20th. Producer, George Jessel. Director, Walter Lang. Color by Technicolor. Based on the play *Burlesque* by George Manker Watters and Arthur Hopkins. Adaptation, Elizabeth Reinhardt. Technicolor Director, Natalie Kalmus. Screenplay, Lamar Trotti. Musical Director, Alfred Newman. Art Directors, Lyle Wheeler, Leland Fuller. Photography, Harry Jackson. Editor, Barbara McLean. Songs: "By the Way" and "What Did I Do?" by Mack Gordon and Josef Myrow; "When My Baby Smiles at Me" by Andrew B. Sterling and Harry Von Tilzer. Previous versions: *Dance of Life* (Paramount, 1929), *Swing High, Swing Low* (Paramount, 1937). 98 minutes

Bonny: Betty Grable, *Skid:* Dan Dailey, *Bozo:* Jack Oakie, *Gussie:* June Havoc, *Harvey:* Richard Arlen, *Lefty:* James Gleason, *Bubbles:* Vanita Wade, *Specialty Dancer:* Kenny Williams, *Sam Harris:* Robert Emmett Keane, *Sylvia Marco:* Jean Wallace, *Woman in Box:* Pati Behrs, *Midget:* Jerry Maren, *Comic:* George "Beetlepuss" Lewis, *Valet:* Tom Stevenson, *Process Server:* Sam Bernard, *Stage Manager:* Mauritz Hugo, *Vendor:* Frank Scannell, *Doorman:* J. Farrell Mac-Donald, *Troupers:* Les Clark, Harry Seymour, *Call Boy:* Lee Mac-Gregor, *Interne:* Charles Tannen, *Attendant:* Robert Karnes, *Conductor:* George Medford, *Girl:* Marion Marshall, *Sailor:* Robert Patten, *Man in Box:* Harry Carter, *Man:* Kit Guard, *Musician:* Tiny

Timbrell, *Sailor:* Ted Jordan, *Chorus Girl:* Bee Stephens, *Tony:* Charles La Torre, *Specialty Dancers:* Dorothy Babb, Joanne Dale, Lu Anne Jones, Noel Neill.

When My Baby Smiles at Me with Betty Grable and Dan Dailey.

WHISPERING SMITH (1948) Par. Associate Producer, Mel Epstein. Directed by Leslie Fenton. Color by Technicolor. Based on the novel by Frank H. Spearman. Screenplay, Frank Butler and Karl Lamb. Score, Adolph Deutsch. Editor, Archie Marshek. Art Directors, Hans Dreier and Walter Tyler. Photography, Ray Rennahan. Song, "Laramie" by Jay Livingston and Ray Evans. 88 minutes.

Luke "Whispering" Smith: Alan Ladd, *Murray Sinclair:* Robert Preston, *Marian Sinclair:* Brenda Marshall, *Barney Rebstock:* Donald Crisp, *Bill Dansing:* William Demarest, *Emmy Dansing:* Fay Holden, *Blake Barton:* Murvyn Vye, *Whitey Du Sang:* Frank Faylen, *George McCloud:* John Eldredge, *Leroy Barton:* Robert Wood, *Bill Baggs:* J. Farrell MacDonald, *Dr. Sawbuck:* Don Barclay, *Sheriff McSwiggin:* Will Wright, *Conductor:* Eddy Waller, *Dog's Master:* Gary Gray, *Gabby Barton:* Bob Kortman.

Whispering Smith with Murvyn Vye and Alan Ladd.

WHITE CHRISTMAS (1954) Par. Producer, Robert Emmett Dolan. Director, Michael Curtiz. VistaVision, Technicolor. Screenplay, Norman Krasna, Norma Panama, Melvin Frank. Art Directors, Hal Pereira, Roland Anderson. Cinematographer, Loyal Griggs. Editor, Frank Bracht. The first film in VistaVision. Songs by Irving Berlin: "White Christmas," "Count Your Blessings," "Love, You Didn't Do

Right by Me," "Choreography," "The Old Man," "Blue Skies," "Minstrel Show and Mandy," "Abraham," "Sisters," "Gee, I Wish I Was Back in the Army," "What Can You Do with a General," "The Best Things Happen While You're Dancing," "Snow." 120 minutes

White Christmas with Danny Kaye and Bing Crosby.

Bob Wallace: Bing Crosby, *Phil Davis:* Danny Kaye, *Betty:* Rosemary Clooney, *Judy:* Vera Ellen, *General Waverly:* Dean Jagger, *Emma:* Mary Wickes, *Joe:* John Brascia, *Susan:* Anne Whitfield, *Adjutant:* Richard Shannon, *General's Guest:* Grady Sutton, *Landlord:* Sig Rumann, *Albert:* Robert Crosson, *Novello:* Herb Vigran, *Asst. Stage Manager:* Dick Keene, *Ed Harrison:* Johnny Grant, *General Carlton:* Gavin Gordon, *Maitre d':* Marcel De La Brosse, *Sheriff:* James Parnell, *Conductor:* Percy Helton, *Fat Lady:* Elizabeth Holmes, *Doris:* Barrie Chase, *Station Master:* I. Stanford Jolley, *Specialty Dancer:* George Chakiris.

The White Cliffs of Dover with Alan Marshal, Irene Dunne and Van Johnson.

THE WHITE CLIFFS OF DOVER (1944) MGM. Producer, Sidney Franklin. Director, Clarence Brown. Author, Alice Duer Miller. Screenplay, Claudine West, Jan Lustig, George Froeschel. Art Director, Cedric Gibbons. Musical Score, Herbert Stothart. Cameraman, George Folsey. Special Effects, Arnold Gillespie, Warren Newcombe. Editor, Robert J. Kern. Based on the poem "The White Cliffs" by Alice Duer Miller, with additional poetry by Robert Nathan. 126 minutes

Susan Ashwood: Irene Dunne, *Sir John Ashwood:* Alan Marshal, *Hiram Porter Dunn:* Frank Morgan, *John Ashwood II as a boy:* Roddy McDowall, *Nanny:* Dame May Whitty, *Colonel:* C. Aubrey Smith, *Lady Jean Ashwood:* Gladys Cooper, *John Ashwood II (age 24):* Peter Lawford, *Sam Bennett:* Van Johnson, *Reggie:* John Warburton, *Rosamund:* Jill Esmond, *Gwennie:* Brenda Forbes, *Mrs. Bland:*

Norma Varden, *Betsy (10 years)*: Elizabeth Taylor, *Betsy (18 years)*: June Lockhart, *Farmer Kenney:* Charles Irwin, *Mrs. Kenney:* Jean Prescott, *American Soldier:* Tom Drake, *Mrs. Bancroft:* Isobel Elsom, *Major Bancroft:* Edmund Breon, *Major Loring:* Miles Mander, *Miss Lambert:* Ann Curzon, *Gerhard:* Steven Muller, *Dietrich:* Norbert Multer, *Helen:* Molly Lamont, *The Vicar:* Lumsden Hare, *Benson:* Arthur Shields, *Plump Lady in Boarding House:* Doris Lloyd, *Immigration Officer:* Matthew Boulton, *Woman on Train:* Ethel Griffies, *Footman:* Herbert Evans, *Duke of Waverly:* Keith Hitchcock, *Duchess:* Vera Graaff, *Miller:* Anita Bolster, *Skipper:* Ian Wolfe, *Billings:* Alec Craig, *Jennings:* Clyde Cook.

Whoopee with Eleanor Hunt and Eddie Cantor.

WHOOPEE (1930) UA. Produced by Samuel Goldwyn and Florenz Ziegfeld. Directed by Thornton Freeland. Color by Technicolor. Dances by Busby Berkeley. Based on the Ziegfeld musical *Whoopee* by William Anthony McGuire, adapted from the comedy *The Nervous Wreck* by Owen Davis. Scenario, William Conselman. Photography, Lee Garmes, Ray Rennahan, Gregg Toland. Editor, Stuart Heisler. Sound, Oscar Lagerstrom. Songs: "Making Whoopee," "A Girl Friend of a Boy Friend of Mine," "My Baby Just Cares For Me," "Stetson" by Walter Donaldson and Gus Kahn; "I'll Still Belong to You" by Edward Eliscu and Nacio Herb Brown. Most of the cast of the musical is featured. Film debut of Barbara Weeks, 16. Remade as Danny Kaye's *Up in Arms* (RKO, 1944). 94 minutes

Henry Williams: Eddie Cantor, *Sally Morgan:* Eleanor Hunt, *Wanenis:* Paul Gregory, *Sheriff Bob Wells:* Jack Rutherford, *Mary Custer:* Ethel Shutta, *Jerome Underwood:* Spencer Charters, *Black Eagle:* Chief Caupolican, *Chester Underwood:* Albert Hackett, *Andy McNabb:* Will H. Philbrick, *Judd Morgan:* Walter Law, *Harriett Underwood:* Marilyn Morgan (Marian Marsh), *Dancer:* Barbara Weeks, The George Oslen Band.

Who's Afraid of Virginia Woolf? with Elizabeth Taylor and Richard Burton.

WHO'S AFRAID OF VIRGINIA WOOLF? (1966) WB. Produced by Ernest Lehman. Directed by Mike Nichols. Screenplay, Ernest Lehman, from the play by Edward Albee. Camera, Haskell Wexler. Editor, Sam O'Steen. Music composed and conducted by Alex North. Assistant director, Bud Grace. Sets, George James Hopkins. Costumes, Irene Sharaff. Hair Styles, Sydney Guilaroff and Jean Burt Reilly. Make-up, Gordon Bau and Ronnie Berkeley. 131 minutes

Martha: Elizabeth Taylor, *George:* Richard Burton, *Nick:* George Segal, *Honey:* Sandy Dennis.

The Wild Angels with Bruce Dern and Peter Fonda.

THE WILD ANGELS (1966) American International. Produced and directed by Roger Corman. Panavision and Pathé Color. Screenplay, Charles B. Griffith. Camera, Richard Moore. Associate Producer, Laurence Cruikshank. Music, Mike Curb. Assistant Director, Paul Rapp. Editor, Monty Helman. Assistant to the Director, Peter Bogdanovich. Art Director, Leon Erickson. Music produced by Group IV Productions. The last film of Art Baker. 93 minutes

Heavenly Blues: Peter Fonda, *Mike:* Nancy Sinatra, *Loser (Joey Kerns):* Bruce Dern, *Gaysh:* Diane Ladd, *Joint:* Lou Procopio, *Bull Puckey:* Coby Denton, *Frankenstein:* Marc Cavell, *Dear John:* Buck Taylor, *Medic:* Norm Alden, *Pigmy:* Michael J. Pollard, *Mama Monahan:* Joan Shawlee, *Suzie:* Gayle Hunnicutt, *Thomas, Undertaker:* Art Baker, *Preacher:* Frank Maxwell, *Hospital Policeman:* Frank Gertsle, *Nurse:* Kim Hamilton, *Mother:* Barboura Morris, *Rigger:* Dick Miller, *Bits:* Hal Bokar, Gina Grant, Jack Bernardi, Members of Hell's Angels of Venice, California.

The Wild One with Ray Teal (bartender) and Marlon Brando.

THE WILD ONE (1954) Col. Producer, Stanley Kramer. Director, Laslo Benedek. Author, Frank Rooney (from *The Cyclists' Raid*). Screenplay, John Paxton. Art Director, Walter Holscher. Cinematographer, Hal Mohr. Editor, Al Clark. 79 minutes.

Johnny: Marlon Brando, *Kathie:* Mary Murphy, *Harry Bleeker:* Robert Keith, *Chino:* Lee Marvin, *Sheriff Singer:* Jay C. Flippen, *Mildred:* Peggy Maley, *Charlie Thomas:* Hugh Sanders, *Frank Bleeker:* Ray Teal, *Bill Hannegan:* John Brown, *Art Kleiner:* Will Wright, *Ben:* Robert Osterloh, *Wilson:* Robert Bice, *Simmy:* William Vedder, *Britches:* Yvonne Doughty, *Gringo:* Keith Clarke, *Mouse:* Gil Stratton, Jr., *Dinky:* Darren Dublin, *Red:* Johnny Tarangelo, *Dextro:* Jerry Paris, *Crazy:* Gene Peterson, *Pigeon:* Alvy Moore, *Go Go:* Harry Landers, *Boxer:* Jim Connell, *Stinger:* Don Anderson, *Betty:* Angela Stevens, *Simmonds:* Bruno VeSoto, *Sawyer:* Pat O'Malley, *Dorothy:* Eve March, *Cyclist:* Wally Albright, *Chino Boy No. 1:* Timothy Carey, *Official:* John Doucette.

Wild River with Lee Remick and Montgomery Clift.

WILD RIVER (1960) 20th. Producer, Elia Kazan. Director, Elia Kazan. CinemaScope, De Luxe Color. Based on the novels *Mud on the Stars* by William Bradford Huie and *Dunbar's Cove* by Borden Deal. Filmed in Cleveland, Tennessee. Screenplay, Paul Osborn. Art Directors, Lyle R. Wheeler, Herman A. Blumenthal. Music composed and conducted by Kenyon Hopkins. Cinematographer, Ellsworth Fredricks. Editor, William Reynolds. 107 minutes

Chuck Glover: Montgomery Clift, *Carol Garth Baldwin:* Lee Remick, *Ella Garth:* Jo Van Fleet, *R. J. Bailey:* Albert Salmi, *Hamilton Garth:* Jay C. Flippen, *Cal Garth:* James Westerfield, *Betty Jackson:* Barbara Loden, *Walter Clark:* Frank Overton, *Sy Moore:* Malcolm Atterbury, *Ben:* Robert Earl Jones, *Jack Roper:* Bruce Dern, *Joe John Garth:* Big Jeff Bess, *Barbara Baldwin:* Judy Harris, *Jim Baldwin, Jr.:* Jim Menard, *Mayor Tom Maynard:* Jim Steakley, *Mattie:* Patricia Perry, *Todd:* John Dudley, *Thompson:* Alfred E. Smith, *Winters:* Mark Menson.

WILSON (1944) 20th. Producer, Darryl F. Zanuck. Director, Henry King. Color by Technicolor. Screenplay, Lamar Trotti. Director of Photography, Leon Shamroy. Technicolor Director, Natalie Kalmus. Associate, Richard Mueller. Music, Alfred Newman. Technical Advisers, Ray Stannard Baker, Miles McCahill. Orchestral Arrangements, Edward Powell. Art Direction, Wiard Ihnen, James Basevi. Set Decorations, Thomas Little. Associate, Paul S. Fox. Film Editor, Barbara McLean. Costumes, Rene Hubert. Make-up Artist, Guy Pearce. Special Photographic Effects, Fred Sersen. Sound, E. Clayton Ward, Roger Heman. 154 minutes

Woodrow Wilson: Alexander Knox, *Prof. Henry Holmes:* Charles Coburn, *Edith Wilson:* Geraldine Fitzgerald, *Joseph Tumulty:* Thomas Mitchell, *Ellen Wilson:* Ruth Nelson, *Senator Henry Cabot Lodge:* Sir Cedric Hardwicke, *William Gibbs McAdoo:* Vincent Price, *George Felton:* William Eythe, *Eleanor Wilson:* Mary Anderson, *Margaret*

Wilson with Geraldine Fitzgerald and Alexander Knox.

Wilson: Ruth Ford, *Josephus Daniels:* Sidney Blackmer, *Jessie Wilson:* Madeleine Forbes, *Admiral Grayson:* Stanley Ridges, *Eddie Foy:* Eddie Foy, Jr., *Colonel House:* Charles Halton, *Senator B. H. Jones:* Thurston Hall, *Edward Sullivan:* J. M. Kerrigan, *Jim Beeker:* James Rennie, *Helen Bones:* Katherine Locke, *Secretary Lansing:* Stanley Logan, *Clemenceau:* Marcel Dalio, *William Jennings Bryan:* Edwin Maxwell, *Lloyd George:* Clifford Brooke, *Von Bernstorff:* Tonio Selwart, *Senator Watson:* John Ince, *Senator Bromfield:* Charles Miller, *Barney Baruch:* Francis X. Bushman, *McCoombs:* George Macready, *Granddaughter:* Phyllis Brooks, *Charles F. Murphy:* Cy Kendall, *Ike Hoover:* Roy Roberts, *Jennie, the Maid:* Anne O'Neal, *Secretary Lane:* Arthur Loft, *Secretary Colby:* Russell Gaige, *Secretary Payne:* Jamesson Shade, *Secretary Baker:* Reginald Sheffield, *Secretary Garrison:* Robert Middlemass, *Secretary Burleson:* Matt Moore, *Secretary Houston:* George Anderson, *Chief Justice White:* Joseph J. Greene, *Secretary William B. Wilson:* Larry McGrath, *Senator:* Gibson Gowland, *Champ Clark:* Davison Clark, *Jeannette Rankin:* Hilda Plowright, *Usher:* Reed Hadley, *La Follette:* Ralph Dunn, *General Bliss:* Major Sam Harris.

Winchester '73 with James Stewart, Millard Mitchell, Tony Curtis, Charles Drake and Jay C. Flippen.

WINCHESTER '73 (1950) Univ. Producer, Aaron Rosenberg. Director, Anthony Mann. From a story by Stuart N. Lake. Screenplay, Robert L. Richards and Borden Chase. Art Directors, Bernard Herzbrun, Nathan Juran. Musical Director, Joseph Gershenson. Photography, William Daniels. Editor, Edward Curtiss. Filmed in Tucson. Remade by Universal as a 1967 TV feature, also with Duryea. 92 minutes

Lin McAdam: James Stewart, *Lola Manners:* Shelley Winters, *Waco Johnny Dean:* Dan Duryea, *Dutch Henry Brown:* Stephen McNally,

High Spade: Millard Mitchell, *Steve Miller:* Charles Drake, *Joe La-mont:* John McIntire, *Wyatt Earp:* Will Geer, *Sgt. Wilkes:* Jay C. Flippen, *Young Bull:* Rock Hudson, *Jack Riker:* John Alexander, *Wesley:* Steve Brodie, *Wheeler:* James Millican, *Latigo Means:* Abner Biberman, *Doan:* Anthony Curtis, *Crater:* James Best, *Mossman:* Gregg Martell, *Cavalryman:* Frank Chase, *Long Tom:* Chuck Roberson, *Dudeen:* Carol Henry, *Marshall Noonan:* Ray Teal, *Mrs. Jameson:* Virginia Mullens, *Roan Daley:* John Doucette, *Masterson:* Steve Darrell, *Indian:* Chief Yowlachie, *Clerk:* Frank Conlan, *Charles Bender:* Ray Bennett, *Virgil:* Guy Wilkerson, *Bassett:* Bob Anderson, *Boy at Rifle Shoot:* Larry Olsen, *Target Watcher:* Edmund Cobb, *Target Clerk:* Forrest Taylor, *Station Master:* Ethan Laidlaw, *Man:* Bud Osborne, *Bunny Jameson:* Gary Jackson, *Betty Jameson:* Bonnie Kay Eddy, *Stagecoach Driver:* Jennings Miles, *Indian Interpreter:* John War Eagle.

Winged Victory with Barry Nelson, Edmond O'Brien and Mark Daniels.

WINGED VICTORY (1944) 20th. Producer, Darryl F. Zanuck. Director, George Cukor. Screenplay, Moss Hart. Musical Score, David Rose. Art Directors, Lyle Wheeler, Lewis Creber. Cameraman, Glen MacWilliams. Special Effects, Fred Sersen. Editor, Barbara McLean. Song by Tod B. Galloway, Meade Minnigerode and George S. Pomeroy, "The Whiffenpoof Song." Based on the play by Moss Hart. Presented in association with the U. S. Army Air Forces. 130 minutes

Frankie Davis: Private Lon McCallister, *Helen:* Jeanne Crain, *Irving Miller:* Sergeant Edmond O'Brien, *Jane Preston:* Jane Ball, *Alan Ross:* Sergeant Mark Daniels, *Dorothy Ross:* Jo-Carroll Dennison, *Danny "Pinky" Scariano:* Corporal Don Taylor, *Doctor:* Corporal Lee J. Cobb, *Ruth Miller:* Judy Holliday, *O'Brian:* T/Sergeant Peter Lind Hayes, *Major Halper:* Corporal Alan Baxter, *Mrs. Ross:* Geraldine Wall, *Whitey:* Corporal Red Buttons, *Mr. Scariano:* George Humbert, *Bobby Crills:* Corporal Barry Nelson, *Dave Anderson:* Sergeant Rune Hultman, *Jimmy Gardner:* Corporal Richard Hogan, *Colonel Gibney:* Corporal Phillip Bourneuf, *Captain McIntyre:* Corporal Gary Merrill, *Colonel Ross:* Corporal Damian O'Flynn, *Lieutenant Thompson:* Sergeant George Reeves, *Barker:* Private First Class George Petrie, *Milhauser:* Private First Class Alfred Ryder, *Adams:* Corporal Karl Malden, *Gleason:* Private First Class Martin Ritt, *Cadet Peter Clark:* Corporal Harry Lewis, *Officer:* Captain Ray Bidwell, *Flight Surgeon:* Corporal Henry Rowland, *Captain Speer:* Lieutenant Carroll Riddle, *Carmen Miranda:* S/Sergeant Sascha Branstoff, *Master of Ceremonies:* Corporal Archie Robbins, *Andrews Sisters:* Corporal Jack Slate, Corporal Red Buttons, Private First Class Henry Slate, *Irving Jr.:* Timmy Hawkins, *Mrs. Gardner:* Moyna Macgill, *Man:* Don Beddoe (AAF), *WAC:* Frances Gladwin, *Cigarette Girl:* Sally Yarnell.

WINTERSET (1936) RKO. Produced by Pandro S. Berman. Directed by Alfred Santell. From the Guthrie McClintic Production of the play by Maxwell Anderson. Screenplay, Anthony Weiler. Music Director,

Winterset with Burgess Meredith, Eduardo Ciannelli, Maurice Moscovich and Edward Ellis.

Nathaniel Shilkret. Music Arrangements, Maurice De Packh. Camera, Peverell Marley. Editor, William Hamilton. Film debuts of Burgess Meredith, Paul Guilfoyle, Myron McCormick. 78 minutes

Mio: Burgess Meredith, *Miriamne:* Margo, *Trock:* Eduardo Ciannelli, *Garth:* Paul Guilfoyle, *Romagna:* John Carradine, *Judge Gaunt:* Edward Ellis, *Shadow:* Stanley Ridges, *Esdras:* Maurice Moscovitch, *Carr:* Myron McCormick, *A Policeman:* Willard Robertson, *A Radical:* Mischa Auer, *A Girl:* Barbara Pepper, *A Hobo:* Alec Craig, *Mrs. Romagna:* Helen Jerome Eddy, *Piny:* Fernanda Eliscu, *Lucia:* George Humbert, *Louie:* Murray Alper, *Joe:* Paul Fix, *A Sailor:* Alan Curtis, *District Attorney:* Arthur Loft, *Elderly Man:* Otto Hoffman, *Woman:* Grace Hayle, *Gangster:* Al Hill, *Girl:* Lucille Ball.

With a Song in My Heart with Susan Hayward (center).

WITH A SONG IN MY HEART (1952) 20th. Producer, Lamar Trotti. Director, Walter Lang. Color by Technicolor. Author, Lamar Trotti. Screenplay, Lamar Trotti. Musical Director, Alfred Newman. Art Directors, Lyle Wheeler, Earle Hagen. Cinematographer, Leon Shamroy. Editor, J. Watson Webb. Technicolor Consultant, Leonard Doss. Songs: "Blue Moon" and "With a Song in My Heart" by Lorenz Hart and Richard Rodgers; "That Old Feeling" by Lew Brown and Sammy Fain; "I've Got a Feeling You're Fooling" by Arthur Freed and Nacio Herb Brown; "Tea for Two" by Irving Caesar and Vincent Youmans; "Deep in the Heart of Texas" by June Hershey and Don Swander; "Carry Me Back to Old Virginny" by James Bland; "Dixie" by Dan Emmett; "They're Either Too Young or Too Old" by Frank Loesser and Arthur Schwartz; "It's a Good Day" by Peggy Lee and Dave Barbour; "I'll Walk Alone" by Sammy Cahn and Jule Styne; "Give My Regards to Broadway" by George M. Cohan; "Alabamy Bound" by Bud Green, B. G. DeSylva and Ray Henderson; "California Here I Come" by B. G. DeSylva, Al Jolson and Joseph Meyer; "Chicago" by Fred Fisher; "America the Beautiful" by Katherine Lee Bates and Samuel A. Ward; "I'm Through with Love" by Gus Kahn, Fred Livingston and Matty Malneck; "Embraceable You" by Ira and George Gershwin; "On the Gay White Way" by Leo Robin and Rainger; "The Right Kind of Love" by Don George and Charles Henderson; "Montparnasse" by Alfred Newman and Eliot Daniel; "Maine Stein Song" by E. A. Fenstad and Lincoln Colcord; "(Back Home Again In) Indiana" by Ballard MacDonald and James F. Hanley; "Get Happy" by Ted Koehler and Harold Arlen; "Hoe That Corn" by Max Showalter and Jack Woodford; "Jim's Toasted Peanuts" and "Wonderful Home Sweet Home" by Ken Darby. 117 minutes

Jane Froman: Susan Hayward, *John Burn:* Rory Calhoun, *Don Ross:* David Wayne, *Clancy:* Thelma Ritter, *G. I. Paratrooper:* Robert Wagner, *Jennifer March:* Helen Westcott, *Sister Marie:* Una Merkel, *Dancer:* Richard Allan, *Guild:* Max Showalter (Casey Adams), *Radio Director:* Lyle Talbot, *General:* Leif Erickson, *Diplomat:* Stanley Logan, *Specialty:* Ernest Newton, *General:* Paul Maxey, *Kansas:* Robert Easton, *U. S. O. Man:* Eddie Firestone, *Texas:* Frank Sully, *Muleface:* George Offerman, *U. S. O. Girl:* Beverly Thompson, *Sister Margaret:* Maude Wallace, *Colonel:* Douglas Evans, *Doctors:* Carlos Molina, Nestor Paiva, Emmett Vogan.

Without Love with Spencer Tracy and Katharine Hepburn.

WITHOUT LOVE (1945) MGM. Producer, Lawrence A. Weingarten. Director, Harold S. Bucquet. Screenplay, Donald Ogden Stewart. Score, Bronislau Kaper. Art Directors, Cedric Gibbons, Harry McAfee. Cameraman, Karl Freund. Special Effects, A. Arnold Gillespie, Danny Hall. Editor, Frank Sullivan. From Philip Barry's Theatre Guild play. 111 minutes

Pat Jamieson: Spencer Tracy, *Jamie Rowan:* Katharine Hepburn, *Kitty Trimble:* Lucille Ball, *Quentin Ladd:* Keenan Wynn, *Paul Carrell:* Carl Esmond, *Edwina Collins:* Patricia Morison, *Professor Grinza:* Felix Bressart, *Anna:* Emily Massey, *Flower Girl:* Gloria Grahame, *Caretaker:* George Davis, *Elevator Boy:* George Chandler, *Sergeant:* Clancy Cooper, *Professor Thompson:* Wallis Clark, *Professor Ellis:* Donald Curtis, *Colonel Braden:* Charles Arnt, *Driver:* Eddie Acuff, *Porter:* Clarence Muse, *Headwaiter:* Franco Corsaro, *Pageboy:* Ralph Brooks, *Doctor:* William Forrest, *Soldier:* Garry Owen, *Soldier:* Joe Devlin, *Soldier:* William Newell, *Sergeant:* James Flavin, *Girl on Elevator:* Hazel Brooks.

WITNESS FOR THE PROSECUTION (1957) UA. Produced by Arthur Hornblow. Directed by Billy Wilder. Based on the story and play by Agatha Christie. Screenplay, Billy Wilder and Harry Kurnitz. A Theme Pictures Production, presented by Edward Small. Song, "I May Never Go Home Anymore" by Ralph Arthur Roberts and Jack Brooks. Filmed at Goldwyn Studios. 114 minutes

Leonard Vole: Tyrone Power, *Christine Vole:* Marlene Dietrich, *Sir Wilfrid Robarts:* Charles Laughton, *Miss Plimsoll:* Elsa Lanchester, *Brogan-Moore:* John Williams, *Mayhew:* Henry Daniell, *Carter:* Ian Wolfe, *Janet McKenzie:* Una O'Connor, *Mr. Myers:* Torin Thatcher, *Judge:* Francis Compton, *Mrs. French:* Norma Varden, *Inspector*

Witness for the Prosecution with Henry Daniell, Tyrone Power and Charles Laughton.

Hearne: Philip Tonge, *Diana:* Ruta Lee, *Miss McHugh:* Molly Roden, *Miss Johnson:* Ottola Nesmith, *Miss O'Brien:* Marjorie Eaton, *Shorts Salesman:* J. Pat O'Malley.

THE WIZARD OF OZ (1939) MGM. Produced by Mervyn LeRoy. Directed by Victor Fleming. Color by Technicolor, opening and closing scenes in Sepia. Adapted from the book by L. Frank Baum. Screenplay, Noel Langley, Florence Ryerson, Edgar Allan Wolfe. Art Directors, Cedric Gibbons and William A. Horning. Sets, Edwin B. Willis. Musical numbers staged by Bobby Connolly. Music Score, Herbert Stothart. Songs by E. Y. Harburg and Harold Arlen: "Over the Rainbow," "Follow the Yellow Brick Road," "If I Only Had a Brain," "We're Off to See the Wizard," "Merry Old Land of Oz," "Laugh a Day Away," "If I Were King," "Courage," "Welcome to Munchkinland," "Ding Dong, The Witch Is Dead," "If I Only Had a Heart," and "The Jitterbug." Special Effects, Arnold Gillespie. Editor, Blanche Sewell. Associate Conductor, George Stoll. Orchestral and Vocal Arrangements, George Bassman, Murray Cutter, Paul Marquardt, Ken Darby. Character Make-ups, Jack Dawn. Photography, Harold Rosson. Film debut of Jerry Maren, 19, 3'6". 101 minutes

Dorothy: Judy Garland, *Professor Marvel (The Wizard):* Frank Morgan, *Hunk (Scarecrow):* Ray Bolger, *Zeke (Cowardly Lion):* Bert Lahr, *Hickory (Tin Woodman):* Jack Haley, *Glinda:* Billie Burke, *Miss Gulch (The Witch):* Margaret Hamilton, *Uncle Henry:* Charley Grapewin, *Nikko:* Pat Walshe, *Auntie Em:* Clara Blandick, *Toto:* Toto, *Munchkins:* The Singer Midgets, *A Munchkin:* Jerry Marenghi (Jerry Maren).

The Wizard of Oz with Margaret Hamilton and Judy Garland.

Woman of the Year with Henry Roquemore, Katharine Hepburn, Fay Bainter and Spencer Tracy.

WOMAN OF THE YEAR (1942) MGM. Produced by Joseph L. Mankiewicz. Directed by George Stevens. Original Screenplay, Ring Lardner, Jr. and Michael Kanin. Music, Franz Waxman. Art Director, Cedric Gibbons. Associate Art Director, Randall Duell. Hair Styles, Sydney Guilaroff. Gowns, Adrian. Sets, Edwin B. Willis. Photography, Joseph Ruttenberg. Sound, Douglas Shearer. Editor, Frank Sullivan. The first Tracy–Hepburn film. Film debut of William Bendix. 112 minutes

Sam Craig: Spencer Tracy, *Tess Harding:* Katharine Hepburn, *Ellen Whitcomb:* Fay Bainter, *Clayton:* Reginald Owen, *William Harding:* Minor Watson, *Pinkie Peters:* William Bendix, *Flo Peters:* Gladys Blake, *Gerald:* Dan Tobin, *Phil Whittaker:* Roscoe Karns, *Ellis:* William Tannen, *Dr. Martin Lubbeck:* Ludwig Stossel, *Matron at Refugee Home:* Sara Haden, *Alma:* Edith Evanson, *Chris:* George Kezas, *Radio M.C. (Voice):* Gerald Mohr, *Reporter:* Jimmy Conlin, *Justice of the Peace:* Henry Roquemore, *Harding's Chauffeur:* Cyril Ring, *Punchy:* Ben Lessy, *Pal:* Johnny Berkes, *Reporter:* Ray Teal, *Football Player:* Duke York, *Adolph:* Edward McWade.

The Women with Joan Crawford, Aileen Pringle, Mariska Aldrich, Joan Fontaine, Norma Shearer, Rosalind Russell and Phyllis Povah.

THE WOMEN (1939) MGM. Producer, Hunt Stromberg. Director, George Cukor. From the play by Clare Boothe. Screenplay, Anita Loos, Jane Murfin. Art Director, Cedric Gibbons. Musical Score, Edward Ward, David Snell. Cameramen, Oliver T. Marsh, Joseph Ruttenberg. Editor, Robert J. Kerns. Song by Chet Forrest, Bob Wright and Ed Ward: "Forevermore." Fashion show sequence in Technicolor. Remade as *The Opposite Sex* (MGM, 1956). 132 minutes

Mary Haines: Norma Shearer, *Chrystal Allen:* Joan Crawford, *Sylvia Fowler:* Rosalind Russell, *Countess Delave:* Mary Boland, *Miriam Aarons:* Paulette Goddard, *Peggy Day:* Joan Fontaine, *Mrs. Moorehead:* Lucile Watson, *Edith Potter:* Phyllis Povah, *Nancy Blake:* Florence Nash, *Little Mary:* Virginia Weidler, *Miss Watts:* Ruth Hussey, *Jane:* Muriel Hutchison, *Mrs. Wagstaff:* Margaret Dumont, *Olga:* Dennie Moore, *Maggie:* Mary Cecil, *Lucy:* Marjorie Main, *Ingrid:* Esther Dale, *Dolly Dupuyster:* Hedda Hopper, *Helene (French Maid):* Mildred Shay, *First Hairdresser:* Priscilla Lawson, *Second Hairdresser:* Estelle Etterre, *Exercise Instructress:* Ann Morriss, *Miss Trimmerback:* Mary Beth Hughes, *Sadie (Old Maid In Powder Room):* Marjorie Wood, *Pat:* Virginia Grey, *Mrs. Van Adams:* Cora Witherspoon, *Olive:* Theresa Harris, *Receptionist:* Virginia Howell, *Receptionist:* Barbara Jo Allen (Vera Vague), *Saleslady:* Aileen Pringle, *Model:* Judith Allen, *Singing Teacher:* Mariska Aldrich.

Wonder Bar with Al Jolson, Dick Powell and Dolores Del Rio.

WONDER BAR (1934) WB. Director, Lloyd Bacon. Adaptation and screenplay by Earl Baldwin. Based on the play by Geza Herczeg, Karl Farkas, and Robert Katscher. Dances by Busby Berkeley. Songs by Harry Warren and Al Dubin: "At the Wonder Bar," "I'm Going to Heaven on a Mule," "Why Do I Dream Those Dreams?" "Don't Say Goodnight" (Valse Amoureuse), "Vive La France," "Fairer on the Riviera," "Tango Del Rio," "Dark Eyes" (O Tchorniya). Editor, George Amy. Cameraman, Sol Polito. 84 minutes

Al Wonder: Al Jolson, *Inez:* Dolores Del Rio, *Harry:* Ricardo Cortez, *Liane Renaud:* Kay Francis, *Tommy:* Dick Powell, *Henry Simpson:* Guy B. Kibbee, *Corey Pratt:* Hugh Herbert, *Captain Von Ferring:* Robert Barrat, *Ella Simpson:* Ruth Donnelly, *Pansy Pratt:* Louise Fazenda, *Mitzi:* Fifi D'Orsay, *Claire:* Merna Kennedy, *Mr. Renaud:* Henry Kolker, *Richards:* Henry O'Neill, *Ilka:* Kathryn Sergava, *First Detective:* Gordon De Main, *Second Detective:* Harry Woods, *Maid:* Marie Moreau, *Broker:* George Irving, *Concierge:* Emil Chautard, *Operator:* Pauline Garon, *Artist:* Mahlon Norvell, *Doorman:* Alphonse Martel, *Gee-Gee:* Mia Ichioka, *Bartender:* William Granger, *Waiter:* Rolfe Sedan, *Frank:* Eddie Kane, *Captain:* Edward Keane, *Baroness:* Jane Darwell, *First Young Man:* Demetrius Alexis, *Second Young Man:* John Marlow, *Call Boy:* Billy Anderson, *Bartender:* Bud Jamison, *Drunk:* Hobart Cavanaugh, *Chorus Boy:* Dave O'Brien, *Extra at Bar:* Dennis O'Keefe, *Waiter:* Gino Corrado, *Fat Dowager:* Grace Hayle, *Norman:* Gordon Elliott (later Bill Elliott), *Chester:* Paul Power, *Page Boy:* Dick Good, *Count:* Michael Dalmatoff, *First Chorus Girl:* Renee Whitney, *Second Chorus Girl:* Amo Ingraham, *Third Chorus Girl:* Rosalie Roy, *Wardrobe Woman:* Lottie Williams, *First Businessman:* Clay Clement, *Second Businessman:* William Stack, *Pete:* Spencer Charters, *Gendarme:* Gene Perry, *Cook:* Louis Ardizoni, *Police Officer:* Robert Graves, *Night Watchman:* Alfred P. James, *Himself:* Hal LeRoy.

The Wonderful World of the Brothers Grimm with Laurence Harvey and Karl-Heinz Boehm.

WONDERFUL WORLD OF THE BROTHERS GRIMM (1962) MGM. Producer, George Pal. Director, Henry Levin. Cinerama, Technicolor. Fairy tales directed by George Pal. Screenplay, David P. Harmon, Charles Beaumont, William Roberts. Story, David P. Harmon. Based on "Die Brüder Grimm" by Dr. Hermann Gerstner. Music, Leigh Harline. Assistant Director, Al Jennings. Songs by Bob Merrill and Charles Beaumont: "The Wonderful World of the Brothers Grimm," "The Singing Bone," "Gypsy Fire," "Christmas Land," "Above the Stars," "Dancing Princess," "Ab-Oom," "Dee-Are-A-Gee-O-En." Choreography, Alex Romero. Costumes, Mary Wills. Locations filmed in Germany. 135 minutes

THE BOOK *Wilhelm Grimm:* Laurence Harvey, *Jacob Grimm:* Karl Boehm, *Dorothea Grimm:* Claire Bloom, *Stossel:* Walter Slezak, *Greta Heinrich:* Barbara Eden, *The Duke:* Oscar Homolka, *Rumpelstiltskin:* Arnold Stang, *Story Teller:* Martita Hunt, *Gruber:* Ian Wolfe, *Miss Bettenhausen:* Betty Garde, *Mrs. von Dittersdorf:* Cheerio Meredith, *Friedrich Grimm:* Bryan Russell, *Pauline Grimm:* Tammy Marihugh, *Priest:* Walter Rilla.

THE DANCING PRINCESS *The Princess:* Yvette Mimieux, *The Woodsman:* Russ Tamblyn, *The King:* Jim Backus, *The Gypsy:* Beulah Bondi, *The Prime Minister:* Clinton Sundberg.

THE COBBLER AND THE ELVES *The Cobbler:* Laurence Harvey, *The Mayor:* Walter Brooke, *The Ballerina:* Sandra Gale Bettin, *The Hunter:* Robert Foulk, And The Puppetoons.

THE SINGING BONE *Ludwig:* Terry-Thomas, *Hans:* Buddy Hackett, *The King:* Otto Kruger, *The Shepherd:* Robert Crawford, Jr., *The Spokesman:* Sydney Smith.

Wonder Man with Vera-Ellen and Danny Kaye.

WONDER MAN (1945) RKO. Producer, Samuel Goldwyn. Director, Bruce Humberstone. Color by Technicolor. Original Story, Arthur Sheekman. Screenplay, Don Hartman, Melville Shavelson, Philip Rapp. Dances, John Wray. Art Directors, Ernest Fegte, McClure Capps. Musical Director, Louis Forbes. Technicolor Director, Natalie Kalmus. Musical Numbers, Ray Heindorf. Cameramen, Victor Milner, William Snyder. Special Effects, John Fulton. Editor, Daniel Mandell. Adaptation, Jack Jevne and Eddie Moran. Musical numbers: "So in Love" by Leo Robin and David Rose; "Bali Boogie" by Sylvia Fine. Film debut of Vera-Ellen. 98 minutes

Buzzy Bellew/Edwin Dingle: Danny Kaye, *Ellen Shanley:* Virginia Mayo, *Midge Mallon:* Vera-Ellen, *Chimp:* Allen Jenkins, *Torso:* Edward S. Brophy, *Schmidt:* S. Z. Sakall, *Ten Grand Jackson:* Steve Cochran, *Monte Rossen:* Donald Woods, *District Attorney O'Brien:* Otto Kruger, *Assistant D. A. Grosset:* Richard Lane, *Mrs. Hume:* Natalie Schafer, *The Prima Donna:* Alice Mock, *Girl on Bench (in Park):* Virginia Gilmore, *Goldwyn Girls:* Ruth Valmy, Alma Carroll, Georgia Lange, Karen Gaylord, Mary Moore, Gloria Delson, Deannie Best, Margie Stewart, Mary Meade, Martha Montgomery, Ellen Hall, Phyllis Forbes, Mary Jane Woods, Katherine Booth, Chili Williams, *Prompter:* Luis Alberni, *Opera Conductor:* Aldo Franchetti, *Stage Manager:* Maurice Cass, *Acrobatic Dancer:* Barbara La Rene, *Dancer:* Carol Haney, *Customer:* Byron Foulger, *Mrs. Schmidt:* Gisela Werbiseck, *Sailor:* Huntz Hall, *Cop in the Park:* Ed Gargan, *Specialty Dancer:* Al Ruiz, *Specialty Dancer:* Willard Van Simons, *Drunk at Table:* Jack Norton, *Drunk at Bar:* Charles Irwin, *Bartender:* Frank Orth, *Barker:* Cecil Cunningham, *Meek Man on Bus:* Chester Clute, *Bus Driver:* James Flavin, *D. A.'s Secretary:* Mary Field, *Headwaiter:* Eddie Kane, *Ticket Taker:* Ray Teal, *Pianist:* Leon Belasco.

The World of Henry Orient with Peter Sellers.

THE WORLD OF HENRY ORIENT (1964) UA. Producer, Jerome Hellman. Director, George Roy Hill. Screenplay, Nora Johnson, Nunnally Johnson. Based on the novel by Nora Johnson. Music, Elmer Bernstein. Photography, Boris Kaufman, Arthur J. Ornitz. Costumes, Ann Roth. Assistant Directors, Michael Hertzberg, Roger Rothstein. Concerto, Kenneth Lauber. A Pan Arts Co. Presentation In Panavision and De Luxe Color. Filmed in New York. Later a Broadway musical, "Henry, Sweet Henry." 106 minutes

Henry Orient: Peter Sellers, *Stella:* Paula Prentiss, *Isabel Boyd:* Angela Lansbury, *Frank Boyd:* Tom Bosley, *Mrs. Gilbert:* Phyllis Thaxter, *Valerie Boyd:* Tippy Walker, *Marian Gilbert:* Merrie Spaeth, *Boothy:* Bibi Osterwald, *Joe Byrd:* Peter Duchin, *Sidney:* John Fiedler, *Store Owner:* Al Lewis, *Doctor:* Fred Stewart, *Emma:* Philippa Bevans, *Kafritz:* Jane Buchanan.

THE WORLD OF SUZIE WONG (1960) Par. Producer, Ray Stark. Director, Richard Quine. Screenplay, John Patrick. Adapted from the novel by Richard Mason and play by Paul Osborn. Music, George

Duning. Song, James Van Heusen and Sammy Cahn. Assistant Director, Gus Agosti. In Technicolor. 129 minutes

Robert Lomax: William Holden, *Suzie Wong:* Nancy Kwan, *Kay:* Sylvia Syms, *Ben:* Michael Wilding, *O'Neill:* Laurence Naismith, *Gwenny Lee:* Jacqui Chan, *Ah Tong:* Andy Ho, *Otis:* Bernard Cribbins, *Minnie Ho:* Yvonne Shima, *Wednesday Lu:* Lier Hwang, *Dancing Sailor:* Lionel Blair, *Barman:* Robert Lee, *Waiter:* Ronald Eng.

The World of Suzie Wong with William Holden and Nancy Kwan.

WRITTEN ON THE WIND (1956) Univ. Producer, Albert Zugsmith. Director, Douglas Sirk. Technicolor. Based on the novel by Robert Wilder. Screenplay, George Zuckerman. Art Directors, Alexander Golitzen, Robert Clatworthy. Music, Frank Skinner. Music Supervision, Joseph Gershenson. Cinematographer, Russell Metty. Special Photography, Clifford Stine. Editor, Russell Schoengarth. Title song by Victor Young and Sammy Cahn, sung by The Four Aces. 99 minutes

Mitch Wayne: Rock Hudson, *Lucy Moore Hadley:* Lauren Bacall, *Kyle Hadley:* Robert Stack, *Marylee Hadley:* DorothyMalone, *Jasper Hadley:* Robert Keith, *Biff Miley:* Grant Williams, *Dan Willis:* Robert J. Wilke, *Doctor Paul Cochrane:* Edward C. Platt, *Hoak Wayne:* Harry Shannon, *Roy Carter:* John Larch, *Sam:* Roy Glenn, *Bertha:* Maidie Norman, *Blonde Girl:* Dani Crayne, *Woman Beer Drinker:* Jane Howard, *Man Beer Drinker:* Floyd Simmons, *Waitress:* Cynthia Patrick, *College Girl:* Colleen McClatchey, *Brunette Girl:* Joanne Jordan, *Reporter:* William Schallert, *Hotel Manager:* Robert Brubaker, *Court Clerk:* Bert Holland, *Taxi Starter:* Don C. Harvey, *Bartender:* Carl Christian, *R. J. Courtney:* Joseph Granby, *Hotel Floorlady:* Gail Bonney, *Maitre d':* Paul Bradley, *Marylee as a girl:* Susan Odin, *Kyle as a boy:* Robert Lyden, *Mitch as a boy:* Robert Winans, *Secretary:* Dorothy Porter, *Hotel Proprietor:* Robert Malcolm.

Written on the Wind with Rock Hudson, Lauren Bacall, Robert Stack and Dorothy Malone.

WUTHERING HEIGHTS (1939) UA. Producer, Samuel Goldwyn. Director, William Wyler. From the novel by Emily Brönte. Screenplay, Ben Hecht, Charles MacArthur. Musical Director, Alfred Newman. Cameraman, Gregg Toland. Editor, Daniel Mandel. 103 minutes

Cathy: Merle Oberon, *Heathcliffe:* Laurence Olivier, *Edgar:* David Niven, *Dr. Kenneth:* Donald Crisp, *Nellie:* Flora Robson, *Hindley:* Hugh Williams, *Isabella:* Geraldine Fitzgerald, *Mr. Earnshaw:* Cecil Kellaway, *Joseph:* Leo G. Carroll, *Judge Linton:* Cecil Humphreys, *Lockwood:* Miles Mander, *Cathy as a child:* Sarita Wooton, *Heathcliffe as a child:* Rex Downing, *Hindley as a child:* Douglas Scott, *Robert:* Romaine Callender, *Miss Hudkins:* Helena Grant, *First Guest:* Susanne Leach, *Little Boy:* Tommy Martin, *Little Boy:* Schuyler Standish, *Little Girl:* Diane Williams, *Beadle:* Harold Entwistle, *Heathcliffe Servant:* Frank Benson, *Cathy's Partner:* Philip Winter, *Dancer:* William Stelling, *Frau Johann:* Alice Ahlers, *Giles:* Vernon Downing, *Linton Servant:* Eric Wilton.

Wuthering Heights with Merle Oberon and Laurence Olivier.

YANKEE DOODLE DANDY (1942) WB. Producers, Jack L. Warner, Hal B. Wallis. Associate Producer, William Cagney. Director, Michael Curtiz. Author, Robert Buckner. Original Story, Robert Buckner. Screenplay, Robert Buckner, Edmund Joseph. Musical Director, Leo F. Forbstein. Cameraman, James Wong Howe. Montage, Don Siegel. Editor, George Amy. Songs: "I Was Born in Virginia," "The Warmest Baby in the Bunch," "Give My Regards to Broadway," "Mary's a Grand Old Name," "So Long Mary," "Yankee Doodle Boy," "Over There," "Harrigan," "Forty-Five Minutes From Broadway" and "You're a Grand Old Flag" by George M. Cohan; "All Aboard for Old Broadway" by Jack Scholl and M. K. Jerome. 126 minutes

George M. Cohan: James Cagney, *Mary:* Joan Leslie, *Jerry Cohan:* Walter Huston, *Sam Harris:* Richard Whorf, *Dietz:* George Tobias, *Fay Templeton:* Irene Manning, *Nellie Cohan:* Rosemary De Camp, *Josie Cohan:* Jeanne Cagney, *Schwab:* S. Z. Sakall, *Erlanger:* George Barbier, *Manager:* Walter Catlett, *Singer:* Frances Langford, *Albee:* Minor Watson, *Eddie Foy:* Eddie Foy, Jr., *Goff:* Chester Clute, *George M. Cohan (age 13):* Douglas Croft, *Josie (age 12):* Patsy Lee Parsons, *Franklin D. Roosevelt:* Captain Jack Young, *Receptionists:* Audrey Long and Ann Doran, *Madame Bartholdi:* Odette Myrtil, *Butler:* Clinton Rosemond, *Stage Manager:* Spencer Charters, *Sister Act:* Dorothy Kelly and Marijo James, *George M. Cohan (age 7):* Henry Blair, *Josie Cohan (age 6):* Jo Ann Marlow, *Stage Manager:* Thomas Jackson, *Fanny:* Phyllis Kennedy, *Magician:* Leon Belasco, *Star Boarder:* Syd Saylor, *Stage Manager:* William B. Davidson, *Dr. Lewellyn:* Harry Hayden, *Dr. Anderson:* Francis Pierlot, *Teenagers:* Charles Smith, Joyce Reynolds, *Sergeant:* Frank Faylen, *Theodore Roosevelt:* Wallis Clark, *Betsy Ross:* Georgia Carroll.

Yankee Doodle Dandy with Rosemary De Camp, Walter Huston, Jeanne Cagney, James Cagney.

The Yellow Rolls-Royce with Jeanne Moreau and Rex Harrison.

THE YEARLING (1946) MGM. Producer, Sidney Franklin. Director, Clarence Brown. Color by Technicolor. Based on the novel by Marjorie Kinnan Rawlings. Art Directors, Cedric Gibbons, Paul Groesse. Music, Herbert Stothart. Cameramen, Charles Rosher, Leonard Smith. Editor, Harold F. Kress. Screenplay, Paul Osborn. Film debut of Claude Jarman, Jr. 134 minutes

Pa Baxter: Gregory Peck, *Ma Baxter:* Jane Wyman, *Jody Baxter:* Claude Jarman, Jr., *Buck Forrester:* Chill Wills, *Pa Forrester:* Clem Bevans, *Ma Forrester:* Margaret Wycherly, *Mr. Boyles:* Henry Travers, *Lem Forrester:* Forrest Tucker, *Fodderwing:* Donn Gift, *Millwheel:* Daniel White, *Gabby:* Matt Willis, *Pack:* George Mann, *Arch:* Arthur Hohl, *Twink Weatherby:* June Lockhart, *Eulalie:* Joan Wells, *Oliver:* Jeff York, *Doc Wilson:* B. M. Chick York, *Mr. Ranger:* Houseley Stevenson, *Mrs. Saunders:* Jane Green, *Captain:* Victor Killian, *Mate:* Robert Porterfield, *Deckhand:* Frank Eldredge.

The Yearling with Gregory Peck, Claude Jarman, Jr. and Jane Wyman.

THE YELLOW ROLLS-ROYCE (1965) MGM. Producer, Anatole De Grunwald. Director, Anthony Asquith. Screenplay, Terence Rattigan. Director of Photography, Jack Hildyard. Music, Riz Ortolani. Assistant Director, Kip Gowans. Associate Producer, Roy Parkinson. Clothes, Castillo of Paris, Edith Head, Pierre Cardin. In Panavision and MetroColor. 122 minutes

Marquess of Frinton: Rex Harrison, *Marchioness of Frinton:* Jeanne Moreau, *John Fane:* Edmund Purdom, *Lady St. Simeon:* Moira Lister, *Duchesse d'Angouleme:* Isa Miranda, *Norwood:* Roland Culver, *Harmsworth:* Michael Hordern, *His Assistant:* Lance Percival, *Taylor:* Harold Scott, *Mae Jenkins:* Shirley MacLaine, *Paolo Maltese:* George C. Scott, *Stefano:* Alain Delon, *Joey:* Art Carney, *Bomba:* Riccardo Garrone, *Mrs. Gerda Millett:* Ingrid Bergman, *Davich:* Omar Sharif, *Miss Hortense Astor:* Joyce Grenfell, *Ferguson:* Wally Cox, *Mayor:* Guy Deghy, *Mrs. Millett's Chauffeur:* Carlo Groccolo.

YELLOW SKY (1948) 20th. Producer, Lamar Trotti. Director, William A. Wellman. Based on a story by W. R. Burnett. Screenplay, Lamar Trotti. Art Directors, Lyle Wheeler, Albert Hogsett. Photography, Joe MacDonald. Editor, Haromon Jones. Music Director, Alfred Newman. 98 minutes

Stretch: Gregory Peck, *Mike:* Anne Baxter, *Dude:* Richard Widmark, *Bull Run:* Robert Arthur, *Lengthy:* John Russell, *Half Pint:* Henry Morgan, *Grandpa:* James Barton, *Walrus:* Charles Kemper, *Jed:* Robert Adler, *Bartender:* Victor Kilian, *Drunk:* Paul Hurst, *Banker:* William Gould, *Bank Teller:* Norman Leavitt, *Colorado:* Chief Yowlachie, *Woman:* Eula Guy.

Yellow Sky with Robert Arthur and Gregory Peck.

YOU CAN'T HAVE EVERYTHING (1937) 20th. Produced by Darryl F. Zanuck. Associate Producer, Laurence Schwab. Directed by Norman Taurog. Original story by Gregory Ratoff. Screenplay, Harry Tugend, Jack Yellen, and Karl Tunberg. Dances, Harry Losee. Music Director, David Buttolph. Art Director, Duncan Cramer. Photography, Lucien Andriot. Editor, Hansen Fritch. Songs by Mack Gordon and Harry Revel: "You Can't Have Everything," "Afraid to Dream," "The Loveliness of You," "Please Pardon Us We're in Love," and "Danger—Love At Work"; "Rhythm on the Radio" by Louis Prima; "It's a Southern Holiday" by Louis Prima, Jack Loman and Dave Franklin. 99 minutes

Judith Poe Wells: Alice Faye, *Ritz Brothers:* Themselves, *George McCrea:* Don Ameche, *Sam Gordon:* Charles Winninger, *Lulu Riley:* Louise Hovick (Gypsy Rose Lee), *David Rubinoff:* Himself, *Bobby Walker:* Tony Martin, *Bevins:* Arthur Treacher, *Evelyn Moore:* Phyllis Brooks, *Orchestra Leader:* Louis Prima, *Specialty Dancing Act:* Tip, Tap and Toe (Samuel Green, Ted Fraser, Ray Winfield) *Romano:* George Humbert, *Jerry:* Wally Vernon, *Mr. Whiteman:* Jed Prouty, *Waiter:* George Davis, *Accordion Player:* Frank Yaconelli,

Guitar Player: Nick Moro, *Waiter:* Frank Duglia, *Blonde:* Dorothy Christy, *Alderman Barney Callahan:* Robert Murphy, *Tony:* Howard Cantonwine, *Truck Driver:* Paul Hurst, *Mrs. Romano:* Inez Palange, *Lulu's Bathing Companion:* Gordon (Bill) Elliott, *Publicity Agent:* Sam Ash, *Matron in Y.W.C.A.:* Claudia Coleman, *Miss Barkow:* Margaret Fielding, *Townswoman:* Clara Blandick, *Joan:* Lynne Berkeley, *Bagpiper:* William Mathieson, *Cab Driver:* Hank Mann, *Copilot:* Robert Lowery, *Girl in Y.W.C.A.:* June Gale.

You Can't Have Everything with Alice Faye and Don Ameche.

YOU CAN'T TAKE IT WITH YOU (1938) Col. Produced and directed by Frank Capra. Based on the play by George S. Kaufman and Moss Hart. Screenplay, Robert Riskin. Music Score, Dimitri Tiomkin. Music Director, Morris Stoloff. Art Director, Stephen Goosson. Associate, Lionel Banks. Miss Arthur's Gowns, Bernard Newman and Irene. Photography, Joseph Walker. Editor, Gene Havlick. Sound, Ed Bernds. Assistant Director, Arthur Black. Film debut of xylophonist Dub Taylor. 127 minutes

Alice Sycamore: Jean Arthur, *Martin Vanderhof:* Lionel Barrymore, *Tony Kirby:* James Stewart, *Anthony P. Kirby:* Edward Arnold, *Kolenkhov:* Mischa Auer, *Essie Carmichael:* Ann Miller, *Penny Sycamore:* Spring Byington, *Paul Sycamore:* Samuel S. Hinds, *Poppins:* Donald Meek, *Ramsey:* H. B. Warner, *DePinna:* Halliwell Hobbes, *Ed Carmichael:* Dub Taylor, *Mrs. Anthony Kirby:* Mary Forbes, *Rheba:* Lillian Yarbo, *Donald:* Eddie Anderson, *John Blakely:* Clarence Wilson, *Professor:* Josef Swickard, *Maggie O'Neill:* Ann Doran, *Schmidt:* Christian Rub, *Mrs. Schmidt:* Bodil Rosing, *Henderson:* Charles Lane, *Judge:* Harry Davenport, *Attorneys:* Pierre Watkin, Edwin Maxwell, Russell Hicks, *Kirby's Assistant:* Byron Foulger, *Kirby's*

You Can't Take It With You with Mary Forbes, James Stewart, Jean Arthur, Irving Bacon, Robert Greig and John Hamilton.

Secretary: Ian Wolfe, *Henry:* Irving Bacon, *Hammond:* Chester Clute, *Jailer:* James Flavin, *Inmates:* Pert Kelton, Kit Guard, *Strongarm Man:* Dick Curtis, *Detectives:* James Burke, Ward Bond, *Board Member:* Edward Keane, *Court Attendant:* Edward Hearn, *Diners:* Robert Greig, John Hamilton.

The Young Doctors with Ben Gazzara, Fredric March, Dick Clark and Eddie Albert.

THE YOUNG DOCTORS (1961) UA. Producers, Stuart Millar, Lawrence Turman. Director, Phil Karlson. Screenplay, Joseph Hayes. Music, Elmer Bernstein. Costumes, Ruth Morley. A Drexel Films-Millar-Turman Production. Cinematographer, Arthur J. Ornitz. Based on the novel by Arthur Hailey, *The Final Diagnosis,* presented originally on TV as *No Deadly Medicine* (Studio One, 1957). Filmed in New York City. Narrated by Ronald Reagan. 100 minutes.

Dr. Joseph Pearson: Fredric March, *Dr. David Coleman:* Ben Gazzara, *Dr. Alexander:* Dick Clark, *Cathy Hunt:* Ina Balin, *Dr. Charles Dornberger:* Eddie Albert, *Mrs. Alexander:* Phyllis Love, *Bannister:* Edward Andrews, *Dr. Lucy Grainger:* Aline MacMahon, *Tomaselli:* Arthur Hill, *Miss Graves:* Rosemary Murphy, *Dr. Kent O'Donnell:* Barnard Hughes, *Dr. Shawcross:* Joseph Bova, *Dr. Howard:* George Segal, *Dr. Rufus:* Matt Crowley, *Operating Intern:* Dick Button, *Bits:* Dolph Sweet, Ella Smith, Nora Helen Spens, *X-Ray Technician:* William Hansen, *Board Physician:* Addison Powell.

THE YOUNG LIONS (1958) 20th. Producer, Al Lichtman. Director, Edward Dmytryk. CinemaScope. Based on the novel by Irwin Shaw. Screenplay, Edward Anhalt. Art Directors, Lyle R. Wheeler, Addison Hehr. Music, Hugo Friedhofer. Music conducted by Lionel Newman.

The Young Lions with Marlon Brando and Maximilian Schell.

Cinematographer, Joe MacDonald. Special Photographic Effects, L. B. Abbott. Editor, Dorothy Spencer. 167 minutes

Lieutenant Christian Diestl: Marlon Brando, *Noah Ackerman:* Montgomery Clift, *Michael Whiteacre:* Dean Martin, *Hope Plowman:* Hope Lange, *Margaret Freemantle:* Barbara Rush, *Gretchen Hardenberg:* May Britt, *Captain Hardenberg:* Maximilian Schell, *Simone:* Dora Doll, *Sergeant Rickett:* Lee Van Cleef, *Francoise:* Liliane Montevecchi, *Brant:* Parley Baer, *Lieutenant Green:* Arthur Franz, *Private Burnecker:* Hal Baylor, *Private Cowley:* Richard Gardner, *Captain Colclough:* Herbert Rudley, *Cafe Manager:* Gene Roth, *Colonel Mead:* Robert Burton, *General Rockland:* Harvey Stephens, *Corporal Kraus:* John Alderson, *Private Faber:* Sam Gilman, *Private Donnelly:* L. Q. Jones, *Private Brailsford:* Julian Burton, *German Major:* Stephen Bekassy, *German Colonel:* Ivan Triesault, *British Colonel:* Clive Morgan, *Maier:* Ashley Cowan, *Private Abbott:* Paul Comi, *Private Hagstrom:* Michael Pataki, *Mr. Plowman:* Vaughn Taylor, *Burn:* John Gabriel, *Emerson:* Kendall Scott, *Acaro:* Stan Kamber, *Rabbi:* Robert Ellenstein, *Drunk:* Jeffrey Sayre, *Camp Commandant:* Kurt Katch, *Physician:* Milton Frome, *Bavarian:* Otto Reichow.

Young Mr. Lincoln with Marjorie Weaver, Alice Brady, Arleen Whelan and Henry Fonda.

YOUNG MR. LINCOLN (1939) 20th. Producer, Kenneth Macgowan. Director, John Ford. Original Screenplay, Lamar Trotti. Cameraman, Bert Glennon. Editor, Walter Thompson. 100 minutes

Lincoln: Henry Fonda, *Abigail:* Alice Brady, *Mary Todd:* Marjorie Weaver, *Hannah:* Arleen Whelan, *Eph:* Eddie Collins, *Ann Rutledge:* Pauline Moore, *Matt:* Richard Cromwell, *Felder:* Donald Meek, *Carrie Sue:* Judith Dickens, *Adam:* Eddie Quillan, *Judge Bell:* Spencer Charters, *Palmer Cass:* Ward Bond, *Douglas:* Milburn Stone, *Sheriff:* Cliff Clark, *Mr. Edwards:* Charles Tannen, *Frank:* Francis Ford, *Scrub White:* Fred Kohler, Jr., *Mrs. Edwards:* Kay Linaker, *Woodridge:* Russell Simpson, *John Stuart:* Edwin Maxwell, *Hawthorne:* Charles Halton, *Mr. Clay:* Robert Homans, *Juror:* Steven Randall, *Matt as a boy:* Jack Kelly, *Adam as a boy:* Dickie Jones, *Barber:* Harry Tyler, *Court Clerk:* Louis Mason, *Buck:* Jack Pennick, *Loafers:* Paul Burns, Frank Orth, George Chandler, Dave Morris, *Women:* Dorothy Vaughan, Virginia Brissac.

YOU ONLY LIVE TWICE (1967) UA. Produced by Harry Saltzman and Albert R. Broccoli. Directed by Lewis Gilbert. Panavision and Technicolor. An Eon-Danjaq Production. Based on the novel by Ian Fleming. Screenplay by Roald Dahl. Production Design, Ken Adam. Art Director, Harry Pottle. Sets, David Ffolkes. Music by John Barry. Title song by John Barry and Leslie Bricusse, sung by Nancy Sinatra. Second unit directed by Peter Hunt. Action scenes directed by Bob Simmons. Assistant Director, William P. Cartlidge. Production Supervisor, David Middlemas. Additional Story Material, Harry Jack Bloom. Photography, Freddie Young. Second Unit Photography, Bob Huke. Aerial Photography, John Jordan. Underwater Photography, Lamar Boren. Technical Adviser, Kikumaru Okuda. Titles,

You Only Live Twice with Tetsuro Tamba and Sean Connery.

Maurice Binder. Special Effects, John Stears. Editor, Peter Hunt. Sound, John Mitchell. Filmed in Japan. The sixth James Bond film, fifth with Sean Connery. 117 minutes

James Bond: Sean Connery, *Aki:* Akiko Wakabayashi, *Tiger Tanaka:* Tetsuro Tamba, *Kissy Suzuki:* Mie Hama, *Osato:* Teru Shimada, *Helga Brandt:* Karin Dor, *Miss Moneypenny:* Lois Maxwell, *Q:* Desmond Llewelyn, *M:* Bernard Lee, *Henderson:* Charles Gray, *Chinese Girl:* Tsai Chin, *Ernst Stavro Blofeld:* Donald Pleasence, *American President:* Alexander Knox, *President's Aide:* Robert Hutton, *Spectre 3:* Burt Kwouk, *Spectre 4:* Michael Chow, *Double:* Diane Cilento.

ZIEGFELD FOLLIES (1946) MGM. Producer, Arthur Freed. Director, Vincente Minnelli. Color by Technicolor. Dance Director, Robert Alton. Musical Adaptation, Roger Edens. Musical Director, Lennie Hayton. Art Directors, Cedric Gibbons, Merrill Pye, Jack Martin Smith. Cameramen, George Folsey, Charles Rosher. Editor, Albert Akst. Orchestration, Conrad Salinger and Wally Heglin. Songs: "This Heart of Mine" by Arthur Freed and Harry Warren; "There's Beauty Everywhere" by Arthur Freed and Earl Brent; "Love" by Ralph Blane and Hugh Martin; "Limehouse Blues" by Philip Braham and Douglas Furber; "Bring on the Wonderful Men" by Earl Brent and Roger Edens; "Here's to the Girls" by Ralph Freed and Roger Edens; "The Babbitt and the Bromide" by Ira and George Gershwin. 110 minutes

ZIEGFELD DAYS Fred Astaire, Bunin's Puppets.

MEET THE LADIES Fred Astaire, Lucille Ball.

DEATH AND TAXES *Jimmy Durante:* Himself, *Mr. Huggins:* Edward Arnold, *Inspector McGrath:* Horace McNally (Stephen McNally), *Inspector Ramrod:* Douglas Cowan, *Third Inspector:* Russ Clark, *Secretary:* Kay Williams.

IF SWING GOES I GO, TOO Fred Astaire.

THE BURGLAR *Baby Snooks:* Fannie Brice, *The Father:* Hanley Stafford, *The Burglar:* B. S. Pully, *Officer Todd:* Harry Shannon.

LOVE Lena Horne.

THIS HEART OF MINE *The Imposter:* Fred Astaire, *The Princess:* Lucille Bremer, *The Duke:* Count Stefenelli, *The Duchess:* Naomi Childers, *The Countess:* Helen Boice, *Retired Dyspeptic:* Robert Wayne, *The Major:* Charles Coleman, *The Lieutenant:* Feodor Chaliapin, *The Flunky:* Sam Flint.

WE WILL MEET AGAIN Esther Williams, James Melton.

THE INTERVIEW *Judy Garland:* Herself, *The Butler:* Rex Evans.

WHEN TELEVISION COMES Red Skelton.

THE BABBIT AND THE BROMIDE Fred Astaire, Gene Kelly.

TRAVIATA James Melton, Marion Bell.

LIZA Lena Horne, Avon Long.

THE SWEEPSTAKES TICKET *Norma:* Fannie Brice, *Monty:* Hume Cronyn, *Martin:* William Frawley, *Telegraph Boy:* Arthur Walsh.

LIMEHOUSE BLUES *Tai Long:* Fred Astaire, *Moy Ling:* Lucille Bremer, *Men:* Captain George Hill, Jack Deery.

PAY THE TWO DOLLARS *Victor Moore:* Himself, *Edward Arnold:* Himself, *Special Officer:* Ray Teal, *Judge:* Joseph Crehan, *Presiding Judge:* William B. Davidson, *Warden:* Harry Hayden, *Officer:* Eddie Dunn, *Second Officer:* Garry Owen.

THE PIED PIPER *Pied Piper:* Jimmy Durante, *Mailman:* Alex Pollard, *Pedestrian:* Jack Perrin, *Maitre D'Hotel:* Eddie Kane, *Waiter:* Jack Chefe.

THE COWBOY James Melton.

FINALE—There's Beauty Everywhere.

Ziegfeld Follies with Judy Garland.

ZIEGFELD GIRL (1941) MGM. Produced by Pandro S. Berman. Directed by Robert Z. Leonard. Musical numbers directed by Busby Berkeley. In Sepia. Story, William Anthony McGuire. Screenplay, Marguerite Roberts, Sonya Levien. Score, Herbert Stothart. Music Director, Georgie Stoll. Vocals and Orchestrations, Leo Arnaud, George Bassman, Conrad Salinger. Musical Presentation, Merrill Pye. Art Director, Cedric Gibbons. Art Associate, Daniel B. Cathcart. Sets, Edwin B. Willis. Gowns and Costumes, Adrian. Make-up, Jack Dawn. Photography, Ray June. Sound, Douglas Shearer. Editor, Blanche Sewell. Songs: "You Stepped Out of a Dream" by Gus Kahn and Nacio Herb Brown; "Whispering" by John Schonberger, Richard Coburn, Vincent Rose; "Mr. Gallagher and Mr. Shean" by Edward

Gallagher and Al Shean; "I'm Always Chasing Rainbows" by Joseph McCarthy and Harry Carroll; "Caribbean Love Song" by Ralph Freed and Roger Edens; "You Never Looked So Beautiful Before" by Walter Donaldson; (from *The Great Ziegfeld*, 1936) "Minnie from Trinidad," "Ziegfeld Girls," and "Laugh? I Thought I'd Split My Sides" by Roger Edens: "You Gotta Pull Strings" (from *The Great Ziegfeld*, 1936) by Harold Adamson and Walter Donaldson. 131 minutes

Gilbert Young: James Stewart, *Susan Gallagher:* Judy Garland, *Sandra Kolter:* Hedy Lamarr, *Sheila Regan:* Lana Turner, *Frank Merton:* Tony Martin, *Jerry Regan:* Jackie Cooper, *Geoffrey Collis:* Ian Hunter, *Pop Gallagher:* Charles Winninger, *Noble Sage:* Edward Everett Horton, *Franz Kolter:* Philip Dorn, *John Slayton:* Paul Kelly, *Patsy Dixon:* Eve Arden, *Jimmy Walters:* Dan Dailey, Jr., *Al:* Al Shean, *Mrs. Regan:* Fay Holden, *Mischa:* Felix Bressart, *Mrs. Merton:* Rose Hobart, *Nick Capalini:* Bernard Nedell, *Mr. Regan:* Ed McNamara, *Jenny:* Mae Busch, *Annie:* Renie Riano, *Perkins:* Josephine Whittell, *Native Dancer:* Sergio Orta, *Ziegfeld Girls:* Jean Wallace, Myrna Dell, Lorraine Gettman (Leslie Brooks), Georgia Carroll, Louise La Planche, Nina Bissell, Virginia Cruzon, Alaine Brandes, Frances Gladwin, Patricia Dane, Irma Wilson, Anya Tarana, Madeline Martin, Vivien Mason.

Ziegfeld Girl with Lana Turner and Judy Garland.

ZORBA THE GREEK (1964) International Classics. Produced, directed and written by Michael Cacoyannis. Based on the novel by Nikos Kazantzakis. Camera, Walter Lassaly. Music, Mikis Theodorakis. 142 minutes.

Alexis Zorba: Anthony Quinn, *Basil:* Alan Bates, *The Widow:* Irene Papas, *Madame Hortense:* Lila Kedrova, *Mavrandoni:* George Foundas, *Lola:* Eleni Anousaki, *Mimithos:* Sotiris Moustakas, *Manolakas:* Takis Emmanuel, *Pavlo:* George Voyadjis, *Soul:* Anna Kyriakou.

Zorba the Greek with Anthony Quinn and Alan Bates.

CHAPTER IV

THE DIRECTORS

The Sullivans with Selena Royle, John Campbell, Edward Ryan, Trudy Marshall, Thomas Mitchell, James Cardwell, George Offerman, Jr., and John Alvin. (*Bacon*)

LLOYD BACON Born January 16, 1890; died November 15, 1955; *The Singing Fool*, 1928; *Honky Tonk*, 1929; *A Notorious Affair*, 1930; *Moby Dick*, 1930 (plus codirected with Michael Curtiz a separate German version, 1930); *Kept Husbands*, 1931; *Honor of the Family*, 1931; *You Said a Mouthful*, 1932; *42nd Street* (with Busby Berkeley), 1933; *Picture Snatcher*, 1933; *Mary Stevens, M.D.*, 1933; *Footlight Parade* (with Busby Berkeley), 1933; *Wonder Bar* (with Busby Berkeley), 1934; *He Was Her Man*, 1934; *Here Comes the Navy*, 1934; *Devil Dogs of the Air*, 1935; *In Caliente* (with Busby Berkeley), 1935; *Broadway Gondolier*, 1935; *The Irish in Us*, 1935; *Frisco Kid*, 1935; *Sons O' Guns*, 1936; *Cain and Mabel*, 1936; *Gold Diggers of 1937* (with Busby Berkeley), 1936; *Marked Woman*, 1937; *San Quentin*, 1937; *Submarine D-1*, 1937; *A Slight Case of Murder*. 1938; *Cowboy from Brooklyn*, 1938; *Boy Meets Girl*, 1938; *Racket Busters*, 1938; *Wings of the Navy*, 1939; *The Oklahoma Kid*, 1939; *Indianapolis Speedway*, 1939; *Invisible Stripes*, 1939; *A Child Is Born*, 1940; *Three Cheers for the Irish*, 1940; *Brother Orchid*, 1940; *Knute Rockne, All American*, 1940; *Honeymoon for Three*, 1941; *Footsteps in the Dark*, 1941; *Affectionately Yours*, 1941; *Navy Blues*, 1941; *Larceny, Inc.*, 1942; *Wings for the Eagle*, 1942; *Action in the North Atlantic*, 1943; *The Sullivans*, 1944; *Sunday Dinner for a Soldier*, 1944; *I Wonder Who's Kissing Her Now*, 1947; *You Were Meant for Me*, 1948; *Give My Regards to Broadway*, 1948; *Don't Trust Your Husband*, or *An Innocent Affair*, 1948; *Mother Is a Freshman*, 1949; *It Happens Every Spring*, 1949; *Miss Grant Takes Richmond*, 1949; *Kill the Umpire*, 1950; *The Good Humor Man*, 1950; *The Fuller Brush Girl*, 1950; *Call Me Mister* (with Busby Berkeley), 1951; *The Frogmen*, 1951; *Golden Girl*, 1951; *The I Don't Care Girl*, 1953; *The Great Sioux Uprising*, 1953; *Walking My Baby Back Home*, 1953; *The French Line*, 1954; *She Couldn't Say No*, 1954.

Two Weeks With Love with Jane Powell, Ann Harding, Debbie Reynolds, Carleton Carpenter, Ricardo Montalban, Gary Gray, Phyllis Kirk and Tommy Rettig. (*Berkeley*)

BUSBY BERKELEY Born November 29, 1895; *Whoopee* (with Thornton Freeland), 1930; *Kiki* (with Samuel Taylor), 1931; *Palmy Days* (with Edward Sutherland), 1931; *Flying High* (with Charles Riesner), 1931; *Night World* (with Hobart Henley), 1932; *Bird of Paradise* (with King Vidor), 1932; *The Kid from Spain* (with Leo McCarey), 1932; *42nd Street* (with Lloyd Bacon), 1933; *Gold Diggers of 1933* (with Mervyn LeRoy), 1933; *She Had to Say Yes*, 1933; *Footlight Parade* (with Lloyd Bacon), 1933; *Roman Scandals* (with Frank Tuttle), 1933; *Wonder Bar* (with Lloyd Bacon), 1934; *Fashions of 1934* (with William Dieterle), 1934; *Twenty Million Sweethearts* (with Ray Enright), 1934; *Dames* (with Ray Enright), 1934; *Gold Diggers of 1935*, 1935; *Go Into Your Dance* (with Archie Mayo), 1935; *Bright Lights*, 1935; *In Caliente* (with Lloyd Bacon), 1935; *I Live for Love*, 1935; *Stars Over Broadway* (with William Keighley), 1935; *Stage Struck*, 1936; *Gold Diggers of 1937* (with Lloyd Bacon), 1936; *The Go-Getter*, 1937; *The Singing Marine* (with Ray Enright), 1937; *Varsity Show* (with William Keighley), 1937; *Hollywood Hotel*, 1937; *Men Are Such Fools*, 1938; *Gold Diggers in Paris* (with Ray Enright), 1938; *Garden of the Moon*, 1938; *Comet Over Broadway*, 1938; *They Made Me a Criminal*, 1939; *Broadway Serenade* (with Robert Z. Leonard), 1939; *Babes in Arms*, 1939; *Fast and Furious*, 1939; *Forty Little Mothers*, 1940; *Strike Up the Band*, 1940; *Blonde Inspiration*, 1941; *Ziegfeld Girl* (with Robert Z. Leonard), 1941; *Lady Be Good* (with Norman Z. McLeod), 1941; *Babes on Broadway*, 1941; *Born to Sing* (with Edward Ludwig), 1941; *For Me and My Gal*, 1942; *Girl Crazy* (with Norman Taurog), 1943; *The Gang's All Here*, 1943; *Cinderella Jones*, 1946; *Take Me Out to the Ball Game*, 1949; *Two Weeks With Love* (with Roy Rowland), 1950; *Call Me Mister* (with Lloyd Bacon), 1951; *Two Tickets to Broadway* (with James V. Kern), 1951; *Million Dollar Mermaid* (with Mervyn LeRoy), 1952; *Small Town Girl* (with Leslie Kardos), 1953; *Easy to Love* (with Charles Walters), 1953; *Rose Marie* (with Mervyn LeRoy), 1954; *Jumbo*, or *Billy Rose's Jumbo* (with Charles Walters), 1962.

FRANK CAPRA Born May 19, 1897; *Flight*, 1929; *Ladies of Leisure*, 1930; *Rain or Shine*, 1930; *Dirigible*, 1931; *Miracle Woman*, 1931; *Platinum Blonde*, 1931; *Forbidden*, 1932; *American Madness*, 1932; *The Bitter Tea of General Yen*, 1933; *Lady for a Day*, 1933; *It Happened One Night*, 1934; *Broadway Bill*, 1934; *Mr. Deeds Goes to Town*, 1936; *Lost Horizon*, 1937; *You Can't Take It With You*, 1938; *Mr. Smith Goes to Washington*, 1939; *Meet John Doe*, 1941; *Arsenic and Old Lace*, 1944; *It's a Wonderful Life*, 1946; *State of the Union*, 1948; *Riding High*, 1950; *Here Comes the Groom*, 1951; *A Hole in the Head*, 1959; *Pocketful of Miracles*, 1961.

Dirigible with Hobart Bosworth and Ralph Graves. *(Capra)*

ROGER CORMAN Born April 5, 1926; *The Monster From the Ocean Floor* (producer only), 1954; *The Fast and the Furious* (producer only), 1954; *Highway Dragnet* (producer only), 1954; *Five Guns West*, 1955; *Apache Woman*, 1955; *The Day the World Ended*, 1956; *Swamp Woman*, 1956; *Oklahoma Woman*, 1956; *Gunslinger*, 1956; *It Conquered the World*, 1956; *Not of This Earth*, 1957; *The Undead*, 1957; *She-Gods of*

The Raven with Boris Karloff and Peter Lorre. *(Corman)*

Shark Reef, 1957; *Naked Paradise*, 1957; *Attack of the Crab Monsters*, 1957; *Rock All Night*, 1957; *Teenage Doll*, 1957; *Carnival Rock*, 1957; *The Little Guy* (uncompleted), 1957; *Reception* (uncompleted), 1957; *Sorority Girl*, 1958; *Viking Women and the Sea Serpent*, 1958; *War of the Satellites*, 1958; *Machine Gun Kelly*, 1958; *Teenage Caveman*, 1958; *I, Mobster*, 1958; *Bucket of Blood*, 1959; *Cry Baby Killer*, 1959; *Wasp Woman*, 1959; *Ski Troop Attack*, 1960; *The Fall of the House of Usher*, 1960; *The Little Shop of Horrors*, 1960; *Last Woman on Earth*, 1960; *Creature from the Haunted Sea*, 1961; *Atlas*, 1961; *The Pit and the Pendulum*, 1961; *The Intruder*, 1961; *The Premature Burial*, 1962; *Tales of Terror*, 1962; *Tower of London*, 1962; *The Young Racers*, 1963; *The Raven*, 1963; *The Terror*, 1963; *X—The Man With the X-Ray Eyes*, 1963; *The Haunted Palace*, 1963; *The Secret Invasion*, 1964; *The Masque of the Red Death*, 1964; *The Tomb of Ligeia*, 1965; *The Wild Angels*, 1966; *The Saint Valentine's Day Massacre*, 1967; *The Trip*, 1967; *What's in It for Harry?*, 1968.

JOHN CROMWELL Born December 23, 1888; *The Dummy*, 1929; *The Mighty*, 1929; *The Dance of Life* (with Edward Sutherland), 1929; *Close Harmony* (with Edward Sutherland), 1929; *Street of Chance*, 1930; *Tom Sawyer*, 1930; *The Texan*, 1930; *For the Defense*, 1930; *Scandal Street*, 1931; *Rich Man's Folly*, 1931; *Vice Squad*, 1931; *Unfaithful*, 1931; *The World and the Flesh*, 1931; *Sweepings*, 1933; *The Silver Cord*, 1933; *Double Harness*, 1933; *Ann Vickers*, 1933; *Spitfire*, 1934; *This Man Is Mine*, 1934; *Of Human Bondage*, 1934; *The Fountain*, 1934; *Jalna*, 1935; *Village Tale*, 1935; *I Dream Too Much*, 1935; *Little Lord Fauntleroy*, 1936; *To Mary—With Love*, 1936; *Banjo on My Knee*, 1936; *The Prisoner of Zenda*, 1937; *Algiers*, 1938; *Made for Each Other*, 1939; *In Name Only*, 1939; *Abe Lincoln in Illinois*, 1940; *Victory*, 1940; *So Ends Our Night*, 1941; *Son of Fury*, 1942; *Since You Went Away*, 1944; *The Enchanted Cottage*, 1945; *Anna and the King of Siam*, 1946; *Dead Reckoning*, 1947; *Night Song*, 1947; *Caged*, 1950; *The Company She Keeps*, 1951; *The Racket*, 1951; *Hidden Fear*, 1957; *The Goddess*, 1958; *A Matter of Morals*, 1961.

Night Song with Ethel Barrymore and Merle Oberon. *(Cromwell)*

A Woman's Face with Conrad Veidt, Joan Crawford, Donald Meek and Connie Gilchrist. *(Cukor)*

GEORGE CUKOR Born July 7, 1899; *Grumpy* (with Cyril Gardner), 1930; *Virtuous Sin* (with Louis Gasnier), 1930; *The Royal Family of Broadway* (with Cyril Gardner), 1930; *Tarnished Lady*, 1931; *Girls About Town*, 1931; *One Hour With You* (with Ernst Lubitsch), 1932; *What Price Hollywood*, 1932; *A Bill of Divorcement*, 1932; *Rockabye*, 1932; *Our Betters*, 1933; *Dinner at Eight*, 1933; *Little Women*, 1933; *David Copperfield*, 1935; *Sylvia Scarlett*, 1935; *Romeo and Juliet*, 1936; *Camille*, 1936; *Holiday*, 1938; *Zaza*, 1939; *Gone With the Wind* (replaced by Sam Wood, then Victor Fleming), 1939; *The Women*, 1939; *Susan and God*, 1940; *The Philadelphia Story*, 1940; *A Woman's Face*, 1941; *Two-Faced Woman*, 1942; *Her Cardboard Lover*, 1942; *Keeper of the Flame*, 1942; *Gaslight*, 1944; *Winged Victory*, 1944; *Desire Me* (uncredited), 1947; *A Double Life*, 1947; *Edward, My Son*, 1948; *Adam's Rib*, 1949; *A Life of Her Own*, 1950; *Born Yesterday*, 1950; *The Model and the Marriage Broker*, 1951; *The Marrying Kind*, 1952; *Pat and Mike*, 1952; *The Actress*, 1953; *It Should Happen to You*, 1953; *A Star Is Born*, 1954; *Bhowani Junction*, 1956; *Les Girls*, 1957; *Wild Is the Wind*, 1957; *Heller in Pink Tights* (with Arthur Rosson), 1960; *Song Without End* (replaced the late Charles Vidor), 1959; *Let's Make Love*, 1960; *The Chapman Report*, 1962; *My Fair Lady* 1964; *The Nine-Tiger Man* (uncompleted), 1967.

MICHAEL CURTIZ Born December 24, 1888; died April 11, 1962; *The Glad Rag Doll*, 1929; *Madonna of Avenue A*, 1929; *The Gamblers*, 1929; *Hearts in Exile*, 1929; *Noah's Ark*, 1929; *Mammy*, 1930; *Under a Texas Moon*, 1930; *The Matrimonial Bed*, 1930; *A Soldier's Plaything*, 1930; *Bright Lights*, 1930; *River's End*, 1930; *God's Gift to Women*, 1931; *The Mad Genius*, 1931; *The Woman From Monte Carlo*, 1932; *The Strange Love of Molly Louvain*, 1932; *Alias the Doctor*, 1932; *Cabin in the Cotton* (with William Keighley), 1932; *Doctor X*, 1932; *20,000 Years in Sing Sing*, 1933; *The Mystery of the Wax Museum*, 1933; *The Keyhole*, 1933; *Private Detective 62*, 1933; *Goodbye Again*, 1933; *The Kennel Murder Case*, 1933; *Female*, 1933; *Mandalay*, 1934; *Jimmy the Gent*, 1934; *The Key*, 1934; *British Agent*, 1934; *Black Fury*, 1935;

I'll See You in My Dreams with Doris Day and Danny Thomas. *(Curtiz)*

The Case of the Curious Bride, 1935; *Captain Blood*, 1935; *Little Big Shot*, 1935; *Front Page Woman*, 1935; *The Walking Dead*, 1936; *The Charge of the Light Brigade*, 1936; *Stolen Holiday*, 1937; *Mountain Justice*, 1937; *Kid Galahad*, 1937; *The Perfect Specimen*, 1937; *Gold Is Where You Find It*, 1938; *Sons of Liberty*, 1938; *The Adventures of Robin Hood* (with William Keighley), 1938; *Four's a Crowd*, 1938; *Four Daughters*, 1938; *Angels With Dirty Faces*, 1938; *Dodge City*, 1939; *Daughters Courageous*, 1939; *The Private Lives of Elizabeth and Essex*, 1939; *Four Wives*, 1939; *Virginia City*, 1940; *The Sea Hawk*, 1940; *Santa Fe Trail*, 1940; *The Sea Wolf*, 1941; *Dive Bomber*, 1941; *Captains of the Clouds*, 1942; *Yankee Doodle Dandy*, 1942; *Casablanca*, 1942; *Mission to Moscow*, 1943; *This Is the Army*, 1943; *Passage to Marseilles*, 1944; *Janie*, 1944; *Roughly Speaking*, 1945; *Mildred Pierce*, 1945; *Night and Day*, 1946; *Life With Father*, 1947; *The Unsuspected*, 1947; *Romance on the High Seas*, 1948; *My Dream Is Yours*, 1949; *Flamingo Road*, 1949; *The Lady Takes a Sailor*, 1949; *The Breaking Point*, 1950; *Bright Leaf*, 1950; *Young Man With a Horn*, 1950; *Force of Arms*, 1951; *Jim Thorpe, All American*, 1951; *I'll See You in My Dreams*, 1952; *The Story of Will Rogers*, 1952; *The Jazz Singer*, 1952; *Trouble Along the Way*, 1953; *The Boy From Oklahoma*, 1954; *The Egyptian*, 1954; *White Christmas*, 1954; *We're No Angels*, 1955; *The Vagabond King*, 1956; *The Scarlet Hour*, 1956; *The Best Things in Life Are Free*, 1956; *The Helen Morgan Story*, 1957; *King Creole*, 1958; *The Proud Rebel*, 1958; *The Hangman*, 1959; *The Man in the Net*, 1959; *A Breath of Scandal*, 1959; *The Adventures of Huckleberry Finn*, 1960; *Francis of Assisi*, 1961; *The Comancheros*, 1961;

DELMER DAVES Born July 24, 1904; *Destination Tokyo*, 1943; *The Very Thought of You*, 1944; *Hollywood Canteen*, 1944; *Pride of the Marines*, 1945; *This Love of Ours*, 1945; *The Red House*, 1947; *Dark Passage*, 1947; *To the Victor*, 1948; *A Kiss in the Dark*, 1949; *Task Force*, 1949; *Broken Arrow*, 1950; *Bird of Paradise*, 1951; *Return of the Texan*, 1952; *Treasure of the Golden Condor*, 1953; *Never Let Me Go*, 1953; *Demetrius and the Gladiators*, 1953; *Drumbeat*, 1954; *Jubal*, 1956; *The Last Wagon*, 1956; *3 : 10 to Yuma*, 1957; *Cowboy*, 1958; *Kings Go Forth*, 1958; *The Badlanders*, 1958; *The Hanging Tree*, 1959; *A Summer Place*, 1959; *Parrish*, 1961; *Susan Slade*, 1961; *Rome Adventure*, 1962; *Spencer's Mountain*, 1963; *Youngblood Hawke*, 1964; *The Battle of the Villa Fiorita*, 1965.

Drum Beat with Anthony Caruso, Marisa Pavan and Alan Ladd. *(Daves)*

CECIL B. DE MILLE Born August 12, 1881; died January 21, 1959; *The Godless Girl*, 1929; *Dynamite*, 1929; *Madame Satan*, 1930; *The Squaw Man*, 1931; *The Sign of the Cross*, 1932; *This Day and Age*, 1933; *Four Frightened People*, 1934; *Cleopatra*, 1934; *The Crusades*, 1935; *The Plainsman*, 1936; *The Buccaneer*, 1938; *Union Pacific*, 1939; *North West Mounted Police*, 1940; *Reap the Wild Wind*, 1942; *The Story of Dr. Wassell*, 1944; *Unconquered*, 1947; *Samson and Delilah*, 1949; *The Greatest Show on Earth*, 1952; *The Ten Commandments*, 1956; *The Buccaneer* (producer only), 1958.

Four Frightened People with Mary Boland, Claudette Colbert, Herbert Marshall, William Gargan and Leo Carrillo. *(DeMille)*

WILLIAM DIETERLE Born July 15, 1893; *Kismet* (separate German version), 1930; *The Last Flight*, 1931; *Her Majesty, Love*, 1931; *Man Wanted*, 1932; *Jewel Robbery*, 1932; *The Crash*, 1932; *Scarlet Dawn*, 1932; *Lawyer Man*, 1932; *Six Hours to Live*, 1932; *Grand Slam*, 1933; *From Headquarters*, 1933; *Fashions of 1934*, 1934; *Concealment*, 1934; *Firebird*, 1934; *Madame Du Barry*, 1934; *Fog Over Frisco*, 1934; *A Midsummer Night's Dream* (with Max Reinhardt), 1935; *Satan Met a Lady*, 1936; *The Story of Louis Pasteur*, 1935; *Dr. Socrates*, 1935; *The Great O'Malley*, 1936; *Another Dawn*, 1937; *The White Angel*, 1936; *The Life of Emile Zola*, 1937; *Blockade*, 1938; *Juarez*, 1939; *The Hunchback of Notre Dame*, 1939; *Dr. Ehrlich's Magic Bullet*, 1940; *A Dispatch from Reuters*, 1940; *All That Money Can Buy*, 1941; *Syncopation*, 1942; *Tennessee Johnson*, 1942; *Kismet*, 1944; *I'll Be Seeing You*, 1944; *Love Letters*, 1945; *This Love of Ours*, 1945; *The Searching Wind*, 1946; *Duel in the Sun* (with King Vidor), 1946; *A Portrait of Jennie*, 1948; *The Accused*, 1948; *Rope of Sand*, 1949; *Paid in Full* or *Bitter Victory*, 1949; *Volcano*, 1949; *September Affair*, 1950; *Dark City*, 1950; *Red Mountain*, 1951; *Peking Express*, 1951; *Turning Point*, 1952; *Boots Malone*, 1952; *Salome*, 1953; *Elephant Walk*, 1954; *Joseph and His Brethren* (unreleased), 1954; *Magic Fire*, 1956; *The Loves of Omar Khayyam*, 1957; *Friday the Thirteenth* (unreleased), 1957; *John Paul Jones*, 1959; *Dubrowsky* (shot initially in Italy), 1960.

Another Dawn with Kay Francis and Ian Hunter. *(Dieterle)*

EDWARD DMYTRYK Born August 4, 1908; *The Hawk*, 1935; *Television Spy*, 1939; *Emergency Squad*, 1940; *Golden Gloves*, 1940; *Mystery Sea Raider*, 1940; *Her First Romance*, 1940; *Secrets of the Lone Wolf*, 1941; *The Devil Commands*, 1941; *Under Age*, 1941; *Sweetheart of the Campus*, 1941; *The Blonde from Singapore*, 1941; *Confessions of Boston Blackie*, 1941; *Counter-Espionage*, 1942; *Seven Miles From Alcatraz*, 1942; *Hitler's Children*, 1943; *The Falcon Strikes Back*, 1943; *Captive Wild Woman*, 1943; *Behind the Rising Sun*, 1943; *Tender Comrade*, 1943; *Murder, My Sweet*, 1944; *Back to Bataan*, 1945; *Cornered*, 1945;

Till the End of Time, 1946; *Crossfire*, 1947; *So Well Remembered*, 1947; *Give Us This Day*, 1949; *The Hidden Room*, 1949; *Mutiny*, 1952; *The Sniper*, 1952; *Eight Iron Men*, 1952; *The Juggler*, 1953; *The Caine Mutiny*, 1954; *Broken Lance*, 1954; *The End of the Affair*, 1955; *Soldier of Fortune*, 1955; *The Left Hand of God*, 1955; *The Mountain*, 1956; *Raintree County*, 1957; *The Young Lions*, 1958; *Warlock*, 1959; *The Blue Angel*, 1959; *A Walk on the Wild Side*, 1962; *The Reluctant Saint*, 1962; *The Carpetbaggers*, 1964; *Mirage*, 1965; *Alvarez Kelly*, 1966; *Anzio*, 1968.

Mirage with Diane Baker and Gregory Peck. *(Dmytryk)*

ALAN DWAN Born April 3, 1885; *Frozen Justice*, 1929; *South Sea Rose*, 1929; *What a Widow*, 1930; *Man to Man*, 1930; *Chances*, 1931; *Wicked*, 1931; *While Paris Sleeps*, 1932; *Her First Affair*, 1933; *I Spy*, 1933; *Counsel's Opinion*, 1933; *The Morning After*, 1934; *Black Sheep*, or *Star for a Night*, 1935; *Navy Wife*, or *Beauty's Daughter*, 1935; *The Song and Dance Man*, 1936; *Human Cargo*, 1936; *High Tension*, 1936; *15 Maiden Lane*, 1936; *Woman Wise*, 1937; *That I May Live*, 1937; *One Mile From Heaven*, 1937; *Heidi*, 1937; *Rebecca of Sunnybrook Farm*, 1938; *Josette*, 1938; *Suez*, 1938; *The Three Musketeers*, 1939; *The Gorilla*, 1939; *Frontier Marshal*, 1939; *Sailor's Lady*, 1940; *Young People*, 1940; *Trail of the Vigilantes*, 1940; *Look Who's Laughing*, 1941; *Rise and Shine*, 1941; *Here We Go Again*, 1942; *Friendly Enemies*, 1942; *Around the World*, 1943; *Up in Mabel's Room*, 1944; *Abroad With Two Yanks*, 1944; *Brewster's Millions*, 1945; *Getting Gertie's Garter*, 1945; *Rendezvous With Annie*, 1946; *Calendar Girl*, 1947; *Northwest Outpost*, 1947; *Driftwood*, 1947; *The Inside Story*, 1948; *Angel in Exile* (with Philip Ford), 1948; *Sands of Iwo Jima*, 1949; *Surrender*, 1950; *Belle Le Grand*, 1951; *The Wild Blue Yonder*, 1951; *I Dream of Jeannie*, 1952; *Montana Belle* (shot in 1948), 1952; *The Woman They Almost Lynched*, 1953; *Sweethearts on Parade*, 1953; *Flight Nurse*, 1953; *Silver Lode*, 1954; *Passion*, 1954; *Cattle Queen of Montana*, 1954; *Escape to Burma*, 1955; *Pearl of the South Pacific*, 1955; *Tennessee's Partner*, 1955; *Slightly Scarlet*, 1956; *Hold Back the Night*, 1956; *The River's Edge*, 1957; *The Restless Breed*, 1957; *Enchanted Island*, 1958; *The Most Dangerous Man Alive* (shot in 1958), 1961.

Look Who's Laughing with Fibber McGee, Lucille Ball, Edgar Bergen and Molly McGee. *(Dwan)*

JOHN FORD Born February 1, 1895; *Black Watch*, 1929; *Salute*, 1929; *Men Without Women*, 1930; *Born Reckless*, 1930; *Up the River*, 1930; *The Seas Beneath*, 1931; *The Brat*, 1931; *Arrowsmith*, 1931; *Air Mail*, 1932; *Flesh*, 1932; *Pilgrimage*, 1933; *Doctor Bull*, 1933; *The Lost Patrol*, 1934; *The World Moves On*, 1934; *Judge Priest*, 1934; *The Whole Town's Talking*, 1935; *The Informer*, 1935; *Steamboat Round the Bend*, 1935; *The Prisoner of Shark Island*, 1936; *Mary of Scotland*, 1936; *The Plough and the Stars*, 1936; *Wee Willie Winkie*, 1937; *The Hurricane* (with Stuart Heisler), 1937; *Four Men and a Prayer*, 1938; *Submarine Patrol*, 1938; *Stagecoach*, 1939; *Young Mr. Lincoln*, 1939; *Drums Along the Mohawk*, 1939; *The Grapes of Wrath*, 1940; *The Long Voyage Home*, 1940; *Tobacco Road*, 1941; *How Green Was My Valley*, 1941; *They Were Expendable* (with Robert Montgomery), 1945; *My Darling Clementine*, 1946; *The Fugitive* (with Emilio Fernandez), 1947; *Fort Apache*, 1948; *Three Godfathers*, 1948; *Mighty Joe Young* (producer only), 1949; *Pinky* (replaced by Elia Kazan), 1949; *She Wore a Yellow Ribbon*, 1949; *When Willie Comes Marching Home*, 1950; *Wagonmaster*, 1950; *Rio Grande*, 1950; *What Price Glory*, 1952; *The Quiet Man*, 1952; *The Sun Shines Bright*, 1953; *Mogambo*, 1953; *Hondo*, 1953; *The Long Gray Line*, 1955; *Mister Roberts* (with Mervyn LeRoy), 1955; *The Searchers*, 1956; *The Wings of Eagles*, 1957; *The Rising of the Moon*, 1957; *The Last Hurrah*, 1958; *Gideon's Day*, 1959; *The Horse Soldiers*, 1959; *Sergeant Rutledge*, 1960; *The Alamo* (with John Wayne), 1960; *Two Rode Together*, 1961; *The Man Who Shot Liberty Valance*, 1961; *How the West Was Won:* "The Civil War" episode, 1962; *Donovan's Reef*, 1963; *Cheyenne Autumn*, 1964; *Young Cassidy* (replaced by Jack Cardiff), 1964, *7 Women*, 1965.

Rio Grande with John Wayne and Maureen O'Hara. *(Ford)*

JOHN FRANKENHEIMER Born February 19, 1930; *The Young Stranger*, 1957; *The Young Savages*, 1961; *All Fall Down*, 1962; *Bird Man of Alcatraz*, 1962; *The Manchurian Candidate*, 1962; *Seven Days in May*, 1964; *The Train* (replaced Arthur Penn, with Bernard Farrel), 1965, *Seconds*, 1966; *Grand Prix* (replaced John Sturges), 1967; *The Extraordinary Seaman*, 1968; *The Fixer*, 1968.

Seconds with Rock Hudson. *(Frankenheimer)*

TAY GARNETT Born 1905; *The Flying Fool*, 1929; *Oh Yeah!*, 1930; *Officer O'Brien*, 1930; *Her Man*, 1930; *Bad Company*, 1931; *Prestige*, 1932; *One Way Passage*, 1932; *Okay America*, 1932; *Destination Unknown*, 1933; *S.O.S. Iceberg*, 1933; *She Couldn't Take It*, 1935; *China Seas*, 1935; *Professional Soldier*, 1935; *Love Is News*, 1937; *Slave Ship*, 1937; *Stand-In*, 1937; *The Joy of Living*, 1938; *Trade Winds*, 1938; *Eternally Yours*, 1939; *Slightly Honorable*, 1940; *Seven Sinners*, 1940; *Cheers for Miss Bishop*, 1941; *Unexpected Uncle* (producer only), 1941), *Weekend for Three* (producer only), 1941; *My Favorite Spy*, 1942; *Bataan*, 1943; *The Cross of Lorraine*, 1943; *Mrs. Parkington*, 1944; *The Valley of Decision*, 1945; *The Postman Always Rings Twice*, 1946; *Wild Harvest*, 1947; *A Connecticut Yankee in King Arthur's Court*, 1949; *The Fireball*, 1950; *Cause for Alarm*, 1951; *Soldiers Three*, 1951; *One Minute to Zero*, 1952; *Main Street to Broadway*, 1953; *The Black Knight*, 1954; *Cinerama's Seven Wonders of the World*, India Sequence, 1956; *A Terrible Beauty*, or *The Night Fighters*, 1960; *Cattle King*, 1963.

Seven Sinners with John Wayne and Marlene Dietrich. *(Garnett)*

EDMUND GOULDING Born March 20, 1891; died December 24, 1959; *Paramount on Parade* (among various directors), 1930; *The Devil's Holiday*, 1930; *Reaching for the Moon*, 1931; *The Night Angel*, 1931; *Flesh*, 1932; *Grand Hotel*, 1932; *Blondie of the Follies*, 1932; *Riptide*, 1934; *The Flame Within*, 1935; *That Certain Woman*, 1937; *The Dawn Patrol*, 1938; *White Banners*, 1938; *Dark Victory*, 1939; *The Old Maid*, 1939; *We Are Not Alone*, 1939; *Till We Meet Again*,

The Flame Within with Henry Stephenson, Herbert Marshall and Ann Harding. *(Goulding)*

1940; *The Great Lie*, 1941; *Forever and a Day* (among various directors), 1943; *The Constant Nymph*, 1943; *Claudia*, 1943; *Of Human Bondage*, 1946; *The Razor's Edge*, 1946; *Nightmare Alley*, 1947; *Everybody Does It*, 1949; *Mister 880*, 1950; *We're Not Married*, 1952; *Down Among the Sheltering Palms* (completed 1951), 1953; *Teenage Rebel*, 1956; *Mardi Gras*, 1958.

HENRY HATHAWAY Born March 13, 1898; *Wild Horse Mesa*, 1933; *Heritage of the Desert*, 1933; *Under the Tonto Rim*, 1933; *Sunset Pass*, 1933; *Man of the Forest*, 1933; *To the Last Man*, or *Law of Vengeance*, 1933; *The Last Round-Up*, 1934; *Thundering Herd*, 1933; *The Witching Hour*, 1934; *Come On, Marines!*, 1934; *Now and Forever*, 1934; *Peter Ibbetson*, 1935; *Lives of a Bengal Lancer*, 1935; *The Trail of the Lonesome Pine*, 1936; *Go West, Young Man*, 1936; *Souls at Sea*, 1937; *Spawn of the North*, 1938; *The Real Glory*, 1939; *Johnny Apollo*, 1940; *Brigham Young—Frontiersman*, 1940; *The Shepherd of the Hills*, 1941; *Sundown*, 1941; *Ten Gentlemen From West Point*, 1942; *China Girl*, 1942; *Wing and a Prayer*, 1944; *Home in Indiana*, 1944; *Nob Hill*, 1945; *The House on 92nd Street*, 1945; *The Dark Corner*, 1946; *13 Rue Madeleine*. 1946; *Kiss of Death*, 1947; *Call Northside 777*, 1948; *Down to the Sea in Ships*, 1949; *The Black Rose*, 1949; *You're in the Navy Now*, 1951; *Rawhide*, 1951; *14 Hours*, 1951; *The Desert Fox*, 1951; *Diplomatic Courier*, 1952; *White Witch Doctor*, 1953; *Niagara*, 1953; *Prince Valiant*, 1954; *Garden of Evil*, 1954; *The Racers*, 1955; *The Bottom of the Bottle*, 1956; *23 Paces to Baker Street*, 1956; *Legend of the Lost*, 1957; *From Hell to Texas*, or *Man Hunt*, 1958; *Woman Obsessed*, 1959; *Seven Thieves*, 1960; *North to Alaska*, 1960; *How the West Was Won* (three to the five episodes; other two: John Ford and George Marshall), 1962; *Circus World*, 1964; *Of Human Bondage* (replaced Ken Hughes), 1964; *The Sons of Katie Elder*, 1965; *Nevada Smith*, 1966; *The Last Safari*, 1967.

Man's Favorite Sport? with Rock Hudson and Paula Prentiss. (Hawks)

Murder, 1930; *The Skin Game*, 1931; *Rich and Strange*, 1932; *Number Seventeen*, 1932; *Lord Camber's Ladies* (producer only), 1932; *Waltzes From Vienna*, 1933; *The Man Who Knew Too Much*, 1934; *The Thirty-Nine Steps*, 1935; *The Secret Agent*, 1936; *Sabotage*, 1936; *Young and Innocent*, 1937; *The Lady Vanishes*, 1938; *Jamaica Inn*, 1939; *Rebecca*, 1940; *Foreign Correspondent*, 1940; *Mr. and Mrs. Smith*, 1941; *Suspicion*, 1941; *Saboteur*, 1942; *Shadow of a Doubt*, 1943; *Lifeboat*, 1944; *Bon Voyage*, 1944; *Adventure Malgache*, 1944; *Spellbound*, 1945; *Notorious*, 1946; *The Paradine Case*, 1947; *Rope*, 1948; *Under Capricorn*, 1949; *Stage Fright*, 1950; *Strangers on a Train*, 1951; *I Confess*, 1953; *Dial M For Murder*, 1954; *Rear Window*, 1954; *To Catch a Thief*, 1955; *The Trouble With Harry*, 1955; *The Man Who Knew Too Much*, 1956; *The Wrong Man*, 1956; *Vertigo*, 1958; *North by Northwest*, 1959; *The Wreck of the Mary Deare* (replaced by Michael Anderson), 1959; *Psycho*, 1960; *The Birds*, 1963; *Marnie*, 1964; *Torn Curtain*, 1966.

China Girl with George Montgomery, Philip Ahn and Gene Tierney. (Hathaway)

Saboteur with Priscilla Lane, Robert Cummings and Otto Kruger. (Hitchcock)

HOWARD HAWKS Born May 30, 1896; *The Dawn Patrol*, 1930; *The Criminal Code*, 1931; *The Crowd Roars*, 1932; *Scarface, Shame of the Nation*, 1932; *Tiger Shark*, 1932; *Today We Live*, 1933; *Viva Villa!* (with Jack Conway), 1934; *Twentieth Century*, 1934; *Barbary Coast*, 1935; *Ceiling Zero*, 1936; *The Road to Glory*, 1936; *Come and Get It* (with William Wyler), 1936; *Bringing Up Baby*, 1938; *Only Angels Have Wings*, 1939; *His Girl Friday*, 1939; *The Outlaw* (with Howard Hughes; shot in 1943), 1946; *Sergeant York*, 1941; *Ball of Fire*, 1941; *Air Force*, 1943; *Corvette K-225* (producer only), 1943; *To Have and Have Not*, 1944; *The Big Sleep*, 1946; *Red River*, 1948; *A Song Is Born*, 1948; *I Was a Male War Bride*, 1949; *The Thing* (producer only), 1951; *The Big Sky*, 1952; *O. Henry's Full House:* "The Ransom of Red Chief" episode, 1952; *Monkey Business*, 1952; *Gentleman Prefer Blondes*, 1953; *Land of the Pharaohs*, 1955; *Rio Bravo*, 1959; *Hatari!*, 1962; *Man's Favorite Sport?*, 1963; *Red Line 7000*, 1965.

ALFRED HITCHCOCK Born August 13, 1899; *Blackmail*, 1929; *Elstree Calling*, two episodes, 1930; *Juno and the Paycock*, 1930;

JOHN HUSTON Born August 5, 1906; *The Maltese Falcon*, 1941; *In This Our Life*, 1942; *Across the Pacific*, 1942; *Report From the Aleutians*, 1943; *The Battle of San Pietro*, 1944; *Let There Be Light*, 1945; *The Stranger* (producer only, under Sam Spiegel), 1946; *The Treasure of Sierra Madre*, 1948; *Key Largo*, 1948; *We Were Strangers*, 1949; *The Asphalt Jungle*, 1950; *The Prowler* (producer only, under Sam Spiegel), 1951; *The Red Badge of Courage*, 1951; *The African Queen*, 1951; *Moulin Rouge*, 1952; *Beat the Devil*, 1953; *Moby Dick*, 1956; *Heaven Knows, Mr. Allison*, 1957; *A Farewell to Arms* (replaced by Charles Vidor), 1957; *The Barbarian and the Geisha*, 1958; *The Roots of Heaven*, 1958; *The Unforgiven*, 1960; *The Misfits*, 1960; *Freud, the Secret Passion*, 1962; *The List of Adrian Messenger*, 1963; *The Night of the Iguana*, 1964; *The Bible*, 1966; *Casino Royale* (David Niven footage only; 38 minutes), 1967; *Reflections in a Golden Eye*, 1967; *Sinful Davey*, 1968.

ELIA KAZAN Born September 7, 1909; *It's Up to You*, 1941; *A Tree Grows in Brooklyn*, 1945; *Sea of Grass*, 1947; *Boomerang*, 1947; *Gentle-*

The Maltese Falcon with Humphrey Bogart, Peter Lorre, Mary Astor and Sydney Greenstreet. *(Huston)*

man's Agreement, 1947; *Pinky*, 1949; *Panic in the Streets*, 1950; *A Streetcar Named Desire*, 1951; *Viva Zapata!*, 1952; *Man on a Tightrope*, 1953; *On the Waterfront*, 1954; *East of Eden*, 1955; *Baby Doll*, 1956; *A Face in the Crowd*, 1956; *Wild River*, 1960; *Splendor in the Grass*, 1961; *America America*, 1963.

Man on a Tightrope with Alex D'Arcy and Terry Moore. *(Kazan)*

HENRY KING Born January 24, 1896; *Hell's Harbor*, 1930; *Eyes of the World*, 1930; *Lightning*, 1930; *Merely Mary Ann*, 1931; *Over the Hill*, 1931; *The Woman in Room 13*, 1932; *State Fair*, 1933; *I Loved You Wednesday*, 1933; *Carolina*, 1934; *Marie Galante*, 1934; *One More Spring*, 1935; *Way Down East*, 1935; *The Country Doctor*, 1936; *Ramona*, 1936; *Lloyds of London*, 1936; *Seventh Heaven*, 1937; *In Old Chicago*, 1938; *Alexander's Ragtime Band*, 1938; *Jesse James*, 1939; *Stanley and Livingstone*, 1939; *Little Old New York*, 1940; *Maryland*, 1940; *Chad Hanna*, 1940; *A Yank in the R.A.F.*, 1941; *Remember the Day*, 1941; *The Black Swan*, 1942; *The Song of Bernadette*, 1943; *Wilson*, 1944; *A Bell for Adano*, 1945; *Margie*, 1946; *The Captain From Castile*, 1947; *Deep Waters*, 1948; *The Prince of Foxes*, 1949; *Twelve O'Clock High*, 1949; *The Gunfighter*, 1950; *I'd Climb the Highest Mountain*, 1951; *David and Bathsheba*, 1951; *Wait Till the Sun Shines, Nellie*, 1952; *O. Henry's Full House:* "The Gift of the Magi" episode, 1952; *The Snows of Kilimanjaro*, 1952; *King of the Khyber Rifles*, 1953; *Untamed*, 1955; *Love Is a Many-Splendored Thing*, 1955; *Carousel*, 1956; *The Sun Also Rises*, 1957; *The Old Man and the Sea* (replaced Fred Zinnemann; replaced by John Sturges), 1958; *The Bravados*, 1958; *This Earth Is Mine*, 1959; *Beloved Infidel*, 1959; *Tender Is the Night*, 1961.

Little Old New York with Henry Stephenson and Brenda Joyce. *(King)*

HENRY KOSTER Born May 1, 1905; *Three Smart Girls*, 1936; *One Hundred Men and a Girl*, 1937; *The Rage of Paris*, 1938; *First Love*, 1939; *Three Smart Girls Grow Up*, 1939; *It Started With Eve*, 1941; *Spring Parade*, 1940; *Between Us Girls*, 1942; *Music for Millions*, 1944; *Two Sisters From Boston*, 1946; *The Bishop's Wife*, 1947; *Luck of the Irish*, 1948; *Come to the Stable*, 1949; *The Inspector General*, 1949; *My Blue Heaven*, 1949; *Wabash Avenue*, 1950; *Harvey*, 1950; *No Highway in the Sky*, 1951; *Mr. Belvedere Rings the Bell*, 1951; *O. Henry's Full House:* "The Cop and the Anthem" episode, 1952; *Stars and Stripes Forever*, 1952; *My Cousin Rachel*, 1952: *The Robe*, 1953; *Desiree*, 1954; *A Man Called Peter*, 1955; *The Virgin Queen*, 1955; *Good Morning, Miss Dove*, 1955; *D-Day, The Sixth of June*, 1956; *The Power and the Prize*, 1956; *My Man Godfrey*, 1957; *Fraulein*, 1958; *The Naked Maja*, 1959; *The Story of Ruth*, 1960; *Flower Drum Song*, 1961; *Mr. Hobbs Takes a Vacation*, 1962; *Take Her, She's Mine*, 1963; *Dear Brigitte*, 1965; *The Singing Nun*, 1966.

My Blue Heaven with Dan Dailey, Betty Grable and Mitzi Gaynor. *(Koster)*

FRITZ LANG Born December 5, 1890, *Fury*, 1936; *You Only Live Once*, 1937; *You and Me*, 1938; *The Return of Frank James*, 1940; *Western Union*, 1941; *Man Hunt*, 1941; *Confirm or Deny* (replaced by Archie Mayo), 1941; *Moontide* (replaced by Archie Mayo), 1942; *Hangmen Also Die*, 1943; *The Ministry of Fear*, 1944; *The Woman in the Window*, 1944; *Scarlet Street*, 1945; *Cloak and Dagger*, 1946; *The Secret Beyond the Door*, 1948; *The House by the River*, 1950; *American Guerrilla in the Philippines*, 1950; *Rancho Notorious*, 1952; *Clash by Night*, 1952; *The Blue Gardenia*, 1953; *The Big Heat*, 1953; *Human Desire*, 1954; *Moonfleet*, 1955; *While the City Sleeps*, 1956; *Beyond a Reasonable Doubt*, 1956.

MITCHELL LEISEN Born October 6, 1899; *Cradle Song*, 1933; *Death Takes a Holiday*, 1934; *Murder at the Vanities*, 1934; *Behold My Wife*, 1935; *Four Hours to Kill*, 1935; *Hands Across the Table*, 1935; *13 Hours by Air*, 1936; *The Big Broadcast of 1937*, 1936; *Swing High, Swing Low*, 1937; *East Living*, 1937; *The Big Broadcast of 1938*, 1938;

The Ministry of Fear with Marjorie Reynolds and Ray Milland *(Lang)*

Artists and Models Abroad, 1938; *Midnight*, 1939; *Remember the Night*, 1940; *Arise, My Love*, 1940; *I Wanted Wings*, 1941; *Hold Back the Dawn*, 1941; *The Lady Is Willing*, 1942; *Take a Letter, Darling*, 1942; *No Time For Love*, 1943; *Lady in the Dark*, 1944; *Frenchman's Creek*, 1944; *Practically Yours*, 1944; *Kitty*, 1945; *Masquerade in Mexico*, 1945; *To Each His Own*, 1946; *Suddenly It's Spring*, 1947; *Golden Earrings*, 1947; *Dream Girl*, 1948; *Bride of Vengeance*, 1949; *Song of Surrender*, 1949; *No Man of Her Own*, 1950; *Captain Carey, U.S.A.*, 1950; *The Mating Season*, 1951; *Darling, How Could You!*, 1951; *Young Man with Ideas*, 1952; *Tonight We Sing*, 1953; *Bedevilled*, 1955; *The Girl Most Likely*, 1957; *Las Vegas by Night*, or *Here's Las Vegas*, 1963.

The Lady Is Willing with Marlene Dietrich and Sterling Holloway (man without flowers at window). *(Leisen)*

MERVYN LEROY Born October 15, 1900; *Dramatic School* (producer only), 1938; *Flying Romeos*, 1928; *Harold Teen*, 1928; *Naughty Baby*, 1929; *Hot Stuff*, 1929; *Broadway Daddy*, 1929; *Showgirl in Hollywood*, 1930; *Little Johnny Jones*, 1930; *Playing Around*, 1930; *Numbered Men*, 1930; *Top Speed*, 1930; *Little Caesar*, 1930; *Gentlemen's Fate*, 1931; *Five Star Final*, 1931; *Broad-Minded*, 1931; *Too Young to Marry*, 1931; *Local Boy Makes Good*, 1931; *Tonight or Never*, 1931; *Two Seconds*, 1932; *Heart of New York*, 1932; *Big City Blues*, 1932; *Three on a Match*, 1932; *I Am a Fugitive From a Chain Gang*, 1932; *High Pressure*, 1932; *Gold Diggers of 1933* (with Busby Berkeley), 1933; *Tugboat Annie*, 1933; *Elmer the Great*, 1933; *Hard to Handle*, 1933; *The World Changes*, 1933; *Heat Lightning*, 1934; *Sweet Adeline*, 1934; *Happiness Ahead*, 1934; *Hi, Nellie!*, 1934; *Page Miss Glory*, 1935; *Oil for the Lamps of China*, 1935; *I Found Stella Parish*, 1935; *Anthony Adverse*, 1936; *The King and the Chorus Girl*, 1937; *They Won't Forget*, 1937; *Fools for Scandal*, 1938; *A Day at the Circus* (producer only), 1939; *The Wizard of Oz* (producer only), 1939; *Escape*, 1940; *Waterloo Bridge*, 1940; *Blossoms in the Dust*, 1941; *Unholy Partners*, 1941; *Johnny Eager*, 1941; *Random Harvest*, 1942; *Madame Curie*, 1943; *Thirty Seconds Over Tokyo*, 1944; *Without Reservations*, 1946; *Homecoming*, 1948; *Little Women*, 1949; *In the Good Old Summertime*,

1949; *Any Number Can Play*, 1949; *East Side, West Side*, 1949; *Quo Vadis*, 1951; *Lovely to Look At* (with Vincente Minnelli), 1952; *Million Dollar Mermaid* (with Busby Berkeley), 1952; *Latin Lovers*, 1953; *Rose Marie* (with Busby Berkeley), 1954; *Strange Lady in Town*, 1955; *Mister Roberts* (with John Ford), 1955, *Toward the Unknown*, 1956; *The Bad Seed*, 1956; *No Time for Sergeants*, 1958; *Home Before Dark*, 1958; *The FBI. Story*, 1959; *Wake Me When It's Over*, 1960; *The Devil at Four O'Clock*, 1961; *A Majority of One*, 1962; *Gypsy*, 1962; *Mary, Mary*, 1963; *Moment to Moment*, 1965.

Latin Lovers with Lana Turner and Ricardo Montalban. *(LeRoy)*

ANATOLE LITVAK Born May 10, 1902; *The Woman I Love*, 1937; *Tovarich*, 1937; *The Amazing Dr. Clitterhouse*, 1938; *The Sisters*, 1938; *Confessions of a Nazi Spy*, 1939; *The Roaring Twenties* (replaced by Raoul Walsh), 1939; *Castle on the Hudson*, 1940; *All This, and Heaven Too*, 1940; *City for Conquest*, 1940; *Out of the Fog*, 1941; *One Foot in Heaven* (replaced by Irving Rapper), 1941; *Blues in the Night*, 1941; *This Above All*, 1942; "Why We Fight" series features: *The Nazis Strike*, 1942; *Divide and Conquer*, 1943; *The Battle of Russia*, 1943; *The Battle of China*, 1944; *War Comes to America* (with Frank Capra), 1945; *Operation Titanic*, 1943; *New Orleans* (replaced by Arthur Lubin), 1947; *The Long Night*, 1947; *Sorry, Wrong Number*, 1948; *The Snake Pit*, 1949; *Decision Before Dawn*, 1951; *Act of Love*, 1954; *The Deep Blue Sea*, 1955; *Anastasia*, 1956; *The Journey*, 1959; *Goodbye Again*, 1961; *Five Miles to Midnight*, 1963; *A Shot in the Dark* (replaced by Blake Edwards), 1964; *10: 30 P. M. Summer* (producer only), 1966; *The Night of the Generals*, 1967.

The Journey with Yul Brynner and Deborah Kerr. *(Litvak)*

FRANK LLOYD Born February 2, 1889; died 1960; *Weary River*, 1929; *Drag*, 1929; *Young Nowheres*, 1929; *The Dark Streets*, 1929; *Son of the Gods*, 1930; *The Lash*, 1931; *East Lynne*, 1931; *Right of Way*, 1931; *Age for Love*, 1931; *Passport to Hell*, 1932; *Cavalcade*, 1933; *Berkeley Square*, 1933; *Hoopla*, 1933; *Servants' Entrance*, 1934; *Mutiny on the Bounty*, 1935; *A Tale of Two Cities*, 1935; *Under Two Flags*, 1936; *Maid of Salem*, 1937; *Wells Fargo*, 1937; *If I Were King*, 1938; *Rulers of the Sea*, 1939; *The Howards of Virginia* (producer only), 1940; *The Lady from Cheyenne*, 1941; *This Woman Is Mine*, 1941; *The Spoilers* (producer only), 1942; *Invisible Agent* (producer only), 1942; *Saboteur* (co-producer only), 1942; *Forever and a Day* (among various directors), 1943; *Blood on the Sun*, 1945; *Shanghai Story*, 1954; *The Last Command*, 1955.

If I Were King with Ronald Colman, Henry Wilcoxon, William Haade, Jean Fenwick, Sidney Toler, Stanley Ridges, Francis McDonald and Adrian Morris. *(Lloyd)*

LEO McCAREY Born October 30, 1894; *The Sophomore*, 1929; *Red Hot Rhythm*, 1929; *Wild Company*, 1930; *Let's Go Native*, 1930; *Part Time Wife*, 1930; *Indiscreet*, 1931; *The Kid From Spain* (with Busby Berkeley), 1932; *Duck Soup*, 1933; *Six of a Kind*, 1934; *Belle of the Nineties*, 1934; *Ruggles of Red Gap*, 1935; *The Milky Way*, 1936; *Make Way for Tomorrow*, 1937; *The Awful Truth*, 1937; *Love Affair*, 1939; *My Favorite Wife*, 1940; *Once Upon a Honeymoon*, 1942; *Going My Way*, 1944; *The Bells of St. Mary's*, 1945; *Good Sam*, 1948; *My Son John*, 1952; *An Affair to Remember*, 1957; *Rally 'Round the Flag, Boys!*, 1958; *Satan Never Sleeps*, 1961.

Satan Never Sleeps with William Holden, France Nuyen and Clifton Webb. *(McCarey)*

ROUBEN MAMOULIAN Born October 8, 1898; *Applause*, 1929; *City Streets*, 1931; *Dr. Jekyll and Mr. Hyde*, 1932; *Love Me Tonight*, 1932; *The Song of Songs*, 1933; *Queen Christina*, 1933; *We Live Again*, 1934; *Becky Sharp* (replaced Lowell Sherman, who died during shooting), 1935; *The Gay Desperado*, 1936; *High, Wide and Handsome*, 1937;

Golden Boy, 1939; *The Mark of Zorro*, 1940; *Blood and Sand*, 1941; *Rings on Her Fingers*, 1942; *Summer Holiday*, 1948; *The Wild Heart* (replaced Michael Powell, but uncredited), 1951; *Silk Stockings*, 1957; *Porgy and Bess* (replaced by Otto Preminger), 1959.

Rings on Her Fingers with Henry Fonda and Gene Tierney. *(Mamoulian)*

JOSEPH L. MANKIEWICZ Born February 11, 1909; *The Three Godfathers* (producer only), 1936; *Fury* (producer only), 1936; *The Gorgeous Hussy* (producer only), 1936; *Love on the Run* (producer only), 1936; *The Bride Wore Red* (producer only), 1937), *Double Wedding* (producer only), 1937); *Mannequin* (producer only), 1937; *Three Comrades* (producer only), 1938; *The Shopworn Angel* (producer only), 1938; *The Shining Hour* (producer only), 1938; *A Christmas Carol* (producer only), 1938; *The Adventures of Huckleberry Finn* (producer only), 1939; *Strange Cargo* (producer only), 1940; *The Philadelphia Story* (producer only), 1940; *The Wild Man of Borneo* (producer only), 1941); *The Feminine Touch* (producer only), 1941; *Woman of the Year* (producer only), 1942; *Cairo* (producer only), 1942; *Reunion in France* (producer only), 1942; *The Keys of the Kingdom* (producer only), 1944; *Dragonwyck*, 1946; *Somewhere in the Night*, 1946; *The Late George Apley*, 1947; *The Ghost and Mrs. Muir*, 1947; *Escape*, 1948; *A Letter to Three Wives*, 1949; *House of Strangers*, 1949; *No Way Out*, 1950; *All About Eve*, 1950; *People Will Talk*, 1951; *Five Fingers*, 1952; *Julius Caesar*, 1953; *The Barefoot Contessa*, 1954; *Guys and Dolls*, 1955; *The Quiet American*, 1958; *I Want to Live!* (co-producer only), 1958; *Suddenly, Last Summer*, 1959; *Cleopatra* (replaced various directors), 1963; *The Honey Pot*, 1967.

People Will Talk with Cary Grant and Jeanne Crain. *(Mankiewicz)*

ANTHONY MANN Born June 30, 1906; died April 29, 1967; *Dr. Broadway*, 1942; *Moonlight in Havana*, 1942; *Nobody's Darling*, 1943;

My Best Gal, 1944; *Strangers in the Night*, 1944; *The Great Flamarion*, 1945; *Two O'Clock Courage*, 1945; *Sing Your Way Home*, 1945; *Strange Impersonation*, 1946; *The Bamboo Blonde*, 1946; *Desperate*, 1947; *Railroaded*, 1947; *T-Men*, 1947; *Raw Deal*, 1948; *Reign of Terror*, 1949; *Follow Me Quietly*, 1949; *Border Incident*, 1949; *Side Street*, 1949; *Devil's Doorway*, 1950; *Winchester '73*, 1950; *The Furies*, 1950; *Quo Vadis* (as second-unit director under Mervyn LeRoy), 1951; *The Tall Target*, 1951; *Bend of the River*, 1952; *The Naked Spur*, 1953; *Thunder Bay*, 1953; *The Glenn Miller Story*, 1954; *The Far Country*, 1955; *Strategic Air Command*, 1955; *The Man From Laramie*, 1955; *The Last Frontier*, 1956; *Serenade*, 1956; *Men in War*, 1957; *The Tin Star*, 1957; *God's Little Acre*, 1957; *Man of the West*, 1958; *Spartacus* (replaced by Stanley Kubrick), 1960; *Cimarron*, 1960; *El Cid*, 1961; *The Fall of the Roman Empire*, 1964; *Heroes of Telemark*, 1965; *A Dandy in Aspic* (shot February 20, 1967 through Mann's death mid-shooting April 29, 1967; completed by Laurence Harvey, 1968).

Thunder Bay with James Stewart and Gilbert Roland. *(Mann)*

LEWIS MILESTONE Born September 30, 1895; *New York Nights*, 1929; *All Quiet on the Western Front*, 1930; *Hell's Angels* (with Howard Hughes), 1930; *The Front Page*, 1931; *Rain*, 1932; *Hallelujah, I'm a Bum*, 1933; *The Captain Hates the Sea*, 1934; *Paris in the Spring*, 1935; *Anything Goes*, 1936; *The General Died at Dawn*, 1936; *Night of Nights*, 1939; *Of Mice and Men*, 1939; *Lucky Partners*, 1940; *My Life With Caroline*, 1941; *Edge of Darkness*, 1943; *North Star*, or *Armored Attack*, 1943; *The Purple Heart*, 1944; *A Walk in the Sun*, 1945; *The Strange Love of Martha Ivers*, 1946; *Guest in the House* (replaced John Brahm), 1945; *No Minor Vices*, 1948; *Arch of Triumph*, 1948; *The Red Pony*, 1949; *The Halls of Montezuma*, 1950; *Kangaroo*, 1952; *Les Miserables*, 1952; *Melba*, 1953; *They Who Dare*, 1954; *The Widow*, 1955; *King Kelly* (uncompleted), 1957; *Pork Chop Hill*, 1959; *Ocean's 11*, 1960; *Mutiny on the Bounty* (replaced Carol Reed), 1962; *PT-109* (replaced by Leslie H. Martinson), 1963; *The Dirty Game* (replaced by Terence Young, 1965), 1966.

Anything Goes with Charlie Ruggles, Bing Crosby and Ethel Merman. *(Milestone)*

VINCENTE MINNELLI Born February 28, 1906; *Cabin in the Sky*, 1943; *I Dood It*, 1943; *Meet Me in St. Louis*, 1944; *The Clock*, 1945; *Yolanda and the Thief*, 1945; *Ziegfeld Follies*, 1946; *Undercurrent*, 1946; *The Pirate*, 1948; *Madame Bovary*, 1949; *Father of the Bride*, 1950; *An American in Paris*, 1951; *Father's Little Dividend*, 1951; *The Bad and the Beautiful*, 1952; *Lovely to Look At* (with Mervyn LeRoy), 1952; *The Band Wagon*, 1953; *The Story of Three Loves:* "Mademoiselle" sketch, 1953; *The Long, Long Trailer*, 1953; *Brigadoon*, 1954; *The Cobweb*, 1955; *Kismet*, 1955; *Lust for Life*, 1956; *Tea and Sympathy*, 1956; *Designing Woman*, 1957; *The Seventh Sin* (replaced Ronald Neame), 1957; *Gigi*, 1958; *The Reluctant Debutante*, 1958; *Some Came Running*, 1958; *Home from the Hill*, 1960; *Bells are Ringing*, 1960; *The Four Horsemen of the Apocalypse*, 1962; *Two Weeks in Another Town*, 1962; *The Courtship of Eddie's Father*, 1963; *Goodbye Charlie*, 1964; *The Sandpiper*, 1965.

I Dood It with Red Skelton and Eleanor Powell. *(Minnelli)*

JEAN NEGULESCO Born February 29, 1900; *Kiss and Make Up*, 1934; *Crash Donovan*, 1936; *Singapore Woman*, 1941; *The Mask of Dimitrios*, 1944; *The Conspirators*, 1944; *Three Strangers*, 1946; *Nobody Lives Forever*, 1946; *Humoresque*, 1946; *Deep Valley*, 1947; *Johnny Belinda*, 1948; *Roadhouse*, 1948; *The Forbidden Street*, 1949; *Under My Skin*, 1950; *Three Came Home*, 1950; *The Mudlark*, 1950; *Take Care of My Little Girl*, 1951; *Phone Call From a Stranger*, 1952; *Lydia Bailey*, 1952; *Lure of the Wilderness*, 1952; *O. Henry's Full House:* "The Last Leaf" episode, 1952; *Titanic*, 1953; *Scandal at Scourie*, 1953; *How to Marry a Millionaire*, 1953; *Three Coins in the Fountain*, 1954; *Woman's World*, 1954; *Daddy Long Legs*, 1955; *The Rains of Ranchipur*, 1955; *Boy on a Dolphin*, 1957; *Dry Martini* (uncompleted), 1957; *The Gift of Love*, 1958; *A Certain Smile*, 1958; *Count Your Blessings*, 1959; *The Best of Everything*, 1959; *Jessica*, 1962; *The Pleasure Seekers*, 1964.

Scandal at Scourie with Greer Garson, Walter Pidgeon and Donna Corcoran. *(Negulesco)*

OTTO PREMINGER Born December 5, 1906; *Under Your Spell*, 1936; *Danger, Love at Work*, 1937; *Margin for Error*, 1943; *In the Meantime, Darling*, 1944; *Laura*, 1944; *A Royal Scandal*, 1945; *Fallen Angel*, 1945; *Centennial Summer*, 1946; *Forever Amber*, 1947; *Daisy Kenyon*, 1947; *That Lady in Ermine* (replaced Ernst Lubitsch), 1948; *The Fan*, 1949; *Whirlpool*, 1949; *Where the Sidewalk Ends*, 1950; *The Thirteenth Letter*, 1951; *Angel Face*, 1952; *The Moon Is Blue*, 1953; *River of No Return*, 1954; *Carmen Jones*, 1954; *The Court-Martial of Billy Mitchell*, 1955; *The Man with the Golden Arm*, 1955; *Saint Joan*, 1957; *Bonjour, Tristesse*, 1958; *Porgy and Bess* (replaced Rouben Mamoulian), 1959; *Anatomy of a Murder*, 1959; *Exodus*, 1960; *Advise and Consent*, 1962; *The Cardinal*, 1963; *In Harm's Way*, 1965; *Bunny Lake Is Missing*, 1965; *Hurry Sundown*, 1967.

Bunny Lake Is Missing with Clive Revill, Carol Lynley, Laurence Olivier and Keir Dullea. *(Preminger)*

MARK ROBSON Born December 4, 1913; *The Seventh Victim*, 1943; *Ghost Ship*, 1943; *Youth Runs Wild*, 1944; *Isle of the Dead*, 1945; *Bedlam*, 1946; *Roughshod*, 1949; *Champion*, 1949; *Home of the Brave*, 1949; *My Foolish Heart*, 1949; *Edge of Doom*, 1950; *Bright Victory*, 1951; *I Want You*, 1952; *Return to Paradise*, 1953; *Hell Below Zero*, 1954; *Phffft*, 1954; *The Bridges at Toko-Ri*, 1954; *A Prize of Gold*, 1955; *Trial*, 1955; *The Harder They Fall*, 1956; *The Little Hut*, 1957; *Peyton Place*, 1957; *The Inn of the Sixth Happiness*, 1958; *From the Terrace*, 1960; *Lisa* (producer only), 1962; *Nine Hours to Rama*, 1963; *The Prize*, 1963; *Von Ryan's Express*, 1965; *Lost Command*, 1966; *Valley of the Dolls*, 1967.

The Harder They Fall with Nehemiah Persoff, Humphrey Bogart, Jan Sterling and Rod Steiger. *(Robson)*

ROBERT ROSSEN Born May 16, 1908; died February 18, 1966; *Johnny O'Clock*, 1947; *Body and Soul*, 1947; *The Undercover Man* (producer only), 1949; *All the King's Men*, 1949; *No Sad Songs for Me* (producer only), 1950; *The Brave Bulls*, 1951; *Mambo*, 1955; *Alexander* the Great, 1956; *Island in the Sun*, 1957; *They Came to Cordura*, 1959; *The Hustler*, 1961; *Lilith*, 1964.

The Brave Bulls with Mel Ferrer, Eugene Iglesias (hand on gate). *(Rossen)*

GEORGE SEATON Born April 17, 1911; *Diamond Horseshoe* or *Billy Rose's Diamond Horseshoe*, 1945; *Junior Miss*, 1945; *The Shocking Miss Pilgrim*, 1947; *Miracle on 34th Street*, 1947; *Apartment for Peggy*, 1948; *Chicken Every Sunday*, 1949; *The Big Lift*, 1950; *For Heaven's Sake*, 1950; *Rhubarb* (producer only, with William Perlberg), 1951; *Aaron Slick from Punkin' Crick*, 1952; *Anything Can Happen*, 1952; *Somebody Loves Me*, 1952; *Little Boy Lost*, 1953; *The Bridges at Toko-Ri* (producer only, with William Perlberg), 1954; *The Country Girl*, 1955; *The Proud and the Profane*, 1956; *Williamsburg, Story of a Patriot*, 1957; *The Tin Star* (producer only, with William Perlberg), 1957; *Teacher's Pet*, 1958; *But Not for Me* (producer only, with William Perlberg), 1959; *The Rat Race* (producer only, with William Perlberg), 1960; *The Pleasure of His Company*, 1961; *The Counterfeit Traitor*, 1962; *The Hook*, 1963; *Twilight of Honor* (producer only, with William Perlberg), 1963; *36 Hours*, 1965.

The Shocking Miss Pilgrim with Dick Haymes and Betty Grable. *(Seaton)*

ROBERT SIODMAK Born August 8, 1900; *West Point Widow*, 1941; *Fly-By-Night*, 1942; *The Night Before the Divorce*, 1942; *My Heart Belongs to Daddy*, 1942; *Someone to Remember*, 1943; *Son of Dracula*, 1943; *Cobra Woman*, 1944; *Phantom Lady*, 1944; *Christmas Holiday*, 1944; *The Suspect*, 1945; *The Strange Affair of Uncle Harry*, 1945; *The Spiral Staircase*, 1946; *The Killers*, 1946; *The Dark Mirror*, 1946; *Time Out of Mind*, 1947; *Cry of the City*, 1948; *Criss Cross*, 1949; *The Great Sinner*, 1949; *The File on Thelma Jordan*, or *Thelma Jordan*, 1949; *Deported*, 1950; *The Whistle at Eaton Falls*, 1951; *The Crimson Pirate*, 1952; *Escape from East Berlin*, 1962; *Custer of the West*, 1967.

The Crimson Pirate with Eva Bartok and Burt Lancaster. (Siodmak)

GEORGE STEVENS Born December 18, 1904; *Cohens and Kellys in Trouble*, 1933; *Bachelor Bait*, 1934; *Kentucky Kernels*, 1934; *Laddie*, 1935; *The Nitwits*, 1935; *Alice Adams*, 1935; *Annie Oakley*, 1935; *Swing Time*, 1936; *Quality Street*, 1937; *A Damsel in Distress*, 1937; *Vivacious Lady*, 1938; *Gunga Din*, 1939; *Vigil in the Night*, 1940; *Penny Serenade*, 1941; *Woman of the Year*, 1942; *The Talk of the Town*, 1942; *The More the Merrier*, 1943; *I Remember Mama*, 1948; *A Place in the Sun*, 1951; *Shane*, 1953; *Giant*, 1956; *The Diary of Anne Frank*, 1959; *The Greatest Story Ever Told* (initially with David Lean), 1965; *The Stalking Moon*, 1968.

I Remember Mama with Irene Dunne, Rudy Vallee, Oscar Homolka and Steve Brown. (Stevens)

JOHN STURGES Born January 3, 1910; *Thunderbolt* (with William Wyler), 1945; *The Man Who Dared*, 1946; *Shadowed*, 1946; *Alias Mr. Twilight*, 1947; *For the Love of Rusty*, 1947; *Keeper of the Bees*, 1947; *Best Man Wins*, 1948; *Sign of the Ram*, 1948; *The Walking Hills*, 1949; *Mystery Street*, 1950; *The Capture*, 1950; *The Magnificent Yankee*, 1950; *Right Cross*, 1950; *Kind Lady*, 1951; *The People Against O'Hara*, 1951; *It's a Big Country:* "The Census Takers" sketch, 1951; *The Girl in White*, 1952; *Jeopardy*, 1953; *Escape from Fort Bravo*, 1953; *Bad Day*

The Scarlet Coat with Anne Francis and Cornel Wilde. (Sturges)

at Black Rock, 1954; *Underwater*, 1955; *The Scarlet Coat*, 1955; *Backlash*, 1956; *Gunfight at the O.K. Corral*, 1957; *The Obsessed* (uncompleted), 1957; *The Spirit of St. Louis* (replaced by Billy Wilder), 1957; *The Old Man and the Sea* (replaced various directors), 1958; *The Law and Jake Wade*, 1958; *Never So Few*, 1959; *Last Train from Gun Hill*, 1959; *The Magnificent Seven*, 1960; *By Love Possessed*, 1961; *Sergeants Three*, 1962; *A Girl Named Tamiko*, 1963; *The Great Escape*, 1963; *The Satan Bug*, 1965; *The Hallelujah Trail*, 1965; *Grand Prix* (replaced by John Frankenheimer), 1966; *Ice Station Zebra*, 1968.

NORMAN TAUROG Born February 23, 1899; *The Diplomats*, 1928; *The Farmer's Daughter*, 1928; *Lucky Boy*, 1929; *Sunny Skies*, 1930; *Hot Curves*, 1930; *Follow the Leader*, or *Manhattan Mary*, 1930; *Finn and Hattie* (with Norman Z. McLeod), 1931; *Skippy*, 1931; *Newly Rich*, 1931; *Huckleberry Finn*, 1931; *Sooky*, 1931; *Hold 'Em Jail*, 1932; *The Phantom President*, 1932; *If I Had a Million*, 1932; *A Bedtime Story*, 1933; *The Way to Love*, 1933; *We're Not Dressing*, 1934; *Mrs. Wiggs of the Cabbage Patch*, 1934; *College Rhythm*, 1934; *The Big Broadcast of 1936*, 1935; *Strike Me Pink*, 1936; *Rhythm on the Range*, 1936; *You Can't Have Everything*, 1937; *Mad About Music*, 1938; *The Adventures of Tom Sawyer*, 1938; *Boys Town*, 1938; *The Girl Downstairs*, 1938; *Lucky Night*, 1939; *Broadway Melody of 1940*, 1940; *Young Tom Edison*, 1940; *Little Nellie Kelly*, 1940; *Men of Boys' Town*, 1941; *Design for Scandal*, 1941; *A Yank at Eton*, 1942; *Presenting Lily Mars*, 1943; *Girl Crazy* (with Busby Berkeley), 1943; *The Hoodlum Saint*, 1946; *The Beginning, or the End*, 1947; *The Bride Goes Wild*, 1948; *Big City*, 1948; *Words and Music*, 1948; *That Midnight Kiss*, 1949; *Please Believe Me*, 1950; *The Toast of New Orleans*, 1950; *Mrs. O'Malley and Mr. Malone*, 1950; *Rich, Young and Pretty*, 1951; *Room for One More*, 1952; *Jumping Jacks*, 1952; *The Stooge*, 1952; *The Stars Are Singing*, 1953; *The Caddy*, 1953; *Living It Up*, 1954; *You're Never Too Young*, 1955; *The Birds and the Bees*, 1956; *Pardners*, 1956; *Bundle of Joy*, 1956; *The Fuzzy Pink Nightgown*, 1957; *Onionhead*, 1958; *Don't Give Up the Ship*, 1959; *Visit to a Small Planet*, 1960; *G. I. Blues*, 1960; *Blue Hawaii*, 1961; *Girls! Girls! Girls!*, 1962; *It Happened at the World's Fair*, 1963; *Palm Springs Weekend*, 1963; *Tickle Me*, 1965; *Sergeant Deadhead, the Astronut*, 1965; *Dr. Goldfoot and the Bikini Machine*, 1965; *Spinout*, 1966; *Double Trouble*, 1967; *Speedway*, 1967.

Please Believe Me with Robert Walker, Peter Lawford, Deborah Kerr and Mark Stevens. (Taurog)

JACQUES TOURNEUR Born November 12, 1904; *The Winning Ticket* (with Chuck Reisner), 1935; *A Tale of Two Cities* (with Jack Conway), 1935; *They All Come Out*, 1939; *Nick Carter, Master Detective*, 1939; *Phantom Raiders*, 1940; *Doctors Don't Tell*, 1941; *Cat People*, 1942; *I Walked With a Zombie*, 1943; *The Leopard Man*, 1943; *Days of Glory*, 1944; *Experiment Perilous*, 1944; *Canyon Passage*, 1946; *Out of the Past*, 1947; *Berlin Express*, 1948; *Easy Living*, 1949; *Stars in My Crown*, 1950; *The Flame and the Arrow*, 1950; *Circle of Danger*, 1951; *Anne of the Indies*, 1951; *Way of a Gaucho*, 1952; *Appointment in Honduras*, 1953; *Stranger on Horseback*, 1955; *Wichita*,

1955; *Great Day in the Morning*, 1956; *Nightfall*, 1956; *Night of the Demon*, 1957; *The Fearmakers*, 1958; *Timbuktu*, 1959; *The Giant of Marathon*, 1959; *The Comedy of Terrors*, 1963; *War Gods of the Deep*, 1965.

The Fearmakers with Veda Ann Borg and Dana Andrews. *(Tourneur)*

FRANK TUTTLE Born August 6, 1882; died 1963; *The Studio Murder Mystery*, 1929; *The Greene Murder Case*, 1929; *Sweetie*, 1929; *Only the Brave*, 1930; *The Benson Murder Case*, 1930; *Paramount on Parade* (among various directors), 1930; *True to the Navy*, 1930; *Love Among the Millionaires*, 1930; *Her Wedding Night*, 1930; *No Limit*, 1931; *It Pays to Advertise*, 1931; *This Is the Night*, 1932; *Big Broadcast*, 1932; *Roman Scandals* (with Busby Berkeley), 1933; *Ladies Should Listen*, 1934; *Springtime for Henry*, 1934; *The Glass Key*, 1935; *College Holiday*, 1936; *Waikiki Wedding*, 1937; *Dr. Rhythm*, 1938; *I Stole a Million*, 1939; *This Gun for Hire*, 1942; *Lucky Jordan*, 1942; *Hostages*, 1943; *The Hour Before Dawn*, 1944; *The Great John L.*, 1945; *Don Juan Quilligan*, 1945; *Suspense*, 1946; *Swell Guy*, 1946; *The Magic Face*, 1951; *Hell on Frisco Bay*, 1955.

The Glass Key with George Raft and Guinn "Big Boy" Williams. *(Tuttle)*

CHARLES VIDOR Born July 27, 1900; died June 5, 1959; *The Bridge*, 1931; *The Mask of Fu Manchu*, 1932; (*not* Charles Brabin, as appears in many sources); *Sensation Hunters*, 1933; *Double Door*, 1934; *Strangers All*, 1935; *The Arizonian*, 1935; *His Family Tree*, 1935; *Muss 'Em Up*, 1936; *A Doctor's Diary*, 1937; *The Great Gambini*, 1937; *She's No Lady*, 1937; *Romance of the Redwoods*, 1939; *Those High Grey Walls*, 1939; *My Son, My Son*, 1940; *The Lady in Question*, 1940; *New York Town*, 1941; *Ladies in Retirement*, 1941; *The Tuttles of Tahiti*, 1942; *The Desperadoes*, 1943; *Cover Girl*, 1944; *Together Again*, 1944; *A Song to Remember*, 1945; *Over 21*, 1945; *Gilda*, 1946; *The Guilt of Janet Ames*, 1947; *The Loves of Carmen*, 1948; *The Man From Colorado* (replaced by

Henry Levin), 1948; *It's a Big Country* (among various directors), 1951; *Hans Christian Andersen*, 1952; *Thunder in the East*, 1953; *Rhapsody*, 1954; *Love Me or Leave Me*, 1955; *The Swan*, 1956; *The Joker Is Wild*, 1957; *A Farewell to Arms* (replaced John Huston), 1957; *Song Without End* (died during shooting; completed by George Cukor), 1960.

Rhapsody with Vittorio Gassman and Elizabeth Taylor. *(Charles Vidor)*

KING VIDOR Born February 8, 1896; *Show People*, 1928; *The Political Flapper*, or *The Patsy*, 1928; *Hallelujah!*, 1929; *Not So Dumb*, 1930; *Billy the Kid*, 1930; *Street Scene*, 1931; *The Champ*, 1931; *Bird of Paradise* (with Busby Berkeley), 1932; *Cynara*, 1932; *The Stranger's Return*, 1933; *Our Daily Bread*, 1934; *The Wedding Night*, 1935; *So Red the Rose*, 1935; *The Texas Rangers*, 1936; *Stella Dallas*, 1937; *The Citadel*, 1938; *Northwest Passage*, 1940; *Comrade X*, 1940; *H. M. Pulham, Esq.*, 1941; *An American Romance*, 1944; *Duel in the Sun* (with William Dieterle), 1946; *On Our Merry Way* (with Leslie Fenton), 1948; *The Fountainhead*, 1949; *Beyond the Forest*, 1949; *Lightning Strikes Twice*, 1951; *Japanese War Bride*, 1952; *Ruby Gentry*, 1952; *Man Without a Star*, 1955; *War and Peace*, 1956; *Solomon and Sheba*, 1959.

Comrade X with Clark Gable and Hedy Lamarr. *(King Vidor)*

RAOUL WALSH Born March 11, 1892; *In Old Arizona* (with Irving Cummings), 1929; *The Cock-Eyed World*, 1929; *Hot for Paris*, 1929; *The Big Trail*, 1930; *The Man Who Came Back*, 1931; *Women of All Nations*, 1931; *The Yellow Ticket*, 1931; *Wild Girl*, 1932; *Me and My Gal*, 1932; *Sailor's Luck*, 1933; *The Bowery*, 1933; *Going Hollywood*, 1933; *Under Pressure*, 1935; *Baby Face Harrington*, 1935; *Every Night at Eight*, 1935; *Klondike Annie*, 1936; *Big Brown Eyes*, 1936; *Spendthrift*, 1936; *You're in the Army, Now!*, 1937; *When Thief Meets Thief*, 1937; *Artists and Models*, 1937; *Hitting a New High*, 1937; *College*

Swing, 1938; *Saint Louis Blues*, 1939; *The Roaring Twenties* (replaced Anatole Litvak), 1939; *Dark Command*, 1940; *They Drive by Night*, 1940; *High Sierra*, 1941; *The Strawberry Blonde*, 1941; *Manpower*, 1941; *They Died With Their Boots On*, 1941; *Desperate Journey*, 1942; *Gentleman Jim*, 1942; *Background to Danger*, 1943; *Northern Pursuit*, 1943; *Uncertain Glory*, 1944; *San Antonio* (with David Butler), 1945; *Objective Burma*, 1945; *Salty O'Rourke*, 1945; *The Horn Blows at Midnight*, 1945; *The Man I Love*, 1946; *Stallion Road* (with James V. Kern), 1947; *Pursued*, 1947; *Cheyenne*, 1947; *Silver River*, 1948; *Fighter Squadron*, 1948; *One Sunday Afternoon*, 1948; *Colorado Territory*, 1949; *White Heat*, 1949; *Along the Great Divide*, 1951; *Captain Horatio Hornblower*, 1951; *Distant Drums*, 1951; *Glory Alley*, 1952; *The World in His Arms*, 1952; *The Lawless Breed*, 1952; *Blackbeard the Pirate*, 1952; *Sea Devils*, 1953; *A Lion Is in the Streets*, 1953; *Gun Fury*, 1953; *Saskatchewan*, 1954; *Battle Cry*, 1955; *The Tall Men*, 1955; *The Revolt of Mamie Stover*, 1956; *The King and Four Queens*, 1956; *Band of Angels*, 1957; *The Naked and the Dead*, 1958; *The Sheriff of Fractured Jaw*, 1958; *A Private's Affair*, 1959; *Come September* (producer only), 1960; *Esther and the King*, 1960; *Marines, Let's Go!*, 1961; *A Distant Trumpet*, 1964.

Northern Pursuit with Errol Flynn (center). *(Walsh)*

ORSON WELLES Born April 6, 1915; *Citizen Kane*, 1941; *The Magnificent Ambersons*, 1942; *It's All True* (unreleased), 1942; *Journey into Fear* (with Norman Foster), 1942; *The Stranger*, 1946; *The Lady From Shanghai*, 1948; *Macbeth*, 1948; *Othello*, 1952; *Confidential Report*, or *Mr. Arkadin*, 1955; *Touch of Evil*, 1958; *The Trial*, 1962; *Chimes at Midnight*, 1965.

Macbeth with Orson Welles and Jeanette Nolan. *(Welles)*

WILLIAM WELLMAN Born February 29, 1896; *Chinatown Nights*, 1929; *The Man I Love*, 1929; *Woman Trap*, 1929; *Dangerous Paradise*, 1930; *Young Eagles*, 1930; *Maybe It's Love*, 1930; *The Steel Highway*, or *Other Men's Women*, 1930; *Public Enemy*, 1931; *The Star Witness*, 1931; *Night Nurse*, 1931; *Safe in Hell*, 1931; *The Conquerors*, 1932;

The Hatchet Man, 1932; *Love Is a Racket*, 1932; *So Big*, 1932; *The Purchase Price*, 1932; *Frisco Jenny*, 1933; *Central Airport*, 1933; *Lilly Turner*, 1933; *Wild Boys of the Road*, 1933; *College Coach*, 1933; *Heroes for Sale*, 1933; *Lady of the Night*, or *Midnight Mary*, 1933; *Looking for Trouble*, 1934; *Stingaree*, 1934; *The President Vanishes*, 1934; *Call of the Wild*, 1935; *Robin Hood of El Dorado*, 1936; *Small Town Girl*, 1936; *A Star Is Born*, 1937; *Nothing Sacred*, 1937; *Men With Wings*, 1938; *Beau Geste*, 1939; *The Light That Failed*, 1939; *Reaching for the Sun*, 1941; *Roxie Hart*, 1942; *The Great Man's Lady*, 1942; *Thunder Birds*, 1942; *Lady of Burlesque*, 1943; *The Ox-Bow Incident*, 1943; *Buffalo Bill*, 1944; *Air Ship Squadron #4*, 1944 (Service film later exhibited to public); *This Man's Navy*, 1945; *The Story of G.I. Joe*, 1945; *Gallant Journey*, 1946; *Magic Town*, 1947; *The Iron Curtain*, 1948; *Yellow Sky*, 1948; *Battleground*, 1949; *The Next Voice You Hear*, 1950; *The Happy Years* (completed in 1948), 1950; *It's a Big Country* (among various directors), 1951; *Across the Wide Missouri*, 1951; *Westward the Women*, 1951; *My Man and I*, 1952; *Island in the Sky*, 1953; *The High and the Mighty*, 1954; *Track of the Cat*, 1954; *Blood Alley*, 1955; *Goodbye, My Lady*, 1956; *Darby's Rangers*, 1958; *Lafayette Escadrille*, 1958.

Roxie Hart with George Montgomery and Ginger Rogers. *(Wellman)*

BILLY WILDER Born June 22, 1906; *The Major and the Minor*, 1942; *Five Graves to Cairo*, 1943; *Double Indemnity*, 1944; *The Lost Week-End*, 1945; *The Emperor Waltz*, 1948; *A Foreign Affair*, 1948; *Sunset Boulevard*, 1950; *The Big Carnival*, or *Ace in the Hole*, 1951; *Stalag 17*, 1953; *Sabrina*, 1954; *The Seven Year Itch*, 1955; *The Spirit of St. Louis* (replaced John Sturges), 1957; *Love in the Afternoon*, 1957; *Witness for the Prosecution*, 1957; *Some Like It Hot*, 1959; *The Apartment*, 1960; *One, Two, Three!*, 1961; *Irma La Douce*, 1963; *Kiss Me, Stupid*, 1964; *The Fortune Cookie*, 1966.

The Fortune Cookie with Jack Lemmon. *(Wilder)*

ROBERT WISE Born September 10, 1914; *The Curse of the Cat People* (with Gunther von Fritsch), 1944; *Mademoiselle Fifi*, 1944; *The Body Snatchers*, 1945; *The Game of Death*, 1945; *Criminal Court*, 1946; *Born to Kill*, 1947; *Mystery in Mexico*, 1948; *Blood on the Moon*, 1948; *The Set-Up*, 1949; *Three Secrets*, 1950; *Two Flags West*, 1950; *The House on Telegraph Hill*, 1951; *The Day the Earth Stood Still*, 1951; *Captive City*, 1952; *Something for the Birds*, 1952; *Destination Gobi*, 1953; *The Desert Rats*, 1953; *So Big*, 1953; *Executive Suite*, 1954; *Helen of Troy*, 1955; *Tribute to a Bad Man*, 1956; *Somebody Up There Likes Me*, 1956; *This Could Be the Night*, 1957; *Until They Sail*, 1957; *Bannon* (uncompleted), 1957; *Run Silent, Run Deep*, 1958; *I Want to Live!*, 1958; *Odds Against Tomorrow*, 1959; *West Side Story* (with Jerome Robbins), 1961; *Two for the Seesaw*, 1962; *The Haunting* 1963; *The Sound of Music*, 1965; *The Sand Pebbles*, 1966; *Star*, 1968.

The Day the Earth Stood Still with Lock Martin, Michael Rennie and Patricia Neal. *(Wise)*

WILLIAM WYLER Born July 1, 1902; *The Shakedown*, 1929; *The Love Trap*, 1929; *Come Across*, 1929; *Evidence*, 1929; *Hell's Heroes*, 1929; *The Storm*, 1930; *A House Divided*, 1932; *Tom Brown of Culver*, 1932; *Her First Mate*, 1933; *Counsellor at Law*, 1933; *Glamour*, 1934; *The Good Fairy*, 1935; *The Gay Deception*, 1935; *Come and Get It* (with Howard Hawks), 1936; *Dodsworth*, 1936; *These Three*, 1936; *Dead End*, 1937; *Jezebel*, 1938; *Wuthering Heights*, 1939; *The Westerner*, 1940; *The Letter*, 1940; *The Little Foxes*, 1941; *Mrs. Miniver*, 1942; *The Memphis Belle*, 1943 (this and the three films following were Service feature films later exhibited to the public); *The Fighting Lady*, 1944; *Glory for Me*, 1945; *Thunderbolt* (with John Sturges), 1945; *The Best Years of Our Lives*, 1946; *The Heiress*, 1949; *Detective Story*, 1951; *Carrie*, 1952; *Roman Holiday*, 1953; *The Desperate Hours*, 1955; *Friendly Persuasion*, 1956; *Thieves' Market* (uncompleted), 1957; *The Big Country*, 1958; *Ben-Hur*, 1959; *The Children's Hour*, 1962; *The Collector*, 1965; *How to Steal a Million*, 1966; *Funny Girl*, 1968.

Come and Get It with Walter Brennan, Edward Arnold and Frances Farmer. *(Wyler)*

FRED ZINNEMANN Born April 29, 1907; *Redes* (with Emilio Gomez Muriel), 1934; *Kid Glove Killer*, 1942; *Eyes in the Night*, 1942; *The Seventh Cross*, 1944; *Little Mr. Jim*, 1946; *My Brother Talks to Horses*, 1946; *The Search*, 1948; *Act of Violence*, 1948; *The Men*, 1950; *Teresa*, 1951; *High Noon*, 1952; *Member of the Wedding*, 1952; *From Here to Eternity*, 1953; *Oklahoma!*, 1955; *A Hatful of Rain*, 1957; *The Old Man and the Sea* (replaced by Henry King, then John Sturges), 1958; *The Nun's Story*, 1959; *The Sundowners*, 1960; *Behold a Pale Horse*, 1963; *Hawaii* (replaced by George Roy Hill), 1966; *A Man for All Seasons*, 1966.

Teresa with Pier Angeli. *(Zinnemann)*

CHAPTER V

THE PRODUCERS

No Sad Songs for Me with Wendell Corey and Margaret Sullavan.

(Adler)

BUDDY ADLER Born June 22, 1906; died July 12, 1960; *The Dark Past*, 1949; *A Woman of Distinction*, 1950; *No Sad Songs for Me*, 1950; *Saturday's Hero*, 1951; *Last of the Comanches*, 1952; *Salome*, 1953; *From Here to Eternity*, 1953; *On the Waterfront*, 1954; *Violent Saturday*, 1955; *Soldier of Fortune*, 1955; *Love Is a Many-Splendored Thing*, 1955; *The Left Hand of God*, 1955; *House of Bamboo*, 1955; *The Lieutenant Wore Skirts*, 1956; *The Bottom of the Barrel*, 1956; *The Revolt of Mamie Stover*, 1956; *Bus Stop*, 1956; *Anastasia*, 1956; *Heaven Knows, Mr. Allison*, 1957; *A Hatful of Rain*, 1957; *South Pacific*, 1958; *The Inn of the Sixth Happiness*, 1958; *The Story of Ruth* (died after preparing production), 1960; *Cleopatra* (died after preparing production), 1963.

SAMUEL Z. ARKOFF Born June 12, 1918; *Voodoo Woman*, 1957; *Rock All Night*, 1957; *Dragstrip Girl*, 1957; *Invasion of the Saucer Men*, 1957; *Reform School Girl*, 1957; *Sorority Girl*, 1957; *Motorcycle Gang*, 1957; *How to Make a Monster*, 1958; *Suicide Battalion*, 1958; *Attack of the Puppet People*, 1958; *The Bonnie Parker Story*, 1958; *War of the Colossal Beast*, 1958; *Terror From the Year 5000*, 1958; *High School Hellcats*, 1958; *Paratroop Command*, 1959; *House of Usher*, 1960; *The Pit and the Pendulum*, 1961; *The Master of the World*, 1961; *Tales of Terror*, 1962; *Panic in Year Zero*, 1962; *The Premature Burial*, 1962; *The Comedy of Terrors*, 1963; *Beach Party*, 1964; *War Gods of the Deep*, 1965; *How to Stuff a Wild Bikini*, 1965; *Beach Blanket Bingo*, 1965; *Ski Party*, 1965; *Sergeant Deadhead, the Astronut*, 1965; *Die, Monster, Die!*, 1965; *Dr. Goldfoot and the Bikini Machine*, 1965; *The Big T-N-T Show*, 1966; *The Ghost in the Invisible Bikini*, 1966; *Fireball 500*, 1966; *Thunder Alley*, 1967; *Wild in the Streets*, 1967.

ROBERT ARTHUR Born November 1, 1909; *Buck Privates Come Home*, 1947; *The Wistful Widow of Wagon Gap*, 1947; *Are You With It?*, 1948; *Abbott and Costello Meet Frankenstein*, 1948; *Mexican Hayride*, 1948; *For the Love of Mary*, 1948; *Bagdad*, 1949; *The Big*

The Premature Burial with Richard Ney (center) and Ray Milland.

(Arkoff)

566

A Man Could Get Killed with James Garner, Anthony Franciosa and Roland Culver. *(Arthur)*

Heat (under Jerry Wald), 1953; *The Black Shield of Falworth*, 1954; *The Long Gray Line* (under Jerry Wald), 1955; *Pillars of the Sky*, 1955; *Kelly and Me*, 1957; *The Midnight Story*, 1957; *Man of a Thousand Faces*, 1957; *A Time to Love and a Time to Die*, 1958; *Flood Tide*, 1958; *The Perfect Furlough*, 1958; *Operation Petticoat*, 1959; *The Great Impostor*, 1961; *Come September*, 1961; *Lover Come Back*, 1962; *That Touch of Mink*, 1962; *The Spiral Road*, 1962; *For Love or Money*, 1963; *Captain Newman, M.D.*, 1963; *Father Goose*, 1964; *Bedtime Story*, 1964; *The Brass Bottle*, 1964; *Shenandoah*, 1965; *A Very Special Favor*, 1965; *A Man Could Get Killed*, 1966.

ROBERT BASSLER Born September 26, 1903; *My Gal Sal*, 1942; *The Black Swan*, 1942; *The Lodger*, 1944; *Hangover Square*, 1945; *Thunderhead, Son of Flicka*, 1945; *Smoky*, 1946; *The Homestretch*, 1947; *Thunder in the Valley*, 1947; *The Green Grass of Wyoming*, 1948; *The Snake Pit*, 1948; *Rope of Sand*, 1949; *Thieves' Highway*, 1949; *A Ticket to Tomahawk*, 1950; *The Halls of Montezuma*, 1950; *The House on Telegraph Hill*, 1951; *Kangaroo*, 1952; *Night Without Sleep*, 1952; *My Wife's Best Friend*, 1952; *Beneath the 12-Mile Reef*, 1953; *The Girl Next Door*, 1953; *Suddenly!*, 1954; *Gentlemen Marry Brunettes*, 1955; *Gunsight Ridge*, 1957; *Stranger at Soldier Springs* (uncompleted), 1957.

A Ticket to Tomahawk with Anne Baxter, Will Wright and Dan Dailey. *(Bassler)*

PANDRO S. BERMAN Born March 28, 1905; *Way Back Home*, 1932; *Ann Vickers*, 1933; *What Price Hollywood*, 1932; *The Gay Divorcee*, 1934; *Of Human Bondage*, 1934; *Roberta*, 1935; *Alice Adams*, 1935; *Top Hat*, 1935; *Mary of Scotland*, 1936; *Sylvia Scarlett*, 1936; *Winterset*, 1936; *Stage Door*, 1937; *A Damsel in Distress*, 1937; *Room Service*, 1938; *Vivacious Lady*, 1938; *The Flying Irishman*, 1939; *Gunga Din*, 1939; *Love Affair*, 1939; *The Hunchback of Notre Dame*, 1939; *The Story of Vernon and Irene Castle*, 1939; *Ziegfeld Girl*, 1941; *Honky Tonk*, 1941; *Dragon Seed*, 1944; *The Seventh Cross*, 1944; *National Velvet*, 1944; *The Picture of Dorian Gray*, 1945; *Undercurrent*, 1946; *Sea of Grass*, 1947; *Living in a Big Way*, 1947; *If Winter Comes*, 1947;

The Bribe, 1949; *The Three Musketeers*, 1948; *The Doctor and the Girl*, 1949; *Madame Bovary*, 1949; *Father of the Bride*, 1950; *Soldiers Three*, 1951; *Father's Little Dividend*, 1951; *The Light Touch*, 1951; *The Prisoner of Zenda*, 1952; *Lovely to Look At*, 1952; *Ivanhoe*, 1952; *The Knights of the Round Table*, 1953; *Battle Circus*, 1953; *All the Brothers Were Valiant*, 1953; *The Long, Long Trailer*, 1954; *The Blackboard Jungle*, 1955; *Quentin Durward*, 1955; *Bhowani Junction*, 1956; *Tea and Sympathy*, 1957; *Something of Value*, 1957; *Jailhouse Rock*, 1958; *The Brothers Karamazov*, 1958; *The Reluctant Debutante*, 1958; *All the Fine Young Cannibals*, 1960; *Butterfield 8*, 1960; *Sweet Bird of Youth*, 1962; *The Prize*, 1963; *Honeymoon Hotel*, 1964; *A Patch of Blue*, 1965.

If Winter Comes with Deborah Kerr and Walter Pidgeon. *(Berman)*

SAMUEL BISCHOFF Born August 11, 1890; *The Last Mile* (producer and director), 1932; *The Rich Are Always With Us*, 1932; *The Dark Horse*, 1932; *Three on a Match*, 1932; *The Big Shakedown*, 1934; *Front Page Woman*, 1935; *The Golden Arrow*, 1936; *The Charge of the Light Brigade*, 1936; *Kid Galahad*, 1937; *San Quentin*, 1937; *Swing Your Lady*, 1938; *Racket Busters*, 1938; *Angels With Dirty Faces*, 1938; *A Slight Case of Murder*, 1938; *The Oklahoma Kid*, 1939; *You Can't Get Away with Murder*, 1939; *The Roaring Twenties* (with Hal B. Wallis), 1939; *The Kid From Kokomo* (with Hal B. Wallis), 1939; *Castle on the Hudson*, 1940; *You'll Never Get Rich*, 1941; *Texas*, 1941; *A Night to Remember*, 1943; *None Shall Escape*, 1944; *A Thousand and One Nights*, 1945; *Best of the Bad Men*, 1948; *Pitfall*, 1948; *Mrs. Mike*. 1949; *Sealed Cargo*, 1951; *The Las Vegas Story*, 1952; *Macao*, 1952; *The Half-Breed*, 1952; *The System*, 1953; *South Sea Woman*, 1953; *The Bounty Hunter*, 1954; *A Bullet for Joey*, 1955; *The Phoenix City Story*, 1955; *Screaming Eagles*, 1956; *Operation Eichmann*, 1961; *King of the Roaring Twenties*, 1961; *The Strangler*, 1963.

Mrs. Mike with Evelyn Keyes, Dick Powell and J. M. Kerrigan. *(Bischoff)*

HENRY BLANKE Born December 30, 1901; *Female*, 1933; *Convention City*, 1933; *Bureau of Missing Persons*, 1933; *Fashions of 1934*, 1934; *The Story of Louis Pasteur*, 1935; *A Midsummer Night's Dream*, 1935; *Satan Met a Lady*, 1936; *The Petrified Forest*, 1936; *Green Pastures*, 1936; *The Life of Emile Zola*, 1937; *Jezebel* (under Hal B. Wallis), 1938; *Adventures of Robin Hood*, 1938; *Juarez* (under Hal B. Wallis), 1939; *The Old Maid* (under Hal B. Wallis), 1939; *The Sea Hawk*, 1940; *The Maltese Falcon* (under Hal B. Wallis), 1941; *The Great Lie* (under Hal B. Wallis), 1941; *Blues in the Night*, 1941; *Old Acquaintance*, 1943; *Edge of Darkness*, 1943; *The Mask of Dimitrios*, 1944; *Deception*, 1946; *Winter Meeting*, 1948; *June Bride*, 1948; *The Treasure of Sierra Madre*, 1948; *The Fountainhead*, 1949; *Beyond the Forest*, 1949; *Lightning Strikes Twice*, 1951; *Come Fill the Cup*, 1951; *The Iron Mistress*, 1952; *So Big*, 1953; *King Richard and the Crusaders*, 1954; *The McConnell Story*, 1955; *Sincerely Yours*, 1955; *Serenade*, 1956; *Too Much, Too Soon*, 1958; *Westbound*, 1959; *The Nun's Story*, 1959; *The Miracle*, 1959; *Cash McCall*, 1959; *Ice Palace*, 1960; *The Sins of Rachel Cade*, 1961; *Hell Is for Heroes*, 1962.

Cash McCall with James Garner and Natalie Wood. *(Blanke)*

JULIAN C. BLAUSTEIN Born May 30, 1913; *Broken Arrow*, 1950; *Mister 880*, 1950; *Half Angel*, 1950; *The Day the Earth Stood Still*, 1951; *Take Care of My Little Girl*, 1951; *Don't Bother to Knock*, 1952; *The Outcasts of Poker Flat*, 1952; *Desiree*, 1954; *The Racers*, 1955; *Storm Center*, 1956; *Guard of Honor* (uncompleted), 1957; *Bell, Book and Candle*, 1958; *The Wreck of the Mary Deare*, 1959; *Two Loves*, 1961; *The Four Horsemen of the Apocalypse*, 1962; *Khartoum*, 1966.

Mister 880 with Edmund Gwenn, Dorothy McGuire and Burt Lancaster. *(Blaustein)*

BENEDICT E. BOGEAUS Born c. 1910; *Shanghai Gesture*, 1941; *The Bridge of San Luis Rey*, 1944; *Dark Waters*, 1944; *Captain Kidd*, 1945; *Diary of a Chambermaid*, 1946; *Mr. Ace*, 1946; *The Macomber Affair*, 1947; *Christmas Eve*, 1947; *On Our Merry Way, or A Miracle*

Can Happen, 1948; *Lulu Belle*, 1948; *Girl From Manhattan*, 1948; *Johnny One Eye*, 1950; *My Outlaw Brother*, 1951; *One Big Affair*, 1952; *Count the Hours*, 1953; *Appointment in Honduras*, 1953; *Silver Lode*, 1954; *Passion*, 1954; *Cattle Queen of Montana*, 1954; *Escape to Burma*, 1955; *Pearl of the South Pacific*, 1955; *Tennessee's Partner*, 1955; *Slightly Scarlet*, 1956; *The River's Edge*, 1957; *Enchanted Island*, 1958; *From the Earth to the Moon*, 1958; *Jet Over the Atlantic*, 1959; *The Most Dangerous Man Alive*, 1958–1961.

Escape to Burma with Robert Ryan and Barbara Stanwyck. *(Bogeaus)*

CHARLES BRACKETT Born November 26, 1892; *Five Graves to Cairo*, 1943; *The Uninvited*, 1944; *The Lost Weekend*, 1945; *To Each His Own*, 1946; *The Emperor Waltz*, 1948; *A Foreign Affair*, 1948; *Miss Tatlock's Millions*, 1948; *Sunset Boulevard*, 1950; *The Mating Season*, 1951; *The Model and the Marriage Broker*, 1951; *Niagara*, 1953; *Titanic*, 1953; *Garden of Evil*, 1954; *Woman's World*, 1954; *The Girl in the Red Velvet Swing*, 1955; *The Virgin Queen*, 1955; *The King and I*, 1956; *D-Day, Sixth of June*, 1956; *Teenage Rebel*, 1956; *The Wayward Bus*, 1957; *The Gift of Love*, 1958; *Ten North Frederick*, 1958; *The Remarkable Mr. Pennypacker*, 1958; *Blue Denim*, 1959; *Journey to the Center of the Earth*, 1959; *High Time*, 1960; *State Fair*, 1962.

The Girl in the Red Velvet Swing with Ray Milland and Joan Collins. *(Brackett)*

SAMUEL BRONSTON *The Adventures of Martin Eden*, 1942; *Jack London*, 1943; *A Walk in the Sun*, 1945; *John Paul Jones*, 1959; *King of Kings*, 1961; *El Cid*, 1961; *55 Days at Peking*, 1963; *Circus World*, 1964; *The Fall of the Roman Empire*, 1964.

HARRY JOE BROWN Born September 22, 1893; *Madison Square Garden*, 1932; *Dangerous*, 1935; *Captain Blood*, 1935; *The Florentine Dagger*, 1935; *I Found Stella Parish*, 1935; *Ceiling Zero*, 1935; *Hearts Divided*, 1936; *The Great O'Malley*, 1937; *Alexander's Ragtime*

Jack London with Michael O'Shea. *(Bronston)*

Band (under Darryl F. Zanuck), 1938; *The Gorilla* (under Darryl F. Zanuck), 1939; *The Rains Came*, 1939; *Johnny Apollo*, 1940; *Down Argentine Way*, 1940; *Four Sons* (with Darryl F. Zanuck), 1940; *Young People*, 1940; *Moon Over Miami*, 1941; *Western Union*, 1941; *The Desperados*, 1943; *Sahara*, 1943; *Coroner Creek*, 1948; *The Untamed Breed*, 1948; *The Doolins of Oklahoma*, 1949; *Fortunes of Captain Blood*, 1950; *The Nevadan*, 1950; *Stage to Tucson*, 1950; *The Lady and the Bandit*, 1951; *Santa Fe*, 1951; *Man in the Saddle*, 1951; *Hangman's Knot*, 1952; *The Stranger Wore a Gun*, 1953; *Three Hours to Kill*, 1954; *Ten Wanted Men*, 1955; *A Lawless Street*, 1955; *Seventh Cavalry*, 1956; *The Guns of Fort Petticoat*, 1957; *The Tall T*, 1957; *Decision at Sundown*, 1957; *Screaming Mimi*, 1958; *Buchanan Rides Alone*, 1958; *Ride Lonesome*, 1959; *Comanche Station*, 1960; *The Son of Captain Blood*, 1963; *Duel at the Rio Grande*, 1964.

The Nevadan with Kate Drain Lawson (center) and Randolph Scott. *(Brown)*

MERIAN C. COOPER Born October 24, 1893; *The Four Feathers*, 1929; *The Phantom of Crestwood*, 1932; *King Kong*, 1933; *Lucky Devils*, 1933; *Morning Glory*, 1933; *Melody Cruise*, 1933; *Professional Sweetheart*, 1933; *Ann Vickers*, 1933; *Ace of Aces*, 1933; *Little Women*, 1933; *Flying Down to Rio*, 1933; *The Lost Patrol*, 1934; *She*, 1935; *The Last Days of Pompeii*, 1935; *The Toy Wife*, 1938; *The Jungle Book* (pre-production), 1942; *Eagle Squadron* (pre-production), 1942; *The Fugitive*, 1947; *Fort Apache*, 1948; *She Wore a Yellow Ribbon*, 1949; *Three Godfathers*, 1949; *Mighty Joe Young*, 1949; *Rio Grande*, 1950; *Wagonmaster*, 1950; *The Quiet Man*, 1952; *The Sun Shines Bright*, 1953; *This Is Cinerama*, 1952; *The Searchers*, 1956; *The Best of Cinerama*, 1963.

She with Nigel Bruce, Helen Mack and Randolph Scott. *(Cooper)*

JACK CUMMINGS *The Winning Ticket*, 1935; *Born to Dance*, 1936; *Broadway Melody of 1938*, 1937; *Honolulu*, 1939; *Broadway Melody of 1940*, 1940; *Go West*, 1940; *Ship Ahoy*, 1942; *I Dood It*, 1943; *Bathing Beauty*, 1944; *Romance of Rosy Ridge*, 1947; *Fiesta*, 1947; *Neptune's Daughter*, 1949; *The Stratton Story*, 1949; *Two Weeks With Love*, 1950; *Three Little Words*, 1950; *Excuse My Dust*, 1951; *Texas Carnival*, 1951; *Lovely to Look At*, 1952; *Sombrero*, 1953; *Give a Girl a Break*, 1953; *Kiss Me, Kate!*, 1953; *Seven Brides for Seven Brothers*, 1954; *The Last Time I Saw Paris*, 1954; *Many Rivers to Cross*, 1955; *Interrupted Melody*, 1955; *The Teahouse of the August Moon*, 1956; *The Blue Angel*, 1959; *Can Can*, 1960; *The Second Time Around*, 1961; *Bachelor Flat*, 1962; *Viva Las Vegas*, 1964.

Give a Girl a Break with Debbie Reynolds, Bob Fosse and Lurene Tuttle. *(Cummings)*

SAMUEL G. ENGEL Born December 29, 1904; *My Darling Clementine*, 1946; *Sitting Pretty*, 1948; *Deep Waters*, 1948; *The Street With No Name*, 1948; *Come to the Stable*, 1949; *Mr. Belvedere Goes to College*, 1949; *The Jackpot*, 1950; *Rawhide*, 1951; *Follow the Sun*, 1951; *Red Skies of Montana*, 1951; *The Frogmen*, 1952; *Belles on Their Toes*, 1953; *A Man Called Peter*, 1955; *Daddy Long Legs*, 1955; *Good Morning, Miss Dove*, 1956; *Bernadine*, 1957; *Boy on a Dolphin*, 1957; *The Story of Ruth*, 1960; *The Lion*, 1962.

Good Morning, Miss Dove with Robert Stack, Jennifer Jones and Biff Elliot. *(Engel)*

Private Lives with Reginald Denny and Norma Shearer. *(Franklin)*

SIDNEY FRANKLIN Born March 21, 1893.

Primarily a Director: *The Last of Mrs. Cheney*, 1929; *Devil May Care*, 1929; *The Lady of Scandal*, 1930; *A Lady's Morals*, or *Jenny Lind*, 1930; *The Guardsman*, 1931; *Smilin' Through*, 1932; *Reunion in Vienna*, 1933; *The Barretts of Wimpole Street*, 1934; *Private Lives*, 1934; *The Dark Angel*, 1935; *The Good Earth*, 1937; *Goodbye, Mr. Chips*, 1939.

Primarily a Producer: *On Borrowed Time*, 1939; *Waterloo Bridge*, 1939; *Mrs. Miniver*, 1942; *Random Harvest*, 1942; *Madame Curie*, 1943; *The White Cliffs of Dover*, 1944; *The Yearling*, 1946; *Homecoming*, 1948; *Command Decision*, 1948; *The Miniver Story*, 1950; *Young Bess*, 1953; *The Story of Three Loves*, 1953; *The Barretts of Wimpole Street* (producer and director), 1957.

ARTHUR FREED Born September 9, 1894; *The Wizard of Oz* (with Mervyn LeRoy), 1939; *Babes in Arms*, 1939; *Strike Up the Band*, 1940; *Little Nellie Kelly*, 1940; *Lady Be Good*, 1941; *Babes on Broadway*, 1941; *Panama Hattie*, 1942; *For Me and My Gal*, 1942; *Cabin in the Sky*, 1943; *Du Barry Was a Lady*, 1943; *Girl Crazy*, 1943; *Best Foot Forward*, 1943; *Meet Me in St. Louis*, 1944; *The Clock*, 1945; *Yolanda and the Thief*, 1945; *The Harvey Girls*, 1946; *Ziegfeld Follies*, 1946; *Till the Clouds Roll By*, 1946; *Good News*, 1947; *Summer Holiday*, 1948; *The Pirate*, 1948; *Easter Parade*, 1948; *Words and Music*, 1948; *Take Me Out to the Ball Game*, 1949; *The Barkleys of Broadway*, 1949; *Any Number Can Play*, 1949; *On the Town*, 1949; *Annie Get Your Gun*, 1950; *Crisis*, 1950; *Pagan Love Song*, 1950; *Royal Wedding*, 1951; *Show Boat*, 1951; *An American in Paris*, 1951; *Belle of New York*, 1952; *Singin' in the Rain*, 1952; *The Band Wagon*, 1953; *Brigadoon*, 1954; *It's Always Fair Weather*, 1955; *Kismet*, 1955; *Invitation to the Dance*, 1956; *Silk Stockings*, 1957; *Gigi*, 1958; *Bells Are Ringing*, 1960; *The Subterraneans*, 1960; *Light in the Piazza*, 1962.

Pagan Love Song with Charles Mauu, Rita Moreno, Howard Keel and Esther Williams. *(Freed)*

WILLIAM GOETZ Born March 24, 1903; *The Bowery*, 1933; *The Man From Laramie*, 1955; *Autumn Leaves*, 1956; *Sayonara*, 1957; *Me and the Colonel*, 1958; *They Came to Cordura*, 1959; *The Mountain Road*, 1960; *Song Without End*, 1960; *Cry for Happy*, 1961; *Assault on a Queen*, 1966.

Autumn Leaves with Cliff Robertson and Joan Crawford. *(Goetz)*

SAMUEL B. GOLDWYN Born August 27, 1884; *Bulldog Drummond*, 1929; *Condemned*, 1929; *Raffles*, 1930; *Whoopee*, 1930; *One Heavenly Night*, 1930; *The Devil to Pay*, 1930; *Street Scene*, 1931; *The Unholy Garden*, 1931; *Palmy Days*, 1931; *Tonight or Never*, 1931; *Arrowsmith*, 1931; *The Greeks Had a Word for Them*, 1932; *Cynara*, 1932; *The Kid From Spain*, 1932; *The Masquerader*, 1933; *Roman Scandals*, 1933; *Nana*, 1934; *We Live Again*, 1934; *Kid Millions*, 1934; *The Wedding Night*, 1935; *The Dark Angel*, 1935; *Barbary Coast*, 1935; *Splendor*, 1935; *Strike Me Pink*, 1936; *These Three*, 1936; *Dodsworth*, 1936; *Come and Get It*, 1936; *Beloved Enemy*, 1936; *Woman Chases Man*, 1937; *Hurricane*, 1937; *Stella Dallas*, 1937; *Dead End*, 1937; *The Adventures of Marco Polo*, 1938; *The Goldwyn Follies*, 1938; *The Cowboy and the Lady*, 1938; *The Real Glory*, 1939; *Wuthering Heights*, 1939; *They Shall Have Music*, 1939; *Raffles*, 1940; *The Westerner*, 1940; *The Little Foxes*, 1941; *Ball of Fire*, 1941; *The Pride of the Yankees*, 1942; *They Got Me Covered*, 1943; *The North Star*, or *Armored Attack*, 1943; *Up in Arms*, 1944; *The Princess and the Pirate*, 1944; *Wonder Man*, 1945; *The Kid From Brooklyn*, 1946; *The Best Years of Our Lives*, 1946; *The Secret Life of Walter Mitty*, 1947; *The Bishop's Wife*, 1947; *A Song is Born*, 1948; *Enchantment*, 1948; *Roseanna McCoy*, 1949; *My Foolish Heart*, 1949; *Our Very Own*, 1950; *Edge of Doom*, 1950; *I Want You*, 1951; *Hans Christian Andersen*, 1952; *Guys and Dolls*, 1955; *Porgy and Bess*, 1959.

JAMES EDMUND GRAINGER Born October 1, 1906; *A Holy Terror*, 1931; *Diamond Jim*, 1935; *Love Before Breakfast*, 1936; *Magnificent Brute*, 1936; *Sutter's Gold*, 1936; *The Road Back*, 1937; *The Road to*

Cynara with Kay Francis and Ronald Colman. *(Goldwyn)*

Reno, 1938; *The Crime of Dr. Hallet*, 1938; *The Jury's Secret*, 1938; *The Lady With Red Hair*, 1940; *Riders of the Purple Sage*, 1941; *International Squadron*, 1941; *Flying Tigers*, 1942; *The Fabulous Texan*, 1947; *Wake of the Red Witch*, 1948; *Sands of Iwo Jima*, 1949; *Flying Leathernecks*, 1951; *The Racket*, 1951; *One Minute to Zero*, 1952; *Blackbeard the Pirate*, 1952; *Split Second*, 1953; *Second Chance*, 1953; *Devil's Canyon*, 1953; *The French Line*, 1954; *The Treasure of Pancho Villa*, 1955; *Great Day in the Morning*, 1956; *Bundle of Joy*, 1956; *Ten Days in August* (uncompleted), 1957; *The Sheepman*, 1958; *Torpedo Run*, 1958; *Green Mansions*, 1959; *Never So Few*, 1959; *Home From the Hill*, 1960; *Cimarron*, 1960.

The French Line with Mary McCarty and Jane Russell. *(Grainger)*

HAROLD HECHT Born June 1, 1907; *The Flame and the Arrow*, 1950; *Ten Tall Men*, 1951; *The First Time*, 1952; *The Crimson Pirate*, 1952; *His Majesty O'Keefe*, 1953; *Apache*, 1954; *Vera Cruz*, 1954; *Marty*, 1955; *The Kentuckian*, 1955; *Trapeze*, 1956; *The Bachelor Party*, 1957; *Sweet Smell of Success*, 1957; *Tell It on the Drums* (uncompleted), 1957; *Run Silent, Run Deep*, 1958; *Separate Tables*, 1958; *The Devil's Disciple*, 1959; *The Unforgiven*, 1960; *The Young Savages*, 1961; *Taras Bulba*, 1962; *Bird Man of Alcatraz*, 1962; *Wild and Wonderful*, 1964; *Flight From Ashiya*, 1964; *Cat Ballou*, 1965; *The Way West*, 1967.

Marty with Ernest Borgnine and Esther Miniciotti. *(Hecht)*

MARK HELLINGER Born March 21, 1903; died December 21, 1947; *It All Came True* (under Hal B. Wallis), 1940; *Torrid Zone*, 1940; *Brother Orchid* (under Hal B. Wallis), 1940; *They Drive by Night* (under Hal B. Wallis), 1940; *High Sierra* (under Hal B. Wallis), 1941; *The Strawberry Blonde*, 1941; *Manpower* (with Hal B. Wallis), 1941; *Rise and Shine*, 1941; *Moontide*, 1942; *Thank Your Lucky Stars*, 1943; *The Horn Blows at Midnight*, 1945; *The Killers*, 1946; *The Two Mrs. Carrolls*, 1947; *Brute Force*, 1947; *The Naked City*, 1948.

Moontide with Jean Gabin and Ida Lupino. *(Hellinger)*

ARTHUR HORNBLOW, JR. Born March 15, 1893; *The Pursuit of Happiness*, 1934; *Mississippi*, 1935; *Ruggles of Red Gap*, 1935; *Wings in the Dark*, 1935; *The Princess Comes Across*, 1936; *Easy Living*, 1937; *Swing High, Swing Low*, 1937; *High, Wide and Handsome*, 1937; *Waikiki Wedding*, 1937; *Man About Town*, 1939; *Midnight*, 1939; *The Cat and the Canary*, 1939; *Arise, My Love*, 1940; *Nothing But the Truth*, 1941; *Hold Back the Dawn*, 1941; *I Wanted Wings*, 1941; *The Major and the Minor*, 1942; *The Heavenly Body*, 1943; *Gaslight*, 1944; *Weekend at the Waldorf*, 1945; *Desire Me*, 1947; *The Hucksters*, 1947; *Cass Timberlane*, 1947; *The Asphalt Jungle*, 1950; *Million Dollar Mermaid*, 1952; *Remains to Be Seen*, 1953; *Oklahoma!*, 1955; *Witness for the Prosecution*, 1957; *The War Lover*, 1962.

The Heavenly Body with William Powell, Hedy Lamarr and Connie Gilchrist. *(Hornblow)*

HOWARD HUGHES Born December 24, 1905; *Hell's Angels*, 1930; *The Front Page*, 1931; *Scarface*, 1932; *Sky Devils*, 1932; *The Outlaw* (Hughes personally replaced Howard Hawks as director around 1940), 1943—released 1946; *Vendetta* (directors Howard Hughes and Stuart Heisler replaced Max Ophüls), 1950; *Two Tickets to Broadway*, 1951; *The Racket*, 1951; *His Kind of Woman*, 1951; *Jet Pilot*, 1952, released 1957; *Double Dynamite*, 1952; *The Las Vegas Story*, 1952; *Montana Belle*, 1948, released 1952; *The French Line*, 1953; *Macao*, 1953; *Underwater*, 1955; *Son of Sinbad*, 1955.

ROSS HUNTER *A Guy, a Girl and a Gob*, 1945; *Take Me to Town*, 1953; *All I Desire*, 1953; *Tumbleweed*, 1953; *Taza, Son of Cochise*, 1954; *Magnificent Obsession*, 1954; *Naked Alibi*, 1954; *The Yellow Mountain*, 1954; *Captain Lightfoot*, 1955; *One Desire*, 1955; *All That Heaven Allows*, 1955; *The Spoilers*, 1955; *There's Always*

Macao with Robert Mitchum and Jane Russell. *(Hughes)*

Tomorrow, 1956; *Battle Hymn*, 1956; *Tammy and the Bachelor*, 1957; *Interlude*, 1957; *My Man Godfrey*, 1957; *This Happy Feeling*, 1958; *The Restless Years*, 1958; *Stranger in My Arms*, 1959; *Imitation of Life*, 1959; *Pillow Talk*, 1959; *Portrait in Black*, 1960; *Midnight Lace*, 1960; *Tammy, Tell Me True*, 1961; *Flower Drum Song*, 1961; *Back Street*, 1961; *If a Man Answers*, 1962; *The Thrill of It All*, 1963; *Tammy and the Doctor*, 1963; *The Chalk Garden*, 1964; *I'd Rather Be Rich*, 1964; *The Art of Love*, 1965; *Madame X*, 1966; *The Pad (and How to Use It)*, 1966; *Thoroughly Modern Millie*, 1967.

Stranger in My Arms with June Allyson, Charles Coburn and Mary Astor. *(Hunter)*

NUNNALLY JOHNSON Born December 5, 1897; *The Prisoner of Shark Island* (with Darryl F. Zanuck), 1936; *The Road to Glory* (with Darryl F. Zanuck), 1936; *The Grapes of Wrath* (with Darryl F. Zanuck), 1940; *The Pied Piper*, 1942; *Roxie Hart*, 1942; *The Moon Is Down*, 1943; *Holy Matrimony*, 1943; *The Woman in the Window*, 1944; *Casanova Brown*, 1944; *The Senator Was Indiscreet*, 1947; *Three Came Home*, 1950; *The Gunfighter*, 1950; *The Desert Fox*, 1951; *Phone Call From a Stranger*, 1952; *We're Not Married*, 1952; *My Cousin Rachel*, 1952; *How to Marry a Millionaire*, 1953; *The Black*

Oh Men! Oh Women! with Dan Dailey and Ginger Rogers. *(Johnson)*

Widow (producer and director), 1954; *How to Be Very, Very Popular* (producer and director), 1955; *The Three Faces of Eve* (producer and director), 1957; *Oh Men! Oh Women!* (producer and director), 1957; *The Man Who Understood Women* (producer and director), 1959.

SAM KATZMAN Born July 7, 1901; *Spotlight Serenade*, 1943; *Voodoo Man*, 1944; *Freddie Steps Out*, 1946; *Last of the Buccaneers*, 1950; *Purple Heart Diary*, 1951; *The Golden Hawk*, 1952; *California Conquest*, 1952; *Siren of Bagdad*, 1953; *Rock Around the Clock*, 1956; *Earth vs. the Flying Saucers*, 1956; *Rumble on the Docks*, 1956; *The Werewolf*, 1956; *Don't Knock the Rock*, 1957; *Utah Blaine*, 1957; *The Man Who Turned to Stone*, 1957; *Zombies of Mara-Tau*, 1957; *The Giant Claw*, 1957; *Calypso Heat Wave*, 1957; *The Night the World Exploded*, 1957; *The Tijuana Story*, 1957; *Escape From San Quentin*, 1957; *Crash Landing*, 1958; *Going Steady*, 1958; *The World Was His Jury*, 1958; *Life Begins at 17*, 1958; *The Last Blitzkrieg*, 1959; *Juke Box Rhythm*, 1959; *The Flying Fontaines*, 1959; *The Enemy General*, 1960; *The Wizard of Bagdad*, 1960; *The Pirates of Tortuga*, 1961; *Twist Around the Clock*, 1961; *The Wild Westerners*, 1962; *Don't Knock the Twist*, 1962; *Let's Twist Again*, 1961; *Hootenanny Hoot*, 1963; *Kissin' Cousins*, 1964; *Get Yourself a College Girl*, 1964; *Your Cheatin' Heart*, 1964; *Harum Scarum*, 1965; *When the Girls Meet the Boys*, 1965; *Hold On*, 1966; *Riot on the Sunset Strip*, 1967; *A Time to Sing*, 1968.

Your Cheatin' Heart with George Hamilton. *(Katzman)*

FRED KOHLMAR Born August 10, 1905; *The Lone Wolf Strikes*, 1940; *Take a Letter, Darling*, 1942; *The Glass Key*, 1942; *That Night in Rio*, 1945; *The Late George Apley*, 1947; *The Ghost and Mrs. Muir*, 1947; *Kiss of Death*, 1947; *You Were Meant for Me*, 1948; *When Willie Comes Marching Home*, 1950; *You're in the Navy Now*, 1951; *Elopement*, 1951; *Call Me Mister*, 1951; *It Should Happen to You*, 1953; *Phffft*, 1954; *Three Stripes in the Sun*, 1955; *My Sister Eileen*, 1955; *Picnic*, 1955; *The Solid Gold Cadillac*, 1956; *Full of Life*, 1957; *Pal Joey*, 1957; *The Great Sebastians* (uncompleted), 1957; *Lost Horizon* (remake uncompleted), 1957; *Gunman's Walk*, 1958; *The Last*

Dear Brigitte with John Williams, Glynis Johns and James Stewart. *(Kohlmar)*

Angry Man, 1959; *The Devil at Four O'Clock*, 1961; *The Notorious Landlady*, 1962; *Bye Bye Birdie*, 1963; *Dear Brigitte*, 1965; *How to Steal a Million*, 1966; *A Flea in Her Ear*, 1968.

STANLEY KRAMER Born September 29, 1913; *So Ends Our Night*, 1941; *The Moon and Sixpence*, 1942; *So This Is New York*, 1948; *Home of the Brave*, 1949; *Champion*, 1949; *The Men*, 1950; *Cyrano de Bergerac*, 1950; *High Noon*, 1952; *Death of a Salesman*, 1951; *The Sniper*, 1952; *The Happy Time*, 1952; *My Six Convicts*, 1952; *Member of the Wedding*, 1952; *The Wild One*, 1954; *The Caine Mutiny*, 1954; *Not as a Stranger* (producer and director), 1955; *The Pride and the Passion* (producer and director), 1957; *The Defiant Ones* (producer and director), 1958; *On the Beach* (producer and director), 1959; *Inherit the Wind* (producer and director), 1960; *Judgment at Nuremberg* (producer and director), 1961; *Pressure Point*, 1962; *A Child Is Waiting*, 1962; *It's a Mad, Mad, Mad, Mad World* (producer and director), 1963; *Invitation to a Gunfighter*, 1964; *Ship of Fools*, 1965; *Guess Who's Coming to Dinner* (also directed), 1967.

The Happy Time with Linda Christian, Louis Jourdan, Bobby Driscoll, Charles Boyer and Marsha Hunt. *(Kramer)*

CARL LAEMMLE, JR. Born April 28, 1908; *Show Boat*, 1929; *All Quiet on the Western Front*, 1930; *Bad Sister*, 1931; *The Spirit of Notre Dame*, 1931; *Frankenstein*, 1931; *Waterloo Bridge*, 1931; *Back Street*, 1932; *Once in a Lifetime*, 1932; *Air Mail*, 1932; *They Just Had to Get Married*, 1933; *Out All Night*, 1933; *Don't Bet on Love*, 1933; *Only Yesterday*, 1933; *By Candlelight*, 1934; *The Countess of Monte Cristo*, 1934; *Glamour*, 1934; *Little Man, What Now?*, 1934; *The Good Fairy*, 1935; *The Bride of Frankenstein*, 1935.

Out All Night with Slim Summerville, Billy Barty and ZaSu Pitts. *(Laemmle)*

SOL LESSER Born February 17, 1890; *Breaking the Ice*, 1938; *Tarzan the Fearless*, 1933; *Thunder Over Mexico* ("assembler"), 1933; *Peck's Bad Boy*, 1934; *The Dude Ranger*, 1934; *The Cowboy Millionaire*, 1935; *Hard Rock Harrigan*, 1935; *Thunder Mountain*, 1935; *O'Malley of the Mounted*, 1936; *Let's Sing Again*, 1936; *The Border Patrolman*, 1936; *King of the Royal Mounted*, 1936; *Wild Brian Kent*, 1936; *Rainbow on the River*, 1936; *The Californian*, 1937; *Make a Wish*, 1937; *Western Gold*, 1937; *Hawaii Calls*, 1938; *Peck's Bad Boy With the Circus*, 1938; *Tarzan's Revenge*, 1938; *Fisherman's Wharf*, 1939; *Way Down South*, 1939; *Everything's on Ice*, 1939; *Our Town*, 1940; *That Uncertain Feeling*, 1941; *The Tuttles of Tahiti*, 1942; *Tarzan Triumphs*, 1943; *Stage Door Canteen*, 1943; *Tarzan's Desert Mystery*, 1943; *Tarzan and the Leopard Woman*, 1946; *Tarzan and the Huntress*, 1947; *The Red House*, 1947; *Tarzan and the Mermaids*, 1948; *Tarzan's Magic Fountain*, 1949; *Tarzan's Peril*, 1951; *Kon-Tiki* ("assembler"), 1951; *Tarzan and the She-Devil*, 1953; *Vice Squad*, 1953; *Tarzan's Hidden Jungle*, 1955; *Tarzan and the Lost Safari*, 1957.

Peck's Bad Boy with Jackie Searl, Jackie Cooper and Gertrude Howard. *(Lesser)*

ROBERT LORD Born May 1, 1902; *Loose Ankles*, 1930; *Playing Around*, 1930; *The Flirting Widow*, 1930; *20,000 Years in Sing Sing*, 1933; *Fog Over Frisco*, 1934; *The Girl From Tenth Avenue*, 1935; *Oil for the Lamps of China*, 1935; *Black Legion*, 1936; *Tovarich* (under Hal B. Wallis), 1937; *Brother Rat*, 1938; *Dawn Patrol*, 1938; *The Amazing Dr. Clitterhouse*, 1938; *Dodge City*, 1939; *Confessions of a Nazi Spy*, 1939; *The Private Lives of Elizabeth and Essex* (under Hal B. Wallis), 1939; *The Letter* (under Hal B. Wallis), 1940; *High Wall*, 1947; *Knock on Any Door*, 1949; *Tokyo Joe*, 1949; *In a Lonely Place*, 1950; *Sirocco*, 1951; *The Family Secret*, 1951.

Oil for the Lamps of China with Josephine Hutchinson and Pat O'Brien. *(Lord)*

573

WALTER M. MIRISCH Born November 8, 1921; *Fall Guy*, 1947; *Bamba the Jungle Boy*, 1949; *The Hidden City*, 1950; *Bomba on Panther Island*, 1950; *The Lost Volcano*, 1950; *Country Fair*, 1950; *Elephant Stampede*, 1951; *Cavalry Scout*, 1951; *Flight to Mars*, 1951; *The Lion Hunters*, 1951; *The Maze*, 1953; *Wichita*, 1955; *The Warriors*, 1955; *The First Texan*, 1956; *The Oklahoman*, 1957; *The Tall Stranger*, 1957; *Man of the West*, 1958; *Fort Massacre*, 1958; *Cast a Long Shadow*, 1959; *The Gunfight at Dodge City*, 1959; *The Magnificent Seven*, 1960; *By Love Possessed*, 1961; *West Side Story*, 1961; *Town Without Pity*, 1961; *Two for the See-Saw*, 1962; *The Children's Hour*, 1962; *Kid Galahad*, 1962; *The Great Escape*, 1963; *Toys in the Attic*, 1963; *Stolen Hours*, 1963; *The Pink Panther*, 1964; *The Satan Bug*, 1965; *The Hallelujah Trail*, 1965; *A Rage to Live*, 1965; *Return From the Ashes*, 1965; *Hawaii*, 1966; *Cast a Giant Shadow*, 1966; *The Russians Are Coming, The Russians Are Coming*, 1966; *Return of the Seven*, 1966; *The Fortune Cookie*, 1966; *In the Heat of the Night*, 1967; *Fitzwilly*, 1967.

The Warriors with Yvonne Furneaux. *(Mirisch)*

ALAN J. PAKULA Born April 7, 1928; *Fear Strikes Out*, 1957; *To Kill a Mockingbird*, 1962; *Love With the Proper Stranger*, 1963; *Baby, the Rain Must Fall*, 1965; *Inside Daisy Clover*, 1965; *Up the Down Staircase*, 1967.

Baby, the Rain Must Fall with Kimberly Black, Lee Remick, Steve McQueen and Estelle Hemsley. *(Pakula)*

GEORGE PAL Born February 1, 1900; *The Great Rupert*, 1950; *Destination Moon*, 1950; *When Worlds Collide*, 1951; *Houdini*, 1953; *War of the Worlds*, 1953; *The Naked Jungle*, 1954; *The Conquest of Space*, 1955; *Captain Cook* (uncompleted), 1957; *tom thumb* (producer and director), 1958; *The Time Machine* (producer and director), 1960; *Atlantis, the Lost Continent* (producer and director, with Henry Levin), 1961; *The Wonderful World of the Brothers Grimm* (producer

The Time Machine with Yvette Mimieux and Rod Taylor. *(Pal)*

and director), 1962; *The Seven Faces of Dr. Lao* (producer and director), 1964.

JOE PASTERNAK Born September 17, 1901; *Three Smart Girls*, 1936; *One Hundred Men and a Girl*, 1937; *Mad About Music*, 1938; *Youth Takes a Fling*, 1938; *That Certain Age*, 1938; *Three Smart Girls Grow Up*, 1939; *The Under-Pup*, 1939; *Destry Rides Again*, 1939; *It's a Date*, 1940; *A Little Bit of Heaven*, 1940; *Seven Sinners*, 1940; *Nice Girl?*, 1941; *It Started With Eve*, 1941; *Flame of New Orleans*, 1941; *Seven Sweethearts*, 1942; *Presenting Lily Mars*, 1942; *Thousands Cheer*, 1943; *Song of Russia*, 1943; *Two Girls and a Sailor*, 1944; *Music for Millions*, 1944; *Anchors Aweigh*, 1945; *Her Highness and the Bellboy*, 1945; *Two Sisters from Boston*, 1946; *Holiday in Mexico*, 1946; *No Leave, No Love*, 1946; *Unfinished Dance*, 1947; *This Time for Keeps*, 1947; *Three Daring Daughters*, 1948; *The Kissing Bandit*, 1948; *On an Island With You*, 1948; *Luxury Liner*, 1948; *Big City*, 1948; *A Date With Judy*, 1948; *In the Good Old Summertime*, 1949; *That Midnight Kiss*, 1949; *Nancy Goes to Rio*, 1949; *The Duchess of Idaho*, 1950; *Summer Stock*, 1950; *The Toast of New Orleans*, 1950; *The Great Caruso*, 1951; *Rich, Young and Pretty*, 1951; *The Strip*, 1951; *Skirts Ahoy!*, 1952; *The Merry Widow*, 1952; *Because You're Mine*, 1952; *Small Town Girl*, 1953; *Latin Lovers*, 1953; *Easy to Love*, 1953; *The Flame and the Flesh*, 1954; *The Student Prince*, 1954; *Athena*, 1954; *Hit the Deck*, 1955; *Love Me or Leave Me*, 1955; *Meet Me in Las Vegas*, 1956; *The Opposite Sex*, 1956; *Ten Thousand Bedrooms*, 1957; *This Could Be the Night*, 1957; *Party Girl*, 1958; *Ask Any Girl*, 1959; *Please Don't Eat the Daisies*, 1960; *Where the Boys Are*, 1960; *The Horizontal Lieutenant*, 1961; *Billy Rose's Jumbo*, 1962; *The Courtship of Eddie's Father*, 1963; *A Ticklish Affair*, 1963; *Looking for Love*, 1964; *Girl Happy*, 1965; *Made in Paris*, 1966; *Spinout*, 1966; *Penelope*, 1966; *The Sweet Ride*, 1968.

Holiday in Mexico with Jose Iturbi, Jane Powell and Walter Pidgeon. *(Pasternak)*

WILLIAM PERLBERG Born October 22, 1899; *The King Steps Out*, 1936; *Golden Boy*, 1939; *Son of Fury*, 1942; *The Song of Bernadette*, 1943; *Miracle on 34th Street*, 1947; *Forever Amber* (with Darryl F. Zanuck), 1947; *The Shocking Miss Pilgrim*, 1947; *Escape*, 1948; *Apartment for Peggy*, 1948; *Forbidden Street*, 1949; *It Happens Every Spring*, 1949; *Slattery's Hurricane*, 1949; *For Heaven's Sake*, 1950; *The Big Lift*, 1950; *Wabash Avenue*, 1950; *I'll Get By*, 1950; *Rhubarb* (with George Seaton), 1951; *Anything Can Happen*, 1952; *Little Boy, Lost*, 1953; *The Bridges at Toko-Ri* (with George Seaton), 1954; *The Country Girl*, 1954; *The Proud and Profane*, 1956; *The Tin Star* (with George Seaton), 1957; *Teacher's Pet*, 1958; *But Not for Me* (with George Seaton), 1959; *The Rat Race* (with George Seaton), 1960; *The Pleasure of His Company*, 1961; *The Counterfeit Traitor*, 1962; *The Hook*, 1963; *Twilight of Honor* (with George Seaton), 1963; *36 Hours*, 1964; *Half a Sixpence*, 1967.

The Hook with Nehemiah Persoff (T-shirt), Robert Walker, Jr., Nick Adams and Kirk Douglas. *(Perlberg)*

AARON ROSENBERG Born August 26, 1912; *Johnny Stool Pigeon*, 1949; *Outside the Wall*, 1950; *Winchester '73*, 1950; *Air Cadet*, 1951; *Cattle Drive*, 1951; *The Iron Man*, 1951; *Here Come the Nelsons*, 1952; *Bend of the River*, 1952; *The World in His Arms*, 1952; *Red Ball Express*, 1952; *Gunsmoke*, 1953; *Thunder Bay*, 1953; *Man From the Alamo*, 1953; *All American*, 1953; *Wings of the Hawk*, 1953; *The Glenn Miller Story*, 1954; *Saskatchewan*, 1954; *The Far Country*, 1955; *Six Bridges to Cross*, 1955; *Man Without a Star*, 1955; *The Shrike*, 1955; *Foxfire*, 1955; *The Benny Goodman Story*, 1955; *To Hell and Back*, 1955; *Backlash*, 1956; *The World in My Corner*, 1956; *Walk the Proud Land*, 1956; *Four Girls in Town*, 1956; *Joe Butterfly*, 1957; *Night Passage*, 1957; *The Badlanders*, 1958; *Never Steal Anything Small*, 1959; *It Started With a Kiss*, 1959; *Go Naked in the World*, 1961; *Mutiny on the Bounty*, 1962; *Move Over, Darling*, 1963; *Fate Is the Hunter*, 1964; *Shock Treatment*, 1964; *The Saboteur, Code Name—Morituri*, 1965; *The Reward*, 1965; *Do Not Disturb*, 1965; *Smoky*, 1966; *Caprice*, 1967; *The Detective*, 1968.

Do Not Disturb with Rod Taylor and Doris Day. *(Rosenberg)*

VICTOR SAVILLE Born 1897.
Primarily a Director: *Sunshine Susie*, 1931; *Hindle Wakes*, 1931; *Michael and Mary*, 1932; *Love on Wheels*, 1932; *The Faithful Heart*, 1933; *The Good Companions*, 1933; *I Was a Spy*, 1934; *Friday the Thirteenth*, 1934; *Evensong*, 1934; *The Iron Duke*, or *Me and Marlborough*, 1934; *Evergreen*, 1935; *Loves of a Dictator*, 1935; *First a Girl*, 1935; *It's Love Again*, 1936; *Storm in a Teacup* (with Ian Dalrymple), 1937; *Dark Journey* (producer and director), 1937.
Primarily a Producer: *Action for Slander* (producer and director), 1938; *South Riding* (producer and director), 1938; *The Citadel*, 1938; *Goodbye, Mr. Chips*, 1939; *The Earl of Chicago*, 1940; *The Mortal Storm*, 1940; *Bitter Sweet*, 1940; *A Woman's Face*, 1941; *Dr. Jekyll and Mr. Hyde*, 1941; *Smilin' Through*, 1941; *The Chocolate Soldier*, 1941; *White Cargo*, 1942; *Keeper of the Flame*, 1942; *Forever and a Day* (director, among various others), 1943; *Above Suspicion*, 1943; *Tonight and Every Night* (producer and director), 1945; *The Green Years* (producer and director), 1946; *Green Dolphin Street* (producer and director), 1947; *If Winter Comes* (director), 1947; *The Conspirator* (director), 1949; *Kim* (producer and director), 1950; *Calling Bulldog Drummond* (producer and director), directed 1949, released 1951, 1951; *24 Hours of a Woman's Life* (director), 1952; *I, the Jury*, 1953; *Affair in Monte Carlo* (director), 1953; *The Long Wait* (director), 1954; *The Silver Chalice* (producer and director), 1954; *Kiss Me, Deadly*, 1955; *The Greengage Summer*, 1961.

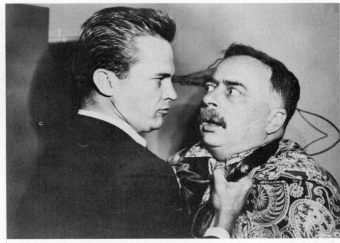

Kiss Me Deadly with Ralph Meeker and Silvio Minciotti. *(Saville)*

DORE SCHARY Born August 31, 1905; *Joe Smith, American*, 1942; *The War Against Mrs. Hadley*, 1942; *Journey for Margaret*, 1942; *Bataan*, 1943; *Lassie, Come Home*, 1943; *Lost Angel*, 1943; *I'll Be Seeing You*, 1944; *The Spiral Staircase*, 1946; *Till the End of Time*, 1946; *The Farmer's Daughter*, 1947; *Crossfire*, 1947; *The Bachelor and the Bobby-Soxer*, 1947; *Berlin Express*, 1948; *Mr. Blandings Builds His Dream House*, 1948; *The Set-Up*, 1949; *The Window*, 1949; *Battleground*, 1949; *The Next Voice You Hear*, 1950; *Go for Broke*, 1951; *It's a Big Country*, 1951; *Westward the Women*, 1951; *Washington*

Joe Smith, American with Marsha Hunt and Robert Young. *(Schary)*

Story, 1952; *Plymouth Adventure*, 1952; *Dream Wife*, 1953; *Take the High Ground*, 1953; *Bad Day at Black Rock*, 1954; *The Last Hunt*, 1956; *The Swan*, 1956; *Designing Woman*, 1957; *Lonelyhearts*, 1958; *Sunrise at Campobello*, 1960; *Act One* (producer and director), 1963.

SOL C. SIEGEL Born March 30, 1903; *Army Girl*, 1938; *Dark Command*, 1940; *Three Faces West*, 1940; *Among the Living*, 1941; *Hostages*, 1943; *Kiss and Tell*, 1945; *Blue Skies*, 1946; *Welcome Stranger*, 1947; *House of Strangers*, 1949; *A Letter to Three Wives*, 1948; *I Was a Male War Bride*, 1949; *Panic in the Streets*, 1950; *Fourteen Hours*, 1951; *Dream Boat*, 1952; *Deadline, U.S.A.*, 1952; *What Price Glory*, 1952; *Monkey Business*, 1952; *Call Me Madam*, 1953; *Gentlemen Prefer Blondes*, 1953; *Broken Lance*, 1954; *Three Coins in the Fountain*, 1954; *There's No Business Like Show Business*, 1954; *High Society*, 1956; *Man on Fire*, 1957; *Les Girls*, 1957; *Merry Andrew*, 1958; *Some Came Running*, 1958; *The World, the Flesh and the Devil*, 1959; *Home From the Hill*, 1960; *Walk, Don't Run*, 1966; *Alvarez Kelly*, 1966; *No Way to Treat a Lady*, 1968.

High Society with Grace Kelly, Frank Sinatra and Celeste Holm.
(Siegel)

DAVID O. SELZNICK Born May 10, 1902; died June 22, 1965; *What Price Hollywood*, 1932; *A Bill of Divorcement*, 1932; *The Animal Kingdom*, 1932; *Bird of Paradise*, 1932; *Our Betters*, 1933; *Topaze*, 1933; *Dinner at Eight*, 1933; *Night Flight*, 1933; *Dancing Lady*, 1933; *Little Women*, 1933; *Viva Villa!*, 1934; *Mahattan Melodrama*, 1934; *David Copperfield*, 1935; *Anna Karenina*, 1935; *A Tale of Two Cities*, 1935; *Little Lord Fauntleroy*, 1936; *The Garden of Allah*, 1936; *A Star Is Born*, 1937; *Nothing Sacred*, 1937; *The Prisoner of Zenda*, 1937; *The Adventures of Tom Sawyer*, 1938; *Intermezzo*, 1939; *Gone With the Wind*, 1939; *Rebecca*, 1940; *Claudia*, 1943; *Jane Eyre*, 1944; *The Keys of the Kingdom*, 1944; *Since You Went Away*, 1944; *I'll Be Seeing You*, 1944; *Spellbound*, 1945; *The Spiral Staircase*, 1946; *Notorious*, 1946; *Duel in the Sun*, 1946; *The Farmer's Daughter*, 1947; *The Bachelor and the Bobby-Soxer*, 1947; *The Paradine Case*, 1948; *Portrait of Jennie*, 1948; *The Third Man* (assisted Alexander Korda

Duel in the Sun with Lionel Barrymore and Harry Morgan.
(Selznick)

and Carol Reed), 1949; *The Wild Heart*, or *Gone to Earth*, 1952; *Stazione Termini* (financed only), 1953; *A Farewell to Arms*, 1957.

EDWARD SMALL Born February 1, 1891; *The Gorilla*, 1931; *I Cover the Waterfront*, 1933; *Palooka*, 1934; *The Count of Monte Cristo*, 1934; *Transatlantic Merry-Go-Round*, 1934; *Let 'em Have It*, 1935; *Red Salute*, 1935; *The Melody Lingers On*, 1935; *The Last of the Mohicans*, 1936; *Sea Devils*, 1937; *New Faces of 1937*, 1937; *Super Sleuth*, 1937; *The Toast of New York*, 1937; *The Duke of West Point*, 1938; *King of the Turf*, 1939; *The Man in the Iron Mask*, 1939; *My Son, My Son*, 1940; *South of Pago Pago*, 1940; *Kit Carson*, 1940; *The Son of Monte Cristo*, 1940; *International Lady*, 1941; *The Corsican Brothers*, 1941; *A Gentleman After Dark*, 1942; *Twin Beds*, 1942; *Miss Annie Rooney*, 1942; *Friendly Enemies*, 1942; *Up in Mabel's Room*, 1944; *Abroad With Two Yanks*, 1944; *Brewster's Millions*, 1945; *Getting Gertie's Garter*, 1945; *Temptation*, 1946; *The Return of Monte Cristo*, 1946; *T-Men*, 1947; *Red River*, 1948; *Scandal Sheet*, 1952; *Kansas City Confidential*, 1952; *Bandits of Corsica*, 1953; *Gun Belt*, 1953; *99 River Street*, 1953; *Steel Lady*, 1953; *Wicked Woman*, 1953; *Overland Pacific*, 1954; *Southwest Passage*, 1954; *Lone Gun*, 1954; *Down Three Dark Streets*, 1954; *Khyber Patrol*, 1954; *New York Confidential*, 1955; *The Naked Street*, 1955; *Top Gun*, 1955; *Witness for the Prosecution*, 1957; *Solomon and Sheba*, 1959; *Timbuktu*, 1959; *Jack, the Giant Killer*, 1962; *Diary of a Madman*, 1963; *Twice Told Tales*, 1963; *The Quick Gun*, 1964; *Apache Rifles*, 1964; *I'll Take Sweden*, 1965; *Frankie and Johnny*, 1966; *Boy, Did I Get a Wrong Number!*, 1966; *The Wicked Dreams of Paula Schultz*, 1968; *Hostile Witness*, 1968.

Palooka with Stuart Erwin and Marjorie Rambeau. *(Small)*

HUNT STROMBERG Died 1968; *Our Blushing Brides*, 1930; *Guilty Hands*, 1931; *The Wet Parade*, 1932; *Letty Lynton*, 1932; *Red Dust*, 1932; *The White Sister*, 1933; *Penthouse*, 1933; *The Thin Man*, 1934; *Treasure Island*, 1934; *Hide-Out*, 1934; *The Painted Veil*, 1934; *Chained*, 1934; *Naughty Marietta*, 1935; *Ah, Wilderness*, 1935; *Rose Marie*, 1936; *Wife vs. Secretary*, 1936; *Small Town Girl*, 1936; *The Great Ziegfeld*, 1936; *After the Thin Man*, 1936; *Maytime*, 1937; *Night Must Fall*, 1937; *The Firefly*, 1937; *Sweethearts*, 1938; *Marie Antoinette*, 1938; *Idiot's Delight*, 1939; *The Women*, 1939; *Susan and God*, 1940; *Northwest Passage*, 1940; *Pride and Prejudice*, 1940; *They Met in Bombay*, 1941; *Shadow of the Thin Man*, 1941; *Lady of Burlesque*, 1943; *Guest in the House*, 1944; *The Strange Woman*, 1946; *Dishonored Lady*, 1947; *Lured*, 1947; *Too Late for Tears*, 1949.

WILLIAM C. THOMAS Born August 11, 1903; *Tokyo Rose*, 1945; *Follow That Woman*, 1945; *Scared Stiff*, 1945; *Hot Cargo*, 1946; *Swamp Fire*, 1946; *People Are Funny*, 1946; *Big Town*, 1947; *Fear in the Night*, 1947; *Danger Street*, 1947; *Jungle Flight*, 1947; *Seven Were Saved*, 1947; *I Cover the Big Town*, 1947; *Adventure Island*, 1947; *Big Town After Dark*, 1947; *Waterfront at Midnight*, 1948; *Speed to Spare*, 1948; *Shaggy*, 1948; *Mr. Reckless*, 1948; *Caged Fury*, 1948; *Big Town Scandal*, 1948; *Albuquerque*, 1948; *Disaster*, 1948; *Dynamite*, 1949; *El Paso*,

Idiot's Delight with Edward Arnold and Norma Shearer. *(Stromberg)*

1949; *Special Agent*, 1949; *Manhandled*, 1949; *Captain China*, 1949; *The Lawless*, 1950; *The Eagle and the Hawk*, 1950; *Crosswinds*, 1951; *Hong Kong*, 1951; *Blazing Forest*, 1952; *Carribbean*, 1952; *The Vanquished*, 1953; *Jamaica Run*, 1953; *Sangaree*, 1953; *Jivaro*, 1954; *Hell's Island*, 1955; *Run for Cover*, 1955; *Far Horizons*, 1955; *Lucy Gallant*, 1955; *Nightmare*, 1956; *The Big Caper*, 1957; *Bailout at 43,000*, 1957.

El Paso with John Payne, Gail Russell and Sterling Hayden. *(Thomas)*

JERRY WALD Born September 16, 1911; died July 13, 1962; *Navy Blues*, 1941; *All Through the Night*, 1942; *The Man Who Came to Dinner* (under Hal B. Wallis), 1942; *Larceny, Inc.*, 1942; *Juke Girl*, 1942; *Across the Pacific*, 1942; *Desperate Journey*, 1942; *George Washington Slept Here*, 1942; *Casablanca*, 1942; *The Hard Way*, 1942; *Air Force* (no screen credit), 1943; *Action in the North Atlantic*, 1943; *Background to Danger*, 1943; *Destination Tokyo*, 1943; *In Our Time*, 1944; *Shine On, Harvest Moon*, 1944; *The Very Thought of You*, 1944; *To Have and Have Not* (no screen credit), 1944; *Objective Burma*, 1945; *Pride of the Marines*, 1945; *Rhapsody in Blue*, 1945; *Humoresque*, 1946; *The Unfaithful*, 1947; *Possessed*, 1947; *Dark Passage*, 1947; *To the Victor*, 1948; *Key Largo*, 1948; *Johnny Belinda*, 1948; *One Sunday Afternoon*, 1948; *The Adventures of Don Juan*, 1948; *John Loves Mary*, 1949; *Flamingo Road*, 1949; *Look for the Silver Lining*, 1949; *Task Force*, 1949; *Always Leave Them Laughing*, 1949; *The Inspector General*, 1949; *Young Man With a Horn*, 1950; *Perfect Strangers*, 1950; *The Damned Don't Cry*, 1950; *Caged*, 1950; *The Breaking Point*, 1950; *The Glass Menagerie*, 1950; *Storm Warning*, 1951; *Behave Yourself* (this film and the three following were produced with Norman Krasna; Wald did the production work), 1951; *The Blue Veil*, 1951; *Clash by Night*, 1952; *The Lusty Men*, 1952; *From Here to Eternity*, 1953; *The Big Heat*, 1953; *Miss Sadie Thompson*, 1953; *The Caine Mutiny*, 1954; *Phffft*, 1954; *Cell 2455, Death Row* (Wald was the actual working producer), 1955; *The Queen Bee*, 1955; *Picnic*, 1955; *The Last Frontier*, 1955; *The Harder They Fall*, 1956; *Jubal*, 1956; *The Eddy Duchin Story*, 1956; *The Solid Gold Cadillac*, 1956; *You Can't Run Away from It*, 1956; *An Affair to Remember*, 1957; *No Down Payment*, 1957; *Kiss Them for Me*, 1957; *Peyton Place*,

1957; *The Hard-Hats* (uncompleted), 1957; *The Long Hot Summer*, 1958; *In Love and War*, 1958; *Mardi Gras*, 1958; *Beloved Infidel*, 1959; *The Sound and the Fury*, 1959; *Hound-Dog Man*, 1959; *The Best of Everything*, 1959; *The Story on Page One*, 1959; *Sons and Lovers*, 1960; *Let's Make Love*, 1960; *Hemingway's Adventures of a Young Man*, 1962; *The Stripper* (prepared the production and died before completion), 1963.

John Loves Mary with Ronald Reagan and Jack Carson. *(Wald)*

HAL B. WALLIS Born September 14, 1899; *Little Caesar*, 1930; *I Am a Fugitive From a Chain Gang*, 1932; *The Story of Louis Pasteur*, 1935; *A Midsummer Night's Dream*, 1935; *Green Pastures*, 1936; *The Life of Emile Zola*, 1936; *The Go-Getter*, 1937; *Marked Woman*, 1937; *Kid Galahad*, 1937; *That Certain Woman*, 1937; *It's Love I'm After*, 1937; *Tovarich* (with Robert Lord), 1937; *The Sisters*, 1938; *Jezebel* (with Henry Blanke), 1938; *The Adventures of Robin Hood*, 1938; *Invisible Stripes*, 1939; *Dark Victory*, 1939; *Juarez* (with Henry Blanke), 1939; *The Old Maid* (with Henry Blanke), 1939; *The Kid From Kokomo* (with Samuel Bischoff), 1939; *They Made Me a Criminal*, 1939; *The Roaring Twenties* (with Samuel Bischoff), 1939; *The Private Lives of Elizabeth and Essex* (with Robert Lord), 1939; *Virginia City*, 1940; *It All Came True* (with Mark Hellinger), 1940; *Brother Orchid* (with Mark Hellinger), 1940; *They Drive by Night* (with Mark Hellinger), 1940; *The Letter* (with Robert Lord), 1940; *City for Conquest*, 1940; *All This, and Heaven Too*, 1940; *The Sea Hawk*, 1941; *Footsteps in the Dark*, 1941; *Manpower* (with Mark Hellinger), 1941; *Sergeant York*, 1941; *The Maltese Falcon* (with Henry Blanke), 1941; *High Sierra* (with Mark Hellinger), 1941; *The Great Lie* (with Henry Blanke), 1941; *The Bride Came C.O.D.*, 1941; *One Foot in Heaven* (with Robert Lord), 1941; *The Man Who Came to Dinner* (with Jerry Wald), 1941; *Now, Voyager*, 1942; *In This Our Life*, 1942; *Desperate Journey*, 1942; *Casablanca*, 1942; *Yankee Doodle Dandy*, 1942; *Air Force*, 1943; *Watch on the Rhine*, 1943; *Passage to Marseille*, 1944; *The Affairs of Susan*, 1945; *Saratoga Trunk*, 1945; *Desert Fury*, 1947; *I Walk Alone*, 1947; *The Perfect Marriage*, 1947; *So Evil My Love*, 1948; *Sorry, Wrong Number*, 1948; *The Accused*, 1948; *My Friend Irma*, 1949; *Rope of Sand*, 1949; *Paid in Full*, 1949; *Thelma Jordan*, 1949; *September Affair*, 1950; *My Friend Irma Goes West*, 1950; *The Furies*, 1950; *Dark City*, 1950; *Red Mountain*, 1951; *That's My Boy*, 1951; *Sailor Beware*, 1951; *Peking Express*, 1951; *The Stooge*, 1952; *Jumping Jacks*, 1952; *Come Back, Little Sheba*, 1952; *Scared Stiff*, 1953; *Money From Home*, 1953; *About Mrs. Leslie*, 1954; *Three Ring Circus*, 1954; *Artists and Models*, 1955; *The Rose Tattoo*, 1955; *Hollywood or Bust*, 1956; *The Rainmaker*, 1956; *The Sad Sack*, 1957; *Gunfight at the O. K. Corral*, 1957; *Loving You*, 1957; *Wild Is the Wind*, 1957; *The Obsessed* (uncompleted), 1957; *Hot Spell*, 1958; *King Creole*, 1958; *Rock-A-Bye Baby*, 1958; *The Last Train From Gun Hill*, 1959; *Career*, 1959; *Don't Give Up the Ship*, 1960; *Visit to a Small Planet*, 1960; *G.I. Blues*, 1960; *All in a Night's Work*, 1961; *Summer and Smoke*, 1961; *Girls, Girls, Girls*, 1962; *A Girl Named Tamiko*, 1962; *Wives and Lovers*, 1963; *Fun in Acapulco*, 1963; *Becket*, 1964; *Roustabout*, 1964; *The Sons of Katie Elder*, 1965; *Boeing-Boeing*, 1965; *Paradise, Hawaiian Style*, 1966; *Barefoot in the Park*, 1967; *Easy Come, Easy Go*, 1967.

The Sisters with Bette Davis. *(Wallis)*

WALTER WANGER Born July 11, 1894; *The Cocoanuts*, 1929; *Washington Merry-Go-Round*, 1932; *The Bitter Tea of General Yen*, 1933; *Gabriel Over the White House*, 1933; *Another Language*, 1933; *Going Hollywood*, 1933; *Queen Christina*, 1933; *The President Vanishes*, 1934; *Private Worlds*, 1935; *Shanghai*, 1935; *Every Night at Eight*, 1935; *Mary Burns, Fugitive*, 1935; *The Trail of the Lonesome Pine*, 1936; *The Moon's Our Home*, 1936; *Big Brown Eyes*, 1936; *Palm Springs*, 1936; *Spendthrift*, 1936; *Fatal Lady*, 1936; *Sabotage*, 1936; *You Only Live Once*, 1937; *History Is Made at Night*, 1937; *Vogues of 1938*, 1937; *Stand-In*, 1937; *52nd Street*, 1937; *Blockade*, 1938; *Algiers*, 1938; *Trade Winds*, 1938; *Winter Carnival*, 1939; *Stagecoach*, 1939; *Eternally Yours*, 1939; *Slightly Honorable*, 1940; *The House Across the Bay*, 1940; *Foreign Correspondent*, 1940; *The Long Voyage Home*, 1940; *Sundown*, 1941; *Eagle Squadron*, 1942; *Arabian Nights*, 1942; *We've Never Been Licked*, 1943; *Gung Ho!*, 1943; *Ladies Courageous*, 1944; *Salome, Where She Danced*, 1945; *Scarlet Street*, 1945; *A Night in Paradise*, 1946; *Canyon Passage*, 1946; *Smash-up—the Story of a Woman*, 1947; *The Lost Moment*, 1947; *The Secret Beyond the Door*, 1948; *Tap Roots*, 1948; *Joan of Arc*, 1948; *Tulsa*, 1949; *Reign of Terror*, 1949; *The Reckless Moment*, 1949; *Aladdin and His Lamp*, 1952; *The Lady in the Iron Mask*, 1952; *Battle Zone*, 1952; *Kansas Pacific*, 1953; *Fort Vengeance*, 1953; *Riot in Cell Block 11*, 1954; *The Adventures of Hajji Baba*, 1954; *The Invasion of the Body Snatchers*, 1956; *The Quiet American*, 1958; *I Want to Live!*, 1958; *Cleopatra* (replaced by Darryl F. Zanuck), 1963.

A Night in Paradise with Merle Oberon and Turhan Bey. *(Wanger)*

LAWRENCE WEINGARTEN *Broadway Melody*, 1929; *Libeled Lady*, 1936; *A Day at the Races*, 1937; *I Love You Again*, 1940; *Escape*, 1940; *When Ladies Meet*, 1941; *Without Love*, 1945; *Adam's Rib*, 1949; *Invitation*, 1952; *Pat and Mike*, 1952; *The Actress*, 1953; *Rhap-*

sody, 1954; *The Tender Trap*, 1955; *I'll Cry Tomorrow*, 1955; *Don't Go Near the Water*, 1957; *Cat on a Hot Tin Roof*, 1958; *The Gazebo*, 1959; *Ada*, 1961; *The Honeymoon Machine*, 1961; *Period of Adjustment*, 1962; *The Unsinkable Molly Brown*, 1964; *Signpost to Murder*, 1965; *The Impossible Years*, 1968.

Invitation with Van Johnson and Dorothy McGuire. *(Weingarten)*

DARRYL F. ZANUCK Born September 5, 1902; *Noah's Ark*, 1929; *The Bowery*, 1933; *Moulin Rouge*, 1934; *The House of Rothschild*, 1934; *The Mighty Barnum*, 1934; *Cardinal Richelieu*, 1935; *Clive of India*, 1935; *Les Miserables*, 1935; *Prisoner of Shark Island*, (with Nunnally Johnson), 1936; *A Message to Garcia*, 1936; *Lloyds of London*, 1936; *One in a Million*, 1936; *The Road to Glory* (with Nunnally Johnson), 1936; *Wee Willie Winkie*, 1937; *Seventh Heaven*, 1937; *Alexander's Ragtime Band* (with Harry Joe Brown), 1938; *In Old Chicago*, 1938; *Suez*, 1938; *Kentucky*, 1938; *Four Men and a Prayer*, 1938; *Submarine Patrol*, 1938; *The Gorilla* (with Harry Joe Brown), 1939; *The Story of Alexander Graham Bell*, 1939; *Jesse James*, 1939; *Stanley and Livingston*, 1939; *The Rains Came*, 1939; *Young Mr. Lincoln*, 1939; *Drums Along the Mohawk*, 1939; *The Grapes of Wrath* (with Nunnally Johnson), 1940; *The Return of Frank James*, 1940; *The Mark of Zorro*, 1940; *Four Sons* (with Harry Joe Brown), 1940; *Tobacco Road*, 1941; *Western Union*, 1941; *How Green Was My Valley*, 1941; *Blood and Sand*, 1941; *A Yank in the R.A.F.*, 1941; *Son of Fury*, 1942; *This Above All*, 1942; *Winged Victory*, 1943; *The Purple Heart*, 1944; *Wilson*, 1944; *Anna and the King of Siam*, 1946; *The Razor's Edge*, 1946; *Dragonwyck*, 1946; *Forever Amber* (with William Perlberg), 1947; *Gentleman's Agreement*, 1947; *Pinky*, 1949; *Twelve O'Clock High*, 1949; *All About Eve*, 1950; *No Way Out*, 1950; *David and Bathsheba*, 1951; *People Will Talk*, 1951; *The Snows of Kilimanjaro*, 1952; *Viva Zapata!*, 1952; *The Egyptian*, 1954; *The Man*

Kentucky with Eddie "Rochester" Anderson, Walter Brennan, Loretta Young and Willard Robertson. *(Zanuck)*

in the Gray Flannel Suit, 1956; *Island in the Sun*, 1957; *The Sun Also Rises*, 1957; *Crime of the Century* (uncompleted), 1957; *Parris Island* (uncompleted), 1957; *The Roots of Heaven*, 1958; *Crack in the Mirror*, 1960; *Sanctuary*, 1961; *The Big Gamble*, 1961; *The Longest Day*, 1962; *The Chapman Report*, 1962; *Cleopatra* (replaced Walter Wanger), 1963; *The Visit*, 1964.

SAM ZIMBALIST Died November 4, 1958; *Tarzan Escapes*, 1936; *Married Before Breakfast*, 1937; *Navy Blue and Gold*, 1937; *The Crowd Roars*, 1938; *Tarzan Finds a Son*, 1939; *Boom Town*, 1940; *Tortilla Flat*, 1942; *Thirty Seconds Over Tokyo*, 1944; *Killer McCoy*, 1947; *Side Street*, 1949; *King Solomon's Mines*, 1950; *Too Young to Kiss*, 1951; *Quo Vadis*, 1951; *Mogambo*, 1953; *Beau Brummel*, 1954; *Tribute to a Bad Man*, 1956; *The Catered Affair*, 1956; *I Accuse!*, 1958; *Ben-Hur* (died during preparation), 1959.

(Zugsmith)

Platinum High School with Yvette Mimieux and Mickey Rooney.

ALBERT ZUGSMITH Born April 24, 1910; *Sword of Venus*, 1953; *Female on the Beach*, 1955; *The Square Jungle*, 1955; *Star in the Dust*, 1956; *Raw Edge*, 1956; *Red Sundown*, 1956; *Written on the Wind*, 1956; *The Tattered Dress*, 1957; *Slaughter on Tenth Avenue*, 1957; *The Incredible Shrinking Man*, 1957; *The Girl in the Kremlin*, 1957; *The Tarnished Angels*, 1957; *Man in the Shadow*, 1957; *Touch of Evil*, 1958; *The Female Animal*, 1958; *High School Confidential*, 1958; *The Beat Generation*, 1959; *The Big Operator*, 1959; *Girl's Town*, 1959; *Night of the Quarter Moon*, 1959; *Platinum High School*, 1960; *College Confidential*, 1960; *Sex Kittens Go to College*, 1960; *Dondi*, 1960; *The Private Lives of Adam and Eve*, 1960; *Confessions of an Opium Eater*, 1962; *Fanny Hill: Memoirs of a Woman of Pleasure*, 1965; *Movie Star American Style*, or *LSD I Hate You*, 1966; *The Chinese Room*, 1967; *The Ghost Riders*, 1967.

Side Street with Farley Granger and Jean Hagen. *(Zimbalist)*

The Oscar

CHAPTER VI

THE AWARDS

THE ACADEMY AWARDS

BY ARTHUR FREED
Former President, Academy of Motion
Picture Arts and Sciences

Recognition of achievement by his peers is probably the most satisfying reward anyone engaged in creative work can receive. Our experience has demonstrated that few rewards provide greater incentive for excellence than such recognition.

It was largely for these reasons that the Academy of Motion Picture Arts and Sciences, at its founding in 1927, established the annual Awards of Merit as one of our major activities.

During the past 40 years, the "Oscar" has become the ultimate symbol of excellence in the world of motion pictures. Its prestige has grown consistently, and long ago spread beyond the boundaries of the American industry. Today the Academy Awards have international significance, acknowledged by film makers everywhere.

"Oscar's" growth in worldwide prestige has not come about accidentally. It is the result, rather, of Academy foresight in maintaining the integrity, character and intent of the Awards in the face of numerous attempts to change or modify the original purposes.

In a word, the Academy Awards always have been and remain "different" from the hundreds of other prizes bestowed in the motion picture industry and other fields. Our Awards honor artistic achievement, with little regard for popularity, box-office success or other yardsticks applied by critics or the general public.

The presentation of "Oscar" is not something in which the entire industry participates. Only the approximately 3,000 top men and women who have been elected to Academy membership because of their recognized competence take part in the balloting. In fact, only specialists in 13 phases of picture-making determine the nominated achievements in their fields, but the entire membership votes the final award. Their votes are based objectively upon their knowledge of standards of attainment in the motion picture medium.

The Academy recognizes that it requires the blending of people with many varied skills to produce today's motion picture. These include not only actors, actresses and directors, but also cinematographers, musicians, soundmen, writers and many others. Thus, each "Oscar" awarded, no matter in what category, conveys equal honor to its recipient.

There are many ways of determining the benefits gained by maintaining our basic policies and not deviating from our original purposes. One of the most dramatic is the steadily increasing international interest in the Awards, as measured by the growing size of the television and radio audience that each year "looks in" on the presentation of the "Oscars" and the widening press coverage of the event.

In its first year, 1927, the presentation was a private affair, attended only by members of the motion picture industry. Public demand brought about radio coverage of the event the following year. The 1953 presentation was the first to be televised.

In the past three years the television broadcast of the Awards has been presented in color. The 38th Awards show in 1966, the 39th Awards last April 10, 1967 and the 40th Awards on April 10, 1968 drew the three largest single-network television audiences in history. Additional millions heard them over the radio. At the same time, international publicity in newspapers and magazines reached unprecedented heights.

Other vital Academy services such as its world-renowned research library, outstanding theater, players directory and periodic credit bulletins reached new levels of usage within the industry.

All in all, the "Oscar" is the motion picture industry's most valuable public relations vehicle.

FIRST YEAR 1927–28

Best Picture: *Wings*, Par. Other nominees: *The Last Command, The Racket, Seventh Heaven, The Way of All Flesh*. **Actor:** Emil Jannings in *The Way of All Flesh* and *The Last Command*, Par. Other nominees: Richard Barthelmess in *The Noose* and *The Patent Leather Kid*, Charles Chaplin in *The Circus*. **Actress:** Janet Gaynor in *Seventh Heaven, Street Angel* and *Sunrise*, Fox. Other nominees: Louise Dresser in *A Ship Comes In*, Gloria Swanson in *Sadie Thompson*. **Directing:** Frank Borzage, *Seventh Heaven*. **Directing—Comedy:** Lewis Milestone, *Two Arabian Knights*, UA. **Art Direction:** *The Dove, The Tempest*, UA. William Cameron Menzies, Art Director. **Artistic Quality of Production:** *Sunrise*. **Cinematography:** Charles Rosher, Karl Struss, *Sunrise*. **Engineering Effects:** Roy Pomeroy, *Wings*. **Writing—Adaptation:** Benjamin Glazer, *Seventh Heaven*. **Writing—Original Story:**

Sunrise with Janet Gaynor and Charles Farrell.

Ben Hecht, *Underworld*, Par. **Writing—Title:** Joseph Farnham, *The Fair Co-Ed, Laugh, Clown, Laugh, Telling the World*, MGM. **Special Awards:** Warner Brothers, for producing *The Jazz Singer*, the pioneer talking picture, which has revolutionized the industry. Charles Chaplin, for versatility and genius in writing, acting, directing and producing *The Circus*.

SECOND YEAR 1928–29

Best Picture: *Broadway Melody*, MGM. Other nominees: *Alibi, Hollywood Revue, In Old Arizona, The Patriot*. **Actor:** Warner Baxter in *In Old Arizona*, Fox. Other nominees: George Bancroft in *Thunderbolt*, Chester Morris in *Alibi*, Paul Muni in *The Valiant*, Lewis Stone in *The Patriot*. **Actress:** Mary Pickford in *Coquette*, UA. Other nominees: Ruth Chatterton in *Madame X*, Betty Compson in *The Barker*, Jeanne Eagels in *The Letter*, Bessie Love in *The Broadway Melody*. **Directing:** Frank Lloyd, *The Divine Lady*, WB. **Art Direction:** *The Bridge of San Luis Rey*, MGM. Cedric Gibbons, Art Director. **Cinematography:** Clyde De Vinna, *White Shadows in the South Seas*, MGM. **Writing—Achievement:** Hans Kraly, *The Patriot*, Par.

Broadway Melody with Mary Doran, Anita Page, Bessie Love and Charles King.

THIRD YEAR 1929–30

Best Picture: *All Quiet on the Western Front*, Univ. Other nominees: *The Big House, Disraeli, The Divorcee, The Love Parade*. **Actor:** George Arliss in *Disraeli*, WB. Other nominees: George Arliss in *The Green Goddess*, Wallace Beery in *The Big House*, Maurice Chevalier in *The Love Parade* and *The Big Pond*, Ronald Colman in *Bulldog Drummond* and *Condemned*, Lawrence Tibbett in *The Rogue Song*. **Actress:** Norma Shearer in *The Divorcee*, MGM. Other nominees: Norma Shearer in *Their Own Desire*, Nancy Carroll in *The Devil's Holiday*, Ruth Chat-

Disraeli with Anthony Bushnell, George Arliss and Joan Bennett.

terton in *Sarah and Son*, Greta Garbo in *Anna Christie* and *Romance*, Gloria Swanson in *The Trespasser*. **Directing:** Lewis Milestone, *All Quiet on the Western Front*. **Art Direction:** *King of Jazz*, Universal. Herman Rosse, Art Director. **Cinematography:** Joseph T. Rucker, Willard Van Der Veer, *With Byrd at the South Pole*, Par. **Sound Recording:** *The Big House*, Metro-Goldwyn-Mayer Sound Department. Douglas Shearer, Sound Director. **Writing—Achievement:** Frances Marion, *The Big House*.

FOURTH YEAR   1930–31

Best Picture: *Cimarron*. RKO. Other nominees: *East Lynne*, *The Front Page*, *Skippy*, *Trader Horn*. **Actor:** Lionel Barrymore in *A Free Soul*, MGM. Other nominees: Jackie Cooper in *Skippy*, Richard Dix in *Cimarron*, Fredric March in *The Royal Family of Broadway*, Adolphe Menjou in *The Front Page*. **Actress:** Marie Dressler in *Min and Bill*, MGM. Other nominees: Marlene Dietrich in *Morocco*, Irene Dunne in *Cimarron*, Ann Harding in *Holiday*, Norma Shearer in *A Free Soul*. **Directing:** Norman Taurog, *Skippy*. **Art Direction:** *Cimarron*. Max Ree, Art Director. **Cinematography:** Floyd Crosby, *Tabu*, Par. **Sound Recording:** Paramount Studio Sound Department. **Writing—Adaptation:** Howard Estabrook, *Cimarron*. **Writing—Original Story:** John Monk Saunders, *The Dawn Patrol*, WB. **Scientific and Technical Awards:** Electrical Research Products, Inc., RCA-Photophone, Inc., and RKO Radio Pictures, Inc., for noise-reduction recording equipment. DuPont Film Manufacturing Corp. and Eastman Kodak Co., for supersensitive panchromatic film. Fox Film Corp., for effective use of synchro-projection composite photography. Electrical Research Products, Inc., for moving-coil microphone transmitters. RKO Radio Pictures, Inc., for reflex-type microphone concentrators. RCA-Photophone, Inc., for ribbon microphone transmitters.

Skippy with Jackie Cooper and Mitzi Green.

Cimarron with Irene Dunne and Richard Dix.

Transatlantic with Edmund Lowe and Myrna Loy.

FIFTH YEAR   1931–32

Best Picture: *Grand Hotel*, MGM. Other nominees: *Arrowsmith*, *Bad Girl*, *The Champ*, *Five Star Final*, *One Hour With You*, *Shanghai Express*, *Smiling Lieutenant*. **Actor:** Fredric March in *Dr. Jekyll and Mr. Hyde*, Par, and Wallace Beery in *The Champ*, MGM. Other nominee: Alfred Lunt in *The Guardsman*. **Actress:** Helen Hayes in *The Sin of Madelon Claudet*, MGM. Other nominees: Marie Dressler in *Emma*, Lynne Fontanne in *The Guardsman*. **Directing:** Frank Borzage, *Bad Girl*, Fox. **Art Direction:** *Transatlantic*, Fox. Gordon Wiles, Art Director. **Cinematography:** Lee Garmes, *Shanghai Express*, Par. **Short Subjects—Cartoon:** *Flowers and Trees*, Disney, UA. **Short Subjects—Comedy:** *The Music Box*, roach, MGM. **Short Subjects—Novelty:** *Wrestling Swordfish*, Sennett, Educational. **Sound Recording:** Paramount Studio Sound Department. **Writing—Adaptation:** Edwin Burke, *Bad Girl*. Writing—**Original Story:** Frances Marion, *The Champ*. **Special Award:** Walt Disney, for the creation of Mickey Mouse. **Scientific and Technical Awards:** Technicolor Motion Picture Corp., for their color cartoon process. Eastman Kodak Co., for the Type II-B Sensitometer.

Dr. Jekyll and Mr. Hyde with Miriam Hopkins and Fredric March.

SIXTH YEAR   1932–33

Best Picture: *Cavalcade*, Fox. Other nominees: *A Farewell to Arms*, *Forty-Second Street*, *I Am a Fugitive from a Chain Gang*, *Lady for a Day*, *Little Women*, *The Private Life of Henry VIII*, *She Done Him Wrong*, *Smilin' Thru*, *State Fair*. **Actor:** Charles Laughton in *The Private Life of Henry VIII*, London Films, UA. Other nominees: Leslie Howard in *Berkeley Square*, Paul Muni in *I Am a Fugitive from a Chain*

Little Women with Paul Lukas and Katharine Hepburn.

Gang. **Actress:** Katharine Hepburn in *Morning Glory*, RKO. Other nominees: May Robson in *Lady for a Day*, Diana Wynyard in *Cavalcade*. **Directing:** Frank Lloyd, *Cavalcade*. **Art Direction:** *Cavalcade*. William S. Darling, Art Director. **Assistant Dirctors:** William Tummel, Fox; Charles Dorian, Metro-Goldwyn-Mayer; Charles Barton, Paramount; Dewey Starkey, RKO Radio; Fred Fox, United Artists; Scott Beal, Universal; Gordon Hollingshead, Warner Brothers. **Cinematography:** Charles Bryant Lang, Jr., *A Farewell to Arms*, Par. **Short Subjects—Cartoon:** *Three Little Pigs*, Disney, UA. **Short Subjects—Comedy:** *So This Is Harris*, RKO. **Short Subjects—Novelty:** *Krakatoa*, Educational. **Sound Recording:** *A Farewell to Arms*, Paramount Studio Sound Department. Franklin Hansen, Sound Director. **Writing—Adaptation:** Sarah Y. Mason, Victor Heerman, *Little Women*, RKO. **Writing—Original Story:** Robert Lord, *One Way Passage*, WB. **Scientific and Technical Awards:** Electrical Research Products, Inc., for their wide-range recording and reproducing system. RCA-Victor Co., Inc., for their high-fidelity recording and reproducing system. Fox Film Corp., Fred Jackman and Warner Bros. Pictures, Inc., and Sidney Sanders of RKO Studios, Inc., for their development and effective use of the translucent cellulose screen in composite photography.

One Way Passage with William Powell and Kay Francis.

Cleopatra with Henry Wilcoxon and Claudette Colbert.

SEVENTH YEAR   1934

Best Picture: *It Happened One Night*, Col. Other nominees: *The Barretts of Wimpole Street, Cleopatra, Flirtation Walk, The Gay Divorcee, Here Comes the Navy, The House of Rothschild, Imitation of Life, One Night of Love, The Thin Man, Viva Villa!, The White Parade.* **Actor:** Clark Gable in *It Happened One Night*. Other nominees: Frank Morgan in *Affairs of Cellini*, William Powell in *The Thin Man*. **Actress:** Claudette Colbert in *It Happened One Night*. Other nominees: Grace Moore in *One Night of Love*, Norma Shearer in *The Barretts of Wimpole Street*. **Directing:** Frank Capra, *It Happened One Night*. **Art Direction:** *The Merry Widow*, MGM. Cedric Gibbons, Frederic Hope, Art Directors. **Assistant Director:** John Waters, *Viva Villa!*, MGM. **Cinematography:** Victor Milner, *Cleopatra*, Par. **Film Editing:** Conrad Nervig, *Eskimo*, MGM. **Music—Score:** *One Night of Love*, Columbia Studio Sound Department. Louis Silvers, Head of Department. Thematic music composed by Victor Schertzinger and Gus Kahn. **Music—Song:** "Continental" from *The Gay Divorcee*, RKO. Music by Con Conrad. Lyrics by Herb Magidson. **Short Subjects—Cartoon:** *The Tortoise and the Hare*, Disney. **Short Subjects—Comedy:** *La Cucaracha*, RKO. **Short Subjects—Novelty:** *City of Wax*, Educational. **Sound Recording:** *One Night of Love*, Columbia Studio Sound Department. John Livadary, Sound Director. **Writing—Adaptation:** Robert Riskin, *It Happened One Night*. **Writing—Original Story:** Arthur Caesar, *Manhattan Melodrama*, MGM. **Special Award:** Shirley Temple, a miniature statuette presented in grateful recognition of her outstanding contribution to screen entertainment during the year 1934. **Scientific and Technical Awards:** Electrical Research Products, Inc., for their development of the vertical-cut disc method of recording sound for motion pictures (hill-and-dale recording). Columbia Pictures Corp., for their application of vertical-cut disc method (hill-and-dale recording) to actual studio production, with their recording of the sound on the picture *One Night of Love*. Bell and Howell Co., for their development of the Bell and Howell fully automatic sound and picture printer.

Eskimo with Peter Freuchen and Mala (hands on gun).

EIGHTH YEAR   1935

Best Picture: *Mutiny on the Bounty*, MGM. Other nominees: *Alice Adams, Broadway Melody of 1936, Captain Blood, David Copperfield, The Informer, Les Miserables, Lives of a Bengal Lancer, A Midsummer Night's Dream, Naughty Marietta, Ruggles of Red Gap, Top Hat.* **Actor:** Victor McLaglen in *The Informer*, RKO. Other nominees: Clark Gable in *Mutiny on the Bounty*, Charles Laughton in *Mutiny on the Bounty*, Franchot Tone in *Mutiny on the Bounty*. **Actress:** Bette Davis in *Dangerous*, WB. Other nominees: Elisabeth Bergner in *Escape Me Never*, Claudette Colbert in *Private Worlds*, Katharine Hepburn in *Alice Adams*, Miriam Hopkins in *Becky Sharp*, Merle Oberon in *The Dark Angel*. **Directing:** John Ford, *The Informer*, RKO. **Art Direction:** *The Dark Angel*, Goldwyn, UA. Richard Day, Art Director. **Assistant Directors:** Clem Beauchamp, Paul Wing, *Lives of a Bengal Lancer*, Par. **Cinematography:** Hal Mohr, *A Midsummer Night's Dream*, WB. **DanceDirection:** Dave Gould, "I've Got a Feeling You're Fooling" number from *Broadway Melody of 1936*, MGM. "Straw Hat" number from *Folies Bergere*, 20th, UA. **Film Editing:** Ralph Dawson, *A Midsummer Night's Dream*. **Music—Score:** *The Informer*, RKO Radio Studio Music Department. Max Steiner, Head of Department. Score composed by Max Steiner. **Music—Song:** "Lullaby of Broadway" from *Gold Diggers of 1935*, WB. Music by Harry Warren. Lyrics by Al Dubin. **Short Subjects—Cartoon:** *Three Orphan Kittens*, Disney, UA. **Short Subjects—Comedy:** *How to Sleep*, MGM. **Short Subjects—Novelty:** *Wings over Mt. Everest*, Gaumont-British, Educational. **Sound Recording:** *Naughty Marietta*, Metro-Goldwyn-Mayer Studio Sound Department. Douglas Shearer, Sound Director. **Writing—Original Story:** Ben Hecht, Charles MacArthur, *The Scoundrel*, Par. **Writing—Best Written Screenplay:** Dudley Nichols, *The Informer*. **Special Award:** David Wark Griffith, for his distinguished creative achievements as director and producer and his invaluable initiative and lasting contributions to the progress of the motion picture arts. **Scientific and Technical Awards:** Agfa Ansco Corp., for their development of the Agfa infrared film. Eastman Kodak Co., for their development of the Eastman Pola-Screen. Metro-Goldwyn-Mayer Studio, for their development of antidirectional negative and positive development by means of jet turbulation, and the application of the method to all negative and print processing of the entire product of a major producing company. William A. Mueller of Warner Brother–First National Studio Sound Department, for his method of dubbing, in which the level of the dialogue automatically controls the level of the accompanying music and sound effects. Mole-Richardson Co., for their development of the "Solar-spot" spot lamps. Douglas Shearer and Metro-Goldwyn-Mayer Studio Sound Department, for their automatic control system for cameras and sound-recording machines and auxiliary stage equipment. Electrical Research Products, Inc., for their study and development of equipment to analyze and measure flutter resulting from the travel of film through the mechanisms used in the recording and reproduction of sound. Paramount Productions, Inc., for the design and construction of the Paramount transparency air turbine developing machine. Nathan Levinson, Director of Sound Recording for Warner Brother–First National Studio, for the method of intercutting variable-density and variable-area sound tracks to secure an increase in the effective volume range of sound recorded for motion pictures.

The Dark Angel with Fredric March, Merle Oberon and Herbert Marshall.

Dodsworth with Ruth Chatterton and Walter Huston.

NINTH YEAR   1936

Best Picture: *The Great Ziegfeld*, MGM. Other nominees: *Anthony Adverse, Dodsworth, Libeled Lady, Mr. Deeds Goes to Town, Romeo and Juliet, San Francisco, The Story of Louis Pasteur, A Tale of Two Cities, Three Smart Girls.* **Actor:** Paul Muni in *The Story of Louis Pasteur*, WB. Other nominees: Gary Cooper in *Mr. Deeds Goes to Town*, Walter Heuston in *Dodsworth*, William Powell in *My Man Godfrey*, Spencer Tracy in *San Francisco*. **Actress:** Luise Rainer in *The Great Ziegfeld*. Other nominees: Irene Dunne in *Theodora Goes Wild*, Gladys George in *Valiant Is the Word for Carrie*, Carole Lombard in *My Man Godfrey*, Norma Shearer in *Romeo and Juliet*. **Supporting Actor:** Walter Brennan in *Come and Get It*, Goldwyn, UA. **Supporting Actress:** Gale Sondergaard in *Anthony Adverse*, WB. **Directing:** Frank Capra, *Mr. Deeds Goes to Town*, Col. **Art Direction:** *Dodsworth*, Goldwyn, UA. Richard Day, Art Director. **Assistant Director:** Jack Sullivan, *The Charge of the Light Brigade*, WB. **Cinematography:** Tony Gaudio, *Anthony Adverse*, **Dance Direction:** Seymour Felix, "A Pretty Girl Is Like a Melody" number from *The Great Ziegfeld*. **Film Editing:** Ralph Dawson, *Anthony Adverse*. **Music—Score:** *Anthony Adverse*, Warner Brothers Studio Music Department. Leo Forbstein, Head of Department. Score composed by Erich Wolfgang Korngold. **Music—Song:** "The Way You Look Tonight" from *Swing Time*, RKO. Music by Jerome Kern. Lyrics by Dorothy Fields. **Short Subjects—Cartoon:** *Country Cousin*, Disney, UA. **Short Subjects—Color:** *Give Me Liberty*, WB. **Short Subjects—One-Reel:** *Bored of Education*, Roach, MGM. **Short Subjects—Two-Reel:** *The Public Pays*, MGM. **Sound Recording:** *San Francisco*, Metro-Goldwyn-Mayer Studio Sound Department. Douglas Shearer, Sound Director. **Writing—Original Story:** Pierre Dollings, Sheridan Gibney, *The Story of Louis Pasteur*. **Writing—Best Written Screenplay:** Pierre Collings, Sheridan Gibney, *The Story of Louis Pasteur*. **Special Awards:** The March of Time, for its significance to motion pictures and for having revolutionized one of the most important branches of the industry—the newsreel. W. Howard Greene and Harold Rosson, for the color cinematography of the Selznick International production, *The Garden of Allah*. **Scientific and Technical** Awards: Douglas Shearer and the Metro-Goldwyn-Mayer Studio Sound Department, for the development of a practical two-way horn system and a biased class A push-pull recording system. E. C. Wente and the Bell Telephone Laboratories, for their multicellular high-frequency horn and receiver. RCA Manufacturing Co., Inc., for their rotary stabilizer sound head. RCA Manufacturing Co., Inc., for their development of a method of recording and printing sound records utilizing a restricted spectrum (known as ultraviolet light recording). Electrical Research Products, Inc., for the ERPI "Type Q" portable recording channel. RCA Manufacturing Co., Inc., for furnishing a practical design and specifications for a non-slip printer. United Artists Studio Corp., for the development of a practical, efficient and quiet wind machine.

TENTH YEAR   1937

Best Picture: *The Life of Emile Zola*, WB. Other nominees: *The Awful Truth, Captains Courageous, Dead End, The Good Earth, In Old Chicago, Lost Horizon, One Hundred Men and a Girl, Stage Door, A Star Is Born.* **Actor:** Spencer Tracy in *Captains Courageous*, MGM. Other

The Good Earth with Luise Rainer and Paul Muni.

nominees: Charles Boyer in *Conquest*, Fredric March in *A Star Is Born*, Robert Montgomery in *Night Must Fall*, Paul Muni in *The Life of Emile Zola*. **Actress:** Luise Rainer in *The Good Earth*. MGM. Other nominees: Irene Dunne in *The Awful Truth*, Greta Garbo in *Camille*, Janet Gaynor in *A Star Is Born*, Barbara Stanwyck in *Stella Dallas*. **Supporting Actor:** Joseph Schildkraut in *The Life of Emile Zola*. **Supporting Actress:** Alice Brady in *In Old Chicago*, 20th. **Directing:** Leo McCarey, *The Awful Truth*, Col. **Art Direction:** *Lost Horizon*, Columbia. Stephen Goosson, Art Director. **Assistant Director:** Robert Webb, *In Old Chicago*. **Cinematography:** Karl Freund, *The Good Earth*. **Dance Direction:** Hermes Pan, "Fun House" number from *A Damsel in Distress*, RKO. **Film Editing:** Gene Milford, Gene Havlick, *Lost Horizon*. **Music—Score:** *One Hundred Men and a Girl*, Universal Studio Music Department, Charles Previn, Head of Department. **Music—Song:** "Sweet Leilani" from *Waikiki Wedding*, Par. Music and lyrics by Harry Owens. **Short Subjects—Cartoon:** *The Old Mill*, Disney, RKO. **Short Subjects—Color:** *Penny Wisdom*, MGM. **Short Subjects—One-Reel:** *Private Life of the Gannets*, Educational. **Short Subjects—Two-Reel:** *Torture Money*, MGM. **Sound Recording:** *The Hurricane*, Samuel Goldwyn Studio Sound Department. Thomas T. Moulton, Sound Director. **Writing—Original Story:** Robert Carson, William A. Wellman, *A Star Is Born*, Selznick International, UA. **Writing—Best Written Screenplay:** Norman Reilly Raine, Heinz Herald, Geza Herczeg, *The Life of Emile Zola*. **Irving G. Thalberg Memorial Award:** Darryl F. Zanuck. **Special Awards:** Mack Sennett, "for his lasting contribution to the comedy technique of the screen,

Lost Horizon with Ronald Colman and Sam Jaffe.

the basic principles of which are as important today as when they were first put into practice, the Academy presents a Special Award to the master of fun, discoverer of stars, sympathetic, kindly, understanding comedy genius—Mack Sennett." Edgar Bergen, for his outstanding comedy creation, Charlie McCarthy. The Museum of Modern Art Film Library, for its significant work in collecting films dating from 1895 to the present and for the first time making available to the public the means of studying the historical and aesthetic development of the motion picture as one of the major arts. W. Howard Greene, for the color photography of *A Star Is Born*. **Scientific and Technical Awards:** Agfa Ansco Corp., for Agfa Supreme and Agfa Ultra Speed pan motion picture negatives. Walt Disney Productions, Ltd., for the design and application to production of the Multi-Plane Camera. Eastman Kodak Co., for two fine-grain duplicating film stocks. Farciot Edouart and Paramount Pictures, Inc., for the development of the Paramount dual-screen transparency camera setup. Douglas Shearer and the Metro-Goldwyn-Mayer Studio Sound Department, for a method of varying the scanning width of variable sound tracks (squeeze tracks) for the purpose of obtaining increased noise reduction. John Arnold and the Metro-Goldwyn-Mayer Studio Camera Department, for their improvement of the semi-automatic follow focus device and its application to all of the cameras used by the Metro-Goldwyn-Mayer Studio. John Livadary, Director of Sound Recording for Columbia Pictures Corp., for the application of the biplanar light valve to motion picture sound recording. Thomas T. Moulton and the United Artists Studio Sound Department, for the application to motion picture sound recording of volume indicators that have peak reading response and linear decibel scales. RCA Manufacturing Co., Inc., for the introduction of the modulated high-frequency method of determining optimum photographic processing conditions for variable-width sound tracks. Joseph E. Robbins and Paramount Pictures, Inc., for an exceptional application of acoustic principles to the soundproofing of gasoline generators and water pumps. Douglas Shearer and the Metro-Goldwyn-Mayer Studio Sound Department, for the design of the film-drive mechanism as incorporated in the ERPI 1010 reproducer.

ELEVENTH YEAR   1938

Best Picture: *You Can't Take It With You*, Col. Other nominees: *The Adventures of Robin Hood, Alexander's Ragtime Band, Boys Town, The Citadel, Four Daughters, Grand Illusion, Jezebel, Pygmalion, Test Pilot.* **Actor:** Spencer Tracy in *Boys Town*, MGM. Other nominees: Charles Boyer in *Algiers*, James Cagney in *Angels With Dirty Faces*, Robert Donat in *The Citadel*, Leslie Howard in *Pygmalion*. **Actress:** Bette Davis in *Jezebel*, WB. Other nominees: Fay Bainter in *White Banners*, Wendy Hiller in *Pygmalion*, Norma Shearer in *Marie Antoinette*, Margaret Sullavan in *Three Comrades*. **Supporting Actor:** Walter Brennan in *Kentucky*, 20th. **Supporting Actress:** Fay Bainter in *Jezebel*. **Directing:** Frank Capra, *You Can't Take It With You*. **Art Direction:** *The Adventures of Robin Hood*, WB. Carl Weyl, Art Director. **Cinematography:** Joseph Ruttenberg, *The Great Waltz*, MGM. **Film Editing:** Ralph Dawson, *The Adventures of Robin Hood*. **Music—Best Score:** Alfred Newman, *Alexander's Ragtime Band*, 20th. **Music—Original Score:** Erich Wolfgang Korngold, *The Adventures of Robin Hood*. **Music—Song:** "Thanks for the Memory" from *The Big Broadcast of 1938*, Par. Music by Ralph Rainger. Lyrics by Leo Robin. **Short Subjects—Cartoon:** *Ferdinand the Bull*, Disney, RKO. **Short Subjects—One-Reel:** *That Mothers Might Live*, MGM. **Short Subjects—Two-Reel:** *Declaration of Independence*, WB. **Sound Recording:** *The Cowboy and the Lady*, Samuel Goldwyn Studio Sound Department. Thomas T. Moulton, Sound Director. **Writing—Adaptation:** W. P. Lipscomb, Cecil Lewis, Ian Dalrymple, *Pygmalion*, MGM. **Writing—Original Story:** Dore Schary, Eleanore Griffin, *Boys Town*. **Writing—Best Written Screenplay:** George Bernard Shaw, *Pygmalion*. **Irving G. Thalberg Award:** Hal B. Wallis. **Special Awards:** Deanna Durbin and Mickey Rooney, for their significant contribution in bringing to the screen the spirit and personification of youth, and as juvenile players setting a high standard of ability and achievement. Harry M. Warner, in recognition of patriotic service in the production of historical short subjects presenting significant episodes in the early

You Can't Take It With You with Mary Forbes, Jean Arthur and Ann Miller.

struggle of the American people for liberty. Walt Disney, for *Snow White and the Seven Dwarfs*, recognized as a significant screen innovation which has charmed millions and pioneered a great new entertainment field for the motion picture cartoon. Oliver Marsh and Allen Davey, for the color cinematography for the Metro-Goldwyn-Mayer production *Sweethearts*. For outstanding achievement in Special Photographic and Sound Effects in the Paramount production *Spawn of the North*. Special Effects by Gordon Jennings, assisted by Jan Domela, Dev Jennings, Irmin Roberts and Art Smith. Transparencies by Farciot Edouart, assisted by Loyal Griggs. Sound Effects by Loren Ryder, assisted by Harry Mills, Louis H. Mesenkop and Walter Oberst. J. Arthur Ball, for his outstanding contributions to the advancement of color in motion picture photography. **Scientific and Technical Awards:** John Aalberg and the RKO Radio Studio Sound Department, for the application of compression to variable-arearecording in motion picture production. Byron Haskin and the Special Effects Department of Warner Bros. Studio, for pioneering the development and for the first practical application to motion picture production of the triple-head background projector.

TWELFTH YEAR 1939

Best Picture: *Gone With the Wind*, Selznick International, MGM. Other nominees: *Dark Victory, Goodbye, Mr. Chips, Love Affair, Mr. Smith Goes to Washington, Ninotchka, Of Mice and Men, Stagecoach, Wizard of Oz, Wuthering Heights.* **Actor:** Robert Donat in *Goodbye, Mr. Chips*, MGM. Other nominees: Clark Gable in *Gone With the Wind*, Laurence Olivier in *Wuthering Heights*, Mickey Rooney in *Babes in Arms*, James Stewart in *Mr. Smith Goes to Washington.* **Actress:** Vivien Leigh in *Gone With the Wind.* Other nominees: Bette Davis in *Dark Victory*, Irene Dunne in *Love Affair*, Greta Garbo in *Ninotchka*, Greer Garson in *Goodbye, Mr. Chips.* **Supporting Actor:** Thomas Mitchell in *Stagecoach*, Wanger, UA. **Supporting Actress:** Hattie McDaniel in *Gone With the Wind.* **Directing:** Victor Fleming, *Gone With the Wind.* **Art Direction:** *Gone With the Wind.* Lyle Wheeler, Art Director. **Cinematography—Black-and-White:** Gregg Toland, *Wuthering Heights*, Goldwyn, UA. **Cinematography—Color:** Ernest Haller, Ray Rennahan, *Gone With the Wind.* **Film Editing:** Hal C. Kern, James E. Newcom, *Gone With the Wind.* **Music—Best Score:** Richard Hageman, Franke Harling, John Leipold, Leo Shuken, *Stagecoach.* **Music—Original Score:** Herbert Stothart, *The Wizard of Oz*, MGM. **Music—Song:** "Over the Rainbow" from *The Wizard of Oz.* Music by Harold Arlen. Lyrics by E. Y. Harburg. **Short Subjects—Cartoon:** *The Ugly Duckling*, Disney, RKO. **Short Subjects—One-Reel:** *Busy Little Bears*, Par. **Short Subjects—Two-Reel:** *Sons of Liberty*, WB. **Sound Recording:** *When Tomorrow Comes*, Universal Studio Sound Department. Bernard B. Brown, Sound Director. **Special Effects:** *The Rains Came*, 20th. Fred Sersen, E. H. Hansen. **Writing—Original Story:** Lewis R. Foster, *Mr. Smith Goes to Washington*, Col. **Writing—Best Written Screenplay:** Sidney Howard, *Gone With the*

Wind. **Irving G. Thalberg Memorial Award:** David O. Selznick. **Special Awards:** Douglas Fairbanks (Commemorative Award). Recognizing the unique and outstanding contribution of Douglas Fairbanks, first President of the Academy, to the international development of the motion picture. The Motion Picture Relief Fund, acknowledging the outstanding services to the industry during the past year of the Motion Picture Relief Fund and its progressive leadership. Presented to Jean Hersholt, President; Ralph Morgan, Chairman of the Executive Committee; Ralph Block, First Vice-President; Conrad Nagel. The Technicolor Company, for its contributions in successfully bringing three-color feature production to the screen. Judy Garland, for her outstanding performance as a screen juvenile during the past year. William Cameron Menzies, for outstanding achievement in the use of color for the enhancement of dramatic mood in the production *Gone With the Wind.* **Scientific and Technical Awards:** George Anderson of Warner Bros. Studio, for an improved positive head for sun arcs. John Arnold of Metro-Goldwyn-Mayer Studio, for the MGM mobile camera crane. Thomas T. Moulton, Fred Albin and the Sound Department of the Samuel Goldwyn Studio, for the origination and application of the Delta db test to sound recording in motion pictures. Farciot Edouart, Joseph E. Robbins, William Rudolph and Paramount Pictures, Inc., for the design and construction of a quiet portable treadmill. Emery Huse and Ralph B. Atkinson of Eastman Kodak Co., for their specifications for chemical analysis of photographic developers and fixing baths. Harold Nye of Warner Bros. Studio, for a miniature incandescent spot lamp. A. J. Tondreau of Warner Bros. Studio, for the design and manufacture of an improved sound track printer. Multiple Award for important contributions in cooperative development of new improved Process Projection Equipment: E. R. Abbott, Haller Belt, Alan Cook and Bausch & Lomb Optical Co., for faster projection lenses; Mitchell Camera Co., for a new type process projection head; Mole-Richardson Co., for a new type automatically-controlled projection arc lamp; Charles Handley, David Joy and National Carbon Co., for improved and more stable high-intensity carbons; Winton Hoch and Technicolor Motion Picture Corp., for an auxiliary optical system; Don Musgrave and Selznick International Pictures, Inc., for pioneering in the use of coordinated equipment in the production *Gone With the Wind.*

Wuthering Heights with Geraldine Fitzgerald and Laurence Olivier.

THIRTEENTH YEAR 1940

Best Picture: *Rebecca*, Selznick International, UA. Other nominees: *All This, and Heaven Too, Foreign Correspondent, The Grapes of Wrath, The Great Dictator, Kitty Foyle, The Letter, The Long Voyage Home, Our Town, The Philadelphia Story.* **Actor:** James Stewart in *The Philadelphia Story*, MGM. Other nominees: Charles Chaplin in *The Great Dictator*, Henry Fonda in *The Grapes of Wrath*, Raymond Massey in *Abe Lincoln in Illinois*, Laurence Olivier in *Rebecca.* **Actress:** Ginger Rogers in *Kitty Foyle*, RKO. Other nominees: Bette Davis in *The Letter*, Joan Fontaine in *Rebecca*, Katharine Hepburn in *The Philadelphia Story*, Martha Scott in *Our Town.* **Supporting Actor:**

The Westerner with Walter Brennan and Gary Cooper.

Walter Brennan in *The Westerner*, Goldwyn, UA. **Supporting Actress:** Jane Darwell in *The Grapes of Wrath*, 20th. **Directing:** John Ford, *The Grapes of Wrath*. **Art Direction—Black-and-White:** *Pride and Prejudice*, MGM. Cedric Gibbons, Paul Groesse, Art Directors. **Art Direction—Color:** *The Thief of Bagdad*, Korda, UA. Vincent Korda, Art Director. **Cinematography—Black-and-White:** George Barnes, *Rebecca*. **Cinematography-Color:** George Perrinal, *The Thief of Bagdad*. **Film Editing:** Anne Bauchens, *North West Mounted Police*, Par. **Music—Best Score:** Alfred Newman, *Tin Pan Alley*, 20th. **Music—Orignial Score:** Leigh Harline, Paul J. Smith, Ned Washington, *Pinocchio*, Disney, RKO. **Music—Song:** "When You Wish Upon a Star" from *Pinocchio*. Music by Leigh Harline. Lyrics by Ned Washington. **Short Subjects—Cartoon:** *Milky Way*, MGM. **Short Subjects—One-Reel:** *Quicker 'n a Wink*, MGM. **Short Subjects—Two-Reel:** *Teddy, the Rough Rider*, WB. **Sound Recording:** *Strike Up the Band*, Metro-Goldwyn-Mayer Sound Department. Douglas Shearer, Sound Director. **Special Effects:** *The Thief of Bagdad*. Lawrence Butler (Photographic); Jack Whitney (Sound). **Writing—Original Screenplay:** Preston Struges, *The Great McGinty*, Par. **Writing—Original Story:** Benjamin Glazer, John S. Toldy, *Arise, My Love*, Par. **Writing—Best Written Screenplay:** Donald Ogden Stewart, *The Philadelphia Story*. **Special Awards:** Bob Hope, in recognition of his unselfish services to the motion picture industry. Colonel Nathan Levinson, for his outstanding service to the industry and the Army during the past nine years, which has made possible the present efficient mobilization of the motion picture industry facilities for the production of Army Training Films. **Scientific and Technical Awards:** 20th Century-Fox Film Corp., for the design and construction of the 20th Century Silenced Camera, developed by Daniel Clark, Grover Laube, Charles Miller and Robert W. Stevens. Warner Bros. Studio Art Department and Anton Grot, for the design and perfection of the Warner Bros. water ripple and wave illusion machine.

FOURTEENTH YEAR   1941

Best Picture: *How Green Was My Valley*, 20th. Other nominees: *Blossoms in the Dust, Citizen Kane, Here Comes Mr. Jordan, Hold Back the Dawn, The Little Foxes, The Maltese Falcon, One Foot in Heaven, Sergeant York, Suspicion*. **Actor:** Gary Cooper in *Sergeant York*. WB. Other nominees: Cary Grant in *Penny Serenade*, Walter Huston in *All That Money Can Buy*, Robert Montgomery in *Here Comes Mr. Jordan*, Orson Welles in *Citizen Kane*. **Actress:** Joan Fontaine in *Suspicion*, RKO. Other nominees: Bette Davis in *The Little Foxes*, Olivia De Havilland in *Hold Back the Dawn*, Greer Garson in *Blossoms in the Dust*, Barbara Stanwyck in *Ball of Fire*. **Supporting Actor:** Donald Crisp in *How Green Was My Valley*. **Supporting Actress:** Mary Astor in *The Great Lie*, WB. **Directing:** John Ford, *How Green Was My Valley*. **Art Direction—Blck-and-White:** *How Green Was My Valley*. Richard Day, Nathan Juran, Art Directors. Thomas Little, Interior Decorator. **Art Direction—Color:** *Blossoms in the Dust*, MGM. Cedric Gibbons, Urie McCleary, Art Directors. Edwin B. Willis, Interior Decorator. **Cinematography—Black-and-White:** Arthur Miller, *How Green Was My Valley*. **Cinematography Color:** Ernest Palmer, Ray Rennahan, *Blood and Sand*, 20th. **Film Editing:** William Holmes, *Sergeant York*. **Music—Scoring Musical**

Suspicion with Joan Fontaine and Cary Grant.

Picture: Frank Churchill, Oliver Wallace, *Dumbo*, Disney, RKO. **Music—Music Score of a Dramatic Picture:** Bernard Herrmann, *All That Money Can Buy*, RKO. **Music—Song:** "The Last Time I Saw Paris" from *Lady Be Good*, MGM. Music by Jerome Kern. Lyrics by Oscar Hammerstein II. **Short Subjects—Cartoon:** *Lend a Paw*, Disney, RKO. **Short Subjects—One-Reel:** *Of Pups and Puzzles*, MGM. **Short Subjects—Two-Reel:** *Main Street on the March*, MGM. **Sound Recording:** *That Hamilton Woman*, Korda, UA. General Service Studio Sound Department. Jack Whitney, Sound Director. **Special Effects:** *I Wanted Wings*, Paramount. Farciot Edouart, Gordon Jennings (Photographic); Louis Mesenkop (Sound). **Writing—Original Screenplay:** Herman J. Mankiewicz, Orson Welles, *Citizen Kane*, Mercury, RKO. **Writing—Original Story:** Harry Segall, *Here Comes Mr. Jordan*, Col. **Writing—Best Written Screenplay:** Sidney Buchman, Seton I. Miller, *Here Comes Mr. Jordan*. **Irving G. Thalberg Memorial Award:** Walter E. Disney. **Special Awards:** *Churchill's Island*, Canadian National Film Board. Citation for distinctive achievement in short subjects documentary production. Rey Scott, for his extraordinary achievement in producing *Kukan*, the film record of China's struggle, including photography with a 16-mm camera under the most difficult and dangerous conditions. The British Ministry of Information, for its vivid and dramatic presentation of the heroism of the R.A.F. in the documentary film, *Target for Tonight*. Walt Disney, William Garity, John N. A. Hawkins and the RCA Manufacturing Company, for their outstanding contribution to the advancement of the use of sound in motion pictures through the production of *Fantasia*. Leopold Stokowski and his associates, for their unique achievement in the creation of a new form of visualized music in Walt Disney's production *Fantasia*, thereby widening the scope of the motion picture as entertainment and as an art form. **Scientific and Technical Awards:** Electrical Research Products Division of Western Electric Co., Inc., for the development of the precision integrating sphere densitometer. RCA Manufacturing Co., for the design and development of the MI-3043 Uni-directional microphone. Ray Wilkinson and the Paramount Studio Laboratory, for pioneering the use of and for the first practical application to release printing of fine-grain positive stock. Charles Lootens and the Republic Studio Sound Department, for pioneering the use of and for the first practical application to motion picture production of Class B push-pull variable-area recording. Wilber Silvertooth and the Paramount Studio Engineering Department, for the design and computation of a relay condenser system applicable to transparency process projection, delivering considerably more usable light. Paramount Pictures, Inc., and 20th Century-Fox Film Corp., for the development and first practical application to motion picture production of an automatic scene-slating device. Douglas Shearer and the Metro-Goldwyn-Mayer Studio Sound Department, and Loren Ryder and the Paramount Studio Sound Department, for pioneering the development of fine-grain emulsions for variable-density original sound recording in studio production.

FIFTEENTH YEAR   1942

Best Picture: *Mrs. Miniver*, MGM. Other nominees: *The Invaders, Kings Row, The Magnificent Ambersons, The Pied Piper, The Pride of the Yankees, Random Harvest, The Talk of the Town, Wake Island, Yankee Doodle Dandy*. **Actor:** James Cagney in *Yankee Doodle Dandy*, WB. Other nominees: Ronald Colman in *Random Harvest*, Gary Cooper in *The Pride of the Yankees*, Walter Pidgeon in *Mrs. Miniver*, Monty Woolley in *The Pied Piper*. **Actress:** Greer Garson in *Mrs. Miniver*. Other nominees: Bette Davis in *Now, Voyager*, Katharine Hepburn in *Woman of the Year*, Rosalind Russell in *My Sister Eileen*, Teresa Wright in *The Pride of the Yankees*. **Supporting Actor:** Van Heflin in *Johnny Eager*, MGM. **Supporting Actress:** Teresa Wright in *Mrs. Miniver*. **Directing:** William Wyler, *Mrs. Miniver*. **Art Direction—Black-and-White:** *This Above All*, 20th. Richard Day, Joseph Wright, Art Directors. Thomas Little, Interior Decorator. **Art Direction—Color:** *My Gal Sal*, 20th. Richard Day, Joseph Wright, Art Directors. Thomas Little, Interior Decorator. **Cinematography—Black-and-White:** Joseph Ruttenberg, *Mrs. Miniver*. **Cinematography—Color:** Leon Shamroy, *The Black Swan*, 20th. **Film Editing:** Daniel Mandell, *The Pride of the Yankees*, Goldwyn, RKO. **Music—Scoring Musical Picture:** Ray Heindorf, Heinz Roemheld, *Yankee Doodle Dandy*. **Music—Music Score of a Dramatic or Comedy Picture:** Max Steiner, *Now, Voyager*, WB. **Music—Song:** "White Christmas" from *Holiday Inn*, Par. Music and lyrics by Irving Berlin. **Short Subjects—Cartoon:** *Der Fuehrer's Face*, Disney, RKO. **Short Subjects—One-Reel:** *Speaking of Animals and Their Families*, Par. **Short Subjects—Two-Reel:** *Beyond the Line of Duty*, WB. **Sound Recording:** *Yankee Doodle Dandy*, Warner Brothers Studio Sound Department. Nathan Levinson, Sound Director. **Special Effects:** *Reap the Wild Wind*, Par. Gordon Jennings, Farciot Edouart, William L. Pereira (Photographic); Louis Mesenkop (Sound). **Writing—Original Screenplay:** Ring Lardner, Jr., Michael Kanin, *Woman of the Year*, MGM. **Writing—Original Story:** Emeric Pressburger, *The Invaders*, Ortus, Columbia (British). **Writing—Best Written Screenplay:** Arthur Wimperis, George Froeschel, James Hilton, Claudine West, *Mrs. Miniver*. **Irving G. Thalberg Memorial Award:** Sidney Franklin. **Documentary:** *Battle Of Midway*, U.S. Navy, 20th. *Kokoda Front Line*, Australian News Information Bureau. *Moscow Strikes Back*, Artkino (Russian). *Prelude to War*, U.S. Army Special Services. **Special Awards:** Charles Boyer, for his progressive cultural achievement in establishing the French Research Foundation in Los Angeles as a source of reference for the Hollywood Motion Picture Industry. Noel Coward, for his outstanding production achievement, *In Which We Serve*. Metro-Goldwyn-Mayer Studio, for its achievement in representing the American Way of Life in the production of the *Andy Hardy* series of films. **Scientific and Technical Awards:** Carroll Clark, F. Thomas Thompson and the RKO Radio Studio Art and Miniature Departments, for the design and construction of a moving cloud and horizon machine. Daniel B. Clark and the 20th Century-Fox Film Corp., for the development of a lens calibration system and the application of this system to exposure control in cinematography. Robert Henderson and the Paramount Studio Engineering and Transparency Departments, for the design and construction of adjustable light bridges and screen frames for transparency process photography. Daniel J. Bloomberg and the Republic Studio Sound Department, for the design and application to motion picture production of a device for marking action negatives for pre-selection purposes.

SIXTEENTH YEAR   1943

Best Picture: *Casablanca*, WB. Other nominees: *For Whom the Bell Tolls, Heaven Can Wait, The Human Comedy, In Which We Serve, Madame Curie, The More the Merrier, The Ox-Bow Incident, The Song Of Bernadette, Watch on the Rhine*. **Actor:** Paul Lukas in *Watch on the Rhine*, WB. Other nominees: Humphrey Bogart in *Casablanca*,

Watch on the Rhine with George Coulouris, Paul Lukas and Bette Davis.

Gary Cooper in *For Whom the Bell Tolls*, Walter Pidgeon in *Madame Curie*, Mickey Rooney in *The Human Comedy*. **Actress:** Jennifer Jones in *The Song of Bernadette*, 20th. Other nominees: Jean Arthur in *The More the Merrier*, Ingrid Bergman in *For Whom the Bell Tolls*, Joan Fontaine in *The Constant Nymph*, Greer Garson in *Madame Curie*. **Supporting Actor:** Charles Coburn in *The More the Merrier*, Columbia. **Supporting Actress:** Katina Paxinou in *For Whom the Bell Tolls*, Par. **Directing:** Michael Curtiz, *Casablanca*, WB. **Art Direction—Black-and-White:** *The Song of Bernadette*. James Basevi, William Darling, Art Directors. Thomas Little, Interior Decorator. **Art Direction—Color:** *The Phantom of the Opera*, Univ. Alexander Golitzen, John B. Goodman, Art Directors. Russell A. Gausman, Ira S. Webb, Interior Decorators. **Cinematography—Black-and-White:** Arthur Miller, *The Song of Bernadette*. **Cinematography—Color:** Hal Mohr, W. Howard Greene, *The Phantom of the Opera*. **Film Editing:** George Amy, *Air Force*, WB. **Music—Scoring Musical Picture:** Ray Heindorf, *This Is the Army*, WB. **Music—Music Score of a Dramatic or Comedy Picture:** Alfred Newman, *The Song of Bernadette*. **Music—Song:** "You'll Never Know" from *Hello, Frisco, Hello*, 20th. Music by Harry Warren. Lyrics by Mack Gordon. **Short Subjects—Cartoon:** *Yankee Doodle Mouse*, MGM. **Short Subjects—One-Reel:** *Amphibious Fighters*, Par. **Short Subjects—Two-Reel:** *Heavenly Music*, MGM. **Sound Recording** *This Land Is Mine*, RKO Radio Studio Sound Department. Stephen Dunn, Sound Director. **Special Effects:** *Crash Dive*, 20th. Fred Sersen (Photographic); Roger Heman (Sound). **Writing—Original Screenplay:** Norman Krasna, *Princess O'Rourke*, WB. **Writing—Original Story:** William Saroyan, *The Human Comedy*, MGM. **Writing—Best Written Screenplay:** Julius J. Epstein, Philip G. Epstein, Howard Koch, *Casablanca*. **Irving G. Thalberg Memorial Award:** Hal B. Wallis. **Documentary—Feature:** *Desert Victory*, British Ministry of Information. **Documentary—Short Subject:** *December 7th*, U.S. Navy. **Special Award:** George Pal, for the development of novel methods and techniques in the production of the short subjects known as *Puppetoons*. **Scientific and Technical Awards:** Farciot Edouart, Earle Morgan, Barton Thompson and the Paramount Studio

The Phantom of the Opera with Claude Rains and Susanna Foster.

Engineering and Transparency Department, for the development and practical application to motion picture production of a method of duplicating and enlarging natural color photographs, transferring the image emulsions to glass plates and projecting these slides by specially designed stereopticon equipment. Photo Products Department, E. I. duPont de Nemours and Co., Inc., for the development of fine-grain motion picture films. Daniel J. Bloomberg and the Republic Studio Sound Department, for the design and development of an inexpensive method of converting Moviolas to Class B push-pull reproduction. Charles Galloway Clarke and the 20th Century-Fox Studio Camera Department, for the development and practical application of a device for composing artificial clouds into motion picture scenes during production photography. Farciot Edouart and the Paramount Studio Transparency Department, for an automatic electric transparency cueing timer. Willard H. Turner and the RKO Radio Studio Sound Department, for the design and construction of the phono-cue starter.

A Tree Grows in Brooklyn with Peggy Ann Garner and James Dunn.

SEVENTEENTH YEAR   1944

Best Picture: *Going My Way*, Par. Other nominees: *Double Indemnity, Gaslight, Since You Went Away, Wilson.* **Actor:** Bing Crosby in *Going My Way.* Other nominees: Charles Boyer in *Gaslight*, Barry Fitzgerald in *Going My Way*, Cary Grant in *None But the Lonely Heart*, Alexander Knox in *Wilson.* **Actress:** Ingrid Bergman in *Gaslight*, MGM. Other nominees: Claudette Colbert in *Since You Went Away*, Bette Davis in *Mr. Skeffington*, Greer Garson in *Mrs. Parkington*, Barbara Stanwyck in *Double Indemnity.* **Supporting Actor:** Barry Fitzgerald in *Going My Way.* **Supporting Actress:** Ethel Barrymore in *None But the Lonely Heart*, RKO. **Directing:** Leo McCarey, *Going My Way.* **Art Direction—Black-and-White:** *Gaslight*, MGM. Cedric Gibbons, William Ferrari, Art Directors, Edwin B. Willis, Paul Huldschinsky, Interior Decorators. **Art Direction—Color:** *Wilson*, 20th. Wiard Ihnen, Art Director. Thomas Little, Interior Decorator. **Cinematography—Black-and-White:** Joseph LaShelle, *Laura*, 20th. **Cinematography—Color:** Leon Shamroy, *Wilson.* **Music—Scoring Musical Picture:** Morris Stoloff, Carmen Dragon, *Cover Girl*, Col. **Music—Music Score of a Dramatic or Comedy Picture:** Max Steiner, *Since You Went Away*, Selznick International, UA. **Music—Song:** "Swinging on a Star" from *Going My Way*, Music by James Van Heusen. Lyrics by Johnny Burke. **Short Subjects—Cartoon:** *Mouse Trouble*, MGM. **Short Subjects—One-Reel:** *Who's Who in Animal Land*, Par. **Short Subjects—Two-Reel:** *I Won't Play*, WB. **Sound Recording:** *Wilson*, 20th Century-Fox Studio Sound Department. E. H. Hansen, Sound Director. **Special Effects:** *Thirty Seconds Over Tokyo*, MGM. A. Arnold Gillespie, Donald Jahraus, Warren Newcombe (Photographic); Douglas Shearer (Sound). **Writing—Original Screenplay:** Lamar Trotti, *Wilson.* **Writing—Original Story:** Leo McCarey, *Going My Way.* **Writing—Best Written Screenplay:** Frank Butler, Frank Cavett, *Going My Way.* **Irving G. Thalberg Memorial Award:** Darryl F. Zanuck. **Documentary—Feature:** *The Fighting Lady*, U.S. Navy, 20th. **Documentary—Short Subject:** *With the Marines at Tarawa*, U.S. Marine Corps. **Special Awards:** Margaret O'Brien, outstanding child actress of 1944. Bob Hope, for his many services to the Academy, a Life Membership in The Academy of Motion Picture Arts and Sciences. **Scientific and Technical Awards:** Stephen Dunn and the RKO Radio Studio Sound Department and Radio Corporation of America, for the design and development of the electronic compressor-limiter. Linwood Dunn, Cecil Love and Acme Tool Manufacturing Co., for the design and construction of the Acme-Dunn Optical Printer. Grover Laube and the 20th Century-Fox Studio Camera Department, for the development of a continuous-loop projection device. Western Electric Co., for the design and construction of the 1126A Limiting Amplifier for variable-density sound recording. Russell Brown, Ray Hinsdale and Joseph E. Robbins, for the development and production use of the Paramount floating hydraulic boat rocker. Gordon Jennings, for the design and construction of the Paramount nodal point tripod. Radio Corporation of America and the RKO Studio Sound Department, for the design and construction of the RKO reverberation chamber. Daniel J. Bloomberg and the Republic Studio Sound Department, for the design and development of a multi-interlock selector switch. Bernard B. Brown and John P. Livadary, for the design and engineering of a separate soloist and chorus recording room. Paul Zeff, S. J. Twining and George Seid of the Columbia Studio Labora-

tory, for the formula and application to production of a simplified variable-area sound negative developer. Paul Lerpae, for the design and construction of the Paramount traveling matte projection and Photographing device.

EIGHTEENTH YEAR   1945

Best Picture: *The Lost Weekend*, Par. Other nominees: *Anchors Aweigh, The Bells of St. Mary's, Mildred Pierce, Spellbound.* **Actor:** Ray Milland in *The Lost Weekend.* Other nominees: Bing Crosby in *The Bells of St. Mary's*, Gene Kelly in *Anchors Aweigh*, Gregory Peck in *The Keys of the Kingdom*, Cornel Wilde in *A Song to Remember.* **Actress:** Joan Crawford in *Mildred Pierce*, WB. Other nominees: Ingrid Bergman in *The Bells of St. Mary's*, Greer Garson in *The Valley of Decision*, Jennifer Jones in *Love Letters*, Gene Tierney in *Leave Her to Heaven.* **Supporting Actor:** James Dunn in *A Tree Grows in Brooklyn*, 20th. **Supporting Actress:** Anne Revere in *National Velvet*, MGM. **Directing:** Billy Wilder, *The Lost Weekend.* **Art Direction—Black-and-White:** *Blood on the Sun*, Cagney, UA. Wiard Ihnen, Art Director. A. Roland Fields, Interior Decorator. **Art Direction—Color:** *Frenchman's Creek*, Paramount. Hans Dreier, Ernst Fegte, Art Directors, Sam Comer, Interior Decorator. **Cinematography—Black-and-White:** Harry Stradling, *The Picture of Dorian Gray*, MGM. **Cinematography—Color:** Leon Shamroy, *Leave Her to Heaven*, 20th. **Film Editing:** Robert J. Kern, *National Velvet.* **Music—Scoring Musical Picture:** Georgie Stoll, *Anchors Aweigh*, MGM. **Music—Music Score of a Dramatic or Comedy Picture:** Miklos Rozsa, *Spellbound*, Selznick, UA. **Music—Song:** "It Might as Well Be Spring" from *State Fair*, 20th. Music by Richard Rodgers. Lyrics by Oscar Hammerstein II. **Short Subjects—Cartoon:** *Quiet, Please*, MGM. **Short Subjects—One-Reel:** *Stairway to Light*, MGM. **Short Subjects—Two-Reel:** *Star in the Night*, WB. **Sound Recording:** *The Bells of St. Mary's*, RKO Studio Sound Department. Stephen Dunn, Sound Director. **Special Effects:** *Wonder Man*, Beverly, RKO. John Fulton (Photographic); Arthur W. Johns (Sound). **Writing—Original Screenplay:** Richard Schweizer, *Marie-Louise*, Praesens (Swiss). **Writing—Original Story:** Charles G. Booth, *The House on 92nd Street*, 20th. **Writing—Best Written Screenplay:** Charles Brackett, Billy Wilder, *The Lost Weekend.* **Documentary—Feature:** *The True Glory*, Governments of Great Britain and the U.S. **Documentary—Short Subject:** *Hilter Lives?*, WB. **Special Awards:** Walter Wanger, for his six years' service as President of the Academy. Peggy Ann Garner, outstanding child actress of 1945. *The House I Live In*, tolerance short subject. Produced by Frank Ross and Mervyn LeRoy. Directed by Mervyn LeRoy. Screenplay by Albert Maltz. Song, "The House I Live In." Music by Earl Robinson. Lyrics by Lewis Allen. Starring Frank Sinatra. Released by RKO Radio. Republic Studios, Daniel J. Bloomberg and the Republic Studios Sound Department, for the building of an outstanding musical scoring auditorium which provides optimum recording conditions and combines all elements of acoustic and engineering design. **Scientific and Technical Awards:** Loren L. Ryder, Charles R. Daily and the Paramount Studio Sound Department, for the design, construction and use of the first dial-controlled step-by-step sound channel line-up and test circuit. Michael S. Leshing, Benjamin C. Robinson, Arthur B. Chatelain and Robert

C. Stevens of 20th Century-Fox Studio and John G. Capstaff of Eastman Kodak Co., for the 20th Century-Fox film processing machine.

NINETEENTH YEAR 1946

Best Picture: *The Best Years of Our Lives*, Goldwyn, RKO. Other nominees: *Henry V, It's a Wonderful Life, The Razor's Edge, The Yearling*. **Actor:** Fredric March in *The Best Years of Our Lives*. Other nominees: Laurence Olivier in *Henry V*, Larry Parks in *The Jolson Story*, Gregory Peck in *The Yearling*, James Stewart in *It's a Wonderful Life*. **Actress:** Olivia De Havilland in *To Each His Own*, Par. Other nominees: Celia Johnson in *Brief Encounter*, Jennifer Jones in *Duel in the Sun*, Rosalind Russell in *Sister Kenny*, Jane Wyman in *The Yearling*. **Supporting Actor:** Harold Russell in *The Best Years of Our Lives*. **Supporting Actress:** Anne Baxter in *The Razor's Edge*, 20th. **Directing:** William Wyler, *The Best Years of Our Lives*. **Art Direction—Balck-and-White:** *Anna and the King of Siam*, 20th. Lyle Wheeler, William Darling, Art Directors. Thomas Little, Frank E. Hughes, Interior Decorators. **Art Direction—Color:** *The Yearling*, MGM. Cedric Gibbons, Paul Groesse, Art Directors, Edwin B. Willis, Interior Decorator. **Cinematography—Black-and-White:** Arthur Miller, *Anna and the King of Siam*. **Cinematography—Color:** Charles Rosher, Leonard Smith, Arthur Arling, *The Yearling*. **Film Editing:** Daniel Mandell, *The Best Years of Our Lives*. Music—Scoring Musical Picture: Morris Stoloff, *The Jolson Story*, Col. **Music—Music Score of a Dramatic or Comedy Picture:** Hugo Friedhofer, *The Best Years of Our Lives*. **Music—Song:** "On the Atchison, Topeka and Santa Fe" from *The Harvey Girls*, MGM. Music by Harry Warren. Lyrics by Johnny Mercer. **Short Subjects—Cartoon:** *The Cat Concerto*, MGM. **Short Subjects—One-Reel:** *Facing Your Danger*, WB. **Short Subjects—Two-Reel:** *A Boy and His Dog*, WB. **Sound Recording:** *The Jolson Story*, Columbia Studio Sound Department. John Livadary, Sound Director. **Special Effects:** *Blithe Spirit*, Rank-Coward-Cineguild, United Artists (British). Thomas Howard (Photographic). **Writing—Original Screenplay:** Muriel Box, Sydney Box, *The Seventh Veil*, Rank-Box-Ortus, Universal (British). **Writing—Original Story:** Clemence Dane, *Vacation From Marriage*, London, Metro-Goldwyn-Mayer (British). **Writing—Best Written Screenplay:** Robert E. Sherwood, *The Best Years of Our Lives*. **Documentary—Short Subject:** *Seeds of Destiny*, U.S. War Department. **Irving G. Thalberg Memorial Award:** Samuel Goldwyn. **Special Awards:** Laurence Olivier, for his outstanding achievement as actor, producer and director in bringing *Henry V* to the screen. Harold Russell, for bringing hope and courage to his fellow veterans through his appearance in *The Best Years of Our Lives*. Ernst Lubitsch, for his distinguished contributions to the art of the motion picture. Claude Jarman, Jr., outstanding child actor of 1946. **Scientific and Technicl Awards:** Harlan L. Baumbach and the Paramount West Coast Laboratory, for an improved method for the quantitative determination of hydroquinone and metol in photographic developing baths. Herbert E. Britt, for the development and application of formulas and equipment for producing cloud and smoke effects. Burton F. Miller and the Warner Bros. Studio Sound and Electrical Departments, for the design and construction of a motion picture arc-lighting generator filter. Carl Faulkner of the 20th Century-Fox Studio Sound Department, for the reversed bias method, including a double bias method, for light valve and galvanometer density recording. Mole-Richardson Co., for the Type 450 super-high-intensity carbon arc lamp. Arthur F. Blinn, Robert O. Cook, C. O. Slyfield and the Walt Disney Studio Sound Department, for the design and development of an audio finder and track viewer for checking and locating noise in sound tracks. Burton F. Miller and the Warner Bros. Studio Sound Department, for the design and application of an equalizer to eliminate relative spectral energy distortion in electronic compressors. Marty Martin and Hal Adkins of the RKO Radio Studio Miniature Department, for the design and construction of equipment providing visual bullet effects. Harold Nye and the Warner Bros., Studio Electrical Department, for the development of the electronically controlled fire and gaslight effect.

TWENTIETH YEAR 1947

Best Picture: *Gentleman's Agreement*, 20th. Other nominees: *The Bishop's Wife, Crossfire, Great Expectations, Miracle on 34th Street.*

Actor: Ronald Colman in *A Double Life*, Kanin, Univ. Other nominees: John Garfield in *Body and Soul*, Gregory Peck in *Gentleman's Agreement*, William Powell in *Life with Father*, Michael Redgrave in *Mourning Becomes Electra*. **Actress:** Loretta Young in *The Farmer's Daughter*, RKO. Other nominees: Joan Crawford in *Possessed*, Susan Hayward in *Smash Up—The Story of a Woman*, Dorothy McGuire in *Gentleman's Agreement*, Rosalind Russell in *Mourning Becomes Electra*. **Supporting Actor:** Edmund Gwenn in *Miracle on 34th Street*, 20th. **Supporting Actress:** Celeste Holm in *Gentleman's Agreement*. Directing: Elia Kazan, *Gentleman's Agreement*. **Art Direction—Black-and-White:** *Great Expectations*, Rank, Universal-International (British). John Bryan, Art Director. Wilfred Shingleton, Set Decorator. **Art Direction—Color:** *Black Narcissus*, Rank, Universal-International (British). Alfred Junge, Art Director and Set Decorator. **Cinematography—Black-and-White:** Guy Green, *Great Expectations*. **Cinematography—Color:** Jack Cardiff, *Black Narcissus*. **Film Editing:** Francis Lyon, Robert Parrish, *Body and Soul*, Enterprise, UA. **Music—Scoring Musical Picture:** Alfred Newman, *Mother Wore Tights*, 20th. **Music—Music Score of a Dramatic or Comedy Picture:** Dr. Miklos Rozsa, *A Double Life*. **Music—Song:** "Zip-A-Dee-Doo-Dah" from *Song of the South*, Disney, RKO. Music by Allie Wrubel. Lyrics by Ray Gilbert. **Short Subjects—Cartoon:** *Tweetie Pie*, WB. **Short Subjects—One-Reel:** *Goodbye Miss Turlock*, MGM. **Short Subjects—Two-Reel:** *Climbing the Matterhorn*, Mon. **Sound Recording:** *The Bishop's Wife*, Samuel Goldwyn Studio Sound Department. Gordon Sawyer, Sound Director. **Special Effects:** *Green Dolphin Street*, MGM. A. Arnold Gillespie, Warren Newcombe (Visual); Douglas Shearer, Michael Steinore (Audible). **Writing—Original Screenplay:** Sidney Sheldon, *The Bachelor and the Bobby-Soxer*, RKO. **Writing—Original Story:** Valentine Davies, *Miracle on 34th Street*. **Writing—Best Written Screenplay:** George Seaton, *Miracle on 34th Street*. **Documentary—Feature:** *Design for Death*, RKO. **Documentary—Short Subject:** *First Steps*, United Nations. **Special Awards:** *Bill and Coo*, for a novel and entertaining use of the medium of motion pictures. *Shoe-Shine*, an Italian production of superlative quality made under adverse circumstances. Colonel William N. Selig, Albert E. Smith, George K. Spoor and Thomas Armat, motion picture pioneers, for their contributions to the development of the film industry. James Baskett, for his characterization of Uncle Remus in *Song of the South*. **Scientific and Technical Awards:** C. C. Davis and Electrical Research Products, Division of Western Electric Co., for the development and application of an improved film-drive filter mechanism. C. R. Daily and the Paramount Studio Film Laboratory, Still and Engineering Departments, for the development and first practical application to motion picture and still photography of a method of increasing film speed as first suggested to the industry by E. I. duPont de Nemours & Co. Nathan Levinson and the Warner Bros. Studio Sound Department, for the design and construction of a constant-speed sound editing machine. Farciot Edouart, C. R. Daily, Hal Corl, H. G. Cartwright and the Paramount Studio Transparency and Engineering Departments, for the first application of a special antisolarizing glass to high-intensity background and spot arc projectors. Fred Ponedel of Warner Bros. Studio, for pioneering the fabrication and practical application to motion picture color photography of large translucent photographic backgrounds. Kurt Singer and the RCA-Victor Division of the Radio Corporation of America, for the design and development of a continuously variable band elimination filter. James Gibbons of Warner Bros. Studio, for the development and production of large dyed plastic filters for motion picture photography.

TWENTY-FIRST YEAR 1948

Best Picture: *Hamlet*, Rank-Two Cities, Universal-International (British). Other nominees: *Johnny Belinda, The Red Shoes, The Snake Pit, Treasure of Sierra Madre*. **Actor:** Laurence Olivier in *Hamlet*. Other nominees: Lew Ayres in *Johnny Belinda*, Montgomery Clift in *The Search*, Dan Dailey in *When My Baby Smiles at Me*, Clifton Webb in *Sitting Pretty*. **Actress:** Jane Wyman in *Johnny Belinda*, WB. Other nominees: Ingrid Bergman in *Joan of Arc*, Olivia De Havilland in *The Snake Pit*, Irene Dunne in *I Remember Mama*, Barbara Stanwyck in *Sorry, Wrong Number*. **Supporting Actor:** Walter Huston in *Treasure of Sierra Madre*, WB. **Supporting Actress:** Claire Trevor in

The Snake Pit with Minna Gombell, Olivia De Havilland, Leo Genn and Mark Stevens.

Key Largo, WB. **Directing:** John Huston, *Treasure of Sierra Madre*. **Foreign Language Film Award:** *Monsieur Vincent* (French). **Art Direction—Black-and-White:** *Hamlet*. Roger K. Furse, Art Director. Carmen Dillon, Set Decorator. **Art Direction—Color:** *The Red Shoes*, Rank-Archers, Eagle-Lion (British). Hein Heckroth, Art Director. Arthur Lawson, Set Decorator. **Cinematography—Black-and-White:** William Daniels, *The Naked City*, Hellinger, Univ. **Cinematography—Color:** Joseph Valentine, William V. Skall, Winton Hoch, *Joan of Arc*, Sierra, RKO. **Costume Design—Black-and-White:** Roger K. Furse, *Hamlet*. **Costume Design—Color:** Dorothy Jeakins, Karinska, *Joan of Arc*. **Film Editing:** Paul Weatherwax, *The Naked City*. **Music—Scoring Musical Picture:** Johnny Green, Roger Edens, *Easter Parade*, MGM. **Music—Music Score a of Dramatic or Comedy Picture:** Brian Easdale, *The Red Shoes*. **Music—Song:** "Buttons and Bows" from *The Paleface*, Par. Music and lyrics by Jay Livingston and Ray Evans. **Short Subjects—Cartoon:** *The Little Orphan*, MGM. **Short Subjects—One-Reel:** *Symphony of a City*, 20th. **Short Subjects—Two-Reel:** *Seal Island*, Disney, RKO. **Sound Recording:** *The Snake Pit*, 20th Century-Fox Studio Sound Department. Thomas T. Moulton, Sound Director. **Special Effects:** *Portrait of Jennie*, Selznick. Paul Eagler, J. McMillan Johnson, Russell Shearman, Clarence Slifer (Visual); Charles Freeman, James G. Stewart (Audible). **Writing—Motion Picture Story:** Richard Schweizer, David Wechsler, *The Search*, Praesens, Metro-Goldwyn-Mayer (Swiss). **Writing—Best Written Screenplay:** John Huston, *Treasure of Sierra Madre*. **Documentary—Feature:** *The Secret Land*, U.S. Navy, MGM. **Documentary—Short Subject:** *Toward Independence*, U.S. Army. **Irving G. Thalberg Memorial Award:** Jerry Wald. **Special Awards:** Ivan Jandl, for the outstanding juvenile performance of 1948 in *The Search*. Sid Grauman, master showman, who raised the standard of exhibition of motion pictures. Adolph Zukor, for his services to the industry over a period of forty years. Walter Wanger, for distinguished service to the industry in adding to its moral stature in the world community by his production of the picture, *Joan of Arc*. **Scientific and Technical Awards:** Victor Caccialanza, Maurice Ayers and the Paramount Studio Set Construction Department, for the development and application of "Paralite," a new lightweight plaster process for set construction. Nick Kalten, Louis J. Witti and the 20th Century-Fox Studio Mechanical Effects Department, for a process of preserving and flame-proofing foliage. Marty Martin, Jack Lannon, Russell Shearman and the RKO Radio Studio Special Effects Department, for the development of a new method of simulating falling snow on motion picture sets. A. J. Moran and the Warner Bros. Studio Electrical Department, for a method of remote control for shutters on motion picture arc-lighting equipment.

TWENTY-SECOND YEAR   1949

Best Picture: *All the King's Men*, Col. Other nominees: *Battleground*, *The Heiress*, *A Letter to Three Wives*, *Twelve O'Clock High*. **Actor:** Broderick Crawford in *All the King's Men*. Other nominees: Kirk Douglas in *Champion*, Gregory Peck in *Twelve O'Clock High*, Richard

Todd in *The Hasty Heart*, John Wayne in *Sands of Iwo Jima*. **Actress:** Olivia De Havilland in *The Heiress*, Par. Other nominees: Jeanne Crain in *Pinky*, Susan Hayward in *My Foolish Heart*, Deborah Kerr in *Edward, My Son*, Loretta Young in *Come to the Stable*. **Supporting Actor:** Dean Jagger in *Twelve O'Clock High*, 20th. **Supporting Actress:** Mercedes McCambridge in *All the King's Men*. **Directing:** Joseph L. Mankiewicz, *A Letter to Three Wives*, 20th. **Foreign Language Film Award:** *The Bicycle Thief* (Italian). **Art Direction—Black-and-White:** *The Heiress*. Harry Horner, John Meehan, Art Directors. Emile Kuri, Set Decorator. **Art Direction—Color:** *Little Women*, Metro-Goldwyn-Mayer. Cedric Gibbons, Paul Groesse, Art Directors. Edwin B. Willis, Jack D. Moore, Set Decorators. **Cimematography—Black-and-White:** Paul C. Vogel, *Battleground*, MGM. **Cinematography—Color:** Winton Hoch, *She Wore a Yellow Ribbon*, Argosy, RKO. **Costume Design—Black-and-White:** Edith Head, Gile Steele, *The Heiress*. **Costume Design—Color:** Leah Rhodes, Travilla, Marjorie Best, *Adventures of Don Juan*, WB. **Film Editing:** Harry Gerstad, *Champion*, Screen Plays, UA. **Music—Scoring Musical Picture:** Roger Edens, Lennie Hayton, *On the Town*, MGM. **Music—Music Score of a Dramatic or Comedy Picture:** Aaron Copland, *The Heiress*. **Music—Song:** "Baby, It's Cold Outside" from *Neptune's Daughter*. Music and lyrics by Frank Loesser. **Short Subjects—Cartoon:** *For Scent-Imental Reasons*, WB. **Short Subjects—Two-Reel:** *Aquatic House-Party*, Par. **Short Subjects—Tw-Reel:** *Van Gogh*, Cinema Distributors. **Sound Recording:** *Twelve O'Clock High*, 20th. Studio Sound Department. Thomas T. Moulton, Sound Director. **Special Effects:** *Mighty Joe Young*, Argosy, RKO. **Writing—Motion Picture Story:** Douglas Morrow, *The Stratton Story*, MGM. **Writing—Best Written Screenplay:** Joseph L. Mankiewicz, *A Letter to Three Wives*. **Writing—Story and Screenplay:** Robert Pirosh, *Battleground*. **Documentary—Feature:** *Daybreak in Udi*, British Information Services. **Documentary—Short Subject:** *A Chance to Live*, March of Time, 20th Century-Fox. *So Much for So Little*, Warner Brothers Cartoons, WB. **Special Awards:** Bobby Driscoll, as the outstanding juvenile actor of 1949. Fred Astaire, for his unique artistry and his contribution to the techniques of musical pictures. Cecil B. De Mille, distinguished motion picture pioneer, for 37 years of brilliant showmanship. Jean Hersholt, for distinguished service to the motion picture industry. **Scientific and Technical Awards:** Eastman Kodak Co., for the development and introduction of an improved safety base motion picture film. Loren L. Ryder, Bruce H. Denney, Robert Carr and the Paramount Studio Sound Department, for the development and application of the supersonic playback and public address system. M. B. Paul, for the first successful large-area seamless translucent backgrounds. Herbert Britt, for the development and application of formulas and equipment producing artificial snow and ice for dressing motion picture sets. Andre Coutant and Jacques Mathot,

Twelve O'clock High with Dean Jagger, Gary Merrill and Hugh Marlowe.

for the design of the Eclair Camerette. Charles R. Daily, Steve Cstillag and the Paramount Studio Engineering, Editorial and Music Departments, for a new precision method of computing variable tempo-click tracks. International Projector Corp., for a simplified and self-adjusting take-up device for projection machines. Alexander Velcoff, for the application to production of the infrared photographic evaluator.

TWENTY-THIRD YEAR   1950

Best Picture: *All About Eve*, 20th. Other nominees: *Born Yesterday*, *Father of the Bride*, *King Solomon's Mines*, *Sunset Boulevard*. **Actor:** José Ferrer in *Cyrano de Bergerac*, Kramer, UA. Other nominees: Louis Calhern in *The Magnificent Yankee*, William Holden in *Sunset Boulevard*, James Stewart in *Harvey*, Spencer Tracy in *Father of the Bride*. **Actress:** Judy Holliday in *Born Yesterday*, Col. Other nominees: Anne Baxter in *All About Eve*, Bette Davis in *All About Eve*, Eleanor Parker in *Caged*, Gloria Swanson in *Sunset Boulevard*. **Supporting Actor:** George Sanders in *All About Eve*. **Supporting Actress:** Josephine Hull in *Harvey*, Univ. **Directing:** Joseph L. Mankiewicz, *All About Eve*. **Foreign Language Film Award:** *The Walls of Malapaga* (Franco-Italian). **Art Direction—Black-and-White:** *Sunset Boulevard*, Par. Hans Dreier, John Meehan, Art Directors. Sam Comer, Ray Moyer, Set Decorators. **Art Direction—Color:** *Samson and Delilah*, De Mille, Par. Hans Dreier, Walter Tyler, Art Directors. Sam Comer, Ray Moyer, Set Decorators. **Cinematography—Black-and-White:** Robert Krasker, *The Third Man*, Selznick, London Films (British). **Cinematography—Color:** Robert Surtees, *King Solomon's Mines*, MGM. **Costume Design—Black-and-White:** Edith Head, Charles Le Maire, *All About Eve*. **Costume Design—Color:** Edith Head, Dorothy Jeakins, Elois Jenssen, Gile Steele, Gwen Wakeling, *Samson and Delilah*. **Film Editing:** Ralph E. Winters, Conrad A. Nervig, *King Solomon's Mines*. **Music—Scoring Musical Picture:** Adolph Deutsch, Roger Edens, *Annie Get Your Gun*, MGM. **Music—Music Score of a Dramatic or Comedy Picture:** Franz Waxman, *Sunset Boulevard*. **Music—Song:** "Mona Lisa" from *Captain Carey*, *USA*, Par. Music and lyrics by Ray Evans and Jay Livingston. **Short Subjects—Cartoon:** *Gerald McBoing-Boing*, UPA, Col. **Short Subjects—One-Reel:** *Granddad of Races*, WB. **Short Subjects—Two-Reel:** *In Beaver Valley*, Disney, RKO. **Sound Recording:** *All About Eve*, 20th Century-Fox Studio Sound Department. Thomas T. Moulton, Sound Director. **Special Effects:** *Destination Moon*, Pal, ELC. **Writing—Motion Picture Story:** Edna Anhalt, Edward Anhalt, *Panic in the Streets*, 20th. **Writing—Screenplay:** Joseph L. Mankiewicz, *All About Eve*. **Writing—Story and Screenplay:** Charles Brackett, Billy Wilder, D. M. Marshman, Jr., *Sunset Boulevard*. **Documentary—Feature:** *The Titan: Story of Michelangelo*, Michelangelo, Classics. **Documentary—Short Subject:** *Why Korea?*, 20th Century-Fox

Harvey with Josephine Hull, James Stewart, Grace Mills and Victoria Horne.

Movietone. **Irving G. Thalberg Memorial Award:** Darryl F. Zanuck. **Honorary Awards:** George Murphy, for his services in interpreting the film industry to the country at large. Louis B. Mayer, for distinguished service to the motion picture industry. **Scientific and Technical Awards:** James B. Gordon and the 20th Century-Fox Studio Camera Department, for the design and development of a multiple-image film viewer. John Paul Livadary, Floyd Campbell, L. W. Russell and the Columbia Studio Sound Department, for the development of a multi-track magnetic rerecording system. Loren L. Ryder and the Paramount Studio Sound Department, for the first studio-wide application of magnetic sound recording to motion picture production.

TWENTY-FOURTH YEAR   1951

Best Picture: *An American in Paris*, MGM. Other nominees: *Decision Before Dawn*, *A Place in the Sun*, *Quo Vadis*, *A Streetcar Named Desire*. **Actor:** Humphrey Bogart, *The African Queen*, Horizon, UA. Other nominees: Marlon Brando in *A Streetcar Named Desire*, Montgomery Clift in *A Place in the Sun*, Arthur Kennedy in *Bright Victory*, Fredric March in *Death of a Salesman*. **Actress:** Vivien Leigh in *A Streetcar Named Desire*, Feldman, WB. Other nominees: Katharine Hepburn, *The African Queen*, Eleanor Parker in *Detective Story*, Shelley Winters in *A Place in the Sun*, Jane Wyman in *The Blue Veil*. **Supporting Actor:** Karl Malden in *A Streetcar Named Desire*. **Supporting Actress:** Kim Hunter in *A Streetcar Named Desire*. **Directing:** George Stevens, *A Place in the Sun*, Par. **Foreign Language Film Award:** *Rashomon* (Japanese). **Art Direction—Black-and-White:** *A Streetcar Named Desire*. Richard Day, Art Director. George James Hopkins, Set Decorator. **Art Direction—Color:** *An American in Paris*. Cedric Gibbons, Preston Ames, Art Directors. Edwin B. Willis, Keogh Gleason, Set Decorators. **Cinematography—Black-and-White:** William C. Mellor, *A Place in the Sun*. **Cinematography—Color:** Alfred Gilks, John Alton, *An American in Paris*. **Costume Design—Black-and-White:** Edith Head, *A Place in the Sun*. **Costume Design—Color:** Orry-Kelly, Walter Plunkett, Irene Sharaff, *An American in Paris*. **Film Editing:** William Hornbeck, *A Place in the Sun*. **Music—Scoring Musical Picture:** Johnny Green, Saul Chaplin, *An American in Paris*. **Music—Music Score of a Dramatic or Comedy Picture:** Franz Waxman, *A Place in the Sun*. **Music—Song:** "In the Cool, Cool, Cool of the Evening" from *Here Comes the Groom*, Paramount. Music by Hoagy Carmichael. Lyrics by Johnny Mercer. **Short Subjects—Cartoon:** *Two Mouseketeers*, MGM. **Short Subjects—One-Reel:** *World of Kids*, WB. **Short Subjects—Two-Reel:** *Nature's Half Acre*, Disney, RKO. **Sound Recording:** *The Great Caruso*, Metro-Goldwyn-Mayer Studio Sound Department. Douglas Shearer, Sound Director. **Writing—Motion Picture Story:** Paul Dehn, James Bernard, *Seven Days to Noon*, Boulting, Mayer-Kingsley, Distinguished (British). **Writing—Screenplay:** Michael Wilson, Harry Brown, *A Place in the Sun*. **Writing—Story and Screenplay:** Alan Jay Lerner, *An American in Paris*. **Documentary—Feature:** *Kon-Tiki*, Artfilm, RKO (Norwegian). **Documentary—Short Subject:** *Benjy*, Paramount. **Special Effects:** *When Worlds Collide*, Par. Irving G. Thalberg Memorial Award: Arthur Freed. **Honorary Awards:** Gene Kelly, in appreciation of his versatility as an actor, singer, director and dancer, and specifically for his brilliant achievements in the art of choreography on film. **Scientific and Technical Awards:** Gordon Jennings, S. L. Stancliffe and the Paramount Studio Special Photographic and Engineering Departments, for the design, construction and application of a servo-operated recording and repeating device. Olin L. Dupy of Metro-Goldwyn-Mayer Studio, for the design, construction and application of a motion picture reproducing system. Radio Corporation of America, Victor Division, for pioneering direct positive recording with anticipatory noise reduction. Richard M. Haff, Frank P. Herrnfeld, Garland C. Misener and the Ansco Film Division of General Aniline and Film Corp., for the development of the Ansco color scene tester. Fred Ponedel, Ralph Ayres and George Brown of Warner Bros. Studio, for an air-driven water motor to provide flow, wake and white water for marine sequences in motion pictures. Glen Robinson and the Metro-Goldwyn-Mayer Studio Construction Department, for the development of a new music wire and cable cutter. Jack Gaylord and the Metro-Goldwyn-Mayer Studio Construction Department, for the development of balsa falling snow. Carlos Rivas of Metro-Goldwyn-Mayer Studio, for the development of an automatic magnetic film splicer.

TWENTY-FIFTH YEAR 1952

Best Picture: *The Greatest Show on Earth*, De Mille, Par. Other nominees: *High Noon, Ivanhoe, Moulin Rouge, The Quiet Man.* **Actor:** Gary Cooper in *High Noon*, Kramer, UA. Other nominees: Marlon Brando in *Viva Zapata!*, Kirk Douglas in *The Bad and the Beautiful*, José Ferrer in *Moulin Rouge*, Alec Guinness in *The Lavender Hill Mob.* **Actress:** Shirley Booth in *Come Back, Little Sheba*, Wallis, Par. Other nominees: Joan Crawford in *Sudden Fear*, Bette Davis in *The Star*, Julie Harris in *The Member of the Wedding*, Susan Hayward in *With a Song in My Heart.* **Supporting Actor:** Anthony Quinn in *Viva Zapata!*, 20th. **Supporting Actress:** Gloria Grahame in *The Bad and the Beautiful*, MGM. **Directing:** John Ford, *The Quiet Man*, Argosy, Rep. **Foreign Language Film Award:** *Forbidden Games* (French). **Art Direction—Black-and-White:** *The Bad and the Beautiful.* Cedric Gibbons, Edward Carfagno, Art Directors. Edwin B. Willis, Keogh Gleason, Set Decorators. **Art Direction—Color:** *Moulin Rouge*, Romulus, UA. Paul Sheriff, Art Director. Marcel Vertes, Set Decorator. **Cinematography—Black-and-White:** Robert Surtees, *The Bad and the Beautiful.* **Cinematography—Color:** Winton C. Hoch, Archie Stout, *The Quiet Man.* **Costume Design—Black-and-White:** Helen Rose, *The Bad and the Beautiful.* **Costume Design—Color:** Marcel Vertes, *Moulin Rouge.* **Film Editing:** Elmo Williams, Harry Gerstad, *High Noon.* **Music—Scoring Musical Picture:** Alfred Newman, *With a Song in My Heart*, 20th. **Music—Music Score of a Dramatic or Comedy Picture:** Dimitri Tiomkin, *High Noon.* **Music—Song:** "High Noon" from *High Noon.* Music by Dimitri Tiomkin. Lyrics by Ned Washington. **Short Subjects—Cartoon:** *Johann Mouse*, MGM. **Short Subjects—One-Reel:** *Light in the Window*, Art Films, 20th. **Short Subjects—Two Reel:** *Water Birds*, Disney, RKO. **Sound Recording:** *Breaking the Sound Barrier*, London Films Studio Sound Department (British). **Writing—Motion Picture Story:** Fredric M. Frank, Theodore St. John, Frank Cavett, *The Greatest Show on Earth.* **Writing—Screenplay:** Charles Schnee, *The Bad and the Beautiful.* **Writing—Story and Screenplay:** T. E. B. Clarke, *The Lavender Hill Mob*, Rank, Ealing, Universal-International (British). **Documentary—Feature:** *The Sea Around Us*, RKO. **Documentary—Short Subject:** *Neighbours*, National Film Board of Canada, Mayer-Kingsley (Canadian). **Special Effects:** *Plymouth Adventure*, MGM. **Irving G. Thalberg Memorial Award:** Cecil B. De Mille. **Honorary Awards:** George Alfred Mitchell, for his design and development of the camera which bears his name and for his continued and dominant presence in the field of cinematography. Joseph M. Schenck, for long and distinguished service to the motion picture industry. Merian C. Cooper, for his many innovations and contributions to the art of motion pictures. Harold Lloyd, master comedian and good citizen. Bob Hope, for his contribution to the laughter of the world, his service to the motion picture industry, and his devotion to the American premise. **Scientific and Technical Awards:** Eastman Kodak Co., for the introduction of Eastman color negative and Eastman color print film. Ansco Division, General Aniline and Film Corp., for the introduction of Ansco color negative and Ansco color print film. Technicolor Motion Picture Corp., for an improved method of color motion picture photography under incandescent light. Projection, Still Photographic and Development Engineering Departments of Metro-Goldwyn-Mayer Studio, for an improved method of projecting photographic backgrounds. John G. Frayne and R. R. Scoville and Westrex Corp., for a method of measuring distortion in sound reproduction. Photo Research Corp., for creating the Spectra color temperature meter. Gustav Jirouch, for the design of the Robot automatic film splicer. Carlos Rivas of Metro-Goldwyn-Mayer Studio, for the development of a sound reproducer for magnetic film.

TWENTY-SIXTH YEAR 1953

Best Picture: *From Here to Eternity*, Col. Other nominees: *Julius Caesar, The Robe, Roman Holiday, Shane.* **Actor:** William Holden in *Stalag 17*, Par. Other nominees: Marlon Brando in *Julius Caesar*,

From Here to Eternity with Montgomery Clift and Frank Sinatra.

Richard Burton in *The Robe*, Montgomery Clift in *From Here to Eternity*, Burt Lancaster in *From Here to Eternity.* **Actress:** Audrey Hepburn in *Roman Holiday*, Par. Other nominees: Leslie Caron in *Lili*, Ava Gardner in *Mogambo*, Deborah Kerr in *From Here to Eternity*, Maggie McNamara in *The Moon Is Blue.* **Supporting Actor:** Frank Sinatra in *From Here to Eternity.* **Supporting Actress:** Donna Reed in *From Here to Eternity.* **Directing:** Fred Zinnemann, *From Here to Eternity.* **Art Direction—Black-and-White:** *Julius Caesar*, MGM. Cedric Gibbons, Edward Carfagno, Art Directors. Edwin B. Willis, Hugh Hunt, Set Decorators. **Art Direction—Color:** *The Robe*, 20th. Lyle Wheeler, George W. Davis, Art Directors. Walter M. Scott, Paul S. Fox, Set Decorators. **Cinematography—Black-and-White:** Burnett Guffey, *From Here to Eternity.* **Cinematography—Color:** Loyal Griggs, *Shane*, Par. **Costume Design—Black-and-White:** Edith Head, *Roman Holiday.* **Costume Design—Color:** Charles Le Maire, Emile Santiago, *The Robe.* **Film Editing:** William Lyon, *From Here to Eternity.* **Music—Scoring Musical Picture:** Alfred Newman, *Call Me Madam*, 20th. **Music—Music Score of a Dramatic or Comedy Picture:** Bronislau Kaper, *Lili*, MGM. **Music—Song:** "Secret Love" from *Calamity Jane*, WB. **Short Subjects—Cartoon:** *Toot, Whistle, Plunk and Boom*, Disney. **Short Subjects—One-Reel:** *The Merry Wives of Windsor Overture*, MGM. **Short Subjects—Two-Reel:** *Bear Country*, Disney, RKO. **Sound Recording:** *From Here to Eternity*, Columbia Studio Sound Department. John P. Livadary, Sound Director. **Writing—Motion Picture Story:** Ian McLellan Hunter, *Roman Holiday.* **Writing—Screenplay:** Daniel Taradash, *From Here to Eternity.* **Writing—Story and Screenplay:** Charles Brackett, Walter Reisch, Richard Breen, *Titanic*, 20th. **Documentray—Feature:** *The Living Desert*, Disney. **Documentary—Short Subject:** *The Alaskan Eskimo*, Disney, RKO. **Special Effects:** *War of the Worlds*, Par. **Irving G. Thalberg Memorial Award:** George Stevens. **Honorary Awards:** Pete Smith, for his witty and pungent observations on the American scene in his series of *Pete Smith Specialties.* The 20th Century-Fox Film Corporation, in recognition of their imagination, showmanship and foresight in introducing the revolutionary process known as CinemaScope. Joseph I. Breen, for his conscientious, open-minded and dignified management of the Motion Picture Production Code. Bell and Howell Company, for their pioneering and basic achievements in the advancement of the motion picture industry. Scientific and Technical Awards: Professor Henri Chretien and Earl Sponable, Sol Halprin, Lorin Grignon, Herbert Bragg and Carl Faulkner of 20th Century-Fox Studios, for creating, developing and engineering the equipment, processes and techniques known as CinemaScope. Fred Waller, for designing and developing the multiple photographic and projection systems that culminated in Cinerama. Reeves Soundcraft Corp., for their development of a process of applying stripes of magnetic oxide to motion picture film for sound recording and reproduction. Westrex Corp., for the design and construction of a new film-editing machine.

On the Waterfront with Marlon Brando and Eva Marie Saint.

TWENTY-SEVENTH YEAR   1954

Best Picture: *On the Waterfront*, Horizon-American, Col. Other nominees: *The Caine Mutiny, The Country Girl, Seven Brides for Seven Brothers, Three Coins in the Fountain.* **Actor:** Marlon Brando in *On the Waterfront.* Other nominees: Humphrey Bogart in *The Caine Mutiny*, Bing Crosby in *The Country Girl*, James Mason in *A Star Is Born*, Dan O'Herlihy in *Adventures of Robinson Crusoe.* **Actress:** Grace Kelly in *The Country Girl*, Perlberg-Seaton, Par. Other nominees: Dorothy Dandridge in *Carmen Jones*, Judy Garland in *A Star Is Born*, Audrey Hepburn in *Sabrina*, Jane Wyman in *The Magnificent Obsession.* **Supporting Actor:** Edmond O'Brien in *The Barefoot Contessa*, Figaro, UA. **Supporting Actress:** Eva Marie Saint in *On the Waterfront.* **Directing:** Elia Kazan, *On the Waterfront.* **Foreign Language Film Award:** *Gate of Hell* (Japanese). **Art Direction—Black-and-White:** *On the Waterfront.* Richard Day, Art Director. **Art Direction—Color:** 20,000 *Leagues Under the Sea*, Disney. John Meehan, Art Director. Emile Kuri, Set Decorator. **Cinematography—Black-and-White:** Boris Kaufman, *On the Waterfront.* **Cinematography—Color:** Milton Krasner, *Three Coins in the Fountain*, 20th. **Costume Design—Black-and-White:** Edith Head, *Sabrina*, Par. **Costume Design—Color:** Sanzo Wada, *Gate of Hell*, Daiei, Harrison (Japanese). **Film Editing:** Gene Milford, *On the Waterfront.* **Music—Scoring Musical Picture:** Adolph Deutsch, Saul Chaplin, *Seven Brides for Seven Brothers*, MGM. **Music—Music Score of a Dramatic or Comedy Picture:** Dimitri Tiomkin, *The High and the Mighty*, Wayne-Fellows, WB. **Music—Song:** "Three Coins in the Fountain" from *Three Coins in the Fountain.* Music by Jule Styne. Lyrics by Sammy Cahn. **Short Subjects—Cartoon:** *When Magoo Flew*, UPA, Col. **Short Subjects—One-Reel:** *This Mechanical Age*, WB. **Short Subjects—Two-Reel:** *A Time Out of War*, Carnival. **Sound Recording:** *The Glenn Miller Story*, Universal-International Studio Sound Department. Leslie I. Carey, Sound Director. **Special Effects:** 20,000 *Leagues Under the Sea.* **Writing—Motion Picture Story:** Philip Yordan, *Broken Lance*, 20th. **Writing—Screenplay:** George Seaton, *The Country Girl.* **Writing—Story and Screenplay:** Budd Schulberg, *On the Waterfront.* **Documentary—Feature:** *The Vanishing Prairie*, Disney. **Documentary—Short Subject:** *Thursday's Children*, World Wide-Morse, British Information Service (British). **Honorary Awards:** The Bausch & Lomb Optical Company, for their contributions to the advancement of the motion picture industry.

Kemp R. Niver, for the development of the Renovare Process which has made possible the restoration of the Library of Congress Paper Film Collection. Greta Garbo, for her unforgettable screen performances. Danny Kaye, for his unique talents, his service to the Academy, the motion picture industry, and the American people. Jon Whiteley, for his outstanding juvenile performance in *The Little Kidnappers.* Vincent Winter, for his outstanding juvenile performance in *The Little Kidnappers.* **Scientific and Technical Awards:** Paramount Pictures, Inc., Loren L. Ryder, John R. Bishop and all the members of the technical and engineering staff, for developing a method of producing and exhibiting motion pictures known as VistaVision. David S. Horsley and the Universal-International Studio Special Photographic Department, for a portable remote-control device for process projectors. Karl Freund and Frank Crandell of Photo Research Corp., for the design and development of a direct reading brightness meter. Wesley C. Miller, J. W. Stafford, K. M. Frierson and the Metro-Goldwyn-Mayer Studio Sound Department, for an electronic sound-printing comparison device. John P. Livadary, Lloyd Russell and the Columbia Studio Sound Department, for an improved limiting amplifier as applied to sound-level comparison devices. Roland Miller and Max Goeppiner of Magnascope Corp., for the design and development of a cathode-ray magnetic sound-track viewer. Carlos Rivas, G. M. Sprague and the Metro-Goldwyn-Mayer Studio Sound Department, for the design of a magnetic sound-editing machine. Fred Wilson of the Samuel Goldwyn Studio Sound Department, for the design of a variable multiple-band equalizer. P. C. Young of the Metro-Goldwyn-Mayer Studio Projection Department, for the practical application of a variable focal length attachment to motion picture projector lenses. Fred Knoth and Orien Ernest of the Universal-International Studio Technical Department, for the development of a hand-portable, electric, dry oil-fog machine.

TWENTY-EIGHTH YEAR   1955

Best Picture: *Marty*, Steven, UA. Other nominees: *Love Is a Many-Splendored Thing, Mister Roberts, Picnic, The Rose Tattoo.* **Actor:** Ernest Borgnine in *Marty.* Other nominees: James Cagney in *Love Me or Leave Me*, James Dean in *East of Eden*, Frank Sinatra in *The Man with the Golden Arm*, Spencer Tracy in *Bad Day at Black Rock.* **Actress:** Anna Magnani in *The Rose Tattoo*, Wallis, Par. Other nominees: Susan Hayward in *I'll Cry Tomorrow*, Katharine Hepburn in *Summertime*, Jennifer Jones in *Love Is a Many-Splendored Thing*, Eleanor Parker in *Interrupted Melody.* **Supporting Actor:** Jack Lemmon in *Mister Roberts*, Orange, WB. **Supporting Actress:** Jo Van Fleet in *East of Eden*, WB. **Directing:** Delbert Mann, *Marty.* **Foreign Language Film Award:** *Samurai* (Japanese). **Art Direction—Black-and-White:** *The Rose Tattoo.* Hal Pereira, Tambi Larsen, Art Directors. Sam Comer, Arthur Krams, Set Decorators. **Art Direction—Color:** *Picnic*, Columbia. William Flannery, Jo Mielziner, Art Directors. Robert Priestley, Set Decorator. **Cinematography—Black-and-White:** James Wong Howe, *The Rose Tattoo.* **Cinematography—Color:** Robert Burks, *To Catch a Thief*, Paramount. **Costume Design—Back-and-White:** Helen Rose, *I'll Cry Tomorrow*, MGM. **Costume Design—Color:** Charles Le Maire, *Love Is a Many-Splendored Thing*, 20th. **Film Editing:** Charles Nelson, William A. Lyon, *Picnic.* **Music—Scoring Musical Picture:** Robert Russell Bennett, Jay Blackton, Adolph Deutsch, *Oklahoma!*, Rodgers & Hammerstein, Magna. **Music—Music Score of a Dramatic or Comedy Picture:** Alfred Newman, *Love Is a Many-Splendored Thing.* **Music—Song:** "Love Is a Many-Splendored Thing" from *Love Is a Many-Splendored Thing.* Music by Sammy Fain. Lyrics by Paul Francis Webster. **Short Subjects—Cartoon:** *Speedy Gonzales*, WB. **Short Subjects—One-Reel:** *Survival City*, 20th. **Short Subjects—Two-Reel:** *The Face of Lincoln*, USC, Cavalcade. **Sound Recording:** *Oklahoma!* Todd-AO Sound Department. Fred Hynes, Sound Director. **Special Effects:** *The Bridges at Toko-Ri*, Par. **Writing—Motion Picture Story:** Daniel Fuchs, *Love Me or Leave Me*, Metro-Goldwyn-Mayer. **Writing—Screenplay:** Paddy Chayefsky, *Marty.* **Writing—Story and Screenplay:** William Ludwig, Sonya Levien, *Interrupted Melody*, MGM. **Documentary—Feature:** *Helen Keller in Her Story*, Hamilton. **Documentary—Short Subject:** *Men Against the Arctic*, Disney. **Scientific and Technical Awards:** National Carbon Co., for the development

Anastasia with Ingrid Bergman and Yul Brynner.

and production of a high-efficiency yellow-flame carbon for motion picture color photography. Eastman Kodak Co., for Eastman Tri-X panchromatic negative film. Farciot Edouart, Hal Corl and the Paramount Studio Transparency Department, for the engineering and development of a double-frame, triple-head background projector. 20th Century-Fox Studio and Bausch & Lomb Co., for the new combination lenses for CinemaScope photography. Walter Jolley, Maurice Larson and R. H. Spies of 20th Century-Fox Studio, for a spraying process that creates simulated metallic surfaces. Steve Krilanovich, for an improved camera dolly incorporating multidirectional steering. Dave Anderson of 20th Century-Fox Studio, for an improved spotlight capable of maintaining a fixed circle of light at constant intensity over varied distances. Loren L. Ryder, Charles West, Henry Fracker and Paramount Studio for a projection film index to establish proper framing for various aspect ratios. Farciot Edouart, Hal Corl and the Paramount Studio Transparency Department, for an improved dual stereopticon background projector.

TWENTY-NINTH YEAR   1956

Best Picture: *Around the World in 80 Days*, Todd, UA. Other nominees: *Friendly Persuasion, Giant, The King and I, The Ten Commandments.* **Actor:** Yul Brynner in *The King and I*, 20th. Other nominees: James Dean in *Giant*, Kirk Douglas in *Lust for Life*, Rock Hudson in *Giant*, Laurence Oliver in *Richard III*. **Actress:** Ingrid Bergman in *Anastasia*, 20th. Other nominees: Carroll Baker in *Baby Doll*, Katharine Hepburn in *The Rainmaker*, Nancy Kelly in *The Bad Seed*, Deborah Kerr in *The King and I*. **Supporting Actor:** Anthony Quinn in *Lust for Life*, MGM. **Supporting Actress:** Dorothy Malone in *Written on the Wind*, Univ. **Directing:** George Stevens, *Giant*, WB. **Art Direction—Black-and-White:** *Somebody Up There Likes Me*, Metro-Goldwyn-Mayer. Cedric Gibbons, Malcolm F. Brown, Art Directors. Edwin B. Willis, F. Keogh Gleason, Set Decorators. **Art Direction—Color:** *The King and I*. Lyle R. Wheeler, John De Cuir, Art Directors. Walter M. Scott, Paul S. Fox, Set Decorators. **Cinematography—Black-and-White:** Joseph Ruttenberg, *Somebody Up There Likes Me*. **Cinematography—Color:** Lionel Lindon, *Around the World in 80 Days*. **Costume Design—Black-and-White:** Jean Louis, *The Solid Gold Cadillac*, Col. **Costume Design—Color:** Irene Sharaff, *The King and I*. **Film Editing:** Gene Ruggiero, Paul Weatherwax, *Around the World in 80 Days*. **Foreign Language Film Award:** *La Strada*, Ponti-DeLaurentiis, Trans-Lux (Italian). **Music—Scoring Musical Picture:** Alfred Newman, Ken Darby, *The King and I*. **Music—Music Score of a Dramatic or Comedy Picture:** Victor Young, *Around the World in 80 Days*. **Music —Song:** "Whatever Will Be, Will Be" ("Que Sera, Sera") from *The Man Who Knew Too Much*, Filwite, Paramount. Music and lyrics by Ray Evans and Jay Livingston. **Short Subjects—Cartoon:** *Mister Magoo's Puddle Jumper*, UPA, Col. **Short Subjects—One-Reel:** *Crashing the Water Barrier*, WB. **Short Subjects—Two-Reel:** *The Bespoke Overcoat*, Romulus, Arthur. **Sound Recording:** *The King and I*, 20th Century-Fox Studio Sound Department. Carl Faulkner, Sound Director. **Special Effects:** *The Ten Commandments*, MPA, Paramount. John Fulton. **Writing—Motion Picture Story:** *The Brave One*, King Brothers, RKO. **Writing—Screenplay-Adapted:**

James Poe, John Farrow, S. J. Perelman, *Around the World in 80 Days*. **Writing—Screenplay-Original:** Albert Lamorisse, *The Red Balloon*, Montsouris, Lopert (French). **Documentary—Feature:** *The Silent World*, Columbia (French). **Documentary—Short Subject:** *The True Story of the Civil War*, Camera Eye. **Irving G. Thalberg Memorial Award:** Buddy Adler. **Jean Hersholt Humanitarian Award:** Y. Frank Freeman. **Honorary Awards:** Eddie Cantor, for distinguished service to the film industry. **Scientific and Technical Awards:** Richard H. Ranger of Rangertone, Inc., for the development of a synchronous recording and reproducing system for quarter-inch magnetic tape. Ted Hirsch, Carl Hauge and Edward Reichard of Consolidated Film Industries, for an automatic scene counter for laboratory projection rooms. The Technical Departments of Paramount Pictures Corp., for the engineering and development of the Paramount lightweight horizontal-movement VistaVision camera. Roy C. Stewart and Sons of Stewart-Trans Lux Corp., Dr. C. R. Dally and the Transparency Department of Paramount Pictures Corp., for the engineering and development of the Hitrans and Para-HiTrans rear-projection screens. The Construction Department of Metro-Goldwyn-Mayer Studio for a new hand-portable fog machine. Daniel J. Bloomberg, John Pond, William Wade and the Engineering and Camera Departments of Republic Studio, for the Naturama adaptation to the Mitchell camera.

THIRTIETH YEAR   1957

Best Picture: *The Bridge on the River Kwai*, Horizon, Col. Other nominees: *Peyton Place, Sayonara, 12 Angry Men, Witness for the Prosecution.* **Actor:** Alec Guinness in *The Bridge on the River Kwai*. Other nominees: Marlon Brando in *Sayonara*, Anthony Franciosa in *A Hatful of Rain*, Charles Laughton in *Witness for the Prosecution*, Anthony Quinn in *Wild Is the Wind*. **Actress:** Joanne Woodward in *The Three Faces of Eve*, 20th. Other nominees: Deborah Kerr in *Heaven Knows, Mr. Allison*, Anna Magnani in *Wild Is the Wind*, Elizabeth Taylor in *Raintree County*, Lana Turner in *Peyton Place*. **Supporting Actor:** Red Buttons in *Sayonara*, Goetz, WB. **Supporting Actress:** Miyoshi Umeki, *Sayonara*. Directing: David Lean, *The Bridge on the River Kwai*. **Art Direction:** *Sayonara*. Ted Haworth, Art Director. Robert Priestley, Set Decorator. **Cinematography:** Jack Hildyard, *The Bridge on the River Kwai*. **Costume Design:** Orry-Kelly, *Les Girls*, Siegel, MGM. **Film Editing:** Peter Taylor, *The Bridge on the River Kwai*. **Foreign Language Film Award:** *The Nights of Cabiria*, De Laurentiis (Italian). **Music—Scoring:** Mal-

Les Girls with Gene Kelly and Mitzi Gaynor.

596

colm Arnold, *The Bridge on the River Kwai*. **Music—Song:** "All the Way" from *The Joker Is Wild*, A.M.B.L., Paramount. Music by James Van Heusen. Lyrics by Sammy Cahn. **Short Subjects—Cartoon:** *Birds Anonymous*, WB. **Short Subjects—Live Action:** *The Wetback Hound*, Disney. **Sound Recording:** *Sayonara*, Warner Brothers Studio Sound Department. George R. Groves, Sound Director. **Special Effects:** *The Enemy Below*, 20th. Walter Rossi (Audible). **Writing—Screenplay** based on material from another medium: Pierre Boulle, *The Bridge on the River Kwai*. **Writing—Original Story and Screenplay:** George Wells, *Designing Woman*, Metro-Goldwyn-Mayer. **Documentray—Feature:** *Albert Schweitzer*, Hill-Anderson, De Rochemont. **Jean Hersholt Humanitarian Award:** Samuel Goldwyn. **Honorary Awards:** Charles Brackett, for outstanding service to the Academy. B. B. Kahane, for distinguished service to the motion picture industry. Gilbert M. ("Broncho Billy") Anderson, motion picture pioneer, for his contributions to the development of motion pictures as entertainment. The Society of Motion Picture and Television Engineers, for their contributions to the advancement of the motion picture industry. Scientific and Technical Awards: Todd-AO Corp. and Westrex Corp., for developing a method of producing and exhibiting wide-film motion pictures known as the Todd-AO System. Motion Picture Research Council, for the design and development of a high-efficiency projection screen for drive-in theaters. Societe D'Optique et de Mecanique de Haute Precision, for the development of a high-speed vari-focal photographic lens. Harlan L. Baumbach, Lorand Wargo, Howard M. Little and the Unicorn Engineering Corp., for the development of an automatic printer light selector. Charles E. Sutter, William B. Smith, Paramount Pictures Corp. and General Cable Corp., for the engineering and application to studio use of aluminum lightweight electrical cable and connectors.

THIRTY-FIRST YEAR   1958

Best Picture: *Gigi*, Freed, MGM. Other nominees: *Auntie Mame*, *Cat on a Hot Tin Roof*, *The Defiant Ones*, *Separate Tables*. **Actor:** David Niven in *Separate Tables*, Clifton, UA. Other nominees: Tony Curtis in *The Defiant Ones*, Paul Newman in *Cat on a Hot Tin Roof*, Sidney Poitier in *The Defiant Ones*, Spencer Tracy in *The Old Man and the Sea*. **Actress:** Susan Hayward in *I Want to Live!*, Figaro, UA. Other nominees: Deborah Kerr in *Separate Tables*, Shirley MacLaine in *Some Came Running*, Rosalind Russell in *Auntie Mame*, Elizabeth Taylor in *Cat on a Hot Tin Roof*. **Supporting Actor:** Burl Ives in *The Big Country*, Anthony-Worldwide, UA. **Supporting Actress:** Wendy Hiller in *Separate Tables*. **Directing:** Vincente Minnelli, *Gigi*. Art Direction: *Gigi*, William A. Horning, Preston Ames, Art Directors. Henry Grace, Keogh Gleason, Set Decorators. **Cinematography—Black-and-White:** Sam Leavitt, *The Defiant Ones*, Kramer, UA. **Cinematography—Color:** Joseph Ruttenberg, *Gigi*. **Costume Design:** Cecil Beaton, *Gigi*. **Film Editing:** Adrienne Fazan, *Gigi*. **Foreign Language Film Award:** *My Uncle*, Specta-Gray-Alter, Films del Centaure (French). **Music—Scoring Musical Picture:** Andre Previn, *Gigi*. **Music—Music Score of a Dramatic or Comedy Picture:** Dimitri Tiomkin, *The Old Man and the Sea*, Hayward, WB. **Music—Song:** "Gigi" from *Gigi*. Music by Frederick Loewe. Lyrics by Alan Jay Lerner. **Short Subjects—Cartoon:** *Knighty Knight Bugs*, WB. **Short Subjects—Live Action:** *Grand Canyon*, Disney. **Sound:** *South Pacific*, Todd-AO Sound Department. Fred Hynes, Sound Director. **Special Effects:** *Tom Thumb*, Pal, MGM. Tom Howard (Visual). **Writing—Screenplay** based on material from another medium: Alan Jay Lerner, *Gigi*. **Writing—Original Story and Screenplay:** Nathan E. Douglas, Harold Jacob Smith, *The Defiant Ones*. **Documentary—Feature:** *White Wilderness*, Disney. **Documentary—Short Subject:** *Ama Girls*, Disney. **Irving G. Thalberg Memorial Award:** Jack L. Warner. **Honorary Award:** Maurice Chevalier, for his contributions to the world of entertainment for more than half a century. **Scientific and Technical Awards:** Don W. Prideaux, Leroy G. Leighton and the Lamp Division of General Electric Co., for the development and production of an improved 10-kilowatt lamp for motion picture set lighting. Panavision, Inc., for the design and development of the Auto Panatar anamorphic photographic lens for 35-mm. CinemaScope photography. Willy Borberg of the General Precision Laboratory Inc., for the development of a high-speed intermittent movement for

Some Like It Hot with Tony Curtis and Marilyn Monroe.

35-mm motion picture theater projection equipment. Fred Ponedel, George Brown and Conrad Boye of the Warner Bros. Special Effects Department, for the design and fabrication of a new rapid-fire marble gun.

THIRTY-SECOND YEAR   1959

Best Picture: *Ben-Hur*, MGM. Other nominees: *Anatomy of a Murder*, *The Diary of Anne Frank*, *The Nun's Story*, *Room at the Top*. **Actor:** Charlton Heston in *Ben-Hur*. Other nominees: Laurence Harvey in *Room at the Top*, Jack Lemmon in *Some Like It Hot*, Paul Muni in *The Last Angry Man*, James Stewart in *Anatomy of a Murder*. **Actress:** Simone Signoret in *Room at the Top*, Romulus, Continental (British). Other nominees: Doris Day in *Pillow Talk*, Audrey Hepburn in *The Nun's Story*, Katharine Hepburn in *Suddenly, Last Summer*, Elizabeth Taylor in *Suddenly, Last Summer*. **Supporting Actor:** Hugh Griffith in *Ben-Hur*. **Supporting Actress:** Shelley Winters in *The Diary of Anne Frank*, 20th. **Directing:** William Wyler, *Ben-Hur*. **Art Direction—Black-and-White:** *The Diary of Anne Frank*. Lyle R. Wheeler, George W. Davis, Art Directors. Walter M. Scott, Stuart A. Reiss, Set Decorators. **Art Direction—Color:** *Ben-Hur*. William A. Horning, Edward Carfagno, Art Directors. Hugh Hunt, Set Decorator. **Cinematography—Black-and-White:** William C. Mellor, *The Diary of Anne Frank*. **Cimematography—Color:** Robert L. Surtees, *Ben-Hur*. **Costume Design—Black-and-White:** Orry-Kelly, *Some Like tI Hot*, Ashton, Mirisch, UA. **Costume Design—Color:** Elizabeth

Pillow Talk with Doris Day and Rock Hudson.

Haffenden, *Ben-Hur*. **Film Editing:** Ralph E. Winters, John D. Dunning, *Ben-Hur*. **Foreign Language Film Award:** *Black Orpheus*, Dispatfilm, Gemma (France). **Music—Scoring Musical Picture:** Andre Previn, Ken Darby, *Porgy and Bess*, Goldwyn, Col. **Music—Music Score of a Dramatic or Comedy Picture:** Miklos Rozsa, *Ben-Hur*. **Music—Song:** "High Hopes" from *A Hole in the Head*, Sincap, UA. Music by James Van Heusen. Lyrics by Sammy Cahn. **Short Subjects—Cartoon:** *Moonbirds*, Storyboard, Harrison. **Short Subjects—Live Action:** *The Golden Fish*, Les Requins, Columbia (French). **Sound:** *Ben-Hur*, Metro-Goldwyn-Mayer Studio Sound Department. Franklin E. Milton, Sound Director. **Special Effects:** *Ben-Hur*. A. Arnold Gillespie, Robert MacDonald (Visual); Milo Lory (Audible). **Writing—Screenplay based on material from another medium:** Neil Paterson, *Room at the Top*. **Writing—Original Story and Screenplay:** *Pillow Talk*, Arwin, Universal-International. Story: Russell Rouse, Clarence Greene. Screenplay: Stanley Shapiro, Maurice Richlin. **Documentary—Feature:** *Serengeti Shall Not Die*, Okapia, Transocean (German). **Documentary—Short Subject:** *Glass*, Netherlands Government, Arthur-Go (The Netherlands). **Jean Hersholt Humanitarian Award:** Bob Hope. **Honorary Awards:** Lee de Forest, for his pioneering inventions which brought sound to the motion picture. Buster Keaton, for his unique talents which brought immortal comedies to the screen. **Scientific and Technical Awards:** Douglas G. Shearer of Metro-Goldwyn-Mayer, Inc., and Robert E. Gottschalk and John R. Moore of Panavision, Inc., for the development of a system of producing and exhibiting wide-film motion pictures known as Camera 65. Wadsworth E. Pohl, William Evans, Werner Hopf, S. E. Howse, Thomas P. Dixon, Stanford Research Institute and Technicolor Corp., for the design and development of the Technicolor electronic printing timer. Wadsworth E. Pohl, Jack Alford, Henry Imus, Joseph Schmit, Paul Fassnacht, Al Lofquist and Technicolor Corp., for the development and practical application of equipment for wet printing. Dr. Howard S. Coleman, Dr. A. Francis Turner, Harold H. Schroeder, James R. Benford and Harold E. Rosenberger of the Bausch & Lomb Optical Co., for the design and development of the Balcold projection mirror. Robert P. Gutterman of General Kinetics, Inc., and the Lipsner-Smith Corp., for the design and development of the CF-2 Ultra-sonic Film Cleaner. Ub Iwerks of Walt Disney Prods., for the design of an improved optical printer for special effects and matte shots. E. L. Stones, Glen Robinson, Winfield Hubbard and Luther Newman of the Metro-Goldwyn-Mayer Studio Construction Department, for the design of a multiple-cable remote-controlled winch.

THIRTY-THIRD YEAR   1960

Best Picture: *The Apartment*, Mirisch, UA. Other nominees: *The Alamo, Elmer Gantry, Sons and Lovers, The Sundowners*. **Actor:**

Elmer Gantry with Shirley Jones and Burt Lancaster.

Spartacus with Charles Laughton, Peter Ustinov and Jean Simmons.

Burt Lancaster, *Elmer Gantry*, Lancaster-Brooks, UA. Other nominees: Trevor Howard in *Sons and Lovers*, Jack Lemmon in *The Apartment*, Laurence Olivier in *The Entertainer*, Spencer Tracy in *Inherit the Wind*. **Actress:** Elizabeth Taylor in *Butterfield 8*, Afton-Linebrook, MGM. Other nominees: Greer Garson in *Sunrise at Campobello*, Deborah Kerr in *The Sundowners*, Shirley MacLaine in *The Apartment*, Melina Mercouri in *Never on Sunday*. **Supporting Actor:** Peter Ustinov in *Spartacus*, Byrna, Univ. **Supporting Actress:** Shirley Jones in *Elmer Gantry*. Directing: Billy Wilder, *The Apartment*. **Art Direction—Black-and-White:** *The Apartment*. Alexander Trauner, Art Director. Edward G. Boyle, Set Decorator. **Art Direction—Color:** *Spartacus*, Alexander Golitzen, Eric Orbom, Art Directors. Russell A. Gausman, Julia Heron, Set Decorators. **Cinematography—Black-and-White:** Freddie Francis, *Sons and Lovers*, Company of Artists, 20th. **Cinematography—Color:** Russell Metty, *Spartacus*. **Costume Design—Black-and-White:** Edith Head, Edward Stevenson, *The Facts of Life*, Panama-Frank, UA. **Costume Design—Color:** Valles, Bill Thomas, *Spartacus*. **Film Editing:** Daniel Mandell, *The Apartment*. **Foreign Language Film Award:** *The Virgin Spring*, Svensk (Swedish). **Music—Scoring Musical Picture:** Morris Stoloff, Harry Sukman, *Song Without End* (*The Story of Franz Liszt*), Goetz-Vidor, Col. **Music—Music Score of a Dramatic or Comedy Picture:** Ernest Gold, *Exodus*, Carlyle-Alphina, UA. **Music—Song:** "Never on Sunday" from *Never on Sunday*, Melinafilm, Lopert (Greek). Music and lyrics by Manos Hadjidakis. **Short Subjects—Cartoon:** *Munro*, Rembrandt, Film Representations. **Short Subjects—Live Action:** *Day of the Painter*, Little Movies, Kingsley-Union. **Sound:** *The Alamo*, Samuel Goldwyn Studio Sound Department, Gordon E. Sawyer, Sound Director. Todd-AO Sound Department. Fred Hynes, Sound Director. **Special Effects:** *The Time Machine*, Galaxy, MGM. Gene Warren, Tim Baar (Visual). **Writing—Screenplay based on material from another medium:** Richard Brooks, *Elmer Gantry*. **Writing—Original Story and Screenplay:** Billy Wilder, I. A. L. Diamond, *The Apartment*. **Documentary—Feature:** *The Horse With the Flying Tail*, Disney. **Documentary—Short Subject:** *Giuseppina*, Hill, Schoenfeld (British). **Jean Hersholt Humanitarian Award:** Sol Lesser. **Honorary Awards:** Gary Cooper, for his many memorable screen performances and the international recognition he, as an individual, has gained for the motion picture industry. Stan Laurel, for his creative pioneering in the field of cinema comedy. Hayley Mills, for *Pollyanna*, the most outstanding juvenile performance of 1960. **Scientific and Technical Awards:** Ampex Professional Products Co., for the production of a well-engineered multipurpose sound system combining high standards of quality with convenience of control, dependable operation and simplified emergency provisions. Arthur Holcoms, Petro Vlahos and Columbia Studio Camera Department, for a camera flicker-indicating device. Anthony Paglia and the 20th Century-Fox Studio Mechanical Effects Department, for the design and construction of a miniature flak gun and ammunition. Carl Hauge, Robert Grubel and Edward Reichard of Consolidated Film Industries, for the development of an automatic developer-replenisher system.

THIRTY-FOURTH YEAR   1961

Best Picture: *West Side Story*, Mirisch, B & P, UA. Other nominees: *Fanny, The Guns of Navarone, The Hustler, Judgment at Nuremberg*. **Actor:** Maximilian Schell in *Judgment at Nuremberg*, Kramer, UA.

598

West Side Story with Natalie Wood and Rita Moreno.

Other nominees: Charles Boyer in *Fanny*, Paul Newman in *The Hustler*, Spencer Tracy in *Judgment at Nuremberg*, Stuart Whitman in *The Mark*. **Actress:** Sophia Loren in *Two Women*, Embassy (Italo-French). Other nominees: Audrey Hepburn in *Breakfast at Tiffany's*, Piper Laurie in *The Hustler*, Geraldine Page in *Summer and Smoke*, Natalie Wood in *Splendor in the Grass*, **Supporting Actor:** George Chakiris in *West Side Story*. **Supporting Actress:** Rita Moreno in *West Side Story*. **Directing:** Robert Wise, Jerome Robbins, *West Side Story*. **Aert Direction—Black-and-White:** *The Hustler*, Rossen, 20th. Harry Horner, Art Director. Gene Callahan, Set Decorator. **Art Direction—Color:** *West Side Story*. Boris Leven, Art Director. Victor Q. Gangelin, Set Decorator. **Cinematography—Black-and-White:** Eugen Shuftan, *The Hustler*. **Cinematography—Color:** Daniel L. Fapp, *West Side Story*. **Costume Design—Black-and-White:** Piero Gherardi, *La Dolce Vita*, Riama, Astor (Italian). **Costume Design—Color:** Irene Sharaff, *West Side Story*. **Film Editing:** Thomas Stanford, *West Side Story*. **Foreign Language Film Award:** *Through a Glass Darkly*, Svensk (Swedish). **Music—Scoring Musical Picture:** Saul Chaplin, Johnny Green, Sid Ramin, Irwin Kostal, *West Side Story*. **Music—Music Score of a Dramatic or Comedy Picture:** Henry Mancini, *Breakfast at Tiffany's*, Jurow-Shepherd, Par. **Music—Song:** "Moon River" from *Breakfast at Tiffany's*. Music by Henry Mancini. Lyrics by Johnny Mercer. **Short Subjects—Cartoon:** *Ersatz*, Zagreb, Herts-Lion (Yugoslavian). **Short Subjects—Live Action:** *Seawards the Great Ships*, Templar, Schoenfeld (British). **Sound:** *West Side Story*, Todd-AO Sound Department. Fred Hynes, Sound Director. Samuel Goldwyn Studio Sound Department. Gordon E. Sawyer, Sound Director. **Special Effects:** *The Guns of Navarone*, Foreman, Col. Bill Warrington (visual); Vivian C. Greenham (audible). **Writing—Screenplay based on material from another medium:** Abby Mann, *Judgment at Nuremberg*. **Writing—Original Story and Screenplay:** William Inge, *Splendor in the Grass*, NBI, WB. **Documentary—Feature:** *Le Ciel et la Boue* (*Sky Above and Mud Beneath*), Ardennes, Arthur Rank (French). **Documentary—Short Subject:** *Project Hope*, Klaeger. **Irving G. Thalberg Memorial Award:** Stanley Kramer. **Jean Hersholt Humanitarian Award:** George Seaton. Honorary Awards: William L. Hendricks, for his outstanding patriotic service in the conception, writing and production of the Marine Corps film, *A Force in Readiness*, which has brought honor to the Academy and the motion picture industry. Jerome Robbins, for his brilliant achievements in the art of choreography on film. Fred L. Metzler, for his dedication and outstanding service to the Academy of Motion Picture Arts and Sciences. **Scientific and Technical Awards:** Sylvania Electric Products, Inc., for the development of a handheld high-power photographic lighting unit known as the Sun Gun Professional. James Dale, S. Wilson, H. E. Rice, John Rude, Laurie

The Miracle Worker with Patty Duke and Anne Bancroft.

Atkin, Wadsworth E. Pohl, H. Peasgood and Technicolor Corp., for a process of automatic selective printing. 20th Century-Fox Research Department, under the direction of E. I. Sponable and Herbert E. Bragg, and Deluxe Laboratories, Inc., with the assistance of F. D. Leslie, R. D. Whitmore, A. A. Alden, Endel Pool and James B. Gordon, for a system of decompressing and recomposing CinemaScope pictures for conventional aspect ratios. Hurletron, Inc., Electric Eye Equipment Division, for an automatic light-changing system for motion picture printers. Wadsworth E. Pohl and Technicolor Corp., for an integrated sound and picture transfer process.

THIRTY-FIFTH YEAR   1962

Best Picture: *Lawrence of Arabia*, Horizon, Spiegel, Lean, Col. Other nominees: *The Longest Day*, *The Music Man*, *Mutiny on the Bounty*, *To Kill a Mockingbird*. **Actor:** Gregory Peck in *To Kill a Mockingbird*, Univ., Pakula-Mulligan-Brentwood. Other nominees: Burt Lancaster in *Bird Man of Alcatraz*, Jack Lemmon in *Days of Wine and Roses*, Marcello Mastroianni in *Divorce—Italian Style*, Peter O'Toole in *Lawrence of Arabia*. **Actress:** Anne Bancroft in *The Miracle Worker*, Playfilms, UA. Other nominees: Bette Davis in *What Ever Happened to Baby Jane*, Katharine Hepburn in *Long Day's Journey into Night*, Geraldine Page in *Sweet Bird of Youth*, Lee Remick in *Days of Wine and Roses*. **Supporting Actor:** Ed Begley in *Sweet Bird of Youth*, Roxbury, MGM. **Supporting Actress:** Patty Duke in *The Miracle Worker*. **Directing:** David Lean, *Lawrence of Arabia*. **Art Direction—Black-and-White:** *To Kill a Mockingbird*. Alexander Golitzen, Henry Bumstead, Art Directors. Oliver Emert, Set Decorator. **Art Direction—Color:** *Lawrence of Arabia*. John Box, John Stoll, Art Directors. Dario Simoni, Set Decorator. **Cinematography—Black-and-White:** Jean Bourgoin, Walter Wottitz, *The Longest Day*, Zanuck, 20th.

Sweet Bird of Youth with Rip Torn and Ed Begley.

Cinematography—Color: Fred A. Young, *Lawrence of Arabia*. **Costume Design—Black-and-White:** Norma Koch, *What Ever Happened to Baby Jane*, Seven Arts, Aldrich, WB. **Costume Design—Color:** Mary Wills, *The Wonderful World of the Brothers Grimm*, MGM. **Film Editing:** Anne Coates, *Lawrence of Arabia*. **Foreign Language Film Award:** *Sundays and Cybele*, Terra-Fides-Orsay-Trocadero (French). **Music—Music Score, Substantially Original:** Maurice Jarre, *Lawrence of Arabia*. **Music—Scoring of Music, Adaptation or Treatment:** Ray Heindorf, *The Music Man*, WB. **Music—Song:** "Days of Wine and Roses" from *Days of Wine and Roses*, Manulis-Jalem, Warner Brothers. Music by Henry Mancini. Lyrics by Johnny Mercer. **Short Subjects—Cartoon:** *The Hole*, Storyboard, Brandon. **Short Subjects—Live Action:** *Heureux Anniversaire* (*Happy Anniversary*), CAPAC, Atlantic (French). Sound: *Lawrence of Arabia*, Shepperton Studio Sound Department (British). John Cox, Sound Director. **Special Effects:** *The Longest Day*. Robert MacDonald (visual); Jacques Maumont (audible). **Writing—Screenplay** based on material from another medium: Horton Foote, *To Kill a Mockingbird*. **Writing—Original Story and Screenplay:** Ennio de Concini, Alfredo Giannetti, Pietro Germi, *Divorce—Italian Style*, Lux-Vides-Galatea, Embassy (Italian). **Documentray—Feature:** *Black Fox*, Image, Heritage. **Documentary—Short Subject:** *Dylan Thomas*, TWW, Janus (Welsh). **Jean Hersholt Humanitarian Award:** Steve Broidy. **Scientific and Technical Awards:** Ralph Chapman, for the design and development of an advanced motion picture camera crane. Albert S. Pratt, James L. Wassell and Hans C. Wohlrab of the Professional Division, Bell & Howell Co., for the design and development of a new and improved automatic motion picture additive color printer. North American Philips Co., Inc., for the design and engineering of the Norelco Universal 70/35-mm motion picture projector. Charles E. Sutter, William Bryson Smith and Louis C. Kennell of Paramount Pictures Corp., for the engineering and application to motion picture production of a new system of electric-power distribution. Electro-Voice, Inc., for a highly directional dynamic line microphone. Louis G. Mackenzie for a selective sound effects repeater.

THIRTY-SIXTH YEAR   1963

Best Picture: *Tom Jones*, Woodfall, UA, Lopert. Other nominees: *America America*, *Cleopatra*, *How the West Was Won*, *Lilies of the Field*. **Actor:** Sidney Poitier in *Lilies of the Field*, Rainbow, UA. Other nominees: Albert Finney in *Tom Jones*, Richard Harris in *This Sporting Life*, Rex Harrison in *Cleopatra*, Paul Newman in *Hud*. **Actress:** Patricia Neal in *Hud*, Salem-Dover, Par. Other nominees: Leslie Caron in *The L-Shaped Room*, Shirley MacLaine in *Irma La Douce*, Rachel Roberts in *This Sporting Life*, Natalie Wood in *Love with the Proper Stranger*. **Supporting Actor:** Melvyn Douglas in *Hud*. **Supporting Actress:** Margaret Rutherford in *The V.I.P.s*, MGM. **Directing:** Tony Richardson, *Tom Jones*. **Art Direction—Black-and-White:** *America America*, Athena, Warner Brothers. Gene Callahan, Art Director. **Art Direction—Color:** *Cleopatra*, 20th. John De Cuir, Jack Martin Smith, Hilyard Brown, Herman Blumenthal, Elven Webb, Maurice Pelling, Boris Juraga, Art Directors. Walter M. Scott, Paul S. Fox, Ray Moyer, Set Decorators. **Cinematography—Black-and-White:** James Wong Howe, *Hud*. **Cinematography—**

Hud with Patricia Neal, Melvyn Douglas and Brandon De Wilde.

Color: Leon Shamroy, *Cleopatra*. **Costume Design—Black-and-White:** Piero Gherardi, *8½*, Cineriz, Embassy. **Costume Design—Color:** Irene Sharaff, Vittorio Nino Novarese, Renie, *Cleopatra*. **Film Editing:** Harold F. Kress, *How the West Was Won*, MGM, Cinerama. **Foreign Language Film Award:** *8.5*, Federico Fellini, Cineriz (Italy). **Music—Music Score, Substantially Original:** John Addison, *Tom Jones*. **Music—Scoring of Music, Adaptation or Treatment:** Andre Previn, *Irma La Douce*, Mirisch-Phalanx, UA. **Music—Song:** "Call Me Irresponsible" from *Papa's Delicate Condition*, Amro, Paramount. Music by James Van Heusen. Lyrics by Sammy Cahn. **Short Subjects—Cartoon:** *The Critic*, Pintoff-Crossbow, Col. **Short Subjects—Live Action:** *An Occurrence at Owl Creek Bridge*, Centaure-Filmartic, Cappagariff-Janus. **Sound:** *How the West Was Won*, Metro-Goldwyn-Mayer Studio Sound Department. Franklin E. Milton, Sound Director. **Sound Effects:** *It's a Mad, Mad, Mad, Mad World*, Casey, United Artists. Walter G. Elliott. **Special Effects:** *Cleopatra*. Emil Kosa, Jr. **Writing—Screenplay based on material from another medium:** John Osborne, *Tom Jones*. **Writing—Original Story and Screenplay:** James R. Webb, *How the West Was Won*. **Documentary—Feature:** *Robert Frost: A Lover's Quarrel With the World*, WGBH Educational Foundation. **Documentary—Short Subject:** *Chagall*, Auerbach-Flag. **Irving G. Thalberg Memorial Award:** Sam Spiegel. **Scientific and Technical Award:** Douglas G. Shearer and A. Arnold Gillespie of Metro-Goldwyn-Mayer Studios, for the engineering of an improved Background Process Projection System.

THIRTY-SEVENTH YEAR   1964

Best Picture: *My Fair Lady*, WB. Other nominees: *Becket, Dr. Strangelove or: How I Learned to Stop Worrying and Love the Bomb, Mary Poppins, Zorba the Greek*. **Actor:** Rex Harrison in *My Fair Lady*. Other nominees: Richard Burton in *Becket*, Peter O'Toole in *Becket*, Anthony Quinn in *Zorba the Greek*, Peter Sellers in *Dr. Strangelove*. **Actress:** Julie Andrews in *Mary Poppins*, Disney. Other nominees: Anne Bancroft in *The Pumpkin Eater*, Sophia Loren in *Marriage Italian Style*, Debbie Reynolds in *The Unsinkable Molly Brown*, Kim Stanley in *Seance on a Wet Afternoon*. **Supporting Actor:** Peter Ustinov in *Topkapi*, Filmways, UA. **Supporting Actress:** Lila Kedrova in *Zorba the Greek*, International. **Directing:** George Cukor, *My Fair Lady*. **Foreign Language Film Award:** *Yesterday, Today and Tomorrow*, Champion-Concordia (Italian). **Art Direction—Black-and-White:** *Zorba the Greek*. Vassilis Fotopoulos, Art Director. **Art Direction—Color:** *My Fair Lady*. Gene Allen, Cecil Beaton, Art Directors. George James Hopkins, Set Decorator. **Cinematography—Black-and-White:** Walter Lassally, *Zorba the Greek*. **Cinematography—Color:** Harry Stradling, *My Fair Lady*. **Costume Design—Black-and-White:** Dorothy Jeakins, *The Night of the Iguana*, Seven Arts, MGM. **Costume Design—Color:** Cecil Beaton, *My Fair Lady*. **Film Editing:** Cotton Warburton, *Mary Poppins*. **Music—Original Score:** Richard M. Sherman, Robert B. Sherman, *Mary Poppins*. **Music—Scoring, Adaptation or Treatment:** Andre Previn, *My Fair Lady*. **Music—Song:** "Chim Chim Cher-ee" from *Mary Poppins*. Music and lyrics by Richard M. Sherman, Robert B. Sherman. **Short Subjects—Cartoon:** *The Pink Phink*, Mirisch-Geoffrey, UA. **Short Subjects—Live Action:** *Casals Conducts: 1964*, Thalia. **Sound:** *My Fair Lady*. Warner Brothers Studio Sound Department. George R. Groves, Sound Director. **Sound Effects:** *Goldfinger*, Eon, United Artists. Norman Wanstall. **Special Visual Effects:** Peter Ellenshaw, Hamilton Luske, Eustace Lycett, *Mary Poppins*. **Writing—Screenplay adapted from another medium:** Edward Anhalt, *Becket*, Wallis, Paramount. **Writing—Original Story and Screenplay:** *Father Goose*, Universal. Story: S. H. Barnett. Screenplay: Peter Stone, Frank Tarloff. **Documentary—Feature:** *World Without Sun*, Col. **Documentary—Short Subject:** *Nine From Little Rock*, USIA, Guggenheim. **Honorary Award:** William Tuttle, for his outstanding make-up achievement for *7 Faces Of Dr. Lao*. **Scientific and Technical Awards:** Petro Vlahos, Wadsworth E. Pohl and Ub Iwerks, for the conception and perfection of techniques for Color Traveling Matte Composite Cinematography. Sidney P. Solow, Edward H. Reichard, Carl W. Hauge and Job Sanderson of Consolidated Film Industries, for the design and development of a versatile Automatic 35-mm. Composite Color Printer. Pierre Angenieux for the development of a ten-

Topkapi with Peter Ustinov and Maximilian Schell.

to-one Zoom Lens for cinematography. Milton Forman, Richard B. Glickman and Daniel J. Pearlman of ColorTran Industries, for advancements in the design and application to motion picture photography of lighting units using quartz iodine lamps. Stewart Filmscreen Corporation, for a seamless translucent Blue Screen for Traveling Matte Color Cinematography. Anthony Paglia and the 20th Century-Fox Studio Mechanical Effects Department, for an improved method of producing Explosion Flash Effects for motion pictures. Edward H. Reichard and Carl W. Hauge of Consolidated Film Industries, for the design of a Proximity Cue Detector and its application to motion picture printers. Edward H. Reichard, Leonard L. Sokolow and Carl W. Hauge of Consolidated Film Industries, for the design and application to motion picture laboratory practice of a Stroboscopic Scene Tester for color and black-and-white film. Nelson Tyler, for the design and construction of an improved Helicopter Camera System.

THIRTY-EIGHTH YEAR   1965

Best Picture: *The Sound of Music*, Argyle, 20th. Other nominees: *Darling, Doctor Zhivago, Ship of Fools, A Thousand Clowns.* **Actor:** Lee Marvin in *Cat Ballou*, Hecht, Columbia. Other nominees: Richard Burton in *The Spy Who Came In From the Cold*, Laurence Olivier in *Othello*, Rod Steiger in *The Pawnbroker*, Oskar Werner in *Ship of Fools*. **Actress:** Julie Christie in *Darling*, Anglo-Amalgamated, Embassy. Other nominees: Julie Andrews in *The Sound of Music*, Samantha Eggar in *The Collector*, Elizabeth Hartman in *A Patch of Blue*, Simone Signoret in *Ship of Fools*. **Supporting Actor:** Martin Balsam in *A Thousand Clowns*, Harrell, UA. **Supporting Actress:** Shelley Winters in *A Patch of Blue*, Berman-Green. **Directing:** Robert Wise, *The Sound of Music*. **Art Direction—Black-and-White:** *Ship of Fools*, Columbia. Rebert Clatworthy, Art Director. Joseph Kish, Set Decorator. **Art Direction—Color:** *Doctor Zhivago*, MGM. John Box, Terry Marsh, Art Directors. Dario Simoni, Set Decorator. **Cinematography—Black-and-White:** Ernest Laszlo, *Ship of Fools*. **Cinematography—Color:** Freddie Young, *Doctor Zhivago*. **Costume Design—Black-and-White:** Julie Harris, *Darling*. **Costume Design—Color:** Phyllis Dalton, *Doctor Zhivago*. **Film Editing:** William Reynolds, *The Sound of Music*. **Foreign Language Film Award:** *The Shop on Main Street*, Ceskoslovensky (Czechoslovakian). **Music—Original Score:** Maurice Jarre, *Doctor Zhivago*. **Music—Scoring of Music, Adaptation or Treatment:** Irwin Kostal, *The Sound of Music*. **Music—Song:** "The Shadow of Your Smile" from *The Sandpiper*, Filmways-Venice, MGM. Music by Johnny Mandel. Lyrics by Paul Francis Webster. **Short Subjects—Cartoon:** *The Dot and the Line*, MGM. **Short Subjects—Live Action:** *The Chicken* (*Le Poulet*), Renn, Pathé Contemporary. **Sound:** *The Sound of Music*. 20th Century-Fox Studio Sound Department. James P. Corcoran, Sound Director. Todd-AO Sound Department. Fred Hynes, Sound Director. **Sound Effects:** *The Great Race*, Patricia-Jalem-Reynard, WB. **Special Visual Effects:** *Thunderball*, Broccoli-Saltzman, UA. John Stears. **Writing—Screenplay based on material from another medium:** Robert Blot, *Doctor Zhivago*. **Writing—Original Story and Screenplay:** Frederick Raphael, *Darling*. **Documentary—Feature:** *The Eleanor Roosevelt Story*, Glazier, AIP. **Documentary—Short Subject:** *To Be Alive!*, Johnson Wax. **Irving G. Thalberg Memorial Award:** William Wyler. **Jean Hersholt Humanitarian Award:** Edmond L. DePatie. **Honorary**

Award: Bob Hope, for unique and distinguished service to our industry and the Academy. **Scientific and Technical Awards:** Arthur J. Hatch of The Strong Electric Corporation, subsidiary of General Precision Equipment Corporation, for the design and development of an Air Blown Carbon Arc Projection Lamp. Stefan Kudelski, for the design and development of the Nagra portable 1/4″ tape-recording system for motion picture sound recording.

THIRTY-NINTH YEAR   1966

Best Picture: *A Man for All Seasons*, Highland Films, Col. Other nominees: *Alfie, The Russians Are Coming, the Russians Are Coming, The Sand Pebbles, Who's Afraid of Virginia Woolf?* **Actor:** Paul Scofield in *A Man for all Seasons*. Other nominees: Alan Arkin in *The Russians Are Coming, the Russians Are Coming;* Richard Burton in *Who's Afraid of Virginia Woolf?*, Michael Caine in *Alfie*, Steve McQueen in *The Sand Pebbles*. **Actress:** Elizabeth Taylor in *Who's Afraid of Virginia Woolf?*, Chenault, WB. Other nominees: Anouk Aimée in *A Man and a Woman*, Ida Kaminska in *The Shop on Main Street*, Lynn Redgrave in *Georgy Girl*, Vanessa Redgrave in *Morgan*. **Supporting Actor:** Walter Matthau in *The Fortune Cookie*, Phalanx-Jalem-Mirisch, UA. **Supporting Actress:** Sandy Dennis in *Who's Afraid of Virginia Woolf?* **Directing:** Fred Zinnemann, *A Man for All Seasons*. **Art Direction—Black-and-White:** *Who's Afraid of Virginia Woolf?*, Richard Sylbert, Art Director. George James Hopkins, Set Decorator. **Art Direction—Color:** *Fantastic Voyage*, 20th. Jack Martin Smith, Dale Hennesy, Art Directors. Walter M. Scott, Stuart A. Reiss, Set Decorators. **Cinematography—Black-and-White:** Haskell Wexler, *Who's Afraid of Virginia Woolf?* **Cinematography—Color:** Ted Moore, *A Man for All Seasons*. **Costume Design—Black-and-White:** Irene Sharaff, *Who's Afraid of Virginia Woolf?* **Costume Design—Color:** Elizabeth Haffenden, Joan Bridge, *A Man for All Seasons*. **Film Editing:** Fredric Steinkamp, Henry Berman, Stewart Linder, Frank Santillo, *Grand Prix*, MGM. **Foreign Language Film:** *A Man and a Woman*, Les Films 13 (France). **Music—Scoring, Substantially Original:** John Barry, *Born Free*, Col. **Music—Scoring, Adaptation or Treatment:** Ken Thorne, *A Funny Thing Happened on the Way to the Forum*, Melvin Frank, UA. **Music—Song:** "Born Free" from *Born Free*. Music by John Barry. Lyrics by Don Black. **Short Subjects—Cartoon:** *Herb Alpert and the Tijuana Brass Double Feature*, Hubley, Par. **Short Subjects—Live Action:** *Wild Wings*, British Transport, Manson. **Writing—Screenplay based on material from another medium:** Robert Bolt, *A Man for All Seasons*. **Writing—Original Story and Screenplay:** *A Man and a Woman*. Story by Claude Lelouch. Screenplay by Pierre Uytterhoeven, Claude Lelouch. **Documentary—Feature:** *The War Game*, BBC, Pathé. **Documentary—Short Subject:** *A Year Toward Tomorrow*, Sun Dial, Office of Economic Opportunity. **Sound:** Metro-Goldwyn-Mayer Studio Sound Department, *Grand Prix*. Franklin E. Milton, Sound Director. **Sound Effects:** Gordon Daniel, *Grand Prix*. **Special Visual Effects:** Art Cruickshank, *Fantastic Voyage*. **Irving G. Thalberg Memorial Award:** Robert Wise. **Jean Hersholt Humanitarian Award:** George Bagnall. **Honorary Awards:** Y. Frank Freeman, for unusual and outstanding service to the Academy during his thirty years in Hollywood. Yakima Canutt, for creating the profession of stuntman as it exists today and for the development of many safety devices used by stuntmen everywhere. **Scientific and Technical Awards:** Mitchell Camera Corp., for design and development of the Mitchell Mark II 35-mm. portable motion picture reflex camera. Arnold and Richter K.G., for the design and development of the Arriflex 35-mm. portable reflex motion picture camera. Panavision, Inc., for the design of the Panatron Power Inverter and its application to motion picture camera operation. Carroll Knudson, for production of a composer's manual for motion picture music synchronization. Ruby Raskin, for production of a composer's manual for motion picture music synchronization.

FORTIETH YEAR   1967

Best Picture: *In the Heat of the Night*, Mirisch, UA. Other nominees: *Bonnie and Clyde, Doctor Dolittle, The Graduate, Guess Who's Coming to Dinner.* **Actor:** Rod Steiger in *In the Heat of the Night*. Other nominees: Warren Beatty in *Bonnie and Clyde*, Dustin Hoffman in *The Graduate*, Paul Newman in *Cool Hand Luke*, Spencer Tracy in *Guess*

Who's Coming to Dinner. **Actress:** Katharine Hepburn in *Guess Who's Coming to Dinner*, Col. Other nominees: Anne Bancroft in *The Graduate*, Faye Dunaway in *Bonnie and Clyde*, Dame Edith Evans in *The Whisperers*, Audrey Hepburn in *Wait Until Dark*. **Supporting Actor:** George Kennedy in *Cool Hand Luke*, Jalem, WB-7Arts. **Supporting Actress:** Estelle Parsons in *Bonnie and Clyde*, Tatira-Hiller, WB-7Arts. **Directing:** Mike Nichols, *The Graduate*. **Art Direction:** *Camelot*, WB-7Arts. John Truscott, Edward Carrere, Art Directors. John W. Brown, Set Decorator. **Cinematography:** Burnett Guffey, *Bonnie and Clyde*. **Costume Design:** John Truscott, *Camelot*. **Film Editing:** Hal Ashby, *In the Heat of the Night*. **Foreign Language Film Award:** *Closely Watched Trains*, Barrandov, Sigma III. *Music— Original Score:* Elmer Bernstein, *Thoroughly Modern Millie*, Univ. **Music—Adaptation or Treatment:** Alfred Newman, Ken Darby, *Camelot*. **Music—Song:** *Talk to the Animals* from *Doctor Dolittle*, Apjac, 20th, Music and lyrics by Leslie Bricusse. **Short Subjects— Cartoon:** *The Box*, Murikami, Wolf, Brandon. **Short Subjects—Live Action:** *A Place to Stand*, T.D.F., Col. **Writing—Screenplay based on material from another medium:** Stirling Silliphant, *In the Heat of the Night*. **Writing—Original Story and Screenplay:** William Rose, *Guess Who's Coming to Dinner*. **Documentary—Feature:** *The Anderson Platoon*, French Broadcasting System. **Documentary—Short Subject:** *The Redwoods*, King. **Sound:** *In the Heat of the Night*, Samuel Goldwyn Studio Sound Department. **Sound Effects:** John Poyner, *The Dirty Dozen*, MKH, MGM. **Special Visual Effects:** L.B. Abbott, *Doctor Dolittle*. **Irving G. Thalberg Memorial Award:** Alfred Hitchcok. **Jean Hersholt Humanitarian Award:** Gregory Peck. **Scientific and Technical Awards:** Electro-Optical Division of the Kollmorgen Corporation, for the design and development of a series of motion picture projection lenses. PanvisionInc., for a variable speed motor for motion picture cameras. Fred R. Wilson, Samuel Goldwyn Studio Department, for an audio level clamper. Waldon O. Watson and the Universal City Studio Sound Department, for new concepts in the design of a music scoring stage.

NATIONAL BOARD OF REVIEW AWARDS

The National Board of Review Committee, consisting of about 175 public-spirited men and women with an interest in motion pictures and a mature sense of social responsibility, votes on the pictures to be recommended to the Board's Committee on Exceptional Films; and this Committee, composed of men and women with critical experience and flair, vote on the "Ten Best."

Just what the Committee on Exceptional Films cites annually has evolved through the years. In 1930–31, for example, the Committee listed its "Ten Best" alphabetically. In 1932 it picked a best film of the year (*I Am a Fugitive From a Chain Gang*) and listed its nine other choices alphabetically. The following year it arranged its "Ten Best" according to the number of votes each film received. In 1937 it began citing the year's best performances, and in 1945 it refined this to naming the best actress and actor, adding, in 1954, the best supporting actress and supporting actor. For a time the Committee considered documentaries separately from fiction films, but during World War II there were so many documentaries that the Committee abandoned a distinction which was, at bottom, only formal. Toward the end of the war, and for a few years after it, the Committee did not use separate categories for American and foreign films.

1930

American: 1) *All Quiet on the Western Front;* 2) *Holiday;* 3) *Laughter;*

4) *The Man From Blankley's;* 5) *Men Without Women;* 6) *Morocco;* 7) *Outward Bound;* 8) *Romance;* 9) *The Street of Chance;* 10) *Tol'able David.*

Foreign: 1) *High Treason;* 2) *Old and New;* 3) *Soil;* 4) *Storm Over Asia;* 5) *Zwei Herzen im 3/4 Takt.*

1931

American: 1) *Cimarron;* 2) *City Lights;* 3) *City Streets;* 4) *Dishonored;* 5) *The Front Page;* 6) *The Guardsman;* 7) *Quick Millions;* 8) *Rango;* 9) *Surrender;* 10) *Tabu.*

Foreign: 1) *Die Dreigroschenoper (The Three Penny Opera);* 2) *Das Lied vom Leben;* 3) *Le Million;* 4) *Sous les Toits de Paris;* 5) *Vier vom der Infanterie (Comrades of Westfront 1918).*

1932

American: 1) *I Am a Fugitive from a Chain Gang;* 2) *As You Desire Me;* 3) *A Bill of Divorcement;* 4) *A Farewell to Arms;* 5) *Madame Racketeer;* 6) *Payment Deferred;* 7) *Scarface;* 8) *Tarzan the Ape Man;* 9) *Trouble in Paradise;* 10) *Two Seconds.*

Foreign: 1) *A Nous la Liberte;* 2) *Der Andere;* 3) *The Battle of Gallipoli;* 4) *Golden Mountains;* 5) *Kameradschaft;* 6) *Madchen in Uniform;* 7) *Der Raub der Mona Lisa;* 8) *Reserved for Ladies;* 9) *Road to Life;* 10) *Zwei Menschen.*

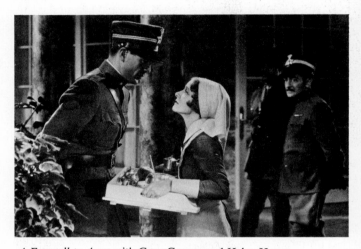

A Farewell to Arms with Gary Cooper and Helen Hayes.

1933

American: 1) *Topaze;* 2) *Berkeley Square;* 3) *Cavalcade;* 4) *Little Women;* 5) *Mama Loves Papa;* 6) *The Pied Piper* (cartoon); 7) *She Done Him Wrong;* 8) *State Fair;* 9) *Three-Cornered Moon;* 10) *Zoo in Budapest.*

Cavalcade with Herbert Mundin and Bonita Granville.

Foreign: 1) *Hertha's Erwachen;* 2) *Ivan;* 3) *M;* 4) *Morgenrot;* 5) *Niemandsland (Hell on Earth);* 6) *Poil de Carotte;* 7) *The Private Life of Henry VIII;* 8) *Quatorze Juillet;* 9) *Rome Express;* 10) *Le Sang d'un Poet (Blood of a Poet).*

1934

American: 1) *It Happened One Night;* 2) *The Count of Monte Cristo;* 3) *Crime Without Passion;* 4) *Eskimo;* 5) *The First World War;* 6) *The Lost Patrol;* 7) *Lot in Sodom* (a nontheatrical short); 8) *No Greater Glory;* 9) *The Thin Man;* 10) *Viva Villa!*

Foreign: 1) *Man of Aran;* 2) *The Blue Light;* 3) *Catherine the Great;* 4) *The Constant Nymph;* 5) *Madame Bovary.*

It Happened One Night with Clark Gable and Claudette Colbert.

1935

American: 1) *The Informer;* 2) *Alice Adams;* 3) *Anna Karenina;* 4) *David Copperfield;* 5) *The Gilded Lily;* 6) *Les Miserables;* 7) *The Lives of a Bengal Lancer;* 8) *Mutiny on the Bounty;* 9) *Ruggles of Red Gap;* 10) *Who Killed Cock Robin* (cartoon).

Foreign: 1) *Chapayev;* 2) *Crime et Chatimen (Crime and Punishment);* 3) *Le Dernier Milliardaire;* 4) *The Man Who Knew Too Much;* 5) *Marie Chapdelaine;* 6) *La Maternelle;* 7) *The New Gulliver;* 8) *Peasants;* 9) *Thunder in the East;* 10) *The Youth of Maxim.*

1936

American: 1) *Mr. Deeds Goes to Town;* 2) *The Story of Louis Pasteur;* 3) *Modern Times;* 4) *Fury;* 5) *Winterset;* 6) *The Devil Is a Sissy;* 7) *Ceiling Zero;* 8) *Romeo and Juliet;* 9) *The Prisoner of Shark Island;* 10) *Green Pastures.*

Foreign: 1) *La Kermesse Heroique (Carnival in Flanders);* 2) *The New Earth;* 3) *Rembrandt;* 4) *The Ghost Goes West;* 5) *Nine Days a Queen;* 6) *We Are from Kronstadt;* 7) *Son of Mongolia;* 8) *The Yellow Cruise;* 9) *Les Miserables* (with Harry Baur); 10) *The Secret Agent.*

1937

American: 1) *Night Must Fall;* 2) *The Life of Emile Zola;* 3) *Black Legion;* 4) *Camille;* 5) *Make Way for Tomorrow;* 6) *The Good Earth;* 7) *They Won't Forget;* 8) *Captains Courageous;* 9) *A Star Is Born;* 10) *Stage Door.*

Foreign: 1) *The Eternal Mask;* 2) *The Lower Depths;* 3) *Baltic Deputy;* 4) *Mayerling;* 5) *The Spanish Earth;* 6) *Golgotha;* 7) *Elephant Boy;* 8) *Rembrandt;* 9) *Janosik;* 10) *The Wedding of Palo.*

Best Acting (alphabetically): Harry Baur, *The Golem;* Humphrey Bogart, *Black Legion;* Charles Boyer, *Conquest;* Nikolai Cherkassov,

Captains Courageous with Freddie Bartholomew and Spencer Tracy.

Baltic Deputy; Danielle Darrieux, *Mayerling;* Greta Garbo, *Camille;* Robert Montgomery, *Night Must Fall;* Maria Ouspenskaya, *Conquest;* Luise Rainer, *The Good Earth;* Joseph Schildkraut, *The Life of Emile Zola;* Mathias Wieman, *The Eternal Mask;* Dame May Whitty, *Night Must Fall.*

1938

English Language: 1) *The Citadel;* 2) *Snow White and the Seven Dwarfs;* 3) *The Beachcomber;* 4) *To the Victor;* 5) *Sing You Sinners;* 6) *The Edge of the World;* 7) *Of Human Hearts;* 8) *Jezebel;* 9) *South Riding;* 10) *Three Comrades.*

Foreign: 1) *La Grande Illusion;* 2) *Ballerina;* 3) *Un Carnet de Bal;* 4) *Generals Without Buttons;* 5) *Peter the First.*

Best Acting (alphabetically): Lew Ayres, *Holiday;* Pierre Blanchar, Harry Baur, Louis Jouvet and Raimu, *Un Carnet de Bal;* James Cagney, *Angels with Dirty Faces;* Joseph Calleia, *Algiers;* Chico, *The Adventures of Chico;* Robert Donat, *The Citadel;* Will Fyffe, *To the Victor;* Pierre Fresnay, Jean Gabin, Dita Parlo and Erich von Stroheim, *La Grande Illusion;* John Garfield, *Four Daughters;* Wendy Hiller, *Pygmalion;* Charles Laughton and Elsa Lanchester, *The Beachcomber;* Robert Morley, *Marie Antoinette;* Ralph Richardson, *South Riding* and *The Citadel;* Margaret Sullavan, *Three Comrades;* Spencer Tracy, *Boys Town.*

1939

English Language: 1) *Confessions of a Nazi Spy;* 2) *Wuthering Heights;* 3) *Stagecoach;* 4) *Ninotchka;* 5) *Young Mr. Lincoln;* 6) *Crisis;* 7) *Goodbye, Mr. Chips;* 8) *Mr. Smith Goes to Washington;* 9) *The Roaring Twenties;* 10) *U-Boat 29.*

Foreign: 1) *Port of Shadows;* 2) *Harvest;* 3) *Alexander Nevsky;* 4) *The End of a Day;* 5) *Robert Koch.*

Best Acting (alphabetically): James Cagney, *The Roaring Twenties;* Bette Davis, *Dark Victory* and *The Old Maid;* Geraldine Fitzgerald, *Dark Victory* and *Wuthering Heights;* Henry Fonda, *Young Mr. Lincoln;* Jean Gabin, *Port of Shadows;* Greta Garbo, *Ninotchka;* Francis Lederer and Paul Lukas, *Confessions of a Nazi Spy;* Thomas Mitchell, *Stagecoach;* Laurence Olivier, *Wuthering Heights;* Flora

Goodbye, Mr. Chips with Robert Donat and Greer Garson.

Robson, *We Are Not Alone;* Michel Simon, *Port of Shadows* and *The End of a Day.*

1940

American: 1) *The Grapes of Wrath;* 2) *The Great Dictator;* 3) *Of Mice and Men;* 4) *Our Town;* 5) *Fantasia;* 6) *The Long Voyage Home;* 7) *Foreign Correspondent;* 8) *The Biscuit Eater;* 9) *Gone With the Wind;* 10) *Rebecca.*

Foreign: *The Baker's Wife.*

Best Acting (alphabetically): Jane Bryan, *We Are Not Alone;* Charles Chaplin, *The Great Dictator;* Jane Darwell, *The Grapes of Wrath;* Betty Field, *Of Mice and Men;* Henry Fonda, *The Grapes of Wrath* and *Return of Frank James;* Joan Fontaine, *Rebecca;* Greer Garson, *Pride and Prejudice;* William Holden, *Our Town;* Vivien Leigh, *Gone With the Wind* and *Waterloo Bridge;* Thomas Mitchell, *The Long Voyage Home;* Raimu, *The Baker's Wife;* Ralph Richardson, *The Fugitive;* Ginger Rogers, *The Primrose Path;* George Sanders, *Rebecca;* Martha Scott, *Our Town;* James Stewart, *The Shop Around the Corner;* Conrad Veidt, *Escape.*

Best Documentary: *The Fight for Life.*

1941

American: 1) *Citizen Kane;* 2) *How Green Was My Valley;* 3) *The Little Foxes;* 4) *The Stars Look Down;* 5) *Dumbo;* 6) *High Sierra;* 7) *Here Comes Mr. Jordan;* 8) *Tom, Dick and Harry;* 9) *The Road to Zanzibar;* 10) *The Lady Eve.*

Foreign: *Pepe le Moko.*

Best Acting (alphabetically): Sara Allgood, *How Green was My Valley;* Mary Astor, *The Great Lie* and *The Maltese Falcon;* Ingrid Bergman, *Rage in Heaven;* Humphrey Bogart, *High Sierra* and *The Maltese Falcon;* Gary Cooper, *Sergeant York;* Donald Crisp, *How Green Was My Valley;* Bing Crosby, *The Road to Zanzibar* and *Birth of the Blues;* George Coulouris, *Citizen Kane;* Patricia Collinge and Bette Davis, *The Little Foxes;* Isobel Elsom, *Ladies in Retirement;* Joan Fontaine, *Suspicion;* Greta Garbo, *Two-Faced Woman;* James Gleason, *Meet John Doe* and *Here Comes Mr. Jordan;* Walter Huston, *All That Money Can Buy;* Ida Lupino, *High Sierra* and *Ladies in Retirement;* Roddy MacDowell, *How Green Was My Valley;* Robert Montgomery, *Rage in Heaven* and *Here Comes Mr. Jordan;* Ginger Rogers, *Kitty Foyle* and *Tom, Dick and Harry;* James Stephenson, *The Letter* and *Shining Victory;* Orson Welles, *Citizen Kane.*

Citizen Kane with Joseph Cotten and Orson Welles.

1942

English Language: 1) *In Which We Serve;* 2) *One of Our Aircraft Is Missing;* 3) *Mrs. Miniver;* 4) *Journey for Margaret;* 5) *Wake Island;* 6) *The Male Animal;* 7) *The Major and the Minor;* 8) *Sullivan's Travels;* 9) *The Moon and Sixpence;* 10) *The Pied Piper.*

Foreign: None were cited.

Documentary: *Moscow Strikes Back.*

Best Acting (alphabetically): Ernest Anderson, *In This Our Life;* Florence Bates, *The Moon and Sixpence;* James Cagney, *Yankee Doodle Dandy;* Charles Coburn, *H. M. Pulham, Esq.; In This Our Life* and *Kings Row;* Jack Carson, *The Male Animal;* Greer Garson, *Mrs. Miniver* and *Random Harvest;* Sidney Greenstreet, *Across the Pacific;* William Holden, *The Remarkable Andrew;* Tim Holt, *The Magnificent Ambersons;* Glynis Johns, *The Invaders;* Gene Kelly, *For Me and My Gal;* Diana Lynn, *The Major and the Minor;* Ida Lupino, *Moontide;* Bernard Miles and John Mills, *In Which We Serve;* Agnes Moorehead, *The Magnificent Ambersons;* Hattie McDaniel, *In This Our Life;* Thomas Mitchell, *Moontide;* Margaret O'Brien, *Journey for Margaret;* Susan Peters, *Random Harvest;* Edward G. Robinson, *Tales of Manhattan;* Ginger Rogers, *Roxie Hart* and *The Major and the Minor;* George Sanders, *The Moon and Sixpence;* Ann Sheridan, *Kings Row;* William Severn, *Journey for Margaret;* Rudy Vallee, *The Palm Beach Story;* Anton Walbrook, *The Invaders;* Googie Withers, *One of Our Aircraft Is Missing;* Monty Woolley, *The Pied Piper;* Teresa Wright, *Mrs. Miniver;* Robert Young, *H. M. Pulham, Esq., Joe Smith, American* and *Journey for Margaret.*

1943

English Language: 1) *The Ox-Bow Incident;* 2) *Watch on the Rhine;* 3) *Air Force;* 4) *Holy Matrimony;* 5) *The Hard Way;* 6) *Casablanca;* 7) *Lassie Come Home;* 8) *Bataan;* 9) *The Moon Is Down;* 10) *The Next of Kin.*

Foreign: None Cited.

Documentary: 1) *Desert Victory;* 2) *Battle of Russia;* 3) *Prelude to War;* 4) *Saludos Amigos;* 5) *The Silent Village.*

Best Direction: William A. Wellman, *The Ox-Bow Incident;* Tay Garnett, *Bataan* and *The Cross of Lorraine;* Michael Curtiz, *Casablanca* and *This Is the Army.*

Best Actresses: Gracie Fields, *Holy Matrimony;* Katina Paxinou, *For Whom the Bell Tolls;* Teresa Wright, *Shadow of a Doubt.*

Best Actors: Paul Lukas, *Watch on the Rhine;* Henry Morgan, *The Ox-Bow Incident* and *Happy Land;* Cedric Hardwicke, *The Moon Is Down* and *The Cross of Lorraine.*

1944

English Language: 1) *None But the Lonely Heart;* 2) *Going My Way;* 3) *The Miracle of Morgan's Creek;* 4) *Hail the Conquering Hero;* 5) *The Song of Bernadette;* 6) *Wilson;* 7) *Meet Me in St. Louis;* 8) *Thirty Seconds Over Tokyo;* 9) *Thunder Rock;* 10) *Lifeboat.*

Foreign: None cited.

Documentaries: 1) *The Memphis Belle;* 2) *Attack! The Battle for New Britain;* 3) *With the Marines at Tarawa;* 4) *Battle for the Marianas;* 5) *Tunisian Victory.*

Best Acting (alphabetically): Ethel Barrymore, *None But the Lonely Heart;* Ingrid Bergman, *Gaslight;* Eddie Bracken, *Hail the Conquering Hero;* Humphrey Bogart, *To Have and Have Not;* Bing Crosby, *Going My Way;* June Duprez, *None But the Lonely Heart;* Barry Fitzgerald, *Going My Way;* Betty Hutton, *The Miracle of Morgan's Creek;* Margaret O'Brien, *Meet Me in St. Louis;* Franklin Pangborn, *Hail the Conquering Hero.*

1945

The Ten Best (including documentaries as well as feature-films, and British as well as American): 1) *The True Glory;* 2) *The Lost Weekend;* 3) *The Southerner;* 4) *The Story of G.I. Joe;* 5) *The Last Chance;* 6)

Colonel Blimp; 7) *A Tree Grows in Brooklyn;* 8) *The Fighting Lady;* 9) *The Way Ahead;* 10) *The Clock.*

Foreign: None cited.

Best Director: Jean Renoir, *The Southerner.*

Best Actress: Joan Crawford, *Mildred Pierce.*

Best Actor: Ray Milland, *The Lost Weekend.*

1946

The Ten Best: 1) *Henry V;* 2) *Open City;* 3) *The Best Years of Our Lives;* 4) *Brief Encounter;* 5) *A Walk in the Sun;* 6) *It Happened at the Inn;* 7) *My Darling Clementine;* 8) *The Diary of a Chambermaid;* 9) *The Killers;* 10) *Anna and the King of Siam.*

Best Director: William Wyler, *The Best Years of Our Lives.*

Best Actress: Anna Magnani, *Open City.*

Best Actor: Laurence Olivier, *Henry V.*

The Best Years of Our Lives with Dana Andrews and Harold Russell.

1947

The Ten Best: 1) *Monsieur Verdoux;* 2) *Great Expectations;* 3) *Shoe-Shine;* 4) *Crossfire;* 5) *Boomerang!;* 6) *Odd Man Out;* 7) *Gentleman's Agreement;* 8) *To Live in Peace;* 9) *It's a Wonderful Life;* 10) *The Overlanders.*

Best Director: Elia Kazan, *Boomerang!* and *Gentleman's Agreement.*

Best Actress: Celia Johnson, *This Happy Breed.*

Best Actor: Michael Redgrave, *Mourning Becomes Electra.*

1948

The Ten Best: 1) *Paisan;* 2) *Day of Wrath;* 3) *The Search;* 4) *Treasure of Sierra Madre;* 5) *Louisiana Story;* 6) *Hamlet;* 7) *The Snake Pit;* 8) *Johnny Belinda;* 9) *Joan of Arc;* 10) *The Red Shoes.*

Best Director: Roberto Rossellini, *Paisan.*

Best Actress: Olivia De Havilland, *The Snake Pit.*

Best Actor: Walter Huston, *Treasure of Sierra Madre.*

Best Script: John Huston, *Treasure of Sierra Madre.*

1949

The Ten Best: 1) *The Bicycle Thief;* 2) *The Quiet One;* 3) *Intruder in the Dust;* 4) *The Heiress;* 5) *Devil in the Flesh;* 6) *Quartet;* 7) *Germany, Year Zero;* 8) *Home of the Brave;* 9) *Letter to Three Wives;* 10) *The Fallen Idol.*

Best Director: Vittorio de Sica, *The Bicycle Thief.*

The Search with Montgomery Clift, Ivan Jandl and Wendell Corey.

Best Actress: None.

Best Actor: Ralph Richardson, *The Heiress* and *The Fallen Idol.*

Best Script: Graham Greene, *The Fallen Idol.*

1950

American: 1) *Sunset Boulevard;* 2) *All About Eve;* 3) *The Asphalt Jungle;* 4) *The Men;* 5) *Edge of Doom;* 6) *Twelve O'Clock High;* 7) *Panic in the Streets;* 8) *Cyrano de Bergerac;* 9) *No Way Out;* 10) *Stage Fright.*

Foreign: 1) *The Titan;* 2) *Tight Little Island;* 3) *The Third Man;* 4) *Kind Hearts and Coronets;* 5) *Paris 1900.*

Best Director: John Huston, *The Asphalt Jungle.*

Best Actress: Gloria Swanson, *Sunset Boulevard.*

Best Actor: Alec Guinness, *Kind Hearts and Coronets.*

1951

American: 1) *A Place in the Sun;* 2) *Red Badge of Courage;* 3) *An American in Paris;* 4) *Death of a Salesman;* 5) *Detective Story;* 6) *A Streetcar Named Desire;* 7) *Decision Before Dawn;* 8) *Strangers on a Train;* 9) *Quo Vadis;* 10) *Fourteen Hours.*

Foreign: 1) *Rashomon;* 2) *The River;* 3) *Miracle in Milan;* 4) *Kon-Tiki;* 5) *The Browning Version.*

Best Director: Akira Kurosawa, *Rashomon.*

Best Actress: Jan Sterling, *The Big Carnival.*

Best Actor: Richard Basehart, *Fourteen Hours.*

Best Script: T. E. B. Clarke, *The Lavender Hill Mob.*

All About Eve with Bette Davis, Gary Merrill, Anne Baxter and George Sanders.

1952

American: 1) *The Quiet Man;* 2) *High Noon;* 3) *Limelight;* 4) *Five Fingers;* 5) *The Snows of Kilimanjaro;* 6) *The Thief;* 7) *The Bad and the Beautiful;* 8) *Singin' in the Rain;* 9) *Above and Beyond;* 10) *My Son John.*

Foreign: 1) *Breaking the Sound Barrier;* 2) *The Man in the White Suit;* 3) *Forbidden Games;* 4) *Beauty and the Devil;* 5) *Ivory Hunter.*

Best Director: David Lean, *Breaking the Sound Barrier.*

Best Actress: Shirley Booth, *Come Back, Little Sheba.*

Best Actor: Ralph Richardson, *Breaking the Sound Barrier.*

1953

American: 1) *Julius Caesar:* 2) *Shane;* 3) *From Here to Eternity;* 4) *Martin Luther;* 5) *Lili;* 6) *Roman Holiday;* 7) *Stalag 17;* 8) *Little Fugitive;* 9) *Mogambo;* 10) *The Robe*

Foreign: 1) *A Queen Is Crowned;* 2) *Moulin Rouge;* 3) *The Little World of Don Camillo;* 4) *Strange Deception;* 5) *Conquest of Everest.*

Best Director: George Stevens, *Shane.*

Best Actress: Jean Simmons, *Young Bess, The Robe* and *The Actress.*

Best Actor: James Mason, *Face to Face, The Desert Rats, The Man Between* and *Julius Caesar.*

Stalag 17 with Robert Strauss, William Holden and Harvey Lembeck.

1954

American: 1) *On the Waterfront;* 2) *Seven Brides for Seven Brothers;* 3) *The Country Girl;* 4) *A Star Is Born;* 5) *Executive Suite;* 6) *The Vanishing Prairie;* 7) *Sabrina;* 8) *20,000 Leagues Under the Sea;* 9) *The Unconquered;* 10) *Beat the Devil.*

Foreign: 1) *Romeo and Juliet;* 2) *The Heart of the Matter;* 3) *Gate of Hell;* 4) *Diary of a Country Priest;* 5) *The Little Kidnappers;* 6) *Genevieve;* 7) *Beauties of the Night;* 8) *Mr. Hulot's Holiday;* 9) *The Detective;* 10) *Bread, Love and Dreams.*

Best Director: Renato Castellani, *Romeo and Juliet.*

Best Actress: Grace Kelly, *The Country Girl, Dial M for Murder* and *Rear Window.*

Best Actor: Bing Crosby, *The Country Girl.*

Best Supporting Actress: Nina Foch, *Executive Suite.*

Best Supporting Actor: John Williams, *Sabrina* and *Dial M for Murder.*

Special Citations: For the choreography of Michael Kidd in *Seven Brides for Seven Brothers;* the modernization of traditional Japanese acting by Machiko Kyo in *Gate of Hell* and *Ugetsu;* for the new methods of moving puppets in *Hansel and Gretel.*

1955

American: 1) *Marty;* 2) *East of Eden;* 3) *Mister Roberts;* 4) *Bad Day at Black Rock;* 5) *Summertime;* 6) *The Rose Tattoo;* 7) *A Man Called Peter;* 8) *Not as a Stranger;* 9) *Picnic;* 10) *The African Lion.*

Foreign: 1) *The Prisoner;* 2) *The Great Adventure;* 3) *The Divided Heart;* 4) *Diabolique;* 5) *The End of the Affair.*

Best Director: William Wyler, *The Desperate Hours.*

Best Actress: Anna Magnani, *The Rose Tattoo.*

Best Actor: Ernest Borgnine, *Marty.*

Best Supporting Actress: Marjorie Rambeau, *A Man Called Peter* and *The View from Pompey's Head.*

Best Supporting Actor: Charles Bickford, *Not as a Stranger.*

Special Citation: For the aerial photography in *Strategic Air Command.*

1956

American: 1) *Around the World in 80 Days;* 2) *Moby Dick;* 3) *The King and I;* 4) *Lust for Life;* 5) *Friendly Persuasion;* 6) *Somebody Up There Likes Me;* 7) *The Catered Affair;* 8) *Anastasia;* 9) *The Man Who Never Was;* 10) *Bus Stop.*

Foreign: 1) *The Silent World;* 2) *War and Peace;* 3) *Richard III;* 4) *La Strada;* 5) *Rififi.*

Best Director: John Huston, *Moby Dick.*

Best Actress: Dorothy McGuire, *Friendly Persuasion.*

Best Actor: Yul Brynner, *The King and I, Anastasia* and *The Ten Commandments.*

Best Supporting Actress: Debbie Reynolds, *The Catered Affair.*

Best Supporting Actor: Richard Basehart, *Moby Dick.*

1957

American: 1) *The Bridge on the River Kwai;* 2) *Twelve Angry Men;* 3) *The Spirit of St. Louis;* 4) *The Rising of the Moon;* 5) *Albert Schweitzer;* 6) *Funny Face;* 7) *The Bachelor Party;* 8) *The Enemy Below;* 9) *A Hatful of Rain;* 10) *A Farewell to Arms.*

Foreign: 1) *Ordet;* 2) *Gervaise;* 3) *Torero!;* 4) *The Red Baloon;* 5) *A Man Escaped.*

Best Director: David Lean, *The Bridge on the River Kwai.*

Best Actress: Joanne Woodward, *The Three Faces of Eve* and *No Down Payment.*

Best Actor: Alec Guinness, *The Bridge on the River Kwai.*

Best Supporting Actress: Dame Sybil Thorndike, *The Prince and the Showgirl.*

Best Supporting Actor: Sessue Hayakawa, *The Bridge on the River Kwai.*

Special Citation: For the photographic innovations in *Funny Face.*

1958

American: 1) *The Old Man and the Sea;* 2) *Separate Tables;* 3) *The Last Hurrah;* 4) *The Long Hot Summer;* 5) *Windjammer;* 6) *Cat on a Hot Tin Roof;* 7) *The Goddess;* 8) *The Brothers Karamazov;* 9) *Me and the Colonel;* 10) *Gigi.*

Foreign: 1) *Pather Panchali;* 2) *Rouge et Noir;* 3) *The Horse's Mouth;* 4) *My Uncle;* 5) *A Night to Remember.*

Best Director: John Ford, *The Last Hurrah.*

Best Actress: Ingrid Bergman, *The Inn of the Sixth Happiness.*

Best Actor: Spencer Tracy, *The Old Man and the Sea* and *The Last Hurrah.*

Best Supporting Actress: Kay Walsh, *The Horse's Mouth.*

Best Supporting Actor: Albert Salmi, *The Brothers Karamazov* and *The Bravados.*

Special Citation: For the valor of Robert Donat's last performance in *The Inn of the Sixth Happiness.*

1959

American: 1) *The Nun's Story;* 2) *Ben-Hur;* 3) *Anatomy of a Murder;* 4) *The Diary of Anne Frank;* 5) *Middle of the Night;* 6) *The Man Who Understood Women;* 7) *Some Like It Hot;* 8) *Suddenly, Last Summer;* 9) *On the Beach;* 10) *North by Northwest.*

Foreign: 1) *Wild Strawberries;* 2) *Room at the Top;* 3) *Aparajito;* 4) *The Roof;* 5) *Look Back in Anger.*

Best Director: Fred Zinnemann, *The Nun's Story.*

Best Actress: Simone Signoret, *Room at the Top.*

Best Actor: Victor Seastrom, *Wild Strawberries.*

Best Supporting Actress: Dame Edith Evans, *The Nun's Story.*

Best Supporting Actor: Hugh Griffith, *Ben-Hur.*

Special Citations: To Ingmar Bergman for the body of his work; to Andrew Marton and Yakima Canutt for their direction of the chariot race in *Ben-Hur.*

1960

American: 1) *Sons and Lovers;* 2) *The Alamo;* 3) *The Sundowners;* 4) *Inherit the Wind;* 5) *Sunrise at Campobello;* 6) *Elmer Gantry;* 7) *Home from the Hill;* 8) *The Apartment;* 9) *Wild River;* 10) *The Dark at the Top of the Stairs.*

Foreign: 1) *The World of Apu;* 2) *General Della Rovere;* 3) *The Angry Silence;* 4) *I'm All Right, Jack:* 5) *Hiroshima, Mon Amour.*

Best Director: Jack Cardiff. *Sons and Lovers.*

Best Actress: Greer Garson, *Sunrise at Campobello.*

Best Actor: Robert Mitchum, *Home from the Hill* and *The Sundowners.*

Best Supporting Actress: Shirley Jones, *Elmer Gantry.*

Best Supporting Actor: George Peppard, *Home from the Hill.*

Sons and Lovers with Dean Stockwell and Wendy Hiller.

1961

American: 1) *Question 7;* 2) *The Hustler;* 3) *West Side Story;* 4) *The Innocents;* 5) *The Hoodlum Priest;* 6) *Summer and Smoke;* 7) *The Young Doctors;* 8) *Judgment at Nuremberg;* 9) *One, Two, Three;* 10) *Fanny.*

Foreign: 1) *The Bridge;* 2) *La Dolce Vita;* 3) *Two Women;* 4) *Saturday Night and Sunday Morning;* 5) *A Summer to Remember.*

Best Director: Jack Clayton, *The Innocents.*

Best Actress: Geraldine Page, *Summer and Smoke.*

Best Actor: Albert Finney, *Saturday Night and Sunday Morning.*

Best Supporting Actress: Ruby Dee, *A Raisin in the Sun.*

Best Supporting Actor: Jackie Gleason, *The Hustler.*

1962

Ten Best in English: 1) *The Longest Day:* 2) *Billy Budd;* 3) *The Miracle Worker;* 4) *Lawrence of Arabia;* 5) *Long Day's Journey into Night;* 6) *Whistle Down the Wind;* 7) *Requiem for a Heavyweight;* 8) *A Taste of Honey;* 9) *Birdman of Alcatraz;* 10) *War Hunt.*

Best in Foreign Languages: 1) *Sundays and Cybele;* 2) *Barabbas;* 3) *Divorce—Italian Style;* 4) *The Island:* 5) *Through a Glass Darkly.*

Best Director: David Lean, *Lawrence of Arabia.*

Best Actress: Anne Bancroft, *The Miracle Worker.*

Best Actor: Jason Robards, Jr., *Long Day's Journey into Night* and *Tender Is the Night.*

Best Supporting Actress: Angela Lansbury, *The Manchurian Candidate* and *All Fall Down.*

Best Supporting Actor: Burgess Meredith, *Advise and Consent.*

1963

Ten Best in English: 1) *Tom Jones;* 2) *Lilies of the Field;* 3) *All the Way Home;* 4) *Hud;* 5) *This Sporting Life;* 6) *Lord of the Flies;* 7) *The L-Shaped Room;* 8) *The Great Escape:* 9) *How the West Was Won;* 10) *The Cardinal.*

Best in Foreign Languages: 1) *8.5;* 2) *The Four Days of Naples;* 3) *Winter Light;* 4) *The Leopard;* 5) *Any Number Can Win.*

Best Director: Tony Richardson, *Tom Jones.*

Best Actress: Patricia Neal, *Hud.*

Best Actor: Rex Harrison, *Cleopatra.*

Best Supporting Actress: Margaret Rutherford, *The V.I.P.'s*

Best Supporting Actor: Melvyn Douglas, *Hud.*

1964

Ten Best in English: 1) *Becket;* 2) *My Fair Lady;* 3) *Girl with Green Eyes;* 4) *The World of Henry Orient;* 5) *Zorba the Greek;* 6) *Topkapi;* 7) *The Chalk Garden;* 8) *The Finest Hours;* 9) *Four Days in November;* 10) *Seance on a Wet Afternoon.*

Best in Foreign Languages: 1) *World Without Sun;* 2) *The Organizer;* 3) *Anatomy of a Marriage;* 4) *Seduced and Abandoned;* 5) *Yesterday, Today and Tomorrow.*

Best Director: Desmond Davis, *The Girl With Green Eyes.*

Best Actress: Kim Stanley, *Seance on a Wet Afternoon.*

Best Actor: Anthony Quinn, *Zorba the Greek.*

Best Supporting Actress: Edith Evans, *The Chalk Garden.*

Best Supporting Actor: Martin Balsam, *The Carpetbaggers.*

1965

Ten Best in English: 1) *The Eleanor Roosevelt Story;* 2) *The Agony and the Ecstasy;* 3) *Doctor Zhivago;* 4) *Ship of Fools;* 5) *The Spy Who Came in from the Cold;* 6) *Darling;* 7) *The Greatest Story Ever Told;* 8) *A Thousand Clowns;* 9) *The Train;* 10) *The Sound of Music.*

Best in Foreign Languages: 1) *Juliet of the Spirits;* 2) *The Overcoat;* 3) *La Boheme;* 4) *La Tia Tula;* 5) *Gertrud.*

Best Director: John Schlesinger, *Darling.*

Best Actress: Julie Christie, *Darling* and *Doctor Zhivago.*

Best Actor: Lee Marvin, *Cat Ballou* and *Ship of Fools.*

Best Supporting Actress: Joan Blondell, *The Cincinnati Kid.*

Best Supporting Actor: Harry Andrews, *The Agony and the Ecstasy* and *The Hill.*

1966

Ten Best in English: 1) *A Man for All Seasons;* 2) *Born Free;* 3) *Alfie;* 4) *Who's Afraid of Virginia Woolf?;* 5) *The Bible;* 6) *Georgy Girl;* 7)

The Bible . . . In The Beginning with John Huston.

Years of Lightning, Day of Drums; 8) *It Happened Here;* 9) *The Russians Are Coming, The Russians Are Coming;* 10) *Shakespeare Wallah.*

Best in Foreign Languages: 1) *The Sleeping Car Murders;* 2) *The Gospel According to St. Matthew;* 3) *The Shameless Old Lady;* 4) *A Man and a Woman;* 5) *Hamlet.*

Best Director: Fred Zinnemann, *A Man for All Seasons.*

Best Actress: Elizabeth Taylor, *Who's Afraid of Virginia Woolf?*

Best Actor: Paul Scofield, *A Man for All Seasons.*

Best Supporting Actress: Vivien Merchant, *Alfie.*

Best Supporting Actor: Robert Shaw, *A Man for All Seasons.*

1967

Ten Best in English: 1) *Far From the Madding Crowd;* 2) *The Whisperers;* 3) *Ulysses;* 4) *In Cold Blood;* 5) *The Family Way;* 6) *The Taming of the Shrew;* 7) *Doctor Dolittle;* 8) *The Graduate;* 9) *The Comedians;* 10) *Accident.*

Best in Foreign Languages: 1) *Elvira Madigan;* 2) *The Hunt;* 3) *Africa Addio;* 4) *Persona;* 5) *The Great British Train Robbery.*

Best Director: Richard Brooks, *In Cold Blood.*

Best Actress: Edith Evans, *The Whisperers.*

Best Actor: Peter Finch, *Far From the Madding Crowd.*

Best Supporting Actress: Marjorie Rhodes, *The Family Way.*

Best Supporting Actor: Paul Ford, *The Comedians.*

THE NEW YORK FILM CRITICS AWARDS

The purpose of The New York Film Critics is to represent, as an impartial organized working unit, the profession of screen criticism to signify the recognition of the highest creative achievements in the field of motion pictures; and to uphold the dignity and significance of film criticism.

Membership in the organization is restricted to film critics (assistant critics and official substitute critics) of New York daily (or equivalent) newspapers.

The primary function of The New York Film Critics is the annual selection of outstanding screen achievements and the presentation of awards for these selections.

The basic awards of The New York Film Critics are for Best Picture, Best Actor, Best Actress and Best Director (of an English-language feature) and Best Import (originating in a foreign language), all of the current calendar year.

All awards are selected under the following special voting procedure. Voting in each category is restricted to six ballots. Any nominee may be named on the first two ballots. After the first two ballots, only nominees receiving two or more votes are retained on the nomination list.

After any ballot, a nominee receiving two-thirds of the votes (of members present or represented by proxy) is declared the winner. If this has not occurred after the sixth ballot, the winner is chosen by plurality of the votes cast by voting members.

If a majority present consents, a seventh ballot may be cast in case of ties. Voting on awards is by secret ballot. Only the actual vote totals given various nominees are revealed officially.

1935 **Best Motion Picture:** *The Informer* (RKO); **Best Male Performance:** Charles Laughton, *Mutiny on the Bounty* (MGM) and *Ruggles of Red Gap* (Par.); **Best Feminine Performance:** *Greta Garbo, Anna Karenina* (MGM); **Best Direction:** John Ford, *The Informer* (RKO).

Mutiny on the Bounty with Charles Laughton and Clark Gable.

1936 **Best Motion Picture:** *Mr. Deeds Goes to Town* (Col.); **Best male Performance:** Walter Huston, *Dodworth* (Goldwyn-United Artists); **Best Feminine Performance:** Luise Rainer, *The Great Ziegfeld* (MGM); **Best Direction:** Rouben Mamoulian, *The Gay Desperado* (Lasky-United Artists); **Best Foreign Film:** *La Kermesse Heroique* (American Tobis).

1937 **Best Motion Picture:** *The Life of Emile Zola* (WB); **Best Male Performance:** Paul Muni, *The Life of Emile Zola* (WB); **Best Feminine Performance:** Greta Garbo, *Camille* (MGM); **Best Direction:** Gregory La Cava, *Stage Door* (RKO); **Best Foreign Film:** *Mayerling* (Pax Film).

1938 **Best Motion Picture:** *The Citadel* (MGM); **Best Male Performance:** James Cagney, *Angels with Dirty Faces* (WB); **Best Feminine Performance:** Margaret Sullavan, *Three Comrades* (MGM); **Best Direction:** Alfred Hitchcock, *The Lady Vanishes* (Gaumont-British); **Best Foreign Film:** *La Grande Illusion* (World Films); **Special Award:** *Snow White and the Seven Dwarfs* (Disney-RKO).

1939 **Best Motion Picture:** *Wuthering Heights* (Goldwyn-United Artists); **Best Male Performance:** James Stewart, *Mr. Smith Goes to Washington* (Col.); **Best Feminine Performance:** Vivien Leigh, *Gone With the Wind* (Selznick, MGM); **Best Direction:** John Ford, *Stagecoach* (Wanger-United Artists); **Best Foreign Film:** *Harvest* (French Cinema Center).

1940 **Best Motion Picture:** *The Grapes of Wrath* (20th); **Best Male Performance:** Charles Chaplin,* *The Great Dictator* (Chaplin-United Artists); **Best Feminine Performance:** Katharine Hepburn, *The Philadelphia Story* (MGM); **Best Direction:** John Ford, *The Grapes of Wrath* (20th) and *The Long Voyage Home* (Wanger-United Artists);

Gone With the Wind with Vivien Leigh and Leslie Howard.

Best Foreign Film: *The Baker's Wife* (Baker's Wife, Inc.); **Special Award:** Walt Disney, *Fantasia* (Disney-RKO).

*Award refused.

1941   Best Motion Picture: *Citizen Kane* (RKO); **Best Male Performance:** Gary Cooper, *Sergeant York* (WB); **Best Feminine Performance:** Joan Fontaine, *Suspicion* (RKO); **Best Direction:** John Ford, *How Green was My Valley* (20th).

How Green Was My Valley with Roddy McDowell, Donald Crisp and Sara Allgood.

1942   Best Motion Picture: *In Which We Serve* (Noel Coward-United Artists); **Best Male Performance:** James Cagney, *Yankee Doodle Dandy* (WB); **Best Feminine Performance:** Agnes Moorehead, *The Magnificent Ambersons* (RKO); **Best Direction:** John Farrow, *Wake Island* (Par.).

1943   Best Motion Picture: *Watch on the Rhine* (WB); **Best Male Performance:** Paul Lukas, *Watch on the Rhine;* **Best Feminine Performance:** Ida Lupino, *The Hard Way* (WB); **Best Direction:** George Stevens, *The More the Merrier* (Col.).

1944   Best Motion Picture: *Going My Way* (Par.); **Best Male Performance:** Barry Fitzgerald, *Going My Way;* **Best Feminine Perfor-**

The More the Merrier with Richard Gaines, Jean Arthur, seated, Charles Coburn and Joel McCrea.

mance: Tallulah Bankhead, *Lifeboat* (20th.); **Best Direction:** Leo McCarey, *Going My Way* (Par.).

1945   Best Motion Picture: *The Lost Weekend* (Par.); **Best Male Performance:** Ray Milland, *The Lost Weekend;* **Best Feminine Performance:** Ingrid Bergman, *Spellbound* (Selznick-United Artists) and *The Bells of St. Mary's* (Rainbow-RKO); **Best Direction:** Billy Wilder, *The Lost Weekend;* **Special Awards:** *The True Glory* and *The Fighting Lady,* U. S. documentaries.

The Lost Weekend with Ray Milland.

1946   Best Motion Picture: *The Best Years of Our Lives* (Goldwyn-RKO); **Best Male Performance:** Laurence Olivier, *Henry V* (J. Arthur Rank-United Artists); **Best Feminine Performance:** Celia Johnson, *Brief Encounter* (J. Arthur Rank-Universal); **Best Direction:** William Wyler, *The Best Years of Our Lives;* **Best Foreign Film:** *Open City* (Mayer-Burstyn).

1947   Best Motion Picture: *Gentleman's Agreement* (20th); **Best Male Performance:** William Powell, *Life With Father* (WB); **Best Feminine Performance:** Deborah Kerr, *The Adventuress* (J. Arthur Rank-Eagle Lion); **Best Direction:** Elia Kazan, *Gentleman's Agreement* and *Boomerang!* (20th); **Best Foreign Film:** *To Live in Peace* (Times Pictures).

1948   Best Motion Picture: *Treasure of Sierra Madre* (WB); **Best Male Performance:** Laurence Olivier, *Hamlet* (Rank–Universal-International); **Best Feminine Performance:** Olivia De Havilland, *The Snake Pit* (20th); **Best Direction:** John Huston, *Treasure of Sierra Madre;* **Best Foreign Film:** *Paisan* (Mayer-Burstyn).

1949   Best Motion Picture: *All the King's Men* (Col.); **Best Male**

Treasure of Sierra Madre with Tim Holt, Humphrey Bogart and Walter Huston.

Performance: Broderick Crawford, *All the King's Men;* **Best Feminine Performance:** Olivia De Havilland, *The Heiress* (Par.); **Best Direction:** Carol Reed, *The Fallen Idol* (British-Selznick Releasing Organization); **Best Foreign Film:** *The Bicycle Thief* (Mayer-Burstyn).

1950 **Best Motion Picture:** *All About Eve* (20th); **Best Male Performance:** Gregory Peck, *12 O'Clock High* (20th); **Best Feminine Performance:** Bette Davis, *All About Eve;* **Best Direction:** Joseph L. Mankiewicz, *All About Eve;* **Best Foreign Film:** *Ways of Love* (Burstyn).

1951 **Best Motion Picture:** *A Streetcar Named Desire* (WB); **Best Male Performance:** Arthur Kennedy, *Bright Victory* (Univ.); **Best Feminine Performance:** Vivien Leigh, *A Streetcar Named Desire;* **Best Direction:** Elia Kazan, *A Streetcar Named Desire;* **Best Foreign Film:** *Miracle in Milan* (Burstyn).

High Noon with Gary Cooper and Grace Kelly.

1952 **Best Motion Picture:** *High Noon* (Stanley Kramer-United Artists); **Best Male Performance:** Ralph Richardson, *Breaking the Sound Barrier* (London Films-United Artists); **Best Feminine Performance:** Shirley Booth, *Come Back, Little Sheba* (Hal Wallis-Paramount); **Best Direction:** Fred Zinnemann, *High Noon;* **Best Foreign Film:** *Forbidden Games* (Times Film Corp.).

1953 **Best Motion Picture:** *From Here to Eternity* (Col.); **Best Male Performance:** Burt Lancaster, *From Here to Eternity;* **Best Feminine Performance:** Audrey Hepburn, *Roman Holiday* (Par.); **Best Direction:** Fred Zinnemann, *From Here to Eternity;* **Best Foreign Film:** *Justice Is Done* (Burstyn, Inc.).

1954 **Best Motion Picture:** *On the Waterfront* (Horizon Pictures-Columbia); **Best Male Performance:** Marlon Brando, *On the Waterfront;* **Best Feminine Performance:** Grace Kelly, *The Country Girl* (Par.), *Rear Window* (Par.), *Dial M for Murder* (WB); **Best Direction:** Elia Kazan, *On the Waterfront;* **Best Foreign Film:** *Gate of Hell* (Daiei-Harrison).

The Country Girl with Grace Kelly, Bing Crosby and William Holden.

1955 **Best Motion Picture:** *Marty* (Hecht-Lancaster–United Artists); **Best Male Performance:** Ernest Borgnine, *Marty;* **Best Feminine Performance:** Anna Magnani, *The Rose Tattoo* (Hal Wallis-Paramount); **Best Direction:** David Lean, *Summertime* (Lopert-United Artists); **Best Foreign Film:** *Umberto D.* (Harrison), and *Diabolique* (UMPO).

1956 **Best Motion Picture:** *Around the World in 80 Days* (Mike Todd-United Artists); **Best Male Performance:** Kirk Douglas, *Lust for Life* (MGM); **Best Feminine Performance:** Ingrid Bergman, *Anastasia* (20th); **Best Direction:** John Huston, *Moby Dick* (Moulin-Warner Bros.); **Best Writing:** S. J. Perelman, *Around the World in 80 Days;* **Best Foreign Film:** *La Strada* (Trans-Lux).

Lust for Life with Kirk Douglas and Anthony Quinn.

1957 Best Motion Picture: *The Bridge on the River Kwai* (Spiegel-Columbia); **Best Male Performance:** Alec Guinness, *The Bridge on the River Kwai;* **Best Feminine Performance:** Deborah Kerr, *Heaven Knows, Mr. Allison* (20th); **Best Direction:** David Lean, *The Bridge on the River Kwai;* **Best Foreign Film:** *Gervaise* (Continental).

1958 Best Motion Picture: *The Defiant Ones* (Kramer-United Artists); **Best Male Performance:** David Niven, *Separate Tables* (UA); **Best Feminine Performance:** Susan Hayward, *I Want to Live!* (UA); **Best Direction:** Stanely Kramer, *The Defiant Ones;* **Best Writing:** Nathan E. Douglas and Harold Jacob Smith, *The Defiant Ones;* **Best Foreign Film:** *My Uncle* (Continental).

I Want to Live! with Susan Hayward.

1959 Best Motion Picture: *Ben-Hur* (Zimbalist-MGM); **Best Male Performance:** James Stewart, *Anatomy of a Murder* (Col.); **Best Feminine Performance:** Audrey Hepburn, *The Nun's Story* (WB); **Best Direction:** Fred Zinnemann, *The Nun's Story;* **Best Writing:** Wendell Mayes, *Anatomy of a Murder;* **Best Foregin Film:** *The 400 Blows* (Zenith International).

1960 Best Motion Picture: Tie, *Sons and Lovers* (Wald–20th Century-Fox) and *The Apartment* (Wilder-United Artists); **Best Male**

The Apartment with Jack Lemmon and Shirley MacLaine.

Performance: Burt Lancaster, *Elmer Gantry* (United Artists); **Best Feminine Performance:** Deborah Kerr, *The Sundowners* (Warner Bros.); **Best Direction:** Tie, Jack Cardiff, *Sons and Lovers,* and Billy Wilder, *The Apartment;* **Best Writing:** Billy Wilder and I.A.I. Diamond, *The Apartment;* **Best Foreign Film:** *Hiroshima, Mon Amour* (Zenith International).

1961 Best Motion Picture: *West Side Story* (Wise-United Artists); **Best Male Performance:** Maximilian Schell, *Judgment at Nuremberg* (UA); **Best Feminine Performance:** Sophia Loren, *Two Women* (Embassy); **Best Direction:** Robert Rossen, *The Hustler* (20th); **Best Foreign Film:** *La Dolce Vita* (Astor).

1962 No awards presented.

1963 Best Motion Picture: *Tom Jones* (United Artists-Lopert); **Best Male Performance:** Albert Finney, *Tom Jones;* **Best Feminine Performance:** Patricia Neal, *Hud* (Par.); **Best Direction:** Tony Richardson, *Tom Jones;* **Best Foreign Film:** *8.5* (Embassy).

1964 Best Motion Picture: *My Fair Lady* (WB.); **Best Male Performance:** Rex Harrison, *My Fair Lady* (WB); **Best Feminine Performance:** Kim Stanley, *Seance on a Wet Afternoon* (Artixo); **Best Direction:** Stanley Kubrick, *Dr. Strangelove or: How I Learned to Stop Worrying and Love the Bomb* (Col.); **Best Writing:** Harold Pinter, *The Servant* (Landau Releasing); **Best Foreign Film:** *That Man From Rio* (Lopert); **Special Citation:** *To Be Alive!* (Johnson's Wax).

1965 Best Mtoion Picture: *Darling* (Embassy); **Best Male Performance:** Oskar Werner, *Ship of Fools* (Col.); **Best Feminine Performance:** Julie Christie, *Darling;* **Best Direction:** John Schlesinger, *Darling;* **Best Foreign Film:** *Juliet of the Spirits* (Rizzoli).

1966 Best Motion Picture: *A Man for All Seasons* (Highland, Columbia). **Best Male Performance:** Paul Scofield in *A Man for All Seasons;* **Best Feminine Performance:** Tie, Elizabeth Taylor in *Who's Afraid of Virginia Woolf?* (Chenault, Warner Brothers) and Lynn Redgrave in *Georgy Girl* (Col.); **Best Direction:** Fred Zinnemann, *A Man for All Seasons;* **Best Foreign Film:** *The Shop on Main Street* (Czechoslovakian).

1967 Best Motion Picture: *In The Heat of the Night* (United Artists). **Best Male Performance:** Rod Steiger in *In The Heat of the Night.* **Best Feminine Performance:** Edith Evans in *The Whisperers.* **Best Direction:** Mike Nichols, *The Graduate* (Nichols-Turman, Embassy). **Best Foreign Language Film:** *La Guerre Est Finie* (French). **Best Screen Writing:** David Newman and Robert Benton, *Bonnie and Clyde* (Warner Brothers). **Special Award:** Bosley Crowther, for his 27 years service as a film critic.

THE PATSY AWARDS

"PATSY" is a double-duty abbreviation. It can mean either PICTURE ANIMAL TOP STAR OF THE YEAR or PERFORMING ANIMAL TELEVISION STAR OF THE YEAR.

The PATSY Awards signify skill and ability in animal-handling and compliance with the American Humane Association standards in treatment of these animals. The AHA launched PATSY Awards in 1951 to recognize noteworthy performances by animals in motion pictures. The original idea is credited to a publicity man, who, at lunch one day in Hollywood, said, "What we should have is OSCARS for the animals." The idea was developed by the AHA Hollywood staff in cooperation with studio executives. The nation's first PATSY winner was "Francis," the talking mule, then film land idol of the animal set.

The PATSY Awards—and their attendant publicity—help to call attention to the value of kindness toward animals—household pets or Hollywood "stars"—as far superior to punishment, brutality and fear. Further, they demonstrate the importance of animals in motion pictures and television and have helped to create the impetus for even better animal stories.

After seven years and with the increasing importance of television, the American Humane Association established an identical set of honors for animal "actors" appearing in this medium. This was in 1958, for performances during 1957, and a long-time favorite, "Lassie," came out on top.

Each year, the AHA polls many hundreds of entertainment editors, writers and critics to determine the winner of the coveted first-place PATSY trophy and the second- and third-place animal stars in both motion pictures and television. Additional awards of excellence are presented when the vote indicates deserving performances.

Motion picture animals are eligible for the PATSY Award when they appear in a feature film meeting AHA standards.

1951 First Place: FRANCIS, mule, *Francis* (Univ.). Second Place: CALIFORNIA, horse, *The Palomino* (Col.). Third Place: PIERRE, chimp, *My Friend Irma Goes West* (Hal Wallis-Paramount). Craven Award: JERRY BROWN, falling horse (Ace Hudkins, owner and trainer). Awards of Excellence: FLAME, dog, My Pal series (RKO); LASSIE, dog, *Challenge to Lassie* (MGM); BLACK DIAMOND, horse, *Black Midnight* (Lindsley Parsons-Monogram); JACKIE, lion, *Samson and Delilah* (Par.).

1952 First Place: RHUBARB, cat, *Rhubarb* (Par.). Second Place: FRANCIS, mule, *Francis Goes to the Races* (Univ.). Third Place: CHETA, chimp, *Tarzan's Peril* (Sol Lesser). Craven Award: SMOKY, fighting stallion (Fat Jones, owner and trainer). Awards of Excellence: CHINOOK, dog, *Yukon Manhunt* (Mon.). DIAMOND, horse, *Flame of Araby* (Univ.). CORKY, dog, *Behave Yourself* (Wald-Krasna–RKO).

1953 First Place: JACKIE, lion, *Fearless Fagan* (MGM). Second Place: BONZO, chimp, *Bonzo Goes to College* (Univ.). Third Place: TRIGGER, horse, *Son of Paleface* (Par.). Craven Award: FRANCIS, mule, *Francis Goes to West Point* (Univ.). Awards of Excellence; TRAMP, JR., dog, *Room for One More* (WB). CHETA, chimp, *Tarzan's Savage Fury* (Sol Lesser). CHINOOK, dog, *Yukon Gold* (Wm. F. Broidy Productions).

1954 First Place: SAM, dog, *Hondo* (Wayne-Fellows Productions). Second Place: FRANCIS, mule, *Francis Covers the Big Town* (Univ.). Third Place: JACKIE, lion, *Androcles and the Lion* (RKO). Craven Award: COCAINE, falling horse (Chuck Roberson, owner and trainer). Awards of Excellence: BARON, dog, *Back to God's Country* (Univ.). PEGGY, chimp, *Valley of the Headhunters* (Esskay Productions-Columbia). JACKIE, lion, *White Witch Doctor* (Fox).

1955 First Place: GYPSY, horse, *Gypsy Colt* (MGM). Second Place: FRANCIS, mule, *Francis Joins the WACS* (Univ.). Third Place: ESMERALDA, seal, *20,000 Leagues Under the Sea* (Walt Disney Productions). Craven Award: FLASH, falling and lay-down horse (Henry Wills, owner and trainer). Awards of Excellence: SHEP, dog, *A Bullet is Waiting* (Howard Welsch Productions). SATIN, tiger, *Demetrius and the Gladiators* (Fox). OUTLAW, horse, *Black Horse Canyon* (Univ.). BEAUTY, horse, *Outlaw Stallion* (Col.).

1956 First Place: WILDFIRE, dog, *It's a Dog's Life* (MGM). Second Place: FRANCIS, mule, *Francis Joins the Navy* (Univ.). Third Place: FARO, dog, *The Kentuckian* (Hecht-Lancaster Productions). Craven Award: FLAME, dog (Frank Barnes, owner and trainer).

1957 First Place: SAMANTHA, goose, *Friendly Persuasion* (AA).

Second Place: WAR WINDS, horse, *Giant* (WB). Third Place: FRANCIS, mule, *Francis in the Haunted House* (Univ.). Craven Award: KING COTTON, horse (Ralph McCutcheon, owner and trainer). Awards of Excellence: SILVER, horse, *The Lone Ranger* (WB). LADY, dog, *Goodbye, My Lady* (Batjac Productions). BASCOM, dog, *Hollywood or Bust* (Par.).

1958 First Place (Motion Picture): SPIKE, dog, *Old Yeller* (Walt Disney Productions). First Place (Television): LASSIE, dog, "Lassie" series (Jack Wrather Productions). Second Place (M.P.): BEAUTY, horse, *Wild Is the Wind* (Par.). Second Place (TV): CLEO, dog, *The People's Choice* (Norden Productions). Third Place (M.P.): KELLY, dog, *Kelly and Me* (Univ.). Third Place (TV): RIN-TIN-TIN, dog, *Adventures of Rin-Tin-Tin* (Herbert B. Leonard Productions). Craven Award: TRIGGER, horse (Roy Rogers, owner; Glenn Randall, trainer). Awards of Excellence: (M.P.) TONY, horse, *Hoofs and Goofs*, short subject (Col.). (TV): FLICKA, horse, "My Friend Flicka" (Fox TV).

1959 First Place (Motion Picture): PYEWACKET, cat, *Bell, Book and Candle* (Col.). First Place (Television): LASSIE, dog, "Lassie" series (Jack Wrather Productions). Second Place (M.P.): TONKA, horse, *Tonka* (Walt Disney Productions). Second Place (TV): ASTA, dog, "The Thin Man" (MGM-TV). Third Place (M.P.): HARRY, rabbit, *The Geisha Boy* (Par.). Third Place (TV): RIN-TIN-TIN, dog, "Adventures of Rin-Tin-Tin" (Screen Gems). Craven Award: BALDY, rearing horse (Fat Jones Stables, owner; William "Buster" Trow, trainer). Awards of Excellence: (M.P.) KING, dog, *The Proud Rebel* (Formosa Productions). (TV): JASPER, dog, "Bachelor Father" (Bachelor Productions).

1960 First Place (Motion Picture): SHAGGY, dog, *The Shaggy Dog* (Walt Disney Productions). First Place (Television): ASTA, dog, "The Thin Man" (MGM-TV). Second Place (M.P.): HERMAN, pigeon, *The Gazebo* (MGM). Second Place (TV): LASSIE, dog, "Lassie" series (Jack Wrather Productions). Third Place (M.P.): NORTH WIND, horse, *The Sad Horse* (Fox). Third Place (TV) Tied: FURY, horse, "Fury" series (TPA Productions) and JASPER, dog, "Bachelor Father" (Bachelor Productions). Craven Award: SHARKEY, DEMPSEY, CHOCTAW and JOKER, four-up team of horses (Hudkins Bros. Stables, owners).

1961 First Place (Motion Picture): KING COTTON, horse, *Pepe* (Col.). First Place (Television): TRAMP, dog, "My Three Sons" (Don Fedderson Productions). Second Place (M.P.): SPIKE, dog, *Dog of Flanders* (Fox). Second Place (TV): LASSIE, dog, "Lassie" series (Jack Wrather Productions). Third Place (M.P.) Tied: MR. STUBBS, monkey, *Toby Tyler* (Walt Disney Productions) and SKIP, dog, *Visit to a Small Planet* (Hal Wallis Productions). Third Place (TV): FURY, horse, "Fury" series (Jack Wrather Productions).

1962 First Place (Motion Picture): CAT, *Breakfast at Tiffany's* (Par.) First Place (Television): MISTER ED, horse, "Mister Ed" series (Mister Ed Company). Second Place (M.P.): PETE, dog, *The Silent Call* (Fox). Second Place (TV): LASSIE, dog, "Lassie" series (Jack Wrather Productions). Third Place (M.P.): FLAME, horse, *The Clown and the Kid* (UA). Third Place (TV): TRAMP, dog, "My Three Sons" series (Don Fedderson Productions).

1963 First Place (Motion Picture): BIG RED, dog, *Big Red* (Walt Disney Productions). First Place (Television): MISTER ED, horse, "Mister Ed" series (Mister Ed Company). Second Place (M.P.): SYDNEY, elephant, *Jumbo* (MGM). Second Place (TV): LASSIE, dog, "Lassie" series (Jack Wrather Productions). Third Place (M.P.): ZAMBA, lion, *The Lion* (20th). Third Place (TV): TRAMP, dog, "My Three Sons" series (Don Fedderson Productions). Craven Award: MICKEY O'BOYLE, trained "fighting" horse.

1964 First Place (Motion Picture): TOM DOOLEY, dog, *Savage Sam* (Walt Disney Productions). First Place (Television): LASSIE, dog, "Lassie" series (Jack Wrather Productions). Second Place (M.P.): PLUTO, dog, *My Six Loves* (Par.). Second Place (TV): MISTER ED, horse "Mister Ed" series (Mister Ed Company). Third Place (M.P.): RAUNCHY, jaguar, *Rampage* (WB). Third Place (TV): TRAMP, dog, "My Three Sons" series (Don Fedderson Productions).

1965 First Place (Motion Picture): PATRINA, tiger, *A Tiger Walks*

(Walt Disney Productions). First Place (TV): FLIPPER, dolphin, "Flipper" series (Tors–MGM-TV). Second Place (M.P.): STORM, dog, *Goodbye Charlie* (Fox). Second Place (TV): LASSIE, dog, "Lassie" series (Jack Wrather Productions). Third Place (M.P.): JUNIOR, dog, *Island of the Blue Dolphins* (Radnitz-Universal). Third Place (TV): MISTER ED, horse, "Mister Ed" series (Filmways). Craven Award: LUCKY BUCK, trained lay-down horse.

1966   First Place (Motion Picture): SYN CAT, cat, *That Darn Cat* (Walt Disney Productions). First Place (Tevevision): FLIPPER, dolphin "Flipper" series (Tors–MGM-TV). Second Place (M.P.): CLARENCE, lion, *Clarence, the Cross-Eyed Lion* (Tors-MGM). Second Place (TV): LORD NELSON, dog, "Please Don't Eat the Daisies" series (MGM-TV). Third Place (M.P.): JUDY, chimpanzee, *The Monkey's Uncle* (Walt Disney Productions). Third Place (TV): HIGGINS, dog, "Petticoat Junction" series (Filmways). Craven Award: SMOKEY, horse, *Cat Ballou* (Col.).

FILM DAILY TEN BEST PICTURES OF THE YEAR

Selected by more than 450 motion picture critics of America in an annual poll conducted by *The Film Daily*, the national trade journal of the motion picture industry.

1922   *Orphans of the Storm* (UA); *Grandma's Boy* (Associated Exhibitors); *Blood and Sand* (Par.); *The Prisoner of Zenda* (Metro); *When Knighthood Was in Flower* (Par.); *Nanook of the North* (Pathé); *Smilin' Through* (WB); *Tol'able David* (WB); *Robin Hood* (UA)*; *Oliver Twist* (WB).

1923   *Covered Wagon* (Par.); *Merry-Go-Round* (Univ.); *The Hunchback of Notre Dame* (Univ.); *Robin Hood* (UA)*; *The Green Goddess* (Goldwyn); *Scaramouche* (Metro); *Safety Last* (Pathé); *Rosita* (UA); *Down to the Sea in Ships* (Hodkinson); *Little Old New York* (Goldwyn, Cosmopolitan).

1924   *The Thief of Bagdad* (UA); *The Sea Hawk* (WB); *Monsieur Beaucaire* (Par.); *Beau Brummel* (WB); *Secrets* (WB); *The Marriage Circle* (WB); *The Ten Commandments* (Par.); *Girl Shy* (Pathé); *Abraham Lincoln* (WB); *America* (UA).

1925   *The Gold Rush* (UA); *The Unholy Three* (Metro-Goldwyn); *Don Q, Son of Zorro* (UA); *The Merry Widow* (Metro-Goldwyn); *The Last Laugh* (Univ.); *The Freshman* (Pathé); *The Phantom of the Opera* (Univ.); *Lost World* (WB); *The Big Parade* (Metro-Goldwyn)*; *Kiss Me Again* (WB).

1926   *Variety* (Par.); *Ben-Hur* (MGM)*; *The Big Parade* (MGM)*; *The Black Pirate* (UA); *Beau Geste* (Par.)*; *Stella Dallas* (UA); *The Volga Boatman* (PDS); *What Price Glory* (Fox)*; *The Sea Beast* (WB); *La Boheme* (MGM).

1927   *Beau Geste* (Par.)*; *The Big Parade* (MGM)*; *What Price Glory* (Fox)*; *The Way of All Flesh* (Par.); *Ben-Hur* (MGM)*; *Seventh Heaven* (Fox); *Chang* (Par.); *Underworld* (Par.); *Resurrection* (UA); *The Flesh and the Devil* (MGM).

   *During the early stages of *The Film Daily* polls, certain productions were selected twice. The voting system has been altered so that critics now vote from a ballot supplied by *The Film Daily*.

1928   *The Patriot* (Par.); *Sorrell and Son* (UA); *The Last Command* (Par.); *Four Sons* (Fox); *Street Angel* (Fox); *The Circus* (UA); *Sunrise* (Fox); *The Crowd* (MGM); *The King of Kings* (Pathé); *Sadie Thompson* (UA).

1929   *Disraeli* (WB); *The Broadway Melody* (MGM); *Madame X* (MGM); *Rio Rita* (RKO); *Gold Diggers of Broadway* (WB); *Bulldog Drummond* (UA); *In Old Arizona* (Fox); *The Cock-Eyed World* (Fox); *The Last of Mrs. Cheyney* (MGM); *Hallelujah* (MGM).

Seventh Heaven with Charles Farrell and Janet Gaynor.

The Patriot with Emil Jannings.

1930   *All Quiet on the Western Front* (Univ.); *Abraham Lincoln* (UA); *Holiday* (Pathé); *Journey's End* (Tiff.); *Anna Christie* (MGM); *The Big House* (MGM); *With Byrd at the South Pole* (Par.); *The Divorcee* (MGM); *Hell's Angels* (UA); *Old English* (WB).

1931   *Cimarron* (RKO); *Street Scene* (UA); *Skippy* (Par.); *Bad Girl* (Fox); *Min and Bill* (MGM); *The Front Page* (UA); *Five Star Final* (WB); *City Lights* (UA); *A Free Soul* (MGM); *The Sin of Madelon Claudet* (MGM).

1932   *Grand Hotel* (MGM); *The Champ* (MGM); *Arrowsmith* (UA); *The Guardsman* (MGM); *Smilin' Through* (MGM); *Dr. Jekyll and Mr. Hyde* (Par.); *Emma* (MGM); *A Bill of Divorcement* (RKO); *Back Street* (Univ.); *Scarface* (UA).

1933   *Cavalcade* (Fox); *42nd Street* (WB); *The Private Life of Henry VIII* (UA); *Lady for a Day* (Col.); *State Fair* (Fox); *A Farewell to Arms* (Par.); *She Done Him Wrong* (Par.) *I Am a Fugitive From a Chain Gang* (WB); *Madchen in Uniform* (Filmchoice); *Rasputin and the Empress* (MGM).

Bad Girl with Minna Gombell and Sally Eilers.

1934 *The Barretts of Wimpole Street* (MGM); *The House of Rothschild* (UA); *It Happened One Night* (Col.); *One Night of Love* (Col.); *Little Women* (RKO); *The Thin Man* (MGM); *Viva Villa!* (MGM); *Dinner at Eight* (MGM); *The Count of Monte Cristo* (UA); *Berkeley Square* (Fox).

1935 *David Copperfield* (MGM); *The Lives of a Bengal Lancer* (Par.); *The Informer* (RKO); *Naughty Marietta* (MGM); *Les Miserables* (UA); *Ruggles of Red Gap* (Par.); *Top Hat* (RKO); *Broadway Melody of 1936* (MGM); *Roberta* (RKO); *Anna Karenina* (MGM).

1936 *Mutiny on the Bounty* (MGM); *Mr. Deeds Goes to Town* (Col.); *The Great Ziegfeld* (MGM); *San Francisco* (MGM); *Dodsworth* (United Artists, Samuel Goldwyn); *The Story of Louis Pasteur* (WB); *A Tale of Two Cities* (MGM); *Anthony Adverse* (WB); *The Green Pastures* (WB); *A Midsummer Night's Dream* (WB).

Snow White and the Seven Dwarfs.

1940 *Rebecca* (UA); *The Grapes of Wrath* (20th); *Ninotchka* (MGM); *Foreign Correspondent* (UA); *All This, and Heaven Too* (WB); *Abe Lincoln in Illinois* (RKO); *Boom Town* (MGM); *Northwest Passage* (MGM); *Our Town* (UA); *The Mortal Storm* (MGM).

Anthony Adverse with Claude Rains, Fredric March, Fritz Leiber, Gale Sondergaard and Donald Woods.

1937 *The Life of Emile Zola* (WB); *The Good Earth* (MGM); *Captains Courageous* (MGM); *Lost Horizon* (Col.); *A Star Is Born* (UA, Selznick International); *Romeo and Juliet* (MGM); *Stage Door* (RKO); *Dead End* (United Artists, Samuel Goldwyn); *Winterset* (RKO); *The Awful Truth* (Col.).

1938 *Snow White and the Seven Dwarfs* (RKO); *You Can't Take It with You* (Col.); *Alexander's Ragtime Band* (20th); *Boys' Town* (MGM); *Marie Antoinette* (MGM); *In Old Chicago* (20th); *The Adventures of Robin Hood* (WB); *The Citadel* (MGM); *Love Finds Andy Hardy* (MGM); *The Hurricane* (United Artists, Samuel Goldwyn).

1939 *Goodbye, Mr. Chips* (MGM); *Mr. Smith Goes to Washington* (Col.); *Pygmalion* (MGM); *Wuthering Heights* (United Artists, Goldwyn); *Dark Victory* (WB); *The Women* (MGM); *The Wizard of Oz* (MGM); *Juarez* (WB); *Stanley and Livingston* (20th); *The Old Maid* (WB).

The Grapes of Wrath with Charles Grapewin, Russell Simpson, Jane Darwell and Henry Fonda.

1941 *Gone With the Wind* (Metro-Goldwyn-Mayer, Selznick International); *Sergeant York* (WB); *The Philadelphia Story* (MGM); *Citizen Kane* (RKO); *Here Comes Mr. Jordan* (Col.); *The Little Foxes* (RKO); *Kitty Foyle* (RKO); *The Great Dictator* (UA); *Meet John Doe* (WB); *Blossoms in the Dust* (MGM).

1942 *Mrs. Miniver* (MGM); *How Green Was My Valley* (20th); *Kings Row* (WB); *Wake Island* (Par.); *The Pride of the Yankees* (RKO, Goldwyn); *The Man Who Came to Dinner* (WB); *One Foot in Heaven* (WB); *Suspicion* (RKO); *Woman of the Year* (MGM); *The Pied Piper* (20th).

Woman of the Year with Spencer Tracy and Katharine Hepburn.

1943 *Random Harvest* (MGM); *For Whom the Bell Tolls* (Par.); *Yankee Doodle Dandy* (WB); *This Is the Army* (WB); *Casablanca* (WB); *The Human Comedy* (MGM); *Watch on the Rhine* (WB); *In Which We Serve* (UA); *So Proudly We Hail!* (Par.); *Stage Door Canteen* (United Artists, Sol Lesser).

1944 *Going My Way* (Par.); *The Song of Bernadette* (20th); *Since You Went Away* (United Artists, Selznick); *Madame Curie* (MGM); *Dragon Seed* (MGM); *The White Cliffs of Dover* (MGM); *Gaslight* (MGM); *A Guy Named Joe* (MGM); *The Story of Dr. Wassell* (Par.); *Lifeboat* (20th).

The Song of Bernadette with Marcel Dalio, Mary Anderson, Jennifer Jones and Anne Revere.

1945 *Wilson* (20th); *A Tree Grows in Brooklyn* (20th); *The Keys of the Kingdom* (20th); *The Valley of Decision* (MGM); *A Song to Remember* (Col.); *Laura* (20th); *The Story of G. I. Joe* (United Artists, Lester Cowan); *The Corn Is Green* (WB); *National Velvet* (MGM); *Anchors Aweigh* (MGM).

1946 *The Lost Weekend* (Par.); *The Green Years* (MGM); *Anna and the King of Siam* (20th); *The Bells of St. Mary's* (RKO, Rainbow); *Spellbound* (UA); *Saratoga Trunk* (WB); *Henry V* (United Artists, Twin Cities); *Notorious* (RKO); *Leave Her to Heaven* (20th); *Night and Day* (WB).

1947 *The Best Years of Our Lives* (RKO, Goldwyn); *The Jolson Story* (Col.); *Life With Father* (WB); *The Yearling* (MGM); *Miracle on 34th Street* (20th); *Great Expectations* (Universal, J. Arthur Rank); *Crossfire* (RKO); *Boomerang!* (20th); *Brief Encounter* (Universal, J. Arthur Rank); *Odd Man Out* (Universal, J. Arthur Rank).

The Yearling with Claude Jarman, Jr., and Jane Wyman.

1948 *Gentleman's Agreement* (20th); *Johnny Belinda* (WB); *I Remember Mama* (RKO); *Treasure of Sierra Madre* (WB); *Hamlet* (Universal, J. Arthur Rank); *The Naked City* (Univ.); *Sitting Pretty* (20th); *State of the Union* (MGM); *Call Northside 777* (20th); *The Bishop's Wife* (RKO, Goldwyn).

1949 *The Snake Pit* (20th); *The Red Shoes* (Eagle Lion, J. Arthur Rank); *A Letter to Three Wives* (20th); *Champion* (UA); *The Stratton Story* (MGM); *Come to the Stable* (20th); *Home of the Brave* (UA); *Command Decision* (MGM); *The Heiress* (Par.); *Pinky* (20th).

1950 No Awards

1951 *A Place in the Sun* (Par.); *A Streetcar Named Desire* (WB); *An American in Paris* (MGM); *Detective Story* (Par.); *Born Yesterday* (Col.); *Cyrano de Bergerac* (UA); *Death of a Salesman* (Col.); *Quo Vadis* (MGM); *Bright Victory* (Univ.); *The Great Caruso* (MGM).

A Place in the Sun with Montgomery Clift and Shelley Winters.

1952   *High Noon* (UA); *The Quiet Man* (Rep.); *The Greatest Show on Earth* (Par.); *The African Queen* (UA); *Ivanhoe* (MGM); *Come Back, Little Sheba* (Par.); *The Lavender Hill Mob* (Univ.); *Singin' in the Rain* (MGM); *With a Song in My Heart* (20th); *Five Fingers* (20th).

1953   *From Here to Eternity* (Col.); *Shane* (Par.); *The Robe* (20th); *Roman Holiday* (Par.); *Moulin Rouge* (UA); *Lili* (MGM); *Stalag 17* (Par.); *The Moon Is Blue* (UA); *Little Boy Lost* (Par.); *The Cruel Sea* (Univ.).

Shane with Alan Ladd, Van Heflin, Jean Arthur and Brandon de Wilde.

1954   *The Caine Mutiny* (Col.); *On the Waterfront* (Col.); *Rear Window* (Par.); *The Country Girl* (Par.); *The High and the Mighty* (WB); *Seven Brides for Seven Brothers* (MGM); *Sabrina* (Par.); *Executive Suite* (MGM); *The Glenn Miller Story* (Univ.); *Three Coins in the Fountain* (20th).

Gigi with Leslie Caron and Louis Jourdan.

1955   *Mister Roberts* (WB); *Marty* (UA); *East of Eden* (WB); *Blackboard Jungle* (MGM); *Bad Day at Black Rock* (MGM); *A Man Called Peter* (20th); *Trial* (MGM); *Love Me or Leave Me* (MGM); *Summertime* (UA); *Love Is a Many-Splendored Thing* (20th).

1956   *The King and I* (20th); *Giant* (WB); *War and Peace* (Par.); *Friendly Persuasion* (AA); *Anastasia* (20th); *Moby Dick* (WB); *Picnic* (Col.); *The Ten Commandments* (Par.); *Tea and Sympathy* (MGM); *The Rose Tattoo* (Par.).

1957   *Around the World in 80 Days* (UA); *Sayonara* (WB); *12 Angry Men* (UA); *Peyton Place* (20th); *A Hatful of Rain* (20th); *Les Girls* (MGM); *A Face in the Crowd* (WB); *Heaven Knows, Mr. Allison* (20th); *Don't Go Near the Water* (MGM); *The Pajama Game* (WB).

1958   *The Bridge on the River Kwai* (Col.); *Cat on a Hot Tin Roof* (MGM); *Gigi* (MGM); *Auntie Mame* (WB); *The Defiant Ones* (UA); *Witness for the Prosecution* (UA); *Separate Tables* (UA); *The Long Hot Summer* (20th); *The Young Lions* (20th); *The Big Country* (UA).

1959   *Anatomy of a Murder* (Col.); *The Diary of Anne Frank* (20th); *The Nun's Story* (WB); *Pillow Talk* (Univ); *North by Northwest* (MGM); *Room at the Top* (Continental); *Some Like It Hot* (UA); *Compulsion* (20th); *I Want to Live!* (UA); *Some Came Running* (MGM).

1960   *The Apartment* (UA); *Elmer Gantry* (UA); *Ben-Hur* (MGM); *Inherit the Wind* (UA); *Sunrise at Campobello* (WB); *The Dark at the Top of the Stairs* (WB); *Suddenly, Last Summer* (Col.); *Spartacus* (Univ.); *Sons and Lovers* (20th); *Midnight Lace* (Univ.).

1961   *The Guns of Navarone* (Col.); *The Hustler* (20th); *Breakfast at Tiffany's* (Par.); *Fanny* (WB); *West Side Story* (UA); *Judgment at Nuremberg* (UA); *The Parent Trap* (Walt Disney-Buena Vista); *Exodus* (UA); *Splendor in the Grass* (WB); *The Mark* (Continental).

1962   *The Manchurian Candidate* (UA); *The Music Man* (WB); *The Miracle Worker* (UA); *The Longest Day* (20th); *To Kill a Mockingbird* (Univ.); *Requiem for a Heavyweight* (Col.); *Birdman of Alcatraz* (UA); *Lawrence of Arabia* (Col.); *Billy Budd* (AA); *A Taste of Honey* (Continental).

The Music Man with Shirley Jones and Robert Preston.

1963   *Tom Jones* (UA); *Hud* (Par.); *Lilies of the Field* (UA); *David and Lisa* (Continental); *Cleopatra* (20th); *Charade* (Univ.); *Irma La Douce* (UA); *The L-Shaped Room* (Col.); *America America* (WB); *The Great Escape* (UA).

1964   *My Fair Lady* (WB); *Becket* (Par.); *Mary Poppins* (BV); *Dr. Strangelove or: How I Learned to Stop Worrying and Love the Bomb* (Col.); *Topkapi* (UA); *A Hard Day's Night* (UA); *The Americanization of Emily* (MGM); *The Unsinkable Molly Brown* (MGM); *The Chalk Garden* (Univ.); *Seven Days in May* (Par.).

1965 *The Sound of Music* (20th); *Ship of Fools* (Col.); *The Pawn-broker* (Landau–Unger–AIP); *Darling* (Embassy); *The Collector* (Col.); *Those Magnificent Men in Their Flying Machines* (20th); *The Spy Who Came in from the Cold* (Par.); *Doctor Zhivago* (MGM); *The Ipcress File* (Univ.); *The Great Race* (WB).

1966 *Who's Afraid of Virginia Woolf?* (WB); *The Russians Are Coming, The Russians Are Coming* (UA); *Alfie* (Par.); *Born Free* (Col.); *Harper* (WB); *A Man for All Seasons* (Col.); *The Professionals* (Col.); *Georgy Girl* (Col.); *The Bible . . . In the Beginning* (20th); *How to Steal a Million* (20th).

1967 *In The Heat of the Night* (UA); *Bonnie and Clyde* (WB); *Cool Hand Luke* (Col.); *To Sir, With Love* (Col.); *The Dirty Dozen* (MGM); *Up the Down Staircase* (WB-7Arts); *Ulysses* (Reade-Strick, Continental); *The Family Way* (WB); *Thoroughly Modern Millie* (Univ.); *Wait Until Dark* (WB-7Arts).

PHOTOPLAY GOLD MEDAL AWARD

Photoplay magazine's annual Gold Medal Awards were developed over 48 years ago and they have now become a classic in the entertainment industry.

The Gold Medal Award is unique: it is the oldest award in the industry and only award in which the viewing public has the opportunity to speak its mind. The votes are cast by *Photoplay's* multi-million audience. This enables *Photoplay* to attach a personal barometer to the true feelings of the American movie-going public toward the movie product.

It has also offered *Photoplay* the opportunity to express its feelings of appreciation to the talent of the industry and the ability to gauge exactly how effective the efforts of various studios have been throughout the years.

1920—*Humoresque;* **1921**—*Tol'able David;* **1922**—*Robin Hood;* **1923**—*Covered Wagon;* **1924**—*Abraham Lincoln;* **1925**—*The Big Parade;* **1926**—*Beau Geste;* **1927**—*Seventh Heaven;* **1928**—*Four Sons;* **1929**—*Disraeli;* **1930**—*All Quiet on the Western Front;* **1931**—*Cimarron;* **1932**—*Smilin' Through;* **1933**—*Little Women;* **1934**—*Barretts of Wim-*

San Francisco with Clark Gable and Jeanette MacDonald.

pole Street; **1935**—*Naughty Marietta;* **1936**—*San Francisco;* **1937**—*Captains Courageous;* **1938**—*Sweethearts;* **1939**—*Gone With the Wind;* **1940–1943**—no awards. **1944**—Actor, Bing Crosby; Actress, Greer Garson; Film, *Going My Way.* **1945**—Actor, Bing Crosby; Actress, Greer Garson; Film, *The Valley of Decision.* **1946**—Actor, Bing Crosby; Actress, Ingrid Bergman; Film, *The Bells of St. Mary's.* **1947**—Actor, Bing Crosby; Actress, Ingrid Bergman; Film, *The Jolson Story.* **1948**—Actor, Bing Crosby; Actress, Ingrid Bergman; Film, *Sitting Pretty.* **1949**—Actor, James Stewart; Actress, Jane Wyman; Film, *The Stratton Story.* **1950**—Actor, John Wayne; Actress, Betty Hutton; Film, *Battleground.* **1951**—Actor, Mario Lanza; Actress, Doris Day; Film, *Show Boat.* **1952**—Actor, Gary Cooper; Actress, Susan Hayward: Film, *With a Song in My Heart.* **1953**—Actor, Alan Ladd; Actress, Marilyn Monroe; Film, *From Here to Eternity.* **1954**—Actor, William Holden; Actress, June Allyson; Film, *Magnificent Obsession.* **1955**—Actor, William Holden; Actress, Jennifer Jones; Film, *Love is a Many-Splendored Thing.* **1956**—Actor, Rock Hudson; Actress, Kim Novak; Film, *Giant.* **1957**—Actor, Rock Hudson;

Giant with Elizabeth Taylor and James Dean.

Actress, Deborah Kerr; Film, *An Affair to Remember.* **1958**—Actor Tony Curtis; Actress, Debbie Reynolds; Newcomers, Edd Byrnes, David Nelson, Sandra Dee; Film, *Gigi.* **1959**—Actor, Rock Hudson; Actress, Doris Day; Newcomers, Troy Donahue, Millie Perkins; Film, *Pillow Talk.* **1960**—no awards. **1961**—Actor, Troy Donahue; Actress, Connie Stevens; Newcomers, Warren Beatty, Deborah Walley, Paula Prentiss; Film, *Splendor in the Grass.* **1962**—Actor, Richard Chamberlain; Actress, Bette Davis; Newcomers, Gary Clarke, Suzanne Pleshette; Film, *The Miracle Worker.* **1963**—Actor, Richard Chamberlain; Actress, Connie Stevens; Newcomers, Robert Walker, Tippi Hedren; Film, *How the West Was Won.* **1964**—Actor, Richard Chamberlain; Actress, Ann-Margret; Newcomers, Robert Goulet, Barbara Parkins; Film, *The Unsinkable Molly Brown.* **1965**—Actor, Robert Vaughn; Actress, Dorothy Malone; Newcomers, Chris Connelly, Pat Morrow; Film, *The Sound of Music.* **1966**—Actor, David Janssen; Actress, Barbara Stanwyck; Newcomers, Marlo Thomas, Noel Harrison; Film, *The Russians Are Coming, The Russians Are Coming* **1967**—Actor, Paul Newman; Actress, Barbara Stanwyck; Newcomers, Tina Cole, Henry Darrow. Comedy Star, Carol Burnett. Special Gold Medal Award, Glenn Ford. Film, *The Dirty Dozen.*

TOP GROSSING FILMS

The following list of top-grossing films has been garnered from the records of *The Motion Picture Herald, Motion Picture Daily* and *Film Daily.* For each year, the films have been listed in alphabetical order. When a film was a top-grosser for more than one year, only the first year is listed.

1930–31 *Animal Crackers* (Par.); *Check and Double Check* (RKO);

Cimarron (RKO); *City Lights* (UA); *A Connecticut Yankee*, (Fox); *Daddy Long Legs* (Fox); *Hell's Angels* (UA); *Little Caesar* (WB); *The Man Who Came Back* (Fox); *Min and Bill* (MGM); *Morocco* (Par.); *Politics* (MGM); *Reducing* (MGM); *Strangers May Kiss* (MGM); *Trader Horn* (MGM).

1932   *Arrowsmith* (UA); *Bring 'Em Back Alive* (RKO); *Business and Pleasure* (Fox); *Delicious* (Fox); *Dr. Jekyll and Mr. Hyde* (Par.); *Emma* (MGM); *Frankenstein* (Univ.); *Grand Hotel* (MGM); *Hell Divers* (MGM); *Man Who Played God* (WB); *Mata Hari* (MGM); *One Hour With You* (Par.); *Shanghai Express* (Par.); *Shopworn* (Col.); *Tarzan the Ape Man* (MGM).

1933   *Animal Kingdom* (RKO); *Be Mine Tonight* (Univ.); *Cavalcade* (Fox); *42nd Street* (WB); *Gold Diggers of 1933* (WB); *I'm No Angel* (Par.); *The Kid From Spain* (UA); *Little Women* (RKO); *Rasputin and the Empress* (MGM); *State Fair* (Fox); *Tugboat Annie* (MGM).

1934   *Barretts of Wimpole Street* (MGM); *Belle of the Nineties* (Par.); *Chained* (MGM); *It Happened One Night* (Col.); *Judge Priest* (Fox); *Kentucky Kernels* (RKO); *The Lost Patrol* (RKO); *One Night of Love* (Col.); *Queen Christina* (MGM); *Riptide* (MGM); *Roman Scandals* (UA); *She Loves Me Not* (Par.); *Son of Kong* (RKO); *Sons of the Desert* (MGM); *Wonder Bar* (WB).

1935   *China Seas* (MGM); *David Copperfield* (MGM); *Forsaking All Others* (MGM); *Goin' to Town* (Par.); *Les Miserables* (UA); *Lives of a Bengal Lancer* (Par.); *A Midsummer Night's Dream* (WB); *Mutiny on the Bounty* (MGM); *Roberta* (RKO); *She Married Her Boss* (Col.); *Steamboat 'Round the Bend* (20th); *Top Hat* (RKO).

1935–36   *Anna Karenina* (MGM); *The Bride Comes Home* (Par.); *Broadway Melody of 1936* (MGM); *Bullets or Ballots* (WB); *Captain Blood* (WB); *The Country Doctor* (20th); *The Crusades* (Par.); *Follow the Fleet* (RKO); *The Great Ziegfeld* (WB); *Green Pastures* (WB); *In Old Kentucky* (20th); *The King Steps Out* (Col.); *The Littlest Rebel* (20th); *Magnificent Obsession* (Univ.); *Modern Times* (UA); *Mr. Deeds Goes to Town* (Col.); *A Night at the Opera* (MGM); *Rhythm on the Range* (Par.); *Rose Marie* (MGM); *San Francisco* (MGM); *Show Boat* (Univ.); *The Story of Louis Pasteur* (WB); *A Tale of Two Cities* (MGM); *Thanks a Million* (20th); *These Three* (UA).

1936–37   *After the Thin Man* (MGM); *Anthony Adverse* (WB); *Artists and Models* (Par.); *The Big Broadcast of 1937* (Par.); *Born to Dance* (MGM); *Captains Courageous* (MGM); *The Charge of the Light Brigade* (WB); *College Holiday* (Par.); *Come and Get It* (UA); *Dodsworth* (UA); *The Good Earth* (MGM); *The Gorgeous Hussy* (MGM); *Green Light* (WB); *I Met Him in Paris* (Par.); *The Last of Mrs. Cheyney* (MGM); *Libeled Lady* (MGM); *Lloyds of London* (20th); *Lost Horizon* (Col.); *Love Is News* (20th); *Maytime* (MGM); *Mountain Music* (Par.); *My Man Godfrey* (Univ.); *One in a Million* (20th); *On the Avenue* (20th); *Pigskin Parade* (20th); *The Plainsman* (Par.); *Rainbow on the River* (RKO); *The Road Back* (Univ.); *Romeo and Juliet* (MGM); *Shall We Dance* (RKO); *Slave Ship* (20th); *A Star is Born* (UA); *Swing High, Swing Low* (Par.); *Swing Time* (RKO); *Wake Up and Live* (20th); *Waikiki Wedding* (Par.); *Wee Willie Winkie* (20th); *You Can't Have Everything* (20th).

1937–38   *The Adventures of Robin Hood* (WB); *Adventures of Tom Sawyer* (UA); *Alexander's Ragtime Band* (20th); *The Buccaneer* (Par.); *The Firefly* (MGM); *Girl of the Golden West* (MGM); *The Goldwyn Follies* (UA); *Happy Landing* (20th); *Holiday* (Col.); *The Hurricane* (UA); *In Old Chicago* (20th); *Rosalie* (MGM); *Snow White and the Seven Dwarfs* (RKO); *Test Pilot* (MGM); *Wells Fargo* (Par.).

1938–39   *Angels with Dirty Faces* (WB); *Boys' Town* (MGM); *Dodge City* (WB); *Goodbye, Mr. Chips* (MGM); *Gunga Din* (RKO); *Hardys Ride High* (MGM); *Jesse James* (20th); *Juarez* (WB); *Out West with the Hardys* (MGM); *Pygmalion* (MGM); *Stagecoach* (UA); *Sweethearts* (MGM); *That Certain Age* (Univ.); *Three Smart Girls Grow Up* (Univ.); *Union Pacific* (Par.); *You Can't Take It with You* (Col.).

1939–40   *All This, and Heaven Too* (WB); *Another Thin Man* (MGM) *Babes in Arms* (MGM); *Destry Rides Again* (Univ.); *Drums Along the Mohawk* (20th); *The Fighting 69th* (WB); *Gone with the Wind* (MGM); *Grapes of Wrath* (20th); *Gulliver's Travels* (Par.); *Hollywood Cavalcade* (20th); *The Hunchback of Notre Dame* (RKO); *Lillian Russell* (20th); *Mr. Smith Goes to Washington* (Col.); *My Favorite Wife* (RKO); *Ninotchka* (MGM); *Northwest Passage* (MGM); *The Old Maid* (WB); *The Rains Came* (20th); *Rebecca* (UA); *Road to Singapore* (Par.); *The Women* (MGM).

1940–41   *Aloma of the South Seas* (Par.); *Blood and Sand* (20th); *Boom Town* (MGM); *The Bride Came C.O.D* (WB); *Caught in the Draft* (Par.); *Charley's Aunt* (20th); *Dive Bomber* (WB); *The Great Dictator* (UA); *Hold That Ghost* (Univ.); *I Wanted Wings* (Par.); *The Lady Eve* (Par.); *Life Begins for Andy Hardy* (MGM); *Meet John Doe* (WB); *North West Mounted Police* (Par.); *The Philadelphia Story* (MGM); *Road to Zanzibar* (Par.); *The Sea Wolf* (WB); *Strawberry Blonde* (WB); *That Hamilton Woman* (UA); *This Thing Called Love* (Col.); *The Ziegfeld Girl* (MGM).

1941–42   *Ball of Fire* (RKO); *Captains of the Clouds* (WB); *Eagle Squadron* (Univ.); *Holiday Inn* (Par.); *Honky Tonk* (MGM); *How Green Was My Valley* (20th); *In This Our Life* (WB); *Kings Row* (WB); *Louisiana Purchase* (Par.); *The Man Who Came to Dinner* (WB); *Mrs. Miniver* (MGM); *My Favorite Blonde* (Par.); *My Gal Sal* (20th); *Pride of the Yankees* (RKO); *Reap the Wild Wind* (Par.); *Sergeant York* (WB); *Somewhere I'll Find You* (MGM); *This Above All* (20th); *To the Shores of Tripoli* (20th); *Woman of the Year* (MGM); *Yankee Doodle Dandy* (WB).

1942–43   *Air Force* (WB); *Behind the Rising Sun* (RKO); *Casablanca* (WB); *Claudia* (20th); *Commandos Strike at Dawn* (Col.); *Coney Island* (20th); *Dixie* (Par.); *Heaven Can Wait* (20th); *Hello, Frisco, Hello* (20th); *Hers to Hold* (Univ.); *Hitler's Children* (RKO); *Immortal Sergeant* (20th); *In Which We Serve* (UA); *Keeper of the Flame* (MGM); *Lucky Jordan* (Par.); *Mr. Lucky* (RKO); *The More the Merrier* (Col.); *Now, Voyager* (WB); *Random Harvest* (MGM); *Road to Morocco* (Par.); *So Proudly We Hail!* (Par.); *Stage Door Canteen* (UA); *Star Spangled Rhythm* (Par.); *This is the Army* (WB).

1943–44   *Arsenic and Old Lace* (WB); *Cover Girl* (Col.); *Destination Tokyo* (WB); *Dragon Seed* (MGM); *For Whom the Bell Tolls* (Par.); *The Gang's All Here* (20th); *Girl Crazy* (MGM); *Going My Way* (Par.); *Guadalcanal Diary* (20th); *A Guy Named Joe* (MGM); *Lady in the Dark* (Par.); *Let's Face It* (Par.); *Madame Curie* (MGM); *The Miracle of Morgan's Creek* (Par.); *Mr. Skeffington* (WB); *The North Star* (RKO); *See Here, Private Hargrove* (MGM); *Since You Went Away* (UA); *The Song of Bernadette* (20th); *Story of Dr. Wassell* (Par.); *Sweet Rosie O'Grady* (20th); *Thank Your Lucky Stars* (WB); *Thousands Cheer* (MGM); *White Cliffs of Dover* (MGM); *Wilson* (20th).

1944–45   *The Affairs of Susan* (Par.); *Along Camet Jones* (RKO); *Anchors Aweigh* (MGM); *And Now Tomorrow* (Par.); *Casanova Brown* (RKO); *Christmas in Connecticut* (WB); *Diamond Horseshoe* (20th); *Frenchman's Creek* (Par.); *God Is My Co-Pilot* (WB); *Here Come the Waves* (Par.); *Hollywood Canteen* (WB); *I'll Be Seeing You* (UA); *Incendiary Blonde* (Par.); *Irish Eyes Are Smiling* (20th); *The Keys of the Kingdom* (20th); *Meet Me in St. Louis* (MGM); *Mrs. Parkington* (MGM); *Music For Millions* (MGM); *National Velvet* (MGM); *Nob Hill* (20th); *The Princess and the Pirate* (RKO); *Rhapsody in Blue* (WB); *Salty O'Rourke* (Par.); *A Song to Remember* (Col.); *Thirty Seconds Over Tokyo* (MGM); *Thrill of Romance* (MGM); *Thunderhead, Son of Flicka* (20th); *To Have and Have Not* (WB); *A Tree Grows in Brooklyn* (20th); *The Valley of Decision* (MGM); *Winged Victory* (20th); *Without Love* (MGM); *Wonder Man* (RKO).

1945–46   *Adventure* (MGM); *Anna and the King of Siam* (20th); *Bandit of Sherwood Forest* (Col.); *The Bells of St. Mary's* (RKO); *Caesar and Cleopatra* (Rank); *Canyon Passage* (Univ.); *The Dolly Sisters* (20th); *Dragonwyck* (20th); *Duffy's Tavern* (Par.); *Easy to Wed* (MGM); *Gilda* (Col.); *The Green Years* (MGM); *The Harvey Girls*

(MGM); *The House on 92nd Street* (20th); *Kid From Brooklyn* (RKO); *Kitty* (Par.); *Leave Her to Heaven* (20th); *The Lost Weekend* (Par.); *Love Letters* (Par.); *Mildred Pierce* (WB); *Miss Susie Slagle's* (Par.); *Monsieur Beaucaire* (Par.); *My Reputation* (WB); *Night and Day* (WB); *Notorious* (RKO); *Road to Utopia* (Par.); *San Antonio* (WB); *Saratoga Trunk* (WB); *The Spanish Main* (RKO); *Spellbound* (UA); *The Stork Club* (Par.); *They Were Expendable* (MGM); *Tomorrow Is Forever* (RKO); *Two Sisters from Boston* (MGM); *Weekend at the Waldorf* (MGM); *Ziegfeld Follies of 1946* (MGM).

1946–47 *The Bachelor and the Bobby-Soxer* (RKO); *The Best Years of Our Lives* (RKO); *Blue Skies* (Par.); *California* (Par.); *Dear Ruth* (Par.); *Duel in the Sun* (Selznick); *The Farmer's Daughter* (RKO); *The Hucksters* (MGM); *Humoresque* (WB); *I Wonder Who's Kissing Her Now* (20th); *It's a Wonderful Life* (RKO); *The Jolson Story* (Col.); *Life With Father* (WB); *Margie* (20th); *My Favorite Brunette* (Par.); *No Leave, No Love* (MGM); *Nora Prentiss* (WB); *The Perils of Pauline* (Par.); *Possessed* (WB); *The Razor's Edge* (20th); *Till the Clouds Roll By* (MGM); *The Time, the Place and the Girl* (WB); *Two Years before the Mast* (Par.); *Variety Girl* (Par.); *Welcome Strangers* (Par.); *The Yearling* (MGM).

1947–48 *Abbott and Costello Meet Frankenstein* (Univ.); *The Bishop's Wife* (RKO); *Body and Soul* (UA); *Captain from Castile* (20th); *Cass Timberlane* (MGM); *A Date With Judy* (MGM); *Easter Parade* (MGM); *The Emperor Waltz* (Par.); *A Foreign Affair* (Par.); *Forever Amber* (20th); *Fort Apache* (RKO); *The Foxes of Harrow* (20th); *The Fuller Brush Man* (Col.); *Gentleman's Agreement* (20th); *Green Dolphin Street* (MGM); *Homecoming* (MGM); *I Remember Mama* (RKO); *Key Largo* (WB); *Mr. Blandings Builds His Dream House* (Selznick); *My Wild Irish Rose* (WB); *The Naked City* (Univ.); *The Paradine Case* (Selznick); *Road to Rio* (Par.); *Secret Life of Walter Mitty* (RKO); *Sitting Pretty* (20th); *State of the Union* (MGM); *Tap Roots* (Univ.); *Unconquered* (Par.); *Voice of the Turtle* (WB).

1948–49 *Apartment for Peggy* (20th); *The Barkleys of Broadway* (MGM); *Command Decision* (MGM); *A Connecticut Yankee in King Arthur's Court* (Par.); *Every Girl Should Be Married* (RKO); *Family Honeymoon* (Univ.); *Flamingo Road* (WB); *Hamlet* (Rank); *Joan of Arc* (RKO); *Johnny Belinda* (WB); *Julia Misbehaves* (MGM); *A Letter to Three Wives* (20th); *Little Women* (MGM); *Look for the Silver Lining* (WB); *Mr. Belvedere Goes to College* (20th); *Neptune's Daughter* (MGM); *The Paleface* (Par.); *Red River* (UA); *The Red Shoes* (Eagle Lion); *The Snake Pit* (20th); *Sorrowful Jones* (Par.); *The Stratton Story* (MGM); *Take Me Out to the Ball Game* (MGM); *The Three Musketeers* (MGM); *Wake of the Red Witch* (Rep.); *When My Baby Smiles at Me* (20th); *Whispering Smith* (Par.); *Words and Music* (MGM); *Yellow Sky* (20th).

1949–50 *Adam's Rib* (MGM); *Annie Get Your Gun* (MGM); *Battleground* (MGM); *The Black Rose* (20th); *Broken Arrow* (20th); *Cheaper by the Dozen* (20th); *Cinderella* (RKO); *Colt.45* (WB); *Fancy Pants* (Par.); *Father of the Bride* (MGM); *Flame and the Arrow* (WB); *Francis* (Univ.); *I Was a Male War Bride* (20th); *Jolson Sings Again* (Col.); *My Friend Irma* (Par.); *On the Town* (MGM); *Our Very Own* (RKO); *Pinky* (20th); *Samson and Delilah* (Par.); *Sands of Iwo Jima* (Rep.); *She Wore a Yellow Ribbon* (RKO); *Summer Stock* (MGM); *Sunset Boulevard* (Par.); *Task Force* (WB); *Tea for Two* (WB); *Three Little Words* (MGM); *Twelve O'Clock High* (20th); *Winchester '73* (Univ.).

1950–51 *Alice in Wonderland* (RKO); *All About Eve* (20th); *A War with the Army* (Par.); *Born Yesterday* (Col.); *Branded* (Par.); *Captain Horatio Hornblower* (WB); *David and Bathsheba* (20th); *Father's Little Dividend* (MGM); *Francis Goes to the Races* (Univ.); *Go for Broke* (MGM); *The Great Caruso* (MGM); *Halls of Montezuma* (20th); *Harvey* (Univ.); *Here Comes the Groom* (Par.); *Kim* (MGM); *King Solomon's Mines* (MGM); *The Lemon Drop Kid* (Par.); *On Moonlight Bay* (WB); *On the Riviera* (20th); *Operation Pacific* (WB); *Royal Wedding* (MGM); *Show Boat* (MGM); *That's My Boy* (Par.).

1951–52 *Affair in Trinidad* (Col.); *The African Queen* (UA); *An American in Paris* (MGM); *Bend of the River* (Univ.); *Clash by Night* (RKO); *Decision Before Dawn* (20th); *Detective Story* (Par.); *The Greatest Show on Earth* (Par.); *High Noon* (UA); *Just for You* (Par.); *The Merry Widow* (MGM); *The Miracle of Fatima* (WB); *Pat and Mike* (MGM); *A Place in the Sun* (Par.); *The Quiet Man* (Rep); *Quo Vadis* (MGM); *Sailor Beware* (Par.); *Singin' in the Rain* (MGM); *Son of Paleface* (Par.); *Story of Robin Hood* (RKO); *A Streetcar Named Desire* (WB); *Sudden Fear* (RKO); *With a Song in My Heart* (20th).

1952–53 *The Bad and the Beautiful* (MGM); *The Band Wagon* (MGM); *Bwana Devil* (UA); *Call Me Madam* (20th); *The Charge at Feather River* (WB); *Come Back, Little Sheba* (Par.); *Fort Ti* (Col.); *From Here to Eternity* (Col.); *Gentlemen Prefer Blondes* (20th); *Hans Christian Andersen* (RKO); *House of Wax* (WB); *Ivanhoe* (MGM); *Million Dollar Mermaid* (MGM); *The Mississippi Gambler* (Univ.); *Moulin Rouge* (UA); *The Naked Spur* (MGM); *Niagara* (20th); *Peter Pan* (RKO); *Road to Bali* (Par.); *Roman Holiday* (Par.); *Salome* (Col.); *Scared Stiff* (Par.); *Shane* (Par.); *The Snows of Kilimanjaro* (20th); *Stalag 17* (Par.); *Titanic* (20th.).

1953–54 *Apache* (UA); *The Caine Mutiny* (Col.); *Demetrius and the Gladiators* (20th); *Dial M for Murder* (WB); *Executive Suite* (MGM); *The Glenn Miller Story* (Univ.); *The High and the Mighty* (WB); *Hondo* (WB); *How to Marry a Millionaire* (20th); *Johnny Guitar* (Rep.); *Knights of the Round Table* (MGM); *Knock on Wood* (Par.); *Little Boy Lost* (Par.); *The Long, Long Trailer* (MGM); *Magnificent Obsession* (Univ.); *Mogambo* (MGM); *Money From Home* (Par.); *On the Waterfront* (Col.); *Rear Window* (Par.); *The Robe* (20th); *Saskatchewan* (Univ.); *Seven Brides for Seven Brothers* (MGM); *Susan Slept Here* (RKO); *This is Cinerama* (Cinerama); *Three Coins in the Fountain* (20th).

1954–55 *The Barefoot Contessa* (UA); *Battle Cry* (WB); *Blackboard Jungle* (MGM); *The Bridges at Toko-Ri* (Par.); *Brigadoon* (MGM); *Carmen Jones* (20th); *The Country Girl* (Par.); *Daddy Long Legs* (20th); *Dragnet* (WB); *The Far Country* (Univ.); *Interrupted Melody* (MGM); *The Long Gray Line* (Col.); *Love Is a Many-Splendored Thing* (20th); *Love Me or Leave Me* (MGM); *A Man Called Peter* (20th); *The Man From Laramie* (Col.); *Marty* (UA); *Mister Roberts* (WB); *Not as a Stranger* (UA); *Sabrina* (Par.); *Seven Year Itch* (20th); *A Star is Born* (WB); *Strategic Air Command* (Par.); *To Hell and Back* (Univ.); *20,000 Leagues under the Sea* (BV); *Vera Cruz* (UA); *White Christmas* (Par.).

1955–56 *Away All Boats* (Univ.); *The Benny Goodman Story* (Univ.); *Bhowani Junction* (MGM); *Bus Stop* (20th); *Carousel* (20th); *The Court Jester* (Par.); *The Court-Martial of Billy Mitchell* (WB); *The Eddy Duchin Story* (Col.); *Guys and Dolls* (MGM); *Helen of Troy* (WB); *High Society* (MGM); *I'll Cry Tomorrow* (MGM); *The King and I* (20th); *Man in the Gray Flannel Suit* (20th); *The Man with the Golden Arm* (UA); *Moby Dick* (WB); *Oklahoma!* (Magna); *The Phoenix City Story* (AA); *Picnic* (Col.); *Rebel Without a Cause* (WB); *The Rose Tattoo* (Par.); *The Searchers* (WB); *To Catch a Thief* (Par.); *Trapeze* (UA);

1956–57 *An Affair to Remember* (20th); *Anastasia* (20th); *Around the World in 80 Days* (UA); *Attack!* (UA); *The Bad Seed* (WB); *Battle Hymn* (Univ.); *The Delicate Delinquent* (Par.); *Friendly Persuasion* (AA); *Giant* (WB); *Gunfight at the O.K. Corral* (Par.); *Heaven Knows, Mr. Allison* (20th); *Island in the Sun* (20th); *Jeanne Eagels* (Col.); *Love Me Tender* (20th); *Lust for Life* (MGM); *Man of a Thousand Faces* (UA); *The Pride and the Passion* (UA); *The Solid Gold Cadillac* (Col.); *The Spirit of St. Louis* (WB); *The Teahouse of the August Moon* (MGM); *The Ten Commandments* (Par.); *12 Angry Men* (UA); *War and Peace* (Par.); *Written on the Wind* (Univ.).

1957–58 *The Bridge on the River Kwai* (Col.); *Cat on a Hot Tin Roof* (MGM); *Don't Go Near the Water* (MGM); *A Farewell to Arms* (20th); *The Fly* (20th); *Gigi* (MGM); *God's Little Acre* (UA); *Indiscreet* (WB); *The Joker Is Wild* (Par.); *Les Girls* (MGM); *The Long Hot Summer* (20th); *Marjorie Morningstar* (WB); *No Time for Sergeants* (WB); *Old Yeller* (BV); *Pal Joey* (Col.); *Paris Holiday* (UA); *Peyton*

Place (20th); *Raintree County* (MGM); *The Sad Sack* (Par.); *Sayonara* (WB); *South Pacific* (Magna); *Teacher's Pet* (Par.); *Ten North Frederick* (20th); *The Vikings* (UA); *Witness for the Prosecution* (UA); *The Young Lions* (20th);

1958–59   *Anatomy of a Murder* (Col.); *Auntie Mame* (WB); *Bell, Book and Candle* (Col.); *Blue Denim* (20th); *The Defiant Ones* (UA); *The Diary of Anne Frank,* (20th); *The Five Pennies* (Par.); *Hercules* (WB); *A Hole in the Head* (UA); *Horse Soldiers* (UA); *Houseboat* (Par.); *I Want to Live* (UA); *Imitation of Life* (Univ.); *The Inn of the Sixth Happiness* (20th); *North By Northwest* (MGM); *The Nun's Story* (WB); *Porgy and Bess* (Col.); *Rally 'Round the Flag, Boys!* (20th); *Rio Bravo* (WB); *Say One for Me* (20th); *Separate Tables* (UA); *The Seventh Voyage of Sinbad* (Col.); *The Shaggy Dog* (BV); *Some Came Running* (MGM); *Some Like It Hot* (UA); *This Earth Is Mine* (Univ.);

1959–60   *The Apartment* (UA); *Bells Are Ringing* (MGM); *Ben-Hur* (MGM); *The Best of Everything* (20th); *Can Can* (20th); *Elmer Gantry* (UA); *The FBI Story* (WB); *From the Terrace* (20th); *Hell to Eternity* (AA); *Home from the Hill* (MGM); *It Started with a Kiss* (MGM); *Journey to the Center of the Earth* (20th); *The Last Angry Man* (Col.); *Never So Few* (MGM); *Ocean's 11* (WB); *On the Beach* (UA); *Operation Petticoat* (Univ.); *Our Man in Havana* (Col.); *Pillow Talk* (Univ.); *Please Don't Eat the Daisies* (MGM); *Portrait in Black* (Univ.); *Psycho* (Par.); *Sink the Bismark!* (20th); *Solomon and Sheba* (UA); *The Story of Ruth* (20th); *Strangers When We Meet* (Col.); *Suddenly, Last Summer* (Col.); *A Summer Place* (WB).

1960–61   *The Absent-Minded Professor* (BV); *The Alamo* (UA); *Butterfield 8* (MGM); *Exodus* (UA); *Fanny* (WB); *Midnight Lace* (Univ.); *The Misfits* (UA); *North to Alaska* (20th); *One-Eyed Jacks* (Par.); *One Hundred and One Dalmatians* (BV); *The Parent Trap* (BV); *Spartacus* (Univ.); *Swiss Family Robinson* (BV); *World of Suzie Wong* (Par.).

1961–62   *Advise and Consent* (Col.); *Back Street* (Univ.); *Bird Man of Alcatraz* (UA); *Blue Hawaii* (Par.); *Breakfast at Tiffany's* (Par.); *El Cid* (AA); *The Comancheros* (20th); *Come September* (Univ.); *The Counterfeit Traitor* (Par.); *Flower Drum Song* (Univ.); *The Guns of Navarone* (Col.); *Hatari!* (Par.); *The Hustler* (20th); *The Interns* (Col.); *Judgment at Nuremberg* (UA); *King of Kings* (MGM); *Lolita* (MGM); *Lover Come Back* (Univ.); *The Music Man* (WB); *Pocketful of Miracles* (UA); *The Road to Hong Kong* (UA); *Splendor in the Grass* (WB); *Summer and Smoke* (Par.); *That Touch of Mink* (Univ.); *West Side Story* (UA).

1962–63   *The Birds* (Univ.); *Bye Bye Birdie* (Col.); *Cleopatra* (20th); *Come Blow Your Horn* (Par.); *David and Lisa* (Continental); *Days of Wine and Roses* (WB); *Diamond Head* (Col.); *Dr. No* (UA);

55 Days at Peking (AA); *For Love or Money* (Univ.); *Gigot* (20th); *The Great Escape* (UA); *Gypsy* (WB); *Hud* (Par.); *Irma La Douce* (UA); *It's Only Money* (Par.); *The Longest Day* (20th); *The Manchurian Candidate* (UA); *The Miracle Worker* (UA); *Mutiny on the Bounty* (MGM); *Nutty Professor* (Par.); *Son of Flubber* (BV); *Spencer's Mountain* (WB); *Summer Magic* (BV); *The Thrill of It All* (Univ.); *To Kill a Mockingbird* (Univ.); *Toys in the Attic* (UA); *What Ever Happened to Baby Jane?* (WB).

1963–64   *Becket* (Par.); *The Best Man* (UA); *Captain Newman, M.D.* (Univ.); *The Carpetbaggers* (Par.); *The Chalk Garden* (Univ.); *Charade* (Univ.); *Circus World* (Par.); *Dr. Strangelove or: How I Learned to Stop Worrying and Love the Bomb* (Col.); *Fall of the Roman Empire* (Par.); *4 For Texas* (WB); *From Russia with Love* (UA); *Good Neighbor Sam* (Col.); *A Hard Day's Night* (UA); *How the West Was Won* (MGM); *It's a Mad, Mad, Mad, Mad World* (UA); *Lilies of the Field* (UA); *Love with the Proper Stranger* (Par.); *McLintock!* (UA); *The New Interns* (Col.); *The Night of the Iguana* (MGM); *The Pink Panther* (UA); *The Prize* (MGM); *Robin and the 7 Hoods* (WB); *Seven Days in May* (Par.); *A Shot in the Dark* (UA); *Take Her, She's Mine* (20th); *Tom Jones* (UA); *The Unsinkable Molly Brown* (MGM); *The V.I.P.'s* (MGM); *The Victors* (Col.); *What a Way to Go!* (20th); *The Wheeler Dealers* (MGM).

1964–65   *The Americanization of Emily* (MGM); *Cat Ballou* (Col.); *Cheyenne Autumn* (WB); *The Collector* (Col.); *Father Goose* (Univ.); *Goldfinger* (UA); *The Great Spy Mission* (*Operation Crossbow*) (MGM); *The Greatest Story Ever Told* (UA); *Harlow* (Par.); *Help!* (UA); *How to Murder Your Wife* (UA); *Hush . . . Hush, Sweet Charlotte* (20th); *In Harm's Way* (Par.); *Lilith* (Col.); *Mary Poppins* (BV); *My Fair Lady* (WB); *The Pawnbroker* (AIP); *The Sandpiper* (MGM); *Send Me No Flowers* (Univ.); *Shenandoah* (Univ.); *Ship of Fools* (Col.); *Sons of Katie Elder* (Par.); *The Sound of Music* (20th); *Those Magnificent Men in Their Flying Machines* (20th); *Topkapi* (UA); *The Train* (UA); *Von Ryan's Express* (20th); *What's New Pussycat?* (UA); *Yellow Rolls-Royce* (MGM); *Zorba the Greek* (20th);

1965–1966   *The Agony and the Ecstasy* (20th); *Arabesque* (Univ.); *Bambi* (BV); *Battle of the Bulge* (WB); *Beach Party* (AIP); *Bikini Beach* (AIP); *Born Free* (Col.); *Boy, Did I Get a Wrong Number!* (UA); *Cat Ballou* (Col.); *Darling* (Embassy); *Dr. Zhivago* (MGM); *Fantastic Voyage* (20th); *The Great Race* (WB); *Harper* (WB); *My Fair Lady* (WB); *Nevada Smith* (Par.); *Our Man Flint* (20th); *Patch of Blue* (MGM); *The Professionals* (Col.); *The Russians Are Coming, The Russians Are Coming* (UA); *The Silencers* (Col.); *The Singing Nun* (MGM); *The Sound of Music* (20th); *The Ten Commandments* (Par); *That Darn Cat* (BV); *Those Magnificent Men in Their Flying Machines* (20th); *Thunderball* (UA); *Torn Curtain* (Univ.); *The Trouble With Angels* (Col.); *The Ugly Duckling* (BV); *Walk, Don't Run* (Col.); *The Wild Angels* (AIP); *Who's Afraid of Virginia Woolf?* (WB).

BIBLIOGRAPHY

Academy of Motion Picture Arts and Sciences, Research Council. *Motion Picture Sound Engineering.* New York: Van Nostrand, 1938.

Agee, James. *Agee on Film: Five Film Scripts.* Boston: Beacon, 1964.

Alicoate, Charles, ed. *Film Daily Year Book of Motion Pictures.* New York: *Film Daily* Annual.

Arliss, George. *My Ten Years in the Studios.* Boston: Little, Brown & Co., 1940.

Arnheim, Rudolf. *Film as Art.* Berkeley: University of California Press, 1957.

Bardeche, Maurice, and Brasillach, Robert. *The History of Motion Pictures.* New York: Norton, 1938.

Benoit-Levy, Jean. *The Art of the Motion Picture.* New York: Coward-McCann, 1946.

Bluestone, George. *Novels into Films.* Baltimore: Johns Hopkins Press, 1957.

Callenbach, Ernest. *Our Modern Art, the Movies.* Chicago: Center for Study of Liberal Education for Adults, 1955.

Catalog of Copyright Entries, cumulative series. Motion Pictures, 1912-1939. Washington, D. C.: Copyright Office, Library of Congress, 1951.

Catalog of Copyright Entries, cumulative series. Motion Pictures, 1940-1949. Washington, D. C.: Copyright Office, Library of Congress, 1953.

Catalog of Copyright Entries, cumulative series. Motion Pictures, 1950-1959. Washington, D. C.: Copyright Office, Library of Congress, 1963.

Catalog of Copyright Entries: Motion Pictures. Washington, D. C.: Copyright Office, Library of Congress. Semi-annual.

Ceram, C. W. *Archaeology of the Cinema.* New York: Harcourt, 1965.

Clason, W. E. *Dictionary of Cinema, Sound and Music.* New York: Van Nostrand, 1956.

Cogley, John. *Report on Blacklisting.* v. 1, Movies. New York: Fund for the Republic, 1956.

621

Conant, Michael. *Antitrust in the Motion Picture Industry.* Berkeley and Los Angeles: University of California Press, 1960.

Cooke, David C. *Behind the Scenes in Motion Pictures.* New York: Dodd, 1960.

Crowther, Bosley. *Hollywood Rajah: The Life and Times of Louis B. Mayer.* New York: Holt, 1960.

Crowther, Bosley. *Lion's Share: The Story of an Entertainment Empire.* New York: Dutton, 1957.

Dale, Edgar. *The Content of Motion Pictures.* New York: Macmillan, 1935.

Dale, Edgar, and Morrison, John. *Motion Picture Discrimination. An Annotated Bibliography.* Columbus, Ohio: Bureau of Educational Research, Ohio State University, 1951.

Dimmitt, Richard B. *A Title Guide to the Talkies: A Comprehensive Listing of 16,000 Feature-length Films from October 27, 1927, until December 1963.* 2 vols. New York: Scarecrow, 1965.

Dixon, Campbell, ed. *International Film Annual,* No. 1, 1957. New York: Doubleday.

Doyle, G. R. *Twenty-five Years of Films.* London: Mitre Press, 1936.

Everson, William K. *The American Movies.* New York: Atheneum, 1963.

Fenin, George N., and Everson, William K. *The Western: From Silents to Cinerama.* New York: Orion Press, 1962.

Field, Robert D. *The Art of Walt Disney.* New York: Macmillan, 1942.

Franklin, Harold B. *Sound Motion Pictures: From the Laboratory to Their Presentation.* New York: Doubleday, Doran & Co., 1929.

Fulton, A. R. *Motion Pictures: The Development of an Art from Silent Films to the Age of Television.* Norman: University of Oklahoma Press, 1960.

Goldwyn, Samuel. *Behind the Screen.* New York: Doran, 1923.

Green, Abel, and Laurie, Joe, Jr. *Show Biz, from Vaude to Video.* New York: Henry Holt & Co., 1951.

Griffith, Richard, and Mayer, Arthur. *The Movies.* New York: Simon and Schuster, 1957.

Hampton, Benjamin B. *A History of the Movies.* New York: Covici-Friede, 1931.

Handel, Leo A. *Hollywood Looks at Its Audience.* Urbana: University of Illinois Press, 1950.

Hays, Will H. *See and Hear: A Brief History of Motion Pictures and the Development of Sound.* New York: Motion Picture Producers and Distributors of America, 1929.

Holaday, Perry W., and Stoddard, George D. *Getting Ideas from the Movies.* New York: Macmillan, 1933.

Huaco, George A. *The Sociology of Film Art.* New York: Basic Books, 1965.

Hughes, Elinor. *Famous Stars of Filmdom.* Boston: L. C. Page & Co., 1932.

Inglis, Ruth A. *Freedom of the Movies: A Report on Self-regulation from the Commission on Freedom of the Press.* Chicago: University of Chicago Press, 1947.

International Film Guide. London: Tantivy Press. Annual.

Jacobs, Lewis. *The Rise of the American Film: A Critical History.* New York: Harcourt, Brace & Co., 1939.

Jacobs, Lewis, ed. *Introduction to the Art of the Movies: An Anthology of Ideas on the Nature of Movie Art.* New York: Noonday Press, 1960.

Kael, Pauline. *I Lost It at the Movies.* Boston: Atlantic-Little, 1965.

Kiesling, Barrett C. *Talking Pictures: How They Are Made, How to Appreciate Them.* New York: Johnson Pub. Co., 1937.

Knight, Arthur. *Liveliest Art: A Panoramic History of the Movies.* New York: Macmillan, 1957.

Lee, Norman. *Film Is Born: How 40 Film Fathers Bring a Modern Talking Picture into Being.* London: Jordan & Sons, 1945.

LeRoy, Mervyn. *It Takes More Than Talent*, as told to Alyce Canfield. New York: Alfred A. Knopf, 1953.

McAnany, Emile G. *The Film Viewer's Handbook.* Glen Rock: Paulist Press, 1965.

Mayer, Arthur. *Merely Colossal.* New York: Simon and Schuster, 1953.

Michael, Paul. *The Academy Awards: A Pictorial History.* Indianapolis: Bobbs-Merrill, 1964.

Michael, Paul. *Humphrey Bogart: The Man and His Films.* Indianapolis: Bobbs-Merrill, 1965.

Miller, Diane Disney. *The Story of Walt Disney.* New York: Holt, 1957.

New York City. Works Progress Administration. *The Film Index, a Bibliography.* New York: Museum of Modern Art Film Library, 1941.

Pitkin, Walter B., and Marston, William M. *The Art of Sound Pictures.* New York: Appleton, 1930.

Rideout, Eric H. *The American Film.* London: Mitre Press, 1937.

Sadoul, Georges. *Histoire Generale du Cinema.* 2 vols. Paris: Denocl., 1947. *1888-1949: A Pictorial Survey of World Cinema*, new enl. ed. London: Studio Publications, 1950.

Schary, Dore. *Case History of a Movie.* New York: Random House, 1950.

Schickel, Richard. *Movies: The History of an Art and an Institution.* New York: Basic Books, 1964.

Speed, F. M. *Movie Cavalcade: The Story of the Cinema, Its Stars, Studios and Producers.* London: Raven Books, 1944.

Talbot, Daniel, ed. and comp. *Film: An Anthology.* New York: Simon and Schuster, 1959.

Taylor, John R. *Cinema Eye, Cinema Ear: Some Key Film-Makers of the Sixties.* New York: Hill & Wang, 1964.

Thrasher, Frederic, ed. *Okay for Sound: How the Screen Found Its Voice.* New York: Duell, Sloan & Pearce, 1946.

Tyler, Parker. *Magic and Myth of the Movies.* New York: Henry Holt & Co., 1947.

Wagenknecht, Edward. *The Movies in the Age of Innocence.* Norman: University of Oklahoma Press, 1962.

Warshow, Robert. *The Immediate Experience: Movies, Comics, Theatre, and Other Aspects of Popular Culture.* Garden City: Doubleday, 1964.

Winchester's Screen Encyclopedia. London: Winchester Pub., 1948.

Zinsser, William K. *Seen Any Good Movies Lately?* New York: Doubleday, 1958.

Zukor, Adolph. *The Public Is Never Wrong: The Autobiography of Adolph Zukor,* with Dale Kramer. New York: G. P. Putnam's Sons, 1953.

INDEX

Page numbers in **boldface** indicate photographs.

Holden, William, 15, 25, 26, **26**, 28, 35, **78**, **95**, 132, **132**, 260, 279, **282**, 305, 310, 325, 370, **385**, **411**, 426, 451, 499, 507, 546, 559, 606, 610

Holliday, Judy, 25, 27, 132, **132**, 154, 249, 279, 491

Holm, Celeste, 132, **132**, 253, 307, 342, 576

Hope, Bob, 20, 21, 27, 38, 132–3, **133**, 150, 206, 292, 326, 400, 433, 452, 454, 460, 469, 470, 494, 495

Hopkins, Miriam, 11, 133, **133**, 167, 316, 444, 484, 489, 514, 526, 583

Horton, Edward Everett, 133–4, **133**, 409, 483

Howard, Leslie, 12, 13, 134, **134**, 257, 271, 444, 455, 489, 609

Hudson, Rochelle, 134, **134**, 400

Hudson, Rock, 25, 32, 35, 36, 134–5, **134**, 156, 229, 245, 270, 301, 327, 343, 414, 546, 555, 556, 597

Hunt, Marsha, 135, **135**, 300, 573, 575

Hunter, Jeffrey, 135, **135**, 395

Hunter, Kim, 23, 135–6, **135**

Hunter, Tab, 136, **136**, 157, 268

Hussey, Ruth, 136, **136**, 456

Huston, Walter, 15, 136, **136**, 146, 248, 318, 451, 547, 585, 610

Hutton, Betty, 21, 137, **137**, 259, 353, 364, 378, 424, 500

Hutton, Jim, 137, **137**, 202

Hyer, Martha, 137, **137**

Ireland, John, 137–8, **138**, 254, 467

Jaffe, Sam, 9, 28, **262**, 356, 586

Jagger, Dean, 138, **138**, 325, 435, 454, 471, 527, 592

Jean, Gloria, 138, **138**

Johnson, Rita, 138–9, **139**

Johnson, Van, 14, **15**, **88**, 139, **139**, 174, 207, 268, 282, 286, 347, 439, 501, 516, 520, 539, 578

Jolson, Al, 1, **2**, 3, 6, 139, **139**, 387, 488, 544

Jones, Carolyn, 139–40, **141**, 366

Jones, Jennifer, 15, 17, 21, 25, **83**, 140, **140**, 153, 269, 321, 411, 417, 487, 492, 569, 615

Jones, Shirley, 140, **140**, 290, 444, 598, 616

Jory, Victor, 30, 140–1, **140**

Karloff, Boris, 9, 13, 14, 22, 36, **96**, 141, **141**, 208, 281, 330, 337, 352

Karns, Roscoe, 141–2, **141**, 204, 215

Kaye, Danny, 20, 21, 27, 142, **142**, 330, 359, 393, 397, 449, 480, 539, 545

Keaton, Buster, 3, 27, 142, **142**, 261

Keel, Howard, 26, 142, **142**, 570

Keeler, Ruby, 143, **143**, 331, 335

Kellaway, Cecil, 143, **143**, 239, 337

Kelly, Gene, 20, 26, **114**, **124**, 143–4, **143**, 255, 257, 282, 305, 400, 449, 488, 505, 509, 517, 519, 596

Kelly, Grace, 26, 27, 29, **99**, 144, **144**, 313, 365, 426, 466, 521, 576, 610

Kelly, Patsy, 144, **144**, 457, 459, 512, 534

Kelly, Paul, 144–5, **144**

Kennedy, Arthur, 28, 145, **145**, 282, 294

Kennedy, Edgar, 145, **145**, 192

Kerr, Deborah, 25, 146, **146**, 250, 362, 395, 438, 480, 506, 519, 558, 562, 567

Keyes, Evelyn, 118, 146, **146**, 567

Kibbee, Guy, 146–7, **146**, 160, 288, 333, 344, 348

Kruger, Otto, **108**, 147, **147**, 365, 498, 556

Ladd, Alan, 14, 16, 27, **57**, **106**, 147–8, **147**, 171, 280, 413, 483, 516, 528, 539, 553, 616

Lake, Arthur, 11, 148, **148**

Lake, Veronica, 148, **148**, 516

Lamarr, Hedy, 12, 17, 20, 21, 148–9, **149**, 279, 476, 563, 571

Lamour, Dorothy, 21, **137**, 149, **149**, 293, 316, 375, 433, 469, 470

Lancaster, Burt, 17, 18, 19, 24, **24**, 26, 28, 30, 32, 34, 35, 149, **149**, 260, 274, 301, 323, 331, 339, 394, 461, 482, 525, 531, 562, 568, 598

Lanchester, Elsa, 14, **142**, 149–50, **150**, 269, 281, 398

Landi, Elissa, 150, **150**, 487

Landis, Carole, 18, 22, 150, **150**, **385**

Landis, Jessie Royce, 144, 150–1, **150**

Lane, Priscilla, 151, **151**, 261, 336, **556**

Lange, Hope, 151, **151**, 271

Lansbury, Angela, 53, 151, **151**, 216, 501

Lanza, Mario, 151–2, **151**, 179, 352

Laughton, Charles, 9, 11, 13, 17, **51**, 152, **152**, 374, 431, 474, 475, 543, 598, 608

Laurel, Stan, and Oliver Hardy, 5, 13, 21, 27, 152, **152**, 494

Laurie, Piper, 152, **152**, 337

Lawford, Peter, 152–3, **153**, 322, 443, 562

Leigh, Janet, 25, 32, 35, **137**, 153, **153**, 223, 285, 416, 436, 462

Leigh, Vivien, 11, 153, **153**, 349, 504, 513, 609

Lemmon, Jack, 27, 34, **114**, 154, **154**, 170, 260, 269, 350, 373, 383, 425, 455, 492, 528, 564, 611

Leslie, Joan, 154, **154**, 359, 491, 513

Lewis, Jerry, 21, 27, 34, 154, **154**, 263, 270, 406, 426, 443, 475

Lindfors, Viveca, 154–5, **155**

Lindsay, Margaret, 155, **155**

Lockhart, Gene, 93, 155–6, **155**, 350

Lollobrigida, Gina, 25, 156, **156**, 491, 525

Lombard, Carole, 8, 17, 20, 156, **156**, 434, 508, 527

Loren, Sophia, 30, 32, 35, 156–7, **157**, 198, 261, 371, 449

Lorre, Peter, 12, **13**, 22, 157, **157**, 527, 554, 557

Louise, Anita, 157–8, **157**, 418

Lovejoy, Frank, 28, 158, **158**

Loy, Myrna, **5**, 6, 8, 12, 16, **16**, 77, 158, **158**, 251, 257, 259, 261, 264, 272, 296, 303, 324, 339, 412, 429, 463, 512, 515, 583

Lugosi, Bela, 12, 13, **13**, **141**, 158–9, **158**, 319

Lukas, Paul, 16, 159, **159**, 394, 535, 584, 589

Lupino, Ida, 150, 159–60, **159**, 243, 359, 365, 571

Lynn, Diana, 137, 160, **160**, 424

MacDonald, Jeannette, 6, **77**, 160, **160**, 329, 345, 412, 421, 436, 473, 477, 507, 617

MacLaine, Shirley, 26, 34, **62**, 125, 160, **160**, 182, 260, 261, 288, 341, 383, 538, 611

MacMahon, Aline, 160–1, **161**, 348, 416, 479

MacMurray, Fred, 9, 18, 161, **161**, 213, **223**, 233, 248, 278, 281, 286, 315, 319, 332, 483, 493, 508

Macready, George, 25, 161–2, **161**

McCambridge, Mercedes, **123**, 162, **162**, 254, 343

McCrea, Joel, 6, 10, 14, 21, 34, **148**, 162, **162**, 310, 334, 427, 529, 537, 609

McDaniel, Hattie, 162–3, **163**

McDowall, Roddy, 163, **163**, 372, 398, 457, 520, 609

McGuire, Dorothy, 28, 163, **163**, 224, 298, 308, 338, 505, 509, 525, 526, 568, 578

McHugh, Frank, 163–4, **164**, 222, 422

McLaglen, Victor, 9, 26, **54**, 122, 164, **164**, 222, 299, 356, 379, 409

McQueen, Steve, 30, 31, 164–5, **164**, 202, 235, 297, 413, 476, 574

Main, Marjorie, 165, **165**

Malden, Karl, 23, 24, 28, 165, **165**, 216, 358, 372, 445

Malone, Dorothy, 165–6, **165**, 546

Manners, David, 166, **166**

Mara, Adele, 166, **166**

March, Fredric, 6, 8, 14, 16, 17, 28, 32, 166–7, **167**, 258, 259, 267, 272, 284, 311, 316, 324, 379, 422, 482, 487, 499, 548, 583, 585, 614

Margo, 72, 167, **167**, 269, 306

Marshall, Herbert, 6, 14, **101**, 167, **167**, 187, 332, 334, 405, 554, 555, 585

Martin, Dean, 21, 27, 34, 35, 168, **168**, 263, 406, 426, 472, 475, 481, 492, 524

Marvin, Lee, 28, 34, 37, 168, 291, 314, 461, 485

Marx Brothers, 5, 8, 27, **100**, 168, **168**, 231, 257, 309, 438

Mason, James, 24, 25, 169, **169**, 330, 391, 392

Massey, Illona, **102**, 169, **169**

Massey, Raymond, 14, 15, **15**, 169–70, **169**, 247, 346, 459

Matthau, Walter, 170, **170**, 325, 502

Mature, Victor, 18, 20, 22, **117**, 170, **170**, 311, 323, 385, 423, 471, 476

Maxwell, Marilyn, 170, **170**

Mayo, Virginia, 16, 20, **162**, 170–1, **171**, 331

Medina, Patricia, 171, **171**

Meek, Donald, **120**, **135**, 171–2, **171**, 368, 497, 553

Menjou, Adolphe, 28, **166**, 172, **172**, 231, 339, 348, 405, 427, 498, 499, 501

Meredith, Burgess, 15, 172, **172**, 444, 542

Merkel, Una, 172–3, **173**, 279, 307, 470

Merman, Ethel, 173, **173**, 286, 514, 560

Michael, Gertrude, **116**, 173, **173**

Miles, Vera, 173–4, **174**

Milland, Ray, 9, 15, 17, 36, **156**, 174, **174**, 313, 398, 409, 415, 465, 515, 558, 566, 568, 609

Miller, Ann, 26, 174–5, **174**, 177, 449, 587

Mills, Hayley, 175, **175**

Mineo, Sal, 30, 38, 175, **175**

Miranda, Carmen, **59**, 175, **175**, 308

Mitchell, Thomas, 19, **151**, 175–6, **176**, 365, 408, 415, 451, 516, 551

Mitchum, Robert, 15, 19, 22, 28, 176, **176**, 324, 362, 441, 502, 516, 538, 572

Monroe, Marilyn, 24, 26, 28, 32, 176, **176**, 285, 343, 372, 424, 437, 482, 492, 597

Montalban, Ricardo, 176–7, **177**, 268, 437, 488, 551, 558

Montez, Maria, 177, **177**

Montgomery, Robert, 6, 12, 18, 20, **167**, 177, 177, 363, 438

Moore, Ida, 177–8, **178**

Moore, Terry, 178, **178**, 557

Moorehead, Agnes, **50**, 178–9, **178**, 195, 215, 487

Moreland, Mantan, 179, **179**

Moreno, Rita, 179, **179**

Morgan, Dennis, 179–80, **179**, 193, 346, 396, 435, 513, 521

Morgan, Frank, **120**, 160, 180, **180**, 370, 503

Morgan, Ralph, 180, **180**, 498

Morris, Chester, 181, **181**, 253, 273, 315

Morris, Wayne, 181, **181**, 385

Muni, Paul, 6, 12, 15, 182, **182**, 302, 350, 376, 391, 479, 493, 502, 586

Murphy, Audie, 182, **182**

Murphy, George, **88**, 143, 182, **182**, 516

Murray, Don, 182–3, **183**, 264, 361

Naish, J. Carroll, **55**, 179, 183, **183**, 223, 259, 269, 394, 495

Natwick, Mildred, 183–4, **183**

Neal, Patricia, 29, **121**, 184, **184**, 325, 565, 600

Newman, Paul, 24, 28, 30, 34, 35, **51**, 184, **184**, 186, 292, 304, 339, 360, 376, 406, 464, 491, 507

Niven, David, 11, 25, 184–5, **184**, 243, 261, 275, 329, 459, 461, 480

Nolan, Lloyd, 12, 185, **185**, 361

Novak, Kim, 26, 29, 34, 185, **185**, 269, 280, 322, 418, 452

Oakie, Jack, **141**, 185–6, **185**, 352

Oberon, Merle, 11, 186, **186**, 493, 514, 546, 552, 578, 585

O'Brien, Edmond, 18, 28, 186, **186**, 542

O'Brien, George, **5**, 186–7, **187**, 335, 435

O'Brien, Margaret, 76, 187, **187**, 390, 421

O'Brien, Pat, 181, 187, **187**, 293, 339, 573

O'Brien, Virginia, 188, **188**, 360

O'Connell, Arthur, 188, **188**, 219, 456

O'Connor, Donald, 7, 188–9, **188**, 207, 337, 488, 489, 514

O'Connor, Una, 189, **189**

O'Hara, Maureen, 16, **17**, 26, 189, **189**, 374, 462, 524, 555

O'Keefe, Dennis, **59**, **84**, 189–90, **189**, 501

Oland, Warner, 12, 190, **190**

Oliver, Edna May, 190–1, **190**, 406, 509

Olivier, Laurence, 11, 20, 35, **140**, 191, **191**, 466, 513, 546, 561, 587

O'Sullivan, Maureen, 9, 10, 191, **191**, 237, 309, 510

O'Toole, Peter, 33, 191, **191**, 269, 399, 409

Ouspenskaya, Maria, 15, 192, **192**, 410, 463

Owen, Reginald, **152**, 153, 192, **192**, 494

DIRECTORS

Aldrich, Robert, 28, 35
Allen, Lewis, 29
Anger, Kenneth, 38
Averbach, Hy, 38

Bacon, Lloyd, **3**, 551
Beaumont, Harry, 1
Berkeley, Busby, **6**, 552
Brooks, Richard, 33
Browning, Tod, 14

Capra, Frank, 8, 552
Chabrol, Claude, 37
Clarke, Shirley, 38
Collinson, Peter, 39
Coppola, Francis Ford, 39
Corman, Roger, 29–30, 35, 36, 552
Cromwell, John, 15, **15**, 552
Cukor, George, 10, 18, 33, 553
Curtiz, Michael, **5**, 553

Daves, Delmer, 27, 553
Del Ruth, Roy, 6
De Mille, Cecil B., **4**, 8–9, **9**, 10, 14, 25, **25**, 553
Dieterle, William, 12, 554
Dmytryk, Edward, 554
Donen, Stanley, 26
Dwan, Allan, 554

Edwards, Blake, 34

Fleischer, Richard, 32, 37
Fleming, Victor, 8
Ford, John, 9, 10, 11, 16, 21, 26, 27, 34, 555
Foster, Norman, 15
Frankenheimer, John, 32, 33, 35, 36, 555

Garnett, Tay, 555
Goldstone, James, 38
Goulding, Edmund, 555–6
Grauman, Walter, 39
Griffith, D.W., 3

Harvey, Anthony, 39
Hathaway, Henry, 15, 556
Hawks, Howard, 8, 15, 21, 22, 27, 29, 33, 556
Hecht, Ben, 38
Hitchcock, Alfred, 14, 18, **18**, 20, 29, 35, 36, 556
Hunter, Ross, 33
Huston, John, 28, 37, **608**, 556

Jewison, Norman, 35

Kanin, Garson, 15
Kazan, Elia, 17, 19, 23, 24, 28, 30, 32, 39, 556–7
King, Henry, 557
Korda, Zoltan, 15
Koster, Henry, 557
Kubrick, Stanley, 28, 32
Kulik, Buzz, 35

Landis, James, 38
Lang, Fritz, 14, 15, 18, 557
Lean, David, 37
Leisen, Mitchell, 557–8
LeRoy, Mervyn, 8, 558
Lewin, Albert, 17
Lewis, Herschel G., 38
Litvak, Anatole, 12, 16, 20, 31, 558
Lloyd, Frank, 559
Logan, Joshua, 32
Losey, Joseph, 29
Lubitsch, Ernst, 8, 12

Lumet, Sidney, 24, 30, 32, 36, 39
Lupino, Ida, 33

McCarey, Leo, 8, 559
Mamoulian, Rouben, 2, 559
Mankiewicz, Joseph L., 17, 32, 37, 559
Mann, Anthony, 27, 559–60
Mart, Paul, 38
Marton, Andrew, 37
Mekas, Adolfas and Jonas, 38
Meyer, Russ, 38
Minnelli, Vincente, 20, 26, 32, 560
Mishkin, William, 38
Moxey, John, 38
Mulligan, Robert, 31

Negulesco, Jean, 560
Nyby, Christian, 29

Penn, Arthur, 30, 35, 36, 39
Preminger, Otto, 24, 25, 30, **31**, 35, 39, 561

Reed, Carol, 15
Richter, Hans, 38
Robson, Mark, 22, 561
Rossen, Robert, 32, 561
Rydell, Mark, 37

Schaffner, Franklin, 32
Seaton, George, 561
Seitz, George, 16
Siegel, Don, 37
Siodmak, Robert, 561
Stevens, George, 27, 32, 562
Strick, Joseph, 39
Sturges, John, 27–8, 562
Sturges, Preston, 16, 27

Taurog, Norman, 11, 562
Thorpe, Richard, 38
Toth, Andre de, 30
Torre Nilsson, Leopoldo, 37
Tourneur, Jacques, 22, 562–3
Truffaut, François, 37
Tuttle, Frank, 563

Vidor, Charles, 563
Vidor, King, 2, 21, 29, 563
Visconti, Luchino, 37

Walsh, Raoul, 563–4
Welles, Orson, 15, 17, **17**, 564
Wellman, William, 15, 21, 564
Wilder, Billy, 17, 33, 564
Wise, Robert, 22, 28, 33, 34, 36, 565
Wyler, William, 15, 16, 29, 32, 565

Young, Terence, 37

Zinneman, Fred, 565

PRODUCERS

Adler, Buddy, 566
Arkoff, Samuel Z., 566
Arthur, Robert, 566–7

Bassler, Robert, 567
Berman, Pandro S., 567
Bischoff, Samuel, 567
Blanke, Henry, 568
Blaustein, Julian C., 568

Bogeaus, Benedict E., 568
Brackett, Charles, 568
Bronston, Samuel, 32, 568
Brown, Harry Joe, 568–9

Castle, William, 35, 36, 39
Cooper, Merian C., 569
Cummings, Jack, 569
Curtis, Dan, 37

Disney, Walt, 2, 13, 22, 29, 30, 32, 33

Engel, Samuel G., 569

Franklin, Sidney, 570
Freed, Arthur, 570

Goetz, William, 570
Goldwyn, Samuel B., 5, 11, 15, 16, 570
Grainger, James Edmund, 570–1

Hecht, Harold, 571
Hellinger, Mark, **19**, 571
Hornblow, Arthur, Jr., 571
Huggins, Roy, 38
Hughes, Howard, 9, 571
Hunter, Ross, 571–2

Johnson, Nunnally, 572

Katzman, Sam, 572
Kohlmar, Fred, 572–3
Kramer, Stanley, 24, 25, 28, 30, 31, 34, 573

Laemmle, Carl, Sr., 13
Laemmle, Carl, Jr., 573
Lesser, Sol, 573
Lewton, Val, 22
Lord, Robert, 573

Mirisch, Walter M., 574

Oboler, Arch, 23, 25, 39

Pakula, Alan J., 574
Pal, George, 36, 574
Pasternak, Joe, 574
Perlberg, William, 575

Ray, Nicholas, 32
Rosenberg, Aaron, 575
Rowland, Roy, 35

Saville, Victor, 575
Schary, Dore, 575–6
Seigel, Sol C., 576
Selznick, David O., 10, 21, 576
Small, Edward, 576
Spiegel, Sam, 30, 31
Stromberg, Hunt, 576

Thomas, William C., 576–7

Wald, Jerry, 27, 577
Wallis, Hal B., 5, 577
Wanger, Walter, 578
Warhol, Andy, 38
Warner, Jack, 12
Warner, Sam, 1
Weingarten, Lawrence, 578
Wilder, W. Lee, 36

Zanuck, Darryl F., 578–9
Zimbalist, Sam, 579
Zugsmith, Albert, 579